Library of Congress Catalog Card Number: 83–61459
ISBN: 0–88207–812–7

© 1983, SP Publications, Inc. All rights reserved
Printed in the United States of America

15   16   17   18   19   20   Printing/Year   94   93   92

Contents

Maps, Charts, and Diagrams

Maps, Charts, and Diagrams

Preface

The Bible Knowledge Commentary is an exposition of the Scriptures written and edited solely by Dallas Seminary faculty members. It is designed for pastors, laypersons, Bible teachers, serious Bible students, and others who want a comprehensive but brief and reliable commentary on the entire Bible.

Why another Bible commentary when so many commentaries are already available? Several features make this volume a distinctive Bible study tool.

First, *The Bible Knowledge Commentary* is written by faculty members of one school—Dallas Theological Seminary. This volume interprets the Scriptures consistently from the grammatical-historical approach and from the pretribulational, premillennial perspective, for which Dallas Seminary is well known. At the same time, the authors often present various views of passages where differences of opinion exist within evangelical scholarship.

Second, this is the first single-volume commentary to be based on the *New International Version of the Holy Bible* (1978 ed.). The NIV is widely accepted as a translation that faithfully renders the biblical text into clear modern-day English. *The Bible Knowledge Commentary* thus becomes immediately useful as a companion to one's personal Bible study.

Third, this commentary has features that not all one-volume commentaries include. (a) In their comments on the biblical text, the writers discuss how the purpose of the book unfolds, how each part fits with the whole and with what precedes and follows it. This helps readers see why the biblical authors chose the material they did as their words were guided by the Holy Spirit's inspiration. (b) Problem passages, puzzling Bible-time customs, and alleged contradictions are carefully considered and discussed. (c) Insights from the latest in conservative biblical scholarship are incorporated in this volume. (d) Many Hebrew, Aramaic, and Greek words, important to the understanding of certain passages, are discussed. These words are transliterated for the benefit of readers not proficient in the biblical languages. Yet those who do know these languages will also appreciate these comments. (e) Dozens of maps, charts, and diagrams are included; they are placed conveniently with the Bible passages being discussed, not at the end of the volume. (f) Numerous cross references to related or parallel passages are included with the discussions on many passages.

The material on each Bible book includes an *Introduction* (discussion of items such as authorship, date, purpose, unity, style, unique features), *Outline, Commentary,* and *Bibliography.* In the *Commentary* section, summaries of entire sections of the text are given, followed by detailed comments on the passage verse by verse and often phrase by phrase. All words quoted from the NIV appear in boldface type, as do the verse numbers at the beginning of paragraphs. The *Bibliography* entries, suggested for further study, are not all endorsed in their entirety by the authors and editors. The writers and editors have listed both works they have consulted and others which would be useful to readers.

Personal pronouns referring to Deity are capitalized, which often helps make it clear that the commentator is writing about a Member of the Trinity. The word Lord, as in the NIV, is the English translation of the Hebrew YHWH, often rendered *Yahweh* in English. *Lord* translates *'Ădōnāy.* When the two names stand together as a compound name of God, they are rendered "Sovereign Lord," as in the NIV.

The New Testament Consulting Editor, Dr. Stanley D. Toussaint, has added to the quality of this commentary by reading the manuscripts and offering helpful suggestions. His work is greatly appreciated. We also express thanks to Lloyd Cory, Victor Books Reference Editor, to Barbara Williams, whose careful editing enhanced the material appreciably, to hardworking Production Coordinator Myrna Jean Hasse, and to the many manuscript typists at Scripture Press and Dallas Theological Seminary for their diligence.

This volume is an exposition of the Bible, an explanation of the text of Scripture, based on careful exegesis. It is not primarily a devotional commentary, or an exegetical work giving details of lexicology, grammar, and syntax with extensive discussions of critical matters pertaining to textual and background data. May this commentary deepen your insight into the Scriptures, as you seek to have "the eyes of your heart . . . enlightened" (Eph. 1:18) by the teaching ministry of the Holy Spirit.

This book is designed to enrich your understanding and appreciation of the Scriptures, God's inspired, inerrant Word, and to motivate you "not merely [to] listen to the Word" but also to "do what it says" (James 1:22) and "also . . . to teach others" (2 Tim. 2:2).

John F. Walvoord
Roy B. Zuck

Editors

John F. Walvoord, A.B., M.A., Th.M., Th.D., D.D., Litt.D.
    Chancellor and Minister at Large
    Professor of Systematic Theology, Emeritus
    Dallas Theological Seminary

Roy B. Zuck, A.B., Th.M., Th.D.
    Vice-President for Academic Affairs
    Academic Dean
    Professor of Bible Exposition
    Editor, *Bibliotheca Sacra*
    Dallas Theological Seminary

Consulting Editors

Old Testament:
Kenneth L. Barker, A.B., Th.M., Ph.D.
    Executive Director, NIV Translation Center
    (A Ministry of International Bible Society)
    (Formerly Chairman and Professor of
    Old Testament Studies, 1968–81,
    Dallas Theological Seminary)

Eugene H. Merrill, A.B., M.A., M.Phil., Ph.D.
    Professor of Old Testament Studies
    Dallas Theological Seminary

New Testament:
Stanley D. Toussaint, A.B., Th.M., Th.D.
    Chairman and Senior Professor of Bible Exposition
    Dallas Theological Seminary

Contributing Authors*

Louis A. Barbieri, Jr., A.B., Th.M., Th.D.
Pastor, La Grange Bible Church
La Grange, Illinois
(Formerly Dean of Students and
Assistant Professor of Bible Exposition,
1976–86, Dallas Theological Seminary)
Matthew

J. Ronald Blue, A.B., Th.M., Ph.D.
Chairman and Professor of World Missions
James

Edwin A. Blum, B.S., Th.M., Th.D., D.Theol.
Vice-president of Personnel,
Pacific Construction Co., Honolulu, Hawaii
(Formerly Adjunct Teacher of Historical
Theology, 1969, 1971–74, 1976–87,
Dallas Theological Seminary)
John

Donald K. Campbell, A.B., Th.M., Th.D., D.D.
President
Professor of Bible Exposition
Galatians

Thomas L. Constable, A.B., Th.M., Th.D.
Director of D.Min. Studies
Professor of Bible Exposition
1, 2 Thessalonians

Edwin C. Deibler, A.B., Th.M., Ph.D.
Professor of Historical Theology, Emeritus
(retired 1982)
Philemon

**Kenneth O. Gangel, A.B., M.A., M.Div.,
S.T.M., Ph.D., Litt.D.**
Chairman and Senior Professor of
Christian Education
2 Peter

Norman L. Geisler, Th.B., A.B., M.A., Ph.D.
Dean of Evangelical Seminary
Charlotte, North Carolina
(Formerly Professor of Systematic Theology,
1979–89, Dallas Theological Seminary,
Trinity Evangelical Divinity School,
and Liberty University)
Colossians

John D. Grassmick, A.B., Th.M., Ph.D. Cand.
Associate Professor of New
Testament Studies
Mark

Zane C. Hodges, A.B., Th.M.
Pastor, Victory Street Bible Chapel,
Dallas, Texas
(Formerly Professor of New Testament,
1959–86, Dallas Theological Seminary)
Hebrews, 1, 2, 3 John

Harold W. Hoehner, A.B., Th.M., Th.D., Ph.D.
Director of Th.D. Studies Chairman and
Professor of New Testament Studies
Ephesians

Robert P. Lightner, Th.B., M.L.A., Th.M., Th.D.
Professor of Systematic Theology
Philippians

A. Duane Litfin, B.S., Th.M., Ph.D.
Pastor, First Evangelical Church,
Memphis, Tennessee
(Formerly Associate Professor of
Pastoral Ministries, 1974–83,
Dallas Theological Seminary)
1, 2 Timothy, Titus

David K. Lowery, A.B., Th.M., Ph.D.
Professor of New Testament Studies
1, 2 Corinthians

John A. Martin, A.B., Th.M., Th.D., Ph.D.
President, Central College, McPherson, Kansas
(Formerly Dean of Faculty and Professor of
Bible Exposition, 1978–90,
Dallas Theological Seminary)
Luke

**Edward C. Pentecost, A.B., M.A., Th.M.,
D.Miss.**
Associate Professor of World Missions,
Emeritus (retired 1987)
Jude

Roger M. Raymer, A.B., Th.M.
Pastor, Spring Branch Community Church,
Houston, Texas
(Formerly Director of Alumni and Church
Relations, Director of Continuing
Education, and Assistant Professor of
Pastoral Ministries, 1980–82, 1985–91,
Dallas Theological Seminary)
1 Peter

Stanley D. Toussaint, A.B., Th.M., Th.D.
Chairman and Senior Professor of
Bible Exposition
Consulting Editor, *The Bible Knowledge
Commentary*
Acts

**John F. Walvoord, A.B., M.A., Th.M., Th.D.,
D.D., Litt.D.**
Chancellor and Minister at Large
Professor of Systematic Theology, Emeritus
(Formerly President, 1952–86,
Dallas Theological Seminary)
Revelation

**John A. Witmer, A.B., M.A., M.S.L.S.,
Th.M., Th.D.**
Associate Professor of Systematic Theology,
Emeritus (retired 1987)
Romans

*All authors are either present or former members of the faculty of Dallas Theological Seminary.

Abbreviations

A. *General*

act.	active	n., nn.	note(s)
Akk.	Akkadian	n.d.	no date
Apoc.	Apocrypha	neut.	neuter
Aram.	Aramaic	n.p.	no publisher, no place of
ca.	*circa*, about		publication
cf.	*confer*, compare	no.	number
chap., chaps.	chapter(s)	NT	New Testament
comp.	compiled, compilation,	OT	Old Testament
	compiler	p., pp.	page(s)
ed.	edited, edition, editor	par., pars.	paragraph(s)
eds.	editors	part.	participle
e.g.	*exempli gratia*, for example	pass.	passive
Eng.	English	perf.	perfect
et al.	*et alii*, and others	pl.	plural
fem.	feminine	pres.	present
Gr.	Greek	q.v.	*quod vide*, which see
Heb.	Hebrew	Sem.	Semitic
ibid.	*ibidem*, in the same place	sing.	singular
i.e.	*id est*, that is	s.v.	*sub verbo*, under the word
imper.	imperative	trans.	translation, translator,
imperf.	imperfect		translated
lit.	literal, literally	viz.	*videlicet*, namely
LXX	Septuagint	vol., vols.	volume(s)
marg.	margin, marginal reading	v., vv.	verse(s)
masc.	masculine	vs.	versus
ms., mss.	manuscript(s)	Vul.	Vulgate
MT	Masoretic text		

B. *Abbreviations of Books of the Bible*

Gen.	Ruth	Job	Lam.	Jonah
Ex.	1, 2 Sam.	Ps., Pss. (pl.)	Ezek.	Micah
Lev.	1, 2 Kings	Prov.	Dan.	Nahum
Num.	1, 2 Chron.	Ecc.	Hosea	Hab.
Deut.	Ezra	Song	Joel	Zeph.
Josh.	Neh.	Isa.	Amos	Hag.
Jud.	Es.	Jer.	Obad.	Zech.
				Mal.

Matt.	Acts	Eph.	1, 2 Tim.	James
Mark	Rom.	Phil.	Titus	1, 2 Peter
Luke	1, 2 Cor.	Col.	Phile.	1, 2, 3 John
John	Gal.	1, 2 Thes.	Heb.	Jude
				Rev.

C. *Abbreviations of Bible Versions, Translations, and Paraphrases*

ASV	American Standard Version
JB	Jerusalem Bible
KJV	King James Version
NASB	New American Standard Bible
NEB	New English Bible
NIV	New International Version
NKJV	New King James Version
Ph.	New Testament in Modern English (J.B. Phillips)
RSV	Revised Standard Version
Sco.	New Scofield Reference Bible
Wms.	The New Testament (Charles B. Williams)

Transliterations

Hebrew

Consonants

א	– '	ד	– $\underline{d}$	י	– y	ס	– s	ר	– r
ב	– b	ה	– h	כ	– k	ע	– '	שׂ	– $ś$
ב	– $\underline{b}$	ו	– w	כ	– $\underline{k}$	פ	– p	שׁ	– $š$
ג	– g	ז	– z	ל	– l	פ	– $\underline{p}$	ת	– t
ג	– $\underline{g}$	ח	– $ḥ$	מ	– m	צ	– $ṣ$	ת	– $\underline{t}$
ד	– d	ט	– $ṭ$	נ	– n	ק	– q		

Daghesh forte is represented by doubling the letter.

Vocalization

בָה	– bâh	בָ	– bā	בֹ	– bo[1]	בְ	– bĕ
בוֹ	– bô	בֹ	– bō	בֻ	– bu[1]	בְ	– b^e
בוּ	– bû	בָ	– bū	בֶ	– be	בָה	– bāh
בֵי	– bê	בֵ	– bē	בִ	– bi[1]	בָא	– bā'
בֶ	– be	בִ	– bī	בַ	– bă	בֵה	– bēh
בִי	– bî	בַ	– ba	בֳ	– bŏ	בֶה	– beh

[1] In closed syllables

Greek

α, ᾳ	– a	ξ	– x	γγ	– ng
β	– b	ο	– o	γκ	– nk
γ	– g	π	– p	γξ	– nx
δ	– d	ρ	– r	γχ	– nch
ε	– e	σ, ς	– s	αἰ	– ai
ζ	– z	τ	– t	αὐ	– au
η, ῃ	– $ē$	υ	– y	εἰ	– ei
θ	– th	φ	– ph	εὐ	– eu
ι	– i	χ	– ch	ηὐ	– $ēu$
κ	– k	ψ	– ps	οἰ	– oi
λ	– l	ω, ῳ	– $ō$	οὐ	– ou
μ	– m	ῥ	– rh	υἱ	– hui
ν	– n	῾	– h		

Groupings of New Testament Books

I. **History**
   A. Four Gospels
   B. Acts

II. **Epistles**
   A. Pauline

   Journey Epistles
   $\left\{\begin{array}{l}\text{Galatians} \\ \text{1 and 2 Thessalonians} \\ \text{1 and 2 Corinthians} \\ \text{Romans}\end{array}\right.$

   Prison Epistles
   $\left\{\begin{array}{l}\text{Ephesians} \\ \text{Philippians} \\ \text{Colossians} \\ \text{Philemon}\end{array}\right.$

   Pastoral Epistles
   $\left\{\begin{array}{l}\text{1 Timothy} \\ \text{Titus} \\ \text{2 Timothy}\end{array}\right.$

   B. General

   Hebrew Christians
   $\left\{\begin{array}{l}\text{Hebrews} \\ \text{James}\end{array}\right.$

   Others
   $\left\{\begin{array}{l}\text{1 and 2 Peter} \\ \text{1, 2, and 3 John} \\ \text{Jude}\end{array}\right.$

III. **Visions**
   Revelation

MATTHEW

Louis A. Barbieri, Jr.

INTRODUCTION

It is fitting that the New Testament begins with four accounts of the life of Jesus Christ. These accounts present the "good news" concerning the Son of God, telling of His life on earth and His death on the cross for the sin of mankind. The first three Gospels take a similar view of the facts surrounding this Person, while the Fourth Gospel is unique in its presentation. Because of this common view of Jesus Christ the first three New Testament books are called the Synoptic Gospels.

The Synoptic Problem

1. *The problem stated.* "Synoptic" comes from the Greek adjective *synoptikos,* which is from two words *syn* and *opsesthai,* "to see with or together." While Matthew, Mark, and Luke have distinctive purposes, they nevertheless view the life of Jesus Christ in a common way. However, some differences in the Gospel narratives must also be accounted for. These similarities and differences raise the question of the sources of the Gospels, thus positing a "Synoptic problem."

Most conservative scholars acknowledge that the Gospel writers made use of various sources. For example, the genealogical records of both Matthew and Luke may have come from temple records or oral tradition. Luke stated at the beginning of his Gospel (Luke 1:1) that many had written down the facts concerning the Lord Jesus. This implies that Luke could have drawn on a number of written accounts. That the individual writers may have used different sources for their material is a valid conclusion. However, this is not what critical scholars mean when they talk about sources. Most critical scholars view the "sources" as extensive writings which were joined together by skilled editors to produce

their own accounts. This conclusion has led to several explanations of these sources.

a. The Urevangelium theory. Some scholars conclude that an original Gospel (known in German as the *Urevangelium*) now lost, was the source for the biblical editors as they compiled their accounts. The major objection to this view is that no trace of such a writing has ever been discovered. No scholar can point to a document as the possible *Urevangelium.* Also, while such an explanation would account for the similarities, it in no way explains the differences in the Gospel stories of the same events.

b. The oral tradition theory. Some have concluded that the basic sources for the Gospels came from oral tradition, an oral testimony that developed around Jesus Christ. Normally such a testimony involved four steps: (1) The event occurred. (2) The event was told and repeated often enough so that it became widely known. (3) The event became fixed so that it was then told exactly the same way. (4) The event was written down in an account. An objection to this view is similar to the *Urevangelium* theory: this view accounts for similarities in the stories but it fails to account for the differences. Furthermore, why would an eyewitness of the events limit himself to stories from oral tradition?

c. The document theory. A popular view today is that the biblical editors made use of various written sources to compile their accounts. This viewpoint usually posits the following: (1) The first written account was the Gospel of Mark. A major reason for this position is that only 7 percent of the Gospel of Mark is unique, as 93 percent of Mark can be found in Matthew and Luke. (2) In addition to

Mark a second written document existed which basically contained discourse material. This document is known as "Q", an abbreviated form of the German word for source, *Quelle.* The approximately 200 verses common to Matthew and Luke which are not found in Mark must have come from "Q". (3) The editors used at least two other sources. One source reflects verses in Matthew not found in either Mark or Luke, and the other source reflects verses in Luke not found in either Matthew or Mark. This theory with its lines of dependence could be charted in this way:

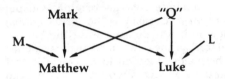

This theory has several problems. First, it has difficulty with tradition. Conservative scholars have generally held that Matthew was the first of the written Gospels. While not all conservatives agree, this tradition does have some weight behind it and should not be shrugged off as "mere tradition" as sometimes tradition is correct. Second, this theory cannot account for the fact that occasionally Mark made a comment that neither Matthew nor Luke included. Mark wrote that the rooster crowed a second time (Mark 14:72), but neither Matthew nor Luke included that fact. Third, if Mark were the first Gospel, written after Peter's death around A.D. 67–68, then Matthew and Luke would probably have been written later after the destruction of Jerusalem in A.D. 70. One would then expect that destruction to have been mentioned as a fitting climax to the Lord's words in Matthew 24–25 or Luke's statement in 21:20-24; however, neither mentioned the event. Fourth, the greatest problem is the whole speculation about the existence of "Q". If such a document existed and were thought of so highly by Matthew and Luke that they quoted extensively from it, why did not the church also regard it highly and preserve it?

d. *The form critical theory.* This widely held view assumes the document theory, but takes it a step further. When the Gospel accounts were compiled, a multiplicity of documents existed, not simply four documents (Matthew, Mark, Luke, and "Q"). Interpreters today seek to discover and classify these documents, called "forms," and also to get behind the forms and discover exactly what the first-century church was seeking to communicate through them. The literal facts communicated in the forms are not sufficient in themselves; the truth is discovered by going behind the literal story. The facts in the stories are considered "myths" which the church built up around Jesus Christ. By scraping away the myths or "demythologizing," kernels of truth concerning Jesus are discovered.

While this theory is widely held, it has some serious problems. It is virtually impossible to classify the "forms" into exact categories. It is doubtful if any two interpreters would agree on the classifications. Furthermore, this view says that the first-century church caused these stories to be told the way they were, but the view never adequately explains what caused the church. In other words, this view has purposefully overlooked the living witness of Jesus Christ and the true impact His life and death made on first-century believers.

2. *A proposed solution.* The similarities and differences in the Gospel accounts can be solved through a composite viewpoint. First, the Gospel writers of the first century had extensive personal knowledge of much of the material they recorded. Matthew and John were disciples of Jesus Christ who spent a considerable amount of time with the Lord. Mark's account may be the reflections of Simon Peter near the end of his life, and Luke could have learned many facts through his relationship with Paul and others. These facts would have been used in writing the four accounts.

Second, oral tradition was involved. For example, Acts 20:35 refers to a saying of Christ not recorded in the Gospels. Paul in 1 Corinthians 7:10 gave a quotation from the Lord; when Paul wrote this, possibly none of the Gospels had yet been written. Third, written documents told some of the stories about Jesus Christ. Luke acknowledged this fact as he began his Gospel (Luke 1:1-4). None of these facts, however, gives the dynamic needed to record an inspired account of Jesus Christ's life that is free from all error. Fourth, another element must be included to help solve the Synoptic problem, namely, the dynamic of the Holy Spirit's ministry of inspiration as the Gospel writers recorded the accounts. The Lord promised the disciples that the Holy Spirit would teach them all things and remind them of all Jesus had told them (John 14:26). This dynamic guarantees accuracy, whether the author was making use of his memory, passed-down oral traditions, or written accounts available to him. Whatever the source, the direction of the Holy Spirit assured an accurate text. The better one understands the various stories about the Lord, the clearer the "difficulties" become, for there was a divine superintendence over the authors regardless of the sources they used.

The Authorship of the First Gospel. When one deals with the question of who wrote a particular Bible book, the evidence is normally twofold: evidence outside the book ("external evidence") and evidence within the book itself ("internal evidence"). External evidence strongly supports the view that the Apostle Matthew wrote the Gospel that bears his name. Many early church fathers cited Matthew as its author, including Pseudo Barnabas, Clement of Rome, Polycarp, Justin Martyr, Clement of Alexandria, Tertullian, and Origen. (For further attestation see Norman L. Geisler and William E. Nix, *A General Introduction to the Bible.* Chicago: Moody Press, 1968, p. 193.) Matthew was certainly not one of the more prominent apostles. One might think the First Gospel would have been written by Peter, James, or John. But the extensive tradition that Matthew wrote it strongly commends him as its author.

Internal evidence also supports the fact that Matthew was the author of the First Gospel. This book has more references to coins than any of the other three Gospels. In fact this Gospel includes three terms for coins that are found nowhere else in the New Testament: "The two-drachma tax" (Matt. 17:24); "a four-drachma coin" (17:27), and "talents" (18:24). Since Matthew's occupation was tax collecting, he had an interest in coins

and noted the cost of certain items. The profession of tax collector would necessitate an ability to write and keep records. Matthew obviously had the ability, humanly speaking, to write a book such as the First Gospel.

His Christian humility comes through as well, for Matthew alone continually refers to himself throughout his Gospel as "Matthew the tax collector." But Mark and Luke do not continually use that term of contempt when speaking of Matthew. Also, when Matthew began to follow Jesus, he invited his friends to a "dinner" (Matt. 9:9-10). Luke, however, called the dinner "a great banquet" (Luke 5:29). The omissions from the First Gospel are significant too, for Matthew omitted the Parable of the Pharisee and the Tax Collector (Luke 18:9-14) and the story of Zacchaeus, a tax collector who restored fourfold what he had stolen (Luke 19:1-10). The internal evidence concerning the authorship of the First Gospel points to Matthew as its most likely author.

The Original Language of the First Gospel. While all the extant manuscripts of the First Gospel are in Greek, some suggest that Matthew wrote his Gospel in Aramaic, similar to Hebrew. Five individuals stated, in effect, that Matthew wrote in Aramaic and that translations followed in Greek: Papias (A.D. 80-155), Irenaeus (A.D. 130-202), Origen (A.D. 185-254), Eusebius (fourth century A.D.), and Jerome (sixth century A.D.). However, they may have been referring to a writing by Matthew other than his Gospel account. Papias, for example, said Matthew compiled the sayings (*logia*) of Jesus. Those "sayings" might have been a second, shorter account of the Lord's words, written in Aramaic and sent to a group of Jews for whom it would have been most meaningful. That writing was later lost, for no such version exists today. The First Gospel, however, was probably penned by Matthew in Greek and has survived until today. Matthew's *logia* did not survive, but his Gospel did. This was because the latter, part of the biblical canon and thus God's Word, was inspired and preserved by the Spirit of God.

The Date of the First Gospel. Pinpointing the writing of the First Gospel to a specific year is impossible. Various dates for the book have been suggested by conservative scholars. C.I. Scofield in the original *Scofield Reference Bible* gave A.D. 37 as a possible date. Few scholars give a date after A.D. 70, since Matthew made no reference to the destruction of Jerusalem. Furthermore, Matthew's references to Jerusalem as the "Holy City" (Matt. 4:5; 27:53) imply that it was still in existence.

But some time seems to have elapsed after the events of the Crucifixion and the Resurrection. Matthew 27:7-8 refers to a certain custom continuing "to this day," and 28:15 refers to a story being circulated "to this very day." These phrases imply the passing of time, and yet not so much time that the Jewish customs had ceased. Since church tradition has strongly advocated that the Gospel of Matthew was the first Gospel account written, perhaps a date somewhere around A.D. 50 would satisfy all the demands mentioned. It would also be early enough to permit Matthew to be the first Gospel account. (For further discussion and an alternate view [that Mark was the first of the four Gospels] see "Sources" under the *Introduction* to Mark.)

The Occasion for Writing the First Gospel. Though the precise occasion for the writing of this account is not known, it appears Matthew had at least two reasons for writing. First, he wanted to show unbelieving Jews that Jesus is the Messiah. Matthew had found the Messiah, and he wanted others to come into that same relationship. Second, Matthew wrote to encourage Jewish believers. If indeed Jesus is the Messiah, a horrible thing had occurred. The Jews had crucified their Messiah and King. What would now become of them? Was God through with them? At this point Matthew had a word of encouragement, for though their act of disobedience would bring judgment on that generation of Israelites, God was not through with His people. His promised kingdom would yet be instituted with His people at a future time. In the meantime, however, believers are responsible to communicate a different message of faith in this Messiah as they go into all the world to make disciples among all nations.

Some Outstanding Characteristics of the First Gospel

1. The Book of Matthew places great emphasis on the teaching ministry of Jesus Christ. Of the Gospel accounts Matthew has the largest blocks of discourse material. No other Gospel contains so much of Jesus' teachings. Matthew 5-7 is commonly referred to as the Sermon on the Mount; chapter 10 includes Jesus' instructions to His disciples as they were sent out to minister; chapter 13 presents the parables of the kingdom; in chapter 23 is Jesus' "hot" denunciation of the religious leaders of Israel; and chapters 24-25 are the Olivet Discourse, a detailed explanation of future events relating to Jerusalem and the nation.

2. Some of the material in Matthew is arranged logically rather than chronologically. As examples, the genealogical tables are broken into three equal groups, a large number of miracles are given together, and the opposition to Jesus is given in one section. Matthew's purpose is obviously more thematic than chronological.

3. The First Gospel is filled with Old Testament quotations. Matthew includes approximately 50 direct citations from the Old Testament. In addition about 75 allusions are made to Old Testament events. This is undoubtedly because of the audience for whom the book was intended. Matthew primarily had Jews in mind as he wrote, and they would have been impressed by the many references to Old Testament facts and events. In addition, if this Gospel was written around A.D. 50, not many New Testament books were available for Matthew to have cited. Those books may not have been known to his readers or even to Matthew himself.

4. The First Gospel shows that Jesus Christ is the Messiah of Israel and explains God's kingdom program (Stanley D. Toussaint, *Behold the King: A Study of Matthew*, pp. 18-20). "If indeed Jesus is Messiah," a Jew would ask, "what has happened to the promised kingdom?" The Old Testament clearly taught that the Messiah would bring in a glorious utopian reign on the earth in which the nation Israel would have a prominent

position. Since the nation rejected its true King, what happened to the kingdom? The Book of Matthew includes some "mysteries" about the kingdom, which had not been revealed in the Old Testament. These "mysteries" show that the kingdom has taken a different form in the present Age, but that the promised Davidic kingdom will be instituted at a future time when Jesus Christ returns to earth to establish His rule.

5. The First Gospel has a summary statement in its first verse: "A record of the genealogy of Jesus Christ the Son of David, the Son of Abraham." Why does David's name appear before Abraham's? Would not Abraham, the father of the nation, be more significant to a Jewish mind? Perhaps Matthew listed the name of David first because the King who would rule over the nation was to come through David (2 Sam. 7:12-17). Jesus Christ came with a message for His own nation. But in the plan of God, His message was rejected. Therefore a universal message reaches out to the entire world. The promise of blessings for all the nations of the world came through Abraham and the covenant God made with him (Gen. 12:3). It is significant that Matthew did include Gentiles, such as the Magi from the East (Matt. 2:1-12), the centurion with his great faith (8:5-13), and the Canaanite woman who had greater faith than Christ had seen in all Israel (15:22-28). Also the book concludes with the Great Commission to "go and make disciples of *all nations*" (28:19).

OUTLINE

I. Introduction of the King (1:1-4:11)
   A. Presentation by ancestry (1:1-17)
   B. Presentation by advent (1:18-2:23)
   C. Presentation by an ambassador (3:1-12)
   D. Presentation through approval (3:13-4:11)
II. Communications from the King (4:12-7:29)
   A. Beginning proclamations (4:12-25)
   B. Continuing pronouncements (chaps. 5-7)
III. Credentials of the King (8:1-11:1)
   A. His power over disease (8:1-15)
   B. His power over demonic forces (8:16-17, 28-34)
   C. His power over men (8:18-22; 9:9)
   D. His power over nature (8:23-27)
   E. His power to forgive (9:1-8)
   F. His power over traditions (9:10-17)
   G. His power over death (9:18-26)
   H. His power over darkness (9:27-31)
   I. His power over dumbness (9:32-34)
   J. His power to delegate authority (9:35-11:1)
IV. Challenge to the King's Authority (11:2-16:12)
   A. Seen in the rejection of John the Baptist (11:2-19)
   B. Seen in the condemnation of the cities (11:20-30)
   C. Seen in the controversies over His authority (chap. 12)
   D. Seen in the change in the kingdom program (13:1-52)
   E. Seen in various rejections (13:53-16:12)
V. Cultivation of the King's Disciples (16:13-20:34)
   A. The revelation in view of rejection (16:13-17:13)
   B. The instruction in view of rejection (17:14-20:34)
VI. Climax of the King's Offer (chaps. 21-27)
   A. The official presentation of the King (21:1-22)
   B. The religious confrontation with the King (21:23-22:46)
   C. The national rejection of the King (chap. 23)
   D. The prophetic anticipation of the King (chaps. 24-25)
   E. The national rejection of the King (chaps. 26-27)
VII. Confirmation of the King's Life (chap. 28)
   A. The empty tomb (28:1-8)
   B. The personal appearance (28:9-10)
   C. The "official" explanation (28:11-15)
   D. The official commissioning (28:16-20)

COMMENTARY

I. Introduction of the King (1:1–4:11)

A. Presentation by ancestry (1:1-17) (Luke 3:23-38)

1:1. From the very first words of his Gospel, Matthew recorded his central theme and character. **Jesus Christ** is the main character in Matthew's presentation, and the opening verse connected Him back to two great covenants in Jewish history: the Davidic (2 Sam. 7) and the Abrahamic (Gen. 12; 15). If Jesus of Nazareth is the fulfillment of these two great covenants, is He related to the rightful line? This is a question the Jews would have asked, so Matthew traced Jesus' lineage in detail.

1:2-17. Matthew gave Jesus' lineage through His legal father, **Joseph** (v. 16). Thus this genealogy traced Jesus' right to the throne of **David**, which must come through **Solomon** and his descendants (v. 6). Of particular interest is the inclusion of **Jeconiah** (v. 11) of whom Jeremiah said, "Record this man as if childless" (Jer. 22:30). Jeremiah's prophecy related to the actual occupation of the throne and the reception of blessing while on the throne. Though Jeconiah's sons never occupied the throne, the line of rulership did pass through them. If Jesus had been a *physical* descendant of Jeconiah, He would not have been able to occupy David's throne. Luke's genealogy made it clear that Jesus was a physical descendant of David through another son named Nathan (Luke 3:31). But Joseph, a descendant of Solomon, was Jesus' *legal* father, so Jesus' right to the throne was traced through Joseph.

Matthew traced Joseph's line from Jeconiah through the latter's son **Shealtiel** and grandson **Zerubbabel** (Matt. 1:12). Luke (3:27) also refers to Shealtiel, the father of Zerubbabel, in Mary's line. Does Luke's account, then, mean that Jesus was a physical descendant of Jeconiah, after all? No, because Luke's Shealtiel and Zerubbabel were probably different persons from those two in Matthew. In Luke Shealtiel was the son of Neri, but Matthew's Shealtiel was the son of Jeconiah.

Another interesting fact about Matthew's genealogy is the inclusion of four Old Testament women: **Tamar** (Matt. 1:3), **Rahab** (v. 5), **Ruth** (v. 5), and Solomon's **mother** (v. 6), Bathsheba. All of these women (as well as most of the men) were questionable in some way. Tamar and Rahab were prostitutes (Gen. 38:24; Josh. 2:1), Ruth was a foreigner, a Moabitess (Ruth 1:4), and Bathsheba committed adultery (2 Sam. 11:2-5). Matthew may have included these women in order to emphasize that God's choices in dealing with people are all of His grace. Perhaps also he included these women in order to put Jewish pride in its place.

When the fifth woman, **Mary** (Matt. 1:16), was mentioned in the genealogy, an important change occurred. The genealogy consistently repeated, **the father of,** until it came to Mary. At that point Matthew changed and said **of whom was born Jesus.** The "of whom" is a feminine relative pronoun (*ex hēs*), clearly indicating that Jesus was the physical Child of Mary but that Joseph was not His physical father. This miraculous conception and birth are explained in 1:18-25.

Matthew obviously did not list every individual in the genealogy between **Abraham** and **David** (vv. 2-6), between **David** and **the Exile** (vv. 6-11), and between **the Exile** and Jesus (vv. 12-16). Instead he listed only **14 generations** in each of these time periods (v. 17). Jewish reckoning did not require every name in order to satisfy a genealogy. But why did Matthew select 14 names in each period? Perhaps the best solution is that the name "David" in Hebrew numerology added up to 14. It should be noted that in the period from the Exile to the birth of Jesus (vv. 12-16) 13 new names appeared. Many scholars feel that Jeconiah (v. 12), though repeated from verse 11, provides the 14th name in this final period.

Matthew's genealogy answered the important question a Jew would rightfully ask about anyone who claimed to be King of the Jews. Is He a descendant of David through the rightful line of succession? Matthew answered yes!

B. Presentation by advent (1:18–2:23) (Luke 2:1-7)

1. HIS ORIGIN (1:18-23)

1:18-23. The fact that Jesus was born "of Mary" only, as indicated in the genealogical record (v. 16), demanded

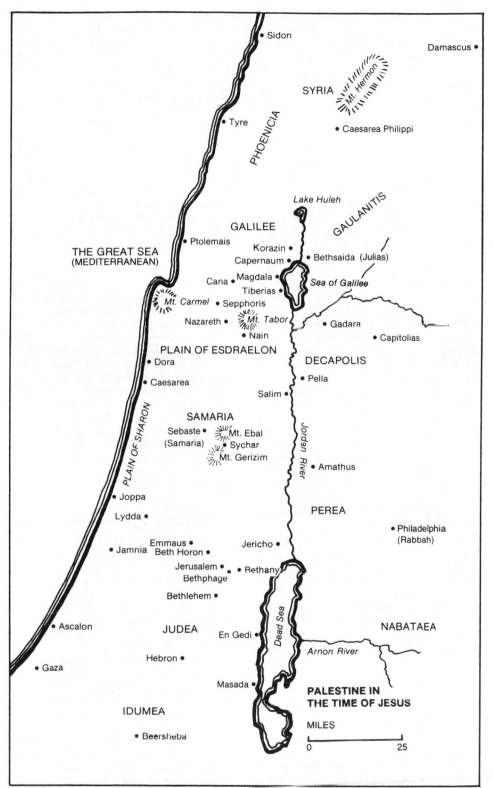

Sidon

Damascus ●

SYRIA

Mt. Hermon

● Tyre

PHOENICIA

● Caesarea Philippi

Lake Huleh

GALILEE

GAULANITIS

THE GREAT SEA
(MEDITERRANEAN)

● Ptolemais

Korazin ●
Capernaum ●

● Bethsaida (Julias)

Cana ● ● Magdala
Tiberias ●

Sea of Galilee

Mt. Carmel ● Sepphoris

Nazareth ● Mt. Tabor

● Nain

● Gadara

● Capitolias

PLAIN OF ESDRAELON

● Dora

DECAPOLIS

● Caesarea

● Pella

Salim ●

PLAIN OF SHARON

SAMARIA

Sebaste ● Mt. Ebal
(Samaria) ● Sychar
Mt. Gerizim

Jordan River

● Amathus

● Joppa

PEREA

Lydda ●

● Philadelphia
(Rabbah)

Emmaus ●
● Jamnia Beth Horon ●

Jericho ●

Jerusalem ●
Bethphage

● Bethany

Bethlehem ●

Dead Sea

● Ascalon

JUDEA

En Gedi ●

NABATAEA

Hebron ●

Arnon River

● Gaza

Masada ●

**PALESTINE IN
THE TIME OF JESUS**

IDUMEA

MILES

● Beersheba

0   25

further explanation. Matthew's explanation can best be understood in the light of Hebrew marriage customs. Marriages were arranged for individuals by parents, and contracts were negotiated. After this was accomplished, the individuals were considered married and were called husband and wife. They did not, however, begin to live together. Instead, the woman continued to live with her parents and the man with his for one year. The waiting period was to demonstrate the faithfulness of the pledge of purity given concerning the bride. If she was found to be with child in this period, she obviously was not pure, but had been involved in an unfaithful sexual relationship. Therefore the marriage could be annulled. If, however, the one-year waiting period demonstrated the purity of the bride, the husband would then go to the house of the bride's parents and in a grand processional march lead his bride back to his home. There they would begin to live together as husband and wife and consummate their marriage physically. Matthew's story should be read with this background in mind.

Mary and Joseph were in the one-year waiting period when Mary **was found to be with child.** They had never had sexual intercourse and Mary herself had been faithful (vv. 20, 23). While little is said about Joseph, one can imagine how his heart must have broken. He genuinely loved Mary, and yet the word came that she was pregnant. His love for her was demonstrated by his actions. He chose not to create a public scandal by exposing her condition to the judges at the city gate. Such an act could have resulted in Mary's death by stoning (Deut. 22:23-24). Instead he decided **to divorce her quietly.**

Then **in a dream** (cf. Matt. 2:13, 19, 22), **an angel** told **Joseph** that Mary's condition was not caused by a man, but through **the Holy Spirit** (1:20; cf. v. 18). The Child Mary carried in her womb was a unique Child, for He would be **a Son** whom Joseph should **name Jesus** for **He would save His people from their sins.** These words must have brought to Joseph's mind the promises of God to provide salvation through the New Covenant (Jer. 31:31-37). The unnamed angel also told Joseph that this was in keeping with God's eternal plan, for the

Prophet Isaiah had declared 700 years before that **the virgin will be with Child** (Matt. 1:23; Isa. 7:14). While Old Testament scholars dispute whether the Hebrew *'almâh* should be rendered "young woman" or "virgin," God clearly intended it here to mean virgin (as implied by the Gr. word *parthenos*). Mary's miraculous conception fulfilled Isaiah's prophecy, and her **Son** would truly be **Immanuel . . . God with us.** In light of this declaration **Joseph** was not to **be afraid** to take **Mary** into his **home** (Matt. 1:20). There would be misunderstanding in the community and much gossip at the well, but Joseph knew the true story of Mary's pregnancy and God's will for his life.

2. HIS BIRTH (1:24-25)

1:24-25. As soon as **Joseph** awakened from this dream, he obeyed. He violated all custom by immediately taking **Mary** into his **home** rather than waiting till the one-year time period of betrothal had passed. Joseph was probably thinking of what would be best for Mary in her condition. He brought her home and began to care and provide for her. But there was **no** sexual relationship between them **until** after the **birth** of this Child, Jesus. Matthew simply noted the birth of the Child and the fact that He was named **Jesus,** whereas Luke, the physician (Col. 4:14), recorded several details surrounding the birth (Luke 2:1-7).

3. HIS INFANCY (CHAP. 2)

a. In Bethlehem (2:1-12)

2:1-2. Though not all scholars agree on the timing of the arrival of the **Magi from the East,** they apparently came some time **after** the birth of **Jesus.** Jesus and Mary and Joseph, though still in Bethlehem, were now in a house (v. 11), and Jesus was called a Child (*paidion*, vv. 9, 11) rather than a newborn Infant (*brephos*, Luke 2:12).

The exact identity of the Magi is impossible to determine, though several ideas have been suggested. They have been given traditional names and identified as representatives of the three groups of peoples that descended from Noah's sons, Shem, Ham, and Japheth. More likely they were Gentiles of high position from a country, perhaps Parthia, northeast of Babylon, who were given a special

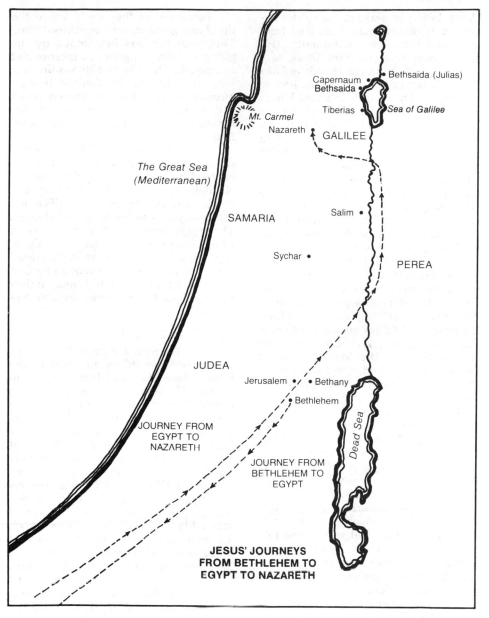

The Great Sea
(Mediterranean)

Bethsaida (Julias)

Capernaum
Bethsaida

Tiberias • *Sea of Galilee*

Mt. Carmel

Nazareth

GALILEE

SAMARIA

Salim •

Sychar •

PEREA

JUDEA

Jerusalem •/ • Bethany

• Bethlehem

JOURNEY FROM
EGYPT TO
NAZARETH

JOURNEY FROM
BETHLEHEM TO
EGYPT

Dead Sea

**JESUS' JOURNEYS
FROM BETHLEHEM TO
EGYPT TO NAZARETH**

revelation by God of the birth of the **King of the Jews.** This special revelation may simply have been in the sky, as might be indicated by their title "Magi" (specialists in astronomy) and by the fact they referred to a **star** which they **saw.** Or this revelation could have come through some contact with Jewish scholars who had migrated to the East with copies of Old Testament manuscripts. Many feel the Magi's comments reflected a knowledge of Balaam's prophecy concerning the

"star" that would "come out of Jacob" (Num. 24:17). Whatever the source, they came to Jerusalem **to worship** the new-born King of the Jews. (According to tradition three Magi traveled to Bethlehem. But the Bible does not say how many there were.)

2:3-8. It is no surprise that **King Herod . . . was disturbed** when the Magi came to **Jerusalem** looking for the One who had been "born King" (v. 2). Herod was not the rightful king from the line of

David. In fact he was not even a descendant of Jacob, but was descended from Esau and thus was an Edomite. (He reigned over Palestine from 37 B.C. to 4 B.C. See the chart on the Herods at Luke 1:5.) This fact caused most of the Jews to hate him and never truly to accept him as king, even though he did much for the country. If someone had been rightfully born king, then Herod's job was in jeopardy. He therefore **called** the Jewish scholars **together** and inquired **where the Christ was to be born** (Matt. 2:4). Interestingly Herod connected the One "born king of the Jews" (v. 2) with "the Christ," the Messiah. Obviously Israel had a messianic hope and believed that the Messiah would be born.

The answer to Herod's question was simple, because Micah **the prophet** had given the precise location centuries before: the Messiah would be born in **Bethlehem** (Micah 5:2). This answer from **the people's chief priests and teachers of the Law** (scribes, KJV) was apparently carried back to **the Magi** by **Herod** himself. Then Herod asked them when they had first seen their **star** (Matt. 2:7). This became critical later in the account (v. 16); it showed that Herod was already contemplating a plan to get rid of this young King. He also instructed the Magi to return and tell him the location of this King so that he might come **and worship Him.** That was not, however, what he had in mind.

2:9-12. The journey of the Magi from Jerusalem wrought a further miracle. **The star they had seen in the East** now reappeared and led them to a specific **house** in Bethlehem where they found **the Child** Jesus. Bethlehem is about five miles south of Jerusalem. "Stars" (i.e., planets) naturally travel from east to west across the heavens, not from north to south. Could it be that "the star" which the Magi saw and which led them to a specific house was the Shekinah glory of God? That same glory had led the children of Israel through the wilderness for 40 years as a pillar of fire and cloud. Perhaps this was what they saw in the East, and for want of a better term they called it a "star." All other efforts to explain this star are inadequate (such as a conjunction of Jupiter, Saturn, and Mars; a supernova; a comet; etc.).

Nevertheless they were led to the Child and going in, they **worshiped Him.** Their worship was heightened by the giving of **gifts . . . gold . . . incense and . . . myrrh.** These were gifts worthy of a king and this act by Gentile leaders pictures the wealth of the nations which will someday be completely given to the Messiah (Isa. 60:5, 11; 61:6; 66:20; Zeph. 3:10; Hag. 2:7-8).

Some believe the gifts had further significance by reflecting on the character of this Child's life. Gold might represent His deity or purity, incense the fragrance of His life, and myrrh His sacrifice and death (myrrh was used for embalming). These gifts were obviously the means by which Joseph took his family to Egypt and sustained them there until Herod died. The wise men were **warned** by God **not to** return and report **to Herod,** so **they returned to their** homes **by another route.**

b. In Egypt (2:13-18)

2:13-15. After the visit of the Magi, Joseph was warned by **an angel of the Lord** to take Mary and Jesus and flee **to Egypt.** This warning was given **in a dream** (the second of Joseph's four dreams: 1:20; 2:13, 19, 22). The reason was **Herod** would be searching **for the Child to kill Him.** Under cover of darkness, Joseph obeyed, and his family **left** Bethlehem (see map) and journeyed into **Egypt.** Why Egypt? The Messiah was sent to and returned from Egypt so that the prophet's words, **Out of Egypt I called My Son,** might be **fulfilled.** This is a reference to Hosea 11:1, which does not seem to be a prophecy in the sense of a prediction. Hosea was writing of God's calling Israel out of Egypt into the Exodus. Matthew, however, gave new understanding to these words. Matthew viewed this experience as Messiah being identified with the nation. There were similarities between the nation and the Son. Israel was God's chosen "son" by adoption (Ex. 4:22), and Jesus is the Messiah, God's Son. In both cases the descent into Egypt was to escape danger, and the return was important to the nation's providential history. While Hosea's statement was a historical reference to Israel's deliverance, Matthew related it more fully to the call of the Son, the Messiah, from Egypt. In that sense, as

Matthew "heightened" Hosea's words to a more significant event—the Messiah's return from Egypt—they were "fulfilled."

2:16-18. As soon as **Herod** learned that **the Magi** had not complied with his orders to give him the exact location of the newborn King, he put into action a plan **to kill all the** male children **in Bethlehem.** The age of **two . . . and under** was selected in compliance **with the time . . . the Magi** saw "the star" in the East. Perhaps this time reference also indicated that when the Magi visited Jesus, He was under two years of age.

This slaughter of the male children is mentioned only here in the biblical record. Even the Jewish historian Josephus (A.D. 37–?100) did not mention this dastardly deed of putting to death innocent babies and young children. But it is not surprising that he and other secular historians overlooked the death of a few Hebrew children in an insignificant village, for Herod's infamous crimes were many. He put to death several of his own children and some of his wives whom he thought were plotting against him. Emperor Augustus reportedly said it was better to be Herod's sow than his son, for his sow had a better chance of surviving in a Jewish community. In the Greek language, as in English, there is only one letter difference between the words "sow" (*huos*) and "son" (*huios*).

This event too was said to be the fulfillment of a prophecy by **Jeremiah.** This statement (Jer. 31:15) referred initially to the **weeping** of the nation as a result of the death of **children** at the time of the Babylonian Captivity (586 B.C.). But the parallel to the situation at this time was obvious, for again children were being slaughtered at the hands of non-Jews. Also, Rachel's tomb was near Bethlehem and Rachel was considered by many to be the mother of the nation. That is why she was seen weeping over these children's deaths.

c. In Nazareth (2:19-23)

2:19-23. After Herod died . . . **Joseph** was again instructed by **an angel of the Lord.** This was the third of four times an angel appeared to him **in a dream** (cf. 1:20; 2:13, 19, 22). He was made aware of Herod's death and told to **return to the land** (v. 20). Joseph obediently followed the Lord's instruction and

was planning to return **to the land of Israel,** perhaps to Bethlehem. However, a son of Herod, **Archelaus, was** ruling over the territories of **Judea,** Samaria, and Idumea. Archelaus, noted for tyranny, murder, and instability, was probably insane as a result of close family intermarriages. (He ruled from 4 B.C. to A.D. 6. See the chart on the Herods at Luke 1:5). God's warning to Joseph (again **in a dream,** Matt. 2:22; cf. 1:20; 2:13, 19) was not to return to Bethlehem, but instead to move back to the northern **district of Galilee** to the **town** of **Nazareth.** The ruler of this region was Antipas, another son of Herod (cf. 14:1; Luke 23:7-12), but he was a capable ruler.

The fact that the family moved to Nazareth was once again said to be in fulfillment of prophecy (Matt. 2:23). However, the words **He will be called a Nazarene,** were not directly spoken by any Old Testament prophet, though several prophecies come close to this expression. Isaiah said the Messiah would be "from [Jesse's] roots" like "a Branch" (Isa. 11:1). "Branch" is the Hebrew word *neṣer,* which has consonants like those in the word "Nazarene" and which carry the idea of having an insignificant beginning.

Since Matthew used the plural **prophets,** perhaps his idea was not based on a specific prophecy but on the idea that appeared in a number of prophecies concerning Messiah's despised character. Nazareth was the town which housed the Roman garrison for the northern regions of Galilee. Therefore most Jews would not have any associations with that city. In fact those who lived in Nazareth were thought of as compromisers who consorted with the enemy, the Romans. Therefore to call one "a Nazarene" was to use a term of contempt. So because Joseph and his family settled in Nazareth, the Messiah was later despised and considered contemptible in the eyes of many in Israel. This was Nathanael's reaction when he heard Jesus was from Nazareth (John 1:46): "Can anything good come from there?" This concept fit several Old Testament prophecies that speak of the lowly character of the Messiah (e.g., Isa. 42:1-4). Also the term "Nazarene" would have reminded Jewish readers of the similar-sounding word "Nazirite" (Num. 6:1-21). Jesus was more devoted to God than the Nazirites.

C. Presentation by an ambassador (3:1-12)
(Mark 1:1-8; Luke 3:1-9, 15-18; John 1:19-28)

3:1-2. In Matthew's story of the Messiah-King, he skipped the next 30 years or so of Jesus' life. Matthew picked up the story with the introductory ministry of **John the Baptist,** the "ambassador" of the King. In the Scriptures several men were named John, but only one had the distinguishing name John the Baptist, that is, the Baptizer. While self-imposed proselyte baptism was known to the Jews, John's baptism was unusual for he was the first person who came baptizing others.

John's ministry was conducted **in the Desert of Judea,** barren and rugged land west of the Dead Sea. His message was forthright and had two parts: (1) a soteriological aspect, **repent,** and (2) an eschatological aspect, **for the kingdom of heaven is near.** The concept of a coming kingdom was well known in Old Testament Scriptures. But the idea that repentance was necessary in order to enter this kingdom was something new and became a stumbling block to many Jews. They thought that as children of Abraham they would automatically be granted entrance into Messiah's kingdom. John's message, however, was that a change of mind and heart (*metanoeite,* "repent") was necessary before they could qualify for the kingdom. They did not realize how far they had drifted from God's Law and the requirements laid down by the prophets (e.g., Mal. 3:7-12).

The eschatological aspect of John's message has caused modern-day commentators greater problems. Not all scholars agree on John's meaning; in fact even conservative scholars are divided. What was John preaching? He announced a coming kingdom, which simply means "a coming rule." This rule was to be heaven's rule: "the kingdom of heaven." Does that mean God would then begin to rule in heavenly spheres? Obviously not, for God has always ruled over heavenly spheres since Creation. John must mean that God's heavenly rule was about to be extended directly to earthly spheres. God's rule over the earth had drawn near and was about to be instituted through the person of the Messiah for whom John

was preparing the way. No one hearing John preach asked him what he was talking about, for the concept of Messiah's rule over the kingdom of earth was a common thread in Old Testament prophecy. The requirement for that institution, however, was that the nation repent.

3:3-10. John's message was a fulfillment of the prophecy in Isaiah 40:3 with reflections of Malachi 3:1. All four Gospels relate John the Baptist to Isaiah's words (Mark 1:2-3; Luke 3:4-6; John 1:23). **Isaiah** 40:3, however, refers to "highway construction workers" who were called on to clear the way in the desert for the return of the Lord as His people, the exiles, returned to Judah from the Babylonian Captivity in 537 B.C. In similar fashion, John the Baptist was in the desert preparing the way for the Lord and His kingdom by calling on people to return to Him.

John was thus **a voice of one calling in the desert** to **prepare** a remnant to receive the Messiah. His preaching "in the Desert of Judea" (Matt. 3:1) suggests that he came to separate people from the religious systems of the day. He dressed similarly to Elijah (**clothes . . . of camel's hair and . . . a leather belt;** cf. 2 Kings 1:8; Zech. 13:4). And he ate **locusts and wild honey.** Locusts were eaten by the poor (Lev. 11:21). Like Elijah he was a rough outdoorsman with a forthright message.

Large numbers of **people . . . from Jerusalem and all Judea** went to hear John the Baptist. Some accepted his message and confessed **their sins,** submitting to water baptism, the identifying sign of John's ministry. John's baptism was not the same as Christian baptism, for it was a religious rite signifying confession of sin and commitment to a holy life in anticipation of the coming Messiah.

However, not all believed. **The Pharisees and Sadducees,** who came to see what he was doing, rejected his appeal. Their feelings were summed up in John's words to them (Matt. 3:7-10). They believed that they, as physical sons of **Abraham,** were automatically qualified for Messiah's kingdom. John completely repudiated Pharisaic Judaism and said that **God,** if necessary, could **raise up . . . stones** to become His **children.** God could take outsiders, Gentiles, if necessary to find individuals to follow Him. Judaism was in danger of being removed. Unless there was productive **fruit in keeping with repentance** (v. 8), God would remove the **tree.**

3:11-12. The relationship of John the Baptist to the coming Messiah was clearly seen. John believed he was not even worthy **to carry** (or untie) the **sandals** of the **Coming One.** John was simply an introducer who was preparing a remnant for the Messiah, and who was baptizing in **water** those who responded. The Coming One would **baptize** them **with the Holy Spirit and with fire.** Those hearing John's words would have been reminded of two Old Testament prophecies: Joel 2:28-29 and Malachi 3:2-5. Joel had given the promise of the outpouring of the Holy Spirit on Israel. An actual outpouring of the Spirit did occur in Acts 2 on the day of Pentecost, but experientially Israel did not enter into the benefits of that event. She will yet experience the benefits of this accomplished work when she turns in repentance at the Lord's Second Advent. The baptism "with fire" referred to the judging and cleansing of those who would enter the kingdom, as prophesied in Malachi 3. This symbolism was carried through by John who spoke of the separation that occurs when a **winnowing fork** tosses up grain, **wheat** is then gathered **into the barn,** and **chaff** is burned **up.** John was saying that the Messiah, when He came, would prepare a remnant (wheat) for the kingdom by empowering and cleansing the people. Those who reject Him (chaff) would be judged and cast into eternal **unquenchable fire** (cf. Mal. 4:1).

D. Presentation through approval (3:13–4:11)

1. BY BAPTISM (3:13-17)

    (MARK 1:9-11; LUKE 3:21-22)

3:13-14. After years of silence in Nazareth, **Jesus** appeared among those listening to John's preaching and presented Himself as a candidate for baptism. Only Matthew recorded John's opposition to this act: **I need to be baptized by You, and do You come to me?** John recognized Jesus did not fit the requirements for his baptism, since his baptism was for repentance from sin. Of what did Jesus have to repent? He had never sinned (2 Cor. 5:21; Heb. 4:15; 7:26;

1 John 3:5), so He could not be officially entering into John's baptism even though He was seeking **to be baptized by John.** Some feel Jesus was confessing the sins of the nation as Moses, Ezra, and Daniel had done on previous occasions. However, another possibility is suggested in Matthew 3:15.

3:15. Jesus' response to John was that it was fitting for Him to take part in John's baptism at this time in order **to fulfill all righteousness.** What did Jesus mean? The Law included no requirements about baptism, so Jesus could not have had in view anything pertaining to Levitical righteousness. But John's message was a message of repentance, and those experiencing it were looking forward to a coming Messiah who would be righteous and who would bring in righteousness. If Messiah were to provide righteousness for sinners, He must be identified with sinners. It was therefore in the will of God for Him to be baptized by **John** in order to be identified (the real meaning of the word "baptized") with sinners.

3:16-17. The significant thing about the baptism of **Jesus** was the authentication from **heaven.** As Jesus came up **out of the water . . . the Spirit of God** came down on Him in the form of **a dove.** As One **went up,** the Other came down. A **voice from heaven**—the voice of God the Father—**said, This is My Son, whom I love; with Him I am well pleased** (cf. Eph. 1:6; Col. 1:13). God repeated these words about Christ on the Mount of Transfiguration (Matt. 17:5). All three Persons of the Godhead were present at this event: the Father who spoke of His Son, the Son who was being baptized, and the Spirit who descended on the Son as a dove. This verified for John that Jesus is the Son of God (John 1:32-34). It was also in keeping with Isaiah's prophecy that the Spirit would rest on the Messiah (Isa. 11:2). The descent of the Holy Spirit empowered the Son, the Messiah, for His ministry among people.

2. BY TEMPTATION (4:1-11)

    (MARK 1:12-13; LUKE 4:1-13)

4:1-2. After being baptized, **Jesus was led** immediately **by the Spirit** of God **into the desert** (traditionally near Jericho; see map) for a period of testing. This period of time was a necessary period

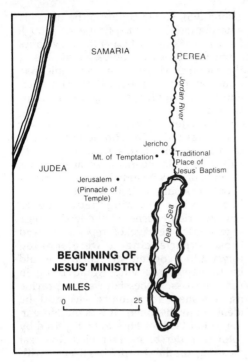

SAMARIA

PEREA

Jordan River

JUDEA

Jericho
Mt. of Temptation • • Traditional
Place of
Jesus' Baptism

Jerusalem •
(Pinnacle of
Temple)

Dead Sea

**BEGINNING OF
JESUS' MINISTRY**

MILES

0   25

under God's direction—a time in which the Son obeyed (Heb. 5:8). **After fasting 40 days,** when the Lord **was hungry,** the tests began. From God's standpoint the tests demonstrated the quality of the Lord. It was impossible for the divine Son to sin, and that fact actually heightened the tests. He could not give in to the tests and sin, but He had to endure until the tests were completed.

4:3-4. The first test pertained to the matter of sonship. Satan assumed that if He were the Son, perhaps He could be persuaded to act independently of the Father. Satan's test was subtle for since He is **the Son of God,** He has the power to turn the **stones** all around Him into **bread.** But that was not the will of His Father for Him. The Father's will was for Him to be hungry in the desert with no food. To submit to Satan's suggestion and satisfy His hunger would have been contrary to God's will. Jesus therefore quoted Deuteronomy 8:3, which affirms that **man does not live on bread alone, but** by God's **Word.** It is better to obey God's Word than to satisfy human desires. The fact that Jesus quoted from Deuteronomy showed that He recognized the inerrant authority of that book, one often criticized by scholars.

4:5-7. The second test by Satan appealed to personal display or popularity. This test built on the first, for if He is **the Son of God** and the Messiah, nothing could harm Him. Satan **took Him to . . . the highest point of the temple.** Whether this was actual or simply a vision cannot be determined dogmatically. Here Satan made a subtle suggestion to Jesus as the Messiah. In effect he was reminding Jesus of Malachi's prophecy (Mal. 3:1), which had led to a common belief among the Jews that Messiah would suddenly appear in the sky, coming down to His temple. Satan was saying, in essence, "Why don't You do what the people are expecting and make some marvelous display? After all, the Scripture says **His angels** will protect You and You won't even hurt a **foot** as You come down." Satan may have thought if Jesus could quote Scripture to him, he could quote it too. However, he purposely did not quote Psalm 91:11-12 accurately. He left out an important phrase, "in all Your ways." According to the psalmist, a person is protected only when he is following the Lord's will. For Jesus to cast Himself **down** from the pinnacle of the temple in some dramatic display to accommodate Himself to the people's thinking would not have been God's will. Jesus responded, again from Deuteronomy (6:16), that it would not be proper to **test . . . God** and expect Him to do something when one is out of His will.

4:8-11. Satan's final test related to God's plan for Jesus. It was and is God's design that Jesus Christ rule the world. Satan **showed** Jesus **the kingdoms of the world** with all **their splendor.** These kingdoms presently are Satan's, as he is "the god of this Age" (2 Cor. 4:4) and "the prince of this world" (John 12:31; cf. Eph. 2:2). He had the power to **give** all these kingdoms to Jesus at that time—**if** only Jesus would **bow down and worship** him. Satan was saying, "I can accomplish the will of God for You and You can have the kingdoms of this world right now." This of course would have meant Jesus would never have gone to the cross. He supposedly could have been the King of kings without the cross. However, this would have thwarted God's plan for salvation and would have meant Jesus was worshiping an inferior. His response, once again from Deuteronomy (6:13 and 10:20), was that **God** alone should be

Satan's Temptations of Eve and of Jesus

Temptation	Genesis 3	Matthew 4
Appeal to physical appetite	You may eat of any tree (3:1).	You may eat by changing stones to bread (4:3).
Appeal to personal gain	You will not die (3:4).	You will not hurt Your foot (4:6).
Appeal to power or glory	You will be like God (3:5).	You will have all the world's kingdoms (4:8-9).

worshiped and served. Jesus resisted this temptation also.

Interestingly Satan's temptations of Eve in the Garden of Eden correspond to those of Jesus in the desert. Satan appealed to the physical appetite (Gen. 3:1-3; Matt. 4:3), the desire for personal gain (Gen. 3:4-5; Matt. 4:6), and an easy path to power or glory (Gen. 3:5-6; Matt. 4:8-9). And in each case Satan altered God's Word (Gen. 3:4; Matt. 4:6). Satan's temptations of people today often fall into the same three categories (cf. 1 John 2:16). The One who had identified Himself with sinners by baptism and who would provide righteousness proved He is righteous, and revealed His approval by the Father. Satan then **left** Jesus. At that moment God sent **angels** to minister to His needs.

II. Communications from the King (4:12–7:29)

A. Beginning proclamations (4:12-25)

1. BY WORD (4:12-22)
   (MARK 1:14-20; LUKE 4:14-15)

a. His sermon (4:12-17)

4:12-16. Matthew presented an important time factor in his account when he noted **Jesus** did not officially begin His public ministry until **John** the Baptist **had been put in prison.** The reason for John's imprisonment was not presented here, but it was stated later (14:3). When Jesus learned of John's imprisonment, He went from **Nazareth** and settled **in Capernaum** (Luke 4:16-30 explains why He left Nazareth). This region was the area settled by the tribes **of Zebulun and Naphtali** after the conquest of Joshua's time. **Isaiah** had prophesied (Isa. 9:1-2) that **light** would come to this region, and Matthew saw this movement of Jesus as fulfillment of this prophecy. One of Messiah's works was to bring **light** into **darkness,** for He would be a light to both Jews and Gentiles (cf. John 1:9; 12:46).

4:17. When John was imprisoned, **Jesus began to preach.** His words had a familiar ring: **Repent, for the kingdom of heaven is near** (cf. 3:2). The twofold message of John was now proclaimed by the Messiah. The work of God was rapidly moving toward the establishing of the glorious kingdom of God on earth. If one wanted to be a part of the kingdom, he must repent. Repentance was mandatory if fellowship with God was to be enjoyed.

b. His summons (4:18-22)
   (Mark 1:16-20; Luke 5:1-11)

4:18-22. Since Jesus is the promised Messiah, He had the right to call men from their normal pursuits of life to **follow** Him. This was not the first time these men had met Jesus, for the Fourth Gospel relates Jesus' first meeting with some of the disciples (John 1:35-42). Jesus now **called** these **fishermen** to leave their profession behind and to begin following Him permanently. He would take them from fishing for fish and **make** them **fishers of men.** The message of the coming kingdom needed to be proclaimed widely so that many could hear and could become, by repentance, subjects of His kingdom. The calling carried with it a cost, for it involved leaving not only one's profession but also one's family responsibilities. Matthew noted that **James** and **John . . . left** not only their fishing, but also **their father** to begin following Jesus.

2. BY DEEDS (4:23-25)
(LUKE 6:17-19)

4:23. The work of the Lord was not limited to preaching. His deeds were as important as His words, for a great question in the minds of the Jews would be, "Can this One claiming to be Messiah perform the works of Messiah?" Matthew 4:23 is an important summary statement crucial to Matthew's theme (cf. 9:35, almost identical to 4:23). Several important elements are included in this verse. (1) **Jesus went throughout Galilee, teaching in their synagogues.** The ministry of this One who claimed to be King of the Jews was conducted among the Jews. He ministered in synagogues, places of Jewish gatherings for worship. (2) This One was involved in "teaching" and **preaching.** He thus was involved in a prophetic ministry for He is "the Prophet" announced in Deuteronomy 18:15-19. (3) He was proclaiming **the good news of the kingdom.** His message was that God was moving to fulfill His covenantal program with Israel and to establish His kingdom on the earth. (4) He was **healing every disease and sickness among the people** (cf. "teaching," "preaching," and "healing" in Matt. 9:35). This authenticated that He is indeed the Prophet, for His words were backed up by authenticating signs. All these actions should have convinced the Jewish people that God was moving in history to accomplish His purposes. They were responsible to get ready by repenting from their sins and acknowledging Jesus as the Messiah.

4:24-25. The ministry of Jesus—and probably also the ministry of the four men he called (vv. 18-22)—was dramatic for multitudes of people heard of Jesus and began to flock to Him. The **news about Him spread all over Syria,** the area north of Galilee. As people came, they brought many who were afflicted with a variety of illnesses and Jesus **healed them** all. No wonder **large crowds** began to follow Jesus **from Galilee,** from **the Decapolis** (lit., "10 cities"; an area east and south of the Sea of Galilee), from **Jerusalem** and **Judea, and the region across** (west of) **the Jordan** River (see map, p. 19).

B. Continuing pronouncements (chaps. 5–7)

1. THE SUBJECTS OF HIS KINGDOM (5:1-16)
a. Their character (5:1-12)
(Luke 6:17-23)

5:1-12. As the multitudes continued to flock to Jesus (cf. 4:25), **He went up on a mountainside and sat down.** It was the custom of Rabbis to sit as they taught. **His disciples came to Him and He began to teach them.** Matthew 5–7 is commonly called "the Sermon on the Mount" because Jesus delivered it on a mountain. Though the mountain's exact location is unknown, it was undoubtedly in Galilee (4:23) and was apparently near Capernaum on a place which was "level" (Luke 6:17). "Disciples" refers not to the Twelve, as some suggest, but to **the crowds** following Him (cf. Matt. 7:28, "the crowds were amazed at His teaching").

Jesus instructed them in view of His announcement of the coming kingdom (4:17). Natural questions on the heart of every Jew would have been, "Am I eligible to enter Messiah's kingdom? Am I righteous enough to qualify for entrance?" The only standard of righteousness the people knew was that laid down by the current religious leaders, the scribes and Pharisees. Would one who followed that standard be acceptable in Messiah's kingdom? Jesus' sermon therefore must be understood in the context of His offer of the kingdom to Israel and the need for repentance to enter that kingdom. The sermon did not give a "Constitution" for the kingdom nor did it present the way of salvation. *The sermon showed how a person who is in right relationship with God should conduct his life.* While the passage must be understood in the light of the offer of the messianic kingdom, the sermon applies to Jesus' followers today for it demonstrates the standard of righteousness God demands of His people. Some of the standards are general (e.g., "You cannot serve both God and money" [6:24]); some are specific (e.g., "If someone forces you to go one mile, go with him two miles" [5:41]); and some pertain to the future (e.g., "many will say to Me on that day, 'Lord, Lord, did we not prophesy in Your name?' " [7:22]).

Jesus began His sermon with "the Beatitudes," statements beginning with

Blessed are. "Blessed" means "happy" or "fortunate" (cf. Ps. 1:1). The qualities Jesus mentioned in this list, "the poor in spirit," "those who mourn," "the meek," etc., obviously could not be products of Pharisaic righteousness. The Pharisees were concerned primarily with external qualities, but the qualities Jesus mentioned are internal. These come only when one is properly related to God through faith, when one places his complete trust in God.

The poor in spirit (Matt. 5:3) are those who consciously depend on God, not on themselves; they are "poor" inwardly, having no ability in themselves to please God (cf. Rom. 3:9-12). **Those who mourn** (Matt. 5:4) recognize their needs and present them to the One who is able to assist. Those who are **meek** (v. 5) are truly humble and gentle and have a proper appreciation of their position. (*Praeis*, the Gr. word rendered "meek," is translated "gentle" in its three other usages in the NT: 11:29; 21:5; 1 Peter 3:4.) **Those who hunger and thirst for righteousness** (Matt. 5:6) have a spiritual appetite, a continuing desire for personal righteousness. **The merciful** (v. 7) extend mercy to others, thus demonstrating God's mercy which has been extended to them. **The pure in heart** (v. 8) are those who are inwardly clean from sin through faith in God's provision and a continual acknowledging of their sinful condition. **The peacemakers** (v. 9) show others how to have inward peace with God and how to be instruments of peace in the world. They desire and possess God's **righteousness** even though it brings them persecution (v. 10).

These qualities contrast sharply with Pharisaic "righteousness." The Pharisees were not "poor in spirit"; did not "mourn" in recognition of their needs; were proud and harsh, not humble and gentle; they felt they had attained righteousness and therefore did not have a continual appetite or desire for it; they were more concerned with "legalities" of God's and their own laws than with showing mercy; were pure ceremonially but not inwardly; created a rift, not peace in Judaism; and certainly did not possess true righteousness. Jesus' followers who possess these qualities become heirs of **the kingdom** (vv. 3, 10) on **earth** (v. 5), receive spiritual comfort (v. 4) and

satisfaction (v. 6), receive **mercy** from God and others (v. 7), **will see God** (v. 8), that is, Jesus Christ, who is God "in a body" (1 Tim. 3:16; cf. John 1:18; 14:7-9). His followers were known as God's **sons** (Matt. 5:9; cf. Gal 3:26) for they partook of His righteousness (Matt. 5:10).

People possessing these qualities would naturally stand out in the crowd and would not be understood by others. Thus they would be **persecuted;** others would speak **evil** of them (v. 11). However, Jesus' words encouraged His followers, for they would be walking in the train of **the prophets,** who also were misunderstood and **persecuted** (v. 12; cf. 1 Kings 19:1-4; 22:8; Jer. 26:8-11; 37:11-16; 38:1-6; Dan. 3; 6; Amos 7:10-13).

b. Their circle of influence (5:13-16)
(Mark 9:50; Luke 14:34-35)

5:13-16. To demonstrate the impact these people would make on their **world,** Jesus used two common illustrations: **salt** and **light.** Jesus' followers would be like salt in that they would create a thirst for greater information. When one sees a unique person who possesses superior qualities in specific areas, he desires to discover why that person is different. It is also possible that salt means these people serve as a preservative against the evils of society. Whichever view one takes, the important quality to note is that salt ought to maintain its basic character. If it fails to be **salty,** it has lost its purpose for existence and should be discarded.

A **light** is meant to **shine** and give direction. Individuals Jesus described in verses 3-10 would obviously radiate and point others to the proper path. Their influence would be evident, like **a city on a hill** or **a lamp . . . on its stand.** A concealed lamp, placed **under a bowl** (a clay container for measuring grain) would be useless. Light-radiating people live so that others **see** their **good deeds** and give praise not to them but to their **Father in heaven.** (V. 16 includes the first of 15 references by Jesus in the Sermon on the Mount to God as "your [or 'our' or 'My'] Father in heaven," "your heavenly Father," "your Father." Also see vv. 45, 48; 6:1, 4, 6, 8-9, 14-15, 18, 26, 32; 7:11, 21. One who stands in God's righteousness by faith in Him has an intimate spiritual relationship to Him, like that of a child to his loving father.)

2. THE SUBSTANCE OF HIS MESSAGE (5:17-20)

5:17-20. This section presents the heart of Jesus' message, for it demonstrates His relationship to the Law of God. Jesus was not presenting a rival system to the Law of Moses and the words of the Prophets, but a true fulfillment of **the Law** and **the Prophets**—in contrast with the Pharisees' traditions. "The Law and the Prophets" refer to the entire Old Testament (cf. 7:12; 11:13; 22:40; Luke 16:16; Acts 13:15; 24:14; 28:23; Rom. 3:21). **I tell you the truth** is literally, "Surely (or Verily, KJV) I say to you." "Surely" renders the word "Amen" (Gr. *amēn*, transliterated from the Heb. *'āman*, "to be firm, true"). This expression, "I tell you the truth," points to a solemn declaration that the hearers should note. It occurs 31 times in Matthew alone. (In the Gospel of John this Gr. word always occurs twice: "Amen, Amen." Cf. comments on John 1:51.)

Jesus' fulfillment would extend to the **smallest** Hebrew **letter,** the "jot" (lit., *yôd*), and even to the smallest **stroke** of a Hebrew letter, the "tittle." In English a jot would correspond to the dot above the letter "i" (and look like an apostrophe), and a tittle would be seen in the difference between a "P" and an "R". The small angled line that completes the "R" is like a tittle. These things are important because letters make up words and even a slight change in a letter might change the meaning of a word. Jesus said He would **fulfill** the **Law** by obeying it perfectly and would fulfill the prophets' predictions of the Messiah and His kingdom. But the responsibility of the people was made clear. The **righteousness** they were currently seeking—**that of the Pharisees and the teachers of the Law**—was insufficient for entrance into **the kingdom** Jesus was offering. The righteousness He demanded was not merely external; it was a true inner righteousness based on faith in God's Word (Rom. 3:21-22). This is clear from what follows.

3. THE SUBSTANTIATION OF HIS MESSAGE (5:21-7:6)

a. Rejection of Pharisaic traditions (5:21-48)

Jesus rejected the traditions of the Pharisees (vv. 21-48) and their practices (6:1-7:6). Six times Jesus said, "You have heard that it was said. . . . But I tell you" (5:21-22, 27-28, 31-32, 33-34, 38-39, 43-44). These words make it clear that Jesus was presenting (a) what the Pharisees and teachers of the Law were saying to the people and, by contrast, (b) what God's true intent of the Law was. This spelled out His statement (v. 20) that Pharisaic righteousness is not enough to gain entrance into the coming kingdom.

5:21-26. Jesus' first illustration pertained to an important commandment, **Do not murder** (Ex. 20:13). The Pharisees taught that murder consists of taking someone's life. But the Lord said the commandment extended not only to the act itself but also to the internal attitude behind the act. Of course, murder is wrong, but the anger prompting the act is also as wrong as plunging in a knife. Furthermore, becoming **angry** and assuming a position of superiority over another by calling him a derogatory name (such as the Aram. **Raca** or **You fool!**) demonstrates sinfulness of the heart. A person with such a sinful heart obviously is a sinner and therefore is headed for **the fire of hell** ("hell" is lit., "Gehenna"; cf. Matt. 5:29-30; 10:28; 18:9; 23:15, 33; 7 of the 11 references to Gehenna are in Matt.). "Gehenna" means valley of Hinnom, the valley south of Jerusalem where a continually burning fire consumed the city refuse. This became an apt name for the eternal punishment of the wicked.

Such wrongful attitudes should be dealt with and made right. Reconciliation between brothers must be accomplished whether the "innocent" (5:23-24) or the "offending" (vv. 25-26) brother takes the first step. Without such reconciliation, gifts presented **at the altar** mean nothing: Even **on the way** to a **court** trial a defendant should seek to clear up any such problem. Otherwise the Sanhedrin, the Jewish court of 70 members, would send him to **prison** and he would be penniless.

5:27-30. A second practical illustration dealt with the problem of **adultery** (Ex. 20:14). Once again the Pharisees' teaching was concerned only with the outward act. They said the only way one could commit adultery was through an act of sexual union. They correctly quoted the commandment, but they missed its point. **Adultery** begins within one's heart (looking **lustfully**) and follows in the act. The lustful desire, **in the heart,** as wrong as the act, indicates that one is not rightly related to God.

Jesus' words recorded in Matthew 5:29-30 have often been misunderstood. Obviously Jesus was not teaching physical mutilation, for a blind man could have as much of a problem with lust as a sighted person, and a man with only one **hand** might use it also **to sin.** Jesus was advocating the removal of the inward cause of offense. Since a lustful heart would ultimately lead to adultery, one's heart must be changed. Only by such a change of heart can one escape **hell** ("Gehenna"; cf. v. 22).

5:31-32 (Matt. 19:3-9; Mark 10:11-12; Luke 16:18). Among the Jewish leaders were two schools of thought regarding the matter **of divorce** (Deut. 24:1). Those who followed Hillel said it was permissible for a husband to divorce **his wife** for any reason at all, but the other group (those following Shammai) said divorce was permissible only for a major offense. In His response, the Lord strongly taught that marriage is viewed by God as an indissoluble unit and that marriages should not be terminated by divorce. The "exception clause," **except for marital unfaithfulness** (*porneias*), is understood in several ways by Bible scholars. Four of these ways are: (a) a single act of adultery, (b) unfaithfulness during the period of betrothal (Matt. 1:19), (c) marriage between near relatives (Lev. 18:6-18), or (d) continued promiscuity. (See comments on Matt. 19:3-9.)

5:33-37. The matter of making **oaths** (Lev. 19:12; Deut. 23:21) was next addressed by the Lord. The Pharisees were notorious for their oaths, which were made on the least provocation. Yet they made allowances for mental reservations within their oaths. If they wanted to be relieved of oaths they had made **by heaven . . . by the earth . . . by Jerusalem,** or **by** one's own **head,** they could argue that since God Himself had not been involved their oaths were not binding.

But Jesus said oaths should not even be necessary: **Do not swear at all.** The fact that oaths were used at all emphasized the wickedness of man's heart. Furthermore, swearing "by heaven," "by the earth," or "by Jerusalem" *is* binding, since they are **God's throne . . . footstool,** and **city,** respectively. Even the color of the hair on their heads was determined by God (Matt. 5:36). However, Jesus later in His life responded to an oath (26:63-64), as did Paul (2 Cor. 1:23). The Lord was saying one's life should be sufficient to back up one's words. A **yes** always ought to mean **yes,** and a **no** should mean **no.** James seems to have picked up these words of the Lord in his epistle (James 5:12).

5:38-42 (Luke 6:29-30). The words **Eye for eye, and tooth for tooth** come from several Old Testament passages (Ex. 21:24; Lev. 24:20; Deut. 19:21); they are called the *lex talionis,* the law of retaliation. This law was given to protect the innocent and to make sure retaliation did not occur beyond the offense. Jesus pointed out, however, that while the rights of the innocent were protected by the Law, the righteous need not necessarily claim their rights. A righteous man would be characterized by humility and selflessness. Instead he might go "the extra mile" to maintain peace. When wronged by being struck on a **cheek,** or sued for his **tunic** (undergarment; a **cloak** was the outer garment), or forced to travel with **someone** a **mile,** he would not strike back, demand repayment, or refuse to comply. Instead of retaliating he would do the opposite, and would also commit his case to the Lord who will one day set all things in order (cf. Rom. 12:17-21). This was seen to its greatest extent in the life of the Lord Jesus Himself, as Peter explained (1 Peter 2:23).

5:43-48 (Luke 6:27-28, 32-36). The Pharisees taught that one should **love** those near and dear to him (Lev. 19:18), but that Israel's enemies should be hated. The Pharisees thus implied that their hatred was God's means of judging their **enemies.** But Jesus stated that Israel should demonstrate God's love even to her enemies—a practice not even commanded in the Old Testament! God loves them; **He causes His sun to rise on** them and He **sends rain** to produce their crops. Since His love extends to everyone, Israel too should be a channel of His love by loving all. Such love demonstrates that they are God's **sons** (cf. Matt. 5:16). Loving only **those who love you** and greeting **only your brothers** is no more than **the tax collectors** and **pagans do**—a cutting remark for Pharisees!

Jesus concluded this section by saying, **Be perfect therefore, as your heavenly Father is perfect.** His message demonstrated God's righteous standard, for God Himself truly is the "standard" of righteousness. If these individuals are to be righteous, they must be as God is, "perfect," that is, mature (*teleioi*) or holy. Murder, lust, hate, deception, and retaliation obviously do not characterize God. He did not lower His standard to accommodate humans; instead He set forth His absolute holiness as the standard. Though this standard can never be perfectly met by man himself, a person who by faith trusts in God enjoys His righteousness being reproduced in his life.

b. Rejection of Pharisaic practices (6:1–7:6)

The Lord then turned from the Pharisees' teachings to examine their hypocritical deeds.

6:1-4. Jesus first spoke of the Pharisees' almsgiving. **Righteousness** is not primarily a matter between a person and others, but between a person and God. So one's **acts** should not be demonstrated **before** others for then his **reward** should come from them (vv. 1-2). The Pharisees made a great show of their giving **to the needy . . . in the synagogues and on the streets,** thinking they were thus proving how righteous they were. But the Lord said that in giving one should **not** even **let** his **left hand know what** his **right hand is doing,** that is, it should be so **secret** that the giver readily forgets what he gave. In this way he demonstrates true righteousness before God and not before people, so God in turn **will reward** him. One cannot be rewarded, as the Pharisees expected, by *both* man and God.

6:5-15 (Luke 11:2-4). Jesus then spoke about the practice of prayer, which the Pharisees loved to perform publicly. Rather than making prayer a matter between an individual and God, the Pharisees had turned it into an act **to be seen by men**—again, to demonstrate their supposed righteousness. Their prayers were directed not to God but to other men, and consisted of long, repetitive phrases (Matt. 6:7).

Jesus condemned such practices. Prayer should be addressed **to your Father, who is unseen** (cf. John 1:18; 1 Tim. 1:17) and who **knows what you**

need (Matt. 6:8); it is not "to be seen by men." But Jesus also presented a model prayer for His disciples to follow. This prayer is commonly called "the Lord's Prayer," but it is actually "the disciples' prayer." This prayer, which is repeated by many Christians, contains elements that are important for all praying: (1) Prayer is to begin with worship. God is addressed as **Our Father in heaven.** Worship is the essence of all prayer. (In vv. 1-18 Jesus used the word "Father" 10 times! Only those who have true inner righteousness can address God in that way in worship.) (2) Reverence is a second element of prayer, for God's **name** is to be **hallowed,** that is, revered (*hagiasthētō*). (3) The desire for God's kingdom—**Your kingdom come**—is based on the assurance that God will fulfill all His covenant promises to His people. (4) Prayer is to include the request that His **will be** accomplished today **on earth as it is** being accomplished **in heaven,** that is, fully and willingly. (5) Petition for personal needs such as **daily** food is also to be a part of prayer. "Daily" (*epiousion,* used only here in the NT) means "sufficient for today." (6) Requests regarding spiritual needs, such as forgiveness, are included too. This implies that the petitioner has already forgiven those who had offended him. Sins (cf. Luke 11:4), as moral **debts,** reveal one's shortcomings before God. (7) Believers recognize their spiritual weakness as they pray for deliverance from **temptation** to **evil** (cf. James 1:13-14).

Jesus' words in Matthew 6:14-15 explain His statement about forgiveness in verse 12. Though God's forgiveness of **sin** is not based on one's forgiving others, a Christian's forgiveness *is* based on realizing he has been forgiven (cf. Eph. 4:32). Personal fellowship with God is in view in these verses (not salvation from sin). One cannot walk in fellowship with God if he refuses to **forgive** others.

6:16-18. Fasting was a third example of Pharisaic "righteousness." The Pharisees loved to **fast** so that others would see them and think them spiritual. **Fasting** emphasized the denial of the flesh, but the Pharisees were glorifying their flesh by drawing attention to themselves. The Lord's words emphasized once again that such actions should be done **in secret** before God. Nor was one to follow the

Pharisees' custom of withholding olive oil from his **head** during fasting. As a result, God alone would know and would **reward** accordingly.

In all three examples of Pharisaic "righteousness"—almsgiving (vv. 1-4), praying (vv. 5-15), and fasting (vv. 16-18)—Jesus spoke of **hypocrites** (vv. 2, 5, 16), public ostentation (vv. 1-2, 5, 16), receiving **their reward in full** when their actions are done before men (vv. 2, 5, 16), acting **in secret** (vv. 4, 6, 18), and being rewarded by the **Father, who sees** or "knows," when one's actions are done secretly (vv. 4, 6, 8, 18).

6:19-24 (Luke 12:33-34; 11:34-36; 16:13). One's attitude toward wealth is another barometer of righteousness. The Pharisees believed the Lord materially blessed all He loved. They were intent on building great **treasures on earth.** But treasures built here are subject to decay (**moth** destroys cloth and **rust** destroys metal; cf. James 5:2-3) or theft, whereas **treasures** deposited **in heaven** can never be lost.

The Pharisees had this problem because their spiritual **eyes** were diseased (Matt. 6:22). With their **eyes** they were coveting money and wealth. Thus they were in spiritual **darkness.** They were slaves to the master of greed, and their desire for money was so great they were failing in their service to their true Master, **God. Money** is the translation of the Aramaic word for "wealth or property," *mamōna* ("mammon," KJV).

6:25-34 (Luke 12:22-34). If a person is occupied with the things of God, the true Master, how will he care for his ordinary needs in life, such as food, clothing, and shelter? The Pharisees in their pursuit of material things had never learned to live by faith. Jesus told them and us **not** to **worry about** these things, for **life** is **more important than** physical things. He cited several illustrations to prove His point. **The birds of the air** are fed by the **heavenly Father, and the lilies of the field grow** in such a way that their **splendor** is greater than **even** Solomon's. Jesus was saying God has built into His Creation the means by which all things are cared for. The birds are fed because they diligently work to maintain their lives. They do not **store** up great amounts of food, but continually work. And believers are far **more valuable** to God

than birds! The lilies grow daily through a natural process. Therefore an individual need not be anxious about his existence (Matt. 6:31), for **by worrying** he **can** never **add** any amount of time, not even **a single hour, to his life.** Rather than being like **the pagans** who are concerned about physical needs, the Lord's disciples should be concerned about the things of God, **His kingdom and His righteousness.** Then **all these needs will be** supplied in God's timing. This is the life of daily faith. It does no good to worry— **do not worry** occurs three times (vv. 25, 31, 34; cf. vv. 27-28)—or be concerned **about tomorrow for** there are sufficient matters to attend to **each day.** Worrying shows that one has "little faith" in what God can do (v. 30; cf. **you of little faith** in 8:26; 14:31; 16:8). As a disciple cares each day for the things God has trusted to him, God, his **heavenly Father** (6:26, 32), cares for his daily needs.

7:1-6 (Luke 6:41-42). A final illustration of Pharisaic practices pertains to judging. The Pharisees were then judging Christ and finding Him to be inadequate. He was not offering the kind of kingdom they anticipated or asking for the kind of righteousness they were exhibiting. So they rejected Him. Jesus therefore warned them against hypocritical judging.

This passage does not teach that judgments should never be made; Matthew 7:5 *does* speak of removing **the speck from your brother's eye.** The Lord's point was that a person should not be habitually critical or condemnatory of a **speck of sawdust** in someone else's **eye** when he has **a plank**—a strong hyperbole for effect—**in his own eye.** Such action is hypocritical (**You hypocrite,** v. 5; cf. "hypocrites" in 6:2, 5, 16). Though judgment is sometimes needed, those making the distinctions (*krinō,* **judge,** means "to distinguish" and thus "to decide") must first be certain of their own lives.

Furthermore when seeking to help another, one must exercise care to do what would be appreciated and beneficial. One should never entrust holy things (**what is sacred**) to unholy people (**dogs;** cf. "dogs" in Phil. 3:2) or **throw . . . pearls to pigs.** Dogs and pigs were despised in those days.

4. THE SUMMONS TO THE LISTENERS (7:7-29)

7:7-11 (Luke 11:9-13). Earlier in this sermon Jesus had given the disciples a model prayer (Matt. 6:9-13). Now He assured them that God welcomes prayer, and urged them to come to Him continuously and persistently. This is emphasized by the present tenses in the verbs: "keep on asking"; "keep on seeking"; "keep on knocking" (7:7). Why? Because **your Father in heaven** (v. 11) delights in giving **good gifts** (cf. James 1:17) to those who persist in prayer. (Luke substitutes "the Holy Spirit" for "good gifts," Luke 11:13.) No decent father would give **his son . . . a stone** instead of a round loaf of **bread** (which looked like a stone), or **a snake** instead of a similar-appearing **fish.** If an earthly father, with his sinful (**evil**) nature, delights to do right materially for his **children,** it makes sense that the righteous, heavenly **Father** will **much more** reward His children spiritually for their persistence.

7:12. This verse is commonly referred to as "the Golden Rule." The principle is that what people ordinarily want **others** to **do** for them should be what they practice toward those others. This principle summarizes the essential teachings of **the Law and the Prophets.** But such a principle cannot be consistently practiced by a natural person. Only a righteous person is able to practice this rule and thereby demonstrate the spiritual change that has come about in his life. An individual who is able to live this kind of life obviously possesses the righteousness Jesus demanded (5:20). Such a person's righteous acts do not save him, but because he has been delivered he is able to demonstrate true righteousness toward others.

7:13-14 (Luke 13:24). Elaborating on the Golden Rule, Jesus presented the clear way of access into righteousness. The righteousness He demanded (Matt. 5:20) does not come through the **wide . . . gate** and the **broad . . . road.** Rather it comes **through** the **small . . . gate** and the **narrow . . . road.** In light of the whole sermon, it was obvious Jesus was comparing the wide gate and the broad road to the outward righteousness of the Pharisees. If those listening to Jesus followed the Pharisees' teachings, their path would lead **to destruction** (*apōleian*, "ruin"). The **narrow gate** and road referred to Jesus' teaching, which emphasized not external requirements but internal transformation. Even the Lord Jesus acknowledged that **few would find** the true way, the way **that leads to life** (i.e., to heaven, in contrast with ruin in hell).

7:15-23 (Luke 6:43-44; 13:25-27). After presenting the true way of access into His anticipated kingdom, Jesus gave a warning about **false prophets.** He referred to these advocates of the broad way as **ferocious wolves** who appear harmless as sheep. How can one determine the character of false teachers? He need only look at the **fruit** they produce. **Grapes** and **figs** do not grow on **thornbushes** or **thistles. Good** fruit trees produce **good fruit,** but **bad** fruit trees produce **bad fruit.** In Jesus' evaluation, the Pharisees were obviously producing **bad fruit;** the only thing to do with **bad** trees is to **cut** them **down** and destroy them. If they do not fulfill their purpose for existence, they should be removed.

Those hearing this sermon must have wondered about the religious leaders, who seemed to be good men, teaching spiritual truths about Messiah and His kingdom. Jesus made it clear they were not good for they were leading others astray. Even if they were doing supernatural deeds—prophesying in His **name,** driving **out demons,** and performing **many miracles,** they were not obedient to the **Father,** continually doing His **will** (Matt. 7:21). They would be refused admission to **the kingdom** because Jesus had no personal relationship with them (vv. 21, 23).

7:24-27 (Luke 6:47-49). In conclusion Jesus presented the two options open to His listeners. They were now responsible for what they had heard and must make a choice. They could build on one of two foundations. One **foundation** was likened to a big **rock** and the other to **sand.** The foundation determines the ability of a structure to withstand the elements (**rain** and **winds**). The **rock** foundation represented the Lord Himself and the truths He had been presenting, especially the truth concerning inner transformation. The **sand** spoke of Pharisaic righteousness which the people knew and on which many were basing their hopes. In storms the first would give stability; the second would result in

The Parables of Jesus

1.	The Two Houses	Matthew 7:24-27 (Luke 6:47-49)
2.	The New Cloth and New Wineskins	Matthew 9:16-17
3.	The Sower	Matthew 13:5-8 (Mark 4:3-8; Luke 8:5-8)
4.	The Weeds	Mathew 13:24-30
5.	The Mustard Seed	Matthew 13:31-32 (Mark 4:30-32; Luke 13:18-19)
6.	The Yeast	Matthew 13:33 (Luke 13:20-21)
7.	The Hidden Treasure	Matthew 13:44
8.	The Pearl of Great Price	Matthew 13:45-46
9.	The Fishing Net	Matthew 13:47-50
10.	The Unforgiving Servant	Matthew 18:23-35
11.	The Workers in the Vineyard	Matthew 20:1-16
12.	The Two Sons	Matthew 21:28-32
13.	The Wicked Vinegrowers	Matthew 21:33-46 (Mark 12:1-12; Luke 20:9-19)
14.	The Wedding Banquet	Matthew 22:1-14
15.	The Two Servants	Matthew 24:45-51 (Luke 12:42-48)
16.	The 10 Virgins	Matthew 25:1-13
17.	The Talents	Matthew 25:14-30
18.	The Seed Growing Secretly	Mark 4:26-29
19.	The Doorkeeper	Mark 13:34-37
20.	The Rude Children	Luke 7:31-35
21.	The Two Debters	Luke 7:41-43
22.	The Good Samaritan	Luke 10:25 37
23.	The Friend at Midnight	Luke 11:5-8
24.	The Rich Fool	Luke 12:16-21
25.	The Barren Fig Tree	Luke 13:6-9
26.	The Great Banquet	Luke 14:15-24
27.	The Unfinished Tower and the King's Rash War	Luke 14:28-33
28.	The Lost Sheep	Matthew 18:12-14 (Luke 15:4-7)
29.	The Lost Coin	Luke 15:8-10
30.	The Prodigal Son	Luke 15:11-32
31.	The Shrewd Manager	Luke 16:1-9
32.	The Servant's Reward	Luke 17:7-10
33.	The Unjust Judge	Luke 18:1-8
34.	The Pharisee and the Tax Collector	Luke 18:9-14
35.	The Pounds	Luke 19:11-27

Jesus' "Proverbs"

Statements

"A city on a hill cannot be hidden" (Matt. 5:14).

"Only in his hometown and in his own house is a prophet without honor" (Matt. 13:57).

"If a blind man leads a blind man, both will fall into a pit" (Matt. 15:14).

"A student is not above his teacher" (Luke 6:40).

"The worker deserves his wages" (Luke 10:7).

"Wherever there is a carcass, there the vultures will gather" (Matt. 24:28).

Questions

"You are the salt of the earth. But if the salt loses its saltiness, how can it be made salty again?" (Matt. 5:13)

"Do you bring in a lamp to put it under a bowl or a bed?" (Mark 4:21)

"Do people pick grapes from thornbushes, or figs from thistles?" (Matt. 7:16)

Command

"Physician, heal yourself!" (Luke 4:23)

---

destruction. Thus hearing and heeding Jesus' words is **wise;** one who does not is **foolish.** Only two courses of action are possible—two kinds of roads and gates (Matt. 7:13-14), two kinds of trees and fruit (vv. 15-20), two kinds of foundations and builders (vv. 24-27).

7:28-29. After recording Jesus' "Sermon on the Mount," Matthew wrote, **When Jesus had finished saying these things.** Five times Matthew wrote such a statement (identical or similar words), each time following a collection of Jesus' sayings: v. 28; 11:1; 13:53; 19:1; 26:1. These serve as turning points or shifts in the book's structure.

As a result of this sermon, **the crowds** of people following Jesus **were amazed at His teaching.** "Amazed" (*exeplēssonto,* lit., "struck out") means "overwhelmed." It suggests a strong, sudden sense of being astounded, and is stronger than *thaumazō* ("to wonder or be amazed"). Matthew used *exeplēssonto* four times (7:28; 13:54; 19:25; 22:33). Jesus had just demonstrated the inadequacies of the Pharisees' religious system. The righteousness they knew was not sufficient for entering His kingdom. The **authority** of Jesus is what amazed them, for He taught as a Spokesman from God—**not as the teachers** of His time who were simply reflecting the authority **of the Law.** The contrast between Jesus and the religious leaders was most pronounced.

III. Credentials of the King (8:1–11:1)

By word and deed Jesus Christ had authenticated Himself as the Messiah (chaps. 3–4). In a long sermon He announced the standards for entrance into His kingdom and clearly presented the way of access to it (chaps. 5–7). But the Jews still had questions on their minds. Could this One be the Messiah? If so, could He bring about the changes necessary to institute the kingdom? Did He have the power to bring about change? Matthew therefore presented a number of miracles to authenticate the King to Israel and to prove that He is able to perform His Word. These miracles demonstrated various realms in which Christ has authority.

A. His power over disease (8:1-15)

1. LEPROSY (8:1-4)

   (MARK 1:40-45; LUKE 5:12-16)

8:1-4. Significantly the first healing Matthew recorded was that of **a man with leprosy.** But Jesus had performed several miracles before that (see the list of Jesus' miracles at John 2:1-11). He **came** to Jesus, acknowledging His authority as **Lord** (cf. 7:21; 8:6). **Jesus** healed him—He **touched** the leper! (v. 3)—and then told him to **go . . . to the priest and offer the** proper sacrifice for cleansing from leprosy, as **Moses** prescribed (Lev. 14; two birds, wood, yarn, and hyssop on the first day [Lev. 14:4-8]; and on the eighth day two male lambs, a ewe lamb, flour, and oil [Lev. 14:10]). Jesus told him not to **tell anyone** before he went to the priest. Apparently Jesus wanted the priest to be the first to examine him.

Jesus said this would be **a testimony to the priests.** And so it was, for in the entire history of the nation there was no record of any Israelite being healed from leprosy other than Miriam (Num. 12:10-15). One can imagine the dramatic impact when this man suddenly appeared at the temple and announced to the priests he had been cured of leprosy! This event should have led to an examination of the circumstances surrounding the healing. Jesus in effect was presenting His "calling card" to the priests, for they would have to investigate His claims. (The healed man, however, disobeyed Jesus' orders to tell no one, for he "began to talk freely" [Mark 1:45]. Presumably, however, the man eventually made his way to the temple.)

2. PARALYSIS (8:5-13)
   (LUKE 7:1-10)

8:5-13. The second miracle dealing with disease also reflected on Jesus' authority. As He **entered Capernaum,** a Roman **centurion came . . . asking for help** (see Luke 7:2 for comments on centurions). This Gentile approached Jesus as **Lord** (as did the leper, Matt. 8:2) and requested healing for a **servant** of his. Luke has *doulos* ("slave"), whereas Matthew has *pais* ("boy"), which may suggest the slave was young. He was **paralyzed** and **suffering** intensely, and he was near death (Luke 7:2).

When **Jesus said** He would **go and heal him, the centurion replied** that would not be necessary. As **a man** who was used to giving orders, he understood the principle of **authority.** One with authority does not need to be present to accomplish a task. Orders may be carried out by others even at a distance. Jesus marveled at the centurion's **great faith** (cf. Matt. 15:28), for this was the kind of faith He was vainly looking for **in Israel.** Faith such as this made entrance into His **kingdom** possible, regardless of national, racial, or geographical residence (**the East and the West**). (Eating at a banquet often pictured being in the kingdom; cf. Isa. 25:6; Matt. 22:1-14; Luke 14:15-24.) But

those who thought they would automatically gain entrance because of their religious backgrounds (they considered themselves **subjects** [lit., "sons"] **of the kingdom**) would not find entrance (Matt. 8:12). Instead they would be cast into judgment (**thrown outside, into the darkness;** cf. 22:13). Regarding **weeping and gnashing of teeth,** see comments on 13:42. In light of this centurion's faith, Jesus **healed** his servant **at that very hour.**

3. FEVER (8:14-15)
   (MARK 1:29-31; LUKE 4:38-39)

8:14-15. As **Jesus** entered **Peter's house** in Capernaum, **He saw Peter's mother-in-law lying in bed with a fever.** Jesus' touch brought healing from **the fever,** but a further miracle was also evident. The woman was also given strength to get **up** from her bed and immediately be involved in work, waiting (*diēkonei,* "serving") **on** the Lord and the many disciples who were still actively following Him. Usually when a fever leaves, one's body is weak for some time, but that was not true here.

B. *His power over demonic forces (8:16-17, 28-34)*

Jesus was capable not only of bringing healing from physical sickness, but also of exercising power over demonic forces.

8:16-17 (Mark 1:32-34; Luke 4:40-41). As Jesus stayed in Peter's home, **many . . . demon-possessed** people were **brought to Him.** Matthew simply recorded that Jesus **healed** them **all,** in fulfillment of words **spoken through . . . Isaiah** (Isa. 53:4). His taking **our infirmities** (*astheneias*) **and** carrying **our diseases** (*nosous*) was finally accomplished on the cross in His death. But in anticipation of that event, Jesus performed many definite acts of healing in His ministry. By casting out demons, Jesus demonstrated His power over Satan, ruler of the demon world (cf. Matt. 9:34; 12:24).

8:18-27. These verses are discussed later, after verse 34.

8:28-34 (Mark 5:1-20; Luke 8:26-39). A more detailed account of Jesus' authority in the demonic realm is seen in these verses. Jesus **arrived . . . in the region of the Gadarenes.** The name "Gadarenes" comes from the town of Gadara, the capital of the region about eight miles southeast of the southern tip of the Sea of Galilee. Mark and Luke wrote that the place was "the region of the Gerasenes" (Mark 5:1; Luke 8:26). For an explanation of this difference, see comments on those two verses. There Jesus met . . . two demon-possessed men. Mark and Luke wrote of one demon-possessed man, but they did not say *only* one. Presumably one of the two was more violent than the other.

The influence of the demons on these men was obvious for they were wild, violent men, forced out of the city and living in a graveyard (tombs). The demons' two questions implied they knew who Jesus is—the Son of God—and also that His coming would ultimately mean their doom (Matt. 8:29). Rather than being forced to become disembodied spirits, the demons requested permission to enter a nearby large herd of pigs. Mark stated that this herd numbered "about 2,000" (Mark 5:13).

As soon as the demons entered them, the whole herd rushed down the steep bank into the lake, the Sea of Galilee, and drowned. Obviously, those keeping the herd were frightened and went into the nearby town to report this incredible event. The people of the town went out, and because of fear (Luke 8:37), pleaded with Jesus . . . to leave their region.

C. *His power over men (8:18-22; 9:9)*

In this section Matthew gave three illustrations to demonstrate the right of the King to ask servants to follow Him and to deny requests from those who were motivated improperly.

8:18-20 (Luke 9:57-58). A teacher of the Law (a scribe) came to Jesus and, seemingly without thinking, blurted out, Teacher, I will follow You wherever You go. Though Jesus desired disciples who would follow Him and work in His harvest fields, He wanted only those who were properly motivated. Jesus' reply to this scribe demonstrated His lowly character for He, in contrast with animals such as foxes and birds, did not even have a place where He could lay His head at night. He had no permanent home. The Lord obviously knew the heart of this person and saw that he desired fame in following a prominent Teacher. Such was not Jesus' character. This is the

first of numerous times Jesus referred to Himself or was called by others the Son of Man (29 times in Matt., 14 in Mark, 24 in Luke, 13 in John). It points to Jesus as the Messiah (cf. Dan. 7:13-14).

8:21-22 (Luke 9:59-60). A second man, already a disciple of Jesus, requested that he be permitted to return home and bury his father. This man's father was not dead or even at the point of death. This disciple was simply saying he wanted to return home and wait until his father died. Then he would return and follow Jesus. His request demonstrated he felt discipleship was something he could pick up or lay down at will. He put material concerns ahead of Jesus, for he apparently wanted to receive the estate when his father died.

Jesus' response, Let the dead bury their own dead, showed that following Him carried with it the highest priority. Jesus said that the physically dead could be cared for by those who are spiritually dead.

8:23–9:8. These verses are discussed after 9:9.

9:9 (Mark 2:13-14; Luke 5:27-28). While it is not clear from either of the two preceding illustrations whether those men did follow Jesus, the third illustration is perfectly clear. The Lord met a man named Matthew sitting in a tax collector's booth. He collected taxes on customs paid at ports, in this case, Capernaum. To him Jesus issued the command, Follow Me. Immediately Matthew got up and began following Jesus. As King, Jesus had the right to select His disciples. Matthew was no doubt profoundly impressed with Jesus' person, teaching, and authority.

D. *His power over nature (8:23-27)*
(Mark 4:35-41; Luke 8:22-25)

8:23-27. Another realm over which Jesus has authority is nature. This was proved as Jesus and His disciples started across the Sea of Galilee, a sea notorious for sudden storms that swept across it. However, in the midst of a furious storm (lit., "great earthquake," i.e., great turbulence), Jesus was asleep. The disciples, fearful of imminent death, awakened Jesus. First He rebuked them: You of little faith (cf. 6:30), why are you so afraid? Then He . . . rebuked the winds and the waves and there was absolute **calm.** His disciples who were seasoned fishermen had been through storms on this sea that had suddenly ceased. But after the wind would pass, the waves would continue to chop for a while. No wonder Matthew recorded their amazement as they wondered **what kind of Man** He **is.** They **were amazed** (*ethaumasan;* cf. 9:33) at the supernatural character of the One whose rebuke was sufficient to bring nature into perfect peace. This the Messiah will do when He institutes His kingdom, as He did when He revealed Himself to His disciples.

8:28-34. See comments on these verses under "B. His power over demonic forces (8:16-17, 28-34)."

E. His power to forgive (9:1-8) (Mark 2:1-12; Luke 5:17-26)

9:1-8. Returning from the eastern side of the Sea of Galilee, **Jesus** went **to His own town,** Capernaum. There the faith of **some men** was evident when **a paralytic, lying on a mat** was brought to Jesus. Mark explained that four men lowered him through the roof (Mark 2:3-4). Several religious leaders were present and heard **Jesus** tell this man, **Take heart, son; your sins are forgiven.** (The words "Take heart" are from the Gr. word *tharseō*, used here for the first of seven times in the NT [Matt. 9:2, 22; 14:27; Mark 6:50; 10:49; John 16:33; Acts 23:11]. It means "to take courage or cheer up.") Apparently the illness had resulted from his sin. Jesus was claiming divine authority, for only God can forgive sins (Mark 2:7; Luke 5:21). The leaders stumbled over this and **said to themselves,** Jesus **is blaspheming!** This was the first opposition of the religious leaders to Jesus. **Knowing their thoughts, Jesus** asked them whether it **is easier to say** one's **sins are forgiven, or to** tell him to arise and walk. While either statement could be *spoken* with ease, the first would be "easier" in that it could not be disproved by onlookers. If, however, Jesus had first said, **Get up and walk,** and the man remained paralyzed on his mat, it would be clear Jesus was not who He claimed to be. Jesus therefore spoke not only the easier words, but He also spoke of healing, thereby proving He has power to perform both acts, healing and forgiving sin. As a result **the crowd** was **filled with awe** (this word *ephobēthēsan* differs

from the word for "amazed" [*ethaumasan,* from *thaumazō*], the disciples' reaction after the storm [Matt. 8:27]). They recognized the **authority** behind such actions, and **they praised God.**

9:9. See comments on this verse under "C. His power over men (8:18-22; 9:9)."

F. His power over traditions (9:10-17)

9:10-13 (Mark 2:15-17; Luke 5:29-32). After Matthew began to follow the Lord (Matt. 9:9), he held a **dinner at** his **house.** Since he had invited many of his associates to this dinner, **many tax collectors and "sinners"** were present. Perhaps this was to introduce them to the Savior. The Jews hated tax collectors, for they collected money to support the Romans, and tax collectors often took in more than necessary and pocketed the difference. Thus **the Pharisees,** who would never eat with such people, **asked** Jesus' **disciples why** *He* was eating with them. The Lord's response demonstrated that His ministry is directed toward those who realize they have a need: Only **sick** people **need a doctor.** The Pharisees did not think they were **sinners** (sick) so they would never have sought out the Lord (the Physician). The Pharisees always brought the proper sacrifices, but they were totally lacking in compassion toward sinners. When **mercy** is lacking, then religious formalities are meaningless (cf. Hosea 6:6).

9:14-17 (Mark 2:18-22; Luke 5:33-39). Not only did **the Pharisees** question Jesus' participation in this feast with tax collectors and "sinners," but **disciples** of John the Baptist also **came and asked** Jesus a question about taking part in such feasts. It was right for John and his disciples to **fast,** for they were calling people to repentance and to the coming kingdom. But John's disciples asked why Jesus' men were not fasting too.

Jesus answered that the kingdom is like a great feast (cf. Matt. 22:2; Isa. 25:6), in this case a wedding banquet. Since the King was now present, it was inappropriate for Him or His disciples to fast. At a wedding, people are happy and are eating, not mourning or fasting. Jesus did, however, anticipate His rejection for He added that a **time** would **come when the bridegroom** would **be taken** away.

Then He pictured the relationship between His ministry and that of John the Baptist. John was a reformer seeking to bring about repentance among those steeped in the traditions of Judaism. Jesus, however, was not out to **patch** up an old system, like sewing a new **unshrunk cloth on an old garment,** which would then **tear,** or pouring **new wine into old wineskins,** which would then **burst.** His purpose was to bring in something **new.** He had come to lead a group out of Judaism into the kingdom based on Him and His righteousness. True righteousness is not built on the Law or on Pharisaic traditions.

G. His power over death (9:18-26) (Mark 5:21-43; Luke 8:40-56)

9:18-26. In this section two miracles are described. A **ruler** (of the synagogue [Mark 5:22] probably at Capernaum), called Jairus in Mark and Luke, came to Jesus and requested healing for his **daughter** who, Luke added, was 12 years old (Luke 8:42). She had **just died,** Jairus said, but he believed Jesus could give her life. In the parallel Gospel accounts the father said she was "dying," not is "dead" (Mark 5:23; Luke 8:42). This apparent discrepancy is explained by the fact that while Jesus was speaking to Jairus, someone came from his house to tell him the girl had died. Matthew did not mention that detail, and therefore included the report of the girl's death in Jairus' request.

As **Jesus . . . went** on the way to deal with Jairus' daughter, He was interrupted by **a woman who** was **healed** as she in **faith** reached out and touched Jesus' **cloak.** Interestingly the duration of her hemorrhaging was the same as Jairus' daughter's age—**12 years.** The woman was ceremonially unclean (Lev. 15:19-30). Jesus stopped and called her **Daughter** (*thygatēr*, an affectionate term; cf. "the girl" [Matt. 9:24], *korasion*, possibly also an affectionate word like the Eng. "maiden"). Jesus said her faith was the reason she was **healed.** Undoubtedly Jairus' heart must have been encouraged by this act, for he too had faith in Jesus. On the words "take heart" (from *tharseō*) see comments on verse 2.

When the party arrived at Jairus' home, **the flute players and the noisy crowd** (of mourners, Luke 8:52) had already assembled to weep for the family. They believed the child was **dead,** for when **Jesus** said **the girl** was merely **asleep . . . they laughed.** Jesus was not denying that she was actually dead. He was simply comparing her dead condition to sleep. Like sleep, her death was temporary, and she would rise from it. **After the crowd** was dismissed, Jesus restored the girl to life. Such power truly belongs only to God, and **news of** the event spread throughout the land (cf. Matt. 9:31).

H. His power over darkness (9:27-31)

9:27-31. As **Jesus** traveled **on,** He was **followed** by **two blind men** who appealed to Him on the basis of the fact that He is the **Son of David** (cf. 12:23; 15:22; 20:30-31). This title clearly related Jesus to the messianic line (cf. 1:1). The persistence of **the blind men** was seen as they followed Jesus into a house where He miraculously **restored** their **sight.** Their faith was genuine for they truly believed He was **able to** heal them (9:28). They affirmed His deity for they acknowledged Him as **Lord.** Their sight was restored in keeping with their **faith.** In spite of Jesus' warning to tell no one **about this** event, His fame continued to **spread** throughout the **region** (cf. v. 26; 12:16). His warning was probably given to keep multitudes from thronging to Him merely for the purpose of physical healing. While Jesus did heal many from physical diseases, His miracles were for the purpose of authenticating His claims. Jesus came primarily for spiritual healing, not physical healing.

I. His power over dumbness (9:32-34)

9:32-34. As the two former blind men were leaving the house, a **demon-possessed** man **was brought to Jesus.** The demon had prevented the man from speaking. Jesus immediately healed him. When the **dumb** man **spoke, the crowd** marveled (*ethaumasan;* cf. 8:27) **and said, Nothing like this has ever been seen in Israel.** However, the religious leaders did not draw the same conclusion. They believed that Jesus was performing His miracles by the power of Satan, **the prince of demons** (cf. 10:25; 12:22-37).

**J. His power to delegate authority
(9:35–11:1)**

1. THE WORK OBSERVED (9:35-38)

9:35-38. In verse 35 Matthew summarized Jesus' threefold ministry (see comments on 4:23, with its almost identical wording). **Jesus had been going through all the towns and villages** of Israel, **teaching** and **preaching** about **the kingdom.** His **healing** ministry was for the purpose of authenticating His Person. The spectacular nature of Jesus' ministry attracted large **crowds.**

As Jesus observed the crowds, **He had compassion** toward **them.** The verb "to have compassion" (*splanchnizomai*) is used in the New Testament only by the Synoptic Gospel writers: five times in Matthew (9:36; 14:14; 15:32; 18:27; 20:34), four in Mark (1:41; 6:34; 8:2; 9:22), and three in Luke (7:13; 10:33; 15:20; see comments on Luke 7:13). Suggesting strong emotion, it means "to feel deep sympathy." The related noun *splanchna* ("sympathy, affection, or inward feelings") is used once by Luke (1:78), eight times by Paul, and once by John (1 John 3:17).

Jesus saw that the people **were harassed and helpless, like sheep without a shepherd.** Like sheep bothered by wolves, lying down and unable to help themselves, and having no shepherd to guide and protect them, the people were maligned by the religious leaders, helpless before them, and wandering about with no spiritual guidance. The religious leaders, who should have been their shepherds, were keeping the sheep from following the true Shepherd. In response to the people's "helpless" condition, Jesus encouraged **His disciples to beseech the Lord of the harvest,** namely, God the Father, **to send out** additional **workers** (cf. Luke 10:2). **The harvest** was ready; for the kingdom was at hand (Matt. 4:17). But additional laborers were necessary to complete the harvest.

2. THE WORKERS NOTED (10:1-4)
   (MARK 3:13-19; LUKE 6:12-16)

10:1-4. It is not surprising that a listing of laborers follows Jesus' injunction in 9:38 to ask the Father for laborers. **Twelve** of the **disciples** (10:1) who were following Jesus (a "disciple," *mathētēs,* was a learner; cf. 11:29) were designated as "apostles." These Twelve were specifi-

cally sent forth ("apostle" means "one sent forth to represent an official") by Jesus and given His **authority to** cast **out** demons **and** heal **every kind of disease and sickness. The 12 Apostles** were here named in pairs and probably were sent out in that fashion ("He sent them out two by two" [Mark 6:7]).

Each time the 12 Apostles are listed, Peter is mentioned first (because of his prominence) and Judas, last. Jesus had changed Simon's name to **Peter** (John 1:42). Soon after the brothers Peter and **Andrew** followed Jesus, another set of brothers—**James and John**—did the same (Matt. 4:18-22). **Philip,** like Andrew and Peter, was from Bethsaida by the Sea of Galilee (John 1:44). Nothing is known about **Bartholomew,** except that he was possibly known as Nathanael (John 1:45-51). **Thomas** was called "Didymus" (twin) in John 11:16; he was one who questioned Jesus' resurrection (John 20:24-27). **Matthew** referred to himself by his former dubious occupation of **tax** collecting (whereas Mark and Luke simply listed him as Matthew). **James son of Alphaeus** is mentioned only in the lists of apostles; **Thaddaeus** may be the same as Judas, son of James (Luke 6:16; Acts 1:13). **Simon the Zealot** had been a member of the revolutionary Jewish Zealots, a political party that sought to overthrow the Roman Empire. And **Judas Iscariot,** of course, later **betrayed** the Lord (Matt. 26:47-50). "Iscariot" may mean "from Kerioth," a Judean town.

3. THE WORKERS INSTRUCTED (10:5-23)

*a. The appropriate message (10:5-15)
   (Mark 6:7-13; Luke 9:1-6)*

10:5-15. The message the 12 Apostles were to give concerning **the kingdom** (v. 7) was identical to John the Baptist's message (3:1) and Jesus' message (4:17). In addition Jesus told them to limit their proclamation to the nation Israel. In fact He specifically told them **not to go to the Gentiles or** to the **Samaritans.** The latter were half-breeds, part Jewish and part Gentile, whose origin began soon after 722 B.C. when Assyria conquered the Northern Kingdom and moved conquered peoples of northern Mesopotamia into Israel where they intermarried. The apostles were to **go only to the lost sheep of Israel** (cf. 15:24) because the kingdom **message** was for God's covenant people.

She needed to accept her King, who had arrived. If she did the nations would then be blessed through her (Gen. 12:3; Isa. 60:3).

The apostles' message, like their Lord's, would be authenticated by miracles (Matt. 10:8; cf. 9:35). They were not to make elaborate provisions for their travel, thus avoiding the impression they were engaged in a business enterprise. Included in the list of items they were **not** to **take** was **a staff** (cf. Luke 9:3). Mark, however, recorded that the apostles *could* take a staff (Mark 6:8). This problem is solved by observing that Matthew said they were not to "procure" (*ktēsēsthe*) extra items (Matt. 10:9), but Mark wrote that they could "take" (*airōsen*) any staffs they already had.

As the apostles ministered, they in turn were to be ministered to by their recipients. In every **town or village** they were to find a **worthy person . . . and stay** with that individual. Such "worthiness" would obviously be determined by a favorable response to the message preached. Those who rejected the message and failed to **welcome** the apostles were to be passed by. Shaking **the dust off** their **feet** as they left an inhospitable place symbolized their rejection of the Jewish city as if it were a despised Gentile city, whose very dust was unwanted. The Lord said that judgment on such people would be greater than that on **Sodom and Gomorrah** (Gen. 19) when the final **day of judgment** comes. (**I tell you the truth** occurs in Matt. 10:15, 23, 42; cf. comments on 5:18.)

b. The anticipated response (10:16-23) (Mark 13:9-13; Luke 21:12-17)

10:16-23. The Lord's words to the apostles concerning the response to their ministry were not encouraging. Their task would be difficult for they would be **like sheep among wolves** (cf. 7:15, where false prophets are spoken of as "ferocious wolves"). It would be essential for them to **be as shrewd as snakes and as innocent as doves,** that is, wise in avoiding danger but harmless in not forcibly opposing the enemy. "Innocent" translates *akeraioi* (lit., "unmixed, pure"). It is used only twice elsewhere in the New Testament: Romans 16:19 and Philippians 2:15. In carrying out their ministries the apostles would be taken before their own Jewish leaders and flogged (cf. Acts 5:40) and **be brought before** Roman **governors and** Herodian **kings.** But the messengers need **not worry,** for the Holy Spirit, called here **the Spirit of your Father,** would give them words to say that would free them from **arrest.**

Even if the persecutions went to the point of betrayal of family members (Matt. 10:21) and extreme hatred (v. 22), Jesus promised them ultimate deliverance. The apostles were to continue their ministries, moving from **place** to place. But even though they moved out for the Lord, they would not be able to reach all **the cities of Israel before the Son of Man** would come.

These words of the Lord probably had an application beyond His own lifetime. What was proclaimed here was more fully demonstrated in the apostles' lives after the day of Pentecost (Acts 2) in the spread of the gospel in the church (e.g., Acts 4:1-13; 5:17-18, 40; 7:54-60). But these words will find their fullest manifestation in the days of the Tribulation when the gospel will be carried throughout the entire world before Jesus Christ returns in power and glory to establish His kingdom on the earth (Matt. 24:14).

4. THE WORKERS COMFORTED (10:24-33) (LUKE 12:2-9)

10:24-33. Jesus reminded the apostles He was not asking something of them He Himself had not already experienced. In reaction to His casting out a demon, the religious leaders had claimed He was working by the prince of the demons (cf. 9:34). If they accused Jesus (**the Head of the house**) of demonic power, surely they would say the same thing of His servants (**the members of His household**). **Beelzebub** (the Gr. has *Beezeboul*) was a name for Satan, the prince of the demons, perhaps derived from Baal-Zebub, god of the Philistine city of Ekron (2 Kings 1:2). "Beelzebub" means "lord of the flies," and "Beezeboul" or "Beelzeboul" means "lord of the high place."

However, the apostles need not fear the religious leaders who could destroy only **the** physical **body** (Matt. 10:28). The leaders' true motives will be revealed in the judgment (v. 26). Obedience to God, who ultimately is in charge of physical as well as spiritual life, is far more crucial.

The message they had received from the Lord privately (**in the dark . . . whispered**), they were to proclaim publicly without fear (**speak in the daylight . . . proclaim from the [flat] housetops**), for their Father was truly concerned for them and aware of their circumstances. He is aware of the death of a sparrow which is worth so little. **Two sparrows** were **sold for a** mere **penny** (*assarion,* a Gr. copper coin worth about 1/16 of a Roman *denarius,* a day's wages). God the **Father** also knows the number of **hairs** on a person's **head** (v. 30). The apostles were instructed not to fear for they, being far **more** valuable to God than **sparrows,** were seen and known by Him. Instead they were faithfully to confess (**acknowledge,** *homologēsei*) Jesus **before men** (v. 32). This would result in the Lord's acknowledging His servants **before** His **Father;** but failure to confess Him would result in His denial of them. Of the original 12 Apostles, only one, Judas Iscariot, fell into the latter category.

5. THE WORKERS ADMONISHED (10:34-39)
   (LUKE 12:51-53; 14:26-27)

10:34-39. Jesus said He had **come** at this time **not . . . to bring peace to the earth . . . but a sword** which divides and severs. As a result of His visit to earth, some children would be set against parents and **a man's enemies** might be those within **his own household.** This is because some who follow Christ are hated by their family members. This may be part of the cost of discipleship, for love of family should not be greater than love for the Lord (v. 37; cf. comments on Luke 14:26). A true disciple must **take his cross and follow** Jesus (cf. Matt. 16:24). He must be willing to face not only family hatred, but also death, like a criminal carrying his cross to his own execution. In addition, in those days a criminal carrying his cross was tacitly admitting that the Roman Empire was correct in executing its death sentence on him. Similarly Jesus' followers were admitting His right over their lives. In so doing one would **find his life** in return for having given it up to Jesus Christ (cf. comments on 16:25).

6. THE WORKERS REWARDED (10:40-11:1)
   (MARK 9:41)

10:40-11:1. Those who faithfully served the Lord and who faithfully received these workers were promised rewards. To receive **a prophet** and his message was tantamount to receiving Jesus Christ. (Here the apostles were called prophets for they were recipients and communicators of God's message; cf. 10:27.) Therefore even **a cup of cold water** given **to one of these little ones,** these insignificant disciples of Jesus, would be detected by the One who keeps accounts. The **reward** is in keeping with the act performed. With these words of instruction, Jesus departed **to teach and preach in . . . Galilee** (11:1). With the **Twelve** having received delegated authority from the Lord, it may be assumed that they departed and carried out Jesus' instructions. The words, **After Jesus had finished instructing,** indicate another turning point in the book (cf. 7:28; 13:53; 19:1; 26:1).

IV. Challenge to the King's Authority (11:2–16:12)

A. Seen in the rejection of John the Baptist (11:2-19) (Luke 7:18-35)

1. JOHN'S INQUIRY (11:2-3)

11:2-3. Matthew had recorded (4:12) that John the Baptist had been put **in prison.** The cause for his imprisonment was stated by Matthew later (14:3-4). **When John heard** of all Jesus **was doing, he sent** some of **his disciples to ask** Jesus, **Are You the One who was to come, or should we expect someone else?** The words "the One who was to come" are a messianic title based on Psalms 40:7 and 118:26 (cf. Mark 11:9; Luke 13:35). John must have thought, *If I am Messiah's forerunner and Jesus is the Messiah, why am I in prison?* John needed reassurance and clarification, for he had expected the Messiah to overcome wickedness, judge sin, and bring in His kingdom.

2. JESUS' ANSWER (11:4-6)

11:4-6. **Jesus** did not answer John with a direct yes or no. Instead, He told John's disciples, **Go back and report to John what** they heard and saw taking place. Among the notable events occurring were **the blind** being given **sight . . . lame** people walking, lepers being **cured, the deaf** hearing, **the dead** being given life, **and the good news** being **preached to the poor.** These works would, of course, indicate that Jesus indeed is the Messiah (Isa. 35:5-6; 61:1). Those who did not miss the true character of the Lord would be truly **blessed.** Though He will ultimately bring judgment to this world by judging sin when He brings in His kingdom, the timing then was not appropriate. Israel's rejection of Him was causing a postponement in establishing the physical kingdom. But all, including John, who truly perceived the person and work of Christ would be blessed.

3. JESUS' DISCOURSE (11:7-19)

11:7-15. John's question prompted **Jesus** to give a discourse **to the crowd.** Perhaps some began to wonder **about** John's commitment to the Messiah in light of his question. So Jesus explained that **John** was not weak and vacillating. He was not a papyrus **reed** that could be shaken by every breeze that blew. Nor was he **a man dressed in fine clothes,** the kind worn **in kings' palaces.** In fact John the Baptist wore the opposite (3:4). John was a true **prophet** who proclaimed the message that God demanded repentance. In fact he was even **more than a prophet,** for he, in fulfillment of Malachi 3:1, was Jesus' own **messenger** or forerunner. Mark in his Gospel (Mark 1:2-3) combined this prophecy from Malachi 3:1 with Isaiah's prophecy (Isa. 40:3) concerning the one who would **prepare** Jesus' **way.** Jesus added that of all men who had lived on earth, none was **greater than John the Baptist.** And **yet** one **who is least in the kingdom** will be **greater than** John. The privileges of Jesus' disciples sharing in the kingdom will be far greater than anything anyone could experience on earth.

But **the kingdom** had been subject to violence and evil men were trying to take it by force (Matt. 11:12). The religious leaders of Jesus' day **(forceful men)** were resisting the movement introduced by John, Jesus, and the apostles. **Forcefully advancing** (*biazetai*) could be rendered in the passive, "is violently treated." (The verb **lay hold of** [*harpazousin*] means "to grasp" in the sense of resisting or laying claim to it on their own). Those leaders wanted a kingdom, but not the kind Jesus was offering. So they were resisting the message and attempting to establish their own rule. But John's message was true, and **if** the nation would **accept it,** and

consequently accept Jesus, John would fulfill the prophecies of Elijah. Only if they accepted the message would John the Baptist be **the Elijah who was to come** (cf. Mal. 4:5). Because the nation rejected the Messiah, Elijah's coming is still future (cf. Mal. 4:6 with Acts 3:21).

11:16-19. Jesus compared that **generation** to a group of little **children sitting in the marketplaces** who could not be pleased by anything. Like children rejecting the suggestions to "play" wedding **(flute . . . dance)** or funeral **(dirge . . . mourn)** music, the people rejected both **John** and Jesus. They were not satisfied with John the Baptist because he did not eat or drink, or with Jesus who did eat and drink with sinners. **They** said John had **a demon,** and they rejected Jesus as **a glutton and a drunkard and a friend of tax collectors and "sinners."** Though that generation was not happy with anything, the **wisdom** of the approach of both John and Jesus would be **proved right** by the results, namely, that many people would be brought into the kingdom.

B. Seen in the condemnation of the cities (11:20-30) (Luke 10:13-15, 21-22)

11:20-24. Though it was not Jesus' primary thrust in His First Advent to pronounce judgment, He did **denounce** sin. Here He specifically pronounced condemnation against **the cities in which** some of His **most** significant **miracles had** occurred—**Korazin . . . Bethsaida,** and **Capernaum,** all three near the Sea of Galilee's northwest shore. By contrast, three terribly wicked Gentile cities—**Tyre and Sidon** (v. 22), cities on the Phoenician coast 35 and 60 miles, respectively, from the Sea of Galilee (cf. 15:21), and **Sodom** (11:23), more than 100 miles south— **would have repented if** they had seen Jesus' **miracles.** Their judgment, though terrible, is less than that on the Jewish cities. All three Galilean cities, in spite of their greater "light," rejected the Messiah, and are today in ruins. Though Jesus lived in Capernaum for some time, it would not **be lifted up to the skies,** or exalted. Instead its inhabitants would **go down to the depths,** literally, to hades, the place of the dead.

11:25-30. In contrast with His condemnation on the three Galilean cities

(vv. 20-24), **Jesus** issued a great call to those who in faith would turn to Him. Jesus had previously condemned that generation for their childish reactions (vv. 16-19). Here He declared that true discipleship can be enjoyed only by those who come to Him in childlike faith. God in His **good pleasure** (cf. Eph. 1:5) had **hidden** the great mysteries of His wise dealings **from the wise and learned** (the leaders of that day) but had **revealed them to little children.** This was possible because God the **Son** and God the **Father** know each other perfectly in the intimacy of the Trinity (Matt. 11:27). ("Father" occurs five times in vv. 25-27.) Hence the only ones who can know **the Father** and the things He has revealed are those **whom the Son chooses** (cf. John 6:37).

Therefore Jesus issued a call to **all . . . who are weary** (*hoi kopiōntes,* "those tired from hard toil") **and burdened** (*pephortismenoi,* "those loaded down"; cf. *phortion,* "load," in Matt. 11:30) to **come to** Him. People's weariness comes from enduring their burdens, probably the burdens of sin and its consequences. Rather, they should come and yoke themselves with Jesus. By placing themselves under His **yoke** and learning **from** Him, they may **find rest for** their **souls** from sins' burdens. By yoking, they become true disciples of Jesus and join Him in His proclamation of divine wisdom. To **learn** (*mathete*) from Him is to be His disciple (*mathētēs*). People can trade their heavy, tiring burdens for His **yoke** and **burden** (*phortion,* "load"), which by contrast are **easy** and **light.** To serve Him is no burden, for He, in contrast with those who reject Him, is **gentle** (*praus;* cf. 5:5) **and humble.**

C. Seen in the controversies over His authority (chap. 12)

1. SABBATH CONTROVERSIES (12:1-21)

a. Working on the Sabbath (12:1-8) (Mark 2:23-28; Luke 6:1-5)

12:1-8. As **Jesus** and **His disciples** were going **through the grainfields on the Sabbath,** His disciples **began to pick** the wheat **and eat the grain. The Pharisees** immediately jumped on this "violation" of the Law (Ex. 20:8-11) and accused the **disciples** of working **on the Sabbath.** According to the Pharisees, plucking wheat from its stem is reaping, rubbing the wheat heads between one's palms is threshing, and blowing away the chaff is winnowing!

Jesus, however, disputed the Pharisees' claim, using three illustrations. First, he cited an event in the life of **David** (Matt. 12:3-4). As he fled from Saul, David was given **the consecrated bread which** had been removed from the tabernacle (1 Sam. 21:1-6), and was normally reserved **for the priests** alone (Lev. 24:9). David believed that preserving his life was more important than observing a technicality. Second, **the priests in the temple** were involved in work on the Sabbath (Matt. 12:5; cf. Num. 28:9-10, 18-19), **yet** they were considered blameless. Third, Jesus argued that He Himself was **greater than the temple** (Matt. 12:6; cf. "One greater" in vv. 41-42), for He **is Lord of the Sabbath,** that is, He controls what can be done on it, and He did not condemn the disciples **(the innocent)** for their action. The Pharisees were splitting hairs with their technicalities about reaping, threshing, and winnowing. They failed to understand compassion for people's basic needs (in this case, the disciples' hunger; cf. Deut. 23:24-25), but were intense in their concern for the sacrifices. Jesus reminded them of the words in Hosea 6:6, **I desire mercy, not sacrifice,** that is, inner spiritual vitality, not mere external formality.

b. Healing on the Sabbath (12:9-14) (Mark 3:1-6; Luke 6:6-11)

12:9-14. The first controversy (vv. 1-8) was barely over when Jesus arrived in the **synagogue.** Since it was **the Sabbath** Day, one would expect Jesus to be in the synagogue. **A man with a shriveled hand was there.** Since **the Pharisees** were continually **looking for** some way **to accuse Jesus, they** undoubtedly planted this man in the synagogue to create an incident. The Pharisees raised the question, **Is it lawful to heal on the Sabbath?** Jesus answered their question, as He often did, with another question. If one's **sheep** would fall **into a pit on the Sabbath,** would he **not . . .** lift the sheep **out** of the pit, even though this might be construed as work? An act of mercy toward an animal was perfectly in order. Since people are **much more valuable** than animals, mercy should be extended toward them even on Sabbath Days. Jesus thus removed any possible objection to what He was going to do, for Scripture did not forbid it and His logic was flawless. His healing **the man,** however, did not prompt faith in the Pharisees for they **went out and plotted how they might kill Jesus.**

c. Jesus' reaction (12:15-21)

12:15-21. Jesus knew what the Pharisees were trying to do through these Sabbath controversies. As **many** people continued to follow **Him . . . He healed all their sick** but warned **them not to tell who He** is (cf. 9:30). To publicize that He is the Messiah would only invite more opposition. **This was to fulfill** the prophecy in **Isaiah** (42:1-4), obviously a messianic passage. "It suits Matthew's argument well. First, it shows how the withdrawal of the King fits the work of the Messiah. He shall not wrangle or cry out in the streets. It is also a fitting picture of His compassion, for he will not break a battered reed or put out a smoldering wick. . . . A second argument presented by the prophecy is the divine approval of the Messiah. Though He does not cry out or engage in open conflicts, He is still God's Servant who shall carry out God's program" (Toussaint, *Behold the King,* p. 161).

The Trinity appears in Matthew 12:18 (quoting from Isa. 42:1). God the Father spoke of Christ as **My Servant,** and His **Spirit** was **on** the Messiah, who proclaimed **justice.** In Christ **the nations . . . hope** (Matt. 12:21).

2. SATANIC CONDEMNATION (12:22-37) (MARK 3:20-30; LUKE 11:14-23; 12:10)

12:22-24. Though the text does not state who **brought** this **demon-possessed man to Jesus . . . they** (v. 22) may refer to **the Pharisees** (cf. v. 14). Probably the Pharisees discovered this man and realized the difficult nature of his case. He **was** both **blind and mute,** so communication with him was almost impossible. The man could not see what someone might want him to do, and while he could hear instructions, he would not be able to respond. Jesus immediately **healed him** by removing the demon, and the man **both** spoke and saw. **The people** (lit., "all the crowds") **were astonished** (*existanto,* "were beside themselves"; cf. comments

on 7:28 on other words for amazement) and asked, **Could this be the Son of David?** In other words, "Is not this the promised Messiah, David's Descendant (cf. 2 Sam. 7:14-16) who has come to rule over us and bring healing to our nation?" While the people were asking this question, the Pharisees were concluding that Jesus' power must be attributed to **Beelzebub, the prince of demons** (cf. Matt. 9:34; on the meaning of "Beelzebub" see comments on 10:25; Mark 3:22).

12:25-29. Knowing what the Pharisees were thinking, **Jesus** defended His authority. This was one of the few times He did so, but the issue was clear. Jesus gave three arguments to answer the claim that He was working by Satan's power. First, He said if He were casting out a demon by Satan's power, then **Satan** would be working **against himself** (vv. 25-26). Why would **Satan** let Jesus cast out a demon and free a man who was already under his control? To do so would divide Satan's **kingdom** and bring it to destruction.

Second, Jesus asked them about contemporary Jewish exorcists, those who were able to cast **out demons** by the power of God (v. 27). The apostles had been given that authority (10:1) and others were thought to possess such power. Jesus was saying in essence, "If you believe exorcists work by the power of God in casting out demons, why do you not think I have that same divine power?"

Third, by driving **out demons,** He was proving He was greater than Satan. He was able to go into Satan's realm (the **strong man's house**), the demonic world, and come away with the spoils of victory (12:29). Since He could do this, He was able to institute **the kingdom of God** among them (v. 28). If He were driving out demons by Satan's power, He certainly could not be offering the people God's kingdom. That would be contradictory. The fact that He was coming to establish the kingdom clearly showed that He worked by the power of **the Spirit of God,** not by Satan's power.

12:30-37. Jesus then invited the people to make a clear decision. They must either be **with** Him or **against** Him. He gave a strong warning to those moving away from Him. Understandably some would not comprehend who Jesus is. A divine Person living among men would naturally not be appreciated fully. That was why allowances for such actions were made: **Anyone who speaks a word against the Son of Man will be forgiven.** But while the person of Jesus was not fully comprehended, the power evidenced through Him should never have been misunderstood, especially by religious leaders.

The nation, because of its leaders, was on the brink of making a decision that would bring irreversible consequences. They were about to attribute incorrectly to Satan the power of **the Holy Spirit** exercised through Jesus and thus to commit **the blasphemy against the Spirit.** This specific sin cannot be reproduced today, for it required Jesus' presence on earth with His performing miracles through the Spirit's power. If, however, the leaders, acting on behalf of the nation, concluded that Jesus was empowered by Satan, they would commit a sin that would never find national or individual forgiveness (**in this Age or in the Age to come**). The consequences would bring about God's judgment on the nation and on any individual who persisted in that view.

The contrasts Jesus made between the **good tree and its fruit** and the **bad tree and its fruit** demonstrated the choices (cf. 7:16-20). Jesus condemned the Pharisees as a **brood of vipers** who could never **say anything good** because their hearts were **evil.** People are responsible for all their actions and **words,** which will acquit or condemn them **on the day of judgment.**

3. SIGN-SEEKERS (12:38-50)

12:38-42 (Luke 11:29-32). Though Jesus had just performed a significant sign-miracle, the religious leaders asked for **a miraculous sign** (cf. Matt. 16:1). Their statement implied that they rejected the many signs given so far. In effect they were saying, "We would just like to see *one* good sign from You." The Lord suggested that signs should not be necessary for faith, even though He had given them many signs. Only **a wicked and adulterous generation** asked for signs (cf. 16:4). ("Adulterous" [*moichalis*] suggests that Israel was spiritually unfaithful to God by its religious formality and its rejection of the Messiah.)

But no more signs would **be given to** that generation **except the sign of the Prophet Jonah** (cf. 16:4). **As Jonah was . . . in the belly of a huge fish for three days and three nights . . . the Son of Man** would be **in the heart of the earth** for **three days and three nights.** (Since the Jews reckoned part of a day as a full day, the "three days and three nights" could permit a Friday crucifixion.) Of course, by giving this sign Jesus was demonstrating that they had already decided to reject Him. For Him to fulfill this sign, He would have to be rejected, die, and be buried. By the time this sign would be accomplished, it would be too late for them to accept His right to rule over the nation as King.

The generation He addressed had an unusual privilege, afforded to no previous generation. **The men of Nineveh . . . repented at the preaching of a mere man, Jonah. The Queen of the South** (i.e., the Queen of Sheba; 1 Kings 10:1-13) **came . . . to listen to the wisdom** of a man, **Solomon.** The response of the Ninevites and of the Queen was commendable. But **One greater than** Jonah and Solomon (cf. Matt. 12:6) was with this generation, and instead of accepting Him, they were rejecting Him. (The words **One greater than** should be trans. "something greater than," referring to the kingdom, for the word *pleion* ["greater than"] is neuter, not masc.) Their judgment will be certain when they stand before the Judge in the final day. Again pagan peoples were more responsive than the Jewish nation itself (cf. 11:20-24).

12:43-45 (Luke 11:24-26). This generation of sign-seekers stood condemned in the final judgment. To show what their condition on earth would be if they persisted in unbelief, Jesus compared them to **a man** who had found deliverance from a demon (**an evil spirit**), perhaps through a Jewish exorcist (cf. Matt. 12:27). After the man was delivered, he tried by every natural means to **clean** up his life and set things **in order.** But mere "religion" is never effective so the man lacked a supernatural conversion. Consequently he was subject to possession again with more serious ramifications. Instead of one demon possessing him, he became possessed by **seven other spirits.** His latter **condition** was **worse than** his former. The Pharisees

New Testament "Mysteries" (previously unknown, but now-revealed truths)

Matthew 13:11—"the secrets [mysteries] of the kingdom of heaven"

Luke 8:10—"the secrets [mysteries] of the kingdom of God"

Romans 11:25—"this mystery . . . Israel has experienced a hardening in part"

Romans 16:25-26—"the mystery hidden for long ages past, but now revealed"

1 Corinthians 4:1—"servants of Christ . . . entrusted with the secret things [mysteries] of God"

Ephesians 1:9—"the mystery of His will"

Ephesians 3:2-3—"the administration of God's grace . . . the mystery made known to me by revelation"

Ephesians 3:4—"the mystery of Christ"

Ephesians 3:9—"this mystery, which for ages past was kept hidden in God"

Ephesians 5:32—"a profound mystery . . . Christ and the church"

Colossians 1:26—"the mystery . . . kept hidden for ages and generations, but . . . now disclosed"

Colossians 1:27—"this mystery, which is Christ in you"

Colossians 2:2—"the mystery of God, namely, Christ"

Colossians 4:3—"the mystery of Christ"

2 Thessalonians 2:7—"the secret power [mystery] of lawlessness is already at work"

1 Timothy 3:9—"keep hold of the deep truths [mysteries] of the faith"

1 Timothy 3:16—"the mystery of godliness is great"

Revelation 1:20—"the mystery of the seven stars . . . is this: [they] are the angels"

Revelation 10:7—"the mystery of God will be accomplished"

Revelation 17:5—"Mystery, Babylon the Great"

and other religious leaders were in danger of that happening to them for their attempts at reformation, without the power of God, were sterile. They clearly did not understand God's power, for they had just confused the power of the Spirit with the power of Satan (vv. 24-28). Thus they were wide-open targets for Satan.

12:46-50 (Mark 3:31-35; Luke 8:19-21). As Jesus concluded His statements, **His mother and brothers** desired to communicate with **Him.** The Apostle John made it clear that His brothers (actually half brothers, born to Mary after Jesus was born) did not believe in Him before His resurrection (John 7:5). Perhaps here they were trying to attach themselves to Jesus and receive special favors through family ties. Jesus stated that true discipleship comes not through physical relationships but only through obedience to **the will of** the **Father.** Mere religion (Matt. 12:43-45) and family relationships (vv. 46-50) cannot obtain merit before God. Following God's will makes one a disciple (cf. 7:21).

D. Seen in the change in the kingdom program (13:1-52)

The previous chapter (12) is probably the major turning point in the book. The King had authenticated His power by various miracles. But growing opposition to the King climaxed when Israel's leaders concluded that Jesus worked not by divine power but by satanic power (9:34; 12:22-37). While their full rejection of Him did not occur until later, the die was cast. Therefore Jesus turned to His disciples and began to instruct them along different lines. This is one of several major discourses in the Gospel of Matthew (others are in chaps. 5–7; 10; 23–25).

1. THE PARABLE OF THE SOWER (13:1-23)

13:1-9 (Mark 4:1-9; Luke 8:4-8). As **Jesus** continued to minister to **crowds** of people, He did something He had not done before. For the first time in Matthew's Gospel, Jesus told **parables.** The word "parable" comes from two Greek words (*para* and *ballō*), which together mean "to throw alongside." A parable, like an illustration, makes a comparison between a known truth and an unknown truth; it throws them alongside each other. In the first of seven parables in this chapter Jesus told about **a farmer** who sowed **seed** in his field. The emphasis in the story is on the results of the sowing, for the seed **fell** on four kinds of soil: **along the path** (Matt. 13:4), **on rocky places** (v. 5), **among thorns** (v. 7), **and on good soil** (v. 8). So the farmer had four kinds of results.

13:10-17 (Mark 4:10-12; Luke 8:9-10). The disciples immediately noticed a change in Jesus' method of teaching. They **came** and **asked** Him directly **why** He was speaking **in parables.** The Lord gave three reasons. First, He was communicating through parables in order to continue to reveal truth to His disciples (Matt. 13:11-12a). The Lord said He was making known to them **the secrets of the kingdom of heaven.** The word "secrets" is translated "mysteries" in other Bible versions and in most of its other NIV occurrences. This term in the New Testament referred to truths not revealed in the Old Testament but which now were made known to those instructed.

Why did Matthew frequently use the term "kingdom of heaven" whereas Mark, Luke, and John used only "kingdom of God" and never "kingdom of heaven"? Some scholars answer that "heaven" was a softened reference to God by Jews who, out of reverence, avoided saying the word "God." However, Matthew did occasionally write "kingdom of God" (12:28; 19:24; 21:31, 43). And he used the word "God" almost 50 times. A distinction seems intended: The "kingdom of God" never includes unsaved people, but the "kingdom of heaven" includes both saved people and also others who profess to be Christians but are not. This is seen in the Parable of the Wheat and Weeds (see comments on 13:24-30, 36-43), the Parable of the Mustard Seed (see comments on vv. 31-35), and the Parable of the Net (see comments on vv. 47-52).

Significantly Jesus did not speak of any "mysteries" concerning the kingdom of heaven until the nation had made its decision concerning Him. That decision was made by the leaders when they attributed His divine power to Satan (9:34; 12:22-37). Now Jesus unveiled certain additional facts not given in the Old Testament about His reign on earth. Many Old Testament prophets had predicted that the Messiah would deliver the nation Israel and establish His kingdom on the earth. Jesus came and offered the kingdom (4:17), but the nation rejected Him (12:24). In view of that rejection what would happen to God's kingdom? The "secrets" of the kingdom now reveal that an entire Age would intervene between Israel's rejection of the King and her later acceptance of Him.

Second, Jesus spoke in parables to hide the truth from unbelievers. The secrets of the kingdom would be given to the disciples, but would be hidden from the religious leaders who rejected Him (13:11b, **but not to them**). In fact, even what they had previously known would no longer be clear to them (v. 12). Jesus' parabolic instruction thus carried with it a judgmental aspect. By using parables in public, Jesus could preach to as many individuals as before, but He could then draw the disciples aside and explain to them fully the meaning of His words.

Third, He spoke in parables in order to fulfill Isaiah 6:9-10. As **Isaiah** began his ministry, God told him that people would not comprehend his message. Jesus experienced the same kind of response. He preached the Word of God and many people saw but they did not truly perceive; they heard but did **not . . . understand** (Matt. 13:13-15).

By contrast, the disciples were **blessed** because they were privileged to **see** (understand) and **hear** these truths (v. 16), truths that people in Old Testament times **longed to** know (v. 17; cf. 1 Peter 1:10-11). Jesus' disciples heard the same truths as the national leaders, but their response was entirely different. The disciples saw and believed; the leaders saw and rejected. Since the leaders turned from the light they had been **given**, God gave them no additional light.

13:18-23 (Mark 4:13-20; Luke 8:11-15). In Jesus' interpretation of **the Parable of the Sower,** He compared the four results of sowing to four responses to the **kingdom** message. This was **the message** preached by John, Jesus, and the apostles. First, when one **hears** the message but **does not understand it, the** devil (**evil one;** cf. Matt. 13:38-39; 1 John

5:19) **snatches away** the Word that **was sown. This is seed sown on the path.** The next two results—represented by seed **on rocky places** that had **no root,** and by seed **among the thorns (worries** and **wealth)** that **choke it** out—speak of hearers' *initial* interest, but with no genuine heartfelt response. The seed on rocky soil speaks of a person who hears the Word but **falls away** (lit., "is offended," *skandalizetai;* cf. Matt. 13:57; 15:12) when he faces **trouble** for having expressed interest in the Word. Only the seed that fell **on good soil** had an abiding result and the production of **a crop** that increased **100, 60, or 30 times** what had been **sown.** The one who believes Jesus' word **(the man who hears the Word and understands it)** will then receive and understand even more (cf. 13:12).

The difference in these results was not in the seed but in the soil on which the seed fell. As the gospel of the kingdom was presented, the good news was the same. The difference was in the individuals who heard that Word. The Lord was not saying that an exact 25 percent of those who heard the message would believe. But He was saying that a majority would not respond positively to the good news. In this parable Jesus demonstrated why the Pharisees and religious leaders rejected His message. They were not "prepared soil" for the Word. The "mystery" concerning the kingdom Jesus presented here was the truth that the good news was rejected by the majority. This had not been revealed in the Old Testament.

2. THE PARABLE OF THE WHEAT AND THE WEEDS (13:24-30, 36-43)

13:24-30. In the second **parable,** Jesus again used the figure of the sower, but with a different twist. After a farmer **sowed** his wheat **seed,** an **enemy came** at night and **sowed weeds** on the same soil. As a result, **the wheat** and **the weeds** grew together and would continue to do so till the time of **harvest,** for removing **the weeds** early would result in destroying **the wheat** (vv. 28-29). Therefore they must **grow together until the harvest** when **the weeds** would **first** be gathered out and destroyed. **Then . . . the wheat** would be gathered **into the barn.**

13:31-35. These verses are discussed later, after verse 43.

13:36-43. As Jesus and **His disciples** came **into a house** away from **the crowd** they asked for an explanation of this "wheat and weeds" **parable.** First, He said, the sower of **the good seed is the Son of Man,** the Lord Himself. This fact is an important starting point for understanding parables. The parables cover the time beginning with the Lord Himself on earth ministering and proclaiming the good news.

Second, **the field is the world** into which the good news is spread.

Third, **the good seed** represents **the sons of the kingdom.** The good seed in this parable corresponds to the seed in the first parable that produced a fruitful crop. **The weeds are the sons of the evil one** (cf. v. 19) that had been sown among the wheat by **the enemy . . . the devil.** This condition of the kingdom was never revealed in the Old Testament, which spoke of a kingdom of righteousness in which evil would be overcome.

Fourth, **the harvest is the end of the Age, and the harvesters are angels** (cf. v. 49). This fact gives the ending of the time period suggested by these parables. "The end of the Age" represents the conclusion of the present Age before Christ establishes the messianic kingdom. Thus the parables in Matthew 13 cover the period of time from Christ's work on earth to the time of the judgment at His return. At His second coming, the **angels** will gather the wicked and **throw them into** judgment (vv. 40-42; cf. vv. 49-50; 2 Thes. 1:7-10; Rev. 19:15).

At that time **there will be weeping and gnashing of teeth.** Matthew frequently mentioned this reaction to judgment (Matt. 8:12; 13:42, 50; 22:13; 24:51; 25:30), and Luke mentioned it once (Luke 13:28). Each time it is used, it refers to judgment on sinners before the Millennium is established. "Weeping" suggests sorrow and grief (emotional agony of the lost in hell), and grinding of one's teeth speaks of pain (physical agony in hell). These are some of the many references in Matthew to judgment. **Then the righteous will shine like the sun in the kingdom of their Father** (Matt. 13:43; cf. Dan. 12:3).

In this period between Jesus' rejection and His future return He the King is absent but His kingdom continues, though in a newly revealed form. This

Age is broader than but includes the Church Age. The church did not begin until the day of Pentecost, and it will conclude at the Rapture, at least seven years before the end of this Age. This "mystery period" is characterized by profession of faith but also by a counter-profession that cannot be separated until the final judgment. This mystery period does not involve a universal triumph of the gospel, as postmillennialists affirm, nor does it include Christ's earthly reign. It simply is the time between His two Advents, before He returns to institute the kingdom promised to David through his greater Son.

3. THE PARABLE OF THE MUSTARD SEED
(13:31-32)
(MARK 4:30-32; LUKE 13:18-19)

13:31-32. Another parable Jesus presented to the crowd likened **the kingdom of heaven** to **a mustard seed.** This seed was in fact the smallest of the garden seeds known. (Orchard seeds, though smaller, were unknown in that part of the world.) Also "small as a mustard seed" was a proverb by which people then referred to something unusually small (e.g., "faith as small as a mustard seed," 17:20).

Though its seed is so small, a mustard plant grows to a great height (12-15 feet!) in one season, and is a nesting place for **the birds of the air.** Jesus did not directly interpret this parable. However, its meaning may be that the sphere of professing followers, sometimes called Christendom, which Jesus mentioned in the second parable, would have a small beginning but would grow rapidly into a large entity. This group could include both believers and unbelievers, as indicated by the birds lodging in the branches of the tree. Other interpreters feel, however, that the presence of the birds is not an indication of evil but simply an expression of prosperity and bounty.

4. THE PARABLE OF THE YEAST (13:33-35)
(MARK 4:33-34; LUKE 13:20)

13:33-35. In this fourth **parable** Jesus compared **the kingdom of heaven** to **yeast** (leaven) which, when **mixed into a large amount of flour,** continues to work till all **the dough** is permeated. Many expositors teach that the yeast here represents evil present in the interval of time between the Advents of the King. In the Bible yeast often represents evil (e.g., Ex. 12:15; Lev. 2:11; 6:17; 10:12; Matt. 16:6, 11-12; Mark 8:15; Luke 12:1; 1 Cor. 5:7-8; Gal. 5:8-9). However, if the yeast in this parable represents evil, the idea would be redundant for evil was already represented by the weeds in the second parable. Therefore some feel that Jesus had in mind here the dynamic character of yeast. The nature of yeast is such that once the process of leavening begins, it is impossible to stop. Perhaps Jesus was implying that those who profess to belong to the kingdom would grow in numbers and nothing would be able to stop their advance. This idea fits with the nature of yeast and makes sense in the flow of these parables.

Matthew added (Matt. 13:34-35) that is in keeping with Jesus' earlier statements (cf. vv. 11-12). By speaking **in parables** Jesus was fulfilling Scripture (Ps. 78:2) and at the same time was teaching truths not previously revealed.

13:36-43. See comments on these verses under "2. The Parable of the Wheat and the Weeds (13:24-30, 36-43)."

5. THE PARABLE OF THE HIDDEN TREASURE
(13:44)

13:44. In a fifth parable Jesus compared **the kingdom of heaven** to **treasure hidden in a field. A man** having discovered the treasure, then **bought that field** in order to have the treasure for himself. Since the Lord did not interpret this parable, a variety of interpretive views are held. In the flow of this chapter, it seems best to understand this to be a reference to Israel, God's "treasured possession" (Ex. 19:5; Ps. 135:4). One reason Jesus came into the world was to redeem Israel, so that He could be viewed as the One who sold all He had (viz., the glories of heaven; cf. John 17:5; 2 Cor. 8:9; Phil. 2:5-8) in order to purchase the treasure.

6. THE PARABLE OF THE PEARL (13:45-46)

13:45-46. This parable, also not interpreted by the Lord, may be linked with the previous one. The pearl **of great value** may represent the church, the bride of Jesus Christ. **Pearls** are uniquely formed. "Its formation occurs because of an irritation in the tender side of an

Parables of the Kingdom in Matthew 13

Parables	References	Meanings
1. The Sower	13:1–23	The good news of the gospel will be rejected by most people.
2. The Wheat and the Weeds	13:24–30, 36–43	People with genuine faith and people with a false profession of faith will exist together between Christ's two Advents.
3. The Mustard Seed	13:31–32	Christendom, including believers and unbelievers, will grow rapidly from a small beginning.
4. The Yeast	13:33–35	People who profess to belong to God will grow in numbers without being stopped.
5. The Hidden Treasure	13:44	Christ came to purchase (redeem) Israel, God's treasured possession.
6. The Pearl	13:45–46	Christ gave His life to provide redemption for the church.
7. The Net	13:47–52	Angels will separate the wicked from the righteous when Christ comes.

oyster. There is a sense in which the church was formed out of the wounds of Christ and has been made possible by His death and sacrifice" (John F. Walvoord, *Matthew: Thy Kingdom Come*, p. 105). The **merchant** who **sold everything he had** in order to buy the highly valued pearl represents Jesus Christ who through His death provided redemption for those who would believe. These two parables in close proximity—the treasure and the pearl—teach that within the period of time when the King is absent, Israel would continue to exist and the church would be growing.

7. THE PARABLE OF THE NET (13:47-52)

13:47-50. Jesus' seventh parable compares **the kingdom of heaven** to **a net that was let down into the lake** so that a great catch **of fish** was hauled in. **The fishermen pulled** the full net to **shore** and sorted out the **fish,** collecting **the good** ones **in baskets** and throwing **the bad** ones **away.** Jesus said this sorting represents the angelic separation of **the wicked from the righteous** at **the end of the Age** (v. 49; cf. vv. 37-43). This separation will occur when Jesus Christ returns to establish His kingdom on earth (cf. 25:30).

13:51-52. Jesus asked the disciples if they had **understood all** He told them. Their **yes** answer is surprising, for they could not have known the full implications of these parables. In fact the disciples' subsequent questions and actions proved that they did not really comprehend the parables. Jesus, however, was performing the function of an **owner of a house** who could bring **new** and **old** treasures **out of his storeroom.**

In these seven parables He presented some truths they were well aware of and others that were new to them. They knew about a kingdom over which Messiah would rule and reign, but they did not know it would be rejected at the time it was offered. They knew the kingdom would include righteousness, but they did not know it would also include evil. Jesus pointed up a new truth that the period between His rejection and His second coming would be characterized by professing followers, both good and evil. This era would have a small beginning, but it would grow into a great "kingdom" of professors. Once this process began, it could not be stopped, and within it God is maintaining His people Israel and creating His church. This interadvent period will end with a time of judgment in which God will separate the wicked from the righteous and the righteous will then enter the earthly kingdom to rule and reign with Christ. Through these parables Jesus answered the question, What happened to the kingdom? The answer: God's kingdom will be established on earth at Jesus' second coming; meanwhile good and evil coexist.

E. Seen in various rejections (13:53–16:12)

1. REJECTION IN THE CITY OF NAZARETH (13:53-58)

(MARK 6:1-6)

13:53-58. After instructing His disciples, **Jesus** returned to **His hometown** (Nazareth; Luke 1:26-27; Matt. 2:23; 21:11; John 1:45) and taught **the people in their synagogue.** On a previous visit to Nazareth, the populace had rejected His teaching and attempted to throw Him over a cliff (Luke 4:16-29). This time the people were impressed with His **powers** and teachings, but they rejected Him. They remembered Him as **the carpenter's Son** (Matt. 13:55). They mentioned four (half) **brothers** (not cousins) of Jesus, children born to **Mary** and Joseph after the birth of Jesus Christ. Three of these sons—**James . . . Simon, and Judas**—are not to be confused with three of the Twelve by the same names. The people of Nazareth refused to believe in Jesus Christ and hampered His ministry there. Nazareth's problem was the danger of the familiar for the city's residents could not see beyond the young Man who had grown up among them. Surely One so "ordinary" could not be the promised Messiah. Consequently they rejected the Messiah and **took offense at Him.** Jesus was not surprised, for He cited what has become a common proverb, namely, that **a prophet** is not honored **in his** own **hometown** and family. As a result of **their lack of faith,** Jesus performed few **miracles there.**

2. REJECTION IN THE ACTIONS OF HEROD (CHAP. 14)

a. The execution of John the Baptist (14:1-12)
(Mark 6:14-29; Luke 3:19-20; 9:7-9)

14:1-12. As the news concerning **Jesus** and His mighty works spread, **Herod** heard about Jesus and His miraculous powers. This was Herod Antipas, who ruled over a fourth of Palestine (hence the title **the tetrarch**), including Galilee and Perea. He ruled from 4 B.C. to A.D. 39. His father Herod the Great had killed the Bethlehem babies (2:16). Herod Antipas judged Jesus when He was on trial (Luke 23:7-12). (See the chart on the Herods at Luke 1:5.)

Herod concluded that Jesus was **John the Baptist . . . risen from the dead** (cf. Luke 9:7). Matthew's last reference to John the Baptist was John's sending messengers to Jesus to inquire about Him (Matt. 11:2-14). The story concerning John was now completed by Matthew. **Herod** Antipas **had arrested John . . . because of Herodias. John** had publicly condemned Herod, who was living with Herodias, his sister-in-law. She was **his brother Philip's wife** so this was an immoral relationship. **Herod** Antipas **wanted to execute John but** was fearful, for **the people** loved John and thought **him** to be **a prophet.** Therefore he only removed John from the public by placing him **in prison.** But at a **birthday** celebration Salome, Herodias' **daughter . . . danced.** She so delighted Herod **that he** foolishly **promised** her anything she wanted. Her request, **Give me here on a platter the head of John the Baptist,** was not her idea, for she was **prompted by her mother** Herodias. Though this request greatly **distressed** (*lypētheis* means to be grieved or sad to the point of distress; cf. 18:31; 19:22) Herod, he was caught in a trap for his **oath** was at stake (14:9). So he **granted** the wish and **John** was **beheaded.**

John's disciples gave his **body** a decent burial, and reported to **Jesus** what had happened. Herod's act was another illustration of the rejection of Jesus, for Matthew so connected the ministries of these two men that what happened to one was viewed as having a direct effect on the other. Herod, by rejecting the King's forerunner, was rejecting the King who followed him.

b. The exit of Jesus (14:13-36)

When Jesus learned of John the Baptist's death, He withdrew with His disciples to a remote place. From this time on, the ministry of Jesus was directed primarily toward His disciples. His goal seemed to be to instruct them in light of the fact that He would be leaving them. He said almost nothing more to the nation to convince them He is the Messiah.

53

14:13-21 (Mark 6:30-44; Luke 9:10-17; John 6:1-14). The people anticipated where **Jesus** and His disciples were going. **The crowds,** by walking along the north shore of the Sea of Galilee, joined Jesus. Feeling **compassion** (*esplanchnisthē;* cf. comments on Matt. 9:36), **Jesus . . . healed their sick.** When **evening** came, **the disciples** wanted to **send the crowds away** for there were no supplies in that **remote place** (cf. **a solitary place,** 14:13) to feed so many people. But the Lord said, **They do not need to go away. You give them something to eat.** However, they had **only five loaves of bread and two fish.** With these elements in Jesus' hands, a miracle occurred. The bread and fish continually multiplied so that **all** present **ate and were satisfied.** More than enough was available, for **12 basketfuls of broken pieces . . . were left over. About 5,000 men** were fed on this occasion, plus many **women and children,** perhaps 15,000 to 20,000 in all.

This miracle took place at Bethsaida (see comments on Luke 9:10) just before the Passover (John 6:4). This is the only miracle of Jesus which is recorded in all four Gospels. The significance of this miracle was intended primarily for the disciples. Jesus was illustrating the kind of ministry they would have after His departure. They would be involved in feeding people, but with spiritual food. The source for their feeding would be the Lord Himself. When their supply ran out, as with the bread and fish, they would need to return to the Lord for more. He would supply them, but the feeding would be done through them. The people Jesus fed sensed that He was the anticipated Prophet (John 6:14-15; Deut. 18:15) and tried to make Him King. Surely One who could heal their physical diseases and provide food so abundantly must be the King. But the timing was not correct, for the nation's leaders had decided against Jesus (Matt. 12:24), and His official rejection would soon come.

14:22-36 (Mark 6:45-56; John 6:15-21). Jesus sent **the disciples** away in **a boat.** After dismissing **the crowd . . . He went up into the hills** alone **to pray** (cf. John 6:15). Sending the disciples **into the boat** did two things: it got them away from the crowd, and it gave them opportunity to ponder the significance of what had just happened through them.

But soon they were in a storm. Somewhere between 3 and 6 in the morning (**the fourth watch of the night), Jesus** joined **them, walking on the lake** to their boat—a distance of "three or three and a half miles" (John 6:19). His power over the elements was obvious, but there was also a lesson in faith for the disciples in this experience. Their **fear** of seeing a **ghost** (Matt. 14:26) was relieved when **Jesus** announced that it was He.

But **Peter** wanted greater assurance that it was really the Lord. He said, **Lord, if it's You . . . tell me to come to You on the water.** The Lord's reply was a simple **Come.** Peter's initial response demonstrated his faith for he stepped **out of the boat and** began walking toward the Lord. (Only Matthew recorded Peter's walk on the water.) In all recorded history only two men ever **walked on . . . water,** Jesus and Peter. **But** Peter's faith was challenged **when he saw the wind,** that is, when he saw its effect on the water. As he sank, he **cried** to the **Lord** for help. **Immediately** the Lord **caught him. Jesus** rebuked Peter for his lack of **faith** (cf. 6:30; 8:26; 16:8), which had caused him to sink.

When they reached **the boat,** the storm calmed and the amazed disciples **worshiped Him.** Their concept of Jesus had been expanded and they acknowledged Him as **the Son of God.** Their view of Jesus was in direct contrast with **the men** of **Gennesaret** (14:34), a fertile plain southwest of Capernaum. When these men learned Jesus had arrived, they **brought all their sick** for healing. Their touching **His cloak** recalls a hemorrhaging woman in that area who had touched His garment (9:20). Though they acknowledged Jesus as a great Healer, they did not fully comprehend who He is. The disciples, however, were growing continually in their comprehension of His true identity.

3. REJECTION IN THE CONTROVERSIES WITH THE RELIGIOUS LEADERS (15:1–16:12)

a. *The first controversy and result (chap. 15)*

15:1-9 (Mark 7:1-13). News of Jesus' teaching and His mighty acts had spread throughout the land. The officials in **Jerusalem** were aware of all **Jesus** was doing, for a delegation arrived in Galilee **from** Jerusalem to interrogate Jesus over a matter of Jewish **tradition.** Their attack was directed against Jesus' **disciples, who** were accused of failing to observe the elders' tradition of the ceremonial washing of **hands before** eating. This tradition (Rabbinic, not Mosaic) was an elaborate washing ritual involving not only one's hands but also cups, pitchers, and kettles (Mark 7:3-4).

Jesus immediately took the offensive against the religious leaders and asked why they continued to **break the** direct **command of God.** He cited the fifth commandment concerning honoring one's **father and mother** (Matt. 15:4; Ex. 20:12). The Jews considered honoring of parents so important that anyone who cursed **his** parents was to **be put to death** (Ex. 21:17; Lev. 20:9).

Jesus showed how these religious leaders had in effect nullified this commandment (Matt. 15:6). They could simply affirm that a particular item had been **a gift devoted to God.** Then the item could not be used by an individual but was kept separate. This was simply a clever way of keeping things from passing to one's parents. The person would of course continue to keep those things in his own home where they had been supposedly set aside for God. Such action was condemned by Jesus as being hypocritical (v. 7), for while it appeared to be spiritual, it actually was done to keep one's possessions for himself. Thus this failure to help one's parents deliberately violated the fifth commandment of the Decalogue. Such action had been described by **Isaiah** centuries before (Isa. 29:13). Their religion had become a matter of action and man-made rules. **Their hearts** were **far from** God and consequently their **worship** was **in vain** (*matēn*, "fruitless, futile," an adjective used only here [Matt. 15:9] and in the parallel passage, Mark 7:7; it is a variation of the more common adjective *mataios*, "without results, futile").

15:10-20 (Mark 7:14-23). Jesus then turned and warned **the crowd** against the religious leaders' teachings. He said a man is not defiled by what goes **into** his **mouth,** but rather his defiled condition is evidenced by **what comes out of his mouth.** The Pharisees were wrong in thinking their washings kept them spiritually clean.

The disciples reported to Jesus **that** **the Pharisees were offended** (cf. Matt. 13:21, 57) by what He had just said, sensing that His words were directed against them. Jesus added that since the Pharisees had **not** been **planted** by His **heavenly Father** (another of the many times in Matt. where Jesus referred to God as "Father"), they were headed for uprooting (judgment). Jesus said to **leave them** alone, for they had chosen their path and nothing would deter them. **They** were **blind guides,** trying to lead **blind** people; they would **fall into a pit.**

Peter asked for further clarification about Jesus' teaching (**the parable** refers to Jesus' words in 15:11; cf. Mark 7:15-17). So Jesus enlarged on His previous statement. Defilement of a person does not come from the outside. What comes from the outside is simply passed through the digestive system and is eventually eliminated. **But** what comes **out of the mouth** represents what is actually inside one's **heart,** and these may **make** him (or, show him to be) **unclean** (*koinoi,* "common, ceremonially impure"). Evil (*ponēroi*) **thoughts, murder, adultery** (*moicheiai*), **sexual immorality** (*porneiai*), **theft, false testimony, slander**—such actions and words rise from within one's evil heart. **These** matters— **not** whether one eats food **with unwashed hands**—reveal spiritual uncleanness.

15:21-28 (Mark 7:24-30). To get away from the questionings of the religious leaders, **Jesus withdrew** from Israel and went north into **the region of Tyre and Sidon,** the Gentile coastal region of Phoenicia. Tyre was 35 miles from Galilee and Sidon was 60. There He met **a Canaanite woman.** Centuries earlier that area's inhabitants were called Canaanites (Num. 13:29). She pleaded with Him to **have mercy** on her demon-possessed **daughter.** She addressed Him as **Lord, Son of David** (cf. Matt. 9:27; 20:30-31), a messianic title. But even that appeal could not help her, for the timing was not appropriate. When **Jesus** failed to **answer** her and she persisted with her appeal, **the disciples . . . urged** Jesus to **send her away.** They seemed to be asking, "Lord, why don't You go ahead and help this woman? She isn't going to give up until You do."

Jesus reminded them, **I was sent only to the lost sheep of Israel** (cf. 10:6).

He had come to offer to His own people the kingdom promised through David centuries before. Thus it was inappropriate for Him to bring blessings on Gentiles before blessings fell on Israel. But **the woman** was not easily discouraged. She saw in Jesus the only chance for help for her child. On her knees she pleaded, **Lord, help me!** Jesus' reply caused her to realize her position, for He said it would **not be right to take the children's bread and toss it to their dogs.** He was picturing a family gathered at mealtime around a table, eating food provided by the head of the household. The Gentile woman saw herself in this picture. She was not a child in the family (of Israel) eligible for the choicest morsels of food. But she saw herself as a household dog (a Gentile; the Jews often called Gentiles "dogs") eligible to receive **crumbs that** might **fall from the master's table.** She was not wanting to deprive Israel of God's blessings. She was simply asking that some of the blessing be extended to her in her need. In light of such **great faith** (cf. 8:10), the kind of faith Jesus was looking for in Israel, He **granted** her **request. Her daughter was healed . . . that very hour.** This Gentile woman's faith contrasted with Israel's leaders who were rejecting Jesus.

15:29-39 (Mark 7:31–8:10). Jesus, returning from Tyre and Sidon, **went near the Sea of Galilee . . . into the hills** (cf. Matt. 14:23) where He **sat down. Great crowds** of people brought a multitude of sick people **to Him.** In view of Mark 7:31-37, the crowds referred to in Matthew 15:30-31 may have been Gentiles (also cf. Mark 8:13 with Matt. 15:39). Jesus **healed** their physical illnesses, and people **praised the God of Israel.** Jesus was thus demonstrating what He will do for Gentiles as well as for Jews when His rightful millennial rule will be established on earth.

This ministry lasted about **three days. Jesus** had **compassion for** them (*splanchnizomai;* cf. comments on 9:36; Luke 7:13). He did **not want to send them** home without food. The **disciples** questioned how **in this remote place** (cf. Matt. 14:15) they could buy **enough** food **to feed** them all. When Jesus asked them about their present resources, they said they had **seven** bread **loaves** and **a few small fish.** The disciples must have anticipated that Jesus was going to use

them again to feed this multitude, as He had done earlier (14:13-21). Jesus **told the crowd to sit down,** gave **thanks** for **the seven loaves and the fish,** and divided the food among **the disciples,** who distributed it **to the people.** After the crowd—estimated this time at **4,000** men, **besides women and children—ate and were satisfied . . . seven basketfuls of broken pieces** were **picked up.**

This miracle demonstrated that the Lord's blessings through His disciples would fall not only on Israel (14:13-21) but also on Gentiles. This is perhaps most clearly seen in Acts 10–11 when Peter shared the good news of salvation with Cornelius and his Gentile household. **After Jesus had** dismissed **the crowd,** He returned to the western shore of the Sea of Galilee to the city of **Magadan,** a variant spelling of Magdala, just north of Tiberias. Mary Magdalene (Matt. 27:56) was from Magdala, also called Dalmanutha (Mark 8:10).

b. The second controversy and result (16:1-12)

16:1-4 (Mark 8:11-13; Luke 12:54-56). As **Jesus** returned to Israel, He was again confronted by religious leaders, **the Pharisees and Sadducees.** They **tested Him by asking** for **a sign from heaven.** By this they were again saying that they rejected all the signs Jesus had performed before their eyes (cf. Matt. 12:38). They were in effect asking Jesus to give them a sign more spectacular than healings, so they could believe. Jesus' response was again condemnatory for He called them **a wicked and adulterous generation** (16:4; cf. 12:39). They were careful observers of **weather** signs and could fairly well forecast whether the weather would be good or threatening. Yet they had been surrounded by spiritual signs relating to the person of Jesus Christ and had missed them all. Such a wicked generation would not receive any special treatment. Jesus was not a sign-worker simply for the sake of working signs. He was not a puppet on strings to perform at their command. The only **sign** they would receive was **the sign of Jonah,** which He had previously given them (12:38-42), but they would not recognize that sign until it was too late.

16:5-12 (Mark 8:14-21). As **Jesus** left the religious leaders, He warned His disciples . . . **against the yeast of the Pharisees and Sadducees,** to whom He had just spoken. Jesus' mention of yeast caused the disciples to think He referred to their having forgotten to **bring** along **bread.** But Jesus explained that He was not referring to their lack of **bread.** He reminded them of previous occasions when He had multiplied **loaves** and fish so that food was left over (Matt. 14:13-21; 15:29-38). The amount of food was not the issue, for **Jesus** could care for such a need if it arose. Because they were not trusting Him for that, they were, He said, **of little faith** (16:8; three other times in Matt. Jesus spoke of "little faith"; 6:30; 8:26; 14:31). He then simply repeated His warning: **Be on your guard against the yeast of the Pharisees and Sadducees** (cf. 16:6). Their **teaching** was like pervasive **yeast,** penetrating and corrupting the nation.

V. Cultivation of the King's Disciples (16:13–20:34)

A. The revelation in view of rejection (16:13–17:13)

1. THE PERSON OF MESSIAH (16:13-16) (MARK 8:27-30; LUKE 9:18-21)

16:13-16. **Jesus** and the **disciples** removed themselves from the region around the Sea of Galilee and went north about 30 miles to **Caesarea Philippi,** that is, Caesarea in the tetrarchy of Herod Philip, Antipas' brother. There Jesus questioned the disciples about their faith in Him. **He asked** them what the **people** were saying about Him. Their replies were all flattering, for people were identifying Jesus with **John the Baptist . . . Elijah . . . Jeremiah, or one of the prophets.** His teachings were certainly similar to theirs. All these answers, of course, were wrong. He then asked the disciples, **But what about you? Who do you say I am?**

Speaking for the disciples, **Peter** spoke his now-famous words, **You are the Christ, the Son of the living God.** As "the Christ," He is the Messiah. *Ho christos* is the New Testament equivalent of the Old Testament *māšîaḥ,* which means "the anointed One." In Him are fulfilled all the promises of God to the nation. And as the Old Testament made clear, the Messiah is more than a human being; He is God (Isa. 9:6; Jer. 23:5-6;

Micah 5:2). Peter thus acknowledged Jesus' deity as the Son of the living God. The disciples had come to this conclusion as they observed the Lord Jesus over a period of time, witnessed His miracles, and heard His words.

2. THE PROGRAM OF MESSIAH (16:17-26)

16:17-20. Peter's words brought a word of commendation from the Lord. **Peter** was **blessed** because he had come to a correct conclusion about the person of Christ and because great blessing would be brought into his life. The Lord added, however, this was **not** a conclusion Peter had determined by his own or others' ability. God, the **Father in heaven,** had **revealed** it to him. Peter was living up to his name (it means "rock") for he was demonstrating himself to be a rock. When the Lord and Peter first met, Jesus had said Simon would be named Cephas (Aram. for "rock") or Peter (Gr. for "rock"; John 1:41-42).

But his declaration about Messiah's person led to a declaration of Messiah's program. **Peter** (*Petros,* masc.) was strong like a rock, but Jesus added that on this **rock** (*petra,* fem.) He would build His church. Because of this change in Greek words, many conservative scholars believe that Jesus is now building His church on Himself. Others hold that the church is built on Peter and the other apostles as the building's foundation stones (Eph. 2:20; Rev. 21:14). Still other scholars say that the church is built on Peter's testimony. It seems best to understand that Jesus was praising Peter for his accurate statement about Him, and was introducing His work of building the church on Himself (1 Cor. 3:11).

Building His church was a yet-future work of Jesus Christ, for He had not yet started the process. He said, **I will build** (future tense) **My church,** but His program for the nation Israel had to be concluded before another program could be set in motion. This is probably why Jesus said not even **the gates of hades** would **overcome** this program. Jews would understand hades' gates to refer to physical death. Jesus was thus telling the disciples His death would not prevent His work of building the church. Later (Matt. 16:21) He spoke of His imminent death. He was therefore anticipating His death

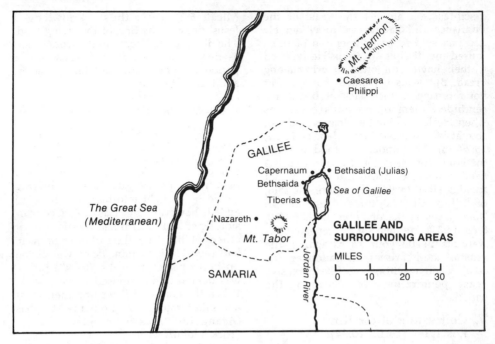

GALILEE AND SURROUNDING AREAS

and His victory over death through the Resurrection.

His church would *then* begin to be built, starting on the day of Pentecost, and Peter and the other apostles would have important roles in it. He declared that Peter would be given significant authority, **the keys of the kingdom of heaven.** A "key" was a sign of authority, for a trusted steward kept the keys to his master's possessions and dispensed them accordingly (cf. "the keys of death and hades" [Rev. 1:18] and "the key of David" [Rev. 3:7], which Jesus possesses). Peter was told he would possess the keys and be able to **bind** and **loose** people. These were decisions Peter was to implement as he received instruction from **heaven,** for the binding and loosing occurred there first. Peter simply carried out God's directions. This privilege of binding and loosing was seen in Peter's life as he had the privilege on the day of Pentecost to proclaim the gospel and announce to all those who responded in saving faith that their sins had been forgiven (Acts 2). He was able to do the same thing with the household of Cornelius (Acts 10–11; cf. Acts 15:19-20). The same privilege was given all the disciples (John 20:22-23).

After making this great declaration about His future church program, Jesus

told the **disciples not to tell anyone that He** is **the Christ,** the Messiah. The Lord knew it was too late for the nation to respond to His offer, and His rejection was drawing near. There was no reason for His disciples to be trying to convince a nation that had already turned from Him.

16:21-26 (Mark 8:31-38; Luke 9:22-25). Jesus explained **to His disciples that** His death was near. It would be necessary for Him to **go to Jerusalem and** there **suffer many things at the hands of the** religious leaders. Eventually He would **be killed,** but He would rise again from the dead **on the third day.** This is Matthew's first prediction of Jesus' death. Other predictions follow in Matthew 17:22-23 and 20:18-19.

Peter, hearing these words, **took the** Lord **aside and began to rebuke Him.** The disciple who had just been blessed by the Master obviously did not fully comprehend the Master's plan. Peter could not understand how Jesus could be Messiah and yet die at the hands of the religious leaders. Peter probably was so shocked to hear Jesus speak of His death that he failed to hear Him mention His resurrection. Peter's rebuke, however, brought a rebuke from the Lord, for **Peter** was playing the role of **Satan. Jesus** directly addressed Satan, who was seeking to use Peter as his instrument.

Jesus had previously told Satan to get away from Him (4:10); He now repeated that order. Peter was trying to keep the Lord from dying, but that was a primary reason why Jesus came into the world. Trying to thwart the Crucifixion, as Satan had earlier tried to do (4:8-10), resulted from not thinking from God's viewpoint.

Though Peter wanted Jesus to follow *his* plan, the Lord showed that discipleship involves a cost. Discipleship does not mean one enjoys glory immediately. A person who **would** follow Jesus **must deny himself** and all his ambitions. He must **take up his cross and follow** Jesus (cf. 10:38). In the Roman Empire a convicted criminal, when taken to be crucified, was forced to carry his own cross. This showed publicly that he was then under and submissive to the rule he had been opposing. Likewise Jesus' disciples must demonstrate their submission to the One against whom they had rebelled. The path Jesus and His followers would travel would be a road of sorrow and suffering. But in so losing one's **life,** one would truly **find** a better **life.** Jesus' similar words (in 10:38-39) were stated in connection with one's attitudes toward his family; here (16:24-25) Jesus spoke in relation to Peter's misunderstanding about His program and the cost of discipleship.

If it were possible for an individual, in preserving his own life, to gain **the whole world,** but in the process lose **his soul,** of what value then would be the possessions of the world? True discipleship involves following Christ and doing His will, wherever that path might lead.

3. THE PICTURE OF MESSIAH'S KINGDOM (16:27–17:13)

16:27-28 (Mark 9:1; Luke 9:26-27). As Jesus continued to instruct His disciples, He spoke prophetically of His second coming when He, **the Son of Man,** would return **in His Father's glory with His angels** (cf. Matt. 24:30-31; 2 Thes. 1:7). As "the Son of . . . God" (Matt. 16:16) He possesses a divine nature, and as "the Son of Man" He possesses a human nature (cf. comments on 8:20). At that time the Lord **will reward** His servants for their faithfulness. Speaking of His return led Him to state that some disciples **standing** there with Him would be permitted to view **His** coming **kingdom** before they experienced **death.** This statement has caused many to misunderstand the kingdom program, for they wonder how the disciples saw the Lord coming in His kingdom. The explanation is found in the following event, the transfiguration (17:1-8).

17:1-8 (Mark 9:2-13; Luke 9:28-36). This chapter division in Matthew is an unfortunate break in the flow of this biblical passage. Jesus had just said that some standing with Him would not die before they saw the Son of Man coming in His kingdom (Matt. 16:28). The continuing story occurred **six days** later when **Jesus took . . . Peter, James, and John** with Him **up a high mountain by themselves.** Luke wrote that this event occurred "about eight days after" (Luke 9:28), which includes the beginning and ending days as well as the six days between. The high mountain may have been Mount Hermon, near Caesarea Philippi (see map), for Jesus was in that region (Matt. 16:13).

There Jesus **was transfigured** (*metemorphōthē*, "changed in form"; cf. Rom. 12:2; 2 Cor. 3:18) **before** this inner circle of disciples (Matt. 17:2). This was a revelation of Jesus' glory. The radiance of His glory was evidenced in **His face** and in His garments that **became as white as the light. Moses and Elijah** appeared from heaven in some visible form and talked **with Jesus** (thus demonstrating that conscious existence follows death). Luke wrote that Moses and Elijah talked with Jesus about His coming death (Luke 9:31).

Why were Moses and Elijah, of all Old Testament people, present on this occasion? Perhaps these two men and the disciples suggest all the categories of people who will be in Jesus' coming kingdom. The disciples represent individuals who will be present in physical bodies. Moses represents saved individuals who have died or will die. Elijah represents saved individuals who will not experience death, but will be caught up to heaven alive (1 Thes. 4:17). These three groups will be present when Christ institutes His kingdom on earth. Furthermore the Lord will be in His glory as He was at the transfiguration, and the kingdom will take place on earth, as this obviously did. The disciples were thus enjoying a foretaste of the kingdom the Lord promised (Matt. 16:28).

Peter seemed to sense the significance of the event for he suggested that he erect **three shelters,** for Jesus, **Moses, and . . . Elijah.** He saw in this event the fulfillment of the Jewish Feast of Tabernacles which looked two ways: backward to the wanderings in the wilderness for 40 years, and forward to Israel's full enjoyment of God's blessings when He would gather His people to the land. Peter was correct in his understanding of what was taking place (he saw the kingdom) but he was wrong in his timing.

While Peter **was still speaking,** a more important **voice** spoke from **a bright cloud** that had **enveloped them.** This voice **said, This is My Son, whom I love; with Him I am well-pleased. Listen to Him!** (cf. 3:17) This authentication of the Son of God by the voice of God carried great significance for the disciples. Years later when Peter wrote his second epistle he referred to this event (2 Peter 1:16-18). This authentication of Jesus by the Father caused the terrified **disciples** to **fall on their faces. When the Lord** Himself told the disciples to **get up . . . they saw no one except Jesus,** for Moses and Elijah had departed.

17:9-13. As this small group returned from **the mountain, Jesus** told the three not to **tell anyone what** they had witnessed **until** after He had risen **from the dead** (cf. 16:20). Some people had already tried to make Jesus King by force, and if news of this event had become commonly known, perhaps others would have attempted to make Jesus King.

This event was a taste of the kingdom, but the disciples were puzzled. Many were teaching that before Messiah could come, **Elijah must** return. **Jesus** explained that **Elijah** must in fact come and **restore all things** (cf. Mal. 4:5), but **Elijah** had **already come** in the person of **John the Baptist** and his ministry was not recognized. Instead of receiving John the Baptist, the religious leaders had rejected him. As they refused to acknowledge John's ministry and instead rejected him, Jesus too would be rejected. At the first announcement concerning the birth of John, Zechariah his father had been told that he would go before the Lord "in the spirit and power of Elijah" (Luke 1:17). The Lord's earlier words concerning John

(Matt. 11:14) affirmed that he would have been the predicted Elijah *if* the nation had responded in saving faith. Everything necessary to bring in Messiah's kingdom had been performed. The only contingency was the acceptance by the nation of her rightful King.

B. The instruction in view of rejection (17:14–20:34)

1. INSTRUCTION CONCERNING FAITH (17:14-21)
(MARK 9:14-29; LUKE 9:37-43A)

17:14-21. When **Jesus** and the inner circle returned to the other disciples, a **crowd** was gathered because **a man** with **an epileptic** son had sought healing help from the nine **disciples.** They, however, had not been able to drive out **the demon** (v. 18) that possessed **the boy** and caused his epilepsy. The father appealed to Jesus, kneeling **before Him** and addressing Him as **Lord.** The boy's epilepsy had caused him much **suffering** and physical danger; the convulsions even caused him to fall uncontrollably **into the fire** and **into the water.** Mark mentioned the boy's foaming at the mouth (Mark 9:18, 20). **Jesus** asked for **the boy** to be brought to Him, and He rebuked not only the disciples but also the entire crowd for their lack of faith. He immediately drove the demon **out of** the boy and restored him completely **from that moment** (cf. Matt. 15:28).

When **the disciples** inquired why they had not been able to heal the boy, Jesus said their problem was their **little faith** (cf. the "great faith" of the Roman centurion [8:10] and of the Canaanite woman [15:28]). Even a small amount of **faith, as small as a mustard seed** (cf. comments on the mustard seed in 13:31), is adequate to **move** a huge **mountain,** assuming, of course, that the "move" is in God's will. **Nothing** is **impossible** with God (cf. 19:26; Luke 1:37). (Some Gr. mss. add Matt. 17:21, "But this kind does not go out except by prayer and fasting," based on Mark 9:29.) Jesus was instructing the disciples about their future ministries. Their problem often would be lack of faith and failure to seek their Lord's direction. His Word would be sufficient to produce the desired healing but their actions would necessitate great faith and constant contact with the Lord through prayer. When these elements are combined, there is no limit to the works the disciples could accomplish, following His will.

2. INSTRUCTION CONCERNING HIS DEATH (17:22-23)
(MARK 9:30-32; LUKE 9:43B-45)

17:22-23. Again the Lord reminded the disciples that He was to be betrayed and wicked men would kill Him. One could never say that death took Jesus by surprise. He was in control of His life and no one took it from Him (John 10:11, 15, 17-18). He also told the disciples that death would not be the end for Him. Again He said He would rise on the third day. Unlike before (Matt. 16:21-23) this announcement of His death was not met by any recorded opposition from the disciples. But they were filled with grief over the Lord's words. One wonders if they heard the complete message or simply the part about His death.

3. INSTRUCTION CONCERNING RESPONSIBILITY TO GOVERNMENT (17:24-27)

17:24-27. When Jesus and the disciples arrived back in Capernaum, tax collectors were waiting for them. According to custom every Jew 20 years old and above was required to pay a temple tax of half a shekel or two drachmas each year to help support the temple (cf. Ex. 30:13-15; Neh. 10:32). Both Peter and Jesus had apparently not yet paid their tax (Matt. 17:27b) for that year, so the collectors sought Peter out. Their question about the Lord's not paying His tax implied that He was not keeping the Law. Peter responded that the Lord would pay the tax in compliance with the Law.

Before Peter spoke to the Lord about this matter, Jesus asked him if kings . . . collect duty and taxes from their own sons, or from others. Peter replied that kings do not collect taxes from family members, for they were exempt, but they do collect from others. The Lord was demonstrating to Peter that not only should He as King be tax-free, but also His disciples, as sons of the kingdom, should be free from such taxes (v. 26). They too had a privileged position, and the King should provide all they needed. However, the Lord did not intend at this time to make an issue (offend them, v. 27) over such a small point. The religious leaders were looking for accusations to use against Jesus. Peter was told to do something he really enjoyed: the Lord sent him fishing. He was to throw out his line and a special catch would be brought in. This fish would have in its mouth a specific four-drachma coin that would be the exact amount Peter needed to pay the tax for himself and for the Lord.

While Matthew did not record the rest of the story, it may be assumed Peter did as he was commanded, caught the fish, found the money, and paid the tax. The Lord thereby demonstrated His submission to ruling authority.

4. INSTRUCTION CONCERNING HUMILITY (18:1-6)
(MARK 9:33-37, 42; LUKE 9:46-48)

18:1-6. While still in the city of Capernaum, the disciples asked Jesus a question they had undoubtedly been pondering among themselves: Who is the greatest in the kingdom of heaven? The disciples were still anticipating an earthly kingdom and wondering what great positions they would have. In response Jesus took a little child (*paidion*), who had no rights according to the Law, and stood him in their midst. He told the disciples a change in their thinking was necessary. Greatness in the kingdom was not based on great works or words, but on childlike humility of spirit.

Jesus' reply indicated they were asking the wrong question. They should have been concerned about serving the Lord, not asking about positions in the kingdom. Their service needed to be directed toward people, for Jesus spoke about welcoming a little child . . . in His name. Little thought was directed in those days toward children, but Jesus did not overlook them. In fact, He gave a stern warning concerning any who might place a stumbling block before one of these little ones who believe in Him. (Interestingly little children can—and do—believe in Jesus!) Causes . . . to sin translates the verb *skandalisē*, "to offend, or cause to fall," a verb Matthew used 13 times. It would be better for such an offender to have a large millstone hung around his neck and to be drowned in the depths of the sea. A truly humble person does not concern himself with position or power, but is concerned about active service, especially toward those who are most in need.

5. INSTRUCTION CONCERNING OFFENSES (18:7-14)

18:7-11 (Mark 9:43-48). Jesus continued the previous discussion by talking about those who **cause** offenses. It was obvious such individuals were present in Jesus' time, but the judgment of God (**woe,** twice, Matt. 18:7; **eternal fire,** v. 8; **the fire of hell,** v. 9; cf. 6:22) would fall on them because they were failing to deal with the basic cause of their **sin.** Jesus was not teaching self-mutilation, cutting **off** one's **hand** or **foot** or gouging **out** one's **eye** (cf. 5:29-30). Doing that would not remove the source of offense, which is the heart (cf. 15:18-19). Jesus was saying one must remove whatever offends. To keep from offending, radical changes are often necessary. The disciples were reminded of the value the Lord places on **these little ones** (*mikrōn toutōn;* cf. 18:6, 14). Children are important to God. It may be God has entrusted the care of little children to a specific group of His angelic beings (**their angels**) who are in constant touch with the heavenly **Father** (cf. Ps. 91:11; Acts 12:15). (Some Gr. mss. add the words of Matt. 18:11, "The Son of Man came to save what was lost," perhaps inserted from Luke 19:10.)

18:12-14 (Luke 15:3-7). In order to demonstrate the importance God attaches to little children, the Lord gave the disciples an illustration. Suppose **a man** who **owns 100 sheep** suddenly discovers only **99** are present. **Will he not leave** them and search **for the one** until he **finds it? In the same way** God (**your Father in heaven;** cf. Matt. 18:10) is concerned about **these little ones** (cf. vv. 6, 10) and does not want to lose **any of** them. Great care must be exercised to avoid all offense.

6. INSTRUCTION CONCERNING DISCIPLINE (18:15-20) (LUKE 17:3)

18:15-20. The Lord had just spoken about offenses; now He talked about what should be done when known sin occurs. When a **brother sins against** another, **the two of** them should discuss the matter. If the matter can be settled at that level, there is no need for it to go any further. But if the sinning brother **refuses to listen**

. . . **two or three witnesses** should be taken **along** for a clear **testimony.** This was in keeping with Old Testament precedents, as in Deuteronomy 19:15. If the sinning brother still failed to recognize his error, the situation should be told before **the** entire **church,** or "assembly." The disciples probably would have understood Jesus to mean the matter should be brought before the Jewish assembly. After the establishment of the church, on the day of Pentecost, these words would have had greater meaning for them. One who **refuses** to acknowledge his sin is then to be treated **as an** outsider (**a pagan or a tax collector**).

This corporate action was entrusted to the entire apostolic group. Their actions of binding and loosing were to be directed by **heaven** (Matt. 18:18; cf. comments on 16:19). Clearly all are addressed for the **you** pronouns are plural. Besides their binding and loosing, they were also to engage in corporate prayer. Whenever they came **together in** the **name** of the Lord, He would be **with them.** And if **two or three** would **agree** together **about anything** it would **be done** for them **by the Father in heaven.**

7. INSTRUCTION CONCERNING FORGIVENESS (18:21-35)

18:21-22. Peter then asked **Jesus . . . Lord, how many times shall I forgive my brother when he sins against me? Up to seven times?** Peter was being generous here, for the traditional Rabbinic teaching was that an offended person needed to forgive a brother only three times. Jesus' reply was that forgiveness needs to be exercised to a much greater extent. **Not** just **7 times,** but "70 times 7" (NIV marg.), that is, 490 times. Jesus meant that no limits should be set. Then to complete the idea, He told a parable.

18:23-35. Jesus told about **a king who wanted to settle accounts with his servants.** One servant owed a large amount, **10,000 talents.** This probably equaled several million dollars, for a talent was probably a measure of gold, between 58 and 80 pounds. When he could **not . . . pay, the master ordered that** the servant **and his wife . . . children, and** possessions **be sold** so he could **repay** as much of **the debt** as possible. **The servant** pleaded with his master, begging for time to repay his master. The **master took pity on** the servant, **canceled the debt, and** set him free.

But shortly thereafter this **servant went out** and **found** another servant **who owed him** a much smaller amount, **100 denarii.** A denarius was a Roman silver coin, worth about 16 cents; it represented a laborer's daily wages. The first servant **demanded** payment and refused to show mercy toward his debtor. In fact he had the second servant **thrown into prison until he** paid **the debt. The other servants,** aware of all that **had happened . . . were greatly distressed** (*elypēthēsan,* "grieved or sad to the point of distress"; cf. 14:9; 19:22) by this turn of events and **told their master** what had transpired. **The master called** back **the** first **servant** and jailed him for failing to show mercy to a fellow servant when he had been forgiven a much greater debt.

The Lord was teaching that forgiveness ought to be in direct proportion to the amount forgiven. The first servant had been forgiven all, and he in turn should have forgiven all. A child of God has had all his sins forgiven by faith in Jesus Christ. Therefore when someone sins against him, he ought to be willing to **forgive . . . from** the **heart** no matter how many times the act occurs (cf. 18:21-22; Eph. 4:32).

8. INSTRUCTION CONCERNING DIVORCE (19:1-12)

(MARK 10:1-12)

19:1-12. Jesus . . . left Galilee for the last time and headed for Jerusalem through **the region of Judea to the** east **side of the Jordan** River. That area was known as Perea. There, as often before, He was **followed** by **large crowds** of needy people, and **He healed them.** But **some Pharisees** sought **to test** Jesus through a question: **Is it lawful for a man to divorce his wife for any and every reason?** The nation was divided over this issue. Followers of Hillel felt a man could divorce his wife for almost any reason, but others, following Shammai, thought one could not divorce his wife unless she were guilty of sexual offense. Without getting involved in the Hillel-Shammai controversy Jesus reminded the religious leaders of God's original purpose in establishing the marriage bond. God made people **male and female** (v. 4; Gen.

1:27). In marriage He joins them **together** in an inseparable bond. This bond is a higher calling than the parent-child relationship, for **a man** is to **leave his father and mother and be** joined **to his wife** in a one-flesh relationship (Gen. 2:24). **Therefore what God has joined together,** men ought **not separate** (*chōrizetō;* in 1 Cor. 7:10 this word means "to divorce").

The Pharisees, realizing that Jesus was speaking of the permanence of the marital relationship, asked why **Moses** made a provision for **divorce** for people in his time (Matt. 19:7). The Lord's answer was that **Moses** granted this permission because people's **hearts were hard** (cf. Deut. 24:1-4). "Because your hearts were hard" is literally, "toward your hardness of heart" (*sklērokardian;* from *sklēros,* "hardness," comes the Eng. "sclerosis," and from *kardian* comes the Eng. "cardiac"). But that was not God's intention for marriage. God intended husbands and wives to live together permanently. Divorce was wrong **except for marital unfaithfulness** (cf. Matt. 5:32).

Bible scholars differ over the meaning of this "exception clause," found only in Matthew's Gospel. The word for "marital unfaithfulness" is *porneia.*

(1) Some feel Jesus used this as a synonym for adultery (*moicheia*). Therefore adultery by either partner in a marriage is the only sufficient grounds for a marriage to end in divorce. Among those holding this view, some believe remarriage is possible but others believe remarriage should never occur.

(2) Others define *porneia* as a sexual offense that could occur only in the betrothal period when a Jewish man and woman were considered married but had not yet consummated their coming marriage with sexual intercourse. If in this period the woman was found pregnant (as was Mary; 1:18-19), a divorce could occur in order to break the contract.

(3) Still others believe the term *porneia* referred to illegitimate marriages within prohibited degrees of kinship, as in Leviticus 18:6-18. If a man discovered that his wife was a near relative, he would actually be involved in an incestuous marriage. Then this would be a justifiable grounds for divorce. Some say this

meaning of *porneia* is found in Acts 15:20, 29 (cf. 1 Cor. 5:1).

(4) Another view is that *porneia* refers to a relentless, persistent, unrepentant lifestyle of sexual unfaithfulness (different from a one-time act of illicit relations). (In the NT *porneia* is broader than *moicheia*). Such a continued practice would thus be the basis for divorce, since such unfaithful and unrelenting conduct would have broken the marriage bond. (On the subject of divorce and remarriage, see comments on 1 Cor. 7:10-16.)

Whatever view one takes on the exception clause, **Jesus** obviously affirmed the permanence of marriage. Those who heard His words understood Him in this way, for they reasoned that if there were no grounds for divorce one would be **better** off never **to marry.** But this was not what Jesus intended, for God has given marriage to people for their betterment (Gen. 2:18). Marriage should be a deterrent to lustful sin and to unfaithfulness (1 Cor. 7:2). But a few either do not have normal sexual desires (they were born **eunuchs** or were castrated), or are able to control those desires for the furtherance of God's program on the earth (Matt. 19:12; cf. 1 Cor. 7:7-8, 26). But **not** all are able to **accept** the single role (Matt. 19:11). Many marry and carry out God's purposes, extending His work in the world.

9. INSTRUCTION CONCERNING CHILDREN (19:13-15)

(MARK 10:13-16; LUKE 18:15-17)

19:13-15. Many parents were bringing **children ... to Jesus for Him to place His hands on them and pray for them.** But the disciples felt this was a waste of Jesus' time. They began rebuking those bringing their children. Apparently the disciples had already forgotten what Jesus said earlier about the worth of children and the seriousness of causing them to fall (cf. 18:1-14). **Jesus** rebuked the disciples, telling them to **let the little children come** and **not hinder them. The kingdom** of heaven is not limited to adults who might be considered to be worth more than children. Anyone who comes to the Lord in faith is a worthy subject for the kingdom. This implies (19:15) that Jesus had time for all the children, for He did not depart from the region till He had blessed them all.

10. INSTRUCTION CONCERNING RICHES (19:16-26)

(MARK 10:17-31; LUKE 18:18-30)

19:16-22. A man who was **young** (v. 20), wealthy (v. 22) and a ruler (Luke 18:18; perhaps of the Sanhedrin) **came** and **asked** Jesus, **Teacher, what good thing must I do to get eternal life?** This ruler was not asking how he could earn salvation. Instead, he wondered how he could be assured of entering Messiah's kingdom. He wanted to know what "good thing" (work) would demonstrate that he was righteous and therefore qualified for the kingdom. **Jesus** replied, **There is only One who is good,** namely, God. Perfection is required (Matt. 5:48; cf. 19:21); therefore one must be as good as God. He must have God's righteousness, which comes through faith in Him (Rom. 4:5). Perhaps Jesus then waited for a response from the ruler to see if he would affirm his belief that Jesus is God, that Jesus, being one with the Father, is good (*agathos,* "intrinsically good").

When the man did not reply, Jesus indicated that **life** (i.e., life in God's kingdom) can be entered only if one gives *evidence* that he is righteous. Since the official standard of righteousness was the Law of Moses, Jesus told the man to **obey the commandments.** The ruler was perceptive for he immediately asked, **Which ones?** Other standards of righteousness were being promoted by the Pharisees, who had added to Moses' commandments far beyond God's intention. The young man was in effect asking Jesus, "Must I keep all the Pharisees' commandments?" **Jesus replied** by repeating several of the commandments from the second table of the Law, the 5th through the 9th commandments forbidding **murder ... adultery,** stealing, giving **false testimony,** and also the positive command to honor one's parents (Ex. 20:12-16). Jesus did not mention the 10th commandment (Ex. 20:17) concerning coveting, but He did add the summary statement, **Love your neighbor as yourself** (cf. Lev. 19:18; Matt. 22:39; Rom. 13:9; Gal. 5:14; James 2:8).

The young man affirmed he had **kept** all **these** things, but he **still** sensed a **lack** (Matt. 19:20). Whether he had truly kept these commands, only God knows. The young man believed he had and yet he knew something was missing in his life. Jesus put His finger on his problem when He told him to **go, sell** all his **possessions and give to the poor, and** he would then **have treasure in heaven.** Such mercy toward the poor would demonstrate inner righteousness. If he were righteous (based on faith in Jesus as God), he should have given his wealth to the poor and followed Jesus. But instead, the **man . . . went away sad** (*lypoumenos,* "grieved or sad to the point of distress"; cf. 14:9; 18:31) for **he had great wealth.** His unwillingness to relinquish his wealth showed he did not love his neighbor as himself. Thus he had not kept all the commandments, and he lacked salvation. Nothing more was written about this young man; probably he never left all and followed Jesus. He loved his money more than God, and thus he violated even the first commandment (Ex. 20:3).

19:23-26. The incident with the young ruler prompted a brief message from **Jesus to His disciples.** He remarked how difficult it is **for a rich man to enter the kingdom of heaven.** In fact Jesus said **it is easier for a camel to go through the eye of a needle.** Since the man was trusting his riches rather than the Lord to save him, he could no more enter the kingdom than a camel (one of the largest animals used by Jews) could go through "the eye of a needle" (*rhaphidos,* a sewing needle; *not* a small gate within another gate as is sometimes suggested). This needle's eye was an extremely small opening. The **astonished** disciples **asked, Who then can be saved?** This showed the Pharisees' influence on them, for the Pharisees said God bestows wealth on those He loves. So if a wealthy person cannot make it into the kingdom, seemingly no one can! **Jesus** answered that salvation is a work of God. What appears to be **impossible** with men is what **God** delights to do (cf. 17:20).

11. INSTRUCTION CONCERNING SERVICE AND REWARDS (19:27–20:16)

19:27-30. In the previous incident Jesus told the rich young man to sell all he had and **follow** Him. This was exactly what the disciples had done, as expressed by **Peter. We have left everything to follow You! What then will there be for us?** Whereas the young ruler did not leave his possessions (v. 22), Peter and the other disciples had (4:18-22; 9:9; cf. 16:25). Surely then, Peter reasoned, God would bless them for they were not trusting in their wealth! The Lord explained there would be a **renewal** (*palingenesia,* "rebirth") **of all things.** Though the nation was then rejecting His offer of the kingdom, the kingdom would come, with its extensive remaking of things spiritual (Isa. 2:3; 4:2-4; 11:9b), political (Isa. 2:4; 11:1-5, 10-11; 32:16-18), and geographical and physical (Isa. 2:2; 4:5-6; 11:6-9; 35:1-2). Christ will then sit **on His glorious throne** (cf. Matt. 25:31; Rev. 22:1).

The disciples will have a special place in the kingdom, sitting **on thrones** and **judging the 12 tribes of Israel** (cf. Rev. 21:12-14). In fact all who leave their homes and relatives **for the Lord's sake will receive** physical blessings that will more than compensate for their losses (Matt. 19:29). This will be in addition to their **eternal life** in His kingdom. While it might appear they are giving up everything now and **are the last,** they will be given everything eternally and **will be first.** Conversely those, like the rich young ruler, who appear to have everything now (the **first**) will discover one day they have lost everything (they **will be last;** cf. 20:16).

20:1-16. Continuing this discussion, Jesus told a parable in which **a landowner . . . went out early in the morning** and hired **men to work in his vineyard** for the day, at an agreed price of one **denarius,** the normal daily pay for a laborer. Later, **about the third hour** (around 9 A.M.) the landowner encouraged others **in the marketplace** also to **work in** the vineyard, not for a stipulated wage but **for whatever is right.** The landowner employed more laborers **about the sixth hour** (about noon) **and** at **the ninth hour** (3 P.M.), and even some at **the eleventh hour** (5 P.M.) when only one hour was left for labor.

When it **came** time (**evening,** i.e., 6 P.M.) for the landowner to **pay** the **workers,** he began with those who had worked the shortest amount of time and paid **each** of them one **denarius.** When those who had worked the entire day came for their reckoning, they thought they would **receive more** than **a denarius.** They had labored all day and **borne the burden of the work and the heat of the**

day. They had agreed, however, to work for a stipulated amount and that is what they received (v. 13). The landowner argued that he had **the right to do what he chose with his money.** He reminded them they should not be **envious** of his generosity toward those who had labored only briefly.

By this illustration, Jesus was teaching that the matter of rewards is under the sovereign control of God, the "Landowner" in the parable. God is the One before whom all accounts will be settled. Many who have prominent places will someday find themselves demoted. And many who often find themselves at the end of the line will find themselves promoted to the head of the line: **The last will be first, and the first will be last.** (This supports what Jesus had said in 19:28-30.) In the final accounting, the Lord's analysis will carry the greatest and only important weight.

12. INSTRUCTION CONCERNING HIS DEATH
(20:17-19)
(MARK 10:32-34; LUKE 18:31-34)

20:17-19. One could never say **Jesus** did not prepare His **disciples** for His **death.** At least three times already He had announced that He was going to die (12:40; 16:21; 17:22-23). He was now on the road **to Jerusalem** (cf. Jesus' movements geographically: 4:12; 16:13; 17:24; 19:1; 21:1). Once again **He** told the disciples that death awaited Him in that city. Here He spoke for the first time of His betrayal, mocking, flogging, and crucifixion. But He also reminded them that death was not the end for Him, for He would rise again **on the third day** (cf. 16:21; 17:23). The disciples gave no response to the Lord's words. Perhaps they could not bring themselves to believe the Lord was indeed going to be treated in that way.

13. INSTRUCTION CONCERNING AMBITION
(20:20-28)
(MARK 10:35-45)

20:20-23. Jesus' recent discussion about "the renewal of all things" (19:28) prompted the following incident. **The mother of** James and John **came to Jesus with her** two **sons** and bowed before **Him.** When Jesus inquired **what** her request was, she asked that her **two sons** might be granted places of favor **in His**

kingdom, one seated **at** His **right** hand **and** one **at** His **left.** Perhaps she had heard Jesus say His disciples would be seated on thrones (19:28), and she, with typical motherly pride, felt her sons deserved the two best locations.

Jesus did not correct her as to the fact of His coming kingdom. His only question was addressed to the two sons (**you** is pl.), who apparently had urged their mother to make the request. He asked if they could **drink the cup** He was about **to drink.** Jesus was speaking of His coming trials and death as He would be betrayed and die on a cross (26:39, 42). **They** both replied, **We can.** Jesus indicated they would **indeed** share the **cup** of suffering and death with Him. James suffered death early in the Church Age at the hands of Herod Agrippa I (Acts 12:1-2), and John is thought to have died a martyr's death near the end of the first century.

However, granting positions of honor to His **right** and **left** in the kingdom is **not** His prerogative. Those **places** will be filled by **those . . . whom** the **Father,** the gracious and generous Judge (cf. Matt. 20:1-16), will appoint (v. 23). This account illustrates again that the disciples did not understand Jesus' teaching about humility (cf. 18:1-6). Peter's question (19:27) also demonstrated a desire for position. This the disciples continued to discuss, even to the point of the Lord's death.

20:24-28. When the 10 disciples **heard about** the request by James and John's mother, **they** became **indignant.** They were probably sorry they had not thought of it first! (cf. 18:1) **Jesus** was of course aware of the friction evident within the group. So He **called** the Twelve **together and** reminded them of some important principles. While some people (**rulers** and **high officials) lord it over** others, the disciples were **not** to do **so.** Greatness in the Lord's kingdom does not come through rulership or authority but through service (20:26-27). Their goal should be serving, not ruling. Those most highly esteemed will be those who serve, those who are humble.

There was no greater example of this principle than the Lord Himself. He **did not come** into the world **to be served, but to serve, and to give His life as a ransom for many.** Here was the first clue as to what the death of Christ would accomplish. He had told them on a number of occasions He would die. But He had not indicated the reason for His death. Now it was clear that His death would be to provide a "ransom" (*lytron*, "payment") "for" (*anti*, "in place of") "many" (see the chart, "New Testament Words for Redemption" at Mark 10:45). His death would take the place of many deaths, for only His death could truly atone for sin (John 1:29; Rom. 5:8; 1 Peter 2:24; 3:18). He was the perfect Sacrifice, whose substitutionary death paid the price for sin.

14. INSTRUCTION CONCERNING AUTHORITY (20:29-34)

(MARK 10:46-52; LUKE 18:35-43)

20:29-34. In a final display of His authority before He reached Jerusalem, **Jesus** healed **two blind men** near the city of **Jericho.** The other Synoptic writers (Mark and Luke) repeat this story with a few differences. Matthew wrote of two men; Mark and Luke spoke of one. Mark included the name of the blind man, Bartimaeus. Undoubtedly two men were there and Bartimaeus was the more noticeable of the two. Matthew and Mark said the men were healed when Jesus left Jericho, but Luke said the healing occurred when Jesus approached Jericho. This can be explained by the fact that there were two Jerichos then, an old city and a new one. Jesus was leaving old Jericho (Matt. and Mark) and approaching new Jericho (Luke) when the miracle occurred.

The blind men cried out for help **when they heard . . . Jesus was** passing **by.** Their appeal to Him was based on the fact that He is the **Lord, Son of David.** Earlier two other blind men called Jesus "Son of David" (Matt. 9:27; cf. 15:22). By using this title, they were appealing to Him as Messiah. They persisted in spite of the rebuke from **the crowd** until **Jesus stopped and called them** out. When **He asked** what they wanted, they simply replied they wanted their **sight. Jesus had compassion** (*splanchnistheis*; cf. comments on 9:36) **on them and** exercising His authority as the Messiah, the **Son of David,** He healed them **immediately.** It is interesting that this extended section (17:14-20:34), in which Jesus was teaching the disciples things they would need after His death, ended with a demonstration of

His authority. Truly He is to be believed for He is the Son of David, the Messiah of Israel.

VI. Climax of the King's Offer (chaps. 21-27)

A. The official presentation of the King (21:1-22)

1. THE TRIUMPHAL ENTRY (21:1-11)

(MARK 11:1-11; LUKE 19:28-42; JOHN 12:12-14)

21:1-5. Jesus and the **disciples** were approaching **Jerusalem** from the east as they came up the road from Jericho. When they reached the town of **Bethphage on** the eastern slopes of **the Mount of Olives,** Jesus **sent two** disciples ahead to **find a donkey** and its **colt.** Though all four Gospel accounts include the Triumphal Entry, only Matthew mentioned a donkey along with the colt. A simple explanation of what some call a contradiction is that when Jesus rode the colt, the mother donkey naturally went along. Perhaps He rode each animal part of the distance (v. 7).

Jesus told the disciples to **bring** the animals **to** Him. **If anyone** questioned their actions, they were to say **the Lord** needed **them.** As Messiah He had the right to request whatever He needed. Matthew mentioned (vv. 4-5) that this act fulfilled a prophecy, namely, Zechariah 9:9 (cf. Isa. 62:11), which spoke to the nation of the coming of her **King** in a **gentle** manner **riding on . . . a colt, the foal** (lit., son) **of a donkey.** This was not the normal manner in which kings arrived, for they usually came as conquerors riding on horses. A colt was a symbol of peace.

21:6-8. The disciples got the animals, threw **their** garments **on them** to make saddles, and people in the **large crowd spread their cloaks** (cf. 2 Kings 9:13) and tree **branches on the road.** Most of these people were pilgrims from Galilee on their way to Jerusalem to celebrate the Passover. They were familiar with Jesus and the many miracles He had performed in Galilee.

21:9. As the people walked along, some before Jesus and some behind **Him,** they were probably singing some of the pilgrim psalms. Matthew noted that they (including children, v. 15) **shouted** the words of Psalm 118:26, **Blessed is He**

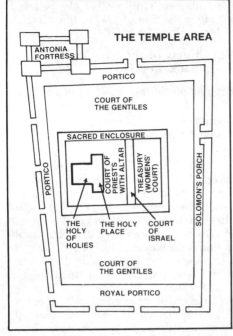

THE TEMPLE AREA

ANTONIA FORTRESS

PORTICO

COURT OF THE GENTILES

SACRED ENCLOSURE

PORTICO

COURT OF PRIESTS WITH ALTAR

TREASURY (WOMENS' COURT)

SOLOMON'S PORCH

THE HOLY OF HOLIES

THE HOLY PLACE

COURT OF ISRAEL

COURT OF THE GENTILES

ROYAL PORTICO

who comes in the name of the Lord. To Him they shouted, **Hosanna to the Son of David.** "Hosanna" is from the Hebrew *hôšî'âh nā'*, "Save (us), we pray," taken from Psalm 118:25. It came to be a note of praise as well as petition.

While the crowd did not fully understand the significance of this event, they seemed to be acknowledging that this One is the promised Seed of David who had come to grant them salvation. Both their actions and words bestowed honor on this One coming into the city, at last presenting Himself publicly as their King.

21:10-11. As **Jesus entered Jerusalem, the** entire **city was** moved **and asked, Who is this?** Since Jesus had usually avoided the city, its inhabitants did not know Him. Those accompanying Jesus from out of town kept answering, **This is Jesus, the Prophet from Nazareth in Galilee** (cf. v. 46). As *the* Prophet, He is the One promised by Moses (Deut. 18:15). Luke recorded that Jesus wept over the city (Luke 19:41) and told the religious leaders that the day was a significant time for the nation: "If you, even you, had only known on this day what would bring you peace—but now it is hidden from your eyes" (Luke 19:42). Jesus may well have had in mind the

significant prophecy of Daniel concerning the time of Messiah's coming and that He had arrived in Jerusalem at the very time predicted by Daniel over 500 years previously (Dan. 9:25-26). This event marked the official presentation of Jesus Christ to the nation of Israel as the rightful Son of David.

2. THE MESSIANIC AUTHORITY (21:12-14)
   (MARK 11:15-19; LUKE 19:45-48)

21:12-14. While Matthew's account seems to imply **Jesus entered the temple** immediately after His entry into Jerusalem, the other accounts state that Jesus returned to Bethany after the entry. The cleansing of the temple probably occurred the next morning when Jesus returned to Jerusalem from Bethany (Mark 11:11-16).

As Messiah Jesus entered the temple **area,** His indignation was directed toward those who had changed the character of the temple from a place **of prayer** into a place of corrupt commercialism. Many were making their living from the temple and the sacrifices purchased there. They insisted that in the temple the people could not use money that had been circulating in society, but had to change their money into temple money first, for a fee, and then use the temple money to purchase animals for sacrifice, at inflated prices. Since such extortion was completely contrary to the temple's purposes, the Lord **overturned** their **tables** and **benches** in the outer court of the Gentiles (see sketch) while quoting parts of two Old Testament verses, Isaiah 56:7 and Jeremiah 7:11. (Jesus had previously cleared the temple at the beginning of His ministry [John 2:14-16].)

Jesus further demonstrated His authority by healing **the blind and the lame** who **came to Him** at the temple. (Only Matthew recorded this fact.) Normally such individuals were excluded from the temple, but Jesus' authority brought many changes.

3. THE OFFICIAL INDIGNATION (21:15-17)

21:15-17. As Jesus healed those who came to Him in the temple, **children** ascribed praise to Him, **shouting . . . Hosanna to the Son of David,** clearly a messianic title (cf. comments on v. 9). **The chief priests and the teachers of the Law** were angered by Jesus' works and the children's praises. **Were indignant** comes from a verb meaning "to be stirred up in anger," used only in the Synoptic Gospels (cf. 20:24; 26:8; Mark 10:14, 41; 14:4; Luke 13:14). Their question to Jesus, **Do You hear what these children are saying?** implied a request that Jesus make them stop. Probably many of the "children" **in the temple** were there for the first time, celebrating their becoming men in the society. Such influence on young minds was not thought to be in the best interests of the nation. Jesus replied by quoting from Psalm 8:2, which spoke of **praise** coming **from the lips of children and infants.** By receiving their praise, Jesus was declaring He was worthy of praise as their Messiah. The religious leaders, in rejecting Jesus, did not even have the insights of children, who were receiving Him (cf. Matt. 18:3-4). Consequently Jesus **left** the leaders and departed from the temple. He returned **to** the town of **Bethany,** about a two-mile walk over the Mount of Olives, **where He spent the night,** probably in the home of Mary, Martha, and Lazarus.

4. THE SYMBOLIC REJECTION (21:18-22)
(MARK 11:12-14, 20-25)

21:18-22. As Jesus was making His **way back to the city** of Jerusalem the next **morning . . . He was hungry.** He saw a **fig tree by the road** and noticed it was covered with **leaves.** As He drew closer, He discovered there was no fruit on the tree. Fig trees **bear fruit** first and then the leaves appear, or both appear about the same time. Since the tree was in leaf, figs should have been on it. When Jesus **found** none, He cursed the tree and it **immediately . . . withered.** Mark indicated that the disciples heard Jesus curse the tree, but did not notice the withered condition till they returned to Jerusalem the next morning (Mark 11:13-14, 20). The **disciples** marveled (*ethaumasan*) that the **tree** withered **so quickly.**

Jesus used this event to teach a lesson in **faith,** for if they had genuine faith in God they not only would be able to do miracles such as cursing the **tree,** but they would be able to move mountains (cf. Matt. 17:20). If they truly believed, they would **receive whatever** they prayed **for.** The Lord was teaching the importance of faith rather than doubting or simply marveling. By con-

trast the nation of Israel had failed to exercise faith in Him.

This event may have meaning beyond the lesson in faith, however. Many believe that Jesus saw this fig tree as a symbol of Israel at that time. They too were professing to be fruitful, but a closer examination of the nation revealed they were fruitless. By cursing that generation, Jesus was showing His rejection of them and predicting that no fruit would ever come from them. Within a few days, that generation would reject their King and crucify Him. This ultimately led to judgment on that generation. In A.D. 70 the Romans came, demolished the temple, overran the country of Israel, and ended Israel's political entity (Luke 21:20). Perhaps in cursing the fig tree, Jesus was setting aside that generation. Of course the entire nation was not set aside (cf. Rom. 11:1, 26).

B. The religious confrontation with the King (21:23–22:46)

1. CONFRONTATION WITH THE PRIESTS AND ELDERS (21:23–22:14)
(MARK 11:27–12:12; LUKE 20:1-19)

a. The attack (21:23)

21:23. **Jesus** returned to **the temple courts** He had just recently claimed for His Father. In these courts He confronted various religious groups in the nation. The debate began as **the chief priests and the elders** asked Jesus, **By what authority are You doing these things? And who gave You this authority?** By "these things" they probably meant His Triumphal Entry into the city, His reception of praise from the people, His clearing of the temple, His healing of the blind and the lame (vv. 8-14), and His teaching (v. 23). The leaders understood Jesus was claiming authority as Messiah and wanted to know where He got such authority. He certainly had not received it from them!

b. The response (21:24–22:14)

(1) The baptism of John (21:24-32). **21:24-27 (Mark 11:29-33; Luke 20:3-8).** In response to the religious leaders' question, **Jesus** asked another **question,** promising that if they answered His question, He would answer theirs. He asked, **John's baptism—where did it come from? Was it from heaven, or from**

men? Though this question seemed fairly simple, it prompted a debate among the religious leaders. If they answered that John's baptism was from heaven, they knew Jesus would respond, Then why didn't you believe him? On the other hand if they responded that John's baptism was from men, they knew the people would be upset with them. John was regarded as a great prophet by the populace. Jesus thus put them in a position in which *they* had tried to place *Him* on many occasions. They finally responded that they did not know the answer to Jesus' question. In keeping with His word, Jesus therefore refused to answer their question. Instead He gave a parable.

21:28-32. In Jesus' parable a man asked his two sons to go . . . work in the vineyard. The first son said he would not go but later he changed his mind and went. The other immediately said he would go and work but he never showed up. Jesus then asked, Which of the two did what his father wanted? The obvious answer was that the first son obeyed. Jesus immediately applied this to the religious leaders. While some seemingly accepted the ministry of John the Baptist (John 5:35), their actions (Luke 7:29-30) proved they were like the second son. On the other hand many tax collectors and prostitutes received the message of John and did the will of the Father. Therefore they would be allowed entrance into the kingdom of God. But the religious leaders who did not repent and believe would be denied entrance. These religious leaders stood condemned. They must have been stunned by Jesus' words that despised, immoral people such as tax collectors and prostitutes were entering the kingdom and they, the religious leaders, were not!

(2) The Parable of the Landowner (21:33-46; Mark 12:1-12; Luke 20:9-19). **21:33-39.** In another parable Jesus continued to demonstrate the response of the nation to His ministry. He told of a landowner who went to great expense to make a vineyard productive. He rented out the vineyard to farmers who were to care for it. When harvesttime came, the landowner sent his servants . . . to collect what was rightfully his. But the tenant farmers mistreated the servants, beating one, killing another, and stoning a third.

Other servants were sent with the same results. Finally the landowner sent his son, thinking they would respect him. The farmers, however, reasoned that if they killed the son, the land would be theirs. Therefore they threw him out of the vineyard and killed him.

It seems clear that Jesus was speaking of the nation of Israel that had been carefully prepared by God to be His fruitful vineyard (cf. Isa. 5:1-7). The care of the vine had been committed to the nation's religious leaders. But they had failed to acknowledge the Master's right over them and had treated His messengers and prophets badly. They ultimately would even kill His Son, Jesus Christ, outside Jerusalem (cf. Heb. 13:12).

21:40-46. Jesus posed a natural question when He asked His listeners what they thought the landowner would do to those unfaithful farmers. Obviously he would not let them continue to operate the vineyard, but he would bring judgment on them. The land would be taken away from them and used by other tenants who would give him his rightful share of the harvest. This was in keeping with the Scriptures, for Jesus quoted Psalm 118:22-23, which refers to the rejected stone which will become the capstone.

By way of application Jesus said the kingdom of God was being taken away from those who heard Him, and it would be given to the people who would produce its fruit. The word for "people" (*ethnei*) is usually translated "nation." (It appears here without an article.) Two interpretations of this verse are often presented. One is that Jesus was saying the kingdom had been taken from the Jewish nation and would be given to Gentile nations who would produce the proper fruit of genuine faith. It is argued that since *ethnei* is singular, not plural, the word refers to the church which is called a nation in Romans 10:19 and 1 Peter 2:9-10. But the kingdom has not been taken completely away from Israel forever (Rom. 11:15, 25). And the church is not now inheriting the kingdom.

A better interpretation is that Jesus was simply saying the kingdom was being taken away from the nation Israel at that time, but it would be given back to the nation in a future day when that nation would demonstrate true repentance and faith. In this view Jesus was using the term "nation" in the sense of generation (cf. Matt. 23:36). Because of their rejection, that generation of Israel would never be able to experience the kingdom of God (cf. comments on 21:18-22). But a future generation in Israel will respond in saving faith to this same Messiah (Rom. 11:26-27), and to that future generation the kingdom will be given. By rejecting Jesus **the Stone,** these **builders** (Matt. 21:42) suffered judgment (**he on whom it** [the Stone] **falls will be crushed**). The religious leaders (then **the chief priests and the Pharisees,** v. 45; cf. v. 23) realized Jesus' remarks were directed toward **them,** and **they** tried their best **to arrest Him. But they were afraid of the . . . people** (cf. v. 26), who thought Jesus **was a Prophet** (cf. v. 11), so they were unable to act.

(3) The Parable of the Wedding Feast (22:1-14; Luke 14:15-24). **22:1-7.** In a third parable addressed to the religious leaders (cf. the other two parables in 21:28-32 and 21:33-44) **Jesus** again referred to God's work in offering **the kingdom.** The figure of **a wedding banquet** here portrays the Millennial Age (cf. 9:15; Isa. 25:6; Luke 14:15). The **king** in this parable had made plans for a wedding banquet **for his son.** His **servants** had told those **invited** that it was time **for the banquet,** but the invitation was ignored and the guests **refused to come.** Further effort was put forth to extend the invitation but the same result followed. Since the offer was rejected to the point of mistreating and killing the servants, **the king was enraged. He sent his army and destroyed those murderers and burned their city.**

Jesus had in mind the effect of the nation's rejection of Him. God had made plans for His Son's millennial reign and the invitation had been extended. But the preaching of John the Baptist, Jesus, and the disciples had largely been ignored. The nation would even kill those extending the offer. Finally in A.D. 70 the Roman army would come, kill most of the Jews living in Jerusalem, and destroy the temple.

22:8-14. The wedding banquet, however, was prepared. Since **those** who were first **invited** had rejected the invitation, opportunity to attend was then given to a broader group. Though the invitation was extended to **both good and bad,** individual preparation was still necessary. This was evidenced by the fact that one guest at the banquet had not made adequate preparation. He had failed to appropriate what the king provided for he **was not wearing** the proper **wedding clothes.** (Apparently the king gave them all wedding clothes as they arrived, for they came off **the streets** [v. 10]. A person must respond not only outwardly, but also he must be rightly related to God the King by appropriating all the King provides.) Consequently this guest was cast out into a place of separation and suffering. (For comments on **weeping and gnashing of teeth,** see 13:42.) While the kingdom had now been expanded to include individuals from all races and backgrounds (**many are invited**), there is an election (**few are chosen**). And yet individual response is essential.

2. CONFRONTATION WITH THE PHARISEES AND THE HERODIANS (22:15-22) (MARK 12:13-17; LUKE 20:20-26)

22:15-17. This incident illustrates that controversy often makes strange bedfellows. The religious leaders of Israel had one goal: to get rid of Jesus of Nazareth. They would do this through any means possible, even if it meant cooperating with lifelong enemies. **The Pharisees** were the purists of the nation who opposed Rome and all attempts by Rome to intrude into the Jewish way of life. But **the Herodians** actively supported the rule of Herod the Great and favored making changes with the times as dictated by Rome. But those issues were less important to them than the pressing issue of getting rid of Jesus. So they sent a delegation to try to trick Jesus.

They began by saying several nice things about Him, but their hypocrisy was obvious for they really did not believe in Him. Their question was, **Is it right to pay taxes to Caesar or not?** Their cleverly devised question appeared to have no clear-cut answer. They thought they had trapped Jesus. If He answered that it was right to pay taxes to Caesar, He would be siding with the Romans against Israel and most Jews, including the Pharisees, would consider Him a traitor. If, however, He said taxes should not be paid to Rome, He could be accused of being a rebel who opposed the authority of Rome, and the Herodians would be against Him.

22:18-22. Jesus was aware of the hypocrisy in their approach and also of the implications of His answer. He therefore answered their question by demonstrating that government does have a rightful place in everyone's life and that one can be in subjection to government and God at the same time. He asked them to give Him a **coin used** to pay **the tax.** A Roman **denarius,** with its image of Caesar, the Roman emperor, made it obvious they were under Roman authority and taxation. (One coin inscription reads, "Tiberius Caesar Augustus, son of the Divine Augustus.") Therefore the taxes must be paid: **Give to Caesar what is Caesar's.**

But Jesus also reminded them that a sphere of authority belongs to God: Give **to God what is God's.** Individuals are to be subject *also* to His authority. Man has both political *and* spiritual responsibilities. **Amazed** at Jesus' answer, both the Pharisees and the Herodians were silenced.

3. CONFRONTATION WITH THE SADDUCEES (22:23-33)

(MARK 12:18-27; LUKE 20:27-40)

22:23-28. The Sadducees were the next religious group to try to discredit Jesus and His ministry. The Sadducees were the "religious liberals" of their day for they said **there is no resurrection** or angels or spirits (Acts 23:8). Purposely their question centered on the doctrine of resurrection and its implications in a particular case. They cited the story of a woman who **married** a man who later **died.** In accordance with the levirate law (Deut. 25:5-10), her husband's **brother** took her as **his wife** (in order to perpetuate the dead brother's line). But he too died shortly thereafter. This happened with **seven brothers.**

The Sadducees' question therefore was, **At the resurrection, whose wife will she be of the seven, since all of them were married to her?** The Sadducees implied that heaven was simply an extension of things on earth men most enjoy, such as marital relationships. But if this woman had seven husbands, how could her marital relationship be possible? The Sadducees were trying to make the resurrection appear ridiculous.

22:29-33. The Sadducees' problems arose, Jesus said, because they did **not know the Scriptures or the power of God.** This was a strong denunciation of religious leaders, for of all people certainly they should have known God's Word and His power. God's Word taught the resurrection, and His power can bring people back to life. Jesus then corrected the Sadducees' two false notions: (1) **Heaven,** He said, is not simply an extension of the pleasures people enjoy on earth. In fact in the eternal state **marriage** will be unnecessary. Once individuals have received glorified bodies no longer subject to death, the need for procreation, one of the basic purposes for marriage, will no longer exist. Believers in glorified bodies **will be like the angels in** that regard, for angels do not reproduce themselves. (He did not say people will *become* angels.) Jesus did not answer all the questions about the eternal state and the eternal relationship of those married in this life. But He did answer the immediate question raised by the Sadducees. (2) A more important issue raised by the Sadducees pertained to **the resurrection.** If they had read and understood the Old Testament Scriptures, they would have clearly seen there is a future life and that when a person dies he continues to exist. To the Sadducees the resurrection was ridiculous because they believed death ended man's existence. But Jesus quoted a statement God had made directly to Moses at the burning bush: **I am the God of Abraham, the God of Isaac, and the God of Jacob** (Ex. 3:6). If the Sadducees were correct and Abraham, Isaac, and Jacob had died and were no longer present anywhere, the words "I am" should have been "I was." The use of the present tense, "I am," implied that God is still the God of these patriarchs for they are alive with God and ultimately will share in the resurrection of the righteous. As a result of this encounter, **the crowds . . . were astonished** (*exeplēssonto;* cf. comments on Matt. 7:28; and cf. *ethaumasan* in 22:22) all the more **at His teaching.** Jesus thus successfully answered and defeated these religious experts.

4. CONFRONTATION WITH THE PHARISEES (22:34-46)

(MARK 12:28-37; LUKE 10:25-28)

a. Their interrogation of Jesus (22:34-40)

22:34-40. When **the Pharisees** heard that **Jesus had** answered **the Sadducees,** they quickly sent a representative, a well-versed **expert in the Law,** to Jesus with a **question . . . Which is the greatest commandment in the Law?** This question was being debated among the religious leaders at the time and various commandments were being championed as the greatest. Jesus' quick reply summarized the entire Decalogue. He replied that the **greatest commandment** is to **love the Lord . . . God with all** one's **heart . . . soul, and . . . mind** (cf. Deut. 6:5). He added that **the second** commandment **is** to **love** one's **neighbor as** oneself (cf. Lev. 19:18). The first summarizes the first table of the Law, and the second summarizes the second table. Jesus said, **All the Law and the Prophets hang on these two commandments,** that is, all the Old Testament develops and amplifies these two points: love for God and love for others, who are made in God's image.

Mark reported that the teacher of the Law said Jesus had correctly answered the question, and that love for God and one's neighbor is more important than burnt offerings and sacrifices (Mark 12:32-33). The light was beginning to shine into his heart. He was not far, Jesus said, from the kingdom of God. Mark also added, "From then on no one dared ask Him any more questions" (Mark 12:34). The reason was obvious. Jesus was answering them as no had ever done. In fact in this last incident, the questioner was close to leaving the Pharisees and accepting Jesus. Perhaps they felt they should stop before they would lose any more people to Jesus' cause.

b. Jesus' interrogation of them (22:41-46)
(Mark 12:35-37; Luke 20:41-44)

22:41-46. Since **the Pharisees** refused to ask **Jesus** any further questions, He took the offensive and posed a question to **them.** His question sought to solicit their views concerning Messiah. He asked, **What do you think about the Christ? Whose Son is He?** Their answer came quickly for they knew the Messiah was to come from the line of David. Jesus' reply (vv. 43-45) demonstrated that the

Messiah had to be more than simply a human **son of David,** as many in that time were thinking. If the Messiah were simply an earthly son of David, why did David ascribe deity to Him? Jesus quoted from a messianic psalm (Ps. 110:1), in which David referred to the Messiah as **my Lord.** "Lord" translates the Hebrew *'ădōnāy*, used only of God (e.g., Gen. 18:27; Job 28:28). If David called this Son "Lord," He certainly must be more than a human son.

The complexities of this theological discussion were too much for the Pharisees who were not ready to acknowledge the deity of this Son of David. **No one . . . dared** answer His question or debate points of practice or theology with Jesus. All His opponents had been silenced, including the chief priests and elders (Matt. 21:23-27), the Pharisees and the Herodians together (22:15-22), the Sadducees (vv. 23-33), and the Pharisees (vv. 34-36).

C. The national rejection of the King (chap. 23)
(Mark 12:38-40; Luke 11:37-52; 20:45-47)

1. HIS WARNING TO THE MULTITUDES (23:1-12)

23:1-12. The hypocrisy and unbelief of the nation's religious leaders, evidenced in chapter 22, prompted a strong message from **Jesus.** He turned **to the crowds and to His disciples,** who were in the temple listening to His debates with the various religious leaders. He warned them about their teachings saying that their *authority* was to be recognized (they **sit in Moses' seat,** i.e., they teach the Law), but their *practices,* being hypocritical, should not be followed. They placed **heavy** burdens **on** people but were not righteous **themselves** (23:4). All their works were performed to be observed by **men. Their phylacteries,** small leather pouches containing strips of parchment with Old Testament verses (Ex. 13:9, 16; Deut. 6:8; 11:18), tied to their left arms and foreheads, were **wide** and thus conspicuous. **And the tassels of their prayer shawls** (Num. 15:38) were **long** and noticeable. **They loved places of honor** and to be called **Rabbi,** implying they were scholars. Such was not to be the attitude of Jesus' followers. Titles (such as **Rabbi . . . father . . . teacher)** and position were not to be sought; instead there should be a brotherly relationship among the disciples (Matt. 23:8).

Jesus was not saying there would be no lines of authority among them. But He was emphasizing that service for Him— the one Master (didaskalos, lit., "teacher") and one Teacher (kathēgētēs, "an authoritative guide," used only here in the NT)— was more important than human positions of honor. Leadership positions should never be a goal in and of themselves, but should always be viewed as opportunities to serve others. The Pharisees, who exalted themselves, would be humbled, and Jesus' followers, by humbling themselves in service, would someday be exalted.

2. HIS WARNINGS TO THE LEADERS (23:13-39)

23:13. In warning the **teachers of the Law** and the **Pharisees** of their ultimate destruction if they continued in their present path, Jesus pronounced seven denunciations, each beginning with **Woe to you.** "Those woes, in contrast to the Beatitudes, denounce false religion as utterly abhorrent to God and worthy of severe condemnation" (Walvoord, *Matthew: Thy Kingdom Come*, p. 171). In six of the seven, Jesus called the leaders **you hypocrites.**

His first denunciation concerned the fact that the Pharisees were preventing others from entering **the kingdom.** Their antagonism toward Jesus had caused many to turn away from Him. Many Jews were looking to their leaders for direction. Their failure to accept Jesus as Messiah had placed a stumbling block in the paths of their countrymen. For this they stood condemned.

23:14. The NIV and some Greek manuscripts omit this verse. It may have been added because of Mark 12:40 and Luke 20:47. If it is authentic here, the number of woes is eight. This "woe" demonstrated the inconsistency of the religious leaders for they made long "prayers" to impress people with their spirituality, but also oppressed widows, whom they should have helped.

23:15. This **woe** addressed the zealous activity of the religious leaders for they actively traveled not only **over land** but also over the **sea to** make even **a single convert** (prosēlyton, "proselyte") to Judaism. The problem with this was that by their actions they were condemning many individuals to eternal damnation. By imposing external restrictions of Rabbinic traditions on their converts, they were preventing these people from seeing the truth. In fact, such a convert became **twice as much a son of hell as** the Pharisees, that is, he became more pharisaic than the Pharisees themselves! "A son of hell" (lit., "of Gehenna"; cf. v. 33), was one deserving eternal punishment.

23:16-22. In the third **woe** Jesus pointed out the tricky character of the leaders. (In the first two woes Jesus spoke of the leaders' effects on others; in the other five woes He spoke of the leaders' own characters and actions.) When taking oaths, they made fine lines of distinction that could possibly invalidate their oaths. If one swore **by the temple,** or **by the altar** of the temple, it meant nothing to them. While thus appearing to be making a binding oath, they inwardly had no intention of keeping it. **But if** one swore **by the gold of the temple** or **the gift on** the altar, **he** would be **bound by** the **oath.** But Jesus said they were wrong in suggesting that **gold** was **greater** than **the temple** and a **gift** greater than **the altar.** Jesus pointed out that any oath based on **the temple** or things in it was binding for behind the temple was **the One who dwelt in it.** This was parallel to making an oath **by God's throne,** for that oath was also binding because of the One who sat on the throne. Such distinctions by the religious leaders were condemned by Jesus, for they were clearly deceptive and dishonest. Jesus denounced those leaders as **blind guides** (v. 16), **blind fools** (v. 17), and **blind men** (v. 19; cf. vv. 24, 26).

23:23-24. The fourth **woe** related to the pharisaic practice of meticulously tithing all their possessions. They went so far as to carry the practice down to the smallest **spices** from plants: **mint, dill, and cummin.** While meticulously following **the Law** in this area (Lev. 27:30), they failed to manifest the **justice, mercy, and faithfulness** demanded by the Law. They were majoring on minors, straining **out a gnat,** while minoring on majors, swallowing **a camel.** Being so busy with small details, they never dealt with the important matters. Jesus was not saying tithing was unimportant; He was saying they were completely **neglecting the** one area at the expense of the other. They **should have** been doing both. Since they were not, they were **blind guides.**

23:25-26. The fifth **woe** emphasized the hypocritical nature of the **Pharisees.** They were concerned with external cleanliness, such as **the outside of the cup and dish** from which they would eat. **But in their hearts were greed and self-indulgence.** Their cleansing was primarily for the sake of being seen by men. But they were not above robbery and excesses in their own lives. If cleansing would take place internally, their **outside** would **also be** affected.

23:27-28. In the sixth **woe** Jesus continued the thought of the previous statement about external purification. The fifth woe stressed their actions; the sixth, their appearances. He called the **teachers of the Law and the Pharisees . . . whitewashed tombs.** A custom then was to keep tombs painted white **on the outside** so they would appear **beautiful.** But **inside** the tombs was the decaying flesh of dead people. Similarly, while the Pharisees appeared beautiful **on the outside** because of their religious conformity, they were corrupt and decaying **inside.** They were **full of hypocrisy and wickedness** (*anomias*, "lawlessness").

23:29-32. The final **woe** also emphasized the religious leaders' hypocrisy. They spent time building **tombs** and decorating **the graves of the righteous.** They were quick to **say** that **if they had lived in the** time **of the prophets,** they would never have been involved **in shedding the blood** of these righteous men. Jesus knew they were already in the process of planning His death. By that act they would demonstrate they were just like the former generations **who murdered the prophets.** By rejecting the Prophet, they would be following in the footsteps of their forefathers and "filling up" their ancestors' **sin.**

23:33-36. In severe language Jesus condemned the religious leaders, calling them **snakes** and a **brood of vipers,** whose eternal destiny was **hell** (lit., "Gehenna"), the place of eternal punishment (cf. v. 15; cf. comments on Gehenna in 5:22). The evidence that they were deserving of hell would be their continual rejection of the truth. The Lord promised to send them **prophets and wise men and teachers,** but the leaders would reject their words and even **kill** some and **flog** and **pursue** others. Their response to the proclaimed truth would justify the judgment coming on them. **Abel** was the first **righteous** martyr mentioned in the Hebrew Scriptures (Gen. 4:8) and **Zechariah** was the last martyr (2 Chron. 24:20-22), 2 Chronicles being last in the Hebrew Bible. (In this statement Jesus attested the Old Testament canon.) In 2 Chronicles 24:20, Zechariah is called the "son of Jehoiada," whereas in Matthew he is the **son of Berakiah.** "Son of" can mean descendant; thus Jehoiada, being a priest, could have been Zechariah's grandfather. Or Jesus may have had in mind the Prophet Zechariah who *was* the son of Berakiah (Zech. 1:1). On that **generation** (*genean*) of Jews, who were guilty because they were following their blind (Matt. 23:16-17, 19, 24, 26) leaders, would fall God's judgment for their involvement in shedding innocent **blood.** The Lord was anticipating the nation's continuing rejection of the gospel. Their refusal of the Messiah ultimately led to the destruction of the temple in A.D. 70.

23:37-39 (Luke 13:34-35). In a final lament over the city of **Jerusalem,** Jesus stated His desire for that nation. **Jerusalem,** the capital, represented the entire nation, and people there had killed **the prophets and** stoned **those sent to** them (cf. Matt. 23:34; 21:35). He **longed to gather** the nation **together** much **as a hen gathers her chicks under her wings.** The nation, unlike chicks that naturally run to their mother hen in times of danger, willfully refused (**you were not willing**) to turn to the Lord. They were responsible to make a choice and their choice brought condemnation. The result was their **house** was **left . . . desolate,** or alone. Their "house" could mean their city; this is probably the most commonly accepted view. Or Jesus might have meant the temple or even the Davidic dynasty. Perhaps all these are involved.

But Jesus is not through with the nation and the city of Jerusalem. Though He would soon depart (John 13:33), at a future time He will be seen **again** (Zech. 12:10) and will be accepted, not rejected. In that day the nation will say, **Blessed is He who comes in the name of the Lord,** a quotation of Psalm 118:26. Jesus was speaking of His return to the earth to establish His millennial kingdom. This statement led to the following discussion.

D. The prophetic anticipation of the King (chaps. 24–25)

1. THE INQUIRY TO JESUS (24:1-3)
(MARK 13:1-4; LUKE 21:5-7)

24:1-3. Having completed His discussions and debates with the religious leaders, **Jesus left the temple** to return to Bethany (cf. 26:6) by way of **the Mount of Olives** (24:3). The words Jesus had just uttered were still burning in **His** disciples' ears. He had denounced the nation and said it would be "desolate" (23:38). If Jerusalem and the temple were destroyed, how would there be a nation for Messiah to rule? The **disciples** pointed out the **buildings** of the temple area to Jesus as if to impress Him with their magnificence. What could possibly happen to such impressive buildings, especially to the temple of God? Jesus' response brought them consternation: **Not one stone here will be left on another; every one will be thrown down.** The temple would be destroyed and Jerusalem with it. This, however, prompted **the disciples** to ask when all this would take place. As Jesus reached the Mount of Olives in His walk to Bethany, He sat down and the disciples **came to Him.** Four disciples, Peter, James, John, and Andrew (Mark 13:3), plainly asked Jesus two questions: (1) **When will this happen?** That is, when will the temple be destroyed and not one stone left on another? (2) **What will be the sign of Your coming and of the end of the Age?**

These two questions prompted the following discussion by Jesus, commonly called the Olivet Discourse (Matt. 24–25). The questions related to the destruction of the temple and Jerusalem, and the sign of the Lord's coming and the end of the Age. They have nothing to do with the church, which Jesus said He would build (16:18). The church is not present in any sense in chapters 24 and 25. The disciples' questions related to Jerusalem, Israel, and the Lord's second coming in glory to establish His kingdom. Actually Matthew did not record Jesus' answer to the first question, but Luke did (Luke 21:20). The disciples felt that the destruction of Jerusalem, of which Jesus had spoken, would usher in the kingdom. They were thinking, no doubt, of Zecha-

riah 14:1-2. (The destruction Jesus referred to in Matt. 23:38 occurred in A.D. 70, a destruction separate from the final one in Zech. 14.)

2. THE COMING TIME OF TROUBLE (24:4-26)

24:4-8 (Mark 13:5-8; Luke 21:8-11). Jesus began to describe the events leading up to His return in glory and to indicate signs of that return. In this section (Matt. 24:4-8) He described the first half of the seven-year period preceding His second coming. That period is called the Seventieth Week of Daniel (Dan. 9:27). (However, some premillenarians hold that Christ in Matt. 24:4-8 spoke of general signs in the present Church Age and that the time of trouble begins at v. 9. Others hold that Christ spoke of general signs in vv. 4-14, with the Tribulation beginning at v. 15.) The events described in verses 4-8 correspond somewhat to the seven seals in Revelation 6. (Walvoord, however, holds that all seven of the seal judgments will occur in the second half of the seven-year period; see comments on Rev. 6.)

That period will be characterized by (a) false Christs (Matt. 24:4-5; cf. Rev. 6:1-2; the first seal is Antichrist), (b) **wars and rumors of wars** (Matt. 24:6; cf. Rev. 6:3-4; the second seal is warfare) in which nations **will rise** up **against** each other on a global scale (Matt. 24:7a), and (c) unusual disturbances in nature including **famines** (v. 7b; cf. Rev. 6:5-6; the third seal is famine; the fourth and fifth seals are death and martyrdom [Rev. 6:7-11]) **and earthquakes** (Matt. 24:7b; cf. Rev. 6:12-14; the sixth seal is an earthquake). **These** things, Jesus said, will be **the beginning of birth pains.** As a pregnant woman's birth pains indicate that her child will soon be born, so these universal conflicts and catastrophes will mean the end of this interadvent Age is near.

24:9-14 (Mark 13:9-13; Luke 21:12-19). Jesus began His words (Matt. 24:9) with a time word, **Then.** At the middle point of the seven-year period preceding Christ's second coming, great distress will begin to be experienced by Israel. The Antichrist, who will have risen to power in the world and will have made a protective treaty with Israel, will break his agreement at that time (Dan. 9:27). He will bring great persecution on Israel (Dan. 7:25) and even establish his own center of worship in the temple in Jerusalem (2 Thes. 2:3-4). This will result in the **death** of many Jews (Matt. 24:9) and **many** people departing **from the faith.** Believing Jews **will** be betrayed by nonbelievers (v. 10), and **many** will be deceived by rising **false prophets** (cf. v. 5; Rev. 13:11-15). **Wickedness** will **increase,** causing **the love of most** people (for the Lord) to **grow cold.**

Those who remain faithful to the Lord until **the end** of that period of time **will be saved,** that is, delivered (Matt. 24:13). This does not refer to a personal self-effort at endurance that results in one's eternal salvation, but to physical deliverance of those who trust in the Savior during the Tribulation. They will enter the kingdom in physical bodies.

Also the **gospel of the kingdom will be preached in the whole world** during this period **as a testimony to all nations.** Though this will be a terrible time of persecution, the Lord will have servants who will witness and spread the good news concerning Christ and His soon-coming kingdom. This message will be similar to that preached by John the Baptist, Jesus, and the disciples at the beginning of Matthew's Gospel, but this message will clearly identify Jesus in His true character as the coming Messiah. This is not exactly the same message the church is proclaiming today. The message preached today in the Church Age and the message proclaimed in the Tribulation period calls for turning to the Savior for salvation. However, in the Tribulation the message will stress the coming kingdom, and those who then turn to the Savior for salvation will be allowed entrance into the kingdom. Apparently many will respond to that message (cf. Rev. 7:9-10).

24:15-26 (Mark 13:14-23; Luke 21:20-26). Having given a brief overview of the entire Tribulation period prior to His return, Jesus then spoke of the greatest observable sign within that period, **the abomination that causes desolation.** This abomination was **spoken of** by **Daniel** (Dan. 9:27). It referred to the disruption of the Jewish worship which will be reinstituted in the Tribulation temple (Dan. 12:11) and the establishment of the worship of the world dictator, the Antichrist, in the temple. He will make the temple abominable (and there-

fore desolate) by setting up in the temple an image of himself to be worshiped (2 Thes. 2:4; Rev. 13:14-15). Such an event will be clearly recognizable by everyone.

When that event occurs, **those . . . in Judea** should **flee to the mountains.** They should not be concerned about taking **anything** with them or returning from **the field** for possessions, not even for a **cloak.** The time following this event will be a time of **great distress, unequaled from the beginning of the world . . . and never to be equaled again** (Jer. 30:7). The awful character of the Tribulation period cannot be truly grasped by anyone. This was why Jesus pointed out how difficult the time would be **for pregnant women and nursing mothers** (Matt. 24:19). He encouraged people to **pray that** their escape would **not** have to be **in the winter** when it would be difficult **or on the Sabbath** when travel would be limited.

There was an encouraging note, however, for the Lord declared that **those days** would be **cut short** (v. 22). This meant there will be a termination of this period of time, not that the days will be fewer than 24 hours. If it were to go on indefinitely, **no one would survive. But** the period will come to an end **for the sake of the elect,** those who will be redeemed in the Tribulation and who will enter the kingdom. The elect of this Church Age will have already been raptured before the Tribulation. Much misinformation will be disseminated then **for false Christs** will be all around (vv. 23-24). They all will be preaching messages of salvation and performing **signs and miracles,** seeking to **deceive even the elect.** The Lord warned the disciples **ahead of time** not to be fooled for He would not be on earth working in that way.

3. THE COMING OF THE SON OF MAN (24:27-31)

(MARK 13:24-27; LUKE 21:25-28)

24:27-31. The Lord will not be on the earth bodily at that time, but He will return to earth. And His **coming** will be like **lightning** flashing **from the east . . . to the west;** it will be a splendorous, visible event. **Wherever there is a carcass** (physical corruption), **vultures will** go there to eat it. Similarly, where there is spiritual corruption judgment will follow. The world will have become the domain of Satan's man, the Antichrist, the lawless one (2 Thes. 2:8), and many people will have been corrupted by false prophets (Matt. 24:24). But **the Son of Man** will come quickly in judgment (v. 27).

Immediately following **the distress of** that period, the Lord will return. His return will be accompanied by unusual displays in the heavens (v. 29; cf. Isa. 13:10; 34:4; Joel 2:31; 3:15-16) and by the appearing of His "sign" **in the sky** (Matt. 24:30). The appearance of the sign will cause **all the nations** to **mourn** (cf. Rev. 1:7), probably because they will realize the time of their judgment has come.

Exactly what **the sign of the Son of Man will** be is unknown. The sign of the setting aside of the nation of Israel was the departure of the glory from the temple (Ezek. 10:3, 18; 11:23). Perhaps the sign of the Lord's return will again involve the Shekinah glory. Some believe the sign may involve the heavenly city, New Jerusalem, which may descend at this time and remain as a satellite city suspended over the earthly city Jerusalem throughout the Millennium (Rev. 21:2-3). Or the sign may be the lightning, or perhaps the Lord Himself. Whatever the sign, it will be visible for all to see, for the Lord will return **on the clouds . . . with power and great glory** (cf. Dan. 7:13). **He will** then **send His angels forth** to regather **His elect from the four winds,** which relates to the earth (cf. Mark 13:27), **from one end of the heavens to the other.** This involves the gathering of those who will have become believers during the Seventieth Week of Daniel and who will have been scattered into various parts of the world because of persecution (cf. Matt. 24:16). This gathering will probably also involve all Old Testament saints, whose resurrection will occur at this time, so that they may share in Messiah's kingdom (Dan. 12:2-3, 13).

4. THE CONFIRMATION BY PARABLES (24:32-51)

In the previous portion of this sermon (24:4-31) Jesus had spoken directly about His return to earth. Then He gave some practical applications and instructions in light of His return. One should keep in mind that the primary application of this section is directed toward the future generation that will experience the days of the Tribulation and will be looking forward to the immediate coming of the King in glory. A secondary application of this passage, as with much of Scripture, is to believers living today who comprise the body of Christ, the church. The church is not in view in these verses. But just as God's people in a future time are told to be prepared, watchful, and faithful, so too believers today should also be faithful and alert.

a. The fig tree (24:32-44)

24:32-35 (Mark 13:28-31; Luke 21:29-33). Jesus' words, **Now learn this lesson,** show that He was beginning to apply what He had been teaching. When the **twigs** of **fig** trees begin to **get tender** and put forth **leaves,** that is a sure sign **summer is** not far away (cf. Matt. 21:18-20). Just as a fig tree was a harbinger of summer, so these signs (24:4-28) Jesus had been speaking of clearly indicated that His coming would follow shortly. The Lord's emphasis fell on the fact that **all these things** would be necessary. While various events throughout history have been pointed to as the fulfillment of this prophecy, clearly *all* these things (pertaining to the Great Tribulation) have never occurred. The completion of all these events is yet future. The **generation** (*genea*) of people living in that future day will see the completion of all the events. Jesus was not referring to the generation listening to Him then, for He had already said the kingdom had been taken from that group (21:43). That first-century generation would experience God's judgment. But the generation that will be living at the time these signs begin to take place will live through that period and will see the Lord Jesus coming as the King of glory. This promise is sure, for it would be easier for **heaven and earth** to **pass away** than for Christ's **words** to fail (cf. 5:18).

24:36-41 (Mark 13:32-33; Luke 17:26-37). The precise moment of the Lord's return cannot be calculated by anyone. When the Lord spoke these words, that information was said to be known by **only the Father.** Christ was obviously speaking from the vantage of His human knowledge (cf. Luke 2:52), not from the standpoint of His divine omniscience. But the period before His coming will be like the time **in the days of Noah. People** then were enjoying the normal pursuits of life, with no awareness of imminent judgment. Life continued normally for the people of Noah's day for they **were eating, drinking, marrying, and giving in marriage.** But **the Flood came and took them all away.** It was sudden and they were unprepared.

As it was in Noah's day, **so it will be** before the glorious **coming of the** Lord. **Two men will be in the field; one will be taken and the other left. Two women will be grinding with a hand mill; one will be taken and the other left.** Analogous to Noah's day, the individuals who will be "taken" are the wicked whom the Lord will take away in judgment (cf. Luke 17:37). The individuals "left" are believers who will be privileged to be on the earth to populate the kingdom of Jesus Christ in physical bodies. As the wicked were taken away in judgment and Noah was left on the earth, so the wicked will be judged and removed when Christ returns and the righteous will be left behind to become His subjects in the kingdom.

Clearly the church, the body of Christ, cannot be in view in these statements. The Lord was not describing the Rapture, for the removal of the church will not be a judgment on the church. If this were the Rapture, as some commentators affirm, the Rapture would have to be posttribulational, for this event occurs immediately before the Lord's return in glory. But that would conflict with a number of Scriptures and present other problems that cannot be elaborated on here (cf., e.g., comments on 1 Thes. 4:13-18 and Rev. 3:10). The Lord's warning emphasized the need to be prepared, for judgment will come at a time when people will least expect it.

24:42-44. The Lord encouraged His disciples to **keep watch** (*grēgoreite,* the word rendered "be alert" in 1 Thes. 5:6), **because** they could **not know on what day** the Lord would **come** (cf. Matt. 25:13). The limits of the Tribulation period are known to God, for the Seventieth Week of Daniel will have a definite starting time and a definite ending time. But the people living then will only know in generalities the limits of the time. Therefore watchfulness is important. If a person knows the approximate **time** a **thief** may come to break into **his house,** he takes precautions and prepares accordingly. Likewise believers in the Tribulation, who will be looking forward to the coming of the Lord of glory, should be alert. They will know generally, from the signs of the end, when He will return, but they will not know the exact time.

b. The faithful servant (24:45-51)
(Mark 13:34-37; Luke 12:41-48)

24:45-51. The coming of the Lord will be a test of servants. As **the master** in Jesus' story entrusted all his possessions to his **servant,** so God has entrusted the care of all things in this earth to His servants. The responses of the servants are indications of their inward conditions. The Lord wants to find His servants, like the first steward, faithfully carrying out His will (vv. 45-46). Such a **servant** will be rewarded for his faithful service when the Lord returns (v. 47). But a **servant** who fails to carry out his stewardship will be judged severely. Such a servant, concluding that his **master** was not returning for **a long time,** took advantage of others (he **beat his fellow servants**) and lived wickedly (eating and drinking **with drunkards**). Like the wicked people of Noah's day (vv. 37-39), he was unaware of the sudden coming judgment (v. 50). But the judgment **will come** and he will be dealt with as one would deal with a hypocrite, which is precisely what an unfaithful servant is. His separation will result in eternal judgment (**weeping and gnashing of teeth;** cf. comments on 13:42) apart from his master. Likewise the judgment of the wicked at the Lord's second coming will separate them eternally from God.

5. THE COMING JUDGMENT ON ISRAEL
(25:1-30)

25:1-13. When Christ returns in glory, further separations will occur, as indicated by the Parable of the **10 Virgins.** While various interpretations have been given to this parable, it seems best to understand it as a judgment on living Jews soon after the Lord's return in glory. The context clearly points to that event (24:3, 14, 27, 30, 39, 44, 51). The judgment of the Gentiles (sheep and goats) will occur when the Lord returns (25:31-46). Also at His glorious return,

Israel will be judged as a nation (Ezek. 20:33-44; Zech. 13:1).

Israel therefore is pictured as 10 virgins who are awaiting the return of **the bridegroom.** In wedding customs in Jesus' day, the bridegroom would return from the house of the bride in a procession leading to his own home where a wedding banquet would be enjoyed. In Jesus' parable, He as King will return from heaven with His bride, the church, in order to enter into the Millennium. The Jews in the Tribulation will be some of the invited guests privileged to share in the feast.

But preparation is necessary. In the parable, **five of** the virgins had made adequate preparation for they possessed the necessary **lamps** and extra **oil in jars** (Matt. 25:4). Five others had **lamps but** no extra **oil. At midnight . . . the bridegroom** arrived. The **lamps** of the five virgins without extra oil were **going out.** So they had to go searching for **oil** and missed the arrival of **the bridegroom.** When they returned and found the **wedding** feast in progress, they sought admission but were denied (vv. 10-12).

Israel in the Tribulation will know that Jesus' coming is near, but not all will be spiritually prepared for it. His coming will be sudden, when it is not expected (24:27, 39, 50). Though this passage does not specifically interpret the meaning of the oil, many commentators see it as representing the Holy Spirit and His work in salvation. Salvation is more than mere profession for it involves regeneration by the Holy Spirit. Those who will merely profess to be saved, and do not actually possess the Spirit, will be excluded from the feast, that is, the kingdom. Those who fail to be ready when the King comes, cannot enter His kingdom. Since **the day** and **hour** of His return are unknown, believers in the Tribulation should **keep watch** (*grēgoreite*), that is, be alert and prepared (cf. 24:42).

25:14-30 (Luke 19:11-27). In another parable on faithfulness, Jesus told the story of a master with three **servants.** The master went **on a journey** and **gave** each servant a specific amount of money, **talents.** The talents were of silver (**money** in Matt. 25:18 is *argyrion*, which means silver money). A **talent** weighed between 58 and 80 pounds. Thus the master entrusted his servants with considerable amounts of money. The amounts were in keeping with the men's abilities.

Two of the servants were **faithful** in caring for the master's money (vv. 16-17) and were accordingly rewarded for their faithfulness with additional wealth, additional responsibilities, and sharing of the **master's** joy (vv. 20-23). The third servant, having **received the one talent,** reasoned that his **master** might not be coming back at all. If he did return someday, the servant could simply return the talent to his master without loss from any poor investment (v. 25). But if he failed to return, the servant wanted to be able to keep the talent for himself. He did not want to deposit the talent in a bank where it would be recorded that the talent belonged to the master (v. 27). His reasoning indicated he lacked faith in his master; he proved to be a **worthless servant.** As a result, he lost what he had (v. 29; cf. 13:12), and was cast into judgment. Like the unworthy servant in 24:48-51, he too would be eternally separated from God. On **weeping and gnashing of teeth** see comments on 13:42. The Parable of the 10 Virgins (25:1-13) stressed the need for preparedness for the Messiah's return. This Parable of the Talents stressed the need to serve the King while He is away.

6. THE COMING JUDGMENT ON GENTILES (25:31-46)

When the Lord returns "in His glory," He will judge not only the nation Israel (as in the Parable of the 10 Virgins [vv. 1-13] and the Parable of the Talents [vv. 14-30]) but also the Gentiles. This is not the same as the great white throne judgment, which involves only the wicked and which follows the Millennium (Rev. 20:13-15). The judgment of the Gentiles will occur 1,000 years earlier in order to determine who will and will not enter the kingdom.

25:31-33. The words **the nations** (*ta ethnē*) should be translated "the Gentiles." These are all **people,** other than Jews, who have lived through the Tribulation period (cf. Joel 3:2, 12). They will be judged individually, not as national groups. They are described as a mingling of **sheep** and **goats,** which the Lord will separate.

25:34-40. The King "on His throne" (v. 31) will extend an invitation **to those**

on His right hand, the sheep, to enter **the kingdom** God had **prepared . . . since the Creation of the world.** The basis of their entrance is seen in their actions, for they provided food, **drink,** clothing, and care for the King (vv. 35-36). The King's statement will prompt the sheep to respond that they do not recall ever having ministered directly to the King (vv. 37-39). **The King will** answer that they performed these services for **the least of these brothers of Mine,** and by so doing were ministering to the King (v. 40).

The expression "these brothers" must refer to a third group that is neither sheep nor goats. The only possible group would be Jews, physical brothers of the Lord. In view of the distress in the Tribulation period, it is clear that any believing Jew will have a difficult time surviving (cf. 24:15-21). The forces of the world dictator will be doing everything possible to exterminate all Jews (cf. Rev. 12:17). A Gentile going out of his way to assist a Jew in the Tribulation will mean that Gentile has become a believer in Jesus Christ during the Tribulation. By such a stand and action, a believing Gentile will put his life in jeopardy. His works will not save him; but his works will reveal that he is redeemed.

25:41-46. To the goats **on His left** hand (cf. v. 33) the King will pronounce judgment. They will be told, **Depart . . . into the eternal fire prepared** not for men but **for the devil and his angels** (cf. "the kingdom prepared," v. 34). The basis of their judgment will be their failure to extend mercy to the remnant of Jewish believers during the Tribulation. Their lack of righteous works will evidence their unconcern (vv. 42-44; cf. vv. 35-36). Such individuals will sympathize with the world dictator and support his cause. They will be removed from the earth and will be cast into "eternal fire" (v. 41) to undergo **eternal punishment** (v. 46). With all wickedness removed in the various judgments at the Second Advent, the kingdom will begin on earth with only saved individuals in physical bodies constituting the earthly kingdom as the King's subjects. Glorified saints from Old Testament times and the church, the bride of Christ, will also be present to share in the reign of the King of kings.

In this extended prophetic sermon, Jesus answered His disciples' questions about the sign of His coming and the end of the Age (24:4-31). He also presented practical lessons for those who will be living at that time (24:32-51), encouraging them to faithfulness, watchfulness, and preparedness. By way of application these lessons are relevant to all believers in any Age. He concluded by pointing out the establishment of the kingdom and the judgment of Jews (25:1-30) and of Gentiles (vv. 31-46).

E. The national rejection of the King (chaps. 26–27)

1. THE PRELIMINARY EVENTS (26:1-46)

a. The developing of the plot (26:1-5) (Mark 14:1-2; Luke 22:1-2; John 11:45-53)

26:1-5. The words, **When Jesus had finished saying all these things,** are the last of five such turning points in the book (cf. 7:28; 11:1; 13:53; 19:1). As soon as Jesus completed the Olivet Discourse, He reminded the **disciples** that **the Passover** feast was only **two days away** and that He would **be handed over to be crucified.** The events in 26:1-16 occurred on Wednesday. Though there is no record of the disciples' reactions to the Lord's words, Matthew did record the plot that developed among the religious leaders to **kill Him. In the palace of the high priest . . . Caiaphas,** the plan was begun **to arrest Jesus in some sly way** but **not** until **the Feast** had passed. Their thinking was to wait until the many pilgrims who had converged on Jerusalem for the Passover had gone home. Then they would dispose of Jesus in a quiet way. Their timing was not God's timing, however, and the advancement in the timetable was due in part to the willingness of Judas Iscariot who volunteered to betray the Lord.

b. The anointing by perfume (26:6-13) (Mark 14:3-9; John 12:1-8)

26:6-9. During the final week of His life before the Cross, the Lord spent the nights in **Bethany,** east of Jerusalem on the south slopes of the Mount of Olives. Matthew recorded an event that took place one evening **in the home of . . . Simon the Leper.** John described the same event in greater detail (John 12:1-8), giving the names of the individuals. The **woman** who **poured** the oil **on** Jesus' **head** was Mary (John 12:3), and the disciple who first objected to the action was Judas Iscariot (John 12:4). The **perfume** was **very expensive** (Matt. 26:7), worth "a year's wages" (John 12:5; lit., "300 denarii"). Obviously this act of love was costly for Mary.

26:10-13. The Lord was aware of the disciples' comments ("Why this waste?" v. 8) and their heart attitude ("they were indignant," v. 8; cf. 20:24; 21:15) behind their words. Judas Iscariot was not motivated by his concern for **the poor** (John 12:6). He was a thief and was concerned about the money not being put in their common purse which he controlled. Jesus reminded them that because **the poor** would **always** be **with** them they would have many opportunities to show kindness, but He would **not always** be among them.

Mary's **beautiful** act prepared His body **for burial** (Matt. 26:12). Jesus had spoken several times of His coming death (e.g., 16:21; 17:22; 20:18), but the disciples did not seem to believe His words. Mary believed and performed this act as a testimony of her devotion to Him. As a result her sacrificial act is often proclaimed **throughout the world.** Perhaps it was this act and the Lord's approval of it that made Judas willing to betray the Lord. From this scene Judas went to the chief priests and offered to betray Jesus.

c. The plan for betrayal (26:14-16)
(Mark 14:10-11; Luke 22:3-6)

26:14-16. Judas Iscariot must have been viewed by the religious leaders as an answer to their prayers. Judas' offer **to the chief priests** to betray Jesus Christ was more than agreeing to point out Jesus to arresting officers. Judas was offering his services as a witness against Jesus when He would be brought to trial. He would do anything to gain more money (cf. John 12:6). The offer was made in exchange for funds, probably paid out immediately to Judas. **Thirty silver coins** were the redemption price paid for a slave (Ex. 21:32). This same amount was also prophesied as the price for the services of the rejected Shepherd (Zech. 11:12). The exact value of the agreed price cannot be determined because the coinage was not identified; it was simply called "silver"

(*argyria*; cf. Matt. 25:18). But it could have been a substantial amount. The bargain had been struck and **Judas** was now being looked to by the religious leaders as their deliverer from their biggest problem, Jesus of Nazareth. Judas knew he had to follow through, for his word had been given and money had been exchanged.

d. The celebrating of the Passover
(26:17-30)

26:17-19 (Mark 14:12-16; Luke 22:7-13). Most Bible students believe that the events recorded in Matthew 26:17-30 took place on Thursday of Passion Week. This was **the first day of the** seven-day **Feast of Unleavened Bread.** On that first day Passover lambs were sacrificed (Mark 14:12). The Feast of Unleavened Bread followed immediately after the Passover; the entire eight-day event was sometimes called the Passover Week (cf. Luke 2:41; 22:1, 7; Acts 12:3-4; see comments on Luke 22:7).

The disciples who were sent to make preparations for **the Passover** meal were Peter and John (Luke 22:8). The place of the Passover celebration is not designated in any of the Gospels, though it took place in **the city** (Matt. 26:18), that is, Jerusalem, probably in the home of someone who acknowledged Jesus as Messiah. That he willingly opened his home indicated he had an awareness of Jesus and His claims. Besides finding the location, **the two disciples . . . prepared the Passover,** that is, they purchased and prepared the food, which probably took them the greater part of the day.

26:20-25 (Mark 14:17-21; Luke 22:14-23; John 13:21-30). When evening came, Jesus entered the prepared room, an "upper" (upstairs) room (Luke 22:12), and partook of the Passover supper **with the Twelve.** During the celebration, Jesus said that **one of** those sitting with Him was about to **betray** Him. This revealed Jesus' omniscience (cf. John 2:25; 4:29). Surprisingly no disciple pointed to another with an accusing finger, but each became **very sad and began to** ask if he would be the betrayer. **Jesus** added that **the one** betraying Him had been sharing close fellowship with Him; they had eaten out of **the** same **bowl.** Jesus said He would **go** (i.e., die) **just as it** had been **written** by prophets (e.g., Isa. 53:4-8; cf. Matt. 26:56). **But woe to the one who**

would betray Him. **It would be better for that one if he had never been born.** Jesus was pointing out to Judas the consequences of his betrayal, for while he had already taken the money to betray Jesus the act was not yet accomplished. When **Judas** asked the Lord, **Surely not I, Rabbi? Jesus** clearly pointed him out as the betrayer. Not surprisingly, Judas called Him "Rabbi," not "Lord" as did the other disciples (v. 22; cf. v. 49).

The Lord's words were not understood by the other disciples, as John made clear (John 13:28-29). If they had understood, it is doubtful they would have let Judas leave the room. Since they did not understand, Judas departed (John 13:30).

26:26-30 (Mark 14:22-26; Luke 22:19-20). Jesus then instituted something new in the Passover feast. **While they were eating,** He **took bread** and **gave** it a special meaning. **Then** taking **the cup** of wine, He **gave** it a special meaning too. Jesus said the bread was His **body** (Matt. 26:26) and the wine was His **blood of the** New **Covenant** (v. 28). While Christians disagree on the meanings of these words, it appears Jesus was using these elements as visible reminders of an event about to take place.

The bread and wine represented His body and blood about to be shed, in keeping with the remission of sins promised in the New Covenant (Jer. 31:31-37; 32:37-40; Ezek. 34:25-31; 36:26-28), a covenant that would replace the old Mosaic Covenant. His blood was soon to be shed **for many** (cf. Matt. 20:28) **for the forgiveness of sins.** This portion of the Passover supper has been followed by Christians and called the Lord's Supper or Communion. Jesus committed this ordinance to the church to be followed as a continual reminder of His work in their salvation. It is to be commemorated until He returns (1 Cor. 11:23-26). Jesus told the disciples He would **not** eat this meal again with them **until** the institution of His **Father's kingdom** on earth. After the Passover meal, Jesus and the disciples together sang **a hymn,** left the home, and **went out to the Mount of Olives.**

e. The prayerful vigil (26:31-46)

26:31-35 (Mark 14:27-31; Luke 22:31-38; John 13:36-38). As **Jesus** and the disciples headed for the Mount of Olives, He reminded **them** that soon they would all forsake Him. This would be in keeping with the words of Zechariah who prophesied that **the Shepherd** would be struck down, **and the sheep . . . scattered** (Zech. 13:7). This is one of numerous times Matthew quoted from and alluded to the Book of Zechariah. **But** Jesus promised victory over death, for He said He would rise from the dead and **go ahead of** them **into Galilee** (Matt. 26:32; cf. 28:7). All the disciples were from Galilee and they had ministered with Jews in Galilee.

Whether **Peter** heard the Lord's words concerning Resurrection cannot be known. But he strongly reacted against the idea that he would forsake Jesus. Peter affirmed he would **never** deny the Lord, **even if all** the others did. But **Jesus** predicted that Peter would deny Him **three times** that **very night before** the crowing of **the rooster** in the early morning. **Peter** could not believe he would forsake Jesus; again he affirmed his devotion even if it meant death (26:35). This was the feeling of **all the other disciples** too; they could not believe they would deny the Lord. They would not betray Him (v. 22), so why would they deny Him?

26:36-46 (Mark 14:32-42; Luke 22:39-46; John 18:1). Jesus then **went . . . to a place** known as **Gethsemane,** which means "an oil press." In a field covered with olive trees, oil presses were used to extract oil from the fruit. An olive grove was in that place (John 18:1). There Jesus left **His disciples**—except for **Peter** and **two** of Zebedee's **sons** (James and John, Matt. 4:21) who went **with Him, and He began to** pray. He was experiencing sorrow (*lypeisthai,* "to be grieved or sad to the point of distress"; cf. 14:9; 17:23; 18:31; 19:22) and trouble such as He had never known in His earthly life. He asked the three disciples to **stay** and **keep watch with** Him (26:38). In this hour of His greatest need the Lord wanted those with a sympathetic understanding to be praying with Him.

Separating Himself then from the three, He **prayed** to His **Father,** asking that if **. . . possible . . . this cup be taken** away **from** Him. The "cup" probably referred to His imminent death. He also may have had in mind His coming separation from the Father (27:46) and

---

Jesus' Six Trials

Religious Trials

Before Annas	John 18:12-14
Before Caiaphas	Matthew 26:57-68
Before the Sanhedrin	Matthew 27:1-2

Civil Trials

Before Pilate	John 18:28-38
Before Herod	Luke 23:6-12
Before Pilate	John 18:39–19:6

His coming contact with sin as He became sin for mankind (2 Cor. 5:21). A cup, figuratively in the Old Testament, refers to wrath. The significant thing about this prayer, however, was that the Lord submitted His **will** to the **will** of His Father (Matt. 26:39).

When Jesus **returned to** the three, He **found them** asleep. He awakened them and reprimanded **Peter** (not the three) for his inability to bear with Him in prayer. Only a short time before, Peter had twice said he would never forsake the Lord (vv. 33, 35) and yet he could not even pray with Him in His greatest need. Jesus encouraged them (the imperatives and the word **you** are pl.) to keep watching and praying, but He did acknowledge the weakness of the human flesh (v. 41).

As Jesus prayed **a second time,** He recognized that the **cup** (cf. v. 39) could not pass **away unless** He "drank" of **it.** He affirmed a second time that God's **will** must be accomplished whatever the cost (v. 42; cf. v. 39). He returned and **found** the three disciples asleep **again,** but this time He did not wake them.

A **third time** He **prayed** the **same** prayer while the disciples slept on. Their **sleeping and resting** was in stark contrast to His agonizing (v. 37) and praying to the point of exhaustion and perspiration (Luke 22:43-44). He was lonely, for though the disciples were nearby, they were useless in their intercession. And yet He evidenced unswerving obedience—determination to follow the Father's will regardless of the cost. When Jesus **returned to the disciples** the third time, He awakened them with the news His **betrayer** was coming and they must **go** meet him.

2. THE ARREST IN THE GARDEN (26:47-56)
   (MARK 14:43-50; LUKE 22:47-53; JOHN 18:2-12)

26:47-56. As Jesus spoke, **Judas . . . arrived** in the garden. He was accompanied by **a large crowd,** including both Roman soldiers (John 18:3) and Jews from the temple guard (Luke 22:52) dispatched **by the chief priests and the elders.** The crowd had **swords and clubs** (Matt. 26:47; Mark 14:43) and torches and lanterns (John 18:3). The large group was considered necessary to make sure Jesus did not get away. Perhaps the leaders felt the pilgrims present for the Passover feast in Jerusalem might somehow try to prevent the arrest.

Judas **had arranged a** sign **with** the officials. **The One** he kissed would be the One to **arrest.** As he approached **Jesus,** he **said, Greetings, Rabbi!** (cf. Matt. 26:25) **and kissed Him.** Jesus' response to Judas indicated that He still loved him, for Jesus addressed him as **Friend** (*hetaire,* "companion" or "associate," used only three times in the NT, each time in Matt. [20:13; 22:12; 26:50]). With this the arresting soldiers probably pushed Judas out of the way and grabbed **Jesus.**

Peter was not to be outdone. (Only John identified him by name [John 18:10].) Having just awakened and perhaps still not fully aware of what was going on, he grabbed **his sword** and attempted to defend Jesus by striking out at one of those in the arresting group. He struck Malchus, **the servant of the high priest** (John 18:10).

The Lord immediately stopped the violence and reprimanded Peter for his efforts. He did not need anyone's defense, for He could have called **on** His **Father** who would have sent **12 legions of angels** to defend Him. A Roman legion numbered about 6,000 soldiers. Such angelic protection (of about 72,000 angels!) could easily have defended Jesus from any opposition. But it was not God's will for Jesus to be rescued. Jesus' arrest occurred because He permitted it. Though Matthew did not mention it Luke, the physician, noted that Jesus healed the man's severed ear (Luke 22:51).

Matthew did record a brief speech by **Jesus** to His captors. He asked them why they had come out in this manner to **arrest** Him. He had been in their midst daily, **teaching** in **the temple courts.** Arrest had been possible at any time. Obviously these religious leaders feared the people's acknowledgment of Him. But the will of the Father was being **fulfilled** as well as **the writings of the prophets** who spoke of His death.

At that point **all the disciples deserted Him and fled** into the night—though they had vowed they would never do so! (Matt. 26:33, 35) The sheep were scattering (v. 31).

3. THE TRIALS OF THE KING (26:57–27:26)

a. The trial before the Jewish authorities (26:57–27:10)

26:57-58 (Mark 14:53-54; Luke 22:54; John 18:15-16). After **Jesus** was **arrested** in Gethsemane, He was led by the soldiers **to Caiaphas, the high priest** (see the chart on Jesus' six trials). But first there was a brief trial before the former high priest, Annas, who was Caiaphas' father-in-law (cf. comments on John 18:12-13, 19-24; see chart at Acts 4:1). That delaying tactic apparently gave Caiaphas time to assemble the "Sanhedrin" quickly (Matt. 26:59; cf. Acts 4:15 for comments on the Sanhedrin). **Peter followed** the Lord **at a distance** and came into **the courtyard of the high** priest's home **to** await **the outcome.**

26:59-68 (Mark 14:55-65; Luke 22:63-65). The purpose of Jesus' trials was to find some legal basis on which to condemn **Him to death.** Judas' testimony was crucial to the religious leaders' case, but he was nowhere to be found. As a result witnesses were sought **against Jesus,** a highly unusual court procedure, attempting to **find** anything that would make Him worthy of death. While **many false witnesses** volunteered, none of them could agree on anything against Jesus (Matt. 26:60). **Finally two** witnesses agreed that Jesus had once **said, I am able to destroy the temple of God and rebuild it in three days.** Jesus had said that approximately three years earlier at the outset of His ministry (John 2:19), referring not to the temple building, but to His body. It is interesting that this statement was here recalled soon before His crucifixion and resurrection. **Jesus refused to answer** any of the charges brought against Him because He was never officially charged with any crime.

Then **the high priest** attempted to get Jesus to respond to the accusations brought against Him (Matt. 26:62). Still Jesus remained silent until **the high priest** placed Him **under** sacred **oath.** Once the high priest charged Jesus under an oath **by the living God,** Jesus had to answer truthfully. Caiaphas insisted that Jesus answer **if** He was **the Christ** (the Messiah), **the Son of God** (v. 63). Jesus answered in the affirmative, adding that **in the future** He would sit **at the right hand of the Mighty One** (cf. 25:31) and He would return **on the clouds of heaven** (cf. 24:30). Here was a clear statement of His deity, clearly understood as such by **the high priest,** who immediately **tore his clothes,** which he was forbidden to do by the Law (Lev. 21:10), and declared that Jesus had **spoken blasphemy** (Matt. 26:65). He said there was no further need of **witnesses** for the Lord's lips had revealed His guilt.

The people had only two choices. One was to acknowledge that Jesus spoke the truth, and fall down and worship Him as Messiah. The other was to reject Him as a blasphemer and put Him to **death.** They chose the latter, thus sealing their rejection of the One who came as their Messiah-King.

No further evidence was examined at this point. No one defended Jesus or pointed to the works He had performed among them during the past three years. It appeared that the Sanhedrin had Jesus where they wanted Him. He had just spoken words of blasphemy which all heard. Contrary to all Jewish and Roman law, they took it on themselves to begin to punish the accused. **They spit in His face . . . struck Him with their fists,** and **slapped Him.** They asked Him to **proph-**

esy, telling, if He could, who had just hit Him. These actions they continued doing, seemingly enjoying every moment of it. The Lord remained silent throughout this terrible ordeal, submitting Himself to His Father's will (cf. Isa. 53:7; 1 Peter 2:23).

26:69-75 (Mark 14:66-72; Luke 22:55-62; John 18:17-18, 25-27). While Jesus was undergoing His trial before the Sanhedrin, **Peter** was also undergoing a testing. He had followed the Lord and gained entrance into the house of the high priest (John 18:15-16). As he sat **in the courtyard** (cf. Matt. 26:58) awaiting the outcome of the trial, he had three opportunities to speak up for his Lord. All three times he denied he ever knew the Accused or was in any way ever connected with Him. The first denial occurred when **a servant girl** said in front of the others that he was one of those who had been **with Jesus** (v. 69). **Another girl** at the gate of the courtyard more directly pointed Peter out as one who had indeed been **with Jesus** (v. 71). Finally a number of those present came and accused **Peter** of being **one** who had been with Jesus **for** his Galilean **accent** gave him **away** (v. 73). With the third accusation, Peter **began to call down curses on himself and he swore** (v. 74). The calling of curses on himself was a legal way of seeking to affirm one's innocence; if the calamities did not follow, he would be assumed innocent (cf. Job 31).

As he publicly denied his Lord the third time, **immediately a rooster crowed.** That triggered in his thinking the words of the Lord, **Before the rooster crows, you will disown Me three times** (cf. Matt. 26:34). Peter knew immediately he had failed the Lord. Though he had affirmed that he would never forsake the Lord, he had publicly denied the One he loved. Filled with remorse, he left the courtyard **and wept bitterly.** His tears were tears of true repentance for having forsaken and denied the Lord.

27:1-2 (Mark 15:1). Jesus' first Jewish trials occurred under the cover of darkness. Since Jewish law required trials to be conducted during the day, the chief priests and the elders of the people realized an official trial was necessary. The brief trial recorded in Matthew 27:1 was simply for the court to reaffirm what had taken place earlier. The court decided that **Jesus** must die, but they did not have the power to put that decision into action (John 18:31). To get a death sentence, they needed to take the case **to Pilate, the governor,** the procurator of Judea and Samaria, A.D. 26–36 (cf. Luke 3:1). Jesus was therefore **bound** and brought by the Jews to Pilate. Pilate's home was in Caesarea, but at this festival time, he was in his Jerusalem palace.

27:3-10. When **Judas** Iscariot realized the outcome of the deliberations, **he was** filled **with remorse and** went back to the officials. He had not envisioned this as the outcome of his betrayal, but what he had hoped to accomplish is not mentioned in the biblical text. He knew he had **betrayed innocent blood** for he admitted Jesus was not worthy of death. The religious leaders were unsympathetic, pointing out that that was his problem, not theirs. **Judas** decided he had to get rid of **the money** he had received for betraying the Lord. The money was apparently a continual reminder of his action and convicted him of his sin. He went to the temple and **threw the money into the temple** (*naos,* the holy place itself, not the temple precincts). Unlike Peter, however, Judas' remorse did not include repentance, for **he went** from the temple **and hanged himself.** (More details of his action were given by Luke, Acts 1:18-19.)

Judas' act of throwing the betrayal money into the temple caused the religious leaders some problems. They did not feel the money should be **put** into the temple coffers **since it** was **blood money,** money paid to bring about a man's death. Yet they had had no scruples about giving it out in the first place (Matt. 26:15). **They decided to** take **the money** and **buy** a parcel of land (apparently in Judas' name, Acts 1:18) in which to bury **foreigners.** The parcel, which was a **potter's field,** a place where potters dug for clay, became known as **the Field of Blood** (Matt. 27:8), or *Akeldama* in Aramaic (Acts 1:19).

Matthew viewed these events as the fulfillment of a prophecy of **Jeremiah.** But the prophecy Matthew quoted was primarily from Zechariah, not Jeremiah. There is a close resemblance between Matthew 27:9-10 and Zechariah 11:12-13. But there are also similarities between Matthew's words and the ideas in Jeremiah 19:1, 4, 6, 11. Why then did

Matthew refer only to Jeremiah? The solution to this problem is probably that Matthew had both prophets in mind but only mentioned the "major" prophet by name. (A similar situation is found in Mark 1:2-3, where Mark mentioned the Prophet Isaiah but quoted directly from both Isaiah and Malachi.) In addition, another explanation is that Jeremiah, in the Babylonian Talmud (*Baba Bathra* 14b), was placed first among the prophets, and his book represented all the other prophetic books.

b. The trial before the Roman authorities (27:11-26)

27:11-14 (Mark 15:2-5; Luke 23:1-5; John 18:28-38). Compared with the other Gospels, Matthew's record of Jesus' trial before Pilate is rather brief. Luke even mentioned that Pilate sent Jesus to Herod when he learned Jesus was a Galilean (Luke 23:6-12). That gesture brought about a friendship between Pilate and Herod that had not existed before. Matthew mentioned only one trial before Pilate and the one "accusation" that **Jesus** is the King of the Jews. The kingship of Jesus of course was Matthew's main theme. When Pilate asked Jesus, **Are You the King of the Jews?** the answer came in the affirmative. But as John recorded, Jesus' kingdom at that time was not a political kingdom to rival Rome (John 18:33-37). Jesus was no threat to Roman rule. Pilate realized that and sought to release Jesus.

While other accusations were presented **by the chief priests and the elders,** Jesus did not **answer** them, and **Pilate** was greatly surprised (*thaumazein,* "to be amazed"). Jesus need not answer those charges, for He was not being tried for those accusations. Instead He was on trial because they said He claimed to be the King of the Jews, the Messiah (Matt. 26:63-64). Since Pilate had also declared Jesus' innocence (John 18:38), there was no reason for Him to answer the accusations.

27:15-23 (Mark 15:6-14; Luke 23:13-24; John 18:39-40). Pilate had been warned by **his wife** to be careful how he dealt with this prisoner, for He was an **innocent Man** (Matt. 27:19). She had **suffered a great deal** through **a dream** concerning Jesus and shared her experience with her husband. To speculate beyond the words of the text on the content of her dream would be useless. Since **Pilate** believed Jesus was innocent, he tried to have Him released. It was a **custom** of the governor **to release a prisoner** each year at the Passover in order to gain acceptance with the Jews. His plan to bring about the **release** of **Jesus** involved a notorious prisoner named **Barabbas,** an insurrectionist (John 18:40) and murderer (Mark 15:7). **Pilate** thought that surely the people of the nation loved Jesus, their King, and that only the leaders were envious of Him and of the people's acclaim of Him (Matt. 27:18). He reasoned that if the people had a choice they surely would release **Jesus,** not the notorious **Barabbas.**

However, **Pilate** failed to grasp the determination of the religious leaders to do away with Jesus, for they **persuaded the crowd to ask for Barabbas and to have Jesus executed.** When Pilate asked the crowd **what he should do . . . with Jesus who is called Christ . . . they all answered, Crucify Him!** The Greek text shows their cry was one word, "Crucify" (*staurōthētō*). One can almost picture this scene, somewhat like a football stadium in which the crowd shouts "Defense!" Their cheer was "Crucify, crucify!" When Pilate sought further information from the crowd as to Jesus' crimes, the crowd simply **shouted . . . louder, Crucify!**

27:24-26 (Mark 15:15; Luke 23:25; John 19:6-16). **Pilate** realized **he was getting nowhere** with the crowd, and their threats to report him to Caesar (John 19:12) concerned him. His record with Caesar was not good, and he did not want word of a rival king to reach Caesar's ears, especially if Pilate had released that king. **He** therefore **took water and washed his hands in front of the crowd,** symbolizing his desire to absolve himself from being involved in putting an innocent man to death (Deut. 21:6-9). But his words, **I am innocent of this Man's blood,** did not make him innocent (Acts 4:27). Such an act did not remove Pilate's guilt from this travesty of justice.

When Pilate turned the **responsibility** over to the Jews (Matt. 27:24), however, they readily accepted it. They said, **Let His blood be on us and on our children!** Their words sadly came to pass as the judgment of God came on many of them and their children in A.D. 70 when

HARMONY OF EVENTS AT JESUS' CRUCIFIXION

1. Jesus arrived at Golgotha (Matt. 27:33; Mark 15:22; Luke 23:33; John 19:17).
2. He refused the offer of wine mixed with myrrh (Matt. 27:34; Mark 15:23).
3. He was nailed to the cross between the two thieves (Matt. 27:35-38; Mark 15:24-28; Luke 23:33-38; John 19:18).
4. He gave His first cry from the cross: "Father, forgive them, for they do not know what they are doing" (Luke 23:34).
5. The soldiers took Jesus' garments, leaving Him naked on the cross (Matt. 27:35; Mark 15:24; Luke 23:34; John 19:23).
6. The Jews mocked Jesus (Matt. 27:39-43; Mark 15:29-32; Luke 23:35-37).
7. He conversed with the two thieves (Luke 23:39-43).
8. He gave His second cry from the cross, "I tell you the truth; today you will be with Me in paradise" (Luke 23:43).
9. He spoke the third time, "Woman, here is your son" (John 19:26-27).
10. Darkness came from noon to 3 P.M. (Matt. 27:45; Mark 15:33; Luke 23:44).
11. He gave His fourth cry, "My God, My God, why have You forsaken Me?" (Matt. 27:46-47; Mark 15:34-36)
12. His fifth cry was, "I am thirsty" (John 19:28).
13. He drank "wine vinegar" (John 19:29).
14. His sixth cry was, "It is finished" (John 19:30).
15. He drank wine vinegar from a sponge (Matt. 27:48; Mark 15:36).
16. He cried a seventh time, "Father, into Your hands I commit My spirit" (Luke 23:46).
17. He dismissed His spirit by an act of His own will (Matt. 27:50; Mark 15:37; Luke 23:46; John 19:30).
18. The temple curtain was torn in two (Matt. 27:51; Mark 15:38; Luke 23:45).
19. Roman soldiers admitted, "Surely He was the Son of God" (Matt. 27:54; Mark 15:39).

the Romans destroyed the nation and the temple. In spite of Pilate's four declarations of Jesus' innocence (Luke 23:14, 20, 22; John 19:4), he fulfilled his commitment to the Jews by releasing **Barabbas** and turning **Jesus** over for crucifixion after He had been **flogged.**

4. THE CRUCIFIXION OF THE KING (27:27-56)

27:27-31 (Mark 15:16-20; John 19:1-5). Jesus was brought **into the Praetorium,** the common meeting courtyard crowded with Roman **soldiers.** The Praetorium may have been at Pilate's residence, the Castle of Antonia, though others suggest Herod's palace. The Praetorium was a large area, for 600 soldiers were there ("company of soldiers" is lit., "cohort," one-tenth of a legion).

There **they** removed His clothing and mocked Him by (a) putting **on Him** a **scarlet robe,** clothing for a king, (b) placing **a crown of thorns . . . on His head,** and (c) giving Him **a staff** for a

"scepter." They **knelt** before **Him and mocked Him** by saying, **Hail, King of the Jews!** What a tragic figure Jesus presented at that moment. They degraded Him further by spitting **on Him,** and striking **Him on the head again and again** with **the staff.** Unknown to them, their actions fulfilled Isaiah's prophecy concerning the Savior's marring (Isa. 52:14). Because of the known cruelty of Roman soldiers, Jesus was probably beaten to the point where few would have recognized Him. Yet He silently bore the unjust treatment, submitting to the will of His Father (cf. 1 Peter 2:23). With their sport completed, the soldiers again dressed Jesus in **His own clothes** and **led Him away to** be crucified.

27:32-38 (Mark 15:21-28; Luke 23:26-34; John 19:17-27). Matthew recorded only a few of the events that occurred when Jesus was taken to the place of crucifixion. **Simon** of **Cyrene,** a city in North Africa populated with many Jews, was **forced . . . to carry the cross**

(actually the crossbeam) when Jesus could no longer carry it Himself, being weak from the beatings. Eventually the procession **came to a place** known as **Golgotha,** which in Aramaic **means the Place of the Skull.** This was not a place of skulls, a cemetery, or place of execution, but a hill that in some way resembled a skull. This was located either at the site of the present Church of the Holy Sepulchre, which was then outside Jerusalem's walls, or at Gordon's Calvary.

Jesus was then **offered . . . wine . . . mixed with gall,** a drink given to dull the senses and make the pain of crucifixion somewhat easier to bear. Jesus **refused to drink** the mixture, for He wanted to be in complete control of His senses even while hanging on the cross. The actual crucifixion was briefly noted by Matthew. He made no reference to the nails being driven into the Lord's hands and feet, but he did record the dividing of **His clothes (by casting lots)** by those crucifying Him. A few Greek manuscripts add to Matthew 27:35 that this action fulfilled Psalm 22:18. Though this probably was not part of Matthew's original account, John pointed out that same prophecy (John 19:24).

Over the **head** of a person being **crucified** was **written** an inscription containing the **charge** that brought him there. Over Jesus' head, was written THIS IS JESUS, THE KING OF THE JEWS, for that truly was the charge for which Jesus was dying. Though each Gospel account presents a slight variation in the wording, the sign probably included a combination of all the accounts. Thus it would have read, "This is Jesus of Nazareth, the King of the Jews." John noted that Pilate had the charge written there in Aramaic, Latin, and Greek (John 19:20). The words "the King of the Jews" offended the chief priests, but Pilate refused to change what he had written (John 19:21-22). Jesus was **crucified** between **two robbers** (Matt. 27:38), whom Luke called "criminals" (Luke 23:33).

27:39-44 (Mark 15:29-32; Luke 23:35-43). While Jesus was hanging on the cross, He was subject to continual verbal abuse by **those** passing **by.** In mockery, they recalled what Jesus had said earlier about destroying **the temple** and raising **it** up **three days** later (John

2:19; cf. Matt. 26:61). Surely He must be a false leader, they thought, because His alleged ability **to destroy** the temple was now gone! If He were **the Son of God,** then He ought to be able to perform a miracle and **come down from the cross.** His inability to do that proved, they reasoned, that His claim was false. He had previously **saved others . . . but now He** could not **save Himself;** in this way too He was disqualified, they alleged. They said that if He came **down . . . from the cross,** they would **believe in Him.** One wonders, however, if even such an act as this would have prompted them to believe. They claimed if He were really **the Son of God . . . God** would **rescue Him.**

Besides the passersby (27:39-40) and the religious leaders (vv. 41-43), **the robbers . . . crucified with Him also** insulted **Him** (v. 44). Luke, however, recorded that a change of heart took place in one of the robbers (Luke 23:39-43). The irony of this scene was that Jesus could have done the things the crowd was shouting for Him to do. He could have come down from the cross and physically saved Himself. He did not lack the power to accomplish His deliverance. But it was not in the Father's will to do that. It was necessary that the Son of God die for others. He therefore patiently bore their insults.

27:45-50 (Mark 15:33-37; Luke 23:44-46; John 19:28-30). Matthew made no reference to the time when the crucifixion began. But Mark indicated that it began at the "third hour" (Mark 15:25), around 9 A.M. Matthew noted specifically that **from the sixth hour,** noon, **until the ninth hour,** 3 P.M., **darkness came over all the land.** In this period of darkness Jesus became the Sin-offering for the world (John 1:29; Rom. 5:8; 2 Cor. 5:21; 1 Peter 2:24; 3:18) and as such was forsaken by the Father. Near the end of this period of time, **Jesus** could bear the separation no longer and **cried out in a loud voice, Eloi, Eloi, lama sabachthani?** These Aramaic words mean, **My God, My God, why have You forsaken Me?** (a quotation of Ps. 22:1) Jesus sensed a separation from the Father He had never known, for in becoming sin the Father had to turn judicially from His Son (Rom. 3:25-26).

Some of those standing near the cross misunderstood Jesus' words. They **heard "Eloi,"** but thought Jesus was trying to call for **Elijah** (Matt. 27:47). In Greek the word "Elijah" sounds more like "Eloi" than it does in English. Thinking His lips and throat had become dry, someone thought a **drink** of **wine vinegar** would moisten His vocal cords so He could speak plainly. Others, however, **said** to **leave** Jesus **alone** and **see if** Elijah would come and deliver **Him.** Their jeers were obviously still being directed against Jesus.

With one last cry **Jesus . . . gave up His spirit,** committing it into the hands of His Father (Luke 23:46). Jesus was in complete control of His life and died at the precise moment He determined by dismissing His spirit. No man took Jesus' life from Him, as He had said (John 10:11, 15, 17-18). He laid His life down in keeping with God's plan and He was involved in taking it back up again in His resurrection.

27:51-53 (Mark 15:38; Luke 23:44-45). At the time of Jesus' death, three momentous events occurred. First, **the curtain of the temple was torn in two from top to bottom.** This curtain separated the holy place from the holy of holies in the temple (Heb. 9:2-3). The fact that this occurred from top to bottom signified that God is the One who ripped the thick curtain. It was not torn from the bottom by men ripping it. God was showing that the way of access into His presence was now available for everyone, not simply the Old Testament high priest (Heb. 4:14-16; 10:19-22).

Second, at Christ's death a strong earthquake occurred, splitting **rocks** (Matt. 27:51). Truly the death of Christ was a powerful, earthshaking event with repercussions affecting even the creation. A third event mentioned was recorded only by Matthew. **The tombs** of **many holy** (righteous) **people** (v. 52) were opened, probably at a Jerusalem cemetery. The NIV suggests that these saints were resurrected when Jesus died and then went into Jerusalem **after Jesus' resurrection.** A number of commentators agree with this view. Many others, however, say that since Christ is the firstfruits of the dead (1 Cor. 15:23), their resurrection did not occur till He was raised. In this view, the phrase "after Jesus' resurrection" goes with the words **were raised to life** and **came out of the tombs.** This is possible in the Greek, and is suggested in the KJV and the NASB. The tombs, then, **broke open** at Christ's death, probably by the earthquake, thus heralding Christ's triumph in death over sin, but the bodies were not raised till Christ was raised.

These people returned to Jerusalem, **(the Holy City)** where they were recognized by friends and family. Like Lazarus (John 11:43-44), Jairus' daughter (Luke 8:52-56), and the widow of Nain's son (Luke 7:13-15), they too passed through physical death again. Or some say they may have been raised with glorified bodies like the Lord's. Walvoord suggests this event was "a fulfillment of the Feast of the Firstfruits of harvest mentioned in Leviticus 23:10-14. On that occasion, as a token of the coming harvest, the people would bring a handful of grain to the priest. The resurrection of these saints, occurring after Jesus Himself was raised, is a token of the coming harvest when all the saints will be raised" (Walvoord, *Matthew: Thy Kingdom Come,* p. 236).

27:54-56 (Mark 15:39-41; Luke 23:47-49). A Roman **centurion** (cf. Matt. 8:5; see Luke 7:2 for comments on centurions) and other Roman guards were impressed and **terrified** with the unusual circumstances surrounding the death of this Man, for such accompanying signs had never been observed in previous crucifixions. Their response was, **Surely He was the Son of God!** The momentous events of the day struck fear into the soldiers' hearts.

Also some **women were there,** observing **from a distance** the Lord's death. These women **had followed Jesus from Galilee** and had been caring **for His needs. Among** this group **were Mary Magdalene** (cf. Matt. 28:1; Mark 16:9; John 20:18), **Mary the mother of James and Joseph** (perhaps the same as "Mary the wife of Clopas," John 19:25), **and the mother of Zebedee's sons,** James and John (Matt. 4:21; 10:2). John mentioned that Mary, Jesus' mother, and Mary's sister were also present at the foot of the cross (John 19:25-27). While Matthew made no reference to what the women may have said or how they felt, their hearts must have been broken as they observed the death of their Lord, whom

FORTY DAYS—from Resurrection to Ascension

SUNDAY MORNING

1. An angel rolled away the stone from Jesus' tomb before sunrise (Matt. 28:2-4).
2. Women who followed Jesus visited Jesus' tomb and discovered Him missing (Matt. 28:1; Mark 16:1-4; Luke 24:1-3; John 20:1).
3. Mary Magdalene left to tell Peter and John (John 20:1-2).
4. The other women, remaining at the tomb, saw two angels who told them about the Resurrection (Matt. 28:5-7; Mark 16:5-7; Luke 24:4-8).
5. Peter and John visited Jesus' tomb (Luke 24:12; John 20:3-10).
6. Mary Magdalene returned to the tomb and Jesus appeared to her alone in the garden (Mark 16:9-11; John 20:11-18): *His first appearance.*
7. Jesus appeared to the other women (Mary, mother of James, Salome, and Joanna) (Matt. 28:8-10): *His second appearance.*
8. Those who guarded Jesus' tomb reported to the religious rulers how the angel rolled away the stone. They were then bribed (Matt. 28:11-15).
9. Jesus appeared to Peter (1 Cor. 15:5): *His third appearance.*

SUNDAY AFTERNOON

10. Jesus appeared to two men on the road to Emmaus (Mark 16:12-13; Luke 24:13-32): *His fourth appearance.*

SUNDAY EVENING

11. The two disciples from Emmaus told others they saw Jesus (Luke 24:33-35).
12. Jesus appeared to 10 apostles, with Thomas absent, in the Upper Room (Luke 24:36-43; John 20:19-25): *His fifth appearance.*

THE FOLLOWING SUNDAY

13. Jesus appeared to the 11 Apostles, including Thomas, and Thomas believed (John 20:26-28): *His sixth appearance.*

THE FOLLOWING 32 DAYS

14. Jesus appeared to seven disciples by the Sea of Galilee and performed a miracle of fish (John 21:1-14): *His seventh appearance.*
15. Jesus appeared to 500 (including the Eleven) at a mountain in Galilee (Matt. 28:16-20; Mark 16:15-18; 1 Cor. 15:6): *His eighth appearance.*
16. Jesus appeared to His half-brother James (1 Cor. 15:7): *His ninth appearance.*
17. At Jerusalem Jesus appeared again to His disciples (Luke 24:44-49; Acts 1:3-8): *His 10th appearance.*
18. On the Mount of Olives Jesus ascended into heaven while the disciples watched (Mark 16:19-20; Luke 24:50-53; Acts 1:9-12).

they loved and had served. With the approach of night, they apparently returned to the city and lodged there, for in a few days they were seeking to assist in the preparation of Jesus' body for burial (Matt. 28:1; Mark 16:1-3; Luke 24:1).

5. THE BURIAL OF THE KING (27:57-66)

27:57-61 (Mark 15:42-47; Luke 23:50-56; John 19:38-42). No known preparation had been made for Jesus' burial; normally the body of a crucified criminal would simply have been discarded without ceremony. However, a **rich man from Arimathea** (a town east of Joppa), **named Joseph,** asked Pilate . . . **for Jesus' body.** Joseph, a member of the Sanhedrin, had not agreed with the council's decision to crucify Jesus (Luke 23:51). Instead he was one who had been looking for the kingdom of God and was a believer in Jesus. **Pilate** granted his request, surprised that Jesus was already dead (Mark 15:44-45). Another account reported Joseph was assisted in the burial by Nicodemus (John 19:39; cf. John 3:1-21). These two men **took the body** of Jesus and following burial customs of the time, **wrapped** the body in **linen** with a mixture of myrrh and aloes, spices used in burial (John 19:40; cf. Matt. 2:11). This procedure was done rapidly in order to be completed before the Sabbath began at nightfall. Joseph **placed** the wrapped body **in his own new tomb . . . cut out of the rock** near the place of crucifixion. Why Joseph of Arimathea would own a tomb in Jerusalem cannot be determined. Possibly Jesus had made arrangements ahead of time with him and he had purchased the tomb especially for this occasion. Joseph and Nicodemus **rolled a big stone** across the tomb's **entrance.**

Matthew noted that **Mary Magdalene and the other Mary** sat **across from the tomb** (27:61), no doubt in mourning. Interestingly these women accompanied Jesus' body right up to the minute it was buried, whereas Jesus' disciples had all abandoned Him (26:56).

27:62-66. It is a little surprising that a group of unbelievers would remember Jesus' prediction that He would **rise again** on the third day, while the believing disciples seemingly forgot. **The** very **next day** after His death, that is, on the Sabbath, **the chief priests and the Pharisees went to Pilate** and informed him of Jesus' words. While they did not believe in Jesus (whom they blasphemously called **that deceiver**), they feared **His disciples** might **come . . . steal the body, and** attempt to fabricate a resurrection lie. If this were to happen, the **deception would be worse than** anything Jesus had accomplished in His life. The Resurrection was the one thing these leaders feared, so they suggested **the tomb . . . be made secure until the third day.**

Pilate agreed with their suggestion and ordered that **a guard** be sent to **the tomb** to **make** it **as secure as** possible. The Roman guard not only sealed the tomb (presumably with the official Roman **seal** and with a cord and wax, which if tampered with, could be detected) but also continued to keep a **guard** at the scene. Their presence made stealing the body impossible.

VII. Confirmation of the King's Life (chap. 28)

A. The empty tomb (28:1-8) (Mark 16:1-8; Luke 24:1-12; John 20:1-20)

1. THE OCCASION (28:1-4)

28:1-4. At dawn on the first day of the week, several women **went** to **the tomb** of Jesus. They knew where the Lord had been laid for they had seen Joseph and Nicodemus roll the stone over the door of the tomb (27:56). The women were returning to the tomb on Sunday morning, now that **the Sabbath** was over, to anoint Jesus' body for burial (Mark 16:1). **There was,** however, **a violent earthquake** associated with **an angel** coming **from heaven and** rolling away **the stone** from the door of **the tomb. The appearance** of the angel **was like lightning, and his clothes were white as snow.** The Roman soldiers guarding the tomb **were so** frightened by the angel **that they shook** and apparently fainted. They had been sent there to seal and guard the tomb, but their power was useless before this angelic messenger.

2. THE PROCLAMATION (28:5-8)

28:5-8. Though the soldiers were afraid, **the angel** had a special message for **the women.** To them he announced the fact of the Resurrection, for the One they sought was no longer there, but had **risen just as He said.** He had told them several times He would rise on the third day (16:21; 17:23; 20:19). If He had failed to rise, He would have been a deceiver unworthy of further devotion. One proof He had risen was the empty tomb. The women were encouraged to **come and see the place where** the Lord had been lying. Then the angel told them to **go quickly and tell** the **disciples** that **He** had **risen from the dead and** would be **going ahead** of them **into Galilee,** just as He had said (26:32). They would **see Him . . . there,** and indeed they did (28:16-20; John 21:1-23). But these words did not preclude His appearing to them on other occasions, as He did later that day (John 20:19-25). **The women** obeyed the angel's instructions for they **hurried away from the tomb,** intending to find the **disciples** and **tell** them the good news. They were filled with joy over the fact of the Resurrection, but they were fearful for they could not possibly comprehend the full implications of this momentous event.

B. The personal appearance (28:9-10)

28:9-10. As the women were on their way to tell the disciples what had happened, **suddenly Jesus met them.** Hearing His greeting, they recognized Him immediately and they fell at **His feet and worshiped Him.** By His appearance Jesus alleviated their fears and repeated the same message the angel had previously given: **Do not be afraid** (v. 10; cf. v. 5). He told them to **tell** the disciples (**My brothers) to go to Galilee** where He would appear before them. The Galilean ministry of Jesus was prominent in Matthew's account and it was natural for Jesus to meet His disciples there. They were all from Galilee and would be returning to Galilee after the Feast. There Jesus would meet them.

C. The "official" explanation (28:11-15)

28:11-15. While the women were running to find the disciples and tell them of the Resurrection, another group was moving rapidly to counteract the truth. Some of those who had been guarding the tomb overcame their fear, **went into the city, and reported to the chief priests** all **that had** transpired. It was imperative that the priests have an explanation to counter the truth. After deliberation **the chief priests** and **elders . . . devised a plan. They gave the soldiers** who had guarded the tomb **a large sum of money** and told **them** what to report to their superiors. The fabricated lie was that the **disciples** of Jesus had come **during the night and** had stolen **away the body of** Jesus **while** the soldiers **were asleep.** Such a report would not have been well received by the officials for a soldier who fell asleep on guard duty would be put to death (Acts 12:19). The Jewish leaders realized this as well, but promised to make things right with the superiors. When this was brought to the attention of **the governor,** they promised to **satisfy him and keep** the soldiers **out of trouble.** Such satisfaction obviously would involve the payment of another large sum of money. **The soldiers took the money** offered by the Jewish leaders **and did as they were instructed.**

As a result, **this story** was **widely circulated among the Jews,** and many believed the disciples had really stolen Jesus' body. But the logic of the explanation does not hold up. If the soldiers were asleep, how would they have known what had happened to the body of Jesus? And why would they admit "sleeping on the job"? The disciples' courage during this period was not sufficient to carry out such a plot. They were afraid and had scattered when Jesus was arrested. To execute this kind of plot was beyond their ability. But the truth is often harder for a person to believe than a lie, and many still swallow this lie.

D. The official commissioning (28:16-20) (Luke 24:36-49)

28:16-20. Matthew did not record the meeting of **Jesus** with the 10 disciples later that same day (John 20:19-23) or the appearance 8 days later to **the 11 disciples** (John 20:24-29). But he did record an appearance occurring some time later in **Galilee,** where He promised He would meet them (Matt. 26:32; cf. 28:7, 10) at a **mountain.** Which mountain He specified is unknown. When Jesus appeared **they worshiped Him, but some doubted.** Since Jesus had appeared to them earlier and verified Himself to them, they were not doubting the Resurrection. There was probably simply a brief question among some of them as to whether this was truly Jesus appearing to them. There was no indication that any miraculous element was involved in His being there and since unusual circumstances had occurred with previous visits, perhaps they wondered.

Their doubts were quickly dispelled, for **Jesus** spoke **to them** claiming **all authority in heaven and on earth.** This authority (*exousia*, "official right or power") had been given to Jesus by the Father and now He was instructing the disciples to **go** on the basis of that authority. Their field was to include **all nations,** not just Israel (see comments on 10:5-6). They were to **make disciples** by proclaiming the truth concerning Jesus. Their hearers were to be evangelized and enlisted as Jesus' followers. Those who believed were to **be baptized** in water **in the name of the Father and of the Son**

and of the Holy Spirit. Such an act would associate a believer with the person of Jesus Christ and with the Triune God. The God whom they served is one God and yet is three Persons, Father, Son, and Holy Spirit. Those who respond are also to be taught the truths Jesus had specifically communicated to the Eleven. Not all that Jesus taught the disciples was communicated by them but they did teach specific truths for the new Church Age as they went abroad. Jesus' commission, applicable to all His followers, involved one command, "Make disciples," which is accompanied by three participles in the Greek: "going," **baptizing,** and **teaching.**

The final words of the Lord recorded by Matthew were a promise that He would **be with** them **always** until **the very end of the Age.** Though the Lord did not remain physically with the Eleven, His spiritual presence was with them until their tasks on earth were finished. These final words of the Lord were carried out by the apostles as they went everywhere, proclaiming the story of their Messiah, Jesus Christ, the King of the Jews.

BIBLIOGRAPHY

Boice, James Montgomery. *The Sermon on the Mount.* Grand Rapids: Zondervan Publishing House, 1972.

Criswell, W.A. *Expository Notes on the Gospel of Matthew.* Grand Rapids: Zondervan Publishing House, 1961.

Edersheim, Alfred. *The Life and Times of Jesus the Messiah.* Reprint (2 vols. in 1). Grand Rapids: Wm. B. Eerdmans Publishing Co., 1971.

Gaebelein, A.C. *The Gospel of Matthew: An Exposition.* Reprint (2 vols. in 1). Neptune, N.J.: Loizeaux Brothers, 1961.

Hendriksen, William. *Exposition of the Gospel according to Matthew.* New Testament Commentary. Grand Rapids: Baker Book House, 1973.

Ironside, Henry Allen. *Expository Notes on the Gospel of Matthew.* Neptune, N.J.: Loizeaux Brothers, 1948.

Kelly, William. *Lectures in the Gospel of Matthew.* 5th ed. Neptune, N.J.: Loizeaux Brothers, 1943.

Morgan, G. Campbell. *The Gospel according to Matthew.* New York: Fleming H. Revell Co., 1929.

Pentecost, J. Dwight. *The Sermon on the Mount.* Portland, Ore.: Multnomah Press, 1980.

—————. *The Words and Works of Jesus Christ.* Grand Rapids: Zondervan Publishing House, 1981.

Plummer, Alfred. *An Exegetical Commentary on the Gospel according to St. Matthew.* 1915. Reprint. Grand Rapids: Baker Book House, 1982.

Scroggie, W. Graham. *A Guide to the Gospels.* London: Pickering & Inglis, 1948.

Tasker, R.V.G. *The Gospel according to Matthew.* The Tyndale New Testament Commentaries. Grand Rapids: Wm. B. Eerdmans Publishing Co., 1961.

Thomas, W.H. Griffith. *Outline Studies in the Gospel of Matthew.* Grand Rapids: Wm. B. Eerdmans Publishing Co., 1961.

Toussaint, Stanley D. *Behold the King: A Study of Matthew.* Portland, Ore.: Multnomah Press, 1980.

Walvoord, John F. *Matthew: Thy Kingdom Come.* Chicago: Moody Press, 1974.

Wiersbe, Warren, W. *Meet Your King.* Wheaton, Ill.: Scripture Press Publications, Victor Books, 1980.

MARK

John D. Grassmick

INTRODUCTION

Mark is the shortest of the four Gospels. From the 4th till the 19th centuries it was largely neglected by scholars because it was commonly regarded as an abridgment of Matthew. But by the end of the 19th century the theory that Mark was the *first* Gospel written gained widespread acceptance. Since then Mark has been the object of intense interest and study.

Authorship. Technically Mark's Gospel is anonymous since it does not name its author. The title "according to Mark" (*Kata Markon*) was added later by a scribe some time before A.D. 125. However, sufficient evidence is available from early church tradition (external evidence) and from information within the Gospel itself (internal evidence) to identify the author.

The unanimous testimony of the early church fathers is that Mark, an associate of the Apostle Peter, was the author. The earliest known statement of this comes from Papias (ca. A.D. 110), who quoted the testimony of John the elder, probably an alternate designation for the Apostle John. Papias' quotation named Mark as author and included the following information about Mark: (1) He was not an eyewitness follower of Jesus. (2) He accompanied the Apostle Peter and heard his preaching. (3) He wrote down accurately all that Peter remembered of Jesus' words and works "but not in order," that is, not always in chronological order. (4) He was Peter's "interpreter," probably meaning he explained Peter's teaching to a wider audience by writing it down rather than translating Peter's Aramaic discourses into Greek or Latin. (5) His account is wholly reliable (cf. Eusebius *Ecclesiastical History* 3. 39. 15).

This early evidence is confirmed by testimony from Justin Martyr (*Dialogue* 106. 3; ca. A.D. 160), the *Anti-Marcionite Prologue* to Mark (ca. A.D. 160–180), Irenaeus (*Against Heresies* 3. 1. 1-2; ca. A.D. 180), Tertullian (*Against Marcion* 4. 5; ca. A.D. 200), and the writings of Clement of Alexandria (ca. A.D. 195) and Origen (ca. A.D. 230), both cited by Eusebius (*Ecclesiastical History* 2. 15. 2; 6. 14. 6; 6. 25. 5). Thus the external evidence for Marcan authorship is early and is derived from various centers of early Christianity: Alexandria, Asia Minor, Rome.

Though not explicitly stated, most interpreters assume that the Mark mentioned by the church fathers is the same person as the "John (Hebrew name), also called Mark" (Latin name) referred to 10 times in the New Testament (Acts 12:12, 25; 13:5, 13; 15:37, 39; Col. 4:10; 2 Tim. 4:11; Phile. 24; 1 Peter 5:13). Objections raised against this identification are not convincing. No evidence exists for "another" Mark who had close connections with Peter nor is it necessary to suggest an "unknown" Mark in light of the New Testament data.

Internal evidence, though not explicit, is compatible with the historical testimony of the early church. It reveals the following information: (1) Mark was familiar with the geography of Palestine, especially Jerusalem (cf. Mark 5:1; 6:53; 8:10; 11:1; 13:3). (2) He apparently knew Aramaic, the common language of Palestine (cf. 5:41; 7:11, 34; 14:36). (3) He understood Jewish institutions and customs (cf. 1:21; 2:14, 16, 18; 7:2-4).

Several features also point to the author's connection with Peter: (a) the vividness and unusual detail of the narratives, that suggest that they were derived from the reminiscences of an "inner-circle" apostolic eyewitness such as Peter (cf 1:16-20, 29-31, 35-38; 5:21-24,

35-43; 6:39, 53-54; 9:14-15; 10:32, 46; 14:32-42); (b) the author's use of Peter's words and deeds (cf. 8:29, 32-33; 9:5-6; 10:28-30; 14:29-31, 66-72); (c) the inclusion of the words "and Peter" in 16:7, which are unique to this Gospel; and (d) the striking similarity between the broad outline of this Gospel and Peter's sermon in Caesarea (cf. Acts 10:34-43).

In light of both external and internal evidence it is reasonable to affirm that the "John/Mark" in Acts and the Epistles authored this Gospel. He was a Jewish Christian who lived in Jerusalem with Mary his mother during the early days of the church. Nothing is known about his father. Their home was an early Christian meeting place (cf. Acts 12:12). Perhaps it was the location of Jesus' last Passover meal (cf. comments on Mark 14:12-16). Mark was probably the "young man" who fled away naked after Jesus' arrest in Gethsemane (cf. comments on 14:51-52). Peter's calling him "my son" (cf. 1 Peter 5:13) may mean Mark became a Christian through Peter's influence.

During the church's early days in Jerusalem (ca. A.D. 33-47) Mark no doubt became familiar with Peter's preaching. Later he went to Antioch and accompanied Paul and Barnabas (Mark's cousin; cf. Col. 4:10), as far as Perga on their first missionary journey (cf. Acts 12:25; 13:5, 13; ca. A.D. 48-49). For an unstated reason he returned home to Jerusalem. Because of this desertion Paul refused to take him on his second journey. Instead Mark served with Barnabas on the island of Cyprus (cf. Acts 15:36-39; ca. A.D. 50-?). Sometime later, perhaps by A.D. 57, he went to Rome. He was a fellow worker with Paul during Paul's first Roman imprisonment (cf. Col. 4:10; Phile. 23-24; ca. A.D. 60-62). After Paul's release Mark apparently remained in Rome and served with Peter on his arrival in "Babylon," Peter's code word for Rome (cf. 1 Peter 5:13; ca. A.D. 63-64). (Some, however, take Babylon to refer to the city on the Euphrates River; cf. comments on 1 Peter 5:13.) Probably because of severe persecution under Emperor Nero and Peter's martyrdom, Mark left Rome for a time. Finally Paul, during his second imprisonment in Rome (ca. A.D. 67-68), requested Timothy who was in Ephesus to pick up Mark who was presumably somewhere in Asia Minor and bring him to Rome because Paul considered him useful in his ministry (cf. 2 Tim. 4:11).

Sources. To say that Mark was the author of this Gospel does not mean he created the material in it. A "Gospel" was a unique literary form in the first century. It was not simply a biography of Jesus' life, a chronicle of His "mighty deeds," or a set of reminiscences by His followers, though it contains elements of all these. Rather it is a theological proclamation to a particular audience of God's "good news" centered in the historical events of Jesus' life, death, and resurrection. In line with his purpose Mark arranged and adapted the historical material he acquired from his sources.

His major source was the preaching and instruction of the Apostle Peter (cf. comments under "Authorship"). Presumably he heard Peter preach many times in Jerusalem in the early days (ca. A.D. 33-47) and may have taken notes. He also probably had personal conversations with him. Mark also had contact with Paul and Barnabas (cf. Acts 13:5-12; 15:39; Col. 4:10-11). Presumably Mark included at least one reminiscence of his own (cf. Mark 14:51-52). Other sources of information include: (a) units of oral tradition that circulated in the early church individually or as a topical (e.g., 2:1–3:6) or temporal/geographical (e.g., chaps. 14–15) series of events forming a continuous narrative; (b) independent traditional sayings of Jesus linked together by "catch words" (e.g., 9:37-50); and (c) oral tradition which Mark summarized (e.g., 1:14-15; 3:7-12; 6:53-56). Under the oversight of the Holy Spirit Mark used these sources to compose a historically accurate and trustworthy Gospel.

There is no certain evidence that Mark used *written* sources, though the Passion narrative (chaps. 14–15) may have come to him at least partially written. This raises the problem of Mark's relationship to Matthew and Luke.

Many scholars believe that Mark was the first Gospel written and that Matthew and Luke used it as a primary source document along with material from other sources. Luke, in fact, stated that he used other documents (Luke

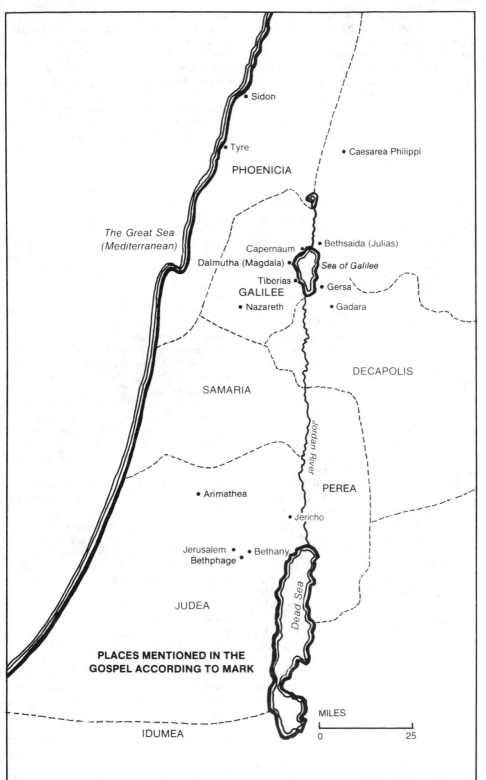

PLACES MENTIONED IN THE GOSPEL ACCORDING TO MARK

Sidon

Tyre

PHOENICIA

Caesarea Philippi

The Great Sea
(Mediterranean)

Capernaum

Bethsaida (Julias)

Dalmutha (Magdala)

Sea of Galilee

Tiberias

Gersa

GALILEE

Nazareth

Gadara

DECAPOLIS

SAMARIA

Jordan River

PEREA

Arimathea

Jericho

Jerusalem
Bethphage

Bethany

Dead Sea

JUDEA

MILES

0   25

IDUMEA

1:1-4). Several arguments support the priority of Mark: (1) Matthew incorporates about 90 percent of Mark, and Luke over 40 percent—over 600 of Mark's 661 verses are found in Matthew and Luke combined. (2) Matthew and Luke usually follow Mark's order of events in Jesus' life, and where either of them differs for topical reasons the other always holds to Mark's order. (3) Matthew and Luke hardly ever agree *against* the content of Mark in passages where they all deal with the same subject. (4) Matthew and Luke often repeat Mark's exact words but where they differ in wording, the language of one or the other is simply grammatically or stylistically smoother than Mark's (cf., e.g., Mark 2:7 with Luke 5:21). (5) Matthew and Luke seem to alter Mark's wording in some instances to clarify his meaning (cf. Mark 2:15 with Luke 5:29) or to "tone down" some of his strong statements (cf., e.g., Mark 4:38b with Matt. 8:25; Luke 8:24). (6) Matthew and Luke sometimes omit words and phrases from Mark's "full" descriptions to make room for additional material (cf., e.g., Mark 1:29 with Matt. 8:14; Luke 4:38).

Five major objections have been raised against the theory of Marcan priority: (1) Matthew and Luke agree with each other against the content of Mark in some passages dealing with the same subject. (2) Luke omits all reference to the material in Mark 6:45–8:26 which is unusual if he used Mark. (3) Mark occasionally has bits of information not found in the same incident reported in Matthew or Luke (cf. Mark 14:72). (4) The early church fathers apparently believed in the priority of Matthew instead of Mark. (5) Marcan priority practically requires the view that Matthew and/or Luke were written after the destruction of Jerusalem in A.D. 70.

In response to the first objection, the agreements of Luke and Matthew against Mark involve a very small number of passages (ca. 6%) and are probably due to common sources (i.e., oral tradition) which they used in addition to Mark. The second objection falters on the commonly acknowledged fact that the Gospel writers selected material from their sources in line with their purposes. Luke may have omitted reference to material in Mark 6:45–8:26 in order not to interrupt the development of his own journey-to-Jerusalem theme (cf. Luke 9:51). This also answers the third objection in addition to the fact that Mark had Peter as an eyewitness source. The fourth objection stems from the arrangement of the Gospels in the New Testament canon. To infer from this that the early fathers believed Matthew was *written* first is not valid. They were concerned about the apostolic authority and apologetic value of the Synoptic Gospels, not their historical interrelationships. Thus Matthew, written by an apostle and beginning with a genealogy that linked it nicely to the Old Testament, was given first place. Furthermore, if Matthew were the first Gospel written and it were used by Mark and Luke, one would expect to find places where Luke follows Matthew's order of events and Mark does not—but this does not occur. It is also more difficult to explain why Mark would shift from Matthew's order than vice versa. Displacement of order favors Marcan priority. In response to the fifth objection, Marcan priority does not necessitate dating Matthew and/or Luke after A.D. 70 (cf. comments on "Date").

Some literary dependence seems to be the only way to explain adequately the close relationship between the Synoptic Gospels. The priority-of-Mark theory, though not without problems, accounts best for the basic outline of events and the detailed similarities between the Synoptic Gospels. The differences are probably due to a combination of oral and written traditions which Matthew and Luke used independently in addition to Mark. (For further discussion and an alternate view on the Synoptic problem [priority of Matt.] see the *Introduction* to Matt.)

Date. Nowhere does the New Testament have any explicit statement regarding the date of Mark. The discourse centered around Jesus' prediction of the destruction of the Jerusalem temple (cf. comments on 13:2, 14-23) suggests that Mark's Gospel was written before A.D. 70, when the temple was destroyed.

Early testimony from the church fathers is divided on whether Mark wrote his Gospel before or after the martyrdom of Peter (ca. A.D. 64–68). On one hand, Irenaeus (*Against Heresies* 3. 1. 1) declared that Mark wrote *after* the "departure" (*exodon*) of Peter *and* Paul (thus after A.D. 67 or 68). By the word *exodon* Irenaeus probably meant "departure in death." The word is used this way in Luke 9:31 and 2 Peter 1:15. This is clearly supported by the *Anti-Marcionite Prologue* to Mark which asserts, "After the death of Peter himself, he [Mark] wrote down this same Gospel. . . ." On the other hand, Clement of Alexandria and Origen (cf. Eusebius *Ecclesiastical History* 2. 15. 2; 6. 14. 6; 6. 25. 5) placed the writing of Mark's Gospel *during* Peter's lifetime stating, in fact, that Peter participated in its production and ratified its use in the church.

Because of conflicting external evidence the question of date remains problematic. Two options are available. One view is that the Gospel can be dated between A.D. 67–69 if one accepts the tradition that it was written after the deaths of Peter *and* Paul. Advocates of this view usually hold either that Matthew and Luke were written after A.D. 70 or that they were written before Mark. A second view is that the Gospel can be dated prior to A.D. 64–68 (when Peter was martyred) if one accepts the tradition that it was written during Peter's lifetime. On this view one can accept the priority of Mark (or Matt.) and still hold that all the Synoptic Gospels were written before A.D. 70.

The second view is preferred for these reasons: (1) Tradition is divided though the more reliable evidence supports this view. (2) The priority of Mark (cf. comments under "Sources"), particularly Mark's relationship to Luke, which antedates Acts (cf. Acts 1:1), points to a date before A.D. 64. The fact that Acts closes with Paul still in prison prior to his first release (ca. A.D. 62) pushes the date for Mark before A.D. 60. (3) It is historically probable that Mark (and perhaps Peter also for a short time) could have been in Rome during the latter part of the 50s (cf. comments under "Authorship" and under "Place of Origin and Destination"). Thus a plausible dating would seem to be A.D. 57–59 during the early part of Emperor Nero's reign (A.D. 54–68).

Place of Origin and Destination. The almost universal testimony of early church fathers (cf. references under "Authorship") is that Mark's Gospel was written in Rome primarily for Gentile Roman Christians.

The following evidence from the Gospel itself supports this: (1) Jewish customs are explained (cf. 7:3-4; 14:12; 15:42). (2) Aramaic expressions are translated into Greek (cf. 3:17; 5:41; 7:11, 34; 9:43; 10:46; 14:36; 15:22, 34) (3) Several Latin terms are used rather than their Greek equivalents (cf. 5:9; 6:27; 12:15, 42; 15:16, 39). (4) The Roman method of reckoning time is used (cf. 6:48; 13:35). (5) Only Mark identified Simon of Cyrene as the father of Alexander and Rufus (cf. 15:21; Rom. 16:13). (6) Few Old Testament quotations or references to fulfilled prophecy are used. (7) Mark portrayed a particular concern for "all the nations" (cf. comments on Mark 5:18-20; 7:24–8:10; 11:17; 13:10; 14:9), and at a climactic point in the Gospel a Gentile Roman centurion unwittingly proclaimed Jesus' deity (cf. 15:39). (8) The tone and message of the Gospel are appropriate to Roman believers who were encountering persecution and expecting more (cf. comments on 9:49; 13:9-13). (9) Mark assumed that his readers were familiar with the main characters and events of his narrative, so he wrote with more of a theological than a biographical interest. (10) Mark addressed his readers as Christians more directly by explaining the meaning for them of particular actions and statements (cf. 2:10, 28; 7:19).

Characteristics. Several features make Mark's Gospel unique among the Gospels. First, it emphasizes Jesus' actions more than His teaching. Mark recorded 18 of Jesus' miracles but only four of His parables (4:2-20, 26-29, 30-32; 12:1-9) and one major discourse (13:3-37). Repeatedly Mark wrote that Jesus taught without recording His teaching (1:21, 39; 2:2, 13; 6:2, 6, 34; 10:1; 12:35). Most of the teaching he did include came out of Jesus' controversies with the Jewish religious leaders (2:8-11, 19-22, 25-28; 3:23-30; 7:6-23; 10:2-12; 12:10-11, 13-40).

Second, Mark's writing style is vivid, forceful, and descriptive, reflecting an eyewitness source such as Peter (cf., e.g., 2:4; 4:37-38; 5:2-5; 6:39; 7:33; 8:23-24; 14:54). His use of Greek is nonliterary, close to the everyday speech of that time with a recognizable Semitic flavoring. His use of Greek tenses, especially the "historical present" tense (used over 150 times), simple sentences linked by "and," frequent use of "immediately" (euthys; cf. comments on 1:10), and the use of forceful words (e.g., lit., "impelled," 1:12) lend vividness to his narrative.

Third, Mark portrayed his subjects with unusual candor. He emphasized the responses of Jesus' hearers with various expressions of amazement (cf. comments on 1:22, 27; 2:12; 5:20; 9:15). He related the concern of Jesus' family over His mental health (cf. 3:21, 31-35). He candidly and repeatedly drew attention to the disciples' lack of understanding and failures (cf. 4:13; 6:52; 8:17, 21; 9:10, 32; 10:26). He also highlighted Jesus' emotions such as His compassion (1:41; 6:34; 8:2; 10:16), His anger and displeasure (1:43; 3:5; 8:33; 10:14), and His sighs of distress and sorrow (7:34; 8:12; 14:33-34).

Fourth, Mark's Gospel is dominated by Jesus' movement toward the Cross and the Resurrection. From Mark 8:31 onward Jesus and His disciples were "on the way" (cf. 9:33; 10:32) from Caesarea Philippi in the north through Galilee to Jerusalem in the south. The rest of the narrative (36%) was devoted to events of the Passion Week—the eight days from Jesus' entry into Jerusalem (11:1-11) to His resurrection (16:1-8).

Theological Themes. Mark's portrait of Jesus and its meaning for discipleship stand at the center of his theology. In the opening verse Jesus Christ is identified as "the Son of God" (1:1). This was confirmed by the Father (1:11; 9:7) and affirmed by demons (3:11; 5:7), by Jesus Himself (13:32; 14:36, 61-62), and by a Roman centurion at Jesus' death (15:39). It was also confirmed by His authoritative teaching (1:22, 27) and His sovereign power over disease and disability (1:30-31, 40-42; 2:3-12; 3:1-5; 5:25-34; 7:31-37; 8:22-26; 10:46-52), demons (1:23-27; 5:1-20; 7:24-30; 9:17-27), the domain of nature (4:37-39; 6:35-44, 47-52; 8:1-10), and death (5:21-24, 35-43). All this was convincing proof that "the kingdom of God"—His sovereign rule—had come near to people in Jesus, both in His words and works (cf. comments on 1:15).

Yet paradoxically Mark stressed Jesus' demand that the demons be silent (1:25, 34; 3:12) and that His miracles not be publicized (1:44; 5:43; 7:36; 8:26). He stressed Jesus' use of parables in teaching the crowds (4:33-34) because His kingly rule was then veiled, a mystery, recognized only by people of faith (4:11-12). Mark stressed the disciples' slowness to understand the meaning of Jesus' presence with them despite private instruction (4:13, 40; 6:52; 7:17-19; 8:17-21). He stressed Jesus' demand for silence even from the disciples following Peter's confession of His identity (8:30). Jesus did this because of the Jews' misleading views about the Messiah, which were contrary to the purpose of His earthly ministry. He did not want His identity declared openly till He had made clear to His followers the kind of Messiah He was and the character of His mission.

Mark recorded Peter's confession, "You are the Christ" (8:29), in its simplest, most direct form. Jesus did not accept or reject this title but turned the disciples' attention from the question of His identity to that of His activity (8:31, 38). He used the preferred designation "Son of Man" and taught His disciples that He must suffer, die, and rise again. The title, Son of Man, used 12 times by Jesus in Mark versus His one use of the title "Christ" ("the Messiah," 9:41), was especially suited to His total messianic mission—present and future (cf. comments on 8:31, 38; 14:62). He was the suffering Servant of Yahweh (Isa. 52:13–53:12) who gave up His life for others in submission to God's will (Mark 8:31). He was also the Son of Man who will come in glory to render judgment and establish His kingdom on earth (8:38–9:8; 13:26; 14:62). But before the glorious triumph of His messianic reign He must first suffer and die under the curse of God for human sin (14:36; 15:34) as a ransom for many (10:45). This had important implications for all who would follow Him (8:34-38).

It was hard for Jesus' 12 disciples to grasp this. They envisioned a reigning Messiah, not One who would suffer and die. In his special discipleship section (8:31-10:52) Mark portrayed Jesus "on the way" to Jerusalem teaching His disciples what it meant to follow Him. The prospect was not attractive. But in

His transfiguration He gave three of them a reassuring preview of His future coming in power and glory (9:1-8). At the same time the Father confirmed Jesus' sonship and commanded them to obey Him. Throughout this section the disciples "saw" but not as they ought (8:22-26). Again Mark emphasized that they followed Jesus with amazement, misunderstanding, and even fear of what lay ahead (9:32; 10:32). At Jesus' arrest they all deserted Him (14:50). With restraint Mark recorded Jesus' crucifixion and the accompanying phenomena that elucidated its meaning (15:33-39).

But Mark emphasized the empty tomb and the angel's message that Jesus was alive and was going ahead of His disciples into Galilee (14:28; 16:7), the place of their initial ministry (6:6b-13). His abrupt conclusion dramatically declared that Jesus is alive to lead His disciples and care for their needs as He had done previously. Thus their "journey" of discipleship was to go on in light of and determined by Jesus' death and resurrection (9:9-10).

Occasion and Purpose. Mark's Gospel contains no direct statement about this, so that information must be derived from a study of its contents and presumed historical setting. Because such assessments differ, various views have been given.

Some suggested purpose statements: (a) to present a biographical portrait of Jesus as the Servant of the Lord, (b) to win converts to Jesus Christ, (c) to give instruction to new Christians and strengthen their faith in the face of persecution, (d) to provide material for evangelists and teachers to use, and (e) to correct false ideas about Jesus and His messianic mission. These suggestions, though helpful, seem either to exclude portions of the Gospel from consideration or fail to account for Mark's emphases.

Mark's purpose was basically *pastoral*. The Christians in Rome had already heard and believed the good news of God's saving power (Rom. 1:8) but they needed to hear it again with a new emphasis to catch afresh its implications for their lives in a dissolute and often hostile environment. They needed to understand the nature of discipleship— what it meant to follow Jesus—in light of

who Jesus is and what He had done and would keep doing for them.

Like a good pastor, Mark presented "the gospel about Jesus Christ, the Son of God" (1:1) in a way that would meet this need and continue to shape his readers' lives. He achieved this through his portraits of Jesus and the 12 disciples with whom he expected his readers to identify (cf. comments under "Theological Themes"). He showed how Jesus Christ is the Messiah because He is the Son of God, and His death as the suffering Son of Man was God's plan for people's redemption. In light of this he showed how Jesus cared for His disciples and taught them about discipleship in the context of His death and resurrection— the same kind of care and teaching needed by all who follow Jesus.

OUTLINE

COMMENTARY

I. The Title (1:1)

1:1. The opening verse (a verbless phrase) stands as the book's title and theme. The word **gospel** (*euangeliou*, "good news") does not refer to Mark's book, known as "the Gospel of Mark." Instead it refers to the good news **about Jesus Christ.**

Those acquainted with the Old Testament knew the importance of the word "gospel" (cf. Isa. 40:9; 41:27; 52:7; 61:1-3). "News" meant that something significant had happened. When Mark used the word, it had become a technical term signifying Christian preaching about Jesus Christ. "The gospel" is the proclamation of God's power through Jesus Christ to save all who believe (Rom. 1:16). It was an important term in the theological shaping of Mark's narrative (Mark 1:14-15; 8:35; 10:29; 13:9-10; 14:9).

For Mark, **the beginning of the** gospel was the historical facts of the life, death, and resurrection of Jesus. Later the apostles proclaimed it, beginning (e.g., Acts 2:36) where Mark ended.

The gospel is "about Jesus Christ," **the Son of God.** "Jesus," His divinely given personal name (cf. Matt. 1:21; Luke 1:31; 2:21), is the Greek equivalent of the Hebrew *y^hôšûa'* ("Joshua"), "Yahweh is salvation."

"Christ" is the Greek equivalent of the Hebrew title *Māšîaḥ* ("Messiah, Anointed One"). It was used specifically of the Deliverer anticipated in the Jewish world who would be God's Agent in fulfilling Old Testament prophecies (e.g., Gen. 49:10; Pss. 2; 110; Isa. 9:1-7; 11:1-9; Zech. 9:9-10). The anticipated Messiah is Jesus. Though the title "Christ" became part of Jesus' personal name in early Christian usage, Mark intended its full titular force as shown by his usage (cf. Mark 8:29; 12:35; 14:61; 15:32).

The title "Son of God" points to Jesus' unique relationship to God. He is a Man (Jesus)—and God's "Special Agent" (Messiah)—but He is also fully divine. As the Son He depends on and obeys God the Father (cf. Heb. 5:8).

II. Introduction: The Preparation for Jesus' Public Ministry (1:2-13)

Mark's brief introduction presents three preparatory events that are necessary for a proper understanding of Jesus' life-mission: the ministry of John the Baptist (vv. 2-8), Jesus' baptism (vv. 9-11), and Jesus' temptation (vv. 12-13). Two recurring words bind this section together: "the desert" (erēmos; vv. 3-4, 12-13) and "the Spirit" (vv. 8, 10, 12).

A. Jesus' forerunner, John the Baptist (1:2-8)

(Matt. 3:1-12; Luke 3:1-20; John 1:19-37)

1. JOHN'S FULFILLMENT OF OLD TESTAMENT PROPHECY (1:2-3)

1:2-3. Mark began by putting his account in its proper scriptural context. Aside from Old Testament quotations by Jesus this is the only place Mark referred to the Old Testament in his Gospel.

Verse 2 blends Exodus 23:20 (LXX) and Malachi 3:1 (Heb.), and Mark 1:3 is from Isaiah 40:3 (LXX). Mark adopted a traditional understanding of these verses so he could use them without explanation. In addition he emphasized the word "way" (hodos, lit., "road, highway"), an important theme in Mark's explanation of discipleship (Mark 8:27; 9:33; 10:17, 32, 52; 12:14).

Mark prefaced this composite quotation from three Old Testament books with the words: **It is written in Isaiah the prophet.** This illustrates a common practice by New Testament authors in quoting several passages with a unifying theme. The common theme here is the "wilderness" (desert) tradition in Israel's history. Since Mark was introducing the ministry of John the Baptist in the desert, he cited Isaiah as the source because the Isaiah passage refers to "a voice . . . calling" **in the desert.**

Under the Holy Spirit's guidance Mark gave those Old Testament texts a messianic interpretation by altering "the way before Me" (Mal. 3:1) to **Your way,** and "the paths of our God" (Isa. 40:3, LXX) to **paths for Him.** Thus the speaker, **I,** was God who **will send** His **messenger** (John) **ahead of You** (Jesus) **who will prepare** Your (Jesus') way. John was **a voice** urging the nation of Israel to **prepare** (pl. verb) **the way for the Lord** (Jesus) and to **make straight** "paths for Him" (Jesus). The meaning of these metaphors is given in John's ministry (Mark 1:4-5).

2. JOHN'S ACTIVITY AS A PROPHET (1:4-5)

1:4. In fulfillment of the preceding prophecy, **John came** (egeneto, "appeared") on the stage of history as the last Old Testament prophet (cf. Luke 7:24-28; 16:16), signaling a turning point in God's dealings with mankind. John was **baptizing in the desert region** (erēmō, dry, uninhabited country) **and preaching a baptism of repentance.** The word "preaching" (kēryssōn) could be rendered "proclaiming as a herald," appropriate in light of the prediction in Mark 1:2-3.

John's baptism was no innovation since Jews required Gentiles wanting to be admitted into Judaism to be baptized by self-immersion. The startling new element was that John's baptism was designed for God's covenant people, the Jews, and it required their repentance in view of the coming Messiah (cf. Matt. 3:2).

This baptism is described as one relating to or expressive of repentance **for** (eis) **the forgiveness of sins.** The Greek preposition eis could be referential ("with reference to") or purpose ("leading to") but probably not cause ("on account of"). "Repentance" (metanoia) occurs in Mark only here. It means "a turn about, a deliberate change of mind resulting in a change of direction in thought and behavior" (cf. Matt. 3:8; 1 Thes. 1:9).

"Forgiveness" (aphesin) means "the removal or cancellation of an obligation or barrier of guilt." It refers to God's gracious act whereby "sins" as a debt are canceled, based on Christ's sacrificial death (cf. Matt. 26:28). Forgiveness was not conveyed by the outward rite of baptism, but baptism was a visible witness that one had repented and as a result had received God's gracious forgiveness of sins (cf. Luke 3:3).

1:5. Using hyperbole (cf. also vv. 32-33, 37), Mark showed the great impact John made on all areas of Judea and **Jerusalem.** The people **went out** and **were baptized by** John **in the Jordan River** (cf. v. 9) as they confessed **their sins** to God. The imperfect tense of the Greek verbs portrays in motion-picture fashion the continual procession of people who kept going out to hear John's preaching and to be baptized by **him.**

The verb "baptize" (*baptizō*, intensive form of *baptō*, "to dip") means "to immerse, submerge." Being baptized by John in the Jordan marked the "turn" of a Jew to God. It identified him with the repentant people who were preparing for the coming Messiah.

Included in the performance of the baptismal rite was the people's open confession of sins. The verb "confessing" (*exomologoumenoi*, "agree with, acknowledging, admitting"; cf. Acts 19:18; Phil. 2:11), is intensive. They openly agreed with God's verdict on their sins (*hamartias*, "failure to hit the mark," i.e., God's standard). Every Jew familiar with the nation's history knew they had fallen short of God's demands. Their willingness to be baptized by John in the desert was an admission of their disobedience and an expression of their turning to God.

3. JOHN'S LIFESTYLE AS A PROPHET (1:6)

1:6. John's attire and diet marked him as a man of the desert and also depicted his role as God's prophet (cf. Zech. 13:4). In this way he resembled the Prophet Elijah (2 Kings 1:8), who was equated in Malachi 4:5 with the messenger (Mal. 3:1) cited earlier (cf. Mark 1:2; 9:13; Luke 1:17). **Locusts** (dried insects) **and wild honey** were the common diet in desert regions. Locusts are listed in Leviticus 11:22 among the "clean" foods.

4. JOHN'S MESSAGE AS A PROPHET (1:7-8)

1:7. The opening words are literally, "And he was proclaiming as a herald, saying . . . " (cf. v. 4). Mark summarized John's **message** in order to focus on its main theme, the announcement of a greater Person still to come who would baptize people with the Holy Spirit (v. 8).

The words, **After me** (in time) **will come One** echo Malachi 3:1 and 4:5, but the precise identity of the Coming One remained hidden even to John till after Jesus' baptism (cf. John 1:29-34). No doubt Mark avoided the term "Messiah" because of popular misconceptions associated with it. Mark 1:8 suggests why the Coming One is **more powerful than** John.

John emphasized the importance of the Coming One and showed his own humility (cf. John 3:27-30) by declaring that he was **not worthy to stoop down** (words recorded only by Mark) **and untie the thongs** (leather straps) used to fasten His **sandals.** Even a Hebrew slave was not required to do this menial task for his master!

1:8. This verse contrasts I with **He.** John administered the outward sign, **water** baptism; but the Coming One would actually bestow the life-giving Spirit.

When used in connection with water, the word "baptize" normally indicated a literal immersion (cf. vv. 9-10). When used with the words **Holy Spirit** it metaphorically means coming under the Spirit's life-giving power.

I **baptize** is literally "I baptized," probably indicating that John was addressing those he had already baptized. His baptism **with** (or "in") "water" was limited and preparatory. But those who received it pledged to welcome the Coming One who would **baptize** them **with the** Holy Spirit (cf. Acts 1:5; 11:15-16). The bestowal of the Spirit was an expected feature of the Messiah's coming (Isa. 44:3; Ezek. 36:26-27; Joel 2:28-29).

B. *Jesus' baptism by John the Baptist (1:9-11)*
(Matt. 3:13-17; Luke 3:21-22)

1. JESUS' BAPTISM IN THE JORDAN (1:9)

1:9. Mark abruptly introduced the Coming One (v. 7) as **Jesus.** In contrast with "all the people" from Judea and Jerusalem (v. 5), He **came** to **John** in the desert region **from Nazareth in Galilee.** Nazareth was an obscure village never mentioned in the Old Testament, the Talmud, or the writings of Josephus, the well-known first-century Jewish historian. Galilee, about 30 miles wide and 60 miles long, was the populous northernmost region of the three divisions of Palestine: Judea, Samaria, and Galilee.

John **baptized** Jesus **in** (*eis*) **the Jordan** River (cf. v. 5). The Greek prepositions *eis* ("into," v. 9) and *ek* ("out of," v. 10) suggest baptism by immersion. Jesus' baptism probably occurred near Jericho. He was about 30 years old at this time (Luke 3:23).

In contrast with all others, Jesus made no confession of sins (cf. Mark 1:5) since He is without sin (cf. John 8:45-46; 2 Cor. 5:21; Heb. 4:15; 1 John 3:5). Mark did not state why Jesus submitted to John's baptism; however, three reasons may be suggested: (1) It was an act of obedience, showing that Jesus was in full agreement with God's overall plan and the role of John's baptism in it (cf. Matt. 3:15). (2) It was an act of self-identification with the nation of Israel whose heritage and sinful predicament He shared (cf. Isa. 53:12). (3) It was an act of self-dedication to His messianic mission, signifying His official acceptance and entrance into it.

2. THE DIVINE RESPONSE FROM HEAVEN (1:10-11)

1:10. Mark used the Greek adverb *euthys* ("immediately, at once") here for the first of 42 occurrences in his Gospel (the NIV omits it here). Its meaning varies from the sense of immediacy (as here) to that of logical order ("in due course, then"; cf. 1:21 ["when"]; 11:3 ["shortly"]).

Three things set **Jesus** apart from all others who had been baptized. First, **He saw heaven being torn open.** The forceful verb, "being torn open" (*schizomenous*, "split") reflects a metaphor for God's breaking into human experience to deliver His people (cf. Pss. 18:9, 16-19; 144:5-8; Isa. 64:1-5).

Second, He saw **the Spirit descending on Him like a dove,** in a visible dovelike form, not in a dovelike way (cf. Luke 3:22). The dove imagery probably symbolized the Spirit's creative activity (cf. Gen. 1:2). In Old Testament times the Spirit came on certain people to empower them for service (e.g., Ex. 31:3; Jud. 3:10; 11:29; 1 Sam. 19:20, 23). The coming of the Spirit on Jesus empowered Him for His messianic mission (cf. Acts 10:38) and the task of baptizing others with the Spirit, as John predicted (Mark 1:8).

1:11. Third, Jesus heard **a voice . . . from heaven** (cf. 9:7). The Father's words, expressing His unqualified approval of Jesus and His mission, echoed three verses: Genesis 22:2; Psalm 2:7; Isaiah 42:1.

In the first declaration, **You are My Son,** the words "You are" affirm Jesus' unique sonship with the Father. The significance of these words is found in Psalm 2:7 where God addressed the anointed King as His Son. At His baptism Jesus began His official role as God's Anointed One (cf. 2 Sam. 7:12-16; Ps. 89:26; Heb. 1:5).

The second clause, **whom I love,** is literally, "the Beloved One" (*ho agapētos*). This is either a title ("the Beloved") or a descriptive adjective ("beloved" Son). As a title it stresses the intensity of love between God the Father and the Son without losing its descriptive force. As an adjective, it can be understood in the Old Testament sense of an "only" Son (cf. Gen. 22:2, 12, 16; Jer. 6:26; Amos 8:10; Zech. 12:10), equivalent to the Greek adjective *monogenēs* ("only, unique"; cf. John 1:14, 18; Heb. 11:17). This more interpretive rendering points to Jesus' preexistent sonship.

The words **with You I am well pleased** point to the kind of kingly Son Jesus was to be in His earthly mission. The verb *eudokēsa* is in the past tense ("I was well pleased"). Timeless in force, it is rendered in English in the present tense to indicate that God is pleased with His Son at all times. God's delight never had a beginning and will never end.

These words come from Isaiah 42:1 in which God addressed His Servant whom He had chosen, the One in whom He delights, and on whom He had put His Spirit. Isaiah 42:1 begins the first of a series of four prophecies about the true Servant-Messiah in contrast with the disobedient servant-nation of Israel (cf. Isa. 42:1-9; 49:1-7; 50:4-9; 52:13–53:12). The true Servant would suffer greatly in fulfilling God's will. He would die as a "guilt offering" (Isa. 53:10), and He Himself would serve as the sacrificial Lamb (cf. Isa. 53:7-8; John 1:29-30). At His baptism Jesus began His role as the Lord's suffering Servant. Mark gives prominence to this feature of Jesus' messianic mission (Mark 8:31; 9:30-31; 10:32-34, 45; 15:33-39).

Jesus' baptism did not change His divine status. He did not *become* the Son of God at His baptism (or at the transfiguration, 9:7). Rather, His baptism showed the far-reaching significance of His acceptance of His messianic vocation as the suffering Servant of the Lord as well as the Davidic Messiah. Because He is the Son of God, the One approved by the Father and empowered by the Spirit, He is the Messiah (not vice versa). All three Persons of the Trinity are involved.

C. Jesus' temptation by Satan (1:12-13)
(Matt. 4:1-11; Luke 4:1-13)

1:12. After His baptism Jesus went forward in the power of the Spirit and **at once** (*euthys*, "immediately") **the Spirit sent Him** farther **out into the desert** region. The word "sent" is from a strong verb (*ekballō*) meaning "drive out, expel, send away." Mark used it to denote the expulsion of demons (vv. 34, 39; 3:15, 22-23; 6:13; 7:26; 9:18, 28, 38). Here it reflects Mark's forceful style (cf. "led," Matt. 4:1; Luke 4:1). The thought is that of strong moral compulsion by which the Spirit led Jesus to take the offensive against temptation and evil instead of avoiding them. The desert (*erēmos*; cf. Mark 1:4) region, dry uninhabited places, was viewed traditionally as the haunt of evil powers (cf. Matt. 12:43; Luke 8:29; 9:24). The traditional temptation site is northwest of the Dead Sea immediately west of Jericho.

1:13. Jesus **was in the desert** for **40 days.** Despite possible appeal to various Old Testament verses (Ex. 34:28; Deut. 9:9, 18; 1 Kings 19:8), the closest parallel is that of the victory of David over Goliath who had opposed Israel 40 days (1 Sam 17:16).

Jesus was **being tempted by Satan.** "Tempted" is a form of *peirazō*, which means "put to the test, make trial of" in order to discover the kind of person someone is. It is used either in a good sense (God's testing, e.g., 1 Cor. 10:13; Heb. 11:17) or in a bad sense of enticement to sin by Satan and his cohorts. Both senses are involved here. God put Jesus to the test (the Spirit led Him to it) to show He was qualified for His messianic mission. But also Satan tried to draw Jesus away from His divinely appointed mission (cf. Matt. 4:1-11; Luke 4:1-13). Jesus' sinlessness does not rule out the fact that He was actually tempted; in fact, it bears witness to His true humanity (cf. Rom. 8:3; Heb. 2:18).

The tempter was Satan, the adversary, the one who opposes. Mark did not use the term "the devil" (slanderer; Matt. 4:1; Luke 4:2). Satan and his forces are in constant, intense opposition against God and His purposes, especially Jesus' mission. Satan tempts people to turn aside from God's will, accuses them before God when they fall, and seeks their ruin. Jesus encountered the prince of evil personally before confronting his forces. He entered on His ministry to defeat him and set his captives free (Heb. 2:14; 1 John 3:8). As the Son of God, He battled Satan in the desert, and the demons confessed Him as such (cf. Mark 1:24; 3:11; 5:7).

The reference to **wild animals** is recorded only by Mark. In Old Testament imagery, "the wilderness" was the place of God's curse—a place of desolation, loneliness, and danger where frightening, ravenous animals lived (cf. Isa. 13:20-22; 34:8-15; Pss. 22:11-21; 91:11-13). The presence of wild animals stresses the hostile character of the desert region as Satan's domain.

In contrast with the dangerous wild animals is God's protecting care through the **angels** who **attended** (lit., "were serving," *diēkonoun*) Jesus throughout the temptation period (though the verb could be rendered "began to serve Him," i.e., after the temptation). They supplied general aid and the assurance of God's presence. Mark did not mention fasting (cf. Matt. 4:2; Luke 4:2), probably because Jesus' stay in the desert region clearly implied it.

Mark's temptation account is brief (in contrast with Matt. and Luke). He said nothing about the temptation's content, its climactic end, or Jesus' victory over Satan. His concern was that this began an ongoing conflict with Satan who kept attempting through devious means to get Jesus to turn aside from God's will (cf. Mark 8:11, 32-33; 10:2; 12:15). Because of the vocation Jesus accepted in His baptism, He faced a confrontation with Satan and his forces. Mark's Gospel is the record of this great encounter which climaxed at the Cross. At the outset Jesus established His personal authority over Satan. His later exorcisms of demons were based on His victory in this encounter (cf. 3:22-30).

III. Jesus' Early Galilean Ministry (1:14–3:6)

The first major section of Mark's Gospel includes a summary statement of Jesus' message (1:14-15); the calling of the first disciples (1:16-20); Jesus' exorcising and healing ministry in and around Capernaum (1:21-45); five controversies with Jewish religious leaders (2:1–3:5), and a plot by the Pharisees and Herodians to kill Jesus (3:6). Throughout the section Jesus demonstrated His authority over all things both by His words and deeds.

A. Introductory summary: Jesus' message (1:14-15)
(Matt. 4:12-17; Luke 4:14-21)

Jesus began His ministry in Galilee (cf. Mark 1:9) after John the Baptist was arrested by Herod Antipas (see chart on the Herods at Luke 1:5) for the reason stated in Mark 6:17-18. Before entering Galilee, Jesus ministered in Judea for about a year (cf. John 1:19–4:45), which Mark did not mention. This shows that Mark's purpose was not to give a complete chronological account of Jesus' life.

1:14. The words **was put in prison** translate *to paradothēnai*, from *paradidomi*, "deliver up or hand over." The verb is used of Jesus' betrayal by Judas (3:19), suggesting that Mark set up a parallel between John's and Jesus' experiences (cf. 1:4, 14a). The passive voice without a stated agent implies that God's purpose was being fulfilled in John's arrest (cf. parallel to Jesus, 9:31; 14:18) and that the time for Jesus' ministry in Galilee had now come (cf. comments on 9:11-13).

Jesus came **into Galilee proclaiming** (*kēryssōn*; cf. 1:4) **the good news** (*euangelion*; cf. v. 1) **of** (from) **God.** Possibly the words "of the kingdom" (kjv) should be included before "of God" because of their presence in many Greek manuscripts.

1:15. Jesus' two declarations and two commands summarize His message. The first declaration, **The time has come,** emphasizes the distinctive note of fulfillment in Jesus' proclamation (cf. Luke 4:16-21). God's appointed time of preparation and expectation, the Old Testament era, now stood fulfilled (cf. Gal. 4:4; Heb. 1:2; 9:6-15).

The second declaration, **The kingdom of God is near,** presents a key feature of Jesus' message. "Kingdom" (*basileia*) means "kingship" or "royal rule." Involved in the term is the sovereign authority of a ruler, the activity of ruling, and the realm of rule including its benefits (*Theological Dictionary of the New Testament* [hereafter tdnt]. Grand Rapids: Wm. B. Eerdmans Publishing Co., s.v. "*basileia*," 1:579-80). Thus "the kingdom of God" is a dynamic (not static) concept that refers to *God's* sovereign activity of ruling over His Creation.

This concept was familiar to the Jews of Jesus' day. In light of Old Testament prophecy (cf. 2 Sam. 7:8-17; Isa. 11:1-9; 24:23; Jer. 23:4-6; Micah 4:6-7; Zech. 9:9-10; 14:9) they were expecting a future messianic (Davidic) kingdom to be established on earth (cf. Matt. 20:21; Mark 10:37; 11:10; 12:35-37; 15:43; Luke 1:31-33; 2:25, 38; Acts 1:6). So Jesus' hearers naturally understood His reference to the kingdom of God to be the long-awaited messianic kingdom.

Jesus said God's rule "is near" (*ēngiken*, "has come near" or "has arrived"; cf. same verb form in Mark 14:42 ["Here comes"]). But it was not near in the form the Jews expected. Rather it had arrived in the sense that Jesus, the Agent of God's rule, was present among them (cf. Luke 17:20-21). This was "the good news from God."

The required response to which Jesus summoned His hearers was a double command: **Repent and believe the good news!** Repentance and faith (belief) are bound together in one piece (not temporally successive acts). To "repent" (*metanoeō*; cf. Mark 1:4) is to turn away from an existing object of trust (e.g., oneself). To "believe" (*pisteuō*, here *pisteuete en*, the only NT appearance of this combination) is to commit oneself wholeheartedly to an object of faith. Thus to believe in the good news meant to believe in Jesus Himself as the Messiah, the Son of God. He is the "content" of the good news (cf. v. 1). Only by this means can one enter into or receive (as a gift) the kingdom of God (cf. 10:15).

As a nation Israel officially rejected these requirements (cf. 3:6; 12:1-12; 14:1-2, 64-65; 15:31-32). Furthermore Jesus taught that His earthly Davidic reign would not come immediately (cf. Luke 19:11). After God completes His present purpose of saving Jews and Gentiles and building His church (cf. Rom. 16:25-27; Eph. 3:2-12), Jesus will return and set up His kingdom on this earth (Matt. 25:31, 34; Acts 15:14-18; Rev. 19:15; 20:4-6). The nation of Israel will be restored and redeemed (Rom. 11:25-29).

So the kingdom of God has two aspects, both centering in Christ (cf. Mark 4:13-31): (1) It is already present, though veiled, as a spiritual realm (Mark's emphasis; cf. 3:23-27; 10:15, 23-27; 12:34). (2) It is still future when God's rule will be openly established on earth (cf. 9:1; 13:24-27).

B. Jesus' call of four fishermen (1:16-20)
(Matt. 4:18-22; Luke 5:1-11)

Jesus' call of four fishermen, to be His followers comes immediately after the summary of His message. So Mark made clear that to repent and believe in the gospel (Mark 1:15) is to break with one's old way of life and to follow Jesus, to make a personal commitment to Him in response to His call. With this call Jesus began His work in Galilee. This anticipated His appointing and sending out the Twelve (3:13-19; 6:7-13, 30).

1:16. The **Sea** (a Semitic label) **of Galilee,** a warm-water lake about 7 miles wide, 13 miles long, and 685 feet *below* sea level, was the scene of a thriving fishing industry. It was geographically central to Jesus' Galilean ministry.

As He was walking along the shore, **Jesus . . . saw Simon** (surnamed Peter) and **Andrew,** his **brother,** each throwing out a circular casting **net** (10–15 feet diameter) **into the lake.** The significant thing about this, Mark explained (*gar,* for), is that **they were fishermen** by trade.

1:17-18. The words **Come, follow Me** are literally, "Come after Me," a technical expression that meant "Go behind Me as a disciple." Unlike a Rabbi whose pupils sought him out, **Jesus** took the initiative and called His followers.

The call included Jesus' promise: **and I will make you** to become (*genesthai*) **fishers of men.** He had "caught" them for His kingdom; now He would equip them to share His task, to become (*genesthai* implies preparation) fishers who catch "men" (generic for "people"; cf. 8:27).

The fishing metaphor was probably suggested by the brothers' occupation but

also had an Old Testament background (cf. Jer. 16:16; Ezek. 29:4-5; Hab. 1:14-17). Though the prophets used this figure to express divine judgment, Jesus used it positively as a means to avoid divine judgment. In view of the impending righteous rule of God (cf. Mark 1:15) Jesus summoned these men to the task of gathering people out of the "sea" (OT imagery for sin and death, e.g., Isa. 57:20-21).

At once (*euthys*; cf. Mark 1:10) Simon and Andrew **left their nets** (their old calling) **and followed Him.** In the Gospels the verb "follow" (*akoloutheō*), when referring to *individuals,* expresses the call and response of discipleship. Later events (cf. vv. 29-31) show that their response meant not a repudiation of their homes but rather giving Jesus their full allegiance (cf. 10:28; 1 Cor. 7:17-24).

1:19-20. On the same occasion Jesus **saw James** and **John,** the sons **of Zebedee** (cf. 10:35), **in their boat, preparing** (from *katartizō,* "put in order, make ready") **their nets** for another night's fishing. They were partners to Simon (cf. Luke 5:10). **Without delay** (*euthys*) Jesus **called them** to follow Him. **They left** behind their old way of life (fishing boat and nets) and prior claims (**their father Zebedee** and **the hired** helpers) **and followed** (lit., "went away after") **Him** as disciples.

Mark did not mention any previous contact with Jesus by these fishermen (cf. John 1:35-42). Later Jesus gathered the Twelve around Himself in a Teacher-pupil relationship (Mark 3:14-19). Mark abbreviated historical events (1:14-20) to emphasize Jesus' authority over people and the obedience of His followers.

Discipleship is prominent in Mark's Gospel. Jesus' call would pose two questions in the minds of Mark's readers: "Who is this One who calls?" and "What does it mean to follow Him?" Mark gave them an answer in his Gospel. He assumed similarities between the Twelve (cf. comments on 3:13; 13:37) and his readers. Discipleship is the expected norm for all who believe the gospel (cf. 1:15).

C. Jesus' authority over demons and disease (1:21-45)

The authoritative nature (v. 22) and importance (vv. 38-39) of Jesus' word already experienced by the four fishermen was demonstrated further by His powerful deeds. Verses 21-34 describe a single, perhaps typical, Sabbath Day's activities in Capernaum: His power over demons (vv. 21-28), the healing of Peter's mother-in-law (vv. 29-31), and the healing of others after sunset (vv. 32-34). Then verses 35-39 present a brief withdrawal for prayer and a summary of a preaching tour in Galilee. One significant event on that tour was the healing of a leper (vv. 40-45). Jesus' authoritative words and deeds provoked both amazement and alarm and set the stage for controversies (2:1-3:5).

1. THE CURE OF A DEMONIAC (1:21-28)
   (LUKE 4:31-37)

1:21-22. The four disciples accompanied Jesus into nearby **Capernaum** (cf. 2:1; 9:33), on the northwestern shore of the Sea of Galilee. It was their hometown and became the hub of Jesus' Galilean ministry (cf. Luke 4:16-31). In due course (*euthys;* cf. Mark 1:10), on **the Sabbath** (Saturday) **Jesus** attended the regular worship service in **the synagogue,** a Jewish place of assembly and worship (cf. vv. 23, 29, 39; 3:1; 6:2; 12:39; 13:9). No doubt by invitation from the ruler of the synagogue, He **began to teach** (cf. Acts 13:13-16). Mark often referred to Jesus' **teaching** ministry (Mark 2:13; 4:1-2; 6:2, 6, 34; 8:31; 10:1; 11:17; 12:35; 14:49), but recorded little of what Jesus taught.

His hearers **were amazed** (*exeplēssonto,* lit., "astounded, struck out of their senses, overwhelmed"; also in 6:2; 7:37; 10:26; 11:18) at the manner and the content (cf. 1:14-15) of Jesus' teaching. **He taught** with direct **authority** from God and had the power to evoke decisions. This contrasted sharply with **the teachers of the Law** (lit., "scribes") who were schooled in the written Law and its oral interpretation. Their knowledge was derived from scribal tradition, so they simply quoted the sayings of their predecessors.

1:23-24. Just then (*euthys;* cf. v. 10), the presence of Jesus and His authoritative teaching **in the synagogue** provoked a strong outburst from **a man** under control of **an evil spirit** (lit., "an unclean spirit," Semitic for "demon"; cf. v. 34).

The demon spoke through the man who **cried out, What do You want with us. . .?** These words translate a Hebrew idiom which expresses the incompatibility of opposing forces (cf. 5:7; Josh. 22:24; Jud. 11:12; 2 Sam. 16:10; 19:22).

This question, in the NIV, could be punctuated more forcefully as a declaration: **"You** have **come** (into the world) **to destroy** (ruin, not annihilate) **us."** The pronoun "us" in both sentences indicates that this demon perceived the significance of Jesus' presence (cf. Mark 1:15) to all the demonic forces. Jesus was the ultimate threat to their power and activity.

The demon, in contrast with most people, recognized Jesus' true character and identity as **the Holy One of God** (cf. 3:11; 5:7), the One empowered by the Holy Spirit. Thus the evil spirit knew the explanation for Jesus' authority.

1:25-26. In a few direct words (no incantations) **Jesus sternly** rebuked (*epetimēsen;* cf. 4:39) the evil spirit and ordered the demon to **come out of** the man. The words **Be quiet** translate the forceful *phimōthēti,* "be muzzled or silenced" (cf. 4:39). Submitting to Jesus' authority, **the evil spirit** convulsed (cf. 9:26) **the** possessed **man, and with a** loud **shriek,** left **him.**

Jesus did not accept the demon's defensive utterance (1:24) because doing so would have undermined His task of confronting and defeating Satan and his forces. His authority over evil spirits was evidence that God's rule had come in Jesus (cf. v. 15). This initial exorcism set the pattern for the sustained conflict Jesus had with demons—an important element in Mark's account. (See the list of Jesus' miracles at John 2:1-11.)

1:27-28. All **the people** were greatly **amazed** (*ethambēthēsan,* "surprised, astonished"; cf. 10:24, 32). Their question, **What is this?** referred both to the nature of Jesus' teaching and His expulsion of a demon with only a word of command. His **teaching** was qualitatively **new** (*kainē*) **and** came **with authority** (cf. 1:22) that extended even to demonic forces who were forced to **obey** (submit to) **Him** (cf. 4:41). In summary, Mark declared that very soon (*euthys;* cf. 1:10) all **Galilee** heard the **news about Him.**

2. THE HEALING OF SIMON'S MOTHER-IN-LAW (1:29-31)
   (MATT. 8:14-15; LUKE 4:38-39)

1:29-31. Immediately (*euthys;* cf. v. 10) after leaving **the synagogue** Sabbath service, Jesus and the four disciples **went to the** nearby **home of Simon** (Peter) **and Andrew.** This house became something of a headquarters for Jesus when He was in Capernaum (cf. 2:1; 3:20; 9:33; 10:10).

He was promptly (*euthys*) **told** that **Simon's mother-in-law was** lying **in bed** burning **with a fever.** In compassionate response **Jesus** stood beside her and without a word simply grasped **her hand and** raised **her up. The fever left** completely, and without weakness **she began to** serve (*diēkonei*, imperf.) her guests.

3. THE HEALING OF MANY PEOPLE AT
   SUNSET (1:32-34)
   (MATT. 8:16-17; LUKE 4:40-41)

1:32-34. This summary portrays the excitement in Capernaum generated by the miracles on that Sabbath. The double time reference, **that evening after sunset,** made it clear that **the people** of Capernaum waited until the Sabbath Day was over (sunset) before moving the sick lest they break the Law (cf. Ex. 20:10) or Rabbinic regulations which prohibited burden-bearing on that day (cf. Mark 3:1-5).

The townspeople **brought** (lit., "kept carrying," imperf.) **to Jesus all the** physically **sick and demon-possessed** (not "possessed with devils," KJV, since there is only one devil). Again, a clear distinction is maintained between physical sickness and demon possession (cf. 6:13). It seemed as if **the whole town** (hyperbole; cf. 1:5) had **gathered at the door** of Simon's house. In compassionate response to this human need **Jesus healed many** (a Heb. idiom meaning "all who were brought"; cf. v. 32; 10:45; Matt. 8:16) **who had** a wide variety of **diseases. He also drove out** (*exebalen*, from *ekballō*; cf. Mark 1:12, 39) **many demons, but** as before (vv. 23-26) He repeatedly silenced their cries of recognition, showing that they were powerless before Him.

The miracles accompanying Jesus' preaching increased His popularity. He performed miracles not to impress people with His power but to authenticate His message (cf. v. 15).

4. A WITHDRAWAL FOR PRAYER AND A
   PREACHING TOUR IN GALILEE (1:35-39)
   (LUKE 4:42-44)

1:35. Despite a full day of ministry (vv. 21-34), **Jesus got up** the next morning

very early, before daybreak (about 4 A.M.) **and went** out **to a solitary** (*erēmon,* "uninhabited, remote") **place** (cf. v. 4) **where He** spent time praying. He withdrew from the acclaim of the Capernaum crowds to a wilderness place—the kind of place where He initially confronted Satan and withstood his temptations (cf. vv. 12-13).

Mark selectively portrayed Jesus at prayer on three crucial occasions, each in a setting of darkness and aloneness: near the beginning of his account (v. 35), near the middle (6:46), and near the end (14:32-42). All three were occasions when He was faced with the possibility of achieving His messianic mission in a more attractive, less costly way. But in each case He gained strength through prayer.

1:36-37. The crowds, returning to Simon's door and expecting to find Jesus, discovered He was gone. **Simon and his companions** (cf. v. 29) **went** out **to look for Him** (lit., "to hunt Him down," from *katadiōkō,* occurring only here in the NT). Their exclamation, **Everyone is looking for You!** implied some annoyance because they thought Jesus was failing to capitalize on some excellent opportunities in Capernaum.

1:38-39. Jesus' reply showed that they too did not understand Him or His mission. His plan was to **go** elsewhere— **to the nearby villages,** populous market towns, **so** that He could **preach** (cf. vv. 4, 14) **there also,** in addition to Capernaum. His explanatory statement, **That** ("to preach") **is why I have come,** probably does not refer to leaving Capernaum (He left to pray, v. 35) but rather to His coming from God on a divine mission. His purpose was to proclaim "the good news of God" (v. 14) and confront people with the demand to "repent and believe" it (v. 15). Since the Capernaum crowds sought Him as a Miracle-worker, He deliberately departed to preach elsewhere.

Verse 39 summarizes His tour **throughout Galilee** (cf. v. 28) which probably lasted several weeks (cf. Matt. 4:23-25). His main activity was **preaching** (cf. Mark 1:14-15) **in** the local **synagogues, and** His **driving out** (*ekballōn;* cf. v. 34) **demons** dramatically confirmed His message.

5. THE CLEANSING OF A LEPER (1:40-45)
(MATT. 8:1-4; LUKE 5:12-16)

1:40. On Jesus' Galilean tour, **a man with leprosy came to Him** (a bold move for a leper). "Leprosy" included a variety of serious skin diseases ranging from ringworm to true leprosy (Hanson's bacillus), a progressively disfiguring disease. This man experienced a pitiful existence due not only to the physical ravages of the disease but also to ritual uncleanness (cf. Lev. 13–14) and exclusion from society. Leprosy brought anguish at all levels: physical, mental, social, and religious. It serves as an illustration of sin.

The Rabbis regarded leprosy as humanly incurable. Only twice does the Old Testament record that God cleansed a leper (Num. 12:10-15; 2 Kings 5:1-14). Yet this leper was convinced that Jesus could cleanse him. Without presumption **(If You are willing)** and without doubting Jesus' ability **(You can make me clean)**, he humbly **begged** Jesus to heal him.

1:41-42. Moved by **compassion** (*splanchnistheis*, "having deep pity"), **Jesus . . . touched the** untouchable and **cured** the incurable. His touch showed that Jesus was not bound by Rabbinic regulations regarding ritual defilement. Both this symbolic touch (cf. 7:33; 8:22) and Jesus' authoritative pronouncement— **I am willing** (pres. tense), **be clean** (aorist pass., decisive act received)—constituted the cure. It was immediate (*euthys*; cf. 1:10), complete, visible to all who saw him.

1:43-44. The forceful words, **sent him away** (*exebalen*; cf. v. 12), **at once** (*euthys*; cf. v. 10), and **a strong warning** (cf. 14:5) emphasize the need for prompt obedience to the instructions in 1:44.

First, Jesus sternly warned (same verb in 14:5) him: **Don't tell this** (his cure) **to anyone.** This could be a temporary prohibition that was in force till the man had been pronounced clean by **the priest.** However, Jesus often commanded silence and sought to minimize the proclaiming of His true identity and miraculous powers (cf. 1:25, 34; 3:12; 5:43; 7:36; 9:9). Why did Jesus do this? Some contend that Mark and the other Gospel writers inserted these commands for silence as a literary device to explain why the Jews did not recognize Jesus as the Messiah during His earthly ministry.

This view is called "the messianic secret," that is, Jesus' messiahship was kept secret.

A more satisfactory view is that Jesus wanted to avoid misunderstandings that would precipitate a premature and/or erroneous popular response to Him (cf. comments on 11:28). He did not want His identity declared till He had made the character of His mission clear (cf. comments on 8:30; 9:9). Thus there was a progressive withdrawal of the veil from His identity until He openly declared it (14:62; cf. 12:12).

Second, Jesus instructed the former leper to **show** himself **to** the priest, who alone could declare him ritually clean, **and** to **offer the sacrifices** prescribed by **Moses** (cf. Lev. 14:2-31).

This demand is qualified by the phrase as (*eis*, "for") **a testimony to them.** This phrase could be understood in a positive sense ("a convincing witness") or negative sense ("an incriminating witness") to either the people in general or the priests in particular. In this context, as in the two other occurrences of this phrase (Mark 6:11; 13:9), the negative sense is preferred. Thus "testimony" means an item of proof which can serve as incriminating evidence (cf. TDNT, s.v. "*martys*," 4:502-4) and "them" refers to the priests.

The cleansing of the leper was an undeniable messianic sign (cf. Matt. 11:5; Luke 7:22) that God was working in a new way. If the priests declared the leper clean but rejected the One who cleansed him, their unbelief would be incriminating evidence against them.

1:45. Instead of obeying Jesus' command to silence, the man **went out and began to talk freely** (lit., "to proclaim [*kēryssein*] it much"), making known the story of his cure far and wide. Mark did not say whether he obeyed Jesus' command to show himself to the priest.

As a result, Jesus' preaching ministry in the synagogues of Galilee (cf. v. 39) was interrupted. He **could** not **enter a town openly** without encountering large crowds seeking special favors. Even when He withdrew to **lonely** (*erēmois*, "uninhabited, remote"; cf. v. 35) **places . . . the people** kept coming **from** all directions.

The deliverance Jesus brought transcended the Mosaic Law and its regulations. Though the Law provided for the ritual purification of a leper, it was powerless to cleanse a person from the disease or to effect inward spiritual renewal.

D. Jesus' controversies with Jewish religious leaders in Galilee (2:1-3:5)

Mark brought together the five episodes in this section because of the common theme of conflict in Galilee between Jesus and the Jewish religious leaders. Thus they are not in strict chronological order. A similar unit of five controversies in the temple at Jerusalem is recorded in 11:27-12:37.

The conflict here concerned Jesus' authority over sin and the Law. The first incident is introduced by a summary statement (2:1-2) of Jesus' preaching. Mark often used this literary device to summarize Jesus' activity and keep his narrative moving on to events that suited his purpose (cf. 1:14-15, 39; 2:1-2, 13; 3:7-12, 23; 4:1, 33-34; 8:21-26, 31; 9:31; 10:1; 12:1).

1. THE HEALING OF A PARALYTIC MAN AND FORGIVENESS (2:1-12)

(MATT. 9:1-8; LUKE 5:17-26)

2:1-2. A few days later when Jesus returned to **Capernaum** (cf. 1:21), it was reported that **He** was at **home** (probably Peter's house; cf. 1:29). In the freedom of Jewish custom **many** uninvited people crowded into the house and around **the door,** thus preventing access. Jesus was speaking (imperf., *elalei*) **the Word** (cf. 1:14-15; 4:14, 33) **to them.**

2:3-4. Four **men** brought **a paralytic** (paralyzed man) **on a mat** (poor man's "bed," KJV), hoping to **get him to Jesus. But they could not . . . because of the crowd.** Like many Palestinian dwellings, this house probably had an outside stairway leading to a flat **roof.** So the men went onto the roof. **After digging through it** (a composite of grass, clay, clay tiles, and laths), **they made an opening . . . above Jesus** and **lowered** the **paralyzed man** before Him (probably using fishing ropes that lay at hand).

2:5. Jesus viewed the determined effort of the four as visible evidence of **their faith** in His power to heal this man. He did not rebuke this interruption to His teaching but unexpectedly told **the paralytic, Son** (an affectionate term), **your sins are forgiven.**

In the Old Testament disease and death were viewed as the consequences of man's sinful condition, and healing was predicated on God's forgiveness (e.g., 2 Chron. 7:14; Pss. 41:4; 103:3; 147:3; Isa. 19:22; 38:16-17; Jer. 3:22; Hosea 14:4). This does not mean there is a corresponding sin for each occurrence of sickness (cf. Luke 13:1-5; John 9:1-3). Jesus simply showed that this man's physical condition had a basic spiritual cause.

2:6-7. The teachers of the Law (lit., "scribes"; cf. 1:22; Luke 5:17) who were present were offended by Jesus' veiled pronouncement. Only God **can forgive sins** (cf. Ex. 34:6-9; Pss. 103:3; 130:4; Isa. 43:25; 44:22; 48:11; Dan. 9:9). In the Old Testament forgiveness of sins was never attributed to the Messiah. The scribes regarded such **talk** by **this fellow** (contemptuous tone) as a pretentious affront to God's power and authority, blasphemy against **God,** a serious offense punishable by death from stoning (Lev. 24:15-16). In fact such a charge became the basis for a formal condemnation later (cf. Mark 14:61-64).

2:8-9. Immediately (*euthys*; cf. 1:10) **Jesus** perceived **in His spirit** (inwardly; cf. 14:38) their hostile thoughts **and He** confronted them directly with pointed counterquestions (a rhetorical device in Rabbinic debate; cf. 3:4; 11:30; 12:37).

The scribes expected a physical healing, but Jesus pronounced the man's **sins . . . forgiven.** They probably thought that a pronouncement of forgiveness was **easier** than one of healing because healing was visible and immediately verifiable.

2:10. This verse presents an interpretive problem due to the awkward change of addressee in the verse's middle. Jesus seemed to be addressing the scribes (v. 10a) but there is an abrupt break in the verse after which He addressed **the paralytic.** Another problem in light of the overall emphasis of Mark is the public use of the title **Son of Man** by Jesus in the presence of unbelieving hearers so early in His ministry (cf. 9:9; 10:33). Apart from 2:10 and 28, this title does not occur in Mark's account until after Peter's confession (8:29). After that it occurs 12 times and is crucial to Jesus' self-disclosure *to His disciples* (cf. 8:31, 38; 9:9, 12, 31;

10:33, 45; 13:26; 14:21 [twice], 41, 62; see comments on 8:31).

In light of these difficulties 2:10a is probably a parenthetical, editorial comment by Mark (cf. similarly, vv. 15c, 28; 7:3-4, 19; 13:14). He inserted it into the narrative to explain the significance of this event for his readers: that Jesus as the risen Son of Man **has authority** (*exousian,* the right and power) **on earth to forgive sins,** something the scribes did not fully recognize. Only here in the Gospels is the forgiveness of sins attributed to the Son of Man.

This view contributes to the literary unity of the passage: forgiveness is declared (2:5), questioned (vv. 6-9), validated (v. 11), and recognized (v. 12). The initial words in verse 10, **But that you may know,** could thus be translated, "Now you (Mark's readers) should know that. . . ." The last clause signals the end of Mark's comment and a return to the incident itself.

2:11-12. Jesus commanded the paralytic to **get up** (a test of his faith), **take** his **mat, and go home** (demand of obedience). The man was enabled to do this immediately (*euthys;* cf. 1:10) **in full view of them all,** including Jesus' critics. They were forced to recognize that the man had received God's forgiveness. This showed the character of salvation Jesus brought, namely, healing whole persons. **Everyone** (probably including the scribes) was **amazed** (*existasthai,* lit., "out of their minds"; cf. 3:21; 5:42; 6:51) and **praised** (ascribed glory to) **God** because of Jesus' display of supernatural power.

2. THE CALL OF LEVI AND EATING WITH
   SINNERS (2:13-17)
   (MATT. 9:9-13; LUKE 5:27-32)

2:13. Jesus went out from Capernaum to **the lake** (Sea of Galilee) **once again** (cf. 1:16). To summarize His activity, Mark stated that Jesus was teaching **a large crowd** which kept on coming **to hear Him.** His withdrawal from populous centers is a recurring pattern in Mark (cf. 1:45; 2:13; 3:7, 13; 4:1; 5:21; etc.) and recalls the "wilderness" theme (cf. 1:4, 12-13, 35, 45).

2:14. Capernaum was a customs post on the caravan route from Damascus to the Mediterranean Sea. **Levi** (surnamed Matthew; cf. 3:18; Matt. 9:9; 10:3) was a Jewish **tax** official in the service of Herod Antipas, the ruler of Galilee (see the chart on the Herods at Luke 1:5). For such service, often involving fraudulent practices, these officials were despised by the Jews. Yet Jesus extended to Levi a gracious call to **follow** Him and leave his old calling behind (cf. Mark 1:17-18).

2:15-16. Shortly afterward, Levi gave a **dinner** for **Jesus** and **His disciples.** This is the first mention (of 43) in Mark of the "disciples" as a distinct group. Mark added an editorial comment explaining that **there were** many (disciples) **who followed** Jesus, not just the five mentioned so far in Mark's Gospel.

Eating with Jesus were **many tax collectors** (Levi's former associates) **and "sinners,"** a technical term for common people regarded by the Pharisees as untaught in the Law, who did not abide by rigid pharisaic standards. For Jesus and His disciples to share a meal (an expression of trust and fellowship) with them offended **the Law** teachers **who were Pharisees.** The Pharisees, the most influential religious party in Palestine, were deeply devoted to the Mosaic Law. They strictly regulated their lives by the supposedly binding interpretations of it passed down in oral tradition and were meticulous about maintaining ceremonial purity (cf. 7:1-5). They criticized Jesus for not being a separatist, for failing to observe their pious distinction between "the righteous" (they themselves) and "the **sinners."**

2:17. Jesus answered their criticism with a well-known proverb (recognized as valid by His opponents) and a statement of His mission which vindicated His conduct. The words, **the righteous,** are used ironically to refer to those who saw themselves as such, namely, the Pharisees (cf. Luke 16:14-15). They saw no need to repent and believe (cf. Mark 1:15). But Jesus knew that everyone, including "the righteous," are sinful. He came (into the world) to call **sinners,** those who humbly acknowledge their need and receive His gracious forgiveness, to God's kingdom. This was why Jesus ate with sinners (cf. 2:5-11, 19-20).

3. THE DISCUSSION ABOUT FASTING AND
   THE NEW SITUATION (2:18-22)
   (MATT. 9:14-17; LUKE 5:33-39)

2:18. Mark's initial statement explained that **John's disciples** (John the

Baptist's remaining followers) **and the Pharisees** (and their disciples or adherents) **were fasting,** presumably while Jesus and His disciples were feasting at Levi's house. The Old Testament prescribed fasting for all Jews only on the annual Day of Atonement, as an act of repentance (Lev. 16:29), but the Pharisees promoted voluntary fasts on every Monday and Thursday (cf. Luke 18:12) as an act of piety. In response to a critical inquiry, **Jesus** showed the incongruity of **fasting** for His disciples (Mark 2:19-22), though He allowed it if practiced properly (cf. Matt. 6:16-18).

2:19-20. Jesus' counterquestion set up a comparison and a veiled analogy to Himself. As it is inappropriate for **guests** (lit., "sons of the bridal chamber," the groom's attendants) to **fast** (an expression of sorrow) in the presence **of the bridegroom,** so it was inappropriate for Jesus' disciples to fast (in sorrow) **while He** was **with them.**

His presence with them constituted a situation as joyous as a wedding festival. **But** this situation would change, for **the time** (lit., "days") would **come when the Bridegroom** (Jesus) would **be taken** (*aparthē,* implying violent removal; cf. Isa. 53:8) **from them and on that day** (His crucifixion) the disciples would **fast** in the metaphorical sense of experiencing sorrow in place of joy. This allusion to His coming death is the first hint of the Cross in Mark's Gospel.

2:21-22. For the first time Mark used two of Jesus' parables, both of which had broader relevance than to fasting. Jesus' presence with His people was a time of newness (fulfillment) and signaled the passing of the old.

An attempt to bind the newness of the gospel to the old religion of Judaism is as futile as trying to **patch** an **old** (*palaion,* "worn out by use") **garment** with a new, **unshrunk** piece of **cloth.** When **the new** (*kainon,* "qualitatively new") **piece** (*plērōma,* "fullness") becomes wet, it **will** shrink, **pull away from the old,** and make a larger hole.

It is equally disastrous to pour **new** (*neon,* "fresh"), not fully fermented **wine into old** (*palaious,* "worn out by use," with no elasticity, brittle) **wineskins.** Inevitably, as **the** new **wine** ferments (expands), it **will burst the skins and both the wine and the wineskins will be**

ruined. Salvation, available through Jesus, was not to be mixed with the old Judaistic system (cf. John 1:17).

4. THE PICKING AND EATING OF GRAIN ON THE SABBATH (2:23-28)
(MATT. 12:1-8; LUKE 6:1-5)

2:23-24. While walking on a footpath **through** someone's **grainfields** one **Sabbath,** Jesus' **disciples . . . began** picking **some heads of grain** to eat. This was legitimate (Deut. 23:25), but **the Pharisees** viewed it as reaping, an act of work forbidden **on the Sabbath** (cf. Ex. 34:21), so they demanded an explanation from **Jesus.**

2:25-26. In response Jesus appealed to Scripture and a precedent set by **David** and **his companions** when they **were hungry and in need** (1 Sam. 21:1-6). The words "his companions" and "in need" are key elements in this incident. David **entered the** tabernacle court, requested **the consecrated bread** (cf. Lev. 24:5-9) which was restricted by Mosaic legislation to **the priests** (cf. Lev. 24:9) and **gave some to his** men. Jesus used this action which God did not condemn, to show that the Pharisees' narrow interpretation of the Law blurred God's intention. The spirit of the Law in respect to human need took priority over its ceremonial regulations.

Mark stated that David's action occurred **in the days of Abiathar the high priest,** but the high priest was actually Ahimelech, his father (1 Sam. 21:1). A plausible explanation is to render the introductory phrase: "in the passage about Abiathar, the high priest" (cf. parallel phrase in Mark 12:26). This was a customary Jewish way of indicating the section of the Old Testament where a desired incident could be found. Abiathar became high priest shortly after Ahimelech and proved more prominent than he, thus justifying the use of his name here.

2:27-28. With the words, **Then He said to them,** Mark appended two principles: (1) He quoted Jesus' words that **the Sabbath was** instituted (by God) **for** mankind's benefit and refreshment, **not** that people were made to keep burdensome regulations pertaining to it. (2) Mark concluded (**so,** in light of vv. 23-27) with an editorial comment (cf. v. 10) on the meaning of Jesus' statement for his readers. **The Son of Man** (cf. 8:31) **is Lord** (Master) **even of the Sabbath;** He has sovereign authority over its use, as the next incident demonstrates.

5. THE HEALING OF THE MAN WITH A WITHERED HAND ON THE SABBATH (3:1-5) (MATT. 12:9-14; LUKE 6:6-11)

3:1-2. On **another** Sabbath occasion in **the synagogue** (probably Capernaum; cf. 1:21) Jesus saw **a man with a shriveled hand** (his "right" one; cf. Luke 6:6). **Some of them** (Pharisees, cf. Mark 3:6) **were** watching **Jesus** closely to see what He would do so they might find **a reason to accuse** Him. They permitted healing on the Sabbath only if a life was in danger. This man's problem was not life-threatening and could wait till the next day; so if Jesus healed him, they could accuse Him of being a **Sabbath**-violator, an offense punishable by death (cf. Ex. 31:14-17).

3:3-4. Jesus commanded the man, **Stand up** so the whole gathering could see his **shriveled hand. Then** He **asked** the Pharisees a rhetorical question concerning which of two kinds of action was really consistent with the purpose of **the Sabbath** in the Mosaic Law. The obvious answer is: **to do good** and **to save life** (psychēn, "soul"; cf. 8:35-36). Yet failure to use the Sabbath to meet this man's need (cf. 2:27) was **to do evil** (harmful misuse of its purpose) and, as ultimately happened, their malicious plotting on the Sabbath (cf. 3:6) led them **to kill.** The moral (not legal) issue of "doing good" on the Sabbath was at stake, and the Pharisees refused to debate it.

3:5. Jesus **looked around** (from periblepomai, an all-inclusive penetrating look; cf. v. 34; 5:32; 10:23; 11:11) at the Pharisees **in anger.** This is the only explicit reference to Jesus' anger in the New Testament. It was nonmalicious indignation coupled with deep sorrow (grief) at their obstinate insensitivity (pōrōsei, "hardening"; cf. Rom. 11:25; Eph. 4:18) to God's mercy and human misery.

When the man held out **his hand** at Jesus' command, it was instantly and **completely restored.** Jesus did not use any visible means that might be construed as "work" on the Sabbath. As Lord of the Sabbath (Mark 2:28) Jesus freed it from legal encumbrances, and in grace delivered this man from his distress.

E. *Conclusion: Jesus' rejection by the Pharisees (3:6)*

3:6. This verse climaxes the section on Jesus' conflicts in Galilee with the religious establishment (2:1–3:5). It is Mark's first explicit reference to Jesus' death, which now began to cast its shadow over His mission. **The Pharisees** conspired immediately (euthys; cf. 1:10) **with the Herodians** (cf. 12:13), influential political supporters of Herod Antipas, in an unprecedented common effort to destroy Jesus (cf. 15:31-32). His authority confronted and overwhelmed their authority, so He must be killed. Their problem was how.

IV. Jesus' Later Galilean Ministry (3:7–6:6a)

The second major section of Mark's Gospel begins and concludes structurally like the first one (cf. 1:14-15 with 3:7-12; 1:16-20 with 3:13-19; 3:6 with 6:1-6a). It shows the development of Jesus' mission in the context of opposition and unbelief.

A. *Introductory summary: Jesus' activity around the Sea of Galilee (3:7-12) (Matt. 12:14-21)*

3:7-10. This summary passage is similar in context and character to 2:13. An added element is that **Jesus withdrew with His disciples** (emphatic first position in Gr.), who shared in both the hostility and the popular acclaim directed toward Jesus.

Many people **from Galilee followed** (nontechnical sense, "went along with") and, attracted by **all He was doing** (i.e., healing miracles), **many . . . came** from areas outside Galilee—from the south, **Judea, Jerusalem, Idumea;** the east, Transjordan (Perea); and the north, the coastal cities of **Tyre and Sidon** (in Phoenicia). Jesus spent time in all these areas (except Idumea; 5:1; 7:24, 31; 10:1; 11:11). So intense was the impact of Jesus' healing ministry and the desire of **those with diseases** (mastigas, "scourges," cf. 5:29 ["suffering"], 34) **to touch Him** that **He told His disciples to have a small boat ready** to escape the rush of the crowds. Only Mark reported this detail, suggesting the memory of an eyewitness such as Peter.

3:11-12. In the crowds were demoniacs, people whose speech and behavior were dominated by **evil spirits.** They recognized Jesus' true status as **the Son of God** and were greatly threatened by His presence. Jesus did not accept their repeated (imperf. verbs) cries of recognition, and ordered (cf. 1:25; 4:39; 8:30, 32-33; 9:25) them **not to tell who He was** (cf. 1:24-25, 34). In silencing their untimely cries Jesus reaffirmed His submission to God's plan for the *progressive* disclosure of His identity and mission.

B. *Jesus' appointment of the Twelve (3:13-19)*
(Matt. 10:1-4; Luke 6:12-16)

3:13. From the lakeside lowlands **Jesus went up into the hills** (of central Galilee; cf. 6:46). Taking the initiative, He summoned to Himself **those He wanted,** namely the Twelve (3:16-19), **and they came** from the crowd **to Him** (cf. Luke 6:13). Mark had already said that Jesus had many other disciples (cf. Mark 2:15).

3:14-15. He appointed (lit., "made") 12 for two reasons: (a) so they could **be with Him** (immediate association for training) and (b) be sent **out** by Him **to preach** (cf. 1:4, 14) **and to have** (delegated) **authority to drive out** (*ekballein;* cf. 1:34, 39) **demons** (their future mission; cf. 6:7-13). Mark devoted attention to their association with Jesus and preparation for their ministries.

Nearly all major ancient Greek manuscripts and most early versions omit the phrase, **designating them apostles.** This seems preferable; its inclusion in a few early manuscripts was probably due to the influence of Luke 6:13 and because Mark used the term "apostles" only in Mark 6:30 where it is appropriate in a nontechnical sense.

The number 12 corresponds to the 12 tribes of Israel, thus expressing Jesus' claim on the whole nation. "The Twelve" became an official designation or title for those appointed by Jesus on this occasion (cf. 4:10; 6:7; 9:35; 10:32; 11:11; 14:10, 17, 20, 43). Though significantly linked with Israel, they are never called a new or spiritual "Israel." Rather they were the nucleus of a coming new community, the church (cf. Matt. 16:16-20; Acts 1:5-8).

3:16-19. These verses give a traditional list of the names of the appointed Twelve. **Simon** (cf. 14:37) heads the list. Jesus surnamed him **Peter** (cf. John 1:42), the Greek equivalent of the Aramaic *Cephas,* which means a "stone or rock." This probably described his leadership role during Jesus' ministry and in the early church (cf. Matt. 16:16-20; Eph. 2:20), and did not refer to his personal character. **James** and **John,** Zebedee's sons, are surnamed **Boanerges,** a Hebrew idiom Mark interpreted as **Sons of Thunder** (cf. Mark 9:38; 10:35-39; Luke 9:54), though a more complimentary meaning (now unknown) may have been intended by Jesus.

Apart from **Andrew** (cf. Mark 1:16; 13:3), **Judas Iscariot** (cf. 14:10, 43), and possibly **James son of Alphaeus** as "James the younger" (cf. 15:40), the remaining names do not occur again in Mark: **Philip** (cf. John 1:43-45), **Bartholomew** (Nathanael; John 1:45-51), **Matthew** (Levi; cf. Mark 2:14), **Thomas** (cf. John 11:16; 14:5; 20:24-28; 21:2), James son of Alphaeus (probably not Levi's brother; cf. Mark 2:14), **Thaddaeus** (Judas son of James; cf. Luke 6:16; Acts 1:13), and **Simon the Zealot** ("Zealot" probably indicated his zeal for God's honor, not an extreme nationalism). In contrast was Judas Iscariot (a "man from Kerioth," the only non-Galilean; cf. John 6:71; 13:26), **who betrayed** Jesus to His enemies (cf. Mark 14:10-11, 43-46).

C. *The Beelzebub accusation and Jesus' identity of His true family (3:20-35)*

This section has a "sandwich" structure in which the account concerning Jesus' family (vv. 20-21, 31-35) is divided by the Beelzebub accusation (vv. 22-30). This deliberate literary device is used several times by Mark (cf. 5:21-43; 6:7-31; 11:12-26; 14:1-11, 27-52) for different reasons. Here Mark pointed out a parallel in the charges made against Jesus (cf. 3:21 and 30) but at the same time made a distinction between general opposition to Jesus and a distortion of the Holy Spirit's work through Him.

1. THE CONCERN OF JESUS' FAMILY FOR HIM (3:20-21)

3:20-21. These verses are unique to Mark. After **Jesus entered a house** (in

Capernaum; cf. 2:1-2), such a large **crowd** demanded His attention **that He and His disciples** had no time **to eat** (cf. 6:31). **When His family** (lit., "those with Him," a Gr. idiom for kinsmen, not "friends," KJV; cf. 3:31) **heard** that His ceaseless activity prevented proper care for His needs, **they** came (probably from Nazareth) **to take charge of Him** (*kratēsai*, a word used for making an arrest; cf. 6:17; 12:12; 14:1, 44, 46, 51) **for** (*gar*; cf. "for" in 1:16) the people kept saying **He** was **out of His mind,** a mentally unbalanced religious fanatic (cf. Acts 26:24; 2 Cor. 5:13).

2. JESUS' REFUTATION OF THE BEELZEBUB ACCUSATION (3:22-30)
(MATT. 12:22-32; LUKE 11:14-23; 12:10)

3:22. Meanwhile a delegation of Law **teachers** (scribes) **came down from Jerusalem** to investigate Jesus. They repeatedly charged (a) that **He** was **possessed by Beelzebub** (demon-possessed; cf. v. 30), and (b) that **He** was **driving out demons** through a power alliance with Satan, **the prince** (ruler) of **demons** (cf. v. 23).

The spelling "Beelzebub" came into English translations from the Latin Vulgate which derived it from the Hebrew "Baalzebub" meaning "Lord of the flies," the name of an ancient Canaanite deity (cf. 2 Kings 1:2). But the spelling "Beelzeboul" (NIV marg.) has better Greek manuscript support. It reflects the later Hebrew "Baalzebul" (not used in the OT) meaning: "Lord of the dwelling place (temple)," that is, of evil spirits in the New Testament contexts (cf. Matt. 10:25; Luke 11:17-22).

3:23-27. Jesus summoned His accusers and refuted their charges **in parables** (short proverbial sayings, not stories). He dealt with the second accusation first (vv. 23-26) by showing the absurdity of their underlying assumption that **Satan** acts against **himself.** He used two illustrations to make the self-evident point that if a **kingdom** or a **house** (household) is **divided against itself** in purpose and goals, it **cannot stand.** The same applies to Satan if it is assumed that **Satan opposes** himself **and his realm is divided.** This would mean that **his end has come,** that is, his power, not his personal existence. Clearly this is false, for Satan remains strong (cf. v. 27; 1 Peter 5:8). So

the charge that Jesus' exorcisms were due to Satan's power was false.

The analogy in Mark 3:27 refuted their first accusation (v. 22) showing in fact (lit., "on the contrary") that the opposite was true. Satan is **the strong man.** His **house** is the realm of sin, sickness, demon possession, and death. **His possessions** are people who are enslaved by one or more of these things, and demons are his agents who carry out his diabolical activity. **No one can enter** his realm to **carry off** (*diarpasai*, "plunder") his possessions **unless he first** binds the strong man (shows he is more powerful). **Then he can rob** (*diarpasei*, "plunder") the realm, releasing the enslaved victims. At His temptation (cf. 1:12-13) and through His exorcisms Jesus demonstrated that He is the Stronger One, empowered by the Holy Spirit (cf. 3:29). His mission is to confront and overpower (not cooperate with) Satan and to deliver those enslaved by him.

3:28-30. In light of the preceding charges Jesus issued a strong warning. The words, **I tell you the truth** (lit., "Amen [truly], I say to you"), are a recurring formula of solemn affirmation (13 times in Mark) found only in the Gospels and always spoken by Jesus.

Jesus declared, **All the sins and blasphemies** (derogatory words vs. God) **of men** (generic, "people") are open to God's gracious forgiveness (cf. 1:4) with one exception—blasphemies **against the Holy Spirit.** In light of the context this refers to an attitude (not an isolated act or utterance) of defiant hostility toward God that rejects His saving power toward man, expressed in the Spirit-empowered person and work of Jesus. It is one's preference for darkness even though he has been exposed to light (cf. John 3:19). Such a persistent attitude of willful unbelief can harden into a condition in which repentance and forgiveness, both mediated by God's Spirit, become impossible. This person **is guilty** (*enochos,* "liable to, in the grasp") **of an eternal sin** (sing., the ultimate sin because it remains forever unforgiven; cf. Matt. 12:32). Judas Iscariot (cf. Mark 3:29; 14:43-46) proved the reality of these words.

Mark explained that Jesus **said all this because they** (the Law teachers, 3:22) kept **saying He** was demon-possessed (v. 22b). Jesus did not actually say the scribes had committed this unpardonable sin; but they came perilously close by attributing His exorcisms to satanic power when they really were accomplished by the Holy Spirit. They were close to calling the Holy Spirit "Satan."

3. JESUS' TRUE FAMILY (3:31-35)
(MATT. 12:46-50; LUKE 8:19-21; 11:27-28)

3:31-32. The arrival of **Jesus' mother** (Mary; cf. 6:3) **and** His **brothers** (cf. 6:3) resumes the narrative suspended in 3:21. **Standing outside** the house, **they sent someone** through the **crowd . . . around Him,** requesting a private conversation in an attempt to restrain His activity.

3:33-35. Jesus' rhetorical question (v. 33) was not a repudiation of family relationships (cf. 7:10-13). He was highlighting the far deeper issue of a person's relationship to Him. It is qualitative in force: **"Who are** the sort of people who are **My mother and My brothers?"** Then looking (from *periblepomai*; cf. 3:5) **at those seated in a circle around Him** (His disciples in contrast with those standing outside, v. 31), Jesus asserted that their kinship went beyond natural family ties.

Jesus broadened the reference beyond those present by stating that **whoever does God's will is** a member of His family. The words **brother and sister and mother,** all occurring without an article in Greek (thus qualitative), figuratively denote Jesus' spiritual family. Doing God's will (e.g., 1:14-20) characterizes those who are Jesus' spiritual kinfolk.

D. Jesus' parables depicting the character of God's kingdom (4:1-34)

This group of parables constitutes the first of two lengthy units in Mark's Gospel devoted to Jesus' teaching (cf. also 13:3-37). Mark selected these parables (as implied in 4:2, 10, 13, 33) from a larger collection to depict the character of God's kingdom (cf. 4:11 with 1:15).

They were given in a climate of growing hostility and opposition (cf. 2:3–3:6, 22-30), but also enormous popular acclaim (cf. 1:45; 2:2, 13, 15; 3:7-8). Both responses showed people's failure to grasp who Jesus really is.

"Parable" is a transliteration of the Greek *parabolē*, "comparison." It can designate a variety of figurative forms of speech (e.g., 2:19-22; 3:23-25; 4:3-9, 26-32; 7:15-17; 13:28). But usually a parable is a short discourse that conveys spiritual truth by making a vivid comparison. The truth to be taught is compared to something in nature or a common-life experience. A parable usually expresses a single important truth, though occasionally a subordinate feature expands its total meaning (cf. 4:3-9, 13-20; 12:1-12). A parable draws its hearers to take part in a situation, evaluate it, and apply its truth to themselves. (See the list of Jesus' 35 recorded parables at Matt. 7:24-27.)

1. INTRODUCTORY SUMMARY (4:1-2)
(MATT. 13:1-2)

4:1-2. Once again (cf. 2:13; 3:7) **Jesus** was teaching a large crowd **by the lake** (Sea of Galilee). **The crowd** was **so large that He** was forced to sit in **a boat . . . out on the lake** and teach those who lined the shore. This time **He taught them many things by parables.**

2. THE PARABLE OF THE SOILS (4:3-20)

a. Jesus' statement of the Soils Parable (4:3-9)
(Matt. 13:3-9; Luke 8:4-8)

Both before and after Jesus told this parable, He urged the crowd to listen carefully (cf. Mark 4:3, 9, 23).

4:3-9. As **a farmer** (lit., "one who sows") scattered **seed** over his unplowed field, **some fell along the** well-trodden foot **path** (cf. 2:23). **Some fell on rocky places** having no depth of **soil** because limestone was close to the surface. **Other seed fell among thorns** (ground containing unearthed thorn plant roots). And **still other** seeds **fell on good soil.**

Not all the seed produced a crop. **Birds . . . ate** the seed that fell on the path (4:4). **The sun . . . scorched** the tender plants that **quickly** (*euthys*; cf. 1:10) sprouted in the **shallow** rocky soil **and they withered** (4:6). Thorns **grew up and choked** other **plants,** making them unproductive (v. 7).

By contrast, the seed on the good soil took root, **grew, and produced** an abundant harvest. It brought yields up to **30, 60,** and **even 100 times** (v. 8) the seed sown, depending on the fertility of the soil. Back then a yield of 10 to 1 was considered a fine crop.

b. Jesus' explanation for teaching in parables (4:10-12)
(Matt. 13:10-17; Luke 8:9-10)

4:10. The change of scene here is significant. Verses 10-20 occurred later (cf. vv. 35-36; Matt. 13:36), but Mark put them here to illustrate the principle stated in Mark 4:11, 33-34, and thereby show the importance of parables. **When** Jesus **was alone** with **the Twelve and the others around Him** (other true disciples; cf. 3:34), they **asked Him about the parables** in general, and the Parable of the Soils in particular (cf. 4:13).

4:11-12. These verses must be viewed in the context of unbelief and hostility (cf. 3:6, 21-22, 30). To those who believed, **to you** (emphatic first position in Gr.), the disciples, God had **given the secret of the kingdom of God** (cf. 1:15). **But to those on the outside** (of the circle of disciples, the unbelieving crowd) **everything,** His whole message and mission, was stated **in parables.** The word "parables" here has the special sense of "enigmatic speech." The crowd did not really understand Jesus.

Both groups were confronted by Jesus and His message (cf. 1:14-15). God enabled the disciples to see in Him the "secret" (*mystērion*) about the kingdom. This refers to the disclosure of God's *present* kingdom plan which is to be an Age of "seed-sowing" (cf. 4:13-20; 13:10). It was previously hidden to the prophets, but now was revealed to people of His choice (cf. Rom. 16:25-26).

The basic "secret," common to all the kingdom parables, is that in Jesus, God's rule (kingdom) has come into human experience in a new spiritual form. The disciples had believed in Jesus. God had already given (*dedotai,* perf. pass.) them this "secret," though so far they understood little of its full impact.

On the other hand those blinded by unbelief saw in Jesus nothing but a threat to their existence. They rejected Him and did not come to know the "secret" of God's kingdom. Jesus' parables served to conceal its truths from them.

They were like the Israelites in Isaiah's day (Isa. 6:9-10). Isaiah said that this spiritual blindness and deafness that comes to people is God's judgment. He particularly referred to Israel as a nation (cf. Mark 6:9, "this people") for rejecting

God's revelation, especially as expressed in Jesus. They would see or hear the imagery of a parable but they would not understand its spiritual meaning. **Otherwise** (*mēpote,* "lest perhaps") **they might turn** to God (repent) **and be forgiven** by Him.

Jesus' audiences were not denied the opportunity to believe in Him. But after they persistently closed their minds to His message (cf. 1:15), they were excluded from further understanding of it by His use of parables. Yet even the parables, which veiled the truth, were meant to provoke thought, enlighten, and ultimately reveal it (cf. 12:12). They uniquely preserved people's freedom to believe, while demonstrating that such a decision is effected by God's enabling (cf. 4:11a).

c. Jesus' interpretation of the Soils Parable (4:13-20)
(Matt. 13:18-23; Luke 8:11-15)

4:13. The two questions here emphasize the importance of the Soils Parable. If Jesus' disciples did not **understand** (*oidate,* "intuitively comprehend") its meaning, then they would not **understand** (*gnōsesthe,* "comprehend by experience") **any** of the kingdom parables.

4:14-20. The farmer (sower) is not identified, but the context indicates he probably represents Jesus and all who sow (proclaim) **the Word** (message) of God, which is the **seed** (cf. 1:15, 45; 2:2; 6:12). In 4:15-20 a change occurs: the kinds of soil represent various types of hearers in whom the **seed** is sown.

Many **people** give one of three negative responses to Jesus' message. **Some . . . hear** the **Word** with hardhearted indifference. **Satan** (like the birds) **comes** immediately (*euthys;* cf. 1:10) **and takes** it **away.** In effect, there was no response.

Others . . . hear the **Word** with a hasty (*euthys*), enthusiastic, but shallow profession of acceptance. However, **they last only a short time** because the Word takes **no root** in them. **When trouble** (lit., "hardships") **or persecution comes** (like a hot sun) on account **of the Word, they quickly** (*euthys*) **fall away** (*skandalizontai,* "are repelled"; cf. comments on 14:27). Their profession proves not to be genuine.

Still others . . . hear the Word but are preoccupied with the cares and riches of this life. Three competing concerns—distracting **worries of this life** (lit., "the present Age"); **the deceitfulness** (deceptive lure) **of wealth;** and **desires for** all sorts of **other things** in place of the Word—enter into their lives (like thriving thorn plants). These things **choke the Word, making it** (the Word, *not* the hearer) **unfruitful** (cf. 10:22), indicating they are not true believers.

By contrast, **others . . . hear the Word, accept it** (*paradechontai,* "welcome it for themselves"), **and produce a crop,** or bear spiritual fruit. These are genuine disciples. In the future harvest they will have fruitful yields of varying amounts: **30, 60, or . . . 100** (cf. 4:24-25 with Matt. 25:14-30; Luke 19:11-27).

Giving out the news of God's kingdom is like sowing seed on various kinds of soil. At Jesus' first coming and in the present Age the kingdom is largely veiled in the face of satanic opposition and human unbelief. But despite this, God's rule takes hold in those who accept Jesus' message and His rule manifests itself in spiritual fruitfulness. But God's kingdom will be openly established on earth at Jesus' second coming with a glory yet undisclosed (cf. Mark 13:24-27). Then there will be an abundant harvest. Thus the parable displayed God's kingdom as both *present but veiled* and *future but openly glorious* (cf. 1:14-15).

3. THE PARABLE OF THE LAMP AND THE MEASURE (4:21-25)

(LUKE 8:16-18; MATT. 5:15 AND LUKE 11:33; MATT. 7:2 AND LUKE 6:38; MATT. 10:26 AND LUKE 12:2; MATT. 13:12; 25:29 AND LUKE 19:26)

Jesus used the parabolic sayings of these verses on various occasions (cf. above references). Mark put them here because their message reinforced the message of Jesus' kingdom parables and demonstrated the need for a proper response to them. Mark 4:23-24a recalls verses 3 and 9, indicating that Mark understood these words to be part of Jesus' parabolic teaching to all (cf. vv. 26, 30) rather than the continuation of Jesus' private address to His disciples.

4:21-23. In this parable Jesus pointed out the self-evident fact that **a lamp,** a lighted wick in a shallow clay bowl full of oil, was not meant to be lit and then hidden **under a** measuring **bowl** (as was done at bedtime) **or a bed** (lit., "dining couch"). Rather, **it** was to be placed **on its stand** where it would give light. Then Jesus explained (*gar,* **for) whatever** was **hidden** or **concealed** (during the night) was **meant to be brought out into the open** (for use in the day). This story from everyday life conveyed a spiritual truth for **anyone** willing to learn from it.

4:24-25. If a person accepts His proclamation (cf. 1:15), God will give him a share in His kingdom now **and even more** will be added in its future manifestation (cf. 4:21-23). But if one rejects His Word, that one suffers absolute loss because even the opportunity he has for a share in the kingdom now **will** someday **be taken** away **from him.**

4. THE PARABLE OF THE EARTH BEARING FRUIT BY ITSELF (4:26-29)

This is Mark's only unique parable. Like the Soils Parable, it presents a comprehensive picture of the coming of God's kingdom: sowing (v. 26), growing (vv. 27-28), and harvesting (v. 29), with emphasis on the growing phase. Only one person, the sower (not identified), appears in all three phases.

4:26. The initial words in this parable could be rendered: "**The kingdom of God** is as follows: it **is like. . . .**" In phase one, the sower **scatters seed on the ground.**

4:27-28. In phase two the sower appears but is not active. After planting **the seed,** he leaves it and goes about his duties **night and day** without anxious thought for the seed. Meanwhile it germinates, **sprouts, and grows** in a way **he** did **not know** and cannot explain.

The soil (lit., "the earth") **produces grain** which develops to maturity in successive stages. The soil does this **all by itself** (*automatē;* cf. the Eng. "automatic"). This key Greek word (emphatic by position) could be translated "without visible cause" implying "without human agency," and thus refers to work done by God (cf. similar situations in Josh. 6:5; Job 24:24; Acts 12:10). God works in the life-bearing seed which, when planted in good soil, grows stage by stage and produces grain without human intervention.

4:29. The sower's ultimate interest is phase three, the harvest. Whenever (future) **the grain is ripe, he** immediately (*euthys*; cf. 1:10) **puts the sickle to it** (lit., "sends forth the sickle," a figure of speech for "sending forth the reapers"; cf. Joel 3:13) **because the harvest has come** (*parestēken*, "stands ready").

Some interpreters view this parable as a picture of evangelism. Some take it as depicting spiritual growth in a believer. Others see it as a picture of the coming of God's kingdom by the mysterious, sovereign work of God. Its emphasis is on growth under God's initiative in the interim phase between the proclamation by Jesus (the lowly Sower) and His disciples and the ultimate manifestation of the kingdom by Jesus (the mighty Harvester). The third view is preferred in light of Mark 4:26a and the overall context of the kingdom parables.

5. THE PARABLE OF THE MUSTARD SEED (4:30-32)

(MATT. 13:31-32; LUKE 13:18-19)

4:30-32. This parable has an elaborate double-question introduction which states in essence that the emergence of God's **kingdom** is similar to what happens to **a mustard seed** (the common black mustard, *sinapis nigra*) after it is sown on **the ground.** In Jewish thinking, its small size was proverbial since it was **the smallest** of all the seeds sown in the field. It took 725–760 mustard seeds to weigh a gram (28 grams equal one ounce). The mustard shrub is an annual plant which, growing from seed, **becomes the largest of all garden plants** (*ta lachana*, "large, fast-growing annual shrubs") in Palestine, reaching a height of 12-15 feet in a few weeks. **Birds of the air** (undomesticated fowl) are attracted by its seed and the **shade** of its large **branches** (cf. TDNT, s.v. "*sinapi*," 7:287-91). This parable emphasizes the contrast between the smallest of the seeds growing into the tallest of the shrubs. It contrasts the insignificant, even enigmatic beginning of God's kingdom, embodied in the presence of Jesus, with the greatness of the end result to be established at His Second Advent when it will surpass all the earth's kingdoms in power and glory.

The reference to the birds may simply indicate the surprising size of the end result. Or perhaps they represent evil forces (cf. v. 4), but this would indicate an abnormal development of God's kingdom. Probably they represent the incorporation of the Gentiles into God's kingdom program (cf. Ezek. 17:22-24; 31:6). What God had promised to do (Ezek. 17), He began to do in Jesus' mission. (The kingdom, however, is not to be identified with the church; cf. comments on Mark 1:15.)

6. CONCLUDING SUMMARY (4:33-34)

4:33-34. These verses summarize the purpose and approach of Jesus' parabolic teaching (cf. vv. 11-12). His practice was to speak **the Word** (cf. 1:15) **to them,** the crowds plus the disciples, through parables which He adapted to their levels of understanding.

Because of misconceptions about God's kingdom, **Jesus . . . did not** teach about it **without using a parable** (in figurative speech). **But to His own disciples** privately (*kat'idian*; cf. 6:31-32; 7:33; 9:2, 28; 13:3) **He explained** (lit., "kept on explaining") **everything** about His mission as it related to God's kingdom. This dual approach, illustrated here in chapter 4, is assumed throughout the rest of the Gospel.

E. *Jesus' miracles demonstrating His sovereign power (4:35–5:43)*

Mark's selection of parables is followed by a series of miracles, indicating that what Jesus *did* (His works) authenticated what He *said* (His words). Both relate to the presence of God's sovereign rule (kingdom) in Jesus.

With only three exceptions Mark put all the miracles he recorded before 8:27. (Cf. the list "The Miracles of Jesus" at John 2:1-11.) This was to highlight the fact that Jesus would not tell His disciples about His coming death and resurrection until they openly acknowledged Him as God's Messiah.

This section contains four miracles that clearly show Jesus' sovereign authority over various hostile powers: a storm at sea (4:35-41); demon possession (5:1-20); incurable physical illness (5:25-34); and death (5:21-24, 35-43).

1. THE CALMING OF THE STORM ON THE LAKE (4:35-41)

(MATT. 8:23-27; LUKE 8:22-25)

4:35-37. The vivid details indicate

that Mark recorded an eyewitness report, probably from Peter. On the **evening** of **that day** of teaching by the lake (cf. v. 1), Jesus took the initiative and decided to cross **over to the other** (east) **side** of the Sea of Galilee with **His 12 disciples.** Though not stated, He probably desired relief from the crowds and rest. Perhaps also He sought a new sphere of ministry (cf. 1:38). Even so, **other boats,** carrying those who wanted to remain with Jesus, tagged along.

His disciples, several of them experienced fishermen, took charge of the voyage. The words, **just as He was,** refer back to 4:1 and link Jesus' teaching in a boat with His miracle-work in a boat (cf. the disciples' address, "Teacher," v. 38).

The journey was interrupted by **a** sudden **furious squall,** common on this lake, surrounded by high hills and narrow valleys that functioned as wind tunnels. A storm in the evening was especially dangerous, and on this occasion the boisterous **waves broke over** (lit., "kept spilling over into") **the boat so that it was nearly swamped.**

4:38-39. Exhausted from a full day of teaching, **Jesus** was **sleeping . . . in the stern,** on a sailor's leather rowing **cushion. The** panic-stricken **disciples woke Him** with a cry of reproach (cf. 5:31; 6:37; 8:4, 32) at His apparent indifference to their situation. Though they called Him **Teacher** (Gr. for the Heb. *Rabbi*), they did not yet understand His teaching.

Jesus **rebuked** (lit., "ordered"; cf. 1:25) **the wind and said to the waves,** "Be silent! Be muzzled and remain so!" (the force of the Gr. perf. tense, *pephimōso*) This verb, "be muzzled," was somewhat of a technical term for dispossessing a demon of his power (cf. 1:25) and may suggest that Jesus recognized demonic powers behind the ferocious storm. But at His command **the wind** stopped and **the lake** became **completely calm.**

4:40-41. Jesus rebuked **His disciples** for being **afraid** (*deiloi*, "cowardly fear") in a crisis. Despite Jesus' tutoring (vv. 11, 34) it still had not dawned on them that God's authority and power were present *in Jesus.* This is what He meant by His second question, **Do you still have no faith?** (cf. 7:18; 8:17-21, 33; 9:19)

In stilling the storm Jesus assumed the authority exercised only by God in the Old Testament (cf. Pss. 89:8-9; 104:5-9; 106:8-9; 107:23-32). That is why the disciples **were terrified** (lit., "feared a great fear") when they saw that **even the** forces of nature did **obey Him.** The verb "terrified" (from *phobeomai*, "have awe;" cf. *deilos*, "cowardly fear," in Mark 4:40) refers to a reverence that overtakes people in the presence of supernatural power (cf. 16:8). However, their question to one another, **Who is this?** indicated that they did not fully comprehend the significance of it all.

2. THE CURE OF THE GERASENE DEMONIAC (5:1-20)

(MATT. 8:28-34; LUKE 8:26-39)

a. *A description of the demoniac (5:1-5)*

5:1. Jesus and His disciples **went** to the east side of **the lake** (Sea of Galilee) into **the region of the Gerasenes.** Greek manuscripts are divided on the precise location involved, citing three names: Gadarenes (Matt. 8:28), Gergesenes (from Origen), and Gerasenes. (See comments on Luke 8:26.) Reliable evidence favors the name Gerasenes which probably referred to the small town Gersa (modern Khersa) located on the lake's eastern shore. Most of its inhabitants were Gentiles (cf. Mark 5:11, 19).

5:2-5. The vivid details of this whole account reflect both an eyewitness report and the report of townspeople who had long been familiar with this demoniac. As soon as (*euthys*; cf. 1:10) **Jesus got out of the boat,** He encountered **a man with an evil spirit** (cf. 5:8, 13 with 1:23) **from** (*ek*, "out of") **the tombs.** These were probably cavelike rooms cut into the rocks of nearby hills which served as tombs and sometimes as haunts for demented people. Matthew mentioned demoniacs, whereas Mark and Luke focused attention on one, probably the worst case.

Mark 5:3-5 elaborately describes his pathetic condition. He **lived in the tombs** (an outcast); he was uncontrollable for **no one could . . . subdue** (from *damazō*, "to tame a wild animal") **him,** not even with fetters for his feet or **a chain** for his hands. He went about **night and day** shrieking wildly and cutting **himself with** sharp **stones,** perhaps in a demonic form of worship.

Such behavior shows that demon possession is not mere sickness or insanity but a desperate satanic attempt to distort and destroy God's image in man (cf. TDNT, s.v. "daimōn," 2:18-19).

b. The command to the demon (5:6-10)

5:6-7. The brief statement of Jesus' encounter with the demoniac (v. 2) is now related in more detail. Three things indicate that the demon possessing the man was fully aware of Jesus' divine origin and superior power: he knelt before **Him** (in homage, not worship); he used Jesus' divine name in an attempt to gain control over Him (cf. 1:24); and he brazenly appealed to **Jesus** not to punish him. The words, **Most High God,** were used in the Old Testament, often by Gentiles, to refer to the superiority of the true God of Israel over all man-made gods (cf. Gen. 14:18-24; Num. 24:16; Isa. 14:14; Dan. 3:26; 4:2; cf. comments on Mark 1:23-24).

The plea, **Swear to God,** was used in exorcisms and should be rendered, "I implore you by (I appeal to) God." The demon did not want Jesus to **torture** him by sending him to his final punishment then (cf. 1:24; Matt. 8:29; Luke 8:31).

5:8. This verse is a brief explanatory (gar, **for**) comment by Mark (cf. 6:52). **Jesus was** commanding **him,** the demon, to leave the **man.** Throughout this section there is fluctuation between the personality of the man and the demon who possessed him.

5:9-10. These verses resume the conversation of verse 7. The demon said through the man, **My name is Legion for we are many.** Many evil powers controlled this man and subjected him to intense oppression. They tormented him as one combined force under the leadership of one demon, their spokesman. This accounts for the alternating singular ("my") and plural ("we") pronouns. Repeatedly the leading demon begged **Jesus** earnestly **not to send them out of the area** (lit., "region"; cf. v. 1) into a lonely exile where they could not torment people.

The Latin word "Legion," commonly known in Palestine, denoted a Roman army regiment of about 6,000 soldiers, though it probably also meant a very large number (cf. v. 15). To people under Roman domination the word no doubt suggested great strength and oppression.

c. The loss of the herd of pigs (5:11-13)

5:11. The Jews considered **pigs** "unclean" animals (cf. Lev. 11:7). But the farmers on the east side of the Sea of Galilee with its predominantly Gentile population raised pigs for the meat markets in the Decapolis, "the 10 cities" of that region (cf. Mark 5:20).

5:12-13. **The demons** (cf. v. 9) specifically **begged Jesus to send** them **among** (eis here suggests movement toward) **the pigs** so that they might **go into them** as their new hosts. They knew they were subject to Jesus' command, and in a desperate attempt to avoid being consigned to a disembodied state until final judgment, they made this appeal.

Jesus **gave them permission** to do so. When the demons left the man and entered **the pigs, the** whole **herd, about 2,000 in number,** stampeded **down the steep bank into the lake and were drowned** (lit., "one after another they drowned themselves"). The "sea" perhaps symbolized the satanic realm.

d. The plea of the townspeople (5:14-17)

5:14-15. The herdsmen **tending the pigs** fled in fear **and reported this** startling event **in the town** (probably Gersa; cf. v. 1) **and** the surrounding **countryside.** The report was so unbelievable that many **people went** to investigate the incident for themselves. **They saw the** former demoniac **sitting there, dressed** (cf. Luke 8:27) **and in his right mind,** rational and self-controlled (contrast Mark 5:3-5). So complete was the transformation that the townspeople **were afraid** (awed; cf. 4:41).

5:16-17. The herdsmen (and perhaps the disciples) rehearsed **what had happened to the . . . man—and** to **the pigs,** a detail Mark emphasized to show that this economic loss (not the man) was the people's major concern. As a result the townspeople **began** urging Jesus to leave. Apparently they feared further losses if He stayed. There is no record that He ever returned to that area.

e. The request of the restored man (5:18-20)

5:18-20. In contrast with the local inhabitants (cf. v. 17), **the man who had been demon-possessed** was begging (parekalei, the same word used by the demon, v. 10) **to go with Jesus.** Jesus' miracles repelled some (vv. 15-17) and attracted others (vv. 18-20).

The words, "to go with Him" (lit., "in order that he might be with Him"), recall a similar clause in 3:14 that describes one of the purposes for which Jesus called the Twelve. It is in this sense that Jesus refused the man's request.

Jesus told **him** to **go** to his **home** (immediate family) and **family** (lit., "to yours," your own people) from whom he had been estranged and report to **them** all that **the Lord,** the Most High God (cf. 5:7; Luke 8:39) had **done for** him **and how He** had shown **mercy on** him. **The man** obeyed and began to proclaim (cf. Mark 1:4, 14) **in the Decapolis** (a league of 10 Gr. cities all but one east of the Jordan) the wonderful things **Jesus** (cf. "Lord," 5:19) **had done for him.** Those who heard him **were amazed** (*ethaumazon,* cf. "astonished"; 6:6a; 12:17; 15:5, 44).

Since this man was a Gentile and his preaching activity was confined to a Gentile area where Jesus was not welcome, Jesus did not give His usual injunction to silence (cf. 1:44; 5:43; 7:36).

3. THE HEMORRHAGING WOMAN AND JAIRUS' DAUGHTER (5:21-43)
(MATT. 9:18-26; LUKE 8:40-56)

This section, like Mark 3:20-35, has a "sandwich" structure. The account of the raising of Jairus' daughter from the dead (5:21-24, 35-43) is divided by the incident of the woman with a hemorrhage (5:25-34). What appeared to be a disastrous delay in the healing of the woman actually assured the restoration of Jairus' daughter. It was providentially ordered to test and strengthen Jairus' faith.

a. *Jairus' earnest request (5:21-24)*
(Matt. 9:18-19; Luke 8:40-42)

5:21-24. **Jesus** and His disciples returned **to the other** (west) **side of the** Sea of Galilee, probably to Capernaum. As before in this area, **a large crowd gathered around** Jesus **while He was** still **by the lake.**

On this occasion, **Jairus came** to Him. As **one of the synagogue rulers,** he was a lay official responsible for the physical management of the synagogue building and the worship services. He was a respected leader in the community.

Not all the religious leaders were hostile to Jesus.

Jairus' **little daughter** (an only daughter, Luke 8:42) was **dying** (lit., "was at the point of death"). Matthew's abbreviated treatment of this event (135 words whereas Mark used 374) accounts for his statement that the girl had already died (Matt. 9:18). In humility, Jairus **pleaded earnestly** (lit., "begged much"; cf. Mark 5:10) **with** Jesus to **come and put** His **hands on her so that she** might **be healed** (lit., "saved," delivered from physical death) **and live.** The practice of "laying on of hands" in healing symbolized the transfer of vitality to a needy recipient; it was popularly associated with Jesus' healings (cf. 6:5; 7:32; 8:23, 25). Jairus probably knew about Jesus' power from previous associations (cf. 1:21-28) and was confident that He could save his daughter's life.

As **Jesus went with** Jairus, **a great crowd followed** them **and pressed** ("kept thronging," from *synthlibō*; cf. v. 31) **around Him.**

b. *The healing of the woman with a hemorrhage (5:25-34)*
(Matt. 9:20-22; Luke 8:43-48)

5:25-27. An unnamed **woman** with an incurable condition joined the crowd. **She had suffered** (lit., "was in") **bleeding for 12 years** (cf. v. 42). This may have been a chronic menstrual disorder or a uterine hemorrhage. Her condition made her ritually unclean (cf. Lev. 15:25-27), excluding her from normal social relations since any who came in contact with her would become "unclean."

She had suffered greatly from various treatments by **many doctors.** She **had spent all she** owned in a desperate attempt to get well. Nothing helped; in fact her condition **grew worse.**

But because **she** had **heard about** Jesus' healing power (which aroused her faith), **she came up behind Him in the crowd and touched His cloak** (outer garment). She did this despite her "uncleanness" and with a desire to avoid an embarrassing public disclosure of her malady.

5:28. She kept telling herself that **if** she could **just touch His clothes,** she would **be healed** and then she could slip away unobserved. Perhaps her faith was mixed with a popular notion that a healer had power in his clothing, or she may have known someone who had been healed in this way (cf. 3:10; 6:56).

5:29. When the woman touched Jesus' garment, **immediately** (*euthys*; cf. 1:10) **her bleeding stopped. She felt** (lit., "knew," from *ginōskō*, "know experientially"; cf. 5:30) by a physical sensation **in her body that she was freed** (lit., "had been healed") **from her suffering.** The healing occurred without overt participation by Jesus.

5:30. Yet **Jesus** immediately (*euthys*) **realized** in Himself (from *epiginōskō*, "know fully"; cf. v. 29) **that power had gone out from Him** or, more literally, "power from Him (on account of who He is) had gone out."

This unusual expression has been understood in two ways. One view maintains that God the Father healed the woman and Jesus was not aware of it till afterward. The other view is that Jesus Himself, wishing to honor the woman's faith, willingly extended His healing power to her. The latter view is more consistent with Jesus' healing ministry. Power did not leave Him without His knowledge and will. However, He exercised it only at the Father's bidding (cf. 13:32). The touch of the garment had no magical effect.

Aware of *how* the miracle took place, Jesus **turned around . . . and asked, Who touched My clothes?** He wanted to establish a personal relationship with the healed person, untainted with quasi-magical notions.

5:31-32. Jesus' question seemed absurd to **His disciples** (the Twelve; cf. Luke 8:45) because the crowd was pressing (from *synthlibō*; cf. Mark 5:24) in and many **people** were touching Him. This emphasized Jesus' ability to distinguish the touch of one who in faith expected deliverance from the inadvertent touch of those **crowding against** Him. There was, and still is, a great difference between the two. So **Jesus kept looking around** (*perieblepeto*; "was looking penetratingly"; cf. 3:5, 34) at the people surrounding Him in order **to see who had** touched Him in this way.

5:33-34. Then the woman, the only one who understood Jesus' question, **came** in humility, and **trembling with fear** (from *phobeomai*, "to have awe, reverence"; cf. 4:41) because she knew

what had happened to her, in courage and gratitude told Him everything.

The affectionate title, **Daughter** (its only recorded use by Jesus) signified her new relationship with Him (cf. 3:33-35). Jesus attributed her cure to her **faith** rather than the touch of His clothing. Her faith **healed** her (lit., "has saved or delivered you"; cf. 5:28; 10:52) in that it caused her to seek healing *from Jesus.* Faith, confident trust, derives its value not from the one who expresses it, but from the object in which it rests (cf. 10:52; 11:22).

Jesus said, **Go in peace and be freed** (lit., "be healthy") **from your suffering** (cf. 5:29). This assured her that her healing was complete and permanent. In her extremity of need—incurable illness and socio-religious isolation—she was a living "dead" person for 12 years. Her restoration to wholeness of life anticipated the dramatic raising of Jairus' daughter who died after living for 12 years.

c. The raising of Jairus' daughter to life (5:35-43)
(Matt. 9:23-26; Luke 8:49-56)

5:35-36. The delay (cf. vv. 22-24) caused by the woman's healing (vv. 25-34) was a severe test of Jairus' faith. His fears that his little **daughter** would die before **Jesus** got there were confirmed by the report of **some men** (unidentified friends and relatives) **from** his **house** that she had died. They concluded that her death ended any hope that Jesus could help so they suggested that it was futile to **bother** (lit., "trouble") **the Teacher** (cf. 4:38) **any** further.

Jesus overheard the message but refused to accept its implications. This is the force of the verb translated **ignoring** (*parakousas*), which means "refuse to listen" (cf. Matt. 18:17). The present imperatives in Jesus' reassuring words to **Jairus** could be rendered: "Stop fearing (i.e., in unbelief); just keep on believing." He had already exercised faith in coming to Jesus, he had seen the relationship between faith and Jesus' power (Mark 5:25-34); now he was exhorted to **believe** that Jesus could restore his lifeless daughter.

5:37-40a. Including Jairus, Jesus let only three disciples—**Peter, James, and John**—accompany Him **to the** house as witnesses (cf. Deut. 17:6). These three disciples served as legal witnesses here in anticipation of Jesus' resurrection, then at His transfiguration (Mark 9:2), and in Gethsemane (14:33).

At the house the elaborate ritual of Jewish mourning had already begun. The **commotion** (*thorybon*, "an uproar") included the activity of hired mourners (cf. Jer. 9:17; Amos 5:16), weeping, and antiphonal **wailing.**

Jesus entered the house and rebuked the mourners because, **He** told **them . . . the child** was **not dead but asleep.** Did Jesus mean she was just in a coma? Friends and relatives (cf. Mark 5:35) as well as the professional mourners who **laughed** scornfully at His words, knew she was dead (cf. Luke 8:53). Was Jesus simply describing death as sleep, implying a state of "sleep" between death and resurrection? This is not supported elsewhere in the New Testament (cf. Luke 23:42-43; 2 Cor. 5:6-8; Phil. 1:23-24). Probably He was saying that in this case death was *like* sleep. From a mourner's point of view, the girl's death would turn out to be like "a sleep" from which she was awakened. Her condition was not final and irrevocable (cf. Luke 8:55; John 11:11-14).

5:40b-42. After He put . . . **out** all the mourners, Jesus **took the** girl's parents **and the** three **disciples** (cf. v. 37) **with Him** into her room. Then **He took her . . . hand and** spoke the Aramaic words, ***Talitha koum!*** This was a command, not a magical formula. Mark translated it for his Greek-speaking readers, **Little girl . . . get up,** adding the clause **I say to you** to emphasize Jesus' authority over death. Since Galileans were bilingual, Jesus spoke both Aramaic, His mother tongue—a Semitic language related to Hebrew—and Greek, the *lingua franca* of the Greco-Roman world. He likely also spoke Hebrew.

At Jesus' command, **immediately** (*euthys*; cf. 1:10) **the girl** got **up and** began walking around for (*gar*), Mark explained, **she was 12 years old.** The parents and three disciples **were completely astonished** (from *existēmi*, lit., "out of their minds with great amazement"; cf. 2:12; 6:51).

5:43. Jesus then gave two **orders.** The first was a **strict** injunction to silence. Jesus did not want the miracle to attract people to Him for the wrong reasons (cf. comments on 1:43-45).

The second command, that the girl be given food, displayed His compassion and also confirmed that she was restored to good health. Her body had been resuscitated, returned to natural life, but was still subject to death, and needed to be sustained by food. This contrasts with a *resurrected* body (cf. 1 Cor. 15:35-57).

F. Conclusion: Jesus' rejection at Nazareth (6:1-6a) (Matt. 13:53-58)

6:1. From Capernaum **Jesus** went about 20 miles southwest **to His hometown,** Nazareth (cf. 1:9, 24), where He had lived and ministered previously (cf. Luke 4:16-30). He was **accompanied by His disciples,** returning as a Teacher (Rabbi) surrounded by His students. This was a public mission, and He was preparing His disciples by example for their own missions (cf. Mark 6:7-13).

6:2-3. On **the Sabbath . . . He** taught **in the synagogue** (cf. 1:21), probably expounding on the Law and the Prophets. **Many . . . were amazed** (*exeplēssonto*, "astounded, struck out, overwhelmed"; cf. 1:22; 7:37; 10:26; 11:18) at His teaching.

But some asked disparaging questions about the origin of (a) **these things,** His teaching, (b) the **wisdom . . . given Him** (lit., "to this One"), and (c) His power to do **miracles** elsewhere (cf. 6:5). Only two answers were possible: His source was God, or Satan (cf. 3:22).

Despite His impressive words and deeds, He was too ordinary for them. The derogatory question, **Isn't this the carpenter?** implied, "He is a common laborer like the rest of us." All His immediate family—mother, brothers, and sisters—were known to the townspeople, and they were ordinary people. The phrase **Mary's Son** was also derogatory since a man was not described as his mother's son in Jewish usage even if she was a widow, except by insult (cf. Jud. 11:1-2; John 8:41; 9:29). Their words, calculated insults, also suggested they knew there was something unusual about Jesus' birth.

His brothers and **sisters** (cf. Mark 3:31-35) were most likely children of Joseph and Mary born after Jesus' birth rather than Joseph's children by a previous marriage or Jesus' cousins. **James** became a leader in the early church at Jerusalem (cf. Acts 15:13-21), and authored the Epistle of James (James 1:1). **Judas** was probably Jude, author of the Epistle of Jude (Jude 1). Nothing more is known of **Joses** and **Simon** or His sisters. Perhaps Joseph was not mentioned because he was already dead.

Thus since the townspeople could not explain Jesus, **they took offense** (from *skandalizomai*, "to be caused to stumble, to be repelled"; cf. comments on Mark 14:27) **at Him,** finding no reason to believe He was God's Anointed One.

6:4. **Jesus** responded to their rejection with the proverb that a prophet is not appreciated at **home.** He was like an Old Testament **prophet** (cf. v. 15; 8:28) whose words were often rejected and who was dishonored most by those who knew Him best (cf. 6:17-29).

6:5-6a. Because of such persistent unbelief Jesus **could not do any miracles there except** to **lay His hands on** (cf. 5:23) **a few sick people and heal them.** There was no limitation on His power, but His purpose was to perform miracles in the presence of faith. Only a few here had faith to come to Him for healing.

Even Jesus **was amazed** (*ethaumasen*, "astonished"; cf. 5:20; 12:17; 15:5, 44) **at their** unbelief, their unwillingness to believe that His wisdom and power were from God. So far as is known, He never returned to Nazareth.

The people of Nazareth represent Israel's blindness. Their refusal to believe in Jesus pictured what the disciples would soon experience (cf. 6:7-13) and what Mark's readers (then and now) would experience in the advance of the gospel.

V. Jesus' Ministry in and beyond Galilee (6:6b–8:30)

The third major section of Mark's Gospel begins structurally like the first two sections (cf. 6:6b with 1:14-15 and 3:7-12; 6:7-34 with 1:16-20 and 3:13-19), but concludes with Peter's confession of Jesus as Messiah (8:27-30) instead of a statement of rejection (cf. 3:6; 6:1-6a). During this phase of His ministry Jesus directed more attention to His disciples. In the face of opposition, He revealed to them by both words and deeds who He really is. Much of this time was spent outside of Galilee.

A. Introductory summary: Jesus' teaching tour of Galilee (6:6b) (Matt. 9:35-38)

6:6b. This statement summarizes Jesus' third tour of Galilee (for the first, cf. 1:35-39; Mark did not mention the second, cf. Luke 8:1-3). Despite His rejection at Nazareth, **Jesus** was going **around** the neighboring villages **teaching** (cf. Mark 1:21). This set the stage for the Twelve's mission.

B. Jesus' sending forth of the Twelve and John the Baptist's death (6:7-31)

This section has a "sandwich" structure (cf. 3:20-35; 5:21-43). The narrative of the mission of the Twelve (6:7-13, 30-31) is divided by the account of John the Baptist's death (6:14-29). This indicates that the death of John the messenger did not silence his message. The forerunner's death prefigured Jesus' death. And Jesus' message would still be proclaimed by His followers.

1. THE MISSION OF THE TWELVE (6:7-13)
   (MATT. 10:1, 5-15; LUKE 9:1-6)

6:7. In order to extend His ministry on this Galilean tour, Jesus **sent** (from *apostellō;* cf. 3:14; 6:30) **the Twelve out two by two,** a common practice in that day for practical and legal reasons (cf. 11:1; 14:13; John 8:17; Deut. 17:6; 19:15).

The Twelve were His authorized representatives in keeping with the Jewish concept of *š^elûhîm,* that is, a man's representative (*šâlîah*) was considered as the man himself (cf. Matt. 10:40 and TDNT, s.v. "*apostolos,*" 1:413-27). They were to fulfill a *special* commission and bring back a report (cf. Mark 6:30); so Jesus' unusual instructions (vv. 8-11) pertained only to that particular mission.

He **gave them authority** (*exousian;* the "right" and the "power"; cf. 2:10; 3:15) **over evil spirits.** This power to exorcise demons (cf. 1:26) would authenticate their preaching (cf. 6:13; 1:15).

6:8-9. The urgency of their mission required that they travel lightly. They were to **take a staff** (*rhabdon,* "walking stick") and to **wear sandals** (ordinary footwear). **But** they were **not** to take **bread** (food), a **bag** (probably a traveler's bag for provisions, not a beggar's bag), **money** (small copper coins easily tucked in their cloth **belts**), or **an extra tunic,**

additional inner garment used as a covering at night. They were to depend on God to provide food and shelter through the hospitality of Jewish households.

The two concessions of a staff and sandals are unique to Mark. Both are forbidden in Matthew 10:9-10, and the staff is forbidden in Luke 9:3. Matthew used *ktaomai* ("to procure, acquire"), instead of *airō* ("to take"); so the disciples were not to acquire *additional* staffs or sandals—but to use the ones they already had. Mark and Luke both use *airō*, "to take or carry along." But Luke says, "Take nothing for the journey—no staff (*rhabdon*)," presumably no additional staff; while Mark says, "Take nothing for the journey *except* (cf. Mark 6:5) a staff (*rhabdon*)," presumably the one already in use. Each writer stressed a different aspect of Jesus' instructions.

6:10-11. Whenever the disciples entered **a house** as invited guests, they were to **stay there** making it their base of operations **until** they left the **town.** They were not to impose on the hospitality of many people or accept more attractive offers once they were settled.

They should also expect rejection. **If any place** (a household, synagogue, village) would **not** offer hospitality **or listen to** their message, they were to **leave** there and to **shake the dust off** their **feet.** Devout Jews did this when they left Gentile (alien) territory to show that they were dissociating themselves from it. This would tell Jewish hearers they were acting like pagans in rejecting the disciples' message.

This was to be done **as a testimony** (cf. 1:44; 13:9) **against** the citizens. It warned them that the disciples' responsibility to them had been fulfilled and those who rejected the message would have to answer to God for themselves (cf. Acts 13:51; 18:6). No doubt it provoked serious thought and perhaps repentance by some. The KJV statement regarding Sodom and Gomorrah is not in the earliest Greek manuscripts of Mark's text (cf. Matt. 10:15).

6:12-13. In obedience the Twelve **preached** repentance (cf. 1:4, 14-15), **drove out many demons** (cf. 1:32-34, 39), and healed **many sick people** (cf. 3:10). As Jesus' representatives (cf. 6:7; 9:37) they learned that His power extended beyond His personal presence. Their mission showed the coming of God's kingdom (cf. 1:15).

Anointing the sick **with oil** is unique to Mark. This use of olive oil was both because of its medicinal properties (cf. Luke 10:34; James 5:14) and its symbolic value indicating that the disciples acted by Jesus' authority and power, not their own.

2. THE BEHEADING OF JOHN THE BAPTIST (6:14-29)
(MATT. 14:1-12; LUKE 3:19-20; 9:7-9)

a. *Popular explanations of Jesus' identity (6:14-16)*

6:14-16. The miraculous activity of Jesus and the Twelve throughout Galilee caught the attention of **Herod** Antipas, son of Herod the Great (see the chart on the Herods at Luke 1:5). Herod Antipas was *tetrarch* (ruler of a fourth part of his father's kingdom) of Galilee and Perea under the aegis of Rome from 4 B.C. to A.D. 39 (cf. Matt. 14:1; Luke 3:19; 9:7). Officially he was not a **king** but Mark's use of the title probably reflected local custom in view of Herod's covetous ambitions.

Mark 6:14b-15 presents three opinions which attempt to account for Jesus' **miraculous powers;** He was (a) **John the Baptist** (cf. 1:4-9) risen **from the dead,** (b) **Elijah** (cf. Mal. 3:1; 4:5-6), or (c) a **prophet,** resuming the suspended line of Israel's **prophets.**

Despite other opinions **Herod,** troubled by a guilty conscience, remained convinced that Jesus was **the man** he had **beheaded.** Herod believed **John** the Baptist was risen **from the dead** and was using miraculous powers. Mark 6:17-29 explains verse 16 in a "flashback."

b. *Flashback: the execution of John the Baptist (6:17-29)*

Mark included this section not only to supplement 1:14 and further clarify 6:16, but also to provide a "passion narrative" of Jesus' forerunner that foreshadowed and paralleled Jesus' own suffering and death. Mark focused on what Herod and Herodias did to John. Perhaps he included so many details to draw a parallel to the Elijah-Jezebel conflict since Jesus later identified John as Elijah (9:11-13).

6:17-18. Mark explained (*gar*, **for**) that **Herod himself had** ordered **John** to be **put in prison.** According to Josephus, this prison was at the fortress-palace of Machaerus near the northeastern shore of the Dead Sea (*The Antiquities of the Jews* 18. 5. 2). Herod **did this because of Herodias,** an ambitious woman who was his second **wife.** Herod had first married a daughter of the Arabian king, Aretas IV. Then he became enamored with his half-niece Herodias (daughter of his half-brother, Aristobulus) who was married to Herod's half-brother (**brother** means half-brother) Philip (her half-uncle; cf. Josephus *The Antiquities of the Jews* 18. 5. 1-2). They had a daughter, Salome. Herod divorced his wife in order to marry Herodias who had divorced Philip (not the Philip of Luke 3:1). **John had** repeatedly denounced this marriage as unlawful (cf. Lev. 18:16; 20:21).

6:19-20. John's bold rebuke infuriated **Herodias** who **nursed a grudge against** him (lit., "had it in for him"). Not satisfied with John's imprisonment, she **wanted to kill him, but** her plans were thwarted **because Herod feared John** (had a superstitious dread of him), whom he knew was **a righteous and holy man.** So he **protected** John from Herodias' murderous intentions by keeping him in prison—a shrewd compromise.

In spite of his immoral lifestyle, **Herod** was fascinated by John. He had a certain attraction for John's preaching, but it left him **greatly puzzled.** The words "greatly puzzled" (*polla ēporei*) have good manuscript support and are preferred on contextual grounds to the reading "he did many things" (*polla epoiei*; NIV marg.; KJV), a reading that may reflect an error of hearing by scribes who copied the text as it was read to them. Herod's conflict between his passion for Herodias and his respect for John showed his vacillating moral weakness.

6:21-23. Finally (cf. v. 19) Herodias found an opportunity to carry out a murderous scheme. The occasion was Herod's **birthday . . . banquet,** a luxurious celebration he gave **for his high officials** (in civil government), **military commanders, and the leading men** (prominent citizens) **of Galilee.** Herodias deliberately sent (implied by vv. 24-25) her **daughter,** Salome, into the banquet room to dance in a way that would win Herod's approval.

Salome was a young woman of marriageable age (*korasion*, "girl"; cf. Es. 2:2, 9; Mark 5:41-42), probably in her middle teens. Her skillful and provocative dance **pleased Herod and his . . . guests,** and led him to make her an ostentatious, rash offer as a reward. **He** arrogantly **promised her** anything she wanted and sealed it **with an oath** (cf. Es. 5:6) which included the words **up to half my kingdom** (cf. Es. 7:2). Actually Herod had no "kingdom" (realm) to give (cf. comments on Mark 6:14). He used a proverbial saying for generosity which Salome knew was not to be taken literally (cf. 1 Kings 13:8).

6:24-25. When Salome asked **her mother what** she should **ask for,** Herodias replied with premeditated promptness, **The head of John the Baptist.** She wanted proof that he was dead. **At once** (*euthys*; cf. 1:10) Salome **hurried** back **to the king with** her macabre **request.** She demanded that the deed be done **right now** (*exautēs*, "at once") before Herod could find a way to avoid it. She added the words **on a platter,** suggested perhaps by the festive occasion.

6:26-28. Salome's request deeply grieved (cf. 14:34) Herod. **But because of his oaths** (considered irrevocable) and to save face before **his dinner guests** (cf. 6:21) **he did not** have the courage to reject it. **So he immediately** (*euthys*) ordered the request to be fulfilled.

An executioner (*spekoulatora*, a Latin loanword, probably a bodyguard) **beheaded John in the prison** of the fortress, **brought . . . his head on a platter** to Salome in the banquet hall. **She** in turn **gave it to** Herodias (cf. 9:12-13). John had been silenced, but his message to Herod still stood.

6:29. When **John's disciples** (cf. Matt. 11:2-6) heard about his death, they **came . . . took his body, and put** it **in a tomb.**

3. THE RETURN OF THE TWELVE (6:30-31)
(LUKE 9:10A)

6:30-31. The apostles (*apostoloi*, "delegates, messengers") returned to **Jesus,** probably at Capernaum by prearrangement, **and reported to Him all they had done** (they mentioned their "works"

129

first) **and taught** ("words") in fulfilling their commission (cf. vv. 7-13). The designation "apostles" for the Twelve occurs only twice in Mark (cf. 3:14). It is used in a nontechnical sense to describe their function as "missionaries" (cf. 6:7-9; Acts 14:14) rather than to denote an official title (cf. Eph. 2:19-20).

Jesus directed them to **come with** Him for a brief, well-earned **rest.** This was necessary **because so many people were coming and going that they** had no time **to eat** (cf. Mark 3:20). They were to come **by** themselves (*kat' idian;* cf. 4:34) **to a quiet** (*erēmon,* "remote"; cf. 1:35, 45) **place** (cf. 6:32).

C. Jesus' self-disclosure to the Twelve in word and deed (6:32–8:26)

This section highlights a period in Jesus' ministry when He made several withdrawals from Galilee to minister elsewhere (cf. 6:31; 7:24, 31; 8:22). During this time He showed the Twelve and Mark's readers how He cares for His own.

1. THE FEEDING OF THE 5,000 (6:32-44)
   (MATT. 14:13-21; LUKE 9:10B-17; JOHN 6:1-14)

6:32-34. These verses are a transition from the successful mission of the Twelve to the resultant presence of **a large crowd** in a remote place. Two phrases in the fulfillment of Jesus' directive provide the connecting links: **by themselves** (*kat' idian,* Gr. idiom meaning "privately"), a phrase Mark used for Jesus' private instruction of individuals (cf. 4:34a; 6:31-32; 7:33; 9:2, 28; 13:3); and **to a solitary** (*erēmon,* "remote") **place** (cf. 1:3-4, 12-13, 35, 45; 6:31-32, 35). The place where they sailed, though unnamed by Mark, was near Bethsaida Julias, a city across the Jordan River on the northeast side of the Sea of Galilee (cf. Luke 9:10).

Many people anticipated their destination and arrived there **on foot . . . ahead of them.** Their planned rest was interrupted by people in need.

When Jesus . . . saw the large crowd, **He** felt **compassion** (not annoyance) toward **them.** This inner emotion moved Him to help them (cf., e.g., Mark 6:39-44). He viewed them as **sheep without a shepherd,** lost and helpless, without guidance, nourishment, or protection. In several Old Testament pas-

sages (Num. 27:17; 1 Kings 22:17; Ezek. 34:5, 23-25) the sheep/shepherd image is associated with the "wilderness" (*erēmos;* cf. Mark 6:31-32). This crowd, representing the nation of Israel, received compassion, extensive **teaching** concerning God's kingdom (cf. Luke 9:11), and the provision of their needs (Mark 6:35-44) from Jesus, the true Shepherd (cf. John 10:1-21).

6:35-38. These verses present a significant dialogue between Jesus and the Twelve after He had taught the crowd all **day.** Since **it was late** (after 3 P.M. Jewish time) and they were in **a remote** (*erēmos;* cf. vv. 31-32) **place,** the **disciples** asked Jesus to dismiss **the people . . . so they** could **buy** food in **the surrounding . . . villages** before sunset.

Unexpectedly, Jesus told them to feed the crowd. He emphasized the word **you** (*hymeis*). The disciples' caustic reply showed the inadequacy of their resources and the impossibility of meeting His demand. According to their calculations, to feed such a crowd would take, literally, 200 denarii (NIV marg.). The denarius, the basic Roman silver coin used in Palestine, was the average daily wage for a farm laborer. Consequently 200 denarii was roughly equivalent to **eight months of a man's wages,** a sum beyond the disciples' means.

Jesus insisted they find **out** what bread was available, probably back at the boat and also in the crowd. The disciples returned with the answer: a mere **five** loaves of bread **and two fish** (salted and dried or roasted).

6:39-44. Mark's vivid description of the miracle indicates an eyewitness report, perhaps Peter's.

To insure orderly distribution, **Jesus** commanded the disciples **to have** everyone **sit down in groups on the green grass** (suggesting springtime). The words "in groups" in verse 39 could be rendered "table company by table company" (*symposia symposia,* lit., "drinking or eating parties"). But the words "in groups" in verse 40 are literally, "garden plot by garden plot" (*prasiai prasiai*); they are used figuratively, picturing well-arranged plots of people, perhaps colorfully dressed, seated on the grass **in groups of 100s and 50s.** The command was a challenge to faith for both the disciples and the crowd.

Jesus, serving as Host, spoke the customary Jewish blessing over **the five loaves** (round wheat or barley cakes) and **two fish** (cf. Lev. 19:24; Deut. 8:10). The words **gave thanks** are from *eulogeō* (lit., "to praise, extol" [God], or "to bless"; cf. Mark 14:22). The object of the blessing in such a prayer was not the food, but God who gave it. Jesus looked **up to heaven,** regarded as where God is (cf. Matt. 23:22), in dependence on the Father for a miraculous provision of food.

Then He **broke the loaves** into pieces, **divided** the fish into portions, and **gave** (lit., "kept giving") **them to His disciples to set before the people.** How the miracle itself took place is not stated, but the imperfect tense of the verb "gave" indicates the bread multiplied in Jesus' hands (cf. Mark 8:6).

The provision was miraculous and abundant. Mark emphasized that **all ate and were** fully **satisfied.** This was confirmed by the fact that **the disciples** collected **12 basketfuls** (*kophinoi*, small wicker baskets; contrast 8:8, 20) of leftovers, probably a basket for each disciple. The count of 5,000 men (*andres*, "males"), a very large crowd by local standards, did not include women and children (cf. Matt. 14:21), who were probably grouped separately for the meal according to Jewish custom.

The usual theme of astonishment at the close of a miracle story is not included here. This, plus subsequent comments in Mark 6:52 and 8:14-21 on this event, indicate that Mark regarded it as an important disclosure to Jesus' disciples of who He is. But they failed to understand its meaning (cf. 6:52).

2. JESUS' WALKING ON THE WATER (6:45-52)
(MATT. 14:22-33; JOHN 6:15-21)

6:45-46. Immediately (*euthys*; cf. 1:10) after feeding the 5,000, **Jesus made** (lit., "compelled") **His disciples** return to their **boat and** set sail (lit., "go before [Him] to the other side") to **Bethsaida** ("house of fishing"). The verb "made" implies an unexplained urgency; but John 6:14-15 states that the people recognized Jesus as the promised future Prophet (cf. Mark 6:14-15) and were determined to make Him King, by force if necessary. Jesus sensed the potential danger of this "messianic enthusiasm" and its effect on the disciples, so He compelled them to

embark **while He dismissed the crowd.**

There is a geographical difficulty about the location of "Bethsaida" (cf. 6:32; Luke 9:10; John 12:21). The simplest solution seems to be that Bethsaida Julias (east of the Jordan) spread across to the western side of the Jordan and was called "Bethsaida in Galilee" (cf. John 12:21; 1:44; Mark 1:21, 29), a fishing suburb of Capernaum (cf. John 6:17). The disciples sailed for this town from the northeastern shore of the Sea of Galilee but were blown off course southward, eventually landing at Gennesaret on the western shore (cf. Mark 6:53).

After dismissing the excited crowd, Jesus **went** up on a nearby hillside **to pray** (cf. comments on 1:35).

6:47. At **evening** (sunset till darkness) **the** disciples' **boat was** well out **in the . . . lake** (not the geographical middle) and Jesus **was alone on land.** When He was absent (or appeared to be), the disciples often experienced distress and demonstrated a lack of faith (cf. 4:35-41; 9:14-32).

6:48. Jesus continued praying well past midnight. Meanwhile **the disciples** had made little headway out on the lake **because** a strong north **wind** blew **against them.** In the dim light of early dawn, **the fourth watch of the night** (by Roman reckoning, 3 to 6 A.M.; cf. 13:35), Jesus **saw** them **straining at the oars** and **went out to them, walking on the** choppy water's surface. The words **He was about to pass by them** do not mean He was going "to bypass" them. He intended "to pass beside" them in the sense of an Old Testament theophany (cf. Ex. 33:19, 22; 1 Kings 19:11; Mark 6:50b) to reassure them.

6:49-50a. The disciples **cried out** (cf. 1:23) with terror at Jesus' appearance on the water. **They thought He was a ghost** (*phantasma*, a water phantom). Mark explained that they responded this way **because they all saw Him** (not a hallucination by a few) **and were terrified.**

6:50b-52. Immediately (*euthys*; cf. 1:10) Jesus calmed their fears and spoke words of reassurance. **Take courage!** (*tharseite*) **Don't be afraid** (lit., "stop fearing") are familiar Old Testament words to people in distress (cf. the LXX of Isa. 41:10, 13-14; 43:1; 44:2). The first command occurs seven times in the New Testament, always on the lips of Jesus except for Mark 10:49 (cf. Matt. 9:2, 22; 14:27; Mark 6:50; John 16:33; Acts 23:11). The words **It is I** (lit., "I am," *egō eimi*) may simply convey self-identification ("It is I, Jesus"), but they are probably intended here to echo the Old Testament formula of God's self-revelation: "I am who I am" (cf. Ex. 3:14; Isa. 41:4; 43:10; 51:12; 52:6).

When Jesus joined the disciples **in the boat . . . the wind died down** (*ekopasen,* "stopped, rested"; cf. Mark 4:39), an additional demonstration of His mastery over nature (cf. 4:35-41).

The disciples **were completely amazed** (*existanto,* lit., "out of their minds"; cf. 2:12; 5:42) among themselves at this revelation of Jesus' presence and power. Mark alone explained (*gar,* **for**) **they had not** caught on to the meaning of **the loaves** miracle (cf. 6:35-44) as a pointer to His true identity. So they did not recognize Him when He walked on the water; they were spiritually imperceptive (cf. 3:5).

3. SUMMARY STATEMENT: JESUS' HEALING MINISTRY AT GENNESARET (6:53-56)
(MATT. 14:34-36)

This summary statement marks the climax of Jesus' Galilean ministry just before His departure for the coastal region around Tyre and Sidon (cf. Mark 7:24).

6:53. Jesus and His disciples **had crossed over** the Sea of Galilee from the northeast to the west (cf. v. 45) **and anchored** (moored) **at Gennesaret,** a fertile, populous plain (two miles wide and four miles long), south of Capernaum on the northwestern shore of the lake. Rabbis called this plain "the Garden of God" and "a paradise." A small town there was also called Gennesaret.

6:54-56. Immediately (*euthys;* cf. 1:10) **people recognized Jesus.** As He moved through the **region,** they **carried the sick on mats to** Him for healing. **Everywhere He went . . . the sick** were **placed** in **marketplaces** (open spaces). Several medicinal mineral springs in this area made it a resort for invalids.

They kept begging again and again (*parekaloun;* cf. 5:10, 23) to **touch even the edge of His cloak** as He passed by. The "edge" or "fringe" was a border of blue tassels worn by a loyal Jew on his outer cloak (cf. Num. 15:37-41; Deut. 22:12).

All who touched Him were healed (lit., "were being saved"; cf. Mark 5:28). These words iterate Mark's earlier reference to a personal faith relationship between Jesus and a sick person (cf. 3:7-10; 5:25-34). Healing was not effected by a touch but by the gracious action of Jesus who honored this means of expressing their faith in Him.

4. THE CONTROVERSY WITH THE RELIGIOUS LEADERS CONCERNING DEFILEMENT (7:1-23)
(MATT. 15:1-20)

This passage returns to the theme of conflict between Jesus and the religious leaders (cf. Mark 2:1–3:6). It emphasizes the rejection Jesus encountered in Israel (cf. 3:6, 19-30; 6:1-6a) despite His public popularity (cf. 6:53-56). It serves as a fitting prelude for His ministry to Gentiles (7:24–8:10). The words "unclean" (7:2, 5, 15, 18, 20, 23) and "tradition" (vv. 3, 5, 8, 9, 13) bind the section together.

a. The charge by the religious leaders (7:1-5)
(Matt. 15:1-2)

7:1-2. The Pharisees (cf. 2:16; 3:6) **and some** Law **teachers** (cf. 1:22) **from Jerusalem** (cf. 3:22-30) came to investigate **Jesus** and His followers again, presumably at Capernaum (cf. 7:17).

They critically observed **some of** Jesus' **disciples eating food with "unclean" . . . hands.** "Unclean" (*koinais,* "common"), as Mark explained for his Gentile readers, meant **ceremonially unwashed.** It was a technical term among Jews denoting whatever was contaminated according to their religious rituals and thus was unfit to be called holy or devoted to God.

7:3-4. These verses constitute an extended parenthesis in which Mark explained (*gar;* cf. 1:16), **for** the benefit of his Gentile readers who lived outside Palestine, the common Jewish practice of **ceremonial washing.**

The ritual washing regulations were observed by **the Pharisees and all the Jews** (a generalization depicting their custom) as part of **the tradition of the elders** which they followed scrupulously. These interpretations, designed to regulate every aspect of Jewish life, were considered as binding as the written Law and were passed on to each generation by faithful Law teachers (scribes). Later, in the third century A.D., the oral tradition was collected and codified in the Mishnah which, in turn, provided the foundation for and structure of the Talmud.

The most common ritual cleansing was the washing of one's hands with a handful of water, a formal practice required before eating food (cf. TDNT, s.v. "katharos," 3:418-24). This was especially important after a trip to **the marketplace** where a Jew would likely come in contact with an "unclean" Gentile or such things as money or utensils.

The comment that the Jews observed **many other traditions,** some of which Mark named, indicates that the issue under discussion involved the whole detailed question of ritual cleansing. For a loyal Jew, to disregard these regulations was a sin; to follow them was the essence of goodness and service to God.

7:5. The religious leaders directed their critical inquiry to **Jesus** who, as the disciples' Teacher, was held responsible for their conduct (cf. 2:18, 24). The Jewish leaders thought that the disciples' failure to observe ritual washing was a symptom of a deeper problem. Their concern was that the **disciples,** and Jesus, did not **live according to the tradition of the elders** (cf. 7:3).

b. Jesus' response and countercharge to His critics (7:6-13) (Matt. 15:3-9)

In reply Jesus made no reference to His disciples' conduct. Rather He addressed two issues underlying the inquiry: (a) the true source of religious authority—tradition or Scripture (Mark 7:6-13), and (b) the true nature of defilement—ceremonial and moral (vv. 14-23).

7:6-8. Jesus quoted Isaiah 29:13 (almost verbatim from the LXX) and applied Isaiah's description of his contemporaries to His questioners whom He called **hypocrites** (occurring only here in Mark).

They were "hypocrites" because they made an outward profession of worshiping God but gave Him no genuine **worship** from **their hearts,** the hidden centers of their thoughts and decisive choices (cf. Mark 7:21; 12:30). Their

worship (a pious act) of God was **in vain** (*matēn,* "futile") because like the Jews of Isaiah's day they were teaching the **rules of men** as authoritative (divine) teachings.

Consequently Jesus charged them with abandoning **the commands of God,** His Law, and instead adhering **to the traditions of men.** He redefined their oral tradition (cf. 7:3, 5), emphasizing its human origin (cf. vv. 9, 13), and He straightforwardly rejected its authority.

7:9. Jesus restated His charge that the religious leaders were clever at sidestepping God's Law **in order to observe** their **own traditions** (cf. v. 8). He supported this verdict by citing a striking illustration (vv. 10-12) which exposed their sin.

7:10. Moses clearly set forth the divine command (cf. v. 13) regarding a person's duty toward his parents. He stated it positively (Ex. 20:12, LXX, the fifth commandment; cf. Deut. 5:16) and negatively (Ex. 21:17, LXX; cf. Lev. 20:9). Such responsibility included adequate financial support and practical care for their needs in their old age (cf. 1 Tim. 5:4, 8). A person who treated his parents with contempt would face the **death** penalty.

7:11-12. Jesus quoted a scribal tradition that sidestepped the divine command. The words, **But you say,** are emphatic, showing the contrast with Moses' words (v. 10). In their "tradition" it was possible for a person to declare all his possessions to be **Corban** and thereby absolve himself from the fifth commandment.

"Corban" is the Greek (and Eng.) transliteration of a Hebrew term used to refer to **a gift devoted to God.** It was a dedicatory formula pronounced over money and property donated to the temple and its service by an inviolable vow. Such gifts could only be used for religious purposes.

If a son declared that the resources needed to support his aging parents were "Corban" then, according to scribal tradition, he was exempt from this command of God, and his parents were legally excluded from any claim on him. The scribes emphasized that his vow was unalterable (cf. Num. 30) and held priority over his family responsibilities. So they **no longer let him do anything for** his parents.

7:13. By their tradition they nullified the Word of God. Nullify translates *akyrountes*, from *akyroō*, used in the papyri for annulling contracts. To sanction religious donations at the expense of violating God's command regarding one's duty to parents was to set human tradition above God's Word.

The "Corban" vow was only one example of **many** other **things like** it (e.g., restrictive Sabbath rules; cf. 2:23–3:5) where scribal tradition distorted and obscured the Old Testament.

c. Jesus' explanation of real defilement (7:14-23) (Matt. 15:10-20)

At this point Jesus gave a more direct reply to the defilement question (cf. Mark 7:5). He addressed the crowd first (vv. 14-15) and gave a general principle applicable to everyone. Then He explained the principle to His disciples privately (vv. 17-23).

7:14-16. Following a solemn call to attentive hearing and careful consideration by **everyone** (cf. 4:3), **Jesus** disclosed to **the crowd** the true source of defilement. Negatively, **Nothing outside a man** (generic, "person") by going into him **can make him "unclean"** (cf. 7:2). Jesus spoke in a moral not a medical sense. A person is *not* defiled morally by what he eats even if his hands are not ceremonially washed.

Positively **What comes out of a man** (person; cf. vv. 21-23) **makes him "unclean."** A person *is* defiled morally by what he thinks in his heart even though he may scrupulously observe outward purity rituals. So Jesus contradicted the Rabbinic view by stating that sin proceeds from within and not from without (cf. Jer. 17:9-10). He also demonstrated the true spiritual intent of the laws regarding clean and unclean food in the Mosaic Law (cf. Lev. 11; Deut. 14). A Jew who ate "unclean" food was defiled not by the food, but by His disobeying God's command.

7:17. After they left the crowd and entered the house (probably in Capernaum; cf. 2:1-2; 3:20), **His disciples asked** for an explanation of the **parable** given in 7:15. Their failure to understand Jesus' words and works is emphasized throughout 6:32–8:26 and is traced to their hardness of heart (cf. 6:52; 8:14-21).

7:18-19. Jesus' question, **Are you so dull?** is literally, "So then are you *also* without understanding?" It showed that they, like the crowd, did not comprehend His teaching despite the instruction He already gave them.

Jesus amplified the negative truth that **nothing . . . from the outside** of a person **can** defile **him** morally (cf. v. 15a). The reason is that food (or any other item) does not enter **his heart,** the control center of the human personality, and thereby affect his moral nature. Rather, it enters **his stomach** (a nonmoral agent).

The concluding sentence of verse 19 is an editorial comment by Mark (cf. 2:10, 28; 3:30; 13:14), to emphasize the significance of Jesus' statement for his Christian readers in Rome, some of whom may have been confused over Jewish food laws (cf. Rom. 14:14; Gal. 2:11-17; Col. 2:20-22). He simply pointed out that **Jesus declared all foods "clean"** for Christians. The early church was slow to grasp this truth (cf. Acts 10; 15).

7:20-23. Jesus repeated and amplified the positive truth that **what comes out of a** person **is what** defiles **him** morally (cf. v. 15b). This is confirmed by noting what things come **from within, out of** a person's heart (cf. v. 19).

The general term translated **evil thoughts** precedes the verb in the Greek text and is viewed as the root of various evils which follow. Evil thoughts generated in a heart unite with one's will to produce evil words and actions.

The catalog of evil Jesus gave has a strong Old Testament flavor and consists of 12 items. First, there are six *plural* nouns (in Gr.) depicting wicked acts viewed individually: **sexual immorality** (*porneiai,* "illicit sexual activities of various kinds"); **theft** (*klopai*); **murder** (*phonoi*); **adultery** (*moicheiai,* illicit sexual relations by a married person); **greed** (*pleonexiai,* "covetings"), insatiable cravings for what belongs to another; **malice** (*ponēriai,* "wickednesses"), the many ways evil thoughts express themselves.

Second, there are six singular nouns depicting evil dispositions: **deceit** (*dolos*), cunning maneuvers designed to ensnare someone for one's personal advantage; **lewdness** (*aselgeia;* cf. Rom. 13:13; Gal. 5:19; Eph. 4:19; 2 Peter 2:2, 7), unrestrained and unconcealed immoral behavior; **envy** (*opthalmos poneros*, lit., "an evil eye," a Heb. expression for stinginess; cf. Prov. 23:6), a begrudging, jealous attitude toward the possessions of others; **slander** (*blasphēmia*), injurious or defaming speech against God or man; **arrogance** (*hyperēphania*, used only here in the NT), boastfully exalting oneself above others who are viewed with scornful contempt; **and folly** (*aphrosynē*), moral and spiritual insensitivity.

All these evils defile a person, and have their source **from inside,** from one's heart. So Jesus took the focus of attention away from external rituals and placed it on the need for God to cleanse one's evil heart (cf. Ps. 51).

5. THE CURE OF THE SYROPHOENICIAN WOMAN'S DAUGHTER (7:24-30)

(MATT. 15:21-28)

This is the first of three events Mark recorded from Jesus' third excursion beyond the borders of Galilee (for the three excursions see Mark 4:35; 5:20; 6:32-52; 7:24–8:10). On this journey He actually went out of Palestine, apparently for the only time. These events in Gentile territory are an appropriate sequel to Jesus' teaching in verses 1-23 and a fitting preview of the proclamation of the gospel to the Gentile world (cf. 13:10; 14:9).

7:24. Jesus left that place, probably Capernaum **and went to the vicinity of Tyre,** a Mediterranean seaport city in Phoenicia (modern Lebanon) about 40 miles northwest of Capernaum. Because of excellent, early Greek manuscript support, the words "and Sidon" (cf. NIV marg.) should be included (cf. v. 31).

Jesus went there not to minister publicly to the people but to secure privacy, previously interrupted (cf. 6:32-34, 53-56), in order to instruct His disciples. That is why He **did not want anyone to know** He was there. But **He could not** conceal **His presence** since news of His healing power had preceded Him (cf. 3:8).

7:25-26. An unnamed **woman, whose little daughter was** demon-possessed (cf. 1:23; 5:2), **came** immediately (*euthys;* cf. 1:10) **and fell at His feet,** an expression of deep respect as well as personal grief over her daughter's condition (cf. 9:17-18, 20-22, 26). She kept asking **Jesus to drive the demon out of her daughter.**

Mark stressed the woman's non-Jewish identity: she **was a Greek,** not from Greece, but a Gentile by culture and religion. She was a Syrophoenician **born** in **Phoenicia,** part of the province of Syria. Matthew called her a "Canaanite woman" (Matt. 15:22).

7:27. Jesus' reply was appropriate to His purpose for being there (cf. v. 24), and was on a level the Gentile woman could grasp. It was cast in figurative language: **the children** represented His disciples (cf. 9:35-37); **the children's bread** represented the benefits of His ministry to them; and the **dogs** (lit., "little dogs," house pets, not outdoor scavengers) represented the Gentiles (not in a derogatory sense here).

Jesus was telling the woman that His first priority in being there was to instruct His disciples. It is not appropriate to interrupt a family meal to give the dogs food from the table. So it was not appropriate for Him to interrupt His ministry to His disciples to give His services to her, a Gentile. But Jesus' reluctance to help stimulated her faith.

Other interpreters understand a broader theological meaning in Jesus' words: the children (unbelieving Israel) must be fed (Jesus' mission); their bread (special privileges including first claim on Jesus' ministry) must not be thrown to the dogs (Gentiles) because their time for feeding (worldwide proclamation of the gospel) had not yet come. Though this view is true theologically, it overplays Mark's point.

7:28. The woman accepted Jesus' statement with the words, **Yes, Lord** ("Sir," a title of respect). She realized He had the right to refuse her request. However, feeling no insult in the analogy He used, she pressed it a little further: **Even the dogs under the table eat the children's crumbs.**

Her point was that the dogs get some food *at the same time* as the children and thus do not have to wait. There need be no interruption in His instructing the disciples for all she humbly requested was a crumb, a small benefit of His grace for her desperate need.

7:29-30. Because of **such a reply,** which demonstrated her humility and faith, Jesus told **her** to go home (cf. 2:11; 5:34; 10:52), and assured her that **the demon** had **left** her **daughter.** The words "has left" (perf. tense) indicate the cure was already complete.

When she returned home, she found that her child was resting peacefully and the demon was gone. This is the only miracle recorded in Mark that Jesus performed at a distance without giving any vocal command.

6. THE HEALING OF THE DEAF MAN WITH DEFECTIVE SPEECH (7:31-37)

This miracle is recorded only by Mark. It concludes a narrative cycle, 6:32–7:37, with the people's confession about Jesus (7:37). This event prefigured the opening of the disciples' "ears" (cf. 8:18, 27-30). A second narrative cycle begins in 8:1 and climaxes in the disciples' confession (8:27-30).

7:31-32. Jesus left . . . Tyre (cf. v. 24) and went north 20 miles through Sidon, a coastal city, and then turned southeastward, avoiding Galilee, to a place on the eastern side of the Sea of Galilee within the region of the Decapolis (cf. 5:20).

Some people there begged Jesus to place His hand (cf. 5:23) on a man who was deaf and could hardly talk (mogilalon, "speaking with difficulty"). This rare word occurs only here and in the Septuagint of Isaiah 35:6, a passage promising the coming of God's rule on earth. This promised intervention was already taking place in Jesus' ministry (cf. Mark 7:37; 1:15).

7:33-35. In healing this man, Jesus used sign language and symbolic acts (which Mark did not explain) that uniquely suited the man's needs and caused him to exercise faith. Jesus took him aside privately (cf. 6:32) in order to communicate one-to-one with him apart from the crowd. By touching his ears and tongue, spitting (on the ground) and looking up to heaven (to God; cf. 6:41), Jesus conveyed what He was going to do. His deep sigh may have reflected compassion for the man but it was likely Jesus' strong emotion as He battled the satanic powers that enslaved the suffering man.

Then Jesus gave the Aramaic command Ephphatha! meaning Be opened! (lit., "be completely opened") This word could easily be lip-read by a deaf person. This Aramaic word may indicate that the man was not a Gentile.

Immediately (euthys; cf. 1:10) at Jesus' command the man's ears were opened, his tongue was loosened, and he could speak clearly. Defective speech usually results from defective hearing, both physically and spiritually.

7:36. The more Jesus commanded (lit., "kept commanding") the people to be silent, the more they kept proclaiming the news (cf. 1:44-45; 5:20, 43). He wanted to minister in the Decapolis region without being regarded as a popular "Miracle-worker."

7:37. Jesus' miracle left the people overwhelmed with amazement (exeplēssonto; "struck out, overwhelmed"; cf. 1:22; 6:2; 10:26; 11:18) beyond all measure (hyperperissōs, a forceful adverb used only here in the NT).

The crowd's climactic confession is a general statement about their understanding of Jesus, based on previous reports (cf. 3:8; 5:20). The words the deaf and the dumb are plural in Greek, viewing them as two classes of people. Even should be rendered "both." Mark probably intended an allusion to Isaiah 35:3-6 in the crowd's confession.

7. THE FEEDING OF THE 4,000 (8:1-10) (MATT. 15:32-39)

In Mark 8:1-30 Mark presented a series of events that parallels his sequence in 6:32–7:37. Despite the replay of events and teaching, the disciples were still slow to "see and hear" who Jesus really is (cf. 8:18). In both narrative cycles the feeding of a multitude played an important role (cf. 6:52; 8:14-21).

8:1-3. During Jesus' ministry in the Decapolis region (cf. 7:31), another large crowd gathered (cf. 6:34), probably both Jews and Gentiles.

After listening to Jesus' teaching three days, they had nothing to eat. They were weakened by hunger so that if Jesus would send them home hungry, they would collapse on the way as some had come a long distance.

Jesus had compassion on them in their physical need (cf. 6:34) and called the disciples' attention to it (contrast 6:35-36). He took the initiative to feed the multitude who chose to forgo food in order to be nourished by His words.

8:4-5. The disciples' question highlighted their slowness in comprehending the significance of Jesus' presence with them in a new crisis. It also showed their inadequacy to meet the need; yet they indirectly referred the matter back to Jesus (contrast 6:37).

Jesus' question concerning the amount of **bread** available clearly indicated His intentions, and was an invitation for the **disciples** to use the resources they had—**seven** loaves. They also had "a few small fish" (cf. 8:7; Matt. 15:34).

8:6-7. The feeding of this crowd occurred much like the feeding of the 5,000 (cf. 6:39-42). The Greek participles translated **taken** and **given thanks** (*eucharistēsas*; cf. 14:23), and the verb **broke** are in the aorist tense, expressing decisive acts, whereas the verb **gave** is in the imperfect, showing that Jesus "kept on giving" the bread **to His disciples** for distribution (cf. 6:41). He did the same thing with **a few small fish.**

8:8-9a. In abrupt fashion Mark stressed the sufficiency of the miracle (all **ate and were satisfied**), the abundance of the provision (**seven basketfuls of** food remained), and the large size of the crowd (**about 4,000 men** besides women and children; cf. Matt. 15:38).

The baskets (*spyridas*) on this occasion differed from those used in feeding the 5,000 (*kophinoi*, Mark 6:43; cf. 8:19-20). They were rope or mat baskets sometimes large enough to carry a man (cf. Acts 9:25). Thus the 7 basketfuls (perhaps a basket for each loaf used) of Mark 8:8 likely held more than the 12 basketfuls of 6:43.

8:9b-10. Dismissing the crowd, Jesus immediately (*euthys*; cf. 1:10) entered a **boat with His disciples** and crossed the Sea of Galilee **to the region of Dalmanutha,** a town (also called Magadan; cf. Matt. 15:39) near Tiberias on the lake's western side (cf. Mark 8:13, 22).

8. THE PHARISEES' DEMAND FOR A SIGN (8:11-13)
(MATT. 16:1-4)

8:11. The religious authorities (cf. 3:22-30; 7:1-5) **came and began to question** (*syzētein*, "to dispute, debate") Him. They wished **to test** (from *peirazō*; cf. 1:13; 10:2; 12:15) Him, to get Him to prove the source of His authority (cf. 3:22-30; 11:30; Deut. 13:2-5; 18:18-22). They were seeking (from *zēteō*; cf. Mark 11:18; 12:12; 14:1, 11, 55) from Him a **sign from heaven,** one with divine

authorization. In the Old Testament a "sign" was not so much a demonstration of power as an evidence that an utterance or action was authentic and trustworthy (cf. TDNT, s.v. *"sēmeion,"* 7:210-6, 234-6). The Pharisees did not demand a spectacular miracle, but that Jesus give unmistakable proof that He and His mission were authorized by God. They believed quite the opposite (cf. 3:22).

8:12. Jesus **sighed deeply** (cf. 7:34) and asked a rhetorical question that reflected His distress at their obstinate unbelief. The words **this generation** denoted the nation of Israel represented by those religious leaders (cf. 8:38; 9:19; 13:30). They continually rejected God's gracious dealings with them (cf. Deut. 32:5-20; Ps. 95:10). **Miraculous** is not in the Greek text.

With a solemn introductory formula **(I tell you the truth;** cf. Mark 3:28) and a Hebrew idiom of strong denial (cf. Ps. 95:11; Heb. 3:11; 4:3, 5), Jesus rejected their demand: **No sign will be given to** "this generation." Matthew cited the only exception, "the sign of Jonah" (Matt. 16:4), that is, Jesus' resurrection (cf. Matt. 12:39-40).

In Mark, there is a distinction between a miracle (*dynamis*) and a sign (*sēmeion*). The former evidences God's presence and power in Jesus. An appeal for a miracle can be a legitimate expression of one's faith (e.g., Mark 5:23; 7:26, 32). But such an appeal is illegitimate if it arises out of unbelief, as was true of the Pharisees.

8:13. Jesus' indignation was evident by His abrupt departure. He **crossed** the Sea of Galilee **to the** northeastern shore once more. This ended His public ministry in Galilee.

9. THE DISCIPLES' FAILURE TO UNDERSTAND JESUS' WORDS AND DEEDS (8:14-21)
(MATT. 16:5-12)

8:14. Their hasty departure (v. 13) probably accounts for the disciples' failure **to bring bread.** They had no food in the boat **except for one loaf,** a sufficient amount with Jesus on board (cf. 6:35-44).

8:15. With the encounter near Tiberias (vv. 11-13; the site of Herod's palace) still fresh in His mind, **Jesus warned** (lit., "kept giving orders to"; cf. 7:36) **them to be** continually on guard against **the yeast**

of the Pharisees and that of Herod Antipas.

A small amount of yeast can affect a large amount of bread dough when they are mixed. Yeast was a common Jewish metaphor for an invisible, pervasive influence. It often, as here, connoted a corrupting influence. In this context the yeast referred to a gradual increase of unbelief. This lay behind the Pharisees' request for a sign even though their minds were already made up (cf. 8:11-12; 3:6). So it was with Herod (cf. 6:14-16; Luke 13:31-33; 23:8-9). As indicated by Jesus' question (Mark 8:12), this attitude had affected the whole nation of Israel, and He warned His disciples against it. In contrast, He called them to faith and understanding without signs (cf. vv. 17-21).

8:16. The disciples totally ignored Jesus' reference to the Pharisees and Herod. They heard "yeast" and assumed Jesus spoke of their **bread** shortage.

8:17-18. Jesus' rebuke is expressed in five penetrating questions that showed their persistent lack of spiritual understanding (cf. 4:13, 40; 6:52). Since He was **aware of their discussion** (cf. 8:16), His rebuke was not because of their failure to grasp the meaning of His warning (v. 15), but at their failure to **understand** the meaning of His presence with them. Their **hearts** were **hardened** (cf. 6:52). They had **eyes but** failed **to see and ears but** failed **to hear** (cf. Jer. 5:21; Ezek. 12:2). In this sense, they were no better than those "outside" (cf. Mark 4:11-12). They also had short memories.

8:19-20. The questions about the two miraculous feedings (cf. 6:35-44; 8:1-9) indicated that the disciples had failed to comprehend the meaning of what they had seen, and to discern who Jesus really is.

8:21. The climactic question, **Do you still not understand?** was more of an appeal than a rebuke. The emphasis on "understanding" (vv. 17-18, 21) expressed the goal of Jesus' words and works which had not yet been reached.

10. THE HEALING OF THE BLIND MAN AT
    BETHSAIDA (8:22-26)

This miracle and its structural parallel (7:31-37) are the only miracles recorded in Mark alone. It is the only recorded two-stage miracle which Jesus

performed. Sight was a widely used metaphor for understanding. This miracle depicts the correct but incomplete understanding of the disciples.

8:22. When **Jesus** and the disciples arrived in **Bethsaida** Julias (cf. v. 13; 6:32), **some people brought a blind man and begged** Him **to touch him** with healing (cf. 5:23; 7:32).

8:23-24. Jesus **led** the man **outside the village,** probably to establish a one-to-one relationship with him (cf. 7:33) and to avoid publicity (8:26). In general Jesus' miracles were public events (cf. 1:23-28; 32-34; 3:1-12; 6:53-56; 9:14-27; 10:46-52). But there are three exceptions in Mark (5:35-43; 7:31-37; 8:22-26). The latter two may teach that a true understanding of Jesus comes through a personal relationship with Him apart from the crowd's opinions.

The touch of saliva and Jesus' **hands** (cf. 7:33) conveyed His intentions and stimulated the blind man's faith. At first the healing was only partial: **He looked up** (cf. 8:25) **and** saw **people** (lit., "the men," perhaps the Twelve) moving in a blur **like trees walking around.** Jesus' unusual question, **Do you see anything?** indicated that this was intentional on His part (not a weakness in the man's faith). It was a fitting follow-up to His rebuking the disciples (vv. 17-21). The man was no longer totally blind, but his sight was still poor. How like him were the disciples!

8:25. Then **Jesus put His hands on the man's eyes** again. He looked intently (from *diablepō;* v. 24 has a form of *anablepō*); **his sight was restored, and he** began to see (from *emblepō*) **everything clearly.** Now his sight was perfect. This was the outcome the disciples could anticipate despite difficulties in the process.

8:26. Apparently the man did not live in Bethsaida since **Jesus sent him** home with the admonition, **Don't go into the village** (i.e., "Don't go there first"). This is likely another instance of a command for silence in order to safeguard His planned activity (cf. 1:44-45; 5:43; 7:36).

D. Conclusion: Peter's confession that Jesus is the Christ (8:27-30) (Matt. 16:13-20; Luke 9:18-21)

At the center of his Gospel Mark placed Peter's confession that Jesus is the

Messiah. Up to this point the underlying question had been, "Who is He?" After Peter's declaration on behalf of the Twelve, Mark's narrative is oriented toward the Cross and the Resurrection. From now on, the underlying double question was, "What kind of Messiah is He, and what does it mean to follow Him?" This crucial passage is the point to which the first half of the book leads and from which the second half proceeds.

8:27. Jesus took His disciples about 25 miles north of Bethsaida (cf. v. 22) **to the villages around Caesarea Philippi,** a city located at the source of the Jordan River on the southern slopes of Mount Hermon. It was in the tetrarchy of Herod Philip, who gave it his own name to distinguish it from the Caesarea on the Mediterranean coast.

On the way (en tē hodō; cf. 1:2; 9:33-34; 10:17, 32, 52) Jesus **asked** the disciples what **people** were saying about Him. Often Jesus' questions were springboards for new teaching (cf. 8:29; 9:33; 12:24-25).

8:28. Their response was the same as that given in 6:14-16: **John the Baptist . . . Elijah . . . one of the prophets.** All three responses were wrong, indicating that Jesus' identity and mission remained veiled from the people.

8:29. Then more directly and personally Jesus **asked** the disciples, **Who do you say I am?** The emphasis is on **you,** those He had chosen and trained. **Peter,** acting as the Twelve's spokesman (cf. 3:16; 9:5; 10:28; 11:21; 14:29), declared openly, **You are the Christ,** the Messiah, God's Anointed One (cf. 1:1).

Their open confession of Him at this point (cf. John 1:41, 51) was necessary because people in general were failing to discern His true identity, the religious leaders were strongly opposed to Him, and He was about to give the disciples additional revelation about Himself that would have costly implications for them. It was essential that the question of His identity be firmly settled. This affirmation of faith in Jesus was the anchor of their discipleship despite their temporary failures and defections (cf. Mark 14:50, 66-72).

Mark gave Peter's confession in its simplest, most direct form (cf. Matt. 16:16-19) to focus on Jesus' teaching on

the nature of His messiahship (cf. Mark 8:31; 9:30-32; 10:32-34, 45).

8:30. Jesus sternly **warned** (lit., "ordered"; cf. 1:25; 3:12) **them not to tell anyone** He is the Messiah. People had thought up many false ideas about the concept of the "Messiah." The promised Davidic Messiah (cf. 2 Sam. 7:14-16; Isa. 55:3-5; Jer. 23:5) was commonly thought to be a political, nationalistic figure destined to free the Jews from Roman domination (cf. Mark 11:9-10). But Jesus' messianic mission was broader in scope and far different in nature. So He was reluctant to use this title (cf. 12:35-37; 14:61-62), and the disciples were not yet ready to proclaim the true meaning of His messiahship.

Jesus knew He is God's Anointed One (cf. 9:41; 14:62), so He accepted Peter's declaration as correct. However, because of the disciple's misunderstandings (cf. 8:32-33), He commanded silence (cf. 1:44) until He could explain that as Messiah it was necessary for Him to suffer and die in obedience to God's will (cf. 8:31).

VI. Jesus' Journey to Jerusalem (8:31–10:52)

The fourth major section of Mark's Gospel is set in the framework of His journey from Caesarea Philippi in the north, where Jesus was confessed as Messiah, to Jerusalem in the south, where He fulfilled His messianic mission (cf. 8:27; 9:30; 10:1, 17, 32; 11:1; also cf. 14:28; 16:7).

Jesus explained the nature of His messianic vocation and its implications for those who wish to follow Him. There is a balanced tension between His veiledness in suffering and His future revelation in glory. The structure of this section revolves around three Passion predictions: 8:31–9:29; 9:30–10:31; 10:32-52. Each unit includes a prediction (8:31; 9:30-31; 10:32-34); a reaction by the disciples (8:32-33; 9:32; 10:35-41); and one or more lessons in discipleship (8:34–9:29; 9:33–10:31; 10:42-52).

A. The first Passion prediction unit (8:31–9:29)

1. JESUS' FIRST PREDICTION OF HIS DEATH AND RESURRECTION (8:31)
(MATT. 16:21; LUKE 9:22)

8:31. After Peter declared that Jesus

is the Messiah (v. 29), **He . . . began to teach them** what this meant. This marked a turning point to new content in His teaching.

Contrary to popular messianic expectations, Jesus had not come to establish an earthly messianic kingdom *at that time.* Instead He declared **that the Son of Man must suffer many things** (cf. Isa. 53:4, 11), **be rejected by the** Jewish authorities, **be killed, and after three days** ("on the third day"; cf. Matt. 16:21; Luke 9:22) **rise again** (Isa. 52:13; 53:10-12). This introduced to the disciples a new element in God's kingdom program for which they were not prepared (cf. Mark 8:32). "Must" (*dei*, "it is necessary") denotes compulsion. In this context it refers to the compulsion of God's will, the divine plan for Jesus' messianic mission (cf. 1:11). This prediction shows His submission to it (cf. 14:35-36).

Three groups—the **elders** (influential lay leaders), **chief priests** (Sadducees, cf. 12:18, including former high priests), **teachers of the Law** (scribes, mostly Pharisees)—constituted the Sanhedrin, the Jewish supreme court which met in Jerusalem (cf. 11:27; 14:53).

Though Peter identified Him as "the Christ" (8:29), Jesus did not discuss the title or the issue of His identity. Rather, He focused on His mission and used the designation "the Son of Man." This expression has appeared only twice before in Mark (cf. 2:10, 28). Both times Mark used it to show the significance of an event for his Christian readers. From now on it occurs more often but only when Jesus talked about Himself (cf. 8:31, 38; 9:9, 12, 31; 10:33, 45; 13:26; 14:21 [twice], 41, 62).

This title especially suited Jesus' total mission. It was free of political connotations, thus preventing false expectations. Yet it was sufficiently ambiguous (like a parable) to preserve the balance between concealment and disclosure in Jesus' life and mission (cf. 4:11-12). It combined the elements of suffering and glory in a way no other designation could. It served to define His unique role as Messiah.

2. PETER'S REBUKE AND JESUS'
   COUNTERREBUKE (8:32-33)
   (MATT. 16:22-23)

8:32-33. In contrast with previously veiled allusions (cf. 2:10), Jesus **spoke plainly,** in unambiguous terms, **about** the need for His death and resurrection.

Peter clearly understood Jesus' words (8:31), but could not reconcile his view of "Messiah" (v. 29b) with the suffering and death Jesus predicted. So Peter **began to rebuke Him** for this defeatist approach.

Peter's reaction, which the other disciples probably shared, was a satanic attempt similar to the wilderness temptation (cf. 1:12-13), to divert Jesus from the Cross. **Jesus . . . rebuked** (cf. 8:32) **Peter** for the benefit of them all. This was not a personal attack. The words, **Out of My sight,** are literally, "Go away behind (after) Me." This is probably not a command to Peter to take his proper place as a disciple (contrast 1:17; 8:34), for Jesus named **Satan** as the source of Peter's thoughts.

Peter was an unwitting spokesman for Satan because he was setting his **mind** (*phroneō* means "to have a mental disposition for"; cf. Col. 3:2) **not** on **the things of God,** His ways and purposes (cf. Isa. 55:8-9), **but** on **the things of men,** human values and viewpoints. The way of the Cross was God's will and Jesus refused to abandon it.

3. JESUS' TEACHING ON THE MEANING OF
   DISCIPLESHIP (8:34–9:1)
   (MATT. 16:24-28; LUKE 9:23-27)

A suffering Messiah had important implications for those who would follow Him. This section contains a series of short sayings concerning personal allegiance to Jesus (cf. Mark 9:43-50; 10:24-31). The main statement (8:34) is followed by four explanatory (*gar*, "for") clauses (vv. 35-38) and a concluding assurance (9:1). This instruction was part of the disciples' preparation for future ministry. It also provided encouragement for Mark's readers who were facing persecution in Rome.

8:34. Jesus summoned **the crowd,** interested onlookers (cf. 4:1, 10-12; 7:14-15), **along with His disciples and** addressed them both. His words, **If anyone** (not just the Twelve) **would come after Me** (cf. 1:17) indicated that Jesus was talking about their following Him as disciples (cf. 1:16-20). He then stated two requirements which, like repent and believe (cf. 1:15), are bound together.

Negatively, one **must deny himself** decisively ("deny" is an aorist imper.) saying no to selfish interests and earthly securities. Self-denial is not to deny one's personality, to die as a martyr, or to deny "things" (as in asceticism). Rather it is the denial of "self," turning away from the idolatry of self-centeredness and every attempt to orient one's life by the dictates of self-interest (cf. TDNT, s.v. *"arneomai,"* 1:469-71). Self-denial, however, is only the negative side of the picture and is not done for its own sake alone.

Positively, one must **take up his cross,** decisively ("take up" is also an aorist imper.) saying yes to God's will and way. Cross-bearing was not an established Jewish metaphor. But the figure was appropriate in Roman-occupied Palestine. It brought to mind the sight of a condemned man who was forced to demonstrate his submission to Rome by carrying part of his cross through the city to his place of execution. Thus "to take up one's cross" was to demonstrate publicly one's submission/obedience to the authority against which he had previously rebelled.

Jesus' submission to God's will is the proper response to God's claims over self's claims. For Him it meant death on the cross. Those who follow Him must take up *their* (not His) cross, whatever comes to them in God's will as a follower of Jesus. This does not mean suffering as He did or being crucified as He was. Nor does it mean stoically bearing life's troubles. Rather, it is obedience to God's will as revealed in His Word, accepting the consequences without reservations for Jesus' sake and the gospel (cf. 8:35). For some this includes physical suffering and even death, as history has demonstrated (cf. 10:38-39).

In Jesus' words, **Follow Me,** "follow" is a present imperative: "(So) let him keep following Me" (cf. 1:17-18; 2:14; 10:21, 52b; cf. "daily" in Luke 9:23). Saying no to self and yes to God is to continue all through one's following Jesus (cf. Rom. 13:14; Phil. 3:7-11).

8:35. Verses 35-38 each begin with the explanatory Greek *gar* (**for,** trans. only once in the NIV). These verses explain Jesus' requirements in verse 34, focusing on entrance into discipleship, leaving one's old allegiance to this life (the crowd), and pledging allegiance to Jesus as a disciple.

Paradoxically a person **who wants to save** (from *sōzō,* "preserve") **his life** (*psychēn,* "soul, life") **will lose it;** he will not be saved to eternal life. But a person who **loses** (lit., "will lose") **his life** (*psychē*) **for** the sake of Jesus and **the gospel** (cf. 1:1) **will save** (from *sōzō,* "preserve") **it;** he will be saved to eternal life (cf. comments on 10:26-27; 13:13).

Jesus made a word play on the terms "lose" and "life" (*psychē*). The *psychē* on one hand is one's natural physical life but it also refers to one's true self, the essential person that transcends the earthly sphere (cf. 8:36; Matt. 10:28; TDNT, s.v. *"psychē,"* 9:642-4). One who decides to maintain a self-centered life in this world by refusing Jesus' requirements (Mark 8:34) will ultimately lose his life to eternal ruin. Conversely a person who will "lose" (give over, "deny himself") his life (even literally, if necessary) in loyalty to Jesus and the gospel (cf. 10:29) by accepting His requirements (8:34) will actually preserve it forever. As a follower of Jesus, he is heir to eternal life forever with God (cf. 10:29-30; Rom. 8:16-17).

8:36-37. Jesus used penetrating rhetorical questions and economic terms to show the supreme value of eternal life and to reinforce the paradox of verse 35.

For (*gar,* confirming v. 35) **what good** (lit., "benefit, profit") **is it for a man** (generic, "person") **to gain the whole world,** all earthly pleasures and possessions, if this were possible, and **yet forfeit** (lit., "suffer the loss of") **his soul** (*psychēn*) not gaining eternal life with God? The expected answer: "It is no good!" (Cf. Ps. 49, esp. vv. 16-20.)

For (*gar,* confirming Mark 8:36) **what can a man** (generic, "person") **give in exchange for his soul** (*psychēs*), for eternal life with God? The answer: Nothing, because having "gained the world" he has in the end irrevocably lost eternal life with God, with nothing to compensate for it.

8:38. Structurally this verse parallels and complements verse 35 by carrying the thought to its ultimate consequence.

For (*gar,* confirming v. 35) a person who **is ashamed of** (denies) Jesus **and His words** (cf. 13:31) **in this adulterous** (spiritually unfaithful) **and sinful genera-**

tion (*genea*; cf. 8:12; Matt. 12:39; Isa. 1:4; Hosea 1:2), **the Son of Man** (cf. comments on Mark 8:31) **will** also **be ashamed of him when** (lit., "whenever") **He comes in His Father's glory** (visibly invested with God's splendor), **with the holy angels** (cf. 13:26-27).

Clearly Jesus (cf. "Me, My") and the Son of Man are the *same* Person (cf. 14:41b-42, 62). The veiled reference to His future role as Judge was appropriate because of the crowd's presence.

To be "ashamed" of Jesus is to reject Him (cf. 8:34-35a) and to retain allegiance to "this generation" because of unbelief and fear of the world's contempt. In return, when Jesus comes in glory as the awesome Judge, He will refuse to claim those as His own (cf. Matt. 7:20-23; Luke 13:22-30), and they will experience shame (cf. Isa. 28:16; 45:20-25; Rom. 9:33; 10:11; 1 Peter 2:6, 8).

9:1. This verse is the positive side of 8:38 (cf. Matt. 10:32-33; Luke 12:8-9) and provides a reassuring conclusion to this section (Mark 8:34–9:1).

The words **And He said to them** (cf. 2:27) introduce an authoritative statement by Jesus. He predicted that **some who** stood there listening to Him would **not** (lit., "by no means," *ou mē*) **taste death before** (lit., "until") **they** saw a powerful display of God's kingdom. The words "taste death" are a Hebrew idiom for experiencing physical death, like a fatal poison that all must take sooner or later (cf. Heb. 2:9).

Several interpretations have been suggested for the meaning of **the kingdom of God come with power:** (a) Jesus' transfiguration, (b) Jesus' resurrection and Ascension, (c) the coming of the Holy Spirit at Pentecost (Acts 2:1-4) and the spread of Christianity by the early church, (d) the destruction of Jerusalem by Rome in A.D. 70, and (e) the second coming of Jesus Christ.

The first of these is the most reasonable view in this context. The specific time reference in the following account of Jesus' transfiguration (Mark 9:2a) indicates that Mark understood a definite connection between Jesus' prediction (v. 1) and this event. Jesus' transfiguration was a striking preview and guarantee of His future coming in glory (cf. 2 Peter 1:16-19).

4. JESUS' TRANSFIGURATION (9:2-13) (MATT. 17:1-13; LUKE 9:28-36)

a. His glory displayed (9:2-8)

This event confirmed Peter's confession (8:29) and fulfilled Jesus' prediction (9:1). It also served as a prelude to Jesus' Passion (14:1–16:8). Despite His impending death (8:31-32), He assured them by this event that His return in glory (8:38b) was certain and that their commitment to Him was well-founded (8:34-37). Future glory would follow present suffering for Him *and* them.

9:2-4. The words, **after six days** link the transfiguration to Jesus' prediction in verse 1. The event occurred on the *seventh* day after the prediction—a day reminiscent of fulfillment and special revelation (cf. Ex. 24:15-16).

Matthew gave the same time sequence but Luke stated that the transfiguration occurred "about eight days" later (Luke 9:28). Luke's general reference reflects an alternate method of measuring time in which part of a day was counted as a whole day (see comments on Luke 9:28).

Jesus selected **Peter, James, and John** (cf. Mark 5:37; 14:33) **and** took **them up a high mountain where they were all alone** (*kat' idian*; cf. 4:34). The unnamed location was probably a southern ridge of Mount Hermon (ca. 9,200 feet) about 12 miles northeast of Caesarea Philippi (cf. 8:27; 9:30, 33). This is preferable to Mount Tabor in Galilee. The "high mountain" was an appropriate site in view of God's previous self-disclosure to Moses and Elijah on Mount Sinai (Horeb; cf. Ex. 24:12-18; 1 Kings 19:8-18).

Jesus **was transfigured** in the presence of the three disciples (cf. 2 Peter 1:16). "Transfigured" (*metemorphōthē*, cf. Eng. "metamorphosis") means "to be changed into another form," not merely a change in outward appearance (cf. Rom. 12:2; 2 Cor. 3:18). For a brief time Jesus' human body was transformed (glorified) and the disciples saw Him as He will be when He returns visibly in power and glory to establish His kingdom on earth (cf. Acts 15:14-18; 1 Cor. 15:20-28; Rev. 1:14-15; 19:15; 20:4-6). This was dramatically portrayed by the supra-earthly whiteness of **His clothes**—a comment unique to Mark, probably reflecting Peter's eyewitness report.

Two significant Old Testament men, **Elijah and Moses,** appeared miraculously and were conversing **with Jesus** (cf. Luke 9:31). Mark's mentioning Elijah first is likely due to his emphasis on Elijah in this context (cf. Mark 8:28; 9:11-13). Moses, in the role of Israel's deliverer and lawgiver, represented the Law. Elijah, defender of Yahweh worship and the future restorer of all things (Mal. 4:4-5), represented the Prophets. Both were prominent mediators of God's rule to the nation of Israel (cf. Ex. 3:6; 4:16; 7:1; Deut. 18:15-18; 1 Kings 19:13; Acts 7:35). Their presence attested Jesus' role as the Messiah.

9:5-6. Peter's impulsive response, using the Hebrew title **Rabbi** (cf. 11:21; 14:45; also cf. "Teacher" in 4:38; 9:17; 10:35; 13:1), indicates that he did not understand this event. He said it was **good for them to be** there, implying that he wished to prolong the glorious experience. His idea that they build **three shelters** (tents of meeting, booths; cf. Lev. 23:33-43), **one** each for Jesus, **Moses,** and **Elijah,** confirms this and may imply that he viewed all three as being equal in importance. Thinking the kingdom had come, **Peter** felt it appropriate to build booths for the Feast of Tabernacles (Zech. 14:16). Unwittingly or not, Peter (cf. Mark 8:32) was again resisting the suffering which Jesus had said would precede the glory.

Mark's explanatory (*gar*, "for") comment is set off as a parenthesis. It shows that Peter, as spokesman, responded inappropriately because (*gar*) **they were so frightened** (*ekphoboi*, "terrified," a strong adjective used only here and in Heb. 12:21 where it is trans. "fear"; cf. the verb *phobeomai*, "be afraid," in Mark 4:41; 16:8) by this dazzling display of supernatural glory.

9:7-8. God the Father's response to Peter's suggestion set forth the true meaning of this event. The **cloud** that **enveloped them** (Jesus, Moses, Elijah) signified God's awesome presence (cf. Ex. 16:10; 19:9) and from it came His commanding **voice.** Once again, as at Jesus' baptism, the Father placed His unqualified endorsement on His beloved **Son** (cf. comments on Mark 1:11). Jesus' sonship

sets Him above all other men including Moses and Elijah.

Listen to Him (pres. imper.), actually means, "Be obedient to Him." This reflects the prophecy of Deuteronomy 18:15 (cf. Deut. 18:19, 22 also) and serves to identify Jesus as the new and final Mediator of God's rule in its present and future form (cf. Ps. 2:4-7; 2 Peter 1:16-19). Jesus succeeded Moses and Elijah, who suddenly disappeared leaving no one **except Jesus.** Their work was done and they were superseded. Jesus, not Moses or Elijah, is now God's authorized Ruler and Spokesman.

b. His command to silence (9:9-10)

9:9. On their descent from **the mountain Jesus** told the three disciples to keep silent about **what they had seen** till after His resurrection. Their misunderstanding of His messianic mission (8:29-33) was still evident at the transfiguration (cf. 9:5-6, 10; and comments on 8:30).

This was Jesus' last command to silence recorded by Mark and the only one on which He set a time limit. This implied that a time of proclamation (cf. 13:10; 14:9) would follow this period of silence. Only from the perspective of the Resurrection would they understand the transfiguration and thus be able to proclaim its meaning correctly.

9:10. The three disciples were perplexed by Jesus' command. **They kept** discussing among **themselves . . . what "rising from the dead" meant.** They believed in a future resurrection, but were puzzled by the unexpected announcement of Jesus' death and resurrection.

c. His declaration about Elijah (9:11-13)

9:11. The presence of Elijah at the transfiguration (v. 4), the confirmation of Jesus as Messiah (8:29; 9:7), and His reference to the Resurrection (v. 9) suggested that the end of all things was near. If so, where was **Elijah** who **must come first** to prepare the nation spiritually for the Messiah's coming? (cf. Mal. 3:1-4; 4:5-6) Perhaps the disciples thought Elijah's work of renewal would mean the Messiah would not need to suffer.

9:12-13. In reply, **Jesus** made two things clear. First, He acknowledged on the one hand that **Elijah does come** (lit., "is coming") **first** (before the Messiah) and restores ("is going to restore") **all things** through spiritual renewal (Mal. 4:5-6). On the other hand this does not remove the necessity for **the Son of Man** to **suffer much and be rejected** (cf. Ps. 22; Isa. 53, esp. v. 3).

Second, however **(but** in Gr. is a strong adversative), Jesus declared that indeed **Elijah has come** already. In a veiled way Mark recorded how Jesus identified John the Baptist as the one who fulfilled at Jesus' First Advent the role function expected of the end-time Elijah (cf. Mark 1:2-8; Matt. 17:13; Luke 1:17). Jesus gave John his true significance which John did not even recognize about himself (cf. John 1:21; comments on Matt. 11:14).

The expression, **They have done to him everything they wished,** denotes the ruthless, arbitrary suffering and death John experienced at the hands of Herod Antipas and Herodias (cf. Mark 6:14-29). In like manner Elijah suffered persecution at the hands of Ahab and Jezebel (cf. 1 Kings 19:1-3, 10). What these antagonists did to Elijah and John, people hostile to God would do to Jesus.

John the Baptist fulfilled the Elijah prophecy (Mal. 4:5-6) typically at Christ's First Advent. Yet Malachi's prophecy (Mal. 4:5-6) indicates that Elijah himself will also appear just before Christ's Second Advent (cf. Rev. 11).

5. THE CURE OF A DEMON-POSSESSED BOY (9:14-29)

(MATT. 17:14-21; LUKE 9:37-43)

This episode of desperate human need and the disciples' failure contrasts sharply with the glory of the transfiguration. It shows the reality of living in the world in the absence of Jesus.

The disciples from whom help could be expected (cf. Mark 6:7) were powerless. Mark 9:28-29 provides the key to understanding this incident. In Jesus' absence they must live and work by faith in God, expressed through prayer. The extended account (in contrast with Matt. and Luke) and the vivid details once again suggest the input of Peter's eyewitness report.

9:14-15. When Jesus and the three disciples (cf. v. 2) returned **to the other nine disciples, they saw a large crowd** gathered **around** the nine and Law

teachers **arguing with them.** The subject of the dispute is not stated.

As soon as (*euthys;* cf. 1:10) the crowd **saw Jesus** they became greatly amazed (*exethambēthēsan,* "alarmed"; cf. 14:33; 16:5-6) **and ran to greet Him.** Their astonishment was not due to some afterglow from the transfiguration (cf. 9:9) but to the unexpected yet opportune presence of Jesus in their midst.

9:16-18. Jesus **asked** the nine **what** the argument was **about. A man in the crowd,** the father of the demon-possessed boy, explained the situation to Jesus. Respectfully addressing Jesus as **Teacher** (cf. v. 5), the father said he had **brought** his **son** to Jesus for healing because the boy was **possessed by a spirit** (cf. comments on 1:23-24) who deprived **him** of his power of **speech** (and hearing; cf. 9:25). Also the demon often convulsed him with violent seizures symptomatic of epilepsy. The demon's attempts to destroy the lad (cf. vv. 18, 21-22, 26) show again the purpose of demon possession (cf. comments on 5:1-5).

The father's appeal to **the disciples to** exorcise **the** demon was legitimate because Jesus had given them authority over evil spirits (cf. 6:7).

9:19. Jesus addressed the crowd but especially His disciples with deep emotion (cf. 3:5; 8:12). **O unbelieving generation** emphasizes the characteristic cause of all spiritual failure—lack of faith in God (cf. 9:23; 10:27). The rhetorical questions further reflect Jesus' continued distress over His disciples' spiritual dullness (cf. 4:40; 6:50-52; 8:17-21). Yet He intended to act with power where they had failed, so He commanded, **Bring the boy to Me.**

9:20-24. When the demonic **spirit saw Jesus,** he **immediately** (*euthys;* cf. 1:10) **threw the** lad **into a** violent seizure, reducing him to utter helplessness (cf. 9:18).

In reply to Jesus' compassionate inquiry, the **father** said his son had experienced such pathetic and near-fatal convulsions **from childhood.** The lad's condition was long-standing and critical. The words, **If You can do anything,** indicate that the disciples' inability to expel the demon (v. 18) had shaken the father's faith in Jesus' ability.

Jesus took up the father's words of doubt, **If You can,** to show that the point was not His ability to heal the boy but the father's ability to trust in God who can do what is humanly impossible (cf. 10:27). Jesus then challenged the father not to doubt: **Everything is possible for him who believes** (cf. 9:29). Faith sets no limits on God's power and submits itself to His will (cf. 14:35-36; 1 John 5:14-15).

The father's response was immediate (*euthys*). He declared his faith (**I do believe**), but also acknowledged its weakness: **Help me overcome my unbelief!** This brings out an essential element of Christian faith—it is possible only with the help of the One who is its Object.

9:25-27. When Jesus saw that a curious **crowd was** converging on **the scene** (apparently He had withdrawn briefly), **He rebuked** ("ordered"; cf. 1:25) **the evil** (lit., "unclean"; cf. 1:23, 34) **spirit** with two commands: **come out . . . and never enter him again.**

With a final burst of violence on his victim and a scream of rage (cf. 1:26), the demon fled. **The boy** lay limp in utter exhaustion looking **like a corpse so that many** concluded, **He's dead. But Jesus . . . lifted him . . . up.** Mark's parallel wording in the account of the raising of Jairus' daughter (cf. 5:39-42) suggests that breaking from Satan's power is like passing from death to life. To accomplish this in a final, irreversible sense necessitated the death and resurrection of Jesus Himself.

9:28-29. These verses conclude this incident and explain why the disciples failed. **After** going **indoors** (lit., "into the house"; cf. 7:17; the location is unnamed) the **disciples asked** Jesus **privately** (*kat' idian;* cf. 4:34) **why** they could not expel the demon.

Jesus explained, **This kind**—probably demonic spirits in general rather than a special type of demon—**can come out only** (lit., "is not able to come out by anything except . . .") **by prayer.** The disciples had failed because they had not prayerfully depended on God's power. Apparently they had trusted in past successes (cf. 6:7, 13) and had failed.

Nearly all major ancient Greek manuscripts have "prayer and fasting" at the end of 9:29 (NIV marg.). Perhaps the words were added early by some scribes to the textual tradition to support asceticism. But the words, if original, refer to a practical means of focusing one's atten-

tion more fully on God for a specific purpose, for a limited period of time.

B. The second Passion prediction unit (9:30–10:31)

1. JESUS' SECOND PREDICTION OF HIS DEATH AND RESURRECTION (9:30-31) (MATT. 17:22-23A; LUKE 9:43B-44)

9:30-31. Jesus and His disciples **left that place** (cf. vv. 14, 28, probably near Caesarea Philippi) **and** were passing **through** northeastern **Galilee** (cf. 1:9), heading toward Capernaum (9:33). This was the first leg of their final journey southward to Jerusalem. **Jesus** wanted to keep their presence from becoming known **because** His public ministry in Galilee had ended and now **He** wished to prepare **His disciples** for the future.

His coming death was a constant theme of His **teaching** on this journey. He said that He, **the Son of Man** (cf. 8:31) would **be betrayed** to both Jews and Gentiles. "Betrayed" (*paradidotai*) means "deliver up" or "hand over." It was used both of Judas' betrayal of Jesus (3:19; 14:41; Luke 24:7) and of God's delivering up Jesus to death for the redemption of sinners (Isa. 53:6, 12; Acts 2:23; Rom. 8:32). The latter idea is probably intended here, suggesting that the implied Agent of the passive verb is God, not Judas.

2. THE DISCIPLES' LACK OF UNDERSTANDING (9:32) (MATT. 17:23B; LUKE 9:45)

9:32. The disciples failed to **understand what** Jesus **meant** (cf. v. 10) **and were afraid to** inquire further. Perhaps this was because they remembered Jesus' rebuke of Peter (8:33) or, more likely, because His words had a devastating effect on their hopes for a reigning Messiah.

3. JESUS' LESSONS ON THE MEANING OF DISCIPLESHIP (9:33–10:31)

This section has two geographical settings. First, Jesus taught His disciples in a house in Capernaum, Galilee (9:33-50). Second, Jesus resumed a public as well as a private teaching ministry in Judea and Perea (10:1-31).

a. The essence of true greatness (9:33-37) (Matt. 18:1-5; Luke 9:46-48)

9:33-34. Jesus and His disciples **came to Capernaum** for the last time after

145

an absence of several months (cf. 8:13, 22, 27). **When** they were **in the house** (cf. 2:1-2; 3:20; 7:17) Jesus candidly **asked them what** they were . . . **arguing about on the road** (*en tē hodō*, "on the way"; cf. comments on 1:2). Once again His pointed question opened the way for additional teaching (cf. 8:27, 29).

The disciples were ashamed to admit **they had argued about who was the greatest** among them. Matters of rank were important to the Jews (cf. Luke 14:7-11) so it was natural for the disciples to be concerned about their status in the coming messianic kingdom. Perhaps the privileges given to Peter, James, and John (cf. Mark 5:37; 9:2) fueled the argument. Whatever its cause, it showed that the Twelve did not understand or accept what Jesus' Passion prediction (cf. v. 31) meant for them.

9:35. After **sitting down,** the recognized position of a Jewish teacher (cf. Matt. 5:1; 13:1), **Jesus summoned the Twelve.** He taught them the essence of true greatness: **If anyone wants** (cf. Mark 8:34) **to be first,** to have the highest position among the "great" in God's kingdom, **he must be the very last** (lit., "he shall be last of all," by deliberate, voluntary choice) **and the servant of all.** Here "servant" (*diakonos*) depicts one who attends to the needs of others freely, not one in a servile position (as a *doulos*, a slave). Jesus did not condemn the desire to improve one's position in life but He did teach that greatness in His kingdom was not determined by status but by service (cf. 10:43-45).

9:36-37. To illustrate servanthood Jesus set **a little child** from the home (cf. v. 33, perhaps Peter's child) **among** the disciples. To be a "servant of all" included giving attention to a child, the least (cf. "the very last," v. 35) significant person in Jewish as well as Greco-Roman society which idealized the mature adult (cf. TDNT, s.v. "*pais*," 5:639-52).

Jesus took the child **in His arms** (cf. 10:13-16). To welcome, that is, to serve or show kindness to (cf. 6:11; Luke 9:53) **one of these little children,** who represented the lowliest disciple (cf. Mark 9:42), **in** Jesus' **name** (on His behalf) is equivalent to welcoming Jesus Himself (cf. Matt. 25:40 and comments on Mark 6:7). But to do this was not to **welcome** Jesus *only* but also the heavenly Father **who sent** Him to earth (cf. John 3:17; 8:42). This gives dignity to the task of serving others.

b. The rebuke of a sectarian attitude (9:38-42)
(Luke 9:49-50)

9:38. Jesus' words (v. 37) prompted **John** (cf. 3:17; 5:37; 9:2), addressing Him as **Teacher** (cf. 4:38; 9:5), to report an attempt by the disciples **to stop** an anonymous exorcist from **driving out demons in** Jesus' **name** (cf. comments on 1:23-28; 5:6-7). They did this **because he was not one of** them; he was a disciple but not one of the Twelve commissioned by Jesus to do this work (cf. 6:7, 12-13). It was not the man's misuse of Jesus' name (as in Acts 19:13-16) that troubled them but rather his *unauthorized* use of the name. Furthermore, he was successful (in contrast with the nine; Mark 9:14-18). This incident revealed the Twelve's narrow exclusivism.

9:39-40. Jesus told them to **stop** hindering this exorcist because **no one** performs **a miracle** (*dynamin,* a mighty "deed") **in** His **name** and then immediately turns around and publicly speaks evil of Him.

Jesus' acceptance of this man was reinforced by the maxim, **Whoever is not against us is for us** (cf. the reverse of this in Matt. 12:30). "Against us" and "for us" leave no room for neutrality. If one is working for Jesus, in His name (cf. Mark 9:38), he cannot work against Him at the same time.

Though this man did not follow Jesus in exactly the same way as the Twelve, he nevertheless followed Him truly and stood against Satan.

9:41. With a solemn affirmation (**I tell you the truth**; cf. 3:28) Jesus broadened His words (in 9:39-40) to include activity besides exorcism. Even one who performs the smallest act of hospitality in Jesus' name (cf. v. 37), such as giving **a cup of water** to someone **because** he belongs **to Christ will certainly not** (*ou mē,* emphatic negation) **lose his reward.** He will ultimately be recompensed by participation in God's kingdom (cf. v. 47; 10:29-30; Matt. 25:34-40), not on the basis of merit (a good deed) but because of God's gracious promise to people of faith (cf. Luke 12:31-32). Jesus' use of the title "Christ" instead of "Son of Man" is rare in the Synoptic Gospels.

9:42. This verse concludes the thought in verses 35-41 and sets the stage for verses 43-50. Jesus sternly warned **anyone** who would deliberately turn somebody away from believing in Him. The punishment for such an offense was so severe that **it would be better for him to be** drowned in **the sea** before he could cause **one of these little ones who believe in** Jesus (i.e., lowly disciples, including children, who are immature in faith; cf. vv. 37, 41) **to sin.**

The verb "cause to sin" (*skandalisē*; cf. v. 43) must be understood from a future judgment viewpoint (cf. vv. 43-48). It refers to enticing or provoking a disciple to turn away from Jesus, resulting in serious spiritual damage. The undeveloped faith of the exorcist (v. 38) or anyone else who acts in Jesus' name (v. 41) should be encouraged rather than ruined by harsh criticism or sectarian bias.

The **large millstone** (*mylos onikos*, lit., "donkey millstone") was a heavy, flat stone turned by a donkey when it was grinding grain; this differed from the small hand mill (*mylos*) used by women (Matt. 24:41). Punishment by drowning someone this way was no doubt familiar to Jesus' disciples (cf. Josephus *The Antiquities of the Jews* 14. 15. 10).

c. The snare of sin and the radical demands of discipleship (9:43-50) (Matt. 18:7-9)

9:43-48. These strong words warn disciples about the danger of letting *themselves* be led astray. Jesus reinforced the demands of discipleship (cf. 8:34-38; 10:24-31) in hyperboles (cf. TDNT, s.v. "*melos*," 4:559-61).

If (*ean*, "whenever," indicating a real possibility) the activity of **your hand,** an instrument of inward inclinations (cf. 7:20-23), **causes you to sin** (*skandalisē*, "should entice you to fall away"; cf. 9:42) then **cut it off.** Jesus meant a disciple should take prompt, decisive action against whatever would draw him away from his allegiance to Him. The same is true of the **foot** and the **eye,** for temptations come through various means. Whatever *tempts* a disciple to cling to this world's life must be removed much as a surgeon amputates a gangrenous limb.

It is better to be a disciple and **to enter** eternal **life** (cf. 10:17, 30) in God's future **kingdom** (9:47), and to do so **maimed,** minus earthly possessions that have been renounced, **than to** be an unbeliever. An unbeliever retains his allegiance to this world, refuses eternal **life** with God on His terms, **and** so will be **thrown into hell** (*geennan*; vv. 45, 47).

The Greek word *geenna* ("Gehenna," trans. "hell") is transliterated from two Hebrew words meaning "Valley of Hinnom," a place south of Jerusalem where children were once sacrificed to the pagan god Molech (2 Chron. 28:3; 33:6; Jer. 7:31; 19:5-6; 32:35). Later, during the reforms of Josiah (2 Kings 23:10) the site became Jerusalem's refuse dump where fires burned continually to consume regular deposits of worm-infested garbage. In Jewish thought the imagery of fire and worms vividly portrayed the place of future eternal punishment for the wicked (cf. the apocryphal Judith 16:17 and Ecclesiasticus 7:17). Jesus used the word *geenna* in 11 of its 12 New Testament occurrences (the one exception is James 3:6).

Where the fire never goes out is probably Mark's explanation of Gehenna for his Roman readers. The **worm** (internal torment) and **the** unquenchable **fire** (external torment) (quoted from the LXX of Isa. 66:24) vividly portray the unending, conscious punishment that awaits all who refuse God's salvation. The essence of hell is unending torment and eternal exclusion from His presence.

9:49. This enigmatic statement, unique to Mark, is difficult to interpret. About 15 possible explanations have been suggested.

An explanatory "for" (*gar*, not trans. in the NIV) and the word "fire" link this verse to verses 43-48. **Everyone** may be explained in one of three ways: (1) It could refer to every unbeliever who enters hell. They **will be salted with fire** in the sense that as salt preserves food so they will be preserved throughout an eternity of fiery judgment. (2) "Everyone" could refer to every disciple living in this hostile world. They will be "salted with fire" in the sense that Old Testament sacrifices were seasoned with salt (Lev. 2:13; Ezek. 43:24). Disciples, living sacrifices (cf. Rom. 12:1), will be seasoned with purifying fiery trials (cf. Prov. 27:21;

Isa. 48:10; 1 Peter 1:7; 4:12). The trials will purge out what is contrary to God's will and preserve what is consistent with it. (3) "Everyone" could refer to every person in general. All will be "salted with fire" in a time and manner appropriate to their relationship with Jesus—for nonbelievers, the preserving fire of final judgment; for disciples, the refining fire of present trials and suffering. This last view seems preferable.

9:50. "Salt" links this verse to verse 49. **Salt is good,** useful. Salt as a condiment and a preservative was common in the ancient world. It was a necessity of life in Palestine, so it had commercial value.

The main source of salt in Palestine was from the area southwest of the Dead (Salt) Sea. The coarse, impure salt from the saline deposits of this area was susceptible to deterioration, leaving savorless saltlike crystals as residue. If (*ean*, "whenever"; cf. v. 43) **it loses its saltiness,** its savory quality, it cannot be regained so such salt is worthless.

Have salt in yourselves (pres. imper.) points to the disciples' need to "have salt" which is good (not worthless) *within* themselves continually. Here "salt" depicts what distinguishes a disciple from a nondisciple (cf. Matt. 5:13; Luke 14:34). A disciple is to maintain his allegiance to Jesus at all costs and to purge out destructive influences (cf. Mark 9:43-48).

The second command, **Be at peace** (pres. imper.) **with each other** is based on the first command and rounds out the discussion provoked by the disciples' strife (vv. 33-34). In essence Jesus said, "Be loyal to Me and then you will be able to maintain peace with one another instead of arguing about status" (cf. Rom. 12:16a; 14:19).

d. The permanence of marriage (10:1-12)
(Matt. 19:1-12; Luke 16:18)

10:1. On Jesus' final journey to Jerusalem, He **left that place,** Capernaum in Galilee (cf. 9:33), **and went into . . . Judea** west of the Jordan River **and** then **across the Jordan** into Perea on the east side.

Because of His popularity in these areas (cf. 3:8) He drew **crowds of people** around Him **again** and **as was His custom** (cf. 1:21-22; 2:13; 4:1-2; 6:2, 6b, 34; 11:17; 12:35) **He taught them** again. The second "again," left untranslated in the NIV, was included for emphasis. Thus He resumed His public ministry (cf. 9:30-31).

Though Jesus' later Judean and Perean ministries covered a span of about six months, Mark recorded only some of the closing events which probably occurred in Perea (cf. 10:2-52 with Luke 18:15–19:27).

10:2. A group of **Pharisees** questioned Jesus about **divorce** in order to test (from *peirazō*; cf. 8:11; 12:15b) **Him.** They wanted Him to give a self-incriminating answer that would arouse opposition against Him. Perhaps He would contradict Deuteronomy 24:1-4 (cf. Mark 10:4). All Pharisees agreed that this Old Testament passage permitted divorce, that only the husband could initiate it, and that divorce implied the right to remarry. But they disagreed on the grounds of divorce. The strict view of Rabbi Shammai allowed divorce only if a wife were guilty of immorality; the lenient view of Rabbi Hillel allowed a husband to divorce his wife for almost any reason (cf. Mishnah *Gittin* 9. 10). Perhaps Jesus would take sides in this dispute and thereby split the ranks of His followers. Or perhaps He would offend Herod Antipas as John the Baptist had done (cf. 6:17-19) and be arrested since He was under Herod's jurisdiction in Perea. Herod had married his half-niece Herodias despite the decrees in Leviticus 18.

10:3-4. Jesus' counterquestion set aside the casuistry of Rabbinic interpretation and directed the Pharisees to the Old Testament (cf. 7:9, 13). The verb **command** indicates **He** asked about Mosaic legislation on the divorce issue.

In response, they summarized Deuteronomy 24:1-4, the basis for their divorce practices. They believed that **Moses permitted a** husband to divorce his wife if he protected her from the charge of adultery by writing out **a certificate of divorce** in the presence of witnesses, signing it, and giving it to her (cf. Mishnah *Gittin* 1. 1-3; 7. 2). In ancient Israel adultery was punishable by death, usually stoning (cf. Lev. 20:10; Deut. 22:22-25), when guilt was clearly established (cf. Num. 5:11-31). By Jesus' time (ca. A.D. 30) the death penalty was dropped (cf. Matt. 1:19-20; TDNT, s.v.

"moicheuō," 4:730-5), but Rabbinic law compelled a husband to divorce an adulterous wife (cf. Mishnah *Sotah* 1. 4-5; *Gittin* 4. 7).

10:5. Moses wrote . . . this Law (Deut. 24:1-4), **Jesus** said, in view of their hardheartedness, their obstinate refusal to accept God's view of marriage. Moses *acknowledged* the presence of divorce in Israel but did not institute or authorize it.

10:6-8. Jesus then contrasted their view of marriage with God's view **from the beginning of Creation** (Jesus quoted both Gen. 1:27 and 2:24). **God made them,** the first couple, Adam and Eve, distinctly **male and female** yet fully complementary to each other. **A man shall leave** behind **his** parents, shall **be united to his wife, and the two**—man and woman—**will become one flesh.** As "one flesh" they form a new unit comprising a sexually intimate, all-encompassing couple just as indissoluble in God's present Creation order as a blood relationship between parent and child.

So (*hōste,* "so then") **they are no longer two, but one** (lit., "one flesh," a one-flesh unit). Marriage is not a contract of temporary convenience which can be readily broken; it is a covenant of mutual fidelity to a lifelong union made before God (cf. Prov. 2:16-17; Mal. 2:13-16).

10:9. Jesus then added a prohibition. **Therefore,** in light of verses 6-8, **what God has joined together** as one flesh, **let man not separate** (*chōrizetō,* pres. tense; cf. this Gr. verb in 1 Cor. 7:10, 15). "Man" (*anthrōpos,* probably meaning the husband) is to stop disrupting marriage through divorce. Marriage is to be a monogamous, heterosexual, permanent one-flesh relationship. Jesus indirectly confirmed John the Baptist's courageous pronouncement (cf. Mark 6:18), contradicting the Pharisees' lax views.

10:10-12. Later, **when** Jesus' **disciples** questioned Him privately **about this** subject **in the house** (cf. 7:17), **He** added, **Anyone who divorces** (*apolysē,* "releases," same word in 15:6, 9, 15) **his wife and marries another woman commits adultery against her,** his first wife (cf. Ex. 20:14, 17). According to Mark 10:12, which is unique to Mark, the same applies to a woman who **divorces her husband and marries another man.** These words were significant for Mark's

Roman readers since under Roman law a wife could initiate divorce. Though not allowed under Jewish law such action was sometimes practiced in Palestine (e.g., Herodias, 6:17-18).

Divorce violates God's Creation ordinance, but does not dissolve it. Jesus left open the possibility of divorce for sexual immorality as demanded by Jewish law in New Testament times (10:4). But remarriage, though permitted under Rabbinic law, was here forbidden by Jesus (cf. TDNT, s.v. *"gameō, gamos,"* 1:648-51; *"moicheuō,"* 4:733-5). (Many interpreters believe that Jesus gave one exception to this. See comments on Matt. 5:32; 19:1-12.) God's desire for a "broken" marriage is forgiveness and reconciliation (cf. Hosea 1-3; 1 Cor. 7:10-11).

e. The reception of God's kingdom in childlike trust (10:13-16)
   (Matt. 19:13-15; Luke 18:15-17)

This episode complemented Jesus' teaching on marriage and offset the Pharisees' opposition (Mark 10:2-12). It probably took place "in the house" (v. 10). The incident came to be used in later church history in connection with infant baptism but without clear warrant from the passage.

10:13. People—mothers, fathers, older children, and others—**were bringing little children** (*paidia,* those ranging from babies to preteens, cf. same word in 5:39; a different word *brephē,* meaning infants and young children, is used in Luke 18:15) **to Jesus** in order that He might **touch them,** a visible means of conveying God's blessing on their future lives (cf. Mark 10:16). **The disciples rebuked them** (cf. 8:30, 32-33) and tried to keep them from going to Jesus. They probably thought children were unimportant (cf. 9:36-37) and should not waste His time—another instance where they thought only in human-cultural categories (cf. 8:32-33; 9:33-37).

10:14. Jesus . . . was indignant (cf. v. 41) at the disciples' interference (cf. 9:38). This verb of strong emotional reaction is unique to Mark who highlighted Jesus' emotions more than the other Gospel writers (cf. 1:25, 41, 43; 3:5; 7:34; 8:12; 9:19). Jesus' sharp double command—**Let** (lit., "start allowing") **the little children come to Me, and do not hinder** (lit., "stop preventing") them—was a rebuke to the disciples (who had rebuked the people!).

Jesus welcomed the children because the kingdom of God, God's present spiritual rule in people's lives (cf. comments on 1:14-15), belongs as a possession to such as these. All, including children, who come to Jesus in childlike trust and dependence, are given free access to Jesus.

10:15. In a solemn pronouncement (I tell you the truth; cf. 3:28) Jesus developed the truth in 10:14. Whoever will not receive God's kingdom as a gift now with the trustful attitude of a child will never (emphatic negative, ou mē, "by no means") enter it. He will be excluded from its future blessings, specifically eternal life (cf. vv. 17, 23-26). God's kingdom is not gained by human achievement or merit; it must be received as God's gift through simple trust by those who acknowledge their inability to gain it any other way (cf. comments on 1:15).

10:16. Jesus' loving action (cf. 9:36) vividly illustrated that His blessing is freely given to those who receive it trustingly. The intensive compound verb blessed (kateulogei, imperf., occurring only here in the NT) emphasizes the warmhearted fervor with which Jesus blessed each child who came to Him.

f. The rejection of God's kingdom by trust in riches (10:17-27)
(Matt. 19:16-26; Luke 18:18-27)

This event probably took place as Jesus was leaving the house (cf. Mark 10:10) somewhere in Perea. The rich man illustrated those who fail to acknowledge their own inability to gain eternal life and to receive it as God's gift (cf. vv. 13-16).

10:17. As Jesus was setting out on His way (cf. comments on 8:27) to Jerusalem (10:32) a man, influential, wealthy, and young (cf. Matt. 19:20, 22; Luke 18:18), came running to Him. His eager approach, kneeling posture, sincere form of address (Good Teacher, not used by Jews to address a Rabbi), and profound question revealed his earnestness and respect for Jesus as a spiritual Guide.

This man's question indicated that he viewed eternal life as something to be achieved by doing good (in contrast with Mark 10:15; cf. Matt. 19:16) and also that he felt insecure about his future destiny. References to eternal life (mentioned in

Mark only in 10:17, 30), "entering God's kingdom" (vv. 23-25), and being "saved" (v. 26) all focus on the future possession of life with God, though a person enters it now by accepting God's rule in his earthly life. John's Gospel emphasizes the *present* possession of eternal life.

10:18. Jesus challenged the man's faulty perception of good as something measured by human achievement. No one is good, absolutely perfect, except God alone, the true Source and Standard of goodness. The man needed to see himself in the context of God's perfect character. Jesus' response did not deny His own deity but was a veiled claim to it. The man, unwittingly calling Him "good," needed to perceive Jesus' true identity. (Later, however, he dropped the word "good," v. 20.)

10:19-20. In answering the man's question directly, Jesus quoted five commandments from the so-called "second table" of the Decalogue (cf. Ex. 20:12-16; Deut. 5:16-20) but in a different order. Obedience to those commands dealing with human relationships are more easily verified in a person's conduct than are the earlier commands (Ex. 20:3-8). The command, Do not defraud, not a part of the Decalogue and occurring only in Mark, may represent the 10th commandment (Ex. 20:17). But more likely, it is an appropriate supplement to the 8th and/or 9th commandments (Ex. 20:15-16) applicable to a wealthy person (cf. Lev. 6:2-5; Mal. 3:5).

The man's reply shows he firmly believed he had kept these commandments perfectly (cf. Phil. 3:6) since he was a boy, since age 12 when he assumed personal responsibility for keeping the Law as a "son of the Law" (bar Mitzvah; cf. Luke 2:42-47). Perhaps he had expected Jesus to prescribe something meritorious that he needed to do to make up for any lack.

10:21-22. With a penetrating look (from emblepō; cf. 3:5), Jesus saw beneath the rich man's religious devotion to his deepest need and loved him, something mentioned only in Mark (cf. comment on 10:14). The one necessary thing he lacked was unrivaled allegiance to God, since wealth was his god (v. 22). He was devoted to it rather than God, thereby breaking the first commandment (Ex. 20:3).

Jesus commanded two things: (1) The man was to go, sell all his assets, and give to the poor, thereby removing the obstacle blocking him from eternal life, namely, self-righteous achievement coupled with a love for money. (2) Also Jesus told him to follow (pres. imper.) Him to Jerusalem and the Cross. The way to eternal life was in turning from trust in self-attainments and earthly securities to trust in Jesus (cf. Mark 10:14-15).

The man, saddened by Jesus' directives, went away. This particular *form* of self-denial—to sell all—was appropriate in this situation but is not a requirement for all prospective disciples.

10:23-25. When Jesus told the disciples that it is hard . . . for the rich to enter God's kingdom, they were amazed (*ethambounto*, "surprised"; cf. 1:27; 10:32) because in Judaism riches were a mark of God's favor and thus an advantage, not a barrier, in relation to God's kingdom. Only here in the Synoptic Gospels did Jesus address the Twelve as children (cf. John 13:33), reflecting their spiritual immaturity.

In light of their surprise Jesus repeated and clarified His original statement. If the words "for those who trust in riches" (NIV marg.) are omitted, Mark 10:24 (which is unique to Mark) applies to everybody who is confronted with the demands of God's kingdom. If included, they explain the rich man's difficulty and expose the danger of trusting in riches.

The humorous comparison (v. 25) employs a memorable Jewish proverb to depict the impossible. It is easier by comparison for a camel, the largest animal in Palestine at that time, to go through the eye of a common sewing needle (the smallest opening) than for a rich man who trusts in his riches to enter God's kingdom.

10:26-27. Jesus' statement (v. 25) greatly amazed (*exeplēssonto*, "astounded, struck out of their senses, overwhelmed"; cf. 1:22; 6:2; 7:37; 11:18) the disciples. They carried it to its logical conclusion: If it is impossible for a rich man to enter God's kingdom, Who then can be saved? (delivered to life eternal; cf. 10:17, 30)

Jesus offset their concern by declaring that salvation is impossible with men—beyond their human merit or achievement—but not with God. It is not beyond His power to bring about because

all things necessary for people's salvation—rich and poor alike—are possible with God (cf. Job 42:2). What people cannot effect, God can and does by His grace (cf. Eph. 2:8-10).

g. The rewards of discipleship (10:28-31) (Matt. 19:27-30; Luke 18:28-30)

10:28. Acting as spokesman (cf. 8:29) Peter presumptuously reminded Jesus that the Twelve, unlike the rich man (we is emphatic in Gr., suggesting the contrast), had left everything to follow Him (cf. 1:16-20; 2:14; 10:21-22). The implication was, "What recompense shall we get?" (cf. Matt. 19:27) Again this reflected the disciples' tendency to think of material honors in God's kingdom (cf. Mark 9:33-34; 10:35-37; Matt. 19:28-29).

10:29-30. In another solemn affirmation (I tell you the truth; cf. v. 15; 3:28) Jesus acknowledged that their allegiance to Him and the gospel (cf. 1:1; 8:35) entailed a break with old ties—home, loved ones, or property (fields), as the case may be (cf. 13:11-13; Luke 9:59-62). But to everyone who makes the break Jesus promised that all these things will be replaced a hundredfold by new ties with fellow disciples (cf. Mark 3:31-35; Acts 2:41-47; 1 Tim. 5:1-2) in this present Age, the time period between Jesus' First and Second Advents. Then in the Age to come, the future Age following Jesus' return (from a NT viewpoint), each will receive the ultimate recompense—eternal life (cf. Mark 10:17).

In verse 30 the word "father" (cf. v. 29) is omitted since God is the Father of the new spiritual family (cf. 11:25). The words with them (the rewards), persecutions are added realistically by Mark alone. As Jesus said later (10:43-45) discipleship involves service, which often includes suffering. This was relevant to Mark's Roman readers who faced persecution. This fact helped remove the temptation to associate with Jesus simply for the rewards (cf. v. 31).

10:31. This "floating saying" (cf. these same words in other contexts: Matt. 20:16; Luke 13:30) could be intended as (a) a warning against Peter's presumption (Mark 10:28), (b) a confirmation of Jesus' promise (vv. 29-30), or most likely, (c) a summary of Jesus' teaching about the servant nature of discipleship (cf. 9:35;

10:43-45). Rewards in God's kingdom are not based on earthly standards such as rank, priority, or duration of time served, personal merit, or sacrifice (cf. Matt. 20:1-16), but on commitment to Jesus and following Him faithfully.

C. The third Passion prediction unit (10:32-45)

1. JESUS' THIRD PREDICTION OF HIS DEATH AND RESURRECTION (10:32-34)
(MATT. 20:17-19; LUKE 18:31-34)

10:32a. Jesus and His disciples continued **on their way up** from the Jordan Valley (cf. v. 1) **to Jerusalem,** the first mention of their destination. **Jesus** was **leading** them, in accord with Rabbinic custom. This detail unique to Mark points to Jesus as the One who leads His people both in suffering and in triumph (the same verb is trans. "go[ing] ahead of" in 14:28 and 16:7).

His steadfast determination in the face of impending danger **astonished** (*ethambounto,* "surprised"; cf. 10:24; 1:27) **the disciples; indeed those who followed** were afraid (*ephobounto*; cf. 4:40-41; 6:50; 11:18; 16:8). Here Mark probably had *one* group—the Twelve—in mind. In 10:46, he indicated the presence of another group.

10:32b-34. Once **again** Jesus gathered **the Twelve** (cf. 3:13-15) around Him **and** revealed **what** would soon **happen to Him.** This third prediction is the most precise and comprehensive of the three Mark recorded (cf. comments on 8:31; 9:30-31; also see 9:12). Because He understood the Old Testament (cf. Ps. 22:6-8; Isa. 50:6; 52:13–53:12; Luke 18:31) and was aware of the contemporary religio-political climate (cf. Mark 8:15), He was well capable of making this explicit prediction.

Jesus used eight future-tense verbs, implying certainty, in describing the coming events. The new elements were that **the Son of Man** (cf. comments on 8:31) **will be betrayed** (cf. 9:31) into the hands of the *Jewish* leaders, the Sanhedrin (cf. 8:31). **They** would **condemn Him to death** (cf. 14:64) at the hands of **the Gentiles** (the Romans) since the Sanhedrin lacked the power to exercise capital punishment (cf. 15:1, 9-10). Before executing Him (15:24-25), the Romans would **mock Him** (cf. 15:18, 20), **spit on**

Him (cf. 15:19), and **flog Him** (cf. 15:15)—indications that His death would be by crucifixion (cf. Matt. 20:19). But the promise of resurrection offered hope for the future.

2. THE ESSENTIAL MEANING OF DISCIPLESHIP (10:35-45)
(MATT. 20:20-28)

10:35-37. James and John (cf. 1:19; 5:37; 9:2) approached Jesus privately, addressing **Him** as **Teacher** (cf. 4:38; 9:5). They asked for the places of highest honor and authority **in** His **glory,** the messianic kingdom rule which they expected He was about to establish openly (cf. 8:38; 9:1-2; 13:26). One of them wished to **sit at** His **right,** the highest assigned position, **and the other at** His **left,** the next highest place in a royal court (Josephus *The Antiquities of the Jews* 6. 11. 9).

Matthew added that their mother came with them and spoke for them (Matt. 20:20-21). She was Salome, probably a sister of Jesus' mother (cf. Matt. 27:56; Mark 15:40; John 19:25). If so, then James and John were Jesus' first cousins. Perhaps they hoped their family ties would help their cause.

10:38-39. Jesus told them they did **not** realize **what** was involved in their ambitious request. To ask for a place of honor in His glory was also a request to share His suffering since the one is a requisite to the other.

Jesus' question called for a negative response because the sufferings and death facing Him were unique to fulfilling His messianic mission. **The cup** was a common Jewish metaphor either for joy (cf. Pss. 23:5; 116:13) or for divine judgment against human sin, as here (cf. Ps. 75:7-8; Isa. 51:17-23; Jer. 25:15-28; 49:12; 51:7; Ezek. 23:31-34; Hab. 2:16; Zech. 12:2). Jesus applied this figure to Himself for He was to bear the wrath of God's judgment against sin in place of sinners (cf. Mark 10:45; 14:36; 15:34). He would **drink** the "cup" voluntarily.

The figure of **baptism** expresses a parallel thought. Being under water was an Old Testament picture of being overwhelmed by calamity (cf. Job 22:11; Ps. 69:2, 15; Isa. 43:2). Here the "calamity" Jesus faced was bearing the burden of God's judgment on sin which involved

New Testament Words for Redemption

Greek Words	English Meanings	References
agorazō (verb)	To buy, to purchase in the market (or slave market)	(1 Cor. 6:20; 7:23; 2 Peter 2:1; Rev. 5:9; 14:3-4)
exagorazō (verb)	To buy out, to purchase out of the market (or slave market)	(Gal. 3:13; 4:5; Eph. 5:16; Col. 4:5)
lytron (noun)	Ransom, price of release	(Matt. 20:28; Mark 10:45)
lytroomai (verb)	To ransom, to free by paying a ransom price	(Luke 24:21; Titus 2:14; 1 Peter 1:18)
lytrōsis (noun)	Act of freeing by paying a ransom price	(Luke 1:68; 2:38; Heb. 9:12)
apolytrōsis (noun)	A buying back, a setting free by paying a ransom price	(Luke 21:28; Rom. 3:24; 8:23; 1 Cor. 1:30; Eph. 1:7, 14; 4:30; Col. 1:14; Heb. 9:15; 11:35)

overwhelming sufferings culminating in His death (cf. Luke 12:50). He was to be baptized by God who placed these sufferings on Him (Isa. 53:4b, 11). James and John may have thought Jesus was describing a messianic battle and their confident reply, We can, showed their willingness to fight in it. But their reply also showed that they had not understood Jesus' words. So Jesus applied the same cup and baptism figures to them but in a different sense. In following Him they would share His sufferings (cf. 1 Peter 4:13) even to death but not in a redemptive sense. His prediction was fulfilled: James was the first apostle to be martyred (cf. Acts 12:2), whereas John, who endured many years of persecution and exile, was the last apostle to die (cf. John 21:20-23; Rev. 1:9).

10:40. Jesus denied their request for positions of honor. Such places were not within His jurisdiction to give. But He assured James and John that God the Father (cf. Matt. 20:23) will assign those positions to those for whom the places of honor have been prepared.

10:41-44. When the other 10 disciples found out about James and John's private attempt to gain preferential status, they became indignant (cf. v. 14) with them. This jealous reaction indicates that they also harbored those selfish ambitions. To avert disharmony among the Twelve and to reemphasize the meaning of true greatness (cf. 9:33-37) Jesus contrasted greatness in this world's kingdoms with that in God's kingdom. The contrast is not between two ways of ruling but between ruling (good or bad) and serving.

Gentile rulers . . . lord it over them, dominating and oppressing their subjects, and exercise authority over them, exploiting them. But it is not to be this way with Jesus' followers who are under God's rule. Whoever aspires to become great among you, let him be your (pl.) house servant (*diakonos*), one who voluntarily renders useful service to others.

Whoever aspires **to be first** (lit., "first among you") let him **be a slave** (*doulos*), one who forfeits his own rights in order to serve any and **all** (cf. comments on 9:35-37). A disciple is to serve others, not his own interests, voluntarily and sacrificially.

10:45. Jesus Himself is the supreme Example of true greatness (in contrast with v. 42). **The Son of Man** (cf. comments on 8:31) voluntarily veiled His glory (cf. 8:38; 13:26) and came as God's Servant (cf. Ps. 49:5-7; Isa. 52:13-53:12; Phil. 2:6-8) **not . . . to be served** by others **but to serve** them (cf. Mark 2:17; 10:46-52; Luke 22:27). The climax of His service was His death **as a ransom for many.** He did this voluntarily, sacrificially, vicariously, and obediently (cf. comments on Mark 15:34).

"Ransom" (*lytron*) occurs only here and in Matthew 20:28 in the New Testament. As "the price of release" it refers to a payment to effect the release of slaves or captives from bondage. It also includes the concept of substitution (cf. TDNT, s.v. "*lyō*," 4:328-35). People are captives under the power of sin and death (cf. Rom. 5:12; 6:20) from which they cannot free themselves. Jesus' substitutionary death paid the price that sets people free (cf. Rom. 6:22; Heb. 2:14-15). (See the chart, "New Testament Words for Redemption.")

The preposition "for" (*anti*), used in Mark only here, reinforces the idea of substitution. It means "instead of, in the place of" (cf. Matt. 2:22; Luke 11:11; 1 Peter 3:9). Jesus gave His life (*psychēn*) in the place of many (cf. Mark 14:24 where *hyper*, "for," is used).

"Many" is used in the inclusive sense of "all" (cf. 1:32-34; Isa. 53:10-12). It emphasizes how a large number derive redemptive benefit from the single sacrifice of the One Redeemer (cf. Rom. 5:15, 18-19). Jesus' death as a ransom extended beyond His own people to all peoples (cf. 1 Tim. 2:5-6).

D. Conclusion: The faith of blind Bartimaeus (10:46-52)
(Matt. 20:29-34; Luke 18:35-43)

This is the last healing miracle Mark recorded. It concludes his special section on discipleship (Mark 8:31–10:52) and is an excellent illustration of its meaning (cf.

10:52b). It also signifies that the disciples, despite their misunderstandings (cf. 8:32-33; 9:32; 10:35-41), would have clear sight (i.e., understanding) as Jesus opened their eyes to the full implications of His messiahship.

The vividness of the account (e.g., v. 50) suggests that it was an eyewitness report from one such as Peter. The three Synoptic Gospels record this event with some divergent details. Matthew mentioned two blind men (Matt. 20:30), and Luke placed the incident at Jesus' approach to Jericho instead of His exit (Luke 18:35). Probably two blind men were involved but Mark and Luke focused on one, perhaps the more vocal or well known. Also there were two Jerichos—an old and a new city—and the healings could have occurred as the crowd was leaving old Israelite Jericho (Matt. 20:29; Mark 10:46) and entering new Herodian Jericho (Luke 18:35), though the evidence that old Jericho was inhabited at that time is not certain.

10:46. Jesus and His disciples left Perea (cf. v. 1), crossed the Jordan, and **came to Jericho** in Judea. The Jericho of New Testament times, built by Herod the Great as the site for his winter palace, was about 5 miles west of the Jordan River, 1 mile south of the Old Testament city (Josh. 6; 2 Kings 2:4-5, 15-18), and 18 miles northeast of Jerusalem.

As they and **a large crowd,** probably Passover pilgrims en route to Jerusalem (cf. Ps. 42:4; Mark 14:1-2), **were leaving** Jericho, presumably **the** old **city,** they saw **a blind** beggar, **Bartimaeus,** an Aramaic name meaning **the Son of Timaeus.** Only Mark recorded his name, suggesting that perhaps Bartimaeus was known in the early church. He **was sitting** beside **the** road **begging,** a common sight near wealthy Jericho.

10:47-48. When Bartimaeus was informed that **Jesus of Nazareth** (cf. 1:24) was passing by, he clamored for His attention and relentlessly shouted for **Jesus** to **have mercy on** him (cf. Pss. 4:1; 6:2). No doubt he had heard reports that Jesus restored sight. When **many** people kept rebuking (cf. Mark 10:13) **him** to silence him, he cried out **more** intensely. They probably regarded him as a nuisance and may have resented any possible delay. They may also have been opposed to what he was shouting.

Son of David, occurring here for the first time in Mark, designated the Messiah as David's Descendant (2 Sam. 7:8-16) and became a recognized title of the Messiah-King (cf. comments on Mark 12:35-37; also cf. Isa. 11:1-5; Jer. 23:5-6; Ezek. 34:23-24; Matt. 1:1; 9:27; 12:23; 15:22; Rom. 1:3). Bartimaeus' using that title probably indicated that despite his physical blindness he believed Jesus of Nazareth was Israel's Messiah, in contrast with the blind unbelief of most Jews. Later he addressed Jesus more personally ("Rabbi," Mark 10:51) and followed Him (cf. v. 52b). Jesus did not silence him, implying He accepted the title.

10:49-52a. Jesus did not ignore Bartimaeus but directed that he be called, a reproof to those (perhaps including the disciples) who were attempting to silence him (cf. v. 14). In Jesus' determined movement toward Jerusalem He had time to serve someone in need (cf. vv. 43-45).

The crowd encouraged the beggar: **Cheer up!** (*tharsei,* "be courageous"; cf. 6:50) **On your feet!** (lit., "rise") **He's calling you.** This motivated Bartimaeus to toss aside his outer **cloak** which was spread before him to collect alms, jump up, **and** come **to Jesus.**

Jesus' question was not designed to get information but to encourage Bartimaeus to articulate his need and express his faith. Bartimaeus' simple response, **Rabbi, I want to see,** declared his confident trust in Jesus' ability. "Rabbi" (*Rhabbouni*) is an emphatic, personal form meaning, "My Lord, my Master" (cf. John 20:16).

Jesus acknowledged his faith: **Go . . . your faith has healed** (*sesōken,* "saved") **you.** Faith was the necessary means, not the efficient cause of his healing (cf. comments on Mark 5:34). Bartimaeus' physical "salvation" (i.e., deliverance from darkness [blindness] to light [sight]) was an outward picture of his spiritual "salvation" (cf. Ps. 91:14-16; Luke 3:4-6).

10:52b. Immediately (*euthys,* cf. 1:10; contrast 8:22-26) Bartimaeus **received his sight and** began to follow **Jesus along the road** (*en tē hodō,* "on the way"; cf. comments on 1:2). Though he accompanied Jesus to Jerusalem, perhaps to offer a thanksgiving sacrifice in the temple, he also became a "follower" in the sense of a loyal disciple (cf. 8:34). Bartimaeus pictured discipleship clearly.

He recognized his inability, trusted Jesus as the One to give him God's gracious mercy, and when he could "see" clearly he began to follow Jesus.

VII. Jesus' Ministry in and around Jerusalem (11:1-13:37)

The fifth major section of Mark's Gospel presents Jesus' ministry in and around Jerusalem. He denounced the Jewish religious leaders for rejecting God's messengers, especially the last One, God's Son. Jesus also warned of God's impending judgment on Jerusalem and the nation.

The section revolves around three or four days (11:1-11, Sunday; 11:12-19, Monday; 11:20-13:37, Tuesday and probably Wednesday). Precise temporal links are missing between 11:20 and 13:37, suggesting that Mark arranged this material topically, not in strict chronological order (cf. 2:1-3:6). If so, he intended it to be a select summary of Jesus' teaching, some of which took place on Tuesday and some on Wednesday of His Passion Week (cf. 14:49). The Passion narrative opens with a new chronological starting point (cf. 14:1). The chronological framework for 11:1-16:8 is one week, extending from Palm Sunday to Easter Sunday.

A. Jesus' entry into Jerusalem (11:1-11) (Matt. 21:1-11; Luke 19:28-44; John 12:12-19)

Mark's account of this event exhibits vivid detail but is somewhat restrained in proclaiming Jesus as the Messiah (cf. comments on Mark 1:43-44; 8:30-31). Only later (probably after Jesus' resurrection) did His disciples fully understand.

11:1a. Less than a mile southeast of **Jerusalem** was the village of **Bethphage** (lit., "house of unripe figs") **and** about two miles out was **Bethany** (lit., "house of dates or figs") on the eastern side of **the Mount of Olives,** a high ridge about two miles long known for its many olive trees. In Bethany, the last stopping place on the desolate and unsafe road from Jerusalem to Jericho (cf. 10:46), was the home of Mary, Martha, and Lazarus (John 11:1), which generally served as Jesus' abode when He was in Judea (cf. Mark 11:11). Bethany was also the home of Simon the Leper (14:3-9).

11:1b-3. Jesus sent two . . . disciples (cf. 14:13) into **the village ahead of** (*katenanti*, "opposite," perhaps across the Mount of Olives from Bethany) them, presumably Bethphage, to find immediately (*euthys*; cf. 1:10) on entry, an unbroken **colt** of a donkey. They were to **untie it and bring it** to Jesus. Matthew included mention of the mother with her colt (see comments on Matt. 21:2).

If anyone challenged them they were to say, **The Lord needs it and will send it back here** (to the village) **shortly** (*euthys*, "without delay"; cf. Mark 1:10). It is generally assumed that Jesus here referred to Himself by the title "Lord" (*kyrios*; cf. 5:19) not to the colt's owner.

11:4-6. Mark recorded the disciples' carrying out Jesus' instructions (cf. vv. 2-3), demonstrating the detailed accuracy of His prediction. This highlighted the **untying** of the **colt,** which **Jesus** may have intended as a messianic sign (cf. Gen. 49:8-12).

Had Jesus made prearranged plans with the colt's owner, or did this event reflect His supernatural knowledge? A later parallel situation (cf. Mark 14:13-16) may support the first view, but the large amount of detail Mark included on securing the colt (11:2-6) convincingly favors the second view. Even so, the colt's owner probably had had previous contact with Jesus.

The amount of detail Mark recorded here implies an eyewitness report; possibly Peter was one of the two disciples sent on this errand (cf. *Introduction*).

11:7-8. The disciples put **their** outer **cloaks** on **the colt** as a makeshift saddle. **Jesus** mounted the previously unridden colt and began His ride into Jerusalem. **Many people** entered into the excitement of the moment and spontaneously paid Him tribute by spreading **their** outer **cloaks** before Him on the dusty **road** (cf. 2 Kings 9:12-13). **Others spread** green **branches** (*stibadas,* "leaves or leafy branches") **cut** from surrounding **fields.** Palm branches are mentioned in John 12:13.

11:9-10. The chiastic (*a-b-b'-a'*) arrangement of these verses suggests antiphonal chanting by two groups— **those who went ahead** of Jesus **and those who followed** Him. They chanted Psalm 118:25-26. At the annual Passover festival (cf. Mark 14:1), the Jews chanted the six "ascent" psalms (Pss. 113-118) to express thanksgiving, praise, and petitions to God.

Hosanna, a transliteration of the Greek word which is itself a transliteration of the Hebrew *hôšî 'âh nā',* originally was a prayer addressed to God, meaning "O save us now" (cf. Ps. 118:25a). Later it came to be used as a shout of praise (like "Hallelujah!") and then as an enthusiastic welcome to pilgrims or to a famous Rabbi. **Hosanna in the highest,** in highest places, likely means "Save us, O God, who lives in heaven." Its use here probably reflects a mixture of all these elements due to the nature of the crowd.

The acclamation, **Blessed** (lit., "May . . . be blessed") calls for God's gracious power to attend someone or to effect something. **He who comes in the name of the Lord** (as God's representative and with His authority) originally referred to a pilgrim coming to the festival. Though these words are not a messianic title, this crowd of pilgrims applied them to Jesus, perhaps with messianic overtones (cf. Gen. 49:10; Matt. 3:11) but they stopped short of identifying Jesus as the Messiah.

The coming kingdom (cf. comments on Mark 1:15) in association with **David** reflected the peoples' messianic hope for the restoration of the Davidic kingdom (cf. 2 Sam. 7:16; Amos 9:11-12). But their enthusiasm was for a ruling Messiah and a political kingdom, not realizing and not accepting the fact that the One peaceably riding on the colt was their Messiah (cf. Zech. 9:9), the suffering Messiah whose kingdom stood near because of His presence with them. For most people, then, this moment of jubilation was simply part of the traditional Passover celebration—it did not alarm the Roman authorities or initiate a call for Jesus' arrest by the Jewish rulers.

11:11. After entering **Jerusalem Jesus . . . went to the temple** (*hieron,* "the temple precincts"; cf. vv. 15, 27), not the central sanctuary (*naos;* cf. 14:58; 15:29, 38). **He** carefully surveyed the premises to see if they were being used as God intended. This led to His action the next day (cf. 11:15-17). **Since it was** near sunset when the city gates were closed, Jesus **went out to Bethany** (cf. v. 1a) **with the Twelve** for the night.

B. Jesus' prophetic signs of God's judgment on Israel (11:12-26)

This section has a "sandwich" structure (cf. 3:20-35; 5:21-43; 6:7-31). The account of Jesus' judgment on the fig tree (11:12-14, 20-26) is divided by the account of His cleansing the temple precincts (vv. 15-19). This structure suggests that each episode helps explain the other. Like the fig tree, Israel flourished with the "leaves" of ritual religion but lacked the "fruit" of righteousness God demanded. Both episodes signify God's impending judgment on Israel for religious hypocrisy (cf. comments on 7:6). Matthew telescoped the incidents into two separate, successive accounts without the precise time intervals Mark noted (Matt. 21:12-17, 18-22).

1. JESUS' JUDGMENT ON THE UNPRODUCTIVE FIG TREE (11:12-14) (MATT. 21:18-19)

11:12-13. Next day, early Monday morning, after **leaving Bethany** for Jerusalem (cf. v. 1a) **Jesus was** (lit., "became") **hungry.** From a distance Jesus saw a wayside **fig tree in leaf,** with full green foliage, and **went to** see **if it had any fruit.** But it had **nothing but leaves.** Mark explained that **it was not the season for figs.**

The time of year was Passover (cf. 14:1), the middle of the month of Nisan (April). In Palestine fig trees produced crops of small edible buds in March followed by the appearance of large green leaves in early April. This early green "fruit" (buds) was common food for local peasants. (An absence of these buds despite the tree's green foliage promising their presence indicated it would bear no fruit that year.) Eventually these buds dropped off when the normal crop of figs formed and ripened in late May and June, the fig season. Thus it was reasonable for Jesus shortly before Passover (mid-April) to expect to find something edible on that fig tree even though it was not the season for figs.

11:14. Jesus' strong denunciation of the tree, which Peter later regarded as a curse (v. 21), was a dramatic prophetic sign of God's impending judgment on Israel, not an angry reaction because Jesus was hungry and found no food. The

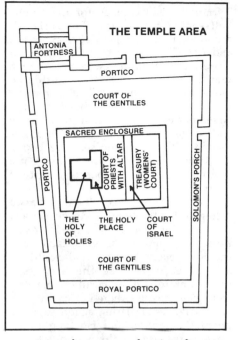

THE TEMPLE AREA

ANTONIA FORTRESS

PORTICO

COURT OF THE GENTILES

SACRED ENCLOSURE

PORTICO

COURT OF PRIESTS WITH ALTAR

TREASURY (WOMENS' COURT)

SOLOMON'S PORCH

THE HOLY OF HOLIES

THE HOLY PLACE

COURT OF ISRAEL

COURT OF THE GENTILES

ROYAL PORTICO

promising but unproductive fig tree symbolized Israel's spiritual barrenness despite divine favor and the impressive outward appearance of their religion (cf. Jer. 8:13; Hosea 9:10, 16; Micah 7:1). This is aptly illustrated in Mark 11:27–12:40.

2. JESUS' JUDGMENT ON THE MISUSE OF THE TEMPLE (11:15-19) (MATT. 21:12-17; LUKE 19:45-46)

This event is recorded in all three Synoptic Gospels. John recorded an earlier cleansing of the temple at the beginning of Jesus' public ministry (cf. comments on John 2:13-22).

11:15-16. When **Jesus** arrived in **Jerusalem,** He went into **the temple area** (*hieron*; cf. v. 11), the large outer court of the Gentiles surrounding the inner sacred courts of the temple itself. (See the sketch of the temple.) No Gentile was allowed beyond this outer court. In it the high priest Caiaphas had authorized a market (probably a recent economic innovation) for the sale of ritually pure items necessary for temple sacrifice: wine, oil, salt, approved sacrificial animals and birds.

Money from three sources circulated in Palestine in New Testament times: imperial money (Roman), provincial money (Greek), and local money (Jewish). Money changers provided the required

Tyrian (Jewish) coinage for the annual half-shekel temple tax (Ex. 30:12-16) required of all male Jews 20 years of age and up. This was in exchange for their Greek and Roman currency, which featured human portraits considered idolatrous. Though a small surcharge was permitted in these transactions, dealings were not free from extortion and fraud. In addition (according to Mark 11:16) people loaded with **merchandise** were taking shortcuts **through** this area, making it a thoroughfare from one part of the city to another.

Jesus was outraged by this blatant disregard for the temple area specifically set apart for Gentile use. So He **overturned the** money changers' **tables** and **the** dove-sellers' **benches, and would not allow** people to use the area as a thoroughfare. Other certified markets were available elsewhere in the city.

11:17. Jesus' daring action captured peoples' attention and **He taught** (lit., "began teaching") them about God's purpose for the temple. Using a question expecting a positive answer, He appealed to Old Testament authority for His action (quoting Isa. 56:7b verbatim from the LXX).

Only Mark extended the quotation from Isaiah to include the words **for all nations.** God desired that both Gentiles and Jews use the temple as a place of worship (cf. John 12:20). This was especially relevant to Mark's readers in Rome.

By contrast **you** (emphatic), the insensitive Jews, **have made it,** the court of the Gentiles, **a den of robbers.** It was a refuge for fraudulent traders (cf. Jer. 7:11) instead of **a house of prayer** (cf. 1 Kings 8:28-30; Isa. 60:7) for both Jews and Gentiles.

By this action Jesus as the Messiah claimed greater authority over the temple than that of the high priest (cf. Hosea 9:15; Mal. 3:1-5).

11:18-19. When the religious leaders (cf. comments on 8:31; 11:27; 14:1, 43, 53) **heard** about **this, they began** seeking (cf. 12:12; 14:1, 11) the best **way to kill Him** without creating a major uprising. Mark alone explained (*gar,* **for**) that **they** were afraid of **Him because** of His authoritative appeal to the crowds. **The whole crowd** of Passover pilgrims from all parts

of the ancient world **was amazed** (*exeplēsseto,* "astounded, struck out of their senses, overwhelmed"; cf. 1:22; 6:2; 7:37; 10:26) **at** the content of **His teaching** (cf. 1:27). His popularity with the people kept the Jewish authorities from arresting Him immediately. That **evening** (Monday) **they,** Jesus and the Twelve, left Jerusalem and presumably went to Bethany (cf. 11:11).

3. THE WITHERED FIG TREE AND A LESSON ON FAITH AND PRAYER (11:20-26)
(MATT. 21:20-22)

11:20-21. These verses form the sequel to verses 12-14. Next **morning,** Tuesday, **as** Jesus and His disciples were returning to Jerusalem, **they saw the** same **fig tree** (v. 13) but it was **withered from the roots,** completely dried up, fulfilling Jesus' words (v. 14).

Addressing **Jesus** as **Rabbi** (cf. 9:5), **Peter** spoke of the tree's condition with great surprise probably because the tree's total destruction was much more severe than Jesus' words the previous day (11:14) indicated. Though Jesus did not explain the meaning of the event, many believe that it was a vivid picture of God's impending judgment on Israel (cf. comments on vv. 12-14).

11:22-24. Jesus exhorted the disciples, **Have faith in God.** Faith that rests in God is unwavering trust in His omnipotent power and unfailing goodness (cf. 5:34).

Following a solemn introduction (**I tell you the truth;** cf. 3:28), Jesus said in a hyperbole that whoever **says to this mountain,** the Mount of Olives representing an immovable obstacle, **Go, throw yourself** (lit., "be uprooted" and "be thrown") **into the sea** (the Dead Sea, visible from the Mount of Olives), **it will be done for him** by God. The one condition is, negatively, absence of **doubt** and positively, belief, unwavering trust in God, that the petition will be granted. Such faith contrasted with Israel's lack of faith.

Therefore, because believing **prayer** taps God's power to accomplish the humanly impossible (cf. 10:27), Jesus exhorted His disciples to **believe that** they **have** already **received** whatever they request **in** prayer. Faith accepts it as good as done even though the actual answer is still future.

Jesus made this promise on the recognized premise that petitions must be in harmony with God's will (cf. 14:36; Matt. 6:9-10; John 14:13-14; 15:7; 16:23-24; 1 John 5:14-15). This enables faith to receive the answers God gives. God is always ready to respond to obedient believers' prayers, and they can petition Him knowing that no situation or difficulty is impossible for Him.

11:25-26. A forgiving attitude toward others as well as faith in God is also essential for effective prayer. When a believer stands to pray, a common prayer posture among Jews (cf. 1 Sam. 1:26; Luke 18:11, 13), and **if** he has **anything against anyone,** a grudge against an offending believer or nonbeliever, he is to **forgive** that one of the offense.

This is to be done in order that his **Father in heaven** (the only Marcan occurrence of this phrase, but frequent in Matt.) **may** "also" (*kai* in Gr.) **forgive** him his **sins** (lit., *paraptōmata,* "trespasses," only occurrence in Mark), acts that sidestep or deviate from God's truth.

Divine forgiveness toward a believer and a believer's forgiveness toward others are inseparably linked because a bond has been established between the divine Forgiver and the forgiven believer (cf. Matt. 18:21-35). One who has accepted God's forgiveness is expected to forgive others just as God has forgiven him (Eph. 4:32). If he does not, he forfeits God's forgiveness in his daily life.

C. Jesus' controversy with the Jewish religious leaders in the temple courts (11:27–12:44)

Mark likely packaged the five episodes in 11:27–12:37 around the theme of conflict between Jesus and various influential religious groups (similarly, cf. 2:1–3:5). A contrast between self-righteous religion and wholehearted devotion to God concludes the section (12:38-44). The temple area was the focal point of Jesus' ministry during His final week (cf. 11:11, 15-17, 27; 12:35, 41; 13:1-3; 14:49). The controversies serve as a summary of Jesus' teaching during Tuesday and Wednesday of that week. They depict the religious leaders' growing hostility toward Him.

1. THE QUESTION CONCERNING JESUS' AUTHORITY (11:27–12:12)

Jesus' credentials were questioned by representatives of the Sanhedrin. His response placed them in an embarrassing dilemma (11:27-33) and His Vineyard Parable exposed their rejection of God's messengers (12:1-12).

a. Jesus' counterquestion about John's baptism (11:27-33)

11:27-28. On Tuesday morning (cf. v. 20) Jesus and His disciples entered **Jerusalem** again (cf. vv. 11-12, 15). **In the temple courts** (*heirō;* cf. vv. 11, 15) **Jesus** was confronted by representatives of the Sanhedrin (cf. comments on 8:31; 14:43, 53; 15:1). As guardians of Israel's religious life they asked two questions: (1) **What** was the nature of His **authority** (cf. 1:22, 27); what were His credentials? (2) **Who** was the source of His **authority?** Who authorized Him **to do this?** "This" (lit., **these things**) refers to His purging the temple the previous day (cf. 11:15-17) and probably more generally to all His authoritative words and deeds which drew much popular acclaim (cf. v. 18; 12:12, 37). Their questions indicate that Jesus had not openly stated that He is the Messiah, a significant point in view of Mark's "secrecy motif" (cf. comments on 1:43-45; 12:1, 12).

11:29-30. Jesus' counterquestions, a common Rabbinic debating technique (cf. 10:2-3), made His answer to them depend on their answer to Him. It focused the issue: Was **John's baptism** and his whole ministry (cf. 1:4-8; 6:14-16, 20) **from heaven** (of divine origin; cf. 8:11), **or from men?** (of human origin) Jesus implied that His own authority came from the same source as John's which indicates there was no rivalry between them. The leaders' conclusion about John would reveal their conclusion about Him.

11:31-32. Jesus' question placed these religious leaders in a dilemma. **If** they answered, **From heaven,** they would incriminate themselves for not believing John and supporting his ministry (cf. John 1:19-27). They would stand self-condemned for rejecting God's messenger. They would also be forced to acknowledge that Jesus' authority came from God (cf. Mark 9:37b). This answer, though true, was unacceptable because of their unbelief.

But if they answered, **From men** (lit., "But shall we say, 'From men'?"), the implications were obvious: they would deny that John was commissioned by God and discredit themselves before the people. Mark explained, **They feared the people** (cf. 12:12) because **everyone** regarded **John** as a genuine **prophet,** God's spokesman (cf. Josephus *The Antiquities of the Jews* 18. 5. 2). The people viewed Jesus this way too (cf. Matt. 21:46). This latter answer, though false, was the one they preferred but found unacceptable because of the people.

11:33. Since neither option was acceptable they pleaded ignorance in an attempt to save face. So **Jesus** was not obligated to answer their question. His question (cf. v. 30) implied that His **authority,** like John's, was from God.

By suspending judgment, these religious leaders showed that they really rejected John and Jesus as God's messengers. Throughout their history most leaders of Israel repeatedly rejected God's messengers, a point Jesus made in the following parable (12:1-12).

b. Jesus' Parable of the Vineyard Owner's Son (12:1-12)
(Matt. 21:33-46; Luke 20:9-19)

This parable reflects the social situation of first-century Palestine, especially Galilee. Wealthy foreign landlords owned large land estates which they leased to tenant farmers. The tenants agreed to cultivate the land and care for the vineyards when the landlords were away. A contract between them designated that a portion of the crop was to be paid as rent. At harvesttime the owners sent agents to collect the rent. Inevitably tension arose between the absentee owners and the tenants.

12:1a. This brief summary statement (cf. introduction to 2:1-2) introduces the single parable (cf. introduction to 4:1-2) Mark recorded here. Jesus addressed it **to them,** the Sanhedrin interrogators who were plotting against Him (cf. 11:27; 12:12). It exposed their hostile intentions and warned them of the consequences.

12:1b. The details of the vineyard's construction are derived from Isaiah 5:1-2 (part of a prophecy of God's judgment on

Israel), as the vineyard is a familiar symbol for the nation of Israel (cf. Ps. 80:8-19).

A man, a landlord (cf. Mark 12:9), **planted a vineyard,** analogous to God's relationship to Israel. The **wall** for protection, **a pit** beneath **the winepress** to gather the juice of the pressed grapes, and **a watchtower** for shelter, storage, and security, show the owner's desire to make this a choice vineyard. **Then he** leased it **to** tenant **farmers,** vinegrowers, representing Israel's religious leaders, **and went away on a journey** probably to live abroad. He was an absentee owner.

12:2-5. The owner sent three servants—agents representing God's servants (the prophets) to Israel—**to the** tenant farmers to receive a share **of the fruit** as rent **at harvesttime** (lit., "at the right time," i.e., the vintage season of the fifth year; cf. Lev. 19:23-25). **But** the tenant farmers behaved violently. **They seized** the first **servant . . . beat him, and sent him away empty-handed. They** seriously wounded the second **servant** and insulted him. **They killed** the third **servant.**

The long-suffering owner also **sent many others, some of** whom were beaten **and others . . . killed.** Time and again God had sent prophets to Israel to gather fruits of repentance and righteousness (cf. Luke 3:8) but His prophets were abused, wounded, and killed (cf. Jer. 7:25-26; 25:4-7; Matt. 23:33-39).

12:6-8. The owner still **had one** messenger **to send, a son, whom he loved** (lit., "a beloved son"—a designation representing God's Son, Jesus; cf. 1:11; 9:7). **Last of all,** a phrase unique to Mark, **he sent** his **son,** expecting the tenant farmers to give *him* the honor denied his servants.

The son's arrival may have caused **the tenants** to assume that the owner had died and **this** son was his only **heir.** In Palestine at the time, a piece of land could be possessed lawfully by whoever claimed it first if it was "ownerless property," unclaimed by an heir within a certain time period (cf. Mishnah *Baba Bathra* 3. 3). The tenant farmers assumed that if they killed the son they could acquire the vineyard.

So they conspired together **and killed him and threw him out of the vineyard.** Some say this predicts what would happen to Jesus: He would be crucified outside of Jerusalem, expelled from Israel in a climactic expression of the leaders' rejection of Him. But this presses the parable's details too far here. It is better to see the throwing of the son's dead body over the wall without burial as a climax to their wicked indignities. Mark's emphasis of their rejection and murder of the son took place *within* the vineyard, that is, within Israel.

12:9. Jesus' rhetorical question invited His audience to share in deciding what action **the owner** should take. He affirmed his listeners' answer (cf. Matt. 21:41) by alluding to Isaiah 5:1-7 again. This was a strong appeal for those plotting His death to consider the serious consequences of their actions. He saw Himself as the "only Son" sent by God (John 3:16).

The rejection of the owner's son was really a rejection of the owner who would **come** with governmental authority **and kill** the murderous **tenants and give the vineyard to others.** Likewise the Jewish leaders' rejection of John the Baptist and of Jesus, God's final Messenger, was a rejection of God Himself. This would inevitably bring His judgment on Israel and would transfer their privileges to others temporarily (cf. Rom. 11:25, 31).

12:10-11. Jesus sharpened the application of the parable to Himself as the Son and extended its teaching by quoting verbatim Psalm 118:22-23 (Ps. 117 in the LXX), a familiar text recognized as messianic elsewhere (Acts 4:11; 1 Peter 2:4-8). The figure changed from the son/tenants of the parable to the stone/builders of the psalm, making possible a parabolic allusion to Jesus' resurrection and exaltation. A slain son cannot be revived but a rejected stone can be retrieved and used.

The quotation begins where the parable ended. **The stone** (Jesus, like the son), which **the builders** (the Jewish religious leaders, like the tenant farmers) **rejected has become the capstone** ("cornerstone," NIV marg.; lit., "head of the corner"). This was considered the most important stone of a building. This dramatic reversal of the builders' decision and exaltation of the rejected stone was God's sovereign doing, a remarkable thing. God overrules in amazing ways

rebellious human attempts to block His purposes.

12:12. **They,** the Sanhedrin representatives (11:27), were seeking (cf. 11:18) **to arrest Him because they** realized Jesus **had** addressed **the parable against them** ("with reference to" or directed "toward" them). **But** fearing **the** excitable Passover **crowd, they left Him** alone **and** departed.

The fact that Jesus' adversaries understood this parable is a new development (cf. 4:11-12), suggesting that at Jesus' initiative the "secret" of His true identity would soon be openly declared (cf. comments on 1:43-45; 14:62).

2. THE QUESTION CONCERNING THE POLL TAX (12:13-17) (MATT. 22:15-22; LUKE 20:20-26)

12:13. Despite Jesus' warning to His Sanhedrin adversaries in the preceding parable, **they** continued their campaign against Him by sending some . . . **Pharisees** (cf. 2:16) **and Herodians** (cf. 3:6) **to catch Him in His words** (lit., "by means of a word," i.e., an unguarded statement they could use against Him; cf. 10:2). The word translated "catch" (*argeusōsin,* found only here in the NT) was used to describe catching wild animals with a trap. **Later** (NIV), though implied, is not in the Greek text; no time reference is given.

12:14-15a. Addressing Jesus as **Teacher** (cf. 4:38; 9:5), they used carefully chosen remarks designed to hide their true motives and to prevent Jesus from evading their difficult question. They acknowledged He was honest and impartial, courting no one's favor, **because** He paid **no attention to who they are** (lit., "You do not look at the face of men," a Heb. expression; cf. 1 Sam. 16:7). Then they asked, **Is it right,** legally permitted by God's Law (cf. Deut. 17:14-15), **to pay taxes to Caesar,** the Roman emperor, **or not? Should we pay** (*dōmen,* "Shall we give") **or shouldn't we?**

"Taxes" (*kēnson*) was a Latin loanword meaning "census." It referred to the annual poll tax (head tax) demanded by the Roman emperor from all Jews since A.D. 6, when Judea became a Roman province (Josephus *The Antiquities of the Jews* 5. 1. 21). The money went directly into the emperor's treasury. This tax was unpopular because it typified the Jews' subjugation to Rome (cf. Acts 5:37).

161

The Pharisees objected to the tax, but expediently justified its payment. They were concerned about the *religious* implications of their question. The Herodians supported foreign rule through the Herods and favored the tax. They were concerned about the *political* implications of their question. Obviously the question was designed to place Jesus in a religious and political dilemma. A yes answer would antagonize the people and discredit Him as God's Spokesman. No messianic claimant could sanction willing submission to pagan rulers. A no answer would invite retaliation from Rome.

12:15b-16. Jesus immediately detected **their hypocrisy,** the malicious intent beneath their pretense of an honest inquiry. He exposed it with a rhetorical question about **why** they were **trying to trap** (*peirazete,* "test"; cf. 10:2) Him. Then **He asked** them to **bring** Him **a denarius** (cf. 6:37) so He might **look at it,** to use it as a visual aid. **The** common Roman denarius, a small silver **coin,** was the only coin acceptable for imperial tax payments.

When Jesus **asked them** to tell Him **whose portrait** and **inscription** were on it, they replied, **Caesar's.** The portrait (*eikōn,* "image") was probably that of Tiberius Caesar (reigned A.D. 14–37; see the list of Roman emperors at Luke 3:1) and the inscription read in Latin: "Tiberius Caesar Augustus, Son of the Divine Augustus" and on the reverse side: "Chief Priest." This inscription originated in the imperial cult of emperor worship and was a claim to divinity, which was particularly repulsive to Jews.

12:17. But to use Caesar's coinage was to acknowledge his authority and the benefits of the civil government it represented and consequently the obligation to pay taxes. So **Jesus** declared, **Give** (*apodote,* "give back"; cf. v. 14) **to Caesar what is Caesar's** (lit., "the things belonging to Caesar"). This tax was a debt they owed to Caesar for use of his money and the other benefits of his rule.

Jesus had made His point but significantly He added, **and** give back **to God what is God's** (lit., "the things belonging to God"). This could refer to "paying" God the temple tax due Him (cf. Matt. 17:24-27), but Jesus probably meant it as a protest against the emperor's claim to deity. Indeed the emperor must receive

his due, but not more than that; he must not receive the divine honor and worship he claimed. Those are due only to God. People are "God's coinage" because they bear His image (cf. Gen. 1:27) and they owe Him what belongs to Him, their allegiance. This, not the poll tax, was the crucial issue to Jesus. His questioners continued to be greatly **amazed** (*exethaumazon,* imperf. tense of a strong compound verb found only here in the NT) **at Him.** This incident was especially relevant to Mark's Roman readers for it indicated that Christianity did not foster disloyalty to the state.

3. THE QUESTION CONCERNING THE RESURRECTION (12:18-27) (MATT. 22:23-33; LUKE 20:27-40)

12:18. The Sadducees . . . came to Jesus **with a question** in another attempt to discredit Him (cf. 11:27; 12:13). It is generally believed that they were the Jewish aristocratic party whose members came largely from the priesthood and the upper classes. Though less numerous and popular than the Pharisees, they occupied influential positions on the Sanhedrin, the Jewish supreme court and generally cooperated with the Roman authorities. They denied the truths of the **resurrection,** future judgment, and the existence of angels and spirits (cf. Acts 23:6-8). They accepted only the Books of Moses (the Pentateuch) as authoritative and rejected the oral traditions observed as binding by the Pharisees. This is Mark's only reference to the Sadducees.

12:19-23. After formally addressing Jesus as **Teacher** (cf. v. 14), they gave a free rendering of the Mosaic regulation concerning levirate (from Latin, *levir,* "husband's brother") marriage (cf. Deut. 25:5-10). If a husband died without leaving a male heir his (unmarried) **brother** (or, if none, his nearest male relative) was to **marry his widow.** The first son of that union was given the name of the dead **brother** and was considered **his** child. This was to prevent extinction of a family line and thereby kept the family inheritance intact.

The Sadducees made up a story about **seven brothers** who successively fulfilled the duty of levirate marriage to their first brother's wife but all seven **died** childless. Then **the woman died** also. They asked Jesus, **At the resurrection**

whose wife will she be? Clearly they were ridiculing belief in the resurrection.

12:24. Using a two-pronged counterquestion expecting a positive answer in Greek, **Jesus** cited two reasons why they were **in error** (*planasthe*, "you are deceiving yourselves"; cf. v. 27): (a) they did **not know the Scriptures**—their true meaning, not merely their contents; and (b) they did not know **the power of God**—His power to overcome death and give life. Then Jesus amplified each reason starting with the second (v. 25) and then the first (vv. 26-27).

12:25. The Sadducees wrongly assumed that marriages would be resumed after the resurrection. In resurrection-life people **will neither marry** (contract a marriage) **nor be given in marriage** (have a marriage arranged by parents). Rather, **like the angels in heaven** they will be immortal beings in God's presence.

Marriage is necessary and suitable for the present world order, in which death prevails, in order to continue the human race. But angels, whose existence the Sadducees denied (cf. Acts 23:8), are deathless and live in a different order of existence where they have no need for marital relations or reproduction of offspring. Their lives center totally around fellowship with God. So it will be in the afterlife for human beings rightly related to God.

The Sadducees did not grasp that God will establish a whole new order of life after death and resolve all apparent difficulties connected with it. In short, their question was irrelevant.

12:26-27. The Sadducees wrongly alleged that the idea of a resurrection was absent from the Pentateuch. But Jesus, using a question expecting a positive answer, appealed to **the Book of Moses,** the Pentateuch, and spoke of **the** burning **bush** (Ex. 3:1-6).

In this passage God identified Himself to Moses, affirming, **I am the God of Abraham . . . Isaac, and . . . Jacob** (Ex. 3:6). God implied that the patriarchs were still alive and that He had a continuing relationship with them as their covenant-keeping God, even though they had died long before. This demonstrates, Jesus concluded, that **He is not the God of the dead,** in the Sadducean understanding of death as extinction, **but of the living.** He is still the patriarchs' God which would

not be true had they ceased to exist at death, that is, if death ends it all. And His covenant faithfulness implicitly guarantees their bodily resurrection.

Jesus' answer clearly affirmed the fact of life after death. Apparently He assumed that this was enough to prove that the resurrection of the body will occur as well. In Hebrew thought people are regarded as a unity of the material (body) and immaterial (soul/spirit). One is incomplete without the other (cf. 2 Cor. 5:1-8). Thus authentic human existence in the eternal order of life demands the union of soul/spirit with the body (cf. Phil. 3:21). Both bodily resurrection and life after death depend on the faithfulness of "the God of the living."

Jesus' final remark, recorded only by Mark, emphasized how seriously **mistaken** (*planasthe*, "you are deceiving yourselves"; cf. Mark 12:24) they were to deny the resurrection and life after death.

4. THE QUESTION CONCERNING THE GREATEST COMMANDMENT (12:28-34) (MATT. 22:34-40)

12:28. One of the Law **teachers** (cf. 1:22), had **heard** Jesus' discussion with the Sadducees (12:18-27) and was impressed with His **good answer to them.** This suggested he was probably a Pharisee.

He came with no apparent hostile or hidden motive to appraise Jesus' skill in answering a much-debated subject in scribal circles. Traditionally the scribes spoke of 613 individual commandments of the Mosaic Law—365 negative ones and 248 positive ones. While they believed all were binding, they assumed a distinction between weightier and lighter statutes and often attempted to sum up the whole Law in a single unifying command.

In light of this debate, this **Law** teacher **asked** Jesus, **Which** (*poia*, "what kind of") commandment **is the most important** (*prōtē*, "first") of them all?

12:29-31. Jesus' reply went beyond the debated lighter/weightier classifications to a statement of **the most important** command and its inseparable companion, which together summarize the whole Law.

He began with the opening words of the *Shema* (from Heb., "Hear!" [*šᵉma*ʻ], the first word of Deut. 6:4). This creed

(Num. 15:37-41; Deut. 6:4-9; 11:13-21) was recited twice daily—morning and evening—by devout Jews. It asserted the basis of Jewish faith: **The Lord** (Heb., *Yahweh*), namely, **our God,** Israel's covenant-keeping God, **the Lord is One,** that is, unique (cf. Mark 12:32).

The command, **Love** (lit., "you shall love") **the Lord your God** (Deut. 6:5), calls for a volitional commitment to God that is personal, comprehensive, and wholehearted. This is emphasized by the repeated words **with** (*ex*, "out of," denoting source), **all** (*holēs*, "the whole of"), **your** (sing.), and the various terms relating to the human personality—**heart** (control center; cf. Mark 7:19), **soul** (self-conscious life; cf. 8:35-36), **mind** (thought capacity), and **strength** (bodily powers). The Hebrew text does not mention "mind"; the Septuagint omits "heart"; but Jesus included both terms, stressing the comprehensive nature of the command (cf. 12:33; Matt. 22:37; Luke 10:27).

Jesus then spoke of a similar commitment to one's neighbor by quoting a **second** inseparable (cf. 1 John 4:19-21) and complementary command. **Love** (lit., "you shall love") **your neighbor** (*plēsion*, "one who is nearby," a generic term for fellowman) **as**, in the same way as, **yourself** (Lev. 19:18). The love a person has naturally for himself is not to focus solely on himself—a constant tendency—but should be directed equally toward others.

No (Gr., "no other") **commandment** is **greater than these** two because wholehearted love to God and one's neighbor is the sum and substance of the Law and the Prophets (cf. Matt. 22:40). To fulfill these commands is to fulfill all others.

12:32-34a. These verses are unique to Mark. Apparently they instructed his readers who struggled with the relationship between spiritual reality and ceremonial ritual (cf. comments on 7:19).

The scribe (cf. 12:28) recognized the accuracy of Jesus' answer and voiced his approval, viewing Him as an excellent **Teacher** (cf. vv. 14, 19). He restated Jesus' answer, carefully avoiding mention of **God** (not in the Gr. text but supplied in the NIV) in keeping with the typical Jewish practice of avoiding unnecessary use of the divine name out of great respect for it. The words, **There is no other but Him,**

come from Deuteronomy 4:35. He also substituted the word **understanding** for "soul" and "mind" (cf. Mark 12:30).

He made the bold statement that the double command of love **is** much **more important than all burnt offerings** (fully consumed sacrifices) **and sacrifices** (those partly consumed and partly eaten by worshipers; cf. 1 Sam. 15:22; Prov. 21:3; Jer. 7:21-23; Hosea 6:6; Micah 6:6-8).

He had responded **wisely,** and **Jesus** probably stimulated further thought by declaring, **You are not far** ("not far" is emphatic in Gr.) **from the kingdom of God** (cf. Mark 1:15; 4:11; 10:15, 23). This man had the kind of spiritual understanding (cf. 10:15) and openness to Jesus that brought him near to embracing God's kingdom, His spiritual rule over those related to Him by faith. Whether he entered this relationship is not known.

12:34b. Jesus had effectively thwarted all attempts to discredit Him and had exposed the hostile motives and errors of His opponents so skillfully that nobody else **dared ask Him any more questions.**

5. JESUS' QUESTION CONCERNING MESSIAH'S SONSHIP (12:35-37)
(MATT. 22:41-46; LUKE 20:41-44)

12:35. Later while **teaching in the temple courts** (*tō hierō*; cf. 11:11), **Jesus** asked what **the** Law **teachers** meant when they said **that the Christ,** the expected Messiah, **is** ("simply" is implied) **the Son** (Descendant) **of David,** who would be the triumphant Deliverer (cf. 10:47). The Davidic sonship of the Messiah was a standard Jewish belief (cf. John 7:41-42) firmly based on the Old Testament Scriptures (cf. 2 Sam. 7:8-16; Ps. 89:3-4; Isa. 9:2-7; 11:1-9; Jer. 23:5-6; 30:9; 33:15-17, 22; Ezek. 34:23-24; 37:24; Hosea 3:5; Amos 9:11). Jesus added that it is equally true that the Messiah is David's Lord. The Law teachers' view was correct but incomplete (cf. similarly, Mark 9:11-13). The scriptural view held far more than just their narrow nationalistic hopes.

12:36-37a. To prove that the Messiah is David's Lord, Jesus quoted what **David himself speaking by** (under the controlling influence of) **the Holy Spirit declared** in Psalm 110:1. This clearly argues for both the Davidic authorship and the divine inspiration of this psalm. He said: **The Lord** (Heb., *Yahweh*, God the Father; cf. Mark 12:29) **said to my** (David's) **Lord** (Heb., '*Aḏōnāy*, the Messiah): **Sit at My** (the Father's) **right hand,** the place of highest honor and authority, **until** (or "while"; cf. 9:1; 14:32) **I** (the Father) **put Your** (the Messiah's) **enemies under Your** (the Messiah's) **feet,** bringing about their subjugation (cf. Josh. 10:24; Heb. 10:12-14).

The unassailable fact was that **David** called the Messiah **Lord.** This raised a problem: **How then,** or in what sense, **can** (*estin*, "is") **He** (the Messiah, David's Lord) **be his** (David's) **Son?** Jesus' rhetorical question pointed His listeners to the only valid answer: the Messiah is David's Son *and* David's Lord at the same time. This strongly implies that the Messiah is both God (David's Lord) and man (David's Son; cf. Rom. 1:3-4; 2 Tim. 2:8). He will restore the future Davidic kingdom on earth (2 Sam. 7:16; Amos 9:11-12; Matt. 19:28; Luke 1:31-33).

No doubt Jesus deliberately raised this issue so that His listeners might relate it to Him. It carried a bold yet veiled reference to His true identity which the Jewish leaders probably caught but did not accept (cf. comments on Mark 12:12; 14:61-62). (Interestingly the NT has more references and allusions to Ps. 110 than to any other single OT passage [cf., e.g., Acts 2:29-35; Heb. 1:5-13; 5:6; 7:17, 21].)

12:37b. In contrast with the Jewish leaders who had been trying to trap Jesus with subtle questions (cf. v. 13), **the large** Passover **crowd** was listening all along to His teaching **with delight,** though not necessarily with comprehension.

6. CONCLUSION: JESUS' CONDEMNATION OF HYPOCRISY AND COMMENDATION OF TRUE COMMITMENT (12:38-44)

Jesus' denunciation of the Law teachers' conduct (vv. 38-40) concludes Mark's account of His public ministry and signals Jesus' final break with the Jewish religious authorities. This contrasts sharply with His recognition of a widow's genuine devotion to God (vv. 41-44) which resumes His teaching to His disciples (cf. v. 43) and forms a transition to His prophetic discourse (chap. 13).

a. Jesus' condemnation of hypocrisy (12:38-40) (Matt. 23:1-39; Luke 20:45-47)

12:38-39. Jesus kept warning people to **Watch out** (cf. 8:15) **for** those (implied in the Gr. construction) Law **teachers** who sought praise from men and abused their privileges. Many but not all Law teachers acted this way (cf. 12:28-34).

They liked **to** (a) go **around in flowing robes,** long white linen garments with fringes worn by priests, Law teachers, and Levites; (b) **be greeted in the marketplaces** with formal titles—Rabbi (teacher), master, father (cf. Matt. 23:7; Luke 20:46)—by the common people who respected them highly; (c) **have the most important** synagogue **seats,** those reserved for dignitaries, situated in front of the chest containing the sacred scrolls of Scripture and facing the whole congregation; **and** (d) have **the places of honor at banquets,** special evening meals at which they were seated next to the host and received preferential treatment.

12:40. Since first-century Law teachers got no pay for their services (Mishnah *Aboth* 1. 13; *Bekhoroth* 4. 6) they depended on the hospitality extended to them by many devout Jews. Unfortunately there were abuses. The charge, **they devour widows' houses,** was a vivid figure of speech for exploiting the generosity of people of limited means, especially widows. They unethically appropriated people's property. In addition, they made **lengthy prayers** in order to impress people with their piety and gain their confidence.

Jesus condemned their ostentatious conduct, greed, and hypocrisy. Instead of pointing people's attention to God they claimed it for themselves under the pretense of piety. Teachers such as these **will be punished most severely** (lit., "will receive greater condemnation"; James 3:1) at God's final judgment.

b. Jesus' commendation of a widow's commitment to God (12:41-44) (Luke 21:1-4)

12:41-42. From the court of the Gentiles (cf. 11:15) where He conducted His public teaching, **Jesus** entered the court of the women. Against the wall of this court were 13 trumpet-shaped collection receptacles for receiving worshipers' freewill **offerings** and contributions (Mishnah *Shekalim* 6. 5).

From a vantage point **opposite** (*katenanti*; cf. comments on 11:2) one of these receptacles Jesus was observing how (*pōs*, "in what way") the Passover **crowd** was **putting their money into the temple treasury** (lit., "the receptacle").

In contrast with **many** wealthy **people** who gave **large amounts** (lit., "many coins" of all kinds—gold, silver, copper, and bronze), one unnamed **poor widow** gave **two** *lepta* (Gr.). A *lepton* was the smallest bronze Jewish coin in circulation in Palestine. Two *lepta* were worth ¹⁄₆₄ of a Roman denarius, a day's wage for a laborer (cf. 6:37). For his Roman readers Mark stated their value in terms of Roman coinage, namely, **a fraction of a penny.**

12:43-44. With solemn introductory words (**I tell you the truth;** cf. 3:28) **Jesus said** that she had given **more . . . than all the others.** The reason was (*gar*, "for, because") the others **gave out of their** material **wealth** at little cost to them, **but** the widow **out of her poverty** gave **everything.** Proportionally she had given the most—**all she had to live on.** In giving to God sacrificially she completely entrusted herself to Him to provide her needs.

She could have kept back one coin for herself. A Rabbinic rule stating that an offering of less than two *lepta* was not acceptable related to charitable gifts and does not apply here. Jesus used her example to teach His disciples the value God places on wholehearted commitment. Their own commitment to Jesus would soon be severely tested (cf. 14:27-31). This incident also illustrates Jesus' total self-giving in death.

D. Jesus' prophetic Olivet Discourse to His disciples (chap. 13) (Matt. 24:1–25:46; Luke 21:5-36)

This chapter, known as the Olivet Discourse as Jesus gave it on the Mount of Olives, is the longest unit of His teaching recorded by Mark (cf. Mark 4:1-34).

Jesus predicted the destruction of the temple in Jerusalem (13:2) which prompted the disciples to inquire about the timing of "these things" (v. 4). Apparently they associated the destruction of the temple with the end of the Age (cf. Matt. 24:3). In reply Jesus skillfully wove together into a unified discourse a prophetic scene involving two perspectives: (a) the near event, the destruction of Jerusalem (A.D. 70); and (b) the far event, the coming of the Son of Man in clouds with power and glory. The former local event was a forerunner of the latter universal event. In this way Jesus followed the precedent of Old Testament prophets by predicting a far future event in terms of a near future event whose fulfillment at least some of His hearers would see (cf. Mark 9:1, 12-13).

This indicates Jesus anticipated a period of historical development between His resurrection and His second coming (cf. 13:10; 14:9). Nearly two millennia have passed since the fall of Jerusalem, and the end has not yet come. This prophetic information was set within a framework of (a) warnings against deception and (b) exhortations to vigilant obedience during the intervening time of missionary outreach, persecution, and socio-political upheavals. There are 19 imperatives in 13:5-37, and in each case the hortatory element (second person verbs: vv. 5b, 7a, 9a, et al.) arises out of Jesus' instruction about the future (third person indicative verbs: vv. 6, 7b-8, 9b-10, et al.). The verb "be on guard" (*blepete*) occurs four times at significant points throughout the discourse (vv. 5 ["Watch out," NIV], 9, 23, 33). This was to encourage His followers to maintain steadfast faith and obedience to God throughout the present Age.

In Mark's narrative, the Olivet Discourse is a bridge between Jesus' controversies with the religious authorities (11:27–12:44) and the Passion narrative (14:1–15:47) which culminated in His arrest and death. It disclosed to His disciples that the religious establishment which opposed Him and would eventually condemn Him to death would itself fall under God's judgment.

1. SETTING: JESUS' PREDICTION OF THE TEMPLE'S DESTRUCTION (13:1-4) (MATT. 24:1-3; LUKE 21:5-7)

13:1. As Jesus **was leaving the temple** area (*hierou*; cf. 11:11) probably on Wednesday evening of Passion Week (cf. the introduction to 11:1–13:37) **one of His disciples** addressed **Him** as **Teacher**

(cf. 4:38; 9:5) and with awe and admiration called attention to the **massive stones** (lit., "Behold, what manner of stones") and the **magnificent buildings** in the temple, that is, the sanctuary itself with its various courts, balconies, colonnades, and porches.

The Jerusalem temple (not fully completed until ca. A.D. 64) was built by the Herodian dynasty to win Jewish favor and to create a lasting Herodian monument. It was considered an architectural wonder of the ancient world. It was built with large white stones, polished and generously decorated with gold (Josephus *The Antiquities of the Jews* 15. 11. 3-7). It covered about 1/6 of the land area of old Jerusalem. To the Jews nothing was as magnificent and formidable as their temple.

13:2. Jesus' response was a startling prediction of the total destruction of **all these great buildings.** The whole complex would be completely leveled— literally, **"stone will** certainly **not** (*ou mē*) **be left** here upon stone." Jesus' use of the emphatic double negative (*ou mē*) twice stressed the certainty of His words' fulfillment.

This ominous prediction is the sequel to Jesus' judgment on the misuse of the temple (cf. 11:15-17; Jer. 7:11-14). As in Jeremiah's day so again the destruction of the temple by a foreign power would be God's judgment on rebellious Israel.

This prediction was fulfilled literally within the span of a generation. In A.D. 70, after the temple area was burned contrary to Titus' directives, he ordered his Roman soldiers to demolish the whole city and level its buildings to the ground (Josephus *Jewish Wars* 7. 1. 1).

13:3-4. Going across the Kidron Valley to the top of **the Mount of Olives** (cf. 11:1a), **Jesus** and His disciples sat down **opposite the temple.** The Mount of Olives rises about 2,700 feet above sea level but is only about 100 feet higher than Jerusalem. West of the mount lay the temple and the city.

The four disciples Jesus called first (cf. 1:16-20) **asked Him privately** (*kat' idian*; cf. 6:32) for more information about His prediction. Only Mark recorded their names. Often in Mark a question from the disciples introduced a section of Jesus' teaching to them (cf.

4:10-32; 7:17-23; 9:11-13, 28-29; 10:10-12).

The disciples' question, perhaps voiced by **Peter** (cf. 8:29), is expressed in two parts: (a) **When will these things** (destruction of the temple [13:2] and other future events [note the pl.]) **happen, and** (b) **What will be the sign that they** (lit., "these things") **are all about to be fulfilled?** The verb "fulfilled" (*synteleisthai*, "be accomplished") denotes the final consummation, the end of the present Age (cf. v. 7; Matt. 24:3).

Having only the perspective of Old Testament prophecy (e.g., Zech. 14), the disciples saw no long interval between the temple's destruction and the end-time events climaxing in the coming of the Son of Man. They assumed that the destruction of Jerusalem and the temple were some of the events at the end of the present Age and would inaugurate the messianic kingdom. They wanted to know *when* this would happen and *what* visible sign would indicate that fulfillment was about to take place.

2. PROPHETIC DISCOURSE IN JESUS' ANSWER TO HIS DISCIPLES' QUESTIONS (13:5-32)

The conditions associated with the impending local crisis of Jerusalem's fall foreshadow those connected with the worldwide end-time crisis. Thus Jesus' words, relevant to His first disciples, remain so for all disciples who face similar conditions throughout this Age.

He first answered their *second* question regarding "the sign" (v. 4b) in two ways: negatively, by warning them against false signs of the end (vv. 5-13), and positively, by stating the notable event that inaugurates unparalleled tribulation and by describing the Second Advent (vv. 14-27). Then He answered their *first* question regarding "when" (v. 4a) in a parable (vv. 28-32).

a. His warnings against deception (13:5-8)
  (Matt. 24:4-8; Luke 21:8-11)

13:5-6. Watch out (*blepete*, "take heed, be on guard") is a call to vigilance repeated throughout the discourse (cf. vv. 9, 23, 33; v. 35 has a different verb). **Jesus** warned His disciples to be on guard against messianic impostors. **Many** false messiahs (cf. v. 22) **will** arise in crisis times, making use of His **name** (His title and authority), **claiming, I am He** (lit., *egō eimi*, "I am"). This claim to deity is expressed in the formula of God's own self-revelation (cf. 6:50; Ex. 3:14; John 8:58). They **will** lead **many** people astray (cf. Acts 8:9-11).

13:7-8. Second, Jesus warned His disciples against misinterpreting contemporary events such as **wars** and natural disasters as indications that the end is at hand. They were **not** to **be alarmed** and thereby diverted from their work whenever they would **hear of** wars (sounds of battle close at hand) **and rumors** (lit., "reports") **of wars** far away. It is necessary (*dei*, by divine compulsion; cf. 8:31; 13:10) that these things come about. They fall within God's sovereign purposes, which include permitting wars as a consequence of human rebellion and sin. **But the end**—of the present Age and the establishing of God's rule on earth—**is still to come** (lit., "is not yet").

This is confirmed (*gar*, "for") and expanded: **Nation will rise** (lit., "shall be raised," i.e., by God; cf. Isa. 19:2) in armed aggression **against nation.** In addition **there will be earthquakes** and **famines,** suggesting divine judgment. Yet **these** ("these things") **are** just **the** (lit., "a") **beginning of birth pains.** The words "birth pains," the sharp pains preceding childbirth, picture divine judgment (cf. Isa. 13:6-8; 26:16-18; Jer. 22:20-23; Hosea 13:9-13; Micah 4:9-10). They refer to the period of intense suffering preceding the birth of the new Age, the messianic kingdom.

This emphasis—"the end is still to come" (Mark 13:7d) and "these [things] are the beginning of birth pains" (v. 8c)—suggests that an extended period of time will precede "the end." Each generation will have its own wars and natural disasters. Yet all these events fall within God's purposes. Human history is heading toward the birth of the new Messianic Age.

b. His warnings about personal dangers while under persecution (13:9-13) (Matt. 24:9-14; Luke 21:12-19)

These "floating sayings" (cf. their use in other contexts: Matt. 10:17-22; Luke 12:11-12) are linked by the word *paradidōmi* ("to hand over," Mark 13:9, 11 ["arrested," NIV], 12 ["betray," NIV]).

Jesus probably said these words several times, not just here on the Mount of Olives. His purpose here was to prepare His disciples for suffering because of their allegiance to Him.

13:9. With the admonition, **Be on your guard** (*blepete*; cf. v. 5), Jesus warned His disciples to be alert against wrongful retaliation under persecution. They would **be handed over** for trial **to the local councils** (lit., "sanhedrins"), local Jewish courts held in the synagogues. **And** they would be publicly **flogged,** that is, beaten with 39 strokes (cf. 2 Cor. 11:24), **in the synagogues** as heretics (cf. Mishnah *Makkoth* 3. 10-14). Because of their loyalty to Jesus Christ they **will stand** (lit., "be made to stand") **before** Gentile civil authorities, that is, provincial rulers (cf. Acts 12:1; 23:24; 24:27), **as witnesses to them** (cf. comments on Mark 1:44; 6:11). Their witness to the gospel during their defenses would become, in God's final judgment, incriminating evidence against their persecutors.

13:10. The gospel **must** (*dei*, "out of [divine] necessity"; cf. v. 7; 8:31) **first be preached** ("proclaimed") **to all nations** (emphatic word position in Gr.), all peoples worldwide (cf. 11:17; 14:9).

In proclaiming the gospel the disciples would be persecuted but they must not despair and give up. Despite all opposition, it is a priority in God's plan for this Age and will be accomplished in accordance with His purposes. It is the responsibility of each generation (cf. Rom. 1:5, 8; 15:18-24; Col. 1:6, 23). But preaching the gospel worldwide does not require or guarantee its worldwide acceptance before or at the end of the Age (cf. Matt. 25:31-46).

13:11. **Whenever** the disciples **are arrested** (from *paradidōmi*; cf. v. 9) **and brought to trial** for preaching the gospel, they are **not** to be anxious **beforehand about what to say** in giving a defense. They are to speak **whatever** God (implied) gives them to say **at that moment** (cf. Ex. 4:12; Jer. 1:9). **The Holy Spirit** would do the **speaking;** He would enable them to say the right things at the right times with boldness despite their natural fears. This assistance, however, did not guarantee acquittal.

13:12-13. Opposition will come through official channels (vv. 9, 11) and also through close personal relationships.

It will be so severe that family members—**brother** versus **brother, father** versus **child,** and **children** versus **parents—will betray** (from *paradidōmi*; cf. vv. 9, 11) each other to hostile authorities, thereby causing Christian members to be **put to death.** Because of their allegiance to Jesus (lit., "on account of My name"; cf. v. 9), His disciples will be hated continually by **all men,** that is, all kinds of people, not just hostile authorities or family members (cf. Phil. 1:29; 3:11; Col. 1:24; 1 Peter 4:16). **He who stands firm** (lit., "he who has endured," viewing one's life as completed), who has remained loyal to Jesus Christ and the gospel (cf. Mark 8:35) **to the end** (*eis telos,* adverbial phrase; an idiom meaning "completely, to the limit"; cf. John 13:1; 1 Thes. 2:16) of his life on earth, **will be saved** (cf. Mark 8:35; 10:26-27). This "saved" one will experience God's salvation in its final form—glorification (contrast usage in 13:20; cf. Heb. 9:27-28). Perseverance is a result and outward sign, not the basis, of spiritual genuineness (cf. Rom. 8:29-30; 1 John 2:19). A person genuinely saved by grace through faith (cf. Eph. 2:8-10) endures to the end and will experience the consummation of his salvation.

These words of warning were pertinent to Mark's Roman readers who were threatened by persecution for their allegiance to Jesus. Such suffering could be more readily endured when viewed in the context of God's plan for worldwide evangelism and vindication. (Cf. comments on Matt. 24:13.)

c. Jesus' portrayal of the coming crisis (13:14-23)
(Matt. 24:15-28; Luke 21:20-24)

Jesus then answered the disciples' second question (Mark 13:4b) positively (vv. 14-23).

Some interpreters limit the events of this section to the chaotic years preceding Jerusalem's fall (A.D. 66-70). Others relate them exclusively to the Great Tribulation at the end of this Age. But the details suggest that *both* events are in view (cf. Matt. 24:15-16, 29-31; Luke 21:20-28). The conquest of Jerusalem is theologically (not chronologically) attached to the end-time events (cf. Dan. 9:26-27; Luke 21:24). The expression "the abomination that causes desolation" is the link between the historical and eschatological

perspectives (cf. Dan. 11:31 with Dan. 9:27; 12:11). These "near" tribulations foreshadowed the "far" Tribulation of the end time.

13:14. The sign that "these things" were about to be fulfilled (cf. v. 4b) was the appearance of **the abomination that causes desolation** (lit., "the abomination of desolation"; cf. Dan. 9:27; 11:31; 12:11; Matt. 24:15), **standing where it does not belong,** a reference to the temple sanctuary. More precise identification may have been politically dangerous for his readers. Mark's exhortation, **Let the reader understand,** was a decoding signal urging them to recognize the significance of Jesus' words in light of their Old Testament context (cf., e.g., Dan. 9:25-27).

The word "abomination" denoted pagan idolatry and its detestable practices (Deut. 29:16-18; 2 Kings 16:3-4; 23:12-14; Ezek. 8:9-18). The phrase "the abomination of desolation" referred to the presence of an idolatrous person or object so detestable that it caused the temple to be abandoned and left desolate.

Historically, the first fulfillment of Daniel's prophetic use of the expression (Dan. 11:31-32) was the desecration of the temple in 167 B.C. by the Syrian ruler Antiochus Epiphanes. He erected an altar to the pagan Greek god Zeus over the altar of burnt offering and sacrificed a pig on it (cf. apocryphal 1 Maccabees 1:41-64; 6:7; and Josephus *The Antiquities of the Jews* 12. 5. 4).

Jesus' use of "the abomination of desolation" referred to another fulfillment—the temple's desecration and destruction in A.D. 70. **When** (lit., "whenever") His disciples, those present and future, **see** this desecration take place, it is a signal for people **in Judea** to escape **to the mountains** beyond the Jordan River in Perea.

Josephus recorded the occupation and appalling profaning of the temple in A.D. 67-68 by Jewish Zealots, who also installed a usurper, Phanni, as high priest (Josephus *Jewish Wars* 4. 3. 7-10; 4. 6. 3). Jewish Christians fled to Pella, a town located in the Transjordanian mountains (Eusebius *Ecclesiastical History* 3. 5. 3).

The events of 167 B.C. and A.D. 70 foreshadow a final fulfillment of Jesus' words just prior to His Second Advent (cf. Mark 13:24-27). Mark used the *masculine* participle "standing" (*hestēkota,* masc. perf. part.) to modify the *neuter* noun "abomination" (*bdelygma*; v. 14). This suggests that "the abomination" is a future person "standing where he (NIV marg.) does not belong."

This person is the end-time Antichrist (Dan. 7:23-26; 9:25-27; 2 Thes. 2:3-4, 8-9; Rev. 13:1-10, 14-15). He will make a covenant with the Jewish people at the beginning of the seven-year period preceding Christ's second coming (Dan. 9:27). The temple will be rebuilt and worship reestablished (Rev. 11:1). In the middle of this period (after 3½ years) the Antichrist will break his covenant, stop temple sacrifices, desecrate the temple (cf. Dan. 9:27), and proclaim himself to be God (Matt. 24:15; 2 Thes. 2:3-4; Rev. 11:2). This launches the terrible end-time events of the Great Tribulation (Rev. 6; 8-9; 16). Those who refuse to be identified with the Antichrist will suffer severe persecution and be forced to flee for refuge (Rev. 12:6, 13-17). Many—both Jews and Gentiles—will be saved during this period (Rev. 7) but many will also be martyred (Rev. 6:9-11).

13:15-18. When this crisis breaks, the person **on the roof of his house** (cf. 2:2-4) must not take time to **go** inside to retrieve any possessions. The person working out **in the field** must not take time to **go back** to another part of the field or his house **to get his cloak,** an outer garment that protected against cold night air.

Jesus expressed compassion **for pregnant women and nursing mothers** forced to flee under such difficult circumstances. He exhorted His disciples (cf. 13:14) to **pray that this** (lit., "it"; cf. v. 29)—the coming crisis necessitating their flight—**will not** happen during the **winter,** the rainy season when swollen streams would be difficult to cross.

13:19. The reason their flight was urgent and hopefully would be unhindered is that **those** (lit., "those days") **will be days of distress** (lit., "will be a tribulation," *thlipsis*; cf. v. 24) **unequaled from the beginning** of Creation **until now . . . never** (*ou mē*; cf. v. 2) **to be equaled again.** At no time in the past, present, or future has there been or will there be such a severe tribulation as this.

This unprecedented distress was true of but not restricted to the destruction of Jerusalem (cf. Josephus *Jewish Wars* preface; 1. 1. 4; 5. 10. 5). Jesus looked beyond A.D. 70 to the final Great Tribulation (*thlipsis*; cf. Rev. 7:14) prior to the Second Advent. This is supported by these facts: (a) Mark 13:19 echoes Daniel 12:1, an end-time prophecy; (b) the words "never to be equaled again" indicate that another crisis will never be like this one; (c) "those days" link the "near" future with the "far" future (cf. Mark 13:17, 19-20, 24; Jer. 3:16, 18; 33:14-16; Joel 3:1) (d) the days will be terminated (Mark 13:20).

13:20. If the Lord (*Yahweh* God; cf. 12:29), **had not** already decided in His sovereign plan to **cut short** (terminate, not reduce the number of) **those days** (lit., "the days"; cf. 13:19), **no one would survive** (*esōthē*, "would be saved"; cf. 15:30-31), that is, be delivered from physical death; this is in contrast with 13:13. **But** God set limits on the duration of the end-time Tribulation, because **of the elect,** those redeemed during "those days," **whom He has chosen** for Himself (cf. Acts 13:48). While all this proved true indirectly in A.D. 70, the language of this verse suggests God's *direct* intervention in judgment, an unmistakable characteristic of the end-time Tribulation (cf. Rev. 16:1).

13:21-22. At that time (*tote*, "then"; cf. vv. 26-27) in the middle of "those days" (cf. v. 19) of severe affliction and flight, **if** someone should claim that **the Christ** (Messiah) was **here** or **there,** His disciples were **not** to **believe it** (the fallacious claim, or possibly "him," the person), and turn aside from taking refuge. Jesus explained that many **false Christs** (messiahs; cf. v. 6) **and false prophets** would **appear and perform** miraculous deeds that would seem to validate their claims. Their purpose would be **to** mislead **the elect** (cf. v. 20), believers in the true Messiah. The clause **if that were possible** shows that they will not succeed.

13:23. Again Jesus exhorted His disciples, **Be on . . . guard** (*blepete*; cf. vv. 5, 9) for deceptive pitfalls in crisis days.

d. Jesus' portrayal of His triumphant return (13:24-27)
(Matt. 24:29-31; Luke 21:25-28)

13:24-25. The word **But** (*alla*) introduces a sharp contrast between the appearance of false messiahs who will perform miraculous signs (v. 22) and the dramatic coming of the true Messiah **in those days** (cf. vv. 19-20; Joel 2:28-32) **following that distress** (*thlipsin*, "tribulation"; cf. Mark 13:19). These phrases indicate a close connection with verses 14-23. If these verses apply exclusively to the events of A.D. 70 then Jesus Christ should have returned shortly thereafter. That He did not return then supports the view that verses 14-23 refer to both the destruction of Jerusalem and the future Great Tribulation before Christ will return.

A variety of cosmic disorders involving **the sun . . . moon,** and **stars** will immediately precede the Second Advent. Jesus' description is fashioned from Isaiah 13:10 and 34:4 without His quoting exactly from either passage. This vividly refers to observable celestial changes in the physical universe.

The last statement—**the heavenly bodies** (lit., "the powers that are in the skies") **will be shaken**—may refer to: (a) physical forces controlling the movements of the celestial bodies which will be thrown out of their normal course, or (b) spiritual forces of evil, Satan and his cohorts, who will be greatly disturbed by these events. The first view is preferred.

13:26. At that time (*tote*, "then"; this Gr. word is also used in vv. 21, 27 though the NIV does not trans. it in v. 27) when the cosmic events just mentioned have taken place, **men** (generic, "people") living on the earth then **will see the Son of Man** (cf. 8:31, 38) **coming in clouds** or "with clouds." The "clouds of heaven" signify divine presence (cf. 9:7; Ex. 19:9; Ps. 97:1-2; Dan. 7:13; Matt. 24:30b). He will exercise **great power and** display heavenly **glory** (cf. Zech. 14:1-7). This is Jesus' personal, visible, bodily return to the earth as the glorified Son of Man (cf. Acts 1:11; Rev. 1:7; 19:11-16). Jesus described it in the familiar but elusive language of Daniel 7:13-14. His triumphant return will bring an end to the veiled nature of God's kingdom in its present form (cf. comments on Mark 1:15; 4:13-23).

13:27. Also at that time (*tote*, "then," omitted in the NIV; cf. vv. 21, 26) the Son of Man **will send** forth (cf. 4:29) **His angels** (cf. 8:38; Matt. 25:31) **and gather His elect** (cf. Mark 13:20, 22) **from the four winds.** The "four winds" means from all directions, a reference to people living in all parts of the world, as emphasized by the last two phrases (v. 27). None of the elect will be left out. Though not stated, this would appear to include a resurrection of Old Testament saints and believers martyred during the Tribulation (cf. Dan. 12:2; Rev. 6:9-11; 20:4). Nothing is said here about those not among the elect (cf. 2 Thes. 1:6-10; Rev. 20:11-15).

The Old Testament often mentioned God's regathering of dispersed Israelites from the remotest parts of the earth to national and spiritual unity in Palestine (Deut. 30:3-6; Isa. 11:12; Jer. 31:7-9; Ezek. 11:16-17; 20:33-35, 41). At the time of the Second Advent Israelites will be regathered around the triumphant Son of Man, judged, restored as a nation, and redeemed (Isa. 59:20-21; Ezek. 20:33-44; Zech. 13:8-9; Rom. 11:25-27). Also all the Gentiles will be gathered before Him (Joel 3:2) and like a shepherd He will separate "the sheep" (the elect) from "the goats" (Matt. 25:31-46). These redeemed Jews and Gentiles will enter the millennial kingdom, living on the earth in natural bodies (Isa. 2:2-4; Dan. 7:13-14; Micah 4:1-5; Zech. 14:8-11, 16-21).

Identifying "the elect" in this context as Gentiles and Jews who come to believe in Jesus as the Messiah *during* the final Tribulation period (cf. Rev. 7:3-4, 9-10) is compatible with a pretribulational view of the Rapture of the church, the body of Christ (cf. 1 Cor. 15:51-53; 1 Thes. 4:13-18). Since the church will be spared from God's final judgment on the earth (cf. 1 Thes. 1:10; 5:9-11; Rev. 3:9-10), the church will not go through the Tribulation. This preserves the imminence of the Rapture for present-day believers and gives added emphasis to Jesus' exhortation, "Watch!" (cf. Mark 13:35-37) But since Jesus' disciples had no clear understanding of the coming church (cf. Matt. 16:18; Acts 1:4-8), He did not mention this initial phase of God's end-time program separately.

Some interpreters, however, hold to a posttribulational view of the Rapture. They identify "the elect" here as the redeemed of all ages—past, present, and future. This requires the resurrection of all the righteous dead at the end of the Tribulation and together with all living believers they will be caught up (raptured) to meet the returning Son of Man who descends to the earth at that time. Thus the church, the body of Christ, *remains* on earth during the Tribulation period, is supernaturally protected as an entity through it, is raptured at the end of it, and immediately returns to the earth to participate in the Millennium. But in light of the preceding discussion on Mark 13:17 and the following discussion on verse 32, the pretribulational viewpoint is preferred.

e. His parabolic lesson from the fig tree (13:28-32)
(Matt. 24:32-36; Luke 21:29-33)

13:28. The disciples' first question (v. 4a) was, "When will these things happen?" Jesus exhorted them to **learn a lesson** (lit., "the parable"; cf. introduction to 4:1-2) **from the fig tree.** Though the fig tree was sometimes used as a symbol for Israel (11:14), Jesus did not intend such a meaning here (in Luke 21:29 the words "and all the trees" are added). In contrast with most of Palestine's trees, fig trees lose their leaves in winter and bloom later in the spring. Thus whenever the stiff, dry, winter **twigs** become **tender,** softened due to the rising sap, and **leaves** appear, then observers **know that** winter is past and **summer is near.**

13:29. This verse applies the lesson of verse 28. Whenever **you** (emphatic position in Gr.), the disciples in contrast with others, **see these things** (cf. vv. 4, 23, 30), the events described in verses 14-23, then **you know that** the impending crisis (cf. v. 14) **is near** in time, in fact, **right at the door.** This was a common figure for an imminent event. If alert to these events the disciples have sufficient insight to discern their true meaning.

The unstated subject of the Greek verb "is" could be rendered "He" (the Son of Man) or preferably **it** ("the abomination that causes desolation," v. 14).

13:30-31. With solemn introductory words (**I tell you the truth;** cf. 3:28) Jesus declared that **this generation will certainly not** (*ou mē*, emphatic double negative; cf. 13:2) come to an end **until** (lit., "until which time") **all these things** (cf. vv. 4b, 29) **have** taken place. "Generation" (*genea*) can refer to one's "contem-

poraries," all those living at a given time (cf. 8:12, 38; 9:19), or to a group of people descended from a common ancestor (cf. Matt. 23:36). Since the word "generation" is capable of both a narrow and a broad sense, it is preferable in this context (cf. Mark 13:14) to understand in it a double reference incorporating both senses. Thus "this generation" means: (a) the Jews living at Jesus' time who later saw the destruction of Jerusalem, and (b) the Jews who will be living at the time of the Great Tribulation who will see the end-time events. This accounts best for the accomplishment of "all these things" (cf. vv. 4b, 14-23).

Jesus' assertion (v. 31) guarantees the fulfillment of His prophecy (v. 30). The present universe will come to a cataclysmic end (cf. 2 Peter 3:7, 10-13) **but** Jesus' **words**—including these predictions—**will never** (*ou mē*; cf. Mark 13:2, 30) **pass away.** They will have eternal validity. What is true of God's words (cf. Isa. 40:6-8; 55:11) is equally true of Jesus' words, for He is God.

13:32. Though it will be possible for some to discern the proximity of the coming crisis (vv. 28-29), yet **no one knows** the precise moment when **that day or hour** will arrive (cf. v. 33) except **the Father. Not even the angels** (cf. 1 Peter 1:12) **nor the Son** know. This openly expressed limitation on Jesus' knowledge affirms His humanity. In His Incarnation Jesus voluntarily accepted human limitations, including this one (cf. Acts 1:7), in submission to the Father's will (cf. John 4:34). On the other hand Jesus' use of "the Son" title (only here in Mark) instead of the usual "Son of Man" revealed His own awareness of His deity and sonship (cf. Mark 8:38). Nevertheless He exercised His divine attributes only at the Father's bidding (cf. 5:30; John 8:28-29).

The words "that day or hour" are widely understood to refer to the Son of Man's second coming (Mark 13:26). But that event will climax a series of preliminary events. In light of Old Testament usage and this context (vv. 14, 29-30) it is preferable to understand "that day" as referring to "the day of the Lord."

The "day of the Lord" includes the Tribulation, the Second Advent, and the Millennium (cf. Isa. 2:12-22; Jer. 30:7-9; Joel 2:28-32; Amos 9:11; Zeph. 3:11-20;

Zech. 12–14). It will begin suddenly and unexpectedly (cf. 1 Thes. 5:2), so no one except the Father knows the critical moment.

In the pretribulational view of the future (cf. comments on Mark 13:27) the coming of the Lord for His own (the Rapture) will occur before the 70th week of Daniel. The Rapture is not conditioned by any preliminary events. It is therefore an imminent event for each generation. The Parable of the Absent House Owner (vv. 34-37) along with Matthew's corresponding account (cf. Matt. 24:42-44) support this view. It precludes all date-setting and lends urgency to Jesus' exhortations to be watching and working till His return.

3. JESUS' EXHORTATION TO VIGILANCE (13:33-37)

(MATT. 24:42-44; LUKE 21:34-36)

13:33. Because no one knows **when** (cf. v. 4a) **that time,** the appointed time of God's intervention ("that day," v. 32), **will come,** Jesus repeated His admonition, **Be on guard!** (*blepete;* cf. vv. 5, 9, 23) and added, **Be alert!** (*agrypneite,* "be constantly awake")

13:34-37. The Parable of the Absent House Owner, unique to Mark, reinforces the call to constant vigilance and defines it as a faithful fulfillment of assigned tasks (cf. Matt. 25:14-30; Luke 19:11-27).

Before **going away** on a journey the Owner put **his servants** (collectively) **in charge of** carrying on the work of **his house.** He gave **each** one **his** own **task** and ordered the doorkeeper who controlled all access to the house **to keep watch** (*grēgoreite,* pres. tense; cf. Mark 13:33).

Jesus applied this parable to His disciples (vv. 35-37) without distinguishing between the doorkeeper and the other servants. They all are responsible to **keep watch,** to be alert to spiritual dangers and opportunities (cf. vv. 5-13) **because** no one knows **when** (cf. v. 33) **the Owner** (*kyrios*) **of the house,** who indirectly represents Jesus Himself, **will** return. The night represents the time of the Owner's (Jesus') absence (cf. Rom. 13:11-14). He could return at any time, so they should be constantly watching in view of the danger that if (lit., "when") the Owner, Jesus, **comes suddenly,** He should **find**

them **sleeping** (spiritually negligent), not watching for His return. Such vigilance is the responsibility not only of the Twelve (cf. Mark 13:3) but also of every believer in every generation during this present Age. Believers should be watching and working (cf. v. 34) in light of the certainty of His return, though its time is unknown except to the Father.

The reference to the four watches corresponds to the Roman system of reckoning time. **The evening** was 6–9 P.M.; the **midnight** watch was 9 P.M. till midnight; **when the rooster crows** was the third watch (midnight till 3 A.M.); and **dawn** was 3–6 A.M. (These names of the watches were derived from their termination points.) This differs from the Jewish system of dividing the night into three watches. Mark used the Roman system for his readers' benefit (cf. 6:48).

VIII. Jesus' Suffering and Death in Jerusalem (chaps. 14–15)

The sixth major section of Mark's Gospel, the Passion narrative, includes Jesus' betrayal, arrest, trial, and death by crucifixion. It provides the necessary historical and theological perspective for various themes mentioned earlier in the Gospel: (a) Jesus as the Christ, the Son of God (1:1; 8:29); (b) His conflicts with the religious authorities (3:6; 11:18; 12:12); (c) His rejection, betrayal, and abandonment by those close to Him (3:19; 6:1-6); (d) His disciples' failure to understand His messianic office clearly (8:31–10:52); (e) His coming as the Son of Man to give His life a ransom for many (10:45).

The narrative reflects how the early Christians turned to the Old Testament (esp. Pss. 22; 69; Isa. 53) to understand the meaning of Jesus' suffering and death and to explain the ignominious course of events to their Jewish and Gentile contemporaries (cf. 1 Cor. 1:22-24).

A. Jesus' betrayal, the Passover meal, and His disciples' desertion (14:1-52)

This division consists of three cycles of events (vv. 1-11, 12-26, 27-52).

1. THE PLOT TO KILL JESUS AND HIS ANOINTING IN BETHANY (14:1-11)

Like other passages in Mark the first cycle of events in this division also has a "sandwich" structure (cf. 3:20-35; 5:21-43; 6:7-31; 11:12-26; 14:27-52). The account of the conspiracy by the religious leaders and Judas (vv. 1-2, 10-11) is divided by the account of Jesus' anointing in Bethany (vv. 3-9). In this way Mark emphasized the striking contrast between the hostility of those who plotted His death and the loving devotion of one who recognized Him as the suffering Messiah.

a. The leaders' plot to arrest and kill Jesus (14:1-2)
(Matt. 26:1-5; Luke 22:1-2)

14:1a. Mark's Passion narrative begins with a new chronological starting point (cf. introduction to 11:1-11), the first of several time notations that link the following events. The chronology of the Passion Week events is complicated partly because two systems of reckoning time were in use, the Roman (modern) system in which a new day starts at midnight and the Jewish system in which a new day begins at sunset (cf. 13:35).

The Passover, observed in Jerusalem (cf. Deut. 16:5-6), was an annual Jewish festival (cf. Ex. 12:1-14) celebrated on Nisan (March-April) 14-15 (which most say was Thursday-Friday of Jesus' Passion Week). Preparations for the Passover meal (cf. Mark 14:12-16)—the highlight of the festival—included the slaughter of the Passover lamb which took place near the close of Nisan 14 by Jewish reckoning, Thursday afternoon. The Passover meal was eaten at the beginning of Nisan 15, that is, between sunset and midnight Thursday evening. This was followed immediately by the festival **of Unleavened Bread** celebrated from Nisan 15-21 inclusive, to commemorate the Jews' exodus from Egypt (cf. Ex. 12:15-20).

These two Jewish festivals were closely related and in popular usage were often designated as the "Jewish Passover Feast" (an eight-day festival, Nisan 14-21 inclusive; cf. Mark 14:2; John 2:13, 23; 6:4; 11:55). So Nisan 14, the day of preparation, was commonly called "the first day of the Feast of Unleavened Bread" (cf. Mark 14:12; Josephus *The Antiquities of the Jews* 2. 15. 1). The words **only two days away** are literally, "after two days." To the Jews, with their inclusive way of counting, "after two days" would mean

"on the day after tomorrow." Reckoning from Nisan 15 (Friday) two days prior would be Nisan 13 (Wednesday), and "after two days" means "after Wednesday and Thursday."

14:1b-2. The Jewish religious leaders, Sanhedrin members (cf. 8:31; 11:27; Matt. 26:3), had already decided that **Jesus** must be put to death (cf. John 11:47-53). But their fear of a popular uprising kept them from seizing Him openly. So they kept seeking (*ezētoun,* imperf. tense; cf. Mark 11:18; 12:12) **for some sly way** (lit., "how to seize Him by deceit"), by a cunning covert strategy, to do it. However, because of the large Passover crowds it was still unwise to risk a **riot** by many potential supporters of Jesus, especially impetuous Galileans. So the leaders determined **not** to seize Him **during the Feast,** the full eight-day festival, Nisan 14-21 inclusive (cf. 14:1a). Apparently they planned to arrest Him after the crowds had gone, but Judas' unexpected offer (cf. vv. 10-11) expedited matters. Thus God's timetable was followed.

b. Jesus' anointing in Bethany (14:3-9)
(Matt. 26:6-13; John 12:1-8)

This anointing episode is not to be equated with an earlier anointing in Galilee (Luke 7:36-50). However, it is the same episode recorded in John 12:1-8 though there are some significant differences. One difference concerns when the event occurred. John stated that it happened "six days before the Passover," that is, the beginning of the Passover festival, Nisan 14 (Thursday). This means it occurred the previous Friday. Mark's placement seems to suggest that the episode occurred on Wednesday of Passion Week (cf. Mark 14:1a). In light of this it seems reasonable to follow John's chronology and to conclude that Mark used the incident thematically (cf. introduction to 2:1-12; 11:1-11) to contrast the responses of this woman and Judas. Consequently the time reference in 14:1 governs the leaders' concern to arrest Jesus, not *this* event.

14:3. While . . . in Bethany (cf. comments in 11:1a) Jesus was being honored with a festive meal **in the home of . . . Simon the Leper,** a man apparently cured by Jesus previously (cf. 1:40) and well known to the early disciples. The unnamed **woman** was Mary, sister of Martha and Lazarus (cf. John 12:3). She **came with an alabaster jar,** a small stone flask with a long slender neck, containing about a pint of costly **perfume** (lit., "ointment") **made of pure** (unadulterated) **nard,** an aromatic oil from a rare plant root native to India.

Mary **broke** the slender neck of **the** stone flask **and poured the perfume** over Jesus' **head.** John wrote that she poured it on Jesus' feet and wiped them with her hair (cf. John 12:3). Both are possible since Jesus was reclining on a dining couch at the table (cf. Mark 14:18). Anointing a guest's head was a common custom at festive Jewish meals (cf. Ps. 23:5; Luke 7:46) but Mary's act had a greater meaning (cf. Mark 14:8-9).

14:4-5. **Some** of the disciples, led by Judas (cf. John 12:4), voiced angry (cf. Mark 10:14) criticism of this apparent wasteful extravagance. In their view the act was uncalled for because the **perfume . . . could have been sold for more than a year's wages** (lit., "more than 300 denarii," roughly a year's wages; cf. comments on 6:37) **and the money given to the poor.** This was a legitimate concern (cf. John 13:29), but here it concealed the disciples' insensitivity and Judas' greed (cf. John 12:6). So they were scolding (same verb in Mark 1:43) **her,** a comment unique to Mark.

14:6-8. **Jesus** rebuked Mary's critics and defended **her** action, calling it **a beautiful thing** (lit., "a good [kalon, 'noble, beautiful, good'] work"). Unlike them, He saw it as an expression of love and devotion to Him in light of His approaching death as well as a messianic acclamation.

The contrast in verse 7 is not between Jesus and **the poor** but between the words **always** and **not always.** Opportunities to **help** the poor will always be present and the disciples should take advantage of them. But Jesus would not be in their midst much longer and opportunities to show Him love were diminishing rapidly. In a sense **she** had anointed His **body beforehand** in preparation for its **burial.**

14:9. Prefaced by a solemn introductory saying (**I tell you the truth;** cf. 3:28) Jesus promised Mary that **wherever the gospel** (cf. 1:1) **is preached throughout the world** (cf. 13:10) her deed of love would **also be told** along with the gospel **in memory of her.** This unique promise looked beyond His death, burial, and resurrection to the present period of time when the gospel is being preached.

c. Judas' agreement to betray Jesus (14:10-11)
(Matt. 26:14-16; Luke 22:3-6)

14:10-11. These verses complement verses 1-2 and heighten the contrast with verses 3-9. **Judas Iscariot** (cf. 3:19), **one of the Twelve** (cf. 3:14), **went to the** influential **chief priests** (cf. 14:1) and offered **to betray** (paradoi; cf. v. 11; 9:31) **Jesus to them.** He suggested doing it "when no crowd was present" (Luke 22:6). This would avoid a public disturbance, which was the priests' primary concern (cf. Mark 14:2). **They** welcomed this unexpected offer, one they would have never dared solicit. They **promised to give him money** (30 pieces of silver, in response to his demand; cf. Matt. 26:15). So Judas was seeking (ezētei; cf. Mark 14:1) the right **opportunity,** without the presence of a crowd, **to hand Him over** (paradoi; cf. v. 10; 9:31) into their custody.

Why did Judas offer to betray Jesus? Various suggestions have been made, each of which may contain an element of truth: (1) Judas, the only non-Galilean member of the Twelve, may have responded to the official notice (John 11:57). (2) He was disillusioned by Jesus' failure to establish a political kingdom and his hopes for material gain seemed doomed. (3) His love for money moved him to salvage something for himself. Ultimately he came under satanic control (cf. Luke 22:3; John 13:2, 27).

In Judas' life one finds an intriguing combination of divine sovereignty and human responsibility. According to God's plan Jesus must suffer and die (Rev. 13:8); yet Judas, though not compelled to be the traitor, was held responsible for submitting to Satan's directives (cf. Mark 14:21; John 13:27).

2. THE PASSOVER MEAL AS THE LAST SUPPER (14:12-26)

The second cycle of events in this chapter also has three parts (vv. 12-16, 17-21, 22-26).

a. The preparation of the Passover meal (14:12-16)
(Matt. 26:17-19; Luke 22:7-13)

14:12. The time designation, **on the first day of the Feast of Unleavened Bread,** would be Nisan 15 (Friday), strictly speaking. However, the qualifying clause (a common feature in Mark's time notations; cf. 1:32, 35; 4:35; 13:24; 14:30; 15:42; 16:2) referring to the day **Passover** lambs were slaughtered indicates that Nisan 14 (Thursday) was meant (cf. comments on 14:1a).

Since the Passover meal had to be eaten within Jerusalem's walls, the **disciples asked** Jesus **where** He wanted them **to go and make preparations** (cf. v. 16) **for** the meal. They assumed they would eat this "family feast" with Him (cf. v. 15).

14:13-15. This episode is structurally parallel to 11:1b-7. It may reflect another instance of Jesus' supernatural knowledge. However, the need for security (cf. 14:10-11), the disciples' question (v. 12), and Jesus' subsequent directives seem to indicate that He had carefully reserved a place in advance where they could eat the Passover meal together undisturbed.

Jesus and **His disciples** were probably in Bethany (cf. 11:1a, 11). Thursday morning **He sent two of** them—Peter and John (cf. Luke 22:8)—into Jerusalem with instructions for locating the reserved room. For security reasons (cf. Mark 14:11; John 11:57) the participants remained anonymous and the location was kept secret.

A man carrying a jar of water would **meet** the two disciples, presumably near the eastern gate. This unusual, eye-catching sight suggests that it was a prearranged signal because normally only women carried water jars (men carried wineskins). They were to **follow** this man, apparently a servant, who would lead them to the right **house.** They were to tell the **owner . . . The Teacher** (cf. Mark 4:38) **asks: Where is My guest room. . . ?** The single self-designation "Teacher" implies Jesus was well known to the owner and the possessive pronoun "My" implies His prior arrangement to use the room.

He (*autos,* the owner "himself") would **show** them **a large Upper Room,** built on the flat ceiling, **furnished** (with a dining table and reclining couches), and set up for a banquet meal. The owner also may have secured the necessary food including the Passover lamb. The two disciples were to prepare the meal for Jesus and the other disciples (cf. 14:12) **there.** Tradition claims this was Mark's home (cf. comments on vv. 41-52; also Acts 1:13; 12:12) and the owner was Mark's father.

14:16. Presumably preparing **the Passover** meal involved roasting the lamb, setting out the unleavened bread and wine, and preparing bitter herbs along with a sauce made of dried fruit moistened with vinegar and wine and combined with spices.

These Passover preparations on Nisan 14 (Thursday) imply that Jesus' last meal with His disciples was the regular Passover meal held that evening (Nisan 15 after sunset) and that He was crucified on Nisan 15 (Friday). This is the consistent witness of the Synoptic Gospels (cf. Matt. 26:2, 17-19; Mark 14:1, 12-14; Luke 22:1, 7-8, 11-15). The Gospel of John, however, indicates that Jesus was crucified on "the day of preparation" (John 19:14). This was the Passover proper and also the preparation for the seven-day Feast of Unleavened Bread, which was sometimes called the Passover Week (cf. Luke 22:1, 7; Acts 12:3-4; see comments on Luke 22:7-38).

b. Jesus' announcement of His betrayal (14:17-21)
(Matt. 26:20-25; Luke 22:21-23; John 13:21-30)

14:17. That (Thursday) **evening,** the beginning of Nisan 15 (cf. v. 1a), **Jesus** and **the Twelve** arrived in Jerusalem to eat the Passover meal which began after sunset and had to be finished by midnight. Mark abbreviated the events of the meal (cf. Luke 22:14-16, 24-30; John 13:1-20) in order to focus attention on two incidents: (a) Jesus' announcement of His betrayal as they dipped bread and bitter herbs into a bowl of fruit sauce together (Mark 14:18-21), and (b) His new interpretation of the bread and wine just after the meal (vv. 22-25).

14:18-20. It was customary to recline on dining couches during a festive meal (cf. 14:3; John 13:23-25); in fact, it was a first-century requirement for the Passover meal, even for the poorest people (cf.

Mishnah *Pesachim* 10. 1). **While they were . . . eating,** dipping bread into the bowl (cf. Mark 14:20) before the meal itself, Jesus, with solemn introductory words (**I tell you the truth;** cf. 3:28), announced that **one of** the Twelve would **betray** Him (cf. 14:10-11).

The added words, **one who is eating with Me,** unique to Mark, allude to Psalm 41:9 where David laments that his trusted friend Ahithophel (cf. 2 Sam. 16:15–17:23; 1 Chron. 27:33), who shared **table** fellowship with him, had turned against him. To eat with a person and then betray him was the height of treachery.

This thought is reinforced in Mark 14:19-20. The disciples were deeply grieved. **One by one** (even Judas; cf. Matt. 26:25) **they** sought to clear themselves. The form of their question in Greek (lit., "It is **not I,** is it?") expects a reassuring negative answer from Jesus. But He declined to name the offender to the group. (The identification in Matt. 26:25 was doubtless made only to Judas.) Jesus repeated His disclosure that His betrayer was **one of the Twelve . . . one who** was dipping **bread into the** same **bowl with** Him. His announcement emphasized the treachery of the betrayal and also gave the betrayer an opportunity to repent.

14:21. On the one hand (Gr., *men*) **the Son of Man** (cf. 8:31) **will go,** that is, He must die, in fulfillment of Scripture (e.g., Ps. 22; Isa. 53). His death was according to God's plan not simply because of the betrayer's action. **But** on the other hand (Gr., *de*) **woe,** a lament denoting heartfelt pity, **to that man,** literally, "through whom **the Son of Man** is being betrayed." The betrayer was acting as Satan's agent (cf. Luke 22:3; John 13:2, 27). So awful a destiny awaited him that **it would** have been **better for him if he** (lit., "that man") **had not been born.** Though he acted within God's plan, the betrayer remained morally responsible (cf. Mark 14:10-11). This woe contrasts sharply with Jesus' promise in verse 9.

c. *The institution of the Lord's Supper (14:22-26)*

(Matt. 26:26-30; Luke 22:19-20)

This is the second key incident Mark selected from the events of the Passover meal (cf. comments on Mark 14:17). Before this meal was eaten in Jewish homes the head of the house explained its meaning regarding Israel's deliverance from slavery in Egypt. As host, Jesus probably did so to prepare His disciples for a new understanding of the bread and wine.

14:22. **While they were eating** (cf. v. 18), apparently before the main part of the meal but after Judas had left (John 13:30), **Jesus took bread** (*arton,* an unleavened flat cake), **gave thanks** (*eulogēsas;* cf. Mark 6:41), **broke it** to distribute it, **and gave it to** them with the words, **Take it** (and "eat" implied); **this is My body.**

Jesus spoke of literal things—the bread, wine, His physical body (*sōma*), and blood—but the relationship between them was expressed figuratively (cf. John 7:35; 8:12; 10:7, 9). The verb "is" means "represents." Jesus was physically present as He spoke these words, so the disciples did not literally eat His body or drink His blood, something abhorrent to Jews anyway (cf. Lev. 3:17; 7:26-27; 17:10-14). This shows the impropriety of the Roman Catholic view of the eucharist (transubstantiation), that the bread and wine are changed into Christ's body and blood.

14:23. Similarly, after the meal (cf. 1 Cor. 11:25), Jesus **took the cup** containing red wine mixed with water, **gave thanks** (*eucharistēsas;* cf. Mark 8:6-7; hence the word "eucharist"), **and offered** (lit., "gave") **it to them, and they all drank from it.** Assuming Jesus followed the established Passover ritual this was the third of four prescribed cups of wine ("the cup of thanksgiving"; cf. 1 Cor. 10:16) which concluded the main portion of the meal. Presumably He did not drink the fourth cup, the cup of consummation. Its significance still lies in the future when Jesus and His followers will be together again in His kingdom (Luke 22:29-30; see comments on Mark 14:25).

14:24. Jesus explained the meaning of the cup: **This** (the wine) **is** (represents) **My blood of** (i.e., which inaugurates) **the covenant, which** (blood) **is poured out for** (*hyper,* "in behalf of, instead of") **many,** a reference to His vicarious, sacrificial death for mankind (cf. 10:45). Just as sacrificial blood ratified the Old (Mosaic) Covenant at Sinai (cf. Ex.

24:6-8), so Jesus' blood shed at Golgotha inaugurated the New Covenant (Jer. 31:31-34). This promises forgiveness of sins and fellowship with God through the indwelling Spirit to those who come to God by faith in Jesus.

The word *diathēkē* ("covenant") refers not to an agreement between two equals (denoted by *synthēkē*) but rather to an arrangement established by one party, in this case God. The other party—man—cannot alter it; he can only accept or reject it. The New Covenant is God's new arrangement in dealing with people, based on Christ's death (cf. Heb. 8:6-13). The spiritual blessings Israel expected God to grant in the last days are *now* mediated through Christ's death to all who believe. The *physical* blessings promised to Israel, however, are not being fulfilled now. They will be fulfilled when Christ returns and establishes His millennial reign with Israel in her land.

14:25. Jesus seldom spoke about His death without looking beyond it. Using solemn introductory words (**I tell you the truth;** cf. 3:28) He vowed that He would **not** (*ouketi ou mē*, "certainly not any more"; cf. 13:2) **drink again of the fruit of the vine,** in this festive way **until that day** (cf. 13:24-27, 32) in the future **when** He will **drink it anew.** He will enjoy renewed table fellowship with His followers in a qualitatively new (*kainon*) existence (cf. Isa. 2:1-4; 4:2-6; 11:1-9; 65:17-25) **in the kingdom of God** (cf. comments on Mark 1:15), the Millennium established on earth when Jesus Christ returns (cf. Rev. 20:4-6).

14:26. The Hallel (praise) Psalms were **sung** or chanted antiphonally in connection with the Passover—the first two (Pss. 113–114) before the meal, the remaining four (Pss. 115–118) after it to conclude the evening observance. Such verses as Psalm 118:6-7, 17-18, 22-24 gain added significance on Jesus' lips just before His suffering and death.

Since their conversation after the meal included Jesus' discourse and prayer (John 13:31–17:26), it was probably near midnight when He and the Eleven (minus Judas) finally left the Upper Room and the city. **They** crossed the Kidron Valley (cf. John 18:1) **to the** western slopes of the **Mount of Olives** (cf. Mark 11:1a) where Gethsemane was located (14:32).

3. JESUS' PRAYER BEFORE HIS ARREST AND THE DISCIPLES' DESERTION (14:27-52)

The third cycle of events in this division has a "sandwich" structure like many other passages in Mark (cf. 3:20-35). The account of Jesus' prediction of His disciples' desertion (14:27-31) and its fulfillment at His arrest (vv. 43-52) is interrupted by the account of Jesus' prayer in Gethsemane (vv. 32-42). In this way Mark emphasized that Jesus faced His final hour of testing alone with His Father, without human sympathy or support.

a. Jesus' prediction of the disciples' desertion and Peter's denial (14:27-31) (Matt. 26:31-35; Luke 22:31-34; John 13:36-38)

Whether this episode took place in the Upper Room (as Luke and John indicate) or on the way to Gethsemane (as Matt. and Mark imply) is difficult to determine. Mark apparently used it thematically without an explicit chronological connection in anticipation of the subsequent events he wished to highlight (e.g., Mark 14:50-52, 66-72). Matthew, however, included a temporal connection (Matt. 26:31, *tote*, "then"). Perhaps Jesus gave this prediction in the Upper Room relating it only to Peter (as in Luke and John), and repeated it on the way to Gethsemane (as in Matt.) telling it to the Eleven and especially to Peter.

14:27. The verb translated **fall away** (*skandalisthēsesthe*) means to take offense at someone or something and thereby turn away and fall into sin (cf. 4:17; 6:3; 9:42-47). **Jesus** predicted that **all 11** disciples would take offense at His sufferings and death. To avoid the same treatment they would "fall away," denying association with Him (cf. 14:30) and desert Him (cf. v. 50). Their loyalty would temporarily collapse.

Jesus applied Zechariah 13:7 to this situation: I (God the Father) **will strike** (put to death) **the Shepherd** (Jesus), **and the sheep** (the disciples) **will be scattered** in all directions. The interpretive change from the command "Strike" (Zech. 13:7) to the assertion "I will strike" suggests that Jesus viewed Himself as God's suffering Servant (cf. Isa. 53: esp. Isa. 53:4-6).

14:28. Jesus immediately countered His desertion prediction with the promise of a post-Resurrection reunion (cf. 16:7; Matt. 28:16-17). As the **risen** Shepherd He would precede His flock **into Galilee,** where they had lived and worked and were called and commissioned by Jesus (Mark 1:16-20; 3:13-15; 6:7, 12-13). They were to "follow" the risen Lord who would continue to lead His people in their future tasks (cf. 13:10; 14:9).

14:29-31. As before (cf. 8:32) **Peter** focused on the first part of Jesus' prediction (14:27), ignoring the second part (v. 28). He insisted that he was an exception—**all** the rest might **fall away** as Jesus predicted (v. 27) but he would **not** (lit., "but not I," the word "I" is emphatic by position). Peter claimed greater allegiance to Jesus than all the others (cf. "more than these"; John 21:15).

Prefaced by solemn introductory words (**I tell you the truth**; cf. Mark 3:28) **Jesus** emphatically told Peter that his failure would be greater than the others despite his good intentions. That same night **before the rooster crows twice,** before dawn, Peter would not only desert Jesus but actually **disown** (*aparnēsē,* "deny"; cf. 8:34) Him **three times.** The "cockcrow" was a proverbial expression for early morning before sunrise (cf. 13:35). Only Mark mentioned the rooster crowing twice, a detail probably due to Peter's clear recollection of the incident. (The major Gr. ms. evidence is split over including the word "twice" but the more strongly attested words "the second time" in 14:72 provide confirmation that Mark wrote "twice" here.)

Jesus' pointed reply caused **Peter** to protest even more **emphatically** (an adverb used only here in the NT) that he would **never** (*ou mē,* emphatic negation) **disown** Jesus **even if** he must (*dei;* cf. 8:31) **die with** Jesus. **The others** echoed Peter's affirmation of loyalty. They implied Jesus' prediction was wrong, but a few hours later they showed He was right (14:50, 72).

b. Jesus' prayer in Gethsemane (14:32-42)
(Matt. 26:36-47; Luke 22:39-46)

This is the third time Mark portrayed Jesus in prayer (cf. Mark 1:35; 6:46). In each case Jesus reaffirmed His commitment to God's will. Though Satan is not mentioned directly, he was no doubt present, giving the event the character of a temptation scene (cf. 1:12-13). The Synoptics give five renderings of Jesus' prayer, all similar but with minor variations. Jesus probably repeated the same request in different ways (cf. 14:37, 39).

14:32-34. Jesus and the 11 disciples came to **Gethsemane** (lit., "press of oils," i.e., a press for crushing oil out of olives). It was a gardenlike enclosure in an olive orchard near the foot of the Mount of Olives (cf. v. 26; John 18:1). This secluded spot known also to Judas was one of their favorite meeting places (cf. Luke 22:39; John 18:2).

Jesus told **His disciples**—perhaps as He often had done—to **sit** down near the entrance and wait, literally, "until I have prayed." Then **He** selected **Peter, James, and John** (cf. Mark 5:37; 9:2) to go **along with Him.**

As the four walked into the "garden" Jesus became noticeably **distressed** (from *ekthambeō,* "to be alarmed"; cf. 9:15; 16:5-6) **and troubled** (from *adēmoneō,* "to be in extreme anguish"; cf. Phil. 2:26). He told the three that His **soul** (*psychē,* inner self-conscious life) was **overwhelmed** with such **sorrow** (*perilypos,* "deeply grieved"; cf. Mark 6:26) that it threatened to extinguish His life. This prompted Him to tell them to remain where they were **and keep watch** (*grēgoreite;* cf. 14:38), be alert. The full impact of His death and its *spiritual* consequences struck Jesus and He staggered under its weight. The prospect of alienation from His Father horrified Him.

14:35-36. Moving forward a short distance from the three and gradually prostrating Himself on **the ground** (cf. Matt. 26:39; Luke 22:41) Jesus **prayed** (*proseucheto,* "was praying") aloud with great emotion (Heb. 5:7). His prayer lasted at least an hour (cf. Mark 14:37) but Mark recorded only a brief summary of it, first in narrative form (v. 35b), then in a direct quotation (v. 36).

In essence Jesus requested that **if possible the hour might pass from Him.** The words "if possible" (first-class condition in Gr.) do not express doubt but a concrete supposition on which He based His request. He made His request on the assumption that the Father was able to grant it. The issue remained whether it was God's will to do so (cf. Luke 22:42).

The metaphor "the hour" denoted God's appointed time when Jesus would suffer and die (cf. Mark 14:41b; John 12:23, 27). The corresponding metaphor, **this cup,** referred to the same event. The "cup" means either human suffering and death or more likely, God's wrath against sin, which when poured out includes not only physical but also spiritual suffering and death (cf. Mark 10:38-39; 14:33b-34). In bearing God's judgment the sinless Jesus endured the agony of being "made sin" (cf. 15:34; 2 Cor. 5:21).

The double title *Abba* (Aram., "My Father") **Father** (Gr., *patēr*) occurs only two other times (Rom. 8:15; Gal. 4:6). "Abba" was a common way young Jewish children addressed their fathers. It conveyed a sense of familial intimacy and familiarity. The Jews, however, did not use it as a personal address to God since such a familar term was considered inappropriate in prayer. Thus Jesus' use of *Abba* in addressing God was new and unique. He probably used it often in His prayers to express His intimate relationship with God as His Father. *Abba* here suggests that Jesus' primary concern in drinking the cup of God's judgment on sin necessarily disrupted this relationship (cf. Jesus' words of address, Mark 15:34).

What did Jesus mean by requesting that the hour "might pass" and that the Father **take** the cup **from** Him? The traditional answer is that Jesus asked to avoid "the hour" hoping, if possible, that it would bypass Him and that the cup would be removed *before* He must drink it. According to this view Jesus prayed a prayer of submission to God's will as He went to the cross. Some interpreters, however, contend that Jesus asked to be restored following "the hour," hoping, if possible, that it would pass on by *after* it came and that the cup would be removed *after* He had drained it (cf. Isa. 51:17-23). In this view, Jesus prayed a prayer of faith that the Father would not abandon Him forever to death under divine wrath but would remove it and resurrect Him.

Though not problem-free (e.g., John 12:27), the traditional view is preferred in light of the contextual factors just discussed, other passages (Matt. 26:39, 42; Luke 22:41-42; Heb. 5:7-8), and the final qualifying statement in Mark 14:36: **Yet** (lit., "but") the final answer, is **not what I** (emphatic) **will but what You** (emphatic) **will.** Jesus' human will was distinct from but never in opposition to the Father's will (cf. John 5:30; 6:38). So He acknowledged that the answer to His request was not governed by what He desired but by what the Father willed. God's will entailed His sacrificial death (cf. Mark 8:31) so He resolutely submitted Himself to it. His deep distress passed from Him but "the hour" did not (cf. 14:41b).

14:37-41a. The emphasis in Mark's narrative now shifts from Jesus' prayer to the three disciples' failure to stay awake (cf. vv. 33-34). Thrice Jesus interrupted His praying and **returned to** where they were only to find **them sleeping.** The first time He addressed **Peter** as **Simon,** his old name (cf. 3:16), and chided him for his failure to **watch for** even **one hour.** Then Jesus exhorted all three, **Watch,** be alert to spiritual dangers, **and pray,** acknowledge dependence on God, **so that you will not fall** (lit., "come") **into temptation.** This anticipated the testings they would face at His arrest and trial (cf. 14:50, 66-72). On the one hand (Gr., *men*) **the spirit** (one's inner desires and best intentions) **is willing** or eager (e.g., Peter, vv. 29, 31), **but** on the other hand (Gr., *de*) **the body** (lit., "flesh"; a person in his humanness and inadequacies) **is weak,** easily overwhelmed in action (e.g., Peter, v. 37).

After going back and praying **the same** petition (cf. v. 36) Jesus returned and **again found them sleeping.** To His words of rebuke they had nothing appropriate **to say** (cf. 9:6).

Following **a third** prayer session, Jesus returned and again found them sleeping. His words (**Are you still sleeping and resting?**) could be a convicting question (NIV), an ironic but compassionate command (KJV), or an exclamation of surprised rebuke. In light of verses 37, 40, the first option seems preferable. Three times Peter failed to watch and pray; three times he would fall into temptation and disown Jesus. This warning applies to all believers, for all are susceptible to spiritual failure (cf. 13:37).

14:41b-42. Probably a short time occurred between verse 41a and 41b. Jesus' word **Enough!** (i.e., of sleeping) aroused the disciples. Then He announced, **The hour** (cf. v. 35) **has come. The Son of Man** (cf. 8:31) was about to be **betrayed** (cf. 9:31) **into the hands**

(control) **of sinners,** specifically, hostile Sanhedrin members. His **betrayer,** Judas, had arrived. Instead of fleeing, Jesus and the three disciples (no doubt now joined by the other eight) advanced to meet Judas. The issue that prompted Jesus' prayer had been settled (cf. 14:35-36).

c. Jesus' betrayal and arrest and the disciples' desertion (14:43-52) (Matt. 26:47-56; Luke 22:47-53; John 18:2-12)

14:43. Immediately (*euthys;* cf. 1:10), while Jesus **was** still **speaking** to His disciples, **Judas** came **with . . . a crowd** of Roman soldiers (cf. John 18:12) **armed with** short hand **swords and** the temple police armed with **clubs** (cf. Luke 22:52). Judas had guided them to Gethsemane (cf. John 18:2) and to Jesus (cf. Acts 1:16) at night so He could be arrested without commotion (cf. Mark 14:1-2). The Sanhedrin (cf. comments on 8:31) issued the warrant for His arrest. The high priest likely secured the aid of the Roman troops.

14:44-47. Judas had given the armed band **a signal** (a **kiss**) that would identify the One they were to **arrest.** They were to **lead Him away under guard** to prevent His escape. When **Judas** entered the "garden," he **at once** (*euthys;* cf. 1:10) **went to Jesus,** greeted Him as **Rabbi** (cf. 4:38; 9:5) **and kissed Him** fervently (intensive compound verb). A kiss on the cheek (or hand) was a common gesture of affection and reverence given to a Rabbi by his disciples. But Judas used it as a token of betrayal.

Since **Jesus** offered no resistance He was easily **seized** and **arrested.** No charges are stated in Mark's account; nevertheless the legality of His arrest according to Jewish criminal law was assumed since the Sanhedrin authorized it. His apparent defenselessness continued to veil His true identity publicly.

Mark recorded a single-handed attempt at armed resistance by an unnamed bystander (Peter; cf. John 18:10). The Greek wording implies Mark knew who it was. As one of two disciples with a **sword** (cf. Luke 22:38), Peter **drew** it **and struck** Malchus, **the servant of the high priest,** Caiaphas. But Peter managed to cut **off** only **his** right **ear** (cf. John 18:10, 13). Only Luke recorded that Jesus

restored it (cf. Luke 22:51). Peter's attempted defense of Jesus was a wrong deed in a wrong place.

14:48-50. Though He offered no resistance **Jesus** did protest to the religious authorities for the excessive display of armed force marshaled against Him as if He had been **leading a rebellion** (lit., "as though they came out against an armed robber"). He was not a revolutionary who acted in stealth but a recognized religious Teacher. **Every day** that week He appeared openly among them in Jerusalem **teaching** (cf. 11:17) **in the temple courts** (*hierō;* cf. 11:11) but they **did not arrest** Him (cf. 12:12; 14:1-2). Their arresting Him like a criminal at night in a secluded place showed their cowardice. But this happened so that **the Scriptures** would **be fulfilled** (cf. Isa. 53:3, 7-9, 12).

When Jesus' response made it clear that He would not resist His arrest, the disciples' loyalty and their confidence in Him as the Messiah collapsed. **Everyone** ("all," emphatic by position) **deserted Him and fled** (cf. Mark 14:27). No one remained with Jesus to share His suffering—not even Peter (cf. v. 29).

14:51-52. This unusual episode, unique to Mark, supplements verse 50 emphasizing the fact that all fled, leaving Jesus completely forsaken. Most interpreters believe that this **young man** (*neaniskos,* a person in the prime of life, between 24 and 40 years of age) was Mark himself. If so, and if he was the son of the house owner (vv. 14-15; cf. Acts 12:12) that night's events may have occurred as follows. After Jesus and His disciples left Mark's father's house after the Passover, Mark removed his outer cloak (cf. Mark 13:16) and went to bed wrapped in **a linen** sleeping **garment** (lit., "cloth"). Shortly afterward a servant may have aroused him with the news about Judas' treachery since Judas and the arresting force had come there looking for Jesus. Without stopping to dress Mark rushed to Gethsemane perhaps to warn Jesus, who had already been arrested when Mark arrived. After all the disciples fled, Mark **was following Jesus** and His captors into the city **when** some of them **seized** Mark, perhaps as a potential witness, but **he fled** from them **naked, leaving his** linen sleeping **garment** in someone's hands. So no one remained with Jesus—not even a courageous young man who intended to follow Him.

B. Jesus' trials, crucifixion, and burial (14:53–15:47)

This division also consists of three cycles of events: Jesus' trials (14:53–15:20), crucifixion (15:21-41), and burial (15:42-47).

1. JESUS' TRIALS BEFORE THE SANHEDRIN AND PILATE (14:53–15:20)

Jesus was tried first by the religious authorities and then by the political authorities. This was necessary because the Sanhedrin did not have the power to exercise capital punishment (John 18:31). Each of the two trials had three hearings. (See the chart, "Jesus' Six Trials," at Matt. 26:57-58.)

a. Jesus' trial before the Sanhedrin and Peter's threefold denial (14:53–15:1a)

Jesus' trial before the Jewish religious authorities included a preliminary hearing by Annas (John 18:12-14, 19-24), an arraignment before Caiaphas, the high priest, and the Sanhedrin at night (Matt. 26:57-68; Mark 14:53-65), and a final verdict by the Sanhedrin just after dawn (cf. Matt. 27:1; Mark 15:1a; Luke 22:66-71).

(1) Jesus in the high priest's residence and Peter in the courtyard (14:53-54; Matt. 26:57-58; Luke 22:54; John 18:15-16, 18, 24). **14:53.** Jesus' captors led Him under guard from Gethsemane back into Jerusalem **to the** residence of the **high priest,** Joseph Caiaphas (cf. Matt. 26:57), who held this office from A.D. 18 to 36 (see the chart on Annas' family at Acts 4:5-6).

The 71-member Sanhedrin (cf. comments on Mark 8:31), including the presiding high priest, was hastily assembled in an upstairs room (cf. 14:66) for a plenary night session. This was an "informal" trial that required a "formal" ratification after dawn (cf. 15:1) to satisfy strict Jewish legal procedure allowing trials only in the daytime. A quorum consisted of 23 members (Mishnah Sanhedrin 1. 6) but on this occasion the majority were probably there even though it was around 3 A.M. on Nisan 15 (Friday), a feast day.

This hasty night meeting was deemed necessary because: (1) In Jewish criminal law it was customary to hold a trial immediately after arrest. (2) Roman legal trials were usually held shortly after sunrise (cf. 15:1) so the Sanhedrin needed a binding verdict by daybreak in order to get the case to Pilate early. (3) With Jesus finally in custody they did not want to delay proceedings, thereby arousing opposition to His arrest. Actually they had already determined to kill Him (cf. 14:1-2); their only problem was getting evidence that would justify it (cf. v. 55). Perhaps also they wished to have the Romans crucify Jesus to avoid the people's blaming the Sanhedrin for His death.

Some have questioned the legality of a capital trial on a feast day in light of certain Rabbinic legal ordinances. However, the Rabbis justified the trial and execution of serious offenders on a major feast day. That way, they argued, "all the people will hear and be afraid" (Deut. 17:13; cf. Deut. 21:21; cf. TDNT, s.v. "pascha," 5:899-900). Normally in capital cases a conviction verdict could not be legally determined until the following day.

14:54. Peter (cf. vv. 29, 31, 50) regained enough courage to follow Jesus **at a distance, right** inside **the courtyard of the high priest.** This was a central quadrangle with the high priest's residence built around it (cf. John 18:15-18). Peter **sat** there **with the guards,** the temple police, and **warmed himself at** a charcoal **fire** (lit., "facing the light" of the fire, so his face was illuminated; cf. Mark 14:67) because of the cold night air. He wanted to know what would happen to Jesus (cf. Matt. 26:58).

(2) Jesus' trial before the Sanhedrin (14:55-65; Matt. 26:59-68). The material in this section probably rests on the report of one or more Sanhedrin members who were secretly sympathetic to Jesus or who were against Him originally but later came to believe in Him (cf. Acts 6:7).

14:55-56. The **Sanhedrin** began their deliberations by seeking **evidence** (lit., "testimony") **against Jesus** in order to justify a **death** sentence **but they** found none (lit., "were **not** finding **any**"). They did not lack witnesses because **many** were testifying **falsely against Him, but their** testimony was invalid because their statements (lit., "testimonies") **did not agree** (lit., "were not equal"). Various unverified charges were made and numerous discrepancies arose in testimony on the same charge. Perhaps these witnesses were already on call prior to Jesus' arrest but did not coordinate their stories. In Jewish trials the witnesses served as the prosecution, giving their testimonies separately. Convicting a person for a crime, the Mosaic Law required precise agreement in the testimony of at least two witnesses (Num. 35:30; Deut. 17:6; 19:15).

14:57-59. In due time **some** witnesses ("two"; cf. Matt. 26:60) declared they had heard Jesus say: **I** (*egō*, emphatic) **will destroy this man-made temple** (*naon*, "the sanctuary"; cf. Mark 11:11), **and in three days will build another** (*allon*, "another" of a different kind), **not made by man.** Yet even in this **testimony** there were unspecified discrepancies, so Mark labeled it **false.**

Jesus had made a cryptic statement similar to this (John 2:19) but He was referring to the "temple" of His body (cf. John 2:20-22). These witnesses, like those present at the time, misinterpreted His words as a reference to the Jerusalem temple. Destruction of a worship place was a capital offense in the ancient world (Josephus *The Antiquities of the Jews* 10. 6. 2). Though their testimony was invalid, it opened the way for questions about Jesus' identity (Mark 14:61) and led to the taunt recorded in 15:29.

14:60-61a. The high priest Caiaphas **asked Jesus** two questions to get information that could be used against Him. In Greek the first question expects a positive answer: "**You are going to answer** Your accusers, aren't You?" The second question expected an explanation from Him: "**What is** the meaning of the charges **these** witnesses **are** making **against You?**" But **Jesus remained silent** and gave no defense (cf. Isa. 53:7). His silence frustrated the court and brought its proceedings to a standstill.

14:61b-62. The high priest changed tactics and **asked** (lit., "kept asking") Jesus pointedly, **Are You** (emphatic) **the Christ** (the Messiah; cf. 1:1; 8:29), **the Son of the Blessed One?** The title "Blessed One," found in this sense only here in the New Testament, is a Jewish substitute for "God" (cf. Mishnah *Berachoth* 7. 3). These two titles of Jesus both refer to His claim to be the Messiah.

Jesus unequivocally answered, **I am,** that is, "I am the Messiah, the Son of God." This is the first time in Mark's Gospel that He openly declared He is the Messiah (cf. comments on 1:43-44; 8:29-30; 9:9; 11:28-33; 12:12). In proof of this—something the Jews expected the true Messiah to provide—Jesus made a startling prediction. Applying words from Psalm 110:1 and Daniel 7:13 to Himself, He stated, **And you** (His human judges) **will see the Son of Man** (cf. Mark 8:31, 38) **sitting at the right hand,** exalted to the place of highest honor and authority (cf. 12:36), **of the Mighty One** (lit., "the Power"), a Jewish substitute title for "God" (cf. 14:61), **and coming on** (lit., "with") **the clouds of heaven** to judge (cf. 8:38; 13:26). The fact that they "will see" this did not mean Jesus would return in their lifetimes. Rather it referred indirectly to bodily resurrection in judgment before the exalted Son of Man who will one day judge those who were judging Him. Then it will be unmistakably clear that He is God's Anointed One, the Messiah.

14:63-64. By tearing **his clothes,** probably his inner garments rather than his official robes, **the high priest** showed that he regarded Jesus' bold declaration as **blasphemy.** To him, Jesus' words dishonored God by claiming rights and powers belonging exclusively to God (cf. 2:7). This symbolic expression of horror and indignation was required of the high priest whenever he heard blasphemy. His reaction also expressed relief since Jesus' self-incriminating answer removed the **need for more witnesses.**

The Mosaic Law prescribed death by stoning for blasphemy (Lev. 24:15-16). Without further investigation the high priest called for a verdict from the Sanhedrin. Since there were no objections **they all condemned Him** (cf. Mark 10:33) **as worthy** (*enochon*, "guilty, liable"; cf. 3:29) **of death.**

14:65. **Some** Sanhedrin members showed their contempt through mockery and physical abuse. To **spit** in someone's face was an act of total repudiation and gross personal insult (cf. Num. 12:14; Deut. 25:9; Job 30:10; Isa. 50:6). On account of His messianic claims **they blindfolded Him, struck Him with their**

fists and demanded that He **prophesy** who hit Him. This reflects a traditional test of messianic status based on a Rabbinic interpretation of Isaiah 11:2-4. The true Messiah could judge such matters without the benefit of sight (cf. Babylonian Talmud *Sanhedrin* 93b). But Jesus refused to submit to their test and remained silent (cf. Isa. 53:7; 1 Peter 2:23). When He was returned to the temple **guards** (cf. Mark 14:54), they followed their superiors' example and continued beating **Him** with open-handed slaps on the face (cf. Luke 22:63-65).

(3) Peter's threefold denial of Jesus (14:66-72; Matt. 26:69-75; Luke 22:55-62; John 18:15-18, 25-27). All four Gospels record this episode with variations, but without contradicting each other. Mark's vivid account probably came from Peter. It resumes Mark 14:54, showing that Peter's ordeal coincided with Jesus' interrogation before the Sanhedrin. After this denial account Mark resumed his report of the Sanhedrin's action (cf. 15:1a).

14:66-68. One of the high priest's **servant girls,** presumably the inner courtyard's doorkeeper (cf. John 18:16) approached **Peter** while he warmed himself by the fire **in the courtyard** (cf. Mark 14:54; 15:16) which apparently **was below** the upstairs room where Jesus' trial was taking place. After **she looked closely** (from *emblepō;* cf. 10:21) **at him,** she blurted out contemptuously, **You** (emphatic sing. pronoun) **also** (John was there too; cf. John 18:15) **were with** (cf. Mark 3:14) **that Nazarene** (cf. 1:24; 10:47), **Jesus.**

Her charge correctly identified Peter as a disciple **but he denied** (*ērnēsato;* cf. 8:34; 14:30) **it,** refusing to acknowledge his relationship to Jesus out of fear for his safety. His denial was a common Jewish legal expression, literally, "I neither **know** nor **understand what** you (emphatic) are saying." To avoid further exposure he **went out into the entryway,** the covered passageway leading to the street.

Nearly all major ancient Greek manuscripts and early versions include the words "and the rooster crowed" (NIV marg.; KJV) at the end of verse 68. This evidence plus the strongly attested words "the second time" in verse 72 favor inclusion of these words. Since only one

rooster-crowing is mentioned in the parallel passages (cf. Matt. 26:74; Luke 22:60; John 18:27) these words were probably omitted from Mark very early by some scribes to conform to the parallels. But Mark was simply more specific than the other Gospels, probably because of Peter's vivid recollection. Apparently this first rooster-crowing held no significance for Peter since it happened every morning (cf. Mark 13:35b; 14:72).

14:69-71. The same **servant girl** along with others (cf. Matt. 26:71; Luke 22:58) **saw** Peter in the entryway and **again** identified him **to** the bystanders as **one of** Jesus' disciples. **Again he denied** (lit., "kept denying," imperf.) **it.**

About an hour later (cf. Luke 22:59) the bystanders (again, in Gr.) confronted **Peter** with the charge, **Surely** (lit., "truly," despite his denials) **you are one of them** (the disciples), **for** ("because") **you are** ("also," in Gr.) **a Galilean.** Galileans spoke an Aramaic dialect with noticeable differences in pronunciation (cf. Matt. 26:73). So they concluded he was a follower of that heretic Galilean, Jesus.

The fact that Peter **began to call down curses on himself and** that **he swore to them** does not mean he used profanity. Rather he placed himself under God's curse if he were lying to them and put himself under oath, as in a courtroom, to confirm the veracity of his denial. Carefully avoiding the use of Jesus' name Peter emphatically denied any knowledge of **this Man** they were **talking about.**

14:72. Peter's third denial in less than two hours was **immediately** (*euthys;* cf. 1:10) punctuated by the rooster's **second** crowing (cf. 14:68, NIV marg.). This time he suddenly **remembered** Jesus' prediction of his denial made earlier that night (vv. 29-31). Peter also saw **Jesus** looking down at him (Luke 22:61). Overwhelmed, **he broke down and wept.**

In contrast with Judas (Matt. 27:3-5) Peter's remorse opened the way for true repentance and a reaffirmation of his loyalty to Jesus as the risen Lord (cf. Mark 16:7; John 21:15-19). Peter had a faith in Jesus that could be renewed, but Judas did not.

(4) The Sanhedrin's verdict at dawn (15:1a; Matt. 27:1; Luke 22:66-71). **15:1a.** Immediately (*euthys;* cf. 1:10) after daybreak—between 5 and 6 A.M., prob-

ably on Friday, April 3, A.D. 33—**the whole Sanhedrin** (cf. 14:53) led by **the chief priests** formalized their condemnation of Jesus and **reached a decision,** a plan of action for getting a guilty verdict from the Roman governor.

Though the Sanhedrin could pronounce a death sentence it could not exercise capital punishment. So a condemned prisoner had to be turned over to the Roman authorities for a death sentence to be carried out (cf. John 18:31; TDNT, s.v. "*synedrion,*" 1:865-6). The Roman governor could either ratify or rescind the Sanhedrin's death sentence (cf. John 19:10). If rescinded, a new trial had to be conducted before a Roman court in which the Sanhedrin had to prove that the defendant had committed a capital crime under Roman law. Since the charge of blasphemy (cf. Mark 14:64) was not punishable by Roman law it was not mentioned in the following trial. In its place the Sanhedrin substituted a charge of treason, turning Jesus' acknowledgment that He was the Messiah into a traitorous political claim that He is "the King of the Jews" (cf. 15:2; Luke 23:2). The Roman court surely could not ignore that charge.

b. Jesus' trial before Pilate and the Roman soldiers' abuse (15:1b-20)

Jesus' trial before the Roman political authorities also had three hearings: (a) an initial interrogation by Pilate (cf. Matt. 27:2, 11-14; Mark 15:1b-5; Luke 23:1-5; John 18:28-38); (b) an interrogation by Herod Antipas (cf. Luke 23:5-12); (c) a final arraignment before Pilate, Barabbas' release, and the crucifixion verdict (cf. Matt. 27:15-26; Mark 15:6-20; Luke 23:13-25; John 18:39–19:16).

Before the Sanhedrin Jesus was condemned for blasphemy under Jewish law, but here He was tried for treason under Roman law. On both occasions He was sentenced to die, in conformity with God's will (cf. Mark 10:33-34).

(1) Pilate's interrogation and Jesus' silence (15:1b-5; Matt. 27:2, 11-14; Luke 23:1-5; John 18:28-38). **15:1b.** The Sanhedrin had Jesus **bound** and led through the city from Caiaphas' residence (cf. 14:53) probably to Herod's palace where they **handed Him over to Pilate** for execution of the death sentence.

Pontius Pilate, the fifth Roman prefect (a title later changed to "procurator," i.e., imperial magistrate) of Judea held office A.D. 26-36. He was a harsh governor who despised the Jews (cf. Luke 13:1-2). Normally he resided in Caesarea by the Mediterranean Sea, but he came to Jerusalem on special occasions such as the Passover festival to help maintain order. Presumably he stayed in Herod's palace as was customary for provincial governors rather than in the Antonia Fortress near the temple. If so, Jesus' civil trial was held there.

15:2. Pilate had sole responsibility for the Roman court's decisions. The proceedings, usually held in public, opened with an indictment by the plaintiff followed by the magistrate's interrogation and further testimony from the defendant and other witnesses. When all the evidence was in, the magistrate usually consulted with his legal advisers and then pronounced the sentence, which had to be carried out immediately.

Instead of confirming the Sanhedrin's death sentence (cf. John 18:29-32) Pilate insisted on hearing the case. Only one of three accusations that had already been made (cf. Luke 23:2) merited Pilate's attention, namely, Jesus' alleged claim to be "a king." So Pilate **asked** Jesus, **Are You** (emphatic) **the King of the Jews?** To Pilate such a claim was tantamount to treason against Caesar, a crime punishable by death.

Jesus gave a cryptic reply, literally, **You** (emphatic) **say** (so), that is, "The designation is yours." It is best understood as a **yes** answer but with a qualification attached. As Messiah, Jesus is the King of the Jews but His concept of kingship differed from that implied in Pilate's question (cf. John 18:33-38).

15:3-5. Since Jesus' initial response provided no solid basis for a capital conviction under Roman law Pilate returned to His accusers to gain more information. **The chief priests** (cf. v. 1a) seized the opportunity to bolster their case by pressing multiple charges against Jesus.

Again Pilate tried to get Jesus to respond to His accusers and defend Himself against their charges **but** to his utter amazement **Jesus** remained absolutely silent (cf. Isa. 53:7; lit., "He answered no longer nothing"; *ouketi ouden*, emphatic negative). Such silence was rare in a Roman court. It seemed to confirm Pilate's initial feeling that Jesus was not guilty.

Mark included only two short utterances by Jesus—one to Caiaphas (Mark 14:62) and one to Pilate (15:2). Jesus' silence highlights the fact that He, the Son of Man, suffered and died within God's sovereign plan (cf. comments on 8:31).

Learning that Jesus was a Galilean and hoping to avoid making a judgment against Him, Pilate sent Him to Herod Antipas, governor of Galilee (cf. 6:14), also in Jerusalem at the time. But Herod soon returned Him to Pilate. Only Luke recorded this middle phase of the civil trial (cf. Luke 23:6-12).

(2) Pilate's futile attempts to gain acquittal for Jesus (15:6-15; Matt. 27:15-26; Luke 23:13-25; John 18:39-40; 19:1, 13-16). **15:6.** Each year during the Passover festival **it was the** governor's **custom** as a sign of goodwill **to release a prisoner** selected by **the people** (cf. v. 8). Though no explicit reference to the custom occurs outside the New Testament it was consistent with Rome's conciliatory attitude toward subject peoples on local matters. Instead of granting Jesus an acquittal, Pilate chose to grant the customary Passover amnesty, thinking the people would request Jesus' release (cf. v. 9).

15:7. While suppressing an **uprising** in Jerusalem, the Roman authorities had arrested **Barabbas** (from *Bar Abba*, "son of the father"), a notorious freedom fighter, robber (John 18:40), and murderer, along **with** other **insurrectionists.** He may have been a Zealot, a nationalist who stirred up opposition against Rome. Now he was awaiting execution.

15:8-11. During the trial proceedings a sizable **crowd** had gathered in the palace forum (cf. v. 16). The people approached Pilate's elevated judgment seat **and asked** him **to** grant the annual Passover amnesty (cf. v. 6). Many of them were probably supporters of Barabbas.

Pilate saw this as an opportunity to show his contempt for the Jews, especially their leaders. He offered **to release to** them **the King of the Jews** (cf. v. 2). He recognized **that the chief priests had** turned **Jesus over to him** not out of loyalty to Rome but **out of envy** and

hatred. **Pilate** hoped to achieve Jesus' release and thus undo the religious leaders' scheme.

But Pilate's plan did not work. **The chief priests** incited **the** emotional **crowd** to pressure him into releasing **Barabbas instead** of Jesus. Apparently they knew that the Sanhedrin had already condemned Jesus (cf. 14:64). Strangely, Pilate failed to consider that the crowd would never side with him against their own leaders (cf. John 19:6-7).

15:12-14. Since the crowd had rejected Pilate's offer and requested the release of Barabbas, he inquired ("again" is in the Gr.) about **what** they wanted done **with the One** they called **the King of the Jews. Pilate** did not accept this title for Jesus but his question implied he was willing to release Jesus *also* if they wished. But without hesitation **they shouted** back, **Crucify Him!** The punishment that once awaited Barabbas was now thrust on Jesus.

Pilate challenged them to state the **crime** which made Jesus guilty enough to be crucified. **But they** persistently cried out **all the louder, Crucify Him!** Pilate considered the clamor of the crowd an acclamation, legally indicating a decision by popular demand. Thus Jesus must be pronounced guilty of high treason, a capital offense normally punishable by crucifixion in Roman provinces.

15:15. Though he believed Jesus was innocent (cf. v. 14) **Pilate** followed political expedience rather than justice. Wishing **to satisfy the** people lest they complain to Emperor Tiberius—thereby putting his position in jeopardy (cf. John 19:12)—Pilate **released Barabbas to them . . . had Jesus flogged, and** sentenced **Him** to death by crucifixion.

A Roman flogging was a brutal beating that always preceded the execution of a capital sentence on male offenders, though it could also be a separate punishment (cf. TDNT, s.v. "*mastigoō*," 4:517-9). The prisoner was stripped, often tied to a post, and beaten on the back by several guards using short leather whips studded with sharp pieces of bone or metal. No limit was set on the number of blows. Often this punishment was fatal.

Pilate had Jesus flogged in hope that the people would take pity and be satisfied. But this also failed; they still insisted He be crucified (cf. John 19:1-7).

(3) The Roman soldiers' mockery of Jesus (15:16-20; Matt. 27:27-31; John 19:2-12). **15:16.** After the flogging of **Jesus,** presumably outside in the public square, **the** Roman **soldiers** took Him, battered and bleeding, **into** (*esō*, "inside") **the palace** (lit., "courtyard"; cf. same word in 14:54, 66). The rendering "palace" is justified due to Mark's explanatory comment, **that is, the Praetorium,** equating the two places. The Latin loanword, *Praetorium,* meant the governor's official residence (cf. Matt. 27:27; John 18:28, 33; 19:9; Acts 23:35).

Once inside they summoned **the whole company** (*speiran,* Gr. for the Latin "cohort") **of soldiers.** Ordinarily a cohort was 600 men, 1/10 of a 6,000-soldier legion. But in this case it may have been an auxiliary battalion of 200-300 soldiers that had accompanied Pilate to Jerusalem from Caesarea.

15:17-19. In ludicrous imitation of a vassal king's regal robes and gilded head-wreath, the soldiers dressed Jesus in **a purple robe,** a faded military cloak, and pressed **a crown of thorns,** perhaps palm spines, on His head. With this "crown" the soldiers unwittingly pictured God's curse on sinful humanity being thrust on Jesus (cf. Gen. 3:17-18). Matthew noted that they also placed a staff in His hand as a mock scepter (Matt. 27:29).

Then they ridiculed Him with contemptuous words and insulting actions in mock homage to a king. The derisive greeting **Hail** (Rejoice), **King of the Jews,** paralleled the formal Roman plaudit, "Ave, Caesar." The NIV words, **again and again** reflect the imperfect tense of the Greek verbs. The soldiers kept striking Jesus **with a staff,** probably His mock scepter, on His thorn-crowned **head.** They kept spitting **on Him** (cf. Mark 14:65) and bending **their knees** in mock submission to royalty. In all this they acted out of contempt not so much for Jesus personally but for their subject nation which had long desired a king of its own.

15:20. The soldiers then removed the mock royal attire and dressed Him in **His own clothes. Then they,** a four-soldier execution squad (cf. John 19:23) under the command of a centurion, **led Him** outside the city **to crucify Him.**

Jesus' suffering before the Roman authorities was exemplary for Mark's readers who would be subjected to similar ridicule before pagan authorities (cf. comments on Mark 13:9-13).

2. JESUS' CRUCIFIXION AND DEATH (15:21-41)

Death by crucifixion was one of the cruelest forms of capital punishment ever devised. Mark's account of Jesus' physical sufferings is vivid but restrained. They were secondary to His overwhelming spiritual anguish (cf. 14:36; 15:34). (For the order of events, see the "Harmony of Events at Jesus' Crucifixion," at Matt. 27:32-38.)

a. *Jesus' crucifixion and the crowd's mockery (15:21-32)*
(*Matt. 27:32-44; Luke 23:26-43; John 19:17-27*)

15:21-22. Customarily a condemned man carried the *patibulum* of his own cross, that is, the crossbeam weighing about 100 pounds, through the city streets out to the place of crucifixion. Jesus started to carry His (cf. John 19:17) but was so weak from being flogged that His strength gave out near the city gate. The soldiers randomly seized **a** passerby named **Simon** and **forced him to carry the** beam the rest of the way.

Simon was a native of **Cyrene,** an important coastal city of North Africa that had a large Jewish colony (Acts 2:10). He was either an immigrant living near Jerusalem or more likely, a pilgrim who had come to Jerusalem for the Passover festival but had to stay in **the country** at night because there was no room in the city. Only Mark mentioned Simon's sons, **Alexander and Rufus,** suggesting that they were disciples known to his readers in Rome (cf. Rom. 16:13).

The soldiers took **Jesus to the place** outside but near the city wall (cf. John 19:20) **called Golgotha,** a Greek transliteration of an Aramaic word meaning **The Place of the Skull.** The word "Calvary" comes from the Latin Vulgate rendering *Calvaria,* a variation of *calva,* "a skull." Golgotha was a rounded, rocky knoll (not a hill or mountain) vaguely resembling the shape of a human skull. Its exact location is uncertain. It was either at the present Church of the Holy Sepulchre, the traditional site dating from the fourth century, or "Gordon's Calvary," a more recent suggestion. The traditional site is more probable.

15:23-24. According to Rabbinic tradition certain Jerusalem women provided sedative drinks for those about to be crucified, to decrease their pain (cf. Prov. 31:6-7). On arrival at Golgotha, **they,** presumably the Roman soldiers, **offered** (lit., "were attempting to give") Jesus such a drink, **wine mixed with myrrh,** a plant's sap having anesthetic properties. But after He had tasted it (cf. Matt. 27:34) He refused it, choosing rather to face suffering and death in full control of all His faculties.

With restrained simplicity Mark wrote, **And they crucified Him.** His Roman readers needed no elaboration and he offered none. Normally a condemned man was stripped (except possibly for a loincloth), laid on the ground, and both outstretched forearms were nailed to the crossbeam. Then this beam was raised and fastened to an upright post already stuck in the ground and the victim's feet were nailed to it. A wooden peg partway up the post on which the victim sat helped support his body. Death from extreme exhaustion and thirst was painful and slow and usually came after two or three days. Sometimes death was hastened by breaking the victim's legs (John 19:31-33).

A victim's personal belongings became the property of the execution squad. In Jesus' case the four-man squad (cf. John 19:23) **cast lots,** probably dice, for **His clothes**—an inner and outer garment, a belt, sandals, and perhaps a head covering—**to see what each one would get.** Unwittingly they fulfilled Psalm 22:18, another aspect of Jesus' humiliation.

15:25. Using the Jewish method of counting hours from sunrise (and sunset) Mark alone recorded that Jesus' crucifixion took place at **the third hour,** that is, 9 A.M. This seems to conflict with the time reference "the sixth hour" in John 19:14. But John probably used the Roman (modern) method of counting hours from midnight (and noon); thus he put Jesus' trial before Pilate at "about the sixth hour," that is, approximately 6 A.M. The interval between 6 and 9 A.M. was filled with the soldiers' mockery (cf. Mark 15:16-20), Pilate's verdict on the two robbers (cf. 15:27), and preparations for the crucifixions.

15:26. It was a Roman custom to write the name of the condemned man and a description of his crime on a board and attach it to his cross (John 19:19). All four Gospels record the words of Jesus' notice but with minor variations, probably because it was written in three languages (John 19:20). Mark recorded only **the** official **charge against Him . . .** THE KING OF THE JEWS (cf. Mark 15:2, 12). Pilate's wording was intended as an insult to Jewish aspirations for independence (cf. John 19:21-22).

15:27-28. Pilate had Jesus **crucified** between **two robbers** who, like Barabbas, were perhaps guilty of insurrection (cf. v. 7; John 18:40). They may have been convicted of treason at the same time as Jesus because they were familiar with His case (Luke 23:40-42).

Unwittingly Pilate's action fulfilled Isaiah 53:12, which is cited in Mark 15:28 (NIV marg.; KJV; cf. Luke 22:37).

15:29-30. Again Jesus was subjected to verbal abuse (cf. 14:65; 15:17-19). Passersby **hurled insults at Him** (lit., "kept slandering Him"). **Shaking their heads** refers to a familiar gesture of derision (cf. Pss. 22:7; 109:25; Jer. 18:16; Lam. 2:15). They taunted Him for His alleged claim regarding **the temple** (cf. Mark 14:58). If He could rebuild the temple **in three days** (a great feat), then surely He could **save** (from *sōzō*, "deliver or rescue"; cf. 5:23, 28, 34) Himself from death by coming **down from the cross** (a lesser feat).

15:31-32. Similarly the Jewish religious leaders **mocked** Jesus indirectly in conversations **among themselves.** Their long-standing desire to kill Him was successful at last (cf. 3:6; 11:18; 12:12; 14:1, 64; 15:1, 11-13). Their words **He saved** (from *sōzō*) **others** refer to His healing miracles, which they could not deny (cf. 5:34; 6:56; 10:52). **But** they ridiculed Him because **He** seemed powerless to **save** (from *sōzō*; cf. 15:30) **Himself.** Ironically their words expressed a profound spiritual truth. If Jesus was to save others, delivering them from the power of sin, then He could not save (rescue)

Himself from the sufferings and death appointed to Him by God (cf. 8:31).

They also mocked Jesus' messianic claims (cf. comments on 14:61-62) replacing Pilate's words "King of the Jews" (cf. 15:26) with **King of Israel.** They challenged Him to prove His messianic claim by a miraculous descent **from the cross** so they could **see** the compelling evidence **and believe** that He is God's Messiah. The issue, however, was not lack of evidence but unbelief.

The two men **crucified with** Jesus **also** joined in reviling Him. But one of them soon stopped and asked Jesus to remember him in His kingdom (Luke 23:39-43).

b. *Jesus' death and the accompanying phenomena (15:33-41)*
(Matt. 27:45-56; Luke 23:44-49; John 19:28-30)

Climactically Mark recorded five phenomena that accompanied Jesus' death: (a) darkness (Mark 15:33), (b) Jesus' cry, "My God . . ." (v. 34), (c) Jesus' loud cry (v. 37), (d) the temple curtain torn from top to bottom (v. 38), and (e) the Roman centurion's confession (v. 39).

15:33. Jesus hanged on the cross for three hours in the daylight (9 A.M. till noon) and then **at the sixth hour** (noon) total **darkness** engulfed **the whole land** (Palestine and environs) **until the ninth hour** (3 P.M.; cf. comments on v. 25). The darkness, whether caused by a sudden dust-laden wind, or thick clouds, or, more likely, a miraculous solar eclipse, was probably a cosmic sign of God's judgment on human sin (cf. Isa. 5:25-30; Amos 8:9-10; Micah 3:5-7; Zeph. 1:14-15) which was placed on Jesus (cf. Isa. 53:5-6; 2 Cor. 5:21). Specifically it pictured God's judgment on Israel who rejected His Messiah, the Sin-Bearer (cf. John 1:29). The darkness visualized what Jesus' cry (Mark 15:34) expressed.

15:34. Mark (and Matthew) recorded only this one of Jesus' seven sayings from the cross. **At the ninth hour** (3 P.M.), **Jesus cried . . . Eloi, Eloi** (Aram. for the Heb., *'Ēlî, 'Ēlî*), **lama sabachthani?** (Aram.; from Ps. 22:1) Mark translated the saying into Greek for his readers, **which** in English **means, My God, My God, why** (lit., "for what [reason]") **have You forsaken** (lit., "did You abandon") **Me?**

This was more than the cry of a righteous Sufferer affirming His faith that God would cause Him to triumph (contrast Ps. 22:1 with Ps. 22:28). Nor did Jesus merely *feel* abandoned. Instead, Jesus' cry combined (a) abandonment by God the Father in a judicial not relational sense, and (b) a genuine affirmation of Jesus' relationship to God. Bearing the curse of sin and God's judgment on sin (cf. Deut. 21:22-23; 2 Cor. 5:21; Gal. 3:13) He experienced the unfathomable horror of separation from God, who cannot look on sin (cf. Hab. 1:13). This answers Jesus' question, "Why?" Dying for sinners (Mark 10:45; Rom. 5:8; 1 Peter 2:24; 3:18), He experienced separation from God.

Also Jesus' cry affirmed His abiding trust, reflected in the words, "My God, My God." This is the only one of Jesus' recorded prayers in which He did not use the address "Abba" (cf. Mark 14:36). Far from renouncing Him, Jesus claimed the Father as His God. He died forsaken by God so that His people might claim God as their God and never be forsaken (cf. Heb. 13:5).

15:35-36. **Some** Jewish bystanders apparently misunderstood or more likely, as a mockery, deliberately misinterpreted Jesus' cry as a call to **Elijah.** Popular Jewish belief held that Elijah came in times of distress to deliver righteous sufferers.

Probably in response to Jesus' additional words "I thirst" (John 19:28-29) a bystander, likely a Roman soldier, soaked **a sponge with wine vinegar** diluted with a mixture of eggs and water, a common inexpensive beverage, and raised **it on a stick** to Jesus' mouth so He could extract some refreshment from it (cf. Ps. 69:21). Jesus' cross was probably higher than normal, holding Him two or three feet off the ground. If the drink prolonged His life, the spectators would have a chance to **see if Elijah** would **take Him down.**

In Mark the words **Leave Him alone** were spoken by the soldier to the bystanders just before he offered a drink to Jesus. The verb is plural, "You (pl.) leave. . . ." In Matthew 27:49 the same words are spoken by bystanders to the soldier apparently while he was giving Jesus the drink. The verb is singular, "You (sing.) leave. . . ." Both expressed the taunt about Elijah coming to rescue Him

189

15:37. Jesus' **loud cry** (Luke 23:46) before He **breathed His last** indicated that He did not die the ordinary death of one who was crucified (cf. Mark 15:39). Normally such a person suffered extreme exhaustion for a long period (often two or three days) and then lapsed into a coma before dying. But Jesus was fully conscious to the end; His death came voluntarily and suddenly. This accounts for Pilate's surprise (cf. v. 44).

15:38. Simultaneous with Jesus' death **the curtain** (veil) **of the temple** (*naou,* "sanctuary"; cf. 11:11) **was torn in two from top to bottom.** The passive verb and the direction of the tear indicate that this was God's action. It was no doubt observed and reported by the priests (cf. Acts 6:7) who at that moment were conducting the Jewish evening sacrifice. This could have been the outer curtain hung between the sanctuary itself and the forecourt (Ex. 26:36-37) or the inner curtain separating the holy place from the most holy place (Ex. 26:31-35). If it was the outer curtain, then the tear was a public sign confirming Jesus' words of judgment on the temple, later fulfilled in A.D. 70 (cf. Mark 13:2). Probably the inner curtain was torn, for it was a sign that Jesus' death ended the need for repeated sacrifices for sins, and opened a new and living way of free and direct access to God (Heb. 6:19-20; 9:6-14; 10:19-22).

15:39. **The centurion who stood** nearby facing **Jesus** and observing these unusual happenings (cf. vv. 33-37) was the *Gentile* Roman officer in charge of the execution squad (cf. v. 20) and thus accountable to Pilate (cf. v. 44). Only Mark used the Greek word *kentyriōn* ("centurion"), a transliteration of the Latin word referring to a commander of 100 soldiers (also vv. 44-45). All other New Testament writers used the equivalent Greek word *hekatontarchos,* also translated "centurion" (e.g., Matt. 27:54). This provides additional evidence that Mark wrote to a Roman audience (see *Introduction*).

The manner of Jesus' death, especially His last loud **cry** (cf. Mark 15:37), prompted the centurion to declare, **Surely** (lit., "truly," despite all insults to the contrary; cf. Matt. 27:40; John 19:7), **this Man was,** from the centurion's perspective, **the Son of God.**

The Roman officer probably did not use the phrase "the Son of God" in its distinctive Christian sense, as a reference to Jesus' deity (cf. Luke 23:47). Because of his pagan background he probably viewed Jesus as an extraordinary "divine man" much like the Roman emperor who was acclaimed "son of God" (cf. comments on Mark 12:16). Consequently some interpreters translate the phrase with an indefinite article, "a son of God" (NIV marg.). However, Mark regarded the declaration in its distinctive Christian sense; the centurion unwittingly said more than he knew.

The centurion's confession is the climax of Mark's revelation of Jesus' identity (cf. comments on 1:1; 8:29-30). This confession by a *Gentile* Roman officer contrasts with the mocking response of those mentioned in 15:29-32, 35-36. This Gentile's confession also exemplifies the truth of the torn curtain.

15:40-41. In addition to the mocking crowd and the Roman soldiers, **some** devoted **women were** also (in Gr.) carefully observing **from a distance** all that occurred. Earlier in the day— probably before the sixth hour (noon; v. 33)—they had stood "near the cross" (John 19:25-27).

Mary Magdalene's surname indicates she was from Magdala, a village on the Sea of Galilee's western shore. Jesus had released her from demon possession (Luke 8:2; she is not the sinful woman of Luke 7:36-50). The second **Mary** (the "other Mary"; Matt. 27:61) is distinguished from the others by the names of her sons **James the younger** (lit., "the small one," in stature and/or age) and **Joses,** who apparently were well known in the early church. **Salome,** whose name appears only in Mark (Mark 15:40; 16:1), was the mother of Zebedee's sons, the disciples James and John (Matt. 20:20; 27:56). She was probably the sister of Jesus' mother whom Mark did not mention (John 19:25).

When Jesus was in **Galilee these** three **women** used to follow (imperf. tense) **Him** from place to place and used to care **for** ("serve," imperf.) **His** material **needs** (cf. Luke 8:1-3). **Many other women who** did not accompany Him regularly **were also there.** They had **come . . . to Jerusalem** for the Passover festival with Jesus, perhaps hoping He would establish His messianic kingdom (cf. Mark 10:35-40; 15:43).

Mark mentioned the women as eyewitnesses of the Crucifixion in anticipation of their eyewitness role at Jesus' burial (15:47) and His resurrection (16:1-8). Their devotion surpassed that of the 11 disciples who had deserted Him (14:50). Mark may have intended these words as an encouragement to faithful discipleship among women in the church at Rome.

3. JESUS' BURIAL IN A NEARBY TOMB (15:42-47)

(MATT. 27:57-61; LUKE 23:50-56; JOHN 19:38-42)

15:42-43. Jesus' burial officially confirmed His death, an important point in early Christian preaching (cf. 1 Cor. 15:3-4). The designation **Preparation Day** is used here as a technical name for Friday, **the day before the Sabbath** (Saturday) as Mark explained to his non-Jewish readers. Since no work was allowed on the Jewish Sabbath, Friday was used to prepare for it. This reference confirms that Jesus was crucified on Friday, Nisan 15 (cf. comments on Mark 14:1a, 12, 16). "Evening" referred to the hours between mid-afternoon (3 P.M.) and sunset, when Friday ended and the Sabbath began.

Under Roman law the release of a crucified man's corpse for burial was determined only by the imperial magistrate. Usually such a request by a victim's relatives was granted, but sometimes a body would be left on a cross to decay or be eaten by predatory animals or birds and the remains were thrown into a common grave. Jewish law required a proper burial for all bodies, even those of executed criminals (cf. Mishnah *Sanhedrin* 6. 5). It also dictated that those hanged were to be taken down and buried before sunset (cf. Deut. 21:23).

Aware of these regulations, **Joseph of Arimathea** went **to Pilate and** requested **Jesus' body** for burial. He did this **as evening approached** (lit., "when evening had already arrived," i.e., probably about 4 P.M.). This gave urgency to his intended action.

Though Joseph probably lived in Jerusalem he was originally from Arimathea, a village 20 miles northwest of the city. He was **a** wealthy (Matt. 27:57), reputable **member of the Council** (*bouleutēs*), a non-Jewish designation for the Sanhedrin. He had not approved of the Sanhedrin's decision to kill Jesus (Luke 23:51). He **was** personally **waiting for the kingdom of God** (cf. Mark 1:15) which suggests he was a devout Pharisee. He regarded Jesus as the Messiah though so far he was a secret disciple (John 19:38).

But he took courage and **went** to Pilate **boldly,** a description unique to Mark. His action was bold because: (a) he was not related to Jesus; (b) his request was a favor that would likely be denied on principle since Jesus had been executed for treason; (c) he risked ceremonial defilement in handling a dead body; (d) his request amounted to an open confession of personal loyalty to the crucified Jesus which would doubtless incur his associates' hostility. He was a secret disciple no longer—something Mark impressed on his readers.

15:44-45. Pilate **was** amazed (*ethaumasen,* "astonished"; cf. 5:20) **that** Jesus had **already** died (cf. comments on 15:37). He summoned **the centurion** in charge of the Crucifixion (v. 39) to find out from a trusted source if the report were true. Once he was assured that Jesus was **dead,** Pilate **gave** (lit., "gave as a gift," i.e., without requiring a fee) **the body** (to *ptōma,* "the corpse") **to Joseph.** Pilate's favorable response to Joseph's request was exceptional; perhaps it arose from his belief that Jesus was innocent (cf. vv. 14-15). Only Mark recorded Pilate's questioning of the centurion, thereby highlighting to his Roman readers that Jesus' death was confirmed by a Roman military officer.

15:46-47. Joseph undoubtedly had servants help him to accomplish a proper burial before sunset, a time span of about two hours. Nicodemus, a fellow Sanhedrin member, joined in, presumably by prearrangement (John 19:39-40).

After Jesus' body was removed from the cross, it was probably washed (cf. Acts 9:37) before it was wrapped tightly in strips of **linen cloth** with aromatic spices placed between the wraps. All this was in accord with Jewish burial customs (John 19:39-40).

Then the body was carried to a nearby garden **and placed** on a stone shelf inside Joseph's own previously unused **tomb** (Matt. 27:60; John 19:41-42) hewn **out of rock.** The tomb was sealed shut with a circular flat **stone** that rolled down a sloping groove till it was securely in front of the entrance to keep out intruders. To roll that stone back up again would require the strength of several men.

Two women who had witnessed Jesus' death (cf. Mark 15:40) **saw** (lit., "were observing," imperf. tense) with interest **where He was** buried. Apparently the other women had returned home to prepare for the Sabbath, a day on which they rested (Luke 23:56).

IX. Jesus' Resurrection from the Dead near Jerusalem (16:1-8) (Matt. 28:1-8; Luke 24:1-12; John 20:1-10)

The four Gospel accounts of the Resurrection contain various differences in recorded details (e.g., the number and names of the women who came to the tomb, the number of angelic messengers who appeared, and the women's reactions to the Resurrection announcement). None of the writers reported all the data; they were free (within veritable limits) to summarize, particularize, and emphasize different aspects of the same event. The various recorded differences reflect the natural effect of this unique event on different eyewitnesses, thereby confirming the Resurrection as a historical event. (See the chart, "Forty Days—from Resurrection to Ascension," at Matt. 28:1-4.)

A. The women's arrival at the tomb (16:1-5)

16:1. The Sabbath, Saturday (Nisan 16), concluded at sunset and the new Jewish day, Sunday (Nisan 17), began. That evening after sunset the women who had witnessed Jesus' death and burial (cf. 15:40, 47) **bought spices,** aromatic oils, **to anoint Jesus' body** (lit., "Him") the next morning. This indicates that they did not expect Jesus to rise from the dead (cf. 8:31; 9:31; 10:34).

Spices were poured over a dead body to counteract the odor of decay and as a symbolic expression of loving devotion. Embalming was not a Jewish custom.

16:2-3. Very early on the first day of the week (Sunday, Nisan 17) **just after sunrise** the women went **to the tomb.** They left home while it was still dark (cf. John 20:1) and got to the tomb shortly after sunrise.

Two of them knew that a large **stone** had been rolled in front of the tomb's **entrance** (cf. Mark 15:47). Only Mark recorded their concern over the practical problem of getting it rolled back. Evidently they were not aware of the official sealing of the tomb or the posting of a guard (cf. Matt. 27:62-66).

16:4-5. When the women arrived on the scene, **they looked up** toward the tomb and immediately noticed **that the stone . . . had been** removed, for (*gar;* cf. 1:16) it **was very large** and thus easily seen.

The women **entered the** tomb's outer room that led to the inner burial chamber. They were startled to see **a young man** (*neaniskon;* cf. 14:51) **sitting** to their **right** probably in front of the burial chamber. The unique circumstances, the accompanying description, and the revelatory message (16:6-7) indicate that Mark viewed him as an angelic messenger sent from God even though Mark called him a young man, as he appeared to the women. The **white robe** pictured his heavenly origin and splendor (cf. 9:3).

Luke (24:3-4) and John (20:12) mentioned the presence of two angels, the number necessary for a valid witness (cf. Deut. 17:6); but Matthew (28:5) and Mark referred to only one, presumably the spokesman.

The women **were alarmed** (*exethambēthēsan;* cf. Mark 9:15; 14:33) when they encountered the divine messenger. This compound verb of strong emotion (used only by Mark in the NT), expresses overwhelming distress at what is highly unusual (cf. 16:8).

B. The angel's announcement (16:6-7)

16:6. Sensing the women's distress, the angel commanded them, **Don't be alarmed** (cf. same verb, v. 5). They were **looking for** (*zēteite,* "seeking") the dead body of **Jesus, the** Man from Nazareth **who** had been **crucified,** expecting to anoint it (cf. v. 1). But the angel announced, **He has risen!** ("He was raised"; *ēgerthē,* pass.) indicating that the Resurrection was God's act, a New Testament emphasis (cf. Acts 3:15; 4:10; Rom. 4:24; 8:11; 10:9; 1 Cor. 6:14; 15:15; 2 Cor. 4:14; 1 Peter 1:21). His body was **not** there as they could easily see. The tomb was empty!

The angel's message clearly identified the Risen One as the Crucified One, both referring to the same historical Person, and it revealed the meaning of the empty tomb. The certainty of the Resurrection rests on the angel's message from God which people then and now are called on to believe. The historical fact of the empty tomb confirms it.

16:7. The women were given a task. They were to **go** and **tell** Jesus' **disciples** that they would be reunited with Him in **Galilee.** The words **and Peter,** unique to Mark, are significant since much of Mark's material likely came from Peter. He was singled out not because of his preeminence among the disciples but because he was forgiven and still included in the Eleven despite his triple denial (cf. 14:66-72).

The message that Jesus was **going ahead of** (from *proagō*) them **into** Galilee recalled the reunion He had promised (cf. the same verb in 14:28). His followers would **see Him** there which implies a Resurrection appearance (cf. 1 Cor. 15:5). This does not refer, as some say, to His second coming. Mark's journey motif (cf. introduction to Mark 8:31; also 10:32a) did not end with Jesus' death, for the risen Jesus continued to lead His followers.

These women were the first to hear the news of Jesus' resurrection but their reports were disregarded initially as women were not considered eligible witnesses under Jewish law. The disciples did not go to Galilee immediately. Jesus' additional appearances to them in the Jerusalem vicinity were necessary to convince them of the reality of His resurrection (cf. John 20:19-29).

C. The women's response to the news of Jesus' resurrection (16:8)

16:8. The women . . . **fled from the tomb** because (*gar;* cf. 1:16) they were **trembling** (*tromos,* a noun) **and bewildered** (astonishment, *ekstasis;* cf. 5:42). For a time **they said nothing to anyone** (Matt. 28:8) a double negative expression in Greek unique to Mark, **because** (*gar*) **they were afraid** (*ephobounto;* cf. Mark 4:41; 5:15, 33, 36; 6:50-52; 9:32; 10:32).

Their response was similar to Peter's at the transfiguration (cf. 9:6). The object of their fear was the awesome disclosure of God's presence and power in raising Jesus from the dead. They were overwhelmed with reverential fear and reduced to silence.

Several interpreters believe that Mark concluded his Gospel at this point. The abrupt ending is consistent with Mark's style and punctuates his development of the themes of fear and astonishment throughout his Gospel. The reader is left to ponder with awe the meaning of the empty tomb as interpreted by the angel's revelatory message (cf. the following comments on 16:9-20).

X. Disputed Epilogue (16:9-20)

The last 12 verses of Mark (16:9-20) known as "the longer ending of Mark" constitute one of the most difficult and most disputed textual problems in the New Testament. Were these verses included or omitted in Mark's original text? Most modern English translations call attention to the problem in some way such as adding an explanatory footnote at verse 9 (NASB), setting this section apart from verse 8 with an explanatory note (NIV), or printing the whole section in the margin (RSV).

The *external* evidence includes the following: (1) The two earliest (fourth century) uncial manuscripts (Sinaiticus and Vaticanus) omit the verses though their respective scribes left some blank space after verse 8, suggesting that they knew of a longer ending but did not have it in the manuscript they were copying. (2) Most all other manuscripts (fifth century on) as well as early versions support the inclusion of verses 9-20. (3) Several later manuscripts (seventh century on) and versions supply a "shorter ending" after verse 8 which is clearly not genuine but all these manuscripts (except one) continue on with verses 9-20. (4) Early patristic writers—such as Justin Martyr (*Apology* 1. 45, ca. A.D. 148), Tatian (*Diatessaron,* ca. A.D. 170), and Irenaeus who quoted verse 19 (*Against Heresies* 3. 10. 6)—support the inclusion of these verses. However, Eusebius

(*Questions to Marinus 1*, ca. A.D. 325) and Jerome (*Epistle* 120. 3; *ad Hedibiam*, ca. A.D. 407) said verses 9-20 were missing from Greek manuscripts known to them. (5) An Armenian manuscript of the 10th century attributed verses 9-20 to "the presbyter Ariston," probably Aristion, a contemporary of Papias (A.D. 60–130) who was purportedly a disciple of the Apostle John. (6) If Mark ended abruptly at verse 8, then it is easy to see why some early copyist(s) wanted to provide a "suitable" ending for the Gospel from other authoritative sources. However, if verses 9-20 were part of the original, it is difficult to see why the early copyists would have omitted it.

Internal evidence includes this data: (1) The transition from verse 8 to verse 9 involves an abrupt change of subject from "women" to the presumed subject "Jesus" since His name is not stated in verse 9 of the Greek text. (2) Mary Magdalene is introduced with a descriptive clause in verse 9 as though she had not been mentioned already in 15:40, 47 and 16:1. (3) About ⅓ of the significant Greek words in verses 9-20 are "non-Marcan," that is, they do not appear elsewhere in Mark or they are used differently from Mark's usage prior to verse 9. (4) The Greek literary style lacks the vivid, lifelike detail so characteristic of Mark's historical narrative. (5) Mark would have been expected to include a Resurrection appearance to the disciples in Galilee (14:28; 16:7), but the appearances in verses 9-20 are in or near Jerusalem. (6) Matthew and Luke parallel Mark until verse 8 and then diverge noticeably, suggesting that Mark began its literary existence without verses 9-20.

Equally astute and conscientious interpreters differ widely in their evaluations of this data and reach opposing conclusions. Those who include these verses in light of the preponderance of early and widespread external support must still account satisfactorily for the internal evidence which appears to distinguish these verses from the rest of the Gospel. And those who omit these verses must still account for their early and widespread attestation externally and give a suitable reason for Mark's seemingly abrupt conclusion at verse 8. Four possible solutions for this have been suggested: (1) Mark finished his Gospel but the original ending was lost or destroyed in some way now unknown before it was copied. (2) Mark finished his Gospel but the original ending was deliberately suppressed or removed for some reason now unknown. (3) Mark was unable to finish his Gospel for some reason now unknown—possibly sudden death. (4) Mark purposely intended to end his Gospel at verse 8.

Of these options, numbers 1 and 2 are unlikely even though the view that the original ending was accidentally lost is widely accepted. If Mark's Gospel was a scroll manuscript rather than a codex (leaf form of book) the ending would normally be on the inside of the scroll and less likely to be damaged or lost than the beginning of the scroll. If the incompleteness of Mark is assumed, number 3 is the most probable option but due to its very nature it cannot be confirmed. In light of Mark's use of the theme "fear" in relation to Jesus' followers (cf. v. 8), many modern interpreters incline toward option 4.

A final conclusion to the problem probably cannot be reached on the basis of presently known data. A view which seems to account for the relevant evidence and to raise the least number of objections is that (a) Mark purposely ended his Gospel with verse 8 and (b) verses 9-20, though written or compiled by an anonymous Christian writer, are historically authentic and are part of the New Testament canon (cf. similarly the last chapter of Deut.). In this view, very early in the transmission of Mark's Gospel (perhaps shortly after A.D. 100) verses 9-20 were added to verse 8 without any attempt to match Mark's vocabulary and style. Possibly these verses were brief extracts from the post-Resurrection accounts found in the other three Gospels and were known through oral tradition to have the approval of the Apostle John who lived till near the end of the first century. Thus the material was included early enough in the transmission process to gain recognition and acceptance by the church as part of canonical Scripture. These verses are consistent with the rest of Scripture. The development of the theme of belief and unbelief unifies the passage.

A. Three of Jesus' post-resurrection appearances (16:9-14)

This section contains three of Jesus' post-resurrection appearances before His Ascension. (See the chart, "Forty Days— from Resurrection to Ascension," at Matt. 28:1-4.)

1. HIS APPEARANCE TO MARY MAGDALENE AND HIS FOLLOWERS' UNBELIEF (16:9-11) (JOHN 20:14-18)

16:9-11. These verses turn abruptly to **Mary** Magdalene's return visit to the tomb while it was still **early** (cf. "very early," v. 2) that same morning. Though mentioned three times previously in Mark (cf. 15:40, 47; 16:1), she was described here for the first time as the Mary **out of whom** Jesus **had** expelled **seven demons** (cf. Luke 8:2). Jesus **appeared,** made Himself visible, to her **first.** This suggests that people could not recognize **Jesus** in His resurrected state unless He deliberately revealed Himself to them (cf. Luke 24:16, 31).

Mary **went and told those who had been with Him** that she had seen Jesus. This designation for Jesus' followers was not used earlier in Mark or in the other Gospels (but cf. Mark 3:14; 5:18). The clause probably refers to Jesus' disciples in general (cf. 16:12), not just the Eleven (cf. Acts 1:21). They all **were mourning and weeping** over Jesus' death, a description unique to this account.

On hearing **that Jesus was alive and . . . had been seen** (*etheathē,* not used elsewhere in Mark) by Mary, the disciples refused to **believe** (*epistēsan,* a verb not used elsewhere in Mark) her report (cf. Luke 24:11). Apparently a short time later Jesus appeared to the other two women, confirming the angel's announcement and urging them to tell His disciples (cf. Matt. 28:1, 9-10).

2. HIS APPEARANCE TO TWO FOLLOWERS AND THE UNBELIEF OF THE REST (16:12-13)

16:12-13. These verses summarize the story about the two Emmaus disciples (Luke 24:13-35). The words **two of them** indicate that they were part of the group who disbelieved Mary's report (cf. Mark 16:10-11). **While they were** out **walking,** going from Jerusalem into **the country,**

Jesus **appeared** (cf. v. 9) to them **in a different form** (*hetera morphē,* "a form of a different kind"). This could mean that He took on a form different from that in which He appeared to Mary Magdalene or, more likely, that He appeared to them in a form different from that in which they had previously recognized Him as **Jesus.** When they **returned** to Jerusalem **and reported** the event **to the rest** of the disciples, **they did not believe** their report **either** (cf. v. 11). Apparently, despite affirmative statements (cf. Luke 24:34), the disciples initially seemed to regard Jesus' post-resurrection appearances as apparitions (cf. Luke 24:37).

3. HIS APPEARANCE TO THE ELEVEN AND HIS REBUKE OF THEIR UNBELIEF (16:14) (LUKE 24:36-49; JOHN 20:19-25)

16:14. Later (*hysteron,* a comparative adverb not used elsewhere in Mark) on the evening of the same day (cf. v. 9) **Jesus appeared to the Eleven** themselves while **they** sat **eating** (their evening meal is implied in Luke 24:41-43). **He rebuked** (*oneidisen,* a strong verb not used of Jesus elsewhere) their unbelief and hardness of heart (*sklērokardian;* cf. Mark 10:5) because they refused **to believe** the testimony of eyewitnesses to His resurrection earlier that day. By hearing about Jesus' resurrection (before seeing **Him**) they learned what it was like to believe the testimony of eyewitnesses. This would be necessary for all those to whom they would preach in their coming missionary outreach.

B. Jesus' commission to His followers (16:15-18) (Matt. 28:16-20)

16:15. Later Jesus gave His disciples His great missionary commission: **Go into all** (*hapanta,* "the whole," emphatic form) **the world and preach** (*kēryxate,* "proclaim"; cf. 1:4, 14) **the good news** (*euangelion,* "gospel"; cf. 1:1) **to all creation,** that is, to all people.

16:16. In response to the preaching of the gospel, **whoever believes and is baptized,** a baptized believer (lit., "the one who believed and was baptized"), **will be saved** (*sōthēsetai;* cf. comments on 13:13) by God (implied) from spiritual death, the penalty of sin. A single Greek article governs both substantival participles, linking them together in describing the inward, efficacious reception of the gospel by faith (believing) and the outward, public expression of that faith in water baptism.

Though the New Testament writers generally assume that under normal circumstances each believer will be baptized, 16:16 does not mean that baptism is a necessary requirement for personal salvation. The second half of the verse indicates by contrast that one who **does not believe** the gospel **will be condemned** by God (implied) in the day of final judgment (cf. 9:43-48). The basis for condemnation is unbelief, not the lack of any ritual observance. Baptism is not mentioned because unbelief precludes one's giving a confession of faith while being baptized by water. Thus the only requirement for personally appropriating God's salvation is faith in Him (cf. Rom. 3:21-28; Eph. 2:8-10).

16:17-18. These verses list five kinds of **signs** (*sēmeia*; cf. comments on 8:11) which would attend **those who believe.** "Signs" are supernatural events attesting the divine origin of the apostolic message (cf. 16:20). The signs authenticated the faith the early believers proclaimed, not the personal faith that any one of them exercised. In light of this and historical evidence it is reasonable to conclude that these authenticating signs were normative only for the apostolic era (cf. 2 Cor. 12:12; Heb. 2:3-4).

In fulfilling their commission (cf. Mark 16:15) believers would be given the ability to do miraculous things **in Jesus' name** (cf. comments on 6:7, 13; 9:38-40). **They** would **drive out demons,** thereby demonstrating Jesus' victory over Satan's realm. The Twelve (cf. 6:13) and the Seventy had already expelled demons, and this ability continued in the apostolic church (cf. Acts 8:7; 16:18; 19:15-16). **They** would **speak in new tongues,** presumably a reference to intelligible foreign languages not previously known to the speakers. This was demonstrated at Pentecost (cf. Acts 2:4-11) and later in the life of the early church (cf. Acts 10:46; 19:6; 1 Cor. 12:10; 14:1-24).

In the Greek the first two clauses in Mark 16:18 may be understood as conditional clauses with the third clause

as the conclusion. An interpretive rendering would be, "And if **they** be compelled to **pick up snakes with their hands and** if **they** should be compelled to **drink deadly poison, it** shall by no means (*ou mē*, emphatic negative; cf. 13:2) harm **them.**" This promise of immunity by divine protection in either situation refers to occasions when persecutors would force believers to do these things. This does not warrant voluntary snake-handling or drinking of poison, practices not attested in the early church. Since Paul's encounter with a snake at Malta was unintentional (cf. Acts 28:3-5), the New Testament records no actual instance of either of the experiences described here.

As a final kind of authenticating sign **they** would put **their hands on sick people and they** would **get well.** Healing by this means is mentioned in Acts 28:8 and the gift of healing was exercised in the early church (cf. 1 Cor. 12:30).

C. Jesus' Ascension and the disciples' ongoing mission (16:19-20) (Luke 24:50-51; Acts 1:9-11)

16:19-20. These verses consist of two closely related parts. On the one hand (Gr., *men*) **the Lord Jesus**—a compound title not found in the Gospels except in Luke 24:3—**after** His post-resurrection ministry (a 40-day period; cf. Acts 1:3) **was taken up into heaven** (by God the Father, implied). There **He sat** down **at the right hand of God,** His place of honor and authority (cf. comments on Mark 12:36-37a). The reality of this was confirmed to the early believers by Stephen's vision (cf. Acts 7:56). In one sense Jesus' work on earth was finished.

On the other hand (Gr., *de*) His work on earth in another sense continued through **the disciples** who **went out** from Jerusalem **and preached** (*ekēryxan*, "proclaimed"; cf. Mark 1:4, 14; 16:15) the gospel **everywhere.** At the same time **the** risen **Lord** was working **with them** by empowering them, **and** confirming **His Word,** the gospel message, **by the signs** (cf. 16:17-18) **that accompanied it.** The signs authenticated their message (cf. Heb. 2:3-4). This task of proclaiming the gospel still goes on through disciples empowered by the risen Lord.

BIBLIOGRAPHY

Alford, Henry. *Alford's Greek Testament.* Vol. 1. Reprint. Grand Rapids: Baker Book House, 1980.

Anderson, Hugh. *The Gospel of Mark.* The New Century Bible Commentary. Grand Rapids: Wm. B. Eerdmans Publishing Co., 1976.

Burdick, Donald W. "The Gospel according to Mark." In *The Wycliffe Bible Commentary.* Chicago: Moody Press, 1962.

Cole, R.A. *The Gospel according to St. Mark.* The Tyndale New Testament Commentaries. Grand Rapids: Wm. B. Eerdmans Publishing Co., 1961.

Cranfield, C.E.B. *The Gospel according to Saint Mark.* Cambridge Greek Testament Commentary. Rev. ed. New York: Cambridge University Press, 1972.

Earle, Ralph. *Mark: the Gospel of Action.* Everyman's Bible Commentary. Chicago: Moody Press, 1970.

Hendriksen, William. *Exposition of the Gospel according to Mark.* New Testament Commentary. Grand Rapids: Baker Book House, 1975.

Hiebert, D. Edmond. *Mark: A Portrait of the Servant.* Chicago: Moody Press, 1974.

Lane, William L. *The Gospel according to Mark.* The New International Commentary on the New Testament. Grand Rapids: Wm. B. Eerdmans Publishing Co., 1974.

Lenski, R.C.H. *The Interpretation of St. Mark's Gospel.* Reprint. Minneapolis: Augsburg Publishing House, 1961.

Martin, Ralph P. *Mark: Evangelist and Theologian.* Grand Rapids: Zondervan Publishing House, 1973.

_____. *Mark.* Knox Preaching Guides. Atlanta: John Knox Press, 1981.

Stonehouse, Ned B. *The Witness of the Synoptic Gospels to Christ.* 1944. Reprint. Grand Rapids: Baker Book House, 1979.

Swete, Henry Barclay. *The Gospel according to St. Mark.* 3rd ed. 1909. Reprint. Grand Rapids: Kregel Publishing Co., 1978.

Swift, C.E. Graham. "Mark." In *The New Bible Commentary: Revised.* Grand Rapids: Wm. B. Eerdmans Publishing Co., 1970.

Taylor, Vincent. *The Gospel according to St. Mark.* 2nd ed. Thornapple Commentaries. 1966. Reprint. Grand Rapids: Baker Book House, 1981.

Vos, Howard F. *Mark: A Study Guide Commentary.* Grand Rapids: Zondervan Publishing House, 1978.

Wilson R. McL. "Mark." In *Peake's Commentary on the Bible.* New York: Thomas Nelson & Sons, 1962.

LUKE

John A. Martin

INTRODUCTION

Author. The two books attributed to Luke (Luke and Acts) make up about 28 percent of the Greek New Testament. Luke is not mentioned by name in either book. The only places where his name occurs in the New Testament are in Colossians 4:14; 2 Timothy 4:11; and Philemon 24. Luke also referred to himself directly in the "we" sections of Acts (16:10-17; 20:5-21:18; 27:1-28:16).

Luke must have been a Gentile for Paul differentiates him from the Jews (Col. 4:10-14). Paul wrote that, of his fellow-workers, Aristarchus, Mark, and John were the only ones who were Jews. The others (Epaphras, Luke, and Demas) were therefore probably Gentiles. Paul referred to Luke as a physician (Col. 4:14), a fact which many try to corroborate from passages in Luke and Acts. Until modern times church tradition uniformly has held Luke to be the author of Luke and Acts. According to tradition Luke was from Antioch, but it is impossible to verify this claim.

Sources. Luke claimed to be a historian (Luke 1:1-4). He carefully researched his material for specific reasons. He consulted eyewitnesses for information (1:2). He may have gathered certain details, such as facts on Jesus' youth, from Mary herself (cf. 2:51). Luke also seemed to have had contacts with the Herodian court (cf. 3:1, 19; 8:3; 9:7-9; 13:31; 23:7-12). Scholars do not agree on which sources Luke used in writing his Gospel. He may have reworked various source materials at his disposal in order to create a unified whole, written in his style, which reflected his purpose. All this, of course, was done under the inspiration of the Holy Spirit.

Date and Place. A number of dates have been suggested for the writing of Luke. If Acts were written before the time of Nero's persecution (A.D. 64)—which seems evident by the fact that Acts closed with Paul still alive and in prison—then the Book of Luke must have been written several years before that, for Acts was subsequent to Luke. Though it is impossible to pinpoint a specific date, a time of composition between A.D. 58 and 60 fits well.

Luke gave no clues as to the place where he wrote his Gospel. Thus any statement on the matter would be mere speculation. Some suggest that Luke wrote from either Caesarea or Rome.

Purposes. Luke had two purposes in writing this book. One was to confirm the faith of Theophilus, that is, to show that his faith in Christ rested on firm historical fact (1:3-4). His other purpose was to present Jesus as the Son of Man, who had been rejected by Israel. Because of this rejection, Jesus was also preached to Gentiles so that they could know the kingdom program of God and attain salvation.

Gentile Character of the Book. Several lines of evidence point to the conclusion that Luke wrote primarily for Gentiles. First, Luke frequently explained Jewish localities (4:31; 8:26; 21:37; 23:51; 24:13). This would be unnecessary if he were writing to Jews. Second, he traced Jesus' genealogy (3:23-38) all the way back to Adam (rather than to Abraham, as in Matthew's Gospel). The implication is that Jesus was representing all mankind rather than just the Jewish nation. Third, Luke referred to Roman emperors in designating the dates of Jesus' birth (2:1) and of John the Baptist's preaching (3:1). Fourth, Luke used a number of words which would be more familiar to Gentile readers than the comparable Jewish terms

199

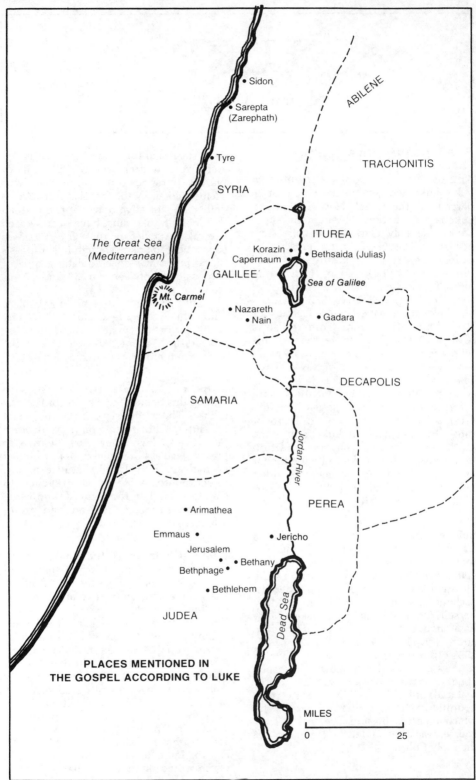

**PLACES MENTIONED IN
THE GOSPEL ACCORDING TO LUKE**

found in Matthew's Gospel. An example is Luke's use of the Greek *didaskalos* rather than *rabbi* for "teacher."

Fifth, Luke used the Septuagint when quoting from the Old Testament. He has relatively few direct quotations, though the book is filled with allusions. The quotations and references are in 2:23-24; 3:4-6; 4:4, 8, 10-12, 18-19; 7:27; 10:27; 18:20; 19:46; 20:17, 28, 37, 42-43; 22:37. All these except 7:27 are based on the Septuagint. The quotation in 7:27 appears to be taken neither from the Greek Septuagint nor the Hebrew Masoretic text but from some other text. Sixth, little is said about Jesus' fulfilling prophecies because that theme was not nearly so important to Gentile readers as it was to Jewish readers. Luke has only five direct references to fulfillment of prophecy and all but one (3:4) are found in the teaching of Jesus to Israel.

Luke's Relationship to Matthew and Mark. Luke is one of the Synoptic Gospels, having much material in common with Matthew and Mark. However, Luke has a lengthy section in which much of the material is unique to his book (9:51–19:27). He also presented unique material in the birth narratives of John and Jesus and the record of Jesus at age 12 (1:5–2:52). It is assumed that Luke knew of and used both Matthew and Mark or sources common to Matthew and/or Mark. The differences in narrative sequence and accounts presented can be explained on the basis of the purposes of the various authors. Though the accounts are historical, the purpose of each of the writers was theological. (For more on the relationships of the Synoptic Gospels see the *Introduction* to the Book of Matt. and the *Introduction* to the Book of Mark.)

Characteristics of the Book. 1. Luke emphasized the universal message of the gospel more than the other Gospel writers. He often wrote about sinners, the poor, and outcasts from Jewish society. He also referred many times to Gentiles who shared in the blessings of the Messiah. Samaritans were presented as coming to faith in the Messiah. And Luke wrote frequently of women and children and their faith.

2. Luke's Gospel gives a reader a more comprehensive grasp of the history of the period than the other Gospels. He presented more facts about the earthly life of Jesus than did Matthew, Mark, or John.

3. Luke emphasized forgiveness (3:3; 5:18-26; 6:37; 7:36-50; 11:4; 12:10; 17:3-4; 23:34; 24:47).

4. Luke emphasized prayer. At many points in His ministry Jesus prayed (3:21; 5:16; 6:12; 9:18, 29; 22:32, 40-41).

5. Luke noted the individual's place in coming to repentance. He stressed the action which must come from each individual who followed Jesus. Examples include Zechariah, Elizabeth, Mary, Simeon, Anna, Martha, Mary, Simon, Levi, the centurion, the widow of Nain, Zacchaeus, and Joseph of Arimathea.

6. Luke said more about material things than did any other author in the New Testament. He did not always present the poor as being righteous, but he did say that the self-sufficient rich, who regarded riches more highly than Jesus, were unable to enter into the salvation Jesus offered.

7. Luke often spoke of joy that accompanies faith and salvation (1:14; 8:13; 10:17; 13:17; 15:5, 9, 32; 19:6, 37).

OUTLINE

COMMENTARY

I. The Prologue and Purpose of the Gospel (1:1-4)

1:1-4. Luke is the only one of the four Gospel writers who stated his method and purpose at the beginning of his book. He was familiar with other writings about Jesus' life and the message of the gospel (v. 1). His purpose was to allow **Theophilus** to **know the certainty of the things** he had **been taught** by writing out **an orderly account** (v. 3; cf. v. 1) of the events in Christ's life.

Luke carefully identified himself with the believers (v. 1). Some have suggested that Luke may have been among the 72 Jesus sent out on the missionary journey (10:1-24) because of his notation that the things were **fulfilled among us.** However, the next statement that these "things" (i.e., accounts and teachings) **were handed down** orally by the **eyewitnesses** of Jesus would negate that possibility. Luke implied that he was not an eyewitness but a researcher. He was thorough and exact in his research, having **investigated** for his account **everything from the beginning,** that is, from the first of Christ's life.

"Theophilus" (lit., "lover of God") was a common name during the first century. Who this man was is open to

conjecture. Though it has been suggested that Luke used the name for all who are "lovers of God" (i.e., the readers of his Gospel narrative), it is better to suppose that this was a real individual who was the first recipient of Luke's Gospel and who then gave it wide circulation in the early church. Apparently he was an official of some kind, for he was called **most excellent** (cf. Acts 23:26; 24:3; 26:25, which use the same Gr. term, *kratiste*).

II. The Births and Maturations of John and Jesus (1:5–2:52)

A. The announcements of the births (1:5-56)

Luke arranged the material in this section and the following sections in a form which compared John's birth and maturation with Jesus' birth and maturation. In both cases the parents were introduced (vv. 5-7 and 26-27), an angel appeared (vv. 8-23 and 28-30), a sign was given (vv. 18-20 and 34-38), and a woman who had no children became pregnant (vv. 24-25 and 42).

1. THE ANNOUNCEMENT OF THE BIRTH OF JOHN (1:5-25)

a. The introduction of John's parents (1:5-7)

1:5-7. John's parents were **a priest named Zechariah** and **Elizabeth,** who **was also a descendant of Aaron.** John therefore was by lineage one who was to become a priest. His parents lived when **Herod** the Great ruled as **king of Judea,** from 37 to 4 B.C. (See chart on the Herods.) They were godly people, or **upright** (*dikaioi*, "righteous"), **observing all the Lord's commandments.** They were **both well along in years** and thus had no prospect of children. This fact was a constant embarrassment to Elizabeth as is evident from her statement later on (v. 25). God's allowing a barren woman to have children occurred several times in the Old Testament (e.g., the mothers of Isaac, Samson, and Samuel).

b. The angel's announcement to Zechariah (1:8-23)

1:8-9. Luke recorded that **Zechariah's division was on duty.** This division was one of 24 groups of priests, drawn up in David's time (1 Chron. 24:7-18). The priests in each division were on duty twice a year for a week at a time.

Herod the Great
King of Palestine, 37–4 B.C. (Luke 1:5)
Killed Bethlehem baby boys (Matt. 2:1-17)

Antipater	Alexander	Herod Aristobulus	**Herod Philip I**	**Herod Antipas**	**Herod Archelaus**	**Herod Philip II**
			4 B.C.–A.D. 34 (Matt. 14:3b; Mark 6:17). Married his niece Herodias.	Tetrarch of Galilee and Perea, 4 B.C.–A.D. 39 (Luke 3:1). Called a "fox" by Jesus (Luke 13:31-33). Had John the Baptist beheaded (Mark 6:14-29). Judged Jesus at His trial (Luke 23:7-12).	Ethnarch of Judea, Samaria, and Idumea, 4 B.C.–A.D. 6 (Matt. 2:22).	Tetrarch of Iturea and Trachonitis 4 B.C.–A.D. 34 (Luke 3:1). Married Herodias' daughter, Salome.

Herod of Chalcis	**Herod Agrippa I**	**Herodias**
A.D. 41–48	King over Palestine, A.D. 37–44. Killed the Apostle James (Acts 12:1-2). Imprisoned Peter (Acts 12:3-11).	Married (1) her uncle Herod Philip I (Matt. 14:3), (2) her uncle Herod Antipas (Mark 6:17).

Herod Agrippa II	**Drusilla**	**Bernice**
Tetrarch of Chalcis and northern territory, A.D. 50-70. Paul was on trial before him (Acts 25:13-26:32).	Wife of *Felix,* procurator of Judea, A.D. 52-59, before whom Paul was tried (Acts 23:26–24:27).	Married her uncle Herod Chalcis. Was with her brother Herod Agrippa II at Paul's trial (Acts 25:13; 26:30).

Names in boldface appear in the New Testament.

Zechariah was of the division of Abijah (Luke 1:5; cf. 1 Chron. 24:10).

Zechariah **was chosen by lot** (*elache*) to be the **priest** who offered the **incense.** Because of the large number of priests this would be the only time in Zechariah's life when he was allowed to perform this task. As elsewhere in Scripture (e.g., Es. 3:7), the sovereignty of God is stressed even in matters which seem like chance, as in the casting of a lot.

1:10-11. While Zechariah was inside at the altar of **incense,** a crowd gathered to pray. The incense for which Zechariah was responsible symbolized the prayers of the entire nation. At that particular

moment Zechariah was thus the focal point of the entire Jewish nation.

At that unique moment in Zechariah's life **an angel of the Lord appeared . . . standing** where Zechariah was praying beside **the altar of incense.**

1:12-13. The purpose of the appearance of the **angel** of the Lord was to announce the birth of **a son** to **Zechariah** and **Elizabeth.** Zechariah **was gripped with fear** (lit., "fear fell on him"). In Luke, many people responded with fear or awe (*phobos*) when confronted with mighty acts of God (cf. 1:30, 65; 2:9-10; 5:10, 26; 7:16; 8:25, 37, 50; 9:34, 45; 12:4-5, 32; 21:26; cf. 23:40). Because of the angel's response, **Do not be afraid, Zechariah; your prayer has been heard,** it may be inferred that Zechariah was praying for a son, or possibly even for the coming of the Messiah and that the birth of John would be a partial answer to his prayer. The angel told Zechariah what to name his son. This was also the case when the angel appeared to Mary (1:31).

1:14-17. The angel not only gave the name of the son, but also detailed six aspects of John's character.

1. **He will be a joy and delight to you** (v. 14). Luke frequently used the word "joy" in his accounts in Luke and Acts, often linking it closely with salvation. An illustration of this is in Luke 15, where three times joy and rejoicing came because something lost had been found, a picture of salvation. And John the Baptist's ministry brought joy to the Israelites who believed his message of repentance for the forgiveness of sins (3:3).

2. **He will be great in the sight of the Lord.** The expression "in the sight of" (*enōpion*) is characteristic of Luke. Though it appears 35 times in Luke and Acts, it is used only one other time in the other Gospels (John 20:30).

3. **He is never to take wine or other fermented drink.** Later John voluntarily took on himself a Nazirite vow, refusing to drink anything fermented (Num. 6:1-21). Luke did not specifically state that John would fulfill all aspects of the Nazirite vow. Instead, John would avoid taking any wine perhaps to support his contention that his message was urgent. Another way he emphasized the urgency of his message was to dress, act, and eat like Elijah the prophet (cf. Matt. 3:4; 2 Kings 1:8).

4. **He will be filled with the Holy Spirit even from birth.** "From birth" is literally "from his mother's womb." When Mary visited Elizabeth before John was born, the baby leaped in her womb. The ministry of the Holy Spirit was important to Luke, and he often went to great length to show His empowering and enabling ministry. Both of John's parents were filled with the Spirit (Luke 1:41, 67).

5. **Many of the people of Israel would he bring back to . . . God.** Crowds of Israelites did turn to the Lord through John's ministry (Matt. 3:5-6; Mark 1:4-5).

6. **He will go on before the Lord.** John the Baptist was the Lord's forerunner, announcing His coming **in the spirit and power of Elijah.** Luke here referred to two passages in Malachi which speak of messengers: a messenger was to be sent to clear the way before the Lord (Mal. 3:1), and Elijah's return was promised before the day of the Lord (Mal. 4:5-6) to restore **the hearts of the fathers to their children.** Zechariah apparently understood that the angel was identifying John the Baptist with the messenger in Malachi 3:1, for in his song of praise he noted that John would "go on before the Lord to prepare the way for Him" (Luke 1:76; cf. 3:4-6). Jesus affirmed that John was the fulfillment of Malachi 3:1 (Matt. 11:10) and stated that John *would have* fulfilled Malachi 4:5-6 if the people had accepted his message (Matt. 11:14).

1:18-20. Zechariah had doubts that such a thing could take place because both he and Elizabeth were **old.** But **the angel,** identifying himself as **Gabriel,** reassured Zechariah that this **good news** was from the Lord. When Gabriel appeared twice to Daniel (Dan. 8:16; 9:21), both times he gave Daniel instruction and understanding. He did the same here with Zechariah, as can be inferred from the song of praise and trust which Zechariah uttered later (Luke 1:67-79). Zechariah's inability **to speak** till the fulfillment of Gabriel's message was, to some degree, a punishment for his unbelief. But it was also a sign. A sign in the Old Testament was often associated with a confirming observable phenomenon which accompanied a word of prophecy. For the next nine months Zechariah's attempts to speak would prove the reality of Gabriel's message.

1:21-23. When **Zechariah** finally **came out** of **the temple,** he was able to make the waiting **people** realize that **he had seen a vision.** He then **returned home** in Judah's hill country after completing his temple duty.

c. Elizabeth's pregnancy (1:24-25)

1:24-25. After . . . **Elizabeth became pregnant . . . for five months** she **remained in seclusion.** Most likely, this was because of the excitement of the surrounding **people** to her pregnancy

(v. 25). Mary may have been the first person other than Zechariah and Elizabeth to know the news which the angel had delivered (v. 36).

Luke did not say in verse 25 if Elizabeth knew about the destiny of her son at this time. However, because she knew that his name was to be John (v. 60) even before Zechariah was able to speak, he probably communicated his entire vision in writing. Elizabeth was overjoyed that she was finally able to have a baby.

2. THE ANNOUNCEMENT OF THE BIRTH OF JESUS (1:26-56)

a. The introduction of Mary and Joseph (1:26-27)

1:26-27. In the sixth month, that is, when Elizabeth was in her sixth month of pregnancy, **God sent . . . Gabriel to Nazareth.**

Mary had not yet had sexual contact with a man, for Luke called her **a virgin** (parthenon; cf. 1:34) and noted that she was **pledged to be married to . . . Joseph** (cf. 2:5). In Jewish culture then a man and woman were betrothed or pledged to each other for a period of time before the actual consummation of their marriage. This betrothal was much stronger than an engagement period today, for the two were considered husband and wife except that they did not live together till after the wedding.

b. The angel's announcement of Jesus' birth to Mary (1:28-38)

1:28-31. The angel said that **Mary** was **highly favored** (kecharitōmenē, a part. related to the noun charis, "grace"; the verb charitoō is used elsewhere in the NT only in Eph. 1:6). Also Mary had **found favor** (charis, "grace") **with God.** Obviously God had bestowed a special honor on her. She was a special recipient of His grace.

Gabriel's admonition (Luke 1:30-31) was the same as to Zechariah: **Do not be afraid,** for **you will** have **a Son** (cf. v. 13). As with John (v. 13b), the naming was by the angel (v. 31).

1:32-33. The angel predicted five things about Mary's Son.

1. **He will be great.**
2. He **will be called the Son of the Most High** (cf. v. 76). The Septuagint often used the term "Most High" (hypsistou) to translate the Hebrew 'elyôn (cf. v.

76). Mary could not have missed the significance of that terminology. The fact that her Baby was to be called the "Son of the Most High" pointed to His equality with Yahweh. In Semitic thought a son was a "carbon copy" of his father, and the phrase "son of" was often used to refer to one who possessed his "father's" qualities (e.g., the Heb. trans. "son of wickedness" in Ps. 89:22 [KJV] means a wicked person).

3. He will be given **the throne of His father David.** Jesus, as David's descendant, will sit on David's throne when He reigns in the Millennium (2 Sam. 7:16; Ps. 89:3-4, 28-29).

4. **He will reign over the house of Jacob forever.** Jesus' reign over the nation Israel as her King will begin in the Millennium and continue on into the eternal state.

5. **His kingdom will never end.** These promises must have immediately reminded Mary of the promise of Yahweh to David (2 Sam. 7:13-16). David understood the prophecy as referring not only to his immediate son (Solomon) who would build the temple, but also to the future Son who would rule forever. David stated that Yahweh had spoken of the distant future (2 Sam. 7:19). Mary would have understood that the angel was speaking to her of the Messiah who had been promised for so long.

1:34-38. Mary did not seem surprised that the Messiah was to come. Rather, she was surprised that she would be His mother since she was **a virgin** (lit., "since I do not know a man"). But **the angel** did not rebuke Mary, as he had rebuked Zechariah (v. 20). This indicates that Mary did not doubt the angel's words but merely wanted to know how such an event would be accomplished. The answer was that **the Holy Spirit** would creatively bring about the physical conception of Jesus (v. 35). This miraculous conception and Virgin Birth of Jesus Christ was necessary because of His deity and preexistence (cf. Isa. 7:14; 9:6; Gal. 4:4).

Like Zechariah, Mary was given a sign: **Elizabeth . . . is going to have a child.** Mary affirmed her part in her Son's subsequent birth by assenting to the plan of God: **May it be to me as You have said.** She willingly submitted to God's plan, calling herself **the Lord's servant** (doulē, "slave"; cf. Luke 1:48).

c. Mary's visit to Elizabeth and her return home (1:39-56)

1:39-45. After learning of the sign, **Mary . . . hurried** to see **Elizabeth.** Elizabeth and Zechariah lived in **a town in the hill country,** which probably referred to the hilly region surrounding Jerusalem. As Mary arrived, Elizabeth's baby **leaped in her womb** for joy, **and Elizabeth was filled with the Holy Spirit.** Zechariah also was later filled with the Holy Spirit (v. 67). Prior to the day of Pentecost, believers were filled with the Holy Spirit for specific tasks.

Elizabeth's loudly spoken words, **Blessed** (*eulogēmenē*, lit., "well spoken of") **are you among women,** carry the idea that Mary is the most honored of all women. Elizabeth called her **the mother of my Lord.** In Luke the term "Lord" (*kyrios*) often describes Jesus. It has a double meaning. "Lord" would be more important for a Greek reader than would the term "Christ" (meaning "Messiah"), for the Gentiles had not been anxiously awaiting the Messiah. On the other hand the Septuagint often used the word "Lord" (*kyrios*) to translate Yahweh. Again (v. 45) Elizabeth said Mary was **blessed** (*makaria,* "happy") because she **believed** what God had told **her.** This suggests that Mary visited Elizabeth not with a skeptical attitude but rather joyously, to confirm what had been announced to her.

1:46-55. In response to the situation at hand **Mary** recited a song which praised God's favor on her and her people. "The Magnificat," as the song is called, consists almost entirely of Old Testament allusions and quotations. The same is true of the songs of Zechariah and Simeon (vv. 1:68-79; 2:29-32). Mary's song has similarities to Hannah's song (1 Sam. 2:1-10). First, Mary praised God for His special favor on her (Luke 1:46-50). Mary saw herself as part of the godly remnant that had served Yahweh. She called God **my Savior** (*sōtēri mou*) showing an intimate acquaintance with Him. She spoke of His faithfulness (v. 48), power (v. 49), holiness (v. 49), and mercy (v. 50). Second, Mary praised God for His special favor on Israel (vv. 51-55). Through the Child that she was to bear, God was being **merciful to Abraham and his descendants.** Mary was aware that the birth of her Child was a fulfillment of the covenant promises to Abraham and his people.

1:56. Mary stayed with Elizabeth for about three months, apparently until John was born (cf. v. 36). Mary **then returned home.** The Greek has the words "her home," indicating that she was still a virgin and was not yet married to Joseph.

B. The births and boyhoods of John and Jesus (1:57-2:52)

As in the previous section (1:5-56) here also the records of the births were arranged by Luke in a parallel fashion. The emphasis is on the birth of Jesus, which is described in greater detail than the birth of John.

1. THE BIRTH AND MATURATION OF JOHN (1:57-80)

a. John's birth (1:57-66)

1:57-66. The record of John's birth is given in a single verse (v. 57), with friends sharing in the **joy.** Several verses then focus on and emphasize the obedience of Zechariah and Elizabeth. The old couple was careful to follow the Law in the circumcision of the boy. Though others objected, Elizabeth said that he was to be named **John,** which Zechariah confirmed in **writing.** The fact that Zechariah **immediately** was able **to speak** amazed the crowd. As was true of each person in the account, Zechariah was praising (*eulogōn,* "was blessing"; cf. *eulogēmonē* in v. 42) **God.** Word then spread through **the** whole **hill country** (in the Jerusalem area) that this was an unusual child. The people continued to note that **the Lord's hand was with him.** Years later, when John began his preaching ministry, many went out from this district who no doubt remembered the amazing events surrounding his birth (Matt. 3:5).

b. Zechariah's prophecy and psalm (1:67-79)

1:67-79. This psalm, known as "the Benedictus," is filled with Old Testament quotations and allusions. Zechariah expounded four ideas.

1. **Zechariah** gave an exhortation to **praise . . . God** (v. 68a).

2. Zechariah noted the reason God should be praised—**He has come and has redeemed His people** (v. 68b).

3. Zechariah described the deliver-

Roman Emperors in New Testament Times

Augustus (27 B.C.—A.D. 14)
Ordered the census that involved Joseph and Mary going to Bethlehem (Luke 2:1)

Tiberius (A.D. 14–37)
Jesus ministered and was crucified under his reign (Luke 3:1; 20:22, 25; 23:2; John 19:12, 15)

Caligula (A.D. 37–41)

Claudius (A.D. 41–54)
An extensive famine occurred in his reign (Acts 11:28). He expelled Jews from Rome, including Aquila and Priscilla (Acts 18:2).

Nero (A.D. 54–68)
He persecuted Christians, including the martyrdoms of Paul and Peter. He is the Caesar to whom Paul appealed for a fair trial (Acts 25:8, 10-12, 21; 26:32; 27:24; 28:19).

Galba (A.D. 68–69)

Otho (A.D. 69)

Vitellius (A.D. 69)

Vespasian (A.D. 69–79)
Crushed the Jewish revolt, and his son Titus destroyed the Jerusalem temple in A.D. 70.

---

ance for Israel through the Messiah (vv. 69-75). The Messiah was to be Israel's **horn of salvation** (v. 69). The horns of an animal symbolized its power. Thus the Messiah would be strong and would deliver the nations **from her enemies** (v. 74). Of special import in these verses is the mention of **His holy covenant, the oath** God **swore to our father Abraham** (vv. 72-73; cf. Gen. 22:16-18).

4. Zechariah prophetically described the ministry John would have (Luke 1:76-79). Zechariah had understood the message of the angel, so he foretold that John would be the one to **go on before the Lord to prepare the way for Him** (cf. Isa. 40:3; Mal. 3:1). He would be **a prophet of the Most High** (Luke 1:76; cf. v. 32). Verse 77 may refer to the Lord rather than to John. However, John did preach the same message of **forgiveness of . . . sins** (cf. 3:3).

c. John's growth and seclusion (1:80)

1:80. As John **grew,** he **became strong in spirit,** that is, in human spirit he had an inner vitality and fortitude. His living **in the desert** till the time of his public appearance was not normal for a young person. But because of the special mission which John knew from an early age he would perform, he chose to follow the role of Elijah (cf. v. 17) by living in a desolate area. For in only a brief period of time John's ministry would catapult him into prominence.

2. THE BIRTH AND MATURATION OF JESUS (CHAP. 2)

a. Jesus' birth (2:1-7)

2:1-2. Jesus' birth was dated by Luke as falling in the reign of **Caesar Augustus,** who was officially made the ruler of the Roman Empire in 27 B.C. and ruled to A.D. 14. (See the list of Roman emperors.) Because Herod the Great's reign ended in 4 B.C., Jesus was born before that time. The mention of **Quirinius** as **governor of Syria** poses a problem. He was governor in A.D. 6-7, much too late for Jesus' birth. Therefore does the word **first** (*prōtē*) refer, as in the NIV, to a first, that is, an earlier, **census** by Quirinius? If so, one would have to posit a previous governorship for Quirinius at about 4 B.C. Perhaps a better solution is to take "first" to mean "before," as it does, for example, in John 15:18. Luke 2:2 would then read, "this was the census that took place before Quirinius was governor of Syria" (i.e., before A.D. 6).

2:3-5. For the census **Joseph** and **Mary went to Bethlehem,** Joseph's ancestral home. Joseph was a descendant **of David** (cf. 1:27), who was born in Bethlehem. Some have argued that it seems strange that people were not registered in the places where they currently lived. However, other instances of the same practice are known (see I. Howard Marshall, *The Gospel of Luke,* pp. 101-2). Mary accompanied Joseph for several reasons. The couple knew she would have the Baby during the time Joseph was gone, and they most likely did not want to be separated at that event. Also both of them knew that the Child was the Messiah. They also would have known that the Messiah was to be born in Bethlehem (Micah 5:2).

2:6-7. The Child was born during their time in Bethlehem. The fact that Jesus was called Mary's **firstborn** implies that later she had other children. The couple was housed in quarters which were not private. According to tradition, they were in a cave near the inn. The Child was **placed . . . in a manger,** from which livestock fed. Being wrapped **in strips of cloth** was important, for this was the way the shepherds would recognize the infant (v. 12). Some infants were bound up in that way to keep their limbs straight and unharmed.

b. The shepherd's worship of the baby (2:8-20)

2:8-14. An announcing **angel** and other angels appeared **at night** to a group of **shepherds** and heralded the birth of the **Savior in the town of David,** that is, Bethlehem (v. 4). The shepherds may have been caring for lambs which were destined for sacrifice during the time of Passover. The appearance of the angel and of the radiant **glory of the Lord . . . terrified** them. The Greek for "terrified" (lit., "they feared a great fear") stresses the intensity of this fear.

The angels' message was comforting. The shepherds were told **not to be afraid** (cf. 1:13, 30). The message was that "a Savior," **Christ the Lord,** was **born.** This was **good news of great joy.** Throughout Luke "joy" (*chara*) is often associated with salvation. This news was to be

proclaimed to **all the people.** These were specifically the people of Israel, but perhaps Luke also hinted that the Savior would be for all mankind. The **angel** was then joined by **a great company** of other angels engaged in **praising God** in the highest. The NIV's **on earth peace to men on whom His favor rests** is preferred to the KJV's "good will toward men." God's peace is not given to those who have good will, but to those who are recipients of God's good will or favor.

2:15-20. The **shepherds** went to see **the Baby,** and they told what **the angels** had related to them. The shepherds understood that the angels were speaking for **the Lord.** They believed the message and went to confirm it for themselves. This was much like the action of Mary after she had heard the message of Elizabeth. Such an attitude contrasts sharply with that of the religious leaders who knew where the Baby was to be born but did not take the time or the effort to confirm it for themselves (Matt. 2:5).

After seeing the Baby, the shepherds were the first messengers to proclaim the arrival of the Messiah: **they spread the word.** Those **who heard . . . were amazed** (*ethaumasan*). The theme of amazement at the proclamation of the Messiah runs throughout the Book of Luke. (The Gr. verb *thaumazō*, "to be amazed, to wonder, to be astonished," occurs in Luke 1:21, 63; 2:18, 33; 4:22; 8:25; 9:43; 11:14, 38; 20:26; 24:12, 41. Two other words for amazement were also used by Luke; see 2:48.) **Mary** reflected on this momentous event in history. Of all the women of Israel *she* was the mother of the Messiah! The **shepherds returned glorifying and praising God,** much as the angels had done (vv. 13-14).

c. Jesus' circumcision (2:21)

2:21. Mary and Joseph carried out the pronouncement of **the angel** by naming their Son according to the word which had come to her before the Baby's conception (1:31) and to him after the Baby's conception (Matt. 1:18-21). The name **Jesus** is very fitting for it is the Greek form of the Hebrew name Joshua which means "Yahweh is salvation" (cf. Matt. 1:21). As was the custom, Jesus was circumcised **on the eighth day** (Lev. 12:3), perhaps in Bethlehem.

d. The presentation of Jesus to the Lord (2:22-38)

(1) Mary and Joseph's offering. **2:22-24.** The couple was required by the Law not only to have Jesus circumcised (Lev. 12:3), but also to present their **firstborn** to God (Ex. 13:2, 12) 33 days later and to bring an offering for Mary's **purification** after childbirth (Lev. 12:1-8).

The offering which they presented for her purification showed that they were a poor couple. They could not afford a lamb, so they bought a pair of doves or pigeons, which were all they could afford. They traveled the short distance from Bethlehem **to Jerusalem** for the presentation and purification at the temple.

(2) Simeon's prophecy and blessing of the family (2:25-35). **2:25-26.** Simeon had been told **by the Holy Spirit that he would not die** till he had seen the Messiah. Simeon was **righteous** (dikaios) **and devout** (eulabēs, "reverent") before God. Unlike the religious leaders, **he was waiting for the consolation of Israel,** that is, the Messiah, the One who would bring comfort to the nation (cf. "the redemption of Jerusalem," v. 38). The notation that **the Holy Spirit was upon** Simeon reminds one of the Old Testament prophets on whom the Holy Spirit came. Since Anna was "a prophetess" (v. 36), Simeon was probably also in the godly prophetic tradition of Israel. The special revelation from the Holy Spirit about seeing the Messiah was apparently unique and perhaps came because of Simeon's intense desire for the Promised One.

2:27-32. On seeing **the Child** and picking Him up, **Simeon . . . praised God,** the response of godly people toward the Messiah throughout the Gospel of Luke. He then uttered a psalm of praise extolling God for fulfilling His promise by bringing **salvation.** The Messiah is the Source of salvation, as His name Jesus indicates. In all three of the hymns of thanksgiving and praise recorded by Luke in his first two chapters (1:46-55, 68-79; 2:29-32) lie the deep significance of the births of John and Jesus for the salvation of Israel and the world. Simeon noted that the Messiah was to be for **the Gentiles** as well as for **Israel.** The idea of salvation for the Gentiles is set forth many times in the Gospel of Luke.

2:33. The words of Simeon caused Mary and Joseph to marvel (thaumazontes; cf. comments on v. 18). Though they had been told that their Son was the Messiah, perhaps they had not comprehended the scope of His ministry to the entire world—to the Gentiles as well as to the people of Israel.

2:34-35. Simeon revealed **to Mary** that her Son would be opposed (**a sign . . . spoken against**) and that she would be hurt greatly. Her grief would be like **a sword** piercing her **soul.** The Son would **cause the falling and rising of many in Israel.** Throughout His ministry Jesus proclaimed that the only way to the kingdom, something the nation had long sought, was to follow Him. The ones who did so would receive salvation; they would "rise." But the ones who did not believe Him would not receive salvation; they would "fall." These consequences would reveal what they thought about Mary's Son.

(3) Anna's thanks to God. **2:36-38.** This godly woman from the prophetic tradition continued the work Simeon had started. Anna **was 84** years old and had devoted herself completely to the Lord's service in **the temple** since her husband had died years before. She announced **to all who were looking forward to the redemption of Jerusalem** (cf. v. 25) that the Messiah had come. The word about Jesus was likely known throughout the entire city as people either believed or disbelieved the words of the old prophet and the widowed prophetess.

e. Jesus' growth in Nazareth (2:39-40)

2:39-40. Joseph and Mary then **returned** with Jesus to their home in **Nazareth** of **Galilee,** about 65 miles north of Jerusalem, where Jesus **grew** up. Luke omitted Jesus' sojourn in Egypt from his account (cf. Matt. 2:13-21) since it was not his purpose to show the early rejection of the Messiah. In Nazareth He was first rejected after He publicly declared that He was the Messiah. The preparation for His ministry took place in that town as He continued to grow up. Luke noted that He **became strong** and **was filled with wisdom** (sophia). His growth in wisdom was mentioned later (Luke 2:52). Luke also portrayed Jesus as the Source of wisdom for His followers (21:15). Jesus had **the grace** or favor (charis) **of God . . .**

upon Him. Luke also reiterated that characteristic in 2:52. The wisdom and favor from God were evident before He reached the age of 12.

f. Jesus' visit to the temple (2:41-50)

2:41-50. By the time Jesus **was 12 years old,** He understood His mission on earth. As was their custom, Mary and Joseph went yearly **to Jerusalem** to observe **the Feast of the Passover.** The one-day Passover was followed by the seven-day Feast of Unleavened Bread (Ex. 23:15; Lev. 23:4-8; Deut. 16:1-8). The entire eight-day festival was sometimes called the Passover (Luke 22:1, 7; John 19:14; Acts 12:3-4). On the return home from their trip to Jerusalem, **His parents** did not realize He was not with them until they had gone some distance. **After three days they found Him in the temple courts.** The "three days" refer to the time since they had left the city. They had traveled one day's journey away from the city (Luke 2:44); it took them a second day to get back; they found Him on the following day. When Jesus was found, He was interacting with the **teachers** of the Law, **listening** and **asking** intelligent **questions. Everyone . . . was amazed** (*existanto,* "beside themselves in amazement"; cf. 8:56) **at His understanding and His answers.** When Mary and Joseph **saw Him, they were astonished** (*exeplagēsan,* "struck out of their senses," perhaps with joy; cf. 4:32; 9:43). In response to Mary's question about why He had **treated** them in this manner, Jesus drew a sharp distinction between them and God, His true Father (2:49). His statement confirmed that He knew His mission and that His parents also should have known about His mission. However, His parents **did not understand** this.

g. Jesus' continued growth (2:51-52)

2:51-52. Luke was careful to point out that Jesus **was obedient to** Joseph and Mary in case his readers would think otherwise from the previous paragraph. **Mary treasured all these things in her heart,** reflecting on and remembering her 12-year-old's words, even though she did not understand them. Perhaps Luke received these details about the early years of Jesus from Mary herself or from someone in whom she had confided. Jesus continued to grow (*proekopten,* lit., "cut one's way forward," i.e., "increased") in every way (spiritually, mentally, and physically) and had **favor with God and men** (cf. v. 40).

III. The Preparation for Jesus' Ministry (3:1–4:13)

This section paves the way for the major message of the Gospel of Luke— Jesus' ministry in Galilee and His ministry on the way to Jerusalem (4:14–19:27).

A. The ministry of John the Baptist (3:1-20)
(Matt. 3:1-12; Mark 1:1-8)

As noted earlier (Luke 1:80) John the Baptist lived a life of seclusion till his meteoric rise in public prominence and his sudden fall by the edict of Herod.

1. THE INTRODUCTION OF JOHN (3:1-6)

3:1-2. John's message began **in the 15th year of the reign of Tiberius Caesar,** that is, A.D. 29. Tiberius ruled over the Roman Empire from A.D. 14 to A.D. 37. **Pontius Pilate was** appointed **governor of Judea** in A.D. 26 and ruled to A.D. 36. He was generally opposed to the Jewish people over whom he ruled. The **Herod** here is Herod Antipas who ruled from Tiberius over **Galilee** from 4 B.C. to A.D. 39. **His brother Philip** ruled to the east of the Jordan from 4 B.C. to A.D. 34. (See chart on the Herods at 1:5.) Herod's capital was at Caesarea Philippi. Little is known about **Lysanias** who ruled in **Abilene,** northwest of Damascus. John's ministry also began in the time **of Annas and Caiaphas.** Annas was the high priest from A.D. 6 to A.D. 15 but was deposed by the Roman authorities. Eventually his son-in-law, Caiaphas, was placed in the position (A.D. 18-36). The Jews continued to recognize Annas as the rightful high priest though Caiaphas functioned in that role (cf. comments on Acts 4:5-6, and see chart there on Annas' family; also cf. comments on Luke 22:54; Acts 7:1).

Luke noted that **the word of God came to John . . . in the desert.** The Old Testament is filled with similar phrases as God called specific prophets to perform tasks. Luke had previously noted that John remained in the desert until his public appearance (1:80).

3:3-6. John's message was **a baptism of repentance for the forgiveness of sins.** John's baptism was associated with repentance, that is, it outwardly pictured an inner change of heart. The word "for" (*eis*) refers back to the whole "baptism of repentance." The baptism did not save anyone, as is clear from what follows (vv. 7-14). Repentance was "unto" (lit. rendering of *eis*; cf. comments on Acts 2:38) or resulted in sins forgiven. Since John's function was to be Christ's forerunner, so also his baptism prefigured a different baptism (Luke 3:16). Luke noted that John's baptizing work was in **the country around** (*perichōron*) **the Jordan.** Because John was visibly taking on himself the role of Elijah, it is possible that he picked this area on the lower Jordan because that was where Elijah spent his last days (cf. 2 Kings 2:1-13). Luke quoted from Isaiah 40:3-5 concerning John's ministry. **Isaiah** was writing of God's smoothing the way for the return of the exiles from Babylon to Judah. But all three Synoptic Gospel writers applied Isaiah's words to John the Baptist.

Isaiah wrote, "A voice of one calling: 'In the desert, prepare the way for the Lord.'" But Matthew, Mark, and Luke each wrote, **A voice of one calling in the desert**—the words "in the desert" going with the "voice" rather than with the preparing of the way. Why? Because they quoted from the Septuagint. Of course both are true—the voice (of John the Baptist) was in the desert, and the desert was to be smoothed.

When a king traveled the desert, workmen preceded him to clear debris and smooth out the roads to make his trip easier. In Luke the leveling of the land was a figurative expression denoting that the way of the Messiah would be made smooth because through John a large number of people were ready to receive Jesus' message (cf. Luke 1:17).

Typical of Luke's emphasis on the universal availability of the gospel are his words in 3:6, **And all mankind will see God's salvation.**

2. THE MESSAGE OF JOHN (3:7-14)

Luke recorded the message of John in ethical terms. John's teaching was that one's life proves whether or not he has truly repented (cf. the Book of James). Ethical teaching was important to Luke for he wrote frequently about helping the oppressed and the poor.

3:7-9. **John** challenged the people to bring forth **fruit** as an indication of their belief. John's address to the people was harsh: **You brood of vipers!** Apparently some were coming with the belief that baptism alone could insure salvation. John was alerting them to the stark realities of life. One must face the fact that **wrath** was **coming.** John was clear that being a member of the nation of Israel would not save anyone (v. 8; cf. John 8:33-39; Rom. 2:28-29). An **ax** is ready to **cut down** trees that do not bear **good fruit** so they can be burned. Likewise judgment was extremely close to anyone who did not evidence ("produce good fruit") a genuine **repentance** (Luke 3:8).

3:10-14. The crowd, tax collectors, and soldiers all asked, **What should we do** (vv. 10, 12, 14) to give evidence of genuine repentance? (Cf. similar questions in 10:25; 18:18.) In response John told the people to be (a) generous (3:11), (b) honest (v. 13), and (c) content (v. 14).

A person showed his repentance by being generous with the necessities of life—clothing and food. A tunic (*chitōn*) was a shirtlike garment. Often people wore two if they had them.

Tax collectors, notorious for their dishonesty in collecting more than required and pocketing it for themselves (cf. 5:27-32), exemplified the need for honesty. And **soldiers,** known and hated for always trying to get more **money** (by extorting it and blaming others for it), were examples of the need to be **content** and gentle.

3. THE ROLE OF JOHN (3:15-17)

3:15-17. Luke had previously explained what John's function was to be (1:17, 76). But the crowds who thronged out to hear John began to wonder if **John might possibly be the Christ.** John distinguished between his own baptism and the Messiah's baptism: John's baptism was **with water,** but the Messiah would baptize **with the Holy Spirit and with fire.** The Apostle John presented Jesus not only as the Spirit-baptized One but also as the baptizing One (John 20:22). Ultimately the fulfillment of the baptizing work of the Spirit was seen on the day of Pentecost (Acts 2:1-4). The baptizing "with fire" may refer to the purifying aspect of the baptism of the Spirit (Acts 2:3), or it may refer to the purifying work of judgment that the

Messiah will accomplish (Mal. 3:2-3). The latter seems more probable in view of the work of judgment described in Luke 3:17 (cf. v. 9).

4. THE PREACHING AND IMPRISONMENT OF JOHN (3:18-20)

3:18-20. Scholars debate the dates of John the Baptist's imprisonment and death. It is likely that John began his ministry about A.D. 29 (cf. v. 1), that he was imprisoned the following year, and that he was beheaded not later than A.D. 32. His entire ministry lasted no more than three years—about one year out of prison and two years in prison. (For details on John's imprisonment and death by beheading see Matt. 14:1-12; Mark 6:14-29; Luke 9:7-9, 19-20.)

B. *The baptism of Jesus (3:21-22)*
   (Matt. 3:13-17; Mark 1:9-11;
   John 1:29-34)

All four Gospels record this momentous occasion in the life of Jesus which signaled the beginning of His public ministry. Luke condensed the account more than the other Gospel writers. The purpose of the baptism was to anoint Jesus with the Spirit and to authenticate Him by the Father for beginning His ministry. Each Person of the Godhead was involved in the activity of the Son on earth, including His baptism. The Son was baptized, the Holy Spirit descended on Him, and the Father spoke approvingly of Jesus. In His baptism Jesus identified Himself with sinners though He was not a sinner.

3:21. Only Luke stated that at Jesus' baptism **He was praying.** Luke presented Jesus as praying in or before many occasions in His life (v. 21; 5:16; 6:12; 9:18, 29; 22:32, 40-44; 23:46). When Luke recorded that **heaven was opened,** he was conveying the idea that God was breaking into human history with revelation—sovereignly declaring that Jesus is His Son.

3:22. Since the dove was a symbol of peace or freedom from judgment (Gen. 8:8-12), the Holy Spirit's presence **like a dove** signified that Jesus would bring salvation to those who turn to Him. The **voice** of God authenticated Jesus by alluding to Psalm 2:7 and Isaiah 42:1.

C. *The genealogy of Jesus (3:23-38)*
   (Matt. 1:1-17)

The genealogy of Jesus, recorded by Luke immediately after His authentication in baptism by the Father, further shows the sovereign hand of God in preparing the events of the world so that the Messiah could accomplish the Father's will.

3:23. Luke recorded that **Jesus . . . was about 30 years old when He began His ministry.** Luke was not unsure of the age of Jesus when the ministry began. Luke had carefully investigated everything from the beginning (1:3), so it is unlikely that he would not have uncovered the age at which Jesus began His ministry. Though Bible students debate when Jesus' ministry began, the year A.D. 29 may be the best. Luke apparently used the term "about 30" to indicate that He was well prepared for ministry. In the Old Testament 30 was often the age when one's ministry began (Gen. 41:46; Num. 4; 2 Sam. 5:4; Ezek. 1:1). Luke's clarity on the fact of the Virgin Birth is seen in his notation that Jesus **was the Son, so it was thought, of Joseph.**

3:24-38. Verses 23-38 list 76 names including Jesus and Adam and excluding God. Contrary to Matthew's genealogy, Luke's genealogy begins with Jesus and works back to God. Matthew began with Abraham and worked forward to Jesus in three sets of 14 generations. Other differences exist between the two genealogies. Luke included 20 names prior to Abraham, and he stated that Adam was "the son of God."

In addition Luke's and Matthew's lists from David to Shealtiel (during the time of the Exile) differ. That is because the lists trace different lines. Luke traced David's line through Nathan, whereas Matthew traced it through Solomon. Following Shealtiel's son, Zerubbabel, the lists once again differ until both lists unite at Joseph whom, Luke noted, was "thought" to be the father of Jesus. Little doubt exists that Matthew's genealogy traced the kingly line of David—the royal legal line. The question is, What is the significance of Luke's genealogy? Two main possibilities exist.

1. Luke was tracing the line of Mary. Many interpreters argue that Luke was giving the genealogy of Mary, showing

that she also was in the line of David and that therefore Jesus was qualified as the Messiah not only through Joseph (since he was the oldest legal heir) but also through Mary.

2. Luke was tracing the actual line of Joseph. This view maintains that the legal line and the actual line of David through which Jesus came met at Joseph, the supposed father of Jesus. In this view Jacob, Joseph's uncle, would have died childless and therefore Joseph would have been the closest living heir. Thus Joseph and then Jesus would have been brought into the royal line.

Both views have problems which are difficult to answer, not the least of which is the fact that the two genealogies meet at Shealtiel and Zerubbabel and then split a second time only to come together at Joseph and Jesus. (Cf. comments on Matt. 1:12.) Regardless of one's view it is important to note an important aspect of the theology Luke expressed in his genealogy. He related Jesus not only to Abraham but all the way back to Adam and to God. This is an indication of the universal offer of salvation, which is common to his Gospel—that Jesus came to save all people—Gentiles as well as the nation of Israel (cf. Luke 2:32).

D. The temptation of Jesus (4:1-13) (Matt. 4:1-11; Mark 1:12-13)

1. JESUS' LEADING BY THE SPIRIT INTO THE DESERT (4:1-2)

4:1-2. Luke then picked up the account of the preparation of the Lord's ministry where he left off in 3:23. **Jesus was full of the Holy Spirit** (cf. 3:22; 4:14, 18). Interestingly **the Spirit** led Him into **the desert, where for 40 days He was tempted by the devil.** The traditional site of Jesus' temptation is a barren area northwest of the Dead Sea. The "40 days" motif is prominent in the Old Testament (cf. Gen. 7:4; Ex. 24:18; 1 Kings 19:8; Jonah 3:4). It is not by accident that Jesus' temptation continued for 40 days, just as Israel's wanderings and temptation continued for 40 years in the wilderness. Jesus' responses to Satan's temptations by quoting from Deuteronomy, chapters 6 and 8, confirm that He was thinking about the experience of the nation in the wilderness. And yet, though the Israelites were miraculously fed in the desert, Jesus **ate nothing.**

2. JESUS' TEMPTATION IN THE AREA OF PHYSICAL NEED (4:3-4)

4:3-4. Since Jesus was extremely hungry and in need of food (v. 2), it is not surprising that **the devil** first tempted Jesus to turn a **stone** into **bread** for His sustenance. Jesus countered this temptation by quoting Deuteronomy 8:3, in which Moses had reminded the people of the manna which God had given them. Though the manna was on the ground, it still was a test of faith for the people. They had to believe that God's Word was trustworthy for their existence. If it was not God's will for them to live they certainly would have died; therefore they did not live by bread alone. Likewise **Jesus,** knowing God's Word, knew of the plan which was before Him and was trusting in the Father and His Word for sustenance. Jesus knew He would not die in the wilderness.

3. JESUS' TEMPTATION IN THE AREA OF GLORY AND DOMINION (4:5-8)

4:5-8. What Matthew recorded as the second and third temptations were reversed by Luke. This may indicate that there were continual temptations in these areas. The second temptation Luke recorded was an appeal to Jesus to be in control of **all the kingdoms of the world.** The condition was that Jesus must **worship** (*proskynēsēs*, lit., "bend the knee to") the devil. Though Jesus would have world rulership, He would be depending on Satan—rather than on God the Father and His plan. Jesus again referred to Moses to combat a temptation. In that passage (Deut. 6:13) Moses warned the people about their attitude when they finally were to get into the land and achieve some glory and dominion. The temptation for them would be to praise themselves and forget to worship God. **Jesus,** by quoting the verse, showed that He would not make that mistake. He would give **God** the credit and not take it for Himself. He would not fail as Israel had failed.

4. JESUS' TEMPTATION IN THE AREA OF THE TIMING OF HIS MINISTRY (4:9-12)

4:9-12. **The devil** tried to get Jesus to change the timing and structure of His ministry. Jesus knew He must go to the cross and die for the sins of the world. He knew that He was the Suffering Servant (Isa. 52:13–53:12). The devil challenged Jesus to throw Himself off **the highest point of the temple.** This was perhaps at the southeastern corner of the wall overlooking the deep Kidron Valley below. Satan meant that the nation, seeing Jesus' miraculous protection from such a jump, would immediately accept Him. The devil even quoted Psalm 91:11-12 to show that the Messiah would be kept safe from harm.

However, Jesus was aware of the implication. To receive the acceptance of the people without going to the cross would be to question whether God was really in the plan at all. That was exactly the situation Moses wrote about in Deuteronomy 6:16, which Jesus quoted. Moses referred back to a time when the people wondered whether God was really with them (Ex. 17:7). But Jesus was confident of the fact that God was with Him and that the Father's plan and timing were perfect. So Jesus would not fall for Satan's temptation.

5. SATAN'S DEPARTURE FROM JESUS (4:13)

4:13. **The devil** departed, not permanently, but only **until** a latter more **opportune time.**

IV. The Ministry of Jesus in Galilee (4:14–9:50)

Jesus' early ministry was primarily in Galilee, though from John 1–4 it is known that He did have an early ministry in Judea and Jerusalem before His Galilean ministry. Two purposes of the Galilean ministry were to authenticate Jesus and to call the disciples who would follow Him.

A. The initiation of Jesus' ministry (4:14-30) (Matt. 4:12-17; Mark 1:14-15)

These 17 verses serve as Luke's summary of what happened throughout the entire ministry of Jesus: Jesus declared Himself to be the Messiah (Luke 4:21); the Jewish hearers proved themselves to be unworthy of God's blessings (vv. 28-29), and the gospel would also go to the Gentiles (vv. 24-27).

1. JESUS' RECEPTION IN GALILEE (4:14-15)

4:14-15. Returning **to Galilee,** Jesus was **in the power** (*dynamei,* "spiritual ability") **of the Spirit.** The Spirit had descended on Him (3:21-22), He had been led by the Spirit into the desert (4:1), and now He ministered "in the power of the Spirit." The Spirit's power was the source of Jesus' authority, which Luke set forth in chapters 4–6. The initial response was positive. The **news about Him spread** and as they heard Him teach **in their synagogues . . . everyone praised Him.**

2. JESUS' REJECTION IN HIS HOMETOWN, NAZARETH (4:16-30) (MATT. 13:53-58; MARK 6:1-6)

4:16-30. Jesus initially was a popular Teacher, so when He went back to His hometown, it was natural for Him to teach in synagogues. It was the custom in the synagogue for a man to stand while he was reading the Scriptures but then to sit while explaining the portion he had read. The portion of Scripture Jesus read was **Isaiah 61:1-2,** a messianic passage. He concluded His reading with the words, **to proclaim the year of the Lord's favor**—stopping in the middle of the verse without reading the next line in Isaiah 61:2 about God's vengeance. When Jesus added, **Today this Scripture is fulfilled in your hearing,** the implication was clear. Jesus was claiming to be the Messiah who could bring the kingdom of God which had been promised for so long—but His First Advent was not His time for judgment. The crowd was fascinated at His teaching—**The eyes of everyone . . . were fastened on Him** (Luke 4:20). Jesus' words plainly stated that the offer of the favorable year of the Lord (i.e., the kingdom time) was being made to them through Him (v. 21).

The people **were amazed** (*ethaumazon,* "wondered, marveled"; cf. comments on 2:18) at His **gracious words** (lit., "words of grace"), but they immediately began to question the authority with which He could say these things. How could **Joseph's Son**—the Boy they saw grow up in their town—be the Messiah? Jesus, sensing their opposition (4:23-24), noted two instances in which God's prophets ministered miraculous acts of grace to Gentiles while Israel was in unbelief—**Elijah** and the **widow of Zarephath** (vv. 25-26; cf. 1 Kings 17:8-16), and **Elisha** and **Naaman the Syrian** leper (Luke 4:27; cf. 2 Kings 5:1-19).

Jesus' mention of Gentiles rather than Jews having God's blessing caused the people to be furious (Luke 4:28). They attempted to kill Him, but He walked right through the crowd (v. 30). Luke no doubt described a miraculous escape from the angry crowd. This pattern is seen throughout the rest of Jesus' ministry: Jesus went to the Jews; they rejected, Him; He told of Gentile participation in the kingdom; some Jews wanted to kill Him. But He was not killed until the proper time, when He chose to die (23:46; cf. John 10:15, 17-18).

B. The authentication of Jesus' authority (4:31–6:16)

The people of Nazareth and others in Galilee who heard of Him wondered by what authority He made His statements. So Jesus authenticated His authority by healing and teaching. And because of who He is and what He taught, He had the authority to call disciples. In this section Jesus performed three sets of healings, and after each one He called one or more disciples (5:1-11, 27-32; 6:12-16).

1. JESUS' DEMONSTRATION OF HIS AUTHORITY BY HEALING AND TEACHING (4:31-44)

a. Jesus' healing of a man with an unclean spirit (4:31-37)
(Mark 1:21-28)

4:31-37. Jesus went . . . to Capernaum, which He later made His home since His own hometown, Nazareth, had rejected Him. Capernaum was also the home of Peter and Andrew (v. 38). Again the people were amazed (exeplēssonto, lit., "struck out of their senses" [also used in 2:48; 9:43]; cf. ethaumazon, "wondered, marveled," 4:22, cf. v. 36) at His teaching (v. 32) for His message had authority. To authenticate that authority, Jesus performed a series of healing miracles which showed that His teaching in Nazareth was true (cf. vv. 18-19). A man with a demon, an evil spirit, was in the synagogue. It has been suggested that since Luke was most likely writing to people with a Greek background, he was clarifying the fact that this demon was evil since the Greeks thought there were both good and evil demons. This demon recognized Jesus, calling Him not only Jesus of Nazareth but also the Holy One of God (v. 34). In the Gospels crying out with a loud voice seems to be characteristic of those who were demon-possessed. Jesus'

exorcism of the demon (v. 35) amazed the crowd (lit. "amazement [thambos] came on all," v. 36). The crowd noted that Jesus had authority (exousia) and power (dynamei) over demons (cf. 9:1), and this caused His fame to spread (4:37). This was Jesus' third miracle. (See the list of His miracles at John 2:1-11.)

b. Jesus' healing of Simon's mother-in-law (4:38-39)
(Matt. 8:14-15; Mark 1:29-31)

4:38-39. Both Mark and Luke related that the next miracle occurred immediately after the first miracle in the synagogue. Simon's mother-in-law had a severe fever. At Jesus' word the fever . . . left her. In each of these cases the cause of the difficulty was removed and the person had no side effects. The demon left without hurting the man (v. 35), and the fever left so that Simon's mother-in-law could immediately serve them (v. 39). She was not left in a weakened condition.

c. Jesus' healing of the sick and the demon-possessed (4:40-41)
(Matt. 8:16-17; Mark 1:32-34)

4:40-41. The news about Jesus' authority over sickness spread quickly so that same night people began coming to Him for healing. They came when the sun was setting, when the Sabbath Day was ending. It would have been unlawful to carry the sick before then. As the demons came out of many people, they were shouting, You are the Son of God! The reason for Jesus' rebuke was that He did not come to earth so that demons could acknowledge Him as the Christ, that is, the Messiah. Instead, He came to be acknowledged by people.

d. Jesus' statement about His wider ministry (4:42-44)
(Mark 1:35-39)

4:42-44. Jesus pointed out to the people that He had a ministry to fulfill (cf. v. 18). He had a mission to the rest of the nation of Israel. The reception Jesus received at Capernaum contrasted greatly with His reception in His hometown of Nazareth. The people of Capernaum wanted Him to stay, but He needed to preach the good news of the kingdom of God elsewhere also.

The main emphasis in Jesus' ministry was on preaching, not healing. Though

He had compassion on people, His healing ministry was usually to authenticate what He was saying (cf. Matt. 11:2-6). Luke's point that **He kept on preaching in the synagogues of Judea** should be interpreted in that light. "Judea" (*Ioudaias*) probably refers to the whole nation (the land of the Jews), not just the southern portion. Luke's point was that wherever Jesus went He constantly taught that He was the Messiah who had come to proclaim the favorable year of the Lord (Luke 4:18-19).

2. JESUS' DEMONSTRATION OF HIS AUTHORITY BY CALLING HIS FIRST DISCIPLES (5:1-11)

(MATT. 4:18-22; MARK 1:16-20)

The incident recorded here is obviously not the first time Jesus had been in contact with the men whom He called to be His disciples. Luke already had stated that Jesus had healed Simon's mother-in-law which denotes previous contact with Simon and Andrew. This seems to be at least the third time Jesus had contact with these men. In John 1:41 Andrew told Peter that he had found the Messiah. Apparently the men at first did not follow Jesus on a "full-time" basis, for in Mark 1:16-20 (also Matt. 4:18-22) Jesus called Simon, Andrew, James, and John. Mark recorded that that call was before Jesus entered the synagogue in Capernaum and healed a man who was demon-possessed. It is no wonder Peter invited Jesus home after the synagogue incident.

Now, sometime later, Peter and the others were still fishermen. It was at this point, now that Jesus had established His authority (Luke 4:31-44), that He called these men to full-time discipleship.

5:1-3. The large throng **crowding around** Jesus prevented His teaching effectively as He stood **by the Lake of Gennesaret,** another name for the Sea of Galilee, by a village on the northwest shore. So He went out a short distance in the water in Simon's boat so that they could all listen **to the Word of God.**

5:4-7. On Jesus' request, **Simon** put out his **nets** and **caught . . . a large** amount **of fish.** Though **Simon,** an experienced fisherman, was sure he would not catch anything at that time of the day when the fish were deeper in the lake, he obeyed Jesus' word. This showed a significant amount of faith. The result-ing catch **began to break the nets,** so they **filled** Simon's and another **boat** with the fish till **both boats . . . began to sink.**

5:8-11. The miracle of the fish brought two responses in **Peter** and the others. They **were astonished** (lit., "amazement [*thambos*] seized him and all those with him," v. 9; cf. 4:36) **at the** large **catch of fish,** and Peter realized his sinfulness before Jesus (5:8). The result was that Jesus made the fishermen fishers of **men.** Jesus' teaching, combined with His miraculous acts, showed that He had the authority to call the men and have them respond by leaving **everything.**

3. JESUS' DEMONSTRATION OF HIS AUTHORITY BY FURTHER HEALING (5:12-26)

The next two healings brought about a confrontation with the religious establishment—the first such conflict recorded in Luke. Both healings authenticated Jesus' claim to be the Messiah (cf. 4:18-21).

a. Jesus' healing of a leper (5:12-16)
(Matt. 8:1-4; Mark 1:40-45)

5:12-16. Jesus encountered **a man . . . covered with leprosy** (lit., "full of leprosy"). Perhaps he was in the final stages of leprosy—a fact which would have been easily discernible in the man's home community. The Law (Lev. 13) commanded strict segregation of a person who had leprosy, for it was a graphic picture of uncleanness. A leprous person could not worship at the central sanctuary; he was ceremonially unclean and therefore cut off completely from the community.

This leper addressed **Jesus** as **Lord** (*kyrie*) as Simon had also done (Luke 5:8). Though the term was often used as one would today use "sir," it seems to have stronger import here. The leper did not doubt the ability of Jesus to heal him, for he said, **If You are willing You can make me clean.** His only reservation seemed to be Jesus' willingness. According to the Mosaic Law one who was leprous was not to be touched by anyone who was ceremonially clean. When someone clean touched something unclean, the clean became unclean. Luke, in describing Jesus' actions, showed that Jesus was the Source of ceremonial cleansing. If He was the Source of cleansing for that leper, He would also be the Source of ceremonial cleansing for the nation. This theme is carried on into the next healing (vv. 17-26) and into the call of Levi (vv. 27-39). At the touch of Jesus, **immediately the leprosy left him.** The immediacy of the healing brings to mind 4:35 and 4:39. Healing from leprosy was rare. The Scriptures record only Miriam (Num. 12) and Naaman (2 Kings 5) as having been healed of leprosy (cf. Moses; Ex. 4:6-7). Thus it would have been extremely unusual for a person to present himself before **the priest and offer the sacrifices . . . for . . . cleansing.** Instructions for an offering for cleansing from leprosy are given in Leviticus 14:1-32. Luke 5:14 emphasized the phrase **as a testimony to them.** The fact that a man would go to the priest claiming healing from leprosy would alert the religious leaders that something new was afoot in Israel. Why did **Jesus** command **him** not to **tell anyone?** Perhaps for two reasons: (a) The man was to go immediately to the priest to be a testimony. (b) When **the news** of Jesus' healing power **spread,** He was constantly besieged by people, which caused Him to have to withdraw (vv. 15-16).

b. *Jesus' healing and forgiveness of a*
   paralytic (5:17-26)
   (Matt. 9:1-8; Mark 2:1-12)

5:17-26. The healing and forgiving of a paralyzed man was further evidence of Jesus' authority and power to make others ceremonially clean. Luke noted that a number of religious officials were present at the occasion, including some from **Jerusalem** who perhaps were the most influential. Luke did not portray this healing as happening immediately after the preceding event he had recorded. It is evident that he placed the two accounts side by side as a development in his argument.

The statement, **the power** (*dynamis*, "spiritual ability") **of the Lord was present for Him to heal the sick,** is unique to Luke (cf. Matt. 9:1-8; Mark 2:1-12). Luke used *dynamis* on several occasions to describe Jesus' healing (cf. Luke 4:36; 6:19; 8:46). A large number of people now accompanied Jesus everywhere because of His works of healing. Thus a group of **men** who were **carrying a paralytic** had to take him to **the roof** of

the house, remove some **tiles,** and let him down **in front of Jesus. Jesus** linked **faith** with the miracle (5:20), which was also the case in 7:9; 8:25, 48, 50; 17:19; and 18:42. Presumably the faith of which **Jesus** spoke (i.e., **their** faith) also included the paralyzed man (5:20).

Surprisingly Jesus did not immediately heal the man's body; instead, He first forgave his **sins.** This is extremely important for the argument of this section, for Luke's point was that Jesus had the authority to call disciples, including people (such as Levi) who were not thought of as being righteous (vv. 27-39). The religious leaders immediately began to think that Jesus' words were **blasphemy** for they rightly associated forgiveness with **God** (cf. 7:49). Jesus pointed out that the religious leaders were absolutely right. His subsequent healing of the man was incontrovertible proof that He did have the **authority . . . to forgive sins** and therefore should be accepted as God. Anyone could *say,* **Your sins are forgiven.** In that sense it was **easier** than saying, **Get up and walk,** for if He did not have the power to heal, all would know it **immediately.** The result of the forgiveness and the healing was that **everyone was amazed** (lit., "received amazement") and was full of awe (*phobou,* "reverential fear,") realizing that they had seen remarkable **things** (*paradoxa,* "things out of the ordinary").

4. JESUS' DEMONSTRATION OF HIS
   AUTHORITY BY CALLING A TAX
   COLLECTOR (5:27-39)
   (MATT. 9:9-17; MARK 2:13-22)

5:27-39. The call of **Levi** was the culmination of the previous two miracles. (Levi is named Matthew in Matt. 9:9.) Jesus had shown that He had the authority to make a person ceremonially clean and to forgive sins. Now those two authorities were brought to bear on one who was to become His disciple.

Luke did not mention Levi's duties as a **tax collector.** But his position alienated him from the religious community of his day (cf. Luke 5:29-31). He was seen as one who betrayed his nation for material gain, for tax collectors gathered money from the Jews to give to the Romans, who were Gentiles, who then did not have to work (cf. 3:12-13). Seemingly Levi would be an unlikely candidate for a disciple of the One who claimed to be the Messiah. Jesus simply spoke the words, **Follow Me.** Levi broke with his way of life; he **left everything and followed** Jesus. Levi's response was the same as that of the fishermen (5:11).

Luke's point would have been clear even if he had stopped with the account of Levi's decision to follow Jesus. But in order to drive the point home Luke related events which occurred at a reception which Levi, Jesus' new follower, gave for Jesus. Levi must have been a wealthy man, for **a great banquet** was prepared at his house and many guests were invited, including **a large crowd of tax collectors.** The same group of religious leaders who had previously questioned Jesus' authority (v. 21) questioned the propriety of Jesus' association **with tax collectors and "sinners."** Not only was Jesus associating with people to whom the Pharisees objected, but He also was eating and drinking with them. Eating and drinking with others denotes a fellowship or camaraderie with them. Though the religious leaders **complained to** Jesus' **disciples . . . Jesus answered** their objections (vv. 31-32). He noted that it was not His purpose **to call the righteous, but sinners to repentance.** Here Jesus was not concerned about discussing who were "the righteous." His point was simply that His mission was to those in need of "repentance"—a change of heart and a change of life (cf. 3:7-14). **The Pharisees** sensed no need for such a change. Because He had shown authority in the two healings which preceded this account, the implication is that He was also able to fulfill His mission to sinners.

The sentence addressed to Jesus in 5:33 causes some difficulty. If the Pharisees and religious leaders were still talking, it seems strange that they would refer to their own disciples as **disciples of the Pharisees.** It is possible that this teaching of Jesus is from a different setting but that Luke included it here because it continued the purpose of this section. The accusation was that Jesus and His disciples refused to fast, in contrast with the disciples of John and of the Pharisees, who were seen as righteous people. Jesus' response was that the new way (His way) and the old way (the way of John and the Pharisees) simply do not mix. He gave three examples.

1. A bridegroom's **guests** (cf. John 3:29) do not **fast while he is with them** because it is a joyous occasion. They **fast** later after he is gone.

2. A **new** unshrunk **patch** of cloth is not put on an **old** garment because it will shrink and the tear will be worse.

3. **New wine** is not put **into old wineskins** for as it ferments it will break **the** old **skins,** which have lost their elasticity, and both the **wine** and the skins **will be ruined.**

In each case two things do not mix: a time of feasting and a time of fasting (vv. 34-35), a new patch and an old garment (v. 36), and new wine and old wineskins (vv. 37-38). Jesus was noting that His way and the way of the Pharisees simply are unmixable. The Pharisees would refuse to try the new way for they assumed that their old way was better. Jesus' teaching was considered by the Pharisees and religious leaders to be like **new** wine, and they wanted no part in it (v. 39).

5. JESUS' DEMONSTRATION OF HIS
   AUTHORITY OVER THE SABBATH (6:1-11)

In 6:1-11 Luke recorded two incidents that occurred on the Sabbath: " One Sabbath" (v. 1) and "On another Sabbath" (v. 6). Luke's point in bringing the accounts together to form a unit was to show that Jesus had authority over the Sabbath.

a. *The disciples' picking of grain on the Sabbath (6:1-5)*
   (Matt. 12:1-8; Mark 2:23-28)

6:1-5. Jesus' **disciples began to pick some heads of grain, rub them in their hands, and eat.** God allowed people to pick grain from a neighbor's field as they passed through (Deut. 23:25). But **the Pharisees,** interpreting the Law strictly, held that rubbing the heads together in order to eat the grain constituted threshing, which was not allowed **on the Sabbath. Jesus** responded to the Pharisees' objection by referring to 1 Samuel 21:1-9. **David** had approached the priests at Nob and asked for bread. The only food available at the moment was the **consecrated bread** that **only** the **priests** were allowed **to eat.** David was given the bread, and **he** and **his companions** ate it. The parallel in Jesus' teaching was clear. In the interest of survival David and his companions were allowed to be above the

Law with the priest's blessing. Christ and His companions were also above the man-made law which the Pharisees proclaimed. Another parallel implicit in Jesus' teaching should not be missed. David, as God's anointed, was being hounded by the forces of a dying dynasty—the dynasty of Saul. Jesus was God's new Anointed One who was being hounded by the forces of a dying dynasty (cf. Luke 5:39). The ultimate conclusion was that Jesus **is Lord of the Sabbath,** that is, He has authority even over matters of the Law.

b. Jesus' healing of a man on the Sabbath (6:6-11)
(Matt. 12:9-14; Mark 3:1-6)

6:6-11. This second contention about the **Sabbath** (cf. the first one in vv. 1-5) seems to have been brought about purposely by **the Pharisees and the teachers of the Law.** As Jesus **was teaching** in the **synagogue,** He encountered **a man . . . whose right hand was shriveled.** The religious leaders were observing Jesus because they **were looking for a reason to accuse** Him. As was the case when He was opposed previously by religious leaders, **Jesus knew what they were thinking** (5:22). He used the situation to show that He has authority over **the Sabbath. Jesus said . . . I ask you, which is lawful on the Sabbath: to do good or to do evil, to save life or to destroy it?** By this question He showed that refusing to do good on the Sabbath was tantamount to doing evil. If suffering is not alleviated, then one is doing evil to the sufferer.

As the man stretched out his **hand** at Jesus' command, it **was completely restored. Jesus** performed no "work" on the Sabbath—He simply spoke a few words and a hand was completely restored. He humiliated the religious leaders and healed the man all at the same time without even breaking the Pharisees' law. It is no wonder that the religious establishment was **furious** and sought a way to get rid of Him.

6. JESUS' DEMONSTRATION OF HIS AUTHORITY BY CALLING THE TWELVE (6:12-16)
(MATT. 10:1-4; MARK 3:13-19)

6:12-16. Before **Jesus** chose the 12 **disciples,** He **spent** an entire **night** in prayer. Jesus had a large number of disciples and from those He picked **12** who were to be close **to Him.** These were specifically called **apostles** (apostolous) as opposed to the term disciples (mathētas). Disciples were followers, but apostles were those sent out as messengers with delegated authority (cf. "apostles" in 9:10; 17:5; 22:14; 24:10). In Luke's list of the Twelve (as well as Matthew's and Mark's lists) **Peter** is listed first and **Judas Iscariot** is last. **Bartholomew** must be Nathanael (John 1:45), Levi and **Matthew** are the same man, and Thaddaeus (Mark 3:18) is **Judas, son of James.** They were now willing to be sent out as apostles, being with Jesus on a full-time basis.

C. Jesus' sermon on the level place (6:17-49)
(Matt. 5-7)

1. INTRODUCTION TO THE SERMON (6:17-19)

6:17-19. The sermon recorded in verses 17-49 is a shorter version of the Sermon on the Mount recorded in Matthew 5-7. Both sermons are addressed to disciples, begin with beatitudes, conclude with the same parables, and have generally the same content. However, in Luke the "Jewish parts" of the sermon (i.e., the interpretation of the Law) are omitted. This fits well with Luke's purpose. The problem in seeing these accounts as reflecting the same sermon is the place in which the sermon was given. Matthew recorded that Jesus was "on a mountainside" (Matt. 5:1), whereas Luke said Jesus was **on a level place** (Luke 6:17). The sequence of events solves the problem easily. Jesus went up in "the hills" near Capernaum to pray all night (v. 12). He called 12 disciples to be His apostles. He then went down on a level place to talk and to heal **diseases** (vv. 17-19). Following that, He went up higher to get away from the crowds and to teach His disciples (Matt. 5:1). The multitudes (Matt. 7:28; Luke 7:1) climbed the mountain and heard His sermon, which explains Jesus' words at the end of the sermon (Matt. 7:24; Luke 6:46-47).

2. THE BLESSINGS AND THE WOES (6:20-26)

Jesus began His sermon with a series of blessings and woes on His listeners. The items are placed in two sets of four—

four blessings and four woes which parallel each other.

a. The blessings (6:20-23)

6:20-23. The term "blessed" (*makarioi*) was common in the Gospels; it occurs more than 30 times. All but 2 of the occurrences are in Matthew and Luke. Originally in Greek usage the word described the happy estate of the gods above earthly sufferings and labors. Later it came to mean any positive condition a person experienced. Unlike the biblical authors, the Greek authors drew happiness from earthly goods and values. In the Old Testament the authors recognized that the truly blessed (or happy) individual is one who trusts God, who hopes for and waits for Him, who fears and loves Him (Deut. 33:29; Pss. 2:12; 32:1-2; 34:8; 40:4; 84:12; 112:1). A formal beatitude was an acknowledgement of a fortunate state before God and man (Ps. 1:1; Prov. 14:21; 16:20; 29:18).

Beatitudes in the New Testament have an emotional force. They often contrast a false earthly estimation with a true heavenly estimation of one who is truly blessed (Matt. 5:3-6, 10; Luke 11:28; John 20:29; 1 Peter 3:14; 4:14). All secular goods and values are subservient to one supreme good—God Himself. This is a reversal of all human values. The Beatitudes present the present in the light of the future (cf. Luke 23:29).

Jesus spoke of four conditions in which people are blessed or happy when they are following Him. **Blessed are you who are poor . . . blessed are you who hunger now . . . blessed are you who weep now,** and **blessed are you when men hate you** (6:20-22). In each case a clause is added that explains why such a person is blessed or happy. A poor person is happy because his **is the kingdom of God.** Matthew referred to "the poor in spirit" (Matt. 5:3), but Luke simply wrote "poor." Jesus' hearers were physically poor. Luke already mentioned twice that those who followed Jesus left everything (Luke 5:11, 28).

Jesus' explanation about their inclusion in "the kingdom of God" is mentioned because they were following the One who was proclaiming His ability to bring in the kingdom. They were staking everything they had on the fact that Jesus

was telling the truth. They were following His new way (5:37-39). Jesus' words were not a promise that every poor person had a part in the kingdom of God; instead His words were a statement of fact for His followers. They were poor and theirs was the kingdom of God. They were much better off being poor, following Jesus, and having a part of the kingdom of God than being rich and not having a part of the kingdom. That is why they were blessed.

The next two explanatory phrases have future fulfillments. The hungry **will be satisfied,** and the ones who weep **will laugh.** The apostles who would hunger and weep because they followed Jesus would eventually be vindicated for their faith in Him.

The final beatitude concerned persecution **because of the Son of Man.** This was to become a natural course of events for the apostles. They would be hated, excluded, insulted, and rejected. Yet they would be happy ("blessed") because of their **reward in heaven** and because they were following in the train of **the prophets** (i.e., those who spoke for God; cf. 6:26).

b. The woes (6:24-26)

6:24-26. In contrast with the disciples who had given up everything to follow Jesus were the people who would refuse to give up anything to follow Him (cf. 18:18-30). These were the **rich,** the **well-fed,** the ones **who laugh,** who were popular. They did not understand the gravity of the situation which confronted them. They refused to follow the One who could bring them into the kingdom, and therefore Jesus pronounced woes on them. These woes were the exact reversal of their temporal benefits. And they are the exact opposites of the blessings and rewards of Jesus' followers, cited in 6:20-23.

3. TRUE RIGHTEOUSNESS (6:27-45)

a. True righteousness revealed by love (6:27-38)

6:27-38. Jesus mentioned seven aspects of unconditional love. These actions, not done naturally by human nature, require supernatural enabling— and are thus proof of true righteousness:

(1) **Love your enemies.**
(2) **Do good to those who hate you.**
(3) **Bless those who curse you.**

(4) **Pray for those who mistreat you.**

(5) Do not retaliate (v. 29a).

(6) Give freely (vv. 29b-30).

(7) Treat **others** the way you want to be treated (v. 31).

This kind of **love** marks one off as distinctive (vv. 32-34), and as having the same characteristics as the heavenly Father (v. 35).

Jesus then taught His followers a fundamental principle of the universe—what one sows he will reap (vv. 36-38; cf. Gal. 6:7). Jesus outlined five areas which were proof of the sowing and reaping theme, mentioned so often in Scripture: (1) Mercy will lead to mercy (Luke 6:36). The disciples were exhorted to have the same merciful attitude God displayed toward them.

(2) Judgment will lead to judgment (v. 37a).

(3) Condemnation will lead to condemnation (v. 37b).

(4) Pardon will lead to pardon (v. 37c).

(5) Giving will lead to giving (v. 38). It is simply a fact of life that certain attitudes and actions often reflect back on the individual.

b. True righteousness revealed by one's actions (6:39-45)

6:39-45. Jesus explained that a person is not able to hide his attitude toward righteousness. It is obvious that if a person is **blind** he will lead another **into a pit** (v. 39). He will not be able to hide the fact that he is not righteous for he will lead others astray. Jesus also noted that a person becomes like the one whom he emulates (v. 40). Therefore His disciples should emulate Him. One must rid himself of a sin before he can help his **brother** with that sin (vv. 41-42). And often one's own sin is greater than the one he criticizes in someone else—a **plank** compared with a **speck of sawdust.** The point is that one cannot help someone else become righteous if he is not righteous himself. To seek to do so is to be a **hypocrite.**

Jesus also pointed out that a man's words will eventually tell what kind of **man** he is (vv. 43-45). Just as people know the kind of **tree** by the **fruit** it **bears,** so people know from what a person says whether he is righteous or not. In this case **fruit** stands for what is said, not

what is done: **out of the overflow of his heart his mouth speaks.**

4. TRUE OBEDIENCE (6:46-49)

6:46-49. Outward expression is not nearly so important as obedience (v. 46). It is not enough to call Jesus **Lord, Lord.** A believer must do what He says. Those who hear His words and act on them are secure—**like a man building a house . . . on rock** (vv. 47-48), and those who hear His words and do not act on them are destroyed—**like a man who built a house . . . without a foundation** (v. 49). The disciples had already acted on His words to some extent by following Him. (This is the first of Jesus' parables recorded in the Gospel of Luke. See the list of Jesus' 35 parables at Matt. 7:24-27.)

D. Jesus' ministry in Capernaum and surrounding cities (chaps. 7–8)

In this section is an interchange between the ministry of Jesus in miraculous signs (which again authenticated that He is the Messiah: 7:1-17, 36-50; 8:22-56) and His teaching (which has authority based on the message He was proclaiming: 7:18 35; 8:1-21). Luke emphasized His teaching, which has authority because of the symbolic miraculous events which show that Jesus is the Messiah.

1. JESUS' MINISTRY IN THE MIDST OF SICKNESS AND DEATH (7:1-17)

Here Luke recorded two miracles—a centurion's servant healed and a dead boy raised—as a basis for belief in authority (vv. 22-23).

a. Healing a centurion's servant (7:1-10) (Matt. 8:5-13; John 4:43-54)

7:1-10. After Jesus' sermon (chap. 6), which was given outside of town, **He entered Capernaum,** His adopted hometown where He performed many of His messianic signs. **A centurion** in the Roman army was a commander of a century, a group of 100 soldiers. This centurion in Capernaum, unlike most Roman soldiers, was well liked and respected by the Jewish people in and around Capernaum because he loved them and **built** them a **synagogue** (7:4-5). This **centurion's servant . . . was** extremely **sick and about to die** (v. 2). **The centurion** had faith that **Jesus** would **heal** the servant. Perhaps the reason he sent

Jewish **elders** to present his request was that he doubted that Jesus would have heeded a Roman soldier's request. Matthew 8:5-13 records the same event, but Matthew did not record the sending of messengers. He presented the account as if the centurion were present himself. Matthew was reflecting what the centurion meant when he noted that his messengers do his bidding as if he were there himself (Luke 7:8).

The centurion realized that his request was brash and that he really was not **worthy to** see Jesus (v. 7). Jesus **was amazed** (*ethaumasen*; cf. comments on 2:18) at the centurion and said, **I have not found such great faith even in Israel.** The concept of faith is extremely important throughout chapters 7 and 8. It is vital to believe who Jesus is (i.e., the Messiah) and what He said. The exercise of faith by Gentiles also becomes prominent later in Luke's book.

b. Raising a widow's son (7:11-17)

7:11-17. Luke recorded the raising of the widow's son from the dead so that the ensuing interchange between Jesus and John the Baptist's disciples (vv. 18-23) would have more force.

A large crowd went along with Jesus as He traveled from Capernaum to **Nain** (v. 11). Nain was about 25 miles southwest of Capernaum. **A large crowd** was also with the funeral procession carrying the coffin of a **dead** young man, **the only son of his mother.** The woman was now completely alone and seemingly unprotected, without a close male relative. Help for widows is a major theme in both the Old and the New Testaments, especially under the covenant as related in Deuteronomy. Jesus' **heart went out to her** and He immediately began to comfort her. The verb "heart went out" translates *esplanchnisthē*, a verb used numerous times in the Gospels to mean pity or sympathy. It is related to the noun *splanchna*, "inner parts of the body," which were considered the seat of the emotions. This noun is used 10 times (Luke 1:78; 2 Cor. 6:12; 7:15; Phil. 1:8; 2:1; Col. 3:12; Phile. 7, 12, 20; 1 John 3:17). The woman and the others in the funeral procession must have had faith in Jesus for when **He touched the coffin . . . those carrying it stood still.** At Jesus' command the previously **dead man sat up and**

began to talk—solid proof that he was truly alive. As a result the people **were all filled with awe** (*phobos*; cf. comments on 1:12), they **praised God,** they thought Jesus was **a great prophet** (thinking, no doubt, of the ministries of Elijah and Elisha), they noted that God had **come to help His people** (cf. Isa. 7:14), and the **news about Jesus spread.**

2. JESUS' TEACHING THAT HIS DEEDS AUTHENTICATE HIS MINISTRY (7:18-35) (MATT. 11:2-19)

Luke's purpose in recording the two previous miracles (7:1-17) was to lead up to the interchange between John's disciples and Jesus. It was important for people to believe in Jesus—His works and His words—for both showed that He is the Messiah.

a. John the Baptist's request for clarification of Jesus' ministry (7:18-23)

7:18-23. This event happened while John was in prison (Matt. 11:2). John had had a meteoric ministry which lasted for no more than a year. John expected that the Messiah would set up the kingdom as he had been announcing. But suddenly John found himself in prison and in danger of being put to death, and still the kingdom had not come. Thus John was anxious concerning the Messiah. He knew the Old Testament well and knew of the works of the Messiah—but he did not see the kingdom coming. He sent two **disciples** to ask Jesus, **Are You the One who was to come, or should we expect someone else?** The disciples of John approached Jesus at the **very time Jesus cured many who had diseases, sicknesses, and evil spirits, and gave sight to many who were blind.** Jesus, who was performing messianic miracles, reminded John's disciples of Isaiah 61:1-2 which He had read in Nazareth. Jesus' miraculous deeds pointed to the fact that He is the Messiah. His point was that one should not **fall away** (*skandalisthē*, lit., "to be trapped" and thus "to let oneself be ensnared away from") **on account of** Him. One had to have faith in His message and His works. Neither Matthew nor Luke recorded the reaction of John the Baptist after his disciples returned to him.

b. Jesus' condemnation of Israel for rejecting John's ministry and His ministry (7:24-35)

7:24-28. **Jesus** used the occasion of John the Baptist's inquiry to teach the people about John's ministry and to commend him. He noted that John was not convictionless, like a **reed** blowing in **the wind.** Nor was he **dressed** luxuriously. Instead, he was rightly understood by the people to be **a prophet.** Jesus added that John was **more than a prophet** in that he, as prophesied in Malachi 3:1, was also the Messiah's forerunner. In Malachi 3:1-2 two messengers are spoken of. One is the forerunner, revealed here as John the Baptist, and the other is "the Messenger of the Covenant" who will purify His people, that is, the Messiah Himself.

Jesus paid John a great compliment by stating that **no one** was **greater than John.** And **yet the one who is least in the kingdom of God is greater than he.** Jesus was not declaring that John was not a part of "the kingdom of God," for John had been preaching the same message of repentance for the forgiveness of sins. Jesus was saying that being a great prophet is not nearly so great as being a member of the kingdom. Implied also is the fact that citizens of the kingdom have a distinct advantage over the prophets who were seen as great men of God in the Old Testament. Citizens of the kingdom will be under the New Covenant and have the Law of God written on their hearts (Jer. 31:31-34). Even the least person in the kingdom will have a greater spiritual capacity than John the Baptist himself.

7:29-30. Luke showed deep division in the thinking of **the people** who listened to **Jesus' words.** Those who **had been baptized by John,** that is, had repented of their sins and had been baptized to show their sincerity, agreed with Jesus and **acknowledged that God's way was right.** In contrast, **the Pharisees and experts in the Law rejected God's purpose for themselves.** By refusing to be **baptized by John** they showed that they did not accept his message of repentance or accept the kingdom. Thus they rejected God's plan of salvation for them. The ironic fact was that the Pharisees and the experts in the Law were the ones who should have known best about the ministry of the forerunner (John) and the Messiah (Jesus).

7:31-35. The editorial interjection by Luke (vv. 29-30) into the narrative account explains the following five verses. Since the religious leaders were rejecting the message of John and of Jesus, the Lord told a short parable to explain their treatment. When Jesus mentioned the **people** (*anthrōpous*) **of this generation** He was not speaking of the people (*laos*) mentioned in verse 29 who accepted His message. Instead the people in His parable were the religious leaders of verse 30, the rejecters of John and Jesus. Jesus described them as capricious **children** who wanted others to respond to their music. They were not satisfied with the behavior of either **John** or Jesus. John was too much of an ascetic, and Jesus was too much of a libertine (in the Pharisees' definition of the term). Neither extreme could make the religious leaders happy. Jesus applied the parable by stating that **wisdom is proved right by all her children.** The ones who were following Jesus and John were proof enough of the correctness of their teaching.

3. JESUS' MINISTRY TO A SINFUL WOMAN (7:36-50)

This passage illustrates the principle Jesus laid down in verse 35. A Pharisee named Simon is contrasted with a sinful woman, who received forgiveness (v. 47) and salvation (v. 50).

7:36-38. Simon (v. 40), a Pharisee, invited **Jesus to . . . dinner,** perhaps to trick Him in some way. It was the custom of the day when one had a dinner party to provide for the guests' feet to be cleaned before the meal. Because most roads were unpaved and the normal foot attire was sandals, it was common for people's feet to be dusty or muddy. As pointed out later in the episode, Simon did not provide for Jesus' feet to be cleaned at the beginning of the dinner party (v. 44). For special dinner parties recliners or couches were provided for the guests to use while eating.

A woman arrived at the dinner after she **learned that Jesus was eating** there. She **had lived a sinful life,** and was probably a prostitute in the community. Her life was known enough for the Pharisee to characterize her as a sinner (v. 39). She was not an invited guest at the dinner gathering, but came in anyway with a **jar of perfume.** Her presence was not unusual for when a Rabbi was invited to someone's house others could stop by and listen to the conversation. As the woman **stood behind** Jesus, **her tears** began to fall on **His feet.** It was a normal sign of respect to pour oil or **perfume** on someone's head. Perhaps the woman felt unworthy to anoint Jesus' head, so she anointed His feet. Such an act would have amounted to a large financial outlay for the woman who apparently was not wealthy. She also bent over Jesus and **wiped** her tears off **His feet . . . with her hair.** She constantly **kissed** His feet (the Gr. verb *katephilei* is the imperf. tense suggesting continuous past action), a sign of the utmost respect, submission, and affection. Jesus pointed out later that the host, in contrast, had done none of these things to His head (v. 46) or even given Him water for His feet (v. 44), whereas the woman was constantly anointing His feet.

The passage does not state why she was weeping. It may have been because she was seeking repentance. Or she may have been weeping for joy at the opportunity of being around the One she obviously considered to be the Messiah.

7:39. The host thought that Jesus could not possibly be **a prophet,** for if He were **He would** have known that the **woman** was **a sinner.** And He then would not have let her touch Him, for a touch by a sinner brought ceremonial uncleanness.

7:40-43. Jesus, knowing Simon's thoughts (cf. 5:22), taught in a parable that a person who is forgiven much loves more than a person who is forgiven little. In the parable one man was forgiven a debt 10 times greater than another man— **500 denarii** compared with **50** denarii. These were huge debts, for one denarius coin was worth a day's wages. When asked **which** one would **love** the lender **more, Simon** rightly responded that **the one who** was forgiven the larger **debt** would naturally be more inclined to greater love. Jesus then applied the parable to the woman.

7:44-50. The woman had been **forgiven** much and therefore **she loved** Jesus very **much.** Jesus was not implying that the Pharisee did not have much need for forgiveness. His point was that "a sinner" who is forgiven is naturally going

to love and thank the One who has forgiven her. Simon's treatment of Jesus differed vastly from the woman's. She was evidencing that she loved Jesus for she realized that she had been forgiven much. She realized that she was a sinner and in need of forgiveness. In contrast, Simon saw himself as pure and righteous and therefore did not need to treat Jesus in a special manner. In fact, he did not even extend to Jesus the normal courtesies of that day: greeting a male by **a kiss** on the cheek, and anointing a guest's **head** with a small portion of **oil.** In effect he did not seem to think Jesus could do anything for him, for he did not consider Jesus a prophet (v. 39).

But the woman was not forgiven because of her love; rather, she loved because she was forgiven (vv. 47-48). Her faith brought her salvation: **Your faith has saved you; go in peace** (cf. 8:48). Her faith in turn caused her to respond in love. **The other** dinner **guests** wondered **who** Jesus **is** since He forgave **sins** (cf. 5:21). Though Jesus in this interchange with Simon never explicitly stated His claim to be the Messiah, He spoke as He did because He is the Messiah.

4. JESUS' TEACHING ABOUT VARIOUS RESPONSES TO HIS MINISTRY (8:1-21)

a. *A close band of followers who responded positively (8:1-3)*

8:1-3. Much as the woman had responded positively to **Jesus,** in contrast with Simon the Pharisee (7:36-50), so others responded positively to the message **of the kingdom** which Jesus was **proclaiming** and some responded negatively (8:4-15). The believers included **the Twelve** and a number of **women** who had been recipients of Jesus' healing power, including **Mary (called Magdalene;** i.e., Mary from Magdala in Galilee) **from whom seven demons had come out.** Often in Scripture the number seven is used to denote completion. Apparently Mary had been totally demon-possessed. **Joanna,** who was the **wife of** one **of Herod's** officials, was also singled out, as was **Susanna.** These three and many other **women were helping to support them** (i.e., Jesus and the Twelve) **out of their own means.** This would have been viewed as a scandalous situation in Palestine in that day. However, like the forgiven woman (7:36-50), these women had also been forgiven much and they loved much. They were responding positively to Jesus' message about His kingdom.

b. Various responses illustrated by the Parable of the Sower (8:4-15) (Matt. 13:1-23; Mark 4:1-20)

8:4. Jesus gave this parable and its explanation to show that a number of responses are possible to the Word of God. Luke noted that **a large crowd was gathering** from many towns. The crowd presumably included people who would respond in the four different ways which Jesus was going to set forth in the **parable.** This parable is perhaps a warning to His hearers that obstacles would be ahead of them.

8:5-8. Farmers sowed seed by scattering it by hand over plowed soil. The **seed** of this **farmer** landed on four kinds of soil. **Some** of the seed **fell along the path** and was eaten by **birds.**

Other seed **fell on rock** (i.e., thin soil covering a ledge of rock) and therefore **withered** (v. 6).

Still **other seed fell** on soil which also supported **thorns** and therefore the **plants** were **choked** out (v. 7).

Still **other seed fell on good soil** and brought forth a good **crop** (v. 8).

Jesus ended His parable by calling out, **He who has ears to hear, let him hear.** The term **called out** denotes that Jesus was making the major point of His short discourse. Jesus used "He who has ears to hear, let him hear" on several occasions when telling parables (Matt. 11:15; 13:9, 43; Mark 4:9, 23; Luke 8:8; 14:35). The expression describes the fact that spiritual people can discern the intended spiritual meaning of a parable. The implication is that unspiritual people would understand no more than the parable's surface meaning.

8:9-10. Jesus' disciples had asked Him **what** the **parable meant.** But before He told them its meaning, He explained why He used the parabolic form of teaching. People who were spiritually discerning, that is, were following Him and acknowledging His message as true (such as those in 7:36-8:3) would have **the knowledge of the secrets of the kingdom of God.** But others who were not responding to Jesus' message of the kingdom would not understand the parable

(cf. 1 Cor. 2:14). In support of this Jesus quoted Isaiah 6:9—the people heard what He said but did **not understand** it. Jesus' speaking **in parables** was actually an act of grace to those listening to Him. If they refused to acknowledge Him as Messiah, their judgment would be less severe than if they had understood more (cf. Luke 10:13-15).

8:11-15. Jesus explained **the parable** to His disciples. **The seed is the Word of God.** The words which were being preached by the Living Word, Jesus, was the same message John the Baptist had been preaching. The people's responsibility was to accept the message which both Jesus and John were preaching.

Four kinds of people are represented by the four soils. All four kinds receive the same news. The first group consists of those **who hear** but do not **believe** at all, because of the work of the devil (v. 12).

The second group are those who listen and rejoice **but** then do not stick with the truth of the message for **they have no root** (v. 13). The fact that **they believe for a while but . . . fall away** means that they only accept the facts of the Word mentally and then reject it when "the going gets rough." It does not mean they lose their salvation, for they had none to lose.

The third group are those who listen but never come to maturity (v. 14). These may be those who are interested in Jesus' message but who cannot accept it because of their devotion to material things— **life's worries, riches, and pleasures.**

The fourth group consists of those who listen, **retain** the Word, **and . . . produce a crop** (v. 15), that is, they bear spiritual fruit, evidence of their spiritual life. Their hearts were changed for they were **noble and good.**

As Jesus' ministry progressed, it was evident that each of these groups surfaced: (1) The Pharisees and religious leaders refused to believe. (2) Some people rallied around Jesus because of His miracles of healing and feeding but refused to stay with His message (e.g., John 6:66). (3) Others, such as the rich ruler (Luke 18:18-30), were interested in Jesus but would not accept Him because of the strong pull of materialism. (4) Others followed Him and were committed to His Word regardless of the cost (e.g., 8:1-3).

c. The need to respond positively to His teaching (8:16-18)
(Mark 4:21-25)

8:16-18. This short parable is a logical extension of the Parable of the Sower. The emphasis is once again on hearing or, as it is put here, on listening (v. 18). If one understands the Word of God his life should reflect that understanding (cf. v. 15). Just as one does not light **a lamp** in order to hide **it** (cf. 11:33-36), so also a person is not **given** "the secrets of the kingdom of God" (8:10) in order to keep them secret. The disciples were to make **known** the things Jesus was telling them. The people who followed Jesus were to **consider carefully** (v. 18) **how** they listened. If they heard and responded with genuine belief (cf. v. 15), then they would receive **more** truth. If they did not receive what they heard, they would lose it.

d. The response of Jesus' earthly family (8:19-21)
(Matt. 12:46-50; Mark 3:31-35)

8:19-21. The logical outcome of the preceding teaching (vv. 1-18) is that a person who understands (and therefore puts into practice) the things Jesus was saying was rightly related to Him. **Jesus' mother and brothers** arrived **to see Him.** These brothers were undoubtedly sons of Mary and Joseph who were born after Jesus. Joseph had no sexual relations with Mary until after the birth of Jesus (Matt. 1:25). The implication is that after Jesus' birth Mary and Joseph engaged in normal marital relations and had a number of children. Thus these "brothers" were Jesus' half-brothers.

Jesus was informed that some blood relatives wanted **to see** Him (Luke 8:20). In His answer Jesus did not negate His relationship with His family. Rather, He positively stated that His affiliation with those **who hear** the Word of God **and put it into practice** is like a family relationship. In addition, Jesus' remarks showed that the gospel is not limited to a people, the Jews, but is for all who believe, including Gentiles. Once again the importance of hearing **God's Word** is central; this time, however, the admonition is that the Word must be "put . . . into practice." James, Jesus' half brother, must have learned the lesson well, for he wrote about obeying the Word instead of merely listening to it (James 1:22-23).

5. JESUS' MINISTRY THROUGH A SERIES OF MIRACLES (8:22-56)

Luke had previously recorded events that authenticated Jesus' authority (4:31–6:16). Here again an authentication was necessary. Jesus had been teaching that one must listen carefully to His words and carry them out. Now He authenticated His words in ways that only the Messiah could do. Jesus showed His power over three aspects of the created world: the natural realm (8:22-25), the demonic realm (vv. 26-39), and sickness and death (vv. 40-56).

a. Jesus' power over the natural realm (8:22-25)
(Matt. 8:23-27; Mark 4:35-41)

8:22-25. While **Jesus** and **His disciples** were sailing across the Sea of Galilee to a less-inhabited area, a storm arose which caused their boat to take on water and to be in peril. Sudden storms would whip the lake into a frenzy very quickly. Jesus was **asleep** so **the disciples went and woke Him** for they were afraid of drowning. Jesus **rebuked** the storm, and chided them for their fear and their lack of **faith** in Him. He had already told them they would be crossing **over to the other side of the lake** (v. 22). This was an excellent opportunity for them to act on God's Word that Jesus had been teaching (vv. 1-21). When Jesus rebuked the storm, the lake calmed immediately (which normally does not occur after a storm). The disciples were in **fear and amazement** (cf. vv. 35, 37).

b. Jesus' power over the demonic realm (8:26-39)
(Matt. 8:28-34; Mark 5:1-20)

8:26. Whereas Matthew wrote that Jesus met two demon-possessed men (Matt. 8:28-34), Luke wrote about only one of the two. There is some confusion as to the place where the miracle occurred. What is meant by **the region of the Gerasenes?** Apparently the area was named for the small town Gersa (now the ruins of Khersa) on the eastern shore, **across the lake from Galilee.** Matthew mentioned "the region of the Gadarenes" (Matt. 8:28), which was named for the town Gadara, about six miles southeast of the lower tip of the Sea of Galilee. Perhaps the territory around Gersa belonged to the city of Gadara (cf. comments on Mark 5:1).

8:27-29. When Jesus stepped ashore, He was confronted **by a man** who was **demon-possessed.** The man's manner of life showed that he was totally under the demon's control. He did not take part in normal human amenities (v. 27) and was often forced **by the demon** to go **into solitary places** (v. 29). As with most "demonized" individuals in the Gospels, this man was **shouting at the top of his voice.** The demon recognized **Jesus,** for the man called Him **Jesus, Son of the Most High God.** The words, **Don't torture me** show that the demon recognized that Jesus had control over him even though men could not (v. 29).

8:30-33. In answer to **Jesus** the demon said that his **name** was **Legion,** a Latin term denoting a group of about 6,000 Roman soldiers. The point of the name was that a large number of demons were inhabiting the man. The demons asked that Jesus not torment them (Matt. 8:29 adds "before the appointed time") by asking that they not be sent **into the abyss,** which was thought of as a place of the dead. The abyss was also thought of as a "watery place," which made the outcome of this encounter all the more ironic and climactic. At the request of **the demons** Jesus let them enter into **a large herd of pigs** nearby which immediately **rushed** over a cliff **into the lake** and were **drowned.** Thus the request not to be sent into the abyss was granted by Jesus, but they were sent to a watery place anyhow.

8:34-37. The effect of the miracle on **the people** of the area was **fear** (vv. 35, 37; cf. 7:16; 8:25). This fear was enough to cause them to ask **Jesus to leave.**

8:38-39. In contrast with those people the previously demon-possessed **man** was, on Jesus' command, spreading the news of what had happened to him. This was the first recorded witness of Jesus in a Gentile area.

c. Jesus' power over sickness and death (8:40-56)
(Matt. 9:18-26; Mark 5:21-43)

This section (chaps. 7–8) begins with Jesus ministering to people in sickness

and death (7:1-17). It closes with the same theme. However, the healings described in 8:40-56 bring the section to a climax because of the rich symbolism concerning Jesus' ability to make others clean while not becoming ceremonially unclean Himself.

8:40-42. Jairus, a ruler of the synagogue, pled with Jesus for the life of **his only daughter,** who **was dying.** The fact that a ruler of a synagogue would come to Jesus showed that people were beginning to acknowledge who Jesus is—that He is indeed the Messiah. A synagogue ruler was in charge of the synagogue services and was responsible for maintaining and cleaning the building. Other synagogue rulers in the New Testament were Crispus (Acts 18:8) and Sosthenes (Acts 18:17).

8:43-48. The story of Jairus is momentarily broken off by Luke who recorded what happened on the way to heal Jairus' daughter. **A woman** in the crowd **had been subject to bleeding for 12 years.** Interestingly, Jairus' only daughter was about 12 years old, and this woman's illness had extended for 12 years. Her hemorrhaging made the woman ceremonially unclean (Lev. 15:25-30), and anyone who touched her would also be ceremonially unclean. In contrast to the fact that **no one could heal her** is the fact that when she **touched** Jesus' **cloak . . . immediately her bleeding stopped.** Jesus' question, **Who touched Me?** does not imply that He was ignorant of the situation. He wanted the woman to reveal herself and openly express the faith which caused her to touch Him. The woman's faith became public when she **fell at His feet.** (This reminds one of another woman who expressed her faith at the feet of Jesus [Luke 7:36-50].) The woman's **faith** had **healed** her (8:48)—faith that Jesus could make her ceremonially clean and therefore faith that He really is the Messiah. Jesus told her, **Go in peace,** just as He had recently said to a sinful woman (7:50).

8:49-56. The story now returned to **Jairus.** Jesus had just been touched by someone who was considered ceremonially unclean. In spite of the fact that Jairus was informed that his **daughter** had died, he had faith that she would be resurrected (v. 50). That faith was partly expressed in the fact that he allowed Jesus to come into his **house** after He had touched an unclean woman.

After Jesus had raised Jairus' daughter from the dead, she was given **something to eat.** This proved that she was restored to normal health and not to a long convalescence (cf. a similar situation with Peter's mother-in-law; 4:39). In this case the **parents were astonished** (*exestē-san*, "beside themselves in amazement"; cf. 2:47), but were not fearful. Jesus' command **not to tell** others about the miracle must have stemmed from His desire not to be openly proclaimed as the Messiah until His formal proclamation in Jerusalem.

E. Jesus' teaching of His disciples (9:1-50)

Luke's section on Jesus' Galilee ministry closes with several important events through which Jesus taught His disciples. For Luke, the events in this chapter, though important, are not the crux of his argument. Jesus' journey to Jerusalem is, for Luke, the highlight of His ministry. The events recorded in this chapter form a climax to this portion of Jesus' ministry (4:14–9:50) and a bridge to His journey to Jerusalem, which begins in 9:51.

1. THE SENDING OF THE TWELVE (9:1-6) (MATT. 10:5-15; MARK 6:7-13)

9:1-6. Jesus gave the **Twelve** two assignments on the mission to which He sent them. They were **to preach the kingdom of God and to heal the sick.** They were able to carry out that mission because Jesus **gave them power** (*dynamin*, "spiritual ability"; cf. 4:14, 36; 5:17; 6:19; 8:46) **and authority** (*exousian*, "the right to exercise the power") over the demonic realm and the physical realm of **diseases.** Jesus had just shown His power over both of these realms (8:26-56). Their healing ministry was to authenticate their preaching ministry. The fact that the Twelve healed in Jesus' authority and power showed that He was the Messiah who could bring in the kingdom. Therefore it was necessary that people believe the Twelve. People would evidence their belief in the Twelve—and thus in the Messiah—by showing hospitality to these men who were ministering in Jesus' authority.

This helps explain Jesus' rather strange instructions (9:3-5) concerning a method of their ministry. The mission was not to be long—they came back to report to Jesus (v. 10). Why were the Twelve not to take supplies or **money** with them? This was because of the brevity of their mission and also because people's reactions to them would indicate whether or not the nation was accepting Jesus' claim as the Messiah. People who believed the message and the messianic healings would be glad to share with the Twelve. People who did not believe would be judged (vv. 4-5). If a **town** rejected the Twelve the latter were to **shake the** town's **dust off** their **feet.** When Jews returned home from a Gentile country, they would shake the dust off their feet to signify their breaking ties with the Gentiles. In this way the Twelve signified that certain Jewish townspeople were like Gentiles who would not listen or believe. Jesus was thus giving the entire area opportunity to believe His message and mission. Luke stated that the Twelve **went . . . everywhere,** presumably everywhere in the Galilean region rather than everywhere in the nation.

2. HEROD'S QUERY ABOUT JESUS (9:7-9) (MATT. 14:1-2; MARK 6:14-29)

9:7-9. As the Twelve went through the villages and towns, their ministry attracted much attention. Even **Herod** who was responsible for the region of Galilee as **tetrarch** (cf. 3:1), **heard about** their ministry but did not understand it. Herod, who apparently did not believe in resurrection, knew that Jesus could not be **John** the Baptist for he had previously killed John. **Others** were saying **that** Jesus might be **Elijah** or another of **the** Old Testament **prophets** raised from the dead. Luke's point in the account seems to be that everyone, even in the highest levels of government, was talking about the ministry of Jesus and the Twelve.

3. JESUS' FEEDING OF THE 5,000 (9:10-17) (MATT. 14:13-21; MARK 6:30-44; JOHN 6:1-14)

The feeding of the 5,000 is the only miracle of Jesus which is recorded in all four Gospels. In many ways it is the climax of Jesus' ministry of miracles. It was designed to produce faith in His disciples.

9:10-11. Luke now called the Twelve **apostles** (*apostoloi*). **Jesus** had so named them previously (6:13). Presumably the apostles **returned** to Jesus' home base at Capernaum. Jesus **took them** to **Bethsaida,** across the Jordan River to the northeast on the Sea of Galilee. (Others, however, say Bethsaida was a town now known as Tabgha, southwest of Capernaum.) As usual, **the crowds . . . followed Him.** Jesus continued to preach the message of **the kingdom of God.** He had sent the Twelve to preach, and He **healed those who needed healing.** The miracle which immediately followed showed climactically that Jesus is the Messiah, fully able to provide for His people. Herod had raised the issue as to who Jesus is (9:7-9). Later Jesus again raised the same issue (vv. 18-20). The feeding of the 5,000 (vv. 10-17) clinched the truth for the disciples that Jesus truly is the Messiah.

9:12-17. The people who had gathered were apparently not local people for the disciples wanted Jesus to **send the crowd away so** that **they** could **find food and lodging.** This would not have been necessary if the people had lived nearby and could have returned to their homes. When Jesus told His disciples to **give** the people **something to eat,** He was showing His men that it was humanly impossible to satisfy the crowd. The disciples admitted this and noted that **food** would have to be bought for the people if they were to feed them. The disciples stated that there were only **five loaves of bread and two fish,** clearly inadequate for such a large group of people. The **5,000 men** (*andres,* "males") is no doubt a round figure, not counting the women and children who were present (Matt. 14:21). If the latter were also counted, the total might have been over 10,000.

After having the people **sit down in groups of** 50s, for ease in distributing the food, Jesus thanked God the Father and gave out the food, using the disciples as waiters. **Twelve basketfuls of broken** food **pieces** were collected at the end of the meal, perhaps thus providing a basket of food for each disciple to eat. The word used for baskets (*kophinoi*) was considered typical of Jewish commerce. The seven baskets from the feeding of the 4,000 (Mark 8:8) were a different kind of basket. Jesus, by this act of provision, had shown Himself sufficient for the nation Israel. He is the One who could provide prosperity if the people would believe His message. This miracle is reminiscent of Elisha when he spoke the Word of the Lord and a small amount of food fed many people, with some left over (2 Kings 4:42-44).

4. JESUS' TEACHING ABOUT HIS IDENTITY AND MISSION (9:18-27) (MATT. 16:13-28; MARK 8:27–9:1)

For the first time in this section Jesus taught His disciples about His ultimate mission—the fact that He had to die.

9:18-21. On this occurrence, which Mark said was on the way north to Caesarea Philippi (Mark 8:27), Jesus initiated the questioning about **who** people said He was (cf. Luke 9:7-9). Jesus was specifically interested in who the **disciples** thought He was. **Peter,** answering for the entire group, affirmed that He is **the Christ** (i.e., the Messiah) **of God.** Though some time had passed since the incident of the loaves and fish, the implication from Luke seems to be that it was Jesus' sufficiency in that instance which clinched His identification as Messiah in the disciples' minds. Jesus did not want others to know of this (v. 21) because it was not time for Him to be proclaimed publicly as Messiah. The public proclamation would come about at a later time and it was that proclamation which Jesus spoke about next.

9:22-27. The subject of these verses is death—Jesus' death and His followers' deaths. He pointed out that the Jewish leaders would play a prominent part in His death (v. 22). Jesus also gave His first indication that He would be resurrected (v. 22). Jesus then discussed the deaths of His followers. They were to have the same attitude toward death and life that He had. Each one **must deny himself,** that is, not think about his own good. Also he must **take up his cross daily,** that is, admit that the One for whom he carried the cross was right (see comments on 14:27). And he must **follow** Jesus, even to death.

The words Jesus spoke in this setting must be understood in their historical context. Not long before this the disciples had been actively engaged in telling the nation about the Messiah and His kingdom program. No doubt many thought the disciples were throwing their lives away. They had given up their sources of income and were in danger because they associated with Jesus. Jesus assured His disciples that they were doing the right thing. They had chosen the proper values (9:24-25). People were to respond in faith and identify with that program (v. 4). Those who did not identify with the kingdom program would be rejected (v. 5). In the same manner Jesus noted that if one **is ashamed of** Him (i.e., will not identify with Him or believe on Him) **and** His **words** (i.e., His message), **the Son of Man will be ashamed of him** in the future. It was vital that the people of that generation side with Jesus and His disciples in order to escape future judgment. That judgment will occur **when He comes in His glory and in the glory of the Father and of the holy angels** (cf. 2 Thes. 1:7-10).

Jesus added, **Some who are standing here will not taste death before they see the kingdom of God.** Over the centuries many views on this statement have been suggested. The four most common views are these: (1) Jesus was talking about the beginning of Christian missions at Pentecost. Surely most of the apostles did see the activities on the day of Pentecost for only Judas was dead at that time. However, to identify Pentecost with the kingdom violates much of the Old Testament teaching about the kingdom. (2) Jesus was speaking about the destruction of Jerusalem. However, it is difficult to see in what way that would even symbolize the kingdom of God. (3) Jesus meant that the disciples would not die with Him but would continue to spread the gospel after His death. But it is difficult to see how this would be related to the kingdom in light of the Old Testament with which the disciples were familiar. (4) Jesus was speaking of the three apostles who would accompany Him up the mountain of transfiguration. The transfiguration was a foretaste of the glories of the kingdom. This seems the best view. Luke linked this teaching (Luke 9:27) with the transfiguration account (vv. 28-36).

5. JESUS' TRANSFIGURATON BEFORE THREE DISCIPLES (9:28-36)
(MATT. 17:1-8; MARK 9:2-8)

9:28-31. About eight days later **Jesus . . . took** three of His apostles **up onto a mountain to pray.** But Mark wrote that the event occurred after *six* days (Mark 9:2). The two accounts are not contradictory if one understands Mark as speaking of the intervening days and Luke as including the days of Jesus' teaching as well as the day on which the transfiguration took place. The transfiguration may have occurred on Mount Hermon near Caesarea Philippi (cf. Mark 8:27), though some say it was Mount Tabor. At the transfiguration three events occurred:

1. Jesus' **face** and **clothes became as bright as a flash of lightning.** This would have immediately reminded those present of Moses' face shining with a bright light when he received the tablets of the Law (Ex. 34:29-35).

2. **Moses and Elijah appeared** and spoke **with Jesus.** The bodies of Moses and Elijah were never found. God buried Moses' body (Deut. 34:5-6), and Elijah did not die but was taken up to heaven (2 Kings 2:11-12, 15-18). These two men represent the beginning and the end of Israel, for Moses, as the Lawgiver, founded the nation, and Elijah is to come back before the great and terrible day of the Lord (Mal. 4:5-6).

3. Moses and Elijah **spoke about His departure** (*exodon*, "going out or away") **which He was about to bring to fulfillment at Jerusalem.** "Departure" referred to Jesus' leaving the world through which He would bring salvation—much as Yahweh had brought deliverance to Israel in its Exodus (departure) from Egypt. This departure was to be fulfilled in Jerusalem. From this point on, Jesus indicated several times that He was headed toward Jerusalem (Luke 9:51, 53; 13:33; 17:11; 18:31). Jesus did not want His miracles widely publicized at that time, for the fulfillment had to be at Jerusalem. This was confirmed by Elijah's and Moses' words.

9:32-33. Three disciples were with Jesus. This number is reminiscent of Moses' three companions—Aaron, Nadab, and Abihu—who saw God (Ex. 24:9-11). **Peter,** James, and John **were very sleepy** at the beginning of the transfiguration. Later these three and the others fell asleep while Jesus was praying in the garden (Luke 22:45). As the disciples woke up, they were overwhelmed with the **glory** of the situation.

They realized they were in a kingdom setting which triggered Peter's idea that they build **three shelters. Peter** may have been thinking of the Feast of Booths, a feast of ingathering long associated with the coming kingdom (cf. Zech. 14:16-21). Peter seemed to have assumed that the kingdom had arrived.

Luke editorially inserted that Peter **did not know what he was saying.** The thought is not that Peter misunderstood the significance of the kingdom setting—he was correct in that. The problem was that he forgot Jesus' prediction that He would suffer (Luke 9:23-24).

9:34-36. While Peter **was speaking, a cloud . . . enveloped them.** Grammatically the word "them" could refer to the three disciples or to all six people (Jesus, Moses, Elijah, and the three disciples). But more likely it refers to Jesus and the heavenly visitors, with the disciples being those who **were afraid.** A **cloud** was often a symbol of God's divine presence (Ex. 13:21-22; 40:38). Perhaps the disciples thought Jesus was being taken away from them, and they would never see Him again.

As was the case at Jesus' baptism (Luke 3:22), so here a voice spoke to those witnessing the event: **This is My Son, whom I have chosen; listen to Him.** Those familiar with the Old Testament, as the disciples were, doubtless immediately recognized the reference (in the words "listen to Him") to Deuteronomy 18:15 with its messianic prediction of a Prophet greater than Moses. The people were to listen to (i.e., obey) the Prophet.

Suddenly **the disciples** saw **that Jesus was alone.** At that time they did not tell anyone **what they had seen.** The experience at the transfiguration fulfilled Jesus' prediction (Luke 9:27). Three of the disciples did see a manifestation of the kingdom of God before they died (cf. 2 Peter 1:16-19).

6. JESUS' HEALING OF THE EPILEPTIC BOY (9:37-43)

(MATT. 17:14-18; MARK 9:14-27)

9:37-43. The transfiguration may have occurred at night, for Luke noted that **the next day** the four descended **from the mountain** and a **crowd met** Jesus. A **man** begged Jesus **to look** at his demon-possessed **son,** whom the other **disciples** had been unable to help. In

stark contrast with the disciples, only Jesus could help the boy—just as He is the only One who can help the world. The disciples were powerless without Him. After the boy was healed, the crowd was **amazed** (*exeplēssonto,* "struck out of their senses"; cf. 2:48; 4:32) **at the greatness of God.**

7. JESUS' TEACHING OF HIS DEATH (9:44-45)

9:44-45. In the midst of the amazement by the crowd, Jesus taught the disciples a second time that He would die by being **betrayed into the hands of men. But they did not understand as it was hidden from them.** Apparently the disciples were still confused as to how Jesus, with His glorious power, could experience a humiliating death. Nor could they put together the crowd's reaction to His miracles and His prediction that the nation would turn against Him and kill Him.

8. JESUS' TEACHING ABOUT GREATNESS (9:46-50)

(MATT. 18:1-5; MARK 9:33-40)

9:46-50. This section (9:1-50) ends with Jesus' teaching concerning the disciples' attitude toward greatness. He had been revealed to them as the Messiah who would bring in the kingdom. Perhaps this fact precipitated the disciples' argument about their greatness in that kingdom. Jesus set forth the principle that the one who is **the greatest** is the one **who is least among you.** This same attitude of service characterized Him, the Messiah who was willing to go to the cross for all people.

Coupled with this discussion on greatness was John's attempt **to stop** someone else who was **driving out demons** in Jesus' name. John's reason was that the **man** was **not one of us.** John must have thought that the disciples' own greatness was diminished if others who were not of the Twelve could also cast out demons. Jesus' reply, **Whoever is not against you is for you,** suggested that the Twelve were not to see themselves as God's exclusive representatives. Rather they should have rejoiced that the power of God was being manifested on earth by others as well. If they manifested that attitude, it would show that they were truly trying to be of service to the Messiah.

V. The Journey of Jesus toward Jerusalem (9:51-19:27)

This lengthy section of Luke comprises two parts: (1) the rejection of Jesus by most on His journey toward Jerusalem (9:51-11:54) and (2) Jesus' teaching His followers in view of that rejection (12:1-19:27).

The previous section (4:4-9:50) dealt with Jesus' authentication in His Galilean ministry. In this next section authentication was no longer the issue. The issue was now acceptance. Jesus was not accepted by most of the nation. Therefore He began to teach His followers how they should live in the face of opposition.

A. The rejection of Jesus by most on His journey toward Jerusalem (9:51-11:54)

This section begins with Jesus' rejection by people in a Samaritan village (9:51-56). Of course it was expected that Samaritans would reject Him, but that rejection set the pattern for what followed. The rejection climaxed when Jesus was accused of having demonic power (11:14-54).

1. JESUS AND THE SAMARITANS (9:51-10:37)

a. Jesus' rejection by a Samaritan city (9:51-56)

9:51-56. After the transfiguration (vv. 9:28-36), in which Moses and Elijah spoke with the Lord concerning His departure *from* Jerusalem, **Jesus resolutely set out *for* Jerusalem.** Jesus made several trips to Jerusalem, but Luke telescoped them to make his point that Jesus had to get to Jerusalem to present Himself as the Messiah and then depart. On His way, **He sent messengers on ahead,** but the Samaritans **did not welcome Him, because He was heading for Jerusalem.** Conflict between Jews and Samaritans had been going on for several hundred years. The reaction of **the disciples, James and John** in particular, was **to destroy them** by **fire . . . from heaven.** They were thinking, no doubt, of Elijah (2 Kings 1:9-12), who destroyed by fire those who were opposing God's work. Jesus, on the other hand, called for tolerance. The implication is not that it was right to oppose Jesus and His followers. The Samaritans who rejected Jesus would be judged for their rejection.

However, there were more important things to take care of. Jesus had to move along toward Jerusalem.

b. Jesus' teaching that discipleship takes radical commitment (9:57-62) (Matt. 8:19-22)

Luke introduced three people who wanted to join Jesus on His journey to Jerusalem.

9:57-58. A **man** approached and wanted to **follow** where they were going. Jesus' response was that a person desiring to follow Him must give up what others consider necessities. Jesus had no home of His own nor did His followers. They were on their way to Jerusalem where Jesus would be put to death.

9:59-60. Jesus called the next **man** with the same words with which He had called His disciples (5:27). The man's reply that he **first** wanted to **go and bury** his **father** has been variously interpreted. Some maintain that the man's father was dead already. It would seem strange if that was the case for he would certainly have been engaged in the burial procedure already. It is more likely that the man's father was ready to die. His request was to let him wait just a little while before following Jesus. Perhaps the man also wanted to receive the inheritance from his father's estate. Jesus' response, **Let the dead bury their own dead,** implies that the spiritually dead can bury the physically dead. The point was that proclaiming **the kingdom of God** was so important that it could not wait. Of course if the man had left and followed Jesus, it would have caused a scandal in the community. But that was less important than proclaiming the kingdom and following the Messiah. A disciple must make a radical commitment.

9:61-62. The third man simply wanted to **go home** and **say good-by to** his **family.** Elijah had allowed Elisha to do this very thing when Elisha was plowing (1 Kings 19:19-20). Jesus' words underscore the fact that His message of the kingdom of God was more important than anything else—even family members. The message and the Messiah cannot wait. Jesus' message was more important than Elijah's message and demanded total allegiance. Jesus' servants should not have divided interests, like a farmer who begins plowing **and looks**

back. Since Jesus was on His way to Jerusalem, the man had to make up his mind right then as to what he was going to do. Interestingly Luke did not record the outcome of any of Jesus' conversations with the three men.

c. Jesus' sending of the messengers to spread the Word (10:1-24)

This section contains instructions similar to those given to the Twelve in 9:1-6. On His way to Jerusalem Jesus was sending out messengers to all the towns in order to give people opportunities to accept His message. Only Luke records this incident.

(1) The choosing of the 72 (10:1-16). **10:1-12.** Jesus gave instructions to the **72.** Some Greek manuscripts in verses 1 and 17 have "70" and others have "72." Both readings have strong support. The 72 were people other than the Twelve, who apparently remained with Jesus on His journey. The 72 were to prepare the way so that when Jesus came into a **town,** it would be ready for Him. When Jesus stated, **Ask the Lord . . . to send out workers,** He implied that the ones asking were also to be workers (v. 2). Their mission was dangerous (v. 3) and required haste (v. 4). The 72 were supported by those who accepted their message (v. 7). Through hospitality people would show whether or not they believed the message of the kingdom. To the believing cities the message was to be, **The kingdom of God is near you.** The Messiah was coming, and He could bring in the kingdom. Even the cities that rejected the message were to be told that **the kingdom** was **near.** (For the meaning of wiping **dust** off their **feet,** see comments on 9:5).

10:13-16. Jesus warned the surrounding towns against rejecting the 72 because that meant rejecting Jesus and the Father (v. 16). Jesus singled out two cities—**Korazin** and **Bethsaida,** both of which were located in the area of Jesus' early ministry of miracles on the north side of the Sea of Galilee. He also singled out His adopted hometown, **Capernaum,** which also had been a site of His miraculous works. The message was clear: those cities (no doubt representative of others as well) were to be more severely judged than pagan cities, such as **Tyre and Sidon** (cf. Sodom, v. 12) which did not have the benefit of the Lord's miraculous works and words.

(2) The return of the 72. **10:17-20.** When the messengers came back, they were excited that **even the demons** had submitted **to** them **in** Jesus' **name.** This was true because of the **authority** Jesus had **given** them. They had such authority because Satan's power had been broken by Jesus. He answered them, **I saw Satan fall like lightning from heaven.** Jesus was not speaking of Satan being cast out at that precise moment, but that his **power** had been broken and that he was subject to Jesus' authority. However, Jesus said the cause for their **joy** should not be what they could do in His name but in the fact **that** their **names** were **written in heaven.** The personal relationship of a believer with God should be the cause of his joy. The authority given to these workers and the promise of no harm from **snakes and scorpions** was given for this particular situation.

(3) Jesus' rejoicing in the Spirit (10:21-24; Matt. 11:25-27). **10:21-24.** Jesus was **full of joy through the Holy Spirit** (cf. the joy of the 72, v. 20). Luke frequently mentioned the Holy Spirit's ministry in Jesus' life. The three Persons of the Godhead are clearly seen: Jesus **the Son** was doing the Father's will in the power of the Holy Spirit. Each had a specific function (vv. 21-22).

The people who were following Jesus were not the important people of the nation; they were not considered **the wise and learned.** They had become like **little children** to enter into the kingdom, and thus they knew **the Son** and **the Father.** The disciples were living in an opportune day which **many** Old Testament **prophets and kings** longed **to see**—the day of the Messiah.

d. Jesus' teaching on one's neighbor (10:25-37)

10:25-37. The Parable of the Good Samaritan is perhaps the most well-known Lucan parable. It must be interpreted on two levels. The first level is the plain teaching that a person, like the Samaritan, should help others in need (v. 37). If one has the heart of a **neighbor,** he will see and help a neighbor. However, in the context of the rejection of Jesus, it should also be noted in this parable that the Jewish religious leaders rejected the man who fell among the robbers. A Samaritan, an outcast, was the only one who helped the man. Jesus was like the Samaritan. He was the outcast One, who was willing to seek and to save people who were perishing. He was directly opposed to the religious establishment. The theme is reminiscent of Jesus' words to the Pharisees (7:44-50). The theme of Jesus' going to those who needed Him became more and more evident.

An expert in the Law asked Jesus, **Teacher . . . what must I do to inherit eternal life?** This question surfaced on several occasions (Matt. 19:16-22; Luke 18:18-23; John 3:1-15). The question in this case was not sincere, as can be seen from two points in the text: (1) The lawyer wanted **to test Jesus.** (He called Jesus "Teacher," *didaskale,* Luke's equivalent of a Jewish Rabbi.) (2) After Jesus answered the man's question, Luke recorded that the man wished **to justify himself** (Luke 10:29).

Jesus answered his question with two other questions (v. 26), driving the Law expert back to **the** Old Testament **Law.** The expert answered **correctly** by quoting from Deuteronomy 6:5 and Leviticus 19:18. One must **love . . . God** and one's fellowman in order to keep the Law properly. **Jesus** affirmed that if the man did **this,** he would **live.**

The man's response should have been to ask, "How can I do this? I am not able. I need help." Instead, he tried "to justify himself," that is, to defend himself against the implications of Jesus' words. So he tried to move the focus off himself by asking, **And who is my neighbor?**

Jesus answered by telling the Parable of the Good Samaritan. The road **from Jerusalem to Jericho** descends approximately 3,000 feet in about 17 miles. It was a dangerous road to travel for **robbers** hid along its steep, winding way. **A priest,** one expected to love others, avoided **the** wounded **man,** probably a fellow Jew.

Levites were descendants of Levi but not of Aaron, and they assisted the priests (Aaron's descendants) in the temple.

The Samaritans were scorned by the Jews because of their mixed Jewish and Gentile ancestry. It is ironic, then, that **a Samaritan** helped the **half-dead** man, dressing **his wounds,** taking **him to an inn,** and paying his expenses. By asking

Which . . . was his **neighbor?** (Luke 10:36) Jesus was teaching that a person should be a neighbor to anyone he meets in need. The ultimate Neighbor was Jesus, whose compassion contrasted with the Jewish religious leaders who had no compassion on those who were perishing. Jesus wrapped up His teaching with the command that His followers were to live like that true neighbor (v. 37).

2. JESUS' TEACHING THAT ATTENTION TO HIM IS THE MOST IMPORTANT THING IN LIFE (10:38-42)

10:38-42. The focus of this passage is not that people should be unconcerned with household chores, but that the proper attitude toward **Jesus** is to listen to Him and obey His words. The **village** where **Martha opened her home to Him** was Bethany (John 11:1–12:8), a few miles east of Jerusalem. Jesus stayed in Bethany during His final week on earth. A sharp contrast was portrayed between the two sisters. **Mary . . . sat** and listened to Jesus, while **Martha** made **preparations** for a meal. The phrase, **only one thing is needed** (Luke 10:42), refers to listening to His words, which **Mary** had **chosen** to do. The same theme is seen in 8:1-21.

3. JESUS' TEACHING ABOUT PRAYER (11:1-13)

11:1. Jesus prayed at every major crisis point in His life. He prayed at the time of His baptism (3:21), and at the time of the choosing of His disciples (6:12). He **was** often alone **praying** (5:16; 9:18) and also prayed with others around (9:28-29). He prayed for Simon (22:32), and He prayed in the garden before His betrayal (22:40-44). He even prayed on the cross (23:46). **One of His disciples,** impressed with Jesus' life of prayer, asked Jesus to **teach** them **to pray.**

a. Jesus' model prayer (11:2-4)
(Matt. 6:9-15)

11:2-4. In this model prayer Jesus began with an intimate direct address, **Father.** This was somewhat characteristic of the way Jesus referred to God in His prayers (cf. 10:21). He then made five requests. The first two dealt with God's interests. The first request was that God's **name** be **hallowed** (*hagiasthētō,* from *hagiazō,* "to set apart or sanctify" or, as here, "to treat as holy"). Thus the request was for God's reputation to be revered by men.

The second request was **Your kingdom come.** John the Baptist, Jesus, the Twelve, and the 72 had been preaching about the coming of God's kingdom. When a person prays for the coming of the kingdom, he is identifying with the message of Jesus and His followers.

The third request was for **daily bread.** Bread is a general term denoting nourishing and filling food. Thus the request is for food that is necessary to sustain life for the day.

The fourth request concerned man's relationship to God—the forgiveness of **sins.** Luke had already linked the forgiveness of sins to faith (7:36-50). In asking for forgiveness of sins a person expresses his faith that God will forgive him. Such a person then evidences his faith by forgiving others.

The fifth request is, **lead us not into temptation.** But why pray such a prayer since God does not want people to sin? The meaning is that Jesus' followers are to pray that they be delivered from *situations* that would cause them to sin. His disciples, contrary to the Law experts (10:25-29), realized that they were easily drawn into sin. Therefore Jesus' followers need to ask God for help to live righteous lives.

b. Jesus' teaching about prayer through two parables (11:5-13)

11:5-8. The first parable concerns **persistence** in prayer. It is common in Luke for good lessons to be taught from bad examples (cf. 16:1-9; 18:1-8). In contrast with the man who did not want to be bothered, God wants His people to pray to Him (11:9-10). So Jesus encouraged people to be persistent in prayer—not to change God's mind but to be steadfast in praying and to receive their **needs.**

11:9-13. The second parable noted that the heavenly Father gives His children what is **good** for them, not what harms them. Jesus encouraged the people of God to **ask.** He noted that natural **fathers** give **good** food to their children rather than something that would harm them (some **fish** may look like snakes, and the body of a large white **scorpion** could be mistaken **for an egg**). How

much more will the heavenly **Father** give what is good to His children.

Jesus stated that this good gift is **the Holy Spirit,** the most important gift that followers of Jesus would receive (cf. Acts 2:1-4). The heavenly Father gives both heavenly gifts and earthly gifts. Believers today are not to pray for the Holy Spirit because this prayer of the disciples (for the Holy Spirit) was answered at Pentecost (cf. Rom. 8:9).

4. THE INCREASED REJECTION OF JESUS (11:14-54)

This section contains a record of the high point of the rejection of Jesus and His message. After the record of this rejection Luke began to record Jesus' words as to how disciples should live in the midst of rejection.

a. Jesus accused of demonic power (11:14-26) (Matt. 12:22-30; Mark 3:20-27)

In Luke the terms "demon" and "demons" occur 16 times and "evil spirit(s)" ("unclean spirit[s]" in KJV) occurs 8 times. Jesus always had authority over the demons—a sign of His messianic power (7:21; 13:32). The demons themselves recognized that authority (4:31-41; 8:28-31), and Jesus' enemies did too (11:14-26). Jesus gave others power over demons (9:1), and His authority over demons amazed the crowds (4:36; 9:42-43).

11:14-16. After seeing **Jesus** cast **out a demon** from a person who **was mute . . . some** among **the crowd** suggested that He did it by demonic power, that is, by the power of **Beelzebub.** This name given to **the prince of demons,** clearly Satan, originally meant "lord of the princes," but had been corrupted to a pun denoting "lord of the flies" (cf. 2 Kings 1:2). The charge was that Jesus was possessed by Satan himself. A second group wanted Jesus to show **a sign from heaven.** They were probably not sincere in their request as Luke linked them with the former group and noted that they were testing Him.

11:17-20. Jesus gave a twofold response. First, He said it would be ridiculous for **Satan** to **drive out** his own **demons,** for then he would be weakening his position and **kingdom.** Second, Jesus pointed out the double standard of those who were accusing Him. If their **followers** drove **out** demons, they claimed it was done by the power of God. Thus since Jesus cast **out demons,** it too must be **by** God's **finger,** that is, His power. Therefore **the kingdom of God has come to you.**

11:21-22. Jesus' parable of the **strong man** and the **stronger** man has been variously interpreted. In view of the context (vv. 17-20) the strong man refers to Satan, and the stronger man to Christ Himself. When it was that Christ attacked and overpowered Satan is not stated by Luke. Luke may have had in mind Jesus' temptation experience, or the Resurrection, or perhaps the ultimate binding of Satan. The point of the parable, however, is that Jesus is the stronger One, and therefore He has the right to divide **up the spoils.** In this case the spoils include formerly demon-possessed people who no longer belong to Satan.

11:23-26 (Matt. 12:43-45). Jesus stated that it was impossible to be neutral in the battle between Christ and Satan. The people who were watching had to make up their minds. If they thought Jesus was casting out demons by the power of Satan, then they were actively **against** Him.

Jesus' words recorded in Luke 11:24-26 are difficult. Probably He was referring to the man who was formerly demon-possessed and was making him a symbol of everyone who was demon-possessed. It was vital that this man also accept what Jesus was saying about His being the Messiah, or he would end up in a **condition . . . worse than the first.** Matthew recorded that Jesus compared this situation to what would happen to the generation of people who were listening to Him (Matt. 12:45).

b. *Jesus' teaching on the observance of God's Word (11:27-28)*

11:27-28. This teaching is similar to that in 8:19-21. Family relationships are not the most important things in life. A **woman** noted that it must have been wonderful to have been Jesus' **mother.** The idea of physical relationship was more important in that day. The whole nation took pride in the fact that they descended from Abraham (cf. John 8:33-39). **Jesus** pointed out that a physical relationship was unimportant compared

with hearing and obeying **the Word of God.** As Luke emphasized, the gospel is not limited to Israel but is for all who trust in Christ.

c. *Jesus' refusal to give a sign (11:29-32) (Matt. 12:38-42; Mark 8:11-12)*

11:29-32. The Pharisees asked Jesus for a sign (Matt. 12:38; Mark 8:11) which Luke did not mention. A **sign** was a confirming miracle which showed that the spoken message was true. The crowds were not willing to believe Jesus' words without external confirmation.

Jesus' response was that no sign would **be given . . . except the sign of Jonah** (Luke 11:29). This sign has been interpreted in at least two ways: Many say it was the physical appearance of Jonah, for perhaps his skin was bleached white by the sea monster's inner juices. However, nothing in the context hints at this. "The sign of Jonah" must have been the words (cf. "preaching," v. 32) Jonah spoke about his miraculous preservation by God when he was at the point of death. The people **of Nineveh** believed what Jonah said, even if they had no physical evidence. Jesus' words about **the Queen of the South** lend strength to this interpretation. The queen traveled a great distance **to listen to Solomon's wisdom** (1 Kings 10). She acted on what she heard, without any external confirmation. The point is clear: the generation that was listening to Jesus' words did not have as much faith as some Gentiles who listened to the words of God in previous eras. Therefore even Gentiles **will stand up at the judgment with this generation and condemn it.** Jesus affirmed that something (neut., not masc.) **greater than Solomon** (Luke 11:31) and **greater than Jonah** was present (v. 32). That something was the kingdom of God, present in the person of Jesus. Thus the people should listen and believe without a sign.

d. *Jesus' stress on responding to His teachings (11:33-36)*

11:33-36. Jesus often taught His disciples through parables. Because they had been listening to Him they had **light** shining **on** them (v. 36). Thus they should share that **light** (v. 33). When a person's eyes (like lamps) react properly to **light,** he can function normally. Being receptive to Jesus' teachings would show that they were **full of light** (vv. 34, 36) and were benefiting from His teachings (cf. comments on 8:16-18).

e. *Jesus accused and questioned by the Pharisees (11:37-54)*
(Matt. 23:1-36; Mark 12:38-40)

11:37-41. A Pharisee invited Jesus to dinner. **Jesus did not** engage in the ritual washing **before the meal,** which completely **surprised . . . the Pharisee.** Jesus focused on **greed,** a characteristic of the Pharisees, and said that they should be as concerned with the cleansing of **the inside** as they were with washing **the outside** of the body. One indication that they were clean on the inside would be their willingness to give material things **to the poor.** This meant not that their act of giving would atone for their sins, but that it would show a proper relationship to the Law and to God.

11:42-44. Jesus next pronounced three woes (pronouncements of condemnation) on the **Pharisees** for disregarding **justice and the love of God.** They were bound up in the ritual of the Law, tithing even small **garden herbs.** This made them hypocrites (cf. 12:1). They were filled with pride, loving **the most important seats in the synagogues.** And rather than guiding the people aright, they caused people who followed them to be contaminated, just as **unmarked graves,** when walked on, would defile a Jew without his knowing it (Num. 19:16). The Pharisees feared contamination from ritual uncleanness, but Jesus pointed out that their greed, pride, and wickedness contaminated the entire nation.

11:45-52. Jesus then pronounced three woes on the **Law . . . experts** (vv. 46-47, 52). They placed **burdens** on others which effectively kept them away from the way of knowledge. And they built **tombs for the prophets,** thus identifying with their **forefathers who killed . . . the prophets.** Outwardly they seemed to honor the prophets, but God knew that inwardly they were rejecting the prophets. So they would **be held responsible for the blood of all the prophets. The blood of Abel and the blood of Zechariah** refers to the killing of innocent men involved in serving God. Abel was the first innocent victim (Gen. 4:8), and Zechariah the priest (not the writing prophet, though see Matt. 23:35) was the last martyr in the Old Testament (2 Chron. 24:20-21; Chron. was last in the OT Heb. order). Jesus' indictment became even more severe when He noted that not only were they themselves staying away from **knowledge** (i.e., Jesus' teaching) but were also taking **away the key,** that is, they were keeping the knowledge from others (cf. Luke 13:14).

11:53-54. The Pharisees and lawyers **began to oppose** Jesus fiercely. They were constantly questioning Him, plotting against Him, and hoping **to catch Him** saying something wrong.

B. *Jesus' teaching of His followers in view of the rejection (12:1–19:27)*

Jesus first taught several truths to His inner circle of disciples (12:1-53), and then taught several things to the multitudes (12:54–13:21). Jesus taught about people of the kingdom (13:22–17:10), and about the attitude of the disciples in view of the coming kingdom (17:11–19:27).

1. JESUS TEACHING HIS INNER CIRCLE OF DISCIPLES (12:1-53)

a. *Jesus' teaching about witnessing without fear (12:1-12)*

12:1-3. Jesus first stated that it is foolish to be hypocritical because eventually everything will **be made known** (cf. 8:17). So the disciples should be open, not two-faced, about the way they lived. He warned them to **guard against the yeast of the Pharisees,** that is, their teaching, for it **is hypocrisy.** In the Scriptures yeast often refers to something evil (cf. Mark 8:15).

12:4-12 (Matt. 10:28-31). Jesus went on to teach that His disciples (**My friends**) should be fearless (Luke 12:4, 7; cf. v. 32) because God would take care of them. Instead of fearing men who could kill their bodies (cf. 11:48-50), they should **fear** God, the One who **has the power to throw** one **into hell.** This follows as a natural corollary of 12:2-3—God knows everything. The disciples were far more valuable to **God** than **sparrows,** which were sold for a small amount (**five birds for two pennies**). The word for "penny" is *assarion,* a Roman copper coin worth about $1/16$ of a denarius (a day's wage), and used only here and in Matthew 10:29. Since God takes care of common little birds (cf. Luke 12:22), He will also care for His own, even knowing the number of their **hairs.**

The point of verses 8-10 is that disciples must make a choice. To **acknowledge** denotes the fact that the disciples recognized Him as the Messiah and therefore they had access to the way of salvation. Those who did not acknowledge Him were denying themselves the way of salvation. Jesus carried the logic one step further, noting that one **who blasphemes against the Holy Spirit will not be forgiven.** In Matthew 12:32 Jesus linked this activity with the Pharisees who were rejecting the work of Jesus. Apparently the Pharisees were being convicted by the Holy Spirit that Jesus was indeed the Messiah, but were rejecting His witness. They could never be forgiven because they were rejecting God's only means of salvation. (In contrast to that, a number of Jesus' own brothers who initially rejected Him [John 7:5] later came to faith [Acts 1:14] and were forgiven even though they had spoken **against the Son of Man.**)

Jesus then promised the disciples (Luke 12:11-12) that when they were arraigned and **brought before** officials because of their preaching and teaching (cf. Acts 4:1-21), **the Holy Spirit** would **teach** them **what** to **say.** In contrast to Jesus' enemies, who blasphemed the Holy Spirit, Jesus' followers would be helped by the Holy Spirit.

b. Jesus' teaching about greed (12:13-21)

12:13-21. This passage explains Jesus' teaching to **guard against all kinds of greed.** Someone wanted Jesus to instruct his **brother to divide** up the **inheritance** which was due him in an equitable way. Jesus' point was that **life does not consist in** having many **possessions.** The disciples needed to learn the lesson that life is more important than material things. To explain this teaching Jesus told a parable about a **rich man** who continued to build **bigger** and bigger **barns** to **store all** his **grain and . . . goods.** His attitude was that he would have an easy life because he had everything he could possibly want or need. God's response in the parable was that the man was foolish (**You fool!**) because when he died that **night** his goods would do

nothing for him. They would simply pass on to someone else. Such a person **is not rich toward God** (cf. 1 Tim. 6:6-10; James 1:10). Luke returned to this subject in chapter 16.

c. Jesus' teaching about anxiety (12:22-34) (Matt. 6:25-34)

The section builds to a climax in verse 31 when the disciples were instructed to seek God's kingdom. In building to that climax Jesus said three things about anxiety.

12:22-24. Jesus first noted that anxiety is foolish because **life** consists of far **more** than what one eats or wears (cf. v. 15). Jesus again referred to **birds** (cf. vv. 6-7) to point out that since His disciples were **more valuable** than **ravens,** which **God feeds,** He cares for them. (Unlike sparrows, ravens were not sold for they are scavengers.)

12:25-28. Jesus next pointed out that **worry** is foolish because it cannot change the situation. Not one **hour** can be added to one's **life** so it is ridiculous to worry. Again Jesus went to the natural realm (**lilies** and **grass**) to point out that **God** takes care of what belongs to Him.

12:29-31. Finally Jesus pointed out that **worry** is foolish because worry is the attitude of pagans. **The pagan world** is concerned with the material things of life and not with life's ultimately important spiritual realities. On the other hand one who pursues spiritual matters (seeking God's **kingdom**) will also receive from God material provisions.

12:32-34. Jesus then told His disciples not to fear (cf. vv. 4, 7). He compared them to a **little flock,** a seemingly defenseless group which could be preyed on. To make them even more defenseless Christ instructed, **Sell your possessions and give to the poor.** (Luke later came back to this subject in chaps. 16 and 19.) This is also what the early church did (Acts 2:44-45; 4:32-37). Jesus' point was that if His followers had a treasure on earth they would think about it. But if they instead had **a treasure in heaven,** which is safe from theft and decay by moths, and were "rich toward God" (Luke 12:21), they would be concerned with matters pertaining to **the kingdom** and therefore would not be in a state of anxiety.

d. Jesus' teaching about readiness
(12:35-48)
(Matt. 24:45-51)

In this section Jesus told two parables (vv. 35-40 and 42-48) which were joined by a question by Peter (v. 41). The second parable expands and explains the first.

12:35-40. Jesus taught that the disciples should **be ready because the Son of Man will come** at a time when they will **not** be expecting **Him.** The parable describes a scene in which several servants were **waiting for their master to return from a wedding banquet.** The point was that they had to remain constantly vigilant so that the **master** would be able to come into the house whenever he might arrive at home. If they are **watching** (v. 37) and **ready** (v. 38), their master will **serve** them. **The second** watch was from 9 P.M. to midnight, and the **third watch** was from midnight to 3 A.M. The point of the words about **the thief** (v. 39) is the same—the disciples must "be ready" for "the Son of Man will come" unexpectedly.

12:41. Peter's question holds the two parables together. **Peter** wanted to know the extent of the first parable's meaning. Was it addressed only to the disciples **or to everyone?**

12:42-48. Jesus did not answer Peter's question directly. Instead these verses indicate that He was talking primarily about the leadership of the nation at that time. The religious leaders were supposed to be managing the nation for God until He brought in the kingdom. However, they failed in that task; they were not looking expectantly toward the kingdom. Because of the penalty exacted (vv. 46-47), Jesus must not have been speaking about believers who were not **ready.** He seems to have been referring to the nation's leaders who would be present at the time of the coming of the Son of Man. Faithless ones (v. 47) will be judged more severely than those who, though wicked, do **not know** about the coming of the Son of Man (v. 48a). Unbelievers with a great knowledge of God's revelation will have to answer for their lack of response to that revelation.

e. Jesus' teaching about being
misunderstood (12:49-53)
(Matt. 10:34-36)

12:49-53. To be Jesus' disciple might mean being misunderstood even by one's own **family.** Ultimately His ministry would bring not **peace . . . but division** because some would accept what He was saying and others would reject it. His ministry would be like a **fire** which devours (v. 49). Jesus longed for the purpose of His ministry to be accomplished. His life and death would be the basis for His judging Israel. That judgment, like fire, would purify the nation. The **baptism** He spoke of no doubt referred to His death which He said would be **completed** (v. 50). Jesus' mission actually did result in the kind of family divisions of which He spoke here (vv. 52-53). Families have been **divided** and loyalties broken. Jewish believers are still ostracized from their families and friends. However, to be a disciple one must be willing to undergo such problems.

2. JESUS' TEACHING OF THE MULTITUDES (12:54–13:21)

After Jesus spoke directly to His disciples, He turned His attention to the multitudes. In this section six events occurred in which the crowds played a major part. They were now the focal point in Jesus' ministry.

a. Jesus' teaching about signs (12:54-56)
(Matt. 16:2-3)

12:54-56. Jesus taught the crowds that they needed to be sensitive **to interpret** the things they were seeing. Though they had been observing His ministry they were not able to ascertain that He was truly the Messiah. He made the point that they, with no trouble, could **interpret** natural signs (western clouds and **south** winds—**the appearance of the earth and the sky**). But they could not discern spiritual signs. They should discern what was going on right in their midst—He was offering the kingdom and they were not responding properly to His offer.

b. Jesus' illustration of the law court
(12:57-59)

12:57-59. Jesus used an illustration of a law court to drive home the point that people need to be rightly related to God. Even in the earthly sphere it makes sense to **try hard to be reconciled** with an

239

opponent—even **on the way . . . to the magistrate**—in order to avoid being thrown **into prison** and having to pay **the last penny.** How much more important it is to "be reconciled" when the opponent is God! (The word for "penny" is *leptos,* used only here and in Mark 12:42; Luke 21:2. It was a Jewish copper coin worth about ⅛ of a cent.)

c. Jesus' teaching on perishing (13:1-5)

13:1-5. Jesus taught the crowds that calamity can happen to anyone because all are human. **Jesus** cited two common instances about destruction. The first concerned some **Galileans** who were killed by **Pilate** while they were offering **sacrifices.** The second concerned **18** seemingly innocent bystanders **in Siloam** who were killed when a **tower . . . fell on them.** Jesus' point was that being killed or not being killed is no measure of a person's unrighteousness or righteousness. Anyone can be killed. Only God's grace causes any to live. This point is brought out in verses 3 and 5—**unless you repent, you too will all perish.** Death is the common denominator for everyone. Only repentance can bring life as people prepare to enter the kingdom.

d. Jesus' parable of the fig tree (13:6-9)

13:6-9. To illustrate His point Jesus taught in a **parable** that if **fruit** does not show in one's life, judgment will come. A **fig tree** requires **three years** to bear figs, but since this one did not produce, the owner said, **Cut it down.** His **vineyard** keeper asked him to give it **one more year.** This parable illustrates the point made in verses 1-5 that judgment comes on those who do not repent. Here Jesus took the thought one step further and noted that **fruit** must be present (cf. Matt. 3:7-10; 7:15-21; Luke 8:15). A visible change must be seen in the life of one who claims to trust the Messiah. If there is no visible change that person, like the figless fig tree, is judged.

e. Jesus' healing of a woman (13:10-17)

Jesus illustrated His teaching by healing a woman on a Sabbath. This episode is the last time in the Gospel of Luke Jesus taught in a synagogue. The term "hypocrites" is extremely important in the narrative. Toward the beginning of this section (12:54–13:21) Jesus had called the crowds and the leaders of the people "hypocrites" (12:56). Here at the end of the section He again called them "hypocrites" (13:15). Jesus' point was that the crowds and the leaders were not really interested in what God could and would do in their lives.

13:10-13. Luke described the **woman** as one **who had been crippled by a spirit for 18 years** and "bound" by "Satan" (v. 16). Without denying the historicity of the event, it must be pointed out that there is obvious symbolic value in Luke's placing this miracle at this point in the narrative. It was Jesus' mission among the people of the nation to loose them from crippling influences and bring them to uprightness. Here was a graphic example of Jesus' touch, bringing the woman to a position of uprightness. Jesus healed **her** by His words (**Woman, you are set free from your infirmity**) and by touching **her. Immediately she straightened up and praised God.** This act of praising God was the proper response to the work of Jesus (cf. 2:20; 5:25-26; 7:16; 17:15; 18:43; 23:47). It showed that people were understanding His mission.

13:14. In contrast to the proper response which the woman evidenced, **the synagogue ruler** was **indignant because Jesus had** not followed the Law as that ruler interpreted it. He appealed to the crowd to reject Jesus' miracle. This attitude supports what Jesus had already said about religious leaders keeping others from entering the kingdom (11:52).

13:15-17. Jesus pointed out that a person is much more important than an animal, and His enemies saw nothing wrong in helping their animals **on the Sabbath** (cf. 14:5). The total hypocrisy and foolishness of the thinking of the religious leaders was obvious. As a result Jesus' **opponents were humiliated but the** crowds **were delighted.**

f. Jesus' teaching about the kingdom of God (13:18-21)
(Matt. 13:31-33; Mark 4:30-32)

13:18-21. This passage is actually a hinge between Jesus' teaching of the multitudes (12:54–13:21) and His teaching about the people of **the kingdom** (13:22–17:10). Some feel that in these brief parables about the **Mustard Seed** (a mustard tree, from a tiny seed, grows as tall as 12-15 feet in one season!) and the

Yeast Jesus was teaching something positive about the kingdom. It seems better, however, to understand these parables as teaching something undesirable. Like pervading yeast, evil will enter the Age and become all-pervasive. This seems to be true since Luke placed this teaching immediately after the synagogue leader's rejection of Jesus' work on the Sabbath.

3. JESUS' TEACHING ABOUT THE PEOPLE OF THE KINGDOM (13:22–17:10)

In this section Luke recorded Jesus' teachings concerning who is and who is not a member of the kingdom. Throughout this section the theme of entering into the kingdom is often symbolized as taking part in a feast or banquet (13:29; 14:7-24; 15:23; 17:7-10). The kingdom was yet to come. Those who enter are those who respond positively to God by accepting the Messiah and His kingdom message.

a. Jesus' teaching that most of Israel will be excluded from the kingdom (13:22-35)

13:22-30. Jesus taught that many from Israel will not be in **the kingdom** whereas many from outside Israel will be. **Someone asked** Jesus if **only a few people** were **going to be saved.** Apparently His followers were somewhat discouraged that His message of the kingdom was not sweeping the nation as they thought it would. They saw that Jesus continually met opposition as well as acceptance. Jesus' teaching was clear—a person must accept what He was saying in order to enter the kingdom. To a Jewish mind salvation was related to the kingdom, that is, a person was saved in order to enter into God's kingdom.

Jesus responded to the person's question with a story of a man who was giving a **feast** (symbolic of the kingdom, v. 29). After he closed **the door** to the banquet, no one else could come in for they were too late (v. 25). In fact, the host of the feast actually called them **evildoers** (v. 27). The latecomers responded that they had eaten and drunk with the host and that he had **taught in** their **streets** (v. 26), an obvious reference to Jesus' ministry among the people of that generation. Jesus' point in telling the story was that the people had to respond to His

invitation at that time, for a time would come when it would be too late and they would not be allowed in the kingdom.

Jesus spoke directly, telling the crowds that judgment would come on those who refused His message: **There will be weeping . . . and gnashing of teeth** and they will be **thrown out,** that is, not allowed to enter the kingdom. (On "weeping and gnashing of teeth" see comments on Matt. 13:42.) But godly ones in the nation (represented by **Abraham, Isaac, and Jacob, and all the prophets**) will be in **the kingdom of God.**

These remarks were revolutionary to Jesus' hearers. Most of them assumed that because they were physically related to Abraham they would naturally enter into the promised kingdom. However, His next words were even more revolutionary—in fact devastating—to those who assumed that *only* the Jewish nation would be involved in the kingdom. Jesus explained that Gentiles would be added to the kingdom in place of Jewish people (Luke 13:29-30). **People** coming from the four corners of the world represent various population groups. Those listening to Jesus' words should not have been surprised by this teaching because the prophets had often said the same thing. However, Jews in Jesus' day believed that Gentiles were inferior to them. When Jesus had begun His ministry in Nazareth, His teaching of Gentile inclusion had so maddened the crowd that they tried to kill Him (4:13-30). The Jewish people considered themselves to be **first** in every way, but they would be **last,** that is, they would be left out of the kingdom. In contrast, some Gentiles, considered **last,** would be in the kingdom and would really be **first** in importance (13:30).

13:31-35 (Matt. 23:37-39). In response to a warning from **some Pharisees . . . Jesus** said that He had to reach **Jerusalem** because He was appointed to **die** there. There is debate concerning the Pharisees' report about **Herod** wanting **to kill** Jesus. Throughout Luke, the Pharisees are presented in a negative light. Why would the Pharisees have wanted to protect Jesus in this instance? It seems best to understand the incident as the Pharisees' pretext to get rid of Jesus. Jesus had publicly stated that His **goal** was to reach Jerusalem, and He was well on His way. Thus the Pharisees were apparently trying to deter Him from His task, to scare Him into setting aside His goal.

Jesus' response, **Go tell that fox,** indicates that He saw the Pharisees as Herod's messengers who would report back to him. Jesus stated that He had a mission to perform (Luke 13:32). This Herod was Herod Antipas (see the chart on the Herods at 1:5).

When Jesus said, **Today and tomorrow and the next day,** He was not saying that He would arrive in Jerusalem in three days. The point was that He had a mission in mind and that He would continue on the schedule He had set for Himself. The goal was Jerusalem where He would die. He must present Himself publicly to the religious authorities and then be put to death.

It was at this point that Luke recorded the rejection of **Jerusalem** (representing the nation) by Jesus (13:34-35). Jesus lamented for the city and **longed to** protect it **as a hen gathers her chicks under her wings,** that is, tenderly and lovingly, even though the people **were not willing.** His entire ministry up to this point had been to offer the kingdom to the nation. But since the nation, which had even killed **the prophets,** had rejected His words, He would now reject them. Jesus stated, **Your house is left to you desolate** (*aphietai,* "abandoned"). "House" probably refers not to the temple, but to the whole city. Though He would continue to offer Himself as the Messiah, the die was now cast. The city was abandoned by the Messiah.

Jesus noted (quoting Ps. 118:26) that the people of the city would **not see** Him **again** till they said that He was the Messiah. The crowd did quote this verse when Jesus entered the city in His Triumphal Entry (Luke 19:38), but their religious leaders disapproved. Ultimately this truth will be proclaimed when Jesus **comes** again and enters the city as the millennial Ruler.

b. *Jesus' teaching that many outcasts and Gentiles will be in the kingdom (14:1-24)*

This section continues the thought of 13:22-35 but explains it from another angle. Rather than the excluded ones being the main subject, the ones included in the kingdom are now discussed. Contrary to His hearers' expectations, Jewish outcasts and Gentiles will make up a large portion of the kingdom's population.

14:1-6. **Jesus** had been invited **to eat** on the **Sabbath** at **the house of a prominent Pharisee** where there **was** also **a man** who was **suffering from dropsy.** Dropsy is a condition of excess fluid in the tissues of the body, caused perhaps by a type of cancer or possibly liver or kidney problems. The man was probably invited to the Pharisee's house in order to see what Jesus would do. **Jesus** immediately took the initiative in the situation and asked the host and other guests whether it would be **lawful to heal** the man **on the Sabbath.** Apparently Jesus' question disarmed the crowd, for all of them **remained silent.** Jesus went ahead and **healed** the man. He said the guests would help **a son or an ox** in distress **on the Sabbath,** so it was totally appropriate to heal this poor individual. Jesus was setting the stage for the discussion to follow concerning those who were considered ceremonially unclean and therefore unable to enter the kingdom.

14:7-11. Looking around, Jesus **noticed how the guests picked the places of honor.** The closer a person was to the host, the greater was that guest's position of honor. As people entered the room in the Pharisee's house where the table was spread, they must have scrambled for seats at the head of the table. The parable Jesus then told was designed to get them to think about spiritual realities in relation to the kingdom message He had been preaching.

Verse 11 records the point of Jesus' parable: **Everyone who exalts himself will be humbled, and he who humbles himself will be exalted.** This recalls Jesus' earlier statement that those who are last will be first and those who are first will be last (13:30). The Pharisees, assuming they would have important positions in the kingdom, would be **humiliated** if they were pushed aside for someone else (14:9). However, if they would humble themselves, then they would perhaps be honored (v. 10).

14:12-14. Then **Jesus** spoke **to His host,** telling him that if he would **invite** the outcasts of society (**the poor, the crippled, the lame, the blind**)—people who could never **repay** him for his generosity—this would show that he was ministering to them for the Lord's sake and not his own (cf. Matt. 6:1-18; James 1:26-27). He would be laying up for himself treasures in heaven (Matt. 6:20) and would be becoming rich toward God (Luke 12:21). Inviting the outcasts would not make the man righteous; it would testify that he was in a righteous standing before God. This is shown by Jesus' statement that the repayment would not come at the present time but **at the resurrection of the righteous.**

14:15-24 (Matt. 22:1-10). Jesus then told a parable about **a great banquet.** One of the diners expressed a blessing on everyone who would **eat . . . in the kingdom.** This person was assuming that he and the other people present would all be present in the kingdom. **Jesus** took the opportunity to use the feast motif to explain that many of the people there would *not* be present in God's kingdom. In their places would be many outcasts and Gentiles. The host in the parable **invited many guests.** However **all** those invited **began to give excuses** for not going. The excuses were supposedly valid—the need to **see** about a recently purchased **field,** or to **try** out recently purchased **oxen,** or to be with one's recently **married** bride (Luke 14:18-20).

The host **became angry** and commanded that people in **the streets and alleys of the town . . . the poor, the crippled, the blind, and the lame**—be invited. Jesus was referring to those members of the Jewish community who were considered inferior and ceremonially unclean as was the man with dropsy He had just healed (vv. 2-4).

When the host learned that there was **still room** for more, he commanded that others be invited from **the roads and country lanes** (v. 23). These people outside the city were probably Gentiles, those outside the covenant community. The host then stated that none of the originally invited guests would **get a taste of** his **banquet.**

This parable at a banquet about another banquet reinforced His previous teaching that He would abandon Jerusalem (13:34-35). The people who originally had been offered a share of the kingdom had rejected it, so now the message was going out to others including Gentiles. The excuses seemed good to those who

gave them, but they were inadequate for refusing Jesus' kingdom offer. Nothing was so important as accepting His offer of the kingdom, for one's entire destiny rests on his response to that offer.

c. Jesus' warning against thoughtless discipleship (14:25-35)

14:25-27. The setting then changed: **large crowds were traveling with Jesus.** Jesus intended to impress on the people their need to examine their resolve to follow Him. He was on His way to die on the cross. Ultimately everyone did desert Him when He was alone in the garden and then arrested and put on trial.

To emphasize that discipleship is difficult, Jesus said that one must **hate his** own family and **even his own life** in order to **be** His disciple. Literally hating one's family would have been a violation of the Law. Since Jesus on several occasions admonished others to fulfill the Law, He must not have meant here that one should literally hate his family. The stress here is on the priority of love (cf. Matt. 10:37). One's loyalty to Jesus must come before his loyalty to his family or even to life itself. Indeed, those who did follow Jesus against their families' desires were probably thought of as hating their families.

The second difficult qualification Jesus stressed was that one must **carry his** (i.e., his own) **cross and follow** Jesus (Luke 14:27; cf. 9:23). When the Roman Empire crucified a criminal or captive, the victim was often forced to carry his cross part of the way to the crucifixion site. Carrying his cross through the heart of the city was supposed to be a tacit admission that the Roman Empire was correct in the sentence of death imposed on him, an admission that Rome was right and he was wrong. So when Jesus enjoined His followers to carry their crosses and follow Him, He was referring to a public display before others that Jesus was right and that the disciples were following Him even to their deaths. This is exactly what the religious leaders refused to do.

14:28-33. Using two illustrations, Jesus then taught that discipleship must include planning and sacrifice. The first illustration concerned **a tower** (vv. 28-30). Before a person begins **to build,** he should be sure he will be able to pay the full **cost** of the project. Jesus' followers must also be sure they are willing to pay the full price of discipleship.

The second illustration concerned **a king** who went out to battle. The king should be willing to sacrifice a desired victory if he senses he is unable to win. This principle of sacrifice is also important in the realm of discipleship: one must be willing to **give up everything** for Jesus. The people who were following Jesus throughout the countryside of Israel had done that. They had given up possessions and employment, knowing that the message Jesus was proclaiming was the most important thing on earth.

14:34-35. Jesus climaxed His teaching on discipleship by proclaiming that **salt is good** only as long as it contains the characteristics of saltiness. If **it loses its saltiness,** it has no value at all and is **thrown out.** The same is true of disciples. They must contain the characteristics of discipleship—planning and willing sacrifice—or they are of no value at all.

d. Jesus' teaching about the hopeless and sinners in the kingdom (chap. 15)

Jesus combated the religious leaders by teaching again that some who were considered to be hopeless and sinners will be in the kingdom. Here are perhaps the best known of Jesus' parables—The Lost Sheep, The Lost Coin, and The Prodigal Son. All three parables teach the same message—that God is vitally concerned with the repentance of sinners. But the third story goes beyond the others, applying that truth to the situation in which Jesus found Himself—being accepted by the outcasts of society while being rejected by the religious leaders.

15:1-2. Much to the disgust of the religious leaders, Jesus associated with those who were thought of as hopeless and **"sinners."** The opposition to Jesus was once again, as almost always in Luke, **the Pharisees and the teachers of the Law.** Because of this opposition Jesus told three parables. All three speak of things or a person being lost and then found, and of rejoicing when the lost is found.

Some view these parables as teaching a believer's restoration to fellowship with God. One cannot lose something he does not own, they reason, so the first two parables must represent children of God who come back to Him. Also, a son is already a son, so the third parable must be teaching that people who are believers can be restored to fellowship with God.

Others understand the parables to teach that lost people (i.e., people who are not believers) can come to Christ. This view seems preferable for two reasons: (1) Jesus was speaking to Pharisees who were rejecting the message of the kingdom. Their objection was that sinners were coming to Jesus and believing His message. In no way could these two groups be adequately represented in the third parable if the point of the parable is a restoration to fellowship by a believer. (2) Verse 22 indicates that the son who came back received a new position which he did not have before. The Jews were God's "children" in the sense that they had a special covenant relationship to Him. But each individual still had to become a believer in God. It was their responsibility to accept the message Jesus was preaching—that He was the Messiah and that He would bring in the kingdom for the nation.

15:3-7. The Parable of the Lost Sheep teaches that **there is . . . rejoicing in heaven** when a **sinner . . . repents.** Jesus was not saying **the** other **99** sheep were not important. Instead, He was emphasizing that the one **sheep** not in the fold corresponded with the sinners with whom Jesus was eating (vv. 1-2). The **99 righteous persons** refer to the Pharisees who *thought* themselves righteous and therefore in no **need to repent.**

15:8-10. The Parable of the Lost Coin teaches that **there is rejoicing in the presence of the angels** when a **sinner . . . repents.** This is the same message as the first but it emphasizes the thoroughness of the search. The woman continued to **sweep the house and search carefully until she** found the **coin** which was a thing of great value. A *drachma,* a Greek silver coin referred to only here in the New Testament, equaled about a day's wages. The point would have been clear to Jesus' listeners: the sinners with whom He was associating were extremely valuable to God. (Cf. similar wording in vv. 6, 9.)

Jesus then told the Parable of the Lost Son and His Older Brother to explain that God is inviting *all* people to enter the kingdom.

15:11. A man . . . had two sons; the

contrast between his sons is the point of the parable.

15:12-20a. This section of the parable describes the actions of **the younger** son. He requested an unusual thing when he asked **his father** to **give** him his **share of the estate.** Normally an estate was not divided and given to the heirs until the father could no longer manage it well. This father acquiesced to his son's demand and gave him his share of the inheritance. **The younger son** took that wealth, went far away, and **squandered it in wild living,** involving himself presumably, as his older brother said, with prostitutes (v. 30). The hearers immediately would have begun to understand the point of the story. Jesus had been criticized for associating with sinners. The sinners were considered people who were far away from God, squandering their lives in riotous living. In contrast with the younger son, the older son continued to remain with the father and did not engage in such practices.

A **famine** occurred and the second son ran out of money so that he had to work for a foreigner feeding **pigs,** something detestable to a Jew. Perhaps the far **country** was east of the Sea of Galilee where Gentiles tended **pigs** (cf. 8:26-37). In his hunger he **longed** for the **pods**—the food he fed **the pigs.** As a Jew, he could have stooped no lower. The pods were probably carob pods, from tall evergreen carob trees.

In this low condition, **he came to his senses** (15:17). He decided to **go back to** his **father** and work for him. Surely he would be better off to work for his **father** than for a foreigner. He fully expected to be **hired** by **his father** as a servant, not to be taken back as his son.

15:20b-24. The third section of the parable describes the father's response. He had been waiting for his son to return, for **while he was still a long way off** the **father saw him.** The father, full of **compassion for** his son, **ran to** him, and hugged **and kissed him.** The father would not even listen to all of the young son's rehearsed speech. Instead **the father** had **his servants** prepare a banquet to **celebrate** the son's return. He gave the son a new position with a **robe . . . a ring . . . and sandals.** Jesus intentionally used the banquet motif again. He had previously spoken of a banquet to symbolize the

coming kingdom (13:29; cf. 14:15-24). Jesus' hearers would have easily realized the significance of this feast. Sinners (whom the young son symbolized) were entering into the kingdom because they were coming to God. They believed they needed to return to Him and be forgiven by Him.

15:25-32. The parable's final section describes the attitude of the older brother, who symbolized the Pharisees and the teachers of the Law. They had the same attitude toward the sinners as **the older son** had toward the younger son. **The older brother,** coming home from working **in the field** and hearing what was happening, got **angry.** Similarly the Pharisees and teachers of the Law were angry with the message Jesus was proclaiming. They did not like the idea that people from outside their nation as well as outcasts and sinners in the nation were to be a part of the kingdom. Like the older son who **refused to go** to the feast, the Pharisees refused to enter the kingdom Jesus offered to the nation.

Interestingly the **father went out and pleaded with** the older brother to go to the feast. Likewise, Jesus ate with Pharisees as well as sinners. He did not desire to exclude the Pharisees and teachers of the Law from the kingdom. The message was an invitation to everyone.

The older brother was angry because he had **never** been honored with a feast even though, as he said, **All these years I've been slaving for you and never disobeyed your orders** (v. 29). Those words betrayed the fact that the older brother thought he had a relationship with his father because of his work. He served his father not out of love but out of a desire for reward. He even thought of himself as being in bondage to his father.

The father pointed out that the older son had had the joy of being in the house all the time, and now he should rejoice with the father in his brother's return. The words, **You are always with me and everything I have is yours,** suggest the religious leaders' privileged position as members of God's Chosen People. They were the recipients and guardians of the covenants and the Law (Rom. 3:1-2; 9:4). Rather than feeling angry, they should rejoice that others were joining them and would be a part of the kingdom.

e. Jesus' teaching about wealth and the kingdom (chap. 16)

This chapter includes two parables about wealth. The first parable (vv. 1-13) was spoken primarily to the disciples (v. 1). The second parable (vv. 19-31) was addressed to the Pharisees because of their response (vv. 14-18) to the first parable.

16:1-8a. Jesus told this Parable of the Unjust Manager to teach that His disciples must use their wealth for kingdom purposes. The application (vv. 8b-13) follows the parable (vv. 1-8a).

In the parable **a rich man . . . called** his **manager** to **give an account of** his dealings. The rich man had heard that the manager was not handling the wealthy owner's finances wisely. In Jesus' day managers were often hired by wealthy people to care for the finances of their estates. Such a manager would be comparable to a modern-day financial planner or trustee who controls the finances of an estate for the purpose of making more money for that estate. The money did not belong to the manager but was his to use for the estate. Apparently the manager was **wasting** those goods as the younger son had wasted his father's goods (15:13).

At the beginning of the parable the rich man viewed his manager as irresponsible rather than dishonest (16:2). The manager was fired. But then, in order to make friends who might later hire him, the ex-manager charged the rich man's two **debtors** less than what they actually owed—**400** instead of **800 gallons of olive oil,** and **800** instead of **1,000 bushels of wheat.** The manager's thinking was reflected in his statement, **When I lose my job here, people will welcome me into their houses** (v. 4).

When the rich man heard what he had done, **he commended the dishonest manager because he had acted shrewdly.** The dishonest manager had not done a good thing. But he *had* been careful to plan ahead, using material things to insure a secure future. Jesus was not teaching that His disciples should be dishonest. He was teaching that they should use material things for future spiritual benefit. This was a good lesson from a bad example.

16:8b-13. In three ways Jesus applied the parable to His disciples who had to live with nonbelievers in the world. First, one should use money to win people into the kingdom (vv. 8b-9). Jesus said, **The people of this world are more shrewd in dealing with their own kind than are the people of the light.** Here Jesus set His disciples apart from the dishonest manager. The dishonest manager was a person of "this world," seeking a way to make his life more comfortable. The disciples, "the people of the light" (cf. 11:33-36; Eph. 5:8), should act in a shrewd (wise, not dishonest) manner. Jesus plainly taught that the people of light should **use worldly wealth** (Luke 16:9). Jesus also used the word "wealth" (*mamōna*) later (v. 13) when He affirmed that one "cannot serve both God and money." In verse 9 Jesus was saying that one is to use wealth, not store it up or be a servant of it. Wealth should be a disciple's servant, not vice versa. The disciples were to use wealth **to gain friends,** the same reason the dishonest manager used the rich man's wealth. The disciples would then **be welcomed into eternal dwellings.** The disciples' wise use of wealth would help lead others to believe the message of the kingdom and bring them to accept that message.

Jesus' second application is in verses 10-12. If one is faithful in his use of money, then he **can be trusted** with greater things. **True riches** (v. 11) seem to refer to the kingdom's spiritual riches of which the disciples will partake.

The third application Jesus drew from the parable was that a person **cannot serve both God and money** (v 13). As masters the two are mutually exclusive. Love for money will drive one away from God (1 Tim. 6:10); conversely, loving God will cause one not to make money his primary concern in life.

16:14-18. The Pharisees, who loved money, reacted negatively to Jesus' teaching about it. They **were sneering at Jesus** because they saw Him as a poor man being followed by other poor men and yet having the nerve to teach about money. Jesus responded that **God knows** the **hearts** of people and is not impressed with their outward appearances or their wealth. Though the Pharisees justified themselves (v. 15; cf. 15:7) **God,** who judges the inward man, will be the ultimate Judge. The Pharisees misunderstood the blessings of God's covenant.

They apparently assumed that a person's wealth was God's blessing in return for his righteous conduct. They completely neglected the fact that many righteous people in the Old Testament lacked material things, while many unrighteous people had plenty.

Luke 16:16-18 is included with Jesus' teaching about money to the Pharisees because it illustrates what Jesus had just said about the Pharisees justifying themselves but really being judged by God. Jesus stated that since the time of **John** the Baptist, He had been announcing God's **kingdom.** People, including the Pharisees (cf. 14:15 and comments on Matt. 11:12), were attempting to force their **way into it.**

However, in spite of justifying themselves, the Pharisees were still not living according to **the Law.** Jesus spoke of divorce as an example. To divorce and remarry constituted **adultery.** (Jesus gave one exception to this. See comments on Matt. 5:32; 19:1-12.) Some Pharisees took a loose view of divorce. It was acknowledged that a **man** should not commit adultery. But if a man wanted another **woman,** many of the Pharisees condoned divorcing his present wife for no good reason and marrying the desired woman. In this way they thought **adultery** did not take place. However, as Jesus pointed out, this was a perfect example of justifying themselves in the eyes of men but not being justified before God (Luke 16:15). The religious leaders were not actually living according to the Law. Jesus pointed out the importance **of the Law** (v. 17), which showed that the people should live by it.

16:19-21. Jesus then told the Parable of the Rich Man and Lazarus to show that being rich should not be equated with being righteous. The **rich man** had everything he wanted. **Purple** referred to clothes dyed that color, **and fine linen** was worn for underclothes; both were expensive.

A poor man, **a** crippled **beggar named Lazarus,** had nothing. One **lived in luxury** for himself, the other in abject poverty with hunger and poor health (**sores**). Perhaps Jesus picked the name Lazarus because it is the Greek form of the Hebrew name which means "God, the Helper." Lazarus was righteous not

because he was poor but because he depended on God.

16:22-23. In the course of **time** both men **died.** Lazarus went **to Abraham's side** while **the rich man . . . was buried** and was **in hell,** a place of conscious torment (vv. 24, 28). *Hadēs,* the Greek word often translated "hell," is used 11 times in the New Testament. The Septuagint used *hadēs* to translate the Hebrew *šᵉʾôl* (the place of the dead) on 61 occasions. Here *hadēs* refers to the abode of the unsaved dead prior to the great white throne judgment (Rev. 20:11-15). "Abraham's side" apparently refers to a place of paradise for Old Testament believers at the time of death (cf. Luke 23:43; 2 Cor. 12:4).

16:24-31. The rich man was able to converse with **Abraham.** He first begged to have **Lazarus** sent over to give him some **water. Abraham replied** that that was not possible and that he should **remember that** during life he had everything he wanted **while Lazarus** had had nothing. Even so, the rich man had never helped Lazarus during the course of his life. Furthermore, **a great chasm** separated paradise and hades so that no one could **cross** from one to the other. The rich man next begged that **Lazarus** be sent to earth to **warn** his **brothers.** It was his contention that if one came back **from the dead** then his brothers would **listen** (v. 30). **Abraham** replied that if they refused to **listen to** the Scriptures (**Moses and the Prophets** represent all the OT; cf. v. 16), then they would refuse to listen to one who came back **from the dead.**

Jesus was obviously suggesting that the rich man symbolized the Pharisees. They wanted signs—signs so clear that they would compel people to believe. But since they refused to believe the Scriptures, they would not believe any sign no matter how great. Just a short time later Jesus did raise a man from the dead, another man named Lazarus (John 11:38-44). The result was that the religious leaders began to plot more earnestly to kill both Jesus and Lazarus (John 11:45-53; 12:10-11).

f. Jesus' teaching about obligations toward men and God (17:1-10)

17:1-4. Jesus taught about the obligations **His disciples** had toward other people (vv. 1-4) and God (vv. 6-10). Followers of Jesus are not to **cause people to sin.** In this life sin cannot be eradicated—such things **are bound to come.** But a disciple would be better off drowned by **a millstone** (a heavy stone for grinding grain) **tied around his neck, than** to bring spiritual harm (*skandalisē*, "to cause to sin") to **these little ones** (people who, like little children, are helpless before God; cf. 10:21; Mark 10:24). Presumably the sinning referred to is lack of faith in the Messiah. Jesus had already noted that the Pharisees were not only refusing to enter the kingdom but were also keeping others from entering (Luke 11:52).

Not only are Jesus' followers not to cause others to sin; they also are to counteract sin by forgiving others (17:3-4). One should **rebuke** a **brother** if he **sins. If he repents,** he is to be forgiven even if he **sins** and repents over and over. The words **seven times in a day** denote a completeness—as often as it happens.

17:5-10. Jesus also taught that His followers have responsibilities toward God. The first responsibility is to **have faith.** When the disciples asked Jesus for more **faith,** He answered that they needed not more faith but the right kind of faith. Even the smallest amount of faith (like **a mustard seed,** the smallest seed; cf. 13:19) could do amazingly miraculous things, such as uprooting a **mulberry tree,** a tree with deep roots (17:6).

The disciples' second responsibility toward God was humble service (vv. 7-10). They should not expect special praise for doing things they were expected to do. **A servant** does not get special praise from his master for doing his job. Likewise disciples have certain responsibilities which they are to fulfill in humility as God's **unworthy** (*achreioi*, "good for nothing," used elsewhere only in Matt. 25:30) **servants.**

4. JESUS' TEACHING ABOUT THE KINGDOM AND THE ATTITUDES OF HIS DISCIPLES (17:11–19:27)

In this section Luke brought together a series of events in the life of Jesus on His way to Jerusalem. The events teach the kind of attitude disciples should have in view of the coming kingdom.

a. *A leper returned (17:11-19)*

17:11-14. Jesus was **on His way to Jerusalem . . . along the border between Samaria and Galilee.** When asked for help by **10** lepers, He healed them from a **distance.** This was the second time in the Book of Luke that lepers were healed (cf. 5:12-16). As in the former case, Jesus instructed the men to **show** themselves to **the priests.** On their way **they were cleansed** from the disease and were made ceremonially clean.

17:15-19. Only **one of** the men—a **foreigner,** that is, **a Samaritan**—came back to thank Jesus. This one understood the significance of what had been done for him. He was **praising God** and **he threw himself at Jesus' feet,** a posture of worship. He apparently understood that Jesus is God, for he placed **faith** in Him. Whether or not he understood that Jesus is the Messiah is not mentioned by Luke. The lack of gratitude by **the other nine** was typical of the rejection of His ministry by the Jewish nation. He alone had the power to cleanse the nation and make it ceremonially clean. However, the nation did not respond properly to Him. The nation accepted the things that Jesus could do (such as heal them and feed them), but it did not want to accept Him as Messiah. However, those outside the nation (such as this Samaritan leper—a person doubly repulsive to the Jews) were responding.

b. *Jesus's teaching about the presence of the kingdom (17:20-37) (Matt. 24:23-28, 37-41)*

17:20-21. Jesus was **asked by the Pharisees when the kingdom of God would come.** This was a logical question to ask, for He had been preaching for quite some time that the kingdom was at hand. **Jesus** responded to the question in two ways. First, He said that the Pharisees would not be able to tell of the coming of **the kingdom** through their observations. Second, he told them that the **kingdom** was in their midst. The term **within you** is often misunderstood. The Pharisees were rejecting Him as the Messiah and were not believers. (They were distinct from the disciples Jesus addressed beginning in v. 22.) Thus it would not make sense for Jesus to have told the Pharisees that the kingdom of God was within them as if it were some sort of spiritual kingdom. It is better to translate the phrase "within you" (*entos hymōn*) as "in your midst." Some feel that the force of the expression is "within your possession or within your reach." Jesus' point was that He was standing right in their midst. All they needed to do was acknowledge that He is indeed the Messiah who could bring in the kingdom—and then the kingdom would come.

17:22-25. Jesus then gave **His disciples** several facts about the kingdom. First, He said that a **time** would come when the disciples would **long to see** Him return, but they would not see it (v. 22). Second, He said that when the kingdom would come everyone would know it (vv. 23-24). It will not be a hidden (i.e., only an inner, spiritual) kingdom. It will be a kingdom that the whole world will know. His appearing **will be like the lightning** (cf. Matt. 24:27, 30). Third, Jesus told the disciples **He must suffer** before the kingdom comes (Luke 17:25).

17:26-27. Next Jesus compared the coming of the kingdom to the coming of the flood in Noah's day and to the coming of judgment on Sodom (v. 29). By bringing up these two events, Jesus was stressing the judgmental aspect of the kingdom. When He will establish His kingdom, people will be judged to see if they will be allowed to enter it. In this section (17:26-35) Jesus was not speaking about the Rapture but about the judgment before entering the kingdom.

Jesus reminded His disciples that people in Noah's day were not prepared for **the Flood,** and therefore they were completely **destroyed** (Gen. 6). The same problem will exist when the kingdom comes—people will not be ready.

17:28-33. In **the same** way the materialistic, indifferent **people** of **Sodom** (**eating and drinking, buying and selling, planting and building**) were not prepared for God's judgment (Gen. 19). They were living in sin, oblivious to God. Therefore they were **destroyed.** Jesus reminded His followers that people should not be attached to their material things at the time of the coming of the kingdom for they, like **Lot's wife,** will be judged accordingly. People who are working or relaxing on their roofs (many of which are flat in Palestine) should not try to get things out of their houses. Nor

should those working in the fields go to their houses to save their possessions. Any delay could be fatal. Thus **whoever tries to keep his life** (Luke 17:33) by going back for his goods (v. 31) **will lose it.**

17:34-36. Jesus stated that some will be **taken** into judgment. In some parts of the world it will be nighttime (**people will be in . . . bed**); in other parts it will be daytime (people will be doing daily tasks, such as **grinding grain**). The taking away means **taken** into judgment, not taken up in the Rapture. The ones left are those who will enter into the kingdom. (Some mss. add the words of v. 36, "Two men will be in the field; one will be taken and the other left." Most likely the verse was inserted to harmonize this passage with Matt. 24:40.)

17:37. The disciples questioned **where** these people would be taken. Jesus' cryptic answer, **Where there is a dead body, there the vultures will gather**—has been interpreted variously. It seems best to understand that Jesus was reaffirming that these people would be taken into judgment. Much as a dead body causes vultures to "gather" on it, so dead people are consigned to judgment if they are not ready for the kingdom (cf. Matt. 24:28; Rev. 19:17-19).

c. Jesus' teaching about prayer (18:1-14)

These verses include two of Jesus' parables about prayer. One was addressed to the disciples (vv. 1-8), and the other (vv. 9-14) to "some who were confident of their own righteousness."

18:1-8. **Jesus told** the **Parable** of the Unjust Judge to teach persistence in prayer: **that they,** His disciples, **should always pray and not give up.** Verses 2-5 contain the parable itself. **A widow** continued to go before an unjust **judge** to plead for **justice** in her case. **He** continually **refused** to "hear" her case, **but finally he** decided to give her **justice so that she** would not **wear** him **out with her** complaining. Jesus interpreted the parable (vv. 6-8), pointing out that if **the unjust judge** would give **justice,** then imagine how **God** (the just Judge) **will see that they get justice, and quickly.** Jesus' question, **When the Son of Man comes, will He find faith on the earth?** was not spoken out of ignorance. Nor was He questioning whether all believers would be gone when He returns. Instead, He asked the question to spur the disciples on to faithfulness in prayer, to encourage them to keep on in their praying. This is another good lesson from a bad example (cf. 16:1-13).

18:9-14. The purposes of the **Parable** of the Prayers of the **Pharisee** and the **Tax Collector** were to show that one cannot trust in himself for **righteousness** and should not view others with contempt (v. 9). The Pharisee's prayer was concerned with telling **God** what a good man he was, for not only did he keep the Law by fasting and tithing (v. 12), but also he considered himself better than other people (v. 11). He was using other people as his standard for measuring righteousness.

On the other hand **the tax collector** used **God** as his standard for measuring righteousness. He realized that he had to throw himself on the **mercy** of **God** for forgiveness.

Jesus' application of the parable echoed His teaching in 13:30. It is necessary for people to humble themselves before God to gain forgiveness, and those who are proud (**everyone who exalts himself**) will be brought low (**humbled**) by God.

d. Jesus' teaching about childlikeness (18:15-17)
(Matt. 19:13-15; Mark 10:13-16)

18:15-17. Luke placed this short section here to follow up on the message of the previous parable. **Jesus** had taught that it was necessary to be humble before God. In these verses He compared that humility to childlikeness: **Let the little children come to Me, and do not hinder them, for the kingdom of God belongs to such as these.** In these words Jesus was stating that a person must come to Him in humility in order to enter **the kingdom. Children** come with expectation and excitement. They come realizing that they are not sufficient in themselves. They depend totally on others. If these same attitudes are not present in adults, they can **never enter** into the kingdom.

e. Jesus' teaching that wealth is a hindrance to the important issues of life (18:18-30)
(Matt. 19:16-30; Mark 10:17-31)

18:18-20. A **certain ruler** (who was

very wealthy, v. 23) came to **Jesus** to talk about how **to inherit eternal life.** This man was perhaps a member of the Sanhedrin or perhaps an official in a local synagogue. "To inherit eternal life" meant to enter the kingdom of God (cf. John 3:3-5). The man wanted to know what actions (**what must I do**) would make him right with God.

The man had called Jesus **Good Teacher.** Jesus responded that **God alone** is **good,** that is, only God is truly righteous. Apparently the man thought Jesus had gained a measure of status with God by His good works. Jesus was implying that if He were truly good, then it would be because He is God. This, then, is another of Jesus' claims of deity.

Jesus responded to the man's question by instructing him to keep the seventh, sixth, eighth, ninth, and fifth commandments (Ex. 20:12-16), each of which pertain to man's relationship to man. (The first four of the Ten Commandments pertain to man's relationship with God.)

18:21-22. The ruler's reply that **he had kept** all these since childhood was probably correct. He may have been a model citizen.

Jesus then told the man **one** other **thing** he needed to do: he needed to **follow** Jesus, and in order to do that he had to **give** the money from his possessions **to the poor.** This action would touch on the 10th commandment against coveting, which included the idea of greed and holding onto things which are one's own as well as wanting things that belong to others. It was at this point that the man faltered.

Jesus' reasoning was clear: (a) one must keep the Law perfectly in order to inherit eternal life (cf. James 2:10). (b) Only God was good—truly righteous. (c) Therefore nobody can obtain eternal life by following the Law (cf. Rom. 3:20; Gal. 2:21; 3:21). The only course of action left to an individual is to follow Jesus in order to obtain eternal life.

18:23-25. The ruler was not prepared to take that step (but contrast Zacchaeus, 19:8). The ruler was more attached to his wealth than to the idea of obtaining "eternal life" which he had so nobly asked about at the beginning of his conversation with the Lord. **Jesus** responded that riches are a hindrance to one's obtaining eternal life. Riches often cloud a person's thinking about what is truly important in life. Jesus used a common hyperbole of something that is impossible—**a camel** going **through the eye of a needle** (*belonēs*, a sewing needle, not a small door in a city gate). Likewise it is most difficult (but not impossible; cf. Zacchaeus, 19:1-10) for a **rich** person to be saved.

18:26-27. The disciples were dumbfounded. They had the mistaken impression, like the Pharisees, that wealth was a sign of God's blessing. If a person such as the ruler could not be saved, **Who then can be saved?** Jesus, by His reply, did not rule out all wealthy people from salvation. He noted that **God** can do the **impossible.**

18:28-30. In response to the disciples' sacrifice in following Him, expressed by **Peter,** Jesus affirmed that they would be amply rewarded. Though they had **left** their families (cf. 14:26-27), their reward would consist of **many times as much in this age and** also **eternal life.** Jesus was obviously referring to the community of believers who would share with the disciples during their ministries. Those believers became a closely knit family, all sharing together, so that none had any need (Acts 2:44-47; 4:32-37).

f. Jesus' teaching about His resurrection (18:31-34)
(Matt. 20:17-19; Mark 10:32-34)

18:31-34. Each time Jesus . . . **told** His followers about what would happen to Him in **Jerusalem,** He got more explicit. At this point He laid out the events which would come to pass. He clearly stated the involvement of **Gentiles** in His trial and death. This was important because Luke did not want his readers to think that the Gentiles were guiltless in Jesus' death. The whole world was guilty of the death of the Savior. But **the disciples** could **not** comprehend any of this. They still thought the kingdom would come almost immediately. So **they did not know what He was talking about.**

g. Jesus and a blind man (18:35-43)
(Matt. 20:29-34; Mark 10:46-52)

In this passage and the next (Luke 19:1-10) are two examples of how the nation should have responded to the

Messiah. In each case the person who did respond was an outcast from the mainstream of Judaism.

18:35-38. Near **Jericho a** certain **blind man,** hearing all the commotion around him as **Jesus** was **passing by . . . asked** those around him **what was** going on. When he was **told** it was **Jesus of Nazareth,** he immediately realized that the Messiah was there, for his words, **Jesus, Son of David, have mercy on me!** presupposed that he knew Jesus is the Messiah.

Great symbolic value is here in Luke's account. The man was a beggar **sitting by the** side of the road, waiting for something to happen. He was blind and could do nothing to improve his condition. The Messiah came through his town (as He had walked through many towns). Immediately the blind man recognized Him as the Messiah, the One who could save him from his blindness. Spiritual outcasts, unable to help themselves, far more readily recognized the Messiah and asked for His help than did the Jewish religious leaders.

18:39. Those in front tried to make **him keep quiet.** Similarly the religious leaders tried to keep people from believing on Jesus. **But** the opposition caused the man to be even more adamant in his faith.

18:40-43. In stating his desire **to see,** the man was confident that **Jesus,** the Messiah, had the power to heal him. When Jesus said, **Your faith has healed you,** He was not saying that the man's faith possessed some power. The man had faith in the Messiah, and it was the Messiah's power that had healed him (cf. 7:50; 17:19). In the same way, if the nation had faith in the Messiah, their faith would have healed them of their spiritual blindness. As a result of the man's healing, **he** and **all the people** who **saw** the miracle **praised God.**

h. Jesus and Zacchaeus (19:1-10)

A second person in Jericho came to faith in Jesus. Zacchaeus, like the blind man, was considered outside the normal Jewish system because of his activities for Rome as a tax collector (cf. 5:27; 18:9-14). Zacchaeus responded to Jesus' message in precisely the opposite way the rich ruler had responded (18:18-25). Zacchaeus, also wealthy (19:2), knew he was a sinner.

When Jesus called on him, he responded with a greater enthusiasm than Jesus had asked for. This account is also a commentary on Jesus' words that with God all things are possible (18:25-27), for Zacchaeus was a wealthy person who found salvation.

19:1-4. This incident seems ludicrous. Here was **Zacchaeus,** a **wealthy** and probably influential man, running **ahead** of **the crowd** and climbing **a sycamore-fig tree** (cf. Amos 7:14) to get a chance **to see . . . Jesus.** Luke may have been presenting Zacchaeus' actions as a commentary on Jesus' words that unless people become like little children they cannot enter the kingdom of God (Luke 18:17).

19:5-6. Jesus already knew Zacchaeus' name and all about him. He instructed the tax man to **come down immediately** for Jesus wanted to **stay at** his **house.** This was more than Zacchaeus had hoped for, so he **welcomed Him gladly.** The word "gladly" (*chairōn*) is literally "rejoicing." Luke used this verb (and the noun *chara*) nine times (1:14; 8:13; 10:17; 13:17; 15:5, 9, 32; 19:6, 37) to denote an attitude of joy accompanying faith and salvation.

19:7-10. As usual, many complained (**began to mutter**) because Jesus had **gone to be the guest of a** "**sinner**" (cf. 15:1). But **Zacchaeus stood up and** voluntarily announced that he would **give half of** what he owned **to the poor** and repay fourfold all he had wronged. He publicly wanted the people to know that his time with Jesus had changed his life. Interestingly he parted with much of his wealth, similar to what Jesus had asked the rich ruler to do (18:22).

Jesus' words, **Today salvation has come to this house,** did not imply that the act of giving to the poor had saved Zacchaeus, but that his change in lifestyle evidenced his right relationship before God. Zacchaeus, **a son of Abraham** by birth, had a right to enter the kingdom because of his connection with **Jesus.** That was Jesus' mission—**to seek and to save** those who are **lost** (cf. 15:5, 9, 24).

i. *Jesus' teaching on stewardship of responsibilities (19:11-27)*
(Matt. 25:14-30)

This parable brings to a close the section of Jesus' teaching in response to rejection (Luke 12:1–19:27). It also concludes the subsection of Jesus' teaching about the coming kingdom and the attitudes of His disciples (17:11–19:27). Jesus' disciples should be like the grateful ex-leper (17:11-19), persistent in prayer (18:1-14), childlike (18:15-17), like the former blind man (18:35-43), and like Zacchaeus (19:1-10) as opposed to the rich ruler (18:18-25).

This Parable of the 10 Minas sums up Jesus' teaching to the disciples. Each disciple had duties given to him by Jesus, and each was to carry out his responsibilities. But the parable was addressed not only to disciples. It was also addressed to the nation at large, to show that it too had responsibilities. If the nation did not turn to Jesus, it would be punished.

19:11. Jesus gave this **parable because . . . the people** with Him **thought** He was **going to** reinstitute **the kingdom** immediately. Since they were close to **Jerusalem,** Jesus wanted to dispel any disappointment on the part of His followers.

19:12-14. The **man of noble birth** obviously represented Jesus. Because His followers thought the kingdom was to be set up immediately, Jesus said the nobleman in the parable had to go **to a distant country to have himself appointed king and then to return.** He would have to leave them before the kingdom would be set up. Before leaving, **he called 10 of his servants and gave them 10 minas,** 1 apiece. A mina was about three months' wages, so its value was considerable. They were to invest the **money** while he was gone. Another group of people, **His subjects,** did not **want** him **to be . . . king.** Obviously this group represented the religious leaders in particular and the nation in general.

19:15-26. When the **king . . . returned,** he called **the servants** in **to find out what they had** done with **the money** he had entrusted to them. **The first** two servants had used the money to be productive for the king. One had earned another **10** minas (v. 16), and the second had earned another **5** minas (v. 18). Each of these servants was commended by the king and given a reward commensurate with the amount of money earned (vv. 17, 19).

Another servant had done nothing with the **mina** given to him. His **words** to the king, **You are a hard man; you take out what you did not put in and reap what you did not sow,** were used against him by the **master** (v. 22). If he were right then he should have at least banked the **money**—then the king would have received his money back **with interest.** The implication was that the servant did not really expect the king to come back. He was not at all concerned about the king's return so he did not bother with the king's business. Matthew related that the third servant was thrown out of the kingdom (Matt. 25:30). This indicates that this servant really belonged to the group of people who did not want the king to reign over them (Luke 19:14). His money was taken away and given **to the one who** had done the most for the king.

19:27. In contrast with the two servants who had expected the king's return, the **enemies** of the **king** were put to death in the king's presence. The analogy of this parable was clear to Jesus' hearers. Jesus was going away to receive a kingship. When He returned, He would establish His kingdom. Until that time His followers were to fulfill the responsibilities He gave them. On His return He would reward the faithful commensurate with their service to Him, and His enemies would be judged before Him.

VI. The Ministry of Jesus in Jerusalem (19:28–21:38)

Jesus' goal was to go to Jerusalem to present Himself to the religious leaders as the Messiah. Now he arrived in Jerusalem and ministered there. This section is divided into two parts: (1) Jesus entered Jerusalem and was presented as the Messiah (19:28-44); (2) He entered the temple and taught there for several days (19:45–21:38). Those present would have clearly understood that He was presenting Himself as the Messiah, capable of bringing in the kingdom.

A. Jesus' entry into Jerusalem as Messiah (19:28-44) (Matt. 21:1-11; Mark 11:1-11; John 12:12-19)

Up to this time Jesus had not sought to be openly called Messiah. But now He allowed it and even encouraged it. Everything He did over the course of these days was designed to call attention to the fact that He is the Messiah.

1. THE PREPARATION FOR ENTRY (19:28-34)

19:28-34. Luke noted that it was now time for **Jesus** to go **up to Jerusalem** and He prepared His way for the entry. Jesus had come from Jericho (18:35–19:10) and was a short distance from Jerusalem at **Bethphage and Bethany.** At that point He stopped until the way could be prepared so that when He entered the city people would know He was presenting Himself as the Messiah. His command to **two of His disciples** was to **find a colt** and **bring it here.** Jesus was fulfilling Zechariah 9:9-10, which predicted the Messiah would ride on a donkey (cf. comments on Matt. 21:2, which refers to a donkey *and* a colt). As is evident (Luke 19:38) the crowds would understand the message behind the symbolism. Apparently even the **owners** of **the colt** understood for they allowed the donkey to go with the disciples when they were told, **The Lord needs it.**

2. JESUS' ADVANCE INTO THE CITY (19:35-40)

19:35-40. Jesus advanced **down** the west side of **the Mount of Olives** (v. 37) toward the city and was praised by the crowd as their Messiah. The act of spreading **their cloaks on the road** (v. 36) in front of **Jesus** was a sign of respect. **The whole crowd of disciples** (*mathētōn*) **began joyfully to praise God . . . for all the miracles** (*dynameōn,* "evidences of spiritual power") **they had seen.** These believers quoted (v. 38a) from Psalm 118:26, a messianic psalm of praise. **The Pharisees** understood the meaning of what was going on, for they told **Jesus** to **rebuke** His followers, so they would stop calling him Messiah or King.

Jesus responded that there must be some proclamation that He is the Messiah. If not, even inanimate objects (**stones**) would be called on to testify for Him. All history had pointed toward this single, spectacular event when the Messiah publicly presented Himself to the nation, and God desired that this fact be acknowledged.

3. JESUS' PROPHECY ABOUT JERUSALEM (19:41-44)

19:41-44. Jesus showed compassion on **Jerusalem** but He also foretold that days would come when it would lie in ruins. Jesus rejected Jerusalem because Jerusalem rejected Him. **He wept over** the city because its people did not understand the significance of what was going on that day—that national acceptance of Him on that day **would bring** them **peace.** Because the people **did not recognize the time of God's coming to** them (v. 44), the city would be totally destroyed. Roman soldiers did this starting in A.D. 70.

B. Jesus in the temple (19:45–21:38)

Jesus cleansed the temple, disputed there with the religious leaders (20:1–21:4), and then told His disciples what would happen in the end times (21:5–36).

1. JESUS' CLEANSING OF THE TEMPLE (19:45-46)
(MATT. 21:12-13; MARK 11:15-17)

19:45-46. Jesus cleansed **the temple** twice—once at the beginning of His ministry (John 2:13-22), and again at the end of His ministry. Matthew, Mark, and Luke recorded the latter but said nothing of the former. Because of Jesus' role as Messiah, His bringing ceremonial cleanliness to the nation was logical at both the beginning and the end of His ministry. In both cases His teaching in the temple was disregarded by the religious leaders.

Jesus quoted from Isaiah 56:7 and Jeremiah 7:11 as **He** was **driving out** the **people who were selling** in the temple. Mark adds that the buyers and money changers were also driven out, as well as people who were apparently taking shortcuts through the temple compound in their business dealings (Mark 11:15-16). Money changing was done because only certain coinage was then accepted in the temple from those who bought animals for sacrifices. The religious leaders made money off the system of buying and selling animals for sacrifice (thus making the temple **a den of robbers**). Also they led the people into mere formalism. A pilgrim traveling to Jerusalem could go to the temple, buy an animal, and offer it as a sacrifice without ever having anything to do with the animal. This led to an impersonalization of the sacrificial system. The commercial system was apparently set up in the area of the temple which had been designated for devout Gentiles to pray and so was

disrupting Israel's witness to the surrounding world.

2. JESUS' TEACHING IN THE TEMPLE (19:47-21:38)

The two parts of this section—Jesus disputing in the temple (20:1–21:4) and His teaching His disciples (21:5-36)—are bracketed by an introduction (19:47-48) and a conclusion (21:37-38). The introduction and conclusion show that the people were amazed at His teaching and liked to listen to Him, whereas in contrast the chief priests, leaders, and teachers of the Law wanted to kill Him (19:47).

a. The crowd's delight (19:47-48)

19:47-48. Jesus taught daily in **the temple** to the delight of the crowds. They **hung on His words,** but the religious **leaders** wanted **to kill Him. Yet they** feared the crowds (cf. 20:19; 22:2; Acts 5:26).

b. Jesus' disputing in the temple (20:1–21:4)
(Matt. 21:23–23:37; Mark 11:27–12:44)

As a logical outcome of Jesus' cleansing of the temple, the religious leaders again rejected Him, and conflict arose. Jesus had upset the normal "religious" atmosphere of the temple, which led the religious leaders to question His authority.

20:1-8 (Matt. 21:23-27; Mark 11:27-33). The religious leaders asked Jesus where His authority came from. **The chief priests** were the temple officials; **the teachers of the Law,** often called "scribes," were made up of both Pharisees and Sadducees; and **the elders** may have been laymen who were political leaders. They asked two questions: **By what authority** was He acting, and **who gave** Him **this authority?** (Luke 20:2) The first question dealt with the kind of authority Jesus was using. Was He a prophet, a priest, or a king? No doubt the words **doing these things** referred to His cleansing the temple. The second question dealt with who was backing Him. Did Jesus believe that He was acting on His own or was He acting for some group?

Jesus responded with **a question.** He asked them about the authority behind

John's baptism. The religious leaders had disapproved the baptizing work of John, for John had humiliated them and had taken away some allegiance from their religious system (Matt. 3:7-10). Because the crowds venerated John the Baptist, the religious leaders were afraid to deny his authority and therefore refused to answer Jesus' question (Luke 20:7; cf. 19:48). So **Jesus** therefore refused to **tell . . . by what authority** He had cleansed the temple. The implication was that He was doing His work with the same authority—God in heaven—by which John the Baptist baptized.

20:9-19 (Matt. 21:33-46; Mark 12:1-12). Jesus then told a **parable** to describe His authority. A parable about a vine was not new for Israelites. Isaiah had used the figure to refer to the nation (Isa. 5:1-7), and the symbolism would have been clear to the hearers. The owner of **a vineyard** sent three servants to gain **fruit** from his **vineyard** (Luke 20:10-12). But the tenant **farmers . . . beat** each of the three. Finally he sent his **son,** whom they **killed** so that they could gain **the inheritance** (vv. 13-15). Jesus then asked his listeners a rhetorical question, **What then will the owner of the vineyard do to them?** He answered His own question—**He** would **kill those tenants and give the vineyard to others** (v. 16).

This culminated all of Jesus' messages concerning the fact that Gentiles and outcasts would be added to the kingdom whereas many from Israel would not be allowed to enter. The crowd responded with a strong statement of negation—**May this never be!** (*mē genoito;* used several times by Paul in Rom.) They understood the implications of what Jesus was saying: the Jewish system was being set aside because the religious leaders were rejecting Him. Luke pointed out the seriousness of the situation by recording that **Jesus looked directly at them** and quoted from Psalm 118:22, a verse which noted that a seemingly insignificant thing (a **stone** thrown away by stone masons) was really the most important thing (this stone became **the capstone**).

Jesus' point was that He, the most important element in the Jewish nation, was being rejected, but ultimately would be supreme. He also would be the means of judgment (Luke 20:18). The severity of Jesus' words struck home. **The teachers of the Law and the chief priests** wanted to kill Him **because they knew He had spoken this parable against them. But** again **they** feared to take any action because **of the people** (cf. 19:47-48; 22:2).

20:20-26. Since the religious leaders were afraid to do anything to Jesus because of the people (v. 19), they kept **a close watch on Him. They** were hoping **to catch** Him in some teaching that the crowds would not like, which would allow them to prosecute Him legally. Some **spies** asked Jesus a question about taxes: **Is it right for us to pay taxes to Caesar or not?** But this question was not merely about money. It pertained to politics and religion as well. If Jesus gave either a yes or a no answer He would lose support. If He said it was proper to pay taxes to Caesar, a foreign ruler (viz., Tiberius Caesar, A.D. 14-37), the zealots (who opposed Roman rule and favored Jewish autonomy) would be offended by His answer. If He answered that it was not proper to pay taxes (which the religious leaders might have suspected because He had been teaching about the kingdom), then the Romans would be displeased and the religious leaders would be able to turn **Him over to** their **authority.**

Jesus, pointing to the **portrait and inscription** of Caesar on **a denarius** coin (cf. 7:41; 10:35), answered in the affirmative: **Give to Caesar what is Caesar's.** But He also used the occasion to teach that one should give to God the thing that bears His image—oneself (**and to God what is God's**).

This astonishing answer silenced the spies (20:26). Interestingly the religious leaders used this incident against Jesus in His trial. But they totally misrepresented His position, charging that Jesus opposed payment of taxes to Caesar (23:2).

20:27-40. The **Sadducees** denied all supernatural occurrences including **resurrection** (v. 27; cf. Acts 23:8). Their **question** on resurrection, therefore, was not to elicit information but to find a way to make **Jesus** look foolish by presenting an extreme hypothetical case. They posited a situation in which **a woman** married each of **seven brothers** after each previous brother had died. The idea behind such an occurrence was the Hebrew concept of the Levirate marriage (Deut. 25:5-10) in which an unmarried man would marry his dead brother's **widow** who was **childless** in order to **have children** in his name. Then the Sadducees asked, **At the resurrection whose wife will she be?**

First, Jesus said, there will be no **marriage** in **the resurrection** (Luke 20:34-36). This showed (a) that the present **Age** contrasts sharply with the **Age** to come; and (b) when **people** are resurrected, **they** will be **like the angels,** being **God's children** and **children of the resurrection.** Jesus did not say that resurrected people become angels. His point was that they, like angels, will be immortal. Thus there will be no further need for procreation, and the marriage relationship will not be necessary.

Second, Jesus pointed out that there certainly will be a resurrection (vv. 37-38). He referred to an incident when the Lord told Moses that He is the God of the patriarchs (Ex. 3:6). Jesus appealed to **Moses** because the Sadducees wrongly taught that Moses' teachings did not reveal a resurrection. The statement that **the Lord** is **the God of** the patriarchs should have shown the Sadducees that the patriarchs were still alive (**He is . . . the God . . . of the living**), even though those words were uttered several hundred years after the last patriarch's death. **God** was preserving them **alive** for future resurrection.

The teachers of the Law and the Sadducees were at odds with each other because of conflicting beliefs. The former applauded Jesus' refutation of the Sadducees' doctrine (Luke 20:39). The result of the conversation was that everyone was afraid **to ask** Jesus **any more questions.**

20:41-44. Jesus then took the offensive and asked a question of the people around Him. The question concerned the nature of the Messiah—**How is it that they say the Christ is the Son of David?** Jesus then quoted from Psalm 110:1, in which **David** called the Messiah **my Lord** and said that He was exalted by being at Yahweh's **right hand,** the place of prominence. Two points are evident in these words of Jesus. First, the Son of David is also David's **Lord** (Luke 20:44) by the power of the resurrection. (In Acts 2:34-35 Peter used the same verse from Ps. 110 to prove that Jesus' superiority is based on His resurrection.) Second, David must have realized that the Son, who was

to be the Messiah, would be divine, for David called **Him Lord.**

20:45-47. Jesus' words were designed not only to teach **His disciples** but also to instruct the crowds (v. 45). Jesus pointed out the dichotomy between what **the teachers of the Law** taught and what they practiced. Their lives were bound up in greed and pride—they desired: (a) display (**flowing robes**), (b) attention (**greeted in the marketplaces**), (c) prominence (**important seats in the synagogues and . . . at banquets**), and (d) more money, taking from those who did not have much (e.g., widows). Their pompous **lengthy prayers** were thus hypocritical. Jesus stated that these teachers would **be punished most severely.** Those who have greater knowledge are held more accountable (James 3:1).

21:1-4. Following naturally what **Jesus** had just said about the teachers of the Law and their attitude toward widows, He pointed to **a poor widow** who was putting into the collection all her meager resources (**two** *lepta,* each worth about ⅛ cent; cf. 12:59; Mark 12:42). The percentage of what she gave was larger than **all the others.** So Jesus' point was that her gift, though small, was more because she gave **out of her poverty . . . all she had to live on.**

c. Jesus' teaching in the temple about the end times (21:5-36)
(Matt. 24:1-44; Mark 13:1-31)

In this section, which parallels the Olivet Discourse (Matt. 24–25), Jesus taught His followers what would happen immediately before His return to set up the kingdom. Being ready for the kingdom was the purpose of this teaching (Luke 21:34-36); thus the Rapture is not in view in this passage. As with all prophecy in Scripture, the teaching had immediate application to the hearers. They were to live righteous lives because of events which would occur in the future.

21:5-7. Some of the **disciples** were impressed with **the temple** and were **remarking** about its **beautiful** craftsmanship. Jesus' comment that a **time** was coming **when not one stone will be left on another** immediately brought a question to the disciples' minds. Their question, recorded by Luke, concerned the destruction of the temple (v. 7). Matthew also recorded another question about the signs of the end of the Age (Matt. 24:3). The disciples wanted to know **what** things would **take place** before the temple complex fell.

21:8-19. Jesus told His disciples about three things that would start to occur before the destruction of the temple, by Titus and the Roman army in A.D. 70, and one that would occur later.

First, Jesus said others would claim to be Messiah (v. 8). He gave this warning so that the disciples would **not** be **deceived.**

Second, Jesus said that **wars** would occur (vv. 9-10). When **these things** happened, the disciples were **not** to be **frightened,** for **the end** would **not come right away.**

Third, Jesus added that tremendous **earthquakes** would occur, causing **famines** (*loimoi*) **and pestilences** (*limoi;* v. 11). But these events do not fit between Jesus' day and the fall of Jerusalem. These **fearful events and great signs from heaven** refer to the Great Tribulation which will precede the return of the Lord to the earth.

Fourth, Jesus taught that persecution of believers would be common and severe. The disciples did undergo persecution by the authorities (cf. Acts 2–4). Because of Jesus' prediction in Luke 21:9-11, it seems that His words in verses 12-17 refer not only to the situation which would confront the disciples before the fall of Jerusalem but also to what will confront believers during the time of the Great Tribulation (cf. vv. 25-36). The same kinds of persecution would be present at both times—imprisonment (vv. 12-15), betrayal (v. 16), and hatred (v. 17). The persecution the original disciples would experience was a precursor to the ultimate persecution which future disciples would undergo.

Jesus' next two statements **(But not a hair of your head will perish,** and **By standing firm you will save yourselves;** vv. 18-19) have confused many. Some interpret these phrases as speaking of spiritual realities in a believer's life. Ultimately even though a believer dies, he or she will be protected eternally by God. However, it appears that Jesus was speaking here of salvation as entering into the kingdom alive (cf. Matt. 24:9-13). To "save yourselves" by "standing firm" means that believers show that they are

members of the believing community in opposition to those who turn away from the faith during times of persecution (Matt. 24:10). The ones who are saved are those who are preserved by God's sovereign power (cf. Matt. 24:22).

21:20-24. Jesus then returned to the disciples' original question about when the temple would be destroyed. In these five verses He noted that Gentile domination included the destruction of **Jerusalem** which would come about when the city was **surrounded by armies.** Gentile domination would continue **until the times of the Gentiles are fulfilled** (v. 24). The times of the Gentiles' domination over Jerusalem actually began when the Babylonians took the city and the nation into Captivity in 586 B.C. Jerusalem will again fall under Gentile domination in the Tribulation (Zech. 14:1-2) just before the Messiah returns to restore Jerusalem. It is that restoration of which Jesus spoke next (Luke 21:25-28).

21:25-28. Here Jesus first noted that cosmic **signs** will precede the **coming** of **the Son of Man** and will cause people to be terrified. The **sun, moon, and stars . . . will be shaken,** and **the sea** will roar and toss, signifying that the world will be in a chaotic state, out of control. Second, Jesus told about the coming of the Son of Man Himself. He drew His terminology from Daniel 7:13-14, in which Daniel saw "one like a Son of Man" coming with clouds and **glory** and receiving the kingdom from the Ancient of Days (i.e., God the Father). Jesus' point was that the Son of Man will come to receive the kingdom— the same kingdom He had been proclaiming since the beginning of His ministry. When these things **begin to** occur, His followers will **lift up** their **heads,** a symbol of rejoicing, **because** their **redemption** (i.e., safety in the kingdom brought by the returning King) will be **drawing near.**

21:29-33. In the **Parable** of **the Fig Tree** Jesus taught that one can tell what is coming by watching the signs. By looking at fig **leaves** sprouting in April, they know **that summer is near.** Similarly when the Great Tribulation comes, people will **know that the kingdom of God is near.**

The clause, **this generation** (*genea*) **will certainly not pass away until all these things have happened,** has caused much controversy. Some think Jesus was telling His disciples that their generation would see the destruction of the temple. That interpretation stems primarily from verses 5-7 in which the discussion pertained to the temple's destruction. However, because of verse 31 (in which Jesus spoke of the coming of the kingdom of God), and because of Matthew 24:34, it seems preferable to say His words refer to the generation living at the time of the cosmological events that will just precede His second coming. That generation will actually see the founding of the kingdom of God—something every generation of Jewish citizens has longed for throughout the nation's history.

21:34-36. Jesus warned His disciples to be ready at all times. Though a believer will be able to anticipate the coming of the kingdom by the signs, it is possible to get so entangled with the affairs **of life** that some will not be ready for the kingdom when it comes—**unexpectedly** (v. 34) and universally (v. 35)—and therefore will not enter the kingdom. It was against this wrong attitude that Jesus said, **Be careful** (v. 34) and **be always on the watch** (v. 36).

d. The crowd's reaction (21:37-38)

21:37-38. The crowd reacted to Jesus' **teaching** with amazement. Jesus spent the nights on **the Mount of Olives,** and each morning returned to **the temple** in Jerusalem to teach. The people were so taken with His teaching that they would arrive **early in the morning** to get an opportunity **to hear Him.** Apparently they were understanding His teachings about the coming of the kingdom in a way they had not understood before.

VII. The Death, Burial, and Resurrection of Jesus (chaps. 22–24)

A. The death and burial of Jesus (chaps. 22–23)

In this section Luke brought out the highpoint of the Messiah's rejection by the religious leaders of the nation, acting for the entire nation and for the world. Luke also emphasized Jesus' innocence in a number of ways not mentioned by the other Gospel writers: (a) Luke recorded that Pilate three times declared Jesus' innocence (23:4, 14, 22). (b) To Pilate's words Luke added the witness of Herod

(23:15). (c) Luke contrasted Jesus with Barabbas, who had been put into prison because of insurrection and murder (23:25). (d) Jesus was declared to be innocent by the thief who confessed his sin and the justice of his own punishment (23:39-43). (e) The centurion confessed that Jesus was righteous (23:47). (f) The multitude beat their breasts, an act which showed that they knew He was innocent (23:48).

1. THE AGREEMENT BY JUDAS TO BETRAY JESUS (22:1-6)

   (MATT. 26:1-5, 14-16; MARK 14:1-2, 10-11; JOHN 11:45-53)

22:1-6. Luke recorded that the death of Christ occurred at the time of **the Passover,** the annual celebration of the time lambs had been slain in Egypt, when God spared the Israelites but punished the Egyptians (Ex. 12:1-28). On the relationship of **the Feast of Unleavened Bread** to the Passover, see comments on Luke 22:7 and John 19:14. The religious leaders **were afraid of the people** (cf. Luke 19:47-48; 20:19), but were still trying **to get rid of Jesus.** The initiative for the betrayal rested on Judas. **Satan entered Judas** (cf. John 13:27) and he was willing to **betray Jesus** for **money.** Satan's taking part in Jesus' death was actually his own downfall, for through dying Jesus conquered Satan and death (Col. 2:15; Heb. 2:14).

2. THE PREPARATION BY JESUS FOR DEATH (22:7-46)

Luke's account of Jesus' preparation for His death includes two parts: Jesus' final ministry to His close disciples at the Passover meal (vv. 7-38), and Jesus' final hours praying alone in the garden (vv. 39-46).

a. Jesus at the Passover meal (22:7-38) (Matt. 26:17-35; Mark 14:12-31; John 13:1-38)

The Synoptic Gospels speak of the meal Jesus ate with His disciples as the Passover meal. But the Gospel of John indicates Jesus died on the cross at the exact time that lambs were slain in preparation for the nation's Passover meals (John 19:14). But this can be explained by the fact that the Feast of Unleavened Bread was a seven-day feast following the one-day Feast of the

Passover, but sometimes all eight days were called "the Passover" (Luke 2:41; 22:1; Acts 12:3-4) or the seven days were the "Passover Week" (John 19:14) A different explanation is that Jews in the first century followed two calendars in observing the Passover. According to this view Jesus and His disciples observed one date, eating the Passover meal before His crucifixion, whereas most of the nation, including the Pharisees, followed the other calendar in which the Passover lambs were slain on the very day of Jesus' death.

(1) The disciples' preparation for the meal. **22:7-13.** Even during these final preparations for His death **Jesus** was doing miraculous things. In this instance He told **Peter and John** exactly what they would find when they went about the **preparations** of **the Passover.** It would be easy to recognize **a man carrying a jar of water** because women usually carried the water from the wells to their houses. The two disciples were to tell the person who owned **the house** that **the Teacher** wanted to use **the guest room** to **eat the Passover with** His **disciples.** The owner of the house must have been a believer in Jesus, for he let the disciples **make preparations** for the meal at his house.

(2) Jesus' teaching during the meal (22:14-38). **22:14-20.** Jesus taught His men that His death would mean the beginning of the **New Covenant.** The symbolism about the **bread** and **the fruit of the vine** was given to show that Jesus' **body** and **blood** were necessary to institute the New Covenant.

Jesus' final teaching about the kingdom occurred at this final feast. Throughout the Book of Luke feasting has symbolic value. **Jesus and His** disciples, now called **apostles** (cf. 6:13; 9:10; 17:5; 24:10), were **reclined at the table.**

Jesus enjoyed the fellowship of those men who had believed His message of the kingdom. They were the ones who had followed Him, knowing that He was truly the Messiah. They were the ones who had left everything in order to follow Him. They had been called to a radical form of discipleship. Jesus announced that this was the last **Passover** He would **eat** with them **until** all that **it** means would find **fulfillment in the kingdom of God** (22:16; cf. v. 18). Many events in the Old Testament, including the Passover, pointed toward the ministry of Jesus and the kingdom He was to inaugurate. When His kingdom would arrive, the Passover would be fulfilled for God would have brought His people safely into their rest.

The bread and the wine were common, not only at Passover meals but also at every meal in that culture. Those elements symbolized His "body," the sacrifice for the entire nation, and His "blood." He was the sacrificial Lamb who was to take away the sin of Israel and of the entire world (John 1:29). The New Covenant (spoken of many times in the OT but highlighted in Jer. 31:31-34), which was a prerequisite for the Kingdom Age, was instituted by Jesus' sacrifice (Luke 22:20). The New Covenant provided for the regeneration of the Israelite nation and the Holy Spirit's indwelling individuals in the nation. Believers in the Church Age also participate in those spiritual blessings of regeneration and the indwelling Spirit (1 Cor. 11:25-26; 2 Cor. 3:6; Heb. 8:6-7).

22:21-23. Jesus now revealed that the betrayer was one of the gathered disciples who was eating the Passover meal. Judas' accountability and God's sovereign plan for Jesus' death are seen together (v. 22). Jesus had to die, for His death was the basis of salvation for all mankind and the only means for lifting the curse of sin. But the betrayer was accountable for his actions. Apparently the disciples had trusted Judas completely, for they had no idea **who would do** such a thing (v. 23).

22:24-30. The disciples' arguing about **which of them was considered to be greatest** is surprising in view of what Jesus had just said about one of them betraying Him. **Jesus** then told them that such thinking is like that of pagans. The followers of the Messiah should not think about such things. Rather than wanting to be **the greatest,** His followers should each desire to be **the one who serves.** For Jesus was **among** them **as One who serves** (*diakonōn,* "serves in a lowly way," v. 27). The disciples should desire to be like Jesus. Ultimately they will have places of honor in the **kingdom** because they were with Jesus **in** His **trials.** They will fellowship with Him, **and sit on thrones judging** Israel's **12 tribes** (cf. Matt. 19:28).

22:31-34. Jesus revealed that **Peter** would deny Him three times that same night, **before the rooster crows.** However, He assured Peter that in spite of Satan's desire to **sift** the disciples (**you** is pl. in the Gr.) like **wheat** (i.e., to put them through difficult times), Peter's faith would not fail. He would be restored (**turned back**), and would be the leader of the disciples (i.e., the leader of the group of **brothers**). Peter protested, thinking that he was strong, stating that he would even go **to prison** or **to death** for Jesus.

22:35-38. Jesus pointed out to His disciples that they had never lacked **anything** while they were with Him and were sent out to minister for Him (cf. 9:3). However, now that He was to be taken away from them, they would have to make preparations for their ministries including **a purse . . . a bag, and . . . a sword** for personal protection. Jesus was about to die and be **numbered with the transgressors,** a quotation from Isaiah 53:12.

When the disciples responded that they had **two swords,** Jesus replied, **That is enough.** This response has been interpreted in at least four ways: (1) Some understand the words as a rebuke to the disciples. If that were the case, then Jesus was saying, "Enough of this kind of talk!" (Leon Morris, *The Gospel according to St. Luke: An Introduction and Commentary,* p. 310) (2) Others understand the words to denote the fact that even two swords are enough to show human inadequacy at stopping God's plan for the death of Christ. Swords could not stop God's purpose and plan. (3) Jesus may simply have been saying that two swords were adequate for the 12 of them. (4) Others see the clause in conjuction with the quotation from Isaiah and understand Jesus to mean that by possessing two swords they would be classified by others as transgressors or criminals. This fourth view seems preferable.

b. Jesus on the Mount of Olives (22:39-46)

(Matt. 26:36-46; Mark 14:32-42)

The account of Jesus' praying in Gethsemane is recorded in the Synoptic Gospels but not in John. However, John recorded that Jesus went to "an olive grove" because Jesus "often met there with His disciples" and Judas "knew the place" (John 18:1-2). There may be deep signficance to the fact that in some of His final hours Jesus faced temptation (Luke 22:46) in a garden. Man fell into sin because of temptation in a garden (Gen. 3). And man's deliverance from sin comes about in spite of further temptation in a garden. Jesus, the "last Adam" (1 Cor. 15:45), did not fall into temptation but followed the will of God which the first Adam failed to do.

22:39-44. Luke says the place was **the Mount of Olives.** Matthew and Mark refer to the place as Gethsemane, which means "olive press." The "garden" was a grove of olive trees on the Mount of Olives (John 18:1, 3).

Jesus . . . prayed fervently for the trial to pass, but He submitted Himself to His **Father.** Because the **disciples** slept, Jesus was alone praying and being buffeted by the temptation to forsake the Father's plan, which was that the Son must go to death and bear the sins of the whole world. The words of His prayer showed that He was concerned **not** with His own interests but with the interests of the Father (Luke 22:42). Only Luke recorded that **an angel** ministered to Jesus in the garden (v. 43). Jesus was **in anguish** with His **sweat** being **like drops of blood falling to the ground.** Luke may have been alluding to God's words to Adam that he would earn his food by the sweat of his brow (Gen. 3:19).

22:45-46. Jesus **found** His **disciples . . . asleep, exhausted from sorrow.** The disciples were most depressed because of Jesus' teaching that He would die. They were not only in physical danger, which was bound to come on them, but also they may have faced spiritual danger as the temptation raged in the garden. Twice Jesus told them to pray that *they* would **not fall into temptation** (vv. 40, 46).

3. THE BETRAYAL OF JESUS (22:47-53)
    (MATT. 26:47-56; MARK 14:43-50; JOHN 18:3-11)

22:47-53. Luke recorded three elements in the betrayal and arrest of Jesus. First, **Jesus** knew that **Judas** would betray Him (vv. 47-48). A large **crowd** including the religious leaders (v. 52) and soldiers (John 18:12) came into the grove with Judas **leading them.** Judas had agreed on a sign for the people who had come with him—he would **kiss** the One they were to arrest. Jesus, by His words, showed that

He already knew all about the betrayal, including Judas' secret sign.

Second, **Jesus** had compassion for people even in the midst of His own arrest (Luke 22:49-51). After Peter cut off the ear of the high priest's servant (named Malchus, John 18:10), using one of the two swords the disciples possessed (Luke 22:38), Jesus **healed** the man.

Third, **Jesus** pointed up the hypocrisy of the religious leaders (vv. 52-53). Jesus asked them why they had not arrested Him during the **day** as He taught **in the temple.** The reason was obvious, that out of fear of the people they looked for a way to arrest Him secretly (19:48; 20:19; 22:2). Thus He could tell them, **This is your hour—when darkness reigns** (v. 53). Not only were they coming out under the cover of darkness, but they were also acting as the forces of darkness to kill the Messiah. The garden experience must have ended by about 2:30 A.M., for the six trials of Jesus were completed by morning and Jesus was on the cross by 9:00 A.M. The arrest in the garden was illegal for it was done at night and was accomplished through a hired accuser.

4. THE TRIALS OF JESUS (22:54–23:25)

Jesus faced six trials in all: three before Jewish officials, and three before Roman officials (see the list of these trials at Matt. 26:57-58). Luke recorded only two of the three Jewish trials.

a. At the house of the high priest
(22:54-65)
(Matt. 26:57-75; Mark 14:53-54,
65-72; John 18:12-18, 25-27)

22:54. Jesus was taken **into the house of the high priest,** who was Caiaphas (Matt. 26:57; John 18:13; cf. comments on Luke 3:2, and see the chart on Annas' family at Acts 4:5-6). But Jesus first was taken to Caiaphas' influential father-in-law, Annas (John 18:13). **Peter,** remaining true to his word up to this point (Luke 22:33), **followed** the Lord even though it could have meant death for him.

22:55-62. Within several hours **Peter** denied Jesus three times, as He had foretold (v. 34). Peter's denials got progressively more vehement (vv. 57-58, 60). After **the rooster crowed,** Jesus **turned and looked straight at Peter.** The

combination of events along with Jesus' look caused Peter to remember the words Jesus spoke earlier in the evening. Peter realized what he had done. His bitter weeping showed he was heartbroken over the fact he had **denied** Jesus.

22:63-65. While at the house of the high priest, **Jesus** began to be mistreated by **the men who were guarding** Him. They mocked Him and beat Him. Blindfolding Him, they mockingly asked Him to **prophesy** by telling **who hit** Him. Apparently they knew of His claims, but they had a misunderstanding of true prophecy.

b. At the council of the elders (22:66-71)
(Matt. 26:59-66; Mark 14:55-64;
John 18:19-24)

22:66-67a. The council of the elders (also known as the Sanhedrin) was the Jewish nation's official judicial body. This council was their final court of appeals. If the council found **Jesus** guilty, it was the last word—the nation found Him guilty. They met **at daybreak** since it was illegal to assemble at night. The council wanted to know if **Jesus** was **the Christ,** that is, if Jesus was truly presenting Himself as the Messiah. At this point they were not interested in other charges. Since the council knew that Jesus had been presenting Himself as the Messiah, they may have been giving Him an opportunity to recant. Or perhaps they were trying to shame Him in front of His followers.

22:67b-70. Jesus affirmed His authority as Messiah, the One who, after His death, resurrection, and Ascension, would **be seated at the right hand of the mighty God,** the place of honor (cf. Ps. 110:1; Acts 2:33; 5:31; Eph. 1:20; Col. 3:1; Heb. 1:3; 8:1; 10:12; 12:2; 1 Peter 3:22). Also He plainly told the council that He is **the Son of God.**

22:71. The council decided they had received all the **testimony** they needed. In their view Jesus was guilty of blasphemy. So they were ready to hand Him over to the Roman authorities. The council could give a guilty verdict, but the Jews at that time were not allowed to impose the death penalty. Only Rome could sentence to death. Even though Jesus had performed messianic miracles, the leaders of the nation refused to believe. They acted on behalf of the nation in rejecting Christ.

c. *Before Pilate (23:1-7)*
(*Matt. 27:1-2, 11-14; Mark 15:1-5;*
John 18:28-38)

23:1-7. The council agreed to take Jesus to the Roman authorities. On arriving before **Pilate,** governor of Judea (3:1; cf. 13:1), the Jewish authorities charged Him falsely. They said He opposed paying **taxes to Caesar,** but Jesus had said the opposite (20:25). And the blasphemy charge—He **claims to be Christ, a king**—was worded to sound as if Jesus was an insurrectionist (23:2). Pilate stated clearly that Jesus was innocent (v. 4). However, because the Jewish leaders kept insisting that Jesus was guilty, Pilate **sent Him to Herod,** "tetrarch of Galilee" (3:1), **who was also in Jerusalem at that time.**

d. *Before Herod (23:8-12)*

23:8-12. Jesus had told Pilate who He is (v. 3), but He repeatedly refused to answer **Herod** who merely wanted **to see Him perform some miracle.** Herod showed his true feelings toward Jesus by joining in the mockery, dressing Him up as a false king. Herod then **sent** Jesus **back to Pilate,** without passing any judgment on the case.

e. *Before Pilate for sentencing (23:13-25)*
(*Matt. 27:15-26; Mark 15:6-15; John 18:39–19:16*)

23:13-17. **Pilate** told **the people** there was really nothing he could do but **punish** Jesus and **release Him** because he **found no basis for** the **charges against Him.** Jesus had **done nothing to deserve death.** (V. 17, missing from many mss., is not in the NIV.)

23:18-25. In spite of the fact that Jesus had been proved by the Roman authorities to have done nothing deserving of death, the Jews yelled out that a known insurrectionist, **Barabbas,** should be **released** in place of Jesus. Amazingly the people were willing to have an insurrectionist and a murderer in their midst rather than the Messiah. They would rather be with a well-known sinner than with the One who could forgive their sins. **Pilate** desired **to release Jesus,** affirming His innocence for a **third time,** but he finally gave in to **their demand . . . and surrendered Jesus to their will.**

5. THE CRUCIFIXION OF JESUS (23:26-49)
(MATT. 27:32-56; MARK 15:21-41; JOHN 19:17-30)

Crucifixion was a common method of carrying out the death sentence in the Roman Empire. It was probably the most cruel and painful method of death the Romans knew. Crucifixion was reserved for the worst criminals; by law a Roman citizen could not be crucified. Crucifixion was usually a long slow process, but Jesus died in a remarkably short period of time for He voluntarily "breathed His last" (v. 46).

23:26-31. A man named **Simon, from** the town of **Cyrene** in North Africa, was forced to carry Jesus' **cross** part of the way to the Crucifixion site. On the way Jesus warned the people of their coming persecution. Because Jesus was going to the cross, the kingdom was being postponed and times of tribulation would come on the nation (cf. Hosea 10:8; Rev. 6:15-17). Jesus' message was being rejected when He was physically present. How much more it would be rejected in coming years! (Luke 23:31)

23:32-43. Luke did not state, as did Matthew and John, how the events of Jesus' death fulfilled Old Testament Scriptures. Luke's purpose, instead, was to show that **Jesus** was the forgiving Messiah even as He died. Jesus asked the **Father** to **forgive** those who were killing Him (v. 34), and He forgave one of the men sentenced to die with Him (v. 43). Even in death Jesus had power to make people right with God. And yet **the rulers . . . sneered** (v. 35) **the soldiers . . . mocked** (vv. 36-37), and **one of the criminals** crucified with Him insulted **Him** (v. 39).

23:44-49. Luke noted four things that occurred at the time Jesus died. First, two symbolic events took place while Jesus was on the cross. **Darkness came over the whole land** for three hours, from **the sixth hour** (noon) **until the ninth hour** (3:00 P.M.). Jesus had already told those who arrested Him that "this is your hour—when darkness reigns" (22:53). Darkness was reigning because of His crucifixion. The other symbolic event was the tearing **in two** of **the curtain of the temple,** which separated the holy of holies from the rest of the temple. The curtain divided people from the place where God had localized His presence. The tearing from top to bottom (Matt. 27:51) symbolized the fact that now, because of Jesus' death, people had freer access to God as they no longer had to go through the sacrificial system (cf. Rom. 5:2; Eph. 2:18; 3:12). Jesus was the only Sacrifice needed to enable people to have a proper relationship with God.

Second, Luke noted that Jesus' death occurred because He willed it. Breathing **His last** (Luke 23:46), He voluntarily gave up His life (John 10:15, 17-18).

Third, even a Roman **centurion** noted that Jesus **was a righteous Man,** that is, not guilty (Luke 23:47). He too **praised God,** as did many others in Luke's Gospel.

Fourth, **the people** who witnessed His death mourned (vv. 48-49).

6. THE BURIAL OF JESUS (23:50-56)
(MATT. 27:57-61; MARK 15:42-47; JOHN 19:38-42)

23:50-56. All four Gospel writers presented details about Jesus' burial in order to demonstrate that Jesus was truly dead. All the preparations for His burial would have been unnecessary if Jesus had not really died. The death of the Messiah was needed or there could not have been the Resurrection.

Interestingly whereas **the council** had demanded Jesus' death one **member . . . Joseph,** disagreed. **Waiting for the kingdom of God,** he believed that Jesus is the Messiah. He was a secret disciple of Jesus (Matt. 27:57; John 19:38). Out of love for Jesus, he buried Him in his own **tomb** (Matt. 27:60).

Jesus died on the **Preparation Day** (which most assume was Friday) before **the Sabbath.**

B. *The resurrection and appearances of Jesus (chap. 24)*

The final chapter of Luke records the experiences of a number of people who had firsthand experiences with the risen Messiah. In each case the people were depressed because of Jesus' death. But after meeting with Him, they were joyful and praised God. (See the list of Jesus' post-resurrection events at Matt. 28:1-4.)

1. THE WOMEN AND THE APOSTLES (24:1-12)
(MATT. 28:1-10; MARK 16:1-8; JOHN 20:1-10)

24:1-9. The first people to learn of the resurrection of Jesus were **the women** who had been faithful in following Him. They found out about the Resurrection first because of their devotion to Him. For after His death they brought more **spices** for His burial **on the first day of the week** (cf. 23:55-56). **They did not find the body** they were looking for. Instead they saw **two men in clothes that gleamed like lightning,** an obvious reference to angelic beings. These **men** reminded them of the words Jesus had spoken about His crucifixion and resurrection (9:31; 18:31-34). The women went to report to the apostles and **others** what they had seen (24:9).

24:10-12. The apostles **did not believe** the report **the women** brought them **because their words seemed . . . like nonsense.** This was because they had seen Jesus' death and had seen His body placed in the grave. But **Peter ran to the tomb** and found what the women had described. Still he did not understand **what had happened.**

2. JESUS' APPEARANCES TO HIS FOLLOWERS (24:13-49)

In these two appearances—to two men (vv. 13-35) and to the gathered disciples (vv. 36-49)—Jesus taught His followers from the Old Testament the things that had been accomplished among them. It was not until after Jesus had explained from the Old Testament that the Messiah had to die that His followers began to understand what had occurred the past few days.

a. *Jesus' appearance to the two men (24:13-35)*
(Mark 16:12-13)

24:13-16. Two of Jesus' followers were walking to **Emmaus,** which is **about seven miles** (northwest) **from Jerusalem.** They were talking . . . about the things **that had happened,** that is, the report that Jesus had been resurrected (vv. 19-24). When **Jesus** joined them, they did not recognize **Him.**

24:17-24. When Jesus asked them to tell Him what they were **discussing,** the men related the view about Jesus that most of the nation believed at that time. The men, **one of** whom was **Cleopas,** said they were talking **about Jesus of Nazareth.** Cleopas commented that their fellow companion must be **the only one**

living in all of Jerusalem who did not know what had happened. By this question Luke got across the point that Jesus' ministry and death were known to everyone in the city and in most of the nation. The entire nation was responsible to accept the Messiah.

The two men added that the chief priests and our rulers handed Him over to . . . death. Along with many others these two men thought that Jesus was the One who was going to redeem Israel, that is, be the Messiah and bring in the kingdom (cf. Simeon's words in 2:30 and Anna's in 2:38). They even related that they had heard a report of the Resurrection directly from some . . . women. But despite all this, their faces were downcast (24:17).

24:25-27. Jesus chided them for not understanding and believing. He explained from Moses and all the Prophets what had been said about Him. He implied that these disciples should have understood from the Old Testament what had happened.

24:28-35. It was not until after Jesus had broken bread with them that their eyes were opened and they recognized Him. Their experience with Jesus caused them to hurry back to Jerusalem (seven miles) and affirm the Resurrection to the Eleven and others who were meeting together. The two men now acknowledged the truth of the reports about Jesus' resurrection for they had recognized Him themselves. The disciples who were meeting together now had at least three reports of the Resurrection: the women, Peter, and Cleopas and his companion. But still they did not understand (cf. v. 38).

b. Jesus' appearance to the gathered
followers (24:36-49)
(Matt. 28:16-20; Mark 16:14-18;
John 20:19-23)

In this appearance three things about Jesus are evident.

24:36-43. First, Jesus proved to His followers that He had really been resurrected. Not only did He stand in their presence so they could see Him and His wounds (vv. 39-40), but He also ate food (a piece of broiled fish) before them to show that He was not a ghost.

24:44-47. Second, Jesus showed His followers all the facts written . . . in the

Old Testament about the Messiah. The Law of Moses, the Prophets, and the Psalms are the three divisions of the Old Testament sometimes referred to in Jesus' day. (More often, however, Moses and the Prophets were said to comprise the OT; e.g., v. 27.) In other words He showed them from different parts of the Old Testament (e.g., Deut. 18:15; Pss. 2:7; 16:10; 22:14-18; Isa. 53; 61:1) that He is the Messiah and that He must suffer and rise from the dead (Luke 24:46; cf. v. 26). Because of His death and resurrection, the message of repentance and forgiveness of sins could be preached in His name to all nations, beginning at Jerusalem for they were witnesses of His death and His rising from the dead. This became the outline for Luke in his second book (cf. Acts 1:8).

24:48-49. Jesus commanded His followers to remain in the city of Jerusalem until they had received power from on high, a clear reference to the Holy Spirit (cf. Acts 1:8), who was promised by the Father.

3. JESUS' PARTING FROM HIS FOLLOWERS
(24:50-53)
(MARK 16:19-20)

24:50-53. In the vicinity of Bethany, that is, on the Mount of Olives, Jesus was taken up into heaven (cf. Acts 1:9-11). The disciples responded with worship and great joy and kept praising God in the temple. As seen frequently in Luke, believers repeatedly responded to Jesus with joy (cf. comments on Luke 2:18) and praise. This attitude set the stage for Luke's next volume which began with Jesus' followers remaining in Jerusalem until the Holy Spirit came (Acts 1:4-14).

BIBLIOGRAPHY

Caird, G.B. Saint Luke. Westminster Pelican Commentaries. Philadelphia: Westminster Press, 1978.

Danker, Frederick W. Jesus and the New Age according to St. Luke: A Commentary on the Third Gospel. St. Louis: Clayton Publishing House, 1980.

Ellis, E. Earle. The Gospel of Luke. The New Century Bible Commentary. Rev. ed. Grand Rapids: Wm. B. Eerdmans Publishing Co., 1974.

Fitzmyer, Joseph A. *The Gospel according to Luke (I–IX)*. The Anchor Bible. Garden City, N.Y.: Doubleday & Co., 1981.

Geldenhuys, J. Norval. *Commentary on the Gospel of Luke*. Grand Rapids: Wm. B. Eerdmans Publishing Co., 1951.

Godet, F. *A Commentary on the Gospel of Saint Luke*. 2 vols. 5th ed. Reprint. Greenwood, S.C.: Attic Press, 1976.

Hendriksen, William. *Exposition of the Gospel according to Luke*. New Testament Commentary. Grand Rapids: Baker Book House, 1978.

Ironside, H.A. *Addresses on the Gospel of Luke*. 2 vols. New York: Loizeaux Brothers, 1946.

Marshall, I. Howard. *The Gospel of Luke*. The New International Greek Testament Commentary. Grand Rapids: Wm. B. Eerdmans Publishing Co., 1978.

Morgan, G. Campbell. *The Gospel according to Luke*. Old Tappan, N.J.: Fleming H. Revell Co., 1931.

Morris, Leon. *The Gospel according to St. Luke: An Introduction and Commentary*. The Tyndale New Testament Commentaries. Grand Rapids: Wm. B. Eerdmans Publishing Co., 1974.

Plummer, Alfred. *A Critical and Exegetical Commentary on the Gospel according to St. Luke*. The International Critical Commentary. Edinburgh: T. & T. Clark, 1901. Reprint. Greenwood, S.C.: Attic Press, 1977.

Safrai, S., and Stern, M., eds. *The Jewish People in the First Century*. 2 vols. Assen: Van Gorcum & Co., 1974, 1976.

JOHN

Edwin A. Blum

INTRODUCTION

Authorship

Internal evidence. In the strict sense of the term, the Fourth Gospel is anonymous. No name of its author is given in the text. This is not surprising because a Gospel differs in literary form from an epistle or letter. The letters of Paul each begin with his name, which was the normal custom of letter writers in the ancient world. None of the human authors of the four Gospels identified himself by name. But that does not mean one cannot know who the authors were. An author may indirectly reveal himself within the writing, or his work may be well known in tradition as coming from him.

Internal evidence supplies the following chain of connections regarding the author of the Fourth Gospel. (1) In John 21:24 the word "them" refers to the whole Gospel, not to just the last chapter. (2) "The disciple" in 21:24 was "the disciple whom Jesus loved" (21:7). (3) From 21:7 it is certain that the disciple whom Jesus loved was one of seven persons mentioned in 21:2 (Simon Peter, Thomas, Nathanael, the two sons of Zebedee, and two unnamed disciples). (4) "The disciple whom Jesus loved" was seated next to the Lord at the Last Supper, and Peter motioned to him (13:23-24). (5) He must have been one of the Twelve since only they were with the Lord at the Last Supper (cf. Mark 14:17; Luke 22:14). (6) In the Gospel, John was closely related to Peter and thus appears to be one of the inner three (cf. John 20:2-10; Mark 5:37-38; 9:2-3; 14:33). Since James, John's brother, died in the year A.D. 44, he was not the author (Acts 12:2). (7) "The other disciple" (John 18:15-16) seems to refer to the "disciple whom Jesus loved" since he is called this in 20:2. (8) The "disciple whom Jesus loved" was at the cross (19:26), and 19:35 seems to refer to him.

(9) The author's claim, "We have seen His glory" (1:14), was the claim of someone who was an eyewitness (cf. 1 John 1:1-4).

Putting all of these facts together makes a good case for the author of the Fourth Gospel having been John, one of the sons of a fisherman named Zebedee.

External evidence. The external evidence is the traditional ascription of authorship which has been well known in the church. Polycarp (ca. A.D. 69–ca. A.D. 155) spoke of his contact with John. Irenaeus (ca. 130–ca. 200), the bishop of Lyons, heard Polycarp and testified that "John, the disciple of the Lord, who also had leaned upon His breast, had himself published a Gospel during his residence in Ephesus in Asia" (*Against Heresies* 3. 1). Polycrates, Clement of Alexandria, Tertullian, and other later fathers support this tradition. Eusebius was specific that Matthew and John of the apostles wrote the two Gospels which bear their specific names (*The Ecclesiastical History* 3. 24. 3-8).

Place of Origin. The external tradition is strong that John came to Ephesus after Paul had founded the church and that he labored in that city for many years (cf. Eusebius *The Ecclesiastical History* 3. 24. 1). Supporting this tradition is the evidence of Revelation 1:9-11. When John was in exile on Patmos, an island off the coast of Asia Minor, he wrote to seven Asian churches, the first of which was Ephesus. That the Fourth Gospel was originally published at Ephesus is a good probability.

Date. The date for the Gospel of John was probably between A.D. 85 and 95. Some critics have attempted to assign a date as late as A.D. 150 on the basis of the book's alleged similarities to Gnostic writings or because of a supposed long development of church theology. Archeological finds supporting the authenticity of the text of John (e.g., John 4:11; 5:2-3), word studies (e.g., *synchrōntai*, 4:9), manuscript discoveries (e.g., P52), and the Dead Sea Scrolls have given powerful support to an early dating for John. So it is common today to find nonconservative scholars arguing for a date as early as A.D. 45-66. An early date is possible. But this Gospel has been known in the church as the "Fourth" one, and the early church fathers believed that it was written when John was an old man. Therefore a date between 85 and 95 is best. John 21:18, 23 require the passing of some time, with Peter becoming old and John outliving him.

Purpose. The purpose of the Gospel of John, stated in 20:31, was to record Jesus' "signs" so that readers would come to believe in Him. Doubtless the author had other purposes as well. Some have argued that John wrote against synagogue Judaism, or the Gnostics, or the followers of John the Baptist. Some think John wrote to supplement the other Gospels. John's Gospel has a clear evangelistic purpose (as do the other Gospels), so it is no accident that it has been greatly used in the history of the church for that purpose.

The Glory of the Fourth Gospel. In introductions to the Fourth Gospel many writers have a section entitled "The Problem of the Fourth Gospel." The Fourth Gospel has been *the* great problem in modern New Testament studies. But what is that problem? One critic claimed many years ago that Jesus in the Synoptics (Matthew, Mark, Luke) is historical but not divine, and that in the Fourth Gospel He is divine but not historical. This, however, is clearly an unwarranted distinction, for the Gospel of John begins with a plain statement of the full deity of the Word made flesh (1:1, 14). And the Gospel nearly ends with Thomas' confession, "My Lord and my God" (20:28). Jesus Christ is both "divine" (Deity) and historical (One who actually lived on the earth). So what is a problem to many critics is actually the chief glory of the church.

Also, contrary to what some have argued, the Synoptic writers, as well as John, present a divine Messiah. But John's Gospel is so clear and pointed in his Christology that his theology has greatly enriched the church. The text, "the Word became flesh" (1:14), became the central focal point of the early church fathers' meditation and study. John presented the Incarnation—God manifest in the flesh—as the foundation of the gospel. This is the "glory," not the "problem," of the Fourth Gospel.

John's Distinctive Portrait. When one compares the Gospel of John with the other three Gospels, he is struck by the distinctiveness of John's presentation. John does not include Jesus' genealogy, birth, baptism, temptation, casting out of demons, parables, transfiguration, instituting of the Lord's Supper, His agony in Gethesemane, or His Ascension. John's presentation of Jesus stresses His ministry in Jerusalem, the feasts of the Jewish nation, Jesus' contacts with individuals in private conversations (e.g., chaps. 3-4; 18:28-19:16), and His ministry to His disciples (chaps. 13-17). The major body of the Gospel is contained in a "Book of Signs" (2:1-12:50) which embraces seven miracles or "signs" which proclaim Jesus as the Messiah, the Son of God. This "Book of Signs" also contains great discourses of Jesus which explain and proclaim the significance of the signs. For example, following the feeding of the 5,000 (6:1-15), Jesus revealed Himself as the Bread of Life which the heavenly Father gives for the life of the world (6:25-35). Another notable and exclusive feature of the Fourth Gospel is the series of "I am" statements that were made by Jesus (cf. 6:35; 8:12; 10:7, 9, 11, 14; 11:25; 14:6; 15:1, 5).

The distinctiveness of this Gospel must be kept in perspective. The Gospels were not intended as biographies. Each Gospel writer selected from a much larger pool of information the material which would serve his purpose. It has been estimated that if all the words from the lips of Jesus cited in Matthew, Mark, and Luke were read aloud, the amount of time taken would be only about three hours. Since the ministry of Jesus lasted about three years, a three-hour sample of His teaching is a small amount. Each Gospel records certain miracles or parables and

Jesus' Seven "Signs" in the Gospel of John

1. Changing water into wine in Cana (2:1-11)
2. Healing an official's son in Capernaum (4:46-54)
3. Healing an invalid at the Pool of Bethesda in Jerusalem (5:1-18)
4. Feeding the 5,000 near the Sea of Galilee (6:5-14)
5. Walking on the water of the Sea of Galilee (6:16-21)
6. Healing a blind man in Jerusalem (9:1-7)
7. Raising dead Lazarus in Bethany (11:1-45)

Jesus' Seven "I Am's" in the Gospel of John

1. "I am the Bread of Life" (6:35).
2. "I am the Light of the world" (8:12).
3. "I am the Gate for the sheep" (10:7; cf. v. 9).
4. "I am the Good Shepherd" (10:11, 14).
5. "I am the Resurrection and the Life" (11:25).
6. "I am the Way and the Truth and the Life" (14:6).
7. "I am the true Vine" (15:1; cf. v. 5).

omits others. The focus of the Gospels is the good news of Jesus' death and resurrection. The Gospels have been called "Passion narratives with extended introductions." That is, they center on Christ's death (e.g., Mark 11–16) with only enough information (e.g., Mark 1–10) to explain the nature of the One who ministered and died.

The following facts are known about John's relationship to the Synoptic Gospels. John, Zebedee's son, was Peter's co-worker in Jerusalem during the early years of the church (Acts 3:1–4:23; 8:14; 12:1-2). Further, John was called one of the "reputed . . . pillars" of the Jerusalem church (Gal. 2:9). The Jerusalem church was led by the apostles, and James the brother of Jesus with Peter and John often took the initiative (Acts 3:1; 4:3-21; 8:14-24; 15:7-11, 13-21). During the early years of the Jerusalem church a certain fixed core of apostolic teaching and preaching developed. After a great multitude were converted, "they devoted themselves to the apostles' teaching" (Acts 2:42). Later the number of men who believed grew to about 5,000 (Acts 4:4). It would be necessary for a system of instruction to be set up. This would center around Jesus' messianic fulfillment of Old Testament prophecies, particularly His ministry and Passion. In particular the commands of Jesus—His "oral Torah"—were to be taught (Matt. 28:20).

According to fairly strong church tradition, Mark's Gospel is directly related to Peter's preaching. Acts 10:36-43 seems to reinforce this tradition, for many have seen the Marcan outline in this example of Peter's preaching. Since Peter's preaching is basically the outline and content of the Gospel of Mark, John—having been with Peter for many years—would have been completely familiar with this body of truth.

This core of early apostolic Jerusalem preaching and teaching came to be written down by Mark who helped Peter in his later ministry. After John was in Jerusalem for many years (perhaps 20) he went to Asia Minor and settled in Ephesus. When John wrote his Gospel he provided, by the Spirit of God, a rich supplement to the early Jerusalem core. Thus John's distinctive portrait of Jesus contains 93 percent original material in comparison to the Synoptics. As John wrote, he was aware that even his contribution contained only a small fraction of what could be said (John 20:30-31; 21:25). (For more on the interrelatedness of the Gospels see the *Introduction* to Matthew and the *Introduction* to Mark.)

The Text. The Greek text of the Fourth Gospel, as well as that of the entire New Testament, is in very good condition. The reader of the NIV will notice certain changes in some places in comparison to the KJV. This reflects the fact that in the years since the publication of the KJV in 1611 new manuscripts and new theories pertaining to textual transmission have enabled scholars to do a better job in ascertaining what the original writings, though not extant, actually said. The two most notable places where the NIV varies from the KJV in John are 5:3b-4 (which is in the NIV marg.) and 7:53–8:11 (which is set off from the main body of the NIV text). These will be discussed in the commentary.

The Structure and Theme. The key word in the Gospel of John is "believe" (*pisteuō*), which occurs 98 times. The Greek noun "faith" (*pistis*) does not occur. (A few times, however, the NIV translates the Gr. verb with the Eng. "put . . . faith in.") The Greek verb *pisteuō* is frequently used in the present tense and in participial forms. Apparently John wanted to stress an active, continuous, and vital trust in Jesus. The book can be divided into the following main sections: Prologue (1:1-18), Book of Signs (1:19–12:50), Farewell Instructions (chaps. 13–17), Passion and Resurrection (chaps. 18–20), Epilogue (chap. 21). The Prologue sets forth the theological introduction, which enables readers to understand that the words and deeds of Jesus are the words and deeds of God manifest in the flesh. The Book of Signs records seven miracles which reveal the Father's glory in the Son. The miracles with their explanatory discourses progressively draw out two responses: faith, and unbelief and hardening in sin.

As Jesus' public ministry closed, irrational unbelief was the people's major response (12:37). Jesus in His farewell instructions prepared His own for His coming death and His followers' future ministry. The culmination of unbelief is evident in the Passion section, and the faith of the disciples is evident in the Resurrection account. The Epilogue completes the Gospel by showing the plans of the Lord for His disciples.

OUTLINE

COMMENTARY

I. The Prologue (1:1-18)

All four Gospels begin by placing Jesus within a historical setting, but the Gospel of John is unique in the way it opens. The Book of Matthew begins with the genealogy of Jesus that connects Him to David and Abraham. Mark starts with the preaching of John the Baptist. Luke has a dedication of his work to Theophilus and follows that with a prediction of the birth of John the Baptist. But John begins with a theological prologue. It is almost as if John had said, "I want you to consider Jesus in His teaching and deeds. But you will not understand the good news of Jesus in its fullest sense unless you view Him from this point of view. Jesus is God manifest in the flesh, and His words and deeds are those of the God-Man."

The prologue contains many of the major themes of the Gospel which are later reintroduced and developed more fully. The key terms include "life" (v. 4), "light" (v. 4), "darkness" (v. 5), "witness" (v. 7), "true" (v. 9), "world" (v. 9), "Son" (v. 14), "Father" (v. 14), "glory" (v. 14), "truth" (v. 14). Two other key theological terms are "the Word" (v. 1) and "grace" (v. 14), but these important words are used in John only in this theological introduction. "Word" (*Logos*) does occur elsewhere in the Gospel but not as a Christological title.

A. The Logos in eternity and time (1:1-5)

1:1. As far back as man can think, **in the beginning . . . the Word** was existing. The term "Word" is the common Greek word *logos*, which meant "speaking, a message, or words." "Logos" was widely used in Greek philosophical teaching as well as in Jewish wisdom literature and philosophy. John chose this term because it was familiar to his readers, but he invested it with his own meaning, which becomes evident in the prologue.

The Word was with God in a special relationship of eternal fellowship in the Trinity. The word "with" translates the Greek *pros*, which here suggests "in company with" (cf. the same use of *pros* in 1:2; 1 Thes. 3:4; 1 John 1:2). John then added that **the Word was God.** Jehovah's Witnesses translate this clause, "The Word was a god." This is incorrect and logically is polytheism. Others have translated it "the Word was divine," but this is ambiguous and could lead to a faulty view of Jesus. If this verse is correctly understood, it helps clarify the doctrine of the Trinity. The Word is eternal; the Word is in relationship to God (the Father); and the Word is God.

1:2. The Word has always been in a relationship **with God** the Father. Christ did not at some point in time come into existence or begin a relationship with the Father. In eternity past the Father (God) and the Son (the Word) have always been in a loving communion with each other. Both Father and Son are God, yet there are not two Gods.

1:3. Why is there something rather than nothing? That is a great question in philosophy. The Christian answer is God. He is eternal, and He is the Creator of **all things.** And the Word was the agent of Creation (cf. 1 Cor. 8:6; Col. 1:16; Heb. 1:2). All Creation was **made** by the Word in relation with the Father and the Spirit. John stressed the work of the Word. He came to reveal the Father (John 1:14, 18); and the work of revelation began in Creation for Creation reveals God (Ps. 19:1-6; Rom. 1:19-20).

1:4. Life is man's most important asset. To lose life is tragic. John affirmed that in the ultimate sense, **life** is **in** Christ. Man's spiritual and physical **life** come from Him. (For John's teaching on life, cf. 5:26; 6:57; 10:10; 11:25; 14:6; 17:3; 20:31.) Jesus, the Source of "life" (cf. 11:25), is also **the light of men** (cf. 8:12). Light is commonly used in the Bible as an emblem of God; darkness is commonly used to denote death, ignorance, sin, and separation from God. Isaiah described the coming of salvation as the people living in darkness seeing a great light (Isa. 9:2; cf. Matt. 4:16).

1:5. Light's nature is to shine and dispel **darkness.** Darkness is almost personified in this verse: darkness is unable to overpower light. By this, John summarized his Gospel record: (a) **Light** will invade the dominion of **darkness.** (b) Satan the ruler and his subjects will resist the light, but they will be unable to frustrate its power. (c) The Word will be victorious in spite of opposition.

B. The witness of John the Baptist (1:6-8)

1:6. In addition to the eternal Word, **a man** came on the stage of history: **his name was John.** This John did not author this Gospel but was the great forerunner of Jesus known as John the Baptist. He **was sent from God,** which was the secret of his importance. Like the Old Testament prophets he was equipped and commissioned by God for special ministry.

1:7. The word **witness** (both as a noun [martyria] and verb [martyreō]) is important in this Gospel (cf. v. 15, 32, 34; 3:11, 26; 5:31-32, 36-37; 18:37; 19:35; etc). (See the chart with the comments on 5:33-34.) John the Baptist was sent for people's benefit to be an additional pointer to the truth of Jesus, the Revealer of the Father. People in sin are in such darkness that they need someone to tell them what is **light.** John's goal was that **all men might** come to trust in Jesus.

1:8. John the Baptist was great, but **he . . . was not the Light.** Some evidence suggests that the movement begun by John the Baptist continued after his death and even after the death and resurrection of Jesus (4:1; cf. Mark 6:29; Luke 5:33). Twenty years after Jesus' resurrection (cf. Acts 18:25; 19:1-7) Paul found about 12 disciples of John the Baptist in Ephesus. A Mandaean sect still continues south of Baghdad which, though hostile to Christianity, claims an ancestral link to the Baptist.

C. The coming of the Light (1:9-13)

1:9. This has been called the Quaker's text because of that group's erroneous use of it and their stress on the "inner light." The words **was coming** (erchome-non) may refer to every man (as in the NIV marg.) or to Christ, **the true Light** (as in the NIV text). The latter is preferred, for it suggests the Incarnation.

Christ **gives light to every man.** This does not mean universal salvation or general revelation or even inner illumination. Instead, it means that Christ as the Light shines (phōtizei) on each person either in salvation or in illuminating him with regard to his sin and coming judgment (3:18-21; 9:39-41; cf. 16:8-11).

1:10. The world (kosmos) means the world of men and human society which is now in disobedience to God and under the rulership of Satan (cf. 14:30). The Logos came among people in the Incarnation, but mankind **did not recognize** its Maker (cf. Isa. 1:2-3). The failure to recognize (egnō, "know") **Him** was not because God's nature was somehow "hidden" in people, as some suggest. Rather, it is because of human ignorance and blindness, caused by sin (John 12:37).

1:11. In some ways this is one of the saddest verses in the Bible. The Logos went to **His own** home **but** He had no welcome. Jesus went to **His own** people, the nation Israel, but they as a whole rejected Him. In rejecting **Him,** they refused to accept Him as the Revelation sent by the Father and refused to obey His commands. Isaiah long before had prophesied of this Jewish national unbelief: "Who has believed our message?" (Isa. 53:1)

1:12. That unbelief, however, was not universal. Some **received** Jesus' universal invitation. **To all who** accepted Jesus as the Revealer of the Father's will and as the Sacrifice for sin, **He gave the right to become children of God.** The word "right" (exousian) is a needed improvement over the KJV's "power," and "children" (tekna) is better than the KJV's "sons." People are not naturally children of God but can become so by receiving the gift of the new birth.

1:13. The new birth does **not** come by **natural descent** (lit., "of bloods"), **nor** is it the result **of a human decision** (lit., "the will of the flesh," i.e., the natural human desire for children), nor is it the result of **a husband's will.** The birth of a child of God is not a natural birth; it is a supernatural work **of God** in regeneration. A person welcomes Jesus and responds in faith and obedience to Him, but the mysterious work of the Holy Spirit is "the cause" of regeneration (3:5-8).

D. The Incarnation and revelation (1:14-18)

1:14. The Word (*Logos*; cf. v. 1) **became flesh.** Christ, the eternal *Logos*, who is God, came to earth as man. Yet in doing so, He did not merely "appear" like a man; He became one (cf. Phil. 2:5-9). Humanity, in other words, was added to Christ's deity. And yet Christ, in becoming "flesh," did not change; so perhaps the word "became" (*egeneto*) should be understood as "took to Himself" or "arrived on the scene as."

"Flesh" in this verse means a human nature, not sinfulness or weakness. In the Greek the words **lived for a while among us** recall God's dwelling with Israel in the Old Testament. The word "lived" is *eskēnōsen*, from *skēnē* ("tabernacle"). Much as God's presence was in the tabernacle (Ex. 40:34), so Jesus dwelt among people.

We have seen most naturally implies that the author was an eyewitness. **His glory** refers to the unique splendor and honor seen in Jesus' life, miracles, death, and resurrection. **The one and only Son** (*monogenous*; cf. John 1:18; 3:16, 18; 1 John 4:9) means that Jesus is the Son of God in a sense totally different from a human who believes and becomes a child of God. Jesus' sonship is unique for He is eternal and is of the same essence as **the Father.** The glorious revelation of God which the *Logos* displayed was **full of grace and truth,** that is, it was a gracious and truthful revelation (cf. John 1:17).

1:15. John the Baptist gave a continuing testimony to Jesus. The present tense of the Greek verbs **testifies** and **cries out** stresses this. Jesus was younger and began His ministry later than John. But John said that because of His preexistence (and thus His true nature) **He . . . has surpassed me.**

1:16. The Word made flesh is the source of grace (*charin*), which is the sum total of all the spiritual favors God gives to people. The words **we . . . all** refer to Christians and include John the author. Because of **the fullness of His grace . . . one blessing after another** (*charin anti charitos*, lit., "grace in place of grace") comes to Christians as waves continue to

come to the shore. The Christian life is the constant reception of one evidence of God's grace replacing another.

1:17. The greatness of the old dispensation was the giving of **the Law** by God **through** His servant **Moses.** No other nation has had such a privilege. But the glory of the church is the revelation of God's **grace and truth . . . through Jesus Christ** (cf. v. 14).

1:18. The statement **No one has ever seen God** (cf. 1 John 4:12) may seem to raise a problem. Did not Isaiah say, "My eyes have seen the King, the LORD Almighty"? (Isa. 6:5) God in His essence is invisible (1 Tim. 1:17). He is One "whom no one has seen or can see" (1 Tim. 6:16). But John 1:18 means, "no one has ever seen God's essential nature." God may be seen in a theophany or anthropomorphism but His inner essence or nature is disclosed only in Jesus.

God the only Son is literally "the unique God" or "the only begotten God" (*monogenēs theos*; cf. *monogenous*, "the one and only" in v. 14). John was probably ending his prologue by returning to the truth stated in verse 1 that the Word is God. Verse 18 is another statement affirming Christ's deity: He is unique, the one and only God. The Son **is at the Father's side,** thus revealing the intimacy of the Father and the Son (cf. the Word was "with God," vv. 1-2). Furthermore, the Son **has made . . . known** (*exēgēsato,* whence the Eng. "exegeted") the Father. The Son is the "exegete" of the Father, and as a result of His work the nature of the invisible Father (cf. 4:24) is displayed in the Son (cf. 6:46).

II. Jesus' Manifestation to the Nation (1:19–12:50)

This major part of John's Gospel describes the public ministry of Jesus to the nation Israel. It is a "book of signs," a narrative of seven of Jesus' miracles that point to Him as the Messiah. Along with the signs are public discourses explaining the significance of the signs and two long private interviews (chaps. 3–4).

A. Jesus' early ministry (1:19–4:54)

1. EARLY TESTIMONIES TO JESUS (1:19-34)

a. John's first witness (1:19-28)

1:19. As in the Synoptic Gospels, the ministry of John the Baptist was so influential that the authorities in **Jerusalem** decided to investigate him. **The Jews** is the author's title for the city's leaders. The **priests and Levites** went **to ask** about his baptism and what he claimed for himself.

1:20-21. John said, **I am not the Christ** (i.e., the Messiah). (See comments on vv. 40-41 about the meaning of the title "Messiah.") This was his confession, as stressed by the repetition of the verb (in Gr.) **confessed.**

Interestingly in response to their questions John's answers were progressively shorter: "I am not the Christ" (v. 20); **I am not** (v. 21); **No** (v. 21). He did not want to talk about himself, for his function was to point to Another. John had an Elijah-type ministry. He appeared on the scene suddenly and even dressed like **Elijah.** He sought to turn people back to God as Elijah did in his day. And Malachi had predicted that Elijah would return before Messiah's coming (Mal. 4:5). Therefore many speculated that John was Elijah. **The Prophet** was expected because of Deuteronomy 18:15 (referring to Christ; cf. John 1:45). Some wrongly understood that the coming "prophet" was to be distinct from the Messiah (v. 24; 7:40-41).

1:22-23. John replied that he was not any of the expected prophetic figures. He explained, however, that his ministry was described in the Old Testament. He was **the voice** (*phōnē*), while Jesus is the Word (*Logos*). John's function was one of preparation, and it was carried on in **the desert.** (On the meaning of John's quotation from Isa. 40:3, see the comments on Matt. 3:3.)

1:24-25. The **Pharisees** were an important sect of Judaism. They numbered about 6,000 and were most influential. They held a strict interpretation of the Law and embraced many oral traditions. The Pharisees were the only minor group to survive the Jewish war of A.D. 66-70, and their teachings formed the basis for Talmudic Judaism. Their question to the Baptizer was, in essence, "Since you have no official title, **why** are you baptizing?"

1:26-27. John knew that his baptizing work was only anticipatory. He explained that another **One** was coming who was unknown to them. That coming **One** is so great that John considered himself unworthy to do even the lowliest service for Him (such as untying His sandals).

1:28. The site of **Bethany on the other side of the Jordan** River is now unknown. (It is not to be confused with another Bethany, home of Mary, Martha, and Lazarus, near Jerusalem.) As early as A.D. 200, Origen, when visiting Palestine, could not find it. A probable site is opposite Jericho.

b. John's second witness (1:29-34)

1:29. John's second witness started at the beginning of a series of days (cf. **The next day** in vv. 29, 35, 43; and "On the third day" in 2:1) when Jesus' first disciples were called and came to faith. **John** identified **Jesus** as **the Lamb of God** (cf. 1:36; 1 Peter 1:19). The connection to the Old Testament sacrifices is probably general. The sin offering which bore the sins of the nation on the Day of Atonement was a goat (Lev. 16). Daily offerings were normally lambs, but they did not atone for sin. The Passover lamb (Ex. 12) and Isaiah's mention of the Messiah's likeness to a lamb (Isa. 53:7) may have been in John's mind. John, by the Holy Spirit, saw Jesus as the sacrificial Victim who was to die for **the sin of the world** (cf. Isa. 53:12).

1:30-31. John repeated here what he had said earlier about Jesus (vv. 15, 27). John's fame was to be superseded by that of Jesus, whose priority stems from His preexistence: **He was before me.** But why did John say, **I myself did not know Him?** Though John and Jesus were related, as Mary and Elizabeth were relatives (Luke 1:36), nothing is known of any contacts between them in their years of childhood and adolescence. John did not know that Jesus was the coming One until He was revealed by the Father. All John knew was that he was to prepare the way for Him by **baptizing with water.** God would send His Man **to Israel** in His good time.

1:32. The baptism of Jesus is not recorded in John's Gospel, but the material of the Synoptic Gospels is assumed (see "John's Distinctive Portrait" in the *Introduction*). The Fourth Gospel does not state that this descent of **the Spirit** like **a dove** occurred at Jesus' baptism. The significant thing is that the invisible Spirit came **from heaven** and manifested Himself in a bodily (dovelike) form. John saw the Spirit as a dove **remain on** Jesus (cf. Isa. 11:2; Mark 1:10).

1:33. John had been **told** by God **(the One who sent** him) that when this sign of the dove would occur, the Person so marked out by the Spirit's coming and presence would be the One who would **baptize** by that same **Holy Spirit.** Cleansing by water is one thing, but the cleansing produced by the Spirit is of another order. Later at Pentecost, 50 days after Jesus' resurrection, the baptism with the Holy Spirit brought in a new Age (Acts 1:5; 2:1-3), the Church Age, the "Age of the Spirit" (cf. 1 Cor. 12:13).

1:34. John's testimony was **that this is the Son of God.** The prophesied Davidic King was God's Son (2 Sam. 7:13), and the messianic King is uniquely the Son of God (Ps. 2:7). The title "Son of God" goes beyond the idea of obedience and messianic King to that of Jesus' essential nature. In the Fourth Gospel this title is not applied to believers. They are called "children" (*tekna*; e.g., John 1:12) while "Son" (*hyios*) is used only of Jesus.

2. THE DISCIPLES OF JESUS (1:35-51)

a. *Jesus' first disciples (1:35-42)*

1:35-36. The next day refers to the second day in this series (cf. vv. 29, 35, 43; 2:1). The most likely reason for this chronological notation is that the author had a particular interest in narrating how some disciples came from their positions as adherents in John's party to faith in **Jesus.** The verb tenses in 1:35-36 are unusual. **John was there** (lit., "stood," perf. tense) while Jesus was **passing by** (pres. tense). The action in God's economy was shifting from John's baptism to the ministry of Jesus. John pointed **his disciples** to Jesus as God's **Lamb** (cf. comments on v. 29).

1:37. Two of John's **disciples heard** the witness of the Baptist and **followed Jesus.** The word "followed" probably has a double meaning here. They followed Him in the sense of literal walking and also as His disciples, that is, they turned their allegiance to Jesus that day.

1:38. The first words the disciples heard from **Jesus** were, **What do you want?** In one sense Jesus was asking a simple question and the disciples responded with a request for information as

to **where** He lived. But the author seemed to imply more. Perhaps Jesus was also asking, "What are you seeking in life?" The word translated **staying** (*menō*) is a favorite word of John's. This Greek word occurs here in his writings for the first time. Of the 112 New Testament passages in which it occurs, 66 are in his writings— 40 in the Gospel of John, 23 in 1 John, and 3 in 2 John (William F. Arndt and F. Wilbur Gingrich, *A Greek-English Lexicon of the New Testament and Other Early Christian Literature.* Chicago: University of Chicago Press, 1957, pp. 504-5). Sometimes, as here, it means "to stay or dwell" in a place; a few times it means "to last or continue"; but more often it has a theological connotation: "to remain, continue, abide" (e.g., John 15:4-7).

1:39. Jesus' words of invitation were, **Come . . . and you will see.** A person must first come to Him; then he will see. In addition to their seeing where He stayed, these words may possibly also have a deeper theological implication. The two disciples remained with Him **that day,** beginning at **the 10th hour.** That hour was 4 P.M. or 10 A.M., depending on whether the Fourth Gospel counted days from 6 A.M. (as the Synoptics customarily did) or from midnight or noon. The 10 A.M. times seems better and was the official Roman usage (cf. comments on 4:6; 19:14).

1:40-41. Andrew, one of the two disciples who **followed Jesus,** was the first proclaimer of Jesus as **the Messiah.** In Hebrew, "Messiah" means "the anointed One," which in Greek is translated **Christ** (*ho Christos*). The idea of "the anointed One" comes from the Old Testament practice of anointing priests and kings with oil. This was symbolic of the Spirit and pointed to the future One who would come (cf. Isa. 61:1). The title "Messiah" came to be used of the future Davidic King (cf. Matt. 1:1; John 6:15). In bringing **his brother Simon** Peter to Christ, no man did the church a greater service than Andrew. Andrew appeared two more times in John (6:4-9; 12:20-22); both times he was bringing someone to Jesus. The unnamed disciple is commonly held to be John the son of Zebedee, a brother of James and author of this Gospel. In Mark 1:16-20 two pairs of brothers (Simon and Andrew, James and John) who were fishermen were called by Jesus.

1:42. When **Jesus . . . looked at** Simon (cf. v. 47), He knew the man's character and destiny. Jesus gave him the Aramaic name **Cephas. Peter** is the Greek translation of Cephas ("rock"). Simon's name in Hebrew was probably Simeon (Gr. in Acts 15:14; 2 Peter 1:1; cf. NIV marg.). No reason is given here for the change of his name from Simon to Cephas. The common understanding is that his name indicates what God by His grace would do through him. He would be a rock-like man in the church during its early years (cf. Matt. 16:18; Luke 22:31-32; John 21:15-19; Acts 2-5; 10–12).

b. Jesus' call of Philip and Nathanael (1:43-51)

1:43-44. Though the first disciples were from Galilee, **Jesus** had called them in Judea where they were with the Baptist. On His way north to **Galilee, He** called **Philip** to be His disciple. Philip's hometown **of Bethsaida** was on the northeast side of the Sea of Galilee (called "Bethsaida in Galilee" in 12:21). Also **Andrew and Peter** were born there. Politically, Bethsaida was in lower Gaulonitis in the territory of Herod Philip (Josephus *The Antiquities of the Jews* 18. 2. 1). Philip's name is Greek but his nationality cannot be inferred from that fact.

1:45. Philip's testimony to **Nathanael** stressed that Jesus is **the** Promised **One** of whom **Moses** (Deut. 18:18-19; cf. John 1:21, 25) and **the prophets** (Isa. 52:13–53:12; Dan. 7:13; Micah 5:2; Zech. 9:9) **wrote.** Surprisingly Philip called **Jesus . . . the son of Joseph.** But this is what the disciples would have believed at this time. Yet Nathanael would soon recognize that He is "the Son of God" (John 1:49).

1:46. Nathanael momentarily stumbled over the lowly origin of the Messiah. **Nazareth! Can anything good come from there?** Nathanael knew of the poor reputation of Nazareth. Surely the Messiah would come from Jerusalem, Hebron, or some other prominent city. Jesus' condescension still remains a puzzle to many people. How can the *Logos* be a Man? **Philip** was wise enough not to argue, he gently invited his friend to meet Jesus: **Come and see.** He knew that Nathanael's questions would then be resolved.

1:47. Jesus, having supernatural knowledge (cf. v. 42), called **Nathanael . . . a true Israelite, in whom there is nothing false** (*dolos,* "deceitful") unlike Jacob (cf. v. 51 with Gen. 28:12).

1:48. Nathanael was puzzled as to **how** Jesus knew about him. **Jesus** said He knew exactly what Nathanael was doing **before Philip** came up to him; he was **under the fig tree.** This expression often meant to have safety and leisure (cf. 1 Kings 4:25; Micah 4:4; Zech. 3:10). Perhaps here the fig tree was a place for meditation (cf. comments on John 1:50-51). Psalm 139 elaborates on the theme of God's knowledge of a person's life in every detail.

1:49. Jesus' supernatural knowledge moved **Nathanael** to confess Him as **the Son of God** and **the King of Israel.** This does not mean that Nathanael at this early date fully understood the Trinity or the Incarnation. Rather He understood Jesus to be the Son of God in the messianic sense (cf. Ps. 2:6-7). This future Davidic King would have God's Spirit on Him (Isa. 11:1-2) and thus would have supernatural knowledge.

1:50-51. Jesus promised Nathanael a **greater** basis for belief, probably referring to the miracles in chapters 2–13. From 1:48, 51 it can be inferred that Nathanael was meditating on Jacob's life, particularly on the incident recorded in Genesis 28:12. Jacob saw the angels going up and down a ladder. But Nathanael would **see . . . the angels of God ascending and descending on the Son of Man.** Just as Jacob saw angels from heaven communicating with earth, so Nathanael (and the others; though **you** is sing. in John 1:50, the **you** in v. 51 is pl.) would see Jesus as the divine Communication from heaven to earth. The Son of Man, replacing the ladder, is God's link with earth (cf. Dan. 7:13; Matt. 26:64). Perhaps Jesus was also indicating that He is the new "Bethel," God's dwelling place (Gen. 28:17; John 1:14).

As the Son of Man, Jesus left heaven to come to the earth. Jesus used the term "Son of Man" of Himself more than 80 times. It speaks of His humanity and suffering and His work as "the ideal Man." **I tell you the truth** ("Verily, verily," KJV; lit., "Amen, Amen") occurs

THE MIRACLES OF JESUS

Order	Miracle	Place	Matthew	Mark	Luke	John
1	Turning water into wine	Cana				2:1-11
2	Healing an official's son	Capernaum				4:46-54
3	Delivering a demoniac in the synagogue	Capernaum		1:21-28	4:33-37	
4	Healing Peter's wife's mother	Capernaum	8:14-15	1:29-31	4:38-39	
5	First miraculous catch of fish	Sea of Galilee			5:1-11	
6	Cleansing a leper	Galilee	8:2-4	1:40-45	5:12-15	
7	Healing a paralytic	Capernaum	9:1-8	2:1-12	5:17-26	
8	Healing an infirm man at the Pool of Bethesda	Jerusalem				5:1-15
9	Healing a withered hand	Galilee	12:9-13	3:1-5	6:6-11	
10	Healing a centurion's servant	Capernaum	8:5-13		7:1-10	
11	Raising a widow's son	Nain			7:11-17	
12	Casting out a blind and dumb spirit	Galilee	12:22-32		11:14-23	
13	Stilling a storm	Sea of Galilee	8:18-27	4:35-41	8:22-25	
14	Delivering a demoniac of Gadara	Gadara	8:28-34	5:1-20	8:26-39	
15	Healing a woman with a hemorrhage	Capernaum	9:20-22	5:25-34	8:43-48	
16	Raising Jairus' daughter	Capernaum	9:18-26	5:22-43	8:41-56	
17	Healing two blind men	Capernaum	9:27-31			
18	Casting out a dumb spirit	Capernaum	9:32-34			
19	Feeding the 5,000	Near Bethsaida	14:13-21	6:32-44	9:10-17	6:1-14
20	Walking on the water	Sea of Galilee	14:22-33	6:45-52		6:15-21
21	Casting out a demon from a Syrophoenician's daughter	Phoenicia	15:21-28	7:24-30		
22	Healing a deaf person with a speech impediment	Decapolis		7:31-37		
23	Feeding the 4,000	Decapolis	15:32-38	8:1-9		
24	Healing a blind man of Bethsaida	Bethsaida		8:22-26		
25	Casting out a demon from a lunatic boy	Mount Hermon	17:14-21	9:14-29	9:37-42	
26	Finding money in a fish's mouth	Capernaum	17:24-27			
27	Healing a man born blind	Jerusalem				9:1-7
28	Healing a woman infirm for 18 years	Perea(?)			13:10-17	
29	Healing a man with dropsy	Perea			14:1-6	
30	Raising Lazarus	Bethany				11:1-44
31	Cleansing 10 lepers	Samaria			17:11-19	
32	Healing blind Bartimaeus	Jericho	20:29-34	10:46-52	18:35-43	
33	Cursing a fig tree	Jerusalem	21:18-19	11:12-14		
34	Healing Malchus' ear	Jerusalem			22:49-51	
35	Second miraculous catch of fish	Sea of Galilee				21:1-13

25 times in John and always calls attention to important affirmations: 1:51; 3:3, 5, 11; 5:19, 24-25; 6:26, 32, 47, 53; 8:34, 51, 58; 10:1, 7; 12:24; 13:16, 20-21, 38; 14:12; 16:20, 23; 21:18. Interestingly this double "Amen" does not occur in the Synoptic Gospels.

3. JESUS' FIRST SIGN (2:1-11)

Jesus' first miracle in the Gospel of John was a private one, known only to His disciples, some servants, and probably Jesus' mother. If Matthew had not yet been called to be one of the Twelve, this may explain why the miracle is not recorded in the Synoptics. Of the four Gospel writers only John was there. John used the word "signs" (sēmeiōn, v. 11) because he was seeking to draw attention away from the miracles as such and to point up their significance. A miracle is also a "wonder" (teras), a "power" (dynamis), and a "strange event" (paradoxos).

This turning water into wine was the first of 35 recorded miracles Jesus performed. (See the chart listing those miracles, the places where they happened, and the references in the Gospels.)

2:1. On the third day probably means three days after the calling of Philip and Nathanael. (Cf. the sequence of days suggested by "the next day" in 1:29, 35, 43.) It would take a couple of days to reach **Cana in Galilee** from Bethany near Jericho of Judea (1:28). Cana was near Nazareth, though its exact location is unknown. **Jesus' mother was there,** but John did not give her name (cf. 2:12; 6:42; 19:25-27). In his Gospel, John never named himself or the mother of Jesus. (Jesus' mother went to the home of the beloved disciple John [19:27].)

2:2-3. Oriental wedding feasts often lasted seven days. The feast followed the groom's taking of his bride to his home or his father's house, before the consummation of the marriage. When the supply of **wine** was used up, Mary turned to Jesus in hope that He could solve the problem. Did Mary expect a miracle? In the light of verse 11 this is not likely. Mary had not yet seen any miracles done by her Son.

2:4-5. The word **woman** applied to His mother may seem strange to a modern reader, but it was a polite, kind expression (cf. 19:26). However, the clause, **Why do you involve Me?** was a common expression in Greek that referred to a difference in realms or relations. Demons spoke these words when they were confronted by Christ ("What do You want with us?" [Mark 1:24]; "What do You want with me?" [Mark 5:7]). Mary had to learn a painful lesson (cf. Luke 2:35), namely, that Jesus was committed to God the Father's will and the time for His manifestation was in the Father's hand. **My time has not yet come** or similar words occur five times in John (2:4; 7:6, 8, 30; 8:20). Later the fact that His time had come is mentioned three times (12:23; 13:1; 17:1). Mary's response **to the servants (Do whatever He tells you)** revealed her submission to her Son. Even though she did not fully understand, she trusted Him.

2:6-8. The water in the **six . . . water jars** (of **20 to 30 gallons** each) was **used** for Jewish purification rites before and after meals (cf. Matt. 15:1-2). The contrast between the old order and the new way is evident (cf. John 4:13; 7:38-39).

Probably the water jars were outside. **The master of the banquet,** in charge of the festivities, would not know he was drinking from the purification jars. For a Jew this would be unthinkable. The servants dipped out the water, which had become wine.

2:9-10. As **the master of the banquet tasted the . . . wine,** he found it to be superior to what they had been drinking. In contrast with a common custom in which the best **wine** was served **first** and the lesser quality later, he affirmed that this wine, served last, was the **best.** The significance of this miracle is that Christianity is an advance over Judaism. God has kept the best gift—His Son—until **now.**

2:11. The significance of the miracle was explained by John as a manifestation of Christ's **glory.** In contrast with the ministry of Moses who turned water into blood as a sign of God's judgment (Ex. 7:14-24), Jesus brings joy. His first miracle was a gracious indication of the joy which He provides by the Spirit. The sign points to Jesus as the Word in the flesh, who is the mighty Creator. Each year He turns water to wine in the agricultural and fermentation processes. Here He simply did the process immediately. The 120 gallons of fine wine were His gift to the young couple. The first miracle—a transformation—pointed to the kind of transforming ministry Jesus would have (cf. 2 Cor. 5:17). The **disciples put their faith in Him.** This initial faith would be tested and developed by a progressive revelation of Jesus, the *Logos.* At this point they did not understand His death and resurrection (John 20:8-9) but they did know His power.

4. JESUS' CAPERNAUM VISIT (2:12)

2:12. Jesus' move **to Capernaum** on the northwest shore of the Sea of Galilee **for a few days** marks an interlude in His life. Though Capernaum is northeast of Cana, **He went down** because of the decline in land elevation toward the sea. Capernaum became His home base (cf. Matt. 4:13; Mark 1:21; 2:1). From this point on He seemed to be alienated from His family (Mark 3:21, 31-35; John 7:3-5) and His hometown of Nazareth (Mark 6:1-6; Luke 4:14-30).

5. JESUS' FIRST MINISTRY IN JERUSALEM
   (2:13–3:21)

a. *Jesus' cleansing of the temple (2:13-25)*

John recorded a cleansing of the temple at the beginning of Jesus' ministry whereas the three Synoptics recorded a temple cleansing toward the end of His public ministry (Matt. 21:12-13; Mark 11:15-16; Luke 19:45-46). Probably there were two cleansings, for there are differences in the narrations. John was undoubtedly aware of the Synoptics, and he supplemented them. The first cleansing caught the people by surprise. The second cleansing, about three years later, was one of the immediate causes of His death (cf. Mark 11:15-18).

2:13-14. As was the custom for the **Jewish** people (Ex. 12:14-20, 43-49; Deut. 16:1-8) **Jesus went up to Jerusalem** to celebrate the **Passover** (cf. two other Passover feasts—one in John 6:4 and one in John 11:55; 12:1; 13:1). This reminded them of God's grace in delivering them from the bondage in Egypt. It was a fitting time for His ministry.

The temple courts refer to a large courtyard, the Court of the Gentiles, surrounding the temple enclosure. (See the sketch of the temple.) The buying and **selling** of animals in the area was probably rationalized as a convenience for the pilgrims coming into Jerusalem. But abuses developed, and the pilgrim

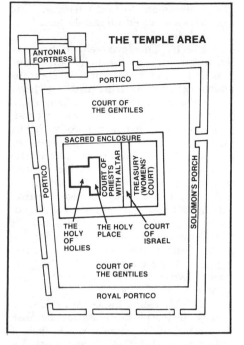

traffic became a major source of income for the city. With **money** to be made, worship easily became corrupted. The money changers were another convenience for the pilgrims. Temple dues had to be paid in the acceptable Tyrian coinage, and a high percentage was charged for changing coins.

2:15. Malachi predicted that One would come suddenly to **the temple** to purify the religion of the nation (Mal. 3:1-3). In moral indignation Jesus started a small stampede of the **sheep and cattle,** and **overturned** the **tables.**

2:16. Jesus protested the turning of His **Father's house into a market.** He did not protest the sacrificial system itself. The purpose of the sacrifices was in danger of being lost. In the second cleansing of the temple toward the end of His ministry, Jesus' attack was sharper. Then He called the temple area "a den of robbers" (Luke 19:46; cf. Jer. 7:11). Jesus frequently referred to God as "My Father." Only through Jesus can the Father be known. "No one knows the Father except the Son and those to whom the Son chooses to reveal Him" (Matt. 11:27).

2:17. Jesus' **disciples remembered** Psalm 69:9, which speaks of the fact that the Righteous One would pay a price for

His commitment to God's temple. This **zeal for** God would ultimately lead Him to His death.

2:18-19. The Jews—either the Jewish authorities or the merchants—**demanded** some proof for His right **to** challenge the existing order ("Jews demand miraculous signs," 1 Cor. 1:22). But instead of giving in to their demand, **Jesus** gave a veiled saying. As with His parables in the Synoptics, one purpose of an enigmatic saying was to puzzle the hearers who opposed Him. He desired that His hearers ponder the saying in order to perceive its significance. **Destroy this temple** is in the form of a command, but the sense is ironic or conditional. At Jesus' trial He was accused of saying He could destroy the temple and **raise it again in three days** (Matt. 26:60-61). A similar charge was made against Stephen (Acts 6:14).

2:20-21. Herod the Great decided to replace the temple of Zerubbabel because it was not of the same glory as that of Solomon's (Hag. 2:3). Since work on Herod's **temple** began in 20 or 19 B.C., **46 years** bring the date to A.D. 27 or 28. The work on the whole temple complex continued until around A.D. 63. The statement of **the Jews** meant either that the sanctuary was completed in 46 years or else one phase had been completed. How then, the Jews asked, could He rebuild **it in three days?** That would be impossible! The Greek words for **and You** are emphatic, suggesting their contempt for Him. Of course by **the temple** Jesus meant **His body** which, after his death, would be resurrected in three days.

2:22. Even Jesus' own **disciples** did not understand His enigmatic saying at first. It took the light of the Resurrection to illuminate it. They did not see the need for His death, so they did not think along these lines until after the event. Nor did they understand the Scriptures which speak of the Messiah's suffering and death (Isa. 52:12–53:12; Luke 24:25-27).

2:23. While . . . **in Jerusalem** during the **Passover,** Jesus did other **signs** which John chose not to describe. The effect of these miracles (which were probably healings) was to elicit faith on the part of **many people.** They **believed in His name,** that is, they trusted in Him. This was not necessarily saving faith as the

next verse implies. They believed He was a great Healer, but not necessarily a great Savior from sin.

2:24-25. Jesus knew that a temporary excitement or a faith based on signs was not sufficient. Many of the early followers later turned back when He did not take up the role of a political king (cf. 6:15, 60, 66). Until His death and resurrection and the coming of the Holy Spirit, the foundation for faith was not fully laid. Having supernatural knowledge, Jesus does **not need** human help to evaluate **men.** As God, He sees beyond the superficial to people's hearts (1 Sam. 16:7; Ps. 139; Acts 1:24). John 3 and 4 give illustrations of this truth. He knew Nicodemus' need, and He told the Samaritan woman about her past (4:29). The connection of chapter 3 to chapter 2 is evident (cf. **in a man** [2:25], and "Now there was a man" [3:1]).

b. *Jesus' interview with Nicodemus (3:1-21)*

3:1. Nicodemus represented the best in the nation. He was a teacher (v. 10), a Pharisee, and **a member of** the Sanhedrin, **the Jewish ruling council.** The Sanhedrin had 70 members who were responsible for religious decisions and also, under the Romans, for civil rule. Two Sanhedrin members who appear in a favorable light in the New Testament are Joseph of Arimathea (19:38) and the Rabbi Gamaliel (Acts 5:34-39; 22:3). The Sanhedrin put Jesus on trial (Luke 22:66). Nicodemus later rebuked the Pharisees for condemning Jesus without hearing Him (John 7:50-51), and he helped Joseph of Arimathea bury Jesus (19:39-40).

3:2. Why did Nicodemus go **to Jesus at night?** Because of fear? Because it was the normal time for visits? Because he wanted a time of uninterrupted conversation without the distractions of the ever-present crowds? John did not say why. And yet nighttime has a sinister tone in the Fourth Gospel (cf. 9:4; 11:10; 13:30; 19:39). Nicodemus began, **Rabbi, we know You are a Teacher who has come from God.** "We" probably means the favorable ones on the council. The titles "Rabbi" and "Teacher" are polite and flattering on one hand, but they showed Nicodemus' inadequate comprehension of who Jesus is. The words "from God" are in an emphatic position in the Greek.

The **signs** had pointed out Jesus as God's Man (**God** was **with Him**), and Nicodemus wanted to talk to Him as one Rabbi to another.

3:3. But **Jesus** was not on the same level with Nicodemus. He is "from above" (*anōthen*; v. 31); therefore Nicodemus must be born "from above" (v. 3, NIV marg.; *anōthen*). To be **born again** or born "from above" (*anōthen* has both meanings; e.g., "from above" in 19:11 and "again" in Gal. 4:9) is to have a spiritual transformation which takes a person out of the kingdom of darkness into **the kingdom of God** (cf. Col. 1:13). The kingdom is the sphere or realm of God's authority and blessing which is now invisible but will be manifested on earth (Matt. 6:10).

3:4. Nicodemus was certain Jesus did not mean something absurd (such as a reincarnation or a **second** physical birth), but yet he did not grasp the nature of regeneration.

3:5. Various views are given to explain Jesus' words about being **born of water and the Spirit:** (1) The "water" refers to the natural birth, and the "Spirit" to the birth from above. (2) The "water" refers to the Word of God (Eph. 5:26). (3) The "water" refers to baptism as an essential part of regeneration. (This view contradicts other Bible verses that make it clear that salvation is by faith alone; e.g., John 3:16, 36; Eph. 2:8-9; Titus 3:5.) (4) The "water" is a symbol of the Holy Spirit (John 7:37-39). (5) The "water" refers to the repentance ministry of John the Baptist, and the "Spirit" refers to the application by the Holy Spirit of Christ to an individual.

The fifth view has the merit of historical propriety as well as theological acceptability. John the Baptist had stirred the nation by his ministry and stress on repentance (Matt. 3:1-6). "Water" would remind Nicodemus of the Baptist's emphasis. So Jesus was saying that Nicodemus, in order to **enter the kingdom,** needed to turn to Him (repent) in order to be regenerated by the Holy Spirit.

3:6-7. There are two distinct realms: one is of fallen man (the **flesh**) and the other is of God (**the Spirit**). A fallen person cannot regenerate himself; he needs a divine operation. Only God's Holy Spirit can regenerate a human spirit.

People should not stumble at or reject the importance of Jesus' words. They **must be born** from above. The necessity is absolute and is universally binding.

3:8. This verse contains a wordplay which cannot be adequately expressed in English. The Greek word *pneuma* means both wind and Spirit. The work of **the Spirit** (*pneuma*) is invisible and mysterious like the blowing of **the wind** (*pneuma*). Man controls neither.

3:9-10. Nicodemus asked . . . how this spiritual transformation takes place. **Jesus** answered that Nicodemus, as the **teacher** of Israel (the Gr. has the article "the"), ought to know. The Old Testament prophets spoke of the new Age with its working of the Spirit (Isa. 32:15; Ezek. 36:25-27; Joel 2:28-29). The nation's outstanding teacher ought to **understand** how God by His sovereign grace can give someone a new heart (1 Sam. 10:6; Jer. 31:33).

3:11. But Nicodemus was ignorant of the realm of which Jesus spoke. He represented the nation's unbelief and lack of knowledge. Jesus, like the prophets, spoke to the nation about divine themes but the Jews rejected His witness. "Witness" (or **testimony**; *martyrian*) is a common word in John's Gospel (see the chart at 5:33-34).

3:12. Since Nicodemus could not grasp the basic teaching of regeneration which Jesus presented in **earthly** analogies, how could he understand and **believe** the more abstract **heavenly** matters such as the Trinity, the Incarnation, and Jesus' coming glorification?

3:13. No one has ever gone into heaven and then come back to earth, able to give clear teaching about divine matters. The one exception is Jesus who is **the Son of Man** (cf. 1:50-51; Dan. 7:13; Matt. 26:64). He is the "Ladder" between heaven and earth with access to both realms (cf. comments on John 1:50-51). He "descended" in the Incarnation and "ascended" in the Ascension. He also was in **heaven** before the Incarnation, and therefore knows the divine mysteries.

3:14-15. The thought of elevation to heaven (v. 13) leads to the thought of Jesus being **lifted up** (cf. 8:28; 12:32). **Moses** raised a bronze **snake** on a pole as a cure for a punishment due to disobedience (cf. Num. 21:4-9). **So** Jesus would **be**

lifted up on a cross for people's sin, so **that** a look of faith gives **eternal life** to those doomed to die.

3:16. Whether this verse was spoken by John or Jesus, it is God's Word and is an important summary of the gospel. God's motivation toward people is love. God's love is not limited to a few or to one group of people but His gift is for **the** whole **world.** God's love was expressed in the giving of His most priceless gift—**His** unique **Son** (cf. Rom. 8:3, 32). The Greek word translated **one and only,** referring to the Son, is *monogenē,* which means "only begotten," or "only born-one." It is also used in John 1:14, 18; 3:18; and 1 John 4:9. On man's side, the gift is simply to be received, not earned (John 1:12-13). A person is saved by believing, by trusting in Christ. **Perish** (*apolētai*) means not annihilation but rather a final destiny of "ruin" in hell apart from God who is life, truth, and joy. **Eternal life** is a new quality of life, which a believer has now as a present possession and will possess forever (cf. 10:28; 17:3).

3:17. Though light casts shadows, its purpose is to illuminate. Though those who do not believe are condemned, God's purpose in sending **His Son** is salvation **(to save),** not damnation **(to condemn).** God does **not** delight in the death of the wicked (Ezek. 18:23, 32). He desires that everyone be saved (1 Tim. 2:4; 2 Peter 3:9).

3:18. The instrumental means of salvation is believing in the finished work of Jesus on the cross. But people who reject the light of the *Logos* are in the dark (1:5; 8:12) and are therefore **already** under God's judgment. They stand **condemned.** They are like those sinful, dying Israelites who willfully rejected the divine remedy (Num. 21:4-9). A believer in Christ, on the other hand, is under "no condemnation" (Rom. 8:1); he "will not be condemned" (John 5:24).

3:19. Men love **darkness** not for its own sake but because of what it hides. They want to continue undisturbed in their **evil** (*ponēra,* "wicked"; cf. v. 20 which has a different word for evil) **deeds.** A believer is also a sinner (though a redeemed one), but he confesses his sin and responds to God (cf. 1 John 1:6-7). In the ultimate sense, man's love of darkness rather than God the **Light** (John 1:5, 10-11; 1 John 1:5) is his love for idols. He

worships and serves "created things rather than the Creator" (Rom. 1:25).

3:20. Just as natural light shows up what is otherwise unseen, so Christ **the Light** exposes people's deeds as "evil." (The word "evil" here is *phaula* ["worthless"], also used by John in 5:29.) Unbelievers have no ultimate meaning of life, no worthy motivation, no adequate goal, and a destiny of doom. Yet **everyone who does evil hates the light** (as well as loves darkness, 3:19). He fears that if he comes to the light **his deeds will be** seen as worthless, and he would need to turn from them.

3:21. Jesus is like a magnet. His people are drawn to Him and welcome His revelation. Though **the light** rebukes their sin, they respond in repentance and faith. They live **by the truth** (cf. 2 John 1-2, 4; 3 John 1, 4). By regeneration they live differently than their former lives of darkness. Their new lives are by faith in Jesus and His Word. And the Spirit, working in their lives, gives them new power, goals, and interests (2 Cor. 5:17; Eph. 2:10).

6. THE FINAL TESTIMONY OF JOHN THE BAPTIST (3:22-30)

3:22-24. For a short time the ministry of **John** the Baptist overlapped Jesus' ministry. Thus **the Judean countryside** must have been alive with the teaching of both these great preachers of repentance and God's kingdom. Both John and **Jesus** had **disciples,** large crowds followed both of them, and both **baptized.** The statement that Jesus "baptized" (vv. 22, 26) probably means He was overseeing the baptizing done by His disciples (4:2). The site of **Aenon near Salim** is unknown today but a likely location is about midway between the Sea of Galilee and the Dead Sea (and about three miles east of Shechem). Both groups were baptizing and thus two "reform" movements were popular. **This was before John was put in prison** (3:24). This statement reveals how the Fourth Gospel supplements the Synoptics. It implies that readers knew about John's imprisonment from reading the other Gospels (Matt. 14:1-12; Mark 6:14-29; Luke 3:19-20) or from common church tradition.

3:25. The zealous **disciples** of John the Baptist found themselves at a disadvantage in **an argument. A certain Jew**

asked why he should join **John's** group. He (and others; cf. "They" in v. 26) argued about **ceremonial washing.** Since there were Essene lustrations and Pharisaic washings, why should Jews follow another washing, John's baptism? Besides, the group following Jesus was larger (v. 26).

3:26. John's disciples may have been angry and jealous. (They were interested in John's movement and were not committed to Jesus.) They complained that Jesus, of whom **John** had **testified,** had now captured the nation's attention. They longed for the former days when **everyone** went to hear John (Mark 1:5).

3:27. John's greatness is revealed in his reply. He said, **A man can receive only what is given him from heaven.** God is sovereign in bestowing His blessings on one's ministry. If Jesus' movement was expanding, then it must have been in the will of God. This principle of God's sovereignty is stressed in John (cf. 6:65; 19:11) as well as elsewhere in the New Testament (e.g., 1 Cor. 4:7).

3:28. John also reminded his disciples that they were forgetting part of his teaching. For he had clearly taught that he was **not the** promised Messiah **but** was only **sent ahead** by God to do a work of preparation for the Messiah (1:8, 15, 20, 23).

3:29-30. In Jesus' growing influence, John found his own **joy** fulfilled. He illustrated this for his disciples by referring to a custom at Near Eastern weddings. **The friend** of **the bridegroom** was only an assistant, not the main participant in the marriage. The assistant acted on behalf of **the bridegroom** and made the preliminary arrangements for the ceremony. His **joy** came when he heard the bridegroom coming for his bride. John the Baptist's work was to prepare for the arrival of Christ, the "Groom." John baptized only with water, not with the Spirit. Therefore Jesus **must become greater** and John **must become less.** This was not merely advisable or fortuitous; it was the divine order. John willingly and with **joy** accepted Jesus' growing popularity as God's plan.

7. THE TESTIMONY OF JOHN THE EVANGELIST (3:31-36)

The quotation marks in the text of the NIV are a modern innovation and the judgment of translators. The original Greek manuscripts did not have any quotation marks. As the NIV margin indicates, the closing quotation marks could be placed after verse 30 rather than at the end of verse 36. It seems better to view this section (vv. 31-36) as the testimony of John the Evangelist because the theological exposition about the Father and the Son is more a feature of Christian theology than a part of John the Baptist's testimony.

3:31. Here John the Evangelist developed the theme about the supremacy of Jesus, which John the Baptist spoke of to his followers (vv. 28-30). Since Jesus has come from heaven, His words surpass those of any religious teacher. Each human teacher is limited by his earthly boundaries (he **belongs to the earth and** is **from the earth**). But the *Logos* **from heaven is above all;** He is preeminent (Col. 1:18).

3:32. What Jesus spoke came from His previous vision of and communion with the Father in heaven (cf. 1:1, 14). Yet in spite of this clear reliable witness, mankind as a whole has rejected His message (cf. 1:11).

3:33. The message of Jesus has not been universally rejected as verse 32 by itself might indicate. One who receives it gives his attestation or certification to the fact **that God is truthful** (cf. v. 21). To reject this testimony is to call God a liar (1 John 5:10).

3:34. Jesus gives the perfect truth of God as He **speaks the words of God,** because He has the full endowment of the Holy Spirit, **the Spirit without limit.** The Old Testament prophets had the Spirit only for limited times and for limited purposes.

The Apostle John referred to Jesus as **the One whom God has sent.** Thirty-nine times the Gospel of John refers to Jesus being sent from God (vv. 17, 34; 4:34; 5:23-24, 30, 36-38; 6:29, 38-39, 44, 57; 7:16, 28-29; 8:16, 18, 26, 29, 42; 9:4; 10:36; 11:42; 12:44-45, 49; 13:16, 20; 14:24; 15:21; 16:5; 17:3, 18, 21, 23, 25; 20:21). This affirms Jesus' deity and heavenly origin, as well as God's sovereignty and love in initiating the Son's Incarnation (cf. Gal. 4:4; 1 John 4:9-10, 14).

3:35. The relationship between **the Son** and **the Father** is one of loving

CONTRASTS BETWEEN NICODEMUS AND THE SAMARITAN WOMAN (JOHN 3–4)

	Nicodemus	Samaritan Woman
PLACE	(Jerusalem) Judah	Samaria
TIME	By night	About 6 P.M.
OCCASION	Planned visit	By chance
CONTENT	Theological	Practical
INITIATOR	Nicodemus	Jesus
ETHNIC GROUP	Jew	Samaritan (mixed blood)
SOCIAL STATUS	Highly respected ruler, teacher	Despised woman (immoral)
SEX	Male	Female
ATTITUDE	Polite, calling Jesus Rabbi	First hostility, then respect
FORM	Nicodemus faded out, dialogue became monologue	Dialogue carried to the end
RESULT	Not mentioned	Woman converted, witnessed, and people came to believe

intimacy and complete confidence. The Son is endowed with all authority to accomplish the Father's purposes (5:22; Matt. 28:18).

3:36. Man has only two options: trust **in the Son** or reject **the Son** (cf. vv. 16, 18). Unbelief is tragic ignorance but it is also willful disobedience to clear light. **God's wrath** is mentioned only here in the Fourth Gospel (but cf. Rev. 6:16-17; 11:18; 14:10; 16:19; 19:15). "Wrath," God's necessary righteous reaction against evil, **remains** (*menei*) on the unbeliever. This wrath is future but it also exists now. Endless sin and disobedience will result in endless punishment (Matt. 25:46).

8. JESUS' MINISTRY IN SAMARIA (4:1-42)

a. Jesus' interview with a Samaritan woman (4:1-26)

4:1-3. In Greek these verses are one long sentence, introducing the reader to a second long interview by Jesus. The words, **When the Lord learned of this** (v. 3), are actually the first phrase in Greek in verse 1. The sudden prominence of **Jesus,** evidenced by the growth of His followers, caused **the Pharisees** to take special notice of Him. Since Jesus was working on God's schedule, He knew

how His ministry would end. Until that appointed time, He must live carefully, so He withdrew from the conflict until His "hour" (7:6, 8, 30; 8:20; cf. 12:23; 13:1; 17:1). **He left Judea** (cf. 3:22) **and went back . . . to Galilee.**

This second interview is another illustration of the fact that "He knew what was in a man" (2:25). The Samaritan woman contrasts sharply with Nicodemus. He was seeking; she was indifferent. He was a respected ruler; she was an outcast. He was serious; she was flippant. He was a Jew; she was a despised Samaritan. He was (presumably) moral; she was immoral. He was orthodox; she was heterodox. He was learned in religious matters; she was ignorant. Yet in spite of all the differences between this "churchman" and this woman of the world, they both needed to be born again. Both had needs only Christ could meet.

4:4. He had to go through Samaria. This was the shortest route from Judea to Galilee but not the only way. The other route was through Perea, east of the Jordan River. (See the two routes on the map.) In Jesus' day the Jews, because of their hatred for the Samaritans, normally took the eastern route in order to avoid Samaria. But Jesus chose the route through Samaria in order to reach the despised people of that region. As the Savior of the world He seeks out and saves the despised and outcasts (cf. Luke 19:10).

"Samaria" in New Testament times was a region in the middle of Palestine, with Judea to the south and Galilee to the north. Samaria was without separate political existence under the Roman governor. The people were racially mixed and their religion resulted from syncretism and schism from Judaism. Its center of worship was Mount Gerizim. Even today in Israel, a small group of Samaritans maintain their traditions.

4:5-6. The village of **Sychar** was **near** Shechem. Most identify the site with modern Akar but others point to Tell-Balatah. Sychar was between Mount Ebal and Mount Gerizim. A well near Sychar today may be the same as **Jacob's well. The plot of ground** which **Jacob** gave to **Joseph** is mentioned in Genesis 48:21-22. Jacob had purchased it years earlier (Gen. 33:18-20). **Jesus, tired** from walking, **sat down by the well. It was about the sixth hour,** which according to Roman time reckoning would have been 6 P.M. (See comments on John 1:39; 19:14.) Jesus being truly human, experienced thirst, weariness, pain, and hunger. Of course He also possesses all the attributes of Deity (omniscience, omnipotence, etc.).

4:7-8. With His **disciples** in the city buying **food,** Jesus did a surprising thing: He spoke to **a Samaritan woman,** whom He had never met. She was of the region of Samaria, not the town of Samaria. The woman was shocked to hear a Jewish man ask for **a drink** from her. The normal prejudices of the day prohibited public conversation between men and women, between Jews and Samaritans, and especially between strangers. A Jewish Rabbi would rather go thirsty than violate these proprieties.

4:9. Surprised and curious, the **woman** could not understand **how** He would dare **ask** her **for a drink,** since **Jews** did **not associate with Samaritans.** The NIV margin gives an alternate translation to the Greek sentence with the word *synchrōntai* ("associate" or "use together"): the Jews "do not use dishes Samaritans have used." This rendering may well be correct. A Rabbinic law of A.D. 66 stated that Samaritan women were

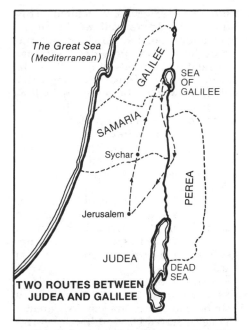

The Great Sea (Mediterranean)

GALILEE

SEA OF GALILEE

SAMARIA

Sychar

PEREA

Jerusalem

JUDEA

DEAD SEA

TWO ROUTES BETWEEN JUDEA AND GALILEE

considered as continually menstruating and thus unclean. Therefore a Jew who drank from a Samaritan woman's vessel would become ceremonially unclean.

4:10. Having captured her attention and stimulated her curiosity, **Jesus** then spoke an enigmatic saying to cause her to think. It was as if He had said, "Your shock would be infinitely greater if you really knew who I am. *You*—not I— would be asking!" Three things would have provoked her thinking: (1) **Who** is He? (2) What is **the gift of God?** (3) What is **living water?** "Living water" in one sense is running water, but in another sense it is the Holy Spirit (Jer. 2:13; Zech. 14:8; John 7:38-39).

4:11-12. She misunderstood the "living water" and thought only of water from **the well.** Since Jacob's **well** was so **deep** how could Jesus **get this living water?** Today this well is identified by archeologists as one of the deepest in Palestine. **Are You greater than our father Jacob?** she asked. In Greek this question expects a negative answer. She could not conceive of Him as greater than Jacob. Her claim "our father Jacob" is interesting in light of the fact that the Jews claim him as the founder of *their* nation. That well had great tradition behind it but, she wondered, *What does this Stranger have?*

4:13-14. **Jesus** began to unveil the

truth in an enigmatic statement. **This water** from Jacob's well would satisfy only bodily thirst for a time. But **the water** Jesus gives provides continual satisfaction of needs and desires. In addition one who **drinks** His living water **will** have within **him a spring of** life-giving **water** (cf. 7:38-39). This inner spring contrasts with the water from the well, which required hard work to acquire. Jesus was speaking of the Holy Spirit who brings salvation to a person who believes and through Him offers salvation to others.

4:15. The woman could not grasp this dark saying because of her sin and materialism. All she could understand was that if she had a spring she would not **get thirsty and** would not have to work so hard.

4:16-18. Since she was not able to receive His truth (1 Cor. 2:14), Jesus dealt with her most basic problem. (Apparently she never served Him a drink. He forgot His own physical need in order to meet her spiritual need.) Jesus suggested she get her **husband and** bring him **back** with her. This suggestion was designed to show her that He knew everything about her (cf. John 2:24-25). Her marital history was known to this Stranger, including the fact that she was living in sin. Thus in a few words **Jesus** had revealed her life of sin and her need for salvation.

4:19-20. Her response was most interesting! Jesus was not just a passing Jewish Rabbi. Since He had supernatural knowledge, He must be **a prophet** of God. But instead of confessing her sin and repenting, she threw out an intellectual "red herring." Could He solve an ancient dispute? Samaritan religion held that the one place of divinely ordered **worship** was **on** top of nearby Mount Gerizim, whereas the **Jews** said it was on the temple mount **in Jerusalem.** Who was right in this controversy?

4:21. A time is coming (cf. v. 23) referred to the coming death of **Jesus** which would inaugurate a new phase of worship in God's economy. In the Church Age, because of the work of the Spirit, **worship** is no longer centered in temples like those on Mount Gerizim and Mount Zion.

4:22. Jesus was firm in His declaration of the issues involved. The Samaritan religion was confused and in error: **You Samaritans worship what you do not know.** They were not the vehicle for the salvation of mankind. Israel was the nation chosen by God to have great privileges (Rom. 9:4-5). When Jesus said, **Salvation is from the Jews,** He did not mean that all Jews were saved or were especially pious. "Salvation is from the Jews" in the sense that it is available through Jesus, who was born of the seed of Abraham.

4:23. With the advent of the Messiah the **time** came for a new order of **worship. True worshipers** are those who realize that Jesus is the Truth of God (3:21; 14:6) and the one and only Way to the Father (Acts 4:12). To worship **in truth** is to worship God through Jesus. To worship **in Spirit** is to worship in the new realm which God has revealed to people. **The Father** is seeking true **worshipers** because He wants people to live in reality, not in falsehood. Everybody is a worshiper (Rom. 1:25) but because of sin many are blind and constantly put their trust in worthless objects.

4:24. God is Spirit is a better translation than the KJV's "God is a Spirit." God is not one Spirit among many. This is a declaration of His invisible nature. He is not confined to one location. **Worship** of God can be done only through the One (Jesus) who expresses God's invisible nature (1:18) and by virtue of the Holy **Spirit** who opens to a believer the new realm of the kingdom (cf. 3:3, 5; 7:38-39).

4:25. The Samaritans expected a coming messianic leader. But they did not expect Him to be an anointed king of the Davidic line, since they rejected all the Old Testament except the Pentateuch. Based on Deuteronomy 18:15-18, they expected a Moses-like figure who would solve all their problems. The Samaritan **woman** now understood a part of what Jesus said. She wistfully longed for the messianic days when the **Messiah** would **explain everything.**

4:26. This self-declaration by Jesus Himself—**I . . . am He** (the Messiah)—is unusual. Normally in His ministry in Galilee and Judea (cf. 6:15) because of political implications, He veiled His office and used the title "Son of Man." But with this Samaritan the dangers of revolt by national zealots were not a problem.

*b. Jesus' instruction of His disciples
(4:27-38)*

4:27-30. The woman, excited by Jesus' statement about Himself and because of the arrival of the **disciples,** left and **went** to the village. In her joy of discovery she forgot **her water jar.** It was more important to her now to share her new faith. Her words **A Man who told me everything I ever did,** were bound to stir interest. Perhaps in that village some who heard her had been partners in her past life. Perhaps they wondered, *Could this One also know about us?*

Could this be the Christ? she asked them. More literally, her question was, "This couldn't be the Messiah, could it?" The question expected a tentative negative answer. She framed the question this way, in all probability, because she knew the people would not respond favorably to a dogmatic assertion from a woman, especially one of her reputation. Just as Jesus had captured her attention by curiosity, so she raised the people's curiosity. They decided to investigate this matter.

4:31-32. As the **disciples** spoke with Jesus, they sensed something had happened. Before, He was tired and thirsty. But now food and drink were not important to Him. His mood had changed. They offered Him food, but He gave them instruction. **I have food to eat that you know nothing about** is another of His enigmatic statements.

4:33-34. The disciples' misunderstanding set the stage for Him to clarify His statement. As usual, the **disciples** were confined to thinking materialistically. **Jesus said, My food . . . is to do the will of Him who sent Me.** This does not mean Jesus had no need of physical **food,** but rather that His great passion and desire was to do God's will (cf. 5:30; 8:29). He knows that man does not live by bread alone, but "by every word that comes from the mouth of the Lord" (Deut. 8:3). His priority is spiritual, not material. It is the Father's **work** which must be done (cf. John 17:4).

4:35. Farmers have a period of waiting between their sowing and their reaping. **Four months more and then the harvest** was probably a local proverb. But in the spiritual realm there is no long wait. Jesus has come so now it is the day

of opportunity. All that is needed is spiritual vision and perception. If the disciples would **look** around, they would see people with spiritual hunger. The Samaritans in their white garments coming from the village (v. 30) may have visually suggested a wheat field **ripe for harvest.**

4:36-38. As reapers, the disciples had the great and rewarding privilege of leading people to faith in Christ. **Others** had already **done** the **work** of sowing. This perhaps refers to the ministry of the Old Testament prophets or to John the Baptist's ministry of preparation. Both kinds of workers—**the sower and the reaper**—get their pay. Reapers harvest **the crop for eternal life,** that is, Jesus' disciples were involved in ministry to others, in the issue of death and life (2 Cor. 2:15-16).

Harvesttime in the ancient world was a time of joy (Ruth 3:2, 7; Isa. 9:3). There is also great joy at the time of salvation (cf. Luke 15:7, 10, 32). The disciples had the greater joy of seeing the completion of the process (John 4:38). A sower has a harder time because he sees no immediate fulfillment. John the Baptist stirred a nation to repent but he died before the day of Pentecost, when the disciples in great joy saw thousands come to faith in Jesus.

*c. The repentance of the Samaritans
(4:39-42)*

4:39. The little revival among **the Samaritans** is notable because the theme of natural rejection by Israel had been sounded (1:11) as well as the note of a wider ministry (3:16; cf. Acts 1:8). The **testimony** of the woman, though, from one point of view was unnecessary ("not that I accept human testimony," John 5:34); yet it was effective. That Jesus knows what is in a person and that He has comprehensive knowledge of one's life is an indication of His deity (Ps. 139; John 1:47-49; 2:24-25).

4:40-41. The witness of the woman led to the Samaritans' personal confrontation with Jesus. **He stayed** with them **two days.** The word "stayed" (from *menō,* "to remain, to abide") is a favorite Johannine theological term (cf. 3:36; 6:56; 15:4; etc.; and comments on 1:38). **Because of His words many more became believers.**

"Words" is singular in Greek ("His word"). His message was the cause of their faith. Personal testimony plus the message of Jesus is still God's means of salvation.

4:42. Faith based simply on the testimony of another is only secondary. True faith moves to its own experience and confrontation with Jesus. **We have heard for ourselves** is the more adequate basis. Jesus **is the Savior of the world,** not in the sense that everyone will be saved (universalism) but that His light shines for all (1:9). The light is not limited to the nation Israel, but is for "every nation, tribe, people, and language" (Rev. 7:9).

9. THE OFFICIAL'S SON (4:43-54)

4:43-45. After His **two-day** ministry in Samaria, Jesus and His disciples continued north into **Galilee. Now Jesus Himself had pointed out that a prophet has no honor in his own country.** This proverbial saying mentioned by Jesus (cf. Matt. 13:57; Mark 6:4) is cited by the author John. Is His "own country" Judea or Galilee? Or is His "own country" heaven, with His being rejected in His "own land" Israel? Generally Galilee was more favorable to Him, but even there men tried to kill Him (Luke 4:18-30). John was perhaps preparing his readers for the upcoming rejection; he may have been saying that even with the warm reception Jesus received **in Galilee,** He still was not really accepted (cf. John 2:24-25; 4:48). They had been impressed by His clearing the temple **at the Passover feast** (2:13-22) and His miracles (2:23). But the people's enthusiasm for the Healer (cf. Mark 5:21, 24b) did not always indicate they had faith in Him (Mark 6:1-6).

4:46-47. The **certain royal official** is not identified. He could have been a Gentile or a Jew, a centurion, or a minor official in Herod's court. Possibly he was a Jew because Jesus included him among the people who desire signs and wonders (v. 48; cf. 1 Cor. 1:22). **His son** had been **sick,** and undoubtedly he had exhausted all the local means at his disposal. Failure of position and money to solve his problem drove him from **Capernaum** to the village of **Cana,** 20 to 25 miles away, hoping that the Healer would save his **son** from **death.**

4:48. Jesus' address to him, though sharp, was necessary. A faith built only on miraculous signs is not a complete faith (cf. 2:23-25). Many **(you people)** hesitate to **believe** in Jesus apart from seeing **miraculous signs** (*sēmeia*) **and wonders** (*terata*). Faith in **Jesus** is absolutely necessary, but not all believers are given public portents (cf. Matt. 16:1-4; 1 Cor. 1:22).

4:49. The **official** was in no position emotionally to argue his case theologically. All he could plead for was mercy, for his **child** was at the point of death.

4:50. Jesus' calm reply to the official's desperate request created a crisis. **Jesus** announced, **You may go. Your son will live.** If the official really believed that Jesus could make a difference in Capernaum, he must also believe Him now in Cana. So he **took Jesus at His word and left.**

4:51-53. On the way back the official must have pondered Jesus' promise every step of his journey. **His servants met him with good news. His boy was living.** The official asked **when his son** recovered. The healing was no accident, for it occurred at **the exact** moment Jesus made His promise to him. It was **at the seventh hour,** which by Roman time was 7:00 in the evening. The man's faith grew, and he brought **all his household** to faith. The lesson of this incident is that Jesus' power is able to save from death even at a great distance. His Word has power to work; people are simply to believe His Word.

4:54. Both signs **in Galilee** (changing the water into wine [2:1-11] and healing the official's son) demonstrate that Jesus is the Promised One. Yet both signs had a certain hidden aspect to them. Only the disciples and some servants saw His miracle at the wedding, and this healing was not in public view.

B. Jesus' controversy in Jerusalem (chap. 5)

1. JESUS' HEALING OF A PARALYTIC (5:1-15)

5:1. Jesus . . . **later** returned **to Jerusalem for a feast.** The feast is not named (some mss. read "the feast"), but it may have been the Passover. Jesus attended three other Passovers (2:23; 6:4; 11:55). John probably intended only to give a reason why Jesus was in Jerusalem.

5:2. To the north of the temple area was **a pool . . . called Bethesda** (see the map showing the pool's location). The excavations of a pool **near the Sheep Gate** have uncovered **five** porticoes or **covered colonnades,** confirming the accuracy of the description given here in the Fourth Gospel. The pool was actually two pools next to each other.

5:3a. The **great number of disabled people** pictures the sad spiritual plight of the world.

5:3b-4. The earliest manuscripts omit these words which appear to be a late insertion to explain why the pool water was "stirred" (v. 7). People believed that an angel came and stirred it. According to local tradition, the first one in the water would be healed. But the Bible nowhere teaches this kind of superstition, a situation which would be a most cruel contest for many ill people. No extant Greek manuscript before A.D. 400 contains these words.

5:5. Jesus picked a certain invalid on a Sabbath Day (v. 9) at a feast time, a man who had been afflicted **for 38 years.** John did not say what kind of physical problem he had or if he was **an invalid** from birth. In any case his condition was hopeless.

5:6. The word **learned** does not mean that **Jesus** received facts from others. It means that He perceived the situation by His knowledge (the Gr. is *gnous,* "knowing"; cf. 1:48; 2:24-25; 4:18). Jesus' seemingly strange question, **Do you want to get well?** was designed to focus the man's attention on Him, to stimulate his will, and to raise his hopes. In the spiritual realm man's great problem is that either he does not recognize he is sick (cf. Isa. 1:5-6; Luke 5:31) or he does not want to be cured. People are often happy, for a while at least, in their sins.

5:7. The man replied that he lacked not the desire but the means to be healed. Without strength and without friends, he could not be helped **when the** pool **water was stirred.** He had tried but without success.

5:8. Jesus then said . . . **Get up! Pick up your mat and walk.** His command carried with it the required enablement. As with dead Lazarus (11:43), Jesus' word accomplished His will. This illustrates conversion. When people obey His command to believe, God works in and through His Word.

5:9-10. God's supernatural power

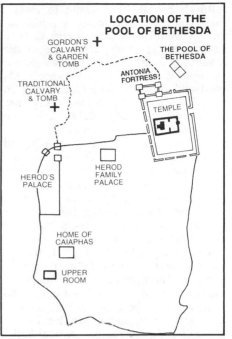

LOCATION OF THE POOL OF BETHESDA

GORDON'S CALVARY & GARDEN TOMB

THE POOL OF BETHESDA

ANTONIA FORTRESS

TRADITIONAL CALVARY & TOMB

TEMPLE

HEROD'S PALACE

HEROD FAMILY PALACE

HOME OF CAIAPHAS

UPPER ROOM

was evident in the man's instantaneous cure. **He picked up his mat and walked.** Muscles long atrophied were completely restored. Isaiah prophesied that in the days of the Messiah the lame would "leap like a deer" (Isa. 35:1-7). Here in Jerusalem was a public sign that the Messiah had come.

The Sabbath was a central issue in the conflicts between Jesus and His opponents (cf. Mark 2:23; 3:4). The Mosaic Law required that work cease on the seventh day. Additional laws were added by later Jewish religious authorities, which became very complicated and burdensome. These human traditions often obscured the divine intention in God's Law. "The Sabbath was made for man" (Mark 2:27) so that he could have rest and a time for worship and joy. The Jews' rigid tradition (not the Old Testament) taught that if anyone carried anything from a public place to a private place on the Sabbath intentionally, he deserved death by stoning. In this case the man who was healed was in danger of losing his life.

5:11. The healed man realized this difficulty and tried to evade any responsibility for violating tradition by saying he was just following orders.

5:12-13. The authorities were naturally interested in the identity of **this**

fellow who told the invalid to violate their rules. But **the man . . . had no** knowledge of Jesus. This seems to be a case in which healing was done in the absence of faith. The invalid was chosen by **Jesus** as an act of grace because of his need and also to display God's glory in him. Jesus then **had slipped away into the crowd** (cf. 8:59; 10:39; 12:35), so momentarily He was unknown.

5:14-15. Jesus later **found** the healed man in **the temple** area. This implied that Jesus sought him out in order to speak to him. The ex-paralytic seemed to have no gratitude to Jesus: his conduct put him in a bad light. Jesus' warning (**Stop sinning or something worse may happen to you**) does not mean that his paralysis was caused by any specific sin (cf. 9:3), though all disease and death come ultimately from sin. The warning was that his tragic life of 38 years as an invalid was no comparison to the doom of hell. Jesus is interested not merely in healing a person's body. Far more important is the healing of his soul from sin.

2. THE DISCOURSE (5:16-47)

5:16. **Jesus was doing these things on the Sabbath.** In addition to the case of the invalid's healing (5:1-15), John later recorded the cure of a blind man on the Sabbath (chap. 9). The grain-picking (Mark 2:23-28), the healing of a shriveled hand (Mark 3:1-5), curing a woman who had been crippled for 18 years (Luke 13:10-17), and healing a man with dropsy (Luke 14:1-6)—all these took place on the Sabbath. As seen in these passages, Jesus' theology or philosophy of the Sabbath differed from that of His opponents. His opponents in the controversy were progressively humiliated while the crowds favored Him. The opponents' response was to persecute Jesus by opposing Him and trying to kill Him (John 5:16, 18; 7:19, 25).

5:17. God rested on the seventh day (Gen. 2:2-3) from His work of Creation. But Jesus pointed to the continuous **work** of God as a justification for His Sabbath activity. God sustains the universe, begets life, and visits judgments. It is not wrong for His Son to do works of grace and mercy on the Sabbath. The words **My Father** should be noted. Jesus did not say "your Father" or even "our Father." His

opponents did not miss His claim to Deity.

5:18. **The Sabbath** controversy was enough to cause them to hate Jesus, but the implication of His claim that God is **His own Father** was impossible for them to accept. To them, God has no equals. Jesus' claim, in their thinking, was a monstrous blasphemy. To be **equal with God** suggested, they thought, two gods and therefore polytheism. To make oneself "equal with God" was a claim of arrogant independence. In the Talmud four persons were branded as haughty because they made themselves equal to God: pagan rulers Hiram, Nebuchadnezzar, Pharaoh, and the Jewish King Joash.

5:19. **Jesus** explained that He is not independent of or in opposition to **the Father.** His activity is not self-initiated. The **Father** directs and has sent **the Son.** The Son's activity imitates the Father, and the Two always work together. (See comments on 1:51 for the clause **I tell you the truth.**)

5:20. **The Son** is in no way independent of or in rebellion against **the Father.** Their relationship is one of continuous love. The Son is not doing simply a part of God's will; He has a full disclosure of all the Father's works. By the Father, the Son will do even more amazing works **than** physical healings.

5:21. One of the prerogatives of Deity is the right over **life** and death. (A king of Israel asked Naaman, "Am I God? Can I kill and bring back to life?" [2 Kings 5:7]) One of Jesus' "greater" works (John 5:20) is the giving of life. **The Son gives life to whom He is pleased to give it,** just as He chose to heal one man out of a crowd of disabled people. The giving of life includes spiritual (eternal) life and a resurrected body. The resuscitation of Lazarus (chap. 11) would illustrate both.

5:22. The Son's ability to give life is coupled with His right to judge mankind (cf. v. 27). **The Father** has placed this eschatological prerogative in Jesus' hands.

5:23. Jesus' unity with His **Father** is so complete that the **honor** of God is tied to Jesus. To reject or dishonor God **the Son** is to reject and dishonor God **the Father.**

5:24. Since Jesus has the unity and divine prerogatives mentioned in verses 19-23, to trust His message and His Father is to have in the present time eternal life (cf. 3:36). No judgment will come in the future (he **will not be condemned** [cf. 3:18; Rom. 6:13; 8:1] because he has already passed **from** one realm—**death**—into another—**life** [cf. Eph. 2:1, 5]). Only once elsewhere (in 1 John 3:14) is the phrase "passed from death to life" used.

5:25. Jesus' life-giving power can call a person out of the grave (11:43), everyone from their tombs (5:28-29), or anyone in spiritual death (v. 24) to eternal life. (The words, **a time is coming,** occur four times in John: 4:21, 23; 5:25, 28.)

5:26-27. Jesus' discourse now returned to the two central prerogatives of God: **life** (vv. 21, 24-26) and judgment (cf. vv. 22, 24-25, 27). Jesus has both because **the Father . . . has given Him** both. This giving is both eternal and temporal. In Himself Christ, the *Logos*, has life as an eternal gift of the Father (1:4), but in the Incarnation **authority to judge** was also delegated to Jesus. As **the Son of Man** (cf. Dan. 7:13), authority is given to Him.

5:28-29. Jesus said His hearers should **not be amazed at** His claim that right now those who believe pass from death into life (v. 24), because in the future there will be a universal physical resurrection at His command. This universal resurrection is clearly taught in Daniel 12:1-2. Other passages show that the resurrection to life, "the first resurrection," will occur in stages (the church at the Rapture, and Tribulation saints at the Lord's second coming at the end of the Tribulation), and that the resurrection of those who will **be condemned** will occur at the end of the Millennium (Rev. 20:11-15). John 5:28-29 is one of the few passages in this Gospel which expressly teaches eschatology.

The words **those who have done good** and **those who have done evil** (*tu phaula,* "worthless things"; cf. 3:20) by themselves might imply a salvation by good deeds or damnation because of evil deeds, but a consideration of John's theology as a whole forbids this (cf. 3:17-21; 6:28-29). Those who are truly born again do live a different kind of life. They obey Him (14:15), they abide in Him (15:5-7), and they walk in the light (8:12; 1 John 1:7). They are saved by the Lamb of God who, as their substitutionary Sacrifice, takes away the penalty of their sin. Salvation is by faith in Christ. Damnation is because of rejection of God's Son (John 3:36).

5:30. This verse is transitional; it concludes the section on Jesus' unity with the Father (vv. 19-30). The section ends the way it began, with the point that the Son **can do nothing** apart from the Father (cf. v. 19). His **judgment,** as everything He does, **is** from the express will of the Father. He is the perfect Spokesman for the Father and His effective Executive. Jesus' will is to do the Father's will (cf. 4:34; 8:29), which shows that He has the same nature.

5:31-32. The thought in this discourse moves from that of Jesus' unity with the Father to that of the Father's witness to Jesus. John 5:31 and 8:14 appear to be contradictory. But they speak to different issues. In 5:31, Jesus' point was that if He bore witness to Himself, this witness would not be accepted by the Jewish authorities. They would see it as an arrogant claim of self-exaltation. Yet in another setting (8:14), self-authentication is perfectly valid because an individual is the only one who knows his own full experience. Jesus affirmed that He did not seek an independent self-authentication. He was content to submit to the Father's will and to let the Father authenticate Him.

Number of Occurrences of "Testimony" and "Testify" (in Gr.) in John's Writings

	Gospel	Epistles	Revelation	Total	Total Occurrences in the NT
Noun	14	7	9	30	60
Verb	33	10	4	47	76
Totals	47	17	13	77	136

5:33-34. As stated earlier (see 1:7), the concept of witness or **testimony** is important in John's Gospel. The chart on the preceding page reveals John's stress on this subject in his various writings.

John the Baptist's function was that of a witness. A good witness tells the truth as he knows it. John's witness to Jesus had an abiding character (**has testified** in the Gr. is in the perf. tense). Jesus did not need **human testimony,** but John's work helped people because in their darkness he pointed them to the light. John's work was **that you may be saved.** His great popular movement was only an anticipatory one, in which he pointed to Jesus as the Lamb of God.

5:35. John was only **a lamp,** not the true Light (1:9). The Jewish nation **for a short time** was stirred by and rejoiced in his ministry. For a moment they thought the Messianic Age was dawning. Even though his preaching had some stinging rebukes, there was a great popular excitement about his message. The people thought that though Israel might be disciplined, their enemies would be destroyed.

5:36. Though **John** the Baptist was a great voice for God, he did not do any miracles (10:41). The "signs" were specific works which God had assigned for the Son to do. These miracles were predicted in the Old Testament (Isa. 35:5-6). Jesus' **work** was a clear manifestation that God was with Him and that He worked through Him (cf. Nicodemus' words [John 3:2]; Jesus' logic [Mark 3:23-29]; and the lesson from an ex-blind man [John 9:30-33]).

5:37-38. Jesus' witness is His Father. **The Father . . . has Himself testified concerning Me.** But when and how did or does the Father give this witness? The possibilities include: (1) at Jesus' baptism (Matt. 3:17), (2) at the transfiguration (Matt. 17:5), (3) at the Triumphal Entry (John 12:28), (4) in Jesus' works (3:2), (5) in people's minds or hearts (6:45). Most likely Jesus was referring to the inner work of God in which He impresses on people's consciences that Jesus is the Truth (6:45; 1 John 5:9-12). Jesus' opponents are ignorant of God. They have no vision of God and no communication with Him. **His Word** is His message of salvation. This message had not been received by them (does not **dwell** [*menonta*, from *menō*, "remain, abide"] **in** them) because they had rejected Jesus.

5:39-40. The Jewish religious leaders studied the Old Testament with great diligence. They believed that if one could comprehend the words of the text, he would gain a share in the world to come. They considered those ignorant of the Law to be under a curse (7:49). Similarly many people today think Bible study is an end in itself rather than a function leading to the knowledge of God and godliness. Somehow a veil was over the minds of these Jewish scholars (2 Cor. 3:15), and they failed to see that Jesus is the Promised One. He is the fulfillment of the Old Testament sacrificial system, the true righteous Servant of Yahweh, the coming Prophet, the Son of Man, the Davidic King, and the promised Son of God and great High Priest. In spite of the clarity of the revelation, they refused **to come to** Him for **life** (cf. John 3:19-20).

5:41-42. The Jews may have thought that Jesus was upset because He was not officially endorsed by the leaders. But He denied that idea. They thought they knew His motivation, but in contrast He knew them and the cause of their unbelief (cf. 2:24-25): they did **not have the love of God** (i.e., love for God, not love from God) **in** their **hearts.** The great command is that people should love God (Ex. 20:4; Deut. 6:5); the great sin is that they reject Him and love and serve "created things" (Rom. 1:25).

5:43-44. Two things evidenced their lack of love for God. (1) They rejected Christ, the **Father's** "Representative." To insult or reject one's ambassador is the same as rejecting him. (2) They accepted false teachers or prophets. This reveals a lack of affinity with the truth. An additional failure was their desire for acceptance and approval from sinful men while ignoring the favor and the will of **the only God.** True faith was impossible because they were seeking the wrong object: man, not God.

5:45-47. Jesus came as the Savior, not as the Judge (cf. 3:17). It was unnecessary for Him to **accuse** the people. **Moses,** whom they claimed to follow, would condemn them because they had broken the covenant he instituted and missed the Person **he wrote about. On whom your hopes are set**

implies that they thought salvation would come by their good deeds in keeping the Law.

If the Jews really believed Moses, they would believe Christ, for Moses **wrote** about Him. Jesus here did not refer to any specific passage (cf. Gen. 3:15; 22:18; 49:10; Num. 24:17; Deut. 18:15) or to any specific types (such as the Passover, the manna, the rock, the offerings, or the high priesthood). He simply assumed the Old Testament clearly points to Him. Since Moses' revelation was rejected (cf. Luke 16:29-31), Jesus' words were rejected also. Later Jesus said that Isaiah had written about Him (John 12:41).

C. Jesus' revelation in Galilee (6:1–7:9)

1. JESUS' SIGNS ON THE LAND AND THE LAKE (6:1-21)

a. Jesus' feeding of the 5,000 (6:1-15)

The miracle of the feeding of the 5,000 is the only sign recorded in all four Gospels (besides Jesus' resurrection). This fact alone points to its importance. The significance of the sign was expounded by the Lord in a long discourse (vv. 22-71). The miracle was spectacular, and it caused a peak in the people's messianic expectations. But in its aftermath many of His followers no longer followed Him (v. 66).

6:1-2. Though **some time after this** is indefinite, it can be learned from the Synoptics that Herod Antipas had killed John the Baptist (Mark 6:14-29; cf. John 3:24), the disciples had preached throughout Galilee (Mark 6:7-13, 30-31), multitudes of people were curious about Jesus, and Herod Antipas was seeking Jesus (Luke 9:7-9). So the time between the events in John 5 and 6 was probably six months. From verses 1-2 it seems that Jesus had gone to the northeast side of **the Sea of Galilee** with His disciples for rest. This lake was also called **the Sea of Tiberias** (cf. 21:1), named for a town on the lake's west shore built by Herod Antipas. But a **crowd** gathered even in this "solitary" (cf. Matt. 14:13; Mark 6:32) and "remote place" (Matt. 14:15).

6:3-4. The mention of **the hillside** or "the mountain" (NASB) may indicate an intended parallel to Moses' experience on Mount Sinai (cf. vv. 31-32). The notice

that **the Jewish Passover feast was near** is theological and only secondarily chronological. The people were thinking in terms of blood, flesh, lambs, and unleavened bread. They longed for a new Moses who would deliver them from Roman bondage.

Since this was the second Passover John mentioned (cf. 2:13, 23), and since he mentioned at least one other Passover (13:1 [5:1 refers to an unnamed feast of the Jews]), Jesus' ministry extended for about three years. The events in chapter 6, then, took place about one year before He was crucified.

6:5-6. Jesus' question **to Philip— Where shall we buy bread for these people to eat?**—was not for information but was part of His program of educating the disciples. Philip was from Bethsaida (1:44) which was the closest town, and he would know the local resources. The answer to Jesus' question was that it was impossible, humanly speaking, for thousands of people to get bread late in the day from the little neighboring villages. John wrote, as he thought back on the incident, that Jesus was asking this **to test** Philip. God tests people to refine their faith, never to tempt them to do evil (cf. Gen. 22:1-18; James 1:2, 13-15; 1 Peter 1:7).

6:7. The amount needed was a large sum of money: literally, "200 denarii." One denarius was the wage for a day's work; this would have been **eight months' wages.** Even if the bread had been available, the disciples did not have nearly that much money. The disciples were supported by people who responded to Jesus' ministry (cf. Mark 6:7-13).

6:8-9. Andrew, in contrast with Philip, had gone into the crowd to determine its resources (cf. Jesus' command, "Go and see"; Mark 6:38). All he could come up with was a little boy's lunch. Man's inability set the stage for a manifestation of Jesus' compassion and power. The **barley loaves** recall the Prophet Elisha's feeding of 100 men with 20 barley loaves (2 Kings 4:42-44). But here was One far greater than Elisha.

6:10-11. As the Good Shepherd, Jesus made the "sheep" (Mark 6:34) **sit down** in green pastures (cf. Ps. 23:2). According to Mark 6:40, the people were seated in groups of 50 and 100. This made the crowd easy to count and the food easy to distribute. **Five thousand men** were there, plus women and children (Matt. 14:21). Thus probably more than 10,000 people were fed.

Since the area was desolate and the time was Passover, **Jesus** was like Moses with the people in the wilderness who needed a miraculous feeding. The miracle itself was not described by John. **Jesus . . . gave thanks,** but no eucharistic implications are obvious as many argue in this chapter. Among devout Jews the giving of thanks was the norm before and after meals. As Jesus **distributed** the food (with the aid of the disciples [Mark 6:41]), the miraculous multiplication took place.

6:12-13. The words, **when they had all had enough to eat,** show that John intended to stress that a miracle took place. Some scholars try to explain away the miracle by saying that this was merely a sacramental or symbolic meal. Others say the "miracle" was in the people's sharing. But these rationalizations are far from the clear meaning of John's words.

The disciples' gathering of the **12 baskets** of fragments was part of their education, to show them that He is more than adequate for their needs. Later He appealed to their spiritual stupidity (cf. Mark 8:17-21). Even though the disciples were closer to Jesus than the crowds, they too were in spiritual blindness (Mark 6:52).

6:14-15. Seeing this **miraculous sign** (*sēmeion*), the people recalled Moses' prediction that a **Prophet** like him would arise (Deut. 18:15). Moses had fed the people. Moses had led them out of bondage. Jesus had fed the people. Jesus could lead the people out of the hated Roman bondage.

The people saw His sign, but they did not perceive its meaning. They wanted to seize Him **and make Him King.** This marks the highpoint of Jesus' popularity and a great temptation for Him. Could He have the kingdom without the Cross? No. Jesus' kingdom would be given to Him by the Father (cf. Ps. 2:7-12; Dan. 7:13-14). It will not come from this world (John 18:36). The path of the Father's will lies in another direction. Before He can be the reigning Lion of Judah, He must be the Lamb who bears the sin of the world (1:29).

b. His walking on the water (6:16-21)

6:16-17. According to Mark 6:45, Jesus compelled His disciples to get **into the boat** and go to Bethsaida while He dismissed the crowds. From Bethsaida they went on toward **Capernaum.** Both villages are at the north end of the Sea of Galilee. **His disciples went down to the lake,** for the land is hilly and high on the east side. As they got out on the lake, the sun went down and the wind picked up. Jesus was up in the hills praying while watching them in their toil (Mark 6:45-48).

6:18-19. The west **wind,** which often picks up at evening, caught them in the open water. They were headed directly into it and found themselves making little progress. They were "straining at the oars" (Mark 6:48). The Sea of Galilee is notable for its sudden and severe storms. **They had rowed three or three and a half miles,** so they were in the middle of the lake. **They were terrified** to see a figure **walking on the water.** They thought it was a ghost (Mark 6:49). Rational explanations have included the idea that Jesus was walking on the sand by the shore or floating on a large beam or log, but neither notion does justice to the text. This occurred in the "fourth watch" of the night, that is, between 3 and 6 o'clock in the morning (Matt. 14:25; Mark 6:48).

6:20-21. The clause **It is I** is literally "I Am," and was used by Jesus (in 8:58) with strong theological meaning. In this setting it seems to mean only that Jesus was identifying Himself. When the disciples recognized Him, they welcomed **Him into the boat.** By the words **and immediately the boat reached the shore** another miracle is probably intended. The two signs on the land and the lake reveal Jesus as the Provider of a "bread" which gives life (as the next section will expound) and as the Savior who intercedes for and protects His own. He intervenes in their times of troubles and brings them to safety.

2. HIS THEOLOGICAL DISCOURSE (6:22-71)

6:22-25. The crowd who had been fed were still on the eastern **shore** of the sea. They saw Jesus compel **His disciples** to get into the **one boat** which was there. But since **Jesus** did not get into the boat, the crowd supposed that He had stayed in the area. After some time they **realized** He was no longer **there. Some boats from Tiberias landed,** so the people decided to seek Jesus in the **Capernaum** region and **got into the boats.** The people's question, **When did You get here?** introduces His long discourse in Capernaum (v. 59). Jesus did not explain how or when He crossed the lake, for His walking on the water was a private sign for the disciples only.

6:26. Jesus began with the solemn words, **I tell you the truth** (cf. comments on 1:51). Jesus spoke these words four times in this discourse (6:26, 32, 47, 53). This drew attention to the importance of what He was about to teach. He rebuked them for their materialistic motivation and their lack of spiritual perception. They **saw miraculous signs,** but to them it was only an easy meal. They failed to see what it signified.

6:27. When Jesus said, **Do not work for food that spoils,** He was not condoning laziness. Rather He was saying that people should expend their efforts for what will last forever. "Man does not live on bread alone, but on every word that comes from the mouth of God" (Matt. 4:4). Physical **food** is short-lived but spiritual **food** leads **to eternal life. The Son of Man** (who has access to heaven [John 3:13]) **will give** people this spiritual food, which is ultimately Christ Himself (6:53). **God the Father** Himself authenticated Jesus' claim that He is true heavenly "food."

6:28. The people recognized that Jesus was saying God had a requirement for them. They would do God's requirement if He would inform them what it was. They believed that they could please **God** and thus obtain eternal life by doing good **works** (cf. Rom. 10:2-4).

6:29. Jesus' response to their question was a flat contradiction of their thinking. They could not please God by doing good works. There is only one **work of God,** that **is,** one thing God requires. They need to put their trust **in the One** the Father **has sent.** Because of their sin people cannot please God by doing good works for salvation (Eph. 2:8-9; Titus 3:5). God demands that people recognize their inability to save themselves and receive His gift (Rom. 6:23).

6:30-31. In response the people demanded a **miraculous sign** (*sēmeion;* cf. "Jews demand miraculous signs" [1 Cor. 1:22]). They thought God's order is **see** and **believe.** But the divine order is believe and see (cf. John 11:40). They did not have faith or spiritual perception, but they understood that Jesus was proclaiming something new.

His coming was claimed as an advance over Moses. They reasoned, "If You are more than Moses, do more than Moses." The crowd that asked for a sign from Jesus must have felt that the feeding of the 5,000 did not compare with Moses' gift of **bread from heaven.** They remembered the divine gift of **manna** (Ex. 16; Num. 11:7). They thought Jesus' feeding was less significant because manna fed the whole nation for 40 years. But they missed two things. First, many of the Israelites who were fed 40 years did not believe. The important thing is not the magnitude of the sign but the perception of its significance (cf. Luke 16:29-31). Second, both Moses and Jesus were authenticated by God's signs; therefore both should be listened to and believed.

6:32. In a solemn revelation (**I tell you the truth,** cf. vv. 26, 47, 53) **Jesus** corrected their ideas in three ways. (1) The Father, **not Moses,** gave the manna. (2) The **Father,** was still giving "manna" then, not merely in the past. (3) **The true Bread from heaven** is Jesus, not the manna. Thus the supposed superiorities of Moses and his sign vanish. Manna was food for the body, and it was useful. But Jesus is God's full provision for people in their whole existence. Jesus repeatedly said He had come down from heaven (vv. 32-33, 38, 41-42, 50-51, 58).

6:33. God is the Source of all life. The Son has life in Himself (1:4; 5:26) and He has come to give real and lasting life to people. Sin cuts them off from God, who is Life, and they die spiritually and physically. Christ has come **down from heaven** to give **life to the world.** Jesus is thus the genuine **Bread of God.**

6:34. As yet, the crowd did not perceive that Jesus is the genuine **Bread** which He had been describing. Like the woman at the well (4:15), they asked for **this** better food. And they wanted it continually (**from now on**), not like the manna which lasted for 40 years.

6:35. I am the Bread of Life. This corrected two more errors in their thinking: (1) The food of which He spoke refers to a Person, not a commodity. (2) And once someone is in right relationship to Jesus, he finds a satisfaction which is everlasting, not temporal. This "I am" statement is the first in a series of momentous "I am" revelations (cf. 8:12; 10:7, 9, 11, 14; 11:25; 14:6; 15:1, 5). "Bread of Life" means bread which provides life. Jesus is man's necessary "food." In Western culture, bread is often optional, but it was an essential staple then. Jesus promised, **He who comes to Me will never go hungry, and he who believes in Me will never be thirsty.** The "nevers" are emphatic in Greek.

6:36. Jesus then rebuked the crowd for their lack of faith. They had the great privilege of seeing Him and yet they did **not believe.** Seeing does not necessarily lead to believing (cf. v. 30).

6:37. Jesus then gave the ultimate explanation of their lack of faith: **the Father** works sovereignly in people's lives. There is an election of God which is the Father's gift to the Son. The Son has no concern that His work will be ineffective, for the Father will enable people to come to Jesus. Jesus has confidence. But people may have confidence also. (Cf. the crippled man's response to Jesus' question, "Do you want to get well?" [5:6-9]) One who comes to Jesus for salvation will by no means be driven **away** (cf. 6:39).

6:38-39. Jesus then repeated His claim about His heavenly origin. The reason He **came down from heaven** was **to do the will of** the Father **who sent** Him. The Father's **will is that** those whom He gives to the Son will not suffer a single loss and **all** will be raised to life in the resurrection (cf. vv. 40, 44, 54). This passage is strong in affirming the eternal security of the believer.

6:40. This verse repeats and reinforces the ideas of the previous verses. One who **looks** and **believes** on Jesus for salvation has his destiny secure. The divine decree has insured it (cf. Rom. 8:28-30). He has **eternal life** (John 6:47, 50-51, 54, 58) and **will be raised at the last day** (cf. vv. 39, 44, 54).

6:41-42. The Jews, hostile unbelievers, grumbled because of Jesus' proclamation of His heavenly origin. Like their ancestors in the wilderness, these Jews murmured (Ex. 15:24; 16:2, 7, 12; 17:3; Num. 11:1; 14:2, 27). Their thinking was seemingly logical: one **whose** parents are known could not be **from heaven** (cf. Mark 6:3; Luke 4:22). They were ignorant of His true origin and full nature. They said He was **the son of Joseph,** but they did not know of the Virgin Birth, the Incarnation. He had come **down** from heaven because He is the *Logos* (John 1:1, 14).

6:43-44. Jesus made no attempt to correct their ignorance other than to rebuke their **grumbling** and to point them to the drawing and teaching ministry of God. They are not in a position to judge Him. Without God's help any assessment of God's Messenger will be faulty. **No one can come to** Jesus or believe on Him without divine help. People are so ensnared in the quicksand of sin and unbelief that **unless** God **draws** them (cf. v. 65), they are hopeless. This drawing of God is not limited to a few. Jesus said, "I . . . will draw all men to Myself" (12:32). This does not mean that all will be saved but that Greeks (i.e., Gentiles; 12:20) as well as Jews will be saved. Those who will be saved will also be resurrected (cf. 6:39-40).

6:45. In support of this doctrine of salvation by God's grace, Jesus cited the Old Testament. The quotation, **They will all be taught by God,** is from **the Prophets,** probably Isaiah 54:13, though Jeremiah 31:34 has the same thought. This "teaching" of God refers to His inner work that disposes people to accept the truth about Jesus and respond to Him. **Everyone who listens to** and **learns from** God will come to and believe in Jesus.

6:46. Yet this secret teaching of God is not a mystical connection of people with God directly. Knowing **God** comes only through Jesus, the *Logos* of God (cf. 1:18). As one is confronted by Him and hears His words and sees His deeds, **the Father** works within him.

6:47-48. These two verses summarize Jesus' teaching in the debate. **I tell you the truth** occurs here for the third of four times in this passage (cf. vv. 26, 32, 53). **He who believes** is in Greek a participial construction in the present tense, meaning that a believer is characterized by his continuing trust. He **has everlasting life,** which is a present and abiding possession. Jesus then repeated His affirmation, **I am the Bread of Life** (see comments on v. 35).

6:49-50. Manna met only a limited need. It provided temporary physical life. The Israelites came to loathe it, and ultimately **they died.** Jesus is a **Bread** of a different kind. He is **from heaven** and gives life. A person who eats of that Bread will **not die.**

6:51. Since Jesus is the **Bread** of Life, what does "eating" this **Bread** mean? Many commentators assume that Jesus was talking about the Lord's Supper. This passage may well illuminate the meaning of the Lord's Supper, in relation to Christ's death. But since the Last Supper occurred one year later than the incidents recorded in this chapter, eating His flesh and drinking His blood should not be thought of as sacramentalism. "Eating" **the living** Bread is a figure of speech meaning to believe on Him, like the figures of coming to Him (v. 35), listening to Him, (v. 45), and seeing Him (v. 40). To eat of this Bread is to **live forever** (cf. vv. 40, 47, 50, 54, 58). Jesus' revelation about the Bread was then advanced in that not only is the Father giving the Bread (Jesus), but also Jesus is giving Himself: **This Bread is My flesh, which I will give for the life of the world.** Salvation is by the sacrificial death of the Lamb of God (1:29). By His death, life came to the world.

6:52. As often happens, Jesus' teaching was not understood (cf. 2:20; 3:4; 4:15; 6:32-34). A violent argument started in the crowd regarding what He meant. Their perception remained at a materialistic level. They wondered, **How can this Man give us His flesh to eat?**

6:53-54. This revelation by **Jesus** is marked out as important by the fourth use of the phrase, **I tell you the truth** (cf. vv. 26, 32, 47). Sacramental interpretations appeal to the words **eat the flesh of the Son of Man and drink His blood** as evidence that Jesus was speaking of the eucharist. As stated earlier, the basic objection to this approach is historical: Jesus did not institute the Communion service until a year later. Drinking "His blood" is another bold figure of speech. The Jews knew the command, "You must not eat . . . any blood" (Lev. 3:17; cf. Lev. 17:10-14). And yet blood was the means of atonement. It is the blood that makes atonement for one's **life** (Lev. 17:11). Jesus' hearers must have been shocked and puzzled by His enigmatic words. But

the puzzle is unlocked by understanding that Jesus was speaking of His making atonement by His death and giving life to those who personally appropriate Him (cf. John 6:63). Faith in Christ's death brings **eternal life** (cf. vv. 40, 47, 50-51) and (later) bodily resurrection (cf. vv. 39-40, 44).

6:55. Just as good food and drink sustain physical life, so Jesus, the **real** (reliable) spiritual **food** and **drink,** sustains His followers spiritually. His **flesh** and **blood** give eternal life to those who receive Him.

6:56-57. One who partakes of Christ enjoys a mutual abiding relationship with Christ. He **remains** (*menei*) in Christ, and Christ remains **in him.** *Menō* is one of the most important theological terms in John's Gospel (cf. comments on 1:38). The Father "remains" in the Son (14:10), the Spirit "remains" on Jesus (1:32), and believers "remain" in Jesus and He in them (6:56; 15:4). The implications of this "remaining" are many. A believer enjoys intimacy with and security in Jesus. Just as He has His life from **the Father, so** believers have life **because of Jesus.**

6:58-59. Jesus gave this discourse on the **Bread** of Life **in the synagogue in Capernaum.** He often spoke in Jewish synagogues, where men had opportunities to give expositions and exhortations (Mark 6:1-6; Luke 4:16-28; Acts 13:15-42). The services were not as formal as those of traditional American churches; "laymen" usually spoke. The conclusion to Jesus' exposition and exhortation, based on the **manna** incident from Exodus 16, repeats the major themes: Moses' bread did not give lasting life (salvation does not come by the Law); God has given the genuine life-giving **Bread . . . from heaven;** those who trust Jesus have eternal life.

6:60. As the people began to understand His teaching, they found it to be totally unacceptable. Besides the hostile Jewish leaders, **many of** the Galilean **disciples** turned away from Him. The popular enthusiasm for Jesus as a political Messiah (v. 15) was then over. They saw that He was not going to deliver them from Rome. He might be a great Healer, but His words were **a hard** (i.e., harsh) **teaching. Who** could **accept it,** that is, obey it? How could they personally appropriate Him?

6:61-62. Jesus knew **His** audience (cf. 1:47; 2:24-25; 6:15). **Aware that** they **were grumbling** (cf. v. 41), He asked what was so offensive to **them. (Offend** in Gr. is *skandalizei.*) Paul wrote that the crucified Messiah was a "stumbling block" (*skandalon*) to the Jews (1 Cor. 1:23). The Ascension of **the Son of Man** is also an offense. But His glorification is His heavenly vindication. He was crucified in weakness but He was raised in power (1 Cor. 15:43).

6:63. After His Ascension Jesus gave the Holy Spirit (7:38-39; Acts 1:8-9). **The** Holy **Spirit,** poured out in the world, **gives life** (salvation) to those who believe. Without the Holy Spirit, man **(flesh)** is utterly unable to understand Jesus' person and His works (John 3:6; 1 Cor. 2:14). Though the crowds assessed Jesus' words as "hard" (John 6:60), actually His **words . . . are spirit and . . . life.** That is, by the work of the Holy Spirit in an individual, Jesus' words provide spiritual life.

6:64. The life **Jesus** gives must be received by faith. The words do not work automatically. From the start Jesus knew **which** followers were believers and which ones were unbelievers. This is another evidence of His supernatural knowledge (cf. 1:47; 2:24-25; 6:15).

6:65. Jesus had taught that divine enablement was necessary for people to **come to** faith (v. 44). The apostasy here (v. 66) should not be surprising. Believers who remain with Jesus evidence the Father's secret work. The unbelieving crowds are evidence that "the flesh counts for nothing" (v. 63).

6:66. His rejecting their desire to make Him their political king; His demand for personal faith; His teaching on atonement; His stress on total human inability and on salvation as a work of God—all these proved to be unpalatable for **many** people. They gave up being **His disciples** ("disciples" here refers to followers in general, not to the 12 Apostles; this is evident in v. 67).

6:67. You do not want to leave too, do you? He framed this question to encourage their weak faith. **The Twelve** were affected by the apostasy of the many, and **Jesus** used that occasion to refine their faith. They did not fully understand His words either and would not until after the Resurrection (20:9).

6:68-69. Peter, as a spokesman, gave his confession of faith. The path may be difficult, but he was convinced that Jesus' **words** lead to life. No one else has the gift **of eternal life.** "We have believed and have known" is a better translation of the Greek perfect tenses (NIV: **We believe and know**). Peter was confident of the apostles' commitment to Jesus as **the Holy One of God.** This title is unusual (a demon addressed Jesus that way; Mark 1:24). It suggests Jesus' transcendence ("the Holy One") and His representation of the Father ("of God"); thus it is another way of confessing Him as Messiah. Peter knew this by a special work of the Father (cf. Matt. 16:17).

6:70-71. Jesus then asked, **Have I not chosen you, the Twelve?** John's Gospel does not record Jesus' choice of the Twelve. He assumed his readers knew the Synoptics or common church tradition (cf. Mark 3:13-19). This choice was not election to salvation, but was Jesus' call to them to serve Him. **Yet,** He said, **one of you is a devil!** In the light of John 13:2, 27, Satan's working in Judas was tantamount to Judas being the devil. In 6:70 the Greek does not have the indefinite article "a," so it could be translated "one of you is Satan (devil)." Jesus' knowledge of **Judas** (who was called Judas Iscariot because his father was **Simon Iscariot)** was still another example of His omniscience (cf. 1:47; 2:24-25; 6:15, 61). **Later** in the Upper Room, Jesus again said **one of the Twelve** would **betray Him** (13:21). John called Judas "the traitor" (18:5). The disciples later could reflect on this prophecy of His and be strengthened in their faith. Judas was a tragic figure, influenced by Satan; yet he was responsible for his own evil choices.

3. THE MINISTRY IN GALILEE (7:1-9)

This section prepares the way for another confrontation of Jesus with His opponents in Jerusalem. This ministry in relative obscurity in Galilee provides a delay in the coming conflict.

7:1. After this is a vague time reference. Since the events recorded in chapter 6 took place shortly before the Passover (6:4), that is, in April, and the Feast of Tabernacles (in October) was now near (7:2), about six months were spent by **Jesus** in His ministry **in Galilee.** Galilee was safer because His enemies were in **Judea** . . . **waiting to take His life.**

7:2. The **Feast of Tabernacles** was one of the three great **Jewish** feasts. Josephus called it their holiest and greatest feast (*The Antiquities of the Jews* 8. 4. 1). This feast, also called the Feast of Ingathering, was a time of thanksgiving for harvest. It was a happy time; devout Jews lived outdoors in booths made of tree branches for seven days as a reminder of God's provision in the desert during their forefather's wanderings. The feast also signified that God dwells with His people.

7:3. Jesus' brothers, sons of Mary and Joseph after Jesus' birth, were at this time unbelievers (cf. Mark 3:21, 31-35; 6:3; John 7:5). They logically argued that the messianic question could not be settled in Galilee, as Jerusalem was the religious capital. The popular Feast of Tabernacles would be the right time for Jesus to present Himself as the Messiah. If He would display His powers in **Judea,** He might be able to recapture the lost crowds.

7:4-5. It did not seem rational to Jesus' brothers for Him not to show off His glory. If He really was what He claimed to be, they reasoned, He should publicly demonstrate it. They advised Him to display Himself in a powerful, brilliant way: **Show Yourself to the world.** But God's way was a public display on a cross of humiliation. John explained that **even His own brothers did not believe in Him.** This sad note sounds again (cf. 1:10-11; 12:37). Proximity to Jesus, either in a family or as a disciple, does not guarantee faith.

7:6-7. Jesus responded that His time differed from theirs. They could **come** and go without any significance; **for them any time is right.** But He always pleased the Father, so His time movements were those the Father desired. It was not yet time for the public manifestation (the Cross). Several times John noted that Jesus' **time** had **not yet come** (2:4; 7:6, 8, 30; 8:20). Then in His intercessory prayer, just before the Cross, He began, "Father, the time has come" (17:1; cf. 12:23, 27; 13:1).

The world was not dangerous to the brothers of Jesus because they were part of it (**the world cannot hate you**). But the world hated Jesus **because** He is not of it.

He had come into it as Light and pointed out its sin and rebellion against the Father. The world has its religions, its programs, its plans, its values, but Christ witnessed **that** is all **evil** (*ponēra,* "wicked"). Partly because of this, He lived carefully in order to fulfill the Father's will.

7:8-9. I am not yet going up to this Feast is clearly the thought in light of verse 10. However, most Greek editions of the New Testament omit the word "yet," because it is considered a difficult reading, but it is more likely in the original. If Jesus said, "I am not going up to the Feast," was He lying since He *did* go to the Feast? (v. 10) No, He simply meant that He was not going up to the Feast "right then," as they suggested. Jesus then for a time **stayed in Galilee,** doing the tasks of ministry which the Father had ordained.

"Going up" may have a geographical meaning (since Jerusalem is in the hills) as well as a theological meaning (going back to the Father).

D. Jesus' return to Jerusalem and the resumption of hostility (7:10-10:42)

1. THE FEAST OF TABERNACLES (7:10-8:59)

a. The anticipation of the feast (7:10-13)

7:10. Because of plots to kill Him (vv. 1, 25) Jesus made a covert entry into the city. It was not yet the time for His messianic manifestation (the Cross).

7:11-13. While Jesus' enemies **were** searching **for Him,** people were debating this controversial Teacher. The opposition against Jesus was growing. A **widespread whispering** (lit., "grumbling"; cf. 6:41, 61), occurred. (Cf. the Israelites' grumbling in the wilderness.) The charge, **He deceives the people,** had ominous tones for the penalty for this, according to Talmudic law, was death by stoning. Since the whole crowd was Jewish, **fear of the Jews** meant fear of the religious leaders.

b. Jesus at the feast (7:14-36)

7:14-15. The first three days passed without anyone seeing **Jesus.** The crowds wondered if He would come and perhaps claim to be the Messiah. Then **halfway through the Feast** He began teaching in **the temple courts.** As the official religious leaders listened to Him along with the crowds they **were amazed** (cf. Mark 1:22). His teaching was learned and spiritually penetrating. Yet He had never been a disciple in any Rabbinic school. They wondered how this could be possible.

7:16-17. The religious authorities figured that either a person studied in a traditional school or else he was self-taught. But Jesus' reply pointed to a third alternative. His **teaching** was **from** God who had commissioned Him (cf. 12:49-50; 14:11, 24). **Jesus** was God-taught, and to know Jesus properly one must be God-taught (6:45). In order to evaluate Jesus' claim, one must desire **to do God's will.** Since Jesus is God's will for man, people must believe in Him (6:29). Faith is the prerequisite for understanding. Without faith it is impossible to please God (Heb. 11:6).

7:18. If Jesus were only self-taught (speaking **on His own**) or a genius, then His ministry would be self-exalting. But He did not seek **honor for Himself.** The true goal of man should be to glorify (**honor**) God and enjoy Him forever. Jesus is what man ought to be. His purpose is to represent His Father correctly (1:18). He **is a Man of truth** (i.e., reliable; cf. 6:28; 8:26) without any injustice.

7:19. The audience boasted in Moses' **Law** (9:28). Jesus attacked their self-confident religion. They assumed they were Law-keepers. But their hearts (inner thoughts) were full of evil (Mark 7:6-7, 20-22; Matt. 5:21-22). He knew them (John 2:24-25), and that their hatred would lead to murder.

7:20. Instead of repenting because His light had rebuked their darkness (3:19-20), they insulted Him, saying He was **demon-possessed.** People had said the same of John the Baptist (Matt. 11:18). Jesus had told His half-brothers the world hated Him (John 7:7), because "everyone who does evil hates the light" (3:20). To call Jesus, who is sent from God, demon-possessed is to call light darkness (cf. 8:48, 52; 10:20). They denied His accusation that they were **trying to kill** Him. But earlier they were in fact trying to do that very thing (5:18). (Cf. Peter who denied he would deny Jesus; Mark 14:29.)

7:21-23. The **one miracle** (lit., "work") Jesus referred to was His healing of the paralytic at the pool of Bethesda, which He had performed in Jerusalem at His last visit (5:1-18). This started a fierce controversy. Circumcision is a religious rite that predated **Moses.** Abraham circumcised as a sign of the covenant (Gen. 17:9-14). But **Moses gave** Israel **circumcision** in the sense of establishing it as part of the Levitical system. Under the Mosaic Law, "On the eighth day the boy is to be circumcised" (Lev. 12:3). If that day fell on a Sabbath, circumcising a boy would seemingly violate the Sabbath Law of rest. Yet the Jews circumcised **on the Sabbath.** Therefore, Jesus argued, if care for one part of the body was permitted, then certainly the **healing** of a **whole** body (that of the paralytic) should be allowed **on the Sabbath.** Hence they had no reason to be **angry** with Him.

7:24. Their problem was that they understood the Scriptures only superficially. They majored in minors and missed the intents of many passages (cf. Matt. 23:23; John 5:39-40). They were **judging by mere appearances.** Their superficial understanding was caused by their hostility against God's Representative. In their darkness they erred. Jesus called them to **make a right judgment;** ultimately this was a call for them to repent.

7:25-26. Some of the local people were amazed at His bold public teaching. They knew of a plot **to kill** Him. Yet the leaders were **not** doing what **they** said they would do. Why? Had **the authorities** changed their minds? People were confused over the lack of leadership in the nation. They felt that if He was a deceiver, He should be locked up, or if He was the Messiah, they should accept Him.

7:27. The crowds assumed that Jesus **(this Man)** was only a Galilean carpenter from the city of Nazareth. They also believed that the Messiah **(the Christ)** would be unknown until His public appearing. A reader of the Gospels recognizes the irony. Jesus is more than a Galilean; He is the *Logos* who was virgin-born in Bethlehem. Yet He was relatively unknown until His manifestation (the Cross and the Resurrection).

7:28-29. Cried out introduced a solemn announcement (cf. 1:15; 7:37; 12:44). He responded to their supposed knowledge of Him (7:27) with irony. He is **from** the Father. God **is true** ("reliable"; cf. v. 18; 8:26) and had **sent** Jesus.

Whereas His enemies did **not know** Jesus or God (1:18; cf. Matt. 11:27), Jesus knows the Father **because** of His origin (John 1:1, 14, 18) and divine mission.

7:30. Jesus' rebuke of the Jerusalemites stirred them to attempt **to seize** (*piazō*, "arrest"; cf. vv. 32, 44; 8:20; 10:39) **Him. But** the Father had ordered a **time** and place for His manifestation (His death), and until then all things would work in concert toward that goal. They could not lay **a hand on Him because** the Father's hand was over Him.

7:31. The exposure of Jesus and His teaching moved **many in the crowd** to believe on **Him.** They logically thought that His **miraculous signs** marked Him out as unusual. Certainly the Messiah could not do any more miracles **than this Man.** But the crowd's faith in Jesus as Messiah was tentative and was not linked to belief in His atoning death.

7:32. Since many in **the crowd** were turning to Jesus, they would set aside the Pharisees' traditional teachings (cf. Mark 7:1-23). **The Pharisees,** as the guardians of Jewish traditions (see comments on the Pharisees, John 1:24-25), realized something needed to be done about Jesus soon. **The chief priests** were leading priests, not just high priests. **Arrest** is the same Greek word (*piazō*) as "seize" in 7:30, 44; 8:20; 10:39.

7:33. While the plan to arrest Him proceeded, **Jesus** continued to teach. The nation had **only a short time** to decide about Him. This time was determined not by the authorities but by God. When He had completed God's plan for His earthly life, He would return to the Father.

7:34. You will look for Me is a prophecy that the Jewish nation will long for her Messiah. She is doing this now, not knowing that Jesus is her Messiah. Later she will weep for Him (Zech. 12:10-13; Rev. 1:7). The time of spiritual opportunity is now. A time will come when it is too late. He went bodily to heaven where unbelievers **cannot come** (cf. John 8:21). So people today do not have the unique opportunity people had when Jesus was speaking to them face to face.

7:35. Once more the words of Jesus were an enigma to **the Jews** (cf. vv. 15, 31, 41-42). **Where** could He possibly **go that** they could not **find Him?** Because they were of the earth, they could think only earthly thoughts (cf. Isa. 55:8). During some of that period the Jewish people lived in Palestine whereas others migrated throughout the Roman Empire and beyond, as far east as Babylonia. They were **scattered among the Greeks.** "Greeks" means not just people of Greece or Greek-speaking peoples but generally non-Jews or heathen (cf. "Greek" and "Jew" in Col. 3:11). The question then was, Will Jesus go **teach the** heathen? Without the Jews realizing it, this question was prophetic of the spread of the gospel after Jesus' Ascension.

7:36. The crowd, after pondering what Jesus meant, simply repeated their questions. They did not understand His words.

c. The last day of the Feast (7:37-52)

7:37. The Feast of Tabernacles was celebrated with certain festival rituals. One was a solemn procession each day from the temple to the Gihon Spring. A priest filled a gold pitcher with water while the choir sang Isaiah 12:3. Then they returned to the altar and poured out the water. This ritual reminded them of the water from the rock during the wilderness wanderings (Num. 20:8-11; Ps. 78:15-16). It also spoke prophetically of the coming days of Messiah (cf. Zech. 14:8, 16-19). The Feast's seventh and **last** day was its **greatest** (cf. Lev. 23:36). **Jesus stood,** in contrast with the Rabbis' usual position of being seated while teaching. **Said in a loud voice** (cf. John 1:15; 7:28; 12:44) was a way of introducing a solemn announcement. His offer, **Come to Me and drink,** was an offer of salvation (cf. 4:14; 6:53-56).

7:38. Streams of living water will flow from within one who **believes in** Jesus. That is, he will have a continual source of satisfaction, which will provide life continually (cf. 4:14). When Jesus added, **As the Scripture has said,** He did not identify the Old Testament passage(s) He had in mind. But He may have thought of Psalm 78:15-16 and Zechariah 14:8 (cf. Ezek. 47:1-11; Rev. 22:1-2).

7:39. John explained that the "living water" (v. 38) was the coming gift of **the** Holy **Spirit.** The Spirit within a believer satisfies his need of God, and provides him with regeneration, guidance, and empowerment. In the earliest Greek manuscripts, the words, **Up to that time the Spirit had not been given,** are simply, "for there was not yet Spirit." This cannot be taken in an absolute sense since the Spirit had actively worked among people in the Old Testament era. Jesus referred to the special baptizing, sealing, and indwelling work of the Spirit in the Church Age, which would start on the day of Pentecost (Acts 1:5, 8). Jesus said He would "send the Spirit" to His followers (John 15:26; 16:7). "The Spirit had not [yet] been given" to indwell believers permanently (cf. Ps. 51:11). That happened after **Jesus** was **glorified,** that is after His death, resurrection, and Ascension. "Glorified," "glory," and "glorify" are used frequently in John's Gospel (John 7:39; 11:4; 12:16, 23, 28; 13:31-32; 14:13; 15:8; 16:14; 17:1, 4-5, 10).

7:40-41. The crowd continued to debate Jesus' identity. **Some** saw Him as **the Prophet** mentioned by Moses (Deut. 18:15, 18). He would speak God's words to people but not in the awesome display of Mount Sinai from which Moses spoke. Jesus is indeed that predicted Prophet (Acts 3:22), but many rejected Him as such. Some said Jesus **is the Christ,** that is, the Messiah, but **others** rejected that idea because He came **from Galilee** (cf. John 7:52).

7:42. According to Samuel and Isaiah (2 Sam. 7:16; Isa. 11:1) the Messiah was to be born into a Davidic **family.** Micah predicted that He would be born in **Bethlehem . . . David's** hometown (Micah 5:2). Jesus *is* from a Davidic family (Matt. 1:1-17; Luke 3:23-38; Rom. 1:3) and *was* born in Bethlehem (Matt. 2:1-6), but the crowd ignorantly overlooked those facts.

7:43-44. The crowd's **divided** opinion about **Jesus** enabled Him to continue His ministry without immediate arrest (**seize,** *piazō,* is the same word for "arrest" in v. 32, and is also used in v. 30; 8:20; 10:39). Many of the people held a favorable opinion of Jesus even though they did not personally commit themselves to Him (cf. 7:12, 31, 40-41). His enemies had to be careful lest a riot would result. So for a time, **no one** touched **Him.** Twice later the Jews were again divided over Jesus (9:16; 10:19-21).

7:45-46. The temple guards, who were sent to arrest Jesus (v. 32) returned without Him. Responding to the question

Why? the guards answered, **No one ever spoke the way this Man does.** Literally this is, "Never spoke thus a man," which implies that the guards sensed that He was most unusual or perhaps more than a man. The Gospels often reveal Jesus as a most impressive Teacher and Speaker (e.g., Matt. 7:29; 22:46). Though Jesus was opposed, many of those who heard Him were moved by Him (cf. John 7:15; 12:19).

7:47-48. The Pharisees' question to the guards, **Has any of the rulers or of the Pharisees believed in Him?** reveals their pride. They thought they were too educated (v. 15) to be taken in by a deceiver. Ironically a number of the rulers *did* believe (12:42; 19:38-39). The Pharisees were jealous of Jesus' great popularity ("The whole world has gone after Him" [12:19]).

7:49. The Pharisees explained Jesus' popularity among the populace by suggesting that the people were too ignorant to recognize Jesus as a deceiver. The crowd **(this mob),** according to the Pharisees, did not know **the Law.** They did not study it, so they could not obey it. And since they did not obey it, they were under God's **curse** (Deut. 28:15). The irony of the situation was that the Pharisees, not the mob, were under God's wrath because they rejected God's revelation in Jesus (John 3:36).

7:50-51. The Mosaic Law (Deut. 1:16-17) and Rabbinic law stipulated that a person accused of a crime should get a fair **hearing.** Nicodemus appeared as a fair-minded man who did not want the Sanhedrin to make a false or hasty judgment. He had personally spoken with **Jesus** and knew He was from God (John 3:1-3; cf. 12:42; 19:38-39).

7:52. Even though Nicodemus was a respected teacher in the nation (3:10), he was insulted by the other members of the Sanhedrin. Their prejudice and hatred against Jesus were already strong enough to overthrow reason. The Sanhedrin accused Nicodemus of being as ignorant as the Galileans. **A prophet does not come out of Galilee,** they argued. So the messianic Prophet cannot be a Galilean (cf. 7:41).

Note on 7:53–8:11

7:53–8:11. Almost all textual scholars agree that these verses were not part of the original manuscript of the Gospel of John. The NIV states in brackets that

"The earliest and most reliable manuscripts do not have John 7:53–8:11." The style and vocabulary of this passage differ from the rest of the Gospel, and the passage interrupts the sequence from 7:52–8:12. It is probably a part of true oral tradition which was added to later Greek manuscripts by copyists. For more discussion on the subject and an exposition of the passage, see the *Appendix* before the John *Bibliography*.

d. The Light of the world discourse (8:12-59)

A major feature of the Feast of Tabernacles was the lighting of giant lamps in the women's court in the temple (see the diagram). The wicks were made from the priests' worn-out garments. The light illuminated the temple area and the people gathered to sing praises and dance. The light reminded the Jewish people of how God was with them in their wanderings in the wilderness in a pillar of cloud which turned to fire at night (Num. 9:15-23).

8:12. This discourse continues Jesus' public teaching in the city of Jerusalem in the temple area. How fitting that during the Feast of Tabernacles, when the large lamps were burning, **Jesus . . . said, I am the Light of the world** (cf. 1:4, 9; 12:35, 46). The world is in darkness, a symbol of evil, sin, and ignorance (Isa. 9:2; Matt. 4:16; 27:45; John 3:19). "Light" in the Bible is a symbol of God and His holiness (Acts 9:3; 1 John 1:5). Jesus is "*the* Light," not merely a light or another light among many lights. He is the only Light, "the true Light" (John 1:9), for the whole world. When Jesus said, **Whoever follows Me,** He meant whoever believes and obeys Him (cf. 10:4-5, 27; 12:26; 21:19-20, 22). Jesus was speaking of salvation.

Coming to Christ for salvation results in a different kind of life. A believer **will never walk in darkness,** that is, he will not live in it (cf. 12:46; 1 John 1:6-7). He does not remain in the realm of evil and ignorance (John 12:46) for he has Christ as his **Light** and salvation (cf. Ps. 36:9).

8:13. Again **the Pharisees challenged** His claim. Since He appeared **as** His **own witness,** they said His **testimony** was **not valid.** Self-authentication is sometimes unacceptable. The Law required two witnesses to establish a fact in

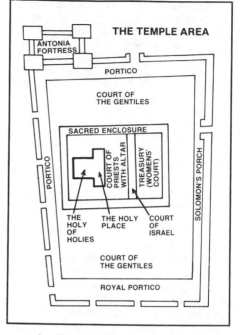

THE TEMPLE AREA

ANTONIA FORTRESS

PORTICO

COURT OF THE GENTILES

SACRED ENCLOSURE

PORTICO

COURT OF PRIESTS WITH ALTAR

TREASURY (WOMENS' COURT)

SOLOMON'S PORCH

THE HOLY OF HOLIES

THE HOLY PLACE

COURT OF ISRAEL

COURT OF THE GENTILES

ROYAL PORTICO

capital offenses (Deut. 17:6; 19:15; John 8:17). Rabbinic tradition rejected self-testimony.

8:14. Sometimes, however, self-authentication is the only way to truth. Sometimes an individual is the only one who knows the facts about himself. And only God can give **testimony** to Himself. **Jesus** was competent to give a true witness of Himself because as God He has a comprehensive knowledge of His origin and destiny (7:29). In spite of what the Pharisees thought they knew about Jesus, they were ignorant of His heavenly origin and destiny (cf. 7:33-34), and thus were invalid judges of Him.

8:15. The Pharisees, Jesus said, judged **by human standards,** that is, they were limited by superficial appearances. They saw only His flesh, not His deity, so they misjudged Him. By contrast, Jesus did not come to **judge** people but to save them (3:17). When He does judge in the future, He will simply execute the Father's will according to truth and the Law (cf. 5:27, 45). He Himself will **pass judgment on no one.**

8:16. Jesus' judging was totally unlike theirs. Theirs was biased and limited. His was not His own because of His unique union **with the Father.** Nor was His witness **alone;** He spoke with divine authority.

8:17-18. In your own Law may refer to Deuteronomy 17:6; 19:15 (or to Rabbinic laws), which speak of the necessity of **two** witnesses. In Jesus' case only God could authenticate Him. God the Son and God **the Father** are the required two Witnesses. The Father **sent** Jesus and authenticated Him by the signs (miracles) He performed.

8:19. Jesus' teaching on God as His **Father** was unique (cf. 5:18), and the Jews were puzzled by His familiar way of talking about Him. The Pharisees **asked Him, Where is Your Father?** Was He talking about God, or (as they supposed) His human father? Their ignorance of Jesus showed their ignorance of God, for Jesus is the Revelation of the **Father** (cf. 1:14, 18; 14:7, 9).

8:20. Jesus **spoke these words while teaching in the temple area near the place where the offerings were put.** This was probably in the women's court (see the diagram at 8:12; cf. Mark 12:41-42). Jesus went there and instructed the people. **No one seized** (*piazō*, "arrested") **Him** (cf. John 7:30, 32, 44, 10:39) **because,** as John repeatedly pointed out, Jesus was working on God's **time** schedule to accomplish the Father's will (cf. 2:4; 7:6, 30; 12:23, 27; 13:1; 17:1).

8:21. Just as His time was short, so their opportunity for trusting in Him was limited. Soon He would go back to His Father and they could not follow Him there (cf. 7:33-34). **You will die in your sin.** The singular "sin" is that of rejecting the One who offers salvation (cf. 16:9). They would "die" because they continued living in the realm of sin, remaining under its power. Physical death would be their prelude to eternal separation from God.

8:22. Their question, **Will He kill Himself?** was both a misunderstanding and an ironic prophecy. They wondered if He would commit suicide and thus be unreachable. (Earlier they thought He meant He would go teach non-Jews in other lands [7:35].) Though Jesus did not kill Himself, He did lay down His own life (10:11, 18).

8:23. Jesus pointed out His heavenly origin and His real home (**from above . . . not of this world**). They belong here (**from below . . . of this world**), but He does not.

8:24. Jesus said twice they **would die**

in their **sins** (cf. this pl. with the sing. "sin" in v. 21). If they would reject the Sin-Bearer (1:29), they would continue in the realm of sin. If they would reject Jesus as the revelation of God, they would miss their only hope for salvation. **I am the One I claim to be** in Greek is the enigmatic "I Am," which is a self-designation for God in certain contexts (cf. Isa. 43:10-11, LXX).

8:25. This revelation of Jesus as "I Am" only confused the Jews. And His words about their sins probably angered them. **Who are You? they asked.** He replied, **Just what I have been claiming all along.** This is the NIV's translation of a problematic Greek sentence. (Other translations make it a question or an exclamation.)

8:26-27. Jesus could have said much more and even condemned His hearers, but His purpose in coming was to give them and **the world** the message from the One **who sent** Him. This message is certainly true because the Sender **is reliable** (cf. 7:18, 28). John added that the people **did not understand that** Jesus **was** referring to the **Father.** God was unknown to them so they missed Jesus (cf. 1:18).

8:28. Jesus was now unknown to them. Only the Crucifixion (when **the Son of Man** would be **lifted up;** cf. 3:14; 12:32) would enable them to see Him for **who** He really is. He did not mean that all will be saved, but that the Cross would reveal that Jesus is God's Word (the *Logos*) to man, and that what He taught was **just what the Father . . . taught** Him.

8:29. Jesus' union with the Father is one of love and continual obedience (cf. 4:34; 5:30). Though people reject Jesus, the Father will never abandon Him. Jesus is never **alone,** and even on the cross the Father glorified Him (cf. 16:32; 17:5).

8:30. In spite of widespread unbelief and official rejection, the ministry of Jesus did bring many to faith (cf. 7:31). Yet this faith would need to be tested and refined. The words **many put their faith in Him** contrast with the next verse. Though large numbers of people responded to Jesus, many people fell away.

8:31-32. Jews who had believed Him indicates that some paid attention to Jesus' words without necessarily committing themselves to Him personally (cf. 6:53). It was possible to "believe" in the message of repentance and the coming kingdom without being born again. Continuing in the truth is the sign of true followers and learners (**disciples**). If they really grasped His message, they would find salvation **truth.** Knowing this salvation truth would liberate them from their bondage in sin.

8:33. Their response indicated that they had not grasped Christ's message. Even though they were under Rome, they insisted that as **Abraham's descendants** they were **free** men. How could Jesus free them when they were not **slaves?** They had no sense of their bondage to sin.

8:34. Three times in this chapter (vv. 34, 51, 58) **Jesus** said, **I tell you the truth** (cf. comments on 1:51). The very act of committing **sin** reveals that the one doing the act is under the power and authority of sin. Sin is personified as a cruel master. Paul used the same illustration (Rom. 6:15-23).

8:35. Just as Ishmael, Abraham's **slave** son, was cast out of the house (Gen. 21:8-21), so those in sin are in danger. Isaac was **a son** who belonged and therefore remained in the house. Were they like Ishmael, or Isaac? The issue was not physical genealogy but spiritual kinship.

8:36. Jesus is **the** true **Son** and seed of Abraham (Gal. 3:16). He remains in the house and is over it (Heb. 3:6). People can become truly **free** by becoming sons of God by faith in Christ, *the* Son (Gal. 3:26).

8:37. Physically the Jews of course **are** the **descendants** of Abraham. Yet this same crowd was seeking **to kill** Jesus, Abraham's true Son, thus showing that they were not Abraham's *spiritual* descendants (cf. Rom. 2:28-29; 9:6, 8; Gal. 3:29). They were rejecting His message (**My word**).

8:38. Jesus spoke what He had **seen in the Father's presence** (cf. v. 28). Thus His words are God's truth. But the people had no affinity for His words because they listened to *their* **father** (Satan; v. 44) and followed him. As yet Jesus had not identified their father, but the implication was becoming plain.

8:39. To counter the thrust of Jesus' argument, the Jews claimed **Abraham** as their spiritual **father.** But **Jesus** responded by stating that spiritual descendants of Abraham **do what Abraham did,** that is, they believe and obey God. They should

respond in faith to the heavenly messenger and do what He says. John the Baptist had earlier warned the Jews against the danger of trusting in their Abrahamic lineage (Luke 3:8).

8:40. But they were rejecting the heavenly Messenger and seeking **to kill** the One who **told** them God's Word. **Abraham did not do** that; he was obedient to God's commands (cf. Gen. 12:1-9; 15:6; 22:1-19).

8:41. The Jews' works were different, so their **father** (cf. v. 38) must also be different. They could seek to evade Jesus' logic only by denying an illegitimate human paternity and claiming a heavenly one. In their denial, **We are not illegitimate children,** they may have been casting aspersions on Jesus' birth.

8:42. Love is a family affair (1 John 5:1). If the Jews really had **God** as their **Father** and really loved Him (the Gr. assumes they did not), then they **would** have loved **Jesus** because He **came from God.** Jesus again affirmed His position as God's Representative: the Father **sent** Him.

8:43. Jesus the *Logos* speaks to people, but their fundamental opposition to Him caused them to misunderstand His **language. Unable to hear** means a spiritual inability to respond. The rendering **what I say** is literally, "My word" (*logos*). Paul later wrote that "the man without the Spirit does not accept the things that come from the Spirit of God, for they are foolishness to him" (1 Cor. 2:14).

8:44. The devil is the enemy of life and **truth.** By a lie he brought spiritual and physical death to mankind (cf. Gen. 3:4, 13; 1 John 3:8, 10-15.) He still distorts truth (**there is no truth in him . . . he is a liar and the father of lies**) and seeks to lead people away from God, the Source of truth and life (2 Cor. 4:4). Since these Jews wanted Jesus' death and since they rejected the truth and embraced the lie, their family solidarity with Satan and his desires was certain. How different from having Abraham as their father!

8:45. Jesus, in contrast with them, lives in **truth** and proclaims it. Since unbelievers love darkness not light (cf. 3:19-20), and falsehood not reality, they reject Jesus.

8:46. Many accusations had been made against Jesus (cf. 7:12b, 20). But He is so committed to doing God's will ("I always do what pleases Him" [8:29]) that it is impossible to show any connection between Jesus and sin: **Can any of you prove Me guilty of sin?** Since this is so, they should have recognized His divine origin. His second question, **Why don't you believe Me?** is answered in the next verse.

8:47. Belonging **to God** is the basis for hearing Him. To **hear** God is **not** a matter of being able to discern audible sounds but of obeying the heavenly commands. Jesus' hearers absolute rejection of the heavenly Word was a clear reflection **that** they did **not belong to God** (lit., "are not of God").

8:48. Samaritans were a mixed race with a religion the Jews considered apostate (cf. comments on 4:4). To call Jesus **a Samaritan** was to use a term of abuse, referring to a heretic or one with a faulty worship. Their charge that Jesus was **demon-possessed** (cf. 7:20; 8:52; 10:20) suggested they thought He was mad, unclean, and evil. How ironic that after He said their father was the devil (8:44), they said He was demon-possessed!

8:49-50. Jesus' claims were not those of a demon-**possessed** person. He was seeking not self-exaltation but the **honor** of His **Father.** Their attempt to **dishonor** Him was an attack on His Father. (Cf. Hanun's attack on David's messengers, which was an insult against the king; 2 Sam. 10:1-6.)

When accused, Jesus did not seek to justify Himself (cf. John 8:54). He committed His case to the heavenly **Judge,** knowing that even if people judge the Son falsely, the Father will reverse their verdict and vindicate Him.

8:51. Again Jesus said, I **tell you the truth** (cf. comments on 1:51). **Keeps My Word** is another way of expressing a positive response to His revelation. (Similar expressions are "hear" His Word [5:24] and "hold" to His teaching [8:31].) It means to observe, pay attention to, or to fulfill. A person who obeys Jesus **will never see death,** that is, **he** will not be eternally separated from God (cf. 3:16; 5:24).

8:52-53. His opponents thought that He meant physical death. To **taste death** means to experience death (Heb. 2:9). So they concluded that since **Abraham and**

the prophets had **died,** He must be insane or **demon-possessed** (cf. John 7:20; 8:48; 10:19). In Greek their first question in 8:53 expected a negative answer: "You are not **greater than our father Abraham** who died, **are You?"** The irony is that of course He is. But He had not come to proclaim His greatness.

8:54. If He honored Himself (cf. v. 50), His **glory** would have no value. The **Father . . . is the One who** will do the work of vindication. Yet the hostile unbelievers claimed a relationship to God. It is obvious that they were in error. Jesus' Father is God; their father was Satan.

8:55. In the deepest intimacy Jesus has a relationship and union wih God but His enemies did not. Jesus knows (*oida*, "to know inherently or intuitively") the Father, but they did **not know** (*ginōskō*, "to come to know by experience or observation") Him. For Him to deny this would be to lie just as they were lying. Jesus did **know** the Father and obey Him (keep His Word; cf. v. 52).

8:56. The unbelieving Jews were not Abraham's descendants spiritually (v. 39). But here when Jesus referred to **your father Abraham** He meant they were physically related to him. Abraham **rejoiced** to see **My day,** that is, the messianic salvation which God promised ("all peoples on earth will be blessed through you"; Gen. 12:3). Abraham by faith was granted a son Isaac, through whom the Seed (Christ) would come. How much of the messianic times God revealed to His friend Abraham is unknown. But it is clear that he knew of the coming salvation and he rejoiced in knowing about it and expecting it.

8:57. The unbelievers objected that one so young (**not yet 50 years old**) could not have **seen Abraham.** (Nothing should be inferred about Jesus' age from this remark.) They could not understand how Abraham and Jesus could have possibly had any visual contact.

8:58. Jesus then affirmed His superiority over the prophets and Abraham. **Abraham** came into being; but when he **was born,** Jesus was already existing. I **Am** is a title of Deity (cf. Ex. 3:14; Isa. 41:4; 43:11-13; John 8:28); the Jews' response (v. 59) showed they understood it that way. Jesus, because of His equality with God (5:18; 20:28; Phil. 2:6; Col. 2:9), existed from all eternity (John 1:1).

8:59. Jesus' clear affirmation of His deity evoked a crisis. They had to decide whether He was what He claimed or was a blasphemer (cf. 5:18). Stoning was the normal punishment for this sin. The words, **but Jesus hid Himself,** could refer to a supernatural means of escape. The NIV's **slipping away** (lit., "He went out") implies ordinary means (cf. 5:13; 10:39; 12:36). Once again His time had not yet come (cf. 2:4; 7:6, 8, 30; 8:20).

2. THE HEALING OF A MAN BORN BLIND (CHAP. 9)

Isaiah predicted that in messianic times various signs would occur. The Messiah would "open eyes that are blind" (Isa. 42:7; cf. Isa. 29:18; 35:5). Jesus often healed the blind (cf. Matt. 9:27-31; 12:22-23; 15:30; 20:29-34; 21:14). This miracle in John 9 is notable because Jesus had just proclaimed Himself as "the Light of the world" (8:12). As a public demonstration of His claim, He gave sight to a man born blind.

9:1. As He went along in the city of Jerusalem, Jesus **saw a man** with congenital blindness. Jesus' choice of this individual is significant (cf. 5:5-6). He is Sovereign in His works. That the man was **blind from birth** pointed out his seeming hopelessness. This illustrates man's spiritual blindness from birth (9:39-41; 2 Cor. 4:4; Eph. 2:1-3).

9:2-3. The **disciples** faced a theological problem. Believing that sin directly caused all suffering, how could a person be *born* with a handicap? Therefore either **this man . . . sinned** in his mother's womb (Ezek. 18:4) **or his parents** sinned (Ex. 20:5). **Jesus** therefore answered, **Neither this man nor his parents sinned.** These words do not contradict the universal sinfulness of man (cf. Rom. 3:9-20, 23). Instead Jesus meant that this man's blindness was not caused by some *specific* sin. Instead the problem existed **so that . . .** God could display His glory in the midst of seeming tragedy (cf. Ex. 4:11; 2 Cor. 12:9).

9:4-5. **Day** means the time allotted for Jesus to do God's will (to **do the work of Him who sent Me**). **We** includes the disciples and by extension all believers. **Night is** the limit set to do God's works. In Jesus' case it was His coming death. As

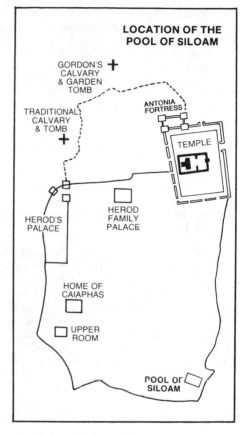

LOCATION OF THE POOL OF SILOAM

GORDON'S CALVARY & GARDEN TOMB

ANTONIA FORTRESS

TRADITIONAL CALVARY & TOMB

TEMPLE

HEROD'S PALACE

HEROD FAMILY PALACE

HOME OF CAIAPHAS

UPPER ROOM

POOL OF SILOAM

the **Light of the world** Jesus gives people salvation (cf. 8:12). After His death, His disciples would be His lights (cf. Matt. 5:14; Eph. 5:8-14), bringing Christ to others.

9:6-7. Jesus placed clay (**mud with . . . saliva**) **on the man's eyes.** Interestingly man was made from this same substance—the dust of the earth (Gen. 2:7). Jesus probably used the clay as an aid to develop the man's faith, not as a medicine. Jesus' making of clay broke the Rabbinic regulations against kneading clay on the Sabbath (cf. John 9:14). Jesus then **told the man, Wash in the pool of Siloam (this word means Sent).** This is located at the southeast corner of Jerusalem (see the map), where Hezekiah's tunnel channeled water inside the city walls from the Gihon Spring. The man was "sent" there and Jesus was the One "sent" by the Father. **The man . . . washed and** went **home seeing!**

9:8-9. People argued over whether he was **the same man who used to sit and beg.** If so, it was incredible that he could see. Perhaps, they said, it was a case of mistaken identity. **But he himself insisted, I am the man.**

9:10-12. But if he were the same man, **how** was this possible? He gave a simple and factual account of how the miracle occurred. He referred to the Lord as **the Man they call Jesus.** Since he was blind at the time of the miracle, he had no idea **where** Jesus went.

9:13-14. Since this miracle was so unusual, the people **brought** the man **to the Pharisees,** who were highly respected in religious matters. To the Pharisees, healing (unless life was in danger) and making or kneading clay violated the **Sabbath** Law.

9:15-16. When **the Pharisees . . . asked him** about his situation, he briefly told what happened (cf. v. 11). **The Pharisees** believed that since Jesus "violated" the Sabbath He was a false prophet turning the people away from God (Deut. 13:3-5). So they concluded, **This Man is not from God.** Later they said Jesus was "a sinner" (John 9:24). **Others** concluded that the **signs** were so impressive that **a sinner** could not do them. (Of course a false prophet could do deceptive signs [cf. 2 Thes. 2:9].) The Pharisees then **were divided** (cf. John 7:43; 10:19).

9:17. The healed **blind** man's opinion was that Jesus **is a prophet.** Old Testament prophets sometimes performed miracles which marked them out as God's men.

9:18-20. The Jews still could **not believe** this man **had been blind.** Surely some mistake had been made. So **they sent for** his **parents,** who affirmed that **he** was their **son** who had been **born blind.**

9:21-23. But the **parents . . . were afraid** to hazard any opinions about the cure or the Healer. The Pharisees and other Jewish authorities (**the Jews**) had **already . . . decided that** Jesus was not the Messiah. Those who held such a heresy would be excommunicated from **the synagogue.** (Some scholars argue that this verse was added later by an editor, but there is nothing unthinkable about this kind of persecution during Jesus' ministry.) The **parents** shifted the pressure from themselves by noting that their son was **of** legal **age** to testify for himself (vv. 21, 23).

9:24. The authorities tried to pressure the healed **man** into withdrawing his testimony about Jesus: **Give glory to God** (cf. Josh. 7:19; 1 Sam. 6:5; Jer. 13:16) was a call to admit his guilt in siding with Jesus, whom they called **a sinner.** When they said **We know,** they were pressuring him. Unbelief often claims to be scientific, but here it was just stubborn and willful.

9:25-26. His witness was clear, and he refused to deny what he knew for certain: **I was blind, but now I see! They asked him** to go over the story again, hoping to find some contradiction in the man's report.

9:27. The ex-blind man got impatient. He had already **told** how he was healed (v. 15), but they **did not listen** to him. That is, they rejected it. He sarcastically asked if their request for him to repeat his report indicated that they had changed their hearts. Were they inquiring because they were interested in becoming Jesus' disciples?

9:28-29. The idea of this illiterate beggar sarcastically suggesting they were interested in Jesus was more than their pride could take. They insulted **him** and then claimed that they were Moses' **disciples.** Jesus to them was an unknown. **We don't even know where He comes from.** Yet they claimed to know **Moses** who, Jesus said, wrote about Him (5:46).

9:30-33. The beggar proceeded to teach them since they admitted ignorance of Jesus' origin. The irony is strong for the reader knows His origin (1:14, 18). According to the beggar's logic, this miracle was notable and unique. He said that no one had **ever heard of . . . a man born blind** receiving sight. He reasoned that **God** grants **not** the requests of **sinners** but those of the righteous (cf. Elijah, James 5:16-18). Therefore **this Man,** he said, is **from God.** Otherwise He could do no miracles.

9:34. Upstaged by a beggar, they could only insult him again and throw **him out** of the synagogue (cf. v. 22). They reasoned that his blindness must have been due to some specific "sin" (they forgot the Book of Job). But they were irrational. How could anybody be **steeped in sin at birth?** Everybody is born with a sinful nature (Ps. 51:5; Rom. 5:12), but a baby can hardly commit numerous acts of sin moments after it is born!

9:35. Taking the initiative again (cf. v. 6), **Jesus** found the former blind man.

Do you (emphatic in the Gr.) **believe in the Son of Man?** This was a call to commitment. "Son of Man" is a title of Messiah which includes a rich background (cf. Dan. 7:13; and comments on Mark 2:10).

9:36-37. The beggar responded that he was willing to **believe** but he was ignorant. **Jesus** then disclosed Himself and gave the beggar the necessary knowledge for faith. Faith involves an act of the will, based on information.

9:38. After Jesus revealed that *He* is the Son of Man, **the man** responded in faith (**Lord, I believe**) and **worshiped Him.** His worship of Jesus replaced his worship in the synagogue. The Jews had cast him out of the synagogue, but Jesus does not cast out those who come to Him (6:37). One goal of salvation is worship of the One who saves (4:23).

9:39. Does this verse contradict 3:17? According to that verse (and 12:47) Jesus was *not* sent "to condemn the world." But here Jesus said, **For judgment I have come into this world.** Jesus meant He came to pronounce decisions on the ungodly, like a judge (cf. 5:22, 27). **The blind** who come to sight are those who, admitting their helplessness and inability, trust Jesus for salvation. **Those who see** and **become blind** are those whose self-trust and pride blinds them to the wonders of Jesus. He does not condemn them by *making* them blind; they blind themselves by rejecting Him and Satan contributes to that blinding (2 Cor. 4:4).

9:40-41. **Some** of the **Pharisees . . . asked,** literally, "**We also are not blind, are we?**" They expected a negative answer because they assumed that certainly they, of all men, possessed spiritual perception. Sin constantly deceives people so they live in falsehood. Jesus replied, If the Pharisees **were blind** to spiritual things absolutely, they might have claimed ignorance as a defense. But their claims and pretentions of spiritual insight (**you claim you can see**) and leadership made them culpable. They were responsible for their sins because they sinned willfully. It is dangerous to be a teacher of spiritual truths (cf. 3:10; Rom. 2:19-24; James 3:1).

3. THE GOOD SHEPHERD DISCOURSE
   (10:1-21)

The discourse on the Good Shepherd continues the same setting as in chapter 9. Comparing people to a shepherd and his sheep was common in the Middle East. Kings and priests called themselves shepherds and their subjects sheep. The Bible makes frequent use of this analogy. Many of the great men of the Old Testament were shepherds (e.g., Abraham, Isaac, Jacob, Moses, David). As national leaders, Moses and David were both "shepherds" over Israel. Some of the most famous passages in the Bible employ this motif (cf. Ps. 23; Isa. 53:6; Luke 15:1-7).

Jesus developed this analogy in several ways. The connection with the preceding chapter is seen in Jesus' contrast of the Pharisees with the man born blind. The Pharisees—spiritually blind while claiming insight (John 9:41)—were false shepherds. As the True Shepherd, Jesus came to seek and to heal. His sheep hear and respond to His voice.

10:1-2. Verses 1-5 describe a morning shepherding scene. A **shepherd** enters through a **gate** into a walled enclosure which has several flocks in one **sheep pen.** The enclosure, with stone walls, is guarded at night by a doorkeeper to prevent thieves and beasts of prey from entering. Anyone who would climb the wall would do it for no good purpose.

10:3-4. By contrast, the shepherd has a right to enter the sheep pen. **The watchman opens the gate,** and the shepherd comes in to call **his own sheep by name** (out from the other flocks). Shepherds knew their sheep well and gave them names. As **sheep** hear the sound of their owner's familiar **voice,** they go to him. He **leads them out** of the pen till his flock is formed. Then he goes **out** toward the fields with **the sheep** following **him.**

10:5-6. If **a stranger** enters the pen, the sheep **run away from him because** his **voice** is not familiar. The point of **this figure of speech** consists in how a shepherd forms his flock. People come to God because He calls them (cf. vv. 16, 27; Rom. 8:28, 30). Their proper response to His call is to follow Him (cf. John 1:43; 8:12; 12:26; 21:19, 22). But this spiritual lesson was missed by those who heard Jesus, even though they certainly understood the local shepherd/sheep relationship. In their blindness, they could not see Jesus as the Lord who is the Shepherd (cf. Ps. 23).

10:7-9. Jesus then developed the shepherd/sheep figure of speech in another way. After a shepherd's flock has been separated from the other **sheep,** he takes them to pasture. Near the pasture is an enclosure for the sheep. The shepherd takes his place in the doorway or entrance and functions as a door or **gate.** The sheep can go out to the pasture in front of the enclosure, or if afraid, they can retreat into the security of the enclosure. The spiritual meaning is that Jesus is **the** only **Gate** by which people can enter into God's provision for them.

When Jesus said, **All who ever came before Me were thieves and robbers,** He referred to those leaders of the nation who cared not for the spiritual good of the people but only for themselves. Jesus the Shepherd provides security for His flock from enemies **(whoever enters through Me will be saved,** or "kept safe"). He also provides for their daily needs (the sheep **come in and go out, and find pasture).**

10:10. The thief, that is, a false shepherd, cares only about feeding himself, not building up the flock. He steals sheep in order to **kill** them, thus destroying part of the flock. But Christ has **come** to benefit the sheep. He gives **life** which is not constricted but overflowing. The thief takes life; Christ gives **it to the full.**

10:11. Jesus then developed the sheep/shepherd figure in a third way. When evening settled over the land of Palestine, danger lurked. In Bible times lions, wolves, jackals, panthers, leopards, bears, and hyenas were common in the countryside. The life of a shepherd could be dangerous as illustrated by David's fights with at least one lion and one bear (1 Sam. 17:34-35, 37). Jacob also experienced the labor and toil of being a faithful shepherd (Gen. 31:38-40). Jesus said, **I am the Good Shepherd** (cf. John 10:14). In the Old Testament, God is called the Shepherd of His people (Pss. 23:1; 80:1-2; Ecc. 12:11; Isa. 40:11; Jer. 31:10). Jesus is this to His people, and He came to give **His life for** their benefit (cf. John 10:14, 17-18; Gal. 1:4; Eph. 5:2, 25; Heb. 9:14). He is also the "Great Shepherd" (Heb. 13:20-21) and "the Chief Shepherd" (1 Peter 5:4).

10:12-13. In contrast with **the** Good **Shepherd, who owns,** cares, feeds, protects, and dies for His **sheep,** the one who works for wages—**the hired hand**—does not have the same commitment. He is interested in making money and in self-preservation. If a **wolf attacks** (harpazei, lit., "snatches away"; cf. this same verb in v. 28), he **runs away** and his selfishness causes **the flock** to be scattered. Obviously he **cares nothing for the sheep.** Israel had many false prophets, selfish kings, and imitation messiahs. The flock of God suffered constantly from their abuse (Jer. 10:21-22; 12:10; Zech. 11:4-17).

10:14-15. In contrast with a hired workman, **the Good Shepherd** has an intimacy with and personal interest in the sheep (cf. vv. 3, 27). **I know My sheep** stresses His ownership and watchful oversight. **My sheep know Me** stresses their reciprocal knowledge of and intimacy with Him. This intimacy is modeled on the loving and trusting mutual relationship of **the Father** and the Son. Jesus' care and concern is evidenced by His prediction of His coming death for the flock. Some shepherds have willingly died while protecting their sheep from danger. Jesus willingly gave His **life for** His **sheep** (vv. 11, 15, 17-18)—on their behalf as their Substitute (Rom. 5:8, 10; 2 Cor. 5:21; 1 Peter 2:24; 3:18). His death gives them life.

10:16. The other sheep . . . not of this flock refers to Gentiles who would believe. His coming death would **bring them also** to the Father. **They too will listen to My voice.** Jesus continues to save people as they hear His voice in the Scriptures. Acts 18:9-11 illustrates how this works out in the history of the church. "I have many people in this city" (i.e., Corinth), the Lord told Paul. **One flock and one Shepherd** speaks of the church with believers from Jewish and Gentile "sheep pens" in one body with Christ as Head (cf. Eph. 2:11-22; 3:6).

10:17-18. Again Jesus predicted His death, saying four times that He would voluntarily **lay down His life** (vv. 11, 14, 17-18). The **Father** has a special love for Jesus because of His sacrificial obedience to the will of God. Jesus predicted His resurrection twice (He would **take . . . up** His life **again** [vv. 17-18]) and His sovereignty **(authority)** over His own destiny. His death was wholly voluntary: **No one takes it from Me.** Jesus was not a helpless pawn on history's chessboard.

10:19-21. For the third time Jesus' teaching **divided** the people (cf. 7:43; 9:16). **Many** in this hostile crowd judged Him to be **demon-possessed and raving mad** (cf. 7:20; 8:48, 52). **But others** figured that He was not demon-possessed, for how could **a demon open the eyes of the blind?** (cf. 9:16)

4. THE FINAL PUBLIC TEACHING (10:22-42)

John then recorded a final confrontation of Jesus with the hostile Jerusalem crowd (vv. 22-39), followed by His withdrawal beyond Jordan (vv. 40-42) because of attempts to kill Him.

10:22-23. The Feast of Dedication is nowadays called Hanukkah or the Feast of Lights. It commemorates the reconsecration of the temple by Judas Maccabeus in 165 B.C. after its desecration in 168 B.C. by Antiochus IV (Epiphanes). The time for the eight-day feast was in December. **It was winter.** The feast reminded the Jewish people of their last great deliverance from their enemies. **Solomon's Colonnade** was a long covered walkway on the east side of **the temple.** Two months had elapsed since Jesus' last confrontation with the Jews (7:1–10:21) at the Feast of Tabernacles (7:2), which was in October. Jesus again returned to the temple **area.**

10:24. The Jews gathered around Him. Actually they "closed in (*ekyklōsan*) on Him." The hostile Jerusalem leaders were determined to pin Him down so they surrounded Him. His enigmatic sayings plagued them, and they wanted Him to declare Himself on their terms. **How long will You keep us in suspense?** they asked. "Keep us in suspense" is literally "hold up our soul." They insisted, **If You are the Christ, tell us plainly.**

10:25-26. Jesus responded that **the miracles** (lit., "works"; cf. vv. 32, 38) He had done are clear evidence that He is from the Father (cf. Isa. 35:3-6; John 3:2; 9:32-33). He is the One the Father sent, but He did not match their expectations. He was no Judas Maccabeus nor would His ministry be like Moses'. Their problem was a lack of spiritual perception and faith. **But you do not believe because you are not My sheep** is a simple statement of fact about their conduct. It also reminds one of the ultimate mystery of God's election (cf. 6:37).

10:27. Jesus' flock is responsive to His teaching. They **listen to** His **voice** (vv. 3-5, 16). They have an intimacy with Jesus (**I know them;** cf. vv. 3, 14), they understand His message of salvation, **and they follow** Him (vv. 4-5). To follow Him means to obey the Father's will as Jesus did.

10:28. This is one of the clearest statements in the Bible that one who believes in Jesus for salvation will never be lost. Believers sin and stumble, but Jesus as the perfect Shepherd loses none of His flock (cf. Luke 22:31-32). **Eternal life** is a gift (John 3:16, 36; 5:24; 10:10; Rom. 6:23). If one has it, he has it eternally. **They shall never perish** is a strong affirmation in the Greek: *ou mē apolōntai eis ton aiōna* ("they will indeed not ever perish"; cf. John 3:16, *mē apolētai,* "never perish"). The security of the sheep is found in the ability of the Shepherd to defend and preserve His flock. Such security does not depend on the ability of the frail sheep. **No one can** even **snatch** His sheep **out of** His **hand.** "Snatch" is *harpasei,* related to *harpax* ("ravenous wolves, robbers"). This is a fitting word here for the same verb (*harpazei*) is used in 10:12, "the wolf attacks" (lit., "snatches away").

10:29. My Father, who has given them to Me, is greater than all. That is, **no one** is strong enough to **snatch** any of Jesus' flock from the **Father's hand** (or from Jesus' hand, v. 28). As the NIV margin states, verse 29a in many early Greek manuscripts reads, "What My Father has given Me is greater than all." The thought of the verse in either case is that the Father who is omnipotent secures the flock by His power and protection. God's plan of salvation for Jesus' flock cannot be aborted.

10:30. When Jesus said, **I and the Father are One,** He was not affirming that He and the Father are the same Person. The Son and the Father are two Persons in the Trinity. This is confirmed here by the fact that the word "One" is neuter. Instead, He was saying They have the closest possible unity of purpose. Jesus' will is identical to the Father's regarding the salvation of His sheep. And yet absolute identity of wills involves identity of nature. Jesus and the Father are One in will (and also in nature for both are God; cf. 20:28; Phil. 2:6; Col. 2:9).

10:31-32. The hostile crowd reacted and attempted **to stone** Jesus (cf. 8:59) because they understood the implications of His claim. Jesus' courage was displayed in His calm question: **Which of** His **many great miracles** (lit., "works"; cf. 10:25, 38) **from the Father** was their reason for wanting to **stone** Him?

10:33. They claimed that they found no objection in His works. (Yet His healings on the Sabbath had angered them [5:18; 9:16].) They said they objected **because** He, **a mere man,** claimed **to be God.** This, they said, was **blasphemy.** And yet, ironically, Jesus, who *is* God, did become Man (1:1, 14, 18). Jesus did not walk around Palestine saying "I am God," but His interpretation of the Sabbath and His words about His union with the Father revealed His claim of oneness in nature with God.

10:34. Jesus' response to their objection requires a bit of insight into the methods of argument common in Rabbinic discussions. He first directed them to the Old Testament: **in your Law.** Normally "the Law" refers to the first five books. But here it means all the Old Testament, for Jesus quoted from the Psalms. It was "your" Law in the sense that they gloried in their possession of it, and also in the sense that they should submit to its authority over them. Psalm 82 speaks of God as the true Judge (Ps. 82:1, 8) and of men, appointed as judges, who were failing to provide true judgment for God (Ps. 82:2-7). "Gods" in Psalm 82:1, 6 refers to these human judges. In this sense, God **said** to the Jews, **You are gods.** In no way does this speak of a divine nature in man.

10:35. As seen in verse 34, Jesus argued that in certain situations (as in Ps. 82:1, 6) men were **called . . . "gods."** The Hebrew word for **God** or gods is *'ĕlōhîm.* This word is used elsewhere (e.g., Ex. 21:6; 22:8) to mean human judges. Jesus added to His argument the words, **and the Scripture cannot be broken,** so that no one could evade its force by saying an error was in the Scriptures. This important text clearly points up the inerrancy of the Bible.

10:36. Jesus now completed His argument. Since the inerrant Bible called

their judges "gods," the Jews could not logically **accuse** Him **of blasphemy** for calling Himself **God's Son** since He was under divine orders (**set apart**) and on God's mission (**sent into the world**).

10:37-38. Though the Jews were reluctant to **believe** Jesus' words, God was giving them **miracles** (lit., "works"; cf. vv. 25, 32), which he was doing through Jesus. These signs were given for their learning so that by pondering their significance they might recognize Jesus' oneness with the **Father (the Father is in Me, and I in the Father).** Nicodemus had recognized this for he said, "No one could perform [those] miraculous signs . . . if God were not with Him" (3:2).

10:39. Again an attempt was made **to seize** (from *piazō*) **Him** (cf. 7:30, 32, 44; 8:20), perhaps to bring Him to trial. Once again, since it was not God's time, **He escaped** (cf. 5:13; 8:59; 12:36). No explanation is given as to how He escaped.

10:40-42. Because of their hostility, **Jesus went . . . across the Jordan to** Perea, which had been the location of **John** the Baptist's activity (1:28). Jesus' ministry here was received much more favorably, probably because the Baptist had prepared the people there. **John,** even though dead, was still having influence in people's lives as they remembered his witness. **Though John never performed a miraculous sign** (*sēmeion*), the people **believed** his witness **about** Jesus. By contrast, the hostile Jerusalem crowd had seen His signs and yet disobeyed. In Perea **many** trusted **Jesus** as Savior.

E. The great sign at Bethany (11:1-44)

This climactic miracle of raising Lazarus from the dead was Jesus' public evidence of the truth of His great claim, "I am the Resurrection and the Life." Death is the great horror which sin has produced (Rom. 5:12; James 1:15). Physical death is the divine object lesson of what sin does in the spiritual realm. As physical death ends life and separates people, so spiritual death is the separation of people from God and the loss of life which is in God (John 1:4). Jesus has come so that people may live full lives (10:10). Rejecting Jesus means that one will not see life (3:36) and that his final destiny is "the second death," the lake of fire (Rev. 20:14-15).

11:1-2. This **Lazarus** is mentioned in the New Testament only in this chapter and in chapter 12. **Bethany** (cf. 11:18) is on the east side of the Mount of Olives. Another Bethany is in Perea (cf. 1:28). Luke added some information on the two sisters **Mary** and **Martha** (Luke 10:38-42). **This Mary . . . was the same one who** later (see John 12:1-10) **poured perfume on the Lord and wiped His feet with her hair.** However, John may be assuming that the original readers of his Gospel already had some knowledge of Mary (cf. Mark 14:3-9).

11:3. The **sisters** assumed, because of the Lord's ability and His **love** for Lazarus, that He would immediately respond to their **word** about Lazarus' illness and come.

11:4. Jesus did not go immediately (see v. 6). But His delay was not from lack of love (cf. v. 5), or from fear of the Jews. He waited till the right moment in the Father's plan. Lazarus' **sickness** would **not end in death,** that is, in permanent death. Instead Jesus would **be glorified** in this incident (cf. 9:3). This statement is ironic. Jesus' power and obedience to the Father were displayed, but this event led to *His* death (cf. 11:50-53), which was His true **glory** (17:1).

11:5-6. In spite of Jesus' love for all three **(Martha and her sister and Lazarus), He** waited **two more days.** Apparently (vv. 11, 39) Lazarus was already dead when Jesus heard about him. Jesus' movements were under God's direction (cf. 7:8).

11:7-10. His disciples knew that His going **to Judea,** would be dangerous (10:31). So they tried to prevent Him from going. **Jesus** spoke in a veiled way to illustrate that it would not be too dangerous to go to Bethany. In one sense He was speaking of walking (living) in physical **light** or darkness. In the spiritual realm when one lives by the will of God he is safe. Living in the realm of evil is dangerous. As long as He followed God's plan, no harm would come till the appointed time. Applied to people then, they should have responded to Jesus while He was in the world as its Light (cf. 1:4-7; 3:19; 8:12; 9:5). Soon He would be gone and so would this unique opportunity.

11:11-12. Jesus then said, **Our friend Lazarus has fallen asleep.** The word "friend" has special significance in Scripture (cf. 15:13-14; James 2:23). This "sleep" is the sleep of death. Since the coming of Christ the death of a believer is regularly called a sleep (cf. Acts 7:60; 1 Cor. 15:20; 1 Thes. 4:13-18). Dead Christians are asleep not in the sense of an unconscious "soul sleep," but in the sense that their bodies appear to be sleeping. The **disciples** wrongly assumed that Jesus meant Lazarus had not died, but was sleeping physically (cf. John 11:13) and was on his way to recovery: **If he sleeps, he will get better.**

11:13-15. As was often the case in the Gospels, **Jesus** was **speaking** about one thing **but** the **disciples** were thinking about another. The words **Lazarus is dead, and for your sake I am glad I was not there** seem shocking at first. But if Lazarus had not died, the disciples (and readers of all ages) would not have had this unique opportunity to have their faith quickened. Lazarus' death was **so that you may believe.**

11:16. Didymus means "twin." **Thomas** is often called "doubting Thomas" because of the incident recorded in 20:24-25. But here he took the leadership and showed his commitment to Christ, even to death. **That we may die with Him** is ironic. On one level it reveals Thomas' ignorance of the uniqueness of Christ's atoning death. On another level it is prophetic of many disciples' destinies (12:25).

11:17. Apparently **Lazarus had** died soon after the messengers left. **Jesus** was then a day's journey away. Since Palestine is warm and decomposition sets in quickly, a person was usually buried the same day he died (cf. v. 39).

11:18-19. The fact that **Bethany was less than two miles from Jerusalem** points up two things. It explains why **many Jews** from Jerusalem were at the scene of this great miracle (vv. 45-46). It also prepares the reader for the coming climax which was to take place in the great city. When a person died, the Jews mourned for a prolonged period of time. During this period it was considered a pious duty **to comfort** the bereaved.

11:20-22. Martha, the activist, **went . . . to meet** Jesus while **Mary,** the contemplative sister, waited. (Cf. Luke 10:39-42 for a similar portrayal of their personalities.) Martha's greeting is a confession of faith. She really believed that Jesus could have healed her brother if He **had been** there. No criticism of Jesus seems to be implied since she knew her **brother** was dead before the messengers got to Jesus. Her words **But I know . . . God will give You whatever You ask** might imply by themselves that she was confident Lazarus would be resuscitated. But her actions in protest at the tomb (John 11:39) and her words to Jesus (v. 24) contradict that interpretation. Her words may be taken as a general statement of the Father's blessing on Jesus.

11:23-24. Your brother will rise again. Since the word "again" is not in the Greek it is better to omit it in the translation. This promise sets the stage for Jesus' conversation with **Martha.** She had no thought of an immediate resuscitation but she did believe **in the** final **resurrection at the last day.**

11:25-26. I am the Resurrection and the Life. This is the fifth of Jesus' great "I am" revelations. The Resurrection and the Life of the new Age is present right now because Jesus is the Lord of life (1:4). Jesus' words about life and death are seemingly paradoxical. A believer's death issues in new life. In fact, the life of a believer is of such a quality that he **will never die** spiritually. He has eternal life (3:16; 5:24; 10:28), and the end of physical life is only a sleep for his body until the resurrection unto life. At death the spiritual part of a believer, his soul, goes to be with the Lord (cf. 2 Cor. 5:6, 8; Phil. 1:23).

11:27. Martha gave a great confession of faith in Christ. She agreed with Jesus' exposition about eternal life for those who **believe** in Him. Then she confessed three things about Jesus. He is (a) **the Christ** ("Messiah"), (b) **the Son of God**—which is probably a title of the Messiah (cf. 1:49; Ps. 2:7)—and (c) the **One who was to come into the world** (lit., "the Coming One"; cf. John 12:13). She believed that Jesus is the Messiah who came to do God's will, but as yet she had no hint of the coming miracle regarding her brother.

11:28-30. Martha then told **Mary** that Jesus **the Teacher** was **asking for** her. He evidently wanted to have a private conversation with Mary. His purpose was probably to comfort and instruct her. "The Teacher" is a notable title for it was unusual for a Jewish Rabbi to instruct a woman (cf. 4:1-42).

11:31-32. Mary's sudden departure to see Jesus caused the crowd of Jewish comforters to follow **her.** So a private session with Jesus became impossible. Reaching **Jesus,** Mary **fell at His feet.** This is significant, for on a previous occasion she had sat at Jesus' feet listening to His teaching (Luke 10:39). Her greeting to Jesus was the same as her sister's (John 11:21). She felt the tragedy would have been averted **if** He **had been** present. Her faith was sincere but limited.

11:33-34. In great contrast with the Greek gods' apathy or lack of emotion, Jesus' emotional life attests the reality of His union with people. **Deeply moved** may either be translated "groaned" or more likely "angered." The Greek word *enebrimēsato* (from *embrimaomai*) seems to connote anger or sternness. (This Gr. verb is used only five times in the NT, each time of the Lord's words or feelings: Matt. 9:30; Mark 1:43; 14:5; John 11:33, 38.)

Why was **Jesus** angry? Some have argued that He was angry because of the people's unbelief or hypocritical wailing. But this seems foreign to the context. A better explanation is that Jesus was angry at the tyranny of Satan who had brought sorrow and death to people through sin (cf. 8:44; Heb. 2:14-15). Also Jesus was **troubled** (*etaraxen,* lit., "stirred" or "agitated," like the pool water in John 5:7; cf. 12:27; 13:21; 14:1, 27). This disturbance was because of His conflict with sin, death, and Satan.

11:35-37. Jesus' weeping differed from that of the people. His quiet shedding of tears (*edakrysen*) differed from their loud wailing (*klaiontas,* v. 33). His weeping was over the tragic consequences of sin. The crowd interpreted His tears as an expression of love, or frustration at not being there to heal Lazarus.

11:38-39. Disturbed emotionally (cf. comments on **deeply moved,** in v. 33), He **came to the tomb.** Tombs were often cut into limestone making **a cave** in the side of a wall of rock. **A stone** was placed over **the entrance. Jesus** commanded that **the stone** door be taken **away.** To do so was to risk defilement. But obedience was necessary if Jesus' purpose was to be realized. The scene was highly dramatic. The crowd watched and listened. Mary was weeping and **Martha** objected because after **four days** putrefaction had set in.

11:40. Jesus reminded Martha of His earlier promise (vv. 25-26; cf. v. 4). **If** she **believed** His word that He is the Resurrection and the Life and trusted Him, **God** would be glorified. But unless the sisters had trusted Jesus, permission would not have been given to open the tomb.

11:41-42. With **the stone** taken **away,** the tension mounted. What would **Jesus** do? He simply thanked His **Father** for granting His request. He knew He was doing the Father's will in manifesting His love and power. His prayer of thanksgiving was public, not so that He would be honored as a Wonder-Worker but so He would be seen as the Father's obedient Son. The granting of His request by the Father would give clear evidence to the people that He had been **sent** by the Father and would cause the people to **believe** (cf. Elijah's prayer; 1 Kings 18:37).

11:43-44. On other occasions **Jesus** had said that men would hear His voice and come out of their graves (5:28) and that His sheep hear His voice (10:16, 27). After His brief prayer He **called** (*ekraugasen*, lit., "shouted loudly") **in a loud voice.** This verb is used only nine times in the New Testament, eight of them in the Gospels (Matt. 12:19; Luke 4:41; John 11:43; 12:13; 18:40; 19:6, 12, 15; Acts 22:23).

Jesus shouted only three words: **Lazarus come out!** Augustine once remarked that if Jesus had not said Lazarus' name all would have come out from the graves. Immediately, **the dead man came out.** Since he was **wrapped** in **strips of linen,** a special work of God's power must have brought him out. Jesus' directive to the people, **Take off the grave clothes,** enabled Lazarus to move on his own and at the same time gave evidence that he was alive and not a ghost.

This event is a marvelous picture of God's Son bringing life to people. He will do this physically at the Rapture for church saints (1 Thes. 4:16), and at His return for Old Testaments saints (Dan. 12:2) and Tribulation saints (Rev. 20:4, 6). Also He now speaks and calls spiritually dead people to spiritual life. Many who are dead in sins and trespasses believe and come to life by the power of God (Eph. 2:1-10).

F. The plot to kill Jesus (11:45-57)

11:45-47a. Jesus' revelation of Himself always produces two responses. For **many of the Jews,** this miracle was clear proof of Jesus' claim. In response they trusted **Him. But** others were only hardened in sin or confused. They **went to** His enemies, **the Pharisees, and** reported **what** had happened. This miraculous sign was so significant that **the chief priests and the Pharisees** decided to call an emergency session **of the Sanhedrin** (see comments on 3:1 on the Sanhedrin). Doubtless they felt that Jesus was some kind of magician who by secret arts was deceiving the people.

11:47b-48. The council expressed its inability to solve the problem by continuing to do what they had been doing. Official disapproval, excommunication, and counterteaching were not stopping Jesus' influence. The outcome would be insurrection and **the Romans** would crush the Jewish revolt; taking **away both our place** (i.e., the temple) **and our nation.**

11:49-50. Caiaphas was the **high priest that year** (cf. 18:13-14, 24, 28). Originally the high priest held his position for a lifetime, but the Romans were afraid of letting a man gain too much power. So the Romans appointed high priests at their convenience. Caiaphas had the office from A.D. 18 to 36. His contempt was expressed in his words, **You know nothing at all!** His judgment was **that** this **Man** must be sacrificed if the **nation** was to continue in Rome's favor. The alternative was destruction of the Jewish nation in war (11:48). But their rejection of Jesus did not solve the problem. The Jewish people followed false shepherds into a war against Rome (A.D. 66-70), which did in fact destroy their nation.

11:51-53. John by God's Spirit recognized a deep irony in Caiaphas' words. **As the high priest,** Caiphas pointed to the last sacrificial Lamb in a prophecy he did not even know he made. Caiphas meant **Jesus** had to be killed, but God intended the priest's words as a reference to His substitutionary atonement. Jesus' death would abolish the old system in God's eyes by fulfilling all its types and shadows. His death was not only for Jews but also for the world, thus making a new body from both (cf. Eph.

2:14-18; 3:6). The Sanhedrin then decided to kill Jesus.

11:54. Jesus . . . withdrew from Bethany **to a village** 15 or so miles to the north **called Ephraim.** The little village provided a place for rest and it was close to the wilderness of Judea in case it was necessary to escape.

11:55-57. Jewish pilgrims **went up to the Passover** feast at **Jerusalem** and looked **for Jesus.** Previously (2:13-25) He had attended the national festivals during which time He publicly taught **in the temple area.** Would He continue this pattern of ministry? Large crowds gathering in the city **kept looking for** Him. The religious authorities gave **orders** for **anyone** to **report** if he **found out where Jesus was** so **they** could **arrest Him.**

G. The conclusion of Jesus' public ministry (12:1-36)

1. THE ANOINTING (12:1-8)

John in chapter 12 concluded his record of Jesus' public ministry with (a) the account of Mary's anointing of Jesus (which set the stage for His coming sacrifice), (b) His Triumphal Entry, and (c) the prediction of His death.

12:1-2. The time schedule now was more definite and critical: It was **six days before the Passover. Jesus** went back from Ephraim (11:54) to **Bethany, where Lazarus lived,** and attended **a dinner** in His honor. Mark wrote that the place was Simon the Leper's home (Mark 14:1-11). The dinner must have been a joyous occasion with Mary, **Martha,** and **Lazarus** there. The relationship of this family to Simon is not known, but it must have been close since Martha **served.**

12:3. The **pure nard** was a fragrant oil prepared from the roots and stems of an aromatic herb from northern India. It was **an expensive perfume,** imported in sealed alabaster boxes or flasks which were opened only on special occasions. Mary's lavish gift (**a pint**) expressed her love and thanks to Jesus for Himself and for His restoring Lazarus to life. **The house was filled with the fragrance.** This is one of John's many side comments which indicate that he was an eyewitness of much of Jesus' ministry.

12:4-5. Judas Iscariot . . . objected to this lavish waste (in his viewpoint). His objection—that **money** from the sale of the **perfume** should have been **given to**

the poor—was not honest (cf. v. 6). According to Mark (14:4-5) the other disciples picked up his criticism and rebuked her harshly. Evil quickly spreads, and even leaders can be carried along by Satan's tools. The value of the perfume was **a year's wages** (lit., "300 denarii") perhaps a lifetime of savings.

12:6. John with the hindsight of history was able to state why Judas said **this.** Judas, evidently the group's treasurer (cf. 13:29), would pocket some of the benevolence **money** for **himself.** Whereas Mary gave openly and sacrificially, Judas wanted to hoard money for himself secretly and selfishly. He even betrayed Jesus for money—30 pieces of silver (the price of a gored slave; cf. Ex. 21:32; Zech. 11:12-13).

12:7-8. Normally anointing was something festive. But in this case the anointing was in anticipation of His **burial.** Living by God's Word, **Jesus** knew that as the suffering Servant, He must endure pain, die, and be buried (cf. Isa. 53:9).

So He immediately defended Mary's act of love and devotion. **You will always have the poor among you** is not a divine endorsement of poverty or an encouragement to do nothing about poverty. Instead, Jesus was saying that the causes of poverty are many and people will always have occasions to help the poor (Mark 14:7). But the opportunity to show love to Jesus on earth was limited. **You will not always have Me,** that is, here on earth (cf. John 12:35; 13:33; 14:3-4).

2. THE TRIUMPHAL ENTRY (12:9-19)

12:9-11. Jesus was such a controversial Person that it was impossible for Him to be near Jerusalem and remain unnoticed. From all over the country, people came to the Passover feast. Many sought out **Jesus** (cf. 11:56) and **also . . . Lazarus.** Because Lazarus had been restored, **many . . . Jews** believed in **Jesus. So the chief priests** planned **to kill** two men—Jesus and **Lazarus!**

12:12-13. A wild enthusiasm over **Jesus** broke out. Thousands of Galilean pilgrims **had come** to the Passover, and they had seen many of His mighty works. Previously He had rejected the role of a political Messiah (6:15) but, they thought, perhaps now was the right moment. **Jerusalem** was the city of the great King and He was coming to it. Waving their **palm branches,** symbols of victory, the people were **shouting** (*ekraugazon;* cf. comments on 11:43) **Hosanna!** "Hosanna" in Hebrew means "Please save" or "Save now" (cf. Ps. 118:25). It came to be a shout of praise. Quoting Psalm 118:26, they ascribed messianic titles to Him: **He who comes** (lit., "the Coming One"; cf. John 11:27) and **the King of Israel.**

12:14-15. Jesus' riding into the city on **a young donkey** was a sign of peace (cf. comments on Matt. 21:2, which speaks of Jesus riding on a donkey *and* a colt). He did not ride a war horse or carry a sword or wear a crown. Nor did He ride in a wheeled vehicle, as did many kings. His manner of entry fulfilled Zechariah's prophecy which contrasted Jesus' coming (Zech. 9:9) with the coming of Alexander the Great (Zech. 9:1-8). **Daughter of Zion** is a poetic way of referring to the people of Jerusalem, the city built on Mount Zion. Here, in quoting Zechariah 9:9, John called Jesus Israel's **King.**

12:16. The **disciples,** though close to Jesus and participants in these events, **did not understand** them. They lacked the perspective of the Cross and the Resurrection (when He **was glorified**). They were unaware that Zechariah's prophecy **had been written about Him.** Their faith was weak and they needed the ministry of the Holy Spirit (16:12-14).

12:17-18. The size of **the crowd** kept increasing. The news of the great **miraculous sign—Lazarus** raised **from the dead**—spread through the city, and other groups surged **out to meet Him.** It was a day of great popular acclaim, but sadly the people had little spiritual perception.

12:19. The mass reception of Jesus made the plans of **the Pharisees** impossible. They "were looking for some sly way to arrest Jesus and kill Him. 'But not during the Feast,' they said, 'or the people may riot' " (Mark 14:1-2). Pessimistically they acknowledged, **The whole world has gone after Him.** Irony is again evident, for most of those people did not really believe in Jesus.

3. THE GREEKS AT THE FEAST (12:20-36)

12:20. The mention of **Greeks** is significant. They were the wanderers of the ancient world and the seekers of truth. These Greeks were probably God-fearers who attended Jewish synagogues and feasts. Their coming was symbolic of the coming of Gentiles **to worship** God through Christ (cf. 10:16).

12:21-22. Why did the Greeks approach **Philip** about seeing **Jesus?** Perhaps because Philip had a Greek name. Or he may have had some contact with Greeks from the Decapolis area. **Philip went to . . . Andrew, and Andrew and Philip . . . told Jesus.** Since crowds of people probably wanted to speak with Jesus, the disciples may have tried to do some screening (cf. Luke 18:15-16).

12:23-24. **Jesus** had been moving toward His decisive hour (cf. 2:4; 4:21, 23; 7:6, 8, 30; 8:20). The coming of the Greeks confirmed that **the hour has come for the Son of Man to be glorified** (cf. 12:23; 13:1; 17:1). For most people death is their humiliation. But for Jesus death was His means of entry into glory. His willingness to die for others' sins in obedience to the Father (Isa. 53:10, 12) brought Him renown (glory; cf. John 12:16; 17:1, 5). **I tell you the truth** introduces a solemn affirmation. The analogy of **a kernel of wheat** "dying" in **the ground** and producing **many seeds** teaches that death is necessary for a harvest.

12:25-26. The wheat analogy (v. 24) illustrates a general paradoxical principle: death is the way to life. In Jesus' case, His death led to glory and life not only for Himself but also for others.

In the case of a disciple of Jesus, the principle is similar. A disciple must hate **his life in this world.** To "hate his life" means to be so committed to Christ that he has no self-centeredness, no concern for himself. On the other hand **the man who loves his life will lose it.** Anything in life can become an idol including goals, interests, and loves (cf. Luke 12:16-21; 18:18-30). A believer should undergo a spiritual death to self (Rom. 6:1-14; 2 Cor. 5:14-15; Gal. 6:14).

Being a servant of Jesus requires following Him. Many of Jesus' original servants *did* follow Him—in death. According to tradition, the early disciples died as martyrs. Jesus' word was thus a prophecy and also a promise. His true disciples (those who serve Him) **follow** Him in humiliation and later in **honor** or glory (Rom. 8:17, 36-39; 2 Tim. 2:11-13).

12:27-28a. Jesus instructed His disciples on the cost of commitment to the Father's will by disclosing His emotions. He was in turmoil (*tetaraktai*, "stirred, agitated"; cf. 11:33; 14:1) because of the prospect of being made sin (2 Cor. 5:21) in His death. In view of His turmoil, should He shrink back and ask for deliverance **from this hour?** Certainly not, for His Incarnation **was for** the **very** purpose of bringing Him **to this hour** (cf. John 12:23; 13:1; 17:1). Jesus willingly expressed His submission to the will of the Father in the words, **Father, glorify Your name!** So also believers in difficulty should stand and embrace His will—desiring that His name be glorified—in spite of conflicting emotions.

12:28b-29. The Father then spoke **from heaven** in **a** thunderous **voice,** confirming His working in Jesus both in the past and in the future. The voice was audible but not all understood it (cf. v 30; Acts 9:7; 22:9).

12:30-31. The **voice** from heaven confirmed faith in the spiritually perceptive but to the unspiritual it was only a noise (1 Cor. 2:14). Jesus' death on the cross was a **judgment on** the **world.** Evil was atoned for. The world's goals, standards, and religions were shown to be folly. The Cross was also the means of Satan's defeat (Rev. 12:10). **The prince of this world** (i.e., Satan; cf. John 14:30; 16:11), **Jesus** said, **will be driven out.** His power over people by sin and death was defeated and they can now be delivered out of his domain of spiritual darkness and slavery to sin (Col. 1:13-14; Heb. 2:14-15).

12:32-33. Jesus' words, **When I am lifted up from the earth,** refer not to His Ascension but to His crucifixion (cf. 3:14; 8:28). He knew how He would die—by being "lifted up" on a cross. Jews, however, normally stoned those they considered worthy of death (cf. Stephen's death, Acts 7:58-60).

Jesus said that at the cross He would **draw all men to** Himself. He did not mean everybody will be saved for He made it clear that some will be lost (John 5:28-29). If the drawing by the Son is the same as that of the Father (6:44), it means He will draw indiscriminately. Those saved will include not only Jews, but also those from every tribe, language, people, and nation (Rev. 5:9; cf. John 10:16; 11:52).

12:34. The **crowd** was puzzled. If the Messiah is **the Son of Man,** then He

should be here **forever,** they reasoned. Daniel 7:13-14 spoke of the Son of Man's everlasting dominion. Perhaps the people wondered if He was making a distinction between the Messiah (**Christ**) and **the Son of Man.** Did He use the term "Son of Man" differently than its sense in Daniel 7:13? They seemed to understand that Jesus was predicting His death, but they could not see how that was possible, if He was the Messiah.

12:35-36. The crowd thought on intellectual difficulties, but **Jesus** confronted them with the fact that the issue was moral. Their time of opportunity was limited. He is **the Light** for the world (1:4, 9; 8:12; 12:46), but the day of His public ministry was almost over (v. 23). The **darkness** of night was coming in which evil powers would hold sway over people. **The man who walks in the dark** means an unbeliever who stumbles through life without knowing what life is all about and **where** it **is** headed (cf. 3:19; 8:12; 1 John 1:6). Their privilege was to **trust in the Light** (i.e., in Jesus) and **become sons of Light** (i.e., His disciples; cf. Rom. 13:12; Eph. 5:8, 14; Col. 1:13-14; 1 Thes. 5:5; 1 John 1:7; 2:10). Once again **Jesus** supernaturally vanished **from them** (cf. John 5:13; 8:59; 10:39).

H. Jewish national unbelief (12:37-50)

1. JOHN'S EXPLANATION (12:37-43)

12:37. John from the beginning of his Gospel (1:11) had sounded the theme of national unbelief. John now explained that in spite of **all** Jesus' **miraculous signs** (*sēmeia*), **they still would not believe in Him.** Their unbelief was irrational, as sin always is.

12:38. The Jews' national, irrational unbelief had been predicted by **Isaiah the prophet.** The clearest Old Testament passage concerning the suffering Servant (Isa. 53:1-12) began by stating that Israel would not perceive God's revelation in and through the Servant. **Who has believed our message and** seen His **arm . . . revealed?** implies that only a few have believed (quoting Isa. 53:1).

12:39-40. Then John again quoted from **Isaiah** (6:10) to explain that the nation as a whole was *unable* to believe. Because they constantly rejected God's revelation, He had punished them with judicial blindness **and deadened . . . hearts.** People in Jesus' day, like those in

Isaiah's day, refused to believe. They "would not believe" (John 12:37); therefore **they could not believe** (v. 39). Similar illustrations of God's punishing of persistent sin by hardening are common (Ex. 9:12; Rom. 1:24, 26, 28; 2 Thes. 2:8-12).

12:41. In a vision **Isaiah . . . saw** "the Lord Almighty" (lit., "Yahweh of hosts," or "Yahweh of armies"; Isa. 6:3). John wrote that this glory Isaiah saw was **Jesus' glory.** The implication is startling: Jesus is Yahweh! (Cf. John 1:18; 10:30; 20:28; Col. 2:9.) Jesus in His nature is God (but God the Son is distinct in person from God the Father and God the Spirit). Isaiah **spoke about Him,** for many of Isaiah's prophecies predicted the coming Messiah, Jesus of Nazareth (e.g., Isa. 4:2; 7:14; 9:6-7; 11:1-5, 10; 32:1; 42:1-4; 49:1-7; 52:13–53:12; 61:1-3). Earlier Jesus had said that Moses wrote about Him (John 5:46).

12:42-43. In spite of massive national unbelief, the situation was not hopeless. God always has a remnant. **Many** individuals in high places did believe **in** Jesus, but **for fear** of being **put out of the synagogue** they did **not** openly **confess** Him. They feared men's opinions and **loved** men's **praise . . . more than** God's **praise.**

2. JESUS' EXHORTATION (12:44-50)

When and where Jesus spoke these words is not indicated. This seems to be a general summary of Jesus' manifestation of Himself to the nation.

12:44-46. Cried out (*ekraxen,* "called out," *not* wept; cf. 1:15; 7:28, 37) indicates the importance of the issues before the nation. **Jesus** is the perfect manifestation of God, **the One who sent** Him (1:18; Col. 1:15; Heb. 1:3), so that to **believe in** Jesus is to believe in God. People do not have two objects of faith: God and/or Jesus. When one sees Jesus, he **sees** the Father **who sent** Him (cf. John 12:41; 14:9). Jesus came to lead people out of Satan's kingdom of **darkness** into God's kingdom of love and **light** (cf. 1:4, 9; 8:12; 12:35; Col. 1:13-14).

12:47-50. Since Jesus is God's Word (*Logos*) to people, God **spoke** decisively and finally in Him (Heb. 1:1-3). The issue is the command of **the Father.** To obey **the Father** is to come **to eternal life** (John 12:50). To reject the Father's word—

which is Jesus' **very word** (v. 48; cf. v. 50b; 7:16; 14:10, 24)—is to abide in death. Moses predicted the coming of the great Prophet (One who would speak for God). Moses said, "You must listen to Him" (Deut. 18:15). Condemnation **at the last day** is the penalty for rejecting the One whom the Father sent (Deut. 18:18-19; John 3:18, 36; 5:24).

The purpose of God's revelation in Jesus is positive: He came **to save,** not **to judge** (12:47; cf. 3:17 and comments on 9:39). But rejection of God's Revelation inevitably brings a hardening in sin and ultimately God's judgment.

In speaking of Jewish national unbelief John balanced his theological explanation with Jesus' serious exhortation to the nation to repent. In the words of Moses, these "are not just idle words for you—they are your life" (Deut. 32:47).

III. Jesus' Preparation of His Disciples (chaps. 13–17)

A. The Last Supper (13:1-30)

1. JESUS' WASHING OF HIS DISCIPLES' FEET (13:1-17)

John's Gospel reports more of the content of Jesus' instructions to His disciples than do the other three Gospels. Chapters 13–17 concentrate on His teachings on that fateful night in which He was arrested. Before the instruction, Jesus washed His disciples' feet and predicted His betrayal.

13:1. Jesus knew that the time had come (cf. 2:4; 7:6, 8, 30; 12:23, 27; 17:1) **for Him to leave this world and go to the Father.** Jesus' death and resurrection were now imminent. He had come to die in obedience to the Father's will. His coming was also an act of love for all mankind (3:16). But He has a special love for His sheep: He **loved His own.** Then He **showed them the full extent of His love.** His humble service (13:1-17), His teaching (13:18–17:26), and finally His death (chaps. 18–19) are in view. All three revealed His love.

13:2-4. At **the evening meal** before the Passover, **the devil had already prompted Judas Iscariot . . . to betray Jesus. Jesus** had predicted this (6:70-71). Later Satan actually entered Judas (13:27). Yet **God** was in control of all events leading to Jesus' death. Jesus **knew** (cf. vv.

1, 18) His sovereign authority, His origin, and coming destiny; yet He voluntarily took the place of a slave, washing the feet of His disciples. His action contrasts sharply with their self-seeking (cf. Matt. 20:20-24; Mark 9:33-34; Luke 22:24-30) and pictures His whole ministry on earth (cf. Phil. 2:5-8).

13:5. Foot-washing was needed in Palestine. The streets were dusty and people wore sandals without socks or stockings. It was a mark of honor for a host to provide a servant to wash a guest's feet; it was a breach of hospitality not to provide for it (cf. 1 Sam. 25:41; Luke 7:40-50; 1 Tim. 5:10). Wives often washed their husbands' feet, and children washed their parents' feet. Most people, of course, had to **wash** their own **feet.**

13:6-8. **Peter** sensing Jesus' reversing of their natural roles, asked why He, Peter's **Lord,** should **wash** the **feet** of His servant Peter. In Peter's question the word **You** is emphatic in the Greek. **Jesus** said that **later** (after His death and resurrection) Peter would **understand.**

No . . . You shall never wash my feet, Peter replied. Apparently he did not feel that Jesus should act like a servant toward Peter. This is another case of Peter's thoughtless speech (cf. Mark 8:32; 9:5). **Jesus** responded, **Unless I wash you, you have no part with Me.** This does not mean, "Unless you are baptized you cannot be saved," but, "Unless I wash your sins away by My atoning death (cf. Rev. 1:5) you have no real relationship to Me" (cf. 1 John 1:7).

13:9-10. Peter continued to miss the spiritual lesson, but he was certain of his desire to be joined to Jesus. Therefore he asked Jesus to wash his **hands** and **head as well** as his **feet. Jesus answered, A person who has had a bath needs only to wash his feet; his whole body is clean.** (Some Gr. mss. omit the words "his feet.") Roman Catholics sometimes have interpreted verse 10 to mean that after infant baptism only penance is needed. A preferable interpretation is that after salvation all one needs is confession of sins, the continual application of Jesus' death to cleanse one's daily sins (cf. 1 John 1:7; 2:1-2). When Jesus added that **not every one of you** is **clean,** He was referring to Judas (cf. John 13:11, 18). This suggests that Judas was not converted.

13:11. Judas had rejected the life-giving, cleansing words of Jesus (cf. 6:63; 15:3), so he was yet in his sins. Judas did have his feet literally washed, but he did not enter into the meaning of the event. John stressed Jesus' supernatural knowledge (cf. 2:25; 4:29) of Judas' deception.

13:12-14. After giving this object lesson in humility the Lord questioned the disciples in order to draw out the significance of the lesson: **Do you understand what I have done for you? He asked them** (cf. v. 7). **Teacher** (*didaskalos*) **and Lord** (*kyrios*) show that Jesus is on a higher level than they. Yet He had done a humble service for them. Meeting others' needs self-sacrificially is what they ought to do too.

13:15-16. The foot-washing was **an example** (*hypodeigma,* "pattern"). Many groups throughout church history have practiced literal foot-washing as a church ordinance. However, present culture in many lands does not call for the need to wash dust from the feet of one's guests. Whereas the Lord's Supper was practiced by the early church as an ordinance, it apparently did not practice foot-washing as an ordinance in church gatherings. This passage emphasizes inner humility, not a physical rite. A Christian widow's practice of "washing the feet of the saints" (1 Tim. 5:10) speaks not of her involvement in a church ordinance but of her humble slavelike service to other believers. Not to follow the example of Jesus is to exalt oneself above Him and to live in pride. **No servant is greater than his master** (cf. John 12:26).

13:17. God blesses His servants not for what they **know** but for their responses to what they know. Christian happiness (**you will be blessed**) comes through obedient service (**if you do them,** i.e., **these things** Jesus commanded).

2. JESUS' PREDICTION OF HIS BETRAYAL (13:18-30)

13:18-19. Jesus had just said that blessedness comes through obedience (v. 17). Now He added that there would be no blessedness for one of the disciples. His selection of Judas was not an accident or a failure in God's plan. Jesus chose a betrayer among His 12 disciples (cf. 6:70-71) in order **to fulfill the Scripture,** namely, Psalm 41:9. As David was betrayed by his trusted table companion Ahithophel, who then hanged himself

(2 Sam. 16:20–17:3, 23), so Judas, Jesus' close companion, betrayed Him and then hanged himself. Though Judas' deed was foreknown by God, he was fully culpable. The fact that Jesus knew all this in advance (before it happens) and that it fit the Scriptures helped the disciples after the fact to believe God sent Jesus (John 13:19; cf. 14:29).

13:20. As Jesus has a high and holy dignity because of His commission from the Father, so the disciples represented Jesus. Anyone who accepted the disciples was thus accepting Jesus, the One they represented, and in turn that person was also accepting the Father.

13:21. Jesus was troubled in spirit. The word "troubled" is etarachthē ("stirred or agitated"), the same word used of Jesus in 11:33; 12:27 (also used by Jesus in 14:1, 27). Being human, Jesus was troubled over Judas' soon betrayal of His love and friendship. Being divine, Jesus knew in advance that it would happen. Jesus sensed the spiritual hardness and deadness which sin had produced in Judas. The word testified and the formula I tell you the truth stress the solemn announcement of Jesus' words.

13:22. That anyone in this close fellowship could do this to Jesus was almost beyond comprehension. Judas had covered his tracks so well that none of the others suspected him.

13:23-24. Simon Peter, the leader and perhaps the most emotional disciple, wanted to deal with the traitor. Luke (22:38, 49-50) mentioned that the disciples had two swords! The disciple whom Jesus loved was evidently John, the author of this Gospel (cf. Introduction). John and Judas were reclining next to Jesus, but Peter's position at the table was not near enough to ask Jesus privately. So he motioned to John and asked him to ask Jesus whom He meant.

13:25-27. By leaning John could touch Jesus, so he asked . . . Lord, who is it? Giving the morsel of recognition to John was an uncaught sign of recognition to John, but it was also the Lord's final extension of grace to Judas. A host's giving a morsel of bread to a guest was a sign of friendship. How ironic that Jesus' act of friendship to Judas signaled Judas' betrayal of friendship.

Satan entered into him (cf. v. 2) is one of the most terrible expressions in the Scriptures. Satan now used Judas as his tool to accomplish his will. Do quickly is literally "do it more quickly," which may imply Jesus' words spurred Judas to act in God's proper timing.

13:28-30. Since no one grasped the significance of Jesus' words, even the beloved disciple must have missed the intent of the sop until later. As Judas . . . went out, no one thought anything but good of him. They assumed that he, as the group's treasurer (cf. 12:6), was going to buy food for the Passover feast or to give something to the poor. He had deceived his peers but not Jesus. And it was night in any other Gospel might simply be a time notice, but in John's Gospel it probably also has symbolic significance. Judas was leaving the Light (8:12; 12:35, 46) and going out into the darkness of sin (3:19).

B. Jesus' coming departure (13:31-38)

13:31-32. After the departure of Judas, the events leading to Jesus' death fell into place quickly. Jesus was then free from the tension which Satan in Judas had produced. Also the long tension building up toward His death (Luke 12:50) would soon be over. The words glorified and glorify occur five times in these two verses. Jesus' unique glory was revealed in His death. The Father was also glorified in Jesus' death because God's love, His condescension, and His righteousness were made known (cf. John 1:14; Rom. 3:21-26). The words God . . . will glorify Him at once looked ahead to the Resurrection and the Ascension.

13:33. My children translates teknia, ("little children"; the diminutive of tekna, "children"). This term of love expressed Jesus' concern for them. It is used only here by Jesus in this Gospel. John used it seven times in his first epistle (1 John 2:1, 12, 28; 3:7, 18; 4:4; 5:21), and Paul used it once (Gal. 4:19). Jesus announced once again that He would be gone and they would not be able to find Him (cf. Matt. 23:29; John 7:34; 8:21; 12:8, 35). This was true in both His death and His Ascension.

13:34-35. The 11 disciples would survive in His absence by obeying His example of love. The command is new in that it is a special love for other believers based on the sacrificial love of Jesus: As I have loved you, so you must love one another. Christians' love and support for one another enable them to survive in a hostile world. As Jesus was the embodiment of God's love, so now each disciple should embody Christ's love. This love is a sign to the world as well as to every believer (1 John 3:14).

13:36-38. Peter, quick to speak, picked up on what Jesus had said about going away (v. 33). He wanted to know **where** Jesus was **going** (cf. Thomas' similar request; 14:5). Peter's love was such that he wanted to be with Jesus. But **Jesus replied** that it was not possible right then for Peter to be with Him. **Peter** could not conceive of any situation that would make Jesus' words necessary. He was certain that his love and courage were up to any challenge, including death. **I will lay down my life for You,** he affirmed. But Peter did not know himself as well as he thought, nor did he know the satanic power at work against him (cf. Luke 22:31-32). Jesus' prediction of Peter's defection (**you will disown Me three times**) must have completely shocked the other disciples. They may have wondered if Peter was the traitor (cf. John 13:21-25).

C. *Jesus, the Way to the Father (14:1-14)*

The disciples were completely bewildered and discouraged. Jesus had said He was going away (7:34; 8:21; 12:8, 35; 13:33), that He would die (12:32-33), that one of the Twelve was a traitor (13:21), that Peter would disown Him three times (13:38), that Satan was at work against all of them (Luke 22:31-32), and that all the disciples would fall away (Matt. 26:31). The cumulative weight of these revelations must have greatly depressed them.

14:1-2. To comfort the disciples, Jesus gave them several exhortations along with promises. **Do not let your hearts be troubled,** He said. "Troubled" is *tarassesthō* ("stirred, agitated") from the same verb translated "troubled" in 11:33; 13:21; 14:27. One's heart is the center of his personality. Each believer is responsible for the condition of his heart (cf. Prov. 3:1, 3, 5; 4:23; 20:9). By a firm trust in God the Father and Jesus the Son, they could relieve their soul-sorrow and be sustained in their coming tests. When Jesus said, **Trust in God; trust also in Me,** He was probably giving commands, not making statements (see NIV marg.). Death should not be a terror to them because

Jesus was leaving **to prepare a place for** them in heaven, the **Father's house.**

14:3-4. I will come back refers here, not to the Resurrection or to a believer's death, but to the Rapture of the church when Christ will return for His sheep (cf. 1 Thes. 4:13-18) and they will be **with** Him (cf. John 17:24). Jesus said nothing about the nature of the place where He was going. It is sufficient that believers will be with the Father and Jesus (cf. 2 Cor. 5:8; Phil. 1:23; 1 Thes. 4:17). The disciples knew how to get to heaven. He told them, **You know the way to the place where I am going.** Throughout His ministry, Jesus had been showing them the way, but as Thomas indicated (John 14:5), they did not fully understand.

14:5-6. Thomas' statement (**We don't know where You are going**) and his question (**So how can we know the way?**) reflected the perplexity of the Eleven (cf. Peter's similar question; 13:36). They would remain puzzled until His death and resurrection and until the advent of the Spirit. They had all the information but they could not put it together.

Jesus' words, **I am the Way and the Truth and the Life,** are the sixth of Jesus' seven "I am" statements in the Gospel of John (6:48; 8:12; 10:9, 11; 11:25; 14:6; 15:1). Jesus is the "Way" because He is the "Truth" and the "Life." As the Father is Truth and Life, Jesus is the embodiment of God so people can come to the Father (cf. 1:4, 14, 18; 11:25). By His words, **No one comes to the Father except through Me,** Jesus stressed that salvation, contrary to what many people think, is *not* obtainable through many ways. Only one Way exists (cf. Acts 4:12; 1 Tim. 2:5). Jesus is the only access to the Father because He is the only One from the Father (cf. John 1:1-2, 51; 3:13).

14:7. The first sentence in this verse may either be a promise ("If you really knew Me, you *will* know My Father as well") or a rebuke (**If you really knew Me, you would know My Father as well**). The Lord seems to be rebuking them for a failure to understand His person and mission (cf. 8:19). The following dialogue (14:8-9) indicates a failure on the disciples' part. **From now on, you do know Him** is a promise, which looks beyond the Cross and the

Resurrection (cf. 20:28, "My Lord and my God").

14:8-9. Philip expressed a universal desire of mankind: to see God (cf. Ex. 33:18). In a perverted form this desire leads to idolatry. Philip was probably longing for a theophany (cf. Ex. 24:9-10; Isa. 6:1) or some visible display of God's glory. Jesus' statement, **Anyone who has seen Me has seen the Father** (cf. John 12:45), is one of the most staggering claims He ever made. The Father is in Jesus and Jesus perfectly reveals Him (1:18). Hence no theophany was necessary, for by seeing Jesus they *were* seeing the Father!

14:10-11. The proof of the union of Jesus and His Father is threefold. They should **believe** Jesus (a) because of His character (**I am in the Father** [cf. v. 20] **and . . . the Father is in Me**); (b) because His words are the Father's (**The words I say to you are not just My own** (cf. 7:16; 12:49-50; 14:24); and (c) because the miracles reveal God's working through Him (**the Father, living in Me . . . is doing His work. . . . believe on the evidence of the miracles themselves;** cf. 5:36). One of the key elements in John's Gospel is the stress on the signs as gracious pointers to faith (cf. 5:36; 10:25, 38; 11:47; 12:37; 20:30-31).

14:12-14. The apostles would not necessarily do more stupendous miracles than Jesus did (e.g., feeding 5,000) but their outreach would be greater (e.g., Peter in one sermon had 3,000 converts). This was possible **because** Jesus had gone **to the Father** and had sent the Spirit. Miracles are important, but some evangelists have done **even greater things than these** by preaching the good news to many thousands of people.

In My name (vv. 13-14) is not a magical formula of invocation. But the prayers of believers, as Christ's representatives doing His business, will be answered. John expanded this teaching in his first epistle. He wrote, "If we ask anything according to His will . . . we have what we asked of Him" (1 John 5:14-15). To **ask Me for anything in My name** means to ask according to His will (cf. "in My name" in John 15:16; 16:23-24, 26). The word "Me" is omitted in some Greek manuscripts but it is probably correct here. Prayers in the New Testament are usually addressed to God

the Father, but prayer addressed to **the Son** is proper also (e.g., Stephen's prayer to the "Lord Jesus" [Acts 7:59]). The goal of answered prayers is to **bring glory to the Father.** Also bearing fruit glorifies the Father (John 15:8).

D. Jesus' promise of the Counselor (14:15-31)

14:15. The disciples' **love** for Christ is revealed in their obeying His commands (cf. vv. 21, 23; 1 John 2:3; 3:22, 24; 5:3). Christ has set the pattern of love and obedience (John 14:31); His disciples are expected to follow (13:15-16).

14:16-17. This is the first of several passages on the Holy Spirit in the Upper Room Discourse. Up to this point in John's Gospel, little has been said about the Holy Spirit. The words to Nicodemus (3:5-8) were private and 7:39 pointed ahead to Pentecost. The Holy Spirit is to be the **Counselor** (*paraklētos;* also used in 14:26; 15:26; 16:7; for its meaning see comments on 16:7). In a sense He has now replaced Jesus' physical presence; and He mediates God to believers. The Spirit is in a believer **forever** (cf. Rom. 8:9). He is also **the Spirit of Truth** (lit., "Spirit of *the* truth"; cf. John 15:26; 16:13) and thus would guide the apostles. He is invisible (**the world cannot accept Him because it neither sees Him nor knows Him**), yet He is real and active. Without a radio, radio waves go unnoticed. The Holy Spirit is unnoticed by the unsaved who have no spiritual life. The disciples had some experience with the Spirit (doubtless in preaching and miracle-working) but now His working would be much more intimate.

Why did Jesus say that the Holy Spirit **will be** (fut. tense) **in** them? Because in Old Testament times the Spirit came on some believers for special enablement, but after Pentecost He indwells every believer permanently (Rom. 8:9; 1 Cor. 12:13).

14:18-19. What did Jesus mean when He said, **I will come to you?** Was He referring to (1) His resurrection, (2) the Rapture, (3) the death of a believer, (4) a mystical experience, or (5) the Holy Spirit's coming at Pentecost? Views 1 and 5 seem best. Verse 19 favors view 1 since the disciples did see Him after His resurrection. His resurrection is also the pledge of their resurrection (**Because I**

live, you also will live; cf. 1 Cor.
15:20-21) and the foundation of a new
life.

14:20-21. On that day refers to the
day of Pentecost when the outpoured
Spirit gave evidence of Jesus' Ascension
to the **Father.** (Some, however, take the
"day" to refer to Jesus' resurrection, the
basis for believers' assurance.) The Spirit
would come into believers (v. 17), and
would teach them of their union with
Jesus (you are in Me, and I am in you)
while He manifested Christ in them.

Christian love is manifested as a
believer **obeys** the Lord's words (cf. vv.
15, 23). The rewards of loving Him are
great: (a) the **Father** will show His love to
him (cf. v. 23), and (b) the Son **will love
him and show** Himself to him. This
passage does not teach a "works"
religion, but rather that one who believes
and obeys Christ's Word is loved by the
Lord. Saving faith results in obedience (cf.
"the obedience that comes from faith,"
Rom. 1:5).

14:22. Judas (not Judas Iscariot)
may have been the same man called
Thaddaeus (Matt. 10:3; Mark 3:18). He
was puzzled that Jesus would manifest
Himself to them **and not to the world** (cf.
John 14:19a).

14:23-24. Jesus answered that He
and the **Father** will not manifest themselves to those who are disobedient to His
teaching. Obedience grows out of **love**
for Jesus and His Word (cf. vv. 15, 21;
1 John 2:3; 3:22, 24; 5:3). And as a result,
the Father and the Son abide **(make Our
home) with him.** "Home" is *monēn*, the
singular of plural *monai*, translated
"rooms" in John 14:1. This word occurs in
the New Testament only in those two
verses. To rebel against Jesus' word is to
rebel against God **the Father who sent**
Him. Jesus' **words** were **not** His **own,** as
He had said previously (12:49; 14:10).

14:25-26. What Jesus said in the
days of His earthly ministry was only
partially understood. Three things were
needed for the apostles to understand
Jesus' person and mission: (1) His death
had to occur. (2) He had to rise again to
vindicate His claim and demonstrate His
victory. (3) The **Spirit** had to come (He
would be sent by **the Father . . . in My
name,** i.e., in Jesus' place and for Him)
and interpret the meanings of Jesus'
words and deeds. The Spirit, Jesus said,

will teach you all things and will remind
you of everything I have said to you.
This verse is addressed to the apostles.
The context limits the "all things" to the
interpretation and significance of His
person and work. The Spirit worked in
their minds, reminding them of His
teaching and giving them insight into its
meaning (cf. 2:22; 7:39; 20:9).

14:27. In New Testament times the
normal way to say good-bye was **Peace**
(*šālôm* in Heb.). In His death Jesus
provided a legacy for His disciples: **My
peace I give you.** They would have
"peace with God" (Rom. 5:1) because
their sins were forgiven and the "peace of
God" (Phil. 4:7) would guard their lives.
The world is unable to **give** this kind of
peace. Fear of death (Heb. 2:14-15) and
fear of the future are removed as Jesus'
followers trust in Him. Thus they need
not **be troubled** (cf. John 11:33; 13:21;
14:1).

14:28. If the disciples had been more
mature in their love for Jesus, they **would**
have been **glad** for His departure. But
their love was still selfish at this point.
Jesus was in His humiliation on earth, but
by **going** back **to the Father** He would be
exalted in glory (cf. 13:31-32) and He will
come **back** (cf. 14:3).

Arians and Jehovah's Witnesses
argue from the statement, **The Father is
greater than I,** that Jesus is a lesser god.
But this would make Jesus a created being
or would lead to polytheism, both of
which are clearly unbiblical. The Father
and the Son share the same essence (cf.
1:1-2; 14:9; 20:28). The Father and the Son
are "One" in purpose and essence
(10:30). Thus the Father is greater in office
or glory than the Son was in His humiliation.

14:29-31. Fulfilled prophecy is a
great comfort and support to believers (cf.
Isa. 46:8-10). Jesus had predicted His
death and resurrection many times (e.g.,
Mark 8:31-32; 9:31). When this came to
pass, after their initial shock, it would
greatly help their faith. His teaching time
was now limited because Satan, **the
prince of this world** (cf. John 12:31;
16:11), was moving his forces against
Jesus through Judas (cf. 13:2, 27). And yet
Satan had **no hold on** Jesus. Sin leads to
death (Rom. 5:12, 21a; 6:16), and sin and
death give Satan a hold over people (cf.
Heb. 2:14-15; Rev. 12:10). But since Jesus

is sinless, Satan cannot claim Him for his kingdom of darkness. Satan thought Jesus' death was a victory for him, but actually it was Jesus' victory over Satan (John 16:11; Col. 2:15).

Because Jesus loves **the Father,** He did **exactly what** the Father . . . **commanded** (cf. John 10:18; 12:49-50) including being "obedient to death" (Phil. 2:8). Then He said, **Come now; let us leave.** Jesus had been with the disciples in the Upper Room. He now prepared to go to the Garden of Gethsemane on the Mount of Olives. Whether Jesus' words in John 15-17 were spoken in the room or on the way to the garden is uncertain, but probably they were given in the room.

E. The Vine and the branches (15:1-10)

Jesus now instructed His disciples on three vital relationships. Disciples are to be rightly related to Jesus (vv. 1-10), to each other (vv. 11-17), and to the world (vv. 18-16:4). Disciples have three respective duties: to remain (abide), to love each other, and to testify.

15:1. I am the true Vine (cf. v. 5). This is the last of the seven great "I am" statements in John (cf. comments on 6:35). Israel was God's choice vine on which he lavished care and attention (Ps. 80:8; Isa. 5:1-7; Jer. 2:21; 6:9; Ezek. 15; 17:5-10; 19:10-14; Hosea 10:1; 14:8). He longed for fruit, but the vine (Israel) became degenerate and produced rotten fruit. Therefore Jesus, as "the true Vine," fulfills what God had intended for Israel. The **Father is the Gardener** who cultivates and protects the Vine.

15:2. He (i.e., the Gardener, the Father) desires **fruit,** which is mentioned eight times in this chapter (vv. 2 [thrice], 4 [twice], 5, 8, 16). A progression is seen: **fruit** (v. 2), **more fruitful** (v. 2), and "much fruit" (vv. 5, 8). The fruit which God desired from Israel was loving obedience, righteousness, and justice (Isa. 5:1-7). **Every branch in Me that** does not bear fruit **He cuts off.** The phrase "in Me" does not mean the same thing as Paul's words "in Christ." Here it is part of the metaphor of the Vine and seems to mean, "every person who professes to be My disciple (a 'branch') is not necessarily a true follower." A branch **that bears no** fruit is obviously dead. Therefore, like Judas, it is cut off. (See comments on John

15:6.) Every year in Palestine gardeners prune their vines. They cut off the dead wood which has no life in it and trim the living branches so that their yield will be greater.

15:3. The disciples had been cleansed by Jesus and His message, but one, Judas, was not cleansed (cf. 13:10-11).

15:4. Fruitfulness is the result of the Son's life being reproduced in a disciple. The disciple's part is to **remain.** The word **remain,** a key word in John's theology, is *menō* which occurs 11 times in this chapter, 40 times in the entire Gospel, and 27 times in John's epistles. What does it mean to **remain?** It can mean, first, to accept Jesus as Savior (cf. 6:54, 56). Second, it can mean to continue or persevere in believing (8:31 ["hold" is remain]; 1 John 2:19, 24). Third, it can also mean believing, loving obedience (John 15:9-10). Without faith, no life of God will come to anyone. Without the life of God, no real **fruit** can be produced: **Neither can you bear fruit unless you remain in Me.**

15:5-6. A disciple's continual abiding with Jesus (**If a man remains in Me**)—and the indwelling of Jesus in a believer (**and I in him**)—result in abundant **fruit** (cf. v. 8). But those who do not believe face disaster. A **branch** without life is dead and cut off (v. 2). It is worthless and therefore is **thrown into the fire and burned.** What did Jesus mean by these symbolic words about vine branches being burned? These words have been interpreted in at least three ways: (1) The "burned" branches are Christians who have lost their salvation. (But this contradicts many passages, e.g., 3:16, 36; 5:24; 10:28-29; Rom. 8:1.) (2) The "burned" branches represent Christians who will lose rewards but not salvation at the judgment seat of Christ (1 Cor. 3:15). (But Jesus spoke here of *dead* branches; such a branch **is thrown away and withers.**) (3) The "burned" branches refer to professing Christians who, like Judas, are not genuinely saved and therefore are judged. Like a dead branch, a person without Christ is spiritually dead and therefore will be punished in eternal fire (cf. Matt. 25:46). Judas was with Jesus; he seemed like a "branch." But he did not have God's life in him; therefore he departed; his destiny was like that of a dead branch.

15:7-8. In contrast with verse 6, the emphasis in these verses is positive: **remain** with Jesus and **bear much fruit.** Effective prayer is based on faith in Christ and on His **words** remaining in believers. Christ's words condition and control such a believer's mind so that his prayers conform to the Father's will. Since his prayer is in accord with God's will, the results are certain—**it will be given you** (cf. 1 John 5:14-15). Fulfilled prayers bring **glory** to the Father because, like Jesus, His **disciples** are doing the heavenly Father's will (cf. "Your kingdom come, Your will be done on earth" [Matt. 6:10]).

15:9-10. A believer is motivated by the wonder of Jesus' **love,** which is patterned after the Father's **love** in its quality and extent. **Remain in My love** might seem to be mystical but Jesus makes it very concrete. Obedience to the **Father's commands** is the same for a disciple as it was for the Son (cf. 14:15, 21, 23; 1 John 2:3; 3:22, 24; 5:3). Active dependence and loving obedience are the proper paths for all of God's children.

F. Jesus' friends (15:11-17)

15:11. Jesus had great **joy** in pleasing His Father by living a fruitful life (cf. Heb. 12:2). The purpose of His teaching is to give man an abundant life, not a joyless existence (John 10:10). The commands for His disciples to obey are for their **joy** (cf. 17:13).

15:12. One primary **command** was given by Jesus to believers: they must have mutual love (**Love each other;** this is repeated in v. 17). Christians grow by caring for and nurturing each other. The standard for that love is Christ's example of humble sacrificial service: **as I have loved you.**

15:13-14. The most a person can do for his friend is to die for him; such a death is a clear demonstration of **love.** Jesus demonstrated His love (v. 12b) by dying **for His friends,** those who obey Him. Abraham was called God's "friend" (2 Chron. 20:7; Isa. 41:8) because he obeyed God. Like close friends, Abraham and God communicated well with each other (cf. Gen. 18:17).

15:15-17. A **servant** (lit., "slave") **does not** have a close relationship with his master, as friends do. Normally, a slave does what he is told without understanding **his master's** mind or **business.** Since Jesus had opened Himself to His disciples, the title "slave" did not fit their relationship. (When Paul spoke of himself as "a servant [lit., slave] of God" [Rom. 1:1], he had a different idea in mind. He meant he willingly and humbly served and obeyed God.) Jesus **called** His disciples **friends** because He had disclosed His Father's revelation to them.

Jesus then reminded them that contrary to the common practice of disciples picking a teacher, Jesus had chosen them (cf. John 15:19). The purpose of His choosing was so that they would produce lasting **fruit.** He **chose** them for a mission, and His **Father** would answer their requests in order to accomplish that mission (**whatever you ask in My name;** cf. v. 7; cf. "in My name" in 14:13-14; 16:23-24, 26). Friendship with Jesus involves the obligation of brotherly love: **Love each other** (cf. 15:12).

G. The world's hatred (15:18–16:4)

15:18. Friendship with God results in enduring the world's hatred. Conversely, being friends with the world is to be God's enemy (James 4:4). Jesus alerted His disciples to the fact of the world's hatred. **The world** in John's Gospel is the system of organized society hostile to God, which is under Satan's power (John 14:30). Believers might be surprised by this hostility (1 Peter 4:12-13), but they should remember that Jesus was **hated** from His birth (when Herod the Great sought to kill Him) to His death on the cross.

15:19. A fundamental reason for the world's hatred of a Christian lies in their differences (cf. 1 Peter 4:4; Rom. 12:2). A believer, having left the kingdom of darkness and having been transferred into the kingdom of God's Son (Col. 1:13), has a different joy, purpose, hope, and love. He now has certainty, truth, and a standard for life. Christians **have** been **chosen** (cf. John 15:16) **out of the world** system by Christ and they now belong to Him. Since they **do not belong to the world . . . the world hates** them.

15:20-21. Jesus reminded His disciples of a statement He had made earlier: **No servant is greater than his master** (cf. 13:16). Previously He was referring to their need to imitate His humble service. But the principle has other applications. Christians are to identify so closely with Jesus that they share in His sufferings (**they will persecute you also**). On the positive side, some people followed and **obeyed** Jesus' **teaching,** so they **also** responded to the apostles' message. The root cause of the world's hatred against the disciples is their identification with Jesus. They hate Jesus because they are ignorant of God, **the One who sent** Him.

15:22-23. Jesus came as the Revelation of God. If Jesus **had not come,** their sin would not be so great. The statement, **they would not be guilty of sin** (cf. v. 24), must not be taken absolutely as 16:9 shows (cf. 3:19; 9:41). Before Jesus' coming people might have pleaded ignorance as an excuse for sin (cf. Acts 17:30). But now that the Light has come, those who willfully reject it **have no excuse.** The revelation in Jesus and by Jesus is so tied to the **Father** that to hate Jesus is to hate God (cf. John 15:24b).

15:24-25. These two verses amplify the thought in verses 22-23. Jesus' **miracles** were so distinctive that their import was unmistakable. The Jewish nation should have honestly confessed, "No one could perform the miraculous signs You are doing if God were not with Him" (3:2). But the nation as a whole rejected **both** Jesus **and** the **Father** because in their sins they loved darkness rather than light (3:19). The nation thought it was serving God in rejecting Jesus (16:2-3) but in reality it was serving Satan (8:44). Sin is basically irrational. Their hatred of Jesus was **without** any rational cause which also fits the pattern of hatred for righteous people, as seen in those who hated David (Pss. 35:19; 69:4; 109:3).

15:26-27. In the face of the opposition and hatred of the world a believer might be tempted to try to escape from the world or to be silent in it. Monasticism, extreme separation, and lack of witnessing have been too common in the church's history. Jesus encouraged His disciples by the promise of the Spirit's work in the world. As the work of Jesus was to promote the Father and not Himself, so the Spirit will witness to Jesus as the Messiah (**He will testify about Me**). And what He says is true for He is **the Spirit of Truth** (cf. 16:13). As **the**

Counselor (cf. 14:26; 16:7), He presents God's truth to the world. The Spirit is sent **from the Father** (cf. 14:26), just as the Son was sent from the Father. Yet this mysterious work of the Spirit is not done in isolation from the church. The apostles were to bear witness to the facts that they came to know: **You also must testify.** As the apostles witnessed, the Holy Spirit persuaded, and people were saved. The same combination of human obedience to the divine command (Acts 1:8) coupled with the witness of the Spirit is needed in every generation.

16:1-2. The disciples may have wondered why Jesus was telling them about the world's hatred and persecution. Jesus, anticipating this question, indicated that expecting trouble beforehand would help them remain in the path of God's will. (He gave a second reason in v. 4.) The disciples would face excommunication and even death. Remembering that Jesus was ostracized and martyred and that He had predicted the same for His apostles would help fortify them. The earliest Christians were Jews (Acts 2:11, 14, 22), but quite soon after the church began to grow and spread, it was quickly thrust outside **the synagogue** (ca. A.D. 90). Persecution unto death occurred in the case of Stephen (Acts 7:59), James (Acts 12:2), and others (Acts 9:1-4). Some people throughout church history have been motivated to persecute believers because of a misguided zeal for God. They **think** they are **offering a service to God** (cf. Rom. 10:2).

16:3-4. The world will persecute Jesus' followers **because they have not known the Father or Me.** They do not recognize the Father at work in the words and deeds of Jesus. The Jewish people, for example, had a certain knowledge of God through the Law, but that knowledge was not a saving knowledge for God said their "hearts go astray and they have not known My ways" (Ps. 95:8-10).

Jesus gave this warning to His disciples about coming persecution in order to strengthen their faith. By recognizing His knowledge of the future they would grow in their confidence in Him. Jesus **did not** give them **this** warning before because the world's hatred was directed against Him. He shielded them with His personal presence, but now they would be His body on earth (Eph. 1:22-23).

H. The Spirit's work (16:5-15)

16:5-6. Learning of Jesus' departure brought depression to the disciples. They were obsessed by their coming personal loss of His immediate physical presence. If they could have understood why He was going and to whom He was going, then they would have rejoiced. Later (v. 22) Jesus predicted that their time of sorrow would be suddenly transformed into great joy. Jesus' statement, **Now I am going to Him who sent Me,** should have led the disciples to ask questions, but they didn't (Even Thomas [14:5] did not ask, **Where are You going?**) Their preoccupation with their own problems prevented their understanding the crucial nature of the time ("now") and the momentous significance of the events (His death, burial, resurrection, and Ascension).

16:7. The departure of Jesus was necessary—though painful and difficult—for the disciples. In fact, His leaving was profitable and beneficial (the meaning of the Gr. *sympherei*, here rendered **good**). Without His departing (which included His death, burial, resurrection, and Ascension) there would have been no gospel. Atonement for sin was necessary for Jesus to save His people from their sins (Matt. 1:21). Also **unless he departed** there would have been no glorified Lord to **send . . . the Counselor** (the Holy Spirit) to apply the atonement. "The Counselor" translates the Greek *paraklētos.* This word was used of legal assistants who pleaded a cause or presented a case. This Counselor is the promised Spirit who came into the world in a new and distinctive sense on the day of Pentecost.

16:8. One of the Spirit's new ministries was to **convict the world of guilt in regard to sin and righteousness and judgment.** Conviction is not the same as conversion but is necessary to it. The words "convict . . . of guilt" translate the one word *elenxei,* "to present or expose facts, to convince of the truth." The Spirit works on the minds of the unsaved to show them the truth of God for what it is. Normally this process includes human aid (cf. 15:26-27).

16:9. Sin is rebellion against God and this rebellion reached its climax in the crucifixion of Jesus. Today the greatest sin is the failure to **believe in** Jesus (cf. 3:18; 15:22, 24). Most people do not readily admit to being guilty of sin. They will admit to failures or vices or even crimes. However, sin is against God, and people have suppressed the truth of God (cf. Rom. 1:18, 21, 25, 28). The mighty working of the Holy Spirit is necessary to convince and convict people of their desperate plight.

16:10. In crucifying Jesus, the Jewish people showed that they thought He was unrighteous, that only a wicked person would be hanged on a tree and thus be under God's curse (Deut. 21:23; Gal. 3:13). But the Resurrection and the Ascension vindicated Jesus as God's righteous Servant (Acts 3:14-15; Isa. 53:11). The Spirit convicts men of their faulty views of Jesus when the gospel with its stress on the Resurrection is proclaimed (1 Cor. 15:3-4).

16:11. The third area of the Holy Spirit's convicting work concerns **judgment.** The death and resurrection of Jesus were a condemnation of Satan (12:31; Col. 2:15), **the prince of this world** (cf. John 14:30). By Jesus' death, He defeated the devil, who held "the power of death" (Heb. 2:14). (Though defeated at the Cross, Satan is still active [1 Peter 5:8]. But, like a condemned criminal, his "execution" is coming [Rev. 20:2, 7-10].)

People in rebellion should take note of Satan's defeat and fear the Lord who holds the power to judge. As the fact of coming judgment (both Satan's and man's) is proclaimed, the Spirit convicts people and prepares them for salvation (cf. Acts 17:30-31).

16:12-13. The disciples were not able to receive any **more** spiritual truth at that time. Their hearts were hardened, their concern was for their own preeminence in an earthly kingdom, so they saw no need for Jesus' death. Sorrow over His departure and dismay over the prophecy of a traitor among them, along with the prediction of their own desertion, rendered them insensitive to more spiritual truth. **But . . . the Spirit of Truth** (cf. 15:26) would come after Jesus' death to lead the apostles **into** the **truth** about Jesus and His work.

The Spirit, Jesus said, would **not** teach the disciples **on His own** (i.e., on His own initiative) but would teach **only** what He hears from the Father. This points up the interdependence of the Persons in the Trinity. The Father would tell the Spirit what to teach the apostles about the Son.

Also the Spirit would teach **what is yet to come.** This statement helps one understand the promise, **He will guide you into all truth** (lit., "all *the* truth"). This was a promise to the apostles that their partial understanding of the person and work of Jesus as the Messiah would be completed as the Spirit would give them insight into the meanings of the soon-to-come Cross and the Resurrection as well as truths about Jesus' return (cf. 1 Cor. 2:10). The New Testament books are the fulfillment of this teaching ministry of the Spirit.

16:14-15. Because Jesus is the *Logos,* the revelation of the Father (or as Paul expressed it, "the image of the invisible God" [Col. 1:15]), **all that belongs to the Father is** also the Son's. The Spirit of Truth brought **glory to Jesus as** He revealed to the apostles things pertaining to the person and work of the *Logos* **(taking from what is Mine and making it known to you).** The Spirit worked in the apostles' minds so that they could perceive, understand, and teach about the Savior.

I. The prediction of changes (16:16-33)

Jesus' instruction of His disciples shifted at this point from the Spirit's future work to what the immediate future would hold for them. Someday Jesus will reappear, but sorrow, pain, and spiritual failure would be the apostles' lot first. Then, however, joy, prayer, and peace will be their portion.

16:16. The words **in a little while** were bewildering to the disciples (and also possibly to the initial readers of John's Gospel). Also the prediction, **you will see Me,** was not immediately understood. Did Jesus refer (a) to the coming of the Holy Spirit or (b) to His Second Advent or (c) to His brief, 40-day ministry between His resurrection and His Ascension? The last interpretation fits this passage best.

16:17-18. The **disciples** were confused about the time interval. The words **they kept asking** (Gr. imperf. tense) indicate that considerable dialogue took place among the disciples without their arriving at an answer. They could not reconcile Jesus' statements because He said: (a) **In a** short time they would not **see** Him, (b) they *would* **see** Him, and (c) He was **going to the Father.** Only His death, resurrection, post-resurrection ministry, and Ascension would make it all clear.

16:19-20. As a Master Teacher, **Jesus** understood the confusion among His students. He did not clarify His teaching; He knew it would all come into focus with the passage of time and with the aid of the Spirit's teaching ministry (cf. vv. 12-13). **I tell you the truth** (cf. comments on 1:51) introduces a solemn prediction that their coming grief would be followed by joy. His death would be bitter agony for them but **the world** would be happy over it. However, the very event, the death of the Messiah, which would cause them to **weep and mourn** would bring them gladness: **your grief will turn to joy.** His resurrection and the Spirit's work of interpretation would enable them to know that He had to die so that they could have forgiveness of sins. Later the church would rejoice in His death (cf. 1 Cor. 1:23; 2:2).

16:21-22. Jesus illustrated the truth of **pain** replaced by **joy** by the pain of childbirth followed by the joy of new life when **a child is born.** The disciples were entering the process of pain **(your time of grief), but** the light of **joy** was just ahead. When they saw Him after His resurrection, their joy erupted—joy that will never end since He died to sin once but now lives forever (cf. Rom. 6:9-10; Luke 24:33-52; Heb. 7:24-25).

16:23-24. The forthcoming events brought about changed relations. Since Jesus would not be with them physically **(in that day** means after His Ascension), they would not be able to **ask** Him questions. But the Holy Spirit would help them (vv. 13-15).

I tell you the truth again introduced an important statement. They would be His ambassadors and therefore had the right to **ask** the **Father** for **whatever** they needed to accomplish His will. The words **in My name** are not a magical formula which enable the user to get *his* will done; instead those words tied the requests to the work of the Son in doing the *Father's* will (cf. "in My name" in 14:13-14; 15:16; 16:24, 26). Up to this point the disciples had **not** prayed **in** the **name** of Jesus. Now they are to do this since Jesus' death and the Spirit's coming would enable them to enter into God's new program of the Church Age. Answered prayer brings complete **joy** (cf. 15:11; 16:22) because God is at work in them.

16:25. Though Jesus was a Master Teacher and taught His disciples for three years by example and word, yet their perception of His revelation of the Father remained limited (14:9; cf. 2:22; 6:60; 13:7, 15-17). Veiled utterances (His **speaking figuratively**) would give way to plain speech. In His post-resurrection teaching (cf. Acts 1:3) the Son spoke **plainly about** the **Father** (cf. John 14:25-26).

16:26-27. The coming new **day** would give the disciples intimacy with **the Father** and clarity of understanding. The disciples would have direct personal access to **the Father** by the **name** of, that is, through Jesus (cf. "in My name" in 14:13-14; 15:16; 16:24). Jesus would no longer need to pray **on** their **behalf** since they could ask for themselves. This truth does not negate the promise of Christ's intercessory work in overcoming a believer's sin (cf. Rom. 8:34; 1 John 2:1-2). The disciples were now in a personal love-and-faith relationship with the Father. Only children have this privilege of access to their Father (Rom. 5:2).

16:28. Jesus summarized His mission in one sentence: His Incarnation (**I came from the Father**), His humiliation (**and entered the world**), and His resurrection, Ascension, and exaltation (**now I am leaving the world and going back to the Father**). This is what the disciples had come to believe.

16:29-30. The response of the **disciples** to the Lord's teaching was that **now** they understood and believed. They felt the teaching was so plain that recognizing Jesus' omniscience (**You know all things**) and divine origin (**You came from God**) was their only proper response.

16:31-32. Though the disciples were honest and sincere in their affirmations of faith (v. 30), **Jesus** knew their limitations far better than they did (cf. 2:24-25). The words **You believe at last!** could also be translated "Do you now believe?" (NIV marg.) This seems to capture the thought better. They did believe but it was not complete faith or strong faith until after

the death and resurrection of Jesus and the advent of the Spirit. **You will be scattered** is a fulfillment of Zechariah's words which spoke of the Shepherd (the Messiah) smitten by decree of the Lord Almighty, which resulted in the scattering of the sheep (Zech 13:7). In spite of the disciples' loyalty, faith, and love, they soon failed Him miserably. His prediction, **You will leave Me all alone,** was fulfilled by all His disciples deserting Him (Matt. 26:56) when He was arrested and by Peter's denial (John 18:17, 25-26). Yet the Father had not forsaken Him; **I am not alone for My Father is with Me** (cf. 8:29; Pss. 23:4; 73:25-26), though the Father did forsake Jesus when He was on the cross (Matt. 27:46).

16:33. Jesus' instructions about **these things** (chaps. 14–16) were intended to sustain them, to give them **peace** in Him. Believers have a dual existence: they are **in** Christ and **in this world**. In union with Jesus, His disciples have peace, but the world exerts a hostile pressure. The world system, the enemy of God and His people, opposed Jesus' message and ministry (cf. 1:5, 10; 7:7). **But** Jesus won the victory over the system; He has **overcome the world.** As the "strong man" who came and ruined Satan's kingdom (Matt. 12:25-29), Jesus is the Victor. Jesus wanted the disciples to remember this fact and to rejoice in His victory. **Take heart!** means "Be courageous." (In the NT the word *tharseō* ["take heart, be courageous, cheer up"] was spoken only by the Lord [Matt. 9:2, 22; 14:27; Mark 6:50; 10:49; John 16:33; Acts 23:11].) Because He won they, in union with Him, can win also (Rom. 8:37).

J. Jesus' intercession (chap. 17)

1. JESUS' REQUESTS FOR HIMSELF (17:1-5)

Following the symbolic washing of the disciples' feet (13:1-30) and His private instruction of the apostles (14–16), Jesus prayed. This prayer in John 17 has been called "the Lord's high-priestly prayer," and "the Lord's prayer."

Jesus had ended His teaching of the disciples with a shout of victory: "I have overcome the world" (16:33). This was in anticipation of His work on the cross. Throughout His ministry Jesus' work was done in obedience to the Father's will (cf. Luke 4:42; 6:12; 11:1; Matt. 26:36). As He turned again to His Father, He prayed first for Himself (John 17:1-5), then for His apostles (vv. 6-19), and finally for future believers (vv. 20-26).

17:1. **Jesus** could approach God in prayer because of Their Father-Son relationship. He began His prayer with the word **Father** (cf. Matt. 6:9) and used that word three other times in this prayer (John 17:5, 21, 24) as well as "Holy Father" (v. 11) and "Righteous Father" (v. 25). **The time,** Jesus said, **has come.** The divine plan of redemption was at God's appointment. Several times before this Jesus' time had *not* come (2:4; 7:6, 8, 30; 8:20). But now it had arrived (cf. 12:23; 13:1).

Jesus then prayed, **Glorify Your Son** (cf. 17:5). This request for glorification included sustaining Jesus in suffering, accepting His sacrifice, resurrecting Him, and restoring Him to His pristine glory. The purpose of the request was **that** the Father would be glorified by the **Son,** that God's wisdom, power, and love might be known through Jesus. Believers too are to glorify God (v. 10); in fact, this is the chief end of man (Rom. 11:36; 16:27; 1 Cor. 10:31; Eph. 1:6, 12, 14; cf. *Westminster Larger Catechism*, Question 1).

17:2. The words, **You granted Him authority over all people,** indicate that Jesus' prayer request was in accordance with the Father's plan. The Father has ordained the rule of the Son over the earth (cf. Ps. 2). So the Son has the authority to judge (John 5:27), to take up His life (10:18), and to **give eternal life to all those** whom the Father gave Him. Five times in this prayer Jesus referred to His own as those the Father gave Him (17:2, 6 [twice], 9, 24).

17:3. **Eternal life,** as defined here by **Jesus,** involves the experience of knowing **the only true God** through His Son (cf. Matt. 11:27). It is a personal relationship of intimacy which is continuous and dynamic. The word **know** (*ginōskōsin*) here in the present tense, is often used in the Septuagint and sometimes in the Greek New Testament to describe the intimacy of a sexual relationship (e.g., Gen 4:1, "lay"; Matt. 1:25, "had . . . union"). Thus a person who knows God has an intimate personal relationship with Him. And that relationship is eternal, not temporal. Eternal life is not simply endless existence. Everyone will exist

somewhere forever (cf. Matt. 25:46), but the question is, In what condition or in what relationship will they spend eternity?

17:4-5. Jesus' prayer for Himself was based on His completed **work** (cf. 4:34)— **I have brought You glory** (cf. 17:1)— which assumed His obedience to death (Phil. 2:8). Even though the Cross was future, it was a certainty. He repeated His request for a return to His pristine **glory** with the Father (cf. John 17:1) based on the certainty of the finished work on the cross.

This "work" the Father gave Him **to do** is one of five things in Jesus' prayer which the Father "gave" the Son: (a) work (v. 4), (b) believers (vv. 2, 6, 9, 24), (c) glory (vv. 5, 24), (d) words (v. 8), and (e) a name (vv. 11-12). The Son, in turn, gave believers God's words (vv. 8, 14) and God's glory (vv. 22, 24).

2. JESUS' INTERCESSION FOR THE APOSTLES (17:6-19)

Jesus prayed for His disciples before He chose them (Luke 6:12), during His ministry (John 6:15), at the end of His ministry (Luke 22:32), here (John 17:6-19), and later in heaven (Rom. 8:34; Heb. 7:25). This prayer of intercession reveals Jesus' concern and love for His apostles.

17:6-8. The little flock of disciples was given by the Father to the Son (cf. vv. 2, 9, 24). They had been separated **out of the world** ("world" occurs 18 times in this chap.: vv. 5-6, 9, 11 [twice], 13, 14 [thrice], 15, 16 [twice in the Gr.], 18 [twice], 21, 23-25). This separation was by the electing work of the Father, in which the apostles had been given as a gift to Jesus Christ (cf. 6:37). With the words, **They have obeyed Your Word,** Jesus praised His disciples for responding to the message of God in Jesus Christ. The disciples were not perfect, but they had the right commitment. Their faith in Jesus was a trust in His union with the Father (17:8). This faith in Jesus was manifested in their obedience to His words because **they believed** in His divine mission (cf. 16:27).

17:9-10. Christ's prayer (in vv. 6-19) was particularly for the Eleven, though it applies to all believers (cf. v. 20). At this point He was **not praying for the world** in its hostility and unbelief. This prayer is for two things: (a) the disciples' preservation ("protect them," v. 11) and (b) their sanctification ("sanctify them," v. 17). The world is not to be preserved in its rebellion or sanctified in its unbelief. Jesus prayed this request because of God's ownership of them by creation and election (**they are Yours**). Jesus' words, **All I have is Yours, and all You have is Mine,** reveal His claim to unity, intimacy, and equality with the Father.

In the old economy, God dwelt among people and showed His glory. In Jesus, God's glory was displayed (cf. 1:14). Then Christ's disciples glorified Him: **Glory has come to Me through them.** And now in the Church Age the Holy Spirit glorifies the Son (16:14) and believers are also to glorify the Son (Eph. 1:12).

17:11. Jesus would soon depart to the Father and leave His disciples **in the world. They** had to stay in the world to carry out God's plan in spreading the good news of redemption and in planting the church. With the formation of the church, the history of the world has become, in a sense, "a tale of two cities": the city of God and the city of man.

Since the disciples would be **in the world,** Jesus prayed for their protection. The hostility against God which fell on Jesus would now fall on the tiny band of apostles, and subsequently on many of Jesus' followers. Jesus, in calling on His **Holy Father,** pointed up God's distinction from sinful creatures. This holiness is the basis for believers' separation from the world. He would **protect them** from the sin and enmity of the world **by the power of** His **name** (cf. Prov. 18:10). In Bible times a person's name stood for the person. (In John 17:6, 26 the NIV translates the Gr. "Your name" by the word "You.")

Why did Jesus pray for their preservation? It was to promote the unity of the believers, patterned after the unity of the Father and the Son: **so that they may be one as We are One** (cf. vv. 21-22). The unity here seems to be that of will and purpose. By being protected from the world they would be unified in their desires to serve and glorify the Son.

17:12. As the Good Shepherd, Jesus took care of the flock entrusted to Him by the Father. But Judas was an exception. He is here called **the one doomed to destruction** (lit., "the son of perdition").

Judas was never a sheep and his true character was finally manifested (cf. 13:11; 1 John 2:19). He was a "dead branch" (cf. comments on John 15:2, 6). Judas did what he wanted (he sold Jesus). Yet he was an unwitting tool of Satan (13:2, 27). Even people's volitionally free acts fit into God's sovereign plan (cf. Acts 2:23; 4:28). Thus Judas' betrayal of Jesus **fulfilled** (i.e., filled up in a larger sense) the words in Psalm 41:9 about David's betrayal by his friend.

17:13. The words of comfort spoken by Jesus (**I say these things**) to His disciples were of great benefit to them. Following His Passion, **they** would recall His words and experience **the full measure of** His **joy.** Joy came to them because they knew from His words that He had conquered the evil one and brought eternal life to them.

17:14. Jesus' intercession for the disciples continued with a reminder of (a) their value and (b) their coming danger. They were valuable because they had received the Word of God: **I have given them Your Word** (cf. "I gave them the words You gave Me," v. 8). They were in danger because the satanic **world** system **hated them.** It hated them because **they are not** a part **of** it. As believers share Jesus Christ, "Everything in the world— the cravings of sinful man, the lust of his eyes, and the boasting of what he has and does" (1 John 2:16) loses its attractiveness. A believer's commitment shows the world's values to be trash or dung (cf. Phil. 3:8). Therefore **the world** hates the exposure of its sham values (cf. John 3:20).

17:15. God's plan was **not** to remove the disciples from danger and opposition (**take them out of the world**) **but** to preserve them in the midst of conflict. Though Jesus would soon be taken out of the world (v. 11), His followers are to remain in it. Like Daniel in Babylon (Dan. 1-2; 4-6) and the saints in Caesar's household (Phil. 4:22), God intends for His followers to be witnesses to truth in the midst of satanic falsehood. Satan, **the evil one** (cf. Matt. 5:37; 1 John 5:19), as head of the world system, seeks to do everything possible to destroy believers (cf. Rev. 2:10; 12:10) but God's plan will prevail. Christians must not take themselves out of the world but remain in meaningful contact with it, trusting in

God's protection while they witness for Jesus.

17:16-17. Just as Jesus did not belong to the satanic world system (**I am not of it;** cf. v. 14), so believers do not. They belong to the heavenly kingdom (Col. 1:13) because of their new births (cf. John 3:3). Jesus had prayed for protection for His disciples (17:11). Now His second petition for them was for their sanctification. **Sanctify** means "set apart for special use." A believer is to be distinct from the world's sin, its values, and its goals.

The means of this sanctifying work is God's **truth. The truth** is communicated in the **Word,** which is both personal and propositional. As the message about Jesus was heard, believed, and understood, the disciples' hearts and minds were captured. This change in their thinking resulted in changes in their living. The same is true of believers today. As they appropriate God's Word to their lives, they are sanctified—set apart for God and changed in their living in order to honor God (cf. 15:3). God's message set the apostles apart from **the world** so that they would do His will, not Satan's.

17:18. Jesus is the model for every believer. He was in the world but He was not of the world (vv. 14b, 16b). He was **sent . . . into the world** on a mission by His Father. So believers are **sent . . . into the world** on a mission by the Son, to make the Father known (cf. 20:21). Inasmuch as Jesus' prayer for the disciples was not limited to the immediate apostles (cf. 17:20), this passage is similar to the Great Commission (Matt. 28:18-20). Each Christian should view himself as a missionary whose task is to communicate God's truth to others.

17:19. For the benefit of the disciples, Jesus sanctified Himself. In what sense did Jesus need to **sanctify** Himself? Was He not already set apart to God and distinct from the world? Yes, but *this* sanctification refers to His being separated and dedicated to His *death.* And the pupose of His death was **that they too may be truly sanctified.** The words "truly sanctified" are literally "sanctified in truth." This probably means that God's truth is the means of sanctification (cf. comments on v. 17). The purpose of the death of Christ is to dedicate or separate believers to God and His program.

3. JESUS' INTERCESSION FOR FUTURE BELIEVERS (17:20-26)

17:20. The final portion of Jesus' **prayer** (vv. 20-26) was for future believers who would come to Him **through** the **message** of the apostles. In the Church Age all Christians have come to Christ directly or indirectly through the apostles' witness. Jesus knew His mission would succeed. He would die and be raised, He would send forth the Spirit, the apostles would preach, people would be converted, and the church would be formed. As each high priest of Israel bore the names of the tribes before the presence of God in the tabernacle and the temple (cf. Ex. 28:9-12, 21-29), so now Jesus, the great High Priest, carried future believers into the holy presence of His heavenly Father (cf. Heb. 4:14–5:12; 7:24–8:2).

17:21. Jesus requested unity for future believers (cf. vv. 11, 22). This verse is a favorite of promoters of the present ecumenical movement. Admittedly the divided church is in many ways a scandal. The cure, however, is not institutional union. Jesus was not praying for the unity of a single, worldwide, ecumenical church in which doctrinal heresy would be maintained along with orthodoxy. Instead, He was praying for a unity of love, a unity of obedience to God and His Word, and a united commitment to His will. There are great differences between uniformity, union, and unity.

All believers belong to the **one** body of Christ (1 Cor. 12:13) and their spiritual unity is to be manifest in the way they live. The unity Christ desires for His church is the same kind of unity the Son has with the Father: **just as You are in Me and I am in You** (cf. John 10:38; 17:11, 23). The Father did His works through the Son and the Son always did what pleased the Father (5:30; 8:29). This spiritual unity is to be patterned in the church. Without union with Jesus and the Father (**they . . . in Us**), Christians can do nothing (15:5). The goal of their lives is to do the Father's will.

The disciples' union with Jesus as His body will result in people in **the world** believing in the Father: **that You have sent Me** (cf. 17:23).

17:22-23. The glory which Christ **gave** the church may refer to the glory of the Cross (cf. vv. 1-5). As the church

333

received and pondered the significance of Jesus' atoning work, it would be united in God's purposes and redemptive plan. Again the union of Christians (that they may be one) is likened to the unity the Son has with the Father (as We are One; cf. vv. 11, 21). This union is further linked by Christ's indwelling of believers (I in them).

The goal of the unity of believers with each other and with God is twofold: (a) that the world will believe in the Son's divine mission (know that You sent Me), and (b) that the world will sense that God's love for believers is deep, intimate, and lasting as is His love for His unique Son (cf. v. 26).

17:24. The communion and fellowship which disciples have with Jesus in this life will increase in eternity. The goal of a believer's salvation is future glorification which includes being with Jesus (cf. 14:3; Col. 3:4; 1 Thes. 4:17). Jesus' last testament and will (I want, *thelō*) is that His disciples enter into (see) His glory (Heb. 2:10). This glory was what Jesus had from the Father and would again have (John 17:5). His testament was sealed by His death and resurrection. Since His will is identical to the Father's (4:34; 5:30; 6:38), it will certainly come to pass.

17:25-26. Jesus' prayer for believers ends with a call to the Righteous Father. The word translated "righteous" here does not occur often in John's Gospel (cf. 5:30; 7:24). Its significance here seems to be in Jesus' praise of the Father for His work of revelation (cf. Matt. 11:25-26). The Father is right (righteous) and the world is in the wrong (the world does not know You). Jesus has known, revealed (John 17:6), and glorified (v. 4) the Father, and so should Christians. The essence of God is love (1 John 4:8). Jesus made the Father and His love known to the world by His death. And the Father made known His love for the Son by raising Him to glory. Jesus' purpose in revealing the Father was that Christians would continue to grow in that love (that the Father's love for the Son may be in them) and to enjoy the personal presence of Jesus in their lives (that I Myself may be in them).

Jesus' petitions for believers are four: preservation (John 17:11), sanctification (v. 17), unity (vv. 11, 21-22), and partici-pation in Jesus' glory (v. 24). This prayer is sure to be answered (cf. 11:42; 1 John 5:14).

IV. Jesus' Passion and Resurrection (chaps. 18–20)

A. The arrest of Jesus (18:1-11)

18:1. Jesus left the room where He ate the Last Supper with His disciples and crossed the Kidron Valley, to the east. The Kidron, the modern Wodi en-Nar, is a valley or torrent bed which starts north of Jerusalem and passes between the temple mount and the Mount of Olives on its way to the Dead Sea. David was betrayed by a friend (Ahithophel) while crossing the Kidron and going up to the Mount of Olives (2 Sam. 15:23, 30-31). So too Jesus was betrayed by His "trusted friend" Judas while crossing the Kidron and going to the Mount of Olives. The olive grove was a place where Jesus and His disciples came each night to bivouac when they were in Jerusalem (Luke 21:37). During festival times (e.g., the Passover) thousands of Jews flocked to the Holy City and most of them had to stay in tents or other temporary shelters.

18:2-3. "The love of money is a root of all kinds of evil" (1 Tim. 6:10). So it is not surprising that Judas . . . betrayed Jesus for money (John 12:4-6; Matt. 26:14-16). Judas was not an unusual monster but a common man caught in a common sin (greed) which Satan used to accomplish his purpose. Judas knew the habits of Jesus, and his deed stands out in black contrast with Jesus' unselfish love. The soldiers . . . officials from the chief priests, and Pharisees united in their hostility toward Jesus. The detachment of Roman soldiers was a cohort (*speiran*, 10th part of a legion), which here included about 600 men. They were probably commanded to pick up this insurrectionist who claimed to be some kind of king.

18:4. Jesus was conscious of all the events coming on Him. He was not taken by surprise, but was a willing voluntary sacrifice (10:14, 17-18). Earlier in His ministry Jesus was unwilling to be made a popular king (6:15). The scene in 18:4 is one of intense drama and irony. Judas came with soldiers and religious leaders to take Jesus by force. But Jesus stood alone (the disciples had fallen asleep; Luke 22:45-46); though unarmed, He was in command. In the darkness of the night, He could have fled as all the disciples would soon do (cf. Mark 14:50). But instead He gave Himself up.

18:5-6. His words **I am He** (lit., "I Am") startled them and **they . . . fell backward to the ground,** struck no doubt by the majesty of His words (cf. 7:45-46). The phrase **I am** is ambiguous and could refer to Jesus' deity (Ex. 3:14; John 8:58). Or it may simply have been Jesus' way of identifying Himself (as in 9:9).

18:7-9. As the Good Shepherd, Jesus laid down His life for the sheep (10:11). His protection of the apostles was a perfect illustration of His substitutionary atonement. He died not only for them but instead of them. As the Good Shepherd He did not lose any of His sheep but fulfilled His Father's will for the apostles (6:38) and fulfilled His own prophetic Word (6:39).

18:10. Peter had promised that he would die for Jesus (Matt. 26:33-35) and he thought he perhaps could save Jesus or at least go down fighting. Undoubtedly he was better at fishing than at swordplay, for he no doubt tried to take off the head of **the high priest's servant . . . Malchus** not just his ear. Both Luke (22:50) and John recorded that it was his **right ear** which is an incidental evidence of the historical reliability of these Gospel books. (Luke added that Jesus healed the man's ear [Luke 22:51], an amazing touch of love for His enemies!) Peter's blind loyalty was touching, but it missed God's plan. Zeal without knowledge in religion often leads men astray (cf. Rom. 10:2).

18:11. Earlier that same night **Jesus** had rebuked **Peter** (13:6-11). Now He rebuked him again, this time for not understanding God's will. In spite of constant teaching about His approaching death (3:14; 8:28; 12:32-33; cf. Luke 9:22) the disciples did not understand its need (cf. Luke 24:25). The cup which the Father had given Jesus refers to the suffering and death He would experience under God's wrath against sin (Ps. 75:8; Isa. 51:17, 22; Jer. 25:15; Ezek. 23:31-33). The words **the cup the Father has given Me** indicated that Jesus saw all the things coming on Him as part of God's sovereign plan. His rhetorical question to Peter was designed to prod Peter's thinking. Jesus had come to do the Father's will and so He must now embrace it.

B. The religious trial and Peter's denials (18:12-27)

18:12-14. When **Jesus** was **arrested,** it was dark and late at night. Jesus had already had a long day. His disciples were so exhausted by the schedule and the pressures that they had fallen asleep. But for Jesus, the time while they were sleeping was a deep crisis in prayer and agony (Mark 14:33-41; Luke 22:44). Now Jesus was **bound** and in the hands of His enemies. He was alone since His disciples had been scattered (Matt. 25:56; John 16:32).

The religious trial began (cf. the list of Jesus' six trials at Matt. 26:57). The words, **They . . . brought Him first to Annas,** provide information not given in the other Gospels. Annas had been appointed high priest by Quirinius, governor of Syria, in A.D. 6 and remained until he was deposed by Valerius Gratus, procurator of Judea, in A.D. 15. According to the Jewish law the high priestly office was for life, but the Romans did not like the concentration of power in one person so they frequently changed high priests. Annas was succeeded by five of his sons and by his son-in-law **Caiaphas** (see the chart at Acts 4:6; cf. Luke 3:2). Evidently Annas remained the power behind the throne; a preliminary investigation was carried out by him before Jesus' formal religious trial. **Caiaphas** was **the high priest that year,** that is, that fateful year of Jesus' death. John reminded his readers of Caiaphas' unconscious prophecy (John 11:49-52).

18:15-16. After the immediate fright in the olive grove, when the mob took **Jesus** and the disciples ran, two disciples returned and followed the Lord and His enemies back across the Kidron and into the city. They were **Simon Peter and another disciple.** The other disciple is unknown but he may well have been John, son of Zebedee (cf. 20:2; 21:20, 24). **This disciple** knew **the high priest** and therefore had access **into the high priest's courtyard.** Thus he was in a unique position to know what was going on and to enable **Peter** to get into the courtyard.

18:17-18. Peter's denial before the servant **girl** was a striking contradiction to his earlier boast to lay down his life for Jesus (13:37), and his show of offense in cutting off Malchus' ear (18:10). Evidently the other disciple was also in danger (perhaps greater) but he did not deny Jesus. **Peter** stood by the **fire . . . warming himself** in the **cold** spring evening, Jerusalem being about 2,500 feet above sea level. This little detail about the cold evening is another indication that the author of this book was an eyewitness.

18:19. The events in the narrative in verses 12-27 are like a drama presented on two stages. Stage one was set (vv. 12-14) while the action on stage two went on (vv. 15-18). Then the action shifted back to stage one (vv. 19-24), and then returned to the other stage (vv. 25-27).

The preliminary investigation of Jesus may be likened to what might happen today when an arrested person is first brought into a police station. Annas **questioned Jesus about** people who held His views and about the nature of **His teaching.** If an insurrection was feared (cf. 11:48), these would be normal questions.

18:20-21. Jesus responded that He had no secret cult or organization. He had an inner circle of disciples but the character of His teaching was not private. He **taught** in the open and in public places (**in synagogues or at the temple**). The people knew **what** He taught so if there was a **question** concerning what He taught, answers were readily available. Jesus did not have two kinds of truths or teaching. He was innocent unless proven guilty. Therefore they should produce witnesses if they had something substantial against Him. Of course, they had no clear accusation so they sought some way to trick Him or catch Him in a trap.

18:22-24. One of Annas' assistants did not like Jesus' answer so he **struck Him in the face.** The preliminary hearing had several illegalities, and this was one of them. It was improper to try to induce self-accusation, and it was wrong to hit an unconvicted person. Jesus' response concerned not the manner of His speech (**Is that any way . . . ?**) but the substance of His teaching (**If I said something wrong . . .**). It was easier to evade **the truth** or to silence the One who spoke the truth than to attempt to answer the truth. Truth has a self-evident power of persuasion and those who oppose it find it difficult to deny. **Jesus** pressed this point and exposed their hypocrisy. They knew the truth but loved error. They saw the light but loved darkness (cf. 3:19; Rom. 1:18). Following this preliminary interview, **Annas sent** Jesus on to his son-in-law **Caiaphas** (cf. John 18:13). (The NIV text is more probable than the NIV marg.)

18:25-27. In this section **Peter** denied the Lord for the second and third times. Peter's betrayal is reported in all four Gospels, which indicates something of the importance the Gospel writers saw in this defection of the disciples' leader. Since all men fail and even many noted Christians stumble greatly, the record of Peter's denials (and his subsequent restoration; cf. chap. 21) is of great pastoral comfort. The final denial was prompted by a question by **a relative of the man** Malchus, whom **Peter had** tried to kill in the garden. Just after Peter denied Jesus the third time, the Lord looked on him (Luke 22:61) and he went out weeping bitterly (Luke 22:62). Then a **rooster began to crow** (cf. Matt. 26:72-74), which fulfilled Jesus' prophecy (John 13:38). (Mark wrote that a rooster crowed twice; see comments on Mark 14:72.) A rooster crowing and Baalam's donkey speaking reveal God's sovereignty and the movement of all things in His plan and timing.

C. The civil trial (18:28–19:16)

18:28-29. Each of the Gospel writers had a special emphasis in his presentation of Jesus' trial, death, and resurrection. John seems to supplement the material of the first three Gospels. Only he reported the interview with Annas, and he reported the interview with Pilate in much more detail and psychological insight. John did not report the trial before the Jewish Sanhedrin (Mark 14:55-64) with the charge of blasphemy. (See the list of Jesus' six trials at Matt. 26:57.)

Since the Jewish council did not have the legal right to put Jesus to death, the case had to be brought before the Roman governor, Pontius Pilate (A.D. 26–36). Normally the governor lived in Caesarea, but during the great feasts it was prudent for him to come to Jerusalem in case a riot or insurrection took place. **Passover** was particularly dangerous because emotions ran high as the Jews remembered their deliverance from bondage.

The location of **the palace of the Roman governor** is disputed. It could have been at the Antonia Fortress on the north side of the temple area or at one of Herod's two palaces on the west of the city. **The Jews** would **not enter** a Gentile house (in this case **the** governor's **palace**), but they could go into the courtyard or under the colonnades. It is ironic that the Jewish leaders were concerned with ritual **uncleanness** while they planned murder! **So Pilate came out to** the Jews (probably to a courtyard) and began an informal inquiry.

18:30-31. The Jews' reply to **Pilate** revealed the hostility between them. (Pilate was hated by them for his harshness and the fact that he was a Gentile ruling over them. Pilate despised them and eventually in the year A.D. 36 they were able to get Pilate recalled to Rome.) At this time Pilate refused to be their executioner. He knew what was going on. He had seen the Triumphal Entry a few days earlier. He knew that envy was the cause of their accusation against Jesus (Matt. 27:18). So Pilate decided to play a game with the Jews with Jesus' life as the prize. He refused to do anything without a sufficient charge. The Jews' accusation of blasphemy would be difficult to prove and would not impress Pilate as worthy of death under Roman civil law. The Jews seem to have lost the official **right to execute** but in certain cases people were stoned (cf. Acts 6:8–7:60). Jesus was popular, and the Sanhedrin wanted Him dead and, if possible, killed by the Romans. The Sanhedrin could condemn, but only the Romans could execute legally.

18:32. John explained why **Jesus** was delivered by the Jews to the Romans. Jewish executions were normally by stoning, which broke bones. The Roman method of execution was crucifixion. It was necessary for three reasons for Jesus to be crucified by the Romans at the instigation of the Jews: (a) to fulfill prophecies (e.g., that none of His bones be broken; cf. 19:36-37); (b) to include both Jews and Gentiles in the collective guilt for the deed (cf. Acts 2:23; 4:27); (c) by crucifixion, Jesus was "lifted up" like "the snake in the desert" (cf. comments on John 3:14). A person under God's curse was to be displayed (hanged) on a tree as a sign of judged sin (Deut. 21:23; Gal. 3:13).

18:33-34. Pilate had a private interview with **Jesus** (vv. 33-38a). He realized that the Jews would not normally turn over one of their own to the hated Romans so something was strange about this case. According to Luke (23:2) they accused Jesus of three things: subverting the nation, opposing payment of taxes to Caesar, and claiming to be "Christ, a King." Pilate began by asking Jesus if He was **the King of the Jews.** Jesus asked Pilate if he had that **idea** on his **own** or if **others** (Jews) talked **to** him. Jesus here asked Pilate if he was concerned that He was some political threat to Rome, that is, a revolutionary.

18:35-36. Pilate sarcastically **replied** with a question as to whether he was **a Jew** or not. Of course he was not interested in Jewish questions, but only in matters pertaining to civil government. It must have hurt Jesus deeply to have Pilate press the point that **it was** the Jews, His own **people,** and their own religious leaders **who** had accused Him. In his prologue John had sounded this sad theme, "He came to that which was His own, but His own did not receive Him" (1:11). **Jesus** replied that Rome need not fear a political insurrection. He was not a zealot or a revolutionary guerrilla leader. His **kingdom** is not like that. It **is not of this world;** it **is from another place,** that is, heaven. Therefore it comes not by rebellion but by submission to God. Its source was not from men's acts of violence but from a new birth from heaven which transferred a person out of Satan's kingdom into God's **kingdom** (cf. Col. 1:13; John 3:3).

18:37. Since Jesus spoke of a kingdom, **Pilate** seized on the word "king." **You are a king, then?** Jesus answered that question in the affirmative, and then clarified that His kingdom is not like Rome's. It is a kingdom of truth which overshadows all kingdoms. He said, **Everyone on the side of truth listens to Me.** Jesus in a few words asserted His divine origin (**I was born . . . I came into the world**) and ministry (**to testify to the truth**). Later *He* became Pilate's judge.

18:38. Pilate's question, **What is truth?** has echoed down through the centuries. How his question was intended is problematic. Was it a wistful desire to know what no one could tell him? Was it philosophical cynicism concerning the problem of epistemology? Was it indifference to anything so impractical as abstract thought? Or was it irritation at Jesus' response? These are all possible interpretations of his words. But the significant thing is that he suddenly turned away from the *One* who is "the Truth" (14:6) without waiting for an answer. Pilate's declaration of Jesus' innocence is important. He would die like a Passover lamb, a male in its prime without blemish (Ex. 12:5).

18:39-40. Having displayed a lack of interest in truth, Pilate then revealed a lack of commitment to justice. He lacked the courage of his convictions. If Jesus was innocent of all charges, then Pilate should have set Him free. Instead, Pilate began a series of compromising moves to avoid dealing with an inconvenient truth in a difficult circumstance. First, when Pilate found out Jesus was from Galilee, he sent Him to Herod (Luke 23:6-7). Second, Pilate tried to appeal to the crowd (John 18:38), hoping to bypass the desire of the chief priests and elders. Knowing Jesus was popular, he thought the crowd would prefer Jesus to **Barabbas.** But the leaders proved to be persuasive (cf. Matt. 27:20). The offer **to release . . . Barabbas** who was guilty of murder and insurrection showed poor judgment for a person responsible for Rome's interests.

19:1-3. Third, **Pilate . . . had him flogged.** Pilate's action, according to Luke (23:16), was another attempt at compromise. He hoped the crowd would be satisfied with a little blood. Roman flogging was done with a leather whip with bits of metal at the ends. Such flogging often killed a person. The flogging, the mocking **crown of thorns** and **purple robe,** the ridiculing in hailing Him **King of the Jews,** and the physical blows on His **face**—these were all part of Jesus' deep humiliation as He was identified with human sin as the Servant of the Lord (cf. Isa. 50:6; 52:14–53:6). (Matthew and Mark added that the soldiers spit on Jesus [Matt. 27:30; Mark 15:19].) The thorns **on His head** are mindful of the curse of thorns caused by human sin (Gen. 3:18).

19:4-5. Again Pilate's attempt to free Jesus by an appeal to the crowd missed the mark. Their taste for His blood was beyond recall. Pilate's words, **Here is the Man!** (KJV, "Behold the Man!" Latin, *Ecce*

homo) have become famous. It is strange that several of Pilate's statements have become immortal. **Jesus** by that time must have appeared as a pathetic figure, bloody and **wearing the crown of thorns and the purple robe.**

19:6-7. The Jewish leaders displayed their hatred of Jesus and **shouted** for His death. Crucifixion was a shameful death, usually reserved for criminals, slaves, and especially revolutionaries. **Pilate** at first refused to be the executioner, but then the leaders brought forth their real reason: **He claimed to be the Son of God. According to the Law** the charge of blasphemy (Lev. 24:16) called for death, if it could be proven. About the same time Pilate's wife sent him strange words: "Don't have anything to do with that innocent Man, for I have suffered a great deal today in a dream because of Him" (Matt. 27:19).

19:8-11. Pilate's response was one of fear. As a pagan he had heard stories of humanlike gods who visited men and judged them. Perhaps the solemn majesty of **Jesus** with His claims of truth began to convict his conscience. Jesus' refusal to **answer** Pilate's question, **Where do You come from?** fulfilled the words of prophecy in Isaiah 53:7.

Pilate had his opportunity for truth and was found wanting. Disturbed by Jesus' silence, he asked, **Don't You realize I have power . . . ?** True, Pilate had some power, but he was a pawn. Yet he was responsible for his decisions (cf. Acts 4:27-28; 1 Cor. 2:8). In reality, God is the only One who has ultimate and full power. Pilate, Jesus said, was under God and therefore responsible to Him: **The one who handed Me over to you is guilty of a greater sin.** In this statement was Jesus referring to Judas, Satan, Caiaphas, the priests, or the Jewish people? Perhaps Caiaphas is the best choice since he is the one who handed Jesus over to Pilate. Pilate was guilty (cf. the words in the Apostles' Creed, "suffered under Pontius Pilate"). But Jesus put more weight on Caiaphas as the responsible one (cf. John 11:49-50; 18:13-14).

19:12-13. **Pilate,** probably under conviction, wanted to **free** Jesus **but the Jews** now tried a new attack. To let **Jesus** go free, they argued, would be disloyalty to **Caesar.** The title **friend of Caesar** (Latin, *amicus Caesaris*) was an important consideration. Tiberius was on the throne and he was sick, suspicious, and often violent. Pilate had plenty to cover up and he did not want an unfavorable report to go to his boss. If he had to choose between showing his loyalty to Rome or siding with a despised and strange Jew, there was no question in his mind. The dilemma had to be resolved so **Pilate** made the official decision.

19:14-16. The sixth hour, by Roman reckoning of time, could indicate 6 A.M. (some scholars, however, take it to mean noon; cf. comments on 1:39; 4:6). This **was the day of preparation** for the **Passover Week** (i.e., Friday). That day was the Passover proper, the day on which Christ died. But it was also the preparation for the seven-day Feast of Unleavened Bread, which followed immediately after the Day of Passover, and which was sometimes called the Passover Week (cf. Luke 2:41; 22:1, 7; Acts 12:3-4; see comments on Luke 22:7-38).

Pilate said, **Here is your King** (KJV, "Behold your King!"). This is another example of irony. (John is the only Gospel writer who mentioned this incident.) Pilate did not believe Jesus was their King, but to spite the Jews he called Jesus the King of the Jews. John saw this as significant, for Jesus would die for His people as the King of His people, as the Messiah. Pilate could not resist goading the Jews: **Shall I crucify your King?** As if Rome would *not* crucify a Jewish king! The Jewish rejoinder, **We have no king but Caesar,** was full of irony. The rebellious Jews claimed loyalty to Rome while disclaiming their Messiah (cf. Ps. 2:1-3).

D. The Crucifixion (19:17-30)

19:17-18. Carrying His own cross, Jesus **went out.** These words fulfill two Old Testament symbols or types. Isaac carried his own wood for the sacrifice (Gen. 22:1-6) and the sin offering used to be taken outside the camp or city (cf. Heb. 13:11-13). So Jesus was made sin (2 Cor. 5:21). **Golgotha** in **Aramaic (The place of the skull)** was probably called this because the hill with its stony barren top looked like a skull. The **two others** who were crucified with Jesus are mentioned to make understandable the following sequel in which their legs were

broken but not those of Jesus (cf. John 19:32-33). Luke added that the two were "criminals" (Luke 23:32-33), and Matthew called them "robbers" (Matt. 27:44).

19:19-20. The game between **Pilate** and the priests continued with the writing of the **notice** (Gr., *titlon;* Latin, *titulus)* which was usually attached to a criminal's **cross. It read,** JESUS OF NAZARETH, THE KING OF THE JEWS. Since **the sign was written in** three languages—**Aramaic, Latin, and Greek**—and the Crucifixion was in a public **place,** all who could **read** saw a clear proclamation.

19:21-22. The chief priests naturally did not want this to be proclaimed as a fact. They wanted Jesus to die for *claiming* to be the Jews' **King.** So they **protested to Pilate** to change the superscription. **Pilate** refused to do so. Doubtless he felt he had done enough dirty work for the leaders of the nation, and he enjoyed his little joke against them. His haughty answer, **What I have written, I have written,** completes a series of amazing utterances by Pilate (cf. 18:38; 19:5, 14-15; Matt. 27:22). Irony was also shown by John, who recognized that Pilate wrote those words but that God wanted His Son to die with this proclamation on His cross. The words in another sense are a fitting judgment on the life of Pilate. He had played his part and had his moment of truth. He, a Gentile, would be judged accordingly by the King of the Jews!

19:23-24. The soldier's activity in stripping **Jesus** and dividing **His clothes** was part of the customary cruelty of those times. Clothes were handmade and therefore expensive in comparison with clothes today. The executioners received the pieces as their due. The **seamless** tunic (**undergarment**) may be significant as the type of garment which the high priest wore, yet John did not expound on this point. John saw the significance in the fulfillment of Psalm 22:18, in which the poetic parallelism in that verse was fulfilled in two separate acts: (a) **They divided My garments** and (b) they **cast lots for My clothing.** That Jesus died naked was part of the shame which He bore for our sins. At the same time He is the last Adam who provides clothes of righteousness for sinners.

19:25-27. In stark contrast with the cruelty and indifference of the soldiers, a group of four women watched with love and grief. The anguish of Jesus' **mother** fulfilled a prophecy of Simeon: "A sword will pierce your own soul too" (Luke 2:35). Seeing her sorrow **Jesus** honored **His mother** by consigning her into the care of John, **the** beloved **disciple.** His brothers and sisters being in Galilee, were not in a position to care for or comfort her. The words of Jesus to Mary and the beloved disciple were His third saying from the cross (the first one recorded by John). In the other Gospels Jesus had already given a respite to the Roman executioners (Luke 23:24) and a pardon to one thief (Luke 23:42-43).

19:28-29. Jesus' fourth of seven sayings from the cross, "My God, My God, why have You forsaken Me?" is not recorded by John (cf. Matt. 27:46; Mark 15:34). John recorded the fifth saying, **I am thirsty.** The wording in John 19:28 indicated that Jesus was fully conscious and was aware of fulfilling the details of prophecies (Pss. 42:1-2; 63:1). The paradox of the One who is the Water of life (John 4:14; 7:38-39) dying in thirst is striking. Giving Him **wine vinegar,** a sour wine, fulfilled Psalm 69:21. Putting the vinegar-soaked **sponge** on the end of a **hyssop plant** stalk seems odd. Perhaps this detail points to Jesus dying as the true Lamb at Passover, for hyssop was used in the Passover ceremonies (cf. Ex. 12:22).

19:30. The sixth word or saying that **Jesus** spoke from the cross was the single Greek work *tetelestai* which means **It is finished.** Papyri receipts for taxes have been recovered with the word *tetelestai* written across them, meaning "paid in full." This word on Jesus' lips was significant. When He said, "It is finished" (not "I am finished"), He meant His redemptive work was completed. He had been made sin for people (2 Cor. 5:21) and had suffered the penalty of God's justice which sin deserved. Even in the moment of His death, Jesus remained the One who gave up His life (cf. John 10:11, 14, 17-18). **He bowed His head** (giving His seventh saying, "Father, into Your hands I commit My spirit" [Luke 23:46]) **and** then dismissed **His spirit.** This differs from the normal process in death by crucifixion in which the life-spirit would ebb away and then the head would slump forward.

E. The burial (19:31-42)

19:31-32. In the only known archeological find of a crucifixion, which came to light in 1968, the skeletal remains revealed that the lower legs had been shattered by a single blow. This illustrates this passage. **Because** of the Law (Deut. 21:22-23) a body was not to remain exposed on a tree (or cross) overnight and certainly not on a **Sabbath.** A person so executed was under God's curse and his body if left exposed would defile the land (cf. Deut. 21:23; Gal. 3:13).

The smashing of the lower leg bones was called in Latin the *crurifragium.* This caused death to occur fairly quickly by shock, loss of blood, and inability to breathe (the chest cavity would bear the pressure of the body's weight after the legs were broken). Without this procedure, a person could live for many hours or even days. This *crurifragium* was done to the two thieves on each side of Jesus.

19:33-34. Jesus had **already** died so **His legs** were not broken. **Instead,** just to make sure, a soldier **pierced Jesus' side with a spear.** The result was **a sudden flow of blood and water.** This flow has been interpreted in various ways. Some have seen this as evidence that Jesus died of a broken heart so that His pericardium was full of blood and serum. Others see a symbolic or sacramental significance of the stream which heals people. More likely, it indicates that Jesus was a real human who died a real death. Possibly the spear struck the stomach and the heart, which accounted for the flow. The one who saw this (v. 35) saw saving significance in the sign. At the time of the writing of this Gospel, Gnosticism and Docetism were current problems. These ideologies denied the reality of the Incarnation and of His death. But the blood and water are firm answers against those heresies.

19:35-37. This section relates the **testimony** of the eyewitness who is also most probably the writer of this Gospel, John the disciple (cf. 13:23; 21:20-24). The value of His **testimony is** an important claim of **truth,** given so that others may grasp the facts and discern their significance (cf. 20:31). John explained that soldiers not administering the *crurifragium* to Jesus but simply piercing His side **fulfilled** two specific prophecies or types.

Jesus, as the true Passover Lamb, did not have any **of His bones . . . broken** (Ex. 12:46; Num. 9:12; Ps. 34:20) and people in the future **will look on** the **pierced** One (Zech. 12:10; cf. Rev. 1:7).

19:38-39. Joseph of Arimathea was rich (Matt. 27:57) and was waiting for the kingdom (Mark 15:43). (Arimathea was about 20 miles northwest of Jerusalem.) Though a member of the Sanhedrin, the Jewish council, he was "a good and upright man who had not consented to their decision" (Luke 23:50-51). After a crucifixion the Romans usually left the dead body to the beasts of prey. This lack of proper burial was the final humiliation in a crucifixion. But Jews removed exposed bodies (cf. comments on John 19:31-32).

Joseph got **permission** to bury Jesus' **body.** He along with another influential man **(Nicodemus;** cf. 3:1; 7:51) made the necessary arrangements. **About 75 pounds** of **myrrh and aloes** was an extensive amount of spices, used in preparing the body for burial. Perhaps Nicodemus now understood the teaching of Jesus that He would be lifted up and that a man could look in faith to Him and live (cf. 3:14). Both men who had been secret disciples now became manifest.

19:40-42. Because it was almost **the Sabbath** (which began at sundown) the burial had to take place quickly. **Jewish burial customs** did not involve mummification or embalming, which took out the blood and body organs. Their normal process was to wash a body and cover it with cloth and aromatic oils or **spices.** The NIV translation of *othoniois* as **strips of linen** has some support (cf. William F. Arndt and F. Wilbur Gingrich, *A Greek-English Lexicon of the New Testament and Other Early Christian Literature.* Chicago: University of Chicago Press, 1957, p. 558). However, some Roman Catholic scholars argue for the translation "cloth wrappings" since Matthew refers to a linen cloth in which Jesus' body was wrapped (Matt. 27:59, *sindōn*).

Recent discussion on the Shroud of Turin has raised considerable controversy. The translation "strips of linen" would argue against the authenticity of the shroud. But at this time, because of the uncertainties of Jewish burial practices, the meaning of *othoniois*, and the Shroud of Turin, dogmatism should be avoided. Jesus' body was placed in **a new tomb** in **a** private **garden,** not in a cemetery. Matthew wrote that this was Joseph's "own new tomb that he had cut out of the rock" (Matt. 27:60). Isaiah prophesied that the Messiah, the suffering Servant, though despised and rejected by men, would be with the rich in His death (Isa. 53:9).

The burial of Jesus is part of the gospel ("He was buried," 1 Cor. 15:4). Its significance lies in the fact that it was the completion of Jesus' suffering and humiliation. It also pointed up the reality of His death and set the stage for His coming bodily resurrection. Also, in Jesus' burial He identified with believers who will die and be buried.

Joseph and Nicodemus' act of love and respect for the body of Jesus was for them dangerous, costly, and without any personal gain. The service of Christians for their living Lord should be equally courageous and sacrificial, for their labor is not in vain (1 Cor. 15:58).

F. The empty tomb (20:1-9)

John's Gospel comes to a conclusion with a proclamation of Jesus' victory over death (chap. 20) followed by an epilogue (chap. 21). Each Gospel writer stressed certain aspects of the events. John began with a testimony of how he came to personal faith in the Resurrection by considering the evidence found in the open tomb.

20:1-2. The first day of the week, Sunday, **Mary of Magdala** and other women (cf. **we** in v. 2) came **to the tomb.** "Mary of Magdala" is a translation of the same Greek words which elsewhere are rendered "Mary Magdalene" (Matt. 28:1; Mark 16:1, 9; Luke 24:10). Her devotion to Jesus, living and dead, was based on her gratitude for His delivering her from bondage to Satan. She had been an observer at the cross and now was the first person at the grave. This tomb had been closed with a large rock door (Mark 16:3-4) and had been sealed by the authority of the Roman governor Pontius Pilate (Matt. 27:65-66). The women were amazed to see an open and apparently empty tomb. They ran and told **Peter and the** beloved **disciple** (cf. John 19:26) that a terrible thing had occurred. They assumed that grave robbers had desecrated the tomb.

20:3-9. Peter and John started a footrace to **the tomb.** John beat Peter to the garden and looked in **the tomb.** It was not quite empty for John saw the grave clothes. Perhaps his first thought was that the women had made a mistake! **He bent over and looked** (*blepei*) **in** but **did not** enter the tomb, probably for fear of defilement. When **Peter . . . arrived** he rushed in and **saw** (*theōrei*, "beheld attentively") the grave clothes and the **separate** burial **cloth.** He must have remained inside puzzled at what he saw. After a period of time John **went** in and **saw** (*eiden*, "perceived"—the third Gr. word for "see" in these verses) the significance of the grave clothes **and believed.** Peter must have been thinking, "Why would a grave robber have left the clothes in this order? Why take the body of Jesus?" But John perceived that the missing body and the position of the grave clothes was not due to a robbery. He realized that Jesus had risen from the dead and had gone through the grave clothes. The tomb was open not to let Jesus' body out but to let the disciples and the world see that He rose.

This section of John's Gospel (20:1-9) is a powerful eyewitness testimony which strikes the perceptive reader as being psychologically and historically true. John commented (v. 9) that even after a long period of teaching by Jesus the disciples **still did not understand from Scripture that Jesus had to rise from the dead** (cf. Pss. 16:10-11; 110:1, 4; Isa. 53:11-12).

G. Jesus' appearance to Mary (20:10-18)

20:10-14. Jesus' first resurrection appearance was to **Mary** of Magdala, out of whom He had cast seven demons (Luke 8:2). (For a list of His resurrection appearances see Matt. 28.) **The disciples returned to their homes** while Mary remained **outside the tomb crying.** John must not have yet told her that Jesus was risen. He probably was too stunned and puzzled to say anything significant. Mary looked **into the tomb and saw two** individuals who were **angels.** In the Bible when angels appeared to people, the angels looked like men; they did not have halos or wings. In certain visions, winged beings appeared (e.g., Isa. 6) but the norm for angels was that they were in human-like forms.

Because of her grief Mary did not notice anything unusual. Their question and her answer set the stage for the greatest "recognition scene" in all of history (perhaps the second greatest is "I am Joseph"; cf. Gen. 45:1-3). The appearance of **Jesus** to Mary was so unexpected that **she did not realize that it was Jesus.** The fact that He appeared to Mary rather than to Pilate or Caiaphas or to one of His disciples is significant. That a woman would be the first to see Him is an evidence of Jesus' electing love as well as a mark of the narrative's historicity. No Jewish author in the ancient world would have invented a story with a woman as the first witness to this most important event. Furthermore, Jesus may have introduced Himself to Mary first because she had so earnestly sought Him. She was at the cross while He was dying (John 19:25), and she went to His tomb early on Sunday morning (20:1).

20:15-16. Mary talked with Jesus but still did not realize who He was. Some suggest that Jesus' appearance was changed; others say she had a temporary "blindness" as did the Emmaus Road disciples who "were kept from recognizing Him" (Luke 24:16) until His act of disclosure. Others say that possibly the tears in her eyes kept her from recognizing Him.

Jesus said to her, Mary. As the Good Shepherd, He calls His sheep by name (cf. John 10:3) and "they know His voice" (10:4). Immediately she recognized Him! She responded with the cry **Rabboni! (which means** my **Teacher)**

20:17-18. She may have embraced Him physically, for the Lord responded, **Do not hold on to Me, for I have not yet returned to the Father. Go instead to My brothers and tell them. . . .** These words spoke of a new relationship, new relatives, and a new responsibility. Many wanted to "hold onto" Jesus. The KJV translation "Touch Me not," has caused many interpreters to wonder why He could not be "touched." The NIV translation is more accurate, for He certainly was not untouchable (cf. Matt. 28:9; John 20:27). Mary had lost Jesus once before (at His crucifixion) and it was natural to fear the loss of His presence again.

Jesus said, in effect, "This (the physical contact) is not My real presence for the church. A *new relationship* will begin with My Ascension and the gift of the Holy Spirit to the church." Jesus then explained the fact of the *new relatives*. He called His disciples His brothers. Earlier He had said they were friends: "I no longer call you servants . . . instead, I have called you friends" (15:15). Believers in Jesus become a part of Jesus' family with God as their Father (cf. Heb. 2:11-12; Rom. 8:15-17, 29; Gal. 3:26). Mary's *new responsibility* was to testify to His risen presence. She was the recipient of four special graces: to see angels; to see Jesus risen; to be the first to see Him alive; and to be a proclaimer of the good news. Christians today are also the recipients of special grace; they too are given this new responsibility to witness to the world (cf. Matt. 28:16-20).

Jesus' words, **I am returning to My Father** indicate His unique sonship. **Mary** and the other women told **the news** to **the disciples,** but according to Luke, they did not believe her or the other women "because their words seemed to them like nonsense" (Luke 24:11; cf. Luke 24:23).

H. Jesus' appearance to His disciples (20:19-23)

20:19-20. The disciples had almost been arrested with Jesus. They remained under the **fear of** death at the hands of **the Jews** (i.e., the Jewish authorities), so they met in secret at night, with fear, behind locked doors. (What a contrast with their boldness about seven weeks later on the day of Pentecost!) **Jesus** passed through the door, as indicated by the fact that when the **doors** were **locked, He came and stood among them** (cf. v. 26). This showed the power of His new resurrection body. But His body had substantial form and continuity with His pre-Cross body (cf. v. 27). His first words, **Peace be with you!** were a conventional greeting similar to *šālôm* in Hebrew. But the words were now invested with a deeper and fuller meaning (cf. 14:27; 16:33; Rom. 5:1; Phil. 4:7).

Seeing the wounds in **His** pierced **hands and side,** they **were overjoyed** (though at first they were frightened, as Luke stated [Luke 24:37-44]). What a change from their fear and despondency!

20:21-23. Jesus then recommissioned the disciples as His apostles: He was **sending** them as His representatives, **as the Father** had **sent** Him (cf. 17:18).

They were sent with His authority to preach, teach, and do miraculous signs (Matt. 28:16-20; Luke 24:47-49). For their new commission they needed spiritual power. So **He breathed on them and said, Receive the Holy Spirit.** The image and wording of breathing on them recalls God's creative work in making Adam (Gen. 2:7). Now this post-Resurrection "breathing" was a new kind of creative work for they would soon become new creations (Eph. 2:8-10). This reception of the Spirit was in anticipation of the day of Pentecost and should be understood as a partial limited gift of knowledge, understanding, and empowerment until Pentecost, 50 days later.

Forgiveness of **sins** is one of the major benefits of the death of Jesus. It is the essence of the New Covenant (cf. Matt. 26:28; Jer. 31:31-34). Proclaiming the forgiveness of sins was the prominent feature of the apostolic preaching in the Book of Acts. Jesus was giving the apostles (and by extension, the church) the privilege of announcing heaven's terms on how a person can receive forgiveness. If one believes in Jesus, then a Christian has the right to announce his forgiveness. If a person rejects Jesus' sacrifice, then a Christian can announce that that person is **not forgiven.**

I. Jesus' appearance to Thomas (20:24-29)

20:24-29. In his Gospel, John has traced the development of unbelief, which culminated in Jesus' enemies crucifying Him. Conversely, John also traced the disciples' development of faith, which was now climaxed in **Thomas. The disciples** were affirming Jesus' resurrection to Thomas (**told** in v. 25 is *elegon,* an imperf. tense which indicates their continual activity). But **he** remained unconvinced. He wanted bodily proof of Jesus' risen state. The reappearance of Jesus **a week later** provided the opportunity Thomas wanted. **Again . . . Jesus** miraculously entered a room with **locked** doors (cf. v. 19). He asked **Thomas** to touch Him (cf. "showed" in v. 20) and to **stop doubting and believe.** This was a forthright challenge to a personal commitment.

Thomas' response, **My Lord and My God!** is the high point of the Gospel. Here was a skeptical man, confronted by the evidence of Jesus' resurrection. He announced that Jesus, the Man of Galilee, is God manifest in the flesh. Thus the truths in the first chapter were realized personally in this apostle (1:1, 14, 18). The Resurrection (a) demonstrated that what Jesus predicted about His being raised was true (Mark 8:31; 9:9, 31; 10:34; John 2:19), (b) proved that Jesus is the Son of God (Rom. 1:4) and was sent by God ("vindicated by the Spirit," 1 Tim. 3:16), (c) testified to the success of His mission of salvation (Rom. 4:25), (d) entitled Jesus to a position of glory (1 Peter 1:11), and (e) proclaimed that Jesus is the "Lord" (Acts 2:36).

Jesus then pronounced a blessing on all who would come to faith without the help of a visible, bodily manifestation to them (John 20:29; cf. 1 Peter 1:8). This blessing comes to all who believe on the basis of the proclaimed gospel and the evidences for its validity. Believers living today are not deprived by not seeing Him physically; instead, they are the recipients of His special blessing: **Blessed are those who have not seen and yet have believed.**

J. The purpose of the book (20:30-31)

20:30-31. John explained His purpose in writing this Gospel, that people might contemplate and perceive the theological significance of Jesus' miracles (*sēmeia*, "signs"). Many people today ignore, deny, or rationalize Jesus' miracles. Even in Jesus' day some people attributed them to God whereas others attributed them to Satan (3:2; 9:33; Matt. 12:24). To ignore, deny, or rationalize them in that day was impossible because the miracles were manifold and manifest. John indicated He was aware of the Synoptic miracles: **Jesus did many other miraculous signs.** In fact, 35 different miracles are recorded in the four Gospels (see the list at John 2:1-11). John selected 7 for special consideration in order that people might come to **believe that Jesus is the Christ,** the promised Messiah, and **the Son of God.** (The NIV marg. reading, "may continue to believe," is probably not the correct textual reading; the NIV text correctly renders the Gr. by the words **may** believe.)

V. The Epilogue (chap. 21)

John's purposes in this final chapter are (a) to reveal how Jesus reinstated Peter after his great fall, and (b) to correct a serious error about the Lord's return. The chapter also provides additional clues to the identity of the author. Some critics have argued that this chapter is anticlimactic after the great conclusion in chapter 20, and therefore was written by another (anonymous) writer. But the linguistic evidence does not support this notion. In addition, other great books of Scripture have appendixes after reaching a grand climax (cf., e.g., Rom. 16 following Rom. 15:33). Thus John 21 is neither without value nor out of harmony with other Bible books.

A. Jesus' appearance by the lake (21:1-14)

21:1-3. An angel had promised that **Jesus** would meet with **His disciples** in Galilee (Matt. 28:7). It was significant evidence for Jesus to manifest Himself in a different location and at a later time (cf. Acts 1:3). (**The Sea of Tiberias** is another name for the Sea of Galilee; cf. comments on John 6:1.) The **disciples** had gone to Jerusalem and had experienced a tumultuous series of events: the Triumphal Entry, the expectation of a new kingdom, a betrayal by a trusted friend, near arrest, denial of Jesus by their leader Peter, the agonizing crucifixion of Jesus, the Resurrection, and the manifestations of the risen Lord. Understandably they were confused and unsure of the future.

Peter went fishing since he may have misunderstood the Lord's commission (20:22). **Peter** also had a family to support and undoubtedly had a sense of failure over his sin in denying the Lord. His leadership quality is evident in that six other disciples went **with** him. Their lack of success without Jesus' aid (cf. 15:5) and their great catch with His help gave them direction for their new lives.

21:4-6. Early in the morning the **disciples** failed to recognize **Jesus . . . on the shore** either because of distance or lack of light. **He called out to them, Friends, haven't you any fish?** The word "friends" (*paidia*) is literally, "little children" or perhaps "lads." In response to His authoritative voice and instruction (v. 6), they hauled in a huge catch **of fish** (cf. v. 11). This similarity to an earlier miracle (Luke 5:1-11) enabled the disciples to identify the Lord and to recognize

His ability to do great signs after His resurrection.

21:7-9. This revelation of **Jesus** and His power to His disciples dawned first in the beloved **disciple,** who exclaimed, **It is the Lord!** (cf. 20:28) John had also been first to discern the significance of the grave clothes (20:8). Hearing John's word, **Peter** immediately **jumped into the water,** and apparently swam to Jesus. This is typical of his impulsive nature (he went first into the tomb; 20:6). This psychological insight into Peter's character reinforces the historical reliability of John's eyewitness testimony. Peter's action contrasts strikingly with the time he started to sink in the water (Matt. 14:30). Jesus had prepared a breakfast of charcoaled **fish** with **bread** for the hungry disciples.

21:10-11. Mention of the **large fish, 153** in all, has given rise to all kinds of allegorical and symbolic interpretations. But probably John mentioned the number as a matter of historical detail. With a group of men fishing, the common procedure would be for them to count the fish they caught and then divide them equally among the fishermen. A spiritual lesson here is that great blessing comes to one's efforts when he follows the Lord's will.

21:12-14. When **Jesus** invited them to eat with Him, **none of** them asked **who** He was for **they knew it was the Lord.** The fact that both Mary (20:14) and the Emmaus Road disciples (Luke 24:13-35) did not immediately identify the Lord may indicate some difference in the Lord's resurrection appearance here. Yet the identification was so certain that all the disciples knew it was **Jesus.** Their meal together stamped an indelible impression on their minds. Years later in his preaching Peter spoke of himself as a reliable witness who ate and drank with Jesus after His resurrection (Acts 10:41). **The third time** means Jesus' third appearance to the apostles, which John narrated (cf. John 20:19, 24 for the other two appearances).

B. Jesus' reinstating of Peter (21:15-23)

21:15-17. Earlier **Peter** had denied Jesus beside a fire (18:18, 25). Now beside another fire he was restored publicly. **Jesus** called him **Simon Son of John,** as He had when He first met Peter (1:42). Jesus asked him, **Do you truly love Me more than these?** What did Jesus mean by "these"? Jesus probably was referring to the disciples, in light of Peter's proud statement that he never would fall away no matter what others did (Matt. 26:33, 35; Luke 22:33; John 13:37). Jesus' threefold question and threefold commission of apostolic mission contrast directly with Peter's three denials. Three times Peter said he did not even know the Lord (18:17, 25, 27); now three times he said he loved the Lord (21:15-17). No matter how great a person is, he may fall (cf. 1 Cor. 10:12). But God's grace and forgiveness will restore the repentant. This provision of grace would be important, for the church would soon face great persecution and even church leaders would waver in their commitments.

Three times **Jesus** commissioned **Peter** to care for the flock: **Feed My lambs;** (v. 15); **Take care of My sheep** (v. 16); **Feed My sheep** (v. 17). Some Roman Catholics assume that this asserts Peter's primacy, but this is foreign to the passage (cf. 1 Peter 5:2). In Jesus' three questions of **love** (*agapas, agapas,* and *phileis*) and His three commands of duty (*boske,* "tend"; *poimaine,* "herd, lead to pasture"; *boske*) various Greek synonyms are used. Since it is difficult to see any consistent distinctions that John intended, most scholars see these as stylistic variations.

21:18-19. I tell you the truth (cf. comments on 1:51) introduces a solemn prediction of Peter's coming crucifixion. In old age **Peter** was tied to a cross and had his hands stretched out (cf. 1 Clement 5:4; 6:1; Eusebius *The Ecclesiastical History* 2. 25). Obedience to Jesus' command, **Follow Me,** is the key issue in every Christian's life. As Jesus followed the Father's will, so His disciples should follow their Lord whether the path leads to a cross or to some other difficult experience.

21:20-23. Peter, having been informed about God's plan for his life, naturally wondered what the future held for his friend John, **the disciple whom Jesus loved.** Jesus sharply rebuked Peter for being curious about God's will for another's life: **What is that to you? You must follow Me.** Some disciples can be easily distracted by unnecessary questions about God's secret will; as a result they neglect God's plainly revealed will. God's plans for Christians vary and His reasons are not often made known. Peter was to commit himself to God's plain commands to him.

John then corrected a faulty inference made by some believers that John **would not die.** Interestingly Jesus' last words recorded by John in this Gospel refer to His **return.** Of course, Jesus gave no indication *when* He would return. **The false rumor** about Jesus' words to Peter show the possibility of misunderstanding God's promises. Christians must seek to understand God's Word accurately.

C. The colophon (21:24-25)

21:24-25. The Fourth Gospel ends with information about its composition. The beloved **disciple** is identified as the author (cf. comments on "Authorship" in the *Introduction*). The first sentence in verse 24 may have been someone other than John, but the wording sounds Johannine (cf. 19:35). **These things** most likely refer to the entire Gospel. The words, **We know that his testimony is true,** were probably written by someone other than John. They are an endorsement, perhaps by the Ephesian church, or a testimony from the early church as a whole. They were certainly in a position to know the facts better than any generation since then.

The final verse—with its statement about the world **not** having **room for** all **the books that** could **be written** about Jesus' deeds—may seem at first glance to be an exorbitant overstatement. (The I seems to suggest John as the author of this verse though that is uncertain.) Yet the Gospels record only a small sample of Jesus' words and works. Someone has estimated that a person can read aloud Jesus' words recorded in the Gospels in only about three hours. But if all that the infinite Son of God said and did in His Incarnation were pondered, the resulting commentary would be endless.

APPENDIX

The Story of the Adulteress (7:53–8:11)

Five questions need to be considered before commenting on this story: (1) Is it Scripture? (2) Was it written by John? (3) Is it ancient and true, that is, historical? (4) Is it canonical? (5) If it was not originally part of John's Gospel, why is the material placed before 8:12 in most English Bible versions? Questions 1 and 4 are closely related but are not identical. As to question 1, the consensus of New Testament textual scholars is that this section was not part of the original text. For Protestants who accept that judgment, this fact settles the issue of canonicity (question 4): the passage is not part of the biblical canon. However, for Roman Catholic scholars canonicity means that this passage is authoritative because it is in the Vulgate. So even though the passage may not have been part of John's original manuscript, Catholics nevertheless accept the passage as having God's authority because the Vulgate includes it. Question 2, on the passage's Johannine origin, is also tied to question 1. Not only do many Greek manuscripts lack these verses, but those that do include them often mark them with asterisks or obeli. In addition various ancient Greek manuscripts include the passage in five different locations (after John 7:36, after 7:44, after 7:52, after 21:25, and after Luke 21:38). Both the textual evidence and stylistic data in the passage indicate that this is non-Johannine material.

Most commentators answer question 3 (Is it historical?) by yes. If this judgment is correct, then this is a rare extrabiblical authentic tradition about Jesus. John alluded to other things Jesus did (John 21:25) so this story may be one of those events. The answer to the fifth question seems to be that the material was placed before 8:12 in most Bible versions because the contents of this section relate well to two statements of Jesus in chapter 8 ("I pass judgment on no one" [8:15], and "Can any of you prove Me guilty of sin?" [8:46]).

7:53. This verse shows that this story was a continuation of some other material. The original connection is now lost.

8:1-2. Since **Jesus** regularly taught **in the temple courts . . . the people** daily **gathered** to hear **Him.** As Luke wrote, "Each day Jesus was teaching at the temple, and each evening He went out to spend the night on the hill called the Mount of Olives, and all the people came early in the morning to hear Him at the temple" (Luke 21:37-38).

8:3-6a. Jesus' teaching was interrupted by some **teachers of the Law and . . . Pharisees.** They held a strict application of **the Law** to life. The **woman,** who may have been married, was **caught in adultery.** According to the Law there had to be two witnesses to confirm the guilt of a person accused of a crime (Deut. 19:15). Being **caught in the act** of intercourse normally seems unlikely, so the religious leaders may have deliberately planned to catch her in the act. The man should have been brought in with the woman, but perhaps he had escaped. The purpose of bringing this woman before **Jesus** was to discredit Him as a **Teacher.** If He condemned her, He would lose favor with the common people. If He did not, He would be disagreeing with **Moses.**

8:6b-8. Many have tried to guess what **Jesus** wrote **on the ground.** Some suggest He wrote the sins of the accusers. Others propose that He wrote the words of Exodus 23:1, "Do not [be] a malicious witness." Still others say He simply traced **His finger** in the dust while preparing to respond, but that seems unlikely. Since it is impossible to know, any conjecture is fruitless. His response— that only **one** who **is without sin** can judge—pointed to their own sinfulness and at the same time to Himself as the only competent Judge because of His sinlessness (cf. John 8:16). Then He **wrote on the ground** again.

8:9-10. While **Jesus** was still stooped down, His authoritative word (cf. Matt. 7:28-29) struck conviction of sin in their hearts. **The older ones** left **first,** perhaps because they had the wisdom to recognize the sin in their hearts and lives. Since the witnesses and the accusers left, the legal case against the woman was dropped.

8:11. Jesus' words again reveal Him as the Master Teacher. He rebuked **sin** but He gave the woman hope for a new **life.** Theologically Jesus could forgive her sin because he has that authority (cf. Mark 2:8-12) and because He is the Lamb of God who bore "the sin of the world" (John 1:29). Besides having the divine ability to forgive her sin, His manner of dealing with her was gracious. He was revealed to her as the One who is "full of grace" (1:14).

BIBLIOGRAPHY

Barrett, C.K. *The Gospel according to John.* 2d ed. Philadelphia: Westminster Press, 1978.

Bernard, J.H. *A Critical and Exegetical Commentary on the Gospel according to St. John.* The International Critical Commentary. 2 vols. Edinburgh: T. & T. Clark, 1928. Reprint. Naperville, Ill.: Allenson & Co., 1953.

Brown, Raymond E. *The Gospel according to John.* 2 vols. The Anchor Bible. Garden City, N.Y.: Doubleday & Co., 1966, 1970.

Gaebelein, Arno C. *The Gospel of John.* Rev. ed. Neptune, N.J.: Loizeaux Bros., 1965.

Godet, Frederic. *Commentary on the Gospel of John.* Reprint (2 vols. in 1). Grand Rapids: Kregel Publications, 1979.

Hendriksen, William. *Exposition of the Gospel according to John.* New Testament Commentary. 2 vols. in 1. Grand Rapids: Baker Book House, 1953, 1954.

Kent, Homer A., Jr. *Light in the Darkness: Studies in the Gospel of John.* Grand Rapids: Baker Book House, 1974.

Lightfoot, R.H. *St. John's Gospel: A Commentary.* Edited by C.F. Evans. London: Oxford University, Press, 1956.

Lindars, Barnabas. *The Gospel of John.* New Century Bible. London: Marshall, Morgan & Scott, 1972.

Morgan, G. Campbell. *The Gospel according to John.* New York: Fleming H. Revell Co., n.d.

Morris, Leon. *The Gospel according to John.* The New International Commentary on the New Testament. Grand Rapids: Wm. B. Eerdmans Publishing Co., 1971.

————. *Studies in the Fourth Gospel.* Grand Rapids: Wm. B. Eerdmans Publishing Co., 1969.

Sanders, J.N., and Mastin, B.A. *A Commentary on the Gospel according to St. John.* Harper's New Testament Commentaries. New York: Harper & Row, Publishers, 1968.

Schnackenburg, Rudolf. *The Gospel according to St. John.* Vol. 1: *Introduction and Commentary on Chapters 1–4.* 1968. New York: Seabury Press, 1980. Vol. 2: *Commentary on Chapters 5–12.* 1979. New York: Crossroad Publishing Co. 1982.

Tasker, R.V.G. *The Gospel according to St. John: An Introduction and Commentary.* The Tyndale New Testament Commentaries. Grand

Rapids: Wm. B. Eerdmans Publishing Co., 1960.

Tenney, Merrill C. "John." In *The Expositor's Bible Commentary*, vol. 9. Grand Rapids: Zondervan Publishing House, 1981.

_____. *John: The Gospel of Belief.* Grand Rapids: Wm. B. Eerdmans Publishing Co., 1948.

Turner, George Allen, and Mantey, Julius R. *The Gospel according to St. John.* The Evangelical Commentary on the Bible. Grand Rapids: Wm. B. Eerdmans Publishing Co., n.d.

Westcott, B.F. *The Gospel according to St. John: The Greek Text with Introduction and Notes.* 2 vols. London: John Murray, 1903. Reprint (2 vols. in 1). Grand Rapids: Baker Book House, 1980.

ACTS

Stanley D. Toussaint

INTRODUCTION

Among the New Testament writings, Acts stands out as singular and unique. This claim is made on the basis of several considerations. For one, it is the only historical sequel to the four Gospels in the canonical writings. No other narrative in the New Testament continues the accounts given by the four evangelists.

Furthermore, this book forms a background and setting for most of Paul's writings. Bruce writes, "But it is Luke that we have to thank for the coherent record of Paul's apostolic activity. Without [Acts], we should be incalculably poorer. Even with it, there is much in Paul's letters that we have difficulty in understanding; how much more there would be if we had no Book of Acts" (F.F. Bruce, *Commentary on the Book of the Acts*, p. 27).

The Book of Acts gives today's Christians basic information and insights into the early church. Luke portrays the tensions, persecutions, frustrations, theological problems, and hopes confronting the neophyte bride of Christ. How great would be the church's lack without the material in Acts!

In addition, Acts marks the transition from the work of God provincially among the Jews to His establishment of the universal church. In a real sense the reader goes from Jerusalem to the uttermost part of the world in these 28 chapters.

Besides all these, Acts presents a stimulating challenge to every Christian today. The zeal, the faith, the joy, the commitment, and the obedience of those early saints is an example to all believers. It is crucial for followers of Jesus Christ to be as intimately acquainted with this book as possible. As Rackham affirms, "We can hardly overestimate the importance of the Acts of the Apostles" (Richard Belward Rackham, *The Acts of the Apostles*, p. xiii).

Title of the Book. The earliest extant evidence for the name "Acts" is found in an anti-Marcionite Prologue to the Gospel of Luke, a work dated between A.D. 150 and 180. How or why it received this title is open to speculation.

It must be conceded that "Acts" is not an accurate title because the book by no means contains all the acts of all the apostles. Only Peter and Paul are emphasized. The great Apostle John is mentioned, but none of his words are recorded. The death of John's brother James is given in one brief sentence (Acts 12:12).

The work more accurately could be titled "Certain Acts of Certain Apostles." However, the title "The Acts of the Apostles" is so well established it identifies this work of Luke very well.

Purpose of Acts. Under the inspiration of the Holy Spirit Luke certainly had a purpose in writing. What was he intending to accomplish? To put it another way,

Miracles by Peter and Paul	
Peter	
Acts 3:1-11	Healed a man lame from birth
5:15-16	Peter's shadow healed people
5:17	Success caused Jewish jealousy
8:9-24	Dealt with Simon, a sorcerer
9:36-41	Raised Dorcas to life
Paul	
14:8-18	Healed a man lame from birth
19:11-12	Handkerchiefs and aprons from Paul healed people
13:45	Success caused Jewish jealousy
13:6-11	Dealt with Bar-Jesus, a sorcerer
20:9-12	Raised Eutychus to life

why did he select the materials he chose for the book? To this question there are two answers.

On the one hand some say the primary purpose is a historical one; on the other hand some say the goal is apologetic, that is, it is a written defense. All acknowledge there are subsidiary ends, but the question revolves around its primary purpose.

The view that the purpose of Acts is a Pauline apologetic is buttressed by the amazing set of parallels between Peter and Paul (see chart "Miracles by Peter and Paul").

Perhaps Luke intended in this way to defend Paul's apostleship; Paul certainly did not rate behind Peter in power and authority. This may also account for the *three* accounts of Paul's conversion (chaps. 9; 22; 26). But though there are striking parallels between Peter's and Paul's ministries, the vindication of Paul's apostleship can hardly be the book's primary purpose. There is just too much in the book that would be extraneous to this goal. How does the appointment of the Seven in Acts 6 or the detailed description of the shipwreck in Acts 27 further that end?

Most recognize that Acts shows the universality of Christianity. Is this its primary purpose? The gospel goes to Samaritans, the Ethiopian eunuch, Cornelius, Gentiles at Antioch, poor and wealthy, educated and uneducated, women and men, the high and lofty as well as those in humble positions. This approach also helps explain the emphasis on the Jerusalem Council described in Acts 15. However, this again does not explain certain elements in the book such as the choice of Matthias in Acts 1 or the selection of the Seven in Acts 6.

The question remains, what is the primary purpose of Acts? F.F. Bruce, a representative of those who believe the goal is an apologetic one, affirms, "Luke is, in fact, one of the first Christian apologists. In that particular type of apologetic which is addressed to the secular authorities to establish the law-abiding character of Christianity he is absolutely the pioneer" (Bruce, *Acts*, p. 24; cf. F.J. Foakes Jackson and Kirsopp Lake, eds., *The Beginnings of Christianity*, vol. 2, *Prolegomena II: Criticism*. Grand Rapids: Baker Book House, 1979, pp.

177-87). There is much in Acts to substantiate the idea that the book was written to defend Christianity before Roman rulers.

The persecution in Acts is always religious except in two locations—Philippi (chap. 16) and Ephesus (chap. 19). In both of these the opposition was due to vested interests. In every other case the persecutions arose from Jewish sources.

It may be debated, however, whether the primary purpose of Acts is apologetic, even though much in the book substantiates that view. Why include the shipwreck of Acts 27, for instance? Another objection to the concept of an apologetic purpose is the close association of Luke's Gospel with Acts. It is patently clear that Luke-Acts is a two-part work; Acts 1:1 is evidence enough of this. Acts, then, can hardly be apologetic in its primary purpose because there is little in the Gospel of Luke which reveals such an intention.

By far the most popular view of the purpose of Acts is the one which states that it is a historical one. According to this approach Luke's goal was to record the spread of the gospel message from Jerusalem to Judea to Samaria and to the ends of the earth (1:8). Barclay asserts, "Luke's great aim was to show the expansion of Christianity, to show how that religion which began in a little corner of Palestine had in a little more than 30 years reached Rome" (William Barclay, *The Acts of the Apostles*, p. xvii). This explains the transition from a Jewish ministry to a Gentile one, and from Peter to Paul. In addition, this view suits the historical outlook of Acts 1:1 with Luke 1:1-4. The prologue of Luke 1:1-4 is that of a historian like Herodotus, Thucydides, or Polybius. It is quite clear that Luke was writing history in both books.

But is Luke only a historiographer? Luke-Acts is history but it is also intensely theological and especially eschatological. The Book of Acts opens with an eschatological question (1:6) and concludes with eschatological terminology ("the kingdom of God," 28:31). In addition there is a stress on God's sovereignty. In spite of intense opposition of every kind, the Word of God spreads and people respond. Nothing can stop the steady growth of Christianity. The purpose of the Book of Acts may be stated as follows: *To explain with the Gospel of Luke the orderly and sovereignly directed progress of the kingdom message from Jews to Gentiles, and from Jerusalem to Rome.* In Luke's Gospel the question is answered, "If Christianity has its roots in the Old Testament and in Judaism, how did it become a worldwide religion?" The Book of Acts continues in the vein of the Gospel of Luke to answer the same problem.

Alongside this worldwide progression there is an emphasis on eschatology in both Luke and Acts. The prophetic expression *kingdom of God* occurs in Luke 32 times and in Acts 6 times besides the allusions to God's kingdom in 1:6 and 20:25 (cf. 1:3; 8:12; 14:22; 19:8; 28:23, 31). In addition there are many references to eschatology in other terminology and by inference (1:11; 2:19-21, 34-35; 3:19-25; 6:14; 10:42; 13:23-26, 32-33; 15:15-18; 17:3, 7, 31; 20:24-25, 32; 21:28; 23:6; 24:15-17, 21, 25; 26:6-8, 18; 28:20). Obviously, the church in the present Age is heavily accented, but the church also is seen as an heir of the kingdom. It may be concluded, then, that Luke shows how the kingdom message moved from mostly Jews to mostly Gentiles and from Jerusalem to Rome.

This progression is directed in an orderly and sovereign way. One theme that runs as a heavy cord in the fabric of the book is God's sovereignty. In spite of strong opposition, under the Lord's direction the Word of the Lord grew and spread. Thus the purpose of Luke in writing Acts is to show how it is God's intention for His millennial kingdom to include a population of believers taken from Jews and Gentiles during this Age.

If this purpose statement is accepted, it does not rule out the previous suggestions. It includes both Peter and Paul as prime characters, Peter the minister to the circumcised, and Paul to the uncircumcised. The universality of the gospel is part of Luke's emphasis in both his Gospel and here in Acts. Certainly the progression of the book, declared in 1:8, fits into this statement. All of these contribute to the overall purpose of Luke in penning this work.

Sources Luke May Have Used. Under the inspiration of the Holy Spirit Luke probably used a number of sources. First and primary were his own personal experiences. This is most clearly seen in the "we" sections of Acts (16:10-40; 20:5-28:31). A second source of information would have been Paul, with whom Luke spent much time. The apostle's conversion and his experiences in ministry undoubtedly would have been discussed by the two in their time together. A third source is seen in the other witnesses whom Luke contacted (cf. 20:4-5; 21:15-19). In Acts 21:18-19 James is mentioned as being one with whom Luke met. James certainly would have been able to convey information about the very first chapters in Acts! In fact, the early chapters of Acts seem to betray an Aramaic source. Furthermore, while Paul was incarcerated for two years in Caesarea (24:27), Luke would have been free to carry out thorough investigative work in Palestine (Luke 1:2-3). Having carefully researched eyewitness accounts, Luke, by the Spirit's direction, penned the Book of Acts.

Date of the Book. The writing of Acts must have taken place before the destruction of Jerusalem in A.D. 70. Certainly an event of such magnitude would not have been ignored. This is especially true in light of one of the basic themes of the book: God's turning to the Gentiles from the Jews because of the Jews' rejection of Jesus Christ.

Luke scarcely would have omitted an account of Paul's death, traditionally dated from A.D. 66–68, if it had occurred before he wrote Acts.

Nor did Luke mention the Neronian persecutions which began after the great fire of Rome in A.D. 64.

Furthermore, a defense of Christianity before Nero by using the Book of Acts to appeal to what lower officials had ruled regarding Paul would have had little point at the time of the Neronian antagonism. At that time Nero was so intent on destroying the church, the defense set forth in Acts would have had little effect in dissuading him.

The date usually accepted by conservative scholars for the writing of Acts is around A.D. 60–62. Accordingly the place of writing would be Rome or possibly both Caesarea and Rome. At the time of writing Paul's release was either imminent or had just taken place.

Outline of the Book. The outline used in this study is the result of using two keys in Acts. The first and most obvious one is the theme verse, Acts 1:8, "But you will receive power when the Holy Spirit comes on you; and you will be My witnesses in Jerusalem, and in all Judea and Samaria, and to the ends of the earth."

The second key is the use Luke makes of "progress reports" which are sprinkled throughout the book (cf. 2:47; 6:7; 9:31; 12:24; 16:5; 19:20; 28:30-31). Because Luke does not use a precise formula there is some debate as to the location of other progress reports (cf. 2:41; 4:31; 5:42; 8:25, 40; etc.). However, these other statements either do not have the same sense of summary or they lack finality.

The beautiful correlation of these two factors—the key verse of Acts 1:8 and the seven progress reports—form the basis of the following outline.

OUTLINE

I. The Witness in Jerusalem (1:1–6:7)
  A. The expectation of the chosen (chaps. 1–2)
    1. The introduction (1:1-5)
    2. The internment at Jerusalem (1:6-26)
    3. The inception of the church (chap. 2)
Progress report no. 1: "And the Lord added to their number daily those who were being saved" (2:47).
  B. The expansion of the church at Jerusalem (3:1–6:7)
    1. Opposition to the church (3:1–4:31)
    2. Correction in the church (4:32–5:11)
    3. Progression in the church (5:12-42)
    4. Administration in the church (6:1-7)
Progress report no. 2: "So the Word of God spread. The number of disciples in Jerusalem increased rapidly" (6:7).

II. The Witness in all Judea and Samaria (6:8–9:31)
  A. The martyrdom of Stephen (6:8–8:1a)
    1. The arrest of Stephen (6:8–7:1)
    2. The address of Stephen (7:2-53)
    3. The attack on Stephen (7:54–8:1a)
  B. The ministry of Philip (8:1b-40)
    1. In Samaria (8:1b-25)
    2. To the Ethiopian eunuch (8:26-40)
  C. The message of Saul (9:1-31)
    1. The conversion of Saul (9:1-19a)
    2. The conflicts of Saul (9:19b-31)
Progress report no. 3: "Then the church throughout Judea, Galilee, and Samaria . . . was strengthened; and [it was] encouraged by the Holy Spirit, it grew in numbers, living in the fear of the Lord" (9:31).

III. The Witness to the Extremity of the Earth (9:32–28:31)
  A. The extension of the church to Antioch (9:32–12:24)
    1. The preparation of Peter for a universal gospel (9:32–10:48)
    2. The preparation of the apostles for a universal gospel (11:1-18)
    3. The preparation of the church at Antioch for a universal gospel (11:19-30)
    4. The persecution of the church at Jerusalem (12:1-24)
Progress report no. 4: "But the Word of God continued to increase and spread" (12:24).
  B. The extension of the church in Asia Minor (12:25–16:5)
    1. The call and dedication of Barnabas and Saul (12:25–13:3)
     [First missionary journey, chaps. 13–14]
    2. The circuit in Asia Minor (13:4–14:28)
    3. The conference at Jerusalem (15:1-35)
    4. The confirmation of the churches in Asia Minor (15:36–16:5)
     [Second missionary journey, 15:36–18:22]

Progress report no. 5: "So the churches were strengthened in the faith and grew daily in numbers" (16:5).

C. The extension of the church in the Aegean area (16:6–19:20)

1. The call to Macedonia (16:6-10)
2. The conflicts in Macedonia (16:11–17:15)
3. The crusade in Achaia (17:16–18:18)
4. The conclusion of the second missionary journey (18:19-22)
5. The conquest of Ephesus (18:23–19:20)
   [Third missionary journey, 18:23–21:16]

Progress report no. 6: "In this way the Word of the Lord spread widely and grew in power" (19:20).

D. The extension of the church to Rome (19:21–28:31)

1. The completion of the third journey (19:21–21:16)
2. The captivity at Jerusalem (21:17–23:32)
3. The captivity at Caesarea (23:33–26:32)
4. The captivity at Rome (chaps. 27–28)

Progress report no. 7: "Paul . . . welcomed all who came to see him. Boldly and without hindrance he preached the kingdom of God and taught about the Lord Jesus Christ" (28:30-31).

COMMENTARY

I. The Witness in Jerusalem (1:1–6:7)

A. The expectation of the chosen (chaps. 1–2)

1. THE INTRODUCTION (1:1-5)

1:1-2. In the first two verses of this book Luke looked back to his Gospel. **Theophilus** may have been Luke's patron who financed the writing of Luke and Acts. At any rate he was a believer in Christ. These two books would confirm and instruct Theophilus, as well as the church of Christ, in the faith (cf. Luke 1:1-4).

The verb **began** indicates that Acts continues the account of the ministry and teaching Christ began on earth. He is still working and teaching through His people today.

The reference to the Lord's Ascension in Acts 1:2 looks back to Luke 24:51.

Two commandments were given by the Lord before He returned to heaven: (1) the apostolic band was to remain in Jerusalem (Acts 1:4; cf. Luke 24:49); (2) they were to go into the world as witnesses (Acts 1:8; cf. Luke 10:4; 24:47). These **instructions** may have seemed contradictory but they were to be obeyed sequentially.

1:3. The Lord's post-resurrection appearances attested the reality of the Resurrection. Christ **gave many convincing proofs** of this. The word "proofs" (*tekmēriois*) occurs only here in the New Testament and looks at demonstrable evidence in contrast with evidence provided by witnesses. In other words, the Resurrection was proven by touch, sight, and feel (cf. Luke 24:39-40; 1 John 1:1).

For **40 days** after His resurrection the Lord **appeared** to the apostles and discussed **the kingdom of God** with **them.** What is meant by this term? God has always ruled over the world and especially in Israel (Dan. 2:47; 4:3, 25-26, 32, 34-37; 5:21; 6:25-27; Pss. 5:2; 84:3; 89:6-18; 103; etc.). However, a time is coming, commonly called the Millennium, when God will burst into human history in a spectacular way to establish His rule on earth. This is what is meant by the term "kingdom of God" (cf. comments on Matt. 3:2; 13:10-16). Though this topic was the subject of much of the Lord's teaching and preaching before the Cross, He saw fit to discuss it further during His 40 days of post-resurrection ministry.

1:4. The promised **gift** from the **Father,** also anticipated in Luke 24:49, was quite obviously the Holy Spirit (cf. Acts 1:5; John 14:16; 15:26; 16:7).

1:5. Indeed **John** had predicted a Spirit baptism by the Lord Jesus. The greatness of Christ was seen in the fact that John identified people with himself by **water** baptism; Christ Jesus would join His followers to Himself by **the Holy Spirit.** The word **baptized,** which normally means "dipped or immersed," here has the idea of "uniting with" (cf. 1 Cor. 10:1-2). The Lord made the same prediction of Spirit baptism that John made (Matt. 3:11; Mark 1:8; cf. Acts 11:16).

2. THE INTERNMENT AT JERUSALEM (1:6-26)

a. The Ascension (1:6-11)

1:6. The disciples' question, **Lord are You at this time going to restore the kingdom to Israel?** is most illuminating. The sentence is introduced by the connective **so** (*men oun*), which associates the thought of verse 6 with verse 5. In the disciples' minds the outpouring of the Holy Spirit and the coming of the promised kingdom were closely associated. And well they should be, because the Old Testament frequently joined the two (cf. Isa. 32:15-20; 44:3-5; Ezek. 39:28-29; Joel 2:28–3:1; Zech. 12:8-10). When Christ told the disciples of the soon-coming Spirit baptism, they immediately concluded that the restoration of Israel's kingdom was near in time (cf. comments on "restore" in Acts 3:21).

1:7. Some conclude from the Lord's response that the apostles had a false concept of the kingdom. But this is wrong. Christ did not accuse them of this. If the followers of the Lord Jesus had an incorrect view, this would have been the time for Him to correct it. The fact is, Christ taught the coming of an earthly, literal kingdom (cf. Matt. 19:28; Luke 19:11-27; 22:28-30). Acts 1:3 states that the Lord instructed the disciples about the kingdom; He certainly gave them the right impression as to its character and future coming. What Jesus discussed here (v. 7) was the *time* of the coming of the kingdom. The Greek word for **times** (*chronous*) basically describes duration of times, and the word for **dates** (*kairous*) refers to both length of times and kinds of times (as in, e.g., "hard times"). The disciples were **not . . . to know** either the times or the critical periods **the Father** had **set by His . . . authority.** Later, further revelation would be made concerning these (cf. 1 Thes. 5:1).

1:8. This verse contrasts (*alla*, **but**) with verse 7. Instead of knowing the times or dates, the apostles were to be Christ's witnesses **to the ends of the earth.** This they were to do after they had been supernaturally empowered by **the Holy Spirit.**

The meaning of the clause **you will be My witnesses** is subject to question. Is this a command, or is it a simple statement of fact? Grammatically the words may be taken either way, but because of 10:42 (cf. 4:20) it is clearly an imperative in the future tense.

Probably "the ends (sing., 'end' in the Gr. text) of the earth" looks to Rome, the proud center of world civilization in the Apostolic Age, a significant distance from Jerusalem (more than 1,400 miles, as the crow flies).

1:9-11. These verses describe the Lord's Ascension but they also anticipate His return. He will come back in **a cloud,** bodily, in view of people (Rev. 1:7), and to the Mount of Olives (Zech. 14:4)—**the same way** the apostles saw **Him go.**

The Ascension of Christ marked the conclusion of His ministry on earth in His bodily presence. It also exalted Him to the right hand of the Father (Acts 2:33-36; 5:30-31; Heb. 1:3; 8:1; 12:2). At the same time the Ascension meant that the continuing work of Christ on earth was now placed in the hands of His disciples (Acts 1:1-2, 8).

It was imperative that the Ascension occur so that the promised Comforter could come (cf. John 14:16, 26; 15:26; 16:7; Acts 2:33-36). The Holy Spirit would empower the disciples as they ministered the gospel and waited for the kingdom.

b. The supplication in the Upper Room (1:12-14)

1:12-14. **A Sabbath Day's walk** was about 3,000 feet or a bit more than half a mile (cf. Ex. 16:29; Num. 35:5). **The Mount of Olives** is this short distance east of Jerusalem.

The apostles were gathered **upstairs.** Large groups normally would meet in upper stories because the largest rooms were upstairs (cf. Acts 20:8-9). The lower stories had smaller rooms so that their walls would bear the weight of the upper stories.

The **prayer** (1:14) may be specific prayer for the promise referred to in verse 4. In the Greek "prayer" has the article. The disciples were following the instruction suggested by Jesus (Luke 11:13). However, since the day of Pentecost, it is not necessary for Christians to pray for the Holy Spirit (cf. Rom. 8:9).

Evidently the Lord's resurrection led to the conversion of the **brothers** of Jesus

SERMONS AND SPEECHES IN ACTS

| Speakers | | | Occasions and/or | | |
Peter	Paul	Others	Hearers	Cities	References
1. Peter			Selection of successor to Judas	Jerusalem	1:16-22
2. Peter			Signs on the day of Pentecost	Jerusalem	2:14-36
3. Peter			Healing of lame man in the temple	Jerusalem	3:12-26
4. Peter			Before the Sanhedrin for preaching the resurrection of Christ	Jerusalem	4:8-12
		Gamaliel	Before the Sanhedrin, regarding Peter and others	Jerusalem	5:35-39
		Stephen	Before the Sanhedrin, after Stephen was arrested	Jerusalem	7:2-53
5. Peter			At Cornelius' house, to present the gospel to Gentiles there	Caesarea	10:34-43
6. Peter			Defense to the church about what happened in Caesarea	Jerusalem	11:4-17
	1. Paul		Sabbath sermon to Jews in the synagogue	Antioch of Pisidia	13:16-41
	2. Paul and Barnabas		Crowd who wanted to worship them	Lystra	14:15-17
7. Peter			Church council	Jerusalem	15:7-11
		James	Church council	Jerusalem	15:13-21
	3. Paul		Athenians on Mars' Hill	Athens	17:22-31
		Demetrius	Workmen who were disturbed at Paul's preaching	Ephesus	19:25-27
		Town clerk	Riot at Ephesus	Ephesus	19:35-40
	4. Paul		Gathering of Ephesian elders	Miletus	20:18-35
	5. Paul		Mob of people who tried to kill Paul	Jerusalem	22:1-21
	6. Paul		Defense before the Sanhedrin	Jerusalem	23:1-6
	7. Paul		Defense before Felix	Caesarea	24:10-21
	8. Paul		Defense before Festus	Caesarea	25:8, 10-11
	9. Paul		Defense before Herod Agrippa II	Caesarea	26:1-23
	10. Paul		Shipmates in a violent storm	Mediterranean Sea, between Crete and Malta	27:21-26
	11. Paul		Testimony to Jewish leaders	Rome	28:17-20, 25-28

(cf. John 7:5; 1 Cor. 15:7). If so, this is the only recorded appearance Christ made to unsaved people after His resurrection.

c. The completion of the apostolate (1:15-26)

1:15. Peter, leader of the apostolic band, **stood up among the** group of some **120** who were gathered together in Jerusalem. Obviously there were far more followers elsewhere (cf. 1 Cor. 15:6).

1:16-17. Peter's allusion to the Old Testament shows his high view of the Scriptures. The Psalms were inspired by **the Holy Spirit** speaking **through the mouth of David.** Peter's assessment was that **the Scripture had to be fulfilled.** The verb "had to" is from *dei,* which is used of logical or divine necessity.

Peter said that David prophesied of **Judas.** But when did David discuss Judas Iscariot? Certainly he did not refer to him directly or name him. In the Psalms the Messiah is anticipated as the ideal King; therefore the royal psalms, which discuss the King of Israel, often anticipate Christ. Likewise the enemies of the royal psalmist became the enemies of the Messiah. Therefore Judas was predicted in Psalms 69:25 and 109:8 as Acts 1:20 states. Both of these psalms are royal imprecatory psalms (cf. Ps. 41:9).

1:18-19. Though **Judas** himself did not personally buy **a field,** he did so indirectly. The priests used the betrayal money Judas flung into the temple to make this purchase in Judas' name (Matt. 27:3-10).

The account of Judas' violent end in Acts 1:18 seems to contradict Matthew 27:5, which starkly says he "hanged himself." One explanation is that Judas' **intestines** quickly became swollen and distended after he hanged himself, so he **burst open.** Another explanation, more probable, is that Judas hanged himself over a cliff and the rope or branch of the tree he was using broke. When he fell to the rocks below, he "burst open."

Akeldama is Aramaic for **Field of Blood.** The exact location of that field is unknown, but traditionally it is believed to be near the Greek Orthodox Church and Convent of Saint Oniprius, where the Valley of Hinnom joins the Kidron Valley, southeast of Jerusalem (see map).

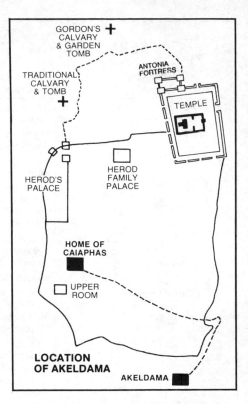

1:20. On Peter's quotation of Psalms 69:25 and 109:8 in reference to Judas, see comments on Acts 1:16-17.

1:21. Once again (cf. v. 16) Luke used the verb *dei,* translated **it is necessary,** to show logical or divine necessity. Interestingly the apostolate saw fit to replace the vacancy left by Judas, but later when the Apostle James died (12:2) no record was given of a successor being appointed. Evidently it was necessary to replace Judas' position because he had vacated his place of promise, referred to in Matthew 19:28. There **the Lord** promised the apostles they would sit on 12 thrones reigning over Christ's kingdom of Israel when He returns to reign on Planet Earth (cf. Rev. 21:14).

1:22. The importance of the Resurrection is seen in the requirement that the replacement **must** be **a witness . . . of His resurrection.** The resurrection of the Lord **Jesus** is a cornerstone of the Christian faith (cf. 1 Cor. 15).

1:23-26. With **two men** to choose from, **Joseph** (alias **Barsabbas** and **Justus**) **and Matthias,** the apostles did two things: **they prayed** (acknowledging the Lord's omniscience; cf. Ps 139:1-6; John 2:25;

4:29) and **they drew lots.** Probably the two names were written on stones placed in a container. When the stones were shaken out of the container, the first stone to fall out was considered the Lord's choice.

This is the last time in the Bible lots were said to be used to determine God's will. A couple of observations are in order. First, no moral question was involved here. It was a matter of making a choice between two men who were apparently equally qualified. Second, this procedure may have come from Proverbs 16:33 which says the decision of lots is from the Lord.

Some feel the choice of Matthias was a wrong one. It is contended that this was a poor method of choosing and Paul should have filled the vacancy left by Judas' apostasy. However, those who believe Matthias was a proper selection argue that Matthew 19:28 is Jewish in its orientation and Paul was to minister to Gentiles (Gal. 2:9). Furthermore Luke, Paul's friend and companion, acknowledged the Twelve as an official group (Acts 2:14; 6:2). Finally, there is no sense or spirit of censure in the Acts account on the selection of Matthias.

3. THE INCEPTION OF THE CHURCH (CHAP. 2)

a. The descent of the Holy Spirit (2:1-13)

2:1. The day of Pentecost was an annual feast that followed the Feast of Firstfruits by a week of weeks (i.e., seven weeks, or 49 days) and therefore also was called the Feast of Weeks (cf. Lev. 23:15-22). The name "Pentecost," of Greek derivation, means 50 because it was the 50th day after the Firstfruits feast (Lev. 23:16).

Where the followers of Christ were gathered at this time is not definitely known. Luke simply wrote, **They were all together in one place.** Perhaps they were in the temple precincts. However, the place is called a "house" (Acts 2:2), an unlikely designation for the temple, though it may be referred to as a house (cf. 7:47). If they were not assembled at the temple, they must have been near it (cf. 2:6).

2:2-3. The references to "wind" and "fire" are significant. The word for "Spirit" (*pneuma*) is related to *pnoē*, the word translated "wind" here. It also means breath. Both nouns—"spirit" and "wind" or "breath"—are from the verb *pneō*, "to blow, to breathe." The **sound like the blowing of a violent wind . . . from heaven** points to the power of the Holy Spirit and the fullness of His coming.

The **tongues of fire** portray the presence of God. Several times in the Old Testament God displayed Himself in the form of flames (Gen. 15:17; Ex. 3:2-6; 13:21-22; 19:18; 40:38; cf. Matt. 3:11; Luke 3:16).

No believer there was exempt from this experience, for the flames **separated and came to rest on each of them.**

2:4. The filling **with the Holy Spirit** is separate from the baptism of the Spirit. The Spirit's baptism occurs once for each believer at the moment of salvation (cf. 11:15-16; Rom. 6:3; 1 Cor. 12:13; Col. 2:12), but the Spirit's filling may occur not only at salvation but also on a number of occasions after salvation (Acts 4:8, 31; 6:3, 5; 7:55; 9:17; 13:9, 52).

An evidence of the baptism of the Holy Spirit was **other tongues** (*heterais glōssais*; cf. 11:15-16). These were undoubtedly spoken living languages; the word used in 2:6, 8 is *dialektō*, which means "language" and not ecstatic utterance. This gives insight into what is meant by "tongues" in chapters 2; 10; 19; and in 1 Corinthians 12–14.

This event marked the beginning of the church. Up to this point the church was anticipated (Matt. 16:18). The church is constituted a body by means of Spirit baptism (1 Cor. 12:13). The first occurrence of the baptism of the Spirit therefore must indicate the inauguration of the church. Of course Acts 2:1-4 does not state that Spirit baptism took place at Pentecost. However, 1:5 anticipates it and 11:15-16 refers back to it as having occurred at Pentecost. The church, therefore, came into existence then.

2:5-13. Jews of the "diaspora" (dispersion; cf. James 1:1; 1 Peter 1:1) **were . . . in Jerusalem** for the feast. Perhaps they were bilingual, speaking both Greek and their native languages. They were dumbfounded to hear Jews from Galilee speaking the languages of peoples surrounding the Mediterranean Sea.

It is a question whether only the Twelve spoke in **tongues** or all 120.

Several factors support the idea of only the Twelve being involved in this phenomenon: (1) They are referred to as **Galileans** (Acts 2:7; cf. 1:11-13). (2) Peter stood up with "the Eleven" (2:14). (3) The nearest antecedent of "they" in verse 1 is the "apostles" in 1:26. However, a problem with this view is that the number of languages listed in 2:9-11 is more than 12. But one apostle could have spoken more than one language, in sequence. Still it is possible that all 120 spoke in tongues. Since the majority of them were from Galilee they could have been called Galileans. The references to the Twelve would have indicated they were the leaders of the 120.

The topic the people discussed in all these languages was **the wonders of God.** It seems they were praising God. Their message was not one of repentance; it was not the gospel.

Unable to explain this miracle away, the Jewish unbelievers were puzzled, and some resorted to scoffing and asserted, **They have had too much wine.** The word "wine" (*gleukous*) means new sweet wine.

b. *The discourse of Peter (2:14-40)*

This sermon has basically one theme: Jesus is the Messiah and Lord (v. 36). Peter's discourse may be outlined as follows:

I. This is the fulfillment of prophecy (vv. 15-21)
   A. A defense (v. 15)
   B. An explanation (vv. 16-21)
II. Jesus is the Messiah (vv. 22-32)
   A. His works attest that He is the Messiah (v. 22)
   B. His resurrection attests that He is the Messiah (vv. 23-32)
III. Jesus, the glorified Messiah, poured forth the Holy Spirit (vv. 33-36)
IV. Application (vv. 37-40)

2:14-15. Peter began with a rebuttal of their accusation of drunkenness. It was **only 9 in the morning** (lit., "the third hour of the day"; days began at 6 A.M.), far too early for a group of revelers to be inebriated!

2:16-21. Instead of being drunk the believers were experiencing what was described in Joel 2. In Peter's words, **This is what was spoken by the Prophet Joel.** This clause does not mean, "This is *like*

that"; it means Pentecost fulfilled what Joel had described. However, the prophecies of Joel quoted in Acts 2:19-20 were not fulfilled. The implication is that the remainder would be fulfilled if Israel would repent. This aspect of contingency is discussed more fully in the comments on 3:19-23.

2:22. Jesus' **miracles,** Peter said, were God's way of verifying Jesus' claims **to you,** the Jews (cf. 1 Cor. 1:22; 14:22).

2:23. The point of this verse is clear: the Crucifixion was no accident. It was in **God's set purpose** (*boulē,* "plan") and was God's determined will, not merely His inclination. It was a divine necessity (cf. 4:28). When Peter referred to **you,** he meant Jews; and by **wicked men** he perhaps meant Gentiles because the word "wicked" means lawless (*anomōn*). Both Gentiles and Jews were implicated in Christ's **death.** Many times the apostles accused the Jews of crucifying Jesus (2:23, 36; 3:15; 4:10; 5:30; 7:52; 10:39; 13:28), though the apostles also held the Gentiles culpable (2:23; 4:27; cf. Luke 23:24-25).

2:24. The resurrection of the Lord is a basic doctrine in Acts (v. 32; 3:15, 26; 4:10; 5:30; 10:40; 13:30, 33-34, 37; 17:31; 26:23). Here is another indication that He is the Messiah for **it was impossible for death to keep its hold on Him** (John 20:9).

2:25-35. These verses include four proofs of the Lord's resurrection and Ascension: (a) The prophecy of Psalm 16:8-11 and the presence of David's **tomb** (Acts 2:25-31), (b) the witnesses of the Resurrection (v. 32), (c) the supernatural events of Pentecost (v. 33), and (d) the Ascension of David's greater Son (Ps. 110:1; Acts 2:34-35).

The word translated **grave** in verses 27 and 31 is *hadēs,* which means either the grave (as here) or the underworld of departed spirits.

Peter's point is that since **David,** the **patriarch** and prophet **was** dead and **buried,** he could not have been referring to himself in Psalm 16:8-11; hence he was writing about **the Christ** ("Messiah") and His **resurrection.** The **oath** (Acts 2:30) looks back to Psalm 132:11 (cf. 2 Sam. 7:15-16). **God . . . raised . . . Jesus to life,** and **exalted** Him (cf. Acts 3:13; Phil. 2:9) **to** the Father's **right hand** (cf. Acts 5:30-31; Eph. 1:20; Col. 3:1; Heb. 1:3; 8:1; 10:12; 12:2; 1 Peter 3:22). Thus Jesus had the authority to send **the promised Holy Spirit** (Acts 1:5, 8; John 14:16, 26; 15:26; 16:7), whose presence was evidenced by what they saw ("tongues of fire," Acts 2:3) and heard ("a violent wind," v. 2), and the apostles speaking in other languages (vv. 4, 6, 8, 11).

Just as David was not speaking of himself in Psalm 16:8-11, so in Psalm 110:1 he was not speaking of himself. David was not resurrected (Acts 2:29, 31) nor **did** he **ascend to heaven** (v. 34). **The Lord** is Yahweh God who spoke **to my** (David's) **Lord,** who is Christ, God's Son.

On five occasions in Acts some of the apostles said they were **witnesses of** the resurrected Christ (v. 32; 3:15; 5:32; 10:39-41; 13:30-31). They knew whereof they spoke!

2:36. Here is the conclusion of Peter's argument. The noun **Lord,** referring to **Christ,** probably is a reference to Yahweh. The same word *kyrios* is used of **God** in verses 21, 34, and 39 (cf. Phil. 2:9). This is a strong affirmation of Christ's deity.

2:37. Verses 37-40 contain the application of Peter's sermon. The verb **cut** (*katenygēsan*) means "to strike or prick violently, to stun." The convicting work of the Spirit (cf. John 16:8-11) in their hearts was great.

Their question had a ring of desperation about it (cf. Acts 16:30). If the Jews had crucified their Messiah and He was now exalted, what was left for them to do? **What** could and must they **do?**

2:38-39. Peter's answer was forthright. First they were to **repent.** This verb (*metanoēsate*) means "change your outlook," or "have a change of heart; reverse the direction of your life." This obviously results in a change of conduct, but the emphasis is on the mind or outlook. The Jews had rejected Jesus; now they were to trust in Him. Repentance was repeatedly part of the apostles' message in Acts (v. 38; 3:19; 5:31; 8:22; 11:18; 13:24; 17:30; 19:4; 20:21; 26:20).

A problem revolves around the command "be baptized" and its connection with the remainder of 2:38. There are several views: (1) One is that both repentance and baptism result in remission of sins. In this view, baptism is essential for salvation. The problem with this interpretation is that elsewhere in Scripture forgiveness of sins is based on faith alone (John 3:16, 36; Rom. 4:1-17; 11:6; Gal. 3:8-9; Eph. 2:8-9; etc.). Furthermore Peter, the same speaker, later promised forgiveness of sins on the basis of faith alone (Acts 5:31; 10:43; 13:38; 26:18).

(2) A second interpretation translates 2:38, "Be baptized . . . on the basis of the remission of your sins." The preposition used here is *eis* which, with the accusative case, may mean "on account of, on the basis of." It is used in this way in Matthew 3:11; 12:41; and Mark 1:4. Though it is possible for this construction to mean "on the basis of," this is not its normal meaning; *eis* with the accusative case usually describes purpose or direction.

(3) A third view takes the clause **and be baptized, every one of you, in the name of Jesus Christ** as parenthetical. Several factors support this interpretation: (a) The verb makes a distinction between singular and plural verbs and nouns. The verb "repent" is plural and so is the pronoun "your" in the clause **so that your sins may be forgiven** (lit., "unto the remission of your sins," *eis aphesin tōn hamartiōn hymōn*). Therefore the verb "repent" must go with the purpose of forgiveness of sins. On the other hand the imperative "be baptized" is singular, setting it off from the rest of the sentence. (b) This concept fits with Peter's proclamation in Acts 10:43 in which the same expression "sins may be forgiven" (*aphesin hamartiōn*) occurs. There it is granted on the basis of faith alone. (c) In Luke 24:47 and Acts 5:31 the same writer, Luke, indicates that repentance results in remission of sins.

The gift of the Holy Spirit is God's **promise** (cf. 1:5, 8; 2:33) to those who turn to the Lord, including Jews and their descendants and those **who are far off,** that is, Gentiles (cf. Eph. 2:13, 17, 19). Acts 2:38-39 put together the human side of salvation ("repent") and the divine side (**call** means "to elect"; cf. Rom. 8:28-30).

2:40. Peter's **words** in this verse look back to verses 23 and 36. Israel was guilty of a horrendous sin; individual Jews could be spared from God's judgment on that **generation** if they would repent (cf. Matt. 21:41-44; 22:7; 23:34–24:2). They would be set apart to Christ and His church if only they would be disassociated from Israel.

359

c. The description of the first church
(2:41-47)

2:41. Three thousand who believed were baptized, thus displaying their identification with Christ. This group of people immediately joined the fellowship of believers.

2:42. The activity of this early church was twofold. The believers first continued steadfastly (proskarterountes, "persisting in or continuing in"; cf. 1:14; 2:46; 6:4; 8:13; 10:7; Rom. 12:12; 13:6; Col. 4:2) in the apostles' teaching or doctrine. The second was fellowship, which is defined as the breaking of bread and . . . prayer. The omission of "and" between "fellowship" and "to the breaking of bread and to prayer" indicates the last two activities are appositional to fellowship.

Perhaps the breaking of bread included both the Lord's Table and a common meal (cf. Acts 2:46; 20:7; 1 Cor. 10:16; 11:23-25; Jude 12).

2:43. Wonders (terata, "miracles evoking awe") and miraculous signs (sēmeia, "miracles pointing to a divine truth") authenticated the veracity of the apostles (cf. 2 Cor. 12:12; Heb. 2:3-4). The apostles performed many such "signs and wonders" (Acts 4:30; 5:12; 6:8; 8:6, 13; 14:3; 15:12). Christ too had performed many "wonders" and "signs"—and also "miracles" (dynameis, "works of power").

2:44-45. The selling of property and the common possession of the proceeds may imply that the early church expected the Lord to return soon and establish His kingdom. This may explain why the practice was not continued. Holding everything in common was not socialism or communism because it was voluntary (cf. 4:32, 34-35; 5:4). Also their goods were not evenly distributed but were given to meet needs as they arose.

2:46-47. The activities described in verses 42-47 would tend to separate the church from traditional Judaism even though every day (cf. v. 47) they continued (proskarterountes; cf. v. 42) to meet together in the temple courts.

One of the subthemes of Acts is joy, because a victorious church is a joyful one. This is seen in verses 46-47 and numerous other times (5:41; 8:8, 39; 11:23; 12:14; 13:48, 52; 14:17; 15:3, 31; 16:34; 21:17). In their fellowship they broke bread in their homes and ate together (cf. 2:42) with joy. (The word praising [ainountes] is used only nine times in the NT, seven of them by Luke: Luke 2:13, 20; 19:37; 24:53; Acts 2:47; 3:8-9; Rom. 15:11; Rev. 19:5).

With the first of seven summary progress reports (cf. Acts 6:7; 9:31; 12:24; 16:5; 19:20; 28:30-31) Luke brought this section of Acts to a close: each day others were being saved. The church grew rapidly right from the start!

B. The expansion of the church at Jerusalem (3:1–6:7)

1. OPPOSITION TO THE CHURCH (3:1–4:31)

a. The occasion (chap. 3)

3:1. Apparently there were several times for prayer at the Jerusalem temple—9 A.M., 12 noon, and 3 P.M. Perhaps the hour of 3 P.M. is stated here because it helps explain 4:3.

3:2. The description of a man crippled from birth emphasizes his hopeless condition. He was more than 40 years old (4:22). People carried him every day to the temple gate named Beautiful so that he could beg. This may have been the eastern gate of the temple area that led from the court of the Gentiles into the women's court.

3:3-11. God's supernatural healing of the crippled man through Peter and John (v. 7), together with his exuberant response (v. 8), attracted a crowd amazed (filled with wonder and amazement) at what had taken place. They ran and assembled at Solomon's Colonnade, a portico of columns running the length of the east side of the outer court (cf. 5:12). Two other cripples were healed in Acts (9:32-34; 14:8-10).

3:12. Peter assessed the situation and used it as an opportunity to preach. His message included: (a) an explanation (vv. 12-16) and (b) an exhortation (vv. 17-26).

3:13-15. Peter attributed the power for healing to Jesus, here described as God's Servant (cf. v. 26; 4:27, 30). This term recalls the title "Servant of Yahweh" in Isaiah 42:1; 49:6-7; 52:13; 53:11. Interestingly forms of the verb handed . . . over (paradidōmi) are used twice in Isaiah 53:12 in the Septuagint. This lowly Servant (cf. Phil. 2:6-8) was exalted (glorified; cf. John 12:23; 17:1; Acts 2:33; Phil. 2:9; Heb. 1:3-4, 8) by the God of the Jews' ancestors, Abraham, Isaac, and Jacob (cf. Gen. 32:9; Ex. 3:6, 16; Matt. 22:32; Mark 12:26; Luke 20:37; Acts 7:32). Peter emphasized with sledgehammer effect three contradictions in the people's conduct (3:13-15). First, he said the Jews demanded Christ's death when Pilate . . . had decided to let Him go. Second, the Jews disowned the Holy and Righteous One and demanded the release of a murderer. Third, Israel killed the Author of life but God raised Him from the dead. Peter's titles of Christ are interesting: "His Servant Jesus," "the Holy and Righteous One" (cf. Heb. 7:26), and "the Author of life" (cf. John 10:10). In the third title the irony is strong: they *killed* the Author of *life* but He was raised to *life* from the dead! (On Jesus' resurrection, see comments on Acts 2:24. On witnesses of the Resurrection, see 2:32.)

3:16. The crippled man's healing came because of his faith in the name of Jesus. Faith was also evident in many of those whom Jesus healed (e.g., Mark 5:34; 10:52; Luke 17:19). In Bible times a person's name represented him and his characteristics. In Acts, Luke spoke of "the name" (of Jesus) at least 33 times (cf. Acts 2:21, 38; 3:6, 16; 4:7, 10, 12, 17-18; 5:28, 40-41; etc.).

3:17-18. Peter's exhortation begins here. The people with their leaders (cf. Luke 23:13) had acted in ignorance (cf. Acts 17:30; Eph. 4:18; 1 Peter 1:14) in the sense that they did not recognize who Jesus really is. So God gave them further opportunity to repent. Though they crucified Him in ignorance, the suffering of Christ fulfilled Old Testament prophecies (cf. Acts 17:3; 26:23).

3:19-21. Peter's exhortation, as in his Pentecost sermon (2:38), was to repent. Was Peter saying here that if Israel repented, God's kingdom would have come to earth? This must be answered in the affirmative for several reasons: (1) The word restore (3:21) is related to the word "restore" in 1:6. In 3:21 it is in its noun form (*apokatastaseōs*), and in 1:6 it is a verb (*apokathistaneis*). Both occurrences anticipate the restoration of the kingdom to Israel (cf. Matt. 17:11; Mark 9:12). (2) The concept of restoration parallels regeneration when it is used of the kingdom (cf. Isa. 65:17; 66:22; Matt. 19:28; Rom. 8:20-22). (3) The purpose clauses are different in Acts 3:19 and 20. In verse 19 a so that translates *pros to* (some mss. have *eis to*) with the infinitive. This points to a near purpose. The two occurrences of that in verses 19b and 20 are translations of a different construction (*hopōs* with subjunctive verbs), and refer to more remote purposes. Thus repentance would result in forgiveness of sins, the near purpose (v. 19a). Then if Israel as a whole would repent, a second more remote goal, the coming of the kingdom (times of refreshing at the second coming of Christ) would be fulfilled. (4) The sending of the Christ, that is, Messiah (v. 20) meant the coming of the kingdom. (5) The Old Testament "foretold these days" (v. 24; cf. v. 21). The Old Testament prophets did not predict the church; to them it was a mystery (Rom. 16:25; Eph. 3:1-6). But the prophets often spoke of the messianic golden age, that is, the Millennium.

This offer of salvation and of the Millennium pointed both to God's graciousness and to Israel's unbelief. On the one hand God was giving the Jews an opportunity to repent after the sign of Christ's resurrection. They had refused the "pre-Cross" Jesus; now they were being offered a post-Resurrection Messiah. On the other hand Peter's words underscore Israel's rejection. They had been given the sign of Jonah but still they refused to believe (cf. Luke 16:31). In a real sense this message confirmed Israel's unbelief.

Some Bible scholars oppose the view that the kingdom was offered by Peter. They do so on the basis of several objections: (1) Since God knew Israel would reject the offer, it was not a legitimate offer. But it was as genuine as the presentation of the gospel to any nonelect person. (2) This puts kingdom truth in the Church Age. However, church truth is found before the church began at Pentecost (cf. Matt. 16:18; 18:17; John 10:16; 14:20). (3) This view leads to ultradispensationalism. But this is not a necessary consequence if this offer is seen as *a transition within the Church Age*. Acts must be seen as a hinge book, a transition work bridging the work of Christ on earth with His work through the church on earth.

In conclusion, Acts 3:17-21 shows that Israel's repentance was to have had two purposes: (1) for *individual* Israelites there was forgiveness of sins, and (2) for *Israel as a nation* her Messiah would return to reign.

3:22-23. Here Jesus is portrayed as the "New Testament Moses" in fulfillment of Deuteronomy 18:15-19 (cf. John 6:14). Christ will come not only with deliverance as Moses did, but He will also judge as Moses did (cf. Lev. 23:29 with Deut. 18:19; also cf. Num. 14:26-35).

3:24-25. Peter's mention of **Samuel** as the next prophet after Moses (cf. 13:20) clearly implies that Joshua did not fulfill Deuteronomy 18:15.

All the prophets (cf. Acts 3:18, 21) in one way or another wrote about **these days,** that is, the Messianic Age. The Jews were **heirs of the prophets** of the Abrahamic **Covenant** given to **Abraham** (Gen. 12:2-3; 15:18-21; 17:1-8; 22:18) and confirmed to the Jews' **fathers** (e.g., Isaac [Gen. 26:41]). The Jews then could be blessed if they, like Abraham, believed (cf. Rom. 3:28-29; 4:3; Gal. 3:6-7). In fact **all peoples** would **be blessed** through Abraham (cf. Gen. 12:3; Rom. 4:12, 16; Gal. 3:29; Eph. 3:6).

3:26. Jesus, God's **Servant** (cf. v. 13; 4:27, 30), was **sent . . . first to you,** that is, to the Jews. This chronological pattern was followed throughout the Gospels and Acts (cf., e.g., Matt. 10:5; Acts 13:46; Rom. 1:16). The reason for this is that the establishing of the kingdom depended and still depends on Israel's response (cf. Matt. 23:39; Rom. 11:26).

b. The incarceration (4:1-22)

4:1-2. Involved in this apprehension of Peter, John, and the healed man (v. 14), were **the priests and the captain of the temple guard and the Sadducees.** Since the captain of the temple guard was responsible for maintaining order in the temple, it is no surprise that he, along with the priests and Sadducees, interrupted **Peter and John** in order to disband the mob (cf. 3:11).

The priests were primarily Sadducees in their religious affiliation (5:17); so the principal accusers were Sadducees. These people were distinguished by several characteristics: (a) a disbelief in a bodily resurrection and a denial of the existence of angels or spirits (23:8); (b) loyalty to the Roman government; (c) a desire to maintain the status quo; (d) an association with the wealthy class; and (e) adherence only to the Pentateuch. The Sadducees **were greatly disturbed** by Peter and John's preaching **because** it directly opposed the Sadducees' denial of **the resurrection** and would also shake the establishment.

4:3. The two apostles were incarcerated overnight **because it was** already **evening,** that is, late afternoon (cf. 3 P.M. in 3:1), too late for a trial.

4:4. One of the subthemes of Acts is the growth of God's Word in spite of opposition. Like a juggernaut the message irresistibly moved ahead. Two leading apostles were bound, but the Word of God cannot be bound! (Cf. 28:30-31; Phil. 1:12-14.)

Annas' Family

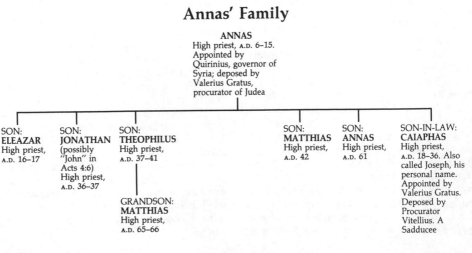

ANNAS
High priest, A.D. 6–15.
Appointed by Quirinius, governor of Syria; deposed by Valerius Gratus, procurator of Judea

SON: **ELEAZAR** High priest, A.D. 16–17

SON: **JONATHAN** (possibly "John" in Acts 4:6) High priest, A.D. 36–37

SON: **THEOPHILUS** High priest, A.D. 37–41

GRANDSON: **MATTHIAS** High priest, A.D. 65–66

SON: **MATTHIAS** High priest, A.D. 42

SON: **ANNAS** High priest, A.D. 61

SON-IN-LAW: **CAIAPHAS** High priest, A.D. 18–36. Also called Joseph, his personal name. Appointed by Valerius Gratus. Deposed by Procurator Vitellius. A Sadducee

4:5-6. Luke's careful description of the Jewish leaders underscores the pomp and power of this assembly. Simple fishermen were in the midst of the highest leaders in the land! **The rulers, elders, and teachers of the Law** included the Sanhedrin, the Jewish supreme court (cf. v. 15). **Annas** was Caiaphas' father-in-law. Annas had been **high priest** from A.D. 6 to 15, and was deposed. His son-in-law **Caiaphas** was priest from A.D. 18 to 36. But apparently Annas, being something of a priestly statesman, was still thought of by the Jews as their high priest. (See the chart on Annas' family. Cf. comments on Luke 3:2; John 18:13; Acts 7:1.) The assembly had examined Jesus on trial; now, ironically, they were facing two of Jesus' prominent—and bold—followers! Nothing is known of the **John** and **Alexander** mentioned here.

4:7-10. When **Peter and John** were **brought before** the Sanhedrin, and were asked the basis of their authority, **Peter,** the spokesman, was **filled with the Holy Spirit** (cf. 2:4). This is Peter's fourth speech already in the Book of Acts! Speaking with irony, he said, in effect, "Are we on trial for doing a good deed **to a cripple?**" The miracle was done not in their power, but **by the name of Jesus Christ** (cf. 3:16; 4:7, 12, 17-18). Though they had **crucified** Jesus, **God** had **raised** Him **from the dead** (cf. 2:23-24; 3:15).

4:11. The One who healed the cripple was **the Stone** which the **builders rejected.** Here Peter quoted Psalm 118:22. The background of this verse is disputed. The rejected stone (Ps. 118) may be (a) an actual building stone, (b) the nation of Israel, or (c) David. Or it may also be a proverb with no specific application. Most probably, to David the rejected stone in Psalm 118:22 meant Israel, a nation spurned by other nations. At any rate, the verse finds its ultimate fulfillment in Christ Jesus who is the "ideal" Israel (cf. Isa. 5:1-7; Matt. 2:15; 21:42; Mark 12:10; Luke 20:17; 1 Peter 2:7). The rejected Stone (Christ rejected by the nation in their crucifying Him) is **the Capstone,** the resurrected Lord.

4:12. The word **salvation** goes back to Psalm 118 which Peter had just quoted, for it is a prominent theme there. Verses 22-29 in that psalm anticipate millennial

deliverance. In Acts 4:12 Peter was speaking not only of individual justification, but also of national salvation, predicted in Psalm 118.

The rulers were thus put on the defense! They had rejected the only Savior of Israel and they were preventing the completion of God's building. Thus no other way of salvation is available to people (cf. John 14:6; 1 Tim. 2:5).

4:13-14. The authorities **were astonished** (cf. 3:10) that **Peter and John . . . unschooled** (agrammatoi, "illiterate") and **ordinary** (idiōtai) **men,** spoke with such **courage.** Courage (parrēsia, "boldness" or "courage to speak openly and frankly") is another theme prominent in Acts (2:29; 4:13, 29, 31; 28:31; cf. the verb "to speak boldly" in 9:27-28; 13:46; 14:3; 18:26; 19:8; 26:26). The Sanhedrin, realizing that Peter and John **had been with Jesus** (cf. John 7:15), were silenced. The apostles were thus experiencing what Christ had promised (Matt. 10:19-20; Luke 12:11-12; 21:12-15).

4:15-17. Significantly the authorities could not and did not **deny** the reality of the **miracle.** They deliberately refused to mention the word "Jesus"; they referred to Him as **this name** (cf. the high priest's same refusal in 5:28).

Perhaps Luke obtained this information about what went on behind the closed doors from someone such as Nicodemus or Paul. Even though Paul was not a Sadducee, he probably would have had access to such information.

The Sanhedrin, the supreme court and administrative body of the Jews, consisted of 71 members, including the high priest. Most of them were Sadducees. In Acts this was the first of four times some of Jesus' followers were brought before the Sanhedrin (cf. Peter and the apostles, 5:27; Stephen, 6:12; and Paul, 22:30).

4:18-22. When **Peter and John** were **commanded . . . not to speak or teach at all in the name of Jesus,** they rejoined that they must **obey** God **rather than** human authorities (cf. 5:29). They were simply being witnesses as Christ had commanded them (1:8). The authorities threatened them (apparently with punishment if they continued to preach Jesus) and released them. They were afraid to punish them then **because all the people were praising God** (cf. 3:9; 5:26).

c. The supplication (4:23-31)

Three movements may be discerned in this prayer of the early church: (1) God is sovereign (v. 24). (2) God's plan includes believers' facing opposition against the Messiah (vv. 25-28). (3) Because of these things they petitioned God to grant them boldness to preach (vv. 29-30).

4:23-24. Interestingly the believers (Peter and John's **own people**), faced with persecution, acknowledged God's **sovereign** creative power.

4:25-27. The words **by the Holy Spirit through the mouth of . . . David** point up, as do many passages, the divine inspiration of Scripture through human agents (cf. 28:25). Acts 4:25-26 contains a quotation from Psalm 2:1-2, which is prophetic of the Tribulation. In a *preliminary* sense Peter saw the opposition to the Messiah, God's **Anointed One** (*tou Christou*; cf. "anointed," Acts 4:27)—predicted by David in Psalm 2—as fulfilled in the early church. The parallels are obvious.

Nations (*ethnē*, Acts 4:25) compare with **Gentiles** (*ethnesin*, v. 27); **peoples** (*laoi*, v. 25) compare with **people of Israel** (*laois Israēl*, v. 27); **kings** (v. 26) compare with **Herod** (v. 27); and **rulers** (v. 26) compare with **Pontius Pilate** (v. 27).

4:28-30. Just as God's sovereign **power and will had decided beforehand** that Christ should be opposed, so now Peter and John prayed for God's power to be manifested in **great boldness** for the apostolic church. They also petitioned the Lord for supernatural ability **to heal** and to **perform miraculous signs** (*sēmeia*; cf. 2:43) **and wonders** (*terata*; cf. 2:43) **through the name of . . . Jesus.**

4:31. The Lord's answer to the believers' prayer for boldness was preceded by a shaking of their **meeting** place. The answer also included a supernatural filling **with the Holy Spirit** (cf. v. 8). When Luke, as here, used a verb form to refer to believers being filled with the Spirit, he usually said the filling was bestowed sovereignly by **God.** This is in distinction to the imperative in Ephesians 5:18 which states that Christians are responsible for being Spirit-filled.

2. CORRECTION IN THE CHURCH (4:32–5:11)

a. The division of goods (4:32-37)

Luke had two reasons for including this passage here. For one thing he used it to introduce Barnabas to his readers. A common technique of Luke was to introduce a character quickly in a minor role and then later bring him on stage in a major role. This he did with Barnabas.

Luke's second purpose in these verses was to show how Barnabas and the rest of the church contrasted with Ananias and Sapphira (chap. 5). The generosity of the church and especially Barnabas differed markedly from the selfishness of that husband-wife team.

4:32-35. **The believers were** unified not only spiritually (**one in heart and mind**) but also materially (cf. 2:44-45 and comments there). Their selling of their goods was voluntary and the distribution was according to **need.** The Lord answered their prayer for boldness (4:29) for **the apostles** kept on testifying of Christ's **resurrection. Grace** (v. 33) is one of numerous times that word occurs in Acts (e.g., 6:8; 11:23; 13:43; 14:3, 26; 15:11, 40; 18:27; 20:24, 32; etc.).

4:36-37. Joseph was nicknamed **Barnabas which means Son of Encouragement,** evidently because of his character and ability to encourge those who were downhearted.

How could **a Levite** own property as Barnabas did? Were not Levites prohibited from owning property? (Num. 18:20, 24) The answer may be that whereas the Levites were not to hold land in Israel, they could own land elsewhere. Apparently Barnabas, being **from** the island of **Cyprus,** owned land there. It is also possible that his wife owned land in Israel and that they together sold it. Most probably the restriction in Numbers 18:20, 24 was no longer observed, as seen in the case of Jeremiah (cf. Jer. 1:1; 32:6-15).

b. The deceit of Ananias and Sapphira (5:1-11)

This story is reminiscent of Achan in Joshua 7 (cf. Num. 15:32-36; 16:1-35).

5:1-2. The sin of **Ananias** and **his wife Sapphira** is explained in verses 3-4, 9. They could have retained the proceeds from their sale **of property,** of course, but in collusion with each other they had lied, saying they had given all the money when actually they had given only a **part of the money.**

The phrase **the apostles' feet** is the same as in 4:35, 37 and throws Ananias' action into bold contrast with Barnabas' action.

5:3. In response **Peter** accused **Ananias** by saying, **Satan has . . . filled your heart.** The verb translated "filled" is *eplērōsen*, from *plēroō*, which here has the idea of control or influence. The same verb is used in the command, "Be filled with the Spirit" (Eph. 5:18). Ananias, a believer, was influenced by Satan, not the Spirit! The fact that Peter asked, **How is it. . .?** implies that Satan had gained control because Ananias had not dealt with some previous sin in his life.

5:4. Peter referred to Ananias' lying "to the Holy Spirit" (v. 3); now Peter referred to his lying **to God.** This is an affirmation of the Holy Spirit's deity.

The fact that believers had the right to keep their money shows that this was not Christian socialism. It was a free-will arrangement for the support of the church, used only temporarily because evidently the early church expected Christ to come in their generation.

5:5-6. When Ananias heard this, he fell down and died. As Peter wrote later, judgment begins "with the family of God" (1 Peter 4:17). This is a case of "sin that leads to death" (1 John 5:16). This discipline was severe because it was an example, as Achan was an example to Israel (cf. 1 Cor. 10:6).

5:7-10. Then Sapphira, not aware of her husband's sudden death, also lied about the amount they **got for the land.**

Peter accused Sapphira of agreeing with Ananias **to test the Spirit of the Lord.** "To test the Holy Spirit" is to see how much one can get away with before He judges; it means to presume on Him, to see if He will perform His Word, or to stretch Him to the limits of judgment (cf. Deut. 6:16; Matt. 4:7).

5:11. As a result of the discipline of this couple, **all** the believers and unbelievers **who heard about** it felt **great fear,** a consequence already stated in verse 5 and repeated here for emphasis (cf. 19:17).

The purpose of this account in the narrative is manifold: (1) It revealed God's displeasure with sin, particularly dishonesty, in His body, the church. (2) It marked the church off as distinct from Israel, for such discipline was not seen in Israel. The word **church** (used here for the first time in Acts) refers to the universal church here and in 9:31 and 20:28, and to local congregations in 11:26 and 13:1. (3) It indicated God was at work in this new group.

3. PROGRESSION IN THE CHURCH (5:12-42)

a. *The authentication of the apostles (5:12-16)*

This paragraph prepares readers for what follows. Such activity could hardly go unnoticed!

5:12. Once again **the apostles** were used by God to perform **many miraculous signs and wonders** (cf. comments on 2:43). Interestingly the regular meeting place of the early Jerusalem church was in the temple at **Solomon's Colonnade,** where people gathered after they had heard of the lame man's healing (3:11).

5:13. This verse probably means that no hypocrite or unbeliever **dared joined them.** The case of Ananias and Sapphira frightened them too much!

The words **no one else** are literally, "none of the rest" (*tōn loipōn oudeis*). The words "the rest" are used of the lost (trans. "others" in Luke 8:10; cf. Rom. 11:7; Eph. 2:3; 1 Thes. 4:13; 5:6).

5:14. In spite of the reluctance of the unsaved to join the group of believers, **more and more men and women believed in the Lord and were added to their number.** Rapid numerical growth was a phenomenon of the early church (cf. 2:41, 47; 4:4; 6:1, 7; 9:31).

5:15-16. Miraculous signs (cf. v. 12) confirmed the Word of God in the midst of the young church. This shows God's sovereign sanction of the church, following His discipline of it. Many **people** revealed not only their confidence in the apostles to heal, but also their superstition. They thought it was **Peter's shadow** itself which fell **on the sick** that would heal **them.**

The apostles' divinely given power to heal and to exorcise demons accords with the Lord's promise to them (Matt. 10:8; Mark 16:17-18).

b. The second detention and release of the apostles (5:17-20)

5:17-20. After this second apprehension and incarceration of **the apostles**—apparently all 12 of them—God supernaturally released them and commanded them by means of **an angel** to continue the public proclamation (**in the temple courts,** near the church's gathering place; cf. v. 12) of **the full message of this new life** (lit., "all the words of this life," an unusual way to refer to the gospel). In Acts this is the first of three miraculous jail miracles (cf. Peter, 12:6-10; Paul and Silas, 16:26-27).

c. The examination and defense of the apostles (5:21-32)

5:21a. The obedience of the apostles to the angel's directive (v. 20) is evident. Though their sleep was abbreviated the preceding night, **at daybreak they entered the temple courts** (cf. v. 20).

5:21b-25. The facts recorded in these verses are filled with irony: (1) **The guards** were carefully keeping empty **jail** cells secured (vv. 21b-23). (2) The highest powers **of Israel** were gathered to judge prisoners they did not have. (3) While the frenzied leaders were deliberating as to what had happened to **the men** who had been in their custody, they were told the apostles were preaching in the **courts** of the **temple. The captain of the temple guard and the chief priests** (cf. 4:1) **were puzzled** (*diēporoun*, lit., "were perplexed," or "were at a loss") as to how to explain the **locked** but empty cells. Perhaps they also wondered **what would come of** them for losing their prisoners! (Cf. 16:27-28.)

5:26-27. The **captain** and the jail officers carefully recaptured **the apostles** (without using **force,** for fear of arousing the anger of the populace) and **brought the apostles . . . before the Sanhedrin** for questioning. (On the Sanhedrin, see comments on 4:15; cf. 6:12; 22:30.)

5:28. Use of the pronoun **this** twice underscores the high priest's reluctance to pronounce the name of Jesus (cf. "this name," 4:17). Obviously his hatred of Christ Jesus was great!

5:29. Here **Peter** reiterated a basic principle already affirmed in 4:19-20. The converse is also true: Christians are to **obey** their governments unless it is a sin to do so (cf. Rom. 13:1-7; 1 Peter 2:13-17).

5:30-31. This response by Peter and the apostles about Jesus' resurrection must have infuriated the Sadducees (cf. 4:1-2; 5:17; 23:8). Yet it was the same message Peter, once again the apostles' spokesman, had preached before: (a) they had **killed** Jesus, but **God . . . raised** Him **from the dead** (cf. 2:23-24, 36; 3:15; 4:10); (b) they could have **forgiveness of sins** (cf. 2:38; 10:43; 13:38; 26:18) by turning to Him in **repentance** (cf. 2:38; 3:16; 4:12; 8:22).

5:32. The apostles were well aware of their responsibility for they asserted, **We are witnesses of these things** (*rhēmatōn,* "words, sayings," or "things"). Furthermore, **the Holy Spirit** was corroborating their testimony by supernaturally enabling them to preach with boldness and to perform miracles. This same Spirit is **given to** all who believe in Christ (Rom. 8:9).

d. The liberation of the apostles (5:33-42)

5:33. The fury of the leaders toward the apostles could have been expected. The leaders **wanted to put them to death.** Their opposition followed the same pattern as their hostility to the Lord a few weeks earlier. Characteristically opposition grows, and so it did here.

5:34-35. The venerated **Gamaliel,** a **Pharisee** and **teacher,** influenced **the Sanhedrin** not to oppose the apostles. He spoke not from sympathy for the church, but from insight into God's sovereign working on earth (cf. v. 39).

5:36. Nothing is known of this **Theudas** with his **400** insurrectionists, whose cause came to naught. Though Josephus, a Jewish historian of the first century, described a rebellion led by a Theudas, that insurrection was later and much larger. Furthermore, that rebellion *followed* the one led by the Judas described in verse 37.

5:37. The insurrection led by **Judas the Galilean** was Gamaliel's second illustration. Josephus gave a rather full account of this movement which led to the execution of Judas, but also spawned further rebellion.

5:38-39. Here is the conclusion and main thrust of Gamaliel's speech. Seeing what would come of this movement would tell them if it were **of human origin** or **from God.** Interestingly this speech was, in one sense, an apologetic for the church of Jesus Christ given by a representative of the church's enemies: to try to stop God's work would be like fighting against God!

5:40. Not considering it adequate simply to admonish **the apostles,** the council **had them flogged** and **ordered them not to speak in the name of Jesus** (on Jesus' "name" see comments on 3:16). The flogging was evidently punishment for the apostles' disobedience to their earlier prohibition (cf. 4:18, 21; 5:28).

5:41-42. In spite of the bloody beating, **the apostles left the Sanhedrin, rejoicing.** Here again the theme of joy is evident in the Book of Acts (cf. comments on 2:46-47). A victorious church rejoices in God's working in spite of persecution—and even on account of it, as here. The apostles were honored to be **suffering disgrace for the name** (on "the name" see 3:16; cf. 1 Peter 4:14, 16). Later, Peter encouraged Christians to "rejoice" when they would "participate" in sufferings on behalf of Christ (1 Peter 4:13; cf. 1 Peter 2:18-21; 3:8-17).

Luke's object in writing Acts 5:17-42 was to show how Israel as a nation was continuing down its tragic path of rejecting Jesus as its Messiah.

4. ADMINISTRATION IN THE CHURCH (6:1-7)

6:1. The Grecian Jews could not speak Aramaic, the native tongue of Jews living in Israel. They probably were reared outside the land and were bilingual, speaking both Greek and their native tongues (cf. 2:5-11). Probably Gentile proselytes to Judaism who later became Christians were also in this group. The native Jews were also bilingual in that they spoke Aramaic and Greek (cf. 21:40). In the Jewish world tensions existed between the Grecian Jews and **the Aramaic-speaking** Jews; tragically these strains were brought into the church.

6:2. The **tables** (*trapezais*) may refer to tables used for serving food or to money tables, that is, banks. Probably it was used here to refer to the place where funds and supplies were administered for the widows.

The Twelve recognized their proper priorities in **the ministry of the Word of God** and prayer (cf. v. 4).

6:3-4. The apostles mentioned three qualifications for those who would be enlisted to serve: they must (a) **be full of the Spirit and** (b) be full of **wisdom** (cf. v. 10). In addition they were to (c) be **known** for these things, that is, the previous two qualifications were to be their reputations. All three were necessary for the handling of finances. (Faith, v. 5, is not another qualification, for belief is simply the means of being filled with the Holy Spirit.)

Selecting **seven men** may go back to the tradition in Jewish communities where seven respected men managed the public business in an official council.

By choosing these seven, the Twelve could **give** their **attention to prayer and the ministry of the Word** (cf. v. 2).

6:5. The suggestion of the Twelve **pleased the whole group** of the disciples. Significantly all seven men had Greek names, implying they were Hellenists. **Nicolas,** the last one named, was not even a Jew but was **a convert to Judaism** and then to Christianity. The early church evidently felt the problem of the unintentional neglect of Grecian Jewish widows would be best solved by the Hellenistic Jews; certainly they would not neglect the Aramaic-speaking widows.

The introduction of these seven (cf. 21:8) prepares readers for the ministries of **Stephen** and **Philip,** the first two men listed. Furthermore, the reference to Grecian Jews looks ahead to the wider spread of the gospel outside the circle of Jerusalem and Judea. (Nothing else is known about the other four: **Procorus, Nicanor, Timon, Parmenas.**)

6:6. Though the Christian community selected the Seven, they were commissioned by **the apostles.** This was done by prayer and the laying on of **hands.** The practice of laying hands on others was a gesture signifying commissioning and granting of authority (cf. 8:17-19; 13:3; 19:6; 1 Tim. 4:14; 5:22; Heb. 6:2).

Were these the first deacons? Which church office is in view here? Three answers are given to these questions.

(1) Some say these were the first deacons. Several factors are used to support this viewpoint. First, the office of deacon is assumed in Paul's letters (cf. Phil. 1:1). If Acts 6:1-6 is not an account

of their beginning, it is argued, when and where did deacons originate? Second, several words related to deacon (*diakonos*) are found here: "distribution" (lit., "service") in verse 1 is *diakonia*, and "to wait" in verse 2 is *diakonein*. However, these men were never called "deacons" (*diakonoi*) as such. Much later they were called "the Seven" (21:8). Furthermore, the words "distribution" and "wait" do not seem to have a technical sense here. These words in the Greek New Testament are commonly used in a nonspecialized sense.

(2) Others hold that these were precursors to the office of elder. This is not a common interpretation, but it gains its support from 11:30, which refers to relief money being given to the elders. If deacons handled these funds earlier (chap. 6), it is argued, they must have later become the elders (chap. 11). However, the office of elder has its origin in the Jewish synagogue.

(3) A third view is that these seven men held a temporary position for the purpose of meeting a specific need. This seems to be the best approach for a couple of reasons. First, these men were chosen for a particular task, not an overall one. Second, they were in a temporary responsibility because of the communal nature of the church at Jerusalem. Even so, these men do illustrate the role and function of the office of deacons.

6:7. This verse contains another of Luke's progress reports. The church was rapidly growing in numbers (cf. 2:41, 47; 4:4; 5:14; 6:1; 9:31), with even many Jewish **priests** becoming believers (**obedient to the faith;** cf. Rom. 1:5). With the appointment of these men, readers are prepared for the work of Stephen and Philip and the proclamation of the gospel outside Jerusalem.

II. The Witness in All Judea and Samaria (6:8–9:31)

A. The martyrdom of Stephen (6:8–8:1a)

1. THE ARREST OF STEPHEN (6:8–7:1)

Stephen's ministry, arrest, and trial are strikingly similar to the Lord's.

6:8. Like Christ and the apostles, **Stephen** was **full of God's grace and power** (cf. 4:33; Luke 2:40, 52). Interest-ingly Stephen was "full of" or controlled by five factors: the Spirit, wisdom, faith, grace, power (Acts 6:3, 5, 8). What an outstanding leader! Furthermore, he **did great wonders and miraculous signs** (cf. 2:22; Luke 24:19; also cf. Acts 2:43). These evidences of God's grace were in addition to his responsibilities in the daily ministration to the widows.

6:9-11. The Synagogue of the Freedmen was perhaps comprised of those who themselves or whose forebears had been set free from being prisoners of war or from slavery. Precisely who they were is not known for sure.

The members of this synagogue were from three divergent areas—North Africa (**Cyrene and Alexandria** were two of its leading cities), **Asia** (the western portion of modern-day Turkey), and **Cilicia.** Possibly this was the assembly Paul attended because Tarsus was located in the province of Cilicia.

Besides being one of the Seven and a wonder-worker, Stephen was also a skilled debater. His opponents **could not stand up against his wisdom or the Spirit by which he spoke** (cf. "full of the Spirit and wisdom" in v. 3 and "full of . . . the Holy Spirit" in v. 5 and 7:55).

To remove Stephen, the men of the synagogue covertly induced men to make an accusation against him. Like those who complained against the Lord Jesus, they charged **Stephen** with **blasphemy** (cf. Matt. 26:65).

6:12-14. These words were sufficient to arouse the laity and leaders to apprehend **Stephen** and accuse **him before the Sanhedrin.** This is the third of four times in Acts when the Lord's followers stood before this Jewish court; the others were Peter and John (4:15), Peter and the apostles (5:27), and Paul (22:30).

The **false witnesses** were not necessarily outright liars. Stephen had probably said the things they accused him of; however, they misrepresented the intentions and imports of his statements (cf. Matt. 26:61; Mark 14:58; John 2:19). The Lord Himself predicted the destruction of the temple (Matt. 24:1-2; Mark 13:1-2; Luke 21:5-6), though He never said *He* would do it. The other half of the allegation against Stephen involved the temporary nature of the Mosaic system. Undoubtedly he saw the theological implications of justification by faith and the fulfillment of the Law in Christ. Furthermore, if the gospel was for the whole world (Acts 1:8), the Law had to be a temporary arrangement.

6:15. All . . . the Sanhedrin—all 71 of them—**looked intently at Stephen** to see his response. **They saw that his face was like** that **of an angel.** Evidently his face glowed with glory (cf. Moses' face, Ex. 34:29, 35).

7:1. The high priest mentioned here possibly is Caiaphas, the same one who presided over the trials of the Lord (Matt. 26:57; Mark 14:54; Luke 22:53; John 18:13, 24; cf. comments on Acts 4:5-6).

2. THE ADDRESS OF STEPHEN (7:2-53)

7:2-53. This is the longest recorded message in Acts, which shows the importance Luke attached to it. Stephen, a Grecian Jew, by his life and words prepared the way for the gospel to reach outside the pale of Judaism.

But what did Stephen say in this powerful discourse that resulted in his death? Though he touched on the accusations made against him, Stephen did not give a legal defense of himself. Rather, he set forth Israel's past history and God's past workings in order to vindicate Christianity.

In this discourse three ideas run like cords through its fabric:

1. *There is progress and change in God's program.* God was creative and innovative in His dealings with humans and particularly with Israel. Stephen developed this thought in five points: (a) The promise to **Abraham** (vv. 2-8). From working with the entire human race, the Lord sovereignly called Abraham, father of the Jews, from **Mesopotamia** to the land of promise, and gave him 12 great-grandsons who became the progenitors of Israel's 12 tribes. (b) The sojourn of **Joseph** (vv. 9-16). This move to **Egypt** was the fulfillment of God's prediction recorded in verses 6-7. It too was a radical change for Jacob's descendants. (c) The deliverance under **Moses** (vv. 17-43). A major portion of Stephen's discourse pertained to **Moses** and the Exodus, another important aspect of Israel's history. (d) The building of **the tabernacle** (vv. 44-46). Constructing the tabernacle so that it was portable implied it was

temporary. (It was called **the tabernacle of Testimony** because it testified to God's presence among them.) (e) The construction of the temple (vv. 47-50). Even the temple was to be a symbol of God's presence and not the very home of God.

In God's workings with the nation from Abraham to Solomon there was innovation and change. The point is clear: If God changed so many things in Israel's history, who is to say that the Law and the temple were permanent?

2. *The blessings of God are not limited to the land of Israel and the temple area.* Some of Israel's greatest favors were bestowed apart from the temple and the land.

Stephen gave four examples: (a) Israel's patriarchs and leaders were blessed *outside* the land. **Abraham** was called in Mesopotamia and given promises **before he lived in Haran** (vv. 2-5). In **Egypt . . . Joseph** found favor with **Pharaoh** because **God was with him** (vv. 9-10). **Moses** was commissioned by God in **Midian** (vv. 29-34). To substantiate the fact that God blessed Moses while he was in Midian, Stephen carefully recounted that **two sons** were born to Moses there. (b) The Law itself was given outside the land: Moses **was in the congregation in the desert** (v. 38). (c) The tabernacle was built in the desert. The tabernacle was **with them in the desert** (v. 44). In fact the Jews **brought it with them when they took the land** (v. 45). (d) Even the temple, though in the land, was not to be limited in its theology. How could the temple be God's dwelling place when the Scripture declares, **Heaven is My throne, and the earth is My footstool?** (v. 49; Isa. 66:1)

3. *Israel in its past always evidenced a pattern of opposition to God's plans and His men.* This is the main point of Stephen's discourse, as its climax affirms (Acts 7:51-53). **You are just like your fathers: You always resist the Holy Spirit!** This theme is seen throughout the message, but there are some definite specifics. (a) Instead of going directly from Mesopotamia to the Promised Land, **Abraham** tarried **in Haran** (vv. 2-4). (b) **Joseph** was **sold** by his brothers into slavery in **Egypt** (v. 9). (c) **Moses** was rejected by the Israelites (vv. 23-29). It is highly significant that both Joseph and Moses were not accepted until their *second* appearances

(vv. 13, 35-36). The parallel with Christ could not have escaped Stephen's hearers. (d) Israel rejected true worship by turning to idols (vv. 39-43). Her blatant unbelief was seen in idolatry, a sin which the Jews of the Apostolic Age particularly abhorred. As a result God judged the nation by sending her **into Exile** in **Babylon** (v. 43). (e) The people of Israel missed the point of the temple (vv. 48-50). The strong and clear assertion of Stephen (v. 48) implies that the Jews believed the temple was God's dwelling place on earth, the Jewish counterpart to Mount Olympia. Indeed the temple was to be a place of worship and prayer; but it was not God's home (cf. 1 Kings 8:23-53).

Stephen's three main points in this discourse fit together. Since there is progression in God's program and since His blessings are not limited to the temple, Israel had better be careful not to "resist" (Acts 7:51) His workings as they had in the past. They would withstand God's purpose by refusing to see His work in the church and His blessing outside the borders of Israel. This defense related specifically to the accusation made against Stephen in 6:11-14.

A chronological problem exists in 7:6, where Stephen said Israel would be **enslaved and mistreated 400 years.** For in Galatians 3:17 Paul implied that the period of time from the Abrahamic promise in Genesis 15:13-16 to Mount Sinai was 430 years. The difference between the 400 and 430 years can easily be accounted for by understanding that Stephen used round numbers. Another explanation is that the 400 years was the actual time of bondage whereas the 430 years described the time from the confirming of the covenant in Genesis 35:9-15 to the Exodus, which occurred in 1446 B.C. The main problem, however, is the time Israel spent in bondage in Egypt. If Galatians 3:17 means it was 430 years from the promise given to Abraham (Gen. 15) to the Exodus, the time in Egypt would then be 215 years. However, if Acts 7:6 is taken at face value the bondage was 400 years. Perhaps the best solution is to say Paul was looking at *periods* of time. The promises were given to Abraham, Isaac, and Jacob. These three patriarchs were all recipients of God's promise. The promise was reconfirmed in Genesis 46:1-4 to Jacob at Beersheba as he was on his way to Egypt. From that point (the end of God's giving promises to the patriarchs) to the Exodus was 400 years. (Cf. Harold W. Hoehner, "The Duration of the Egyptian Bondage," *Bibliotheca Sacra* 126. October–December 1969:306-16.)

Another apparent discrepancy in Stephen's discourse is in Acts 7:14. Stephen stated that **75** persons were in Jacob's **family,** but the Hebrew text has "70" in both Genesis 46:27 and Exodus 1:5. In both places the Septuagint has 75. It is commonly said that Stephen, a Greek-speaking Jew, would have used the Septuagint and therefore was making only an "honest" mistake. This difficulty, however, can be resolved in other ways. One of the most widely accepted solutions is to recognize that the Hebrew text includes Jacob, Joseph, and Joseph's two sons, Ephraim and Manasseh (a total of 70), but that the Septuagint omits Jacob and Joseph but includes Joseph's seven grandchildren (mentioned in 1 Chron. 7:14-15, 20-25). This is supported by the Hebrew in Genesis 46:8-26 which enumerates 66 names, omitting Jacob, Joseph, and Joseph's two sons. Another solution is that the Septuagint's 75 includes the 66 plus the 9 wives of Jacob's 12 sons (Judah's and Simeon's wives had died and Joseph's wife was in Egypt).

Acts 7:16 contains another apparent discrepancy. Stephen's words imply that **Jacob** was buried **at Shechem** whereas the Old Testament clearly affirms that he and his wife Leah (and his parents Isaac and Rebekah and his grandparents Abraham and Sarah) were interred in the Cave of Machpelah at Hebron (Gen. 49:29–50:13). However, the bodies buried at Shechem did not include Jacob but did include those of Joseph and his brothers. Joseph was buried first in Egypt but was reburied in Shechem (Gen. 50:26; Ex. 13:19; Josh. 24:32). True, Joshua 24:32 refers only to Joseph's bones, but evidently his brothers were also buried at Shechem (though Josephus states otherwise). The pronoun **their** (Acts 7:16), then, does not include Abraham, Isaac, and Jacob, but looks back to the words **our fathers** in verse 15 and refers to Joseph and his brothers.

Stephen's phrase, **the tomb that Abraham had bought from the sons of**

Hamor at Shechem (v. 16), presents another problem. Actually Jacob, not Abraham, bought the plot of ground (Gen. 33:19). This may be explained by saying that Abraham in a sense did purchase the property in the person of his grandson. Abraham would be given title to Shechem through Jacob.

This favorable allusion to Shechem, the "capital" of the Samaritans, would not please Stephen's audience. But his reference to Samaria prepares readers for the next step in the outreach of the gospel (Acts 8).

3. THE ATTACK ON STEPHEN (7:54–8:1A)

7:54-56. The response of the religious authorities to Stephen's message was easily predictable: **They were furious** (cf. 5:33) **and gnashed their teeth at him.** Instead of being intimidated, **Stephen, full of the Holy Spirit** (cf. 6:3, 5, 10), **saw the glory of God, and Jesus standing at the right hand of God.** The Lord Jesus normally is seated at the Father's right hand (Ps. 110:1; Rom. 8:34; Col. 3:1; Heb. 1:3, 13; 8:1; 10:12; 12:2; 1 Peter 3:22). The standing position may imply that the Lord Christ was standing to welcome Stephen.

Acts 7:56 is a climactic verse in this chapter for several reasons. First, it repeats the claim Christ made at His trial before the high priest (Mark 14:62). Just as His claim resulted in His being accused of blasphemy, so also these words brought a violent response toward Stephen. Second, the term **Son of Man** is filled with significance. This is the last time it is used in the New Testament and it is the only time in the Gospels and Acts when it is not spoken by the Lord Jesus. This expression, Son of Man, shows that Jesus is the Messiah for it comes from Daniel 7:13-14. It is definitely eschatological. (See additional comments on "the Son of Man" at Mark 8:31.) Third, Acts 7:56 combines two great messianic passages—Daniel 7:13-14 and Psalm 110:1. Daniel 7:13-14 emphasizes the universal aspect of the Lord's rule. He is not simply a Jewish ruler; He is Savior of the world. Psalm 110:1 presents the Messiah as being at God's **right hand.** Besides stressing power and position, this also shows acceptance. Christ is therefore the Mediator (cf. 1 Tim. 2:5), thus proving

that people have access to God by means other than the temple and its priests.

7:57-58. The response of the Sanhedrin was immediate and violent. They quickly saw the theological implications of Stephen's doctrine—Israel was guilty; the Law was temporary; the temple must be done away—so they **dragged him out of the city and began to stone him.** Blasphemy was to be punished by death (Lev. 24:16). The Jews' martyring Stephen is ironic because their forefathers, having worshiped "Moloch" (Acts 7:43), should have been put to death, according to Moses (Lev. 20:2).

A young theologue **named Saul** agreed that Stephen should be stoned. **The witnesses laid their clothes at** his **feet.** This meant Saul was giving his approval by guarding their clothes (Acts 8:1; 22:20).

7:59-60. In words reminiscent of the Lord's, **Stephen** committed his **spirit** to the **Lord** and **prayed** for his enemies (cf. Luke 23:34, 46). Luke recorded the fact of his death by simply writing, **he fell asleep.** For a Christian, his body (not his soul) sleeps in death (cf. John 11:11; 1 Thes. 4:13, 15).

8:1a. The words **giving approval** (*syneudokōn*) indicate active approval, not just passive consent (cf. Rom. 1:32). This gives fuller meaning to Saul's deed in Acts 7:58.

B. The ministry of Philip (8:1b-40)

1. IN SAMARIA (8:1B-25)

a. The persecution of the church (8:1b-3)

Chapter 8 is closely linked with chapters 6 and 7. The *subject* of persecution begun in 6 is continued in 8. Furthermore, the *personality* of Saul, introduced in 7, is also found in 8. There is a close connection between Philip (chap. 8) and Stephen (chaps. 6–7) because both belonged to the Seven (6:5). Even the order of their two names in 6:5 is followed in the sequence of the narrative in 6:8–8:40.

8:1b. On that day indicates that the **persecution** of **the church** was signaled by Stephen's martyrdom. It implies that Jewish leaders approved of Stephen's execution. Israel was in the process of confirming its tragic choice to reject Jesus as her Messiah.

371

The fact that **all the Jerusalem** believers **except the apostles were scattered throughout Judea and Samaria** was God's method of fulfilling the mandate of 1:8. The word "scattered" (*diesparēsan*), also used in 8:4, comes from the verb *speirō*, used to refer to sowing seed (Matt. 6:26; 13:3-4, 18; 25:24, 26; Luke 8:5; 12:24; etc.) This statement also prepares the way for the ministry of Philip in Samaria (Acts 8:4-25).

Though Luke refers to "all," he could not have included everyone, for the church continued on in Jerusalem. From the context it may be concluded that the primary objects of persecution were the Greek-speaking Jews. They would have been easily identifiable and would have been associated with Stephen.

Why the apostles did not leave the city is not stated. Perhaps their sense of obligation to the church in Jerusalem kept them there. The Jerusalem church undoubtedly became more Jewish with the evacuation of people who would be more sympathetic with Stephen. At the same time this persecution deepened the cleavage between the church and Judaism.

8:2-3. These verses contrast sharply with each other. **Godly men buried Stephen and mourned deeply for him.** On the other hand **Saul began to destroy the church.** The word for "destroy" (*elymaineto*, used only here in the NT) appears in the Septuagint in Psalm 79:13 (80:13 in Eng. texts) about wild boars that destroy (NIV, "ravage") a vineyard. Saul's zeal was so great against Christians that it was as if he were wildly raging against them (cf. Acts 9:1, 13). In violence **he dragged off men and women** (cf. 9:29; 22:4-5) and beat them (22:19; 26:11). This caused havoc in Jerusalem (9:21). Saul's own later imprisonment as an apostle *for* Christ contrasted with his imprisoning these followers!

Stephen's martyrdom together with the ensuing persecution of the church confirmed Israel's unbelief and her obstinate refusal to accept Jesus as her Redeemer.

b. The proclamation of the message (8:4-8)

8:4. In the Greek this verse begins with "therefore on the other hand" (*men oun*, not trans. in the NIV). Because of persecution believers were **scattered** (cf. v. 1) and **the Word** of God spread (cf. Rom. 8:28; 2 Cor. 2:14; Phil. 1:12-14). This is another evidence of God's sovereign control; in spite of opposition the Word of God grew (cf. Acts 12:24; 19:20).

8:5. Philip, a Grecian Jew and therefore more broadminded than Aramaic-speaking Jews in Israel (cf. 6:1), went to the Samaritans. Samaria is north of Jerusalem, but Luke said Philip **went down** because **Samaria** is lower in elevation than Jerusalem. The significance of Philip's ministry in this unnamed city is seen when Matthew 10:5-6; Luke 9:52-54; and John 4:9 are compared with Acts 8:5.

8:6-7. Philip's proclamation of Christ was confirmed by **miraculous signs** (*sēmeia;* cf. v. 13) so that **they all paid close attention to what he said.** The miracles (casting out **evil spirits,** i.e., demons, and healing **paralytics and cripples** [cf. 3:1-10]) authenticated his message (cf. 2:43).

8:8. Once again the gospel resulted in **great joy** (cf. comments on 2:46-47).

c. The professions of faith (8:9-13)

8:9-10. Many traditions revolve around **Simon** the sorcerer. It is alleged: (a) that he was the founder of the Gnostic heresies, (b) that he went to Rome and perverted Christian doctrine there, and (c) that he became involved in a miracle contest with Peter and lost. At any rate, this Simon of Samaria did practice **sorcery in the city and amazed all the people of Samaria.** Because of his "sorcery," the ability to exercise control over nature and/or people by means of demonic power, **people** called him the **Great Power.** They may or may not have thought of him as possessing deity. At any rate Simon **boasted that he was someone great,** and the people of Samaria believed him. Furthermore, he accepted their adulation.

8:11-12. Simon's **magic** means his sorcery, his demonic powers (the Gr. words for "practiced sorcery" and "magic" are related). When **Philip** came to Samaria, **he preached the good news of the kingdom of God and the name** (cf. 3:16) **of Jesus Christ.** The term "the kingdom of God" refers to the coming kingdom (cf. 1:3, 6). "The name of Jesus

Christ" looks to His position as Messiah (cf. 8:5, "the Christ," lit., the Messiah). In other words, the message meant that some Samaritans would become heirs of the Millennium by faith in Jesus, the Messiah.

As an evidence of their faith the Samaritans **were baptized, both men and women** (cf. "men and women" in v. 3). The contrasts and comparisons between Simon and Philip are striking. Both performed miracles, Simon by demonic power and Philip by divine power. Simon boasted and welcomed acclaim to himself, but Philip proclaimed Christ. People were amazed at Simon's magic, but people were converted to Christ by Philip's ministry.

8:13. Amazingly **Simon himself believed and was baptized.** Now rather than people following Simon, **he followed Philip!** His response must have had a profound effect on his own followers.

Was Simon saved? Luke did not specify this clearly, so it is difficult to be dogmatic. But seven facts suggest that Simon probably was not born again: (1) The verb "believe" (*pisteuō*) does not always refer to saving faith. Simon's faith could have been like that of the demons in James 2:19, merely intellectual assent. (2) Furthermore, faith based on signs is not a trustworthy faith (cf. John 2:23-25; 4:48). (3) In addition, Luke never stated that Simon received the Holy Spirit (Acts 8:17-18). (4) Simon continued to have a self-centered interest in the display of miraculous power (vv. 18-19). (5) The verb "repent" (*metanoeō*) used in verse 22 is normally addressed to lost people. (6) The word "perish" (*eis apōleian*) employed in verse 20 is strong. It is related to the word "perish" in John 3:16. (7) The description of Simon in Acts 8:23 is a better description of a lost man than of one who is saved (cf. Deut. 29:18). Still one cannot be dogmatic on this point. The Lord knows those who are His (2 Tim. 2:19).

d. The proof of the work (8:14-17)

8:14-17. It was necessary for **the apostles in Jerusalem** to commission **Peter and John** to Samaria for several reasons. Normally **the Holy Spirit** baptizes, indwells, and seals at the moment of faith, but in this instance the delay served several purposes: (1) Peter and John's prayer (for bestowing of **the Holy Spirit**) and their laying **on** of **hands** (resulting in the coming of the Spirit) confirmed Philip's ministry among the Samaritans. This authenticated this new work to the Jerusalem apostles. (2) Also this confirmed Philip's ministry to the Samaritans. This message Philip had preached was validated by the coming of the Spirit, a mark of the coming kingdom (cf. v. 12; Jer. 31:31-34; Ezek. 36:23-27; Joel 2:28-32). (3) Perhaps the most important aspect of God's withholding the Spirit till apostolic representatives came from the Jerusalem church was to prevent schism. Because of the natural propensity of division between Jews and Samaritans it was essential for **Peter and John** to welcome the Samaritan believers officially into the church. The contrast between John's attitude here and in Luke 9:52-54 is significant.

e. The perversion of the truth (8:18-24)

8:18-19. The clause **Simon saw that the Spirit was given** implies there was some external manifestation to evidence the coming of **the Holy Spirit.** Possibly it was speaking in tongues, though the Scripture does not say so (cf. 2:4; 10:45-46; 19:6).

The term *simony,* which is the buying or selling of things considered religious or sacred such as an ecclesiastical office, comes from Simon's desire to purchase the **ability** to impart the Holy Spirit to others.

Luke's purpose in including this incident with Simon was to show the superiority of Christianity over the occult and demoniacs. Several times this kind of conflict took place in Acts, and Christ was always the Victor (13:6-12; 16:16-18; 19:13-20; 28:1-6).

8:20. Peter's response to Simon's request was one of outrage. **May your money perish with you!**

The reason for such strong language was Simon's failure to understand grace, the free nature of God's salvation and blessings. Peter explained his strong language by saying, **You thought you could buy the gift of God with money!**

8:21-22. The language of this verse, **You have no part or share in this**

ministry (*logō*, "word, matter"), implies Simon was not a Christian. (For similar terminology see Deut. 12:12; 14:27. Just as the Levites had no inheritance in the Promised Land, so also Simon had no portion in the matter of salvation.) The adverb **perhaps** does not mean **God** is reluctant to forgive sin. The question was whether Simon would **repent of** his heart's intention.

8:23-24. The allusion to **bitterness** (lit., "gall of bitterness," *cholēn pikrias*) seems to refer to Deuteronomy 29:18, which speaks of idolatry and bitter apostasy (cf. Heb. 12:15). **Simon** had been captivated by false doctrine and sin. Simon's response may have been genuine or simply an outcry of fear. At least he was apprehensive about the outcome of his tragic request (Acts 8:18-19).

f. The promotion of the work (8:25)

8:25. **Peter and John** were so convinced of God's working among the Samaritans that when they **returned to Jerusalem** they too shared **the gospel** with Samaritans, in fact, **in many Samaritan villages**. This was a remarkable thing for these Jewish apostles to do!

2. TO THE ETHIOPIAN EUNUCH (8:26-40)

a. The command (8:26)

8:26. Though Luke gave no record of God's commanding **Philip** to preach to the Samaritans (v. 5), God did sovereignly direct Philip toward Gaza (see the map at Acts 9). The highway is referred to as **the desert road**. The expression may refer to a desert road or a desert city. Ancient Gaza was destroyed in 93 B.C. and the city was rebuilt nearer the Mediterranean in 57 B.C. The old city was called Desert Gaza. The Greek for the angel's command could be translated, "Arise and **go to the south to the road . . . that goes down from Jerusalem to Gaza.** This is desert." This reference to the road in 8:36 may imply that the road, not the city, was in a deserted area.

b. The contact (8:27-30)

8:27. The **Ethiopian eunuch** is described rather fully as **an important official in charge of all the treasury of Candace, queen of the Ethiopians.** "Ethiopia" here refers not to modern-day Ethiopia but to ancient Nubia, the region

from Aswan in southern Egypt to Khartoum, Sudan. Candace was a title given to the queen-mother, as Pharaoh was used of the king of Egypt. Governmental power rested in the hands of Candace, for the royal son, worshiped as an offspring of the sun, was therefore above such mundane activities as ruling over a nation. Rulership was therefore vested with the queen-mother. The fact that **this** eunuch **had gone to Jerusalem to worship** is interesting. The Law prohibited eunuchs from entering the Lord's assembly (Deut. 23:1). However, Isaiah 56:3-5 predicts great blessing for eunuchs in the Millennial Age. Evidently this eunuch was a worshiper of Yahweh though not a full-fledged proselyte.

8:28-30. The eunuch's wealth is revealed in the simple description **sitting in his chariot**. As this finance officer was riding, he was **reading** from **the Book of Isaiah**. Since it was customary to read aloud, **Philip** could have easily **heard the** portion of Scripture the eunuch was **reading** (v. 30). Interestingly **Philip** was guided first by an angel (v. 26) and then by **the Holy Spirit** (v. 29).

c. The conversion (8:31-35)

8:31-35. The quotation from Isaiah 53:7-8 was perplexing to the eunuch. Welcoming the opportunity to have **Philip** explain the passage, **he invited** the apostle into his chariot. The Ethiopian knew the passage described an individual, but was it Isaiah **or someone else?** **Philip** seized the opportunity to present **the good news about Jesus** from Isaiah 53 (cf. John 5:39).

d. The consequences (8:36-40)

8:36-39. The first consequence of Philip's evangelization was the eunuch's conversion. His response, **Why shouldn't I be baptized?** indicates that **water** baptism was the seal of a personal decision to trust in Christ (cf. Matt. 28:19). The second result was joy, for **the eunuch . . . went on his way rejoicing.** A third result was a further outreach of the gospel to one who was neither Jew nor Samaritan, but a Gentile (African) worshiper of Yahweh who was not a full-fledged proselyte to Judaism. Possibly the eunuch was uncircumcised. (As indicated in the NIV marg., Acts 8:37 is included only in late Gr. mss. and therefore was probably not in the original ms.)

When the baptism was completed **the Spirit of the Lord suddenly took Philip away, and the eunuch did not see him again.** Whatever happened to the Ethiopian eunuch after that is unknown.

8:40. Philip, however, appeared at Azotus. This city is the same as Ashdod, an ancient Philistine capital. As he **traveled** to **Caesarea** he proclaimed **the gospel in all the towns** along the way (see Azotus and Caesarea on the map at chap. 9). Evidently Philip then settled in Caesarea for he was still there about 20 years later (cf. 21:8). Significantly an evangelist may be resident or itinerary; Philip carried on both types of ministries.

The area around Azotus and Caesarea was later visited by Peter (9:32-43). Even though Philip the evangelist resided in Caesarea, the Lord called Peter from Joppa to give the gospel to Cornelius in Caesarea (chaps. 10–11).

C. The message of Saul (9:1-31)

The conversion of Saul (Paul) is believed by some to be the most important event in the church since Pentecost. Luke certainly considered Saul's conversion significant for he recorded it three times in Acts (chaps. 9, 22, 26).

The record of Saul's conversion at this juncture prepares readers for the gospel going to Gentiles (chap. 10). The apostle to the Gentiles (Gal. 2:8; Eph. 3:8) was preceded in this ministry by Peter's evangelization of Cornelius and his household.

The account of Saul's Damascus Road experience may be recorded here also to relate it to Stephen's martyrdom. Stephen's discourse seemed to have spurred Saul to renewed efforts to stamp out Christianity (Acts 8:1-3). If the doctrine propagated by Stephen was correct, then the Law was in jeopardy. So Saul, zealous as he was, went on persecuting the church (cf. Gal. 1:13; Phil. 3:6).

But Saul the persecutor was about to become Paul the apostle of Jesus Christ! His background and qualifications suited him eminently for the work to which God had called him: (1) He knew the Jewish culture and language well (Acts 21:40; Phil. 3:5). (2) Because he was reared in Tarsus he was well acquainted with the

Greek culture and its philosophies (Acts 17:22-31; Titus 1:12). (3) He possessed all the privileges of a Roman citizen (Acts 16:37; 22:23-29; 25:10-12). (4) He was trained and skilled in Jewish theology (Gal. 1:14). (5) Because he was capable in a secular trade he was able to support himself (Acts 18:3; 1 Cor. 9:4-18; 2 Cor. 11:7-11; 1 Thes. 2:9; 2 Thes. 3:8). (6) God gave him zeal, leadership qualities, and theological insight.

1. THE CONVERSION OF SAUL (9:1-19A)

a. The conviction of Saul (9:1-9)

9:1a. The adverb **still** looks back to 8:3. While the gospel was reaching farther outside of Jerusalem, **Saul** was continuing his relentless persecution of the church.

9:1b-2. So great was Saul's hatred for the church that **he went to the high priest and asked him for letters to the synagogues in Damascus.** Damascus (see its location on the map) was not under the control of Judea, Galilee, or the Decapolis. What jurisdiction would the high priest have over synagogues in Damascus? This is usually answered by saying Rome recognized the right of extradition when the high priest in **Jerusalem** demanded it. But this can also be explained in another way. At that time Damascus may have been under the Nabatean king, Aretas IV (cf. 2 Cor. 11:32-33). In order to gain favor with the anti-Roman Jews, Aretas, who hated the Romans, would have conceded this favor to the high priest.

The mention of "synagogues in Damascus" indicates that Christianity was still closely associated with Judaism (in James 2:2 the word "meeting" renders the Gr. *synagōgēn*, "synagogue"). Mention of Damascus shows that Christianity had spread rapidly.

Strangely, Saul referred to Christianity as **the Way,** a term used only in Acts (19:9, 23; 22:4; 24:14, 22).

9:3-4. Saul both **heard** the **voice** of the Lord Jesus and saw Him (cf. 9:17, 27; 22:14; 26:16; 1 Cor. 9:1; 15:8). Though there is no explicit statement of Saul's seeing Christ, it is implicit in the reference to **a light from heaven.** It was fundamental to Saul's apostleship that he saw the resurrected Lord (cf. 1 Cor. 9:1).

The question, **Why do you persecute Me?** (cf. Acts 9:5) is filled with signif-

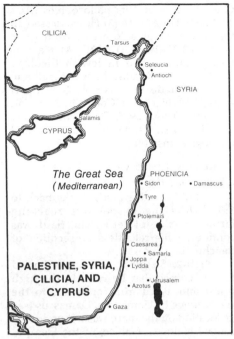

CILICIA

Tarsus

Seleucia

Antioch

SYRIA

Salamis

CYPRUS

The Great Sea
(Mediterranean)

PHOENICIA

• Sidon   • Damascus

• Tyre

• Ptolemais

• Caesarea

• Samaria

PALESTINE, SYRIA,
CILICIA, AND
CYPRUS

• Joppa
• Lydda

• Jerusalem

• Azotus

• Gaza

icance for it shows the union of Christ with His church. The Lord did not ask, "Why do you persecute My church?" The reference to "Me" gave Saul his first glimpse into the great doctrine of Christians being in Christ. This same truth was implied earlier by Luke when he wrote that the Lord continues His work on earth in the church (1:1). Also Ananias' lie to Peter was a lie to the Holy Spirit (5:3). Luke, with Paul, saw Christ and the church as the Head and its body.

9:5. Some interpret "Lord" in Saul's question, **Who are You, Lord?** (*kyrie*) as "Sir." It is possible for this noun to have this meaning, as it does in Matthew 13:27; 27:63; John 4:11; Acts 10:4; and elsewhere. However, there is too much that is supernatural in this passage to use the mere human vocative, "Sir." Even though **Saul** did not immediately recognize this One as Jesus, he must have acknowledged a supernatural being. Jesus then identified Himself to Saul: **I am Jesus** (cf. 9:17).

The words, "It is hard for thee to kick against the pricks" (kjv), are not in the better and earlier Greek manuscripts. But this statement *is* found in Acts 26:14.

9:6. The resurrected Lord commanded Saul, **Go into the city and you will be told what you must do.** This does

not mean that Ananias (v. 10) taught Saul the doctrine of justification, as some claim. Instead, Saul was told he must proclaim the gospel, which would involve suffering (vv. 15-16; 22:10, 15; 26:16-20). The Lord Himself gave Saul the truth of justification by faith on the Damascus Road; Acts 26:18 is clear on that point (cf. Gal. 1:11-12).

9:7. An apparent discrepancy stands between verse 7 and 22:9. In 9:7 Luke recorded that **the men** who traveled **with Saul . . . heard the sound** (*phōnēs*), but in 22:9 Luke wrote that "they did not understand the voice" (*phōnēn*). Literally, that clause in 22:9 may be translated, "They did not hear the sound." The NIV correctly translates the verse, because the verb "to hear" with the genitive case may mean "to hear a sound" and with the accusative case "to hear with understanding." The genitive case is employed in 9:7, and the accusative is used in 22:9. So the travelers with Saul heard the sound (9:7) but did not understand what Christ said (22:9).

9:8. If Saul's "thorn in the flesh" was eye trouble (cf. comments on 2 Cor. 12:7), this may have been the prelude of it. At any rate there is a sharp contrast between **Saul** in Acts 9:1 and 8. One moment he was storming up the road, determined to capture and imprison Christians. Soon thereafter he was **led** like a child **by the hand into Damascus.** God's grace is often displayed in great powerful acts and in apparent catastrophes.

9:9. The **three days** of blindness, fasting, and praying (v. 11) were a time of waiting. Saul still had not received the message God had promised him (v. 6).

b. The contrition of Saul (9:10-19a)

9:10-14. By means of **a vision** God instructed a reluctant **Ananias** to **restore** Saul's **sight.** He was to go to **Saul** where he was staying with a man named **Judas** whose **house** was **on Straight Street.** It was one of the two parallel streets that ran from the western to the eastern wall. The first reference to Saul's birthplace—**Tarsus**—is given in verse 11 (see the map; cf. comments on v. 30).

Interestingly believers were first called **saints** in the Book of Acts here (v. 13). The church is comprised of "set-apart ones" (*hagiois*; cf. "saints" in Rom.

1:1; Eph. 1:1; Phil. 1:1). From Acts 9:14 it is evident that the news of Saul's coming to persecute believers in Damascus had preceded his arrival, and **Ananias** feared what Saul might do.

9:15. The Lord assured **Ananias . . . This man is My chosen instrument to carry My name before the Gentiles and their kings and before the people of Israel.** Saul was to become Paul, the apostle to the uncircumcised (Rom. 11:13; Gal. 2:2, 7-8; Eph. 3:8), including kings (cf. Governor Felix [Acts 24:1-23], Governor Porcius Festus [24:27–25:12], King Herod Agrippa II [25:13–26:32], and possibly Emperor Nero [25:11]). The apostle, of course, also ministered to "the people of Israel" (cf. 9:20; 13:5, 14; 14:1; 17:2, 10, 17; 18:4, 19; 19:8; 26:17-20; Rom. 1:16). How amazing that the one who persecuted Christians so violently should himself be transformed into a witness of the gospel—and such a dynamic, forceful witness at that!

9:16. The partial fulfillment of this prediction is seen in Saul's inventory of his suffering (2 Cor. 11:23-27).

Three times in as many verses the conversation between Ananias and the Lord included the word **name** (Acts 9:14-16; cf. 3:16).

9:17. Brother Saul—what words of encouragement these must have been to **Saul!** The first recorded man to call Saul a Christian brother was **Ananias.** A more complete statement of Ananias' words is given in 22:14-16. Ananias' apprehension of Saul was turned to love for Saul because of the Lord's directive. Ananias identified with Saul by **placing his hands on** him.

Saul's being **filled with the Holy Spirit** clearly followed his conversion (cf. 4:8, 31; Eph. 5:18).

9:18. In his healing from his blindness **something like scales fell from Saul's eyes, and he could see again.** The word "scales" (*lepides,* from the verb *lepō,* "to peel") was used of the scales of fish and crocodiles. As in several previous conversions recorded in Acts, water baptism followed conversion (8:12, 38).

After this event Ananias disappeared from the narrative and is not mentioned again except in chapter 22 where Paul recounted his own conversion.

9:19a. The three days without food or drink, in addition to the shock of his

"exposure" to the resurrected Christ, left Saul weak. However, several things helped him regain **his strength:** his encounter with Ananias, his healing, his filling with the Spirit, his water baptism, and his **taking some food.**

2. THE CONFLICTS OF SAUL (9:19B-31)

a. *The confession of Saul (9:19b-22)*

9:19b-20. After only a few **days with the** Christians **in Damascus** Saul **began to preach in the synagogues that Jesus is the Son of God.** Preaching to Jews in their synagogues was also his strategy on his missionary journeys (the first journey—13:5, 14; 14:1; the second journey—17:2, 10, 17; 18:4; the third journey—18:19; 19:8). Acts 9:20 includes the only occurrence of the phrase "Son of God" in Acts. On the Damascus Road the first thing Saul learned was who Jesus is.

9:21. The Jews **were astonished.** This response is understandable. The Greek verb *existanto* is literally, "they were beside themselves; they were struck out of their senses"; several other people had the same response to Jesus (Mark 2:12; 5:42; 6:51). This word is used in Acts five times (2:7; 8:13; 9:21; 10:45; 12:16). Saul's intense persecution campaign had **raised havoc in Jerusalem** (cf. 8:3; 22:19; 26:11).

9:22. Saul used his theological training to good advantage in pressing home the truth that the Lord **Jesus is the** Messiah. He had gone to **Damascus** to persecute the church; he ended up preaching Jesus. What a contrast! What grace! No wonder the Damascus **Jews** were **baffled** (*synechynnen,* "bewildered, confused," from *syncheō,* used in the NT only in 2:6; 9:22; 21:27, 31).

b. *The conspiracies against Saul (9:23-31)*

(1) In Damascus. **9:23-25.** One of the themes in Acts, underscored in this paragraph, is the Jewish leaders' opposition to the gospel. It is clear from 2 Corinthians 11:32-33 that this was a joint effort of the Jews and the governor under King Aretas (a Nabatean), though the Jews were the prime movers. Saul's **followers,** aware that **the Jews conspired to kill him . . . lowered him in a basket** outside **the wall** since **the city gates** were guarded. Saul's plans for persecuting Christians in Damascus took a strange

turn; he had entered the city blind and left in a basket! Ironically *he* became the object of persecution.

The reference to "followers" (*mathē-tai*, lit., "disciples") shows that Saul was already having a fruitful ministry. He was a gifted leader.

Luke in compressing the narrative omits Saul's brief sojourn into Arabia, mentioned by Paul in Galatians 1:17. Probably this occurred between Acts 9:22 and 23. The purpose of Paul's time in Arabia is unknown. Possibly he went there to evangelize, but the area was sparsely populated and it was Saul's strategy to go to populous metropolitan centers. He may have left Damascus to reduce the church's persecution. Or, more probably, he went to Arabia to meditate and study.

(2) In Jerusalem (9:26-30). **9:26-28.** **Saul** had left **Jerusalem** an inveterate enemy of Christianity to persecute the church **in Damascus;** but in God's sovereign grace he joined the believers and preached the gospel in that very city. He joined the work in Jerusalem, but the believers there refused to trust him (cf. Ananias' similar fear, v. 13). In Damascus Saul needed a friend, Ananias; in Jerusalem he needed another, **Barnabas.** He whose name means "Son of Encouragement" (4:36) proved to be that for Saul. Barnabas is seen in Acts on four other occasions. (a) 11:22-24; (b) 11:30; 12:25; (c) 13:1-2, 50; 14:12; (d) 15:2, 12, 22, 25, 37. The believers in Jerusalem, convinced by Barnabas that Saul had in fact been converted, allowed **Saul** to stay **with them.** In Damascus he **preached fearlessly in the name of Jesus,** and in **Jerusalem** he was **speaking boldly in the name of the Lord** (cf. comments on "boldly" in 4:31).

9:29. Saul **talked and debated with the Grecian Jews,** thus continuing the work of Stephen (cf. 6:8-10). Evidently Saul's debating ability proved to be too much for the Grecian Jews as they attempted to assassinate him.

9:30. The brothers (cf. v. 17) at Jerusalem then escorted Saul **to Caesarea,** the seaport about 65 miles away by road, **and sent him** to his hometown, **Tarsus.** An ancient city, then over 4,000 years old, Tarsus was an intellectual city in the Roman Empire. (For a brief survey of

significant events in Tarsus' history, see V. Gilbert Beers, *The Victor Handbook of Bible Knowledge.* Wheaton, Ill.: Scripture Press Publications, Victor Books, 1981, p. 555.)

Saul's movements in chapter 9 may be summarized as follows:

1. Jerusalem (vv. 1-2)
2. Damascus (vv. 3-22)
3. Arabia (Gal. 1:17)
4. Damascus (Acts 9:23-25; Gal. 1:17; 2 Cor. 11:32-33)
5. Jerusalem (Acts 9:26-29; Gal. 1:18-20)
6. Caesarea (Acts 9:30)
7. Tarsus (v. 30; Gal. 1:21-24)

(3) The conclusion. **9:31.** In the phrase **the church throughout Judea, Galilee, and Samaria** the word "church" is singular. Luke was obviously speaking of the universal church as it was dispersed in the Holy Land.

So strong was Jewish antagonism to Saul and his ministry that after he left the area the church **enjoyed a time of peace.**

The church was still confined to Jews, half-Jews (the Samaritans), and proselytes to Judaism who became Christians (with the one exception of the eunuch from Ethiopia, 8:26-40). But all was in readiness for the extension of the church to a new segment of the world's population.

With this third of seven progress reports on the spiritual and numerical growth of the church (cf. 2:47; 6:7; 12:24; 16:5; 19:20; 28:30-31), Luke brought this section of his book to a conclusion.

III. The Witness to the Extremity of the Earth (9:32–28:31)

A. The extension of the church to Antioch (9:32–12:24)

1. THE PREPARATION OF PETER FOR A UNIVERSAL GOSPEL (9:32–10:48)

a. Peter at Lydda (9:32-35)

9:32-35. Peter was last mentioned in 8:25 when he was returning to Jerusalem from Samaria with John. Peter was involved in an itinerant mission around Judea which brought him to **Lydda.** Lydda, mentioned only here in the New Testament, is today called Lod; Israel's international airport is just north of the city. Peter later carried on an extensive traveling ministry, evident from 1 Corinthians 9:5. This is also implied from the addressees of his first epistle (1 Peter 1:1). Philip had preceded Peter to the area in and around Caesarea (Acts 8:40).

The miraculous healing of **Aeneas, a paralytic who had been bedridden for eight years,** was the occasion for many to come to faith in Christ. Three times in Acts, Luke used the words **turned to the Lord** to refer to salvation (9:35; 11:21; 15:19). The gospel was beginning to attract a wider audience, for many in this coastal region were Gentiles. **Sharon** is the fertile plain along the coast of Palestine, about 10 miles wide and 50 miles long. Lydda was on the southeastern edge of the plain. This miracle was Peter's second healing of a cripple (cf. 3:1-10; also cf. 14:8-10).

b. Peter at Joppa (9:36-43)

9:36-38. While **Peter was** at Lydda, a well-beloved Christian woman (a disciple) in **Joppa** by the name of **Dorcas . . . died.** Her name means "gazelle" in Greek as does its counterpart **Tabitha** in Aramaic. She was known for her help to **the poor.** Because the cities of **Lydda** and **Joppa** are only about 12 miles apart **two men were sent** from Joppa to call Peter. (For a brief statement on Joppa's history see Beers, *The Victor Handbook of Bible Knowledge,* p. 559.) No one had been raised from the dead in the early church so far as the records of Acts declare, but the faith of the believers was so great they expected the Lord to use Peter to resurrect Dorcas.

9:39-41. When **Peter** arrived, he **sent** the weeping **widows** and other believers out of the **upstairs . . . room,** prayed **on his knees** for Dorcas, and commanded her to arise (cf. Mark 5:41). To avoid ceremonial defilement (cf. Lev. 21:1; Num. 5:2; 9:6-10; 19:11), **Peter** did not touch her until after God restored her to life.

9:42-43. **This** miracle, like previous ones, led **many** to believe **in the Lord** (2:43, 47; 4:4; 5:12, 14; 8:6; 9:33-35). After this miracle **Peter** remained **in Joppa for some time** (lit., "sufficient days") **with a tanner named Simon.** His house was "by the sea" (10:6).

This passage (9:32-43) shows the excellent preparation given Peter for his ensuing experience with Cornelius.

(1) Two outstanding miracles confirmed his ministry; God was with him in a special way. (2) He was ministering in an area that was partially Gentile. (3) His living in the home of Simon the tanner was significant. Tanners were considered to be ceremonially unclean because they were constantly in contact with the skins of dead animals (Lev. 11:40).

c. Peter and Cornelius (chap. 10)

The importance of this event is seen in the fact that Luke recounts it three times—here in Acts 10, again in chapter 11, and finally in 15:6-9. The geographic extension of the gospel in Acts is an initial fulfillment of Jesus' words in Matthew 8:11: "Many will come from the east and the west, and will take their places . . . in the kingdom of heaven."

(1) The vision of Cornelius (10:1-8). **10:1.** By separate visions both Peter and **Cornelius** were prepared for this momentous happening. Cornelius and his vision are described first. Cornelius was **a centurion,** a Roman officer in charge of 100 soldiers, in **the Italian Regiment,** consisting of 600 soldiers. In the New Testament centurions are consistently viewed in a favorable light (cf. Matt. 8:5-10; 27:54; Mark 15:44-45; Acts 22:25-26; 23:17-18; 27:6, 43). Centurion Cornelius became one of the first Gentiles after Pentecost to hear the good news of Jesus Christ's forgiveness.

10:2. From the description of Cornelius as **devout** (*eusebēs,* used only here and in v. 7; 2 Peter 2:9) **and God-fearing** ("righteous and God-fearing," Acts 10:22), it can be inferred he was not a full-fledged proselyte to Judaism (he had not been circumcised, 11:3), but he did worship Yahweh. Evidently he attended the synagogue and to the best of his knowledge and ability followed the Old Testament Scriptures. Nevertheless, he had not entered into New Testament salvation (cf. 11:14).

10:3-6. The time reference, **3 in the afternoon,** may refer to a Jewish time of prayer (cf. 3:1). If so, the Lord approached Cornelius by means of **an angel** while he was at prayer (cf. 10:9). Later Cornelius called this angel "a man in shining clothes" (v. 30). **Cornelius** responded to **the angel** by asking, **What is it, Lord?** Perhaps "Lord" (*kyrie*) here means "Sir" (cf. comments on 9:5). This soldier's piety was evidenced by his **prayers** and his generous giving **to the poor** (cf. 10:2). The angel instructed him to send for **Simon . . . Peter** at the home of **Simon the tanner** (cf. 9:43).

10:7. When the angel who spoke to him had gone, the centurion **called** three of his men—**two servants** and a military aide, also **a devout man** (*eusebē*; cf. v. 2). Undoubtedly these three had been influenced by Cornelius' devotion.

10:8. He told them everything that had happened. Related to the Greek participle used here (*exēgēsamenos*) is the English noun "exegesis." The verb means he "explained" everything.

The three went off **to Joppa,** some 33 miles south of Caesarea (v. 24), to bring Peter back to Cornelius.

(2) The vision of Peter (10:9-16). **10:9.** That **Peter** prayed morning and evening may be assumed, for those were normal times of prayer. In addition he prayed at **noon.** Prayer three times a day was not commanded in the Scriptures, but Peter followed the example of pious men before him (cf. Ps. 55:17; Dan. 6:10). Peter **went up** to the (flat) **roof to pray;** this would have given him privacy.

10:10-12. While **hungry,** Peter **fell into a trance** in which God gave him a vision of a **sheet** coming **down to earth** with **all kinds of . . . animals . . . reptiles . . . and birds.**

10:13-14. When God commanded **Peter** to **eat** of these animals, his response was, **Surely not, Lord!** Significantly his refusal ("surely not") was *mēdamōs,* a more polite and subjective term than *oudamōs* ("by no means," used only in Matt. 2:6). This was the third time in Peter's career that he directly refused God's will (cf. Matt. 16:23; John 13:8).

Peter knew from the Law that he should not eat **unclean** animals (Lev. 11). But could he not have killed and **eaten** the clean animals and left the unclean? Probably Peter understood the command to include them all. Or possibly the large sheet contained only unclean animals.

10:15. Do not call anything impure that God has made clean. This rebuttal gives Mark 7:14-23 more meaning (cf. 1 Tim. 4:4). It is generally recognized that Mark wrote down Peter's words. In retrospect Peter must have recognized that Jesus as the Messiah cleansed all goods from ceremonial defilement.

10:16. Why did Peter refuse **three times** to eat the unclean foods? For one thing, this indicated emphasis. But more than that it revealed certainty and truth. Here was one place where Peter was being scrupulous beyond the will of God. His intentions were good, but he was being disobedient. Also, was there some link here with Peter's threefold denial (John 18:17, 25-27) and with his three affirmations of his love for the Lord? (John 21:15-17)

(3) The visit of the messengers (10:17-23a). **10:17-22.** In marvelous timing and by the coordination of the sovereign God the three messengers and **Peter** met. **The Holy Spirit,** who told Peter about the arrival of the **three men,** may have been the One whose unidentified voice Peter heard earlier (vv. 13, 15).

The men . . . from Cornelius spoke highly of him (cf. vv. 2, 4) and conveyed to **Peter** their purpose in coming.

10:23a. Then Peter invited the men into the house to be his guests. Since Peter had been waiting for his noon meal (cf. v. 10), he undoubtedly now shared it with his visitors. Perhaps he was already beginning to discern the lesson of his vision!

(4) The visitation of Gentiles (10:23b-43). **10:23b.** By the time **Peter** and his guests finished lunch it must have been too late to start back to Caesarea that day. **The next day** they began the almost-two-day trip. (Cornelius' emissaries had left Caesarea after 3 P.M. one day [vv. 3, 8] and arrived at noon two days later [vv. 9, 19]. Cf. "four days ago" in v. 30.)

Peter took with him **some of the brothers from Joppa.** The two-by-two motif is common in the Gospels and Acts; Christian workers often went out by twos. In this debatable situation at least six people accompanied Peter (11:12). So there would be seven witnesses to attest to what would transpire.

10:24. Cornelius was so confident that Peter would come and he was so expectant of Peter's message that he **called together his relatives and close friends.**

10:25-26. When **Peter** arrived, **Cornelius** prostrated himself before the apostle in worship. The verb *prosekynēsen* means "he worshiped" and is here translated **in reverence. Peter,** refusing this kind of obeisance, urged Cornelius to **stand up,** for, **he said, I am only a man myself.**

10:27-29. Peter was well aware of the consequences of his fellowshiping with Gentiles in their homes (cf. 11:2-3), but he had learned the lesson of the vision well. The command to eat unclean animals meant he was **not** to **call any man impure or unclean.** So he **came without** protest.

10:30-33. After **Cornelius** recounted the circumstances that brought **Peter** to his house he said, **Now we are all here in the presence of God to listen to everything the Lord has commanded you to tell us.** What a divinely prepared audience!

10:34-35. These words of **Peter** were revolutionary. They swept away the prejudice and indoctrination of generations of Judaism. However, Gentile salvation certainly was a doctrine known in the Old Testament (cf. Jonah; Gen. 12:3). In the Old Testament the Jews were God's Chosen People, the special recipients of His promises and revelation. Here Peter stated that God's program was reaching out to the world through the church.

There is considerable debate about Peter's words that God **accepts men from every nation who fear Him and do what is right.** This does not teach salvation by works because a person's first responsibility before God is to fear Him, which is tantamount to trusting Him and reverencing Him. It is the New Testament parallel to Micah 6:8. Furthermore, God's acceptance of such people refers to His welcoming them to a right relationship by faith in Christ (cf. Acts 11:14).

10:36-37. Peter then outlined the career of **Christ** (vv. 36-43), the sovereign **Lord of all,** through whom **God sent . . . the good news of peace.** Bible students have often observed how this parallels the Gospel of Mark almost perfectly. Mark began with John's **baptism** and traced the ministry of the Lord Jesus from **Galilee** to **Judea** to Jerusalem and finally to the Crucifixion, Resurrection, and the Great Commission.

10:38. The word *Messiah* means "Anointed One"; so when Peter said,

God anointed Jesus of Nazareth he was saying, "God declared Him the Messiah" (cf. Isa. 61:1-3; Luke 4:16-21; Acts 4:27). This declaration occurred at the Lord's baptism (cf. Matt. 3:16-17; Mark 1:9-11; Luke 3:21-22; John 1:32-34). Isaiah spoke of the Anointed One performing great deeds (Isa. 61:1-3), and as Peter declared, **He went around doing good and healing all who were under the power of the devil.**

10:39-41. Peter affirmed that he and his associates were personal eyewitnesses of all Jesus **did. They,** that is, **the Jews . . . killed Him by hanging Him on a tree,** an ignominious form of execution. Earlier Peter had told Jews **in Jerusalem,** "You killed the Author of life" (3:15); to the rulers he said, "You crucified" Him (4:10); and to the Sanhedrin he replied, "You killed" Him "by hanging Him on a tree" (5:30). And Stephen too told the Sanhedrin, "You . . . have murdered Him" (7:52). On five occasions in Acts, the apostles said they were **witnesses** of the resurrected Christ (2:32; 3:15; 5:32; 10:41; 13:30-31). After Christ's resurrection the disciples **ate and drank with Him** (cf. John 21:13). This was proof that the resurrected Lord Jesus was no bodiless phantom and it explains how Christ was **seen** (Acts 10:40).

10:42-43. Peter made it clear that Christ's ministry results either in judgment (v. 42) or salvation (v. 43). The key phrase is, **Everyone who believes in Him.** This Greek construction consists of a present participle with an article, which is almost the equivalent of a noun (in this case "every believer in Him"). The key element in salvation is faith, belief in Christ. This message of **forgiveness of sins** (cf. 2:38; 5:31; 13:38; 26:18) **through** faith in the Messiah was spoken of by the prophets (e.g., Isa. 53:11; Jer. 31:34; Ezek. 36:25-26).

(5) The vindication by the Spirit (10:44-48). **10:44-45.** Peter's message was rapidly concluded by the sovereign interruption of **the Holy Spirit** who **came on all** those **who heard** Peter's **message** about Jesus and believed. **The** six (cf. v. 23; 11:12) **circumcised believers . . . were astonished** (*exestēsan*; "they were beside themselves"; cf. 9:21) at this evidence of equality of **Gentiles** with Jewish believers.

381

10:46. The sign which God used to validate the reality of Gentile salvation was **speaking in tongues.** (For the significance of tongues-speaking in Acts, see the comments on 19:1-7.)

10:47-48. Peter quickly discerned at least three theological implications of what had happened: (1) He could not argue with God (11:17). (2) Cornelius and his household, though uncircumcised (11:3), were **baptized** because they had believed in **Christ,** as evidenced by their receiving **the Holy Spirit.** The order of these events was believing in Christ, receiving the Holy Spirit, speaking in tongues, and being baptized in water. (3) The reality of Cornelius' conversion was confirmed by Peter's staying with him several **days,** probably to instruct him more fully in his newfound faith.

2. THE PREPARATION OF THE APOSTLES FOR A UNIVERSAL GOSPEL (11:1-18)

a. The accusation (11:1-3)

11:1-2. The response on the part of Jewish Christians was mixed. The expression **circumcised believers** (also used in 10:45) evidently describes Christians who still held to the Law of Moses (cf. 15:5; 21:20; Gal. 2:12).

11:3. The accusation lodged against Peter was that he **went into the house of uncircumcised men and ate with them.** The primary problem was not his preaching to Gentiles but his eating with them (cf. Mark 2:16; Luke 15:2; Gal. 2:12). This gives even greater significance to Peter's vision (Acts 10:9-16). Eating with someone was a mark of acceptance and fellowship (cf. 1 Cor. 5:11). This problem could have caused a serious break in the church.

b. The answer (11:4-17)

11:4-14. Peter recounted to the circumcised believers in Jerusalem briefly what had occurred (cf. chap. 10), including his **vision** (11:5-7), his response to it (vv. 8-10), and the trip to Cornelius' **house** (vv. 11-14).

11:15-16. In recounting what happened next, Peter made an important identification of the day of Pentecost with the Lord's prediction of **Spirit** baptism (1:4-5). Luke did not state specifically in chapter 2 that Pentecost was that fulfillment, but Peter here pointedly said so by

the phrase **at the beginning** (cf. 10:47, "just as we have," and 11:17, "the same gift as He gave us"). The Church Age, then, began on the day of Pentecost.

11:17. Peter's defense did not rest on what he himself did, but on what God did. **God** had made no distinction between Jew and Gentile, so how could Peter?

c. The acquittal (11:18)

11:18. With Peter the saints recognized that the conversion of **Gentiles** was initiated by **God** and that they should not stand in His way. This response had two ensuing and significant results. First, it preserved the unity of the body of Christ, the church. Second, it drove a huge wedge between Church-Age believers and temple-worshipers in Jerusalem. Before this the common Jewish people looked on Christians with favor (cf. 2:47; 5:13, 26), but soon thereafter the Jews opposed the church. This antagonism is attested by Israel's response to the execution of James (12:2-3; cf. 12:11). Perhaps this concourse with Gentiles was a starting point of the Jewish opposition.

3. THE PREPARATION OF THE CHURCH AT ANTIOCH FOR A UNIVERSAL GOSPEL (11:19-30)

a. The cosmopolitan nature of the church (11:19-21)

This is a crucial hinge in the Acts account. For the first time the church actively proselytized Gentiles. The Samaritans of chapter 8 were partly Jewish; the Ethiopian eunuch on his own was reading Isaiah 53 on his return from Jerusalem; and even Cornelius took the initiative in seeking the gospel from Peter's lips. But here the church took the first steps to take the message to uncircumcised Greeks.

11:19. The narrative reaches back to **Stephen** (8:1-2) to point to still another result of his martyrdom. His death had helped move the gospel into Samaria (cf. the similarity between 8:4 and 11:19). Also Stephen's death had incited Saul to persecute the church more vigorously (8:3) and he consequently was converted (9:1-30). Now a third result from Stephen's martyrdom was the spreading of the gospel to Gentile lands (**Phoenicia, Cyprus, and Antioch**).

11:20. The reference to **Antioch** in Syria prepares the reader for the importance of this city in the subsequent narrative. This city, one of many bearing the same name, was the third largest in the Roman Empire behind Rome and Alexandria. Located on the Orontes River 15 miles inland, it was known as Antioch on the Orontes. Beautifully situated and carefully planned, it was a commercial center and the home of a large Jewish community. In spite of the fact that it was a vile city, with gross immorality and ritual prostitution as part of its temple worship, the church at Antioch was destined to become the base of operations for Paul's missionary journeys. The Roman satirist, Juvenal, complained, "The sewage of the Syrian Orontes has for long been discharged into the Tiber." By this he meant that Antioch was so corrupt it was impacting Rome, more than 1,300 miles away.

This amazing step forward for the gospel to the Gentiles (**Greeks** at Antioch) was accomplished by unnamed helpers of the faith. Nevertheless this was a bold and critical move by these believers from **Cyprus,** the island not too far from Antioch, **and Cyrene,** a city in North Africa (cf. Matt. 27:32; Acts 2:10; 6:9; 13:1).

11:21. The clause **believed and turned to the Lord** does not necessarily refer to two separate actions. The Greek construction (an aorist participle with an aorist finite verb) often indicates that the two actions are simultaneous. This clause, then, means, "in believing, they turned to the Lord."

b. The confirmation of the church (11:22-26)

11:22. Such an important move on the part of **the church** could not escape the attention of the mother church in **Jerusalem.** Earlier the Jerusalem apostles sent Peter and John to check up on Philip's ministry in Samaria. Now the Jerusalem saints **sent Barnabas** all the way **to Antioch,** over 300 miles north. The selection of that delegate was of crucial importance; and Barnabas was a wise choice for several reasons. First, he, like some of these Christian ambassadors, was from Cyprus (4:36; 11:20). Second, he

was a generous man (4:37) and therefore thoughtful of others. Third, he was a gracious gentleman as attested by his nickname (4:36) and Luke's testimony about him (11:24).

11:23. Barnabas could not escape the conclusion that **God** was genuinely at work in Antioch, and as Luke often noted there was the response of joy. True to his nickname, Son of Encouragement (4:36), he **encouraged** the believers (cf. 14:22). (Barnabas is also mentioned in 9:27; 11:25, 30; 12:25; 13:1-2, 7, 43, 46, 50; 14:3, 12, 14, 20; 15:2, 12, 22, 25, 35-37, 39; 1 Cor. 9:6; Gal. 2:1, 9, 13; Col. 4:10.)

11:24. Three things were said about Barnabas: **he was a good man,** he was **full of the Holy Spirit, and** he was full of **faith** (Stephen too was full of faith and the Holy Spirit; 6:5). Luke wrote this description of Barnabas *after* the confrontation between Paul and Barnabas, recorded in 15:39. Since Luke was Paul's traveling companion, this statement about Barnabas must have been Paul's assessment as well.

11:25. The work in Antioch grew to such proportions **Barnabas** needed aid, and he could think of no one better suited for the work than **Saul** who was living in **Tarsus** (cf. 9:30). Possibly some of the sufferings and persecutions Paul described in 2 Corinthians 11:23-27 took place while he was in Tarsus. This may also be where Paul had the revelation described in 2 Corinthians 12:1-4. Based on Acts 22:17-21, some think that Saul was already ministering to Gentiles when Barnabas contacted him to bring him to Antioch.

11:26. Barnabas and Saul ministered a full **year** in **Antioch,** teaching **great numbers of people.** The church was continuing to grow numerically (cf. 2:41, 47; 4:4; 5:14; 6:1; 9:31; 11:21, 24).

Jesus' **disciples were first called Christians at Antioch.** The ending "-ian" means "belonging to the party of"; thus "Christians" were those of Jesus' party. The word "Christians" is used only two other times in the New Testament: in 26:28 and 1 Peter 4:16. The significance of the name, emphasized by the word order in the Greek text, is that people recognized Christians as a distinct group. The church was more and more being separated from Judaism.

c. The charity of the church (11:27-30)

11:27. Believers from Jerusalem with the gift of prophecy **came down from Jerusalem to Antioch.** (Though going north, they went "down" because Jerusalem is on a much higher elevation than Antioch.)

11:28. Agabus, also mentioned again in 21:10-11, prophesied **that a severe famine would spread over the entire Roman world.** This was actually a series of severe famines that struck various sections of the Roman Empire **during the reign of** Emperor **Claudius** (A.D. 41–54.) This same Claudius later expelled Jews from Rome (18:2). (See the list of Roman emperors at Luke 2:1.)

11:29-30. The Christians at Antioch, **each according to his ability** (cf. 1 Cor. 16:2; 2 Cor. 9:7), sent money to the believers **in Judea.** This expression of love undoubtedly bound the two churches together (cf. Rom. 15:27).

When **Barnabas and Saul** brought the gift to Judea, they gave the **gift to the elders.** This is the first mention of church elders in Acts and significantly they received finances. Evidently they had ultimate oversight over all aspects of the ministry. Later Paul and his companions presented the offering of the churches of Achaia, Macedonia, and Asia Minor to the elders of the Jerusalem church. This may have happened when Paul arrived in Jerusalem (Acts 21:18; though this verse doesn't refer to offering money).

Though there is some question about it, this famine visit in 11:27-30 is probably the same one referred to in Galatians 2:1-10.

4. THE PERSECUTION OF THE CHURCH AT JERUSALEM (12:1-24)

The purpose of this section of Acts is to confirm Israel's rejection of the Messiah. Luke has skillfully woven this theme throughout the entire book and it can be seen up to this point in 4:1-30 (esp. 4:29); 5:17-40; 6:11–8:3; 9:1-2, 29. This animosity of Israel set the stage for the first missionary journey.

a. The martyrdom of James (12:1-2)

12:1-2. Artfully, Luke contrasted the love of the church at Antioch for the saints at Jerusalem with the coldhearted enmity of **Herod** and the Jews for **the church.**

The Herod mentioned here is Agrippa I, a ruler popular with the Jews for he was partly Jewish, being of Hasmonean descent. His kingdom covered basically the same area as that of his grandfather Herod the Great. He was known for doing everything possible to curry the favor of the Jews, so he found it politically expedient to arrest Christians and to execute **James, the brother of John.** Herod Agrippa I died in A.D. 44. His son, Herod Agrippa II, was king of Judea from A.D. 50–70. Paul was on trial before Agrippa II and his sister Bernice (25:13–26:32). (See the chart on the Herods at Luke 1:5.)

b. The imprisonment and escape of Peter (12:3-19)

This incident clearly indicates that the church was an identifiable group which had become hated and despised by the Jews.

12:3-4. The execution of James **pleased the Jews** so Herod apprehended and incarcerated **Peter . . . during the Feast of Unleavened Bread.** This seven-day spring feast followed immediately after the Passover. **Herod intended to bring** out Peter **for public trial after the Passover.** The "Passover" here referred to the combined eight-day festival, the Passover itself followed by the seven days of unleavened bread. For at least two reasons Herod would find it expedient to execute Peter. First, Peter was known as the leader of the church, and second, he had fraternized with Gentiles.

Herod made certain that Peter's imprisonment was secure by **handing him over to be guarded by four squads of four soldiers each!** Probably this means two were chained to Peter, one on each side and two were standing guard outside (cf. vv. 6, 10). The four squads probably were each on guard for six hours each. Evidently the authorities remembered Peter's earlier escape (cf. 5:19-24) and Herod did not want that to happen again.

12:5. So Peter was kept in prison, **but the church was earnestly praying to God for him.** The contrast is obvious: Peter was bound, but prayer was loosed!

12:6. Peter was so trusting the Lord that he was sound asleep the **night before** his **trial** (cf. 1 Peter 2:23; 5:7). He did not fear for his life because Christ had said he would live to an old age (John 21:18).

12:7-10. This is the second time **an angel** helped Peter escape (cf. 5:17-20). Awakening **Peter,** the angel told him to get dressed **and follow** him **out of the prison.** Supernaturally God caused **the chains** to fall **off** his **wrists,** kept the guards asleep, and opened **the iron gate.**

12:11. One of the subthemes of Acts is the outreach of the gospel in spite of opposition. This is seen in Peter's release. When **Peter came to himself,** braced by the night air, he acknowledged God's deliverance for him **from** Herod and the Jews. He now knew this was no vision (v. 9).

12:12. This verse introduces the reader to John **Mark** who figures prominently in Paul's first missionary journey. Evidently his mother **Mary** was a woman of prominence and means. Probably her house was a principal meeting place of the church, so it must have been spacious. Because John Mark's father is not named, Mary may have been a widow. This same Mark is considered to be the writer of the Gospel bearing his name (cf. Mark 14:51-52; 1 Peter 5:13).

12:13-17. The story of **Peter's** unsuspected arrival at John Mark's home is filled with humor and human interest. Joy in the Book of Acts is also evident here in the **servant girl . . . Rhoda** who answered Peter's knock and **recognized** his **voice.** Though the saints were praying earnestly (v. 5) for Peter's release, they did not expect an answer so soon! When Rhoda insisted, **Peter is at the door!** they replied, **You're out of your mind. It must be his angel.** This statement implies a belief in personal angels, that is, angels who are assigned to individuals (cf. Dan. 10:21; Matt. 18:10). It also suggests a belief that an angel may look like the person with whom he is identified!

When they **saw** Peter, **they were astonished** (exestēsan; cf. 9:21). Peter's mention of **James** indicates that James had a place of prominence in the Jerusalem church. Quite clearly this James was the Lord's half brother.

After making himself known to the brothers, Peter **left for another place.**

Where this was is not known. It is possible, because of 1 Peter 1:1, to say he went to Asia Minor. Later Peter was at Antioch of Syria (Gal. 2:11). Paul referred to Peter's itinerant ministry (1 Cor. 1:12; 9:5).

12:18-19. After an investigation of Peter's escape, **Herod . . . cross-examined the guards and** ruthlessly **ordered** their executions. Herod no doubt justified such harshness by reasoning that guards whose prisoners escape are irresponsible and unreliable. Yet Herod lost 16 guards by his actions (cf. v. 4). **Herod** then left **Judea** to stay for **a while** in **Caesarea,** the capital of the Roman province of Judea, from which Roman governors governed the nation.

c. The death of Herod Agrippa I (12:20-23)

12:20-23. Tyre and Sidon were in Herod's dominion and for some reason had incurred his wrath. Because these cities **depended on** Galilee for grain, they desired to make **peace** with Herod Agrippa. Probably they bribed **Blastus, a trusted personal servant of the king,** to work out a reconciliation. **On the appointed day** when **Herod** was delivering a speech, **the people** honored him as **a god,** and the Lord **God** judged him with death. This was in A.D. 44. This account parallels that given by Josephus in his *Antiquities of the Jews* (19. 8. 2). After Herod's death, Felix and Festus, successively, were the governors of Judea.

Three of Herod's children figure prominently in the later narrative of Acts—Drusilla, the wife of Felix (24:24-26); Bernice (25:13, 23), and Herod Agrippa II (25:13–26:32).

d. The prosperity of the church (12:24)

12:24. But the Word of God continued to increase and spread (cf. similar wording in 6:7; 13:49; 19:20). In spite of opposition and persecution the Lord sovereignly prospered the work of His church. With this progress report Luke brought another section of his work to a conclusion (cf. 2:47; 6:7; 9:31; 12:24; 16:5; 19:20; 28:30-31). From Antioch the gospel message was now ready to go to Asia Minor.

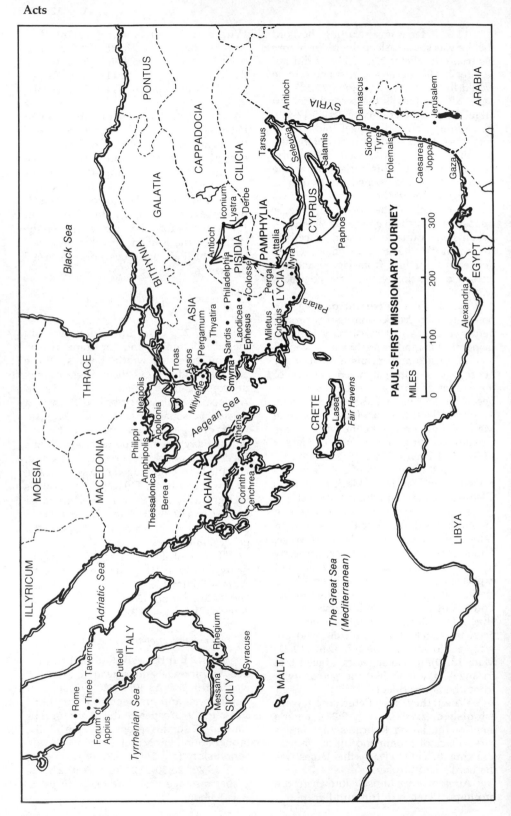

PAUL'S FIRST MISSIONARY JOURNEY

MILES

0   100   200   300

B. The extension of the church in Asia Minor (12:25–16:5)

1. THE CALL AND DEDICATION OF BARNABAS AND SAUL (12:25–13:3)

12:25. After depositing the famine relief money with the elders at **Jerusalem** (11:27-30), **Barnabas and Saul** returned to Antioch. They took **with them John . . . Mark** (cf. 13:5), a cousin of Barnabas (Col. 4:10) from Jerusalem (Acts 12:12).

[First missionary journey, chaps. 13–14]

13:1. **The church at Antioch** now became the base of operation for Saul's ministry. Jerusalem was still the mother church, but the missionary church was Antioch on the Orontes River. Furthermore, Peter was no longer the central figure; Saul became that.

The diversity in the backgrounds of the leaders of the church at Antioch shows the cosmopolitan nature of the church. **Barnabas** was a Jew from Cyprus (4:36). **Simeon** was also a Jew, but his Latin nickname **Niger** not only indicates he was of dark complexion but also that he moved in Roman circles. He could be the Simon of Cyrene who carried Christ's cross (Matt. 27:32; Mark 15:21), but this is highly debatable. **Lucius** was from **Cyrene** in North Africa (cf. Acts 11:20). **Manaen** had high contacts for he **had been** reared **with Herod the tetrarch,** actually Herod Antipas, who beheaded John the Baptist and who treated the Lord so shamefully at His trial (see the chart on the Herod family at Luke 1:5). One in that court (Manaen) became a disciple; the other (Herod) an antagonist! At the end of the list, for he was last on this scene, was **Saul,** a Jew trained in Rabbinical schools. Despite their variegated backgrounds, these men functioned as one.

Perhaps the name of Barnabas appears first in the list because as the delegate from the mother church in Jerusalem he held the priority position.

13:2. Evidently God made His will known by means of the "prophets" in the church (cf. v. 1). Frequently in Acts **the Holy Spirit** gave directives to God's leaders (e.g., 8:29; 10:19; 13:4). Here He directed the five, **while they were worshiping . . . and fasting,** to **set apart** for Him **Barnabas and Saul.** Once again

the principle of two men working together is underscored. The verb "set apart" (*aphorizō*) is used of three separations in Saul's life—at his birth he was separated to God (Gal. 1:15); at his conversion he was set apart for the gospel (Rom. 1:1); and in Antioch he was separated for a specific service (Acts 13:2).

13:3. The church leaders **placed their hands on** Barnabas and Saul **and sent them off.** The laying on of hands identified the church with their ministry and acknowledged God's direction for them (cf. Ananias' identifying himself with Saul by laying hands on him, 9:17). Two of the choicest were sent on this significant mission.

2. THE CIRCUIT IN ASIA MINOR (13:4–14:28)

a. At Cyprus (13:4-12)

13:4. Directed **by the Holy Spirit** (cf. v. 2) they first **went down to Seleucia,** a seaport 16 miles from Antioch, **and sailed from there to Cyprus.** This island, known in the Old Testament as Kittim (Gen. 10:4), was the homeland of Barnabas (Acts 4:36). This implies Barnabas was the leader of the party (cf. the order of names in 13:2, 7).

13:5. **Salamis** was the largest city in the eastern half of Cyprus. Evidently a large number of Jews resided there, for Barnabas and Saul **proclaimed** God's **Word . . . in the . . . synagogues,** not "a" synagogue.

There was wisdom in going to these religious centers: (1) It gave priority in that generation to the Jews receiving the gospel first (cf. Rom. 1:16; Acts 13:46; 17:2; 18:4, 19; 19:8). (2) Gentiles in the synagogues would be a fruitful field for sowing the gospel because they would already be acquainted with the Old Testament and its anticipation of the Messiah.

John Mark, a cousin of Barnabas (Col. 4:10), **was with them as their helper** (cf. Acts 12:25). What is meant by the term "helper" (*hypereten*) is debated. Probably he instructed new converts, assisted in baptisms (cf. 1 Cor. 1:14-17), and helped in any way he could.

13:6. The results of the ministry in Salamis are unstated. **Paphos,** 100 miles southwest of Salamis and the seat of the provincial government, was their next point of ministry. What took place here is of great significance in the progression of the gospel to Gentiles.

At Paphos, Barnabas and Saul **met a Jewish sorcerer and false prophet named Bar-Jesus.** The word "sorcerer" (*magos*) could describe a counselor or honorable gentleman (e.g., the "Magi" in Matt. 2:1, 7, 16) or it could refer to a fraudulent wizard, as here. It is related to the verb "practice sorcery" (*mageuō*) used of Simon (Acts 8:9).

13:7. It so happened that Bar-Jesus **was an attendant of the proconsul, Sergius Paulus.** This sorcerer was greatly threatened by the **intelligent** proconsul's interest in the gospel. Proconsuls were governors appointed by the Roman senate; procurators, on the other hand, were appointed by the emperor. Three Judea procurators are mentioned in the New Testament: Pontius Pilate (A.D. 26–36), Antonius Felix (A.D. 52–59?), and Porcius Festus (A.D. 59–62).

13:8. The sorcerer . . . tried to turn the proconsul from the faith.

The name **Elymas** is something of a problem. Probably it is a Semitic word meaning "sorcerer," which was given or taken by him as a nickname.

13:9. At this juncture **Saul,** now for the first time **called Paul,** stepped to the fore and assumed leadership. He probably was more aggressive and also knew Gentile minds better than Barnabas. From this point on Paul was the leader and his name preceded Barnabas' name except when they were in Jerusalem (15:12, 25) and in 14:14.

Furthermore, the Roman name Paul was used from here on; the Jewish name Saul was used only when he in his personal testimonies referred to his former life (22:7; 26:14).

13:10. In Aramaic, Bar-Jesus means "Son of Jesus." But Paul told him that instead of being a son of Jesus ("Jesus" means "Yahweh is salvation"), Elymas was **a child** (*huie*, lit., "son") **of the devil.** Paul lashed at him with strong language: Bar-Jesus was **an enemy of everything that is right** (lit., "righteousness"), he was **full of . . . deceit** (*dolou*) **and trickery** (*rhadiourgias*, "unscrupulous mischief, work that easily deceives," used only here in the NT) and **perverting the right ways of the Lord.** Sorcery, exercising power by the help and control of demons, had led

him into all kinds of deception of others and distortion of the truth. The occult is indeed dangerous.

This is the second of four incidents of conflict with and victory over demonic powers in the Book of Acts (cf. 8:9-23; 16:16-18; 19:13-17).

13:11-12. In judgment Paul inflicted a temporary blindness on Elymas. This is the first of Paul's recorded miracles and it was performed in conflict with a Jew over giving the gospel to a Gentile.

Seeing this miracle, Sergius Paulus' interest in the Word of God (v. 7) blossomed into genuine faith in Christ. Interestingly the Greek names of this **proconsul** and of the apostle were the same: Paulus.

This incident is significant for three reasons: (1) It marks the beginning of Paul's leadership in this journey; verse 13 refers to "Paul and his companions." (2) From this point on the ministry took on an even more decidedly Gentile slant. (3) It is filled with figurative nuances. A Gentile with the name Paul accepted the message while a Jew opposed it. The Jews' blindness pictured the judicial blinding of Israel (cf. 28:26-27). Luke by this means emphasized the transitional nature of the Book of Acts. On one hand Gentiles became the primary object of the gospel, and on the other God temporarily turned from the Jews and thus judged them.

b. At Pisidian Antioch (13:13-52)

(1) The defection of John Mark. **13:13.** Barnabas' greatness is displayed by his willingness to let Paul be the leader. So **Paul and his companions sailed to Perga in Pamphylia.** But **John** (i.e., John Mark) **left them** and returned **to Jerusalem.** What caused Mark to desert is open to speculation: (1) Perhaps he was disillusioned with the change in leadership. After all, Barnabas, the original leader, was John Mark's cousin. (2) The new emphasis on Gentiles may have been too much of an adjustment for a Palestinian Jew like Mark. (3) Possibly he was afraid of the dangerous road over the Taurus Mountains to Antioch which Paul was determined to travel. (4) There is some evidence Paul became quite ill in Perga, possibly with malaria, as the city of Perga was subject to malarial infections.

Furthermore, Paul preached to the people of Galatia "because of an illness" (Gal. 4:13). The missionary party may have gone inland to higher ground to avoid the ravages of malaria and Mark in discouragement over this may have returned home. (5) Some think Mark was homesick. His mother may have been a widow (Acts 12:12); perhaps Mark became lonesome for her and home. Whatever the reason, Paul considered it a defection and a fault (cf. 15:38).

(2) The discourse on the first Sabbath (13:14-41). **13:14.** This Antioch was actually in Phrygia but was known as **Pisidian Antioch** because it was so near Pisidia. Like other cities—such as Lystra, Troas, Philippi, and Corinth—Antioch was a Roman colony. Paul visited these cities because they were located at strategic points.

13:15. The first opportunity for Paul and Barnabas to preach came in **the synagogue.** In the Sabbath service it was customary to read two portions of the Old Testament—one **from the Law** (the Pentateuch) **and** one from **the Prophets.** "The Law and the Prophets" means the entire Old Testament (cf. Matt. 5:17; 7:12; 11:13; 22:40; Luke 16:16; Acts 24:14; 28:23; Rom. 3:21). Evidently Paul and Barnabas had made themselves known to the **rulers** of the synagogue before the meeting. After the Scripture reading they were invited to share **a message of encouragement for the people.**

13:16-25. Paul seized the opportunity to present the fulfillments of Old Testament expectations of the Messiah in Jesus. Luke recorded a number of "sample sermons" of Paul in Acts (cf. 14:15-17; 17:22-31; 20:18-35). This, the first recorded discourse of Paul and the most completely preserved, illustrated how Paul preached to an audience grounded in the Old Testament.

The message may be divided into three parts by the three occurrences of direct address (13:16, 26, 38) and outlined as follows: (1) the anticipation of and preparation for **the coming of** the Messiah (vv. 16-25), (2) the rejection, crucifixion, and resurrection of the Lord Jesus (vv. 26-37), and (3) the application and appeal (vv. 38-41).

The apostle began with the vocatives, **Men of Israel and you Gentiles who worship God** (v. 16). This address embraced both Jews and Gentiles. Probably the Gentiles were not full-fledged converts to Judaism. And yet, though they revered the Yahweh of Israel (cf. vv. 26, 43), they did not have New Testament salvation. (The phrase trans. "devout converts to Judaism" in v. 43 should be trans. "worshipers." It refers to pagan worshipers but not full-fledged proselytes to Judaism. In Acts the phrase is used in almost a technical sense.)

In surveying the history of Israel, Paul mentioned the key events and people: the **stay in Egypt** (v. 17), the Exodus (v. 17), the 40-year wilderness sojourn (v. 18), the Conquest and possession of Palestine (v. 19; the **seven nations in Canaan** which God **overthrew** are

---

PAUL'S EPISTLES, WRITTEN ON HIS JOURNEYS AND DURING HIS IMPRISONMENTS

Epistle	Number of Epistles	Journeys and Imprisonments
GALATIANS	1	After his first missionary journey
1 THESSALONIANS	2	On his second missionary journey
2 THESSALONIANS		
1 CORINTHIANS	3	On his third missionary journey
2 CORINTHIANS		
ROMANS		
EPHESIANS	4	During his first imprisonment
PHILIPPIANS		
COLOSSIANS		
PHILEMON		
1 TIMOTHY	3	Before and during his second imprisonment
TITUS		
2 TIMOTHY		

listed in Deut. 7:1), the period of the **Judges** (Acts 13:20), and the monarchy under **Saul** and **David** (vv. 21–22). Mention of **David** made an easy transition to refer to **the Savior Jesus** (v. 23) and to His harbinger **John** the Baptist (vv. 24-25). (Cf. Stephen's message in 7:2-47.) The **450 years** (13:20) includes the oppression in Egypt (400 years), the wilderness sojourn (40 years), and the Conquest of Canaan under Joshua (10 years).

13:26-37. Paul, like Peter (2:23, 36; 3:15; 4:10; 5:30; 10:39) and Stephen (7:52), directly blamed the Jews for killing **Jesus.** His resurrection, frequently spoken of by His followers in Acts, was witnessed **for many days.** This is the fifth time in Acts that the apostles stated that they were **witnesses** of the resurrection of Jesus Christ (2:32; 3:15; 5:32; 10:39-41; 13:30-31).

Do the words **by raising up Jesus** (v. 33) refer to His resurrection or to His exaltation? It probably refers to the latter for several reasons: (1) When the Resurrection is mentioned in the next verse it is explained as being **from the dead.** (2) The same verb "raise up" (*anistēmi*) is used in the sense of elevation in 3:22, 26; 7:37 ("send," NIV). (3) A synonym (*egeirō*) is used in 13:22 to refer to David's promotion to kingship. (4) The primary reason for taking it to refer to Jesus' exaltation is the meaning of **Psalm** 2:7. This Old Testament passage, quoted by Paul (Acts 13:33), described the anointing of the King, which will find its ultimate fulfillment in the Millennium.

Paul confirmed the fact of Jesus' resurrection from the dead by quoting from Isaiah 55:3 and Psalm 16:10 (Acts 13:34-35). Earlier Peter had argued similarly from Psalm 16:10 (see comments on Acts 2:25–32).

13:38-39. Forgiveness of sins was mentioned frequently by the apostles in Acts (cf. 2:38; 5:31; 26:18). Acts 13:39 gives the thesis of Paul's Epistle to the Galatians, which was probably written shortly after his first missionary journey and before the Jerusalem Council (Acts 15). (See the chart "Paul's Epistles, Written on His Journeys and during His Imprisonments.")

13:40-41. Habakkuk 1:5, quoted in Acts 13:41, is an appropriate warning

against impending judgment. Judah, the prophet had said, would fall to Babylon (Hab. 1:6), which would be God's doings. Here Paul left unnamed the source of the judgment on the unbelieving Jews in his day. Paul's warning: believe or be judged.

(3) The disputation on the second Sabbath (13:42-52). **13:42-43.** The leaders were interested in Paul's message and desired to hear more. Some were disposed to accept the gospel; **Paul and Barnabas . . . urged them to continue in the grace of God.**

13:44-45. On the next Sabbath . . . the Jews (i.e., Jewish leaders), moved by **jealousy . . . talked abusively against what Paul was saying** ("abusively" renders the Gr. participle *blasphēmountes*).

13:46. To combat this Jewish opposition **Paul and Barnabas answered them boldly, We had to speak the Word of God to you first.** Apostolic preaching was noted for its boldness (cf. comments on 4:13).

It was necessary that the apostles go to the Jews first for a number of reasons. First, the coming of the earthly kingdom depended on Israel's response to the coming of Christ (cf. Matt. 23:39; Rom. 11:26). Second, only after Israel rejected the gospel could Paul devote himself to the Gentiles. Third, the message of Jesus is fundamentally Jewish in that the Old Testament, the Messiah, and the promises are all Jewish. (On "the Jew first," cf. Acts 3:26; Rom. 1:16.)

So Paul turned **to the Gentiles** in Antioch. This pattern was repeated in city after city until Paul reached Rome (cf. Acts 13:50-51; 14:2-6; 17:5, 13-15; 18:6; 19:8-9). There for the final time in the book the Apostle Paul turned from Jews to Gentiles (28:23-28).

13:47. In thus turning to the Gentiles Paul and Barnabas saw an outworking of the prophecy of Isaiah 49:6, **I have made you a light to the Gentiles.** This Old Testament passage has at least three applications—to Israel (Isa. 49:3), to Christ (Luke 2:29-32), and to Paul, the apostle to the Gentiles.

13:48. The Gentiles rejoiced in this turn of events **and all who were appointed for eternal life believed.** It is difficult to miss the doctrine of God's election here; the words "were appointed" come from the verb *tassō*, a military word meaning "to arrange" or "to assign." Luke used it here to show that God's elective decree included Gentiles.

13:49-51. The good news was shared so that **the Word of the Lord spread through the whole region** (cf. 6:7; 12:24; 19:20). But **the Jews** had contacts in high places and used these to stir **up persecution against Paul and Barnabas,** who in conformity with the Lord's instruction (Matt. 10:14) **shook the dust from their feet in protest** and left the city.

13:52. **Joy** was again a fruit of the gospel (cf. v. 48; 2:46). In addition they **were filled . . . with the Holy Spirit** (cf. 2:4).

c. At Iconium (14:1-6)

14:1-2. This paragraph (vv. 1-6) confirms the events which occurred in Pisidian Antioch. The Spirit of God was clearly prospering the apostles' ministry, as evidenced by their preaching **so effectively that a great number of Jews and Gentiles believed. But** again there was opposition (cf. growth and opposition in 13:49-50). The result of that opposition is seen in 14:6.

14:3. The NIV renders the connective *oun* (normally trans. "therefore") with the word **So.** This conjunction is a bit of a problem. It may suggest that the time in which the opposition arose (v. 2) provided further opportunity for preaching. Or it may indicate that the opposition was an evidence of God's working in the hearts of the people (cf. 1 Cor. 16:8-9), thus leading to further preaching. Probably the latter is to be preferred.

Again apostolic boldness is evident (cf. Acts 4:13; 13:46).

The reference to **miraculous signs and wonders** was further confirmation of God's endorsement of this ministry (cf. 2:43; 4:30; 5:12; 6:8; 8:6, 13; 15:12). Later Paul referred to these miracles to validate the reality of the gospel among the Galatians (Gal. 3:5). This, of course, assumes the South Galatian view of the term "Galatia" in that epistle. (See the *Introduction* to Gal. for a discussion of the South and North Galatian views.) On the confirming nature of miracles, see comments on 2 Corinthians 12:12 and Hebrews 2:3-4.

14:4. The apostolic band was referred to as **apostles.** And so they were,

for the word means "those sent with authority as representatives of another," and these men had been sent out by the church of Antioch on the Orontes River (13:3) with the church's authority.

14:5-6. When Paul and Barnabas learned of **a plot . . . to mistreat . . . and stone them,** they fled to **. . . Lystra and Derbe,** cities of Lycaonia. Luke's accuracy as a historian has been vindicated here. Though Iconium was also a **Lycaonian** city its citizens were primarily Phrygian. In location and nature Lystra and Derbe were Lycaonian (cf. "Lycaonian language," v. 11).

d. At Lystra (14:7-20a)

(1) The superstition of the Gentiles (14:7-18). **14:7.** Paul and Barnabas did not go to Lystra and Derbe simply to escape persecution; they also went to preach the gospel. The verbal construction **they continued to preach the good news** emphasizes continuity of action over a period of time.

14:8. **Lystra,** a Roman colony, was the home of at least one hopeless cripple. The dire circumstances of this man are seen in the repeated idea: **crippled in his feet . . . lame from birth . . . had never walked.** Apparently there was no Jewish synagogue in Lystra, so God used a different thrust, the healing of this helpless cripple, to bring the gospel to these people. This is the third time in Acts a cripple was healed (3:1-10; 9:33-35).

14:9-10. Paul's healing of this infirm man closely parallels Peter's healing in chapter 3. In each case the cripple was lame from birth (3:2; 14:8); both Peter and **Paul** gazed at the one **to be healed** (3:4; 14:9); and both healed men responded by jumping and walking (3:8; 14:10). This shows Paul was equal to Peter in his apostleship (cf. *Introduction*).

14:11-13. The response of the **Lycaonian** folk was one of pagan credulity. Because the people spoke in their native **language,** Paul and Barnabas could not understand what they were saying. Attributing deity to **Barnabas** and **Paul** probably can be traced to a legend about **Zeus** and **Hermes** visiting an aged Lystrian couple named Philemon and Baucis, who were abundantly rewarded for their hospitality.

Zeus was the chief god and Hermes the messenger equivalent to the Roman gods Jupiter and Mercury, respectively. Why then would Barnabas be referred to as Zeus when Paul was the leader? The answer is that Paul was the spokesman and would therefore be called Hermes and Barnabas, the more retiring of the two, would be seen as Zeus, the dignified, behind-the-scenes god.

In one spontaneous movement **the priest of Zeus . . . brought bulls and wreaths to the city gates** so the people could **offer sacrifices to** Paul and Barnabas. The wreaths were woolen garlands placed on the sacrificial animals.

14:14. When **the** two **apostles** discerned what was happening, they were horrified. **Their** tearing of **clothes** was a way of showing strong aversion to blasphemy. Usually rips were made four or five inches into the neckline of the garment.

14:15-18. This message, evidently preached by both apostles (pl. verb in the Gr.) is another sample sermon. It illustrates how these early preachers approached superstitious heathen. By contrast, the first of Paul's messages demonstrated how he preached to those well acquainted with the Old Testament (cf. 13:16-41).

After disclaiming their own deity, they urged their hearers **to turn from** their cultic gods **to the** *one* true and **living God.** This God, Creator of all, is therefore supreme over all (cf. 17:24; Rom. 1:19-20). He is recognizable not only from His creating **rain** and **crops** but also by His beneficial providence in giving **food** and **joy.**

Some interpret Acts 14:16 to mean that God will not judge the heathen who lived before the Apostolic Age. However, verse 16 must be taken with verse 17. Up to the time of the church, God gave no direct revelation to the **nations** (i.e., Gentiles) so they were responsible only for their reactions to the general revelation discernible in Creation (cf. comments on 17:27, 30 and Rom. 1:18-20).

(2) The stoning of Paul. **14:19-20a.** Once again some **Jews** proved to be enemies of the gospel of grace, and turned **the crowd,** which had just tried to make Paul and Barnabas gods, against them so **they stoned Paul.** This is the

second of five times a crowd was incited because of Paul's ministry (cf. 13:50; 16:19-22; 17:5-8, 13; 19:25-34). Whether or not Paul was **dead** is not stated; probably he was unconscious and at death's door (cf. 2 Cor. 12:2-4). At any rate his recovery was so rapid as to be miraculous. The reference to Paul's stoning (2 Cor. 11:25) undoubtedly had this incident in view (cf. 2 Tim. 3:11).

e. At Derbe (14:20b-21a)

14:20b-21a. The apostles' ministry here, in the most remote and easterly of the cities reached in Asia Minor on this journey, was successful. The gospel met no great opposition and **a large number of disciples** were **won** over to the Lord Jesus (cf. 20:4).

f. The return to Antioch of Syria (14:21b-28)

14:21b-22. Tarsus, Paul's hometown, was only about 160 miles farther on from Derbe, but the two apostles retraced their steps in Asia Minor in order to confirm the churches so recently established.

By warning and by promise, Paul and Barnabas strengthened (cf. 15:32, 41) and encouraged the believers. Previously Barnabas had encouraged the believers in Antioch of Syria (11:23). The warning consisted of a prediction of **many hardships** and the promise was the anticipation of entering **the kingdom of God.** The latter term certainly describes the eschatological reign of Christ on earth.

14:23. The believers were given not only edification but also organization. **Paul and Barnabas appointed elders for them in each church.** These elders were not novices in the faith (1 Tim. 3:6); they were probably Jews who came out of the synagogues where they had been steeped in the Scriptures. Thus elders from the synagogues became elders in the churches.

14:24-28. When the apostles returned **to Antioch** (retracing their steps through the provinces of **Pisidia** and **Pamphylia** and preaching **in Perga;** cf. 13:13-14), they gave to **the** sending **church** a full report of **all that God had done.** The clause, **how He had opened the door of faith to the Gentiles,** is most important: (a) It shows the gospel had gone to Gentiles. (b) It was a "by-faith" message and not by works of the Law. (c) God did it, for He opened the door.

Thus ends the first missionary journey which lasted between one and two years and in which Paul and Barnabas traversed more than 700 miles by land and 500 miles by sea. But more than that, it demolished the wall between Jews and Gentiles (cf. Eph. 2:14-16). The two apostles **had been committed** by the church at Antioch **to God's grace** (cf. Acts 15:40) and they saw His grace at work (cf. "grace" in 13:43; 14:3).

Probably Paul wrote the Book of Galatians from Antioch shortly after his first missionary journey and before the Jerusalem Council (Acts 15).

3. THE CONFERENCE AT JERUSALEM (15:1-35)

a. *The dissension concerning circumcision (15:1-2)*

15:1-2. The **men** who **came down from Judea to Antioch** may well be the same ones referred to in Galatians 2:12. They insisted circumcision was essential for justification. Perhaps they based their theology on such passages as Genesis 17:14 and Exodus 12:48-49.

At any rate, they were sure to cause a severe schism in the church, so their teaching **brought Paul and Barnabas into sharp dispute and debate with them.**

The men from Judea were dogmatic in their doctrine in spite of the fact they had no authority from the church in Jerusalem. How they explained the case of Cornelius (Acts 10) or the work of Barnabas (11:22-24) is left unstated. Perhaps they felt Cornelius' case was unique and the believers in Antioch in chapter 11 were too insignificant to use as examples. Now the movement was becoming overwhelming and this was their way of protesting.

The church at Antioch felt it was wise to discuss the matter with **the apostles and elders in Jerusalem.** So they commissioned **Paul and Barnabas** for the task and wisely sent **some other believers** along as witnesses. These witnesses would protect Paul and Barnabas against being accused of distorting the facts.

b. *The discussion concerning circumcision (15:3-12)*

15:3-4. As the men in the delegation made **their way** to Jerusalem they reported the good **news** of **Gentile** conversions to the brethren in **Phoenicia and Samaria.** Once again the response of a believing church was joy! (cf. 2:46) Furthermore, **the church** in **Jerusalem** with its leaders **welcomed** Paul and Barnabas; this was scarcely the response of the antagonists.

15:5. The issue was stated forthrightly by **the** believing **Pharisees.** Significantly circumcision also involved keeping **the** whole Old Testament **Law** as Paul later wrote (Gal. 5:3). The method of justification ultimately determines the method of sanctification (cf. Col. 2:6).

15:6-9. The apostles and elders met to consider this question. In addition many other believers were present (cf. vv. 12, 22).

The problem was no small one; there was **much discussion** (*zēteseōs*, meaning "inquiry, debate, questioning"; trans. "debate" in v. 2; "controversies" in 1 Tim. 6:4; "arguments" in 2 Tim. 2:23 and Titus 3:9). **Peter** wisely permitted this to continue for a time lest the impression be given that the results were a foregone conclusion. The date of this council is generally taken to be A.D. 49. When Peter referred to God's **choice** of Cornelius **some time ago** he was looking back about 10 years (Acts 10:1–11:18). The issue of whether to accept **Gentiles** was settled then and there. This was evidenced, Peter said, because **God gave the Holy Spirit to them** (10:44-46) **just as** He did to the Jews (2:4; 11:15). So God **made no distinction between** believing Jews and Gentiles. All are accepted **by faith.**

15:10. Requiring Gentiles to be circumcised to obey the Mosaic Law would have had two results: (a) the Jews would **test** (*peirazete*) **God** (cf. Deut. 6:16) and (b) they would put **on the necks of the disciples** an unbearable **yoke** (cf. Matt. 23:4). To "test" God is to see how far one can go with God (cf. Acts 5:9). Putting a yoke on the disciples' necks was an appropriate way to state the second result, for "taking the yoke" was used to describe Gentile proselytes coming into Judaism. It spoke of an obligation.

In discussing the question Peter referred not only to Gentiles but also to all believers coming under the Law. The term "disciples" was used of both Jews and Gentiles.

15:11. The statement, **We are saved, just as they are,** is amazing. A Jew under the Law would say the opposite and in reverse order ("they are saved as we are"), but one who knew God's **grace,** as Peter did, would not say that. Salvation for anyone—Jew or Gentile—is by God's grace (v. 11) and is by faith (v. 9; cf. Gal. 2:16; Eph. 2:8).

15:12. Barnabas and Paul, who next addressed the assembly, described **the miraculous signs and wonders** (sēmeia and terata; cf. 2:43 [see comments there]; 5:12; 6:8; 8:6, 13; 14:3) that **God had done among the Gentiles through them.** These would especially convince the Jews (cf. 1 Cor. 1:22) so **they listened** in silence. This response implied they would not argue against the testimonies of Peter, Paul, and Barnabas.

c. The decision concerning circumcision (15:13-29)

15:13-14. James, evidently the head of the church at Jerusalem, then took the floor and issued a summary statement. He was Jesus' half brother and wrote the Epistle of James.

He began by discussing Peter's experience (Acts 10). In referring to Peter as **Simon,** James used a name which would be logical in its setting in Jerusalem (actually the Gr. has *Symeōn,* an even more Jewish spelling, used only here and in 2 Peter 1:1 in the NT).

The phrase **at first** is crucial because it affirmed that Paul and Barnabas were not the first to go to **the Gentiles.** As Peter had already said (Acts 15:7-11) the question had actually been settled in principle (chaps. 10–11) *before* Paul and Barnabas went on their first journey.

15:15-18. Quite properly the council desired more than the testimony of experience. They wanted to know how it corresponded with the witness of the Scriptures. This was the ultimate test.

To prove that Gentile salvation apart from circumcision was an Old Testament doctrine, James quoted from Amos 9:11-12. Several problems are involved in this quotation.

One problem involves the text. James here quoted a text similar to the Septuagint (the Gr. OT) that differs from the Hebrew text. The Hebrew of Amos 9:12 may be translated, "That they may possess the remnant of Edom and all the nations who are called by My name." But James used the noun **of men** (or "of mankind"), not "Edom," and the verb **seek,** not "possess."

The Hebrew consonants for "Edom" and for "Adam" are identical ('dm). The confusion in the vowels (added much later) is easy to understand. The only distinction in the Hebrew between "possess" (yāraš) and "seek" (dāraš) is in one consonant. The text James used may well represent the original.

Another problem, the major one, involves interpretation. What did Amos mean when he wrote these verses, and how did James use the passage? Several observations need to be noted before the passage is interpreted: (1) James did not say Amos 9:11-12 was *fulfilled* in the church; he simply asserted that what was happening in the church was in full agreement with the Old Testament prophets. (2) The word "prophets" is plural, implying that the quotation from Amos was representative of what the prophets in general affirmed. (3) James' main point is clear: Gentile salvation apart from the Law does not contradict the Old Testament prophets. (4) The words **After this** are neither in the Masoretic text nor the Septuagint; both have "in that day." Any interpretation of the passage must consider these factors.

Bible students interpret these verses in one of three ways. Those who hold to amillennial theology say the rebuilt house (skēnēn, "tent") of David is the church which God is using to preach to the Gentiles. While this view at first appears plausible, several factors oppose it. (1) The verb **return** (anastrepsō) used in Acts 15:16 means an actual return. Luke used it only in 5:22 ("went back") and here (he did not use it in his Gospel); in both occurrences it describes a literal, bodily return. Since God's Son has not yet returned bodily, this rebuilding has not taken place. (2) Christ's present ministry in heaven is not associated with the Davidic throne elsewhere in the New Testament. He is now seated at the right hand of God (Ps. 110:1; Rom. 8:34; Col. 3:1; Heb. 1:3; 8:1; 10:12; 12:2; 1 Peter 3:22). When He returns He will sit on David's throne (2 Sam. 7:16; Ps. 89:4; Matt. 19:28; 25:31). (3) The church was a mystery, a truth not revealed to Old Testament saints (Rom. 16:25; Eph. 3:5-6;

Col. 1:24-27); so the church would not be referred to in Amos.

A second view of the passage is commonly held by premillenarians. According to this view there are four chronological movements in this passage: the present Church Age ("taking from the Gentiles a people for Himself," Acts 15:14), the return of Christ to Israel (v. 16a), the establishing of the Davidic kingdom (v. 16b), and the turning of Gentiles to God (v. 17). While this does interpret these verses in a logical fashion, this approach has some difficulties. (1) The quotation begins with the words "After this." Premillenarians assert James used this phrase to suit his interpretation of the passage. But since the quotation begins with "after this" James must be quoting the sense of Amos 9:11. Therefore this phrase looks back, not to Acts 15:14, but to Amos 9:8-10, which describes the Tribulation ("a time of trouble for Jacob," Jer. 30:7). (2) If the temporal phrase "after this" refers to the present Age in Amos 9:11, Amos would then have predicted the church in the Old Testament.

A third view, also premillennial, may be more plausible. James simply asserted that Gentiles will be saved in the Millennium when Christ will return and rebuild David's fallen tent, that is, restore the nation Israel. Amos said nothing about Gentiles needing to be circumcised. Several factors support this interpretation: (1) This fits the purpose of the council. If Gentiles will be saved in the Kingdom Age (the Millennium), why should they become Jewish proselytes by circumcision in the Church Age? (2) This approach suits the meaning of "in that day" in Amos 9:11. After the Tribulation (Amos 9:8-10) God will establish the messianic kingdom (Amos 9:11-12). James (Acts 15:16) interpreted "in that day" to mean that "at the time when" God does one (the Tribulation) He will then do the other. In that sense James could say "After this." (3) This interpretation gives significance to the word "first" in verse 14. Cornelius and his household were among the first Gentiles to become members of Christ's body, the church. Gentile salvation will culminate in great blessing for them in the Millennium (cf. Rom. 11:12). (4) A number of prophets predicted Gentile salvation in the Millennium, as James stated in Acts 15:15 (e.g., Isa. 42:6; 60:3; Mal. 1:11).

15:19-21. As a result of this theological discussion James set forth a practical decision. It was his considered **judgment** (*krinō*, lit., "I judge") that the church **should not make it difficult** (*parenochlein*, "to annoy"; used only here in the NT) **for the Gentiles.** This parallels in thought the sentiments of Peter expressed in verse 10. **Instead** (*alla*, "but," a strong adversative conjunction) James suggested they draft a letter affirming an ethic which would not offend those steeped in the Old Testament.

The Gentiles were **to abstain from** three items: (a) **food polluted by idols,** (b) **sexual immorality,** and (c) **the meat of strangled animals and . . . blood.** Many Bible teachers say these are only ceremonial matters. The food polluted by idols is explained in verse 29 as "food sacrificed to idols" (cf. 21:25). This then, it is argued, looks at the same problem Paul discussed (1 Cor. 8-10). The abstinence from sexual immorality is explained as referring to the marriage laws of Leviticus 18:6-20. The prohibition against eating blood is taken to refer to Leviticus 17:10-14. All three prohibitions according to this interpretation look back to the Jewish *ceremonial* Law.

However, it seems better to take these as moral issues. The reference to food polluted by idols should be taken in the sense of Revelation 2:14, 20. It was a usual practice among Gentiles to use an idol's temple for banquets and celebrations. Paul also condemned the practice of Christians participating in these (1 Cor. 10:14-22). Fornication was such a common sin among the Gentiles that it was an accepted practice. The problem of immorality even persisted among Christians all too often, as is witnessed by the New Testament injunctions against it (cf. 1 Cor. 6:12-18, where Paul was evidently answering arguments in favor of immorality). The third prohibition goes back further than Leviticus 17; it looks back to Genesis 9, where God established the Noahic Covenant, a "contract" still in effect today. There God gave people the privilege of eating flesh but the blood was to be drained from it.

All three prohibitions in Acts 15:20 are best taken in an ethical or moral sense. If this be so, they are still the responsibility of Christians today, even to the point of not eating blood sausage and raw meat. By not attending temple banquets, or being involved in fornication, or eating meat with blood in it, the Gentile Christians would be maintaining high moral standards and would keep from offending their Jewish brothers. There were Jews in every city who would be offended by Christians not following these strictures. These Israelites were well acquainted with these moral issues.

15:22. The whole church (cf. v. 12) was permitted to express itself on this issue. Interestingly two witnesses were delegated to attend **Paul and Barnabas** for the protection of both sides (v. 2). They would "confirm by word of mouth" what was written (v. 27). No one could claim there were poor communications about this delicate issue.

Silas was one of these **two men.** This is in keeping with Luke's style of bringing someone on the scene unobtrusively who later becomes a main character (cf. v. 40). These two **leaders**, also "prophets" (v. 32), may have represented two groups in the Jerusalem church—**Judas**, probably a brother of Joseph (cf. 1:23), for the Hebrew section; and Silas, a Roman citizen (cf. 16:37), for the Hellenists.

15:23-29. The **letter**, sent by **the apostles and elders**, confirmed the findings of the council. The church's admiration for **Barnabas and Paul** is evidenced by the words **our dear friends** and their acknowledging that Paul and Barnabas had **risked their lives for the name** (cf. comments on 3:16) **of our Lord Jesus Christ** (cf. 13:50; 14:5, 19). Significantly the letter referred **to the Holy Spirit** as the "Prime Mover" in this discernment of truth.

d. The delegation among the Gentiles (15:30-35)

15:30-35. The contingent from Jerusalem together with Judas and Silas **went down to Antioch** (Antioch is on a lower elevation than Jerusalem) **and delivered the letter.** The brothers in Antioch were encouraged by the letter, and also by **Judas and Silas**, the **prophets**, who encouraged the church still further and strengthened them by a lengthy message.

The saints in Antioch appreciated the ministry of Judas and Silas and **sent** them **off** with blessings. The word **peace** expressed a desire for well-being in all areas of their lives.

Verse 34 is omitted by several important Greek manuscripts. Perhaps a scribe added it later to explain the choice of Silas (v. 40).

In the following months **Paul and Barnabas** continued to minister to the saints **in Antioch.**

4. THE CONFIRMATION OF THE CHURCHES IN ASIA MINOR (15:36–16:5)

[Second missionary journey, 15:36–18:22]

a. The contention between Paul and Barnabas (15:36-41)

15:36-41. Later when **Paul** proposed **to Barnabas** a return trip to confirm the churches established on their first journey, **Barnabas wanted to take . . . Mark with them. Paul** disagreed with this suggestion because Mark **had deserted them** earlier, **in Pamphylia** (cf. 13:13). The argument became **such a sharp disagreement** (*paroxysmos,* "provoking, stirring up, arousing," the root of the Eng. "paroxysm") **that they parted company.** The Lord overruled in this dissension for through it two missionary journeys instead of one were formed—one to **Cyprus** with **Barnabas** and **Mark,** and the other to **Syria and Cilicia** and ultimately Europe with **Paul** and **Silas.** Probably both Paul and Barnabas were right in their assessments of Mark. It may have been too soon for Mark to venture out with such a pro-Gentile apostle as Paul, but Barnabas certainly and correctly saw good raw material in his cousin Mark (cf. Col. 4:10; 2 Tim. 4:11; Phile. 24; 1 Peter 5:13). Paul later spoke of Barnabas in positive terms (1 Cor. 9:6; Col. 4:10). The Apostle Paul owed much to Barnabas and it appears they remained friends despite their contention over Mark.

Neither Mark nor Barnabas are seen again in the Book of Acts; the same is true of Peter following the Jerusalem Council (Acts 15).

Paul's choice of Silas, whose Roman name (in Gr.) was Sylvanus (2 Cor. 1:19; 1 Thes. 1:1; 2 Thes. 1:1; 1 Peter 5:12), was a wise one: (1) He was an official repre-

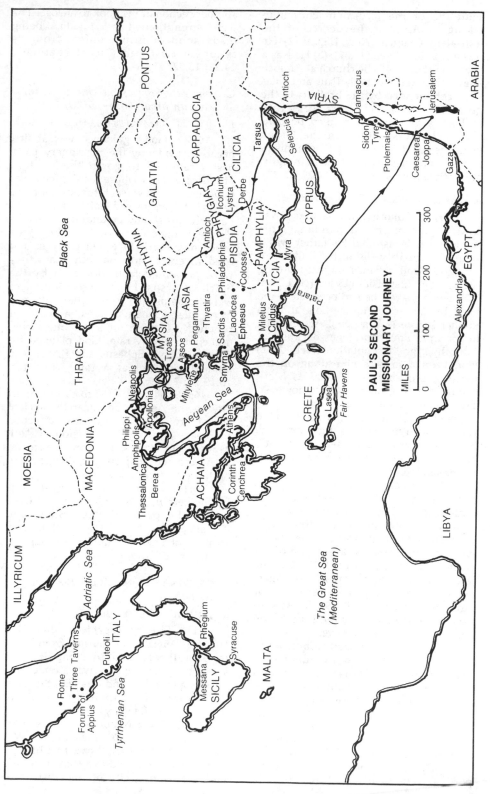

PAUL'S SECOND MISSIONARY JOURNEY

MILES

0   100   200   300

sentative of the Jerusalem church in taking to Antioch the decree of the Jerusalem Council (Acts 15:22). (2) He was a Roman citizen (16:37). (3) He was a prophet (15:32). (4) The church at Antioch knew him well, so both Paul and Silas were **commended by the brothers to the grace of the Lord.** (5) Because Silas served as Peter's amanuensis, it may be concluded he was skilled in the Greek language (cf. 1 Peter 5:12). The ministry of Paul and Silas involved their **strengthening the churches** (cf. Acts 14:22; 15:32).

b. The conscription of Timothy (16:1-5)

16:1-3. Timothy, whose home was **Lystra,** was of mixed parentage; his **mother was** Jewish and his **father was a Greek.** Probably Timothy had been converted under Paul's ministry during the apostle's first visit to Lystra (cf. 1 Tim. 1:2). Some suggest he had been led to the Lord by his grandmother Lois and his mother Eunice (2 Tim. 1:5). At any rate, he became Paul's protegé. Because of Timothy's good reputation (Acts 16:2) **Paul wanted to take him along on the journey,** probably as a helper as Mark had been. There was a problem, however. The Jews to whom Paul would be preaching the gospel would be offended if a man with a Jewish mother was uncircumcised. So Timothy was **circumcised.** Apparently he had been uncircumcised because of his father's influence.

This appears to contradict Paul's thinking in Galatians 2:3-5 where he refused to let Titus be circumcised. The situations, however, were different. In Galatians 2 the issue was the method of justification; here it was a question of not giving offense (cf. 1 Cor. 9:19-23). The Jerusalem Council, of course, had determined circumcision was not necessary for salvation (Acts 15:10-11, 19). In Acts 16 Paul acted as he did for the sake of the ministry; it was a wise move.

16:4. As they traveled from town to town, they delivered the decisions reached by the Jerusalem Council (15:23-29). Assuming Paul wrote Galatians after the first missionary journey, but before the Jerusalem Council, the report of the decision would be strong confirmation of the gospel which he preached and about which he wrote.

16:5. With another "progress report" (cf. *Introduction*), Luke brought

another section of his book to a close. The word **strengthened** (*estereounto*, "being made solid or firm") differs from its synonym *epistērizō* ("to strengthen"; 14:22; 15:32, 41).

C. The extension of the church in the Aegean area (16:6-19:20)

1. THE CALL TO MACEDONIA (16:6-10)

16:6-7. God's guidance was at first negative. Evidently the missionary party first attempted to go to the western **province of Asia** whose leading city was Ephesus. So they went **throughout the region of Phrygia and Galatia** (cf. 18:23). Possibly this should be understood as the Phrygian region of Galatia. **They** then proceeded north to eastern **Mysia** and **tried to enter Bithynia, but** again they were prevented from doing so by **the Spirit of Jesus.** How these hindrances were accomplished is not stated. It may have been circumstances, a word of prophecy, a vision, or some other phenomenon. At any rate, God planned for people in both Ephesus and Bithynia to hear the gospel at a later time (cf. 18:19-21, 24-19:41; 1 Peter 1:1).

16:8-9. Finally, at **Troas,** a seaport city on the Aegean Sea near the ancient site of Troy, God gave positive direction by means of a **night . . . vision to Paul. Macedonia** was a Roman senatorial province, corresponding roughly to northern Greece today.

16:10. The first of the **we** sections begins here in Acts, indicating that Luke joined the party of Paul, Silas, and Timothy. The how, why, and precise location of Luke's joining the group are left unstated.

2. THE CONFLICTS IN MACEDONIA (16:11-17:15)

a. At Philippi (16:11-40)

(1) The conversion of Lydia (16:11-15). **16:11.** The journey **from Troas** to **Samothrace** and **to Neapolis,** the seaport city for Philippi, was a rapid one, implying that the wind was with them (cf. 20:6 where the trip in the opposite direction took five days).

16:12. From Neapolis the missionaries **traveled** the 10 miles on the Via Egnatia, the Egnatian Road **to Philippi,** which Luke described as **a Roman colony and the leading city of that district of**

Macedonia. Quite clearly Luke displayed pride in the city he came to love. Some say he grew up and attended medical school there. Philippi, originally named Crenides ("Fountains"), was taken by Philip of Macedon and renamed after him. In 168 B.C. Philippi became a Roman possession. After Mark Antony and Octavian defeated Brutus and Cassius, the assassins of Julius Caesar, near Philippi in 42 B.C., the city was made into a Roman colony. This gave it special privileges (e.g, fewer taxes) but more importantly it became like a "transplanted" Rome (cf. comments on Philippi in the *Introduction* to Phil.). The primary purpose of colonies was military, for the Roman leaders felt it wise to have Roman citizens and sympathizers settled in strategic locations. So Octavian (who became Caesar Augustus, the first Roman emperor, in 27 B.C.) settled more colonists (primarily former soldiers) at Philippi after his defeat of Antony at Actium, on Greece's west coast, in 31 B.C.

16:13. The Jewish population at Philippi must have been limited, for there was no synagogue there; 10 Jewish males were required for a synagogue. **A place of prayer** (cf. v. 16), which may have been a place in the open air or a simple building, was located by **the** Gangites **River** about a mile and one-half west of town.

To the women . . . gathered there, the missionaries presented the gospel.

16:14. Lydia was a seller of **purple cloth.** This purple color came from a shellfish, the murex, or from the root of a plant. She was from Thyatira, a city known for its commerce in Asia Minor (cf. comments on Thyatira in Rev. 2:18-29). She **was a worshiper of God,** a term used for Gentiles (e.g., Cornelius [Acts 10:2] and those in Thessalonica [17:4] and Athens [17:17]) who were not proselytes to Judaism but who did worship Yahweh. Even so, they were not in the New Testament church, the body of Christ. **The Lord opened her heart** (cf. Luke 24:45) **to respond to Paul's message.** Again Luke stressed the sovereignty of God in salvation (cf. Acts 13:48).

16:15. Lydia was then **baptized,** apparently soon after her faith in Christ. **The members of her household** probably refer to servants as well as to her children, if she was a widow. Other persons in the New Testament who along with their "household" members came to Christ include Cornelius (10:24, 44), the Philippian jailer (16:31), Crispus (18:8), Aristobulus (Rom. 16:10), Narcissus (Rom. 16:11), and Stephanas (1 Cor. 1:16).

That she was a woman of considerable means is evidenced by the size of her **house.** It would have to be ample enough to house four men as well as her household without embarrassment (cf. Acts 16:40).

(2) The deliverance of the soothsayer. **16:16-18.** Some men were exploiting a demon-possessed **slave girl** for her ability to predict the future. The English words, **a spirit by which she predicted the future,** translate two Greek words, "a spirit, a python." This concept goes back to the Greek city of Delphi where the god Apollo was believed to be embodied in a python snake. The original priestess at Delphi was purported to be possessed by Apollo and thereby able to predict the future; therefore anyone possessed by the python spirit could foretell coming events. No doubt an actual demon gave such a person predictive powers. Demons took advantage of people's worship of false gods (cf. 17:23; 1 Cor. 10:20).

The **girl** attached herself to **Paul and the** others and was **shouting** (imperf. tense) who they were (**servants of the Most High God**) and what they preached (**the way to be saved**). Though her statements were true, the gospel of Christ would be damaged by an association with a demon-possessed slave girl. So after **many days . . . Paul** exorcised the demon, speaking directly **to the spirit.** (Other cases of victory over the occult in Acts are recorded in 8:9-24; 13:6-12; 19:13-20.)

(3) The conversion of the jailer (16:19-34). **16:19-21.** Each Roman colony was governed by two leaders called *douviri* in Latin. The term **magistrates** translates *stratēgois,* the Greek equivalent for the Latin word.

The charge of **the** slave girl's **owners** against **Paul and Silas** was obviously prejudicial. Shortly before this incident the Emperor Claudius had expelled the Jews from Rome (18:2). Philippi, a Roman colony, would have caught this flavor of anti-Semitism. This also helps explain why Timothy and Luke were not taken before the authorities. Timothy was a half-Gentile (16:1) and Luke was probably a Gentile.

Furthermore, Paul and Silas were accused of disrupting the **city . . . by advocating customs unlawful for . . . Romans to accept or practice.** Rome permitted the peoples of its colonies to have their own religions but not to proselytize Roman citizens. The civil leaders could not distinguish between Judaism and Christianity (cf. 18:14-15), so they would see the preaching of Paul and Silas as a flagrant infraction of imperial law.

16:22. Impelled by **the crowd . . . the magistrates ordered them to be stripped and beaten.** The verb translated "beaten" is from *rhabdizō,* which means "to beat with a rod." This was one of the three beatings Paul referred to in 2 Corinthians 11:25, the only other place where this verb occurs in the New Testament.

16:23-24. Paul and Silas were **severely flogged** and then **thrown into prison.** What a reception in the first European city where they preached the gospel! **The jailer** with his strict **orders** was not going to take any chances so **he put them in the inner cell** (possibly a dungeon, at least the most secure cell) **and fastened their feet in stocks.**

16:25. Paul and Silas singing in the inner prison gives special significance to the theme of joy in Acts (cf. Ps. 42:8; "at night His song is with me"). Their **praying and singing** was heard not only by God but also by **the other prisoners.**

16:26. This supernatural deliverance reminds the reader of the parallel experiences of Peter (cf. 5:18-20; 12:3-11). This was certainly an unusual midnight experience in a **prison**—the earth quaking, the **prison** shaking, **doors** flying **open . . . chains** falling off.

16:27-28. Because **the jailer** was responsible for any escaped **prisoners** (cf. 12:19), **he drew his sword . . . to kill himself. But Paul,** seeing what was about to happen, reassured him that the prisoners had not **escaped.** Perhaps the other prisoners were so impressed with the God of Paul and Silas that they did not dare flee!

16:29-30. Going into Paul and Silas' cell, **the jailer . . . trembling . . . asked, Men, what must I do to be saved?** This question was filled with significance. He

must have understood what he was asking. Undoubtedly he had heard the story of the slave girl and how she had announced these men to be servants of God with the message of salvation (v. 17). Possibly also the prayers and singing of **Paul and Silas** (v. 25) had reached his ears. The awesome earthquake with the subsequent opportunity for the prisoners to escape and Paul's reassuring words all moved him to ask for the way of salvation.

16:31-32. Verse 31 is a key passage on the message of faith. All that is needed for justification is faith **in the Lord Jesus.** The jailer had asked what he should do. The answer was that he need perform no works; he only needed to **believe** in Jesus who is the Lord.

The words **and your household** mean those members of **his house** who were of sufficient age to believe would be saved (cf. v. 34) as they trusted Christ. Each member had to believe to be saved.

16:33. The jailer . . . washed the **wounds** of Paul and Silas (cf. v. 23)—an amazing thing for a jailer to do for his prisoners. Then by water baptism **he and all his family** gave testimony to the washing away of their sins.

16:34. The jailer took the former prisoners home and fed them! And his **family** was joyful. Once again the evidence of the victorious gospel was joy.

(4) The deliverance of Paul and Silas (16:35-40). **16:35-36.** Apparently **the jailer** brought **Paul** and **Silas** back to prison. What prompted **the magistrates** to change their minds is left unstated. Perhaps the earthquake jarred their senses, or maybe on further reflection they realized how unjust they had been.

16:37-40. Paul's demand that the magistrates **escort** him and Silas **out** of **prison** appears to be vindictive. But it probably was designed to spare the young church in Philippi from further harassment. It certainly would place the believers in a far more secure position before the officials.

But why did **Paul** wait so long to mention his **Roman** citizenship? Perhaps the uproar at the trial (vv. 19-22) kept him from being heard. Or maybe Paul purposely waited till the most propitious time to give out this information. Born a

Roman citizen (22:28), Paul had certain rights, including a public hearing. And no Roman citizen was supposed to be scourged.

In only two places in Acts was Paul harmed or threatened by Gentiles—in Philippi and in Ephesus (19:23-41). In both instances people were losing money in vested interests and in each case Paul was vindicated by a Roman official. **After their prison release, Paul and Silas . . . met with the** believers at **Lydia's house** (cf. 16:15).

With Paul's departure the first **we** section ends, indicating Luke remained on at Philippi (cf. **they** in 16:40).

b. At Thessalonica (17:1-9)

17:1. The journey from Philippi to Thessalonica was about 100 miles with **Amphipolis and Apollonia** at approximately 30-mile intervals on the Via Egnatia. Evidently there were no Jewish synagogues in the two towns where Paul did not stop. A **synagogue** provided an excellent point of contact for the gospel (cf. v. 10) so Paul remained at **Thessalonica,** modern Saloniki, to preach.

17:2. The reference to **three Sabbath days** does not mean the missionary band stayed only three weeks in Thessalonica. Paul carried on the work with a Jewish emphasis for three Sabbaths and then turned to Gentiles and ministered to them for some weeks after that. This was the situation for three reasons: (1) The Philippian church sent money to Paul at least twice during this visit (Phil. 4:15-16), implying a longer lapse of time than three weeks. (2) In addition, Paul supported himself by manual labor (1 Thes. 2:9; 2 Thes. 3:7-10). This may indicate that considerable time elapsed before the aid from Philippi arrived. (3) Most of the converts at Thessalonica were not from the synagogue but were Gentiles steeped in idolatry (cf. 1 Thes. 1:9).

17:3-4. Paul and Silas' ministry in presenting the crucified and resurrected Jesus as **the Christ** (the Messiah) met with response: **some . . . Jews,** many **God-fearing Greeks** (cf. 16:14, where the same Greek word is used of Lydia, who is called "a worshiper of God"; cf. the same word in 17:17), **and not a few prominent women** (cf. v. 12). The gospel message was received by people of various nationalities and social positions.

17:5. Luke evidently included this incident to reemphasize the continued Jewish rejection. Jason probably had provided lodging for **Paul and Silas. The Jews were** intent on finding Paul and Silas **in order to bring them out to the crowd.** Thessalonica was a free city which meant it was sovereign in its local affairs and not subject to provincial administration in such matters. Besides local rulers, Thessalonica also had its own local assembly called the *dēmos,* the word translated "crowd" here (see the NIV marg.; cf. 19:30 ["crowd"], 33 ["people"] where the noun also occurs).

17:6-7. Because the mob could **not find** Paul and Silas **they** grabbed **Jason and some other** believers and accused them **before the city officials** (*politarchas,* lit., "city rulers"). In Macedonian cities these magistrates formed the city council. The charge was specifically against **Jason** (possibly a relative of Paul; cf. Rom. 16:21) for harboring men who had **caused trouble all over the world**—obviously an exaggeration—and defied **Caesar's decrees, saying that there is another King, One called Jesus.** This latter accusation is significant for it shows Jews were behind the whole mob scene (cf. Acts 17:5); only they would have known enough about Paul's theology to make such a charge. (Jews also accused Jesus of claiming to be "a king"; Luke 23:2.) Furthermore it reflects Paul's proclamation. As the Thessalonian Epistles indicate, Paul proclaimed that the messianic kingdom will be established at the return of Christ (1 Thes. 3:13; 5:1-11; 2 Thes. 1:5-10; 2:14; cf. Luke 23:2; John 18:33-37).

17:8-9. The crowd and the politarchs **were** in **turmoil** (*etaraxan,* "agitated, disturbed, troubled"; cf. John 11:33; Acts 16:20) probably because they could not find Paul and Silas (17:6), the source of the city's problem. Probably the bond-posting was to guarantee that Paul and Silas would leave town and not return. If more trouble arose, **Jason and the others** would lose their money. This may explain why Paul was prohibited from returning (1 Thes. 2:18). In spite of this, the Christians at Thessalonica kept on boldly proclaiming the gospel (1 Thes. 1:7-10; cf. 2:14-16).

c. At Berea (17:10-15)

17:10. Under cover of **night** (cf. Paul's other nighttime escape; 9:25) **the brothers sent Paul and Silas away to Berea.** Perhaps Timothy accompanied them or he may have joined them at Berea later (cf. 17:14). Berea was about 46 miles southwest of Thessalonica on the eastern slopes of a mountain. Berea was also on the way to Achaia, the province that corresponds to southern Greece today. Sopater was from Berea (20:4). As usual, Paul and Silas **went to the . . . synagogue** (cf. 17:2, 17; 18:4, 19; 19:8).

17:11-12. The Berean Jews **were of more noble character than the Thessalonians.** They welcomed Paul's **message with great eagerness and examined the Scriptures every day to see if what Paul said was true.** This differed from the Jews in Thessalonica only some of whom believed (v. 4), whereas most of them were jealous of Paul and stirred up trouble. The Bereans' interest in the Word resulted in many conversions of both Jews and Greeks. Interestingly **prominent . . .women** in both Thessalonica and Berea received Christ (vv. 4, 12).

17:13-14. Once again Jewish unbelievers (from **Thessalonica**) forced the expulsion of **Paul. Stirring** is from the same Greek word used in verse 8 to speak of being "in turmoil." **Silas and Timothy** remained **at Berea** to help establish the fledgling church, while **Paul** went on south.

17:15. Whether **Paul** went **to Athens** by boat or by land is not known. In either case some brothers **accompanied** Paul to guarantee his safe arrival. Paul told the friends to instruct **Silas and Timothy to join him** in Athens **as soon as possible.**

It is clear from 1 Thessalonians 3:1-2, 6 that Silas and Timothy did rejoin Paul at Athens. Silas likewise was commissioned by Paul to leave Athens and then meet him at Corinth (cf. Acts 18:1-5).

3. THE CRUSADE IN ACHAIA (17:16–18:18)

a. At Athens (17:16-34)

17:16. The glory of Greece in the fifth and fourth centuries B.C. was fading in Paul's day and even **Athens,** the proud center of Hellenism, was past its bloom. Even so, it was still a vital cultural center with a world-famous university. Many of its famous buildings were built during the days of its leader Pericles (461–429 B.C.). Beautiful as were the architecture and art forms, Paul could not enjoy them because **he was greatly distressed to see that the city was full of idols.** The art of Athens was a reflection of its worship. The intellectual capital of the world was producing idolatry.

17:17. In this city Paul waged spiritual warfare on two fronts, **the synagogue** and **the marketplace.** In the synagogue he no doubt used his normal approach, proving from the Old Testament Scriptures that Jesus is the Messiah (cf. vv. 2-3). In that synagogue were **Jews** and **God-fearing** Gentiles (cf. v. 4). In the marketplace (*agora*, the center of civic life) where philosophers debated and presented their views, Paul **reasoned . . . with those who happened to be there.**

17:18. The primary antagonists of Paul in the *agora* were the **Epicurean and Stoic philosophers.** The Epicureans, who followed Epicurus (341–270 B.C.), said the chief end of man was pleasure and happiness. This pleasure, they believed, is attained by avoiding excesses and the fear of death, by seeking tranquility and freedom from pain, and by loving mankind. They believed that if gods exist they do not become involved in human events.

The Stoics, on the other hand, were followers of Zeno (ca. 320–ca. 250 B.C.) and got their name from the painted portico or *stoa*, where he traditionally taught in Athens. Pantheistic in their view, they felt a great "Purpose" was directing history. Man's responsibility was to fit himself and align himself with this Purpose through tragedy and triumph. Quite obviously this outlook, while it produced certain noble qualities, also resulted in inordinate pride and self-sufficiency.

When these philosophers encountered Paul, they **began to dispute with him. Some of them asked, What is this babbler trying to say?** "Dispute" is *syneballon* (lit., "to throw with," i.e., to toss ideas back and forth). This differs slightly from what Paul did in the synagogues. There he reasoned (*dielegeto*, "discussed, conversed," v. 17; cf. the same word in v. 2; 18:4, 19; 19:8). The word translated "babbler" is *spermologos* (lit., "seed-picker"). It described someone who, like a bird picking up seeds, took some learning here and some there and then passed it off as his own. **Others remarked, He seems to be advocating foreign gods.** This response was due to their inability to grasp Paul's doctrine of Christ and **the Resurrection;** it was totally foreign to their thinking (cf. 17:31-32).

17:19-21. Areopagus, literally, "Hill of Ares," was the **meeting** place of the Council of the Areopagus, the supreme body for judicial and legislative matters in Athens. In the Apostolic Age its power had been reduced to oversight over religion and education.

There is some question as to where this council met in Paul's time. Some think it met on the traditional Mars Hill behind the *agora* and immediately west of the Acropolis. Others say it met in the Stoa Basileios, a building in the *agora*. The council wanted to know about Paul's **new teaching,** which was **strange** to their **ears.** In Athens, the ancient world's intellectual center, **the Athenians and** foreign residents loved **to** debate **the latest ideas.** This openness gave Paul an opportunity to preach his message.

17:22. Beginning with this verse (and continuing through v. 31) is another of Paul's "sample sermons" (cf. 13:16-41; 14:15-18; 20:18-35). This one shows how Paul addressed intellectual pagans. The thrust of his message is clear: the Creator God, who has revealed Himself in Creation, has now commanded all to repent, for everyone must give an account to Jesus Christ whom God raised from the dead.

Paul's discourse includes three parts: (a) the introduction (17:22-23), (b) the unknown God (vv. 24-29), and (c) the message from God (vv. 30-31).

Paul began wisely by acknowledging they were **very religious.** These two words translate the Greek *deisidaimonesterous* from *deidō* ("to fear or revere"), *daimōn* ("deities, evil spirits"), and *stereos* ("firm, hard"). The idea is that the Athenians were firm and rigid in their reverencing of their deities. This was a carefully chosen word. Hearing it, the **men of Athens** would have thought of their deities or gods. But Paul subtly implied that their deities were evil spirits or demons, not gods. Behind idols are demons (cf. comments on 16:16).

17:23. The Athenians, who feared they might overlook venerating some deity they did not know about, dedicated an altar TO AN UNKNOWN GOD. When Paul referred to this, he did not emphasize the **altar** but their ignorance of the true God.

17:24. Because **God** made **everything,** He is supreme over all—**the Lord of heaven and earth** (cf. 14:15; cf. Ps. 24:1). Such a great God **does not live** in humanly constructed **temples,** as the Athenians assumed their Greek gods did (cf. Stephen's words in Acts 7:48-50).

17:25. God is above human temples, but **He** is also self-sufficient and **is not** sustained **by human** provisions. This truth would appeal to the Epicureans who believed that what god or gods existed were above human events.

The last part of the verse, dealing with God's providing people with **life** (cf. v. 28) and material needs (cf. 14:17), suited the Stoic philosophy of aligning their lives with the "Purpose" of the Cosmos. Paul was thus beginning where his listeners were and was leading them from their inadequate concepts of the truth.

17:26. From one man refers back to Adam. This would be a blow to Athenian pride; they were sourced in the same original Creation as everyone else! One purpose of this Creation was to populate the planet (Gen. 1:28).

This sovereign God has omnipotently decreed the history **(the times) and** boundaries **(the exact places)** for the nations (cf. Deut. 32:8). Greece was not the only **nation** on **earth!**

17:27. One of God's purposes in revealing Himself in Creation and history is that people **would seek Him** (cf. Rom. 1:19-20). Though sovereign (Acts 17:24), He is also immanent and not so **far** removed that **He** cannot be found.

17:28. To buttress his point Paul apparently quoted from Epimenides, the Cretan poet (whom Paul also quoted later in Titus 1:12): **For in Him we live** (cf. Acts 17:25), **and move, and have our being.** Also Paul quoted the poet Aratus, from Paul's homeland Cilicia: **We are His offspring.** This second quotation was from Aratus' work *Phainomena.* All people—Athenians along with all others—are God's offspring, not in the sense that they are all His redeemed children or in the sense that they all possess an element of deity, but in the sense that they are created by God and receive their very life and breath from Him (v. 25). The Athenians' very creation and continued existence depended on this one God whom they did not know! No such claim could ever be made of any of the scores of false gods worshiped by the Greeks.

17:29. The conclusion is inevitable: since humans have been created by God, **the divine Being,** He cannot possibly be in the form of an idol, **an image** conceived and constructed by man (cf. Rom. 1:22-23). ("Divine being" translates *theion,* lit., "divine nature," used frequently in classical Gr., but in the NT only here and in 2 Peter 1:3-4). This would be a revolutionary concept to the Athenians, whose city was "full of idols" (Acts 17:16) and "objects of worship" (v. 23).

17:30. God overlooked human **ignorance** revealed in idol-making, that is, He was patient. Though people are under His wrath (Rom. 1:18) and are without excuse because of natural revelation (Rom. 1:19-20), God "in His forbearance (*anochē,* 'holding back, delay') left the sins committed beforehand unpunished" (Rom. 3:25). This parallels Acts 14:16, "In the past, He let all nations go their way" (cf. comments there). All through time the Gentiles were responsible for the general revelation given to them; now with the worldwide proclamation of the gospel, the Gentiles are also responsible to special revelation. That response is to obey God's command **to repent** of their sins.

17:31. At this point Paul introduced a distinctively Christian viewpoint. His reference to **the Man** clearly looks to Daniel 7:13-14 which speaks of the Son of Man. This One, **appointed** by God the Father, **will judge the world with justice** (cf. John 5:22). The authentication of Christ's person and work was His resurrection. Here again the resurrection of Jesus was preached. The idea of resurrection (cf. Acts 17:18, 32) was incompatible with Greek philosophy. The Greeks wanted to get rid of their bodies, not take them on again! A personal judgment was also unpalatable to Greeks. The gospel message struck at the center of the Athenians' needs.

Interestingly Paul (vv. 30-31) discussed the topics of sin ("to repent"), righteousness ("justice"), and judgment ("He will judge"), the same areas in which Jesus said the Holy Spirit would convict people (John 16:5-11).

17:32-34. To a Greek it was nonsense to believe a dead man could be raised from the grave to live forever, so **some of them sneered. Others** with more discretion **said** they wanted **to hear** Paul **again on this subject.** As a result **a few men became followers of Paul and believed,** including even **Dionysius,** an **Areopagus** member (i.e., a council **member;** cf. comments on v. 19), and **a woman named Damaris.** Other women converts in Acts include Lydia (16:14-15), a few prominent women in Thessalonica (17:4), and a number of prominent Greek women in Berea (v. 12).

Was Paul's ministry at Athens a failure? This is difficult to assess. There is no record of a church being founded in Athens. Paul later referred to the household of Stephanas (1 Cor. 16:15) in Corinth as "the first converts" (lit., "firstfruits") of Achaia. (Athens was in Achaia.) How could this be if some were converted in Athens, as Acts 17:34 asserts? Probably the solution is found in thinking of Stephanas as the firstfruits "of a church" in Achaia. Also possibly the term "firstfruits" can be used of more than one person.

If no church was begun in Athens, the failure was not in Paul's message or method but in the hardness of the Athenians' hearts.

b. At Corinth (18:1-18)

18:1. Without explaining the circumstances Luke simply stated, **After this, Paul left Athens and went to Corinth.** The cities of Athens and Corinth, though only 50 miles apart, were quite different. Athens was noted for its culture and learning, Corinth for its commerce and profligacy. Corinth was located just south of a narrow isthmus which joined the peninsula called Peloponnesus to Achaia to the north. Land trade moving north and south went through Corinth as did sea trade going east and west. Corinth possessed two seaport cities—Lechaeum two miles to the west on the Gulf of Corinth which opened to the Adriatic Sea, and Cenchrea, seven miles to the southeast which brought trade from the Aegean Sea. The southern tip of the Peloponnesus Peninsula was dangerous for ocean travel, so ships would put into port at one of Corinth's seaports and have their cargoes carried across to the other side of the isthmus for shipping there.

In 146 B.C. the Romans razed Corinth. However, its strategic location would not permit the city to die. It was rebuilt a century later in 46 B.C.

As one would expect from a city supported by commerce and travelers, Corinth was marked by profligate and licentious living. It was a center for the worship of Aphrodite, the goddess of love, who promoted immorality in the name of religion.

Politically, Corinth was a Roman colony and capital of the province of Achaia.

Some insights into Paul's emotions as he came to Corinth are seen in 1 Corinthians 2:1-5. His acknowledged weakness, fear, and much trembling may have been due to several factors: (1) He came alone. (2) The difficulties he had faced since coming to Macedonia may have filled him with apprehension as to what would happen in Corinth (cf. Acts 18:9-10). (3) Even in a world hardened to profligacy Corinth held a reputation for its sexual license.

The fact that Paul came to Corinth alone *may* account for his having baptized some people in that city, a practice he normally delegated to others (cf. 1 Cor. 1:14-17).

18:2. In Corinth Paul met **Aquila and his wife Priscilla.** Aquila was a Jew, originally from **Pontus,** a province in northeast Asia Minor south of the Black Sea. Displaced from Rome because of an edict in A.D. 49 or 50 from **Claudius** for **all the Jews to leave Rome,** Aquila and Priscilla had come to Corinth to ply their trade. (Claudius reigned from A.D. 41 to 54; see the list of Roman emperors at Luke 2:1.) Suetonius (A.D. 69?–140), a biographer of Roman emperors, described what may have been the occasion for such a decree. In his *Life of Claudius* (25. 4) he referred to the constant riots of the Jews at the instigation of Chrestus.

Possibly the name Chrestus is a reference to Christ.

Whether Aquila and Priscilla were Christians before they met Paul is not known. Because Aquila was called "a Jew" did not mean he knew Christ (cf. Apollos, a Jew; Acts 18:24). Nor can it be argued that Paul lived with them because they were believers; he stayed with them because they were tentmakers (v. 3).

Several times Priscilla's name is given before Aquila's (vv. 18-19, 26; Rom. 16:3). This *may* be due to her noble family background.

18:3. Their mutual trade was **tent-making.** The term used here is *skēnopoioi,* which some say includes working in leather. Perhaps leather was used in the tents as was goat's hair, for which Paul's home province of Cilicia was well known.

As is still common in the Middle East, a workman's shop was downstairs and his living quarters upstairs.

18:4. Once again Paul, according to his custom, began his work of evangelism **in the synagogue** (cf. 9:20; 13:5, 14; 14:1; 17:2, 10, 17; 18:19; 19:8).

18:5. With the arrival of **Silas and Timothy . . . from Macedonia** (cf. 17:14-15), **Paul devoted himself exclusively to preaching.** The verb translated "devoted . . . exclusively" is *syneicheto* (from *synechō*) which here in the passive means "to be constrained." Several factors about Silas and Timothy's arrival encouraged Paul: (1) The pair evidently brought financial aid from Macedonia (cf. 2 Cor. 11:9; Phil 4:15). Because of this monetary gift it was no longer necessary for Paul to pursue a trade and he could give himself totally to the work of the gospel. (2) The good news about the steadfastness of the Thessalonian church refreshed Paul (cf. 1 Thes. 3:6-8). (3) Their companionship would have been an encouragement to the apostle.

His message was the same as the one he learned on the Damascus Road: **Jesus is the Christ,** that is, the Messiah (cf. Acts 2:36; 3:18, 20; 17:3; 18:28).

18:6. Once again is seen the pattern of Jewish opposition to the gospel, followed by Paul's subsequent turning to **the Gentiles** (cf. 13:7-11, 46; 14:2-6; 17:5; 19:8-9; 28:23-28).

Paul's shaking **out his clothes** parallels Paul's and Barnabas' shaking dust

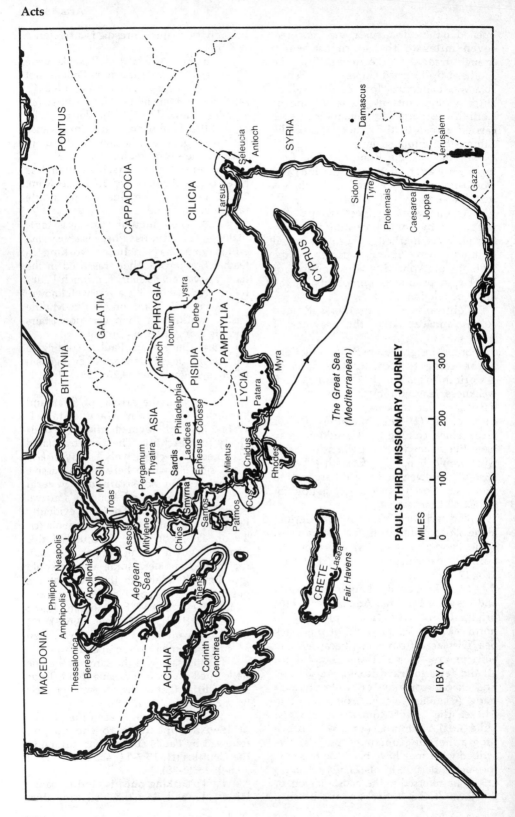

PAUL'S THIRD MISSIONARY JOURNEY

MILES

0   100   200   300

from their feet (13:51). When Paul said, **Your blood be on your own heads,** he was referring to their destruction and their own **responsibility** for it (cf. Ezek. 33:1-6).

18:7-8. After **Paul left the synagogue,** he found a fortunate location for preaching the gospel to the assembly of the saints **next door** in **the house of Titius Justus.** He was probably a Gentile, for he is called **a worshiper of God** (cf. 16:14; 17:4). In addition, **Crispus, the synagogue ruler,** with **his** family **believed.** He would have been well acquainted with the Old Testament Scriptures, and his conversion undoubtedly was an impetus for **many** more **Corinthians** to be converted.

18:9-11. Some threatening circumstances must have prompted this **vision** from **the Lord.** Perhaps this was God's response to Paul's vow (cf. v. 18 and the comments made there). The Lord urged **Paul** to **keep on** ministering in Corinth, assuring him that **no . . . harm** would come. No doubt **Paul** welcomed this word because of recent attacks against him in other cities (cf. 17:5, 13) and in Corinth itself (18:6). Paul obediently followed the Lord's direction and **stayed for a year and a half** (cf. v. 18), second only in length to his two to three years in Ephesus (19:10; 20:31).

Interestingly the word used for **people** in 18:10 is *laos,* often used of God's people Israel. Quite clearly, the Lord's plans for the world meant that the church temporarily was to take the place of His Chosen People, the Jews (cf. Rom. 11:11-21).

18:12. Verses 12-17 form a critical point in Luke's apologetic. It is important first because of who **Gallio** was, a Roman **proconsul,** governor **of Achaia.** Any judgment pronounced by him would establish legal precedent. Furthermore, Gallio was a brother of Seneca (4 B.C.?–A.D. 65), a philosopher of great influence in Rome.

The unbelieving **Jews** were not about to stop opposing **Paul** (cf. v. 6). They **united** and **brought him into court.**

18:13-15. The Jews **charged** Paul with **persuading the people to worship God in ways contrary to the** Roman **law.** Rome did not permit the propagation of new religions. Judaism was an accepted and established belief. These Jews were saying in effect that Christianity was a new and different cult, distinct from Judaism.

However, **Gallio** saw it differently. To him Christianity came under the aegis of Judaism and therefore was not a **matter** to be settled in a civil court. This decision was crucial for it was tantamount to legitimatizing Christianity in the eyes of Roman law.

18:16-17. The spontaneous outburst of violence against **Sosthenes, the synagogue ruler,** betrayed the spirit of anti-Semitism that lay just beneath the veneer of society in Corinth. The Gentiles in Corinth wanted nothing of the Jews' contentions. Sosthenes had evidently become ruler of the synagogue in place of Crispus and had led in the Jews' charge against Paul. He may well be the same Sosthenes who was later converted to Christianity and was referred to in 1 Corinthians 1:1.

Such a minor incident was of **no concern** to **Gallio.** Though there was violence, he was unconcerned about religious matters.

18:18. The actual length of Paul's stay **in Corinth** is unclear because the 18 months (v. 11) may be dated from the time of Paul's vision (vv. 9-10) or it may include all of Paul's **time** in Corinth (from v. 5 on).

Paul then **left** Corinth, heading for his sending church, Antioch on the Orontes River in **Syria.** But **before he left he had his hair cut off at Cenchrea,** Corinth's southeastern port, **because of a vow he had taken.** When Paul made this vow is unstated. He may have made it when he left Troas for Macedonia, or at the beginning of his ministry at Corinth, or more likely, before the Lord gave him the vision (vv. 9-10). During the vow Paul would have let his hair grow. Now the time of the Nazirite vow was over (after about a year and a half), and Paul got a haircut at Cenchrea (cf. Num. 6:1-21).

Josephus wrote about some Jews who immediately after a misfortune, shaved their heads and refused to offer sacrifices for 30 days (*Jewish Wars* 2. 15. 1). If this is the case Paul would have cut his hair at the beginning of his vow. But this is somewhat improbable because there is no mention of an illness or other affliction (unless 2 Cor. 12:7-9 fits in here).

While Paul was at Corinth he penned 1 and 2 Thessalonians (see the chart at Acts 13:38-39).

4. THE CONCLUSION OF THE SECOND
MISSIONARY JOURNEY (18:19-22)

18:19. Priscilla and Aquila accompanied **Paul** as far as **Ephesus.** Evidently Silas and Timothy remained in Macedonia and Achaia to oversee the churches there. Why Priscilla and Aquila moved to Ephesus is not known. Probably it was for the sake of the gospel.

As in every city where there was a **synagogue** Paul **went** in **and reasoned with the Jews** (cf. 9:20; 13:5, 14; 14:1; 17:2, 10, 17; 18:4; 19:8).

18:20-21. Unlike the obstinate refusal of the Jews in other synagogues to believe, those in **Ephesus** desired further interchange with Paul. However, he was more inclined to press on homeward. Some Greek manuscripts add that Paul's desire to go to Jerusalem in haste was to keep a feast. If this is accurate, probably Paul wanted to observe the Passover.

18:22. After landing **at Caesarea** on the Palestinian coast—a voyage of about 500 miles from Ephesus—Paul **went up** (to Jerusalem) **and greeted the church and then went down to Antioch.** "Going up" and "going down" are almost technical terms that refer to going to and leaving Jerusalem's higher elevation.

5. THE CONQUEST OF EPHESUS
(18:23–19:20)

[Third missionary journey, 18:23–21:16]

a. The initiation of Paul's third journey
(18:23)

18:23. With great brevity Luke covered the first part of the apostle's third missionary journey. Obviously Luke's aim was to emphasize Paul's ministry in Ephesus. On Paul's way to Ephesus he ministered in **Galatia and Phrygia** (cf. 16:6), **strengthening all the disciples.** No doubt many of them were converts from his second missionary journey. For this reason the incident of 18:24-28 is used to introduce Paul's work in Ephesus.

b. The instruction of Apollos (18:24-28)

This episode (18:24-28) and the following (19:1-7) underscore the transitional nature of this phase of church history. It may be assumed from 19:1-7 that Apollos had not received Christian baptism and probably had not received the Holy Spirit.

This section of Acts also indicates that Christianity is the logical outgrowth of the Old Testament and of John the Baptist's ministry. In fact, the message of Paul is superior to that of the spiritual giant John the Baptist. Though John's message had reached as far as Alexandria and Ephesus, John's work was brought to fruition only in Christ.

18:24. What took place in verses 24-28 occurred after Paul left **Ephesus**

SPEAKING IN TONGUES IN ACTS

PASSAGE	TONGUES-SPEAKERS	AUDIENCE	RELATED TO SALVATION	PURPOSE
2:1-4	The 12 Apostles and others	Unsaved Jews	After salvation	To validate (for Jews) the fulfillment of Joel 2
10:44-47	Gentiles (Cornelius and his household)	Saved Jews (Peter and others) who doubted God's plan	The same time as salvation	To validate (for Jews) God's acceptance of Gentiles
19:1-7	About 12 Old Testament believers	Jews who needed confirmation of the message	The same time as salvation	To validate (for Jews) Paul's message

(v. 21) and before he returned (19:1). During this interval a church had been started, probably under the influence of Aquila and Priscilla. To this church came the gifted **Apollos** from **Alexandria** in northern Africa. **As a Jew,** he knew **the Scriptures,** that is, the Old Testament, well.

18:25. His doctrine regarding **Jesus** was accurate but deficient. Probably this means Apollos did not know about the Holy Spirit's baptism. John's **baptism** symbolized cleansing by God because of repentance toward God (cf. 19:4). But Christian baptism pictures union with Christ in His death, burial, and resurrection by means of Spirit baptism (cf. Rom. 6:3-10; 1 Cor. 12:13; Gal. 3:27; Col. 2:12).

18:26. Rather than correct Apollos publicly, **Priscilla and Aquila . . . invited him to their home and explained to him the way of God** (cf. "the way of the Lord," v. 25) **more adequately.**

18:27-28. Armed with this new doctrine **Apollos** crossed the Aegean Sea **to Achaia** (probably at Corinth) where he was mightily used. **He vigorously refuted the Jews** demonstrating **from the Scriptures** (which he knew well, v. 24), **that Jesus is the Messiah.** This was Paul's approach as well (v. 5). So forceful was Apollos' ministry that factious believers at Corinth formed an Apollos party (1 Cor. 1:12). There is no indication that Apollos promoted such a faction and Paul nowhere held him accountable for it.

c. The influence of the gospel (19:1-20)

(1) With the 12 (19:1-7). **19:1-2. Ephesus** became Paul's base of operation during his third missionary journey. Ephesus was the home of the Temple of Artemis, one of the seven wonders of the ancient world. The temple, according to its ruins, was 239' wide and 418' long, four times the size of the Parthenon in Athens! As a commercial center, Ephesus was the leading city of the province of Asia. Its present-day extensive ruins reveal the glory of its past. However, the Caÿster River silted its harbor full and the site was later abandoned. During Paul's time the city was approaching its zenith.

Arriving in this metropolitan area from **the interior** road (perhaps a shorter route than others), **Paul . . . found some disciples.** What Luke meant by the term "disciples" is unclear. Normally Luke used it of Christians; it may have that meaning here because Paul's question included the words **when you believed** (i.e., believed in Jesus Christ).

The answer of these disciples is also enigmatic. When they said, **No, we have not even heard that there is a Holy Spirit,** they probably meant they had not heard He had been given or was being given. A similar construction is used in the Greek in John 7:39. Furthermore, John the Baptist had clearly predicted the coming work of the Holy Spirit (Matt. 3:11; Mark 1:8; Luke 3:16; cf. John 1:32-33).

19:3-4. Like Apollos (18:25) these Ephesian disciples knew only of **John's baptism,** a sign **of repentance** toward God (Matt. 3:2, 6, 8, 11; Mark 1:4-5; Luke 3:8). Paul told them that John pointed to Jesus Christ as **the One** in whom they should **believe** (Matt. 3:11-12; Mark 1:7-8; Luke 3:16-17).

19:5. This is the only place in the New Testament that refers to anyone being rebaptized. Quite clearly, John's ministry was anticipatory; Christ is the fulfillment of all things.

19:6. The laying on of **hands** may have been in conjunction with the baptism or more probably afterward. As a result **the Holy Spirit came on** these disciples **and they spoke in tongues and prophesied.** The subject of tongues in Acts confirms Paul's statement that tongues "are a sign . . . for unbelievers" (cf. comments on 1 Cor. 14:22). The purpose of tongues was to overcome unbelief. The accompanying chart compares the usages of tongues-speaking in Acts and points up its purpose.

It should also be noted that the reception of the Holy Spirit in Acts does not follow any set pattern. He came into believers before baptism (Acts 10:44), at the time of or after baptism (8:12-16; 19:6), and by the laying on of apostolic hands (8:17; 19:6). Yet Paul declared (Rom. 8:9) that anyone without the Holy Spirit is not a Christian. Quite obviously the transitional Book of Acts is not to be used as a doctrinal source on how to receive the Holy Spirit (cf. comments on tongues, 1 Cor. 13:8–14:25).

19:7. The reference to **12 men** does not imply, as some have suggested, that the church is the new Israel. If there is any significance to the number, it is that this fullness of the Spirit is yet to be experienced by Israel (cf. Ezek. 36:26-27; Joel 2:28-32; Zech. 12:10-14).

(2) In the synagogue. **19:8.** In accord with his promise (18:21) **Paul** did return to the Ephesus **synagogue and spoke boldly there for three months.** Three months in a synagogue without a riot was something of a record for Paul. Perhaps the cosmopolitan nature of Ephesus caused the Jews there to be more tolerant. On the apostles' boldness, see comments on 4:13.

The topic of his discussion was **the kingdom of God** which obviously included the person and work of Christ but also must have anticipated His millennial reign (cf. 1:3, 6).

(3) In the school of Tyrannus (19:9-12). **19:9.** Once again the old pattern of Jewish opposition arose (cf. 18:6). This time the Jews **publicly maligned the Way** (on "the Way," cf. 9:2; 19:23; 22:4; 24:14, 22). **So Paul left them.**

After he led the believers out of the synagogue he taught **daily in the lecture hall of Tyrannus.** Apparently Tyrannus made his lecture hall available to traveling teachers. One Greek manuscript adds that the school was available from 11 A.M. to 4 P.M., when most people would have their noon meal and an afternoon "siesta." This tradition is probably correct. The rest of each day Paul worked with his own hands (20:34).

19:10. Paul ministered in Ephesus **for two years.** But according to Acts 20:31, he was there for three years. Since it was customary to count part of a unit of time as a whole, his ministry was actually between two and three years.

So effective was this work that the gospel emanated throughout **the province of Asia,** on the west coast of modern-day Turkey. During this time the churches at Colosse, Laodicea, and Hierapolis were founded (Col. 4:13). Some believe all seven churches of Revelation 2-3 were started at this time, but this cannot be asserted dogmatically.

19:11-12. These feats of **Paul** parallel the **miracles** of Peter in 5:15-16. Quite clearly God's hand of blessing and endorsement was on Paul. Apparently the **handkerchiefs and aprons** were tangible symbols of God's power through His apostle; these objects had no magical powers in themselves. Certainly this is no basis for people trying to repeat such miracles today. As seen many times in Acts, miracles confirmed the work of the apostles (2:43; 4:30; 5:12; 6:8; 8:6, 13; 14:3; 15:12; cf. 2 Cor. 12:12; Heb. 2:3-4).

The mention of **evil spirits** bridges this portion with the next incident (Acts 19:13-20).

(4) With exorcism and sorcery (19:13-20). One of the themes of Acts is the victory of Christ over occultism (cf. 8:9-24; 13:6-12; 16:16-18). This incident is another example of His power over demons.

19:13. **Some** itinerant Jewish exorcists who obviously used a variety of chants and methods **tried to invoke** Jesus' **name** over **demon-possessed** people.

19:14. Sceva is said to be **a Jewish chief priest.** But perhaps he merely claimed to be, and Luke simply recorded his boast. Or Sceva may have actually been a chief priest whose **seven sons** had gone astray into exorcism.

19:15. Some significance may be attached to the variation in the verbs for "know" used here by **the evil spirit** (i.e., the demon). He said, **Jesus I know** (*ginōskō*, "to know by interaction and experience"), **and** he added, **Paul I know about** (*epistamai*, "to know about, to understand"). **But** the demon did not know Sceva's sons.

19:16. Instead of being exorcised of this demon, **the** possessed **man** became supernaturally strong and overcame **all** seven (*amphoterōn* normally means "both" but may also signify "all"), **beating** them. The seven **ran out of the house naked and bleeding.** Demons can sometimes cause those they possess to have unusual physical power (cf. Mark 5:3-4).

19:17-18. The result was **fear** (or awe, *phobos*) on the part of both **Jews and** Gentiles (cf. 5:5), and **high** esteem for Jesus' **name** (in contrast with the attempted use of His name for exorcism; cf. 19:13). **Many** Christians had also been involved in sorcery and spiritism and they **openly confessed their evil deeds.** The noun translated "deeds" is *praxeis*, which probably describes magical spells and formulas. Giving out these secrets would cause them to lose their power.

19:19. Furthermore, many publicly **burned** their manuals of **sorcery.** In sorcery, people by the assistance of demons sought to gain power over others. The word translated **drachmas** is actually *argyriou* and simply means "silver"; consequently the value of the coins is unknown. But **50,000** silver coins was a large sum.

19:20. The cleansed church became a powerful and growing church. (The spreading of God's **Word** is also mentioned in 6:7; 12:24; 13:49.) With this sixth "progress report" Luke brought another section of his book to a conclusion (cf. 2:47; 6:7; 9:31; 12:24; 16:5; 28:30-31).

D. The extension of the church to Rome (19:21-28:31)

1. THE COMPLETION OF THE THIRD JOURNEY (19:21-21:16)

a. The disturbance at Ephesus (19:21-41)

19:21. This verse sets the tone for the remainder of the book. Paul's sights were now set on **Rome** (via **Jerusalem**) with the ultimate goal of reaching Spain (Rom. 1:15; 15:22-24). Luke made no reference to Spain because one of his purposes in writing Acts was to trace the spread of the gospel up to Paul's being in Rome, center of the Roman world. Several have observed how Luke's Gospel focuses *in* on Jerusalem, whereas Acts emphasizes the message going *out* from Jerusalem to Rome. These two cities seem to be the focal points of Luke-Acts.

The NIV simply says **Paul decided** whereas the Greek has *etheto ho Paulos en tō pneumati,* "Paul purposed in the spirit." This may mean Paul's own spirit or the Holy Spirit. Since the verb means "purposed," not "was led," it may refer to Paul's human spirit.

First, however, he desired to visit the churches of **Macedonia and Achaia.** The purposes of this itinerary were (a) to confirm the churches and (b) to take up an offering for the saints in Jerusalem.

19:22. Timothy, who was last seen with Paul in Corinth (18:5), once again came on the scene. He **and Erastus** were **sent . . . to Macedonia,** evidently to prepare for Paul's coming. Paul also mentioned Erastus in 2 Timothy 4:20.

19:23-24. Before Paul's departure and as an incentive for him to leave Ephesus there was a riot. On the words **the Way,** see comments on 9:2.

In only two incidents recorded in Acts did Gentiles oppose Paul: (a) here and (b) in the case of the Philippian fortune-teller (16:16-24). In both cases the opposition was because of vested monetary interests.

Actually two goddesses in Asia Minor were named **Artemis.** The one, a goddess worshiped in Greek culture whose counterpart in Rome was Diana, was the virgin goddess of the hunt. The other was Artemis of the Ephesians, a many-breasted goddess of fertility. Probably the original "statue" was a meteorite that resembled a woman with many breasts (cf. 19:35).

Silver **craftsmen** made statues (**silver shrines**) of this Ephesian goddess, but because of the power of the gospel their business had gone bad.

19:25-27. Demetrius (v. 24), a silversmith, assembled the other craftsmen and appealed to them on the basis of both business (**our trade will lose its good name**) and religion (**the temple of the great goddess Artemis will be discredited**). The appeal on the basis of the cult of Artemis was obviously hypocritical; his concern was simply financial. Artemis was worshiped in many cities besides Ephesus. Obviously Paul's view **that man-made** idols are not **gods** would ruin their thriving idol-making **business.**

19:28-29. The silversmiths, enraged at Paul by Demetrius' speech, instigated a riot and **rushed** to **the** Ephesian **theater,** the largest place for an assembly of people in the city, capable of seating 25,000. As tokens of opposition the **people seized Gaius and Aristarchus** (cf. 20:4). Gaius was a common name; so it is doubtful this is the same man mentioned in Romans 16:23 and 1 Corinthians 1:14. Aristarchus is also mentioned in Acts 20:4 and 27:2. Evidently the two escaped with little or no injury.

19:30-31. These verses are important not only for what they directly state but also for what they imply. **Paul** was eager to defend the gospel, ready to take on his opponents! But the Christians did **not let him. Even some of the officials of the province** would not let him get caught in the riot. They were *Asiarchs* (lit., "rulers of Asia"), in charge of the community's political and religious welfare. They would be on good terms with Rome and therefore would evidence Christianity's good standing with the government.

19:32-34. Luke's sense of humor is seen in this passage. Ironically **most of the people did not even know why they were there.** Because the Jews were monotheists and strongly opposed to idols, they thrust **Alexander to the front** in order to issue a disclaimer. The reduction in Artemis' idol business was not their fault! However, anti-Semitism took over, the mob refused to listen to **a Jew, and they** chanted in frenzy **for about two hours, Great is Artemis of the Ephesians!**

19:35-39. The term **city clerk** (*grammateus,* lit., "scribe") does not do justice to this man's position. Actually he was the chief executive officer of the city. When he appeared, the people listened.

He first appealed to the position of **Ephesus** as **the guardian of** Artemis' **temple** and to **her** heaven-sent **image.** The latter assertion may be a subtle rebuttal of the statement (v. 26, "man-made gods are no gods at all"). Artemis, he argued, was *not* man-made. So why should they be concerned with Paul's preaching? Second, the town clerk asserted the innocence of Gaius and Aristarchus, thereby exonerating Paul as well (v. 37). Third, he pointed out the legal methods of obtaining a hearing— through **the courts . . . proconsuls,** and a **legal assembly** (vv. 38-39). *This* assembly was not legal.

19:40-41. Finally, the unnamed official warned of the political implications of the **commotion** in the city. They would be hard-pressed to give Rome a legitimate explanation of this riot, and the city could be deprived of some of its liberties because of it. So Paul was cleared of any misdeeds, religious or political.

While Paul was at Ephesus, he wrote 1 Corinthians as well as an earlier letter to the Corinthians that is not part of the biblical canon (cf. 1 Cor. 5:9). In addition he made a third visit to Corinth which is unrecorded in Acts (cf. 2 Cor. 12:14; 13:1; see "Contacts and Correspondence" in the *Introduction* to 2 Cor.).

b. The departure from Macedonia and Achaia (20:1-6)

20:1-2. This segment of the third missionary journey is covered briefly by Luke. Second Corinthians 2:12-13; 7:5-7 gives further information about Paul's stop at Troas for evangelistic purposes and of his desire to see Titus for a report on the Corinthian church. Subsequently Paul went to **Macedonia** (cf. Acts 19:21), met Titus, and wrote 2 Corinthians.

During this time Paul probably ministered as far as Illyricum, corresponding roughly to modern-day Yugoslavia (Rom. 15:19; cf. 2 Cor. 10:13).

20:3. During the apostle's **three**-month stay in Achaia he wrote Romans (cf. Rom. 15:23–16:2) from Corinth.

The **plot** by **the Jews . . . against** Paul was evidently to assassinate him on board ship and dispose of his body at sea. Somehow the insidious plan became known to Paul and **he decided** not to go directly to the eastern Mediterranean but **to go back through Macedonia.** Possibly he had wanted to be in Jerusalem for Passover; now the best he could hope for would be Pentecost (Acts 20:16).

20:4-6. The mention of these seven men implies what is stated elsewhere: Paul was concerned for the collection for the saints in Jerusalem. As representatives of various churches they carried funds. Three men were from Macedonia (**Sopater . . . Aristarchus, and Secundus**) and four were from Asia Minor (**Gaius . . . Timothy . . . Tychicus** [cf. Eph. 6:21; Col. 4:7; 2 Tim. 4:12; Titus 3:12], **and Trophimus** [cf. Acts 21:29; 2 Tim. 4:20]). Their rendezvous point was **Troas.** In Acts 19:29 Gaius is said to be "from Macedonia," whereas in 20:4 he is said to be **from Derbe.** Probably these are two different men (cf. a third Gaius, from Corinth; 1 Cor. 1:14).

In Acts 20:5-6 Luke resumed another **we** section. Luke was left at **Philippi** in chapter 16 and evidently remained there until this point. Then he rejoined the party to accompany Paul to Jerusalem. **The Feast of Unleavened Bread** was in the spring. They made the 150-mile trip from Philippi to Troas in **five days.**

c. The discourse at Troas (20:7-12)

20:7. This is the clearest verse in the New Testament which indicates that Sunday was the normal meeting day of the apostolic church. Paul stayed in Troas for seven days (v. 6) and the church met **on the first day of the week.** Luke's method of counting days here was not Jewish, which measures from sundown to sundown, but Roman, which counted from midnight to midnight. This can be stated dogmatically because "daylight" (v. 11) was **the next day** (v. 7).

Probably the church met at night because most people had to work during the day. Because Paul was leaving them, possibly for the final time, he prolonged his discourse **until midnight.**

20:8-10. The presence of **many lamps** would contribute to a soporific atmosphere because the lamps consumed oxygen. Probably crowded conditions exacerbated the condition.

A young man named Eutychus (lit., "fortunate") proved to be true to his name. Luke, the physician, affirmed that Eutychus **was picked up dead** after he had fallen from a **third-story** window. It was normal for the larger rooms to be on the top floor of a building (see comments on 1:13). After the manner of Elijah and Elisha (1 Kings 17:21; 2 Kings 4:34-35), **Paul** embraced Eutychus and the young man came **alive.**

20:11-12. As part of the meal they participated in the Lord's Supper (**broke bread and ate;** cf. v. 7), and the meeting continued until dawn. Eutychus, **the** fortunate **young man** (cf. vv. 9-10), was taken **home alive.**

d. The discourse at Miletus (20:13-38)

20:13-15. Evidently **Paul** remained in Troas longer than he originally planned (v. 7). To compensate for the delay he sent the rest of the party **on ahead.** The journey across land from Troas to **Assos** is much shorter than by sea. By this arrangement Paul was able to stay a bit longer in Troas. They sailed from Assos **to Mitylene . . . Chios . . . Samos** and **Miletus.** The voyage to the last three stops took one **day** each.

20:16-17. **Paul** avoided a stop in **Ephesus** because **he was in a hurry to reach Jerusalem, if possible, by the day of Pentecost.** He knew it would take far too long to say good-bye to his many friends in Ephesus. **Miletus** was some 30 miles by land south of **Ephesus,** so he **sent** for **the** Ephesian church's **elders** to come there. Evidently his ship had a layover of several days in the port of Miletus.

20:18. Here begins another "sample sermon" of Paul (cf. 13:16-41; 14:15-17; 17:22-31), this one given to Christian leaders, men he loved deeply. This discourse has three parts: (a) a review of Paul's *past* three-year's ministry in Ephesus (20:18-21), (b) a description of the *present* situation (vv. 22-27), and (c) the *future* responsibilities of the Ephesian elders (vv. 28-35).

20:19. In Ephesus, as elsewhere, **the Jews** had plotted against Paul, though the riot recorded in Acts 19 emphasizes opposition from Gentiles. Here Luke referred to **the plots** by the Jews, but he did not detail them (cf. Paul's words in 1 Cor. 15:30-32; 16:9; 2 Cor. 1:8-10).

20:20. Paul's ministry **from house to house** (cf. 2:46) is contrasted with his public ministry and probably refers to house churches. If so, each elder was possibly the overseer of a house church. Paul both preached and **taught.**

20:21. In the Greek the words **repentance** and **faith** are joined together by one article. This may imply that these two words stress two aspects of trust in Christ (cf. 2:38). When a person places his faith **in Christ,** he is then turning from (repenting of) his former unbelief. This is the same message for **both Jews and Greeks** (i.e., Gentiles; cf. 19:10; Gal. 3:28).

20:22. Here Paul began to describe present circumstances (vv. 22-27). The NIV words, **compelled by the Spirit,** are literally, "bound in the Spirit" (*dedemenos . . . tō pneumati*). Probably this refers to the Holy Spirit's guidance in the apostle's life (cf. Luke 2:27; 4:1; Acts 8:29; 10:19; 11:12; 16:6-7). Paul's reason for **going to Jerusalem,** though not stated, evidently was to take the offering from churches to the poor saints in Jerusalem (24:17; cf. comments on 21:12-14).

20:23. Already Paul had been warned by **the Holy Spirit**—that is, evidently by people with the Spirit-given gift of prophecy—**that prison and hardships** awaited him in Jerusalem. He anticipated troubles in Jerusalem when he wrote Romans 15:30-31. Yet he was determined to go there (cf. Acts 19:21; 20:16).

20:24-25. When these verses are read together, it becomes clear that the **preaching** of **the kingdom** and **the gospel of God's grace** are related. God's work of grace enables believing Gentiles to have both the privilege of salvation and of entering the Lord's millennial reign.

Because of the warning to Paul (v. 23) he concluded that the Ephesian elders would not **see** him **again.** The NIV translation, **none of you,** is a bit strong. The Greek refers to "all" of them (as a group) not seeing Paul again (lit., "all of you [as a group] will never see me again"). He did not say no *one* of them would see him again (cf. the pl. verb in v. 38). His ambition was to **finish the race,** which later he said he did (2 Tim. 4:7).

20:26-27. In conformity with Ezekiel 33:1-6, Paul declared himself to be **innocent of the blood of all men** in Ephesus (cf. comments on Acts 18:6). He preached to "all men" (cf. "all the Jews and Greeks . . . in the province of Asia," 19:10). And the content of His preaching was all of God's **will** (*boulēn,* "purpose, plan"; cf. 2:23; 4:28; 13:36; Eph. 1:11; Heb. 6:17). Interestingly Paul used several words in referring to his role in communicating the gospel: (a) "preach" (Acts 20:20) and **proclaim** (v. 27), both from *anangellō* ("proclaim, announce"); (b) "taught" (from *didaskō,* "teach," v. 20); (c) "declared" (v. 21) and "testifying" (v. 24), both from *diamartyromai* ("solemnly bear witness to"); (d) **declare** (*martyromai,* "testify," v. 26).

20:28. In verses 28-35 Paul turned to the future responsibilities of the elders in Ephesus. First, they were to **guard** (*prosechete,* "attend to" in the sense of taking care of) themselves **and all the flock.** Significantly before they could provide for the flock they had to care for their own spiritual well-being.

Here the elders are described as **overseers** (*episkopous,* from the verb *episkopeō,* "to look for, to care for"). The term "elders" has primarily Jewish antecedents and stresses the dignity of the office, whereas "overseers" is mainly Greek in its derivation and emphasizes the responsibility of the office, namely, "to look after" others.

The value of the flock, over which the elders were to **be shepherds** (*poimainein,* pres. tense infinitive; cf. 1 Peter 5:2), is underscored by Paul's calling it **the church of God** (i.e., the church that is owned by God) and by his referring to its purchase (cf. Ps. 74:2) by **His own blood.**

Nowhere does the Bible speak of the blood of God the Father. The Greek here can read "by the blood of His own," that is, His own Son. The Greek word for **bought** means "acquired, obtained."

20:29-31. These verses explain the need for the command to elders to guard themselves and the flock (v. 28). False teachers, called **savage wolves,** would enter **the flock,** or even some of their **own** would **distort the truth.** This warning is attested by subsequent references to the church at Ephesus (1 Tim. 1:6-7, 19-20; 4:1-7; 2 Tim. 1:15; 2:17-18; 3:1-9; Rev. 2:1-7). Again Paul urged the leaders, **Be on your guard!** He had repeatedly warned them of the danger of doctrinal error. In fact he had done so **with tears** (cf. Acts 20:19).

20:32. Paul then committed them first **to God and** then **to the Word of His grace.** Though trust in God is essential, it must be accompanied by obedience to His Word. This will lead to edification (it will **build you up**) and to **an inheritance among all those who are sanctified** (cf. 26:18; Eph. 1:18; Col. 1:12; 1 Peter 1:4).

20:33-34. Paul worked to provide for himself and for others (cf. 18:3; Eph. 4:28).

20:35. Hard work also enabled Paul to **help the weak** (cf. 1 Thes. 5:14). **The words** of the Lord, **It is more blessed to give than to receive,** are not found in the four Gospels. They represent an oral tradition passed on to the early church.

20:36-38. The elders' deep love for Paul is displayed here. The remainder of the trip to Jerusalem (21:1-25) is filled with details of such expressions of love for Paul. Why did Luke linger on these points? He did this to contrast the response to Paul in Gentile lands with that of the Jews in Jerusalem.

e. *The dissuasions from Miletus to Jerusalem (21:1-16)*

21:1. Each of these stops—from **Cos** to **Rhodes** to **Patara**—evidently represented one day's **sea** journey (cf. 20:13-15).

21:2. Rather than remain on board a boat which put into port each evening Paul boarded **a ship** which evidently was larger and would make the journey **to Phoenicia** with no stops.

21:3-4. Going **south** of **Cyprus** they landed at **Tyre where** the **ship was to unload its cargo,** a task which took a week (v. 4). The persecution of the early church in Jerusalem had scattered the believers to Phoenicia (11:19), so Paul sought out believers there.

Through the Spirit the believers at Tyre **urged Paul not to go on to Jerusalem.** In view of the phrase, "through the Spirit," was Paul wrong in pursuing his course to Jerusalem? Probably he was not violating God's will for several reasons: (1) Acts 20:22 and 21:14 imply it was God's will for Paul to continue on to Jerusalem (cf. 19:21). (2) The comfort given by God (23:11) implies Paul had not stubbornly refused the Lord's will. (3) In 23:1 Paul declared he had lived in all good conscience to that day.

Probably, then, the words "through the Spirit" (21:4) mean they knew through the Spirit that Paul would suffer in Jerusalem (cf. 20:23); therefore, concerned for his safety, they tried to dissuade him.

21:5-6. This was Paul's first contact with this church at Tyre, and yet after only one week there was a strong bond of love. The departure scene is not as poignant as the one at Miletus (20:37), but it was meaningful.

21:7. The ship then proceeded 20 miles south to **Ptolemais,** modern Acre or Akko, for **a** one-**day** stop. Probably the church there began as a result of the persecutions mentioned in 11:19, as did the church in **Tyre.**

21:8-9. The 40-mile trip to **Caesarea** may have been by land or by sea; probably it was the latter because the overland route was rather difficult and the port at Caesarea was commodious.

Paul's host there was **Philip the evangelist.** He was **one of the Seven** (cf. 6:1-5) who ministered to widows in Jerusalem. His evangelistic work was described in chapter 8. Evidently he had settled in Caesarea (cf. 8:40), even though it was the most Roman city in Israel, and had lived there for some 20 years when Paul arrived.

He had four unmarried (*parthenoi,* lit., "virgins") **daughters who had the gift of prophecy.** This spiritual gift, evident in the early church, was not limited to men (cf. 1 Cor. 11:5). Their apparent silence in view of all the other prophecies regarding Paul's suffering in Jerusalem is surprising.

21:10-11. Agabus, a **prophet** introduced in 11:28, **came down from Judea,** evidently from Jerusalem, for it was his home and Caesarea was in the province of Judea. Dramatically he illustrated how Paul would be bound in Jerusalem. Prophets often symbolized their predictions (cf. 1 Kings 11:29-31; Isa. 20:2-4; Jer. 13:1-7; Ezek. 4). The fact that Paul would be imprisoned was known by several including Paul himself (Acts 20:23).

21:12-14. After **the people** heard that prophecy, they **pleaded with Paul not to go up to Jerusalem** (cf. v. 4). Even Luke joined in the plea, as indicated by the use of **we** here. But the apostle **would not be dissuaded.**

Though Luke did not say so, apparently one reason this trip to **Jerusalem** was important to Paul was that he was taking an offering to the Jerusalem believers (cf. 24:17; Rom. 15:25-27; 1 Cor. 16:1-4; 2 Cor. 8:13-14; 9:12-13; Gal. 2:10). **Paul** wanted to make this presentation of money in order to fortify one of his basic doctrines, the unity of Jew and Gentile in Christ (Eph. 2:11-22; 3:6).

21:15-16. The distance **from Caesarea** to **Jerusalem** is about 65 miles, a two-day journey by horse. Some think **the home of Mnason** was at a halfway point **where** Paul and his party may have spent the night. More probably, Mnason was a resident of Jerusalem. Interestingly Mnason was **from Cyprus,** the island where Barnabas was born.

2. THE CAPTIVITY AT JERUSALEM
(21:17–23:32)

a. *The detention of Paul (21:17-36)*

(1) The vow of Paul (21:17-26). **21:17-19.** As soon as possible **Paul and** his party had an audience with **James,** head of the church at Jerusalem (cf. 15:13-21), and with **all** that church's **elders.** Luke only mentioned Paul's report of **what God had done among the Gentiles through his ministry** (cf. 14:27). Obviously Paul at this point also turned the large offering for the saints at Jerusalem (24:17) over to James in the presence of the elders. Probably because Luke's emphasis was on the gospel going from the Jews to the Gentiles, he omitted this matter of money.

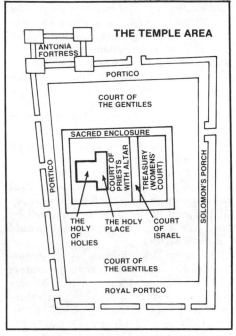

THE TEMPLE AREA

ANTONIA FORTRESS

PORTICO

COURT OF THE GENTILES

SACRED ENCLOSURE

PORTICO

COURT OF PRIESTS WITH ALTAR

TREASURY (WOMENS' COURT)

SOLOMON'S PORCH

THE HOLY OF HOLIES

THE HOLY PLACE

COURT OF ISRAEL

COURT OF THE GENTILES

ROYAL PORTICO

21:20-21. When the leaders of the Jerusalem church **heard** of Paul's ministry among the Gentiles, **they praised God.** Undoubtedly included in this was thanksgiving for the Gentile offering to the believing Jews in Jerusalem (see comments on vv. 12-14).

While there was rejoicing over Paul's report, there was also apprehension about Paul's reputation among believing **Jews** who were **zealous for the Law.** A patently false report had gone out concerning Paul. It was true **Paul** taught **Gentiles** that it was religiously inconsequential whether they circumcised their sons or not and he did not teach them Jewish customs. However, he never taught **Jews . . . not to circumcise their** sons or to disregard Jewish **customs.**

21:22-24. James and the elders suggested that Paul **join in** the **purification rites** of **four men** who had taken a **vow** and **pay their expenses.** This was for the purpose of placating Jewish believers. Whether Paul's actions accomplished this is left unstated. That was beside Luke's purpose.

The details of this vow are unknown; it can only be surmised exactly what Paul was to do. The four men evidently had a Nazirite vow. At the conclusion of their vow some costly sacrifices were required

of each man (cf. Num. 6:13-17). These men evidently were too poor to pay for them. Paul was asked to underwrite the expense of their sacrifices and thereby display his sympathy with the zealots of **the Law.**

Was Paul wrong in entering into this arrangement, which was a specific part of the Law? For several reasons it may be said he was not: (1) Paul himself had previously taken a Nazirite vow (Acts 18:18). (2) Later he unashamedly referred to this incident before Felix (24:17-18). (3) This action on Paul's part only confirmed one of the principles of his ministry which was to become like a Jew to win the Jews, and to become like one under the Law to win those under it (1 Cor. 9:20). (4) One of Paul's goals for the Jerusalem trip, along with relief of the poor, was the unifying of Jews and Gentiles. (5) Paul was not denying the finished work of Christ by offering animal sacrifices. The epistles Paul had already written by this time (Gal., 1 and 2 Thes., 1 and 2 Cor., Rom.) make it clear that such a denial was incomprehensible. He must have looked on these sacrifices as memorials. After all, this will be the significance of millennial sacrifices (Ezek. 43:18–46:24; Mal. 1:11; 3:3-4). (6) Paul later asserted he did not violate his own conscience (Acts 23:1).

21:25-26. The decision of the Jerusalem Council was once again iterated (cf. 15:20, 29). The elders assured **Paul** that their plan (mentioned in 21:23-24) did not conflict with the council's earlier **decision.** Paul then followed the elders' suggestion **and purified himself** with **the** four **men** (vv. 23-24). This did not conflict with Paul's teaching that Jews and Gentiles cannot be brought under the Law to be saved. This was a matter of Jewish custom, not of salvation or of sanctification.

(2) The violence of the people (21:27-36). **21:27.** This opposition to Paul came not from believers but from unbelieving Jews. A riot was instigated by **some Jews from the province of Asia,** a place where the gospel had enjoyed great success. These men, in Jerusalem for the Feast of Pentecost, immediately recognized their old nemesis in **the temple** and incited **the whole crowd and seized him.** This is the sixth time a crowd was incited

because of Paul's ministry (14:19; 16:19-22; 17:5-8, 13; 19:25-34).

21:28-29. The patently false charges they brought against Paul were similar to those raised against Stephen (6:11, 13-14). When they accused Paul of bringing **Greeks into the temple area** they were assuming a falsehood. Such an act in Jewish eyes would have **defiled** their **holy place.** Gentiles were permitted into the court of the Gentiles but no farther. Two inscriptions have been found on a balustrade separating the court of the Gentiles from the rest of the temple area. These warned Gentiles they would have themselves to blame for their deaths which would certainly ensue if they would proceed beyond the barrier (cf. Eph. 2:14).

So deep was this feeling that the Romans gave permission to Jews to fulfill this death sentence, even if the intruder was a Roman citizen.

21:30. The whole city was galvanized into action; they seized **Paul** and **dragged him from the temple.** Here the "temple" evidently refers to the court of the men. After they had brought Paul out, **immediately the gates were shut** so that no one could proceed beyond the court of the Gentiles and thus defile the temple.

21:31-32. Adjoining the temple area to the northwest was the Fortress of Antonia with two flights of steps leading into the outer court of the temple (see the sketch of the temple area and the fortress). **Troops** were stationed there, and more were added during Jewish feast days. They were part of the Roman Tenth Legion. **The commander of the** troops at the fortress, Claudius Lysias (cf. 23:26), **at once took some officers and soldiers and ran down to the crowd.** "Commander" is *chiliarchos,* leader of a thousand soldiers (25:23). The "officers" (*hekatontarchas,* lit., "rulers of hundreds" or centurions) indicates at least 200 **soldiers** were involved since the noun is plural.

21:33-36. These men rescued **Paul,** who was promptly **arrested** (*epelabeto,* "laid hold of," the same verb trans. "seizing" in v. 30) by **the commander** who **ordered him to be bound with two chains. So great** was the confusion and **violence** Paul **had to be carried by the soldiers. The crowd . . . kept shouting, Away with him!** In the same city a crowd

had shouted similar words against the Lord Jesus (Luke 23:18; John 19:15).

b. The defense of Paul (21:37–23:10)

(1) Before the mob (21:37–22:29). **21:37-38. The commander,** surprised that **Paul** could **speak Greek,** had supposed the apostle to be an **Egyptian** insurrectionist who had not yet been apprehended by the Romans. Evidently this Egyptian rebel was unable or refused to speak Greek.

Josephus wrote of an Egyptian impostor who claimed to be a prophet. He said this Egyptian had gathered 30,000 followers (Luke with accuracy states **4,000;** Josephus had a tendency to inflate numbers) and in A.D. 54 came to the Mount of Olives promising his adherents that the walls of Jerusalem would collapse at his command. Instead, the Roman army promptly marched on them, killed some and captured others, while the remainder were scattered. The Egyptian escaped.

Undoubtedly the people of Israel would have liked to lay their hands on this character who had caused so much trouble. When Lysias saw the riot in the temple, he assumed the center of the attention was this Egyptian and that the Jews were venting their wrath on him.

21:39-40. Paul assured the commander he was **a Jew** (with rights to be in the temple) and also **a citizen** of **Tarsus,** where he learned Greek. Tarsus was a city which enjoyed a good reputation, particularly for being an educational center. As yet Paul had not revealed his Roman citizenship (cf. 22:23-29).

When **Paul** was granted **permission** to **speak to the** mob, he addressed **them in Aramaic,** the common language of Palestinian Jews, used throughout the Middle East at that time. He **stood on the** stairs of the fortress overlooking **the crowd** below.

Paul's defense was in three parts: (a) his conduct before his conversion (22:1-5), (b) his conversion (22:6-16), and (c) his commission to minister (22:17-21).

22:1. The vocatives **Brothers and fathers** with which Paul began his speech are those Stephen used (7:2). Stephen's speech and martyrdom had a lasting impression on Paul! (cf. 8:1)

22:2. When they heard him speak to them in Aramaic, they quieted down.

Undoubtedly the Jews in the land were pleased if not surprised that a Jew of the Dispersion, as **Paul** was, could speak Aramaic as well as Greek. So they settled down and listened.

22:3-9. How much of Paul's rearing took place in Jerusalem (cf. 26:4) is not known. The verb translated **brought up** is from *anatrephō*, which may also mean "educate." One of his mentors was the beloved and esteemed **Gamaliel** (cf. 5:34).

Paul's point here is obvious. He had been thoroughly committed to **the Law** and to stamping out Christianity. On the **Way,** see comments on 9:2 (cf. 19:9, 23; 22:4; 24:14). His determination was so deep that only a radically supernatural transformation could change his viewpoint. He recounted the events of his conversion (22:6-9; cf. 9:1-6).

22:10-11. The statement, **There you will be told all that you have been assigned to do** (cf. 9:6), looks ahead to Paul's future ministry and anticipates his words in 22:14-15.

22:12-13. The Jewish viewpoint of this address is seen in Paul's description of **Ananias. He was a devout observer of the Law and highly respected by all the Jews living there.** These facts about him are not given in Acts 9. **Brother** reflects the same outlook seen in 22:5 where Jews in Damascus were called the "brothers" of the Jews in Jerusalem.

22:14-15. The reference to seeing Christ, **the Righteous One,** is important because it qualified Paul to be an apostle (cf. 1 Cor. 9:1; 15:8). The term "Righteous One" was also used by Stephen (Acts 7:52). The **all men** to whom Paul was to present the gospel included Gentiles, kings, and Jews (9:15).

22:16. Two questions revolve about this verse. First, when was Paul saved— on the Damascus Road or at Judas' house? Several factors suggest he was saved on the Damascus Road: (1) The gospel was presented to him directly by Christ (Gal. 1:11-12), not later by Ananias. (2) Already (Acts 22:10) Paul said he had submitted in faith to Christ. (3) Paul was filled with the Spirit *before* his baptism with water (9:17-18). (4) The Greek aorist participle, *epikalesamenos,* translated **calling on His name** refers either to action which is simultaneous with or before that of the main verb. Here Paul's calling on Christ's name (for salvation) preceded his water

baptism. The participle may be translated, "having called on His name."

Second, what then do the words **wash your sins away** mean? Do they teach that salvation comes by water baptism? Because Paul was already cleansed spiritually (see comments in preceding par.), these words must refer to the symbolism of baptism. Baptism is a picture of God's inner work of washing away sin (cf. 1 Cor. 6:11; 1 Peter 3:21).

22:17-18. Paul's departure from **Jerusalem,** according to 9:29-30, was because of the advice of Christian brothers. Actually a combination of divine revelation (22:17-18) and human direction led Paul to go to Tarsus.

22:19-20. Paul's rejoinder to the **Lord** shows he thought the Jews would be impressed by the radical change in his life; after all, he had been most zealous in persecuting believers (8:3; 9:2; 22:4-5; 26:11), even taking part in the martyrdom of **Stephen** (7:58; 8:1).

22:21-22. When **Paul** mentioned his commission to preach **to the Gentiles,** the mob was moved to instant rage and violence. Preaching to Gentiles could not have caused such a response because the religious authorities of Israel had preached to Gentiles (cf. Matt. 23:15). Paul's message that infuriated the mob was that Jews and Gentiles were equal without the Law of Moses (cf. Eph. 2:11-22; 3:2-6; Gal. 3:28).

This response is important to the argument of the Book of Acts. It indicates the Jews in Jerusalem had irrevocably refused the gospel of Jesus Christ and had sealed their fate. Less than 20 years later in A.D. 70 the city of Jerusalem became rubble and ruin (cf. Matt. 24:1-2; 21:41; 22:7). This, of course, does not mean Israel will not be restored in the future (cf. Rom. 11:26).

22:23-24. The people in the mob **threw off their cloaks and** flung **dust into the air** as expressions of intense anger. **The commander** who could not understand Aramaic was confused by everything that was going on. He was determined to get to the bottom of it all, even if it meant flogging **Paul.**

This flogging is different from Paul's beating with rods at Philippi and on two other occasions (2 Cor. 11:25; Acts 16:22-23). Nor was it the same as the Jewish 39 lashes administered with the long whips, a punishment Paul had received five times (2 Cor. 11:24). The Roman scourge was inflicted with shorter whips embedded with pieces of metal or bones and attached to a strong wooden handle. It could kill a man or leave him permanently crippled. This was the punishment Christ received (Matt. 27:26), leaving Him unable to carry His cross.

22:25-27. By law **a Roman citizen** not proven **guilty** of a crime could not be flogged. **Paul** called the centurion's attention to this fact by a question. When this was reported **to the commander** he was incredulous that Paul in his circumstances, the object of such hatred by the Jews, could be **a Roman citizen.**

22:28. During the reign of Emperor Claudius (A.D. 41–54; see the chart on Roman emperors at Luke 2:1) it was possible to purchase Roman **citizenship.** Those in government who sold this privilege could feather their nests with the bribery money. In contrast with **the commander . . . Paul** was **born a citizen** because his parents were citizens.

22:29. The commander, knowing **he had put Paul . . . in chains,** was fearful that Rome would learn he had violated Roman law. The chains probably were those that would hold him for flogging. Paul as a citizen was in chains at a later time (26:29).

Could not anyone avoid flogging by simply claiming to be a Roman citizen? Perhaps; but if a person falsely claimed to be a citizen, he was liable to the death penalty.

(2) Before the Sanhedrin (22:30–23:10). **22:30.** By this time **the commander** knew the accusations against Paul were Jewish (cf. vv. 23–29), and the best way to unearth these was to have a hearing before **the Sanhedrin.** If the prisoner was found innocent he could be released, but if the charges were valid the case could be remitted to the procurator, the Roman governor (cf. 23:26-30).

23:1-2. The setting for this brief trial is given here. After Paul claimed **all good conscience** in his ministry (cf. 24:16; 1 Cor. 4:4), **the high priest Ananias ordered those standing near Paul to strike him on the mouth.** Ananias' response is in keeping with what is known about him from Josephus, who

described him as insolent, hot-tempered, profane, and greedy. Ironically, at the beginning of Paul's ministry another Ananias helped him receive his sight.

23:3-5. Paul's outburst was triggered by the high priest's illegal command. How could the priest **violate the Law** while sitting as **judge** over one who supposedly had transgressed **the Law?** Jewish **law** presumed the accused to be innocent until proven guilty. Like a **whitewashed wall,** Ananias looked all right on the outside but was weak and deteriorating inwardly. Jesus too in His trials was struck on the mouth and challenged the legality of it (John 18:20-23).

Paul's statement, **Brothers, I did not realize that he was the high priest,** presents a problem. This could hardly be because of poor eyesight because Paul had "looked straight (*atenisas,* lit., 'looked intently') at the Sanhedrin" (Acts 23:1). Paul's words could be irony in which he was saying he *could* not recognize such a violent man as priest. However, the word "brothers" (v. 5) renders this interpretation improbable. Possibly there was such confusion the **high priest** was not identifiable. Certainly he was not wearing his priestly garments. It is also probable Paul did not know Ananias personally because the apostle had not had contact with the Sanhedrin for many years. The high priesthood changed hands frequently (see the chart on Annas' family at 4:5-6).

At any rate, Paul recognized the position of the high priest even if he did not respect the priest as a person.

23:6-9. In such a scene justice was impossible. Recognizing this, **Paul** changed his tactics completely and stated his **hope in the resurrection of the dead** along with **the Pharisees** (on this hope, cf. 24:15; 26:6-7; 28:20). This immediately disrupted the proceedings because it started an argument **between the Pharisees and the Sadducees** (cf. 4:1-2). By using this clever tactic, Paul divided his enemy. Amazingly the **Pharisees** defended Paul, a fellow **Pharisee.**

23:10. Paul was in more danger in the midst of the Jews than he was in a Roman prison. So again he was brought up the steps to **the** army **barracks** at the Antonia Fortress (cf. 21:35).

419

c. The danger to Paul (23:11-32)

23:11. The importance of this vision was not only in its comfort and encouragement (cf. 18:9-10) but also in the confirmation it gave of Paul's plans to go to Rome. The gospel of Christ would literally go from **Jerusalem** to **Rome** by means of the Apostle **Paul.** This was the fourth vision **the Lord** gave Paul (cf. 9:4-6; 16:9; 18:9-10).

23:12-13. So great was the hatred for Paul, **the** very **next morning . . . 40** fanatical **Jews formed a conspiracy and bound themselves with an oath not to eat or drink until they had killed** him (cf. the crowd's efforts to kill him; 21:31). The verb for taking an oath is *anathematizō* (whence the Eng. "anathema"), which means a person binds himself under a curse if he does not fulfill his oath. Presumably these men were later released from this oath by lawyers because Paul's circumstances changed through a dramatic series of events.

23:14-15. The complicity of **the chief priests and elders** in this plot reveals both their lack of a legitimate case against Paul and their base characters. The fanatic zeal of the 40 men is also seen because a number of them would certainly be killed in overcoming Paul's guards, should their plan be carried out.

23:16-22. Paul's unnamed nephew somehow **heard** about the **plot** of the **40** and was able to get to **the barracks** to tell **Paul** and then **the commander.** Many unresolved questions come to mind. Was Paul's nephew a Christian? How did he secure this information? Did Paul's **sister** live in Jerusalem? If Paul had relatives living in Jerusalem, why did he not stay with them?

The nephew was a **young man** (vv. 17-19, 22). This Greek word *neanias,* used in verse 17, was earlier used of Paul (7:58) and Eutychus (20:9). It may refer to a man in his twenties or thirties. (*Neaniskos,* a synonym of *neanios,* is used in 23:18 and 22. In v. 19 the NIV has "young man" but the Gr. does not.) When the fortress **commander** heard of this plan, he **cautioned** Paul's nephew not to **tell anyone** he had **reported this.**

23:23-24. The commander decided to get Paul away from this danger spot. So he made every possible provision for Paul's security in his escape. First, he sent **Paul** in the company of more than 470 men—**two . . . centurions . . . 200 soldiers** (a centurion was over 100), **70 horsemen, and 200 spearmen.** Second, they began the journey under cover of nightfall at **9 P.M.** In addition, **Caesarea** would be a far more secure place, not as subject to a riot as was Jerusalem. For the third time(!) Paul left a city surreptitiously, at night (cf. Damascus, 9:25; Thessalonica, 17:10).

23:25-30. When a prisoner was forwarded to a superior, the subordinate officer was required to accompany the subject with a written statement of the case.

This **letter** from **Claudius Lysias** presents the essentials of the case. The commander bent the truth in saying he **rescued Paul** (v. 27) because he actually learned from a subordinate that Paul was a Roman citizen (22:26). He also discreetly omitted any reference to his preparing to have Paul flogged (cf. 22:25, 29).

The importance of this document is seen in 23:29 where the commander declared Paul to be innocent. Compare similar comments by Gallio (18:14-15), the city executive of Ephesus (19:40), Pharisees (23:9), Festus (25:25), and Herod Agrippa II (26:31-32).

23:31-32. The journey to **Antipatris** from Jerusalem was more than 35 miles. This must have been a forced march because they arrived by **the next day.** The terrain from Jerusalem to Lydda or Joppa (modern-day Lod; cf. 9:32-43), seven or eight miles before Antipatris, was difficult and would provide suitable cover for an ambush party. Once the entourage was in Antipatris **the soldiers** were no longer needed. The remaining 27 miles to Caesarea could be traversed with less danger.

3. THE CAPTIVITY AT CAESAREA (23:33–26:32)

a. Paul's defense before Felix (23:33–24:27)

23:33–35. When the cavalry and Paul **arrived,** Felix held a minor preliminary interrogation. Felix was the procurator (**governor**) of Judea about A.D. 52–58. He is one of three Roman procurators mentioned in the New Testament. The others are Pontius Pilate (A.D. 26–36) and Porcius Festus (A.D. 58–62). Felix married Drusilla (24:24), a sister of Herod Agrippa

II, the Agrippa in 25:13–26:32. (See the chart on the Herods at Luke 1:5.)

After Felix learned Paul **was from Cilicia he** determined to **hear the case.** Evidently a case could be tried in the province of the accused or in the province in which his alleged crime took place. The question actually involved "**what** sort of (*poias*) **province**" Paul was from. At this time Cilicia was not a full province but was under the legate of Syria, for whom Felix was a deputy. The legate would not want to be bothered with such a small case as this. Furthermore, Felix would not want to incur the Jews' wrath by forcing them to present their case against Paul in his hometown Tarsus, a city so far away. Felix could make only one decision and that was to hear the case. But witnesses against Paul would have to be present (cf. Acts 23:30).

24:1. The high priest himself **went down to Caesarea** as well as **some of the elders** of the Sanhedrin. They had hired an attorney (*rhētoros*, "a public speaker, orator," used only here in the NT), **Tertullus,** who was to present the case **before** Felix.

24:2-4. The lawyer spent almost as much time on his introduction as he did on the specific charges against **Paul.** His description of **Felix** was obviously fawning flattery, for Felix was known for his violent use of repressive force and corrupt self-aggrandizement. Felix had been a slave, won his freedom, and curried favor with the imperial court. Tacitus, a Roman historian, bitingly summed up Felix's character with the terse comment, "He exercised royal power with the mind of a slave."

24:5-8. The accusations were three: (1) Paul was a worldwide **troublemaker, stirring up riots** everywhere. (2) **He** was a leader **of the Nazarene sect.** (3) He attempted **to desecrate the temple.**

The first charge had political overtones because Rome desired to maintain order throughout its empire.

The second charge was also concerned with the government because Tertullus made it appear that Christianity was divorced from the Jewish religion. Rome permitted Judaism as a *religio licita* (a legal religion), but it would not tolerate any new religions. By describing Christianity as a "sect" (*haireseōs*, "faction,

party, school"; whence the Eng. "heresy") of the Nazarenes, the attorney made Paul's faith appear to be cultic and bizarre.

Desecrating the temple also had political overtones because the Romans had given the Jews permission to execute any Gentile who went inside the barrier of the temple (cf. 21:28). At this point Tertullus modified the original charge made in 21:28. There Paul was accused of bringing a Gentile (Trophimus the Ephesian) into the temple courts; here Paul is said to have attempted desecration. The truth was severely damaged in the clause **so we seized him,** the implication being they took Paul to arrest him. (The NIV marg. gives some words that are added in vv. 6-8 in a few less-reliable Gr. mss.)

24:9-10. After **the Jews** had agreed to the veracity of their prosecuting attorney's charges, **Paul** was given an opportunity to answer.

His introduction was much shorter and truthful. He implied Felix knew the situation in Judea well enough to make an accurate decision.

24:11. Paul gave several points in his own defense. First, he had not been in **Jerusalem** long enough to instigate a riot. In fact one of his purposes for being in Jerusalem was **to worship,** to observe the Feast of Pentecost (20:16). Another reason was developed in 24:17-18.

24:12-13. Second, even Paul's calumniators could **not** cite an instance when he instigated a riot in the city.

24:14-16. Third, he worshiped the **God of** Israel in full conformity **with the Law and . . . the Prophets** (cf. 26:22; 28:23). (On the term "the Law and the Prophets" see Matt. 5:17.) Furthermore his faith was not in **a sect** but in Christianity, which was known as **the Way** (cf. Acts 9:2; 19:9, 23; 22:4; 24:22). His **hope** in the **resurrection** (cf. 23:6; 26:6-7) was **the same** as that of his accusers (Paul assumed a number of them were Pharisees). By this Paul meant Christianity was an outgrowth of the Old Testament. Further, Paul **always** sought **to keep** his **conscience clear** (cf. 23:1). "Clear" translates *aproskopon* (lit., "not causing to stumble, or not offending"), used only two other times in the New Testament, both by Paul (1 Cor. 10:32; Phil. 1:10).

24:17. This is the only time in Acts Paul's goal of bringing an offering to Jerusalem from the Gentile churches is mentioned. Luke did not stress this because it was not a major factor in his argument. However, it was most important to Paul as is evidenced by his frequent allusions to it in his epistles (Rom. 15:25-28; 1 Cor. 16:1-4; 2 Cor. 8:13-14; 9:12-13; Gal. 2:10).

What did Paul mean when he said he went **to Jerusalem . . . to present offerings?** Perhaps he meant he "entered the temple to present offerings" (cf. Acts 24:18). But more probably he meant he offered thank offerings for God's blessings on his ministry.

24:18. Again Paul affirmed that he was not the instigator of a **disturbance** (cf. v. 12); his accusers were!

24:19-21. Finally, Paul said his genuine accusers were not present, the **Jews from the province of Asia** who made the original false allegations and incited the riot in the temple (cf. 21:27). Since **the Sanhedrin** had not found him guilty (23:1-9), Tertullus' speech did not really contain any legitimate charges.

24:22. How **Felix** knew about Christianity can only be surmised. Probably he heard about it from Drusilla, his wife, who was a daughter of Herod Agrippa I and a sister of Herod Agrippa II. Because she was a Jewess (v. 24) she would know about **the Way.** Besides this, Felix could scarcely have ruled in Judea for several years without learning something about the faith of the early church.

Rather than make a decision which would have been unfavorable to the religious authorities he **adjourned the proceedings.** He said, **When Lysias the commander comes . . . I will decide your case.** Whether Claudius Lysias (cf. 23:25-30) ever came to Caesarea or not was beside the point; the case had been postponed indefinitely.

24:23. Felix, evidently aware of Paul's innocence, granted him a limited amount of **freedom** as a prisoner under the guardianship of **the centurion.** Later another centurion gave Paul similar freedom in Sidon (27:3).

24:24-26. Felix must have taken a brief trip **with his wife, Drusilla.** When they returned, Felix **sent for Paul** who **spoke about faith in Christ Jesus.** Felix was brought under conviction when **Paul discoursed on righteousness, self-control, and the judgment to come.** Well he should, for his marriage to Drusilla was his third and he had to break up another marriage to secure her. His regime was marked by injustices that contrasted with the righteousness of God. And he was a man grossly lacking in self-control.

The duplicity and greed of Felix is seen in his desire to be bribed by **Paul.**

24:27. To placate **the Jews,** Felix **left Paul in prison** even though he knew Paul was innocent. **Felix** eventually lost his position because he was cruelly intemperate in putting down a Jewish and Gentile conflict in Caesarea.

b. Paul's defense before Festus (25:1-12)

25:1. This section (vv. 1-12) is crucial because in it Paul appealed to Caesar. It sets the direction for the remainder of the book and also shows how the apostle reached Rome.

Little is known of Porcius **Festus,** Roman procurator of Judea, A.D. 58–62, but what history discloses is favorable. His desire to rule well is attested by his going to Jerusalem **three days after arriving in the province.** No doubt he had heard of the volatile nature of that city!

25:2-3. One item heavy on the minds of the religious authorities was a trial for **Paul.** They knew their case was so weak that the only way they could rid themselves of him was by **ambush** while he was being **transferred** from Caesarea **to Jerusalem.**

25:4-5. Evidently **Festus** felt their request was unreasonable so he promised to reopen the case in **Caesarea.** Paul was already there and Festus was returning **there.**

25:6-7. The scene of previous trials repeated itself. Luke added, however, that the **charges** were **many** and **serious.**

25:8-9. After **Paul** briefly and categorically denied the allegations against him, **Festus** asked the prisoner if he would be **willing to go . . . to Jerusalem** for another **trial.** Festus had changed his mind on this (cf. vv. 4-5), apparently feeling this would be a suitable compromise to placate **the Jews.** Also he was realizing he did not know how to handle this kind of religious case (v. 20).

25:10. Paul would have nothing to do with this switch for several reasons: (1) The journey from Caesarea to Jerusalem would be most dangerous. The 40 Jews who two years before (cf. 24:27) had taken an oath to murder Paul (23:13-14) would probably have gotten out of their oath somehow by then, but they would still want to kill Paul. (2) The possibility of a fair trial in Jerusalem was remote. (3) He had already languished as a prisoner in Caesarea for some two years.

The charges brought against Paul were civil (they said he had done **wrong to the Jews**); therefore the present **court** where Festus represented Caesar, was the proper one.

25:11. The charges were serious enough to demand a **death** penalty. If the accusations were **true,** Paul said, he was willing **to die.** He interpreted Festus' suggestion that he go to Jerusalem (v. 9) as tantamount to delivering Paul over to the **Jews,** even though the trial would be conducted by Festus.

25:12. There is some debate as to whether **Festus** was legally bound to remand the case **to Caesar** (Nero, who reigned from A.D. 54–68), or if he could have chosen to handle the case himself. If Festus had decided to hear the case and made a negative decision, Paul could still have appealed to Caesar. But Festus probably had no alternative but to transfer the case to Rome. So **after** he **had conferred with his council,** he announced that in view of Paul's appeal, he must go **to Caesar.**

c. Paul's defense before Agrippa II (25:13–26:32)

25:13. The **King Agrippa** referred to here was Agrippa II, son of Herod Agrippa I (12:1) and a great-grandson of Herod the Great (Matt. 2:1). (See the chart on the Herods at Luke 1:5.) At this time he was a young man of about 30 years of age and the ruler of territories northeast of Palestine with the title of King. Because he was a friend of the Roman imperial family he was awarded the privilege of appointing the Jewish high priest and also had been made the custodian of the temple treasury. His background made him eminently qualified to hear Paul; he was well acquainted with the Jews' religion (cf. Acts 25:26-27).

Agrippa II and his sister **Bernice,** came to **Caesarea to pay their respects to Festus.** Though Bernice had a tendency to support the Jews she lived a profligate life. She had an incestuous relationship with Agrippa, her brother.

25:14-21. Festus reviewed his dealings with **Paul's case** which had been **left** to him by **Felix.** Festus frankly confessed he was incapable of handling the case (v. 20). In particular he did not understand Paul's insistence on the resurrection of Christ (v. 19).

25:22. The rehearsal of the situation had its desired effect on **Agrippa.** The Herodian family was useful to Rome for its knowledge of Jewish affairs and Agrippa's insights would be helpful **to Festus.**

25:23-24. The petty King **Agrippa and** his sister **Bernice** used this occasion to display their position, clothes, and ceremony. Luke undoubtedly was contrasting the lowly prisoner **Paul** in the audience room with Agrippa and Bernice and **the high-ranking officers and the leading men of the city.** Because five cohorts (each cohort had a thousand soldiers) were stationed at Caesarea, five high-ranking officers were there (*chiliarchoi,* lit., "commanders of a thousand"; cf. 21:31). **Festus** told **Agrippa** that the Jews urged that Paul should die.

25:25-27. The statement in verse 25 is significant because it shows that Festus, like Felix before him, **found** Paul **had done nothing deserving of death** (cf. 23:9, 29; 26:31).

It would look bad for Festus **to send** Paul to Caesar with no clear **charges against him.** Festus believed that **Agrippa,** with his knowledge of Jewish customs and laws, could help Festus **write** out some charges that would be specific enough for Caesar Nero to consider.

Two interesting terms for Roman royalty are found in this chapter, the first of which is *Sebastos* meaning "revered" or "august" and used in the New Testament only in 25:21, 25; 27:1. In chapter 25 it is translated "Emperor" and in 27:1 it is rendered "Imperial."

The other term is *kyrios* meaning "lord." In 25:26 "the lord" is translated **His Majesty.** Both Augustus and Tiberius refused this title for themselves because they felt it exalted them too highly;

however, by the time Paul made his appeal to Caesar, Nero was on the throne and "lord" was used much more commonly of the Caesar. Though Nero did accept the title of "lord," he had not yet gone to the excesses that characterized his reign later. At this juncture Nero was reputed to be a fair-minded ruler.

26:1. Paul had already made **his defense** to Festus (25:6-12), so now the apostle directed his address to **Agrippa.** Furthermore, the purpose of this speech was for Agrippa's information.

The motioning of the **hand** was evidently after the manner of orators of that time. This speech has a number of parts: (1) complimentary remarks (26:2-3), (2) Paul's early life in Judaism (vv. 4-8), (3) his zeal in opposing Christianity (vv. 9-11), (4) his conversion and commission (vv. 12-18), (5) his ministry (vv. 19-23), (6) his verbal jousts with Festus and Agrippa (vv. 24-29).

26:2-3. Paul was sincere in these compliments because he knew **Agrippa** was indeed **well acquainted with all the Jewish customs and controversies,** in addition to being a practicing Jew.

In contrast with Tertullus who promised a brief speech before Felix (24:4), Paul implied his defense might be more lengthy. This is the climax of all Paul's defenses recorded in Acts (cf. 22:1-21; 23:1-8; 24:10-21; 25:6-11).

26:4-8. In summary, Paul asserted that from his early **life he lived . . . according to** and for the **hope** of Israel (vv. 6-7; cf. 23:6; 24:15; 28:20). (On his living **in Jerusalem,** see 22:3.) He stated that this hope involved the resurrection from **the dead.** This is why Christ quoted Moses (Ex. 3:6) to defend the doctrine of the Resurrection (Matt. 22:32). Because Yahweh is the God of Abraham, Isaac, and Jacob, people must be resurrected in order to receive the promise God made to them. Likewise the promises made to the Jews demand they be resurrected in the coming Messianic Age.

Paul's reference to the **12 tribes** of Israel shows the error of British-Israelism with its "10 lost tribes of Israel" (cf. Matt. 19:28; Luke 22:30; James 1:1; Rev. 7:4-8; 21:12).

26:9-11. Besides being committed to Judaism, Paul had also been fanatic in his opposition to Christianity (cf. 8:3; 9:2; 22:4-5, 19). His casting votes **against**

imprisoned Christians does not necessarily mean Paul was a member of the Sanhedrin. It may simply mean he agreed with the Sanhedrin's action (cf. 8:1; 22:20).

When Paul apprehended Christians he **tried to force them to blaspheme,** that is, to recant their belief in Jesus.

26:12-18. As Paul recounted his conversion (cf. 9:1-19; 22:1-21) he once again told of the **light . . . brighter than the** noonday **sun** (22:6). For the first time the reader is informed that the language of the heavenly **voice** was **Aramaic,** though it was implied because the spelling of Saul's name in 9:4 and 22:7 was Aramaic.

Some believe that the statement, **It is hard for you to kick against the goads,** means Paul had guilt feelings and was violating his conscience in persecuting believers in Christ. However, Paul wrote later that in spite of his blaspheming, violence, and persecution of the church he was shown mercy because he was acting in ignorance and unbelief (1 Tim. 1:13). Kicking the goads evidently referred to the futility of his persecuting the church.

The statement of Paul's commission (Acts 26:18) closely resembled the work of the Messiah, predicted in Isaiah 35:5; 42:7, 16; 61:1. As a representative of the Lord **Jesus** Christ, Paul did figuratively what the Lord Jesus will someday do on earth literally. Spiritually Paul had led many **from the darkness** of sin (John 3:19; 2 Cor. 4:4; Eph. 4:18; 5:8; Col. 1:13) **to light** in Christ (John 12:36; 2 Cor. 4:6; Eph. 5:8; Col. 1:12; 1 Thes. 5:5). This salvation releases from Satan's **power** (John 8:44; Heb. 2:14) and gives **forgiveness of sins** (Acts 2:38; 5:31; 10:43; 13:38; Eph. 1:7; Col. 1:14) and a spiritual inheritance (Rom. 8:17; Col. 1:12) with **those who are sanctified,** that is, those who are positionally set apart to God by His redeeming work (cf. 1 Cor. 1:30; Heb. 10:10; 13:12).

26:19-23. Paul's statement in verse 20 is something of a problem. He said he had **preached** to those in **Damascus, then to those in Jerusalem and in all Judea.** But Paul wrote the Galatians he was unknown in the churches of Judea (Gal. 1:22). Many have felt that there was an early textual corruption and that the Greek text should read, "To those in

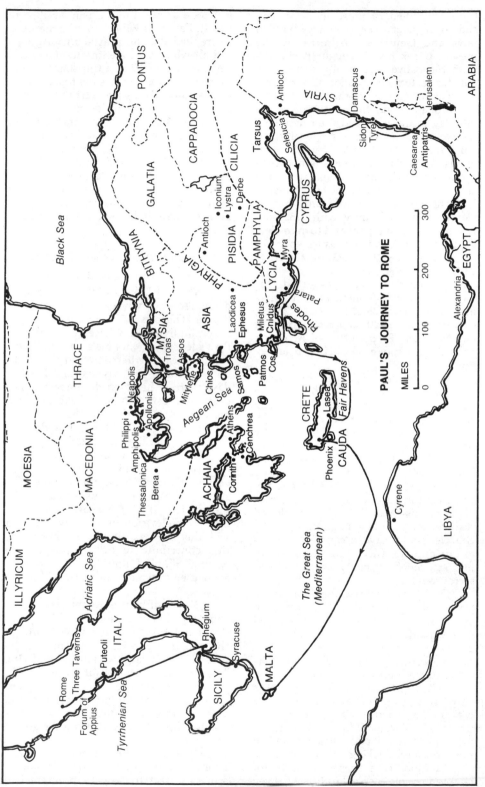

PAUL'S JOURNEY TO ROME

MILES

0   100   200   300

ARABIA

Jerusalem

Damascus

Antioch

SYRIA

Sidon

Tyre

Caesarea

Antipatris

Tarsus

Seleucia

CILICIA

CAPPADOCIA

PONTUS

GALATIA

Iconium

Lystra

Derbe

Antioch

PISIDIA

PHRYGIA

PAMPHYLIA

LYCIA

Myra

Patara

CYPRUS

Rhodes

EGYPT

Alexandria

BITHYNIA

ASIA

Laodicea

Ephesus

Miletus

Cnidus

Cos

Patmos

Samos

Chios

Mitylene

MYSIA

Troas

Assos

THRACE

Black Sea

MOESIA

MACEDONIA

Neapolis

Philippi

Amphipolis

Apollonia

Thessalonica

Berea

Aegean Sea

Athens

Cenchrea

Corinth

ACHAIA

CRETE

Lasea

Fair Havens

Phoenix

CAUDA

Cyrene

LIBYA

The Great Sea
(Mediterranean)

MALTA

SICILY

Syracuse

Rhegium

ITALY

Puteoli

Forum of
Appius

Three Taverns

Rome

Tyrrhenian Sea

Adriatic Sea

ILLYRICUM

Damascus, then to those in Jerusalem, and throughout every country, both to Jews and Gentiles." Admittedly the present Greek text is rough (it changes from the dative case to the accusative), but this textual emendation is extremely speculative and unnecessary.

Probably Paul first summarized his ministry to the Jews and then described his work among **Gentiles.** He affirmed much the same in Acts 26:17-18. In other words Paul's statement here is not to be taken in strict chronological sequence but as a general overview of his ministry. First, he preached to Jews and then to Gentiles, in conformity with 1:8. Both groups needed to **repent and turn to God.** Frequently in Acts the apostles spoke of repentance (2:38; 3:19; 5:31; 8:22; 11:18; 13:24; 17:30; 19:4; 20:21).

Furthermore, Paul asserted, his message was a fulfillment of Old Testament prophecies (26:22; cf. 24:14; 28:23), concerning the death and resurrection of the Messiah. Frequently in Acts, the apostles also spoke of Christ's resurrection.

26:24-29. Festus, with his Greek outlook, thought the doctrine of the Resurrection was impossible (cf. 17:32; 23:6-7), so he **interrupted** Paul, though the apostle had already made his primary points. Festus said that Paul was **out of his mind,** that his education was **driving** him **insane.**

But **Paul** clearly asserted his sanity and then turned once again to **Agrippa. None of this**—that is, Christ's death and resurrection and the beginning of the church—could have **escaped** Agrippa's attention. He was well-schooled in Judaism, and Christianity was no esoteric secret society.

Finally Paul pressed the issue with a forthright question, **King Agrippa, do you believe the prophets?** (cf. 26:22) **I know you do** (cf. Paul's witness to Felix, 24:24).

Now **Agrippa** was in a corner. If he accepted the prophets he would be forced to admit Christ Jesus fulfilled them. His only escape was to parry the question with an interrogative of his own.

The NIV translation of 26:28 catches the spirit of Agrippa's question well. It was probably a joking rebuttal of Paul.

Paul took his response seriously, for he loved people for the Lord's sake. Even

if it took a **long** time to win Agrippa to Christ, Paul was willing to take the time. He replied that he prayed that Agrippa and **all who** were listening to him would **become** like him (i.e., a Christian), **except for these chains.** (This is the first mention of chains on Paul since 22:29.) So Paul's defense came to a conclusion.

26:30-32. Already others had said Paul was innocent: Pharisees (23:9); Claudius Lysias, the commander in Jerusalem (23:29); and Governor **Festus** (25:25). Now **Agrippa,** a man of power, well-trained in Judaism and sympathetic with Jews, stated, **This man could have been set free, if he had not appealed to Caesar.**

4. THE CAPTIVITY AT ROME (CHAPS. 27-28)

a. The sea journey (chap. 27)

Why did Luke go into such lengthy detail about the voyage from Caesarea to Rome? There is no easy answer. (1) It may simply be a device to emphasize Paul's journey to and his arrival at Rome. As the Gospel writers stressed the Lord's final approach to Jerusalem and His last days there to heighten the impact of His death and resurrection, so Luke climaxed his Luke-Acts work with the proclamation of the gospel of the kingdom to Gentiles in the Roman capital.

(2) Luke may have used the example of great ancient epics of his day which commonly employed the theme of a storm and shipwreck. This would parallel the modern use of a chase scene in a movie or television drama. The problem with this view is a simple one. How does this contribute to Luke's purpose in writing? Simply following the example of ancient epics would not really add to the book.

(3) Possibly the writer desired to show a parallel with Jonah and his storm (Jonah 1:4-15). After Jonah lived through the storm by miraculous means he preached to a large Gentile capital city. The comparison with Paul is obvious.

(4) The purpose of this account is to show God's sovereign protection and direction in Paul's ministry. It was God's will for the apostle to minister the gospel in Rome.

(5) It was Luke's intention to show Paul's leadership and thereby to underscore the fact that God's program had

become primarily Gentile and therefore Paul was God's man of the hour. In the account Paul certainly does come off as the one who is in control even in the spheres of ocean travel and shipwreck.

(6) Some think the story is something of an allegory. In the Old Testament the sea was portrayed as an enemy; so here it figures opposition to the spread of the gospel. In spite of all antagonism the good news of the kingdom will survive and will ultimately reach its predetermined goal. But this is so allegorical it is a highly improbable view.

The answer to the question of Luke's great emphasis on the journey to Rome may be a combination of answers 1, 3, 4, and 5, though it is difficult to be dogmatic.

27:1. Who and how many **other prisoners** accompanied **Paul** to Rome is an unanswered question. Nor is the reader informed as to why the others were being taken to the capital city.

The **centurion . . . Julius, who** is a primary character in this account, **belonged to the Imperial Regiment,** an honorary title given to certain troops. "Imperial" translates *Sebastēs*, meaning "revered" (cf. comments on 25:25). A "centurion" commanded 100 soldiers (cf. 10:1; 21:32 ["officers" in NIV]; 22:25-26; 23:17, 23; 24:23).

Use of the pronoun **we** indicates Luke accompanied Paul on this journey.

27:2-3. Adramyttium, the home base of the **ship,** was east-southeast of Troas in northwest Asia Minor. Evidently the ship was making its last journey to its base before the stormy winter sailing season set in. Apparently the centurion wanted to find a ship bound for Rome along the way or to get to the Egnatian Road and use it to transport the prisoners.

Aristarchus evidently accompanied Paul to be his helper. Aristarchus stayed with Paul during his Roman incarceration (Col. 4:10; Phile. 24).

Interestingly **Paul** had **friends** in **Sidon,** the ship's first port of call after leaving Caesarea. The **kindness** of this centurion is mindful of another centurion's kindness (Acts 24:23).

27:4-8. The information in these verses points up the difficulty of sailing from east to west in the Mediterranean Sea. **The** prevailing **winds** blew from the west so the ships would sail to the east **of Cyprus** and proceed with **difficulty** along the southwest coast of Asia Minor and to the east **of Crete.** When Paul sailed in the opposite direction, the ship took a more direct route (21:1-3).

In **Myra,** a port city on the south coast of Asia Minor, **the centurion found an Alexandrian ship sailing for Italy.** This was a grain ship (27:38) large enough to carry 276 passengers (v. 37). Egypt was Rome's breadbasket. The grain ships would commonly sail north to Asia Minor and then make their way west across the Mediterranean using the islands for as much protection as they could obtain from them.

Paul's journey on this second ship took him from Myra toward the island of **Cnidus** and then southwest to the south side of Crete, **to a place called Fair Havens.** The Cretans were known for their laziness and depravity (Titus 1:12). Later Paul wrote to Titus to appoint elders for that island's churches (Titus 1:5).

27:9-12. The Fast referred to here was probably the Day of Atonement which occurred in late September to early October. After that time of year the unsettled weather patterns over the Mediterranean Sea made sailing hazardous. In those days sea traffic ceased by early November.

Paul was perhaps included in the ship's council because of his experiences in travel (cf. 2 Cor. 11:25, "three times I was shipwrecked") and his natural leadership. Contrary to Paul's advice **the majority** (Acts 27:11) **decided** it best to **sail on** to a more commodious **harbor** and to **winter there.** The authority rested ultimately in the hands of **the centurion** because grain ships were considered to be in government service. So they sailed along the southern coast of **Crete.** They hoped **to reach** the harbor of **Phoenix.**

27:13-17. Once caught by a sudden **Northeaster,** a **hurricane**-like **wind,** they could not remain in the protection **of Crete** and **were driven** helplessly into the open sea. **Cauda,** a **small island** 25 miles south of Crete, provided a brief respite from the teeth of the wind. While they were south of the island they hauled in **the lifeboat** which was normally pulled in tow but now was probably full of water.

What is meant by **they passed ropes under the ship itself to hold it together** is not positively clear. It probably means the sailors encircled the boat with ropes so that the beams would not separate and leak more water from the pressure of the sea and storm.

The sandbars of Syrtis were located off Libya of North Africa. The Greek word translated sea anchor is *skeuos* and literally means "vessel" or "equipment," so it could refer to any gear. Probably, however, it was an anchor.

27:18-26. The storm raged on; so the next day they threw the cargo overboard and the day after that the ship's tackle. So awesome was the storm that after many days, they gave up all hope of getting out of the situation alive.

The passengers and probably also the crew had gone . . . without food for a number of days. Perhaps the storm had destroyed much of the supplies; some evidently were seasick; and perhaps many were too discouraged to eat (cf. v. 33). After Paul reminded them of the advice he gave earlier at Crete (cf. v. 10), he encouraged them with a message from God. This was not the first time a vision had lifted Paul's spirits (cf. 18:9-10; 23:11); in fact, in the Jerusalem vision (23:11) God promised Paul not only safety there but ultimately a safe journey to Rome. Here too God (through an angel) promised that Paul would stand trial before Caesar. Twice Paul urged his shipmates (all 275 of them; cf. 27:37) to keep up their courage (vv. 22, 25). The verb "to keep up one's courage" (*euthymeō*) is used only three times in the New Testament—twice here and in James 5:13 ("to be happy"). The verb has the idea of having good feelings or being in good spirits. Even as a prisoner Paul did not hesitate to make known his faith in God.

27:27-32. The Adriatic Sea was a term used in New Testament times of the sea not only between Italy and Greece but also south of Italy and Sicily to Malta. After two weeks in the storm the sailors finally sensed they were coming to some land. The water was becoming shallower (from 120 feet to 90 feet). Their soundings were made by throwing into the water a line with lead on it (*bolisantes*, "took soundings," is lit., "heaving the lead") and thereby judging the water's depth. As they came into even shallower water they dropped four anchors. Paul

warned the centurion that the sailors attempting to escape needed to stay with the ship (cf. v. 24). The soldiers cut . . . the lifeboat loose which meant that all aboard could only depend on the Lord God for deliverance.

27:33-35. Because of Paul's confidence in the Lord to keep them all safe (v. 24), he encouraged them to eat (vv. 33-34). He then took some bread, unashamedly thanked God for it, and broke it and started eating. Though this sounds like an observance of the Lord's Table, it probably was not. Most of those 276 people were not Christians. Rather it was a public testimony by Paul of his faith in the God and Father of the Lord Jesus as well as a practical expedient of eating in order to muster strength for the ordeal ahead.

27:36. Two problems were mentioned in verse 33—the people had "gone without food" for a fortnight and also had "been in constant suspense." But now they were all encouraged (lit., "they became of good spirits," *euthymoi*; cf. vv. 22, 25) and ate some food themselves— solving the two problems in verse 33.

27:37-38. This grain ship not only carried cargo but also had 276 passengers and crew members. The number of prisoners (v. 42) is not stated. This was not an excessively large ship, for Josephus wrote about a ship which he boarded to Italy which carried 600 passengers.

27:39-40. Seeing a bay with a sandy beach at dawn, they decided to try running the ship aground. They cut away the anchors and rudders . . . hoisted the foresail, and headed for the beach. The word "rudders" (*pēdaliōn*) literally describes the blades of oars and refers to paddle rudders extending from the sides of the ship. These were tied while the ship was at anchor.

27:41. The ship struck a sandbar which the sailors had not seen. Because of the beating of the waves, the back of the ship was broken to pieces while the bow was stuck in the sand.

27:42-44. Because soldiers were accountable with their own lives for any prisoners who escaped (cf. 12:19; 16:27) they planned to kill the prisoners to prevent any of them from swimming away and escaping. For the soldiers this was simply a matter of self-preservation.

The centurion, however, **wanted to spare Paul's life.** He saw the value and trustworthiness of this prisoner and so forestalled the soldiers' **plan.** Obviously God was sovereignly at work to spare Paul for ministry at Rome and to guarantee the fulfillment of his prediction (v. 24). In the cold rain (28:2) the passengers (soldiers and prisoners) and crewmen **who could swim** were urged **to** swim ashore, while **the rest** held onto the ship's debris.

As Paul had predicted, the ship was lost (27:22), they ran aground on an island (v. 26), and no one perished (v. 22).

b. The sojourn at Malta (28:1-10)

28:1-2. They were shipwrecked on **Malta,** a small **island** 60 miles south of Sicily. Malta had good harbors and was ideally located for trade. In two weeks the storm had carried them 600 miles west of Fair Havens, Crete. **The islanders** translates *hoi barbaroi* (lit., "the barbarians"), a Greek term used to refer to non-Greek-speaking people. This does not mean the people were savages or uncultured, but that their civilization was not Greek-oriented. They **showed . . . unusual** hospitality to the victims of the shipwreck, building them **a fire** and welcoming them.

28:3. Because the weather was cold (v. 2) a snake would be stiff and lethargic. Of course the heat of **the fire** would drive **a viper** from the flames and also make it more active.

28:4-6. Seeing that **Paul** was bitten by **the snake** the **islanders** concluded he was **a murderer,** now getting **justice.** But when he was unaffected by the viper's bite (with not even any swelling of his hand), the islanders superstitiously **said** that Paul **was a god.** No doubt Paul's response to this, though not recorded, was similar to his reaction at Lystra (14:8-18).

28:7-10. Publius took **Paul** and others (**us** included Luke) to his **estate . . . for three days.** One benefit of Paul's ministry was the healing of Publius' **father** (who had **fever and dysentery**) and **the rest of the sick on the island.** Interestingly Paul, besides not being harmed by the viper, was used by God to heal others. No wonder the islanders **honored** the shipwrecked men **in many**

ways, even giving them **supplies** before they set sail three months later (v. 11). These supplies were no doubt given in gratitude for Paul's services.

c. The summation of service at Rome (28:11-31)

28:11. Since the crew and passengers left Crete in October or November ("after the Fast," 27:9) and were in the storm two weeks, their **three** months' stay on Malta brought them through the winter into February or March. In that time they saw another **ship** docked at the island. Because **it was** of **Alexandrian** origin, it too was probably a grain ship (cf. 27:6, 38) from Egypt that had spent the three months of winter, when it was too dangerous to sail, at a seaport on Malta. Probably it was at the Valletta harbor.

The twin gods Castor and Pollux on the ship's figurehead were the heavenly twin sons of Zeus and Leda according to Greek mythology; supposedly they brought good fortune to mariners. If their constellation, Gemini, was seen during a storm it was an omen of good luck. Possibly Luke included this detail to contrast the superstition of the people of Malta, Rome, Greece, and Egypt with Christianity.

28:12-14. The journey was carefully traced by Luke: from Malta to **Syracuse,** Sicily; to **Rhegium** (today Reggio) on the "toe" of Italy; to **Puteoli** (today Pozzuoli), 152 miles south of Rome; and finally **to Rome** itself. Puteoli was an important commercial seaport halfway between Rhegium and Rome. At Puteoli Paul and his companions **found some brothers.** This is significant because it shows that the gospel had already spread from Rome to this Italian seaport. No doubt a church had been planted in Rome by Roman Jews who had gone to the Pentecost feast, heard Peter's sermon, were saved, and returned home with the good news (2:10). Paul accepted the believers' invitation **to spend a week with them.** Perhaps the centurion was in charge of unloading the ship or else had to spend a week in Puteoli on some other business.

28:15. The Christians at Rome soon **heard** of Paul's **coming,** so **they traveled as far as the Forum of Appius** (a market town 43 miles from Rome) **and the Three Taverns** (33 miles from Rome) **to meet**

him and his companions. The noun *apantēsin*, translated as an infinitive "to meet," was used in Greek literature of an entourage coming out of a city to meet an official going to the city. It is also used in 1 Thessalonians 4:17, which speaks of believers being "caught up . . . to meet (*apantēsin*) the Lord in the air." Like an entourage, believers will go up at the Rapture into the clouds to meet Jesus, their Savior and Lord, coming from heaven to take them to Himself. Paul looked forward to joining that group.

At the sight of these men Paul thanked God and was encouraged (lit., "received courage," *tharsos*; the verb *tharseō* is used in the LXX of people in distress who were then encouraged; cf. comments on Mark 6:50). At last God was bringing Paul to Rome. And the welcome of fellow believers, whom he had never met, uplifted his soul. So they proceeded on the Appian Way, "the queen of the long roads," to the city of Rome.

28:16. Because he was a trusted prisoner, **Paul was allowed to live by himself, with a soldier to guard him.** Paul's residence was in a rented house (v. 30).

28:17-20. The climax of the book is found in these closing verses (vv. 17, 24) which speak of another rejection of the gospel and of Paul's taking the message to Gentiles (v. 28).

As usual **Paul** first spoke with **the Jews** (cf. 9:20; 13:5, 14; 14:1; 17:2, 10, 17; 18:4, 19; 19:8). In this case **he called . . . the leaders** to meet with him because he could not go to their synagogues.

In his presentation Paul made several significant points: (1) He was innocent of damaging **the Jews** or their **customs** (28:17). (2) The Roman authorities in Judea thought Paul was innocent (v. 18; cf. 23:29; 25:25; 26:31-32). (3) Paul's only recourse was **to appeal to Caesar** because the Jews refused to deal with Paul justly (28:19; cf. 25:11). (4) This fourth point is a major one: he was not pressing charges against Israel; he only wanted to be acquitted (28:19). (5) His primary objective in calling the leaders was to **talk with** them about **the hope of Israel.** This term and concept was used by Paul a number of times in the last part of Acts (cf. 23:6; 24:15; 26:6-7). The hope of Israel was more than a resurrection; it meant

fulfillment of the Old Testament promises to Israel (cf. 26:6-7). Paul firmly believed Jesus is the Messiah of Israel who will return someday and establish Himself as the King of Israel and Lord of the nations (cf. 1:6).

28:21-22. The response of the leaders was ambivalent: they said they knew nothing about Paul and their only reports about Christianity (**this sect**) were negative. One wonders if they were being truthful. How could Jewish leaders be unaware of Jews in Rome who had become Christians and also of the existence of tensions between the church and Judaism in Jerusalem? It is quite possible they had heard nothing of Paul, but they probably knew more than they acknowledged about Christianity. They were interested in hearing Paul's **views** since they knew **that people** were **talking against** his message.

28:23-24. In the Jewish leaders' second meeting with **Paul,** they were much more definitive in their responses to the gospel. This time they **came in even larger numbers.** The discussion was also longer. All day long Paul spoke of **the kingdom of God and tried to convince them about Jesus from the Law of Moses and from the Prophets** (cf. 24:14; 26:22).

The term "kingdom of God" includes the death and resurrection of Christ as its basis but also looks ahead to Christ's reign on earth. It is clearly eschatological in significance (cf. 1:3-6; 8:12; 14:22; 19:8; 20:25; Luke 1:33; 4:43; 6:20; 7:28; 8:1, 10; 9:2, 11, 27, 60, 62; 10:9, 11; 11:2, 20; 12:31-32; 13:18, 20, 28-29; 14:15; 16:16; 17:20-21; 18:16-17, 24-25, 29-30; 19:11; 21:31; 22:16, 18, 29-30; 23:42, 51). To the Jews the concept of the Messiah dying for sins as an atonement and the teaching of justification by faith as the way of entering the kingdom sounded strange.

The Jews were divided in their responses. **Some were convinced . . . but others** refused to **believe** (Acts 28:24). In Greek the verb "convinced" is in the imperfect tense and may be rendered, "began to be convinced," that is, they were not fully convinced. The same verb, used in verse 23, is translated, "tried to convince."

28:25-27. The disagreement **among** the Jewish leaders in Rome about Paul's message showed that they were not amenable to the gospel. With prophetic insight **Paul** applied the words of **Isaiah** (6:9-10) to his own contemporaries. Obstinate refusal to believe results in **calloused** hearts, deafened **ears,** and spiritually blinded **eyes.** This had happened to Israel both in Isaiah's day and in Paul's (cf. Rom. 11:7-10). Interestingly Paul ascribed Isaiah's words to the inspiration of **the Holy Spirit** (cf. Acts 4:25).

28:28. At the climax of this book and now for the final time the gospel focus was turned toward **Gentiles.** From Jerusalem to Rome most Jews rejected it and in city after city the message was then directed to non-Jews. Now in the capital of the Roman world the same phenomenon occurred; so it will be until the fullness of Gentiles comes (Rom. 11:19-26).

28:29. Some Greek manuscripts add, "After he said this, the Jews left, arguing vigorously among themselves" (NIV marg.). Probably this verse should not be included in the text, though this undoubtedly was their response (cf. v. 25).

28:30-31. These verses are Luke's final "progress report" (cf. 2:47; 6:7; 9:31; 12:24; 16:5; 19:20). With freedom **in his own rented** quarters **Paul . . . preached** God's **kingdom.** This eschatological expression indicates not only that Jews and Gentiles alike are justified by faith but also that Gentiles with Jews will participate in the millennial kingdom (cf. comments on 28:23).

One question commonly raised pertains to Paul's activities after this two-year captivity. What happened? Perhaps no charges were filed in Rome and Paul was released. The Jews would know they had no case against Paul outside of Judea and so would be reluctant to argue their cause in Rome.

Probably Paul returned to the provinces of Macedonia, Achaia, and Asia and then turned west to Spain according to his original plans (Rom. 15:22-28). Then he ministered once more in the Aegean area where he was taken prisoner, removed to Rome, and executed.

During this two-year period Paul wrote what are commonly called his "Prison Epistles"—Ephesians, Colossians, Philemon, and Philippians (see the chart

"Paul's Epistles, Written on His Journeys and During His Imprisonments," at Acts 13:16-25).

While Paul was in Rome during this incarceration the gospel was not bound. **He** spoke **boldly** (cf. comments on Acts 4:13). The last word in the Greek text of Acts is the adverb *akōlytōs* which means **without hindrance.** Men may bind the preachers, but the gospel cannot be chained!

And so it was that the kingdom message under God's sovereign control went from Jew to Gentile, and from Jerusalem to Rome.

BIBLIOGRAPHY

Alexander, Joseph Addison. *Commentary on the Acts of the Apostles.* New York: Charles Scribner, 1875. Reprint (2 vols. in 1). Grand Rapids: Zondervan Publishing House, n.d.

Barclay, William. *The Acts of the Apostles.* Philadelphia: Westminster Press, 1953.

Bruce, F.F. *Commentary on the Book of the Acts.* The New International Commentary on the New Testament. Grand Rapids: Wm. B. Eerdmans Publishing Co., 1954.

Dunnett, Walter M. *The Book of Acts.* Grand Rapids: Baker Book House, 1981.

Harrison, Everett F. *Acts: The Expanding Church.* Chicago: Moody Press, 1975.

Hiebert, D. Edmond. *Personalities around Paul.* Chicago: Moody Press, 1973.

Jensen, Irving L. *Acts: An Inductive Study.* Chicago: Moody Press, 1968.

Kent, Homer A., Jr. *Jerusalem to Rome: Studies in the Book of Acts.* Grand Rapids: Baker Book House, 1972.

Longenecker, Richard N. "The Acts of the Apostles." In *The Expositor's Bible Commentary,* vol. 9. Grand Rapids: Zondervan Publishing House, 1981.

Lumby, J. Rawson. *The Acts of the Apostles.* Cambridge: At the University Press, 1882.

Marshall, I. Howard. *The Acts of the Apostles: An Introduction and Commentary.* The Tyndale New Testament Commentaries. Grand Rapids: Wm. B. Eerdmans Publishing Co., 1980.

Morgan, G. Campbell. *The Acts of the Apostles.* New York: Fleming H. Revell Co., 1924.

Neil, William. *Acts.* New Century Bible Commentary Series. Rev. ed. Grand Rapids: Wm. B. Eerdmans Publishing Co., 1981.

Rackham, Richard Belward. *The Acts of the Apostles: An Exposition.* London: Methuen & Co., 1901. Reprint. Grand Rapids: Baker Book House, 1978.

Ryrie, Charles Caldwell. *The Acts of the Apostles.* Everyman's Bible Commentary. Chicago: Moody Press, 1967.

Thomas, W.H. Griffith. *Outline Studies in the Acts of the Apostles.* Grand Rapids: Wm. B. Eerdmans Publishing Co., 1956.

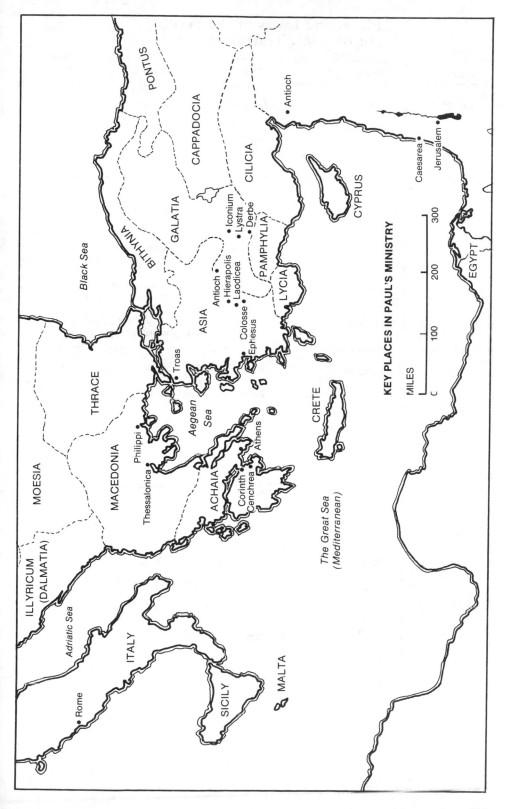

KEY PLACES IN PAUL'S MINISTRY

MILES

0   100   200   300

PONTUS

CAPPADOCIA

CILICIA

Antioch

GALATIA

BITHYNIA

Iconium
Lystra
Derbe

PAMPHYLIA

LYCIA

CYPRUS

Caesarea
Jerusalem

EGYPT

Antioch
Hierapolis
Laodicea

ASIA

Colosse
Ephesus

Black Sea

THRACE

Troas

MOESIA

MACEDONIA

Philippi

Aegean
Sea

Thessalonica

ACHAIA

Corinth
Cenchrea   Athens

CRETE

The Great Sea
(Mediterranean)

ILLYRICUM
(DALMATIA)

Adriatic Sea

ITALY

Rome

SICILY

MALTA

Places and Dates of the Writings
of the New Testament Epistles

Decade	Books	Places	Dates
A.D. 40–49	James	Jerusalem	A.D. 45–48
	Galatians	Antioch of Syria	40–49, after Paul's first missionary journey
50–59	1 Thessalonians	Corinth	50–54, in Paul's second missionary journey
	2 Thessalonians	Corinth	50–54, in Paul's second missionary journey
	1 Corinthians	Ephesus	About 56, in Paul's third missionary journey
	2 Corinthians	Macedonia	About 56, in Paul's third missionary journey
	Romans	Corinth	57, in Paul's third missionary journey
60–69	Ephesians	Rome	60
	1 John	Ephesus	60–65
	2 John	Ephesus	Early 60s
	3 John	Ephesus	Early 60s
	Philippians	Rome	60–61
	Colossians	Rome	60–62
	Philemon	Rome	60–62
	1 Timothy	Macedonia?	63–66
	Titus	Macedonia?	63–66
	1 Peter	Rome?	64
	Jude	?	67–80
	2 Timothy	Rome	67
	2 Peter	Rome?	67–68
	Hebrews	?	68–69

ROMANS

John A. Witmer

INTRODUCTION

This letter is the premier example of the epistolary form of writing, not only in the Pauline body of material and in the New Testament but also in all of ancient literature. It stands first in every list of the Apostle Paul's writings though it was not first in time of composition. This bears witness to the importance of the work both in its theme and in its content. It may also reflect the significance of the location of the letter's first readers, the imperial capital of Rome. In addition a possible tie grows out of the fact that the Book of Acts ends with Paul in Rome so that his letter to the Romans follows naturally in the order of Bible books.

Authorship. That Paul is the author of this letter is denied by almost no one. Even the ancient heretics admitted Romans was written by Paul. So do the modern (19th century and later) radical German critics, who deny many other facts in the Scriptures. Paul identified himself as the author by name, of course (1:1); but that is no guarantee of the acceptance of his authorship, since he did that in all his letters, including those for which his authorship is questioned or denied. In Romans Paul referred to himself by name only once, in contrast with several of his other letters; but a number of other internal details support Paul's authorship. He claimed to be of the tribe of Benjamin (11:1; cf. Phil. 3:5). He sent greetings to Priscilla and Aquila (Rom. 16:3), whom Paul had met in Corinth (Acts 18:2-3) and left in Ephesus (Acts 18:18-19) on his second missionary journey. Paul referred to his journey to Jerusalem with the love gift from the churches in Macedonia and Achaia (Rom. 15:25-27), facts confirmed in the Book of Acts (19:21; 20:1-5; 21:15, 17-19) and the epistles to the Corinthians (1 Cor. 16:1-5; 2 Cor. 8:1-12; 9:1-5). And Paul mentioned several times his intention to visit Rome (Rom. 1:10-13, 15; 15:22-32), a fact also confirmed in the Book of Acts (19:21). These confirming coincidences between Romans and Acts in particular support Paul as the author of this letter.

Unity. Acceptance of the unity and integrity of Romans is another matter, however. A number of critics from Marcion to the present have questioned chapters 15 and 16 or parts of both as belonging to the letter. Chapter 16 is a special target, in part because of Paul's greetings to Priscilla and Aquila (v. 3), who were last seen settled in Ephesus (Acts 18:19, 26). But the couple had previously lived in Italy (Acts 18:2) and had left only because of an imperial decree. Their return to Rome when circumstances permitted is reasonable. The major Greek manuscripts support the unity of the letter, a position endorsed by the overwhelming consensus of scholarship.

Recipients. A valid question does exist concerning the identity of the recipients of this letter. Paul simply addressed it "to all in Rome who are loved by God and called to be saints" (Rom. 1:7); he did not address it to "the church in Rome." That a church did exist in Rome is obvious, because Paul sent greetings to the church that met in the home of Aquila and Priscilla (16:5). Probably several churches were in Rome; perhaps this multiplicity of churches is why Paul addressed the letter to "the saints" instead of to "the church."

Were these believers in Rome Jews or Gentiles in ethnic background? The answer is both. Aquila, for example, was a Jew (Acts 18:2), as were Andronicus, Junias, and Herodion, all three identified as Paul's relatives (Rom. 16:7, 11). According to Josephus and others a large Jewish colony lived in Rome (cf. Acts

28:17-28). But Rome was a Gentile city, the capital of a Gentile empire in which all Jews, believing and unbelieving, formed a small minority. In addition, though Paul never failed to witness and to minister to Jews, his calling from God was to be "the apostle to the Gentiles" (Rom. 11:13; cf. 15:16). So it is reasonable to conclude that his readers were mostly Gentile in background.

This conclusion is supported by evidence in the letter. Paul addressed Jews directly (2:17), and he included Jewish Christians with himself when he spoke of "Abraham, our forefather" (4:1, 12). On the other hand Paul directly said, "I am talking to you Gentiles" (11:13). Several additional passages indicate that Gentile Christians made up a segment of his readers (11:17-31; 15:14-16). In fact the implication from 1:5, 13 is that Paul considered the Christian community in Rome predominantly Gentile.

Since the Apostle Paul had not yet visited Rome, how had the Christian faith been introduced to the city? Apparently no other apostle had yet reached Rome, in the light of Paul's stated purpose to be a pioneer missionary and to open virgin territory to the gospel (15:20). In particular, it is evident that Peter was not in Rome at that time because Paul expressed no greetings to him, a grievous error if Peter indeed were there.

Perhaps a partial answer to the founding of the church at Rome is the fact that "visitors from Rome" (Acts 2:10) were in the crowd that witnessed the miracle of Pentecost and heard Peter's sermon. Some of them probably were among the 3,000 converts that day and returned to Rome as believers in Jesus Christ to propagate their faith. Other believers migrated to Rome through the years since Pentecost, for Rome was a magnet that drew people from all over the empire for business and other reasons. Aquila and Priscilla are good examples. They had lived in Italy before (Acts 18:2), and undoubtedly returned as soon as circumstances permitted. Phoebe (Rom. 16:1-2), apparently the courier of this letter, is another example. She did not go to Rome primarily to deliver Paul's letter; she delivered Paul's letter because she was making a trip to Rome. In fact, Phoebe's planned trip to Rome was undoubtedly the specific occasion for Paul's writing this letter. Humanly speaking, Paul seized this opportunity to communicate with a group of Christians he was deeply interested in and planned to visit as soon as possible.

Just as Paul's absence of greeting to Peter in chapter 16 is evidence that Peter was not in Rome at the time, so his numerous greetings to individuals (28 persons are named or referred to, plus several groups) reveal the impact of Paul's ministry on the establishment and the development of the church in Rome. Many of the believers there were Paul's converts or associates in other parts of the empire. As a result Paul had a proprietary interest in the Christian community of Rome. He considered the church there one of his, as this letter bears witness.

Place and Date. Though Paul never named the city, it is obvious that he wrote this letter from Corinth, Cenchrea (16:1) being its eastern harbor. The letter was written at the close of Paul's third missionary journey during the "three months" he was in Greece (Acts 20:3) just before his return to Jerusalem with the offering from the churches of Macedonia and Achaia for the poor believers there (Rom. 15:26). After leaving Corinth, Paul was in Philippi during the Passover and the Feast of Unleavened Bread (Acts 20:6) and desired to reach Jerusalem by Pentecost (Acts 20:16). The letter was written, therefore, in the late winter or early spring of A.D. 57 or 58.

Purposes. While Phoebe's projected trip to Rome (Rom. 16:2) was undoubtedly the specific occasion for Paul's writing this letter, he had several objectives in writing. The most obvious was to announce his plans to visit Rome after his return to Jerusalem (15:24, 28-29; cf. Acts 19:21) and to prepare the Christian community there for his coming. The believers in Rome had been on Paul's heart and prayer list for a long time (Rom. 1:9-10) and his desire to visit them and to minister to them, unfulfilled to this point, was finally about to be satisfied (1:11-15; 15:22-23, 29, 32). Therefore Paul wanted to inform them of his plans and to have them anticipate and pray for their fulfillment (15:30-32).

A second purpose Paul had for writing this letter was to present a complete and detailed statement of the gospel message he proclaimed. Paul was eager "to preach the gospel also to you who are at Rome" (1:15) and he wanted them to know what it was. As a result in this letter Paul accomplished what Jude desired to do, "to write to you about the salvation we share" (Jude 3). Perhaps Jude was kept from doing this because Paul already had, for Romans certainly is a very full and logical presentation of the Triune Godhead's plan of salvation for human beings, from its beginning in man's condemnation in sin to its consummation in their sharing eternity in God's presence, conformed to the image of God's Son, the Lord Jesus Christ.

A third purpose for writing this letter is not as obvious as the first two. It is related to the tension between the Jewish and the Gentile segments in the Christian community at Rome and a possible conflict between them. Paul was hounded in his ministry by the Judaizers, who followed him from city to city and sought to lead his converts away from liberty in the gospel (Gal. 5:1). The letter to the Galatians is Paul's classic though not his only response to the Judaizers. Their attacks on Paul incorporated physical violence about the time this letter to the Romans was written (Acts 20:3). Whether the Judaizers had reached Rome before Paul or not, the Jew-versus-Gentile issue looms large in this letter. Paul did not take sides, but he carefully set forth both sides of the question. On the one hand he emphasized the historical and chronological priority of the Jews—"first for the Jew, then for the Gentile" (Rom. 1:16; cf. 2:9-10). He also stressed the "advantage . . . in being a Jew" (3:1-2; 9:4-5). On the other hand he pointed out that "since there is only one God" (3:30), He is the God of the Gentiles as well as the God of the Jews (3:29). As a result "Jews and Gentiles alike are all under sin" (3:9) and alike are saved by faith in the Lord Jesus Christ and His redemptive and propitiatory sacrifice. Furthermore, in order to bring believing Gentiles into His program of salvation, extending His grace to all human beings, God temporarily halted His specific program for Israel as a chosen nation, since that nation through its official leaders and as a whole had rejected in unbelief God's Son as the Messiah. During this period God contin-

ues to have a believing "remnant chosen by grace" (11:5) "until the full number of the Gentiles has come in" (11:25) and God takes up again and fulfills His promises to Israel as a nation.

Related to the Jewish-Gentile tension that runs throughout this letter is a muted but definite undertone that questions God's goodness and wisdom and justice as seen in His plan of salvation. No complaints against God are voiced, but they are implied. As a result this letter to the Romans is more than an exposition of Paul's "gospel of God's grace" (Acts 20:24), a declaration of God's plan of salvation for all human beings by grace through faith. It is a theodicy, an apologetic for God, a defense and vindication of God's nature and His plan for saving people. It sets God forth "to be just and the One who justifies the man who has faith in Jesus" (Rom. 3:26). It exults in "the depth of the riches of the wisdom and knowledge of God" (11:33) and challenges the readers, "Let God be true, and every man a liar" (3:4).

Theme. Growing out of Paul's three purposes for writing this letter (especially the latter two purposes), is the theme of the work. In the simplest and most general terms it is "the gospel" (1:16). More specifically it is "a righteousness from God" which "is revealed" in that gospel and is understood and appropriated "by faith from first to last" (1:17). This "righteousness from God" is first the righteousness God Himself possesses and manifests in all His actions; and second, it is the righteousness that God gives to human beings by grace through faith. This involves an imputed righteous standing before God (justification) and an imparted righteous practice and a progressively transformed lifestyle, the latter due to the regenerating and indwelling Holy Spirit of God (regeneration and sanctification). Practice is consummated and conformed to standing (glorification) when a believer in Jesus Christ through death and resurrection or through translation—"our adoption as sons, the redemption of our bodies" (8:23)—stands in the presence of God "conformed to the likeness of His Son" (8:29). God's program of salvation for people will not fail because it is His work, and "He who began a good work in you will carry it on to completion until the day of Christ Jesus" (Phil. 1:6).

OUTLINE

COMMENTARY

I. Introductory Matters (1:1-17)

A. Epistolary greetings (1:1-7)

The customary formula for letters in ancient times included (a) naming and identifying the author, (b) naming and

Paul's Introductions to His Epistles

Epistle	Paul's Titles	Paul's Companions	Addressees	Greetings
Romans	Paul, a servant of Christ Jesus, called to be an apostle and set apart for the gospel	—	To all in Rome who are loved by God and called to be saints	Grace and peace to you from God our Father and from the Lord Jesus Christ.
1 Corinthians	Paul, called to be an apostle of Christ Jesus by the will of God	our brother Sosthenes	To the church of God in Corinth, to those sanctified . . . together with all those everywhere who call on the name of our Lord Jesus Christ.	Grace and peace to you from God our Father and the Lord Jesus Christ.
2 Corinthians	Paul an apostle of Christ Jesus by the will of God	Timothy our brother	To the church of God in Corinth, together with all the saints throughout Achaia	Grace and peace to you from God our Father and the Lord Jesus Christ.
Galatians	Paul an apostle—sent not from men nor by man, but by Jesus Christ and God the Father, who raised Him from the dead	and all the brothers with me	To the churches in Galatia	Grace and peace to you from God our Father and the Lord Jesus Christ.
Ephesians	Paul, an apostle of Christ Jesus by the will of God	—	To the saints in Ephesus, the faithful in Christ Jesus	Grace and peace to you from God our Father and the Lord Jesus Christ.
Philippians	Paul . . . servants of Christ Jesus	Timothy	To all the saints in Christ Jesus at Philippi	Grace and peace to you from God our Father and the Lord Jesus Christ.
Colossians	Paul, an apostle of Christ Jesus by the will of God	Timothy our brother	To the holy and faithful brothers in Christ at Colosse	Grace and peace to you from God our Father.
1 Thessalonians	Paul	Silas and Timothy	To the church of the Thessalonians in God the Father and the Lord Jesus Christ	Grace and peace to you.
2 Thessalonians	Paul	Silas and Timothy	To the church of the Thessalonians in God our Father and the Lord Jesus Christ	Grace and peace to you from God the Father and the Lord Jesus Christ.
1 Timothy	Paul, an apostle of Christ Jesus by the command of God our Savior and of Christ Jesus our hope	—	To Timothy, my true son in the faith	Grace, mercy, and peace from God the Father and Christ Jesus our Lord.
2 Timothy	Paul, an apostle of Christ Jesus by the will of God, according to the promise of life that is in Christ Jesus	—	To Timothy, my dear son	Grace, mercy, and peace from God the Father and Christ Jesus our Lord.
Titus	Paul, a servant of God and an apostle of Jesus Christ	—	To Titus, my true son in our common faith	Grace and peace from God the Father and Christ Jesus our Savior.
Philemon	Paul, a prisoner of Christ Jesus	Timothy our brother	To Philemon our dear friend and fellow worker, to Apphia our sister, to Archippus our fellow soldier, and to the church that meets in your home	Grace to you and peace from God our Father and the Lord Jesus Christ.

identifying the recipient, and (c) a word of salutation. Paul followed this formula in this letter to the Romans despite the lengthy digression precipitated by the word "gospel." The same formula is used in all the New Testament letters except Hebrews and 1 John. (See the chart, "Paul's Introductions to His Epistles.")

1:1. Paul identified himself first as **a servant of Christ Jesus.** "Servant" *(doulos)* means slave, a person owned by another. Paul wore this title gladly (Gal. 1:10; Titus 1:1), reveling in the Old Testament picture of a slave who in love binds himself to his master for life (Ex. 21:2-6).

Paul also identified himself as **an apostle**—one sent with delegated authority (cf. Matt. 10:1-2)—a position to which he was **called.** (Lit., the Gr. is, "a called apostle.") This calling was from God (Acts 9:15; Gal. 1:1), though it was acknowledged by men (Gal. 2:7-9). It involved being **set apart** (from *aphorizō*; cf. Acts 13:2) **for the gospel of God,** the message of good news from God that centered on "His Son" (Rom. 1:2, 9) which Paul was "eager to preach" (v. 15) without shame (v. 16). This setting apart did not keep Paul from making tents to support himself and his companions (Acts 20:34; 1 Thes. 2:9; 2 Thes. 3:8) nor from mingling freely with all levels of pagan society. It was a setting apart to something—a commitment and dedication, not from things in isolation like the Pharisees. (Interestingly the word "Pharisee" means "separated one" in the sense of being isolated and segregated.)

1:2. The phrase **Holy Scriptures** refers obviously to the Old Testament and occurs only here in the New Testament (2 Tim. 3:15 uses different Gr. words for "holy" and "Scriptures"). Paul did not quote any **prophets** where **the gospel** was **promised,** but Philip's use of Isaiah 53:7-8 with the Ethiopian eunuch is a good example (Acts 8:30-35; cf. Luke 24:25-27, 45-47).

1:3-4. God's good news concerns **His Son,** identified as **Jesus Christ our Lord.** This asserts Christ's deity as basic to His person and prior to His Incarnation, since His identification with David's line "came to be," a literal rendering of the participle *genomenou*, translated **was.** He was genuinely **human** too, as His tie

with **David** and **His resurrection from the dead** show. That resurrection **declared** Him **to be the Son of God** because it validated His claims to deity and His predictions that He would rise from the dead (John 2:18-22; Matt. 16:21). This declaration was made **through** (lit., "in accord with") **the Spirit of holiness.** This is the Holy Spirit, and not, as some have suggested, Christ's human spirit.

1:5-7. Paul's ministry from Jesus was **among all the Gentiles,** which included the Romans, whom Paul addressed not as a church but as individual believers. Paul was the human agent (from and **for** Christ he **received grace and apostleship,** i.e., "the grace of apostleship"; cf. 12:3; 15:15) but the calling (God's summons to salvation; cf. 8:28, 30) came from the Lord and set his readers apart as "saints." **Obedience** and **faith** are often linked (cf. 15:18; 16:26; also cf. 1 Peter 1:2). Just as Paul was a "called" apostle, so the believers **in Rome** were **called to belong to Jesus Christ** (lit., "called of Jesus Christ") and **called to be saints** (lit., "called saints").

Paul's salutation like that in all his epistles, expressed the desire that they enjoy God's **grace and peace.**

B. Establishing rapport (1:8-15)

1:8-15. Paul made a practice of beginning his letters with a word of thanks to **God,** a specific prayer, and a personal message to the recipients. For the Romans he rejoiced that news of their **faith** had spread **all over the world,** a hyperbole meaning throughout the Roman Empire. His constant intercession for them (vv. 9-10) had the new note of petition for his projected visit, a heart-desire of long standing that finally was definitely on Paul's agenda (v. 10; cf. 15:23-24). This visit would be **mutually** beneficial spiritually; he desired to minister for three purposes: (a) to the strengthening of the Romans (1:11; to **impart . . . some spiritual gift** means either to exercise his own spiritual gift on their behalf or to bestow on them spiritual favors, i.e., blessings); (b) to see some spiritual fruit (**a harvest,** v. 13) **among** them and, in turn, (c) to be strengthened by them (v. 12). In this sense Paul's ministry at Rome would be the same as in **other** centers of the empire.

As a result of his "apostleship" (v. 5) to the **Gentiles** Paul felt **obligated** (lit., "I am a debtor") to the entire human race to proclaim God's good news (vv. 14-15). The word translated **non-Greeks** is literally, "barbarians," all other human beings from the viewpoint of the **Greeks** (cf. Col. 3:11). Parallel to it is the word **foolish** (*anoētois*; cf. Titus 3:3) in the next couplet, which has the significance of uncultured. Paul's sense of debt to the Gentile world produced an eagerness (**I am so eager,** Rom. 1:15) to evangelize it, including **Rome,** capital of the empire.

C. Emphasizing theme (1:16-17)

1:16. Paul's eagerness to evangelize sprang also from his estimate of his message, **the gospel.** (This is the fourth of five times Paul used the word "gospel" in these opening verses: vv. 1, 9, 15-17.) Many consider this the theme of the letter, which it is in one sense. At least Paul gladly proclaimed it as God's panacea for mankind's spiritual need. He identified it as the infinite resources (*dynamis,* "spiritual ability") **of God** applied toward the goal of **salvation** in the life **of everyone who believes** regardless of racial background. He recognized, however, a priority **for the Jew** expressed in the word **first,** which has sufficient textual support here and is unquestioned in 2:9-10.

Because the Jews were God's Chosen People (11:1), the custodians of God's revelation (3:2), and the people through whom Christ came (9:5), they have a preference of privilege expressed historically in a chronological priority. As the Lord Jesus stated it, "Salvation is from the Jews" (John 4:22). In Paul's ministry he sought out the Jews first in every new city (Acts 13:5, 14; 14:1; 17:2, 10, 17; 18:4, 19; 19:8). Three times he responded to their rejection of his message by turning to the Gentiles (Acts 13:46; 18:6; 28:25-28; cf. comments on Eph. 1:12). Today evangelism of the world must include the Jews, but the priority of the Jews has been fulfilled.

1:17. The theme of the letter is expressed in the phrase **a righteousness from God is revealed.** The subjective genitive (lit., "of God") identifies this as **a righteousness that** God provides for people on the basis of and in response to faith **in the gospel** (cf. 3:22). (NIV's **by**

faith from first to last renders the Gr. *ek pisteōs eis pistin,* lit., "out of faith in reference to faith.") Such a righteousness is totally unachieveable by human efforts. This righteousness is not God's personal attribute, however, since it comes "from God," it is consistent with His nature and standard. Robertson happily calls it "a God kind of righteousness" (A.T. Robertson, *Word Pictures in the New Testament.* Nashville: Broadman Press, 1943, 4:327). In response to faith this righteousness is imputed by God in justification and imparted progressively in regeneration and sanctification, culminating in glorification when standing and state become identical. "Righteousness" and "justify," though seemingly unrelated in English, are related in Greek. "Righteousness" is *dikaiosynē,* and "justify" is *dikaioō.* Paul used the noun many times in his epistles, including 28 times in Romans (1:17; 3:21-22, 25-26; 4:3, 5-6, 9, 11, 13, 22; 5:17, 21; 6:13, 16, 18-20; 8:10; 9:30; 10:3-6 [twice in v. 3], 10; 14:17). And Paul used the Greek verb 15 times in Romans (2:13; 3:4, 20, 24, 26, 28, 30; 4:2, 5; 5:1, 9; 6:7; 8:30 [twice], 33). To justify a person is to declare him forensically (legally) righteous. "Declared righteous" is the way the NIV translates *dikaioō* in 2:13 and 3:20 and "freed" is NIV's rendering in 6:7.

Paul's closing words in 1:17, **The righteous will live by faith,** are a quotation from Habakkuk 2:4, also quoted in Galatians 3:11 and Hebrews 10:38. As a result of faith (cf. "believes" in Rom. 1:16) in Christ, a person is declared "righteous" (cf. 3:22) and is given eternal life. What a marvelous work of God!

II. God's Righteousness Revealed in Condemnation (1:18-3:20)

The first step in the revelation of the righteousness that God provides for people by faith is to set forth their need for it because they are under God's judgment. The human race stands condemned before God and is helpless and hopeless apart from God's grace.

A. Condemnation against pagan humanity (1:18-32)

This section looks at the human race prior to the call of Abram and the establishment of a special people of God. This situation persisted in the pagan world of the Gentiles as distinct from the Jews.

1. REASONS FOR CONDEMNATION (1:18-23)

God never condemns without just cause. Here three bases are stated for His judgment of the pagan world.

a. For suppressing God's truth (1:18)

1:18. This verse serves as a topic sentence for this entire section. In addition, it stands in contrastive parallel to verse 17. The continuing revelation (the verb **is being revealed** is in the pres. tense) of **the wrath of God** is an expression of His personal righteousness (which also "is being revealed," Gr., v. 17) and its opposition to human sinfulness. Therefore people need the continuing revelation of "a righteousness from God" (v. 17) that He provides. God's wrath **is** directed **against all the godlessness** (asebeian, "lack of proper reverence for God") **and wickedness** (adikian, "unrighteousness") **of men,** not against the men as such. (God's wrath will also be revealed in the future; cf. 2:5.) God hates sin and judges it, but loves sinners and desires their salvation.

Failure to give God His due inevitably results in failure to treat people, created by God in His image, the right way. Conversely, people (in their unrighteousness toward others) continue to **suppress** (katechontōn, lit., "holding down") **the truth** (cf. 1:25; 2:8) concerning both God and man. People had God's truth but suppressed it, refusing to heed it. And these wicked ones did this in an attitude of **wickedness** (en adikia). This suppression of the truth is Paul's first reason for God's condemnation of the pagan world.

b. For ignoring God's revelation (1:19-20)

These verses declare that knowledge concerning God is available to all. This knowledge is called natural revelation because it is seen in the created world, is accessible to the entire human race, and is not soteriological, dealing with salvation effected by Christ.

1:19. Paul called this knowledge **plain** (phaneron), which means visible or clear. This is true **because God has made it plain** (ephanerōsen, the verb related to the noun phaneron). Some scholars

translate the phrase **to them** as "in them," insisting that verse 19 is speaking of the knowledge of God within the being of man through conscience and religious consciousness. Preferable is the position that verse 19 states the fact of natural revelation and verse 20 explains the process. One support for this view is the word "for" which begins verse 20 and indicates a tie between the verses.

1:20. "What may be known about God" (v. 19) is now called **God's invisible qualities** and identified as **His eternal power and divine nature.** Since "God is spirit" (John 4:24), all His qualities are invisible to physical eyes and can be **understood** by the human mind only as they are reflected in **what has been made,** that is, in God's creative work. The self-existent God, however, is the Creator of all things, and therefore **since the Creation of the world** His "invisible qualities" **have been clearly seen.** Paul may have intended a play on words between the noun translated "invisible qualities" (aorata) and the verb translated "clearly seen" (kathoratai) because they share a common Greek root. Both the verb "clearly seen" and the participle "being understood" are in the present tense, which emphasizes the continuous nature of the action. The word theiotēs, translated "divine nature," occurs only here in the New Testament and embraces the properties which make God God. Creation, which people see, reveals God's unseen character—the all-powerful Deity. An Old Testament parallel to these verses is Psalm 19:1-6.

Paul's conclusion to this description of natural revelation is important—**men are without excuse.** The witness to God in nature is so clear and so constant that ignoring it is indefensible. Their condemnation is based not on their rejecting Christ of whom they have not heard, but on their sinning against the light they have.

c. For perverting God's glory (1:21-23)

1:21. This reason for God's condemnation of the pagan world builds on the preceding one just as that one built on the first. The relationship is seen in the use of the same Greek connective (dioti) at the beginning of verses 19 and 21, in the latter translated **for.** People's suppression of the truth is seen in their rejecting the clear evidence of God as the sovereign Creator and their perversion of that knowledge into idolatry.

The clause **although they knew God** refers to an original experiential knowledge of God such as Adam and Eve had both before and after the Fall. How long this knowledge of God continued before it was perverted is not stated, but God was known by people. This fact makes human actions all the more reprehensible. One would suppose that to know God would be to honor Him, but these people **neither glorified Him as God nor gave thanks to Him.** They turned from the very purpose for which God made them: to glorify Him for His Person and thank Him for His works. With such willful rebellion against God it is little wonder that **their thinking became futile** (*emataiōthēsan*, lit., "became worthless, purposeless"; cf. Eph. 4:17) **and their foolish** (*asynetos*, "morally senseless"; cf. Rom. 1:31) **hearts were darkened** (cf. Eph. 4:18). When truth is rejected, in time the ability to recognize and to receive truth is impaired (cf. John 3:19-20).

1:22-23. When the true Source of wisdom is rejected (cf. Ps. 111:10), people's claim **to be wise** is an idle boast. Progressively **they became fools** (*emōranthēsun*, lit., "became stupid"), a reality demonstrated by the worship as gods of idols in the forms of people **and animals** (cf. Rom. 1:25). The ultimate irony in humanity's refusal to glorify the true **God** is the insanity or stupidity of idolatry described in Isaiah 44:9-20. Man's refusal to acknowledge and glorify God leads to a downward path: first, worthless thinking; next, moral insensitivity; and then, religious stupidity (seen in idol-worship).

2. RESULTS OF CONDEMNATION (1:24-32)

In a real sense the results of God's condemnation on rebellious humanity are nothing more than the natural consequences of suppressing truth, ignoring revelation, and perverting God's glory. However, God did more than simply let nature take its course. God acted to abandon (the thrice-mentioned "gave them over" [vv. 24, 26, 28] is *paredōken*, "abandoned") people to expressions of a corrupt lifestyle that deserved God's wrath and the sentence of death (v. 32).

a. Abandoned to fornication (1:24-25)

1:24. One aspect of mankind's corruption (to which **God** actively let people go) was **sexual** profligacy. The frequency of live-in lovers, wife-swapping, and group sex parties today only confirms this result of God's abandonment. Sex within marriage is a holy gift from God, but otherwise sex is **impurity** (lit., "uncleanness") and **the degrading of . . . bodies** by using them contrary to God's intent.

1:25. In a sense this verse repeats the truth of verse 23, but it expresses more. **The truth of God** is not only the truth concerning God but also God's truth concerning all things, including mankind. This truth is that people are creatures of God and can find true fulfillment only in worshiping and obediently serving God **the Creator. A lie** (lit., "the lie") on the other hand says that the creature—angelic (Isa. 14:13-14; John 8:44) or human (Gen. 3:4-5)—can exist independent of God, self-sufficient, self-directing, and self-fulfilling. Mankind made himself his god in place of the true God. Because God the Creator **is forever praised** (in contrast with creatures who are undeserving of worship), Paul added **Amen.** This word transliterates in both Greek and English the Hebrew word meaning "so let it be." As an affirmation, not a wish, it places approval on what has just been said (cf. comments on 2 Cor. 1:20).

b. Abandoned to sexual perversion (1:26-27)

1:26-27. Also **God gave them over to shameful lusts** (lit., "passions of disgrace"). This involved, as the text states, both sexes engaging in homosexual instead of heterosexual relationships. **Women** deliberately **exchanged natural relations** (with men in marriage) **for unnatural ones** (with other women). This is the second "exchange" the unregenerate made (cf. v. 25). **Men . . . were inflamed with lust** (*orexei*, "sexual lust," used only here in the NT and differing from the more common word for lust in v. 26).

The words translated **women** and **men** in these verses are the sexual words "females" and "males." Contemporary homosexuals insist that these verses mean that it is perverse for a heterosexual male or female to engage in homosexual relations but it is not perverse for a homosexual male or female to do so since homosexuality is such a person's natural preference. This is strained exegesis unsupported by the Bible. The only natural sexual relationship the Bible recognizes is a heterosexual one (Gen. 2:21-24; Matt. 19:4-6) within marriage. All homosexual relations constitute sexual **perversion** and are subject to God's judgment. Such lustful and **indecent acts** have within them the seeds of punishment **(due penalty)**.

c. Abandoned to depraved lifestyle (1:28-32)

1:28. Pagan humanity's rebellion also included the rejection of **the knowledge** (epignōsei, "full knowledge"; cf. v. 32) **of God.** In a sense they put God out of their minds. God's responding judgment was abandonment (cf. vv. 24, 26) **to a depraved** (adokimon, "disapproved") **mind,** which expressed itself in attitudes and actions that **ought not to be done** (lit., "what is unfitting or improper," a technical Stoic word).

1:29-31. The mental vacuum created by dismissing God was **filled** (the perf. tense implies filled full) **with** four forms of active sin: **wickedness** (adikia; cf. v. 18), **evil** (ponēria), **greed, and depravity** (kakia, "badness or malice"). These four in turn express themselves in 17 more specific types of wickedness. The first two, **envy** and **murder,** sound much alike in Greek: phthonou and phonou. Also the four vices in verse 31 each begin with the Greek letter alpha ("a" in Eng.).

1:32. This whole pattern of evil becomes the lifestyle of people who **continue to do** (pres. tense implies continuing or habitual action) **these very things** in open defiance of God, a defiance aggravated (a) by fully knowing (epignontes; cf. v. 28) that **such things deserve death** and (b) by encouraging others in the same lifestyle. Such extremity of human rebellion against God fully warrants **God's** condemnation.

B. Condemnation according to divine standards (2:1-16)

1. TRUTHFULNESS (2:1-4)

2:1. In any generalization such as the preceding blanket indictment of pagan humanity (1:18-32) exceptions to the rule always exist. Obviously some pagans had high ethical standards and moral lifestyles and condemned the widespread moral corruption of their contemporaries. In addition the Jews morally stood in sharp contrast with the pagan world around them and freely condemned the Gentiles. Both groups of moralists might conclude that God's condemnation did not apply to them because of their higher planes of living. But Paul insisted that they also stood condemned because they were doing **the same things** for which they judged others.

Therefore, Paul declared, **at whatever point you judge the other, you are condemning yourself.** Everyone in the entire human race has turned away from God and commits sins even though there are differences of frequency, extent, and degree. In addition the entire human race, especially moral pagans and the Jews, stood condemned before God (and **have no excuse** [cf. 1:20]) because God's judgment is based on three divine standards—truth (2:2-4), impartiality (vv. 5-11), and Jesus Christ Himself (vv. 12-16)—which are absolute and infinite, condemning every person.

2:2-3. The first divine standard of judgment is **truth.** Nowhere in Scripture is God identified as "Truth" as He is as "Spirit" (John 4:24), "Light" (1 John 1:5) and "Love" (1 John 4:8, 16), though Jesus did call Himself "the Truth" (John 14:6). But God is called "the God of truth" (Ps. 31:5; Isa. 65:16). Truth—absolute, infinite truth—is unquestionably one of God's essential attributes. As a result when **God's judgment** of people is declared to be **based on** (lit. "according to") "truth," no **escape** from that **judgment** is possible for anyone. All are without "excuse" (Rom. 2:1) and without "escape." One may be moral and he may even judge his contemporaries as totally enmeshed in a depraved lifestyle, but yet he is judged by God because he does **the same things** (cf. v. 1).

2:4. By not exacting His divine penalty on sinful humanity immediately, God is displaying **the riches of His kindness** (chrēstotētos, "benevolence in action," also used of God in 11:22; Eph. 2:7; Titus 3:4), **tolerance, and patience** (cf. Acts 14:16; 17:30; Rom. 3:25). God's purpose is to lead people **toward repentance**—a return to Him—through His

kindness. (This word for "kindness" is *chrēstos*, a synonym of *chrēstotētos*, also trans. "kindness," used earlier in the verse.) Both words mean "what is suitable or fitting to a need." *Chrēstos* is used of God in Luke 6:35 and 1 Peter 2:3 and of people in Ephesians 4:32. **Not realizing** (lit., "being ignorant of") **God's** purpose, people showed **contempt for** (*kataphroneis,* "you thought down on") God's attributes and actions (cf. "suppress the truth," Rom. 1:18). People knew of God's Being through natural revelation (1:19-21, 28), but did not know the purpose of His kindness.

2. IMPARTIALITY (2:5-11)

2:5-6. Why are people ignorant of God's intention to be kind? (v. 4) And why do they despise it? It is **because of** their **stubbornness** (lit., "hardness"; *sklērotēta,* whence the Eng. "sclerosis") and their **unrepentant heart**(s). So **God's wrath** against people's sins is being stored up like a great reservoir until **the day** when it will all be poured forth in **His righteous judgment.** On that day **God will give to each person according to what He has done** (quotation of Ps. 62:12 and Prov. 24:12). God's judging will be based on the standard of truth (Rom. 2:2) and it will be impartial (v. 11).

2:7-11. God will bestow **eternal life** on **those who by persistence in doing good seek** (pres. tense, "keep on seeking") **glory, honor, and immortality.** On the other hand **wrath and anger** will be the portion of **the self-seeking . . . who reject** (lit., "keep on disobeying") **the truth and follow** (pres. tense, "keep on obeying") **evil** (*adikia,* "unrighteousness"; cf. 1:18). Each one **who does** ("keeps on producing") **evil** will receive **trouble and distress,** whereas each one **who does** ("keeps on working") **good** will have **glory, honor** (cf. "glory and honor" in 2:7), **and peace.** This just recompense by God is without regard to ethnic background or any other consideration except what each person has done.

A person's habitual conduct, whether good or evil, reveals the condition of his heart. Eternal life is not rewarded for good living; that would contradict many other Scriptures which clearly state that salvation is not by works, but is all of God's grace to those who believe (e.g., Rom. 6:23; 10:9-10; 11:6; Eph. 2:8-9; Titus

3:5). A person's doing good *shows* that his heart is regenerate. Such a person, redeemed by God, has eternal life. Conversely a person who continually does evil and rejects the truth *shows* that he is unregenerate, and therefore will be an object of God's wrath.

The statement **first for the Jew, then for the Gentile** (lit. "Greek") does not imply special consideration for Jews. Instead, in the light of the divine standard of impartiality (**God does not show favoritism**), it emphasizes that the entire human race is dealt with by God.

The phrase "the day of God's . . . judgment" (Rom. 2:5) taken by itself may seem to lend support to the idea of a single general judgment of all humanity. However, the Scriptures do not support such a concept. This phrase must be interpreted in conjunction with passages which clearly indicate that several judgments of different groups occur at different times (cf. judgment of Israel at Christ's Second Advent, Ezek. 20:32-38; the judgment of Gentiles at Christ's Second Advent, Matt. 25:31-46; the great white throne judgment, Rev. 20:11-15). The focus of this passage is on the *fact* that God will judge all peoples, not on the details of who will be judged when.

3. JESUS CHRIST (2:12-16)

2:12. God's impartiality in judgment is also seen in the fact that He will deal with people in accordance with the dispensation in which they live. "The Law was given through Moses" (John 1:17), which marks the beginning of the dispensation of Law. The Law was provided for God's Chosen People Israel, and the Gentiles were considered outside the Law. Therefore Paul declared, **All who** (lit., "as many as") **sin apart from the Law** (lit., "without Law") **will also perish apart from the Law.** Gentiles who sin will perish, but the Law of Moses will not be used as a standard of judgment against them. On the other hand the Jews **who sin under** (lit., "in the sphere of") **the Law will be judged by the Law.** The Gentiles are not excused from God's judgment, but they will not be judged according to the standard (the Mosaic Law) that was not given to them.

2:13. Reading the Mosaic Law was a regular part of each synagogue service, so that Jews were **those who hear the Law.**

445

However, being recognized as **righteous** was not the automatic concomitant of being a Jew and hearing the Law. Those **who will be declared righteous** (a forensic action usually trans. "justified," e.g., 3:24; see comments on 1:17 on "justify") are **those who obey the Law** (lit., "the doers of the Law"). James made the same point (James 1:22-25). Again (cf. comments on Rom. 2:7-10) God does not give eternal life or justification to those who perform good works, but to those who believe (trust) in Him and whose conduct reveals their regenerate hearts.

2:14-15. The Jews looked down on the **Gentiles** partly because they did **not have the** revelation of God's will in the Mosaic **Law.** But, as Paul pointed out, there are moral Gentiles who **do by nature things required by the Law.** Such persons show that the Law is not to be found only on tablets of stone and included in the writings of Moses; it is also inscribed in their hearts and is reflected in their actions, consciences, and thoughts. The Law given to Israel is in reality only a specific statement of God's moral and spiritual requirements for everyone. Moral Gentiles by their actions **show that the requirements** (lit., "the work") **of the Law are written on their hearts.** This is confirmed by **their consciences,** the faculty within human beings that evaluates their actions, along with .**their thoughts** that either accuse or excuse them of sin. This is why Paul called such Gentiles **a law for themselves** (v. 14).

Conscience is an important part of human nature, but it is not an absolutely trustworthy indicator of what is right. One's conscience can be "good" (Acts 23:1; 1 Tim. 1:5, 19) and "clear" (Acts 24:16; 1 Tim. 3:9; 2 Tim. 1:3; Heb. 13:18), but it can also be "guilty" (Heb. 10:22), "corrupted" (Titus 1:15), "weak" (1 Cor. 8:7, 10, 12), and "seared" (1 Tim. 4:2). All people need to trust the Lord Jesus Christ so that "the blood of Christ" might "cleanse [their] consciences" (Heb. 9:14).

2:16. The Greek text of this verse begins with the phrase "in the day." The words **this will take place** are not in the Greek but are supplied to tie this verse back to the main idea of this section (vv. 5-13), namely, God's righteous judgment (v. 5). Verses 14-15 are actually a parenthetic idea (as indicated in the NIV).

This was brought to mind by verse 13 and the Jewish prejudice against the Gentiles. The certainty of divine judgment is emphasized by the words **God will judge** (lit., "God judges"). The Agent of divine judgment is **Jesus Christ** (cf. John 5:22, 27; Acts 17:31). This judgment will deal with **men's secrets** (lit., "the hidden things of men") and will reveal those things and prove God's judgment right (cf. 1 Cor. 4:5). Paul's **gospel** is not the standard of God's judgment. The idea is that the righteous judgment of God is an essential ingredient of the gospel Paul preached and a reason for trusting Jesus' finished redemption.

In this section (2:1-16) God is seen as the Creator-Sovereign of the universe conducting the moral government of His human creatures. God's absolute standards are known. God punishes the wicked and rewards the righteous impartially according to their works, which reveal their hearts. Since no human being—Jesus Christ excepted—can be declared righteous (justified) by God on the basis of his own merit, every human is condemned by God. At this point in Paul's argument the way a person can secure a righteous standing before God has not yet been presented. Here the emphasis is on the justice of God's judgment, leading to the conclusion that nobody on his own can be declared righteous by God.

C. Condemnation against unfaithful Jews (2:17-3:8)

1. CONDEMNATION BECAUSE OF THEIR HYPOCRISY (2:17-24)

2:17-20. Paul undoubtedly had the Jews as well as moral Gentiles in mind in the group he addressed as "you who pass judgment on someone else" (v. 1). But there he did not refer to them by name as he did here—**if you call yourself a Jew** (lit., "if you are named a Jew"). In Greek this is a first-class conditional sentence in which the conditional statement is assumed to be true. Paul was addressing individuals who were truly called Jews and who, in fact, gloried in that name. This fact is followed by a list of eight other moral and religious details in which the Jews gloried in their sense of superiority to the Gentiles, all of these included as part of the "if" clause (vv. 17-21a).

The verbs used in this list are all in the present tense or have the force of the present, which emphasizes the habitual nature of the action: (1) The Jews **rely on the Law**; they put their confidence in the fact that God gave it to them. (2) The Jews **brag about** their **relationship to God** (lit., "boast in God"; cf. v. 23), which means they glory in their covenantal ties with God. As a result of these two things the Jews (3) **know His will** (they have an awareness of God's desires and plan) and they (4) **approve of** (*dokimazeis*, "to test and approve what passes the test") **what is superior** (*diapheronta*, "the things that differ and as a result excel"; the same Gr. word in Phil. 1:10 is trans. "what is best"). They have a concern for spiritually superior standards. These abilities of Jews exist because they (5) **are instructed** (lit., "are being instructed") **by the Law**. Their catechetical lessons as youths and the regular reading of the Law in the synagogues provided this continuing instruction.

Though the next verb (in Rom. 2:19) continues the first-class conditional structure begun in verse 17, it also marks a transition of thought. It is the perfect tense of a verb which means "to seek to persuade," in which tense it has the meaning "to believe." (6) Many Jews were **convinced** and as a result believed certain things about themselves in relationship to Gentiles. Paul listed four of these: **a guide for the blind, a light for those who are in the dark, an instructor** (*paideutēn*, "one who disciplines, a trainer") **of the foolish**, and **a teacher of infants**. (7) This belief by Jews rested in their having **in the Law the embodiment** (*morphōsin*, "outline, semblance"; used elsewhere in the NT only in 2 Tim. 3:5) **of knowledge and truth** (the Gr. has the definite article "the" with both nouns: "the knowledge and the truth").

2:21-24. Without doubt as Paul enumerated this list of moral and religious distinctives, he got repeated affirmative responses from his Jewish readers. The Jews gloried in their special spiritual position, which contrasted with the Gentiles. The apostle then summed up all these distinctives in the clause, (8) **You, then, who teach others.** Then Paul asked the question, **Do you not teach yourself?** This question is followed by a series of questions on specific prohibitions in the

Law—against **stealing,** committing **adultery,** hating **idols**—each of which a Jew ("you" throughout Rom. 2:17-27 is sing., not pl.) was guilty of doing after telling others not to do those things. Paul indicted such a Jew for hypocrisy: **You who brag about** ("are boasting in"; cf. v. 17) **the Law, do you dishonor God by breaking the Law?** An honest Jew would have to respond to Paul's questions by admitting his guilt and his hypocrisy. Paul did not condemn this hypocrisy of the Jews on his own authority; he quoted their own Scriptures (the close of Isa. 52:5, in the LXX). Their hypocrisy dishonored God; also it caused **Gentiles** to blaspheme God. "Why should we honor God," Gentiles may have reasoned, "when His Chosen People do not follow Him?"

2. CONDEMNATION BECAUSE OF THEIR TRUST IN RITES (2:25-29)

The Jews trusted not only in the Law of Moses, as the preceding paragraph shows (vv. 17-24), but also in circumcision as the sign of their special covenantal relationship with God. But Paul argued that trust in the rite itself was meaningless and was a basis for God's judgment.

2:25-27. **Circumcision has value if you observe** ("are practicing") **the Law.** Conversely, **if you break the Law** (and they did), **you have become as though you had not been circumcised.** In the Greek this second part of verse 25 is interesting: "If you are a lawbreaker, your circumcision has become a foreskin." In other words a Jewish lawbreaker is just like a Gentile lawbreaker; the Jews' rite of circumcision counts for nothing.

The opposite is also true. **If those who are not circumcised** (lit., "if the foreskin," a word used by Jews as a slang expression for a Gentile; cf. the comments on v. 25) **keep** (*phyllasē*, "guard" and therefore "keep" or "observe"; cf. 1 Tim. 5:21) **the Law's requirements** (and apparently some Gentiles did), **will they not be regarded as though they were circumcised?** Paul concluded that a Gentile who **obeys** ("fulfills") **the Law** judges a Jew who, despite his having **the written code and circumcision,** is **a lawbreaker.** A Gentile who obeys what the Law requires, even though he does not know the Law (Rom. 2:14) is in God's sight similar to a circumcised Jew. This thought would be revolutionary for Jews who considered themselves far superior to Gentiles (cf. vv. 17-21).

2:28-29. These verses form the conclusion to the entire section that begins with verse 17. Being **a** true or geuine **Jew** is not a matter of **outward** or external things (such as wearing phylacteries, paying tithes, or being circumcised). Genuine **circumcision** is not the physical rite itself. Rather, a genuine Jew **is one inwardly** and true **circumcision is . . . of the heart** and **by the Spirit.** The NIV has rendered the Greek words "in spirit" as "by the Spirit," as though they refer to the Holy Spirit. However, it is better to understand this verse as saying that circumcision of heart fulfills "the spirit" of God's Law instead of mere outward conformity to the Law. Some Jews followed the Law's regulation outwardly, but their hearts were not right with God (Isa. 29:13). A circumcised heart is one that is "separated" from the world and dedicated to God. The true Jew receives his **praise . . . not from men** (as did the Pharisees) **but from God,** who sees people's inward natures (cf. Matt. 6:4, 6) and discerns their hearts (cf. Heb. 4:12).

3. CONDEMNATION BECAUSE OF THEIR
   UNBELIEF (3:1-8)

3:1-2. A characteristic mark of Paul's style, particularly in this letter to the Romans, is to ask and answer an obvious question his discussion has raised in his readers' minds. The natural response to the preceding material (2:17-29) is, **What advantage** (*perrison*, "overplus"), **then, is there in being a Jew?** Expressed in other words the question is, **What value** (*ōpheleia*, "advantage") **is there in circumcision?** The first question pertains to Paul's words in 2:17-24, and the second question to his words in 2:25-29. Paul's response is immediate and direct: **Much in every way!** He was not saying that being a Jew or being circumcised had *no* gains.

By the phrase **First of all** Paul suggested that he was going to list a number of items, though actually he stated only one. He did this same thing elsewhere (1:8; 1 Cor. 11:18). In this case the item he stated is the most important and in a sense includes any others that could have been mentioned. The Jews

have been entrusted (the Gr. past tense could be rendered "were entrusted") **with the very words** (*logia*, pl. of *logos*, "word" or "statement") **of God.** This can refer to the entire Old Testament but here it probably means just the promises and commands of God. Yet, though in that privileged position, the Jews were unable to live up to God's standards.

3:3-4. The fact that the chief benefit of being a Jew was being "entrusted with the very words of God" raised another question. **What if some did not have faith?** This verb "did not have faith" also means "be unfaithful." This is preferred since the same verb is rendered "entrusted" in verse 2. It is true that some Jews did not believe the promises of God, but also some Jews were unfaithful to their trust. **Will their lack of faith** (this noun can also mean "unfaithfulness," which is preferred here) **nullify God's faithfulness?** To that possibility Paul responded, **Not at all** (*mē genoito*, "Let it not be," a frequent exclamation by Paul; cf. vv. 6, 31; 6:1, 15; 7:7, 13; 11:1, 11). Though some Jews did not believe or were unfaithful (evidenced by their sinful conduct mentioned in 2:21-23, 25), God remains faithful to His Word (cf. Deut. 7:9; 1 Cor. 1:9; Heb. 10:23; 11:11; 1 Peter 4:19). This concept of God's faithfulness in spite of Israel's unbelief is developed more fully in Romans 9–11.

Paul continued, **Let God be true and every man a liar.** This means, "Let God keep on being true even though every man becomes a liar." This idea is taken from Psalm 116:11. As still further support, Paul quoted Psalm 51:4.

3:5-6. The apostle then pursued his argument with additional questions. The first is, **What shall we say** to the idea that the Jews' **unrighteousness** served to accentuate **God's righteousness?** Could they conclude that God's **wrath on** Jews **is** therefore **unjust?** Paul immediately interjected, **I am using a human argument,** and responded with the answer, **Certainly not!** (*mē genoito*, the same response as in v. 4; cf. v. 31) **If that were** the case, that **God** were unfair in judging unfaithful Jews, then He would be barred from judging **the world.** And of course, that could not be. So, since God will judge the world (cf. 2:5) He will not be unfair in extending His wrath on guilty Jews (cf. 2:11).

3:7-8. A second question is this: **If** someone's lack of truth enhances **God's truthfulness,** how can God in fairness condemn (lit., "judge") him **as a sinner?** In other words, since sin seemingly benefits God, how could He turn around and judge sinners for their sin? Paul raised these two questions, which are examples of unsaved people's casuistry, because some opponents were falsely accusing him of advancing them and proclaiming, **Let us do evil** (lit., "the evil things") **that good** (lit., "the good things") **may result.** The apostle did not reply to these slanders. He assigned such persons to God and simply observed, **Their condemnation** (*krima,* "judgment") **is deserved.** Later, however, he did discuss a similar question (6:1). To suggest, as did these two questions (3:5, 7), that God is unfair in condemning sin is to blaspheme the very nature of God. Such persons who question God's condemning are therefore themselves condemned!

D. Condemnation against all human beings (3:9-20)

In this section Paul concluded not only his indictment of the Jews but also the first section of his discussion that God's righteousness is revealed in condemnation against the sinful human race.

1. ALL ARE UNDER SIN (3:9-18)

3:9. Paul asked, **What shall we conclude then?** and, **Are we any better?** The exact meaning of this Greek verb *proechometha* (used only here in the NT) is difficult to determine. It seems best to take the question as coming from Jewish readers to whom Paul has just been writing and to translate it, "Are we preferred?" Both the material preceding and Paul's answer (**Not at all!**) support this solution. "Not at all" is literally "not by any means." This is not Paul's characteristic *me genoito,* used in verses 3, 6, 31, and elsewhere. Jews have advantages over Gentiles (2:17-20a; 3:1-2), but God does not give them preferential treatment.

As evidence that the Jews have no preferred position, Paul stated that he had previously accused both **Jews and Gentiles** as **all under sin,** that is, they stand under sin's power and control and under the condemnation that results from it (cf. 1:18; 2:5). The order of accusation was

first Gentiles (1:18–2:16) and then Jews (chap. 2). This order is reversed here because the Jews were most recently discussed.

3:10-12. To validate his accusation that everybody is "under sin" Paul quoted in verses 10-18 from six Old Testament passages. Romans 3:10-12, taken from Psalm 14:1-3, makes the point that all people without exception are not **righteous** (cf. Rom. 1:18, 29-31), do not understand **God** (cf. 1:18b, 28) nor seek (lit., "seek out") Him, **have turned away** from Him (cf. 2:5; Isa. 53:5), are **worthless** (from *achreioō,* "become useless," used only here in the NT), and do not do **good** (*chrēstotēta,* "kindness," or "benevolence in action"; cf. 2 Cor. 6:6; Gal. 5:22; and comments on Rom. 2:4). Apart from the indwelling Holy Spirit people cannot exhibit this fruit of the Spirit (Gal. 5:22). They have no inner spiritual capacity whereby they can normally and automatically exercise genuine kindness toward others. Instead sin causes them to be selfish and self-centered.

These seven condemnatory phrases end with the words **not even one,** which are also in Romans 3:10. This repetition stresses that not a single exception in the human race (except, of course, the Son of God) can be found.

Though Paul did not quote Psalm 14:2, "The Lord looks down from heaven on the sons of men," that verse is significant, for what follows in that psalm is God's indictment of humanity.

3:13-18. These verses describe the vileness and wickedness of various parts of the human body, indicating figuratively that every part contributes to a person's condemnation. In sequence these quotations are taken from Psalm 5:9 (Rom. 3:13a); Psalm 140:3 (Rom. 3:13b); Psalm 10:7 (Rom. 3:14); Isaiah 59:7-8 (Rom. 3:15-17); and Psalm 36:1 (Rom. 3:18). They pertain to three actions: talking (**throats . . . tongues . . . lips . . . mouths;** vv. 13-14), conduct (**feet;** vv. 15-17) and seeing (**eyes;** v. 18). Their speech is corrupt (**open graves;** cf. James 3:6), dishonest (**deceit;** cf. Ps. 36:3), damaging (**poison;** cf. James 3:8), and blasphemous (**cursing and bitterness;** cf. James 3:9-10). From talking of sin, they commit sin, even to the point of quickly murdering (cf. Prov. 1:11-12, 15-16). As a result they and others are destroyed materially and spiritually, are miserable, and **know** no inner **peace** (cf. Isa. 57:21). All this is summarized in Paul's words, **There is no fear of God before their** eyes. Fearing God (i.e., reverencing Him by worship, trust, obedience, and service) is the essence of a godly person (cf. Job 28:28; Prov. 1:7; 9:10; Ecc. 12:13). So for a Jew not to fear God was the height of sin and folly. In these verses (Rom. 3:10-18) Paul left no basis whatsoever for Jewish readers to say that his point that Jews are sinners contradicts the Old Testament!

2. ALL ARE CONSCIOUS OF SIN (3:19-20)

3:19-20. Paul concluded his discussion with a final statement to the Jews concerning the purpose and ministry of **the Law.** He included himself with his Jewish readers when he said, **Now we know.** The principle is obvious: the Law's pronouncements are **to those who are under the Law.** The Law was not a special talisman that the Jews could obey or ignore as they wished; they were "under" it and accountable to God (cf. Jews and Gentiles being "under sin," v. 9). The Law's ministry was **so that every mouth may be silenced** (lit., "stopped"), **and the whole world held accountable** (lit., "become answerable") **to God. No one** can argue in his own defense that he is not under sin. The Law points up God's standards and illustrates people's inability to live up to them.

Finally, **the Law** is not a way for a person to **be declared righteous** (justified) **in His sight** (cf. 3:28). That was not its purpose (Acts 13:39; Gal. 2:16; 3:11). Instead, **the Law** was given so that **through** it **we become conscious** (lit., "through the Law is full knowledge") **of sin** (cf. Rom. 5:20; 7:7-13). The Mosaic Law is an instrument not of justification but of condemnation.

III. God's Righteousness Revealed in Justification (3:21-5:21)

In God's condemnation of the human race His own personal infinite righteousness was revealed along with the fact that not a single human being—the Lord Jesus Christ excepted—has ever or will ever be able to meet that standard and be accepted by God on his own merit. Now in this second major section of Romans Paul discussed God's "provided righteousness" for people through Jesus in justification. Justification is a forensic declaration of righteousness as a result of God's imputing to believers Christ's righteousness, provided by God's grace and appropriated through faith.

A. Provided righteousness explained (3:21-31)

3:21. By the words **but now** Paul introduced a sharp contrast with what preceded. He had just affirmed, "No one will be declared righteous in His [God's] sight by observing the Law" (v. 20). This is now followed by the statement, **Apart from Law** (in the Gr. this phrase is in the emphatic first position) **a righteousness from God . . . has been made known** (i.e., made plain). This in essence repeats the words of 1:17a. But Paul added the fact that **the Law and the Prophets testify** to this fact. What Paul was introducing about God's righteousness was not foreign to the Old Testament. "The Law and the Prophets" was often used of the entire Old Testament (see references at Matt. 5:17), the Law referring to the first five books and the Prophets, the other books. In Romans 4 Paul illustrated this truth from the Law (Abraham: Gen. 15:6; Rom. 4:1-3, 9-23) and from the Prophets (David: Ps. 32:1-2; Rom. 4:4-8).

3:22. The first part of this verse is not a new sentence in the Greek; it is an appositional clause, and could be rendered, "a righteousness from God **through faith.**" These words reminded Paul again of the Jewish insistence on their special position before God. As a result he added, **There is no difference** (cf. 10:12), introduced in the Greek by the word "for" to tie it to what precedes. Any prior privilege the Jews had is gone in this Age when God is offering a righteous standing before Him to all sinful people on the basis of faith in Christ alone. Since all are "under sin" (3:9), salvation is available "to all" on an equal basis.

3:23. Paul explained that "no difference" existed among human beings because **all have sinned.** The Greek is literally, "all sinned" (*pantes hēmarton*). The same two Greek words are used in 5:12 (cf. comments on that verse). Since the entire human race was plunged into sin with Adam, all (whether Jews or Gentiles) are sinners. It is impossible to say there is a "difference," that the Jews' privileges (2:12-21; 3:1) exclude them from God's condemnation.

Not only did all sin, but also all **fall short.** This single Greek verb is in the present tense, stressing continuing action. It can be translated "keep on falling short." The simple fact is that as a sinner not a single human being by his own efforts is able to measure up to **the glory of God.** God's glory is His splendor, the outward manifestation of His attributes. God desires that humans share that splendor, that they become like Him, that is, Christlike (cf. "glory" in 5:2; 2 Cor. 3:18; Col. 1:27; 2 Thes. 2:14). Yet their sin keeps them from sharing it.

3:24. In view of man's sin God has stepped in with His provided righteousness, because all who believe **are justified** (the pres. tense may be trans. "keep on being declared righteous," i.e., each person as he believes is justified). "Justify" (*dikaioō*) is a legal term, meaning "declare righteous" (not "make righteous"; cf. Deut. 25:1). See comments on Romans 1:17 on Paul's frequent use of this verb and its related noun "righteousness."

God's justification of those who believe is provided **freely** (*dōrean*, "as a free gift," i.e., without charge) **by His grace.** God justifies by the instrument of His grace, His unmerited favor. Grace too is a favorite word of Paul's, used by him in Romans 24 times (in the Gr.). But God would not declare a person righteous without an objective basis, without dealing with his sin. That basis is **the redemption that came by Christ Jesus.** The Greek word for "redemption" is *upolytrōsis*, from *lytron*, "a ransom payment." *Apolytrōsis* is used 10 times in the New Testament (Luke 21:28; Rom. 3:24; 8:23; 1 Cor. 1:30; Eph. 1:7, 14; 4:30; Col. 1:14; Heb. 9:15). (See the chart, "New Testament Words for Redemption" at Mark 10:45.) The death of Christ on the cross of Calvary was the price of payment for human sin which secured release from the bondage of Satan and sin for every person who trusts God's promise of forgiveness and salvation.

3:25a. God presented Him, Christ, **as a Sacrifice of atonement.** The Greek word for "Sacrifice of atonement" is *hilastērion,* rendered "propitiation" in the KJV and the NASB. This noun is used elsewhere in the New Testament only in Hebrews 9:5 for the mercy seat (NIV, "the place of atonement") of the tabernacle's ark of the covenant. There a goat's blood was sprinkled on the Day of Atonement to cover (atone) Israel's sins (Lev. 16:15), and satisfy God for another year. Jesus' death is the final sacrifice which completely satisfied God's demands against sinful people, thus averting His wrath from those who believe. (The verb *hilaskomai,* "to satisfy by a sacrifice, to propitiate," is used in Luke 18:13 ["have mercy"] and Heb. 2:17 ["make atonement"]. And the related noun, *hilasmos,* "propitiation," appears in 1 John 2:2; 4:10.)

Christ, God's propitiatory Sacrifice for sin, was "presented" (lit., "set forth"), in contrast with the tabernacle's mercy seat which was hidden from view. This work of Christ is **through faith in His blood** (cf. Rom. 5:9). It is appropriated by faith (cf. 3:22). By the death of Jesus and the shedding of His blood the penalty for sin has been paid and God has been satisfied or propitiated. The phrase "in (or by) His blood" probably should go with "a sacrifice of atonement," not with "through faith." A believer places His faith in Christ, not in His blood as such.

3:25b-26. God's purpose in Christ's death was **to demonstrate His justice** (i.e., God's own judicial righteousness, *dikaiosynēs;* cf. comments on 1:17) **because in His forbearance** (*anochē,* "holding back, delay") **He had left the sins committed beforehand unpunished** (cf. Acts 17:30). Why did God not always punish sins in the past? Does this mean He is not righteous after all? Previously Paul said God was forbearing because He wanted to lead people to repent (Rom. 2:4). Here God is said to be forbearing because He anticipated His provision for sins in the death of Jesus Christ. Such forbearance was an evidence of His grace (cf. Acts 14:16; 17:30), not of His injustice.

Paul was so insistent that God's righteousness be recognized that (Rom. 3:26) he repeated (from v. 25) the words **to demonstrate His justice** (*dikaiosynēs,* "righteousness"). God's purpose in the redemptive and propitiatory death of Jesus Christ was so that He could be seen to be **just** (*dikaion,* "righteous") **and the One who justifies** (*dikaiounta,* "the One who declares righteous") **the man who has faith in Jesus.** God's divine dilemma was how to satisfy His own righteousness and its demands against sinful people, and at the same time how to demonstrate His grace, love, and mercy to restore rebellious, alienated creatures to Himself. The solution was the sacrifice of Jesus Christ, God's incarnate Son, and the acceptance by faith of that provision by individual sinners. Christ's death vindicated God's own righteousness (He is just because sin was "paid for") and enables God to declare every believing sinner righteous.

3:27-28. After explaining God's provided righteousness for sinners, Paul considered five questions (in Gr.) which he anticipated his readers might ask. Two are in verse 27, two in verse 29, and the other in verse 31. The first is, **Where, then is boasting?** How can Jews have any boasting in their special position? (2:17-20, 23) Paul's response was abrupt: **It is excluded** ("completely shut out").

Since justification is by grace (3:24) through faith (vv. 22, 25-26), boasting because of one's accomplishments (works) is ruled out. This prompted a second question: **On what principle?** ("Law" here in the Gr. means "principle.") **On that of observing the Law?** (lit., "through works") Paul's response was, **No** (lit., "not at all," an intensive form), **but on that of faith.** Doing works (i.e., observing the Law) is no basis for boasting for the Law cannot justify. It was not given for that purpose (cf. v. 20). The apostle then summarized, **For we maintain** (the verb *logizometha*, "to reckon," here has the idea of coming to a settled conclusion) **that a man is justified** ("declared righteous") **by faith** (cf. vv. 22, 25-27) **apart from observing the Law** (lit., "apart from works of Law").

3:29-30. The next two questions cover the same issue of Jewish distinctiveness from a different angle. Because the Gentiles worshiped false gods through idols, the Jews concluded that Yahweh, the true and living God (Jer. 10:10), was **the God of Jews only.** That was true in the sense that the Jews were the only people who acknowledged and worshiped Yahweh (except for a few proselyte Gentiles who joined with Judaism). But in reality Yahweh, as the Creator and Sovereign of all people, is the God of all people. Before God called Abraham and his descendants in the nation Israel to be His Chosen People (Deut. 7:6) God dealt equally with all people. And even after God's choice of Israel to be His special people, God made it plain (e.g., in the Book of Jonah) that He is **the God of** everyone, **Gentiles** as well as Jews. And now since there is "no difference" among people for all are sinners (Rom. 3:23) and since the basis for salvation has been provided in the sacrificial death of Jesus Christ, God deals with everyone on the same basis. Thus **there is only one God** (or "God is one"). Paul no doubt had in mind here the "Shema" of Israel: "Hear, O Israel: The Lord [*Yahweh*] our God [*'Ĕlōhîm*], the Lord [*Yahweh*] is One" (Deut. 6:4). This one God over both Jews and Gentiles **will justify** all who come to Him regardless of background (**circumcised** or **uncircumcised**) on the **same** human condition of **faith.**

3:31. The final question is, **Do we, then, nullify the Law by this faith?** Paul responded in his characteristic expletive, **Not at all!** (*mē genoito*, "Let it not be"; cf. comments on v. 4) and then explained, **Rather, we uphold the Law.** The purpose of the Mosaic Law is fulfilled and its place in God's total plan is confirmed when it leads an individual to faith in Jesus Christ (cf. v. 20; Gal. 3:23-25). Paul repeatedly affirmed that faith, not works of the Law, is the way of salvation. He wrote the word "faith" eight times in Romans 3:22-31! (See vv. 22, 25-28, 30 [twice], and 31.)

B. Provided righteousness illustrated (chap. 4)

The Apostle Paul had presented his case that God declares people righteous on the principle of faith instead of works. If his position is true, he should be able to illustrate it from the past. This he did with Abraham, the patriarch of Israel (cf. John 8:39), and David as well (cf. comments on "the Law and the Prophets," Rom. 3:21).

1. BY FAITH NOT WORKS (4:1-8)

4:1. Paul introduced his illustration of Abraham with the first of six occurrences of the question, **What then shall we say?** (6:1; 7:7; 8:31; 9:14, 30) He referred to **Abraham** as **our forefather.** ("Forefather" is used only here in the NT.) Undoubtedly this was to distinguish Abraham's physical ancestry from his spiritual fatherhood, mentioned later in 4:11-12, 16. What had this patriarch **discovered in this matter?** What lesson could Paul's readers learn from the biblical record of Abraham's experience?

4:2-3. The Rabbis taught that **Abraham** had a surplus of merit from his works that was available to his descendants. Paul built on that idea and agreed that, assuming that **Abraham was justified by works, he had something to boast about** (cf. boasting or bragging in 2:17, 23; 3:27). **But,** Paul insisted, his boasting could only be before other people, **not before God.** If a person could establish his finite righteousness by works—though that was impossible—he could never boast of it in God's presence. Paul then turned to an authority his readers would acknowledge and asked, **What does the Scripture say?** He quoted Genesis 15:6, which states that Abraham's faith in God and His promise **was credited to him as righteousness.** Because he believed, God imputed righteousness to his account ("credited," *elogisthē*, from *logizomai*, is an accounting term). Paul had quoted this verse before (Gal. 3:6).

4:4-5. The apostle then discussed the significance of this Scripture quotation. He pointed out that a worker's **wages are** what are owed him because he earned them, and are **not** graciously given **to him as a gift.** Conversely, a person who is not working but is believing (these participles are in the pres. tense) **God who justifies the wicked** (*asebē,* "the ungodly, impious"; cf. 5:6), **his faith is credited as righteousness** (cf. 4:3). Abraham was the latter kind of person as the Scripture stated. He was justified not because he worked for it but because he trusted God.

4:6-8. This fact about Abraham was also true of **David,** whose description of God's gracious dealing with him Paul quoted from Psalm 32:1-2. A person, like David, **to whom God credits righteousness apart from works,** is blessed. Such a person's sins **are forgiven** and **covered.** And instead of his **sin** credited (*logisētai*) to his account, God credits (*logizetai;* cf. Rom. 4:3) righteousness to **him.**

2. BY FAITH NOT RITES (4:9-12)

4:9-10. Paul again raised the question of the Jews' special position (cf.

2:17-21a; 3:1-2). The way the question is worded in the Greek suggests the answer, that **this blessedness** is **for the uncircumcised** (Gentiles) as well as **for the circumcised** (Jews). But in response Paul turned again to the example of Abraham. He repeated the authoritative scriptural declaration that Abraham was declared righteous on the basis of his **faith.** Then Paul asked whether **Abraham's** justification occurred **before** or **after he was circumcised.** Answering his own question, Paul stated, **It was not after, but before!** (The Gr. has lit., "not in circumcision, but in uncircumcision.") Abraham's age when he was declared righteous (Gen. 15:6) is not stated. But later when Hagar bore him Ishmael, he was 86 (Gen. 16:16). After that, God instructed Abraham to perform the rite of circumcision on all his male descendants as a sign of God's covenant with him; this was done when Abraham was 99 (Gen. 17:24). Therefore the circumcision of Abraham followed his justification by faith by more than 13 years.

4:11-12. Therefore, Paul argued, **the sign of circumcision** was **a seal of** Abraham's being declared righteous because of his **faith** which he received **while he was still uncircumcised** (lit.,"in uncircumcision"). Circumcision, as a "sign" or "seal," was an outward token of the justification Abraham had already received. God's purpose was that Abraham be **the father of all who believe** and are thereby justified. This included both the uncircumcised (Gentiles) and the **circumcised** (Jews). Jews must do more than be **circumcised** to be right with God. They must also **walk in the footsteps of . . . faith,** like **Abraham** (cf. 2:28-29). Obviously, then, the rite of circumcision, which many Jews rely on for salvation, contributes in no way to one's status before God. It gives them no special standing before Him because they must be declared righteous on the basis of faith in God.

3. BY FAITH NOT THE LAW (4:13-17)

4:13. The Jews also considered the Mosaic Law, a special revelation of God's standards for human conduct, as the basis for their special standing before God. Therefore Paul turned next to it, declaring, **It was not through Law** ("not" is emphasized by its position at the beginning of the Gr. sentence) **that Abraham and his offspring** (lit., "seed") **received the promise that he would be heir of the world.**

God's promise in Genesis 12:1-3 preceded the giving of the Law by several centuries (cf. Gal. 3:17). Being "heir of the world" probably refers to "all peoples on earth" (Gen. 12:3), "all nations" (Gen. 18:18), and "all nations on earth" (Gen. 22:18), for through Abraham and his descendants all the world is blessed. He is thus their "father" and they are his heirs. These promises of blessing are given to those to whom God has imputed **righteousness,** and this, Paul added once again, is **by faith.** Believers of all ages are "Abraham's seed," for they enjoy the same spiritual blessing (justification) which he enjoyed (Gal. 3:29). (However, God has not abrogated His promises to Abraham about his physical, believing descendants, the regenerate nation Israel, inheriting the land [Gen. 15:18-21; 22:17]. These promises still stand; they will be fulfilled in the Millennium.)

4:14-15. As Paul explained, if Jews could become **heirs** by obeying the **Law,** then **faith has no value** (*kekenōtai*, "it has been made empty"; cf. the noun *kenos*, "empty, without content," in 1 Cor. 15:10, 58). Also **the promise is worthless** (*katērgētai*, "has been made invalid"). The reason this would be true is that **Law brings wrath** (lit., "the Law keeps on producing wrath") as a consequence of disobedience. No one can keep the Law fully; therefore God, in wrath against sin, judges those who disobey.

Paul then stated a related general principle: **And where there is no law, there is no transgression.** A person may still be sinning in his action, but if there is no command prohibiting it his action does not have the character of a transgression, an overstepping of a prohibition (cf. Rom. 5:13).

4:16. Paul then drew his conclusion. **Therefore** (lit., "On account of this") **the promise comes by** (*ek*, "out of") **faith so that it may be by** (*kata*, "according to the standard of") **grace.** Responding in faith to God's promise is not meritorious, since the promise springs from His grace, His disposition of favor toward those who deserve His wrath. The human exercise of faith is simply the prerequisite response of trust in God and His promise. Since faith and grace go together, and since the promise is by grace, the promise can be received only by faith, not by the Law.

Another reason the promise is by faith is so that it **may be guaranteed to all Abraham's offspring, not only** the Jews **(those . . . of the Law) but** to all who exercise **faith** in God. If the promise were fulfilled for those who keep the Law, then no Gentiles (or Jews either) could be saved! But this cannot be, because **Abraham . . . is the father of us all,** that is, all who believe (cf. "our" in v. 1; also cf. Gal. 3:29).

4:17. Paul then supported his conclusion in verse 16 with scriptural authority, quoting God's covenantal promise from Genesis 17:5. The fact that believers in this Church Age are identified with Abraham and God's covenant with him does not mean that the physical and temporal promises to Abraham and his physical descendants are either spiritualized or abrogated. It simply means that God's covenant and Abraham's response of faith to it have spiritual dimensions as well as physical and temporal aspects (cf. comments on Rom. 4:13). The quotation is in effect a parenthesis. Therefore the latter part of verse 17 connects with the close of verse 16: "He is the father of us all . . ." **in the sight of God.** (The words **He is our father** are not in the Gr., but are added in the NIV for clarification.) **God . . . gives life to the dead and calls things that are not** (lit., "the nonexisting things") **as though they were** (lit., "as existing").

Identifying God in this way obviously refers to God's promise in Genesis 17 following the statement quoted above that Abraham and Sarah would have a son of promise when Abraham was 100 and Sarah was 90 (Gen. 17:17, 19; 18:10; 21:5; cf. Rom. 4:19). That he would be the ancestor of many nations seemed impossible in his and Sarah's childless old age.

4. BY FAITH IN GOD'S PROMISE (4:18-25)

4:18. Though humanly there was no hope of ever having a child, the old patriarch believed God's Word. **Against all hope, Abraham in hope believed.** God honored his faith, and he **became the father** (ancestor) **of many nations.** This was in accord with God's promise, **So shall your offspring be** (a quotation of Gen. 15:5).

4:19. Verses 19-21 restate in specific details the first part of verse 18 about Abraham's hope. Abraham **without weakening in his faith . . . faced the fact** (lit., "considered carefully") **that his body was as good as dead** (some Gr. mss. add the word "already"), a reference to the patriarch's advanced age (Gen. 17:17; 21:5). Abraham also considered carefully **that Sarah's womb was also dead.** She was unable to conceive a child, as had been demonstrated through their life together (cf. Gen. 16:1-2; 18:11) and as was certainly true for her at age 90 (Gen. 17:17).

4:20-21. In spite of the humanly impossible situation, Abraham **did not waver through** (lit., "by") **unbelief.** "Waver" (diekrithē) means "to be divided" (sometimes trans. "doubt," as in James 1:6). The patriarch **was strengthened in his faith** (lit., "was empowered [enedynamōthē, from endynamoō] by means of faith"). God, responding to Abraham's faith, empowered him and Sarah physically to generate the child of promise. Also he **gave glory to God,** that is, he praised God by exalting or exclaiming His attributes. Abraham was **fully persuaded that God had power** (dynatos, "spiritual ability") **to do what He had promised.** What confidence in God this spiritual forefather possessed! He "in hope believed" (Rom. 4:18); he was not weak in faith despite insuperable odds (v. 19); he was not divided in his thinking by unbelief (v. 20a); he was empowered by faith (v. 20b); and he was fully persuaded God has the ability to do what He had said (v. 21).

4:22. Paul concluded his illustration about Abraham by saying, **This is why** (dio kai, "wherefore also") **it was credited to him as righteousness.** Abraham's response of faith to God and God's promise to him was the human requirement for God's justifying Abraham, for God's declaring that Abraham stood righteous before Him. No wonder God credited such faith with righteousness!

4:23-24. Verses 23-25 apply the truth about justification and its illustration in Abraham to the apostle's readers—from the believers in Rome who first read this letter to people today. The divine declaration of Abraham's justification was **written not for him alone, but also for us, to whom God will credit**

righteousness. Such an act of justification, however, is not for everyone. It is **for us who believe in Him who raised Jesus our Lord from the dead** (lit., "out from dead ones"; cf. 6:4; 8:11). Repeatedly in this chapter Paul referred to Abraham and other believers having righteousness credited to them because of their faith (4:3, 5-6, 9-11, 23-24).

4:25. Mentioning the Lord Jesus led Paul to state again the Savior's central place in God's program of providing righteousness for sinful people by grace through faith. Both Christ's death and His resurrection are essential to that work of justification. **He was delivered over** (by God the Father; cf. 8:32) **to death for our sins** (lit., "on account of or because of" [dia with the accusative] "our trespasses" [paraptōmata, "false steps"; cf. 5:15, 17, 20; Eph. 2:1]). Though not a direct quotation, these words in substance are taken from Isaiah 53:12 (cf. Isa. 53:4-6). Also He **was raised to life for** ("on account of" or "because of" [dia with the accusative]) **our justification.** Christ's death as God's sacrificial Lamb (cf. John 1:29) was to pay the redemptive price for the sins of all people (Rom. 3:24) so that God might be free to forgive those who respond by faith to that provision. Christ's resurrection was the proof (or demonstration and vindication) of God's acceptance of Jesus' sacrifice (cf. 1:4). Thus because He lives, God can credit His provided righteousness to the account of every person who responds by faith to that offer.

In chapter 4, Paul presented several irrefutable reasons why justification is by faith: (1) Since justification is a gift, it cannot be earned by works (vv. 1-8). (2) Since Abraham was justified before he was circumcised, circumcision has no relationship to justification (vv. 9-12). (3) Since Abraham was justified centuries before the Law, justification is not based on the Law (vv. 13-17). (4) Abraham was justified because of his faith in God, not because of his works (vv. 18-25).

C. Provided righteousness enjoyed
(5:1-11)

5:1. The apostle now turned to a presentation of the experiential results (suggested by the connective oun, trans. **therefore**) of the believers' justification—

God's declaring them righteous—on the basis of faith (cf. 3:21–4:25). The participial clause **since we have been justified** (cf. 5:9) **through faith** describes antecedent action to the main clause, **we have peace** (*echomen*) **with God.** Some of the important Greek manuscripts read, "Let us have peace (*echōmen*) with God." This seems to be the preferred reading. If so, then the sense is, "Let us keep on having (in the sense of enjoying) peace with God." Peace has been made by God **through our Lord Jesus Christ** (cf. Eph. 2:14a), which fact is demonstrated by God's justification. A believer is not responsible for having peace in the sense of making it but in the sense of enjoying it.

5:2. The Lord Jesus, besides being the Agent of the believer's enjoyment of peace with God, is also the One **through whom we have gained access** (*prosagōgēn*, "privilege of approach" to a person of high rank; used elsewhere only in Eph. 2:18; 3:12) **by faith into this grace in which we now stand.** Though the phrase "by faith" is not supported by the best Greek manuscripts, it is the human means of the access. Believers in Christ stand in the sphere of God's grace (cf. "grace" in Rom. 3:24) because Christ has brought them to this position. He is their means of access.

In the Greek text the sentence, **And we rejoice in the hope of the glory of God,** is coordinate to the clause, "We have peace" (5:1). Like that clause, this one too may be translated, "Let us keep on rejoicing." Because of Christ, Christians eagerly anticipate the time when they will share Christ's glory, in contrast with their falling short of it now (3:23). In that sense He is "the hope of glory" (Col. 1:27; cf. Rom. 8:17-30; 2 Cor. 4:17; Col. 3:4; 2 Thes. 2:14; Heb. 2:10; 1 Peter 5:1, 10). Certainly such a prospect is cause for joy and even boasting! (*Kauchōmetha*, "rejoice," is lit., "boast" or "exult," here in a pure sense; this Gr. word is also used in Rom. 5:3, 11 where it is trans. "rejoice.")

5:3-4. Believers can enjoy the peace with God that has been achieved and the glorious future in God's presence that awaits them. But how should they react to the experiences of life that are often adverse and difficult? They are to **rejoice in their sufferings.** The word "rejoice" is *kauchōmetha,* the same word in verse 2. "Sufferings" is *thlipsesin,* "afflictions, distresses, pressures." James wrote along the same line: "Consider it pure joy, my brothers, whenever you face trials of many kinds" (James 1:2). This is more than mere Stoic endurance of troubles, even though endurance or steadfastness is the first result in a chain-reaction outgrowth from distress. This is spiritual glorying in afflictions because of having come to **know** (from *oida,* "to know by intuition or perception") that the end product of this chain reaction (that begins with distress) is **hope. Suffering** brings about **perseverance** (*hypomonēn,* "steadfastness," the ability to remain under difficulties without giving in; cf. Rom. 15:5-6; James 1:3-4). Only a believer who has faced distress can develop steadfastness. That in turn develops **character** (*dokimēn* ["proof"] has here the idea of "proven character"), which in turn results in hope. As believers suffer, they develop steadfastness; that quality deepens their character; and a deepened, tested character results in hope (i.e., confidence) that God will see them through.

5:5. A believer's **hope,** since it is centered in God and His promises, **does not disappoint** him. "Disappoint" means "put to shame because of disappointment" in unfulfilled promises. This affirmation concerning hope in God is a reflection of Psalm 25:3, 20-21 (cf. Ps. 22:5; Rom. 9:33; 1 Peter 2:6). The reason this hope (resulting finally from affliction) does not disappoint is that **God has poured out His love into our hearts.** God's love, so abundant in believer's hearts (cf. 1 John 4:8, 16), encourages them on in their hope. And this love is poured out **by** (better, "through," *dia* with the genitive) **the Holy Spirit, whom He has given us.** The Holy Spirit is the divine Agent who expresses to a believer the love of God, that is, God's love for him. The reality of God's love in a believer's heart gives the assurance, even the guarantee, that the believer's hope in God and His promise of glory is not misplaced and will not fail. This ministry of the Holy Spirit is related to His presence in believers as the seal of God (Eph. 4:30) and as the earnest or down payment of their inheritance in glory

(2 Cor. 1:21-22; Eph. 1:13-14). Later Paul wrote that the Holy Spirit Himself has been poured out in believers (Titus 3:6). Each believer has the Spirit of Christ (Rom. 8:9) in the sense that He is indwelt by the Holy Spirit (cf. 1 John 3:24; 4:13).

5:6-8. Having mentioned the pouring out of God's love, Paul now described the character of God's love, which explains why its pouring out assures believers of hope. God demonstrated His love by the death of His Son, Jesus **Christ.** This demonstration was first, **at just the right time** (cf. Gal. 4:4). Second, it was **when we were still powerless** (*asthenōn*, "without strength, feeble"; cf. John 5:5). Third, it was **for** (*hyper*) **the ungodly** (*asebōn*, "impious"; cf. Rom. 4:5). Clearly Christ's death was a substitutionary death, a death in place of others. The Greek preposition *hyper* often means "on behalf of," but occasionally it means "in place of," its meaning here. This is clear from the statement in 5:7, which also has *hyper*. A person willing to **die for a righteous man** or **for a good man** obviously is offering himself as a substitute so that the righteous or good man can continue to live. This is the highest expression of human love and devotion. However, God's love contrasts with human love in both nature and degree, because **God demonstrates** ("keeps on showing") **His own love for us in this: While we were still sinners, Christ died for us** (*hyper*, "in our place"). Though a few people might possibly be willing to die to save the lives of good people, though that is rare, Christ went well beyond that. He died in the place of the *powerless* ("feeble," v. 6), the *ungodly* (v. 6; 4:5), *sinners* (5:8), and even His *enemies!* (v. 10).

5:9-11. The participle translated **have . . . been justified** ("declared righteous") ties these verses to the argument at the beginning of the chapter (cf. v. 1). The immediate connection, however, is with what preceded (vv. 6-8). God gave proof of His love by having Christ die in the place of humans "while we were still sinners." Because of the sinner's response by faith (v. 1) to Christ's sacrifice on the cross, God has declared him righteous. Certainly that now-declared-righteous person will not be forsaken by God's love, which has been poured out effusively in his heart. Since

the divine dilemma of justification (3:26) has been solved on the basis of Jesus' shed **blood** (cf. 3:25), certainly Jesus Christ will see that justified sinners will **be saved from God's wrath.** Believers will never be condemned to hell (John 5:24; Rom. 8:1) nor will they be the objects of God's coming Tribulation wrath (1 Thes. 1:10; 5:9).

Here this same truth is repeated in different words (Rom. 5:10). Reconciliation, the third great achievement of Jesus' sacrificial death on Calvary, is presented (also v. 11). This great triumvirate—*redemption* (3:24; 1 Cor. 1:30; Gal. 3:13; Eph. 1:7); *propitiation* (Rom. 3:25 [NIV: "sacrifice of atonement"]; 1 John 2:2; 4:10 [NIV: "atoning sacrifice"]); *reconciliation* (Rom. 5:10-11; 2 Cor. 5:18-20; Col. 1:22)—is totally the work of God, accomplished through the death of Jesus Christ. Redemption pertains to sin (Rom. 3:24), propitiation (or satisfaction) pertains to God (3:25), and reconciliation is for people (cf. **we were reconciled**). Reconciliation is the removal of enmity that stands between people and God (cf. "enemies" in 5:10; Col. 1:21). Reconciliation is the basis of restored fellowship between people and God (cf. 2 Cor. 5:20-21).

If (Rom. 5:10) may be rendered "since"; it assumes that the reconciliation **through the death of His Son** is true. In addition, reconciliation was done **when we were God's enemies** (lit., "being enemies"). Since reconciliation was accomplished by Jesus' death, certainly **His life** is able to insure the complete and final salvation of believers. "His life" is His present life (not His life on earth) in which He intercedes (Heb. 7:25) for believers. He died for His enemies; surely He will save those, His former enemies, who are now fellowshiping in Him. Because Christians, God's reconciled ones, share in Christ's life, they will **be saved. Not only is** future salvation assured, **but we also rejoice in God** ("but also boasting [*kauchōmenoi*] in God") here and now. This is what Paul already exhorted believers to do (Rom. 5:1-3). The assurance and guarantee of it all is the fact that **through . . . Christ . . . we have now received reconciliation** (lit., "the reconciliation"). Since God has reconciled godless enemies to Himself, they should enjoy that peace with Him.

D. Provided righteousness contrasted (5:12-21)

5:12. Paul had now finished his description of how God has revealed and applied to humans His provided righteousness on the basis of the sacrificial death of Jesus Christ received by faith. One thing remains to be done—to present the contrastive parallelism between the work of Jesus Christ (and its results in justification and reconciliation) and the work of another man, Adam (and its results in sin and death). Paul began by saying, **Therefore** (lit., "because of this"; cf. 4:16), and started his comparison, **just as;** but he became concerned by other matters and did not return to the comparison until 5:15. Paul explained that **sin** (in Gr., "the sin") **entered** (*eisēlthen,* "entered into") **the world through one man; and,** in accord with God's warning (cf. Gen. 2:16-17), **death** (in Gr., "the death") **through sin.** God's penalty for sin was both spiritual and physical death (cf. Rom. 6:23; 7:13), and Adam and Eve and their descendants experienced both. But physical death, being an outward, visible experience, is in view in 5:12-21. Paul concluded, **And in this way death** ("the death") **came to all men.** "Came" is *diēlthen,* literally "passed or went through" or "spread through." *Eisēlthen,* "entered into" (the first clause in the verse) means that sin went in the world's front door (by means of Adam's sin); and *diēlthen,* "went through," means that death penetrated the entire human race, like a vapor permeating all of a house's rooms. The reason death spread to all, Paul explained, is that **all sinned.**

The Greek past (aorist) tense occurs in all three verbs in this verse. So the entire human race is viewed as having sinned in the one act of Adam's sin (cf. "all have sinned," also the Gr. past tense, in 3:23). Two ways of explaining this participation of the human race in the sin of Adam have been presented by theologians—the "federal headship" of Adam over the race and the "natural or seminal headship" of Adam. (Others say that people merely imitated Adam, that he gave the human race a bad example. But that does not do justice to 5:12.)

The federal headship view considers Adam, the first man, as the *representative* of the human race that generated from him. As the representative of all humans, Adam's act of sin was considered by God to be the act of all people and his penalty of death was judicially made the penalty of everybody.

The natural headship view, on the other hand, recognizes that the entire human race was seminally and *physically* in Adam, the first man. As a result God considered all people as participating in the act of sin which Adam committed and as receiving the penalty he received. Even adherents of the federal headship view must admit that Adam is the natural head of the human race physically; the issue is the relationship spiritually. Biblical evidence supports the natural headship of Adam. When presenting the superiority of Melchizedek's priesthood to Aaron's, the author of Hebrews argued that Levi, the head of the priestly tribe, "who collects the 10th, paid the 10th through Abraham, because when Melchizedek met Abraham, Levi was still in the body of his ancestor" (Heb. 7:9-10).

5:13. Though **sin** entered human experience through the act of Adam's sin (in which the entire human race participated seminally), sin expressed itself repeatedly in people's actions (cf. Gen. 6:5-7, 11-13) from the point of its entrance "until" (not **before,** as the NIV has it) **the Law was given.** However, as Paul had already said, "Where there is no Law there is no transgression" (Rom. 4:15). This does not mean that **sin** does not exist unless there is a Law. It means that sin does not have the character of being a transgression apart from **Law** and therefore **sin is not taken into account** (lit., "imputed, reckoned") as such.

5:14. The fact that sin did exist during the period from Adam to the Law is proved by the fact that **death reigned from the time of Adam to the time of Moses** (lit., "from Adam until Moses"). And death also reigned over people who had not broken **a command as did Adam** (cf. "death reigned," v. 17, and "sin reigned in death," v. 21). Adam had disobeyed a specific command of God (Gen. 2:17) and committed a transgression, something that his descendants did not do when they sinned till other specific commands from God were received. But yet all Adam's descendants had sinned with Adam (Rom. 5:12), and therefore death did reign (cf. Gen. 5:5, 8, 11, 14, 17, 20, 27, 31). Since death was present, that proved all had sinned in Adam (cf. comments on Rom. 5:12).

The mention of Adam by name (cf. "one man," v. 12) brought Paul back to the point of referring to him, **who was a pattern of the One to come.** A parallelism exists between Adam and Jesus Christ as heads of groups of human beings (cf. 1 Cor. 15:45-49), but the parallelism is more contrastive than comparative.

5:15. The details of the parallelism between Adam and Christ (begun by Paul in v. 12 with the words "just as") are given in verses 15-17. The apostle made clear the contrastive nature of the parallelism by stating, **But the gift** (*charisma*, "grace-gift") **is not like the trespass.** What Christ "gives" contrasts with what Adam did, his "trespass" (*paraptōma*, "false step"; also mentioned in 4:25; 5:16-18, 20). The point of the first contrasting parallel is the degree—**how much more.** The trespass of the one man brought physical death to **the many,** in this case the entire human race to date with two exceptions—Enoch and Elijah. By contrast, **God's grace—and the gift** (viz., righteousness, as stated in v. 17; cf. v. 16) **that came by the grace of the one Man, Jesus Christ—abounded to the many!** If this latter "many" is identical with the first (the many who died, which is possible, but is not required by the text) and constitutes the entire human race, then "God's grace and the gift" by means of "grace" abound in the sense of reaching and being available to all people, but not necessarily being appropriated by all.

5:16. Here Paul presented a second contrasting parallelism; this one is different in kind. He began by emphasizing the contrast: **Again, the gift of God is not like the result of the one man's sin.** Literally, the Greek is, "Also not as through the one who sinned is the gift." Obviously here a noun paralleling "the gift" is missing in the text. Some suggest "the judgment" from what follows; others the transgression, or the death, or the condemnation. It seems best to leave it indefinite as does the Greek text and to translate it by "the result" (as does the NIV) of that which happened.

Paul continued, **The judgment followed** ("was out of") **one sin** (lit., "one," i.e., Adam) **and brought condemnation.** God passed judgment (*krima*) on Adam and he (and the entire human race) received condemnation (*katakrima*, "punishment"; *katakrima* occurs elsewhere only in v. 18 and 8:1). **But,** by contrast, **the gift** (*charisma*, "grace-gift," i.e., righteousness, 5:17; cf. v. 15) **followed** ("was out of") **many trespasses and brought justification** (*dikaiōma*, "a declaration of righteousness," also used in 1:32, 2:26; 5:18; 8:4). God's grace, as Paul stated repeatedly, beginning in 3:24, is the basis of a person's being justified, declared righteous. And this was in the face of "many trespasses" (*paraptōmatōn*; cf. 5:15, 17-18, 20). One man (Adam) trespassed (v. 15) God's command, and everyone since has repeatedly overstepped God's instructions.

5:17. The third contrasting parallelism (cf. vv. 15-16) combines the two preceding ones and involves both a difference in degree (**how much more;** cf. v. 15) and a difference in kind ("death" and "life"; cf. v. 16). The first-class condition in the first part of the verse assumes the statement to be true, **if** (since) **death reigned** (cf. v. 20) **through that one man.** This fact is confirmed by verses 12 and 14. Death is a tyrant, ruling over people and bringing every person under its fear and into its grip (cf. Heb. 2:15).

As a result it also is true that **those who receive God's abundant provision of grace and of the gift** (cf. Rom. 5:15) **of righteousness reign in life through the one Man, Jesus Christ.** The Lord Jesus is the Agent of all of God's provision for people. Whereas death reigns like a tyrant over all, believers in Christ, who receive God's grace, reign in life. In the one case people are dying victims under a ruthless ruler; in the other they themselves become the rulers (cf. Rev. 1:6) whose kingdom is one of life! The fact that it is "those who receive" God's grace and gift emphasizes that the provision made for all in Christ's sacrificial death and offered to all by God must be appropriated by an individual by faith to become effective (cf. "received" in John 1:12).

5:18-19. In these verses Paul concludes his basic parallelism between

Adam and Jesus Christ begun in verse 12 and the contrasts between them in verses 15-17. Paul reduced the contrast to the briefest possible statement. **Consequently** (lit., "so then"), **just as the result of one trespass** (*paraptōmatos*, "false step"; cf. vv. 15-17, 20) **was condemnation** (*katakrima*, "punishment"; cf. v. 16) **for all men, so also the result of one act of righteousness was justification that brings life for all men.** The "one righteous act" (lit. Gr.) was Christ's death on the cross. One trespass (Adam's sin) is contrasted with one righteous act (Christ's sacrifice). The result of Adam's sin (everyone under God's condemnation) is contrasted with the result of Christ's work (justification offered to all). One brought death; the other brings life. Once again the "all men" in the first half of the sentence includes the entire human race (cf. "all men" in v. 12, and "the many" in the first half of v. 15). This implies the same dimensions for the "all men" in second half of the verse (cf. "many" in the second halves of vv. 16, 19). The provision in the one righteous act, therefore, is potential and it comes to the entire human race as the offer and opportunity which are applied only to "those who receive" (v. 17).

The same conclusion is stated in different words in verse 19, where Adam's act is called **disobedience** and the sacrificial death of Jesus Christ is called **obedience.** As a result **the many** (cf. first halves of vv. 15, 18) **were made** (lit., "stand constituted as") **sinners** (cf. 11:32). In the second half of 5:19 **the many** means "those who receive" (v. 17; cf. "many" in the second half of v. 16). They are not simply declared righteous (the verb *dikaioō* is not used here), but they **will be made righteous** in the process of sanctification, culminating in glorification in God's presence. The word "made" (from *kathistēmi*) means "stand constituted as," the same verb used in the first half of verse 19 in the words "were made sinners."

5:20-21. A remaining question in this discussion is, Where does the Mosaic Law fit into all this and why? Paul explained, **The Law was added so that the trespass** (*paraptōma,* cf. vv. 15-19) **might increase** ("abound"). The word "added" should be rendered "came in beside," for it translates the verb *pareisēl-*

then. Two similar verbs, *eisēlthen* and *diēlthen,* were used in verse 12. Galatians 2:4 is the only other place in the New Testament that uses the Greek verb for "came in beside."

Is the statement in Romans 5:20a a purpose or a result clause? The coming of the Mosaic Law (clearly meant here in light of vv. 13-14) did *result* in the abounding of "the trespass" (the consequence of any law), but (also in the light of vv. 13-14 and 4:15) the Mosaic Law came in "so that" (*purpose*) abounding sin might be recognized as abounding trespass.

The result was that **where sin increased** (lit., "abounded"; cf. 5:20) **grace increased all the more** ("overflowed superlatively"; cf. "overflow" in v. 15). What a contrast! No matter how great human sin becomes, God's grace overflows beyond it and abundantly exceeds it. No wonder Paul wrote that God's grace "is sufficient" (2 Cor. 12:9). God's goal (*hina,* **so,** introduces a purpose clause) is that His **grace might reign through righteousness** (the righteousness of Christ provided for people) **to bring eternal life through Jesus Christ our Lord.** Once again Paul spoke of reigning in connection with life. In verse 17 those who received God's gift "reign in life" through Christ. Here God's grace is personified as reigning and bringing eternal life.

By the time the Apostle Paul had reached this point he had not only described how God's provided righteousness is revealed in justification but he also was anticipating how it is to be revealed through regeneration and sanctification.

IV. God's Righteousness Revealed in Sanctification (chaps. 6–8)

God's provided righteousness involves more than declaring believers righteous on the basis of faith. In Romans the first clue to this fact is in 5:5: "God has poured out His love into our hearts by the Holy Spirit, whom He has given us." The presence of the Holy Spirit within believers and God's reproduction of an attribute of His (His love) in believers speak of their new natures and their new lives. This new kind of life, with the sanctifying ministry of the Holy Spirit, is now discussed at length by Paul in chapters 6–8.

Contrasts between Adam and Christ in Romans 5:15–21

One Man (Adam)	One Man (Christ)
v. 15 One man's *trespass* → *many* died	One Man's grace → *gift* of grace (righteousness) to *many*
v. 16 One (Adam) → judgment and condemnation	*Many trespasses* → gift → justification
v. 17 Through *one* man's *trespass* → death reigned	Through *one* Man Jesus Christ → believers reign in life
v. 18 One *trespass* → condemnation for *all* men	One act of righteousness → justification offered to *all* men
v. 19 Disobedience of *one* → *many* constituted sinners	Obedience of One → *many* constituted righteous
v. 21 Sin reigned in death	Grace reigns to bring eternal life

→ = led to or results in

A. Ground of sanctification (6:1-4)

6:1-2. The questions that open this section demand reflection. A review of God's provision by grace through Jesus Christ should elicit praise to God. But the teaching on God's justification of sinful people (3:21–5:21) and the statement of 5:20 in particular might lead some to suggest what Paul expressed: **Shall we go on sinning so that grace may increase?** Some may have reasoned that since grace increases "all the more" when sin abounds, then believers ought to sin more so they could experience more grace! The apostle voiced this idea only to reject it vehemently: **By no means!** (*mē genoito;* cf. comments on 3:4) In no way is the abundance of God's grace designed to encourage sin.

Then Paul explained why such a thought cannot be entertained. The fact is, Christians **died to sin** (cf. 6:7, 11). The Greek aorist (past) tense for "died" suggests a specific point when the action occurred, at salvation. Death, whether physical or spiritual, means separation, not extinction (cf. vv. 6-7, 14). Death to sin is separation from sin's power, not the extinction of sin. Being dead to sin means being "set free from sin" (vv. 18, 22). That being true, Paul asked, **How can they live in it any longer?** Obviously believers cannot *live* in sin if they *died* to it.

6:3-4. Paul explained in more detail the spiritual basis for his abrupt declaration, "We died to sin" (v. 2). Whether the Roman Christians knew it or not, the fact is **that all of us who were baptized into Christ Jesus were baptized into His death.** The question here is whether Paul had in mind Spirit baptism (1 Cor. 12:13) or water baptism. Some object to taking Romans 6:3 as Spirit baptism because that verse speaks of being "baptized into Christ" whereas 1 Corinthians 12:13 speaks of Spirit baptism placing the believer into Christ's *body.* Of course, both are true: the believer is "baptized" (placed into) Christ and also into the body of Christ, and both are done by the Holy Spirit.

Others take Romans 6:3 to refer to water baptism, but the problem with that is that it seems to suggest that baptism saves. However, the New Testament consistently denies baptismal regeneration, presenting water baptism as a public attestation to an accomplished spiritual work (cf., e.g., Acts 10:44-48; 16:29-33). The spiritual reality Paul spoke of is that by faith believers are "baptized (placed) into Christ" and thereby are united and identified with Him. This spiritual reality

461

is then graphically witnessed to and pictured by believers' baptism in water. The one baptism (by water) is the visible picture of the spiritual truth of the other baptism (identification with Christ; cf. Gal. 3:27, "baptized into Christ . . . clothed with Christ").

This is supported by the statement, **We were therefore buried with Him through baptism into death.** Christ's burial shows that He actually died (cf. 1 Cor. 15:3-4). Christians' "burial" with Christ shows that they in fact died with Him to their former sinful ways of living. The purpose of their identification with Christ in His death and burial is **that just as Christ was raised from the dead** (lit., "out from dead ones"; cf. Rom. 4:24; 8:11) **through the glory** (a synonym for God's power; cf. Eph. 1:19; Col. 2:12) **of the Father, we too may live a new life** (lit., "so also in newness of life we should walk about"). The Greek word "newness" (*kainotēti*) speaks of life that has a new or fresh quality. The resurrection of Jesus was not just a resuscitation; it was a new form of life. In the same way the spiritual lives of believers in Jesus have a new, fresh quality. Also, a believer's identification with Jesus Christ in His resurrection, besides being the start of new spiritual life now, is also the guarantee of physical resurrection.

This work of God at salvation in identifying a believer with Christ's death, burial, and resurrection—thus separating him from sin's power and giving him a new quality of life—is the basis of the Holy Spirit's continuing work in sanctification.

B. Attitudes for sanctification (6:5-23)

Sanctification begins with regeneration, the implanting of spiritual life in a believer. From that starting point sanctification is God's progressively separating a believer from sin to Himself and transforming his total life experience toward holiness and purity. The process of sanctification for a believer never ends while he is on earth in his mortal body. It is consummated in glorification when that believer through death and resurrection or through the Rapture stands in the presence of God "conformed to the likeness of His Son" (8:29). A believer's identification with Jesus Christ by faith is both the ground and the goal of sanctifi-

cation. The process of translating that identification into the daily experience of progressive sanctification, however, demands three attitudes of mind and action on a believer's part. These Paul discussed in 6:5-23.

1. RECKON (6:5-11)

The first attitude for sanctification demanded of believers is to "count" (pres. imper., "keep on counting") themselves dead to sin but alive to God in Christ Jesus (v. 11). Being able to reckon something as true, however, depends on knowing and believing certain things. These things to know and believe are stated in verses 5-10.

6:5-7. The first clause should be translated, "Since (not **if**) **we have become united** in the likeness of **His death**," because the statement is assumed to be true and is true. It affirms the certainty of the second clause of the sentence, which promises that believers are **united with** Christ **in** the likeness of **His resurrection.** As a result **we know** (*ginōskontes* suggests experimental or reflective knowing, not intuitive knowledge as in *eidotes* in v. 9) **that our old self was crucified with Him.** Literally, the last portion of this sentence is, "our old man was crucified together," obviously with Christ. A believer's "old man" is the person as he was spiritually before he trusted Christ, when he was still under sin (3:9), powerless and ungodly (5:6), a sinner (5:8), and an enemy of God (5:10). ("Old self" or "old man" does not refer to the sin nature as such. The Bible does not teach that the sin nature was eradicated at salvation or is ever eradicated in this life.)

The "old man" was "crucified" with Christ (cf. "baptized into His death," 6:3; and "united with Him in His death," v. 5) **so that the body of sin might be rendered powerless.** The phrase "the body of sin" does not mean that a human body is sinful in itself. It means that one's physical body is controlled or ruled by sin (cf. comments on "body of death" in 7:24). This was the condition of each believer before his conversion. But now at salvation the power of controlling sin is broken; it is "rendered powerless" or ineffective (*katargēthē*; trans. "nullify" in 1 Cor. 1:28).

The next clause (Rom. 6:6b-7) in effect explains the first clause (v. 6a). In his unregenerate state a believer was enslaved **to sin.** But his "old man" was crucified (identified) with Christ, and that is the basis for deliverance from enslavement to sin. **Anyone who has died has been freed from sin.** The words "has been freed" are a loose rendering of *dedikaiōtai,* literally, "has been justified or declared righteous." The perfect tense of this verb describes a past action with a continuing effect or force. Sin no longer has the legal right to force its mastery and control on a believer, for he has died with Christ.

6:8-11. These verses state much the same truth as verses 5-7 and in the same format, beginning with **if** ("since"). Those who by faith receive Jesus Christ and are identified with Him have **died with Christ** (cf. vv. 3, 5). Because this is true, **we believe** (pres. tense, "we keep on believing") **that we will also live with Him.** The sharing of the resurrection life of Christ begins at the moment of regeneration, but it will continue as a believer shares eternity with the Lord. Again as a result **we know** (*eidotes,* "intuitive knowledge," perceiving a self-evident truth [cf. v. 15], not *ginōskontes,* "experimental or reflective knowledge" as in v. 6) that Christ's resurrection was a removal from the sphere of physical death to an unending spiritual form of life. Having experienced physical death once and having been removed from its realm by resurrection life, Jesus **cannot die again** (lit., "dies no more"). In resurrection Jesus Christ was victorious over death (Acts 2:24) and **death no longer has mastery** (*kyrieuei,* "rules as lord"; cf. Rom. 6:14) **over Him** as it does over all other human beings (John 10:17-18).

Paul summarized this discussion by stating that Jesus in His physical **death . . . died to sin** (i.e., in reference to sin) **once for all** (*ephapax;* cf. Heb. 7:27; 9:12; 10:10). This stands in opposition to the doctrine and practice of the so-called perpetual sacrifice of Christ in the Roman Catholic Mass. Contrariwise, **the life He lives, He lives** (pres. tense, "keeps on living") **to God.** Resurrection life is eternal in quality and everlasting in duration. Furthermore, God is its Source and also its Goal. What is true of Jesus Christ in reality and experience, believers

who are identified with Him by faith are commanded to reckon true for themselves. They are to **count** themselves **dead to** (in reference to) **sin but alive to God.** Since they are dead to its power (Rom. 6:2), they ought to recognize that fact and not continue in sin. Instead they are to realize they have new life **in Christ;** they share His resurrection life (cf. Eph. 2:5-6; Col. 2:12-13).

2. YIELD (6:12-14)

6:12. The attitude of mind that a believer has died to sin must be translated into action in his experience. Paul commanded, **Therefore do not let sin reign** (pres. imper., "do not let sin continue to reign") as it did before salvation. The present imperative negative can also be translated, "Stop letting sin reign." When sin reigns in people's lives and bodies, they **obey its evil desires.** Sin enslaves (v. 6), making a person subject to his own desires. *Epithymia* refers to "longings" or "desires," which may be either good or evil, depending on how the word is used. Here, in the case of sin, the desires are evil. **In your mortal body** means that sin manifests itself through one's physical actions in this body. The Greek here stresses that the body is mortal or dying. Perhaps this suggests the foolishness of giving in to the desires of a body that is transitory and decaying. To give in to a dying master is strange indeed.

6:13. Actually this verse repeats the command of verse 12 in more specific terms. **Do not offer** (lit., "do not continue to present," or "stop presenting") **the parts of your body** (lit., "your members"; cf. v. 19) **to sin, as instruments** (*hopla,* frequently in military context, "weapons" or "armor"; cf. 13:12; 2 Cor. 6:7; 10:4) **of wickedness** (*adikias,* "unrighteousness" in contrasting parallelism with righteousness, later in Rom. 6:13). On the contrary, in sharp contrast, Paul commanded, **offer** (aorist imper., "present once and for all"; also used in v. 19) **yourselves to God, as those who have been brought from death to life** (lit., "as if being alive out from dead ones"; cf. John 5:24) **and offer the parts of your body** (lit., "and your members") **to Him as instruments** (*hopla*) **of righteousness** (*dikaiosynēs*). A related passage is Paul's exhortation, "Offer your bodies as living sacrifices . . . to God"

(Rom. 12:1). Because they were once dead in sin (cf. Eph. 2:1) but have been given new life (Rom. 6:11) believers ought to live for God. Their bodies should be used not for sin (v. 12) or unrighteousness (v. 13) but for promoting righteousness (cf. "bodies" and "body"; 7:5, 23; 1 Cor. 6:15).

6:14. God's design is that **sin shall not be your master** (*kyrieusei;* "shall not rule as lord"; cf. v. 9). The reason this should not happen is that **you are not under Law, but under grace.** Paul had already explained that "the Law was added so that the trespass might increase" (5:20), and elsewhere he declared, "The power of sin is the Law" (1 Cor. 15:56). If believers were still under the Law, it would be impossible to keep sin from exercising mastery. But since believers are "under grace," this can be done by following Paul's instructions.

3. SERVE (6:15-23)

6:15-16. The mention that believers are "under grace" (v. 14) raised another aberrant idea that the apostle refuted. The question is, **Shall we sin because we are . . . under grace** instead of the **Law?** The Greek aorist (past) tense here may have the sense of committing an act of sin now and then, in contrast to living a life of sin as stated in verse 1. Paul's response was the same as before (v. 2): **By no means!** (*mē genoito;* cf. comments on 3:4) Again he proceeded to explain why that idea cannot be accepted. He asked, **Don't you know** ("perceive intuitively" a self-evident truth; cf. 6:9) that in effect there is no middle ground between being a slave **to sin** and a slave **to obedience** to God. As the Lord Jesus said, "No one can serve two masters. . . . You cannot serve both God and money" (Matt. 6:24; Luke 16:13). Paul also pointed out that being a slave to sin **leads to death** (cf. Rom. 6:21, 23). This is not physical death only or even spiritual death only, but death in general as the natural consequence and inevitable concomitant of sin (cf. Gen. 2:17). On the other hand being a slave to obedience (to God and His gospel obviously) **leads to righteousness** (again righteousness in the general sense as equivalent to eternal life or glorification). Death is the normal consequence of sin (which is disobeying God); righteousness

is the normal consequence of obeying God and living for Him.

6:17-18. This discussion reminded the Apostle Paul of what the grace of God had already accomplished in his readers' lives and he burst forth in praise. Before they responded to the gospel they had been **slaves to sin,** but they **wholeheartedly** (lit., "out from hearts," thus inwardly and genuinely, not merely externally) **obeyed** (cf. "obedience" in 1 Peter 1:2) **the form of teaching to which** they **were entrusted.** Hearing the teaching of God's Word, they committed themselves to those truths. That commitment was evidenced by their response to the gospel and their being baptized. The result was that they **have been set free from sin and have become slaves** (past tense in Gr.) **to righteousness** (cf. Rom. 6:22). This is positional and must be manifested in daily experience, but it demonstrates again that there is no middle ground. Christians are not to give in to sin because they are dead to it and no longer slaves of it. It is totally contrary to God's plan for slaves of righteousness to become enslaved to sin!

6:19. To talk of being "enslaved" to righteousness and to God is not correct in one sense, Paul wrote, because God does not hold His children in bondage. But the word "slavery" appropriately describes an unregenerate person's relationship to sin and to Satan. So Paul used "slavery" for contrasting the relationship of the believer as well. Before developing this idea further, the apostle in effect apologized for its use—**I put this in human terms** (lit., "I am speaking in human fashion")—**because you are weak in your natural selves** (lit., "your flesh"). Apparently Paul felt that his readers' spiritual perception was feeble so he used this terminology from human experience. Then he basically repeated the ideas of verses 16-17. Unsaved Romans had offered their bodies **to impurity and to ever-increasing wickedness** (lit., "lawlessness"; cf. 1:24-27; 6:13). They had voluntarily become enslaved! But Paul exhorted believers now to offer themselves as slaves **to righteousness leading to holiness** (perfect holiness, as the end of the process [cf. v. 22]) in contrast with their former impurity.

6:20-23. Paul once again stated that slavery **to sin** and to **righteousness** are mutually exclusive (cf. vv. 13, 16). But he went on to indicate the superiority of being enslaved to righteousness and God. The **benefit** (this Gr. word is usually trans. "fruit") of enslavement to sin was that it produced things that a believer is **now ashamed of.** But even worse, "the end of **those things** is **death**" (lit. trans.).

Responding to the gospel by faith and accepting Jesus Christ completely reverses things for an individual. He is **now . . . set free from sin** (cf. v. 18) and has been enslaved **to** God with the result that he has **the benefit** of **holiness** (cf. v. 19), the subject of chapters 6–8. The sinful life gives no benefit (6:21), but salvation gives the benefit of a holy, clean life (v. 22). Whereas the "end" (*telos*) or result of sin is death (v. 21), the "end" of salvation **is eternal life.** Paul then summarized these contrasts. **The wages** (the Gr. word *opsōnia* originally meant a soldier's pay) **of sin is death** (eternal death here, in contrast with "eternal life" in v. 23b). This death is eternal separation from God in hell, in which unbelievers suffer conscious torment forever (Luke 16:24-25). This is the wages they have earned and deserve because of their sin (cf. Rom. 5:12; 7:13). By contrast, **the gift** (*charisma*, "grace-gift") **of God is eternal life** (cf. John 3:16, 36). Eternal life is a gift that cannot be earned (cf. Eph. 2:8-9; Titus 3:5).

Three times in this chapter Paul wrote that sin results in death (Rom. 6:16, 21, 23). But believers have been set free from sin (vv. 18, 22) and are no longer slaves to it (vv. 6, 20) but are "slaves to righteousness" (vv. 16, 18-19; cf. v. 13). Because they are alive to God (v. 11) and have eternal life (v. 23) they should present themselves to Him (vv. 13, 19) and live accordingly, not letting sin master them (vv. 6, 11-14, 22).

C. Conflict in sanctification (chap. 7)

It is one thing for a believer to understand that his identification with Jesus Christ means that he has died to sin (6:2) and to count or reckon that to be true (6:11). But it is something else for him to deal with the sin nature that remains within and its efforts to express itself in his thoughts and actions. This is the internal conflict in the area of sanctification that every believer faces.

1. THE BELIEVER AND THE LAW (7:1-6)

7:1-3. Verses 1-6 relate to 6:14, the intervening verses (6:15-23) being a digression raised by the question in 6:15. The statement that a believer identified with Jesus Christ in His death is no-longer "under Law" (6:14) should not have surprised Paul's readers because they were **men who know the Law.** This statement should not be restricted to Jewish believers in the church at Rome because Gentiles also knew the principle **that the Law has authority** (*kyrieuei*, "rules as lord"; cf. 6:9, 14) **over a man only as long as he lives.** This is a self-evident truth, which Paul then illustrated by marriage. **A married woman** (lit., "the under-a-man woman") **is bound** (perf. tense, "has been bound and stands bound") **to her husband as long as he is alive. But if her husband dies** (in Gr., a third-class condition indicating a real possibility) **she is released** (perf. tense, "has been and stands discharged") **from the law of marriage** (lit., "from the law of the man"). She is bound to him by marriage as her husband while he lives, and obviously his death frees her from that marriage.

Then Paul continued the illustration, pointing out that **if** a wife **marries** (lit., "if she comes to") **another man while her husband is still alive she is called** (future tense, "shall be publicly known as") **an adulteress.** Conversely, on the death of her **husband** she is free from that marriage (cf. 7:2). So she **is not an adulteress if she marries** (lit., **"even though** she comes to") **another man.** A widow who marries again is not guilty of adultery.

7:4-6. In these verses Paul applied his illustration of marriage to a believer and the Law. He said, **You also died** (lit., "you were put to death," as was true of Jesus) **to the Law.** Just as a believer "died to sin" (6:2) and so is "set free from sin" (6:18, 22), so he also died to the Law and is separated and set free from it (6:14; cf. Gal. 2:19). As a wife is no longer married to her husband when he dies, so a Christian is no longer under the Law. This separation was **through the body of Christ,** that is, because of Christ's death on the cross.

As a result Christians **belong to another, to Him who was raised from the** dead (cf. Rom. 6:4, 9). This One of course is the Lord Jesus Christ. In a sense believers are united to Him as His bride (Eph. 5:25). God's purpose in all this is **in order that we might bear fruit to God** (cf. Rom. 6:22; Gal. 5:22-23; Phil. 1:11). Only a person who is spiritually alive can bear spiritual fruit, that is, holy living (cf. John 15:4-5). A person who is married to Christ can bear spiritual progeny. Paul moved from the second person plural (**you**) to the first person plural (**we**), including himself along with his readers.

The apostle continued, **For when we were controlled by the sinful nature** (lit., "For when we were in the flesh"; *sarx* often means sin nature; cf. Rom. 7:18, 25) **the sinful passions aroused by the Law were at work in our bodies.** This describes a believer before he was saved (cf. 6:19). The Law by its prohibitions aroused sinful passions, as explained in 7:7-13. In that sense unsaved Gentiles were "under" the Law. Consequently their progeny was not "fruit to God" (v. 4) but **fruit for death.** Sin, Paul repeatedly affirmed, leads to death (5:15, 17, 21; 6:16, 21, 23; 7:10-11, 13; 8:2, 6, 10, 13).

But now, being identified with Christ, believers are dead to the Law. Like a widow released from marital obligations, so believers are **released from the Law** and its arousal to sin. The purpose of this release "from the Law" is **so that** they may **serve** (a better rendering is "be slaves"; cf. "slave[s]" in 6:6, 16 [thrice], 17-18, 20, 22) **in the new way of the Spirit, and not in the old way of the written code.** The word "Spirit" may be "spirit" (lowercase "s") to contrast with the written document, the Law. The thought then is that believers do not live by the "oldness" of the Law but by the "newness" of a regenerated spirit. Or "Spirit" may refer to the Holy Spirit, the Source of new life. (Cf. comments on "the Spirit" and "the letter," 2 Cor. 3:6.)

2. THE LAW AND SIN (7:7-13)

The involvement of the Mosaic Law in the discussion of a believer's identification with Christ and death to sin raises a question about the Law's relationship to sin.

7:7-8. Is the Law sin? Paul's response again was a vehement denial. **Certainly not!** (*mē genoito*; cf. comments on 3:4) The Law arouses sin (7:5) but that

does not mean the Law itself is sin. In fact, Paul said later, the Law is holy (v. 12) and spiritual (v. 14). Paul went on to explain that the Law made sin **known** (cf. 3:19-20). Then to be specific, he mentioned coveting. The Law's prohibition, **Do not covet** (Ex. 20:17; Deut. 5:21), makes people want **to covet** all the more. Paul knew **sin** as a principle and specifically, covetousness as an expression of it, and that knowledge came **through the Law.** Paul described how it worked. The indwelling principle of **sin, seizing the opportunity** (lit., "taking a start point" [*aphormēn*, a base for military operations or for an expedition]) **afforded by the commandment** (cf. Rom. 7:11), **produced in me every kind of covetous desire.** The Law is not the cause of the act of sin; the principle or nature of sin within an individual is. But the Law's specific commandments stimulate the sin principle into acts that violate the commandments and give those acts the character of transgression (4:15; cf. 3:20; 5:13b, 20a). As Paul concluded, **Apart from Law, sin is dead.** This does not mean that sin has no existence without the Law (cf. 5:13), but that without the Law sin is less active, for the Law arouses "sinful passions" (7:5).

It is significant that, beginning with verse 7 and continuing through this chapter, the Apostle Paul turned to the first person singular, presenting his personal experience. Up to this point he had used the third person, the second person, and even the first person plural. But now he described his own experience, allowing the Holy Spirit to apply the truth to his readers.

7:9-12. Some generalize the words, **Once I was alive apart from Law,** to refer to the experience of mankind in the period between the Fall and the giving of the Mosaic Law. But there is no basis for this. Evidently the apostle was speaking of his personal experience as a child and perhaps even a youth prior to his awareness and understanding of the full impact of God's commandments. The clause, **but when the commandment came,** does not speak of the giving of the Mosaic Law, but the dawning of the significance of the commandment ("Do not covet") on Paul's mind and heart before his conversion. The result was that the principle of **sin** within made its presence and power known (it **sprang to life**) in his violations of the **commandment.** As a result Paul **died** spiritually (cf. 6:23a) under the sentence of judgment by the Law he had broken. The commandment not to covet was given to help people see how to live, but it actually produced **death** because of the sin in human hearts.

Repeating from 7:8 his description of sin's relationship to the commandment, Paul declared that **sin . . . deceived me.** Apart from the Law, the principle of sin was dormant and inactive; but using the commandments of the Law, it demonstrated its controlling force over one's actions. So this sin deceived him (*exēpatēsen,* "led [him] astray"; cf. 2 Cor. 11:3; 1 Tim. 2:14) and **put** him **to death** (lit., "killed" him), not physically but spiritually. Sin is like a personal enemy within (cf. Gen. 4:7). **The Law,** instead of being sin (Rom. 7:7), **is holy, and the commandment** not to covet (which, as a part of the Law, represents the whole) **is holy, righteous, and good.**

7:13. Paul then considered still another possible misunderstanding in his effort to clarify the relationship of sin and the Law. Taking the last-mentioned quality of the commandment ("good"), he asked, **Did that which is good, then, become death to me?** Once again his immediate response was a vehement denial (**By no means!** *mē genoito;* cf. comments on 3:4), followed by an explanation. The principle of **sin,** not the Law, becomes **death** to an individual (5:12). But **sin** uses **the commandment,** the **good** thing, as an agent or instrument to keep on producing **death in** a person and thereby **sin** is seen as **utterly** (lit., "exceedingly") **sinful.** The internal principle or nature of sin uses the specific commandments of the Law of God—in part and in the whole; a "holy, righteous, and good" thing in itself—to manifest its true nature as opposed to God and to demonstrate its power within individuals.

3. THE BELIEVER AND SIN (7:14-25)

7:14. Understanding the conflict in personal sanctification involves seeing the relationship between a believer and his indwelling sin. In verse 14 Paul made a transition from the previous subject (vv. 7-13) to the next one. The statement, **The Law is spiritual** (cf. v. 12), is not only the

conclusion of Paul's previous argument but also an accepted fact among people. The Law comes from God who is Spirit (John 4:24) and expresses God's will for human living. Paul, using himself as the example, said the problem is that **I am unspiritual** (*sarkinos,* "fleshy, made of flesh"). In addition he was **sold as a slave** (perf. tense, "had been sold and remained in that state") **to sin** (lit. "under the sin"; cf. "under sin" in Rom. 3:9).

In relating his personal experience in 7:14-25 Paul consistently used the present tense whereas he had used the imperfect and aorist tenses. Obviously he was describing his present conflict as a Christian with indwelling sin and its continuing efforts to control his daily life. The clause, "sold under sin" (KJV), describes an unregenerate person; but sin also resides in a believer, who is still subject to sin's penalty of physical death. As a result, indwelling sin continues to seek to claim what it considers its property even after one has become a Christian.

7:15-17. At the start Paul confessed, **I do not understand what I do** (lit., "what I am producing I do not know"). He was like a little boy whose honest answer to why he did something wrong is, "I don't know." A person's actions are at the dictate of someone or something besides himself that he really does not understand and cannot explain. Paul continued to present this quandary he faced: **For what I want to do I do not do** (lit., "For what I am wishing, that I am not doing," *prassō*) and conversely, **What I hate I do** (lit., "What I am hating that I am doing," *poiō*). No difference of emphasis can be put in this verse on the two Greek verbs translated "do" (even though such difference is significant elsewhere), because the occurrence of those two verbs is reversed in verse 19. This statement can be made by an unregenerate person in his highest moral and ethical moments, but it can also be said by a regenerate person. There is no reason to conclude that Paul was not describing his experience as a believer at that time. Paul said, **I agree that the Law is good.** Here the Greek word for "good" is *kalos,* "beautiful, noble, excellent," whereas in verse 12 it is *agathē,* "useful, upright." Because of this evidence, Paul concluded, **It is no longer I myself who do it** (lit., "no longer am I myself producing it"; cf. v. 15) **but it is sin living in me** (lit., "but the dwelling-in-me sin"). This does not mean Paul was avoiding personal responsibility for his actions; he was speaking of the conflict between his desires and the sin within him.

7:18-20. Paul's experience convinced him that "the Law is good" (v. 16). But he also concluded, **I know that nothing good lives in me.** Then he hastened to explain that by the phrase "in me" he meant **in my sinful nature** (*sarki*, "flesh"; cf. vv. 5, 25). This is not literal physical or material flesh, but the principle of sin that expresses itself through one's mind and body.

As support for this conclusion Paul explained, **For I have the desire to do what is good** ("For to wish is present with me" [or "is lying beside me"]), **but I cannot carry it out** (lit., "but to produce the good is not"). Paul then repeated in slightly different words the statement of verse 15b, and then in verse 20 he repeated in effect his statement in verse 17. Paul recognized that even as a believer he had an indwelling principle of **sin** that once owned him as a slave and that still expressed itself through him to do things he did **not want to do** and not to do things he desired to do. This is a problem common to all believers.

7:21-23. Paul was a person who tried to learn from his experiences, **so** now he concluded, **I find this law at work.** This is not the Mosaic Law, of course, but a principle drawn from experience. Also in 8:2 "law" (*nomos*) means principle. This law or principle is the reality of ever-present **evil** in an individual whenever he wants **to do good.** Paul held fast to the fact that, as he said, **In my inner being I delight in God's Law** (cf. 7:25). "In my inner being" is literally, "according to the inner man." (The "inner man" is used in the Gr. NT also in 2 Cor. 4:16 and Eph. 3:16.) Delight in God's Law was the psalmist's response, stated repeatedly in Psalm 119 (e.g., vv. 16, 24, 47; cf. Ps. 1:2). Because of regeneration, a believer has a new nature or capacity for loving spiritual truths. Yet, recognizing the facts of experience, Paul said he saw **another law** or principle **at work** within him. This is the principle of sin. Paul called it "sin living in me" (Rom. 7:17, 20), "evil" **right**

there with me (v. 21), and "the sinful nature" (vv. 5, 18, 25).

This principle is continually doing two things: **waging war against the law of** the believer's **mind and making** him **a prisoner of the law of sin at work within** his **members.** The indwelling principle of sin is constantly mounting a military campaign against the new nature, trying to gain victory and control (cf. "slave" in vv. 14, 25 and "slaves" in 6:17, 19-20), of a believer and his actions. The new nature is called "the law" of the "mind" (*noos*; cf. 7:25) because it has the capacity for perceiving and making moral judgments. Further, despite a believer's identification with Jesus Christ's death and resurrection and his efforts to have Christ-honoring attitudes and actions, he cannot in his own power resist his indwelling sin nature. In and of himself he repeatedly experiences defeat and frustration.

7:24-25. Paul expressed that frustration in his exclamation, **What a wretched man I am!** Significantly Paul's description of himself is part of John's picture of the church of Laodicea—"wretched" (Rev. 3:17). The apostle then asked, **Who will rescue me from this body of death?** Paul recognized that as long as he was in his mortal body he would face the conflict with the indwelling sin principle and would have defeat in his own strength. Here he wrote of the "body of death"; in Romans 6:6 he wrote of the "body of sin." These mean that sin works through one's human body (cf. 6:6, 12-13, 19; 7:5, 23), bringing death (6:16, 21, 23; 7:10-11, 13; 8:10). Paul's answer to this question was triumphant and immediate: **Thanks be to God—through Jesus Christ our Lord!** Paul in this answer was looking to the final triumph of Jesus Christ for His people. Just as believers are identified with Him in His death and resurrection by faith here and now, so they will join their resurrected and exalted Lord for all eternity in new bodies, free forever from the presence of sin (8:23; Phil. 3:20-21). Meanwhile, in this life, Paul concluded, **I myself in my mind** (*noi*; cf. *noos* in Rom. 7:23) **am a slave** (lit., "am serving as a slave") **to God's Law, but in the sinful nature** (*sarki*, "flesh"; cf. vv. 5, 18, where *sarki*, from *sarx*, is also trans. "sinful nature") **a slave to the law of sin** (cf. "slave to sin," v. 14). While awaiting freedom from the presence of sin, believers still face conflicts between their regenerated minds (or new natures or capacities) and their sin natures or capacities.

D. Power for sanctification (8:1-17)

8:1. The question naturally arises, Must a believer spend his whole life on earth frustrated by ongoing defeats to indwelling sin? (7:21-25) Is there no power provided to achieve victory? The answer to the first question is no and to the second, yes. In chapter 8, Paul described the ministry of the indwelling Holy Spirit of God who is the source of divine power for sanctification and the secret for spiritual victory in daily living. But first Paul reminded his readers that **therefore**—since deliverance is "through Jesus Christ our Lord" (7:25)—**no condemnation** (*katakrima,* "punishment") awaits **those who are in Christ Jesus,** as a result of their faith and identification with Him (cf. 6:13; John 5:24). They are justified, declared righteous, and therefore stand in His grace (Rom. 5:2) and not under His wrath (1:18), and possess eternal life (5:17-18, 21). Christ is the sphere of safety for all who are identified with Him by faith. In the better Greek manuscripts, 8:1 ends here. The words "who do not live according to the sinful nature but according to the Spirit" were probably transcribed from verse 4.

8:2. The word **because** (*gar,* "for"), connects **through** (lit., "in") **Christ Jesus** in this verse with the identical phrase "in Christ Jesus" in verse 1. (In the Gr. word order of the sentence in v. 2, "in Christ Jesus" follows **the law of the Spirit of life.)** If 7:7-25 is Paul's testimony of his struggle as a believer with indwelling sin, then "the Spirit of life" is the Holy Spirit of God, not the spirit of the new nature each believer receives. The Holy Spirit is the Member of the Godhead who regenerates every believing individual (Titus 3:5) and bestows new life (John 3:5-8), the resurrection life of Christ (Rom. 6:4, 8, 11). Romans 8:2 has the second mention of the Holy Spirit since 5:5, but He is mentioned 18 more times through 8:27. This law ("principle"; cf. 7:23) **set me free** (the Gr. aorist tense suggests a once-for-all act of freedom at salvation) **from the law of sin and death.** That principle is called the principle "of sin and death"

because sin, as Paul said repeatedly, produces death (5:15, 17, 21; 6:16, 21, 23; 7:10-11, 13; 8:6, 10, 13). As the principle of *sin* it contrasts with the Spirit; as the principle that brings *death* it also contrasts with the Spirit who gives life. For the pronoun translated **me** some Greek manuscripts read "us" and others "you" (sing.). The difference is incidental; the truth stated applies to every believer.

8:3-4. Having stated the fact of freedom, Paul then explained how it is achieved. He declared again the impossibility of attaining freedom over sin through **the** (Mosaic) **Law.** It **was powerless to** free from sin. Not that the Law was weak in itself (as many translations suggest), for it was good (7:12). But because of **sinful** human **nature,** the Law could not deliver from sin. The words "sinful nature" translate *sarx* (lit., "flesh"), which can mean either human sinful corruption or human weakness (cf. 7:5, 18, 25; 8:4-5, 8-9, 12-13).

God accomplished deliverance over sin, however, **by sending His own Son in the likeness of sinful man** (lit., "likeness of flesh of sin"). Jesus was sent not in sinful flesh but *in the likeness* of it. His human nature was protected and preserved from the indwelling principle of sin that has plagued all other human beings since Adam (cf. Luke 1:35). He was also sent, literally "concerning or for sin" (*peri harmartias,* not as the NIV has it, **to be a sin offering).** In other words He came to do something about sin. What He did was to condemn it; by His death on the cross, **He condemned sin** (*katakrinen,* "passed a judicial sentence on it"; cf. *katakrima,* "punishment," Rom. 8:1) so that those in Christ are *not* condemned. The goal of this was so **that the righteous requirements of the Law**—a life of holiness (Lev. 11:44-45; 19:2; 20:7)—could **be fully met** as believers **do not live according to the sinful nature but according to the Spirit.** The provision of deliverance from the power of sin is through the death of Jesus Christ, but experiencing it in one's daily conduct comes through the controlling power of the Holy Spirit.

8:5-8. In these verses Paul answered the implied question, What does it mean to **live according to the sinful nature** and according to the Spirit? He explained that the former means having **their minds set on** (*phronousin*, pres. tense, "keep on being mindful of or aspiring for") **what that nature desires.** An unbeliever cares only for his sinful interests and has no regard for God. The exact opposite is true of **those who live** according to **the Spirit.** They aspire for or **have their minds set on what the Spirit desires.** The sinful nature and the indwelling Spirit are in conflict (Gal. 5:17).

But what difference does it make whether a person is mindful of the flesh or of the Spirit? Again Paul explained. **The mind** (*phronēma*, "mind-set, aspirations"; cf. Rom. 8:6b-7) **of sinful man** (*tēs sarkos*, "of the flesh") **is death,** that is, it is equivalent to death, or it leads to death in all its forms (physical and spiritual). On the other hand **the mind** (*phronēma*, "mind-set, aspirations") **controlled by the Spirit** (lit., "of the Spirit") **is life** (eternal resurrection life) **and peace** immediately (5:1) and ultimately. In 8:7-8 Paul focused only on the sinful mind (*phronēma tēs sarkos*, "mind-set, aspirations of the sin nature"; cf. v. 6) to explain why he said (v. 6) that it ends up in death: (1) It **is hostile to God** (cf. 5:10); (2) **it does not submit** (pres. tense, "is not submitting") **to God's Law;** and (3) **it** cannot **do so.** The result is that **those controlled by the sinful nature cannot** (pres. tense, "are not able to") **please God.** The unsaved lead lives that are totally void of spiritual life and ability. A believer, then, who gives in to his sin nature is acting like the unsaved (cf. 1 Cor. 3:3).

8:9-11. After speaking objectively about the two types of persons, Paul now addressed his readers directly. **You, however, are controlled not by the sinful nature but by the Spirit** (lit., "But you are not in the flesh but in the Spirit"), **if** (*eiper*, "if, as is the fact"; cf. v. 17) **the Spirit of God lives** (pres. tense, "is dwelling") **in you** (cf. v. 11). The indwelling Holy Spirit gives a believer a totally different life (2 Cor. 5:17). The opposite, however, is also true: **If anyone does not have the Spirit of Christ, he does not belong to Christ** (lit., "this one is not of Him"). Since only the Holy Spirit gives spiritual life, a person cannot be related to Christ apart from the Spirit.

The interchange of the titles "Spirit of God" and "Spirit of Christ" argues for the deity of Jesus Christ. This statement also makes it clear that the indwelling presence of the Holy Spirit is the identifying mark of a believer in Jesus Christ (cf. 1 John 3:24; 4:13). Another significant fact is that Romans 8:10 equates the indwelling presence of Christ (**Christ is in you**) with the indwelling presence of the Holy Spirit (vv. 9, 11). This adds further support to the biblical doctrine of the Trinity. Verse 10, like verses 9b and 11, is a conditional statement in which in Greek the condition is assumed to be true; **if** can be understood as "since" or "because." As a result of Christ's indwelling presence, **your body is dead** (or, "subject to death"; cf. 7:24) **because of sin, yet your spirit is alive because of righteousness.** Because of God's imputed righteousness, a believer is alive spiritually. The eternal, spiritual life of God is implanted by the indwelling Holy Spirit and Jesus Christ here and now, even though a believer's body is mortal.

Then Paul wrote about an even better promise (8:11). Since God **raised Jesus from the dead** (lit., "out from dead ones"; cf. 4:24; 6:4), God promises believers in whom His **Spirit . . . is living** (cf. 8:9) that He **will also give life to** their **mortal bodies through His Spirit.** In other words, God promises spiritual resurrection life now (6:4, 8, 11) for each believer's mortal body and physical resurrection in the future for that mortal body (6:5; 1 Cor. 6:14; 15:42, 53; 2 Cor. 4:14).

8:12-14. Paul drew a conclusion and made an application from his previous discussion. **Therefore . . . we have an obligation.** Each believer's responsibility is a positive one—to live each day in the control and power of the Holy Spirit. But first Paul expressed this truth negatively—**not to the sinful nature, to live according to it.** Each Christian is to refuse to follow the inclinations and desires of his sin nature. He is to deny the efforts of that nature to impose its lifestyle on him (cf. Titus 2:12). The reason is that a **sinful** manner of life results in death. This does not suggest that a believer who sins will face eternal death in hell; instead, it means he will not enjoy his spiritual life. He will seem like an unsaved person (1 Cor. 3:1-4) and will be unable to enjoy the indwelling presence of the Spirit. **You**

will die is literally, "you are about to die," or "you are at the point of dying." On the other hand, **if by the Spirit you put to death** (pres. tense, "are putting to death") **the misdeeds of the body, you will live.** A few Greek manuscripts have "flesh" instead of "body." But the body is the vehicle by which one's sin-nature expresses itself (cf. Rom. 6:6, 13). Only by the Holy Spirit's power can a believer put to death the sins of his former life (cf. Eph. 4:22-31; Col. 3:5-9). This is what Paul referred to when he said "count yourselves dead to sin" (Rom. 6:11).

Paul then continued his explanation. **Those who are led** (pres. tense, "are being led") **by the Spirit of God are sons of God.** Many Bible students see no difference between the word translated "sons" in 8:14 and the word translated "children" in verse 16. However, in verse 16 the Holy Spirit's indwelling presence attests *the believer's birth relationship to God* (*tekna*, "children," is lit., "born ones"). But in verse 14 the Holy Spirit's control and direction attests *the believer's privileges in God's family* as a "son" (*huios* means a child mature enough to take on adult family privileges and responsibilities). A son in God's family is led by God's Spirit.

8:15-17. In contrast with the control of sin, which enslaves to the point of **fear,** believers have **received the Spirit of sonship.** The word translated "sonship" (*huiothesias*) means "placing as a son" and is frequently translated "adoption" (as in, e.g., v. 23). Believers are adopted sons (Gal. 4:5; Eph. 1:5), not slaves (Gal. 4:7); so they need not be enslaved to sin or in fear. In New Testament times adopted sons enjoyed the same privileges as natural-born sons. So, instead of cowering in slave-like fear, Christians can approach God in an intimate way calling Him **Abba, Father.** "Abba" is a Greek and English transliteration of the Aramaic word for father (used elsewhere in the NT only in Mark 14:36; Gal. 4:6). Besides being adopted into God's family as sons, believers also are His children (*tekna*, "born ones") by the new birth (John 1:12; 1 John 3:1-2). And **the** Holy **Spirit,** who gives believers life, **testifies with** (not to) their **spirit**(s) of the fact of the new birth.

In many families children inherit their parents' estates; each child is an heir and the children together are co-heirs.

Similarly, since Christians **are God's children,** they **are** His **heirs** (cf. Gal. 4:7), **and** they are **co-heirs with Christ.** They are recipients of all spiritual blessings (Eph. 1:3) now, and in the future they will share with the Lord Jesus in all the riches of God's kingdom (John 17:24; 1 Cor. 3:21-23). Sharing with Jesus Christ, however, involves more than anticipating the glories of heaven. For Jesus Christ it involved suffering and abuse and crucifixion; therefore being co-heirs with Christ requires that believers **share in His sufferings** (cf. John 15:20; Col. 1:24; 2 Tim. 3:12; 1 Peter 4:12). In fact believers do share in His sufferings; **if indeed** translates *eiper*, which means "if, as is the fact" (cf. Rom. 8:9). Then after the suffering they will **share in His glory** (2 Tim. 2:12; 1 Peter 4:13; 5:10).

E. Goal of sanctification (8:18-27)

8:18. In one sense this verse is the conclusion of the preceding paragraph in which believers are assured of being heirs of Christ's coming glory. However, Paul reminded his readers that sharing in the glory of Christ in the future required sharing "in His sufferings" in this life. But after careful figuring (*Logizomai*, **I consider**) Paul concluded **that our present sufferings are** far outweighed by **the glory that will be revealed in** (as well as to and through) **us.** This future glory is so great that present sufferings are insignificant by comparison. Also the glory is forever, whereas the suffering is temporary and light (2 Cor. 4:17). Certainly this truth can help believers endure afflictions. Romans 8:18 also serves as a topic sentence for the following discussion on the relationship between believers and the whole Creation, both in their afflictions and in their future glory.

8:19-21. The interrelationship of man with the physical creation of which he is a part and in which he lives was established in God's sentence of judgment on Adam after the Fall (Gen. 3:17-19). In Romans 8:19-21 Paul demonstrated that this relationship has a future aspect in connection with God's program of salvation for people. He declared, **The Creation waits in eager expectation** (lit., "for the strained expectation [*apokarado-kia* is used only one other time in the NT, in Phil. 1:20] of the Creation keeps on eagerly awaiting") **for the sons of God to**

be revealed. The verb for "eagerly waits" (*apekdechomai*) is used seven times in the New Testament, each time to refer to Christ's return (Rom. 8:19, 23, 25; 1 Cor. 1:7; Gal. 5:5; Phil. 3:20; Heb. 9:28). The revealing of the sons of God will occur when Christ returns for His own. They will share His glory (Rom. 8:18; Col. 1:27; 3:4; Heb. 2:10), and will be transformed (Rom. 8:23). All of nature (inanimate and animate) is personified as waiting eagerly for that time.

The reason for this eager anticipation is stated in verse 20. **For the Creation was subjected to frustration.** The Greek word *mataiotēti* ("futility, frailty, purposelessness"; cf. Eph. 4:17; 2 Peter 2:18) describes the change and "decay" (cf. Rom. 8:21) that prevails in all created things. This was not a voluntary subjection because the created world as such had no choice. Instead it was a decree of God, the sovereign Creator, **who subjected it.** (This probably refers to God, not, as some have suggested, to Adam.) And yet it was **in hope,** that is, in anticipation of a coming day when the "frustration" would be removed (cf. vv. 24-25). God judged the totality of His Creation along with people for their sin (Gen. 3:14, 17-19).

When God's program of salvation for people is completed and **the children of God** together experience their **glorious freedom** from sin, Satan, and physical decay, then **the Creation itself will be liberated from its bondage to decay.** God had cursed the physical Creation as a part of His judgment on people for sin because of their position and authority over the Creation as God's representatives (Gen. 1:26-30; 2:8, 15). Similarly, since God's program of salvation for people is one of a new Creation (2 Cor. 5:17; Gal. 6:15), the physical world also will be re-created (Rev. 21:5). This will take place in two stages. First will be the renovation of the present cosmos in conjunction with the return to earth of the Lord Jesus and the establishment of the messianic kingdom on earth (Isa. 11:5-9; 35:1-2, 5-7; 65:20, 25; Amos 9:13). The second stage will be creation of "a new heaven and a new earth" (Rev. 21:1; cf. 2 Peter 3:7-13).

8:22-23. In one sense verse 22 is an appropriate conclusion to the preceding paragraph, summing up the present cursed state of the physical creation. Paul said, **We know** (*oidamen,* continuing state of knowledge that grows out of perception) **that the whole Creation has been groaning as in the pains of childbirth** (lit., "keeps on groaning together and keeps on travailing together") **right up to the present time.** The emphasis on "together" in these verbs does not include believers in Christ, who are specifically mentioned in verse 23, but involves the various parts of the natural Creation. At the same time verse 22 introduces this new paragraph, which sets forth the hope of future deliverance from suffering under the curse of sin.

Paul had begun this section by referring to the believers' "present sufferings" (v. 18), a subject to which he returned in verse 23. Believers are described as the ones having **the first-fruits of the Spirit.** This is an appositional use of the genitive and means that the Holy Spirit *is* "the firstfruits" (*aparchēn*) of God's work of salvation and re-creation in believers. Elsewhere the Holy Spirit is called "a deposit (down payment or earnest) guaranteeing our inheritance" (Eph. 1:14; cf. 2 Cor. 1:22), a similar idea. A farmer's "firstfruits" were the initial harvesting of his first-ripened crops. This first installment was a foretaste and promise that more harvest was to come. Similarly God the Holy Spirit, indwelling believers, is a foretaste that they will enjoy many more blessings, including living in God's presence forever.

Because of "present sufferings" (Rom. 8:18) believers, like the Creation, **groan inwardly** (cf. v. 22; 2 Cor. 5:2) as they **wait eagerly** (from *apekdechomai,* the same word used of the Creation in Rom. 8:19 and of the manifestation of hope in v. 25) **for their adoption as sons,** which is identified as **the redemption of** their **bodies.** The word "adoption" (*huiothesian,* "placing as a son"; trans. "sonship" in v. 15) describes a believer's legal relationship to God as a result of God's grace received by faith. (Regeneration, however, describes a believer's relationship to God as a result of the new birth.) Israel had received adoption by God (9:4), a reality undoubtedly growing out of her covenantal ties with God (Deut. 7:6-9). In one sense each believer has already received the adoption because he has "received the Spirit of sonship" (lit., "adoption," Rom. 8:15) and is a son of God (Gal. 4:6-7). At the same time, as Romans 8:23 states, believers still anticipate their adoption in its completeness, which is said to be "the redemption" (*apolytrōsin*; etymologically the Gr. word describes a release or deliverance or manumission achieved by a ransom payment [*lytron*]; cf. comments on 3:24) of their bodies. This is called the revelation of the sons of God (8:19) and "the glorious freedom of the children of God" (v. 21). It will occur at the Rapture of the church when believers will be raised and transformed with glorious bodies (1 Cor. 15:42-54; 2 Cor. 5:1-5; Phil. 3:20-21; 1 Thes. 4:13-18). Paul called that day "the day of redemption" (Eph. 4:30).

8:24-25. God has promised that a believer's body will finally be delivered from sin and its effects by the work of His Son. Those who respond by faith to that promise have **hope,** a confident expectation of that bodily redemption (cf. Gal. 5:5). This is the final step of salvation and it was in that anticipation that **we were saved.** The redemption of the body (Rom. 8:23) obviously has not yet occurred (**Who hopes for what he already has?**), but it is hoped for and eagerly anticipated (**wait** is from *apekdechomai*; cf. vv. 19, 23) with steadfast endurance (**patiently** is lit., "through endurance") in present sufferings (v. 18).

8:26-27. These verses point out that believers are not left to their own resources in their sufferings (v. 18) and groaning (v. 23). **The Spirit helps** (pres. tense, "keeps on helping") **us in** (the Gr. here does not have the words rendered "us in") **our weakness.** It is not that the Spirit helps in those occasional times *when* Christians are weak; their state is one of weakness and the Spirit continually helps them. The Greek word for weakness (*astheneia*) may include physical, emotional, and spiritual disability (cf. comments on James 5:14) evidenced by inward "groaning" (Rom. 8:23). "Helps" translates *synantilambanetai*, a rich word that pictures someone helping another carry a heavy load. (It is used elsewhere in the NT only in Luke 10:40.)

One evidence of their weakness is the fact that believers **do not know what they ought to pray** (lit., "what we should pray as it is necessary"). In their weakness both the content and the manner of proper prayer eludes them, **but the Spirit Himself** comes to their rescue and **intercedes** (pres. tense, "keeps on interceding") **for us with groans that words cannot express.** Natural Creation groans (Rom. 8:22) and believers groan (v. 23), and so does the Holy Spirit. This has nothing to do with praying in tongues, as some suggest. The groaning is done by the Holy Spirit, not believers, and is not stated in words. The help the Spirit gives (v. 26) is His interceding. "Intercedes" translates *hyperentynchanei*, which occurs only here in the New Testament; it means "approaches or appeals to someone." The One **who searches our hearts** is God (1 Sam. 16:7; Heb. 4:13), and He **knows** (*oiden*, "knows perceptively or intuitively") **the mind of the Spirit, because the Spirit intercedes** (*entynchanei*; cf. Rom. 8:26) **for the saints in accordance with God's will.** Even though the Spirit's words are not expressed, the Father knows what the Spirit is thinking. This is an interesting statement about the Father's omniscience and the intimacy within the Trinity. The Lord Jesus continually intercedes for believers in God's presence (v. 34; Heb. 7:25) and the Holy Spirit also intercedes on their behalf! Though believers are ignorant of what to pray for and how to voice those requests, the Spirit voices their requests for them.

F. Certainty of sanctification (8:28-39)

This section on the doctrine of a believer's sanctification (vv. 28-39) logically follows the discussion of its goal or end (vv. 18-27). To discuss the goal of sanctification—a believer's hope, which he awaits eagerly and steadfastly—is pointless unless realizing that goal is certain. God provided that certainty and confirms the believer's hope, since sanctification from its beginning in regeneration to its completion in glorification is ultimately God's work, which believers appropriate by faith (cf. Phil. 1:6).

8:28. Believers, Paul began, know of sanctification's certainty, and that knowledge is gained by spiritual perception. Christians **know** intuitively (*oidamen*)—though they may not always fully understand and sense it experientially—**that in**

all things God works for the good of those who love Him (lit., "to the ones who love God He works all things together unto good"). The things themselves may not be good, but God harmonizes them together for believers' ultimate good, because His goal is to bring them to perfection in His presence (cf. Eph. 1:4; 5:27; Col. 1:22; Jude 24). Even adversities and afflictions contribute to that end. The active voice present tense of the verb *synergei* ("He works together") emphasizes that this is a continuing activity of God. And His working is on behalf of "those who love Him," who are further identified as the ones **who have been called according to His purpose.** It is significant that a believer's love for God *follows* God's calling of him and is undoubtedly the product of the indwelling Holy Spirit (cf. Rom. 5:5; 1 John 4:19). The word for "purpose" is *prothesin*, God's plan (Paul used the same word in Rom. 9:11; Eph. 1:11; 3:11). "Called" means more than being invited to receive Christ; it means to be summoned to and given salvation (cf. Rom. 1:6; 8:30).

8:29-30. These verses give Paul's explanation of what it means to be one who has "been called according to His purpose" and why God keeps on working all their experiences together to their benefit (v. 28). Believers are those God foreknew. This does not mean simply that God foreknows *what* believers will do, but that God foreknows *them.* Nor does divine foreknowledge merely mean an awareness of or acquaintance with an individual. Instead it means a meaningful relationship with a person based on God's choice (cf. Jer. 1:4-5; Amos 3:2) in eternity before Creation. "He chose us in Him before the Creation of the world" (Eph. 1:4).

This eternal choice and foreknowledge involves more than establishing a relationship between God and believers. It also involves the goal or end of that relationship: **Those God foreknew He also predestined to be conformed to the likeness of His Son** (cf. 1 John 3:2). The entire group that is brought into relationship with God in His eternal plan by divine foreknowledge and choice is **predestined** (*proōrisen*, "predetermined"; cf. Eph. 1:5, 11). God determined beforehand the believers' destiny, namely,

conformity to the image of Jesus Christ. By all saints being made like Christ (ultimate and complete sanctification), Christ will be exalted as **the Firstborn among many brothers.** The resurrected and glorified Lord Jesus Christ will become the Head of a new race of humanity purified from all contact with sin and prepared to live eternally in His presence (cf. 1 Cor. 15:42-49). As the "Firstborn" He is in the highest position among others (cf. Col. 1:18).

Between the start and finish of God's plan are three steps: being **called** (cf. Rom. 1:6; 8:28), being **justified** (cf. 3:24, 28; 4:2; 5:1, 9), and being **glorified** (cf. 8:17; Col. 1:27; 3:4), and in the process not a single person is lost. God completes His plan without slippage. "Glorified" is in the past tense because this final step is so certain that in God's eyes it is as good as done. To be glorified is another way of saying that God's children will be "conformed" to His Son; and that is God's ultimate "purpose." No longer will they "fall short of the glory of God" (Rom. 3:23).

8:31-32. It is astounding to realize that God's plan of salvation for people is a program that reaches from eternity past to eternity future which God will carry out perfectly. Recognizing this, Paul asked and answered (in vv. 31-39) seven questions to drive home the truth that a believer's eternal salvation is completely secure in God's hands. The first question is general, **What, then, shall we say in response to this?** (cf. 4:1; 6:1; 9:14, 30) The obvious response to 8:28-30 would be to say "Hallelujah," or to stand in open-mouthed amazement.

This leads to a series of six more specific questions. The first is, **If God is for us, who can be against us?** Obviously, Satan and his demonic hosts are against believers (cf. Eph. 6:11-13; 1 Peter 5:8), but they cannot ultimately prevail and triumph over believers. God is the self-existent One and the sovereign Creator and, since He is for believers, no one can oppose believers successfully. He is for believers to the extent that **He . . . did not spare His own Son, but gave Him up for us all.** The word "spare" (*epheisato,* from *pheidomai*) is the same word used in the Septuagint in Genesis 22:12 where the NIV translates it "withheld." God said to Abraham, "You have not withheld your son." Then God directed Abraham to spare Isaac and to offer a ram as a substitute (Gen. 22:2-14), whereas God offered His own Son as the Sacrifice for sin (John 1:29). In view of this supreme act of God's grace, **How will He not also, along with Him, graciously give us all things?** Since God gave the greatest Sacrifice of all, His own Son, He will certainly not hesitate to give believers all other things pertaining to and leading to their ultimate sanctification (cf. 2 Peter 1:3).

8:33-34. The next two questions Paul raised and answered are forensic or legal in nature. **Who will bring any charge** (*enkalesei*, "make a formal accusation in court; press charges"; cf. Acts 19:40; 23:29; 26:2) **against those whom God has chosen?** Satan is identified as "the accuser" of God's people (Rev. 12:10; cf. Zech. 3:1). His accusations are valid, because they are based on the believer's sinfulness and defilement. But Satan's accusations will be thrown out of court, because **it is God who justifies.** The Judge Himself declares the accused person righteous on the basis of his faith in Jesus Christ (Rom. 3:24; 5:1). As a result all accusations are dismissed and no one can bring an accusation that will stand.

The related question is, **Who is He that condemns?** The Greek participle *ho katakrinōn* can have a future sense, "will condemn," which seems preferable here. (Cf. *katakrima*, "condemnation, punishment" in 8:1.) Jesus Christ is God's appointed Judge (John 5:22, 27; Acts 17:31), so Paul answered this question by stating, **Christ Jesus.** But Jesus is the very One whom the believer has trusted for salvation. Furthermore, He is the One **who died—more than that** (lit., "but more") **who was raised to life**—who **is at the right hand of God** (cf. Luke 22:69; Acts 2:33; 5:31; Eph. 1:20; Col. 3:1; Heb. 1:3, 13; 8:1; 10:12; 12:2; 1 Peter 3:22) **and is also interceding for us.** The Lord Jesus Christ is indeed the Judge, but He is also the One with whom each believer is identified by faith. As a result he is a believer's Sacrifice for sin (cf. Rom. 5:8; 8:32), his new life (a believer shares in Christ's resurrection life; 6:4, 8, 11; Eph. 2:5-6; Col. 2:13), his Intercessor (cf. Heb. 7:25; also the Holy Spirit intercedes, Rom.

8:26-27) and his Defense (1 John 2:1). Certainly the Judge will not condemn His own who are in Him by faith! (cf. Rom. 8:1)

8:35-37. Paul's final questions are in verse 35: **Who shall separate us from the love of Christ?** The context (vv. 37, 39) shows that "the love of Christ" is His love for believers (not their love for Him; cf. 5:5). The apostle suggested seven things a believer might experience (Paul experienced all of them; 2 Cor. 11:23-28) that some might think could come between a believer and Christ's love—**trouble** (*thlipsis*, "pressure or distress"; mentioned frequently by Paul in 2 Cor.) **or hardship** (*stenochōria*, lit., "narrowness," i.e., being pressed in, hemmed in, crowded) **or persecution or famine or nakedness or danger or sword.** These things—stated in increasing intensity—do not separate Christians from Christ; instead they are part of the "all things" (Rom. 8:28) God uses to bring them to conformity to His Son. Then Paul quoted Psalm 44:22 to remind his readers that in this life the people of God must face much affliction (cf. John 16:33) including even martyrdom for some. In the early days of the church one or more Christians were martyred every day, or faced the possibility of it. Their persecutors valued Christians' lives as nothing more than animals to be butchered.

In all these adversities (cf. "all things" in Rom. 8:28 and "all things" in v. 32 with **all these things** in v. 37), rather than being separated from Christ's love, believers are **more than conquerors** (pres. tense, *hypernikōmen*, "keep on being conquerors to a greater degree" or "keep on winning a glorious victory") **through Him who loved us.** Jesus Christ and His love for believers enable them to triumph (cf. 2 Cor. 2:14).

8:38-39. Paul then ended his discussion on believers' safety in Jesus Christ and the certainty of their sanctification with a positive declaration—**For I am convinced** (perf. tense, "I stand convinced"; cf. 15:14) **that** nothing can **separate** believers **from the love of God** (God's love for them, not their love for God; cf. v. 35). Paul's list of 10 items begins with death, where the list of 7 items in verse 35 ended. These elements in God's universe include the extremes of existence: (1) **death** and (2) **life** (in either death [2 Cor. 5:8-9] or life, believers are in God's presence); the extremes of created spiritual armies: (3) **angels** and (4) **demons** (angels would not and demons could not undo God's relationship with His redeemed ones); the extremes in time: (5) **the present** and (6) **the future** (nothing known now, e.g., the hardships listed in Rom. 8:35, or in the unknown time to come); spiritual enemies: (7) **powers** (perhaps Satan and his demons; cf. Eph. 6:12; or possibly human governments); the extremes in space: (8) **height** and (9) **depth** (nothing overhead or underneath can suddenly come swooping down or up to sever believers from God's love); and (10) everything in the entire created realm. Absolutely nothing in His **Creation** can thwart His purpose for believers **in Christ.** What a climactic way to affirm the certainty of believers' salvation!

V. God's Righteousness Revealed in Sovereign Choice (chaps. 9–11)

Since God is the self-existent Being who is the Creator of everything that exists outside Himself, He is sovereign and can therefore use and dispose of His Creation as He wishes. This sovereignty reveals not only His personal righteousness but also His provided righteousness.

A. God's sovereign choice enunciated (9:1-29)

Paul here discussed God's sovereign choice because of a practical problem. The Jews gloried in the fact that as Israelites they were God's Chosen People (Deut. 7:6; cf. Rom. 2:17-20a; 3:1-2). But now in God's program of salvation in the church, Jewish involvement was decreasing while Gentile participation was becoming dominant. Had God, then, abandoned the Jewish people? This is ultimately explained by God's sovereign choice, a principle which has always been in operation even within the Chosen People of Israel and between Israel and other nations. Now this principle operates in God's purposes for Israel and the church and in His dealings with Jews and Gentiles within the church.

1. ISRAEL'S PRIVILEGES (9:1-5)

9:1-5. By repetition in positive and negative terms (internally attested by the witness of his own **conscience** [cf. comments on 2:15] in the presence of **the Holy Spirit**) Paul affirmed his deep **anguish** of **heart** over the rejection of the gospel by the vast majority of Jews. His desire for their salvation was so strong that he was at the point of wishing (imperf. tense, **I could wish**) **that** he **were cursed and cut off from Christ for** his kinsmen, the Israelites.

Paul then listed seven spiritual privileges which belonged to the people of Israel as God's chosen nation: **the adoption as sons** (cf. Ex. 4:22), **the divine glory** (cf. Ex. 16:10; 24:17; 40:34; 1 Kings 8:11), **the covenants** (Gen. 15:18; 2 Sam. 7:12-16; Jer. 31:31-34), **the receiving of the Law** (Deut. 5:1-22), **the temple worship** (*latreia,* "sacred service," which may also include service in the tabernacle), **and the promises** (esp. of the coming Messiah). Also the Israelites were in the line of promise from its beginning in **the patriarchs** (cf. Matt. 1:1-16; Rom. 1:3) to its fulfillment in the Messiah, **who is God over all, forever praised! Amen.** This is a clear affirmation of the deity of Messiah. Some take these words as a separate sentence (see NIV marg.), but the NIV text seems preferable.

2. THE CHOICE ILLUSTRATED (9:6-18)

a. Isaac over Ishmael (9:6-9)

9:6-9. The failure of the Jews to respond to the gospel of Christ did not mean **God's Word had failed.** Instead this rejection was simply the current example of the principle of God's sovereign choice established in the Old Testament. Paul reminded his readers of a truth he had presented earlier: **For not all who are descended from Israel are Israel,** that is, spiritual Israel (cf. 2:28-29).

Then Paul gave three Old Testament illustrations of God's sovereignty (Isaac and Ishmael, 9:7b-9; Jacob and Esau, vv. 10-13; and Pharaoh, vv. 14-18). The first two show that God made a sovereign choice among the physical descendants of Abraham in establishing the spiritual line of promise. Ishmael, born to Hagar (Gen. 16)—and the six sons of Keturah as well (Gen. 25:1-4)—were Abraham's **descendants** (*sperma*), but they were not counted as **Abraham's children** (*tekna,* "born ones") in the line of promise. Instead, as God told Abraham (Gen. 21:12), **It is** through Isaac that your offspring will be reckoned (lit., "in Isaac seed [*sperma*] will be called to you"). Paul repeated the principle for emphasis in different words: **It is not the natural children** (lit., "the born ones of the flesh") **who are God's children** (*tekna*, "born ones of God"), **but it is the children** (*tekna*) **of the promise who are regarded as Abraham's offspring** (*sperma*). To be a physical descendant of Abraham is not enough; one must be chosen by God (cf. "chosen" in Rom. 8:33) and must believe in Him (4:3, 22-24). God's assurance that **the promise** would come through Isaac, not Ishmael, was given to Abraham: **At the appointed time I will return, and Sarah will have a son** (a somewhat free quotation of Gen. 18:10 from the LXX).

b. Jacob over Esau (9:10-13)

9:10-13. The second Old Testament illustration of God's sovereign choice is drawn from the second generation of Jewish ancestry. Apparently God purposed to establish this principle clearly at the beginning of His relationship with His Chosen People. This illustration emphasizes God's sovereignty even more than the first since it involves God's choice of one twin over another. (In the case of Abraham's sons, God chose the child of one woman over the child of another woman.) In addition, in the case of **Rebecca's children** God's choice was indicated **before the twins were born or had done anything good or bad.** This demonstrated that **God's** sovereign choice was **not by works,** even foreseen works, **but by Him who calls** (cf. "called" in 1:6; 8:28, 30). God's plan (8:28; 9:11), and not man's works (4:2-6), is the basis of His **election.** Rebecca was informed, **The older will serve the younger** (cf. Gen. 25:23), a divine choice confirmed by God's declaration, **Jacob I loved, but Esau I hated** (cf. Mal. 1:2-3). Esau, the older, did not actually serve Jacob, his younger twin; but Esau's descendants, the Edomites, did (cf. 1 Sam. 14:47; 2 Sam. 8:14; 1 Kings 11:15-16; 22:47; 2 Kings 14:7). God's "love" for Jacob was revealed in His choice of Jacob and God's "hatred" for Esau was seen in His rejecting Esau for the line of promise. Hatred in this sense is not absolute but relative to a higher choice (cf. Matt. 6:24; Luke 14:26; John 12:25).

c. Pharaoh (9:14-18)

9:14-18. With the words, **What then shall we say?** (cf. 4:1; 6:1; 8:31) Paul introduced the question undoubtedly in his readers' minds, **Is God unjust** in choosing Isaac over Ishmael, and Jacob over Esau? The Greek negative particle (*mē*) with a question implies a negative response. Paul responded in his usual emphatic way, **Not at all!** (*mē genoito;* cf. comments on 3:4) The issue in such matters is not justice but sovereign decision, as God's word **to Moses** (Ex. 33:19) quoted by Paul indicates. As the sovereign God, He has the right to show **mercy** to whomever He chooses. In fact, He is not under obligation to extend mercy to *anyone.* **Therefore** experiencing His mercy **does not . . . depend on man's desire** (lit., "the one willing") **or effort** (lit., "the one running"). No one deserves or can earn His **mercy.**

The Apostle Paul then presented his third illustration, the Egyptian **Pharaoh** of the Exodus. To him God said through Moses, **I raised you up** (i.e., brought you onto the scene of history) **to display My power in you and that My name might be proclaimed in all the earth** (cf. Ex. 9:16). God's power (cf. Rom. 9:22) was demonstrated as He freed the Israelites from under Pharaoh's hand. And other nations heard about it and were awed (Ex. 15:14-16; Josh. 2:10-11; 9:9; 1 Sam. 4:8). It is significant that Paul introduced this quotation with the words, **For the Scripture says,** for he equated the words of God with the words of Scripture. Paul concluded, **God has mercy on whom He wants to have mercy** (cf. Rom. 9:15) **and He hardens whom He wants to harden** ("make stubborn"; cf. Ex. 4:21; 7:3; 9:12; 10:27; 14:4, 8; cf. 14:17). Because of God's choice, Pharaoh then hardened his own heart (Ex. 7:13-14, 22; 8:15, 19, 32; 9:7, 34-35). All this shows that God chooses and works sovereignly, but not arbitrarily. Yet Pharaoh was responsible for his actions.

3. THE CHOICE EXPLAINED (9:19-29)

9:19-21. Once again Paul anticipated the questioning response of his readers: **Then why does God still blame us?** (The Gr. word trans. "then" probably goes with the preceding statement rather than this question, though this also makes good sense.) **For who resists** (perf. tense, "has taken and continues to take a stand against") **His will?** (*boulēmati*, "deliberate purpose") These questions are still raised by those who reject the biblical doctrine of God's sovereignty. If God makes the choices, how can He hold man responsible? Who can go against what He does?

In response Paul reaffirmed the reality of God's sovereignty and the effrontery of such questions. **But who are you, O man, to talk back to God?** (cf. Isa. 45:9) Man, the created one, has no right to question God, the Creator. Paul then quoted a clause from Isaiah 29:16: **Shall what is formed say to Him who formed it, Why did You make me like this?** Drawing an analogy between the sovereign Creator and a potter, Paul asked, **Does not the potter have the right to make out of the same lump of clay some pottery for noble purposes** (lit., "one vessel [pot or vase] unto honor") **and some for common use?** (lit., "unto dishonor") Obviously a potter from the same pile takes some clay to form a finely shaped and decorated vase and takes other clay to make a cooking pot (cf. Jer. 18:4-6). And the clay has no right to complain! The sovereign Creator has the same authority over His creatures, especially in light of man's origin from dust (Gen. 2:7).

9:22-26. Having stated that God is like a potter, Paul now applied this illustration to God's sovereign purpose for different people. He stated the two alternatives as conditional clauses (**What if. . . ?**) and left unstated the obvious common conclusion: Does not God have that right? The one alternative is that **God . . . bore with great patience** (cf. 2 Peter 3:9) **the objects** (lit., "vessels"; cf. Rom. 9:21) **of His wrath—prepared for destruction** (*apōleian*, "ruin"). The perfect participle "prepared" describes past action with a continuing result or state. "Prepared" may be reflexive ("prepared themselves"), but it seems preferable to take it as passive ("were prepared"). The thought is that they have been and are in a state of readiness or ripeness to receive God's wrath. The objects of God's wrath are the unsaved (1:18), who will suffer eternal judgment (John 3:36). God has patiently endured their antagonism to Him (cf. Acts 14:16; Rom. 3:25), but their judgment is coming. Those who oppose

Him and refuse to turn to Him (Matt. 23:37) are then "prepared" by Him for condemnation. They are "storing up [God's] wrath" against themselves (Rom. 2:5). In hell they will experience **His wrath,** and **His power** will be made known (cf. 9:17). God does not delight in wrath, and He did not choose some people to go to hell. **Choosing** (v. 22) should be rendered "willing." Some are prepared by God for eternal judgment not because He delights to do so, but because of their sin. In view of their sin, which makes them "ripe" for destruction, God is willing to exhibit His wrath, and He will do so at the proper time.

The other alternative relates to God's dealings with **the objects** (lit., "vessels"; cf. v. 21) **of His mercy.** God chose them as such in order **to make the riches of His glory known** and **He prepared** them **in advance for glory** (cf. 8:29-31; Col. 1:27; 3:4). The verb "He prepared in advance" (Rom. 9:23) is *proētoimasen*, "He made ready beforehand," which God does by bestowing salvation. (The word "prepared" in v. 22 is *katērtismena*, "are made or prepared or ripened.")

Up to this point Paul had been speaking conditionally and objectively, but in verse 24 he was more direct—**even us**—because he and his readers were some of the vessels of mercy sovereignly chosen by God. God **not only** chose them but **He also called** them, including **Jews** and **Gentiles.** The point is that God's sovereign choice was manifested not only in the Jews' ancestry (in Isaac and Jacob, vv. 6-13), but also in Paul's generation and today. To back up his conclusion and particularly the part about Gentiles, Paul quoted two verses from **Hosea** (2:23; 1:10). God directed Hosea to give his children symbolic names—one son Lo-Ammi (**not my people**) and the daughter Lo-Ruhamah (**not . . . loved**). These represented God's abandonment of the Northern Kingdom of Israel to the Assyrian Captivity and Exile (Hosea 1:2-9).

God was not permanently casting away the people of Israel, however. In the verses quoted by Paul God promised to restore them as His beloved and as His **people.** By ethnic heritage the Gentiles were **not** God's **people,** so Paul was led by the Spirit of God to apply these verses to Gentiles—and Jews also—who were sovereignly chosen by God and **called** to be His people in Christ. The quotation of Hosea 2:23 is rather free with the order of the clauses reversed to fit the application to Gentiles. Paul was applying these verses from Hosea to the Gentiles, not reinterpreting them. He was not saying that Israel of the Old Testament is part of the church.

9:27-29. Here Paul quoted Old Testament verses to support the fact that God in His sovereign choice and calling always includes a Jewish segment, though it is a minority. The passages quoted (Isa. 10:22-23 and 1:9, both from the LXX) make it clear that in God's judgment on rebellious Israel He by sovereign choice preserves and saves a **remnant.** Those promises were fulfilled in the Captivity and Exile of both Israel and Judah and in the destruction of Jerusalem in A.D. 70 and will also be fulfilled in the national end-time deliverance of Israel (Rom. 11:26-27). Even today the same principle is true. Jews who become members of the church, the body of Christ, are what Paul later called "a remnant chosen by grace" (11:5), which included himself (11:1).

B. God's sovereign choice applied (9:30–10:21)

1. ISRAEL'S STUMBLING (9:30–10:4)

9:30-33. Once again Paul asked his familiar rhetorical question, **What then shall we say?** (cf. 4:1; 6:1; 8:31; 9:14) preparatory to his summation of this situation. His identification of **the Gentiles** (lit., "the nations") as the ones who **have obtained . . . a righteousness that is by** (ek, "out from") **faith** is interesting. As Paul stated later, the church included Jewish as well as Gentile believers (11:1-5), but by the time of Paul's third missionary journey the increasing rejection of the gospel by the Jews and the predominance of Gentiles in the church led the apostle to speak of "the Gentiles" as antithetical to **Israel.** The latter **pursued** ("kept on pursuing") **a Law of righteousness, but has not attained it.** "A Law of righteousness" refers to the Mosaic Law (cf. 7:7, 12, 14). To seek to attain righteousness by observing the Law requires that it be kept perfectly (cf. James 2:10). **Why did Israel not attain it? Because they pursued it not by** (ek, "out from") **faith but as if it were by** (ek, "out from") **works.** The Israelites did not

admit their inability to keep the Law perfectly and turn by faith to God for forgiveness. Instead a few of them kept trying to keep the Law by their own efforts. Consequently **they stumbled** (cf. Rom. 11:11) **over the "stumbling Stone."** The Lord Jesus Christ, "the stumbling Stone" (cf. 1 Peter 2:4-8), did not conform to the Jews' expectations, so they rejected Him instead of responding to Him by faith. To show that God anticipated this, Paul quoted from Isaiah 8:14 and 28:16 (cf. Rom. 10:11), combining the two statements to indicate the two contrasting reactions by **men** to the **Stone** that God placed **in Zion** (cf. "Zion" in 11:26).

10:1-4. Having stated the fact of Israel's stumbling in the preceding verses, Paul now explained the reason for that stumbling. But first, in words reminiscent of the opening verses of chapter 9, the apostle expressed his deep personal spiritual burden for the salvation of the people of Israel. Perhaps with his own experience in mind (cf. Acts 26:11; Gal. 1:13-14; Phil. 3:4-6) Paul affirmed, **For I can testify** (pres. tense, "I testify, bear witness") **about them that they are zealous for God.** Israel was called "the God-intoxicated people." Paul had to acknowledge, however, that **their zeal is not based on** (lit., "according to") **knowledge** (epignōsin, "intensive, full knowledge"). The Jews obviously had knowledge of God but not full knowledge. Otherwise they would not have stumbled over Christ by seeking to gain righteousness on the basis of works.

Paul continued his explanation of Israel's failure and their misguided zeal. **Since they did not know** (the participle agnoountes means "being ignorant," here in the sense of not understanding) **the righteousness that comes from God.** The NIV implies that the people of Israel did not understand the God-provided righteousness expounded in this letter to the Christians in Rome (cf. Rom. 1:17). That may be true, even though they should have known from their own Scriptures (cf. Gen. 15:6; Ps. 32:1-2). But here preferably the righteousness in view is the righteousness God requires for people to be accepted by Him, which is God's own infinite righteousness. The Jews did not really understand God's own infinite righteousness, which is why they were continuing to seek **to establish their own** (cf. Isa. 64:6). Little wonder then that **they did not submit to** ("place themselves under") **God's righteousness,** that is, the righteousness God provides through Christ by faith. The Greek in Romans 10:4 includes the coordinating particle *gar,* "for" (not trans. in the NIV). It introduces a statement that is crucial to Paul's explanation of Israel's stumbling— **Christ is the end of the Law so that there may be righteousness for everyone who believes.** The word translated "end" (*telos*) stands in the emphatic first position in the Greek sentence. It means that Christ is the designed end (termination) or Purpose-Goal of the Law (cf. Gal. 3:24), the Object to which the Law pointed.

The Law did not and could not of itself provide righteousness before God for individuals (cf. Rom. 3:20; 7:7). But Christ fulfilled the Law (Matt. 5:17-18) by keeping it perfectly during His sinless life (cf. John 8:46) and then gave His life in payment for the penalty of sin and the broken Law (cf. Eph. 2:15; Col. 2:13-14). The Law then pointed to Him as the Source of the God-provided righteousness it could not supply (Gal. 3:24). A godly Jew who trusted Yahweh and followed the Levitical system, including the sin offering and the trespass offering, would most likely be inclined to respond to Christ by faith and would receive God's righteousness (i.e., be justified; Acts 13:39; Rom. 3:24; 4:3, 5). He then could meet the requirements of the Law by the indwelling Holy Spirit (8:4). Conversely, a Jew who sought by works to establish his own righteousness would not recognize Christ as "the end of the Law" and would stumble over Him.

2. GOD'S GRACIOUS OFFER (10:5-15)

10:5-8. In presenting God's gracious offer of salvation in Christ and the provision of righteousness by faith, Paul first stated the contrast of the by-works approach to achieving righteousness. He wrote, **Moses describes** (lit., "writes") **the righteousness that is by the Law.** Then Paul quoted Leviticus 18:5, **The man who does these things will live by them.** If a Jew were to receive righteousness by keeping the demands of the Law, that would be human achievement; it would not be from God. However, a Jew would need to keep the entire Law perfectly all

his life—an impossible task (James 2:10). But then Paul also quoted Moses in support of his righteousness-by-faith position centered in Christ as "the end of the Law" and the means by which righteousness is available for everyone who believes. It does not seem appropriate that Paul was merely borrowing Moses' words and applying them to something foreign in Moses' thought. This suggests, then, that **righteousness . . . by faith** is not a new concept, but had been proclaimed to Israel by Moses.

The material Paul quoted in Romans 10:6-8 is taken somewhat freely from Deuteronomy 30:12-14 with clauses quoted here and there. The material in Deuteronomy was part of Moses' charge to the generation of Israel about to enter the land of Canaan. This exhortation was the conclusion of Moses' prophetic description of God's dealing with Israel. Blessing was promised for faith and obedience, and chastisement would result from rejection and disobedience. If Israel forsook God, Moses said, she would face worldwide dispersion and affliction. When the people then finally do turn to God in faith, He will restore them to blessing, prosperity, and prominence among the nations (Deut. 30:1-10). The point of Moses' exhortation (Deut. 30:11) is that the generation to whom he was speaking had the message (it was very **near you** and **in your mouth,** Deut. 30:14) and could respond by faith **(in your heart,** Deut. 30:14) and walk with God in obedience. Since the Israelites in Moses' day had the message, they did not need to ask that it be brought down from heaven or that someone "cross the sea to get it" (Deut. 30:13). Instead, **the word** (Moses' instructions) was "near" them (Deut. 30:14).

In effect, Paul indicated that the same truth applied to his generation, with the added fact that Christ had come in the flesh (John 1:14) and had been resurrected. Therefore there was no need for anyone to ask **to bring Christ down** (in His Incarnation) or **to bring Christ up from the dead;** He had already come and had been resurrected. The message of righteousness by faith in Paul's day was "near" his readers (available to them) and this was "the word" (*rhēma,* "saying") **of faith** he was **proclaiming** (*rhēma,* "the spoken word" is also used in Eph. 5:26;

6:17; 1 Peter 1:25). Thus the gospel, "the word of faith," is available and accessible.

10:9-13. In these verses Paul stated the content of that message concerning faith. Confessing **with the mouth that Jesus is Lord** is mentioned first to conform to the order of the quotation from Deuteronomy 30:14 in Romans 10:8. The confession is an acknowledgement that God has been incarnated in Jesus (cf. v. 6), that Jesus Christ is God. Also essential is **heart-**faith **that God raised Him from the dead** (cf. v. 7). The result is salvation. The true order is given in verse 10: **For it is with your heart that you believe and are justified** (lit., "it is believed unto righteousness"), **and it is with your mouth that you confess and are saved** (lit., "it is confessed unto salvation"). Yet these are not two separate steps to salvation. They are chronologically together. Salvation comes through acknowledging to God that Christ is God and believing in Him.

Paul then (v. 11) supported his position by requoting part of Isaiah 28:16 (cf. Rom. 9:33), adding the Greek word translated **everyone.** God responds with the gift of provided righteousness to each individual who believes. Then Paul reminded his readers of God's impartiality, as he did when discussing human sinfulness (3:22). Just as all who sin will be judged, so all who believe will be saved and **richly** blessed. This conclusion also is supported by a quotation from Joel 2:32: **Everyone who calls on the name of the Lord will be saved.** To **call on** the Lord means to pray in faith for salvation. (On the significance of the "name," see comments on Acts 3:16.)

10:14-15. After proclaiming God's gracious offer in Christ, Paul confronted the natural questions that arise, each additional question building on the key verb from the preceding question. God's promise of salvation to "everyone who calls" on Him (v. 13) begins the process. **How, then, can they call on the One they have not believed in?** Previously, to call on the Lord was equated with trusting Him or believing in Him (cf. vv. 11 and 13), but here it follows the believing. When one believes in Christ, he "calls" on Him. Believing, in turn, is based on hearing, and hearing is based on **someone preaching . . . and how can they preach unless they are sent?** (Since the Gr. word

kēryssō, "preach," means "to be a herald, to announce," it is not limited to proclamation from a pulpit.) Carrying God's gracious offer involves human beings whom God has brought to Himself and then uses as His heralds. They share God's message of salvation because He will save everyone who calls on His name. Paul quoted from Isaiah 52:7 concerning the eagerness of the bearers of **good news.** Those who bear it have **beautiful . . . feet,** that is, their message is welcome. In Isaiah 52:7 the messenger announced to Judah that God had ended their Exile in Babylon (cf. Isa. 40:9-11). But Paul applied Isaiah 52:7 to the Jews of his day to whom the gospel was being given.

3. ISRAEL'S REJECTION (10:16-21)

10:16-18. Paul had made it clear that God's gracious offer of righteousness by faith was given to all, Jews and Gentiles alike (cf. v. 12). His focus in this chapter, however, has been on the people of Israel and their response to that offer (cf. v. 1). Therefore when he wrote, **But not all the Israelites** (the Gr. text simply says "all") **accepted the good news,** he obviously had in mind the Jews' failure to respond. ("Accepted" translates *hypēkousan,* a compound of the verb "to hear." It means "to hear with a positive response," and so "to obey, to submit to.") This is borne out by Paul's confirming quotation of Isaiah 53:1: **Lord, who has believed our message?** This failure of the Jews to respond to the good news was true in Jesus' days on earth (John 12:37-41) and in Paul's day as well. However, the indefinite "all" of the Greek text (Rom. 10:16) is appropriate, because the response to the gospel among the Gentiles was also far less than total. Paul explained, **Consequently, faith comes from hearing the message** (lit., "is out from hearing"; cf. v. 14) **and the message is heard through the word of Christ** (lit., "and the hearing is through the saying [*rhēmatos;* cf. v. 17] concerning Christ"). The Greek word *akoē* ("hearing") can mean the thing heard (the message; v. 16) or the act or sense of hearing (v. 17).

Someone, however, might insist that the Jews were not given adequate opportunity to hear the message. So, Paul said, **But I ask** ("say"), **Did they not hear? He** then quoted Psalm 19:4, concerning God's general revelation in the cosmic heavens (cf. Rom. 1:18-20). However, that psalm also discusses God's special revelation in the Old Testament (Ps. 19:7-11). Paul's obvious answer to his question is that Israel had ample opportunity by both general and special revelation to respond to God. Certainly she heard.

10:19-21. With these verses the argument takes a turn. The apostle anticipated another objection. Someone might argue, "Yes, Israel heard but she did not understand that God purposed to offer righteousness by faith to all mankind, including Gentiles." So Paul wrote, **Again I ask** (lit., "But I say"), **did Israel not understand?** (*egnō*, "know") His answer this time was from two Old Testament quotations, one as early as **Moses** (Deut. 32:21) **and** the second by **Isaiah** (Isa. 65:1). Both Old Testament leaders wrote about God's turning to the Gentiles, whom the Jews thought had **no understanding** (*asynetō*, "senseless"; cf. Rom. 1:21, 31). And yet **concerning Israel,** God has been gracious in spite of her disobedience (a quotation of Isa. 65:2). Israel's continuing rebellious and unbelieving disobedience was judged by God's turning to the Gentiles (Rom. 10:20; cf. Acts 8:1-8, 10). At the same time God has not withheld salvation from Jews. He has **held out** His **hands,** imploring them to return to Him.

C. God's sovereign choice fulfilled (chap. 11)

To this point in this major section of Romans (chaps. 9–11) God's personal righteousness and His provided righteousness for people has been displayed primarily in Israel's rejecting Christ and rebelling against God, and in God's choosing and turning to Gentiles in grace. These themes continue in this chapter, but God's sovereign choice also involves His restoring Israel and His being magnified thereby.

1. IN ELECTION OF GRACE (11:1-10)

11:1-6. Paul's transition from chapter 10 is seen in the repetition of his rhetorical clause "I ask" (10:18-19). **I ask then** is literally, "Therefore, I say." The apostle's question is, **Did God reject His people?** In Greek the question is asked to

elicit a negative reply: "God did not reject His people, did He?" This is reinforced by Paul's characteristic negative ejaculation, **By no means!** (*mē genoito;* cf. comments on 3:4) Then Paul presented himself as his first proof. He had responded by faith to Jesus Christ and had received God's provided righteousness, and yet he was **an Israelite** (cf. Phil. 3:5) and of **the tribe of Benjamin.** Though small, Benjamin was a significant tribe (Saul, Israel's first king, was from Benjamin). If God could save Paul (Acts 9; 22; 26), He certainly could save other Jews (1 Tim. 1:15-16). Then he positively declared, **God did not reject His people** (quoted from 1 Sam. 12:22; Ps. 94:14), **whom He foreknew** (*proegnō,* "had a meaningful relationship with"; cf. Amos 3:2; and cf. comments on Rom. 8:29). God had chosen Israel as His covenant people from eternity past and entered into a relationship with them that will never be destroyed (cf. Jer. 31:37).

Paul's second proof that God has not rejected His people was taken from Israel's history during Elijah's ministry. The prophet was deeply depressed, having fled for his life from Jezebel. Paul said, **Elijah . . . appealed to** (*entynchanei,* "petitioned"; trans. "intercedes" in Rom. 8:27 and "is . . . interceding" in 8:34) **God against Israel.** Paul then quoted part of the prophet's complaint (1 Kings 19:10, 14), reversing the order of the details quoted and concluding with Elijah's lament, **I am the only one left, and they are trying to kill me.** Elijah considered himself the only believing person left in Israel. Paul asked, **And what was God's answer** (lit., "the divine response") **to him?** God was not limited to one fearful, depressed prophet; He had **reserved for** Himself a godly remnant in Israel that numbered **7,000** (1 Kings 19:18). The preservation of the faithful remnant was a work of God.

After the historical illustration Paul drew a conclusion for his day: **So too, at the present time there is a remnant chosen by grace** (lit., "a remnant according to the election of grace has come to be"). Paul was only one of many in his generation elected to faith from the people of Israel. In every generation of the church "a remnant chosen by grace" has been called from among the Jews. Paul added that this choice is totally **by**

God's **grace** (cf. Eph. 2:8-9) and he emphasized the antithesis between **grace** and **works** (cf. Rom. 4:4-5; 9:30-32).

11:7-10. Paul then discussed what "a remnant chosen by grace" out of **Israel** meant for the people as a whole. The situation was ironic. The Jews zealously sought to be accepted by God on the basis of works and the righteousness of the Law (cf. 10:2-3). However, they were not accepted by God; only **the elect** were, because of God's sovereign choice by grace. **The others were hardened** (cf. 11:25). What it means to be hardened is seen from Paul's explanatory and supporting quotations. The first is taken from both Deuteronomy 29:3-4 and Isaiah 29:10, and indicates that hardening involves spiritual drowsiness (**stupor** is the rendering of *katanyxeōs*, "a numbness resulting from a sting"), blindness, and deafness (cf. Isa. 6:9-10). The second quotation (in Rom. 11:9-10) is of Psalm 69:22-23, which predicts that the very things which should have been the source of nourishment and blessing to Israel (**table** means their blessings from the hand of God, which should have led them to Christ; cf. Gal. 3:24) became the occasion for their rejection of God (**a snare and a trap, a stumbling block;** cf. Rom. 9:32-33) and God's judgment (**retribution**) on them. Because they refused to receive God's truth (cf. Isa. 6:9-10; John 5:40) **their backs** will **be bent** under the weight of guilt and punishment **forever.**

2. IN GENTILES (11:11-24)

11:11-12. Paul asked still another question he anticipated from his readers. **Did they stumble** (cf. 9:32) **so as to fall beyond recovery?** Literally, the Greek says simply, "Did they stumble so that they fell?" But the tense of the verb "fell" and its contrast with the verb translated "stumble" imply the idea of falling beyond recovery. Once again the question in Greek was worded to elicit a negative answer, and for the 10th and last time in Romans, Paul responded, **Not at all!** (*mē genoito;* cf. 3:4, 6, 31; 6:2, 15; 7:7, 13; 9:14; 11:1) "They" refers to "the others" (v. 7), the majority of the people of Israel, excluding the "remnant chosen by grace" (v. 5).

Israel experienced not a permanent fall, but a stumbling. It served at least two divine purposes: (a) to offer **salvation . . . to the Gentiles,** and (b) **to make Israel envious** (lit., "to the provoking of them to jealousy"; cf. Deut. 32:21). Twice already in his ministry Paul had turned away from unbelieving Jews to the Gentiles (Acts 13:46; 18:6), and he would do so at least once more in Rome (Acts 28:25-28). In so doing he was fulfilling these purposes of God. But Paul was convinced that Israel's **transgression** (*paraptōma,* "false step," which seems to fit with "stumble"; cf. *paraptōma,* trans. "trespass" in Rom. 5:17-18, 20) was temporary. So he looked beyond its immediate results (**riches for the world and . . . riches for the Gentiles**) to the possibility of its removal (**how much greater riches will their fullness bring!**). "World" here means mankind, not the physical world (cf. "world" in 11:15). Certainly the world has been enriched spiritually because of so many Gentiles coming to Christ (cf. comments on "reconciliation" in v. 15). But even greater riches will be enjoyed by Gentiles after the conversion of Israel at the Lord's return (cf. v. 26). Israel's "fullness" suggests a large-scale conversion (cf. "full number [lit., 'fullness'] of the Gentiles," v. 25).

11:13-15. Paul then singled out a part of the Christian community at Rome, saying, **I am talking to you Gentiles.** Though writing, Paul used terms referring to oral communication, a fact with implications for the inspiration of the Scriptures. Paul then affirmed his special position as **the apostle to the Gentiles** (cf. Acts 9:15; Gal. 1:16; 2:7-8; Eph. 3:8), and declared, **I make much of** (lit., "I glorify" or "I magnify") **my ministry.** Part of Paul's purpose for magnifying his service to the Gentiles was to provoke to jealousy his fellow Jews (Rom. 11:11), resulting in the salvation **of some of them** (cf. 9:1-4; 10:1). Any such Jews won to Christ would be part of the "remnant chosen by grace." Then Paul reminded his Gentiles readers that Israel's **rejection** meant the **reconciliation of the world** in the purpose of God. Because Israel rejected Christ, the gospel was taken to these Gentiles. In Scripture reconciliation is a work of God in the death of Christ which does not *actually* restore an individual to fellowship with God but provides the basis for him to be restored to fellowship (cf. 2 Cor. 5:18-20). This statement serves to explain the meaning of the phrases "riches for the world" and "riches for the Gentiles" in Romans 11:12. (When a person comes to Christ by faith God's work of reconciliation is appropriated to him and he then has fellowship with God and the spiritual enmity is removed.)

Because Paul was convinced that Israel's stumbling is temporary, he asked, **What will their acceptance be but life from the dead?** (lit., "out from dead ones") This question explains the clause, "How much greater riches will their fullness bring" (v. 12). Israel's "acceptance" of Christ is related to "the first resurrection" (Rev. 20:4-6), the resurrection of life (John 5:29, KJV). The first resurrection includes dead saints at the Rapture (1 Thes. 4:13-18), martyred Great Tribulation saints raised at Christ's return (Rev. 20:4, 5b), and believing Old Testament saints (Dan. 12:1-2). The second resurrection will include all the wicked dead to be judged at the great white throne judgment (Rev. 20:5a, 12-13). The teaching that there will be one general resurrection of all humanity at one time fails to take these distinctions into account.

11:16. Paul was convinced that Israel's stumbling is temporary rather than permanent and that the nation will be restored as God's people. With two illustrations Paul showed why he believed this. His first illustration was taken from God's instructions to Israel to take "a cake from the first of [their] ground meal and present it as an offering" (Num. 15:20) after they entered the land of Canaan and reaped their first wheat harvest. This offering was to be repeated each year at their harvests. The cake made from the first ground meal of the wheat harvest was sanctified or made holy by being offered to God. As Paul explained, **If the part of the dough offered as firstfruits** (lit., "If the first-fruits") **is holy, then the whole batch is holy** (lit., "the lump is also"). Paul's second illustration was that of a tree: **If the root is holy, so are the branches.**

In both illustrations the principle is the same: what is considered first contributes its character to what is related to it. With a tree, the root obviously comes first and contributes the nature of that type of tree to the branches that come later. With the cake presented to the Lord, the flour for the cake is taken from the ground meal, but that cake is formed and baked first and presented as a firstfruit. Since it is set apart to the Lord first, it sanctifies the whole harvest. The firstfruits and the root represent the patriarchs of Israel or Abraham personally, and the lump and the branches represent the people of Israel. As a result Israel is set apart (holy) to God, and her "stumbling" (rejection of Christ) must therefore be temporary.

11:17-21. In the apostolic generation God put aside as a whole the people of Israel, an action Paul described as one in which **some of the branches have been broken off.** The apostle then spoke directly to Gentile Christians: **And you** (sing.), **though a wild olive shoot, have been grafted in among the others and now share in the nourishing sap from the olive root** (lit., "have become a co-partner of the root of the fatness of the olive"). To be so blessed by God and His grace, however, is no reason to **boast,** which Paul warned against. Since they were like "a wild olive shoot" grafted to a regular cultivated olive tree, they were indebted to Israel, not Israel to them. "Salvation is from the Jews" (John 4:22).

Normally a branch of a cultivated olive tree is grafted into a wild olive tree, the opposite of what Paul spoke of here. But he knew that grafting the wild into the cultivated was not the norm (though it was done), for later he said it was "contrary to nature" (Rom. 11:24).

To reinforce his warning Paul declared, **You do not support the root, but the root supports you.** The root of the tree is the source of life and nourishment to all the branches, and Abraham is "the father of all who believe" (4:11-12, 16-17). So Gentile believers are linked to Abraham; in one sense they owe their salvation to him, not vice versa.

The apostle anticipated the rebuttal a Gentile believer might make: **Branches were broken off so that I could be grafted in.** Though that was not the real reason the branches were broken off, Paul accepted the statement for the sake of argument. Then he pointed out that the real reason the branches were broken off was Israel's **unbelief** and that any Gentile as a grafted-in branch stands (cf. 5:2) **by faith.** Therefore Paul warned Gentile

Christians individually again, **Do not be arrogant** (lit., "Do not think high" of yourself; cf. 12:16) **but be afraid,** have a proper fear of God.

Paul reminded them, **For if God did not spare the natural branches,** Israel, **He will not spare you either.** In Greek this is a first-class condition in which the conditional statement beginning with "if" is assumed to be true. As clearly stated in the previous verses, this speaks of Israel's "fall" (11:11), "loss" (v. 12), and "rejection" (v. 15), for "the branches have been broken off" (v. 17) "because of unbelief" (v. 20). This section (vv. 11-21) explains the righteousness of God's sovereign choice. If God is righteous in temporarily putting aside Israel as a whole for unbelief, He certainly could put aside the Gentiles for boasting and haughtiness.

11:22-24. In these verses Paul summarized his whole discussion of God's sovereign choice in temporarily putting Israel aside corporately and proclaiming righteousness by faith to all mankind. **Consider** (*ide*, "see, behold") **therefore the kindness** (*chrēstotēta*, "benevolence in action"; also used of God in 2:4; Eph. 2:7; Titus 3:4) **and sternness of God.** "Sternness" translates *apotomian*, used only here in the New Testament (cf. the adverb *apotomōs* in 2 Cor. 13:10 ["be harsh"] and Titus 1:13 ["sharply"]). God's sovereign choice involved severity toward the Jews **who** stumbled (**fell;** cf. Rom. 11:11) in unbelief and were hardened (v. 25), but that same decision displayed the goodness of God toward individual Gentiles. God's continuing His goodness to the Gentiles depends on their continuing **in His kindness.** If Gentiles do not continue in God's kindness, they **also will be cut off.** This does not suggest that a Christian can lose his salvation; it refers to Gentiles as a whole (suggested by the sing. **you**) turning from the gospel much as Israel as a nation had done.

Conversely for the people of Israel, **if they do not persist** (lit., "continue") **in unbelief, they will be grafted in, for God is able to graft them in again.** At issue is not God's ability but God's decision. God sovereignly chose to put Israel aside corporately because of unbelief and to extend righteousness by faith to everyone. This demonstrates His decision to graft Gentiles into the spiritual stock of Abraham (cf. 4:12, 16-17; Gal. 3:14).

Obviously, therefore, if the unbelief which caused Israel's rejection by God is removed, God is able and will graft the people of Israel (**the natural branches**) back into the spiritual stock to which they belong (**their own olive tree**). After all, as Paul wrote earlier, "Everyone who calls on the name of the Lord will be saved" (Rom. 10:13).

The "olive tree" is not the church; it is the spiritual stock of Abraham. Believing Gentiles are included in that sphere of blessing so that in the Church Age both Jews and Gentiles are in Christ's body (Eph. 2:11-22; 3:6). Yet someday Israel as a whole will turn to Christ (as Paul discussed in Rom. 11:25-27). This passage does not teach that the national promises to Israel have been abrogated and are now being fulfilled by the church. This idea, taught by amillenarians, is foreign to Paul's point, for he said Israel's fall is temporary. While believing Gentiles share in the blessings of the Abrahamic Covenant (Gen. 12:3b) as Abraham's spiritual children (Gal. 3:8-9), they do not permanently replace Israel as the heirs of God's promises (Gen. 12:2-3; 15:18-21; 17:19-21; 22:15-18).

3. IN ISRAEL'S SALVATION (11:25-32)

11:25-27. Israel's corporate stumbling, which is temporary, not permanent, is called a **mystery.** In Scripture a mystery is not a truth difficult to understand, but a truth previously unrevealed (and therefore unknown) which is now revealed and publicly proclaimed (cf. Eph. 3:9; Col. 1:26; at Matt. 13:10-16, see the chart that lists NT mysteries). Paul wanted to make sure his Gentile readers knew about the mystery concerning Israel in God's sovereign choice. God's purpose was **so that you may not be conceited** (lit., "wise in yourselves"). God's sovereign plan to put Israel aside temporarily in order to show grace to Gentiles is no basis for conceit on the part of the Gentiles; it is designed to display further the glory of God.

God purposed that some from all nations should by faith receive the righteousness provided by grace. In order to achieve this goal Israel's relationship as God's Chosen People was rescinded for a time and **Israel** is now experiencing **a hardening in part until the full number** (*plērōma*, "fullness") **of the Gentiles has come in.** There is a fullness for Israel (Rom. 11:12) and a fullness for the Gentiles. God is now "taking from the Gentiles a people for Himself" (Acts 15:14).

In Romans 11:25 are two specific facts about Israel's hardening (cf. vv. 7-8): (a) it is partial, "in part" (because throughout this time "there is a remnant chosen by grace," v. 5), and (b) it is temporary (because it will end when God's sovereignly chosen number of Gentiles has been saved).

"Hardening" is *pōrōsis* ("hardening, dulling"); it differs from the verb *sklērynei* ("hardens") used of Pharaoh (9:18) and the noun *sklērotēta* ("stubbornness," lit., "hardening," 2:5). The first noun (*pōrōsis*) refers to dullness, the second suggests stubbornness.

After "the fullness of the Gentiles" (11:25, KJV) the partial hardening of Israel will be removed and **all Israel will be saved,** that is, "delivered" (in the OT "saved" often means "delivered") from the terrible Tribulation by the Messiah, **the Deliverer.** To confirm this, Paul quoted from Isaiah 59:20-21 and 27:9. The statement, "All Israel will be saved" does not mean that every Jew living at Christ's return will be regenerated. Many of them will not be saved, as seen by the fact that the judgment of Israel, to follow soon after the Lord's return, will include the removal of Jewish rebels (Ezek. 20:34-38). Following this judgment God will then remove **godlessness** and **sins** from the nation as He establishes His New Covenant with regenerate Israel (cf. Jer. 31:33-34).

11:28-29. Here Paul summarized God's dealings with Israel and with the Gentiles. In order for God to bring **the gospel** to Gentiles He had to deal with Israel corporately as **enemies.** But in relation to God's choice (**election**) of Abraham and His covenant with him and **the patriarchs,** Israel is beloved. Because God chose Abraham, Isaac, and Jacob (cf. 9:6-13), He loves the nation and will carry through on His promises. This is another reason Israel's hardening must be temporary (cf. 11:15, 22-25) and she must finally be saved corporately: God chose her. And **God's gifts and His call are irrevocable** (lit., "for not repented of are the grace-gifts and the calling of God"). He does

not revoke what He has given or whom He has chosen ("call" means election and salvation; cf. 1:6; 8:30).

11:30-32. The Gentiles to whom Paul wrote **were at one time disobedient to God,** but in this Age of Grace Gentiles (**you**) **have now received mercy.** When Adam disobeyed (5:19) all were constituted sinners because all humanity sinned in Adam (5:12). (Cf. "disobedient" in Eph. 2:2; 5:6; and "disobedience" in Heb. 4:6, 11.) Israel (**they**) is **now** corporately **disobedient** to God so **that** when **God's mercy to** the Gentiles (**you**) reaches its full number (Rom. 11:25), Israel will again **receive mercy** (cf. vv. 26-27). God's ultimate purpose is to **have mercy on . . . all.** To do so justly **God has bound** (*synekleisen,* "enclosed, shut in on all sides") **all men over to disobedience.** "All have sinned and fall short of the glory of God" (3:23). "Jews and Gentiles alike are all under sin" (3:9), so that "there is no difference" (3:22). When the Gentiles rejected God and disobeyed Him (1:17-21), God chose Abraham and his descendants as His special people. Now the disobedience of the Jews enables God to show mercy to the Gentiles. Then, when that purpose is achieved, He will again show mercy to Israel corporately.

4. TO GOD'S GLORY AND PRAISE (11:33-36)

11:33-36. As Paul ended his discussion on the revelation of God's righteousness in His sovereign choice, he burst forth in a doxology of praise to God. He exclaimed, **Oh, the depth of the riches of the wisdom and knowledge of God!** The plan of God for the salvation of all people demonstrates God's infinite knowledge and His ability to use it wisely. God has revealed some of **His judgments and His paths** ("ways") so that people may know them, but it is humanly impossible to exhaust them. **Beyond tracing out** translates the one word *anexichniastoi,* which means "incapable of being traced by footprints." In Ephesians 3:8, its only other use in the New Testament, it is rendered "unsearchable" and refers to the riches of Christ.

The apostle then quoted Isaiah 40:13, which shows that **God** is the sole Designer of His wise plan. No one knows His **mind** or gives Him advice. This is followed by a free quotation from Job

41:11, which testifies to God's sole responsibility for His acts. **God** is indeed the Sovereign of all things, the One to whom all creatures are accountable and whom all should glorify. He is under no obligation to **repay** anyone, for no one **has ever given** Him anything. Paul concluded, **For from Him and through Him and to Him are all things.** God is the first Cause, the effective Cause, and the final Cause of everything. His deep ways are beyond man's discovering (Rom. 11:33); beyond man's knowing (v. 34a), beyond man's counseling (v. 34b), and beyond man's giving (v. 35). "All things" come from Him and by means of Him (John 1:3; Col. 1:16a; Rev. 4:11) and are for Him and His glory (Col. 1:16b). Therefore, **To Him be the glory forever! Amen** (cf. Rom. 15:6; 16:27; 1 Peter 4:11; Rev. 5:12-13). God is the only proper One to magnify (1 Cor. 1:31). The all-sovereign God deserves the praise of all His creatures.

VI. God's Righteousness Revealed in Transformed Living (12:1–15:13)

Paul divided several of his letters into two major sections, a doctrinal portion and a practical one. He followed that pattern in this epistle too, though the doctrinal part is more than twice as long as the practical. (In both Eph. and Col. the doctrinal and the practical sections are about equal in length.)

A. The basic consecration (12:1-2)

12:1-2. The start of this practical section is indicated by Paul's exhortation **I urge** (the first word of v. 1 in the Gr. text). **Therefore** also shows a transition (cf. "therefore" in 3:20; 5:1; 8:1). The basis of Paul's exhortation is **God's mercy** (*oiktirmōn*, rendered "compassion" in 2 Cor. 1:3; Phil. 2:1; Col. 3:12, and "mercy" in Heb. 10:28). God's compassion has been described in detail in the first 11 chapters of Romans. The content of Paul's urging is **to offer your bodies** (cf. Rom. 6:13) **as living sacrifices.** A Christian's body is the temple of the Holy Spirit (1 Cor. 6:19-20). In the KJV "offer" is translated "present" (Rom. 12:1) and "yield" (6:13, 16, 19). The word "bodies," mindful of the Old Testament sacrifices, represents the totality of one's life and

activities, of which his body is the vehicle of expression. In contrast with Old Testament sacrifices this is a "living" sacrifice. Such an offering is **holy** (set apart) **and pleasing** (cf. "pleasing" in 12:2) **to God.** Furthermore, it is **spiritual** (*logikēn*; cf. 1 Peter 2:2) **worship** (*latreian*). *Latreian* refers to any ministry performed for God, such as that of the priests and the Levites. Christians are believer-priests, identified with the great High Priest, the Lord Jesus Christ (cf. Heb. 7:23-28; 1 Peter 2:5, 9; Rev. 1:6). A believer's offering of his total life as a sacrifice to God is therefore sacred service. In the light of Paul's closely reasoned and finely argued exposition of the mercies of God (Rom. 1–11), such an offering is obviously a desirable response for believers.

Paul then stated general implications of a believer's offering his life to God as a sacrifice. Such an offering represents a complete change in lifestyle, involving both a negative and a positive aspect. First, Paul commanded, **Do not conform** (lit., "Do not be conformed"; this Gr. word occurs elsewhere in the NT only in 1 Peter 1:14) **any longer to the pattern of this world** (*aiōni*, "Age"). Living according to the lifestyle of "the present evil Age" (Gal. 1:4; cf. Eph. 1:21) must now be put aside. Then Paul commanded, **But be transformed** (pres. passive imper., "keep on being transformed") **by the renewing of your mind.** The Greek verb translated "transformed" (*metamorphousthe*) is seen in the English word "metamorphosis," a total change from inside out (cf. 2 Cor. 3:18). The key to this change is the "mind" (*noos*), the control center of one's attitudes, thoughts, feelings, and actions (cf. Eph. 4:22-23). As one's mind keeps on being made new by the spiritual input of God's Word, prayer, and Christian fellowship, his lifestyle keeps on being transformed.

Paul added, **Then you will be able to test and approve** (*dokimazein*, "prove by testing" [1 Peter 1:7, "proved genuine"], i.e., ascertain) **what God's will is— His good, pleasing** (cf. Rom. 12:1), **and perfect will.** These three qualities are not attributes of God's will as the NIV and some other translations imply. Rather, Paul said that God's will itself is what is good, well-pleasing (to Him), and perfect. "Good," for example, is not an adjective

(God's "good" will) but a noun (God's will is what is good—good, i.e., for each believer).

As a Christian is transformed in his mind and is made more like Christ, he comes to approve and desire God's will, not his own will for his life. Then he discovers that God's will is what is good for him, and that it pleases God, and is complete in every way. It is all he needs. But only by being renewed spiritually can a believer ascertain, do, and enjoy the will of God.

B. In Christian ministry (12:3-8)

12:3-5. A believer's consecration to God and his transformed lifestyle is demonstrated in his exercising his spiritual gifts in the body of Christ. As an apostle of Christ **(by the grace given me;** cf. 1:5; 15:15-16) he warned his readers individually **(every one of you), Do not think of yourself more highly** (hyperphronein, "think higher") **than you ought.** An inflated view of oneself is out of place in the Christian life. Then Paul encouraged them, **But rather think** (phronein) **of yourself with sober judgment** (sōphronein, "sound thinking"), **in accordance with the measure of faith God has given you.** God has given each believer some faith by which to serve Him. By his involved word play on various forms of the verb phroneō, "to think," Paul emphasized that human pride is wrong (cf. 3:27; 11:18, 20) partly because all natural abilities and spiritual gifts are from God. As a result every Christian should have a proper sense of humility and an awareness of his need to be involved with other members of Christ's body. As Paul explained, a parallelism exists between a believer's physical **body** which has parts with differing functions and the community of believers **in Christ** as a spiritual **body** (cf. 1 Cor. 12:12-27; Eph. 4:11-12, 15-16). The point is that **each member** functions to serve the body, not the body to serve the members. The diversity of the **many** accompanies the unity of the body. Therefore it is important to think soundly about oneself and to evaluate properly God's gifts and their uses.

12:6-8. Paul then applied what he had just said (vv. 3-5) to the exercise of God-given abilities for spiritual service (vv. 6-8). He built on the principle, **We**

have different gifts (cf. v. 4, "not all have the same function"; cf. 1 Cor. 12:4). The grace-gifts (charismata) are **according to** God's **grace** (charis). He listed seven gifts, none of which—with the possible exception of **prophesying**—is a sign gift. The Greek text is much more abrupt than any English translation; **let him** is supplied for smoother English. One's "prophesying" is to be done **in proportion to his faith;** a better translation would be "in agreement to the (not 'his') faith." That is, prophesying—communicating God's message, to strengthen, encourage, and comfort (1 Cor. 14:3)—is to be in right relationship to the body of truth already revealed (cf. "faith" as doctrine in Gal. 1:23; Jude 3, 20). The other six gifts mentioned here are **serving . . . teaching . . . encouraging . . . contributing . . . leadership,** and **showing mercy.** Contributing to people's **needs** is to be done with generosity (en haplotēti), not skimpily (cf. 2 Cor. 8:2; 9:11, 13). Managing, leading, or administering (proistamenos, lit., "standing before"; cf. proistamenous, "who are over," 1 Thes. 5:12) is to be done **diligently** (en spoudē, "in eagerness, earnestness"), not lazily or halfheartedly. And bestowing mercy is to be done **cheerfully** (en hilarotēti, "in gladness"), not with sadness. Three of these seven gifts are mentioned in 1 Corinthians 12:28 (prophets, teachers, administration); two (prophets and pastor-teachers) are included in Ephesians 4:11; and two (administering and serving) are listed in 1 Peter 4:10-11. Whatever one's gift, he should exercise it faithfully as a stewardship from God.

C. In social relationships (12:9-21)

This section consists of a lengthy series of short exhortations or commands. The statements relate to a Christian's relationships to other people, both saved and unsaved.

12:9-10. Paul began these specific exhortations with the key ingredient for success: **Love must be sincere.** This is God's love, which has been ministered to believers by the Holy Spirit (5:5) and must be ministered by them to others in the Holy Spirit's power. "Sincere" translates anypokritos (lit., "without hypocrisy"), also used of love (2 Cor. 6:6; 1 Peter 1:22), of faith (1 Tim. 1:5; 2 Tim. 1:5), and of wisdom (James 3:17).

This first command is followed by a pair of related basic commands—**Hate what is evil; cling to what is good.** Many Bible students consider these two clauses as explanatory of the sincerity of love, translating the verse, "Let love be unfeigned, abhorring the evil and cleaving to the good." Hating various forms of sin is frequently mentioned in Scripture (Pss. 97:10; 119:104, 128, 163; Prov. 8:13; 13:5; 28:16; Heb. 1:9; Rev. 2:6). Turning from evil is to accompany adhering to the good (cf. 1 Peter 3:11).

Divine love is to be exercised with other believers. The Greek adjective *philostorgoi,* translated **devoted,** suggests family affection. As in Romans 12:9, the second clause in verse 10 can be understood as explaining the first command. Verse 10 may be translated, "With **brotherly love** have family affection for **one another,** in **honor** giving place to **one another**" (cf. Phil. 2:3, "consider others better than yourselves").

12:11-12. Paul then provided a series of exhortations concerning a believer's personal attitudes, attitudes that will make him more attractive to others. In verse 11 the key thought is the last clause—**serving** (*douleuontes; diakonian* in v. 7 is trans. "serving") **the Lord**—and the first two clauses explain how a believer is to serve as the Lord's "slave" (*doulos;* cf. 1:1): **never . . . lacking** ("not shrinking, not hesitating, not being lazy") **in zeal** (*en spoudē,* "diligence," rendered "diligently" in 12:8), and being fervent in spirit. **Keep your spiritual fervor** is literally, "being fervent, or boiling (*zeontes,* used only here and in Acts 18:25 of Apollos) in the spirit" (either the Holy Spirit or one's inner life). These two commands also balance each other as negative and positive commands (cf. Rom. 12:9). As believers serve God as His slaves they should be enthusiastic and diligent.

The three exhortations in verse 12 can be understood either as independent items or as additional descriptions of how believers should serve the Lord. They are to **be joyful in hope,** because their hope in Christ is the basis of their rejoicing (5:2-5; 1 Peter 1:6-9). **In affliction** (*thlipsei,* "distress, trouble, pressure"; cf. Rom. 8:35) believers are to be **patient** (*hypomenontes,* "being steadfast, having endurance"; cf. 5:3). Also Christians should continue **in prayer** to God for wisdom,

guidance, and strength (cf. 1 Thes. 5:17). Being **faithful,** NIV's translation of *proskarterountes,* should be rendered "persisting in" or "devoted to" (cf. Acts 1:14; 2:42; Col. 4:2).

12:13. Returning to Christians' responsibilities to other believers, Paul exhorted them, **Share with God's people who are in need** (lit., "sharing [*koinōnountes,* 'having in common'] the needs of the saints"). This characterized the Jerusalem church (Acts 2:44-45; 4:32, 34-37). This concern also motivated the church in Antioch (Acts 11:27-30) and the Apostle Paul (1 Cor. 16:1-4; 2 Cor. 8-9; Rom. 15:25-27) to give to the church in Jerusalem. In the same vein the apostle commanded, **Practice hospitality** (lit., "pursuing friendliness to strangers"). Both ministries, meeting needs and being hospitable, involve helping others.

12:14-16. Paul's exhortations in this section relate to a believer's reactions to the actions and emotions of others, whether Christians or not. The hatred displayed in persecution usually evokes response in kind, but Paul commanded, **Bless those who persecute you; bless and do not curse** (cf. Matt. 5:44). Perhaps Paul thought of Stephen (Acts 7:59-60) and of Jesus Christ (Luke 23:34). They both modeled these words and responded to persecution even to death by praying for God's forgiveness of their persecutors.

Christians should be able to empathize with others, both believers and unbelievers. Paul commanded, **Rejoice with those who rejoice; mourn with those who mourn.** Related to this is the next command, **Live in harmony with one another** (lit., "having the same attitude toward one another"; cf. Rom. 15:5; Phil. 2:2; 1 Peter 3:8). Being in harmony with other Christians is basic to being able to empathize with them. This idea is then presented in negative and positive details: **Do not be proud** (lit., "not thinking highly" of yourself; cf. Rom. 11:20; 12:3) and **be willing to associate with people of low position** (cf. James 2:1-9). These orders are summarized in the command, **Do not be conceited** (lit., "Do not become wise concerning themselves"; cf. Prov. 3:7; Rom. 11:25), an attitude that makes empathy impossible.

12:17-18. The exhortations in verses 17-21 relate primarily to believers' relationships with unbelievers, speaking as they do of those who do evil toward believers (v. 17) and are the "enemy" of believers (v. 20). The Old Testament principle of justice was "eye for eye" (Ex. 21:24), but Paul commanded, **Do not repay anyone evil for evil** (cf. 1 Peter 3:9). On the positive side Christians are **to do what is right** (*kala*, "beautiful," used here in the ethical sense of good, noble, and honorable). Paul then commanded believers, **Live at peace with everyone** (cf. "live in harmony with one another," Rom. 12:16). But recognizing that limits exist, Paul included the words, **If it is possible, as far as it depends on you.** Harmony with others may not always be achievable, but believers should not be responsible for that lack of peace (cf. Matt. 5:9).

12:19-21. Referring again to the negative (cf. v. 17a) Paul then exhorted his readers **not** to **take revenge** after they are misused. Instead they should **leave room for God's wrath** (lit., "for the wrath"), because God has promised to avenge His people: **It is Mine to avenge, I will repay** (Deut. 32:35; cf. Heb. 10:30). David's refusal to kill Saul on two occasions when it seemed that God had delivered Saul into David's hands is a classic biblical example of this principle. In light of God's promise to execute vengeance, a Christian should therefore **feed** his **enemy** and quench his thirst—in short, respond to his evil with Christian love. Heaping **burning coals on his head,** along with the first part of Romans 12:20, is a quotation from Proverbs 25:21-22. The coals on the head may refer to a ritual in Egypt in which a person showed his repentance by carrying a pan of burning charcoal on his head. Helping rather than cursing an enemy may cause him to be ashamed and penitent. As Paul summarized, **Do not be overcome by evil,** giving in to the temptation to retaliate, **but overcome evil with good** (cf. Matt. 5:44, "love your enemies"). Again positive and negative commands are put together (cf. Rom. 12:9, 11, 16-20).

D. In relation to authority (13:1-7)

13:1-3. Rome was the imperial capital, the seat of the empire's civil government. As residents in Rome, Paul's initial readers were aware of both the glory and the shame of that city in the days of Nero, who reigned from A.D. 54 to 68. But they were also citizens of Christ's kingdom (Phil. 3:20; Col. 1:13). Appropriately, therefore, Paul discussed a Christian's relationship to his government and civil rulers. Both in its length and specific details this discussion is the key New Testament passage on the subject (cf. 1 Tim. 2:1-4; Titus 3:1; 1 Peter 2:13-17).

The apostle's basic exhortation is, **Everyone must submit himself to the governing authorities** (lit., "higher authorities"). The basic reason for such submission is that those authorities are **established** by **God** (cf. Dan. 4:17, 25, 34-35). An individual **who rebels against the authority,** therefore, **is rebelling against** (lit., "has taken a stand against") **what God has instituted** (lit., "the ordinance of God"). Such persons are thus actually rebelling against God, and bring civil and/or divine **judgment on themselves.** Those who obey and **do right** need have no fear of authorities; in fact, civil leaders **commend** those who do good.

13:4-5. Furthermore, a civil leader **is God's servant,** a concept often forgotten today. By commending those who do right (v. 3), a civil leader himself does **good** (v. 4). But on the other hand he bears arms (**the sword**) as **God's servant** (the second time in this verse Paul referred to the ruler this way; cf. v. 6), as **an agent of wrath.** Governmental force, properly used, helps prevent tyranny and executes justice; it brings **punishment on the wrongdoer.** A Christian has two reasons to be submissive to civil authorities—to avoid **possible punishment** (lit., "the wrath") and to heed his **conscience,** which prods him to obey God's ordinances.

13:6-7. A Christian's responsibility to civil authorities involves more than obedience (vv. 1, 5). It also includes support by paying **taxes** (cf. Matt. 22:21). This is because the leaders, as **God's servants** (cf. Rom. 13:4), are supposed to **give their full time to governing** and need support through taxes from citizens, Christians included. So a Christian ought to **give everyone what** he owes **him** (lit., "repay everyone his dues"), whether substance (**taxes** and **revenue**) or **respect** and **honor.**

E. In light of the future (13:8-14)

13:8-10. Discussion of believers' obligations to civil authorities evidently triggered Paul's thinking concerning believers' debts to others. He commanded, **Let no debt remain outstanding** (lit., "Do not keep on owing anyone anything") **except the continuing debt to love one another** (lit., "except loving one another"). This is not a prohibition against a proper use of credit; it is an underscoring of a Christian's obligation to express divine love in all interpersonal relationships. A Christian should never fall short, and so be "in debt," in loving others (John 13:34-35; 1 Cor. 16:14; Eph. 5:2; Col. 3:14; 1 John 3:14, 23; 4:7, 11, 21).

The importance of continually showing love is seen in the explanation, **For he who loves his fellow man** (lit., "the other one") **has fulfilled the Law** (cf. Matt. 22:39; Mark 12:31). Love, not mere external conformity to rules, is the essence of the Law (cf. Gal. 5:14).

Paul then quoted various specific commands from the social section of the Ten **Commandments.** These prohibitions—**not** to **commit adultery . . . murder . . . steal** and **covet**—are the 7th, 6th, 8th, and 10th commandments, in that order (Ex. 20:13-15, 17). Paul summed up that entire section of the Law by quoting Leviticus 19:18. The Jewish Rabbis and the Lord Jesus summarized the social section of the Law in the same words (cf. Matt. 22:39). Paul then expressed this principle in other words, **Love does no harm** (lit., "Love does not keep on working evil") **to its neighbor,** and then he repeated (cf. Rom. 13:8) his basic assertion that **love** fulfills **the** Mosaic **Law.** Only in Christ can a person meet this or any of the other requirements of the Law (8:4).

13:11. Expressing divine love is a Christian's constant responsibility, but it is especially crucial in **understanding the present time** (lit., "knowing the season"). Paul was not referring to time in general but to the end-time and to the imminent return of the Lord Jesus. It is a time, therefore, for spiritual vigilance and industriousness: **wake up from your** (some mss. have "our," which conforms to the context) **slumber** (cf. Eph. 5:14; 1 Peter 5:8). This need for alertness is **because our salvation** (ultimate or final salvation realized at the return of the Savior; cf. Rom. 8:23; Heb. 9:28; 1 Peter 1:5) **is nearer now than when we first believed** (cf. James 5:8). Each passing day in the faith brings final salvation and deliverance closer.

13:12. Paul considered the time of Christ's return and the consummation of salvation for believers (v. 11) as the start of a new **day.** The present time, while Christ is absent (John 14:2-3; Acts 1:11) and Satan is at work (2 Cor. 4:4; Eph. 2:2), is described as **the night** (cf. 2 Peter 1:19). Since "the day" **is almost here,** Paul urged his readers to **put aside the deeds of darkness and put on the armor of light.** Christians are soldiers in a conflict who need to be alert and equipped for battle (Eph. 6:10-17; 1 Thes. 5:8). Upright, Christ-honoring living is often referred to as being in the light (John 12:36; Eph. 5:8, 14; Col. 1:12; 1 Thes. 5:5; 1 John 1:7; 2:10).

13:13-14. In verse 13 Paul repeated his exhortation of verse 12, changing the figure from warfare to lifestyle. He charged, **Let us behave decently, as in the daytime** (lit., "day"). Crime, violence, and wickedness are associated with darkness and the night (John 1:5; 3:19-20; 8:12; 12:35, 46; Eph. 5:8, 11; 6:12; 1 Thes. 5:7; 1 Peter 2:9; 1 John 1:5-6; 2:9, 11). Perhaps this contrast was suggested to Paul by his phrase "deeds of darkness" (Rom. 13:12). At any rate the activities and attitudes he listed—**orgies and drunkenness . . . sexual immorality and debauchery . . . dissension and jealousy** (cf. Gal. 5:19-21)—are certainly "deeds of darkness." It is interesting that Paul linked jealousy with immorality. Such actions and attitudes have no place in a Christian's life. He belongs to "the light"; these deeds and thoughts belong to the darkness.

A Christian's lifestyle must be pure and holy, especially in view of Christ's approaching return (cf. Rom. 13:11-12; 1 John 3:3). The secret to living chaste lives is for Christians to **clothe** themselves **with the Lord Jesus Christ** (cf. "put on," Eph. 4:24; Col. 3:10). At salvation they were "clothed with Christ" (Gal. 3:27), so they should conduct themselves accordingly. Also the secret includes **not** thinking **about how to gratify the desires of the sinful nature** (lit., "and do not make forethought [*pronoian*] for the flesh [*sarkos*; cf. Rom.

491

8:3-5, 8-9, 12-13] for lusts"). For a Christian to plan out specific ways to gratify his sinful nature is wrong and out of bounds.

F. In dealing with other Christians (14:1–15:13)

Paul had discussed various aspects of a Christian's responsibilities in interpersonal relationships (12:9-21; 13:8-10), but relationships with other believers loom large and involve special problems that require discussion. Harmonious relationships within the family of God are important.

1. WITHOUT JUDGING (14:1-12)

Christians are at different levels of spiritual maturity. They also have diverse backgrounds that color their attitudes and practices. The first lesson to learn in living harmoniously with other Christians, therefore, is to stop judging others.

14:1-4. The focus in these verses is on **him whose faith is weak** (lit., "the one being weak in faith"), which appears in the emphatic first position in the sentence. Paul commanded believers to **accept** (pres. middle imper., "keep on taking to yourselves"; cf. 15:7) such a person, **without passing judgment on disputable matters** (lit., "but not unto quarrels about opinions"). A believer with certain scruples is not to be welcomed into the fellowship with the intent of changing his views or opinions by quarreling with him about them.

One area of differing scruples pertains to food, in particular the eating of meat. **One man's faith allows him to eat everything, but another man, whose faith is weak, eats only vegetables** (lit., "but the one being weak eats vegetables"). The reason some Christians then were vegetarians is not stated. Since the issue is related to their Christian faith, it could be to insure against eating meat offered to idols (cf. 1 Cor. 8; 10:23-30). The reason for a believer's scruple is not the point, however; its existence alongside a differing opinion was Paul's concern.

In such a situation neither believer should judge the other. **Look down on** (exoutheneitō; also used in Rom. 14:10) should be translated "despise" or "reject with contempt" (cf. "treat . . . with

contempt," Gal. 4:14; 1 Thes. 5:20). The reason a "strong" Christian (cf. Rom. 15:1) should not despise a "weak" one, and the reason that a weak Christian should **not condemn** (krinetō) the strong one is that **God has accepted** (same verb as in 14:1) both of them. (Another reason for not downgrading others is given later in v. 10.) As a believer, he is a servant of God and he is accountable to God, his Judge. Any Christian tempted to judge another believer must face Paul's question, **Who are you to judge** (lit., "the one judging") **someone else's servant?** (Oiketēn, "domestic servant," is not the usual word doulos, "slave.") The present participle, "the one judging," suggests that Paul sensed some judging of others was occurring among the Christians at Rome. But such criticizing is wrong because a domestic servant should be evaluated by **his . . . master,** not by fellow believers. Therefore, Paul concluded, **And he will stand** (lit., "he shall be made to stand"), **for the Lord is able to make him stand.** Even if a believer despises the scruples of another Christian, God can defend the second person.

14:5-8. A second area of differing opinions was the significance of special days. **One man considers one day more sacred than another; another man considers every day alike** (cf. Col. 2:16). Which position a person held meant nothing to the apostle. His concern was that **each one should be fully convinced in his own mind** (cf. Rom. 14:14, 22), examining his heart to be sure he is doing what he feels the Lord would have him do. And he should hold his opinion **to the Lord.** This is true for any issue where an honest difference of opinion exists among Christians, whether in keeping or not keeping **special** days or eating or abstaining from **meat,** or in other matters not prohibited by Scripture. All belongs **to the Lord** and is sanctioned by Him (1 Cor. 10:25-27; 1 Tim. 4:3-5). A believer's individual accountability to the Lord in every area and experience of life is paramount. Each Christian in both life and death is seen by the Lord, and is accountable to Him, not to other Christians. **So whether we live or die, we belong to the Lord.**

14:9-12. In these verses Paul stated the theological basis for his exhortation for Christians to desist from and to resist judging one another. One of the reasons for the Lord Jesus' redemptive death and resurrection is to be **the Lord of both the dead and the living.** Since Jesus is the Lord, Christians should not **judge** (*krineis*) **or . . . look down on** (*exoutheneis,* "despise" or "reject with contempt"; cf. v. 3) one another, their brothers, in such matters. One Christian is not above another as his judge; all are equally under Christ, the Judge.

As Lord, Jesus will one day review and evaluate the ministry of His servants at His **judgment seat** (*bēma;* see comments on 2 Cor. 5:10). Paul affirmed the certainty of this event by quoting Isaiah 49:18 and 45:23, pertaining to everyone standing **before** Christ and confessing Him as Lord (cf. Phil. 2:10-11). At that event **each** believer **will give an account** (lit., "a word") **of himself to God.** Since Paul was writing to the Christians in Rome (Rom. 1:7) and included himself with them in the first personal plural pronoun and verb (*"we* will all stand," 14:10), "God's judgment seat" is only for believers in the Lord. What is here called *God's* judgment seat is the judgment seat of Christ in 2 Corinthians 5:10. Because God judges through His Son (John 5:22, 27), this judgment seat can be said to belong to both the Father and the Son. The issue of the believer's eternal destiny will not be at stake; that was settled by his faith in Christ (cf. Rom. 8:1). Each believer's life of service will be under review in which some loss will be experienced (cf. 1 Cor. 3:12-15), but he will be rewarded for what endures (cf. 1 Cor. 4:4-5). This judgment of believers climactically demonstrates God's lordship.

2. WITHOUT HINDERING (14:13-23)

Paul's warning against judging relates to Christians' attitudes and actions toward the convictions of other believers (vv. 1-12). The other side of the coin is evaluating the impact of one's own convictions and actions on other Christians. In this section Paul warned against causing other Christians to stumble (hindering their spiritual growth) by asserting that one is free to live in accord with convictions not shared by other believers.

14:13-14. Paul's opening sentence is both the final charge on the previous subject and the introduction to the new one: **Therefore, let us stop passing judgment on** (*krinōmen,* "condemning") **one another** (pres. tense subjunctive, "no longer let us keep on judging or condemning one another"). **Instead** a Christian should judge *himself* and his actions so that he does not place a **stumbling block** (*proskomma,* lit., "something a person trips over"; cf. 1 Cor. 8:9 and comments on Rom. 14:20-21) **or obstacle** (*skandalon,* lit., "trap, snare," and hence "anything that leads another to sin"; cf. 16:17) **in** his **brother's way** (lit., "to the brother").

Returning to the subject of food (14:2-3, 6), Paul expressed his own conviction (cf. v. 5) as a Christian **that no food** (lit., "nothing") **is unclean** (*koinon,* "common") **in itself** (cf. Acts 10:15; Rom. 14:20; 1 Cor. 8:8). The problem, however, is that not all Christians—especially some from a Jewish heritage—shared Paul's conviction. Therefore Paul properly concluded, **But if anyone regards** (lit., "but to the one reckoning") **something as unclean** ("common"), **then for him it is unclean** (cf. Titus 1:15). But if someone persisted in holding that conviction, he could bring harm to others. That is the point Paul made next (Rom. 14:15-18).

14:15-18. How should a Christian whose convictions allow him to eat everything respond to one with scruples against certain foods? In Christian love he ought to forgo his liberty in Christ to avoid being a spiritual hindrance to his spiritual **brother.** If he persists in exercising his liberty so that his brother **is distressed** (*lypeitai,* "grieved, hurt"), Paul concluded, then the Christian exercising his liberty is **no longer acting** (lit., "walking") **in love.** Such persistence could cause the spiritual destruction of a **brother for whom Christ died. Destroy** renders the word *apollye,* which often means eternal ruin. Here it may mean temporal ruin; a Christian forced to act contrary to his scruples, even though more strict than necessary, may find himself ruined by his wounded conscience (cf. 1 Cor. 8:10-12). Persisting in one's freedom could also result in his Christian liberty (**what you consider good**) being blasphemed (**spoken of as evil,** *blasphēmeisthō*).

Such things should not happen. After all, food is not that important an issue (1 Cor. 8:8); it is **not** the sum and substance of **the kingdom of God. But . . . righteousness** (upright living), **peace** (cf. Rom. 12:16, 18; 14:19) **and joy in** (the sphere of) **the Holy Spirit** (cf. 15:13) are essentials of Christian fellowship and harmony. A concerned believer insists on right conduct, harmony, and joy rather than forcing his own lifestyle on others. As a result the Christian **who serves** (pres. participle, *douleuōn*, "who keeps on serving as a slave") **Christ in this way**— in Christian love, pursuing righteousness, peace, and joy in the Holy Spirit—**is pleasing** (cf. 12:1; 15:1; Heb. 13:21) **to God and approved by men** (in contrast with being evil spoken of, Rom. 14:16).

14:19-21. Continuing his emphasis on not hindering another Christian's spiritual life, Paul urged his readers, **Let us therefore make every effort** (lit., "Let us keep on pursuing") **to do what leads to peace** (lit., "the things of peace"; cf. v. 17) **and to mutual edification** (lit., "and the things of building up one another"; cf. 15:2; 1 Thes. 5:11). To Paul **food** and one's personal convictions about it were not so important as the spiritual health of a fellow Christian and **the work of God.** Therefore **it is wrong** to insist on one's personal freedom in Christ concerning food (**all food is clean;** cf. Rom. 14:14, "no food is unclean") and drink if it **causes someone else to stumble** (*proskommatos*, "a stumbling block"; cf. vv. 13, 21). **Meat or drink** or **anything else** should be put aside if it causes a **brother to fall** (*proskoptei*, "stumble"; cf. *proskomma*, in vv. 13, 20). At times one's Christian liberty must be relinquished for the sake of others. As Paul wrote to the Corinthians, "Everything is permissible—but not everything is constructive" (1 Cor. 10:23). And "be careful . . . that the exercise of your freedom does not become a stumbling block to the weak" (1 Cor. 8:9).

14:22-23. Concerning personal convictions in areas where different views exist, Paul concluded, **So whatever you believe about these things** (lit., "The faith that you have," or "Do you have faith?") **keep between yourself and God.** A Christian must not insist on influencing a believer with tighter scruples to change his ways. It should be something "in his own mind" (v. 5), for he lives "to the Lord" (v. 8). Paul considered a Christian like himself who had a clear conscience

on such matters **blessed** (lit., "happy"). On the other hand, a Christian **who has doubts is condemned** (perf. pass. verb, "stands condemned") **if he eats.** If a Christian eats food or does anything when he has doubts in his own mind as to whether it is right or wrong before God (one who is "weak" in faith, vv. 1-2), his action does **not** spring **from** (*ek*, "out of") his **faith** or trust in God and is therefore wrong. As Paul generalized, **Everything that does not come from** (*ek*, "out of") **faith is sin.** The principle is, "When in doubt, don't." The "strong" Christian (15:1) is wrong if he causes a weak brother to sin (by doing something while doubting, 14:20), and a weak brother (vv. 1-2) who goes against what he doubts also sins (v. 23).

3. AS IMITATORS OF CHRIST (15:1-13)

Paul had written that Christians should not despise or condemn others (14:1-12) nor should they hinder the conduct of other Christians (14:13-23). Now he gave a third principle to observe when a believer is dealing with fellow Christians: he is to follow the example of the Lord Jesus Christ. Jesus was supremely the Person who ministered on behalf of others, not for Himself. It is fitting, therefore, that those who take His name should imitate Him.

15:1-4. Paul summarized the previous discussion (chap. 14) by saying, **We who are strong** (obviously in convictions and conscience) **ought** (pres. tense, emphasizing continuing obligation; its first position in the sentence underscores its importance) **to bear with the failings** (lit., "infirmities, weaknesses") **of the weak** (lit., "nonstrong"). The strong ought not despise the weak; they ought to bear with them. Also the strong should **not** seek **to please** themselves. This last clause is the key; a Christian should not be self-centered, but should be concerned about the spiritual welfare of others. Pleasing others, however, is not the end in itself, but is **for their good, to build** them **up** (lit., "unto edification"; cf. "edification" in 14:19). This is the example the Lord Jesus **Christ** left. **Even** He **did not please Himself.** He came "to do the will" of the Father who sent Him (John 4:34) and to please Him (John 5:30; 8:29). To support this statement Paul quoted a part of a verse from a messianic psalm (Ps. 69:9).

Christ was insulted by others because of His associations with God the Father.

Then Paul stated a significant principle concerning the purpose and ministry of the Scriptures: **For everything that was written in the past was written to teach us** (lit., "for our instruction"). **The Scriptures** serve to give believers **endurance** (*hypomonēs*, "steadfastness in the face of adversities") and **encouragement** so that they **might have hope** (pres. tense, "keep on having hope"; cf. Rom. 5:3-5). As Christians learn from the *past* (what is written in the OT about others who did not please themselves) they are motivated to endure and be comforted in the *present*, looking ahead in hope (confidence) to the *future*.

15:5-6. The steadfast **endurance and encouragement** a Christian receives from the Scriptures (v. 4) come ultimately from **God** (v. 5), the Author of the Scriptures. Paul prayed that God would give his readers **a spirit of unity** (lit., "to think the same"; 12:16, "live in harmony," has the same Gr. construction) as they **follow Christ Jesus** (lit., "according to Christ Jesus"). The ultimate purpose of this unity was **that with one heart and mouth** (a unity of inward feeling and outward expression) they would **glorify** (pres. tense, "keep on glorifying") **the God and Father of our Lord Jesus Christ** (2 Cor. 1:3; Eph. 1:3; 1 Peter 1:3 have the same wording about God). This is the final purpose of Christians individually and of the church corporately (cf. Rom. 15:7; 1 Cor. 6:20; 2 Thes. 1:12).

15:7. Since the goal of interpersonal relationships among Christians is a unified glorying of God, Paul concluded his commands with **Accept one another** (pres. imper., "keep on accepting or receiving one another"). Significantly this is the same command Paul gave the strong Christians when he opened this entire discussion (14:1). The Model of acceptance for Christians, however, is the Lord Jesus, who **accepted** us. The Lord received believers when they were not only "powerless" (5:6, lit., "weak") but also "ungodly" (5:6), "sinners" (5:8), and "enemies" (5:10). Certainly Christians can receive others who differ with them on nonessential matters. Jesus Christ received them so that they can **bring praise to God** (lit., "unto glory of God"), which

is the purpose of Christian unity (15:6).

15:8-12. Having pointed to the Lord Jesus as the Model for Christians, Paul proceeded to discuss Jesus' ministry and its objectives: **Christ** became **a servant** (the word "deacon" comes from this Gr. noun *diakonon*) **of the Jews** (lit., "to the circumcision"). Jesus was born a Jew as God's Messiah for Israel. God had two objectives to accomplish through Jesus' ministry. The first was **to confirm the promises made to the patriarchs** (cf. 9:4-5). God's second objective in Christ's ministry was **so that** (lit., "and that," because the following clause is coordinate with the preceding one) **the Gentiles may glorify God** (cf. 15:6) **for His mercy.** God had made covenants only with Israel (9:4), not with the Gentiles (cf. Eph. 2:12), so God had no covenantal promises to confirm with the Gentiles. Any spiritual blessings that come to the Gentiles spring solely from the mercy of God. Nevertheless God eternally purposed to bless the Gentiles spiritually through the Lord Jesus as their Messiah and through His covenants with Israel (e.g., Gen. 12:3; cf. John 4:22).

God's two purposes in the ministry of Christ are being achieved now while Israel nationally has been set aside (cf. Rom. 11:1-31) and the church is being formed of both Jews and **Gentiles** (Eph. 2:14-22). And it will be achieved in the future when Israel is restored to her place as head of the nations and becomes a means of blessing to everyone (cf. Deut. 30:1-10).

To demonstrate the validity of his statement concerning the ministry of Christ and its purposes, particularly the one relating to Gentiles, the Apostle Paul quoted four Old Testament passages, introducing the series with the formula, **As it is written** (perf. tense, "it stands written"). Significantly these quotations are taken from all three divisions of the Old Testament—"the Law of Moses, the Prophets, and the Psalms" (Luke 24:44)— and from three great Jewish heroes: Moses, David, and Isaiah. The first quotation (Rom. 15:9) is from David's song of deliverance (2 Sam. 22:50; Ps. 18:49); the second (Rom. 15:10), from Moses' valedictory song to the people of Israel (Deut. 32:43); the third (Rom. 15:11), from both the shortest and the middle chapter of the Bible (Ps. 117:1); and the fourth (Rom. 15:12), from Isaiah's messianic prophecy (Isa. 11:10).

A progression of thought can be traced through the four quotations. In the first, David praised God **among the Gentiles** (Rom. 15:9); in the second, Moses exhorted the Gentiles, **Rejoice . . . with His people** (v. 10); in the third the psalmist commanded the Gentiles to **praise the Lord** (v. 11; cf. v. 7); and in the fourth, Isaiah predicted that **the Gentiles will live under the rule of the Root of Jesse** (the Messiah) and they **will hope in Him** (v. 12). The Old Testament never presented the Gentiles as "heirs together with Israel, members together . . . in the promise in Christ Jesus" (Eph. 3:6), but it certainly did see them as receiving blessing from God's fulfilling His covenantal promises to His people Israel.

15:13. Several times Paul's words sound as if he were ending this epistle (vv. 13, 33; 16:20, 25-27). This verse (15:13) is in effect a benedictory prayer. The description of God as **the God of hope** relates to hope mentioned in the preceding verses and to the promises of God recorded in the Scripture which give hope (v. 4). Paul desired God to **fill** his readers **with all joy and peace** (cf. 14:17). Joy relates to the delight of anticipation in seeing one's hopes fulfilled. Peace results from the assurance that God will fulfill those hopes (cf. 5:1; Phil. 4:7). These are experienced **as** believers **trust in Him** (cf. Heb. 11:1). As a result believers **overflow with hope by the power of the Holy Spirit** (cf. Rom. 15:19). The achievement of all God's purposes for the spiritual welfare of His children comes from the power given by the Spirit of God. What a fitting closing reminder to the apostle's discussion of Christian living.

VII. Concluding Remarks (15:14–16:27)

Though all Paul's letters have closing remarks, he devoted more space to them in Romans than in any other epistle. This was due at least in part to the fact that he had never visited the city and its churches and to his desire to establish personal relationships with his readers. Another factor undoubtedly was his plan to visit Rome in the future.

A. Personal plans (15:14-33)

In writing to a group of people whom he had never met as a group, Paul showed admirable restraint in avoiding personal references to himself. Only once did he use himself as an example (7:7-25), and his other personal remarks are few (1:8-16; 9:1-3; 10:1-2; 11:1). Now as he closed his letter he felt led to discuss his philosophy of ministry and his plans in light of it.

15:14-16. Paul had demonstrated in this letter and elsewhere his ability to be straightforward, even almost blunt, and forceful. Yet he also had a deep concern for the feelings of others and an ability to use effective principles of interpersonal relations. This is seen in his statement, **I myself am convinced** (perf. tense, "I stand convinced"; cf. 8:38), **my brothers, that you yourselves are full of goodness, complete in knowledge** (perf. tense, "having been filled with all knowledge," not in the absolute sense, but in the sense that they had an understanding of the full scope of Christian truth), **and competent** (lit., "being able") **to instruct** (*nouthetein*, "to counsel, admonish"; cf. Col. 1:28; 3:16) **one another.** Paul did not have a low opinion of the Roman Christians; on the contrary he considered them spiritually informed and spiritually mature. Why then did he write on such basic Christian themes? Paul explained, **I have written** (past tense, "I wrote") **you quite boldly on some points** (lit., "in some measure") **as if to remind you of them again.** This was what Peter did as well (2 Peter 1:12; 3:1-2).

Paul was qualified to remind his readers of those points **because** he had his special position as a result of God's **grace** (cf. Rom. 1:5). He was **a minister** (*leitourgon*, a "public servant") **to the Gentiles.** This ministry was carried out as a **priestly duty** (the Gr. verb *hierourgounta* means "to work in sacred things") and involved his **proclaiming the gospel of God** (cf. 1:2-4). Because of his sharing the good news with **Gentiles** (11:13; Gal. 1:16; 2:2, 7-9; Eph. 3:8; Col. 1:27; 2 Tim. 4:17) they became **an offering acceptable** (the words **to God** are not in the text but are obviously understood), **sanctified** (perf. tense, "having been sanctified" or "having been set apart") **by the Holy Spirit** (cf. 1 Peter 1:2). Like a priest, Paul introduced Gentiles to God, and then presented them like an offering to the Lord. God's willingness to accept Gentiles, set apart by the work of the Holy Spirit, shows His plan in the Church Age is to unite Jews and Gentiles in one body (Eph. 3:6).

15:17-19. As a result of his special ministry by God's grace to the Gentiles, Paul affirmed, **Therefore I glory** (lit., "I have boasting") **in Christ Jesus in my service to God** (lit., "in the things relating to God"). This was no boasting in mere human achievements, as Paul explained: **I will not venture to speak of anything except what Christ has accomplished through me in leading the Gentiles to obey God** (lit., "unto the obedience of the Gentiles"). "Obedience" is a synonym for coming to Christ (cf. 1:5; 1 Peter 1:2; cf. "obey" in Rom. 16:26) for God "commands all men everywhere to repent" (Acts 17:30).

Paul recognized that all credit goes to Christ. And yet Paul was involved; God worked **by what** he had **said and done.** The apostle had been used by God to perform **signs** (*sēmeiōn*, miracles that signify theological truths) **and miracles** (*teratōn*, miracles that produce wonder). Luke referred to a miracle God performed through Paul at Cyprus (Acts 13:11, making Elymas blind), "signs and wonders" at Iconium (Acts 14:3; cf. Acts 15:12) and miracles at Lystra (Acts 14:8-10, 19-20), Ephesus (Acts 19:11-12), Troas (Acts 20:9-12), and Malta (Acts 28:1-8). Signs, wonders, and miracles authenticated the work of the apostles (2 Cor. 12:12; Heb. 2:3-4). And all this, Paul said, was **through the power of the Spirit** (cf. Rom. 15:13). Anything Paul achieved that was worthy of praise had God's grace as its source, Jesus Christ as its motivation and goal, and the Holy Spirit as its energy.

The result was that Paul preached the gospel **from Jerusalem all the way around to Illyricum.** Literally, this reads, "from Jerusalem and in a circle (i.e., Jerusalem and its environs) even to Illyricum." "The gospel of God" (v. 16) is here called **the gospel of Christ.** The New Testament records several of Paul's visits to Jerusalem after his conversion (Acts 9:26-28 [cf. Gal. 1:17-19]; Acts 11:27-30; 15:2 [cf. Gal. 2:1]; Acts 18:22). In the last reference Jerusalem is not named, but the words "he went up and greeted the church" obviously refers to the church at Jerusalem. Paul's visit to Illyricum is not mentioned elsewhere in the New Testament. This area, also known as Dalmatia, corresponds approximately to modern-day Yugoslavia. It is west and north of Greece (see the location on the map between Acts and Rom.). At one time Titus went to Dalmatia (2 Tim. 4:10). A logical suggestion is that Paul went into Illyricum from Macedonia while waiting for a response to 2 Corinthians before going on to Corinth (Acts 20:1-3; 2 Cor. 13:1-2, 10). This visit was fresh in his mind since Corinth was the city where he wrote Romans (see the *Introduction* to Rom.).

15:20-22. Reference to the geographical extent of his ministry (v. 19) led Paul to declare something of his philosophy of outreach: **It has always been my ambition to preach the gospel where Christ was not known** (lit., "named"). Paul purposed to be a true pioneer evangelist, opening virgin territory to the good news of God's grace in Jesus Christ. This was so that he **would not be building on someone else's foundation** (cf. 1 Cor. 3:10). Paul then expressed his ministry goal in a quotation of the second half of Isaiah 52:15 and explained, **This is why I have often been hindered** (imperf. tense, "I was being hindered many times") **from coming to you.** Up to this time Paul had always found new areas for ministry in Asia Minor and the Grecian Peninsula so that he had not yet felt free to look beyond to Rome and Spain.

15:23-24. Perhaps his visit to Illyricum convinced Paul that no more virgin territory for the gospel lay in Asia Minor and the Grecian Peninsula. This does not mean that he had visited every center, but the gospel had been introduced and local churches had been established that could complete the work (cf. Acts 19:8-10). At any rate Paul concluded, **There is no more place for me to work in these regions** (lit., "having no more place in these regions"). Coupled with this was his **longing for many years to see** the Roman Christians. At the beginning of this epistle he had expressed this desire to visit them (Rom. 1:10-11, 13). Paul continued, **I plan to do so** (this clause

497

does not occur in the Gr. text, but the idea is implied) **when** (the indefiniteness of the Gr. clause requires "whenever") **I go to Spain** (cf. 15:28). Spain was then a Roman colony where many Jews lived; it was the western limit of the empire. He hoped **to visit** them **while passing through.** Apparently he did not plan a long stay in Rome. They could then **assist** him **on** his **journey there** (lit., "and by you to be sent forward there"); that is, they would encourage him on to Spain. Paul would proceed to Spain only **after** he had **enjoyed** (lit., "I am filled full with," "I am satisfied with") their **company for a while.** Paul paid the Roman believers the sincere compliment that their fellowship would refresh and satisfy him spiritually (cf. 1:13). He also wanted to impart a spiritual gift to them, thereby strengthening them (1:11) and to have some spiritual harvest among them (1:13), that is, to be able to help them grow in Christ.

15:25-27. Paul balanced his tentative plans for the future with the business immediately at hand. **I am on my way to Jerusalem in the service of the saints there** (lit., "ministering [*diakonōn*] to the saints"). Paul's visit to Jerusalem was to deliver the voluntary offering from churches **for the poor among the saints in Jerusalem** (cf. Acts 24:17; 1 Cor. 16:1-4; 2 Cor. 8:13-14; 9:12-13; Gal. 2:10). The churches of Asia Minor contributed to the offering also, but Paul mentioned only **Macedonia and Achaia,** the areas closest to Rome and those on his mind for obvious reasons. (See the location of these two portions of Greece on the map between Acts and Rom.)

The voluntary nature of the **contribution** (*koinōnian,* "fellowship") is stressed by the repetition of the verb, **were pleased** (cf. Rom. 15:26-27; 2 Cor. 8:10-12). At the same time Paul recognized the churches had an obligation: **Indeed they owe it to them** (lit., "and they are debtors to them"). This sense of moral obligation had undoubtedly prompted Paul to suggest the offering. Since **the Gentiles have shared in the Jews' spiritual blessings** (lit., "in their spiritual things"; cf. Rom. 11:11-12, 17-18; 15:12; Gal. 3:14; Eph. 3:6), Gentile Christians certainly ought **to share with** (*leitourgēsai,* "to minister to, serve"; cf. *leitourgon* in Rom. 15:16) the Jews **their**

material blessings (lit., "in fleshly things"; cf. Gal. 6:6).

15:28-29. Again Paul said that **after** going to Jerusalem he would **go to Spain and visit** the Romans **on the way** (cf. v. 24). Paul got to Rome, but not when or in the manner he anticipated! (Acts 27–28) Whether he ever got to Spain no one knows for sure. Christians should plan ahead, but they should also be flexible. Paul, not boastfully but simply confident of God's provision, promised that his visit would be a spiritual blessing to the Roman Christians: **I will come in the full measure of the blessing of Christ,** that is, with Christ's blessing to share with them (cf. Rom. 1:11-13).

15:30-33. The Apostle Paul recognized his need for intercessory prayer support from his readers and asked for it again and again (Eph. 6:19-20; Col. 4:3-4; 1 Thes. 5:25; 2 Thes. 3:1-2; Phile. 22). Here he entreated the Romans **by our Lord Jesus Christ and by the love of the Spirit to join** him **in** his **struggle** through prayer. "The love of the Spirit" is probably the love given by the Spirit (cf. Rom. 5:5), not love for the Spirit. Recognizing that divine love, they would be motivated to pray. A Christian's intercession is a means of sharing in the ministry of others.

Paul's specific request was **that** he would **be rescued from the unbelievers** (lit., "the disobedient") **in Judea and that** his **service** (*diakonia*) **in Jerusalem** would **be acceptable to the saints.** Paul was aware of the problems that lay before him in Jerusalem (Acts 20:23), and he was deeply concerned that the offering from the Gentile Christians be delivered and distributed properly. If these objectives were accomplished, according to Paul, he could then **by God's will** go **to** them **with joy and . . . be refreshed** with them. The word rendered "refreshed" suggests that Paul would be able to rest or relax with them in the knowledge of a job well done. Paul closed this section with a brief benediction: **The God of peace** (cf. Rom. 16:20; also cf. "the God of hope," 15:13) **be with you all. Amen.** This is the third benediction in this chapter (cf. vv. 5, 13).

B. Personal greetings (16:1-16)

The capital city of Rome was a magnet that drew people from all over the empire. In addition Paul's travels to many of the major population centers—Jerusalem, Syrian Antioch, Philippi, Athens, Corinth, Ephesus—brought him into contact with the mobile segment of Roman society. These factors help explain the presence of Paul's many friends in Rome, but his knowledge of their whereabouts remains a tribute to his deep concern for people.

16:1-2. Phoebe (which means "bright, radiant") was Paul's emissary to deliver this letter, so he wrote officially, **I commend to you our sister Phoebe.** The relationship mentioned is spiritual, not familial. Phoebe was **a servant of the church in Cenchrea,** a seaport a few miles east of Corinth (cf. Acts 18:18; and see the map between Acts and Rom.). The word *diakonon,* "servant," is used for the office of deacon (Phil. 1:1; 1 Tim. 3:8, 10, 12) as well as used generally (Rom. 15:8; 1 Cor. 3:5). Use of the word with the phrase "of the church" strongly suggests some recognized position, a fact appropriate for a person serving as Paul's emissary. Paul not only officially commended her (cf. 2 Cor. 3:1), but also asked the Roman Christians **to receive her in the Lord in a way worthy of the saints and to give her any help** (lit., "and to stand by her in whatsoever matter") **she may need from you.** Paul explained, **for she has been a great help** (*prostatis,* "a protectress, succorer") **to many people, including me.** So they should help her since she had helped others.

16:3-5. This list of greetings (vv. 3-16) that Paul wanted conveyed to friends in Rome is the longest in any of his epistles. He mentioned 26 people by name, and referred to many others (vv. 5, 10-11, 13-15). Several women are included in the list: Priscilla (v. 3), Mary (v. 6), Tryphena and Tryphosa (v. 12), Persis (v. 12), Rufus' mother (v. 13), and Nereus' sister (v. 15). Two others are possibly women—Junias (v. 7) and Julia (v. 15).

Paul first met **Priscilla and Aquila** when he arrived in Corinth on his second missionary journey (Acts 18:2) and worked with them at their trade of tentmaking. They had come to Corinth from Rome because of Claudius' decree that all Jews must leave Rome. They accompanied Paul when he left Corinth

(Acts 18:18), but stayed in Ephesus when the party stopped briefly (Acts 18:19). There they ministered to Apollos (Acts 18:26) and undoubtedly to Paul during his stay in Ephesus on his third journey, because they sent greetings to the Corinthian Christians (1 Cor. 16:19). Shortly after that, they must have moved back to Rome and still later returned to Ephesus (2 Tim. 4:19).

Paul paid them great praise, calling them **my fellow workers in Christ Jesus** and revealing that **they risked their lives for me** (lit., "they lay down their own neck for my soul"). In what way they risked their lives is not known. **All** the Gentile **churches,** Paul added, were **grateful to them.** Paul also sent greetings to **the church that** met **at their house.** The Christians in Rome apparently worshiped in numerous homes such as Priscilla and Aquila's. This couple had had a house church in Ephesus (1 Cor. 16:19) and probably wherever they lived. Other churches in homes are mentioned in Colossians 4:15 and Philemon 2.

Epenetus, to whom greetings were sent, is mentioned only here, but is called by Paul **my dear friend** (lit., "the one loved by me"; cf. Stachys, v. 9). He **was the first convert** (lit., "the firstfruits") **to Christ in the province of Asia.** Paul reached Asia, the western portion of modern-day Turkey, on his third missionary journey (Acts 19:10), after having been prevented from going there on his second journey (Acts 16:6).

16:6-7. Mary is identified simply as one **who worked very hard** ("toiled much"; cf. v. 12). Some Greek manuscripts read Mariam, the Hebrew form, which probably identifies this woman as a Jew.

Andronicus and Junias, greeted together, may have been husband and wife; Junias can be either masculine or feminine. Paul called them **my relatives,** which probably refers to a tribal, not a family kinship (cf. 9:3). He also mentioned four other "relatives" (16:11, 21). He said Andronicus and Junias had **been in prison with** him (lit., "my fellow prisoners"); when or where this occurred is not mentioned (cf. 2 Cor. 11:23). Paul commended them as **outstanding** (*episēmoi,* lit., "having a mark [*sēma*] on them," therefore "illustrious, notable, outstand

Paul's Concluding Benedictions in His Epistles

Romans 16:20b	"The *grace of our Lord Jesus* be with you."
1 Corinthians 16:23	"The *grace of the Lord Jesus* be with you."
2 Corinthians 13:14	"May *the grace of the Lord Jesus Christ,* and the love of God, and the fellowship of the Holy Spirit be with you all."
Galatians 6:18	"The *grace of our Lord Jesus Christ* be with your spirit, brothers. Amen."
Ephesians 6:24	"*Grace* to all who love *our Lord Jesus Christ* with an undying love."
Philippians 4:23	"The *grace of the Lord Jesus Christ* be with your spirit."
Colossians 4:18	"*Grace* be with you."
1 Thessalonians 5:28	"The *grace of our Lord Jesus Christ* be with you."
2 Thessalonians 3:18	"The *grace of our Lord Jesus Christ* be with you all."
1 Timothy 6:21b	"*Grace* be with you."
2 Timothy 4:22	"The Lord be with your spirit. *Grace* be with you."
Titus 3:15b	"*Grace* be with you all."
Philemon 25	"The *grace of our Lord Jesus Christ* be with your spirit."

ing") **among the apostles.** The word "apostles" is probably used here in the broader, general sense in which Barnabas, Silas, and others were called apostles (Acts 14:14; 1 Thes. 2:7). Or it could mean the apostles in the limited sense, referring to the reputation this pair had among the Twelve. Paul added, **They were** (perf. tense, "they came to be and still are") **in Christ before I was.** So they had been believers for about 25 years.

16:8-11. Ampliatus was one Paul loved **in the Lord.** This was high praise from the apostle. **Urbanus** was called **our fellow worker in Christ,** and **Stachys** was addressed as **my dear friend** (lit., "the one loved by me"; cf. Epenetus, v. 5). Paul said **Apelles** was **tested and approved** (*ton dokimon,* "the one approved through testing"; cf. the same word trans. "approved," 14:18; the related infinitive *dokimazein* is trans. "to test and approve," 12:2). Without naming other individuals Paul sent greetings to **those who belong to the household of Aristobulus,** perhaps a grandson of Herod the Great. (See the chart on the Herods at Luke 1:5.) A household may have included family members and servants. (However, the Gr. simply has "those out of, belonging to Aristobulus"; cf. Rom. 16:11).

Herodion was greeted as **my relative,** but once again the relationship was probably tribal and not familial (cf. vv. 7, 21). The name may identify this person as belonging to Herod's family. Once again without naming individuals Paul sent greetings to **those in the household of Narcissus** (lit., "those out of, belonging to Narcissus"; cf. v. 10). But Paul restricted his greetings to the ones **who are in the Lord,** which probably indicated Narcissus' family was divided spiritually.

16:12-13. Paul sent greetings jointly to **Tryphena and Tryphosa,** identifying them as **those women who work hard** ("toil") **in the Lord.** Some believe they were sisters, possibly even twins. Then **Persis,** addressed as **my dear friend** (lit., "the one loved"), was **another woman who has worked very hard** ("toiled much") **in the Lord.** Interestingly four women were said to have "worked hard" (cf. Mary, v. 6).

Whether **Rufus** is the same person mentioned in Mark 15:21 or not is uncertain. If so, then he, as a son of Simon of Cyrene, was a North African.

Paul said Rufus was **chosen in the Lord,** a statement true of every believer (cf. Eph. 1:4). Consequently the word translated "chosen" may mean "eminent," since it was given to Rufus as a statement of distinction. The greeting included Rufus' **mother who,** Paul said, had also **been a mother to** him. Paul obviously did not say she was his actual mother, but he had been the recipient of her motherly care.

16:14-16. The next five names mentioned together (v. 14) evidently had something in common, perhaps as leaders of another house church. This may be indicated by the reference to **the brothers with them.** They are all common names, particularly among slaves.

Julia may have been the wife of **Philologus.** Two other husband-wife teams were Priscilla and Aquila (v. 3) and (possibly) Andronicus and Junias (v. 7). **Nereus and his sister** were then greeted, though the sister's name is not given. And finally, greetings were sent to **Olympas and all the saints with** him. This group may have been the leaders of another house church (cf. v. 14).

Of all these individuals only Priscilla and Aquila are mentioned elsewhere in the New Testament for certain; yet Paul knew them all individually and sent personal greetings to them and their associates. Paul cannot properly be charged with not being "a people person." He closed this section with the command, **Greet one another with a holy kiss,** the mode of salutation similar to the handshake today (cf. comments on 1 Cor. 16:20; also cf. 2 Cor. 13:12; 1 Thes. 5:26; 1 Peter 5:14) and with a general word of salutation, **All the churches of Christ send greetings** (lit., "greet you").

C. Final words (16:17-27)

16:17-20. Paul could not resist giving a final word of warning that they **watch out for** spiritual enemies: **those who** are divisive and seek to hinder the Lord's work (who **put obstacles** [skandala, "traps, snares"; cf. 14:13] **in your way that are contrary to the teaching you have learned**). Believers are to **keep away** (pres. imper., "keep on turning away") **from** such false teachers, who were **not serving** (douleuousin, "serving as slaves"; cf. 14:18) **Christ,** but were slaves to **their**

own appetites (lit., "bellies"; cf. Phil. 3:19). They were selfish gluttons. The problem, however, was that **by smooth talk and flattery they** deceived **the minds** (lit., "hearts") **of naive people** (akakōn, "innocent, unsuspecting").

Paul hastened to assure the Romans that he did not consider them naive. Their **obedience** (to Christ; cf. Rom. 1:5; 15:18; 1 Peter 1:2) was well known and Paul was glad for them. But he was concerned that they **be wise about what is good, and innocent about what is evil** (kakon). The word for "innocent" is akeraious, "unmixed, simple, pure." In Greek it was used of wine that was not diluted and of metal that was not weakened in any way. The word is used in the New Testament in only two other places: Matthew 10:16 ("innocent") and Philippians 2:15 ("pure"). Christians should be innocent about evil, not following the ways of the world (Rom. 12:2).

To conclude this warning Paul added the promise, **The God of peace** (cf. 15:33; Heb. 13:20) **will soon crush Satan under your feet** (cf. Gen. 3:15). The false teachers (Rom. 16:17-18) were under Satan's influence, but he will be destroyed and God will establish peace (Rev. 20:1-6). Then Paul gave another benediction (cf. Rom. 15:13, 33) about God's **grace.** (See the chart, "Paul's Concluding Benedictions in His Epistles.")

16:21-24. These few verses contain personal **greetings** from some of Paul's associates: first, **Timothy, my fellow worker,** and then **Lucius, Jason, and Sosipater, my relatives.** Once again these men were not members of Paul's family, but fellow countrymen (cf. vv. 7, 10). These may be the men of the same names mentioned elsewhere (Acts 13:1; 17:5-9; 20:4; cf. 2 Cor. 9:4).

Then **Tertius,** who was Paul's stenographer for this epistle, sent his greetings. So did **Gaius,** Paul's host in Corinth, who apparently had a church meeting in his home. This Gaius was probably not the same Gaius who was from Macedonia and traveled with Paul (Acts 19:29) nor the Gaius who was from Derbe (Acts 20:4). The Gaius mentioned here in Romans was probably Paul's convert whom he baptized (1 Cor. 1:14). **Erastus sent greetings.** He was **the city's** director of public works (lit., "the city's steward," a high position in Corinth). Paul called **Quartus** our **brother,** undoubtedly meaning a spiritual brother, not a physical one. Romans 16:24 (NIV marg.), which repeats the benediction in verse 20b, is not found in a number of the major Greek manuscripts and is not considered genuine.

16:25-27. The apostle finally came to his closing benediction. This letter to the Romans is Paul's longest and most complete statement of the message he proclaimed, what he here called **my gospel** (cf. 2:16; 2 Tim. 2:8) **and the proclamation of** (i.e., concerning) **Jesus Christ.** The truth of this message is the means of spiritual life and stability, as Paul expressed his praise to God **who is able to establish you** (cf. 1 Peter 5:10).

Paul said that aspects of this message (e.g., Rom. 11:25; 1 Cor. 15:51; Eph. 5:32) and in a sense the total message (cf. Eph. 3:3-9; Col. 1:26-27) are **the mystery hidden for long ages past, but now revealed and made known.** The message of the gospel of Christ was "hidden" in the Old Testament, but is revealed in the New. In **the prophetic writings** (of the OT; cf. Rom. 1:2), given **by the command of the eternal God** (1 Tim. 1:17), Christ was referred to (Luke 24:44-45), but even the prophets themselves were not fully aware of all they wrote (1 Peter 1:10-12). **But now** in the Church Age their writings are understood.

The goal of this "revelation of the mystery" (Rom. 16:25) is **that** people of **all nations might believe and obey** Christ (cf. 1:5; 15:18; 1 Peter 1:2). Paul's concern for the geographical spread of the gospel is evident here (cf. Matt. 28:19), appropriate in view of his writing to the believers at the empire's capital city.

Paul then identified specifically the object of his benediction: **To the only wise God.** In the Greek this phrase is followed immediately by the words **through Jesus Christ.** This indicates that the wisdom of God is displayed supremely through Christ (cf. Col. 2:3). According to the Greek text the benediction then ends, to whom **be glory forever! Amen** (cf. Rom. 11:36). God the Father ultimately is the One to be praised and to whom glory belongs (cf. 1 Cor. 15:24-28).

BIBLIOGRAPHY

Barnhouse, Donald Grey. *Exposition of Bible Doctrines Taking the Epistle to the Romans as a Point of Departure.* Reprint (10 vols. in 4). Grand Rapids: Wm. B. Eerdmans Publishing Co., 1952–64.

Barrett, C.K. *A Commentary on the Epistle to the Romans.* Harper's New Testament Commentaries. New York: Harper & Row Publishers, 1957.

Best, Ernest. *The Letter of Paul to the Romans.* Cambridge: Cambridge University Press, 1967.

Black, Matthew. *Romans.* New Century Bible. London: Marshall, Morgan & Scott, 1973.

Bruce, F.F. *The Epistle to the Romans: An Introduction and Commentary.* The Tyndale New Testament Commentaries. Grand Rapids: Wm. B. Eerdmans Publishing Co., 1963.

Cranfield, C.E.B. *A Critical and Exegetical Commentary on the Epistle to the Romans.* The International Critical Commentary. 6th ed. 2 vols. Edinburgh: T. & T. Clark, 1975, 1979.

Godet, Frederic Louis. *Commentary on Romans.* 1883. Reprint. Grand Rapids: Kregel Publications, 1977.

Harrison, Everett F. "Romans." In *The Expositor's Bible Commentary,* vol. 10. Grand Rapids: Wm. B. Eerdmans Publishing Co., 1976.

Hendriksen, William. *Exposition of Paul's Epistle to the Romans.* New Testament Commentary. 2 vols. Grand Rapids: Baker Book House, 1980, 1981.

Hodge, Charles. *Commentary on the Epistle to the Romans.* 1886. Reprint. Grand Rapids: Wm. B. Eerdmans Publishing House, 1950.

Hunter, Archibald MacBride. *The Epistle to the Romans: Introduction and Commentary.* London: SCM Press, 1955.

Ironside, H.A. *Lectures on the Epistle to the Romans.* Neptune, N.J.: Loizeaux Bros., 1928.

Johnson, Alan F. *Romans: The Freedom Letter.* Everyman's Bible Commentary. 2 vols. Chicago: Moody Press, 1976.

Moule, H.C.G. *The Epistle of St. Paul to the Romans.* 1892. Reprint. Minneapolis: Klock & Klock Christian Publishers, 1982.

Murray, John. *The Epistle to the Romans*. 2 vols. Grand Rapids: Wm. B. Eerdmans Publishing Co., 1959, 1965.

Sandlay, William, and Headlam, Arthur C. *A Critical and Exegetical Commentary on the Epistle to the Romans*. The International Critical Commentary. 5th ed. Edinburgh: T. & T. Clark, 1955.

Stifler, James M. *The Epistle to the Romans*. Chicago: Moody Press, 1960.

Thomas, W.H. Griffith. *Romans: A Devotional Commentary*. 3 vols. London: Religious Tract Society, n.d. Reprint (3 vols. in 1). Grand Rapids: Wm. B. Eerdmans Publishing Co., 1946.

Vaughan, Curtis, and Corley, Bruce. *Romans: A Study Guide Commentary*. Grand Rapids: Zondervan Publishing House, 1976.

Wiersbe, Warren W. *Be Right*. Wheaton, Ill.: Scripture Press Publications, Victor Books, 1976.

1 CORINTHIANS

David K. Lowery

INTRODUCTION

According to Greek legend, Sisyphus was a king of Corinth. For defying the gods with his insolent wit he was sentenced to the eternal drudgery of pushing a huge stone up a hill. When he would reach the summit, the stone would roll back to the bottom and force resumption of the task. Camus, a 20th-century philosopher, found in this legend of the Corinthian king a picture of modern man's condition, the purposeless absurdity of life.

If Camus had read the two biblical letters sent to the Corinthians, he would have gotten a different picture, one with a message of purpose and hope for misdirected people. The attitude of these Corinthians, like their legendary king, smacked of proud self-centeredness. But instead of dealing with a capricious Zeus, these first-century Corinthians interacted with the gracious and loving God and His messenger, the Apostle Paul.

Author and Readers. That Paul is this letter's author there is little doubt. Even the most imaginative critics find no objection on this point. The apostle came to Corinth (Acts 18:1-18) on his second missionary journey (probably in the spring of A.D. 51 as the proconsulship of Gallio likely began later that year, in July). There Paul met Aquila and Priscilla who had left Rome in A.D. 49, when Claudius issued an edict ordering the expulsion of Jews from that city. The couple ran a tent-making business, a trade also practiced by Paul. Since no mention is made of their conversions, they were probably Christians when Paul met them. With a kinship along spiritual, ethnic, and vocational lines, Paul was naturally attracted to them.

According to his custom Paul attended the synagogue and took part in its services, seeking to persuade his hearers that Jesus is the Messiah. When the synagogue was closed to Paul, he went next door to the house of a synagogue listener who heard and believed, a Gentile named Titius Justus (Acts 18:7). He was one of many people in Corinth who belonged to the Lord.

From a human point of view Paul probably had reason to wonder if many saints would be found in Corinth. The ancient city had a reputation for vulgar materialism. In the earliest Greek literature it was linked with wealth (Homer *Iliad* 2. 569-70) and immorality. When Plato referred to a prostitute, he used the expression "Corinthian girl" (*Republic* 404d). The playwright Philetaerus (*Athenaeus* 13. 559a) titled a burlesque play *Ho Korinthiastēs*, which may be translated "The Lecher." And Aristophanes coined the verb *korinthiazomai* to refer to fornication (*Fragment* 354). According to Strabo (*Geography* 8. 6-20) much of the wealth and vice in Corinth centered around the temple of Aphrodite and its thousand temple prostitutes. For this reason a proverb warned, "Not for every man is the voyage to Corinth."

For a hundred years after 146 B.C. no one cared to make the voyage to Corinth. The city was destroyed because of its revolt against Rome. Only a few columns in the temple of Apollo survived the razing. All its citizenry was killed or sold into slavery.

But this favorable location did not go unused for long, as Julius Caesar refounded the city as a Roman colony in 46 B.C. In 27 B.C. it became the governmental seat for Achaia, from which seat Gallio as proconsul would allow Paul's proclamation of the gospel. It was onto this new stage, which nonetheless preserved the vices of the old, that Paul stepped in A.D. 51.

Contacts and Correspondence. The nature and number of Paul's contacts and correspondence with the Corinthians after his first visit in A.D. 51 is subject to considerable debate. A defense for the scheme of events to be presented may be found in several of the works cited in the *Bibliography*.

1. The length of Paul's stay on this first tour of ministry was one and one-half years, after which he sailed in the fall of A.D. 52 to Ephesus enroute to Jerusalem. Priscilla and Aquila accompanied Paul to Ephesus where they remained to meet and instruct the gifted Alexandrian Apollos whom they subsequently sent on to Corinth for ministry there (Acts 18:18-28).

2. While Apollos was ministering in Corinth (Acts 19:1), Paul returned to Ephesus on his third missionary journey in the fall of A.D. 53 for a period of about two and one-half years (Acts 19). It was probably during the early part of Paul's ministry in Ephesus that he wrote the letter mentioned in 1 Corinthians 5:9, a letter misunderstood by the Corinthians (5:10-11) and later lost.

3. Paul learned of this misunderstanding and of further problems in the church at Corinth from the household of Chloe (1:11). Then an official delegation—Stephanas, Fortunatus, and Achaicus (16:17)—brought Paul specific questions on issues dividing the church. First Corinthians was written, probably in A.D. 54 or 55, to address these matters.

4. But apparently this did not resolve the problems in the church. It is possible that Timothy was the bearer of this news (4:17; 16:10). Paul then decided to revisit the church which he called in 2 Corinthians 1:15 and 2:1 the "painful" visit (cf. 2 Cor. 13:1, which speaks of a third visit, the last leg of Paul's third missionary journey), because of the action of the man referred to in 2 Corinthians 2:5 and 7:2.

5. After his second visit and return to Ephesus, Paul sent a letter borne by Titus, which it grieved him deeply to write (2 Cor. 2:4) apparently because of its disciplinary nature (2 Cor. 7:8-9).

6. After the silversmiths' riot Paul left Ephesus bound for Troas to meet Titus. Because Paul could not find him there, he anxiously pushed on to Macedonia, apparently with grave concern about Titus' safety (2 Cor. 2:12-13; 7:5). There he met Titus who brought good news about the general well-being of the Corinthian church but bad news about a group opposed to Paul.

7. From Macedonia Paul wrote 2 Corinthians and followed it up with his third visit during the winter of A.D. 56–57 (Acts 20:1-4).

Purpose and Nature of the Letter. If Ephesians is a letter concerned with the universal church, 1 Corinthians is pointedly concerned with the local church. If anyone thinks his church has more than its share of riffraff and woe, he need only turn to this letter (and its companion, 2 Cor.) to put his problems in perspective. First Corinthians provides a glimpse of life inside one first-century church, and far from saintly it was. Yet that is the reason Paul wrote this letter—to make positional sanctification practical. The spirit of the world seemed more influential in the Corinthian church than the Spirit of God, despite the splendidly evident gifts given by the Spirit. Paul wanted to change that. He directed his message along three lines:

1. The first six chapters were an attempt to correct the contentions in the church brought to his attention by Chloe's servants (1:11) and to bring about unity in perspective and practice.

2. Beginning in chapter 7, Paul addressed himself to certain questions (introduced by the phrase *peri de*, "now concerning") about marital issues (7:1, 25), liberty and responsibility (8:1), spiritual gifts and church order (12:1), money for impoverished saints in Jerusalem (16:1), and the availability of Apollos (16:12).

3. In chapter 15 he reaffirmed and defended the doctrine of the Resurrection, which some denied. It is possible that Paul saw this as a fundamental ill affecting all the preceding discussion, so he placed it at the climax of his letter.

Standing above all the issues with which this letter deals is the very existence of a church in Corinth, a testimony to the power of God and the gospel.

OUTLINE

COMMENTARY

I. Introduction (1:1-9)

The introductions to Paul's letters are frequently seedbeds for issues expanded on later; his prefatory words in 1 Corinthians are no exception. He touched on his calling to be an apostle, the Corinthians' calling to be saints, and the unity which is theirs in Christ.

A. Salutation and description of the writer and readers (1:1-3)

1:1. The legitimacy of Paul's apostleship and its denial by some is hinted at in this letter (chap. 9), but receives explicit defense in 2 Corinthians. In the first words in 1 Corinthians **Paul** affirmed his appointment to this position **by the will of God** to represent not his own interests but those **of Christ.**

Sosthenes was probably Paul's amenuensis and may have been the synagogue ruler publicly thrashed by the Jews (Acts 18:17). If so, he illustrates how God can turn the worst circumstances to a believer's ultimate advantage.

1:2. The church belongs to **God,** not man. Had the Corinthians recognized this, their problem of division might not have existed. Those who compose the church have been **sanctified,** set apart by God as His possession. The burden of Paul's letter was that the Corinthians' practice might more nearly approximate their position. **Christ Jesus** as **Lord** was to be obeyed. Herein was unity for Christians not only in Corinth but **everywhere.**

507

1:3. Grace was what brought them together and what they needed to display mutually so that relational **peace** would be maintained. These qualities, especially needed in the Corinthian church, were produced by **God** in those dependent on Him.

B. Thanksgiving for the effects of God's grace (1:4-9)

Thanksgiving for a church so rife with problems may seem a bit strange. If Paul's only resources had been his own, the prospects of reforming a group like the Corinthians would have been dim indeed. But God was at work and that, for Paul, was a matter of thanksgiving.

1:4. However prone the Corinthians may have been to self-exaltation, it was because of God's **grace** alone that they were members of the body which existed **in Christ Jesus.**

1:5. It was only because they were a part of His body that they had been so **enriched** with the **speaking** and **knowledge** gifts such as tongues, prophecy, discernment of spirits, and/or interpretation (12:4-11). These gifts were not given to be abused as the Corinthians had done, but to be used for the good of all the church.

1:6. The presence of these gifts also bore **testimony** to the effectiveness of Paul's message **about Christ.** Though it might have been feebly delivered (2:1-5), God securely implanted His Word.

1:7-8. Because it was God's work, Paul had no question about the outcome. Because the Corinthian believers were justified by God's grace, they would stand before Him **blameless** (anenklētous, "free from accusation"; cf. Col. 1:22) when **Christ** returns. Thus they could **eagerly wait** (apekdechomenous; used seven times in the NT of the return of Christ: Rom. 8:19, 23, 25; 1 Cor. 1:7; Gal. 5:5; Phil. 3:20; Heb. 9:28) for Him.

1:9. This was so because **God . . . is faithful** and He had **called** the Corinthians **into fellowship with His Son Jesus Christ.** But one cannot enjoy fellowship with Christ while being at odds with other members of His body (Matt. 5:23-24). So it is on this note that Paul made his transition from what God had done in the past and will do in the future to what the Corinthians needed to do in the present, namely, mend their divisions.

II. Divisions in the Church (1:10–4:21)

Dissension in their church was the first problem openly addressed by Paul.

A. The reality of division (1:10-17)

1:10. Paul appealed to **brothers,** not to adversaries, in the most authoritative fashion, **in the name of** the **Lord Jesus Christ.** This is the 10th reference to Christ in the first 10 verses, leaving no doubt as to the One Paul believed should be the source and focus of Corinthian unity. His appeal was for harmony, not the elimination of diversity. He desired a unity of all the parts, like a quilt of various colors and patterns blended together in a harmonious whole.

1:11-12. Instead of this unity, however, the fabric was coming apart at the seams, or so **Chloe's** servants said. While the divisions were certainly real, it is possible, on the basis of Paul's remark in 4:6, that he made adaptations with regard to party heads so that the names cited— **Paul, Apollos, Cephas**—were illustrative, in order to avoid worsening an already deplorable situation.

1:13. The three questions in this verse were rhetorical and expected a definite no. The universal body of **Christ** is not **divided,** and neither should its local expression be. No man won salvation for the Corinthians, nor did any of them owe their allegiance to anybody except Christ.

1:14-17. Paul's imitation of Christ apparently touched every aspect of his ministry. According to John 4:2, Jesus did not **baptize,** but left it to His disciples. This was usually Paul's practice too. Could Paul then have believed baptism was necessary for salvation? Such is impossible (cf. 1 Cor. 4:15; 9:1, 22; 15:1-2). Not that baptism is pointless. It was commanded by Christ (Matt. 28:19) and practiced by the early church (Acts 2:41), which makes it, with the Lord's Supper, an ordinance of the church. But it is what an ordinance gives testimony to, not what it effects, that is more important.

Paul's primary charge was **to preach the gospel** (9:16) **not with words of human wisdom.** Brilliantly persuasive eloquence may win a person's mind but not his heart, whereas the unadorned words of the gospel, though seemingly foolish by human standards, are made effective by the Spirit of God (2:4-5).

B. The causes of division (1:18–4:5)

From a human point of view, the message of the gospel, at the heart of which was the suffering and dying Savior, seemed foolishly contradictory. No less so was the principle that he who would be greatest must be the servant of all (Matt. 23:11-12). But this was precisely what Paul meant to affirm in his analysis of the causes of division in Corinth.

1. A MISUNDERSTANDING OF THE MESSAGE (1:18–3:4)

Fundamentally the Corinthians needed a renewal of their minds (Rom. 12:2). They were trying to live their Christian lives on the basis of unsanctified common sense which has self-preservation as its ultimate goal. This kind of life is self-seeking, self-serving, and ultimately self-destructive (Luke 9:24-25).

1:18. It was that very point which Paul wanted to drive home to the Corinthians. **The message of the Cross** cuts to the heart of self-centeredness. Paul saw it as central to salvation which he understood to be a process begun by justification, advanced by sanctification, and climaxed in glorification. Paul spoke most pointedly in this verse and in the letter as a whole to the second of these phases, progressive sanctification. "The message of the Cross" is the message of self-renunciation, of obedience to God which may lead as it did in Jesus' case to humiliation and death, but which ultimately leads not to self-destruction but to preservation (Mark 8:34-35) and exaltation (2 Tim. 2:12; Rev. 22:5). That was the recurring theme in these verses (1 Cor. 1:17-18, 23-24; 2:2, 8), an idea **those who are perishing** consider **foolishness** (cf. Luke 9:23-25).

1:19. As he often did, Paul illustrated his point by an example of Israel who, following humanly wise counsel, formed an alliance with Egypt as a defense against Assyria, when in fact only the miraculous intervention of God was able to save them (cf. Isa. 29:14; 2 Kings 18:17–19:37).

1:20-21. It was the same with all human wisdom, whether of the esteemed Jewish **scholar** or Greek **philosopher.** The

brilliance of man cannot appreciate the plan of God (Isa. 55:8-9). It is not self-confident erudition but self-effacing faith that allows one to enter the narrow way.

1:22-25. It was not on man's terms and initiative but on God's that man found what he needed, **the power of God and the wisdom of God.** In the preaching of **Christ crucified** God **called** people by opening their eyes of faith to believe the gospel.

1:26-31. Were not the situation so grievous, one could almost imagine a smile of incredulity on Paul's face as he wrote these words and urged the Corinthians to survey their own congregation. From a human viewpoint wisdom, influence, and high breeding were apparently in short supply. If God had chosen on the basis of such criteria, He would have passed them by. But when God called, he turned the world's standards upside down and usually chose the ordinary rather than the outstanding in order **that no one may boast before Him** (v. 29) but only in the Lord. For **Christ** alone personified the **wisdom from God** (v. 30) and in Him the Corinthians experienced **righteousness,** that is, justification (Rom. 4:24-25), **holiness,** that is, sanctification (2 Thes. 2:13-15), and **redemption,** that is, glorification (Rom. 8:23; Eph. 4:30). In the wisdom of God the plan of salvation was accomplished by a crucified Christ hidden from the wise and learned but revealed to simple believers (cf. Matt. 11:25-26).

2:1-5. On this note, Paul made his transition to a third point in his illustration of the futility of human **wisdom,** compared with the power and wisdom of **God.** That was seen also in the manner of his ministry which he described as characterized by **weakness and fear and with much trembling** (v. 3). Some see in this a Paul chastened by his encounter with the Athenian philosophers and therefore temporarily shaken and unsure. But that was probably not so. The phrases simply describe a spirit of dependence and subjection to God's authority (cf. Eph. 6:5; Phil. 2:12), which marked his ministry. It was also true that his manner of preaching was unimpressive from a human point of view (2 Cor. 10:10). Paul readily admitted this and even used it as a point in his argument. His preaching was not marked by **eloquence** or **persuasive**

words such as characterized the sophists, the traveling teachers of that day, but was instead the unembellished message of a **crucified Christ** as the only means of salvation. Faith, then, was induced by **a demonstration of the Spirit's power** and was not a product of human ingenuity or rhetorical flourish. Paul wanted to be sure their **faith** would **not rest on men's wisdom, but on God's power.**

2:6. In Paul's disclaimer about his own brilliance he did not mean that God puts a premium on ignorance and rejects **wisdom** of any sort. There was a wisdom taught by the Spirit which Paul wanted his readers to grasp firmly. Some of his readers had done so (no doubt Paul hoped that someday all would do so). He referred to them as **the mature,** probably including the individuals mentioned in 16:15-18. They are the same people he described as spiritual people (2:13, 15). The reason **the rulers of this age** (cf. 1:20) did not understand this wisdom was because they lacked the Spirit (2:14), and thus were **coming to nothing.**

2:7. The message which Paul proclaimed was **God's secret wisdom,** known only by God's revelation (Matt. 11:25). At the heart of this wisdom is the plan of salvation intended **for our glory,** determined **before time began** (Eph. 1:4).

2:8. As did John in his Gospel (John 17:1), Paul linked **glory** with the **crucified Lord,** an utter paradox to both Jews and Gentiles (1 Cor. 1:23) who nonetheless unwittingly (Luke 23:34) took part in that central act of God's plan of salvation.

2:9-10. The blessings of salvation were prepared by the Father, carried out by the Son, and applied by the Spirit (Eph. 1:3-14) to all believers who as a result love God (1 John 4:19). The only way the Corinthians could know this was **by the Spirit,** who knows and reveals these **deep things of God** about salvation.

2:11. Paul illustrated this by pointing out that nobody can fully fathom **the thoughts** of anyone else. How much more necessary, then, is the work of **the Spirit** if **the thoughts of God** are to be known.

2:12. It was for that purpose, in part, that **the Spirit who is from God** came (John 16:13), not just to some Christians but to all (1 Cor. 12:13).

2:13. It was this message of salvation which Paul proclaimed and now expounded further. It did not originate in man but in God and was **taught by the Spirit.** Paul then expressed these **spiritual truths** which were a message of wisdom (cf. v. 6). The Greek word *pneumatikois* may be neuter gender and so translated **spiritual words** as in the NIV ("expressing spiritual truths in spiritual words"). Or it may be masculine gender and translated "spiritual men" ("interpreting spiritual truths to spiritual men," as in the NIV margin). Both senses are possible, but Paul's primary point in this passage was not how the message of wisdom was received but who received it, as suggested by the context: Paul spoke the message of wisdom to "the mature" (v. 6). Thus verse 13 parallels verse 6 and forms a kind of bracket, in keeping with well-written Greek style.

2:14. Since only spiritual people are able to receive spiritual truths, it follows that **the man without the Spirit,** an unregenerate person, would not and could not receive the message of wisdom regardless of his intellectual abilities or accomplishments (1:20). Like a deaf critic of Bach or a blind critic of Raphael is the unregenerate critic of God's Word.

2:15-16. On the other hand a person possessing the Spirit and guided by Him is able to evaluate and apply **all things** the Spirit reveals (v. 10).

The spiritual man can be judged only by God (4:3-5), not by unregenerate people (2:15) or by worldly Christians (3:1-3). To **have the mind of Christ** is to be obedient to God's revelation (Phil. 2:5-8), as were the spiritual people in the Corinthian church.

3:1-4. However, this was not true of all at Corinth. When Paul came and preached Christ to them, they believed. By faith they were justified and granted peace with God (Rom. 5:1-2). No doubt Paul taught them all the blessings that came to them as Christians, what Paul called **milk.** At that time their way of thinking and living was only beginning to be transformed (Rom. 12:2). They were still greatly influenced by worldly thinking and behavior—they were **infants in Christ.**

But "the message of the Cross" (1 Cor. 1:18) concerned more than justification. It also concerned sanctification. It called for a renewal of attitude and action in response to God's revelation. It called for righteousness in thought and deed (Heb. 5:11-14). And this part of the message of "Christ . . . crucified" (1 Cor. 2:2), this **solid food** (3:2), the Corinthians had spurned. As a result they were **still worldly** (v. 3). Instead of mature behavior characterized by humility and concern for others—obedience to God—the Corinthians were infantile, self-centered, and therefore divisive (v. 4; cf. 1:12). They wanted lives of exaltation (4:8) without lives of humiliation (4:9-13) because they did not understand that "Christ . . . crucified" was a message concerned not only with justification but also with sanctification (cf. Phil. 2:1-8). This misunderstanding was at the root of their disunity (cf. 1 Cor. 1:10; 3:4), which error Paul wanted to correct.

2. A MISUNDERSTANDING OF THE MINISTRY (3:5-4:5)

A second and related cause of division in their church concerned the ministry. The Corinthians had focused on men when in fact God alone was the source of blessing (3:5-9) and ministers were only servants accountable to Him (3:10-17). Since that was so, a minister needed to beware of cultivating the praise of men—as certain leaders in the Corinthian church apparently were doing (3:18-23), and needed instead to seek by faithful service to gain the praise of God (4:1-5).

3:5-9. Apollos and **Paul** were given their ministries by Christ (Eph. 4:11). They were the *means,* not the *cause,* whereby the Corinthians believed (cf. 1 Cor. 2:4-5). God alone produced results. **God made** the seed **grow** (3:6). Therefore God alone should get the credit (v. 7). As servants, Paul and Apollos were not competing against each other but were complementing each other's ministries (v. 8). Their purpose was to bring the church to maturity, to Christlikeness (Eph. 4:12-13). In accord with their faithfulness to that task would come their reward (cf. 1 Cor. 4:2-5). For though a minister served the church he was basically responsible to God. Paul and Apollos were fellow workers who belonged to God and worked for Him in His **field,** the church (3:9).

3:10-17. Paul then shifted metaphors for the church from a field to a **building.** Paul used in various ways the metaphor

of Christians individually and collectively as a building in which God dwells, a **temple.** Jesus had referred to His physical body as a temple (John 2:19-22). In another letter Paul applied the same imagery to Christ's spiritual body, the universal church (Eph. 2:21). Paul also called the body of each individual Christian a temple (1 Cor. 6:19). In this passage, however, it was the local church which he described as a building of God, a temple in which God's Spirit lives (3:16).

Paul now further developed the theme of a minister's accountability for his labor (v. 8). Though it was true that every Christian in the Corinthian church was given at least one gift, or ability to minister in some way to other church members (12:11), it was primarily the leading ministers Paul was concerned about, who functioned in a capacity like that of Apollos and himself (cf. 3:5, 21-22).

3:10. Not every minister, however, labored to the same effect in this building process. Paul had **laid a foundation** in Corinth with the message of the Cross. Apollos too had labored beneficially in Corinth (Acts 18:27-28). Apparently so also had Peter, whom Paul here called "Cephas" (1 Cor. 1:12; 3:22). But as Paul wrote, **someone else** was ministering in Corinth, and Paul's words to him and others like him were a warning.

3:11. Jesus Christ alone was the **foundation,** the basis of salvation (Acts 4:12). But others had come to Corinth and preached a different gospel (2 Cor. 11:4). Perhaps such a one was present in Corinth when Paul wrote this letter.

3:12. In verses 12-17 Paul described three kinds of builders or ministers: the expert (v. 14; cf. v. 10), the unwise (v. 15), and the destructive (v. 17).

The materials used in the building may be interpreted in at least four ways: (a) The **gold, silver, costly stones** refer to the enduring quality of the builder's work; and the **wood, hay, or straw** suggest work that is temporary and valueless. This view is supported by "work" (v. 13) and "what he has built" (v. 14). (b) The three expensive materials suggest sound doctrine which the builder "builds" into people's lives, and the three valueless materials are false doctrines. (c) The first three materials refer to the worker's worthy motives, and the other three point to his unworthy motives (cf. 4:5). (d) The "gold, silver, costly stones" refer to believers who constitute the church (this is supported by similar uses of the metaphor in Eph. 2:22; 2 Tim. 2:20; and 1 Peter 2:5), and the "wood, hay, or straw" represent unregenerate people present in the church (*chorton*, rendered "hay" in 1 Cor. 3:12, is used of unbelievers in James 1:10, where the NIV renders it "wild flower").

3:13. **The day** of judgment is when Christ will judge the quality of His servants' **work** (2 Cor. 5:10). It is not a question of salvation which is a gift (Rom. 6:23), or a matter of individual deeds (Eph. 2:8-9), but of service which is judged on the basis of quality not quantity. Considerable apparent success can be had by dint of human effort and wisdom (cf. 1 Cor. 2:4), but unless it is empowered by God in accordance with His plan it cannot last (Ps. 127:1).

3:14-15. The image of fire associated with the coming of Christ is used elsewhere in the New Testament (2 Thes. 1:7; Rev. 18:8). What the **reward** for the expert builder consists of was not detailed, though praise (1 Cor. 4:5) is certainly a part. The inept builder will see the **loss** of his labor, but **he himself will be saved,** like a burning stick snatched from a fire (Amos 4:11; Jude 23). Before such judgment the various materials may coexist and appear indistinguishable (cf. Matt. 13:30).

3:16-17. However, a local church (**you** here is pl.) might come to the point where its structure is so weak that it collapses entirely or exists in name only, that is, it is destroyed. Paul did not want this to happen in Corinth (2 Cor. 11:3, 13). If it did, the false minister would be paid back in kind by God Himself (an application of the OT *lex talionis* [Gen. 9:6; cf. 2 Cor. 11:15]). The destroyer would be destroyed (Matt. 13:41-42). The words **Don't you know** (1 Cor. 3:16) are the first of 10 occurrences of the clause in this letter (cf. 5:6; 6:2-3, 9, 15-16, 19; 9:13, 24; each time it introduces an indisputable statement).

3:18-23. Since this was so, Paul gave a pointed warning to ministers (vv. 18-20) and to the congregation in Corinth (vv. 21-23). Ministers could avoid self-deception by evaluating their ministries

and realizing that **the wisdom of this world** reflects the mind of Satan (Eph. 2:2) and **is foolishness in God's sight** (1 Cor. 3:19). Paul supported this fact by quoting from Job 5:13 and Psalm 94:11. The members needed to see that the practice of **boasting** (1 Cor. 3:21) **about** ministers was similarly a self-centered spirit. Instead, they should boast in **God** (cf. 1:31) to whom they belonged (3:23; cf. 1:2, 15:28) and who was the source of their every blessing (cf. 1:30).

4:1. It follows then that all who minister for Christ are responsible to Him. The word translated **servants** (*hyperetas*) differs from that used in 3:5 (*diakonoi*) and stresses subordination and responsibility to a superior. The **secret things of God** refers to God's wisdom, the message of the Cross known only by the Spirit's revelation (2:7-10).

4:2. Paul was concerned that he and ministers like him proclaim this message faithfully in the interests of their Master.

4:3-4. He was not deflected from this ministry because the worldly wise rejected it. From a human point of view he was not competent to **judge** even his own motives, much less the quality of his service. How then could others decide these matters?

4:5. Therefore premature judgment, whether it led to the exaltation of some ministers (3:21) or to the humiliation of others (4:10), was wrong. Only at the divine bar would all the facts be known and even there grace will be displayed— **each** faithful minister **will receive . . . praise.**

C. The cure of division (4:6-21)

Paul concluded his address to the problem of division in the church by putting his finger unambiguously on their problem: pride (v. 6). He then suggested a practical cure—imitation of him (v. 16).

4:6. Throughout this discussion Paul avoided singling out guilty persons by name. Instead he applied the problem cases to **Apollos** and himself (and Peter and Christ; cf. 1:12; 3:4-6, 22-33). Now Paul and Apollos would serve as curative examples of men under authority who did **not go beyond what** was **written.** They obeyed the Word of God, not their own inclinations or worldly opinions. From the example of their lives Paul hoped the Corinthians would **learn** the lesson of humility. (The verb "learn" is *mathēte*, and the related noun *mathētēs* is translated "disciple," or "one who practices what he is taught.") This was a difficult lesson, for the Greeks believed humility was a despicable trait of a slave, a sign of weakness, not a characteristic of great men (Plato *Laws* 6. 774c).

4:7. But humility is the only acceptable posture of a person in relation to the God who gives a wide variety of gifts (v. 7a) on the basis of grace (v. 7b) and therefore alone is deserving of praise (v. 7c; cf. 1:4-9). Paul underscored these truths in this series of rhetorical questions.

4:8. The posture of humility should be taken by all Christians. Paul set forth the pattern of Christ's life to the Philippians (Phil. 2:5-11). It was marked first by humiliation and then crowned by exaltation. The Corinthians had apparently dispensed with the first half. They wanted their exaltation immediately—no more sickness, no more suffering, no more pain. This is no more possible today than it was when Paul wrote to these self-deluded Corinthians, but nonetheless many follow in their train.

The Corinthians thought they had **all** they wanted (1 Cor. 4:8a), but they should have been hungering and thirsting for the practical righteousness they so desperately needed (Matt. 5:6). They thought of themselves as **kings** in need of nothing when in fact they were as needy as the foolish king in the children's tale of the emperor's new clothes, who blithely paraded nakedly before his subjects (cf. Rev. 3:17-18).

4:9-13. Paul was no fool. He did not like suffering. He wished they were right. But they weren't. The apostles followed the path of Christ's humiliation. As He marched a parade route to His death, so did they (cf. 2 Cor. 2:14). As Christ had suffered deprivation and defamation, so did His servants, and in His Spirit they endured and responded with grace (Luke 23:34). The apostles lived out the message of the Cross. But the Corinthians were complacent and secure with their "theology of the palace" (cf. Amos 6:1-7).

4:14-17. Prompted by love, Paul issued a warning. His purpose in writing the biting irony of the preceding verses was **not** simply **to shame** the Corinthians. But if it did not shame them, they were

calloused indeed. His goal was to bring about a change of heart and manner of life in them. His motivation was love like that of a **father** for his **children.** Many ministers might address, advise, and instruct the Corinthians, but only one had planted the seed that brought them life. More than any guardian (Gal. 3:24) Paul had their interests at heart. For that reason he urged them to **imitate** him (1 Cor. 4:16; cf. vv. 9-13). He had one spiritual child who did just that, namely, **Timothy** (Phil. 2:20). Timothy could **remind** them by precept and example of Paul's **way of life in Christ Jesus,** which was in turn an imitation of their Lord.

4:18-21. Paul anticipated that not all would be moved by his appeal. **Some,** probably the unnamed party leaders (v. 5) or guardians (v. 15), were **arrogant,** which was the cause of the Corinthians' division problem. They might not be swayed by exhortation. They required action. And that, Paul knew, he was capable of meting out in the power of the Spirit (Acts 13:9-11). When he had preached to the Corinthians, he had not depended on his own ability but on the **power** of the Spirit (1 Cor. 2:4-5). He would rely on this same power for discipline (2 Cor. 10:4-6). This was the authority of God's rule (cf. Acts 5:3-11). Though Paul loved the Corinthians he knew that a loving father did not shy away from discipline (cf. Heb. 12:7). If it were needed, he would wield **a whip** (*rabdos,* a "rod"). From the Greco-Roman point of view this "rod" was a symbol of discipline executed by one in authority. Paul himself had been punished by rods more than once (Acts 16:22-23; 2 Cor. 11:25). But he preferred a visit characterized by **love and . . . a gentle spirit.**

III. Disorders in the Church (chaps. 5–6)

In the spirit of love but with the need for their discipline in mind, Paul turned in his letter to deal with certain disorders in the church, including their failures to discipline an immoral brother (chap. 5), to resolve personal disputes in a godly manner (6:1-11), and to maintain sexual purity (6:12-20).

A. Failure to discipline a sinner (chap. 5)

Pride is the opposite of love because it produces self-concern, while love responds to the needs of others. Corinthian pride had produced not only disunity but also indifference and an unwillingness to exercise discipline within the church.

5:1. The issue concerned a Corinthian Christian who was carrying on an incestuous affair with his stepmother, a relationship prohibited both in the Old Testament (Lev. 18:8; Deut. 22:22) and in Roman law (Cicero *Cluentes* 6. 15 and Gaius *Institutis* 1. 63). The fact that Paul said nothing about disciplining the woman suggests that she was not a Christian.

5:2. The shameful situation did not seem to faze the Corinthians in the least. If anything, the affair may have even bloated their arrogant spirits. The godly response would have been **grief** for this brother (cf. 12:26; Gal. 6:1-2), leading to discipline which would exclude him from intimacy with the congregation until he would repent (cf. Matt. 18:15-17).

5:3-5. In view of the Corinthian indifference to the matter, Paul was compelled to act. By the authority vested in him as an apostle, he **passed judgment on** the offender which he asked the church to enact at their next meeting. Here was an example of the power he had earlier referred to (4:20-21). What the exercise of this power accomplished is not certain. The translation of the Greek word *sarkos* by **the sinful nature** suggests the idea that the man's fleshly appetites were to be annulled. However, several factors suggest a different discipline, namely corporeal affliction—with *sarkos* understood as "body" (as in the NIV margin). (The result, of course, is the same—the man's purification.) First, the latter is the usual meaning of the term when it is juxtaposed with **spirit**, which signifies the whole man in his inner and external being. Second, the word translated **destroyed** (*olethron*) is a strong term, the noun form of which (*olethreutou*) occurs elsewhere in this letter (10:10) where it is translated "the destroying angel" who killed men. Third, Paul also spoke in this letter about a discipline which leads to death (11:30) with the same end in view—the ultimate preservation of the person (11:32; cf. 1 Tim. 1:20; 1 John 5:16).

So it seems probable that Paul intended this man should be excluded from the fellowship of the congregation, thus physically expressing his exclusion from God's protection which he formerly enjoyed (cf. Job 1:12) and thrusting him out into the arena of the world (1 John 5:19) where Satan would bring about his death. It thus became a painful example of the price of self-centered indifference and a powerful reminder of the demand for holiness in God's temple (1 Cor. 3:17; 6:19).

5:6. There was, of course, no excuse for the Corinthians' pathetic behavior. Paul reminded them of a truth they already knew but were failing to practice—**a little yeast** soon permeates **the whole batch of dough.** A small sickness can eventually kill a body. The need for church discipline is based on the same principle.

5:7-8. As the literal **yeast** was removed from the house during **the Festival** of Unleavened Bread (Ex. 12:15-20; 13:1-10), so that which it illustrated, sin, was to be removed from the house of God, the local church, during its "Festival of Unleavened Bread," a continual observance for a Christian who has found in Christ's death on the cross the once-for-all sacrifice of the **Passover Lamb** (cf. John 1:29; Heb. 10:10, 14). This was nowhere more true than in the celebration which commemorated that sacrificial act, the Lord's Supper, the quintessential act of fellowship for Christians. Probably Paul meant to exclude the unrepentant Christian from this meal in particular.

5:9-10. In an earlier **letter** Paul had given direction on this subject but the Corinthians had applied it only to those outside the church. Paul showed the absurdity of such a view by noting that such compliance would necessitate **leaving this world.** Paul was certainly no advocate of monasticism (or its separatistic kind in Protestantism).

5:11. What he called for was disciplinary action for **anyone** associated with the church, whether **a brother** or one in name only, who took part in the church while continuing a life of sin. The discipline demanded for such a one was exclusion from fellowship with other members. Certainly the prohibition extended to an exclusion from eating the communal meal, the Lord's Supper. Other social contact might also have been excluded. It was unlikely, however, that the sanctioned individual was barred from all congregational meetings, for the church's ministry might lead to his conviction and repentance (14:24-25).

5:12-13. It was not Paul's **business** to judge **those outside the church** (cf., e.g., his silence about the woman in 5:1); still less was it the business of the Corinthians. But discipline *within* the church was their responsibility.

Those in the world **God will judge** (cf. Acts 17:31). But those within the Christian community who continue in sin with an unrepentant spirit, the church should discipline by expulsion.

B. Failure to resolve personal disputes (6:1-11)

The topic of judgment continued as Paul shifted to another disorder afflicting the Corinthian church. The same laxity in dealing with the immoral brother was found in cases of personal disputes between members which the church refused to adjudicate. It was yet another manifestation of the divisive spirit which racked the congregation.

With the introductory phrase "Do you not know," Paul pointed toward certain truths which should have prevented the problem in the first place. The phrase recurs six times in this chapter alone. (Outside this letter this construction appears only three other times in the NT.) Paul had used it before (3:16; 5:6) and would subsequently use it again (9:13, 24) to the same effect. The implication that they should have known these things must have painfully hit home to a church enamored with its own wisdom and knowledge.

6:1. Paul's chagrin about this issue was great, not only because it further divided the church, but also because it hindered the work of God among the non-Christians in Corinth (cf. 10:32). Those related by faith needed to settle their disputes like brothers, not adversaries (cf. Gen. 13:7-9).

6:2. The first of six **do you not know** phrases in this chapter (cf. vv. 3, 9, 15-16, 19) concerned the role of saints in judging (cf. John 5:22; Rev. 3:21). Paul had probably taught this doctrine in Corinth in the course of his founding the church there, since he cited it as an indisputable proposition.

6:3. Since they were going to judge supernatural beings (the fallen **angels,** 2 Peter 2:4; Jude 6), surely they should handle mundane matters satisfactorily.

6:4. The form of the Greek word (*kāthizete,* **appoint**) may be a statement (indicative) or a command (imper.). The NIV has taken it as a command, making the difficult phrase **men of little account** refer to those in the church not too highly esteemed for their "wisdom"; but Paul considered them more than adequate for the task.

"Appoint" may be indicative (and therefore a question; see alternate trans. in marg.) which seems more likely in view of verse 5. If so, the participle translated "men of little account" would be better rendered "men who have no standing" **in the church,** that is, non-Christians. The sad refrain of verse 1 to which Paul would refer yet a third time in verse 6 was thus heard again.

6:5-6. No doubt the statement in verse 5 reddened some of the **wise** Corinthians' faces. Certainly a part of Paul's concern in this issue was the harmful effect such legal wrangling would have on the cause of the gospel in Corinth (9:23). Such lawsuits certainly did not glorify God (10:31-33).

6:7-8. Because their greed dishonored God, Paul concluded that the important issue was lost before the case had begun. He therefore said that mundane loss was preferable to the spiritual loss which the **lawsuits** produced. As it was, the Corinthian lawsuits seemed not to have been so much a matter of redressing wrong or seeing justice served as a means for personal gratification at the expense of fellow believers. This was "body life" at its worst!

6:9-10. Paul's third reminder (**Do you not know** . . . cf. vv. 2-3) was probably meant to complement the thought of verse 4, but it also illustrated the gap which existed between the Corinthians' future position and their present practice. **The wicked** would have no share in God's future **kingdom** because they were not related to Christ, the Heir (cf. Mark 12:7). The wicked would one day be judged by the saints (1 Cor. 6:2) on the basis of their works (Rev. 20:13) which would condemn them. Yet the saints were acting no differently.

The word *adikoi* ("the wicked") in 1 Corinthians 6:9 was used in verse 1, there translated "the ungodly." The verb form *adikeite* ("do wrong") however, was used in verse 8 to describe the Corinthians' behavior. Their future role should have radically affected their practice in the present (cf. 1 John 3:3). If they thought otherwise, Paul warned, they were **deceived** (cf. 1 Cor. 5:11; Rev. 21:7-8; 22:14-15).

The list of offenders was similar to that noted earlier (1 Cor. 5:10-11), which no doubt corresponded to problems in Corinth and in other large cities of the day (cf. Eph. 5:3-6). Homosexuality and male prostitution, for example, were especially characteristic of Greco-Roman society. Plato lauded homosexual love in *The Symposium* (181B). Nero, emperor at the time Paul wrote this letter, was about to marry the boy Sporus (Suetonius *Lives of the Caesars* 6. 28), an incident bizarre only in its formality, since 14 of the first 15 Roman emperors were homosexual or bisexual.

6:11. **Some** (but not all) the Corinthian Christians had been guilty of the sins listed in verses 9-10, **but** God had intervened. They **were washed . . . by the Spirit** (cf. Titus 3:5), **sanctified** in the Son (cf. 1 Cor. 1:2), and **justified** before God (cf. Rom. 8:33). This fact of justification was an appropriate thought for those judicially carping Corinthians.

C. Failure to practice sexual purity (6:12-20)

The theme of legality continued as Paul turned to another problem troubling the Corinthian assembly. This problem was the issue of freedom from the Old Testament Law in the area of sexual relationships. Paul addressed this issue in the manner of a dialogue, the diatribe style, familiar to his readers. This also enabled him to prepare them for both his subject matter and his approach in the rest of the letter, which concerned answers to questions and objections they had raised.

The issue of the limits of liberty (v. 12) was developed later by Paul in chapters 8–10. To a degree this subject also colored the discussion on public worship in chapters 11–14. The question of a Christian's relationship to food (6:13) was taken up in chapter 8. The resurrection of Christ (6:14) was expounded in chapter 15. The church as the body of Christ (6:15) was enlarged on in chapter 12. The sanctity of sex (6:16), about which Paul quoted Genesis 2:24 on the divine establishment of marriage, occupied his attention in chapter 7.

6:12. The words, **Everything is permissible for me,** had apparently become a slogan to cloak the immorality of some in Corinth. The statement was true but it required qualification. Paul qualified liberty with the principle of love applied to both neighbor and self (cf. Mark 12:31). Liberty which was not **beneficial** but detrimental to someone else was not loving (1 Cor. 8:1; 10:23) and was to be avoided. So too, liberty which became slavery (**I will not be mastered by anything**) was not love but hatred of self.

6:13-14. Food for the stomach and the stomach for food was another slogan by which some Corinthians sought to justify their immorality. They reasoned that "food" was both pleasurable and necessary. When their stomachs signaled hunger, food was taken to satisfy them. So too, they argued, sex was pleasurable and necessary. When their bodies signaled sexual desire, they needed to be satisfied. But Paul drew a sharp line between the stomach and the **body.** The body (*sōma*) in this context (cf. 2 Cor. 12:3) meant more than the physical frame; it referred to the whole person, composed of flesh (the material) and spirit (the immaterial; cf. 2 Cor. 2:13 with 7:5). The "body," therefore, was not perishable but eternal (1 Cor. 6:14), and it was **not meant for sexual immorality** (*porneia*) but for union with the Lord (vv. 15-17), which is reciprocal (cf. Eph. 1:23). The eternality of the body, the future destiny of the individual, was made certain by Christ's resurrection (1 Cor. 6:14; cf. 15:20).

6:15-17. So too the work of the Spirit (cf. 12:13) has affected Christians' present destiny and joined them to Christ (6:15). Could a Christian practice immorality without grieving Christ? (cf. 12:26) **Never!**

The union of two people involves more than physical contact. It is also a union of personalities which, however transient, alters both of them (6:16). Paul quoted Genesis 2:24 (**The two will** become one flesh) not to affirm that a man and a prostitute are married but to indicate the gravity of the sin (cf. Eph. 5:31-32).

A Christian's union with Christ likewise affects both him and the Savior, and one cannot act without affecting the other.

6:18. Corinthian Christians, when faced with immorality, should respond as did Joseph (Gen. 39:12)—they should run. **Flee from sexual immorality.** Immorality was a unique sin but not the most serious (cf. Matt. 12:32). It was, however, an offense against the sinner and those with whom he was related.

It is possible that the statement **All other sins a man commits are outside his body** (the word "other" is a translator's addition and is not represented by any word in the Gr. text) should be taken as a third slogan (cf. 1 Cor. 6:12-13) bandied about by some in Corinth. If so, then Paul's rejoinder (**he who sins sexually sins against his own body**) is a straight-forward denial. The Greek construction is similar to that in verse 13.

6:19-20. Among those grieved was the **Holy Spirit** who indwells every Christian (**who is in you;** cf. 12:13; 1 John 3:24). Also God the Father is grieved, for He seeks **honor** (Matt. 5:16), not shame, from those who are **bought at a price** (cf. 1 Cor. 7:23), that price being "the precious blood of Christ" (1 Peter 1:19).

IV. Difficulties in the Church (chaps. 7:1-16:12)

The note on which Paul concluded chapter 6, "honor God with your body," could well serve as the guiding principle for this fourth section in which he answered questions put to him by the Corinthians on the topics of marriage (chap. 7), personal liberty (8:1–11:1), church order (11:2–14:40) and doctrine (chap. 15).

A. Counsel concerning marriage (chap. 7)

1. MARRIAGE AND CELIBACY (7:1-9)

Paul had spoken in chapter 6 on the dangers of sexuality outside of marriage. Then he turned to the duty of sexuality within marriage. Probably abandonment of marital duties on the part of some in Corinth had contributed to the immorality he had just described.

7:1. The phrase **not to marry** may be an overtranslation of the Greek phrase "not to touch a woman." Paul probably intended it as a euphemism for sexual intercourse (cf. Gen. 20:6; Prov. 6:29). This too may have been a slogan for some in Corinth (cf. 1 Cor. 6:12-13) who argued that even those who were married should abstain from sexual intercourse. All that Paul said, however, was that celibacy was a **good** state and not to be depreciated.

7:2. However, marriage with sexual intercourse was much more common. For an individual to try to maintain a celibate state apart from the enablement of God (cf. v. 7) would lead to **immorality.** For that reason Paul encouraged people to marry.

7:3-4. Paul stressed the equality and reciprocity of the husband and wife's sexual relationship by emphasizing the responsibilities of each to satisfy the other.

7:5. Some in Corinth were trying to practice celibacy within marriage. Apparently this refraining from sex within marriage was a unilateral decision of one partner, not a mutually agreed-on decision (vv. 3-4). Such a practice sometimes led to immorality on the part of the other mate (v. 5b; cf. v. 2). Paul commanded that they stop this sort of thing unless three conditions were met: (a) The abstention from sexual intercourse was to be a matter of **mutual consent** on the part of both husband and wife. (b) They were to agree beforehand on a **time** period at the end of which normal intercourse would be resumed. (c) This refraining was to enable them to **devote** themselves **to prayer** in a concentrated way.

7:6. Paul presented this possibility for temporary abstention from sexual intercourse in marriage **as a concession** if the preceding stipulations were met. He did not want his advice construed as a **command.** The suggestion that Paul was referring to marriage itself as a "concession" is unlikely in view of Genesis 1:28, the first command to mankind in the Bible, and in view of Paul's Jewish background where marriage was obligatory for all men except the sexually impotent (Mishnah *Niddah* 5. 9).

7:7. Paul, however, did not want any stigma to be attached to the single state, so he affirmed, as he had done earlier

(v. 1), that celibacy was good. Paul, in fact, thought it to be an excellent state, and wished that everyone could see the benefits of celibacy from his point of view. He realized, however, that marriage or remaining single was more than a matter of weighing alternative benefits; each was a **gift from God.** It is God who enables each Christian to be married or single (cf. Matt. 19:12).

7:8-9. What Paul wrote in verses 1-2 he now pointedly applied to those in Corinth who were unmarried but were sexually experienced (cf. "virgins," v. 25). **The unmarried** included divorced persons of both sexes as well as widowers, with **widows** mentioned separately (cf. vv. 39-40). For these Paul affirmed the suitability of remaining single, if they had the appropriate enablement from God (v. 7). Paul, no armchair theologian, anticipated the practical question of how a person can know whether he or she is able to remain celibate. Paul gave his judgment; if one lacks sexual **control,** he does not have the gift of celibacy, and should **marry.**

2. MARRIAGE AND DIVORCE (7:10-24)

Paul's advice to married Christians is summed up in verse 24 after he addressed, in turn, individual Christians married to one another (vv. 10-11), Christians married to non-Christians (vv. 12-16), and other external physical and vocational states for Christians (vv. 17-23).

7:10-11. Paul's direction to Christians married to one another was like that of Jesus Himself (Mark 10:2-12): as a rule, no divorce (cf. Matt. 5:32). The difference in language between **separate** (chōristhēnai) on the part of the **wife** (1 Cor. 7:10) and **divorce** (aphienai) on the part of the **husband** (v. 11) was probably due to stylistic variation as the word translated "separate" (chōrizō) was commonly used in the vernacular as a term for divorce (William F. Arndt and F. Wilbur Gingrich, A Greek-English Lexicon of the New Testament, 4th ed. Chicago: University of Chicago Press, 1957, p. 899). When problems occurred in a Christian marriage, the resolution was to be sought in reconciliation (cf. Eph. 4:32), not in divorce.

7:12-13. The rest referred to Christians who were married to non-

Christians. Jesus, in the course of His ministry, never had addressed this issue (cf. vv. 10, 25). But Paul, with no less authority (cf. v. 25) did. Some divorces may have been initiated because of the command of Ezra to the Israelites in Jerusalem after the Exile (Ezra 10:11) to divorce themselves from pagan spouses. Paul affirmed that the same principle should operate in a believer-unbeliever marriage as in a marriage of two Christians: as a rule, no divorce. A Christian husband **must not divorce** (aphietō) an unbelieving **wife,** and a Christian wife **must not divorce** (aphietō) a non-Christian **husband.**

7:14. Divorce was to be avoided because the Christian spouse was a channel of God's grace in the marriage. Within the "one flesh" relationship the blessing of God which came to the Christian affected the family as a whole (cf. Jacob in Laban's household [Gen. 30:27] and Joseph in Potiphar's [Gen. 39:5]; also cf. Rom. 11:16). It is in this sense that **the unbelieving** spouse was **sanctified** and the children were **holy.**

7:15. However, there were exceptions to the rule of no divorce. If **the unbeliever** insisted on a divorce, he was not to be denied (the word trans. **leaves** is chōrizetai, the verb used in v. 10). Should this occur, the Christian was **not bound** to maintain the marriage but was free to marry again (cf. v. 39). Paul did not say, as he did in verse 11, that the Christian in this case should "remain unmarried." (However, some Bible students say that not being "bound" means the Christian is not obligated to prevent the divorce, but that it does not give freedom for remarriage.)

The second part of this verse in which Paul affirmed that **God** had **called** Christians **to live in peace** could be understood as a separate sentence. The same conjunction (de, **but**) which introduced the exception at the beginning of this verse was repeated by Paul, probably to indicate another shift in thought and a return to the main point in this section, namely, the importance for the Christian spouse of preserving the marriage union and living "in peace" with the non-Christian. (For a similar digression in a discourse on the general rule of no divorce, see Matt. 19:9.) Paul's point was that a Christian should strive to preserve the union and to keep the peace, but with the understanding that marriage is a mutual not a unilateral relationship.

7:16. Paul then stated a second (cf. v. 14) and crucial reason why a Christian should stay married to a non-Christian. God might use the Christian mate as a channel of blessing (cf. v. 14), leading ultimately to the point where the unbelieving spouse would believe the message of the Cross and experience salvation (cf. 1 Peter 3:1-2).

7:17. The general principle which Paul affirmed in dealing with decisions affecting a Christian's marital status was again stated three times (vv. 17, 20, 24; cf. also v. 26): in brief, "stay put." The call to conversion radically altered an individual's spiritual relationship but need effect no changes at all in physical relationships that were not immoral.

7:18-19. The external operation of **circumcision** or the obliteration of the same (cf. [apocryphal] 1 Maccabees 1:15-16) was a matter of little importance compared with **keeping God's commands,** which for Paul meant being controlled by the Spirit (cf. Rom. 2:25-29).

7:20-23. Likewise, a Christian's vocational **situation** is a matter of little consequence (if status can be changed, well and good; if not, it is not a matter for worry). What matters is that every Christian should realize he is **Christ's slave** and needs to render obedience to Him. Every vocation then becomes Christian service performed for the Master (cf. Eph. 6:5-8).

7:24. The fact that **God** had **called** each one to a vocation and sought from each one faithful service in that calling elevated and sanctified both the work and the worker. A Christian could then "live in peace" (v. 15) in his calling and carry it out as one **responsible to God.**

3. MARRIAGE AND MINISTRY (7:25-38)

The basic principle Paul had been setting forth (viz., to continue in one's present position) was then applied to those who had never married. Apparently this was in response to a question put to him. Paul urged them to remain single, for three reasons: (a) an impending time of distress for Christians (vv. 26-28), (b) the imminent return of Christ (vv. 29-31), and (c) the opportunity for undistracted service for Christ (vv. 32-35).

7:25. Virgins here were sexually inexperienced people who had never married. Jesus had never specifically addressed the propriety of marriage per se (cf. Matt. 19:10-12, 29) but Paul gave his **judgment** on the issue which they could take as **trustworthy** counsel. (He of course was writing under the inspiration of the Holy Spirit and hence his "judgment" was as authoritative as Christ's words; cf. 1 Cor. 7:40.)

7:26-28. The present crisis may have referred to persecution then being suffered by the Corinthians (cf. John 16:33; 2 Tim. 3:12; 1 Peter 4:12) or to an experience of suffering which Paul anticipated would shortly befall them (in which case the words could be trans. "impending crisis"). In view of his silence in the letter about any present suffering on their part the latter point of view (and trans.) is preferred. (Cf. 1 Cor. 4:8 which intimates a perceived state of well-being or even positive euphoria.) Still, when persecution came, as Paul felt it surely would, its onslaught could be handled more ably by single than by married persons. However fearsome the thought of martyrdom (cf. 13:3) might be to a single person, it was doubly so to a married person responsible for a spouse and children. With these conditions in view marriage would not be wrong (**if you do marry, you have not sinned**), but it would be inexpedient.

7:29-31. The second reason Paul felt the single state was advantageous was the potential it offered for detachment from temporal situations. The phrase **the time is short** referred to the Lord's return (cf. Rom. 13:11), but it was also a summary philosophy of life for Paul who lived not for the temporary but for the eternal (cf. 2 Cor. 4:18). This detachment from temporal matters should characterize all Christians but it was more complex for the married (cf. Mark 13:12) for whom, nonetheless, devotion to their Lord should occupy first place in life (Luke 14:26). Paul certainly was not recommending abandoning marital duties (cf. 1 Cor. 7:3-5).

Instead he was calling for a commitment to eternal matters and a corresponding detachment from the institutions, values, and substance of **this world** which was **passing away** (v. 31). Such a commit-

519

ment was more easily made and enacted by a single person.

7:32-35. Paul's third reason was a development of the second. The single state has potentially fewer encumbrances and distractions than the married state, so it more easily facilitates a spirit of **undivided devotion to the Lord.** In the Sermon on the Mount, Jesus warned His followers against letting concern for the material aspects of this life distract them from devotion to God (Matt. 6:25-34). The poor widow (Mark 12:44) gave all her material sustenance to God as an act of singular devotion. A **married** man or woman with a needful concern for the well-being of his family would have been less likely to do that. The situation illustrates Paul's point that the single life with its greater simplicity in obligations allows a potentially greater commitment of time, resources, and self **to the Lord** than would be possible for a married person dutifully carrying out the marital and familial obligations attached to that state.

7:36-38. The interpretation and translation of this passage is difficult, as the alternate marginal translation indicates. The issue revolves around whether the indefinite pronoun **anyone** (v. 36) refers to a father or to a prospective bridegroom. The NIV translators, following most modern commentators, have adopted the latter point of view but have included the traditional interpretation in the margin. The strength of the bridegroom view lies in the fact that it permits a consistent subject for the verbs used throughout the passage, a strength which the NIV translators forfeited by making the **virgin** the subject of the phrase **getting along in years.** This decision was possibly prompted by the need to explain why the bridegroom might be thought to act improperly (i.e., his delay in consummating the marriage may, with her advancing age, adversely affect her chance of ever getting **married**). The bridegroom view, however, faces a lexical difficulty in the meaning of two verbs (*gameō* and *gamizō*) for marriage. In order to sustain the bridegroom view it is necessary to understand the terms as virtual synonyms, meaning "to marry." But *gamizō* usually means "give in marriage," and *gameō* means simply "marry," as these words do in the other

New Testament passages where they occur together (Matt. 24:38; Mark 12:25). This distinction in meaning continued to be recognized even in the second century (Apollonius Dyscolus *Syntax* 3. 153). So it seems that the marginal reading is to be preferred.

Paul, then, gave advice to a father who in the first-century culture exercised great decision-making authority in matters affecting his family. A father may have decided that his daughter should not marry, possibly due to reasons similar to those Paul had mentioned in 1 Corinthians 7:25-34. But in coming to this decision, the father had not reckoned with the fact that his daughter might not be able to remain single. She might not possess the gift of celibacy (v. 7). If so, Paul recommended that the father should not feel obligated to hold to his previous commitment but instead let his daughter marry. However, the father should feel free to follow through on his conviction to keep his daughter single (v. 37) if three conditions were met: (a) He had a **settled** and firm conviction about the propriety of her celibacy. (b) He was in a position where he was free to exercise his authority, that is, he was not a slave in which case the master could determine the daughter's destiny. (c) He was **under no compulsion** from evidence which suggested that his daughter was not able to remain single but required marriage instead. If these conditions were met, then the father did well **not** to **give her in marriage.**

4. REMARRIAGE AND WIDOWS (7:39-40)

7:39-40. Paul's earlier counsel to widows (vv. 8-9) was to remain single. In that previous context, however, he acknowledged the fact that not all were equipped to do so. The only constraint Paul placed on a widow who sought remarriage was the obligation to marry another Christian (**he must belong to the Lord**)—an obligation which though previously unstated, he no doubt meant to apply to all who sought marriage partners. That point alone, however, affected a widow's options. Within that condition she might choose whom she wanted and find with that husband great happiness, though Paul added that in his **judgment** she would be **happier** if she remained single. This advice was not only from Paul's heart but also guided by **the Spirit of God,** who equipped both single and married Christians (v. 7) for their respective roles.

B. Counsel concerning Christian liberty (chaps. 8–14)

Paul's reply to the Corinthians' question concerning the propriety of eating the meat of an animal offered in a pagan sacrifice touched off an extensive response, probably because he sensed that this particular issue was another manifestation of the Corinthians' self-centeredness, which produced other similar problems in the church.

Two words which seemed to epitomize the Corinthians' point of view were "freedom" (*eleutheros,* 9:1, 19; *eleutheria,* 10:29) and "rights" (*exousia,* 8:9; 9:4-6, 12, 18). Paul used and qualified these words in these chapters by stressing the importance of a love for others which sought their "good" (*symphero, -os,* 10:24, 33; 12:7; cf. 6:12) by "strengthening" or "building" them up (*oikodomeō, -ia,* 8:1, 10; 10:23; 14:3-5, 12, 17, 26). These two themes, "me first" or "you first," and Paul's development of them as they affected believers in relation to pagan worship and Christian worship, unified these chapters. Secondarily Paul showed that the former attitude ultimately brought God's disapproval (*adokimos,* 9:27) and His discipline (10:5-10; 11:30-32).

1. CHRISTIAN LIBERTY IN RELATION TO PAGAN WORSHIP (8:1-11:1)

Ordinarily the Greeks and Romans burned the less desirable portions of an animal in the course of their sacrifices and retained the choicer parts for personal consumption at banquets celebrating the sacrifices. If a sacrifice were made in connection with a state function, the meat which remained was frequently sold in the marketplace. The Corinthians' questions apparently concerned (a) the acceptability of buying and eating meat from one of these sacrificial animals; (b) the acceptability of eating this meat as an invited guest in a friend's home; (c) the acceptability of attending one of these pagan sacrifices and enjoying the meal of celebration which followed in the temple precincts. Paul spoke to each of these issues.

a. The principle of brotherly love (chap. 8)

Paul struck right to the heart of the matter in these preliminary verses by stating a basic principle: love is superior to knowledge (cf. chap. 13).

8:1. Much as he had begun his reply on marital questions, Paul may have quoted a Corinthian sentiment (**we all possess knowledge**) with which he basically agreed but which required qualification. **Knowledge** was essential in correctly responding to their questions but those who thought they had it did not, as Paul would show.

8:2-3. In the first place, knowledge about God was always partial (13:12). In the second place, true knowledge led to **God** and a love for Him which Paul knew must issue in love for others (cf. 1 John 4:20-21).

8:4. With the principle stated it now remained to be applied to the particular instance in question. The statements which follow the two **thats** (**an idol is nothing at all** and **there is no God but One**) may well have been Corinthian affirmations with which Paul could wholeheartedly agree. An "idol" indeed was "nothing" (Ps. 115:4-8), for there is only one God (Deut. 4:35, 39). Hence **eating food sacrificed to idols** was, in itself, inconsequential.

8:5-6. The pantheon of the Greeks and Romans, not to mention the **gods** and **lords** of the mystery religions, were indeed numerous, but one God alone is real (Deut. 10:17). The **Father** is the source of all (Gen. 1:1) and the One for whom the Corinthians should live (1 Cor. 10:31). The **Lord Jesus Christ** was the agent of Creation (Col. 1:16) and the One **through whom** the Corinthians lived (1 Cor. 12:27; Eph. 1:23).

8:7-8. If all Corinthian Christians could have agreed that an idol was nothing and that there was only one God (v. 4), then they might have eaten the idol meat with impunity. However, such was not the case. All, in fact, did *not* possess knowledge. The **conscience** of some Christians was not strengthened on this point by the truth. They were still ignorant and had not come to the point where they could accept eating this kind of meat as a matter of indifference. For them it was wrong, and so to eat it was sin (cf. Rom. 14:23). Paul denied the validity of their scruples, but in the advice which followed he suggested that the solution would be found in love, not in knowledge.

8:9. When knowledge uninformed by love dictated one's behavior, Paul warned that spiritual harm would result. The **exercise of . . . freedom** by the knowledgeable could in certain circumstances become an obstacle, **a stumbling block** in the **weak** Christian's walk with God (cf. v. 13).

8:10. As an illustration Paul posed a situation in which a **weak** Christian saw a knowledgeable brother enjoying a meal **in an idol's temple** and was by this example encouraged to join in, even though he could not do so with the clear conscience before God that the knowledgeable Christian enjoyed.

8:11. As a consequence the conscience of this **weak** believer was seared (cf. 1 Tim. 4:2), and his capacity to distinguish right from wrong was lost (cf. Titus 1:15) leading to his spiritual ruin and physical death (cf. 1 Cor. 10:9-10; Rom. 14:15). *Apollytai*, rendered **is destroyed,** often refers to physical death (e.g., Matt. 2:13; Acts 5:37). The selflessness of **Christ** was an example for the knowledgeable. If Christ loved **this brother** so that he was willing to give up His exalted rights and even His life (Phil. 2:6, 8), surely the strong could give up his right to eat such meat.

8:12. To be arrogantly indifferent to the need of weaker Christians results in **sin** not only against them (for **you . . . wound their weak conscience;** cf. v. 7) but also **against Christ** of whose body they are members (12:26-27; cf. 1:30; Matt. 25:40, 45). Paul experienced this point acutely on the Damascus Road (Acts 9:4-5).

8:13. In summary Paul stressed the priority of brotherly love. He did not demand that the knowledgeable relinquish their right, but he illustrated how he would apply the principle to himself. Paul did not want any **brother to fall** (cf. v. 9) but to be "built up" (cf. v. 1), and knowledge governed by love accomplished that.

As a final note to this chapter it should be understood that Paul did not say that a knowledgeable Christian must abandon his freedom to the ignorant prejudice of a "spiritual" bigot. The

"weak brother" (v. 11) was one who followed the example of another Christian, not one who carped and coerced that knowledgeable Christian into a particular behavioral pattern. Also it was unlikely that Paul saw this weak brother as permanently shackling the freedom of the knowledgeable Christian. The "weak brother" was no omnipresent phantom but an individual who was to be taught so that he too could enjoy his freedom (Gal. 5:1).

b. The regulation of privilege (9:1–10:13)

(1) The positive example of Paul (chap. 9). Paul ended his warning about exercising freedom if it had detrimental effects on a brother with a statement expressing his willingness to be a vegetarian if it would keep a brother from faltering in his faith (8:13). He then illustrated how he practiced what he preached in this matter of rights when applied to food and drink. It seemed that the rumblings of doubt about his apostleship, which would later call forth an extended defense (esp. 2 Cor. 10–13), had already started. Paul neatly illustrated the principle expressed in 1 Corinthians 8 by relating it to the issue which seems to have been a bone of contention concerning his apostleship. That issue was his steadfast refusal to derive material support from those to whom he was ministering, so no one could say he was motivated by money (cf. 2 Cor. 2:17).

9:1-2. Paul affirmed that his position as **an apostle** was like that of the knowledgeable Christian in this matter of freedom and rights. The four questions in these verses were rhetorical and expected an affirmative reply, though some among the Corinthians may have denied one or all of them. The third and fourth questions seem directly related to apostolic authority, but apparently Paul believed that the fourth one was more significant than the third. In the course of an extended defense of his **apostleship** in 2 Corinthians he never mentioned seeing the **Lord** (cf. Acts 1:21) but he returned repeatedly to the theme of this verse (1 Cor. 9:2) that the Corinthians themselves were his vindication (2 Cor. 3:1-3; 5:12; 7:14-16; 8:24).

9:3. Paul's **defense** looked forward (to vv. 4-23) and not back (to vv. 1-2, which guaranteed a right he had willingly forfeited). Paul's defense, then, was an explanation of why he refused to be maintained at the church's expense even though he had a right to such support (vv. 1-2). This served also as a positive example of his counsel to the knowledgeable brother who was concerned about his rights (chap. 8).

9:4-6. The word **right** in these verses is the same word (*exousia*) translated "freedom" in 8:9. It links the chapters, though Paul's subject here was not sacrificial meat but ordinary **food.** To bring out the meaning of these rhetorical questions the phrase "at the expense of the church" could be added to verses 4-5 (cf. Matt. 10:10-11). Paul was not alone in refusing this right but had an ally in **Barnabas.** Commitment to this practice may have marked their first missionary journey together (Acts 13:1–14:28) and apparently continued to characterize their separate ministries.

9:7. Paul saw the right of maintenance as a principle which extended beyond the apostles to others in the church; he illustrated the point along six different lines. The first was custom. The **soldier,** farmer, and shepherd are all supported by their work.

9:8-10. Second, the Old Testament itself substantiated the principle of just remuneration. Paul's illustration and interpretation has perplexed many commentators. Why did Paul, after referring to the practice of not muzzling a graintreading ox, then ask, **Is it about oxen that God is concerned?** Was he changing the sense of the Old Testament passage? Not among the perplexed was Luther who tried to cut this Gordian knot by observing that since oxen cannot read, Paul's point in the passage was transparent. Problems nonetheless remain for less exuberant interpreters. The solution is probably found in the context of Deuteronomy 25:4 which Paul quoted. That chapter contains instructions not about animal husbandry but human relationships. Not muzzling an ox, therefore, was probably a proverbial expression concerning just remuneration, properly understood and interpreted as such by Paul. A modern parallel would be the adage, "You can't teach an old dog new tricks," which is commonly applied in contexts other than canine obedience.

9:11. Paul's third illustration grew out of verse 10 and his discussion of Deuteronomy 25:4, but it concerned a basic principle of community reciprocity: beneficial service should be rewarded. If Paul had been used to bring **spiritual** riches to the Corinthians (1 Cor. 1:5), **material** recompense was surely not **too much** to expect.

9:12. A fourth line of appeal was made to the precedent of other Christian leaders. Paul had earlier alluded to the ministry of Peter (Cephas) (v. 5). Though unattested, it is probable that Peter ministered in Corinth (cf. 1:12; 3:22; 15:5) and was supported during that time by the church. The same was probably also true of Apollos (1:12; 3:4-6, 22; 4:6; 16:12). If the church supported them, their founding father Paul was surely no less deserving.

Yet Paul did not exercise **this right** (cf. 8:9) because he did not want to **hinder** the response of anyone to **the gospel.** Had he been materially recompensed for his ministry, some might have presumed he was simply another itinerant educator motivated by profits (cf. 2 Cor. 2:17) and would have refused him a hearing. To avoid being a "stumbling block" (1 Cor. 8:9) to any, Paul relinquished his right to receive **support from** those to whom he ministered.

9:13. Paul had temporarily interrupted his catalog of illustrations on the right of recompense to underscore the rationale behind his own refusal to exercise that right, despite its general practice by other worthy servants of Christ (v. 5). He then offered a fifth example in support of the right of remuneration by citing the practice of the priesthood. Old Testament priests were remunerated for their service (Num. 18:8-32), and so were the pagan priests with whom the Corinthians were probably more familiar (cf. 1 Cor. 8:10).

9:14. In the sixth place Paul appealed to the weightiest point of all, the instruction of Jesus that those who give out **the gospel** should derive support from it (Luke 10:7).

9:15. With this catalog of arguments completed Paul had convincingly established his **rights** in relation to the Corinthian church. However, he underscored once again (cf. v. 12) his refusal to exercise those rights. He expressed one reason in verse 12, a desire to avoid any hint of mercenary motivation in his ministry. A second and related reason was now stated: the opportunity to affirm the integrity of his commitment to the ministry (cf. 2 Cor. 11:9-12). This was Paul's **boast:** he ministered willingly and freely from his heart (cf. 2 Cor. 2:17).

9:16. Of course Paul's "call" to the ministry was unique. Others have responded voluntarily to the call to follow Christ (Mark 3:13; John 1:37-39), but Paul was flattened by it (Acts 22:6-10). Like Jonah, Paul was **compelled to preach** (cf. 1 Cor. 1:17), and like that prophet, **woe** to him if he shirked his task.

9:17. The condition, **if I preach voluntarily,** was not true of Paul as he had just said, so he had no claim to any special recompense since he was **simply discharging the trust committed to** him (cf. Luke 17:10).

9:18. Did he then not have any **reward?** Yes; two, in fact. First, he had his boast (v. 15) that he offered the gospel **free of charge,** and no one could deny that (cf. 2 Cor. 11:9-10). Second, he had the opportunity to see the gospel at work among those to whom he preached (1 Cor. 9:19, 23), and these results, the believers themselves, were his reward (cf. 2 Cor. 7:3-4). The word translated "reward" (*misthos*) may also refer to a wage. Paul had shunned material recompense, but he was not without a reward or return for his labor. He had the joy of reaping. To widen that harvest he would gladly give up certain **rights,** among them the right to material support, in order to enjoy both the integrity of his boast about his ministry and the results of his ministry (cf. John 4:36).

9:19. Paul had not shackled the exercise of his rights in the area of food and drink alone (as he had intimated the knowledgeable Christians should do, 8:9-13), but he had applied it to numerous facets of his ministry so that **though** he was **free** (*eleutheros;* cf. 8:9; 9:1) he voluntarily became a **slave** (cf. Phil. 2:6-7) for the good of others (1 Cor. 10:33) whom he wanted **to win** (9:22).

9:20. Though Paul was primarily an apostle to the Gentiles (Gal. 2:8), he never lost his concern for the salvation of his own people (Rom. 9:3). He made it his

custom to seek out the synagogue in each town he entered (Acts 17:2) in order **to win the Jews** (Rom. 1:16). No verse points out more starkly Paul's own consciousness of what he was, both before and after meeting Christ. Before, he was the Jew's **Jew,** faultless with regard to legalistic righteousness (Phil. 3:6). Afterward, he was a new man (2 Cor. 5:17; Gal. 2:20), who had found in Christ the righteousness he had sought (Rom. 10:4; 1 Cor. 1:30). He was still a Hebrew (2 Cor. 11:22; Phil 3:5), but he was no longer a Jew living according to the Law (**I . . . am not under the law**). Still, he was willing to subject himself to the scruples of the Jews (e.g., Acts 21:23-36) in order to gain a hearing for the gospel and **to win** them to Christ. Yet he never compromised the essence of the gospel at the heart of which was salvation by faith, not works (Gal. 2:16; Eph. 2:8-9) and freedom from legalism (Gal. 2:4-5).

9:21. In contrast to the Jews, "those under the Law" (v. 20), **those not having the Law** were the Gentiles. Among Gentiles, Paul was willing to abandon past scruples of a morally indifferent sort, such as eating meat offered sacrificially to a pagan god (10:27; cf. Acts 15:29), in order **to win** Gentiles to Christ. But though Paul was a forceful advocate of liberty (Gal. 5:1), he did not suggest he was an advocate of libertinism (cf. 1 Cor. 6:12-20). He was still under authority, but not to the Old Testament Law. He was responsible to God (cf. 3:9) and Christ (cf. 4:1) and was enabled by the Spirit to fulfill the law of love (Rom. 13:8-10; Gal. 5:13-25), the opposite of lawlessness (cf. Matt. 24:12 where lawlessness drives out love). **Christ's law** (Gal. 6:2) was to love God and man (Mark 12:30-31), which law Paul obeyed (1 Cor. 10:31-33).

9:22. In his references to Jews and Gentiles in the preceding verses, Paul explained his voluntary restraint of freedom in order to reach unbelievers with the gospel. Some suggest that **the weak** in this verse refers to Jews and Gentiles together in a state of unbelief and so was intended to summarize Paul's previously stated convictions (cf. Rom. 5:6 where "the weak" are also called "the ungodly"). It is more likely, however, that Paul was referring explicitly to the weak Corinthians described in 1 Corinthians

8:9-11 (cf. Jew, Greeks, and the church of God in 10:32). His concern to win them was not in the preliminary sense of justification as in the case of unbelieving Jews and Gentiles (9:20-21) but to win the Corinthians in terms of sanctification and maturity in Christ (cf. Matt. 18:15)—and so to save them for God's ongoing work in their lives (cf. 1 Cor. 5:5; 8:11). Paul's condescension to the scruples and customs of all men (cf. "everyone" in 9:19) found application on a momentary case-by-case basis since it would be impossible to satisfy simultaneously the penchants of both Jews and Gentiles alike.

9:23. Paul voluntarily did this in order to gain the widest possible hearing for the gospel and so to share in its blessings as God's fellow worker (3:9), reaping the joyful harvest of many won to Christ (cf. John 4:36).

9:24-25. Paul's commitment to this course of ministry did not come easily. It required personal discipline (strict training) like that of an athlete who strove for supremacy in his field (cf. 15:10). To that end Paul willingly gave up certain privileges which might otherwise be his to enjoy so that he could win the prize. The prize for Paul was not the temporary crown (stephanon) bestowed by men (in the biennial games near Corinth the "crown" was a pine wreath) but the eternal crown bestowed by Christ (3:13-14; 2 Cor. 5:10). Paul's crown would be the consummation of the reward (1 Cor. 9:18) he partially enjoyed, the opportunity to glory before Christ in those he had been able to win (2 Cor. 1:14; Phil. 2:16; 1 Thes. 2:19).

9:26-27. Paul's dictum of becoming "all things to all men" (v. 22) could have been construed as the aimless capitulation of an unprincipled man. But it was just the opposite! Every move made in the course of his race was calculated to further his pursuit of the prize (cf. Phil. 3:13-14). Every blow struck was meant to land squarely on his opponent and send him reeling from the contest (cf. Eph. 6:12; James 4:7). To achieve this, Paul would not let his body master him (cf. 1 Cor. 6:12); sometimes he denied even its demand for rightful privileges and pleasures (8:9) for a greater good (10:33).

Paul was competing well himself and had called many to join him (the word preached is kēryxas, the noun form of which signified a herald who summoned contestants to a race), but that did not guarantee him a victorious finish. He held out the possibility that even he could be disqualified for the prize. The single Greek word translated by that phrase (adokimos) literally means "unapproved." In other contexts it was applied to the unsaved (e.g., Rom. 1:28; Titus 1:16). Here Paul was not addressing the issue of salvation, nor for that matter was even the prize specifically in mind. Rather, he seemed concerned with continuance in the race. Like the brother who had indulged in immorality (1 Cor. 5:1-5), Paul's life could be cut short by the disciplinary disapproval of God. God had disciplined in the past (10:6-10), was disciplining in the present (11:30-32), and would discipline in the immediate future (5:5). Paul was concerned that some might not be able to say with him one day, "I have fought the good fight, I have finished the race" (2 Tim. 4:7), but would find themselves cut off in the midst of the contest by the disciplinary action of God.

(2) The negative example of Israel (10:1-13). 10:1. So that the Corinthians might not think God's discipline would be an unlikely eventuality for a people so blessed as they (1:5), Paul cited the illustration of another group of people who were greatly blessed by God but yet experienced His severe discipline. Israel of old was reckless and unrestrained after her physical and spiritual freedom from tyranny in Egypt. As a result God meted out severe discipline by cutting short the lives of many Israelites. They were all in the "race" (9:24), but almost all were disqualified (9:27) in spite of their advantages.

Five advantages were enjoyed by Israel. First, all the liberated Israelites enjoyed the supernatural guidance (Ex. 13:21) and protection (Ex. 14:19-20) of the pillar of cloud in their Exodus from Egypt. The Corinthians had similarly experienced God's guidance (cf. Luke 1:79) and protection (cf. 1 Peter 1:5). Second, all Israelites passed through the sea and experienced a miraculous deliverance from those who sought to take their lives (Ex. 14:21-28). So too had the Corinthians experienced a miraculous deliverance—salvation (cf. Heb. 2:14-15; Gal. 1:4).

10:2. Third, the Israelites **were all baptized into Moses,** that is, united with their spiritual head, God's servant, who became the object of their trust (Ex. 14:31; cf. John 5:45). The Corinthians had been baptized into the body of Christ (1 Cor. 12:13) of which He is the Head (Eph. 1:22) and in whom they trusted (Matt. 12:21; Eph. 1:12).

10:3. As a fourth privilege, the Israelites **all** enjoyed **spiritual food,** the supernatural bread from heaven (Ex. 16:4, 15). The Corinthians too had eaten bread from heaven (cf. John 6:31-34).

10:4. As a fifth advantage, Paul listed the **spiritual drink** enjoyed by Israel in the desert (Ex. 17:6). According to Paul, **Christ** was the source of this supernatural water. Since the incident of the rock which produced water marked the beginning of Israel's wilderness wanderings (Ex. 17:1-7) and happened again near the ending of their wanderings (Num. 20:1-13), Paul concluded that Christ **accompanied them.** Christ too was the source of supernatural water for the Corinthians (cf. John 4:10-14).

It is possible that these five blessings were intended by Paul to reflect the two ordinances of baptism (1 Cor. 10:1-2) and the Lord's Supper (vv. 3-4) which the Corinthians may have thought communicated a magical protection like similar rites in some of the mystery religions. The Corinthians did seem to have a distorted view and practice of both of these ordinances (cf. 11:17-34; 15:29) which required correction.

10:5. The presence of supernatural privileges in the lives of Old Testament Israelites did not produce automatic success. On the contrary, in spite of their special advantages, **most of them** (in fact, all but two members of one generation, Joshua and Caleb) experienced God's discipline, were disqualified, and died in **the desert** (Num. 14:29). In light of this, Paul's avowed need for personal self-discipline (1 Cor. 9:27) was genuine since even Moses was disqualified for the prize (Num. 20:12).

10:6. Since this was so, the Corinthians' complacency in matters of self-discipline and their corresponding penchant for self-indulgence required immediate remedial action. Christian freedom was not meant to lead to self-indulgence

but to selfless service (cf. Gal. 5:13), as the behavior of past Israelites illustrated.

Paralleling the fivefold blessings enjoyed by Israel in their newfound freedom from Egypt, Paul proceeded to recount a fivefold failure experienced by Israel during this time. He began with the Israelites' craving for the pleasures of Egypt, summarized in their plaintive cry, "Give us meat to eat!" (Num. 11:4-34, esp. v. 13) God gave them what they wanted but while the meat was still between their teeth, He struck them with a plague. The Israelites named the cemetery for those who were killed "Kibroth Hattaavah" ("graves of craving"; Num. 11:34). The application to the Corinthian situation was obvious (cf. 1 Cor. 8:13).

10:7. Second, many in Israel failed by participating in idolatry (Ex. 32:1-6) and paid for it with their lives (Ex. 32:28, 35). Apparently some Corinthians were interested in more than meat in the pagan temples (1 Cor. 8:10; 10:14). For those who thought they as Christians could take part in idolatry with impunity, Paul intended, with illustrations like this, to knock out the false props which supported their behavior (v. 12) before God intervened and took their lives.

10:8. A third failure among the privileged Israelites was in the area of **sexual immorality.** In the Israelites' case the immorality was associated with idolatry (Num. 25:1-2), which also characterized much pagan worship in the first century. But the Corinthians indulged in immorality in contexts other than idolatry, as the instances of rebuke in 1 Corinthians 5:1 and 6:18 illustrate. As God had brought death to the immoral among the Israelites (Num. 25:4-9), He could do in Corinth (e.g., 1 Cor. 5:5), a sobering thought for the libertines who said, "Everything is permissible" (6:12; 10:23).

A possible solution to the apparent discrepancy in the death count found in Numbers 25:9 (24,000) and Paul's figure of **23,000** may reside in the phrase **one day.** Moses and most of Israel were mourning the death of those who had been executed by the judges (Num. 25:5) or killed by an ongoing plague. Meanwhile Phineas was dispatching an Israelite man and Moabite woman in their last act of immorality (Num. 25:6-8), which brought to completion God's discipline of the immoral Israelites and ended the death toll by plague at 24,000, a number probably intended as a summary figure.

Another explanation of the 24,000 in Numbers (contra. Paul's 23,000) is that the former included the leaders (cf. Num. 25:4), whereas the latter did not.

10:9. The Israelites' fourth failure was the presuming of some to question the plan and purpose of God on their trek to Canaan. As a result they **were killed by snakes** (Num. 21:4-6). Did the Corinthians think that they knew better than God the path that would bring them to heaven? (cf. 1 Cor. 1:18–3:20)

10:10. Israel's fifth failure, which God disciplined with death, occurred when they spoke rebelliously against God's appointed leaders, Moses and Aaron (Num. 16:41-49). Was Paul facing a similar situation as an outgrowth of the Corinthians' party spirit? (cf. 1 Cor. 1:11; 4:18-19) It is possible that each of these failures found expression in the Corinthian issue of eating food sacrificed to idols.

10:11. God's dealings with Israel were more than a matter of historical curiosity for Paul. They were **examples** (cf. v. 6) and **warnings** for the Corinthians that the God with whom they had to deal, who was bringing His interaction with people to a close in this **fulfillment of the ages,** was the same God who disciplined the Israelites with death and would do so again (cf. 11:30).

10:12. If the Corinthians believed their **standing** in Christ and corresponding freedom could be exercised in sin with impunity, they were wrong, possibly dead wrong.

10:13. After kicking out the props of false security, Paul pointed toward the One on whom the Corinthians could rely. The temptations that **seized** the Corinthians were like those people had always faced. They could be met and endured by depending on **God,** who **is faithful.** Part of the Corinthian problem, of course, was that some in the face of temptation were not looking for **a way out** by endurance, but a way in for indulgence.

c. The application to idolatry (10:14-11:1)

10:14-15. The **therefore** (*dioper*) introduced Paul's application of Christian

freedom to eating food sacrificed to idols. He gave advice in three areas: (a) meat in the pagan temple (vv. 14-22; cf. 8:10); (b) meat in the marketplace (10:25-26); (c) meat in the home (vv. 27-30). His advice on the first count was uncomplicated— **flee from idolatry** (cf. 6:18, "flee from sexual immorality"). He believed that the rhetorical questions which followed would lead **sensible people** like the Corinthians (cf. 4:10) to agree.

10:16-17. Paul's point in these verses about the Lord's Supper was like that made earlier (5:6-8). The collective worship of Christians at the Lord's Supper expressed the unity among the members and their **participation** (*koinōnia*, "fellowship") **in the blood of Christ** and **in the body of Christ.** The one loaf of bread, of which **all partake,** pictured their unity as members of the **one body** of Christ.

10:18. Likewise in the worship of **Israel,** the participants identified with what was sacrificed and with each other.

10:19-21. The same was true of pagan worship. It was true that **an idol** was nothing (8:4; cf. Ps. 115:4-7), but the ultimate reality behind pagan religion was demonic. Pagan **sacrifices** were **offered to demons, not to God.** Through his minions "the god of this age" blinded unbelievers and kept them from the truth (2 Cor. 4:4). There could be no union for good between Christ and Belial (2 Cor. 6:15). So those who were the temple of God (1 Cor. 3:16; 6:19) should shun the temple of idols (cf. 2 Cor. 6:14-18). No magical contamination was conveyed, but the corrupt character of the participants would be harmful for believers (1 Cor. 15:33). Being **participants with demons** was unthinkable for those who are participants with Christ (10:21; cf. v. 16).

10:22. Most importantly such behavior displeased God (cf. Deut. 32:21). Did the "strong" Corinthians (1 Cor. 8:7-10) require the same discipline as Israel? (10:7; Ex. 32:28, 35)

10:23-24. The principle of freedom (**everything is permissible;** cf. 6:12) was to be regulated by love for others. Activities that are not **beneficial** or **constructive** or that do not promote **the good of others** (cf. 10:33) should be avoided.

10:25-26. For a Christian who bought meat at a market with the intent of eating it at home, Paul recommended that selections be made without reservation. No one could contaminate what God had made clean (cf. Acts 10:15) since **everything** belongs to Him (Ps. 24:1).

10:27-30. For a Christian who accepted an invitation to another's home Paul recommended eating from all the fare without scrupulous reservation. But if another Christian guest piped up (cf. 8:7-13) that the food had been part of a pagan **sacrifice,** the knowledgeable Christian should defer to the uninformed scruples of the weaker brother. To exercise his rightful freedom to eat might cause the brother with the scrupulous **conscience** to follow that example and cause him to sin (cf. Rom. 14:14-23).

A knowledgeable Christian did not need to alter his convictions to accord with the conscience of a weaker brother (1 Cor. 10:29b), but he did need to alter his behavior when in the weaker brother's presence. Otherwise the weak brother might act against his conscience and harm himself (cf. 8:11), which would bring denunciation on the strong brother. What the knowledgeable Christian could enjoy privately **with thankfulness** became in the presence of the weaker brother a contemptible act eliciting condemnation (**why am I denounced** [*blasphēmoumai*] **because of something I thank God for?** cf. 8:12; Rom. 14:16, 22). An echo of 1 Corinthians 8:13 concluded the matter.

10:31–11:1. The principle which summarized Paul's response to the question of eating food offered as a pagan sacrifice was an application of the command to love God and neighbors. Christian behavior should be **for the glory of God.** Also it should build up the church of God by leading some to new birth (v. 33b) and others to maturity in the process of salvation (justification, sanctification, glorification; cf. 1:30). Christians should avoid behavior that would cause others—**whether Jews** (cf. 9:20), **Greeks** (cf. 9:21), **or the church of God . . . to stumble** (lit., "fall"; cf. 10:12). (Interestingly this reference to Jews separate from the church shows that the NT church did not replace the Jewish nation. This argues strongly for premillennialism.)

The One who perfectly exemplified love for God and others was Christ (cf. Rom. 15:3; Phil. 2:5-8). Displaying the same spirit in his ministry, Paul urged the Corinthians to **follow** his **example** in this matter of food from a pagan sacrifice. They should allow their freedom to be regulated by love.

2. CHRISTIAN LIBERTY IN RELATION TO CHRISTIAN WORSHIP (11:2–14:40)

The theme of personal freedom exercised without regard for the needs of others or the glory of God (which characterized the issue about eating food sacrificed to idols [8:1–11:1]) seems no less a part of this section which deals with practices affecting the assembly of the church. Here too Paul responded to the Corinthians' spirit of self-indulgence by stressing the principle of glorifying God and building up each other in the church.

a. The state of women in worship (11:2-16)

Paul began (11:2-16) and ended (14:34-35) his discussion of Christian freedom as it pertained to worship with remarks directed primarily at the behavior of women in the Corinthian church. Some have questioned whether his comments in this section refer to the actual meeting of the church or to extrachurch occasions in which a woman might pray or prophesy. The fact that Paul appealed to church practice elsewhere as a feature of his argument in this section (11:16) suggests that he was discussing church meetings. Modern distinctions between meetings of the church for worship and other meetings of Christians seem based more on expediency than biblical evidence.

11:2. The Corinthians had expressed to Paul, either in their letter or via their spokesmen (cf. 1:11; 16:17), that they remained devoted to Paul and to the **teachings,** the central doctrines of the faith, which he had communicated to them (cf. 11:23; 15:1, 3). For this Paul commended them: **I praise you.**

11:3. Paul no doubt appreciated the Corinthians' goodwill toward him. But more importantly, he wanted to see behavior in keeping with a Christian's calling. As a prelude to his exhortation, Paul characteristically laid down a theological basis. In this instance it concerned headship. The word **head** (*kephalē*) seems to express two things:

subordination and origination. The former reflects the more usual Old Testament usage (e.g., Jud. 10:18), the latter that of Greek vernacular (e.g., Herodotus *History* 4. 91). The former is primary in this passage, but the latter may also be found (1 Cor. 11:8). The subordination of Christ to God is noted elsewhere in the letter (3:23; 15:28). His subordination to the Father is also true in His work as the "agent" of Creation (8:6; cf. Col. 1:15-20).

11:4. When a man prayed aloud publicly or exercised the gift of **prophecy** by declaring a revelation from God (cf. 12:10), he was to have his physical **head** uncovered so that he would not dishonor himself and his spiritual **head,** Christ (v. 3).

The alternate translation in the NIV margin, which interprets the man's covering as long hair, is largely based on the view that verse 15 equated the covering with long hair. It is unlikely, however, that this was the point of verse 4 (cf. comments on v. 15).

11:5-6. It cannot be unequivocally asserted but the preponderance of evidence points toward the public head covering of women as a universal custom in the first century in both Jewish culture ([apocryphal] 3 Maccabees 4:6; Mishnah, *Ketuboth* 7. 6; Babylonian Talmud, *Ketuboth* 72a-b) and Greco-Roman culture (Plutarch *Moralia* 3. 232c; 4. 267b; Apuleius *The Golden Ass* 11. 10). The nature of the covering varied considerably (Ovid *The Art of Love* 3:135-65), but it was commonly a portion of the outer garment drawn up over the head like a hood.

It seems that the Corinthian slogan, "everything is permissible," had been applied to meetings of the church as well, and the Corinthian women had expressed that principle by throwing off their distinguishing dress. More importantly they seem to have rejected the concept of subordination within the church (and perhaps in society) and with it any cultural symbol (e.g., a head-covering) which might have been attached to it. According to Paul, for a woman to throw off the covering was an act not of liberation but of degradation. She might as well shave **her head,** a sign of disgrace (Aristophanes *Thesmophoriazysae* 837). In doing so, she **dishonors** herself and **her** spiritual **head,** the man.

11:7-9. The **man,** on the other hand, was not to have **his head** covered because he was **the image and glory of God.** Paul based this conclusion on Genesis 1:26-27. A woman's (a wife's) **glory** and image was derived from (1 Cor. 11:8) and complementary to (v. 9) that of the man (her husband). Man, then, was God's authoritative representative who found in woman a divinely made ally in fulfilling this role (Gen. 2:18-24). In this sense she as a wife is **the glory of man,** her husband. If a married woman abandoned this complementary role, she also abandoned her glory, and for Paul an uncovered woman's head gave symbolic expression to that spirit.

11:10. Paul offered a third reason (the first reason was the divine order— God, Christ, man, woman, vv. 3-6; the second reason was Creation, vv. 7-9) why womanly insubordination in the church should not exist. **Angels** were spectators of the church (4:9; Eph. 3:10; 1 Tim. 5:21; cf. Ps. 103:20-21). For a woman to exercise her freedom to participate in the church without the head covering, the **sign of** her **authority** (*exousia,* a liberating term; cf. 1 Cor. 7:37; 8:9; 9:4-6, 12, 18), would be to bring the wisdom of God (Eph. 3:10) into disrepute.

Other (but less acceptable) explanations have been suggested for the words **because of the** "angels": (a) evil angels lusted after the women in the Corinthian congregation; (b) angels are messengers, that is, pastors; (c) good angels learn from women; (d) good angels are an example of subordination; (e) good angels would be tempted by a woman's insubordination.

11:11-12. Men and women together in mutual interdependence, complementing each other, bring glory to God (cf. 10:31). Neither should be **independent** or think themselves superior to the other. Woman's subordination does not mean inferiority. Man is not superior in being to woman. Eve came from Adam, and each man born in the world comes from a woman's womb (11:12). **God** created them both for each other (Gen. 1:27; 2:18).

11:13-15. Paul had based his previous reasoning for maintaining the **head**

covering as a woman's expression of her subordination on arguments rooted in special revelation. Now he turned to natural revelation (cf. Rom. 1:20) for a fourth argument in support of his recommendation. Mankind instinctively distinguished between the sexes in various ways, one of which was length of hair. Exceptions to this general practice were due either to necessity (e.g., Apuleius *The Golden Ass* 7. 6, "to escape in disguise") or perversity (Diogenes *Laertius, Lives* 6. 65). No abstract length of hair was in mind so much as male and female differentiation. The Spartans, for example, favored shoulder-length hair for men (cf. Lucian *The Runaways* 27) which they tied up for battle (Herodotus *History* 7. 208-9), and no one thought them effeminate.

Long hair was a woman's **glory** because it gave visible expression to the differentiation of the sexes. This was Paul's point in noting that long hair was given **to her as a covering.** Natural revelation confirmed the propriety of women wearing the physical covering (cf. Cicero *On Duties* 1. 28. 100). She has a natural covering, and should follow the custom of wearing a physical covering in a public meeting.

Some Bible students, however, say that the Greek *anti*, rendered "as" (i.e., "for" or "in anticipation of") should be translated in its more normal sense of "instead of." According to that view, a woman's hair was given instead of a physical covering, for it in itself *is* a covering. In this view women should pray with long hair, not short hair. This view, however, does not explain the woman's act of covering or uncovering her head, mentioned in 1 Corinthians 11:5-6.

11:16. Paul's fifth argument for maintaining the status quo on head-coverings came from universal church **practice.** Paul was not trying to foist a new behavioral pattern on the Corinthians but simply to hold the line against self-indulgent individual excess in the name of freedom. As in the case of food offered to idols (8:1–11:1), Paul dealt with the immediate issue but also put his finger on the root of the problem, the Corinthian pursuit of self-interest which was unwilling to subordinate itself to the needs of others (cf. 10:24) or the glory of God (10:31). Throwing off the head

covering was an act of insubordination which discredited God.

Whether women today in church services should wear hats depends on whether the custom of head coverings in the first century is to be understood as a practice also intended for the present day. Many Bible students see that for today the principle of subordination (not the command to wear hats) is the key point in this passage. The intent of the custom of women wearing hats today, for fashion, seems far different from the purpose of the custom in the first century.

b. The state of Christians at the Lord's Supper (11:17-34)

At Jesus' institution of the Lord's Supper with His disciples (Matt. 26:26-29; Mark 14:22-25; Luke 22:15-20) the bread and cup were part of a meal, with the bread probably broken near the beginning (cf. "when He had given thanks," 1 Cor. 11:24) and the cup taken at the end (cf. "after supper," v. 25). By the time Paul wrote, the Lord's Supper was celebrated in two stages which consolidated the partaking of the bread and cup at the end of a communal meal. The worship with the bread and cup came to be called the "Eucharist" (*Didache* 9:1; Ignatius *Letter to the Philadelphians* 4), from the Greek word for "thanksgiving" (*eucharisteō*). The communal meal was called the *Agapē* (Jude 12; Pliny *Letters* 10. 96. 7), a Greek word for "love."

What bothered Paul about the Corinthian celebration was that the *Agapē* meal had become an occasion not marked by love for fellow Christians but one of self-centered indulgence. In the subsequent development of the church the celebrations came to be divided (Ignatius *Letter to the Smyrneans* 8; 1-2; and [apocryphal] Acts of John 84), possibly on the mistaken assumption that Paul had advised the Corinthians to do that (cf. 1 Cor. 11:22, 34).

11:17. As in the preceding discussion on womanly excesses in worship, Paul had no commendation (but cf. v. 2) for the Corinthians when it came to their practice of the Lord's Supper. In fact an experience meant to build up the church was actually having the opposite effect: **your meetings do more harm than good.**

11:18-19. The church was divided at a celebration which was meant to express unity (cf. 10:17). If these **divisions** (*schismata;* 1:10; 12:25) were related to those noted earlier (1:10–4:21), then one factor contributing to those divisions is evident here, namely, economic differences in the church (11:21).

Paul did not want to believe the report about their divisions (v. 18b), but he knew that sin was inevitable (cf. Luke 17:1) and would not pass unnoticed by God. **God's approval** (*dokimoi*) resumed a point Paul had discussed earlier (1 Cor. 9:27–10:10), where he used in 9:27 the contrasting word "disqualified" (*adokimos*).

In the whole nation of Israel, freed from bondage in Egypt and bound for the Promised Land of Canaan, only two of that vast company gained God's approval and entered the land (cf. 10:5). Many in the Corinthian assembly did not have this approval, which His discipline on them demonstrated (cf. 11:30-32). If the Corinthians thought the ordinances of the Lord's Supper and baptism somehow communicated magical protection to the participants (cf. 10:12; 15:24), Paul's excoriation must have been doubly painful since their behavior at this rite was directly linked to their chastisement (11:30-32)—the very thing they sought to avoid.

11:20-21. The Lord's Supper should have been the remembrance of a preeminently selfless act, Christ's death on behalf of others. Instead the Corinthians had turned the memorial of selflessness into an experience of selfishness and had made a rite of unity a riotous disunity. While **one** brother went **hungry** because he lacked the means to eat well, **another** brother drank to excess.

11:22. If the Corinthians wanted private parties they could have them in their **homes.** The meeting of the church was no place for a sectarian spirit of any sort, especially since the Lord's Supper was intended to commemorate just the opposite spirit. To act in a spirit of selfish disregard for the needs of a brother was to **despise the church of God,** composed not of lifeless stones but of living people who could be grievously hurt. Did the Corinthians somehow think their libertarian acts were a matter for **praise?** (cf. 5:1-2) Just the opposite!

11:23-24. Paul proceeded to remind the Corinthians of what they knew but had denied by their actions. Whether this teaching came to Paul directly (by a vision; cf. Gal. 1:12) or indirectly (by men; 1 Cor. 15:1), it came with the Lord's authority. The bread represented the incarnate body of Christ unselfishly assumed (Phil. 2:6-7) and unselfishly given on the cross for the benefit of others (2 Cor. 8:9; Phil. 2:8), that kept needing to be remembered (cf. 1 Cor. 4:8-13).

11:25. The wine was a poignant reminder of Christ's **blood,** without the shedding of which there could be no forgiveness from sin (Heb. 9:22) and through which cleansing and a **new** relationship (**covenant**) with God was made (Heb. 9:14-15). The word "covenant" referred to a relationship in which one party established terms which the other party accepted or rejected. The focus of the Old Covenant was the written Word (Ex. 24:1-8). The focus of the New Covenant is the Living Word (John 1:14-18). Christ intended the **cup** to be a representational (cf. John 10:9; 1 Cor. 10:4) reminder of Him: **do this . . . in remembrance of Me.**

11:26. The Lord's Supper was a visible sermon that proclaimed "the message of the Cross" (1:18, 23; 2:2, 8), that is, the reality of **the Lord's death,** and also the certainty of His return (**until He comes**) (cf. John 14:1-4). Though there apparently was no prescribed schedule for the observance of the Lord's Supper (cf. Ignatius *Letter to the Ephesians* 13:1), **whenever** it was celebrated its message of humiliation and subsequent exaltation (Phil. 2:6-11) went forth. This was a needed reminder to all saints, especially those in Corinth (cf. 1 Cor. 4:8-13).

11:27-29. The Corinthians' despicable behavior at the communal meal was not without result, which Paul proceeded to point out. Nowadays when this passage is read before participation in the Lord's Supper, it is usually intended to produce soul-searching introspection and silent confession to Christ so that no one will sin against the spiritual presence of the Lord by irreverent observance. Paul's application was probably more concrete. No doubt his experience on the Damascus Road (Acts 9:4-5) contributed to this, for the body of Christ is the church, which consists of individual believers (cf.

1 Cor. 12:12, 27). His body, the church, is also pictured by the bread of Communion (5:7; 10:16-17). Thus to sin against another believer is to sin against Christ (8:12). Those **guilty of sinning against the body and blood of the Lord** were those who despised a poorer member by utter disregard for his need (11:21-22). These came to the remembrance of Christ's work of unity and reconciliation (cf. Eph. 2:15-16) with a trail of deeds that had produced disunity and alienation! If these would **examine** (*dokimazetō*, "test to approve," 1 Cor. 11:28) themselves, they would see that they lacked God's approval (*dokimoi*, v. 19) in this behavior. They should seek out the wronged brother and ask his forgiveness. Only then could a true spirit of worship flourish (cf. Matt. 5:23-24 and *Didache* 14. 1-3). Coming to the Lord's Supper without that sin confessed brought **judgment** on the guilty participants. Only by recognizing (*diakrinōn*, "properly judging") the unity of **the body of the Lord**—and acting accordingly—could they avoid bringing "judgment" (*krima*) on themselves.

11:30-32. What that **judgment** entailed was then explained by Paul. In brief, it was sickness and death (cf. 10:1-11). The solution was self-examination (*diekrinomen*, 11:31; cf. vv. 28-29; 5:1-5; 10:12), self-discipline (9:27), and promoting of unity. The alternative was God's judging (*krinomenoi*, 11:32), which was a discipline that they were then experiencing. This was not a loss of salvation, but of life (cf. 5:5).

11:33-34. If the believers were self-disciplined, they should **wait** in the *Agapē* meal till all arrived. This also may have implied sharing the meal with others (cf. v. 22). If the demands of hunger were too great for some, they should satisfy those pangs **at home** before coming to the assembly. The Lord's Supper was a time not for self-indulgence but for mutual edification (v. 26). If the former prevailed, God would continue to discipline severely. Other matters—apparently less serious aberrations related to the Lord's Supper—Paul would attend to when he returned to Corinth (16:5-9).

c. The state of spiritual gifts (chaps. 12–14)

Related to the subject of irregularities in the worship of the Corinthian church, was a question on the nature of spiritual gifts and their exercise in the public assembly. This subject should also be considered under the broader rubric of Christian freedom which Paul had been qualifying and regulating by the principle of love (starting with 8:1). The need for such regulation was certainly evident. A self-indulgent spirit, which debauched the principle of freedom in other areas, found similar expression in the area of spiritual gifts, and produced selfishness and disunity (12:7, 25; 14:4) and apparent chaos in the assembly (14:23, 33, 40).

Paul dealt with the problem by describing the nature and purpose of gifts (12:1-30), the superiority of love (12:31–13:13), and the regulating of the exercise of gifts by love (chap. 14). As in other areas, so in using gifts in the church, believers should promote the glory of God and the good of others instead of self-satisfaction.

(1) Unity and diversity of gifts (12:1-31a). **12:1-3.** Before Paul began his discussion of **spiritual gifts** he thought it necessary to confront, at the outset, any in the Corinthian assembly who might contradict his message (cf. 14:37). It is probably in this regard that 12:3 is to be understood. Many explanations of the verse have been offered (though most commentators "handle" the problem by ignoring it).

Paul apparently believed that some of the Corinthians' problems were due not entirely to their worldly attitudes (3:3) but also to the presence of false teachers who preyed on their spiritual immaturity and exacerbated the problems. The pagan background out of which many had come (and some were still coming; cf. 8:10; 10:14, 20-21) did not help them ascertain the presence of false prophets. When they **were pagans,** they had been **influenced and led astray to dumb idols** (12:2). Certainly lifeless idols are totally helpless in such matters! (In the Corinthians' vaunted wisdom they showed themselves to be unusually gullible [cf. 2 Cor. 11:1-21, esp. 19-20].)

Paul therefore laid down a simple test related to the person of Christ. The false teachers obviously claimed that their visions, revelations, and messages (cf. 2 Cor. 12:1) were from God, but they apparently denied the humanity of Christ, as expressed by the words **Jesus be** cursed. This may have been a factor in the Corinthians' aversion to Paul's "message of the Cross" (1 Cor. 1:10–4:13). It may be surprising today to realize that the earliest Christological heresy (Docetism) denied Jesus' humanity, not His deity. John had to deal with the same problem years later (1 John 4:1-3).

Also Jesus who had suffered was now the Jesus who reigns as Lord, whom Paul represented (1 Cor. 1:1) and who was to be obeyed. Only believers, speaking **by the Holy Spirit,** acknowledge that **Jesus is Lord.** Nonbelievers—including false teachers—deny His sovereign lordship. Thus anyone who tries to controvert Jesus' authority and His Word will suffer the consequences (14:38; 16:22).

12:4-6. Paul had referred to God, Jesus, and the Holy Spirit in verse 3. Now in reverse order he stressed the unity of the Godhead in relation to the different spiritual gifts. The Holy **Spirit** gives a diversity of gifts (cf. "Spirit" in vv. 7-9, 11) so that individuals can serve the Lord and His body, the church, in various ways (cf. vv. 7, 27), all empowered by God and exercised under His aegis (cf. vv. 18, 24). Though there are **different kinds** (dia-ireseis) **of gifts . . . service,** and **working, the same Spirit . . . the same Lord** (Christ), and **the same God** are involved in **all of them.**

12:7-10. The gifts had a unity in source (vv. 4-6), and they also had a unity in purpose. They were given, not for personal enrichment (cf. 14:4; 1 Peter 4:10), but **for the common good** of the body of Christ, the building up of others (1 Cor. 10:24; 14:12). Paul listed some of the gifts here. Others, along with some of these, are given in Romans 12:6-8; 1 Corinthians 12:28-31; Ephesians 4:11; 1 Peter 4:10-11.

The list here includes nine gifts. (1) **Wisdom** refers to insight into doctrinal truth. Paul exercised and expressed this gift in this letter (e.g., 2:6). (2) **Knowledge** refers to the ability to apply doctrinal truth to life. Paul also exercised and expressed this gift in this letter (e.g., 12:1-3; 11:3). (Cf. the recurrence of the phrase "Do you not know" in 3:16; 5:6; 6:2-3, 9, 15-16, 19; 9:13, 24; also cf. 8:1-3, 10-11). (3) **Faith** as a spiritual gift is probably an unusual measure of trust in God beyond that exercised by most

Christians (e.g., 13:2). (4) **Healing** is the ability to restore health (e.g., Acts 3:7; 19:12) and also to hold off death itself temporarily (Acts 9:40; 20:9-10). (5) **Miraculous powers** may refer to exorcising demons (Acts 19:12) or inducing physical disability (Acts 13:11) or even death (Acts 5:5, 9). (6) **Prophecy** is the ability, like that of the Old Testament prophets, to declare a message of God for His people (1 Cor. 14:3). (7) **Ability to distinguish between spirits** is the gift to differentiate the Word of God proclaimed by a true prophet from that of a satanic deceiver (cf. 2 Cor. 11:14-15; 1 John 4:1). If the Corinthians possessed this gift (cf. 1 Cor. 1:7), it was not being put to good use (cf. 12:1-3). (8) **Tongues** refers to the ability to speak an unlearned, living language (e.g., Acts 2:11). (9) **Interpretation** was the ability to translate an unlearned, known language expressed in the assembly (1 Cor. 14:27).

With the possible exception of faith, all these gifts seem to have been confirmatory and foundational gifts for the establishment of the church (cf. Heb. 2:4; Eph. 2:20) and were therefore temporary.

12:11. The gifts were not meant to be selected by individuals or personally solicited by them, but were instead given by **the . . . Spirit . . . as He** determined. "The Spirit" is referred to six times in verses 7-11.

12:12. This verse forms an excellent three-part summary of the rest of the chapter. (a) The human **body is a unit** (cf. v. 13 on the unity of the body of Christ). (b) The human body has **many parts,** with a necessary diversity in its members (cf. vv. 14-20). (c) The parts of the human body work together as **one,** with a dependent mutuality as each part fulfills an important function (cf. vv. 21-26). Likewise the body of Christ has a diversity of parts functioning together (vv. 27-30).

12:13. The One who gave the diverse gifts, the **Spirit,** was also the medium in which, by which, and with which (possible translations of the Gr. preposition en; cf. Matt. 3:11) that unity exists. The baptism of the Spirit is experienced by all who believe, at the moment of salvation (cf. Rom. 8:9). In that baptism, believers, regardless of nationality (**whether Jews or Greeks**) or

533

station of life (**slave or free**), are identified with Christ (**baptized . . . into one body**) and are indwelt by the Spirit (**given the one Spirit to drink;** cf. John 4:14; 7:38-39).

12:14-20. Different parts are needed if a body is to exist (v. 19). So too, no believer should think of himself or his gift as inferior and so desire another member's gift. The gifts were not haphazardly distributed (cf. v. 11) but carefully **arranged** according to the perfect will of God (v. 18).

12:21-26. In the diversity of the bodily parts there was a corresponding mutual dependence. A person with a seemingly greater gift should not imagine that he could function alone since a bodily member cut off from the natural body would cease to exist. More importantly, one thought to possess a lesser gift should in fact be accorded greater attention by the other members of the body (cf. 14:1-5) just as in the natural body special deference in attention to dress is paid to those parts of the body deemed less presentable (12:22-24). Possibly Paul was reaching back in thought beyond the immediate discussion of gifts when he referred to **weaker** members (v. 22; cf. 8:7-13) and **less honorable** ones (12:23; cf. 11:22) who also required special care and consideration. This too was part of God's plan (**God . . . combined the members**), that members of the spiritual body would demonstrate a mutual concern for the well-being of others (12:25b-26; 10:24, 33) so that rivalry would cease (**so that there should be no division in the body;** 1:10; 11:18) and genuine unity would exist (12:26).

12:27-31a. The unifying member in the spiritual **body** is **Christ.** As the Head (Eph. 1:22; cf. 1 Cor. 11:3) He possesses the body and sovereignly expresses His will. His command is that love should prevail among the members (John 15:12). This was the force which would maintain unity within the diversity and to this subject Paul would shortly move (1 Cor. 12:31b-13:13).

For a third time (cf. 12:18, 24, 28), however, Paul stressed the fact that God, not man, assigned the gifts. As he discussed another sample of gifts (some repeated from vv. 7-10 and some new), it was the members, the people so gifted, to whom he referred. Since the gifts included in the two lists in this chapter contain novelty and redundancy (which is the case elsewhere in passages detailing gifts, e.g., Rom. 12:6-8; Eph. 4:11; 1 Peter 4:10-11—the gift of teaching being the only gift which appears in each list), probably no complete catalog existed.

The fact that Paul assigned ordinal numbers (**first . . . second . . . third**) to the first three gifts suggests that these may have been relegated to a lesser role by the Corinthians (cf. 1 Cor. 12:21-24). Those three kinds of gifted members—**apostles . . . prophets . . . teachers**—probably were rated lower than those who had the more spectacular gift of tongues. But the first three gifts may have been **greater** (v. 31) because of their extensive value to the whole body of Christ. This may be why he listed them first and then said that the church should **eagerly desire** (v. 31) the exercise of those **gifts** in the assembly (cf. 14:1-5). Gifted apostles, prophets, and teachers characteristically ministered to a *whole* church, and so would engender unity and mutual edification. The gift of **tongues,** on the other hand, suited the Corinthian penchant for self-expression and the pursuit of personal freedom. This self-centeredness also afflicted the church in other areas (e.g., eating sacrificial foods, women in worship, celebration of the Lord's Supper). Love for others was an essential need in the Corinthian church, and to that fundamental attribute Paul then turned to pay eloquent tribute.

(2) Superiority of love to all gifts (12:31b-13:13). **12:31b.** Though Paul greatly valued spiritual gifts, he valued even more a quality of life which the Spirit produced. Spiritual gifts were variously apportioned to individuals in the church so that no single gift was possessed by every member (cf. vv. 19-30). On the other hand the Holy Spirit sought to produce the fruit of the Spirit in every Christian (Gal. 5:22-23), chief among which was love. This was more important than the gifts, and when displayed it would help correct the Corinthian aberrations which surrounded their possession and use of God's gifts (cf. 1 Cor. 14:1).

The **way** Paul referred to was a manner of life preeminently characterized by love (cf. John 15:9-17). Jesus and John the Baptist followed this way of righteousness (Matt. 3:15; 21:32) by obediently practicing the will of God and exhorting their followers to do the same (Matt. 5:6, 10, 20; 6:33). This same manner of life and consequent conduct Paul called the way of love (1 Cor. 14:1; cf. Rom. 13:8-10), which he followed and exhorted the Corinthians to do the same (1 Cor. 14:1; cf. 11:1).

13:1. Some have suggested that this "hymn to love" (chap. 13) was composed by Paul on a previous occasion (under the Spirit's inspiration, of course) and inserted in the letter at this point (under the Spirit's direction) because of its telling appropriateness. This may be so, for the balance in form and substance reflects Paul at his best (but cf. 1:25-29, a passage which exhibits superb parallelism). Still, these verses so directly touch the many issues raised in this letter that if they were previously composed, the Corinthians and their problems were never far removed from Paul's mind as he wrote.

Eloquence was greatly admired in the first century and the Corinthians were no exception, though they found little of it in Paul (cf. 2:1, 4; 2 Cor. 10:10). This may explain in part their fascination with tongues. Paul's application of this and the following conditional clauses (1 Cor. 13:2-3) to himself was forceful since he could claim exceptional experiences, particularly in regard to the languages of **men** (14:18) **and of angels** (cf. 2 Cor. 12:4). But the statement was probably meant to include every imaginable mode of speech. It was a statement of hyperbole concerning exalted eloquence, which if void of love might be momentarily electrifying like a clash of **gong** or **cymbal** but then vanished just as quickly. **Love** on the other hand produces eternal effects (cf. v. 13).

13:2. Even **the gift of prophecy** (cf. 12:10) which Paul championed as a great gift for the Corinthian church (14:1) or the gifts of wisdom, **knowledge,** and **faith** (cf. 12:8-9) were nothing compared with **love.** Paul was not depreciating those gifts but was appreciating love by showing it to be incomparable.

13:3. Even self-sacrifice can be self-centered (cf. Matt. 6:2), and the ultimate sacrifice, here depicted as self-immolation (cf. Dan. 3:17-18; [apocryphal] 2 Maccabees 7:5; Strabo *Geography* 15. 1. 73) is ultimately futile without **love.**

13:4. Paul shifted from the first person to the third person and replaced himself with a personification of love. Some have seen in verses 4-6 the fruit of the Spirit (Gal. 5:22-23); others have seen here a description of Christ Himself. As different sides of the same coin, both are applicable and provided a solution to the many Corinthian problems. Love, defined by 14 predications (half of them negative, half positive) constituted the "way." **Love,** Paul wrote, **is patient . . . kind . . . does not envy** or **boast,** and **is not proud.**

Patience (*makrothymia*) is the capacity to be wronged and not retaliate. The Corinthian church had many members who had been wronged (e.g., in lawsuits [1 Cor. 6:8] and the poor at communal meals [11:21-22]). The response of love to these wrongs would be a display of kindness and goodness. Envy and boasting seemed to abound as two poles of the same problem (e.g., divisions [1:10; 3:3, 21]; gifts [12:14-25]). The Corinthians had no monopoly on pride though they seemed to. The verb *physioō* occurs only seven times in the New Testament, six of which are found in this letter (cf. 4:6, 18-19; 5:2; 8:1).

13:5. Paul then gave four negative descriptions of love: **It is not rude** nor **self-seeking** nor **easily angered,** and **it keeps no record of wrongs.** Rudeness found expression in the problem of women in worship (11:2-16), the disorders at the Lord's Supper (11:17-22), and the general organization of worship (14:26-33). Self-satisfaction was a pervasive disorder particularly manifested in the eating of food sacrificed to idols (8:9; 10:23-24). People who are not easily angered usually do not start lawsuits (as in 6:1-11). Love does not record wrongs, though there was ample opportunity for doing so in Corinth (e.g., 6:8; 7:5; 8:11).

13:6. Love does not delight in evil (e.g., incest [5:1-2, 8]), **but rejoices** in **truth** (5:8).

13:7. Love **always protects** (cf. 8:13), **trusts** (cf. 15:11), **hopes** (cf. 9:10, 23), and **perseveres** (*hypomenei,* "remains steadfast in the face of unpleasant circumstances"; cf. 9:19-22).

13:8. Following this elaboration of the preeminence (vv. 1-3) and perfections

(vv. 4-7) of love, Paul concluded with a discussion of its permanence (vv. 8-13). **Love never fails,** in the sense it will never come to an end. Positively stated, it is eternal. This is not true of the spiritual gifts. Some of the gifts were foundational (e.g., **prophecies** and **knowledge;** cf. Eph. 2:20) and confirmatory (e.g., **tongues;** cf. 2 Cor. 12:12; Heb. 2:4). Every gift is linked in some way to building up the church to maturity—some (prophecy, knowledge, tongues) functioning in the early years of the Church Age and others continuing on till the church is perfected. When that perfection is achieved, the gifts will have served their purposes and will be rendered obsolete. But this will not happen to love.

13:9-10. As Paul explained it, the gift of knowledge (v. 8), essential as it was, was not exhaustive. The ability to **prophesy,** however crucial for the church's life, was of limited scope. The gifts were temporary blessings in an **imperfect** age. One day they would give way to **perfection,** toward which all the gifts pointed.

What Paul meant when he referred to the coming of perfection is the subject of considerable debate. One suggestion is that perfection described the completion of the New Testament. But verse 12 makes that interpretation unlikely. A few have suggested that this state of perfection will not be reached until the new heavens and new earth are established. Another point of view understands perfection to describe the state of the church when God's program for it is consummated at the coming of Christ. There is much to commend this view, including the natural accord it enjoys with the illustration of growth and maturity which Paul used in the following verses.

13:11. Paul elsewhere described the purpose of gifts by an illustration employing the imagery of growth and maturity. According to Ephesians 4:11-16, the gifts were to be used to bring the church from a state of infancy to adulthood. The word translated "mature" in that passage (Eph. 4:13) is the word translated "perfection" (*teleion*) in 1 Corinthians 13:10. In the Ephesians passage, maturity is defined as "attaining to the whole measure of the fullness of Christ." Such a state will obviously not exist until Christ's second coming.

It would appear that the same perspective was developed in this passage to the Corinthians. Paul applied the illustration to himself (cf. vv. 1-3). The threefold talking, thinking, and reasoning were probably meant to balance the thrice-mentioned gifts (v. 8). With the coming of adulthood, such gifts become passé. Paul's use of the word **became** (*gegona*, a perf. tense verb, probably proleptic; cf. Rom. 13:8; 1 Cor. 14:23) was of course to be understood in the context of the illustration. It does not indicate that he personally or the church collectively had yet arrived at that point (cf. Phil. 3:12). It would not, on the other hand, necessarily rule out a gradual obsolescence of certain gifts as the church progressed toward maturity.

13:12. A city like Corinth, famous for its bronze mirrors, would have particularly appreciated Paul's final illustration. The perfection and imperfection mentioned in verse 10 were deftly likened to the contrasting images obtained by the indirect **reflection** of one's face viewed in a bronze mirror and the same face when viewed directly. Such, Paul said, was the contrast between the imperfect time in which he then wrote and the perfect time which awaited him and the church when the partial reflection of the present would give way to the splendor of perfect vision. Then Paul would **see** God (cf. 15:28; 1 John 3:2) as God now saw Paul. Then partial knowledge (cf. 1 Cor. 8:1-3) would be displaced by the perfect knowledge of God.

13:13. Paul completed his three-paneled portrait of love (vv. 1-3, 4-7, 8-13) with a final triad: **faith, hope, and love.** Much discussion has focused on whether faith and hope were portrayed by Paul as being (with love) eternal. The solution is probably found in verse 7. Faith is an expression of love (the word "trusts," *pisteuei*, v. 7, is the verb form of the noun "faith," *pistis*), as is hope (cf. Gal. 5:5-6). Faith and hope, as manifestations of love, will endure eternally. So too everyone who follows the way of love (1 Cor. 14:1) finds "the most excellent way" (12:31b), because every individual characterized by love carries that mark eternally. The spiritual gifts will one day cease to exist, but love will endure forever.

(3) Priority of prophecy to tongues (14:1-25). Chapter 13 is one of the most sublime digressions in any letter in any language. But it was nonetheless a deviation from the central theme of gifts and their use by the church which Paul began in chapter 12 and then concluded in chapter 14. Paul had intimated in chapter 12 that the Corinthians were perverting the purpose of gifts from a unifying influence on the church to one fostering fragmentation and discord (esp. 12:21-25). A contributing factor to their factious spirit was the Corinthian pursuit of individual freedom and personal enhancement at the expense of other members of the body whose needs may have been trampled or ignored along the way. Manifestations of this self-centeredness affected each of the problem issues taken up since chapter 8.

The focal problem in the matter of the use and abuse of gifts seemed to be the Corinthian fascination with tongues, a gift which apparently lent itself most readily to perversion from something intended "for the common good" (12:7) to something employed for personal enhancement (14:4). Paul's corrective was not to stifle the use of gifts (14:39; cf. 1 Thes. 5:19-20) but to urge that their use be regulated by love. The gifts of the Spirit should be controlled by the fruit of the Spirit, chief among which was love (Gal. 5:22). This would lead to exercising the gifts so they would benefit the church body as a whole (14:5) and also honor God (14:25, 33, 40). By way of illustration and correction, Paul compared and contrasted the Corinthians' preoccupation with tongues with their apparent disinterest in prophecy.

14:1. That chapter 13 was something of a digression, however sublime, may be seen by the way Paul wove together the two strands which concluded chapter 12 (v. 31) and which began chapter 14 (v. 1). He did this in a chiasmus, a common literary style that connected a series of related words, phrases, or ideas by reversing their order of discussion in the second instance, for example, a^1, b^1, b^2, a^2. As a final note to his discussion on the unity and diversity of the gifts, Paul had exhorted the Corinthians to desire (a^1) exercising the gifts which were of greatest benefit to the church as a whole (cf.

12:31). He then affirmed (b^1) that, however splendid and profitable the gifts were, there was a greater way of life (chap. 13). Chapter 14 picked up on this note as Paul urged (b^2) his readers to make this **way of love** (14:1) the definitive characteristic of their own course of life (cf. John 13:34-35). This in turn would lead them to "desire (a^2) the greater gifts," among which was **prophecy** (cf. 1 Cor. 12:31).

14:2. What Paul meant by speaking **in a tongue** is a matter of considerable debate. One common view is to see Paul's use of the word "tongue" (*glōssa*) against the background of first-century pagan religions and thus define it as ecstatic speech similar to that expressed by the sibylla, or female prophetesses. The Cumaen sibyl (cf. Virgil *Aeneid* 6. 77-102) was the most famous of the 10 female prophetesses claimed by various regions. Others see the tongues-speaking in 1 Corinthians as ecstatic speech similar to that of Pythia, the female oracle at Delphi (Plutarch *Moralia* 5. 409e) or similar to the maenads of Dionysus in their ecstatic frenzy (Ovid *Metamorphoses* 3. 534, 710-30; cf. Euripides *Bacchae*). That the Corinthians may have thought of this gift as analogous to the pagan ecstatics is certainly possible, but to suggest that Paul used the term with reference to this pagan background is hardly enlightened scholarship. In fact the seedbed for most of Paul's theological concepts and the usual source of his terms was the Old Testament. This is evident by Paul's use of *glōssa* outside of these three Corinthian chapters. He used the word 21 times in 1 Corinthians 12-14 but only 3 other times in his other letters. Each of Paul's other uses was either in a quotation from the Old Testament (Ps. 5:9 in Rom. 3:13; Isa. 45:23 in Rom. 14:11) or in an allusion to it (Isa. 45:23 in Phil. 2:11). In all three instances he used the word "tongue" as a figure of speech for the statement or confession made. Whether good (Rom. 14:11; Phil. 2:11) or bad (Rom. 3:13) the statement was clearly intelligible.

The same may be said of the meaning of the word *glōssa* elsewhere in the New Testament. Whether it was used literally of the physical organ (e.g., Mark 7:33; James 3:5; Rev. 16:10) or figuratively of human languages (e.g., Acts 2:11; Rev.

5:9; 7:9; 10:11; 11:9; 13:7; 14:6; 17:15), it nowhere referred to ecstatic speech. If it is reasonable to interpret the unknown with the help of the known, the obscure by the clear, then the burden of proof rests with those who find in this term a meaning other than human language.

The context of this verse is the assembled congregation in Corinth (1 Cor. 11:2–14:40, esp. 14:4-5) in which utterance in a tongue was given without the benefit of interpretation (cf. vv. 13, 19). Apparently no native speaker of the tongue was present in the assembly (cf. vv. 10-11), and no one was given supernatural enablement to interpret it. The utterances therefore were **mysteries,** truths requiring a supernatural disclosure which God had not provided the Corinthians in this particular instance. As a result, the expression of tongues became an exercise in futility for the assembly as a whole, with only the speaker deriving some benefit (v. 4) in **his spirit** (cf. v. 14), the sentient aspect of his being (*pneuma;* cf. Matt. 5:3; Acts 17:16; 2 Cor. 2:13).

14:3. One with the gift of prophecy (cf. 12:10), on the other hand, spoke in the tongue of his listeners, in this case Greek, and edified them by proclaiming God's Word in such a way that it gave them **strengthening,** (*oikodomēn,* "edification"), **encouragement,** (*paraklēsin*), **and comfort** (*paramythian,* "consolation," used only here in the NT).

14:4. A person with the gift of tongues (cf. 12:10) who spoke without the benefit of the gift of interpretation (cf. 12:10) could edify **himself** but not others in **the church.** The edification resulted from the fact that the user of a gift experienced the confirmation that he was the individual object of God's grace (cf. 12:18, 28) and able to offer praise to God (14:16). Though he himself would not comprehend the content of that praise, his feelings and emotions would be enlivened, leading to a general exhilaration and euphoria. This was not a bad thing. Paul certainly was no advocate of cold, dispassionate worship. The gifts were not given for personal enrichment, however, but for the benefit of others (12:7; cf. 10:24; 1 Peter 4:10). Personal edification and exhilaration were often natural by-products of the legitimate exercise of one's gift, but they were not the main reasons for its exercise.

14:5. Paul had no intention of depreciating the gift of **tongues;** he was simply interested in appreciating the gift of prophecy. There was nothing wrong with the gift of tongues; in fact Paul thought it would be good if everyone had the gift. Of course he had said the same thing about celibacy (7:7), but in neither instance did he expect universal compliance with his statement. Since both were gifts from God, neither should be despised. In a church gathering, however, the gift of prophecy and its exercise was greatly to be preferred to uninterpreted tongues simply because the former built up others. As already stated, the tongues gift was confirmatory and thus temporary (see comments on 13:8). Thus those instructions, specifically directed to the Corinthians' misuse of tongues, are not directives for the use of tongues today (cf. comments on 14:21-22).

14:6. Two illustrations (in v. 6 and vv. 7-9) made this plain. In the first, Paul used himself with a possible glance back to his initial ministry in Corinth. He could have **come** proclaiming his message in the tongue of a language which they did not know (cf. v. 18), but it would have produced only disinterest at best (v. 11) or at worst, derision (v. 23). As it was, he brought them a **revelation** from God (cf. 2:10) by his ministry of **prophecy** (12:29), or he brought them a word of **knowledge** (cf. 2:12) by his ministry of **instruction** (12:29; cf. 14:26) which they would understand and to which they could respond (cf. vv. 24-25).

14:7-9. The same was true in a musical **tune** or a **call** to **battle.** To be profitable for others the notes of a **flute** or **harp** or **trumpet** needed to be **clear** and **intelligible;** otherwise they amounted to no more than the venting of air with consequences which, besides being annoying (v. 7), might be devastating (v. 8).

14:10-12. Human communication operated on the same principles as instrumental communication. The word **languages** in verse 10 is *phōnōn,* the plural of the same word *phōnēn,* rendered "sounds" of the harp (v. 7) and "call" of the trumpet (v. 8). Human sounds, apart from a shared understanding of their meanings, were worthless. So was the Corinthian preoccupation with uninterpreted tongues. That was why Paul did not discourage their interest in **spiritual gifts** but did encourage them to pursue those gifts that benefited all in **the church** (v. 12; cf. 12:31; 14:1).

14:13. Interpreted tongues, like prophecy, could benefit the assembly (cf. Acts 19:6). Therefore the gift of interpretation should be requested of God. If no one was present who was able to interpret, the tongues-speaker was to keep silent (1 Cor. 14:28).

14:14-15. It was also true that however beneficial the gift of tongues might be to its recipient (cf. v. 4), when coupled with the gift of interpretation it had much more value because it involved not only the feeling aspects of a person, but his mental faculties as well.

14:16-17. If it were true that one who possessed the gift of tongues would find his worship enhanced by the possession and use of the gift of interpretation (v. 15), it was certainly true that anyone listening to him who did not have the same gift could not empathize with the tongues-speaker. At least another person with the gift of tongues could identify with the exhilaration experienced in the exercise of the gift. However, a Christian with a different gift required intelligible communication if he were to gain any benefit from what was said and so have a basis for affirming his agreement by saying an **Amen.** But such comprehension did not exist if the tongue were not interpreted and so the brother was **not edified.**

14:18-19. Paul's concern to harness the enthusiasm for the gift of **tongues** in Corinth was not motivated by sour grapes. When it came to the gift of tongues, he could outtalk them **all.** But Paul was not primarily interested in self-fulfillment. Instead he was concerned with ministering to **others** and thereby glorifying God (cf. 10:31-33). For that reason he did not use his gift of tongues with the assembled **church** but he did exercise his gift of prophecy (14:6). That, in fact, was in accord with God's purpose. Where then did tongues fit into God's purpose? Paul discussed that next.

14:20. The Corinthian infatuation with tongues was for Paul another manifestation of their immaturity and worldliness (cf. 3:1-3). This he hoped would change, especially in regard to an enhanced appraisal of prophecy and a recognition of the importance of this gift for the assembled church. His final words, contrasting prophecy and tongues (14:21-25), were intended to conclude the exhortation begun in verse 1.

14:21-22. This summary argument in verses 21-25 began with the citation of a portion of Isaiah's prophecy against Israel (Isa. 28:11-12). Because Israel refused to **listen** to God's message proclaimed by His prophets, Isaiah predicted that another message would come. This one would be delivered in a foreign tongue unintelligible to the Israelites, yet unambiguous (cf. 2 Kings 17:23). The foreign tongue symbolized God's rejection (cf. Deut. 28:49; Isa. 33:19), His disciplinary response to Israel's stiff-necked rebellion against Him (cf. 2 Kings 17:14; Acts 7:51). Foreigners instead of Israel became the temporary servants of God (cf. Isa. 5:26; Hab. 1:6; Matt. 21:43; Rom. 10:19-21), and their foreign tongue was a punitive **sign** to Israel of what had taken place.

That seems to be the significance which Paul attached to tongues. As such, the primary arena for its exercise was **not** the company of **believers but . . . unbelievers** (cf. Matt. 13:10-15, on parables). Uninterpreted **tongues** had their place but not in the church where **prophecy** benefited **believers** (1 Cor. 14:3).

14:23-25. **Tongues** were of benefit in an assembly of believers only if they were interpreted. But this seems not to have been the Corinthians' practice. Instead they apparently poured forth their gift of tongues in unrestrained fashion. As a result believers with some other gifts were nonplussed by the behavior of the tongues-speakers (v. 16). Furthermore, newcomers (*idiōtai*, those who attended but were not believers) and other **unbelievers** (*apistoi*) who were aware of but as yet unconvinced by the gospel message (unlike those of vv. 21-22 who had forthrightly rejected it) would find their behavior positively ridiculous. **Will they not say that you are out of your mind?** This, Paul suggested, would certainly not advance the cause of Christ in Corinth. But prophecy was desirable because it would not only benefit believers (v. 3) but would also expose unbelievers not to a scene of chaos but to one of conviction (cf. John 16:8) and judgment (1 Cor. 2:15)—which would lead to personal disclosure (**the secrets of his heart will be laid bare**) and the **worship** of God.

(4) Propriety in the use of gifts (14:26-40). In this section Paul drew to a conclusion his discussion of gifts (chaps. 12–14). He also concluded the whole section dealing with Christian liberty in relation to worship (11:2–14:40). What is most striking to a modern reader is the apparent lack of any fixed order of service and the absence of any reference to particular individuals being responsible for specific ministries. The whole church seemed to exercise their gifts by spontaneously ministering to one another.

14:26. As he had done throughout the letter, Paul addressed the Christian community in Corinth as **brothers,** a general term including both sexes (e.g., 1:10; cf. 1 Peter 5:9). When the church met, anyone was free to participate by contributing **a hymn, or a word of instruction** (cf. 1 Cor. 14:6; probably a lesson based on the OT), **a revelation** from one gifted in prophecy (cf. vv. 6, 29-32), or a word from one gifted in **a tongue** followed by **an interpretation** of what was said. The controlling principle in this free participation was the rule of love. All that was said and done was to have as its goal the need of **strengthening** (pros oikodomēn, "edifying") others (cf. vv. 4-5).

14:27-28. Though there was no established order for a service, it was to be conducted in an orderly way (v. 40). The services were to have balanced participation on the parts of gifted members. Those gifted with **a tongue** who wanted to contribute to a service could do so but only **two** or **three** at any one service and then only if individuals gifted in interpretation were present who could translate the language. If **no interpreter** were present, the tongues-speaker was to **keep quiet.** Though his gift was without benefit to the church if uninterpreted, it did have some other benefits (cf. vv. 4, 14-15, 22).

14:29. The directions for those exercising the gift of prophecy did not differ from those for tongues. **Two or three prophets** could **speak** at each

service and what they **said** was to be carefully considered. Since they would speak in Greek **the others** in the congregation would understand and evaluate their messages. (Or perhaps "the others" referred to those with the gift to distinguish between spirits.) The words **weigh carefully** translate the verb diakrinetōsan, related to the noun diakriseis in 12:10, which speaks of distinguishing "between spirits." It was their responsibility to ascertain if the message delivered was indeed from God (cf. 1 John 4:1).

14:30. A prophet might have received **a revelation,** probably in a vision or dream, sometime prior to the meeting of the church at which he subsequently related it. However, a prophet might also experience a revelation during the service. If such occurred, a prophet in the midst of speaking should draw his message to a close to let the other gifted member speak. Whatever the Corinthian services were, they were not dull.

14:31. The principle which regulated the exercise of tongues applied similarly to prophets. What was said was to benefit **everyone** by way of instruction or encouragement in the Christian life (cf. v. 3).

14:32-33a. Paul apparently did not believe the **prophets** were any more restrained than their fellow members gifted in tongues. So he gave the prophets an instruction that was similar to what he gave the tongues-speakers (v. 28). The **spirits** referred to a prophet's spiritual gift, which did not **control** the gifted member, but he controlled it (cf. v. 30). If two or three prophets spoke in a particular service, others gifted and with something to say could do so on another occasion. The church was not a forum for personal pontification or self-glorification; it was a place where people were to be built up and God was to be honored (cf. 10:31-33). The service and those who took part in it should reflect the character of God. He is a **God . . . of peace,** not **disorder,** and His Spirit worked to produce the same fruit (Gal. 5:22) in believers' lives.

14:33b-36. Some of the verses in this section (vv. 34-35) were felt by some early copyists to be out of place at this point in the letter and so were transposed to the end of the chapter. A more drastic

540

approach taken by some recent commentators is to regard these verses as spurious and unworthy of comment. Though the exact meaning of these verses is difficult to determine, neither expedient has much to commend it. In fact it seems that the guiding thread which prompted these comments by Paul about women was the same theme developed in the preceding verses addressed to those gifted in tongues and prophecy. The church members needed to exercise self-control on occasion, a self-control expressed by silence (vv. 28, 30, 34) in order that the assembly might be characterized by peace.

Apparently certain women in the Corinthian assembly needed to hear this refrain. More than uncovered heads were amiss in regard to their participation in worship services (11:2-16), and Paul was not about to dodge the problem.

Whether the admonition for silence was directed to all women (cf. 11:2-16) or only to those who were married may be debated. The word translated **women** (*gynaikes*) was used to refer to women generally (as in all 11 occurrences in 11:3-15), or to unmarried women (e.g., 7:34), or to married women (e.g., 5:1; 9:5; and all 14 occurrences in chap. 7 except once in 7:34). The context alone aided the readers in distinguishing between the alternative meanings.

Two indications strongly suggest that married women were in view in this passage. The first is the word **submission** (*hypotassesthōsan*, v. 34). When it occurs elsewhere in the New Testament with specific reference to a woman, it always refers to a married woman who was to be subject to her husband (Eph. 5:22; Col. 3:18; Titus 2:5; 1 Peter 3:1, 5).

The second indication is the phrase **their own husbands** (1 Cor. 14:35), whom the inquisitive women were to consult if they had questions. This would obviously be a difficult assignment for single women (e.g., 7:34) or those with unbelieving husbands (e.g., 7:13).

First Timothy 2:11-15, which enjoins women to be quiet in worship, is frequently cited as a parallel to this passage. But there too, married women were probably in view, as verse 15 would not apply to an unmarried woman. Also, when Eve is named in the Old Testament,

it is as Adam's wife (Gen. 3:20; cf. 2 Cor. 11:2-3, the only other NT passage besides 1 Tim. 2:13-14 that names Eve), and her submission is rooted in that relationship (Gen. 3:16, the text Paul probably referred to in 1 Cor. 14:34). In addition, the noun *hēsychia* in 1 Timothy 2:11-12 means "quietness, absence of disorder," whereas the verb *sigaō* in 1 Corinthians 14:28, 34 means "remain silent." (See comments on 1 Tim. 2:11-14 and 2 Thes. 3:12).

Paul then wanted silence on the parts of married women whose husbands were present in the assembly, but he permitted the participation of other women when properly adorned (1 Cor. 11:2-16). Such silence would express their subordinate (but not inferior) relationship to their husbands. This contrasts with a disturbance caused by their talking to their husbands during the service.

The Corinthian believers were not to think of themselves as exclusive, independent interpreters or recipients of **the Word of God** (14:36). They, like those in **all the congregations** (v. 33b), were to submit to God's truth by conforming to this standard of conduct.

14:37-40. These verses were Paul's conclusion not only to the immediately preceding directives (vv. 33b-36) but also to all his discussion about Corinthian irregularities in worship and the needed correctives (11:2-14:36). He expected some opposition (cf. 11:16; 14:36), but warned that those who opposed him did so at their own peril (cf. 4:18-21). Anyone who **ignores** the Lord's commands would find **himself . . . ignored** by Him at the last day (cf. 3:17; Gen. 9:6; Matt. 10:32-33), because his actions would show that he never knew the Lord (cf. 1 Cor. 8:3; Matt. 7:22-23; 1 John 4:6).

The conclusion was that the Corinthians should give special attention to the gifts which were most beneficial to the church as a whole (12:31; 14:1) without denigrating the other gifts. They should see that their services were conducted in a **fitting** (cf. 11:2-16; 14:34-36) **and orderly** (cf. 11:17-34; 14:26-33) **way.**

C. Counsel concerning the Resurrection (chap. 15)

Some have suggested that Paul reserved this chapter on the Resurrection till last because he thought that a firm belief in it would help solve many of the Corinthians' problems. Certainly if the message of Christ crucified were foolishness to the Greek mind (1:23), the corollary doctrine of the Resurrection was no less so (cf. Acts 17:31-32). The implicit denial of the Resurrection on the part of some may be seen in the Corinthian conviction that the present era represented the consummation of God's material blessings (1 Cor. 4:8; cf. 6:2) and sexual immorality was a matter of no lasting consequence (5:1; cf. 6:9, 13-14).

Like the problems previously discussed (1:10-6:20), the denial of the Resurrection by some in the church was a matter apparently reported to Paul (15:12) and not something the Corinthians themselves had included among their questions in their letter to him (cf. 7:25; 8:1; 12:1; 16:1, 12). As in his response to the Thessalonian confusion on the Resurrection (1 Thes. 4:13-18), Paul began with a fundamental affirmation of the faith (cf. 1 Cor. 15:3-4; 1 Thes. 4:14) and expanded on it.

1. THE CERTAINTY OF BODILY
   RESURRECTION (15:1-34)

a. *Historical argument (15:1-11)*

15:1-2. The gospel Paul had **preached** in Corinth (2:1-2) had not changed; but he feared that just as there had been declension in the church concerning the message of Christ crucified and its implication for believers, the same was happening with regard to the message of Christ resurrected. As the former message was an essential element in the Corinthians' experience of ongoing salvation (the pres. tense of the verb **saved** focuses on sanctification), so was the latter. To reject bodily resurrection eviscerated "the gospel" and made faith **vain** (*eikē*, "without cause" or "without success"; cf. vv. 14, 17) because it had an unworthy object (cf. 15:13, 17). Believing the gospel includes holding **firmly** to belief in Christ's resurrection. Unless one holds firmly, his belief is "in vain"; cf. Matt. 13:18-22).

15:3-5. Paul included himself in the company of all believers when he spoke of receiving the truth of Christ's death and His resurrection on behalf of sinful people. These verses, the heart of the gospel, were an early Christian confession

which Paul described **as of first importance.** It was really a twofold confession: **Christ died for our sins** and **He was raised.** The reality of this was verified by the Scriptures (e.g., Ps. 16:10; Isa. 53:8-10) and by historical evidence verified by time in the grave and out of it, in the presence of the living. The fact **that He was buried** verified His death, and the fact **that He appeared** to others verified His resurrection. **Peter,** the first male witness, was soon joined by the remaining disciples who composed the Lord's immediate circle.

15:6. Later a much larger company of believers witnessed His resurrection. The **500 . . . brothers** may have formed the audience who received the commission recorded in Matthew 28:18-20 (cf. Acts 1:3-8). Since **most of** those were **still living** when Paul wrote 1 Corinthians, they could be consulted.

15:7-8. Some have debunked this Resurrection appearance as simply the pious vision of believers seeing with the eyes of faith. But Paul could have cited the testimony of two for whom that was not true, **James,** the half brother of Jesus, and himself. Like Paul, James probably came to faith (cf. John 7:5 with Acts 1:14) because of an appearance of the resurrected Christ (Acts 9:3-6; 22:6-11). Paul considered himself **abnormally born** because he lacked the "gestation" period of having been with Christ during His earthly ministry (cf. Acts 1:21-22). It seems that **the apostles** were a body wider than the previously mentioned Twelve (cf. comments on Eph. 4:11), but were all distinguished by having seen the resurrected Christ (1 Cor. 9:1) which made Paul the last of their company.

15:9. Because he was the last, like a runt, untimely born, Paul could call himself **the least of the apostles.** He felt less deserving of the office because he had been an opponent of the **church** (cf. Acts 22:4; 1 Tim. 1:15-16) which he now served (2 Cor. 4:5).

15:10. He realized, however, that his past was simply a backdrop on which to display **the grace of God** (cf. 1:3), the grace to which Paul had been so responsive. Indeed Paul was without peer in his devotion (cf. 9:19-29). The history of the church confirms that his devotion **was not without effect** (*kenē*, "empty"; cf. 15:14). He had **worked harder** than any of the other apostles, as he traveled more, suffered more opposition, wrote more New Testament epistles, and founded more churches. Yet Paul knew and ministered with the recognition that it was not his power but God's (2:4-5) which produced results (3:6).

15:11. In the final analysis it was not the messenger but the message which was important (cf. 1:18-4:5), and in that regard the apostolic message was that the crucified Christ became the resurrected Christ, which message Paul did **preach** and the Corinthians **believed.**

b. Logical argument (15:12-19)

15:12. Paul then turned to consider the claim of some that no one **dead** could experience bodily **resurrection.** He pressed that tenet to its logical consequences within the framework of the Christian faith.

15:13. To deny a bodily resurrection in principle was to deny the **resurrection** of **Christ.** Presumably some in Corinth had done this, and Paul wanted to warn them and others of the serious consequences which would result from such disbelief.

15:14. Not the least of those consequences was the fact that a denial of the Resurrection tore the heart out of the gospel message and left it lifeless. If that were so, the Corinthians' **faith,** however vital, would be **useless** (*kenē,* "empty"; cf. vv. 2, 10, 17) since its object would be a dead man.

15:15-16. Second, the apostles of the church would turn out to be crass charlatans since their message uniformly affirmed the truth of Christ's resurrection (cf. v. 11).

15:17. Third, the Corinthians' salvation would be only a state of mind with no correspondence to reality. Their **faith** would be **futile** (*mataia,* "without results"; cf. *kenē,* "empty," in vv. 10, 14, *eikē,* "without cause" or "without success," v. 2). The Resurrection was God's validation that the redemption paid by Christ on the cross was accepted (Rom. 4:25). Without the Resurrection there could be no certainty of atonement and the Corinthians would remain in a state of alienation and sin.

15:18. Fourth, if Christ were not raised, the loved ones among the Corinthian believers who had died entered not

bliss but perdition. The pagan concept of a liberated spirit was a lie. Without the Resurrection the sting of death would remain, with lasting painfulness (cf. vv. 54-56).

15:19. Fifth, if there were no Resurrection, the pagans would be right. The "foolishness of the Cross" (1:18) would be just that, and men such as Paul and the apostles who had suffered for the gospel (4:9-13) could only be **pitied.** Those who lived for the pleasure of the moment would be right and the sacrifices of Christians would only be cruel, self-inflicted jokes (cf. 15:32).

c. Theological argument (15:20-28)

15:20. Paul had explored the logical negations which followed from a denial of the bodily resurrection of Christ (vv. 12-19). He then considered the theological tenet that the destiny of Christians was bound up in the destiny of Christ, and he set forth the positive consequences of this union. Speculation had given way to affirmation: **Christ has indeed been raised from the dead.** And He is the **firstfruits,** an Old Testament word (e.g., Ex. 23:16, 19) here used in the sense of a preliminary installment of what will be both an example and a guarantee of more to come (cf. Rom. 8:23).

15:21-22. Death came to all those related to Adam by natural birth because of the disobedience of one **man.** As the father of mankind Adam in his sin brought death to everybody (cf. Gen. 3:17-19; Rom. 5:12). But because of the obedience (Phil. 2:8) of another **Man** (1 Tim. 2:5) **resurrection** will come to **all** those related to Him by spiritual birth. Paul would later expand this grand truth in his letter to the Romans (Rom. 5:12-19). Those who are a part of the body of Christ (1 Cor. 12:27) will one day follow the lead of their Head (Col. 1:18), but will not do so immediately.

15:23. There will be a sequence in the unfolding of the final events. Paul was not concerned to detail all future resurrections since he was addressing the church and was primarily interested here in fixing their place in the scheme of things. As he had earlier affirmed (v. 20), Christ was their sample and surety.

As He promised (John 14:2-3) Christ will return for those who compose the church and the dead in Christ will be raised (1 Thes. 4:16). No time frame was indicated in this sequence but a period of almost 2,000 years has now elapsed.

15:24. Following the resurrection of the church, another period intervenes until **the end** when Christ will deliver His **kingdom to God the Father** (cf. Matt. 13:41-43). Some interpreters dispute that an interval of any sort was hinted at by Paul and find instead the coming of Christ and the consummation of all things as virtually simultaneous events. As in the preceding verse, no time frame was specified and the chronological sequences set forth may indeed be almost momentary (1 Cor. 15:5) but then again they may be prolonged (cf. v. 23). If about 2,000 years can elapse between the first and second phases in this selected presentation of events, a lapse of half that time, that is, a millennium, between the second and third phases should cause no consternation.

15:25-26. Death as a personification of Christ's ultimate opponent (cf. v. 55; Heb. 2:14) will be nullified. It is not human bodies which will **be destroyed,** as some in Corinth were saying, but the destroyer of bodies, death itself.

15:27-28. The reprise of these verses is found in verse 57. It is by the power of **God** that the incarnate **Christ** victoriously mediates His authority (cf. Phil. 3:21). This work of **the Son** will find ultimate completion in the glory of the Father (cf. John 17:4-5). That too is the ultimate goal of the church (cf. 1 Cor. 10:31; Eph. 1:6, 12, 14). When God is **all in all** (cf. Rom. 11:36), the new creation will be consummated and the resurrected Christ and His church will share in that experience (cf. Rev. 22:1).

d. Experiential argument (15:29-34)

In this fourth collection of arguments against those who deny the Resurrection, Paul drew on Corinthian practice (v. 29) and also on his own way of life (vv. 30-32).

15:29. Up to 200 explanations have been given of this verse! Most of these interpretations are inane, prompted by a desire to conform this verse to an orthodox doctrine of baptism. It is clear from the context, however, that Paul distinguished his own practice and teaching from that described here. He merely held up the teaching of being **baptized for the dead** as a practice of some who denied the Resurrection.

How the false teachers came to this view may never be known, but just across the Saronic Gulf, north of Corinth, lay Eleusis, the center of an ancient mystery religion lauded by Homer (*Hymn to Demeter* 478-79) and widely popular (cf. Cicero, himself an initiate, in *De Legibus* 2. 14. 36). Part of the rites of initiation into this pagan religion were washings of purification in the sea without which no one could hope to experience bliss in the life hereafter (cf. Pindar *Fragment* 212; Sophocles *Fragment* 753). A vicarious participation in the mysteries was not unknown either (cf. Orphica *Fragment* 245). Given the Corinthian propensity for distortion in matters of church practice (11:2–14:40), it was likely that some in Corinth (possibly influenced by the Eleusinian mystery) were propounding a false view of baptism which Paul took up and used as an argument against those who denied the Resurrection. No interpretation of this text is entirely satisfactory, but this view has as its chief strength the natural reading of the Greek verse, an asset singularly lacking in other explanations. Also it is noteworthy that Paul referred to **those** (not "we") who are "baptized for the dead."

15:30-32. In contrast to the practice of those cited in verse 29, Paul now mentioned his own lifestyle as a forceful statement of his conviction about the certainty of the Resurrection. Some of the Corinthians may have accused Paul of duplicity (cf. 2 Cor. 1:12-14; 2:17; 6:8), but no one thought him a fool even though he affirmed that he would be one if he ministered without certainty of the Resurrection. Many times his life was imperiled (**I die every day;** cf. 2 Cor. 6:4-5; 11:23-28). At least once he thought he would die (2 Cor. 1:8-9), probably referred to here as his fight with **wild beasts** at **Ephesus.** Though this was probably not an arena experience, it was like it in that Paul saw no hope of deliverance. Why face that if this life were all there is? The Epicureans (and less philosophical men before them; cf. Isa. 22:13) would be right—pursue pleasure and avoid pain (cf. Epicurus *Letter to Menoeceus* 128). But Paul knew there was more, and his life testified to that fact (cf. 1 Cor. 9:24-27; 2 Cor. 4:16-18).

15:33-34. Paul's concluding advice with reference to those who continued to deny the Resurrection was like his former counsel concerning immoral people in the church (chap. 5)—don't associate with them. Previously he had compared immorality in the church to yeast in bread (5:6). Here he quoted the pagan writer Menander (*Thais* 218) to the same effect: **Bad company corrupts good character.** False teachers should be avoided (cf. 2 Cor. 6:14–7:1) because though they claimed great knowledge they were in fact **ignorant of God** (cf. 1 Cor. 8:2). Were the wise Corinthians this easily deceived? (cf. 2 Cor. 11:3)

2. ANSWERS TO CERTAIN QUESTIONS (15:35-58)

In the preceding section (vv. 1-34) Paul had taken up the question implicit in verse 12, why believe in the Resurrection? He answered it with arguments rooted in history, logic, theology, and experience. He then addressed two other questions: How is the resurrection achieved? What is the nature of a resurrected body?

a. *Answers about the resurrection of the dead (15:35-49)*

15:35-37. One objection to belief in anyone's resurrection might be its incomprehensibility. This was the point of the questions **How are the dead raised? With what kind of body will they come?** Paul did not consider these sorts of questions a wise person would ask, as is obvious from his response, **How foolish!** (lit., "how senseless or thoughtless") to his imaginary interlocutor. Belief in the Resurrection was like belief in seedtime and harvest. Neither could be completely understood but both were real. As a plant which sprouted from a seed was directly linked to it but remarkably different from it, so too was the relationship of a natural and a resurrected body.

15:38-41. The variety in Creation reflects the will of the Maker (Gen. 1:1-26). The differences in the animate creation (**men . . . animals . . . birds . . . fish**) and inanimate creation (**sun . . . moon . . . stars**) give expression to the splendor of God and bring Him praise (cf. Ps. 148:13). The differences in splendor

between the **earthly bodies** and the **heavenly bodies** suggested to Paul the differences between a natural and a spiritual body (cf. Dan. 12:3 where resurrected saints were compared to stars; also Matt. 13:43).

15:42-44a. An earthly **natural body** is fallen and so is temporal, imperfect, and weak. A heavenly **spiritual body** will be eternal, perfect, and powerful (cf. 2 Cor. 5:1-4). Like a seed sown in the earth and the plant which proceeds from it, there is continuity but a gloriously evident difference.

15:44b-49. Discussion of the contrast between Adam and Christ (mentioned earlier in v. 22) is resumed here. Adam exemplified the earthly (v. 40) natural body (the word trans. **being,** v. 45, *psychē,* is related to *psychikos,* which is trans. **natural** in v. 44). **Adam** gave his nature to all who followed him (the man without the Spirit is the natural [*psychikos*] man; cf. 2:14). **The last Adam,** Christ, exemplifies the heavenly **spiritual** body (15:22) which those who belong to Him (v. 23; cf. 2:15) will likewise assume at His coming from heaven (cf. Phil. 3:20-21). The full harvest will be like the firstfruits (1 Cor. 15:23; cf. Col. 1:18). First the seed must die; then the spiritual body will emerge.

b. *Answers about the Rapture of the living (15:50-58)*

15:50. What about those who are *not* dead at Christ's coming? Paul now turned to answer that unexpressed question. With all that had preceded about the need for the natural body to give way to the spiritual, it followed that **flesh and blood,** the natural body, could not enter the eternal state (cf. vv. 24-28).

15:51-52. Paul had revealed the same truth to the Thessalonians (1 Thes. 4:15-17). The Rapture of the church was a **mystery** (*mystērion*) in that it had not been known in the Old Testament but now was revealed. (Cf. other "mysteries"— now revealed truths—in Matt. 13:11; Luke 8:10; Rom. 11:25; 16:25; 1 Cor. 4:1; Eph. 1:9; 3:3-4, 9; 5:32; Col. 1:26-27; 2:2; 4:3; 2 Thes. 2:7; 1 Tim. 3:9, 16; Rev. 1:20; 10:7; 17:5.) The dead in Christ will first be raised, and then the living will be instantaneously transformed. The **trumpet,** as in the Old Testament, signaled the appearance of God (cf. Ex. 19:16). It is the last blast for the church because this appearance shall never end (cf. 1 Cor. 13:12). (There is no basis for posttribulationists equating this trumpet with the seventh trumpet in Rev. 11:15-19. The trumpets in Rev. pertain to judgments during the Tribulation, whereas the trumpet in 1 Cor. 15:52 is related to the church.)

15:53-54. Like the dead (vv. 42-43), the living will exchange the temporal and imperfect for the eternal and perfect (cf. 13:10). For those who belong to Christ, death's power will be removed.

15:55. As in the allusion to Isaiah 25:8 (1 Cor. 15:54), Paul again recalled an Old Testament passage which prophesied the cessation of death (Hosea 13:14). (The recollections were adapted by Paul and do not correspond exactly to any of the extant Gr. or Heb. texts.) The apparent victories of Satan, in the Garden of Eden (Gen. 3:13) and on Golgotha (Mark 15:22-24) were reversed on the cross (Col. 2:15; Heb. 2:14-15) and vindicated in the resurrection of Christ. From the vantage point of the certain resurrection of the saints, Paul voiced his taunt against **death** and Satan.

15:56-57. As the word **victory** which ended verse 54 led Paul into the exaltation in verse 55, so the word **sting** which ended verse 55 led him into this brief digression in verses 56-57. Like other theological nuggets in this chapter (vv. 21-22), these verses were later given expanded discussion in Paul's letter to the Romans (Rom. 7:7-13). **Death** came as a result of man's rebellion and disobedience against the command of God (Gen. 3:17-19). The **Law,** which epitomized the command of God, was thus the mirror against which human rebellion and disobedience was starkly portrayed. Like the first Adam, all who followed him rebelled (cf. 1 Cor. 2:14). But through the obedience of the last Adam, **our Lord Jesus Christ** (15:45; cf. Rom. 5:19; Phil. 2:8-11), came "victory" and life (1 Cor. 15:22; cf. 2:15-16).

15:58. Paul's doctrinal declarations led to practical directives and this chapter's conclusion was no exception. The Corinthians were urged to **stand firm** in the apostles' teaching (v. 2), unmoved by the denials of false teachers (cf. Eph. 4:14). This certainty, especially concerning the Resurrection, provided an impetus to faithful service (cf. 1 Cor. 3:8; Gal. 6:9) since labor **in the** resurrected **Lord is not** futile (*kenos*, "empty"; cf. 1 Cor. 15:10, 14, 17, 30-32).

D. Counsel concerning the collection for the poor (16:1-4)

The flow of the previous chapter, from a prolonged discourse on doctrinal matters to a concluding exhortation on practical diligence, moved smoothly to a discussion of a practical expression of that faith—care for the needs of others and in particular, the needy in Jerusalem.

16:1. At this appropriate juncture, Paul took up the Corinthian inquiry (cf. 7:1) concerning a proposed **collection for God's people** (cf. 1:2) in Jerusalem (15:3). The Corinthians had apparently heard about the collection through members of **the Galatian churches,** the oldest of all the Pauline-planted churches (Acts 13:14–14:23) in Derbe, Lystra, Iconium, and Pisidian Antioch. Paul's instruction to them was repeated to the Corinthians.

16:2. Paul never used the word "tithe" when he discussed giving, even though he gave more attention to giving than any other New Testament writer. Giving should be a systematic, weekly practice on Sunday when the church meets together. Giving was also to be proportionate—**in keeping with** one's **income** (cf. Acts 11:29). The income of some would permit them to give a greater proportion, while others, due to their few resources and other constraints on them, would be limited to lesser contributions. What was important was that giving be a unified ministry with **each one** participating, regardless of his income. Then when it came time to deliver the contributions to the saints in Jerusalem, no last-minute **collections** would need **to be made,** and the gift could be sent off gladly, not grudgingly (2 Cor. 9:5)—as would be true if it were wrung out by emotional appeals or personal pressure.

16:3-4. Paul's practice in money matters was scrupulously aboveboard. Not only did he avoid solicitation for himself (cf. 9:12, 15), but also when he acted to meet the needs of others he avoided direct involvement in handling the **gift.** He preferred instead that individuals from the various contributing congregations elect representatives to bear their gift (cf. 2 Cor. 8:19-21) whom he might then **accompany** to the presentation.

E. Counsel concerning future visits (16:5-12)

The mention of his planned arrival in connection with the collection sparked another brief digression on the subject of future visits.

16:5. It was Paul's plan to leave Ephesus, his place of ministry at that time (v. 8), and journey **through Macedonia,** the region north of Corinth where the churches of Philippi, Thessalonica, and presumably Berea (cf. Acts 20:4, a delegate from Berea accompanied Paul) flourished. They too were planning to make a contribution to the needy in Jerusalem (cf. 2 Cor. 8:1-4).

16:6-7. On that journey (cf. Acts 19:21) Paul hoped to be able to **spend** some time with the Corinthians, possibly as long as **the winter** since travel by sea in that season was ill-advised (cf. Acts 27:9-44). This, in fact, he eventually did (see the *Introduction*) but not on the schedule here set forth. This change of plans became a source of trouble for him with the Corinthians later (cf. 2 Cor. 1:15-2:1). What Paul meant by the words **you can help me on my journey** is clarified later (1 Cor. 16:11). He desired that his departure be marked by "peace," which would be in keeping with the Lord's will (cf. James 4:15).

16:8-9. For the time being, Paul intended to **stay on at Ephesus** in ministry, where the opportunities and the opposition were both great. One or the other of these situations may have arisen while he was writing this letter (cf. 4:19). It says something about Paul's perception of his ministry that the presence of opposition was a sign to him of the viability of his labor and reason for pressing on, not running away (cf. Acts 19:30-31). Those who opposed him in Corinth (1 Cor. 4:18-21) probably took note of this.

16:10-11. In the meantime Paul intended to send his beloved assistant **Timothy** to Corinth. The younger man sometimes traveled in Paul's place (cf. Phil. 2:19-24). That Timothy might have cause **to fear while** ministering in Corinth confirms, as this letter indicates, that working with the Corinthian church was

no picnic. However, it probably says more about the character of Timothy, a man devoted to Christ (Phil. 2:19-21) but lacking Paul's robust boldness (cf. 1 Tim. 4:12; 2 Tim. 1:7-8; 2:1).

The identity of **the brothers** accompanying Timothy is not clear. It appears that Timothy went out from Ephesus with Erastus (Acts 19:22). They may have been joined by some of the men who later composed Paul's traveling party for delivering the collection (Acts 20:4).

16:12. The last of the Corinthian questions (cf. 7:10) concerned **Apollos.** They apparently inquired about the possibility of a return visit from him. Paul said he had **strongly urged** Apollos to do this but that the gifted Alexandrian had decided to stay on in Ephesus with Paul, and not join Timothy and Erastus in their trip (Acts 19:22). Earlier in the letter, Paul had described himself and Apollos as fellow workers under God (1 Cor. 3:9). This verse bears eloquent tribute to the fact that Paul conducted himself not as a master but as a partner with others who labored in ministry.

V. Conclusion (16:13-24)

A. Exhortation on appropriate conduct and commendation (16:13-18)

16:13-14. Paul began the conclusion with a pointed exhortation along a fivefold line. The command, **Be on your guard** (*grēgoreite*) might be rendered "be diligent" in carrying out the will of God (cf. 15:58, "give yourselves fully to the work of the Lord"). In view of the Corinthians' susceptibility to false teachers (cf. 2 Cor. 11:3) the exhortation to **stand firm in the faith** was a timely reminder (cf. 1 Cor. 15:1, 58). So too were the closing exhortations (similar to the Gr. text of several Pss., e.g., 27:14; 31:24) to **be men of courage** and **be strong,** that is, marked by maturity (cf. 1 Cor. 14:20) and not infants easily swept aside (cf. Eph. 4:14). That sort of diligence and commitment is required if **everything** is to be done **in love** (cf. 1 Cor. 12:31b-14:1).

16:15-16. Achaia was the Roman province extending over central and southern Greece of which Corinth was the capital. Those in **the household of Stephanas** were among the first converts in the region (cf. Acts 17:34, for some in Athens believed), and they were among those who assumed responsibility for the general welfare of the church. Sometimes Paul appointed elders (Acts 14:23) but in this instance members of Stephanas' household voluntarily took on the responsibility (cf. 1 Tim. 3:1). Paul recognized their position as ordained by God and urged others to **submit to** them. As an aside, it may be said that this text argues strongly against the view that infants were in view when a household was referred to. It is difficult to see how infants could be of **service** to **the saints.** One primary qualification for church leadership was a willingness to serve (cf. Matt. 23:11; Luke 22:26). To those who labored with this spirit, submission on the part of others in the church was due.

16:17-18. By their very presence, three men from the Corinthian church—**Stephanas, Fortunatus, and Achaicus**—were able to refresh and encourage Paul despite the fact that they probably also brought confirmation of the bad news earlier reported by Chloe's people (1:11). These men were the probable bearers of the letter to which Paul had responded (7:1 et al.).

B. Salutation, imprecation, and benediction (16:19-24)

16:19. The churches . . . of Asia, perhaps those indicated in Revelation 2-3, joined with Paul in sending **greetings** to their sister church in Corinth (cf. 1 Cor. 1:2). **Aquila and Priscilla** were tentmakers whom Paul met in Corinth and with whom he lived. They had followed Paul to Ephesus and remained there in ministry, making their house available as a meeting place (cf. Rom. 16:3-5). They would, of course, know and be known by many in the Corinthian church.

16:20. All the brothers may refer to those from the Corinthian church in Ephesus at the time of writing (1:11; 16:17), or to believers in Ephesus who met in a house(s) other than that of Aquila and Priscilla, or simply to the collective community of Christians in the province of Asia.

The **holy kiss** (cf. 2 Cor. 13:12; Rom. 16:16; 1 Thes. 5:25; 1 Peter 5:14) was primarily a symbolic expression of the love, forgiveness, and unity which should exist among Christians. As such, it became associated with the celebration of the Lord's Supper as a prelude to its observance (cf. Justin *Apology* 1. 65. 2). It was a mark of the familial bond which united believers. There is no indication that it was restricted to one's own sex in the New Testament era (cf. Luke 7:37, 45). The suggestion to separate the sexes for the exchange of the kiss arose in the late second century due to concern about criticism from non-Christians and the danger of erotic abuse (cf. Athenagorus *Supplication* 32; Clement of Alexandria *Pedagogue* 3. 81. 2-4). By the third century it seems that the sexes were separated (*Apostolic Constitutions* 2. 57. 17), and by the fourth century the clergy and laity were also kept apart (*Apostolic Constitutions* 8. 11. 9). Such, however, was apparently not the case in the New Testament church where love for one another was openly expressed.

16:21. At this point Paul stopped dictating the letter (cf. Rom. 16:22; Gal. 6:11) and wrote the final words himself.

16:22. Paul's personal note began with a passionate warning probably aimed at false teachers (cf. 12:3) whom he believed to be already present in the congregation (cf. 2 Cor. 11:3-4). The verb **love** (*philei*) is related to the noun *philēmati* for "kiss" (1 Cor. 16:20). It expresses adoration and devotion, qualities absent in false brethren. Paul invoked God's wrath on these false teachers (cf. Gal. 1:8-9) and in the same breath appealed to Christ to return (cf. Matt. 7:21-23; Rev. 22:20). **Come, O Lord!** renders the Greek words *marana tha* ("Maranatha"), which transliterate the Aramaic "Lord, come."

16:23-24. To the congregation of Christians in Corinth, Paul invoked what they sorely needed, the continued **grace of the Lord Jesus** (cf. 1:4). He assured them of what they hardly deserved, his fervent though unrequited (cf. 2 Cor. 6:11-13; 12:15) **love** (*agapē*). He embraced the disunited lot of them (cf. 1 Cor. 1:10) as their spiritual father **in Christ Jesus** (4:15).

BIBLIOGRAPHY

Deluz, Gaston. *A Companion to First Corinthians.* Edited and translated by Grace E. Watt. London: Darton, Longman and Todd, 1963.

Godet, Frederic Louis. *Commentary on First Corinthians.* Edinburgh: T. & T. Clark, 1889. Reprint (2 vols. in 1). Grand Rapids: Kregel Publications, 1977.

Gromacki, Robert G. *Called to Be Saints: An Exposition of 1 Corinthians.* Grand Rapids: Baker Book House, 1977.

Grosheide, F.W. *Commentary on the First Epistle to the Corinthians.* The New International Commentary on the New Testament. Grand Rapids: Wm. B. Eerdmans Publishing Co., 1953.

Hodge, Charles. *An Exposition of the First Epistle to the Corinthians.* Reprint. Grand Rapids: Wm. B. Eerdmans Publishing Co., 1974.

Ironside, Henry Allen. *Addresses on the First Epistle to the Corinthians.* New York: Loizeaux Brothers, 1938.

Johnson, S. Lewis, Jr. "1 Corinthians." In *The Wycliffe Bible Commentary.* Chicago: Moody Press, 1962.

Lenski, R.C.H. *The Interpretation of St. Paul's First and Second Epistles to the Corinthians.* Minneapolis: Augsburg Publishing House, 1963.

Mare, W. Harold. "1 Corinthians." In *The Expositor's Bible Commentary,* vol. 10. Grand Rapids: Wm. B. Eerdmans Publishing Co., 1976.

Morris, Leon. *The First Epistle of Paul to the Corinthians.* Tyndale New Testament Commentaries. Grand Rapids: Wm. B. Eerdmans Publishing Co., 1958.

Parry, R. St. John. *The First Epistle of Paul the Apostle to the Corinthians.* Cambridge: At the University Press, 1916.

Redpath, Alan. *The Royal Route to Heaven.* Westwood, N.J.: Fleming H. Revell Co., 1960.

Robertson, Archibald, and Plummer, Alfred. *The First Epistle of St. Paul to the Corinthians.* The International Critical Commentary. Edinburgh: T. & T. Clark, 1914.

2 CORINTHIANS

David K. Lowery

INTRODUCTION

Few portions of the New Testament pose as many problems for translators and interpreters as does 2 Corinthians. Few, therefore, are the preachers who undertake a systematic exposition of its contents. For those undaunted by its demands, however, an intimate picture of a pastor's heart may be found as the Apostle Paul shepherded the wayward Corinthians and revealed a love which comes only from God.

Author and Readers. Apart from certain portions of the letter which are sometimes mentioned as non-Pauline interpolations (e.g., 6:14–7:1) most agree that 2 Corinthians came not from the hand of a pseudonymous writer but from the heart of the Apostle Paul. It was sent to a church which he had founded (Acts 18:1-17) on his second missionary journey. He worked there for one and one-half years. Like its winter seas, Corinth was a tempestuous city. (See its location on the map between Acts and Rom.) But what apprehension Paul may have felt was at least partially allayed by a vision in the night (Acts 18:9-10) in which the Lord assured him not only of his personal safety but also revealed that many in this city were appointed to faith. There was ample reason to doubt both affirmations. Not many months before, Paul had been beaten and jailed in Philippi and subsequently had been hounded out of Thessalonica and Berea by irate Jews. A sizable community of Jews resided in Corinth. Nor would Corinth have seemed a likely field in which the seed of the gospel could find fertile soil. True, new Corinth was not the same city once pilloried by Athenian playwrights and philosophers as the home of lechers, harlots, and fornicators (see *Introduction* to 1 Cor.) but its refounding by Rome in 46 B.C. did little to upgrade its moral climate. When Paul wrote the Romans and described the degraded course of rebellious mankind (Rom. 1:21-32), he did so from Corinth where he likely saw the sad portrayal that he wrote about.

Unhappily, the church in Corinth was not immune to this debauchery and came in for correction in Paul's first letter to them (e.g., 1 Cor. 5–6). But it was not only in sexual matters that the Corinthians were still children of their age. They were also easily impressed by external qualities such as eloquence and superior human wisdom (1 Cor. 2) and spectacular gifts such as tongues (1 Cor. 12–14). They walked by sight rather than by faith (cf. 2 Cor. 5:7), a fact Paul sought to amend by his correspondence and visits.

Contacts and Correspondence. The nature and number of Paul's contacts and correspondence with the Corinthians is a matter not easily agreed on. The controversy concerns how many letters Paul dispatched to Corinth (opinions range from three to five), and how many times (two or three) and when he visited them. A discussion of the alternative reconstructions may be found in the more extensive commentaries noted in the *Bibliography* (e.g., Barrett, Hughes). While not affecting the understanding of 1 Corinthians, the accepted scheme of Paul's visits and letters to Corinth does shape the interpretation of 2 Corinthians. In the following comments on the text, the view is taken that four letters were sent and three visits made.

1. Paul first came to Corinth in the spring of A.D. 51 and ministered there for one and one-half years. He sailed in the fall of A.D. 52 with Priscilla and Aquila to Ephesus where they remained while Paul continued on to Jerusalem. At Ephesus, Priscilla and Aquila met Apollos whom they instructed and subsequently sent to Corinth for a period of ministry (Acts 18:18-28).

2. While Apollos ministered in Corinth (Acts 19:1) in the fall of A.D. 53 Paul returned to Ephesus on his third missionary journey. Paul remained there for two and one-half years, establishing it as a center for evangelizing the surrounding provinces as well (Acts 19). The letter mentioned in 1 Corinthians 5:9 (a letter misunderstood by the Corinthians [1 Cor. 5:9-11] and now lost) was probably written during the early stages of this Ephesian ministry.

3. Paul learned of the misunderstanding and of additional problems in the Corinthian church from members of the household of Chloe (1 Cor. 1:11). He then received an official delegation in the form of Stephanas, Fortunatus, and Achaicus (1 Cor. 16:17), who brought corroborating news and specific questions on issues dividing the church. First Corinthians, Paul's second letter to the church, was written to address these matters.

4. But apparently the problems in the church were still not resolved. It is possible that Timothy (cf. 1 Cor. 4:17; 16:10) was the bearer of this news. Paul then decided to pay the church a second visit, sailing directly from Ephesus to Corinth. This, it seems, was the "painful visit" referred to in 2 Corinthians 2:1, apparently because of the action of the man mentioned in 2:5 and 7:12 and the failure of the Corinthians to support Paul.

5. After this visit and Paul's return to Ephesus he sent a third letter to the Corinthians (now lost, like the first) borne by Titus. It grieved Paul deeply to write this (2 Cor. 2:3-4) because of its stark disciplinary nature (7:8-9). After a riot provoked by silversmiths (Acts 19:23-41) Paul left Ephesus in the spring of A.D. 56, bound for Macedonia (Acts 20:1) with a preliminary stop in Troas where he hoped to rendezvous with Titus (2 Cor. 2:13) and receive news from him about the situation in Corinth. Because he could not find Titus there, he anxiously pushed on to Macedonia, apparently with grave concern about Titus' safety (7:5-6). There he met Titus, who brought good news about the general well-being of the Corinthian church but bad news about a group opposed to Paul.

6. From Macedonia Paul wrote a fourth letter, 2 Corinthians.

7. Paul then made his third visit to Corinth during the winter of A.D. 56–57 (Acts 20:2-3).

These steps, in summary, are: (1) First visit to Corinth. (2) First letter to Corinth (now lost). (3) Second letter to Corinth (1 Cor.). (4) Second visit to Corinth (a "painful visit," 2 Cor. 2:1). (5) Third letter to Corinth (now lost). (6) Fourth letter to Corinth (2 Cor.). (7) Third visit to Corinth.

The two lost letters were obviously not intended by God to be part of the biblical canon.

Purpose and Nature of the Letter. No letter of Paul's is more personal and intimate in nature than 2 Corinthians. In it he bared his soul and professed his abiding love for the Corinthians despite the apparent fickleness of their affection for him.

What concerned Paul preeminently was the presence of false teachers, claiming to be apostles, who had entered the church. They promoted their own ideas and at the same time sought to discredit both the person and message of the apostle. Second Corinthians was written to defend the authenticity of both his apostleship and his message. This was not carried out in a self-protecting spirit but because Paul knew that acceptance of his ministry and message were intimately bound with the Corinthian church's own spiritual well-being.

Who were these opponents of Paul? This is a widely debated issue. One view sees these men as Hellenistic Jews (i.e., Jews whose first language was Gr. either from Palestine, like Stephen, or from the diaspora, like Timothy). Though they claimed to be followers of Christ, they promoted themselves as men in the line of Moses.

A second view is that those claiming to be apostles of Christ were Jews of a Gnostic or Docetic stripe who rejected the earthly sufferings of Jesus in His humiliation and promoted the glory of Jesus in His exaltation as the norm of life in this world. These false teachers were already present when Paul wrote 1 Corinthians (cf. 4:8-21; 12:3), but later they became more vocal in their opposition to Paul and his theology.

A third view is that these opponents were Palestinian Jews claiming to be apostles of Christ. Some who hold this position also feel these opponents were ostensibly concerned to bolster the position of the Jerusalem apostles, James, Peter, and John. They elevated the Law and promoted allegiance to themselves as interpreters of it.

Probably an unequivocal portrait of these opponents will never exist, but there is no disputing the havoc they wreaked in the Corinthian church and the heartaches they brought Paul. Though it is only in the final chapters of 2 Corinthians that Paul challenged them frontally, their influence pervades the entire letter in its threefold development.

1. The first seven chapters are largely a discussion of Paul's ministry as it specifically affected his relationship with the Corinthians and then generally as it reflected the paradoxes that mark the ministry of a servant of Christ. The accusation, no doubt broached by Paul's opponents, that his ministry and message were as suspect as his travel plans, he pointedly rebutted.

2. Chapters 8 and 9 concern the collection for the poor in Jerusalem. The Corinthians had initially welcomed the opportunity to participate but were failing to carry through on their commitment, possibly because Paul's opponents had intimated that he was profiting from their contributions.

3. The final four chapters include (a) a defense of his apostleship and (b) a denunciation of those who opposed him and Christ. Above all else, Paul's identification with Christ marks this letter. His affirmation to the Galatians, "I no longer live, but Christ lives in me" (Gal. 2:20), is graphically portrayed in 2 Corinthians 10–13.

Unity. All of Paul's letters have sections which digress or are discontinuous, but in no letter is this tendency so evident as in 2 Corinthians. The circumstances under which it was composed likely contributed to this but that has not satisfied the numerous advocates who find interpolations rife in 2 Corinthians. Five proposed interpolations may be noted.

1. Second Corinthians 2:14–7:4 is considered by some a separate letter that disrupts the otherwise smooth connection between 2:13 and 7:5.

2. Within the larger unit just noted, 6:14–7:1 is frequently held to be an extraneous section breaking the former bond of 6:13–7:2. According to some, this passage is the previous "letter" mentioned in 1 Corinthians 5:9.

3. Second Corinthians 8 is held by some to be an interpolated portion of a different letter because 9:1 begins as if no comment on the collection preceded it while the transition into that subject in chapter 8 is felt to be unduly abrupt.

4. Some believe chapters 10–13 are a separate letter either preceding 1–9 and forming the "severe letter" or following it by some lapse in time and so forming a fifth and final letter in the Corinthian correspondence.

5. Second Corinthians 11:32-33 seem to be an awkward intrusion in the flow of thought from 11:31–12:1 and is thought to be interpolated by a subsequent reviser of the letter.

While the sections noted are problematic, the proposed resolutions and the resulting truncated letter are even more so. No explanation of how the fragmented lot emerged to form canonical 2 Corinthians has found even minimal acceptance. That, coupled with the fact that not a shred of manuscript evidence exists to support any interpolation, produces a burden no theory can reasonably bear. Thus 2 Corinthians has a cohesive (though digressive) unity.

OUTLINE

A. Examples of liberality (8:1-9)
B. Advice and arrangements for the collection (8:10–9:5)
C. Reward of generosity (9:6-15)
IV. Affirmative Action (10:1–13:10)
A. Appeal for obedience (10:1-6)
B. False apostles confronted (10:7–11:15)
C. Apostolic credentials (11:16–12:10)
D. Recommended response (12:11–13:10)
V. Conclusion (13:11-14)
A. Appropriate conduct (13:11-12)
B. Salutations and benediction (13:13-14)

COMMENTARY

I. Introduction (1:1-11)

Poised in Macedonia, about to travel to Corinth for a third visit, Paul prepared for his coming by sending this letter. The name of the writer and its recipients followed by a greeting conforms to the usual style of letter writing in the first century (cf. Acts 23:26).

A. Salutation and description of writer and readers (1:1-2)

1:1. Though Paul's description of himself as an apostle was not unusual, in no letter was it more controversial than this one. A defense of the fact that he was **an apostle of Christ Jesus** occupied the heart of this letter. Unlike the false apostles who opposed him in Corinth, **Paul** was sent by Christ Jesus (Acts 9:15). Not a station of his own choosing, apostleship was pressed on him by God (Acts 22:14).

One of Paul's much-loved associates in the ministry was **Timothy.** He is also mentioned in the opening verses of other epistles: Philippians, Colossians, 1 and 2 Thessalonians, Philemon. Timothy joined him near the beginning of the second journey (Acts 16:1-3) and proved to be an invaluable colleague (cf. Phil. 2:19-22). Timothy also had experience ministering at Corinth (Acts 18:5; cf. 1 Cor. 16:10-11; 2 Cor. 1:19), so his association with Paul in the greeting was more than a formality. Though Timothy was a protegé of Paul, the apostle considered him a **brother** (as also in Col. and Phile.).

While there was room for concern about the immediate destiny of **the church of God in Corinth** (cf. 2 Cor. 11:3), Paul was confident that those who composed it belonged to God (cf. Acts 18:10) and no power could wrest them from Him (Rom. 8:38-39). This was true not only of the Corinthians, of course, but also of all Christians living in the region surrounding the capital of **Achaia.** They too were **saints,** set apart by God for service to Him, but they were not immune to the controversy in Corinth or its consequences.

1:2. Grace refers to the love of God in action with **peace** its result. Both aspects were displayed in Jesus' ministry (John 1:14; 14:27). Paul hoped that this salutation would find expression in the Corinthians' lives as he shepherded them. (See the chart, "Paul's Introductions to His Epistles" at Rom. 1:1-7.)

B. Thanksgiving for God's comfort (1:3-11)

One of the many paradoxes of the Christian life is that the grace of God is most keenly experienced not in the best but in what seem to be the worst of times. However much a Christian longs for exaltation (cf. 1 Cor. 4:8), it is often in humiliation that he finds grace (cf. 2 Cor. 12:9). That theme pervades this letter and finds poignant expression in Paul's thanksgiving.

1:3-4. Troubles (*thlipsei*, "pressures, distresses") are mentioned nine times by Paul in this letter (vv. 4 [twice], 8; 2:4; 4:17; 6:4; 7:4; 8:2, 13; sometimes the word is trans. "troubles," other times "hardships"). Paul also used the corresponding verb *thlibō* three times in this epistle ("distressed," 1:6; "hard-pressed," 4:8; "harassed," 7:5). Troubles are experienced by all Christians. And the Apostle Paul probably endured more pressures than nearly all his readers. Troubles, Paul said, help Christians shift their perspective from the external and temporal to the internal and eternal (cf. 1:9; 4:17-18).

The source **of all comfort** in the midst of troubles is **God** Himself, to whom Paul gave three titles: the **Father of our Lord Jesus Christ** (cf. identical wording in Eph. 1:3; 1 Peter 1:3), **the Father** (i.e., the Originator) **of compassion, and the God of all comfort.** This same God had sustained Paul through his suffering (2 Cor. 1:8-9) and delivered him from it (v. 10). "Compassion" translates the Greek *oiktirmōn*, used only four other times in the New Testament (rendered "mercy" in Rom. 12:1 and Heb. 10:28, and "compassion" in Phil. 2:1 and Col. 3:12). Just as spiritual gifts are not intended solely for the recipients' benefit but are to be used in turn for the service of others (cf. 1 Peter 4:10), so comfort **received from God** enables believers to **comfort** others. The comfort of God is channeled through people (cf. Acts 9:10-19; 2 Cor. 7:6) and by means of prayer (1:11). (Paul used a form of "comfort" five times in the Gr. [four are trans. in the NIV] in vv. 3-4, and five more times in vv. 5-7!)

1:5-7. The sufferings Paul experienced were a consequence of his relationship to **Christ** (cf. Matt. 5:11; Col. 1:24). As Paul continued to preach the gospel, he suffered at the hands of men (e.g., 2 Cor. 11:23-26) and from privations which were a part of his task (11:27). But Paul's sufferings for Christ were accompanied by a **comfort** that overflowed.

In referring to **the sufferings of Christ** (1:5), **sufferings we suffer** (v. 6), and **our sufferings** (v. 7), the apostle probably had in mind either the suffering he experienced in Asia which he referred to next (v. 8) or the pain brought to him by the problems of the Corinthian church (cf. 11:28-29). Both kinds may be in mind, but if it was primarily the latter to which he referred (cf. 7:5) then the Corinthians' own suffering was similar. Paul's severe letter (7:8) produced in them a profound sorrow as they understood how their reprehensible behavior had grieved Paul (7:9). It had certainly **distressed** him to write it (2:4) but he did it out of love for them, for their **comfort and salvation** (cf. 7:10). The aspect of salvation suggested here is their advance in sanctification, which in fact this letter produced (cf. 7:11). The Corinthians' response brought comfort to both themselves and Paul (7:13) and reaffirmed Paul's **hope** (1:7) that God indeed had His hand on their lives (cf. Heb. 12:7-8). In addition, the Corinthians' comfort produced in them **patient endurance** (*hypomonē*, steadfastness in the face of unpleasant circumstances; cf. 2 Cor. 6:4; Rom. 5:3; Col. 1:11; James 1:3).

1:8-11. The **hope** in God which sustained Paul in his relationship with the Corinthians was also effective in his own life. An experience in Asia (see map between Acts and Rom.) had brought him to the end of himself. Apparently the Corinthians had some knowledge of this hardship, possibly communicated to them by Titus, but they did not appreciate its severity. Rather than gloss over his feeling of despair and helplessness in this situation Paul underscored it forcefully to illustrate how powerless both he and the Corinthians were apart from God and to stress how important is prayer as a means of effecting God's gracious intervention and aid.

Just what **the hardships** were is debated. Commentators in the 19th century and earlier held that the phrase **in the province of Asia** referred to Ephesus. Paul's experience was linked with that mentioned in 1 Corinthians 15:32, in which he mentioned fighting with wild beasts, a possible allusion to the contention instigated by Demetrius and his fellow silversmiths (Acts 19:23-41). However, no mention is made in that account of any harm coming to Paul. Twentieth-century opinion seems more disposed to locating this experience somewhere in the outlying region of the province of Asia (in the western end of what is today Turkey). One such suggested area is the Lycus Valley, where Paul may have experienced a beating by the Jews (cf. 2 Cor. 11:24), which nearly killed him. Or perhaps he contracted a drastic illness with similar devastating results. All such views are merely conjectures. Being unable to be specific in identifying this experience permits believers today to apply this to themselves, especially when they find themselves in desperate circumstances where deliverance seems impossible.

Paul believed he would die. He was **under** such **great pressure** (*thlipseōs*; cf. 1:4) **far beyond** his human **ability to endure, so that** he **despaired even of life** and **felt the sentence of death** (cf. 4:10-12, 16; 11:23-25). Certainly the Christian life was for him no bed of roses! Some suggest that this experience irrevocably altered Paul's perspective on his own destiny. Before this he expressed the hope that he might be numbered among those who would be alive at the coming of Christ (cf. 1 Cor. 15:51-52; 1 Thes.

4:15-17). Now his focus was on the resurrection (cf. Phil. 3:10-11).

What was sure was Paul's trust that God would **deliver** him from the **peril** of death (cf. 2 Cor. 4:8-14) until his course was run (2 Tim. 4:7), and his task completed. Then later God, he knew, would **deliver** him from **the dead** (cf. 1 Cor. 15:55; 2 Cor. 4:14). Paul had a firm hope in the Corinthians (1:7) and also in the Lord (v. 10). **The prayers** (v. 11) **of** the Corinthians were part of this deliverance, a means ordained by God to fulfill His will among people.

II. Apostolic Ministry (1:12–7:16)

One reason Paul wrote this letter was to answer insinuations raised in Corinth about the authenticity of his apostleship, the propriety of his conduct, and the sincerity of his commitment to those Christians. Later (in chaps. 10–13) Paul gave a defense of the genuineness of his apostleship. Questions about the propriety of his conduct, especially as it concerned "the collection," are addressed in chapters 8 and 9. The burden of these preceding chapters (1:12–7:16) is an emotional affirmation by Paul of his sincere commitment to the ministry in general and to the Corinthians in particular.

A. Changed plans defended (1:12–2:11)

Who raised the questions in the Corinthians' minds about Paul's supposed lack of commitment to the church in Corinth or his alleged insincerity? No one knows for sure. But a reasonable conclusion is that they were broached by false apostles (11:4, 13) who hoped to discredit their chief rival. Though Paul reserved his open confrontation with these opponents for the conclusion of his letter, a polemic pervades even these early chapters.

1:12. Paul met questions concerning his motives head-on. He could affirm with confidence—**this is our boast**—that the moral sensibilities of his **conscience** (cf. 4:2; 5:11), intensified by his knowledge of God's Word, were without censure regarding his conduct, **especially in** his **relations with** the Corinthians (cf. 1 Cor. 4:3-4). He said three things about his conduct. (1) It was with a singleness of heart. Instead of **holiness** (*hagiotēti*) Paul probably wrote "simplicity in the sense of

singlemindedness" (*haplotēti*; cf. 2 Cor. 11:3). These two Greek words could easily have been confused by a manuscript copyist. (2) His conduct was in **sincerity** (cf. 1 Cor. 5:8; 2 Cor. 2:17) of purpose that could stand the closest scrutiny. (3) His conduct was **not** in keeping with **worldly** (*sarkikē*, lit., "fleshly," i.e., human) **wisdom,** for that is ultimately self-serving. Instead it was **according to God's grace,** that is, he was guided by a love for others and sought what was in their best interests.

1:13-14. Paul's letters were like his conduct: simple, sincere, not in man-made wisdom but in God's grace. Paul had no hidden meanings or ulterior motives in his correspondence with the Corinthians. He was aboveboard and straightforward in person; and he was the same way in his letters. He felt the Corinthians must acknowledge this to a degree (**in part**). And he hoped that this provisional assent would one day grow into their wholehearted acceptance and endorsement (**understand fully**). That in fact was how Paul viewed them. He was confident of the genuineness of their conversions (cf. 1 Cor. 9:1-2). And he felt they would eventually come to vindicate him and even **boast of** (*kauchēma*, "exult over") him **in the day of the Lord Jesus** (cf. Phil. 2:16), that is, at the judgment seat of Christ (cf. 2 Cor. 5:10-11).

1:15-16. In this spirit of confidence in his relationship with the Corinthians, Paul had proposed a journey from Ephesus that would have permitted him **to visit** them **twice.** This was apparently a change in the plans he had stated earlier (1 Cor. 16:5-7). At that time he hoped to go to Corinth by way of Macedonia and spend the winter with them, a course of action he eventually followed (cf. Acts 20:1-3). The change included the opportunity for two visits: first from Ephesus to Corinth and then on **to Macedonia;** then a second stop as he retraced his route. The two visits were meant to express Paul's affection for them. He wanted to see them as often as possible.

1:17. But Paul changed his mind about this itinerary (cf. 2:1), and his opponents said his vacillating was a sign of a fundamental unreliability, affecting not only where he went but what he said. Paul fervently denied this. He did not make **plans in a worldly** (i.e., self-serving; cf. "worldly" in 1:12) **manner** altering them for reasons of self-interest. Nor did he talk out of both sides of his mouth to further his own ends. He would explain the reason for his change in plans (1:23–2:2), but for the moment he was more concerned with the accusation that his message was equivocal or unreliable.

1:18-20. The source of stability for Paul in his ministry was **God** Himself, who **is faithful,** and the **message** Paul preached was no less certain than God. Since Paul did not vacillate in his message (**Yes and No,** v. 18), he did not vacillate in his plans either (**Yes, yes and No, no,** v. 17). At the heart of that message was the person of **Jesus Christ who** completely affirms all God's **promises** to people. The only proper response to God's message is **Amen** (lit., "let it be so"). It was this response of obedience to God that brought Paul **and Silas and Timothy** to Corinth in the first place and caused them to exalt Christ among the Corinthians in the synagogue (Acts 18:5). In Christ the promises to Abraham and David are fulfilled (Rom. 1:3; 11:5; Gal. 3:16) and the Law was brought to an end (Rom. 10:4), a truth apparently contested by Paul's opponents (cf. 2 Cor. 3). Nevertheless this message proclaimed by Paul and his associates resulted in the Corinthians' salvation and in turn brought **glory** to **God.**

1:21-22. Those who speak the "Amen" in response to the gospel message experience firmness and security **in Christ.** At the moment of belief **God** anoints each believer with the Holy Spirit so that like Christ (*Christos* means "the Anointed One"), he may glorify God by his life (cf. Matt. 5:16). John wrote that believers receive this anointing from God (1 John 2:20, 27). It is a pouring out of the Holy Spirit on the believer, reminiscent of the anointing of priests with oil.

A further consequence of the Spirit's presence is the **seal of ownership** (cf. Eph. 1:13-14) which also is accomplished at the moment of faith. A seal on a document in New Testament times identified it and indicated its owner, who would "protect" it. So too, in salvation, the Holy Spirit, like a seal, confirms that Christians are identified with Christ and are God's property, protected by Him (cf. 1 Cor. 6:19-20). It was probably this thought that caused Paul to describe

himself as a slave of Christ (Rom. 1:1; Phil. 1:1).

A third work of the Spirit at salvation is His confirmation that what God has begun He will complete. Present redemption is only a foretaste of what eternity holds (cf. Rom. 8:23), and the presence of **His Spirit in our hearts** (cf. Rom. 5:5; 2 Cor. 5:5) is like **a deposit, guaranteeing what is to come.** These last seven words are a translation of one Greek word *arrabōna,* a down payment which obligates the payer to make further payments. The same Greek word is used again in 5:5 and Ephesians 1:14 (cf. "the firstfruits of the Spirit," Rom. 8:23).

1:23-24. Paul had earlier begun to explain his change of plans (v. 15). There he had mentioned his "message" (v. 18) in connection with his own integrity, which led to his digression in verses 19-22. He now returned to explain his altered plans.

He understood that his changed plans had caused a problem in Corinth. This is evident from the strength of his declaration, **I call God as my witness** (cf. Rom. 1:9; Phil. 1:8; 1 Thes. 2:5, 10). With a solemn oath (with God as the Judge) Paul staked his life on the truthfulness of his explanation which followed. It was out of consideration for the Corinthians, a desire to avoid disciplinary action (**to spare you**) that Paul had deferred his visit. Even though he had great authority as an apostle (2 Cor. 10:2-8; cf. 1 Cor. 5:4-5; 1 Tim. 1:20) Paul was reluctant to wield it. He did not **lord it over** their **faith,** that is, domineeringly take advantage of the fact that they came to faith in Christ through him. Dictatorial means can produce compliance but not the obedience that comes from faith which he sought. Authoritarian domination is often the manner of false apostles and the kingdom they serve (cf. 2 Cor. 11:13-15), but it was not the way of Christ (Luke 22:25-27) nor of those who stand in His stead (1 Peter 5:3). Paul assured the Corinthians, **We work with you** (lit., "we are fellow workers"; cf. 1 Cor. 3:9); he did not work against them or over them.

2:1-2. A servant of Christ is no stranger to pain and suffering (Matt. 5:10-12; John 15:18-20; 1 Peter 2:21). Paul had his share (cf. 2 Cor. 1:4-10; 11:16-32) which he did not shirk. But he was no fool. If he could avoid it and still accomplish his work he would do so. This belief led to his change of plans with the Corinthians.

When his first **painful visit** occurred is an unsettled issue. It could have taken place after his founding visit but before the writing of 1 Corinthians, as many suggest. It is odd, however, if that was so, that no mention or intimation of such a visit is found in that letter. More likely, he went to Corinth from Ephesus after writing 1 Corinthians. His "painful visit" may be linked to the projected double visit previously mentioned (2 Cor. 1:15-16) and may thus refer to the first part of those unconsummated plans. During that visit some painful event transpired which **grieved** the Corinthians and Paul (see comments on 2:5). To spare further grief for both of them Paul deferred his visit.

2:3-4. He decided instead to write a letter, a daring venture in view of the Corinthians' propensity for misunderstanding (cf. 1 Cor. 5:9-10). If his "painful visit" (2 Cor. 2:1) had occurred before he wrote 1 Corinthians, the letter here referred to (**I wrote as I did**) would be that letter. But if, as seems more likely, the "painful visit" occurred after he **wrote** 1 Corinthians, the letter Paul referred to followed 1 Corinthians and is now lost (not having been intended by God as a part of the inspired Scriptures). (See point 5 under "Contacts and Correspondence" in the *Introduction*.)

What that letter contained can only be conjectured from the comments which follow in 2 Corinthians 2:5-11 and 7:5-12. What is clear was Paul's depth of feelings for the Corinthians and the level of his own discomfort experienced in writing the letter (**great distress** [*thlipseōs*; "troubles or pressures"; cf. 1:4] **and anguish of heart and with many tears**) and in his waiting for news from Titus concerning its reception (cf. 7:5-8).

2:5. The event that made his visit painful (v. 1) and prompted the severe letter seems to have centered around the action of a certain man at Corinth. Whether he was a member of the Corinthian church or someone visiting them is not clear. Paul did, however, regard him as a Christian.

What this individual did to cause grief is uncertain. In the past many writers identified him with the incestuous

man whom Paul had judged (1 Cor. 5). Relatively few now hold this view because of the severity of that judgment (cf. 1 Cor. 5:5) when compared with this situation, and the unlikelihood that 1 Corinthians is the letter referred to in 2 Corinthians 2:3-4.

Paul's diffidence in this verse suggests the more likely alternative that his authority as an apostle was affronted or challenged at some point in the course of his painful visit (v. 1). The Corinthians apparently failed to make the connection between a challenge to Paul's authority and their own spiritual well-being. They had regarded this as a personal problem requiring no action on their parts, a view which Paul had dispelled in his letter and which they now realized.

2:6. Their response had been to discipline the offender. **Punishment** may be too strong a translation of the Greek word *epitimia*. Perhaps "censure" is better. This discipline, whatever it was, was made **by the** church "as a whole" (*hē hypo tōn pleionōn*) rather than the **majority** (cf. 7:11).

2:7-8. Paul had reason to believe that their pendulum might swing too far (cf. 7:11). They were no longer dispassionate spectators of the wrongdoer, and might become impassioned prosecutors. In that case he would **be overwhelmed by excessive sorrow** (lit., "grief"). The offender was apparently penitent so Paul urged the church **to forgive and comfort him** (for in fact it was they who had been wronged, 2:10) and extend "comfort" to him. As a church they were to affirm their **love for** this fellow Christian and admit him to their fellowship (cf. 1 Cor. 5:11). (**Reaffirm** may be too strong for the word *kyrōsai*; it occurs elsewhere in the NT only in Gal. 3:15 where it is trans. "has been duly established.")

2:9-11. Paul's concern in this matter was not simply personal vindication or primarily that an erring brother be brought in line but that the Corinthian congregation could demonstrate the strength of their commitment to Paul (cf. 7:2). Their love and devotion to him would be affirmed by their being **obedient** to his directives (cf. John 15:14).

The expression of their solidarity with him was mutual. As one with him, they could **forgive** this offender who had wronged them by wronging Paul. Like their own sorrow for this wrong (2 Cor. 7:8) repentance resulted (cf. 7:9) so that Paul could offer forgiveness. Otherwise, **Satan might** use a bitterness of spirit to vitiate Paul's or the Corinthians' ministry. It was important that fellowship between Paul, the Corinthians, and the repentant offender be restored so that the incident **not** become an occasion for Satan to drive a wedge between the church and Paul. This was one of Satan's **schemes** (cf. 11:13-14) which Paul had worked so strenuously to thwart.

In sum, his plans had changed. But that was out of concern for the well-being of the Corinthian church. In place of a personal visit Paul had sent Titus with a letter and accomplished his purpose. But he did not know that until he met Titus in Macedonia. The interim was not an easy time for Paul as 2:12-16 indicate.

B. Glorious ministry described (2:12–7:16)

The interim period between Paul's dispatch of Titus with the letter (2:4; 7:6-7) and his return to report on the state of affairs in the Corinthian church was a turbulent time for Paul. He apparently sensed in an acute way his own helplessness and weakness and came to appreciate afresh how utterly dependent he was on God to accomplish anything of lasting value in his ministry. That theme pervades this section. A ministry is glorious because God is in it.

1. TRIUMPHANT IN CHRIST (2:12–3:6)

2:12-13. Paul had planned to rendezvous with **Titus** at **Troas** (see map between Acts and Rom.) and be apprised of the Corinthian situation. Before proceeding to Greece Paul had hoped to minister in Troas, a favored Roman colony. **The Lord had opened a door** (cf. 1 Cor. 16:9; Col. 4:3) for him, that is, had given him a favorable opportunity **to preach the gospel of Christ.**

But those hopes were dashed when Titus failed to appear. In addition to his apprehension about the church in Corinth, Paul was now also concerned about Titus' safety. For all Paul knew Titus might have been carrying with him a portion of the proposed Corinthian collection (cf. 2 Cor. 8:6) and fallen prey to bandits. Why else had he failed to meet Paul in Troas? Thus Paul **had no**

peace of mind (*anesin tō pneumati,* lit., "relief in spirit"; *anesin* is also used in 7:5 and 8:13).

Despairing at his own inability to concentrate on the great potential for ministry in Troas (cf. 7:5-6) Paul **said good-by to** the church there and pushed **on to Macedonia.** The door would remain open for him and on his return (cf. Acts 20:5-11) God used him mightily in their midst, but for the moment Paul departed, unable to rise to the occasion, no doubt feeling like a beaten man (cf. 2 Cor. 4:9).

2:14. At this juncture Paul broke off his narrative to the Corinthians, not to resume it until 7:5. (Cf. "Macedonia" in 2:13 and 7:5.) But this transition is fitting. The defeated Paul drew attention from himself to the triumphant **Christ** in whose train, by the grace of God, he found himself.

Paul's words in 2:14 are based on a Roman **triumphal procession,** the victory parade awarded a conquering general in which enemy prisoners were forced to march. Through Christ, **God** the Victor had vanquished His enemies (cf. Rom. 5:10; Col. 2:15) and Paul, Christ's captive, was now marching in His parade! Paul, who had been "taken captive" by Christ (in Phile. 23 "fellow prisoner" is lit. "fellow captive"; cf. 1 Cor. 4:9), was now led in triumph. This "triumph in defeat," by a slave who was free, was the paradox of the ministry which Paul subsequently amplified (e.g., in 2 Cor. 4:7-12; 6:9-10).

In a Roman triumph processional incense was burned. Paul compared this to **the knowledge of** Christ, which like a **fragrance** was diffused **everywhere** throughout the world via the preaching of the gospel.

2:15-16. The gospel produces paradoxical results. As a bearer of this message Paul was identified with it so that he could refer to himself as **the aroma of Christ.** In the Septuagint the term "aroma" (*euōdia*) was used of Old Testament sacrifices (Gen. 8:21; Ex. 29:18; Lev. 1:9; Num. 15:3). Paul's life was a sacrificial offering (Rom. 12:1), well-pleasing to God. The course of his life in proclaiming God's message while at the same time suffering rejection and attack by many was an extension of Jesus' life as the Servant of God (cf. Col. 1:24).

The heart of the gospel is that

through Jesus' death people may receive life and resurrection (1 Cor. 15). To those who rejected the gospel and disbelieved the message of Christ crucified and raised Paul was like the stench **of death** in their nostrils (Acts 17:32). They continued on the path to destruction. But to those who believe, their salvation leads on to glorification (cf. 2 Cor. 4:17; Rom. 8:18, 30). For them the gospel is like **the fragrance of life.**

This twofold consequence of Paul's ministry staggered him. **Who is equal to such a task?** He answered this question later (2 Cor. 3:5-6). For the moment, however, he recalled the work of the false apostles. They thought themselves more than adequate but it was because their message and motivation differed so radically from Paul's. To that point he needed to respond.

2:17. In Paul's day there was apparently no lack of false apostles (cf. 2 Peter 2:1). According to Paul, the ministry of the **many** false apostles was a matter of self-interest. **Unlike** them, he had ministered in Corinth without charge (cf. 2 Cor. 11:7-12; 12:14), though in principle he had no problem accepting material remuneration for spiritual labor (1 Cor. 9). What characterized the false apostles were their messages and their motives. Like dishonest merchants they selfishly hawked their wares. Paul said they **peddle** God's Word. This word *kapēleuontes,* "to hawk, peddle," is used only here. Paul may have had in mind Isaiah's description of Jerusalem's unscrupulous Israelites who "diluted" their wine with water to increase their profits (Isa. 1:22; cf. Lucian's description [*Hermotimus* 59] of similarly unscrupulous philosophers). So too these false apostles adulterated **the Word of God for profit.** They served themselves, not **God** whom Paul represented. They were "greedy for money" (1 Peter 5:2), an evidence of their falsehood. But Paul ministered **with sincerity** (cf. 2 Cor. 1:12).

3:1-3. Aware of the tactics of his opponents, Paul realized that his swipe at the false apostles and defense of his own ministry might be turned against him. His first question in verse 1 (**Are we beginning to commend ourselves again?**) suggests that this had happened before (cf. 1 Cor. 9).

Related to this, some might suppose

Paul had to commend himself because he could find no one else to do so. His opponents obviously carried **letters of recommendation,** a common practice in the first century (cf. Oxyrhynchus papyri 1. 32). Paul himself followed this practice at various times on behalf of those who served with him (Rom. 16:1-2; 2 Cor. 8:22-24). Paul, however, had reason to doubt the authenticity of their letters (4:2). Unlike those false letters, apparently unavailable to public scrutiny, Paul's letter of commendation could be examined **by everybody.** His "letter" was the Corinthians themselves! And they were **a letter . . . written** by **the Spirit of the living God** dispatched by **Christ** Himself. The false apostles' commendation was human; Paul's was divine (cf. 1 Cor. 2:1-5).

When Paul spoke of that **letter written on our hearts,** "hearts" probably included Timothy and Titus. **On tablets of human hearts** alluded to the nature of the New Covenant (Jer. 31:33). In contrast with the Old Covenant inscribed in stone (Ex. 24:12), the New Covenant is inscribed on human hearts (Ezek. 11:19; 36:26). As the New is far superior to the Old, so was Paul's commendation compared with that of the false apostles.

3:4-6. Paul's **confidence** was founded not on human resources but on divine ones. He was confident in the Corinthians because the Holy **Spirit** had worked in them. Their faith rested on God's power (1 Cor. 2:1-5). Likewise his own sufficiency and **competence** in the ministry was derived wholly **from God** (cf. 1 Tim. 1:12).

Paul's emphasis on the **New Covenant** implies that his opponents were ministers of the Old Covenant. The Mosaic Covenant was a written revelation of the righteousness God asked of Israel (e.g., Ex. 19–23). It was accepted with an oath of obedience and a blood sacrifice (Ex. 24). When Israel proved unable and unwilling to remain faithful to that covenant, God graciously intervened and promised a New Covenant (Jer. 31:31-34; 32:40), new (*kainēs*) both in time and in quality. It was inaugurated by Christ in His sacrifice on the cross (Luke 22:20), and is entered into by faith (Phil. 3:9) and lived out in dependence on the Spirit (Rom. 7:6; 8:4). (However, the physical and national aspects of the New Covenant which pertain to Israel have not been appropriated to the church. Those are yet to be fulfilled in the Millennium. The church today shares in the soteriological aspects of that covenant, established by Christ's blood for all believers [cf. Heb. 8:7-13].)

Reliance on human rather than divine authority in letters of commendation was shortsighted and dangerous (2 Cor. 3:1-3). Even more so was the attempt to fulfill God's righteousness apart from divine enablement. Those who did so found that **the letter kills** (cf. Rom. 7:10-11). But those who trust in Christ find that **the Spirit gives life** (cf. Rom. 8:2).

2. GLORY FROM THE SPIRIT (3:7-18)

In the preceding portion of this letter (2:12-3:6) Paul had begun an explanation and a defense of his ministry. Prompted by the inference that his credentials were inadequate Paul cited the internal attestation of the Spirit as superior to any external human commendation. In so doing he intimated that those challenging him proclaimed an adulterated message based on the Old Covenant, acceptance of which could only lead to death.

To underscore the superiority of the New Covenant to that of the Old, particularly as it was proclaimed by his opponents, Paul discussed Exodus 34:29-35. His point was to show that the Old Covenant, because it came from God, was glorious. But because its fulfillment was based on human initiative, it ultimately was transitory and "fading" (katargeō, 2 Cor. 3:7, 11, 13), needing to be replaced by the New Covenant and the Spirit's ministry which is eternal (Heb. 9:14). To illustrate this, Paul contrasted the fading radiance of God's glory on the face of Moses (2 Cor. 3:7) with the ever-increasing radiance of Christians (v. 18).

3:7. The Old Covenant **ministry** of Moses **brought death** to people. It was not the fault of Moses or the Law, which was "holy, righteous, and good" (Rom. 7:12; cf. 1 Tim. 1:8). It was the fault of human sin (Rom. 7:10-11). Still even this ministry of death had a **glory,** though transitory and **fading** (cf. 2 Cor. 3:11, 13), which was visually illustrated by the Old Covenant's intended obsolescence.

When Moses came down from Mount Sinai with the tablets of the Ten Commandments, his face was so radiant that the people were afraid to approach him (Ex. 34:29-30). The Old Testament, however, does not mention the fading of this radiance. On the contrary, a part of Jewish tradition maintained that Moses carried the glory of that encounter to his grave (Targum Onkelos; Deut. 34:7). It seems unlikely, however, that Paul would have put forth a novel interpretation which might be easily rejected, especially a view central to his argument, when he had exercised such care thus far in developing this letter.

3:8-11. On this point, the fading of Moses' **glory,** Paul proceeded to argue for the superiority of the New Covenant. The ministry of the Old Covenant, by means of the commandments, condemned **men** (cf. Rom. 7:11). The **ministry of** the New, by means of **the Spirit,** leads men to faith in Christ and the imputation of His **righteousness** (Rom. 3:21-22; 4:24). Like a candle before the sun the Old Covenant paled and passed away (Gal. 3:19-25) before the grandeur of the New, which is eternal (Heb. 13:20). If the Old is **glorious,** how **much more glorious** is the New!

3:12. Because the New Covenant is eternal its recipients had the certain **hope** of acceptance by God. This permitted Paul to be **bold** and candid in speech and action.

3:13. In contrast was the ministry of **Moses** who veiled **his face** as he addressed Israel so that they could not see **the radiance** (produced by those meetings with God) **fading away.** Why did he do this? Did Moses believe that the rebellious Israelites would be less inclined to obey God if they witnessed a diminishing of this awesome radiance? Or did Moses consider them unworthy recipients of this display of God's glory and so veiled his face as a commentary on the hardness of their hearts? Perhaps it was the latter.

3:14-16. Whatever was Moses' reason for using the **veil,** his action proved to be prophetic. Not only was ancient Israel unwilling or unable to comprehend **(their minds were made dull)** the transitory and preparatory nature of **the Old Covenant,** but the dullness remained with subsequent generations. The Jews of Paul's day **(to this day)** failed to perceive that the Old Covenant was a preliminary message, not the final word of God's revelation. Though the cloth that veiled

Moses' glory and the Old Covenant was gone, Paul said a perceptible spiritual **veil remains** and **has not been removed** (cf. 4:3-4; Rom. 11:7-8, 25).

The **veil** of unbelief that **covers their hearts** can be **taken away** only **in Christ** (2 Cor. 3:14), that is, **whenever anyone turns to the Lord.** Moses removed his physical veil in the presence of the Lord. So for any Jew—or anyone—who turns in faith to Christ the Lord his spiritual veil is removed. The Lord who mediated the Old Covenant is the same Lord who established the New.

3:17. In the Old Covenant when Moses entered the Lord's presence he removed his veil (Ex. 34:34). In the New Covenant it is the Spirit who removes the veil. The Holy Spirit is the personal "Agent" of Christ; He is **the Spirit of the Lord** (cf. Rom. 8:9). The Two are One in purpose (John 15:26; 16:6-15) and in result (Rom. 8:15; Gal. 5:1). Paul's words **the Lord is the Spirit** (2 Cor. 3:17; cf. v. 18) do not confuse these two Persons of the Godhead. Instead, they affirm the Holy Spirit's deity.

A major result of the New Covenant **is freedom.** Elsewhere Paul compared those under the Old Covenant to children of slavery and those under the New to children of freedom (Gal. 4:24-31). This freedom is possible because Christ has redeemed from the penalty of the Law those who believe so that they become children of God (Gal. 4:5-7). This freedom as children is confirmed by the Spirit, who enables Christians to call God Father (Rom. 8:15; Gal. 4:6).

3:18. The glory evident in Moses' face was a diminishing radiance (vv. 7, 13). By contrast, in the **faces** of Christians is God's **ever-increasing glory** (cf. 4:6). ("Ever-increasing glory" is the NIV's rendering of the Gr. phrase, "from glory into glory," i.e., from one stage of glory to another.) Christians' glory, like that of Moses, is a reflection of **the Lord's glory.** But unlike Moses' transitory glory a believer's glory is eternal. This is because of God's abiding presence through the Holy Spirit (4:17). This glory is the experience of salvation available in the New Covenant and mediated by **the Spirit** who leads Christians from justification through sanctification to glorification. As believers manifest the fruit of the Spirit (Gal. 5:22-23), they are progres-

sively **being transformed** (the same word Paul used in Rom. 12:2) **into His likeness.** Christlikeness is the goal of the Christian walk (Eph. 4:23-24; Col. 3:10). No wonder Paul said the New is far superior to the Old!

3. POWER FROM GOD (4:1-15)

The New Covenant ministry is glorious because of the certain triumph of Christ (2:14) and the transforming work of the Spirit (3:18), but it is not without its hardships. Physically, the demands of Paul's ministry sometimes seemed too much for him to bear (cf. 1:8; 11:23-27). No less excruciating were the spiritual demands (cf. 7:5; 11:28-29) brought on by those he served (e.g., 2:4) and those he opposed (e.g., 2:5). He reflected on these experiences in this passage and pointed to what sustained him, namely, the power of God (4:7).

4:1. The **ministry** (*diakonia*, "service"; also used in 5:18; 6:3; 8:4; 9:1, 12-13; 11:8) of the New Covenant was given to Paul in spite of his past (cf. 1 Cor. 15:9-10; 1 Tim. 1:13) because of **God's** grace and compassion on him. That same **mercy** sustained Paul through the many painful episodes that marked his ministry (cf. 2 Cor. 1:3-11) and enabled him to overcome feelings of despair (cf. 7:6). Thus he could write, **we do not lose heart** (4:1, 16). "Give up" in Luke 18:1 is the same verb translated "lose heart." Though discouraged at times, the great apostle never quit.

4:2. One source of discouragement was the disquieting state of affairs in Corinth. This was caused by the activity of false apostles in the church and the passivity of the Christians. In the face of sharp accusations Paul found it necessary to defend himself before people who should have trusted him implicitly. Already he had adroitly parried the attacks of his accusers several times in the letter (e.g., 1:17; 2:17; 3:1), but he felt forced to do so again (e.g., 6:3; 7:3; 10-13). Some accused him of using the gospel deceitfully to serve his own ends (**deception** translates the Gr. *panourgia*, "trickery, cunning"; in 11:3 this word is used of Satan). Perhaps Paul had the collection in mind (12:16-18; cf. 2:17). In response he pointed to the openness (**we have renounced secret and shameful ways . . . setting forth the truth plainly**) and boldness (cf. 3:12) which character-ized his proclamation of the gospel. Unlike his opponents, he did not **distort** ("falsify") **the Word of God.** Thus he could **commend** himself (cf. 6:4) before others and **God** (cf. **conscience** in 1:12; 5:11).

4:3-4. Of course many people, particularly Jews (3:14-15), did not accept the **gospel.** To them it was **veiled.** But Paul would not change it to make it more palatable, as his opponents had done (11:4). The gospel was rejected by people who were unable and unwilling to accept it (cf. 1 Cor. 1:18; 2:14). They disbelieved and were abetted in their unbelief by Satan, **the god of this Age** (cf. Eph. 2:2) who, though defeated by Christ (Heb. 2:14), continues his hold over the present world (1 Peter 5:8; 1 John 5:19). His blinding of peoples' **minds** makes it impossible for them to **see the light of the gospel.**

The gospel, then, is not obscure. In fact, it points to **Christ** who, as **the image of God** (cf. Col. 1:15), revealed God the Father by His words and actions (cf. John 1:18; 14:9).

4:5. Christ was the Focus of Paul's message and the Object of his concern. Contrary to what Paul's accusers sug-gested (v. 2), he labored to advance the cause of Christ **(for Jesus' sake)** and not his own interests. **Jesus** was the crucified **Christ** and the resurrected **Lord.** Since Paul served Christ, he also served the church, Christ's body (Eph. 1:22-23). While serving the Corinthians, however unworthy they were, Paul was serving his Lord (cf. Matt. 25:40).

4:6. The reason Paul served the church and openly proclaimed the gospel was because of God's work in his life. Much as in creating the world God acted to bring **light . . . out of darkness** (Gen. 1:2-4), so in spiritual creation He brings **light** to the **hearts** of those in darkness (cf. Luke 1:78-79; Acts 26:18). This had been Paul's experience on the Damascus Road, when "a light from heaven flashed around him" (Acts 9:3). Confronted with the risen Lord, he became a new creation (cf. 2 Cor. 5:17). **The light** in believers' lives is **the knowledge of** God's salvation, a **glory** issuing from and seen in **the face of Christ** and reflected by Paul (cf. 3:18). When people were in the darkness of sin, they had no knowledge of God, no

experience of His life and salvation (Eph. 4:18).

4:7. The message of salvation and the results it produces are glorious and divine. By contrast the bearer of the message is a mere mortal person. The contrast is like a great **treasure** contained in common **jars of clay.** A deepening sense of his own unworthiness, compared with the grandeur of his message, characterized Paul's life (cf. Eph. 3:7-9). God intended this sharp contrast so that no one would question the source of the gospel and its **all-surpassing power.** Salvation is the work of **God** not men (cf. 1 Cor. 2:5; 3:7).

4:8-9. In his earlier letter Paul had compared himself and his fellow apostles to "men condemned to die in the arena" (1 Cor. 4:9). The metaphors employed here evoked the same imagery to describe the demands of the ministry, contrasting human helplessness on one hand with divine enablement on the other. The contrasts include physical (cf. 2 Cor. 1:8-9; 6:5, 9) as well as psychological affliction (cf. 6:4, 8; 7:5-6). **Hard-pressed** is the participle *thlibomenoi,* related to *thlipsis* ("trouble, pressure, hardship"; cf. 1:4). Interestingly the words **perplexed** and **in despair** render two similar Greek words: *aporoumenoi* ("despairing") and *exaporoumenoi* ("totally despairing"). Without God's intervention these trou-bles would have broken Paul (cf. 1:8-10).

4:10-11. The paradoxes in verses 8-9 dramatically contrast the weakness which marked the humiliation of Jesus' earthly life and the power associated with His heavenly exaltation (13:4). In 1 Corinthi-ans Paul had said the content of his message is "Christ crucified" (1 Cor. 1:23). In this letter he referred to his own life as a demonstration of this humili-ation, a constant reminder that through human weakness the power of God is seen to greatest effect (2 Cor. 12:9-10). In his own **body** he carried **around . . . the death of Jesus,** that is, he suffered intensely for Jesus and bore physical scars resulting from wounds inflicted by beatings and a stoning because of his testimony **for Jesus' sake** (cf. 1 Cor. 4:11; 2 Cor. 6:5, 9; 11:23-25; Gal. 6:17). He was **always being given over to death,** that is, he constantly faced death (cf. 2 Cor. 1:9). Paul noticed that God usually chose weak people to serve Him (cf. 1 Cor. 1:26-29).

He subsequently argued for the genuineness of his apostleship on the basis of his sufferings (2 Cor. 11:23-24) and his weakness (11:30; 12:5).

However, **the life of Jesus** was also **revealed in** Paul's **body,** that is, it was evident that he was alive spiritually (cf. 4:16). By means of these experiences his transformation into Christlikeness advanced (3:18).

4:12. But though Paul saw suffering as paradoxically beneficial for himself (Phil. 3:10), he was ultimately motivated by the example of his Lord who gave His life on behalf of others (Mark 10:45; cf. Phil. 2:5-8). Paul believed his own sufferings were a means through which God could minister to the Corinthians (2 Cor. 1:5-6; cf. Eph. 3:10; 2 Tim. 2:10). As Christ had brought life to others through His suffering and death, so Paul's suffering (with **death . . . at work in** him [cf. 2 Cor. 4:10-11]) was a means of causing spiritual **life** to be **at work in** others (Col. 1:24).

4:13-14. What enabled Paul to endure in the face of this suffering? His quotation of Psalm 116:10 gives the answer. The psalmist referred to "the anguish of the grave" (116:3), but he affirmed his confidence that God would deliver him "from death" (116:8). That same confidence was Paul's, so with the psalmist he could declare **I believed.** The second part of the quotation, **Therefore I have spoken,** is from the psalmist's words about his own suffering: "Therefore I said, 'I am greatly afflicted.'" Paul did not quote these last words from Psalm 116:10. But he probably expected his readers to understand that he had in mind his own disclosure of suffering in the preceding verses (2 Cor. 4:8-12) and throughout this letter.

Paul could speak of his suffering and death because he was confident that God would deliver him (cf. 1:9-10). This confidence was founded on the resurrection of Christ, the Firstfruit and Guarantee of resurrection for all who place their faith for salvation in Him (1 Cor. 15:12-19; 1 Thes. 4:14).

4:15. **All this** suffering that Paul experienced was for the **benefit** of Christians like the Corinthians (cf. v. 12). And yet Paul had said he suffered "for Jesus' sake " (v. 11). This illustrates how he identified the church with Christ.

Paul's ministry to the church, Christ's body (Eph. 1:22-23), was also a ministry to Christ (cf. Matt. 25:40).

The grace of God, His unmerited goodness and kindness, was extended to **more and more people** through the gospel Paul preached. Those who heard and responded in belief received salvation and gave thanks to God (cf. Eph. 1:6, 12, 14). As more came to the Savior, it caused **thanksgiving to overflow** (or increase). This verse underscores the selflessness of Paul's ministry. It was for the benefit of others and **to the glory of God** (cf. Mark 12:33), not for himself (cf. 2 Cor. 2:5).

4. ETERNAL PERSPECTIVE (4:16–5:10)

Paul well knew what it was to suffer in ministering for Christ. His distress at not finding Titus in Troas had been a part of that suffering. Remembrance of that painful experience (2:12-13) and God's provision of comfort (7:5-6) touched off this intervening meditation (in 2:12–7:4) on the greatness of the New Covenant ministry. The ministry triumphed in Christ (2:12–3:6), was glorious because of the ministry of the Spirit (3:7-18), and received its power from God (4:1-15). Now Paul turned to another aspect of this ministry, its eternal perspective.

4:16. Paul was not immune to discouragement in his ministry (1:8). In fact, Titus' failure to meet him in Troas disturbed him deeply (2:13; 7:5-6). It was just one of many experiences (e.g., 4:8-9; 11:23-29) which wore him down and reminded him of his mortality (4:11). But God had given him "this ministry" (v. 1) and God—the triumphant Son (2:14), the glorious Spirit (3:18), and the powerful Father (4:7)—was at work in it. God was also the assurance of his resurrection (4:14). Because of all this Paul did **not lose heart** (i.e., "give up"; cf. v. 1; Luke 18:1).

True, his earthly mortality was increasingly evident; **outwardly** he was **wasting away** (cf. 2 Cor. 1:8-9; 4:8-12). But his heavenly destiny was also increasingly evident (vv. 17-18). While physically he grew weaker, spiritually he experienced the renewing (cf. Rom. 12:2; Col. 3:10) work of the Holy Spirit **day by day.** He was becoming increasingly like Christ (2 Cor. 3:18), a prelude to what will be (cf. Rom. 8:23; 1 John 3:2).

4:17-18. Part of the means used by God in this transforming, renewing process is suffering (cf. 1 Peter 4:1, 13-14). Paul compared the sufferings he had experienced, severe as they were (2 Cor. 11:23-29), to **light and momentary troubles** (*thlipseōs*, "pressures, hardships"; cf. 1:4). They were nothing in view of the **eternal glory** that would be his when he would be in Jesus' "presence" (4:14) and would be like Him (1 Cor. 15:49; Phil 3:21; 1 John 3:2). This is amazing: all of his heavy, continuous burdens were, he said, "light" (the Gr. *elaphron* means "light in weight, easy to bear"; used in the NT only twice: here and in Matt. 11:30) and "momentary" (the Gr. *parautika* means "brief, for the slight moment, on the spot"). Though, as he wrote in 2 Corinthians 1:8, his hardships were "far beyond" (*hyperbolēn*) his ability to endure, he said his coming **glory . . . far outweighs them all** (*hyperbolēn eis hyperbolēn* is lit., "extraordinary unto the extraordinary").

This eternal perspective and hope in things to come sustained Paul in the midst of the temporary sufferings that marked his ministry. As he elsewhere reminded the Corinthians, the world and its present sufferings are passing away (1 Cor. 7:31). **What is seen** (the material) **is temporary, but what is unseen** (the spiritual) **is eternal.** The temporal will be replaced by a "glory that will never fade away" (1 Peter 5:4), an "eternal glory in Christ" (1 Peter 5:10). Therefore, Paul said, believers should look not on what is seen but, ironically, on what cannot be seen. What the inner man "sees" surpasses what physical eyes see.

5:1. Few chapter divisions are more unfortunate than this one since what follows (5:1-10) details the thought expressed in 4:16-18. Failure to appreciate this fact unduly complicates these already difficult verses by removing their contextual constraints.

Paul had referred to his mortal "body" (4:10-11) as "wasting away" (4:16). Now he compared his body to a worn-out **earthly** (*epigeios*, "on the earth") **tent** (*skēnous*) soon to be **destroyed.** In Christ's incarnate body He "lived (*eskēnōsen*, lit., 'tabernacled or tented') among us" (John 1:14). This is why the eternal perspective (2 Cor. 4:17) should be maintained (the second Gr. word in 5:1 is

gar ["for"; trans. **now** in the NIV], introducing the reason for what preceded). An earthly body is temporary; a heavenly body is **eternal.**

The reference to the heavenly body as **a building from God, an eternal house in heaven, not built by human hands** is reminiscent of Jesus' description of His own resurrection body as a temple "not made by man" (lit., "not made by hand"; Mark 14:58). Second Corinthians 5:1 briefly summarizes what Paul had earlier written to the Corinthians about the nature of the resurrection body (1 Cor. 15:34-54). The confident assertion, **we know,** was based on the argument set forth in 1 Corinthians 15.

5:2-4. Paul had written about fixing his eyes "not on what is seen but on what is unseen" (4:18). These verses express the same sentiment. Paul's present life was "wasting away" (4:16) and he faced "death" (4:11-12). Using a figure of speech (metonymy of the effect [groaning] substituted for the cause [suffering]), Paul twice said **we groan** (5:2, 4; cf. Rom. 8:22-23). But someday, when **our heavenly dwelling** (2 Cor. 5:2, 4) is received, all such groaning and being **burdened** will give place to laughter and exultation (cf. Luke 6:21; 1 Cor. 15:51-55). **What is mortal** will **be swallowed up by life** in immortal, imperishable spiritual bodies in heaven (Phil. 3:21). For Paul his present mortal life was like nakedness, marked by humiliation and privation. Who would want to focus on this abject state in view of the eternal glory that awaited him? (2 Cor. 4:17-18)

A number of commentators and theologians have seen in these verses reference to an "intermediate state," a period between death and resurrection. This view takes one of two forms: (a) Dead (though conscious) believers are without a body while awaiting their resurrection bodies, or (b) dead (though conscious) believers receive an "intermediate body" that somehow differs from their forthcoming resurrected bodies. (According to either of these intermediate-state views, Paul was suggesting that he hoped to live till the return of Christ so that he would not experience an "intermediate state.") These views, however, seem unwarranted. Paul had only two conditions in view since 4:16, the temporal and the eternal. The introduction of a third is therefore unlikely. It seems clear from 5:4 that being **in this tent** (cf. 2 Peter 1:13), and **unclothed** describe mortality while being **clothed** and possessing a **heavenly dwelling** depict immortality, without specifying any intervening stages.

5:5. This present condition of fading mortality, however disquieting it may be, is not without design. As Paul had just written, ordinary mortals, like common jars of clay, are the means through which God displays, by contrast, His own all-surpassing power (4:7).

Equally encouraging is the realization that in the life of each Christian God has begun the transforming process that will one day culminate in possessing a heavenly body and perfect Christlikeness. The surety of that consummation is the Holy **Spirit**, whose presence and transforming work (3:18) forms the beginning and is guaranteeing the completion of God's gracious salvation (Rom. 8:23; Eph. 4:30). (On the words **as a deposit, guaranteeing what is to come,** see comments on the word *arrabōna* in 2 Cor. 1:22.)

5:6-8. With this perspective Paul could be **confident** (5:6, 8; cf. 7:16) and encouraged (cf. 4:1, 16), even in his period of mortality. These verses (5:6-8) recapitulate the theme first discussed in 4:16-18. To be **at home in the body** means to dwell in "the earthly tent" (5:1), to be outwardly "wasting away" (4:16), to be in a state of mortality **away from the** immediate presence of the **Lord** (cf. 1 Cor. 13:12).

What sustained Paul was the realization that this was a temporary and transitory state (2 Cor. 4:18). He focused not on present but on future conditions, not on the seen but the unseen. To live this way is to **live by faith, not by sight.** It is to live in light of ultimate rather than immediate realities (cf. Rom. 8:24-25), to be obedient to God's commands despite the hardships that obedience produces (e.g., 2 Cor. 11:23-29). Such was Paul's life. If the choice were his, he would have seized the opportunity to depart this pilgrimage life and take up residence (be **at home**) **with the Lord** (Phil. 1:21-23). But the constraints of his commission caused him to press on (cf. Phil. 1:24; Eph. 3:1-13).

5:9-10. Motivating Paul in this

perseverance was his **goal to please** his Lord (cf. Gal. 1:10; Col. 1:10), a desire in effect during his earthly sojourn (**at home in the body**), which would be undiminished in heaven (**away from it**) (cf. 2 Cor. 5:6).

Contributing to this goal was Paul's knowledge that he would one day be evaluated by his Master. He wanted to please Him and to hear from Him, "Well done, My good servant!" (Luke 19:17) In his previous letter Paul had mentioned this judgment (1 Cor. 3:12-15) with particular reference to Christian teachers (1 Cor. 4:1-5). Now he affirmed that **all** Christians will be evaluated at **the judgment seat of Christ** (cf. Rom. 14:12), which will follow the Rapture of the church. Believers will be recompensed **for the things** they have **done** in their earthly lives (**while in the body**). Their **good** deeds will evoke one response (cf. 1 Cor. 4:5; Eph. 6:8) and the **bad** (*phaulon,* "worthless") will evoke another (1 Cor. 3:15; Col. 3:25). Salvation is not the issue here. One's eternal destiny will not be determined at the judgment seat of Christ. Salvation is by faith (Eph. 2:8-9), but deeds issuing from that faith (1 Thes. 1:3) will be evaluated.

This perspective on a day of judgment and the prospect of eternity had a salutary effect on Paul. It enabled him to persevere in the face of hardship (2 Cor. 4:7-12). And it motivated him to be faithful in discharging his ministry (5:11; cf. 1 Cor. 4:2-4).

5. MESSAGE OF RECONCILIATION (5:11–6:2)

The description of the ministry sustained by Paul touched on the work of Christ (2:12–3:6), the work of the Spirit (3:7-18), and the work of the Father (4:1-15). He also spoke of the eternal viewpoint required for the ministry to be carried out effectively (4:16–5:10). He now turned to the heart of that ministry, the message.

5:11-12. Though Paul knew that his salvation and eternal destiny were obtained by faith in Christ (Eph. 2:8-9), the thought of one day standing before his Savior (2 Cor. 5:10) awed him. It was the contemplation of that moment that moved Paul **to fear the Lord** and impelled him on in His service (cf. Matt. 10:28). The purpose of his ministry was to

persuade men to "be reconciled to God" (2 Cor. 5:20).

The personal defense which follows (vv. 11-12) indicates that Paul met opposition in carrying out that commission. Understandably, a Christian's message is intimately bound up with his life and ministry (1 Thes. 1:5); the two are hardly separable. Since this is so, Paul had to justify and defend his conduct in order to win a hearing for his message. He followed the tactic used earlier in the letter, affirming before God the sincerity of his motives (cf. 2 Cor. 1:12, 23) and calling on the Corinthians to confirm this by their own experiences with him (cf. 1:14; 4:2).

The apostle, unlike his opponents, put no stock in external credentials or associations (3:1-2; cf. 5:16a). It was not the externality of the Law but the internality of the Spirit that authenticated his ministry (3:3; cf. Rom. 2:28-29). Nor was he concerned simply about his own reputation among the Corinthians (cf. 1 Cor. 3:21; Gal. 1:10; 1 Thes. 2:6). What did concern him was the reception of his message. He needed to be regarded as a servant of Christ so that his message would be regarded as the message of God (cf. 1 Cor. 4:1). If they took **pride** ("exulted") **in** him, the messenger, then they could **answer** his and their opponents, who looked on the outward appearance (**what is seen**) rather than what one is like inwardly (**in the heart;** cf. 1 Sam. 16:7).

5:13. To affirm his sincerity, Paul was willing to be thought a fool (cf. 11:16-17, 21). Who but one **out of** his **mind** ("insane"; cf. 11:23; Mark 3:21) would show such disregard for himself? (cf. 1 Cor. 4:9-13) Would a sane person willingly face a riotous mob intent on destroying him? (Acts 19:30; 21:35-40) Who would be crazy enough to walk back into a city in which he had just been stoned and dragged out? (Acts 14:19-20) Only a person who was utterly devoted to God would show so little regard for himself. Such a man was Paul.

Yet the Corinthians also knew well the prosaic, "sane" side of Paul the teacher (Acts 18:11) and loving father (1 Cor. 4:14-16). Whether they considered him insane or not, his ministry was selfless: **It is for you.** In his own way Paul had expressed the summation of the Law,

loving God with all his heart, soul, and mind, and loving his neighbor as himself (Mark 12:26-31).

5:14-15. Why would Paul live that way? (v. 13) Because Christ had lived that way (cf. Mark 3:21). Though possessing divine prerogatives, He willingly became incarnate and followed the path of obedience to the cross (Phil. 2:6-8), dying **for all** (not just the elect, as some suggest; cf. 1 Tim. 2:6; Heb. 2:9; 1 John 2:2). By faith Paul was identified with Jesus in His death and resurrection (Rom. 6:3-4; Gal. 2:20). And Paul lived with the same selfless abandon the Lord had. **Christ's love,** which had converted him, now compelled him (cf. 1 John 3:16).

Later in discussing "the ministry of reconciliation" (2 Cor. 5:18-19), Paul developed the historical and objective implications of Christ's atonement. His concern in those verses was the subjective application of the Savior's objective work. All those who by faith entered into the benefits of Christ's sacrifice (and now **live** spiritually) should respond by living selflessly and being involved in that ministry of reconciliation. They **should no longer live for themselves but for Him.** Paul was certainly doing this; therefore the Corinthians should exult in him (v. 12).

5:16. As a result of his conversion Paul no longer evaluated people on the basis of externals. He implied that his opponents, and to a certain extent those influenced by them, did (v. 12).

At one time this had been true of Paul also. He had opposed Christ and His followers (Acts 22:4-5; 1 Cor. 15:9) because he had **regarded Christ** (lit., "knew Christ") **from a worldly** (lit., "according to flesh"; cf. 2 Cor. 1:12) **point of view.** He had information about Jesus, but this was not the same as believing in Him. Mere information about Jesus cannot transform a person from self-centeredness to selflessness (5:15). Only conversion could effect that, as it had done for Paul (Acts 9:1-20).

5:17. No one was more able to reflect on that transformation than Paul who switched from a persecutor of Christ to a proclaimer of Christ (Acts 9:5, 20-22). He was **in Christ** (a phrase Paul used repeatedly in his epistles to speak of a believer's spiritual relationship to Christ) because he believed the message of the gospel and was identified by faith with Christ (2 Cor. 5:14-15; cf. Rom. 6:3-4; Gal. 2:20; 6:14). To be in Christ is to be **a new creation** (cf. Gal. 6:15). This new creation is brought about by the Holy Spirit, the Agent of regeneration (Titus 3:5) and the Giver of divine birth (John 3:3, 6-8). God's new creative work, begun in each one who believes in Christ, will one day be consummated on a universal scale (Rev. 21:4-5). The **old** life of slavery to self and sin **has gone** (2 Cor. 5:16; cf. Rom. 6:6-14; Eph. 4:22; Col. 3:9). The **new** life of devotion to Christ means that one has new attitudes and actions (cf. 2 Cor. 5:14-15; Rom. 6:4; Eph. 4:23–5:2).

5:18-19. Like the first Creation (of the universe), the new creation is initiated by God: **All this is from God** (cf. 4:6; 1 John 4:10). Also, like the first Creation, the new creation becomes a reality **through** the work of **Christ** (cf. Col. 1:16). Christ's death on the cross makes possible human reconciliation to **God** (Rom. 5:10-11). Reconciliation involves removing rebellious and sinful man's enmity toward God (Rom. 5:10). This is one of the many marvelous accomplishments of the Godhead on behalf of a person the moment he believes in Christ for salvation from sin. Because Christ bore mankind's sin on the cross (1 Peter 2:24), He made peace possible (Eph. 2:11-19). No longer need people be the objects of God's wrath (Rom. 5:9). By trusting themselves to the **reconciling** work of **Christ** alone, people pass from God's wrath to God's blessing (Acts 16:30-31; Rom. 8:1) and from spiritual death to spiritual life (John 5:24; Eph. 2:1, 5). Then **men's sins** are no longer counted, that is, imputed or reckoned, **against them,** for Christ has taken them on Himself (2 Cor. 5:21; 1 Peter 2:24; 3:18). This is the treasure of the gospel which Paul proclaimed (2 Cor. 4:7), **the message of reconciliation** (5:19) delivered in **the ministry** (cf. 4:1) **of** reconciliation (5:18).

5:20. Few verses more precisely summarize Paul's ministry and message (cf. Acts 26:16-18). As Christ had preached peace to all men (Eph. 2:17) on the basis of what He would accomplish (Eph. 2:16), Paul continued that proclamation in His stead. The immediate representative of God's message of reconciliation was Paul, whose ministry is shared by all who are "in Christ" (2 Cor. 5:17, 19). All believers should serve Christ as His **ambassadors.** Paul's appeal was not a perfunctory pronouncement but an impassioned plea ("we try to persuade men" [v. 11]) addressed to the world **on Christ's behalf: Be reconciled to God** (cf. 1 Tim. 2:3-4).

5:21. Paul now summarized the basis of this message. The Cross epitomized the love of God (John 3:16) and of Christ (John 15:13; Rom. 5:8). The Savior was sinless: He **had no sin.** He was "without sin" (Heb. 4:15), and "in Him is no sin" (1 John 3:5). He took on Himself the sin of the world (John 1:29; 1 Peter 2:24; 1 John 2:2). **God made Him . . . to be sin for us** (cf. Isa. 53:4-6, 10). The sins of the world were placed on Him so that, in turn, His **righteousness** could be given those who trust Him (Rom. 5:17) and are thus **in Him.** That gift of righteousness is obtainable only by faith (Rom. 3:22; 6:23; Eph. 2:8-9; Phil. 3:9).

6:1. How could the Corinthians possibly **receive God's grace in vain?** One sure way was to disbelieve the message Paul had expressed in 5:21. False apostles in Corinth preached a message different from Paul's gospel (11:4). If they were Judaizers (cf. 3:7-11; 11:22), they probably denied Paul's message that the righteousness of God was obtained only by faith. To believe a truncated gospel meant to believe "in vain" (cf. 1 Cor. 15:2). Paul had reason to believe that some in Corinth had done just that (2 Cor. 11:2-3). "Vain" translates *kenon* ("empty, without content, without result, useless"; cf. 1 Cor. 15:14, 58; Gal. 2:2; Phil. 2:16; 1 Thes. 3:5).

6:2. Paul's quotation from Isaiah 49:8 was a rebuttal to Judaizers who wanted to impose the Mosaic Law as a means of obtaining righteousness. In Isaiah God announced that salvation would be universally offered not only to stubborn Israel but also to the Gentiles (Isa. 49:6). The quotation underscored the fact that **salvation** is God's initiative: **in . . . My favor I heard you, and . . . I helped you.** Jesus inaugurated this message of God's grace in His ministry (Luke 4:18-21) and Paul communicated it. **The day of salvation** is the present Age of Grace. Paul urged the Corinthians not to spurn that grace by turning to Judaistic legalism (cf. 2 Cor. 3:12-16; Gal. 3:1-6).

To do so would be "to receive God's grace in vain" (2 Cor. 6:1).

6. MARKS OF THE MINISTRY (6:3-10)

In 5:11-14 Paul began a defense of his ministry which led in turn to an explanation of his message (5:15-21). Now he returned to the topic of his ministry and its problems (6:3-10).

Paul had stressed that the commendation (5:12) the Corinthians should have been looking for in their ministers was not external letters (3:1), self-recommendations (10:18), or religious credentials (11:22) but the internal testimony of the Spirit (cf. Rom. 2:28-29). Now he suggested that there *are* some external credentials that mark a minister of God but they are hardly the sort the Corinthians would think of or his opponents would like to match. Paul's authenticating marks of the ministry were his sufferings as a servant and the sustaining enablement of God to carry on (cf. 2 Cor. 4:8-10). These were valid credentials for "the servants of God" (6:4; cf. 11:16–12:10; 1 Cor. 4:9-13; Gal. 6:17).

6:3. Paul was concerned more about defending his **ministry** (*diakonia*, "service"; cf. 4:1) than defending himself. To that end he scrupulously avoided behavior that would vitiate his ministry as Christ's ambassador (5:20) and God's fellow worker (6:1). Of course Paul knew that the message of the Cross would offend many (2:16; 1 Cor. 1:18). And he knew that many considered him a fool (cf. 2 Cor. 11:16). But he did not want to offend by self-serving conduct that would bring disrepute to God or spiritual ruin to a fellow Christian. (**Stumbling block** is from the Gr. *proskopēn*; in 1 Cor. 8:9 "stumbling block" translates *proskomma*, a synonym of the word in 2 Cor. 6:3).

6:4-5. As servants (*diakonoi*; cf. "service" [*diakonia*] in v. 3) **of God** Paul and his associates faced various trials without regard for themselves. But with God's help they had **great endurance** (*hypomonē*, "steadfastness," also used in 1:6; cf. 4:7-9). This was the sort of commendation the Corinthians should have required for authenticating their ministers (cf. 3:1; 5:12). Paul listed nine trials, in three sets of three each (6:4-5). Then he mentioned nine inner qualities (vv. 6-7), followed by nine pairs of paradoxes (vv. 8-10). In 11:22-27 his

groupings are mostly fours. First he mentioned general difficulties: **troubles** (*thlipsesin*; cf. 1:4), **hardships, and distresses** (lit., "narrow spaces," i.e., circumstances that hem in; in Rom. 8:35 this word is rendered "hardship"). Then the apostle listed three specific kinds of persecution he endured in his ministry: **beatings** (cf. 1 Cor. 4:11; 2 Cor. 6:9; 11:23-24; Gal. 6:17), **imprisonments, and riots.** He experienced all three of these in Philippi (Acts 16:19-23). The third group describes impositions he accepted as part of the demands of ministry. He was not averse to **hard work** (1 Cor. 4:12; Acts 18:3-4) nor a stranger to **sleepless nights** (2 Cor. 11:27) or to **hunger** (1 Cor. 4:11; 2 Cor. 11:27).

6:6. Paul balanced his nine kinds of trials (in three triads) with nine internal qualities. The first eight are given in four couplets. **Purity** referred to practical righteousness, and **understanding** was a practical knowledge which displayed sensitivity in dealing with others. **Patience** (*makrothymia*, lit., "long temper") is the ability to bear up under the oversights and wrongs afflicted by others without retaliating (cf. Gal. 5:22; Eph. 4:2; Col. 1:11; 3:12; 2 Tim. 4:2; James 5:10). **And kindness** (*chrēstotēti*; cf. Gal. 5:22; Col. 3:12) is love in action.

In the Holy Spirit may be a metonymy, a figure of speech in which the cause stands for the effects. If so, then the Holy Spirit represents that which He causes, namely, spiritual fruit (Gal. 5:22-23) or control by the Spirit (Eph. 5:18). Or possibly the phrase (*en pneumati hagiō*) should be translated "in a spirit of holiness" to describe Paul's dedicated attitude. He hoped his **sincere** (*anypokritō*, lit., "without hypocrisy"; cf. "sincere [*anypokritou*] faith" in 1 Tim. 1:5) **love** (cf. Rom. 12:9) would be evident to his readers and would evoke in them a similar response (2 Cor. 6:12-13).

6:7. The apostle's ministry advanced because of his spiritual resources. **In truthful speech** he proclaimed the gospel (4:2) and relied on **the power of God** in the person of the Spirit to produce results (10:4; cf. 1 Cor. 2:4-5). Relying on God, Paul was completely equipped **with weapons of righteousness** to cope with the attacks of the adversary from any quarter (**right** or **left**) and to send him fleeing (cf. 2 Cor. 10:3-6; Eph. 6:11-18; James 4:7).

6:8. In nine pairs of paradoxes (vv. 8-10) Paul spoke of conflicting responses to his ministry (vv. 8-9a), of his own responses to opposition (vv. 9b-10a), and of the results of his labors (v. 10b, c). Some who believed welcomed Paul like Christ Himself (Gal. 4:14) but more often he faced insults and **dishonor** (1 Cor. 4:10; 1 Thes 2:2). He was maligned by outsiders (1 Cor. 4:13) and also by some within the church (Rom. 3:8), who gave him a **bad report.** He and his associates were **genuine** apostles, yet some **regarded** them **as impostors.** So he found it necessary to defend his ministry against the calumnies of opponents (1 Cor. 9:1-2; 2 Cor. 10:7).

6:9. Paul said he was **unknown** perhaps in the sense of people not acknowledging him or his ministry. But he was **known** by God (2 Tim. 2:19). Though he was **dying** (cf. 2 Cor. 1:8-9; 4:10-11; 11:23), **yet** he lived (cf. 1:10; 4:16), and though **beaten** (6:5; 11:23-25) he was **not killed.** He endured (6:4) these agonies because God sustained him (cf. 4:7-9).

6:10. Such a life would seem to lead naturally to sorrow. Yet because of his trust in God Paul was **always rejoicing** (cf. Acts 16:23-25; Phil. 4:4). Being **poor** and bereft of even basic material necessities (cf. 1 Cor. 4:11), Paul could nonetheless dispense spiritual values, **making many rich** (cf. Eph. 3:8). Though materially he had **nothing,** yet he was **possessing everything** by way of spiritual blessings (1 Cor. 3:21-23; Eph. 1:3).

7. ANTICIPATED RESPONSE (6:11-7:16)

In this section Paul pulled together the strands of the discussion about his ministry to the Corinthian church. He had defended his changed plans out of deference and love for them (1:12-2:11). He then turned to a description of his apostolic ministry in which he contrasted his own impotence with the omnipotence of God (2:12-6:10). Not an exercise in self-indulgence, Paul's point was to produce some changes in the Corinthian church: he sought not only an acceptance of his ministry and message but also a rejection of the influence of his opponents, the false apostles. This was not Paul's final word on this subject (cf.

chaps. 10-13) but it was a forceful beginning.

6:11-13. Whatever failings Paul may have had, dissimulation was not one of them. Candor in speech and an unrestrained affirmation of **affection** (*splanchnois*; cf. 7:15; Phil. 1:8; 2:1; Col. 3:12; Phile. 7, 12, 20; 1 John 3:17) had marked his letter to this point (e.g., 2 Cor. 2:3-4). And he wanted the Corinthians to reciprocate. The depth of his feelings is noted by his calling them **Corinthians.** Only rarely did he name his readers in the midst of a letter. When, for example, he was greatly exercised about the declension in the Galatian churches, he sharply rebuked them by name (Gal. 3:1). On the other hand when he recalled the Philippian church's faithful support of him in the early days of his ministry and in his prison experience, he called them by name (Phil. 4:15). Blending frustration and affection, Paul similarly hailed the Corinthians and called for them to respond with unrestrained love (**my children—open wide your hearts;** cf. 2 Cor. 7:2-3).

6:14-15. What hampered the Corinthians' open, loving response, which Paul called for? (v. 13) Answer: rival suitors vied for their affections and allegiance. Though verses 14-15 are often applied to various sorts of alliances (e.g., mixed marriages, improper business associations), Paul's primary association was probably ecclesiastical. The rival suitors were possibly pagan idolaters (cf. 1 Cor. 10:14) or more likely false apostles (cf. 2 Cor. 11:2-4). In censure or affection Paul was equally candid (cf. 6:11).

The solution to the dilemma was for the Corinthians to separate from the false apostles. Whatever may have been their own and others' estimation of their spiritual status, Paul considered the false apostles to be **unbelievers** (cf. 11:13-15) from whom the Corinthians needed to separate. But Paul did not say that Christians should have no contacts whatever with unbelievers. Earlier he argued the absurdity of such a position (1 Cor. 5:9-10). But religious unbelievers might lead believers astray from "sincere and pure devotion to Christ" (2 Cor. 11:3), and the fact concerned Paul greatly. A **believer** can be rightly **yoked** only with **Christ** (Matt. 11:29-30).

To illustrate, Paul asked five rhetorical questions (2 Cor. 6:14-16), posing antitheses that reflect the wide chasm between the kingdom of Christ and the kingdom of Satan (cf. Col. 1:13). **Belial** (the Gr. *Beliar* is a spelling variation) transliterates an Old Testament word that means "worthless person." In Greek it came to mean "a lawless person." It was then used of Satan, the most worthless and lawless of all.

6:16. Paul's fifth rhetorical question provided a transition to his citing several Old Testament verses. Their cumulative effect bolstered Paul's exhortation (v. 14a). The church is **the temple of God** (cf. 1 Cor. 3:16) where the Spirit of God and Christ dwells (cf. Matt. 28:19-20; Eph. 2:22). The promise of **God** to **live** among His people was ultimately fulfilled in Christ (Matt. 1:23).

6:17. Enjoying God's presence requires personal holiness. Paul cited a portion of Isaiah 52:11 and Ezekiel 20:41, passages that speak of Israel's redemption. God's people are redeemed from pagan bondage (**come out from them and be separate**) in order to be clean before God (**touch no unclean thing**) and thus enjoy fellowship with Him (**I will receive you**). In Galatians Paul spoke of the bondage of those who are under the obligation of the Law (Gal. 3:13-14; 4:5; cf. 2 Cor. 3:7-9). Paul wrote to Titus that redemption implied two things: (a) deliverance "from all wickedness" and (b) a purified people who are "His very own, eager to do what is good" (Titus 2:14). Personal purity makes it possible to serve God and be received by Him.

6:18. A redeemed people are brought into a special relationship with God the **Father** as His **sons and daughters** (cf. Isa. 43:6). Those who identify with Christ by faith in Him may call God "Father" (Eph. 2:18; Gal. 4:5-6). From these sons and daughters God wants obedience (Deut. 32:19-21) as He did from David, His people's chief representative, and from David's lineage (2 Sam. 7:14; cf. Ps. 89:30-34).

7:1. **These promises** refer to God's assurances of His presence (6:16) and fellowship (6:17b-18) to those who obey Him. This obedience requires purification (**let us purify ourselves**), which here implies separation (*katharisōmen;* cf. Matt. 8:3; Deut. 19:13) **from everything that contaminates body and spirit** and from

every person who pollutes the truth (cf. 2 Cor. 2:17; 4:2). "Body and spirit" refers to the whole person in his external and internal aspects (cf. 7:5). In an attitude of **reverence for God** (cf. 5:11) which produces obedience, sanctification (**holiness**) can be perfected, that is, completed or matured. This is a maturing, growing holiness, an increased Christlikeness (3:18), a progressive sanctification (not sinless perfection).

7:2. Having given a warning about the rival suitors for the Corinthians' affections (6:14–7:1), Paul resumed his appeal for mutual love, mentioned in 6:11-13. The accusations made about him were unfounded. He could offer disclaimers (e.g., 2:17; 4:2; 6:3), but the Corinthians' conviction of his integrity was his best rejoinder. Unhappily, however, this was yet lacking.

7:3-4. Paul did not blame the Corinthians for their vacillation. His rivals were impressive (11:3-5), much more so than he (10:7-12), at least in externals. The Corinthians' vacillation had not produced disaffection in Paul. On the contrary his love was unabated (cf. 6:13; 7:1) and his **confidence in** them was unimpaired. He had **pride** ("exulting") and **joy** (cf. v. 7) in them **in all** his **troubles** (*thlipsei,* lit., "trouble" [sing.]; cf. 1:4). No doubt this was primarily due to his confidence that God was at work in them (1 Cor. 1:4-9) but also partially due to the news Titus had brought him when the two finally met in Macedonia (2 Cor. 7:5-7).

7:5-7. Paul's frame of mind and **body** before Titus' arrival was far from placid (cf. 2:13). He **had no rest** (*anesin,* "relief"; also used in 2:13; 8:13). The great apostle did not always ride a spiritual crest, which he was not hesitant to admit (cf. 2:4; 6:10). He candidly admitted that his **conflicts . . . fears** and depression (**downcast**) were brought on by apparent opposition or persecution in **Macedonia,** by anxiety about Titus' well-being, by his reception by the Corinthians, and by their response to his letter.

However, the ample **comfort of God** (cf. 1:3-7) more than met his needs through **the coming of Titus** and the good news he brought. Titus had been well received by the Corinthians. They did love Paul and longed for him and were concerned for him. And they were remorseful (they had **deep sorrow**) at their failure to support him during his "painful visit" (2:1). They had responded positively to his severe letter (2:4).

7:8-9. Paul's harsh **letter** (see point 5 under "Contacts and Correspondence" in the *Introduction*) had **hurt** them. It had hurt Paul too. He had not relished his role as a disciplinarian, and in fact he apparently had wished he had not sent it with Titus. Yet because of the results his **regret** was mollified. In **sorrow** the Corinthians acknowledged their failure and redressed the wrong (cf. 2:6).

7:10-11. They had exemplified **repentance**, a change of mind involving action in accord with God's will. As such it was a **godly sorrow** (like Peter's remorse after his denial of Christ). This was not a **worldly sorrow** which **brings death** (like Judas' "sorrow" after he betrayed the Lord; Matt. 27:3-5). The Corinthians' genuine **sorrow . . . produced** several things: (a) an **earnestness** or concerted effort to make amends, (b) an **eagerness to** vindicate themselves, (c) **indignation** against Paul's opponent (2 Cor. 2:5-11), (d) **alarm** at their own passivity and its injurious effects (2:1-4), (e) **longing** and **concern** for Paul (cf. 7:7), and (f) **readiness to see justice done** (2:6).

In all this they **proved** they were **innocent** by virtue of their repentance. They had sinned not so much by doing wrong but by failing to do right (cf. James 4:17) and of this they had repented (2 Cor. 7:10).

7:12. Paul's primary motive in writing the letter (2:3-4) was to benefit the Corinthians. Uppermost in his mind was their well-being which Paul realized was bound up with their acceptance of his message and of him as an apostle. Paul **wrote** that he was **not** concerned about disciplining the offending brother and ameliorating the situation of **the injured party**. But this was apparently a Semitic way of saying that they were not his *primary* concern (Luke 14:26 gives another example of exclusivism as a way of stating priorities). It is doubtful that "the injured party" refers to the incident in 1 Corinthians 5:1 because no offended party was mentioned there. (In fact, the injured party in the incest incident may have been deceased.) Possibly Paul was the injured party (cf. 2 Cor. 2:5), but if so it was a curiously oblique self-designation (cf. Mark 14:51; John 13:23).

7:13-16. The Corinthians' positive response to Paul and his letter had been a great **encouragement** to him (cf. v. 4). Added to this was Titus' elation at the reception he received. Despite Paul's affirmed confidence in the Corinthians, **Titus** might have been understandably hesitant to undertake this mission (cf. 1 Cor. 16:10-11). But any trepidation **Titus** may have felt proved groundless. Actually the Corinthians responded to him with deference, **receiving him with fear and trembling.** They zealously sought to carry out Paul's directives (2 Cor. 7:7, 11). As a result Titus had great **affection** (*splanchna*, "inner emotion"; cf. 6:12; Phil. 1:8; 2:1; Col. 3:12; Phile. 7, 12, 20; 1 John 3:17) **for** the Corinthians. Paul knew this was God's doing (2 Cor. 7:6), but like a good pastor he commended the Corinthians and expressed his **confidence** (5:6, 8) **in** them after their positive response. He could only hope that the subjects he was about to discuss (in chaps. 8–9 and 10–13) would meet with the same spirit.

III. Gracious Giving (chaps. 8–9)

Having explained his changed plans (1:12–2:11) and having described the nature and orientation of his ministry (2:12–7:16), Paul now turned to the subject of gracious giving. This was no abstract topic; it concerned the collection for the poor in Jerusalem which Paul had been organizing for several years (cf. Gal. 2:10; Rom. 15:25-28). The Corinthians, hearing about "the collection," asked Paul what part they might have in it (cf. 1 Cor. 16:1). Paul instructed them concerning these arrangements (1 Cor. 16:2-3). Good intentions had not been translated into fruition, however, so Paul asked Titus to look into the matter (2 Cor. 8:6).

What factors interrupted the Corinthians' good intentions? No one knows. But one likely possibility was the presence of the false apostles who received support from the church and may have diverted to themselves some of the monies intended for that collection (cf. 2:17; 11:20). As a result, Paul's refusal to accept support was a sore point with the Corinthians (cf. 11:7-12; 12:13-18).

Titus had found the Corinthians in need of an encouraging word which Paul delivered in chapters 8–9 of this letter. This—in conjunction with Titus' work and that of unnamed assistants (8:23; cf. Acts 20:1-4), climaxed by Paul's visit (Acts 20:3)—brought the collection in Corinth to a successful conclusion (cf. Rom. 15:26; Acts 24:17).

A. Examples of liberality (8:1-9)

Whenever possible, Paul preferred to motivate and instruct by deed as well as by words. He did not hesitate to urge the Corinthians and others to imitate his manner of life (cf. 1 Cor. 4:16; 11:1a; 1 Thes. 1:6; 2 Thes. 3:7-9). But he was also quick to point to other worthy examples, including Timothy (1 Cor. 4:17; Phil. 2:19-20), Epaphroditus (Phil. 2:18), and of course, Christ (Phil. 2:5; 1 Cor. 11:1b; 1 Thes. 1:6) and God the Father (Eph. 5:1). Paul gave the Corinthians two examples of liberality: the Macedonian churches and Christ.

8:1-2. The Macedonian churches—those in Philippi, Thessalonica, and Berea—had initially experienced **the grace** of **God** in the person of Paul and his proclamation of the gospel (Eph. 3:2-12) during his second missionary journey. In Philippi (Acts 16:12-40), Thessalonica (Acts 17:1-9), and Berea (Acts 17:10-15), the apostle preached the gospel and founded churches. The believers in these places suffered because of their faith (Phil. 1:29-30; 1 Thes. 1:6), but they remained steadfast (Phil. 1:5; 1 Thes. 1:7). They even contributed at that early juncture to Paul's material support (Phil. 4:15).

While their material welfare apparently deteriorated (cf. Phil. 4:10), their spiritual well-being increased commensurately. Paul attributed this to the grace of God, His unmerited favor. They had ample reason to be sorrowful (**severe trial** is lit., "in much testing of troubles" [*thlipseōs*; cf. 2 Cor. 1:4]), but they rejoiced. Though in **extreme poverty,** they could make others **rich.** Though they had nothing, they possessed everything that really matters (6:10). Like Paul, the Macedonian churches had learned that God's grace is sufficient to take their weaknesses and through them to display God's power (4:7-12; 12:9; Phil. 4:13).

8:3-5. The Macedonians were eager channels of **God's** blessing because they lived in accordance with His **will** (v. 5). Their actions revealed their love and devotion to God and others (cf. Mark 12:28-31; Phil. 2:3-8, 20-21; 1 Thes. 4:9-10). **Entirely on their own** initiative the Macedonians became involved in the collection. Paul, perhaps thinking they too were suitable candidates for aid, hesitated to approach them about the need in Jerusalem. However, like the poor widow Jesus commended (Mark 12:41-44), they were undeterred by their own penury and gave selflessly, trusting God to meet their needs (Phil. 4:19). One could wish that today more churches were like the Macedonians who **pleaded . . . for the privilege of sharing.**

8:6-7. In the light of this effusion of God's grace on the Macedonians (vv. 1-5), could the Corinthians, who had benefited so richly from God's grace (excelling **in faith, in speech, in knowledge, in complete earnestness, and . . . love;** cf. 1 Cor. 1:4-7), do any less? Paul thought not, so he dispatched **Titus** to administer the Corinthians' portion of the collection, to give them opportunity to **excel in this grace of giving.** ("Grace of giving" [2 Cor. 8:7] and **act of grace** [v. 6] both translate the one Gr. word "grace." Giving is the essence of grace!) Titus had gained experience in the collection and distribution of charitable monies elsewhere (cf. Acts 11:29-30; Gal. 2:1). But it is unknown when he became involved with the Corinthian collection.

In writing to the Romans Paul had mentioned the gift (God-given spiritual ability) of "contributing to the needs of others" (Rom. 12:8). The right use of this divine gift was to *give* generously. Paul himself had certainly given unsparingly to the Corinthians, and they in turn had professed their affection for him (2 Cor. 8:11). Paul wanted them to **excel** in their "giving" because giving expresses love (1 John 3:11, 16-18).

8:8-9. Paul, ever sensitive to the charge that he dominated the churches he founded (cf. 1:24), preferred that their motivation not stem from external commands (e.g., 8:7b). He wanted them to be motivated by their internal devotion (**the sincerity of your love**) to him and more importantly to the **Lord.** Could the Corinthians face being compared with the Macedonians in this regard? Or could they face being compared with their Lord, who is supremely worthy of emulation?

Few statements surpass verse 9 as a pithy summary of the gospel (cf. 5:21).

From the splendor of heaven **Christ** came to the squalor of earth. The Incarnation was an incomprehensible renunciation of spiritual and material glory. The One who **was rich,** who had everything, **became poor,** making Himself nothing (Phil. 2:7). He assumed mankind's debt of sin and paid for it with His life (Phil. 2:8). The Corinthians had directly benefited from His generosity (**your** and **you** are emphatic). He became what they were (poor) so that they could become what He was and is (rich). Therefore was a material offering to Him (cf. Matt. 25:34-40) too much to ask? (1 Cor. 9:11)

B. Advice and arrangements for the collection (8:10–9:5)

Concluding that the Corinthians would not refuse his appeal, Paul offered a brief rationale for the collection and an explanation of how it should be handled.

8:10-12. Paul's **advice** (cf. v. 8) was, **finish** what you have begun (cf. v. 6). Best wishes—**desire** and **eager willingness**— are no substitute for good deeds (cf. James 2:15-16). An individual's giving should be commensurate with his **means . . . according to what one has;** cf. 1 Cor. 16:2). By that standard the Macedonian gift, like the poor widow's offering (Mark 12:41-44), might in one sense be easy to equal but in another sense be hard to exceed.

8:13-15. A guiding principle for material exchange among churches is **equality.** Paul was not wanting some church to have relief (*anesis;* cf. 2:13; 7:5) while the Corinthians were **hard pressed** (*thlipsis;* cf. 1:4). That would be like robbing Peter to pay Paul!

Paul no doubt approved of the Jerusalem church's early efforts in meeting each others' needs by having everything in common (Acts 2:44). This expressed their mutual concern for all members of the body of Christ (cf. 1 Cor. 12:25). This principle was modeled after a divine pattern. When God gave food to the Israelites in the wilderness He did so equally according to their needs (Ex. 16:16-18). The church should not do less.

8:16-17. Like Timothy (Phil. 2:19-20), **Titus** was genuinely concerned about the welfare of those he served. In a self-centered world, such a **concern** was a distinguishing feature valued by Paul in his associates. No dictator (cf. vv. 8, 23),

Paul had asked Titus to lend his assistance to a project which it seems Titus had eagerly (**with much enthusiasm**) and independently (**on his own initiative**) determined to do.

8:18-21. To accompany Titus was an unnamed, highly respected (**praised by all the churches**) representative probably from the Macedonian churches. He would take their **gift** to its destination in Jerusalem. Paul's motivation in organizing this collection was **to honor the Lord** (cf. Matt. 25:40; Gal. 2:10). To that end he scrupulously worked to avoid bringing any disrepute on His name through charges of mismanagement or avarice (2 Cor. 8:20; cf. 12:17-18).

8:22-24. In addition to the previously mentioned brother (v. 18) and **Titus,** Paul's **partner and fellow worker,** a third member (anonymously called **our brother**) was appointed to join the collection party. He was apparently an appointee of the Macedonian churches. **He** was **zealous,** and he and the other unnamed brother (v. 18) were **an honor to Christ.** His presence served both to help buffer Paul from accusations of personally profiting from the collection and also to spur the Corinthians on toward completing their project. By their giving, the Corinthians could demonstrate (cf. 9:13) their **love** (cf. 8:8).

9:1-2. The Corinthians' need to complete what they had eagerly begun (8:6, 10) concerned Paul. He had not found it necessary **to write** about the need to give aid to Jerusalem Christians. The Corinthians had agreed enthusiastically (8:11) to be involved in **this service** (*diakonias*) **to the saints** (cf. 8:4; 9:12-13). They were eager **to help** (cf. 8:4), a fact that Paul had relayed **to the Macedonians** the year before, which in turn had spurred the Macedonians on (**stirred . . . them to action**). The difference between the Macedonians and the Corinthians, however, lay in their diligence in seeing the project through to completion. Slow starters, the Macedonians finished quickly. But the Corinthians, willing in spirit, needed help in disciplining the flesh (cf. Matt. 26:41; Rom. 6:19).

9:3-4. Therefore Paul was sending Titus and **the** two **brothers** mentioned in 8:18-24 to aid in arranging the details for the Corinthians' consummation of the collection. Paul had boasted (cf. 9:2)

about the Corinthians' enthusiasm to contribute (8:10-11) and hoped that the promising clouds would indeed produce rain (cf. Hosea 6:3-4; Jude 12). If the Corinthian promise to give went unfulfilled, both Paul and the Corinthians themselves **would be ashamed** in the presence of the less able but more noble **Macedonians** who might accompany him on his third visit (2 Cor. 13:1).

9:5. To circumvent that possibility Paul had arranged for Titus and **the brothers** (8:23) to help the Corinthians get their financial house in order. The two "brothers" with Titus may possibly have been the Macedonians Jason of Thessalonica (Acts 17:5) and Sopater of Berea (Acts 20:4; cf. Rom. 16:21). Then when Paul arrived, no collections would have to be made (1 Cor. 16:2) under pressure which might resemble exploitation (cf. 2 Cor. 7:2; 9:7; 12:17-18). Such motivation is unworthy of Christ's servants. Instead, giving should be a willing response to God's grace, **not** something done **grudgingly.** Paul now turned to that subject.

C. Reward of generosity (9:6-15)

In the grace of God Christians are rewarded in three ways for their generosity: (1) the givers are enriched (vv. 6-10); (2) the receivers' needs are met (vv. 11-12); and (3) God, the Source of all blessing, is praised (vv. 13-15).

9:6-7. Why should the Corinthians give generously? (v. 5) Paul gave two reasons. (1) A principle holds true in both the natural and the spiritual spheres: the size of a harvest corresponds to the scope of the sowing (cf. Prov. 11:24-26). A man may enjoy all his grain by eating it, or he may "lose" some of it by sowing it and later reaping a bountiful harvest. A spiritual harvest, of course, may differ in kind from the seed sown. Material seed may reap a spiritual harvest (2 Cor. 9:9; cf. 1 Cor. 9:11). (2) Another reason for giving generously is that God loves generosity. God prizes not the size of the gift (cf. Acts 11:29; 1 Cor. 16:2), but the giver's sincerity (**not reluctantly**), spontaneity (not **under compulsion**), and joyful willingness (**a cheerful giver**).

9:8. Ultimately Christians can dispense only what they have received, whether material (Acts 14:17) or spiritual (Rom. 5:17). The good work is done through God's enabling (cf. Phil. 1:6).

Regardless of how desperate one's circumstances, a person who wants to give can do so in dependence on God (cf. Phil. 4:11-13; e.g., the widow of Zarephath, 1 Kings 17:9-16; and the Macedonians, 2 Cor. 8:1-3). Once again Paul sounded the note that man's inability, by contrast, showcases God's work (4:7). This verse is full of words indicating inclusiveness in God's enabling: **all grace . . . in all things at all times, having all that you need . . . in every good work.** In the words "all things," "all times," and "all . . . you need," the Greek heaps three words one after the other: *panti pantote pasan.* **God** is indeed sufficient! His *"every"* grace *abounds* so that believers can **abound** "in *every* good work."

9:9-10. The abounding grace mentioned in verse 8 refers to more than provision for one's needs of the moment. Charity reaps an eternal reward (cf. Prov. 19:17; Matt. 25:40). A person who "fears the Lord" (Ps. 112:1) and **gives gifts to the poor** (from Ps. 112:9, which Paul quoted) will be vindicated on the last day (cf. Matt. 6:1). Practical **righteousness endures forever** not only through the deeds but in the doer as he is progressively transformed into Christlikeness (2 Cor. 3:18). Ultimately a believer's reward is the culmination of the process (Phil. 3:14, 21). The One who supplies what is needed is God alone (Phil. 2:13). God (**who supplies seed . . . and bread**) enlarges **the harvest** (rewards or blessings) that results from righteous, generous living. The riches of **righteousness** are inestimable (cf. 6:10).

9:11-13. The more one gives to others, the more he is enriched, and thus he **can be generous on every occasion.** Such a generous spirit toward others results in more and more people giving **thanksgiving to God.**

One expression of this generosity was the contribution to the Jerusalem saints, administered by Paul. **Not only** would **this service** (vv. 12-13; cf. 8:4; 9:1) meet the pressing **needs of** Jerusalem Christians **but** it would **also** overflow **in many expressions of thanks to God** and bring **praise** to **God.** The Corinthian participation in this charitable gesture would demonstrate the reality of their **confession** and the vitality of their spiritual lives.

9:14-15. Because the Corinthians

sent material aid, they reaped the intercessory **prayers** of the Jerusalem Christians who in praising **God** invoked His blessings on their Corinthian brethren. This spirit of selflessness is a consequence of God's **surpassing grace** (cf. "grace" in 8:1, 9; 9:8) supremely expressed in the ministry of the Lord Jesus Christ (8:9). This section on giving concludes (9:15) where it began (8:1), with the grace of God. **Thanks** in 9:15 is the word *charis* ("grace, favor"). Believers are to bestow "favor" on **God** because of His favors bestowed on them. **His** greatest **gift** (*dōrea*) is eternal salvation, spiritual riches, through His rich Son who became poor (8:9). Such a gift is **indescribable** (*anekdiēgētō*, "unable to recount or tell fully," used only here in the NT). Those who have benefited from such a spiritual gift (stemming from God's grace) should not hesitate to benefit others with material gifts. The Corinthians finished this work and sent a gift to Jerusalem (Rom. 15:26).

IV. Affirmative Action (10:1–13:10)

Paul had no easy transition to the subject he reserved for last. Because of this, these final four chapters have sometimes been thought to be from a different letter, possibly written earlier (see "Unity" in the *Introduction*) or a fifth letter, dispatched after chapters 1–9 were written and delivered. But transitions to difficult subjects are notoriously awkward and are usually put off to the end of a conversation or letter. Though Paul had been indirectly polemical in the preceding portions (e.g., 2:17; 3:1, 7-18; 4:2-4; 5:12, 16; 6:14), he saved for now the direct confrontation which he could not avoid. The false apostles needed to be challenged openly and the Corinthians' affections needed to be won over to a singular devotion to Christ and His apostle.

A. Appeal for obedience (10:1-6)

The remarks about the collection (chaps. 8–9) amounted to a mild appeal and call to action. In chapter 10 Paul's subject matter and the intensity of his appeal were amplified. Paul believed that the danger of people defecting from him and his gospel were decidedly real. By appealing for obedience, he tested the

confidence that Titus said the Corinthians had in him (7:16).

10:1-2. **Paul** was loath to take stern action, but the situation demanded it. His model for this was **Christ.** Christ's **meekness** (cf. Matt. 11:29) was a strength of spirit that enabled Him to accept calmly the wrongs done against Himself (e.g., Matt. 27:12-14), but to act with a powerful vengeance on behalf of others (e.g., John 2:15-16). Meekness epitomizes the strength that comes from loving others rather than self.

Gentleness (*epieikeias*, "graciousness," occurring in the NT only here and in Acts 24:4) is the active corollary to this meek disposition. This was the attitude in which Paul ministered, a spirit which could easily be construed as weakness and timidity by the world's **standards.** His opponents, the false apostles (2 Cor. 11:13), acknowledged his "bark." In a letter (cf. 1 Cor. 4:19) and through a delegate like Titus, Paul appeared **bold.** But his "bite," they said, lacked teeth, at least by worldly standards.

10:3-5. **The weapons of the world** are learning, personal influence, impressive credentials (1 Cor. 1:26), rhetorical polish (1 Cor. 2:1), and the like. These things Paul had discounted and discarded (Phil. 3:4-8). He did **not wage war as the world does** or use their weapons.

The **weapons** Paul used were the proclaimed Word of God and prayer (Eph. 6:17-18), weapons with **divine power.** In dependence on God (1 Cor. 2:4-5) these weapons, frail by worldly standards, are able **to demolish** the **arguments and every pretension** of the gospel's foes. Neither the god of this Age (2 Cor. 4:4) nor his henchmen (11:15) could oppose **the knowledge** (or power) **of God** on which Paul relied. No **thought** (*noēma*; cf. 2:11), including those of his opponents, is beyond the reach of the One who "catches the wise in their craftiness" and "knows that the thoughts of the wise are futile" (1 Cor. 3:19-20; cf. Job 5:13; Ps. 94:11).

The object of Paul's warfare was to **make** people **obedient.** Paul was not interested in making them subject to himself or any other man after the manner of the world (cf. 2 Cor. 1:24; 11:20; Luke 22:25).

10:6. His approach to this particular confrontation in Corinth was twofold.

First, it was necessary that the Corinthian church express their subjection to Christ by demonstrating loyalty to His representative Paul (5:20; cf. 7:15). In this way their **obedience** would be **complete.** Second, when Paul was sure they had repudiated his opponents (cf. 6:14-18), he could then deal directly with the false apostles, knowing that the church supported him. He was ready **to punish** their acts **of disobedience** to Christ. The word "punish" (*ekdikēsai*) could more forcefully be translated "avenge" (cf. 1 Cor. 3:17). In other contexts it describes the wrath of God directed against the enemies of His people (Num. 31:2; Deut. 32:43; Rev. 19:2).

B. False apostles confronted (10:7–11:15)

Though Paul had parried the accusations of his opponents at previous points in the letter (3:1, 7-18; 4:2-4; 5:12, 16; 6:14), they had not been the direct focal point of his address. Now they were. Who these opponents were can only be answered tentatively. Apparently they were Jews (11:22) but where they came from is not known. They believed themselves apostles of Christ (10:7; 11:23), a claim Paul rejected (11:13). They brought letters of recommendation (3:1), indulged in self-commendation (10:18), and identified themselves with certain so-called "super-apostles" (cf. 11:5).

These false apostles may have been sent out by those who at the Jerusalem Council had urged the circumcision of Gentiles and obedience to the Law of Moses (Acts 15:5). Of course this appeal was largely unheeded by the apostles and elders (Acts 15:23-29). The false apostles claimed to bear a message of righteousness (2 Cor. 11:14) which Paul called a false gospel (11:4). They may have proclaimed a legalistic righteousness based on external conformity to Mosaic legislation (3:7-15). Ultimately they were self-serving, seeking monetary gains from the Corinthians (2:17) and possibly also indulging in sensuality (12:21). Legalism and self-centeredness are two sides of the same coin (Matt. 6:2, 15-16; 23:5-7) with self-indulgence the ultimate result (Matt. 23:25; cf. Phil. 3:2).

10:7-8. A major factor contributing to the Corinthians' dilemma concerning apostolic authority was their superficiality and shallowness. They looked **only on the surface of things.** They were oriented to externalities and worldly wisdom (cf. 1 Cor. 3:1). As a result the false apostles found them fair game. In order to retrieve this indiscriminate church Paul would have to engage in what he found personally repugnant—self-commendation. His goal was not self-enhancement but restoration of the Corinthians. To that end he wielded his **authority** as an apostle of Christ. And he did so **freely** and without being **ashamed of it.** He tore down the "strongholds," "arguments," and every "pretension" of his opponents (2 Cor. 10:4-5) but he built up believers.

10:9-11. Paul anticipated that his previously written words about his apostolic authority (v. 8) or his **letters** might **frighten** the Corinthians. He also anticipated that his words (vv. 4-6) might raise smirks on the lips of the false apostles and a depreciatory remark about his bite not equaling his bark. He did not deny that his public presence was superficially **unimpressive** (cf. v. 1). He was not a polished speaker (11:6) by design as much as by default (cf. 1 Cor. 2:1-5). If the false apostles equated his rhetorical skills with the power granted him by God as an apostle, they would do so at their peril. True, his letters contained awesome commands about handing men over to Satan for the destruction of their flesh (1 Cor. 5:5; cf. Acts 13:11; 1 Tim. 1:20). But his subsequent action would show that he did what he said.

10:12. Paul's opponents (and any who sided with them) could be censured on several counts. The first was the inadequate standard by which they evaluated themselves. The false apostles compared themselves not with the divine standard exemplified by Christ but with other men, using human standards. In doing so, Paul said, no matter how much they vaunted their human wisdom they showed **themselves** to be **not wise,** but fools (cf. 1 Cor. 1:20).

10:13-14. The false apostles were censured on a second count. Even if Paul granted for the moment the legitimacy of their apostleship it was he, not they, who had been designated the apostle to the Gentiles (cf. Gal. 2:8). God had authenticated Paul's commission by producing fruit in Corinth—**we did get as far as you with the gospel of Christ** (cf. 1 Cor. 3:6).

The false apostles had grossly over-stepped their bounds. They had gone **beyond proper limits** (cf. 2 Cor. 10:15) but Paul had **not**.

10:15-16. Paul's third censure concerned the claims of the false apostles. They had overstepped their bounds but they had also exaggerated their accomplishments. The church in Corinth was a result of Paul's ministry not theirs. Unlike his opponents he did not **boast about work already done . . . by others.** The Corinthians may have had many so-called guardians but they had only one "father," Paul (1 Cor. 4:15). He was the one they should imitate (1 Cor. 4:16). **As their faith** grew and they matured, he could then **expand** his **area of activity** by evangelizing other Gentiles **in the regions beyond** them, even as far away as Spain (Rom. 15:23-24). They could take part in this work by prayer (Eph. 6:19-20) and financial support (cf. 1 Cor. 16:6; Phil. 4:15-17). But first they needed to get their own house in order (2 Cor. 10:6).

10:17-11:1. To **boast** in men is ultimately self-impoverishing (cf. 1 Cor. 3:21). However legitimate and necessary the censuring of his opponents was, along with validating his own work, Paul ultimately believed that both were exercises in **foolishness.** Paul had reminded the Corinthians of this in an earlier letter (1 Cor. 1:31) quoting from Jeremiah 9:24, as he did here. Why did the Corinthians continue to be enamored of men, simply a form of self-adulation, when in fact their spiritual vitality was entirely due to the grace of God? (1 Cor. 1:30; 3:7) Paul certainly had not sought the commendation of the Corinthians nor was he seeking to commend **himself.** He knew he would one day stand before the judgment seat of Christ (2 Cor. 5:10). There only the Master's approval (Luke 19:17) will matter. Self-commendation and the praise of men (cf. Matt. 6:2, 6, 16) will count for nothing (Rom. 2:29; 1 Cor. 4:5). Let the Corinthians make no mistake about it: Paul's rebutting his opponents and reviewing his own labor was not for his own benefit. He subjected himself to this "folly" because he loved them and they needed it (2 Cor. 12:11). Such was his love for them that he would willingly be made a fool if by so doing he could rescue them.

11:2-4. While they may have thought otherwise, they were in peril. The tragedy of Eden was ominously close to reenactment. As **Christ** was elsewhere compared with Adam (Rom. 5:14; 1 Cor. 15:21-22, 45), Paul here compared the church in Corinth to **Eve.** Instead of resisting (cf. James 4:7; 1 Peter 5:9) the devil's inducement to disobedience Eve listened and succumbed (Gen. 3:1-6). The serpent enticed her by his **cunning** (*panourgia,* "trickery"; cf. 2 Cor. 4:2). The devil's representatives in Corinth (11:13-15) were also seductive. They should have been spurned (cf. 6:14-15) but instead were tolerated (11:4). Worse still, if the church like Eve obeyed the lie they would be guilty of disobedience to God and disloyalty to Christ, whom they were singlemindedly to love and obey. (**Sincere** renders the Gr. noun *haplotētos,* "simplicity in the sense of singlemindedness"; cf. 1:12).

In Paul's metaphor the church was a **virgin** betrothed **to Christ** at conversion. As the servant of God's grace he acted as their spiritual father (1 Cor. 4:15). Until the marriage was consummated at Christ's coming, exclusive **devotion to** Christ should prevail (cf. Eph. 5:25-27). The Corinthians, however, were perilously close to forsaking that devotion and the spirit of liberty in which it flourished. They were dangerously open to **a different gospel** and **a different spirit** (i.e., bondage to Law; 2 Cor. 3:7-18; cf. Gal. 4:17-5:1).

11:5-6. The Corinthians vacillated in their devotion to the Lord because of the threefold appeal of the false apostles. First, these false teachers apparently associated themselves and their mission with the original apostles. The designation **"super-apostles"** was used by the false apostles of themselves, or was Paul's ironical portrayal of their adulation of the Twelve (or of Peter, James, and John; Gal. 2:9). The false apostles hoped to derive authority by claiming to be associated with the Twelve. Without demeaning the Twelve, Paul affirmed his own status as an apostle of similar rank: I **am** not **in the least inferior** (cf. 2 Cor. 12:11). His basis for this claim would follow shortly (11:22–12:10).

Second, the false apostles appealed to the Corinthians' desires for superiority in rhetorical excellence. Paul admitted he was not an accomplished rhetorician, **a** trained speaker (cf. 10:10). (However, if he were, he was choosing not to use his rhetorical abilities; cf. 1 Cor. 2:1-5). His apostleship was not a matter of show but of substance. *What* Paul said was more important than *how* he said it. The Corinthians could not deny the content of his message and its transforming consequences (cf. 1 Cor. 4:15; 9:1-2).

11:7-9. A third way the false apostles appealed to the Corinthians was in their method of supporting themselves. When Jesus sent out disciples on missionary tours, He directed them to derive shelter and sustenance from those to whom they ministered (Luke 9:3-4; 10:4-7). This apparently became the usual practice for Christian missionaries (1 Cor. 9:4-6; cf. *Didache* 11:4-6), and it was followed by the false apostles in Corinth. However, Paul and those associated with him (e.g., Barnabas, 1 Cor. 9:6) differed by supporting themselves as best they could without ministerial remuneration (cf. 1 Cor. 4:12; 1 Thes. 2:9; 2 Thes. 3:8). Occasionally Paul accepted unsolicited support from **churches** to whom he had ministered (e.g., the Philippian church in **Macedonia;** Phil. 4:15-16). But he did so uneasily (cf. Phil. 4:10-13), calling it "robbery" (2 Cor. 11:8) to take from poor people. He did not want to be **a burden to** them.

11:10-12. Paul had various reasons for adhering to this general practice (e.g., 1 Cor. 9:17-18; 2 Thes. 3:9-10). His main reason may have been his desire to emulate Christ who became poor even as He enriched others (2 Cor. 8:9). An immediate reason in Corinth for maintaining this practice was that it barred the false apostles from any claim of equality to Paul in apostolic ministry (11:12), and so was anathema to them. However, it was not too well received even by the beneficiaries, the Corinthians. They thought that Paul's hesitation to accept remuneration from them showed that he did **not love** them. Paul, nonetheless, stood his **ground.**

11:13-15. Though Paul had been mild in his remarks about the "super-apostles" (v. 5), here he gave the **false apostles** a withering denunciation. They were only shams, claiming to be ambassadors of Christ when in fact they were emissaries (**servants,** *diakonoi*) of **Satan.** Like Satan's masquerade **as an angel of** light, they were **masquerading** (*metaschēmatizomenoi,* "changing the outward form") **as apostles** and **servants of righteousness.** Like whitewashed tombs they may have looked righteous but inside there was only death and decay (cf. Matt. 23:27-28), prefiguring **their** doom (**end;** cf. 1 Cor. 3:17).

Who were these false apostles? Numerous suggestions have been made, ranging from Hellenistic charismatics to Palestinian Gnostics (see J.J. Gunther, *St. Paul's Opponents and Their Background.* Leiden: E.J. Brill, 1973). Several factors suggest, however, that they were Palestinian Jews, members of the Jerusalem church who were false brothers (cf. Gal. 2:4) in Paul's estimation. They carried commendatory letters from the church (2 Cor. 3:1), possibly under the auspices of the Jerusalem Council, to survey compliance with the Jerusalem decree (Acts 15:20-21). That there were self-appointed delegations to enforce Mosaic ordinances before this is certain (Acts 15:24), and it is possible that the false apostles in Corinth were mavericks of this sort. Paul did not contest their appeal to the authority of the "super-apostles." But he did refute the value of such an appeal and the notion that apostolic authority was a matter of human association rather than divine accreditation.

C. Apostolic credentials (11:16–12:10)

Like most people, the Corinthians were slow to absorb the truth that divine standards differ radically from those of the world. Paul had tried to make this clear in his former letter concerning the message of the Cross: the wisdom of God is foolishness to the world (1 Cor. 1:18-25). If, however, the Corinthians persisted in looking at things from the world's point of view, he would accommodate himself to their perspective. But he would still try to lead them to realize that divine accreditation should be seen not against the backdrop of human greatness but human weakness. The marks of an apostle were the marks of Christ, including weakness and suffering (2 Cor. 13:4; cf. Isa. 53:3-4; Mark 9:12). In this passage (2 Cor. 11:16–12:10) Paul recounted his frailties and with poignant irony said, in essence, "These are the credentials of an apostle" (cf. 1 Cor. 4:9-13).

11:16-18. Following the advice of

Proverbs 26:5, Paul again answered the foolish Corinthians according to their folly. He had previously asked them to "put up with" a bit of foolishness (2 Cor. 11:1); he now resumed this approach. He did so not by choice but by necessity because they had tolerated and welcomed the false apostles. The Corinthians received those false teachers because of the latter's external qualifications and self-aggrandizement. This is like valuing a gem on the basis of its size rather than its quality. Paul's challenge to the believers was a "contest of folly," entered into in order to win the Corinthians. The word **fool** (vv. 16-17, 19, 21; 12:6, 11) is from the adjective *aphrōn*, meaning "ignorant," not *mōros*, which means "stupid." In 2 Corinthians Paul frequently spoke of **boasting**, not in a haughty way but in an effort to affirm his claim as an apostle. In his **boasting** he was **not talking as the Lord would**, as the Lord never defended Himself in this way, but Paul chose to, though reluctantly.

11:19-21a. The irony in these verses borders on sarcasm. Its sting is tempered only by Paul's motive which was to correct this wayward church. The Corinthians, thinking themselves **wise . . . put up with fools**—a naive, foolish thing to do! Though Paul may have been accused of "lording it over" the Corinthians (1:24), the false apostles were the ones they should fear. In the name of Christ they would exploit and enslave the Corinthians to gratify themselves. (Here the Gr. word for **exploits** means "devour," like a parasite. This differs from the word rendered "exploit" in 7:2 and 12:17-18.) Jesus accused the legalistic Pharisees of the same rapacious practice (Mark 12:40). Paul said he had been **too weak for that.** He had presented himself to the Corinthians as their servant and Christ as their only Lord (2 Cor. 4:5).

11:21b-22. Paul was now ready to begin comparing the external qualifications apparently believed by the Corinthians and the false apostles to be matters of great importance. It is usually believed that the questions asked and answered by Paul describe himself and the false apostles. It is possible, however, that Paul is comparing himself with the so-called "super-apostles" (v. 5), the Twelve, to whom the false apostles appealed as their source of authority and with whom they

identified. If so, this would strengthen the comparison (noted in v. 5 and 12:11), would accord well with what Paul had previously written about himself and the Twelve (1 Cor. 15:10), and would eliminate the awkwardness of 2 Corinthians 11:23 as applied to the false apostles immediately after what Paul had written in verse 13. So, while these questions may describe the false apostles who claimed to be the proxy of the Twelve, they may also be understood as Paul's comparison of himself with the Twelve and his superiority, from a human point of view, to them.

The designation **Hebrews** may be an ancestral description but in this context (with **Israelites**) it may also be a linguistic distinction. The term is used elsewhere in the New Testament only twice (Acts 6:1; Phil. 3:5). In Acts 6:1 it clearly distinguished the Semitic-speaking Jews from those whose primary or exclusive language was Greek. Though Paul was born in Tarsus, he was apparently reared in a Semitic-speaking home of Jewish parentage whose orientation was to the homeland of Palestine.

As one of the Israelites Paul traced his lineage through the tribe of Benjamin (Phil. 3:5). As one of **Abraham's descendants** he was circumcised on the eighth day (Phil. 3:5; cf. Gen. 17:9-14); more importantly, Paul was Abraham's descendant by faith (cf. Rom. 4:16). From a human viewpoint Paul's credentials were impeccable (cf. Phil. 3:4-6).

11:23. If Paul were comparing himself with the false apostles rather than the Twelve in these verses (cf. comments on vv. 21b-22) then the phrase **servants of Christ** describes their designation of themselves, previously repudiated by Paul (v. 13) but here adopted for the sake of argument. The thrust of his argument was on quantifiable "service," an absurd measurement in itself (in 1 Cor. 3:13 Paul stressed quality in God's evaluation of Christian service). Paul noted the absurdity of this comparison himself (**I am out of my mind;** cf. 2 Cor. 5:13), but the Corinthian preoccupation with comparisons had forced him to it.

In intensity and scope of ministry no apostle or even group of apostles (cf. 1 Cor. 15:10) could match Paul's record of service. What is remarkable about Paul's catalog of achievements is his focus not on what might be called the triumphs of his ministerial experience but on its defeats. He left unmentioned the times when he seemed to be riding a surge of divine power such as at Ephesus (e.g., Acts 19:11) and chronicled instead the experiences in which he seemed to be dashed helpless to the ground. Like his Lord, who displayed the glory of God in His passion and death (John 13:31), Paul boasted in his sufferings and weaknesses (cf. Gal. 6:14).

The details concerning his ministry which Paul disclosed in this verse reveal how fragmentary is his biographical information in the Book of Acts. The writing of this letter coincided with the events mentioned by Luke in Acts 20:2. At this point in Luke's narrative he mentioned only one imprisonment (in Philippi), one beating (also in Philippi; Acts 16:22), and one brush with **death** (the stoning in Lystra; Acts 14:19). Yet in 2 Corinthians Paul referred to numerous incidents of this kind. Perhaps they occurred before his formal missionary journeys (Acts 13-20), or maybe Luke did not find it necessary to record them.

11:24. This verse makes it clear that Paul's statement in Romans 9:3—wishing himself cursed if by so doing Israel could be saved—was no empty declaration. **Five times** Paul **received** the synagogue's punishment (of 39 **lashes** each) in the course of ministering to fellow **Jews.** Death could occur under the 39 lashes because according to the Mishnah the person delivering the scourging was not liable for a victim's death (Makkoth 3.14).

11:25-26. The apostle to the Gentiles **was beaten** by fellow Jews. Also the Romans inflicted their punishment on Paul by beating him **with rods,** though they did so illegally since he was a Roman citizen (Acts 16:37). The acclaimed Roman peace was not much protection for Paul either. Roman law and order in Lystra did little to stop the mob that **stoned** Paul and left him for dead (Acts 14:19). Nor were the Roman highways and seaways placid avenues of travel. In addition to shipwreck (cf. Acts 27:27-44, though future to Paul's writing 2 Cor.) and river crossings with the consequential threat of death from drowning or exposure, Paul's itinerant ministry (he was **constantly on the move**) exposed him to countless dangers. He needed to be wary of professional **bandits** (cf. Luke 10:30),

and attacks by Jews (his **own countrymen**) and **Gentiles** alike (e.g., Acts 14:19; 16:19). He faced dangers everywhere—**in the city . . . in the country . . . at sea** (cf. **open sea,** v. 25). Even within the churches, such as Corinth, he faced the danger of attack instigated by or at the hands of **false brothers.**

11:27. In addition to living with dangers Paul willingly endured numerous privations in discharging his apostolic ministry. His decision to refuse remuneration for his ministry (cf. vv. 7-9) was not made lightly. Working night and day (cf. 1 Thes. 2:9) so as not to burden anyone for the necessities of life (2 Thes. 3:8), Paul still often found himself with insufficient **food,** drink, and clothing to meet even his minimal needs. He experienced sleepless nights, **hunger . . . thirst, and cold.**

Earlier in 2 Corinthians Paul had referred to being persecuted (2 Cor. 4:9), at the point of death (4:10-12), facing "beatings, imprisonments, and riots," and experiencing "hard work, sleepless nights, and hunger" (6:5). Here (11:23-27) his list of sufferings is far more complete.

11:28-29. It is difficult to comprehend the pain Paul must have felt from these physical afflictions and deprivations. But the spiritual struggles of his ministry were an even greater burden.

These verses climax the catalog of his ministerial suffering. **Concern for** others, not for himself, weighed heavily on him. In 1 Corinthians (12:25) Paul had written at length about the church as a body composed of various members knit together by a mutual concern for each other. Here he revealed the daily burden of the concern he experienced not just for the well-being of the Corinthian church, which would have taxed the noblest spirit, but concern for the well-being of **all the churches** established through his ministry.

In 1 Corinthians 12 he noted that in a spiritual body "if one part suffers every part suffers with it" (1 Cor. 12:26). Here he revealed how that sentiment found expression in his own life. He identified with the weak whether physically (cf. Phil. 2:26) or, more likely, spiritually (1 Cor. 9:22), in their pitiable state (cf. 1 Cor. 8:12; Rom. 14:15). **Who is weak, and I do not feel weak?** If anyone was led into sin, Paul so identified with the sinner that he too felt the consequences of the act. **Who is led into sin, and I do not inwardly burn?** David compared his state of sin under God's hand to "the heat of summer" (Ps. 32:4), a likely inspiration for the equally vivid inner "burning" Paul felt at the knowledge of a brother led astray.

11:30. Paul had taken the standards of the Corinthians and false apostles and turned them upside down. His catalog of sufferings could hardly have been what they expected to read. He boasted not in his power but in his **weakness.** (In chaps. 11–13, Paul spoke frequently of being "weak" [11:21, 29; 12:10; 13:4, 9] and of having "weakness[es]" [11:30; 12:5, 9-10; 13:4].) Yet to Paul this was "boasting," not a contrived or ironical account. Paul's **boast** was that his life was like that of Christ. As Jesus had been "a Man of sorrows and familiar with suffering" (Isa. 53:3), so had Paul (2 Cor. 11:23-27). As Jesus "took up our infirmities and carried our sorrows" (Isa. 53:4) so, in a different sense, had Paul (2 Cor. 11:28-29). Paul's **boast** was that he was like the suffering Servant. It was certainly a grand claim though hardly perceived as such by false apostles and worldly Corinthian believers (1 Cor. 3:3).

11:31. Any one of the severe sufferings Paul had described in the preceding verses might kill an average person. But Paul—one man—endured them all.

Paul was aware that his reliability was suspect among the Corinthians (cf. 1:12-18). For that reason he asserted his veracity: **I am not lying** (cf. 1:18; 11:11). His vow of truthfulness applied not only to the preceding sufferings but also to the following description of his incident in Damascus (11:32-33) and the account of his visionary experience (12:1-6).

11:32-33. Paul mentioned this escape from **Damascus,** an event which occurred early in his life as a Christian (cf. Acts 9:19-25), as a typical or quintessential experience in his work as an apostle. It epitomized the transformation that had taken place in his relationship with God, and sharply contrasted his state with that of the false apostles. Like them, he carried commendatory letters from Jerusalem to Damascus (Acts 9:2), but when he was en route God struck him down and he encountered the risen Christ. He had left for Damascus with

great human authority and zeal (Acts 9:1); he departed abjectly conscious of his own weakness. He was hunted by Jew and Gentile alike (Acts 14:5), but delivered by God through the agency of fellow Christians. His exit (by being **lowered in,** of all things, **a basket**), not his entrance, typified the apostolic life (cf. 1 Cor. 4:9-12). How different were the false apostles, who were like the unconverted Saul!

12:1. A second line of comparison the Corinthians insisted on (cf. v. 11) concerned **visions and revelations.** Like Paul's external credentials (11:22-23) he believed this parading of credentials was an exercise in futility (**there is nothing to be gained**) for building up the church (10:8). He did it, however, in the hope that it would silence his critics and enable him to minister freely. He also neatly turned his readers' attention from these irrelevant credentials to those that were an apostle's authentic marks. What distinguished "servants of Christ" (11:23) was their likeness to the suffering Servant (Isa. 53). If one had exalted "visions and revelations" (2 Cor. 12:1), he should have a corresponding appreciation of his own weakness and humility (vv. 9-10).

12:2-4. Paul's indirect reference to himself as **a man in Christ** showed that he regarded this great experience not as a consequence of inherent worthiness or spiritual excellence but because he was "in Christ." As such it anticipated what everyone in Christ will one day experience, the presence of Christ in heaven.

This event occurred **14 years** earlier, sometime in the years A.D. 42–44 before Paul's missionary journeys reported in Acts. Paul was raptured (**caught up** is from the same verb *harpazō* used in 1 Thes. 4:17 of saints at the Rapture) **to the third heaven,** the dwelling place of Christ and the saints, which Jesus called **paradise** (Luke 23:43; cf. Rev. 2:7). Temporal and spatial sensations were absent (**whether** he was **in the body or apart from the body** he did **not know**). What he heard he was forbidden to communicate, possibly because it applied to him alone (cf. Acts 9:16). The experience, however, no doubt contributed to Paul's conviction that "our light and momentary troubles are achieving for us an eternal glory that far outweighs them all" (2 Cor. 4:17).

12:5-6. Paul boasted about **a man** (cf. "a man in Christ," v. 2, and "this man," v. 3) because his accent was on Christ, not himself. The Corinthian preoccupation with the external and the spectacular was regrettable to Paul (cf. 1 Cor. 14:20). He could boast of these things truthfully (2 Cor. 12:6; cf. 1 Cor. 14:18; Phil. 3:4), by which he implied that the claims of other men in Corinth were suspect. But what mattered to Paul was not his achievements but God's work through him and the gospel that he preached.

12:7-9. So that Paul would not forget this, God gave him a constant reminder of his weakness. Countless explanations concerning the nature of his **thorn in the flesh** have been offered. They range from incessant temptation, dogged opponents, chronic maladies (such as ophthalmia, malaria, migraine headaches, and epilepsy), to a disability in speech. No one can say for sure what his was, but it probably was a physical affliction (for the work of **Satan** in this, cf. 1 Cor. 5:5; 10:10). It is understandable that Paul would consider this thorn a hindrance to wider or more effective ministry (cf. Gal. 4:14-16) and that he would repeatedly petition God for its removal (2 Cor. 12:8). But he learned from this experience the lesson that pervades this letter: divine power (**My power,** v. 8; **Christ's power,** v. 9) is best displayed against the backdrop of human **weaknesses** (cf. 4:7) so that God alone is praised (10:17). Rather than removing the problem God gave him **grace** in it. This grace is sufficient (*arkei,* i.e., adequate in the sense of providing contentment). (The Gr. words trans. **to keep me from becoming conceited** occur in 12:7 twice, at the beginning and end of the verse. The NIV translates only the first one.)

12:10. God's grace transformed Paul's perspective. Experiences in his ministry he would naturally abhor, he could welcome supernaturally because the evidence of Christ's power in the midst of them brought glory to Him, not Paul. When Paul came to the end of himself, Christ alone was seen. **When he was weak, then** Christ, by His strength, could make Paul spiritually **strong.** ("Power," *dynamis,* in v. 9, is the word "strength," thus matching "strong," *dynatos,* in v. 10).

D. Recommended response (12:11–13:10)

Paul hoped, when he visited the Corinthians, to see two responses to his letter: (1) repentance (involving obedience to God) for wrong, and (2) an affirmation of loyalty to himself and his associates as authentic servants of Christ.

12:11. The boasting was over. Paul had played the part demanded of him by the Corinthians—the **fool.** Instead of coming to his defense against the innuendos and calumnies of the false apostles, the Corinthians remained passive spectators, forcing Paul to offer his own defense. Paul knew that he was more than equal to stand comparison with even the greatest of the Twelve (cf. 11:5), as shown by the catalog of credentials he had just given. But it was a foolish endeavor because these credentials were ultimately not his but God's. He was **nothing.** As he had written the Corinthians before, "I worked harder than all of them—yet not I, but the grace of God that was with me" (1 Cor. 15:10).

12:12. The supernatural acts accomplished through God's grace should have sufficed to quiet all suspicion about Paul's apostleship. **Signs** (*sēmeiois,* miracles with emphasis on their significance; e.g., Jesus' seven "signs" in John); **wonders** (*terasin,* unusual events that engender awe); **miracles** (*dynamesin,* wonderworks resulting from supernatural power)—all these are the evidences **that mark an apostle** (cf. Acts 2:22, 43; Heb. 2:4). Though no miraculous signs or wonders done in Corinth were recorded in the Acts account of Paul's ministry in that city, such miracles certainly occurred (they **were done among you**). Paul also performed miracles before and after the Corinthian ministry. A demon was cast out of the servant girl in Philippi (Acts 16:18), and Paul's ministry in Ephesus was marked by numerous miracles (Acts 19:11). Of course the greatest miracle was a church in Corinth planted by Paul but given life by God (1 Cor. 3:6). Remarkable too was his **great perseverance,** again a result of the empowerment of God (Acts 18:9-11). All these evidences pointed to Paul as a true apostle and to his opponents as "false apostles" (2 Cor. 11:13).

12:13-15. In only one sense was Paul

different from other true apostles: he was self-supporting and took no remuneration from the Corinthians. And he would not change his way, for he refused to be a **burden** to them (vv. 13-14, 16). His imminent **third** visit would be no different (cf. 13:1; and see points 7 and 8 under "Contacts and Correspondence" in the *Introduction*). Like a father with his spiritual **children** Paul wanted to care for the church without cost to them. While he refused remuneration for different reasons (cf. 11:10; 1 Cor. 9:17) not the least among them was his **love** for the Corinthians. And he would gladly have received the same "coinage" from them (cf. 2 Cor. 6:11-13).

12:16-18. Paul could live with the fact that the Corinthians' recompense of love would be less than his investment of love in them. But he found it intolerable that they charged him and his associates with underhanded self-gratification (when just the opposite was true). Apparently the false apostles suggested that Paul's unwillingness to accept support from the church was simply a cloak to disguise his love of money and the designs he had on the collection. **Titus** was obviously implicated in this, as was one of the two brothers who accompanied him at Paul's recommendation (cf. 8:22). Paul asked the obvious question: What evidence could be mustered to lend the slightest credence to this allegation? Was there any hint of misconduct in the behavior of **Titus** or **our brother?** Were not Paul's actions equally impeccable? Had either of them ever exploited (cf. 2:11; 7:2) the Corinthians? Paul hoped that the absence of evidence would silence his critics (though the history of his relationship with the Corinthian church hardly boded well for such a result).

12:19-21. The motive behind the apologetic which Paul wove through this letter was not self-preservation. Paul's Judge was **God,** not any human court (1 Cor. 4:3-4; 2 Cor. 5:10). On the contrary, he had undertaken this difficult letter out of concern for the Corinthians **(for your strengthening)** in the hope of rectifying the disorders in the church before punishment became necessary (13:2). Like a father with his children, any punishment which he was compelled to administer would grieve him as well

(12:21). It was for just this reason he had canceled his previously projected third visit (1:23–2:4). They had responded well to his earlier letter (7:8-13) but the entrance of the false apostles threatened to revive their former divisiveness.

The eight sins Paul mentioned (12:20) are all explainable in the context of church division, as are the three sins of verse 21 in the climate of lax morality which disunity produces. (See comments on these three in Gal. 5:19.) While the legalistic bent of the false apostles might be thought to quash the sins of the flesh listed in 2 Corinthians 12:21, the sad truth is that legalism and immorality are frequent bedfellows (cf. Phil. 3:3, 19; John 8:3-7).

13:1-3. Paul's second **visit to** Corinth (2:1) had been a humbling experience (12:21), not only because of the offense against him (cf. 2:5-11) but because many in the church were living contrary to the will of God (12:21). Paul had warned them about the consequences of sin then and he did so again in this letter. Following Jesus' application of Deuteronomy 19:15 to errant brethren (Matt. 18:16), Paul promised discipline for the unrepentant. The proof of his apostolic authority which they wanted would be given but in terms they would be wise to avoid (cf. 1 Cor. 5:5). Though Paul was weak, **Christ** whom he served was **not** (cf. 2 Cor. 10:4).

13:4. The paradox of Christ was the paradox of Paul. With **God's power** at His disposal (Matt. 26:53) Christ nonetheless followed the course of **weakness** to the cross. In the Resurrection the magnitude of that untapped power was displayed (Eph. 1:19-21). This side of the grave Paul like Jesus followed the path of "weakness" but as in Jesus' life, a glimmer of **God's power** showed through (e.g., Matt. 4:23; 2 Cor. 12:12). Paul wanted this power to be used for constructive rather than punitive purposes (cf. 13:10; 10:2-6), power that would enable him **to serve** them.

13:5-7. Throughout the letter Paul subjected himself and his ministry to scrutiny. Now he handed the lens to the Corinthians, with the challenge that they consider their own conduct (**yourselves** is in the emphatic position in Gr.). Paul's question is usually construed with regard to positional justification: were they

Christians or not? But it more likely concerned practical sanctification: did they *demonstrate* that they were **in the faith** (cf. 1 Cor. 16:13) and that **Christ** was in them by their obeying His will? To stand **the test** was to do what was right. To **fail** was to be disobedient and therefore subject to God's discipline. The words **fail(ed) the test** (2 Cor. 13:5-6) and **failed** (v. 7) render the Greek word *adokimoi* ("disapproved"; cf. *adokimos* in 1 Cor. 9:27).

Whatever doubts the Corinthians may have had about Paul's conduct (e.g., 2 Cor. 1:17, 2:17; 7:2) he believed that a sober evaluation would lead them to vindicate him. He hoped they would not be disapproved by God; and he hoped they would see that *he* was not disapproved by God. Still it was their reputation or standing, not his, that concerned him.

13:8-10. For himself, Paul knew he was powerless **against the truth,** the will of God. His experience on the Damascus Road had taught him that (Acts 9:1-6). Like Jesus his **Lord,** he was willing to spend and be spent on behalf of others (cf. 2 Cor. 8:9; 12:15). In his weakness he was made **strong** (12:8, 10) and so were they (13:9). He was concerned about the Corinthians' welfare (cf. Phil. 2:20-21). **Perfection** (*katartisin*) may be translated "restoration." This noun occurs only here in the New Testament but is kin to the verb *katartizesthe* translated "aim for perfection" in 2 Corinthians 13:11 and elsewhere used for repairing nets (Matt. 4:21).

As a conclusion to this warning (2 Cor. 12:20-21; 13:5-7), this prayer for restoration of their ways was certainly fitting. Then Paul could be spared the pain of disciplining those he loved (cf. 2:2) and instead he could work with them for their joy (1:24) and **for building** them **up** (13:10).

V. Conclusion (13:11-14)

Did the Corinthians respond positively to Paul's warning? Yes. Paul had conditioned the expansion of his ministry in other areas on the problems in Corinth being resolved (10:15-16). He followed the writing of this letter with a visit of three months during which time he wrote the letter to the Romans. In that letter he wrote "Now . . . there is no more place for me to work in these regions" (Rom. 15:23). His appeal had been heeded. The Corinthians were now obedient.

A. Appropriate conduct (13:11-12)

13:11-12. Paul's final appeal was a call for unity: **Aim for perfection** (i.e., "be restored or complete"; see comments on "perfection" in v. 9), **listen to my appeal, be of one mind** (cf. Phil. 2:2), **live in peace.** This unity could be realized only as they depended on God who supplies **love** (cf. 2 Cor. 13:14) **and peace.** Such unity was expressed by **a holy kiss** (cf. Rom. 16:16; 1 Cor. 16:20 [see comments there]; 1 Thes. 5:26; 1 Peter 5:14).

B. Salutations and benediction (13:13-14)

13:13-14. The saints of Macedonia, with whom Paul was staying at the time he wrote 2 Corinthians (see the *Introduction*), sent **their** unified **greetings.** In closing, Paul invoked the blessing of the Triune God so that **the grace** manifested by **Christ, the love** expressed by **God** the Father (cf. "the God of love," v. 11), and **the fellowship** created by **the Holy Spirit** might be experienced in Corinth.

BIBLIOGRAPHY

Barrett, C.K. *The Second Epistle to the Corinthians.* Harper's New Testament Commentaries. New York: Harper & Row, 1973.

Bruce, F.F. *1 and 2 Corinthians.* London: Oliphants, 1971.

Gromacki, Robert G. *Stand Firm in the Faith: An Exposition of II Corinthians.* Grand Rapids: Baker Book House, 1978.

Hanson, Richard P.C. *2 Corinthians.* London: SCM Press, 1954.

Héring, Jean. *The Second Epistle of Saint Paul to the Corinthians.* London: Epworth Press, 1967.

Hodge, Charles. *An Exposition of the Second Epistle to the Corinthians.* Reprint. Grand Rapids: Baker Book House, 1980.

Hughes, Philip Edgcumbe. *Paul's Second Epistle to the Corinthians.* The New International Commentary on the New Testament. Grand Rapids: Wm. B. Eerdmans Publishing Co., 1962.

Kent, Homer. *A Heart Opened Wide: Studies in II Corinthians*. Grand Rapids: Baker Book House, 1982.

Moule, H.C.G. *The Second Epistle to the Corinthians*. Fort Washington, Pa.: Christian Literature Crusade, 1976.

Plummer, Alfred. *A Critical and Exegetical Commentary on the Second Epistle of St. Paul to the Corinthians*. The International Critical Commentary. Edinburgh: T. & T. Clark, 1915.

Schelke, Karl. *The Second Epistle to the Corinthians*. New York: Herder & Herder, 1969.

Tasker, R.V.G. *The Second Epistle of Paul to the Corinthians: An Introduction and Commentary*. The Tyndale New Testament Commentaries. Grand Rapids: Wm. B. Eerdmans Publishing Co., 1958.

Thrall, Margaret E. *The First and Second Letters of Paul to the Corinthians*. London: Cambridge Press, 1965.

GALATIANS

Donald K. Campbell

INTRODUCTION

Importance of the Epistle. Galatians, though one of Paul's shorter epistles, is highly esteemed as one of his greatest and most influential. Since both Romans and Galatians teach the doctrine of justification by faith, the former has been considered by some to be an expansion of Galatians and the latter has been called "a short Romans."

Like 2 Corinthians the Epistle of Galatians eloquently defends Paul's apostolic authority and contains in summary form what the apostle taught. In particular it contains a clear statement of justification by faith and builds on that foundation a defense of Christian liberty against any form of legalism.

In the early church, as the separation between Judaism and Christianity was taking place, the letter to the Galatians no doubt helped clarify that cleavage. Centuries later it played such a key role in the Reformation that it was called "the cornerstone of the Protestant Reformation." This was because its emphasis on salvation by grace through faith alone was the major theme of the preaching of the Reformers. Luther was especially attached to Galatians and referred to it as his wife. He lectured on the book extensively and his *Commentary on Galatians* was widely read by the common people.

The profound influence of this small epistle continues. It is indeed the "Magna Charta of Christian Liberty," proclaiming to modern generations that salvation from the penalty and power of sin comes not by works but by grace through faith in God's provision.

Authorship. The Pauline authorship of Galatians has, except for a few radical critics, been generally acknowledged. Even when the higher critics of 19th-century Germany were denying apostolic authorship of book after book, the Tübingen school regarded Galatians as Pauline. The reasons for this are based on the clear testimony of both internal and external evidence. Importantly, the author of the letter calls himself Paul both in the salutation (1:1) and later in the body of the letter (5:2). Most of chapters 1 and 2 are autobiographical and harmonize consistently with the events of Paul's life recorded in Acts. The theology of Galatians is the theology of Paul as taught in his other writings such as Romans.

The external evidence for Pauline authorship of Galatians is also convincing. In the second and third centuries Galatians was attributed to Paul and quoted by Irenaeus, Clement of Alexandria, and Origen. Even the heretics of that time, including Marcion, assumed it was written by Paul.

It must be concluded that no real doubt existed in the early church nor should any exist today as to the Pauline authorship of Galatians.

Original Readers. The Epistle of Galatians was addressed "to the churches in Galatia" (1:2). Where was "Galatia," and who were the "Galatians"? (cf. 3:1) This question is complicated by the fact that Galatia had two meanings when this epistle was written. First, it referred to the area in Asia Minor where the Gauls had settled after migrating from western Europe through Italy and Greece. The territory was limited to the north central and east central areas of Asia Minor and its principal cities were Ancyra, Pessinus, and Tavium. But in 25 B.C. this kingdom was converted to a Roman province, and territory was added to the south, including the cities of Antioch, Iconium, Lystra, and Derbe.

A debate has raged for centuries over whether Paul wrote his Galatian letter to

Christians living in northern or southern Galatia. The North Galatian theory held that Paul visited the geographical district of Galatia in the north and established churches there. This church-planting ministry would have taken place on Paul's second missionary journey after he left the southern Galatian region and before he came to Troas (cf. Acts 16:6-8). A second visit to the northern territory is apparently described in Acts 18:23.

The South Galatian theory was advanced by Sir William Ramsay. In this view the churches addressed in the epistle were those of Derbe, Lystra, Iconium, and (Pisidian) Antioch, cities Paul visited initially on his first missionary journey (cf. Acts 13-14). Thus while there is no account in Scripture of churches having been established in North Galatia, even on the second missionary journey, churches were established in South Galatia, according to Acts.

Other arguments which tend to favor the South Galatia theory are that the main roads from Paul's hometown of Tarsus pass directly through the cities of South, not North Galatia; the Judaizers were not likely to bypass the southern cities for the northern cities; a large Jewish element which could be addressed by the Judaizers lived in the southern cities; representatives of South Galatia accompanied the offering for the poor in Jerusalem but none were from North Galatia (cf. Acts 20:4); Barnabas who is mentioned but not introduced (cf. Gal. 2:1, 9, 13) would not have been known by the believers in the northern cities since he traveled with Paul only on the first journey. For these and other reasons many New Testament scholars now favor the view that Paul wrote the Galatian letter to Christians in the cities of South Galatia.

Time and Place of Writing. Those who identify the recipients of Galatians as the believers in the southern cities of Galatia generally consider that the epistle was written from Antioch of Syria in about A.D. 48 just before the Jerusalem Council (Acts 15). While some chronological problems remain with this view, it is perhaps the best of the available options. After the first missionary journey Paul and Barnabas returned to Antioch. Peter came down from Jerusalem to visit them, fellowshiped with them, and then with-drew from the Gentile Christians only to be publicly rebuked by Paul for his inconsistent behavior. Meanwhile, Judaizing false teachers had infiltrated the churches in Galatia, denying Paul's authority as an apostle and teaching that circumcision was necessary for salvation. Reacting quickly and vigorously to Peter's actions and the threatened lapse of the Galatians into legalism, Paul wrote this strong letter prior to attending the Jerusalem Council.

Purpose of the Epistle. The Judaizers in Galatia both discredited Paul and proclaimed a false gospel. It was necessary that Paul vindicate his apostleship and message, a task he undertook in the first two chapters. In this autobiographical section Paul demonstrated convincingly that his apostleship and his message came by revelation from the risen Christ. In chapters 3 and 4 Paul contended for the true doctrine of grace, that is, for justification by faith alone. Finally, to show that Christian liberty does not mean license the apostle, in chapters 5 and 6, taught that a Christian should live by the power of the Holy Spirit and that when he does he manifests in his life not the works of the flesh but the fruit of the Spirit.

Galatians was written to remedy a desperate situation, to call early Christians back from the Mosaic Law to grace, from legalism to faith. It is an emphatic statement of salvation by faith apart from works and is as relevant today as when it was originally penned.

OUTLINE

COMMENTARY

I. Introduction (1:1-10)

A. The salutation (1:1-5)

1:1. The opening of the Galatian epistle is both typical and atypical. Though the salutation includes the usual identification of author and recipient together with a customary greeting, the usual expression of thanksgiving and praise for believers is totally absent. Further, there is an abruptness about the opening words which plunges the reader immediately into one of Paul's major concerns, namely, that his apostolic credentials had been challenged. Though not one of the original Twelve, **Paul** claimed equality with them as **an apostle.** The word *apostolos* connotes authority and refers to a person who has a right to speak for God as His representative or delegate.

Paul's apostleship did not originate with men (it was **not from men**), that is, he was not appointed an apostle by any official body such as the leaders in Jerusalem or Antioch. Neither did his apostleship originate with any one man, however important (**nor by man**) not even Ananias, who assisted Paul in Damascus (cf. Acts 9:10-17), nor Barnabas, who played a strategic role in opening doors of ministry for Paul in both Jerusalem and Antioch (cf. Acts 9:27; 11:25-26). Rather, Paul made the bold claim that his call was of heavenly origin, from **God the Father** and the risen Lord **Jesus Christ.** This is the only direct mention of the resurrection of Christ in the epistle. It emphasizes the importance of that event to Paul's apostleship, for he was not called during the earthly ministry of the Lord but by the resurrected Christ.

1:2. Joining with Paul in the sending, though not the writing, of this letter were **all the brothers with** him. These were the apostle's fellow workers, perhaps Barnabas as well as the prophets and teachers with whom Paul ministered in Antioch (cf. Acts 13:1). Mentioning these colaborers emphasized the fact that the teachings of this epistle were not peculiar to Paul but were held in common with others.

The recipients of the letter were **the churches in Galatia.** (See map before Rom.) This was then a circular letter probably directed to the churches founded during the first missionary journey of Paul and located in Derbe, Lystra, Iconium, and (Pisidian) Antioch.

1:3. The traditional Greek and Hebrew forms of greeting, **grace and peace,** were always used by Paul in his salutations to express the hope that the believing readers might be sustained by daily portions of these blessings. "Grace and peace" find their source in **God our Father and the Lord Jesus Christ.** (See the chart, "Paul's Introductions to His Epistles" at Rom. 1:1-7.)

1:4-5. Paul concluded his salutation with a magnificent statement regarding the work of Christ on the cross and its delivering power, another major emphasis of this epistle. Christ **gave Himself for our sins** (cf. 1 Tim. 2:6; Titus 2:14; 1 Peter 3:18). His death was voluntary and final. It satisfied God's righteous demands against sinners, reconciled people to God, and provided for human redemption. One purpose of Christ's death is **to rescue us from the present evil age.** The gospel is an emancipating message. It delivers believing sinners from the power of the present world system through the power of the indwelling Christ just as certainly as it delivers them from eternal judgment to come. Was Paul hinting that the Old Testament Law, so strongly promoted by the Galatian legalizers, would be impotent to accomplish such great things?

In His redemptive work Christ accomplished **the will of . . . God** (Gal. 1:4c; cf. Heb. 10:7-10). Further, in that obedience the Savior brought **glory** to God (Gal. 1:5; cf. John 17:1). Redeemed saints will in addition give glory to God **forever** because of the redeeming work of Jesus Christ.

Thus Paul had already drawn the lines of battle by touching on two vital concerns. He had affirmed his own apostleship and had declared that the basis of man's salvation lies solely in the work of Christ and not in any human works.

B. The denunciation (1:6-10)

Conspicuous by its absence is Paul's usual expression of thanksgiving to God for his readers. Instead he vented his astonishment and anger over the Galatians' defection. When compared with the opening of 1 Corinthians this is even more striking, for despite the Corinthians' deep moral defection Paul nonetheless expressed commendation. But here in the face of theological departure he did not express thanks, thus emphasizing the more serious nature of doctrinal apostasy.

1:6-7. Paul's astonishment was over an almost inconceivable turn of events—the Galatian believers were in the process of turning away (**deserting,** *metatithesthe,* as in a military desertion) from the truth. Part of the apostle's amazement was because it was happening **so quickly** after his last visit to them, or so soon after the false teachers began their insidious work. The departure was not simply from a system of theology but from God Himself, **the One who** had **called** them **by the grace of Christ** (the dominant theme of the epistle). In exchange they were embracing **a different gospel,** one that was false. Paul insisted that a gospel of legalism which adds work to faith is not the same kind of gospel that he preached and by which they were saved. It was actually an attempt **to pervert the gospel of Christ.** And Paul was aware of the fact that at the very time he was writing this epistle the false teachers were at work troubling or **throwing** the Galatians **into confusion** (cf. Acts 15:24; 20:29-30).

1:8. To emphasize the fact that the true **gospel** of the grace of God cannot be changed, Paul first stated a hypothetical case. If he (a divinely called apostle) **or an angel** (a heavenly messenger) were to alter the gospel message—a highly improbable situation—then **let him be** accursed or **eternally condemned** (*anathema*).

1:9. In this verse Paul seemed to repeat himself, but he actually advanced his thought. Paul and Barnabas had given a warning of judgment when they had preached to the Galatians. Now Paul repeated it. A zealous champion of the purity of the gospel of grace, Paul said it again: **If anybody** were **preaching** a different **gospel** (which the false teachers were), he would come under God's eternal judgment. It is not difficult to understand why Paul reacted so strongly, because the Judaizers were impugning the Cross; for if works were necessary for salvation, then the work of Christ was not sufficient (cf. 2:21). Furthermore a great deal is at stake for lost people. When the gospel message is corrupted, the way of salvation is confused and people are in danger of being eternally lost.

1:10. Apparently the Judaizers had charged Paul with teaching freedom from the Law in order to curry the Gentiles' favor. But the tone of this letter, specifically the harsh language Paul had just used, was hardly calculated **to win the approval of men.** Men-pleasers simply do not hurl *anathemas* against those who proclaim false gospels. Indeed, if the apostle had wanted **to please men,** he would have remained a zealous Pharisee and promoter of the Law rather than becoming **a servant of Christ.** Elsewhere Paul affirmed his purpose to please God, not men (cf. 6:12; 1 Thes. 2:4).

II. Personal: A Defense of Paul's Authority (1:11–2:21)

Paul then took up in more detail the challenge to his authority as an apostle. Was he a self-appointed impostor? Arguing autobiographically, Paul declared that (a) he was an apostle before he met the other apostles; (b) when he did meet them he was received as an equal; (c) and he even found it necessary to rebuke Peter, the reputed chief apostle.

A. He was independent of the apostles (1:11-24)

1. THESIS: PAUL'S GOSPEL WAS A REVELATION (1:11-12)

1:11-12. First, Paul certified that the **gospel** did not originate with **man.** Man-made religions emphasize human merit and the necessity of human works for salvation. Paul's message did not. Second, the apostle declared that he **did not receive** the gospel from any human source. Though he heard Stephen preach and had personal contacts with Ananias and Barnabas, he was not indebted to them for his knowledge of spiritual truth. Third, Paul affirmed he did not receive the gospel he preached by means of some course of instruction. Even though that was the way the Galatians received the gospel (as Paul had instructed them), the apostle on the other hand **received it by revelation from Jesus Christ.** This was the highest authority. How then could the Galatians question his authority and message? And how did they dare deviate from this divinely revealed truth?

2. EVENTS BEFORE PAUL'S CONVERSION (1:13-14)

1:13-14. By appealing to his personal history Paul established beyond any doubt that he did not learn his gospel from men. Beginning with his preconversion life, he showed that his only relationship to the church was that of a fanatic persecutor of it. Standing before Herod Agrippa II, Paul summarized his frenzied oppression of Christians (cf. Acts 26:9-11). Coupled with this was the fact that he was also zealous to advance as a Pharisee **in Judaism.** He felt driven to excel over other **Jews** his **own age.** He loved the Law and was **zealous for the traditions of** his **fathers.** He no doubt spent much time studying the Law of Moses and the accompanying Rabbinical traditions. Thus who could accuse Paul of not being acquainted with the teachings of Judaism when he knew them better than the Judaizers?

3. EVENTS AT PAUL'S CONVERSION (1:15-16A)

1:15-16a. The contrast with the preceding (vv. 13-14) is striking and is occasioned by God's intervention in the life of Saul of Tarsus: **But . . . God.** Nowhere is this intervention more graphically described than in Acts 9. Here Paul simply enumerated three things God did for him. First, God **set** him **apart from**

birth. Paul knew that God had providentially set him apart from birth and that all his life to this point was a preparation for his ministry as a proclaimer of the gospel of God's grace. Second, God **called** Paul **by His grace.** This is a reference to the time of Paul's salvation. He responded to God's efficacious call and received Jesus Christ as Savior. In Romans (8:30) Paul gave the sequence of God's work in salvation: "Those He predestined, He also called; those He called, He also justified; those He justified, He also glorified." Third, God **was pleased to reveal His Son in** Paul. Blinded as he had been to the deity of Jesus Christ and thinking that the Nazarene was a fraud, God gave Paul an outward vision of Christ on the Damascus Road and later an inner revelation concerning the full significance of the person and work of the Savior. The purpose of this revelation was that Paul **might preach Him among the Gentiles.** The Book of Acts gives full account of Paul's ministry to the non-Jewish world on his missionary journeys. He became known as the apostle to the Gentiles (cf. Acts 9:15; 13:46-47; 26:20; Rom. 11:13; 15:16; Eph. 3:8; 1 Tim. 2:7). Thus Paul emphasized that both his conversion and his commission owed nothing to man but were of God. How else could such a transformation—from persecutor to preacher—be explained?

4. EVENTS AFTER PAUL'S CONVERSION (1:16B-24)

1:16b-17. Paul had emphasized that he did not receive his message from men before or at the time of his conversion. Now he affirmed that he was free from human influences afterward as well. Though Paul met other Christians after his conversion he did not **consult** them on doctrine. If he had been uncertain about the gospel, he could readily have gone **to Jerusalem** for a seminar with the apostles, but he did not. Rather he **went immediately into Arabia.** It is doubtful that he went there to evangelize but rather to be away from men and alone with the Lord for personal study, meditation, and to receive further revelation. This zealous student of the Law now pondered the meaning of his conversion and looked for the things concerning Christ in the Old Testament (cf. Luke 24:27). The product of these days in Arabia was the Christian theology that Paul explained in his epistle to the Romans.

The point of Paul's declaration is clear. He formed his theology not by consulting with others, but independently as he sought God's guidance.

1:18-20. Paul then reinforced his previous argument by asserting that he waited **three years** after his conversion to go **to Jerusalem,** time that was spent in Arabia and Damascus (v. 17). Would he have waited that long if he had needed theological instruction from the disciples? When he did go, it was **to get acquainted with Peter,** that is, it was a personal visit lasting only **15 days.** Paul then left because of a plot against his life (cf. Acts 9:29). Meanwhile Paul had had a meaningful time coming to know the noted apostle, but there is no suggestion that Peter gave him theological instruction or apostolic endorsement for his ministry. Of the rest of the apostles Paul met only **James, the Lord's brother,** a leader in the church in Jerusalem (cf. Acts 12:17). To stress the truth of what he had just said— no doubt in the face of a Judaizer's charge that he had misrepresented his relationship to the apostles—Paul put himself on oath, calling God to be his witness that he was telling the truth.

1:21-22. After his abbreviated visit in Jerusalem Paul worked for an extended time in **Syria and Cilicia,** which is why he **was personally unknown to the churches of Judea** (cf. Acts 9:30; 11:25). He was not commissioned for this ministry by the apostles, and because of the distance between him and Jerusalem he could not have been under their authority or subject to their oversight.

1:23-24. The churches in Judea by this time had almost forgotten Paul. The only **report** they had recently **heard** was that this one who had once **persecuted** the church was **now preaching the faith he once tried to destroy.** This would of course include the doctrine of justification by faith apart from circumcision or works. And in the face of this report the Judean believers **praised God because of** Paul. This was a telling blow to the false teachers. The Jewish Christians in Judea rejoiced in the same gospel the Judaizers sought to undermine.

B. He was recognized by the apostles (2:1-10)

While chapter 2 continues Paul's defense of his apostolic authority and the gospel he preached, he focused not on the source of his message but on its content. Further, whereas in chapter 1 he emphasized his independence from the other apostles, he now demonstrated that there was a basic unity between himself and them.

2:1. Much debate has centered on the question of the identification of this trip which Paul took to **Jerusalem** with **Barnabas,** a Jewish believer, and **Titus,** a Gentile believer. The Book of Acts mentions five Jerusalem visits made by Paul after his conversion: (1) the visit after he left Damascus (Acts 9:26-30; Gal. 1:18-20); (2) the famine visit (Acts 11:27-30); (3) the visit to attend the Jerusalem Council (Acts 15:1-30); (4) the visit at the end of the second missionary journey (Acts 18:22); (5) the final visit which resulted in Paul's Caesarean imprisonment (Acts 21:15–23:35). Scholars are divided primarily over whether Galatians 2:1 refers to the famine visit or to the Jerusalem Council visit. But in the context in which he is listing all contacts with human authorities, why would Paul omit reference to his second trip to Jerusalem? And if the reference is to the Council of Acts 15, why did not the apostle allude to its decrees? It seems this passage has the famine visit in view.

2:2. Paul went to Jerusalem on his second visit **in response to a revelation.** That is, he went because God directed him to, not because the Jerusalem leaders had summoned him or called him "on the carpet" for preaching to **the Gentiles.** The reference may well be to Agabus' prophecy of a famine which prompted Paul and Barnabas to go to Jerusalem on a relief mission (cf. Acts 11:27-30). Paul seized this opportunity to consult with the other apostles **privately** concerning the message he was preaching to the Gentiles. This does not mean Paul sought their approval of its truth and accuracy, for he had received the gospel from God by revelation. Rather, he wanted them to consider its relationship to the gospel they were proclaiming. But if the Jerusalem leaders insisted on circumcision and other requirements of the Law for Gentile converts, Paul's labor (**running**) among the Gentiles was **in vain.** It was not that the apostle had any doubts or misgivings about the gospel he had preached for 14 years (Gal. 2:1), but that he feared that his past and present ministry might be hindered or rendered of no effect by the Judaizers.

2:3-5. It now becomes apparent why Paul brought **Titus** along on this Jerusalem trip. He was a test case. Would the Jerusalem apostles force the rite of circumcision on a Gentile believer? Paul knew that both Jews and Gentiles are accepted by God through faith in Jesus Christ without any distinction and that the church should do the same. The apostle declared that this truth was affirmed in Jerusalem because Titus was **not . . . compelled to be circumcised, even though he was a Greek.** But this victory did not come easily. Pressure to have Titus circumcised was brought to bear by certain **false brothers** (cf. 2 Peter 2:1). No doubt these were Judaizers, whose chief slogan is found in Acts 15:1: "Unless you are circumsised according to the custom taught by Moses, you cannot be saved." These "false brothers" ("sham Christians," NEB) were like spies or fifth-column agents who penetrated to search out weak areas of enemy positions. In this case they **infiltrated** (*pareisēlthon*; lit., "sneaked in alongside," used only here and in Rom. 5:20) the **ranks,** that is, they intruded without invitation into the apostles' private conference. Their goals were twofold: first, **to spy on** (*kataskopēsai*, used only here in the NT) **the freedom we have in Christ.** With hostile intent they purposed to observe the apostles' freedom from the Mosaic Law and from the legalism it engenders. Second, they intended to **make** Christians **slaves.** They wanted to bring believers back into bondage, to enslave them to the Law's rules and ceremonies. Specifically they strongly insisted that Titus be circumcised. But Paul stood absolutely firm because **the truth of the gospel** was at stake for the Galatians, and the entire Christian church. To impose circumcision on Titus would be to deny that salvation was by faith alone and to affirm that in addition to faith there must be obedience to the Law for acceptance before God. Thus the basic issue of the gospel was involved and Paul would not deviate or yield **for a moment.**

2:6. Having completed his discussion of Titus, Paul resumed the narrative relating to his conference with the apostles in Jerusalem and declared that they **added nothing to** his **message.** They did not correct or modify Paul's message but recognized its divine source and affirmed its truth and completeness. But why did the apostle speak in what appears to be a derogatory manner about some of the Jerusalem leaders? In verse 2 he referred to them as "those who seemed to be leaders"; in verse 6 he described them as **those who seemed to be important**; and in verse 9 he finally named "James, Peter, and John" as "those reputed to be pillars." In view of the fact that Paul's purpose in this passage was to emphasize his unity with the apostles, it seems best to explain these allusions as stemming from the fact that the Judaizers, in order to disparage Paul, had made much of the Jerusalem leaders. While there may be irony in Paul's expressions, he declared that he was not awed by the past or present stations of James, Peter, and John. Indeed they endorsed Paul's message and received him as an equal.

2:7-9. Further, **James, Peter, and John** recognized that Paul had been divinely commissioned to preach **the gospel to the Gentiles, just as Peter** had **to the Jews.** Thus Paul jolted the Judaists by declaring that the leaders in Jerusalem approved of his mission to the Gentiles.

It should be noted that Peter and Paul did not preach two gospels, as might be inferred from the KJV rendering, "the gospel of the uncircumcision" and "the gospel of the circumcision." There was one gospel though it was preached by different apostles to two distinct groups of people. The reason the apostles concluded that Paul's commission was equal to Peter's was the fact that God gave success to both as they preached. This was sealed by James, Peter, and John in their extending to Paul **and Barnabas the right hand of fellowship.** This was a sign of agreement and trust and an indication to all present that they endorsed the division of labor whereby the Jerusalem apostles were appointed to evangelize the Jews and Paul was entrusted to carry the gospel **to the Gentiles.**

2:10. The only request from the leaders in Jerusalem was that Paul **remember the poor** which he affirmed he **was eager to do.** It had been concern for the poor which brought Paul to Jerusalem in order to bring them financial relief (cf. Acts 11:29-30). It was the same concern which motivated him on his third missionary journey to raise large welfare offerings for needy Christians in Jerusalem (cf. 1 Cor. 16:1-3). Such offerings would alleviate human suffering, but they would also demonstrate genuine concern on the part of Gentile Christians for Jewish Christians. This in turn would help promote unity and love among believers and help prevent the kinds of misunderstandings which were undermining the Galatian churches.

C. He rebuked the reputed chief of the apostles (2:11-21)

In this final historical incident Paul related how he found it necessary to oppose even Peter, the reputed chief of the apostles, for conduct which threatened to compromise the gospel. The contrast with the previous section is dramatic.

2:11. When Paul visited Jerusalem, Peter (and others) gave him "the right hand of fellowship"; but when **Peter** visited **Antioch,** Paul **opposed him to his face.** The time of Peter's trip to Antioch is not known. There is no reference to it in the Book of Acts, but perhaps the visit occurred soon after Paul, Barnabas, and Titus returned to Antioch from Jerusalem. At any rate Peter's conduct in Antioch produced a tense face-to-face confrontation between two Christian leaders. Paul felt compelled to rebuke and condemn Peter for his actions, thus defending the gospel and demonstrating again his own independence and equality as an apostle.

2:12. On arrival at Antioch, Peter found Jewish and Gentile Christians fellowshiping together at mealtimes without regard to Jewish dietary laws. Because of the vision Peter had received at the house of Simon the tanner (Acts 10:9-15, 28), he felt free **to eat with the Gentiles,** and did so on a regular basis. While it lasted, this was a beautiful demonstration of the unity of Jew and Gentile in Christ. **But** a breach occurred when some arrived from Jerusalem who were shocked at Peter's conduct. These emissaries **came from James** and belonged **to the circumcision** party, but it is doubtful that they had James' endorsement. Nonetheless Peter was influenced by their presence and slowly but surely **began to draw back and separate himself from the Gentiles.** The verb tenses (imperf.) indicate a gradual withdrawal, perhaps from one joint meal a day, and then two; or it may be that he began a meal with Gentiles but finished it with only Jewish Christians. By such actions Peter in effect was teaching that there were two bodies of Christ, Jewish and Gentile. And that was heresy. But why did Peter create this breach? Not because of any change in theology, but simply out of fear. Once, after preaching to Gentile Cornelius, Peter courageously defended himself before the Jerusalem leaders (cf. Acts 11:18); but this time he capitulated to some Jewish friends.

2:13. Like falling dominoes the defection of Peter brought the defection of **the other Jews** and finally **even Barnabas.** The pressure must have been great for Barnabas to succumb because he was from Cyprus, a Gentile center, and was involved in a missionary program with Paul to reach Gentiles with the gospel. All of them—Peter, the other Jewish Christians, and Barnabas—were guilty of **hypocrisy** because while confessing and teaching that they were one in Christ with Gentiles, they were denying this truth by their conduct.

2:14. The response of Paul was electric. What Peter had initiated created a public scandal and therefore deserved a public rebuke. Further, the defectors **were not acting** according to **the truth of the gospel,** that is, they were denying by their actions the truth that on the basis of Jesus Christ's death and resurrection Jews and Gentiles who believe are accepted equally by God. Paul therefore asked Peter before them all, "If you, who are a Jew, do not live like a Jew but like a Gentile, why on earth do you try to make Gentiles live like Jews?" (PH) It was a stinging rebuke. Peter's response is not recorded. He stood condemned. He was acting contrary to his own convictions, was betraying Christian liberty, and was casting a slur on fellow believers. Such behavior needed this severe reprimand.

2:15. But how far did the rebuke extend? Considerable discussion has centered on the question as to whether Paul's direct remarks to Peter were limited to verse 14 or whether, as in the NIV, they continued to the end of the chapter. While it is impossible to determine, it would seem that Paul uttered more than one sentence in reproving Peter. The remaining verses of the chapter develop, then, the inconsistency between Peter's behavior and his beliefs. At the same time they form a superb transition and introduction to chapters 3 and 4 in which Paul defended the key doctrine of justification by faith.

Paul's argument was addressed to those who were **Jews by birth,** including Peter and himself, who in spite of their superior advantages were saved by faith. Why then bind the Law on **Gentile sinners** (said in irony because of Peter's actions), who likewise were saved by faith in Christ?

2:16. In this verse, one of the most important in the epistle, the word *justified* occurs for the first time. It is a legal term, borrowed from the law courts and means "to declare righteous." Its opposite is "to condemn." But since people are condemned sinners and God is holy, how can people be justified? In answer, the apostle made a general declaration that negatively **man is not justified by observing the Law,** but positively, justification is **by faith in Jesus Christ.** This is a strong affirmation of Paul, Peter, and the rest—introduced by **We . . . know.** It is followed by a statement in which Paul explained that he had put this doctrine to the test and validated it in his own experience (v. 16b). Finally, in verse 16c the apostle reaffirmed that justification is by faith and not by works (cf. Gen. 15:6).

2:17-18. Paul's opponents argued, however, that since justification by faith eliminated the Law, it encouraged sinful living. A person could believe in Christ for salvation and then do as he pleased, having no need to do good works. Paul hotly denied the charge, especially noting that this made **Christ** the promoter of **sin.** On the contrary, if a believer would return to the Law after trusting Christ alone for salvation, that Law would only demonstrate that he was a sinner, **a lawbreaker.** Though Paul used the first person here, he clearly had in mind Peter, who by his act of withdrawing from

Gentile fellowship was returning to the Law.

2:19-20. Paul then distinguished himself from Peter, contrasting what he did with the Law with what Peter did with the Law. Paul described the transformation in a person who has come to God by faith in Christ in terms of a death and a resurrection. The concept is repeated in both verses and the reference in both cases is to a believer's union with Christ in His death and resurrection. First, Paul stated that **through the Law** he **died to the Law.** The Law demanded death for those who broke it, but Christ paid that death penalty for all sinners. Thus the Law killed Him and those joined to Him by faith, freeing them to be joined to another, to **live for God** (cf. Rom. 7:4).

In Galatians 2:20 Paul enlarged on the meaning of verse 19. He "died to the Law" because he was **crucified with Christ;** he was able "to live for God" because **Christ** lived in him. Basic to an understanding of this verse is the meaning of union with Christ. This doctrine is based on such passages as Romans 6:1-6 and 1 Corinthians 12:13, which explain that believers have been baptized by the Holy Spirit into Christ and into the church, the body of all true believers. Having been thus united to Christ, believers share in His death, burial, and resurrection. Paul could therefore write, **I have been** "crucified with Christ" (lit., "I have been and am now crucified with Christ"). This brought death to the Law. It also brought a change in regard to one's self: **and I no longer live.** The self-righteous, self-centered Saul died. Further, death with Christ ended Paul's enthronement of self; he yielded the throne of his life to Another, to Christ. But it was not in his own strength that Paul was able to live the Christian life; the living Christ Himself took up His abode in Paul's heart: Christ **lives in me.** Yet Christ does not operate automatically in a believer's life; it is a matter of living the new life **by faith in the Son of God.** It is then faith and not works or legal obedience that releases divine power to live a Christian life. This faith, stated Paul, builds on the sacrifice of Christ **who loved** us **and gave Himself for** us. In essence Paul affirmed, "If He loved me enough to give Himself for me, then He loves me enough to live out His life in me."

2:21. Summing up his case against Peter, Paul declared, **I do not set aside the grace of God.** The clear implication is that Peter and the others who followed him were setting aside God's grace. The essence of grace is for God to give people what they have not worked for (cf. Rom. 4:4). To insist on justification or sanctification by works is to nullify the grace of God. Further, such insistence on legal obedience also means **Christ died for nothing.** If righteousness comes by keeping the Law, the Cross was a futile gesture, the biggest mistake in the universe.

III. Doctrinal: A Defense of Justification by Faith (chaps. 3–4)

In the first two chapters of the epistle Paul established the divine origin of his apostleship and his message. Then he turned to the Galatians who were being urged to add works to faith, to keep the Mosaic Law in addition to placing faith in Christ as the grounds of acceptance before God. The Galatian Christians would receive, the Judaizers thought, a more complete salvation and a greater sanctification if they would obey the Law. But, Paul argued, to supplement the work of Christ is to supplant it. There can only be one way of salvation, and that is by faith in Christ alone.

A. Vindication of the doctrine (chap. 3)

1. BY THE EXPERIENCE OF THE GALATIANS (3:1-5)

3:1. Paul's tone was direct and severe as he remonstrated, **You foolish Galatians!** To embrace a doctrine which declared the death of Christ unnecessary was irrational (cf. 2:21). It would almost appear they had been **bewitched,** cast under some evil spell by a malign influence. For this they were, however, without excuse because the Savior had been **clearly portrayed** (*proegraphē;* lit., "to write for public reading" as with the posting of a public announcement) **as crucified** before them. Paul had vividly and graphically proclaimed the crucified Christ to the Galatians; yet their eyes had been diverted from the Cross to the Law. They were without excuse.

In order to demonstrate convincingly that faith alone is God's method of dealing, the apostle asked four questions.

3:2. (1) *How did you receive the Holy Spirit?* This rhetorical question pointed to the time of their conversions, when they received the Holy Spirit (cf. 4:6). Thus Paul did not question their salvation but challenged them to consider whether they were saved and received the Spirit by faith or on the basis of works. It was of course by faith, when they heard Paul preach the gospel. As an essentially Gentile church they did not possess the Mosaic Law anyway.

3:3. (2) *How will you be sanctified?* Presupposing the answer that the Galatians became Christians by faith, Paul asked if they were **so foolish** as to think they could begin the Christian life in one way (by faith) and move on to spiritual maturity in another (by works). This was what the Judaizers promoted (cf. 4:10; 5:2; 6:13), but the means of justification and sanctification were (and are) the same. There was no provision under the Law for the Holy Spirit to do a work of sanctification. The Galatian believers probably thought that keeping the old Law would aid them in their spiritual lives, but it would not.

3:4. (3) *Did you suffer in vain?* The third question looked back on the persecution the apostles and new believers experienced in the region of Galatia. As Paul and Barnabas retraced their steps at the end of the first missionary journey, they warned the Galatian converts that they would suffer as Christians (Acts 14:21-22). Persecution evidently soon followed, and Paul reminded them that if they turned from grace to Law they would brand their former position in error and would then have **suffered so much for nothing.** But the apostle was unwilling to believe that this was so.

3:5. (4) *On what basis did God perform miracles?* That **miracles** were performed among the Galatians by divine power was recorded in the Book of Acts (14:3, 8-11). It was clear, furthermore, that these supernatural works were not the result of the works of **the Law** but from the hearing that leads to faith. The Galatians did not know the Law, and Paul's message was that of justification by faith.

2. BY THE EXAMPLE OF ABRAHAM (3:6-9)

3:6. The Judaizers claimed to have the Old Testament on their side, especially looking to Moses as their teacher. But Paul went centuries farther back and said, **Consider Abraham.** How was he, the father of Jewish people, justified? The answer was simple and direct. Noting Genesis 15:6, Paul declared, **He believed God, and it was credited to him as righteousness.** Abraham's faith in God's ability to perform what He promised was accepted by God as righteousness and so the patriarch was justified—before he was circumcised (cf. Gen. 17:24). How then could the Judaizers insist that circumcision was essential to being accepted by God?

3:7-8. Striking a tremendous blow at the Judaizers, Paul linked the past with the present and declared that just as **Abraham** was saved **by faith** so were those who now claimed to be his **children** (*huioi;* lit., "sons"). Abraham and his spiritual descendants, both Jews and Gentiles, have all been declared righteous by faith. Moreover, this conclusion is in harmony with **the Scripture** which states that **all nations will be blessed through** Abraham (cf. Gen. 12:3). Thus the justification of uncircumcised Gentiles was anticipated in the universal aspect of the Abrahamic Covenant when God **announced the gospel** (lit., "the good news") . . . **to Abraham.** It should not be overlooked that Paul referred to Scripture speaking as though God were speaking, so it can rightly be affirmed that what the Bible says, God says. This and similar verses (e.g., John 10:35b; 2 Tim. 3:16; 2 Peter 1:20-21) provide important support for believing in the absolute and total inspiration and authority of Scripture.

3:9. The apostle concluded this phase of his argument by stating that though provision was made for "all nations" (v. 8), only **those who have faith** receive the blessing of justification. Thus Paul drew a distinction between God's provision and human appropriation.

3. BY THE EFFECT OF THE LAW (3:10-12)

Having established the fact that justification is by faith from the experiences of the Galatians and of Abraham, Paul then showed the illogic of reliance on the Law.

3:10-11. Contrary to what the Judaizers taught, the Law could not justify; it could only condemn. Paul quoted Deuteronomy 27:26 to show that **the Law** demanded perfection and that **a curse** was attached to failure to keep any part of it. The breaking of only one command even once brings a person under the curse; and since everybody fails at some point, all are under the curse. The proposition that a person can gain divine acceptance by human effort is therefore totally destroyed. Quoting the Old Testament again, Paul showed that even during the dispensation of **Law** legal obedience was not the basis for a **justified** standing **before God . . . because,** as the Prophet Habakkuk wrote, **The righteous will live by faith** (Hab. 2:4).

3:12. But perhaps **faith** and **the Law** could be combined; perhaps both are needed. Quoting again from the Old Testament Paul proved this to be scripturally impossible. Law and faith are mutually exclusive. The basic principle of the Law is found in Leviticus 18:5: **The man who does these things will live by them.** Only perfect performance could win divine approval under the Law, but since that was not achievable the Law could only condemn a person (cf. James 2:10) and cause him to cast himself on God in faith.

4. BY THE WORK OF CHRIST (3:13-14)

3:13. The positive side of Paul's argument emphasized that there is hope for all who have broken the Law and are therefore under its curse. That hope is not in man but in **Christ** who **redeemed us from the curse of the Law.** But how did Christ redeem (*exēgorasen,* lit., "buy out of slavery"; cf. 4:5; see chart "New Testament Words for Redemption" at Mark 10:45) man? The answer is **by becoming a curse for us.** This is a strong declaration of substitutionary redemption whereby Christ took the penalty of all guilty lawbreakers on Himself. Thus the "curse of the Law" was transferred from sinners to Christ, the sinless One (cf. 1 Peter 3:18), and He delivered people from it. The confirming quotation from Deuteronomy 21:23 refers to the fact that in Old Testament times criminals were executed (normally by stoning) and then displayed on a stake or post to show God's divine rejection. When Christ was

crucified, it was evidence He had come under the curse of God. The manner of His death was a great obstacle to faith for Jews until they realized the curse He bore was for them (cf. Isa. 53).

3:14. Two purposes for Christ's redemptive work are given, each introduced by the Greek conjunction *hina,* "in order that" (cf. 4:5): (1) **Gentiles** might receive **the blessing given to Abraham;** as already stated (3:8) this is a reference not to personal or national blessings but to the promised blessing of justification apart from works of the Law, available to all who believe; (2) all who thus believe **might receive the promise of the Spirit,** that is, the Holy Spirit, who was promised (cf. v. 2). Again the apostle emphasized that salvation and sanctification come **by faith,** not by works.

5. BY THE PERMANENCE OF FAITH (3:15-18)

3:15-16. Even if Paul's opponents admitted that Abraham was justified by faith, those Judaizers might have argued that the Law, coming at a later time, entirely changed the basis for achieving salvation. To refute this, Paul declared that just as a properly executed Roman **covenant** (or will) cannot arbitrarily be **set aside** or changed (probably reference to ancient Gr. law), so the promises of God are immutable. Further, **the promises . . . spoken to Abraham and to his seed** were not fulfilled before the giving of the Law. Rather, they found fulfillment in Christ and are in effect forever. The blessing of justification by faith is therefore permanent and could not be changed by the Law. The stress on **seed** (cf. Gen. 12:7; 13:15; 24:7), not **seeds,** was made simply to remind the readers that the faithful in Israel had always recognized that blessing would ultimately come through a single individual, the Messiah (cf. Gal. 3:19). And Matthew declared Christ to be *the* Son of Abraham and the true Heir to the First Covenant's promises (Matt. 1:1).

3:17-18. Finally, Paul applied the principle of the permanence of faith by affirming that a covenant made so long before could not possibly be altered by a later giving of the Law. **The Law** was given **430 years** after the promise. When did that lengthy period of time begin? Some have suggested it began with Abraham, in which case the 430 years included the Israelites' time of about 200 years in Canaan and about 200 years in Egypt. The Septuagint supports this view, but this conflicts with the clear statement in Exodus 12:40 that the Egyptian sojourn was 430 years. Another suggestion is that the period began with the confirming of the Abrahamic Covenant with Jacob (Gen. 35:9-12).

A third and perhaps best view is that the period began with the final confirmation of the covenant to Jacob (given in Gen. 46:1-4). Accordingly the 430 years went from the end of one era (the Age of Promise) to the beginning of another (the Age of Law). This seems to fit best with Exodus 12:40. (Gen. 15:13 and Acts 7:6, in referring to the sojourn in Egypt as 400 years, may be using rounded figures.)

During that long interval God blessed the patriarchs on the basis of faith alone, and the coming of the Law could not change this in any way. Additionally the Law could not alter God's dealing with Abraham on the basis of a promise because the two are fundamentally different in nature. They do not comingle; they cannot be combined. Instead, the Inheritance (i.e., justification by faith) was given by God as an unconditional gift to those who believe. Contrary to the claim of the Judaizers, obedience to the Law was not necessary to gain the inheritance. God's way of salvation has always been by grace through faith.

6. BY THE PURPOSE OF THE LAW (3:19-25)

3:19. An indignant Judaizer was sure to respond with objections to Paul's insistence that the Law could not give the Holy Spirit (vv. 1-5); could not bring justification (vv. 6-9); could not alter the permanence of faith (vv. 15-18); but does bring a curse (vv. 10-12). What, then, was the purpose of the Law? Why *was* a change made at Sinai? Paul answered by declaring the purpose and character of the Law. First, it was given because of transgressions, that is, the Law was given to be a means for checking sins. It served as a restrainer of sins by showing them to be transgressions of God's Law which would incur His wrath (cf. 1 Tim. 1:8-11). Second, the Law was temporary and served until the Seed (the Messiah; cf. Gal. 3:16) came, after which it was no longer needed. Third, the Law was inferior because of the manner of its bestowal. While God made promises to Abraham directly, the Law was established by a mediator. There were in fact two mediators, the angels representing God, and Moses representing the people.

3:20. This verse appears to be closely related to the last part of verse 19. A mediator implies a covenant between two parties both of whom have responsibilities, facts true of the Mosaic Covenant. On the other hand God is One, that is, the "promise" (v. 19) was unilateral and was given to man directly without a mediator, God alone having responsibility for fulfilling it.

3:21-22. Another question was raised: Is there conflict between the Law and the promises of God? "Perish the thought" (*mē genoito*), declared the apostle. God gave both the Law and promises, but for different purposes. And it was not the purpose of the Law to give life. Theoretically salvation could have come by the Law if people had been capable of keeping it perfectly, but they could not (Rom. 8:3-4). The life promised to those who sought to obey the Law refers to temporal blessing on earth (Deut. 8:1).

But if the Law is not opposed to the promises, if there is no conflict between them, how can their harmony be demonstrated? By recognizing that while the Law could not justify or give life, it did prepare the way for the gospel. What part then did Law play in this respect? It declared the whole world . . . a prisoner of sin. Referring perhaps to Psalm 143:1-2 or Deuteronomy 27:26, Paul declared that the whole world is trapped and under the dominion of sin (cf. Rom. 3:9, 23). When people recognize this and give up attempts to please God by their own works, the way is prepared for them to receive the promise of salvation through faith in Jesus Christ.

3:23-25. Continuing to comment on the purpose of the Law, Paul used two figures of speech, likening the Law to a prison and to a child-custodian relationship. Before this faith came means before the advent of faith in Jesus Christ (see v. 22). Justifying faith was operative in the Old Testament but faith in the person and work of Christ did not come until He was revealed. Before that, Israel was under the protective custody of the Law,

God thus shielding His people from the evil heathen rites surrounding them. Further, the Law served as a "tutor" (NASB). The word *paidagōgos* is difficult to render into English since there is no exact parallel to this position in modern society. Phillips suggests "a strict governess." The pedagogue here was not a "schoolmaster" (KJV) but a slave to whom a son was committed from age six or seven to puberty. These slaves were severe disciplinarians and were charged with guarding the children from the evils of society and giving them moral training. This was like the Law's function until **Christ** came and people could **be justified by faith** in Him. It is better then to understand that the Law did not *lead us to* Christ but that it was the disciplinarian *until* Christ came. Thus the reign of Law has ended for faith in Christ has delivered believers from the protective custody of the prison and the harsh discipline of the pedagogue.

7. BY THE BELIEVER'S PRESENT POSITION (3:26-29)

Paul's vindication of the doctrine of justification by faith reached a climax in this section as he contrasted the position of a justified sinner with what he had been under the Law. Three changes are noted.

3:26-27. First, **all** who believe in **Christ** become **sons of God.** The change in person from the first to the second **(you)** indicates that Paul turned from looking at Israel as a nation to address the Galatian believers. Under the dispensation of Law, as seen in verse 24, the Law was a discipling pedagogue, and those under its supervision were regarded as children. However, now that Christ had come, the Galatian believers were adult sons **through faith** and were no longer under a Jewish slave-guardian. Why should they seek to revert to their inferior status? The exalted position of "sons of God" is explained in verse 27 to involve a living union with Christ brought about by being **baptized into Christ.** This is the baptism of (or in) the Holy Spirit, which according to Paul (1 Cor. 12:12-13) joins all believers to Christ and unites them within the church, Christ's body. This union with Him means being **clothed with Christ.** In the Roman society when a youth came of age he was given a special toga which admitted him to the full rights of the family and state and indicated he was a grown-up son. So the Galatian believers had laid aside the old garments of the Law and had put on Christ's robe of righteousness which grants full acceptance before God. Who would want to don again the old clothing?

3:28. Second, believers **are all one in Christ Jesus.** Since all believers became one with each other, human distinctions lose their significance. None is spiritually superior over another, that is, a believing Jew is not more privileged before God than a believing Gentile (**Greek,** in contrast to **Jew,** suggests all Gentiles; cf. Col. 3:11); a believing **slave** does not rank higher than a believing **free** person; a believing man is not superior to a believing woman. Some Jewish men prayed, "I thank God that Thou hast not made me a Gentile, a slave, or a woman." Paul cut across these distinctions and stated that they do not exist in the body of Christ so far as spiritual privilege and position are concerned. Elsewhere, while affirming the coequality of man and woman in Christ, Paul did nonetheless make it clear that there is a headship of the man over the woman (cf. 1 Cor. 11:3) and that there are distinctions in the area of spiritual service (cf. 1 Tim. 2:12).

3:29. Third, believers in Christ **are Abraham's seed.** As Paul previously stated, **Christ** is *the* Seed of Abraham (vv. 16, 19); therefore being in Christ makes a believer a part of that seed and an **heir** of **the promise** to Abraham. Any discussion of the seed of Abraham must first take into account his natural seed, the descendants of Jacob in the 12 tribes. Within this natural seed there is a believing remnant of Jews who will one day inherit the Abrahamic promises directed specifically to them (cf. Rom. 9:6, 8). But there is also the spiritual seed of Abraham who are not Jews. These are the Gentiles who believe and become Abraham's spiritual seed. They inherit the promise of justification by faith as Paul explained earlier (cf. Gal. 3:6-9). To suggest, as amillenarians do, that Gentile believers inherit the national promises given to the believing Jewish remnant— that the church thus supplants Israel or is the "new Israel"—is to read into these verses what is not there.

B. Illustration of the doctrine (chap. 4)

1. A LEGAL ILLUSTRATION (4:1-7)

4:1-2. To illustrate the spiritual immaturity of those who lived under the Mosaic Law, Paul reminded the Galatian believers of certain characteristics of an **heir** as a minor **child** (*nēpios*, "infant, young child"; in contrast with *huios*, "son," in 3:7, 26). Though by birthright **he** owned **the whole estate**, nevertheless he was kept in subservience like **a slave** in that he enjoyed no freedom and could make no decisions. In fact the heir as a child was under **guardians** (*epitropous*, different from the *paidagōgos* in 3:24-25) who watched over his person, **and trustees** who protected his estate. This was true until he came of age as a son, an age that varied in the Jewish, Grecian, and Roman societies. Under Roman law the age of maturity for a child was **set by his father** and involved a ceremonial donning of the *toga virilis* and his formal acknowledgement as son and heir.

4:3. Paul applied the illustration in order to show the contrast between the believers' former position and what they now enjoyed. Formerly, in their state of spiritual immaturity (**when we were children,** *nēpioi*), they were like slaves. The scope of that **slavery** was described as being **under the basic principles** (*stoicheia*, "elements") **of the world.** Though often interpreted as a reference to the Mosaic Law, this view does not fit the Galatians, most of whom were Gentile pagans before conversion and were never under the Law. It seems better to understand the "basic principles" to refer to the elementary stages of religious experience, whether of Jews under the Law or Gentiles in bondage to heathen religions (cf. "weak and miserable principles" in v. 9, and "basic principles of this world" in Col. 2:20) Thus all were enslaved until Christ emancipated them.

4:4. But . . . God marks the fact that divine intervention brought hope and freedom to mankind. As a human father chose the time for his child to become an adult son, so the heavenly Father chose **the time** for the coming of Christ to make provision for people's transition from bondage under Law to spiritual sonship. This "time" was when the Roman civilization had brought peace and a road system which facilitated travel; when the

Grecian civilization provided a language which was adopted as the *lingua franca* of the empire; when the Jews had proclaimed monotheism and the messianic hope in the synagogues of the Mediterranean world. It was then that God **sent His Son,** the preexistent One, out of heaven and to earth on a mission. The "Son" was not only Deity; He was also humanity as the expression **born of a woman** indicates. The exclusive reference to His mother harmonizes with the doctrine of the virgin birth as taught in the Gospels (cf. Matt. 1:18). Further, Christ was **born under Law** as a Jew. He kept the Law perfectly, fulfilled it (cf. Matt. 5:17), and finally paid its curse (cf. Gal. 3:13).

4:5. The reasons "God sent His Son" are twofold (again both reasons are introduced by *hina*, "in order that"; cf. 3:14). First, He came **to redeem** (*exagorasē*) **those under Law.** This is not a redemption from the curse of the Law (as in 3:13), but from a slavery to the entire Mosaic system. The emphasis is not on the penalty of the Law as in 3:13, but on its bondage. Since Christ redeemed and set free those who were under the Law, why should Gentile converts now wish to be placed under it? Second, Christ's Incarnation and death secured for believers **the full rights of sons** ("the adoption of sons," KJV). All the enjoyments and privileges of a mature son in a family belong to those who have entered into the benefits of Christ's redemptive work.

4:6. God the Father not only "sent His Son"; He also sent **the Spirit.** Thus the full Trinity is involved in the work of salvation. The Holy Spirit is a gift of God to every believer because of sonship. No sons or daughters lack the Spirit. Further, He is present within each believer's heart to give evidence of that one's position in God's family. The Spirit moves the believer to pray to God, addressing Him as **Abba, Father** (cf. Rom. 8:15). The word "Abba" is the Aramaic word for "Father." It is the diminutive form used by small children in addressing their fathers. It is appropriate to see its similarity to the English word "Daddy." Used by Christ (cf. Mark 14:36), this familiar form indicates intimacy and trust as opposed to the formalism of legalism.

4:7. To conclude, Paul declared that the Galatians were **no longer** slaves, but were sons and heirs. The plural forms in verse 6 were replaced by the singular forms in verse 7 thus making the application to the reader direct and personal. In God's family, sonship carries with it heirship (cf. Rom. 8:17).

2. A PERSONAL PLEA (4:8-20)

The apostle turned from a formal argument to a personal appeal for the Galatians not to return to a slavery similar to their former bondage in paganism.

a. An appeal not to turn to legalism (4:8-11)

4:8-9. Prior to conversion the Galatians, in their ignorance of the one true **God,** were in bondage to false **gods** such as Zeus and Hermes (cf. Acts 14:11-13). But a great change took place and they came to **know God** (salvation from the perspective of man), **or to be known by God** (salvation from God's perspective). Yet having come to know (*gnontes,* from *ginōskō,* lit., "to know intimately and on a personal level") the true God, the Galatians were **turning back.** Paul was amazed and dismayed. Did they understand that they would be going back to a state of religious slavery? Was this their desire? If so, why would they be attracted to a system that was **weak** (it could not justify or energize for godly living) **and miserable** (it could not provide an inheritance). The **principles** (*stoicheia*) of that system are "of the world," as Paul had already said in verse 3.

4:10. Under the influence of the Judaizers the Galatians had at least begun to observe the Mosaic calendar. They kept **special days** (weekly sabbaths), **and months** (new moons), **and seasons** (seasonal festivals such as Passover, Pentecost, and Tabernacles), **and years** (sabbatical and jubilee years). (Cf. Col. 2:16.) They observed these special times, thinking that they would thereby gain additional merit before God. But Paul had already made it clear that works could not be added to faith as grounds for either justification or sanctification.

4:11. Reflecting concern for the Galatians, Paul expressed the **fear** that his **efforts** (*kekopiaka,* lit., "I have labored to the point of exhaustion") would be **wasted** (*eikē,* "in vain"; cf. the same word rendered "for nothing" in 3:4, "Have you suffered so much for nothing?") if their

attachment to legalistic practices continued. The apostle's words disclosed his strong antipathy toward legalistic religion.

b. An appeal to remember their relationship (4:12-16)

4:12. Intensifying his appeal, Paul challenged the Galatians, **Become like me, for I became like you,** that is, "Become free from the Law as I am, for after my conversion I became like the Gentiles, no longer living under the Law." The irony, however, was that the Galatian Gentiles were putting themselves under the Law *after* their conversions.

4:13-14. The last clause of verse 12 belongs with these and the following verses in which Paul related how he was received by the Galatians on his first visit to them (cf. Acts 13–14). At that time he labored under the handicap of **an illness** but remained until he had **preached the gospel to** them. Whatever his infirmity, the Galatians **did not treat** Paul **with contempt or scorn** as a weak messenger but rather received him as one would receive **an angel** or even **Christ Jesus Himself.**

4:15-16. They had received Paul with **joy,** congratulating themselves that the apostle had preached in their midst. Their appreciation knew no limits; they would even have made the sacrifice of their **eyes** for Paul. While some think this is an indication that Paul had a disease of the eyes (his "thorn" in his "flesh," 2 Cor. 12:7), the evidence is not conclusive. This may simply be a bold figure of speech to convey the high esteem the Galatians had had for the apostle—they would have **given** him their most precious possession.

But that had all changed. They no longer contemplated his presence among them with "joy." Rather, they now acted as though he had **become** their **enemy,** for the simple reason that he had been **telling** them **the truth.** How fickle were these Galatians! They were turning against the Lord, the gospel of grace, and the messenger who brought them the news of justification by faith.

c. An appeal to consider Paul's attitude toward them (4:17-20)

4:17-18. While Paul's attitude toward the Galatians was guileless, the legalists had improper motives. The apostle spoke the truth (cf. v. 16); the Judaizers used flattery. They wanted **to alienate** (*ekkleisai*, lit., "to lock out") the Galatians from Paul and his teaching so that they would be shut up instead to the false teachers and their influence. In an interesting double use of the verb "be zealous" Paul said that the Judaizers were **zealous to win . . . over** the Galatians so that the latter would **be zealous for** the Judaizers! Acknowledging that it was good for anyone to be sought after, Paul nonetheless insisted that the intention must be honorable, but in the case of the Judaizers it was not.

4:19-20. The apostle, on the other hand, had always had good motives regarding the Galatians. Addressing them tenderly as **my dear children** (*tekna mou*, an expression found only here in Paul's epistles), Paul compared himself to a mother in the throes of birth pangs. He had experienced this once for their salvation; he was in travail **again** for their deliverance from false teachers.

But a sudden change in metaphors occurred with the expression **until Christ is formed in you.** Paul longed for these believers to be transformed into (*morphōthē*, lit., "take on the form of"; cf. *morphē* in Phil. 2:6-7) the image of Christ. This expression describes the Christian life as a kind of reincarnation of Christ in a believer's life. This is in fact God's ideal and purpose—for Christ to live His life in and then through each believer (cf. Gal. 2:20). Yet the apostle was **perplexed about** the Galatians because he felt their spiritual development was being arrested. He had a deep desire to be **with** them so that he could speak gently, though firmly, concerning his grave concerns.

3. A BIBLICAL ILLUSTRATION (4:21-31)

In a masterful stroke the apostle turned to a scriptural illustration to conclude his theological defense of justification by faith. An Old Testament story from the life of Abraham enabled Paul to review what he had already declared about contrasts between the Mosaic Law and grace, between works and faith. It also provided an opportunity for him to verbalize the pointed charge to the Galatians that they should cast out the legalizers (cf. v. 30).

a. The historical facts (4:21-23)

4:21. The Galatians had not yet submitted to the bondage of **the Law** but they desired to. Paul desperately wanted to stop them and turn them back to a life under grace. As a transition to what would immediately follow, he challenged the Galatians to be **aware of** or to understand what the Law really said.

4:22. By turning again to **Abraham** (Gen., as one of the Books of Moses, was considered a part of the Law) Paul was appealing to the founder of the Jewish nation from whose physical descent the Jews traced their blessings. John the Baptist and Jesus declared that physical descent from Abraham was not enough, however, to guarantee spiritual blessing (cf. Matt. 3:9; John 8:37-44). Paul reminded his readers that Abraham **had two sons** (those born later are not important to his illustration), and that they should consider which of the two they were most like. One son, Isaac, was born of Sarah, **the free woman;** the other, Ishmael, was born of Hagar, **the slave woman.** According to ancient law and custom the status of a mother affected the status of her son.

4:23. A second contrast concerned the manner in which the sons were conceived. Ishmael **was born in the ordinary way,** that is, in the course of nature and requiring no miracle and no promise of God. Isaac, on the other hand, **was born as the result of a promise.** Abraham and Sarah were beyond the age of childbearing, but God miraculously fulfilled His promise in bringing life out of the deadness of Sarah's womb (cf. Rom. 4:18-21).

b. The allegorical interpretation (4:24-27)

In order to emphasize the contrast between Law and grace Paul next used the historical events above as an allegory, that is, he treated those two mothers figuratively (*allēgoroumena*). He did not in any sense deny the literal meaning of the story of Abraham, but he declared that that story, especially the matters relating to the conception of the two sons, had an additional meaning. Thus he compared the narrative to the conflict between Judaism and Christianity.

(This "allegorizing" is a far cry from the practice of "allegorical interpretation"—followed by Origen, Augustine, and many others down through the ages and into the present day—in which the historical facts are relegated to a lower, less significant level and fanciful, hidden meanings unrelated to the text, are considered vastly more important.)

4:24. First, the apostle pointed to **two covenants.** One, the Mosaic, had its origin at **Mount Sinai.** Those under this legal covenant were **slaves.** As **Hagar** brought forth a slave, so does the Law. At this point the reader is expected to understand and supply the implicit reference to the Abrahamic Covenant, a gracious system represented by Sarah which through its messianic promise brought forth children who are free.

4:25-26. Next, Paul pointed to two Jerusalems. **Hagar** also stood for the first-century **city of Jerusalem,** a city enslaved to Rome and **in slavery** to the Law. Sarah, on the other hand, corresponded to the **Jerusalem . . . above,** the **mother** of all the children of grace. This heavenly city, which one day will come to earth (cf. Rev. 21:2), is now the "city of the living God" (cf. Heb. 12:22), the home of departed believers of all ages.

4:27. The quotation from Isaiah 54:1 prophesied the changing fortunes of Israel, which Paul applied to Sarah's history. Israel before her Babylonian Captivity was likened to a woman with **a husband.** The **barren woman** was Israel in Captivity. The woman bearing **more . . . children** may have pictured Israel restored to the land after the Exile, but more particularly it portrays her millennial blessings. Paul applied this passage (he did not claim it was fulfilled) in this context to Sarah, who though previously barren, was later blessed with a child, and who would ultimately enjoy a greater progeny than Hagar.

c. The personal application (4:28-31)

In applying the truth from the biblical illustration, Paul made three comparisons.

4:28. First, Paul compared the birth of **Isaac** to that of Christians. As "Isaac" experienced a supernatural birth and was a child by means of a promise, so each believer experiences a supernatural birth (John 3:3, 5) and is a recipient of the promise of salvation (Gal. 3:9, 22, 29). As **children of promise** Christians are in a

distinct category and should not live as children of bondage.

4:29. Second, the apostle compared Ishmael's persecution of Isaac to the false teachers' opposition to believers. Abraham celebrated the weaning of Isaac with a banquet. On that occasion Ishmael mocked Isaac, laughing derisively at the younger boy, since Ishmael was the elder son and assumed he would be heir to his father's estate (cf. Gen. 21:8-9). That early animosity has been perpetuated in the two peoples which descended from the two sons of Abraham and is seen in the current Arab-Israel tensions. Paul likened the Judaizers to Ishmael as those who were born out of legalistic self-effort; he charged that they continued to persecute the true believers who were **born by the power of the Spirit.** With few exceptions Paul's persecution came from the Jews, the people in bondage to the Law.

4:30. Third, Paul compared the action of Abraham to the obligation of the Galatians. When Sarah observed Ishmael mocking Isaac, she asked Abraham to expel **the slave woman and her son** lest Ishmael become a joint heir with Isaac. And God granted Sarah's request (cf. Gen. 21:10, 12). This reminded the readers that Law observance brought no **inheritance** in the family of God, and it also charged them to excommunicate the Judaizers and those who accepted their false doctrines. A fundamental incompatibility remains between Law and grace, between a religion based on works and a religion based on faith.

4:31. In conclusion, Paul affirmed that he and the Galatian believers were **not children of the slave woman** who was driven away and was denied a share in the inheritance. Rather all believers are children **of the free woman,** "heirs of God and co-heirs with Christ" (Rom. 8:17).

IV. Practical: A Defense of Christian Liberty (5:1–6:10)

Having defended both his authority as an apostle and the doctrine of justification by faith, Paul turned to defend the life of Christian freedom. Would the apostle's teaching lead the Galatians into lawlessness or into godliness? The Christian life is described as a life apart from Law, a life apart from license, a life according to the Spirit, and a life of service.

A. A life apart from Law (5:1-12)

1. TURNING TO LAW RUINS GRACE (5:1-2)

5:1. This verse summarizes chapter 4, where the theme is bondage and freedom. It also serves to introduce chapter 5. Paul declared that **Christ** was the great Liberator who **set** believers **free** from bondage. The apostle then appealed to the Galatians to **stand firm** (cf. 1 Cor. 16:13; Phil. 1:27; 4:1; 1 Thes. 3:8; 2 Thes. 2:15) in that liberty, for having been delivered from **slavery** to heathenism, they were in danger of becoming entangled in slavery to the Mosaic Law.

5:2. Taking up a prime example of such entanglement, namely circumcision, Paul issued a strong warning to the Galatians who were considering submitting to that rite. If they did, and were thereby seeking righteousness by works, Paul declared that **Christ will be of no value to you at all.** It is not that the apostle condemned circumcision in itself, for he had Timothy circumcised (in Galatia) so that the young man would have a wider ministry (Acts 16:1-3). But Paul was strongly opposed to the Judaistic theology which insisted that circumcision was necessary for salvation. Anyone who was circumcised for that reason added works to faith and demonstrated that he had not exercised saving faith in Christ.

2. TURNING TO LAW MAKES MAN A DEBTOR (5:3)

5:3. In addition to the fact that turning to the Law ruins grace, it also creates an entirely new obligation: a person **is obligated to obey the whole Law.** The Law is a unit, and if a person puts himself under any part of it for justification, he is a "debtor" (KJV) to the entire code with its requirements and its curse (cf. 3:10; James 2:10).

3. TURNING TO LAW IS TO FALL AWAY FROM GRACE (5:4-6)

5:4. Turning to the Law and accepting circumcision as a meritorious work has further dire implications which the Galatians were called on to consider. Anyone seeking justification **by Law** has **been alienated** (*katērgēthēte*) **from Christ,** that is, such a person would not be living in a sphere where Christ was operative. The KJV has a helpful rendering, "Christ is become of no effect unto you." In addition, said Paul, they would **have fallen away from grace.** The issue here is not the possible loss of salvation, for "grace" is referred to not as salvation itself but as a method of salvation (cf. 2:21 where "a Law" route is mentioned as an unworkable way to come to Christ). If the Galatians accepted circumcision as necessary for salvation, they would be leaving the grace system for the Mosaic Law system. The same error is repeated today when a believer leaves a church that emphasizes salvation by grace through faith and joins one which teaches that salvation depends on repentance, confession, faith, baptism, and church membership.

5:5. In contrast with legalists, true believers **by faith** (not works) **eagerly await** (*apekdechometha;* used seven times in the NT of the return of Christ: Rom. 8:19, 23, 25; 1 Cor. 1:7; Gal. 5:5; Phil. 3:20; Heb. 9:28) the consummation of their salvation (cf. Rom. 8:18-25). Then **the righteousness for which we hope** will be fully realized (cf. 1 Peter 1:3-4, 13). At the coming of Christ believers will be completely conformed to all the requirements of God's will. The inward and forensic righteousness which began at justification will be transformed into an outward righteousness at glorification. God will then publicly acknowledge all believers' full acceptability with Him.

5:6. For those **in Christ Jesus,** the true sphere of salvation, **neither circumcision nor** the lack of it is of any significance (cf. 3:28; 6:15). What matters **is faith expressing itself through love** (cf. 5:13). Though salvation is by faith apart from works, faith that is genuine does work itself out "through love" (cf. Eph. 2:10; James 2:14-18).

4. TURNING TO LAW HINDERS THE PROGRESS OF BELIEVERS (5:7-10)

5:7. Employing a metaphor he was fond of, Paul described the Galatians' Christian experience as a **race** (cf. 1 Cor. 9:24-26; 2 Tim. 4:7). They had begun their race well, but someone had **cut in on** them, causing them to break stride and stumble. Though many false teachers were disturbing the Galatians, the singular pronoun (**who**) indicates the leader of the Judaizers was in view here. The result was that the believers were no longer **obeying the truth,** but were attempting to complete the race by legalistic self-effort rather than by faith.

5:8-10. Such false teaching as the Galatians were beginning to embrace did not originate in the God who called them (cf. 1:6). He called them by and into grace. They were now being seduced by other voices into following a false gospel. And lest someone would feel that the apostle was making too much of the problem, he quoted a proverb (5:9) to the effect that false teaching, like **yeast,** spreads and permeates. Its converts may have been few but the believers must be on guard lest the error affect the entire church. Paul's point may also have been that one apparently small deviation from the truth could destroy the entire system. If circumcision, for example, were made necessary for salvation, the whole grace system would fall. But Paul was optimistic about the outcome. He was **confident** the Galatians would share his views and that the leading false teacher, whose identity was unknown to Paul, would suffer his due judgment.

5. TURNING TO LAW REMOVES THE OFFENSE OF THE CROSS (5:11-12)

5:11. Apparently Paul was charged with **still preaching circumcision.** Certainly before his conversion he zealously proclaimed circumcision and the Law, and it is easy to see how the apostle's attitude could be interpreted as being in favor of circumcision. Paul countered with a simple question: How is it that he was **still being persecuted** by Judaizers if he preached the same message they did? If Paul were preaching circumcision, **the offense** (*skandalon,* "stumbling block"; cf. 1 Cor. 1:23) **of the Cross** would have ceased to exist in his ministry. But it had not because people still found the gospel message, which proclaims man's total inability to contribute anything to his salvation, offensive. Thus the Cross marked the end of the Law system and rendered circumcision and obedience to the Mosaic Law unnecessary.

5:12. Speaking out of deep concern for the gospel of the grace of God, Paul uttered a strong expression. He wished that the Judaizers, who were so enthusiastic about circumcision, **would go the whole way** and castrate **themselves,** as did the pagan priests of the cult of Cybele in Asia Minor. Perhaps the resulting physical impotence pictured Paul's desire that they also be unable to produce new converts. While circumcision had once been the sign of the covenant in Israel, it now had no more religious meaning than any other ritual of cutting and marking practiced by ancient pagans.

B. A life apart from license (5:13-15)

5:13-14. In verse 1 Paul spoke of the Christian's freedom and warned against the danger of lapsing into slavery. Here the apostle again reminded believers of their freedom in Christ and warned against its being converted into license. Specifically he charged the Galatians not to use their liberty as "a base of operation" for sin to gain a foothold. Rather than liberty being used for lust, the real goal should be **love.** Rather than being in bondage to the Law or to **the sinful nature,** the Galatians were to be in bondage to **one another.** ("Sinful nature" is an appropriate trans. of the Gr. *sarx,* used by Paul in that sense seven times in Gal. 5:13, 16-17 [thrice], 19, 24; 6:8.)

Having discouraged two forms of slavery as burdensome and terrible, he commended another form that was beneficial—a slavery of mutual love. In support, Paul quoted Leviticus 19:18 and stated that **the entire Law** was summarized in this **single command** to **love** their neighbors. Jesus affirmed the same truth (Matt. 22:39; Luke 10:25-28). But Paul also wanted to show that Christian love is the "fulfillment" or "the carrying out" of the Law. The apostle developed this point in Romans 13:8-10.

5:15. That such love needed to be mutually expressed in the Galatian churches is made clear here. As a result of the inroads of the false teachers the church was divided and engaged in bitter strife. The followers of the legalists and those who remained steadfast were **biting and devouring each other.** This was far from the biblical ideal of believers dwelling together in a loving unity, and threatened the churches with destruction, that is, the loss of their individual and corporate testimonies.

C. A life according to the Spirit (5:16-26)

1. THE PROMISE OF VICTORY OVER SIN (5:16-18)

5:16. The answer to the abuses described in the previous verse is to **live by the Spirit.** The verb *peripateite* is a present imperative and is literally translated, "keep on walking." As a believer walks through life he should depend on the indwelling Holy Spirit for guidance and power. But the Spirit does not operate automatically in a believer's heart. He waits to be depended on. When a Christian does yield to the Spirit's control, the promise is that he will not in anywise (the double negative *ou mē* is emphatic) **gratify** (*telesēte*, "complete, fulfill" in outward action) **the desires of the sinful nature.** Thus, while no believer will ever be entirely free in this life from the evil desires that stem from his fallen human nature, he need not capitulate to them, but may experience victory by the Spirit's help.

5:17. Paul next explained the need for a life that is controlled and energized by **the Spirit.** The explanation is found in the fact that each Christian has two natures, a **sinful nature** received at birth, inherited from fallen Adam, and a new nature received at regeneration when said Christian became a participant in the divine nature (cf. 2 Peter 1:4). Both natures have desires, the one for evil and the other for holiness. Thus **they are in conflict with each other,** and the result can be that they keep a believer from doing what he otherwise would. In other words the Holy Spirit blocks, when He is allowed to do so, the evil cravings of the flesh. (Some hold the view that each believer *is* a new person, still possessing the fallen human nature, but not having a new nature. Others prefer to define "nature" as capacity, the old nature being that capacity to serve sin and self and the new nature the capacity to serve God and righteousness.)

5:18. In summary, Paul emphasized that a godly life is not lived **under** the rules of the **Law** but is a life **led by the Spirit.** It was important for the Galatians to know that just as justification is not possible by works so sanctification cannot be achieved by human effort. This of course does not mean that a Christian is totally passive in either case for the response of faith is necessary—faith in Christ to save and in the Holy Spirit to sanctify.

2. THE PERIL TO VICTORY OVER SIN (5:19-21)

Since a Christian has the same sinful nature he possessed before salvation, he may fall prey to the sins that nature produces if he does not live by means of the Spirit.

5:19. The apostle declared that the sins of the flesh **are obvious,** meaning either, as some suggest, that they are public and cannot be hidden, or better, since some are private sins, that they originate with **the sinful nature** and not with the new nature indwelt by the Holy Spirit. The listed sins are commonly seen to fall into four categories. First, three sexual sins are mentioned. **Sexual immorality** (*porneia*) is often translated "fornication." From this word comes the term "pornography." *Porneia* refers to any and all forms of illicit sexual relationships. **Impurity** (*akatharsia*) is a broad term referring to moral uncleanness in thought, word, and deed (cf. Eph. 5:3-4). **Debauchery** (*aselgeia*) connotes an open, shameless, brazen display of these evils (cf. 2 Cor. 12:21 where the same words occur; *aselgeia* is included in Rom. 13:13).

5:20. Following the sexual sins, Paul cited two religious sins. **Idolatry** involved the worship of pagan gods by bowing to idols, and because of its mention just after the listing of sexual sins it probably includes the male and female prostitution so often a part of heathen religion. **Witchcraft** is the translation of the Greek word *pharmakeia* from which the term "pharmacy" comes. In ancient times the worship of evil powers was accompanied by the use of drugs to create trances. This vice will also be prominent in the Tribulation period (cf. Rev. 9:21; 18:23).

Eight societal evils are then listed (the last one in Gal. 5:21). **Hatred** (*echthrai*) is in the plural form, denoting primarily a feeling of enmity between groups. **Discord** (*eris*) is the natural result of "hatred" and no doubt a problem in the Galatian church. **Jealousy** (*zēlos*) refers not to the godly form but to the sinful and self-centered type. (These two words, *eris* and *zelos*, are also listed in Rom. 13:13.) **Fits of rage** (*thymoi*) or outbursts of temper, often come as a final eruption of smoldering jealousy. **Selfish ambition** (*eritheiai*) is a self-aggrandizing attitude which shows itself in working to get ahead at other's expense (cf. Phil. 2:3). **Dissensions** (*dichostasiai*) and **factions** (*haireseis*) describe what happens when people quarrel over issues or personalities, causing hurtful divisions.

5:21. Envy (*phthonoi*) is an evil feeling, a wrongful desire to possess what belongs to someone else. Thus the sinful nature is seen to be responsible for the breakdown of interpersonal relationships in homes, churches, and in public society.

Two sins associated with alcohol fall in a fourth category of evils. **Drunkenness** (*methai*) refers to excessive use of strong drink by individuals, and **orgies** (*kōmoi*) probably refers to the drunken carousings commonly associated with such things as the worship of Bacchus, the god of wine. Finally, to show that this long list was only representative and not exhaustive, Paul added the words **and the like.**

The apostle then solemnly warned the Galatians, as he had done when he was in their midst, that **those who live like this,** who habitually indulge in these fleshly sins **will not inherit the** future **kingdom of God.** This does not say that a Christian loses his salvation if he lapses into a sin of the flesh, but that a person who lives continually on such a level of moral corruption gives evidence of not being a child of God.

3. THE POWER FOR VICTORY OVER SIN
(5:22-23)

5:22-23. There is a pointed contrast here. As verse 16 indicated, there is no need for a believer to display the works of the flesh. Rather, by the Spirit's power he can manifest the nine graces that are now listed. It is important to observe that **the fruit** here described is not produced by a believer, but by **the** Holy **Spirit** working through a Christian who is in vital union with Christ (cf. John 15:1-8). The word "fruit" is singular, indicating that these qualities constitute a unity, all of which should be found in a believer who lives under the control of the Spirit. In an ultimate sense this "fruit" is simply the life of Christ lived out in a Christian. It also points to the method whereby Christ is formed in a believer (cf. 2 Cor. 3:18; Phil. 1:21).

The first three virtues are habits of mind which find their source in God. **Love** (*agapē*) is listed first because it is the foundation of the other graces. God is love and loves the world (cf. 1 John 4:8; John 3:16). Such self-sacrificing love that sent Christ to die for sinners is the kind of love that believers who are Spirit-controlled manifest. **Joy** (*chara*) is a deep and abiding inner rejoicing which was promised to those who abide in Christ (cf. John 15:11). It does not depend on circumstances because it rests in God's sovereign control of all things (cf. Rom. 8:28). **Peace** (*eirēnē*) is again a gift of Christ (cf. John 14:27). It is an inner repose and quietness, even in the face of adverse circumstances; it defies human understanding (cf. Phil. 4:7).

The second triad reaches out to others, fortified by love, joy, and peace. **Patience** (*makrothymia*) is the quality of forbearance under provocation (cf. 2 Cor. 6:6; Col. 1:11; 3:12). It entertains no thoughts of retaliation even when wrongfully treated. **Kindness** (*chrēstotēs*) is benevolence in action such as God demonstrated toward men. Since God is kind toward sinners (cf. Rom. 2:4; Eph. 2:7) a Christian should display the same virtue (cf. 2 Cor. 6:6; Col. 3:12). **Goodness** (*agathōsynē*) may be thought of both as an uprightness of soul and as an action reaching out to others to do good even when it is not deserved.

The final three graces guide the general conduct of a believer who is led by the Spirit. **Faithfulness** (*pistis*) is the quality which renders a person trustworthy or reliable, like the faithful servant in Luke 16:10-12. **Gentleness** (*prautēs*) marks a person who is submissive to God's Word (cf. James 1:21) and who is considerate of others when discipline is needed (cf. "gently" in Gal. 6:1; 2 Tim. 2:25; "gentle" in 1 Cor. 4:21; Eph. 4:2; "gentleness" in Col. 3:12; 1 Peter 3:16). **Self-control** (*enkrateia*; this noun is used in the NT only here and in Acts 24:25; 2 Peter 1:6) denotes self-mastery and no doubt primarily relates to curbing the fleshly impulses just described. Such a quality is impossible to attain apart from the power of God's Spirit (cf. Gal. 5:16). As a final summary statement Paul affirmed that there are no prohibitions (lit., **there is** not a **law**) **against such** virtues. In a *litotes* (understatement) he asserted that obviously no one would make laws against people who practice such things.

4. THE PROVISION FOR VICTORY OVER SIN (5:24-26)

5:24. Paul next explained that believers (lit., "those who are of Christ Jesus") need not be responsive to **the sinful nature** because they **have crucified** it. This does not refer to self-crucifixion or self-mortification. Rather, it refers to the fact that by means of the baptism of the Holy Spirit, Christians were identified with Christ in His death and resurrection. Paul declared that this had been his experience (cf. 2:20) and that of all believers (cf. Rom. 6:1-6; Col. 2:11; 3:9). While co-crucifixion took place potentially at the cross, it becomes effective for believers when they are converted. This does not mean that their sin nature is then eradicated or even rendered inactive but that it has been judged, a fact believers should reckon to be true (cf. Rom. 6:11-12). So victory over the sinful nature's **passions and desires** has been provided by Christ in His death. Faith must continually lay hold of this truth or a believer will be tempted to try to secure victory by self-effort.

5:25-26. Again Paul reminded the Galatians that in addition to a divine judgment of the sinful nature there is a divine enablement in the person of the Holy Spirit. He made the believer alive by regeneration (cf. John 3:5 6), so each believer is exhorted to **keep in step** (*stoichōmen*, trans. "follow" in Gal. 6:16) **with the Spirit.** Step by step one's Christian walk should conform to the Spirit's direction and enablement, lest believers **become conceited, provoking and envying each other.** The latter traits would be true of a walk in the flesh (cf. 5:19-21) and may point to divisions in the Galatian churches occasioned by the Judaizing error (cf. v. 15).

D. A life of service (6:1-10)

A believer is free from the Law of Moses and possesses liberty in the Spirit, but he must fulfill the law of Christ, and this can be done in the power of the Spirit. Such a life involves sacrificial service directed toward sinning Christians, burdened Christians, the pastor-teachers, and all people.

1. TOWARD THE CHRISTIAN WHO HAS SINNED (6:1)

6:1. Paul deals with a hypothetical case of a Christian who is **caught** (*prolēmphthē*) **in a sin,** or better, is "caught by a sin." The thought is that of someone running from sin but sin, being faster, overtakes and catches him. Two passages show how the legalists responded to such (cf. John 8:3-5; Acts 21:27-29). But a Christian should **restore** (*katartizete,* a word used in secular Gr. for setting broken bones and in the NT for mending fishing nets) **him.** The task of restoration is not to be undertaken by fledglings in the faith but by those **who are spiritual,** that is, believers who walk by the Spirit (cf. Gal. 5:16), and who are mature in the faith (cf. 1 Cor. 2:15; Heb. 5:13-14). Furthermore this delicate work must be done **gently** (*prautētos;* cf. Gal. 5:22) and with the consciousness that no one is immune from falling into sin (cf. 1 Cor. 10:12).

2. TOWARD THE CHRISTIAN WHO IS BURDENED (6:2-5)

6:2. A serving Christian lends a helping hand with heavy loads (*barē;* cf. comments on v. 5). Though the principle would apply to all burdens the context has special reference to the heavy and oppressive weight of temptation and spiritual failure. While the "spiritual" do the work of restoring, all believers are to become involved by prayer and encouragement. This, wrote Paul, will fulfill (*anaplērōsete*) **the law of Christ,** that is, the principle of love (cf. 5:14; John 13:34).

6:3-4. Something must be laid aside if a believer is to be a burden-bearer and that is conceit, an attitude that breeds intolerance of error in others and causes one to think he is above failure. The remedy for self-conceit is found in verse 4—everyone is told to **test** (*dokimazetō;* cf. 1 Peter 1:7) **his own actions.** This means that rather than **comparing himself** with others he should step back and take an objective look at himself and his accomplishments. **Then he can take pride in himself** over what God has done in and through his life (cf. Rom. 12:3). The Greek word *kauchēma,* rendered "pride," means personal exultation, not sinful pride.

6:5. The Christian does in fact test himself by carrying **his own load.** This does not contradict verse 2 because the reference there is to heavy, crushing, loads (*barē*)—more than a man could carry without help. In this verse a different Greek word (*phortion*) is used to designate the pack usually carried by a marching soldier. It is the "burden" Jesus assigns to His followers (cf. Matt. 11:30). There are certain Christian responsibilities or burdens each believer must bear which cannot be shared with others. Jesus assured His disciples that such burdens were light.

3. TOWARD THE PASTOR-TEACHER (6:6-9)

6:6. One responsibility of each believer is to shoulder the financial support of the pastor-teachers in the church. Perhaps the Judaizers had influenced some of the believers to slack off in their support of the teachers, a special group who were giving their full time to this ministry and who were reimbursed for their labors (cf. 1 Cor. 9:7-14). This concept of voluntary giving to provide for the Lord's servants was revolutionary since Jews were taxed for the support of their priests and Gentiles paid fees, made vows, etc., to sustain their religions. The admonition is clear that as a teacher shares the good things of **the Word** of God, a believer is to reciprocate by sharing **all good things with his instructor.**

6:7-8. These verses elaborate on the previous exhortation. First, a solemn warning is sounded that **God cannot be mocked.** No man can snub (*myktērizetai*, lit., "turn up the nose at") God whose rule, **a man reaps what he sows,** is immutable. Each sower decides what his harvest will be. If a person **sows to please his sinful nature,** that is, if he spends his money to indulge the flesh, he **will reap** a harvest that will fade into oblivion. On the other hand if he uses his funds to support the Lord's work, or **sows to please the Spirit,** and promotes his own spiritual growth, he **will reap** a harvest that will last forever. Though a broader application of the principle is legitimate it seems clear that Paul was dealing primarily with the question of financial support of Christian workers in the Galatian churches.

6:9. But Christians may become discouraged with spiritual sowing be-cause the harvest is often long in coming. In the face of this reality the apostle charged the Galatians **not** to **become weary** or **give up** because the **harvest** is sure. (Paul included himself as he no doubt contemplated his sometimes frustrating labors on behalf of the Galatian Christians.) The reaping will come at God's **proper time,** which may be only in part in this life and in full in the life to come at the judgment seat of Christ.

4. TOWARD ALL MEN (6:10)

6:10. Christians have a measure of responsibility **to all people** to **do good,** when the occasions arise. When Jesus fed the 5,000, both saved and unsaved participated. So the benevolence of Christians should not be restricted, except that believers are to have the priority. As in a home, family needs are met first, then those of the neighbors.

This passage then speaks clearly about Christian social responsibility, but it should be noted that it is addressed to individual believers. The church is not an agency for social work, though individual Christians are charged to minister in this way as they are able and have opportunity (cf. Rom. 12:17-21).

V. Conclusion (6:11-18)

As Paul brought the Galatian letter to a close, he again emphasized some of the great issues discussed throughout the epistle. The conclusion contains both a summary and final statement of the issues the apostle felt so strongly about.

A. Paul's autograph (6:11)

6:11. At this point Paul took the pen from his scribe and wrote the rest of the letter himself, a practice he often followed (cf. 1 Cor. 16:21; Col. 4:18; 2 Thes. 3:17). The **large letters** he used probably did not refer to the length of the epistle as some have suggested but to the size of the letters he inscribed. It may be that Paul wrote the conclusion in capital letters after the rest of the epistle was penned mostly in lowercase letters. While it has often been suggested that he did so because he was afflicted with weak eyesight, it is more likely, given the tone of the letter, that the apostle sought in this way to give a final emphatic thrust to his message.

B. Paul's adversaries (6:12-13)

6:12-13. The Judaizers who insisted that circumcision was necessary for salvation (cf. Acts 15:1), in summary, (1) were only men-pleasers (cf. Gal. 1:10) seeking **to make a good impression outwardly;** (2) were afraid of persecution (6:12b); (3) wanted to **boast** about the number of Galatians they hoped to win over to circumcision as a religious and merit-earning rite (v. 13). The legalists knew the offense of the Cross would be softened if they openly proclaimed justification by faith *and works* (i.e., circumcision) and if they could claim conversions to that position in Galatia.

C. Paul's boast (6:14-16)

6:14. The contrast is vivid as Paul declared his boasting to be **in the Cross of our Lord Jesus Christ.** For the Judaizers the Cross was an object of shame; for Paul it was the object of glorying. They gloried in the flesh; he gloried in the Savior. The "Cross" speaks of the atonement of Christ with which Paul was identified (cf. 2:20) and by which **the world** was **crucified to** Paul **and he to the world.** The world system with all its allurements, fleshly displays, and religions of human effort was cast aside by Paul. He looked at the world as if it were on a cross—and the world looked at Paul as though he were on a cross.

6:15. In view of the Cross of Christ and a believer's new position with respect to the world, no outward religious symbol or lack of it **means anything** as a way of salvation (cf. 5:6). The only thing that matters is to be a part of the **new creation** by the new birth (cf. 2 Cor. 5:17).

6:16. **Peace and mercy** from God are available to those who walk according to **this rule,** that is, according to the message of salvation by grace through faith alone. This blessing is pronounced on believing Galatians and on believing Jews. (The NIV errs in trans. **even to the Israel of God** rather than "and upon the Israel of God" as in the NASB.) While some believe that "Israel of God" is the church, the evidence does not support such a conclusion. First, the repetition of the preposition ("upon" or "to") indicates two groups are in view. Second, all the 65 other occurrences of the term "Israel" in the New Testament refer to Jews. It would thus be strange for Paul to use "Israel" here to mean Gentile Christians. Third, Paul elsewhere referred to two kinds of Israelites—believing Jews and unbelieving Jews (cf. Rom. 9:6). Lest it be thought that Paul is anti-Semitic, he demonstrated by means of this benediction his deep love and concern for true Israel, that is, Jews who had come to Christ.

D. Paul's benediction (6:17-18)

6:17. Paul's calling as an apostle and the message he preached had been challenged by the Judaizers. He asked for an end to such **trouble,** and he offered as a final proof to his critics **the marks of Jesus** on his **body.** These "marks" (*stigmata*) meant signs of ownership such as were branded on slaves and cattle. Paul referred to the scars on his body, which were caused by persecution for Christ's sake (cf. 1 Cor. 4:11; 2 Cor. 4:10-11; 6:5, 9; 11:24-25), because they demonstrated he was a slave of Christ and not just a people-pleaser.

6:18. Paul's final word of benediction is noteworthy. While no greetings or personal salutations dim the solemnity of the epistle, the apostle ended as he began, expressing his heartfelt desire that **the grace of** God would be their abiding portion (cf. 1:3). And uniquely among all of Paul's epistles he ends with a reminder of his love for them, calling them **brothers.** How could the Galatians fail to respond in obedience to the persuasive and ultimately tender appeal found in this letter?

BIBLIOGRAPHY

Boice, James Montgomery. "Galatians." In *The Expositor's Bible Commentary,* vol. 10. Grand Rapids: Zondervan Publishing House, 1976.

Bruce, F.F. *The Epistle to the Galatians.* The New International Greek Testament Commentary. Grand Rapids: Wm. B. Eerdmans Publishing Co., 1982.

Burton, Ernest DeWitt. *A Critical and Exegetical Commentary on the Epistle to the Galatians.* The International Critical Commentary. Edinburgh: T. & T. Clark, 1921.

Cole, R.A. *The Epistle of Paul to the*

Galatians. Tyndale New Testament Commentaries. Grand Rapids: Wm. B. Eerdmans Publishing Co., 1965.

Gromacki, Robert G. *Stand Fast in Liberty: An Exposition of Galatians.* Grand Rapids: Baker Book House, 1979.

Ironside, H.A. *Expository Messages on the Epistle to the Galatians.* New York: Loizeaux Brothers, 1941.

Lightfoot, J.B. *The Epistle of St. Paul to the Galatians.* Reprint. Grand Rapids: Zondervan Publishing House, 1957.

Luther, Martin. *A Commentary on St. Paul's Epistle to the Galatians.* Reprint. Grand Rapids: Kregel Publications, 1979.

Stott, John R.W. *The Message of Galatians.* Downers Grove, Ill.: InterVarsity Press, 1968.

Strauss, Lehman. *Devotional Studies in Galatians and Ephesians.* New York: Loizeaux Brothers, 1957.

Tenney, Merrill C. *Galatians: The Charter of Christian Liberty.* Revised. Grand Rapids: Wm. B. Eerdmans Publishing Co., 1960.

Vos, Howard F. *Galatians: A Call to Christian Liberty.* Chicago: Moody Press, 1970.

Wuest, Kenneth S. *Galatians in the Greek New Testament for the English Reader.* Grand Rapids: Wm. B. Eerdmans Publishing Co., 1944.

EPHESIANS

Harold W. Hoehner

INTRODUCTION

Authorship. Twice in this epistle Paul referred to himself by name as the author of the book (1:1; 3:1). Yet the Pauline authorship of Ephesians has been greatly disputed in recent years. Some critics think that the book reflects aspects of vocabulary, style, and doctrine that differ from Paul's writings. Though the book has a close affinity with Colossians, critics claim that Ephesians is uncharacteristic of Paul. They suggest that the book was pseudonymous, that is, it was written by someone who did not use his own name but who instead claimed to be Paul.

However, pseudonymity was not practiced by the early Christians. Also this book is regarded by many as the crown of all Paul's writings. Thus it seems strange that a disciple of Paul would be greater than Paul in theological and spiritual perception. Furthermore, Ephesians was extensively and undisputably accepted in the early church as Paul's letter. There is no strong reason for rejecting the Pauline authorship of Ephesians.

Destination. Some scholars view this epistle as encyclical, a circular letter to be distributed to several undesignated local churches in the province of Asia or some other area. This is supported by two observations: (1) the words "in Ephesus" (1:1) do not appear in three early Alexandrian Greek manuscripts, and (2) it is strange for Paul not to mention by name any of the individuals in a church where he had lived and worked for three years (Acts 20:31). However, it seems better to accept "in Ephesus" as genuine because of the wide geographical distribution of the Greek manuscripts that do include those words. Also no manuscripts of this epistle mention any other city, and none have only the word "in" followed by a

space to insert a city's name. The prescript or title "To the Ephesians" appears in all manuscripts of this epistle. Furthermore, all the letters Paul wrote to churches mention their destinations.

With regard to the absence of names of individuals in Ephesus, it may be that Paul did not want to single out certain persons in this short epistle since he knew so many people there.

Even so, the epistle may still be considered a circular letter, with Ephesus being the primary church addressed since Paul had stayed there so long and since it was the capital city of the province of Asia. This helps explain the absence of personal names of Ephesian believers. If this epistle were routed to other churches after the Ephesians read it, it may have gone to Laodicea and Colosse, for Paul in writing Colossians urged the believers there to "read the letter from Laodicea" (Col. 4:16), possibly a reference to the Ephesian epistle. (For the locations of Ephesus, Asia, Laodicea, and Colosse see the map between Acts and Rom.)

Ephesians was probably delivered by Tychicus (Eph. 6:21-22), who also took Paul's letter to the Colossians (Col. 4:7-9).

Ephesus was a leading center in the Roman Empire. Paul had spent a short time in Ephesus on his way back to Antioch from his second missionary journey (Acts 18:19-22). On his third missionary journey he stayed in Ephesus three years (Acts 20:31). Several remarkable things happened in Ephesus. Paul baptized a dozen of John the Baptist's followers (Acts 19:1-7). He had discussions in the hall of Tyrannus (19:8-10). Unusual miracles occurred (19:11-12), strange events took place (19:13-16), sorcerers were converted (19:17-20), and the city rioted over silversmith Demetrius' loss of business because of people who turned to Christ from worshiping the great Ephesian goddess Artemis

(19:23-41). On Paul's return to Jerusalem from his third missionary journey he gave a moving farewell address to the Ephesian elders at the coastal town of Miletus (20:13-35). That was his last time to see them (20:36-38), unless Paul visited Ephesus after he was in Rome (cf. 1 Tim. 1:3 with 3:14).

Place and Date. Paul was a prisoner at the time he wrote this letter (Eph. 3:1; 4:1; 6:20). Scholars differ on whether Paul wrote this letter while he was imprisoned in Caesarea (Acts 24:27) in A.D. 57–59, or in Rome (28:30) in A.D. 60–62. All things considered, the Roman imprisonment seems more likely. Along with Ephesians, the Books of Philippians, Colossians, and Philemon are thought to have been written during the same time period and hence are called the "Prison Epistles" (cf. Phil. 1:7; Col. 4:10; Phile. 9). Since Ephesians gives no hint of his release from prison, as do Philippians (1:19-26) and Philemon (v. 22), it is reasonable to think that he wrote it in the early part of his stay, or about A.D. 60. This would have been when Paul was kept under guard in rental quarters (Acts 28:30). Following his release he traveled, wrote 1 Timothy and Titus, was arrested again, wrote 2 Timothy, and was martyred in Rome.

Purpose. Though no particular problem is raised in the book, the reason for writing this epistle becomes clear when one considers the contacts the apostle had with the Ephesians. On the return from his third missionary journey Paul told the Ephesian elders at Miletus (A.D. 57) to beware of evil teachers from without and of professing believers within who would teach perverse things (Acts 20:29-30). From Revelation one can see that the Ephesian church had succeeded in keeping out the false teachers (Rev. 2:2) but had failed to maintain the vibrancy of their first love for Christ (Rev. 2:4). This is substantiated in 1 Timothy 1:5, when Paul wrote from Macedonia to Timothy at Ephesus (ca A.D. 62) that the goal of his instruction was "love which comes from a pure heart and a good conscience and a sincere faith." Thus the theme of love needed to be stressed for the saints at Ephesus.

This is in harmony with the contents of Ephesians, for the verb form of "love" (*agapaō*) is used 9 times in Ephesians, whereas Paul used it only 23 times in all his other letters. Paul used the noun (*agapē*, "love") 10 times in Ephesians compared with 65 times in his other epistles. Therefore, of the 107 times Paul used the verb or noun "love," 19 are in Ephesians. Thus more than one-sixth of his references to "love" appear in this small epistle to the Ephesians. This letter begins with love (Eph. 1:4, 6) and ends with love (6:23-24).

Also Ephesians teaches that Jewish and Gentile believers are one in Christ, which is demonstrated by their love for one another. This love can come only from God. Possibly Paul, realizing they were starting to forsake their first love, wrote this epistle to encourage them to love both God and their fellow saints.

OUTLINE

G. Prayer for strengthened love
(3:14-21)
1. The approach to prayer
(3:14-15)
2. The appeal in prayer (3:16-19)
3. The ascription of praise
(3:20-21)
II. The Conduct of the Church
(chaps. 4–6)
A. Walking in unity (4:1-16)
1. The basis of unity (4:1-6)
2. The preservation of unity
(4:7-16)
B. Walking in holiness (4:17-32)
1. Presentation of the old man
(4:17-19)
2. Presentation of the new man
(4:20-32)
C. Walking in love (5:1-6)
1. The positive: to love others
(5:1-2)
2. The negative: to abstain from
evil (5:3-6)
D. Walking in light (5:7-14)
1. Not becoming involved with
evildoers (5:7-10)
2. Not becoming involved with
evildoers' works (5:11-13)
3. Conclusion: enlightenment of
Christ (5:14)
E. Walking in wisdom (5:15–6:9)
1. Admonition (5:15-21)
2. Application (5:22–6:9)
F. Standing in warfare (6:10-20)
1. Putting on the armor (6:10-13)
2. Standing with the armor
(6:14-16)
3. Receiving the final pieces of
armor (6:17-20)
G. Conclusion (6:21-24)
1. Information (6:21-22)
2. Salutation (6:23)
3. Benediction (6:24)

COMMENTARY

I. The Calling of the Church (chaps. 1–3)

All knowledge may be divided into two categories: pure or theoretical knowledge and applied or practical knowledge. In most of his letters Paul begins with pure or doctrinal knowledge and ends with applied or practical knowledge. In this epistle the first three chapters deal with doctrine (the calling of the church) and the last three chapters

with application (the conduct of the church).

A. Prologue (1:1-2)

1:1. Paul was made **an apostle of Christ Jesus** through God's **will** or decision. It was not his own choosing or plan. Thus he had God's authority behind him. As an apostle Paul was commissioned and sent by God with the gospel message.

The letter is addressed **to the saints** who resided **in Ephesus.** "Saints" (*hagiois,* "holy ones") are those set apart for God's use. They are a part of the universal church by virtue of their salvation in Christ. The words "in Ephesus" are omitted by some early manuscripts (see "Destination" under *Introduction*), but strong external and internal evidence support their inclusion. If this epistle were a circular letter, it seems that Ephesus, such a strategic city in Asia Minor, would have certainly received it first. **The faithful in Christ Jesus** further defines the "saints" and could be rendered "that is, the believers in Christ Jesus." These saints were in Christ Jesus, not in Adam or the goddess Artemis of Ephesus. While believers have geographical locations (e.g., "Ephesus"), spiritually they are positioned "in Christ" (cf. "in Christ at Colosse" in Col. 1:2). Paul used "in Christ Jesus," "in Christ," or "in Him" quite frequently. In Ephesians 1:1-14 the phrase occurs nine times! Christians have their very life in Christ.

1:2. Paul's extension of **grace** (*charis*) **and peace** is different from the normal Greek letters which had only "greetings" or "greeting" (*chairein;* e.g., the apocryphal 1 Maccabees 10:18, 25; thousands of ancient papyri letters; and Acts 15:23; 23:26; James 1:1). "Grace" expresses God's steadfast love toward man and "peace" shows the relational state as a result of that grace. Paul opened his letter to the church at Ephesus with greetings to the believers there, expressing his wish that God's grace and peace be with them. (See the chart "Paul's Introductions to His Epistles" at Rom. 1:1-7.)

B. Praise for God's planned spiritual blessings (1:3-14)

Paul now moved from his general greeting to the saints at Ephesus to an expanded discussion of the reason God is to be praised—because of the spiritual blessings He has planned for believers in Christ.

In the Greek text, 1:3-14 is one sentence, which is considered by some scholars to be the most cumbersome sentence in the Greek language! In fact, Ephesians has eight lengthy sentences (1:3-14, 15-23; 2:1-7; 3:1-13, 14-19; 4:1-7, 11-16; 6:14-20). However, it is common even today for prayers and doxologies to be lengthy.

1. THE PROVISION OF SPIRITUAL BLESSINGS (1:3)

1:3. Paul stated that God is to **be blessed** or praised. The word for **praise** is *eulogētos*, from a verb that means "to speak well of." In the New Testament it is applied only to God (Mark 14:61; Luke 1:68; Rom. 1:25; 9:5; 2 Cor. 1:3; 11:31; 1 Peter 1:3), whereas in the Septuagint it is sometimes applied to man (Gen. 26:29; Deut. 7:14; Ruth 2:20). The praise should be given **to the God and Father of our Lord Jesus Christ.** In Ephesians 1:2 God is the Father of believers; here in verse 3 God is the Father of Christ (cf. v. 17; cf. similar wording in Rom. 15:6; 2 Cor. 1:3; 1 Peter 1:3). In Ephesians 1:2 the first Person of the Trinity belongs to believers, suggested by the word "our." Here in verse 3 the pronoun "our" shows that believers belong to Christ, the second Person of the Godhead. Since He is the Son of God and believers are connected with Him, they are also related to the Father.

This God who is to be praised is the One **who has blessed us.** This is a verbal form (*ho eulogēsas*) of the adjective "praise" (*eulogētos*), at the beginning of the verse. The verb means "to speak well of, eulogize, extol"; here it means "to benefit, prosper." This word is not used in classical Greek literature. For example, Zeus is not said to have bestowed any specific act of blessing on anyone. Rather he is said to have caused good luck or good fortune. However, the verb *eulogeō* is used over 400 times in the Old Testament, indicating that God bestows benefits to His children in every Age. Mary was said to be "blessed" among women and to be bearing the "blessed" Child (Luke 1:42).

Paul's use of the past tense participle "has blessed" points to this blessing or

prospering of believers as having occurred in eternity past. With what are believers blessed? **With every spiritual blessing** (in the Gr., this phrase precedes the words "in the heavenly realms"). "Every spiritual blessing" (*eulogia*) refers to every spiritual enrichment needed for the spiritual life. Since these benefits have already been bestowed on believers, they should not ask for them but rather appropriate them by faith. Similarly Joshua was not to ask for land since God had already promised it to him (Josh. 1:3-4). But he was to enter into the enjoyment of that provision.

The manner or sphere of this enrichment is **in Christ.** The place of these "blessings" is **in the heavenly realms,** as opposed to the earthly realm of the Ephesian goddess Artemis. Thus these blessings are spiritual not material, heavenly not earthly, eternal not temporal (2 Cor. 4:18; Col. 3:1-4). Five times Paul used the phrase "in the heavenly realms": in Ephesians 1:3, 20; 2:6; 3:10; 6:12.

Ephesians 1:3 tells much about God's blessings on believers: (a) *when:* eternity past; (b) *with what:* every spiritual blessing: (c) *where:* in the heavenly realms; (d) *how:* in Christ.

2. THE BASIS OF SPIRITUAL BLESSINGS (1:4-14)

Paul continued his discussion of believers' spiritual blessings by showing that they are based on the work of the three Persons of the Trinity: the *selection* of the Father (vv. 4-6), the *sacrifice* of the Son (vv. 7-12), and the *seal* of the Spirit (vv. 13-14).

a. God's election for Himself (1:4-6)

1:4. The apostle first told when God's work of election took place: **before the Creation of the world.** The word **for** at the beginning of this verse is not as literal a translation of the Greek adverb *kathōs* as "even as" (ASV, RSV) or "just as" (NASB). "As" suggests that the *way* God blesses believers (v. 3) is through the threefold work of the Trinity. But the adverb can also have a causal sense, and may be rendered "since," "because," or "insofar as" (cf. 4:32). The idea is that spiritual blessings (1:3) for believers are *because of* or on the basis of the work of the Trinity: God blesses believers because of the Father's electing, the Son's dying, and the Spirit's sealing. Both concepts seem to be included: spiritual blessings are the work of the three Persons of the Trinity, and the work of the Trinity is the basis of all a believer's spiritual blessings.

Spiritual blessings begin with and are based on election (**He chose us**), of which God is the subject and believers are the object. Election is God's sovereign work of choosing some to believe (cf. Rom. 8:30; Eph. 1:11; 1 Thes. 1:4; 2 Thes. 2:13; Titus 1:1). Salvation is God's doing, not man's (Eph. 2:8-9). Though it is an act of grace (Rom. 11:5-6; 2 Tim. 1:9), based on His will (Eph. 1:5, 9, 11), a person is responsible to believe (v. 13). "God chose you to be saved . . . through belief in the truth" (2 Thes. 2:13).

In Him indicates the sphere (cf. "in Christ" in Eph. 1:3) of election, as He is the Head and Representative of spiritual humanity (vv. 10, 22; Col. 1:18). The time of election is in eternity past, and the purpose of election is that believers will **be holy and blameless in His sight** for eternity. What God has begun in the past will be accomplished and completed in the future. Christians are "holy" (*hagious*; cf. *hagiois*, "saints," Eph. 1:1), that is, set apart to God, which is the purpose of His electing grace. In addition, the purpose of His election is to make Christians "blameless." This word *amōmous*, "without blemish," is used eight times in the New Testament (v. 4; 5:27; Phil. 2:15; Col. 1:22; Heb. 9:14; 1 Peter 1:19; 2 Peter 3:14; Rev. 14:5). In the Septuagint it is used of sacrificial animals; only those without blemish could be offered to God.

What does the phrase **in love** modify? Some agree with the NIV that it modifies the word "predestined" (Eph. 1:5). If so, then God's love is seen in predestination. More likely, it modifies the words "to be holy and blameless in His sight" for these reasons: (1) In this context the modifying phrases always follow the action words (vv. 3-4, 6, 8-10). (2) The other five occurrences of "in love" in Ephesians (3:17; 4:2, 15-16; 5:2 ["of love"]) refer to human love rather than divine love. (3) Love fits well with holiness and blamelessness, for this would denote a balance between holiness and love. God is love and believers, because of God's electing love, should manifest love with holiness.

1:5. The cause of election is God's predestination of believers unto sonship (cf. "predestined" in v. 11). **Predestined** is from *proorisas*, "marked out beforehand." Thus the emphasis of predestination is more on the *what* than the *who* in that the believers' predetermined destiny is their being **adopted as** full-fledged **sons** of God **through Jesus Christ**, the Agent of the adoption. The concept of adoption is also found in Romans 8:15 (NIV marg.), 23; Galatians 4:4-7. In adoption a son is brought into a family and is given the same rights as a child who is born into that family.

In this context it seems that predestination logically precedes election: after God looked forward to the glorious destiny of adopting believers into His family, He looked down on sinful humanity and chose believers (cf. Rom. 8:30 where "predestined" precedes "called," which refers to His efficacious saving). All this was done **in accordance with His pleasure** (cf. Eph. 1:9) **and will** (cf. vv. 1, 9, 11), that is, He delighted to impart His spiritual benefits to His children.

1:6. The ultimate goal of God's election is that believers will be **to the praise of His glorious grace.** A similar expression of praise is also given after the description of the work of the Son (v. 12) and of the Spirit (v. 14). "His glorious grace" (undeserved favor; cf. v. 7) had been **freely given us.** The words "freely given" translate the verb *echaritōsen*, from the noun "grace" (*charis*). The verb form is used only one other time in the New Testament (Luke 1:28, where Mary is said to be "highly favored"). Literally, Ephesians 1:6a might be rendered "to the praise of His glorious grace which He 'graced' to us." Since salvation is all of God's grace, Christians certainly ought to praise Him for it! And that is why they were chosen: to give Him praise (cf. "Praise be to . . . God," v. 3). **In the One He loves** stresses the manifestation of God's love to His Son (cf. "the Son He loves," Col. 1:13). This reference to Christ also furnishes the transition to the second Person of the Trinity discussed in Ephesians 1:7-12.

God the Father loves His Son; and believers, being in the Son, are also the object of God's love.

b. God's redemption in Christ (1:7-12)

1:7. Redemption (*apolytrōsin*) denotes release or deliverance from a state of slavery (cf. Col. 1:14). The idea of release is seen in some of the other verses where this Greek word appears (Luke 21:28; Rom. 3:24; 8:23; 1 Cor. 1:30; Eph. 1:7, 14; 4:30; Col. 1:14; Heb. 9:15; 11:35). (See the chart "New Testament Words for Redemption" at Mark 10:45.) This redemption is from sin (Heb. 9:15), and thus this work of Christ delivers believers from slavery to sin. This is further defined by **the forgiveness of sins** (cf. Eph. 4:32; Col. 1:14), which is the immediate result of a believer's release from sin's hold. (The word for "sins" is *paraptōma*, lit., "false steps or transgressions," also used in Rom. 4:25; 5:16-17, 20; Eph. 2:1, 5, and elsewhere.) God could not treat sin lightly for it required the sacrifice of blood (cf. Heb. 9:22).

The means of redemption is the sacrificial substitutionary death of Christ **(through His blood;** cf. Eph. 2:13; 1 Peter 1:19), which completely satisfied God's justice (Rom. 3:24-25). This was accomplished **in accordance with the riches of God's grace** (cf. Eph. 1:6; 2:7). The cost of Christ's blood is the measure of the wealth of God's unmerited favor to every believer. It was accomplished not "out of" but "according to" (*kata*) the wealth of His grace (cf. Phil. 4:19). Six times in Ephesians Paul referred to God's riches (1:7, 18; 2:4, 7; 3:8, 16).

1:8-10. God's grace is given to enable believers to understand His will. God gives them **wisdom** (*sophia*; cf. v. 17; 3:10; Col. 1:9, 28; 2:3, 23; 3:16; 4:5), objective insight into the true nature of God's revelation, **and understanding** (*phronēsei*), the subjective apprehension of it. So believers are able to grasp something of the divine purpose of the ages and to see its relevance in the present time. This is accomplished because God **made known to us the mystery of His will** (cf. "will" in Eph.1:1, 5, 11). "Mystery" is a previously hidden truth unveiled by God's revelation (cf. Rom. 16:25; see Matt. 13:11 for a list of "mysteries" in the NT). This mystery (unveiled truth) is God's **good pleasure** (cf. Eph. 1:5) to purpose **in Christ** to **bring all things in heaven and on earth** under His headship in the consummation of time. The words **to be put into effect when the times will have reached their fulfillment** are literally, "unto the

dispensation of the fullness of the times." The "dispensation" (*oikonomia*) is an arrangement or administration. This dispensation is the millennial kingdom when "the times" in God's purposes will be completed (fulfilled), and all things both spiritual and material will be under Christ and His rule (cf. 1 Cor. 15:27; Col. 1:20).

The words "bring all things . . . together under one Head" translate one Greek word (which occurs elsewhere in the NT only in Rom. 13:9), to speak of summing up all the commandments under love. In the Millennium everything will be restored and brought together under Christ, the **one Head.** This does not suggest that everyone will be saved; instead, sin's disorder will be removed and universal peace will be established (Isa. 2:2-4; 11:1-10).

1:11-12. As a result of the spiritual blessing of insight into the mystery of God's will (vv. 8-10) Paul discussed the Jewish believers' inclusion in Christ. The **we** in verse 11 seems to be a distinct group from the anonymous "we/us" in verses 3-10. This is supported by two facts: (1) verse 11 includes the word **also** and (2) verse 13 changes to "you also," which refers to Gentile believers. Though both Jews and Gentiles participate in God's blessings, the Jews were called first (cf. Acts 3:26; Rom. 1:16).

In Ephesians 1:11 **chosen** (*eklērō-thēmen*) is not the same word used in verse 4 (*exelexato*). The word in verse 11 (used only here in the NT) means "to cast a lot" or "to appoint or obtain by lot." In this context it is best rendered "to be chosen, appointed, or destined." Jewish believers were chosen because they were predestined. But this predestination is not a matter of whim or caprice on God's part; it is **according to the plan** (*prothesin*, "purpose"; cf. Rom. 8:28; 9:11; Eph. 3:11) of God, **who works out everything in conformity with the purpose** (*boulēn*, "counsel or deliberation") **of His will** (*thelēmatos*; cf. 1:5, 9). The combination of these words—*prothesin, boulēn, thelēma-tos*—gives a forceful emphasis of God's sovereignty for including the Jewish believers in the church, which is headed up by Christ. The purpose of God's choice of the Jewish believers is that they **might be for the praise of His glory,** which parallels verse 6. The words "for the praise of His glory" serve as a refrain used after a description of the work of each Person of the Trinity (cf. vv. 6, 14). The relative clause, **who were the first to hope in Christ,** further substantiates that verses 11-12 refer to Jewish believers as opposed to Gentile believers because the Jews did precede the Gentiles chronologically in the faith (Acts 1:8; 13:46; 28:25-28; Rom. 1:16 [see comments there]; 2:9-10).

Christ has set the sinner free from his sin and has revealed His will that all things will be headed up in Christ at the end of the ages, including the Jewish believers who first trusted in Him.

c. God's seal with the Spirit (1:13-14)

God's spiritual blessings for believers are based not only on the sovereign election of the Father (vv. 3-6) and the redemptive work of the Son (vv. 7-12), but also on the seal of the Holy Spirit.

1:13-14a. And you also refers to the Gentiles in contrast with the Jews (cf. comments on vv. 11-12). **When** they **heard the Word of truth** (cf. Col. 1:5; 2 Tim. 2:15; James 1:18) which is further described as **the gospel of your salvation,** and **believed,** they **were** sealed with **the promised Holy Spirit.** The KJV says that the sealing occurs "after" the hearing and believing, thus connoting a second work of grace. This is wrong, for believers are sealed at the moment they hear and believe.

The last part of verse 13 is literally, "They were sealed in Him [Christ] with the Holy Spirit of promise." The word "seal" indicates security (Matt. 27:66; Eph. 4:30), authentication and approval (John 6:27), certification of genuineness (John 3:33), and identification of ownership (2 Cor. 1:22; Rev. 7:2; 9:4). God is the One who seals, Christ is the sphere in which the **seal** is done, and the Holy Spirit is the instrument of the seal. "The promised Holy Spirit" refers to Christ's promise to His disciples that He would send the Spirit (Luke 24:49; John 14:16; 15:26; 16:13; Acts 1:5).

The Holy Spirit who seals **is a deposit guaranteeing our inheritance.** The "deposit" is more than a pledge which could be returned; it is a down payment with a guarantee of more to come (cf. "the firstfruits of the Spirit," Rom. 8:23). "A deposit guaranteeing"

translates the Greek *arrabōn* (used elsewhere in the NT only in 2 Cor. 1:22; 5:5). It guarantees believers' "inheritance" of salvation and heaven (cf. 1 Peter 1:4). (See comments on "inheritance" in Eph. 1:18.) In essence, the "deposit" of the Holy Spirit is a little bit of heaven in believers' lives with a guarantee of much more yet to come.

1:14b. The believer is sealed with the Holy Spirit **until the redemption** (*apolytrōsin*; see the chart "New Testament Words for Redemption" at Mark 10:45) **of those who are God's possession.** This redemption is not release from the guilt of sin; that was spoken of in Ephesians 1:7 and the believer is already "God's possession." Instead, this is the believer's ultimate, final release from the presence of sin (cf. Rom. 8:23b; Phil. 3:20-21). The Greek word for "possession" (*peripoiēsis*) is also used in 1 Thessalonians 5:9; 2 Thessalonians 2:14; Hebrews 10:39 (see comments there); and 1 Peter 2:9. Again the doxological refrain, **to the praise of His glory,** is repeated here as it was after the description of the work of the Father (Eph. 1:6) and of the Son (v. 12).

C. Prayer for wisdom and revelation (1:15-23)

1. COMMENDATION (1:15)

1:15. Because of (**For this reason**) the believers' acquisition of every spiritual blessing—including election, predestination, adoption, grace, redemption, forgiveness, wisdom, understanding, knowledge of the mystery of His will, the sealing of the Holy Spirit, and inheritance—Paul now prayed that his readers might know God personally and intimately. Verses 15-23 are one sentence in the Greek, as are verses 3-14.

Paul **heard** of the Ephesians' **faith** in Christ, their vertical relationship, **and** their **love for all the saints,** their horizontal relationship (cf. Col. 1:4; 2 Thes. 1:3). A proper relationship with God should lead to a proper relationship with other Christians. Interestingly Paul wrote about "love with faith" in Ephesians 6:23.

2. SUPPLICATION (1:16-23)

a. The request for wisdom and revelation (1:16-18a)

1:16. Because of the Ephesians' faith

and love, Paul continued to give **thanks for** them (cf. Rom. 1:8; 1 Cor. 1:4; Phil. 1:3; Col. 1:3; 1 Thes. 1:2; 2 Thes. 1:3) and to make requests for them (cf. Phil. 1:4; Col. 1:9; 1 Thes. 1:3).

1:17. The NIV begins a new sentence here, but this verse is actually a continuation of verse 16. Paul addressed his request to **the God of our Lord Jesus Christ** (cf. v. 3), **the glorious Father,** that is, the Father to whom all glory belongs (cf. "the God of glory" in Acts 7:2 and "the Lord of glory" in 1 Cor. 2:8). The content of Paul's request is that God **may give you the Spirit of wisdom and revelation.** Though the NIV translators interpret "Spirit" (*pneuma*) as referring to the Holy Spirit, it is better to see it as disposition or attitude because of the two genitives following it ("of wisdom and [of] revelation"; cf. "a gentle spirit" in 1 Cor. 4:21). On the other hand one cannot obtain a spirit or attitude of wisdom and revelation apart from the Holy Spirit. As Isaiah wrote, "The Spirit of the Lord will rest on Him [Messiah]— the Spirit of wisdom and of understanding, the Spirit of counsel and of power, the Spirit of knowledge and of the fear of the Lord" (Isa. 11:2). "Wisdom" (*sophia*; cf. Eph. 1:8; 3:10) gives insight into the true nature of things, and "revelation" is the unveiling of the object discussed, namely, God Himself. The purpose in having this wisdom and revelation is **that you may know Him,** God, **better.** The Greek is the phrase, "in knowing of Him." This knowing (*epignōsei*) refers not to abstract knowledge of God or objective facts about Him, but knowing Him personally and intimately (cf. "knowledge," *epignōseōs*, in 4:13). It includes an intimate awareness of God's character and will. Philosophy says, "Know thyself," whereas Christianity says, "Know God through Jesus Christ."

1:18a. The NEB, NASB, and NIV state another request: **I pray also that the eyes of your heart may be enlightened.** However, this is not a new sentence in Greek. It seems to be parenthetical, as in the KJV, ASV, and RSV. In other words, Paul had prayed (v. 17) that they might have true spiritual insight into God, and then he included the phrase, "having the eyes of your heart enlightened" (RSV). Paul's request for them to know God was within proper bounds because their

hearts had *been* enlightened (the Gr. perf. tense indicates past action with continuing results), as discussed in verses 3-14, especially 7-9. In the Bible the "heart" is the center of one's personality.

b. The reason for wisdom and revelation (1:18b-23)

Having prayed (vv. 16-17) that they might know God personally, Paul now gave the reason: "that you may know" three facts, which are spelled out in verses 18b-23 (the first is in v. 18b, the second in v. 18c, and the third in vv. 19-23). The word "know" (*eidenai*, v. 18) is factual knowledge—much as a general needs to know the facts about his equipment and men before he goes to battle.

1:18b. The first fact to be ascertained pertains to the past. A believer's present **hope** has its source in the past when he was **called** (cf. Rom. 1:6; 8:30; Eph. 4:1, 4; 2 Tim. 1:9) to salvation. "Hope" in Scripture is the absolute certainty of a believer's victory in God (cf. Rom. 8:23-24; Eph. 4:4; Col. 1:5; 1 Thes. 1:3; 1 Peter 3:15).

1:18c. The second fact Paul wanted his readers to know refers to the future: **the riches of His glorious inheritance in the saints.** At the time of the resurrection of believers ("saints" are those set apart by God to God; cf. v. 1) God will inherit those whom He has purchased at a great price according to the riches of His grace (v. 7). This is the second of six times in Ephesians in which Paul referred to "riches" (1:7, 18; 2:4, 7; 3:8, 16). In 1:14 Paul wrote that the Christians' "inheritance" is their final redemption from the presence of sin. Here in verse 18 he wrote about *God's* inheritance, the saints themselves! Because of the "glorious grace" (v. 6) of "the glorious Father" (v. 17), He will receive "His glorious inheritance" (v. 18).

1:19-23. The third fact Paul wanted believers to know pertains to the present time: **His incomparably great power for us who believe.** The word "power" (*dynamis;* cf. 3:20) means a spiritually dynamic and living force. This power of God is directed toward believers. Paul then used three additional words to describe God's power. It is according to **the working** (*energeian,* "energetic power," from which comes the Eng.

"energy") **of the might** (*kratous,* "power that overcomes resistance," as in Christ's miracles; this word is used only of God, never of believers) of God's inherent **strength** (*ischyos*) **which He** provides (cf. 6:10; 1 Peter 4:11). This magnificent accumulation of words for power underscores the magnitude of God's "great power" available to Christians.

Then Paul mentioned three manifestations of God's power which are seen in Christ (Eph. 1:20-23). First, this energetic power was **exerted** (*enērgēken*) **in Christ when** God **raised Him from the dead and seated Him at His right hand in the heavenly realms.** God's energetic power which resurrected and exalted Christ in the past (cf. Rom. 8:34; Eph. 2:6; Col. 3:1; Heb. 1:3; 8:1; 12:2; 1 Peter 3:22) is the same power available to believers in the present (cf. Phil. 3:10). What an amazing source of spiritual vitality, power, and strength for living the Christian life! (cf. Col. 1:11) Christ's Ascension to the right hand of God involves His being exalted **above** every order of authority (cf. Col. 1:16), human and superhuman (cf. Phil. 2:8-11), whether present **(in the present Age)** or future **(the Age to come;** cf. 1 Cor. 15:23-28). The words **rule and authority, power and dominion** may refer primarily to angelic beings (cf. Rom. 8:38; Eph. 3:10; 6:12; Col. 1:16; 2:15; Titus 3:1).

A second manifestation of God's power in Christ is seen in His placing **all things under** Christ's **feet.** Whereas Adam lost his headship over Creation when he sinned, Christ was made Head over all Creation (cf. Eph. 1:10). This will be fully realized in the future (Ps. 8:6; 1 Cor. 15:27; Heb. 2:6-8).

The third manifestation of God's power in Christ is His appointment of Christ as **Head over . . . the church.** Though the final manifestation of Christ's headship over all Creation will be in the future, He is now Head over the fellowship of believers. He is also called the church's "Head" in Ephesians 4:15; 5:23; and Colossians 1:18. Though the church is implied in Ephesians 1:10, it is specifically mentioned for the first time in Ephesians in verse 22b. The church is **His body** (v. 23; cf. 4:4, 15-16; Col. 1:18). His body, the universal church consisting of all believers, is **the fullness of Him who fills everything in every way.** The meaning of this description of His body is difficult to determine. The verb "fills" can be taken passively, meaning that Christ, the Head of the body, *is filled by* the church. That is, as the church grows it completes Christ. However, it is better to understand the word "fills" as in the Greek middle voice: Christ, the Head of the body, *fills (for Himself)* the church with blessings. The verse could then be rendered, "which is His body, which is being filled by the One who fills all things with all things (blessings)." This interpretation is preferred for these reasons: (1) Nowhere else does the New Testament state that Christ finds fullness from the church. (2) This view fits the context well because the Persons of the Godhead are completing the actions (cf. Eph. 1:10). (3) This view correlates well with 4:10-11 which speaks of Christ giving all things ("the whole universe" is lit., "all things"), namely, gifted people to the church.

This ends Paul's prayer. After demonstrating that believers have all spiritual blessings (1:3-14), Paul prayed that believers would come to know God intimately (v. 17) in order that they might know three facts: (1) the *past* call of salvation that produced hope (v. 18), (2) the *future* inheritance that God has in His saints (v. 18), and (3) the *present* power of God that is available to believers, which (a) was manifested in the past in Christ's resurrection and Ascension, (b) will be manifested in the future in Christ's headship over Creation, and (c) is presently manifested in Christ's headship over the church.

D. New position individually (2:1-10)

In chapter 1 Paul discussed God's eternal plan in choosing those who are predestined to sonship and the fact that all believers on earth and in heaven will be brought together under Christ the Head of the church. Chapters 2–3 explain the execution of this eternal plan by showing how God makes sinners saints and then places them into the church, Christ's body. In 2:1-10 Paul discussed how sinners who deserve nothing but God's wrath can become trophies of His grace.

1. THE OLD CONDITION: DEAD TO GOD (2:1-3)

At the outset it should be noted that

the grammatical subject of this long sentence (vv. 1-7) in Greek is "God" (v. 4) and the three main verbs are "made . . . alive with" (v. 5), "raised . . . up with" (v. 6), and "seated . . . with" (v. 6). The object of each of these verbs is "us," that is, believers (vv. 5-6). Thus the main assertion in verses 1-7 is that God has made believers alive, raised them up, and seated them with Christ. All the other clauses in these verses are subordinate to this main assertion. This is not really clear in the NIV which has included three additional verbs (one in v. 1 and two in v. 3) as well as the three, already mentioned, in verses 5-6.

Verses 1-3 depict the condition of unbelievers before God transformed them.

a. The condition described (2:1)

2:1. Unregenerate persons are **dead in . . . transgressions** (cf. v. 5) **and sins** (Col. 2:13). This death is spiritual, not physical, for unsaved people are very much alive physically. Death signifies absence of communication with the living. One who is dead spiritually has no communication with God; he is separated from God. The phrase "in your transgressions and sins" shows the sphere of the death, suggesting that sin has killed people (Rom. 5:12; 7:10; Col. 2:13) and they remain in that spiritually dead state. "Transgressions" (paraptōmasin, "false steps"; cf. Eph. 1:7; 2:5) and "sins" (hamartiais, "acts of missing the mark"), though slightly different in their root meanings, are basically synonymous. Both suggest deliberate acts against God and His righteousness and thus failure to live as one should. The plural of these two nouns signifies people's repetitious involvement in sin and hence their state of unregeneration.

b. The condition delineated (2:2-3)

2:2-3. Mankind's unregenerate condition is further delineated in three ways: (1) The unregenerate follow **the ways of this world.** Unbelievers follow the lifestyles of other unbelievers; they experience the world's peer pressure. "This world" (kosmos) is the satanically organized system that hates and opposes all that is godly (cf. John 15:18, 23).

(2) The unsaved follow **the ruler of the kingdom of the air,** that is, Satan.

"The whole world is under the control of the evil one" (1 John 5:19), also called "the god of this Age" (2 Cor. 4:4). In the middle of the Tribulation he will be cast down to the earth, no longer to rule the world or have access to God's presence (Rev. 12:9). The unsaved are now in the clutches of this "ruler" and follow in his opposition to God.

(3) The additional description, **the spirit who is now at work in those who are disobedient,** may be a further elaboration of the distant antecedent, "ways of this world," but this seems too remote. Some (e.g., NIV) suggest that it refers to "the ruler," meaning that Satan personally works in sons of disobedience. However, it seems that "the spirit" is the same as "the kingdom (exousias, lit. 'authority') of the air." This is the nearest antecedent and makes sense grammatically. This "spirit" then refers to the impersonal force or atmosphere, which is controlled and directed by Satan (1 John 5:19). This spirit is presently "at work" (energountos) in unbelievers. "In those who are disobedient" is literally, "in the sons of disobedience." The word for sons (huiois) has the idea of a distinctive characteristic. "A son of disobedience" is one who is a distinctly disobedient person. The Greek word translated "disobedience" and "disobedient" is used several times in the New Testament (Rom. 11:30, 32; Eph. 2:2; 5:6; Heb. 4:6, 11). It suggests conscious and active rebellion and opposition against God.

However, the unconverted not only are under the pressure of the world system and Satan's control but they also enjoy it. **All of us also lived among them at one time** is Paul's reminder to his Gentile readers that the Jews ("all of us") also joined in this disobedience. The word "lived" (anestraphēmen; "conducted themselves") differs from "used to live" (periepatēsate) in Ephesians 2:2. The conduct of the unsaved is in the sphere of **the cravings of** their **sinful nature,** in which they follow the **desires and the thoughts** of the flesh. "Sinful nature" translates "the flesh" (sarkos), which is unregenerated nature. This nature can manifest itself in a respectable form as well as in disreputable pursuits. The "thoughts" (dianoiōn, here pl., but usually sing.) suggest that even unbelievers' reasoning processes (or calculations formed by a thinking mind) are perverted. Such false reasoning directs their wills and acts (cf. Rom. 1:21).

Like the rest, we (i.e., both Jews and Gentiles) are **by nature** (naturally and innately) the **objects** (lit. "children") of **wrath.** *Tekna,* the word for "children," suggests a close relationship to one's parents (in contrast with *huioi,* "sons," which speaks of distinctive characteristics). Unbelievers have a close relationship, not with God, but with His wrath! Disobedience and unbelief lead to the wrath of God (Rom. 1:18–2:29; John 3:36). Ephesians 2:1-3 presents a hopeless picture of an unregenerate person who deserves nothing but God's wrath.

2. THE NEW POSITION: ALIVE IN GOD (2:4-10)

The wrath of God, however, is not the entire story. Its dark background contrasts with the glorious exhibition of God's grace toward the unregenerate. Verses 4-10 set forth the grace of God which works on some unbelievers and gives them life (vv. 4-5), raises them (v. 6a), and seats them in heavenly realms with Christ (vv. 6b-10).

a. God made them alive (2:4-5)

2:4-5. The conjunction **but** introduces God's actions toward sinners, in contrast with their plight in verses 1-3. In the Greek text **God** immediately follows "but," thus placing it in an emphatic position. "God" is the subject of the whole passage. Great differences are suggested by the words "But God"! He is described as **rich in mercy.** (Cf. the "riches" of God's grace [1:7; 2:7], of God's glorious inheritance [1:18], of Christ [3:8], and of His glory [3:16].) In the Septuagint "mercy" (*eleos*) translates the Hebrew *ḥesed* ("loyal love"). In the New Testament *eleos* means "undeserved kindness" toward sinners. Thus God, who is rich in exhibiting this undeserved kindness, acts on behalf of sinners **because of His great love for us.** The noun for "love" (*agapē*) comes from the verb *agapaō* that means "to seek the highest good in the one loved." Since sinners are spiritually dead toward God, they have nothing to commend them to God. This is why Paul described this love as being "great."

God's love has done three things: (a) **made us alive with Christ,** (b) "raised us up with Christ" (2:6), and (c) "seated us

with Him in the heavenly realms in Christ Jesus" (v. 6). An unbeliever, spiritually dead, is "made . . . alive" by God "with (in association with) Christ" (cf. Col. 2:13). The "us" includes both Jews and Gentiles (cf. "us" in Eph. 2:3-4). The only way a spiritually dead person can communicate with God is to be made alive, and that must be done by the One who is Himself alive. He is the living God, "who gives life to the dead" (Rom. 4:17).

God is fully aware of the unbelievers' state. It was clearly described in Ephesians 2:1-3 and is repeated here: **even when we were dead in transgressions** (cf. v. 1). This act of God in making the unregenerate alive is an act of grace: **it is by grace you have been saved.** Paul elaborated on this last statement, which is actually parenthetical, in verse 8. The verb "have been saved" is in the perfect tense which expresses the present permanent state as a result of a past action. Because believers have been "made alive" spiritually with Christ, they have been and are saved.

b. God raised them (2:6a)

2:6a. Besides being made alive, former unbelievers also have been **raised . . . up with Christ.** This speaks of their being positionally resurrected. Christ's post-resurrection state was new, powerful, and unique. So too Christians, in whom Christ dwells, have a new, powerful, and unique life and position. This new life, power, and position demand that believers have a new set of values, as Paul stated in his companion letter to the Colossian believers: "Since, then, you have been raised with Christ, set your heart on things above, where Christ is seated at the right hand of God. Set your minds on things above, not on earthly things" (Col. 3:1-2).

c. God seated them (2:6b-10)

2:6b. Not only has God made alive and raised with Christ many who had been unbelievers, but He has also **seated** them **with** Christ **in the heavenly realms** (cf. 1:3, 20; 2:6; 3:10; 6:12) **in Christ Jesus.** Believers are positioned spiritually in heaven, where Christ is. They are no longer mere earthlings; their citizenship is in heaven (Phil. 3:20). He is the exalted Son of God, and they are exalted sons and daughters of God. These actions of

God toward unbelievers are similar to what God did for Christ: "He raised Him from the dead and seated Him at His right hand in the heavenly realms" (Eph. 1:20). Whereas Christ had died physically (1:20), unbelievers were dead spiritually (2:1-3). While Christ was raised physically (1:20), unbelievers are made alive and raised with Christ spiritually (2:5-6). Christ is seated in the heavenly realms physically (in His resurrected, ascended body; 1:20), but believers are seated with Christ in the heavenly realms spiritually (2:6). This divine power that can make an unbeliever have life, be raised, and exalted with Christ is the same power that presently operates in believers.

2:7. In the future eternal state, God will **show** all His Creation **the incomparable riches of His grace.** "Show" is *endeixētai,* which means "display or demonstrate" (cf. Rom. 2:15; 9:17, 22; 2 Cor. 8:24; Titus 2:10; 3:2). This display will be seen in His redeemed ones. The "riches of His grace" has been mentioned in connection with believers' redemption which brought them forgiveness of sins (Eph. 1:7). These "riches of His grace" are **expressed in His kindness to us in Christ Jesus.** This refers to salvation. The word "kindness" (*chrēstotēti*) basically means what is "appropriate or suitable." (The word is also used in Rom. 2:4; 3:12 ["good"]; 11:22; 2 Cor. 6:6; Gal. 5:22; Col. 3:2; Titus 3:4.) The appropriate expression of God's love to those who are spiritually dead is to give them life—this is "the incomparable riches of His grace, expressed in His kindness."

2:8-9. These verses explain "the incomparable riches of His grace" (v. 7), expanding the parenthetical statement in verse 5, **It is by grace you have been saved,** and adding that the means of this salvation is **through faith.** Hence the basis is grace and the means is faith alone (cf. Rom. 3:22, 25; Gal. 2:16; 1 Peter 1:5). Faith is not a "work." It does not merit salvation; it is only the means by which one accepts God's free salvation.

Paul elaborated, **And this** is **not from yourselves, it is the gift of God.** Much debate has centered around the demonstrative pronoun "this" (*touto*). Though some think it refers back to "grace" and others to "faith," neither of these suggestions is really valid because the demonstrative pronoun is neuter whereas "grace" and "faith" are feminine. Also, to refer back to either of these words specifically seems to be redundant. Rather the neuter *touto,* as is common, refers to the preceding phrase or clause. (In Eph. 1:15 and 3:1 *touto,* "this," refers back to the preceding section.) Thus it refers back to the *concept* of salvation (2:4-8a), whose basis is grace and means is faith. This salvation does not have its source in man (it is "not from yourselves"), but rather, its source is God's grace for "it is the gift of God."

Verse 9 reinforces this by showing that the means is **not by works** since its basis is grace (Rom. 3:20, 28; 4:1-5; 11:6; Gal. 2:16; 2 Tim. 1:9; Titus 3:5), and its means is faith (Rom. 4:5). Therefore since no person can bring salvation to himself by his own efforts, **no one can boast** (cf. Rom. 3:27; 1 Cor. 1:29). Their boasting can only be in the Lord (1 Cor. 1:31).

2:10. This verse, beginning with **For,** tells why this salvation is not from man or by his works. The reason is that salvation is **God's workmanship.** The word "workmanship" (*poiēma*), used only here and in Romans 1:20 (where the NIV renders it "what has been made") denotes a work of art or a masterpiece. It differs from human "works" (*ergōn*) in Ephesians 2:9. Believers are God's workmanship because they have been **created** (a work only God can do) **in Christ Jesus** (cf. "in Christ Jesus" in vv. 6-7). The purpose of this creation is that believers will **do good works.** God's workmanship is not achieved by good works, but it is to result in good works (cf. Titus 2:14; 3:8).

In the clause, **which God prepared in advance for us to do,** the word "which" refers back to the "works" in the previous clause. "For us to do" is literally "in order that we might walk in them." The purpose of these prepared-in-advance works is not "to work in them" but "to walk in them." In other words, God has prepared a path of good works for believers which He will perform in and through them as they walk by faith. This does not mean doing a work for God; instead, it is God's performing His work in and through believers (cf. Phil. 2:13). This path of good works is discussed by Paul in Ephesians 4-6.

In conclusion, 2:1-10 demonstrates that though people were spiritually dead and deserving only God's wrath, God, in

His marvelous grace, has provided salvation through faith. Believers are God's workmanship in whom and through whom He performs good works.

E. New position corporately (2:11-22)

Individuals who have received God's gracious salvation are not left alone but are brought into union with other believers. In 2:11-22 Paul developed this concept of the corporate unity of saved Jews and Gentiles in the church, Christ's body (cf. 1:22-23).

1. STATEMENT OF THE UNION (2:11-13)

a. Past disunion (2:11-12)

2:11. Having completed his discussion of believers as God's workmanship (vv. 1-10), Paul began this section with the strongest inferential particle (*dio,* **therefore**) to alert the Ephesians to the unenviable position of having no relationship with God. Paul commanded them to **remember that formerly,** before their conversions, they were **Gentiles by birth and called "uncircumcised"** by Jews. Jews, being circumcised physically (**in the body**) disparaged all non-Jews by calling them the "uncircumcised." This physical difference between Jews and Gentiles affected every area of their lives. A great social and spiritual boundary existed between them.

2:12. The Gentiles' lack of the external sign of circumcision also meant that they lacked five privileges that God had given the nation Israel. First, they **were separate from** (lit., "without") **Christ** not only personally (true also of many Jews) but also in that they had no national hope of the Messiah.

Second, they were **excluded from citizenship in Israel.** They did not belong to the theocratic state of Israel (cf. Rom. 9:4). The word "excluded" is *apēllotriōmenoi,* "alienated" or "estranged." It is used only two other times (Eph. 4:18; Col. 1:21). Though some Gentiles were admitted into Judaism as proselytes, Gentiles as a whole were excluded; they were thus alienated.

Third, they were **foreigners to the covenants of the promise** (cf. Eph. 3:6). They were deprived of direct participation in God's covenants and thus had no hope of future glory and blessing as Israel did. Israel's "covenants" include the brahamic (Gen. 12:1-3; 15:18-21;

17:1-8), the Palestinian (Deut. 28-30), the Davidic (2 Sam. 7:16; Ps. 89:1-4), and the New (Jer. 31:31-34; Ezek. 36:24-30). These covenants—all pointing to "the promise" of the Messiah and of blessings through Him—assured Israel of a national existence, a land, a King, and spiritual blessings.

Fourth, the Gentiles were **without hope.** Unlike Israel they had no expectation of a personal Messiah-Deliverer and the Messianic Age.

Fifth, they were **without God** (*atheoi,* "apart from God") **in the world.** The Gentiles were in a desperate situation. They had no meaning, hope, purpose, or direction in life.

b. Present union (2:13)

2:13. But now in Christ Jesus marks the contrast both temporally ("formerly" [v. 11] as opposed to "now") and positionally ("separate from Christ" [v. 12] as opposed to "in Christ Jesus"). The Gentiles **who once were far away** (cf. v. 17) from both God and the Jews (v. 12) **have been brought near through the blood of Christ** (cf. 1:7). They have come near to God and to the Jews by means of Christ's sacrificial death. Sin separates people from God and only Christ's atonement can remove that sin barrier.

2. EXPLANATION OF THE UNION (2:14-18)

Having stated the fact of the union of Gentiles and Jews (v. 13), Paul then explained what this involves. He discussed two things in this section: the establishment of peace between Gentile and Jewish believers, and the peace between God and the people who believe in Him.

a. Assertion of peace (2:14-16)

2:14. Christ **Himself is the peace** between Jewish and Gentile believers, having **made the two** groups **one and** having **destroyed the barrier, the dividing wall of hostility.** "Peace" is mentioned four times in three verses (vv. 14-15, 17 [twice]). Various interpretations have been given regarding this "dividing wall," which is mentioned only here in the New Testament. Some have thought it refers to the wall in the Jerusalem temple precincts that separated the Court of the Gentiles from the Court of the Jews. But this view is invalid because Paul makes no reference to the temple in Jerusalem and because this wall was still standing when Paul wrote this epistle. Some think it referred to the curtain in the Jerusalem temple between the holy place and the holy of holies. But that was a curtain, not a wall. Others have suggested it meant the "fence" around the Law mentioned by some Rabbis. But that referred more to the protection of the Law than to the hostility mentioned in this context. The structure of the Greek words suggests that the dividing wall describes not a physical barrier, but the spiritual enmity between Jews and Gentiles, which separated them. Since Christ destroyed this enmity (cf. v. 16), Jewish and Gentile believers should have no hostility.

2:15-16. Paul now described how and why this enmity came to an end. The animosity between believing Jews and Gentiles ceased because by Christ's death (**in His flesh** suggests His actual physical death; cf. Col. 1:22) He rendered **the Law** "inoperative" (*katargēsas*) in believers' lives. Jews and Gentiles were enemies because the former sought to keep the Law **with its commandments and regulations** (cf. Col. 2:14, 21-23), whereas Gentiles were unconcerned about them. This difference was like a barrier between them. But now that the Law is inoperative ("Christ is the end of the Law" [Rom. 10:4]), Jewish-Gentile hostility is gone. Some translations (e.g., KJV, NASB) give the idea that the Law was the enmity, but that is wrong; the Law was the cause of the enmity. Christ "destroyed" the barrier (hostility) by making the Law inoperative.

Christ had two purposes in ending the hostility. The first **purpose was to create in Himself one new man out of the two, thus making peace.** The word "new" (*kainon*) means new or fresh in character or quality rather than new in the sense of recent in time (*neos*). This "new man" (Eph. 2:15), or "new humanity," is also called "this one body" (v. 16), the church. In the church, Gentiles do not become Jews, nor do Jews become Gentiles. Instead believing Jews and Gentiles become Christians, a whole new single entity.

Christ's second purpose in destroying the enmity was **to reconcile both** Jewish and Gentile believers to Himself **in . . . one body** (cf. 3:6). This reconciliation was accomplished **through the cross, by which** Christ killed (**put to death**) the enmity between people and God. Though *He* was put to death, He in turn put to death the Jewish-Gentile **hostility.** In 2:14 the reconciliation is between Jewish and Gentile believers, and in verse 16 the reconciliation is between people and God. Reconciliation (removal of enmity) between man and God is mentioned elsewhere by Paul (Rom. 5:10; 2 Cor. 5:18-20; Col. 1:20).

b. Announcement of peace (2:17-18)

2:17-18. Verse 17 begins in Greek with "and" (untranslated in the NIV). This links verse 17 with verse 14. Not only is Christ "our peace" (v. 14), but **He** also **preached peace.** When did Christ do this? Certainly this refers to the preaching of peace by the apostles rather than Christ Himself because Christ preached almost entirely to Jews (Matt. 10:5-6; 15:24-27). Also the peace that was preached was on the basis of Christ's death rather than during His life on earth. **Peace** is supplied both **to those who were far away** (cf. Eph. 2:13), that is, Gentiles (who were without Christ and alienated from Israel and her covenants, v. 12) and **to those who were near,** namely, Jews (who have "the covenants of the promise," v. 12).

As a result of this message of peace both Jewish and Gentile believers **have access to God the Father by one Spirit** (cf. 1 Cor. 12:13). Access can mean "introduction" in the sense that Christ *is* a believer's "introduction" to the Father. But it seems better to understand that Christ *gives* believers access. The Greek word for access (*prosagōgēn*, "approach") is used elsewhere in the New Testament only in Romans 5:2 and Ephesians 3:12. As so often in this book the work of the Trinity is seen. Here believers have access to God the Father through the Holy Spirit because of Christ's death on the cross.

In four ways in 2:14-18 Paul emphasized that the two (Jew and Gentile) have been united: (1) "the two" (*ta amphotera*) are made "one" (v. 14), (2) "one new man" is created "out of the two" (v. 15), (3) "in this *one* body . . . both" (*tous amphoterous*) are reconciled (v. 16), and (4) "both" (*hoi amphoteroi*) "have access . . . by *one* Spirit" (v. 18). Nothing could be clearer than the fact that this new union replaces enmity.

3. CONSEQUENCE OF THE UNION (2:19-22)

Having stated and explained the union of Jewish and Gentile believers Paul then described the consequence of that union.

a. *The fact: a new relationship (2:19)*

2:19. Consequently (*ara oun*) **you,** that is, Gentile believers, **are no longer foreigners** (*xenoi*; cf. v. 12) **and aliens.** Believing Gentiles become **fellow citizens with God's people and members of God's household.** They become a part of the company of the redeemed of all ages beginning with Adam. However, this does not mean that the church inherits the blessings promised to Israel. There are three reasons for this: (1) In the context Paul was discussing the "one new man" (v. 15), the "one body" (v. 16). This does not mean that Gentiles are incorporated into Israel but that believing Jews and Gentiles are incorporated into one new "humanity." (2) Paul specifically stated that Gentiles are incorporated "with God's people" and are in "God's household" (v. 19); he did not use the word "Israel." If Paul meant that the church became "Israel," he would have named both groups, as he did in verse 11. (3) Paul explained that this new relationship is "built on the foundation of the apostles and prophets with Christ Jesus Himself as the chief Cornerstone" (v. 20). This began on the day of Pentecost, not in the Old Testament. True, Gentile believers become a part of the redeemed of all ages (v. 19). But their being incorporated with Jewish believers into the "one new man" distinctly began when the church came into being at Pentecost.

b. *The cause: a new establishment (2:20-22)*

Paul described the church as a great building, a holy temple in which God dwells. This figure of God dwelling in a temple comes from the Old Testament. Paul wrote of the building's foundation (v. 20), formation (v. 21), and function (v. 22).

2:20. Paul first described the foundation of the building. The reason Gentile believers are "fellow citizens" (v. 19) is that they are **built on the foundation of the apostles and prophets.** The "prophets" are of the New Testament era, not the Old Testament. "Prophets" follows the word "apostles" here and in 3:5 and 4:11. These men received the revelation of the mystery of the church in the present Age, which had been hidden in days past, that is, in Old Testament times (3:5).

The words "apostles and prophets" could modify "the foundation." This could mean (a) that the foundation was built by them, or (b) that the foundation came from them, or (c) that they own a foundation or, as seems best, (d) that they are the foundation. The words could be translated, "the foundation which consists of the apostles and prophets." This makes the best sense when one sees in 4:11 that the apostles and prophets were gifted men given to the church as its "foundation." Furthermore, this fits well in the present context, which states that **Christ Jesus Himself** is **the chief Cornerstone,** that is, He is part of the foundation. In ancient building practices "the chief cornerstone" was carefully placed. It was crucial because the entire building was lined up with it. The church's foundation, that is, the apostles and prophets, needed to be correctly aligned with Christ. All other believers are built on that foundation, measuring their lives with Christ.

2:21. Paul then discussed the formation of the building. **In Christ the whole building is joined together.** The ASV has "each several building" (rather than "the whole building"). But it is preferable to understand the Greek to refer to one whole superstructure, perhaps in several parts. The participle translated "is joined together" is *synarmologoumenē*, used only here and in 4:16. It denotes that the various parts of the building are skillfully fitted to each other, not haphazardly thrown together. This structure **rises to become** (lit., "continually grows [pres. tense] into") **a holy temple in the Lord.** This indicates that the church is a living and growing organism, as new believers are included in this temple's superstructure (cf. 4:15-16; 1 Peter 2:5). Both Jewish and Gentile believers are being "joined together" into this one organism labeled "a holy temple" (cf. "one new man" [Eph. 2:15] and "one body" [v. 16]). The word for temple (*naos*) always refers to the sanctuary within the physical structure in Jerusalem, not to the entire temple area with its open courts (*hieron*).

2:22. Paul now discussed the function of the temple. God places individual believers into the structure; thus it is **being built together.** The goal of this temple is **to become a dwelling in which God lives by His Spirit.** In the Old Testament God's glory was in the temple, which represented His presence with the people. In this Age God dwells in His new temple which is constructed not from inanimate materials but of living believers. The Holy Spirit indwells each individual believer (cf. John 14:17; Rom. 5:5; 8:9, 11; 1 Cor. 2:12; Gal. 3:2; 4:6; 1 John 3:24; 4:13), who is thus a "temple" (1 Cor. 6:19). But the temple in Ephesians 2:21-22 refers to the Holy Spirit's *corporate* "dwelling" (cf. 1 Cor. 3:16; 2 Cor. 6:16), His "temple" composed of *all* Jewish and Gentile believers.

"By His Spirit" is literally, "by the Spirit," as it is translated in Ephesians 3:5.

In conclusion, Paul has shown that though the Gentiles were formerly outside God's household, they are now one "new man" with Jewish believers. This new entity is like a temple that is structured on the apostles and prophets, with Christ being the chief Cornerstone; it is indwelt by God through the agency of the Holy Spirit.

F. Parenthetical expansion of the mystery (3:1-13)

Having discussed the union of Jewish and Gentile believers in the church (2:11-22), Paul was about to offer a prayer on behalf of these believers. But he stopped right in the middle of a sentence (at the end of 3:1) and digressed on the subject of the mystery of Christ. He explained this mystery and his responsibility to dispense it. Then he resumed his prayer, starting with verse 14.

1. THE INTRODUCTION (3:1)

3:1. The words **for this reason** (also used in v. 14) specifically point back to 2:11-22, which dealt with the Jewish and Gentile believers being raised to a new plane. But they also more generally refer back to all the first part of the epistle in which Paul discussed God's grace to the Gentiles. The words **I, Paul, the prisoner of Christ Jesus for the sake of you Gentiles,** refer to Paul's imprisonment in Rome because of his service for Christ (cf. 4:1; 2 Tim. 1:8; Phile. 1, 9), and more particularly because of his ministry as the

apostle to the Gentiles (2 Tim. 1:11-12). Because of his faithfulness to the stewardship God had given him among the Gentiles (Eph. 3:2) bitter Jewish opposition arose against him. This resulted in his being attacked in Jerusalem and put on trial in Caesarea and Rome.

2. THE MYSTERY (3:2-6)

a. The dispensation of God's grace (3:2)

3:2. Having broken off in the middle of a sentence in verse 1, Paul began one new long sentence that ended with verse 13 (one of eight lengthy sentences in Eph.; see comments on 1:3-14). It is a conditional sentence with 3:2 serving as its introduction (**Surely** in v. 2 is lit., "If indeed") and verse 13 as its conclusion. Paul wrote of **the administration of God's grace that was given to** him (v. 2) and concluded by asking them not to be discouraged over his imprisonment in Rome (v. 13). The details of his message and ministry are in verses 3-12. Probably the NIV used "surely" because the wording implies certainty that the Ephesians had heard of his responsibility. Now he spoke of it in greater detail. The word "administration" (*oikonomia*; cf. v. 9) has the sense of stewardship or a trust to be dispensed (in 1 Cor. 9:17 *oikonomia* is trans. "trust" and in Col. 1:25 it is rendered "commission"). Paul was to administer "God's grace" (cf. Eph. 3:7), which was given to him. He elaborated on this in verses 3-6. This grace was given to him to dispense to the Gentiles (v. 1) at Ephesus (**for you**), because he was an apostle to the Gentiles (Gal. 2:7; Eph. 3:8).

b. The revelation of the mystery (3:3-5)

3:3. **That is** further explains that **the mystery** is the "grace" mentioned in verse 2. That mystery (a truth hitherto unknown) is not defined till verse 6. The mystery's disclosure was given to Paul **by revelation,** which in fact he had **already written briefly** about, not in another epistle, but in this one (in 2:11-22).

3:4. The Ephesian Christians would **be able to understand** his **insight** (*synesin*; cf. Col. 1:9; 2:2) **into the mystery of Christ** (cf. Col. 1:27; 2:2) by **reading** what he had "already written." Paul's next words (Eph. 3:5-6) would further enhance their understanding of it. His "insight" was not his own discovery; it was revealed by God.

3:5. Paul then revealed the time when the mystery was disclosed. The mystery **was not made known to men in other generations as it has . . . been revealed.** This statement has caused some debate among Bible students. The problem hinges on the comparative adverb "as" (*hōs*). Some take this as restrictive (a comparison of degree), which would mean that the mystery was partially revealed in the Old Testament but is now fully revealed in the Church Age. The thought of the verse should be, God has not revealed this mystery in the past *to the extent* He has now. Others see the adverb "as" to be descriptive (a comparison of kind), which means that no revelation of this mystery was given in the Old Testament but that this mystery was revealed for the first time in the New Testament.

The second view is a better interpretation for five reasons: (1) Though the restrictive sense for "as" is more common, the descriptive sense *is* used sometimes (e.g., Peter said that the disciples were not drunk "as" the Jews thought [Acts 2:15]). (In fact, sometimes "as" could be trans. "because," e.g., the second "as" in 2 Tim. 1:3.)

(2) The context supports this view for Paul wrote that this mystery was hidden in the past (Eph. 3:9).

(3) Colossians 1:26, parallel to Ephesians 3:5, does not use the comparative adverb "as," but clearly states that the mystery was "kept hidden for ages . . . but is now" (*nun de*) made manifest to the saints.

(4) The position of the temporal adverb "now" (*nun*) agrees with Colossians 1:26 in marking the contrast between the two Ages. In the past the mystery was not known but "now" it is. This is substantiated by the same temporal adverb (*nun*) in Ephesians 3:10: "The manifold wisdom of God" (which is the mystery) is "now" to be made known to the heavenly hosts. If the heavenly hosts did not know of the mystery in the Old Testament, how would people have found out about it? Since the heavenly hosts learned of the mystery through the church (which did not exist before Pentecost) certainly people in the Old Testament did not know.

(5) "Revealed" means "to uncover or unveil" something that has previously been completely covered or hidden. Therefore it would be wrong to say the mystery was *partially* uncovered in the Old Testament.

Those who hold the first view ("as" is a comparison of degree) argue that passages such as Isaiah 2:1-4 and 61:5-6 indicate that Gentiles received God's blessings along with Israel. However, these passages speak of the Millennium, not of the concept of Gentiles and Jews being in one body, the church.

This mystery was revealed **by the Spirit** (cf. Eph. 2:22), and its recipients were **God's holy apostles and prophets** (cf. 2:20; 4:11). Some have promoted the idea that this revelation was given to Paul, but 3:5 explicitly states that it was given to the apostles and prophets and that Paul was one who was to disseminate it.

c. The constitution of the mystery (3:6)

3:6. Paul now defined the **mystery.** In three compound nouns he stated that the Gentile believers with the Jewish believers **are** (a) **heirs together** (i.e., "fellow heirs," 2:19, KJV) of God's riches (1:3-14), (b) are **of** the same **body** (cf. 2:16; *syssōma* occurs only in 3:6 in the NT), **and** (c) are **sharers together in the promise** (the messianic promise; cf. 2:12; Gal. 3:29) **in Christ Jesus.** (See comments on Eph. 2:19 and 3:5 regarding the relationship of the church and **Israel.**)

Thus the mystery is not something mysterious, but is a sacred secret hidden in Ages past but now revealed. This is made possible **through the gospel:** believing Jews and **Gentiles** are in **one** body. The mystery is not that Gentiles would be saved, for the Old Testament gave evidence of that, but rather that believing Jews and Gentiles are joined **together.** That was a revolutionary concept for Jews and Gentiles alike!

3. THE MINISTRY (3:7-12)

Having described the mystery (vv. 2-6), Paul now discussed his ministry of dispensing this mystery to the Gentiles.

a. The placement into the ministry (3:7-8a)

3:7-8a. I became a servant of this gospel (cf. "gospel" in v. 6) denotes Paul's rendering of service (cf. Col. 1:23). The word "servant" (*diakonos*) stresses not the idea of subjection (as does *doulos,* "slave") but the idea of service or serving, as one who is a waiter (John 2:5, 9). This service has its basis in **the gift of God's grace** (cf. Eph. 3:2) **given to** Paul **through the working of His power** (cf. 1:19; Col. 1:29). The Greek more clearly implies that Paul's service was initiated by "the gift of God's grace" and continues by "the working (*energeian*) of His power" (*dynameōs*). Ministering **this grace**—by God's strength, not his own—was Paul's responsibility though he considered himself **less than the least of all God's people.** ("God's people" renders *hagiōn*, "saints"; cf. Eph. 1:1, 15). This denotes Paul's deep humility in view of God's incomparably generous grace.

b. *The performance of the ministry (3:8b-9)*

3:8b-9. Two infinitives state Paul's functioning in this ministry. First, he was **to preach to the Gentiles the unsearchable riches of Christ.** Second, he was **to make plain to everyone the administration of this mystery.** Though Paul ministered to both Jews and Gentiles (cf. comments on Acts 9:15), he was especially designated as the apostle "to the Gentiles" (Rom. 11:13; Gal. 1:16; 2:7-8).

The Gentiles can know something of the riches of Christ's blessings (cf. "the riches of God's grace" in Eph. 1:7 and 2:7 and the richness of His mercy in 2:4). Yet Christ's fathomless spiritual wealth can never be fully comprehended (*anexichniaston*, lit., "not capable of being traced by footprints"; used only here and in Rom. 11:33). Paul was to disclose publicly *to everyone,* not just the Ephesians (cf. Eph. 3:2) this stewardship of God's sacred secret (vv. 3-4, 6). This secret had been **hidden in God** (cf. v. 5), the Creator of the universe. Even before creating **all things** God had in mind this wonderful truth as part of His eternal plan (cf. 1:4, 11).

c. *The purpose of the ministry (3:10-12)*

3:10-12. The purpose (*hina*) of Paul's ministry **was that . . . the manifold wisdom** (*sophia*) **of God might be made known to the rulers and authorities in the heavenly realms.** In classical Greek the adjective "manifold" (*polypoikilos*) referred to the beauty of an embroidered pattern or the variety of colors in flowers (cf. *poikilēs,* "in its various forms," in

1 Peter 4:10). The "manifold wisdom of God" does not refer to redemption as such but rather to the new relationship between believing Jews and Gentiles in one body. The medium by which this wisdom is communicated is **the church;** the recipients are the angelic hosts "in the heavenly realms" (cf. Eph. 1:3). These "rulers and authorities" refer to both good and evil angels as seen in 6:12 (cf. 1:21). As the angelic hosts witness the church, they must admit that having Jews and Gentiles in one body is evidence of God's wisdom.

This mystery—that both believing Jews and Gentiles are in one body (3:6)—was revealed to the apostles and prophets (v. 5) and was disseminated by Paul (vv. 7-9). Its **purpose** was that angelic beings might see God's variegated wisdom. This whole plan was in accord with God's **eternal** intent **which He accomplished in Christ Jesus our Lord** (v. 11). This means either that God is now carrying out His eternal purpose, or that He carried it out (accomplished it) in Christ about 2,000 years ago. The latter view is preferable because (a) "accomplished" is in the past tense not the present or perfect tense, and (b) the inclusion of believing Jews and Gentiles in one body was in fact accomplished by Christ's death.

Through faith in Christ Christians have the right of address (**freedom,** *parrēsian,* lit., "courage, boldness"; cf. Heb. 3:6; 4:16; 10:19, 35) and the right of access (**approach,** *prosagōgēn;* cf. Eph. 2:18; Rom. 5:2) to **God with . . . confidence.** Though God's eternal plan was accomplished in Christ nearly two millennia ago, believers can still address God and go to Him freely and confidently.

4. THE INJUNCTION (3:13)

3:13. This verse marks the conclusion of the sentence begun in verse 2. If the Ephesians truly understood "the administration of God's grace that was given to" Paul (v. 2), they should **not . . . be discouraged because of** his **sufferings** for them. His sufferings were for their gain and **glory.** If Paul had not dispensed to the Gentiles the stewardship of God's grace, then Jews would not have been hostile to him and he would not have been imprisoned. His preaching brought salvation to the Gentiles, but it incurred the wrath of many Jews on him. However, many others became members of the church, Christ's body, and this was their glory.

G. Prayer for strengthened love (3:14-21)

Having stated that positionally the Gentile and Jewish believers are "one new man" (2:15), which is the body of Christ, Paul now prayed that they may be united experientially. He desired that they might genuinely know and experience Christ's love and thus exhibit it toward each other.

1. THE APPROACH TO PRAYER (3:14-15)

3:14-15. Verses 14-19 in the Greek are another of Paul's eight long sentences in Ephesians (see comments on 1:3-14). **For this reason** is an expression that is repeated from verse 1 when Paul was about to pray. He then broke off before finishing the sentence in order to elaborate on the mystery, the body of Christ, and on his ministry of dispensing the mystery. Paul's kneeling in prayer is one of several postures for praying (standing, kneeling, lying prostrate) seen in the Scriptures. The shorter reading, **the Father,** is preferred over the longer one found in the KJV, "the Father of our Lord Jesus Christ." The expression **from whom His whole family** means that all Creation including angels and humans are one family under the fatherhood of God. But this is problematic grammatically for the Greek has no pronoun ("His") before the word "whole." This also has problems theologically. A better translation both grammatically and theologically is "from whom every family" (cf. ASV, NASB, RSV). Paul was not saying that God is the Father of all but rather that He is the Prototype of all fatherhood. "Father" is derived from God, not man. He is the first Father, the only One with "underived" fatherhood. Thus every human family **derives its name,** that is, exists as a family with a father, because of Him. It is to this Father that Paul prayed.

2. THE APPEAL IN PRAYER (3:16-19)

Though the sentence begins in verse 14 and ends in verse 19, Paul's request begins in verse 16. In this prayer he asked for only one thing.

a. Petition stated: to be strengthened in the inner man (3:16-17a)

3:16-17a. The first part of Paul's request is that God, **out of** (*kata,* lit., "according to the standard of") **His glorious riches** (cf. 1:7, 18; 2:4, 7; 3:8) might **strengthen** (*krataiōthēnai,* "be strong to overcome resistance," cf. *kratous* in 1:19 and *kratei* in 6:10) believers **with power** (*dynamis,* dynamic living power; cf. 3:20) **through** the Holy **Spirit in** their **inner being**[s] (lit., "in the inner man," i.e., believers' innermost beings). The result of this is that **through faith** Christ **may dwell in** believers' **hearts,** that is, their whole personalities. "Dwell" (*katoikēsai*) refers not to the beginning of Christ's indwelling at the moment of salvation. Instead it denotes the desire that Christ may, literally, "be at home in," that is, at the very center of or deeply rooted in, believers' lives. They are to let Christ become the dominating factor in their attitudes and conduct.

b. Purpose stated: to comprehend Christ's love and to be filled unto God's fullness (3:17b-19)

3:17b-19. Paul continued his prayer by repeating his request that Christ be the center of believers' lives. He stated this in a mixed metaphor of biological and architectural terminology: **being rooted** (like a plant) **and established** (like a building) **in love.** The participles "being rooted and established" are in the perfect tense, indicating a past action with continuing results. They could be translated "having been rooted and established." The purpose of the request is that they **may have power** (*exischysēte,* "have inherent strength"), **together with all the saints, to grasp how wide and long and high and deep is the love of Christ.** These measurements most likely describe not the thoroughness of comprehension but the immensity of the thing to be comprehended.

Interestingly once again—as in (a) 1:13-14; (b) 1:17; (c) 2:18; (d) 2:22; and (e) 3:4-5—Paul spoke of the Trinity: the Father (v. 14), the Spirit (v. 16), and the Son (v. 17).

The content of this comprehension is **to know** experientially the **love** of Christ **that** supersedes all **knowledge** (cf. Phil. 4:7). The more a Christian knows about

Christ, the more amazed he is at Christ's love for him.

The final purpose is **that you may be filled to the measure of all the fullness of God.** The KJV and RSV translations, "that you may be filled with all the fullness of God," wrongly imply that the whole fullness of God can be contained in a believer's life. But this ignores the Greek preposition *eis* which denotes a goal; this is translated accurately in the NIV: "to the measure." The fullness of the Godhead is only in Christ, and only through Him is a believer made complete (Col. 2:9-10). Though in Christ this divine fullness is ideally a believer's already, Paul prayed that it might be experientially realized in each one (cf. Eph. 4:13). Experiencing God's moral excellence and perfection causes Jewish and Gentile believers to love each other. Positionally they are one in Christ; experientially they are to love each other as one in Him.

3. THE ASCRIPTION OF PRAISE (3:20-21)

3:20-21. Paul closed this prayer with a doxology. He praised God **who is able to do** far **more than** one could **ask or imagine, according to** the standard of **His power** (*dynamin*; cf. v. 16; 1:19) **that is at work** (*energoumenēn*; cf. 1:19) **within us.** No human or angel (cf. 3:10) would ever think that Jews and Gentiles could function together in one body. But with God's power of love in each believer's life, Paul was confident that Jewish and Gentile believers can function and love one another. This is astounding and though it is not naturally possible, God is able to accomplish it. Paul therefore ascribed to God **glory** which is to be manifest **in the church,** where the miracle of love will occur, **and in Christ Jesus,** who made the union of Jewish and Gentile believers possible.

Praise to Him for this accomplishment is to continue throughout eternity (cf. Rom. 11:36; 2 Tim. 4:18). This doxology serves as a fitting conclusion not only to this prayer but also to this book's first three chapters.

II. The Conduct of the Church (chaps. 4–6)

After presenting doctrinal content in the first three chapters, Paul then gave in chapters 4–6 some practical applications of those doctrines. His repeated emphasis

on a believer's "walk" (*peripateō*) is the hallmark of this section. The NIV translates "walk" as "live."

A. Walking in unity (4:1-16)

Having explained the unity of Jewish and Gentile believers, and having prayed for that unity through mutually experiencing Christ's love, Paul now showed how they were to walk in the unity of that body. This is accomplished by gifted people given to the church by Christ so that the body of Christ might grow up in all areas.

1. THE BASIS OF UNITY (4:1-6)

a. Exhortation to unity (4:1-3)

4:1. Paul exhorted them to walk **(live a life) worthy** of their **calling.** The NIV gives the impression that this walk should be on the basis that Paul was **a prisoner for the Lord.** However, the Greek does not connote this. Rather it is, "Therefore (rather than **then**) I, the prisoner of the Lord (as already stated in 3:1), beseech you to walk worthy of your calling." Thus on the basis of what Paul wrote in chapters 1–3 he implored them to walk worthily. The word "worthy" (*axiōs*) means "equal weight"; one's calling and conduct should be in balance. "The calling" refers not only to believers' salvation (cf. Rom. 1:5-6; 1 Cor. 1:9) but also to their union in one body. Therefore a Christian's conduct concerns both his personal life and his responsibility to other believers in the church.

4:2-3. Believers' attitudes are also important. Paul listed three virtues that are to enhance a believer's walk. The first of these is humility. In Greek culture, humility was thought of as a vice, to be practiced only by slaves. But Paul stated that saints should **be completely humble** in their daily walks. This is the opposite of pride. On the other hand Christians should not promote false humility, but should recognize who they are in God's program (cf. John 3:30; Rom. 12:3). This virtue is listed first because of Paul's emphasis on unity (pride promotes disunity; humility promotes unity) and to counteract their past pride, so as to facilitate obedience to and dependence on God. Christ was the supreme example of humility (Phil. 2:6-8).

Second, a believer is to be **gentle** or "meek" (*prautētos*; cf. the adverb of this word in Gal. 6:1; 2 Tim. 2:25 and the noun in Gal. 5:23; Col. 3:12; 1 Peter 3:16). This is the opposite of self-assertion, rudeness, and harshness. It suggests having one's emotions under control. But it does not suggest weakness. It is the mean between one who is angry all the time and one who is never angry. One who is controlled by God is angry at the right time but never angry at the wrong time. Moses was known as the meekest of all men (Num. 12:3, KJV). Yet he got angry when Israel sinned against God (Ex. 32). Christ was meek and humble in heart (Matt. 11:29). Yet He became angry because some Jews were using the temple as a place for thieves (Matt. 21:12-13).

Third, believers should exhibit patience (*makrothymias*). Patience is the spirit which never gives up for it endures to the end even in times of adversity (James 5:10). It is the self-restraint which does not hastily retaliate a wrong (cf. Gal. 5:22; Col. 1:11; 3:12; 2 Tim. 4:2).

Attitudes of humility, gentleness, and patience foster unity among Christians. Having stated these three virtues, Paul then stated the manner in which they are to be carried out in one's conduct: **bearing with one another in love** and making **every effort** (the Gr. has a participle, "making every diligent effort") **to keep the unity of the Spirit through the bond of peace.** Christians are not to make unity but to keep or guard what God made in creating the "one new man" (Eph. 2:15-16). They are to keep this unity "through the bond" which consists of "peace." Concern for peace will mean that Christians will lovingly tolerate each other, even when they have differences.

b. *Elements of unity (4:4-6)*

4:4. Without a conjunction Paul listed the seven elements of unity centered on the three Persons of the Trinity. These provide the basis for the spirit of unity that should exist in the body of believers. **One body** refers to the universal church, all believers (1:23; 2:16; 3:6). **One Spirit** is the Holy Spirit who indwells the church (2:22). The words, **just as you were called to one hope when you were called,** indicate that all believers have a common hope regarding their future with God (cf. 1 Peter 1:3; 3:15), a confidence that began at the time

they were "called" to salvation (Eph. 1:4, 18; 2:7; 4:1).

4:5. One Lord (cf. Rom. 10:12) refers to Christ, the Head of the church (Eph. 1:22-23; Col. 1:18). **One faith** speaks, most likely, not of objective faith, that is, the body of truth believed by Christians (as in Acts 6:7; 1 Tim. 3:9; 4:1, 6; Jude 3) but subjective faith which is exercised by all Christians in Christ their Lord (cf. Col. 2:7). **One baptism** may refer to water baptism, the outward symbol of the inward reality, or it may refer to a believer's identification with Christ and His death (Rom. 6:1-11; Gal. 3:27). It seems unlikely that this refers to the latter, Spirit baptism, because it is in the triad of elements that pertain to Christ, the second Person of the Trinity. Also nothing in the broader context (Eph. 4:1-16) suggests that this is the Spirit's baptism. If it refers to water baptism, then the idea is that by this single act believers demonstrate their spiritual unity.

4:6. One God and Father of all who is over all and through all and in all refers to God the Father and His relationship to all believers. The fourfold use of "all" refers to "all believers," not "all mankind." Certainly these characteristics are not common to all people. God is the Father "of" all who believe; they are His children (John 1:12; Gal. 3:26). And He is "over" all them as their Sovereign. He lives "through" them and manifests Himself "in" them.

Two observations should be noted about this list of seven unifying elements (Eph. 4:4-6). First, the Trinity is an integral part of the list. The one body of believers is vitalized by one *Spirit,* so all believers have one hope. That body is united to its one *Lord* (Christ) by each member's one act of faith, and its identity with Him is depicted by one baptism. One *God,* the Father, is supreme over all, operative through all, and resides in all. All seven components are united in the Trinity.

Second, the order in the listing of the three Persons of the Trinity is interesting. Paul began with the Holy Spirit rather than with the Father. The reason for this is that in the preceding verses he was discussing "the unity of the Spirit" (v. 3) and in verses 7-13 he discussed the gifts of the Spirit. The same order of Trinity Members is given in 1 Corinthians 12:4-6, where Paul also discussed the gifts of the Spirit.

2. THE PRESERVATION OF UNITY (4:7-16)

After discussing the basis of unity (vv. 1-6), Paul now analyzed the means of preserving that unity (cf. "keep the unity," v. 3) of the body by means of the various gifts.

a. The distribution of the gifts (4:7-11)

4:7-8. Previously Paul discussed the unity of the entire church (vv. 1-6). Now he discussed the diversity within the church (cf. unity in 1 Cor. 12:12-13, and diversity in 1 Cor. 12:4-11, 14-20). From God **each** believer receives **grace** or enablement (cf. Eph. 3:2, 7-8) **as Christ apportioned it** (lit., "according to the measure [*metron*, also used in 4:13, 16]; of the gift of Christ," i.e., the gift He is pleased to give). Each believer is to function in Christ's body by God's enablement, proportionate to the gift (spiritual ability) bestowed on him, no more and no less. This means that a variety of gifts will be exercised, as seen in verse 11; Romans 12:4-6; and 1 Corinthians 12:4-6. Furthermore, since each believer receives "grace," clergy and laity—to use a common present-day distinction—are on the same level in exercising their gifts.

Ephesians 4:8 includes a quotation from the Old Testament, which confirms God's giving of gifts. Most think it quotes Psalm 68:18 with five minor and two major changes. The two major variations are the change from the second to the third person, and the change of direction from having received gifts from men to the giving of **gifts to men.** However, it is better to think that Paul was not quoting one particular verse of the psalm but rather that he was summarizing all of Psalm 68, which has many words similar to those in Psalm 68:18. The essence of the psalm is that a military victor has the right to give gifts to those who are identified with him. Christ, having captivated sinful people by redeeming them, is Victor and gives them as gifts to the church. Whereas Romans 12 and 1 Corinthians 12 speak of gifts given to believers, Ephesians 4:7 speaks more of gifted believers given to the church (cf. v. 11).

4:9-10. Verses 9-11 serve as a com-

mentary on two words of the quotation in verse 8, namely, **ascended** (vv. 9-10) and "gave" (v. 11). In verses 9-10 Paul commented on the words **He ascended.** These two verses are parenthetical in thought because the issue of the passage is the giving of gifts. Before Christ could ascend He had to descend. What is meant by **to the lower, earthly regions,** literally, "into the lower parts of earth"? The genitive "of" can be taken in three ways: (1) "Into the lower parts, namely, the earth" (a genitive of apposition). This would refer to Christ's incarnation, His "descent" to the earth. (2) "Into the parts lower than the earth" (a genitive of comparison). This would mean that Christ descended into hades between His death and resurrection. (3) "Into the lower parts which belong to the earth" (a genitive of possession). This would refer to Christ's death and His burial in the grave. The third view best fits the context because in His death Christ had victory over sin and redeemed those who would be given as "gifts" to the church.

Christ's ascent above **the heavens, in order to fill the whole universe** probably refers to His regal relationship with the whole world, from which position He bestows gifts as He wills because of His work on the Cross. This fits well with 1:23, which speaks of Christ imparting all the fullness of His blessings to the church and to the universe. Christ, who embodies the fullness of the Godhead (Col. 2:9), fills the universe and is Head over it (cf. Col. 1:18).

4:11. This verse is a commentary on the second part of the quotation in verse 8, namely, Christ's giving gifts to Christians. The gifts to the church are gifted people. The subject **He** is emphatic in the Greek to denote that Christ Himself gives the gifted people. Five kinds of gifted people are listed in the predicate accusative, so the NIV correctly translates, **gave some to be.** The first two, **apostles** and **prophets,** were already mentioned in 2:20 and 3:5 as the foundational gifts to the church. The apostles include the Twelve, who had the office of apostleship by virtue of being with Christ (Acts 1:21-22) and having been appointed by Him (which would also include Paul; 1 Cor. 15:8-9; Gal. 1:1; 2:6-9). But "apostles" also included others who were recognized as apostles, such as James (1 Cor. 15:7; Gal.

1:19), Barnabas (Acts 14:4, 14; 1 Cor. 9:6), Andronicus and Junias (Rom. 16:7), possibly Silas and Timothy (1 Thes. 1:1; 2:7), and Apollos (1 Cor. 4:6, 9). This latter group had the gift of apostleship but not the apostolic "office" as did the Twelve and Paul. Apostles, then, were those who carried the gospel message with God's authority. "Apostle" means "one sent as an authoritative delegate."

New Testament prophets were gifts to the church to provide edification, exhortation, and comfort (1 Cor. 14:3). They probably revealed God's will to the church when the biblical canon was incomplete. Since the apostles and prophets were foundational, they did not exist after the first generation of believers.

Evangelists were those engaged in spreading the gospel, similar to present-day missionaries. **Pastors and teachers** are listed together because they are governed by one article ("the" occurs before "pastors" but not before "teachers") and because the word "and" (*kai*) differs from the other "and's" (*de*) in the verse. This may imply that these are two kinds of gifted people whose ministries are among settled congregations (rather than itinerant ministries like those of the apostles and evangelists). More likely, they refer to two characteristics of the same person who is pastoring believers (by comforting and guiding) while at the same time instructing them in God's ways (overseers or elders are to be able to teach; 1 Tim. 3:2; Titus 1:9).

b. The intention of the gifts (4:12-16)

The purpose of the gifted believers (vv. 7-11) is to equip other believers for the ministry so as to give them stability doctrinally and practically and thus lead them to mutual edification. Like several other passages in Ephesians (1:3-14, 15-23; 2:1-7; 3:1-13, 14-19; 4:1-7; 6:14-20), 4:11-16 is one long sentence in Greek.

4:12. The purpose of the gifted men is **to prepare God's people for works of service.** More literally, this purpose is "for the perfecting or equipping (*katartismon;* cf. the verb *katartizō* in Matt. 4:21, 'mending' or 'preparing' nets; in Gal. 6:1, 'restore' for proper use; cf. 2 Cor. 13:11; Heb. 13:21) of the saints unto the work of the ministry" (*diakonias*). Gifted people (Eph. 4:11) are to minister the Word to others so that they in turn are readied to

get involved in ministering to others (cf. 2 Tim. 2:2). The goal of all this is the building up or edifying of **the body of Christ** (cf. Eph. 4:16). This shows that all saints and not just a few leaders should be involved in the "ministry." All saints are gifted (v. 7) to serve others spiritually.

4:13. Gifted people are to minister till **all** the church attains (**reach** translates *katantēsōmen,* used in Acts of travelers arriving at their destinations) the three goals, each introduced by the Greek preposition (*eis,* "unto"): literally, (1) "unto the **unity** of **the faith** (cf. Eph. 4:5) and full **knowledge** (*epignōseōs;* cf. 1:17) of the Son of God," (2) "unto a **mature man**," and (3) "unto the **measure** (*metron;* cf. 4:7, 16) of the stature **of the fullness of Christ**." As each believer functions in accord with the gift(s) Christ has given him (v. 7) the body as a whole enjoys unity (cf. vv. 3-6) and becomes more spiritually mature (cf. v. 15), more like Jesus Christ in all His fullness (cf. 1:23; 3:19).

4:14-16. Here Paul expressed the ultimate purpose, or perhaps better, the result (*hina*) of gifted people equipping saints to serve the Lord and others. Negatively, believers should not **be** like immature **infants** who are easily swayed and confused, like **waves** being **tossed back and forth** (cf. Luke 8:24; James 1:6) **and blown here and there** (lit., "whirled around," a violent swinging that makes one dizzy) **by every** gust of **wind of teaching . . . by the cunning,** better, "trickery" (*kybeia,* lit., "dice-playing") **of men in their deceitful scheming** (*panourgia,* also used in Luke 20:23; 1 Cor. 3:19; 2 Cor. 4:2; 11:3), moving toward (*pros* indicates goal) a system of error. False teachers cause this kind of confusion regarding the truth in order to try to bring believers into their erroneous schemes. In contrast (*de,* Eph. 4:15) Paul stated positively that by **speaking the truth in love** (lit., "truthing in love," which has the idea of maintaining truth in love in both speech and life) believers may **grow up into Him** with reference to **all things.** Christ, then, is the Source of a believer's growth and also the Aim and Goal of his growth (cf. v. 13). From the Head (cf. 1:22; 5:23; Col. 1:18) the body derives its **whole** capacity for growth and activity (Eph. 4:16). Each member of the body is **joined** (2:21) by being carefully fitted **together,**

and each member is held or brought together by means of **every supporting ligament** (cf. Col. 2:19) according to the standard (*kata*, with the accusative) of the **measured working** (*metrō*, from *metron*) of **each individual.** This causes the body of Christ to grow (cf. Eph. 4:15) and build **itself up** (cf. v. 12) **in love.** The phrase "in love" occurs three times (vv. 2, 15-16), thus pointing to the way unity is maintained. Significantly the word "measure" (*metron*) is also used three times in this context (vv. 7, 13, 16). Each believer is to function in Christ's body by God's enabling grace in accord with the measure of the gift Christ bestowed on him (v. 7). When each believer accomplishes that measure, then the church **grows** properly (v. 16), coming ultimately to the measure of Christlikeness (v. 13). Stunted growth comes when one does not allow his or others' gifts to function.

The preservation of unity is the responsibility of God's gifted people in the church (vv. 7-16). In this unity of structure is variety of function. Paul emphasized body growth, not self-growth. **Each** individual contributes to this unified growth as he allows his particular gift(s) to function.

B. Walking in holiness (4:17-32)

Believers are to walk in holiness as well as unity. Paul first showed negatively how a believer should not walk; then he gave the positive aspects of Christian conduct.

1. PRESENTATION OF THE OLD MAN (4:17-19)

a. His nature (4:17-18)

4:17-18. The Ephesian believers who were Gentiles (2:1-2, 11-12) were not to walk **as the Gentiles do,** or as implied, as they had once walked. Gentiles walked **in the futility of their thinking.** The word for "futility" (*mataiotēti*; cf. Rom. 1:21) suggests being void of useful aim or goal. (This noun is used only here and in Rom. 8:20 [of Creation] and 2 Peter 2:18 [of words]. The verb *mataioō* is used in Rom. 1:21, "their thinking became futile.") Unbelieving Gentiles failed to attain the true purpose of the mind, namely, to receive God's revelation which would guide them in their conduct. Since their minds could not receive God's revelation, **their understanding** was **darkened** (Rom. 1:21; 2 Cor. 4:4), being **separated** (lit.,

"alienated"; cf. Eph. 2:12) **from the life of** (that comes from) **God.** Their alienation is **because of** their **ignorance** of God (cf. 1 Peter 1:14); and this is because of **the hardening of their hearts,** their being insensitive to God and His ways.

b. His practice (4:19)

4:19. Because of their lack of **sensitivity** these Gentiles gave **themselves over** ("abandoned themselves"; cf. Rom. 1:24, 26, 28) **to sensuality** (*aselgeia*, "licentiousness"; cf. Mark 7:22; Rom. 13:13; 2 Cor. 12:21; Gal. 5:19; 1 Peter 4:3; 2 Peter 2:2, 7, 18; Jude 4), a life without concern for personal standards or social sanctions. Their purpose (*eis*) was to practice **every kind of impurity, with a continual lust for more** (lit., "in greed"), indulging in self-gratification without regard for others. This is a horrible picture of sinful people's selfish and perverted ways.

2. PRESENTATION OF THE NEW MAN (4:20-32)

a. His position (4:20-24)

4:20-24. In contrast (*de*) with the "old man" (vv. 17-19) believers **did not come to know** (lit., "learn") **Christ that way.** Their minds are no longer darkened; their lives are no longer alienated from God; their hearts are no longer hardened and impure. Christ is the Subject (**you heard of Him**) and the Sphere (**you were taught in Him**) of a believer's learning. This teaching and learning is **in accordance with the truth,** because He is the Truth (John 14:6). The content of this learning is twofold: (1) A believer has **put off** the **old self which is being corrupted by its deceitful desires** (cf. Eph. 4:17-19). Self-centered lusts are deceitful because they promise joy but fail to provide it. (2) He has **put on the new self** which has been **created to be like God in true righteousness and holiness,** which is based on truth (v. 24). This truth contrasts with the deceitfulness of lustful living (cf. vv. 14-15). Believers have been **made new in the attitude of** their **minds;** they are no longer futile in their thinking, darkened in their understanding, and ignorant (vv. 18-19). These are not commands, for the construction here (and in the parallel passage in Col. 3:9-10) is not imperative. They are facts that believers have learned, as is also seen in Romans 6:2-10 and 2 Corinthians 5:17. Believers are new people in Christ, and hence they can no longer live as Gentiles live, as the next exhortations state.

b. His practice (4:25-32)

Each of the following five exhortations about a believer's conduct has three parts: (1) a negative command, (2) a positive command, and (3) the reason for the positive command.

4:25. Having **put** away **falsehood,** believers are to tell the truth (cf. v. 15). Truth is conforming one's words to reality. The reason for this exhortation is that believers **are all members of one** another in Christ's **body,** the church (cf. vv. 4, 16).

4:26-27. While believers may at times be legitimately angry (with righteous **anger** against sin; cf. John 2:13-16), they are **not** to **sin.** The way to prevent such sin is to "keep short accounts," dealing with the anger before **the sun** goes **down.** The reason is that **the devil** would like to intensify a Christian's righteous anger against sin, causing it to become sin itself. This then gives the devil **a foothold** (lit., "a place"), an opportunity for leading that Christian into further sin. Then anger begins to control the believer rather than the believer controlling his anger.

4:28. Christians are not to **steal,** but are to **work** in order to give to the needy. A thief takes from others for his own benefit, whereas a believer is to work, **doing something useful** (agathon, "beneficial"; cf. v. 29) **with his own hands** for the purpose of sharing **with those in need.** This is true Christian charity. Work has many benefits: it provides for a person's material needs, it gives him something useful to do (something that is beneficial to himself and others), and it enables him to help others materially.

4:29-30. Believers are **not** to speak **unwholesome** (sapros, "rotten") words (cf. 5:4), but **helpful** (agathos, "good, beneficial"; cf. 4:28) words for the purpose of edification. Good words **benefit** (lit., "give grace" or enablement to) the hearers. One's words are to be true and pure and also are to contribute to benefiting others. Besides one's conscience, **the Holy Spirit** also helps guard a believer's speech. The fact that the Holy Spirit may be grieved points to His

personality. His seal of a believer remains until **the day of redemption,** the time that a believer receives his new body (cf. 1:14; Phil. 3:20-21).

4:31-32. Believers are to **get rid of** the six vices of **bitterness, rage** (thymos, "outbursts of anger"), **anger** (orgē, "settled feeling of anger"), **brawling** (kraugē, "shouting or clamor"), **slander** (blasphēmia), and **malice** (kakia, "ill will, wickedness"). Several of these vices are also listed in Colossians 3:8. The positive commands are three: (1) **be kind** (chrēstoi, lit., "what is suitable or fitting to a need"); (2) be **compassionate** (eusplanchnoi; used elsewhere in the NT only in 1 Peter 3:8; cf. splanchnoi, "inner emotions of affection," in 2 Cor. 6:12; 7:15; Phil. 1:8; 2:1; Col. 3:12; Phile. 7, 12, 20; 1 John 3:17); (3) be **forgiving** (lit., "being gracious," charizomenoi, the participle from the verb charizomai, "to give freely" or "to give graciously as a favor"). The reason for these positive commands is that **in Christ God** is kind (Eph. 2:7), compassionate (Mark 1:41), and gracious (Rom. 8:32) to believers.

C. Walking in love (5:1-6)

In applying his doctrines, Paul now for the third time used the term for "walk" (peripateō, trans. "live" in the NIV; 4:1, 17; 5:2). This is thus the third section in his discussion on the conduct of believers. God's children are to walk (live) in unity, in holiness, and in love.

1. THE POSITIVE: TO LOVE OTHERS (5:1-2)

5:1-2. Each Christian should **be** an imitator **of God** because he is God's child. As a child imitates his parents, so ought a believer to imitate God (cf. Matt. 5:48; Luke 6:36).

The **and** should be translated "that is" in order to convey the idea that Ephesians 5:2 explains how a believer is to imitate God: by walking in **love.** The supreme example of this love is Christ's love for His own—He **loved us;** seen graphically in His sacrificing His life on behalf of those who would believe. He willingly **gave Himself up** (cf. v. 25; John 10:11, 15, 17-18; Gal. 1:4; Heb. 9:14). This **offering** was a fragrance pleasing (and thus acceptable) **to God** (cf. Lev. 1:17; 3:16; Isa. 53:10). (The idea of **fragrant** offerings is also spoken of in 2 Cor. 2:15-16; Phil. 4:18.) Christians can imitate

God by loving others, even to the point of death if necessary (1 John 3:16).

2. THE NEGATIVE: TO ABSTAIN FROM EVIL (5:3-6)

a. Responsibility: to abstain from evil practices (5:3-4)

5:3. The self-centered vices in conduct and speech (vv. 3-4) are the opposite of the self-sacrificing love spoken of in verses 1-2. Since these vices portray selfishness and unconcern for others, a believer should **not** have **even a hint of** these sins in his life. **Sexual immorality** (*porneia*), **any kind of impurity,** and **greed are improper for** (lit., "should not be named among") believers. **God's holy people** is literally, "saints" (*hagiois*; cf. 1:1, 15).

5:4. Improprieties in speech—**obscenity** (*aischrotēs,* "shameless talk and conduct"), **foolish talk** (*mōrologia,* lit., "stupid words"), and **coarse** jesting (*eutrapelia,* "vulgar, frivolous wit")—**are out of place** for Jesus' followers, because such vices often harm (cf. 4:29), whereas **thanksgiving** is appreciation for others and is helpful. Paul was not intimating that humor itself is sin, but that it is wrong when it is used to destroy or tear down others.

b. Reason: no inheritance for evildoers (5:5-6)

5:5-6. Paul sternly warned believers that the reason they are to abstain from evil deeds (specifically, immorality, impurity, and greed; cf. vv. 3 and 5) is that those who practice them are not a part of God's kingdom. Those who have no **inheritance in the kingdom** have not been "washed," "sanctified," and "justified" as 1 Corinthians 6:9-11 so clearly demonstrates. A **greedy person . . . is an idolater** (cf. Col. 3:5) in the sense that greed, like idols, puts things before God.

Christians should not be deceived into thinking that this warning is merely **empty words** (*kenois,* trans. "empty" means void of content), for the **disobedient,** that is, the unregenerate (cf. Eph. 2:2) are the objects of **God's wrath** (cf. Col. 3:6). God's view of sin should be taken seriously. Believers should be imitators of God, not evildoers.

D. Walking in light (5:7-14)

The reason for dividing the outline here rather than between verses 5 and 6 (or between vv. 7 and 8) is because of the resumptive inferential particle (*oun,* "therefore") that marks the beginning of each new section: 4:1, 17; 5:1, 7, 15.

1. NOT BECOMING INVOLVED WITH EVILDOERS (5:7-10)

a. Command: do not get involved (5:7)

5:7. Christians, as objects of God's love (vv. 1-2), are inconsistent if they become **partners with** those who are the objects of God's wrath, those who are not "in the kingdom" (v. 5).

b. Reason: Christians are changed persons (5:8a)

5:8a. The reason (*gar,* for) believers should not be partners with the unregenerate is that Christians are no longer part of the **darkness,** in which they used to live (cf. 4:18; John 1:5; 3:19-20) **but . . . are light in the Lord** (Matt. 5:14-16; John 3:21; 8:12; Rom. 13:12; 1 Thes. 5:4-5). They have been rescued out of darkness (Col. 1:13). Now, being "in the Lord," who is the Light (John 8:12), they too are lights.

c. Command: walk as children of light (5:8b-10)

5:8b-10. The behavior of saints should correspond with their positions. Since they are **children of light,** that is, since their very nature is spiritual light, they are to **live** accordingly (Rom. 13:12). Ephesians 5:9 parenthetically explains that **the fruit of the light**—which is **goodness, righteousness** (cf. Phil. 1:11), **and truth**—reflects God's character in a believer's life. (The KJV rendering, "fruit of the Spirit," lacks good textual support.) Sinners, those in darkness, are characterized by the opposite of this fruit: evil, wickedness, and falsehood. The thought in verse 10 expands on verse 8b in that to live as children of light one must discern **what pleases the Lord** (cf. 2 Cor. 5:9; Col. 1:10). The words **find out** translate *dokimazontes,* which is literally, "putting to the test," "approving," or "discerning" (cf. Rom. 12:2).

2. NOT BECOMING INVOLVED WITH EVILDOERS' WORKS (5:11-13)

Those who profess Christ are to walk in light by not being partners with unbelievers (vv. 7-10). Now Paul mentioned that Christians are not to be involved with unbelievers' deeds (vv. 11-13).

a. Command: do not get involved but expose (5:11)

5:11. Christians are forbidden to be "sharers together" (*symmetochoi,* v. 7; cf. *metochoi* in Heb. 1:9 ["companions"]; 3:1, 14 ["share"]; 6:4 ["shared"]) with the sons of disobedience; now they are told not to take part (*synkoinōneite*) with unbelievers' actions. Their ways are **fruitless deeds of darkness** in contrast with "the fruit of the light" (Eph. 5:9). Sins bear no "fruit"; they give no benefits to oneself or others.

Christians, by conducting themselves as "children of light," **expose** the "deeds of darkness." These deeds, however, refer here to the deeds of other believers who are not walking in the light. This is because only God can expose and convict unbelievers' deeds (1 Cor. 5:12-13). Believers, on the other hand, can expose evil deeds among other Christians within the church. This the Corinthians failed to do (1 Cor. 5).

b. Reason: their works are shameful (5:12)

5:12. The things done **in secret** are too **shameful even** to talk about. The term **the disobedient** in the NIV wrongly suggests that this refers to unbelievers. However, the Greek has "what is done *by them,*" thus indicating that Paul may be referring to believers who commit "deeds of darkness."

c. Explanation: light shows the true character of works (5:13)

5:13. When **light** exposes evil deeds, they become **visible,** manifest for what they really are. Seeing them as evil, a believer then cleanses himself of them (1 John 1:5-7), realizing they are detrimental not only to him but also to other believers.

3. CONCLUSION: ENLIGHTENMENT OF CHRIST (5:14)

5:14. The introductory formula, **This is why it is said,** seems to indicate a quotation from the Old Testament, but it is difficult to identify unless it is a combination of passages (e.g., Isa. 26:19; 51:17; 52:1; 60:1). Possibly it is a quota-

tion from an early Christian hymn. A believer who has committed "deeds of darkness," is to **wake up** and **rise from the dead** since he was involved with the deeds of evildoers. Christ's shining on him speaks of His approval, an indication that he is discerning and following what is pleasing to the Lord (Eph. 5:10).

Therefore verses 7-14 deal with church discipline. Believers are to walk in the **light,** and in so doing to expose other believers of any works that are unfruitful so that they too may walk in the light and please their Lord.

E. Walking in wisdom (5:15–6:9)

For a fifth time Paul used the word "walk" (*peripateō*), translated "live" in the NIV (4:1, 17; 5:2, 8, 15). Here Paul instructed believers to be wise in their walk or conduct by being filled by the Holy Spirit.

1. ADMONITION (5:15-21)

a. Proper action: to walk wisely (5:15-16)

5:15-16. The NIV's **Be very careful, then, how you live** is literally, "Look therefore carefully how you walk." Does the adverb "carefully" (*akribōs,* lit. "accurately") modify "look"? If so the first clause in verse 15 could be translated, "Therefore look carefully how you walk." (This is behind the rendering in the ASV, NASB, and NIV.) Or does "careful" modify "walk"? If so, the idea is, "Therefore look that you walk carefully" (cf. KJV). This second alternative is preferred because better Greek manuscripts place *akribōs* closer to the Greek word "walk" and because in the New Testament the Greek imperative "look" (*blepete*) is never modified by an adverb. Believers then, are to walk (**live**) carefully, so as to be **wise** or skillful and thus please the Lord. The *manner* for this careful, precise walk is **making the** right use **of every opportunity** (cf. Col. 4:5), and the *reason* for this careful walk is that **the days are evil.** Many are walking in sin, and since the time is short believers must make full use of their time to help turn them from darkness to light. This necessitates wise conduct.

b. Proper state: to become wise (5:17-21)

5:17. Rather than being **foolish** (*aphrones,* "senseless") or "unwise" (*asophoi,* v. 15), Christians are to **under-**

stand (*syniete,* "comprehend intellectually") **what the Lord's will is.** Only after one understands what pleases God (v. 1) can he carry it out in his life.

5:18. Going from the general to the specific, Paul explained how wisdom, as an intellectual and spiritual capacity, works out in one's conduct. Verse 18 includes a negative command and a positive one. The negative is to abstain from getting **drunk on wine** with which there is incorrigibility. The word *asōtia* is translated **debauchery** (NIV, RSV), "excess" (KJV), "riot" (ASV), and "dissipation" (NASB). All these give the idea of profligate or licentious living that is wasteful. In this verse the literal sense of incorrigibility seems best, for a drunken man acts abnormally. Rather than controlling himself, the wine controls him. Conversely, the positive command is, **Be filled with the Spirit.** Thus a believer, rather than controlling himself, is controlled by the Holy Spirit. It may be more accurate to say that the Holy Spirit is the "Agent" of the filling (cf. Gal. 5:16) and Christ is the Content of the filling (Col. 3:15). Thus in this relationship, as a believer is yielded to the Lord and controlled by Him, he increasingly manifests the fruit of the Spirit (Gal. 5:22-23). The Spirit's indwelling (John 7:37-39; 14:17; Rom. 5:5; 8:9; 1 Cor. 2:12; 6:19-20; 1 John 3:24; 4:13), sealing (2 Cor. 1:22; Eph. 1:13; 4:30), and baptism (1 Cor. 12:13; Gal. 3:27) occur at the time of regeneration and thus are not commanded. However, believers *are* commanded to be filled constantly with the Holy Spirit. Each Christian has all the Spirit, but the command here is that the Spirit have all of him. The wise walk, then, is one that is characterized by the Holy Spirit's control.

5:19-21. Paul then gave four results of being filled with the Spirit. First is communication with **one another with psalms** (*psalmois,* OT psalms sung with stringed instruments such as harps), **hymns** (*hymnois,* praises composed by Christians), **and spiritual songs** (a general term). Second is communication with **the Lord** by singing and making melody (*psallontes,* singing with a stringed instrument) **in the heart.** Church music, then, should be a means of believers' ministering to each other, and singing should be a means of worshiping the

Lord. Third is thanking **God the Father** (cf. 1:2-3, 17; 3:14) continually for all things (cf. Col. 3:17; 1 Thes. 5:18). Fourth, Spirit-controlled believers are to **submit to one another,** willingly serving others and being under them rather than dominating them and exalting themselves. But basic to Christians' attitudes toward others is their **reverence for Christ.** Paul next elaborated on this subject of submission (Eph. 5:22-6:9).

2. APPLICATION (5:22-6:9)

Having admonished believers to be wise by being controlled by the Holy Spirit, Paul now applied this to specific life-relationships. It is relatively easy to exhibit a Spirit-filled life for one or two hours a week in church but it takes the work of the Holy Spirit to exhibit godliness not only on Sundays but also in everyday relationships between wives and husbands, children and parents, and slaves and masters. In each of these three relationships the first partner is commanded to be submissive or obedient (5:22; 6:1, 5). But the second partner is also to show submissiveness by his care and concern for the first partner. Both partners are to act toward one another as a service rendered to the Lord.

a. Wives and husbands (5:22-33)

5:22-24. Wives are to **submit to** their **husbands.** (The verb "submit," absent in Gr. in v. 22, is borrowed from v. 21.) **As to the Lord** does not mean that a wife is to submit to her husband in the same way she submits to the Lord, but rather that her submission to her husband *is* her service rendered "to the Lord" (cf. Col. 3:18). The reason for this submission is that **the husband is the head of the wife** (cf. 1 Cor. 11:3), and this is compared to Christ's headship over the church (Eph. 5:23; cf. 4:15; Col. 1:18). As **Christ is the** Savior **of the church, His body,** so a husband should be the protector of his wife, who is "one flesh" with him (Gen. 2:24). **As the church** is in submission **to Christ, so also** a wife **should** be to her husband. It would be foolish to think of the church being head over Christ. But submission does not mean inferiority. It means that she recognizes that her husband is the head of the home and responds to him accordingly without usurping his authority to herself.

5:25. After speaking of a wife's submission to her husband (vv. 22-24), Paul then stated the measure of the husband's love for his wife (vv. 25-32). **Husbands** are commanded, **Love your wives** (cf. v. 33) **just as Christ loved the church.** The word "love" (*agapaō*) means seeking the highest good for another person (cf. 2:4). This is an unselfish love as seen in Christ's sacrificial death in which He **gave Himself up for** the church (cf. 5:2; John 10:11, 15, 17-18; Gal. 1:4; Eph. 5:25; Heb. 9:14). A wife's submission in no way hints that a husband may lord it over his spouse, as a despot commanding a slave. The "submit-love" relationship is a beautiful mixture of harmonious partnership in marriage.

5:26-27. The purpose of Christ's death was **to make** the church **holy** (*hagiasē*, "to set apart" for Himself as His own forever; cf. Heb. 2:11; 10:10, 14; 13:12) which He did by **cleansing her by the washing with water through the Word.** This is not baptismal regeneration for that would be contrary to Paul's teaching in this book as well as all his other writings and the entire New Testament. Metaphorically, being regenerated is pictured as being cleansed by water (cf. "the washing of rebirth" in Titus 3:5). The "Word" (*rhēmati*) refers to the "preached Word" that unbelievers hear (cf. *rhēma* in Eph. 6:17; Rom. 10:8, 17; 1 Peter 1:25). The ultimate purpose of Christ's death is **to present . . . to Himself** the church as **radiant** or "in splendor" (RSV). This adjective, "glorious," in NEB, is not attributive (as in NIV's "a radiant church"). It is in the predicate position because there is an article before church (to "present the church . . . glorious," NEB).

This purpose is then described negatively (**without stain or wrinkle**— no taint of sin or spiritual decay—**or any other blemish**) and positively (**holy and blameless**). These last two adjectives (*hagia*, "set apart," and *amōmos*, "without blemish," like a spotless lamb) are stated in Ephesians 1:4 as the purpose of God's election: that Christ may present His church to Himself in all its perfection (cf. "make holy" in 5:26; also cf. *hagious* and *amōmous* in Col. 1:22). Whereas human brides prepare themselves for their husbands, Christ prepares His own bride for Himself.

5:28-30. In verses 28-32 Paul applied the truths given in verses 25-27. As the church is the extension of Christ, so is the wife an "extension" of her husband. No one hates **his own body** but takes care of it. **Feeds** (*ektrephei*; cf. "bring them up" in 6:4) **and cares for** (*thalpei*; cf. 1 Thes. 2:7) is literally, "nourishes and cherishes." Thus as Christ loves the church, **His body** (of which all believers are **members;** cf. Eph. 4:25), so should **husbands . . . love their wives as their own bodies** (5:28; cf. v. 33). Men care for their bodies even though they are imperfect and so they should care for their wives though they are imperfect.

5:31-32. Verse 31 is a free rendering of Genesis 2:24, indicating that the bond between husband and **wife** is greater than that between parent and child. The greatness of the **mystery** refers to **the two** becoming **one flesh.** But then Paul returned to mention the wonderful bond between **Christ and the church,** which illustrates the love of a husband for his wife.

5:33. This is a restatement of the responsibilities of the husband and wife toward each other: **love** by the **husband** (cf. v. 25) and **respect** by **the wife.**

b. Children and parents (6:1-4)

The Spirit-controlled life (5:18) is necessary for having a good parent-child relationship.

6:1-3. Children are to **obey** their **parents.** The phrase **in the Lord** does not mean that children are to obey parents only if their parents are believers. As Colossians 3:20 clearly denotes, a child's obedience to his parents is pleasing in the Lord's sight. The reason **for this** is that it **is right** (*dikaion*); it is a proper course to follow in society. Paul then quoted the fifth commandment (Ex. 20:12; Deut. 5:16) to support the need for children to obey parents (Eph. 6:2a, 3). The parenthetical clause states that this **is the first commandment with a promise.** But this is actually the second command with a promise (cf. Ex. 20:6). Some say Paul meant that this is the first command that children need to learn. But the first, not the fifth, of the Ten Commandments should really be learned first. More likely, Paul meant that this is "first" in the sense of being "a primary commandment," that is, of primary importance for children and it also has a promise. The promise for those who obey their parents is **that they enjoy** a prosperous and **long life on the earth.** This states a general principle that obedience fosters self-discipline, which in turn brings stability and longevity in one's life. (Stated conversely, it is improbable that an undisciplined person will live a long life. An Israelite who persistently disobeyed his parents was not privileged to enjoy a long, stable life in the land of Israel. A clear example of this was Eli's sons Hophni and Phinehas [1 Sam. 4:11].) Though that promise was given to Israel in the Old Testament, the principle still holds true today.

6:4. **Fathers** are addressed because they represent the governmental head of the family on whom rests the responsibility of child discipline. Fathers are **not** to **exasperate** (*parorgizete*, "provoke to anger"; used only here and in Rom. 10:19; cf. Col. 3:21) their **children** by unreasonable demands, petty rules, or favoritism. Such actions cause children to become discouraged (Col. 3:21). **Instead,** fathers are to **bring them up,** that is, rear or nourish (*ektrephete*, "provide for physical and spiritual needs"; also used in Eph. 5:29) them **in the training** (*paideia,* "child discipline," including directing and correcting; cf. "training" in righteousness [2 Tim. 3:16] and God's "discipline" of believers [Heb. 12:8]) **and instruction** (*nouthesia;* cf. 1 Cor. 10:11; Titus 3:10) **of the Lord.** Children are to obey "in the Lord" (Eph. 6:1) and parents are to train and instruct "in the Lord." He is to be the center of their relationships and of their teaching and learning.

c. Slaves and masters (6:5-9)

Paul then discussed a third group. Whereas the first two groups were directly involved in family relationships (wives and husbands, children and parents), this group was outside the immediate family. Slavery existed in Paul's day and he did not try to overthrow it (1 Cor. 7:17-24). Apparently these were Christian slaves under Christian masters.

6:5-8. Slaves' responsibilities to their masters are outlined here. **Slaves** were to **obey** (cf. v. 1) their **masters** with (1) **respect** (cf. 5:33), (2) **fear** (lit., "trem-

bling"), (3) **sincerity** (*haplotēti,* from *haplous,* "simple, without folds"), (4) as a service rendered to Christ **(just as you would obey Christ . . . like slaves of Christ, doing the will of God . . . as if you were serving the Lord),** (5) consistently **(not only . . . when their eye is on you,** but all the time), (6) with inner motivation **(of heart** [6:5], and **from your heart** [v. 6], the latter phrase being lit., "from the soul"), and (7) **wholeheartedly** (*met' eunoias,* "with good will or a peaceable spirit"). The reason for such service is **that the Lord will reward** them. He is the One who can accurately and impartially judge their performance and motivation (cf. 1 Peter 1:17).

6:9. Masters were to **treat** their **slaves in the same way,** that is, to please the Lord in their dealings with them. Slaves owners were **not** to keep threatening **them** but to treat them justly and fairly (cf. Col. 4:1; James 5:4) because they themselves were servants, with a **Master** who **is** an example to them. This, of course, is the Lord and He is the Master over both earthly masters and slaves. He shows no partiality, regardless of one's rank (cf. Eph. 6:8).

In conclusion, only a Spirit-controlled believer (5:18) is able to fulfill the obligations given in this section (5:15–6:9). Many of these verses emphasize selflessness, which results in harmony, one evidence of the Spirit's work.

F. Standing in warfare (6:10-20)

Whereas every division of 4:1–6:9 was introduced by the Greek inferential particle *oun* (4:1, 17; 5:1, 7, 15) and the verb "walk" (*peripateō*; 4:1, 17; 5:1, 8, 15), this final division is signaled by "finally" (*tou loipou,* "the rest"). This section discusses a believer's use of God's resources to help him stand against evil powers.

1. PUTTING ON THE ARMOR (6:10-13)

a. What: to be strong in the Lord (6:10)

6:10. Paul exhorted believers to **be strong in the Lord and in** the might (*kratei,* "**power** that overcomes resistance" as used in Christ's miracles) of God's inherent strength (*ischyos;* cf. "the power [*kratous*] of His inherent strength" [*ischyos*] in 1:19). Hence believers can be strengthened not only by the person of the Lord but also by His resources (cf. Phil. 4:13).

b. How: to put on God's armor (6:11a)

6:11a. The form of the Greek imperative **put on** indicates that believers are responsible for putting on God's (not their) **full armor** (*panoplian,* also in v. 13; all the armor and weapons together were called the *hapla;* cf. 2 Cor. 6:7) with all urgency. The detailed description of the armor (given in Eph. 6:14-17) may stem from Paul's being tied to a Roman soldier while in prison awaiting trial (cf. Acts 28:16, 20).

c. Why: to stand against the devil's strategy (6:11b-13)

6:11b-12. The purpose of putting on God's armor is to be able to **stand against** the **schemes** or stratagems (*methodeias,* used in the NT only here and in 4:14) of the devil or adversary (cf. 4:27). Christians are not to attack Satan, or advance against him; they are only to "stand" or hold the territory Christ and His body, the church, have conquered. Without God's armor believers will be defeated by the "schemes" of the devil which have been effective for thousands of years.

The **struggle is not** physical (**against flesh and blood**); it is a spiritual conflict against the spiritual "Mafia." Though the ranks of satanic forces cannot be fully categorized, the first two (**rulers** and **authorities**) have already been mentioned in 1:21 and 3:10. Paul added **the powers of this dark world** (cf. 2:2; 4:18; 5:8) and **the spiritual forces of evil.** Their sphere of activity is **in the heavenly realms,** the fifth occurrence of this phrase, which is mentioned in the New Testament only in 1:3, 20; 2:6; 3:10; 6:12. Satan, who is in the heavens (2:2) until he will be cast out in the middle of the Tribulation (Rev. 12:9-10), is trying to rob believers of the spiritual blessings God has given them (Eph. 1:3).

6:13. Some think this verse implies that a believer, having subdued all, is able to stand in victory. It is preferable to think that this is summarizing what has been stated: that having made all the necessary preparations (with **the full armor of God;** cf. v. 11), one is then ready and **able to stand in** defense. This view fits better with the context because immediately after this verse Paul de-

scribed the armor to be put on. This would be unnatural if he were speaking (in v. 13) of standing in victory. Also, to say that verse 13 refers to standing in victory but that verses 11 and 14 refer to standing in defense is inconsistent. Too, the word **stand** in verse 13 is *antistēnai,* "to withstand or stand against" (cf. James 4:7; 1 Peter 5:9).

2. STANDING WITH THE ARMOR (6:14-16)

a. The mandate: to stand (6:14a)

6:14a. Verses 14-20 make up the eighth long sentence in this epistle. Others are 1:3-14, 15-23; 2:1-7; 3:1-13, 14-19; 4:1-7, 11-16.

The imperative **stand** denotes urgency. This is followed by four Greek participles that denote either the cause or means of standing. The participles are rendered as follows in the NIV: "buckled," "in place," "fitted," "take up" (6:14-16).

b. The method: to arm (6:14b-16)

6:14b. Before a Roman soldier put on his armor, he put a belt **around** his **waist.** This held his garments together and served as a place on which to hang his armor. **The belt of truth** refers not to the facts of the gospel but to subjective truth, a believer's integrity and faithfulness. As a soldier's belt or sash gave ease and freedom of movement, so truth gives freedom with self, others, and God.

6:14c. The breastplate of righteousness refers not to justification, obtained at conversion (Rom. 3:24; 4:5), but to the sanctifying righteousness of Christ (1 Cor. 1:30) practiced in a believer's life. As a soldier's breastplate protected his chest from an enemy's attacks, so sanctifying, righteous living (Rom. 6:13; 14:17) guards a believer's heart against the assaults of the devil (cf. Isa. 59:17; James 4:7).

6:15. This verse does not speak of the spreading of the gospel, for Christians are pictured in vv. 10-16 as standing, not advancing. Instead this refers to a believer's stability or surefootedness **from the gospel** which gives him **peace** so he can stand in the battle.

6:16. The shield in a Roman soldier's attire, made of wood, was about 2 1/2' wide and 4' long. It was overlaid with linen and leather, to absorb fiery arrows. Thus it also protected the other pieces of the armor; hence Paul used the phrase, **in addition to all this. Of faith** is a genitive of content; the shield consists of faith. The idea, then, is that a Christian's resolute faith in the Lord can stop and extinguish **all the flaming arrows of the evil one** aimed at him. (Cf. "evil one" [Satan] in John 17:15; 1 John 5:19.)

3. RECEIVING THE FINAL PIECES OF ARMOR (6:17-20)

a. *The mandate: to receive (6:17)*

6:17. The outline is divided here because the Greek word **take** is an imperative, rather than another participle. This parallels the imperative "stand" in verse 14. The helmet and sword are the last two pieces a soldier takes up. A helmet, being hot and uncomfortable, would be put on by a soldier only when he faced impending danger. Having one's head guarded by a helmet gives a sense of safety, so **the helmet of salvation** refers either to present safety from the devil's attacks or to a future deliverance, "the hope of salvation as a helmet" (1 Thes. 5:8).

Finally, a Roman soldier would take in hand his sword, his only offensive weapon. **Of the Spirit** refers to the source or origin of **the sword;** hence it is "the sword given by the Spirit." "The sword of the Spirit" is specified as **the Word of God.** "Word" (*rhēma*; cf. Eph. 5:26; Rom. 10:8, 17; 1 Peter 1:25) refers to the preached Word or an utterance of God occasioned by the Holy Spirit in the heart. Believers need this "sword" to combat the enemy's assault, much as Christ did three times when tempted by the devil (Matt. 4:1-11).

b. *The method: to care (6:18-20)*

6:18. The manner in which a soldier takes up these last two pieces of armor is suggested by two Greek participles: "praying" and "being alert." When the enemy attacks—and **on all occasions**—Christians are to **pray** continually **in the Spirit** (i.e., in the power and sphere of the Spirit; cf. Jude 20). **With all kinds of prayers and requests** suggests the thoroughness and intensity of their praying. And like reliable soldiers, they are to **be keeping alert,** literally, "in all persistence" (*en pasē proskarterēsei;* the noun is used only here in the NT). Their requests are to be **for all the saints** because of Satan's spiritual warfare against Christ

and the church. In the Greek "all" occurs four times in this verse; three are translated in the NIV and the fourth is rendered as **always** (lit., "in all times" or "every time").

6:19-20. Paul asked his readers not only to **pray** in general for all saints but **also** specifically to pray **for him that** he might **make known the mystery of the gospel.** Here Paul probably did not refer to witnessing or preaching the gospel of Christ. Instead he may have referred to his need to be bold (twice he said **fearlessly**) and clear regarding the "mystery of the gospel" when he would be on trial before Caesar in Rome (when and if the Jewish accusers would make charges against him). The Romans looked on the Christians as a sect of the Jews, and the Jews considered them as a heretical group. In his trial Paul needed to make clear that Christians are neither a Jewish sect nor a heretical group but a new entity, the church, the body of Christ, composed of Jewish and Gentile believers. This recalls Paul's lengthy discussion of this "mystery of the gospel" in 2:11–3:11. For this reason Paul was **an ambassador in chains** (cf. Acts 28:16, 20; Eph. 3:1; 4:1; Phil. 1:7, 13-14, 16; Col. 4:3, 18; Phile. 1, 9-10, 13).

G. *Conclusion (6:21-24)*

1. INFORMATION (6:21-22)

6:21-22. Apparently **Tychicus** was the bearer of this epistle. Paul considered him a **dear brother and faithful servant in the Lord.** In Colossians 4:7 Paul called him by these same titles and added that he was a "fellow servant" (*syndoulos,* "fellow slave"). Tychicus is also mentioned in Acts 20:4; 2 Timothy 4:12; and Titus 3:12. Tychicus was to inform the Ephesians of Paul's welfare—**how he was and what** he was **doing**—in order to **encourage** them (cf. Eph. 3:13).

2. SALUTATION (6:23)

6:23. Three spiritual qualities frequently mentioned by Paul—peace, love, and faith—are referred to in this verse. The phrase **peace to the brothers** is found nowhere else in the New Testament. This **and love with faith** (cf. 1:15) have their sources in God. Paul wanted them to continue their love for other Christians, their spiritual brothers (since they are all "members of one body," 4:25) and to combine that love with their faith in God, for which they were well known. **God the Father and the Lord Jesus Christ** is similar to Paul's wording in 1:2-3, 17; 5:20.

3. BENEDICTION (6:24)

6:24. Grace concludes the letter, just as it had introduced it (1:2). The words **with an undying love** are literally, "in incorruption, incorruptibility, immortality" (*en aphtharsia;* cf. Rom. 2:7; 1 Cor. 15:42, 50, 53-54; 2 Tim. 1:10). It has the idea that believers' **love** for the **Lord Jesus Christ** is to be pure, not corrupted with wrong motives or secret disloyalties. Unfortunately some Ephesian believers later did lose the fervency of their love for Christ (Rev. 2:4). Paul's benediction, though unusual (cf. the chart "Paul's Concluding Benedictions in His Epistles," at Rom. 16:17-20), was certainly fitting.

BIBLIOGRAPHY

Abbott, T.K. *A Critical and Exegetical Commentary on the Epistles to the Ephesians and to the Colossians.* The International Critical Commentary. 1897. Reprint. Edinburgh: T. & T. Clark, 1979.

Barry, Alfred. "The Epistle of Paul the Apostle to the Ephesians." In *Ellicott's Commentary on the Whole Bible.* Reprint (8 vols. in 4). Grand Rapids: Zondervan Publishing House, 1981.

Barth, Markus. *Ephesians.* 2 vols. The Anchor Bible. Garden City, N.Y.: Doubleday & Co., 1974.

Bruce, F.F. *The Epistle to the Ephesians.* Old Tappan, N.J.: Fleming H. Revell Co., 1961.

Chafer, Lewis Sperry. *The Ephesian Letter: Doctrinally Considered.* Findlay, Ohio: Dunham Publishing Co., 1935.

Ellicott, Charles J. *St. Paul's Epistle to the Ephesians.* 5th ed. London: Longmans, Green, & Co., 1884. Reprint. Minneapolis: James Family Publishing Co., 1978.

Foulkes, Francis. *The Epistle of Paul to the Ephesians: An Introduction and Commentary.* The Tyndale New Testament Commentaries. Grand Rapids: Wm. B. Eerdmans Publishing Co., 1963.

Hendriksen, William. *Exposition of Ephesians.* New Testament Commentary. Grand Rapids: Baker Book House, 1967.

Kent, Homer A., Jr. *Ephesians: The Glory of the Church.* Everyman's Bible Commentary. Chicago: Moody Press, 1971.

Mitton, C. Leslie. *Ephesians.* New Century Bible Commentary. Grand Rapids: Wm. B. Eerdmans Publishing Co., 1973.

Moule, H.C.G. *Studies in Ephesians.* Cambridge: University Press, 1893. Reprint. Grand Rapids: Kregel Publications, 1977.

Robinson, J. Armitage. *Commentary on Ephesians.* 2d ed. London: Macmillan & Co., 1904. Reprint. Grand Rapids: Kregel Publications, 1979.

Simpson, E.K., and Bruce, F.F. *Commentary on the Epistles to the Ephesians and the Colossians.* The New International Commentary on the New Testament. Grand Rapids: Wm. B. Eerdmans Publishing Co., 1957.

Vaughan, Curtis. *Ephesians: A Study Guide Commentary.* Grand Rapids: Zondervan Publishing House, 1977.

Westcott, Brooke Foss. *Saint Paul's Epistle to the Ephesians.* Reprint. Grand Rapids: Baker Book House, 1979.

Wiersbe, Warren W. *Be Rich.* Wheaton, Ill.: Scripture Press Publications, Victor Books, 1976.

Wood, A. Skevington. "Ephesians." In *The Expositor's Bible Commentary,* vol. 11. Grand Rapids: Zondervan Publishing House, 1978.

PHILIPPIANS

Robert P. Lightner

INTRODUCTION

On his second missionary journey Paul visited Philippi. Through his ministry there several people trusted Christ as their Savior. Some of these were Lydia and her family and the Philippian jailer and his family (Acts 16:14-34).

Soon after Paul's visit a local church was established in Philippi. The church helped the apostle in different ways so this epistle was written to acknowledge their help, as well as to help them.

Philippians is personal and practical in its tone and teaching. Paul emphasized the need for believers to rejoice in Christ. "Joy" (chara) is used four times (Phil. 1:4, 25; 2:2; 4:1); "rejoice" (chairō) occurs eight times (1:18 [twice]; 2:17-18; 3:1, 4:4 [twice], 10); and "glad" occurs thrice (2:17-18, 28). (In 1:26 the word "joy" is a different Gr. word; there it is the word "glad," "boast," or "glory," [kauchēma], which also occurs in 2:16 and 3:3.) Paul wrote frequently in this epistle about the mind of a child of God. One's manner of life is truly a reflection of what occupies his mind.

The Theme of the Epistle. Though many exhortations and challenges are given, one major theme or emphasis pervades the book. All the teachings are expressions or ramifications of this one central truth. This theme is "living the Christian life."

The Human Author. Most scholars agree that the Apostle Paul wrote the Book of Philippians. Clearly the work purports to come from him (1:1). Reference to Timothy is also significant since he was with the apostle when Philippi was evangelized (cf. Acts 16). Also the information the writer gave about himself (Phil. 3:4-6) harmonizes perfectly with Paul's life. In addition, the writings of the early church fathers attest to Pauline authorship.

The Date of the Epistle. Paul was in bondage when he wrote Philippians. But all do not agree which imprisonment he was experiencing when he wrote the book. Most believe he was in Rome at the time; some suggest he was in Caesarea; and a few argue for Ephesus.

The Scriptures give no clear indication of any imprisonment in Ephesus. As for Caesarea, Paul was confined there for two years, but imminent martyrdom is not suggested in the account which describes this confinement (Acts 23-24). His reference to the palace guard (Phil. 1:13) as well as his concern about facing possible death (vv. 20-26) argue for his writing from Rome. The date of the writing would then be A.D. 61 or 62.

The Historic Occasion. When the Philippian believers heard about Paul's imprisonment at Rome, they sent Epaphroditus, who may have been their pastor, to minister to him. Epaphroditus personally comforted Paul, expressing to him the affection of the saints in Philippi. And he brought Paul a financial contribution from them so that his confinement would be more comfortable (4:18). Three times before—twice when Paul was at Thessalonica, and once when he was at Corinth (Phil. 4:15-16; cf. 2 Cor. 11:9)—the saints ministered to his needs. The Book of Philippians might be called a thank-you note to saints in Philippi for their generous gifts.

While Epaphroditus was in Rome, he became so ill he almost died (Phil. 2:27). After he recovered, he took Paul's letter to the Philippian Christians.

Philippi was a Roman colony (Acts 16:12). After the Battle of Philippi in 42 B.C. some Roman soldiers were ordered by Anthony to live there. Then in 30 B.C. Octavian forced some people in Italy to give up their homes and settle in Philippi and elsewhere. These Philippian residents were given special privileges including the "Italic right." This meant that the colonists, in return for their displacement, were treated as if their land were part of Italian soil. So the residents were citizens of Rome, their "mother city," and enjoyed the full rights of Roman citizenship, including exemption from taxes. So Paul's words (Phil. 1:27) "conduct yourselves" (lit., "live as citizens") and "our citizenship is in heaven" (3:20) had special meaning to the Christians at Philippi.

The Purposes for the Epistle. The initial reason for writing, as indicated, seems to have been to thank the Philippians for their love gift. But Paul also took advantage of this opportunity to address some of the problems in their church. Apparently rivalry and personal ambition were present among some of the saints (2:3-4; 4:2). The Judaizers were also gaining a hearing (3:1-3). In addition, an antinomian tendency was creeping in (3:18-19).

OUTLINE

COMMENTARY

I. Encouragement for Living the Christian Life (1:1-30)

A. Paul's praise of the saints at Philippi (1:1-8)

The Apostle Paul frequently began his epistles with words of greeting, praise, and commendation. Philippians was no exception. The tender tone of the entire letter is apparent at the outset.

1. INTRODUCTION (1:1-2)

1:1. Paul was the author's Gentile name and Saul his Hebrew name. As the apostle to the Gentiles (Gal. 2:7-8) he used his Gentile name. Instead of referring to his apostleship, as he frequently did in the beginning of a book, here Paul called himself a servant of the Lord. **Timothy** had a special interest in the Philippian saints (Phil. 2:20) and was associated with Paul's imprisonment (2:19, 23). Timothy was not a coauthor of this epistle, since he is spoken of in the third person (2:19-24). Both of these men of God, who had been Roman captives, were **servants** (lit., "slaves") **of Christ Jesus.** By calling the Philippian believers saints, Paul was not saying his readers were sinless. The Greek word he used, *hagioi,* means "those set apart." The saints at Philippi were set apart for God. They were **in Christ Jesus** so far as their relationship to God was concerned, though they lived at **Philippi.**

The apostle made special mention of **the overseers and deacons,** who were included among **all the saints.** The "overseers" or bishops, were also called "elders" (Titus 1:5, 7); and they were responsible for shepherding or pastoring the flock (cf. Acts 20:17, 28). The "deacons" were those church leaders who had special service responsibilities in the assembly (cf. Acts 6).

1:2. In his greeting to the Philippians, Paul used two words descriptive of Christian graces: **grace** and **peace.** The order in which he used them is significant. Before there can be any genuine peace there must be a personal response to God's grace, His unmerited favor manifested climactically at Calvary. Both grace and peace find their source in **God our Father and the Lord Jesus Christ.**

2. PRAISE FOR THEIR CONSTANT WITNESS (1:3-6)

1:3. It must have brought great joy to the Philippians' hearts as they read how the apostle often thanked God for them. Here was a letter of commendation from one who was in Roman chains some 800 miles away. About 10 years had passed since Paul had first worked among them. But the passing of time had not diminished his love or his interest in them. Every time Paul thought of them he thanked God for them.

1:4-6. None of the believers was excluded from Paul's prayers. Coming from a prisoner, this is especially signifi-

cant. It was with **joy** that the apostle also besought God on their behalf. Paul's hardships made him better, not bitter. They always do one or the other to a child of God.

The Philippian saints and Paul were partners in the things of Christ. This was true because they shared with him in his need. They gave of themselves to Paul and in turn to the cause of Christ for which he labored. But not only did they share with him in his need as a prisoner. They had also fellowshiped with him **from the first day** they trusted Christ. This brought great joy to the apostle's heart.

Great confidence gripped the apostle as he thought and prayed for the Philippians. The perfect tense of the Greek word translated **being confident** indicates that Paul had come to a settled conviction earlier and that he still was confident it was true. What was he so confident and sure of? It was that God would most certainly continue on to **completion** the **good work** He had begun in them. That good work was their salvation. It may also have included their fellowship and sharing of their bounties with Paul.

Paul had no doubt that God would continue in the Philippians what He had begun to do in them. God would work in them **until the day of Christ Jesus.** In 2:16 Paul called this "the day of Christ." Though Paul did not know when that day would occur—when all believers would be caught up to meet the Lord in the air— he did know that God would continue the work He had begun in His own children.

3. PRAISE FOR THEIR CONCERN FOR THE GOSPEL (1:7)

1:7. The first part of this verse is a sort of apology or defense for the way Paul felt about the Philippians, as expressed in verses 3-6.

The Greek allows for the phrase **since I have you in my heart** to read "since you have me in your heart." Certainly both Paul and the Philippians were in each others' hearts. However, in view of the specific reference to himself (v. 7) it seems better to accept the NIV rendering. His affection for the saints is also stated in 1:8 and 4:16.

It did not matter whether Paul was under arrest (**in chains;** cf. "chains" in 1:13-14, 17) or free; his friends at Philippi shared with him in what God was doing through him. That work concerned primarily the spread of the gospel. It was because of their partnership with him that he could propagate God's grace. Paul praised them for their concern that this good news be spread abroad.

4. PRAISE SHOWN BY HIS LOVE FOR THEM (1:8)

1:8. Paul called on God to witness to his feelings toward the Philippians. Paul was aware—as were his readers—that they could not know his heart. But God knew it perfectly. The **affection** Paul had for his readers was no mere human interest or attraction. It originated with the Lord Jesus Christ Himself. Christ's love had so overwhelmed Paul that His affection was Paul's very own. The fact that Paul told this to the Philippians demonstrates the reality and intensity of his praise for them.

B. Paul's prayer for the saints at Philippi (1:9-11)

1. PRAYER FOR LOVE (1:9-10)

The apostle assured the saints that he prayed regularly for them (v. 3). Now here (v. 9) he reported what it was he prayed for.

1:9. It was Paul's **prayer** that the Philippians' love for other believers would **abound,** run over as a cup or a river overflows. But that love should be more than sentimental; it should be knowledgeable and discerning. Having genuine spiritual **knowledge** (*epignōsis*) of God and **depth of insight** into His ways enables Christians to love God and others more. (This Gr. word for "insight" [*aisthēsis*] occurs only here in the NT.)

1:10. Paul stated two purposes for his prayer. The first is a near purpose: **to discern what is best;** and the second is a remote one: to **be pure and blameless until the day of Christ.** The idea of testing is clearly in view in the Greek word *dokimazō,* translated "discern." The testing is with a view to approving. The word was used in testing metals and coins, to determine whether they met the specified standards.

"Pure" is the translation of a Greek word used only here and in 2 Peter 3:1. It is *eilikrineis,* which comes from the words for "sun" and "to judge," thus indicating purity that is tested by the light of the

sun. Paul wanted his readers to be rightly related to God and in fellowship with Him. Paul also was concerned that their relationships with others be what God would have them to be. The word *aproskopoi,* translated "blameless," also appears in 1 Corinthians 10:32 where the same writer urged, "Do not cause anyone to stumble." Paul's desire for his friends at Philippi ought to be the concern of all believers—to be morally pure, not causing others to stumble.

2. PRAYER FOR THE FRUIT OF RIGHTEOUSNESS (1:11)

1:11. Paul also prayed that the believers in the church at Philippi would be **filled with the fruit of righteousness.** A righteous stand before God, resulting from being clothed in Christ's righteousness, ought to produce fruit for God. Such inner qualities, partially described in Galatians 5:22-23, will be evident to others. The fruit of the Spirit comes **through Jesus Christ,** for it is really His life lived out through believers. Such fruit magnifies God, not self. So a life that exhibits such traits is to **the glory and praise of God.**

C. Paul's presentation of himself to the saints (1:12-30)

The apostle faced opposition from those outside the church and misrepresentation from some within. But this did not dissuade or distract him from fulfilling God's call. Through it all, Christ was being preached, which brought him great delight. So his bonds, instead of hindering his outreach, resulted in a greater spreading of the gospel of Christ. Paul's friends back in Philippi were apparently quite concerned about him, thinking he was discouraged and that God's plan had gone awry. Not so, the apostle responded.

1. STALWART TESTIMONY (1:12-18)

1:12-14. From his own experiences Paul wanted the believers at Philippi to learn an important truth: there are no accidents with God. Instead of Paul's ministry being curtailed because of his bondage, it was being advanced.

The advance came partly because **the whole palace guard,** as well as others, were hearing about Christ (vv. 12-13). The "palace guard" (*praitōriō*) likely refers to the praetorian guard, made up of

Roman soldiers. Though Paul resided in his own rented facility (Acts 28:30), he was guarded by these soldiers all the time. The custom was for a prisoner to be chained at the wrist to a soldier.

All in Rome who came in contact with Paul heard about Christ. It was well known that he was not under guard for being a lawbreaker. Instead he was **in chains for Christ** (Phil. 1:13). In an effort to silence the truth, the authorities had incarcerated the one who spoke it, but their plan did not work.

Paul's incarceration had another effect: it encouraged those who had been reluctant about speaking for Christ (v. 14). Large numbers of believers became bold for Christ when they saw how God was spreading the gospel through Paul. The positive response Paul received in the face of opposition caused others to speak **more courageously and fearlessly** for Christ. Paul's confinement was doing what his circumstances outside of prison could never do.

1:15-18. The people who were emboldened to speak God's Word were of two kinds. Some preached Christ **out of envy and rivalry,** but others preached Him **out of good will** (v. 15). Those who preached out of good will did so **in love** (v. 16), knowing that Paul was in chains because of his **defense of the gospel.** The word "defense" is the Greek *apologia,* also used in verse 7.

The group that preached Christ out of envy and rivalry (v. 15) had **selfish ambition** (v. 17) as their motive. They purposely wanted to **stir up trouble** for Paul while he was in bondage. They were probably not Judaizers, as some suppose, because Paul said they were preaching Christ, though insincerely. The Judaizers believed that keeping the Old Testament Law was a means of salvation. Paul had sternly rebuked them as preachers of "a different gospel" (Gal. 1:6). However, since he did not accuse these in Philippi of presenting "another gospel," it seems that they were believers who for some unknown reason did not love the apostle or appreciate his work. Though they were doctrinally sound, they promoted themselves.

What rejoiced Paul's heart was that Christ was being preached, even though it was from wrong motives by some (Phil. 1:18). Since the content of the preaching was the same for both groups, the apostle could rejoice. He did not **rejoice** because there was a faction among members of Christ's body, for this brought him grief. Instead, it was the preaching of Christ that brought him joy.

2. SETTLED CONVICTIONS (1:19-26)

1:19. As a man of convictions, Paul shared his assurance that his fetters would eventually result in his **deliverance.** The Greek word translated "deliverance" here was used in different ways in the New Testament. It often meant spiritual deliverance—salvation, being born again. Here (v. 19) Paul used the word to refer to either the final stage of his salvation (cf. Rom. 5:9) or future vindication in a Roman court. It seems unlikely that he had his release in mind since in the next two sentences he wrote of the real possibility of his near death.

The bases on which the apostle's assurance rested were the **prayers** of the saints and the **help given by the Spirit of Jesus Christ** (Phil. 1:19). He knew he could count on the Philippians' prayers, and also on the Holy Spirit's ministry (cf. Rom. 8:26-27). "Help" (*epichorēgias*) carries the meaning of "support," much as a ligament provides support in a physical body. (This Gr. word is used in the NT only here and in Eph. 4:16.)

1:20. Paul was not sure whether he would experience release or martyrdom for his faith. He was certain of one thing though, that he wanted Christ to be **exalted** in his **body** either way (cf. "in the body," vv. 22, 24). This was Paul's expectation and hope. The apostle also knew full well that it would take courage to face death with the proper attitude. **Eagerly expect** is the translation of a unique word. It describes straining one's neck to catch a glimpse of something that is ahead. (*Apokaradokia,* a noun, is used only here and in Rom. 8:19.) Paul's concern was not what would happen to him but what testimony would be left for his Lord. Release would allow him to continue preaching Christ. But martyrdom would also advance the cause of Christ.

1:21. Paul's main purpose in living was to glorify Christ. Christ was the essence of his life. Yet Paul knew that if he were martyred, Christ would be glorified through the promotion of the gospel which would result from his testimony in death. And Paul himself would benefit, for death would result in his being with Christ (v. 23). The words **to die** suggest the act of dying, not the state of death.

1:22-24. The apostle's seeming frustration of mind is apparent in these verses. He knew if he could **go on living** there would certainly be fruit from his labor (v. 22). God would bless his work and continue to use him as He had in the past. Yet if Paul had a choice between going on living or dying for Christ, he was at a loss as to how to decide. He simply did not know which to choose. Of course the choice was really not up to him anyway.

Paul was distressed. He was hard-pressed to know which would bring the most glory to God and therefore be to everyone's advantage in the long run. His personal desire was **to depart and be with Christ** (v. 23). This he knew would be **better by far** for him since it would mean his release from the persecutions and other hardships that he suffered. But he also knew that the Philippians needed him. For them it was **more necessary** that he **remain in the body,** or stay alive (v. 24). Paul's selfless attitude is revealed here by his placing his friends' needs above his own desires.

1:25-26. New confidence of his release appears to have come to Paul. (The word **convinced** is the same word rendered "being confident" in v. 6.) By his release and return to them they would **progress . . . in the faith** and would experience great **joy** (v. 25).

The rejoicing of the Philippians would **overflow** (v. 26; the same word is rendered "abound" in v. 9), and that exulting would be **in Christ Jesus,** the source of true joy for all believers. ("Joy" in v. 26 is the word "exulting" [*kauchēma*] which differs from the more common word for "joy" used more often in Phil., including v. 25.) They would exult because the one who had taught them about Christ would be with them again.

3. SOLEMN EXHORTATIONS (1:27-30)

1:27. The apostle had the believers in Philippi on his heart. Regardless of what would happen to him—release from bonds or martyrdom—he wanted them to honor and glorify Christ. The words **conduct yourselves** translate a political word which would mean much to the Philippian believers. Literally it means "live as citizens." Because Philippi was a Roman colony, the Christian inhabitants of the city would appreciate Paul's use of that verb. To live in a way that is **worthy of the gospel of Christ** (cf. Eph. 4:1) is indeed the responsibility of every child of God. This Paul exhorted the Philippians to do.

The saints embraced a common cause, for they each shared in the same body of Christ. Therefore Paul was burdened that they **stand firm** (cf. Phil. 4:1) **in one spirit** and contend **as one man** (lit., "in one soul") **for the faith of the gospel,** the body of truth (cf. "faith," Jude 3). Their **contending** (*synalthountes*) for the faith suggests a joint effort, like that of an athletic team.

1:28. Paul wanted his readers to live courageously for Christ in the midst of opposition and persecution. True, they would be opposed but this should not frighten them **in any way.** Instead they were to be reminded at such times that their own victorious Christian response would be a sign that their opposers would eventually be destroyed. At the same time it would be **a sign** that the saints of God would be delivered **by God** Himself. This assurance would doubtless be the Holy Spirit working in their hearts.

1:29-30. So that being opposed would not come as a surprise, he gave them a reminder. Both believing on **Christ** and suffering **for Him** had been **granted to** them (v. 29). Suffering for Christ was not to be considered accidental or a divine punishment. Paul referred to a kind of suffering that was really a sign of God's favor. The Greek word *echaristhē,* translated "granted," is derived from a word which means "grace" or "favor." Believing on Christ and suffering for Him are both associated with God's grace.

Paul and his readers shared a similar **struggle** (v. 30). So Paul encouraged them as they had him. They wanted to know how he fared in Rome. He told them, so they could also be encouraged as they faced hardships.

II. Examples for Living the Christian Life (2:1-30)

A. *The Son of God whose attitude the believer is to share (2:1-18)*

This passage is a continuation of the exhortation begun in 1:27-30. The entire section (1:27–2:18) states what Paul called the saints at Philippi to do. It includes the famous *kenōsis* or self-emptying passage (2:5-11), in which the Son of God Himself is set forth as the One whose attitude the believer should share.

1. THE DECLARATION (2:1)

2:1. In 1:27 Paul had written about living the Christian life in harmony with the message on which it is based. He followed that message with a call to show forth spiritual unity. This unity is possible because of the reality of the four qualities mentioned in 2:1. The "if" clauses, being translations of first-class conditions in Greek, speak of certainties. So in this passage "if" may be translated "since." Paul wrote here about realities, not questionable things. Paul appealed on the basis of (a) **encouragement from being united with Christ** . . . (b) **comfort from His love** . . . (c) **fellowship with the Spirit** . . . (d) **tenderness and compassion.**

"Encouragement" is from a Greek word related to the one Christ used in referring to the Holy Spirit as "the Counselor" (John 14:16; "Comforter," KJV). It may also be translated "exhortation" in the sense of either rebuke or comfort. Since each believer had received this work of the Spirit, Paul used it as a basis to appeal for their spiritual unity.

Also they each had "comfort from His [God's] love." God's love in people's hearts produces spiritual unity in their lives.

"Fellowship with the Spirit" is a result of the Spirit's permanent indwelling ministry (cf. 1 Cor. 6:19). This may refer, however, to fellowship that comes *from* the Holy Spirit, just as encouragement comes *from* Christ and comfort comes *from* love.

Paul also spoke of "tenderness (*splanchna*; cf. Phile. 7, 20) and compassion." One of the Spirit's ministries is to produce within each believer a concern and love for other members of God's family. This may be received or rejected by a believer, but the Spirit's work is a reality and is a basis for spiritual unity.

2. THE EXHORTATIONS (2:2-4)

2:2. On the basis of what was presented in verse 1, Paul exhorted his readers to show in practical ways the unity which was theirs in Christ. Their expression of that spiritual unity would make his joy complete. Corresponding to the four realities in verse 1 are four specific ways in which their spiritual unity would be realized. They would be **like-minded,** have **the same love,** be **one in spirit** (*sympsychoi*), and be one in **purpose.**

2:3-4. Paul gave further exhortations, also based on the declaration of the fourfold reality expressed in verse 1. The terms the apostle used reveal an underlying problem in the church at Philippi. The situation Paul addressed evidently was prompted by self-centeredness among certain Christians.

Nothing was to be done **out of selfish ambition** (v. 3). The same word (*eritheian*) appears in 1:17 to describe the attitude of those who opposed Paul. Without question such behavior is of the flesh and not the Spirit (cf. Gal. 5:20, which uses the same word). **Vain conceit,** meaning "empty glory," was probably the root cause of their selfish ambition.

The two negatives are followed by a positive exhortation: **in humility consider others better than yourselves. But,** a word of contrast, introduces these words. Humility before God and man is a virtue every child of God needs to strive for. A spirit of pride in human relations indicates a lack of humility before God. Paul exhorted the Philippians to consider others before themselves (cf. 1 Peter 5:5-6). "This will go far toward removing disharmony" (Homer A. Kent, Jr., "Philippians," in *The Expositor's Bible Commentary,* 11:122).

Paul explained how humility can be expressed (Phil. 2:4). Instead of concentrating on self, each believer should be concerned for **the interests of others** in the household of faith (cf. Rom. 12:10). Preoccupation with oneself is sin.

3. THE HUMILIATION OF CHRIST (2:5-8)

Christ is the supreme example of humility and selfless concern for others (vv. 5-8). These verses, along with verses 9-11, constitute a grand statement on Christology.

2:5. Believers are exhorted to have the same attitude—selfless humility—Christ exhibited in His humiliation and condescension. The word here translated **attitude** is translated "like-minded" in verse 2.

2:6-8. The word translated **nature**

(*morphē*) in verses 6 and 7 is a crucial term in this passage. This word (trans. "form" in the KJV and NASB) stresses the inner essence or reality of that with which it is associated (cf. Mark 16:12). Christ Jesus, Paul said, is of the very essence (*morphē*) of God, and in His incarnation He embraced perfect humanity. His complete and absolute deity is here carefully stressed by the apostle. The Savior's claim to deity infuriated the Jewish leaders (John 5:18) and caused them to accuse Him of blasphemy (John 10:33).

Though possessing full deity (John 1:14; Col. 2:9), Christ did not consider His **equality with God** (Phil. 2:6) as **something to be grasped** or held onto. In other words Christ did not hesitate to set aside His self-willed use of deity when He became a man. As God He had all the rights of deity, and yet during His incarnate state He surrendered His right to manifest Himself visibly as the God of all splendor and glory.

Christ's humiliation included His making **Himself nothing,** taking the **very nature** (*morphē*) **of a servant,** and **being made in human likeness** (v. 7). These statements indicate that Christ became a man, a true human being. The words "made Himself nothing" are, literally, "He emptied Himself." "Emptied," from the Greek *kenoō*, points to the divesting of His self-interests, but not of His deity. "The very nature of a servant" certainly points to His lowly and humble position, His willingness to obey the Father, and serve others. He became a man, a true human being. "Likeness" suggests similarity but difference. Though His humanity was genuine, He was different from all other humans in that He was sinless (Heb. 4:15).

Thus it is seen that Christ, while retaining the essence of God, was also human. In His incarnation He was *fully* God and *fully* man at the same time. He was God manifest in human flesh (John 1:14).

Some have wrongly taught that the phrase, **being found in appearance as a man** (Phil. 2:8), means that He only *looked* human. But this contradicts verse 7. "Appearance" is the Greek *schēmati*, meaning an outer appearance which may be temporary. This contrasts with *morphē* ("very nature") in verses 6 and 7, which speaks of an outer appearance that reveals permanent inner quality.

The condescension of Christ included not only His birth—the Incarnation in which He became the God-Man—but also His **death.** And it was the most cruel and despicable form of death—**even death on a cross!** (v. 8) This form of capital punishment was limited to non-Romans and the worst criminals.

No better example of humiliation and a selfless attitude for believers to follow could possibly be given than that of Christ. With this example before them, the saints at Philippi should be "like-minded" (v. 2) and live humbly before their God and each other.

4. THE EXALTATION OF CHRIST (2:9-11)

God the Father is the subject in these verses, whereas in verses 6-8 God the Son was the subject. Christ's obedience was followed by the Father's exaltation of Him to the place of highest honor. God exalted and honored the One men despised and rejected.

2:9. Christ's exaltation and His receiving a **name that is above every name** was the answer to His high-priestly prayer (John 17:5). The exaltation refers to His resurrection, ascension, and glorification at the Father's right hand (Acts 2:33; Heb. 1:3). His "name" is not merely a title; it refers to His person and to His position of dignity and honor.

2:10. In keeping with Christ's exaltation and high **name . . . every knee** will one day **bow** and acknowledge Him for who He really is. Paul stressed the same truth in his letter to the Romans (Rom. 14:11). Both instances reflect Isaiah's prophecy (Isa. 45:23) of the singular greatness of the God of Abraham, Isaac, and Jacob. The extent of Christ's sovereign authority is delineated in the threefold phrase, **in heaven and on earth and under the earth.** No intelligent being—whether angels and saints in heaven; people living on the earth; or Satan, demons, and the unsaved in hell—in all of God's universe will escape. All will bow either willingly or they will be made to do so.

2:11. What all will **confess** is that **Jesus Christ is Lord.** This, the earliest Christian creed, meant that Jesus Christ is Yahweh-God. One day all will be made to acknowledge that Jesus Christ is all He claimed to be—very God of very God. Unfortunately, for many it will be too late for the salvation of their souls. The exalted place the Savior now occupies and the universal bowing in the future in acknowledgement of His lordship is all **to the glory of God the Father.**

5. THE EXHORTATIONS CONTINUED (2:12-18)

In these verses Paul returned to the exhortations which he began earlier in verses 2-4.

2:12-13. Therefore connects these verses with what immediately precedes them. Christ obeyed the Father and carried out His plan even to death on the cross (v. 8). The Philippian Christians needed to obey, to follow Paul's instruction which was drawn from Christ's example.

The exhortation was direct and pointed, but tempered with love, for he called the believers **my dear friends.** This tender expression doubtless reminded them of the experiences they shared with the apostle and Silas when they first came to Christ and established their church (Acts 16:19-40). When Paul was with them, they followed his instructions willingly and quickly. He reminded them of this before he asked them to do the same at the present time, even though he was far from them. He had earlier spoken of his absence (Phil. 1:27).

The special request he had for them, in view of their needs and in view of the example of Christ, is stated forcefully— **continue to work out your salvation with fear and trembling.**

It is commonly understood that this exhortation relates to the personal salvation of the saints at Philippi. They were told to "work out," to put into practice in their daily living, what God had worked in them by His Spirit. They were not told to work *for* their salvation but to work *out* the salvation God had already given them. In view of the apparent problems of disunity and pride among those believers this interpretation seems correct. Some were not doing their work selflessly and with the interests of others ahead of their own (cf. 2:3-4).

Some writers understand Paul's challenge to refer to the corporate life of the whole assembly in Philippi. Those who hold this view find support in the imme-

diate context where Paul argued against their looking exclusively to their own needs (cf. v. 4). In this view "salvation" refers to the whole assembly's deliverance from disunity, pride, and selfishness.

Perhaps it is best to see *both* the outworking of personal salvation and the corporate salvation or deliverance of the whole assembly from whatever held them back from experiencing God's best.

This outworking was to be done "with fear and trembling," with a complete trust in God and not in themselves. The only way this could be realized was through **God** who would enable them to do it (v. 13). Paul told the Philippian saints that God worked in them so that they could do His good pleasure and accomplish **His good purpose.** Both divine enablement and human responsibility are involved in getting God's work done. Believers are partners with God, laboring together with Him. The verb **works** (v. 13) means "energizes" or "provides enablement." God makes His own both willing and desirous to do His work.

2:14-16. These verses give specific instructions on how to work out God's "good purpose" (v. 13) in relation to daily Christian living.

Everything was to be done **without complaining or arguing** (v. 14). The order of the Greek words here places emphasis on everything a believer does. The present tense of the verb **do** suggests that this was to be done continually. "Complaining" is the translation of a word which reflects a bad attitude expressed in grumbling. The apostle may have had in mind the behavior of the Israelites who often complained to Moses and in turn to God (cf. 1 Cor. 10:10). "Arguing" reflects a legal connotation of disputing and may refer, at least in part, to the practice of going to civil courts to settle their differences (cf. 1 Cor. 6:1-11).

The importance of the kind of behavior called for is set forth in Philippians 2:15-16. Before their testimony for Christ could ever be effective in the community where they lived, the Philippians needed to set some things straight in their own assembly.

Evidently the believers were complaining (to God and each other) and arguing (with each other). As a result they were not **without fault** among the unregenerate; they were not shining **like stars** in their world (2:15). The Philippian assembly needed to show themselves as united and as one in Christ. Non-Christians were not being attracted to Him by the saints' strifes and contentions.

Blameless (*amemptoi*, v. 15) means "above reproach." This does not mean sinless perfection. The corporate testimony of the church is in view. All believers are called on to live out the salvation God has worked in them—to progress in their spiritual maturity. The people were to live so that those outside of Christ could not rightfully point an accusing finger at them. **Pure** translates *akeraioi*, a word that was used of wine which had not been diluted and of metal which had not been weakened in any way. Jesus also used the word when He told the Twelve to be "innocent" as doves (Matt. 10:16). The Greek words for "blameless" and "pure" here (Phil. 2:15) differ from those translated "blameless" and "pure" in 1:10 (see comments on 1:10).

The Philippians lived **in a crooked and depraved generation** (2:15). Again it seems that Paul had the unbelieving Israelites in mind. Moses had used similar words to describe Israel who had gone astray (cf. Deut. 32:5). Peter used the same terminology ("corrupt generation," Acts 2:40) that Christ did ("perverse generation," Matt. 17:17).

The world today, like theirs, is unscrupulous and perverted. Most people have turned their backs on God and truth. In this kind of world God's people are to "shine like stars" (Phil. 2:15; cf. Matt. 5:14-16). They are to be **children of God without fault.**

A child of God is in God's family, but the unregenerate are alienated from Him. They are His enemies. God's sovereign plan is to use His Word, administered by God's people, to transform His enemies into His friends by the regenerating work of God's Spirit.

The Greek word *epechontes*, **hold out** (v. 16) means either "hold forth" or "hold firmly." The former fits better here. It was used in secular Greek of offering wine to a guest at a banquet. As the Philippian saints held out (or offered) **the word of life** to others, Paul would then be able to **boast** (glory) **on the day of Christ** that he had not labored in vain with them. The "day of Christ" refers to the Rapture

when the Savior returns and meets His own in the air (1 Thes. 4:13-18). This boasting was not a selfish ambition of Paul's; he was concerned with God's honor.

2:17-18. Paul's stated desire to be able to rejoice when he would see Christ and to be sure he had not labored in vain for the Philippians is followed by a statement about his joy in the midst of suffering. The apostle knew that death as a martyr was a real possibility for him.

Paul viewed himself as **being poured out like a drink offering** on behalf of the Philippians (v. 17). But instead of sorrowing he rejoiced. "Poured out" is from the Greek word *spendomai*, used of a drink offering given as a sacrifice to God. The possibility of release from prison was not uppermost in Paul's mind as it had been before (cf. 1:24-26). He now viewed his death as imminent. Later, near the actual time of his death, he used this same language (2 Tim. 4:6).

The sacrifice and service (perhaps this could be understood as "sacrificial service") stemmed from their faith. Paul used the same word for sacrifice (*thysia*) in Romans 12:1. There the sacrifice the believer-priest offers is his body. "Service" (*leitourgia*) is the same word translated "ceremonies" in Hebrews 9:21 (cf. Phil. 2:25, 30). This means that the work the Philippians did for God was considered an act of worship. All of this brought rejoicing to the apostle's heart even though it resulted in his facing imminent death.

Paul wanted his friends at Philippi to experience the same joy he had (2:18) and to **be glad and rejoice with** him.

B. The servants of God whose manner of life the believer is to follow (2:19-30)

In chapter 2 Paul first discussed the fact that the attitude of Christ, who humbled Himself and became obedient to death, should be shared by believers (vv. 1-18). Then Paul pointed out (vv. 19-30) that choice servants of God also provide examples for others to follow.

1. TIMOTHY AND PAUL (2:19-24)

Paul's incarceration had made it impossible for him to visit the saints at Philippi. He had referred to this fact earlier (v. 12). His deep and abiding concern for his friends' spiritual welfare prompted him to send Timothy to visit and to minister in his place. Timothy was at the time Paul's companion (1:1), though evidently not a prisoner. The letter would be delivered by Epaphroditus and Timothy's visit would follow.

2:19. The concern Paul demonstrated in sending Timothy was an example for the Philippians and all believers to follow. Not only did Paul give them the gospel and lead them to Christ, but he also wanted to be sure they were growing spiritually. His genuine interest in them continued.

Not certain of his own future, the apostle prefaced his desire with the words **I hope in the Lord Jesus.** This was an unusual way to speak of Timothy's proposed journey. Paul was especially aware that his release or death could come at any time.

The intent of Timothy's visit was clearly stated—**that I also may be cheered.** Both Paul's letter and Timothy's visit would certainly encourage the believers at Philippi. But the apostle also wanted to be encouraged as Timothy returned with good news from them.

Another lesson to be learned from Paul's sending Timothy is the need for selflessness. Timothy was close to Paul and dear to his heart. If Paul ever needed Timothy, it was while he was there in Rome under house arrest. Yet he was willing to sacrifice Timothy's companionship so that others could be helped.

2:20. Paul's young son in the faith had a deep interest and concern for the Philippians. In fact, Paul had **no one else** in Rome who was **like him.** Timothy's interest in their **welfare** was unexcelled. He was an excellent example of one who was selfless, more concerned about others than himself (cf. 2:3-4). The believers in the Philippian assembly needed to share Timothy's sincere interest in the welfare of others. The words "no one else like him" are literally "no one of equal soul" (*isopsychon;* cf. "one in spirit," *sympsychoi,* in 2:2).

2:21. This verse appears to make a rather broad claim. Did Paul mean to include everybody he ever knew? Or did he mean that of all who were near him in Rome, none compared to Timothy? Did Paul mean all others whom he might have

contacted to run the errand were more interested in their **own interests** than in those of Christ's? The second suggestion seems correct. Timothy stood out as a rare gem in a world of self-seekers (cf. 1:15, 17).

2:22. The Philippians knew Timothy, so they knew that what the apostle said about him was true. From the start, when he worked with Paul in Philippi, Timothy was faithful (cf. Acts 16). He had been closely associated with Paul since Paul's second missionary journey. The man had often been tested and **proved.** Paul was Timothy's spiritual **father,** and Timothy worked with him as his **son.** Together they both served the Lord as slaves **in the work of the gospel.**

Timothy's qualities were unexcelled. His whole life stands as an example for every child of God. Those in the Philippian assembly who were deficient in any of these qualities must have been pricked in conscience as they read Paul's letter, even as believers are today.

2:23-24. After his grand commendation of Timothy, Paul reaffirmed his intention to send him to them (v. 23). Just as soon as Paul knew how things were going, he would **send him.** Apparently Paul was waiting for some decision in his legal case.

In view of verse 24, Paul must have expected release from his chains. Significantly Paul's confidence was now **in the Lord** (cf. "in the Lord Jesus," v. 19). This phrase may be rendered "if the Lord wills."

Though the Scriptures include no specific statement about Paul's release, it must have occurred since he was imprisoned again in Rome during which time he wrote his last letter, 2 Timothy. Though there is no record of Paul's revisiting Philippi, he may have returned there after his release.

2. EPAPHRODITUS AND PAUL (2:25-30)

It is uncertain whether Epaphroditus was still with Paul at Rome when Paul wrote Philippians or whether Epaphroditus had already left to return to Philippi. Traditionally Epaphroditus has been viewed as the bearer of this letter to the Philippians. He is mentioned only here and in 4:18.

2:25. Since the church had sent **Epaphroditus** to bring Paul "the gifts" (of money, 4:18) and to discover how things were going with him, they probably intended for him to stay and assist Paul indefinitely. However, the apostle chose to send him back to them. But Paul wanted to be doubly sure the believers knew how highly he thought of Epaphroditus. He called him **my brother, fellow worker . . . fellow soldier,** and **messenger.** He shared Paul's spiritual life, labors, and dangers. He willingly took the role of a servant to assist Paul. What an exemplary lifestyle for every believer to follow. This man, whose name means "charming," served the Lord while he served others. The words **take care** translate the noun *leitourgon* ("serve as a priest"), which is related to the word "service" (*leitourgia*) in verse 17 (cf. v. 30). Epaphroditus' ministry to Paul was a priestly kind of service (cf. 4:18).

2:26-27. Epaphroditus had a deep concern for his friends in Philippi. He longed for all of them. He was **distressed because** he knew they had **heard he was ill.** His longing for the Philippians was exactly like Paul's (1:8). And the distress Epaphroditus experienced was similar to the agony Christ experienced in Gethsemane (Matt. 26:37; Mark 14:33).

Whatever illness Epaphroditus suffered was serious because he **almost died** (Phil. 2:27, 30). There is no indication that Paul had the ability to heal him or that he tried to do so. Neither is there any hint that Epaphroditus was sick because of being out of God's will.

Paul praised God for His **mercy** shown to Epaphroditus in restoring him to health and in sparing Paul **sorrow upon sorrow.** Thankfulness filled the apostle's heart. Paul already had sorrow associated with his imprisonment. He loved and needed Epaphroditus, so Epaphroditus' death would have brought Paul additional heaviness.

2:28-30. Paul was indeed selfless. He had the best interests of the Philippian believers and Epaphroditus at heart. They were sorry because their messenger to Paul had been ill and could not do for the apostle what they had hoped. Anticipating what they might think, Paul took full responsibility for sending Epaphroditus home. With haste he arranged for his trip back to Philippi. He did so for two reasons: He wanted them to **be glad,** and he wanted to be relieved of all **anxiety** himself.

The believers in Philippi were not to think wrongly of Epaphroditus for coming home. They were not to think that he had failed when Paul needed him most. He was to be welcomed **in the Lord** and in fact to be honored.

Paul's desire here illustrates how believers ought to relate toward those who may be misunderstood by others. Genuine Christian love, a fruit of the Spirit (Gal. 5:22), is always desirable, for it defends others and overlooks their faults (1 Cor. 13:7).

Paul explained (Phil. 2:30) why the saints should receive Epaphroditus. This messenger from Philippi was so sick he **almost died.** It was while he was serving Christ that he became sick, and if he had died it would also have been for Christ.

The believers from Philippi could not be in Rome helping Paul. Epaphroditus was **risking his life** to do what they **could not** do. He was serving Christ while he served them and Paul. (The word **help** is *leitourgias*, "priestly service," also used in v. 17; cf. v. 25.) As Christians serve Christ, they also serve others. The apostle reminded his readers of this so that they would receive Epaphroditus as they should.

III. Exhortations for Living the Christian Life (3:1-21)

In chapter 1 Paul encouraged the saints at Philippi to go on living the Christian life. In chapter 2 Paul set forth Timothy, Epaphroditus, and himself as examples of how to please God. Exhortations necessary for those who would lead such a life followed in chapter 3.

A. Believers are to have no confidence in the flesh (3:1-14)

1. THE EXHORTATION INTRODUCED (3:1)

3:1. Before stressing the serious danger of placing confidence in the flesh, the apostle called for a spirit of rejoicing in the Lord. His word **finally** was used to introduce a new subject as well as a clue that he had begun to conclude the letter. He used the same phrase again in 4:8. So some feel that chapter 3 is a digression from the author's main theme.

Paul called on believers to **rejoice in the Lord.** The word "rejoice" appears several times in the epistle (1:18 [twice];

2:17-18 [twice]; 3:1; 4:4 [twice], 10). It seems from this repeated emphasis that the Philippian Christians needed this word. Most of God's people need this challenge often. It is easy for believers to let circumstances discourage them. The cure for discouragement is to rivet one's attention on the Lord and rejoice in Him.

It is significant too that a Roman prisoner would beseech people who were free to be joyful in their Savior. It seems that it should be the other way around. Paul learned what every child of God needs to learn—there can be rejoicing in the Lord even when outward circumstances are contrary to a spirit of rejoicing.

Repetition is a vital part of learning. Either orally or in writing (perhaps in 1:27-30) the apostle had given the same truth to the Philippians before. He made no apology for repeating the instruction by writing **the same things to you again.** It was **no trouble** for him to review the essentials again. He felt constrained to do so for their benefit. The instruction was a **safeguard** for them.

2. THE EXAMPLE TO BE AVOIDED (3:2-3)

One particular group in Paul's day was especially guilty of putting confidence in the flesh. These were the Judaizers. They plagued Paul and his converts constantly. Confused about the gospel, they added works of the law to faith in Christ, both for salvation and for Christian living. The Old Testament rite of circumcision was of special concern to them. They insisted that it was necessary for salvation. They did not omit faith in Christ but added works of the flesh. Paul called such men "deceitful workmen" (2 Cor. 11:13).

3:2. Paul also called the Judaizers **dogs, those men who do evil, those mutilators of the flesh.** He considered their work dangerous and not of God. The saints were not to follow these people, but to beware of them, to **watch out** for them.

It was common for some Jews to refer to Gentiles as dogs, which were considered unclean animals. Paul used the term to describe those Jews who mutilated the gospel by insisting on the need to mutilate the flesh in order to be rightly related to God. What they did was

actually evil, even though they may have had good intentions.

3:3. The Old Testament rite of physical circumcision was not only a sign of covenant relationship, but it was also intended to be related to spiritual circumcision of the heart (cf. Deut. 30:6). Writing to Gentiles, Paul made it clear that he and they were the true **circumcision.** This was because they had **no confidence in the flesh** and instead worshiped **by the Spirit of God** and gloried **in Christ Jesus** alone.

Instead of boasting in human accomplishments, as the Judaizers and Jews did, a child of God should glory in Christ Jesus alone. The word **glory** (kauchōmenoi) used here means "boast" or "exult" (cf. 1:26; 2:16; 2 Cor. 10:17).

3. THE EXAMPLE TO BE FOLLOWED (3:4-14)

Paul gave some interesting autobiographical facts in these verses. On the surface it appears he was boasting. However, closer examination reveals that this was precisely what he tried to avoid and warn against. To be sure, there was a time when the apostle had confidence in the flesh. But this was no longer true. To stress that he used to have great boldness and pride in his own achievements, Paul reviewed his past for the Philippians. After this he told about his crisis conversion experience on the road to Damascus.

3:4-6. It cannot be emphasized too strongly that Paul did not place any **confidence in the flesh.** He had gained victory over that temptation of the devil. His presentation in these verses was intended to review for the Philippians the things in which he could have placed confidence if he had wanted to. In fact the list included things in which he did place great value and trust before he met Christ. His intention was to show that in the flesh he had more in which he could have boasted than did any of the Judaizers.

The **anyone else** (v. 4) referred to all who place confidence in the flesh. Paul wrote as though he were challenging the Judaizers to a showdown. His preliminary conclusion before he even got specific was that no matter what advantage was brought forth by his opponents, his advantages exceeded theirs (cf. Gal. 1:14).

Seven advantages listed in Philippians 3:5-6 demonstrate what Paul used to have in the flesh but what he later counted as loss for Christ. Two kinds of advantages are enumerated. First are those things which the apostle had by birth, apart from his choice. Four of these are listed—circumcision, of the stock of Israel, of the tribe of Benjamin, and a Hebrew son of Hebrew parents. Next he named those privileges which he voluntarily chose—being a Pharisee, being a persecutor of the church, and having a flawless external record of **legalistic righteousness.**

Circumcision was named first probably because it was a big issue with the Judaizers. Paul's specific time, **the eighth day,** stressed that he was not a proselyte or an Ishmaelite but a pure-blooded Jew. Proselytes were circumcised later in life and Ishmaelites after age 13 (cf. Gen. 17:25-26).

Paul was **of the people of Israel,** which describes his heritage. His parents were both true Jews, unlike some of the Judaizers. He could trace his family lineage all the way back to Abraham. He was a true member of the covenant people (cf. 2 Cor. 11:22).

He was also a Benjamite, from which tribe came Israel's first king (1 Sam. 9:1-2). This tribe had a special place of honor and was viewed with great esteem. Even after the kingdom was disrupted the tribe of Benjamin remained loyal to the house of David.

Hebrew was Paul's native tongue. Unlike some of the Israelites, he did not adopt Greek customs. He knew thoroughly both the language and customs of the people of God. He was a Hebrew son of Hebrew parents.

In regard to the Law, Paul was **a Pharisee,** a member of the strictest sect among his people. In addition to the Law of Moses the Pharisees added their own regulations which in time were interpreted as equal to the Law.

What greater **zeal** for the Jewish religion could anyone boast of than that he persecuted **the church?** Paul did this relentlessly before his conversion to Christ (Acts 9:1-2). No Judaizer could match such zeal.

In "legalistic righteousness" Paul also excelled. In fact in his own eyes he was **faultless** (*amemptos*; the same word is used in Phil. 2:15 where it is rendered "blameless").

3:7-9. Any of those who troubled the saints at Philippi would have loved to have been able to list to his credit those things Paul did. On the human side these were reasons to have religious self-confidence. But all those things enumerated in verses 5-6 the apostle considered **loss for the sake of Christ** (v. 7).

Consider means to "think through or reflect on." After reflection he considered them loss. This he did at a point in time in the past and that decision was still in effect when he wrote, as connoted by the use of the Greek perfect tense. Doubtless Paul considered his life-transforming conversion on the Damascus Road as the time when he switched from confidence in the flesh to confidence in Christ alone.

It would be hard to find a more forceful refutation of human effort to please God than what Paul presented here (v. 8). Four Greek particles (*alla menoun ge kai*) are translated **what is more** and introduce the strong statements of verse 8. Paul considered as **loss** not only the things already listed (vv. 5-6), but **everything** (v. 8). In exchange for confidence in the flesh Paul gained the **surpassing greatness of knowing Christ Jesus** personally. Christ was now his **Lord.**

His former "gains" (*kerdē*, v. 7) he considered "rubbish" (which can mean food scraps or dung) so that he might **gain** (*kerdēsō*) **Christ.** Nothing else really mattered to him any longer. Having Christ as his Savior and Lord so far surpassed anything he had in Judaism.

Those who "gain Christ" (v. 8) are those **found in Him** (v. 9). Christ is in the believer and the believer is in Christ. Paul wanted his life to demonstrate these truths. Being in Christ, he was not clinging to any **righteousness** of his own doing associated with Law-keeping. Such a righteousness is viewed by God as no righteousness at all but rather as "filthy rags" (Isa. 64:6). The righteousness which saves and in which Paul rested is **through** (*dia*) **faith in Christ.** This is the only kind which **comes from God and is by** (*epi*) **faith.** When a believing sinner responds in faith to the Spirit's work in his heart, he is clothed in the righteousness of Christ (Rom. 3:24-26). In this position he is "accepted in the Beloved" (Eph. 1:6, KJV). Thus robed, the believing sinner stands complete in Christ.

3:10-11. These verses contain an open and honest confession to the Philippians. Paul already knew Christ as his Savior. But he wanted to know Him more intimately as his Lord. **To know** (v. 10) means "to know by experience" (*gnōnai*). The noun (*gnōseōs*) is used in verse 8. The "surpassing greatness of knowing Christ" is now elaborated in verses 10-11. This is how Paul wanted to know Him. More of what he desired in his Christian life follows.

To experience **the power of His resurrection** was also the apostle's goal. The power which brought Christ forth from the dead now operates in believers' lives since they have been "raised with Christ" (Col. 3:1). "Power" (*dynamis*, also used in Acts 1:8; Rom. 1:16) means ability to overcome resistance. By setting forth his own goals and ambitions Paul gave the Philippians an example to follow. His example was, of course, in stark contrast to the Judaizers whose example they were not to follow.

Paul also longed to share in the fellowship of Christ's sufferings and in so doing to become **like Him in His death** (Phil. 3:10). These sufferings were not Christ's substitutionary sufferings on the cross. Paul knew that those could not be shared. But he did desire to participate with Christ, since he was one of His, in suffering for the sake of righteousness (cf. 1:29). God had used Ananias to tell Paul that this is precisely what he would do as a servant of Christ (Acts 9:16). The apostle did indeed suffer for Christ because he represented Him so openly and truly (cf. Rom. 8:36; 2 Cor. 4:10).

The words "becoming like Him" translate *symmorphizomenos*, which means "being conformed inwardly in one's experience to something" (cf. Phil. 3:21), in this case, to Christ's death. As Christ died *for* sin, so a believer has died *to* sin (Rom. 6:2, 6-7; Col. 3:3). He should exhibit that cutting off from his former sinful way by daily being set apart from sin (Rom. 6:1-4, 11-14) and living a new life by means of Christ's resurrection power (Rom. 6:4).

"Resurrection" (Phil. 3:11) is the translation of *exanastasin*, a Greek word used nowhere else in the New Testament. It means a partial resurrection out from among other corpses, literally an "out-re-

surrection." But why did Paul say he wanted **somehow, to attain to the** (out-) **resurrection from the dead?** Did he doubt he would be raised from the dead? Hardly. Perhaps he was using this word to refer to the Rapture, thus expressing the hope that the Lord would return during his lifetime.

3:12-14. Though Paul was a spiritual giant in the eyes of the Philippian saints, he wanted them to know that he had not yet attained the goals stated in verse 10. He was still actively pressing on toward them. He had by no means reached the final stage of his sanctification.

Paul's salvation experience had taken place about 30 years before he wrote to the Philippians. He had won many spiritual battles in that time. He had grown much in those years, but he candidly confessed he had not **obtained all this,** nor was he yet **made perfect** (v. 12). He still had more spiritual heights to climb. This testimony of the apostle reminded the saints at Philippi—and it serves to remind believers today—that there must never be a stalemate in their spiritual growth or a plateau beyond which they cannot climb.

Paul pursued Christlikeness with the enthusiasm and persistence of a runner in the Greek games. Unlike the Judaizers, whose influence was prevalent among the Philippians, the apostle did not claim to have attained spiritual maturity. He was still pressing on, pursuing **that for which Christ Jesus took hold of** him. Nor had he yet **taken hold of it,** that is, he had not yet attained perfection or ultimate conformity to Christ. But he was determined that he would forget the past and, like a runner, press on toward the goal. Paul refused to be controlled or absorbed by his past heritage (vv. 5-7) or his attainments (v. 8).

Vigorously and with concentration Paul sought **to win the prize** to which God had **called** him **heavenward** (v. 14). Again the Greek games must have been on his mind as he wrote of the prize. The winner in those games was called to the place where the judge sat in order to receive his prize. Paul may have referred to ultimate salvation in God's presence, or to receiving rewards at "the judgment seat of Christ" (2 Cor. 5:10).

B. Believers are to have a walk that pleases God (3:15-21)

1. A WALK OF MATURITY (3:15-16)

The second great exhortation in chapter 3 has a positive ring to it—Paul urged Christians to walk, or live lives, pleasing to God (3:15-21). This should first be a mature walk (vv. 15-16).

3:15-16. The apostle called his readers to share with him the pursuit of Christlikeness. What he wanted for himself he also wanted for them. **All of us who are mature should take such a view of things** (v. 15). What view of things? The one he had expressed regarding persistently pressing on toward the goal. One mark of spiritual maturity is a desire to go on with Christ. Paul's appeal here was to maturing believers who shared his ambitions. He trusted God to **make** things **clear** to those who disagreed with him.

No doubt the greatest need among God's people is to live up to what they already have in Christ. Most live far below their exalted position in Christ. Paul's plea to the Philippians was that they **live up to what** they had **already attained,** namely a righteous position in Christ.

2. A WALK OF WATCHFULNESS (3:17-19)

Paul again called on his readers to follow his own example and not that of the Judaizers.

3:17. Having set forth his life ambition to be more Christlike, Paul did not hesitate to tell the Philippians to follow his **example.** He wanted them to imitate him. Surely he did not mean that they should imitate every single area of his life, for he had just stated that he was not sinlessly perfect. But in the matter of relentlessly pursuing after Christlikeness, he did set himself up as an example. Those Philippians who followed him would **join with others** who were already doing so.

3:18-19. These verses give the reasons for the exhortations in verse 17: **many live as enemies of the cross of Christ.** Believers should be able to determine truth from error (cf. 1 John 4:6). Paul was so concerned about the Philippians' spiritual welfare that he warned them often and wept as he did so.

As enemies of God these false teachers were destined for **destruction.** Those Paul warned against were perhaps profligates in incipient Gnosticism who trusted in their own attainments and not in the sufficiency of Christ alone. All who do so are not children of God, so they await destruction. This word (*apōleia*) does not mean annihilation but rather ruination by separation from the presence of God in eternal judgment.

Three further descriptions of these false teachers follow. First, **their god is their stomach.** They had in mind only their own physical desires and unrestrained gluttony (cf. Rom. 16:18).

Second, **their glory is in their shame.** Instead of giving glory to God these teachers heaped praise on themselves. Ironically they prided themselves in the things they should have been ashamed of.

Third, **their mind is on earthly things.** It is certainly not wrong for God's people to care about their earthly affairs. But those Paul warned against here were depending on earthly things to gain merit with God. The apostle frequently alerted the people of God against such a lifestyle (cf. Gal. 4:3, 9-11; Col. 2:21-22).

3. A WALK COMPLETED (3:20-21)

3:20-21. The people of Philippi were living there as colonists while their citizenship was in Rome. Similarly Christians, while living on earth, have their **citizenship** elsewhere—**in heaven.** This contrasts with those in verse 19 whose minds are exclusively on earthly things.

The believer looks with keen anticipation for his Savior's return from heaven. **Eagerly await** translates a word (*apekdechometha*) that suggests a tiptoe anticipation and longing. This word is also used in Romans 8:19, 23, 25; 1 Corinthians 1:7; Galatians 5:5; Hebrews 9:28.

At the Rapture of the church, Christ **will transform** (*metaschēmatisei*, "change the outward form of") **our lowly bodies so that they will be like** (*symmorphon*, "identical in essential character"; cf. the participle *symmorphizomenos* in Phil. 3:10) **His glorious body.** Then every child of God will be made like the Son of God (1 John 3:2), that is, all Christians will receive glorified bodies like His. No more will they have the limitations they now experience in their "lowly" bodies, which are humbled by disease and sin. Their resurrected bodies will be like Christ's, and their sanctification will be completed.

IV. Enablement for Living the Christian Life (4:1-23)

A. Christ at the center (4:1-7)

Paul's love for the Philippians, which is evident throughout this letter, is especially apparent in the opening verses of chapter 4. One of his chief concerns was that these people would be characterized by the fruit of the Spirit. Love, joy, and peace were uppermost in his heart and mind for them. In order to experience these Christian graces Christ must be at the center of a believer's life. Paul made this plain as he wrote to the saints at Philippi.

1. STANDING FAST IN HIM (4:1-3)

In these verses the apostle first gave a general plea for unity and steadfastness and then a specific plea to two women.

4:1. **Therefore** introduces this exhortation and applies what he wrote in chapter 3 about sanctification and glorification. The apostle's affection for this congregation is revealed by his love and longing for them and his calling them his **brothers** (cf. "brothers" in 1:12; 3:1, 13, 17; 4:8), his **joy and crown** (*stephanos*, the runner's wreath or victor's crown; cf. 1 Thes. 2:19-20), and his **dear friends** (cf. Phil. 2:12). These saints were to their spiritual father what victory wreaths were to runners in the Greek races. The believers were exhorted to **stand firm in the Lord** (cf. 1:27, where Paul urged the same steadfastness).

4:2. Two women, **Euodia** and **Syntyche,** did not live up to the meanings of their names. "Euodia" means a "prosperous journey." "Syntyche" means a "pleasant acquaintance." Since Paul pleaded with these two to **agree with each other in the Lord,** it seems that they were causing dissension in the assembly. This helps explain Paul's earlier plea for unity (2:1-4).

4:3. At one time Euodia and Syntyche **contended** at Paul's **side in the cause of the gospel.** But as he wrote they were not in harmony with each other. They were contentious, rather than content.

The exact identity of Paul's **loyal yokefellow** is not known. Some say "yokefellow" (*syzyge*) is a proper name. Paul knew he could count on him to work

with the women and bring them back to fellowship with each other and with the Lord. **Clement** and other **fellow workers** had also contended for the gospel with these women. (This is more likely than supposing the words "along with Clement and the rest of my fellow workers" go with "help," as though Paul were enlisting Clement and others to help Syzygus unite the women.)

2. REJOICING IN HIM (4:4)

4:4. Sometimes the trials and pressures of life make it almost impossible to be happy. But Paul did not tell his readers to be happy. He encouraged them to **rejoice in the Lord.** In fact, he said it twice in verse 4 (cf. 3:1; 1 Thes. 5:16). Christ is the One in whom the sphere of rejoicing was to take place. Surely there are many circumstances in which Christians cannot be happy. But they can always rejoice in the Lord and delight in Him. Paul himself was an excellent example of one who had inner joy when external circumstances—such as persecution, imprisonment, the threat of death—were against him.

3. LIVING IN THE LIGHT OF HIS PRESENCE (4:5-7)

4:5. In addition to joy, believers are to have **gentleness,** which is to **be evident to all.** *Epieikes* ("gentleness") suggests a forebearing, nonretaliatory spirit. Joy, an inner quality in relation to circumstances, may not always be seen; but the way one reacts to others—whether in gentleness or harshness—will be noticed. Why be gentle? Because **the Lord is near.** This probably refers to the Rapture, not to His presence with His own at all times.

4:6-7. Joy and gentleness (vv. 4-5), accompanied with an awareness of Christ's imminent return, should dispel anxiety. Paul's appeal to the Philippians is **do not be anxious about anything.** But this was not a call to a carefree life. To care and be genuinely concerned is one thing. To worry is another. Paul and Timothy cared for the people they ministered to (2 Cor. 11:28; Phil. 2:20), yet they retained trust in God. Jesus warned against worry which obviously eliminates trust in God (Matt. 6:25-33).

Paul exhorted the Philippians to prayer instead of anxiety. Praying with thanksgiving involves trusting God. Four words are used here to describe a believer's communion with God. **Prayer** (*proseuchē*) describes a believer's approach to God. **Petition** (*deēsei*) emphasizes requesting an answer to a specific need. **Thanksgiving** (*eucharistias*) is an attitude of heart which should always accompany one's prayers. **Requests** (*aitēmata*) speak of definite and specific things asked for.

When the exhortations of verses 4-6 are heeded, **the peace of God** (v. 7) will flood one's troubled soul. The Lord Jesus Christ is a believer's peace (Eph. 2:14), and every child of God has peace *with* God through justification by faith (Rom. 5:1). But the peace *of* (or from) God relates to the inner tranquility of a believer's close walk with God.

This peace of God **transcends all understanding,** that is, it is beyond man's ability to comprehend. This peace guards the believers. **Guard** (*phrourēsei*, also used in 1 Peter 1:5) translates a military term which means "to protect or garrison by guarding." Like soldiers assigned to watch over a certain area, God's peace garrisons the **hearts and . . . minds,** that is, the emotions and thoughts, of God's children.

B. God's presence with believers (4:8-9)

1. THINKING WORTHY THOUGHTS (4:8)

4:8. By the word **finally** Paul indicated he was about to conclude the section. Six items are mentioned as objects of a wholesome thought life, and each one is introduced with **whatever.** In the Greek "whatever" is plural, which suggests that several things could be included under each heading.

True (*alēthē*) things are of course the opposite of dishonest and unreliable things (cf. Eph. 4:15, 25). **Noble** refers to what is dignified and worthy of respect (this word *semna* is used in the NT only here and in 1 Tim. 3:8, 11; Titus 2:2). **Right** refers to conformity to God's standards. **Pure** (*hagna*) refers to what is wholesome, not mixed with moral impurity. **Lovely** (*prosphilē*, occurring only here in the NT) speaks of what promotes peace rather than conflict. **Admirable** (*euphēma*, also used only here) relates to what is positive and constructive rather than negative and destructive.

These six objects of thought are then described as **excellent** (*aretē*) and **praiseworthy** (*epainos*).

2. DOING WORTHY DEEDS (4:9)

4:9. The Christian life involves proper thinking (v. 8), but it also includes doing righteous deeds.

Since the Philippians knew Paul well, he could ask them to follow his example. They had **learned . . . received** and **heard from** him, and they had even **seen** the apostle's conduct. As they **put** these things (from Paul's teaching and living) **into practice,** they would enjoy the presence of **the God of peace** (cf. "the peace of God," v. 7).

C. God's supply of human needs (4:10-20)

Epaphroditus was the messenger the Philippians sent to bring their gift to Paul (4:18). It appears that Paul wrote this letter as both a thank-you note and as a word of greeting and exhortation. The apostle could certainly testify that God does supply His people's needs.

1. THE LESSON OF CONTENTMENT (4:10-13)

4:10-13. Paul's heart was made glad **(I rejoice greatly in the Lord)** because of the continued interest the Philippian Christians showed in him. They had not forgotten him; through them God had met his needs. Even before they sent Epaphroditus they were concerned but **had no opportunity to show it.**

Paul did not beg God's people to help him in his work. He just placed the need before them and trusted God to meet it. Too, he had learned the lesson of contentment. Changing circumstances did not affect the inner contentment he enjoyed. The word **content** (*autarkēs*) means "self-sufficient." The Stoics used this word (which occurs only here in the NT) to mean human self-reliance and fortitude, a calm acceptance of life's pressures. But Paul used it to refer to a *divinely* bestowed sufficiency, **whatever the circumstances.**

At times Paul experienced definite financial and material needs, and at other times he had an abundance (v. 12). He learned how to cope with both **need** and plenty. The words **I have learned the secret** translate *memyēmai* (from *myeō*), which occurs only here in the New Testament. In the mystery religions it was a technical term meaning "to initiate (into the mysteries)." Paul used it here to suggest a kind of "initiation" (by his experiences) into being content when either **well fed or hungry,** and either **in plenty or in want.**

Paul said he could **do everything**—including handling poverty and living in abundance—**through Him who** gave him **strength.** This was not an expression of pride in his own abilities but a declaration of the strength provided by Christ.

2. THE BLESSING OF GIVING AND RECEIVING (4:14-20)

4:14-16. Though Paul was content no matter what the circumstances, he was nevertheless grateful for the help the Philippians sent with Epaphroditus.

Because they gave of their means they shared with the apostle in his **troubles;** they did something about his problem.

In the very beginning of their Christian experience (Acts 16) when Paul left Macedonia they alone shared with him **in the matter of giving and receiving.** And again when Paul was in Thessalonica on his second missionary journey (Acts 17:1) and experienced definite need, the Philippians **sent** him **aid** twice.

4:17-20. Others were always uppermost in Paul's mind. He was not **looking for a gift** simply to satisfy his own needs. He wanted credit to come to the **account** of the Philippians.

Since these people had already helped him so much, Paul did not want them to think he was still looking for more from them. He had received from the Philippians full payment, all the money they had sent, so he was then abounding and was **amply supplied.** What they had sent with Epaphroditus (2:25-30) had an effect on both him and God, for the gifts were a **fragrant offering, an acceptable sacrifice, pleasing to God.** The term "fragrant offering" was used in Leviticus (in the LXX) for an offering that pleased God. It also was used in Ephesians 5:2 of Christ's offering of Himself.

God would reciprocate to the Philippians. They had met Paul's needs and now God would meet theirs. God would not only bless them *out of* or *from* His bounty but also *in accordance with* (*kata*) it: **according to His glorious riches in Christ Jesus.**

To our God—his heavenly Father and theirs—the apostle gave thanks and praise.

D. Conclusion (4:21-23)

4:21-23. Final greetings came to the Philippians from Paul, from his fellow workers, and from other believers.

The apostle sent his greetings from **all the saints** (v. 21). He addressed "all the saints" (1:1) in writing the epistle. The **brothers** who were with Paul also sent greetings. Timothy was certainly included in this group. **The saints** (v. 22) who sent greetings were those in the church in Rome (Rom. 16:1-15).

Those who belong to Caesar's household (Phil. 4:22) were probably those who had come to Christ as a result of Paul's house arrest. They probably included soldiers and relatives of Caesar's household. No wonder Paul could say that what had happened to him had advanced the gospel (1:12).

As was his usual practice Paul gave great prominence to Christ's marvelous **grace** as he concluded his letter (cf. Phile. 25).

BIBLIOGRAPHY

Berry, Harold J. *Studies in Philippians. Gems from the Original,* vol. 3. Lincoln, Neb.: Back to the Bible, 1978.

Boice, James Montgomery. *Philippians: An Expositional Commentary.* Grand Rapids: Zondervan Publishing House, 1971.

Getz, Gene A. *A Profile of Christian Maturity.* Grand Rapids: Zondervan Publishing House, 1976.

Gromacki, Robert G. *Stand United in Joy.* Grand Rapids: Baker Book House, 1980.

Hendriksen, William. *Exposition of Philippians.* New Testament Commentary. Grand Rapids: Baker Book House, 1962.

Philippians

Kent, Homer A., Jr. "Philippians." In *The Expositor's Bible Commentary*, vol. 11. Grand Rapids: Zondervan Publishing House, 1978.

Lightfoot, J.B. *Saint Paul's Epistle to the Philippians*. Reprint. Grand Rapids: Zondervan Publishing House, 1953.

Martin, R.P. *The Epistle of Paul to the Philippians: An Introduction and Commentary.* Tyndale New Testament Commentaries. Grand Rapids: Wm. B. Eerdmans Publishing Co., 1959.

Meyer, F.B. *The Epistle to the Philippians.* Grand Rapids: Baker Book House, 1952.

Pentecost, J. Dwight. *The Joy of Living: A Study of Philippians.* Grand Rapids: Zondervan Publishing House, 1973.

Tenney, Merrill C. *Philippians: The Gospel at Work.* Grand Rapids: Wm. B. Eerdmans Publishing Co., 1956.

Vincent, Marvin R. *A Critical and Exegetical Commentary on the Epistle to the Philippians and to Philemon.* International Critical Commentary. Edinburgh: T. & T. Clark, 1897.

Walvoord, John F. *Philippians: Triumph in Christ.* Chicago: Moody Press, 1971.

Wiersbe, Warren W. *Be Joyful: A Practical Study of Philippians.* Wheaton, Ill.: SP Publications, Victor Books, 1974.

Wuest, Kenneth. *Philippians in the Greek New Testament.* Grand Rapids: Wm. B. Eerdmans Publishing, Co., 1951.

COLOSSIANS

Norman L. Geisler

INTRODUCTION

The Book of Colossians was written by the Apostle Paul about A.D. 60–62, while he was imprisoned in Rome. One purpose was to correct the heresy that had sprung up in the Asian city of Colosse.

Author. The Pauline authorship of Colossians is supported by abundant evidence both in and out of the book. Colossians has three personal references to Paul in the first person (1:1; 1:23; 4:18) and numerous references to Paul's associates, such as Tychicus (4:7), Onesimus (4:9), Aristarchus (4:10), Mark (4:10), Justus (4:11), Epaphras (4:12), Luke (4:14), Demas (4:14), and Archippus (4:17). The style and content of Colossians is similar to Ephesians, written about the same time and probably alluded to as "the letter from Laodicea" (4:16).

While 34 Greek words are unique to Colossians, they are characteristic of the theme of the book and fit the thoughts of Paul. Words in this category include "visible" (1:16), "supremacy" (1:18), "fill up" (1:24), "philosophy" (2:8), and "Deity" (2:9).

The conclusion of Ephesians confirms that Tychicus was the carrier of both it and Colossians (Eph. 6:21; cf. Col. 4:7). This helps confirm Paul as the author of the Colossian epistle.

The external evidence for Paul's authorship is strong, despite the claim of some that the heresy combated in the book is second-century Gnosticism. But there is good reason to believe that the heresy addressed in Colossians (at least in its incipient form) had appeared already in Paul's lifetime. And in view of Paul's other encounters with heresies, in books which are unquestionably his, it seems clear that he authored Colossians (cf. 1 Cor. 15; Gal. 1–2; 2 Thes. 2).

Colossians includes some stylistic differences such as unusual genitival combinations: "the hope of glory" (Col. 1:27), "body of . . . flesh" (2:11, NASB), "growth . . . from God" (2:19, NASB), "reward of . . . inheritance" (3:24, NASB). However, as Donald Guthrie correctly observed, "stylistic differences are generally attributable to changing circumstances or subject matter" (*New Testament Introduction*. Downers Grove, Ill.: InterVarsity Press, 1973, p. 553).

One of the strongest lines of evidence that Colossians is a first-century work of the Apostle Paul is its close link to the Book of Philemon, the authenticity of which is virtually impeccable. (1) Both books include Timothy's name with Paul's in the opening greeting (Col. 1:1; Phile. 1). (2) Greetings are sent in both books from Aristarchus, Mark, Epaphras, Luke, and Demas (Col. 4:10-14; Phile. 23-24). (3) Archippus' ministry is referred to in both books (Col. 4:17; Phile. 2). (4) Onesimus the slave is mentioned in both books (Col. 4:9; Phile. 10).

Date and Place of Writing. Colossians was written from Rome during Paul's (first) imprisonment there, as recorded in Acts 28:30. At the same time Paul wrote Ephesians and Philemon (ca. A.D. 60–62). In Philemon 1, 9 Paul referred to himself as "a prisoner of Christ Jesus." Ephesians also contains references to Paul being a "prisoner" (Eph. 3:1; 4:1). And Ephesians refers to Tychicus carrying the epistles from Paul to their destinations (Eph. 6:21; cf. Col. 4:7). Since the record of Acts ends around A.D. 60–62, Colossians was probably written during this two-year imprisonment. And since neither Colossians, Ephesians, nor Philemon mention the outcome of Paul's trial, anticipated in Philippians 1:19-21, it can be assumed that Colossians was written before Philippians.

Colosse was in the Lycus Valley,

about 100 miles east of Ephesus in Asia Minor. Its name is possibly derived from *Colossus*, a large statue, which in turn may have been named for the unusual shape of stony deposits there. Colosse is about 12 miles from Hierapolis and Laodicea, the other two cities of that valley (see the location of these three on the map between Acts and Rom.). The area was rich in mineral deposits and was also subject to frequent earthquakes. Rich pasturelands were nearby. Several references in Colossians indicate that Paul had not visited the city (Col. 1:7; 2:1; 4:12).

Occasion. The circumstance which prompted the writing of Colossians seemed to be the special heresy that arose there. This false teaching seemed to be the beginning of what later (in the second century) developed into Gnosticism. It contained several characteristics. (1) It was Jewish, stressing the need for observing Old Testament laws and ceremonies. (2) It was philosophical, laying emphasis on some special or deeper knowledge (*gnōsis*). (3) It involved the worship of angels as mediators to God (2:18). (4) It was exclusivistic, stressing the special privilege and "perfection" of those select few who belonged to this philosophical elite. (5) It was also Christological. But this seminal Gnosticism denied the deity of Christ, thus calling forth one of the greatest declarations of Christ's deity found anywhere in Scripture (1:15-16; 2:9).

Purposes. Three purposes seem to have been in Paul's mind as he wrote Colossians. First, he sought to show the deity and supremacy of Christ in the face of the Colossian heresy (1:18; 2:9). Second, he wanted to lead believers into spiritual maturity (1:28; 2:6-7). Third, he wanted to inform them about his state of affairs and elicited their prayers on his behalf (4:2-8).

Contents. The epistle may be summarized as follows: "Greetings, brothers (1:1-2). We thank God for your faith and love (1:3-8). And we ask God to fill you with the knowledge of His will. We pray this so that you will be fruitful for Christ who has redeemed you (1:9-14). For Christ, our Creator and Head, is supreme in all things (1:15-20). And through Christ's death God has reconciled you

who were aliens and enemies (1:21-23). So I rejoice that I can suffer for the church so that God's fullness can be known by the Gentiles (1:24-27). To this end we labor that everyone may be perfect in Christ (1:28-29). For all true wisdom and knowledge is found in Christ (2:1-5). Therefore, brothers, just as you began with Christ, continue in Him (2:6-7).

"Now don't be deceived: God's fullness is in Christ alone and not in vain human philosophy (2:8-10). And since you have been identified with Christ in your baptism, you have no need to live under Jewish laws (2:11-17). And don't let anyone rob you of your prize by forsaking Christ your Head (2:18-19). For you died with Christ, so you need not submit to worldly (legalistic) rules (2:20-23). And since you were raised with Christ, you should set your hearts on heavenly things above (3:1-4). So put to death your sinful worldly practices (3:5-11). And clothe yourself with Christ's virtues (3:15-17).

"In view of your new exalted identity with Christ, I exhort wives to submit to their husbands; husbands to love their wives; children to obey their parents; fathers not to embitter their children; slaves to obey their masters; and masters to be fair with their slaves (3:18–4:1).

"Brothers, pray for me that I may preach this message effectively and clearly, and you live wisely toward outsiders (4:2-6). My coworkers in the gospel send greetings to you (4:7-15). Exchange letters with the Laodiceans and exhort Archippus to complete his ministry (4:16-18)."

OUTLINE

I. Doctrinal: Deeper Life in Christ (1:1–2:7)
  A. Greetings (1:1-2)
  B. Thanksgiving (1:3-8)
  C. Petition (1:9-14)
  D. Exaltation of Christ (1:15-20)
  E. Reconciliation by Christ (1:21-23)
  F. Revelation of the mystery of Christ (1:24-27)
  G. Perfection in Christ (1:28-29)
  H. Education (wisdom) in Christ (2:1-5)
  I. Exhortation to live in Christ (2:6-7)

II. Polemical: Higher Life in Christ
(2:8-23)
   A. "Gnosticism" is wrong: deity is
      in Christ (2:8-10)
   B. Legalism is wrong: reality is in
      Christ (2:11-17)
   C. Mysticism is wrong: headship is
      in Christ (2:18-19)
   D. Asceticism is wrong: immunity is
      in Christ (2:20-23)
III. Spiritual: Inner Life in Christ
(3:1-17)
   A. Seeking spiritual values (3:1-4)
   B. Putting off the sins of the old life
      (3:5-11)
   C. Putting on the virtues of the new
      life (3:12-17)
IV. Practical: Outer Life in Christ
(3:18–4:18)
   A. Perfecting one's private life
      (3:18–4:1)
   B. Perfecting one's prayer life
      (4:2-4)
   C. Perfecting one's public life
      (4:5-6)
   D. Perfecting one's personal life
      (4:7-17)
   E. Salutation (4:18)

COMMENTARY

I. Doctrinal: Deeper Life in Christ (1:1–2:7)

A. Greetings (1:1-2)

1:1-2. In all but his two earliest
epistles (1 and 2 Thes.) and his personal
letter to the Philippians, **Paul** began by
designating himself as **an apostle** (see the
chart, "Paul's Introductions to His
Epistles," near Rom. 1:1-7). He was not
one of the 12 Apostles (Acts 1:21-26) who
were with Christ from the beginning of
His earthly ministry (Acts 1:22; Luke 1:2;
John 15:27). Nevertheless he did see the
risen **Christ** (1 Cor. 9:1; 15:8-9), and he
did possess special miraculous powers
given to authenticate apostles (2 Cor.
12:12; cf. Heb. 2:3-4).

Timothy was with Paul here as he
often was (cf. 2 Cor. 1:1; Phil. 1:1; 2 Thes.
1:1). Timothy had a Gentile father (Acts
16:1) but his mother and grandmother
were godly Jewesses (2 Tim. 1:5) from
whom he had learned the Old Testament
Scriptures from childhood (2 Tim. 3:15).
Paul picked up Timothy on his second
missionary journey at Lystra where the

"brothers . . . spoke well of him" (Acts
16:2). Paul spent much time discipling
Timothy and wrote two of his last letters
to him.

Paul addressed the Colossian believers as **the holy and faithful brothers in
Christ.** This phrase marks them as holy
people, chosen and set apart for **God.** It
parallels the Ephesian introduction to
"the saints . . . the faithful in Christ Jesus"
(Eph. 1:1). Paul's characteristic greeting,
grace and peace includes *charis* ("grace"),
a variation of the normal Greek salutation, *chaire* ("Greetings"; cf. Luke 1:28).
Chaire probably suggested the similar-
sounding but richer *charis*. His greeting
also includes the normal Jewish salutation, "peace." So Paul wished for them
God's favor (grace) and a healthy condition of life (peace).

B. Thanksgiving (1:3-8)

1:3-4. Giving continual thanks to
God was characteristic of Paul's prayers
(Rom. 1:8; 1 Cor. 1:14; Eph. 1:6; etc.),
though he omitted this praise in Galatians
and 2 Corinthians. Here **God** is recognized as the cause of goodness in His
people. This thanks, Paul said, is rendered **when we pray.** And thanksgiving
was given **because** Paul had **heard** (from
Epaphras, Col. 1:7; cf. 4:12) about their
growing **faith in Christ Jesus and** their
love . . . for all the saints. Prayer here is
the broader, more inclusive act of
worship including thanksgiving and
intercession (cf. Matt. 6:7; Acts 16:25).

1:5. Paul thanked God for their **faith
and love that spring from . . . hope.**

This trilogy of virtue—faith, love,
and hope—is a favorite of Paul's (cf.
1 Cor. 13:13; 1 Thes. 1:3) and Peter's
(1 Peter 1:3, 5, 22). Faith is the soul
looking *upward* to God; love looks
outward to others; hope looks *forward* to
the future. Faith rests on the past work of
Christ; love works in the present; and
hope anticipates the future. Even though
"without faith it is impossible to please
God" (Heb. 11:6), and "hope does not
disappoint us" (Rom. 5:5), nevertheless
"the greatest of these is love" (1 Cor.
13:13). The Colossians' love extended to
"all the saints" (Col. 1:4), or all believers,
probably not only at Colosse but everywhere (cf. 1 Thes. 1:7-8 for a similar
commendation).

Faith and love "spring from" (*dia,*

lit., are "on account of") "hope," confidence in what God will do in the future. This confidence led to a greater trust in God and a deeper love for others. This confident expectation of Christ's return, called "the blessed hope" (Titus 2:13), influences believers' conduct (cf. 1 Thes. 4:13-18; 1 John 3:3).

This hope is **stored up . . . in heaven** because Christ, the essence of this hope, is there. Without Christ's Ascension to heaven (Acts 1:10-11) and His present intercession there on behalf of believers (Heb. 7:25; 1 John 2:1), they would have no hope (cf. 1 Cor. 15:16-19). This message is **the Word of truth** (cf. Eph. 1:13; 2 Tim. 2:15; James 1:18), **the gospel** as Paul defines it here and elsewhere (cf. 1 Cor. 15:1-3; Rom. 10:9-10).

1:6. Paul thanked God because the **gospel** was spreading **all over the world.** In fact, in an obvious hyperbole, Paul wrote in verse 23 that the gospel was being "proclaimed to every creature under heaven" (cf. Rom. 1:8). But Paul stressed not only the universality of the gospel but also its practicality, for it was **producing fruit and growing.** As a tree bears fruit and grows in size, so the gospel produces spiritual "fruit" in believers' lives (cf. "the fruit of the Spirit," Gal. 5:22-23; "the fruit of righteousness," Phil. 1:11) and spreads to and influences others (cf. the same words "bearing fruit" and "growing" in Col. 1:10). Heresies (such as the one at Colosse) are local and harmful; but truth is universal and helpful. One of the unmistakable characteristics of the true gospel is **God's grace in all its truth.** Some preach a "different gospel—which is really no gospel at all" (Gal. 1:6-7). This is because it is a gospel of grace plus works, or faith plus works. But the true gospel is one of grace alone (Rom. 11:6; Eph. 2:8-9; Titus 3:5-7).

1:7. The Colossians **learned it,** the gospel, **from Epaphras** who apparently founded the church at Colosse (cf. 4:12). Paul called him a **dear fellow servant,** a humble description from a great apostle, and **a faithful minister of Christ,** as opposed, no doubt, to those unfaithful ones who here and elsewhere were disturbing the faith of God's flock (cf. 2 Cor. 11:15; 2 Peter 2:1-3, 12-19). Paul also called Tychicus "a faithful minister and fellow servant in the Lord" (Col. 4:7).

Epaphras was in Rome with Paul, for Paul called him "my fellow prisoner" (Phile. 23). "Epaphras" is a shortening of "Epaphroditus," referred to in Philippians 2:25 and 4:18. These could be the same person or different persons since both names were common.

Epaphras, said Paul, ministered **on our behalf,** probably as Paul's representative (cf. Phil. 2:25; 4:18 for a similar situation). This implies, of course, that Paul had not visited Colosse himself (cf. Col. 2:1). But even though Epaphras was sent by Paul, he was primarily a "minister of Christ."

1:8. Not only did Epaphras carry the good news of Christ to Colosse, but he also brought back to prisoner Paul the good news about their **love in the Spirit** for Christ. Believers are in the Spirit and the Spirit is in them (Rom. 8:9). Thus their "love . . . for all the saints" (Col. 1:4; cf. v. 5) stemmed from the indwelling Holy Spirit. Elsewhere Paul urged that by "the love of the Spirit" (Rom. 15:30) believers manifest the "fruit of the Spirit" (Gal. 5:22).

C. Petition (1:9-14)

1:9. For this reason, because Paul had heard this good report of them from Epaphras, he continued to pray for them. Paul's ceaseless prayer (**we have not stopped praying for you;** cf. 1 Thes. 5:17) does not mean that he prayed without ever stopping but that he never forgot to pray for them when he daily and regularly prayed (cf. Acts 20:31; Eph. 1:16). "Praying" (Col. 1:9) is the general word for prayer (*proseuchomenoi*), also used in v. 3; and **asking** is the word for petitioning or requesting (*aitoumenoi*).

Paul's primary petition was that **God** would **fill** them **with the knowledge of His will.** Paul used two key words, "fill" (*plēroō*) and "knowledge" (*epignōsis,* also used in v. 10 and 3:10). The first suggests a filling out to completeness, and the latter suggests a full, deep understanding. Such knowledge of God's will does not come from a fleshly mind (which "puffs up, " 1 Cor. 8:1), but from the Holy Spirit who enlightens a believer's inner person (1 Cor. 2:5-6, 13), and from the Word of God. God's will, revealed in the Bible, is made known to believers by the Holy Spirit's teaching ministry. To this Paul added, **through all spiritual wisdom** (*sophia;* used six times in Col. 1:9, 28; 2:3, 23; 3:16; 4:5), that is, practical know-how which comes from God (James 1:5; 3:15), **and understanding** (*synesei;* also used in Col. 2:2), which speaks of clear analysis and decision-making in applying this knowledge to various problems. By contrast, the false teachers offered only "an appearance of wisdom" (*sophia;* 2:23), which captivated their minds and lives in legalistic regulations. But true spiritual wisdom is both stabilizing and liberating (Eph. 4:14). Knowledge (or understanding or intelligence) and wisdom are often connected in Scripture (cf. Ex. 31:3 ["skill" in the NIV is the Heb. word for wisdom]; Deut. 4:6; Isa. 11:2; 1 Cor. 1:19). And the fear of the Lord is the beginning of both (cf. Prov. 1:7; 9:10).

1:10. Paul's aim in this petition was practical: **in order that you may live a life worthy of the Lord.** A genuine knowledge of Christ reveals itself in transformed character (cf. Eph. 4:1; 1 Thes. 2:12), in Christlikeness. *Axiōs,* "worthy," means "of equal weight." Believers are to equal the Lord's standards, to be holy as He is holy (cf. 1 Peter 1:15). The aim of believers in all their worthy conduct should be to **please Him in every way,** to anticipate and do His wishes in every aspect of life (cf. Eph. 5:10). Merely pleasing people is incompatible with being a servant of Christ (Gal. 1:10; Eph. 6:6; Col. 3:22; 1 Thes. 2:4). Indeed, Paul made it the ambition of his life to please God (2 Cor. 5:9). Four things, given in participles, result from such a God-pleasing life: "bearing fruit" and "growing" (Col. 1:10), "being strengthened" (v. 11), and "giving thanks" (v. 12). The first two are related: **bearing fruit** and **growing in the knowledge** (*epignōsei*) **of God** (Paul used these same words "bearing fruit" and "growing," trans. "producing," in v. 6). As one manifests the fruit of faith (cf. Matt. 7:16; Gal. 5:22-23), he grows in faith himself (cf. Eph. 4:13). He comes to a deeper "knowledge" (*epignōsis;* cf. Col. 1:9) of God. As Augustine put it, "Faith is understanding's step, and understanding is faith's reward."

1:11. Spiritual strength is a third factor that results from knowing God's will and pleasing Him. **Being strengthened with all power according to His glorious might** includes three

words for strength: "being strengthened" is *dynamoumenoi;* "power" is *dynamei,* spiritual vitality; and "might" is *kratos* ("power that overcomes resistance"; used only of God in the NT). This God-given strength produces **great endurance and patience.** This endurance (trans. "perseverance" in James 1:3) was exemplified by Job (James 5:11). To this endurance Paul added "patience," a word generally connected with gentleness and calm sweetness (as in 1 Cor. 13:4). Endurance and patience are often associated (cf. 2 Cor. 6:4, 6; 2 Tim. 3:10; James 5:10-11). Endurance (*hypomonē,* lit., a "remaining under") implies not easily succumbing under suffering; and patience (*makrothymia,* lit., "long temper"; cf. Col. 3:12) means self-restraint which does not hastily retaliate. A lack of endurance often results in despondency or losing heart, whereas a lack of patience often leads to wrath or revenge (cf. Prov. 15:18; 16:32).

All this is according to God's "glorious might" (lit., "might of His glory"). Glory means manifest excellence. It is an outward manifestation of God's inner character. In Ephesians 1:19-20 Paul wrote of God's "great power" (*dynamis*) and "the working (*energeian*) of His mighty (*kratous*) strength (*ischyos*)," which raised Christ from the dead.

1:12-13. Such patient-producing power should be accompanied by "joyfully," not begrudgingly, **giving thanks to the Father** from whom comes every good and perfect gift (James 1:17).

Thankfulness, a fourth result of following God's will and pleasing Him, is a keynote in the spiritual life. Believers are urged elsewhere by Paul, "Give thanks in all circumstances" (1 Thes. 5:18) and to come before God "in everything, by prayer and petition, with thanksgiving" (Phil. 4:6). Four other times in Colossians (3:15-17; 4:2) Paul enjoined believers to be grateful. Joyfulness too is part of the fruit of the Spirit (Gal. 5:22), made possible by the gospel (cf. Isa. 29:19; John 16:20; Acts 13:52). Here Paul centered thanksgiving on the fact that God has **qualified you** (lit., "made you competent"; cf. 2 Cor. 3:6) **to share in the inheritance of the saints** (i.e., the kingdom treasures that belong to believers; cf. Eph. 1:7). In short, though believers are unfit in themselves, God has

671

fitted them to share in the inheritance of His holy people. This "inheritance" (*tēn merida tou klērou*, lit., "the parcel of the lot") is reminiscent of the way the inheritance of the land of promise was given to the Israelites under Joshua (Josh. 14:2). This inheritance is **in the . . . light** (cf. 2 Cor. 4:6; 1 Peter 2:9). (The NIV, supplying the words "kingdom of," which are not in the Gr., reads "in the kingdom of light.") This light is the spiritual sphere to which believers have been transferred **from the dominion of darkness** (Luke 22:53; Acts 26:18; Eph. 6:12). From this dominion (*exousias*, "power, authority") of darkness (cf. John 3:19-20) believers have been **rescued**, delivered. Through Christ they were brought from a rebel kingdom and placed under the sovereignty of their rightful King. The sovereign Christ is here called **the Son He loves** (lit., "the Son of His love"; cf. 1 John 4:8, 16). J. B. Lightfoot says this means the Son who embodies and manifests God's love (*St. Paul's Epistles to the Colossians and to Philemon*, p. 142). But H.C.G. Moule says it signifies the Son who is "the blessed Object of the Father's love . . . the supremely Beloved One" (*The Epistles of Paul the Apostle to the Colossians and to Philemon*, p. 75). This seems preferable (cf. Eph. 1:6).

1:14. Through Christ, God's "Loved One," Christians **have redemption, the forgiveness of sins.** The parallel passage (Eph. 1:7) adds "through His blood" (as do some mss.) here. "Redemption" (*apolytrōsin*) means "to rescue by ransom" (see the chart, "New Testament Words for Redemption," at Mark 10:45), and "forgiveness" (*aphesin*) means "remission" by the Redeemer. This emancipation is enjoyed only because of the tremendous cost Christ paid on the cross (cf. Rom. 3:24-26).

D. Exaltation of Christ (1:15-20)

From Paul's petition that the Colossians be enlightened about God's redemptive working in their lives, he moved naturally into his epistle's main emphasis—the exaltation and preeminence of Christ. In this paragraph (vv. 15-20) Paul mentioned seven unique characteristics of Christ, which fittingly qualify Him to have "the supremacy" (v. 18). Christ is: (1) the image of God, (2) the Firstborn over Creation, (3) Creator of

the universe, (4) Head of the church, (5) Firstborn from the dead, (6) the fullness of God, and (7) the Reconciler of all things. No comparable listing of so many characteristics of Christ and His deity are found in any other Scripture passage. Christ is the supreme Sovereign of the universe!

1:15. First, Christ **is the image of the invisible God.** Besides the obvious meaning of likeness (cf. 2 Cor. 4:4), "image" implies representation and manifestation. Like the head of a sovereign imprinted on a coin, so Christ is "the exact representation of [the Father's] being" (Heb. 1:3). As Jesus said, "Anyone who has seen Me has seen the Father" (John 14:9). Anyone who saw Christ, the visible manifestation of the invisible God, has thereby "seen" God indirectly. For "no one has ever seen God, but God the only Son . . . has made Him known" (John 1:18). Paul wrote of the "invisible" God (1 Tim. 1:17), but Christ is the perfect visible representation and manifestation of that God. Though the word "image" (*eikōn*) does not always denote a perfect image (cf. 1 Cor. 11:7), the context here demands that understanding. Indeed, like the word "form" (*morphē*; trans. "nature" in Phil. 2:6-7), *eikōn* means the very substance or essential embodiment of something or someone. In Hebrews 10:1 "shadow" and "the very image" (*eikōn*), which is Christ, are contrasted (cf. Col. 2:17). So Christ's supremacy is first shown in His relationship with God the Father. Christ is the perfect resemblance and representation of God.

Second, Christ's supremacy is shown in His relationship to Creation. He is **the Firstborn over all Creation.** Though it is grammatically possible to translate this as "Firstborn *in* Creation," the context makes this impossible for five reasons: (1) The whole point of the passage (and the book) is to show Christ's superiority *over* all things. (2) Other statements about Christ in this passage (such as Creator of all [1:16], upholder of Creation [v. 17], etc.) clearly indicate His priority and superiority over Creation. (3) The "Firstborn" cannot be part of Creation if He created "all things." One cannot create himself. (Jehovah's Witnesses wrongly add the word "other" six times in this passage in their *New World Translation.* Thus they suggest that Christ created all other things after He was created! But the word "other" is not in the Gr.) (4) The "Firstborn" received worship of all the angels (Heb. 1:6), but creatures should not be worshiped (Ex. 20:4-5). (5) The Greek word for "Firstborn" is *prōtotokos.* If Christ were the "first-created," the Greek word would have been *prōtoktisis.*

"Firstborn" denotes two things of Christ: He preceded the whole Creation, and He is Sovereign over all Creation. In the Old Testament a firstborn child had not only priority of birth but also the dignity and superiority that went with it (cf. Ex. 13:2-15; Deut. 21:17). When Jesus declared Himself "the First" (*ho prōtos;* Rev. 1:17), He used a word that means "absolutely first." "Firstborn" also implies sovereignty. The description "firstborn" was not a fairly common Old Testament designation of the Messiah-God. "I will also appoint Him My Firstborn, the most exalted of the kings of the earth" (Ps. 89:27). While this regal psalm refers to David, it also designates the Messiah, as seen in Revelation 1:5, where Christ is called "the Firstborn from the dead (cf. Col. 1:18) and the Ruler of the kings of the earth." So "Firstborn" implies both Christ's priority *to* all Creation (in time) and His sovereignty *over* all Creation (in rank).

1:16-17. The third characteristic of Christ is that **by Him all things were created.** In fact **all things were created by Him** (*di' autou,* instrumental Cause) **and for Him** (*eis auton,* final Cause), and **in Him** (*en autō*) they **hold together** (He is the constituting or conserving Cause). Christ is not only the One through whom all things came to be, but also the One by whom they continue to exist. Two other New Testament verses parallel this description of Christ: "Through Him all things were made" (John 1:3), and Christ the Son is the One "through whom [the Father] made the universe" (Heb. 1:2). The Father, then, is the ultimate Source (efficient Cause), and the Son is the mediating Cause of the world. The Son was the "master Workman" of Creation, "the beginning (*archē*) of the Creation of God" (Rev. 3:14, NASB).

The Son's Creation includes "all" **things in heaven and on earth, visible and invisible.** These indicate the *entire* universe, both material and immaterial. The hierarchy of angelic beings—**thrones** (*thronoi*) **or powers** (*kyriotētes*) **or rulers** (*archai*) **or authorities** (*exousiai*)—indicate a highly organized dominion in the spirit world, a sphere in which the Colossians were engaged in the worship of angels (Col. 2:18) and over which Christ reigns supreme (cf. Eph. 1:21; 3:10; 6:12; Phil. 2:9-10; Col. 2:10, 15).

1:18. Fourth, Christ **is the Head of the body, the church.** Besides being the Lord of the universe He is also the church's Head (cf. Eph. 1:22-23; 5:23). The reference here is to the invisible or universal church into which all believers are baptized by the Holy Spirit the moment they believe in Christ (1 Cor. 12:13). This work of the Spirit began on the day of Pentecost (Acts 1:5; 2:1-2; 11:15-16). It is a special body in which there is "neither Jew nor Gentile" (Gal. 3:28) but a whole new creation of God (Eph. 2:15). The church is a "mystery . . . which was not made known to men in other generations" (Eph. 3:4-5; cf. Rom. 16:25-26; Col. 1:26).

Fifth, Christ **is the Beginning** (*archē*) **and the Firstborn from among the dead** (cf. Rev. 1:5). Christ was the first to rise in an immortal body (1 Cor. 15:20), and as such He heads a whole new order as its Sovereign (cf. "Firstborn" in Col. 1:15). Also Christ's resurrection marked His triumph over death (Heb. 2:14; 1 John 3:8). He was the "Firstfruits" of those who die (1 Cor. 15:20) since, unlike others, He rose never to die again. He "was declared with power to be the Son of God by His resurrection from the dead" (Rom. 1:4). So He continues to live "on the basis of the power of an indestructible life" (Heb. 7:16). All this is **so that in everything He might have the supremacy.** Christ is given first place over all Creation. He is preeminent. The same eternal *Logos* (John 1:1) who "became flesh" (John 1:14) and "humbled Himself" (Phil. 2:8) is now "exalted" by God the Father "to the highest place" and has been given "the name that is above every name" (Phil. 2:9).

1:19. The sixth description of the exalted Christ is that **all** God's **fullness dwell[s] in Him.** Later Paul wrote, "In Christ all the fullness of the Deity lives in bodily form" (2:9). Colossians 1:19 is one of the most powerful descriptions of Christ's deity in the New Testament (cf. Heb. 1:8). "Fullness" (*plērōma*), a key word in Colossians, is used in 1:19 and 2:9. (The verb *plēroō* is used in 1:9, 25; 2:10; and 4:17.) The noun means "completeness" and is used of a wide range of things including God's being (Eph. 3:19), time (Gal. 4:4), and grace in Christ (John 1:16). This full and complete Deity is said to "dwell" (*katoikēsai*, "abide lastingly or permanently") in Christ.

1:20. The seventh feature of Christ is that He is the Reconciler. Through Christ God will **reconcile to Himself all things.** The phrase "all things" is limited to good angels and redeemed people since only **things on earth** and **things in heaven** are mentioned. Things "under the earth" (Phil. 2:10) are not reconciled. On God's restoring of nature, see comments on Romans 8:19-21; and on the reconciling of sinners, see comments on Romans 5:10-11 and 2 Corinthians 5:17-20. It is important to note that people are reconciled to God ("to Himself") not that God is reconciled to people. For mankind has left God and needs to be brought back to Him. In 2 Corinthians 5:19 "reconciliation" was used by Paul in a judicial (vs. an actual) sense in which the whole "world" is made savable through Christ's death. Paul spoke of "the many" (i.e., "those who receive God's abundant provision of grace") being "made righteous" through the Cross (Rom. 5:19). To make **peace through His blood** means to cause God's enemies (Rom. 5:10; Col. 1:21) to become, by faith, His friends and His children (cf. Eph. 2:11-19).

E. Reconciliation by Christ (1:21-23)

1:21. Having struck the note of reconciliation as the seventh characteristic of the exalted Christ, Paul then developed that theme. Reconciliation is necessary because people are **alienated** ("cut off, estranged") **from** life and **God** (Eph. 2:12; 4:18). Before conversion the Colossian believers also **were enemies** or hostile to God **in** their **minds** as well as in their behavior, internally and externally. Sin begins in the heart (Matt. 5:27-28) and manifests itself in overt deeds (Gal. 5:19). ("In the sphere of your evil deeds" is better than NIV's **because of your evil behavior.** People are not inwardly hostile vs. God because of their outward acts of sins; they commit sins because they are inwardly hostile.)

1:22. Reconciliation of sinners to God is **by Christ's physical body through death.** The Gnostic tendency of the Colossian heresy, with its Platonic orientation, denied both Christ's true humanity and His true deity. As John explained, it is necessary to confess "that Jesus Christ has come in the flesh" (1 John 4:2). Spirits cannot die, and "without the shedding of blood there is no forgiveness" (Heb. 9:22). In order to redeem humans, Christ Himself must be truly human (cf. 1 Tim. 2:5; Heb. 2:17). Thus Christ's real physical body and death were necessary for man's salvation (cf. Rom. 7:4; Heb. 10:10).

The result of Christ's death is redemptive—**to present you holy in His sight.** This may mean judicially perfect as to a believer's position, or spiritually perfect as to his condition. Ultimately God envisions both for believers, and Christ's death is the basis for judicial justification (Rom. 3:21-26), progressive sanctification (Rom. 6-7), and even ultimate glorification (Rom. 8). As Paul wrote the Ephesians, "He chose us in Him before the Creation of the world to be holy and blameless in His sight" (Eph. 1:4). Christians are **without blemish** (*amōmous*; correctly translated "blameless" in Eph. 1:4 and Phil. 2:15; cf. "without . . . blemish" in Eph. 5:27 and "without fault" in Jude 24) in Christ, and also are **free from accusation** (*anenklētous*). This latter Greek word is used five times in the New Testament and only by Paul (here and in 1 Cor. 1:8; 1 Tim. 3:10; Titus 1:6-7). It connotes one who is unaccused, free from all charges. Satan is "the accuser of the brethren" (Rev. 12:10, KJV), but Christ is their "Advocate" (1 John 2:1, KJV) or "Defense" (1 John 2:1, NIV) before the Father. Therefore by the merits of Christ believers are free from every charge (cf. Rom. 8:33). In Christ the accused are unaccused and the condemned are freed.

1:23. This reconciliation in Christ comes only by an abiding faith—**if you continue in your faith.** The Colossians had a settled faith—**established** (i.e., "grounded" like a building on a strong foundation) **and firm** (*hedraioi*, "seated or settled"; cf. 1 Cor. 7:37; 15:58), so Paul did not doubt that they would continue. In fact he spoke of **the hope** (confident expectation) which this **gospel** of reconciliation provides not only to them but also to the whole world—**to every creature under heaven.** This is obviously a figure of speech indicating the universality of **the gospel** and its proclamation, not that every person on the globe heard Paul preach. In Acts 2:5 this phrase describes a wide range of people from various countries without including, for example, anyone from North or South America (cf. also Gen. 41:57; 1 Kings 10:24; Rom. 1:8).

F. Revelation of the mystery of Christ (1:24-27)

1:24. This reconciliation by Christ of Jews and Gentiles to God in one body is a mystery revealed only in Christ. Paul rejoiced that he was able to suffer **for them what** was **still lacking in regard to Christ's afflictions.** By this he did not mean that Christ's suffering on the cross was insufficient (cf. Rom. 3:21-26; Heb. 10:10-14). He was speaking not of salvation but of service. Christ's suffering alone procures salvation (1 Peter 1:11; 5:1; Heb. 2:9). But it is a believer's privilege to suffer for Christ (2 Tim. 3:11; 1 Peter 3:13-14; 5:9; Heb. 10:32). The word "affliction" (*thlipsis*)—never used in the New Testament of Christ's death—means "distress," "pressure," or "trouble" (which Paul had plenty of; 2 Cor. 11:23-29). Ordinarily it refers to trials in life, not the pains of death. Christ does indeed continue to suffer when Christians suffer for Him. He asked Saul (later called Paul) on the Damascus Road, "Why do you persecute Me?" (Acts 9:4) Since the church is Christ's body, He is affected when it is affected. For the sake of Christ's body Paul willingly suffered (Phil. 1:29).

1:25-26. He was a God-ordained servant of the precious truth of **the Word of God in its fullness** (cf. 1:9; 2:9). The Colossian heresy boasted of a "fullness" of knowledge possible only through their mystical experience. But Paul declared that the fullness of **the mystery** is found only in Christ. By "mystery" he meant something once concealed but then revealed. This contrasted with the Colossian heretics' notion that a mystery was a secret teaching known only to an exclusive group and unknown to the masses. The church was unknown in the Old Testament because it had **been kept hidden for ages and generations.** In fact,

said Paul, it is only **now disclosed to the saints.** Since the church is Christ's body, resulting from His death on the cross, it could not possibly have been in existence in the Old Testament. Indeed, Jesus, when on earth, said it was yet future (Matt. 16:16-18). Since the church is Christ's body, welded together by the baptism of the Holy Spirit (1 Cor. 12:13), the church's birthday occurred when this baptism took place (Acts 1:5; 2). Soon Saul recognized that this mysterious body of Christ, the church, was in existence and that he was persecuting it (Acts 9:4; cf. Gal. 1:13).

The "mystery" of the church, however, does not mean that Gentile salvation and blessing was unforeseen before Christ (cf. Luke 2:29-32; Amos 9:11-12). The mystery was not *that* Gentiles would be saved but *how* they could be "fellow-heirs" (Eph. 3:6, KJV), on the same level with Jews, with no middle wall of partition between them (Eph. 2:12-14). In the Old Testament Gentiles who believed and became a part of Judaism were still considered lower than Jews. This special union in which there "is neither Jew nor Greek" (i.e., Gentile, Gal. 3:28) was nonexistent before Christ died and the Spirit descended to baptize all believers into this new body. (For a list of other NT "mysteries" see the chart near Matt. 13:10-16.)

1:27. God has chosen to make known this mystery to New Testament saints. He willed in His sovereign mercy to reveal His eternal purpose with all its **glorious riches** (i.e., divine effulgence or blazing splendor). The amazing thing is that this is now revealed **among the Gentiles,** whereas previously God's special revelation was to the Jews (Rom. 2:17; 3:1-2; 9:4). Now those "who once were far away have been brought near through the blood of Christ" (Eph. 2:13). Those "without hope and without God" (Eph. 2:12) have been given a glorious hope **which is Christ in you** (i.e., in you Gentiles; Col. 1:27). Because of "the glorious riches" (lit., "the riches of the glory"), believers are indwelt by Christ, **the hope of glory.** They are thus "in Christ" (2 Cor. 5:17; Eph. 1:4), and Christ is in them (cf. Rom. 8:10; 2 Cor. 13:5). Because of Christ, believers look forward to sharing His glory (Col. 3:4; Rom. 5:2;

8:18, 30; 2 Cor. 4:17; Gal. 5:5; 1 Peter 5:10; also cf. Rom. 8:24).

G. Perfection in Christ (1:28-29)

1:28-29. Paul, in proclaiming this **Christ** who now also dwells in Gentile believers was **admonishing** (*nouthetountes,* "counseling") **and teaching** (*didaskontes,* "instructing") **everyone** (cf. 3:16). No doubt he did this "admonishing" and instructing because of the false teaching about Christ in Colosse. He did so wisely (cf. 4:5-6) since his purpose was not to drive them into the hands of the heretics but to **present everyone perfect** (*teleion,* "mature"; cf. James 1:4) **in Christ.** Paul was interested in believers not remaining spiritual babies (cf. 1 Cor. 3:1-2) but in becoming spiritually mature (cf. Heb. 5:11-14). Elsewhere Paul prayed for complete sanctification of believers (1 Thes. 5:23). Paul preached the "fullness" of the gospel so that believers could have the fullness of life Jesus promised (John 10:10). **To this end** Paul expended all his God-given strength. Developing maturity in believers took great **labor** (*kopiō*) or wearisome toil (cf. 1 Cor. 15:10, 58; Gal. 4:11; 1 Thes. 1:3) and even **struggling** (*agōnizomenos;* cf. Col. 2:1; 4:12) or agonizing like an athlete in an arena (cf. 1 Cor. 9:25; 1 Tim. 6:12). The power for this struggle came from Christ (cf. Phil. 4:13).

H. Education (wisdom) in Christ (2:1-5)

2:1. Paul's labor (*agōna,* **struggling;** cf. 1:29; 4:12) of love was not limited to those he personally knew; it extended to **all who** had **not met him personally.** This is a clear indication that Paul had not started this or other churches in the Lycus Valley. The mention of **Laodicea** (cf. 4:16) indicates that the heresy had spread there too, though it was probably centered in Colosse.

2:2-3. Paul's stated **purpose** was that **they** might **be encouraged in heart and united in love.** Confidence and strength of conviction as well as cohesive unity yield a full understanding of the truth. There is no full knowledge apart from moral commitment. **Complete understanding** (*syneseōs,* "insight") results from complete yielding. And this understanding is Christocentric. This insight into God's ways enables believers to **know** (*epignōsin*) Christ fully. **Christ,** as the true

mystery of God, reveals God to man (cf. John 1:18; Heb. 1:2-3). For in Him **are hidden** (cf. Col. 1:26) **all the treasures of wisdom** (*sophia,* cf. 1:9) **and knowledge.** Knowledge is the apprehension of truth; wisdom is its application to life. Knowledge is prudent judgment and wisdom is prudent action. Both are found in Christ (cf. Rom. 11:33; 1 Cor. 12:8) whose wisdom is foolishness to the world (1 Cor. 1:21-25), but who is the power of God by which a believer receives "righteousness, holiness, and redemption" (1 Cor. 1:30).

2:4-5. Only this full knowledge and wisdom of Christ can keep a believer from being deceived **by fine-sounding arguments** (*pithanologia,* occurring only here in the NT, is lit., "persuasive speech" that uses plausible but false arguments). Truth and persuasion do not always correlate. Error can persuade, and truth can be compelling at times. It all depends on whether one has the *full* truth and a complete *commitment* to it. Hence even **though** Paul was **absent from** the Colossians, he delighted in **how orderly** (cf. 1 Cor. 14:40) **and how firm** (steadfast, solid) their **faith in Christ** was.

I. Exhortation to live in Christ (2:6-7)

2:6-7. These two verses conclude the argument begun in 1:15. Paul's point may be summarized thus: Divine exaltation belongs to Christ (1:15-20); in Him are found (a) reconciliation to God (1:21-23), (b) the revelation of the mystery of Christ (1:24-27), (c) believers' perfection (1:28-29), and (d) education (wisdom) (2:1-5). Therefore believers should continue to live in Him (vv. 6-7).

The Christian life continues as it commenced: **just as you received Christ Jesus as Lord, continue to live in Him.** Paul gave the same kind of exhortation to others (cf. 2 Cor. 11:4; Gal. 1:6). Since their faith initially laid hold decisively on the apostolic gospel, Paul exhorted them not to forsake its divine authority for any human sophistry. For with these divine roots (**rooted . . . in Him**) that began in the past they can be continually **built up** (edified) and **strengthened in the faith.** If they did so they would not be blown to and fro with every wind of doctrine (Eph. 4:14). As believers are "built up" in Christ, they become more grateful and are **overflowing with thankfulness** (cf. Col. 1:12).

II. Polemical: Higher Life in Christ (2:8-23)

After exhorting believers to continue in Christ (2:6-7)—in whom is the fullness of God and who brought complete redemption—Paul then condemned the Colossian heresy that was diverting them from Christ.

A. "Gnosticism" is wrong: deity is in Christ (2:8-10)

2:8. Paul was concerned that no false teacher take the Colossian believers **captive through hollow and deceptive philosophy** (cf. v. 4). He wrote here not against all philosophy but against *false* philosophy, as the Bible also speaks against false religion (James 1:26). The particular false philosophy at Colosse was "hollow" (*kenēs*, "empty"), "deceptive," and based **on human tradition . . . rather than on Christ.** True Christian philosophy "take[s] captive every thought to make it obedient to Christ" (2 Cor. 10:5). Philosophy is the love of wisdom, but if one loves wisdom that is not Christ (the Sum of all wisdom, Col. 2:3), he loves an empty idol. Such a one will be "always learning but never able to acknowledge the truth" (2 Tim. 3:7). This kind of philosophy is based on the world's **basic principles** (*stoicheia*, "elementary principles" or "elemental spirits" [RSV]; cf. Col. 2:20; Gal. 4:3, 9). This may refer to the evil spirits who inspire such heresy and over whom Christ triumphed (cf. 2 Cor. 4:3-4; Eph. 6:11-12). Such a philosophy is demonic and worldly, not godly or Christlike. Unless believers are careful, such philosophy may ensnare them, taking them "captive."

2:9. There is no "fullness" (*plērōma*) in philosophy based on vain human reasoning. **For in Christ all the fullness of the Deity lives.** Hence only in Christ can one have fullness. Apart from Him is emptiness. As philosopher Jean Paul Sartre put it, "Life is an empty bubble on the sea of nothingness" (cf. Ecc. 1:14-18). The word for "Deity" is *theotetos*, a strong word (used only here in the NT) for Christ's essence as God. The full deity of Christ is nonetheless **in bodily form**—a full humanity (cf. Col. 1:22). Both Christ's deity and humanity were challenged by this early Gnostic-like heresy. Those heretics diminished Christ to an angel

whose "body" was only apparent, not real. Paul affirmed here that Christ is both fully God and truly man (cf. 1 John 4:1-6).

2:10. Not only is all the "fullness" (*plērōma*) of God in Christ (v. 9), but also believers **have been given fullness in Christ.** Their fullness of life comes from Christ's fullness. They partake of the divine nature through Christ (2 Peter 1:4), for "from the fullness of his grace we have all received" (John 1:16). This, of course, does not mean believers *become* God but simply share in Him. They *have* or share in the goodness of the nature which He *is*. They share in the body of Him **who is the Head** (cf. Col. 1:18) **over every power** (*archēs*, "ruler") **and authority** (*exousias*, "ruling power") (cf. 1:16; 2:15), including those who would talk the Colossians into living according to the world instead of according to Christ.

B. Legalism is wrong: reality is in Christ (2:11-17)

2:11-12. Paul turned from the theological errors of the false teachers to their practical errors—from "Gnosticism" to legalism. The Gentile Christians in Colosse had no need to conform to Jewish rules and regulations, such as **circumcision.** For in Christ they had been **circumcised.** This spiritual "circumcision" was **done by Christ,** not by man. It was in fact a crucifixion or putting off of the body, a circumcision of the heart (cf. Rom. 2:29; Eph. 2:11). Their **sinful nature** (lit., "the body of the flesh"; cf., lit., "the mind of the flesh," Col. 2:18) was decisively put off by Christ's death and resurrection. What people were in Adam—sinful, fallen, and corrupt—was destroyed by Christ. Now "in Christ" a believer is a new creation (2 Cor. 5:17). And having a new Head a believer has a new authority for his life—not the Law of Moses but the life of Christ.

The words **putting off** are from the noun *apekdysei* ("total breaking away from"), which occurs only here in the New Testament. This putting off of the old life occurs at the moment of salvation, when a believer is **buried with Christ in baptism** by the Spirit (cf. 1 Cor. 12:13) **and is raised with Him** to new life. This co-burial and co-resurrection is pictured in baptism. In water baptism, immersion portrays burial with Christ, and coming out of the water depicts the resurrection by **the power of God** to "live a new life" (Rom. 6:4).

2:13-14. Before a person is liberated to this new life in Christ, he is **dead in** his **sins and in** his **sinful nature** (cf. comments on the "earthly nature" in 3:5 and the "old self" in 3:9). Death means separation, not annihilation. Even the unsaved still bear the image of God (Gen. 9:6; James 3:9), but they are separated from God. Cut off from spiritual life, they still have human life. But now **God made you alive with Christ** (cf. Eph. 2:1-6). The same "power" (*energeias;* cf. "energy" in Col. 1:29) that raised Christ from the dead (2:12) resurrects believing sinners to spiritual life (v. 13).

This new life came when God **forgave us all our sins** for He **canceled the written code.** Before God's written Law, His "written code," people **stood** condemned (cf. Rom. 3:19), so it worked **against** them and **opposed** them. But in Christ the Law is fulfilled (Rom. 8:2) and done away with (Gal. 3:25; Heb. 7:12). Legalism is wrong because believers are dead to the Law in Christ. He fulfilled its demands in His life and by His death, and Christians are *in* Him.

This written code, the Law, was like a handwritten "certificate of debt" (NASB). Since people cannot keep the Law, it is like a bill of indebtedness. So people, unable to pay the debt, are criminals. But Jesus **took . . . away** this criminal charge, this certificate of indebtedness, by His death. It is as if He were **nailing it to the cross** with Him, showing He paid the debt. He wiped the slate clean. As Krishna Ral put it: "Jesus for thee a body takes, thy guilt assumes, thy fetter breaks, discharging all thy dreadful debt; and canst thou then such love forget?"

2:15-17. By fulfilling the demands of the Law, Christ **disarmed the** demonic **powers and authorities** (cf. 1:16; 2:10), **triumphing over them** (cf. 2 Cor. 2:14). As a result believers are delivered from these evil powers which inspire legalistic rules about foods and festivals. No one should **judge you by what you eat or drink** because Christians are free from the Law's legalistic requirements (such as those in Lev. 11; 17; Deut. 14). God does not condemn those who eat everything (Rom. 14:1-4). In fact, God says that all foods may be eaten since they were "created to be received with thanksgiving

by those who believe and who know the truth" (1 Tim. 4:3). The teaching that forbids this, Paul wrote, is "taught by demons" (1 Tim. 4:1) whom Christ has disarmed (Col. 2:15). This liberation of believers pertains also to festivals such as **a New Moon celebration or a Sabbath Day** (cf. Gal. 4:10). Those who would bring Christians under the bondage of the Law make artificial distinctions between the "ceremonial" and "moral" law, and so they say the Sabbath has not passed away. That this is false can be seen from the following: (1) The Sabbath command is the only one of the Ten Commandments not repeated in the New Testament. (2) The early believers, following Christ's resurrection and appearance on Sunday (Mark 16:1; John 20:1), met on Sundays (Acts 20:7; 1 Cor. 16:2). (3) The Bible nowhere distinguishes between the so-called "moral" and "ceremonial" laws (this distinction was not made before the 13th century A.D.) (4) This Colossian passage explicitly condemns those who command Sabbath obedience. (5) As Paul put it, the Old Testament Law (including the Sabbath) was only **a shadow of the things that were to come. The reality** or "substance" (*sōma,* lit., "body"), **however, is** to be **found in Christ** (cf. Heb. 8:5; 10:1). What the Old Testament foreshadowed, Christ fulfilled (cf. Matt. 5:17; Rom. 8:3-4). A "shadow" (*skia*) is only an image cast by an object which represents its form. Once one finds Christ, he no longer needs to follow the old shadow.

C. Mysticism is wrong: headship is in Christ (2:18-19)

2:18. Those who turn believers from the reality in Christ to the shadow of the Law **disqualify** them **for the prize.** That is, they rob (*katabrabeuetō,* "to decide against"; cf. *brabeuetō* in 3:15) believers of their spiritual rewards. As a judge disqualifies those who turn the wrong way in a race, so believers who turn from faithfully following Christ will be "robbed" of their rewards from Him (cf. 1 Cor. 3:10-15). Some heretics who turn believers away from faithful service have a **false humility,** which is only "a form of godliness but denying its power" (2 Tim. 3:5) that is in Christ (Rom. 8:3-4). This artificial godliness of legalists was connected with **the worship of angels**

which Scripture forbids (Ex. 20:3-4; cf. Rev. 22:8-9). In fact, legalism is a teaching inspired by fallen angels (1 Tim. 4:1) who as "elemental spirits" (Gal. 4:3, RSV) would bring men into slavery by their mystical meditations. These legalistic mystics dwell on **what** they have **seen** (in visions), which Paul called **idle notions** (*eikē*, "vain, to no avail"; cf. Gal. 3:4). This phrase may have occasioned the variant (but less preferable) translation "which he hath *not* seen" (KJV). Far from being humble, such a person's **unspiritual mind** (lit., "the mind of the flesh"; cf., lit., "the body of the flesh," v. 19) is puffed with pride in his visions.

2:19. While believing that his mysticism brings him in touch with some "higher" reality, a legal mystic **has** actually **lost connection with the Head** (Christ) who alone supplies life for it to **grow as God causes it to grow** (cf. John 15:1-5). True spirituality does not come by compliance with laws (which are only a shadow) but by connection with the Life (who is the reality). Without a vital connection to its Head, the body of Christ cannot grow. Using a parallel image, Jesus said, "I am the Vine; you are the branches. If a man remains in Me and I in Him, he will bear much fruit; apart from Me you can do nothing" (John 15:5).

D. Asceticism is wrong: immunity is in Christ (2:20-23)

2:20-21. A concomitant of legalism and mysticism is asceticism. It is the pseudo-spiritual position that revels in rules of physical self-denial. **Do not handle! Do not taste! Do not touch!** These prohibitions increase from not handling to not even touching. This same legalism was manifest in Eve's carnal exaggeration, "You must not touch it, or you will die" (Gen. 3:3; cf. Gen. 2:16-17). Asceticism arises out of guilt. But Christ has taken away all human guilt by His death (Col. 2:13-14). So since believers **died with Christ to the basic principles** (*stoicheia*; cf. comments on v. 8) **of this world,** they are no longer obligated (by fleshly inclinations) to obey them. Only those alive to sin (Rom. 6:2-7) need obey it as master. Worldliness is living by the world's rules, including those that have a show of humility and some alleged "angelic" source. Spirituality is living by the power of the Spirit in union with Christ by whom the believer has died to sin. "For we know that our old self was crucified with Him so that the body of sin might be rendered powerless" (Rom. 6:6).

2:22-23. Asceticism is a man-made system of rules (often taken out of context from God's Law) **based on human commands and teachings.** The persistent example of legalism in the New Testament was the Old Testament command of circumcision which God intended for the Jews as a *sign* of faith (Rom. 4:11) but which the legalists wanted to make a *condition* of grace (Gal. 2:21). Living by **such regulations** or self-made religion has a certain **appearance of wisdom** (*sophias*; cf. Col. 1:9; 2:3, 4:5), but it has absolutely no **value in restraining sensual indulgence.** "Sensual indulgence" is literally "the flesh" (*sarkos*; cf. 2:11, 18). For denying the body its desires merely arouses them, as is well known by many who have tried to lose weight by sticking to rigid diets. Neglecting the body, Paul argued, does not nourish the spirit.

III. Spiritual: Inner Life in Christ (3:1-17)

Knowing that all wisdom is in Christ (2:1-5), Paul urged the Colossian Christians to continue in Him (2:6-7), not being deceived by vain philosophies (2:8-10). Since believers are identified with Christ, they are not to live under Jewish laws (2:11-17), for that would only rob them of their rewards (2:18-19). They have died with Christ and hence need not submit to legalistic rules (2:20-23).

Furthermore, they have also been raised with Christ. So they should set their hearts on heavenly things (3:1-4), put to death sinful worldly practices (3:5-11), and clothe themselves with Christ's virtues (3:12-17). Stated in another way, believers are to seek spiritual values (3:1-4), put off the sins of the old life (3:5-11), and put on the virtues of the new life (3:12-17). This in turn should affect their relationships with other members of their families and society (3:18–4:1).

A. Seeking spiritual values (3:1-4)

3:1. Since believers have not only died with Christ but **have** also **been raised with Christ** (cf. Rom. 6:8-10; Col. 2:12-13), they should **set their hearts on**

things above. That is, believers' lives should be dominated by the pattern of heaven, bringing heavenly direction to their earthly duties. "Set" (*zēteite*) means "to seek or strive for earnestly" (cf. Rev. 9:6; 1 Cor. 7:27). Fixing their attention decisively toward "things above" involves centering their lives on the ascended (Eph. 4:10), glorified (John 17:5; Phil. 2:9) **Christ,** who **is seated at the right hand of God** (Ps. 110:1; Luke 22:69; Acts 2:33; 5:31; Rom. 8:34; Eph. 1:20; Heb. 1:3, 13; 8:1; 10:12; 12:2; 1 Peter 3:22). This is His seat of divine authority because He has defeated the forces of evil and death (Heb. 2:14-15).

3:2. Also Paul wrote, **Set your minds on things above, not on earthly things.** That is, concentrate your concern on the eternal, not the temporal. "Fix [your] eyes not on what is seen, but on what is unseen. For what is seen is temporary, but what is unseen is eternal" (2 Cor. 4:18). The similarity of the two commands in Colossians 3:1-2 reinforces their impact. "Set your hearts on things above" is *ta anō zēteite,* and "Set your minds on things above" is *ta anō phroneite.* The first suggests striving; the second suggests concentrating.

Paul was not enjoining an otherworld asceticism; he had just condemned that (2:20-23). He was saying that life *in this world* will be better if it is lived by a power *beyond this world,* the power of the resurrected, ascended, glorified Christ. The "earthly things" (*ta epi tēs gēs,* lit., "things upon the earth," 3:2; the same Gr. words are used in v. 5) to be avoided are moral, not physical (cf. immorality, impurity, lust, etc., in v. 5). Paul was not encouraging a kind of Gnostic disdain for material things. Every physical thing God created, including the body and sex, is good (cf. Gen. 1:27-30; 1 Tim. 4:1-4). However, since having a physical body does give occasion for the works of the (moral) flesh (cf. Rom. 7:4-6), Paul warned against setting one's affections in this area and perverting God's purpose for them.

3:3-4. At the moment of his salvation, a Christian **died** to the evil of the "flesh," the sin nature (Rom. 6:3-8; Col. 2:11), and his **life is now hidden with Christ in God.** "Hidden" implies both concealment and safety; both invisibility and security. He is not yet glorified, but he is secure and safe in **Christ.** In fact, Christ is his very **life.** Christ said He was going where "the world will not see Me anymore" (John 14:19).

But when He will appear at the Rapture (1 Thes. 4:16-18), believers **will appear with Him** and will be glorified. As John put it, "We know that when He appears, we shall be like Him, for we shall see Him as He is" (i.e., believers will be glorified as He is glorified; 1 John 3:2; cf. 1 Cor. 13:12; Col. 1:27). So Paul added a new direction to the believers' focus of attention: they should look *upward* to Christ's reign over them in heaven and also *forward* to His return for them in the clouds.

B. Putting off the sins of the old life (3:5-11)

3:5-6. Paul's imagery moved from death and life to putting clothes on and off. **Put to death . . . whatever belongs to your earthly nature.** The Greek tense in this command suggests a decisive action, as if Paul said, "Mortify it! Do it now! Do it resolutely!" Of course, God has already done it, but Christians are to *know* this, *count* it to be true, and *act* accordingly (Rom. 6:5-14). In other words, they are not to go on living as though they are still alive to sin when in actuality they are not. They are to put away that old life, which springs from their earthly natures. "Whatever belongs to your earthly nature" is literally "the members that are upon the earth" (*ta melē ta epi tēs gēs*). These contrast with the "things above" (Col. 3:1; *ta epi tēs gēs* is also used in v. 2). This "earthly nature" is the "old self" (or "sinful nature" [2:13], or "old man" [KJV]; Eph. 4:22; Col. 3:9). Some take this to mean the persons Christians were before conversion, whereas others take it (more likely) to refer to the evil tendencies in believers today (i.e., their "old natures"). Even if it means the former, the net effect is the same: they should not live as they did before, because they are new creations in Christ (2 Cor. 5:17).

The list of evil activities flowing from man's earthly nature includes **immorality** (*porneia,* "fornication"), **impurity** (a wider perversion), **lust** (*pathos,* "uncontrollable passion"), **evil desires** ("illicit craving"), **and greed** (or coveting), **which is idolatry** (because it seeks satisfaction in things below and not above). Similar lists of sins appear often in Paul's writings (Rom. 1:29-31; 1 Cor. 5:11; 6:9; Gal. 5:19-21; Eph. 5:3-5). Paul added that **because of these** evils **the wrath of God is coming.** The words "is coming" render the present tense *erchetai* (lit., "comes"). This suggests that God's wrath has already begun (cf. John 3:36). It will, of course, culminate in His future climactic visitation on evil (Rom. 2:5; 2 Thes. 1:7-9).

3:7-9. Though the Colossian Christians **used to walk** [live] **in these** evil **ways,** before they came to know Christ, Paul commanded that they do so no more. **Now you must rid yourselves of all such things.** The word "rid" (*apothesthe*) means "to put off" like a suit of clothes. In its ethical use here it means "throw it off like a dirty shirt" (cf. Rom. 13:12; Eph. 4:22, 25; Heb. 12:1; James 1:21; 1 Peter 2:1). In the Bible, behavior is often likened to a garment (e.g., Job 29:14; Ps. 35:26; Isa. 11:5; Rom. 13:12; 1 Thes. 5:8).

Repulsive habits—**anger, rage, malice, slander, and filthy language**—do not fit or suit Christians. They are unbecoming to believers (cf. Eph. 4:17, 31). "Anger" (*orgēn*) is a chronic attitude of smoldering hatred, whereas "rage" (*thymon*) is an acute outburst. *Thymos* elsewhere is rendered "outbursts of anger" (2 Cor. 12:20), "fits of rage" (Gal. 5:20), and "rage" (Eph. 4:31). "Malice" (*kakian*, the vice that lies below anger and rage as their root) is forbidden, as is "slander" (*blasphēmian*, "railing or evil speaking"). "Filthy language" (*aischrologian*) is shameful or abrasive speech. Neither should Christians **lie** (cf. Eph. 4:25) for truthfulness is essential in followers of the One who is "the Truth" (John 14:6).

Lying and all other vices are inappropriate for a Christian for at salvation he discarded his **old self** (lit., "the old man," i.e., the former sinful way of living, characteristic of the unregenerate; Col. 2:11, 13a) **with its practices** (cf. "died" in 2:20; 3:3).

3:10. A Christian is to **put on** (cf. v. 12) **the new self** (new way of life or disposition). Hence his conduct should be in accord with his new position. This "new self" needs constant renewal or refreshing—it **is being renewed** (pres. tense), in order to keep it victorious over sin. Paul also expressed this idea of continual renewal in 2 Corinthians 4:16 ("Though outwardly we are wasting away, yet inwardly we are being renewed day by day"); in Romans 12:2 (being "transformed by the renewing of your mind"); and in Ephesians 4:23 ("to be made new in the attitude of your minds").

This renewal of the new self is **in knowledge** (*eis epignōsin*; cf. Col. 1:9; 2:2). It takes place as a believer comes to a personal, deep knowledge of and fellowship with Christ. And the renewal is in (*kat'*, "according to") **the image of its Creator;** its goal is to make believers like Him, for the "new self [was] created to be like God" (Eph. 4:24). Adam was created in the image of God (Gen. 1:27), which included a moral and intellectual likeness to God. Though this image was not erased (but only effaced) by the Fall (Gen. 9:6; James 3:9), yet it was corrupted and needs to be repaired and renewed. Christians become increasingly like the Lord as they refresh their new natures, yielding to the Holy Spirit's sanctifying work. And in the resurrection believers "shall bear the likeness of the Man [Christ] from heaven" (1 Cor. 15:49). Then the task of restoring God's image will be complete, for "we shall be like Him" (1 John 3:2).

3:11. In Christ distinctions are removed. These include national distinctions (**Greek or Jew;** Jews called all those outside their nation Greeks; cf. Gal. 3:28); religious distinctions (**circumcised or uncircumcised**); cultural distinctions (anyone foreign to Greek culture was a **barbarian,** and a **Scythian** was a wild, savage nomad); and economic or social distinctions (**slave or free**). If a Greek, an uncircumcised person, a barbarian, a Scythian, or a slave became a believer, he was a "new creation" (2 Cor. 5:17), a "new self" (Col. 3:10), just like a Jew or free person who became a Christian. For **Christ is all, and is in all.** That is, normal human distinctions are overruled and transfigured by one's union in Christ.

All barriers are destroyed in Christ, and all believers are truly "created equal." So it is to be expected that each believer—regardless of his nationality, former religion, culture, or economic standing—should do away with his former sinful practices and should live in accord with his "new self."

C. Putting on the virtues of the new life (3:12-17)

Because of their new lives in Christ all believers are called on to clothe themselves in virtue, letting Christ's peace rule their hearts. His Word should dwell in them richly, and they should do everything in the name of the Lord Jesus.

3:12. Again Paul called on believers to take a decisive action: **Clothe yourselves** (*endysasthe*). Because they have "put on (*endysamenoi*) the new self" (v. 10), they should live accordingly, with appropriate attributes and attitudes. In verses 8-9 Paul listed six vices (anger, rage, malice, slander, filthy language, and lying). Now in contrast to them, Christians—**as God's chosen people** (cf. Rom. 8:33; Titus 1:1), **holy** ("separated to God"; cf. Col. 1:2) **and dearly loved** (cf. Rom. 5:8; 1 John 4:9-11, 19)—are to have several virtues. These include **compassion** (*splanchna oiktirmou*, lit., "tender sympathy of heartfelt compassion"—an unusually touching expression; in Phil. 2:1 Paul joined these two nouns with "and"), **kindness** (benevolence in action; cf. 2 Cor. 6:6), **humility** (a lowly attitude toward God; cf. Phil. 2:3; 1 Peter 5:5), **gentleness** (*prautēta*), meekness, a lowly attitude toward others, **and patience** (*makrothymian*, self-restraint, a steady response in the face of provocation; cf. Col. 1:11). The last three of these are mentioned in the Greek in the same order in Ephesians 4:2; and Galatians 5:22-23 in the Greek includes three of them: patience and gentleness, as well as kindness.

3:13. Furthermore, believers are to **bear with each other** (i.e., "put up with each other") with the attitudes just mentioned in v. 12. Also they are to **forgive whatever grievances** (complaints) they **may have against** others. How? By forgiving **as the Lord forgave** them, graciously and freely (Eph. 4:32). Grudges have no place in a Christian's life for they may lead to the sins mentioned in Colossians 3:8-9.

3:14. But **over all these virtues** Christians are to **put on love.** As Paul wrote elsewhere, "The greatest of these is love" (1 Cor. 13:13). In one's catalog of virtues love should be the cover, because it is of supreme importance and is the perfect bond, holding **them all together in perfect unity.**

3:15. Believers are also to **let the peace of Christ rule in their hearts** because they are **called to peace** as **members of one body.** The closer believers are to Christ (and His likeness), the closer they are to each other. In interpersonal relationships "peace" (transcendent, God-given tranquility) should rule (*brabeuetō*, "arbitrate, decide every debate"; a word used only here in the NT; cf. *katabrabeuetō*, "decide against," 2:18). Christ's followers who have put on the virtues Paul listed (3:12-14), are concerned about being arbitrated in every trying circumstance by His peace, not by their wrangling. Also Christians are to be **thankful** (cf. Phil. 4:6; Col. 1:12; 3:16-17; 4:2; 1 Thes. 5:18). An attitude of gratitude contributes to an enjoyment of spiritual tranquility, whereas grumbling makes for inner agitation.

3:16. The new life Christians must "put on" is one in which **the Word of Christ** dwells **richly.** Christ's words were recorded by Spirit-guided apostles (cf. John 14:26; 16:13; 20:31). The words of the Bible, God's written Word, are to **dwell in** believers. That is, by study, meditation, and application of the Word, it becomes a permanent abiding part of one's life. When the words of Christ become part of a believer's nature, they spring forth naturally and daily in **psalms** (songs from the Book of Psalms), **hymns** (other songs of praise), **and spiritual songs** (as opposed to secular odes) **with gratitude** (*en tē chariti*; lit., "in grace"). This can mean either (a) God's grace, (b) graciousness in Christian singing, or (c) Christian thanks. As suggested by the NIV it probably has the third meaning. Such joyful singing is not only to please oneself or others but is to be praise **to God.** Through this Spirit-filled kind of life (cf. Eph. 5:18-19), Christians can **teach** (instruct) **and admonish** ("counsel") **one another** (Col. 3:16; cf. "admonishing and teaching" in 1:28) if it is done **with all wisdom** (*sophia*; cf. 1:9; 2:3; 4:5) and not tactlessly (cf. Gal. 6:1).

3:17. Whatever one does (cf. v. 23)—for there is no sacred-secular split in God's eyes; He is Sovereign over all—**whether in word or deed** (by lip or life) should **all** be done **in the name of the Lord Jesus** (i.e., for His glory; cf. 1 Cor. 10:31) and with a thankful spirit (cf. Phil. 4:6; 1 Thes. 5:18). Three times in three verses Paul mentioned thankfulness: "be thankful" (Col. 3:15) "sing . . . with gratitude" (v. 16), and give **thanks to God the Father** (v. 17).

IV. Practical: Outer Life in Christ (3:18–4:18)

In this last section Paul turned to practical interpersonal relations that should flow from a believer's position in Christ. First, he exhorted each member in human families to perfect (mature in) his *private* life (wives, husbands, children, fathers, slaves, masters; 3:18–4:1). He then reminded believers to perfect their *prayer* lives (4:2-4) and their *public* lives (4:5-6). Then he shared his concern for perfecting the *personal* lives of all the Colossian believers (4:7-18).

A. Perfecting one's private life (3:18–4:1)

In accordance with the theme of Colossians—maturity in Christ (1:28)—Paul exhorted believers to become mature in their private home relationships.

3:18. Wives are to **submit to** their **husbands as** their heads. This command was not limited to Paul's day, as is obvious from two reasons he gave elsewhere: (1) the order of Creation (man was created first, then woman; 1 Tim. 2:13); (2) the order within the Godhead (Christ submits to the Father; 1 Cor. 11:3). Submission or subordination does not mean inferiority; it simply means that the husband, not the wife, is head of the home. If he may be thought of as the "president," she is the "vice-president."

Of course there are moral limits to this submission; it is only **as is fitting in the Lord.** Just as obedience to government is commanded (Rom. 13:1; Titus 3:1; 1 Peter 2:13) but only insofar as government takes its place under God (Ex. 1; Dan. 3; 6), even so a wife's submission to her husband is only "in the Lord." That is, she is not obligated to follow her husband's leadership if it conflicts with specific scriptural commands.

3:19. Husbands are responsible to **love** their **wives** (as Christ loved the church; Eph. 5:28-29). So they are to exercise loving leadership, not dictatorial dominion. Perhaps husbands need this reminder to be tender and loving as much or more than wives need the reminder not to usurp authority over their hus-

bands. Assuming absolute authority will only embitter one's wife, not endear her. The words **be harsh** translate *pikrainesthe,* which is more literally, "make bitter." (A different word is used in Col. 3:21; see comments there.) Wives, like tender and sensitive flowers (cf. 1 Peter 3:7), may wilt under authoritarian dominance but blossom with tender loving care. So in a maturing marriage the husband exercises compassionate care and his wife responds in willing submission to this loving leadership.

3:20. Children are to **obey** their **parents in everything.** Disobedience to parents is designated in the Old Testament as rebellion against God and was severely punished (Ex. 21:17; Lev. 20:9). Jesus set an example for children by obeying Joseph and His mother Mary (Luke 2:51). Obedience to parents **pleases the Lord.** This does not suggest that obeying one's parents merits salvation for a child. Rather, obedience reflects God's design for order in the home. As Paul wrote elsewhere, "It is right" (*dikaion,* "just" or "proper") for children to obey their parents (Eph. 6:1).

3:21. Fathers (and mothers; cf. Prov. 1:8; 6:20) should not presume on this obedience and **embitter** (*erethizete,* "provoke or irritate") their **children** by continual agitation and unreasonable demands. Paul wrote, "Fathers, do not exasperate (*parorgizete*) your children" (Eph. 6:4). This will only make them **become discouraged.** Praise for well-doing rather than constant criticism will, along with loving discipline (cf. Heb. 12:7), help rear children in "the training and instruction of the Lord" (Eph. 6:4).

3:22-25. Slaves are exhorted to **obey** (the same word is directed to children in v. 20) their **earthly masters.** "Earthly" is literally "according to the flesh"; only Christ is master of the *spirits* of believing slaves. This obedience is to be **with sincerity of heart,** not simply when their masters are watching them or **to win their favor.** Also slaves are to work with **reverence for the Lord.** Working with an awareness of God's character and presence enhances the dignity of the labor of even slaves. In fact, **whatever** (cf. v. 17) slaves **do** should be **with all** their **heart**[s] (lit., "out of the soul," i.e., genuine and from within, not merely by outward pretense) and **for the Lord, not for men.**

While slavery was certainly undesirable, Paul's goals did not include restructuring social institutions (cf. 1 Cor. 7:17-24). Principles in Colossians 3:22-25 for Christian slaves may be applied today to Christian employees. If more Christian employees today served their employers with genuine concern and as though they were serving God, quality and productivity would increase dramatically! **It is the Lord Christ** whom all Christians **are serving.** (This is the only place in the NT where the term "the Lord Christ" is used.) After all, the final "payday" (**an inheritance . . . as a reward**) is coming **from the Lord** (cf. 2 Cor. 5:10). He will judge without **favoritism** (cf. Rom. 2:9; Eph. 6:9), that is, in full justice, repaying wrongdoers and rewarding those who serve Him.

In these verses (Col. 3:22-25) Paul made numerous points about the motives, attitudes, and conduct of Christian slaves. Such instruction was remarkable in a master-slave society.

4:1. On the other hand **masters** were to **provide** ("give deliberate care") for their **slaves with what is right** (*dikaion*) **and fair** (*isotēta,* "equitable"). After all, masters themselves are responsible to the Lord, their **Master in heaven,** who treats them fairly. If employers of nonslaves today manifested this kind of compassionate and impartial care for their employees, certainly their employees' motivation to work would radically improve.

B. Perfecting one's prayer life (4:2-4)

4:2. Paul not only practiced a mature prayer life (cf. 1:3-12) but he also prescribed it for all believers. They should **devote** themselves **to** (lit., "persist, continue in"; cf. Rom. 12:12) **prayer.** Prayer is not a spiritual luxury; it is essential for growth. Prayer—as vital to one's spiritual health as breathing is to one's physical health—should be continual (1 Thes. 5:17), not casual. In his praying, a Christian should be **watchful** ("alert, aware") against spiritual drowsiness caused by attention to the world (Matt. 24:42; Acts 20:31; 1 Cor. 16:13; 1 Thes. 5:6) and/or by the wiles of the devil (Eph. 6:16; 1 Peter 5:8). Being **thankful** should always accompany prayer (Phil. 4:6; Col. 1:12; 3:16-17;

1 Thes. 5:18), for it places a believer in the proper attitude before God (cf. Rom. 1:21).

4:3-4. Pray for us was a request Paul often made of his readers (Rom. 15:30; Eph. 6:19; 1 Thes. 5:25; 2 Thes. 3:1). His request was not selfish; it was for an **open . . . door** (cf. 1 Cor. 16:9; 2 Cor. 2:12) through which he could clearly minister the gospel **message . . . the mystery of Christ** (cf. Eph. 3:4; 6:19; Col. 1:26-27; 2:2), **for which** he was **in chains** (cf. Phil. 1:7, 13-14, 16; Col. 4:18; Phile. 1, 9-10, 13). He desired not only an opportunity to preach but also clarity in preaching: **that I may proclaim it clearly, as I should** (i.e., "as I am obligated to"; cf. Rom. 1:14-15).

C. Perfecting one's public life (4:5-6)

4:5-6. Completion or perfection in Christ includes not only one's private (and prayer) life but also one's public life. To perfect this dimension of one's life in Christ, Paul told believers to **be wise in the way** they **act.** This wisdom (*sophia;* cf. 1:9; 28; 3:16), which is God's, not man's (cf. James 3:13, 17), should be evident to **outsiders,** that is, those outside the "household of faith" (cf. 1 Cor. 5:12; 1 Thes. 4:12; 1 Tim. 3:7). Also Paul's readers should **make the most of every opportunity** (lit., "buy up [*exagorazomenoi*] the time"). They should be ready "in season and out of season" (2 Tim. 4:2) to proclaim Christ. In addition, their **conversation** (*logos,* "word, discourse, talking") should **be always full of** (lit., "in") **grace** ("gracious, pleasing"; cf. Col. 3:8-9) and yet **seasoned with salt** (i.e., pure and penetrating; 4:6). In this way they could **answer everyone** who asked "the reason for the hope" (1 Peter 3:15) they had.

D. Perfecting one's personal life (4:7-17)

Paul set an example for mature interpersonal relations. Besides remembering his friends and companions, he expressed genuine concern for them.

4:7-8. Tychicus (a leader in the church and bearer of this letter) was **a dear brother, a faithful minister** (cf. Eph. 6:21), **and a fellow servant** with Paul in the ministry. He was from the province of Asia (Acts 20:4) and was mentioned by Paul also in 2 Timothy 4:12 and Titus

3:12. Paul sent him to Colosse **for the express purpose** of informing them about his state of affairs to **encourage** them.

4:9. Onesimus (a converted runaway slave of Philemon) was also a **faithful and dear brother** (cf. Phile. 16) to Paul and a fellow Colossian: **one of you** (cf. Col. 4:12). He would accompany Tychicus and also report on Paul's circumstances.

4:10. Aristarchus was a Thessalonian who accompanied Paul on his third missionary journey (Acts 19:29; 20:4; 27:2). Being Paul's **fellow prisoner** meant either that Aristarchus attended Paul, or more likely, that he was incarcerated with Paul (probably also for preaching the gospel). Paul also called him a fellow worker (Phile. 24).

Mark, the cousin of Barnabas, was a companion on Paul's first missionary journey (Acts 12:25). He was later Peter's associate ("my son," 1 Peter 5:13; cf. Acts 12:12-13). Though Mark deserted Paul on the first missionary journey (Acts 15:37-39), Paul here commended him (cf. Phile. 24), as he did later (2 Tim 4:11).

4:11. Jesus was a common Jewish name. This companion of Paul's was also **called Justus** ("righteous"), also a common name (Acts 1:23; 18:7). These three—Aristarchus, Mark, and Justus— were **Jews** (lit., "of the circumcision") by either birth or conversion (proselytism). These three **fellow workers for the kingdom of God** comforted or consoled Paul by their loving loyalty to him. **Comfort** is the unusual word *parēgoria* ("relief, consolation"), found only here in the New Testament.

4:12-13. Epaphras, like Onesimus (v. 9), was a Colossian (**one of you**) whom Paul depicted as **a servant of Christ Jesus** who was **always wrestling** (*agōnizomenos*; cf. 1:29) **in prayer** (as Jacob did with the angel; Gen. 32) for the Colossians. His concern was that the Colossians would **stand firm** in **God's will** . . . **mature** (*teleioi*, "perfected") **and fully assured** (Rom. 4:21; 14:5) or fulfilled. This fits the overall theme of Colossians: that believers be mature, perfected in Christ. Epaphras' prayerful concern went to the point of **working hard** (lit., "has much pain"; *ponon*, "pain or distress," is used only here and in Rev. 16:10-11). His painful labor was for all the believers in the Lycus Valley—those in Colosse,

Laodicea, and Hierapolis (see the location of these three on the map between Acts and Rom.).

4:14. Luke, Paul's **dear friend** and **doctor,** stood firm not only in this earlier imprisonment but also in Paul's latter imprisonment, by which time **Demas** (here with Paul) had forsaken him (2 Tim. 4:10). Luke is the author of the Third Gospel and of Acts (cf. Acts 1:1). By tradition he was one of the 72 (Luke 10:1). Some also suggest he was the anonymous disciple on the Emmaus Road (Luke 24:13). Since the only men with Paul who were "of the circumcision" were Aristarchus, Mark, and Jesus (Justus), Luke may have been a Gentile.

4:15. Paul asked that his **greetings** be given **to the brothers at Laodicea and to Nympha** in whose **house** the **church** met. Churches meeting in homes was a common practice then before there were church buildings (Rom. 16:5; 1 Cor. 16:19; Phile. 2).

4:16. Paul urged an exchange of epistles; once they had read Colossians they should send it to Laodicea and **read the letter** (coming) **from Laodicea.** This "Laodicean letter" may be the letter to the Ephesians, which was written about that time, and sent to the same general vicinity.

4:17. Archippus, probably the son of Philemon (cf. Phile. 2), was ministering in Colosse, possibly in Epaphras' absence. Paul exhorted his readers to **tell Archippus to see to** (*blepe,* "look out" for dangers in) **it that he complete the work** (lit., "the ministry") God had given him. Whatever his problem, he was not fulfilling (completing) his work. This was another example of Paul's concern that the Colossians be complete in Christ.

E. Salutation (4:18)

4:18. As was Paul's custom and sign of authenticity, he signed a **greeting** with his **own hand** (cf. 1 Cor. 16:21; Gal. 6:11; 2 Thes. 3:17; Phile. 19). He then asked that his readers **remember** (in prayerful support) his imprisonment (**chains;** cf. Col. 4:3). As with so many of his epistles, his closing was a benediction, a prayer that God's **grace** (cf. 1:2) **be with** them (see the chart, "Paul's Concluding Benedictions in His Epistles" near Rom. 16:20).

BIBLIOGRAPHY

Barry, Alfred. "The Epistle to the Colossians." In *Ellicott's Commentary on the Whole Bible*. Reprint (8 vols. in 4). Grand Rapids: Zondervan Publishing House, 1959.

Calvin, John. "Commentaries on the Epistles of Paul to the Galatians and Ephesians." In *Calvin's Commentaries*, vol. 21. Translated by William Pringle. Reprint. Grand Rapids: Baker Book House, 1981.

Carson, Herbert M. *The Epistle of Paul to the Colossians and Philemon.* The Tyndale New Testament Commentaries. Grand Rapids: Wm. B. Eerdmans Publishing Co., 1960.

Erdman, Charles R. *The Epistle of Paul to the Colossians and to Philemon.* Philadelphia: Westminster Press, 1933.

Gromacki, Robert G. *Stand Perfect in Wisdom: An Exposition of Colossians and Philemon.* Grand Rapids: Baker Book House, 1981.

Kent, Homer A., Jr. *Treasure of Wisdom.* Grand Rapids: Baker Book House, 1978.

Lightfoot, J.B. *St. Paul's Epistle to the Colossians and to Philemon.* London: Macmillan & Co., 1879. Reprint. Grand Rapids: Zondervan Publishing House, 1959.

Moule, H.C.G. *Studies in Colossians and Philemon.* 1893. Reprint. Grand Rapids: Kregel Publications, 1977.

Peake, A.S. "The Epistle to the Colossians." In *The Expositor's Greek Testament*, vol. 3. Grand Rapids: Wm. B. Eerdmans Publishing Co., 1951.

Simpson, E.K., and Bruce, F.F. *Commentary on the Epistles to the Ephesians and the Colossians.* The New International Commentary on the New Testament. Grand Rapids: Wm. B. Eerdmans Publishing Co., 1957.

Thomas, W.H. Griffith. *Studies in Colossians and Philemon.* Grand Rapids: Baker Book House, 1973.

Vaughan, Curtis. "Colossians." In *The Expositor's Bible Commentary*, vol. 11. Grand Rapids: Zondervan Publishing House, 1978.

_____. *Colossians: Bible Study Commentary.* Grand Rapids: Zondervan Publishing House, 1973.

Wiersbe, Warren W. *Be Complete.* Wheaton, Ill.: Scripture Press Publications, Victor Books, 1981.

1 THESSALONIANS

Thomas L. Constable

INTRODUCTION

The City of Thessalonica. The city of Thessalonica flourished for hundreds of years, partly because of its ideal location. It was situated on the banks of a hospitable harbor in the Thermaic Gulf near the northwest corner of the Aegean Sea. In the Apostle Paul's day it was the chief seaport of the Roman province of Macedonia. Thessalonica ranked with Corinth and Ephesus, the main ports of the provinces of Achaia and Asia, as a great shipping center.

Thessalonica also enjoyed another advantage. The Egnatian Way, the main Roman road from Rome to the Orient via Byzantium (modern Istanbul), passed through the city. This put Thessalonica in direct contact with many other important cities by land as well as by sea. It was one of the most important centers of population in Paul's day, occupying a strategic location both governmentally and militarily.

Estimates of the population of Thessalonica in New Testament times place it at near 200,000 (Everett F. Harrison, *Introduction to the New Testament*, Grand Rapids: Wm. B. Eerdmans Publishing Co., 1964, p. 245). Most of the inhabitants were native Greeks, but many Romans also lived there. Orientals and Jews likewise populated the city. Wherever commerce flourished in the ancient world one would find Jewish businessmen. The Jewish synagogue in Thessalonica was influential; many Greek proselytes were present when Paul preached there (Acts 17:4).

First Thessalonians reflects the moral climate of the city. The pagan Greek religion of the largest segment of the population produced many forms of immorality but whetted the appetites of some for spiritual reality. Evidently the higher standards of Judaism attracted disillusioned Greeks, Romans, and Orientals to the synagogue.

Thessalonica was built by Cassander in 315 B.C. near the site of an ancient city called Therma, named for the hot springs in the area. He chose this place for its excellent location and named it after his wife, Thessalonica, who was a half sister of Alexander the Great. Cassander was a Greek general under Alexander.

Many years later, when the Romans conquered the area (168 B.C.), they divided Macedonia into four districts and named Thessalonica the capital of one of these. In 146 B.C. the Romans reorganized Macedonia and made Thessalonica the capital of the new province which encompassed all four of the older districts. In 42 B.C. Thessalonica received the status of a free city from Anthony and Octavian (later called Caesar Augustus) because the Thessalonians had helped these men defeat their adversaries, Brutus and Cassius. The Romans ruled Thessalonica with a loose hand; though the Roman proconsul (or governor) lived there, no Roman troops were garrisoned in the city. The citizens were allowed to govern themselves, as in a Greek city-state, which they did through a group of five or six politarchs, a senate, and a public assembly.

In World War I the Allies based soldiers in Thessalonica, and during the Second World War the Nazis extracted 60,000 Jews from the city and executed them. Thessalonica still exists today with a population near 300,000. It is called Salonica (or Thessaloniki).

The Evangelization of the City. The Apostle Paul first preached the gospel in Thessalonica during his second missionary journey. Having revisited the churches in the province of Asia where Paul and Barnabas had preached on their first journey, Paul, Silas, Timothy, Luke, and perhaps others made their way to

Troas, after unsuccessfully attempting to travel in other directions. In Troas Paul received his vision of a man of Macedonia calling for help. Responding to this call the party crossed into Europe and preached at Philippi, a major city of Macedonia. Through a series of circumstances the missionaries were led to leave Philippi and press on about 100 miles westward along the Egnatian Way to the next major population center, Thessalonica (Acts 17:1-9).

As was his custom, Paul visited the Jewish synagogue in Thessalonica where he knew he would find people who held much in common with him: respect for the Old Testament, theological concepts, and cultural practices. Since Paul was a well-trained teacher, he was allowed to speak in the synagogue. His message, as Luke summarized it, consisted of two points: the Old Testament taught a suffering, dying, resurrected Messiah; and these predictions were fulfilled in Jesus of Nazareth. Though Luke did not say so, Paul also may have taught that Jesus Christ would return to fulfill the remaining messianic prophecies (Acts 17:7). In the Thessalonian Epistles Paul sought to answer questions that had arisen from his teaching. As a result of Paul's preaching several people were converted including (a) some Jews, (b) several Gentile Greeks who had come to the synagogue because they had placed faith in or were interested in more information about the Jews' God, and (c) the wives of some prominent Thessalonian citizens (17:4).

The length of Paul's stay on this occasion is a matter of minor disagreement among students of the Thessalonian Epistles. Some believe that the reference to Paul's presence in the synagogue on three Sabbath Days (17:2) means that he was in Thessalonica for only about 21 days (e.g., James E. Frame, *A Critical and Exegetical Commentary on the Epistles of St. Paul to the Thessalonians*, p. 7). Others feel that Paul was probably there for a longer period of time, perhaps as long as six months (e.g., Richard B. Rackham, *The Acts of the Apostles*, London: Metheun & Co., 1901, p. 296). Those who hold the latter opinion base it on the implications of other passages that may hint at Paul's experiences in Thessalonica during this visit. For example, Paul apparently worked at his craft of tentmaking while in Thessalonica (1 Thes. 2:9; 2 Thes. 3:8). These references may imply a prolonged stay, but they do not require it. Some interpreters contend that Philippians 4:16 suggests that the Philippians sent two gifts to Paul while he was in Thessalonica and that would be unlikely, they say, if he were there just three weeks. Other commentators insist that this verse only says that the Philippians sent two gifts; they claim it does not explicitly say that Paul was in Thessalonica when he received both of them.

The length of Paul's stay is significant because of the doctrinal background of his readers which the Thessalonian Epistles reveal. Of course knowledge of what went on in the Thessalonian church after Paul left as well as while he was there is sketchy at best. But it seems that Paul fed these new believers a rich diet of doctrinal instruction in a fairly brief period of time. Also, Paul wrote as though he left Thessalonica before he really wanted to. Perhaps a stay of a few months in Thessalonica is fairly accurate.

Quite possibly Paul continued his teaching and evangelizing out of Jason's house after the Jews opposed him (Acts 17:5-10). His adversaries regarded Paul's message as a threat to Judaism, as Jews have done since the gospel was first preached in Jerusalem. The non-Christian Jews in Thessalonica resorted to a strategy to get rid of Paul that was similar to that employed by Jesus' enemies and Stephen's accusers. They hired troublemakers and put false accusations in their mouths. Storming Jason's house, but failing to find the missionaries, the mob dragged Jason before the politarchs. The Jews charged Jason with harboring revolutionaries who were promoting treason by teaching the people to disobey Roman law and to follow a king other than Caesar. Though this was a serious charge, especially in a city whose free status could be withdrawn by Rome if it were true, the city rulers saw through the motives of these jealous Jewish zealots. The rulers only required Jason to guarantee that Paul and his friends would not disturb the city's peace any longer. This made it necessary for the missionaries to leave Thessalonica. The Christians who remained continued to feel the heat of Jewish persecution, however, not only from the Jews themselves, but also from the Gentiles whom the unbelieving Jews influenced (1 Thes. 2:14; 2 Thes. 1:4).

The Occasion of the Letter. When Paul and Silas left Thessalonica, they proceeded about 40 miles west along the Egnatian Way to Berea. There they ministered for a short time until the hostile Thessalonian Jews, hearing of Paul's preaching in Berea, tracked down the missionaries and incited the Berean Jews to expel Paul from their city. Paul made his way south to Athens while Silas and Timothy remained in Berea. Paul sent a message to these two companions as soon as he reached Athens, asking them to join him, which they did (Acts 17:10-15; 1 Thes. 2:1-5). The plight of the new Thessalonian converts so concerned Paul that he sent Timothy back to Thessalonica to check on the church's welfare. Timothy rejoined Paul at the next stop, Corinth, with encouraging news (Acts 18:1, 5; 1 Thes. 3:6-7). This led Paul to write 1 Thessalonians.

Some students of this epistle believe that Paul wrote not only to commend the Thessalonian believers for their steadfastness in persecution, but also to answer questions they sent to him through Timothy. Though there is no external evidence for the existence of a document containing these questions, it is obvious from the text that Paul wrote answers to some of their questions (cf. 1 Thes. 4:9; 5:1). These questions may have been relayed orally by Timothy. Another reason for Paul's writing was to correct misinformation and false accusations that circulated after Paul left Thessalonica. Paul also wrote to exhort them to go forward in their faith.

The Purpose of the Letter. Specifically, the Holy Spirit led Paul to pen this inspired epistle in order to meet several needs. He encouraged his children in the faith to persevere despite their persecution. He refuted false charges made by the local enemies of the gospel: that the missionaries had preached in order to fatten their wallets and gain other personal benefits; that Paul had left Thessalonica hurriedly and had not returned because he was a coward and a hypocrite. Paul also wrote to correct some errors that had cropped up in the church: an inclination to moral laxity and laziness, and a tendency not to respect the church's

spiritual leaders. Paul gave instruction too on the subject of what would happen to Christians who would die before the Lord's return.

The Place and Date of Writing. References in Acts 17 and 18 as well as in 1 Thessalonians make it clear that Paul wrote this epistle from Corinth.

Evidently the letter was written shortly after Paul arrived in Corinth (Acts 17:1-10; 18:1). The references to Gallio's proconsulate in Corinth (cf. 18:12) on ancient secular inscriptions make it possible to date Paul's stay in Corinth fairly accurately—in the early 50s (Jack Finegan, *Light from the Ancient Past,* Princeton, N.J.: Princeton University Press, 1969, p. 282). Conservative scholars date 1 Thessalonians between A.D. 50 and 54. This would make the epistle one of Paul's earliest inspired writings, probably his second (after Galatians).

The Authenticity of the Epistle. The Pauline authorship for 1 Thessalonians is not questioned by scholars who take the statements of the book at face value. During the last century objections to Paul's authorship were raised by critics, but these have now been answered satisfactorily (see, e.g., A. Robert and A. Feuillet, eds., *Introduction to the New Testament,* New York: Desclée Co., 1965, p. 390).

OUTLINE

COMMENTARY

I. Salutation and Greeting (1:1)

1:1. Letters written in first-century Greco-Roman culture began with three statements which are found in the opening verse of 1 Thessalonians: the name(s) of the writer(s), the name(s) of the addressee(s), and a word of formal greeting.

The Apostle **Paul** was the writer of this epistle. His name appears first and he spoke of himself in the singular elsewhere in the letter (e.g., 3:5). He was Saul of Tarsus whose Hebrew name means "asked for." His Roman name, Paul, by which he was known more commonly, means "little." **Silas and Timothy** joined Paul in sending 1 Thessalonians; that is, Paul wrote for them as well as for himself. Perhaps Silas served as Paul's amanuensis, or secretary. Frequently in 1 Thessalonians Paul wrote "we" so he was either including these brethren in his thoughts (e.g., 1:2; 2:1; etc.) or using an editorial "we." Silvanus is the Roman form of Silas which Paul used consistently in his writings, as did Peter (1 Peter 5:12). Luke called the same person Silas (Acts 15:22; etc.). Silas was Paul's primary associate on the second missionary journey (Acts 15:40). Timothy, of course, was a young man Paul led to faith in Jesus Christ (1 Tim. 1:2), probably during Paul's visit to Asia Minor on his first missionary journey (Acts 13–14). Timothy's name (which means "honored by God" or "God-honorer") was doubtless given in faith by his God-fearing mother Eunice (2 Tim. 1:5). His father may have been a pagan Greek when Timothy was born (Acts 16:1). This young man had recently returned to Paul from a trip to Thessalonica with news of conditions in that church (1 Thes. 3:1-2, 6). These three men were undoubtedly the best-known and most highly respected Christian missionaries by the believers in Thessalonica.

The addressees are grouped together in the salutation as **the church of the Thessalonians.** A local church is a group of people called out by God from the mass of humanity to a life of separation to Him. The definite article before "Thessalonians" is not found in some ancient copies of 1 Thessalonians. If this is the correct wording, the text further emphasizes the distinction between those in the church and others in the city.

The church is described as being **in God the Father and the Lord Jesus Christ.** To Paul, the Lord Jesus Christ was as much God as the Father. He preached this in Thessalonica (Acts 17:3) and affirmed it again in this epistle. The description of God as Father connotes security, love, and strength. Paul balanced this picture with a reminder that God the Son is also Lord; He is the Sovereign who is to be obeyed. "Jesus" is the Lord's human name, the Greek form of Joshua, "Savior." "Christ" is the Greek translation of the "Messiah" of the Old Testament and means "Anointed One."

The shortened greeting customary in the Pauline Epistles appears here. **Grace** was the common Greek salutation meaning "greetings" or "rejoice." In Greek **peace** is equivalent to the Hebrew *šālôm* meaning "favor," "prosperity," and "well-being." It is interesting that those two words of salutation always occur in this order in the New Testament. Theologically God's grace is the basis for and leads to man's peace.

II. Personal Commendations and Explanations (1:2–3:13)

In general the first three chapters of 1 Thessalonians are personal in nature, and the last two are practical.

A. Thanksgiving for the Thessalonians (1:2-10)

This first chapter deals primarily with the subject of salvation. Several aspects of the Thessalonians' salvation elicited Paul's thanksgiving to God in these verses.

1. SUMMARY STATEMENT (1:2-3)

In these two verses Paul expressed his gratitude to God and set forth in a brief statement why he was thankful for the Thessalonians.

1:2. Paul, Silas, and Timothy rejoiced together in what God had done in their converts' lives. They continually and frequently gave thanks; the Thessalonians were a constant source of joy to them. Whenever these missionaries prayed for the Thessalonians, they gave thanks to **God** for them. Rather than being a source of grief these Christians evoked gratitude. In this they served as models for all Christians.

1:3. Three characteristics of these believers stood out in Paul's mind. First, they had performed an important **work produced by** (lit., "of") **faith** in Christ. Verse 9 mentions that they had turned to the true God from idols. Faith in Christ had produced true repentance. Second, they performed **labor** (*kopou*, "toil") **prompted by** (lit., "of") **love** for Christ. This consisted in their serving the living and true God (v. 9) in the midst of persecution (v. 6). Third, they had **endurance** (*hypomonēs*, lit., "a bearing up patiently under a heavy load"; cf. 2 Thes. 1:4) **inspired by** (lit., "of") **hope** in **Christ.** Specifically they were waiting for God's Son from heaven (1 Thes. 1:10). These three cardinal virtues that should mark every Christian—faith, love, and hope—stood out in the Thessalonian believers' lives (cf. 1 Cor. 13:13). Each of these virtues found its object in Jesus Christ, and each produced praiseworthy behavior. The Thessalonians had exercised saving faith in Christ in the past when they had believed the gospel, they were loving Christ in the present, and they were hoping for His return in the future. Their lives were certainly focused on Jesus Christ. No wonder Paul and his companions gave thanks for them.

2. SPECIFIC REASONS (1:4-10)

1:4. The Thessalonians' response to the preaching of the gospel in their midst constituted indisputable proof of their salvation. Paul rehearsed their response in this verse as he expanded on the idea he had just introduced.

Characteristically Paul addressed his fellow Christians as **brothers.** He used this term (*adelphoi*) 15 times in this one brief epistle (1:4; 2:1, 9, 17; 3:7; 4:1, 10, 13; 5:1, 4, 12, 14, 25-27), and 7 times in 2 Thessalonians (1:3; 2:1, 13, 15; 3:1, 6, 13). He did not claim superiority over them but recognized the equality of all the redeemed in the sight of their heavenly Father, as he taught elsewhere (e.g., 1 Cor. 12:14-27) and as the Lord taught (Matt. 23:9; etc.). Paul had come a long way from being a proud Pharisee to the place where he could consider Gentiles his equals before God. He reminded his readers that they were beloved by God. Even Paul's incidental statements throb with the warm realization of God's presence (1 Thes. 1:3) and love.

The proof of God's love for the Thessalonians was His choice of them unto salvation. From the word translated **chosen** (*eklogēn*) comes the English "election." That God has chosen to bless some individuals with eternal life is clearly taught in many places in both the Old and New Testaments (e.g., Deut. 4:37; 7:6-7; Isa. 44:1-2; Rom. 9; Eph. 1:4-6, 11; Col. 3:12; 2 Thes. 2:13). Equally clear is the fact that God holds each individual personally responsible for his decision to trust or not to trust in Jesus Christ (cf. John 3; Rom. 5). The difficulty in putting divine election and human responsibility together is understanding how both can be true. *That* both are true is taught in the Bible. *How* both can be true is apparently incomprehensible to finite human minds; no one has ever been able to explain this antinomy satisfactorily. This task transcends human mental powers, much as seeing angels transcends human visual powers and hearing very high-pitched sounds transcends human auditory powers. The Thessalonians' response to the gospel message proved that God had chosen them for salvation.

1:5. The response of his converts was a supernatural work of God, not a natural response to a clearly delivered

691

sermon. When Paul preached to them, he did not just share human opinion and philosophy (cf. 1 Cor. 2:1-5). Rather, his message was marked by the **power** of God (cf. Rom. 1:16). **The Holy Spirit** brought it home to their hearts with **deep conviction** (John 16:8). Paul's message was marked by his own certainty that this message would change their lives as it had radically changed his.

Not only did Paul and his traveling companions preach a convincing message, but they also lived lives consistent with that message when they were in Thessalonica. The Thessalonians were fully aware of their teachers' manner of life and that their motive was to benefit the Thessalonians. The message Paul preached—the **gospel** of the grace of God—had entered into the minds and hearts of these Macedonians and they had been saved. From their belief beautiful lives had blossomed.

1:6. The outstanding fruit of faith in the gospel was the Thessalonians' change of behavior. They **became imitators** of their spiritual parents, the missionaries. This is normal Christian experience. But they also went on to imitate **the Lord.** This too is natural, and the order is true to life as well. A new Christian first looks to other believers as his pattern, but then as he matures he realizes that Jesus Christ is his best "model" (cf. 1 Peter 2:21).

Despite **severe suffering** the Thessalonians **welcomed the message.** The Jews among them must have felt the hatred of their unbelieving brothers in the flesh who, as has been pointed out, were especially antagonistic to the gospel in that city. The Gentile converts must have had to swim against the swift current of paganism that flowed like a torrent through the conduit of commercial Thessalonica. And the city's chief men's wives, who had become Christians, had to go home to unbelieving husbands who would not have appreciated their newly sensitized consciences. Yet **in spite of** trials without, the Thessalonian believers possessed **joy** within, the joy of sins forgiven. It is interesting that Christians who have tribulations in their daily walks often seem to have greater joy in the Lord than those who live in more comfortable spiritual climates. A Christian's joy should be determined not by his circumstances but by his relationship with Christ. This was true of the Thessalonians. The source of their joy was the indwelling **Holy Spirit.**

1:7. The testimony of these Christians did not burn brightly merely at home; it also shone abroad to other people in other parts of **Macedonia,** reaching even to **Achaia,** the neighboring province to the south. Having become imitators of the missionaries and their Lord (v. 6) they in turn became the object of imitation by other believers. When Paul wrote to the Corinthians he pointed to these Macedonians as **a model** (*typon*; cf. 2 Thes. 3:9) of sacrificial giving (2 Cor. 8:1-8). He wrote that they had given money to help other believers even though they themselves were poor. One of the most revealing evidences of a Christian's true spirituality is the way he manages his money. In this revealing test the Thessalonians emerged as gold tried in the fire.

1:8. This verse explains how the Thessalonians became examples to other Christians. Having received the gospel (v. 5) they passed it on to others. The word *exēchētai,* translated **rang out,** could be rendered "reverberated." Paul saw the Thessalonians as amplifiers or relay stations that not only received the gospel message but sent it farther on its way with increased power and scope. Paul's preaching in Thessalonica had the effect of speaking into a public address microphone; his words were received and repeated by many different "speakers" in many remote places where his unaided voice could not have reached.

Apparently it was not through an organized evangelistic campaign that their witness went forth, though Paul's preaching in Thessalonica and elsewhere illustrates this approach. But it was through the personal lives and testimonies of these transformed individuals that neighbors heard about their **faith in God.** As they went the gospel was heard **everywhere,** so an apostolic missionary campaign was not needed.

1:9. Other people were telling Paul what had happened after he had preached the gospel in Thessalonica. The events of his visit had become well known in that part of the world, not because Paul had spread the word, but because of the outspoken Thessalonian believers' witness. Their boldness should challenge every true child of God.

These believers had **turned to God,**

the only true God, **from idols.** This strongly suggests that many of those believers had been pagan Gentiles. The Jews, of course, abhorred idolatry. Someone has observed that humans have the freedom to choose who their master will be, but they do not have the freedom to choose **no** master. The Thessalonians had chosen to **serve the living and true God** rather than God's creatures or satanic powers (cf. Rom. 1:18-23). The fact that God is a living Person was precious to the Jews and to Paul; this is the characteristic by which God is most often distinguished from so-called gods in the Old Testament. He is the only living God; all other gods are not alive and therefore not worthy objects of worship.

1:10. Not only had the Thessalonians turned to God in repentance and begun to serve Him, but they were also awaiting the return of **His Son from heaven.** Paul may have had in mind the "heavens" (pl.) through which Jesus Christ passed when He ascended from the earth (Acts 1:9-11), rather than the seat of His heavenly rule at the right hand of the Father in "heaven" (sing., Rev. 4:2-11). If so, he said that the Thessalonians were looking for Jesus' coming through the clouds, literally, "out of the heavens."

But it was not the clouds, or the signs of His coming, or His deliverance which interested these believers; it was the person of **Jesus,** the Son of the living God. He was the object of their hope, the focus of their attention. May Jesus Himself, rather than anything that will accompany Him or characterize His return, always fill the hopes of His saints!

This reference to "Jesus," His human name, is a strong claim to Jesus of Nazareth's deity. He is further described as the Son of God, the One risen from the dead by the living God. The fact of the Resurrection is indisputable proof (cf. 1 Cor. 15:14-19) of the deity of Jesus.

The return of Jesus is a source of hope for Christians for several reasons, but the reason which Paul mentioned here was Jesus' deliverance of the saints **from the coming wrath** of God. The wrath of God will be poured out on unrighteous people because of their failure to trust in Christ (John 3:36; Rom. 1:18). This happens at many times and in many ways, the great white throne judg-

ment being the most awful occasion (Rev. 20:11-15). But the "time of trouble for Jacob" (Jer. 30:4-7), also called "the Great Tribulation" (Rev. 7:14), will be a period in history during which God's wrath will be poured out on the earth as never before (cf. Rev. 6–19).

Was Paul thinking of a specific time in which God's wrath would be poured out (1 Thes. 1:10), or was he referring to the outpouring of God's wrath on unbelievers in a more general sense? Paul, the Thessalonian believers, and Christians today will escape all aspects of God's wrath, general and specific, including the Tribulation period. The clear implication of this verse is that Paul hoped in the Lord's imminent return. Otherwise Paul would have told his readers to prepare for the Tribulation.

In the phrase "from the coming wrath" the word translated "from" means that Christians are kept from it, not taken out of it. The same verb (**rescues**) and preposition (**from**) are used in 2 Corinthians 1:10 where Paul said he was delivered from a deadly peril. Obviously this does not mean Paul died and was resurrected. Christians will be kept away from God's wrath, not just kept safe through it (cf. comments on Rev. 3:10).

This chapter, like every chapter in this epistle, closes with a reference to the return of Jesus Christ (1 Thes. 1:10; 2:19; 3:13; 4:13-18, 5:23).

B. Reminders for the Thessalonians (2:1-16)

Paul's thoughts, led by the Holy Spirit, turned from the Thessalonians' response to his preaching to other events of his recent visit.

1. HOW THE GOSPEL WAS DELIVERED (2:1-12)

The first part of this chapter records Paul's comments about his visit to Thessalonica. His words suggest that people outside the church were charging him with unworthy motives and improper conduct.

2:1. In verses 1-6 Paul reminded his readers of his actions among them and clarified his motives. All of chapter 2 constitutes an expansion of 1:9. **You** is emphatic in the Greek; Paul called on his readers to remember carefully the facts of his **visit** to them. Thinking back, they would recall that Paul's visit was not in vain. It **was not a failure.** Paul had not come merely to give speeches. Changes in the Thessalonian believers' lives testified to the value and success of his visit.

2:2. Paul and his companions were not on a vacation trip. They had come to Thessalonica after having **suffered, been insulted,** beaten, and imprisoned for preaching the gospel **in Philippi** (Acts 16:22-24). This mission had cost them dearly, but God gave them uncommon boldness to stand up in the synagogue at Thessalonica and preach the same message that had brought them persecution in Philippi. And when opposition broke out in Thessalonica the missionaries kept on preaching. This is not the reaction of people who are trying to make money or build personal reputations at the expense of their hearers. Paul called on his readers to remember these actions and to recognize the sincerity behind them. The missionaries' boldness amid **strong opposition** was the sign of God at work in His servants and was proof of their genuineness.

2:3. Paul's actions (which the Thessalonians personally observed) demonstrated both his sincerity and his motives (which they could not observe but which Paul explained here). Paul denied three allegations: (a) his *message* was not deceptive; it was truth, not **error;** (b) his *motivation* was not **impure,** but was clean; (c) his *method* was not to **trick,** mislead, or deceive them, but was straightforward.

2:4. In strong contrast to these improprieties, Paul said he spoke out of the best motives, realizing that God had put his heart to the test. He and his companions spoke **not . . . to please men, but God.** Having been **approved** (*dedokimasmetha,* "shown by testing to be genuine") **by God,** He **entrusted** them **with the gospel.** Paul used the word "gospel" five times in 1 Thessalonians (1:5; 2:2, 4, 8; 3:2). Paul and his fellow missionaries were veterans; they had been tried and tested for years. God would not have blessed their work if their motivation had not been right. Paul saw himself as a steward entrusted by God to carry His message of salvation to lost men and women (cf. 1 Cor. 9:17). Paul did not choose his work; God selected him for the high calling of proclaiming the gospel. This responsibility was most significant to

Paul, who viewed himself as under God's constant scrutiny. So he would not dare serve with the wrong motives.

2:5. Paul's preaching to the Thessalonians was not aimed at making a favorable impression on them. He asked them to remember how he spoke. He never wore a false face, preaching to gain something for himself. Because they could not know this, Paul appealed to **God** as the **witness** of his motives.

2:6. The missionaries were **not** seeking the **praise** of any man but the praise of God. Traveling philosophers and orators were common in the Roman Empire. They itinerated from place to place, entertaining and seeking a personal following for fame and fortune. Paul and his companions had nothing in common with such men! Rather than seeking something for themselves they delighted in giving to others freely.

2:7. In verses 7-9 Paul shifted the emphasis somewhat from the preachers' activities to the hearers' responses. Paul, Silas, and Timothy rightfully could have expected their converts to support them financially and could have called on them to do so (cf. 1 Tim. 5:18). Certainly they had a right to expect esteem. But they chose to minister rather than to be ministered to for the sake of the Thessalonian converts. Paul and his companions cared for their converts as a nursing **mother** gently cares **for her little children.** This instructive illustration provides a good example for all who are responsible for the care of new believers. If a nursing mother does not feed herself, she cannot feed her baby. If she eats certain foods, her baby will get sick. Similarly the spiritual diet of a parent Christian is vitally important to the health of a newer Christian. The gentleness and unselfishness of Paul as a spiritual parent shines through in this illustration.

2:8. Rather than being greedy (v. 5) the missionaries **were delighted to share with** the Thessalonians. They **not only** gave the message of eternal life, **the gospel of God,** but also imparted their own innermost beings (lit., "our own souls") as well. They gave whatever they had in order to help the beloved Thessalonians. The love of Paul and his companions is evident, for genuine love finds expression in giving to people—not only to their spiritual needs, which are primary, but also to their physical needs.

2:9. Paul ministered to his converts by **toil** (*kopon;* cf. the same word for "toil" in 1:3) and suffering **hardship** (*mochthon*) on their behalf. He **worked night and day** so that he would not **burden** them with his needs (cf. 2 Thes. 3:8). Perhaps he made tents, rising early and staying up late, as he did in other cities (Acts 18:3). Probably he **preached the gospel** and taught as much as he could, both in the daytime and at night.

2:10. Verses 10-12 summarize the appeal to the Thessalonians. The apostles called on their readers and God to bear witness to their behavior in both action and motive. Their inner convictions led to devout (**holy,** *hosiōs*) conduct. With reference to God's objective standard their behavior was **righteous,** measuring up to what God expects and requires. Their conduct was unreproachable (**blameless,** *amemptōs;* cf. 5:23), able to stand their critics' scrutiny because it was right. Both they and **God** were **witnesses** (cf. 2:5) of the truthfulness of Paul's claims.

2:11. Having likened the conduct of the missionaries to the loving, unselfish care of a nursing mother (v. 7), Paul also compared their behavior to that of **a father.** Here the implication is that they trained and instructed the Thessalonians as a responsible father disciplines his children. The word *tekna,* translated **children,** emphasizes the believers' immaturity as well as the apostles' affection. This verse is the fifth time Paul wrote **you know** (cf. 1:5; 2:2, 5).

2:12. The training provided included strong positive appeals (**encouraging,** *parakalountes*), soothing encouragement (**comforting,** *paramythoumenoi*), designed to cheer up and to inspire correct behavior, and solemn, earnest entreaty (**urging,** *martyromenoi*). Such a combination of appeals proved effective in moving the Thessalonians to action by the Holy Spirit's convicting power.

The appeal to lead lives **worthy of God** is the highest of all for those who have tasted God's grace in salvation. Paul heightened his exhortation by reminding his readers that they had been specially called by God, called to enter and be partakers in **His kingdom** and called to glorify and share in God's **glory.**

2. HOW THE GOSPEL WAS RECEIVED (2:13-16)

Paul's attitude of rejoicing continues in this section as indicated by the opening **and,** though now his attention turned from how the gospel came to the Thessalonians to how they welcomed it.

2:13. A second reason for Paul's continual rejoicing is identified in this verse. Not only were the fruits of righteousness manifest in the Thessalonian converts' lives (1:3), but also the way they received the preached **Word of God** warmed the apostles' hearts. The "Word of God" here clearly refers to the message spoken by the missionaries. When the Thessalonians heard it they realized that it was not simply the words of man's wisdom, but a message that had its source in **God** (cf. 1:5). Someone has said that the gospel is not the kind of message that man would invent if he could, nor is it a message that he could invent if he would. The Thessalonian Christians sensed the supernatural truthfulness of the gospel Paul preached as the Holy Spirit brought this conviction home to their hearts. When Christians share their faith, they do not merely give their particular viewpoint on life as one among the endless variety of human theories. They announce the divinely revealed truth of God, a word from God.

The spoken Word of God has an inherent power to change. For this reason the Word of God through the Old Testament prophets was recognized as being powerful and not falling to the ground (i.e., lacking sufficient power to hit its mark and accomplish its purpose; cf. 1 Sam. 3:19). The Word of God has the creative power of God behind it and in it (Gen. 1:3). Paul credited the changes in the Thessalonians to this spoken Word of God. Not only had it effected changes in them in the past, but also it was continuing to change them since they continued to believe. (The word **believe** is in the Gr. pres. tense, indicating continuing action.) The truth of God, like a good medicine, will continue to heal sin-sick souls so long as people receive it by faith.

2:14. Paul encouraged his readers to recognize this evidence of God's working as being true of all believers by directing their attention to another experience common to all saints. He included himself again, by addressing them as **brothers**

(cf. 1:4; 2:1). Those whose lives are being changed by God often find themselves the objects of criticism and attack by people in whom there is no divine life. Frequently when Christians suffer persecution they are tempted to think God's blessing has departed. Paul countered this lie of Satan by reminding his readers that their experience duplicated that of their elder brothers and sisters in the faith who had become Christians **in Judea.** They also suffered opposition from their neighbors; and their neighbors were Jews too.

2:15. The Thessalonians were not alone in their suffering; they had abundant and worthy company. Their persecutors had **killed the Lord Jesus** Himself **and the** Old Testament **prophets.** They **drove . . . out** their father in the faith, the Apostle Paul, and his fellow missionaries. Though Paul laid guilt for the death of Christ at the feet of the Jews he did not charge them alone with this crime. The Romans who were involved in Jesus' trial and execution were also guilty (1 Cor. 2:8) as was every human being for whose sins Christ tasted death (Heb. 2:9). Most likely Paul mentioned the murder of Jesus first and his own persecutions last because in his mind the first example was much more serious.

Those who persecute believers in Christ antagonize both God and other men. Paul knew whereof he spoke, having been a persecutor of the church himself and one to whom God had revealed that he was fighting against the Lord he sought to serve (Acts 26:14-15). Those who set themselves against God's people also set themselves against God. And they also hurt other non-Christians. The worst thing about unbelief is not that it damns the unbeliever, but that it hinders the salvation of others. Such people seek to extinguish the lamp of truth and in doing so cause others to stumble.

2:16. An unbeliever who is willing to live and let live with respect to personal convictions regarding God is less dangerous than one who not only disbelieves himself but also tries to keep others from hearing the gospel. The unbelieving Jews in Thessalonica were of the latter variety.

Such people's actions hurt themselves as well as others because they **heap up** additional **sins** for which God will judge them. God will only allow an individual or a group of individuals to accumulate so much sin, and then He will judge. He does not judge before this **limit,** which He alone knows, has been reached (cf. Gen. 15:16). The Thessalonians' persecutors were hastening God's judgment on themselves by their actions.

The manifestation of God's **wrath** that Paul had in mind in this verse is debatable. Perhaps he was referring to the destruction of Jerusalem by the Romans in A.D. 70, just a few years in the future, which Paul may have known was as certain to take place as if it had already happened. Or he may have had in mind God's turning from the Jews to create for Himself a unique body of believers made up of both Jews and **Gentiles** who now stand on equal footing before God (Eph. 2:13-16). Or possibly Paul was thinking of the wrath of God that is on every individual who fails to believe in Christ (John 3:36). Or the wrath may refer to the Tribulation which will assuredly **come upon them** because of their rejection of Jesus Christ. This was probably his thought since in other contexts in this epistle where he speaks of the wrath to come he has the Tribulation in mind. Though it is not known for sure which of these thoughts was in Paul's mind—all of them could have been—it is known that the wrath of God has indeed come on unbelievers who hinder gospel preaching in every one of the ways just mentioned. Perhaps Paul chose a general statement rather than a specific one because he had several things in mind. God's wrath had reached its full limit in regard to those individuals.

Why did Paul get so excited about the fate of the Thessalonians' persecutors? It was not out of personal hatred for them (Rom. 9:1-5). Rather it was to emphasize the seriousness of hindering the preaching of the gospel. This message was transforming the Thessalonian believers, and they were heralding it to others far and wide. These verses illustrate how important it is that the gospel reach everybody (Matt. 28:19-20).

C. Concerns for the Thessalonians (2:17–3:13)

At this point the Holy Spirit directed Paul's thoughts from his visit to Thessalonica to more recent developments in his relationship with that church.

1. PAUL'S PLANS (2:17-20)

Quite obviously, from the extent to which he went in explaining his failure to return to Thessalonica, Paul wanted to give a clear and persuasive explanation of his activities. Evidently some people in Thessalonica were questioning or criticizing his conduct.

2:17. But contrasts Paul's experiences, which he was about to relate (3:1-10), with those of the Thessalonian brethren, which he had just narrated.

This verse is most revealing of Paul's feelings for those believers. He used the term of endearment in addressing them again: **brothers.** He described his departure from them as a turning away forced on him by circumstances beyond his control. The verb (*aporphanisthentes*) means literally "to be orphaned" and is used only here in the New Testament. To Paul it was as though his family were being **torn** apart when he left them. He hoped the separation would be brief, but it broke his heart to leave them as infant babes in Christ. Though he had left them physically, they were still prominent in his thoughts; they were not "out of sight, out of mind."

Paul and his companions had tried to return to Thessalonica on several occasions because of the intense longing they felt for their brethren. The care and feeding of new Christians was not just an obligation those missionaries felt toward God; it was something they longed with all their hearts to be able to do, because of the love of Christ, in spite of the personal danger that faced them in Thessalonica.

2:18. Paul blamed **Satan** for his failure to be able to return. Was Satan responsible, or was God, or were other people? Paul's reason for deciding to return was to provide additional spiritual help for the new converts. This by itself is clearly the will of God in any situation. Seen as such, any hindrance becomes opposition to the will of God. Regardless of who was involved on the human level, the ultimate leader of this kind of opposition is Satan. As John Calvin wrote, "Whenever the ungodly cause us trouble, they are fighting under the banner of Satan, and are his instruments for harassing us" (*The Epistles of Paul the Apostle to the Romans and to the Thessalonians*, p.

351). God permitted this to happen, but He is no more responsible for it than He is for any sin which His creatures commit and which He permits.

It is unusual that Paul inserted his name in the letter at this point; he rarely did so in his inspired writings. The reason here may be that he wished to emphasize again in a different way that it was he himself who truly felt this way. He did not try to return just once, but **again and again** he sought ways to get back to Thessalonica.

2:19-20. Paul's affection rose to its climax in this almost lyrical passage. The Philippian believers were the only others who received such warm words of personal love from Paul.

He voiced a rhetorical question to heighten the intensity of his fervor. In effect he asked what would be the greatest blessing he could possibly receive at the judgment seat of Christ. They were! They were everything that was worth anything to Paul. They were his **hope;** their development was what he lived for as a parent lives to see his children grow up to maturity, to produce and reproduce. They were his **joy,** they filled his life with sunshine as he thought of what they used to be, what they had become, and what they would be by the grace of God. They were his **crown;** they themselves were the symbol of God's blessing on his life and ministry. They were his **glory and joy,** and not only his but also the glory and joy of his companions in labor. Paul said in essence, "When life is over and we stand in the presence of our Lord Jesus at His coming, you Thessalonians will be our source of glory and joy; you mean that much to us."

This profession of affection should have removed any thoughts from the Thessalonian Christians' minds that Paul had not returned because he was unconcerned or selfish.

2. TIMOTHY'S VISIT (3:1-5)

The thought begun in 2:17 continues in this section. Paul again stated his sincere concern for the Thessalonians.

3:1. Circumstances prohibited Paul from returning to Thessalonica personally, so he and Silas decided to send Timothy back to encourage the saints. Evidently Paul traveled from Berea to **Athens** without the companionship of

Timothy and Silas. When he reached Athens he sent word back to Berea (by the Berean Christians who had accompanied him) for Timothy and Silas to join him in Athens as soon as possible (Acts 17:15). Apparently Timothy and Silas did so. Their mutual concern for the Thessalonian church led Paul and Silas to dispatch Timothy to Thessalonica (1 Thes. 3:1-2). Silas also returned to Macedonia shortly after Timothy's departure, probably to check on the Philippian church. Silas and Timothy both returned to Macedonia to rejoin Paul in Corinth, Paul's next port of call after Athens (Acts 18:1, 5).

3:2. Paul's description of **Timothy** seems to imply that the young man needed more than Paul's normal endorsement. Perhaps because of his youth Timothy was not as readily recognized and respected as his older fellow missionaries. Paul called Timothy **our brother,** suggesting equality in the Lord's work with Paul and Silas. In relation to the Lord, Timothy was a hardworking servant, suggestive of his zeal and humility. He was a brother-servant in **spreading the gospel of Christ.**

Timothy's mission was to have been a positive blessing and help to the Thessalonian Christians. He was to **strengthen** (*stērizai;* cf. v. 13) them, to make them firm and solid in the faith. He was also sent to **encourage** (*parakalesai;* cf. 2:12) them by providing what they needed to fight the good fight of **faith,** individually and collectively. Much of the ministry of the apostles was devoted to grounding new converts in the faith, a ministry as necessary today as it was in the first century.

3:3. Another purpose of Timothy's visit was that the Christians would not lose their spiritual balance and stability as a result of the **trials** they were experiencing (cf. 2:14). The word *sainesthai,* translated **unsettled,** is used of a dog wagging its tail and paints a picture of the Thessalonians going back and forth because of their persecutions.

Paul added his own stabilizing reminder that trials are not necessarily a sign of God's disfavor, but are part of every Christian's legacy. When trouble comes, Christians often react by doubting that they are where God wants them to be; they often think that they have done

something wrong and that God must be displeased with them. Even some mature Christians react this way, as evidenced by Paul's words of reassurance to Timothy many years later. "Everyone who wants to live a godly life in Christ Jesus will be persecuted" (2 Tim. 3:12). Yet storms often come to believers to make them able to stand firm, rather than to blow them away (cf. 2 Cor. 4:15-16).

3:4. Paul reminded his readers that when he was **with** them he kept telling them to expect persecution. And circumstances had **turned out** just as he had predicted. This reminder would have helped calm them down.

3:5. Returning to his original thought (cf. v. 2) Paul explained that he had sent Timothy back to Thessalonica because he was genuinely concerned for their spiritual welfare. The condition of the believers' **faith** burdened Paul's heart. Were they still trusting in God or had they abandoned Him and returned to paganism? Paul was not concerned that they had lost their salvation; this they could never do (1:4). They could, however, have ceased to walk by faith, not trusting God in all circumstances of life. Paul's concern was that his labor **might have been** in vain, not that their faith had been in vain. Paul's reference to the **tempter** is mindful of Satan's activity in the Garden of Eden (Gen. 3) and in the Judean wilderness (Matt. 4). Paul saw Satan as using the persecution the Thessalonians were undergoing in order to lure them away from what they knew to be God's will, namely, perseverance in the midst of trials. He was concerned that Satan might snatch away the seed Paul had sown before it had a chance to put down stabilizing, fructifying roots.

3. TIMOTHY'S REPORT (3:6-10)

From 2:1 through 3:5 Paul related what had happened in the last few months. Starting with 3:6 he moved to the present.

3:6. But contrasts Paul's previous anxiety with his present relief at the report of **Timothy** who returned to Paul in Corinth. Rather than bringing bad news that the Thessalonians' faith had wavered, Timothy had brought good news that their **faith** was bearing fruit in **love.** This **good news** was as thrilling to

Paul as the gospel; he used the same Greek word for both messages.

The Thessalonians were strong in faith toward God and love toward His apostles (cf. 1:3). Though Paul did not mention their hope explicitly here, he did so implicitly by referring to their desire **to see** the apostles again; they were looking forward to this. The fact that the Thessalonians looked back on the visit of the missionaries with **pleasant memories** and looked forward to seeing them again evidenced their genuine love for the apostles. Paul loved them too, and reminded them by restating his longing **to see** them again.

3:7. Timothy's report came as sweet relief to the anxious missionaries. They were indeed brethren, bound not only by the bonds of life in Christ, but also by the bonds of love for one another. As Paul and more recently Timothy had been sources of encouragement to the Thessalonians in their **persecution,** so now the babes in Christ had provided encouragement to their elder brethren who had been persecuted by fears about that church's condition.

3:8. Nothing filled the apostles with joy like news that their converts were **standing firm in the Lord.** This was the desired result in all their ministry; in this they found their greatest fulfillment. "Standing firm" (*stēkete;* cf. 2 Thes. 2:15) in the faith is really "standing firm in the Lord." Such a relationship strengthens one to withstand the storms of life.

3:9. The force of Paul's rhetorical question is, "We cannot **thank God enough for you** because of **all the joy** you have brought to our hearts by your endurance in these trials." It is noteworthy that Paul thanked *God* for the Thessalonians' behavior; *he* did not take credit for this. Paul acknowledged that their endurance was really a tribute to the work of God in them (cf. Phil. 2:13). He commended the Thessalonians, but also recognized and acknowledged the hand of God at work in their lives.

3:10. News of the Thessalonians' perseverance did not relieve Paul of his desire to return to them. Though they were enduring a trial of their faith they still needed more instruction and more growth. Paul wanted to **supply what was lacking in** their **faith.** (The word for "supply" is *katartisai;* cf. Eph. 4:12 where

pros ton katartismon is rendered "to prepare" [NIV] and "for the equipping" [NASB].) The Thessalonians were like tender young plants; their tender roots held them firm against the present storm, but they still needed to grow and mature. This is the first explicit reference to deficiencies in their spiritual condition—deficiencies due more to immaturity than to waywardness. Up till now Paul described them as having the characteristics of new Christians. Now he said they were deficient in certain respects, as a child is deficient in comparison with an adult. In chapters 4 and 5 Paul ministered to some of these deficiencies.

This verse gives another glimpse into the Apostle Paul's private life. He prayed **night and day . . . most earnestly** that God would let him **see** them **again.** That is, he prayed by night and by day, not all night and all day. This and other similar references (cf. 1:2; 2:13) demonstrate the truth of the statement, "It is evident from St. Paul's Epistles that a very large part of his private life was occupied in prayer and thanksgiving to God" (G. W. Garrod, *The First Epistle to the Thessalonians,* London: Macmillan & Co., 1899, p. 89).

4. PAUL'S PRAYER (3:11-13)

The first major section of the epistle, largely personal, closes with a statement in the form of a wish, something for which Paul prayed to God. Verses 11-13 amplify verse 10.

3:11. Paul was praying that he could return to Thessalonica (v. 10); here he expressed the same desire more strongly in a wish before God. **God** was the object of his prayer. He is called the **Father** of Paul and his missionary brethren and the Thessalonian believers. The **Lord Jesus** is addressed equally in prayer with the Father. The fact that Jesus is God is further highlighted by Paul's use of a singular verb (trans. "clear") with a plural subject: "may He **clear the way,** even the Father and Jesus," not "may They clear the way." "One can hardly conceive of a stronger way for Paul to indicate his unquestioning acceptance of the lordship of Jesus and His oneness with the Father" (D. Edmond Hiebert, *The Thessalonian Epistles,* p. 154).

3:12. The Thessalonians were already noted for their **love,** but Paul prayed that it might abound—**increase**

(*pleonasai*) **and overflow** (*perisseusai*)—even more. "Genuine Christian love . . . is the one thing in the Christian life which cannot be carried to excess" (Hiebert, *The Thessalonian Epistles,* p. 155). The image of love overflowing its container suggests that Christian love is something that wells up from within a person naturally. Paul was concerned that it overflow to **everyone,** not just to Christians in the church. His love was their model.

3:13. The Thessalonians needed strengthening by God in their inner beings. The word **strengthen** (*stērizai*), used by Paul in verse 2, describes Timothy's strengthening of the Thessalonians in their faith. Paul did not pray that they would be sinless; that was impossible. He prayed that they would **be blameless** (cf. 2:10), that is, that after they sinned they would deal with it as God requires and so be free from any reasonable charge by their fellowmen. Before God they should be **holy,** separated to **God** in their hearts and habits. Paul longed that when Jesus Christ would return He would find them blameless before men and holy before God. The **holy ones** accompanying Christ at His coming are probably the souls of the saints who have departed this life and gone to be with Christ, whose bodies will be resurrected when He comes (4:16). That is, they are Christians rather than angels.

III. Practical Instructions and Exhortations (4:1–5:24)

Chapters 4 and 5 constitute the second major division of 1 Thessalonians. Whereas chapters 1–3 contain personal messages of commendation for the Thessalonians and explanations of the missionaries' activities and motives, chapters 4–5 record practical instruction in matters of the Thessalonians' deficiencies, plus practical exhortations to proper behavior in view of the truth.

A. Christian living (4:1-12)

This section concerns three aspects of proper Christian living: one general, on conduct; and two specific, about sexual purity and brotherly love.

1. GENERAL CONDUCT (4:1-2)

4:1. The word with which Paul began chapter 4, **Finally,** was not intended to announce the conclusion of the epistle,

as is obvious from all that follows (cf. "Finally" in Phil. 3:1, which is followed by two chapters, as it is here in 1 Thes.). It introduces the final major section of the letter. These chapters deal with "what is lacking in your faith" (3:10). Again Paul reminded his readers of his words to them while in Thessalonica. He moved from their present condition to their next stage of spiritual development. They had responded to Paul's teaching on Christian living. Someone has said that everyone lives to please someone: himself, his spouse, his parents, his child, his God, or someone else. Paul focused motivation for correct living on love for God. Many people regard the Christian life as a set of rules to be obeyed, or a list of prohibitions to avoid; but Paul regarded it as the outworking of a loving desire to **please God** who had chosen him (1:4). His attitude helped prepare his readers to respond positively to his following exhortations.

These instructions were not intended to move the readers to behave differently, but to do more of the same. This conduct was so important that Paul not only asked but urged them to press on (**urge** is *parakaloumen,* also used in v. 10; in 2:12 the participle from the same verb is rendered "encouraging" and in 3:2 and 4:18 the verb is translated "encourage"). Paul added even more power to his exhortation by urging them **in the Lord Jesus** (cf. 2 Thes. 3:12); he wrote in the Spirit and with the authority of Jesus Christ. Paul claimed to speak for Christ in this matter. And he asked them to do so **more and more** (cf. 1 Thes. 4:10).

4:2. So they might not miss this rather subtle emphasis, Paul restated it more clearly here. He said they knew the **instructions** (*parangelias*) he had given them in Jesus' **authority** (cf. v. 1). What he and his fellow missionaries had preached to the Thessalonians they had announced as the gospel of Christ (3:2). The present message came to them with the same authority. Sometimes Christians want to hear new truth when what they need is exhortation to excel still more, to press on to greater experiencing of old truths which they are already practicing to a limited degree.

2. SEXUAL PURITY (4:3-8)

The general exhortation of verses 1-2 is followed by two specific exhortations. The first has to do with sexual purity.

4:3. The will of God is clearly set forth in many places in Scripture, even though Christians often seem to have a great deal of difficulty applying it in everyday decision-making (cf. 5:16-18; 1 Peter 2:15). It is **God's** clear **will** that His people **be holy** (*hagiasmos;* cf. 1 Thes. 3:13). This word can mean a state of being set apart from sin to God, or the process of becoming more dedicated to God. Probably the latter meaning was intended by Paul here. He was not referring to the final state of all Christians when they will be separated from the presence of sin as well as its penalty and power. Rather he probably had in mind the progressive sanctification of his readers by which they were conformed to the image of Christ in daily experiences by proper responses to the Word and the Spirit of God. This is evident by the three statements in verses 3b-6a, each beginning with the word **that.**

The first instruction designed to produce greater holiness is abstinence from **sexual immorality.** Paul called his readers to **avoid** it, implying the need for exercising self-discipline, enabled by God's Spirit. Christians are to avoid and abstain from any and every form of sexual practice that lies outside the circle of God's revealed will, namely adultery, premarital and extramarital intercourse, homosexuality, and other perversions. The word *porneia,* translated "sexual immorality," is a broad one and includes all these practices. The Thessalonians lived in a pagan environment in which sexual looseness was not only practiced openly but was also encouraged. In Greek religion, prostitution was considered a priestly prerogative, and extramarital sex was sometimes an act of worship. To a Christian the will of God is clear: holiness and sexual immorality are mutually exclusive. No appeal to Christian liberty can justify fornication.

4:4. Paul emphasized the same truth in a positive way by expanding on this prohibition. One avoids sexual immorality by learning how to **control his own body** with its passions. Self-control in response to one's sexual desires, Paul taught, could and must be learned. Christians are not the victims of circumstances or their fleshly passions. Sexual desire can be controlled by the Christian through God's power. Paul did not specify how to control one's passions. He implied that there may be several ways. But the Christian should choose a method that is both **holy** (*hagiasmō*) **and honorable** (*timē*). That is, the action taken as an alternative to sexual immorality must be behavior that is set apart to the Lord in its motivation and recognized by others as intrinsically worthy of respect (cf. 1 Cor. 6:13-20). Each Christian is responsible for his own body and behavior, not his neighbor's (cf. 1 Cor. 10:13). Every young Christian, like the Thessalonians, **should learn** how to deal appropriately with sexual temptations.

4:5. They were not to deal with it as the **heathen** did, by indulging **in passionate lust** (*en pathei epithymias*). Such behavior is a mark of heathenism. A heathen is one who does **not know God.** Here Paul put his finger on the key to overcoming sexual temptations. A Christian can overcome because he knows God; this makes all the difference! Paul did not say that the heathen do not know *about* God. The reason they behave as they do is because they do not know God personally, even though they may know about Him. When a person comes to know God by faith in Jesus Christ, not only do his attitudes toward sex change, but he also discovers that God gives him the ability to act toward sexual temptation as he could not before. Knowing God is basic to living a holy life. This is why maintaining a vital relationship with God is essential to maintaining a clean walk before God.

4:6. In the previous two verses Paul's appeal was based on the importance of sexual purity for the sake of the Christian himself. In this verse Paul appealed on the basis of the other person involved in the immoral act. The **brother** here is most likely another human, not necessarily another Christian male. This seems clear from the fact that this person is a victim of illicit sex. Sexual immorality wrongs the partner in the forbidden act by involving him or her in behavior contrary to God's will and therefore under His judgment. Two or more people practicing sex out of God's will are calling God's wrath

701

down on themselves (Heb. 13:4). The initiator of the act takes advantage of his partner in sin by fanning the fire of passion till self-control is lost.

Paul then cited two reasons (1 Thes. 4:6b-7) why sexual immorality should be avoided. First, sexual immorality is sin, and God will judge all sin (Rom. 6:23a). **All such sins** refers most likely to the various forms of sexual uncleanness not specifically mentioned in the context but covered by the general term "sexual immorality." Everyone who fears the wrath of God should abstain from immorality because judgment follows such sin as surely as day follows night. That God always judges sin is a basic Christian truth which Paul had taught them and **warned** them about when he was in Thessalonica.

4:7. A second reason to avoid sexual immorality is that it goes against God's calling for a Christian. Paul's first reason (v. 6b) looks forward to the prospect of future punishment, but his second reason looks back to the purpose for which God called each Christian to Himself. God's plan for a Christian includes purifying his life. Sexual immorality frustrates the purpose of God's call. Certain pagan cults promoted unclean ceremonies, but Christ's plans for a Christian are to clean him up. **A holy life** demonstrates God's supernatural power at work overcoming what is natural, and it glorifies God. The Greek noun *hagiasmos* ("holiness") occurs here for the fourth time in eight verses (3:13; 4:3-4). (The verb *hagiazō* ["sanctify"] is used in 5:23.)

4:8. In this verse Paul drew a conclusion based on his preceding arguments. Sexual purity is grounded in the revelations of **God** concerning His judgment of sin and His calling to holiness. Sexual purity is simply a practical application of basic doctrine. Paul's attitudes toward sexual uncleanness did not arise from his background or personal preferences. They were the logical consequences of divine revelation. The Thessalonians and later readers of this epistle should realize that to **reject** these instructions is to reject the Person from whom they came originally, that is, God.

Lest anyone feel that God is asking more than is reasonable of weak mortals, Paul concluded this exhortation with a reminder that God has also given believ-ers His indwelling Spirit. This Person of the Trinity is so characterized by holiness that He is called the **Holy Spirit.** The indwelling Holy Spirit has power enough to enable any Christian to learn how to control his own body, even in a pagan, immoral climate. The exhortation is to avoid sexual immorality; the enablement comes from the Holy Spirit.

3. BROTHERLY LOVE (4:9-12)

The second specific exhortation regarding Christian living accentuates the positive. Though sexual impurity is a danger to be avoided (vv. 3-8), loving other Christians is a practice to be cultivated. Both deal with the general subject of loving one's neighbor as himself, the basic horizontal aspect of Christian living.

4:9. Some instructions for Christians come through their brethren in Christ. But other lessons are **taught by God** to His children directly, things that almost intuitively seem right for a Christian to do. Loving other Christians is such a lesson. Christians quickly learn that there is a real kinship between believers, and they relate to other Christians in a way they do not relate to those outside God's family. The Thessalonians had already learned **to love each other** even though they were new Christians. Paul pointed out that God Himself had **taught** them this.

4:10. Paul did not need to write and tell them to love one another, but he did need to write and urge them to do this **more and more** (cf. v. 1). The evidence that they had learned the lesson of brotherly love was their deep, selfless, giving affection for Christians in others parts of their province of **Macedonia.** These were their neighbors in Philippi, Berea, and perhaps other towns where Christians lived. Paul commended believers for their love when he wrote the churches (cf. 2 Cor. 8:1-5). Yet there was still room for improvement, perhaps in the persistence and consistency of their love.

4:11. Everyday habits of living manifest love of the brethren as do more special demonstrations of affection. It is these habits that Paul suggested the Thessalonians ponder in the light of brotherly love. He suggested these goals as worthy objectives for their maturing love. His words may reflect less than ideal conditions in their church.

First, his readers should lead a restful life. The word translated **quiet** (*hēsychazein*) means quiet in the sense of restfulness (cf. Acts 22:2; 2 Thes. 3:12; 1 Tim. 2:2, 11), rather than quiet as opposed to talkativeness (*sigaō;* cf. Acts 21:40; 1 Cor. 14:34). The former means "undisturbed, settled, not noisy," while the latter means "silent." Paul was telling the Thessalonians to be less frantic, not less exuberant. A person who is constantly on the move is frequently a bother to other people as well as somewhat distracted from his own walk with God. The latter can lead to the former. But a Christian who strives to be at peace with himself and God will be a source of peace to his brethren. Such quietude constitutes a practical demonstration of love for others.

Second, Paul recommended minding one's **own business.** The connection with love for the brethren is obvious (cf. Prov. 25:17).

Third, working with one's own hands demonstrates love for the brethren because a self-supporting person is not a burden to others. Paul himself set the example by working **with** his **hands** when he was in Thessalonica (1 Thes. 2:9). Too restful a life can be a problem also, and Paul guarded against that with this instruction. This verse dignifies manual labor. The reference also suggests that many, perhaps most, in the church came out of the working class. The Greeks deplored manual labor and relegated it to slaves as much as possible. But the Jews held it in esteem; every Jewish boy was taught a trade regardless of his family's wealth. Work itself is a blessing, and working with one's hands should never be despised by Christians. A man who is willing to work with his hands demonstrates his love for his brethren by being willing to humble himself to provide for his own needs so that he does not depend on others but provides for himself.

4:12. There are good reasons for these exhortations. Such behavior does **win the respect** of non-Christians and so glorifies the Christian's God. Love of this kind is appreciated by everyone. Paul placed importance on the testimony of Christians before **outsiders,** unbelievers. This kind of behavior also wins the respect of Christians; people appreciate those who do not take advantage of them.

Paul discouraged the Thessalonians from expecting financial favors from the brethren simply because they were fellow Christians. Nor was he promoting a fierce spirit of independence; he was not saying that every Christian must become completely self-sufficient. He was advocating personal responsibility, as is clear from the context. This is a manifestation of mature Christian love for the brethren.

B. The Rapture (4:13-18)

The Apostle Paul turned his attention to another area of deficiency in the Thessalonians' understanding, which had probably come to his attention through Timothy. Though Paul had already mentioned the future in this letter (1:10; 2:12, 19; 3:13), he turned to it again and devoted considerable space to instruction and exhortations dealing with Christ's return (4:13–5:11). The subject of the rest of chapter 4 is the relationship of the Lord's return to believers who had died. This is the classic passage in the Bible on the Rapture of the church.

4:13. Paul introduced these instructions in such a way as to lay no guilt on the Thessalonians for their lack of knowledge. After all, they were new believers. He again called them **brothers,** emphasizing their equality of standing before God despite their knowledge deficiency.

Those who fall asleep are Christians who die. The figure of sleep for death is common in the New Testament (cf. Mark 5:39; John 11:11). This is not sleep of the soul, however, because Paul wrote elsewhere that a Christian who is absent from his body is present with the Lord (2 Cor. 5:8; cf. Phil. 1:23; 1 Thes. 5:10). It is rather the "sleep" of the body in the earth until it is resurrected, changed into a glorious body, and reunited with the soul (1 Cor. 15:35-57; 2 Cor. 5:1-9).

Paul wanted the Thessalonians to be neither ignorant nor grieving **like the rest of men,** that is, like unbelievers, over the death of fellow believers. Christians do grieve over the loss of loved ones; this is a normal human experience which even Jesus shared (John 11:35). But the grief of Christians differs from that of unbelievers, for the latter **have no hope** of bodily resurrection to glory with Christ (1 Thes. 4:16).

4:14. Two reasons why Christians should not grieve like unbelievers are that

Christians have a revelation from God that gives them hope and they have a glorious future with Christ. Just as certainly as **Jesus died and** was resurrected by the Father, so **God will** unite the resurrected dead in Christ with their Savior at His coming.

The death and resurrection of Jesus Christ are among the best-attested facts of history. Since Christians know these events took place, they can be equally certain, Paul said, that the souls of believers who have died will return with Christ when He comes for His living saints. The prophecy of the Rapture is as sure to be fulfilled as the prophecies of Christ's death and resurrection.

4:15. The revelation of this resurrection came from Jesus Christ Himself. How it came to Paul is not known, but perhaps it was a direct revelation. Not only will the souls of the dead in Christ return with Him (v. 14), but their bodies will also be resurrected at His coming. The bodies of dead Christians will be resurrected immediately before living Christians are conveyed upward.

Clearly Paul believed that he and his Thessalonian readers might well be **alive** when the Lord returned. He believed that the Rapture was imminent, that it could take place at any moment (cf. 1:10; 1 Cor. 7:29, "the time is short"; Phil. 4:5, "The Lord is near"). And this truth of imminency brought comfort (1 Thes. 4:18).

4:16. Jesus Christ now sits at the right hand of God in **heaven** (Rom. 8:34; Eph. 1:20; Col. 3:1; Heb. 1:3). He will leave this position and descend to the earth. By the words **the Lord Himself** Paul emphasized that it would be the same Jesus who had ascended through the clouds (cf. Acts 1:11).

The sounds mentioned in this verse—**a loud command, with the voice of the archangel and with the trumpet call of God**—are difficult to interpret. Who will voice the loud shout? Will it be Jesus Himself (cf. John 11:43), or the archangel Michael (Dan. 10:13; Jude 9), or another angel? Is this a literal trumpet call, or was Paul speaking figuratively in describing the call of God by which He will announce the Advent of His Son? (cf. 1 Cor. 15:52) These three phenomena may all refer to the same thing, but probably they are three separate almost simultaneous announcements heralding

Christ's return. Though one's curiosity about these aspects of the Rapture is not fully satisfied in this passage, one thing is clear: Christ's return for His saints will be announced from heaven forcefully and dramatically.

Then **the dead in Christ will** be resurrected, that is, believers of this dispensation will be raised. Old Testament saints will evidently be raised at the end of the Great Tribulation (Dan. 12:2), for the phrase "in Christ" refers exclusively to Church-Age saints. The bodies of the dead in Christ will **rise** before the living Christians are caught up to meet the Lord in the air (1 Thes. 4:17).

How will God raise the bodies of people who were buried hundreds of years ago? What about the bodies of those Christians who were burned to death and those whose ashes were thrown to the wind, and Christians who perished at sea? The resurrection of the dead poses a great problem to the faith of many. Perhaps that is why Paul stressed that this revelation came from Jesus Christ Himself and that it is as certain of future fulfillment as Jesus' resurrection is a fact of past history. The God who created the universe out of nothing with a word is fully able to reassemble the decayed bodies of all His saints in a moment of time (cf. 1 Cor. 15:35-58).

4:17. Whereas the previous verse explains the future of dead saints at Christ's return, this one deals with what will happen to living believers (cf. 1 Cor. 15:51-52). After the bodies of dead Christians have been raised, those **who are still alive** and have been **left** behind momentarily **will be caught up with them in the clouds to meet the Lord in the air.** Again Paul, by using the word **we** ("we who are still alive and are left"; cf. 1 Thes. 4:15), put himself in the living group; he thought that Christ would probably return in his lifetime, or at least he allowed for its possibility. Only a moment will separate the resurrection of the dead and the translation of the living (1 Cor. 15:51-52). In Latin the word for "caught up" is *rapturo,* from which comes the term "Rapture." This is the Rapture of the church, when Christians are caught up to meet Christ in the clouds (cf. Acts 1:9). The events described here and in the parallel passage, 1 Corinthians 15, differ considerably from those that will accompany Christ's return to the earth to set up His earthly kingdom (Rev. 19:11-21). This difference substantiates the distinction between the Rapture and the Second Coming.

The resurrected or translated bodies of all Christians will be united with Christ and with each other at the Rapture. From that time on and forever thereafter they will be with the Lord. The Lord will take living believers to the place He is presently preparing for them (John 14:2-3). But the place where Christians will be was not so important to Paul as the Person with whom they will be. "The entire content and worth of heaven, the entire blessedness of life eternal, is for Paul embraced in the one thought of being united with Jesus, his Savior and Lord" (Borhemann, quoted by George G. Findlay, *The Epistles of Paul the Apostle to the Thessalonians*, Cambridge: University Press, 1904, p. 103).

4:18. The logical and practical outcome of this revelation is comfort and encouragement. Paul applied his eschatology to life and called on his readers to **encourage** (*parakaleite*; cf. 2:12; 3:2) **each other with these words.** The facts that Christians who have died will be resurrected to join the living saints with the Lord Jesus when He comes, that they will actually precede those who are alive in that day, that those who are alive will be united with them, and that they will all be with the Lord forever, give abundant reasons for rejoicing. Not only do Christians not grieve like unbelievers, but followers of Christ can actually look forward eagerly to that great day. This is the great hope of the church, to see the Lord and be united with Him forever. It is that which every believer in this Age should anticipate. It is a blessed hope (Titus 2:13) with respect to the dead in Christ as well as for the living!

C. Personal watchfulness (5:1-11)

The preceding section (4:13-18) presented a joyful hope; this one gives a solemn warning. The Thessalonians had not heard the first exhortation before (4:18); they had heard this one.

1. THE DAY OF THE LORD (5:1-3)

Paul introduced a new aspect of the subject of the Lord's appearing. His scope of attention broadened from the Rapture to the longer period of history after the Rapture, namely, the day of the Lord. In these verses the emphasis is on the unpredictability of the time of the Lord's return.

5:1. Paul's affectionate tone continues with the word **brothers** again. **Times and dates** refers to the ages (*chronōn*) and events (*kairōn*) preceding the day of the Lord. Paul did not **need to** expound fully on this subject as he had done with the Rapture, since he had already instructed them about the day of the Lord.

5:2. The **day of the Lord** is a future period of time in which God will be at work in world affairs more directly and dramatically than He has been since the earthly ministry of the Lord Jesus Christ. It is a time referred to by many Old Testament prophets (e.g., Isa. 13:9-11; Joel 2:28-32; Zeph. 1:14-18; 3:14-15). As these and other Old Testament verses indicate, the day of the Lord will include both judgment and blessing. That day begins immediately after the Rapture of the church and ends with the conclusion of the Millennium. This day is a major theme of prophecy with its fullest exposition in Revelation 6–19.

This period of history **will come** as a surprise to those on the earth at the time, **like** the visit of **a thief** to a sleeping homeowner (cf. Matt. 24:43-44; Luke 12:39-40). But the thief **in the night** illustration should not be pressed too far. The point is that this day will come unexpectedly, not necessarily that it will take place at night. Obviously it will be night in some parts of the world and daytime in other parts.

5:3. This day will begin when world conditions appear calm rather than calamitous. This peace will come with the signing of the seven-year covenant, predicted in Daniel 9:27. Note that Paul did not include himself and his readers with the group who would see the day of the Lord, as he did when describing the Rapture (1 Thes. 4:15, 17). Evidently **them** refers to those left behind at the Rapture, that is, non-Christians. They will be ignorantly expecting **peace and safety,** but instead **destruction will come on them.** This "destruction" (*olethros*; cf. 2 Thes. 1:9) is not annihilation, but the breaking up of their peace and security through the outpouring of God's wrath on earth in the Great Tribulation. Destruction will come

suddenly. The illustration of the commencement of labor pains suggests both unpredictable suddenness and great personal discomfort (cf. Matt. 24:8; Mark 13:8). The wrath of God that will have been building up over some time will suddenly break forth. The signs of its coming are discernible, even though the moment of its arrival is unpredictable. No more can the world escape the coming wrath of God, when it breaks out on the day of the Lord, than **a pregnant woman** can escape **labor pains.** A strong expression is used in the Greek (a double negative: *ou mē*) to stress that fleeing (*ekphygōsin*) will be futile.

2. CONSEQUENT PREPAREDNESS (5:4-11)

In this section Paul applied the doctrine of the day of the Lord to his readers.

5:4. His readers were not "in the dark" with regard to these things; they had been taught about them before. But Paul meant more than this. His readers were not in the same group who would be surprised by **this day.** Their sphere of life was **not in the darkness,** but in the light (cf. Col. 1:13). Instructed Christians should not be surprised by the dawning of **this day** of the Lord; they have been told it is coming. It will not take believers by surprise because they will by then be with the Lord (1 Thes. 4:13-18).

5:5. Christians live in a different sphere of life from non-Christians; it is the difference between day and night (cf. Eph. 5:8). Christians are **sons of the light;** they are also **sons of the day.** That is, they have illumination, and they also live in a realm characterized by light, warmth, and growth. Paul brought himself into the picture (**we**) to prepare for his following exhortation which would be more true to life and readily received if he included himself, than if he directed it only toward the Thessalonians.

5:6. Paul's exhortation was for his readers to behave in keeping with their enlightened condition and to be prepared in view of the day of the Lord. He presented this exhortation as a logical conclusion from what preceded. Besides being logical to behave this way, it is also a necessary duty. Christians should not be indifferent to the reality of the Lord's return; they should not be **asleep** on the job. The word for "asleep" (*katheudōmen;* cf. v. 10) differs from the one used thrice

in 4:13-15 where it means death (*koimaō*). Here it means spiritual lethargy and insensitivity. This is the condition of the unsaved, the **others.** Christians, on the other hand, should be watchful and soberly waiting for the Lord's return (1 Cor. 1:7; Titus 2:13; Heb. 9:28; 2 Peter 3:12), and **self-controlled** (1 Thes. 5:6), maintaining self-discipline in view of the great events to come.

5:7. Unbelievers are neither awake nor alert to these spiritual realities. Rather they are asleep and controlled by forces outside themselves—like those who are **drunk**—which render them unable to respond as they should. These are the normal characteristics of those who live in the sphere of **night.**

5:8. In keeping with the sober attitude just described, Paul used the metaphor of a soldier, one of his favorite illustrations of the Christian (Rom. 13:12b; Eph. 6:10-18; 1 Tim. 6:12; 2 Tim. 2:3-4; 4:7a). He based his exhortation on the Christians' position: because they **belong to the day,** they should live accordingly. Standing on the threshold of an event that will mean sudden translation for some and sudden destruction for others, Christians should arm themselves for action with self-control. A Roman **breastplate** covered a soldier from his neck to his waist and protected most of his vital organs (cf. Eph. 6:14). That is what Christians' **faith and love** do. Faith in God protects inwardly and love for people protects outwardly. These two graces cannot be separated; if one believes in God he will also love other people (cf. 1 Thes. 1:3; 3:5). These attitudes equip Christians to stand ready for the Rapture. In addition, **the hope of salvation** guards their heads from attacks on their thinking. The salvation they look forward to is deliverance from the wrath to come when the Lord returns, as is clear from the context. It is not a wishful longing that someday they might be saved eternally. Such a thought is entirely foreign to the New Testament. Followers of Christ have a sure hope; they are not as others who have no hope.

5:9. For (*hoti,* "because") introduces another reason why believers should prepare themselves. God's intention for them is not the **wrath** that will come on the earth in the day of the Lord, but the full **salvation** that will be theirs when the

Lord returns for them in the clouds. The wrath of God referred to here clearly refers to the Tribulation; the context makes this apparent. Deliverance from that wrath is God's appointment for believers. This temporal salvation comes through the **Lord Jesus Christ** just as does eternal salvation.

5:10. What did Paul mean by **whether we are awake or asleep?** Did he mean "whether we are alive or dead," or "whether we are spiritually alert or lethargic"? It seems that he meant the latter because he used the same words for "awake" (*grēgorōmen*) and "asleep" (*katheudōmen*) as he used in verse 6, where they clearly mean spiritually alert and spiritually lethargic. If so, then Paul's point is that Christians are assured of life **together with Him,** whether they are spiritually watchful or not. That they might live with Christ was His purpose in dying for them. They *will* escape God's wrath whether they are watchful or not (cf. 1:10). This is a powerful argument for a pretribulational Rapture.

Paul wrote that Christ **died,** not that He was killed. Jesus Christ laid down His life; no man took it from Him (John 10:18). And He died **for us** (cf. 2 Cor. 5:21). This simple statement of the substitutionary nature of the death of Christ required no elaboration for the Thessalonians. Doubtless Paul had emphasized this central doctrine when he first taught them in person; it is foundational.

5:11. The practical exhortation with which Paul concluded this section arose naturally from what he had explained. His readers were to **encourage** and **build up** (edify) **one another.** His own encouragement and edification in this letter were not enough. This new instruction needed constant repetition and reemphasis. It was to be added to the body of truth they already had received, and as they were encouraging each other in their meetings and in private conversations about other revealed truth they were to include this great truth as well. Believers do not need to be hearing something new all the time, but they often do need to remind themselves of what they already know so that they do not forget it. This verse gives some insight into the meetings of the early church. They included opportunity for mutual edification among the believers. Mutual encouragement and edifica-

tion are still needed in every local church. And encouragement and edification with reference to their hope in Christ's return is especially needed.

D. Church life (5:12-15)

In this passage Paul reminded his readers of their present responsibilities as believers in Christ. He turned from instructions regarding the future to exhortations for the present. His cryptic, almost abrupt style in this section may have been intended to bring them back from considerations of the future to the realities of their immediate responsibilities. First he gave them instructions concerning their relationships with their spiritual leaders.

1. ATTITUDE TOWARD LEADERS (5:12-13)

The following directions are addressed to the group as a whole, that is, to all Christians in the church.

5:12. The church leaders are probably the elders of the church in view of how they were described by Paul. These were men who worked **hard** to provide pastoral care for the flock, probably in their spare time since in the early church local church leaders often carried fulltime jobs outside the church. These leaders are further described as being **over you in the Lord.** They had positions of spiritual leadership in the church and were responsible to God for those under their care (cf. Heb. 13:17). This responsibility included providing admonition as needed. Since Paul used the plural **those** to describe their leaders, there was more than one such person in the Thessalonian church, as in other churches to whom Paul wrote (cf. Phil. 1:1).

Paul gave three exhortations to the church regarding their proper attitude toward their leaders. First, they were to **respect** them. This term (*eidenai*) normally means "to know," but here it includes appreciating and respecting them and their work.

5:13. The need to regard leaders highly is further stressed in the second exhortation. Church members are to esteem, value, and respect their leaders for their works' sake. The Greek is strong: **hold them in the highest regard** (*hēgeisthai autous hyperekperissōs*). This should be a continuing attitude. Some church leaders do not command as much personal respect as others, but Paul taught that all should be held in esteem because of the nature of their responsibilities before God. Not just some respect, but the highest respect is due these leaders, and it is to come from an attitude of affection (**in love**) for them, again, **because of their work**, if for no personal reason. Two reasons for this exhortation are the nature of their work and the fact that church leaders do a good service to others.

The third exhortation is to **live in peace with each other**. This results from obeying the former instructions. The idea here is to maintain rather than to initiate peace. Peaceful conditions existed in the Thessalonian church, but they had to continue. The command is imperative. Much dissension in modern churches is traceable to church members disobeying these commands.

2. RELATIONSHIPS AMONG THEMSELVES (5:14-15)

All church members, as well as church leaders, are responsible to minister to each other.

5:14. All Christians have four ongoing and continuous responsibilities to one another: (a) The **idle** need to be warned. Those who neglect their daily duties need to be stirred up to action. (b) The **timid** (*oligopsychous*, lit., "short of soul") need encouragement. These fainthearted people tend to become discouraged and despondent more easily than most. They need cheering up, stimulation to press on, and extra help to live the Christian life. (Interestingly the verbs in these two commands [*parakaloumen* and *paramytheisthe*] are in the same order as the first two participles in 2:12.) (c) The **weak** need **help.** These have not yet learned to lean on the Lord as much as they should for their spiritual needs. Until they do, they need strong support from other believers. Of course all Christians are weak and need the strength that comes from Christian fellowship, but the spiritually weak need it more than most. The fourth responsibility summarizes the preceding three: (d) **Be patient with everyone.** While other Christians are the primary focus of patience in this context, this charge is general enough to include all people. This ability to help others who are in some respect not as strong as

oneself requires nothing short of the love of God produced by the Holy Spirit (1 Cor. 13:4; Gal. 5:22).

5:15. The opposite of patience is retaliation in some form. Retaliation is not an option for a Christian. Even if the wrong done to him is an imposition by a needy brother, or an action springing from evil intent, the offended one never has the right to repay wrong with wrong (cf. Matt. 5:38-48; Rom. 12:17-21; 1 Peter 3:9). One's response should be to show kindness in such instances. Nor is it enough to abstain from evil; one is also to do positive good—**to be kind to each other.** Christians are to do this not in the sense that they will if they can, but in the sense that they earnestly work at it. This kind of response takes effort and must be continued.

E. Holy living (5:16-24)

This final group of instructions contains general exhortations for holy living.

1. PERSONAL LIVING (5:16-18)

These exhortations—dealing with attitudes—are addressed to believers as individuals concerning their personal lives before God.

5:16. God wants His people to be **joyful** and He gives them every reason to be. But Paul knew human nature well enough to sense the need for a reminder to rejoice at all times (cf. Phil. 3:1; 4:4). This is a command. A Christian's joy does not spring from his circumstances, but from the blessings that are his because he is in Christ. "The Christian who remains in sadness and depression really breaks a commandment: in some direction or other he mistrusts God—His power, providence, forgiveness" (A.J. Mason, "The Epistles of Paul the Apostle to the Thessalonians," in *Ellicott's Commentary on the Whole Bible*, vol. 8, p. 145). These two words (*pantote chairete*) constitute the shortest verse in the Greek New Testament.

5:17. Continual prayer is not prayer that prevails without any interruption, but prayer that continues whenever possible. The adverb for **continually** (*adialeiptōs*, also in 1:3) was used in Greek of a hacking cough. Paul was speaking of maintaining continuous fellowship with God as much as possible in the midst of daily living in which concentration is frequently broken.

5:18. The two previous commands deal with one's time ("always" and "continually"); this one deals with his **circumstances.** Christians are to **give thanks** to God in every circumstance of life. The fact that God works everything together for good for those who love Him (Rom. 8:28) is the basis for this entreaty.

These three exhortations in verses 16-18 are not just good advice; they are **God's will for** every Christian. They are not the totality of God's will, but they are a clear and important segment of it. God's will means joy, prayer, and thanksgiving for those who are **in Christ Jesus.**

2. CORPORATE LIVING (5:19-22)

Whereas the preceding verses stress individual responsibility in personal behavior, these deal with life in the assembly of believers. Five commands follow in staccato fashion. Two are negative (vv. 19-20) and three are positive (vv. 21-22).

5:19. The Bible frequently likens the Holy Spirit to a flame (Isa. 4:4; Matt. 3:11; Acts 2:3-4). He warms the heart, enlightens the mind, and empowers people's spirits. It is the effective working of the Holy Spirit that Paul warned against hindering. His **fire** can be diminished or even snuffed **out** if He is resisted. The Holy Spirit's working can be opposed by believers. It is this that Paul warned against. The next verse may give a clue as to how the Spirit was in danger of being quenched by the Thessalonians.

5:20. There may have been a tendency in the early church, and perhaps in the Thessalonian church in particular, to underrate the value of prophetic utterances. The gift of prophecy was the ability to receive and communicate direct revelations from God before the New Testament was completed (1 Cor. 13:8). Sometimes these revelations concerned future events (Acts 11:28), but often they dealt with the present (Acts 13:2). Perhaps people who had not received prophetic revelations were teaching their own views of such things as the Second Advent, with the result that prophetic revelations tended to be evaluated on superficial terms (e.g., the eloquence of the speaker) instead of on the basis of their intrinsic authority.

By way of application, Christians should not disparage any revelation that has come to the church and has been recognized as authoritative and preserved by the Holy Spirit in Scripture. The temptation to put the ideas of men on an equal footing with the Word of God is still present.

5:21. In view of this danger Christians need to **test** what they hear and read, by comparing it with the Word of God, to determine if it is divine in its origin. This is difficult, but it is possible for a spiritual believer (1 Cor. 2:14). Each Christian has the responsibility and ability to do this, though some have more discernment than others (cf. Acts 17:11; 1 John 4:1). What is discovered to be **good** (i.e., in harmony with what has been given by the Holy Spirit in the Word) should be retained.

5:22. On the other hand counterfeit teaching and living should be rejected and avoided. Not only should pseudo-prophecies be discarded but also, as Paul broadened his warning, **every kind** and form **of evil** should be avoided. What may only appear to be bad also falls under this warning. However, "while believers should abstain from actions which will knowingly offend others, it is not always possible to abstain from everything which may appear evil to a narrow and foolish judgment" (Hiebert, *The Thessalonian Epistles,* p. 249).

3. DIVINE ENABLEMENT (5:23-24)

Since these are high requirements, Paul expressed his pious wish that God would enable his readers to attain them.

5:23. To encourage his readers, Paul highlighted God's ability to produce peace. The church at Thessalonica had come to experience peace through the preaching of the gospel. And when Paul wrote this letter, the Thessalonians were enjoying peace with each other. The **God** who had given them **peace** would be their adequate resource for the future as He had been in the past. Paul prayed that God would **sanctify** (set apart) them to Himself in every area of their lives. Paul did not mean they could attain complete sanctification this side of heaven; that is impossible. He also prayed that his readers would be preserved **blameless** (*amemptos,* i.e., with no legitimate ground for accusation; cf. 2:10) in view of and until the appearing (*parousia*) of the **Lord Jesus Christ** for His saints.

Though Paul spoke of the Christian as **spirit, soul, and body,** man is described elsewhere as having two parts— body and spirit (James 2:26; 2 Cor. 7:1), or body and soul (Matt. 10:28). And man is also said to have a heart, mind, conscience, and other parts. Rather than teaching man as having only three parts, Paul was probably using the three terms here to identify the different aspects of personhood he wished to emphasize. The *spirit* is the highest and most unique part of man that enables him to communicate with God. The *soul* is the part of man that makes him conscious of himself; it is the seat of his personality. The *body*, of course, is the physical part through which the inner person expresses himself and by which he is immediately recognized. Paul was saying then that he desired that the Thessalonians would be kept blameless by God in their relationships with Him in their inner personal lives, and in their social contacts with other people.

5:24. The same God who calls a Christian will perform this by the Holy Spirit who indwells him. God **is faithful** to bring to completion the work He has begun in believers (Phil. 1:6). God does not save a person by grace and then leave him alone to work out his Christian growth by works (Gal. 3:3). As God calls and justifies by grace, He sanctifies by grace too.

IV. Conclusion (5:25-28)

This conclusion is like a postscript to the letter. It contains three more exhortations and a benediction.

A. Personal appeals (5:25-27)

Unlike most of Paul's other epistles, this closing section does not state that it was written by him or by an amenuensis.

5:25. This is the first time in the letter that the greeting **brothers** (used 15 times in 1 Thes.; see comments on 1:4) occurs at the beginning of a sentence in the original. It is emphatic in this position. The force of the present tense here is a strong "keep on praying." Paul's appeal for prayer was to those he regarded as his brothers. Doubtless much of the success of his missionary work could be attributed to the prayers of the Thessalonians and other believers. Paul understood both

his personal insufficiency and God's sufficiency (cf. 2 Cor. 3:5). He requested prayer for his fellow workers as well as for himself.

5:26. It was common in Paul's culture as in many cultures today, to **greet** friends with a kiss on the cheek. The men greeted other men this way, and the women did the same with other women. Such a kiss communicated personal affection, not romantic love. By urging this practice Paul was encouraging an outward physical expression of true Christian love in a form that was culturally acceptable in his day. The kiss was to be **holy,** not passionate or fleshly. An acceptable alternative in Western culture today might be an embrace, a pat on the back, or a handshake. J.B. Phillips paraphrased this verse for 20th-century English readers: "Give a handshake all around among the brotherhood."

5:27. The final exhortation strongly urges that this letter be **read to all the brothers,** probably the whole Thessalonian church. The normal usage of the Greek word for "read" (*anagnōsthēnai*) implies that it should be read aloud. Paul's words are surprisingly strong. He put his readers under oath (*enorkizō hymas,* **I charge you**) to do this, suggesting that God would discipline them if they disobeyed. Were there some problems in the church that Paul wanted to get at by having everyone hear his words? Or did he realize that this epistle was written under divine inspiration and was therefore spiritually valuable? Perhaps he had both motives.

B. Benediction (5:28)

5:28. Paul referred to God's grace in each of his epistolary benedictions. **The grace** of God was Paul's great delight (cf. 1:1). He identified it as the grace that comes through **our Lord Jesus Christ.** In Him Christians have all. Obviously the grace of God is always **with** His children, but Paul's concern was that his readers experience and enjoy this grace. All that one has in Christ is due to His grace.

BIBLIOGRAPHY

Barclay, William. *The Letters to the Philippians, Colossians and Thessalonians.* The Daily Study Bible. Edinburgh: Saint Andrews, 1959.

Calvin, John. *The Epistles of Paul the Apostle to the Romans and to the Thessalonians.* Translated by Ross Mackenzie. Grand Rapids: Wm. B. Eerdmans Publishing Co., 1961.

Ellicott, Charles J. *A Critical and Grammatical Commentary on St. Paul's Epistles to the Thessalonians.* Andover: Warren F. Draper, 1864. Reprint. Grand Rapids: Zondervan Publishing House, 1971.

Frame, James Everett. *A Critical and Exegetical Commentary on the Epistles of St. Paul to the Thessalonians.* The International Critical Commentary. Edinburgh: T. & T. Clark, 1912.

Hendriksen, William. *Exposition of I and II Thessalonians.* New Testament Commentary. Grand Rapids: Baker Book House, 1955.

Hiebert, D. Edmond. *The Thessalonian Epistles.* Chicago: Moody Press, 1971.

Hogg, C.F., and Vine, W.E. *The Epistles of Paul the Apostle to the Thessalonians.* Reprint. Grand Rapids: Kregel Publications, 1959.

Lenski, R.C.H. *The Interpretation of St. Paul's Epistles to the Colossians, to the Thessalonians, to Timothy, to Titus and to Philemon.* 1937. Reprint. Minneapolis: Augsburg Publishing House, 1961.

Lightfoot, J.B. *Notes on the Epistles of St. Paul.* Reprint. Grand Rapids: Zondervan Publishing House, 1957.

Mason, A.J. "The Epistles of Paul the Apostle to the Thessalonians." In *Ellicott's Commentary on the Whole Bible,* vol. 8. Reprint. Grand Rapids: Zondervan Publishing House, n.d.

Milligan, George. *St. Paul's Epistles to the Thessalonians.* Reprint. Grand Rapids: Wm. B Eerdmans Publishing Co., 1952.

Morris, Leon. *The Epistles of Paul to the Thessalonians.* The Tyndale New Testament Commentaries. Grand Rapids: Wm. B. Eerdmans Publishing Co., 1957.

————. *The First and Second Epistles to the Thessalonians.* The New International Commentary on the New Testament. Grand Rapids: Wm. B. Eerdmans Publishing Co., 1959.

Ryrie, Charles Caldwell. *First and Second Thessalonians.* Everyman's Bible Commentary. Chicago: Moody Press, 1968.

Thomas, Robert L. "1 Thessalonians" and "2 Thessalonians." In *The Expositor's Bible Commentary,* vol. 11. Grand Rapids: Zondervan Publishing House, 1978.

Walvoord, John F. *The Thessalonian Epistles.* Grand Rapids: Zondervan Publishing House, 1958.

Wiersbe, Warren W. *Be Ready: A Practical Study of 1 and 2 Thessalonians.* Wheaton, Ill.: SP Publications, Victor Books, 1979.

2 THESSALONIANS

Thomas L. Constable

INTRODUCTION

The Writer of the Epistle. This letter claims to have been written by Paul, who wrote 1 Thessalonians under the inspiration of the Holy Spirit (cf. 1 Thes. 1:1). There are no indications among the writings of the early church fathers who lived during and after Paul's lifetime that anyone questioned the authenticity of this letter's claim. In fact several fathers mentioned the Pauline authorship of this epistle in their writings. Not until early in the 19th century were various questions raised about authorship. They came from rationalistic critics who refused to accept the Bible's claim to divine inspiration. But critical questions have not proven devastating because the authenticity of this and other New Testament books has been demonstrable through the ages.

The Place of Writing. Almost all conservative scholars believe that 2 Thessalonians was written from Corinth. The basis for this conclusion is that Paul, Silas, and Timothy were present together in Corinth (Acts 18:5). They are not referred to in the Bible as being together thereafter, though they might have been. Since 1 Thessalonians was written from Corinth (see *Introduction* to 1 Thes.), and since the topics treated in the second epistle seem to grow out of situations alluded to in the first epistle and reflect a very similar situation in the Thessalonian church, Corinth seems the logical site of composition.

The Date of Writing. For the reasons mentioned above, it appears that 2 Thessalonians was written quite soon after 1 Thessalonians, perhaps within 12 months. This would place the date of composition in the early A.D. 50s and would make this epistle the third of Paul's canonical writings (assuming Galatians was his first).

The Occasion and Purpose for Writing. The epistle gives evidence that Paul had recently heard news about conditions in the church. Probably this information came to him from the messenger who delivered 1 Thessalonians and returned to Corinth. Perhaps other people who had news of the church informed the three missionaries (Paul, Silas, and Timothy) also. Some of the news was good: the Thessalonians were continuing to grow and to remain faithful to Christ in spite of persecution. But some was bad: false teaching concerning the day of the Lord had entered the church and was causing confusion and leading some of the Christians to quit their jobs in expectation of the Lord's return.

In view of these reports Paul felt constrained to write this epistle. He commended his children in the faith for their growth, corrected their doctrinal error about the day of the Lord, and warned of its consequences.

OUTLINE

I. Salutation (1:1-2)
II. Commendation for Past Progress (1:3-12)
   A. Thanksgiving for growth (1:3-4)
   B. Encouragement to persevere (1:5-10)
   C. Prayer for success (1:11-12)
III. Correction of Present Error (2:1-12)
   A. The beginning of the day of the Lord (2:1-5)
   B. The mystery of lawlessness (2:6-12)
IV. Thanksgiving and Prayer (2:13-17)
   A. Thanksgiving for calling (2:13-15)
   B. Prayer for strength (2:16-17)
V. Exhortations for Future Growth (3:1-15)
   A. Prayer for the apostles (3:1-2)
   B. Confidence of the apostles (3:3-5)

COMMENTARY

I. Salutation (1:1-2)

1:1. This epistle begins by naming the same three men mentioned in 1 Thessalonians 1:1. As in 1 Thessalonians, **Paul** was the author (directed by the inspiration of the Holy Spirit) for he spoke of himself in the singular (2 Thes. 2:5; 3:17). But **Silas and Timothy** joined him in sending the epistle (Paul frequently used "we": 1:3-4, 11-12, etc.). For more on these three men see the comments on 1 Thessalonians 1:1.

The same assembly of Christians received both letters. **The church** is described as being **in God our Father and the Lord Jesus Christ.** As in so many places in the New Testament Epistles, Jesus Christ is placed on an equal level with God the Father. God is the Father of Christians individually, a revelation given first by Jesus Christ (Matt. 6:9). A church is an assembly of individuals who are in Christ by faith in His atoning death and are therefore the children of God.

1:2. This verse is a word of greeting; the verb "be" must be implied. Paul reminded his readers that they were the recipients of God's **grace and peace,** and he wished that they would experience these blessings in fullest measure. "Grace" is "God's riches at Christ's expense"; it is God's unmerited favor which He freely bestows on all who accept Jesus Christ's substitutionary work for them on the cross by faith. God gives man the opposite of what he deserves: blessing instead of judgment. This is the grace of God. "Peace" is the cessation of hostility which has resulted from Christ's death; God and people can be reconciled because the debt of human sin has been paid by Christ. Christians have peace *with* God through the death of Christ. They also experience the peace *of* God as a result of Christ's work.

Christians can be at peace even in the midst of trials and persecution. This was Paul's desire for the Thessalonians.

Both grace and peace are gifts of God that come to believers through the Lord Jesus Christ.

In both Thessalonian letters Paul gave the greeting "Grace and peace to you," but here (in 2 Thes.) he added **from God the Father and the Lord Jesus Christ.**

II. Commendation for Past Progress (1:3-12)

This section flows smoothly from one subject to the next in a natural, conversational manner. Paul began by thanking God for the spiritual growth the Thessalonian believers had experienced. This led him to encourage them to persevere in their steadfastness. He explained that he and his fellow writers were praying for their spiritual success.

A. Thanksgiving for growth (1:3-4)

The character of, reasons for, and consequences of the apostle's thanksgiving are explained in these verses.

1:3. Paul and his fellow missionaries to Thessalonica had ample reason to **thank God** on behalf of this church, and their thanksgiving was continuous (cf. 1 Thes. 1:2). It was right for them to give thanks because these believers were a cause for thanksgiving. In fact Paul felt obligated to give thanks as though he owed a debt which he paid enthusiastically. Their **faith** had continued to grow (*hyperauxanei*, "to grow exceedingly"; *auxanō* is used in the Gospels of the growth of plants and babies, and in the epistles of spiritual growth [e.g., Eph. 4:15; Col. 1:6, 10], but in the NT *hyperauxanei* is only used here). The faith of Christians should keep **growing** all their lives; they should trust God more consistently and more extensively as they grow older in Christ. Faith in God is not a static thing. Since it is trust in a Person, it is always increasing or decreasing. A growing faith indicates a growing Christian.

Not only were the Thessalonians' relationships with God developing, but so were their relationships with other people. Genuine faith in God is always accompanied by love for others (James 2:14-17). Faith is the root; love is the fruit. The Thessalonians' **love . . . for each other** kept **increasing** (*pleonaxei*). In 1 Thessalonians 3:12 Paul had expressed concern that their love "increase" (*pleonasai*), and now, happily, he said it *was* increasing. Both faith and love were growing like well-fertilized plants, beyond what would have been normally expected. This was an exceptional church.

1:4. Because of such good growth the apostles frequently spoke with justifiable pride to other **churches** about the Thessalonians, using the Thessalonian church as a model to be emulated. In particular, their **perseverance** (*hypomonēs*; cf. 1 Thes. 1:3; 2 Thes. 3:5) in the midst of persecutions was outstanding. The Thessalonians did not react to discomfort the way many Christians do, by running away from their uncomfortable situations. Instead they viewed their circumstances as God's will and determined to brace up under the pressure. Their attitude was not to endure by force of their own strength, however. They had **faith** in God; they looked to Him for grace sufficient to bear up and accepted their circumstances as conditions which He was allowing for His glory. They were patiently **enduring . . . persecutions** (*diōgmois*) from enemies of the gospel who were hostile toward them (cf. 1 Thes. 3:3-4). The **trials** (*thlipsesin*, "pressures, troubles"; cf. 2 Thes. 1:6-7) they were undergoing were painful circumstances that came from both Jewish and Gentile acquaintances (cf. 1 Thes. 1:6; 2:14; Acts 17:5-9). Their persecutions and trials were numerous. Yet, in spite of them all, the Thessalonians kept on standing strong and stable in their faith.

B. Encouragement to persevere (1:5-10)

Paul proceeded to nourish the souls of these beleaguered saints so that they would be able to continue to bear up under the pressures of temptation.

1:5. The present experiences of the Thessalonians, Paul pointed out to them by way of encouragement, illustrated the righteous **judgment** of God, that is, that God is just.

When God would judge the Thessalonians they would be declared **worthy** of God's kingdom. Endurance in trials does not make one worthy of heaven; one does not earn heaven by suffering. But endurance in trials does *demonstrate* one's worthiness. A Christian is made worthy by God's grace, which he receives as a free gift by faith in Jesus Christ. His trials simply expose what is there already and since the character that emerges through the fire of testing is God-given, God receives all the glory. The grace of God that makes it possible for a Christian to withstand the fires of human experience, which destroy non-Christians, is a Christian's only claim to being worthy of God's kingdom. **The kingdom of God** refers to God's rule over all, which Christians share as His children.

The purpose of the Thessalonians' sufferings was to bring glory to God by manifesting His grace in the way they bore up under their trials. Their **suffering** demonstrated that they were considered worthy of God's kingdom. In another sense they were suffering as soldiers of Christ.

1:6. Paul explained how the Thessalonians' suffering demonstrated the justice of God. He first stated the great truth taught from Genesis through Revelation: **God is just.** God will balance the scales of justice. He will mete out **trouble** (*thlipsin*; cf. v. 4) **to those who** troubled (*thlibousin*) the Thessalonians (cf. Gal. 6:7).

1:7. On the other hand God will give relief from the tensions of trials to those who are unjustly persecuted (lit., "troubled, pressured," *thlibomenois*; cf. vv. 4, 6) by their enemies. The Thessalonians, the apostles, and all other Christians who share in these pressures can look forward to this. **Relief** (*anesin*, "relaxation, rest"; used only five times in the NT: here and in Acts 24:23; 2 Cor. 2:13, 7:5; 8:13) will come at the revelation of Jesus Christ. Paul painted the picture of a veil being removed from in front of Jesus Christ; He will be **revealed in blazing fire** (cf. Ex. 3:2; 19:18; 24:17; Ps. 18:12; Isa. 30:27-30; 66:15; Dan. 7:9-10). This is the **Lord Jesus,** the Man in heaven. He will exercise the power then; the Christians' persecutors do so now. Christ's coming will be **with His powerful angels;** His heavenly servants will be with Him to carry out His bidding. If the Rapture had occurred in Paul's lifetime, the enemies of the Thessalonian believers would have been judged shortly (seven years) thereafter, at Christ's second coming.

1:8. At that time the Lord Jesus Christ will **punish** two classes of people: those who are ignorant of **God** (Rom. 1:18-32), and **those who . . . do not obey the gospel** (cf. John 3:36). The guilt of those in the latter group is the greater because their privilege is greater. God's judgment is perfectly just. Willful rejection of God's revelation spurns God.

1:9. The destruction to befall both groups is stated in this verse. **They will be punished** is literally "they will pay a penalty" (*dikēn tisousin*). For their rejection of God's grace they will experience endless or **everlasting** ruin (*olethron aiōnion*). This is "the most express statement in St. Paul's Epistles of the eternity of future punishment" (Edward Headland and Henry B. Swete, *The Epistle to the Thessalonians*, London: Hatchard, 1863, p. 137). The punishment of the wicked will be neither temporary nor will it be annihilation, but it will continue throughout eternity and those being punished will be conscious. It is eternal death as opposed to eternal life (Matt. 25:46). The nature of the **destruction** follows in the next phrase.

Separation from the Lord's **presence** (lit., "face") is the essence of eternal punishment. On the other hand being in the Lord's presence will make heaven heaven. A Christian's hope is to see and be with the Lord; the judgment of unbelievers is to be eternally inaccessible to His presence (cf. Rom. 1:18; 2:5-9; 6:21; Phil. 3:19; 1 Thes. 1:10; 4:17).

The majesty of His power is the visible splendor of the Lord's presence. The Lord's power will be manifest in a majestic display (cf. Rev. 19:11-16). Unbelievers will be forever **shut out** from the Lord's presence and His power.

1:10. This judgment will take place when the Lord **comes** back to earth and is **glorified** through the lives of believers whom He has transformed by making saints out of sinners. This is not the Rapture (1 Thes. 4:13-18; John 14:2-3), for no judgment accompanies the Rapture. Instead, it is the revelation of Jesus Christ in power and great glory (Ps. 2:1-9; Matt. 25:31), when He will set up His earthly kingdom (Rev. 19:11–20:4). At His return He will destroy the Armageddon armies gathered against Him (Rev. 16:12-16; 19:19-21) and will then judge living Jews (Ezek. 20:33-38) and living Gentiles (Matt. 24:31-46). These judgments are the ones just described (2 Thes. 1:9).

The exact date of His return is not given, of course, but it will be a day of judgment for the lost and a day of glory and marveling for believers. Christ will be "glorified in" (not *by*) His saints, that is, His glory will be mirrored in them. Christians will marvel in that they will admire their Lord for what He has done in them. All believers will marvel—not just those living on the earth and those resurrected when Christ returns, but also those who return to earth with Him, those who had been caught up to be with the Lord at the Rapture.

This group, Paul pointed out, would include the Thessalonian believers to whom he wrote this epistle. Because they **believed** Paul's **testimony** they would share in this great day. Such a hope should strengthen any believer who might be buckling under the pressure of persecution by unbelievers (v. 4). This glimpse into the future undoubtedly encouraged Paul's readers and it should encourage believers in their trials today.

C. Prayer for success (1:11-12)

The preceding revelation moved Paul to pray for his Thessalonian brothers and sisters, that they might live lifestyles that were consistent with their calling and destiny.

1:11. Paul and his colleagues habitually prayed for the Thessalonians. Their spiritual welfare was always on the apostles' hearts.

They prayed that their **God** (the apostles' and the Thessalonains') would reckon or declare the readers **worthy** of the **calling** they had received, to come to God through faith in Jesus Christ (cf. Rom. 8:30; Eph. 4:1; 1 Thes. 4:7). Paul consistently made what God has done for believers the basis of his appeals for them to lead lives in keeping with their destiny. Christians do not live worthily in order to obtain salvation but because they have been granted salvation.

A second request was that God would bring to full expression **every good purpose of** theirs to glorify God, and **every act** motivated by their **faith** in God. Both motives and actions have their source in God (Phil. 2:13); thus they are accomplished **by His power.**

1:12. The ultimate purpose of this prayer is the glory of God. Specifically it was that God's glory might be manifested in and through the Thessalonians, both immediately (v. 12) and at the revelation of Jesus Christ (v. 10). When this happens, the vessels that manifest the glory of God are themselves **glorified** by association with Him. In the Bible **the name** stands for the person named, his character, conduct, reputation, and everything else about him. In praying thus, Paul was asking that God would fully glorify Jesus Christ in these saints. This is in keeping with and springs from the **grace of** God, personalized again by Paul as **our God,** and linked with **the Lord Jesus Christ** as an equal (cf. v. 1; 1 Thes. 1:1). Answers to prayers depend on and are traceable to God's grace. Such lofty requests as these can be fulfilled only by God's grace.

III. Correction of Present Error (2:1-12)

This section of verses contains truths found nowhere else in the Bible. It is key to understanding future events and it is central to this epistle. Paul dealt with a doctrinal error concerning eschatology (the last things) that had crept into the Thessalonian church. In chapter 2 he spoke to the theological error, and in chapter 3 to practical problems in the church that grew out of that error.

A. The beginning of the day of the Lord (2:1-5)

Paul had instructed the Thessalonians from the Old Testament concerning the day of the Lord when he preached to them in person. The day of the Lord is the period of history mentioned repeatedly in the Old Testament during which God will bring judgment and blessing on the people of the earth in a more direct, dramatic, and drastic way than ever before (cf. Isa. 13:6, 9; Zeph. 1:14-16). From other New Testament revelation concerning this period of time it is believed that this will begin after the Rapture of the church, and will include the Tribulation and the Millennium.

In his first letter to the Thessalonians Paul had taught them that the day of the Lord would come as a thief in the night (1 Thes. 5:2). This instruction raised a question in his readers' minds. It must have seemed to some of them that the day of the Lord had already come. After all, the persecutions they were experiencing seemed to be what the prophets had predicted when they wrote about the great calamities coming on God's people and the world in the day of the Lord. The

Thessalonians apparently had received instruction from other teachers to the effect that they were indeed experiencing the judgments of the day of the Lord, that is, the Great Tribulation. But if this were so, how could Paul's previous instruction that they would be caught up and escape the wrath of God coming on the earth be true? Paul wrote this section (2 Thes. 2:1-5) to straighten out the matter.

2:1. The preceding comments concerning the coming of Christ (1:5-10) stimulated the readers' thinking about this subject, but now Paul launched into it more particularly. The **coming** (*parousias,* "presence") **of our Lord Jesus Christ and our being gathered to Him** refers to the Rapture. "Beseech," though archaic, is perhaps a more effective word than **ask** (*erōtōmen*) in conveying Paul's attitude of warm personal affection. He lightened their spirits with a reminder that his readers were his **brothers** and sisters in the faith. Paul probably used the full title for God the Son—"our Lord Jesus Christ"—in order to add solemnity to the subject.

2:2. Paul warned his readers against believing the false teaching that was shaking their spiritual equilibrium and triggering their fears. Apparently the theory that they were in **the day of the Lord** was coming to them from several sources (**prophecy, report, or letter**), making the Thessalonians more inclined to accept it as authoritative. Some were saying this teaching had been revealed to them by the Lord. And some were reporting teaching they had heard from others. And the Thessalonians received a letter, which was allegedly from Paul, that taught the same error (cf. 3:17). No wonder the new converts were shaken.

The erroneous message which all these voices echoed was that the day of the Lord had arrived; the Thessalonians were in it. But if this were so, the believers were wondering, how could Paul speak of the Lord's return as preceding the day of the Lord? (1 Thes. 1:10) And what about those promises that they would not see God's wrath? (1 Thes. 1:10; 5:9) It is clear that Paul had taught them a pretribulational Rapture. Their confusion arose because they could not distinguish their present troubles from those of the day of the Lord.

2:3. Having stated the issue and

identified the sources of the false teaching, Paul proceeded to warn his readers against being deceived. The Thessalonians must not be deceived by any person, no matter how credible he might appear to be, or by the way anyone might present his teaching, claiming the authority of God or godly men. New Christians tend to be gullible because they are not yet grounded in the truth of God's Word (cf. Eph. 4:14). But all Christians can be misled by impressive personalities and spectacular appeals. The antidote to poisonous heresy is a good strong dose of the truth which Paul proceeded to administer.

He referred to three events which must occur before the judgments of the day of the Lord took place. They are the apostasy (2 Thes. 2:3), the revealing of **the man of lawlessness** (vv. 3-4, 8), and the removal of restraint against lawlessness (vv. 6-7). (These are not necessarily given in strict chronological order. See the following comments on vv. 3 and 7.)

One major event is **the rebellion** (lit., "the falling away," *hē apostasia*, from whence comes the English word "apostasy"). This is a revolt, a departure, an abandoning of a position once held. This rebellion, which will take place within the professing church, will be a departure from the truth that God has revealed in His Word. True, apostasy has characterized the church almost from its inception, but Paul referred to a specific distinguishable apostasy that will come in the future (cf. 1 Tim. 4:1-3; 2 Tim. 3:1-5; 4:3-4; James 5:1-8; 2 Peter 2; 3:3-6; Jude). He had already told his readers about it (2 Thes. 2:5).

Some interpreters have taken this "departure" as a reference to the Rapture of the church (e.g., E. Schuyler English, *Rethinking the Rapture*, New York: Loizeaux Brothers, 1954, pp. 67-71), but this is not too probable. D. Edmond Hiebert refutes this view that *apostasia* here refers to the Rapture (*The Thessalonian Epistles*, p. 306). Some scholars believe that this apostasy (called by Paul "the" apostasy) will consist of people turning from God's truth to worship the Antichrist, who will set himself up in God's temple and claim to be God (v. 4). If this is so, then the judgments of the day of the Lord will occur in the second half of the seven-year period preceding Christ's second coming.

Another event that must take place before the judgments of the day of the Lord occur is the revelation of "the man of lawlessness" (*ho anthrōpos tēs anomias*). Paul used a tense for the verb **is revealed** which indicates that this revelation will be a decisive act that will take place at a definite moment in history (cf. vv. 6, 8). He will be fully associated with and characterized by "lawlessness" (or "sin," as some mss. and the KJV have it). He is also described as **the man doomed to destruction** (lit., "the son of perdition," KJV). The destruction to which he is destined is the opposition of salvation; it is everlasting torment. It seems probable that the man of sin will be identified by some people living then when he makes a covenant with Israel at the beginning of the 70th week of Daniel (Dan. 9:27a); but when he breaks the covenant three and a half years later (Dan. 9:27b), he will be widely recognized for who he really is (Charles C. Ryrie, *First and Second Thessalonians*, p. 104). This latter event may be the time Paul had in mind for the "revealing" of the man of lawlessness.

2:4. This man is further described as the adversary of God. He will seek to replace the worship of the true God and all false gods with the worship of himself, and will proclaim **himself to be God.** The beast will tolerate the worship of no one or nothing but himself (cf. Rev. 13:5-8). He will set **himself up** on God's throne **in** the inner sanctuary of **God's temple.** This probably refers to a literal temple, but some suggest that it is a figurative reference to his occupying the most holy place in human worship, which rightfully belongs only to God. The early church fathers and several good modern-day commentators accept the literal view. This man is also called the "beast coming out of the sea" (Rev. 13:1-10), "a scarlet beast" (17:3), and simply "the beast" (17:8, 16; 19:19-20; 20:10). He is the Antichrist (1 John 2:18), a pseudo-Christ hostile to the Savior. He will be a real human being, not a principle or a system or a succession of individuals. Such a person has not yet been spotlighted on the stage of human history.

2:5. This teaching was nothing new to the Thessalonians; Paul had taught them about the day of the Lord when he was with them in Thessalonica. He called on them to recall those lessons. For the first time in this epistle Paul wrote that he personally (sing.) had taught them. He said this in order to emphasize the truth of his message, as he was the chief spokesman in Thessalonica. Paul did not regard prophetic truth as too deep or unimportant or controversial for new Christians. He believed it was a vital part of the whole counsel of God, so he taught it without hesitation or apology.

B. The mystery of lawlessness (2:6-12)

The Apostle Paul continued his correction by giving more information about the man of lawlessness in relation to the removal of the One who now partially restrains lawlessness. This removal constitutes a third event referred to by Paul that must take place before the day of the Lord will begin. The theme of lawlessness pervades this whole section of the epistle.

2:6. **And** (kai) connects what precedes with what follows; the same subject continues, but the emphasis shifts to what is presently restraining the revelation of the man of sin. Paul said the Thessalonians knew what it was, but he did not identify it here. Perhaps he had told them in person. Something or Someone is holding back the culmination of lawlessness. Part of the purpose of this restraint is to keep the man of sin from being revealed prematurely.

2:7. This verse explains and expands on verse 6. Paul reminded his readers that **the secret power of lawlessness** was **already at work.** The "secret power" (mystērion, whence "mystery") is one of the mysteries of the New Testament (Rom. 16:26; 1 Cor. 2:6-12; Eph. 1:9; 3:3-5; Col. 1:25-27). A mystery in the New Testament is a new truth previously unknown before its revelation in the present dispensation. In this case the mystery is the revelation of a future climax of lawlessness in the world. Then and now a movement against divine law directed by Satan was and is operative. But it is being restrained somewhat, and this restraining will continue until the time appointed for revealing the man of sin and the climax of lawlessness.

Who or what is restraining the satanically empowered movement against God's law and is postponing the revelation of the man of sin? Some say it is the Roman Empire. But the empire has long vanished and "the holder back" is not yet

revealed. Another suggestion is that this is Satan, but it is difficult to see why he would hold back sin. Others suggest that human governments are holding back sin and the revealing of the Antichrist. But human governments will not end prior to the Antichrist's unveiling. Nor do all governments restrain sin; many encourage it!

The Holy Spirit of God is the only Person with sufficient (supernatural) power to do this restraining. Some object to this being the Holy Spirit on the grounds that to katechon in 2 Thessalonians 2:6 is neuter ("what is holding back"). But this is no problem for two reasons: (a) The neuter is sometimes used of the Holy Spirit (John 14:26; 15:26; 16:13-14). (b) In 2 Thessalonians 2:7 the words are masculine: ho katechōn, **the one who . . . holds it back.** How does He do it? Through Christians, whom He indwells and through whom He works in society to hold back the swelling tide of lawless living. How will He be **taken out of the way?** When the church leaves the earth in the Rapture, the Holy Spirit will be taken out of the way in the sense that His unique lawlessness-restraining ministry through God's people will be removed (cf. Gen. 6:3). The removal of the Restrainer at the time of the Rapture must obviously precede the day of the Lord. Paul's reasoning is thus a strong argument for the pretribulational Rapture: the Thessalonians were not in the Great Tribulation because the Rapture had not yet occurred.

2:8. After the removal of restraint the world will plunge headlong into lawlessness and the man of sin will be revealed (see comments on v. 3). This man's name is never given in the Bible, but he will be known by his actions. He is the same person referred to in verse 3. He is also spoken of in Daniel 9:26-27 and 11:36–12:1. Paul was conscious of the spiritual forces behind this individual, and for this reason described his revelation as something that will take place by the power of another, not himself.

This powerful person will be destroyed by the mere **breath of the Lord Jesus.** Antichrist may control mankind, but he will be no match for Messiah. Jesus is Lord indeed. "The very breathing of the glorified Jesus will slay the lawless one like the blast of a fiery furnace" (Hiebert, The Thessalonian Epistles, p.

315). He will be killed and his work will be destroyed, brought to nothing. The shining forth of Christ's presence when He comes to earth will immobilize the Antichrist's program as certainly as the revelation of the glorified Christ on the Damascus Road stopped Saul in his tracks and terminated his program of fighting against God.

This verse (2 Thes. 2:8), spans the seven-year career of the Antichrist from the time he makes a covenant with Israel soon after the Rapture, till his **overthrow** by Christ at **His** second **coming** at the end of the Tribulation.

2:9. The career of this **lawless** leader is described in more detail in verses 9-12. His career will be empowered by **Satan** (cf. Rev. 13:2b) and characterized by Satan's method: counterfeiting. Satan's desire to **counterfeit** God's miracles in the world can be traced from Genesis through Revelation. Paul employed three terms to describe the supernatural power this man will demonstrate. **Miracles** (*dynamei*) emphasizes the inherent power behind the works he will perform. **Signs** (*sēmeiois*) refers to the fact that they will have significance. **Wonders** (*terasin*) indicates the attitude of awe that they will evoke when people behold them. He will, in short, perform such powerful miracles that it will be evident to all that he has supernatural power, and people will stand in awe of him. One such miracle and the people's awe are mentioned in Revelation 13:2b-4 and 17:8.

2:10. His miracles are not the only thing that will deceive people into thinking he has divine power. Everything he does will mislead people, especially those whose minds are blinded to the truth of who he is and what he is doing because they do not believe God's Word. The meaning of this verse is not that everything he does will be perceived as **evil** by people, but that it will be evil in its essence because it misrepresents **the truth** and leads people away from worshiping God. The same three words used to describe his miracles in verse 9 (miracles, signs, wonders) were used of the miracles of Jesus Christ (Acts 2:22) and the apostles (Heb. 2:4). It will appear to unbelievers living on the earth at that time that he is indeed God. He will be able to pass himself off as God and receive worship as God.

Those who are being deceived by the man of sin **are perishing** (*apollymenois*, pres. part.; the noun "destruction" [*apoleias*] in 2 Thes. 2:3 is related to this part.) as the result of their refusal **to love** the truth of God and accept His gift of salvation. Their own choice brings about their condemnation. In spite of the inherent attractiveness of the saving truth of the gospel, these unbelievers refuse it. **To love the truth** of the gospel indicates true acceptance of it and adherence to it; it does not imply a higher requirement than simply believing it. The truth contrasts with the lies of the man of sin. The consequence of believing and loving the truth is salvation. One's responses to the gospel must be a matter of the heart (love), rather than simply of the head.

2:11. God desires that all be saved and come to the knowledge of the truth (1 Tim. 2:4-6). But when people refuse to entertain the truth, He lets them pursue and experience the consequences of falsehood (cf. Rom. 1:18-25). In fact God, as the Judge of men, begins this judgment at the moment of their rebellion and subjects them to the **powerful delusion** (*energeian planēs*) which comes from choosing error over truth. They choose to **believe the lie** and God sends them the delusion that is inherent in their choice. This powerful judgment from God is justified by the unbelievers' decision to refuse the truth. "The lie" is the claim that the man of lawlessness is God.

2:12. The purpose of God in acting thus is to execute justice (cf. 1:6). Eternal condemnation will be the fate of all who on the one hand choose to disbelieve **the truth** and on the other hand delight **in wickedness.** The opposite of believing the truth is delighting in wickedness; a spiritual decision leads to its moral manifestation. This consequence befalls everyone who disbelieves the gospel. Paul's primary concern here is of course unbelievers who will be living when the man of sin will be revealed. But these principles of God's judgment apply in all ages and can be seen in the 20th century.

Is this passage saying that those who do not believe the gospel before the man of sin is revealed—and who are therefore not caught up to meet the Lord at the Rapture but still live on the earth—cannot be saved after the man of lawlessness has been revealed? Or can people who recognize but knowingly reject the truth of the gospel before the Rapture be saved after the Rapture takes place? The "powerful delusion" (v. 11) that God will bring on these individuals in particular suggests that few if any then living on the earth will be saved after the Rapture. This seems to be a special judgment from God that will occur at this one time in history. The many saints which the Book of Revelation indicates will be living on the earth during the Tribulation may thus be people who did not hear and reject the gospel before the Rapture (cf. Rev. 7:4).

In summing up this section, Paul reminded his readers that the trials and persecutions they were experiencing (1:4) did not indicate that they were suffering the judgments of the day of the Lord. They had not missed the Rapture. Before the judgments of the day of the Lord would come, certain identifiable events must occur. These are the apostasy (extensive turning away from the truth of God), the removal of the Restrainer (the Holy Spirit restraining evil in the world as He works through the church He indwells) at the Rapture, and the unveiling of the Antichrist, the man of lawlessness. Since these events had not (and still have not) occurred, the Thessalonians were not experiencing the judgments accompanying the day of the Lord.

IV. Thanksgiving and Prayer (2:13-17)

This section forms a transition between Paul's teaching on the day of the Lord (2:1-12) and his exhortations for present living in view of that day (3:1-15).

A. Thanksgiving for calling (2:13-15)

The character, grounds, and implications of Paul's thanksgiving are included in these verses.

2:13. In contrast to the unbelievers just mentioned, the Thessalonians were a source of joy to the apostles. Paul felt a strong obligation to **thank God** on their behalf continually. They were his **brothers** (cf. vv. 1, 15) and sisters in the faith, **loved by the Lord** though hated and persecuted by their godless neighbors.

The reason for the apostle's joy and gratitude to God was His choice of the Thessalonian believers for eternal salvation. **From the beginning** (cf. "before the Creation of the world," Eph. 1:4) **God**

chose (*heilato*, past tense of *aireō*, "to take or pick," used only here and in Phil. 1:22) them, not on the basis of their love for Him or any merit on their part, but because of His love for them (cf. 1 Thes. 1:4). Paul consistently taught that the initiative in salvation comes from God, not man. The means God uses to effect salvation is the work of His Holy **Spirit** who sets aside chosen individuals for lives of holiness and separation from sin (cf. John 16:7-11). The Holy Spirit regenerates, indwells, and baptizes Christians into the body of Christ. The human aspect of salvation is **belief in the truth** of the gospel. The Holy Spirit then uses the Word of God to purify the believer's life (John 17:17).

That God chooses to save some though He loves all men should lead believers to thank God for His grace on behalf of the elect.

2:14. God **called** the readers to salvation by using the **gospel** as it was proclaimed by the apostolic missionaries in Thessalonica. God's purpose in doing so was that the believers **might** one day **share** the splendor and honor that **Jesus Christ** now enjoys, seated at the right hand of the Father (cf. 1:10-12).

2:15. In view of their calling, the Thessalonian believers were to maintain their present position of faith in God, care for the brethren, and hope in the imminent return of Jesus Christ (cf. 1 Thes. 1:3). They were to **stand firm** (*stēkete*; cf. 1 Cor. 16:13; 1 Thes. 3:8). Christians are in constant danger of being swept downstream by the currents of ungodly culture. They are also prone to let the truths they know and the relationship they enjoy with God grow cold. They need to vigorously **hold to** what they have been taught by God's servants. The Thessalonians were in danger of loosening their grip on the apostles' teachings which they had received (cf. 2 Thes. 3:6) in person from the missionaries and from their letters. They were in danger of slipping backward in their Christian experience because of the pressures of their trials and the daily negative influences of the world, the flesh, and the devil.

B. Prayer for strength (2:16-17)

In the face of the Thessalonians' need for steadfastness Paul prayed that God would give them encouragement and strength (cf. 1 Thes. 3:2, 13; 2 Thes. 3:3).

2:16. Though the Son and Father are both mentioned, They are regarded as One. God's love and **grace** is the foundation for **eternal** (i.e., unending) **encouragement** (*paraklēsin aiōnian*) in the face of any temporary present distress. Also God gives **hope** for the future. And that hope is **good** (*agathēn*, "beneficial") for it assures believers of the return of their victorious Savior.

2:17. Paul had two desires for the Thessalonians: (a) The Thessalonians needed comfort and encouragement (the verb **encourage** [*parakalesai*] suggests both "comfort" and "encourage"; sometimes it means "urge" as in 1 Thes. 4:1, 10; 2 Thes. 3:12) in view of their recent anxiety created by false information concerning the day of the Lord. (b) They needed God's grace to make them firm and stable (**strengthen** is *stērizai*, also used in 1 Thes. 3:2, 13) in every **good deed** ("good" in the sense of being done as unto the Lord) and **in every . . . word** they spoke in defense and confirmation of the gospel.

V. Exhortations for Future Growth (3:1-15)

This last major section of the epistle called on its readers to live in the light of the truth previously revealed and by the grace of God just invoked.

A. Prayer for the apostles (3:1-2)

Paul and his companions requested the prayer support of their Thessalonian brethren for whom they prayed.

3:1. Finally introduces the last major part of the letter. The Thessalonians needed prayer in their temptations, but they also needed to **pray** for others. Assuming a burden of prayer for others lightens one's own load. The apostles were needy too. Prayer was requested for two matters. The apostles acknowledged that the success of their missionary labors was due to God's blessing His Word as they proclaimed it. In particular, the spreading of the gospel was God's work and its reception among those who heard it was due to His preparing hearts. The Thessalonians knew from their experiences how God works in people's hearts to prepare them to receive the gospel; so they could pray with conviction that God

would honor His Word by causing others who heard it to believe it.

3:2. The second request was for deliverance from enemies of the gospel. As the missionaries itinerated from city to city, opponents of Christianity tried to frustrate their efforts. The Thessalonians knew all about this (Acts 17:5-9). The enemies of the gospel were doing something irrational, namely, resisting the free gift of God. They were also being destructive of the spiritual welfare of others. The hostility of these enemies was due to their lack of **faith** in the message of salvation. They were **wicked** (*atopōn*, "perverse") and **evil** (*ponēron*, "actively harmful"). Verses 1 and 2 show the positive and negative reactions which the preaching of the gospel produce.

B. Confidence of the apostles (3:3-5)

Rather than feeling distraught over the present situation in the Thessalonian church, the apostles were confident.

3:3. The reason for their confidence was the faithfulness of God rather than anything about the Thessalonians. The character of God should be the basis for a Christian's confidence. Because God has promised to supply believers' needs, Paul could rest in the assurance that He would provide strength (cf. 1 Thes. 3:2, 13; 2 Thes. 2:17) to withstand temptation and trials, and protection from the adversary and his emissaries (cf. Phil. 1:6; 1 Thes. 5:24). (Cf. "evil men" in 2 Thes. 3:2 with **the evil one** in v. 3).

3:4. An additional reason for **confidence** was the conviction that the Thessalonians would **continue to** obey the instructions of Paul and his cohorts in this letter. The missionaries were not relying on their readers' inherent power to do what was right; their confidence was that since the believers were **in** Christ, **the Lord** would work in them to react favorably to this epistle.

3:5. This prayer-wish expressed the apostles' petition that Jesus Christ would open up the way for the readers to obey out of a growing appreciation of **God's love** for them and a consequently greater love for God, as well as increasing endurance in the midst of trials which the Lord's example of **perseverance** (*hypomonēn*; cf. 1 Thes. 1:3; 2 Thes. 1:4; Heb. 12:1-2) stimulates within the hearts of believers. Meditation on the love of God and the patient endurance of Christ motivates Christians to obey His Word and to endure trials patiently. The word **direct** (*kateuthynai*) means "clear away the obstacles." It is also used in 1 Thessalonians 3:11.

C. Treatment of the disorderly (3:6-10)

Doctrinal error concerning the day of the Lord had led to disorderly conduct in the church. Paul dealt with the latter problem forcefully in this section. This cause-effect relationship is not stated explicitly in the epistle, but it is a safe deduction.

3:6. That a minority of the church members were misbehaving seems clear in that Paul admonished his readers generally to discipline the erring brethren. The seriousness of the charge is seen in Paul's appeal to **the name of the Lord Jesus Christ.** On behalf of everything that Jesus Christ is, they should do as Paul said. This is a **command,** not a suggestion. When Paul wrote the church earlier, he told them to "warn those who are idle" (1 Thes. 5:14).

Apparently this warning had not been heeded. Now Paul prescribed harsher discipline. Second-degree discipline involved the orderly separating of themselves from the lazy and the disorderly. This may have included excluding them from the life and meetings of the church (cf. 1 Cor. 5:11). This lack of contact would illustrate in a graphic way the spiritual gap that the behavior of the unruly had created. The offense was idleness, deliberate loafing which led some to interfere in the work of others (2 Thes. 3:11) and to expect others to provide for their needs (v. 12). This behavior was in direct disobedience to the apostles' teaching.

3:7. Paul justified this command with the **example** the missionaries had given them while teaching in Thessalonica (vv. 7-10). Paul had commended the church for following his example (1 Thes. 1:6), but when it came to working some were not following it. Quite clearly, Paul regarded the apostles' example as an authoritative model for their converts. They were to imitate behavior as well as to believe teaching. Paul and his associates were never lazy loafers.

3:8. They did not leech off others.

Paul was not saying that they never accepted a gift or a meal from others, but that they were self-supporting. They earned the bread they ate (cf. v. 12). In fact, they **worked** long and hard so as not to be a financial **burden to any of** the Thessalonians (cf. 1 Thes. 2:9).

3:9. The apostles lived this way to give their converts an example (*typon;* cf. 1 Thes. 1:7) of what it means to sacrifice for the good of others. The apostles had every **right to** receive physical **help** for spiritual ministry (cf. 1 Cor. 9:3-14; 1 Tim. 5:18). But they chose to forego this right in order to teach the importance of self-sacrificing love and industry. Paul did not imply that this right should always be sacrificed; he taught elsewhere that it is legitimate, that those who are taught should support their teachers (Gal. 6:6). His point here was that Christians generally should not expect other people to take care of them but should support themselves as much as possible.

3:10. The missionaries had taught the Thessalonians to be industrious as well as giving them a good example. Paul wanted no one to forget exactly what the apostles had said. It was a firm **rule** of Christian conduct. He either quoted it verbatim here or summarized his previous teaching into a single pithy precept. The individuals in view were not those who could **not work** but those who would not work. They were not to be supported by other Christians out of a sense of charity. The loving thing to do for those drones was to let them go hungry so that they would be forced to do right and go to work. No Christian who is able but unwilling to work should be maintained by others who labor on his behalf.

D. Commands for the idle (3:11-13)

Moving from the apostles' example of industry and a general principle to be followed, Paul focused on a specific problem in the church.

3:11. The apostles had heard more than once (this is the force of the pres. tense of **hear,** *akouomen*) that some in the church were not working to support themselves. They were **busybodies** instead of being **busy.** Instead of tending to their own business of earning a living they were meddling in the business of others (cf. 1 Tim. 5:13).

3:12. Paul and his companions both

commanded (*parangellomen*) those in this category and exhorted (*parakaloumen*) them on behalf of their union with **Christ**. With calm and sober minds, in view of what had been written concerning the day of the Lord, they should **settle down** (lit., "be working with quietude" [not noisily or in disorderliness], *hēsychia*; cf. Acts 22:2; 1 Tim. 2:2, 11; and cf. comments on 1 Thes. 4:11) and engage in regular employment to **earn** a living. Then they would earn their own **bread** and not sponge off others. Paul had previously told them to do this (1 Thes. 4:11), but because some disobeyed he gave this sterner command.

3:13. Turning to the faithful majority, Paul urged continuation in doing what they knew to be right regardless of the leeching of the disobedient. When other Christians take easy paths of irresponsibility and seem to prosper in them, it is easy to get discouraged and be tempted to join them. Though one may **tire *in* doing what is right,** he should never tire *of* doing what is right. In addressing the diligent as **brothers** and the idle as such people (v. 12), Paul implied that those who disobeyed this word from God were separating themselves by their behavior.

E. Discipline of the disobedient (3:14-15)

These verses contain even stronger words regarding the idle. This was how the rest of the church should relate to them if they would not repent.

3:14. Having been warned twice (1 Thes. 4:11; 5:14) a disobedient person must be given **special** treatment if he failed to repent. Paul regarded his writings as authoritative for the church; they were to be obeyed because he was an apostle and his inspired words were the Word of God. The idle one was to be identified as such by the members of the church and placed in a distinct category as disobedient. This seems to be what each faithful brother should do individually; no mention is made of public identification and discipline in the church (2 Thes. 3:14-15).

The faithful were not to have social contact with an idle person till he repented. The purpose of this social ostracism was to make the offender **feel ashamed** of himself so that he would repent. The design of divine discipline is

always to produce repentance, not division. Social pressure can be effective in helping an erring person come to his or her senses. This is exactly what Paul advocated in this case. Ostracism from the body of believers should help such a person be ashamed and feel his separation from fellowship with the Head of the body, Jesus Christ.

3:15. Concerned that the Thessalonians might overdo the discipline, Paul quickly urged them to treat the offender **as a brother,** not **as an enemy.** An occasion for discipline should not become an occasion for disobedience by those exercising the discipline. They were not to think of the offender as personally antagonistic toward them, nor were they to feel hostile toward him. His objective relationship to them as a brother in Christ should govern their feelings and actions, rather than subjective feelings that might be aroused by his idleness. They were to **warn** (*noutheteite*) **him,** not denounce him. Whereas they were to have no social contact with him they were not to break off *all* contact. They were patiently to admonish him to forsake the error of his ways.

VI. Conclusion (3:16-18)

The epistle closes with a prayer, a final greeting, and a benediction.

3:16. This is Paul's fourth prayer for the Thessalonians in this epistle (cf. 1:11-12; 2:16-17; 3:5). From correction Paul turned to intercession. Without the Lord's working all exhortations would be ineffective. Paul's concern was for **peace** within the church through the unity of all members obeying the truth. The **Lord** is the source of peace (cf. 1 Thes. 5:23) and Paul prayed that He would bestow this on the Christians in Thessalonica. A Christian and a church enjoy peace when they are rightly related to the will of God. Paul prayed that this would be the Thessalonians' condition **at all times** regardless of their circumstances, even in persecution.

In praying that **the Lord** would **be with** them **all,** Paul was not implying that God is with Christians only some of the time (cf. Matt. 28:20). Rather, he was praying that fellowship with Christ (that Christians can enjoy only as they obey His Word) might be the portion of each believer—not just of the obedient but also of those who were presently disobedient through idle living.

3:17. There is good evidence that **Paul** dictated his epistles to an amanuensis who actually wrote them down for him (cf. Rom. 16:22; 1 Cor. 16:21; Col. 4:18). But here Paul wrote a **greeting** with his **own hand.** Probably he wrote something by hand in most of his letters, to guarantee their authenticity to the recipients. In the case of this epistle such a personal salutation was especially needed (cf. 2 Thes. 2:2). His handwriting was undoubtedly distinguishable from his secretary's and was probably recognized by his readers as Paul's own.

3:18. The same benediction is used here as in 1 Thessalonians 5:28 except that **all** is added here. "All" sounds a final appeal for unity in the church through the obedience of each individual to Paul's instruction and admonitions. Such unity can come about only through **the grace of our Lord Jesus Christ.**

BIBLIOGRAPHY

See the Bibliography on 1 Thessalonians.

1 TIMOTHY

A. Duane Litfin

INTRODUCTION

The Pastoral Epistles. "The Pastoral Epistles" is a term used to designate Paul's two letters to Timothy and one letter to Titus. Two things distinguish these three epistles from Paul's other letters: (1) They are among the last things Paul wrote, reflecting the sort of concerns which burdened the apostle near the end of his ministry. (2) They are ostensibly addressed not to a congregation but to two young men who were functioning in pastoral roles. This does not mean, of course, that the letters were not read before congregations. The epistles show clear signs that their author intended them to be used widely. Nor does this mean that the epistles are mere handbooks on pastoral duties. There is much of general interest in the letters. Yet 1 and 2 Timothy and Titus are distinctive among Paul's letters. They are highly personal, practical, and unsystematic in nature; and they deal with matters of church order which Paul had not hitherto addressed except in passing. The evolving need for structure in the churches, combined with Paul's awareness that his own steadying influence would soon be passing from the scene, prompted him to treat certain ecclesiastical and pastoral subjects which have profited the church immensely ever since.

Authorship. Each of the Pastoral Epistles begins with an explicit identification of the Apostle Paul as its author. Until modern times no significant voices questioned their Pauline authorship. However, early in the 19th century liberal scholars attacked the authenticity of the Pastorals, and that concerted attack has gained momentum. Today the majority of liberal scholars hold that the Pastorals were written not by Paul, but by a "Paulinist," that is, a follower of Paul one or two generations removed from the apostle. According to this view the Pastorals actually reflect a perspective characteristic of the early second century rather than the mid-first century and, more importantly, of Paul's later followers rather than the apostle himself.

The attack on the authenticity of the Pastorals is four-pronged: historical, stylistic, ecclesiastical, and theological.

1. Historical arguments. The historical arguments stem from the fact that chronological references in the Pastoral Epistles do not fit comfortably within the historical framework of the Book of Acts. This is in some ways a strange argument since liberal scholars also commonly attack the chronological and historical reliability of Acts. How then can Acts be used as history to undermine the authenticity of the Pastorals? Yet despite this inconsistency in the liberal position, for those who take seriously both the historicity of Acts and the Pauline authorship of the Pastorals, this is a real problem.

Some have attempted to force the Pastorals into the Acts chronology, but the historical obstacles to doing so seem insurmountable. Many liberal scholars have therefore solved the seeming problems by assuming that the letters were written much later with fictitious references designed to make the epistles appear Pauline. A variation of this is the theory that the Pastorals represent fragments of truly Pauline material interspersed with material written by a later editor. In either case, the chronological distance from the events mentioned is assumed to account for the lack of historical "fit" with Acts.

A more satisfactory solution is to assume that the Pastorals do not fit within the Book of Acts at all, but rather describe a period after the end of Acts. The Book of Acts ends with Paul in jail in Rome (A.D. 61–62). Surely if Paul was executed at the end of his imprisonment,

Luke would have mentioned it. On the other hand, it is entirely credible that Paul could have been released (A.D. 62), perhaps for lack of evidence, and left free for another period of ministry. According to this supposition (which is all it can ever be), Paul traveled widely from A.D. 62 to 67 and was eventually recaptured, tried, and executed in Rome in 67. During this period of travel he would have written 1 Timothy and Titus, and during his final imprisonment, 2 Timothy. If this scenario is correct then one ought not expect the Pastorals to fit into the chronology of Acts, which ends with his first Roman imprisonment, and the historical arguments against the Pastorals' authenticity lose their force.

2. *Stylistic arguments.* Another line of argument against the authenticity of the Pastorals grows out of detailed examinations of their vocabulary. The occurrence of unusually high numbers of words used only once in the New Testament (but more regularly by second-century writers), words used by other New Testament writers but never elsewhere by Paul, and the absence or different use of characteristic Pauline words all combine, so the argument goes, to suggest a writing style of someone other than Paul.

But such word-counting cannot support the weight of the critics' conclusions. To begin with, the entire process is scientifically unsound since the available samples of literature are far too small for any such findings to be statistically valid. Furthermore such studies completely overlook the fact that different subject matter, different experiences, advancing age, changes in environment and companions, different recipients and purposes—all these and more affect a writer's vocabulary. When the same word-counting techniques are applied to uncontested Pauline Epistles, much the same results occur. Thus authenticity cannot be determined by merely counting word usage.

3. *Ecclesiastical arguments.* The ecclesiastical arguments against the Pauline authorship of the Pastorals all claim, in one form or another, that the church structure and order evidenced in those epistles did not emerge until well after the Apostolic Age and into the second century. In fact, it is claimed,

Paul's other writings show that he had no interest in church polity at all, so that it would be out of character for him to have written some of the instructions found in the Pastorals.

But once again the critics' arguments are questionable. The polity of the Pastorals can actually be contrasted with that of the second century, when Ignatian-type "bishops" (*episkopoi*) came to be distinguished from and set in hierarchical authority over elders (*presbyteroi*). The Pastorals describe no such differentiation. The two terms are used interchangeably in the Pastorals (cf. Titus 1:5-7) in a typically Pauline fashion (cf. Acts 20:17, 28). Clearly the emergence of the offices of elder-bishop and deacon had already occurred within Paul's lifetime (cf. Phil. 1:1), no doubt at his own instigation. Nothing about those offices in the Pastoral Epistles requires a second-century date.

The same may be said for the so-called "order of widows." While the second-century church did develop almost an "office" in the church for widows, the list of widows mentioned in 1 Timothy represents no such formalized position. From the beginning there had been an awareness of the church's responsibility to needy widows (cf. Acts 6:1-6), and the instructions in the Pastorals represent nothing one would not expect to find in an apostolic letter dated two or three decades after the church began.

4. *Theological arguments.* The theological objections to Pauline authorship are two. First, critics argue that the heresy combated in the Pastorals is the well-developed Gnosticism of the second century; and, second, the theological perspective of the author, while admittedly basically Pauline, is in some significant ways unlike the great apostle and much like what one would expect of a second-century follower.

As to the first of these objections, it is widely acknowledged that what became a full-fledged heretical movement called Gnosticism in the second century was already "incipient" during the years of Paul's ministry. He often met and dealt with Gnostic tendencies, preeminently in Colosse. Therefore the fact that the Pastorals contain denunciations of false teaching that shows hints of a Gnostic dualism and asceticism does not require a second-century date. Moreover, on closer inspection, the error addressed in the Pastorals looks less and less like a well-formed Gnosticism. The false teachers described in the Pastorals actually show certain eclectic tendencies, drawing on Jewish influences as well (cf. 1 Tim. 1:7; Titus 1:10, 14; 3:9). Furthermore the essential danger of the error described seemed to lie in its irrelevance and worthlessness, a claim that would not be true of the fully formed second-century Gnosticism. Hence, the objections to Pauline authorship based on presumed references to a full Gnosticism in the Pastorals do not stand up under scrutiny.

As to the theological objection—that the theology of the author is in some ways un-Pauline—the same may be said. This does not stand up under close inspection.

According to this critical view the Pastorals supposedly show a lesser mind at work. They say the material is not anti-Pauline, or even non-Pauline, but merely un-Pauline, or perhaps sub-Pauline. Instead of refuting error, the author simply denounced it. Instead of developing the truth, the author was intent merely on conserving and guarding it. He was concerned with mere religion rather than theology, mere orthodoxy rather than creative thought. Right belief is given too much prominence, goes the argument. So they say Paul would never have written such things. Thus when combined with the fact that some of Paul's favorite ideas are missing, slighted, or reshaped (e.g., the ministry of the Holy Spirit, grace, the believers' mystical position "in Christ"), the conclusion is inevitable, according to the critics: Paul did not write the Pastorals.

Yet such a drastic conclusion is unwarranted. All of Paul's favorite themes do occur in the Pastorals, and any differences in their treatment can be fairly explained by the unique characteristics of the Pastorals. These epistles were written under unique circumstances, to unique audiences (first and foremost Timothy and Titus), for unique purposes. One should not expect them to sound exactly like Paul's other epistles. Arguments built on such subtle and in the end flimsy evidence cannot prove a second-century date.

The Pastorals do reflect, of course, a profound concern on the part of the apostle for the conservation of the truth. Paul was in the best sense of the word a "conservative." Having faithfully done all he could to develop and teach the truths of the gospel throughout his ministry, he was concerned near the end of his life that his faithful disciples not change them, but rather entrust them in turn to other faithful Christians, who would in turn entrust them to still others. He viewed this body of truth as a special stewardship from God, to be managed with great care. Since this truth led to godliness by pointing believers to Jesus Christ, it was the most valuable of treasures. It was to be taught faithfully in the congregation, and all attempts to undermine, pollute, or attack it were to be met with stern resistance.

Such a view of objective propositional truth is in serious conflict with modern existential views of truth. Hence it is not surprising that critics seek to dissociate it from Paul and attribute it to second-century followers. Yet to do so requires an unwarranted a priori assumption about the apostle's view of truth. A more objective assessment is that there is nothing in the theology of the Pastorals which requires a late date or which cannot be explained by the fact that these epistles represent Paul's last instructions to his two faithful representatives, Timothy and Titus.

Date. Paul's missionary journeys occupied approximately the years A.D. 48–56. From 56–60 Paul was slowly making his way through the Roman courts, arriving ultimately at Rome. For two years, 61–62, Paul was held under house arrest in Rome, at the end of which time, it can be surmised, he was released. From 62–67 Paul traveled more or less freely, leaving Timothy in Ephesus and Titus in Crete, and then subsequently writing each of them a letter. Thus the approximate dates for 1 Timothy and Titus are perhaps 63–66. After being recaptured and once again imprisoned, Paul wrote Timothy a second letter, 2 Timothy. Thus 2 Timothy, dated approximately A.D. 67, represents the last Pauline Epistle.

The Recipients. 1. Timothy. Timothy was the son of a Greek father and Jewish mother (Acts 16:1). No mention is made of his father being a Christian, but his mother Eunice and grandmother Lois were both known for their sincere faith (2 Tim. 1:5). Timothy was no doubt living at Lystra when Paul visited that city on his first missionary journey (cf. Acts 14:6; 16:1). Whether or not Paul led Timothy to Christ cannot be known with certainty. At any rate Timothy already knew and believed the Old Testament Scriptures, thanks to his mother and grandmother (cf. 2 Tim. 3:15), and Paul took him on as a promising protégé. Paul thus became like a spiritual father to the young man, referring to him as "my true son in the faith" (1 Tim. 1:2) and "my dear son" (2 Tim. 1:2; cf. Phil. 2:22).

Timothy's promise for the ministry was recognized early (1 Tim. 1:18; 4:14; 2 Tim. 4:5). Thus Paul took him on as a companion and he became one of the apostle's most trustworthy fellow-laborers (cf. Rom. 16:21; 1 Cor. 16:10; Phil. 2:19-22; 1 Thes. 3:2). He also became Paul's faithful representative and messenger (Acts 19:22; 1 Cor. 4:17; 2 Cor. 1:19; Phil. 2:19; 1 Thes. 3:2, 6). Six of Paul's epistles include Timothy in the salutations (2 Cor. 1:1; Phil. 1:1; Col. 1:1; 1 Thes. 1:1; 2 Thes. 1:1; Phile. 1; see the chart, "Paul's Introduction to His Epistles" at Rom. 1:1). Timothy had become so dear to Paul that in the apostle's last message was a touching appeal for Timothy to join him in his final days of imprisonment (2 Tim. 1:4; 4:9, 21).

After being released from his first Roman imprisonment Paul, with Timothy by his side, evidently revisited some of the churches in Asia, including Ephesus. On his departure from Ephesus, Paul left Timothy behind to provide leadership to the congregation. Then after an interval Paul wrote Timothy a letter, 1 Timothy, urging him on in that ministry.

Timothy may have been by nature somewhat passive, timid, retiring, and easily intimidated (cf. 2 Tim. 1:7). Thus Paul repeatedly spurred him into action (1 Tim. 1:3; 4:11; 5:7; 6:2; 2 Tim. 3:14; 4:2, 5). He was to let nothing, including his relative youth (1 Tim. 4:12) stand in the way of his performance of duty (2 Tim. 2:1-7; 4:5). Like a good soldier he was to "fight the good fight" (1 Tim. 1:18; 6:12), aggressively protecting and propagating the gospel, using the full range of his gifts (1 Tim. 4:14; 2 Tim. 1:6).

2. *Titus.* Considerably less is known of Titus than of Timothy. Like Timothy he was one of Paul's converts, or at least a protégé (cf. Titus 1:4), but when or where he became a believer is unknown. Nor is anything known about his family or background, except that he was a Gentile (Gal. 2:3).

It is clear, however, that he was a trustworthy co-laborer with Paul. Titus was given one of Paul's most difficult and delicate assignments—to represent the apostle in troubled Corinth (2 Cor. 2:13; 7:6-7, 13-15; 8:6, 16-17). During the time between his two Roman imprisonments, Paul visited Crete with Titus, whom he left behind to further the work the two had begun (cf. Titus 1:5). Sometime later, during Paul's second imprisonment, Titus left Crete to travel to Dalmatia (2 Tim. 4:10), presumably for evangelistic purposes.

OUTLINE

D. Concerning slaves and masters (6:1-2)
E. Concerning the heretical and greedy (6:3-10)
VI. Final Charge to Timothy (6:11-21)
A. Exhortation to godliness (6:11-16)
B. Instructions for the rich (6:17-19)
C. Exhortations to remain faithful (6:20-21)

COMMENTARY

I. The Salutation (1:1-2)

1:1. Paul's typical salutation includes an identification of both author and recipient, combined with a more or less ritualized greeting. Here as in each of his other epistles except Philippians, 1 and 2 Thessalonians, and Philemon, **Paul** identified himself as **an apostle of Christ Jesus.** He no doubt used the term "apostle" in its more restricted sense to refer to those who had been personally commissioned by the risen Christ (cf. 2 Cor. 8:23 ["representatives"]; Phil. 2:25 ["messenger"] for its broader usage). Paul's apostleship was not something he had sought; it had come to him through a heavenly command (Gal. 1:11–2:2; cf. 1 Tim. 2:7). In several of his other epistles Paul commonly made a similar point by stressing his apostolic "calling" according to "the will of God" (1 Cor. 1:1; 2 Cor. 1:1; Eph. 1:1; Col. 1:1; 2 Tim. 1:1). Paul was often in the position of having to defend his authority which came from both God the Father and God the Son. The identification of **God our Savior** has an Old Testament ring to it but is common in the Pastorals (cf. 1 Tim. 2:3; 4:10; Titus 1:3; 2:10; 3:4). **Jesus** is described as **our hope,** a term which directs the reader's attention to the certain fulfillment of God's saving plan in **Christ** (cf. Col. 1:27).

1:2. Though this letter was clearly intended to be read aloud to the congregations in Ephesus and beyond, **Timothy** was identified as its immediate recipient. As Paul's genuine or **true son in the faith,** none could mistake Timothy's special place in Paul's heart. (This is the first of 19 times Paul used the Gr. word *pistis,* "faith," in 1 Tim.) Paul had probably not led him to Christ (cf. 2 Tim. 1:5; 3:15), but he probably had ordained (2 Tim. 1:6) the young minister, and had

great confidence in him. Timothy was issued Paul's fairly standard greeting of **grace, mercy, and peace.**

II. Instructions concerning False Teachers (1:3-20)

A. Warnings against false teachers (1:3-11)

1:3. The moves referred to in this verse cannot be followed clearly. Was Paul leaving **Ephesus** to enter **Macedonia?** Had he given Timothy instructions prior to leaving Ephesus? This is perhaps the best supposition. Timothy was urged, apparently for a second time, to **stay** on in Ephesus, indicating perhaps some inclination on Timothy's part to leave that ministry, perhaps to accompany Paul. Timothy's task in remaining was to stifle **certain men** in the congregation who were teaching **false** (lit., "different"; cf. 6:3) **doctrines**—that is, different from Paul's doctrine (cf. 1:11).

1:4. These false teachers were following after fables (*mythois,* cf. 4:7) and long, involved **genealogies.** Exactly what these fables and genealogies involved is not known. They may have had a Gnostic flavor, but were more likely of Jewish origin (cf. Titus 1:14). Whatever their nature, they were empty of any spiritual value and led only to further speculation, questions, and arguments. Such speculations were to be avoided because they did not further **God's** plan, which is grasped and implemented not by human imaginings, but **by faith.** By contrast, human speculations tend to lead off down endless blind tunnels which serve only to confuse and obscure God's truth.

1:5. Unlike such aimless speculations, the intended result of Paul's instruction to Timothy was **love,** and the purest kind of love at that. It is that love which pours naturally from a cleansed **heart** (cf. 2 Tim. 2:22), untainted **conscience,** and a sincere (*anypokritou,* "unhypocritical"; cf. 2 Tim. 1:5) **faith.** Each member of this beautiful trio speaks of a purity and integrity which produces the most exquisite kind of selfless love, seen in its ultimate form in God's love itself. Whereas the false teachers were motivated by worthless curiosity, Paul's instruction was designed to promote the most magnificent of virtues by maintaining the purity of the church's teaching.

God's truth always purifies the human spirit, while error putrifies it.

1:6. Paul no doubt believed that such love should be the goal of all Christian ministry (cf. 1 Cor. 13:1-3). Yet, sadly, though they should have known better, some teachers in the Ephesian congregation had lost sight of this lofty purpose and had **wandered away** (lit., "missed the aim"; cf. 1 Tim. 6:21; 2 Tim. 2:18) and **turned** aside **to meaningless talk.** Their teaching was *mataiologian,* that is, idle, useless, futile, empty verbiage.

1:7. More specifically, the problem with these false teachers, as is often the case, was a matter of the ego. They wanted to become respected **teachers of the Law.** Yet they were completely incapable of doing so. But instead of recognizing their inadequacies and remaining silent, they went on babbling as if with great authority, never understanding their subject (the Law), or even **what they** were saying about it.

1:8. Paul wanted to be sure that he was not misunderstood. He was not disparaging the Law. Paul viewed the Law as "holy, righteous, and good" (Rom. 7:12). Thus he clarified his point by emphasizing that **the Law is good** provided it is used **properly.** There is an inappropriate, legalistic use of the Law which Paul disavowed; but there is also a proper use of the Law that Paul embraced (cf. Gal. 3:19, 24).

1:9-10. The **Law** is designed to show people their sinfulness. Thus the Law is not for one who had already recognized his sin and turned to Christ. That person is no longer under the Law but should now walk in the Spirit (Gal. 5:13-26). The Law is intended for those who remain unconvinced of their sin.

Paul provided a striking list of examples which seem to be intentionally based on the Ten Commandments (cf. Ex. 20:3-17). The list begins with three pairs corresponding to the *first* table of the Decalogue dealing with offenses against God: (1) **lawbreakers and rebels,** (2) **the ungodly and sinful,** (3) **the unholy** (*anosiois,* "not devout"; cf. *hosious* in 1 Tim. 2:8) **and irreligious** (*bebēlois,* "profane"; cf. 4:7; 6:20; 2 Tim. 2:16). Paul then listed violators of the first five commandments of the *second* table of the Decalogue: **those who kill their fathers or mothers** represent the ultimate viola-

tion of the fifth commandment, and **murderers** the sixth. **Adulterers and perverts** pertain to the seventh commandment, which was generally broadly interpreted to include all forms of sexual sin. **Slave traders** may correspond to the eighth commandment since kidnapping was viewed as the ultimate act of stealing (Ex. 21:16; Deut. 24:7). **Liars and perjurers** clearly pertain to the ninth commandment. Only the 10th commandment ("You shall not covet") is not included (but cf. Rom. 7:7). Paul concluded this inventory of sinners with an all-inclusive reference to any behavior which **is contrary to sound doctrine** (lit., to "healthy teaching"; cf. 2 Tim. 1:13), including no doubt the very behavior of the false teachers themselves. "Doctrine" here is *didaskalia,* "teaching" or "the content taught," used seven times in this epistle: 1 Timothy 1:10; 4:1, 6, 13, 16; 5:17; 6:1.

1:11. Paul's yardstick for measuring what is and is not sound teaching, of course, was the message of God's great good news in Christ with which he had been **entrusted** (cf. 1 Thes. 2:4; Titus 1:3), and which he had faithfully preached in Ephesus (cf. Acts 20:17-27).

B. Paul's experience of grace (1:12-17)

1:12. At this point Paul's inventory of sinners, of which he knew he was the chief—combined with his remembrance of the gospel with which he had been entrusted—triggered within him a powerful surge of gratitude. Literally, the words "Thanks I have"—with "thanks" in the emphatic position—begins this section. Paul's gratitude stemmed from the fact that God in His grace had provided Paul all necessary enablement (cf. Phil. 4:13) and, considering him trustworthy, had pressed him into a privileged place of **service.**

1:13. The reason this was so striking to the apostle was that he knew so well the pit from which he had been dug. When he said he was **a blasphemer and a persecutor and a violent man,** he was not exaggerating for the sake of effect. (See Acts 22:4-5, 19-20; 26:9-11 for the vivid truth.) Yet Paul **was shown mercy because** his actions were the product of **ignorance.** Willful disobedience triggers God's wrath (cf., e.g., Num. 15:22-31; Heb. 10:26). But God deals gently with the ignorant and misguided (Heb. 5:2). The German philosopher Nietzsche said, "If you could prove God to me, I would believe Him all the less." No such willfulness characterized Paul's unbelief.

1:14. Therefore the apostle received God's mercy, not His wrath. God's **grace** far outpaced even Paul's grievous sin. Where there was once only unbelief, God **poured out . . . faith . . . in Christ.** Where there had been violent aggression against God and His people, now God poured out the **love** of Christ. (See comments on 2 Tim. 2:10.) Everything Paul lacked, God's grace had more than amply supplied. (The verb *hyperepleonasen*, used only here in the NT, means "to be present in great or superabundance.") Here may be seen the full measure of what Paul meant when he spoke of the empowering ministry of Christ (1 Tim. 1:12).

1:15. The central thrust of Paul's personal digression, begun in verse 12, now becomes clear. It is a testimony concerning the purpose of the Incarnation of **Christ. Jesus came** not merely to set an example or to show that He cared. He came to salvage **sinners** from their spiritual destitution—and Paul said he was **the worst** of that lot. There must be no misunderstanding of this most fundamental point. It is a truth that is completely **trustworthy** and deserving of **full acceptance.** (Four other passages include this "trustworthy" phrase: 3:1; 4:9; 2 Tim. 2:11; Titus 3:8.)

1:16. In fact it was just for this purpose—that is, to demonstrate God's plan to save sinners—that Paul himself was saved. As **the worst of sinners** (cf. Paul's other descriptions of himself in 1 Cor. 15:9; Eph. 3:8), Paul represents the extreme **example.** If God was patient and gracious enough to save Paul, He is patient and gracious enough to save anyone. All who follow can look back at Paul as a prototype or pattern ("example," *hypotypōsin*; cf. 2 Tim. 1:13). The ultimate sinner became the ultimate saint; God's greatest enemy became His finest servant. Somewhere between these extremes fall all the rest. In studying Paul's pattern, Christians can therefore learn about themselves.

1:17. This contemplation of God's grace as seen in Paul's case prompted him to one of his typical doxologies. It is filled with awe and adoration of the Lord. **King eternal** (lit., "King of the Ages") emphasizes God's sovereignty over all the ebb and flow of human history. **Immortal** and **invisible** speak of two of the central attributes of God: His eternality and His spiritual essence. **The only God** emphasizes His uniqueness in a typical Jewish monotheistic fashion. To this God alone must all **honor and glory** be ascribed, eternally. **Amen** (cf. 6:16).

C. Paul's charge to Timothy (1:18-20)

1:18. Returning from his brief personal digression (vv. 12-17), Paul got back to the specific matters before Timothy in Ephesus, resuming the charge begun in verse 3. **This instruction** (the same word *parangelian* is translated "command" in v. 5) refers to the teaching about the false teachers mentioned in verse 3. Such instructions were in accord with **the prophecies . . . made** earlier concerning Timothy's call and fitness for service in Ephesus. When and by whom these prophecies were made can only be guessed. It is known that the prophecies reinforced Paul's conviction that Timothy was a fit soldier to conduct the battle against error in the Ephesian church (cf. 6:12; 2 Tim. 4:7 for an athletic rather than military metaphor). Timothy was to remember these prophecies and be inspired by them in the struggle.

1:19. Whereas in Ephesians 6:10-17 Paul spelled out in detail to that church the Christian's equipment for spiritual warfare, here he listed only two items: **faith and a good conscience.** These two always seem to travel together (cf. 1 Tim. 1:5; 3:9). Strength in the one is always combined with strength in the other. So also is failure in the one correlated with failure in the other. Thus **some** who **have rejected** (*apōtheō*, "a strong, deliberate thrusting away"; used elsewhere in the NT only in Acts 7:27; Rom. 11:1-2) a good conscience have also found **their faith** destroyed (cf. 1 Tim. 4:1; 6:10). Theological error is often rooted in moral failure.

1:20. Two in Ephesus who illustrate this principle are **Hymenaeus** (cf. 2 Tim. 2:17) **and Alexander.** Whether this is the same Alexander mentioned in Acts 19:33 and 2 Timothy 4:14 is not clear. Probably it is not. Paul's prescription for these two blasphemers was that they be **handed over to Satan,** a phrase which perhaps refers to excommunication from the congregation (cf. 1 Cor. 5:1-5) and abandonment to realms controlled by Satan (2 Cor. 4:4). Paul viewed the congregation as a haven and protection for believers without which they would suffer painful disadvantage. Thus excommunication was designed to chasten the two apostates. Yet Paul's motive was remedial, not punitive (cf. 2 Cor. 2:5-8; 2 Thes. 3:14-15).

III. Instructions concerning Conduct in the Church (2:1–3:13)

A. Instructions concerning prayer (2:1-7)

2:1. From his concerns about false teachers Paul turned to matters relating to the conduct of the church broadly (cf. 3:14-15). Paul began with what he considered most important: prayer. What too often comes last in a church's priorities should actually come first. Not much weight should be placed on the presumed distinctions between **requests, prayers,** and **intercession.** The terms are more likely designed to build on one another for emphasis. It should be noted, however, that **thanksgiving** should have a prominent place in the church's prayer life.

2:2. The Ephesian church was to pray "for everyone" (v. 1, lit., "all men"), but especially for the leaders of civil government. Paul did not specify here the content of these prayers, but almost certainly he was instructing that requests be made for the salvation of the populace and its governors. This can be seen clearly from the following verses. With Nero's growing resentment toward Christians—which came to full bloom after the fire in Rome in July, A.D. 64—and the general disintegration of the Roman Empire due to Nero's profligacy, Christians began to suffer persecution from the Roman authorities. Having recently been released from his Roman imprisonment, Paul was greatly aware of the deteriorating political atmosphere. Thus he urged prayer for the salvation of all men, but especially rulers, so that the stable, noninterfering environment of previous days might be recovered. This is the minimum requirement if Christians are to live **peaceful and quiet lives in all godliness and holiness.** (This is the first of 10 times Paul used the word *eusebia,*

"godliness." These 10 occurrences are all in the Pastoral Epistles: 2:2; 3:16; 4:7-8; 6:3, 5-6, 11; 2 Tim. 3:5; Titus 1:1. Its five other usages are in Acts 3:12; 2 Peter 1:3, 6-7; 3:11.) Times of political and social upheaval are excellent times in which to die for Christ, but hard times in which to live for Him.

2:3. As in modern times, some in the Ephesian church were prepared to question the validity of a prayer for the salvation of all men. Thus Paul defended his instructions by pointing out that such a prayer **is good, and pleases God our Savior** (cf. 1:1). Literally, the Greek says that such a prayer is "acceptable before" (in the presence of) God. Many prayers are unacceptable to God, but not this one.

2:4. The reason this prayer is acceptable to God is that it is a prayer "according to His will" (1 John 5:14). God, who is by nature a Savior, **wants all men to be saved.** Paul repeated the words "everyone" (1 Tim. 2:1) and "all men" (vv. 3, 6). The same Greek word (*pas,* "all") is used in each case, referring all three times to the same group (cf. 4:10). God desires that no one perish (2 Peter 3:9), that the entire human race come to know the truth through a personal relationship with Jesus Christ, who is the Truth (John 14:6). (Of course not all do come to salvation; Paul was not teaching universalism.)

2:5-6. To further buttress his argument Paul cited the commonly accepted teaching about God and His work in Christ. Verses 5-6 may represent a fragment of a familiar confession of the first century. In any case, Paul cited these unquestioned truths of the gospel: (1) **There is** only **one God.** (2) There is only one way for men to approach Him—through **the Man** who was God in the flesh, **Christ Jesus.** (3) This Jesus **gave Himself** up to die on the cross **as a ransom** (*antilytron;* cf. *lytron,* "ransom" for a slave or prisoner, in Matt. 20:28; Mark 10:45) for the human race. (Cf. the chart, "New Testament Words for Redemption," at Mark 10:45.) This act is a clear **testimony,** offered at just the right **time** (Gal. 4:4-5; Heb. 1:1-2), of God's desire to save **all men** (cf. Titus 1:3).

2:7. The exclusivists in the Ephesian church evidently felt that the gospel was only for Jews. This was a common problem, as seen preeminently in the case of Peter (cf. Acts 10:9-43; Gal. 2:11-13). Thus Paul cited his own commission as **apostle . . . to the Gentiles** as a clincher. Paul had been **appointed a herald** (*kēryx*, "messenger"; cf. 2 Tim. 1:11) to take the gospel to the majority of the human race that the Jews had considered beyond the pale. Thus, as Paul reminded the Ephesians, it can be seen that God desires everyone to be saved. Paul's assurances of his truthfulness were stylistic devices designed to stress the importance of his point (cf. Rom. 9:1; 2 Cor. 11:31; Gal. 1:20).

B. Instructions concerning men and women (2:8-15)

2:8. Undoubtedly Paul wanted all Christians to offer up prayers for a widespread spiritual awakening among the populace and its rulers. Yet in the public assembly Paul specified that **men** (*undras*, lit., "males") **everywhere** are to lead the congregation in **prayer.** Moreover, these prayers were to be offered with lifted **hands.** This was a common Old Testament practice (cf., e.g., 1 Kings 8:22; 2 Chron. 6:13; Ezra 9:5; Pss. 28:2; 141:2; Lam. 2:19). It was also common in the pagan mystery religions of the first century and in the early church. Paintings on the walls of the catacombs in Rome portray this posture. The hands were to be **holy** (*hosious*, "devout, undefiled"), signifying an internal cleanness on the part of these spiritual leaders. Further, such leaders must be men of sound relationships, not characterized by **anger** (*orgēs*, "outbursts of temper") **or disputing** (*dialogismou*). Broken human relationships affect one's ability to pray (cf. Matt. 5:22-24; 6:12; 1 Peter 3:7), which would include leading others in prayer.

2:9. Next Paul turned to the females in the congregation. For their adornment they should not emphasize the external, but the internal. They should dress **modestly, with decency and propriety** (cf. v. 15). These terms stress not so much the absence of sexual suggestiveness, though it is included, but rather an appearance that is simple, moderate, judicious, and free from ostentation. The specifics Paul mentioned (**braided hair or gold or pearls or expensive clothes**) are not wrong in themselves, but become inappropriate when they indicate misplaced values (cf. 1 Peter 3:3). In the

Ephesian church these styles may have been associated with the local temple prostitutes. Christians must be careful about letting a pagan culture set their fashions.

2:10. Instead of stressing external beauty, according to the world's standards, Christian women should manifest a different set of values. They should adorn themselves **with** (lit., "by means of") **good deeds.** They should depend on their faithful service in the name of Christ to render them attractive to others. This was no plea for women to make themselves unattractive; it was simply an exhortation to reject the world's yardstick for measuring beauty and adopt heaven's standard (1 Sam. 16:7). One should expect nothing less from **women who profess to worship God.**

2:11-12. In emphasizing godly conduct for women, Paul stressed, with Peter, "the unfading beauty of a gentle and quiet spirit, which is of great worth in God's sight" (1 Peter 3:4). The females in the congregation should receive instruction from the male leadership with **quietness and full submission.** They should not attempt to turn the tables by clamoring for the office of congregational teacher or by grasping for **authority over** men. Rather they should, literally, "be in quietness." The word, *hēsychia*, translated "quietness" in 1 Timothy 2:11 and **silent** in verse 12, does not mean complete silence or no talking. It is clearly used elsewhere (Acts 22:2; 2 Thes. 3:12) to mean "settled down, undisturbed, not unruly." A different word (*sigaō*) means "to be silent, to say nothing" (cf. Luke 18:39; 1 Cor. 14:34).

2:13. Why is such a quiet and submissive spirit "of great worth in God's sight"? (1 Peter 3:4) Because it manifests an understanding and acceptance of His design for the human race. As elsewhere (cf. 1 Cor. 11:8-10), Paul here based his view of male/female relationships in the church on the account of Creation recorded in Genesis 2. He made no reference whatever to the so-called "curse" of Genesis 3:16. Rather, the roles Paul spelled out here are a product of God's fundamental design wherein **Adam was formed first, then Eve** (cf. Gen. 2:7-25). More is involved here than mere chronological priority. Paul saw the priority in time as indicative of the leadership given to the male, to which the woman, the "helper suitable for him" (Gen. 2:18), should respond.

2:14. Further, Paul contrasted the experiences of Adam and Eve. **The woman . . . was deceived and became a sinner,** but **Adam was not the one deceived.** Some chauvinists see Paul arguing here that women, as represented in their archetype Eve, are more gullible and thus more susceptible to error, than men. Thus, they say, females should not be in places of teaching or authority in the church. Others believe Paul was saying, in effect, "Look what happens when the Creation order is reversed and the man abdicates the leadership role to the woman." In any case, Paul was emphatically not excusing or absolving Adam of blame for the Fall. Elsewhere Paul put the responsibility squarely on Adam's shoulders (cf. Rom. 5:12-21).

2:15. This is one of the most difficult verses of the New Testament to intepret. The ambiguous words **kept safe through childbirth** have given rise to several diverse interpretations: (a) preserved (physically) through the difficult and dangerous process of childbirth; (b) preserved (from insignificance) by means of her role in the family; (c) saved through the ultimate childbirth of Jesus Christ the Savior (an indirect reference to Gen. 3:15); and (d) kept from the corruption of society by being at home raising children. The interpretation of the verse is further clouded by the conditional clause at the end: **if they,** that is, mothers, **continue in faith, love, and holiness with propriety.** Whatever one understands the first part of the verse to be affirming, it is contingent on a woman's willingness to abide in these four virtues. Hence the second of the preceding options seems most likely. A woman will find her greatest satisfaction and meaning in life, not in seeking the male role, but in fulfilling God's design for her as wife and mother with all "faith, love, and holiness with propriety" (i.e., self-restraint; cf. 1 Tim. 2:9).

C. *Instructions concerning elders and deacons (3:1-13)*

3:1. Continuing his instructions on how the church should conduct itself, Paul turned to the crucial matter of leadership qualifications. He wanted to encourage respect for the congregation's leaders, so he cited what was apparently a familiar maxim and commended it as a sound one. Two implications emerge: (1) It is valid to aspire to church leadership, and (2) church leadership is **a noble task.** The term **overseer** (*episkopos*), sometimes translated "bishop," is only one of several words used in the New Testament to describe church leaders. "Elders" (*presbyteroi*) is by far the most common. Other terms such as "rulers" (*proistamenoi*, Rom. 12:8; 1 Thes. 5:12), "leaders" (*hēgoumenois*, Heb. 13:17) and "pastors" (*poimenas*, Eph. 4:11; cf. also Acts 20:28; 1 Peter 5:2) are also used. Though each of these terms may describe a different facet of leadership, they all seem to be used interchangeably in the New Testament to designate the same office. This office is different from that of deacons (cf. comments on 1 Tim 3:8).

3:2. More is required of an overseer than mere willingness to serve. In verses 2-7 Paul listed 15 requirements for a church leader: (1) **above reproach.** He must be blameless in his behavior. This Greek word *anepilēmpton,* "above reproach," is used in the New Testament only in this epistle (v. 2; 5:7; 6:14). It means to have nothing in one's conduct on which someone could ground a charge or accusation. It differs slightly in meaning from its synonym *anenklētos* in 3:10 (see comments there). (2) **Husband of but one wife,** literally, a "one-woman man." This ambiguous but important phrase is subject to several interpretations. The question is, how stringent a standard was Paul erecting for overseers? Virtually all commentators agree that this phrase prohibits both polygamy and promiscuity, which are unthinkable for spiritual leaders in the church. Many Bible students say the words a "one-woman man" are saying that the affections of an elder must be centered exclusively on his wife. Many others hold, however, that the phrase further prohibits any who have been divorced and remarried from becoming overseers. The reasoning behind this view is usually that divorce represents a failure in the home, so that even though a man may be forgiven for any sin involved, he remains permanently disqualified for leadership in the congregation (cf. vv. 4-5; 1 Cor. 9:24-27). The most strict interpretation and the one common among the earliest commentators (second and third centuries) includes each of the above but extends the prohibition to *any* second marriage, even by widowers. Their argument is that in the first century second marriages were generally viewed as evidence of self-indulgence. Though Paul honored marriage, he also valued the spiritual benefits of celibacy (1 Cor. 7:37-38) even for those who had lost a mate (1 Tim. 5:3-14). Thus he considered celibacy a worthy goal for those who possessed the self-control to remain unmarried. According to this strict view Paul considered a widower's second marriage, though by no means improper, to be evidence of a lack of the kind of self-control required of an overseer, in much the same way that a similar lack disqualified a widow from eligibility for the list of widows (5:9). Church leaders must also be (3) **temperate** (*nēphalion*, "well-balanced"; used elsewhere only in 3:11; Titus 2:2), (4) **self-controlled** (*sōphrona*, also used in Titus 1:8; 2:5), (5) **respectable**, and (6) **hospitable**. Such characteristics are prerequisites for those who would lead others into these important Christian virtues. The phrase (7) **able to teach** speaks of a leader's ability to handle the Scriptures. He must be able both to understand and to communicate the truth to others, as well as to refute those who mishandle it (cf. Titus 1:9). Not all must necessarily do this publicly, of course; some may conduct this aspect of their ministries more informally in private settings. Yet all leaders must possess an aptitude for handling the Word with skill.

3:3. Four negative phrases follow: (8) **not given to much wine** (cf. Titus 1:7), and (9) **not violent.** His self-control (1 Tim. 3:2) is to extend to his appetites and his anger. By contrast, a church leader must be (10) **gentle,** or forbearing, making room for others. (This word *epieikē* is also used in Phil. 4:5; Titus 3:2; James 3:17; 1 Peter 2:18). Unlike false teachers, an effective church leader is (11) **not quarrelsome** (cf. 1 Tim. 6:4) and (12) **not a lover of money** (cf. 6:5; Titus 1:11). He neither relishes fighting with others nor pursues his ministry for personal gain (cf. 1 Peter 5:2).

3:4. An overseer must (13) **manage his own family well.** Paul's specific focus here was on the children. The most reliable (though not infallible) means of determining the quality of one's potential leadership is by examining the behavior of his children. Do they respect their father enough to submit to his leadership? **With proper respect** (lit., "with all gravity") may refer, however, not to the children's submission, but to the manner in which the father exercises his authority, that is, without due fuss or clamor.

3:5. A rhetorical question forms a parenthetical support for the validity of the preceding qualification. Paul made an analogy between leadership or management of a home and that in a church (Eph. 2:19; 1 Tim. 3:15). Many of the same skills and qualifications are needed for both. Success in a family may well indicate success in a church; likewise, failure in a home raises a red flag about one's ability to lead in a congregation.

3:6. An overseer **must** (14) **not be a recent convert** (*neophyton*, "neophyte"), lest his rapid advancement to leadership fill him with pride and conceit, and he experience the **same** kind of **judgment** that **the devil** incurred for his pride.

3:7. An overseer **must also** (15) **have a good reputation with outsiders** (cf. Col. 4:5; 1 Thes. 4:12). Paul's thought here seems to be that church leaders, as representatives of the congregation, are constantly susceptible to the snares of the devil (cf. 2 Tim. 2:26). Satan likes nothing better than to **disgrace** God's work and God's people by trapping church leaders in sin before a watching world. It is important therefore that overseers achieve and maintain a good reputation before unbelievers.

3:8. Like overseers, **deacons** (cf. Phil. 1:1) must also be men of quality, even though their function in the congregation is significantly different. The word translated "deacon" (*diakonos*) means literally a "humble servant." The role of the deacons is to carry out, under the elders' oversight, some of the more menial tasks of the church so that the elders can give their attention to more important things. (See Acts 6:1-6 for the prototype of what later became the "office" of deacon in the church.) The qualifications for the office of deacon are almost as stringent as for elder because of their public profile in the church and because the servant nature of their work requires strong qualities of maturity and piety. Deacons must therefore **be men worthy of respect**—that is, serious men of dignity, not clowns. (The same Gr. word is used of women in 1 Tim. 3:11.) They must be **sincere** (mē dilogous, lit., "not double-tongued") in the sense of being honest and unhypocritical. Like the overseers (v. 3), deacons must not be heavy **wine** drinkers or greedy chasers after **dishonest gain.**

3:9. Most important of all, deacons **must** be men of spiritual depth (cf. Acts 6:3). Specifically they should be men who understand and **hold fast the deep truths of the faith.** By the phrase **with a clear conscience** Paul (cf. "good conscience" in 1 Tim. 1:5) meant that there must be nothing in the conduct of these men that was glaringly inconsistent with their professed beliefs. In other words they must not profess one thing but practice another.

3:10. Moreover, like the overseers, who are to demonstrate their maturity before being placed in a position of responsibility (v. 6), deacons **must** also **first be tested.** Paul's intent here was not to require some formal testing procedure, but rather that these men "prove" their quality over time in the ordinary activities of life and ministry. After they showed themselves "irreproachable," then **let them serve as deacons.** The words **if there is nothing against them** translate two Greek words, anenklētoi ontes, "being free from accusation." The word anenklētos occurs in the New Testament only in Paul's writings (1 Cor. 1:8; Col. 1:22; 1 Tim. 3:10; Titus 1:6-7). It means one who is unaccused, free from any charge at all. Christlike conduct is required of deacons. (Cf. comments on a synonym, anepilēmpton, in 1 Tim. 3:2.)

3:11. Similarly the gynaikas ("women" or **wives) are to be worthy of respect,** that is, dignified (the same word, semnas, is used of deacons in v. 8), not slanderers (diabolous, from diaballō "to slander"; from this verb comes the noun "devil," the chief slanderer) of others, **but temperate** (nēphalious, "well-balanced; cf. v. 2; Titus 2:2), **and trustworthy** (lit., "faithful") **in everything.** Who are these gynaikas Paul addressed? They were almost certainly not the women of the congregation generally. They were most likely either the wives of the deacons or a group of female deacons (cf. Phoebe, Rom. 16:1). A case can be made for either of these two options, with a slim advantage falling to the first. But being dogmatic about either view is unwarranted by the exegetical data.

3:12. Like the elders, deacons must be "one-women men" (cf. v. 2) and capable managers of their own families. Paul's reasoning behind this latter qualification is spelled out in verses 4-5.

3:13. Though the position of deacon seems by worldly standards to be menial and unattractive, to close followers of Jesus Christ it looks quite different (cf. John 13:11-17; Mark 10:42-45). Those who fulfill their servant roles faithfully **gain** two things: first, **an excellent standing** before fellow Christians who understand and appreciate the beauty of humble, selfless, Christlike service; and second, **great assurance** (parrēsian, "confidence, boldness") **in their faith in Christ Jesus.** Humble service, which lacks all the rewards the world deems important, becomes a true test of one's motives. Here one discovers for himself whether or not his efforts are truly prompted by a Christlike spirit of selfless service. When a deacon has indeed "served well" his ministry builds confidence in the sincerity of his own faith in Christ and of his unhypocritical approach to God (cf. Eph. 3:12; Heb. 10:19).

IV. Instructions concerning Guarding the Truth in the Church (3:14–4:16)

A. The church and its truth (3:14-16)

3:14. If Paul had left Timothy at Ephesus to pastor the church (cf. 1:3), he also hoped to rejoin Timothy there soon. In the meantime, in case of delay Paul wanted the Ephesian pastor and congregation to have **these instructions** in hand. The "instructions" no doubt refer to what has come before as well as the exhortations to follow.

3:15. The clearly stated purpose of these instructions is to inform the Ephesian congregation **how people ought to conduct themselves in God's household.** Again Paul used the analogy of the "household" (oikos) to refer to the church (ekklēsia; cf. v. 5). This merges into an architectural image involving the church as **pillar and foundation of the truth.** The idea of the church as a "building" dedicated to **the living God** is a common one for Paul (cf. 1 Cor. 3:16-17; 2 Cor. 6:16; Eph. 2:20-22). Some people teach that the church as the "foundation of the truth" is the *source* of God's truth, that no one can know the truth unless he depends on the teaching of some organized church or church group. But Paul was simply affirming the crucial role of the universal church as the support and bulwark—not the source—of God's truth. His words should not be stretched beyond this.

3:16. Paul had been discussing proper godly conduct in the church, behavior which is in every way consistent with the truth, rather than "contrary to the sound doctrine" (1:10). In 3:16 he expressed a simple idea which becomes difficult due only to its compactness. This truth about **godliness** being a **mystery** means that it was hidden but now is revealed. Further, it **is a great** (*mega*, "large, important") "mystery" in that it is overwhelmingly large in scope and sublimely important in significance (cf. Eph. 5:32). Paul cited the content of this truth in the form of an excerpt from an early hymn about Christ, who is the essence of the "mystery" (Col. 1:27). Whether the fragment should be divided into two or three parts is disputed. Whichever one chooses, the six elements of the excerpt are as follows: (1) **Appeared in a body** refers to the Incarnation of Christ. (2) **Was vindicated by the Spirit** refers to God's demonstration through the Resurrection (cf. Acts 2:24-36), by the Holy Spirit (cf. Rom. 8:11), that the crucified Jesus is Lord and Messiah. (3) **Was seen by angels** refers to His exaltation before the heavenly realm (cf. Phil. 2:9-11; Col. 2:15; Heb. 1:6). (4) **Was preached among the nations** (cf. Col. 1:23) and (5) **was believed on in the world** refer to the progressive fulfillment of God's redemptive plan through His preordained means (cf. 1 Cor. 1:18-2:5). (6) **Was taken up in glory** refers to the Ascension (Eph. 4:10).

B. Predictions of apostasy (4:1-5)

4:1. As the repository and guardian of the truth, the church must be aware of the strategies of the truth's enemies. It is crucial then for the church to understand what God has revealed about these enemies (cf. 1 Peter 4:1-18; Jude 17-18). By **the Spirit clearly says** Paul was not necessarily referring to any particular revelation but to the repeated teaching of the Lord (e.g., Mark 13:22), the other apostles (e.g., 2 Peter 3:1-18), and Paul himself (e.g., Acts 20:29; 2 Thes. 2:1-12). According to this teaching the situation will degenerate as Christ's return approaches. **In later times** (cf. 2 Tim. 3:1 for a synonym), which Paul viewed as still future though casting their shadow already, **some** people **will abandon the faith** (cf. 1 Tim. 1:19) to **follow** after the false teaching of **deceiving spirits and . . . demons.** Spiritual error is seldom due to innocent mistakes. It is more often due to the conscious strategies of God's spiritual enemies (cf. Eph. 6:12). The teachings (*didaskaliais*) of demons are false doctrines taught by errorists whose views are instigated by demons.

4:2. But God's spiritual enemies do not directly confront their victims with error. Instead they work through **hypocritical liars** (lit., "men who speak lies in hypocrisy"). This is Satan's standard operating procedure (cf. 2 Cor. 11:13-15). He selects likely representatives and renders their **consciences** beyond feeling (cf. Eph. 4:19), **seared** (from *kaustēriazō*, "to brand, cauterize") **as with a hot iron.** In this condition they are ready to do Satan's bidding.

4:3. The false teachers plaguing the Ephesian church were the forerunners of the Gnostics of the second century. Even at this relatively incipient stage, the strong dualism of the Gnostics is clear: spirit is good; matter is evil. They believed all appetites relating to the body are therefore evil and should be rooted out, including normal desires for sex and food. Thus the false teachers **forbid people to marry and order them to abstain from certain foods** (cf. Col. 2:21). But Paul went to the heart of the dualistic error by stating that matter is not inherently evil; it is rather part of what **God created** (cf. 1 Tim. 6:17b). Hence **those who believe and who know the truth** can gratefully (cf. 4:4) receive and use the things God created, which were designed **to be received** (*eis metalēmpsin*, "for partaking").

4:4. Contrary to the teaching of the errorists, **everything God created is good.** Here Paul echoed God's own verdict (Gen. 1:31). Whereas the false teachers were intent on "forbidding" and "abstaining" (1 Tim. 4:3), Paul said that **nothing is to be rejected**—nothing, that is, that God created. Man can abuse what God has created, as adultery is an abuse of the marital sexual relationship, and gluttony is an abuse of a normal appetite for food. Such abuses should certainly be rejected. But God's creations themselves are all good and should be **received with thanksgiving,** not with taboos.

4:5. All the seemingly "ordinary" things of life can then become extraordinary as they are **consecrated by the Word of God and prayer.** In the light of the Scriptures a Christian recognizes God's good hand behind the things provided, and offers thanksgiving to the Lord. In this way the ordinary things so easily taken for granted (some of which are forbidden by errorists) become sanctified as occasions for worship and praise.

C. Responsibilities of a good minister of Christ (4:6-16)

4:6. From his warning of the apostasy to come Paul turned to Timothy, and exhorted him to pass along these same warnings to others in the church. One of the works of **a good minister of Christ Jesus** is that he is a faithful conduit of the truth to other Christians (cf. 2 Tim. 2:2). To do this, however, Timothy first had to keep himself "nourished" (not **brought up**) by (a) the objective **truths of the faith** which, as Jude 3 puts it, were "once for all entrusted to the saints," and (b) the truths **of the good teaching that you have followed.** This latter phrase probably refers to Paul's own instructions to his young disciple, which Timothy had faithfully carried out (didaskalia, "teaching" is also used in 1 Tim. 1:10; 4:1, 13, 16; 5:17; 6:1).

4:7. But since Timothy was to channel God's truth to others, he was to **have nothing to do with godless myths and old wives' tales.** The godless (bebēlous, "profane") and the worthless go hand in hand (cf. 1:9; 6:20; 2 Tim. 2:16) and should be shunned. Instead, Timothy was to devote himself to much more manly pursuits. Paul introduced an athletic image with the words **train yourself.** The verb here is gymnaze, from which comes the English "gymnasium." But Timothy's training was to be for godliness (cf. 1 Tim. 2:2), not physical fitness. Paul

often used athletic analogies to drive home the need for spiritual discipline (cf. esp. 1 Cor. 9:24-27).

4:8. As valuable as **physical** fitness (**training** is gymnasia, "exercise," used only here in the NT) may be (and Paul did not disparage it), spiritual fitness, or godliness, is much more valuable. Physical fitness is profitable only, literally, "for a little." **But godliness** is profitable **for all things,** not merely in this **present** transient **life** but in **the life to come,** that is, for eternity. Godliness colors all aspects of temporal and eternal life, bestowing its blessing on all it touches.

4:9. The **trustworthy saying** formula can point forward, as in 1:15, or backward, as in Titus 3:8. Here it is probably best to see it as reinforcing the proverbial impact of 1 Timothy 4:8 (in contrast with the NIV).

4:10. To this end, said Paul, **we labor and strive**—that is, to develop the godliness of verse 8. The word "strive" translates agōnizometha ("I agonize"), another athletic term. Paul practiced what he had just preached to Timothy (cf. Col. 1:29). **We have put our hope** renders ēlpikamen, a perfect tense denoting an action with the results continuing. The durative quality of Paul's confidence is stressed. Paul knew his struggle was worth it because his hope was set, not on himself, some philosophy of life, other men, or nonexistent gods—but **in the living God, who is the Savior of all men, and especially of those who believe.** The mention of the "living" God picks up the reference in 1 Timothy 3:15; the stress on God as "Savior" picks up 1:1 and 2:3. Again Paul stated that God is the Savior of "all men" (cf. 2:2, 4, 6) since He desires that all be saved and He provided Christ as the ransom (2:6) to make that salvation possible. Yet God is the Savior of those who believe in a special way since only in them has His desire for their salvation come to fruition.

4:11. Timothy, as a young man with perhaps a nonassertive personality, was evidently given to timidity and fear (cf. 1 Cor. 16:10-11). Thus Paul exhorted him to **command** (parangelle, "insist on") **and teach these things.** By "these things" Paul usually meant the contents of his instructions in the immediate context, but the term here seems almost intentionally ambiguous (cf. 1 Tim. 3:14; 4:6, 15; 5:7,

21; 6:2, 11). Paul was prodding Timothy to be firm and courageous in his ministry. Paul used the same Greek word *parangelle* in 5:7 and 6:13.

4:12. At first Paul's instruction that Timothy should not **let anyone** "despise" (KJV) his youth might seem impossible to fulfill since Timothy could not control the attitudes of others. Yet when combined with the latter part of the verse, the thrust of Paul's instruction becomes clear. Timothy must not be intimidated by his relative youthfulness or what others might think of it. Instead he was to demonstrate his maturity by living such a godly life that he would become a pattern for other Christians in every area of his life: **speech . . . life** (i.e., "behavior or conduct," *anastrophē*; cf. "conduct" in 3:15), **love . . . faith, and . . . purity.** The word for "purity" (*hagneia*, "moral cleanness") is used only here and in 5:2.

4:13. After referring again to his own movements (cf. 1:3; 3:14-15), Paul exhorted Timothy to attend to his public ministry as well as his private life. This public ministry was to consist of at least three elements: (1) **Public reading of Scripture.** It has always been the practice of God's people to read the Word of God aloud in the congregation (e.g., Ex. 24:7; Deut. 31:11; Josh. 8:35; 2 Kings 23:2; Neh. 8:7-8; Luke 4:16; Acts 15:21; Col. 4:16; 1 Thes. 5:27). (2) **Preaching;** better yet "exhortation" (*paraklēsei*). This term includes the exposition and application of the passages read. (3) **Teaching.** The distinction between this and the former term is by no means clear-cut. The two merge into each other. Yet "teaching" (*didaskalia*; cf. 1 Tim. 1:10; 4:1, 6, 16; 5:17; 6:1) may refer primarily to a more catechetical treatment of the truths of the Christian faith. The two terms occur in Romans 12:7-8 and are there related to spiritual gifts.

4:14. Timothy's image of himself as a minister was evidently deficient, so Paul reminded him of the fact that God had given him the requisite ability for service. Timothy must not ignore or **neglect** this basic factor (cf. 2 Tim. 1:6). If others were not to look down on Timothy, neither was he to look down on himself. His **gift** had come to him **through a prophetic message** which was delivered at the time of his ordination, and the remembrance of this prophecy was designed to

strengthen Timothy's confidence. The laying on of **hands** is commonly associated in the Bible with a continuity of leadership (cf. Num. 27:18-23; Deut. 34:9; Acts 6:6; 8:18; 13:3; Heb. 6:2). The phrase **body of elders** renders the Greek *presbyteriou*, which speaks of a group or "board" of elders, or "presbytery." These men together constitute a biblically recognized group. The Bible never speaks of a corresponding group identity for deacons. The notion of deacons functioning as a "board" is never mentioned in the Bible.

4:15. Here is the positive side of Paul's negative ("do not neglect. . . .") exhortation of verse 14. The command **be diligent** (*meleta*, from *meletaō*, "give careful thought to") is the converse of the command in the previous verse (*amelei*, from *ameleō*, "give no thought to"). Timothy was to give his careful attention to Paul's instructions; indeed, he was, literally, "to be in them" (or, with the NIV, to **give** himself **wholly to them**). As he would do so his **progress** would be evident to all observers and his problem of low credibility, implied throughout this section, would be alleviated.

4:16. **Watch your life** (lit., "yourself") **and doctrine** (lit., "the teaching"; cf. 1:10; 4:1, 6, 13; 5:17; 6:1) **closely** summarizes 4:6-16. Throughout this epistle Paul had been advising Timothy concerning his private life and public ministry. He was to keep a sharp eye on both, persevering in the instructions Paul had offered in the two realms. In so doing, said Paul, **you will save both yourself and your hearers.** Ultimately only God can save, of course; yet in a secondary sense the New Testament speaks of a person "saving" himself (Phil. 2:12) and others (James 5:19-20; Jude 23). Paul's words are a pointed reminder of the awesome burden of responsibility that congregational leaders carry.

V. Instructions concerning Various Groups in the Church (5:1–6:10)

A. Concerning various age-groups (5:1-2)

From the above instructions about how Timothy was to conduct his personal life and ministry, Paul turned to advice on how to relate effectively to individuals who make up various groups in the church. Paul's overall advice about how to treat various age-groups was that Timothy handle different people as he would corresponding members of his own family.

5:1-2. Older man translates *presbyteros*, the plural of which is rendered "elders" in 4:14. Here, however, Paul was not referring to those who hold the office of overseer. The word denotes "elderly" men, in contrast with **younger men** (cf. Titus 2:2-3 where the same word is used to contrast "older men" and "older women"). Timothy was to appeal to the older men as he would his own **father**— not with rough rebukes but with gentle exhortations. Young men may be treated somewhat more directly, yet with fraternity as if they were Timothy's own **brothers. Older women** were to receive all the respect Timothy would accord his own mother Eunice (2 Tim. 1:5). **Younger women** were likewise to be treated respectfully, **with** the **absolute purity** (*hagneia*; cf. 1 Tim. 4:12) Timothy would grant his own sister. This would safeguard the young minister from reproach.

B. Concerning widows (5:3-16)

Next Paul offered instruction on how Timothy must deal with the widows in the congregation. Throughout the Old and New Testaments widows, along with aliens and orphans, are viewed as special objects of God's mercy. As such they are to be taken under the wing of the congregation (cf. Deut. 10:18; 14:29; 24:17-21; Acts 6:1-7; James 1:27). As early as Acts 6 the church had established a charitable outreach to widows. Now about 30 years later the ministry to widows, of whom there were no doubt many, showed signs of being a major burden to the congregation. Paul was therefore eager in this passage to identify those who did not truly need help in order to leave enough for those who did.

5:3-4. Timothy was instructed to **give proper recognition to** (lit., "honor") those who were truly widows—that is, **widows who** were **really in need.** These Paul contrasted with widows who had lost their husbands but who had **children or grandchildren** still living. Since in God's economy the first responsibility for caring for the needy falls on the **family** (not the church and surely not the state), **these** family members **should learn first of all to put their religion into practice by caring for their own.** In so doing, these family members would repay their "forebears" (*progonois*; cf. 2 Tim. 1:3) part of the debt owed them. Such reciprocity **is pleasing to God.** It is "welfare" as God intended it.

5:5. The widow who is really in need and left all alone has nowhere to look for help but to **God** and His people. Thus one of the marks of a needy widow is that she **puts her hope in God and** therefore **continues** in petition and prayer **night and day.** Such a godly person, dedicated after the death of her husband to the service of the Lord, was deeply respected (cf. the description of the widow-prophetess Anna, Luke 2:37), and was viewed as worthy of the church's support.

5:6. Not all women who became widows gave themselves to such godly service, of course. Some widows used their widowhood to seek after sensual pleasure (**lives for pleasure**); *spatalō,* (used elsewhere in the NT only in James 5:5). Some commentators suggest even the hint of prostitution here. In any case Paul stated that a life devoted to wanton pleasure, in stark contrast to the godly life described in 1 Timothy 5:5, produces a woman who **is dead even while she lives** (cf. Rom. 8:6; Rev. 3:1). One need only witness the spiritual emptiness produced within those who choose such a profligate lifestyle to understand Paul's point. Such women must not be placed on the widows' list.

5:7-8. In 4:11 Paul instructed Timothy to "command . . . these things" (*parangelle tauta*). Now, having added the intervening instructions, Paul repeated the exact words: "Command these things too." Paul wanted Timothy to pass along **these instructions** about the list of widows in order **that no one may be open to blame.** The reference is somewhat ambiguous, but probably refers to the widows in the church. If the wrong women are included on the list their sensual lifestyles (cf. 5:6) will bring reproach on the entire group. But it may also refer to the remaining families of the widows. Failure to **provide** (*pronoei* means "to think ahead, to provide by seeing needs in advance") **for** these family members gives the lie to any claim to know God (cf. Titus 1:16) and becomes de facto a denial of **the faith.** Indeed, such a failure renders the defaulting family member **worse than an unbeliever,** since even many non-Christians understand and fulfill their familial responsibilities.

5:9-10. The "proper recognition" of verse 3 is here made specific. Widows **may be put on the list** if they meet three primary qualifications. What exactly this list involved is not known. It may have been an official order for service in the congregation; more likely it was merely a roll of those **widows** who were to receive assistance from the congregation. In any case, to qualify a woman had to meet these qualifications: (1) She must be **over 60.** Though the age of 60 was more advanced in that day, Paul had his reasons for keeping the younger widows off the rolls (cf. vv. 11-15). (2) She must have **been faithful to her husband.** The Greek here is literally "a one-man woman," the mirror image of the stipulation for both the overseer-elder (cf. 3:2; Titus 1:6) and the deacon (1 Tim. 3:12), and for the same reason (cf. comments on 3:2). The NIV, to be consistent with its renderings of 3:2, 12 and Titus 1:6, should have adopted its footnote reading, "has had but one husband." The translation, "has been faithful to her husband," points to the view that the words merely prohibit promiscuity. (3) **She must be well-known for her good deeds.** As illustrations of the kinds of things he had in mind, Paul cited five examples, which characterize godly women (cf. 1 Tim. 2:10). The examples span the realms of home, church, and community, and include child-raising, **hospitality, washing** saints' **feet** (humble service; cf. comments on John 13:1-15) **helping people in trouble,** and various other **kinds of good deeds.** The women on the widows' roll must be those whose reputations for godly living are well known.

5:11-12. Younger widows, on the other hand, were **not** to be **put on the list.** Paul's reasoning for this was twofold: First, unlike the older women whose active sexual lives would presumably be behind them, the younger women might be faced with normal sexual **desires** which would **overcome their dedication to Christ.** As a result they would **want to** remarry, bringing **judgment on themselves, because** they had **broken their**

first pledge. The pledge Paul referred to was probably a more or less formal commitment, taken on joining the list of widows, wherein the woman vowed to serve Christ entirely without thought of remarriage. In this way she could devote herself without distraction to the Lord (cf. 1 Cor. 7:34-35). Remarriage would involve breaking this vow and a broken vow would incur judgment (cf. Num. 30:2; Deut. 23:21; Ecc. 5:4-5).

5:13-15. Second, younger and more energetic widows would have a more difficult time resisting the temptations connected with idleness. With the congregation supporting them, their time normally given to maintaining a living would be free. Instead of giving this time to the service of Christ in visitation and counseling, **younger widows** would be more susceptible to **going about from house to house** and becoming **idlers . . . gossips** (*phlyaroi*, used only here in the NT; the verb *phlyareō* is used in 3 John 10) **and busybodies, saying things they ought not to.** Too much time with not enough to do is dangerous for anyone except those too old to get into trouble. Hence Paul's **counsel** was that younger widows should not take the vow and be added to the list; instead they should marry, raise a family, **manage their homes,** and by being thus occupied **give the enemy no opportunity for slander.**

The "enemy" here may refer to the church's adversaries who looked for every chance to tear others down (cf. 1 Cor. 16:9), or to the opposition of the devil himself (cf. 1 Tim. 5:15). Perhaps Paul did not see much difference between the two (cf. 4:1). The importance of Paul's counsel was buttressed by the fact that it came too late to preserve the congregation from some who had **in fact already turned away to follow Satan.** No doubt Paul was aware of specific cases in the churches where younger women had been placed on the list and then had broken their vows.

5:16. Paul wanted to be certain that the instructions of verse 8 were understood to include well-situated women as well as men. The men would be the obvious objects of Paul's directions in verse 8, but not necessarily the women. So, as a closing note to his discussion of **widows,** Paul specified that any believing **woman** who possessed the means bore the same responsibilities for widows in her family as would a man in similar circumstances. This would relieve the congregation of the responsibility so that the church could help those widows who were really in need.

C. Concerning elders (5:17-25)

5:17. The elders (*presbyteroi*) refer here, not merely to elderly men (cf. v. 1), but to those who occupy official positions of leadership in the church (cf. 3:1-7; Titus 1:5-9; Acts 20:17-38). The task of the elders is to **direct the affairs of the church.** Elders have the oversight of the affairs of the congregation, with the deacons providing their helpful support wherever appropriate. For their oversight all elders received a stipend; but those who excelled in this ministry of leadership were to be considered **worthy of double honor,** or twice the remuneration as the rest. **Especially** was this true of **those** who labored in **preaching and teaching.** While the leadership needs of a congregation extend far beyond the preaching and teaching of the truth, these are at the core of the ministry and are perhaps most important, which should be reflected by the double value given them by the congregation.

5:18. To support his point—that elders should be paid, and certain ones paid double—Paul quoted two Scripture passages: (1) **Do not muzzle the ox while it is treading out the grain** (Deut. 25:4; cf. also 1 Cor. 9:9). (2) **The worker deserves his wages** probably refers to passages such as Leviticus 19:13 and Deuteronomy 24:15, or perhaps to the teaching of the Lord Jesus Himself (cf. Matt. 10:10; Luke 10:7). Though Paul reserved the right not to receive support from a congregation (cf. 1 Cor. 9:15-23; 1 Thes. 2:9), he clearly believed and repeatedly taught that a congregation did not have the right not to offer it (cf. Gal. 6:6; 1 Cor. 9:14).

5:19-20. Paul was deeply aware of opposition to the ministry. He had already spoken of the need to guard the congregation from the reproach of slanderers (cf. 3:2, 7), and would do so again (6:1). Here he stipulated the procedure for separating valid accusations from false ones. It is the venerable approach of both the Old Testament (cf. Deut. 19:15) and the New (cf. Matt. 18:16; John 8:17; 2 Cor. 13:1), wherein an accusation should be considered only if two or three witnesses swear to it. When such accusations would then prove to be true, Timothy was to rebuke the offenders publicly, that is, before the entire congregation. In this way the remaining members could take warning (lit., "have fear"). Fear of the discipline of God, in this case administered through the congregation, is a healthy thing in a Christian, especially for those in places of leadership. Modern congregations that ignore church discipline do so at the peril of both the offender and themselves.

5:21. Why Paul punctuated his instructions with this strong **charge** can only be guessed. Had Timothy passively avoided unpleasant confrontations, or had he taken a strong stand in some cases but not others? For whatever reasons, Paul strongly adjured the young minister to follow through on (**keep** is lit., "guard") **these instructions without partiality** (lit., "prejudging," used only here in the NT) or **favoritism** (*prosklisin,* lit., "inclination toward someone," used only here in the NT). The strength of Paul's charge is underlined by his invocation of the authority of **God and Christ Jesus** (cf. 2 Tim. 4:1), **and the elect angels,** all of whom are associated with righteous judgment (cf. Matt. 25:31; Mark 8:38; Luke 9:26; Rev. 14:10).

5:22. One way to avoid painful situations involving the disciplining of an elder is to be careful about who is ordained in the first place. Thus Paul counseled Timothy to a judicious reluctance **in the laying on of hands** (cf. 4:14; 2 Tim. 1:6). The words **do not share in the sins of others** may be merely advice for Timothy to guard his own conduct generally (cf. 1 Tim. 4:16; Acts 20:28). But more likely, in light of the context, this is a warning about the implications of hasty ordinations. Those who take part in the premature ordination of an errant elder share some of the blame for the negative consequences to their church. Whichever is the case, Timothy was to **keep** himself free from sin. One cannot deal with sin in another if one's own life is not **pure** (*hagnon*).

5:23. This verse may be only a somewhat disjointed bit of personal advice to Timothy or it may flow more naturally from the reference to purity in verse 22. Perhaps Timothy was inclined to an asceticism which associated purity with total abstention (cf. 4:3-5), which in turn led in Timothy's case to **stomach** ailments and **frequent illnesses,** perhaps due to the poor quality of the **water** he drank. Paul thus qualified his exhortation to purity by encouraging Timothy to drink **a little wine** (*oinō oligō*) for his stomach's sake, because of his "frequent illnesses." This instruction applies only to using wine for medicinal purposes, of course, and therefore contributes little or nothing to either side of the debate over the use of wine as a beverage.

5:24-25. The meaning of these two verses, though at first glance obscure, proves on closer examination to be profound. Verse 23 is a parenthesis. Thus verse 24 picks up the advice of verse 22 and carries the thought forward. All people are heading toward **judgment,** carrying with them either their **sins** or their **good** works. For some, their **sins** or good works go before **them** and **are obvious** to all observers. For others their sins or good works **trail behind,** hidden from view, becoming known only after the individual has passed. Thus Paul emphasized the difficulties inherent in choosing qualified candidates for the ordination. Hasty, superficial assessments, whether positive or negative, are sometimes inaccurate, leading to the enlistment of unqualified men or the overlooking of those whose fine qualities are less obvious. With time, however, a man's true colors will emerge to an astute observer. Thus the perceptive observations of verses 24-25 are designed to underline the warning of verse 22: do not rush to ordain someone.

D. Concerning slaves and masters (6:1-2)

6:1. Under normal circumstances slaves and masters had no associations outside the institution **of slavery.** With the advent of the gospel, however, these two groups found themselves thrown together in the congregation in new ways, creating problems the apostles were forced to address repeatedly (cf. 1 Cor. 7:20-24; Gal. 3:28; Eph. 6:5-9; Col. 3:22-25; Phile.; 1 Peter 2:13-25). Paul's instructions here correspond entirely with what is taught elsewhere in the New Testament on the subject, with one major exception: in this passage he addresses

only slaves. Usually his exhortations to submit to authority were immediately buttressed by warning **masters** against abusing their authority (cf. Eph. 6:5-9; Col. 3:22–4:1).

The matter of the uses and abuses of authority is first and foremost a problem of attitude. Thus Paul wrote repeatedly of how slaves and masters should see themselves and one another. Here he wrote that slaves are to view their masters as **worthy of full respect** (*timēs*, "honor"). The same word is used of God in 1 Timothy 1:17 and 6:16, and of elders in 5:17. Such honor or respect should be granted lest **God's** reputation and the Christian faith (*hē didaskalia*, "the teaching"; cf. 1:10; 4:1, 6, 13, 16; 5:17) **be slandered** (lit., "be blasphemed"). Social goals should always be subordinate to spiritual values.

6:2. Paul's thought here is totally foreign to the world, and can be fully appreciated only by those who view their lives through the eyes of Jesus Christ (cf. Mark 10:42-45). Christian slaves whose **masters** are also believers should redouble rather than reduce their service. This should stem purely from the realization that the one who is receiving the benefits is a beloved brother or sister in Christ. The attitude undergirding this instruction is complete nonsense to anyone who does not understand the Lord Jesus, but it is the genius of Christlikeness and the ultimate source of all meaning and joy in life to those who have eyes to see (cf. John 13:4-17; 15:9-14). Thus Timothy was commanded once again to **teach and urge . . . these things** on the congregation (cf. 1 Tim. 4:6, 11; 5:7).

E. Concerning the heretical and greedy (6:3-10)

6:3. The last group Paul discussed are those with whom he began (cf. 1:3-11): false teachers. Here, like a physician diagnosing a sick patient, Paul described the characteristics of their disease. The objects of Paul's attention show three overlapping symptoms: (1) those who teach **false doctrines** (lit., "anyone who teaches differently"; 1:3 has the same word); (2) those who do **not agree to the sound instruction of our Lord Jesus Christ;** with the word "sound" Paul reintroduced a medical analogy (cf. also 2 Tim. 2:17); he spoke of, literally, the "healthy words or sayings" (*hygiainousin logois*) of Christ; (3) those who do not consent **to godly teaching** (lit., "the teaching which corresponds to godliness," *tē kat' eusebian didaskalia*). The correspondence between truth and godliness, and error and moral deficiency, is one of the recurrent themes in the Pastoral Epistles.

6:4-5. Doctrinal error is seldom merely a case of being innocently mistaken. There is almost always some degree of culpability. The false teachers in Ephesus were **conceited** (lit., "puffed up"), with inflated egos (cf. 1:7). Such a one **understands nothing.** Picking up the medical analogy again, Paul described them as "diseased with" (*noson peri*) **controversies** (*zētēseis*, "debates," perhaps on theological problems; cf. 2 Tim. 2:23; Titus 3:9) **and arguments** (*logomachias*, "battles of words"), out of which come only **envy, quarreling, malicious talk, evil suspicions, and constant friction.** This contrasts strikingly with the *telos* or "end" of Paul's instruction (1 Tim 1:5; cf. also the similar contrast in Gal. 5:16-24). Such evil fruits seem the inevitable external products of false teachers once one understands their true inner motives (Matt. 7:13-23). They are **men:** (1) whose minds have been corrupted (cf. 2 Tim. 3:8); (2) **who have been robbed of the truth** by Satan (cf. Luke 8:5, 12, and the culpability of being "hard ground" rather than "good ground"); (3) **who think that godliness is a means to financial gain.** Greed was their core motivation (cf. Titus 1:11; Jude 12). In that day the stipends associated with ministry were attractive, so that even the best men had to be warned against letting personal gain creep into their motivation (cf. 1 Peter 5:2). Congregational leaders were to be chosen from those known for their "freedom from the love of money" (cf. 1 Tim. 3:3, 8; Titus 1:7). By contrast the moral corruption so often associated with false teaching (cf. Jude 4-16 for the most graphic description in the NT) produced just the opposite.

6:6. Picking up on the words "godliness" and "gain," Paul shifted their meaning in a characteristically Pauline fashion (cf. 1 Cor. 2:5-6 for a similar shift) from the erroneous to the truthful. **Godliness** does not *give* financial gain (1 Tim. 6:5); it itself *is* gain when accompanied with **contentment.** *Autarkeias* literally means "self-sufficiency." Yet the sufficiency of oneself is due to the sufficiency of God (cf. 2 Cor. 9:8; Phil. 4:11, 13 for other uses of the same word). Godliness combined with that inner God-given sufficiency which does not depend on material circumstances (the opposite of the false teachers' greed) is indeed of great gain.

6:7-8. Paul supported his point with a common Jewish and Christian idea (cf. Job 1:21; Ecc. 5:15; Luke 12:16-21) about the complete transiency of material things. They should freely be used and enjoyed to the glory of God if one has them (cf. 1 Tim. 4:3-4; 6:17), but in no way do they contribute to godliness. Christians do have basic material needs for **food and clothing,** of course, like everyone else; but when these are met a godly Christian can be satisified (cf. Heb. 13:5-6). Paul knew whereof he spoke (Phil. 4:10-13).

6:9-10. Paul contrasted the proper attitude of contentment with its opposites: The craving **to get rich** and **the love of money,** two sides of the same coin. The history of the human race, and perhaps especially that of modern Western societies, cries out in support of Paul's point. The grasping after riches leads to: (1) **temptation,** (2) **a trap,** and (3) **many foolish and harmful desires that plunge men into ruin and destruction.** Though not an end in itself, greed **is** actually **a root of all kinds of evil.** It is a crucial chink through which other vices gain access. To illustrate his point Paul referred indirectly to **some people,** undoubtedly known to Timothy, who had fallen into the trap Paul was discussing. **Eager for money,** they **wandered from the faith.** This may mean that they had fallen into heretical teaching (cf. 2 Tim. 2:17-18) or simply that their spiritual fruitfulness had been choked off (cf. Luke 8:14) by their concern for riches. In either case, they had suffered for it, causing themselves to be **pierced . . . with many griefs** (lit., "pains").

VI. Final Charge to Timothy (6:11-21)

A. Exhortation to godliness (6:11-16)

6:11. Paul began this concluding section of the epistle by turning directly to Timothy. The words **but you** are an emphatic contrast with "some people" of verse 10, who chase after riches. Timothy, as a **man of God,** was to do the opposite—to **flee from all this,** but chase instead after personal virtues that are of eternal value: **righteousness, godliness** (*eusebeian;* cf. 2:2; 3:16; 4:7-8; 6:3, 5-6; 2 Tim. 3:5; Titus 1:1), **faith, love, endurance** (*hypomonēn,* "steadfastness under adversity"), **and gentleness.** This list may be compared to both the fruit of the Spirit (Gal. 5:22-23) and the qualifications of elders (1 Tim. 3:1-3).

6:12. Fight the good fight is the language of athletic contests. In 1:18 the same English words translate Greek words that refer to a military conflict. Timothy was to give his best effort to this most worthwhile of struggles, the struggle to further **the faith.** This would involve the complete appropriation (cf. "take hold" in v. 19) at all times of the fact that he possessed eternal life. (Paul's words, **Take hold of . . . eternal life** in no way suggest that Timothy could gain eternal life by his own efforts.) To Paul, Christ's life is the possession of each Christian, not only throughout eternity, but now (cf. 2 Cor. 4:10-12). It is this new life in Christ (2 Cor. 5:17) to which every Christian is **called** and which Christians confess by baptism (Rom. 6:4) and by word (Rom. 10:9-10). Timothy's **good confession in the presence of many witnesses** could refer to his ordination but more likely speaks of his baptism.

6:13. Repeatedly in this letter Paul directly addressed Timothy with personal charges, the second strongest of which is found in 5:21. But here is Paul's strongest, most solemn charge of all (**I charge you,** *parangellō;* cf. 1:3; 4:11; 5:7; 6:14) conjuring up images of perhaps a familiar baptismal formula triggered by the reference in verse 12. **While testifying before Pontius Pilate** is translated by some, "who testified in the time of Pontius Pilate." If translated this way, the qualifying clause is designed to fix the Crucifixion in time, as in the Apostles' Creed. Both translations are possible.

6:14. The content of Paul's charge is that Timothy **keep this commandment without spot or blame.** The "commandment" is probably broader than any single law. It refers to the entire body of sound teaching Paul had been describing throughout the letter. Timothy, by his own godly life and by his faithful ministry, was to preserve this body of truth from stain or reproach **until the appearing** (cf. 2 Tim. 1:10; 4:1, 8; Titus 2:13) **of our Lord Jesus Christ.** Then and only then will the struggle (1 Tim. 6:12) be over.

6:15-16. Early in his ministry Paul was convinced that Christ would return soon. Now near the end of his ministry he showed both an awareness that Christ might not return before he died and a desire to encourage Timothy to leave the timing of this great event up to the Lord. Hence Paul stressed that **God will bring about** Christ's appearing **in His** (or "its") **own time.** The section ends with an inspiring doxology to the **God** who is the cause and object of it all: the ultimate **Ruler** of the universe, **the King of kings and Lord of lords** (cf. Rev. 17:14; 19:16), the only eternal One, who dwells where no man can survive or approach or even see (cf. John 1:18). Such a Lord deserves an awesome reverence combined with complete humility (cf. Job 42:1-6). **To Him be honor and might forever. Amen** (cf. 1 Tim. 1:17).

B. Instructions for the rich (6:17-19)

6:17. Paul had dealt with those who did not possess wealth, but who deeply desired it (vv. 3-10). Now he addressed those who had it, and instructed them as to what their attitude should be toward it. They are **not to be arrogant** as if their wealth is deserved (1 Cor. 4:7-8; 1 Sam. 2:7). Nor must they **put their hope in wealth, which is so uncertain** and transient. This is perhaps the greatest temptation to wealthy Christians, into which category most modern Western believers fit. Christians should **put their hope in God,** who is the Source of material things. Again material possessions are among those things God has given **for our enjoyment.**

6:18-19. Yet Christians must not merely consume material possessions selfishly. Possessions are to be shared with those who have less. Thus Timothy was to charge the well-off **to do good, to be rich,** not ultimately in money, but **in good deeds.** The wealthy should make every effort **to be generous and willing to share** what they have. If they do this **they will lay up treasure for themselves** in heaven. This undoubtedly refers to the sayings of Jesus (cf. Matt. 6:19-21; Luke 12:33-34; 18:22) wherein the transient is exchanged for the eternal. Such eternal treasure becomes **a firm foundation for** the future, recalling in a mixed metaphor perhaps another of the Lord's teachings (cf. Matt. 7:24-27; Luke 6:47-49). Wealthy Christians should invest their riches for eternity. "He is no fool who gives what he cannot keep to gain what he cannot lose" (Jim Elliot). Paradoxically it is in this giving away of the possessions which the world considers the key to the good life that a Christian **may take hold of** (cf. 1 Tim. 6:12) **the life that is truly life.** The alluring but vain and plastic substitutes for life, supplied by an unhealthy attachment to material things, pale into worthlessness when compared with that life which is found in Jesus Christ (cf. Matt. 16:24-26), who is Himself the Life (John 14:6) and whom to know is life everlasting (John 17:3).

C. Exhortations to remain faithful (6:20-21)

6:20-21. One final time Paul exhorted **Timothy** to **guard** (cf. *phylaxon,* "keep," in 5:21) the "deposit" or "trust" Paul had passed on to him (*paratheken,* used elsewhere only in 2 Tim. 1:12, 14), a reference to the body of Christian truth which in some way was under attack in Ephesus. Paul was concerned that Timothy give himself wholly to the truth and reject even the subtle inroads of error. Thus Timothy must **turn away from godless chatter** (lit., "profane empty utterances"; cf. 2 Tim. 2:16), and from **opposing ideas** (*antitheseis,* "counterassertions") **of what is falsely called knowledge.** Such knowledge was the supposed key to the mystery religions which were already aborning and which would mature into a full-fledged Gnosticism during the next century. Their influence was already being felt in Ephesus, so much so that Paul could say that some had gotten so caught up in professing their esoteric *gnosis* that they **wandered from the faith** (lit., "concerning the faith missed the aim"; cf. 1 Tim. 1:6; 2 Tim. 2:18). This does not suggest that true believers lose their salvation but that some believers turn to false doctrines, from the content of their faith. With these exhortations Paul seemed to

have come full circle, back to his concerns in 1 Timothy 1:3-6.

Paul closed his letter with the simple benediction, **Grace be with you.** "You" is in the plural, however, no doubt indicating Paul's awareness that this letter would be read widely in the churches (cf. Col. 4:18; 2 Tim. 4:22; Titus 3:15).

BIBLIOGRAPHY

Barrett, C.K. *The Pastoral Epistles.* Oxford: Clarendon Press, 1963.

Blaiklock, E.M. *The Pastoral Epistles.* Grand Rapids: Zondervan Publishing House, 1972.

Dibelius, Martin, and Conzelmann, Hans. *The Pastoral Epistles.* Translated by Philip Buttolph and Adela Yarbro. Edited by Helmut Koester. Philadelphia: Fortress Press, 1972.

Getz, Gene A. *A Profile for a Christian Life Style: A Study of Titus.* Grand Rapids: Zondervan Publishing House, 1978.

Guthrie, Donald. *The Pastoral Epistles.* Grand Rapids: Wm. B. Eerdmans Publishing Co., 1957.

Hendriksen, William. *Exposition of the Pastoral Epistles.* New Testament Commentary. Grand Rapids: Baker Book House, 1957.

Hiebert, D. Edmond. *First Timothy.* Chicago: Moody Press, 1967.

————. *Titus and Philemon.* Chicago: Moody Press, 1957.

Jensen, Irving L. *1 and 2 Timothy and Titus: A Self-Study Guide.* Chicago: Moody Press, 1973.

Kelly, J.N.D. *A Commentary on the Pastoral Epistles.* London: Adam and Charles Black, 1963. Reprint. Grand Rapids: Baker Book House, 1981.

Kent, Homer A. *The Pastoral Epistles.* Chicago: Moody Press, 1958.

Knight, George W. *The Faithful Sayings in the Pastoral Epistles.* Grand Rapids: Baker Book House, 1979.

Lock, Walter. *A Critical and Exegetical Commentary on the Pastoral Epistles.* The International Critical Commentary. Edinburgh: T. & T. Clark, 1924.

Stott, John R.W. *Guard the Gospel: The Message of 2 Timothy.* Downers Grove, Ill.: InterVarsity Press, 1973.

Wiersbe, Warren W. *Be Faithful.* Wheaton, Ill.: Scripture Press Publications, Victor Books, 1981.

2 TIMOTHY

A. Duane Litfin

INTRODUCTION

Paul was a prisoner in a Roman dungeon when he wrote this, the last of his epistles, to Timothy (cf. 2 Tim. 1:8, 16; 4:6-13). The date, as best it can be established, was approximately A.D. 67. Not long afterward, according to tradition, the apostle was beheaded. (For a more detailed discussion of the authorship and dating of the Pastoral Epistles see the *Introduction* to 1 Tim.)

The purpose of 2 Timothy was to encourage Timothy in his ministry at Ephesus. The primary theme of the letter is the need for faithfulness in the face of hardship.

OUTLINE

COMMENTARY

I. Salutation (1:1-2)

1:1-2. In his typical fashion **Paul** began this letter identifying himself as **an apostle of Christ Jesus,** a reminder Timothy hardly needed. No doubt this is another indication that Paul knew he was writing first to Timothy but ultimately to a much wider audience. In his first letter to the young pastor Paul said his apostleship was "by the command of God" (1 Tim. 1:1). Here Paul said it was **by the will of God.** The two are essentially synonymous. The words **according to the promise of life that is in Christ Jesus** are intentionally vague. They relate to Paul's apostleship (not the will of God), but did they refer to a promise of life Paul personally received, or to a promise he was to proclaim to others? In other words was his apostleship "because of" the promise or "in conformity to" the promise? The Greek word *kata* (here ambiguously trans. "according to") allows the two to merge. The promise of life in Christ, the gospel, was the reason for and the yardstick of Paul's apostleship (cf. Titus 1:2-3). **To Timothy, my dear son** (lit., "child") once again (cf. "my true son" in 1 Tim. 1:2) emphasizes the close fatherly relationship Paul maintained with his protégé, if not his convert. The remainder of the greeting duplicates 1 Timothy exactly (cf. 1 Tim. 1:2). (See the chart, "Paul's Introductions to His Epistles" at Rom. 1:1-7.)

II. Call to Faithfulness (1:3-18)

A. Thanksgiving for Timothy (1:3-7)

1:3. In 1 Timothy Paul expressed thanks for his own salvation and ministry (1 Tim 1:12); here he began by expressing thanks for Timothy's salvation and ministry. In passing, Paul referred to his own upbringing, just before he turned to Timothy's (2 Tim. 1:5). The apostle viewed his own faith in Christ, not as a break with his Jewish **forefathers**, but in continuity with their faith. (Cf. **a clear conscience** with 1 Tim. 1:5, "a good conscience.") As Paul prayed for Timothy **night and day,** his gratitude for Timothy kept welling up anew. Sitting chained in a Roman prison there was little else Paul could do but pray; and Timothy, perhaps Paul's closest companion, ministering to the church that Paul probably knew best, was no doubt the single most common object of his petitions.

1:4. Paul remembered Timothy's **tears** on their last parting, possibly at Paul's second Roman arrest. In this letter he would ask Timothy to join him in Rome (cf. 4:9, 21). Paul had longed for Timothy's companionship which was such a **joy** to him. Even the great apostle at times became lonely, discouraged, and in need of support from fellow Christians.

1:5. So many, it seems, had opposed or deserted Paul (cf. 1:15; 2:17; 3:1-9, 13; 4:3-4, 10-21) that Timothy's **sincere** (*anypokritou*, "unhypocritical"; cf. 1 Tim. 1:5) **faith** stood out in bold relief. Paul attributed Timothy's faith to the influence of his Jewish **mother Eunice** and **grandmother Lois,** both of whom were believers (cf. Acts 16:1). Timothy's father was a Gentile and probably an unbeliever; hence no mention of him is made here. According to this verse, Paul seems to attribute Timothy's conversion to his mother and grandmother (cf. 2 Tim. 3:15). References to Timothy as Paul's son in the faith (cf. 1:2; 2:1; 1 Tim. 1:2) could therefore probably be understood to mean a mentor-protégé relationship.

1:6. Because Paul was persuaded that Timothy possessed true faith (v. 5), something he often refused to take for granted in others (e.g., 1 Thes. 3:5), he urged the young minister **to fan into flame** (or perhaps, "keep at full flame")

his God-given ability for ministry. God's gifts must be used if they are to reach and maintain their full potential. In Timothy's case, Paul wrote (1 Tim. 4:14) that his **gift** (*charisma*) had come "through" (*dia*) a prophetic message, "with" (*meta*) the laying on of the elder board's hands. Here Paul stated that the gift came "through" (*dia*) **the laying on of** his own **hands.** The language is highly imprecise and may reflect nothing more in the apostle's thinking than a general association between Timothy's ordination (which involved both a prophetic message and the laying on of hands by Paul and the elders) and the young man's awareness of his own abilities. Surely the language does not bear the weight of any detailed conclusions about how spiritual gifts are bestowed, much less full-blown theories of apostolic succession or of ordination as a means of grace.

1:7. Why Timothy needed this reminder of his ordination, and the confidence in his own gifts he developed as a result of it, is not clear. In 1 Timothy the reference to Timothy's ordination is associated with problems stemming from his youthfulness (cf. 1 Tim. 4:12). Perhaps he had become somewhat intimidated by the opposition to both Paul and the gospel, even in some ways threatened, defensive, and ashamed (cf. 2 Tim. 1:8) at having to defend a prisoner (cf. 2:9) and the "foolishness" which they both preached about a despised and crucified Jesus (cf. 1 Cor. 1:18–2:5). But such **timidity** (*deilias*, lit., "cowardice," used only here in the NT) has no place in God's service. Instead **God** gives **a spirit of power** (cf. 1 Cor. 2:4), **of love** (cf. 1 Tim. 1:5), **and of self-discipline** (cf. 1 Tim. 4:7). These three virtues, each supplied by the Holy Spirit, should characterize Timothy.

B. Call to courage (1:8-12)

1:8. If Timothy's ministry were marked by power, love, and self-discipline, he would be able to stand tall against his opponents, and would **not be ashamed to testify about our Lord** (cf. 1 Cor. 1:6), **or ashamed of** Paul **His prisoner.** Though Paul was held in a Roman prison (cf. 2 Tim. 1:16; 2:9), yet he called himself Christ's prisoner—that is, a prisoner for Christ's sake and purpose (cf. Eph. 3:1; Phil. 1:12–14; Phile. 1, 9). With this reminder of his own condition, which was far graver than Timothy's, Paul exhorted Timothy to **join** courageously with him **in suffering for the gospel** (cf. 2 Tim. 2:3), for it is just in such circumstances that **the power of God** is made manifest (cf. 2 Cor. 12:9-10).

1:9-10. Having mentioned the gospel, Paul spelled out some of its most important details. God **saved us and called us to a holy life.** This is an accomplished fact, not something yet to come. Timothy could therefore count on God's power in his daily ministry. Moreover, this salvation had nothing to do with a believer's merits **but** was purely **because of His own purpose** (*prothesin*; cf. Rom. 8:28; 9:11; Eph. 1:11; 3:11) **and grace** (cf. 1 Tim. 1:14). This is the very core of the gospel (cf. Eph. 2:8-10). **Before the beginning of time** Christians were granted this unmerited favor, but were only made aware of it **through the appearing** (*epiphaneias*; 2 Thes. 2:8; 1 Tim. 6:14; 2 Tim. 4:1, 8; Titus 2:13) **of our Savior, Christ Jesus.** Here and in Titus 1:4; 2:13; and 3:6 *Christ* is called Savior; in 1 Timothy 1:1; 2:3; 4:10; Titus 2:10; and 3:4 *God* is titled Savior (cf. 2 Peter 1:1 with 3:18). Clearly both are in different senses true. Christ the Son embodied God the Father's saving purpose and plan, by which **death,** the product of sin (cf. Gen. 2:17; Rom. 5:12; 6:23), would be **destroyed** (1 Cor. 15:26), and **life and immortality** (lit., "incorruptibility"; cf. 1 Peter 1:4) would be brought into view.

1:11-12. Little wonder that Paul called this **gospel** "glorious" (1 Tim. 1:11). It is the most important message ever told. Paul had been **appointed** to serve as **a herald and an apostle and a teacher** of this message (cf. 1 Tim. 2:7), three roles which merely reflect different facets of the stewardship entrusted to him (1 Tim. 1:11). Carrying out his stewardship had brought Paul much **suffering,** including his present imprisonment. In the eyes of the world he was a common criminal (cf. 2 Tim. 2:9). Yet he was able to say, **I am not ashamed.** He was trusting his own destiny to the same One who had **entrusted** him with the stewardship of the gospel. Thus, even though he was suffering abuse and humiliation, he was confident of God's complete vindication in the end (cf. 1:18; 4:8). Throughout, of course, Paul was using his own example to bolster Timothy's perhaps flagging courage.

C. Call to guard the truth (1:13-14)

1:13. From the example of his life, Paul turned to the example or **pattern** (*hypotypōsin*; cf. 1 Tim. 1:16) of his teaching. Timothy was to view what he had **heard from** Paul as the essential outline or sketch of **sound teaching** (lit., "healthy doctrine"; cf. 1 Tim. 1:10) and was to **keep** or maintain it. Timothy was to hold the truth **with faith and love in Christ Jesus.** To be balanced, a commitment to the truth always requires faith and love, virtues which ultimately come only from being "in Christ" (1 Tim. 1:14).

1:14. Paul used the notion of a "trust" (*parathēkēn*; cf. 1 Tim. 5:21; 6:20) in two ways in the Pastorals. First, he had been given a trust or stewardship from God (cf. 1 Tim. 1:11); second, he had in turn **entrusted** himself and his destiny to God (2 Tim. 1:12). Here Paul spoke of the first of these two. The stewardship of the truth he had received had now been passed along into the hands of Timothy, who was to pass it on yet again to other faithful Christians, who were to pass it on to still others (2:2). While it was in Timothy's possession, however, he was to **guard** (*phylaxon*; cf. 1 Tim. 5:21; 6:20) **it with the help of the Holy Spirit who lives in us.** It was Timothy's responsibility to preserve sound teaching from becoming corrupted through distortion, dilution, deletion, and addition. Heretical teaching was not only a possibility to Paul; it was a constant threat to be guarded against. Moreover, Timothy could count on the assistance of the indwelling Spirit of God (cf. 1 John 3:24; 4:13) who desires to promote the truth about Christ (John 16:13).

D. Examples of unfaithfulness and faithfulness (1:15-18)

1:15. Nothing is known of **Phygelus and Hermogenes** beyond this single reference. It is fair to conjecture that theirs may have been the most unexpected defections among the group represented by **everyone in the province of Asia,** of which Ephesus was the leading city. (See the location of Asia and of Ephesus on the map between Acts and Rom.) Perhaps they were leaders of some sort. Timothy certainly knew their situation well, in any case, and Paul singled them out. It is unnecessary to assume either (a) that "everyone" means literally every Christian, or (b) that their failure consisted of a total defection from the faith. Verses 16-18 suggest rather that there was a general failure to support the apostle in his personal time of need.

1:16-18. From these sad examples of unfaithfulness, Paul turned to the sparkling instance **of Onesiphorus** (mentioned elsewhere only in 4:19), who had supported Paul not only **in Ephesus** but also **in Rome.** Repeatedly he had gone out of his way to help Paul, even to the point of following him to Rome and painstakingly seeking out his whereabouts. There, despite Paul's imprisonment and the stigma attached to it, Onesiphorus remained unfazed, continuing his faithful ministry without hesitation. For all of this Paul commended him, twice invoking God's **mercy** (1:16, 18) on both the faithful servant and his **household.**

The contrast between the faithful and the unfaithful, the strong and the weak, the trustworthy and the unreliable, is striking. The many in Asia (v. 15) portray the very things Paul had been warning Timothy against—cowardice, shame, self-indulgence, infidelity. Onesiphorus, on the other hand, demonstrated the characteristics Paul had been recommending to Timothy—courage, love, self-discipline, boldness, and faithfulness. Clearly the negative and the positive examples were designed to strengthen Timothy's resolve to be counted among those who were willing to stand shoulder to shoulder with the apostle.

III. Challenge to Endurance (2:1-13)

A. Enduring hardship for Christ (2:1-7)

2:1. After the reminders of Timothy's ordination, his own example, and that of others, Paul addressed Timothy with a direct application: **You then, my son** (*teknon,* "child," an endearing term), **be strong** (lit. "be empowered"; cf. Eph. 6:10). Yet Timothy's strength was not his own; it was a divine "gift" (**grace,** *charis*) found only **in Christ** (Phil. 4:13).

2:2. Traveling with Paul, Timothy had **heard** the apostle address scores of diverse audiences. Among all those groups the essence of Paul's message had not changed. It was the same body of truth Paul had taught Timothy personally. Now, with the apostle nearing the end of his own ministry, what Timothy had heard from Paul he was in turn to **entrust** (cf. 1:14) **to reliable men who will also be qualified to teach others** (cf. 1 Tim. 3:2; Titus 1:9). This has come to be called "the ministry of multiplication," and it is God's method for propagating the good news of Jesus Christ.

2:3-4. Such faithfulness to God's truth would inevitably involve Timothy in suffering, even as it had Paul. Thus without varnishing Timothy's prospects the mentor once again called his protégé to share in **hardship** or suffering (cf. 1:8 for the same word used only in these two places: *synkakopathēson,* "to suffer hardship with someone"; also cf. 4:5) for the sake of Christ (cf. John 15:18-20). Paul introduced three common illustrations to emphasize his point (cf. 1 Cor. 9:7, 24 for the same three): **a . . . soldier,** an athlete, and a farmer (2 Tim. 2:3-6). Military images were common in Paul's thought (cf. 1 Tim. 1:18), no doubt because the word pictures were familiar to his readers (cf. Rom. 6:13 ["instruments" can be trans. "weapons"]; Rom. 7:23; 1 Cor. 9:7; 2 Cor. 6:7; Eph. 6:11-18; Phil. 2:25; Phile. 2). A Roman soldier's single-minded purpose, rigorous discipline, and unquestioning obedience to **his commanding officer** combine to make the figure of a soldier an apt one for a servant of the gospel.

2:5. With a quick change of metaphor Paul switched to **an athlete.** The thought here is similar to 1 Corinthians 9:24-27 (and Heb. 12:1-2). **According to the rules** translates *nomimōs* (lit., "lawfully"). The metaphor clearly draws on athletic games such as the Olympics, but do "the rules" refer to the regulations governing each event or to those governing the training of those qualified to take part? Competitors in the Olympic games, for example, were required to swear that they had trained diligently for at least 10 months. Though the second is in some ways easier to explain, the first is required by Paul's grammar, which suggests that the issue is not whether one is qualified to compete but, among those competing, who will win the **crown.** Every athletic event has its boundaries, its rules; moreover, all who fail to discipline themselves to observe these rules are disqualified. Paul wanted Timothy to run so as to win the crown (cf. 2 Tim. 4:7-8) and not be disqualified. This requires a Christian to have strong qualities of discipline, self-control, endurance, and a certain toughness.

2:6. The final image is that of a **farmer.** The language puts an emphasis on the word **hardworking,** in contrast with idle, lazy workers. The diligence Paul has just described in each case has its reward (cf. vv. 11-12): A diligent soldier gains the approval of his commanding officer; a diligent athlete wins the victory; a diligent farmer wins **the first . . . share of the crops.** The three illustrations have in common the point that success is achieved through discipline (cf. 1:7), hard work, and single-mindedness.

2:7. Paul appealed to Timothy to **reflect on what I am saying,** confident that with meditation and contemplation **the Lord** would grant the young man the **insight** (*synesin*, lit., "understanding") **into** the wisdom of Paul's instructions (cf. James 1:5).

B. Christ's example of endurance (2:8-10)

2:8. Paul rather abruptly introduced the ultimate example of endurance leading to success: **Jesus Christ** (cf. Heb. 12:2-3). The words **raised from the dead, descended from David** may represent a fragment of some familiar creed or catechetical formula (cf. Rom. 1:3-4). The purpose of the fleeting reference is not to expound, but simply to suggest to Timothy a rich subject for his meditation (2 Tim. 2:7), the place of suffering in the life of God's servant (cf. 1 Peter 2:19-24). The quick reference to Jesus' identity (via His ancestral line) and resurrection represents only a portion of Paul's **gospel,** of course, but a central one. The Gospel writers and the messages of the apostles in Acts address both Christ's lineage and His resurrection in great detail.

2:9-10. Preaching the good news about the crucified but resurrected Son of David was what had landed Paul in a Roman jail. Much of the Book of Acts catalogs Paul's suffering for the cause of Christ (cf. 2 Cor. 11:23-33 for a sum-

mary). With every move as he wrote or dictated this letter, the clinking iron reminded him that he was **chained like a criminal** (*kakourgos*, lit., "evildoer"). But though he was chained, **God's Word is not chained** (Paul equated "my gospel" with "God's Word"; cf. 1 Thes. 2:13; 2 Thes. 3:1). God would continue to use it through Timothy, and those to whom Timothy entrusted it. Paul's apparent shame and impotence should be no cause for alarm, discouragement, or faintheartedness. God's Word accomplishes its purpose of calling out God's people, **the elect, that they too may obtain the salvation that is in Christ Jesus, with eternal glory.** If this process required **suffering** from Paul, so be it. He was willing to **endure** (*hypomenō*, "be steadfast under"; cf. 2 Tim. 2:12) **everything for the sake of** "the chosen ones" (*tous eklektous*; cf. Col. 3:12; Titus 1:1). The contrast with Paul's original, natural sentiments could not be more stark (cf. Acts 22:4; 26:9-11; 1 Tim. 1:13), giving full meaning to the apostle's words in 1 Timothy 1:14. The greatest enemy of the saints became their greatest friend, all as a result of the gracious outpouring of Christ's love into his heart.

C. A faithful saying (2:11-13)

2:11-13. Once more Paul used the trustworthy-saying formula, so common in the Pastorals (cf. 1 Tim. 1:15; 3:1; 4:9; Titus 3:8), to introduce a quotation. The formula serves to place Paul's stamp of approval on the content of the quotation, which may have been part of a baptismal ceremony. The quotation sets forth four couplets, the first two of which are positive: (1) **If we died with Him, we will also live with Him** expresses the idea so powerfully portrayed in the rite of baptism and explained in Romans 6:2-23. The reference is not to martyrdom for Christ, but rather to a believer's mystical identification with the death and life of Christ (cf. Col. 3:3). (2) **If we endure** (*hypomenomen*; cf. 2 Tim. 2:10), **we will also reign with Him** furthers the believer's identification with Christ. In the previous couplet the focus is on the contrast between death and life; here the parallel contrast is between suffering and glorification (Rom. 8:17). Christ endured and will one day reign (1 Cor. 15:25), and those saints who endure will one day reign with Him (Rev. 3:21). The last two couplets are negative: (3) **If we disown Him, He will also disown us** speaks of the possibility of apostasy (cf. 1 Tim. 4:1; Heb. 10:38-39; 2 John 9) and the Lord's ultimate rejection of those who professed Christ only temporarily (cf. Matt. 10:33). Instead of identifying with Christ, the apostate finally dissociates himself with Christ. (4) **If we are faithless, He will remain faithful** speaks not of the apostate, but of a true child of God who nevertheless proves unfaithful (cf. 2 Tim. 1:15). Christ **cannot disown Himself;** therefore He will not deny even unprofitable members of His own body. True children of God cannot become something other than children, even when disobedient and weak. Christ's faithfulness to Christians is not contingent on their faithfulness to Him. The significance of these couplets could hardly have been lost on Timothy.

IV. Marks of a Good Workman (2:14-26)

A. Faithfulness in ministry (2:14-19)

2:14. The instruction of the previous verses was not for Timothy only. Timothy was to **keep reminding** others of **these things.** The verb is a present imperative, which means that this was to be Timothy's regular practice. The bulk of preaching to a knowledgeable audience frequently consists of reminding them of what they already know. In the case of the Christians at Ephesus, they were to be solemnly charged in the presence of God (cf. 1 Tim. 5:21) to avoid **quarreling about words** (cf. 1 Tim. 1:3-4; 4:7; 6:4; 2 Tim. 2:23; Titus 3:9), a tendency in the early church (cf. Acts 18:15). Such wrangling **is of no value,** but worse, actually **ruins those who listen** (cf. 2 Tim. 2:16, 18; 3:6), The destructiveness, but especially the worthlessness, of false teaching is a recurrent note in the Pastorals.

2:15. As for Timothy, he was to **do his best** (lit., "be zealous") to be sure he would meet with God's approval, a "laborer" (*ergatēn*; cf. Matt. 20:1, 8) **who does not need to be ashamed.** Paul had spoken of shame before men (2 Tim. 1:8, 12, 16); far worse is shame before God. Timothy need not fear such shame if he would **correctly** handle **the Word of truth**

(cf. Eph. 1:13; Col. 1:5; James 1:18), which for him included both Old Testament Scripture and what he had heard orally from Paul. The Greek *orthotomounta*, "correctly handling," found only here and in the Septuagint in Proverbs 3:6 and 11:5, means literally "to cut straight," but just what image Paul had in mind here is uncertain. Stone masons, plowers, road builders, tentmakers, and (least likely of all) surgeons have all been suggested, but a firm conclusion remains elusive. What is clear is that the shame of God's disapproval awaits those who mishandle His Word.

2:16-18. Timothy was to **avoid godless chatter** (lit., "shun profane empty utterances"; cf. 1 Tim. 6:20) which only advances ungodliness like **gangrene** (*gangraina*). (Such godless chatter contrasts with "the Word of truth" [2 Tim. 2:15] and "the truth" [v. 18].) The medical image is striking. Participating with those who engage in such profane speculations will only, literally, "give their words a feeding place like gangrene." They must be amputated instead. Two who deserved such treatment were **Philetus** about whom nothing is known, and **Hymenaeus,** whom Paul had already "delivered over to Satan" for chastisement (1 Tim. 1:20). These two had **wandered away from the truth** (lit., "concerning the truth missed the mark"; cf. 1 Tim. 1:6; 6:21) regarding the crucial doctrine of **the resurrection.** Greek philosophers typically viewed the soul as immortal and the body as its temporal prison. The idea of the physical resurrection of the body, both Christ's and the Christians', was therefore foreign and difficult for them to grasp. Hence there was a natural tendency toward heresies which rejected bodily resurrection (1 Cor. 15; Acts 17:32). The heresy of Philetus and Hymenaeus probably involved the idea that resurrection was a purely spiritual affair which occurred at conversion or baptism. But bodily resurrection is the keystone of Christian doctrine, as Paul showed (1 Cor. 15). Without it, the entire edifice of the gospel collapses. Little wonder then that Paul said that these two false teachers **destroy the faith of some** (cf. 1 Tim. 1:19).

2:19. Yet the defection of these two, and their followers, must not shake

Timothy's confidence. **God's solid foundation** (i.e., the church; cf. 1 Cor. 3:10-15; Eph. 2:19-22; 1 Tim. 3:15) **stands firm,** with two inscriptions as a "seal" to indicate the structure's authenticity and integrity (cf. Rom. 4:11; 1 Cor. 9:2). The first is a reference to the rebellion of Korah in which the Lord differentiated between the true and the false (Num. 16:5; cf. Jude 11). The second inscription is possibly a loose reference to Numbers 16:26 or more likely some other Old Testament passage such as Isaiah 52:11. The two inscriptions emphasize respectively both God's sovereign control over the church and every Christian's responsibility to turn away from evil. Thus Timothy did not need to fear for the destiny of God's work, but he was to make every effort to keep himself free from the contamination of the false teachers.

B. A clean instrument (2:20-21)

2:20-21. Paul furthered his point about noncontamination by introducing a new but similar metaphor. The image changes from a building to a household (cf. 1 Tim. 3:5, 15). In a **large** and varied household are all sorts of containers. Some are made **of gold and silver** and others **of wood and clay.** More importantly, **some are for noble purposes and some for ignoble.** Clearly the reference so far is to the faithful and the unfaithful within the church. But Paul then shifted the metaphor slightly to show how one can **be an instrument for noble purposes,** by cleansing **himself from the** ignoble vessels. The metaphor is somewhat mixed (one would usually think of cleansing from corruption, not cleansing from the corrupted vessels), but the apostle's point is clear: Timothy was to have nothing to do with the false teachers. In this way he would be a vessel: (1) "for noble purposes" ("unto honor," *timēn*), (2) **made holy** ("set apart"), (3) **useful** ("serviceable") **to the Master, and** (4) **prepared to do any good work** (cf. 2 Tim. 3:16). What is clean and set apart for special use can easily get contaminated and be rendered unusable through contact with the corrupt. Paul was concerned that Timothy, his choicest disciple, keep himself in a usable condition for the Lord.

C. Faithfulness in conduct (2:22-26)

2:22-23. Timothy was still a young man (cf. 1 Tim. 4:12), and even though he was probably mature beyond his years, he might have still displayed some of the characteristics and passions of the young: impatience, intolerance, love of argument, self-assertion, partiality. Timothy was to **flee the evil desires of youth** (probably Paul did not have sexual passions in mind here, at least not primarily), **and pursue** the opposite virtues: **righteousness, faith, love** (cf. 1 Tim. 6:11 for the same trio), **and peace.** The NIV wrongly places a comma after "peace"—the phrase should read straight through: "peace" **along with those who call on the Lord out of a pure heart** (cf. "pure heart" in 1 Tim. 1:5). While Timothy must oppose the false teachers, he was to be at peace with his brethren who were honest before God. The clear implication is that the false teachers were dishonest before God (cf. 1 Tim. 1:5; 4:2; 6:3-5). Timothy must refuse to get caught up in **foolish and stupid arguments** (*zēteseis,* "debates"; cf. 1 Tim. 6:4; Titus 3:9) which only **produce quarrels.**

2:24-26. False teaching will always be divisive, but **the Lord's servant** should **not** be a fighter but a promoter of unity, by being **kind** ("gentle") **to everyone** (cf. 1 Thes. 2:7), **able** or ready **to teach** (cf. 1 Tim. 3:2) those who are willing to learn, and forbearing in the face of differences (*anexikakon,* lit., "ready to bear evil treatment without resentment"; used only here in the NT). He must treat even his opponents with gentle instruction characterized by "meekness," **in the hope that God will grant them repentance** ("a change of heart and conduct") **leading them to a knowledge** (*epignōsin,* "full knowledge"; cf. Col. 1:9; 2 Tim. 3:7) **of the truth.** The goal is always remedial, never punitive, when dealing with brethren (cf. 2 Thes. 3:6, 15). The purpose must always be to edify Christ's body, not tear it down (cf. 1 Cor. 14:26). Thus when brethren fall into false teaching they must be treated with gentleness and Christian love in the hope **that they will come to their senses and escape from the trap of the devil** (cf. Gal. 5:1; 1 Tim. 3:7; 6:9) **who has taken them captive to do his will.** False teaching and all its negative consequences in the church are always the handiwork of Satan, but God in His grace often salvages the situation through the Christlike ministry of His servants.

V. Predictions of Faithlessness (3:1-9)

3:1-5. As in his previous letter, Paul warned Timothy about the collapse predicted for **the last days** (cf. 1 Tim. 4:1-3), a term which includes the entire period between the first century and Christ's return. During this interim, according to the prediction, the world will see **terrible times** of societal degeneration. Paul gave an extraordinary list (cf. Rom. 1:28-32) of 19 general characteristics believers should expect. **People will be:** (1) **lovers of themselves** (*philautoi*, "self-centered, narcissistic"); (2) **lovers of money** (*philargyroi*; cf. 1 Tim. 6:9-10); (3) **boastful**—the outward manifestation of the fact that inwardly they are (4) **proud** ("arrogant"); (5) **abusive** toward others, which translates *blasphēmoi* ("blasphemers"). Several of the words which follow begin in the Greek with the prefix *a-*, meaning "without" (as in moral-amoral, theist-atheist), signifying absence of the designated virtue. Thus people will be (6) **disobedient** (*apeitheis*) **to their parents;** (7) **ungrateful** (*acharistoi*); (8) **unholy** (*anosioi*); (9) **without love** (*astorgoi*, trans. "heartless" in Rom. 1:31, the only other place it is used in the NT); (10) **unforgiving** (*aspondoi*). *Diaboloi*, a word usually translated "devil" (cf. 1 Tim. 3:6-7; 2 Tim. 2:26), is used here with the root meaning (11) **slanderous;** (12) **without self-control** (*akrateis*); (13) **brutal** (*anēmeroi*, lit., "untamed," the opposite of civilized); (14) **not lovers of the good** (*aphilagathoi*; cf. Titus 1:8; Pss. 15:4; 19:8). The next two characteristics begin in the Greek with the prefix *pro-*, indicating an aggressive inclination toward vice: (15) **treacherous** (*prodotai*, "disposed toward betrayal"); (16) **rash** (*propeteis*, "disposed toward recklessness"). The final three characteristics are (17) **conceited** (lit., "puffed up"; cf. 1 Tim. 3:6; 6:4); (18) **lovers of pleasure** (*philēdonoi*) **rather than lovers of God** (*philotheoi*; the Gr. prefix *phil-* here and in characteristics 1, 2, and 14 above signifies "lovers of . . ."); (19) **having a form** (*morphōsin*, "outward shape," used only here and in Rom. 2:20) **of godliness but denying its power** (cf. Titus 1:16).

Though these characteristics are cataloged under the auspices of a prediction about "the last days," it is clear that Paul considered them to be already present in Ephesus. Though they would intensify with time, Timothy had to beware of such people and **have nothing to do with them.** No doubt Paul had in mind here Timothy's official associations, since he had already instructed Timothy to be kind to everyone (cf. 2 Tim. 2:24).

3:6-7. Paul focused on the specific situation in Ephesus. It was from the increasingly large group in society who displayed the preceding characteristics that the false teachers had emerged to plague the church. Their methods were insidious. They would **worm their way into homes and gain control over** those they knew were vulnerable and gullible. In the case of Ephesus the false teachers had crept in via a group of **weak-willed women who** were, literally, "heaped with sin and fed by various lusts." Once more Paul connected false teaching with moral deficiency. Their carnality and immaturity rendered them easy targets for the false teachers (cf. Eph. 4:14). Out of a so-called "openness to learn" they evidently embraced as a fad whatever new heresy came along. Their problem was that they could not recognize the truth when they saw it. (**To acknowledge the truth** is, lit., "to come to a full knowledge of the truth"; cf. 2 Tim. 2:25.)

3:8-9. The reference to **Jannes and Jambres** and their opposition to **Moses** draws not on the Old Testament but on a widespread Jewish legend about two of Pharaoh's magicians who competed against Moses and lost (cf. Ex. 7:11; 9:11). The comparison between the false teachers and the Egyptians, and implicitly therefore Timothy and Moses, must have encouraged the young minister. The opponents were **men of depraved** (lit., "corrupt"; cf. 1 Tim. 6:5) **minds** who **oppose the truth** and were therefore **rejected** (*adokimoi*, "disapproved") by God in regard to any claim to be teaching **the faith** (cf. 1 Tim. 3:9). Consequently, while their influence was temporarily a serious matter in the church, in the long run **they** would **not get very far.** Like Jannes and Jambres, eventually **their folly** would **be clear to everyone** (cf. 1 Tim. 4:15; 5:24-25).

VI. Challenge to Faithful Preaching (3:10–4:8)

A. Faithfulness in the face of opposition (3:10-13)

3:10-11. Paul returned (cf. 1:8, 12; 2:10) to his own example of endurance and faithfulness in another of his direct exhortations to Timothy (cf. 2:1). The contrast with the false teachers is a strong one: **You, however. . . .** Timothy knew intimately of Paul's **teaching** (*didaskalia*, "content") **way of life . . . purpose, faith, patience, love, endurance** (cf. 2:10; 12), **persecutions, sufferings** (cf. 1 Tim. 6:11), along with his various missionary experiences and deliverances, and the elderly apostle was not ashamed to lift them up before his young disciple as exemplary. The references to **Antioch** (of Pisidia), **Iconium, and Lystra** must have stirred Timothy's earliest memories of Paul (cf. Acts 13:14, 51; 14:6, 21; 16:1).

3:12-13. It was important for Timothy, as for all Christians, to realize that persecution awaits **everyone who wants to live a godly life in Christ** (cf. John 15:18-21)—hence Paul's reminder of his own past experience. Yet with the last days again in mind Paul wrote that Timothy could actually expect the situation to get worse and the pressure to intensify. False teaching would increase as **evil men and impostors** (lit., "magicians," but here with the connotation of "charlatans") **go from bad to worse** (lit., "advance further"), **deceiving and being deceived.** Error feeds on itself.

B. Faithfulness to God's Word (3:14–4:5)

3:14-15. Again the strong direct address, **But as for you. . . .** begins this section (cf. 2:1; 3:10; 4:5). The exhortation is to **continue in** the things Timothy had **learned** and **become convinced of** (cf. 1 Cor. 15:1-2). These things had come from two sources, which Paul set side by side as of equal importance: his own testimony, and **the Holy Scriptures,** which at that time of course consisted of the Old Testament. Timothy's complete confidence in both sources would be enough to prevent any slippage in his commitment to the truth. Again these verses seem to imply that Timothy's salvation occurred prior to his acquaintance with Paul (cf. 1 Tim. 1:2; 2 Tim. 1:2, 5; Acts 16:1). The Scriptures bring **salvation** only when one places his **faith in Christ Jesus.**

3:16-17. Paul had just noted that the Scriptures are able to make one wise with regard to salvation, a lesson Timothy had learned long before. But now Paul wanted to reemphasize to Timothy the crucial role of God's inscripturated revelation in his present ministry. Thus Paul reminded Timothy that **all Scripture is God-breathed** (*theopneustos*, "inspired"), that is, God's words were given through men superintended by the Holy Spirit so that their writings are without error. This fact was virtually taken for granted by the Jews. Then Paul asserted the "usefulness" of the Word. For each aspect of Timothy's ministry, whatever it might be— **teaching** (instructing believers in God's truths), **rebuking** those in sin (cf. 1 Tim. 5:20; 2 Tim. 4:2), **correcting** those in error (cf. 2 Tim. 2:25; 4:2), **and training** (*paideian*, lit., "child-training") **in righteousness** (guiding new believers in God's ways)—for all of these and more the written Word of God is profitable. With it **the man of God** (one who must provide spiritual leadership to others) is *artios*—"complete, capable, proficient in the sense of being able to meet all demands." To drive home his point still more emphatically Paul added **equipped** (*exērtismenos*, "furnished") **for every good work** (cf. 2:21). Paul placed heavy burdens of ministry on his young disciple in this letter, but he did not do so irresponsibly. He was confident of Timothy's commitment to and dependence on the Scriptures, and he was even more confident of God's ability to supply all Timothy's needs through the Word.

4:1. It would be difficult to see how Paul could have made his charge to Timothy any more weighty (cf. 1 Tim. 5:21; 6:13). He adjured Timothy, not only **in the** name of **God and of Christ,** but in the light of the coming judgment, Christ's return (*epiphaneian*, **appearing**; cf. 1 Tim. 6:14; 2 Tim. 4:8; Titus 2:13), and the establishment of **His** millennial **kingdom.**

4:2. The content of Paul's charge represents the central thrust of every minister's task: Timothy was to **preach the Word.** All the weight of verse 1 bears on this entreaty. Paul could hardly have emphasized the matter more strongly.

Because the Word is inspired and profitable for all aspects of the ministry, proclaiming that Word was to be Timothy's business **in season and out of season,** that is, he was to stand by this duty whether the opportunity seemed ripe or not. Those in error he was to **correct** (cf. 2:25); those who were sinning he was to **rebuke** (1 Tim. 5:20; 2 Tim. 3:16; Titus 1:13; 2:15); those who were doing well he was to **encourage.** These are the facets of public ministry: proclamation, correction, rebuke, and encouragement—all of which must be done **with great patience and careful instruction.**

4:3-4. The reason Paul's charge to Timothy is so solemn is that **the time will come**—and no doubt was already partially present, in the apostle's opinion—**when men will not put up with sound** (lit., "healthy"; cf. 1 Tim. 1:10; 6:3; 2 Tim. 1:13; Titus 1:9, 13; 2:8) **doctrine. Instead . . . they** would seek out (lit. "heap up") **teachers,** of whom many are always available, who would tell them what they wanted to hear rather than face them with the truth (cf. Rom. 1:18-32). Such teachers merely "tickle the ear" so that they **turn** people **away from the truth** on the one hand and toward **myths** (*mythous;* cf. 1 Tim. 1:4) on the other. Paul's main focus in this passage was on the inclinations of the audience rather than, as was more his custom (but cf. 2 Tim. 3:6-7), the evil intent of the false teachers. For error to flourish both sides of the transaction must cooperate. This is the sixth time Paul used "truth" in this epistle (cf. 2:15, 18, 25; 3:7-8). (He referred to truth five times in 1 Tim. [2:4, 7; 3:15; 4:3; 6:5] and twice in Titus [1:1, 14].) Obviously he was concerned about the dangers of heresies diverting people from God's truth.

4:5. Again Paul used the strong contrast **But you . . .** (cf. 3:10, 14). Timothy must remain cool-headed in the face of difficulties. He must be ready to **endure hardship** (cf. 2:3) as the pressure mounted. He must **do the work of an evangelist,** proclaiming the gospel at every opportunity. (There is no reason to assume, as some suggest, that Timothy was without the gift of evangelism). In every way, Paul wrote, fulfill **your ministry** (*diakonian,* the word for voluntary "service" from which comes "deacon").

C. Faithfulness of Paul (4:6-8)

4:6. What had overshadowed the entire epistle is now stated explicitly: Paul was about to die. The apostle's strong charge in the previous verses takes on added weight with this reminder. The "But you" of verse 5 must therefore be seen in contrast not only with the false teachers of verses 3-4 but also with the **For I** of verse 6. Paul viewed his death now as certain; he was **already being poured out like a drink offering** (cf. Phil. 2:17). This refers to the libation connected with the daily offerings of the lambs (cf. Num. 28:4-7). Paul knew, sitting in a Roman jail, that there would be no release. **The time** had **come for** his **departure** (*analyseōs,* a traveler's term commonly used as a euphemism for death).

4:7. Looking back over his life, the apostle offered a remarkable description few could honestly echo. He had **fought the good fight** (cf. 1 Tim. 6:12) **finished the race** (cf. Acts 20:24), and **kept the faith** (cf. 1 Tim. 6:20). The first two are common Pauline athletic images (cf. 1 Cor. 9:24-27), while the third draws again on the image of faithfulness in one's stewardship of Christian truth (cf. 2 Tim. 1:14).

4:8. As a result of his faithfulness to duty Paul had no fear of facing **the Lord, the righteous Judge,** but only anticipation of reward in the form of a **crown** (*stephanos,* the laurel wreath of the athletic games) **of righteousness which** was already waiting **in store for** him. "Crown of righteousness" can mean either that righteousness itself is the crown or reward, or that this crown is the reward *for* righteousness (cf. 2 Tim. 3:16). In favor of the first view is the fact that James 1:12 and Revelation 2:10 seem to say that the "crown of life" means that life *is* the crown, not that a crown is given because one has life. In either case Paul expected to receive his reward **on that day** (a reference to Christ's return, not Paul's death), side by side with the rest of the faithful **who have longed for His appearing** (cf. Phil. 3:20-21; Titus 2:13).

VII. Reminder of God's Faithfulness in Paul's Adversity (4:9-18)

A. Paul's enemies and friends (4:9-16)

4:9. In this last section of the epistle

Paul twice urged Timothy to join him in Rome (vv. 9, 21). The emphasis is on speed since Paul did not know how much longer he would be allowed to live. The delivery of the epistle, followed by Timothy's travel, would occupy some months as it was; any delay on Timothy's part could make his arrival too late. Paul evidently had reason to believe that his execution was imminent (cf. v. 6).

4:10. Paul's need for Timothy was intensified by the defection of **Demas** who, instead of loving the Lord's appearing (v. 8), **loved this world.** Previously mentioned among Paul's fellow workers (though, perhaps significantly, not commended) in Colossians 4:14 and Philemon 24, Demas **deserted** the apostle to embrace the safety, freedom, or comfort of **Thessalonica.** It should not be surprising that Paul would long for his most faithful disciple Timothy at such a time (cf. Phil. 2:20-22; 2 Tim. 1:4). Of **Crescens** nothing is known. He and **Titus** had evidently been dispatched to the Lord's work elsewhere, Crescens to **Galatia** and Titus to **Dalmatia,** now Yugoslavia. Unlike Demas, there is no hint of any defection on their part.

4:11. Of all Paul's close associates, **only** the "beloved physician" **Luke** (cf. Col. 4:14) was **with** Paul. He had accompanied Paul on many of his travels and had shared the first Roman imprisonment with him (cf. Col. 4:14; Phile. 24). In joining the two of them, Timothy was to pick up **Mark** along the way. It is not known where Mark might have been located. But this one whom Paul had once considered untrustworthy (Acts 15:36-40) was now considered **helpful to** Paul **in** his **ministry.** Barnabas' concern (in opposition to Paul's wishes) to salvage the young John Mark was now paying dividends to Paul himself (cf. Col. 4:10).

4:12. Tychicus, another of Paul's faithful traveling companions (cf. Acts 20:4) and messengers (Eph. 6:21-22; Col. 4:7-9) had been **sent . . . to Ephesus.** The reference is cryptic and evidently self-explanatory to Timothy. Perhaps Tychicus delivered the letter; perhaps he was even, by prior arrangement, to relieve Timothy temporarily (cf. Titus 3:12). In any case Tychicus was another of Paul's absent companions.

4:13. Again little is known of **Carpus** or **the cloak . . . scrolls,** or **parchments** mentioned here. Such glimpses into the daily life of the apostle are intriguing, but any attempts to suggest what the documents might have contained, for example, are purely speculative. Paul may have needed the cloak because winter was coming on and his prison was cold, but even this is uncertain.

4:14-15. Alexander the metalworker may be the same man named in Acts 19:33-34, or more likely, the person in 1 Timothy 1:20. But since the name Alexander was common, one cannot be certain. The Alexander referred to here was well known to Timothy and had done **a great deal of harm** to Paul by opposing his **message.** The apostle had no desire for personal revenge, as may be seen by his reference to Psalm 62:12: **The Lord will repay him for what he has done** (cf. Rom. 12:19). Yet Paul was concerned lest Timothy run afoul of Alexander's attacks. Hence his warning to **be on your guard against him.**

4:16. Paul's **first defense** evidently refers, not to his first Roman imprisonment, about which Timothy would have already known, but to a preliminary hearing leading up to his present trial. At such trials it was common to hear advocates for the accused, but in Paul's case **no one came to** his **support, but everyone deserted** him. The widespread desertion of the apostle may be explained by the fact that, unlike the period of his first imprisonment, it had now become dangerous to be a Christian in Rome. As early as A.D. 59-60 Roman Jews had informed Paul "that people everywhere are talking against this sect" (Acts 28:22). But the situation had gotten far worse after the fire of Rome in July of A.D. 64. Nero made the Christians scapegoats and many were tortured and died. The intensity of the anti-Christian pressure must have eased somewhat by A.D. 67, but the thought of identifying themselves with the fearless and outspoken apostle must have been more than the Roman Christians and even Paul's companions could face. In fact Paul was understanding toward their unfaithfulness, and he expressed the hope that **it not be held against them** (cf. Christ's words on the cross, Luke 23:34).

B. Paul's deliverance by the Lord (4:17-18)

4:17. Paul's courage in proclaiming the gospel was not dampened by the weakness of those around him. The secret to his ministry was his dependence on the strength of God (Phil. 4:13; 1 Tim. 1:12). Though nobody remained with him Paul said, **The Lord stood at my side and gave me strength.** The apostle to the Gentiles had long before discounted his own life for the sake of preaching the gospel (cf. Acts 20:24). This was simply the latest episode of many wherein Paul put his own life on the line **so that through** him **the message might be fully proclaimed and all the Gentiles might hear it.** And once again, at least for the time being, he had been **delivered from the lion's mouth.** Some have seen in this last phrase a metaphorical reference to Nero or a literal reference to the wild animals in the Roman Coliseum. More likely Paul is drawing on a biblical image (cf. Ps. 22:21; Dan. 6:22).

4:18. Paul knew that his fate in the Roman courts was sealed (cf. vv. 6-8), and he was ready to die. Yet he saw his death not as a victory for Rome but as a **rescue** of the Lord. Despite **every evil attack,** he had complete confidence that God would **bring** him **safely to His heavenly kingdom** (cf. v. 1). For this Paul, even in the face of his own death, could do nothing but praise God: **To Him be glory forever and ever. Amen** (cf. Eph. 3:21; 2 Peter 3:18).

VIII. Final Greetings (4:19-22)

4:19-20. Prisca (NIV marg.; elsewhere called **Priscilla) and Aquila,** the well-known couple who taught Apollos in Ephesus (cf. Acts 18:2, 18, 26; Rom. 16:3; 1 Cor. 16:19), **and the** faithful **household of Onesiphorus** (cf. 2 Tim. 1:16) were singled out by the apostle for greeting. **Erastus** was an old associate of Timothy (Acts 19:22) and his whereabouts would presumably be of interest; the same would be true of the information about **Trophimus** (cf. Acts 20:4; 21:29), an Ephesian.

4:21. The appeal in verse 9 is repeated with the addition of the words **before winter.** Paul may have desired his cloak before the weather turned cold (v. 13), but he was more likely concerned about the sailing conditions on the Adriatic Sea. Of the four individuals listed, **Eubulus . . . Pudens, Linus,** and **Claudia,** nothing is known. Though "everyone" had deserted Paul at his first defense, still, in the spirit of forgiveness expressed in verse 16, Paul had not cut the Roman Christians off. The greeting is from **all the brothers.**

4:22. Paul's closing benediction is first directed to Timothy (**your spirit,** sing.) and then to his other readers (**you,** pl.), once again demonstrating that the epistle was designed to be read widely (cf. 1 Tim. 6:21; Titus 3:15). If 2 Timothy were penned during Paul's second Roman imprisonment, these are the last words of the apostle to have survived.

BIBLIOGRAPHY

See Bibliography on 1 Timothy.

TITUS

A. Duane Litfin

INTRODUCTION

Titus was a Gentile convert (Gal. 2:3) who had served and traveled with the Apostle Paul (Gal. 2:1-3). Titus had also functioned as a faithful emissary to the troubled church in Corinth (2 Cor. 7:6-7; 8:6, 16).

In approximately A.D. 63–64, sometime after they left Timothy behind in Ephesus, Paul and Titus traveled on to Crete. After a brief visit Paul then left Titus behind to help provide leadership for the Cretan churches (Titus 1:5). Subsequently the apostle wrote this epistle and had it delivered to Titus. The exact time and place of writing is unknown. (See the *Introduction* to 1 Timothy for a more detailed discussion of the authorship and dating of the Pastoral Epistles.)

The purpose of the epistle to Titus was to instruct him about what he should do and teach in the Cretan churches. A special theme of the letter is the role of grace in promoting good works among God's people (Titus 2:11–3:8).

Paul hoped to join Titus again in Nicopolis for the winter (3:12), but there is no way of knowing whether that meeting ever took place. Titus was last mentioned by Paul (2 Tim. 4:10) as having gone to Dalmatia (Yugoslavia). Tradition has it that Titus later returned to Crete and there served out the rest of his life.

OUTLINE

COMMENTARY

I. Salutation (1:1-4)

1:1. Paul began by identifying himself as **a servant of God.** Usually, no doubt as a result of his Damascus Road experience (Acts 9:1-9), Paul called himself a "servant of Christ Jesus." Only here did he use the term "servant of God." On the other hand **apostle of Jesus Christ** is standard. Both of these titles ("servant" and "apostle") focus on Paul's two main concerns: **the faith of God's elect** (cf. Rom. 8:33; Col. 3:12) **and the knowledge of the truth that leads to godliness** (cf. 1 Tim. 2:4; 2 Tim. 2:25; 3:7). God was using Paul to call out a people for Himself (e.g., 1 Thes. 1:2-10) and to teach them the truth which is conducive to godly living (cf. 1 Tim. 6:3). In other words Paul's ministry was aimed at both the salvation and sanctification of God's people.

1:2-3. In the NIV the **faith and knowledge** (already mentioned in v. 1) are said to be **resting on the hope of eternal life.** "Resting on" is from the single Greek word *epi.* But it is better to understand this word as "with a view to," as in Ephesians 2:10. Thus Paul's thought is that all of his ministry is "with a view to" eternal life. This hope was promised to the elect from eternity past (2 Tim. 1:9) by God, who cannot default on His word. Only in the latter days, however, has the full understanding of that word come to light in the message God gave Paul to preach. As is common in the Pastorals, the apostle referred to God as Savior (cf. 1 Tim. 1:1; 2:3; 4:10; Titus 2:10; 3:4). God's eternal plan to salvage a people for Himself, rather than any this-worldly agenda to liberate social structures or institutions, formed the primary focus of Paul's ministry.

1:4. Titus was the ostensible recipient of the letter even though this epistle, like 1 and 2 Timothy, was designed to be read widely. Titus was called **my true son,** indicating possibly that Paul was responsible for Titus' conversion. The same phrase was also used of Timothy (1 Tim. 1:2). Or the term may denote a mentor-protégé relationship, or both concepts. The greeting **grace and peace from God the Father and Christ Jesus our Savior** is typical (cf. 1 Tim. 1:2; 2 Tim. 1:2) except for the last term which was applied earlier (Titus 1:3) to God the Father. Paul used the term *Savior* in Titus' letter interchangeably for the first two Members of the Godhead (cf. 2:10 and 13; 3:4 and 6).

II. Qualifications of the Elders (1:5-9)

1:5. As with Timothy in Ephesus (1 Tim. 1:3), Paul had left Titus behind to provide leadership to the fledgling church in Crete. Now the apostle reiterated his previous instructions, both for Titus' sake and for the congregation's. The organization of the Cretan church was **unfinished** due to the brevity of Paul's visit. Thus Titus was to **straighten out** (lit., "set in order") the situation by appointing **elders in every town.** Titus was now acting as an apostolic agent (cf. Acts 14:23) in Paul's absence. His authority in the Cretan church was an extension of Paul's own. Such authority ended with the close of the Apostolic Age.

1:6. As in 1 Timothy 3:2-7 Paul listed the qualifications for elders (cf. comments on 1 Tim. 3:1). There the list numbered 15; here 17. Yet both lists cover essentially the same qualities: (1) the elder must be **blameless** (*anenklētos,*

"unreprovable"). In 1 Timothy 3:10 Paul used this same word of deacons, while in 1 Timothy 3:2 he used *anepilēmpton* to express the same thought of the elders. (2) **Husband of but one wife** probably means that the elder should have been married only once (see comments on 1 Tim. 3:2). (3) The elder must have his own household under control. This involves not only the matter of discipline (1 Tim. 3:4-5), but also positive spiritual influence as well. His children must be believers who **are not open to the charge of being wild and disobedient.** The apostle had explained why this requirement is important (1 Tim. 3:5).

1:7. Here Paul switched from the term "elder" (*presbyteros*) to **overseer** (*episkopos,* commonly trans. "bishop"). The two words are plainly interchangeable in the apostle's thinking, referring to the same church office. The term "overseer" is singular here, but this certainly does not mean that there must be only one *episkopos* per congregation. Rather the word is used here in a generic sense. Paul was simply affirming that these qualifications are required of all overseers. The need for blamelessness is repeated from verse 6. The reason this quality is so important is that an overseer serves as a steward of God. Damage to a church leader's reputation is damage to God's reputation. Then Paul resumed his list with five vices which must not characterize an overseer: (4) **not overbearing,** not arrogant and self-willed; (5) **not quick-tempered** (cf. James 1:19-20); (6) **not given to much wine;** (7) **not violent** (cf. 1 Tim. 3:3 for this and the previous vice); (8) **not pursuing dishonest gain** (cf. comments on 1 Tim. 6:5).

1:8. Whereas verse 7 lists negative characteristics to avoid, verse 8 lists positive qualities to be sought. The elder must be (9) **hospitable** (cf. 1 Tim. 3:2); (10) **one who loves what is good** (cf. Ps. 15); (11) **self-controlled,** or temperate and sensible (*sōphrona;* cf. Gal. 5:23; 1 Tim. 3:2; Titus 2:2, 4); (12) **upright** (*dikaion,* "just"); (13) **holy** (these last two are, with blamelessness, two of the characteristics Paul himself had modeled [cf. 1 Thes. 2:10], but neither is mentioned in 1 Tim. 3); and (14) **disciplined** (in contrast to the vices of Titus 1:7; cf. 1 Tim. 4:7-8).

1:9. Not only must an overseer meet moral and spiritual standards in his personal life, but he must also be a reliable man of the Word. (15) He must **hold firmly to the trustworthy message as it has been taught.** This last clause, "as it has been taught," actually comes first in the Greek, for emphasis. According to Paul, an elder is a conservator of the truth, one who must understand it, hold it fast; (16) **encourage others** by teaching it; and (17) **refute those who oppose it.** To be qualified as an elder a man must be a capable handler of the truth (cf. comments on 1 Tim. 3:2).

III. Characteristics of the False Teachers (1:10-16)

1:10. Having mentioned those who oppose the truth, Paul then described them for Titus and offered advice on how to handle them. He noted their three most prominent characteristics: they are **rebellious** (cf. Jude 8), **mere talkers,** and **deceivers.** All three characteristics were also present in Timothy's opponents in Ephesus (cf. 1 Tim. 1:3-11; 6:3-10; 2 Tim. 2:14-18); but in Crete, Titus faced a Jewish element (the **circumcision group,** cf. Acts 11:2; Gal. 2:12) in whom these characteristics stood out prominently.

1:11. These false teachers **must be silenced** because of the damage they were doing to the families of the congregation (cf. 2 Tim. 3:6). No doubt Titus' method of silencing was to be the same as Timothy's: the false teachers were to be instructed not to teach certain things lest they be excommunicated (cf. 1 Tim. 1:3-4; 2 Tim. 3:5). Again Paul condemned the motives of the false teachers—they were interested in **dishonest gain** (cf. comments on 1 Tim. 6:5).

1:12. To emphasize his point Paul quoted from Epimenides, a Cretan poet and philosopher from the sixth century B.C. who was widely believed to be a religious prophet. Though the quotation may originally have referred to a particular lie (viz., that Zeus was buried in Crete, which was especially offensive to those who believed Zeus was still alive), by Paul's day the saying had become a proverb which merely emphasized the low reputations of Cretans generally. So little did others think of the Cretans that the verb *krētizō* was invented to mean "to lie." Of course many noble Christians were in the congregations in Crete, but Paul was frontal in his assertion that the

false teachers possessed these baser Cretan tendencies.

1:13-14. How the congregations reacted to Paul's forthright use of this quotation is not known, but they certainly could not have missed his point: **This testimony is true.** The false teachers fit the Cretan stereotype. Thus their negative influence must be remedied, if at all possible, by salvaging the false teachers themselves. Titus was to **rebuke them sharply, so that they will be sound** ("healthy"; cf. 1 Tim. 1:10; 6:3-4) **in the faith.** The ultimate goal of discipline should be to recover the one who is in error (Gal. 6:1; 2 Thes. 3:14-15). In the present case Paul hoped that Titus' severe rebuke would be enough to bring the errorists around so that they would cease paying **attention to Jewish myths** and **to the commands of those who reject the truth.**

1:15-16. The "commands" of verse 14, especially in light of the Jewish and possibly Gnostic influences, undoubtedly included ascetic rules about eating, drinking, and purification (cf. Col. 2:20-23; 1 Tim. 4:1-5). Paul set the matter straight by reminding his readers of the Lord's teaching that purification is largely a matter of the internal rather than the external (cf. Mark 7:15; Luke 11:39-41). Nothing outside can corrupt one who is internally pure; but someone who is internally impure corrupts all he touches. The problem with the false teachers was that on the inside, in their **minds and consciences,** they were impure. As a result, even though they claimed to know and follow God, their corrupt actions belied their true natures (cf. 1 John 2:4). Their impure interiors thus rendered them externally **detestable** (lit., "abominable") to God, **disobedient** (cf. Titus 1:10), and **unfit** (*adokimoi*, "disapproved"; cf. 1 Cor. 9:27) **for doing anything good** (cf. 2 Tim. 3:17). Once again Paul connected theological error with moral deficiency.

IV. Godly Behavior for Different Groups (2:1-10)

A. Older men (2:1-2)

2:1. Returning to his instructions to Titus, Paul established a strong contrast with the false teachers he had just discussed. **You** translates *sy de,* which should probably be rendered more strongly: "But as for you. . . ." Titus was to teach in the congregation **what is in accord with sound doctrine,** or more literally, "healthy teaching." The notion of healthy teaching is common in the Pastorals (cf. 1 Tim. 1:10; 6:3; 2 Tim. 1:13; 4:3; Titus 1:9, 13; 2:2). So also is the idea that certain behavior befits sound doctrine, and other behavior does not (cf. 1 Tim. 1:10; 6:3). The victims of false teachers (cf. Titus 1:16) were out of harmony with sound doctrine; but now Paul would describe the right sorts of behavior.

2:2. Paul addressed several groups, the first being the **older men.** Titus was to teach them to manifest the characteristics of maturity. Older men are to be **temperate** (*nēphalious*; cf. 1 Tim. 3:2), **worthy of respect** (*semnous*, "serious-minded," i.e., not clowns), and **self-controlled** (*sōphronas*, cf. 1 Tim. 3:2; Titus 1:8; 2:4). These marks of maturity should be complemented by marks of godliness, the three central Christian virtues of **faith . . . love,** and **endurance** (*hypomonē*). This last one may seem to have replaced the familiar virtue "hope" in the trio, but the two are closely aligned (cf. Rom. 5:4; 15:4, 1 Thes. 1:3), especially for those who have lived long lives.

B. Older women (2:3)

2:3. Titus was likewise to teach the **older women** to behave reverently, in a way suitable to sound doctrine. They were **not to be slanderers** (cf. 1 Tim. 3:11) **or addicted to much wine** (cf. 1 Tim. 3:8). Both were real possibilities for women whose families were grown and who may have had too much idle time on their hands (cf. 1 Tim. 5:13-14). Titus was to encourage these older women to develop a ministry of teaching younger women **what is good.** Younger women with children were to keep their primary focus at home (see Titus 2:4-5), but the older women would do well to reach outside their homes and share what they had learned with those who would profit from it most.

C. Younger women (2:4-5)

2:4-5. Paul specified here what he meant by his general reference to "what is good" in verse 3. Older women could help the **younger women** in at least seven areas, a list that no doubt represents the apostle's understanding of a young wife

and mother's proper priorities. This list emphasizes, in the original, first what young wives and mothers are to be, and then only secondarily what they are to do. They are to be (1) lovers of their **husbands;** (2) lovers of their **children;** (3) **self-controlled;** (4) **pure;** (5) **busy at home,** that is (cf. 1:8; 2:2) "domestic" (*oikourgous*, lit., "working at home"); (6) **kind;** and (7) **subject to their husbands.** By (*agathas*, "good") manifesting these qualities, Paul wrote, young Christian wives and mothers would earn the respect of outsiders and thereby prevent God's Word from being maligned. Today, though the opposite is often true, Christian wives and mothers can still be sure that the Lord will honor those who value what He values, and that He will ultimately vindicate both His Word and those who are faithful to it.

D. Younger men (2:6-8)

2:6. Titus was to **similarly** encourage the **young men** to exercise self-control, a virtue in which many young men are deficient. Paul used some form of the word here translated "self-control" with each of the four groups of people (vv. 2, 4, 5, 6). Various forms of the word are prominent in the Pastorals, indicating for all Christians the importance of moderation, sensibleness, and self-restraint.

2:7-8. Titus qualified as a young man too, and so received some direct advice from the apostle. He must strive to "show himself" **an example** (*typos,* "pattern") to all (but esp. to the other young men) in every good work (cf. 1 Tim. 4:15-16). In his public ministry of teaching Titus must show an **integrity, seriousness, and soundness of speech that cannot be condemned.** Paul was always concerned lest **those who oppose** be provided ammunition for their attacks. Far better, said the apostle, that they **be ashamed because they have nothing bad to say about us.** They would not cease their attacks, of course, but they might at least be embarrassed by having to make up their own false accusations.

E. Slaves (2:9-10)

2:9-10. Slaves too, who made up a significant portion of first-century congregations, were responsible to honor God with their lives (see comments on 1 Tim.

6:1). Paul listed five qualities which were to characterize Christians who found themselves serving others. Titus was to teach them (1) **to be subject to their masters in everything;** (2) **to try to please them;** (3) **not to talk back to them;** (4) **not to steal from them;** (5) **to show that they can be fully trusted.** From the world's perspective a slave should not owe any of these things to his master, but from a Christian's perspective the situation looks different. A Christian slave is in fact serving, not his earthly master, but the Lord Christ who will vindicate him in the end (Col. 3:23-24). In the meantime he must avoid giving offense, and must concentrate on following Christ's example in every way (cf. 1 Peter 2:18-25). In this way his life will prove to be an adornment to **the teaching about God our Savior.** Thus Paul drove home again what had been the theme of this entire section (Titus 2:1-10): a believer's behavior is to be in accord with or befitting sound doctrine.

V. Role of Grace in Promoting Godly Behavior (2:11–3:11)

A. The educating power of grace (2:11-14)

2:11-12. Paul had been exploring the affirmation that godly living is demanded by God's truth. Now he changed his focus to explore that central aspect of God's truth which demands godly living: grace. The word **for** (*gar*) suggests that here is the theological foundation for what the apostle had just written.

When fully understood, it is the gospel of **the grace of God** which teaches Christians how to live. This grace has brought salvation to all men, i.e., it is universally *available*. The NIV, however, states that God's grace **that brings salvation has appeared to all men,** thus suggesting a universal *appearance*. The question is whether "to all men" goes with "appeared" (as in the NIV) or with the adjective *sōtērios* ("that brings salvation"). Grammatically "to all men" can be taken either way, but the latter makes better sense and correlates with the clear teaching of 1 Timothy 2:4, 6; 4:10. In each case the reference to God as Savior (cf. 1 Tim. 2:3; 4:10; Titus 2:10) prompted Paul to affirm the universal availability of salvation through Christ. To side with the NIV, on the other hand,

introduces an idea foreign to the New Testament and to common sense, since the gospel itself has patently not "appeared" to all men (unless "all men" means all kinds of people and not every single person). The message of God's grace, when its full implications are seen, leads Christians, negatively, **to say "No" to ungodliness and worldly passions** (cf. Heb. 11:24-26), and positively, **to live self-controlled, upright, and godly lives in this present Age.** All the specific instructions of Titus 2:1-10 can fit into these two negative and positive categories.

2:13-14. The gospel of grace affects one's present behavior, on the one hand, by focusing on God's unmerited favor in the past (see the Lord's parable in Matt. 18:23-35 for the dynamics of how this should work). But the Gospel also promotes godly living by focusing on the future. Christians look forward to **the blessed hope—the glorious appearing of our great God and Savior, Jesus Christ** (cf. 2 Tim. 4:8). It is crucial, moreover, to see that this One whom Christians look forward to meeting is the same One **who gave Himself for us to redeem** (*lytrōsētai,* "set free by payment of a price"; cf. Luke 24:21; 1 Peter 1:18) **us from all wickedness and to purify for Himself a people that are His very own, eager to do what is good.** A holy people was His purpose in paying such a fearful price. Therefore, knowing what all He has done and why He has done it, a Christian who truly loves Christ and looks forward to His return will pay any price to bring his life into conformity with his beloved Lord's will, lest he disappoint Him at His return. This was the Apostle John's thought when he wrote about the hope of Christ's appearing: "Everyone who has this hope in him purifies himself, just as He is pure" (1 John 3:3). A full understanding of these things leads inexorably to godly living. Conversely, ungodly living in a Christian is a clear sign that either he does not fully understand these things or he does not actually believe them.

B. The gracious behavior that results from grace (2:15–3:2)

2:15. Turning again to Titus, Paul told him to teach **these . . . things,** i.e., the specific aspects of godly behavior listed in verses 1-10 and referred to more cryptically in the last phrase of verse 14, "what is good." Like Timothy (e.g., 1 Tim. 4:12; 2 Tim. 4:2), Titus was told to step out aggressively in his public ministry, encouraging those who were doing well, rebuking those who needed to be corrected, being intimidated by no one.

3:1-2. A large part of any pastor's public ministry is reminding people of what they already know. Titus was to **remind** the Christians on Crete to be good citizens within their communities, a virtue in which Cretans were notoriously deficient. Though Paul did not repeat it here, his thought was no doubt that this behavior, like that of a Christian slave, will adorn the gospel and make it attractive to others (cf. 2:10). Paul listed seven qualities expected of Christian citizens: (1) **to be subject to rulers and authorities;** (2) **to be obedient** (cf. Rom. 13:1-7); (3) **to be ready to do whatever is good** (cf. Eph. 2:10; 2 Tim. 3:17); (4) **to slander no one;** (5) **to be peaceable and** (6) **considerate; and** (7) **to show true humility toward all men.** A Christian citizen should be an influence for good in the community in every way, demonstrating the loveliness of Christ to all through courteous and gracious behavior. This is precisely the lifestyle that results from understanding God's grace. In other words the instructions in Titus 2:15–3:2 must be seen as concrete examples of the behavior required of one who understands God's grace (2:11-14).

C. Grace as a motivation for godly living (3:3-8)

3:3. Paul never forgot the sinful condition from which he and his converts had been salvaged (cf. 1 Cor. 6:9-11; Eph. 4:17-24; Col. 3:6-7), and he reminded them of it once more. Instead of the gracious, Christlike people he was encouraging them to be, they once were just the opposite, being **foolish** instead of sensible, **disobedient** instead of submissive, **deceived and enslaved by all kinds of passions and pleasures** instead of self-disciplined and ready for every good work. Far from being peaceable, considerate, and humble, they were characterized by **malice and envy, being hated and hating one another.** Such is the brutish existence of people apart from God. While a veneer of civilization often obscures the bleak truth, the slightest

crack in the surface of society reveals the reality behind the facade. The painful truth is that apart from God people degenerate into little more than animals wrangling over bones.

3:4. But all of that changed **when the kindness and love** (*philanthrōpia*, lit., "love for man") **of God our Savior appeared.** The contrast is startling. In verse 3 man is the actor, but in verses 4-7 man is merely the recipient, and God becomes the actor. What man could in no wise do for himself, God initiated for him. (On the reference to God as Savior, see comments on 1 Tim. 1:1.)

3:5. God in His grace saves those who believe, not because of any righteousness in them (cf. Rom. 3:21-24; Eph. 2:8-9; 2 Tim. 1:9), but **because of His mercy.** The three words, "kindness," "love," and "mercy" (Titus 3:4-5) all represent aspects of God's grace. The dual means of grace through which He accomplished this salvation are (1) the **rebirth** spoken of as a **washing** from the filth of sin, and (2) the **renewal by the Holy Spirit** (cf. 2 Cor. 5:17). No mention is made here of the role of faith in the process because Paul's entire focus was on what God has done, not on human response.

3:6-7. God **poured out** the Holy Spirit on the world **generously through Jesus Christ our Savior.** Jesus was the Mediator of the Spirit (cf. Acts 2:33). The language intentionally conjures up images of the day of Pentecost (Acts 2:17). God's purpose in pouring out the Holy Spirit was **so that, having been justified by His grace,** believers **might become heirs having the hope of eternal life.** The ministry of the Holy Spirit is intimately involved, the New Testament explains, with bringing to fruition God's gracious purposes to save (cf. Rom. 8:15-17; Gal. 4:6-7; Eph. 1:13-14). What God in His grace began, God in His grace will see to the end, through His Spirit.

3:8. The **trustworthy saying** formula so common in the Pastorals (cf. 1 Tim. 1:15; 3:1; 4:9; 2 Tim. 2:11) introduces Paul's return to direct address. Because what he had just been saying is trustworthy, Titus should **stress these things** in order to promote godly behavior in his listeners. Twice before Paul had instructed Titus to teach these things in accordance with sound doctrine (Titus

2:1, 15), and this exhortation is his final reiteration of what is probably the central thrust of the entire epistle. Paul was deeply concerned that God's people **devote themselves to doing what is good** because **these things are excellent and profitable for everyone.** Titus was to promote good works, for they go hand in hand with sound doctrine.

D. Behavior inconsistent with grace (3:9-11)

3:9. If sound teaching is profitable for everyone, **foolish controversies and genealogies and arguments and quarrels about the Law . . . are unprofitable and useless.** This is a repeated theme in the Pastorals (cf. 1 Tim. 1:4; 6:4; 2 Tim. 2:23; Titus 1:14). Titus was to **avoid** (lit., "turn away from") such things.

3:10-11. As to the people who are advocating these useless things and thereby exerting a divisive and otherwise destructive influence in the church (cf. 1:11), Paul's instructions to Titus were direct and specific. He was to give such a person two warnings. If that did not work, he was to **have nothing to do with him.** The assumption is that a failure to respond to two warnings is a clear sign that the offender is **warped and sinful,** and **self-condemned.** Paul's thought here is similar to the Lord's instructions (Matt. 18:15-17), when He taught that after giving an offender three chances to repent, he is then to be cut off (but cf. 2 Thes. 3:14-15).

VI. Final Instructions and Greetings (3:12-15)

3:12. As usual, Paul ended his letter with some personal allusions. Though it is not known where Paul was when he wrote this epistle, he was planning to winter at **Nicopolis** on the Adriatic coast of Greece. Paul exhorted Titus to do his best to join him there as soon as **Artemas**

or **Tychicus** arrived. Evidently Paul intended to send one of the two to relieve Titus in Crete. Of Artemas nothing is known. (On Tychicus, see comments on 2 Tim. 4:12.)

3:13. **Zenas the lawyer** is mentioned nowhere else in the New Testament, and nothing is known about him, not even whether he was Jewish or Roman. But **Apollos** was a familiar fellow worker. The apostle's instructions seem to suggest that both Zenas and Apollos were in Crete and that Titus was in a position to **see that they have everything they need.** Servants of Christ who are called to travel from place to place have always received support from the churches (cf. 3 John 6-8).

3:14. Some have suggested that the Cretan Christians may have manifested some of their countrymen's traits (cf. 1:12) and were therefore unable to **provide for daily necessities,** much less be of use to anyone else. This is probably behind Paul's reference to **unproductive lives.** In any case Paul had been stressing the need for good works, not to earn salvation but to serve others, and he pointedly reiterated it here. He expressed the same thought to the Ephesian congregation (Eph. 4:28).

3:15. It is not known who was included in the phrase **everyone with me. Those who love us in the faith** obviously excluded the false teachers who opposed Paul. The closing greeting, **grace be with you all,** is similar to that in both 1 and 2 Timothy. The plural word **you** indicates an awareness on Paul's part that he was addressing a broader audience than just Titus.

BIBLIOGRAPHY

See Bibliography on 1 Timothy.

PHILEMON

Edwin C. Deibler

INTRODUCTION

Concerning the authenticity of this most personal of Paul's epistles, there has been no question. John Knox wrote, "The genuineness of the letter is so well established as to require little discussion" (*Philemon among the Letters of Paul*, p. 32).

Authorship. Among the church fathers, Ignatius, Tertullian, Origen, and Eusebius give evidence of the canonicity of this brief book. It was also included in the canon of Marcion and in the Muratorian fragment.

Three times in the epistle the author refers to himself as Paul (vv. 1, 9, 19). The style and language remind one of Paul (cf. v. 4 with Phil. 1:3-4). Paul in the introductions of his epistles commonly used the terms "love" and "faith." And these are used here also, in Philemon 5. Too, there is a close association with Colossians, for both epistles mention Archippus, Epaphras, Aristarchus, Demas, and Luke (cf. Col. 4:10, 12, 14, 17).

Date and Place of Writing. Paul was a prisoner when he wrote Philemon (vv. 1, 9). This epistle is therefore included among the so-called "prison epistles," and was written during his first Roman imprisonment, A.D. 61-63. Because Onesimus accompanied Tychicus, who carried the letter to Colosse, it is evident the two epistles were written at about the same time, probably in the summer of A.D. 62.

Destination. Philemon was the recipient. Judging by his ownership of slaves and the size of his home (large enough to house the local church referred to in v. 2), Philemon was a wealthy resident of Colosse. Though it is not known when Philemon first heard Paul, evidently Philemon was a convert of the apostle (v. 19b). It is likely that the two became friends during Paul's three-year ministry in Ephesus (Acts 19). It is commonly believed that Apphia (Phile. 2) was Philemon's wife, and Archippus his son, though this cannot be asserted dogmatically.

Included among the first readers were the members of "the church that meets in [Philemon's] home" (Phile. 2). Possibly Archippus was an official in this church, and Philemon served as a lay worker (vv. 1-2; contrast the terms "fellow worker" and "fellow soldier"). Lightfoot suggests that Archippus was an elder or was on a missionary charge, either of which was an important responsibility in the church. Some suggest that Archippus may have been the pastor. It is possible that Archippus had some official capacity at Colosse (Col. 4:17).

Occasion and Purpose. The occasion for writing is almost identical with the story of the epistle itself. Onesimus, a slave of Philemon, had run away, having evidently robbed his master (Phile. 18). His travels somehow brought him to Rome where, in the providence of God, he came in contact with Paul. Through this contact Paul led Onesimus to know the Savior. Then Onesimus in some way became useful to Paul (vv. 12-13).

But Paul realized that Onesimus had a responsibility to Philemon and should make restitution for his thievery. Thus Paul deemed it right to return Onesimus to Philemon. Tychicus was given the responsibility of carrying Paul's letter from Rome to the Colossians, and Onesimus evidently traveled back with him (Col. 4:7-9).

In this letter to Philemon Paul explained his situation and asked Philemon to treat Onesimus not as a runaway, thieving slave, but now as a beloved brother in Christ (Phile. 15-16; cf. Col. 4:9). In so doing, the apostle gave not only some insight into the institution of slavery in the Apostolic Age but also his

Christian response to it. The reality of Galatians 3:28 becomes evident here in Philemon: "There is neither . . . slave nor free . . . in Christ Jesus." Paul also gave a brilliant cameo of gospel truth in the words, "Charge that to my account" (Phile. 18, NASB).

OUTLINE

COMMENTARY

I. The Salutation of the Letter (vv. 1-7)

A. The writer (v. 1a)

V. 1a. This is the only one of Paul's epistles in which he referred to himself in the salutation as **a prisoner of Christ Jesus.** In seven of his epistles he called himself "an apostle"; in two of them (1 and 2 Thes.) he used no appellation, and in three he referred to himself as Christ's "servant."

Probably Paul refrained from calling himself an apostle here because this epistle is one of entreaty and request, not one of commands that would necessitate its readers' awareness of his apostolic authority. Paul was a prisoner of the Roman Empire, but actually his imprisonment was because of his witness for the Savior. Paul called himself "a prisoner of Christ Jesus" (Phile. 9). Epaphras was his "fellow prisoner" (v. 23).

Adding the words **and Timothy our brother** strengthened the weight of Paul's sympathy and love. Timothy's name was also joined with Paul's in the salutations to five of Paul's other epistles (2 Cor., Phil., Col., 1 and 2 Thes.).

B. The readers (v. 1b-2)

V. 1b. About all that is known of Philemon in the New Testament is disclosed in the words, **To Philemon our dear friend and fellow worker.** He was loved by Paul ("dear friend" is the rendering of *agapētō*, lit., "loved" or "beloved"; cf. v. 16); and Paul considered Philemon on his level as a "fellow worker" (cf. the pl. "fellow workers," v. 24). Philemon was a well-to-do Christian of the Apostolic Age, in whose home at Colosse the church met. "Fellow worker" does not necessarily suggest that Paul and Philemon labored together; more likely, Philemon worked to build up the church in Colosse while Paul served in nearby Ephesus (see "Destination" under the Book of Philemon's *Introduction*). Paul also addressed Philemon as "brother" in verses 7 and 20.

V. 2. **Apphia our sister** was most likely the wife of Philemon. She may have possibly served in a semi-official position in the church in their home. "She is as much a part of the decision as her husband, because according to the custom of the time, she had day-to-day responsibility for the slaves" (Arthur A. Rupprecht, "Philemon," in *The Expositor's Bible Commentary*, 11:458).

Some have surmised that **Archippus our fellow soldier** was Philemon's son. He may likely have been a mission-pastor in Colosse, for Paul gave a brief instruction for the Colossians to pass on to Archippus (Col. 4:17). Perhaps Archippus, because of his position, could have exerted additional influence on Philemon.

The church that meets in your home could also put pressure on Philemon to heed Paul's request. If Paul had not included this church in his salutation, they might have gossiped when they saw Onesimus had returned. The practice of churches meeting in private homes for worship was common up to A.D. 200. Not until the third century did churches meet in separate buildings. Home churches were also mentioned by Paul in Romans 16:5 and Colossians 4:15. The words "your home" may refer, some say, to Archippus' home ("your" is the sing. *sou*), but it is better to take it as referring to Philemon's home since he is addressed first in the salutation. The singular "you" in Philemon 4, 6-8, 10-12, 16, 18-21, 23 obviously refers to Philemon. "You" and "your" is plural only in verses 22 and 25.

C. The salutation (v. 3)

V. 3. This salutation—**Grace to you and peace from God our Father and the Lord Jesus Christ**—is the usual Pauline greeting. It is almost identical in wording to the greeting in six of his other epistles (Rom., 1 and 2 Cor., Gal., Eph., Phil.); the salutation in Paul's six other epistles have only slight variations (Col., 1 and 2 Thes., 1 and 2 Tim., Titus). (See chart, "Paul's Introductions to His Epistles" at Rom. 1:1.)

It is important to note the word order. The word "peace" expresses a spiritual state denoting a proper relationship between God and man; it is the effect of only one cause: the "grace" of God. There can be no peace apart from grace. Peace *with* God, a judicial matter, comes by means of faith (Rom. 5:1). The peace *of* God, an experiential condition, results from the infilling ministry of the Holy Spirit (Eph. 5:18; Gal. 5:22-23). Paul concluded the letter with a similar prayer regarding the "grace of the Lord Jesus Christ" (Phile. 25).

D. The commendation (vv. 4-7)

1. THANKSGIVING (VV. 4-5)

V. 4. Every letter of Paul's except Galatians includes an expression of thanksgiving in the opening. This follows the custom, in both pagan and Christian first-century correspondence, of including a word of thanks in the salutation. The words **I always thank my God as I remember you in my prayers** are almost the same ones Paul used in his other prison epistles (see Eph. 1:15-16; Phil. 1:3-4; Col. 1:3-4). Paul told *when* he gave thanks ("always"), and *to whom* ("God"), and *for whom* ("you," i.e., Philemon).

V. 5. Paul also told *why* (**because I hear about your faith in the Lord Jesus and your love for all the saints**). The coupling of faith in Christ and love for the saints was also true of the Ephesians (Eph. 1:15), the Colossians (Col. 1:4), the Thessalonians (1 Thes. 1:3; 2 Thes. 1:3).

Paul may have heard about Philemon's faith in Christ and love for the saints from Onesimus and Epaphras. Philemon's faith in Christ produced love for all the saints. Since Philemon loved "all" the saints, he surely should include Onesimus, now a saint, in his love!

2. PRAYER (V. 6)

V. 6. Having commended Philemon's faith and love (v. 5) Paul expanded on Philemon's faith (v. 6) and his love (v. 7). Paul's prayer was that Philemon (**you** is sing.) would be **active in sharing his faith** (lit., "active in *the* sharing," *hē koinōnia*). The relationship of the second clause to the first is difficult to translate. The NIV suggests that the second is a *result* of the first: **so that you will have a full understanding of every good thing we have in Christ.** Philemon's sharing of his faith would then lead to a full understanding of his spiritual blessings. However, the NIV words "so that you will have" are simply the one Greek word *en* ("in"). This hints that the first clause results from the second. As Philemon would gain a fuller understanding of his blessings in Christ he would become more active in sharing Him. He would share Christ *in* (i.e., in the sphere of) his full understanding of his blessings. The more a believer comes to comprehend all he has in Christ the more eager he is to share Him with others. The "full understanding" is *epignōsei*, mentioned in Paul's prayers in each of the other prison epistles (Eph. 1:18; Phil. 1:9; Col. 1:9).

3. TESTIMONY (V. 7)

V. 7. Philemon's **love** (cf. vv. 5, 9) resulted in **joy and encouragement** for

Paul, for Philemon had **refreshed the hearts of the saints.** "Refreshed" (*anape-pautai*, cf. v. 20) is the word the Lord used in Matthew 11:28, "Come to Me, all you who are weary and burdened, and I will give you rest" (*anapausō*, "I will refresh you"). Philemon, having been spiritually "refreshed" by Christ, could refresh others. "Hearts" is not the normal Greek word *kardia* for heart, but is *splanchna* (lit., "inner parts of the body"). The emotions stemmed from the inner parts, according to some Greeks. Thus this is a deep emotional term. Paul used it again in Philemon 12 and 20 (cf. Phil. 2:1, kjv).

II. The Body of the Letter (vv. 8-21)
A. The plea (vv. 8-12, 17)

Paul then gave his recommendations regarding the runaway slave Onesimus. Throughout this plea the apostle's words were courteous, and yet they bore a note of authority and earnestness. He revealed a double truth. Onesimus was now a *son* in the faith to Paul (v. 10), and Onesimus was now a *brother* to Philemon (v. 16). The latter forms a Christian reply to the horrible institution of slavery. Onesimus, in the lowest social status in the Roman world—a slave with no rights—was on a spiritual plane equal with his owner Philemon and with the leading apostle!

1. A PLEA, NOT A COMMAND (V. 8)

V. 8. Therefore introduces the application of Paul's prior words (vv. 4-7). Philemon's love, demonstrated to all the saints, should now include Onesimus. As an apostle Paul said he **could be bold and order you to do what you ought to do,** but he refrained. The word "bold" is *parrēsian*, rendered "courage" and "confidence" in Hebrews (3:6; 10:19, 35).

2. A PLEA FOR LOVE'S SAKE (V. 9)

V. 9. Paul's **appeal** was **on the basis of love,** probably Philemon's love (cf. vv. 5, 7). To receive back and forgive Onesimus would be a laudable expression of Philemon's love to both Onesimus and Paul. Further motivation for heeding Paul's plea was that Paul was both **an old man and now also a prisoner of Christ Jesus** (cf. v. 1). Being an "old man" (*presbytēs*) meant that Paul had authority (since older men in those days were considered wise and thus authoritative) and also that Paul's position as an *impris-*

oned old man greatly restricted what he himself could do for Onesimus. Also, the reminder that Paul was imprisoned might appeal to Philemon's sympathy. Thus Onesimus' restitution depended on Philemon. Paul's calling himself an old man undoubtedly was in contrast to Onesimus rather than to Philemon.

3. A PLEA FOR A SPIRITUAL SON (VV. 10-11)

V. 10. The verb **I appeal** (*parakalō*) was repeated from verse 9, thus giving it special force. This plea was for Paul's **son** (*tou emou teknou*, lit., "my own child"), a term of endearment, which Paul used elsewhere only of Timothy and Titus (1 Tim. 1:2; 2 Tim. 1:2; Titus 1:4). Onesimus, having escaped from his owner, somehow met Paul in Rome. Led to the Savior by Paul, Onesimus **became** Paul's **son while** he **was in chains.** Since the slave was converted while Paul was in prison, their relationship was probably stronger. What an encounter it must have been between that slave and that prisoner! But the slave-prisoner relationship became spiritually a son-father relationship. Paul thought of himself as a father to those he won to the Lord (1 Cor. 4:15; cf. 1 Tim. 1:2; 2 Tim. 1:2). A special bond of Christian affection exists between a believer and the person God used to bring him to Christ.

In Greek, the word **Onesimus** is last in Philemon 10, evidently withheld deliberately in order to render Philemon's heart more tender.

V. 11. Onesimus, a common name for slaves, means "useful." But this slave, by running away, had become the opposite of his name. He was then of no use to his owner. The words **but now** suggest a change resulting from his new birth. He who **was useless** (*achrēston*) had **become useful** (*euchrēston*) **both to you and to me.** "St. Paul seems to say, 'He belied his name in days past; he will more than deserve it now'" (Alfred Barry, "The Epistle to Philemon," in *Ellicott's Commentary on the Whole Bible,* 4:273). Onesimus was then doubly useful, to Paul as well as Philemon. This clever play on words on the slave's name no doubt strengthened the force of the apostle's request.

4. A PLEA FROM THE HEART (V. 12)

V. 12. Paul passed the problem on to Philemon: **I am sending him . . . back to**

you. Philemon would not have opportunity to think over Paul's request before seeing Onesimus. Instead, facing Onesimus, the slave owner would need to decide right then. Since this converted slave was, as Paul wrote, **my very heart** (*splanchna*, "emotions"; cf. vv. 7, 20), how could Philemon refuse his friend Paul? The apostle certainly knew the art of friendly persuasion! This verse suggests that Onesimus himself was the bearer of the letter.

5. A PLEA FROM A PARTNER (V. 17)

V. 17. Earlier Paul wrote that his appeal was "for" Onesimus (v. 10), and that Philemon could "have him back for good" (v. 15). But not until verse 17 did Paul explicitly state his request: **welcome him.**

Since Philemon considered Paul a **partner,** he certainly should welcome Onesimus as if he were welcoming Paul himself. The bond between the apostle and the slave owner was that kind of unity which draws fellow workers in the gospel to each other. "Partner" is *koinōnon.* This is from *koinōnia* ("fellowship or partnership"), which Paul used in verse 6. If Philemon rejected Onesimus, it would be like rejecting the apostle, his friend (v. 1), fellow worker (v. 1), brother (vv. 7, 20), and even partner (v. 17). Such would of course be unthinkable.

B. *The relationship (vv. 13-16)*

1. THE PRESENT BROTHERHOOD BETWEEN
   PAUL AND ONESIMUS (V. 13)

V. 13. Paul's estimate of this Christian slave placed the latter on equal footing with Philemon. If Onesimus were kept by Paul—which Paul **would have liked** — Onesimus would have served in **place** of (*hyper*) Philemon. Both were equally capable of helping Paul. And being **in chains for the gospel,** incarcerated because of his testimony for Christ (cf. "prisoner" in vv. 1, 9), Paul could have used some assistance. But duty erased his wish. Knowing that a slave was his master's property, Paul had no choice but to send him back.

2. THE PAST BROTHERHOOD BETWEEN
   PAUL AND PHILEMON (V. 14)

V. 14. Retaining a slave could be done only with the owner's **consent.** Though Paul probably could have talked Philemon into letting him keep Onesimus in Rome, he did not want to take undue advantage of their relationship. Paul preferred that such permission would be **spontaneous** (*hekousion,* "voluntary," used only here in the NT). No one knows whether Philemon freed Onesimus and sent him back to minister to Paul in Rome, but it is an interesting thought.

3. THE FUTURE BROTHERHOOD BETWEEN
   ONESIMUS AND PHILEMON (VV. 15-16)

V. 15. Philemon's temporary loss **(for a little while** is lit., "to an hour") of his slave resulted in his having him returned permanently. Some slaves were able to stay undetected in large cities or isolated areas, never to be returned to their owners. The words **for good,** which translate *aiōnion* (normally rendered "forever"), may mean either permanently in this life or forever in heaven.

V. 16. Paul also contrasted Onesimus' status **as a slave** with his new relationship to Philemon **as a dear brother,** thus placing all three men on the same level. Paul also called Onesimus "dear brother" in Colossians 4:9. The slave was dear to Paul but should be even more so to Philemon (cf. Phile. 11, "useful both to you and me"). For Philemon to take Onesimus back **no longer as a slave but better than a slave** may suggest emancipation (cf. v. 21). On the other hand some say that Philemon's receiving him **as a man** (lit., "in flesh") may point to a retaining of the master-slave relationship along with their new spiritual relationship **in the Lord.** Or these phrases may indicate just the opposite, with "as a man" referring to a person-to-person relationship, not a master-slave relationship.

(The commentary for v. 17 appears after that for v. 12.)

C. *The pledge (vv. 18-21)*

1. PHILEMON TO CHARGE ONESIMUS' DEBT
   TO PAUL (VV. 18-19A)

V. 18. Though Paul did not name Onesimus' offense, it probably involved a monetary loss for Philemon. Onesimus may have stolen some money or goods when he escaped from his owner, or the absence of Onesimus' services may have involved Philemon in financial loss. Paul did not castigate Onesimus for some crime; he simply wrote **if he has wronged you or owes you anything.**

Paul asked Philemon to charge (*elloga*, an accounting term) Onesimus' financial obligation to Paul. This generous act compares in a small way with Christ's substitutionary work on the cross. As Onesimus was in debt to Philemon, so sinners are in debt; they must pay for their sins against God. As Paul was not involved in any way with Onesimus' guilt, so Christ was sinless, separate from sinners (Heb. 4:15; 7:25). And as Paul assumed Onesimus' debt, so Christ took on Himself the sins of the world (Isa. 53:6; John 1:29; Heb. 7:27; 9:26, 28).

V. 19a. Paul stated that he was writing these words **with [his] own hand** (cf. Gal. 6:11), thus placing himself under legal obligation to carry out his commitment. His ability to **pay it back** may have come from the gifts sent to him from Philippi (cf. Phil. 4:14-19).

2. PHILEMON TO CONSIDER HIS OWN DEBT TO PAUL (V. 19B)

V. 19b. You owe me your very self hints that Philemon may have been won to the Lord by Paul, and was thus obligated to him spiritually. If so, this was further evidence that Onesimus and Philemon were on the same spiritual plane; they had both been led to the Savior by the apostle. Such a debt could in one sense cover Onesimus' obligations. And yet Paul chose not to dwell on that fact.

3. PHILEMON TO REFRESH PAUL (V. 20)

V. 20. Receiving and restoring Onesimus would give **some benefit** to Paul **in the Lord** (cf. "in the Lord," v. 16) and would **refresh** his **heart in Christ.** The words "some benefit" translate the Greek *onaimēn*, which is obviously related to the word "Onesimus." Paul was saying in effect, "Let me find in you, as I have found in him, a true Onesimus." "Refresh" (*anapauson*) and "heart" (*splanchna*) recall the words of verse 7. Philemon, who refreshed the hearts of other saints, could hardly refrain from doing the same for Paul.

4. PHILEMON TO GO BEYOND PAUL'S REQUEST (V. 21)

V. 21. Paul was sure that Philemon would heed his request. **Obedience** is stronger than Paul's other more tactful and less direct appeals. Paul was also confident that Philemon would do **even**

more than he asked. What Paul had asked was that Onesimus be welcomed and forgiven. What could be "more than" that? Onesimus' freedom seems to be in mind (cf. v. 16, "no longer as a slave"). Or it may refer to Philemon's returning Onesimus to Paul; but had he not asked already for that, though subtly? (v. 13) If Onesimus were released, this shows an effect of Christianity on slavery through a recognition of true brotherhood in Christ.

III. The Conclusion of the Letter (vv. 22-25)

A. The comfort (v. 22)

V. 22. Paul then requested something for himself: **Prepare a guest room for me,** likely in Philemon's home. The prospect of a visit from the apostle would comfort Philemon but would also spur him to respond quickly to Paul's plea for Onesimus. The "guest room" points to Philemon's financial status. Like Paul, many Christian workers have been encouraged and assisted in their ministries by such provisions.

Paul knew that many were praying for his release (cf. Phil. 1:25-26). (How could Philemon pray for Paul's release and yet refuse to release Onesimus?) By using the plural **you** and **your,** Paul referred back to those mentioned in Philemon 1-2: Philemon, Apphia, Archippus, and all the believers with them.

B. The fraternal greetings (vv. 23-24)

Vv. 23-24. Those who sent greetings to Philemon (**you** in v. 23 is sing.) are five of the six people also mentioned in Colossians 4:10-14, though in a different order: **Epaphras . . . Mark, Aristarchus, Demas, and Luke.** In Colossians Paul also added "Jesus, who is called Justus." In Colossians 4:12-13 Paul highly commended Epaphras, who in Philemon 23 is called **my fellow prisoner for Christ Jesus.**

C. The benediction (v. 25)

V. 25. Paul concluded all 13 of his epistles with a one-sentence benediction similar to the one here: **The grace of the Lord Jesus Christ be with your spirit.** "Your" is plural, pointing back to those addressed in verses 1-2. These believers were already enjoying the grace that brought them salvation, but here and in verse 3 Paul was concerned that they be encompassed with God's enabling grace for their daily walk before others. "Spirit" (cf. "your spirit" in the Gal. 6:18 and 2 Tim. 4:22 benedictions) refers to one's inner spiritual self. What a gracious way for Paul to conclude this touching intimate epistle.

BIBLIOGRAPHY

Barnes, Albert. *Barnes' Notes on the New Testament*. Grand Rapids: Kregel Publications, 1966.

Barry, Alfred. "The Epistle to Philemon." In *Ellicott's Commentary on the Whole Bible*. Reprint (8 vols. in 4). Grand Rapids: Zondervan Publishing House, 1959.

Carson, Herbert M. *The Epistles of Paul to the Colossians and Philemon*. Tyndale New Testament Commentaries. Grand Rapids: Wm. B. Eerdmans Publishing Co., 1960.

Gromacki, Robert G. *Stand Perfect in Wisdom: An Exposition of Colossians and Philemon*. Grand Rapids: Baker Book House, 1981.

Hendriksen, William. *Exposition of Colossians and Philemon*. New Testament Commentary. Grand Rapids: Baker Book House, 1964.

Hiebert, D. Edmond. *Titus and Philemon*. Chicago: Moody Press, 1957.

Jamieson, Robert; Fausset, A.R.; and Brown, David. *A Commentary Critical, Experimental and Practical on the Old and New Testaments*. Grand Rapids: Wm. B. Eerdmans Publishing Co., 1974.

Knox, John. *Philemon among the Letters of Paul*. Chicago: University of Chicago Press, 1935. Reprint. New York: Abingdon Press, 1959.

Lightfoot, J.B. *St. Paul's Epistles to the Colossians and Philemon*. London: Macmillan & Co., 1879. Reprint. Grand Rapids: Zondervan Publishing House, 1979.

Lohse, Eduard. *Colossians and Philemon*. Translated by William R. Poehlmann and Robert J. Harris. Philadelphia: Fortress Press, 1971.

Moule, H.C.G. *The Epistles of Paul the Apostle to the Colossians and to Philemon*. Cambridge Bible for Schools and Colleges. Cambridge: At the University Press, 1906.

Muller, Jacobus J. *The Epistles of Paul to the Philippians and to Philemon*. The New International Commentary on the New Testament. Grand Rapids: Wm. B. Eerdmans Publishing Co., 1955.

Oesterly, W. E. "The Epistle to Philemon." In *The Expositor's Greek Testament*. Grand Rapids: Wm. B. Eerdmans Publishing Co., 1951.

Rupprecht, Arthur A. "Philemon." In *The Expositor's Bible Commentary*, vol. 11. Grand Rapids: Zondervan Publishing House, 1978.

HEBREWS

Zane C. Hodges

INTRODUCTION

The Epistle to the Hebrews is a rich part of the New Testament canon. In a unique fashion it exalts the person and work of the Lord Jesus Christ. In doing so, it makes immensely valuable contributions to the doctrines of His Incarnation, His substitutionary death, and His priesthood. Among the other truths to which the epistle effectively contributes are those involving the relationship between the New Covenant and the Old, the interpretation of the Old Testament, and the life of faith. The church would indeed be incalculably poorer without the teaching of this inspired book.

But despite its unquestioned value, little is known with certainty about its occasion, background, and authorship. Ignorance in these matters, however, does not seriously affect the understanding of the epistle's message. That remains timeless and relevant whatever the circumstances out of which it arose.

Date. In considering the background of Hebrews, it is reasonable to begin with the question of its date. This can be fixed within fairly good limits. The epistle can hardly be later than about A.D. 95 since it was known to Clement of Rome and quoted by him in 1 Clement. In addition it can scarcely be dated after A.D. 70, since there is no reference to the destruction of the Jewish temple in Jerusalem. Had this event already occurred, it would have given the author a definitive argument for the cessation of the Old Testament sacrificial system. Instead he seems to regard this system as still in operation (cf. 8:4, 13; 9:6-9; 10:1-3).

There is no need to regard 2:3 as a reference to second-generation Christians, and the epistle was obviously written during the lifetime of Timothy, whom the author knew (13:23). If the author is not Paul (and on the whole it

seems likely he is not; see the following discussion on *Authorship*), then 13:23 may suggest he had already died. Otherwise, Timothy might have been expected to join Paul on his release from prison. On balance, a date somewhere around A.D. 68 or 69 seems most likely.

Authorship. Many names have been conjectured for the authorship of Hebrews, but the question remains unsolved. The tradition of Pauline authorship is very old and has never been decisively disproved. From the time of Pantaenus (died ca. A.D. 190) it was held in Alexandria that the epistle was in some sense Pauline. Clement of Alexandria thought Paul had written it originally in the Hebrew language and that Luke had translated it into Greek.

On the basis of style, Origen doubted the Pauline authorship but was not willing to set the tradition aside. In a famous statement he admitted that only God knew who had written the book.

The belief in the Pauline authorship of Hebrews belonged chiefly to the East until a later time. Jerome and Augustine seem to have been responsible for popularizing it in the West. In modern times it has usually been felt that the style and internal characteristics of Hebrews rule out Paul as the author. But arguments built on such considerations are notoriously subjective and have also been used to prove highly untenable propositions. Still it must be admitted that when Hebrews is read in Greek and compared with the known letters of Paul, the total impression is that here one meets a spiritual mind clearly attuned to Paul but in subtle ways quite different. This subjective impression, however, would not have prevailed if the early church's tradition had only mentioned Paul.

In fact the other name with early support is that of Paul's former missionary partner, Barnabas. This tradition appeared first in the West in Tertullian (ca. 160/170–215/220). In a polemical passage he quoted from Hebrews and assigned the quotation to an Epistle by Barnabas. Moreover, he did not talk as if this were his own opinion but simply a fact which his readers would know. The view that Barnabas wrote Hebrews was referred to at a later time by Jerome and reappeared in Gregory of Elvira and Filaster, both writers of the fourth century. There is reason to think that in the ancient catalog of canonical books found in the Western manuscript called Codex Claremontanus, the Book of Hebrews went under the name of the Epistle of Barnabas.

The evidence is not extensive, but the fact that it came from the West is perhaps significant. The only geographical reference in Hebrews is to Italy (13:24), and if the tradition about Barnabas is true it is not surprising that it comes from that part of the world. In other respects, Barnabas fits the requirements for authorship of this epistle. Since he was a Levite (Acts 4:36), an interest in the Levitical system, such as the author of Hebrews displayed, would be natural for him. Since he had close ties with Paul, resemblances in Hebrews to Paul's thought would be naturally explained. Moreover, Timothy had been converted in the area of Paul's first missionary journey (Acts 16:1-3) and was therefore most probably known to Barnabas. If Paul were dead at the time of the writing of Hebrews, it would not be surprising if Timothy were to join Paul's former companion (Heb. 13:23). The rift between Paul and Barnabas (Acts 15:37-39) had long since healed and Paul had later spoken warmly of Barnabas' cousin Mark (cf. Col. 4:10; 2 Tim. 4:11).

Of course authorship by Barnabas cannot be proved, any more than authorship by Paul can be disproved. But it has more to commend it than the other alternative suggestions. Among these it may be mentioned that at one time or another the names of Clement of Rome, Luke, Silvanus, Philip the Evangelist, Priscilla, and Apollos have been offered as possible authors. In particular the name of Apollos has found favor with some modern writers. The suggestion is often traced to Martin Luther. But the evidence is tenuous and does not include the early traditional support that the proposal Hebrews was written by Barnabas does. On balance this seems like the best conjecture. If Hebrews were actually authored by Barnabas, then it can claim apostolic origin since Barnabas was called an apostle (Acts 14:4, 14). In any case its divine authority is manifest.

Background and Setting. The identity of the first readers of Hebrews, like the author, is unknown. Nevertheless they were evidently part of a particular community. This appears from several considerations. The readers had a definite history and the writer referred to their "earlier days" (Heb. 10:32-34); he knew about their past and present generosity to other Christians (6:10); and he was able to be specific about their current spiritual condition (5:11-14). Moreover, the author had definite links with them and expressed his intention to visit them, perhaps with Timothy (13:19, 23). He also requested their prayers (13:18).

In all probability the readers were chiefly of Jewish background. Though this has sometimes been questioned, the contents of the epistle argue for it. Of course the ancient title "To the Hebrews" might be only a conjecture, but it is a natural one. When everything is said for a Gentile audience that can be said, the fact remains that the author's heavy stress on Jewish prototypes and his earnest polemic against the permanence of the Levitical system are best explained if the audience was largely Jewish and inclined to be swayed back to their old faith. The heavy and extensive appeal to the authority of the Old Testament Scriptures also was most suitable to readers who had been brought up on them.

As to the locale of which the readers were a part, nothing can be said definitely. The view that Apollos wrote the letter to the churches of the Lycus valley (where Colosse was situated), or to Corinth, is not independent of this view about authorship. The thesis that the readers were an enclave of Jewish Christians within the church at Rome has also found adherents. But apart from the reference to "those from Italy" (13:24), there is not much to suggest a Roman destination. On the view that Barnabas was the author, Cyprus has been proposed as a destination, since Barnabas was a Cypriot. But none of these proposals carries conviction.

The opinion that the epistle had a Palestinian destination has recently been strengthened by the observation that the polemic of the author may be best explained as directed against a sectarian form of Judaism such as that found at Qumran. Many of the alleged parallels are both interesting and impressive and will be mentioned in the following commentary. In particular the author's concern to show that the wilderness experience of ancient Israel was a time of unbelief and failure can be seen as especially pointed if directed at sectarians such as those at Qumran, who idealized the wilderness sojourn. Though not everyone is equally impressed by the data purporting to link Hebrews with sectarian thought, as far as it goes it adds support to a Palestinian location for the epistle's readership.

But there are problems with this view as well. For one thing, the reference to the readers receiving their knowledge of the Lord from those who originally heard Him (2:3) sounds a bit more natural for readers on a mission field. In Palestine, and especially Jerusalem, many of the readers might have heard Christ in person. In addition the reference to the readers' generosity to the poor (6:10) does not sound like Jerusalem at any rate, since poverty was prevalent there at a later time (cf. Acts 11:27-29; Gal. 2:10). If the statement of Hebrews 12:4 means that no martyrdoms had occurred in the community the writer is addressing, then a Palestinian or at least a Jerusalem locale is excluded. But the writer may only have meant that the people in his audience had not yet made such a sacrifice.

If Barnabas is the author of the epistle, one locale which might fit all the requirements is the ancient Libyan city of Cyrene in North Africa. Cyrene had been founded as a Greek colony around 630 B.C., but in the Roman period had a sizable and influential Jewish community. The origins of Christianity there seem to have been quite early, for the church at Antioch in Syria was founded by missionaries from Cyprus and Cyrene (Acts 11:20). The connection between Cyprus and Cyrene in that account is of interest because of Barnabas' Cypriot background. Two of the men with whom

Barnabas later ministered in the Antioch church were "Simeon called Niger" and "Lucius of Cyrene" (Acts 13:1). Since Simeon's other name, Niger, means "black," he may have been from North Africa, as was his companion Lucius. Whether this Simeon was also the man called Simon who bore Jesus' cross (Luke 23:26) is unknown, but he too was from Cyrene. This latter Simon had two sons, Alexander and Rufus (Mark 15:21), who may have been known in the Roman church if that is where that Gospel was first published. In any case, contacts between Christians of the Libyan city of Cyrene and those at Rome and in Italy is most probable. This would explain the reference to Italians in Hebrews 13:24.

If the parallels with some kind of Jewish desert sectarianism are given weight, then the fact that Cyrene stood on the fringes of a wilderness where nomadism was a way of life may also be important. The author's references to the Greek word *oikoumenē* (trans. "world" in 1:6 and 2:5) would have special point in Cyrene. The word was commonly used to denote the Roman Empire and the limits of the Roman *oikoumenē* to the south were not far from Cyrene. Since it is unlikely that the impulse to withdraw from urban life and corrupted Jewish society existed only in Palestine, it would not be surprising if desert enclaves of sectarians existed also in the wilderness of Cyrenaica. That an ascetic Jewish sect had taken up residence on the shores of a lake near Alexandria in Egypt is known from Philo.

On the whole, the most plausible backdrop for the Epistle to the Hebrews might be a Christian church, largely Jewish in membership, in a city such as Cyrene. Under repeated pressures from their unbelieving fellow Jews they were tempted to give up their Christian profession and to return to their ancestral faith. If the form of this faith that allured them particularly was a sectarianism similar to that known at Qumran, then many of the author's appeals would have been especially pertinent, as the commentary will seek to show. The temptation to withdraw from civilized life into a kind of wilderness experience is precisely the kind of temptation the Epistle to the Hebrews would counter so well.

The destiny of the Lord Jesus is precisely to rule the *oikoumenē* (2:5) and those who adhere faithfully to Him will share in that rule (cf. 12:28). They must therefore hold fast to their Christian profession.

In the final analysis, however, the exact destination of the epistle is of as little importance as the identity of its author. Regardless of who wrote it, or where it was first sent, the Christian church has rightly regarded it down through the ages as a powerfully relevant message from God, who has definitively spoken in His Son.

OUTLINE

COMMENTARY

I. Prologue (1:1-4)

In a majestically constructed opening paragraph, the writer introduced his readers at once to the surpassing greatness of the Lord Jesus Christ. The Son, he declared, is the par excellence vehicle for divine revelation. In asserting this, he implicitly contrasted Him with the prophets of old and explicitly contrasted Him with the angels.

1:1-2a. The central assertion of the Prologue is made here. Though **God** has variously (*polymerōs kai polytropōs*, lit., "by various means and in various ways") revealed Himself **in the past,** Old Testament prophetic revelation has now received its end-times climax through God's **Son.** However highly the readership regarded that former revelation, the writer implied they must now listen most closely to the Son.

1:2b-4. In a series of subordinate constructions which are part of a single sentence in the Greek, the author set forth the Son's greatness. The unified structure of the writer's sentence is hidden by the NIV which breaks it down into several sentences. To begin with (v. 2b), the Son is the designated **Heir of all things.** This is obviously as it should be since He is also their Maker—the One **through whom He made the universe** (*tous aiōnas*, lit., "the ages," also rendered "the universe" in 11:3). The reference to the Son's heirship anticipates the thought of His future reign, of which the writer will say much.

But the One who is both Creator and Heir is also a perfect reflection of the God who has spoken in Him. Moreover **His Word** is so **powerful** that all He has made is sustained by that Word. And it is this Person who has **provided purification for sins** and taken His seat **at the right hand of the Majesty in heaven** (cf. 8:1; 10:12; 12:2). In doing so it is obvious He has attained an eminence far beyond anything **the angels** can claim.

As might easily be expected in the Prologue, the writer struck notes which will be crucial to the unfolding of his argument in the body of the epistle. He implied that God's revelation in the Son has a definitive quality which previous revelation lacked. Moreover the sacrifice for sins which such a One makes must necessarily be greater than other kinds of sacrifices. Finally the Son's greatness makes preoccupation with angelic dignities entirely unnecessary. Though the Prologue contains no warning—the writer reserved those for later—it carries with it an implicit admonition: This is God's supremely great Son; hear Him! (cf. 12:25-27)

II. Part I: God's King-Son (1:5–4:16)

The first major unit of the body of the epistle begins at this point and extends through the dramatic appeal of 4:14-16 for the readers to avail themselves of the resources available to them at "the throne of grace" (4:16). The emphasis of the whole unit is on the sonship of Jesus Christ which the writer viewed as a kingly sonship in accord with the Davidic Covenant.

A. The King-Son exalted (1:5-14)

Drawing heavily on the witness of Old Testament revelation, the writer demonstrated the uniqueness of the Son. The title of Son, and the prerogatives it entails, elevate Him above all comparison with the angels. Those who see in Hebrews ties with sectarian Judaism point to the highly developed angelology of the Dead Sea sect. These verses offer an effective rebuttal against any tendency to give excessive prominence to angels.

1:5. The two questions in this verse show that the name **Son** belongs to Messiah in a sense in which it never belonged to **the angels.** Obviously "Son" is the superior name which Jesus "has inherited" (v. 4). But it is clear that the special sense of this name, in its kingly ramifications, is what basically concerns the writer.

The quotation in verse 5a is drawn from Psalm 2:7, while the quotation in Hebrews 1:5b comes from either 2 Samuel 7:14 or 1 Chronicles 17:13. Psalm 2 is an enthronement psalm in which God "adopts" the Davidic King as His "Son." That this is what the writer to the Hebrews understood is confirmed in Hebrews 1:5a by the quotation from the Davidic Covenant. No doubt the "today" in the expression **today I have become Your Father** was understood by the author of Hebrews to refer to Messiah's sitting at the right hand of God (cf. v. 3).

Of course the Lord Jesus Christ has always been the eternal Son of God. In a collective sense, the angels are called "sons of God" in the Old Testament (Job 38:7, marg.), but the writer was thinking of the title **Son** in the sense of the Davidic Heir who is entitled to ask God for dominion over the whole earth (cf. Ps. 2:8). In this sense the title belongs uniquely to Jesus and not to the angels.

1:6. The prerogatives of the One who bears this superlative title are set forth beginning with this verse. Instead of the NIV's **And again, when God brings**

His Firstborn into the world, it would be preferable to translate, "and when He again brings the Firstborn into the world." The reference is to the Second Advent when the kingly prerogatives of the Son will be recognized with open angelic worship (cf. Ps. 97:7 where the LXX rendering "angels" correctly renders the text).

1:7-9. In a pair of contrasting quotations, the author juxtaposed the servanthood of the angels (v. 7) and the eternal dominion of the Son (vv. 8-9). It is possible that, in line with one strand of Jewish thought about angels (cf. 2 Esdras 8:21-22), the writer understood the statement of Psalm 104:4 (quoted in Heb. 1:7) as suggesting that angels often blended their mutable natures with winds or fire as they performed the tasks God gave them. But in contrast with this mutability, the Son's throne is eternal and immutable (v. 8).

The quotation found in verses 8-9 is derived from Psalm 45:6-7 which describes the final triumph of God's messianic King. The writer extended this citation further than the previous ones, no doubt because the statements of the psalmist served well to highlight truths on which the author of Hebrews desired to elaborate. The King the psalmist described had loved righteousness and hated wickedness. This points to the holiness and obedience of Christ while He was on earth, to which reference will be repeatedly made later (cf. Heb. 3:1-2; 5:7-8; 7:26; 9:14). And though this King thus deservedly enjoys a superlative joy, still He has companions in that joy. The reference to "companions" is likewise a significant theme for the writer. The same word metochoi ("companions or sharers") is employed in 3:1, 14 of Christians (it is also used in 12:8). Since the King has attained His joy and dominion through a life of steadfast righteousness, it might be concluded that His companions will share His experience by that same means. This inference will later become quite clear (cf. 12:28).

1:10-12. The immutability of the King-Son is further stressed by the statements now quoted from Psalm 102:25-27. A simple "and" (kai, disguised a bit by NIV's He also says) links the quotation in these verses with that in Hebrews 1:8-9. That the author construed the words of Psalm 102 as likewise addressed to the Son cannot be reasonably doubted. The Son, then, is Lord and has created both earth and the heavens (cf. Heb. 1:2). But even when the present creation wears out like an old garment and is exchanged for a new one, the Son will remain unchanged. The reference here of course is to the transformation of the heavens and earth which will occur after the Millennium and will introduce the eternal state (2 Peter 3:10-13). Yet even after those cataclysmic events the Son's years will never end. This certainly points to His personal eternality, but it is also likely that the word "years" stands for all that they contain for the Son, including an eternal throne and scepter as well as unending joy with His companions. The writer definitely taught that Messiah's kingdom would survive the final "shaking" of the creation (cf. Heb. 12:26-28).

1:13-14. The writer drew this section to a climax with a final Old Testament quotation, one which is crucial to the entire thought of the epistle. It is taken from Psalm 110 which the author later employed in his elaboration of the Melchizedek priesthood of the Lord Jesus. Here he cited verse 1 of the psalm to highlight the final victory of the Son over His enemies. If the Son is to have an eternal throne (Heb. 1:8), such a victory obviously awaits Him. But the victory is His and not the angels'. Their role, by contrast, is to serve those who will inherit salvation.

It should not be automatically assumed that "salvation" here refers to a believer's past experience of regeneration. On the contrary it is something future as both the context and the words "will inherit" suggest. As always, the writer of Hebrews must be understood to reflect the ethos of Old Testament thought, especially so here where a chain of references to it form the core of his argument. And it is particularly in the Psalms, from which he chiefly quoted in this chapter, that the term "salvation" has a well-defined sense. In the Psalms this term occurs repeatedly to describe the deliverance of God's people from the oppression of their enemies and their consequent enjoyment of God's blessings. In the Septuagint, the Greek Bible so familiar to the writer, the word "salvation" (*sōtēria*) was used in this sense in Psalms 3:2, 8; 18:2, 35, 46, 50; 35:3; 37:39; 71:15; 118:14-15, 21; 132:16; and elsewhere. This meaning is uniquely suitable here where the Son's own triumph over enemies has just been mentioned.

That the readers were under external pressure there is little reason to doubt. They had endured persecution in the past and were exhorted not to give up now (Heb. 10:32-36). Here the writer reminded them that the final victory over all enemies belongs to God's King and that the angels presently serve those who are destined to share in that victory, that is, to "inherit salvation."

B. The first warning (2:1-4)

The writer now paused in his exposition to address the readers with the first in a series of five urgent warnings. (The others are in chaps. 3–4; 5:11–6:20; 10:19-39; 12.) This one is the briefest and most restrained of all of them, but is nonetheless solemn.

2:1. The truth he had just enunciated has important implications. The **therefore** shows that this admonition arose directly from the preceding material. Since the Son is so supremely great and is destined for final triumph over His enemies, the readers would do well to **pay more careful attention** to these realities. The danger is that, if they would not, they might **drift away** (*pararyōmen*, a word that occurs only here in the NT). The writer's audience was marked by immaturity and spiritual sluggishness (cf. 5:11-12), and if this trait were not eliminated there was danger of their slipping away from what they had learned. The author may have had the Septuagint rendering of Proverbs 3:21 in mind, where the Greek translators used the word for "drift away" that is found here: "My son, do not slip away, but keep my counsel and intent."

2:2-4. Inasmuch as under the Old Covenant, which was instituted through angelic ministration (Gal. 3:19), there were severe penalties for infractions of its demands, the readers could not suppose there would be no penalties for infractions against the New Covenant. On the contrary, with tantalizing vagueness, the author asked, **How shall we escape** (cf. Heb. 12:25) **if we ignore such a great salvation?** If the readers lost sight of the ultimate victory and deliverance that was promised to them in connection with the Son's own final victory, they could expect retribution. What its nature might be the writer did not spell out, but it would be unwarranted to think he was talking about hell. The "we" which pervades the passage shows that the author included himself among those who needed to pay close attention to these truths.

The "salvation," of course, is the same as that just mentioned in 1:14 (see comments there) and alludes to the readers' potential share in the Son's triumphant dominion, in which He has "companions" (cf. 1:9). The Lord Jesus Himself, while on earth, spoke much of His future kingdom and the participation of His faithful followers in that reign (cf., e.g., Luke 12:31-32; 22:29-30). But **this salvation** experience, **which was first announced by the Lord** had also received confirmation through the various miracles and manifestations of the Spirit which His original auditors, **those who heard Him,** were empowered to exhibit. In speaking like this, the writer of Hebrews regarded these **miracles** as the powers of the coming Age (cf. Heb. 6:5) and, in harmony with the early Christians in the Book of Acts, saw them as expressions of the sovereignty of the One who had gone to sit at God's right hand (cf. "signs," "wonders," and/or "miracles" in Acts 2:43; 4:30; 5:12; 6:8; 8:6, 13; 14:3; 15:12; also cf. 2 Cor. 12:12). That the author was indeed thinking throughout of "the world to come" is made clear in Hebrews 2:5.

C. The King-Son as the perfected Captain (2:5-18)

The author here returned to his main train of thought, the destiny of Jesus in the world to come. But now Jesus' intimate involvement through His Incarnation with those who will share that destiny was brought to the fore.

1. THE DESTINY OF THE CAPTAIN (2:5-9)

2:5. It has been claimed that the Dead Sea Scrolls show that the sectarians of Qumran believed that the coming Age would be marked by the dominion of Michael and his angelic subordinates. The statement here by the writer of Hebrews forcefully refutes this view. **Not . . . angels,** but people, will be awarded this dominion in **the world to come.** That the author was not just now introducing this subject is made plain by the expression **about which we are speaking.** It is obvious that the first chapter, with its manifest stress on the kingship and future reign of the Son, was about this very subject.

2:6-8a. A portion of Psalm 8 was now quoted. While the psalm as a whole is often read as a general statement about the role of man in God's Creation, it is clear in the light of Hebrews 2:5 and the application that follows in verses 8b-9 that the author of Hebrews read it primarily as messianic and eschatological. In doing so he stood well within the New Testament perspective on the Old Testament, a perspective directly traceable to Jesus Himself (cf. Luke 24:25-27, 44-45).

2:8b-9. Whatever might have been the general appropriateness of Psalm 8 to man's current standing in the world, in the view of the writer those words do not now describe the actual state of affairs. Instead, he affirmed, **at present we do not see everything subject to Him.** He was thinking here primarily of Jesus (Heb. 2:9). No doubt the familiar messianic designation "Son of Man" (v. 6) contributed to this understanding. Thus, he asserted, while total dominion over the created order is not yet His, Jesus is at last seen as **crowned with glory and honor because He suffered death.** The One so crowned **was made a little lower than the angels** for the very purpose of dying, that is, **that by the grace of God He might taste death for everyone.** This last statement is best understood as the purpose of the Lord's being made lower than the angels in His Incarnation. The words beginning with "now crowned" and ending with "suffered death" are a parenthesis more easily read as such in the Greek text. The focus of the statement, despite its reference to Jesus' present glory, is on the fact that He became a man in order to die.

2. THE CAPTAIN'S LINK WITH HIS
   FOLLOWERS (2:10-18)

In this section the writer of Hebrews used, for the first time, the Greek word *archēgos* of Jesus (his other use of the word is in 12:2). The word suggests such concepts as "Leader," "Originator," and "Founder" and is almost equivalent in some respects to the English word "Pioneer." The familiar rendering "Captain" (KJV) seems a bit superior to "Author" (2:10). The Lord Jesus, the writer will try to show, is the Captain of that loyal band of people whom God is preparing for glory.

2:10. The author here continued to think of Psalm 8, as his reference to **everything** reveals (cf. Heb. 2:8). Thus the **glory** he mentioned here is also the glory referred to in the psalm, that is, the glory of dominion over the created order (cf. Heb. 2:7-8). Even the expression **many sons** is inspired by the psalmist's mention of "the Son of Man" and suggests that for the writer of Hebrews the messianic title Son of Man probably had a corporate aspect. Jesus is *the* Son of Man, and His brothers and sisters are the many people who are linked with Him in both **suffering** and future glory. They will be the King's "companions" who share His joy in the world to come (cf. 1:9).

In 2:9 the writer had mentioned Jesus' death for the first time. Now he affirmed that such suffering was appropriate for the One who was to serve as the Captain of the many sons. Before He could fittingly lead them to the salvation experience God had in mind for them (i.e., "to glory"), He must be made **perfect** for this role "through suffering." Since His brethren must suffer, so must He if He is to be the kind of Captain they need. By having done so, He can give them the help they require (cf. v. 18).

2:11-13. Accordingly there is a deep unity between the Son and the many sons. By His death He **makes** them **holy,** and those who are thus **made holy are of the same family.** That the writer thought of the sacrifice of Christ as making the many sons holy in a definitive and final way is clear from 10:10, 14 (see comments there). Thus as Psalm 22:22 (quoted in Heb. 2:12) predicts, Jesus can **call them brothers.** He can also speak to them of His own **trust in** God (v. 13a, quoting Isa. 8:17) and can regard them as **the children God has given Me** (Heb. 2:13b, quoting Isa. 8:18). Like an elder brother in the midst of a circle of younger children, the Captain of their salvation can teach them the lessons of faith along the pathway of suffering.

2:14-15. These children, however, were once held in servitude by their enemy, Satan. Since they were human, their Captain had to become human and die for them, in order to rescue them. But by doing so He was able to **destroy . . . the devil.** The author did not mean that Satan ceased to exist or to be active. Rather the word he used for "destroy" (*katargēsē*) indicates the annulment of his power over those whom Christ redeems. In speaking of the devil as wielding **the power of death,** the writer meant that Satan uses people's **fear of death** to enslave them to his will. Often people make wrong moral choices out of their intense desire for self-preservation. The readers were reminded that they were no longer subject to such **slavery** and that they could face death with the same confidence in God their Captain had.

2:16-18. Whatever their needs or trials, their Captain is adequate to help them since He ministers to **Abraham's descendants,** not angels. The expression "Abraham's descendants" (lit., "Abraham's seed") may point to the Jewishness of the writer's audience, but even Gentile Christians could claim to be the "seed of Abraham" in a spiritual sense (Gal. 3:29). The help which the Captain gives to these His followers is again predicated on the fact that **He** was **made like His brothers in every way** (Heb. 2:17), that is, both in terms of becoming incarnate and by virtue of suffering. Here for the first time the writer introduced the thought of His priesthood, which he elaborated on later. For now he was content to affirm that this identification with "His brothers" had made possible a priesthood characterized both by mercy and fidelity **in service to God.** This involved, as its basis, **atonement for the sins of the people.** Of this too the author said more later, but he chose to conclude the section on the profoundly hopeful thought that the Captain, in His role as Priest, is able to aid his readers **who are being tempted** (v. 18) out of the experience of temptation which His own sufferings entailed. Though the discussion of these themes is far from over, the author has already suggested that the Captain has indeed been made perfect for His role in leading them into participation in His future glory.

D. The second warning (chaps. 3–4)

The writer paused again in the course of his exposition to introduce the second warning section. This one is far more extensive and detailed than the brief one in 2:1-4. The real nature of his anxiety for his readers becomes clearer here, as well as the incalculable loss which they faced if they did not attend to his exhortation. The basic text for this section is Psalm 95:7-11 which he quoted (Heb. 3:7-11) and expounded in the remainder of chapter 3 and in 4:1-11. The section closes with a reminder of the judgmental power of God's Word (4:12-13) and with a call to seek the help available through the great High Priest (4:14-16).

1. THE CALL FOR FAITHFULNESS (3:1-6)

3:1. The readers were now addressed as **holy brothers, who share in the heavenly calling.** This form of address gathered up the strands of truth which the author dealt with in chapter 2. They were indeed "brothers" (cf. 3:12; 10:19), not only with one another but with their Captain (2:11-12), and they were "holy" because He had made them so (2:11). They did "share in the heavenly calling" because God was "bringing" them "to glory" (2:10). The words "who share" are rendered "companions" in 1:9 (*metochoi*; this Greek word is also used in this epistle in 3:14; 6:4; 12:8). The author was thinking especially of their high privilege of being invited to participate in the future dominion and joy of God's King-Son.

It was as such people that they were to focus their thinking on the One who is both **the Apostle and High Priest** of their Christian profession. The first of these titles probably points to the Lord Jesus as the One sent forth by God as the supreme Revealer of the Father (cf. 1:1-2), while the second picks up the role just mentioned in 2:17-18.

3:2. The NIV disjoins this verse from the previous one by making it a separate sentence. But connecting it as in the original with verse 1, the statement may read: "Contemplate Jesus . . . being faithful to the One who appointed Him." Taken in this way, the readers are urged to fix their gaze on the person of Christ who is even now **faithful** to God. Thus they would find a model for their own fidelity. The faithfulness of Christ, moreover, has an Old Testament prototype in Moses.

The reference to **Moses** being **faithful in all God's house** was drawn from Numbers 12:7 in which the tabernacle furnished the backdrop. Hence God's "house" in the Old Testament situation would be the tabernacle itself which Moses had constructed in strict obedience to the divine directions. It was a prophetic testimony "to what would be said in the future" (Heb. 3:5).

3:3-6a. But **Jesus** as a **Builder** excels **Moses** in **honor** since Moses was simply a servant carrying out instructions. But what Jesus has built is, in fact, **everything**, for **God is the Builder of** "everything." Implicit here is the Son's role in Creation (cf. 1:2, 10) and indeed His identification as God (cf. 1:8). But beyond this is the thought that **God's house** in which **Moses was faithful** was a kind of miniature representation of "everything," that is, of the greater **house** over which the Son presides at God's right hand in heaven (cf. 1:3 with 4:14). The "holy of holies" in **His** earthly **house** was but a shadow of heaven itself where Christ has now gone "to appear for us in God's presence" (9:24). Moses' fidelity consisted in erecting that shadow house, the tabernacle, so that it could properly prefigure the future order of priestly activity which now has the universe itself as its proper sphere. This is the sphere where the exalted **Christ** sits **faithful** in all His current ministrations as well as past ones, functioning **as a Son over God's house** (3:6a).

3:6b. By a natural semantic shift to which the Greek word for **house** naturally lends itself, the writer moved from the thought of the house as the sphere where priestly activities transpired to the thought of the "house" as consisting of the people who engaged in these activities. His readers, he affirmed, comprise **His** (the Son's) "house" contingent, however, on one important consideration: **if** they **hold on to** their **courage** (parrēsian, used four times in Heb., here and in 4:16; 10:19, 35) **and the hope of which** they **boast.** As in the earlier warning passage (2:1-4), the writer used "we" and thus included himself within the scope of his admonition. As he will shortly state

(3:12), he was concerned that there might be in some of his Christian "brothers" an "unbelieving heart that turns away from the living God." Should any of his readers do this, they would forfeit their roles in the Son's priestly house, which is only maintained by holding firmly to their Christian profession (cf. also v. 14 and 10:23-25, 35-36). The author did not mean, of course, that his readers could forfeit their eternal salvation; it is an error to identify the word "house" with the body of Christ, the true universal church. As the context and the Old Testament background show, the author was thinking in priestly terms. He was also thinking functionally. The exalted Son presides over a priestly apparatus which is an operative reality. As long as the readership held firmly to their Christian commitment, they also functioned within this priestly arrangement. But just as one who was a true Levite by birth could withdraw from participation in the tabernacle of Moses' day, so too one who is truly a Christian by new birth may withdraw from his priestly role within the functioning household. It was precisely this danger which concerned the writer, in the present warning passage as well as in later ones.

2. THE ADMONISHMENT FROM ISRAEL'S FAILURE (3:7-4:11)

3:7-11. To drive home his call to fidelity and to warn of the consequences of unbelieving infidelity, the author referred to the classic failure of Israel at Kadesh Barnea which led to their 40-year detour in the wilderness. Far from being an ideal period of Israel's history, as some sectarians seem to have held, it was an era marked by tragic loss and defeat. The readers were not to repeat such an experience in their own lives.

The text chosen by the writer to enforce the lesson he had in mind was taken from Psalm 95. Verses 7-11 of that psalm are quoted here. The choice of this psalm is highly appropriate in a context that is concerned with worship and priestly activity. For Psalm 95 is, in fact, essentially a call to worship (cf. Ps. 95:1-7). The psalmists' invitation, "Come, let us bow down in worship, let us kneel before the Lord our Maker, for He is our God and we are the people of His pasture, the flock under His care" (Ps.

95:6-7), ideally reflects the author's perspective with regard to his readers. The material quoted in Hebrews immediately follows these words and, most naturally, must be understood against this background.

3:12-13. **See to it, brothers** introduces the author's application of his text to his Christian readership. Neither here nor anywhere else in his letter did the writer betray the slightest suspicion that his audience might contain people who were not real Christians. Instead, they were regarded as "brothers" (as here) or as "holy brothers, who share in the heavenly calling" (v. 1). The widespread view that he was concerned about mere professors of the faith as over against genuine believers is not found in the text.

Each Christian brother, therefore, should be most careful to guard against a **sinful, unbelieving heart** which God's flock in the wilderness displayed, the kind of heart **that turns away from the living God.** One preventative against such a tendency would be a spirit of mutual concern and admonition among the Christian brotherhood. Accordingly they were to **encourage one another daily . . . so that none** would **be hardened by sin's deceitfulness** (v. 13). This exhortation is still completely pertinent to any local congregation at the present time, where the hardening tendencies of sin can often be counteracted by truly concerned fellow Christians. The expression **as long as it is called Today** alludes to the "Today" in Psalm 95:7 and means something like "while you still have opportunity."

3:14. The statement, **we have come to share in Christ** might be more literally rendered, "we are partners with the Christ." The word "the" found in the original probably gives to "Christ" the sense of "the Messiah." In the word "partners" the reader meets again the Greek *metochoi*, used in 1:9 and 3:1 of the "companions" of the messianic King. Once again, the writer reverted to the supreme privilege of being among the "many sons" whom God is bringing to the glory of shared dominion over the created order which Christ is destined to rule. But again too, like the privilege of serving in the priestly house (v. 6), this role is contingent on continuing fidelity: if

we hold firmly to the end the confidence we had at first. In this connection, Revelation 2:26-27 comes readily to mind: "To him who overcomes and does My will to the end, I will give authority over the nations—he will rule them with an iron scepter."

3:15. The renewed quotation of part of the writer's text in Psalm 95 connects with the caution just uttered in Hebrews 3:6. The readers must hold their confidence firmly to the end and not, like the Israelites of old, **harden** their **hearts as . . . in the rebellion.**

3:16-19. Having alluded again to the passage he wished to expound, the author then began doing so. The questions in verse 16 seem more naturally read as statements: "For some, when they had heard, did provoke; howbeit not all that came out of Egypt by Moses." The writer is aware of the notable exceptions of Joshua and Caleb, who did not take part in the general failure. But then he asked, **With whom was** God **angry for 40 years?** The answer is that He was angry **with those** in the wilderness congregation **who sinned** and who died in that wilderness. Their disobedience in refusing to enter the Promised Land caused **God** to **swear that they would never enter His rest.** This meant of course that the sinful generation in **the desert** was permanently excluded from taking possession of their inheritance in Canaan. Naturally it had nothing to do with the question of their going to hell, so it would be wrong to allege that the entire Exodus generation was unregenerate. But exclusion from Canaan was a consequence of their lack of faith in the power of God to bring them into it in victory over their enemies, a failure that in principle might be repeated by the readers of Hebrews if they forgot Messiah's ultimate triumph over His enemies and theirs (cf. 1:13-14). The writer wished his readers to take it to heart that **unbelief,** lack of confidence in God, was the reason God's people did not enter the land.

4:1. It follows from the tragic example of Israel that Christians should also take warning. This is true because **the promise of entering His rest still stands.** The NIV rendering of the last half of the verse is, **let us be careful that none of you be found to have fallen short of it.**

This is possible, but the word "found" cloaks a difficulty in the underlying text, involving a word which usually means "to seem" or "to suppose." Some modern writers (Montefiore, Héring) prefer the meaning, "let us be careful that none of you suppose that he has missed it." Since the following context seems dedicated to demonstrating that God's rest is still open, this understanding is probably preferable.

The writer's concept of "rest" must not be separated from its Old Testament roots. The Septuagint includes notable passages where the word for rest (*katapausis*), in connection with Israel's possession of the land, is clearly paralleled with the word for inheritance (*klēronomia*). Moses showed clearly (Deut. 3:18-20; 12:9-11) that for Israel their rest was their inheritance. In the same way it is natural to suppose that the term "rest" for the writer of Hebrews was a functional equivalent for a Christian's inheritance. That Christians are "heirs" he has already affirmed (Heb. 1:14) and will shortly do so again (6:12, 17; cf. 9:15). How exactly he understood their relationship to this inheritance will unfold as his argument proceeds. But the inheritance itself can hardly be divorced from his presentation of Messiah's kingdom and His "partners'" share in that. If this needed explicit confirmation, it could be found in 12:28.

If, as just suggested, the writer was concerned that none of his readers would think they had missed their "inheritance-rest," it is quite conceivable that he was confronting the problem of the delay in the Second Advent, which Paul himself had also already encountered at Thessalonica. The writer of Hebrews' later call to patience that the readers may "receive what He has promised" is followed by the assurance that "in just a very little while, 'He who is coming will come and will not delay'" (10:36-37). If this was God's concern, it was urgent to show that this promised "rest" is still available.

4:2. Here the writer said that **the gospel** was **preached to us** (lit., "we were evangelized" or "we were given good news"). But this good news does not always refer to the plan of salvation from sin. In some circles the word "gospel" has acquired a sense too technical and narrow to do justice to the writer's ideas here. What was preached to the Israelites of old was, quite clearly, God's offer of rest. This, of course, was "good news" for them just as it is for people now, but it is not exactly what is meant today by "gospel." The Greek verb used, *euangelizomai*, was fully capable of having a nontechnical sense in the New Testament (cf. its use in Luke 1:19; 1 Thes. 3:6), but naturally the writer here did not sharply distinguish the "good news" about rest, which his readers had heard, from the "good news" to which the term "gospel" is more usually applied (cf. 1 Cor. 15:1-4). But as the whole context shows, his concern was with the good news about a future rest for God's people (cf. Heb. 4:10), not with the fundamental facts Paul spoke of in 1 Corinthians 15.

As was already pointed out in reference to the Israelites, **the message they heard** (about rest) **was of no value to them, because** of their lack of **faith** (cf. Heb. 3:19). That is to say, through unbelief they failed to take advantage of God's offer of rest. So it follows that for the readers to profit from this invitation to rest, they had to exercise faith.

4:3. This is precisely what he then affirmed. The words *hoi pisteusantes* should be rendered "we who believe" rather than **we who have believed.** The writer's concern was not about their original faith in the past, but their perseverance in it (cf. 3:6, 14). Faith remains the prerequisite for entrance into rest, since it was to those who failed to exercise faith that God **declared** by **oath** they would not **enter** into His **rest.** This exclusion was definitive despite the fact that this rest had been established as far back as **Creation** itself.

4:4-5. With considerable enrichment of thought, the author then linked God's Sabbath-rest at the time of Creation with the rest that the Israelites missed in the desert. **God rested** when He finished His creative activity and this kind of experience has, ever since, lain open to people who also finish the **work** that is set before them (cf. v. 10). When, as with the nation in the wilderness, a task is left unfinished, of such it must be said, **They shall never enter My rest.**

4:6-7. But the failure of the Israelites did not nullify the truth **that some will**

enter that rest, and accordingly God renewed the offer (in Ps. 95) as late as the time of David. At that time **God again set a certain day, calling it Today,** thus presenting this opportunity to all readers of the psalm for whom the "Today" becomes their own "Today." Already the writer had applied that "Today" to his readers (cf. Heb. 3:14-15).

4:8-10. But the readers were not to suppose that the promise of rest was realized in Joshua's day. Here the author showed himself perfectly aware that the Old Testament might have been quoted to show that the **rest** had already been entered via the conquest of the land in Joshua's time (cf. Josh. 22:4; 23:1). Probably it had been so quoted to his audience. But the writer's rebuttal was simple and sufficient: if this had been so, **God would not have spoken later about another day.** The psalm which forms his text disproves the notion that the rest had already been entered and was no longer open.

Behind this argument lies the undeniable fact that the conquest in Joshua's day did not lead to a permanent possession of the land. Such permanent possession of their promised inheritance had become for Judaism an expectation which would only be realized in Messiah's kingdom. This at least was true in normative Judaism, whatever might have been true in some sectarian thought. It may be suspected that here the author confronted some form of "realized eschatology" which denied the futurity of such a hope. (Cf. the similar view of believers' resurrection which Paul resisted, 2 Tim. 2:17-18.) If so, the Hebrews author regarded Psalm 95 as silencing such a distorted perspective. The rest— the messianic partnership—did indeed lie ahead: **There remains, then, a Sabbath-rest for the people of God.**

But it must now be said clearly that entering into **God's rest** means resting from one's **own work just as God did from His.** The statement is both a reassurance and an admonition. On the one hand it follows up the writer's conclusion (Heb. 4:9) that there is such a rest to be entered. But on the other, it reminds the readers that this is only done by their getting to the end of their task just as did God in His creative activity. In the phrase "rests from His own work," the author employed a kind of word play since the verb for "rest" also signifies "cease" which, against the backdrop of God's own work, clearly suggests successful completion. This thrust is what the writer has had in mind from the beginning of the section. The readers need to model their lives after Jesus Christ who "was faithful to the One who appointed Him" (3:2) and must be careful to "hold firmly till the end the confidence we had at first" (3:14; cf. 3:6). Only thus would they be able to rest from their works *in the joyful possession of their inheritance in the messianic kingdom.*

4:11. It follows logically from this that the readers should, along with the author (note, **Let us**), **make every effort to enter that rest.** Unlike the assurance which all Christians have that they possess eternal life and will be raised up to enjoy it in the presence of God (cf. John 6:39-40), the share of the companions of Messiah in His dominion over creation is attained by doing His will to the end (Rev. 2:26-27). The readers must therefore be warned by Israel's failure in the desert and take care that they not follow Israel's **example of disobedience.**

3. GOD'S WORD AND THE THRONE OF GRACE (4:12-16)

Having completed his exposition of Psalm 95 and Israel's failure to enter rest, the writer brought this section of warning to a conclusion that is both sobering and comforting. God's Word is a solemn instrument of divine judgment, but His throne is both gracious and merciful.

4:12. The lesson he had just taught from the Old Testament Scriptures was not a mere historical tale. Instead, as had already been made clear by much he had said, it was powerfully relevant to his audience. **For the Word of God is living** (*zōn*) **and active** (*energēs*). Not only that, its penetrating power is greater **than any double-edged sword** and reaches the innermost being of a person so that **it judges the thoughts and attitudes of the heart.** In doing this, it is able to discriminate successfully between what is spiritual in man and what is merely "soulish" or natural (**it penetrates even to dividing soul and spirit**), and does so even when these often-contradictory inner elements are interwoven as closely as **joints and**

marrow. The inner life of a Christian is often a strange mixture of motivations both genuinely spiritual and completely human. It takes a supernaturally discerning agent such as the Word of God to sort these out and to expose what is of the flesh. The readers might think that they were contemplating certain steps out of purely spiritual motivations when, as God's Word could show them, they were acting unfaithfully as did Israel of old.

4:13. Let them not suppose, therefore, that their motives would go undetected for **nothing is hidden from God's sight.** Instead, **everything is uncovered and laid bare before . . . Him.** In saying this, the readers were reminded that, like all Christians, they would someday stand before the judgment seat of Christ where they **must give account** to God for their lives (cf. Rom. 14:10-12; 2 Cor. 5:10). If at that time their lives are seen to be marked by the kind of failure they have been warned against, the writer implied they will suffer loss of reward (cf. 1 Cor. 3:11-15). In this context the loss they suffer will be that of their inheritance-rest.

4:14. But this need not be so. On the contrary there is every reason to **hold firmly to the faith we profess** in view of the fact that the believers' **great High Priest . . . has gone through the heavens.** Only once previously (2:1–3:6) had the writer referred explicitly to the priesthood of Jesus, though it was implicit in 1:3, but now he was preparing to undertake an extensive consideration of that truth. But before doing so, he wished to suggest its practical relevance to his readers whom he exhorted to "hold firmly to the faith." They had to know that the priesthood of their Lord offered them all the resources they needed.

4:15. The One who served as **High Priest** on their behalf had been where they were and had **been tempted in every way, just as** they were. Though unlike them He **was without sin** (cf. 7:26; 2 Cor. 5:21; 1 John 3:5), never responding wrongly to any of His temptations (nor could He, being God), yet as a man He could feel their reality (much as an immovable boulder can bear the brunt of a raging sea) and thus He is able to **sympathize** (*sympathēsai*, lit., "to feel or suffer with")* with their and **our weak-**

nesses. It may indeed be argued, and has been, that only One who fully resists temptation can know the extent of its force. Thus the sinless One has a greater capacity for compassion than any sinner could have for a fellow sinner.

4:16. With such a High Priest, it follows that believers should **approach the throne of grace with confidence** (*parrēsias*; cf. 3:6; 10:19, 35). In a book filled with lovely and captivating turns of expression, few excel the memorable phrase "throne of grace." Such a conception of the presence of God into which beleaguered Christians may come at any time, suggests both the sovereignty of the One they approach (since they come to a "throne") and His benevolence. At a point of contact with God like this Christians can fully expect to **receive mercy and find grace to help . . . in . . . time of need.**

III. Part II: God's Priest-Son (chaps. 5–10)

In the first major movement of the epistle (1:5–4:16), the author set forth two major truths: (1) the exalted position and destiny of Him who is uniquely God's King-Son and (2) the salvation-inheritance of those who cleave to Him by faith. Included in the consideration of these themes have been solemn warnings not to neglect or forfeit the inheritance that His exalted station makes so attainable. The Son's future kingship has been at the center of all this discussion.

At the same time, it has been made clear that the King-Son is also a High Priest. The importance of this reality has already been briefly pointed out. Now, however, the Son's priestly role would be considered in detail. In doing so the writer as usual interspersed sections of exposition with passages of exhortation and warning.

A. Introduction: the qualified Priest (5:1-10)

Before enlarging on the ramifications of the priesthood of Christ, the writer took the logical step of showing Christ's qualifications for that role. Though His priesthood has already been assumed, its validity must now be asserted if the admonitions based on it are to carry full weight.

1. THE GENERAL REQUIREMENTS FOR A
HIGH PRIEST (5:1-4)

5:1. If it be asked what a **high priest** really is, the answer is easily drawn from the Old Testament institution with which the readers were familiar. Such a person is one of mankind's own number: he **is selected from among men** and he is also their representative **in matters related to God.** These "matters" include the offering of both **gifts** (*dōra*) **and sacrifices** (*thysias*) **for sins** (cf. 8:3; 9:9).

5:2-3. The high priest must also be a man of compassion as the word *metriopathein,* which underlies the phrase **deal gently,** implies. This is the capacity to moderate one's feelings to avoid the extremes of cold indifference and uncontrolled sadness. For an ordinary high priest of the Old Testament, this sympathy grew out of an awareness that **he** himself was **subject to weakness,** prone to failures of his own. Hence in his sacrificial activities he must make the necessary offerings **for his own** and the peoples' **sins.** In this respect alone, as the author will show later (cf. 7:27), Christ did not exactly correspond to the characteristics described here, since He "was without sin" (4:15). But it is also possible that the writer thought of the compassion of the Son-Priest as being far richer than the moderate gentleness he ascribed to other high priests.

5:4. But one thing is certain. The high-priestly office was a divine appointment and could not simply be entered because one aspired to that **honor. Just as Aaron was,** this High Priest must also be **called by God.**

2. THE SON'S CALL TO PRIESTHOOD (5:5-10)

5:5-6. No one is to suppose, the author insisted, that Christ began His priestly functions without the appropriate call from **God.** On the contrary, the same One who declared **Christ** to be the King-Son, declared Him also to be **a Priest forever, in the order of Melchizedek.** In uniting as the author did here the text of Psalm 2:7, which he had quoted before (Heb. 1:5), and the text of Psalm 110:4, he skillfully joined the two great truths about the Messiah which lie at the heart of this epistle. The declaration of Psalm 2 had proclaimed Him the Davidic Heir whose destiny was to rule the nations (cf. Ps. 2:8). But Psalm 110 had also been earlier quoted to much the same effect (cf. Heb. 1:13). Now, however, a further statement of this latter psalm was cited to show that the future Conqueror is also a Priest of a special order. In this way the author united in the person of Christ the dual offices of Priest and King. In doing so the author was perhaps conscious of countering a sectarian position like that evidently current at Qumran, where both a lay, or kingly, Messiah and a priestly Messiah seem to have been anticipated. In any case the two quotations given here from Psalms 2:7 and 110:4 furnish the concentrated essence of the author's thought about the Lord Jesus Christ. It is likely enough that the writer assigned the proclamations of both psalms to the moment when the Son "sat down at the right hand of the Majesty in heaven" (Heb. 1:3).

5:7. But also in other respects Jesus is qualified for His priesthood. If it is a question of offerings (cf. v. 1), it can be pointed out that when Jesus was on earth **He offered up prayers and petitions.** In the expression "offered up" the writer employed the same verb (*prospherō*) he had used in verse 1. The added description, **with loud cries and tears to the One who could save Him from death,** has often been thought to refer to the experience of Gethsemane. But the Greek here seems to reflect the Septuagint rendering of Psalm 22:24. Since that psalm is messianic for this author (cf. Heb. 2:12), it is probable that he actually has the sufferings of the Cross in mind, as does the psalm. This would be appropriate since the cries of the Savior would then be linked directly with His sacrificial work.

That these "cries and tears" were accepted by God is evidenced by the observation, **He was heard because of His reverent submission** (*eulabeias*). To this also Psalm 22 bears reference in that its latter half are the words of One who has emerged from suffering in triumph and praises God for that (cf. Ps. 22:22-31). In fact the psalm's first note of triumph has already been quoted (i.e., Ps. 22:22 in Heb. 2:12). Thus the "reverent" Sufferer was indeed saved from death, and this by means of rising from the dead. Hence too the Resurrection furnishes the decisive proof of God's acceptance of **Jesus'** sacrificial activity.

5:8-10. The whole experience just referred to was a form of education for Jesus before He served His suffering people. His unique relation to God notwithstanding (**He was a Son**), He had to experience the true meaning of obedience in terms of the suffering it entailed. Having done so, He was thereby **made perfect** for the role He would play as His people's Captain and High Priest. That there is an element of mystery in all this need not be denied, but it is no greater than that found in Luke's words: "Jesus grew in wisdom and stature, and in favor with God and men" (Luke 2:52). In a real sense not fully comprehensible, the Incarnation gave the already infinitely wise and perfect Son of God the experiential acquisition of knowledge about the human condition. Suffering thus became a reality that He tasted and from it He can sympathize deeply with His followers. (The Gr. has an interesting play on words in the verbs **He learned** [*emathen*] and **He suffered** [*epathen*].)

This is what the writer had in mind when he affirmed that **He became the Source** (*aitios*) **of eternal salvation for all who obey Him.** The salvation here referred to cannot be distinguished from that which is termed an inheritance (Heb. 1:14). It is also to be identified with the "eternal inheritance" mentioned in 9:15. It should not be confused with the acquisition of eternal life which is conditioned not on obedience but on faith (cf. John 3:16, etc.). Once again the writer had in mind final deliverance from and victory over all enemies and the consequent enjoyment of the "glory" of the many sons and daughters. This kind of salvation is explicitly contingent on obedience and indeed on an obedience modeled after that of Jesus who also **suffered.** It is thus closely related to the saying of the Lord in which He declared, "If anyone would come after Me, he must deny himself and take up his cross and follow Me. For whoever wants to save his life will lose it, but whoever loses his life for Me and for the gospel will save it" (Mark 8:34-35).

The High Priest has become the "Source" of this kind of salvation experience for those who are willing to live obediently. In describing Him this way, the author was chiefly thinking of all the resources that flow from Christ's priestly activities that make a Christian's life of obedience possible. Whatever one's suffering, the High Priest understands it, sympathizes, and makes available the "mercy" and "grace" which are needed to endure it successfully. As the writer will later say, "He is able to save completely those who come to God through Him, because He always lives to intercede for them" (Heb. 7:25). With precisely this end in view Christ **was designated by God to be High Priest in the order of Melchizedek.**

B. The third warning (5:11–6:20)

The author had barely begun his consideration of the topic of the Melchizedek priesthood of Christ. But he felt constrained to pause for another warning section before proceeding further. This was due to the immaturity and sluggishness of his audience which made him wonder how much exposition they could digest. No doubt he hoped to arouse them to greater attentiveness to the truth he wished to unfold. But at the same time he wanted them to face squarely the danger of remaining where they were, since this could lead to tragic retrogression.

1. THE PROBLEM OF IMMATURITY (5:11-14)

5:11-12. We have much to say about this, he began, referring to the subject of Jesus' Melchizedek priesthood. As it turned out, his subsequent discussion was indeed lengthy (7:1–10:18) as well as deep. Accordingly he anticipated that it would be **hard to explain because** his readers were **slow to learn.** They had been Christians a long time, he reminded them, so that **by this time** they **ought to be teachers.** Others who had been in the faith less time than they should be profiting from their instruction. Instead they needed someone to instruct them again in the basics.

In alluding to **the elementary truths** the writer employed an expression which could refer to the letters of the alphabet as they might be learned by a school child. "You seem to need your ABCs reviewed," his rebuke suggested, but at the same time he had no intention of going over them (6:1). What he apparently had mainly in view was their wavering state of mind in regard to the error that sought to lure them away from the faith. If they were being urged, whether by sectarians or others, to abandon their Christian profession, then clearly this called into question the fundamental truths they should have been firm in. The result was, to all appearances, **you need milk, not solid food!** But what he would shortly offer them would be solid food indeed, by which he evidently hoped to pull them dramatically forward in their Christian experience.

5:13-14. It is unsatisfactory to remain a baby in spiritual matters. This is true because a spiritual **infant, living on milk . . . is not acquainted with the teaching about righteousness.** The words "not acquainted" (*apeiros*) might be better rendered "inexperienced." It is not so much that a spiritual "infant" lacks information—though at first he obviously does—but rather that he has not yet learned to put "the teaching about righteousness" to effective use. He lacks the skill which goes with maturity and which results in the ability to make appropriate moral choices. Such ability is exactly what is possessed by those **who . . . have trained themselves to distinguish good from evil.** That kind of person can handle **solid food.**

Once more the writer betrayed his concern about his readers' ability to reject the false ideas which confronted them. Had they been sufficiently mature they would be able to "distinguish" those ideas as "evil" over against the truths they should have known were "good." But he feared that this capability was not yet really theirs, though he would make every effort to instill it in them.

2. THE SOLUTION TO THE PROBLEM (6:1-3)

6:1-2. Somewhat surprisingly, despite his estimate of their spiritual state, the author declined to go over old ground. Instead he urged them to go beyond **the elementary teachings about Christ and go on to maturity.** To have reviewed the fundamentals would only have left them where they were. The author preferred "radical surgery" and decided to pull them forward as rapidly as he could. Indeed this was the solution to their problem. If they progressed properly, they would avoid the danger of **laying again the foundation of repentance.** If, as verses 4-6 went on to warn, they were to "fall away," then a foundation would have been laid for a new repentance, but such a repentance is "impossible" (cf. vv. 4, 6). So advance was their only real remedy.

Acts that lead to death literally means "dead works," which expression occurs again in a context where it seems to refer to the Levitical ritual (9:14). Here it would be appropriate in the same sense since many of the readers had been converted to Christianity from Judaism. The rituals they had left behind were lifeless ones, incapable of imparting the experiences of life they had found in Christ. The author implied that they should not return to these dead works in any form since to do so would be to lay again a basis for repenting from them—though such repentance would not be easily reached, however appropriate it might be.

But the foundation they would lay in the unhappy event that they fell away would involve other fundamental truths. These are enumerated in the words, **and of faith in God, instruction about baptisms, the laying on of hands, the resurrection of the dead, and eternal judgment.** The author clearly implied that all these matters belong to the "elementary truths" (5:12) on which the readers gave every indication of wavering. It is likely that each of them was a point at issue in one way or another in the readers' confrontation with those of other persuasions. The return to ordinances, whether in normative or sectarian Judaism, would only be a return to "dead works." One who took that backward step would need to be taught all over again that acceptance was obtained by "faith in God," not by rituals.

Moreover the significance of the various "baptisms" which Christianity knew (John's baptism, Christian baptism proper, or even Spirit baptism) would have to be relearned as well as the basic facts about "laying on of hands." In alluding to matters like these, the writer may have been consciously countering sectarian teachings which may well have offered initiations of their own involving "baptisms" and "laying on of hands." If the sectarians or others, in addition to offering their own initiatory rites, likewise denied the normal Christian eschatological expectations (cf. comments on 4:1, 8-10), then the fundamental doctrines of "the resurrection of the dead and eternal judgment" would also have been at issue. To abandon their Christian profession and "fall away" (6:6) would be to abandon all these doctrines. Whatever the readers had previously learned, they would be giving up. In this sense the foundation would have been laid for relearning them all over again, though the writer held out little hope in his subsequent statements for such a process to take place.

6:3. What he wanted them to do was to press forward. But he was perfectly aware that this required more than his effort to challenge his readers to make progress. God must help and He alone could help them achieve these goals. The writer had said, "Let us . . . go on to maturity" (v. 1), but in a spirit of dependence on divine aid he then added, **and God permitting, we will do so.**

3. THE ALTERNATIVE TO PROGRESS (6:4-8)

In an extremely solemn pronouncement, the author then set forth the tragic alternative to the progress he desired his readers to make. If they did not advance, they would retreat. Should anyone so retreat, his situation would be grim indeed.

6:4-6. This passage has been interpreted in four ways: (1) that the danger of a Christian losing his salvation is described, a view rejected because of biblical assurances that salvation is a work of God which cannot be reversed; (2) that the warning is against mere profession of faith short of salvation, or tasting but not really partaking of salvation (*The New Scofield Reference Bible,* p. 1315); (3) that hypothetically *if* a Christian could lose his salvation, there is no provision for repentance (*The Ryrie Study Bible,* p. 1843); (4) that a warning is given of the danger of a Christian moving from a position of true faith and life to the extent of becoming disqualified for further service (1 Cor. 9:27) and for inheriting millennial glory. The latter is the interpretation adopted here. The entirety of these verses constitutes a single sentence in Greek as well as in the English of the NIV. The central assertion is: **It is impossible for those who have . . . to be brought back to repentance.** Following the words "those who" is a description of the persons whom the

writer affirmed cannot possibly be brought back to a state of repentance. The description he gave shows that he had Christians in mind.

To begin with, he described them as individuals **who have once been enlightened.** This is a natural way to refer to the conversion experience (cf. 2 Cor. 4:3-6). The writer's only other use of the verb "enlightened," is Hebrews 10:32, where the reference to true Christian experience can hardly be doubted. In also calling them people **who have tasted the heavenly gift,** he again employed familiar concepts related to initial conversion (cf. John 4:10; Rom. 6:23; James 1:17-18). The effort to evade this conclusion by seeing in the word "tasted" something less than full participation fails—in view of the writer's own use of this word (Heb. 2:9)—to describe Jesus' experience of death. One might also compare 1 Peter 2:3, which quotes Psalm 34:8.

The description is continued with the words **who have shared in the Holy Spirit.** The underlying Greek employs again the word *metochoi,* used in Hebrews 1:9 of the "companions" of the messianic King, and in 3:1, 14 of the Christian readers (and is also used in 12:8). The preceding expression evidently led the author to think about those who had received the gift of the Spirit as a result of their conversions. Finally, there are also those **who have tasted the goodness of the Word of God and the powers of the coming Age.** Here the thought naturally applies to converts whose instruction in "the Word of God" had given them a genuine experience of its "goodness" and who likewise had known the reality of miracles. The word rendered "powers" (*dynameis*) in NIV is the usual one in the New Testament for "miracles" and is an apparent allusion back to the experience mentioned in 2:4. In every way the language fits true Christians with remarkable ease. The effort to see here mere professors of the faith as over against true converts is somewhat forced.

There follows, however, the grim expression **if they fall away.** But the translation does not do full justice to the original language, where there is no hint of a conditional element. The Greek word *parapesontas* is in fact a part of the construction to which the preceding descriptive phrases belong. Thus a more accurate translation would be: "It is impossible for those who have once been enlightened, who have tasted . . . who have shared . . . who have tasted . . . and who have fallen away, to be brought back to repentance." Far from treating the question in any hypothetical way, the writer's language sounds as if he knew of such cases.

Naturally the words "fall away" cannot refer to the loss of eternal life which, as the Gospel of John makes perfectly clear, is the inalienable possession of those who trust Christ for it. But the writer evidently has in mind defection from the faith, that is, apostasy, withdrawal from their Christian profession (cf. Heb. 3:6, 14; 10:23-25, 35-39). The assertion that such a failure is not possible for a regenerate person is a theological proposition which is not supported by the New Testament. Paul knew the dangers of false doctrine to a Christian's faith and spoke of a certain Hymenaeus and Philetus who said "that the resurrection has already taken place, and they destroy the faith of some" (2 Tim. 2:17-18). The author of Hebrews was a solid realist who took assaults against the faith of his readers with great seriousness. And he warned that those who succumb, that is, "fall away," after all of the great spiritual privileges they had experienced, could not be brought back to repentance.

The reason is expressed in the words because to their loss they are crucifying the Son of God all over again and subjecting Him to public disgrace. The words "to their loss" might be better rendered "with respect to themselves." Those who renounce their Christian faith are, with respect to their own conduct and attitude, taking a step that amounts to a fresh public rejection of Christ. When they first trusted Him, they thereby acknowledged that His crucifixion had been unjust and the result of man's sinful rejection of the Savior. But by renouncing this opinion, they reaffirmed the view of Jesus' enemies that He deserved to die on a cross. In this sense, "they [were] crucifying the Son of God all over again." Since the original Crucifixion was especially the work of the Jewish nation, if the readers were Jews being lured back into some form of their ancestral religion, the writer's words made a particular point.

Their apostasy would be like stepping back over the line again and once more expressing solidarity with their compatriots who wanted Jesus put on the cross. That this was most serious was precisely the writer's point. Such persons could not be won back to the state of repentance which marked their original conversion to Christianity. In affirming this, the author's words suggested a deep hardening of their hearts against all efforts to win them back, not to Christian conversion, but to Christian commitment.

6:7-8. An illustration from nature now drives home the writer's point. Whenever **rain**-soaked ground is properly productive, it **receives the blessing of God.** Here the writer compared the spiritual privileges he had just enumerated (vv. 4-5) to a heavenly rain descending on the life of a Christian. Their effect should be a **crop useful to those for whom it is farmed**—a reference perhaps to the way other Christians benefit from the lives of fruitful believers (cf. v. 10). Such productivity brings divine blessings on fruitful believers' lives.

But suppose the land that has received this "rain" is unproductive? Though the NIV introduces the word **land** for a second time in verse 8, the original text seems to relate the statement directly to the "land" mentioned in verse 7. A clearer rendering would be: "But when (or, if) it produces thorns and thistles. . . ." The point is that when a plot of ground that has been rained on is productive, God blesses it. But if it only **produces thorns and thistles, it is worthless** (adokimos, "disapproved"; cf. 1 Cor. 9:27) **and is in danger of being cursed. In the end it will be burned.** The metaphor recalls God's original curse on the ground (Gen. 3:17-19) and suggests that an unproductive Christian life ultimately ("in the end") falls under the severe condemnation of God and is subject to His blazing wrath and judgment (cf. Heb. 10:27).

Naturally the reference to "burned" has caused many to think of hell, but there is nothing in the text to suggest this. God's anger against His failing people in the Old Testament is often likened to the burning of fire (cf., e.g., Isa. 9:18-19; 10:17). Even this writer could say, with intense metaphorical effect, "Our God is a consuming fire" (Heb. 12:29). In fact, to think of hell here is to betray inattention to the imagery employed by the author. The burning of a field to destroy the rank growth it had produced was a practice known in ancient times. Its aim was not the destruction of the field itself (which, of course, the fire could not effect), but the destruction of the unwanted produce of the field. Thereafter the field might be serviceable for cultivation.

By choosing this kind of metaphor, the author showed that he did not totally despair of those who took the backward step he was warning against. To be sure, at least prior to severe divine judgment, all efforts to recall such people to Christian faith are futile (6:4-6), but it cannot be said that the impossibility applies in an absolute sense to God Himself. What the author probably meant is that nothing can deter apostates from the fiery retribution toward which they are headed, but once their "land" has been burned it is another matter. Paul believed that those who "have shipwrecked their faith" could profit by the retributive experiences to which they were exposed as a result (1 Tim. 1:19-20). But of course the writer of Hebrews was reticent about the issue of subsequent restoration. That some might not respond to the chastisement was perhaps in mind, but he was mainly concerned about warning against the course of action which leads to such calamitous divine judgment. Nevertheless his deft choice of this agricultural image serves to disclose that the "burning" is both temporary and essentially hopeful.

4. THE CONCLUDING ENCOURAGEMENT
   (6:9-20)

The author knew that his words were both heavy and solemn, though not to the same degree that subsequent exposition has often made them. He felt that a word of encouragement was then in order. This pattern—stern warning followed by warm encouragement—has already appeared in the previous warning section (3:1–4:16) which concluded in a distinctly positive manner (4:14-16). Similarly the writer drew his warning section here to a conclusion that is alive with hope.

6:9. The author did not want his readers to believe that he had despaired of them. Instead he was convinced **of better things in your case.** The words are

like those of a pastor who, after warning his congregation of a dangerous course of action, might say: "But I am sure you people would never do that!" The words are not a theological proposition, as they are sometimes wrongly taken, but an expression of hope. The "better things" about which he had confidence were the **things that accompany salvation.** The "salvation" referred to should be understood in congruity with its meaning in 1:14. It is that experience of victory and glory which the persevering companions of the King inherit. It is also the inheritance-rest which the persevering are allowed to enter. The writer insisted here that he had every expectation that the readers would persevere to the end and acquire these blessings, even though he felt constrained to warn them against a contrary course.

6:10. The author knew that **God is not unjust.** His readers would not be forsaken. God would remember their **work and the love** they had **shown Him** in their helping other believers. The author's words were a skilled touch on the hearts of his fellow Christians. In speaking of them, he reminded his readers of what they had done for their fellow Christians and were still doing. He thus encouraged them to keep it up while assuring them that God was conscious of all their aid and available to help them in any needed way.

6:11-12. If they would only diligently hold onto the good course they already were pursuing—and of which God was fully mindful—they would thus guarantee the **hope** which is duly awarded to those who so persevere. He added, **We do not want you to become lazy.** The word "lazy" (nōthroi) is the same word rendered "slow" in 5:11 in the phrase "slow to learn." The sluggishness which marked their immaturity was to be shrugged off. (The Gr. of this verse can mean, "We do not want you to be lazy" rather than "become lazy.") Their real goal should be the inheritance that is set before them. They were to be imitators of **those who through faith and patience inherit** God's promises.

6:13-15. If the readers were searching for models to "imitate," there was the case of **Abraham** who received an oath from **God,** the **promise** that assured the multiplication of his seed. In due time his patience was rewarded in that he (lit.) "received the promise." Since the reference is to the promise given in Genesis 22:17 after the offering of Isaac, the author may have been thinking of the reception of the promise itself as the reward. In that case the idea is that after Abraham had patiently endured (the test involving Isaac), he obtained the promise. **Waiting patiently** translates the participle *makrothymēsas*, related to the noun "patience," *makrothymias* in Hebrews 6:12. This word, common in the New Testament, refers to the ability to hold one's feelings in restraint without retaliation against others (cf., e.g., Col. 1:11; 3:12; James 5:7-8, 10). A synonym, *hypomonē*, "endurance, perseverance," means the ability to remain steadfast in the face of undesirable circumstances; cf. Col. 1:11; Heb. 12:1-3, 7; James 5:11).

6:16-18. At this point Abraham is left behind as a model and **the oath** made to him is treated as for the benefit of Christians generally. That the promise of Genesis 22:18 had messianic aspects is clear from these words: "Through your offspring all nations on earth will be blessed." Then the author of Hebrews affirmed that the messianic hope which the promise entailed was sure, not only to Abraham, but also to the Christian **heirs of what was promised.** As in human affairs an oath **puts an end to all arguments,** so too there can be no argument about this expectation since God **confirmed it with an oath.** If anyone, such as a sectarian, denied this eschatological anticipation, he was flying in the face of the strongest possible divine guarantee. Not only was it **impossible for God to lie,** but His ever truthful Word was supported in this case by His oath. These are the **two unchangeable things,** which encourage those who **take hold of the hope.**

6:19-20. The image suggested in verse 18 by the words "fled to take hold" of hope was that of a fortified refuge. By a swift change in his figure, the writer then suggested the thought of a harbor where **the soul** may securely drop **anchor.** That anchor has been carried to the safest point of all—**the inner sanctuary behind the curtain**—by **Jesus, who went before us.** The Greek *prodromos* ("who went before us") suggests a "forerunner," and if the harbor imagery is still in mind it

recalls the role of sailors who leave their ship in a smaller craft in order to carry the anchor forward to a place where it can be firmly lodged. So too the Lord Jesus, by His entrance into the heavenly sanctuary where He functions as **a High Priest forever,** has given to a Christian's hope an anchorage from which it cannot be shaken loose. Since, therefore, the readers' hope was sure, they could cling to it tenaciously right to the very end.

C. The greater Priest and His greater ministry (7:1–10:18)

Here begins the longest single expository passage in the epistle. Its very length suggests its importance. Its theme is the core theme of Hebrews. The real resource of the readership, in the midst of their pressures, is the high priesthood of Christ. They must realize the greatness of that priesthood, its superiority to the Levitical institutions, and the perfect access they have to it on the basis of Christ's death.

1. THE SUPERIOR PRIEST (CHAP. 7)

The writer returned to the theme he had introduced in 5:1-10, but which he doubted his readers would comprehend (cf. 5:11). In the conclusion of his most recent warning (5:11–6:20) he had renewed the subject of the Melchizedek priesthood (6:19-20). The exposition of that theme is now given.

a. The greatness of Melchizedek (7:1-10)

7:1-3. To begin with, the writer set forth the personal greatness of the Old Testament figure **Melchizedek.** As a fit prototype for Christ Himself, Melchizedek was both a **king and a priest.** He both **blessed . . . Abraham** and received his tithes. Melchizedek's name and title suggest the messianic attributes of **righteousness** and **peace.** So far as the Old Testament record is concerned, he was **without father or mother, without genealogy, without beginning of days or end of life.** In saying this, the author is often taken to mean that the silence of the inspired record presents Melchizedek as typologically **like the Son of God.** But though this is possibly true, the statements do not sound like it, particularly the assertion that Melchizedek **remains a priest forever.** The word "forever" translates a phrase (*eis to diēnekes*) that occurs only in Hebrews (here and in 10:12, 14) and means "continuously" or "uninterruptedly."

It seems more natural that the author meant that Melchizedek belonged to an order in which there was no end to the priesthood of those engaged in it. (He later said in 7:8 that Melchizedek "is declared to be living.") If this is correct, Melchizedek may have been an angelic being who reigned for a time at Salem (i.e., Jerusalem). If so, the statement that he was "without beginning of days" would not mean that he was eternal, but simply that he had a pretemporal origin. Nor would this concept of Melchizedek as an angel elevate him to the same level as God's Son, since the author painstakingly asserted the Son's superiority to the angels (1:5-14). There is indeed evidence that, at Qumran, Melchizedek was regarded as an angelic personage. If this is the case in Hebrews, then the Son of God is the *High* Priest in an order in which Melchizedek is simply a priest.

7:4-10. The personal superiority of Melchizedek over the patriarch Abraham is guaranteed by the fact that **Abraham gave him a 10th of the plunder.** And though Melchizedek had no connections with the Levitical order, still he both received this tithe from **Abraham and blessed him.** This act of blessing reinforced his superiority to the patriarch. Moreover, he was evidently superior to the Levites as well, who collected tithes but were nonetheless subject to death. By contrast the tithe collected from Abraham was collected **by him who is declared to be living.** Furthermore, in a sense Levi paid the tithe **through Abraham because . . . Levi was still in the body of his ancestor.** The original expression, rendered **one might even say,** probably means something like "so to speak." The writer knew that Levi did not literally pay tithes to Melchizedek, but on the principle that an ancestor is greater than his descendants, Abraham's act affirmed Melchizedek's superiority even to the Levitical priests themselves. Melchizedek thus has a greatness which the Old Testament record clearly attests.

b. The new priesthood supersedes the old (7:11-19)

Having established Melchizedek's greatness both personally and in comparison with Abraham and Levi, the writer was ready for a new point. This superiority was needed, since the Law was superseded. The inadequacy of the legal and Levitical systems had to be replaced by something better.

7:11-12. In the simplest manner, the author argued for the imperfection of **the Levitical priesthood** on the basis of God's promise (recorded in Ps. 110:4) that a new Priest would arise belonging to an order other than Aaron's. Since there was **a change of the priesthood,** it follows that the whole legal system on which the Levitical institutions were predicated also had to be changed. Here the writer virtually affirmed the Pauline truth that "you are not under Law" (Rom. 6:14), though he approached it from a different angle.

7:13-14. Levitical priesthood was superseded by the fact that **our Lord descended from Judah. That tribe** had no role in the Levitical institutions, and the things God had said about the new Priest applied to One from Judah, which is proof that a change was made.

7:15-19. A further proof **(and what we have said is even more clear)** is found in the consideration that the new Priest has **an indestructible** (*akatalytou*) **life.** Psalm 110:4 was here quoted again to show that such an unending life is an inherent part of the order of Melchizedek. (The author probably had this text in mind when he made the statement about Melchizedek in Heb. 7:8.) Thus the new Priest does not hold His office **on the basis of a regulation as to His ancestry.** This rendering freely translates the original which is more nearly represented by the words "not after the Law of a carnal commandment." The writer seems to mean that the Law which regulated the priestly institution and succession was "carnal" or "fleshly," not in the sense of being evil, but in the sense that it pertained to people of flesh who died. But this **former regulation** has been replaced because of its inherent weakness and uselessness. What has replaced it is the new priesthood which constitutes **a better hope . . . by which we draw near to God.** Thus the writer established the point that **the Law** which **made nothing perfect** was replaced by a priestly institution which *can* accomplish its objectives in those who approach God through it.

c. The superiority of the new Priest (7:20-28)

If, as the author has shown, Melchizedek was greater than Levi (vv. 4-10) and the new priesthood necessarily abrogates the old (vv. 11-19), then the new Priest has to be greater than the Levitical priests.

7:20-22. The priesthood of Christ differs dramatically from the Levitical priesthood in that it was instituted **with an oath.** By contrast, the descendants of Aaron assumed their jobs **without any oath.** The writer then quoted again the divine oath of Psalm 110:4 whose very solemnity argues for the superiority of the new Priest, who was majestically inducted into His role. Moreover, **because of this oath, Jesus** became **the guarantee** (*engyos*, used only here in the NT) **of a better covenant.** In His own person, Jesus assured the superiority of the new order over the old because His oath secured His permanent installation in the priestly office.

7:23-25. No Old Testament priest ever functioned in this permanent way, **since** all were subject to **death.** But the **permanent priesthood** of Jesus gives Him the capacity to carry His saving work to completion. When the writer asserted that **He is able to save completely,** he continued to have in mind the salvation-inheritance first referred to in 1:14. The readers were to hold fast to their professions of faith and to continue numbering themselves among **those who come to God through Him,** knowing that He can see them through every trial and difficulty right to the end of the road **because He always lives to intercede for them.** In saying this, the author reverted again to a truth he had already enunciated (4:14-16) where he had invited the readers to avail themselves boldly of the mercy and grace accessible to them through Jesus' priesthood. As they did so, they would find that their Captain and High Priest could get the job done! He could lead them victoriously into the glory of the many sons. In this way He saves "completely."

7:26-28. After all, He is the kind of **High Priest** who **meets our need.** His character is utterly without blemish and He has been **exalted above the heavens.** Consequently too, He had no need like the Levitical priests **to offer sacrifices day after day, first for His own sins, and then**

for the sins of the people. At first sight verses 27-28 seem to refer to the ritual of the Day of Atonement (Lev. 16), but that was yearly, not "day after day." Probably these verses telescope that ritual with the regular sacrificial routine. There seems to be some evidence from Jewish tradition that a high priest was thought to offer daily sacrifice, and the stipulations of Leviticus 6:12-13 may refer to him.

In any case the new Priest had no need either for sacrifices for Himself or for repeated sacrifices for others. His one act of self-offering was definitive and sufficient. Of this more will be said in Hebrews 9 and 10. Here the author was content to conclude that, in contrast with the Levitical priests, the Son is a perfected High Priest. The reference to the fact that He **has been made perfect forever** recalls 5:8-10. The sufferings of the Son, here referred to as His sacrificial offering of Himself **once for all** (*ephapax*, cf. 9:12; 10:10; also cf. *hapax*, "once" in 9:26, 28), are what have constituted Him "perfect" for His role in God's presence where He intercedes for His followers. Thus **the Law** appointed **as high priests those who** were **weak, but the oath, which came after the Law, appointed** this kind of Priest. Accordingly the readers could go to Him at all times, fully confident of His capacity to serve their every need.

2. THE SUPERIOR SERVICE (8:1–10:18)

In chapter 7, the writer had considered the superiority of the new priesthood. It follows that such a priesthood must have a superior priestly ministry. That it does is unfolded in this section of the epistle. In the process, the letter reveals that the New Covenant underlies this newer priestly service.

a. Introduction to the superior service (8:1-6)

8:1-2. The author of Hebrews opened this passage with a clear transitional statement: **the point of what we are saying is this.** He wished to summarize what he had been teaching and go on to new ideas. By referring to the Lord Jesus as **a High Priest who sat down at the right hand . . . of the Majesty in heaven,** he picked up the wording of 1:3 (cf. 10:12; 12:2). What he meant by this truth is reasonably clear but will be elaborated further in what follows. In the

799

expression **who serves in the sanctuary, the true tabernacle,** he touched on ideas already implicit in his foregoing instruction, yet used new terms to describe them. The idea of service (*leitourgos*, a "minister" in the priestly sense) is in reality the new theme. The "true tabernacle" is the heavenly sphere where that service takes place.

8:3-6. Here is an initial, preliminary elaboration of the new theme. Since the role of a priest involved **gifts** (*dōra*) **and sacrifices** (*thysias*; cf. 5:1; 9:9), it follows that this new High Priest should **have something to offer.** Nevertheless His service cannot be an earthly one since the Levitical ritual of sacrifice continued. (These words imply that the Jewish temple was still standing.) But the **sanctuary** used for that is a mere **copy** (*hypodeigmati*; cf. 9:23-24) **and shadow** (*skia*; cf. 10:1) of the heavenly one in which the new Priest ministers. Its status as a "shadow sanctuary" was secured when Moses erected **the tabernacle** (prototype of the temple) under strict divine direction (8:5). But Jesus' ministry surpasses that of the Levitical priests just as the covenant He mediates supersedes theirs. (The word **Mediator** is used of Jesus by the author three times—8:6; 9:15; 12:24.) The word **ministry** (*leitourgia*, cf. "serves," 8:2) again strikes the pivotal note, but it is now added that the superiority of the new priestly service is related to a superior covenant, which in turn **is founded on better promises.** Both the covenant and its promises will now be considered.

b. The superior covenant (8:7–9:15)

8:7. That there is a promise of a New Covenant the writer will shortly prove by quoting Jeremiah 31:31-34. By doing so, he argued that such a promise demonstrates the inadequacy of the old one.

8:8-12. The promise of a New Covenant was made, the writer pointed out, in a passage where God **found fault with the people.** The Old Covenant failed because of the sinfulness of the nation, for which it had no remedy. The **New Covenant,** however, has such a remedy.

In the passage quoted, there is first the prediction that a New Covenant will be made (v. 8) followed by a strong declaration that it will differ from the previous one (v. 9). Then follows (vv. 10-12) a description of the superior accomplishments, or enablements, of the promised **covenant.** These are: (1) an inner inclination to obey (God will put His **laws in their minds and write them on their hearts),** (2) a firm relationship with God **(I will be their God, and they will be My people),** (3) the knowledge of God **(they will all know Me),** and (4) the forgiveness of sins **(I will forgive their wickedness and will remember their sins no more).** These are the "better promises" alluded to in verse 6.

It is clear that all these benefits belong, in fact, to all the regenerate of every age since the Cross. Though the New Covenant is specifically focused on Israel (cf. **house of Israel** and "house of Judah" in Jer. 31:31), it is clear that Christians of the present time also stand under its blessings (cf. Luke 22:20; 1 Cor. 11:25; 2 Cor. 3:6). This perception does not lead to an inappropriate confusion between Israel and the church. The New Covenant is God's appointed vehicle for fulfilling the Abrahamic blessings to Israel. But the Abrahamic Covenant also promised universal blessing, so the New Covenant becomes as well God's vehicle of salvation for believers since the Cross. To say this is not to say anything more than Jesus did when He declared that "salvation is from the Jews" (John 4:22). In no way should this impede the perception of the Christian church as a unique, interadvent body, closely united to Christ as His bride and significantly distinct from the nation of Israel. But inasmuch as all salvation is through the Cross of Christ, it is also through the blood of the New Covenant.

8:13. From the Old Testament prophecy he had just quoted, the writer then drew the justifiable conclusion that the Old Covenant was **obsolete** (*palaioumenon*) **and aging** and would **soon disappear.** The ceremonies still being conducted under it (cf. vv. 4-5) were spiritually anachronistic and the author's words suggest that he recalled the prophecy of Jesus that the temple in Jerusalem would be destroyed (Matt. 24:1-2). Probably this prophecy was fulfilled soon after Hebrews was written. If so, it was a dramatic confirmation of the writer's thesis about the Old Covenant.

9:1-5. With regard to the "aging" First Covenant, the writer wished to discuss that covenant's **regulations for worship** and its **earthly sanctuary.** These he highlighted in order to contrast them with the superior features of the New-Covenant ministry. How "earthly" (*kosmikon,* v. 1), or mundane, that first sanctuary was, he emphasized by reviewing the material objects associated with it. All these had typological value, but the author could not **discuss these things in detail** at the time (v. 5). He confined himself to the chief features of the comparison he wished to make.

9:6-10. The "regulations for worship" mentioned in verse 1 were now dealt with so that they underlined the insufficiency of the Old-Covenant service. Whereas **the outer room** of the tabernacle could be **entered regularly** by the officiating **priests,** it was only on the Day of Atonement (cf. Lev. 16) that **the high priest entered the inner room** (i.e., the "holy of holies") and then only with sacrificial **blood, which he offered for himself and for the sins the people had committed in ignorance.** This restricted access clearly demonstrated that a true entrance into God's presence (symbolized by **the most holy place) had not yet been disclosed.** That at least was the message **the Holy Spirit** intended to communicate by this arrangement. The Levitical arrangements were designed to convey the idea that the true way to God did not lie in them. What this indicates **for the present time** is that the Old-Covenant sacrificial system did not meet human need at its deepest level. It could not **clear the conscience of the worshiper.** Hence the regulations which formed part of the observant worshiper's adherence to this system were chiefly concerned with externals which were only meant to apply **until the time of the new order.**

The words of Hebrews 9:10 probably refer to sectarians for whom **food** laws and **ceremonial washings** retained great importance. The readers must remember the transitory nature of these things under the "aging" covenant and should not return to them.

9:11-12. The author then brought the discussion which began in 8:7 to a fitting conclusion. He had shown that the Old Testament anticipated a better New Covenant (8:7-13) and that the ritual of the Old Covenant, carried on in an "earthly sanctuary," pointed to its own inadequacy (9:1-10). Now he set forth the superiority of Christ's service as Mediator of the New Covenant (vv. 11-15).

The NIV rendering of verse 11 is questionable. It is not likely the writer meant to say that **Christ . . . went through the greater and more perfect tabernacle,** since this cannot be distinguished from "the most holy place" which He entered according to verse 12. It is probably better to take the original word translated "through" (*dia*) and connect it with **came as High Priest of the good things that are already here** (or, per most Gr. mss., "the good things which were to come"). In that case, instead of "through" the word can be translated "in connection with" and the total statement expresses the idea that Christ's high-priesthood is linked with "the greater and more perfect tabernacle" rather than the "earthly" one previously described (vv. 1-5).

When Christ **entered the most holy place once for all by His own blood** (v. 12; cf. Christ's blood in v. 14; 10:19, 29; 13:20) rather than by animal blood, He likewise demonstrated the superiority of His service because His blood had **obtained eternal redemption.** Thus the value of His sacrifice is immeasurably greater than the animal offerings of the Levitical arrangements. A perfect ransom price had been paid for human "redemption," and because it need not be paid again (this sacrificial act was "once for all," *ephapax;* cf. 7:27; 10:10) that redemption is an "eternal" one.

9:13-14. This "eternal redemption" through which the blessings of the New Covenant (cf. 8:10-12) have reached all believers, should affect the way believers serve God. Old-Covenant rituals served for the **ceremonially unclean** and only made them **outwardly clean.** But **the blood of Christ** can do much more. His was a sacrifice of infinite value because **through the eternal Spirit He offered Himself unblemished to God.** With this lovely assertion, the writer of Hebrews involved all three Persons of the Godhead in the sacrifice of Christ, which magnifies the greatness of His redemptive offering. "Unblemished" (*amōmon*) fittingly describes Christ's perfection (cf. 4:15; 7:26) for it is also used of spotless animals brought for sacrifice.

Such a great accomplishment ought to **cleanse our consciences from acts that lead to death,** but the expression "acts that lead to death" is literally "dead works" which in this context seems to refer to the Levitical rituals that, in contrast with the work of Christ, can never impart spiritual life. As also in 6:1, where such "acts that lead to death" are referred to, the writer wished his readers would give up all thoughts of returning to Old-Covenant rituals. Their consciences ought to be perfectly free from any need to engage in such things and, retaining their confidence in the perfect efficacy of the Cross, they should hold fast their profession and **serve the living God** within the New-Covenant arrangements.

9:15. To do so is to retain the hope of an **eternal inheritance** (cf. "eternal redemption" in v. 12 and "the eternal Spirit" in v. 14) which has been **promised** to recipients of New-Covenant life. **Christ is the Mediator** (cf. 8:6; 12:24) of that **covenant,** and the "inheritance" is available to **those who are called** since the death of the Mediator has freed them from all guilt derived **from the sins committed under the First Covenant.**

The author was here perhaps countering the appeal of the sectarians, or others, to the "guilt feelings" of those Jewish Christians who must often have been charged with deserting their ancestral faith. But the blood of Christ ought to quiet their consciences permanently and lead them to pursue the "eternal inheritance" which the New-Covenant relationship brought them. Of course the writer meant here as elsewhere that it is only "through faith and patience" that his readers could "inherit what has been promised" (6:12); but if they would rest their consciences at the Cross, they could pursue this heirship undistractedly.

c. The superior sacrifice (9:16-28)

The author has made it clear that Christ's death has instituted a better covenant (vv. 11-15) which is superior to animal offerings (vv. 12-14). But the need for such a sacrifice has yet to be explored. So a key word in this subunit is "necessary" (*anankē*, vv. 16, 23). In the process of exploring this point, the author clearly underscored the measureless superiority of the sacrificial death of Christ.

9:16-17. In opening the new unit of thought, the writer employed a swift semantic shift in which he treated the Greek word for "covenant" (*diathēkē*) in the sense of **a will.** While "covenants" and "wills" are not in all respects identical, the author meant that in the last analysis the New Covenant is really a testamentary disposition. Like human wills, all the arrangements are secured by the testator and its beneficiaries need only accept its terms.

Treating the New Covenant in this way, the author argued that its **force**—like that of all human wills—depends on **the death of the one who made it.** That is when it **takes effect.**

9:18-21. The Old **Covenant** was also **put into effect** with **blood.** Drawing on material that may have partly been derived from traditions known to the writer but not specified in the Old Testament, he described the inauguration of the Old Covenant through ceremonies involving the sprinkling of sacrificial **blood.**

9:22. This verse applies to the Old-Covenant institutions, and the words **nearly everything** leave room for the flour offering which a poor Israelite might bring for his sin (Lev. 5:11-13). But the writer was thinking of the system as a whole and the ritual of the Day of Atonement that pertained to the totality of the nation's sins, which showed that **without the shedding of blood there is no forgiveness.** These words also constitute a principle that is true in the New Covenant.

9:23. In connection with the New Covenant, the writer then enunciated his basic principle: the death of Christ **was necessary.** Mere **copies** (*hypodeigmata*; cf. 8:5; 9:24) **of the heavenly things** might be adequately hallowed by animal sacrifices, **but the heavenly things themselves** required more than that. The expression "heavenly things" referred quite generally to the new priestly arrangements, which have heaven as their focal point. These arrangements involve dealing with people's sin and must thus be inaugurated with a sacrifice adequate to "do away" with that sin (cf. v. 26). The death of Christ meets this requirement.

9:24-26. Christ was appointed as High Priest of the New Covenant to represent sinful people in **heaven itself,** that is, in the presence of God. So His sacrifice had to be greater than that which allowed entrance into a mere **man-made sanctuary that was only a copy** (*antitypa*) **of the true one.** Nor could Christ offer repeated sacrifices as in the Levitical institution, for that would have required Him to die **many times since the Creation of the world.** Instead, as is obvious, the heavenly ministry of Christ called for a thoroughly sufficient, one-time sacrifice. This is precisely why He **appeared once for all** (*hapax,* cf. v. 28; also cf. *ephapax* in 7:27; 9:12; 10:10) **at the end of the ages to do away with sin,** which the priests in the old arrangement could not do. By the phrase "end of the ages" the writer evidently meant the climax of the Old Testament eras as well as the imminency of the climax of all things. He will shortly refer to Christ's second advent.

9:27-28. With this observation, eschatological realities come into focus. Humans are sinful creatures **destined to die once, and after that to face judgment.** But this danger is turned aside by the fact that **Christ was sacrificed once** (*hapax,* cf. v. 26) **to take away the sins of many people.** The recurrence of "once" (9:26, 28) and of "once for all" (7:27; 9:12; 10:10) stresses the finality and the singleness of Christ's sacrificial work in contrast with the repeated Levite ministrations. In addition, the "once"-sacrifice of Christ (vv. 26, 28) compares with the "once"-death of each person (v. 27). Now those **who are waiting** (*apekdechomenois;* used seven times in the NT of the return of Christ: Rom. 8:19, 23, 25; 1 Cor. 1:7; Gal. 5:5; Phil. 3:20; Heb. 9:28) **for Him** can look forward to His coming, not with a fearful expectation of judgment, but with the anticipation of **salvation.**

His first advent was to bear sins away—but His second will be **not to bear sin** (lit., "without [reference to] sins").

Deftly the author implied that "those who are waiting for Him" constitute a smaller circle than those whom His death has benefited. They are, as all his previous exhortations reveal, the ones who "hold firmly till the end the confidence we had at first" (3:14). The "salvation" He will bring them at His second coming will be the "eternal inheritance" of which they are heirs (cf. 9:15; 1:14).

d. The superior effect of the new priesthood (10:1-18)

This is the final subsection of the expository unit that began at 7:1. In chapter 7 the author argued for the superiority of Christ, as a Priest after the order of Melchizedek, over the Levitical priests. In 8:1–10:18 he argued the superiority of Christ's priestly ministry which is based on a superior covenant (8:7–9:15) and entailed a superior sacrifice (9:16-28). Now he argued that the superior sacrifice perfects the New-Covenant worshiper.

10:1. By virtue of its anticipatory character, **the Law** could **never . . . make perfect those who draw near to worship.** By "make perfect" the writer did not mean sinless perfection. As the following discussion shows, he was concerned with that definitive removal of guilt which makes free access to God possible for worshipers who trust in the sufficiency of the Cross.

10:2-4. The continous sacrifices of the old order which are "repeated endlessly year after year" (v. 1) testify to the Law's incapacity to "perfect" its **worshipers.** Far from enabling them to achieve a standing before God in which they **would no longer have felt guilty for their sins,** the yearly rituals (of the Day of Atonement) served as a kind of **annual reminder of sins,** since animal blood has no power **to take away sins.**

10:5-7. It was precisely for this reason that an Old Testament prophecy (Ps. 40:6-8) recorded the words of the One who would do what God really wanted. This psalm prophetically anticipated some of Christ's words at his First Advent. The phrase **a body You prepared for Me** is one Septuagint rendering of the Hebrew expression "You have dug ears for Me." The Greek translator whose version the author of Hebrews used (obviously translating with the help of the Holy Spirit), construed the Hebrew text as a kind of figure of speech (technically called synecdoche) in which a part is put for the whole. If God is to "dig out ears" He must "prepare a body." This interpretation is both valid and correct as its quotation in Hebrews proves. In the "body" which He assumed in Incarnation,

Christ could say that He had **come to** achieve what the Old-Covenant sacrifices never achieved, the perfecting of New-Covenant worshipers. In this sense He did God's will.

10:8-10. The writer then expounded the text he had just quoted. In the words **He sets aside the first to establish the second** (v. 9), the author referred to the setting aside of the Old-Covenant sacrifices which did not ultimately satisfy God. What was established was God's will, and it was **by that will** that **we have been made holy through the sacrifice of the body of Jesus Christ once for all** (*epha-pax*; cf. 7:27; 9:12).

The words rendered "made holy" involve a single Greek word (*hēgiasmenoi*) often rendered "sanctify" (cf. 10:14, 29). Here it occurs in a tense that makes it plain, along with the rest of the statement, that the sanctification is an accomplished fact. Nowhere in Hebrews does the writer refer to the "progressive sanctification" of a believer's life. Instead sanctification is for him a functional equivalent of the Pauline concept of justification. By the sanctification which is accomplished through the death of Christ, New-Covenant worshipers are perfected for guilt-free service to God (cf. 2:11).

10:11-14. The truth just stated is reinforced by a contrast with the Levitical priesthood. Levite priests could never sit down on the job since their sacrificial services were never completed. But Christ's sitting **at the right hand of God** (cf. 1:3; 8:1; 12:2) is both a signal that His sacrifice was offered **for all time** and also that He can now confidently await final victory over **His enemies.** The words "for all time" (*eis to diēnekes*) are translated "forever" in verse 14 (see comments on 7:3). Thus by a single sacrifice (**one sacrifice,** 10:12, 14)—in contrast with the many sacrifices offered by the priests **day after day** and **again and again . . . He has made perfect forever those who are being made holy.** The translation "are being made holy" sounds like a continuing process. But this ignores the force of the expression "made holy" in verse 10. A better rendering is, "them who are sanctified" (*tous hagiazomenous*; cf. v. 29). "The sanctified" have a status in God's presence that is "perfect" (cf. 11:40; 12:23) in the sense that they approach

Him with the full acceptance gained through the death of Christ (cf. 10:19-22).

10:15-18. Reverting to his basic text on the benefits of the New Covenant (cf. 8:8-12), the author requoted a portion of it (in 10:16 he quoted Jer. 31:33; and in Heb. 10:17, Jer. 31:34) to drive home his point. The text is a testimony given by God's **Holy Spirit,** and shows that final forgiveness, such as the New Covenant promised, meant that there was no further need for any **sacrifice for sin.** As the writer will shortly show, a person who turns from the one sufficient sacrifice of Christ has no real sacrifice to which he can turn (cf. Heb. 10:26).

D. The fourth warning (10:19-39)

In some ways this warning section is the most pointed and stern of all. It is also climactic. It follows the completion of the epistle's exposition of the high priestly role and service of Jesus Christ, so it gathers up the implications of these truths and drives them home with full force. But as usual, the writer mingled a solemn warning with his words of consolation and encouragement.

1. THE BASIC ADMONITION (10:19-25)

10:19-22. The central assertion of these verses is in the words, **Therefore, brothers** (cf. 3:1, 12) **. . . let us draw near to God.** The intervening material, beginning with the word **since,** gives the basis for the author's call to approach God. The readers are New-Covenant people ("brothers") who should **have confidence** (*parrēsian*; cf. 3:6; 4:16; 10:35) to come into the very presence of God. This idea is enriched by the use of Old-Covenant imagery. God's presence in **the most holy place** and **the curtain** that once was a barrier to man is now no longer so. It symbolized Christ's **body,** so the writer may have had in mind the rending of the temple curtain at the time of Christ's death (Matt. 27:51). At any rate His death gave believers the needed access and route to God, aptly described as **new** (*prosphaton,* "recent," occurring only here in the NT) **and living,** that is, partaking of the fresh and vitalizing realities of the New Covenant.

But in addition, the call to draw near is appropriate **since we have a great Priest over the house of God** with all that this entails in the light of the writer's previous discussion. So the approach of believers should be **with a sincere** (*alēthinēs*, "true, dependable," from *aletheia*, "truth") **heart in full assurance of faith.** There ought to be no wavering in regard to these superlative realities. Rather each New-Covenant worshiper should approach God in the conscious enjoyment of freedom from guilt (**having our hearts sprinkled to cleanse us from a guilty conscience**) and with a sense of the personal holiness that Christ's sacrifice makes possible (**having our bodies washed with pure water**). The writer's words are probably an exhortation to lay hold consciously of the cleansing benefits of Christ's Cross and to draw near to God in enjoying them, putting away inward guilt and outward impurity. These verses approximate 1 John 1:9.

10:23-25. This kind of confident access to God necessarily entails that believers **hold unswervingly to the hope we profess** with full confidence in the reliability of God's promises. The writer revealed in these verses that his concern for fidelity to the faith is not an abstraction, but a confrontation with real danger. There was an urgent need for mutual concern and exhortation (**toward love and good deeds**) within the church he wrote to. His readers were not to abandon **meeting together, as some** were **doing.** Already there seemed to have been defections from their ranks, though his words might have applied to other churches where such desertions had occurred. In any case their mutual efforts to spur one another on should increase **as** they **see the Day approaching** (cf. v. 37; a well-known NT triology is included in these vv.: faith, v. 22; hope, v. 23; love, v. 24).

In referring again to the Second Advent, the writer left the impression he was concerned that genuine believers might cease to hope for the Lord's coming and be tempted to defect from their professions of faith in Christ (cf. comments on 1:13–2:4; 6:9). They must treat their future expectations as certainties (since **He who promised is faithful**). If they would only lift up their eyes, they could "see the Day approaching."

2. THE RENEWED WARNING (10:26-31)

10:26-27. The KJV translation here, "if we sin willfully," is superior to NIV's

if we deliberately keep on sinning, as the words "keep on" overplay the Greek tense. As the context shows (cf. v. 23), the author was concerned here, as throughout the epistle, with the danger of defection from the faith. Most sin is "deliberate," but the writer was here influenced by the Old Testament's teaching about sins of presumption (cf. Num. 15:29-31) which lay outside the sacrificial provisions of the Law. Apostasy from the faith would be such a "willful" act and for those who commit it **no sacrifice for sins is left** (cf. Heb. 10:18). If the efficacious sacrifice of Christ should be renounced, there remained no other available sacrifice which could shield an apostate from God's **judgment** by **raging fire.** A Christian who abandons "the confidence [he] had at first" (3:14) puts himself on the side of God's enemies and, as the writer had already said, is in effect "crucifying the Son of God all over again and subjecting Him to public disgrace" (6:6). Such reprehensible conduct can scarcely be worthy of anything but God's flaming indignation and retribution. This, however, as stated earlier (cf. comments on 6:8), is not a reference to hell (cf. comments on 10:29).

10:28-29. Under the Old Covenant, if an Israelite spurned the Mosaic Law and at least **two or three witnesses** verified his actions, he was put to death. This being true, the author then argued from the lesser to the greater. If defiance of an inferior covenant could bring such retribution, what about defiance of the New Covenant which, as he had made clear, is far superior? The answer can only be that the punishment would be substantially greater in such a case.

In order to show that this is so, the writer then placed defection from the faith in the harshest possible light. An apostate from the New Covenant **has trampled the Son of God underfoot** and **has treated as an unholy thing the blood of the covenant** (cf. "blood of the eternal covenant," 13:20) **that sanctified him.** The words "sanctified him" refer to true Christians. Already the writer to the Hebrews has described them as "made holy (Gr. 'sanctified') through the sacrifice of the body of Jesus Christ once for all" (10:10) and as "made perfect forever" through this sanctifying work (v. 14).

Some seek to evade this conclusion by suggesting that Christ is the One referred to here as "sanctified" or that the person only *claims* to be sanctified. But these efforts are foreign to the writer's thought and are so forced that they carry their own refutation. The author's whole point lies in the seriousness of the act. To treat "the blood of the covenant" (which actually sanctifies believers) as though it were an "unholy" (*koinon,* "common") thing and to renounce its efficacy, is to commit a sin so heinous as to dwarf the fatal infractions of the Old Covenant. To this, an apostate adds the offense of insulting **the Spirit of grace** who originally wooed him to faith in Christ. This kind of spiritual rebellion clearly calls for a much worse punishment than the capital penalty that was inflicted under the Mosaic setup.

But again the writer was not thinking of hell. Many forms of divine retribution can fall on a human life which are worse than immediate death. In fact, Jeremiah made just such a complaint about the punishment inflicted on Jerusalem (Lam. 4:6, 9). One might think also of King Saul, whose last days were burdened with such mental and emotional turmoil that death itself was a kind of release.

10:30-31. No one should regard such a warning as an idle threat. God Himself has claimed the right to take vengeance and to **judge His people.** In saying this, the author quoted twice from Deuteronomy (32:35-36), a chapter which most vividly evokes the picture of God's people suffering His retributive judgments (cf. esp. Deut. 32:19-27). Those familiar with this text, as well as other descriptions of God's wrath against "His people," agree: **it is a dreadful thing to fall into the hands of the living God.**

3. THE RENEWED ENCOURAGEMENT
(10:32-39)

But as was his custom after the most severe admonitions, the writer chose to conclude his warning with a distinct note of encouragement.

10:32-34. An effective way to fortify people against future trials is to remind them of the courage they displayed in past ones. This is precisely what the writer did. His readers knew what it was to stand their **ground in a great contest in the face of suffering.** (The words "stood your ground" [*hypemeinate*] render the verb usually translated "persevered," as in, e.g., v. 36). They knew what it was to be publicly shamed and persecuted, and also to support others who had such experiences (v. 33). They had shown sympathy for brethren who had been imprisoned, and they had suffered property loss with joy because they had an assurance of possessing heavenly wealth (v. 34). They would do well to recall now their steadfastness in the past. Whatever they might now be facing—and the writer suggested it might be something similar—they would be helped if they would **remember those earlier days after** they **had received the light** (cf. "received the knowledge" in v. 26 and "enlightened" in 6:4).

10:35-36. This was no time for them, then, to **throw away** their **confidence** (*parrēsia,* cf. 3:6; 4:16; 10:19). As the author's exposition of the eternal inheritance—the glory of the many sons—had sought to show, that confidence, if retained, **will be richly rewarded.** What the readers needed, therefore, was just what the writer had often said and implied: **to persevere** (lit., "you had need of perseverance," *hypomonēs echete chreian*) so that by thus doing God's **will** (cf. v. 9) they would **receive what** God had **promised.** As much as anything, these words express the central exhortation of the Book of Hebrews.

10:37-38. If their concern was about the delay of the Second Advent, they should rest assured that **in just a very little while, He who is coming will come and will not delay.** These words and those that follow were adapted by the author from the Septuagint of Isaiah 26:21 and Habakkuk 2:3-4. But they were used freely and were not intended as a precise quotation, since no words such as "He says" introduced them. In the phrase **My** (or "the") **righteous one** (only a handful of Gr. mss. read "My"), the author employed Paul's description of a person who is justified by faith. It is likely that the writer of Hebrews understood it similarly. A justified person ought to **live by faith,** which is what the writer had been urging his readers to do. But, **if he shrinks back,** that is, if the "righteous one" commits apostasy, denouncing his

Christian profession, God's favor cannot rest on his life. By understating the serious consequences, the writer softened his words so that he would not distract from his predominant note of encouragement.

10:39. Then he affirmed, **But we are not of those who shrink back and are destroyed.** Here the original text has an emphatic "we," which the writer might have intended as an "editorial we," of which he was quite fond (cf. 2:5; 5:11; 8:1; etc.). Then he would mean: "As far as I am concerned, I am determined not to shrink back and experience the ruin which divine retribution would bring." The words "are destroyed" reflect the Greek *apōleia,* which can refer either to temporal or eternal ruin. In this context the former is correct. Instead of the ruin which an apostate invites, the writer intended to be among **those who believe and are saved.** The NIV rendering should not be misread as a reference to conversion. Though the author's own normal word for salvation does not occur here, the expression "and are saved" somewhat freely translates *eis peripoiēsin psychēs.* A viable rendering of the last half of verse 39 would be: "but [we are] of faith leading to the preservation of the soul" (cf. comments on 1 Peter 2:9). But "soul" here should be understood in the Hebraic sense of the person himself, or his life, and refers in this context to the way in which persistence in the faith preserves an individual from the calamities that overtake those who "shrink back." Even if the writer was speaking primarily of his own purpose of heart, he clearly intended that to be shared by his readers. Thus the concluding statement of his warning passage (10:19-39) amounts to a call for determination and perseverance.

IV. Part III: The Response of Faith (chaps. 11–12)

This section—the final major portion of the epistle—constitutes a call to respond in the only appropriate way, namely, by faith, to the realities the writer has discussed. Though the importance of faith has already been made apparent, the thought of the writer is not complete till its value and worth are more fully considered. As before, there is exposition (chap. 11) followed by warning and exhortation (chap. 12).

A. The life of faith (chap. 11)

In concluding the previous warning section, the writer touched on the theme of living by faith (cf. 10:37-39). What this really means he then expounded in terms his readers could fully appreciate, because it is faith that underlies the experience of the heroes of Old Testament history. Since these people experienced faith, so could his readers.

1. PROLOGUE (11:1-3)

11:1-3. In a brief Prologue the author set forth three fundamental considerations about faith: its basic nature, the honor associated with it, and its way of seeing things. In its essence **faith is being sure** (*hypostasis,* rendered "being" in reference to God in 1:3) . . . **and certain** (*elenchos,* from the verb *elenchō,* "to prove or convince") about unseen hopes and realities. That this is honorable is seen in the fact that Old Testament worthies, **the ancients, were commended for** it. **Faith** is also a way of viewing all experience since it is the way in which believers see **the universe** (*tous aiōnas,* lit., "the ages," also rendered "the universe" in 1:2) for what it is—a creation by God.

2. THE DIVINE ACCEPTANCE OF FAITH (11:4-16)

In the first major movement of his exposition, the author stressed the theme suggested in verse 2. Faith wins acceptance and reward from God.

11:4. **Abel** represents the **righteous man** referred to in 10:38, whose acceptance before God was based on a superior sacrifice. Like Abel, the readers found acceptance before God on the basis of the better sacrifice of the New Covenant. Their unbelieving brethren, like **Cain,** found no such divine approbation. Even death does not extinguish the testimony of a man like Abel.

11:5-6. **Enoch,** on the other hand, reflected the kind of life that pleases God since he walked with God by faith (as the readers also should). If Christ had come in their lifetimes (cf. 10:37), the readers also would **not** have experienced **death.** In any case they could only please God by continued confidence that **He exists and . . . rewards those who earnestly seek Him.**

11:7. That God does reward those who seek Him is suggested by the career of **Noah,** who became an heir of righteousness by faith. What he inherited was, in fact, the new world after the Flood as the readers might inherit "the world to come" (cf. 2:5). The reference here to Noah saving his household recalls the writer's stress on a Christian's salvation-inheritance. It further suggests that a man's personal **faith** can be fruitful in his family, as they share it together.

11:8-10. That the readers should look forward to "the world to come" and treat their present experience as a pilgrimage is a lesson enforced by the life of **Abraham.** This great patriarch lived like **a stranger** in a land **he would later receive as his inheritance.** So also would the readers inherit if they, like this forefather, kept **looking forward to the city with foundations,** a reference to the heavenly and eternal Jerusalem (cf. Rev. 21:2, 9-27).

11:11-12. The NIV introduces the word **Abraham** into these verses. But its marginal reading is preferable: "By faith even Sarah, who was past age, was enabled to bear children because she. . . ." The NIV interpretation is influenced by the opinion that the phrase **to become a father** (*eis katabolēn spermatos*) can refer only to the male parent, but this need not be so. The writer here chose to introduce his first heroine of faith, one who was able to overlook the physical limitation of her own barrenness to become a fruitful mother. Since "she considered Him faithful who had promised" (NASB) so also should the readers (cf. 10:23). Her **faith** in fact, contributed to the startling multiplication of her husband's seed, when old Abraham was **as good as dead.**

11:13-16. In an impressive summary of his discussion thus far, the writer pointed out that people can be **still living by faith** when they die, even if by that time they do **not receive the things promised.** By faith the old saints saw the promised realities **from a distance** and persisted in their pilgrim character, **looking for a country of their own** and refusing to **return** to the land they had left. So too the readers should renounce the **opportunity** to go back to any form of their ancestral religion and should persist in **longing for a better country—a heavenly one.** If they did so they, like the

patriarchs, would be people with whom **God** would **not** be **ashamed** to be associated.

3. THE VARIEGATED EXPERIENCES OF FAITH (11:17-40)

A new movement, the author's exposition of the life of faith, begins here. In a multiplicity of varied experiences faith remains the constant factor by which these experiences are met and understood. Faith constitutes a Christian's true "world view" (cf. v. 3).

11:17-19. The theme of testing emerges here as the writer returned to **Abraham.** The readers can learn from that supreme test in which the patriarch was called on **to sacrifice his . . . son.** Though this seemed to contradict the divine promise, Abraham was able to rise above the trial and trust in the resurrecting power of God. So also Christian readers must sometimes look beyond the experiences of life, in which God's promises do not seem to be fulfilled, and realize that their resurrections will bring those promises to fruition.

11:20-22. The patriarchs mentioned here likewise looked to the future in **faith. Isaac,** trusting God to fulfill His promises to Abraham and his descendants, pronounced blessings on his own two sons **Jacob and Esau** regarding **their future.** So did **Jacob** in regard to **Joseph's sons,** which was for him an act of faith in his old age. The readers too were to maintain their worship right to the end of life, persevering in faith in the future that God had foretold. **Joseph** too, nearing death, expressed confidence that God would in the future deliver **the Israelites from Egypt.** In similar fashion all believers should, in genuine faith, have confidence in the future of God's people.

11:23. With this transition to the life of **Moses,** the writer began to focus on the way faith confronts opposition and hostility, a subject familiar to his readers. It was **by faith** that Moses was hidden by his **parents** and his life was thus preserved. The phrase **because they saw he was no ordinary child** might be better read, "because they saw he was a beautiful child." ("Beautiful" is the Gr. *asteion*, which occurs in the NT only here and in Acts 7:20, which also refers to Moses.) Delighted by the precious gift of a son which God had given them, they evidently believed God had something better for this lovely baby than death. Not fearing Pharaoh's **edict**, they kept him alive, and God rewarded their faith by their son's illustrious career.

11:24-26. In a classic presentation of the way faith chooses between the attractive but temporary **pleasures of sin** and the prospect of **disgrace for the sake of Christ**, the writer showed **Moses** to be a real hero of faith who had an intelligent regard for the eschatological hopes of the nation of Israel. The readers also were to accept "disgrace" and reject "the pleasures of sin," and they would do so if they, like Moses, anticipated their **reward**.

11:27-28. Moreover, at the time of the Exodus, Moses was undeterred by fear of **the king's anger**. By keeping **the Passover**, which included **the sprinkling of blood**, the nation avoided God's judgment. In the same way, the readers should not be afraid of human wrath and should maintain their separateness from the surrounding world. They should persist in the worship experience made possible by the blood of the New Covenant. If they would do so, they would not fall under divine retribution (cf. 10:19-31).

11:29-31. The readers could also look forward to victory over their enemies (cf. 1:13-14). They could learn from the destruction of **the Egyptians** and the collapse of **the walls of Jericho** what triumphs faith can win over its adversaries. If, as seems probable, there were a few Gentiles in the church that received this letter, they could take comfort from the experience of **the prostitute Rahab**, a Gentile who was spared when Jericho was conquered.

11:32-35a. There were far too many heroes of faith for the writer to deal with them all in detail. Swiftly he mentioned the variegated accomplishments of some of them. At the climax of this list stand **women** who **received back their dead, raised to life again**—a truly superlative victory of faith which does not allow death to defeat it (cf. 1 Kings 17:17-24; 2 Kings 4:17-37).

11:35b-38. In a swift transition of thought, the writer moved from faith's obvious triumphs to what seemed to be its defeats. But these defeats were only apparent, not real. Those who **were tortured and refused to be released** did so because they knew their sufferings would lead to a richer and **better resurrection** experience. So the readers might also endure suffering staunchly and expect reward in the future world. Indeed, all manner of physical suffering (vv. 36-37, 38b cite about a dozen kinds of persecution) has been endured by people of faith, as well as ostracism from their homes and countries, treatment that the readers might also have to endure. But in a lovely touch, the writer commented that **the world was not worthy** of those whom it banished.

11:39-40. In a concluding summary the writer pointed out that the great heroes of faith he had spoken of had not yet realized their eschatological hopes. This fact shows that **God had planned something better for** them **and us**. It is indeed "better for us" that the future hopes they strove toward be delayed, since only thus could believers enjoy the present experience of becoming companions of the Messiah who leads them to glory. As a result, the perfecting (cf. 10:14; 12:23) of the Old Testament worthies—that is, the realization of their hopes—awaits that of all believers.

B. The final warning (chap. 12)

The author concluded the basic argument of the epistle with a final admonition and warning. As usual his hortatory section grew directly out of the expository one which preceded it. His discussion of the life of faith now led to another call for perseverance.

1. THE INTRODUCTORY ADMONITION (12:1-2)

12:1-2. The life of faith has been amply attested by this **great cloud of** Old Testament **witnesses**. (This does not mean that they watch believers today.) Hence believers ought to **run with perseverance** (hypomonēs; cf. 10:32, 36; 12:2-3,7) **the race marked out** in their Christian lives, setting aside whatever **hinders and the sin that so easily entangles** (euperistaton, "ambushes or encircles"). Their supreme Model for this continued to be **Jesus**, however admirable any Old Testament figure might be. He is both **the Author and Perfecter of our faith**. The word "author" (archēgon) was used in 2:10 (see comments there) and suggests that Jesus "pioneered" the path of faith Christians should follow. He also "perfected" the way of faith since He reached its end successfully. He kept His eye on **the joy set before Him,** the "joy" alluded to in 1:9 wherein He obtained an eternal throne. The believers' share in that joy must also be kept in view. After enduring (*hypemeinen,* the verb related to the noun *hypomonē* in 12:1; cf. vv. 3, 7) **the cross** and **scorning its shame,** Jesus assumed that triumphant position **at the right hand of the throne of God** (cf. 1:3; 8:1; 10:12) which presages His and the believers' final victory (cf. 1:13-14).

2. THE REMINDER THAT THINGS ARE NOT AS BAD AS THEY SEEM (12:3-11)

Nothing is more natural for a person than to overestimate the severity of his trials. The writer did not want his audience to do that.

12:3-4. If they would **consider** the **opposition from sinful men** which Jesus confronted and **endured** (*hypomemenēkota;* cf. vv. 1-2, 7), they would be encouraged. After all, unlike Him, they had **not yet resisted . . . sin . . . to the point of** bloodshed. By "sin" the author probably primarily meant that of "sinful men" who opposed them, but doubtless also had their own sin in mind, which they had to resist in order to maintain a steadfast Christian profession.

12:5-8. The readers also seemed to **have forgotten the encouragement** found in Proverbs 3:11-12, which presents divine **discipline** as an evidence of divine love. Thus they should not **lose heart** (cf. Heb. 12:3) but should **endure hardship** (*hypomenete,* lit., "persevere"; cf. vv. 1-3) **as discipline** and regard it as an evidence of sonship, that is, that they are being trained for the glory of the many sons (cf. 2:10 and comments there). All God's children are subject to His discipline, and in the phrase **everyone undergoes discipline** the writer for the last time used the Greek *metochoi* ("companions, sharers"), also used in 1:9; 3:1, 14; 6:4. (Lit., the Gr. reads, ". . . discipline, of which all have become sharers.") In speaking of those who **are not disciplined** and **are** thus **illegitimate children,** he was probably thinking of Christians whose disloyalty to the faith resulted in their loss of inheritance (i.e., reward) which is acquired by

the many sons and daughters. (In the Roman world, an "illegitimate child" had no inheritance rights.) What such Christians undergo, the author had shown, is severe judgment. On the other hand believers who undergo God's "discipline" are being prepared by this educational process (*paideia,* "discipline," lit., "child-training"; cf. Eph. 6:4) for millennial reward.

12:9-11. Drawing on the analogy of the discipline of earthly **fathers,** the author encouraged a submissive spirit to the discipline of **the Father of our spirits** which is life-preserving (**and live**) as well as productive of an experience of **His holiness,** which involves a rich **harvest of righteousness and peace.** But Christians must let this discipline have its full effect and be **trained by it.**

3. THE CALL TO RENEWED SPIRITUAL VITALITY (12:12-17)

12:12-13. The author sensed the tendency to spiritual weakness in his readers, and in the light of the truths he had expounded he encouraged them to renew their strength. If they would do this and would pursue the **level paths** which real righteousness entails, the weakest among them (**the lame**) would not be further **disabled, but rather healed.** Their own strength would benefit weaker Christians.

12:14. Peace with all men as well as personal holiness must be vigorously sought since **without holiness** (*hagiasmos*) **no one will see the Lord.** Since no sin can stand in God's presence, Christians must—and will be—sinless when they see the Lord (cf. 1 John 3:2). That realization offers motivation for pursuing holiness here and now. But the author may also have had in mind the thought that one's perception of God even now is conditioned by his real measure of holiness (cf. Matt. 5:8).

12:15-17. As a grim reminder of what can happen among believers, the writer warned that **one** who **misses the grace of God** may become like a **bitter root** whose infidelity to God affects others. Here the author had in mind Deuteronomy 29:18 where an Old-Covenant apostate was called a "root . . . that produces such bitter poison." Such a person would be **godless** (*bebēlos,* "profane, unhallowed, desecrated") **like Esau,**

Jacob's brother, whose loose and profane character led him to sell **his inheritance rights as the oldest son** for the temporary gratification of **a single meal.** He warned the readers not to yield to transitory pressures and forfeit their inheritances. If some did, they would ultimately regret the foolish step and might find their inheritance privileges irrevocably lost as were Esau's. This would of course be true of one who ended his Christian experience in a state of apostasy, which the writer had continually warned against.

4. THE FINAL WARNING ITSELF (12:18-29)

12:18-21. Vividly the writer pictured the situation at Mount Sinai where the Old Covenant was given and its awesomeness and fearful nature were described (cf. Ex. 19:9-23; Deut. 9:8-19).

12:22-24. The realities that pertain to New-Covenant people and to which they **have come** are even more impressive because they are **heavenly.** Not only is there the heavenly **city,** but there are also heaven-related beings, both **angels** and people, associated with it. The term **church of the firstborn** may mean the assembly of those whose inheritance rights are already won (since under the OT Law the "firstborn" was the primary heir; cf. v. 16). They have already gone on to the heavenly regions where the angels are. But above all, it is to **God, the Judge of all men,** that they have come—and there are some who indeed can stand His searching scrutiny of their lives (**the spirits of righteous men made perfect;** cf. 10:14; 11:40)—and **to Jesus the Mediator** (cf. 8:6; 9:15) **of a New Covenant** whose atoning **blood** does not cry for judgment as did Abel's but secures the acceptance of all New-Covenant persons.

If the readers would contemplate these things properly, they would be awed by them and more inclined to fulfill their call to the highest privileges that the New Covenant can provide.

12:25. The contrast between the two covenants is now focused as a contrast between a warning given **on earth** and one that issues **from heaven** itself. Since those who refused the Old Covenant **did not escape,** how could those of the New Covenant who **turn away** expect to do so? (cf. 2:3) Here no doubt the author thought of the Speaker as none other than the Originator of the New Covenant who

now sits "at the right hand of the Majesty in heaven" (1:3).

12:26-27. This is the divine **voice** which once **shook** only **the earth,** but will ultimately **shake not only the earth but also the heavens.** The reference to Haggai 2:6 was understood by the author as speaking of the ultimate remaking of the heavens and earth which will follow the millennial kingdom (cf. Heb. 1:10-12). What remains after this cataclysmic event will be eternal.

12:28-29. And such is the character of the **kingdom** which **we are receiving.** The words **let us be thankful** may be rendered "let us have [or, 'obtain'] grace" (*echōmen charin*) and are likely a final reference to the resources of grace available from the great High Priest (cf. 4:14-16). This is confirmed by the words **and so** (lit., "through which," *di' ēs*) which remind the readers that this grace is required in order to **worship** (better, "serve," *latreuōmen,* also used in 8:5; 9:9; 10:2; 13:10) **God acceptably** within the New-Covenant community. Failure to do so should be deterred by the concluding solemn thought that **our God is a consuming fire** (cf. 10:26-27). A believer who departs from his magnificent privileges will invite God's retribution.

V. Epilogue (chap. 13)

The Epilogue can be distinguished from the body of the epistle in that the latter contains only broad, general admonitions, while the Epilogue contains specific ones. In some ways these specific instructions suggest ways "to worship God acceptably" (cf. 12:28). The Epilogue also contains the writer's personal comments to his readers and his farewell to them.

13:1-6. The first section of the Epilogue contains moral directions for the readers. Obeying these would inculcate personal kindness to **brothers** (v. 1), **strangers** (v. 2), and **prisoners** (v. 3). The writer then called for sexual purity in which **marriage** is held in high regard (v. 4). The readers were also to avoid monetary greed and to **be content with what** they **have** (v. 5; cf. Luke 12:15; Phil. 4:11; 1 Tim. 6:6-10). Even if they had little on the material level, they had the Lord (Heb. 13:5) and His help (v. 6).

13:7-8. Religious directions follow the moral ones and this segment of the

Epilogue extends through verse 17. The call, **Remember your leaders,** perhaps referred to former leaders who had passed away. The **outcome of their way of life** could be contemplated with good effect and the readers were to **imitate their faith.** Those leaders were gone, but **Jesus Christ** of whom they spoke remains continuously **the same.**

13:9. That is why new doctrines which conflict with the unchanging message about Jesus Christ should be rejected. The author's reference here to **all kinds of strange teachings** does not sound at all like a reference to normative Judaism but as if the readers were confronting a peculiar, sectarian variation of that religion (cf. comments under "Background and Setting" in the Heb. *Introduction*).

13:10-14. If those who hawked "strange teachings" tended to idealize the wilderness experience and the tabernacle, the writer's words now make a special point. A Christian has a special **altar** (probably a figure of speech for the sacrifice of Christ) from which he derives spiritual sustenance. **Those who minister at the tabernacle** were not entitled to partake of that kind of spiritual food. If some people preferred a desert way of life and considered themselves "servants" of the ancient tabernacle they were, the writer pointed out, debarred from Christian privileges. Under the old institution the **blood** from sacrifices made on the Day of Atonement was brought **into the most holy place, but the bodies** were **burned outside the camp** (v. 11), a location deemed unholy in the years of the wilderness sojourn. But **Jesus also suffered outside the city gate** (i.e., outside Jerusalem), but the effect of His sacrifice was **to make the people holy.** Far from association with Him being unholy, as some unbelieving Jews regarded it, the readers were in fact "holy" (or sanctified; cf. 2:11; 10:10, 14) and should not hesitate to share in **the disgrace He bore** (cf. 12:2) by abandoning **the camp** of Judaism and identifying with Him. If the readers actually were acquainted with sectarian encampments in their region this exhortation would have had special force. The readers' true home was no camp or city that then existed, but **the city that is to come** (cf. 11:10, 16; 12:22).

13:15-16. No blood sacrifices were needed in the light of Jesus' death, but to **offer . . . praise** and **to do good and to share with others** were indeed **sacrifices** that **God** desired (cf. 10:25).

13:17. If former **leaders** were to be remembered and their teachings retained (vv. 7-8), present ones were to be obeyed. Their responsibility before God was to be recognized and their shepherding tasks should not be complicated by disobedience. (**So that their work will be a joy** possibly should be, "so their accounting [to God for you] may be with joy.")

13:18-19. With that same sense of spiritual humility that led him to use "we" in most of his warning sections, the writer requested the prayers of his readers, and **particularly** that he might **be restored to them soon.** His interest in them was personal, and he was eager to see them.

13:20-21. In a lovely benediction which captures a number of the major themes of the epistle (e.g., **peace, blood, covenant,** Resurrection, **Shepherd, equip**), the writer expressed confidence in **our Lord Jesus** as the **Great Shepherd** of New-Covenant people, through whom God was able to effect His will (equip is *katartisai,* "to prepare, make ready for use"; cf. Eph. 4:12) in the readers and in himself. This indeed is what he prayed for his readers.

13:22-25. Urging once again that his readers **bear with** his **word of exhortation,** he expressed the hope that he and **Timothy** would soon **see** them. After giving them greetings, he committed them to God's **grace.**

BIBLIOGRAPHY

Bruce, F. F. *The Epistle to the Hebrews: The English Text with Introduction, Exposition and Notes.* Grand Rapids: Wm. B. Eerdmans Publishing Co., 1964.

Griffith Thomas, W.H. *Hebrews: A Devotional Commentary.* Grand Rapids: Wm. B. Eerdmans Publishing Co., n.d.

Héring, Jean. *The Epistle to the Hebrews.* Translated by A.W. Heathcote and P.J. Allcock. London: Epworth Press, 1970.

Hewitt, Thomas. *The Epistle to the Hebrews: An Introduction and Commentary.* The

Tyndale New Testament Commentaries. Grand Rapids: Wm. B. Eerdmans Publishing Co., 1961.

Hughes, Philip Edgcumbe. *A Commentary on the Epistle to the Hebrews.* Grand Rapids: Wm. B. Eerdmans Publishing Co., 1977.

Kent, Homer A., Jr. *The Epistle to the Hebrews: A Commentary.* Grand Rapids: Baker Book House, 1972.

Montefiore, Hugh. *A Commentary on the Epistle to the Hebrews.* London: Adam & Charles Black, 1964.

Newell, William R. *Hebrews Verse by Verse.* Chicago: Moody Press, 1947.

Pfeiffer, Charles F. *The Epistle to the Hebrews.* Everyman's Bible Commentary. Chicago: Moody Press, 1968.

Westcott, Brooke Foss. *The Epistle to the Hebrews: The Greek Text with Notes and Essays.* London: Macmillan & Co., 1892. Reprint. Grand Rapids: Wm. B. Eerdmans Publishing Co., 1974.

Wiersbe, Warren W. *Be Confident.* Wheaton, Ill.: Scripture Press Publications, Victor Books, 1982.

JAMES

J. Ronald Blue

INTRODUCTION

Few books of the Bible have been more maligned than the little Book of James. Controversy has waged over its authorship, its date, its recipients, its canonicity, and its unity.

It is well known that Martin Luther had problems with this book. He called it a "right strawy epistle." But it is only "strawy" to the degree it is "sticky." There are enough needles in this haystack to prick the conscience of every dull, defeated, and degenerate Christian in the world. Here is a "right stirring epistle" designed to exhort and encourage, to challenge and convict, to rebuke and revive, to describe practical holiness and drive believers toward the goal of a faith that works. James is severely ethical and refreshingly practical.

Considered one of the General Epistles, James, like the epistles of Peter, John, and Jude, is an encyclical addressed not to individual churches or persons but to a larger sphere of believers. The teaching in these general letters complements the doctrine of Paul. Paul emphasized faith; James stressed conduct; Peter, hope; John, love; and Jude, purity.

Authorship. The human author of this epistle is not easily identified. The New Testament mentions at least four men named James: (1) the son of Zebedee and brother of John (Mark 1:19), (2) the son of Alphaeus (Mark 3:18), (3) the father of Judas (not Iscariot; Luke 6:16), and (4) the half brother of the Lord (Gal. 1:19). Which one wrote the epistle?

James, the son of Zebedee, could not be the author since he suffered martyrdom under Herod Agrippa I before this epistle was written (Acts 12:2).

It is unlikely that the little-known son of Alphaeus was the author though some, especially Roman Catholics, equate

the son of Alphaeus with the Lord's brother. They claim that James was really Jesus' cousin through Mary of Cleopas (Alphaeus), the Virgin Mary's sister. This contention, however, violates a literal interpretation of "brother" and is clearly an attempt to support the invention of the perpetual virginity of Mary. It seems clear from Scripture that children were born to Joseph and Mary after the virgin birth of the Lord Jesus Christ. Jesus is called "her firstborn" (Luke 2:7), implying that others were born thereafter. The Scriptures state that Joseph had no union with Mary, that is, no normal physical relationship, "until" (*heōs*) after the birth of Jesus (Matt. 1:25). Repeated references are made to the Lord's half brothers and half sisters and four of His brothers are named: James, Joseph, Simon, and Judas (Matt. 13:55).

James, the father of Judas (not Iscariot) did not figure as an important person in the early church. He could hardly be the author of this epistle.

It seems clear therefore that the author is James, the half brother of the Lord, who became the recognized leader in the Jerusalem church. This conclusion is supported by the authoritative tone of the letter and by the marked similarities in Greek between this epistle and the speech by James recorded in Acts 15.

Though James was reared in the same home with the Lord Jesus, he apparently did not become a believer until after Christ's resurrection. John wrote, "For even His own brothers did not believe in Him" (John 7:5).

James' encounter with the risen Lord may have brought him to saving faith. Christ "appeared to James, then to all the apostles" (1 Cor. 15:7). Paul later listed James, Peter, and John as "those reputed to be pillars" of the church (Gal. 2:9).

The strongest evidence for the authorship of the Epistle of James clearly favors the half brother of Christ. Furthermore, Origen, Eusebius, Cyril of Jerusalem, Athanasius, Augustine, and many other early writers support this view.

Date. The date of the epistle is related to its authorship. Some deny that James wrote this letter because of its excellent Greek. They place the writing between A.D. 80 and 150. This is hardly justified. James was obviously a gifted Galilean, fluent in both Aramaic and Greek.

Flavius Josephus, first-century historian, records that James was martyred in A.D. 62, so the epistle must have been written prior to that date. Since no mention is made of the Jerusalem Council (A.D. 49) in which James took so active a role, it is likely that the letter was written between A.D. 45 and 48.

James is probably the earliest of the writings of the New Testament and therefore can hardly be seen as a polemic against Paul's letter to the Romans, which was written later. Romans, however, is not a refutation of James. It is apparent from Paul's relationship with James (Acts 15:13; 21:18) and his recognition of James (Gal. 1:19; 2:9, 12) that Paul held James in high respect. Together Paul and James give the full dimension of faith. Paul wrote about inner saving faith from God's perspective. James wrote about outward serving faith from man's perspective. The true seed of saving faith is verified by the tangible fruit of serving faith. James' point is that biblical faith works.

Recipients. Clearly addressed to "the 12 tribes scattered among the nations" (James 1:1), this letter has a marked Jewish flavor. The book has the substance and authority of the Prophets and the style and beauty of the Psalms. He refers to "firstfruits" (1:18; cf. Lev. 23:10), the synagogue or "meeting" (James 2:2), "our ancestor Abraham" (2:21), Gehenna or "hell" (3:6), "the Lord Almighty" (5:4; cf. Gen. 17:1), and to the early and latter or "fall and spring rains" (James 5:7; cf. Deut. 11:14). Though some suggest that the "12 tribes" may be taken metaphorically as the Gentile church scattered throughout the Roman Empire, it is far more logical to take the statement in its normal sense. The letter is definitely to a Jewish constituency. Though the letter demonstrates careful Greek diction, it is nonetheless filled with extensive Hebrew symbolism.

It is likely that Peter wrote to the Jewish Christians scattered to the West (cf. 1 Peter 1:1) and that James addressed the Jewish Christians scattered to the East, in Babylon and Mesopotamia.

Canonicity. It is interesting to note that James was omitted from some of the early versions and collections of sacred books. The earliest known collection, the Muratorian fragment of the second century, does not include Hebrews, James, and the epistles of Peter. It was not until the fourth and fifth centuries that James appears to be consistently included in the canon. It appears that while the churches of Rome and Carthage doubted the canonicity of James, it was nonetheless in use from an early date by the churches of Jerusalem and Alexandria and is included in the collections of scriptural books in Asia Minor. The reason is rather obvious. Written at Jerusalem and addressed to the Jews of the Eastern dispersion, those of the West were not so ready to accept the letter as Scripture. It is clear, however, that God not only superintended the writing of Scripture but its acceptance and authority as well.

Style. The Book of James is as much a lecture as it is a letter. Though it opens with the customary salutation of an epistle, it lacks personal references common in a letter and it has no concluding benediction.

This so-called "epistle" was obviously prepared for public reading as a sermon to the congregations addressed. The tone is clearly authoritative but not autocratic. James included 54 imperatives in his 108 verses—an average of one call for action in every other verse!

James' style is both energetic and vivid, conveying profound concepts with crisp, well-chosen words. The sentences are short, simple, and direct. He used many metaphors and similes with a touch of poetic imagination. In fact, the Book of James probably has more figures of speech, analogies, and imagery from nature (see the chart) than all Paul's epistles together. Exhortations, rhetorical questions, and illustrations from everyday life give spice to this little book.

A striking literary technique employed by James is the practice of linking together clauses and sentences by the repetition of a leading word or one of its cognates. For example, "perseverance" (1:3) and "perseverance" (v. 4); "not lacking anything" (v. 4) and "if any of you lacks" (v. 5); "he should ask" (v. 5) and "when he asks" (v. 6); "he must . . . not doubt" (v. 6) and "he who doubts" (v. 6). (For others see W. Graham Scroggie, *Know Your Bible*, 2 vols. London: Pickering & Inglis, n.d., 2:293.)

In addition to his unique and innovative style, James furnishes an unusual number of references or parallels to other writings. He makes reference to Abraham, Rahab, Job, Elijah, to the Law and the Ten Commandments, and includes allusions to passages in 21 Old Testament books: Genesis through Deuteronomy,

Joshua, 1 Kings, Psalms, Proverbs, Ecclesiastes, Isaiah, Jeremiah, Ezekiel, Daniel, and 7 of the 12 Minor Prophets.

James' teaching strongly resembles that of John the Baptist (e.g., cf. James 1:22, 27 with Matt. 3:8; James 2:15-16 with Luke 3:11; James 2:19-20 with Matt. 3:9; James 5:1-6 with Matt. 3:10-12). Probably James, like Peter, John, and Andrew, had heard John the Baptist preach. Amazing parallelisms exist between James' letter and the Sermon on the Mount in Matthew 5–7 (see the chart on the next p.). James did not actually quote the Lord's words, but he obviously had internalized His teachings and reproduced them with spiritual depth.

In its expressive abruptness and eloquent austerity, James' epistle stands as a literary masterpiece. This book is

---

References to Nature in the Book of James

1:6	"wave of the sea"
1:6	"tossed by the wind"
1:10	"wild flower"
1:11	"sun . . . with scorching heat"
1:11	"the plant . . . blossom falls"
1:17	"the heavenly lights"
1:17	"shifting shadows"
1:18	"firstfruits"
3:3	"bits into the mouths of horses"
3:4	"ships . . . driven by strong winds"
3:5	"a great forest is set on fire by a small spark"
3:6	"a fire"
3:7	"animals, birds, reptiles, and creatures of the sea"
3:8	"deadly poison"
3:11	"fresh water and salt water"
3:12	"can a fig tree bear olives, or a grapevine bear figs?"
3:18	"sow in peace [and] raise a harvest of righteousness"
4:14	"you are a mist"
5:2	"moths have eaten your clothes"
5:3	"gold and silver are corroded"
5:4	"workmen who mowed your fields"
5:4	"the cries of the harvesters"
5:5	"fattened yourselves in the day of slaughter"
5:7	"the farmer waits for the . . . crop"
5:7	"how patient he is for the fall and spring rains"
5:14	"anoint him with oil"
5:17	"prayed . . . that it would not rain"
5:17	"it did not rain on the land"
5:18	"the heavens gave rain"
5:18	"the earth produced its crops"

James' References to Jesus' Sermon on the Mount

James	Sermon on the Mount
1:2	Matthew 5:10-12
1:4	5:48
1:5; 5:15	7:7-12
1:9	5:3
1:20	5:22
2:13	5:7; 6:14-15
2:14-16	7:21-23
3:17-18	5:9
4:4	6:24
4:10	5:3-5
4:11	7:1-2
5:2	6:19
5:10	5:12
5:12	5:33-37

both picturesque and passionate. It combines the rhythmic beauty of Greek with the stern intensity of Hebrew. This letter is beautiful in its expression and bombastic in its impression.

Unity. The alleged lack of unity in James has been a prevalent complaint. Some contend the book bears a loose format like that of Hebrew wisdom literature of the type found in Proverbs. One commentator contends that there is "no discernible plan in the epistle" (C. Leslie Mitton, *The Epistle of James*, p. 235). Another argues that what James wrote "is not so much a reasoned argument as a series of sententious sayings clustered round certain recurring themes" (Frank E. Gaebelein, *The Practical Epistle of James*, p. 14). "Lack of continuity of thought" (Martin Dibelius, *A Commentary on the Epistle of James*, Philadelphia: Fortress Press, 1976, p. 1); "a series of loosely connected paragraphs" (Clayton K. Harrop, *The Letter of James*, p. 14); and "altogether informal and unsystematic" (E.H. Plumptre, *The General Epistle of St. James*, p. 43) are other expressions of commentators' frustrations. However, there is little need for confusion. The epistle demonstrates a marked unity and a clear goal.

The purpose of this potent letter is to exhort the early believers to Christian maturity and holiness of life. This letter deals more with the practice of the Christian faith than with its precepts. James told his readers how to achieve spiritual maturity through a confident stand, compassionate service, careful speech, contrite submission, and concerned sharing. He dealt with every area of a Christian's life: what he is, what he does, what he says, what he feels, and what he has.

With his somewhat stern teaching on practical holiness, James showed how Christian faith and Christian love should be expressed in a variety of actual situations. The seemingly unrelated parts of the book can be harmonized in light of this unified theme. The pearls are not rolling around in some box; they are carefully strung to produce a necklace of priceless beauty.

OUTLINE

I. Stand with Confidence (chap. 1)
   A. Salutation and greeting (1:1)
   B. Rejoice in diverse trials (1:2-12)
      1. Attitude in trials (1:2)
      2. Advantage of trials (1:3-4)
      3. Assistance for trials (1:5-12)
   C. Resist in deadly temptation (1:13-18)
      1. Source of temptation (1:13-14)
      2. Steps in temptation (1:15-16)

COMMENTARY

I. Stand with Confidence (chap. 1)

A. Salutation and greeting (1:1)

1:1. The letter begins with a conventional opening: the name of the writer, the people to whom the letter is addressed, and a word of greeting. James was content with a simple introduction.

The writer introduced himself modestly. He did not indicate his status in the church or that he was the Lord's brother. The lack of title suggests that he was well known and had the authority to send a letter of this kind.

James was actually Jacob (*Iakōbos*). It is not certain why the English translators chose "James" rather than "Jacob." "James," "Jake," and "Jacob" all come from the same root. Bible translations in other languages tend to utilize the transliterated name from the actual Hebrew "Jacob" (*ya'ăqōb*). Could it be that King James desired to see his name in the English translation he authorized?

James, or Jacob, described himself simply as **a servant of God and of the Lord Jesus Christ.** James considered himself a bond-slave (*doulos*). He was the property of God and of the One he could have called his "Brother," the Lord Jesus Christ. Obviously James recognized the deity of Christ by placing Him coequal with God. Furthermore, James used His full name, "the Lord Jesus Christ." "Jesus" means "Savior" and "Christ" is the Greek for "Messiah," the "Anointed." The eternal "Lord" became the Savior, "Jesus," and rose again as everlasting Sovereign, "Christ." The Lord of lords is King of kings (1 Tim. 6:15; Rev. 17:14; 19:16).

The letter is addressed **to the 12 tribes scattered among the nations.** James was writing to the Jews dispersed from their homeland. The technical term "scattered" (*diaspora*) occurs in only two other places in the New Testament (John 7:35; 1 Peter 1:1). It refers to the Jews who were scattered among the Gentiles as their ancestors had been in the days of the Captivity. Though the 12 tribes of Israel are scattered, they are never lost. They are again listed at the close of biblical history in the Book of Revelation: Judah, Reuben, Gad, Asher, Naphtali, Manasseh, Simeon, Levi, Issachar, Zebulun, Joseph, and Benjamin (Rev. 7:5-8; cf. 21:12).

The idiom, **Greetings,** common in thousands of ancient papyri letters, does not stand alone in any other New Testament letter. This is the Greek salutation much like the English "Hello" or "Welcome." (See comments on 2 John 10-11.) It is interesting that James did not add the Jewish salutation "Peace" (*šālôm*). Paul usually included both the Greek and Hebrew greetings, which are translated "grace and peace." James undoubtedly sought to maintain a crisp style and the simple elegance of good Greek even though he wrote to fellow Jews. Furthermore, the play on words between "greetings" (*chairein*) in James 1:1 and "joy" (*charan*) in verse 2 is thus more evident.

In order to attain Christian maturity and holy conduct it is essential to have a firm foundation. The believer must be able to stand with confidence. He dare not be pushed down by trials. He must not be pulled over by temptation. "Push, pull—stick, stick" must be his motto. How can such stamina be achieved? A believer can stand by pursuing, perceiving, and practicing the Word of God. Trials from without and temptations from within are no match for a Christian who stands in the truth from above.

B. Rejoice in diverse trials (1:2-12)

All too often trials prompt groanings and complaints. This kind of response does not contribute to Christian maturity. It only makes matters worse. Trials are not to be seen as tribulations but testings. A test is given to see if a student can pass, not pass out. James gave sound advice on how to score high on every test. One who brings the right attitude to the trial, who understands the advantage of the trial, and who knows where to obtain assistance in the trial will certainly end up on God's honor roll.

1. ATTITUDE IN TRIALS (1:2)

1:2. To persecuted Jewish believers scattered among pagan peoples, James gave the surprising advice, **Consider it pure joy, my brothers, whenever you face trials of many kinds.** Trials should be faced with an attitude of joy. Trials should not be seen as a punishment, a curse, or a calamity but something that must prompt rejoicing. Furthermore they should produce "pure joy" (lit., "all joy"; i.e., joy that is full or unmixed), not just "some joy" coupled with much grief.

Though James' command was direct and forceful, he did not preach at his audience. He identified with them. He addressed them warmly as "my brothers." This mode of address is characteristic of the epistle. He used this familiar form no less than 15 times. James' direct commands are coupled with deep compassion.

It is important to note that James did *not* say that a believer should be joyous *for* the trials but *in* the trials. The verb translated "face" might more literally be expressed as "fall into," *peripesēte*, much as the poor man "fell among robbers" (Luke 10:30). The "trials of many kinds" (*peirasmois . . . poikilois*) were also referred to by Peter, who used the same Greek words, though in reverse order (1 Peter 1:6). When surrounded by these trials, one should respond with joy. Most people count it all joy when they *escape* trials. James said to count it all joy in the midst of trials (cf. 1 Peter 1:6, 8).

It is clear that the reference here is to external trials, or tests of stamina (*peirasmois*) whereas later in the same chapter (James 1:13) the verb form (*peirazomai*) of that noun is used to speak of inner temptations, or solicitations to sin.

Obviously the question arises: How can a person find joy in trials?

2. ADVANTAGE OF TRIALS (1:3-4)

1:3. Christians can face trials with joy because there are rich advantages from these testings. Trials, rightly taken, produce the sterling quality of endurance.

This is no new revelation. It is a simple reminder. James wrote, **because you know,** literally "knowing through experience" (*ginōskontes*). Everyone has experienced both the pain of problems and the ensuing profit of persistence. There is no gain in endurance without some investment in trials.

It is the true part or approved portion of faith that produces perseverance. **The testing** refers more to "approval" than to "proving." The word (*dokimion*) appears only here and in 1 Peter 1:7. **Faith** is like gold; it stands in the test of fire. Without this approved standard of faith, trials would not yield perseverance. There would only be ashes. True faith, like pure gold, endures, no matter how hot the fire. True faith therefore **develops,** or more literally "works" (*katergazetai*), **perseverance** or staying power. The noun "perseverance" (*hypomonēn;* cf. the verbal form in James 1:12) means steadfastness or endurance in the face of difficulties (cf. 5:11).

1:4. Perseverance is only the beginning of benefits. There are more advantages to trials. **Perseverance must finish its work.** Just as tested and true faith works to produce perseverance, so perseverance must be allowed to continue its perfect or finished work to produce the ultimate by-products of maturity and spiritual fulfillment. This, of course, is the lofty goal that serves as this epistle's unifying theme. James' main point was to show how to achieve spiritual maturity.

Two words describe the goal: **mature and complete.** "Mature" (*teleioi*), often translated "perfect" or "finished," is coupled with "complete" (*holoklēroi,* from *holos,* "whole," and *klēros,* "part") to give the idea of perfected all over or fully developed in every part.

Trials can be faced with joy because, infused with faith, perseverance results, and if perseverance goes full-term it will develop a thoroughly mature Christian who lacks nothing. He will indeed be all God wants him to be.

James' argument may seem logical, but it is still difficult to see how trials can be welcomed with an attitude of joy. Where does one turn for help to understand this paradox?

3. ASSISTANCE FOR TRIALS (1:5-12)

1:5. To those who feel confused and frustrated by the high goal of "not lacking anything," James wrote, **If any of you lacks wisdom, he should ask God.** Assistance is readily available from "the giving God" (*tou didontos theou*). To those who lack wisdom, this valuable resource is available for the asking. James assumed his readers would feel the need

for wisdom (*sophias*), not just knowledge. God will not only provide wisdom, but will do so generously, not grudgingly.

1:6-8. However, God's provision has some prerequisites. To receive God's wisdom in trials, the believer must be wise in asking. First, he must ask in faith. **He must believe and not doubt** (*diakrinomenos,* the word for "doubt," suggests vacillating). He dare not come to God **like a wave of the sea, blown** [horizontally] **and tossed** [vertically] **by the wind.** God is not pleased with **a double-minded** (lit., "two-souled," *dipsychos;* cf. 4:8) **man** who is **unstable in all he does,** like an unsteady, staggering drunk. The answer from God depends on assurance in God.

1:9-11. Furthermore one who asks for wisdom needs to evidence hope. Whatever his social or economic position, the believer must see eternal advantages. **The brother in humble circumstances** can be glad in his **high** standing spiritually, and **the one who is rich** can be glad for his human frailty (knowing that he has "eternal glory" in Christ, 2 Cor. 4:17). Social prominence passes away, wealth withers away **like a wild flower** in the hot **sun,** and fame will **fade.** Hope in the eternal is evidence of believing faith.

1:12. Finally, the one who asks for wisdom must be steadfast and infused with love. God blesses someone **who perseveres under trial.** In this verse James returned to the theme with which he opened this passage in verses 2-3; both refer to "trials," "testing," and "perseverance." The Christian who steadfastly endures (*hypomenei*) trials (*peirasmon*) and **has stood the test** (*dokimos genomenos;* cf. *dokimion* in v. 3) . . . **will receive the crown of life.** This "crown" consists of life, that is, the crown *is* life (cf. Rev. 2:10). "The life which is promised is probably life here and now, life in its fullness, life in its completeness" (cf. James 1:4) (Curtis Vaughan, *James: Bible Study Commentary,* p. 28). (Other crowns are referred to in 1 Thes. 2:19; 2 Tim. 4:8; 1 Peter 5:4.) **God** promises such life **to those who love Him.** Love for God enables believers who undergo trials to rest confidently in Him. Their steadfastness reveals their love. (Some, however, say the crown refers not to full life now but to eternal life, for all true believers do in fact love God; 1 John 4:8.) Asking for wisdom with faith (James 1:6-8), hope (vv. 9-11), and love (v. 12) brings not only the blessing of wisdom but also the blessing of winning.

To have the right attitude in trials, one must see the advantage of trials, but if it is difficult to see the advantages, one can ask for aid and, if one asks correctly, God will give him the right attitude in trials. He can rejoice in trials (v. 2) and be **blessed** (v. 12) by enduring them.

C. Resist in deadly temptation (1:13-18)

Believers are in danger of falling before the attacks and pressures of trials. But they are also subject to falling before the attractions and pleasures of temptation. Just as a wrong reaction to testing will obstruct spiritual growth and maturity, so will a wrong response to temptation. James outlined the source of temptation, the steps in temptation, and the solution for temptation.

1. SOURCE OF TEMPTATION (1:13-14)

1:13. James offered a sharp rebuke to those who find an easy excuse for their sinning. To free themselves from responsibility they say, "I am tempted by God," or "from God" (apo theou), denoting the origin, not merely the agency. James made it abundantly clear **God cannot be tempted.** There is nothing in God to which evil can make an appeal. He is literally "untemptable" (apeirastos; cf. comments on Heb. 4:15). Furthermore, He tempts no one. God often tests, but He never tempts.

1:14. The source of temptation is from within a person; it is **his own evil desire,** lust, or inner craving. **He is dragged away and enticed.** This inner craving draws a person out (exelkomenos) like a fish drawn from its hiding place, and then entices him (deleazomenos, from the verb deleazō "to bait, to catch a fish with bait, or hunt with snares"). So a person both builds and baits his own trap.

2. STEPS IN TEMPTATION (1:15-16)

1:15-16. The biological imagery is vivid. The lust or **desire** conceives and from this conception **sin** is born. The unmentioned father is most certainly Satan. The grotesque child, **sin,** then

matures and produces its own offspring, death. The steps are all too clear: unchecked lust yields sin, and unconfessed sin brings death. How strange that sin **gives birth to death.** It may seem strange, but James warned his dear brothers and sisters who were to read this "genealogy" not to be **deceived** or led astray. Just as a right response to trials can result in growth to full spiritual maturity, so a wrong response to lust will result in decline to abject spiritual poverty and ultimately to death itself.

3. SOLUTION FOR TEMPTATION (1:17-18)

1:17-18. In stark contrast with the morbid scene of death that descends from unbridled lust is the bright scene of new life that emanates from **the Word of truth** (v. 18; cf. Eph. 1:13; Col. 1:5). The father of darkness—Satan (Acts 26:18; Col. 1:13)—generates the offspring of sin and death. **The Father of the heavenly lights** (i.e., God, who created the starry universe) gives salvation and life and is unchanging. Shadows from the sun shift, but not the One who made the sun! The words, **every good and perfect gift is from above,** have a poetic cadence in Greek. They are literally, "every good act of giving (dosis) and every perfect gift (dōrēma) is from above."

The solution for temptation is to be found in a close relationship with the Father and a constant response to His Word. One must rest in the unchangeable Lord of light and rely on His life-giving "Word of truth" (cf. Eph. 1:13; Col. 1:5; 2 Tim. 2:15).

There is no reason why one of God's chosen **firstfruits,** or regenerated believers, has to yield to temptation. He must learn to resist its deadly force, or he can never grow into the spiritual maturity God desires of His children of light (Eph. 5:8; 1 Thes. 5:5).

D. Rest in divine truth (1:19-27)

Ultimately the key both to responding to trials and resisting temptation is to be found in one's reaction to God's Word. Receptivity to the Word, responsiveness to the Word, and resignation to the Word are essential to spiritual growth. One must accept God's Word, act on it, and abide by it.

1. RECEPTIVITY TO THE WORD (1:19-21)

1:19-20. Again James identified with his audience, **My dear brothers,** and then made it clear that what was to follow was of great importance: **take note of this,** or "know this" (*iste*). A threefold injunction follows: let **everyone . . . be quick to listen, slow to speak, and slow to become angry.** In an argument, of course, the one who is listening rather than lambasting is the one who is slow to anger (cf. 3:1-12). Anger fails to yield **the righteous life that God desires,** the goal to which this epistle is committed.

1:21. Consequently it is essential to put away, or remove, **all moral filth** (*ryparian,* used only here in the NT; cf. *rypara,* "shabby," in 2:2) and all the abundance of **evil,** and **humbly** (lit., "in meekness") receive the implanted **Word.** "Planted" (*emphyton,* used only here in the NT) contrasts with grafted. The Word is to be ingrown or inborn, rooted in the fertile soil of the soul. It is that Word of God **which can save.**

2. RESPONSIVENESS TO THE WORD (1:22-25)

1:22. It is not sufficient, however, to receive the Word; one must respond to it in active obedience. The command is clear, **Do not merely listen to the Word. . . . Do what it says.** One must "become," or "keep on becoming" (*ginesthe*), a doer of the Word and not just a hearer. The growing numbers of sermon-sippers who flit from one doctrinal dessert to another like helpless hummingbirds are deceiving themselves. "Deceiving" is from a verb used in the New Testament only here and in Colossians 2:4. *Paralogizomai* means "to cheat or deceive by false reasoning." The deception comes from thinking they have done all that is necessary when actually listening to the Word is only the beginning. A fitting illustration of the "sit, soak, and sour" crowd follows.

1:23-24. The one **who listens** and does nothing **is like a man who** glances at **his face in a mirror and** then **forgets what he** saw. It is interesting that James cited a man (*andri*) in this illustration. A woman would probably not give just a cursory glance, and if she saw a flaw she would probably do what she could to cover it or correct it. Not so this man who sees the "face of his birth" (*prosōpon tēs geneseōs*) and then forgets about it.

1:25. To look into the mirror of the Word of God involves an obligation. One must look **intently into the perfect Law that gives freedom.** The intent and sustained look with a ready response is the key to spiritual strength and continued maturity. The word for "looks intently into" (*parakypsas*) literally means "to stoop down" in order to have a good close look.

The "Law that gives freedom" seems like a paradox. Law seems to imply restraint and therefore a lack of freedom. Not so with God's Law. His perfect Law provides true freedom. "Hold to My teaching," Christ said, "then you will know the truth, and the truth will set you free" (John 8:31-32). One who does what God decrees will find full liberty and **will be blessed in what he does.**

3. RESIGNATION TO THE WORD (1:26-27)

Receptivity to the Word and responsiveness to its revelation must be coupled with a new approach to life. One must be resigned to continued obedience and perpetual practice.

1:26. One who is truly **religious** will demonstrate it by controlled speech. The word "religious" (*thrēskos*) refers to external observances. The outward ritualistic practices which a person may think are commendable are considered to be **worthless** (*mataios,* "futile, fruitless, useless") if there is no parallel control, or **tight rein on** the **tongue,** a theme elaborated more fully in 3:1-12. Such a person **deceives himself** (*apatōn kardian heautou,* lit., "misleads or seduces his own heart"; cf. a different word for deceive in 1:22).

1:27. A clean and undefiled religion is one in which one's conduct and character are disciplined in accordance with God's Word. The Greek word *thrēskeia* (**religion**) appears only four times in the New Testament and two of those occurrences are here (cf. Col. 2:18; Acts 26:5). It is apparent that God's emphasis is not on religious ritual but on right living.

James outlined what **God** the **Father** (cf. "Father" in James 1:17) stresses: **look after orphans and widows**—referring to one's conduct, and **keep oneself from being polluted**—referring to one's character. "From being polluted" translates one word *aspilon,* "spotless" (cf. 1 Tim. 6:14; 1 Peter 1:19; 2 Peter 3:14), in contrast with moral filth (James 1:21). A believer with God-pleasing "religion" helps others in need—and thus is **faultless** (lit., "pure, undefiled"), and keeps himself **pure** (lit., "clean"). This is not a definition of religion but rather a contrast to mere acts of worship and ritualistic observances that are commonly called "religion." Again, the goal is a mature Christian walk and practical holiness. What does it take to achieve that goal? The first step is to stand with confidence. Trials or temptations will not topple one who is anchored in God's truth and is applying that truth to his life.

II. Serve with Compassion (chap. 2)

One who is properly related to the Bible is also properly related to the body of Christ. He who stands with confidence serves with compassion. James just made it clear that true religion finds an outlet in service, a service which demands that a believer learn to accept others without prejudice and to assist others without presumption.

A. Accept others (2:1-13)

James became increasingly specific and direct in his admonitions and instructions. He was obviously displeased with the inconsistencies among the brethren. He attacked the attitudes these believers displayed toward others and then complained of their failures to act as they should. He first condemned the attitude of favoritism and gave suggestions on how to combat this obstacle to spiritual maturity. One must learn to accept others, whatever their status or class. He must show courtesy to all, compassion for all, and consistency to all. Equity, love, and fidelity are the vital ingredients.

1. COURTESY TO ALL (2:1-4)

2:1. A transition to a new consideration is evident by James' use of **my brothers.** By "brothers" he meant fellow **believers in our glorious Lord Jesus Christ.** The NIV has done well in showing that it is the faith *in* Christ, not the faith *of* Christ, that is here considered, and in taking the word "glorious" (*doxēs*) in apposition to, and therefore descriptive of, Christ. The key command is likewise clear: **don't show favoritism.** God shows no favoritism (Rom. 2:11; Eph. 6:9; Col. 3:25); therefore neither should Christians.

James condemned prejudice and preferential treatment.

2:2-3. The issue addressed is then illustrated. The illustration's hypothetical nature, evident in the Greek "if clause," is shown with the word **suppose.** The specific situation is then presented. A **gold**-fingered and brilliantly clothed man comes **into** the **meeting** place, here designated as a synagogue which emphasizes the Jewish character of both the epistle and this scene. **A poor man** in dirty **clothes** also enters. The word **shabby** (*rypara*, "dirty" or "vile") is found only here and in Revelation 22:11. (Cf. the word *ryparian*, "moral filth," which James used in 1:21.) **Special attention** (lit., "to gaze upon") and preferential seating is given to the rich man, and standing room only or an inferior seat **on the floor** (lit., "under my footstool") is afforded the **poor man.**

2:4. The illustration is followed by a penetrating inquiry: **Have you not discriminated among yourselves?** The question in Greek assumes an affirmative answer. James' brethren must plead guilty not only to discriminatory divisions but also to assuming the role of **judges with evil thoughts** of partiality.

2. COMPASSION FOR ALL (2:5-9)

2:5-7. With the plea, **Listen, my dear brothers,** James went on to explain why their preferential judgment was wrong. He made his point through four questions, each of which anticipated an affirmative answer. First, **Has not God chosen those** who appear **poor** materially, but are **rich** spiritually, **to inherit** His promised **kingdom?** (cf. 1:9) Second, Are not **the rich** the ones who are consistently guilty of oppression, extortion, and slander (*blasphēmousin*, 2:7, lit., "blasphemy")? Third, **Are they not the ones who are dragging you into court?** Fourth, **Are they not the ones who** slander Jesus' **noble name?** Believers **belong to Him,** not to the rich exploiters. James' readers would have to agree with these contentions, and to recognize that insulting **the poor** and favoring the rich was wrong and totally unreasonable.

2:8-9. The alternatives are clear. Love is right. Favoritism is sin. James was optimistic; the "if-clause," **if you really keep the royal law,** was written in Greek in such a way that an obedient response was anticipated. The "royal law" was given in Leviticus 19:18 and affirmed by Christ (Matt. 22:39): **Love your neighbor as yourself.** The law is royal or regal (*basilikon*, from *basileus*, "king") because it is decreed by the King of kings, is fit for a king, and is considered the king of laws. The phrase reflects the Latin *lex regia* known throughout the Roman Empire. Obedience to this law, nonpreferential love, is the answer to the evident disobedience to God's **Law**, prejudicial **favoritism.**

3. CONSISTENCY IN ALL (2:10-13)

2:10-11. James was aware there would be some who would tend to dismiss their offense of prejudice as a trivial fault. They would hardly consider themselves as lawbreakers. James went on to make it clear that this was no small offense. **Whoever keeps the whole Law and yet stumbles at just one point is guilty of breaking all of it.** There are no special indulgences. Utilizing the extreme instances of **adultery** and **murder,** James showed the absurdity of inconsistent obedience.

2:12-13. Total obedience is the key. One must both habitually **speak and act** (Gr. pres. tense imper.) as those **to be judged by the Law.** God's Law, because of its wise constraints, brings true **freedom** (cf. 1:25). Disobedience to God's Law brings bondage; and to those who have **not been merciful,** God's **judgment** is **without mercy.** Just as love triumphs over prejudice, **mercy triumphs over judgment.** The verb "triumphs" or "exults over" (*katakauchatai*) appears only here, in 3:14, and in Romans 11:18.

God has ordained unalterable laws. Complete and consistent obedience is required if spiritual maturity is to be attained. The believer is commanded to accept his brother with courtesy, compassion, and consistency.

B. Assist others (2:14-26)

Just as the law of love gives no excuse for respect of persons, so the possession of faith gives no license to dispense with good works. A believer must not only demonstrate his love by ready acceptance of others, but he must also demonstrate his faith by responsible aid to others. James went on in his letter to emphasize the expression of true faith, to outline the evidence of true faith, and finally to cite examples of true faith.

1. EXPRESSION OF TRUE FAITH (2:14-17)

2:14. Another shift in the argument of the epistle can be seen by James' use of **my brothers.** He introduced this paragraph with a rhetorical question, **What good is it . . . if a man claims to have faith but has no deeds?** The emphasis is not on the true nature of faith but on the false claim of faith. It is the spurious boast of faith that James condemned. Such "faith" does no "good"; there is no "profit" (*ophelos*, used in the NT only here and in v. 16; 1 Cor. 15:32). It is worthless because it is all talk with no walk. It is only a habitual empty boast ("claims" is in the pres. tense). **Can such faith save him?** A negative answer is anticipated in the Greek. Merely claiming to have faith is not enough. Genuine faith is evidenced by works.

2:15-16. The rhetorical question is followed by a hypothetical but realistic illustration: **Suppose a brother or sister is without clothes and daily food.** (James frequently wrote about the poor: 1:9, 27; 2:2-6, 15.) For one in need of the basics of life, sentimental good wishes do little good, like the common Jewish farewell, **Go, I wish you well** (lit., "Go in peace," cf. Jud. 18:6; 1 Sam. 1:17; 2 Sam. 15:9; Mark 5:34; Luke 7:50). If nothing is done to fill the pressing need for warm clothes and satisfying food, **what good is it?** The same phrase that James used to introduce this paragraph (James 2:14) is repeated for emphasis.

2:17. The vain boast, **faith by itself,** or faith in and of itself with no evidence of **action, is dead.** Workless faith is worthless faith; it is unproductive, sterile, barren, dead! Great claims may be made about a corpse that is supposed to have come to life, but if it does not move, if there are no vital signs, no heartbeat, no perceptible pulse, it is still dead. The false claims are silenced by the evidence.

2. EVIDENCE OF TRUE FAITH (2:18-20)

2:18. This may be one of the most misunderstood sections of the entire epistle. **But someone will say, You have faith; I have deeds.** An imaginary respondent, "someone," was introduced.

He did not object to James' conclusion. He agreed that faith without works is dead. But he wrongly disparaged faith while stressing works (see comments on v. 19).

What follows, **Show me your faith without deeds, and I will show you my faith by what I do,** may be the continuation of the respondent's words. If so, they should be included within quotation marks. (If this were James' response to a contender's "I have deeds," James would have written, "Show me your *deeds* without *faith*.") Though recent translations do not include the second half of verse 18 in the quotation of the respondent (e.g., NEB, NIV, RSV), the NASB correctly considers this entire verse part of his remarks. The Greek, of course, does not include quotation marks, which accounts for the variations in English. It seems, however, that the respondent is throwing down the challenge, "Show me your faith apart from (*chōris*, 'without') works, and I will show you my faith by (*ek*, 'emerging from') my works" (author's trans.).

2:19. It may be well to include even verse 19 as part of the respondent's argument: **You believe that there is one God. Good! Even the demons believe that—and shudder.** If so, he may be a typical Gentile believer who attacked the creedal belief of monotheism accepted by all Jews. He was saying, to "believe" in one God may be good so far as it goes, but it does not go far enough. The demons do that. In fact not only do they believe (the same verb, *pisteuō*); they even "shudder," or "bristle up" (*phrissousin,* an onomatopoeic verb used only here in the NT). The "belief" in one God may not be "trust" in that God. Unless it is "trust," it is not true faith and will not be evidenced in good works.

In other words the respondent is saying, "Faith is not the key; what counts is works." Thus the respondent has gone too far. James did not say that works are *essential* to faith, or that faith is unimportant. His argument was that works are *evidence* of faith.

Other writers understand this passage to mean that James (v. 18b) challenged the "someone" to show his faith without deeds—the point being that it cannot be done! James, however, said that faith can be demonstrated (only) by what

one does (v. 18c). The demons' "belief" in God is inadequate. Such a so-called but unreal faith is obviously unaccompanied by deeds on their parts.

2:20. James did not launch into a lengthy refutation of the respondent. The apostle simply addressed him forcefully, **You foolish man,** and returned to his original argument **that faith without deeds is useless** (*argē,* "lazy, idle, negligent"). The adjective "foolish" (*kene*) is usually translated "vain," "empty," or "hollow" (cf. *mataios,* "worthless, fruitless, useless," in 1:26). Flimsy faith is dead; so are empty, faithless works. James' argument is not pro-works/anti-faith or pro-faith/anti-works. He has simply said that genuine faith is accompanied by good works. Spiritual works are the evidence, not the energizer, of sincere faith.

3. EXAMPLES OF TRUE FAITH (2:21-26)

As a final proof of his thesis, James gave two biblical examples: Abraham, the revered patriarch, and Rahab, the redeemed prostitute. He presented each example in the form of a question, anticipating the reader's ready agreement.

2:21. Was not our ancestor Abraham considered righteous for what he did when he offered his son Isaac on the altar? This question is often held to be directly opposed to Paul's statement that Abraham's faith, not his works, caused God to declare him righteous (Rom. 4:1-5). Paul, however, was arguing for the *priority* of faith. James argued for the *proof* of faith. Paul declared that Abraham had faith, and was therefore justified, or declared righteous (Gen. 15:6), prior to circumcision (Gen. 17:11; cf. Rom. 4:9). James explained that Abraham's faith was evident in his practice of Isaac's sacrifice (Gen. 22:12), and he was therefore justified, or declared righteous. Works serve as the barometer of justification, while faith is the basis for justification.

2:22-24. James emphasized the joint role of **faith and . . . actions . . . working together.** Faith is the force behind the deed. The deed is the finality of the faith. The verb translated **was made complete** (*eteleiōthē*) means to "carry to the end." Faith finds fulfillment in action. So it was with **Abraham.** James and Paul quoted the same passage—Genesis 15:6—to prove their points (cf. Rom. 4:3). Paul said that Abraham was **justified** by faith, and James said that Abraham was justified by faith evidenced **by what he did.**

2:25. In the same way (lit., "and likewise also"; *homoiōs de kai*) **was not even Rahab** declared **righteous for** her actions in welcoming **the spies** (*angelous*, "messengers") and helping them escape? (Josh. 2; 6)

2:26. The conclusion is most clear. **Faith** and **deeds** are as essential to each other as **the body** and **the spirit.** Apart from (*chōris*) the spirit, or the "breath" (*pneumatos*) of life, the body **is dead.** Apart from (*chōris*) the evidence of works, faith may be deemed **dead.** It is *not* the real thing. True faith continually contributes to spiritual growth and development.

Not only is a believer to stand confidently on God's Word even in the midst of trials and temptations (chap. 1), but also he must serve his brothers and sisters in Christ (chap. 2). He is to accept all members of God's family without favoritism (vv. 1-13) and to aid the family with a working faith (vv. 14-26). To gain spiritual maturity a believer must be what God wants him to be and do what God wants him to do.

III. Speak with Care (chap. 3)

Another measure of spiritual maturity is a believer's speech. James devoted a good portion of his letter to attacking a careless and corrupt tongue. He appealed, however, not only for controlled tongues (3:1-12) but also for controlled thoughts (3:13-17). The mouth is, after all, connected to the mind. Winsome speech demands a wise source. Both controlled talk and cultivated thought are necessary.

A. Control talk (3:1-12)

From his discourse on idle faith, James proceeded to discuss idle speech. The failure to bridle the tongue, mentioned earlier (1:26), is now expanded. As disturbing as those who have faith with no works are those Christians who substitute words for works. One's tongue should be controlled. Small though it is, the tongue is powerful and all too prone to perversion and pollution.

1. THE TONGUE IS POWERFUL (3:1-5)

3:1. Again addressing **my brothers,** a sign that a new topic is being considered,

James suggested moderation and restraint in the multiplication of **teachers.** Obviously too many of the new Jewish Christians aspired to teach and thereby carry some of the rank and admiration given to Rabbis. It is doubtful that the reference here is to official teachers of the apostolic or prophetic status. These are the unofficial teachers (*didaskaloi*) in the synagogue meetings of the church family where much latitude was given for even strangers to speak. Paul frequently used this courtesy given visitors. James' complaint was simply that too many believers were overly anxious to speak up and show off (cf. John 3:10; 9:40-41).

Teaching has to be done, but those who teach must understand their responsibility, as those **who teach will be judged more strictly.** A teacher's condemnation is greater because, having professed to have a clear knowledge of duty, he is all the more bound to obey it.

3:2. James did not point a finger at the offenders without including himself: **We all stumble in many ways.** Nothing seems to trip a believer more than a dangling tongue. If a believer **is never at fault** (lit., "stumbles not") **in what he says** (lit., "in word"), **he is a perfect,** fulfilled, mature, complete person (*teleios anēr*). He is **able** to "bridle" **his whole body.** Spiritual maturity requires a tamed tongue.

3:3-5. The tongue may be small but it is influential. Three illustrations make this point clear: the bit and the horse, the rudder and the ship, and the spark and the forest. James' use of imagery drawn from natural phenomena is similar to the Lord's. It is likewise characteristic of Jewish thought. The Greek used in this passage is both ancient and eloquent. James was both steeped in Jewish tradition and well-versed in Greek classics.

The argument is clear. Just as little **bits . . . turn** grown **horses,** small rudders guide large **ships,** and **a small spark** consumes an entire **forest,** so **the tongue is a small part of the body, but it makes great boasts.** The tongue is petite but powerful!

2. THE TONGUE IS PERVERSE (3:6-8)

3:6. The tongue is not only powerful; it is also perverse. It is small and influential but, worse by far, it can be satanic and infectious. **The tongue . . . is a**

fire (cf. Prov. 16:27; 26:18-22), **a world of evil.** The tongue sets itself up *(kathistatai)* among the members, or **parts** of one's anatomy, corrupting, spotting, or staining *(spilousa;* cf. *aspilon,* "spotless," in James 1:27) the whole **body** and inflaming **the whole course of . . . life** (lit., "the wheel of existence" or "wheel of birth," *ton trochon tēs geneseōs).* It is as though the tongue is at the center or hub of the wheel of nature and, like a fireworks display, the wheel is **set on fire** at the center. The more it burns, the faster it revolves until the whole wheel spins in a blaze, spitting fire in all directions. But the tongue is only the fuse; the source of the deadly fire is **hell** itself (lit., "Gehenna," a place in the Valley of Hinnom south of Jerusalem where human sacrifice had been offered [Jer. 7:31] and where continuous burning of rubbish made it a fit illustration of the lake of fire).

3:7. The tongue is not only like an uncontrolled fire. It is also like an untamed beast. Every kind, or all nature *(physis),* of wild beasts—**birds** of the air, **reptiles** on land, and **creatures of the sea**—all **are being tamed and have been tamed by man** (lit., "human nature," *physis;* thus "beastly nature" is tamed by "human nature"). But no human is able to tame the tongue!

3:8. No one **can tame the tongue** because **it is a restless evil,** an unruly, unsteady, staggering, reeling evil (like the "unstable" man of 1:8). Worse yet, the tongue is **full of deadly poison** (cf. Ps. 140:3). Like the poison of a serpent, the tongue is loaded with the venom of hate and death-dealing gossip.

3. THE TONGUE IS POLLUTED (3:9-12)

3:9-10. Similar to the forked tongue of a snake, man's uncontrolled **tongue** both emits **praise** and spews out curses. "Praise," or "saying a good word" *(eulogoumen)* of **our Lord and Father** (this is the only place where the NT uses this title of God) is polluted by a "curse," or "wishing evil" *(katarōmetha)* on **men . . . made in God's likeness** (cf. Gen. 1:27; 9:6; Col. 1:10). That both **praise and cursing** should **come** from **the same mouth** is incongruous. **My brothers, this should not be.**

3:11-12. Again James turned to the natural elements to illustrate his point. Anticipating a negative response, James asked, **Can both fresh** (lit., "sweet," *glyky)* **water and salt** (lit., "bitter," *pikron)* **water flow,** or "bubble up," **from the same spring? Can a fig tree bear olives, or a grapevine bear figs?** Of course not. **Neither** does **salt** *(halykon)* make **water** sweet *(glyky).* The point is clear: a believer's tongue should not be an instrument of inconsistency.

Small and influential, the tongue must be controlled; satanic and infectious, the tongue must be corralled; salty and inconsistent, the tongue must be cleansed.

B. Cultivate thought (3:13-18)

A key to right talk is right thought. The tongue is contained in a cage of teeth and lips, but it still escapes. It is not intelligence that keeps the lock on that cage; it is wisdom—a wisdom that is characterized by humility, grace, and peace.

1. WISDOM IS HUMBLE (3:13)

3:13. James asked the rhetorical question, **Who is wise and understanding among you?** "Wise" *(sophos;* cf. *sophias* in 1:5) describes one with moral insight and skill in the practical issues of life. "Understanding" *(epistēmōn)* refers to intellectual perception and scientific acumen.

Let him show it. Here is an original "show and tell." Wisdom is not measured by degrees but by deeds. It is not a matter of acquiring truth in lectures but of applying truth to life. The **good life** and **deeds** are best portrayed **in the humility** of **wisdom,** or "wise meekness" *(prautēti sophias).* The truly wise man is humble.

2. WISDOM IS GRACIOUS (3:14-16)

3:14. True wisdom makes no room for **bitter envy** ("zealous jealousy") or for **selfish ambition** ("factious rivalry," *erithian,* from *eritheuō,* "to spin wool," thus working for personal gain). This is nothing to glory about. To **boast** (lit., "exult," *katakauchasthe)* in such attitudes is to **deny,** or "lie against," **the truth.**

3:15-16. Envy and strife are clear indicators that one's so-called **wisdom** is not from above (cf. 1:17), **but is earthly, unspiritual** ("natural, sensual," *psychikē),* **and of the devil** ("demonic," *daimoniōdēs).* **Envy and selfish ambition,** or rivalry, can only produce **disorder,** or confusion, and **every evil practice.** A truly wise person does not seek glory or gain; he is gracious and giving.

3. WISDOM IS PEACEABLE (3:17-18)

3:17. Wisdom that comes from heaven (lit., "wisdom from above"; cf. "from above" in 1:17) **is first . . . pure** or "holy" (*hagnē*), then **peace-loving, considerate** or "forbearing," **submissive** or "easy to be entreated" (*eupeithēs*, only used here in the NT), **full of mercy and good fruit, impartial** (lit., "without uncertainty"; cf. "not doubt" in 1:6), **and sincere** ("without hypocrisy").

3:18. Peace is the seed sown that yields **a harvest** (lit., "fruit") **of righteousness.** The truly wise man is a man of peace.

To achieve "righteousness," spiritual maturity, practical holiness—the theme of this book—a believer must learn to speak with care. Winsome speech comes from a wise spirit. A controlled tongue is possible only with cultured thought. A mouth filled with praise results from a mind filled with purity.

A believer should stand confidently (chap. 1), serve compassionately (chap. 2), and speak carefully (chap. 3). He should be what God wants him to be, do what God wants him to do, and speak as God wants him to speak.

IV. Submit with Contrition (chap. 4)

Fights, quarrels, lust, hate, envy, pride, and sin are words that stain this portion of James' letter like inkblots. In stark contrast with the closing words of chapter 3, "peacemakers who sow in peace raise a harvest of righteousness," chapter 4 opens with "fights and quarrels." James confronted this despicable behavior with valor. Furthermore he gave clear advice on how to quell the storms that are so detrimental to spiritual growth and maturity. A believer must turn hatred into humility, judgment into justice, and boasting into belief.

A. Turn hatred into humility (4:1-6)

The appearance of conflict among the followers of Jesus stirred James to intense indignation. The severity of his tone in this section is accented by the absence of the words "my brothers," which James used so frequently in other parts of the letter. He revealed the cause of conflict, outlined the consequences of conflict, and proposed a cure for conflict.

1. CAUSE OF CONFLICT (4:1-2)

4:1. Characteristically, James introduced this new section with a rhetorical question, **What causes fights and quarrels among you?** Where do "fights" (lit., "state of war," *polemoi*) and "quarrels" (lit., individual disputes or "battles," *machai*) come from? James answered his own question: **from your desires that battle within you.** Conflict comes out of (*ek*) inner sensual lusts or pleasures (*hēdonōn;* cf. v. 3). Hedonism, the playboy philosophy that makes pleasure mankind's chief end, still wages battles in people's hearts.

4:2. War is the fruit of illicit wants. Lust brings about murder. Covetousness results in the frustration of not obtaining the hotly pursued desires. It all leads to the "quarrels" and "fights," that "battle" against people, mentioned in verse 1. The last part of verse 2, **You do not have, because you do not ask God,** is best taken with what follows. James did not contend that the reason lust was not gratified was because people failed to ask God to fill those desires. He simply revealed the clear source of conflict deep in covetous human hearts.

2. CONSEQUENCE OF CONFLICT (4:3-4)

4:3. The correct way for Christians to have their legitimate needs met is by asking God. One reason a believer does not receive what he asks for is that he asks **with wrong motives** (lit., "evilly" or "amiss," *kakōs*). The verb **ask** is in the middle voice, meaning, "ask for yourself." The purpose clause that follows further clarifies, **that you may spend what you get on your pleasures.** "Spend" could be translated "squander." "Pleasures" is again the Greek word *hēdonais* (cf. v. 1). God will never provide for "hedonistic squandering"!

4:4. Instead of the customary "my brothers," James bristled with **you adulterous people.** Again he asked a pointed question: **Don't you know that friendship** (*philia*) **with the world** (cf. "world" in 1:27) **is hatred toward God?** Then he added, **Anyone who chooses to be a friend of the world becomes** (lit., "is constituted") **an enemy of God.** The consequence is worse than ending up empty-handed; a rebellious Christian who has an illegitimate relationship with the world is at enmity with God!

3. CURE FOR CONFLICT (4:5-6)

4:5. This is one of the most difficult verses to translate in the entire letter. A very literal translation would be, "Or think you that vainly the Scripture says to envy yearns the spirit which was made to dwell in you, but He gives great grace." Is the "spirit" the Holy Spirit or the human spirit? Is the spirit to be taken as the subject of the verb "yearns" or as its object? Is "envy" to be seen as "unrighteous desire" or as "righteous jealousy"? Numerous translations are possible: (a) "The Spirit who indwells you jealously yearns [for you] and He gives more grace." (b) "He [God] yearns jealously for the Holy Spirit which indwells you and He gives more grace." (c) "The [human] spirit which indwells you yearns to envy, but He [God] gives more grace." The NIV favors the latter idea: **Or do you think . . . that the spirit He caused to live in us tends toward envy,** but "He gives us more grace?" (v. 6)

Not only is the translation of the sentence a problem, but also the apparent indication that it is a part of Scripture poses difficulties. James' question, typically rhetorical, "or do you think Scripture says without reason" (*kenōs*, lit., "vainly"), introduces the section. The ambiguous sentence that follows is not a direct quotation of any passage in Scripture. Rather than assume that James quoted some other sacred book, or some unknown Greek translation of the Old Testament, or that he simply referred to the general sense of Scripture, it seems more reasonable to assume that he focused on the quotation in verse 6, a statement clearly taken from Proverbs 3:34: "God opposes the proud but gives grace to the humble" (also quoted in 1 Peter 5:5).

4:6. Whatever questions remain unresolved about verse 5, there is no question about the clear truth of verse 6. **God opposes the proud.** The word "opposes," or "resists," is *antitassetai*, a military term meaning "to battle against." **To the humble,** however, God **gives grace.** Whether a believer is called to resist his human spirit which tends

toward envy or to rejoice in the Holy Spirit who jealously yearns for each believer's edification, the call is to shun pride and to submit humbly to God's authority. The cure for conflict is a humble spirit which is rewarded by God's unmerited favor. James continued by showing in verses 7-12 how humility is related to peaceful justice.

B. Turn judgment into justice (4:7-12)

Apparently the Jewish believers to whom James wrote tended not only to conflict and jealousy but also to condemnation and judgment. Justice, not judgment, is what God requires. Upright, righteous relationships are essential to spiritual growth. Pointed advice for justice is given, the clear advantage of justice is revealed, and the divine author of justice is named.

1. ADVICE FOR JUSTICE (4:7-9)

4:7. In verses 7-9 a whole series of commands (10 aorist imperatives) are given which, if followed, contribute to harmony and holiness. James called for commitment (v. 7), cleansing (v. 8), and contrition (v. 9).

Like a magnet, the call for commitment has both positive and negative poles: **submit . . . to God** and **resist the devil.** "Submit" is a military term "to be subordinated" or "to render obedience." "Resist" (*antistēte*) means "take a stand against." Take a stand against the devil, **and he will flee.**

4:8. On the other hand draw **near to God and He will come near** in response. To draw near to God, however, demands His cleansing. **Wash your hands, you sinners, and purify your hearts, you double-minded.** Both "wash" and "purify" are verbs that refer to ceremonial cleansing, a figure that spoke eloquently to Jewish converts. The need for cleansing is clear from the way James addressed his readers, "you sinners" and "you double-minded" (*dipsychoi*; cf. 1:8).

4:9. Recognition of the tremendous need for cleansing allows no room for merriment. **Grieve** (lit., "be afflicted"), **mourn, and wail** was James' candid advice. Exchange merriment for **mourning** and gaiety for **gloom** (lit., "a downcast look, lowered eyes"). A contrite spirit of confession is essential for God's cleansing.

2. ADVANTAGE OF JUSTICE (4:10-11)

4:10. The key is humility. **Humble yourselves before the Lord, and He will lift you up.** The way up is down. The lowly one becomes the lifted one. There is a marked advantage to humility—eventually it brings honor.

4:11. To **slander** and **judge one another** is totally incongruous to the humble spirit God desires. Furthermore, to judge another is actually a judgment of God's **Law** itself. His Law is a mandate over all people. No one dares assume a haughty position over the Law. The slanderer is sentenced by the Law; the self-styled judge is jeopardized by the Law; only the humble person is honored. True justice is rendered when a believer subjects himself to God in humility and obedience.

3. AUTHOR OF JUSTICE (4:12)

4:12. Only One is above the Law. He alone has the right to modify or overrule it. God is the **one Lawgiver and Judge.** "Lawgiver" is a compound noun used only here in the New Testament (*nomothetēs*, from *nomos*, "law," and *tithēmi*, "to set, place, constitute, or lay down"). God not only authored the Law; He also administrates the Law. He serves as both the executive and judicial branches of the divine government. God is King; He institutes and declares His Law. God is Judge; He upholds and enforces His Law. He is **the One who is able to save and destroy.** There is one Author of the Law, one Judge over the Law, and but one Savior from the Law's condemnation. This reminder of a truth well known by James' Jewish readers was also a rebuke to their haughty attitudes and judgmental actions. **But you—who are you to judge your neighbor?** is another of James' typical penetrating rhetorical questions. A humble attitude and just actions are essential for spiritual growth. James then went on to show how these qualities of life militate against empty boasting.

C. Turn boasting into belief (4:13-17)

In addition to conflict and a judgmental spirit among the brethren, bragging was also apparently prevalent. James gave an example of a boastful statement, struck a condemnatory sentence on such boasting, and offered a practical solution for boasting.

1. STATEMENT OF BOASTING (4:13)

4:13. James' attack was direct. **Now listen** is literally, "Go now." It is the same construction found in 5:1, a colloquial phrase used only by James in the New Testament. The interjection both goads the reader and gains his undivided attention. The offender attacked by James is a fairly typical businessman who makes his plans apart from God. He is self-assertive in his travel plans: **we will go to this or that city;** self-confident in his time schedule, **spend a year there;** and self-centered in his trade relationships, **carry on business and make money.** "Carry on business" is from a compound verb (*emporeusometha*, from *en*, "in," and *poreuomai*, "to go") from which the English word "emporium" has come. It is related to the noun (*emporos*) which could be translated "merchant," "trader," "drummer," or "one who goes in and gets the trade." A vivid picture of the Jewish merchant James tried to correct is a go-getter salesman out drumming up business for the bottom-line objective: "Make money!"

2. SENTENCE ON BOASTING (4:14)

4:14. To the selfish hustlers James simply stated, **Why, you do not even know what will happen tomorrow.** Man's plans are always tentative. His plans are not his own. Time is not his own. In fact, life is not his own. James then fired another of his famous questions: **What is your life?** The answer is **a mist** ("vapor, a puff of steam"). Believers need this godly perspective on their earthly sojourn. Among other things, it blasts boasting right out of the selfish, proud quagmire from which it emerged.

3. SOLUTION FOR BOASTING (4:15-17)

4:15. The key to avoiding boasting is to maintain a godly perspective. Instead of making big plans on the human plane, one must expand his view to include God in the picture. In place of vain boasting one should **say, If it is the Lord's will, we will live and do this or that.** These are not so much words to be used like some charm but a realistic attitude that affects all of one's being and behavior.

4:16. To make sure his readers understood, James reiterated that to **boast and brag . . . is evil.** Self-centered bragging must be replaced by God-honoring trust. The cure for boasting is belief.

4:17. It is likely that chapter 4's concluding sentence, **Anyone, then, who knows the good he ought to do and doesn't do it, sins,** is related not only to the matter of boasting but also to all the advice given thus far in the epistle. "Then" (lit., "therefore," *oun*) supports this contention. James' readers could not plead ignorance. The letter abounds with exhortations to do good. To fail to comply is clearly sin.

To attain spiritual maturity a believer must do the good he now knows. He must stand confidently on God's Word even in trials and temptations. He must compassionately serve his brethren without prejudicial favoritism but with practical faith. He must speak carefully with a controlled tongue and wise, cultivated thought. He must submit in contrition to his all-powerful Father, Lawgiver, and Judge with a humble spirit, just action, and a trusting heart. He must be what God wants him to be, do what God wants him to do, speak as God wants him to speak, and sense what God wants him to sense.

V. Share with Concern (chap. 5)

James continued his attack on self-centered merchants who seem to succeed in their business plans and not only turn a profit but are considered rich with their hoarded wealth. Such wealth James declared waste. Spiritual access is found in sharing, not hoarding, possessions. To those who may have been the victims of the heartless conduct of the rich, or who may have been tempted to turn to similar shortsighted goals, James recommended patience. Finally, to all believers, whether blessed, burdened, or backslidden, James appealed for praise, prayer, and persuasion.

James' concluding remarks center on sharing—sharing one's possessions, sharing with patience, and sharing in prayer.

A. Share in possessions (5:1-6)

The attack begun in the concluding section of chapter 4 is carried into chapter 5 but with greater concentration and condemnation. The rich are denounced. James appears to have included all rich people, both believers (cf. 1:10) and unbelievers (cf. 2:6). There is no plea for reform, only a grim warning that hoarded wealth brings consternation, ends up in corrosion, and results in condemnation.

1. CONSTERNATION FROM WEALTH (5:1)

5:1. The same exclamatory interjection used in 4:13 introduces this section: **Now listen** (lit., "Go now"). The **rich people,** so often the object of envy, were the object of James' scorn and condemnation. He put down those who placed their arrogant trust in things which were doomed to decay. **Weep and wail,** could be elaborated as "burst into tears" (*klausate;* also in 4:9) and "howl with grief" (*ololyzontes,* an onomatopoeic verb used only here in the NT). Money brings merriment only temporarily; wealth eventually results in **misery** (*talaipōriais,* from *talaō,* "to undergo, endure," and *pōros,* "a callus" or "hardened concretion").

2. CORROSION OF WEALTH (5:2-3)

5:2-3. Riches rot, and fine **clothes** may be chewed up by **moths.** The story is not from "rags to riches" but from "riches to rags." **Gold and silver** are the most sought-after metals and have long been considered the material standards for the world. Though they do not rust, they do become **corroded.** Gold can darken and silver tarnishes. **Their corrosion** (*ios,* or "poison," as in 3:8 and Rom. 3:13) is a testimony to the rich man's folly and will consume his **flesh like fire.** As metals lose their luster, the poison of greed eats up people. The corrosion of **wealth** is testimony to this sickness of the wealthy. Hoarding for **the last days** only gives more fuel for the fire that will consume the lost.

3. CONDEMNATION IN WEALTH (5:4-6)

5:4-5. It is not the wealth itself that is condemned, but the greedy attitude toward it and the grisly actions with which it was obtained. God is not deaf to the cries of injustice that rise both from **wages** withheld in fraud and from the laborers who have been oppressed by the rich. The Jewish converts were well aware of God's Law forbidding holding back on wages (Lev. 19:13; Deut. 24:15) and oppressing the poor (Prov. 3:27-28; Amos 8:4-6; Mal. 3:5). The life of **luxury** (*etryphēsate*, "to lead a soft life," used only here in the NT) **and self-indulgence** (*espatalēsate*, "to live voluptuously or wantonly," used only here and in 1 Tim. 5:6), is like so much fat for the **slaughter.** The sarcastic illustration was vivid for Jewish believers who had seen many fattened sheep and oxen meet their fates in sacrifice.

5:6. In the scramble for more wealth, the rich used their influence in courts of justice, and in the process were guilty of bringing condemnation and even death to **innocent men** who offered no resistance ("innocent men" is lit., "the righteous one" though it probably refers to a class of people rather than to one individual). What began as an interest in money ended as an insensitivity to murder.

A believer who seeks spiritual growth dare not become caught up in the accumulation of wealth for himself. He should share his possessions for God's glory and the good of others.

B. Share in patience (5:7-12)

From the rich, James turned to the restless. For these he again used the friendly address, "brothers." The tone turns from stark condemnation to sensitive consolation. James excoriated the rich but encouraged the receptive. He appealed to his brethren to be patient. He defined the essence of patience, gave some examples of patience, and indicated an evidence of patience.

1. ESSENCE OF PATIENCE (5:7-9)

5:7. Be patient, then (lit., "therefore"), said James as a direct corollary to the coming judgment on the wicked rich. "Be patient" (*makrothymēsate*) comes from a compound of "long" (*makros*) and "temper" (*thymos*). The idea is to set the timer of one's temper for a long run. Think long. Focus on the final lap in the race of life. Have a long fuse. Look ahead to **the Lord's coming.** The essence of patience is furthermore seen in **the farmer** who **waits** patiently (*makrothymōn*) for the needed **rains** and the ultimate **valuable** (lit., "precious") **crop.**

5:8. The application is clear. Just like the farmer, every believer should **be patient and stand firm, because the**

Lord's coming is near. The Lord's return (*parousia*) should stimulate every believer to patience and persistence.

5:9. James called for the believers to stop groaning lest they be judged, because Jesus **the Judge is standing at the door!** In view of the hope of Christ's soon return, believers should cease the petty conflicts to which James alluded in chapter 4. As children in a school classroom look out for their teacher's soon return, God's children should be on guard for Christ's return. In so doing, good behavior and mutual harmony are essential.

2. EXAMPLES OF PATIENCE (5:10-11)

5:10. James reminded his Jewish **brothers** of **the prophets** who endured much **suffering** with **patience** (*makrothymia,* lit., "long-temperedness"; cf. v. 7) as they spoke out **in the name of the Lord.**

5:11. As you know (lit., "behold"), **we consider blessed** (lit. "happy or fortunate"; *makarizomen*) **those who have persevered.** James then presented another well-known and highly revered example of patience, Job. The Lord honored **Job's perseverance** with multiplied blessings (cf. Job 42:12). Interestingly, James did not say that Job had *makrothymia,* "patience," but that he had *hypomonēn,* "steadfastness, endurance, perseverance" (cf. James 1:3; Col. 1:11). Job endured and he was steadfast, though he was impatient with God!

James summed it up: **The Lord is full of compassion and mercy.** "Full of compassion" is a compound adjective (*polysplanchnos,* from *polys,* "much," and *splanchna,* "innermost parts" or "seat of affections"), used only here in the New Testament. "Mercy," also rare (*oiktirmōn,* from the verb *oikteirō,* "to pity") is found only here and in Luke 6:36.

3. EVIDENCE OF PATIENCE (5:12)

5:12. Above all, my brothers, concluded James, **do not swear** or take an empty oath. For those who truly demonstrate the persistence and patience prescribed for believers, there is no need to invoke an oath, whether **by heaven or by earth,** that their word is certain. ("Swear" does not refer to profanity but to taking an oath.) The testimony should be such that when one says **yes,** it means **yes,** and when he says **no,** that is just what he means (cf. Matt. 5:37). The soon return of the Lord, the Judge who stands at the door (James 5:9), is motivation enough for this kind of honesty and trustworthiness, lest one **be condemned** (lit., "fall under judgment").

C. Share in prayer (5:13-20)

A fitting climax to James' letter is his emphasis on prayer. The greatest assistance any believer can offer another is faithful prayer. Prayer is clear evidence of care. Prayer is the "hotline" to the One who can provide for any need no matter how complex or impossible it may seem. To share in prayer, a believer must have a sensitivity to someone's needs, engage in diligent supplication for those needs, and recognize the significance of those needs.

1. SENSITIVITY TO NEEDS (5:13)

5:13. Perhaps the two greatest weaknesses in the average church today are the areas of prayer and praise. The reason for these weaknesses may be traced to insensitivity. There is much need for prayer and much cause to praise. Suffering should elicit prayer. Sufficiency should elicit praise. James used several questions to stress these points. **Is any one of you in trouble?** "In trouble" (*kakopathei*, "suffering ill"; cf. v. 10) relates to suffering from any source. **Is anyone happy? Let him sing songs of praise.** "Praise" (*psalletō*) originally meant "to play on a stringed instrument." The verb is used only four times in the New Testament (cf. Rom. 15:9; 1 Cor. 14:15; Eph. 5:19).

2. SUPPLICATION FOR NEEDS (5:14-18)

5:14-15. James asked a third question and then answered it fully. **Is any one of you sick?** A great deal of misunderstanding has resulted from these verses. Some seem to teach from this passage that full physical health is always just a prayer away. Others have found in this passage justification for "extreme unction" (a practice begun in the eighth century). Still others have tried to relate the process outlined by James to the modern practice of invoking God ("pray over him") and using medicine ("anoint him with oil")—prayer plus a physician.

The heart of the problem lies in just what James meant when he referred to the "sick." Actually there is no reason to consider "sick" as referring exclusively to physical illness. The word *asthenei* literally means "to be weak." Though it is used in the Gospels for physical maladies, it is generally used in Acts and the Epistles to refer to a weak faith or a weak conscience (cf. Acts 20:35; Rom. 6:19; 14:1; 1 Cor. 8:9-12). That it should be considered "weak" in this verse is clear in that another Greek word (*kamnonta*) in James 5:15, translated **sick person,** literally means "to be weary." The only other use in the New Testament (Heb. 12:3) of that word clearly emphasizes this same meaning.

James was not referring to the bedfast, the diseased, or the ill. Instead he wrote to those who had grown weary, who had become weak both morally and spiritually in the midst of suffering. These are the ones who **should call** for the help of **the elders of the church.** The early church leaders were instructed (1 Thes. 5:14) to "encourage the timid" and "help the weak" (*asthenōn*).

James said that the elders should **pray over him and anoint him with oil.** It is significant that the word "anoint" is *aleipsantes* ("rub with oil") not *chriō* ("ceremonially anoint"). The former is the "mundane" word and the latter is "the sacred and religious word" (Richard Chenevix Trench, *Synonyms of the New Testament,* ninth ed. Reprint. Grand Rapids: Wm. B. Eerdmans Publishing Co., 1950, pp. 136-7). "Therefore James is not suggesting a ceremonial or ritual anointing as a means of divine healing; instead, he is referring to the common practice of using oil as a means of bestowing honor, refreshment, and grooming" (Daniel R. Hayden, "Calling the Elders to Pray," *Bibliotheca Sacra* 138. July–September 1981:264). The woman "poured" (*aleiphō*) perfume on Jesus' feet (Luke 7:38). A host "put oil" (*aleiphō*) on the head of his guest (Luke 7:46). A person who is fasting should not be sad and ungroomed, but should "put oil" (*aleiphō*) on his head, and wash his face (Matt. 6:17). Thus James' point is that the "weak" (*asthenei*) and "weary" (*kamnonta*) would be refreshed, encouraged, and uplifted by the elders who rubbed oil on the despondents' heads and prayed for them.

For the fallen, discouraged, distressed weary believer, restoration is assured and the elders' **prayer offered in faith will make the sick person** (lit., "weary one") **well** (i.e., will restore him from discouragement and spiritual defeat), and **the Lord will raise him up.** That the restoration is spiritual, not physical, is further clarified by the assurance, **if he has sinned, he will be forgiven.** Many physically ill Christians have called on elders to pray for them and to anoint them with oil, but a sizable percentage of them have remained sick. This fact suggests that the passage may have been mistakenly understood as physical restoration rather than spiritual restoration.

5:16. The conclusion is clear: **therefore confess your sins to each other and pray for each other.** A mutual concern for one another is the way to combat discouragement and downfall. The cure is in personal confession and prayerful concern. The healing **(that you may be healed)** is not bodily healing but healing of the soul (*iathēte*; cf. Matt. 13:15; Heb. 12:13; 1 Peter 2:24). It is the **powerful and effective . . . prayer of a righteous** person that brings the needed cure from God. This of course relates to the closing two verses of James' letter. If James 5:14-16 refer to physical healing, then those verses seem disjointed with the verses before and after them.

5:17-18. James again gave an example well known to his Jewish audience. First, it was the prophets (v. 10), then Job (v. 11), and now **Elijah.** James identified Elijah as a fellow sufferer. **A man just like us** could be translated "a man of like feeling" or "of similar suffering" (*homoiopathēs*; cf. *kakopathei* in vv. 10, 13). Elijah knew all the frailties of human nature but "in prayer he prayed" (*proseuchē proseyxato*), that is, **he prayed earnestly,** and **rain** was withheld and later restored (1 Kings 17:1; 18:41-46). Earnest and persistent prayer, of course, is essential, whereas halfhearted prayer is self-defeating (cf. James 1:6-8).

3. SIGNIFICANCE OF NEEDS (5:19-20)

5:19-20. James' last appeal to his readers has a touch of tenderness and a clear note of encouragement to those who have helped others who have grown weary and have fallen from the way. **My brothers,** he wrote, "if any one among you strays from the truth, and someone turns him around, let him know that the one who turns him back from his error will save his soul from death and will hide a multitude of sins" (author's trans.).

These who have lost their way are the "sick ones" of the church family. They have wandered away. The Greek word here (*planēthē*) suggests one who has missed his path and is hopelessly lost. "Planet" was taken from this Greek word to convey the idea that the luminaries were "wandering stars" (cf. Jude 13), not "fixed" like the rest.

Wandering ones need to be brought back to the fold. James referred here not to evangelism but to restoration. Revival, not redemption, is in view. The rescue action is of great significance. A lost sheep is saved from destruction and his **sins** (the sins of the restored one, not the restorer) are covered as if a veil were thrown over them (cf. 1 Peter 4:8). He can move ahead again on the path toward spiritual maturity.

James has given clear instructions about how to achieve practical holiness and spiritual maturity. His pointed exhortations were designed to stab the consciences and stir the souls of his beloved Jewish brothers. Stand with confidence, serve with compassion, speak with care, submit with contrition, and share with concern. A believer should be what God wants him to be, do what God wants him to do, say what God wants him to say, sense what God wants him to sense, and share what God wants him to share. Spiritual maturity involves every aspect of life.

BIBLIOGRAPHY

Adamson, James B. *The Epistle of James.* The New International Commentary on the New Testament. Grand Rapids: Wm. B. Eerdmans Publishing Co., 1976.

Barclay, William. *The Letters of James and Peter.* 2d ed. Philadelphia: Westminster Press, 1960.

Davids, Peter H. *The Epistle of James.* The New International Greek Testament Commentary. Grand Rapids: Wm. B. Eerdmans Publishing Co., 1982.

Gaebelein, Frank E. *The Practical Epistle of James*. Great Neck, N.Y.: Doniger and Raughley, 1955.

Harrop, Clayton K. *The Letter of James*. Nashville: Convention Press, 1969.

Hiebert, D. Edmond. *The Epistle of James*. Chicago: Moody Press, 1979.

Manton, Thomas. *A Practical Commentary or An Exposition with Notes on the Epistle of James*. London: John Gladding, 1840.

Mayor, Joseph B. *The Epistle of St. James: The Greek Text with Introduction Notes and Comments*. Reprint. Grand Rapids: Baker Book House, 1978.

Mitton, C. Leslie. *The Epistle of James*. London: Marshall, Morgan & Scott, 1966.

Motyer, J.A. *The Tests of Faith*. London: InterVarsity Press, 1970.

Oesterley, W.E. "The General Epistle of James." In *The Expositor's Greek Testament*, vol. 4. Reprint. Grand Rapids: Wm. B. Eerdmans Publishing Co., 1976.

Plumptre, E.H. *The General Epistle of St. James*. The Cambridge Greek Testament for Schools and Colleges. Cambridge: University Press, 1893.

Reicke, Bo. *The Epistles of James, Peter, and Jude*. The Anchor Bible. Garden City, N.Y.: Doubleday & Co., 1964.

Robertson, A.T. *Studies in the Epistle of James*. New York: George H. Doran, 1915.

Ropes, James H. *A Critical and Exegetical Commentary on the Epistle of St. James*. The International Critical Commentary. Edinburgh: T. & T. Clark, 1916.

Ross, Alexander. *The Epistles of James and John*. The New International Commentary on the New Testament. Grand Rapids: Wm. B. Eerdmans Publishing Co., 1954.

Strauss, Lehman. *James Your Brother*. New York: Loizeaux Brothers, 1956.

Tasker, R.V.G. *The General Epistle of James*. The Tyndale New Testament Commentaries. Grand Rapids: Wm. B. Eerdmans Publishing Co., 1957.

Vaughan, Curtis. *James: Bible Study Commentary*. Grand Rapids: Zondervan Publishing House, 1974.

1 PETER

Roger M. Raymer

INTRODUCTION

First Peter was written to Christians who were experiencing various forms of persecution, men and women whose stand for Jesus Christ made them aliens and strangers in the midst of a pagan society. Peter exhorted these Christians to steadfast endurance and exemplary behavior. The warmth of his expressions combined with his practical instructions make this epistle a unique source of encouragement for all believers who live in conflict with their culture.

Authorship. First Peter 1:1 clearly identifies the author as "Peter, an apostle of Jesus Christ." His given name was Simon, but Jesus, on meeting him, said he would be called Cephas (John 1:42). The Greek translation of the Aramaic word *Cephas* is "petros," and the word in both languages means "stone" or "rock." Jesus' description of Simon's future strength of character became his personal name. Interestingly he is the only man in the New Testament called Peter.

Until relatively recent times the authenticity of the epistle's claim to apostolic authorship went unchallenged. Then some modern scholars noted that Peter was considered by Jewish religious leaders as "unschooled" and "ordinary" (Acts 4:13). The superb literary style and sophisticated use of vocabulary in 1 Peter seem to indicate that its author must have been a master of the Greek language. Those who deny Peter's authorship say that such an artistic piece of Greek literature could not possibly have flowed from the pen of a Galilean fisherman.

Though Peter could be called "unschooled" and though Greek was not his native tongue, he was by no means ordinary. The Jewish leaders saw Peter as unschooled simply because he had not been trained in rabbinical tradition, not because he was illiterate. Luke also recorded (Acts 4:13) that these same leaders were astonished by Peter's confidence and the power of his Spirit-controlled personality. Peter's public ministry spanned more than 30 years and took him from Jerusalem to Rome. He lived and preached in a multilingual world. It is reasonable to believe that after three decades Peter could have mastered the language of the majority of those to whom he ministered.

The rhetorical style and use of metaphor employed in 1 Peter could just as easily be credited to an accomplished public speaker as to a literary scholar. Certainly Peter had the time and talent to become an outstanding communicator of the gospel via the Greek language.

Any further doubts of Petrine authorship based on linguistic style may be answered by the fact that Peter apparently employed Silas as his secretary (1 Peter 5:12). Silas, though a Jerusalem Christian, was a Roman citizen (Acts 16:36-37) and may have had great facility in the Greek language. But whether or not Silas aided Peter with the grammatical Greek nuances, the epistle's content still remains Peter's personal message, stamped with his personal authority.

The parallels between this letter and Peter's sermons recorded in Acts are significant (cf. 1 Peter 1:20 with Acts 2:23 and 1 Peter 4:5 with Acts 10:42). One of the more striking examples is the similarity between 1 Peter 2:7-8 and Acts 4:10-11. In each passage Psalm 118:22 is quoted and applied to Christ. It is interesting that Peter was present when Christ Himself used Psalm 118:22 to refer to His rejection by the Jewish leaders (Matt. 21:42).

Another allusion to Jesus' ministry that strongly supports Peter's authorship is the command to elders in 1 Peter 5:2 to "be shepherds." The only other place in the New Testament where this word is used as a command is in John 21:16, where Jesus gave Peter the same charge. In several other passages the author referred to being an eyewitness of Christ's earthly ministry (1 Peter 1:8; 2:23; 5:1).

This epistle exerted a wide influence on early Christian writings. The letters of Polycarp, Clement, and Irenaeus (to name only a few) show that the early church unquestionably accepted the authenticity of 1 Peter. The letter's content and the witness of church history support beyond any reasonable doubt the simple affirmation made in verse 1. The letter indeed comes from "Peter, an apostle of Jesus Christ."

Date. Peter wrote this epistle apparently just before or shortly after the beginning of Nero's persecution of the church in A.D. 64. Since Peter referred to the government as still functioning (an institution which commends those who do right and punishes those who do wrong; 2:13-14), some believe that the church was not yet facing an organized Roman persecution. Evidently repressive laws had not yet been enacted specifically against Christians. It was still possible for Peter's readers to "honor the king" (2:17). The persecution and suffering that Peter did refer to was primarily social and religious rather than legal. A hostile pagan society would slander, ridicule, discriminate against, and even inflict physical abuse on those whose lifestyles had radically changed because of their faith in Christ.

However, Peter seemed to indicate that greater persecution was imminent. He assured his readers (1:6) that they could rejoice though they "may have had to suffer grief in all kinds of trials." Peter exhorted them to prepare, to be self-controlled (1:13), possibly to suffer as Christians according to God's will (4:19). So perhaps Nero's severe persecution had already begun in Rome and was spreading to the provinces to which Peter was writing. This would place the date of the letter in late A.D. 64 or early 65.

The suggestion that the persecution had already begun in Rome also explains why Peter would refer cryptically to his location as "Babylon" (5:13). Peter was in Rome during the last decade of his life. His martyrdom is dated about A.D. 67. At the time of the writing of 1 Peter he was not in the custody of the Roman officials, and evidently wished to conceal his true location. (Other scholars, however, say that Peter was in the literal city of Babylon, where a Jewish community then flourished.)

Destination. First Peter is addressed to Christians scattered throughout five Roman provinces of the peninsula of Asia Minor. That area today is northern Turkey. The churches in those provinces were made up of both Jews and Gentiles. This epistle is rich in references to and quotations from the Old Testament. Jewish Christians would have found special significance in the term *diasporas*, translated "scattered," used in the salutation (1:1). Jews who lived outside of Jerusalem were referred to as living in the diaspora.

Gentile readers would have noted Peter's exhortation to holy living in light of their background of complete ignorance of God's Word (1:14). Gentile Christians also would have been greatly encouraged by the fact that though they *were* in ignorance, they were now considered "the people of God" (2:10). Clearly Peter carefully included both Jewish and Gentile Christians in his letter of encouragement to the churches of Asia Minor.

Purpose. This epistle could be understood as a handbook written for ambassadors to a hostile foreign land. The author, knowing persecution would arise, carefully prescribed conduct designed to bring honor to the One they represented. The purpose then of 1 Peter was to encourage Christians to face persecution so that the true grace of Jesus Christ would be evidenced in them (5:12).

This epistle gives a theology of practical exhortation and comfort for believers' daily needs. Peter concretely linked doctrine with practice. The *new birth* gives a living hope to those in the midst of persecution. *New conduct* is prescribed because Christ endured unjust suffering. *New behavior* is required to demonstrate the grace of God to an unbelieving and hostile world. And *new responsibilities* are placed on the leaders and members of the body of Christ since they should stand together as living stones against the onrushing tide of persecution.

Those who read 1 Peter are encouraged to lift their eyes from present problems and trials and behold the vistas provided by an eternal perspective. For though believers may for a while suffer grief in trials, they wait for an inheritance that can never perish, spoil, or fade.

OUTLINE

COMMENTARY

I. Customary Salutation (1:1-2)

The introductory greeting is the common form of salutation used in first-century correspondence. Paul's letters usually began in the same manner, identifying both the author and those to whom the letters were addressed.

A. Identification of the author (1:1a)

1:1a. Peter is the Greek translation of the Aramaic Cephas, the name Jesus gave Simon when he was called to be a disciple (John 1:42). Nobody else in the New Testament could be identified as Peter, **an apostle of Jesus Christ.** This bold statement of apostolic authority is supported both by internal evidence in the text and by its early and universal acceptance as a part of the canon of Scripture.

B. Identification of those addressed (1:1b-2)

1:1b-2. Peter immediately, using a careful choice of words, began to comfort and encourage his readers. Christians are **God's elect** not by chance or human design but by God's sovereign, unconditional choice. Once only the nation of Israel could claim this title.

It is not surprising that those who have been **chosen** by God are seen as **strangers in the world** (from the one word *parepidēmois*, that emphasizes both foreign nationality and temporary residence; cf. 2:11). Christians, whose citizenship is in heaven (cf. Phil. 3:20), live in the midst of a pagan society as aliens and sojourners, displaced persons whose thoughts should often turn toward their true home.

The readers were **scattered throughout Pontus, Galatia, Cappadocia, Asia, and Bithynia,** sprinkled like salt throughout five of Asia Minor's Roman provinces. The letter was evidently meant to circulate among the churches in this area. "Scattered" (*diasporas*) had special meaning to the Jewish Christians in these churches. The diaspora referred to Jews who were separated from their homeland. Peter adapted this word which previously described Israel to emphasize the condition of the early church.

Peter elaborated on the descriptive term "God's elect" (cf. 2:9) **who have been chosen according to the foreknowledge of God.** God's choice is part of His predetermined plan, and is not based on any merit in those who are elected, but solely on His grace and love for them before their creation.

As the Williams translation puts it, God's choosing is "in accordance with" (*kata*) or in keeping with His foreknowledge. This seems preferable to the view that election follows or is based on foreknowledge. Moreover the word for foreknowledge (*prognōsin*) means more than a passive foresight; it contains the idea of "having regard for" or "centering one's attention on" (cf. Kenneth S. Wuest, *First Peter in the Greek New Testament for the English Reader*, p. 15). The same word is used in 1:20 of Christ who was "chosen" by the Father before Creation. The Father did more than merely know about His Son ahead of time; He knew Him completely. Thus God chose all those on whom He focused His attention (by His grace, not because of their merit).

The sanctifying work of the Spirit has set these chosen ones apart for service, putting God's choice and purpose into effect. The result of the Spirit's work is **obedience . . . and sprinkling by His blood.** "Obedience" (*hypakoēn*, from *hypakouō*, "to hear under, to hearken") is man's responsibility to be submissive to God's Word (cf. Ex. 24:7; Rom. 1:5; 15:18; 16:26). One living in obedience is constantly being cleansed with Christ's blood and is thus "set apart" from the world (cf. 1 John 1:7, 9). The blood sprinkling is redolent of the Old Testament priestly work at the tabernacle (Lev. 7:14; 14:7, 16, 51; 16:14-15; cf. Heb. 9:13; 12:24), which required obedience on the part of the offerers. However, the only time *people* were sprinkled with blood was at the inauguration of the Mosaic Covenant (Ex. 24:8).

In these words (1 Peter 1:2) Peter laid the theological foundations for this letter of encouragement. "God" **the Father** in His grace had chosen them and God the "Spirit" had sanctified them through the atoning blood of God the Son, **Jesus Christ.** (All three Persons of the Trinity are mentioned in this verse.) Thus Peter greeted his readers with the prayerful wish that they might experience **in abundance** God's **grace** (*charis*) **and peace** (*eirēnē*, equivalent of the Heb. *šālôm*; cf. 5:14). The words (lit.) "Grace to you and peace be multiplied" are also used in 2 Peter 1:2. God's grace was dear to Peter, for he referred to it 10 times in this epistle (1 Peter 1:2, 10, 13; 2:19-20 [trans. "commendable" in these two verses]; 3:7; 4:10; 5:5, 10, 12).

II. Chosen for New Birth (1:3–2:10)

Peter continued to present the theological basis for encouragement in persecution. The stress throughout this section is on God's grace toward believers, evidenced by His sovereign call to salvation and its results in a believer's life. In the midst of trials one's new birth is the source of a living hope and a lifestyle of holiness.

A. The new birth's living hope (1:3-12)

In a doxology of praise to God, Peter encouraged his readers by reminding them that the new birth gave them a living hope in an imperishable future inheritance. The inheritance is sure because believers are shielded by the power of God till it is ready to be revealed. Consequently Christians may rejoice even when they face trials, since trials will prove their faith genuine and thus bring greater glory to Christ. Finally the new birth's hope is based not only on a future inheritance and present blessings but also on the written Word of God.

1. THE FUTURE INHERITANCE (1:3-5)

1:3. The contemplation of God's grace caused Peter to praise God, the Author of salvation and the Source of hope. The words **Praise be to the God and Father of our Lord Jesus Christ** are identical in 2 Corinthians 1:3. The phrase **in His great mercy** refers to God's unmerited favor toward sinners in their hopeless condition. **He has given us new birth;** people can do nothing to merit such a gift. The words "has given . . . new birth" translate *anagennēsas,* from the verb "beget again" or "cause to be born again." It is used twice in the New Testament, both times in this chapter (1 Peter 1:3, 23). Peter may have been recalling Jesus' interview with Nicodemus (John 3:1-21). The "new birth" results in **a**

living hope through the resurrection of Jesus Christ from the dead. The "living hope" is based on the living resurrected Christ (cf. 1 Peter 1:21). The Christian's assurance in Christ is as certain and sure as the fact that Christ is alive! Peter used the word "living" six times (1:3, 23; 2:4-5; 4:5-6). Here "living" means that the believer's hope is sure, certain, and real, as opposed to the deceptive, empty, false hope the world offers.

1:4. The sure hope is of a future **inheritance** (*klēronomian*). This same word is used in the Septuagint to refer to Israel's promised possession of the land (cf. Num. 26:54, 56; 34:2; Josh. 11:23); it was her possession, granted to her as a gift from God. A Christian's inheritance cannot be destroyed by hostile forces, and it will not spoil like overripened fruit or fade in color. Peter used three words, each beginning with the same letter and ending with the same syllable, to describe in a cumulative fashion this inheritance's permanence: **can never perish** (*aphtharton*), **spoil** (*amianton*), **or fade** (*amaranton*). This inheritance is as indestructible as God's Word (cf. 1 Peter 1:23, where Peter again used *aphtharton*). Each Christian's inheritance of eternal life is **kept in heaven** or "kept watch on" by God so its ultimate possession is secure (cf. Gal. 5:5).

1:5. Not only is the inheritance guarded, but heirs who have been born into that inheritance **are shielded by God's power.** "Shielded" (*phrouroumenous*) is a military term, used to refer to a garrison within a city (Phil. 4:7 uses the same Gr. word). What greater hope could be given to those undergoing persecution than the knowledge that God's power guards them from within, to preserve them for an inheritance of salvation that will be completely **revealed** to them in God's presence. Believers possess salvation now (pres. tense) but will sense its full significance at the return of Christ **in the last time.** This final step, or ultimate completion of "the salvation of their souls" (1 Peter 1:9), will come "when Jesus Christ is revealed," a clause Peter used twice (vv. 7, 13).

2. THE PRESENT JOY (1:6-9)

1:6. A living hope results in a present joy. **In this** likely refers to the truths mentioned in verses 3-5. Peter encouraged his readers to put their knowledge into practice. Their response to the tremendous theological truths taught so far should be that they would **greatly rejoice.** Knowledge alone cannot produce the great joy of experiential security and freedom from fear in the face of persecution. God's omnipotent sovereignty needs to be coupled with human responsibility. Christians are responsible to respond in faith. Faith turns sound doctrine into sound practice. Faith acts on the content of theology and produces conduct that corresponds to that content. Faith makes theological security experiential. The Apostle John wrote, "This is the victory that has overcome the world, even our faith" (1 John 5:4). This kind of faith or living hope can enable believers to rejoice even when they are called on **to suffer grief in all kinds of trials.**

Peter stressed that a Christian's joy is independent of his circumstances. James used the same two Greek words (*poikilois peirasmois*, trans. here "all kinds of trials"). The trials themselves are seen as occasions for joy (James 1:2). Though trials may cause temporary grief, they cannot diminish that deep, abiding joy which is rooted in one's living hope in Christ Jesus.

1:7. These various trials—which seem to refer to persecution rather than life's normal problems—have two results: (a) they refine or purify one's faith—much as **gold** is **refined by fire** when its dross is removed, and (b) trials prove the reality of one's **faith.** Stress deepens and strengthens a Christian's faith and lets its reality be displayed. The word *dokimazomenou*, rendered **proved genuine**, means "to test for the purpose of approving" (cf. *dokimion*, "testing," in v. 7 ["the trial of your faith," KJV] and James 1:3, and *dokimon*, "test," in James 1:12).

In addition to *comparing* faith to gold, Peter *contrasted* purified faith with purified gold. Faith is more precious, **of greater worth, than gold.** Even refined gold, though it lasts a long time, eventually perishes (cf. 1 Peter 1:18; cf. James 5:3). It will be valueless in the marketplace of eternity. But faith "purchases" an inheritance that can never perish.

Genuine faith is not only of ultimate value to its possessor, but it will also bring **praise, glory, and honor** to the One whose name Christians bear, when He will return (**is revealed;** cf. 5:1) to claim them as His own. "Is revealed" translates *apokalypsei*, from which comes "apocalypse" (cf. 1:5, 12, and comments on v. 13).

1:8. Here is the climax of the experiential joy that results from faith. God accomplished salvation through the work of His Son Jesus Christ. So the focus of a believer's faith is not on abstract knowledge but on the person of Christ. The apostle's warm heart overflowed as he spoke of the love and belief in Christ of those who, unlike himself, did not see Jesus when He walked on earth. Peter may have had in mind Jesus' words: "Blessed are those who have not seen and yet have believed" (John 20:29). Yet, though Christians **do not** now **see Him,** like Peter they love and **believe in Him,** and are also **filled with an inexpressible and glorious joy.** The verb *agalliasthe* ("are filled with . . . joy") was used by Peter in 1 Peter 1:6, "you greatly rejoice," and *agalliōmenoi* is used in 4:13.

1:9. Believers can rejoice because they **are** (pres. tense) **receiving** (*komizomenoi*, "to receive as a reward") what was promised, namely **salvation,** the **goal** or culmination (*telos,* "end") **of . . . faith.** For those who love and believe in Jesus Christ, salvation is past ("He has given us new birth," v. 3), present ("through faith are shielded by God's power," v. 5), and future (it is their "inheritance," v. 4, which will "be revealed in the last time," v. 5, and is "the goal of your faith," v. 9). Since each day brings believers closer to that final day, they are now "receiving" it. All of this—in spite of persecution which deepens and demonstrates one's faith—is certainly cause for "inexpressible and glorious joy"! (v. 8)

3. THE PAST REVELATION (1:10-12)

1:10-12. The living hope of the new birth springs not only from believers' future inheritance and present experience but also from their faith in God's written Word (v. 11). Peter iterated that faith is not based on the mere writings of men but on the Word of God. **Concerning this salvation** (cf. "salvation" in vv. 5, 9) **the prophets . . . searched intently and with the greatest care** their own Spirit-guided writings. They longed to participate in this salvation and coming period of grace

and tried to discover the appointed **time and circumstances to which the Spirit of Christ in them was pointing.** They pondered how the glorious Messiah could be involved in suffering. Again Peter echoed the teachings of Christ (cf. Matt. 13:17).

In 1 Peter 1:10-12 the apostle gave a practical illustration of the doctrine of the inspiration of Scripture he clearly stated in 2 Peter 1:20-21. The prophets did not fully understand all that the Holy Spirit had authored through them. It was the Spirit who predicted **the sufferings of Christ** (Isa. 53) **and the glories that would follow** (Isa. 11). Peter's readers would be encouraged by this reminder that Christ's suffering was followed by glory. They too would experience glory after their suffering (cf. 1 Peter 5:10).

Peter gave further encouragement (1:12), stating that the prophets understood they were not writing for themselves but for those who would live later, those who would hear **the gospel** proclaimed **by the Holy Spirit** (cf. "the Spirit of Christ," v. 11), and consequently follow Christ. In the ultimate stage of believers' salvation they will experience glory, not suffering. The writer of Hebrews also referred to this "ultimate" salvation (Heb. 1:14; 2:3).

The reality of the Christian's living hope was held in awe and wonder by the angelic hosts of heaven. Prophets and angels alike wondered about "this salvation" in **the grace that was to come** (v. 10).

B. The new birth's holiness (1:13–2:10)

The believers' living hope based on their new birth should lead to a lifestyle of holiness. Those chosen for new birth are also called to be holy. Peter exhorted his readers to prepare to meet the challenge of obedience by adopting a new mind-set. The price paid for a believer's redemption calls for reverence and obedience. Obedience involves purifying oneself and practicing holy living, while offering spiritual sacrifices as a royal priest.

1. THE PREPARATION (1:13-16)

1:13-16. Peter now gave five pointed exhortations: **prepare your minds for action; be self-controlled; set your hope.**

. . . do not conform to . . . evil desires. . . . be holy. Actually in the Greek the first, second, and fourth are participles, which are subordinate to *two* commands: "have hope" and "be holy." The participles either support the commands (i.e., have hope, with a prepared mind and self-control; and be holy, not conforming to evil desires) or they take the role of commands, as in the NIV.

(1) "Prepare your minds for action" (v. 13). Obedience is a conscious act of the will. Christians in conflict need a tough-minded holiness that is ready for action.

(2) "Be self-controlled" (v. 13; cf. 4:7; 5:8; 1 Thes. 5:6, 8). This word *nēphontes*, from the verb *nēphō* ("be sober") is used only figuratively in the New Testament. It means to be free from every form of mental and spiritual "drunkenness" or excess. Rather than being controlled by outside circumstances, believers should be directed from within.

(3) "Set your hope fully" (1 Peter 1:13). Holy living demands determination. A believer's hope is to be set perfectly (*teleiōs*, completely or unchangeably), and without reserve **on the grace** (cf. v. 10) to be bestowed **when Jesus Christ is revealed** (lit., "in the revelation [*apokalypsei*] of Jesus Christ"; cf. the same phrase in v. 7; also cf. the verb "be revealed" [*apokalyphthēnai*] in v. 5). Four times Peter has already spoken of the Savior's return and the accompanying ultimate stage of salvation (vv. 5, 7, 9, 13).

The strenuous mental preparation suggested by the three admonitions in verse 13 is needed so that Christians (4) **do not conform to** (*syschēmatizomenoi*, also used in Rom. 12:1) **the evil desires** (1 Peter 1:14) of their past sinful lives (cf. Eph. 2:3), when they were ignorant of God (cf. Eph. 4:18). Rather **as obedient children** (lit., "children of obedience") they were to mold their characters to (5) "be holy" **in all** they did (1 Peter 1:15). Their lifestyle was to reflect not their former **ignorance** (*agnoia*), but the **holy** (*hagioi*) nature of their heavenly Father who gave them new birth and called them (cf. "called" in 2 Peter 1:3) to be His own. First Peter 1:15-16 do not speak of legal requirements but are a reminder of a Christian's responsibility in his inner life

and outer walk. Though absolute holiness can never be achieved in this life, all areas of life should be in the process of becoming completely conformed to God's perfect and holy will. The quotation in verse 16 was familiar to all who knew the Old Testament (Lev. 11:44-45; 19:2; 20:7).

2. THE PRICE (1:17-21)

The high cost of salvation—the beloved Son's precious blood—calls for believers to live in reverent fear before God. Holy living is motivated by a God-fearing faith which does not take lightly what was purchased at so great a cost.

1:17-19. Obedient children know the holy nature and just character of this One who **judges . . . impartially.** Their right to call God **Father** leads to their obeying Him **in reverent fear.** So they are to live according to His absolute standards, **as strangers** (cf. "aliens" in 2:11) to the world's shifting, situational ethics. "Reverent fear" is evidenced by a tender conscience, a watchfulness against temptation, and avoiding things that would displease God. Children of obedience should also be strangers to their former **empty way of life** (cf. v. 14) **handed down** from their forebears, since they have been **redeemed** (*elytrōthēte*, from *lytroō*, "to pay a ransom") **with the precious** (cf. 2:4, 6-7) **blood of Christ** (cf. 1:2). That redemption is a purchasing from the marketplace of sin, a ransom not paid by silver or gold, which perish (cf. v. 7), but with the priceless blood of a perfect **Lamb.** Similar to the sacrificial lambs which were to be **without . . . defect,** Christ was sinless, uniquely qualified as "the Lamb of God, who takes away the sin of the world" (John 1:29; cf. Heb. 9:14).

1:20-21. This payment for sin was planned **before the Creation of the world** and **revealed** for people's sake through the Incarnation of Jesus Christ. (The pres. Age is **these last times** [v. 20] whereas the coming Age is "the last time" [v. 5].) It is through Christ, whom the Father resurrected (cf. v. 3) and **glorified** in His Ascension (John 17:5; Heb. 1:3) that people may come to know and trust in God. As a result of God's eternal plan and priceless payment for sin, **faith and hope** can be placed in Him. (Cf. "faith" in 1 Peter 1:5, 7, 9; and "hope" in vv. 3, 13.)

3. THE PURIFICATION (1:22–2:3)

The response of holy living that should result from the new birth is now applied to three areas. Obedience to the truth purifies and produces (a) a sincere love for the brethren (1: 22-25), (b) repentance from sin (2:1), and (c) a desire for spiritual growth (2:2).

1:22. Holy living demands purification. A positive result of **obeying the truth** is a purified life (cf. v. 2b). "How can a young man keep his way pure? By living according to Your Word" (Ps. 119:9). As trials refine faith, so obedience to God's Word refines character. One who has **purified** himself by living according to God's Word has discovered the joy of obedience.

A changed life should also be evidenced by a changed relationship with God's other children. A purified life allows one to love purely those who share the same faith. **Sincere** (anypokriton) could also be rendered "without hypocrisy." All evil thoughts and feelings regarding one's **brothers** and sisters in Christ must be removed, for His followers are **to love . . . deeply, from the heart.** This kind of loving (agapēsate, from agapē) can come only from a changed heart, from one whose motives are pure, and who seeks to give more than he takes. This love is to be expressed not shallowly but "deeply" (ektenōs, "at full stretch" or "in an all-out manner, with an intense strain"; cf. ektenē in 1 Peter 4:8).

1:23-25. Peter again reminded his readers that they had experienced the new birth (cf. v. 3): **For you have been born again.** This supernatural event made it possible for them to obey the truth, purify themselves, and love the brethren. This change in their lives would not die, because it took place through God's **Word,** which is **imperishable** (aphthartou, the word in v. 4 that described a believer's inheritance), **living and enduring.** Peter supported his exhortation (v. 22) by quoting Isaiah 40:6-8 (1 Peter 1:24-25). All that is born of perishable seed withers and falls, but God's Word **stands forever.** This imperishable Word was the content of Peter's preaching (cf. v. 12). His hearers must be affected by its life-changing power, as indicated in 2:1-3.

2:1. Repentance was called for: **Therefore, rid yourselves.** Peter then listed five sins of attitude and speech, which if harbored would drive wedges between believers. **Malice** (kakian) is wicked ill-will; **deceit** (dolon) is deliberate dishonesty; **hypocrisy** (hypokriseis), pretended piety and love; **envy** (phthonous), resentful discontent; and **slander** (katalalias), backbiting lies. None of these should have any place in those who are born again. Rather, in obedience to the Word, believers are to make decisive breaks with the past.

2:2. Peter wanted his readers to be as eager for the nourishment of the Word as babies are for **milk.** After believers cast out impure desires and motives (v. 1), they then need to feed on wholesome **spiritual** food that produces growth. (**Pure** [adolon] is deliberately contrasted with "deceit" [dolon] in v. 1. God's Word does not deceive; neither should God's children.) Christians should approach the Word with clean hearts and minds (v. 1) in eager anticipation, with a desire to **grow** spiritually. The words **in your salvation** (lit., "unto salvation") recall the ultimate fulfillment of salvation spoken of in 1:5, 7, 9, 13.

2:3. Quoting Psalm 34:8, Peter continued the milk analogy used in 1 Peter 2:2 and likened their present knowledge of Christ to tasting. They had taken a sample, having experienced God's grace in their new birth, and had found that indeed **the Lord is good.**

4. THE PRACTICE (2:4-10)

Peter then used a new metaphor in his exhortation to holy living. His readers, having purified themselves, were ready for the practice or ministry of holiness. No longer babies, they were to grow up together to offer spiritual sacrifices as a chosen "royal priesthood."

2:4. As you come to Him does not refer to the initial response of a sinner who comes to Christ for salvation. The participle's tense and voice indicate that this coming is a personal, habitual approach. It is an intimate association of communion and fellowship between believers and their Lord.

The first step in practicing holiness is fellowship with Jesus Christ, **the living Stone.** Here Peter used a unique figure of speech. In 1:3 he referred to a "living hope" and in 1:23 to the "living . . . Word"; then in 2:4 he referred to Christ as "the living Stone." Peter developed and explained the metaphor of the stone in the following verses. Here he said this Stone is living. It has life in itself and gives life to others. People may enter into personal, vital relationships with this "living Stone." Whereas Christ was **rejected by men . . . God** had **chosen** Him (cf. 1:20) and held Him **precious** (cf. 1:19; 2:4, 7). Christians rejected by the world may take heart in the knowledge that they are the elect (1:1), valued (1:18) by God.

2:5. Believers are identified with Christ, for He is *the* living Stone and they are **like living stones.** And as they become more like Him, further conformed to His image, they **are being built into a spiritual house.** Jesus told Peter, "On this rock I will build My church" (Matt. 16:18). Now Peter (1 Peter 2:4-5) clearly identified Christ as the Rock on which His church is built. Paul called the church a "temple" (1 Cor. 3:16; Eph. 2:21) and "a dwelling" (Eph. 2:22). Believers not only make up the church but serve in it, ministering as **a holy priesthood, offering spiritual sacrifices.** All believers are priests (cf. 1 Peter 2:9; Heb. 4:16; Rev. 1:6) and need no mediator other than Jesus Christ to approach God directly. Such priestly service requires holiness (cf. 1 Peter 1:16, 22). Praise to God and doing good to others are spiritual sacrifices that please Him (Heb. 13:15). However, "living stones" may also offer themselves as "living sacrifices" (Rom. 12:1), **acceptable to God through Jesus Christ.**

2:6. In verses 6-8 Peter marshaled Old Testament support about the stone from three passages. His first source is Isaiah 28:16, where Christ is the **chosen and precious** (cf. "precious" in 1 Peter 1:19; 2:4, 7) **cornerstone.** A cornerstone is the visible support on which the rest of the building relies for strength and stability. Believers trust in Christ much as a building rests on its cornerstone. Moreover, they **will never be put to shame.** The Greek double negative *ou mē* used here in the subjunctive mood indicates an emphatic negative assertion referring to the future: never indeed will they be shamed. So Peter encouraged his readers with a sure scriptural promise of ultimate victory for those who trust Christ.

2:7-8. These verses present a sharp contrast between those who believe and those who do not. Christ is "precious," of ultimate value, to those who believe. But those who have **rejected** Christ, the Stone (Peter's second quotation is from Ps. 118:22) **stumble** because of their disobedience. This happened to the chief priests and Pharisees Jesus referred to when He quoted Psalm 118:22 (Matt. 21:42; cf. 21:43-46).

Peter's third quotation is from Isaiah 8:14. Rejection of Jesus Christ is fatal and is connected with disobeying **the message** of God's Word (1 Peter 2:8b). To **disobey** the message (cf. 4:17) is to reject it; and to obey it is to believe (cf. obedience in 1:14, 22 and "obedient to the faith" in Acts 6:7). All who do not receive Christ as their Savior will one day face Him as their Judge. Because of sin, all disobedient unbelievers are **destined for** a "stumbling," which will lead to eternal condemnation.

2:9-10. Peter closed this portion of his letter of encouragement with a moving exhortation for his readers to practice holiness. He reminded them that, in contrast with the disobedient who are destined for destruction, they were a **chosen** (*eklekton*; cf. "elect," *eklektois*, 1:1) **people.** Peter again echoed the Old Testament, specifically Isaiah 43:20. "Chosen people," which used to apply only to Israel, was now used of both Jewish and Gentile believers. The responsibility once solely trusted to the nation of Israel has now, during this Age of Grace, been given to the church. At Sinai, God told Moses to tell the people, "You will be for Me a kingdom of priests and a holy nation" (Ex. 19:6). Now believers in the Church Age are called **a royal priesthood, a holy nation, a people belonging to God.** Peter called Christians "a holy priesthood" (1 Peter 2:5) and "a royal priesthood" (2:9; cf. Rev. 1:6). The words "belonging to God" loosely render the words *eis peripoiēsin,* which are literally "unto obtaining or preserving" (also used in Heb. 10:39, where the NIV has "are saved"). Christians are a special people because God has preserved them for Himself. While these descriptions of the church are similar to those used of Israel in the Old Testament, this in no way indicates that the church supplants Israel and assumes the national blessings promised to Israel (and to be fulfilled in the Millennium). Peter just used similar terms to point up similar truths. As Israel was "a chosen people, a royal priesthood, a holy nation, a people belonging to God," so too believers today are chosen, are priests, are holy, and belong to God. Similarity does not mean identity.

God's purpose in choosing believers for Himself is so that they may **declare the praises of Him** before others. "Praises" could also be translated "eminent qualities," "excellencies," or "virtues" (*aretos,* used only four times in the NT: Phil. 4:8; 1 Peter 2:9; 2 Peter 1:3, 5). Believer-priests should live so that their heavenly Father's qualities are evident in their lives. They are to serve as witnesses of the glory and grace of God, who called them **out of darkness into His wonderful light.** Peter (1 Peter 2:10) explained this figure with a quotation from Hosea 2:23. "Darkness" refers to the time when his readers were pagans, ignorant of God's provision of salvation (cf. Col. 1:13), when they were **not a people,** when they **had not received mercy.** His "wonderful light" now illumines **the people of God** because they **have received mercy.** The practice of holiness, in which God's people serve as a holy and royal priesthood offering spiritual sacrifices and extolling His excellencies, is the proper response to the mercy (cf. 1 Peter 1:3) they have received.

III. Challenged to New Behavior (2:11–3:7)

How can Christians, as a people belonging to God, declare His praises before others? In this section Peter answered this question by suggesting specific ways Christians can behave differently before the world, as citizens, as slaves, and as wives and husbands. Even in familiar situations, their conduct should be different.

A. New behavior before the world (2:11-25)

The world Peter had in view refers to the people his readers faced daily as witnesses, citizens, and slaves. Peter challenged Christians to take a stand against sin, to submit to lawful authority, and to endure harsh masters patiently. This kind of conduct would win others to

belief, silence the tongues of foolish people, and bring commendation from God.

1. CHRISTIAN CONDUCT AS WITNESSES (2:11-12)

2:11. Peter warmly addressed his readers as **dear friends** or better, "beloved" (*agapētoi*). Those who are loved by God are exhorted to live **as aliens** (*paroikous,* "those who live in a place that is not their home," used figuratively of Christians, whose real home is in heaven) **and strangers in the world** (cf. comments on "strangers" in 1:1). Just as their Christian values and beliefs are rejected by the world, so they are to live apart from the immorality and **sinful desires** that surround them. **Abstain** (*apechesthai*) is literally "hold oneself constantly back from." Christians are to resist the sinward pull of those worldly desires **which war against** (cf. James 4:1) their spiritual lives. In this real spiritual battle a demonic strategy is to attack believers at their weakest points.

2:12. Christians are to abstain from sinful desires not only for their own spiritual well-being but also in order to maintain an effective testimony before unbelievers. The negative exhortation of verse 11 is now followed by positive instruction. A positive Christian lifestyle is a powerful means of convicting the world of its sin (cf. Matt. 5:16). Peter used the word **good** (*kalos*) twice in this verse to define both Christians' **lives** and their works. A "good" life is composed of **good deeds** (cf. Matt. 5:16; Eph. 2:10; Titus 3:8; James 2:18). Before the critical eyes of slanderous people and their false accusations, the "good deeds" of believers can **glorify God** (cf. Matt. 5:16; Rom. 15:6; 1 Cor. 6:20) and win others to belief. **On the day He visits** is literally "in the day of [His] visitation" (*en hēmera episkopēs*; cf. Luke 19:44). Some say this refers to God's "visiting" or looking on the wicked in judgment, but it probably refers to their salvation (i.e., when God looks in on them in His mercy and brings them to conversion; cf. *epeskepsato,* Acts 15:14).

2. CHRISTIAN CONDUCT AS CITIZENS (2:13-17)

2:13-15. Christians are responsible to obey the law (cf. Rom. 13:1-7; Titus 3:1-2). Peter exhorted his readers to abide by governmental laws, **to submit . . . to every authority** (*ktisei*, lit., "creation" or here "institution" or "law") **instituted among men** (*anthrōpinē*, "made by man, human"). The motivation for obedience is not avoiding punishment but is **for the Lord's sake.** To honor God who ordained human government, Christians are to observe man-made laws carefully as long as those laws do not conflict with the clear teaching of Scripture (cf. Acts 4:19). The general purpose of legal authority is **to punish . . . wrong and to commend . . . right.** Evidently Christians were being slandered and falsely accused of evil, for Peter stressed that **it is God's will** (*thelēma*, a term expressing the result of one's purpose or desire; cf. "God's will" in 1 Peter 3:17; 4:2, 19) that through excellent behavior they **silence** (*phimoun*, lit., "muzzle") **the ignorant talk of foolish men.** Each of the three Greek words rendered "ignorant talk of foolish men" begins with the letter alpha, as do the three Greek words in 1:4 rendered "never perish, spoil, or fade." Apparently Peter enjoyed alliteration!

This section of Peter's argument leads many to believe that the organized persecution through oppressive Roman laws either had not begun or had not yet reached the provinces of Asia Minor. Christians were then facing lies and verbal abuse, not torture and death. Christians were still enjoying the protection of a legal system which commended those who obeyed the law. So a believer's best defense against slanderous criticism was good behavior.

2:16. Submission to lawful authority does not negate Christian liberty (cf. Gal. 5:1, 18). Civil laws should be freely obeyed, not out of fear but because doing so is God's will. Christian freedom is always conditioned by Christian responsibility (cf. Gal. 5:13) and must never be used **as a cover-up** (*epikalymma*, lit., "veil") **for evil.** Christians enjoy true freedom when they obey God and **live as servants** (*douloi*, lit., "slaves"; cf. Rom. 6:22) **of God.** Though living **as free men**, they should also live as God's slaves.

2:17. This section concludes with a four-point summary of Christian citizenship. First, Christians are to **respect** (*timēsate*, "honor, value, esteem"; cf. *timēn*, "respect, honor," in 3:7) . . . **everyone** (cf. Rom. 12:10; 13:7). Believers

should be conscious of the fact that each human has been uniquely created in God's image. Second, Christians are to **love the brotherhood of believers,** their brothers and sisters in Christ. God's family members should love each other. Third, Christians are to **fear God.** The verb "fear" (*phobeisthe*) here does not mean to be in terror, but awe and reverence that leads to obedience (cf. *phobō* in 1 Peter 1:17, *phobou* in 3:16, and *phobon* in 2 Cor. 7:11). One will never truly respect people until he reverences God. Fourth, believers are to **honor the king.** "Honor" is from *timaō*, the verb used at the beginning of this verse. The respect or "honor" due to all is especially to be given to those God has placed in authority (cf. "the king" in 1 Peter 2:13 and "governors" in v. 14; cf. Rom. 13:1).

3. CHRISTIAN CONDUCT AS SLAVES (2:18-25)

Peter's instruction to slaves included two reasons why they should patiently endure personal injustice. First, this found favor with God, and second, it faithfully followed Jesus Christ's example.

2:18. The Greek word for **slaves** here is not *douloi*, the common term for slaves (cf. v. 16), but *oiketai*, which refers to household or domestic servants (cf. Luke 16:13; Rom. 14:4). The word translated **submit** (*hypotassomenoi*) is a nominative participle that continues the idea of submission expressed in 1 Peter 2:13 through the aorist imperative *hypotagēte*. This word of exhortation was relevant to a large number of Peter's first readers. Servants and slaves made up a high percentage of the early church, and undeserved punishment and suffering was common for the underlings. To be sure, there were some **good and considerate** masters. Certainly Christian masters were to be numbered in that category. However, Peter challenged Christian slaves to a new behavior which required them to submit to and respect even **those who are harsh.** "Harsh" is from the Greek *skolios* (lit., "curved," "bent," or "not straight"). The medical term "scoliosis," referring to curvature of the spine, comes from this word.

2:19-20. Peter set forth a principle here that may be applied to any situation where unjust suffering occurs. The **commendable** (lit., "for this is grace") motivation for patiently bearing **up under . . . unjust suffering** is a believer's **conscious** awareness of God's presence. No **credit** accrues for enduring punishment for **doing wrong.** It is respectful submission to *undeserved* suffering that finds favor with God because such behavior demonstrates His grace.

2:21-22. Peter powerfully supported his exhortation to slaves by citing Christ's example of endurance in unjust suffering. The Williams translation renders the opening phrase of this verse, "For you have been called for this purpose," referring to suffering for doing good. Christians are **called** (*eklēthēte;* cf. 1:15; 2:9) to **follow** Christ, to emulate His character and conduct, because He **suffered for** them. The word rendered **an example** (*hypogrammon,* lit., "underwriting"), appearing only here in the New Testament, refers to a writing or drawing that a student reproduces. Peter delineated Christ's example in verse 22 by quoting from Isaiah 53:9. Jesus **committed no sin,** either before or during His suffering (cf. 2 Cor. 5:21; Heb. 4:15; 1 John 3:5). He was completely innocent in both deed and word: **no deceit** (*dolos;* cf. 1 Peter 2:1) **was found in His mouth.**

2:23-25. Christ was the perfect example of patient submission to unjust suffering. **He did not retaliate . . . He made no threats** (cf. Rom. 12:19-20). Humanly speaking, the provocation to retaliate during Christ's arrest, trial, and crucifixion was extreme. Yet He suffered in silence, committing Himself to God. Peter explained (1 Peter 2:24) why the One who could have destroyed His enemies with a word patiently endured the pain and humiliation of the Cross. God was justly judging **our sins** which His Son **bore** (cf. 2 Cor. 5:21). In the Greek the words "our sins" are near the beginning of the verse and thus stand out emphatically, while **He Himself** stresses Christ's personal involvement. His death makes it possible for believers to be free from both the penalty and the power of sin and to live for Him: **so that we might die to sins and live for righteousness** (cf. Rom. 6:2, 13). Christ suffered so it would be possible for Christians to follow His example, both in suffering and in righteous living. Peter made a general reference to salvation: **by His wounds you have been healed** (Isa. 53:5). This

does not refer to physical healing for the verb's past tense indicates completed action, the "healing" is an accomplished fact. The reference is to salvation. Christ's suffering (lit., "wound"; *mōlōpi,* "stripe left by a lash," referred to Jesus' scourging) and death accomplished "healing," the salvation of every individual who trusts Him as his Savior.

Christ not only set the example and provides salvation, but He also gives guidance and protection to those who were headed away (**like sheep going astray**) from Him, but who then "turned about" (rather than **returned**) **to the Shepherd and Overseer** (*episkopon*) **of** their **souls.** "Shepherd" and "Overseer" stress Christ's matchless guidance and management of those who commit themselves to His care (cf. Ezek. 34:11-16).

B. New behavior in the family (3:1-7)

Peter extended the principles of respect and submission to authority, from Christian conduct in the world to Christian conduct in the family. He challenged his readers to new behavior as submissive wives and considerate husbands.

1. CHRISTIAN CONDUCT AS WIVES (3:1-6)

3:1-4. The participle translated **be submissive** (*hypotassomenai,* lit., "being under authority") carries the force of a command (cf. 2:18). This command is for **wives** to submit to their *own* **husbands** (cf. Eph. 5:22; Col. 3:18). The command does not require women to be subordinate to men in general but to their husbands as a function of order within the home. A wife is to accept her place in the family under the leadership of her husband whom God has placed as head in the home. Wives are to be submissive even if their husbands are unbelievers, so those men might be saved **by the behavior of their wives.** The powerful **purity** of a godly woman's life can soften even the stoniest male heart without a word (cf. Titus 2:5).

A woman who wins this kind of victory has a winsome loveliness that comes not **from outward adornment** but from her **inner self, the unfading beauty of a gentle and quiet spirit** (cf. 1 Tim. 2:9-11). This adornment of the spirit **is of great worth in God's sight.** While the world prizes costly clothing and gold jewelry, a woman with a gentle and quiet spirit is precious to God. Peter did not state that women should not wear jewelry and nice clothes, but that Christian wives should not think of outer attire as the source of genuine beauty.

3:5-6. Examples of **holy women** in the Old Testament support Peter's exhortation. Purity of life (v. 2) and a submissive spirit (v. 5) have always been a godly woman's lasting source of beauty and attractiveness. **Sarah** is chosen as a specific example of a woman who was **submissive to** her husband. She **obeyed Abraham and called him her master.** That is, she recognized him as the leader and head of their household (Gen. 18:12). Like other holy women of the past, Sarah put her **hope in God.** This kind of conduct gives women the spiritual heritage of Sarah: **You are her daughters if you do what is right and do not give way to fear** (*ptoēsin*, "terror"—used only here in the NT). Wives who are fearful (perhaps because of disobeying their husbands) are not putting all their trust in God.

2. CHRISTIAN CONDUCT AS HUSBANDS (3:7)

Peter exhorted Christian husbands to give their wives two gifts of love: understanding and respect.

3:7. The words (*kata gnōsin*) translated **considerate** (more lit., "according to knowledge" or "with understanding") point out that husbands should understand and be considerate of their wives' spiritual, emotional, and physical needs. Paul also elaborated on the husband's responsibility to protect and care for his wife, "just as Christ does the church" (Eph. 5:28-30).

Also husbands are to **treat** their wives **with respect as the weaker partner.** "Weaker" (*asthenesterō*) refers to physical or emotional weakness, not intellectual inferiority, for wives are their husbands' fellow **heirs** of God's **gift of life.** If Peter referred here to Christian husbands whose wives were Christians, then "the gracious gift of life" could refer to salvation (cf. Rom. 8:17; Eph. 3:6). If, however, the exhortation were directed to Christian husbands whose wives were unsaved (as 1 Peter 3:1-2 was written to wives with unsaved husbands), then "the gift of life" would refer to sharing the gift of physical life together. Peter added that husbands who do not treat their wives

with consideration and respect (*timēn*, "honor"; cf. 2:17) cannot expect to have their **prayers** answered.

IV. Cautioned for New Persecution (3:8–4:19)

In the first two chapters Peter referred to "all kinds of trials" (1:6), accusations of "doing wrong" (2:12), "the ignorant talk of foolish men" (2:15), and "the pain of unjust suffering" (2:19). All these persecutions seem to have resulted from the natural reactions of a pagan society against Christians who faithfully obeyed Jesus Christ.

Peter then warned that a time of more severe persecution and suffering was close at hand. He cautioned Christians to keep clear consciences when facing injustice, to endure the inevitable suffering with Christlike courage.

A. Overcoming injustice (3:8-22)

Peter used both Christ and Noah to illustrate the principle that in times of rising persecution the right response to injustice results in blessing.

1. A COMPASSIONATE CONDUCT (3:8-12)

3:8-12. Finally introduces a new section rather than giving a summary of the previous exhortations to specific groups (cf. "finally" in Phil. 3:1; 1 Thes. 4:1). Peter now addressed all his readers **(all of you)** and gave practical principles for living peacefully in a hostile pagan culture. First Peter 3:8-9 is Peter's exposition of Psalm 34:12-16, which he then quoted (1 Peter 3:10-12). Peter constructed his thoughts around the three exhortations in the psalm.

Whoever would love life . . . must first **keep his tongue from evil** (3:10). Verse 8 is a listing of Christian characteristics that keep a tongue from evil. **Harmony** (*homophrones*) could be translated "like-minded." Christians are urged to **be sympathetic** (*sympatheis*), to **love as brothers** (*philadelphoi*), to **be compassionate** (*eusplanchnoi*; cf. *splanchna* in Phil. 2:2; Phile. 7, 20), **and humble** (*tapeinophrones*). Of these five characteristics listed in 1 Peter 3:8 only the word for "compassionate" is found more than once in the New Testament and it is only used twice (here and in Eph. 4:32). This unique vocabulary stresses the importance of these Christian virtues which keep one

from deceitful (*dolon*; cf. 1 Peter 2:1, 22) **speech.**

The second exhortation, taken from Psalm 34:14, is foreshadowed by 1 Peter 3:9, **do not repay evil with evil** (cf. Rom. 12:17). Turning **from evil** (1 Peter 3:11) requires that there be no retaliation for ill treatment. Jesus taught this same law of love: "If someone strikes you on the right cheek, turn to him the other also" (Matt. 5:39).

Third, rather than returning evil, Christians are to **seek peace** (*eirenēn*; cf. 1 Peter 1:2; 5:14) **and pursue it** (Ps. 34:14). Peace is pursued by returning a **blessing** (1 Peter 3:9) when an insult is given. "Blessing" (*eulogountes*) here means to speak well of someone. This differs from the word "blessed" (*makarioi*, "fortunate or privileged" in verse 14; cf. 4:14; Matt. 5:3-11). Jesus said, "Pray for those who persecute you" (Matt. 5:44), and Paul wrote, "When we are cursed, we bless" (1 Cor. 4:12). This is the compassionate way that Christians should pursue peace. As a result, believers **inherit a blessing** (1 Peter 3:9; cf. 1:4; 3:7), **for the eyes of the Lord** (v. 12) watch over **the righteous and His ears are attentive to their prayer.** The "eyes" and "ears" of the Lord are figures of speech, anthropomorphisms which attribute human physical characteristics to God. Here the figures emphasize God's watchful oversight and careful attention to His people's needs (cf. 2:25).

2. A CLEAR CONSCIENCE (3:13-22)

Persecution occurred, however, in spite of believers' desires to live peacefully and their eagerness to do good. Peter encouraged his readers with the fact that the right response to undeserved suffering results in blessing. He presented the principle in verses 13-17 and provided examples in verses 18-22.

3:13-14. Who is going to harm you . . .? The context of Peter's question makes it almost rhetorical. Though the adversary, through physical suffering or material hardship, would distress those who were **eager** (*zēlōtai*, lit., "zealots") **to do good,** no real harm can come to those who belong to Christ. For even if suffering should occur, Christians **are blessed** and thus should **not be frightened.** The word here translated "blessed" (*makarioi*; cf. 4:14) was used by Jesus (Matt. 5:3-11). To be "blessed" in this context does not

mean to "feel delighted" but to be "highly privileged." Christians are not to be afraid of what men can do to them (cf. Matt. 10:28). Consequently 1 Peter 3:14 concludes with a quotation from Isaiah 8:12 which, in context, is part of an exhortation to fear God rather than men.

3:15. In their **hearts** Christians are to **set apart Christ as Lord.** Alexander Maclaren wrote, "Only he who can say, 'The Lord is the strength of my life' can go on to say, 'Of whom shall I be afraid?' " (*Expositions of Holy Scriptures,* 16: 42) Christians should overcome fear by sanctifying (*hagiasate,* "make separate from others") Christ as their Lord (*kyrion*). As a result Christians should **always be prepared** (*hetoimoi,* "ready"; cf. 1:5) **to give . . . the reason** (*apologian,* the "defense" which a defendant makes before a judge; cf. Acts 22:1; 25:16) **for** their **hope** in Christ. Such an oral defense should be consistent with one's "set-apart" conduct.

3:16. A believer's testimony should not be given in an arrogant manner but **with gentleness and respect.** ("Respect" here is from *phobos,* "fear," whereas "respect" for one's wife [v. 7] is *timē,* "honor.") Christians who are not afraid in the face of persecution are able to witness respectfully to their faith in Christ. They then keep **a clear** (*agathēn,* "good") **conscience** (*syneidēsin;* cf. 2:19; 3:21). Peter may have been alluding to the occasion when he denied Christ out of fear, in words that were neither gentle nor respectful.

Christians who suffer unjustly and keep a clear conscience put to shame those who **slander** their **good behavior in Christ.** Once again Peter encouraged his readers with the fact that good behavior is their best defense against unjust punishment and persecution.

3:17. However, Peter pointed out that it may be **God's will** (*thelēma;* cf. 2:15; 4:2, 19) for them **to suffer for doing good** (cf. 1:6; 2:15; 4:16, 19). This, as he told them earlier, "is commendable before God" (2:20) and so is **better** than deserved suffering **for doing evil** (cf. 2:14). First Peter 3:17 is an effective summary of the content of 2:15, 19-20.

3:18. In verses 18-22 Peter illustrated the principles given in verses 13-17. Once again Christ provided the perfect example. He suffered for doing what was right

(2:14). His sinless life provoked the unjust hostilities of evil men. However, He did not fear men but trusted Himself to God. Christ clearly stated His purpose and committed Himself to a course of action. He died in mankind's place, keeping His conscience clear (cf. 2:23). As a result He received tremendous blessing and reward in His own resurrection and exultation.

J.M.E. Ross wrote that verse 18 is "one of the shortest and simplest, and yet one of the richest summaries given in the New Testament of the meaning of the Cross of Jesus" ("The First Epistle of Peter," in *A Devotional Commentary.* London: Religious Tract Society, n.d., pp. 151-52). **Christ died for sins** (cf. 2:21, 24). The phrase "for sins" (*peri hamartiōn*) is used in the Septuagint in regard to the sin offering for atonement. However, **once for all** (cf. Rom. 6:10; Heb. 9:26, 28; 10:10) is clearly a contrast with the Old Testament yearly sacrifice on the Day of Atonement and declares the complete sufficiency of Christ's death. The substitutionary nature of Christ's death is indicated by the phrase **the righteous for the unrighteous** (*dikaios hyper adikōn*). Christ, the "righteous One" (*dikaios*), uniquely qualified to die as the substitute for (*hyper*, "for," "in place of," or "instead of") the "unrighteous ones" (*adikōn*). The divine purpose for Christ's sacrificial death was man's reconciliation, **to bring** people **to God.**

Peter concluded his summary of Christ's redemptive work by referring to His resurrection. Though Christ **was put to death in the body** (*sarki*, "flesh"), He was **made alive by the Spirit.** "By the Spirit" translates one word, *pneumati,* which could refer to the third Person of the Trinity as the agent of Christ's resurrection. Or it may refer to Christ's human spirit in contrast with His human body (cf. 1 Peter 4:6).

3:19-20. Through whom . . . He . . . preached to the spirits in prison has been subject to many interpretations. Some believe Peter here referred to the descent of Christ's Spirit into hades between His death and resurrection to offer people who lived before the Flood a second chance for salvation. However, this interpretation has no scriptural support.

Others have said this passage refers to Christ's descent into hell after His crucifixion to proclaim His victory to the imprisoned fallen angels referred to in 2 Peter 2:4-5, equating them with "the sons of God" Moses wrote about (Gen. 6:1-2). Though much commends this view as a possible interpretation, the context seems more likely to be referring to humans rather than angels.

The "spirits" (*pneumasin,* a term usually applied to supernatural beings but also used at least once to refer to human "spirits"; cf. Heb. 12:23) are described in 1 Peter 3:20 as those who were disobedient **when God waited patiently** for **Noah** to finish building **the ark.** They had rebelled against the message of God during the 120 years the ark was being built. God declared He would not tolerate people's wickedness forever, but would extend His patience for only 120 more years (Gen. 6:3). Since the entire human race except Noah (Gen. 6:5-9) was evil, God determined to "wipe mankind . . . from the face of the earth." The "spirits" referred to in 1 Peter 3:20 are probably the souls of the evil human race that existed in the days of Noah. Those "spirits" are now "in prison" awaiting the final judgment of God at the end of the Age.

The problem remains as to *when* Christ preached to these "spirits." Peter's explanation of the resurrection of Christ (3:18) "by the Spirit" brought to mind that the preincarnate Christ was actually in Noah, ministering through him, by means of the Holy Spirit. Peter (1:11) referred to the "Spirit of Christ" in the Old Testament prophets. Later he described Noah as "a preacher of righteousness" (2 Peter 2:5). The Spirit of Christ preached through Noah to the ungodly humans who, at the time of Peter's writing, were "spirits in prison" awaiting final judgment.

This interpretation seems to fit the general theme of this section (1 Peter 3:13-22)—keeping a good conscience in unjust persecution. Noah is presented as an example of one who committed himself to a course of action for the sake of a clear conscience before God, though it meant enduring harsh ridicule. Noah did not fear men but obeyed God and proclaimed His message. Noah's reward for keeping a clear conscience in unjust suffering was the salvation of himself and his family, who **were saved through**

water, being brought safely through the Flood.

3:21. And this (*ho,* relative pronoun—"water" is the understood antecedent) **water symbolizes baptism** (*baptisma*). Baptism represents a complete break with one's past life. As the Flood wiped away the old sinful world, so baptism pictures one's break from his old sinful life and his entrance into new life in Christ. Peter now applied to his readers the principle he set forth in verses 13-17 and illustrated in verses 18-20. He exhorted them to have the courage to commit themselves to a course of action by taking a public stand for Christ through baptism. The act of public baptism would "save" them from the temptation to sacrifice their good consciences in order to avoid persecution. For a first-century Christian, baptism meant he was following through on his commitment to Christ, regardless of the consequences.

Baptism does not save from sin, but from a bad conscience. Peter clearly taught that baptism was not merely a ceremonial act of physical purification, **but** (*alla,* making a strong contrast) **the pledge** (*eperōtēma,* also trans. "appeal"; cf. NASB) **of a good conscience** (*syneidēseōs;* cf. v. 16) **toward God.** Baptism is the symbol of what has already occurred in the heart and life of one who has trusted Christ as Savior (cf. Rom. 6:3-5; Gal. 3:27; Col. 2:12). To make the source of salvation perfectly clear Peter added, **by the resurrection of Jesus Christ** (cf. 1 Peter 1:3).

3:22. Mentioning Christ's resurrection returned Peter's thoughts to his original example, so he concluded his digression and completed his first illustration with a reference to Christ's reward and blessing. Having witnessed Christ's physical Ascension (cf. Mark 16:19; Luke 24:51; Acts 1:6-11), Peter wrote that Christ **has gone into heaven.** The reward for Christ's faithfulness is seen in His exaltation over all things. He is enthroned **at God's right hand** (cf. Ps. 110:1; Heb. 1:13; 8:1; 10:12; 12:2), the seat of supreme honor, to rule and reign over all creation (cf. Col. 1:15-16; 2:14-15).

B. Enduring suffering (chap. 4)

This chapter is the heart of Peter's encouragement for endurance. Here is practical instruction based on Christ's example in undergoing suffering. In order to endure suffering, Christians are to arm themselves with Christlike courage, minister to one another with Christlike service, and commit themselves to God with Christlike faith.

1. CHRISTLIKE ATTITUDE (4:1-6)

Maintaining proper conduct in suffering requires that Christians maintain a Christlike attitude, living for the present in God's will, knowing that they will live for eternity in His presence.

4:1. Therefore (*oun,* an inferential conjunction) Peter referred back to Christ's suffering in 3:18 and applied the principles of patient endurance in unjust suffering to his readers' immediate situation. He exhorted believers to **arm** themselves with **the same** courageous **attitude** or mind-set Christ had regarding suffering. The word translated "arm yourselves" (*hoplisasthe,* used only here in the NT) referred to a soldier putting on armor (cf. Eph. 6:13). With the same determination and care with which a soldier puts on his armor, Christians are to adopt Christ's "attitude" (*ennoian,* lit., "thought"; Heb. 4:12 has the only other biblical usage of this word) toward persecution, an unswerving resolve to do God's will.

Identification with Christ, arming oneself with His attitude, also means sharing in His suffering and death. Christ **suffered in His body,** and a believer suffers **in his body** also. One who has suffered in this way **is done with sin,** that is, his being identified with Christ demonstrates (as does baptism) his break with a sinful life. Because of Christ's death, "we should no longer be slaves to sin, because anyone who has died has been freed from sin" (Rom. 6:6-7).

4:2. As a result Christians who have adopted Christ's mind-set have counted themselves dead to sin. They **live the rest** of their lives not **for evil human desires, but rather for the will of God** (cf. 2:15; 3:17; 4:19).

4:3. Christians were exhorted to live for the present in God's will because old habits were a thing of **the past.** In blunt language Peter stressed that there must be a definite break from **what pagans choose to do** (*boulēma tōn ethnōn,* lit., "desire of the Gentiles"), the wasted years of debauchery, lust, drunkenness, orgies, carousing, and . . . idolatry (cf. Gal. 5:19-21). This exhortation probably had a strong impact on Gentile Christians who used to live in gross sin.

4:4. Christians are to live in the present for the will of God because old acquaintances are now persecutors. Godless men are genuinely surprised by the changed lives of those who once were like they are. **They think it strange** (*xenizontai*, from *xenos*, "stranger"; cf. v. 12). A changed life provokes hostility from those who reject the gospel. Consequently **they heap abuse on** (*blasphē-mountes*, lit., "blaspheme") believers.

4:5. Those who have spent their lives in indulgence and idolatry will someday **give account** (*apodōsousin logon*, lit., "give back a word or an account"; cf. Matt. 12:36; Luke 16:2; Acts 19:40; Heb. 13:17). Peter warned that these people must one day face the One **who is ready** (i.e., willing) **to judge.** No one will escape this final judgment of the words and works of his earthly life, when Christ will judge both **the living** (*zōntas*) **and the dead** (*nekrous*) (cf. Acts 10:42; Rom. 14:9; 1 Thes. 4:15; 2 Tim. 4:1).

4:6. For this . . . reason, because everybody must give an account to God, **the gospel was preached even to those . . . now dead.** This has been interpreted as referring to (a) those who are spiritually "dead in sin," (b) those who heard and believed the gospel but have since died, (c) those who died without hearing or believing the gospel. Barclay preferred the third interpretation, assuming that 3:19 refers to Christ's preaching to the dead. Consequently he believed that here "was a breathtaking glimpse of a gospel of a second chance." This interpretation has no scriptural support and is contrary to orthodox Christian doctrine (cf. v. 5).

In verse 6 Peter, in contrast with verse 5, encouraged his readers with the fact that rather than facing judgment for their sins, those who had heard and believed the gospel of Jesus Christ faced an altogether different future. The penalty for their sin has been paid by Christ on the cross. The last earthly effect of sin is physical death. Believers still die physically; they are **judged . . . in regard to the body** (cf. suffering in this life "in his body," v. 1). But for Christians physical death does not lead to judgment but to eternal life. They **live . . . in regard to the Spirit.** Those armed with a Christlike attitude will live forever in God's presence.

2. CHRISTLIKE SERVICE (4:7-11)

Encouragement to endure suffering comes not only from a believer's future hope but also from the Christlike service of others within His body.

4:7. The end . . . is near (*ēngiken*, lit., "draws near"; the same form is used in James 5:8 to refer to the Second Coming). After mentioning Christians who had died (1 Peter 4:6), Peter then referred to the imminent return of Christ for His church. The shortness of the time remaining is motivation to live for and serve Jesus Christ (v. 2). As a result, Christians are to **be clear-minded** (*sōphronēsate*, lit., "be of sound mind"; cf. Mark 5:15) **and self-controlled** (*nēpsate*, lit., "be sober"; cf. 1 Peter 1:13; 5:8) **so that** they are able to **pray** (cf. Eph. 6:18). Prayer, of high priority in persecution, is to be clear, reasonable, sober communication with God.

4:8-9. Love (*agapēn . . . echontes*) **each other deeply.** "Deeply" (*ektenē*, "stretched" or "strained") was used to describe the taut muscles of an athlete who strains to win a race (cf. *ektenōs* in 1:22). A Christian's unselfish love and concern for others should be exercised to the point of sacrificially giving for others' welfare. **Love covers over** (*kalyptei*, lit., "hides") **a multitude of sins.** This kind of strenuously maintained love is not blind but sees and accepts the faults of others (cf. Prov. 10:12; 1 Cor. 13:4-7). Christian love may be displayed through extending free food and lodging, offering **hospitality** (*philoxenoi*, lit., "being friendly to strangers") **without grumbling** to those who are traveling. During times of persecution, hospitality was especially welcomed by Christians who were forced to journey to new areas.

4:10. Believers should be diligent in using their spiritual gifts. Each **gift** (*charisma*) is to be used **to serve** (*diakonountes*; cf. *diakonos*, "deacon") or "minister to" **others.** The phrase **faithfully administering** (*hōs kaloi oikonomoi*) could also be translated "as good stewards." A "steward" was one who served as a house manager; he had no wealth of his own, but distributed his master's wealth according to his master's will and direction. The "gift" (*charisma*) stems from **God's grace** (*charitos*). His grace is manifested to His church as believers exercise their spiritual gifts in service to each other. His grace is evident **in its various forms,** that is, it is "manifold" (NASB), variegated, rich in variety (*poikilēs*; cf. 1:6, where Peter said trials are *poikilois*, or varied).

4:11. Peter divided Christian service into two general categories: the one who **speaks** (*lalei*) and the one who **serves** (*diakonei*; cf. v. 10). This division relates to the distinction God's leaders made between ministry roles (Acts 6:2-4). These two general ministry functions often overlap. Both groups function through dependence on God's gracious provision. The reason for relying on God's words (cf. Acts 7:38; Rom. 3:2; Heb. 5:12) and **strength** (*ischyos*, "power") is that **God** will receive the praise **through Jesus Christ.** At the mention of Christ's name Peter offered an appropriate word of praise as a benediction: **To Him be the glory and the power** (*kratos*, "might") **forever and ever. Amen.** (Cf. the similar benediction in 1 Peter 5:11.) The praise and credit for Christian ministry should always be given to Christ.

3. CHRISTLIKE FAITH (4:12-19)

Anticipating hardships the believers in Asia Minor were about to undergo, Peter encouraged his readers to endure suffering with Christlike faith so that they might be further identified with Christ, receive a blessing, and trust God completely.

4:12. Peter warned his readers about the coming of a more intense period of persecution. He again stressed mental readiness (cf. 1:13; 4:7): **Do not be surprised** (*xenizesthe*, "amazed"; cf. v. 4) **at the painful trial you are suffering.** The NASB translates this last phrase "the fiery ordeal among you." Literally rendered it could read "the among you burning." The verb *pyrōsei* is from *pyroō*, "to burn." The meaning may be metaphorical as in 1:7 where the context is quite similar. However, the verse could also be aptly applied to the historical reality of the Neronian persecution. Christians were blamed for the burning of Rome. Some

were covered with pitch and used as living torches to light the imperial gardens at night. Peter may have believed that the provincial officials were likely to follow their emperor's example and stake-burn Christians in Asia Minor. Such persecution should not take the Christians by surprise **as though something strange** (*xenou*) were befalling them.

4:13. But rejoice that you participate (*koinōneite*, from *koinōneō*, "to share"; related nouns are *koinōnia*, "communion, fellowship, close relationship," and *koinōnos*, "sharer"; cf. 5:1). Suffering for Christ's sake should cause rejoicing because through suffering Christians further identify with Christ. Sharing in **the sufferings of Christ** results in (a) joy with Christ (the word **overjoyed** is trans. "rejoice" in 1:6), (b) fellowship with Him (Phil. 3:10), (c) being glorified with Him (Rom. 8:17), and (d) reigning with Him (2 Tim. 2:12). The New Testament is clear that those who take part in the suffering of Christ also will take part in **His glory,** when it **is revealed** (*apokalypsei*; cf. 1 Peter 1:7; 5:1). Peter presented this truth as a cause for future hope and present rejoicing while enduring persecution.

4:14. Peter again referred to Jesus' teaching (Matt. 5:11). If a Christian was **insulted** (cf. 1 Peter 3:9) **because of the name of Christ,** he should be considered **blessed** (*makarioi*; cf. 3:14). Anything that we suffer for the sake of Christ is a privilege, not a penalty. **The Spirit of glory and of God** (cf. Isa. 11:2; Matt. 3:16) refers to the Holy Spirit's indwelling presence within all who are identified by "the name of Christ" and thus suffer persecution (cf. 1 Peter 4:16).

4:15. Peter stressed that persecution was no excuse for lawlessness. Christians were not to retaliate (3:9). Physical violence was not to be met by murder. Confiscation of property was not to be compensated for by theft. No matter what their trials, Christians were to do nothing that would justify punishing them as criminals (cf. 2:19; 3:17). They were not to suffer **as a murderer or thief or any other kind of criminal, or even as a meddler.** Even interfering in other people's affairs is out of place for Christians (cf. 1 Tim. 5:13).

4:16. There is no shame if one **suffer**(s) **as a Christian** rather than as a criminal. On the contrary, **that name** should be a source of praise to God for it identifies the bearer with the blessings of salvation (cf. v. 11). The term "Christian" (*Christianos*) occurs only three times in the Bible (here and Acts 11:26; 26:28). It may have been used derisively by unbelievers, as an insult.

4:17-18. Peter had referred to persecution and suffering as trials that refine and prove one's faith (1:6-7) if reacted to in the will of God (3:17). Now he added that God allows persecutions as disciplinary judgment to purify the lives of those in **the family of God.** If believers need disciplinary earthly judgments (**if it begins with us,** a first-class condition which assumes the reality of the premise), how much more will **those who do not obey the gospel** (cf. 2:7) **the ungodly and the sinner,** deserve everlasting judgment? Peter quoted the Septuagint rendering of Proverbs 11:31, **If it is hard for the righteous to be saved,** to emphasize God's disciplinary demands on His children. The vicissitudes of life are a part of God's constant care, yet from a human perspective discipline is always "hard." Peter is not teaching that salvation is earned through personal trials or works, but simply that those who are saved are not exempt from temporal disciplinary judgments which are the natural consequences of sin. The writer of Hebrews also supports Peter: "Endure hardship as discipline; God is treating you as sons" (Heb. 12:7).

4:19. Believers could be sure that they were being called on to **suffer according to God's will** (cf. 2:15; 3:17; 4:2) if, having committed no crimes, they were suffering solely because they bore Christ's name. Peter encouraged suffering saints to endure through the exercise of Christlike faith. Just as Christ trusted Himself to His Father who judges justly (2:23), so should believers **commit** (*paratithesthōsan,* an accounting term, "to deposit or entrust") **themselves** (*psychas autōn,* lit., "their souls") **to their faithful Creator and continue to do good** (cf. 2:15, 20).

V. Charged with New Responsibility (5:1-11)

In the final chapter Peter emphasized new responsibilities within the church in light of the troubled times. He exhorted the elders to shepherd the people, the young men to submit to the elders, and everyone to stand firm in the faith.

A. Elders are to shepherd (5:1-4)

Peter's charge to elders was given in three pairs of negative and positive exhortations. The exhortations reflect Ezekiel (34:1-16), where false shepherds were contrasted with the True Shepherd.

5:1. Peter, in addressing the **elders** (*presbyterous;* cf. Acts 11:30; 20:17), also used a word that identified himself as one who held the same office (*sympresbyteros,* "fellow-presbyter"). As an elder, Peter was speaking from experience. However, Peter's authority came from the fact that he was an apostle (1 Peter 1:1), and **a witness** (*martys;* cf. Acts 3:15; 10:39) **of Christ's sufferings.** Peter also referred to himself as **one who . . . will share** (*koinōnos;* cf. 1 Peter 4:13) **in the glory to be revealed.** Peter had just made the point that those who share in Christ's sufferings will also share in His glory (4:13). Peter further identified with his readers by referring to his own suffering for Christ's sake (Acts 5:40).

5:2. The command **Be shepherds** was also given by Jesus to Peter (John 21:16) The word *poimanate* means "to tend." Besides feeding, it includes caring, leading, guiding, and protecting—all duties and responsibilities a shepherd has for his flock. Related to the participle **serving as overseers** (*episkopountes*) is the noun "overseer" (*episkopos,* used five other times: Phil. 1:1; 1 Tim. 3:1-2; Titus 1:7; 1 Peter 2:25). "Overseer" seems to be interchangeable with "elder" and connotes both a spiritual and physical guardianship. ("Serving as overseers" is not in some Gr. mss.)

Peter, through contrasting exhortations, presented both the motive and the manner of one's ministry. An elder's motive must be from willingness, not from a sense of external compulsion: **not because you must, but because you are willing.** Social or financial pressures should not be substituted for the pure motivation to do God's will and to serve Him freely and eagerly: **not greedy for money, but eager to serve** (cf. 1 Tim. 3:8; Titus 1:7, 11). Shepherds who serve with false motives care only for themselves and devour the flock (Ezek. 34:2-3).

5:3. The word translated **lording it over** (*katakyrieuontes*) includes the idea of domineering as in the rule of a strong person over one who is weak (cf. Matt. 20:25; Mark 10:42; Acts 19:16). Ezekiel indicted false shepherds: "You have ruled them harshly and brutally. So they were scattered because there was no shepherd" (Ezek. 34:4-5). Peter exhorted the elders to be **examples** (*typoi*, "types or patterns"), to serve as models for the people to follow. They were not to drive God's people, but to lead them by their examples of mature Christian character.

5:4. Christ, **the Chief Shepherd** (*archipoimenos*), is "the True Shepherd" (Ezek. 34:11-16), "the Good Shepherd" (John 10:11, 14), and "the Great Shepherd" (Heb. 13:20). When Christ returns, His faithful undershepherds will share in His glory (1 Peter 5:1) and receive unfading crowns (cf. 1:4).

B. Young men are to submit (5:5-7)

Peter then turned his attention from the shepherds to the sheep. Good leaders deserve good followers. Those who are led are responsible to be in subjection to men and to God.

5:5. **Young men . . . be submissive** (*hypotagēte*; cf. 3:1) **to those who are older.** Church leaders were usually older members. The younger members were to place themselves willingly under the authority of those who had been given the responsibility of leadership. Peter exhorted both young and old alike to **clothe** (*enkombōsasthe*, "clothe or tie on oneself"; an *enkombōma* was the apron of a slave) **yourselves with humility.** True humility is attractive dress (cf. 3:8). Peter may have alluded to Christ's girding Himself with a towel and teaching the disciples that humility is the prerequisite for service and service is the practice of humility (John 13:4-15).

Peter quoted Proverbs 3:34 to emphasize God's different attitudes toward the proud and the humble. **God opposes** (lit., "sets Himself against") the arrogant **but** grants favor and acceptance **to the humble.**

5:6-7. Knowing God's attitude should cause Christians not only to be subject to others but also to subject themselves deliberately to **God's** sovereign rule. The command **humble yourselves** (*tapeinōthēte*) could be translated "allow yourselves to be humbled." Those who were suffering persecution for Christ's sake could be encouraged by the fact that the same **mighty hand** that let them suffer would one day **lift** (*hypsōsē*, "exalt") them **up** (cf. James 4:10).

Peter then referred to Christ's classic words of encouragement in the Sermon on the Mount (Matt. 6:25-32), while quoting Psalm 55:22: "Cast your cares on the Lord and He will sustain you." All a believer's anxieties can be **cast . . . on Him.** Christ sustains **because He cares.** A Christian's confidence rests in the fact that Christ is genuinely concerned for his welfare.

C. All are to stand firm (5:8-11)

Though believers should place their confidence in God, they should not be careless. Christians in conflict are to be on the alert, made strong and steadfast by Christ Himself.

5:8. **Be self-controlled** (*nēpsate*; cf. 1:13; 4:7) **and alert** (*grēgorēsate*; cf. 1 Thes. 5:6, 10). Christians should be constantly alert because the **enemy** (*antidikos*, "adversary"), **the devil** (*diabolos*, "slanderer"), is always actively seeking an opportunity for a vicious attack. This verse could also be a veiled allusion to the horrors of the Neronian persecution in the Roman Coliseum, in which lions mauled and devoured Christians. Satan desired to do the same thing spiritually, to defeat believers' testimonies.

5:9. The devil can be and should be resisted. **Resist** (*antistēte*) means "withstand," used also in James 4:7 (cf. *antidikos*, "enemy" in 1 Peter 5:8). It is a term of defense rather than attack. Christians may stand firm against Satan only if they depend wholly on Christ, **standing firm in the faith** (cf. v. 12; Col. 2:5). Peter also encouraged his readers by reminding them that they were not alone in their suffering. The knowledge that other Christians, **your brothers throughout the world,** were suffering, would strengthen their resolve to continue to stand firm.

5:10. Peter had encouraged his readers to endure suffering in such a way that the grace of God would be made manifest in their lives. Now in a closing word of benediction he committed them to **the God of all grace** (cf. 4:10). The benediction briefly summarizes Peter's message of encouragement. Christians' suffering will last only **a little while,** while their **glory in Christ,** to which they were **called,** will be **eternal** (cf. Rom. 8:17-18; 2 Cor. 4:16-18). (This is Peter's last of eight uses of "glory" in this epistle: 1 Peter 1:7,11, 21, 24; 2:20; 4:14; 5:1, 10.) God Himself would **restore** them **and make** them **strong** (stērixei; cf. 2 Thes. 2:17), **firm** (sthenōsei, used only here in the NT), **and steadfast** (themeliosei, "established"; cf. Eph. 3:17; Col. 1:23).

5:11. To Him be the power (kratos, "might") **forever and ever. Amen.** In this benediction, similar to the one in 4:11, Peter praised Christ who has all power for all time (cf. Rom. 11:36; 1 Tim. 6:16). Certainly He has the power to strengthen His own as they undergo persecution.

VI. Conclusion (5:12-14)

5:12. As Paul often did at the close of his epistles, Peter may have penned these last verses himself. Silas served as Peter's amanuensis **(with the help of Silas . . . I have written to you),** and probably personally delivered the letter to the churches of Asia Minor along the predetermined route specified in 1:1. This was probably the same Silas who accompanied Paul on his second missionary journey (Acts 15:40). In the words **encouraging** (parakalōn, "exhorting, appealing"; cf. 1 Peter 5:1) **. . . and testifying** (epimartyrōn, "bearing witness"), Peter summarized the purpose of his letter. He wrote to encourage Christians to endure persecution, to **stand fast,** so that **the true grace of God** (cf. 1:13; 4:10) would be evidenced to the unbelieving world. They were to "stand fast" in His grace (cf. 5:9).

5:13. Some scholars suggest that **she who is in Babylon** refers to Peter's wife (cf. 1 Cor. 9:5). However, since Peter was writing to churches and said she is **chosen together with you,** probably "she" refers to the church (which is a feminine noun ekklēsia). If so, Peter was sending greetings from the church in "Babylon" to the churches in Asia Minor. According to historical evidence, Peter was in Rome during the final years of his life. "Babylon" here might be a disguised reference to Rome, used in order to protect both the Roman church and Peter from the Neronian persecution. (Others suggest, however, that he wrote from the literal

city of Babylon on the Euphrates River.) Greetings were also sent from Peter's **son** in the faith, **Mark.** Paul (Col. 4:10) placed John Mark in Rome on an earlier occasion. Consequently most would agree that John Mark, the cousin of Barnabas, was in Rome at the time 1 Peter was written. This strengthens the view that "Babylon" referred to Rome.

5:14. The number of New Testament references to **a kiss** indicate that it was a common sign of fellowship and Christian love (cf. Rom. 16:16; 1 Cor. 16:20; 2 Cor. 13:12; 1 Thes. 5:26).

Peter closed as he began (1 Peter 1:2), encouraging Christians in the midst of persecution by praying for **peace** (eirēnē), which is abundantly available to all **who are in Christ,** the Prince of Peace.

BIBLIOGRAPHY

Barbieri, Louis A. First and Second Peter. Everyman's Bible Commentary. Chicago: Moody Press, 1977.

Barclay, William. The Letters of James and Peter. The Daily Study Bible. Rev. ed. Philadelphia: Westminster Press, 1976.

Bigg, Charles. A Critical and Exegetical Commentary on the Epistles of St. Peter and St. Jude. The International Critical Commentary. Edinburgh: T. & T. Clark, 1902.

Blum, Edwin A. "1 Peter." In The Expositor's Bible Commentary, vol. 12. Grand Rapids: Zondervan Publishing Co., 1981.

Cranfield, C.E.B. The First Epistle of Peter. London: S.C.M. Press, 1950.

Johnstone, Robert. The First Epistle of Peter: Revised Text, with Introduction and Commentary. Edinburgh: T. & T. Clark, 1888. Reprint. Minneapolis: James Family Publishers, 1978.

Lenski, R.C.H. The Interpretation of the Epistles of St. Peter, St. John, and St. Jude. Minneapolis: Augsburg Publishing House, 1966.

Maclaren, Alexander. Expositions of Holy Scripture, vol. 16. Reprint. Grand Rapids: Baker Book House, 1975.

Robertson, A.T. Word Pictures in the New Testament, vol. 6. Nashville: Broadman Press, 1933.

1 Peter

Selwyn, E.G. *The First Epistle of Peter.* New York: Macmillan Co., 1964.

Stibbs, Alan M. *The First Epistle General of Peter.* Grand Rapids: Wm. B. Eerdmans Publishing Co., 1959.

Wiersbe, Warren W. *Be Hopeful.* Wheaton, Ill.: Scripture Press Publications, Victor Books, 1982.

Wuest, Kenneth S. *First Peter in the Greek New Testament for the English Reader.* Grand Rapids: Wm. B. Eerdmans Publishing Co., 1942.

2 PETER

Kenneth O. Gangel

INTRODUCTION

This epistle may be titled "The Believer's Conflict in the Latter Days." The apostle opened and closed 2 Peter with the theme of victory. But within the epistle he focused primarily on how to live when surrounded by the problems and perplexities of the end time. After painting a landscape (in 2:1–3:10) replete with false teachers, fallen angels, flagrant immorality, and flaccid scoffers, Peter charged his readers "to live holy and godly lives as you look forward to the day of God and speed its coming" (3:11-12). Faithful living in difficult times—that is the lesson Peter would have believers learn through this dynamic letter.

Authorship and Canonicity. For more than 17 centuries this brief but poignant epistle has withstood the blasts of skeptical scholars who have denied the authenticity of its claim to Petrine authorship. The first verse names Simon Peter who stood with James and John as one of the unique eyewitnesses to Christ's transfiguration (1:17-18; cf. Mark 9:2-7). This Peter who had written earlier (1 Peter 1:1), now addressed the same readers (2 Peter 3:1). He was numbered as one of the Twelve (1:1; 3:2), and he knew the Apostle Paul as a "dear brother" (3:15). Peter had heard the manner of his own death foretold by his Lord as they walked together along the shore of the Sea of Galilee (1:14; cf. John 21:18). Yet, despite this internal evidence, as early as the third century Origen (died ca. 253) noted that there was some doubt concerning the true identity of the author of 2 Peter.

During the fourth century, the great church historian Eusebius (260?–340?) listed 2 Peter, along with 2 and 3 John and James, as antilegomena, books whose canonicity was under dispute. Eusebius noted that no long line of church tradition

seemed to support the acceptance of 2 Peter.

Jerome (346–420) included 2 Peter in his well-known translation of the Bible, the Latin Vulgate. Though Jerome accepted the authenticity of the book, he stated that many questioned its Petrine authorship because of the marked difference of style between 1 and 2 Peter.

Through the centuries scholars have added to these early arguments. Some have attempted to identify 2 Peter with the apocryphal or pseudonymous writings which claim apostolic authorship (i.e., the Apocalypse of Peter, the Gospel of Peter, and the Acts of Peter). The strong similarity between 2 Peter and Jude has caused some to doubt Petrine authorship.

Others have pointed out that the mention of Paul's writings (3:16) and the problems raised by the false teachers (specifically the delay of the Lord's return [3:4]), argue for a later author writing sometime during the second century, long after Peter's death. As a result of those and other related arguments, most nonconservative scholars reject the apostolic authorship of 2 Peter.

Yet, while modern opinion may run against the acceptance of the traditional position, none of these problems is insurmountable and none of the arguments is unanswerable.

External evidence. The church literature of the second century includes no direct references to 2 Peter. Consequently critics have stated that there is less external attestation for 2 Peter than for any other book in the New Testament. However, silence argues neither for nor against Petrine authorship. The epistle is short and was probably not widely circulated. Its acceptance may have come slowly because of the suspicion the early church had for letters bearing the names of apostles. The extent of early forgeries is emphasized by Paul's admonition to beware of certain false epistles (2 Thes. 2:2). Also since 2 Peter was written just shortly before the author's death, he could not have been around long to verify its authenticity. However, the silence of second-century authors does not indicate that the church did not accept 2 Peter.

During the third century three men referred directly to the Petrine authorship of 2 Peter. Methodius of Olympus, martyred in the Diocletian persecution, quoted 2 Peter 3:8 to support his argument in *De Resurrectione*. He definitely referred to the Apostle Peter as the author. Firmilian, a bishop of Caesarea in Cappadocia, referred to the Apostle Peter's denunciation of false teachers. First Peter does not refer to false teachers, but 2 Peter devotes an entire chapter to the subject. Thus Firmilian may have been ascribing Petrine authorship to 2 Peter. Finally, Origen, though pointing out a current trend of doubt, seems from the content and frequent references in his other writings to have accepted 2 Peter as authoritative. Though the first statement questioning Petrine authorship was made in the third century, both Methodius and Firmilian affirmed 2 Peter as genuine— and, most likely, Origen did as well.

In the fourth century the Petrine authorship of 2 Peter was strongly affirmed. Two of the great theologians of the early church, Athanasius and Augustine, considered 2 Peter as canonical. The Council of Laodicea (A.D. 372) included the epistle in the canon of Scripture. Jerome placed 2 Peter in the Latin Vulgate (ca. A.D. 404). Also the great third Council of Carthage (A.D. 397) recognized the intrinsic authority and worth of 2 Peter and formally affirmed that it was written by the Apostle Peter.

Though 2 Peter is the least attested book in the New Testament, its external support far surpasses that of many of the other Bible books. The absence of early church tradition supporting 2 Peter certainly could have been due to the letter's brevity and the lack of communication among Christians during times of heavy persecution. Consequently the silence of the second century and the caution of the third century posed no insurmountable problems for the careful scholarship of the canonical councils of the fourth century.

Internal evidence. The question of stylistic differences between 1 Peter and 2 Peter has been debated since Jerome first recorded the problem in the fourth century. Jerome himself explained that the difference in style could easily be attributed to the fact that Peter most likely used an amanuensis other than Silvanus who served Peter in writing his first letter (1 Peter 5:12). If Jerome is right, the differences in style are no greater than might have been expected, considering the different subject matter and different purposes for writing the two letters.

The similarities in style between the two books are just as striking as the differences. Both books are filled with *hapax legomena,* words that occur only once in the New Testament. Of the 686 *hapax legomena* in the New Testament, 1 Peter contains 62 and 2 Peter has 54— more, proportionately, than most New Testament books their size (Homer K. Ebright, *The Petrine Epistles.* Cincinnati: Methodist Book Concern, 1917, pp. 70-5, 121-3; cf. Charles Bigg, *A Critical and Exegetical Commentary on the Epistles of St. Peter and St. Jude,* pp. 224-5). Ebright concludes that the noticeable differences are not between the two Petrine Epistles but between these Epistles and the rest of the New Testament. The prominence of *hapax legomena* in both books may point to a common author who had a rich vocabulary and a public speaker's flare for fresh creative expression.

It should not be considered remarkable, then, that a number of words and phrases are found only in these two epistles. Both books include the unusual salutation, "Grace and peace be yours in abundance" (1 Peter 1:2; 2 Peter 1:2). The term *aretas* ("praises") in 1 Peter 2:9, and *aretē* ("goodness") in 2 Peter 1:3 are forms of the same unique word and refer to the moral excellence and goodness of God. The word *apothesis* is used in the New Testament only in 1 Peter 3:21 and 2 Peter 1:14 and is translated "removal" and "put . . . aside," respectively. The graphic phrase *amōmou kai aspilou,* used in 1 Peter 1:19 to refer to the sinlessness of Christ as One without "blemish or defect," is artfully rephrased in 2 Peter 2:13 as *spiloi kai mōmoi* ("blots and blemishes") to refer to the character of the false teachers. The phrase is used again in 3:14, *aspiloi kai amōmētoi* "spotless and blameless"), to challenge Christians to moral excellence in light of Christ's return. The use of these and other unique words and phrases in these two epistles provides strong evidence of their common authorship.

Second Peter also reflects the unique vocabulary of Peter's sermons recorded in the Book of Acts. One of the best examples is the verb *kolasōntai* ("punish"), found only in Acts 4:21, and *kolazomenous* ("punishment") in 2 Peter 2:9. Other similarities may be noted between 1:3 and Acts 3:12 ("power" and "godliness") and between 2 Peter 2:13, 15 (*misthon adikias*, lit., "wages of wickedness") and Acts 1:18 (*misthou tēs adikias*, lit., "reward of wickedness").

Though differences in style exist between 1 and 2 Peter, the frequent use of *hapax legomena*, the unique vocabulary shared by both books, and the strong resemblance between words in 2 Peter and words in Peter's sermons recorded in Acts, all argue strongly for Petrine authorship.

The problem of other apocryphal or pseudonymous literature bearing Peter's name has caused some scholars to reject the authenticity of 2 Peter. In fact, as already mentioned, the early church was slow in giving 2 Peter unqualified acceptance because of the circulation of spurious pseudonymous epistles. Some have tried to argue that pseudonymity was an accepted second-century literary device (e.g., James Moffatt, *The General Epistles: James, Peter, and Judas*, pp. 173-5, and Montague Rhodes James, *The Second Epistle General of Peter and the General Epistle of Jude*, pp. xxxii-iv). However, the fact that 2 Peter was eventually accepted and that the Apocalypse of Peter, the Gospel of Peter, and the Acts of Peter were rejected as pseudonymous books clearly indicates that pseudonymity was not tolerated. The early church recognized the distinctive character and authority of 2 Peter, as opposed to works of lesser quality that merely copied Petrine thought, mixed in later Jewish and Greek ideas, and added a distinctly Docetic view of the person of Christ (that He only *seemed* to have a human body).

The external and internal evidence, though subject to heavy critical attack, has withstood the test of time. No argument against Petrine authorship is conclusive and no new evidence has successfully refuted the epistle's claim to apostolic authorship.

Relationship to Jude. Even a cursory reading of 2 Peter 2 and Jude 4-18 confirms their striking similarity. However, the exact nature of their dependence on each other and the effect of that dependence on their canonicity and authenticity has been the subject of much debate. Scholars of the early church thought that 2 Peter was written first, and that Jude borrowed from it. The results of German higher criticism have swayed scholars in modern times to the opposite view. Some have even posited that the authors of 2 Peter and Jude used a common third source. All three positions face significant difficulties.

If Jude were written first, it is questioned whether an apostle of Peter's standing would have borrowed so extensively from a writer of lesser reputation. However, perhaps Peter viewed Jude's warning against false teachers as important enough to be reemphasized and reinforced by his own apostolic authority. The priority of Jude does not pose a problem to Petrine authorship as long as it is not dated later than A.D. 68, the traditional date of Peter's martyrdom. The Book of Jude does not provide enough evidence for conclusive dating.

If 2 Peter is given priority, the problem arises as to why Jude would merely repeat what was already available and include so little new material. However, Jude may have abbreviated and clarified Peter's letter or some unknown common source to meet the particular needs of churches that had not yet received the earlier epistle. (Cf. Charles Bigg, *A Critical and Exegetical Commentary on the Epistles of St. Peter and St. Jude*, pp. 216-24.)

Donald Guthrie points out that the order of priority of 2 Peter and Jude need not have any particular bearing on their authenticity, authorship, or inspiration (*New Testament Introduction*. Downers Grove, Ill.: InterVarsity Press, 1970, p. 926). The evidence is inconclusive and either position may be held consistently with a conservative view of the inspiration and authority of Scripture.

Date and Place of Writing. Since Peter mentions Pauline literature and deals with questions regarding the Lord's return, some feel the book demands a second-century date and thus could not have been written by the Apostle Peter.

The mention of Paul's letters in 2 Peter 3:16 has given rise to the assumption that the author was referring to an organized collection of epistles that were recognized by the church at large as authoritative. F. H. Chase has written, "It is impossible to suppose that a collection of St. Paul's epistles had been made and that they were treated as Scripture during the lifetime of St. Peter" (*A Dictionary of the Bible*, ed. James Hastings. New York: Charles Scribner's Sons, 1902, s.v. "Peter," 3:810). However, Peter's statement (2 Peter 3:16) need not refer to the entire body of Pauline literature but merely to those letters with which Peter was familiar. Certainly Peter, living the last few years of his life in Rome itself, would have had occasion to read several of Paul's letters as they circulated among churches throughout the Roman world.

Two references in 2 Peter give some indication of the date of the epistle. In 2 Peter 1:13-15, Peter indicated that the time of his death was near. The traditional date for Peter's death is late A.D. 67 or early A.D. 68. The reference to Paul's epistles in 3:16 would seem to indicate a date some time after A.D. 60. Since 1 Peter is normally dated around A.D. 64, 2 Peter may be conservatively placed some time after the writing of 1 Peter and before Peter's death, between A.D. 64 and 68.

The text of 2 Peter suggests no specific place for its composition. However, since 1 Peter was written in Rome and Rome is traditionally held to be the place of Peter's crucifixion, it is reasonable to assume that 2 Peter was written in Rome as well.

Destination. Peter was writing to Christians (1:1) to whom he had written before (3:1). If 2 Peter 3:1 refers to 1 Peter, then he was writing to the mixed Jewish and Gentile churches of "Pontus, Galatia, Cappadocia, Asia, and Bithynia" (1 Peter 1:1). If, however, he referred to a letter no longer extant, then the destination of 2 Peter cannot be determined.

Occasion and Purpose. Peter was both a concerned pastor and a champion of theological orthodoxy. This final impassioned plea to grow in Christian maturity and guard against false teachers was precipitated by the fact that His time was short (1:13-15) and that these congregations faced immediate danger (2:1-3). He desired to refresh their memories (1:13) and stimulate their thinking (3:1-2) so that they would remember his teaching (1:15). He carefully described the characteristics of mature believers and challenged them to make every effort to grow in grace and knowledge (1:3-11). Credentials of true teachers were given to help the readers be discerning students of God's Word (1:12-21). Peter cautioned them against false teachers and exposed their evil characteristics (chap. 2). And he encouraged his readers with the certainty of Christ's return (3:1-16).

The purpose of 2 Peter is to call Christians to spiritual growth so that they can combat apostasy as they look forward to the Lord's return.

OUTLINE

COMMENTARY

I. Introduction (1:1-2)

A. The salutation (1:1)

1. THE AUTHOR (1:1A)

1:1a. The author is identified as **Simon Peter.** It is ironic that this letter, whose authorship has been so disputed, begins with a textual problem concerning the spelling of its author's name. Some manuscripts have the common Greek spelling (*Simōn*), whereas others have the direct transliteration of the Hebrew (*Symeōn*). The best textual evidence supports the more unusual Hebrew spelling, used elsewhere only in Acts 15:14. This detail provides support for the authenticity of Petrine authorship, for an impostor probably would have used the more widely accepted spelling.

"Peter," the Greek translation of "Cephas" and the name given to Simon by Jesus, is discussed in the *Introduction* of 1 Peter (see also 1 Peter 1:1).

Peter's combining these distinctly Hebrew and Greek names may be an indication of the mixed audience (Hebrew and Greek Christians) he addressed.

Peter adds the term **servant** (*doulos,* lit., "slave"; cf. Matt. 23:11) to his title **apostle of Jesus Christ** (cf. Rom. 1:1; Titus 1:1). Near the close of his life, at the apex of his apostolic authority, he was Christ's servant first, and His apostle second.

2. THE AUDIENCE (1:1B)

1:1b. The recipients of the letter are described only in general terms (cf. 3:1). They are **those who . . . have received a faith as precious as ours.** "Received" is from the unusual verb *lanchanō,* "to obtain by lot" (cf. Luke 1:9; John 19:24). This implies God's sovereign choice rather than anything they might have done to deserve such a gift. The words "as precious" translate the compound word *isotimon,* used only here in the New Testament. It comes from *isos* ("equal") and *timē* ("honor, value"). The word *isotimon* was used for foreigners who had been granted the privileges of citizenship which were equal to those of the native born. The faith given them by God was of equal honor or privilege with that of the apostles' faith. Here Peter foreshadowed his purpose by stressing that the faith of the apostles was no different from the faith of any believer. This contrasted with the pre-Gnostic doctrines of the false teachers who spoke of an inner circle of special knowledge attainable by and available only to a privileged few.

The word "faith" (*pistin*) is used without the article; thus it could refer to the objective content of faith (cf. Jude 3) or, more likely, to the subjective ability to believe. This faith is given **through** (or, on the basis of) **the righteousness** (*dikaiosynē,* "justice" or "uprightness"; cf. Rom. 1:17; 3:22) **of our God and Savior** (Peter called Jesus Savior [Acts 5:31]) **Jesus Christ.** The grammar here clearly indicates that "God and Savior" are one Person, not two (i.e., there is one Gr.

article with two substantives). This passage ranks with the great Christological passages of the New Testament which plainly teach that Jesus Christ is coequal in nature with God the Father (cf. Matt. 16:16; John 1:1; 20:28; Titus 2:13). "Savior" is used of Christ five times in this short epistle (2 Peter 1:1, 11; 2:20; 3:2, 18).

B. The blessing (1:2)

1:2. The first half of this verse corresponds exactly with 1 Peter 1:2b: **Grace and peace** (*charis . . . kai eirēnē*; cf. Pauline usage in Rom. 1:7; 1 Cor. 1:3; 2 Cor. 1:2; etc.) were the characteristic Greek and Hebrew greetings (*eirēnē* being the Gr. trans. of the Heb. *šālôm*). The verb translated **be . . . in abundance** (*plēthyntheiē*; also used in 1 Peter 1:2; Jude 2) is in the optative mood, thus stressing a sincere, prayerful wish for his readers.

This blessing of grace and peace is more than a mere formula of greeting. These virtues come **through the knowledge of God and of Jesus our Lord.** In each of his first two verses Peter mentioned God and Jesus as equal. "Knowledge" (*epignōsei*, "full [*epi*, additional] knowledge") implies an intimate and personal relationship. It is the means by which God's grace and peace may be received and experienced. Peter used this term *epignōsis* again in 2 Peter 1:3, 8; and 2:20. The shorter form (*gnōsis*) is found in 1:5-6 and 3:18. Christians are urged to take advantage of the "full knowledge" available to them through Christ Jesus (each occurrence of *epignōsis* in 2 Peter is related to Christ). In this way they could combat false teachers who claimed to have special knowledge (*gnōsis*) but who openly practiced immorality (cf. Paul's usage of *epignōsis* to combat incipient Gnosticism: Col. 1:9-10; 2:2; 3:10).

II. The Christian's Nature: The Work of God (1:3-11)

Peter challenged believers to take full advantage of the divine power and promise of God which made it possible to *participate* in the divine nature and thus overcome the corruption caused by evil desires (vv. 3-4). Based on this promised power, Peter further challenged Christians to *practice* the characteristics of the divine nature so that they would experi-

ence the assurance of eternal rewards (vv. 5-11).

A. The fact of the divine nature (1:3-4)

1. DIVINE POWER (1:3)

1:3. Christ's **divine power has** provided **everything** believers **need for life and godliness.** "Divine" translates *theias*, which is from *theos* ("God") and is used only three times in the New Testament (here and in Acts 17:29; 2 Peter 1:4). "Power" (*dynameōs*) is one of Peter's favorite words (cf. 1 Peter 1:5; 3:22; 2 Peter 1:16; 2:11). All that believers need for spiritual vitality (life) and godly living (*eusebeian*, "godliness," "piety"; cf. comments on 1:6; 3:11) is attainable **through our knowledge of Him** (Christ). An intimate "full knowledge" (*epignōseōs*; cf. 1:2) of Christ is the source of spiritual power and growth (cf. Phil. 1:9; Col. 1:9-10; 2:2).

Christ **called** (cf. 1 Peter 1:15) **us** to this life of godliness **by His own glory and goodness** (*aretē*, "moral excellence"; trans. "praises" in 1 Peter 2:9 and "goodness" in 2 Peter 1:5). Christ attracts people enslaved by sin (cf. 2:19) by His own moral excellence and the total impact of His glorious Person.

2. DIVINE PROMISES (1:4A)

1:4a. **Through these,** that is, Christ's "glory and goodness" (v. 3), **He has given** believers **His very great and precious promises.** The Greek verb translated "has given" (*dedōrētai*) means "to bestow, to endow." Not the usual word for "give," it carries with it the idea of the worth of the gift. Peter used the same verb in verse 3. In Mark 15:45 the word is used to describe Pilate's "giving" of Jesus' body to Joseph of Arimathea.

The word for "promises" (*epangelmata*, from *epangellō*; used only in 2 Peter 1:4 and 3:13) implies an emphatic public announcement. The promises are appropriately described as "very great and precious" (*timia*, from *timē*, "value"). Peter used "precious" to describe a Christian's faith (1 Peter 2:7; 2 Peter 1:1), Christ's blood (1 Peter 1:19), and here, Christ's promises. The promises Peter had previously written about related to a believer's inheritance (1 Peter 1:3-5) and the return of Christ (1 Peter 1:9, 13).

3. DIVINE PARTICIPATION (1:4B)

1:4b. These promises enable Christians to **participate in the divine nature.** "Participate" is literally "become partners" (*genēsthe . . . koinōnoi*). "Participate" in 1 Peter 4:13 and "share" in 1 Peter 5:1 are from the same word *koinōnoi* ("partners" or "sharers"). "Divine" is *theias,* also used in 2 Peter 1:3. Believers take on God's very nature; each one is a "new creation" (2 Cor. 5:17).

Because they are "partakers" (KJV) of God's nature, Christians can share in His moral victory over sin in this life and share in His glorious victory over death in eternal life. Because of the promise of the new birth (1 Peter 1:3), the promise of God's protecting power (1 Peter 1:5), and the promise of God's enabling power (2 Peter 1:3), believers can "participate in the divine nature," that is, become more like Christ (cf. Rom. 8:9; Gal. 2:20). In addition they can **escape the corruption** (*phthoras,* "moral decay") **in the world** (cf. 2 Peter 2:20; 1 John 2:15-17) **caused by evil desires** (*epithymia,* lit., "lust").

In 2 Peter 1:3-4 Peter employed graphic vocabulary borrowed from the false teachers he warned against. His language must have arrested his readers' attention as he invested words from the pagan and philosophic worlds with new Christian meaning: "godliness" (*eusebeia*), "virtue" (*aretē*), "nature" (*physis*), and "corruption" (*phthoras*).

B. The function of the divine nature (1:5-9)

In this beautiful paragraph Peter orchestrates a symphony of grace. To the melody line of faith he leads believers to add harmony in a blend of seven Christian virtues which he lists without explanation or description. A carnal Christian has spiritual myopia (v. 9), but a spiritual Christian is both effective and productive (v. 8) in his understanding of the Lord Jesus and his application of biblical principles to daily life.

1. CHARACTERISTICS OF THE FUNCTION (1:5-7)

1:5-7. Peter referred back to the divine nature by beginning this new paragraph with the words **for this very reason.** The words **make every effort** translate a participle (*pareisenenkantes,* "applying, bringing to bear alongside of";

used only here in the NT) and *spoudēn pasan* ("all diligence" or "all zeal"; *spoudē* in Rom. 12:11 is rendered "zeal"). It takes every bit of diligence and effort a Christian can muster, along with the enabling power of the Holy Spirit, to "escape the corruption in the world caused by evil desires" (2 Peter 1:4) and to bring in alongside of his faith a complement of virtue. He should work hard at cultivating the seven qualities Peter listed in verses 5-7. As a Christian does so, he becomes more like Christ, participating more fully in God's divine nature.

The word **add,** in the imperative, translates *epichorēgēsate,* from which come the English words "chorus," "choreograph," and "choreography." In ancient Greece the state established a chorus but the director, the *chorēgys,* paid the expenses for training the chorus. Then the word came to be used of one who provides for or supports others or supplies something for them in abundance. A believer is to "furnish, supply, or support" his life with these virtues. (The same word is trans. "supplies" in 2 Cor. 9:10 and "supported" in Col. 2:19. Peter used it again in 2 Peter 1:11 where the NIV renders it "receive.")

Faith in Jesus Christ is what separates Christians from all other people. *Pistis,* trust in the Savior which brings one into the family of God, is the foundation of all other qualities in the Christian life.

1. **To** his faith each believer should add **goodness** (lit., "moral excellency," or "virtue"). In Greek the word is *aretēn,* which Peter also used at the end of verse 3 and in 1 Peter 2:9 ("praises" in the NIV).

2. **Knowledge** (*gnōsin;* cf. 2 Peter 1:2; 3:18) comes not from intellectual pursuits, but is spiritual knowledge which comes through the Holy Spirit and is focused on the person and Word of God.

3. Faith, **goodness,** and spiritual **knowledge** are not enough for a Christian's walk. He must also make every effort to practice **self-control** (*enkrateian;* used only two other times in the NT, in Acts 24:25; Gal. 5:23). This means to have one's passions under control. It contrasts sharply with the anarchy and lack of control on the part of the false teachers whom Peter exposed (chap. 2). In an increasingly anarchistic society Christians

do well to let the music of **self-control** be played in their lives.

4. Believers living in the latter days, especially when surrounded by scoffers and false teachers, also need **perseverance.** This word *hypomenēn* means "staying under." It is frequently used in the New Testament to refer to constancy or steadfast endurance under adversity, without giving in or giving up (cf. Rom. 5:3-4; 15:4-5; 2 Cor. 1:6; 6:4; Col. 1:11; 1 Thes. 1:3; 2 Thes. 1:4; James 1:3).

5. **Godliness** (*eusebian*, also used in 2 Peter 1:3 and 3:11 and 10 times [in the Gr.] in the Pastoral Epistles) refers to piety, man's obligation of reverence toward God. The fourth-century church historian Eusebius was named for this lovely Greek word. How unfortunate that the words "piety" and "pious" have fallen on hard times in current usage.

6. The first five virtues pertain to one's inner life and his relationship to God. The last two relate to others. **Brotherly kindness** translates the Greek *philadelphian*, a fervent practical caring for others (1 John 4:20). Peter already urged this attitude on his readers in his first epistle (1 Peter 1:22; cf. Rom. 12:10; 1 Thes. 4:9; Heb. 13:1).

7. Whereas **brotherly kindness** is concern for others' needs, **love** (*agapēn*) is desiring the highest good for others. This is the kind of love God exhibits toward sinners (John 3:16; Rom. 5:8; 1 John 4:9-11).

Interestingly this "symphony" begins with faith and ends with love. Building on the foundation of faith in Christ, believers are to exhibit Christlikeness by supplying these seven qualities that climax in love toward others (cf. faith and love in Col. 1:4-5; 1 Thes. 1:3; 2 Thes. 1:3; Phile. 5).

2. CONSEQUENCES OF THE FUNCTION (1:8)

1:8. Christian growth (vv. 5-7) results in spiritual effectiveness and productivity. The word **possess** (*hyparchōnta*, lit. "possessing") emphasizes that these spiritual qualities "belong to" Christians. However, Christians are to do more than merely possess these virtues. Effective and productive spirituality comes as **these qualities** are held **in increasing measure.** There is to be a growth in grace. A believer who does not progress in these seven areas is **ineffec-**

tive (*argous*, "idle" or "useless") **and unproductive** (lit., "unfruitful") **in** his **knowledge** (*epignōsin*, "full personal knowledge"; cf. vv. 2-3; 2:20) **of our Lord Jesus Christ.** Unfortunately many Christians know the Lord in salvation but lack the "fruit" of the Spirit and are not advancing spiritually. They remain "infants in Christ" (1 Cor. 3:1), still in need of spiritual "milk" (Heb. 5:12-13). But as Peter urged, believers should "grow in the grace and knowledge (*gnōsei*) of our Lord and Savior Jesus Christ" (2 Peter 3:18).

3. CONTRASTS OF THE FUNCTION (1:9)

1:9. In contrast with a growing Christian, a carnal believer is **blind** (*typhlos*) and **nearsighted** (*myōpazōn*). (The NIV reverses these two words; in Gr. the word "blind" comes first.) *Myōpazōn* (from which comes the word "myopia"), occurs only here in the New Testament. A believer with spiritual myopia is not magnifying the grace of Christ. Since his life is not evidencing the qualities cited in verses 5-7, he seems to be just like a spiritually blind (or unsaved) person (2 Cor. 4:4; cf. John 9:39). Such a person **has forgotten that he has been cleansed from his past** (preconversion) **sins.** Some commentators say this refers to unbelievers. But it seems preferable to say that Peter wrote of Christians who are spiritually immature. After all, they had been cleansed from their sins (cf. Titus 3:5), but had not grown spiritually.

C. *The finality of the divine nature (1:10-11)*

In order to be an effective and productive Christian avoiding spiritual myopia, one must be sure that he is genuinely saved. This is demonstrated by his new life in Christ, which provides evidence that he will reach his eternal home.

1. EXPERIENTIAL FINALITY (1:10)

1:10. Being **eager** (*spoudasate*, also used in vv. 1, 15; 3:14 ["make every effort"]; cf. *spoudēn* in 1:5) **to make** one's **calling and election sure** focuses on the confidence a Christian has about his standing with God. A believer hardly has the authority to assure God of his status; actually the reverse is true. The Greek word for "sure" (*bebaian*) was used in classical Greek to refer to a warranty deed somewhat like those people use today on houses and other pieces of property. One's godly behavior is a warranty deed for himself that Jesus Christ has cleansed him from his past sins and therefore that he was in fact called and elected by God. *Bebaian* is rendered "secure" (Heb. 6:19), "guaranteed" (Rom. 4:16), "firm" (2 Cor. 1:7), "courage" (Heb. 3:6), "confidence" (Heb. 3:14), and "in force" (Heb. 9:17).

"Calling" refers to God's efficacious work in salvation (cf. Rom. 1:7; 8:30; 1 Cor. 1:9), and "election" is God's work of choosing some sinners (by His grace, not their merits) to be saved (Rom. 8:33; 11:5; Eph. 1:4; Col. 3:12; 1 Peter 1:1). Election, of course, precedes calling. A believer shows by his godly life and his growth in the virtues mentioned in 2 Peter 1:5-7 that he is one of God's chosen. Such a believer **will** not **fall** (or "stumble," *ptaisēte*). This word "stumble" does not suggest that a believer loses his salvation, for salvation does not depend on one's spiritual growth. The Greek word for stumble means "to trip up" or "to experience a reversal." Certainly one who is maturing in Christ will not trip up in his spiritual life as readily as one who is immature and nearsighted.

2. ETERNAL FINALITY (1:11)

1:11. The ultimate reward of a growing, Christ-honoring life is the personal "welcome" by the Savior into His kingdom. Stephen experienced it (Acts 7:56); Paul knew when it was imminent for him (2 Tim. 4:7-8, 18); and every believer will experience such a welcome when he enters the Lord's presence in heaven. **You will receive a rich welcome** is, literally, "the entrance will be supplied richly for you." "Supplied" is from the verb *epichorēgeō*, translated "add" in 2 Peter 1:5. The entrance **into the eternal kingdom of our Lord and Savior Jesus Christ** will be supplied with richness; it will be a wonderful "welcome home."

III. The Christian's Nurture: The Word of God (1:12-21)

As Peter made a transition from focusing on the work of God in believers' lives (vv. 3-11) to the Word of God as the instrument of nurture (vv. 16-21) he began with a parenthetical personal note about his readers' need to remember what he wrote (vv. 12-15). His section on the Word of God climaxes in a major statement on revelation and inspiration, reaching a high-water mark in verse 21, Peter's tribute to the Holy Spirit's role in God-breathed Scripture.

A. Memory of God's Word (1:12-15)

1:12. Peter, knowing his days were numbered, wanted his readers to retain all he would write in this epistle. Three times he spoke of this: **I will . . . remind you** (v. 12), "I . . . refresh your memory" (v. 13), "you will . . . be able to remember" (v. 15; cf. 3:1).

Peter was almost apologetic in the second half of 1:12; he did not want his readers to misunderstand his intention. He was not being critical nor did he suggest they were wavering. Instead, he said they did **know** the truths he wrote about **and** he was aware that they were **firmly established in the truth.** He wanted them to stay that way. ("Established" is from *stērizō*, which means "strengthen" or "be firm"; cf. 1 Thes. 3:2, 13; 2 Thes. 2:17; 3:3; 1 Peter 5:10.) A problem in many churches today is not that believers do not know what God expects of them, but they either forget (cf. 2 Peter 1:9) or are unwilling to live out the truth they **now have.**

1:13-14. Expecting he would **soon** be with the Lord, Peter wanted **to refresh** (lit., "keep on refreshing," pres. tense) their memories **as long as** he was allowed by the Lord of life to **live in the tent of his body** (cf. "the earthly tent" and "this tent," 2 Cor. 5:1, 4). Peter would **put** that tent **aside, as** the **Lord** had **made clear to** him. This could refer to Jesus' words to Peter about his death by crucifixion (John 21:18-19) or to his awareness that through old age or the threat of persecution, his life was almost at an end. The image of this earthly body being like a tent fits well with Peter's pilgrimage theme (1 Peter 1:1, 17; 2:11).

1:15. Peter deliberately repeated himself, perhaps for emphasis: **I will make every effort** translates the one word *spoudasō*, also used in verse 10 ("be . . . eager") and in 3:14 ("make every effort"). The word **departure** (*exodon*), though not the usual word for "death," does not veil the clarity of Peter's suggestion that he is about to die. On the Mount of Transfiguration, Jesus, Moses, and Elijah spoke of Jesus' "departure" (*exodon;* Luke 9:31). Interestingly this "exodus" (lit., "going out," i.e., from this body) contrasts with a believer's "entrance" into (*eisodos,* "going into") God's kingdom (2 Peter 1:11).

How could Peter guarantee that after his death his readers would **always be able to remember these things?** Some suggest this is a subtle reference to Peter's aid in preparing the Gospel of Mark, but this is only speculation. More obviously he was laboring to complete this second epistle which, when joined with the first, would provide ongoing written testimony of the truths so close to his heart. Still another possibility is that he referred to his own life and ministry extending into the lives of others, as Silas and Mark, who would carry on his work after he died. One thing is clear—Peter wanted to be sure that the Lord's people would not forget God's work and God's Word.

B. Majesty of God's Word (1:16-18)

1:16. It is important to distinguish between the written Word (the Bible) and the incarnate Word (Christ). They are both major avenues of God's revelation (cf. Ps. 19:7-11; John 1:18; Heb. 1:2) and therefore both come into focus throughout the remainder of this chapter. A Christian's faith does not rest on clever **stories** (*mythois*) as did the doctrines of the false teachers Peter attacked (2 Peter 2). Instead, true faith is founded on historical facts, which **eyewitnesses** corroborated. It appears that Peter introduced a new theme here. He plunged quickly into a mention of the Lord's return: **the power and coming of our Lord Jesus Christ.** He had already talked about that welcome into the eternal kingdom (1:11), and had written about his own departure from this life. His defense of the doctrine of the Second Coming therefore is based on his eyewitness experience on the Mount of Transfiguration at which time he truly saw Christ's **majesty.** Several times in his earlier epistle he spoke of Christ's return (1 Peter 1:5, 13; 4:13). Obviously Peter considered this doctrine of great importance, one his readers should always keep in mind.

But how does the transfiguration argue that the Lord will come again with power? The transfiguration was designed to show the three apostles, Peter, James, and John, what Christ would be like in His glory, to give them a foretaste of His kingdom (cf. Matt. 16:28–17:2; Mark 9:1-8; Luke 9:28-36). This was a glorious demonstration they could never forget.

1:17-18. Peter's lofty language may stem from his burning desire to communicate the true majesty of the Savior which he, a member of the inner band of disciples, was uniquely privileged to see. Peter wanted his readers to look beyond Christ's first coming to the time when He will return with that same **honor and glory** He demonstrated on the mountain. In Peter's preaching during the days of the early church he was firmly committed to the doctrine of the Second Coming (Acts 2:32-33, 36; 3:16, 20-21).

Interestingly Peter was more profoundly impressed by what he **heard** than what he saw **on** that **sacred mountain.** The **voice that came from heaven,** the **voice** of God the Father, called **the Majestic Glory** (an unusual name for God), spoke approvingly of the **Son.**

C. Meaning of God's Word (1:19-21)

1:19. As Peter wrote of that unforgettable transfiguration experience, he was reminded of another form of God's Word, the written Word, given by the prophets. In fact, God's voice on the mountain made **the word of the prophets . . . more certain** (*bebaioteron;* cf. *bebaian,* v. 10) because the transfiguration pictured the fulfillment of their words. Both the prophets and the transfiguration pointed to Jesus' kingdom on earth.

In an exhortation Peter told how to derive meaning from God's Word—**pay attention to it.** As a Light, God's written Word has validity and authority. In today's experience-oriented societies many people, including some Christians, seek to determine or assess truth by the particular way God has worked in their own lives. But for Peter the splendor of his experience (with Christ at His transfiguration) faded as he spoke of the surety of the written revelation of the prophets.

The apostle wrote of illumination (v. 19), revelation (v. 20), and inspiration (v. 21). Old Testament prophecy is a light compared with the darkness of a squalid room. God's prophetic Word is **a Light** (*lychnō,* "an oil-burning lamp"; cf. Ps. 119:105) **shining in a dark place.** Though the world is darkened by sin (cf. Isa. 9:2; Eph. 6:12), God's Word, pointing to the future, enlightens believers about His ways. But **the day** (Christ's return, Rom. 13:12) is coming. In the daytime, lamps are no longer needed. And a lamp is nothing compared with **the Morning Star** (*phōsphoros*, "Light-Bringer"; used only here in the NT). Much as a lamp at night anticipates and is outshined by the bright morning star, so Old Testament prophecy looks ahead to the coming of Christ, "the bright Morning Star" (*astēr;* Rev. 22:16). Until He comes, believers are to let the Scriptures illumine their hearts (though the light which it brings on that great day will be greatly exceeded by the understanding which will be **in** their **hearts**).

1:20. Peter then wrote about revelation. The statement, **No prophecy of Scripture came about by the prophet's own interpretation,** has been interpreted several ways: (1) Scripture should be interpreted only in context, that is, a prophecy cannot stand alone without other prophecies to aid in its understanding. (2) Scripture should not be interpreted according to one's own individual liking. (3) Scripture cannot be correctly interpreted without the Holy Spirit. (4) The prophecies did not originate with the prophets themselves. The word *epilyseōs* ("interpretation," lit., "unloosing") and the word *ginetai* ("came about") favor the fourth view. The Scriptures did not stem merely from the prophets themselves; their writings came from God. Verse 20, then, speaks not of interpretation, but of revelation, the source of the Scriptures.

1:21. This verse also supports the view that Peter wrote in verse 20 about prophecies being born of God, not originating from the prophets themselves. **Prophecy** came not from **the will of man, but men spoke from God as they were carried along by the Holy Spirit.**

As the authors of Scripture wrote their prophecies, they were impelled or borne along by God's Spirit. What they wrote was thus inspired by God (2 Tim. 3:16). "Borne along" or "carried along" translates the word *pheromenoi.* Luke used this word in referring to a sailing vessel carried along by the wind (Acts 27:15, 17). The Scriptures' human authors were controlled by the divine Author, the Holy Spirit. Yet they were consciously involved in the process; they were neither taking dictation nor writing in a state of ecstasy. No wonder believers have a word of prophecy which is certain. And no wonder a Christian's nurture must depend on the Scriptures. They are the very words of God Himself!

IV. The Christian's Warfare: The Attack of False Teachers (chap. 2)

When the Edict of Milan was passed in A.D. 313 the church was then free to move into the world, legally and openly propagating its doctrines. But at the same time, the world also began to move into the church, diluting its message for the next 1,200 years until the Reformation broke forth on the scene. But it is obvious from 2 Peter 2 that the world was already in the church well before the time of Constantine. Believers in all ages must be constantly on guard against its attack.

A. Deliverance from false teachers (2:1-9)

The word "rescue" in verses 7 and 9 speaks of God's willingness and ability to deliver His people from assorted difficulties and dangers even when they themselves (like Lot) do not overtly seek deliverance. But depending on the Lord's ability to rescue is no excuse for failing to enter the warfare against false teachers and false prophets.

1. EXPOSURE OF FALSE TEACHING (2:1-3)

2:1. Satan's counterfeits with their insidious activities are always present. They appeared in Israel during the days of the writing prophets spoken of in 1:19-21, and they were present in the first-century church. Though Peter switched from writing about **false prophets** of the past to **false teachers** in the present, their teaching was the same— heresy. False prophets often rose out of Israel (cf. Jer. 5:31; 23:9-18), not from surrounding peoples. Similarly false teachers appear from the midst of the church. They **secretly introduce** their false teachings which are **destructive heresies.** "Secretly introduce" translates *pareisaxousin,* "bring in alongside" (cf. "infiltrated," which translates the related noun *pareisaktous,* in Gal. 2:4). "Heresies" transliterates the Greek word *haireseis,* which in classical Greek simply meant schools of philosophy. But New Testament writers used it to describe religious parties or sects (e.g., the Sadducees [Acts 5:17] or the Pharisees [Acts 15:5]), or factions probably based on false doctrine (e.g., 1 Cor. 11:19, "differences," NIV; "factions," NASB). Such heresies are "destructive," for they lead people away from Christ and thus to spiritual ruin (apōleias).

The focus of their heresies was **the sovereign Lord,** Christ, whom they denied (cf. Jude 4). This in turn led to their own spiritual **destruction** or ruin (apōleian; cf. 2 Peter 2:3; 3:16), which will be **swift** (tachinēn, "sudden"; cf. tachinē ["soon"] in 1:14). How can these false teachers, who were said to be **among the people,** and whom the Lord had **bought** (agorasanta, "redeem"), end up in everlasting destruction? Several suggestions have been offered: (1) They were saved but lost their salvation. But this contradicts many other Scriptures (e.g., John 3:16; 5:24; 10:28-29). (2) "Bought" means the Lord created them, not that He saved them. But this stretches the meaning of agorazō ("redeem"). (3) The false prophets merely said they were "bought" by Christ. This, however, seems to read into the verse. (4) They were "redeemed" in the sense that Christ paid the redemptive price for their salvation, but they did not apply it to themselves and so were not saved. Christ's death is "sufficient" for all (1 Tim. 2:6; Heb. 2:9; 1 John 2:2), but is "efficient" only for those who believe. This is a strong argument for unlimited atonement (the view that Christ died for everyone) and against limited atonement (the view that Christ died only for those whom He would later save).

2:2. The tragic fact about **many** false teachers is that they are successful—people listen to them and **follow** them and **their shameful ways** (aselgeiais, which Peter also used in 1 Peter 4:3 ["debauchery"]; 2 Peter 2:7 ["filthy"]; v. 18 ["lustful"]). (Cf. aselgeia in Rom. 13:13; 2 Cor. 12:21; Gal. 5:19; Eph. 4:19; Jude 4.) It refers to debased sexually immoral practices.

2:3. Ministerial charlatans and quacks have often troubled the flock of God. **In their greed** (cf. v. 14) they use others for their own mercenary purposes and turn the church into a dirty marketplace. **Exploit** (emporeusontai) means to commercialize ("buy, sell, trade"; cf. emporeusometha, "carry on business," in James 4:13). **Stories they have made up** is literally, "fabricated words" (plastois [whence the Eng. "plastic"] logois). They are artificial, not genuine. And **their** end is **condemnation** (krima, "judgment") and **destruction** (apōleia; used twice in 2 Peter 2:1 and also in 3:16). They fall into the same doom which God has planned for other violators of truth and righteousness (as Peter stated in vv. 4-6). Their destruction **has not been sleeping** (ou nystazei, used only one other time in the NT, to describe the sleepy virgins in Matt. 25:5). God's justice does not sleep and it is never late.

2. EXAMPLES OF HISTORIC JUDGMENT (2:4-6)

In verses 4-10a, Peter gave several illustrations to demonstrate both the Lord's judgment and His deliverance. After citing three examples of punishment (vv. 4-6), Peter then cited a case of deliverance (Lot, v. 7). In fact, verses 4-9 are a single sentence, one of the longest in the New Testament. Peter was intent on demonstrating that God will judge false teachers and others who sin against Him and His Word. History, Peter wrote, gives ample verification of this truth.

2:4. The first example is that of fallen **angels.** This refers either to their fall with Satan in his rebellion against God (Ezek. 28:15) or to the sin of angels in Genesis 6:1-4. Since Peter's other two illustrations in this section are from Genesis (chaps. 7; 19), perhaps this one is too, though it is difficult to be sure. **If God** in His justice punished angels, surely He would not hesitate to punish people. He plunged the angels into **hell,** literally, "tartarus" apparently a prison of custody **(gloomy dungeons)** between the time of the **judgment** and their ultimate consignment to the eternal lake of fire. There will be no future trial for their doom is already sealed. False prophets, Peter argued, will taste the same judgment as the rebellious angels.

2:5. Peter was greatly impressed by the significance of **the Flood** for he referred to it three times in his two epistles (1 Peter 3:20; 2 Peter 2:5; 3:6). **Noah . . . and seven others** is the NIV's rendering of the Greek "Noah, the eighth person." The others were his wife, his three sons (Shem, Ham, and Japheth), and their wives (Gen. 6:10, 18). Noah was a righteous man (Gen. 6:9), an obedient servant of God, and a shipbuilder (Gen. 6:13-22). Peter added that he was also **a preacher** (kēryka, "herald") **of righteousness,** who spoke out against the vile corruption all around him.

The primary focus of 2 Peter 2:5 is the unsparing hand of God on the antediluvian civilization, **the ancient world** with **its ungodly people.** Do false teachers today think they can escape God's judgment because of their large numbers? Peter reminded them and those who are the targets of their delusions that God can judge evil even when it involves the entire human race (with the exception of only eight people). The word **brought** (epaxas, past part. from epagō, "to bring on") suggests the suddenness of God's judgment in the Flood. Peter used the same verb in verse 1 in speaking of heretics who are "bringing" destruction on themselves.

2:6. God's destruction of **Sodom and Gomorrah by** fire is a classic example of universal destruction of the ungodly (Gen. 10:15-29). The participle tephrōsas **(burning them to ashes),** used only here in the New Testament, means "reduce to ashes" or "cover with ashes." Peter concluded this illustration by saying that God **made them an example** (hypodeigma, "model, pattern") **of what is going to happen to the ungodly** (cf. Jude 7). The apostle's purpose here was to cite this historical incident of judgment, not to elaborate on the cause for such severe destruction. In the present day homosexuality, which is scarring so much of Western culture, recalls the same shameful conduct in those two ancient cities (Gen. 19:4-5; cf. Gen. 13:13; Rom. 1:27).

3. EXPLANATION OF DIVINE DELIVERANCE (2:7-9)

2:7-9. Peter had spoken (v. 5) of one deliverance (of Noah and his family); now he cited another, God's rescue of **Lot.** Here again is an interesting New Testament commentary on a familiar Old Testament passage (cf. comments on v. 5). In Genesis 19 Lot hardly comes across as **a righteous man;** possibly godliness was not a consistent mark in his daily conduct. But in his standing before God he was a justified man ("righteous," occurring three times in 2 Peter 2:7-8, is

dikaion, "justified"). This is evidenced by the fact that Lot **was distressed** (kataponoumenon, "tormented, oppressed"; used only here and in Acts 7:24 in the NT) by the enormity of iniquity all around him. The people in those twin cities were **filthy** (en aselgeia, "in sexual debauchery"; in 2 Peter 2:2 aselgeia is trans. "shameful"), **lawless** (athesmōn, "unprincipled"; used only twice in the NT: here and in 3:17), and involved in **lawless** (anomois, "without any standard or law") **deeds.** Besides being distressed, Lot **was** also **tormented** (ebasanizen, "tortured, tormented"; cf. Matt. 8:29) **in his righteous soul** (lit., "he tormented [his] righteous soul"). Seeing and hearing about all their vile ways **day after day** grieved Lot to the point of inner torture.

In 2 Peter 2:9 the point of his words in verses 4-9 unfolds. **The Lord knows how to rescue** the righteous **and to** punish **the unrighteous.** That God can deliver the **godly . . . from trials** is a source of comfort to believers, exemplified by Noah and his seven family members and Lot and his wife and daughters. On the other hand God holds (tērein, "keeps under guard") **the unrighteous for the** coming **day of judgment** (cf. 3:7), the great white throne judgment and the lake of fire (Rev. 20:11-15). Meanwhile God continues **their punishment** in this life (cf. Rom. 1:27b) and in hades after death (Luke 16:23). The participle kolazomenous ("punishing, injuring") is another of Peter's words that occurs only once in the New Testament.

B. Description of false teachers (2:10-16)

False teachers will be judged by God, as certainly as were the angels, the world in Noah's day, and the sinful people of Sodom and Gomorrah. In verses 10-16 (also v. 17) Peter described the true nature of the false teachers plaguing the church in the first century.

1. THEY ARE REBELLIOUS (2:10-12A)

2:10-12a. The apostles and teachers emphasized purity and cleanliness before God. But the false teachers in the church who denied these standards demonstrated their desire to be indulging the flesh (**follow the corrupt** [miasmou, "pollution, defilement"] **desire of the sinful nature**), like the people of Sodom and Gomorrah, and did so in a spirit which held **authority** in contempt (cf. Jude 16, 18). But this was not just any authority; these reckless antinomians **despise**(d) (*kataphronountas*, "think down on") "lordship." *Kyriotētos*, "authority," refers either to angelic powers (Eph. 1:21; Col. 1:16) or perhaps more likely, to the authority of the Lord (*kyrios*) Himself (cf. 2 Peter 2:1). One would expect people of this mentality—who are **bold** (*tolmētai*, "presumptuous") **and arrogant** (*authadeis*, "self-willed"; cf. Titus 1:7)—to **slander** (*blasphēmountes*) even to the point of deliberately speaking untruth about **celestial beings** (*doxas*, possibly fallen angels). It is possible that their blaspheming was the teaching that lustful indulgence is angelic and that God wills man to live under no restraints whatever.

False teachers were doing things **even angels** would not do, namely, slander **such beings.** One might expect **stronger and more powerful** beings (good angels) to criticize less powerful beings (fallen angels), but that is simply not allowed **in the presence of the Lord** (cf. Jude 8-9). Yet so great was the pride of these slanderers that it knew no bounds in their attack on all who disagreed with their teachings. Even so, they were totally ignorant of the very things they blasphemed (2 Peter 2:12a; cf. Jude 10).

2. THEY ARE ANIMALISTIC (2:12B)

2:12b. The false teachers of the first century were **like brute beasts.** They operated from instinct, which was locked into their sin nature, rather than from rational choice. **Creatures of instinct** translates the one Greek word *physika*, "belonging to nature." They followed their natural desires. Like animals in a jungle, their only value was in being **caught and destroyed** (cf. Jude 10). This harsh language from Peter is an indication of how serious he considered these heresies to be. **Like beasts they too will perish** is literally, "in their corruption (*phthora*) they too shall be corrupted" (*phtharēsontai*), an interesting play on words (cf. "corrupted" in Eph. 4:22). Corruption here probably means eternal punishment.

3. THEY ARE DECEITFUL (2:13)

2:13. The wordplay in verse 12b sets up Peter's point in verse 13a, namely, that these false teachers will be caught in their own webs. **They will be paid back with harm** (*adikoumenoi* ["being damaged," or "suffering injustice"] *misthon* ["wages"]) **for the harm** (*adikias*, "injustice" or "wickedness"; cf. v. 15) **they have done.** God will give them what they have done to others (cf. Gal. 6:7). Though the false teachers tried to pass themselves off as spiritual leaders possessing a special level of knowledge, they did not even hide their orgies under the cover of darkness but would **carouse in broad daylight,** while **reveling in their pleasures** (*apatais*, perhaps better trans. "deceptions"). And they did all this while obviously joining in the love feasts of the church (NIV marg.; cf. Jude 12). **They** were **blots** (*spiloi*) **and blemishes** (*mōmoi*; cf. 2 Peter 3:14). Like a stain on a clean shirt or a scratch on a tiny ring, they marred the Lord's Supper by their very presence. This was one of the injustices they did to others.

4. THEY ARE CHRONIC SINNERS (2:14)

2:14. Invective poured from Peter's pen as he summoned staccato phrases to condemn these heretics. Had there been any doubt up to this point about the salvation of these false teachers, Peter closed the door by indicating they were habitual sinners, their eyes consistently looking toward sinning. **With eyes full of adultery** is literally, "having eyes full of an adulteress," that is, thinking only of adultery when they see women. **They never stop sinning** is literally, "unceasing in sin," probably referring to their sinning with their eyes (Matt. 5:28). That such persons should be viewed as believers is diametrically opposed to the Johannine idea that habitual sinning does not mark one who is born of God (1 John 3:9).

Their deceit was aimed at seducing (from *deleazō*, "bait, entice"; used only here and in 2 Peter 2:18) **the** unwary or unsteadfast (cf. 3:16), and **they** had become specialists **in greed** (cf. 2:3; lit., "having a heart exercised in greed"). **Experts** ("exercised," KJV) translates *gegymnasmenēn*, from which comes "gymnasium." They "work out" in covetousness, practicing and sharpening greedy skills. Yet they never have enough. No wonder Peter called them **an accursed brood** (lit., "children of a curse," a Hebraism denoting certain destruction from the hand of God). Sensuality, deception, greed—all are deserving of God's wrath.

5. THEY ARE MERCENARY (2:15-16)

2:15-16. Here Peter invoked a fourth Old Testament illustration, but this time he moved from Genesis to Numbers (chaps. 22–24). These false prophets were like animals (2 Peter 2:12), and their prototype, **Balaam son of Beor,** was reproved by an animal (Num. 22:28, 30). In addition to his mercenary mentality (he **loved the wages** [*misthon*] **of wickedness** [*adikias*]; cf. the same Gr. words in 2 Peter 2:13), Balaam actually urged the Moabites to trick Israelite men into illicit relationships with Moabite women, thereby introducing immorality into the camp (Num. 31:16; cf. Num. 25:1-3; Rev. 2:14). The **donkey . . . spoke** (*phthenxamenon,* "was making a sound"; also used in 2 Peter 2:18), stopping **the** prophet in his **madness** (*paraphronian,* lit., "being apart or away from right thinking"; used only here in the NT). A mere donkey, a dumb animal, was smarter than Balaam! The false teachers, like Balaam, had sinned so long and so intensely that their sin had become a form of insanity. Also today many people have so thoroughly given themselves over to avarice and debauchery that their lifestyles are spiritually insane. Money and sex (even in the name of religion) continue to bring spiritual ruin to many people. This is "the error of Balaam" (Jude 11), his **way** which is diverse from **the straight way.**

C. Destruction by false teachers (2:17-22)

Though the ultimate judgment of heretics is assured, Peter wrote as he did because of the damage they continued to wreak in the church. Certain types of people seemed to be especially selected for recruitment by false teachers. Having explained the avenues of God's *deliverance* from ungodly people and offered a vivid *description* of false teachers, Peter now explained the *destruction* that such false teaching can bring into the church.

1. THE TARGETS OF DESTRUCTION (2:17-18)

2:17-18. The "accursed brood" (v. 14) is able to make an impact because of the deceptive nature of its approach and the vulnerability of its targets. False teachers **are springs without water and mists driven by a storm** (cf. Jude 12-13). In both cases one would look for some benefit or blessing (a cool drink from the spring; a refreshing shower from the clouds) but in each case he is disappointed. The very nature of hypocrisy is that one does not have what he pretends to have. Once again (cf. 2 Peter 2:1, 3, 9, 12-13) Peter wrote of their coming judgment. The **blackest darkness** (lit., "blackness" or "gloominess" [*zophos;* cf. "gloomy" in v. 4] of darkness) **is reserved for them** (cf. Jude 13). This blackness is presumably hell. As in the propagation of all heresy, human speech is the weapon that false teachers aim at their targets: **they mouth** (*phthengomenoi,* "make a sound"; also used in 2 Peter 2:16) **empty** (*mataiotētos,* "futile, worthless, without results"; cf. Eph. 4:17) **boastful** (*hyperonka,* "swollen"; still another *hapax legomenon* by Peter) **words.** Such high-sounding words by which they sought to impress and deceive people were actually worthless, being no different from the sound a donkey makes! These false teachers sought to lure the unstable **by appealing to** (*deleazousin,* "baiting, enticing," also used in 2 Peter 2:14) **the lustful** (*aselgeiais;* cf. v. 7) **desires of sinful human nature.** The teachers themselves were licentious and they tried to encourage Christians to be the same.

Such propaganda and sensual license appeals to some people who are **just** learning the gospel and weighing its claim on their lives. The enticed **people who are . . . escaping from those who live** (lit., "are constantly living," pres. part.) **in error** are not believers, according to most commentators. Some Bible students, however, say the ones enticed by the heretics are already converts to Christ, who by their conversions have recently escaped from their pagan companions who live in falsehood.

2. THE TECHNIQUES OF DESTRUCTION (2:19)

2:19. The techniques of false teachers are only workable with the naive, for the heretics are like a 300-pound man selling diet books—**they promise . . . freedom** but are **themselves** hopelessly enslaved by **depravity** (John 8:34-36). Their empty and boastful promises of liberty are reminiscent of Satan's words to Eve (Gen. 3:5). Slavery is not merely chattel ownership but is the mastery of one's will by any person, idea, or substance (Rom. 6:16; 1 Cor. 6:12b).

3. THE TERMINATION OF DESTRUCTION (2:20-22)

Of whom are these verses speaking? Four views are possible.

(1) Some suggest that the word "they" refers to the false teachers rather than the targets of their attack (e.g., Edwin A. Blum, "2 Peter" in *The Expositor's Bible Commentary*, 12:282).

(2) But the connection between the end of verse 18 ("people who are just escaping from those who live in error") and the beginning of verse 20 ("if they have escaped the corruption of the world") seems to favor a reference to the unstable, unsaved people who were "listeners" of the gospel (v. 18).

(3) Others think the reference might encompass both the false teachers and their "converts," who can lose their salvation. This, however, runs counter to many passages that assure believers of eternal salvation.

(4) Another view is that *new* believers are warned against being "caught up into a life of carnality . . . only to find that there is even less pleasure, less fulfillment than before they were saved" (Duane A. Dunham, "An Exegetical Study of 2 Peter 2:18-22," *Bibliotheca Sacra* 140. January–March, 1983:51).

2:20-21. Whether **they** in verse 20 refers to the teachers or their victims, both groups had available to them knowledge about **Jesus Christ,** which could produce liberty and life. But when that knowledge was rejected, their end was deeper corruption (**again entangled in it and overcome**) and presumably a more severe degree of punishment. Indeed, they **would have been better** off never **to have known** the gospel, **the way of righteousness,** and **the sacred** (holy) **commandment** (i.e., the apostolic message) **than to have known** the truth **and** have deliberately violated it.

2:22. Jews considered both dogs and pigs among the lowest of creatures (cf. Matt. 7:6) so Peter chose these animals to describe people who knew the truth and turned away from it. The first proverb, **A dog returns to its vomit,** is taken from Proverbs 26:11. The second proverb, **A sow that is washed goes back to her wallowing in the mud,** was presumably commonly known by Jews in the first century. The underlying principle of both is the same: these apostates (whether false teachers, their victims, or both) never were what they seemed to be and returned to what they had been all along. Dogs and pigs can be scrubbed but not kept clean, for it is in their very nature to return to unclean living. Such apostates are in a tighter bondage, they are farther from the truth, and they are deeper in spiritual filth than ever before.

Believers today do well to heed Peter's warning against false teachers, to learn how to discern truth for themselves, and to teach it to others. The false teachers will themselves meet destruction and others will be destroyed by them. But Christians can wage spiritual warfare more effectively if they know their spiritual enemies, the techniques that heretics use, and the end result of their deception.

V. The Christian Hope: The Lord's Return (3:1-16)

Few people like to wait, but that is precisely what God calls believers to do as they anticipate the Lord's return. Three times the word *prosdokaō,* "look(ing) forward," appears in this chapter (vv. 12-14). This is the same Greek word translated "expect" in Luke 12:46. Waiting is to be coupled with watching.

First-century Christians were close to the words of the Old Testament prophets about Christ's second coming, to which were added the promises of the Lord Himself and the constant reminders of apostles such as Peter in letters like this. Second Peter 3:1-16 presents five facts about or perspectives on the Lord's return.

A. Believers remember it (3:1-2)

3:1. Addressing his readers as **Dear friends** (*agapētoi,* "beloved, loved ones"; the first of four occurrences in this chapter: vv. 1, 8, 14, 17; cf. Jude 17-18), Peter called this his **second letter to** this group, and said **both** letters are **remind-**

ers. Many scholars assume that the earlier letter is 1 Peter. But some suggest that calling 1 Peter a "reminder" does not suit its contents. Of greater importance, however, is Peter's purpose: **to stimulate you to wholesome thinking.** "As reminders to stimulate you" translates the same Greek words which are rendered "to refresh your memory" in 2 Peter 1:13. The phrase *eilikrinē dianoian* ("wholesome thinking") may also be rendered "sincere mind" or "pure disposition." (*Eilikrinēs* occurs elsewhere in the NT only in Phil. 1:10, where it is trans. "pure.") The English "sincere" is from the Latin words *sine cera,* "without wax." Some pottery salesmen would use wax to cover cracks and weak places in pottery. Such a cover-up could be detected only by holding the jug up to the sun to see if any weaknesses were visible. Such a vase was "sun-judged" (the lit. meaning of the Gr. *eilikrinēs*). God wants His people to have sun-judged minds, not those in which their sin spots have been covered over.

3:2. Peter again reminded his readers of the need to remember (cf. 1:12-15). Others, like Peter, referred to **the holy prophets** (cf. Luke 1:70; Acts 3:21; Eph. 3:5), whose **words** were oracles regarding the day of the Lord and related topics. **The command** of **our Lord and Savior** refers to His teachings, which were then proclaimed by the **apostles** (cf. Jude 17). Peter's linking the prophets and apostles placed them on the same level of authority (cf. Eph. 2:20). This also suits Peter's earlier purpose of distinguishing the true servants of the Lord from the false. Believers do well **to recall the** writings of both Testaments regarding the Lord's return.

B. Scoffers laugh at it (3:3-7)

3:3. Peter understood that he and his readers were living **in the last days,** the period of time between the Lord's First and Second Advents. **First of all** means "above all" (as in 1:20), foremost in importance. **Scoffers** are the false teachers who deny Jesus Christ (2:1) and His return (3:4). Jesus had said these heretics would come (Matt. 24:3-5, 11, 23-26), and Paul had written the same (1 Tim. 4:1-3; 2 Tim. 3:1-9). Peter echoed the warning, adding that their **scoffing** is accompanied

by their . . . **evil desires** (*epithymias,* also used in 2 Peter 1:4; 2:10, 18; Jude 16, 18). Arrogant snobbery and disdain for the idea of a coming judgment led to sexual perversion.

3:4. Their mocking took the form of a stinging question: **Where is this "coming" He promised?** Rejecting this promise, so often repeated in the New Testament (John 14:1-3; Acts 1:11; 1 Cor. 15:23; 2 Cor. 1:14; Phil. 1:6; 1 Thes. 3:13; 4:14-18; 2 Thes. 1:10; 2:1; 1 Tim. 6:14; 2 Tim. 4:8; Titus 2:13; Heb. 9:28; James 5:7) rests on the principle of uniformitarianism. This is the view that the cosmic processes of the present and the future can be understood solely on the basis of how the cosmos has operated in the past. There is almost an incipient deism here which rules out divine intervention in the universal order. In a universe governed by natural laws miracles, mockers argue, simply cannot happen. Therefore they say Jesus Christ could not come again.

The scoffers wanted to push their argument as far back as possible. So they referred to **our fathers** (lit., "the fathers"), that is, Old Testament patriarchs (John 7:22; Acts 3:13; 13:32; Rom. 9:5; 11:28; Heb. 1:1), and to **the beginning of Creation.** Since nothing has happened in all this time, mockers reasoned, why expect the Lord's return now?

3:5-6. Peter met those arguments head on by reviewing some ancient history. Just as water by God's command played a significant role in the early formation of the earth, so **water** also was the agent for destruction of the earth at God's command. **The heavens existed** refers to the expanse or sky created on the second day of Creation (Gen. 1:6-8); **and the earth was formed out of water and with water** refers to the land appearing from the water on the third day of Creation (Gen. 1:9-10).

God the Creator is also God the Judge. In His sovereign will, any change in process can occur at any time for He designed and controls these "natural" processes. The scoffers **deliberately** (*thelontas,* "willingly") **forget** God's Creation and the Flood, an interesting contrast with Peter's constant reminders to his readers to "remember" (2 Peter 1:12-13, 15; 3:1-2, 8). The scoffers deliberately put aside **God's Word** and then complained that God was not doing anything. Interestingly Peter was both a creationist and a believer in the universal Flood (cf. his other references to the Flood: 1 Peter 3:20; 2 Peter 2:5).

At the beginning of 3:6 the words "by water" are literally, "through which." This may refer back to "God's Word" (at the end of v. 5 in Gr.), or it may refer to both water and the Word. But God's use of water in both Creation and destruction seems to lend credence to the NIV rendering. **The world** (kosmos) refers to inhabitants, since the earth itself was not destroyed in the Flood. Similarly in John 3:16 "the world" (kosmos) means the globe's inhabitants (cf. John 1:9; 3:17, 19; 4:42; 6:33; 7:7; 15:18-19; 17:14, 21, 23, 25; 1 John 2:2; 3:13; 4:14).

3:7. Verses 7, 10, and 12 are the only places where the New Testament depicts the future destruction of the world by fire. In the past the world was destroyed in the Flood by God's Word and by water; in the future it will be destroyed **by the same Word** and by **fire.** Having decided to judge the world (cf. 2:3-4, 9, 17), God is simply holding the earth on layaway. It is **reserved** (tethēsaurismenoi, "being stored up like a treasure") **for fire** and **kept** (tēroumenoi, "guarded" or "held") for judgment. Isaiah (66:15-16) and Malachi (4:1) associated fire with the return of the Lord. References to it are also found in the Qumran literature (Dead Sea Scrolls) as well as other sources shortly before and after Christ's birth. "The day of the Lord" (2 Peter 3:10) includes the Tribulation, the Millennium, the great white throne judgment, and the destruction of **the present heavens and earth.** At the great white throne after the Millennium, **ungodly men** (i.e., the wicked dead) will be judged and then thrown into the lake of fire (Rev. 20:11-15). This, as Peter wrote, will be their **day of judgment** (cf. 2 Peter 2:9) **and destruction.** After they are cast into fire, the heavens and the earth will be destroyed by fire. God intervened castastrophically before (in the Flood), and He will do so again.

C. God guarantees it (3:8-9)

3:8-9. Why should the Lord be so long in coming? Peter offered two answers. First, God counts time differently than does man. Once again Peter appealed to their memories (**do not forget this one thing**). The scoffers forget (v. 5), but believers should not. Christians should recall Psalm 90:4, which Peter quoted. People see time against time; but God sees time against eternity. In fact time only seems long because of man's finite perspective. **With the Lord a day is like a thousand years, and a thousand years are like a day.**

Some suggest that this statement argues against premillennialism. They point out that the concept of 1,000 years is not to be taken literally since it is merely a comparative time reference. However, the literal 1,000-year reign of Christ on earth is strongly affirmed in Revelation 20:1-6 (see comments there). Peter was simply using a simile. What to people, including scoffers, may seem like a long time is to the Lord very short. The present Church Age has lasted, in God's eyes, not quite two days!

The second reason the Lord's return seems to be so long in coming is that God wants as many people to be saved as possible (2 Peter 3:9). **The Lord is not slow in keeping His promise.** The words "is . . . slow" translate bradynei ("hesitate, linger, delay"), used only here in the New Testament. Again Peter gave a divine-human comparison (cf. v. 8). God's so-called "tardiness" as viewed by some people (**as some understand slowness**) is only a delay with respect to their time schedules, not His. In fact God's time schedule is modified by patience, a major attribute of the heavenly Father (cf. v. 15; Rom. 2:4; 9:22).

The words **not wanting** (mē boulomenos) **anyone to perish** do not express a decree, as if God has willed everyone to be saved. Universal salvation is not taught in the Bible. Instead those words describe God's wishes or desires; He longs that all would be saved (cf. 1 Tim. 2:4) but knows that many reject Him.

D. Peter describes it (3:10-13)

3:10. When the Lord does **come,** it will be both surprising and catastrophic: **like a thief.** This simile was used by Jesus (Matt. 24:42-44) and repeated by others (1 Thes. 5:2; Rev. 3:3; 16:15). **The day of the Lord** describes end-time events that begin after the Rapture and culminate with the commencement of eternity. In the middle of the 70th week of Daniel the Antichrist will turn against the people of God in full fury (Dan. 9:24-27; see comments on 1 Thes. 5:2; 2 Thes. 2:2-12).

In the catastrophic conflagration at the end of the Millennium, **the heavens** (the earth's atmosphere and the starry sky, not God's abode) **will disappear with a roar,** which in some way will involve fire (2 Peter 3:7, 12). **The elements** (*stoicheia,* either stars or material elements with which the universe is made) **will be destroyed by fire** (and will melt, v. 12), **and the earth and everything in it will be laid bare** (*eurethēsetai*). This Greek word could mean that everything will be exposed for what it really is. Or it could suggest a question: "The earth and everything in it—will they be found?" Others (on the basis of some Gr. mss.; NIV marg.) say the word *eurethēsetai* should be substituted with *katakaēsetai,* "shall be burned up." Perhaps the first of these views is preferable (as rendered in the NIV).

3:11. Peter sees all this as a strong motivational expectation which should provoke holy living. The question, **What kind of people ought you to be?** is rhetorical. But in case someone should miss the point, Peter answered it: **You ought to live holy and godly lives.** "Holy lives" (*en hagiais anastrophais,* lit., "in holy conduct") refers to Christian separation and sanctification apart from the world, apart toward God. "Godly" (*eusebeiais;* also in 1:3, 6-7) refers to piety before God. The word "live" (*hyparchein*) is in the present tense, indicating that these qualities are to be constantly present in light of the Lord's return. Scoffers, questioning the Lord's coming with its ensuing judgment on them, lead ungodly lives (2:7, 10, 12-15, 18-20; 3:3). By contrast, Jesus' followers, anticipating His return, are to be godly (v. 14; cf. Titus 2:12-14; 1 John 3:3).

3:12. Holiness and piety (v. 11) not only cause God's people to **look forward to** (from *prosdokaō,* "expect and anticipate"; cf. vv. 13-14) the Lord's return but also to **speed its coming.** How do believers hasten it? The godly lives of the Lord's people, their praying, and their witnessing help bring others to repentance. Peter then repeated for emphasis

the fact that at the commencement of eternity (here called **the day of God**) **the heavens** will be destroyed **by fire and the elements will melt** (cf. comments on v. 10). That event concludes "the day of the Lord" (v. 10) and commences "the day of God."

3:13. The old cosmic system will then give way to **a new heaven and a new earth** and this is what believers **are looking forward to** (cf. vv. 12, 14), not to the earth's destruction. The new heaven and new earth, given by the **promise** of God, will finally be **the home** or dwelling place **of righteousness** (lit., "in which righteousness dwells permanently"). It will be the home of righteousness because the Righteous One will be there (Jer. 23:5-7; 33:16; Dan. 9:24; Rev. 21:1, 8, 27). What a contrast this will be to the world's unrighteousness!

E. Behavior is changed by it (3:14-16)

3:14. To show that one's behavior is linked to his expectation of the Lord's coming, this paragraph begins with **So then** (*Dio*). What kind of people should believers be? They are to be holy and godly (v. 11), and they also are to **make every effort** (*spoudasate;* cf. 1:10, 15; also cf. *spoudēn,* 1:5) **to be . . . spotless** (*aspiloi,* also used in 1 Tim. 6:14; James 1:27 ["pure"]; 1 Peter 1:19 ["without . . . defect," referring to Christ]), **blameless** (*amōmētoi,* "without [moral] defect" like a sacrificial animal without a blemish; used also in Eph. 1:4; 5:27; Phil. 2:15; Col. 1:22; Heb. 9:14; 1 Peter 1:19; Jude 24; Rev. 14:5), **and at peace with Him** (cf. Rom. 5:1). The false teachers, Peter said, "are blots (*spiloi*) and blemishes" (*mōmoi;* 2 Peter 2:13), but believers are to make it their business to be morally clean (cf. 1:4) like Christ the spotless One (1 Peter 1:19). This is the practical result of the implantation of the divine nature (2 Peter 1:4) in the members of God's family; it is the ringing encore to the symphony of grace described in 1:5-7.

3:15. **The Lord's patience** is because of His desire that people come to **salvation** (cf. v. 9). The seeming procrastination of the Second Coming, far from being negative inaction on God the Father's part is rather a demonstration of His *makrothymian* ("long-suffering"). Now the world has time to repent, but this will not be so when "the day of judgment" (2:9; 3:7) comes. The Lord's patience leads toward repentance, which is precisely the point **Paul** made in Romans 2:4, though this may or may not be the passage Peter had in mind (cf. comments on 2 Peter 3:16). Interestingly Peter called Paul **our dear** (*agapētos*, "beloved"; cf. vv. 1, 8, 14, 17) **brother.** Years before Paul had severely rebuked Peter (Gal. 2:11-14), but this did not sever their love and respect for each other.

3:16. Peter said that Paul wrote about **the same** thing **in all his letters.** Though written with God's "wisdom" (v. 15), Paul's **letters contain some things that are hard to understand.** The Greek word for "hard to understand" (*dysnoēta*, only here in the NT) was sometimes applied in secular Greek literature to oracles that were ambiguous and obscure. Peter himself, as well as the **ignorant** (*amatheis*, "unlearned"), who were neophytes in New Testament doctrine, found some of Paul's statements obscure. These difficult passages (which Peter did not specify) had caused the **unstable** (*astēriktoi*; cf. 2:14) to pervert and **distort** (*streplousin*, "twist, torment"; another word occurring only here in the NT) their real meaning. But that was to be expected since that is how they handled **the other Scriptures.**

The fact that Peter referred to Paul's letters and then to "the other Scriptures" indicates that Paul's writings were then considered authoritative Scripture. Such behavior—twisting the Scripture to suit their own purposes—is met with God's judgment which, in this case, the ignorant and unstable bring on themselves in the form of **destruction** (*apōleian*; cf. 2:1, 3). Believers may not fully understand all the Scriptures, but they certainly ought not twist their obvious meanings.

VI. Conclusion (3:17-18)

3:17. In a warm and loving style (**dear friends** occurs here for the fourth time in this chap.; cf. vv. 1, 8, 14) the Apostle Peter closes this public yet personal epistle with a word of warning (v. 17) and a word of encouragement (v. 18). Both are based on an assumption: **You already know this.** These words translate one Greek word (*proginōskontes*), from which comes the English word "prognosis." When a medical prognosis

is made, a patient is better able to prepare himself for what is ahead and if possible, to correct himself. When a doctor says, "If you continue to eat as much as you do now, you will have serious heart problems in a few years," the patient "knows beforehand" and can therefore change his life in accord with the information he has.

Peter then warned, **Be on your guard** (*phylassesthe*). If Peter were writing today, he might say, "Don't say I didn't warn you." If his readers were not careful they could **be carried away by the error of lawless men** (*athesmōn*; cf. 2:7). The verb "carried away" (*synapachthentes*; trans. "led astray" in Gal. 2:13) emphasizes a group or corporate movement. False teachers are not satisfied with ambushing one or two, now and then, here and there; they want to sweep large groups of people away from the correct doctrine of Christ. Those who keep company with such people are in danger of being led astray (referred to as "falling"; cf. 2 Peter 1:10; Gal. 5:4). This does not refer to losing one's salvation. On the other hand those who have paid attention to the warnings, carefully heeding the prognosis, can maintain their **secure position** in the truth. "Secure position" translates *stērigmou* ("firm position"; cf. the adjective *astēriktos*, "unstable," in 2 Peter 2:14; 3:16, and the verb *stērizei*, "make strong or firm" in 1 Peter 5:10).

3:18. To **grow in . . . grace** is not subjective, based merely on experience and emotional happenings. It is objectively related to Peter's key word **knowledge** (cf. 1:2-3, 5-6, 8, 20 ["understand"]; 2:20-21 [twice in v. 21]; 3:3). This is not just any knowledge; it is knowledge about **our Lord and Savior Jesus Christ** (cf. 1:1-2, 11; 2:20). The verb "grow" is a present imperative, which could be rendered "be continually growing." Believers are to grow "in grace," that is, in the sphere of God's unmerited favor, and in the exercise of spiritual graces which Peter spoke of in 1:5-7. This process of spiritual growth begins by knowing Christ initially in regeneration (cf. John 17:3) and it continues in one's deepening relationship with Him (Eph. 4:15; Phil. 3:10; 1 Peter 2:2). Both are necessary. Without the initial knowledge there is no opportunity for growth. But if there is only that initial knowledge, the struggling new believer forgets "that he has been cleansed from his past sins" (2 Peter 1:9).

Now the apostle, at one time more comfortable in fishing boats than with the parchments of biblical texts, affirmed the oneness of the Father and the Son in a splendid doxology. The One who is "our Lord" is also "our Savior." And glory, which belongs only to God (Isa. 42:8), is also the Son's (cf. 2 Peter 1:17). **To Him be glory** (lit., "the glory") is Peter's praise and prayer (cf. 2 Tim. 4:18). The glory of redemption, the glory of spiritual growth, the glory of manifesting the symphony of grace, the glory of escape from the false teachers, and the glory of His ultimate return—*all* glory belongs to Jesus. And He receives that glory **both now and forever.** "Forever" is literally, "to the day of the Age"—from the moment of the Cross, on through the days of the New Testament, throughout the history of the church, to the present hour, and throughout eternity! No wonder Peter concluded with the affirmative word of praise, **Amen!**

BIBLIOGRAPHY

Barbieri, Louis A., Jr. *First and Second Peter.* Everyman's Bible Commentary. Chicago: Moody Press, 1977.

Barnes, Albert. *Barnes' Notes on the New Testament.* 1962. Reprint. Grand Rapids: Kregel Publications, 1966.

Bigg, Charles. *A Critical and Exegetical Commentary on the Epistles of St. Peter and St. Jude.* The International Critical Commentary. Edinburgh: T. & T. Clark, 1901.

Blum, Edwin A. "2 Peter." In *The Expositor's Bible Commentary,* vol. 12. Grand Rapids: Zondervan Publishing House, 1981.

Calvin, John. "Commentaries on the Second Epistle of Peter." In *Calvin's Commentaries,* vol. 22. Translated by John Owen. Reprint. Grand Rapids: Baker Book House, 1981.

DeHaan, Richard W. *Studies in 2 Peter.* Wheaton, Ill.: Scripture Press Publications, Victor Books, 1977.

Demarest, John T. *Commentary on the Second Epistle of the Apostle Peter.* New York: Sheldon & Co., 1862.

Green, Michael. *The Second Epistle of Peter and the General Epistle of Jude.* The Tyndale New Testament Commentaries. Grand Rapids: Wm. B. Eerdmans Publishing Co., 1968.

James, Montague Rhodes. *The Second Epistle General of Peter and the General Epistle of Jude.* Cambridge: At the University Press, 1912.

Lenski, R.C.H. *The Interpretation of the Epistles of St. Peter, St. John and St. Jude.* Minneapolis: Augsburg Publishing House, 1966.

Lillie, John. *Lectures on the 1st and 2nd Epistles of Peter.* Reprint. Minneapolis: Klock & Klock Christian Publishers, 1978.

Mayor, Joseph B. *The Epistle of St. Jude and the Second Epistle of St. Peter.* London: Macmillan & Co., 1907. Reprint. Minneapolis: Klock & Klock Christian Publishers, 1978.

Moffatt, James. *The General Epistles: James, Peter, and Judas.* New York: Harper & Bros. Publishers, n.d.

Reicke, Bo. *The Epistles of James, Peter, and Jude.* The Anchor Bible. Garden City, N.Y.: Doubleday & Co., 1964.

Ward, J.W.C. *The General Epistles of St. Peter and St. Jude.* Westminster Commentaries. London: Methuen & Co., 1934.

Wuest, Kenneth S. *In These Last Days.* Grand Rapids: Wm. B. Eerdmans Publishing Co., 1954.

1 JOHN

Zane C. Hodges

INTRODUCTION

The First Epistle of John is an intensely practical letter addressed to Christian readers. It warns against the dangers of false teaching and exhorts believers to lives of obedience to God and love for their brothers and sisters. Its controlling theme is fellowship with God the Father and with His Son Jesus Christ (1:3).

Authorship. The epistle has been traditionally ascribed to John the Apostle. The author's name, however, does not occur in the letter. Yet it is plain from the tone of the letter as a whole that the writer possessed spiritual authority. Moreover, he placed himself among the eyewitnesses to the incarnate life of the Lord Jesus (1:1-2). Early Christian writers including Irenaeus, Clement of Alexandria, and Tertullian cited the epistle as John's. There is thus no good reason for denying the traditional belief that the letter is of apostolic authorship.

Background. The letter contains no hint about the identity or location of the readers beyond the fact that they are Christians. Since early church tradition associates John with the Roman province of Asia (in western Turkey), it has often been thought that the readers lived there. This may well be true especially since this association is confirmed by Revelation 2 and 3.

The readers had been confronted with false teachers, whom John called antichrists (1 John 2:18-26). The exact character of these false teachers has been much discussed. Many have thought they were Gnostics who held to a strict dualism in which spiritual and material things were sharply distinguished. Others have seen the letter as directed against Docetism, the belief that Jesus' humanity was not real and that He only appeared to have a physical body. Often too, the letter is thought to refute the heresy of Cerinthus. According to church tradition, Cerinthus lived in Roman Asia and was strongly opposed by the Apostle John. Cerinthus taught that Jesus was only a man and that the divine Christ descended on Jesus at His baptism and left Him before the Crucifixion.

It is not possible to be precise about the exact character of the false teaching which John opposed in his letter. The only certain data is what is found in the epistle itself. It is clear that the antichrists denied that Jesus is the Christ (2:22). The statements in 5:6 may well be intelligible against the backdrop of a teaching like that of Cerinthus. The strong claims made in 1:1-2 about the physical reality of the Incarnation would be appropriate if Docetism were in view. The emphasis on "knowing" God fits the view that the heretics made special claims to "knowledge" as the Gnostics did. But Gnosticism is chiefly known from sources much later than 1 John and many characteristics of later Gnostic thought do not find reflection in the epistle.

It is probably a mistake to attempt to systematize the thought of the heretics whom John opposed in this letter. According to his own statements, he had "many" false teachers in view (2:18; 4:1). There is no reason to think that all of them held exactly the same views. The ancient Greco-Roman world was a babel of religious voices, and it is likely that the readers were confronted by a variety of ideas. Still, the heretics had in common their denials of the person of Christ, though they could have done so in different ways. On the basis of 2:19 it may be suggested that they had originated chiefly in Judea (see comments on 2:19). But beyond this little can be said with certainty about the exact nature of the heresy or heresies that gave rise to John's epistle.

That the initial readers were indeed Christians is clear from 2:12-14, 21; and 5:13. The reference to "the anointing" which they possessed (2:20, 27) that is, the Holy Spirit, might also suggest that the addressees were principally the leaders of the church or churches to which John wrote. In the Old Testament the leaders of Israel—prophets, priests, and kings—were often anointed to their offices. While it is conceivable that 1 John 2:20 and 27 refer to an "anointing" which is true of all Christians, this kind of idea is rare in the New Testament. Even 2 Corinthians 1:21 may refer to Paul's apostolic office. Possibly therefore, in 1 John 2:20 and 27 the writer sought to affirm the competency of the church leaders in the area of spiritual understanding and thus to shore up their authority as over against the false teachers. The leaders did not need to be taught by any human teachers since they were taught by their "anointing," that is, by the Holy Spirit.

It is impossible to be dogmatic on this point. No doubt John knew the addressees when he wrote the epistle. Even if the leaders were primarily in view, the letter would naturally have been read to the entire congregation(s) since only in this way could it perform its purpose of supporting the established teachers' authority. The larger audience could then receive the instruction which the letter contained while at the same time being encouraged to rely on the guidance offered by their Spirit-taught leadership. In the early church one of the chief responsibilities of the elders was to protect the flock from spiritual "wolves" (Acts 20:28-29; Titus 1:9-11). If the false teachers made grandiose claims to spiritual wisdom and authority, it would make good sense for the inspired author to affirm his confidence in the regular church leaders. This would strengthen their hands with their congregation(s) in resisting the inroads of heretical ideas.

It might be thought, however, that the references to "children," "fathers," and "young men" (1 John 2:12-14) point to an audience of people of varying levels of spiritual attainment. If so, the leadership alone can hardly be considered as the principal addressees. On the other hand all the readers were addressed by this writer as "children" (e.g., 2:1, 18) and the terms used in 2:12-14 may simply be ways of addressing the same people viewed from different standpoints. (For further discussion, see the comments on those verses.)

In any case the letter was no doubt intended ultimately for the warning and instruction of the whole church or churches to which it was sent. And its truths are richly applicable to every Christian's experience.

Date. Virtually nothing in the epistle indicates a specific date or period for its writing. Many conservatives suggest a date late in the first century A.D., about the time of or shortly after the writing of the Fourth Gospel. But a good case can be made for dating the Gospel of John sometime prior to A.D. 70. If this is done, there is no particular reason why 1 John may not be assigned to the same period of time. If 2:19 suggests that the false teachers had seceded from the Palestinian churches which the apostles supervised, then this perhaps can be taken to indicate a time before the calamities of the Jewish revolt against the Romans in A.D. 66-70. After this period the influences (both good and bad) of Palestinian Christianity on the Gentile churches must have greatly decreased. If the reference of 2:19 is indeed to Palestine, then John may well have been writing from Jerusalem when he stated, "They went out from us."

These deductions are far from firm, but they might be taken to point to a date for the epistle somewhere between A.D. 60 and 65. But it must be admitted that an even earlier date cannot be excluded. Whatever the actual date of writing, the epistle gives truths of timeless value to the Christian church.

OUTLINE

The First Epistle of John is notoriously difficult to outline. Many different approaches have been offered. The justification for the following outline must be sought in the exposition which the commentary contains.

I. Prologue (1:1–4)
II. Introduction: Basic Principles (1:5–2:11)
    A. Basic principles of fellowship (1:5–2:2)

COMMENTARY

I. Prologue (1:1-4)

The first four verses of the epistle constitute its prologue. Here the writer affirmed the tangible reality of the Incarnation of Christ and announced that the goals of his letter were fellowship and joy.

1:1. The apostle declared his subject to be **that which was from the beginning.** Many have thought that he referred here to an absolute beginning, such as described in Genesis 1:1 and John 1:1. This is possible, but in view of the epistle's concern with the original message about Jesus Christ, it seems more likely that John referred to the beginning of the gospel proclamation. If so, the usage is similar to that found in 1 John 2:7, 24; and 3:11. The writer was then asserting that what he proclaimed was the truth about God's Son that was originally witnessed by the apostles who had direct contact with Him. Numbering himself among these apostolic eyewitnesses, the author described this proclamation as one **which we have heard, which we have seen with our eyes, which we have looked at and our hands have touched.**

With these introductory words, the apostle directed his first shafts at the heresy with which he was concerned. The antichrists brought new ideas, not those which were "from the beginning" of the gospel era. Moreover, their denial of the reality of the incarnate life of Christ could be countered by the experiences of the eyewitnesses whose testimony was founded on actual hearing, seeing, and touching (cf. "look" and "touch" in Luke 24:39). John's message is solidly based on a historical reality.

The exact meaning of the expression **concerning the Word of life** has been variously explained. By capitalizing the term "Word," the NIV interprets this as a title for the Lord like that found in John 1:1, 14. But there this title has no qualifying phrase such as the expression "of life," which is used here. It seems more natural to understand the phrase in the sense of "the message about life" for which Philippians 2:16 furnishes a parallel (see also Acts 5:20). Indeed, as 1 John 1:2 shows, "life," not "word," is personified. Thus John was saying that his subject matter in this epistle deals with the original and well-attested verities that concern "the message about Life"—that is, about God's Son, who is Life (cf. 5:20).

1:2. The Life which the apostles proclaimed is intensely personal. Not only has that Life **appeared,** but **it** is nothing less than **the eternal life, which was with the Father and has appeared to** people. The Incarnation is unquestionably in view.

1:3. The objective John had in mind in writing about these significant realities was **that you,** the readers, **may have fellowship with us,** the apostles. Since he later, in 2:12-14, made it perfectly clear that he regarded the readers as genuine Christians, his goal was obviously not their conversions. It is an interpretive mistake of considerable moment to treat the term "fellowship" as though it meant little more than "to be a Christian." The readers were already saved, but they needed this letter if they were to enjoy real fellowship with the apostolic circle to which the author belonged. In the final analysis that apostolic **fellowship is with the Father and with His Son, Jesus Christ.**

Probably the false teachers denied that the readers possessed eternal life (see comments on 2:25; 5:13). If so, and if the readers would begin to doubt God's guarantees on that point, their fellowship with the Father and the Son would be in jeopardy. This, of course, is not the same as saying that their salvation would be in jeopardy. As believers they could never lose the gift of life which God had given them (cf. John 4:14; 6:32, 37-40), but their fellowship depended on walking in the light (1 John 1:7). The danger to the readers was that they might be allured into darkness by the siren song of the antichrists. How seductive their godless appeal was emerges in this letter. John's aim, therefore, was to furnish his readership with a necessary reaffirmation of the basic truths of their faith so that their fellowship with God would be sustained.

1:4. John rounded off the prologue with a delicate personal touch. If this letter would succeed in fulfilling its aim for the readership, the writer himself (and his fellow apostles) would reap spiritual joy. **We write this to make our joy complete.** This statement is similar to one the same author made in 3 John 4: "I have no greater joy than to hear that my children are walking in the truth." The apostles so shared the heart of Christ for His people that their own joy was bound up in the spiritual well-being of those to whom they ministered. If the readers retained their true fellowship with God and with His apostles, no one would be any happier than John himself.

II. Introduction: Basic Principles (1:5–2:11)

Since fellowship is the objective of John's letter, it was natural for him to begin with a discussion of this subject. So in 1:5–2:11 he enunciated some fundamental principles which lie at the root of all genuine fellowship with God. These principles are of immense practical value to the everyday lives of all Christians. By these principles believers may test the reality of their personal communion with God. They may also discern whether they

have come to know the God with whom they commune.

A. Basic principles of fellowship (1:5–2:2)

1:5. In the prologue the author asserted that he was writing about things he had heard, seen, and touched. Here he began with something he had heard. **This is the message we have heard from Him and declare to you.** By the words "from Him," John no doubt meant from the Lord Jesus Christ whose Incarnation he had just referred to (vv. 1-2). The content of this "message," as John expressed it, is that **God is Light; in Him there is no darkness at all.** This precise statement is not found in the recorded words of Jesus, but the author was an apostle who heard much more than was "written down" (cf. John 21:25). There is no reason to think that John did not mean just what he said. This is a truth he had learned from the Lord.

In describing God as Light, which John frequently did (John 1:4-5, 7-9; 3:19-21; 8:12; 9:5; 12:35-36, 46; Rev. 21:23), he was no doubt thinking of God as the Revealer of His holiness. Both aspects of the divine nature figure in the discussion of sin and fellowship in 1 John 1:6-10. As Light, God both exposes man's sin and condemns it. If anyone walks in darkness, he is hiding from the truth which the Light reveals (cf. John 3:19-20). Thus revelatory terms such as "the truth" and "His Word" are prominent in 1 John 1:6, 8, 10.

It is important that the "message" John had heard is the one he directed to his readers ("we . . . declare to you"). Some scholars have maintained that the false assertions which are condemned in verses 6, 8, and 10 are those of the false teachers, or antichrists, about whom John wrote later. But there is no proof of this. The writer continued to use the word "we" throughout as though both he and his readership were in view. When carefully considered, the kind of claims which John refuted are precisely the kind which may be made by Christians who lose touch with spiritual realities and with God. The effort to find in verses 6-10 the doctrinal beliefs of heretical teachers lacks adequate exegetical foundation.

1:6. Since "God is Light," it follows that a Christian cannot truly claim communion with Him while living in the darkness. As John warned, **If we claim to have fellowship with Him yet walk in the darkness, we lie and do not live by the truth.** John knew, as does every perceptive pastor, that Christians sometimes feign spirituality while engaging in acts of disobedience. The Apostle Paul had to deal with a case of incest in the Corinthian assembly (1 Cor. 5:1-5) and laid down a list of sins for which church members should come under church discipline (1 Cor. 5:9-13). Spurious claims to fellowship with God have been a tragic reality throughout the history of the church.

A Christian who says he is in fellowship with God (who "is Light") but who is disobeying Him (walking "in the darkness") is lying (cf. 1 John 2:4). Ten times John used "darkness" to refer to sin (John 1:5; 3:19; 12:35 [twice]; 1 John 1:5-6; 2:8-9, 11 [twice]).

1:7. There can be only one sphere of real communion with God—the light itself. Thus John insisted that this is where a Christian will find that communion: **But if we walk in the light, as He is in the light, we have fellowship with one another.** It is strange that many commentators have understood the expression "with one another" as a reference to fellowship with other Christians. But this is not what the author is discussing here. The Greek pronoun for "one another" *(allēlōn)* may refer to the two parties (God and the Christian) named in the first part of the statement. John's point is that if Christians live in the light where God is, then there is mutual fellowship between Himself and them. That is, they have fellowship with Him and He has fellowship with them. The light itself is the fundamental reality which they share. Thus true communion with God is living in the sphere where one's experience is illumined by the truth of what God is. It is to live open to His revelation of Himself in Jesus Christ. As John soon stated (v. 9), this entails believers' acknowledging whatever the light reveals is wrong in their lives.

It is significant that John talked of walking *in* the light, rather than *according to* the light. To walk *according to* the light would require sinless perfection and would make fellowship with God impossible for sinful humans. To walk *in* it,

however, suggests instead openness and responsiveness to the light. John did not think of Christians as sinless, even though they are walking in the light, as is made clear in the last part of this verse. For John added that **the blood of Jesus, His Son, purifies us from every sin.** This statement is grammatically coordinate with the preceding one, "We have fellowship with one another." The statement of verse 7, in its entirety, affirms that two things are true of believers who walk in the light: (a) they are in fellowship with God and (b) they are being cleansed from every sin. So long as there is true openness to the light of divine truth, Christians' failures are under the cleansing power of the shed blood of Christ. Indeed, only in virtue of the Savior's work on the cross can there be any fellowship between imperfect creatures and the infinitely perfect God.

1:8. But when a believer is experiencing true fellowship with God he may then be tempted to think or say that he is, at that moment at least, free from sin. John warned against this self-deluding conception. **If we claim to be without sin, we deceive ourselves and the truth is not in us** (cf. v. 6; 2:4). If Christians understand the truth that God's Word teaches about the depravity of the human heart, they know that just because they are not *conscious* of failure does not mean that they are free from it. If the truth is "in" them as a controlling, motivating influence, this kind of self-deception will not take place. Whether someone claims to be "without sin" for a brief period of time or claims it as a permanent attainment, the claim is false.

1:9. In view of verse 8, Christians ought to be ready at all times to acknowledge any failure which God's light may expose to them. Thus John wrote, **If we confess our sins, He is faithful and just and will forgive us our sins and purify us from all unrighteousness.** Though the NIV's translation "our sins" (after the words "forgive us") is quite admissible, "our" is not in the Greek text. The phrase *(tas hamartias)* contains only an article and noun and it is conceivable that the article is the type which grammarians call "the article of previous reference." If so, there is a subtle contrast between this expression and the "all unrighteousness" which follows it. John's thought might be paraphrased: "If we confess our sins, He . . . will forgive the sins we confess and moreover will even cleanse us from *all* unrighteousness." Naturally only God knows at any moment the full extent of a person's unrighteousness. Each Christian, however, is responsible to acknowledge (the meaning of "confess," *homologōmen;* cf. 2:23; 4:3) whatever the light makes him aware of, and when he does so, a complete and perfect cleansing is granted him. There is thus no need to agonize over sins of which one is unaware.

Moreover, it is comforting to learn that the forgiveness which is promised here is both absolutely assured (because God "is faithful") and also is in no way contrary to His holiness (He is "just"). The word used here for "just" *(dikaios)* is the same one which is applied as a title to Christ in 2:1 where it is translated "the Righteous One." *Dikaios* is also used of God (either the Father or the Son) in 2:29 and 3:7. Obviously God is "just" or "righteous" when He forgives the believer's sin because of the "atoning sacrifice" which the Lord Jesus has made (see 2:2). As is already evident from 1:7, a Christian's fellowship with God is inseparably connected with the effectiveness of the blood which Jesus shed for him.

In modern times some have occasionally denied that a Christian needs to confess his sins and ask forgiveness. It is claimed that a believer already has forgiveness in Christ (Eph. 1:7). But this point of view confuses the perfect position which a Christian has in God's Son (by which he is even "seated . . . with Him in the heavenly realms" [Eph. 2:6]) with his needs as a failing individual on earth. What is considered in 1 John 1:9 may be described as "familial" forgiveness. It is perfectly understandable how a son may need to ask his father to forgive him for his faults while at the same time his position within the family is not in jeopardy. A Christian who never asks his heavenly Father for forgiveness for his sins can hardly have much sensitivity to the ways in which he grieves his Father. Furthermore, the Lord Jesus Himself taught His followers to seek forgiveness of their sins in a prayer that was obviously intended for daily use (cf. the expression "give us today our daily bread" preceding "forgive us our debts," Matt. 6:11-12). The teaching that a Christian should not ask God for daily forgiveness is an aberration. Moreover, confession of sin is *never* connected by John with the acquisition of eternal life, which is always conditioned on faith. First John 1:9 is not spoken to the unsaved, and the effort to turn it into a soteriological affirmation is misguided.

It may also be said that so long as the idea of walking in the light or darkness is correctly understood on an experiential level, these concepts offer no difficulty. "Darkness" has an ethical meaning (*Theological Dictionary of the New Testament,* s.v. *"skotos,"* 7:444). When a believer loses personal touch with the God of light, he begins to live in darkness. But confession of sin is the way back into the light.

1:10. However, after a believer sins, he should not deny that sin. **If we claim we have not sinned, we make Him out to be a liar and His Word has no place in our lives.** This statement should be read in direct connection with verse 9. When a Christian is confronted by God's Word about his sins, he should admit them rather than deny them. To deny one's personal sin in the face of God's testimony to the contrary, is to "make" God "out to be a liar." By contradicting His Word, a person rejects it and refuses to give it the proper "place" in his life.

2:1. Some of John's readers might have thought his insistence on the sinfulness of Christians somehow would discourage holiness. The opposite was John's intention as he affirmed: **My dear children, I write this to you so that you will not sin.** He addressed them affectionately as an apostle with a fatherly concern (The Gr. word for "children" ["dear" is not in the Gr.] is *teknia* [lit., "little born ones"], used seven times by John in this epistle [vv. 1, 12, 28; 3:7, 18; 4:4; 5:21] and once in his Gospel [John 13:33]. A similar word *tekna* ["born ones"] occurs in John 1:12; 11:52; 1 John 3:2, 10 [twice]; 5:2; 2 John 1, 4, 13; and 3 John 4. On the other hand *paidia* ["children"] occurs only twice in 1 John [2:13, 18].)

The statements in 1:8, 10 about believers' sinful tendencies do not encourage sin; they actually put perceptive Christians on guard against it. If a believer tries to make the claims denounced in 1:8 and 10, then he is most likely to fail to recognize and reject sin. But sin is nevertheless a reality, however much John wished his readers would not commit it. Accordingly he assured them, **But if anybody does sin, we have One who speaks to the Father in our defense—Jesus Christ the Righteous One.** John did not want his readers to sin, but he knew that none of them was perfect and that all would need the help available from their Advocate.

The words "One who speaks . . . in our defense" translate a single term *(paraklēton)*. Its essential meaning is captured by the KJV's familiar "Advocate." John is the only New Testament writer to use it of the Holy Spirit (four times in his Gospel: John 14:16, 26; 15:26; 16:7). In these four verses the NIV renders it "Counselor" each time (cf. KJV's "Comforter"). The thought here in 1 John 2:1 is of a defense attorney who takes up the case of his client before a tribunal. The way in which the advocacy of the Lord Jesus works for His sinning people is admirably illustrated in His prayer for Peter (Luke 22:31-32). In anticipation of Peter's approaching denial, Jesus asked the Father to prevent Peter's faith from collapsing. He also had in mind Peter's future helpfulness to his Christian brethren. There is no reason to suppose that Christ must ask God to keep a Christian from going to hell as a result of his sin. Eternal life is fully guaranteed to those who have trusted Jesus for it (John 3:16; 5:24; etc.). But the consequences of a believer's failure, his restoration, and future usefulness are all urgent matters which Jesus takes up with God when sin occurs. His own personal righteousness (He is "the Righteous One"; cf. 1 John 1:9, God is "just") is what uniquely suits Christ for His role as a Christian's Advocate after he sins.

2:2. If God extends mercies to a sinning believer—and the believer does not reap the full consequences of his failure in his personal experience—that fact is not due to the merits of that believer himself. On the contrary, the grace obtained through the advocacy of Christ is to be traced, like all of God's grace, to His all-sufficient sacrifice on the cross. Should any sinning believer wonder on what grounds he might secure God's mercy after he has failed, the answer is found in this verse. So adequate is Jesus Christ as God's **atoning Sacrifice** that the efficacy of His work extends **not** merely to the **sins** of Christians themselves, **but also to the sins of the whole world.** In saying this, John was clearly affirming the view that Christ genuinely died for everyone (cf. 2 Cor. 5:14-15, 19; Heb. 2:9). This does not mean, of course, that everyone will be saved. It means rather that anyone who hears the gospel *can* be saved if he so desires (Rev. 22:17). In context, however, John's point is to remind his readers of the magnificent scope of Christ's "atoning sacrifice" in order to assure them that His advocacy as the Righteous One on their behalf is fully consistent with God's holiness.

In recent times there has been much scholarly discussion of the Greek word *hilasmos,* which the NIV renders as "atoning Sacrifice." (The word occurs in the NT only here and in 1 John 4:10.) Some say the term is not the placating of God's wrath against sin, but rather is an "expiation" or "cleansing" of sin itself. But the linguistic evidence for this interpretation is not persuasive. The view has been capably discussed and refuted by Leon Morris in *The Apostolic Preaching of the Cross* (Grand Rapids: Wm. B. Eerdmans Publishing Co., 1965, pp. 125–85).

God's wrath against sin may not be a concept congenial to the modern mind, but it is thoroughly biblical. *Hilasmos* could be fittingly rendered "propitiation" (cf. the noun *hilastērion,* "propitiation," in Rom. 3:25 and the verb *hilaskomai,* "to propitiate," in Luke 18:13 and Heb. 2:17). The Cross has indeed propitiated (satisfied) God and has met His righteous demands so thoroughly that His grace and mercy are abundantly available to both saved and unsaved alike.

B. Basic principles of knowing God (2:3–11)

John's transition (v. 3) to the subject of knowing God may seem more abrupt than it really is. In ancient thought, the concept of "light" readily suggested the idea of "vision," "perception," or "knowledge." It seems obvious that a life of fellowship with God in the light ought to lead to knowing Him. Of course in a sense all true Christians know God (John 17:3), but sometimes even genuine believers can be said not to know God or

Christ (John 14:7-9). Furthermore, Jesus promised His disciples a special self-disclosure that was predicated on their obeying His commands (John 14:21-23). It is clear that such an experience involves the knowledge of God. Finally, fellowship naturally leads to knowing the One with whom that fellowship takes place. Even on the level of human experience this is true. If a father and son live apart, they will not know each other as well as if they lived together, even though their parent-child relationship continues to exist.

It would be wrong, therefore, to read 1 John 2:3-11 as if John had left the subject of fellowship with God behind. On the contrary, the subject of knowing God is its logical continuation.

2:3. For readers who wish to decide whether their experience of fellowship with God has led them really to know Him in a personal way, John gave a simple test: **We know that we have come to know Him if we obey His commands.** The two occurrences of the word "know" (ginōskō) in this verse are the first of 23 times John used this word in this epistle. (A synonym, oida, occurs six times: 3:2; 5:15 [twice], 18-20.) As often in Johannine usage, the word "Him" might refer either to God or to Christ. For John, Jesus is so closely linked with the Father that a precise distinction between the Persons of the Godhead sometimes seems irrelevant. Fellowship is with both the Father and the Son (1:3) and to know One of Them intimately is to know the Other. But obedience is the condition for such knowledge (cf. John 14:21-23). It is also the means by which a Christian can be sure that he has really "come to know" his Lord (cf. "obey His commands" in 1 John 3:22, 24; 5:2-3).

2:4. It follows, therefore, that **the man who says, I know Him, but does not do what He commands is a liar.** As in 1:6, someone may profess a fellowship with God which his life shows he does not possess. John was not afraid to call this kind of claim what it really is: a lie. Furthermore, it may be said of the same person that **the truth is not in him.** The idea is similar to the statements made earlier about false claims (1:6, 8, 10). In such a person the truth is not a dynamic, controlling influence. He is seriously out of touch with spiritual reality.

2:5-6. On the other hand, obedience to God's **Word** ("His commands," v. 3) results in a rich and full experience of God's love: **God's love is truly made complete in him.** The Greek expression "the love of God" (rendered "God's love") could mean either His love for a Christian or a Christian's love for God. But the NIV rendering is perhaps the best, particularly in light of John 14:21-23. In that passage an obedient disciple is promised a special experience of the love of the Father and Son. Since a Christian is already the object of God's saving love, this additional, experiential realization of the divine affection may be properly said to make God's love complete in him (cf. 1 John 4:12, 17). That is to say, an obedient believer has a deep, full-orbed acquaintance with "God's love." Since God is love (4:16), to know God intimately is to know His love intimately.

John then added, **This is how we know we are in Him: Whoever claims to live in Him must walk as Jesus did.** (The translators have supplied the word "Jesus" which is represented in the original by a pronoun.) In these statements, John used two other expressions ("in Him" and "live in Him") which further his thought. As with the connection he makes between obedience and the knowledge of God, here too the Upper Room Discourse (John 13-16) is the seed-plot from which these ideas come. The concept involved is derived especially from the Parable of the Vine and the Branches (John 15:1-8). The vine-branch relationship is an image of the disciple-ship experience. Jesus said, "This is to My Father's glory, that you bear much fruit, showing yourselves to be My disciples" (John 15:8). In 1 John 2:5-6 discipleship is also in view, as is seen from the reference to the imitation of Christ in verse 6. Moreover, the Greek term rendered in the NIV by "live" (menō) is the same verb used in John 15:4 where the NIV translates it "remain."

It would be a mistake to equate the concept of being "in Him" as John uses it here with the Pauline concept of being "in Christ." For Paul, the words "in Christ" describe a Christian's permanent position in God's Son with all its attendant privileges. With John, the kind of relationship pictured in the vine-branch imagery describes an experience that can be ruptured (John 15:6) with a resultant loss of fellowship and fruitfulness. Thus here in 1 John, the proof that a person is enjoying this kind of experience is to be found in a life modeled after that of Jesus in obedience to His Word. In short, 2:5-6 continues to talk about the believer's fellowship with God.

2:7. Verses 3-6 introduce the issue of obedience, though it was surely implicit also in 1:5-10. But John's insistence on obeying God's commands as a test of one's personal intimacy and knowledge of Him leads to a natural question: Which commands did John have in mind? The answer is offered here. John did **not** have in mind some **new** obligation which his readers had never heard. On the contrary the **command** foremost in his mind was **an old one, which you have had since the beginning** (cf. 2 John 5). No doubt John thought here especially of the command to love one another (cf. 1 John 2:9-11). He emphasized his point by adding that **this old command is the message** (logos, lit., "word"; cf. 1:5; 3:11) which **you have heard** (the majority of mss. add again "from the beginning"). Whatever innovations the readers might be confronting because of the doctrines of the antichrists, their real responsibility was to a commandment which they had heard from the very start of their Christian experience (cf. "heard" and "from the beginning" in 1:1; 2:24; 3:11).

John's affectionate concern for them is seen in his use of *Agapētoi*, literally, "Beloved" and here rendered **Dear friends.** He used the same word in 3:2, 21; 4:1, 7, 11 and *Agapēte* ("Dear friend") in 3 John 2, 5, 11.

2:8. Yet Jesus had called that commandment "new" (John 13:34) and John pointed out that it had not lost its freshness. It is really still **a new command** and **its truth is seen in Him and you.** This last assertion, somewhat freely rendered by NIV, seems to mean that the command to love came to realization first in Jesus Himself and then in His followers. The next phrase, **because the darkness is passing and the true light is already shining,** is best related back to the claim that he was after all writing a new command to them. His point was that the command to love (which Jesus and His followers exhibit) belongs to the new Age of righteousness which has begun to dawn. It does not belong to the

old Age of darkness which was passing away. Christ's Incarnation brought a light into the world which can never be extinguished. The love He manifested and taught His disciples to manifest is a characteristic of the Age to come. It is the darkness of the present world and all its hatred which is destined to disappear forever (cf. 1 John 2:17a).

In speaking this way, John gave to the terms "light" and "darkness" a slant differing slightly from what they had in chapter 1. There light was defined in terms of the fundamental character of God (1:5). In that sense, the light has been shining as long as there has been a revelation of God to man. But here John wrote of the Incarnation in particular as the point at which the light began to shine. The new Age has dawned and its true character can now be defined in terms of the special revelation God has made of Himself in His Son. And above all, that revelation is a revelation of divine love.

2:9. It follows that **anyone who claims to be in the light but hates his brother is still in the darkness.** This warning is clearly intended for Christians as the words "his brother" plainly show. An unsaved person can indeed hate a brother of physical kin, but since he has no spiritual kin he cannot really hate his (spiritual) brother. If John thought that no Christian could hate another Christian, there was no need to personalize the relationship with the word "his." But the opinion, held by some, that a true Christian could never hate another Christian is naive and contrary to the Bible and experience. Even so great a man as King David was guilty of murder, which is the final expression of hate. John was warning his readers against a spiritual danger that is all too real (cf. 1:8, 10). And he was affirming that a Christian who can hate his fellow Christian has not genuinely escaped from the darkness of this present passing Age. To put it another way, he has much to learn about God and cannot legitimately claim an intimate knowledge of Christ. If he really knew Christ as he ought, he would *love* his brother.

2:10-11. By contrast, **whoever loves his brother lives in the light** of the new Age which has dawned in Christ (cf. v. 8). **There is nothing in him** (in one who loves his brother) **to make him stumble.** Hatred is a kind of internal "stumbling block" which can lead to disastrous spiritual falls. But the calamities to which hatred leads are avoided by one who loves his brother.

This is not so, however, for one who **hates his brother.** Such a person **walks around in the darkness** and **he does not know where he is going, because the darkness has blinded him** (cf. v. 9). A Christian who harbors hatred for a fellow Christian has lost all real sense of direction. Like a man wandering aimlessly in the dark, he faces potentially grave dangers.

III. The Purpose of the Epistle (2:12-27)

In the prologue John had expressed the general aim and goal of his letter. Now he told his audience the specific concerns which motivated the letter. In that sense he articulated the precise purpose of this epistle.

A. In light of the readers' spiritual conditions (2:12-14)

In the light of all the warnings John gave (1:5–2:11), his readers might think that he was fundamentally dissatisfied with their spiritual conditions. But this was not so. John now assured them that he wrote because of the spiritual assets which they possessed.

2:12-13a. In describing these assets, the author addressed his readers as **dear children . . . fathers,** and **young men.** Some have suggested that John here divided his readers by chronological age-groups. Others say he did so by their spiritual maturity. If either explanation is adopted, the sequence—which makes "fathers" the middle term—is somewhat strange. Moreover, elsewhere John addressed *all* his readers as "children" (vv. 1, 28; 3:7, 18; 5:21). It seems best (with C.H. Dodd and I.H. Marshall) to view the terms of address as referring to all the readers in each case. Then each experience ascribed to them is appropriate to the category named.

Thus, thought of as "children," the readers had experienced the forgiveness that their heavenly Father grants to His own. As "fathers," they had an experience that touches eternity past, since they **have known Him who is from the beginning.** In the light of 2:3-6, this implies they have truly experienced fellowship with God. (Here again [cf. v. 3] the word "Him" could refer to either the Father or the Son; the distinction was not important to John. His readers knew both.) As "young men," the readers had engaged in spiritual warfare and had **overcome the evil one,** Satan (cf. "evil one" in v. 14; 3:12; 5:18-19).

Thought of in this way, the sequence "children," "fathers," and "young men" is meaningful. The readers knew what it was to have sins forgiven and then have fellowship with the Eternal One. As a result they were like vigorous young men who had defeated satanic assaults.

2:13b-14. The attainments of the readers were then reiterated, but with some subtle variations. Thought of as **children** again, it can be said that they **have known the Father.** Unlike newborn infants (*teknia* ["little born ones"], v. 12; see comments on v. 1), who can scarcely recognize their fathers, these people (*paidia*, "children"; cf. v. 18)—through fellowship—have come to know their divine Parent. But what can be added to the experience of knowing the Eternal One? In calling them **fathers** again, John simply repeated the attainment mentioned earlier without changing it. Then viewing them once more as **young men,** the writer implied growth in strength. In verse 13, he had simply spoken of victory over Satan. Now he wrote, **You are strong, and the Word of God lives in you, and you have overcome the evil one.** By repeating the three categories under which he here addressed his audience, John suggested not only that they possessed spiritual attainments worthy of being called children, fathers, and young men, but also that they possessed these attainments in ample measure.

B. In light of the world's allurements (2:15-17)

The writer was not dissatisfied with the spiritual state of his readers. Much less did he question or doubt their salvation, as some expositors of this epistle imply. On the contrary, his readers may even be viewed as having matured in the faith. John wrote precisely because their present state was so good. But he wished to warn them about dangers which always exist, no matter how far one has advanced in his Christian walk.

2:15. He turned now to a warning. **Do not love the world or anything in the world.** The "world" *(kosmos),* thought of here as an entity hostile to God (cf. 4:4), is always a seductive influence which Christians should continually resist (cf. John 15:18-19; James 4:4. In other NT verses "world" *[kosmos]* means people, e.g., John 3:16-17.) The world competes for the love of Christians and one cannot both love it and the Father at the same time. **If anyone loves the world, the love of the Father is not in him.** As James also had told his Christian readers, "Friendship with the world is hatred toward God" (James 4:4).

2:16. The reason love for the world is incompatible with love for God is that **everything in the world . . . comes not from the Father but from the world.** The world thus conceived is a system of values and goals from which God is excluded. In describing "everything in the world," John specified its contents under three well-known phrases that effectively highlight the world's false outlook. Men of the world live for **the cravings of sinful man.** "Cravings" translates *epithymia,* which is used twice in this verse and once in the next verse. The NIV translates it differently each time: "cravings," "lust," "desires." In the New Testament the word usually, though not always, connotes desires that are sinful. The expression "sinful man" translates the Greek *sarx* (lit., "flesh"). The phrase refers particularly to illicit bodily appetites. The expression **the lust** *(epithymia)* **of his eyes** points to man's covetous and acquisitive nature. **The boasting of what he has and does** paraphrases the Greek *hē alazoneia tou biou* (lit., "the pretension of human life"), which signifies a proud and ostentatious way of life. (*Alazoneia* is used only here in the NT.) Christians ought to have nothing to do with such worldly perspectives as these.

2:17. After all, **the world and its desires** *(epithymia)* are temporary and **pass away, but the man who does the will of God lives forever.** The word "lives" renders the characteristic Johannine word *menō* (cf. 1:6). It suggests, as almost always in this epistle, the "abiding life" of fellowship with God. But here is obviously the additional thought that the life lived in God's fellowship, rejecting the sinful things of this passing world, is a life that has no real ending. A person whose character and personality are shaped by obedience to God will not be affected by the passing away of the world and its vain desires. It is a Johannine way of saying, "Only one life, 'twill soon be past; only what's done for Christ will last."

C. In the light of the deceptions of the last hour (2:18-23)

2:18. John's general warning against the world is now followed by a warning against one of its end-time manifestations. The false teachers who were present were worldly to the core (cf. 4:5). The readers knew about the predicted advent of **the Antichrist** and needed to be alerted to the appearance of **many** who would display his traits of hostility toward God's Christ. This is a clear indication that history has entered a climactic era: **the last hour.** Despite the lapse of centuries since John wrote, the climax of all things impends in a special way. The stage has been set for history's final drama.

2:19. Of the false teachers John had in mind, he wrote, **They went out from us.** The word "us" here is most naturally taken as the apostolic first person plural of this epistle (see 1:1-5; 4:6). "Us" contrasts with the "you" in 2:20-21, which referred to the readers. It does not make sense that the false teachers had left the churches to which the readers belonged. If they had, how were they still a problem? On the other hand if, like the legalists of Acts 15, they had seceded from the apostolic churches of Jerusalem and Judea, then they were a particular threat to the readers because they came to them claiming roots in the soil out of which Christianity arose. Thus John was eager to deny any connection with them.

They did not really belong to us paraphrases an expression more literally rendered, "they were not of us." The writer's point was that these men did not really share the spirit and perspective of the apostolic circle, for if they had their secession would not have taken place. Heresy in the Christian church, whether on the part of its saved members or unsaved people in it, always unmasks a fundamental disharmony with the spirit and doctrine of the apostles. A man in touch with God will submit to apostolic instruction (cf. 1 John 4:6).

2:20-21. The readers were well fortified against the antichrists, however, since they had **an anointing from the Holy One** (i.e., from God). The "anointing" is no doubt the Holy Spirit since, according to verse 27, the anointing "teaches." This clearly suggests that the "anointing" is conceived of as a Person. Jesus Himself was "anointed" with the Holy Spirit (cf. Acts 10:38). (For the possibility that the term suggests that the church leaders are in view, see the *Introduction*.) As a result of their "anointing," the readers (perhaps primarily the church leaders) had adequate instruction in **the truth** of God. John wrote them precisely **because** their apprehension of **the truth** was correct and **because . . . the truth** should never be confused with a **lie**.

2:22-23. The antichrists are liars for they deny **that Jesus is the Christ,** that is, God's Son and the appointed Savior (cf. John 4:29, 42; 20:31). This denial involves also a denial of **the Father.** Any claim they might make to having the Father's approval is false. **One** cannot have the **Father** without the **Son.** To reject One is to reject the Other.

D. In light of the readers' responsibilities to abide (2:24-27)

2:24. The readers must **see that what** they **have heard from the beginning** (cf. 1:1; 2:7; 3:11) **remains in** them. **If it does** (NIV paraphrases here), they **will remain in the Son and in the Father.** The term translated "remain" is again *menō,* which the NIV renders as "live" and "lives" in 2:6, 10, 14, 17. John's point was that if the readers would resist the lies of the antichrists and let the truth they had heard from the beginning "abide" (or "be at home") in them, they would continue to "abide" in the fellowship of God the Father and God the Son.

2:25-26. They could also continue to rest on the divine promise of **eternal life.** As John later insisted (5:9-13; cf. 5:20), they could be sure that they possessed this on the basis of God's testimony to that fact. It may well be that the antichrists denied that the readers were actually saved, since John went right on to say, **I am writing these things to you**

about those who are trying to lead you astray (cf. 3:7). Coming as they evidently did from the apostolic churches of Judea, these men apparently sought to undermine the readers' conviction that Jesus is the Christ and that they had eternal life through Him. John's insistence that his readers genuinely know God and know His truth (2:12-14, 21) was part of his strategy for fortifying them against the antichrists.

2:27. The readers did not need teaching from the antichrists or, for that matter, from anyone. Their **anointing . . . received from** God, **remains in** them **and** was a sufficient Teacher. This, along with verses 12-14, may imply that John's readers were relatively spiritually mature, since the immature need human teachers (cf. Heb. 5:12). This is appropriate if John were addressing church leaders, but it would also suit a congregation that had long been in the faith. Unlike the antichrists, who may have claimed some form of inspiration, the readers' **anointing** was **real, not counterfeit.** They needed to **remain** (*menete,* "abide") **in Him** (the pronoun can refer to **the anointing**) and rely fully on His continuing instruction.

IV. The Body of the Epistle (2:28–4:19)

In the section just completed (2:12–27), John wrote both to assure his readers of the validity of their spiritual experiences and to warn them against the antichrists who denied that validity. In what may be described as the body of his letter, John then explored the true character and consequences of that form of experience which the readers already had and needed to maintain.

A. The theme stated (2:28)

2:28. Many commentators see a major break here. The words **continue in Him** involve again the Greek verb *menō* ("abide") which has already occurred 10 times in verses 6–27. (John used *menō* 66 of the 112 times it occurs in the NT: 40 in John, 23 in 1 John, and 3 in 2 John.) In accord with his basic theme about fellowship (1 John 1:3), John once more enjoined the "abiding" life. But now he introduced the new thought of being **confident** before Christ **at His coming.** The Greek words rendered "be confident" are literally "have confidence." The latter is *parrēsia*, a word that can signify a bold freedom of speech. John used it again in 3:21; 4:17; 5:14. If the readers would maintain their fellowship with God, they would enjoy a genuine boldness of speech when they would meet their Lord. How this can be so is the subject of 2:29–4:19. Should a believer fail to abide in Him, however, there is the possibility of shame when Christ comes. This intimates divine disapproval at the judgment seat of Christ, referred to in 4:17-19. The NIV's **unashamed before Him** might be more literally rendered: "not be ashamed before Him." The possibility is real but does not, of course, suggest the loss of salvation.

B. Discerning the children of God (2:29–3:10a)

At this point John began to develop a line of thought which culminates in the acquisition of the boldness of which he had just spoken (2:28; cf. 4:17-19). The fellowship with the apostolic circle and with God which he had in mind (cf. 1:3) requires discerning the way the lives of God's children are manifested in their actions. John was moving toward the thought that when one's life is properly manifested, God Himself is manifested in it (4:12-16).

2:29. This verse introduces for the first time in 1 John the explicit thought of new birth. Since the readers **know that He** (God the Father or God the Son) **is righteous,** they would also **know that everyone who does what is right has been born of Him** (the pronoun here probably refers to God the Father who regenerates). (The phrase "born of God" occurs in 3:9; 4:7; 5:1, 4, 18 [twice].) The statement has nothing to do with the readers' individual assurance of salvation. It is rather an assertion that when they see real righteousness ("what is right" translates *tēn dikaiosynēn*) exhibited, they can be sure that the person who exhibits it is a child of God. This righteousness, of course, for John can only mean the kind that Christ had enjoined. It has nothing to do with mere humanistic kindness and morality. The converse of John's statement does not follow, namely, that everyone who is born of God does righteousness. John knew that Christians can walk in the darkness and are suscep-

tible to sin (1:6, 8; 2:1). He was writing here of the way one can see the new birth in the actions of others.

3:1. This verse begins with the word *idete* ("behold, look at"), not translated in the NIV. The writer had just told the readers how to see the reality of new birth in righteous behavior; now he invited them to contemplate the greatness of the divine love which that reality displays. Behold **how great is the love the Father has lavished on us, that we should be called children of God.** (The words **and that is what we are,** rightly omitted by most mss., are probably a scribal addition.) In the Bible the word "called" indicates that this is what one actually is (cf. "called to be holy," lit., "called saints" [1 Cor. 1:2]). Believers are "called children of God" because they are the born-ones *(tekna)* of "the Father."

The perception to which John invited his readers is, however, lost on the world. Since the **world . . . did not know Him** (God or Christ), it can hardly be expected to recognize believers as His children. This kind of discernment about others is a distinctively Christian perception.

3:2-3. But even for Christians, this perception is a spiritual one. Though **now we are children of God,** there is no physical evidence of this that an eye can see. The physical changes in Christians await the coming of Christ. **But we know that when He appears, we shall be like Him** (cf. 1 Cor. 15:52-54; Phil. 3:21). Such a transformation will result from seeing **Him as He is.** But pending that event it is already true that **everyone who has this hope in Him** (the pronoun probably refers to Christ, the Object of this hope) **purifies himself, just as He is pure.** Here the writer probably continued to refer to the new birth. One who sets his hope by faith on the Son of God experiences an inward purification that is as complete as Christ's own purity ("just as He is pure"). John thus prepared the ground for the assertions he would soon make (1 John 3:6, 9). New birth involves a perfect purification from sin.

3:4. John now wrote about sin which stands in opposition to the purity he had just referred to in verse 3. The NIV renders his statement: **Everyone who sins breaks the law** (*tēn anomian poiei*, "does lawlessness"); **in fact, sin is lawlessness** *(anomia).* Usually in the Greek New

Testament *anomia* is a general term like the English word "wickedness," which has some prominence in eschatological contexts (cf. Matt. 7:23; 13:41; 24:12; 2 Thes. 2:7). So its use here so soon after the references to the antichrists may be significant. The writer probably intended it to be a strongly pejorative description of sin. It seems likely, in view of 1 John 3:7, that the antichrists had a softened view of sin which John wished to refute. A person who sins does what is wicked, and sin *is* wickedness, John was insisting. (Lit., the first clause in v. 4 is, "Everyone who commits wickedness.") Sin must not be taken lightly.

3:5-6. The seriousness of sin is further underscored by the consideration that Christ **appeared so that He might take away our sins. And in Him is no sin.** The Incarnation brought into the world the One who is totally sinless and who had as an objective the removal of sin from the lives of His own (cf. John 1:29; Heb. 9:28a). It follows logically from this that a person who is ("abides") *in* a sinless Person must himself be sinless, for he has a sinless, regenerate nature.

This is the inescapable logic of the text. But a different point is suggested by the NIV's rendering: **No one who lives** (*menōn*, "abides") **in Him keeps on sinning. No one who continues to sin has either seen Him or known Him.** A widely held explanation of this verse is that a believer "does not sin habitually," that is, sin is not his way of life. However, the Greek text has no words to represent phrases such as "keeps on" or "continues to" or "habitually." These phrases are based on an understanding of the Greek present tense which is now widely in dispute among New Testament scholars (see, e.g., S. Kubo, "1 John 3, 9: Absolute or Habitual?" *Andrews University Seminary Studies* 7. 1969:47–56; C.H. Dodd, *The Johannine Epistles,* pp. 78–81; I. Howard Marshall, *The Epistles of John,* p. 180). It cannot be shown anywhere in the New Testament that the present tense can bear this kind of meaning *without the assistance of other words.* Such a view is invalid for this verse and also for 1 John 3:9. Nor is John saying that sinless perfection must be achieved, and that those who fail to do so lose their salvation. Such a notion is foreign to John's argument and to all of Scripture.

John's point is simple and straight-forward. Sin is a product of ignorance and blindness toward God. "No one who sins has seen Him or known Him" (v. 6b).

Sin can never come out of seeing and knowing God. It can never be a part of the experience of abiding in Christ. "No one who abides in Him sins" (v. 6a). But though the meaning of this is not really open to question, there has seemed to be an inconsistency between such assertions and John's earlier insistence that a believer can never claim to be without sin (1:8). The solution to this problem has been suggested by the statement in 3:3 in which the purification of the one "who has this hope in Him" is comparable in its nature to the purity of Christ ("just as He is pure"). From this it follows that the regenerate life is, in one sense, an essentially and fundamentally sinless life. For the believer sin is abnormal and unnatural; his whole bent of life is away from sin.

The fact remains, however, that Christians do not experience the sinless life perfectly on this earth; hence 1:8, 10 remain true. The two ideas are not really incompatible. The Christian still experiences a genuine struggle with the flesh and overcomes its impulses only by the help of the Holy Spirit (cf. Gal. 5:16-26).

Paul's thinking also conforms with this view. In his struggle with sin he was able to conclude, "Now if I do what I do not want to do, it is no longer I who do it, but it is sin living in me that does it" (Rom. 7:20). In this way Paul could perceive sin as not a real part of what he was at the most inward level of his being (cf. Rom. 7:25). When he wrote, "I no longer live, but Christ lives in me" (Gal. 2:20), he implied the same thing. If Christ alone really lives, sin can be no part of that experience. Insofar as God is experienced by a believer, that experience is sinless. (Cf. comments on 1 John 3:9.)

3:7-8. These verses suggest strongly that the doctrine of the antichrists involved a confusion between sin and righteousness. Perhaps the antichrists felt free to sin while at the same time denying their guilt and claiming to behave righteously. John warned against such ideas: **Do not let anyone lead you astray.** (The Gr. verb "lead astray," *planaō,* used also in 2:26, is the same word rendered "deceive" in 1:8.) **He who does what is**

right is righteous, just as He is righteous (cf. 1:9; 2:1, 29). Only righteousness springs from a righteous nature. By contrast, **He who does what is sinful is of the devil.** It would be wrong to water this assertion down. All sin, of whatever kind or degree, is satanic in nature. This is **because the devil has been sinning from the beginning** (cf. John 8:44). Sin originated with Satan and is his constant practice. To take part in sin at all is to take part in his activity. It is also opposing the work of **the Son of God** who came (**appeared;** cf. 1 John 3:5; Heb. 9:28a) **to** put an end (*lysē*, **destroy**) to that activity, **the devil's work.** Even the smallest sin runs counter to the work of Christ. Believers are to *overcome* "the evil one" (1 John 2:13-14), here called "the devil," and not to *participate* in what he is.

3:9. As was pointed out in connection with verse 6, adding such phrases as "continue to" and "go on" to John's statements about sinning is not justified on the basis of the Greek text. As before, the statements are absolute. **One who is born of God** (cf. 2:29; 4:7; 5:1, 4, 18) does not **sin** precisely **because God's seed remains in him,** and he cannot sin **because he has been born of God.** "God's seed" is His nature, given to each believer at salvation (John 1:13; 2 Peter 1:4). The point here is that the child partakes of the nature of his Parent. The thought of a sinless Parent who begets a child who only sins a little is far from the author's mind. As always, John dealt in stark contrasts. All sin is devilish (1 John 3:8); it does not stem from the believer's regenerate nature, God's seed, but the child of God cannot and does not sin. The explanation here is the same as that given in verse 6. The "new man" (or "new self"; Eph. 4:24; Col. 3:10) is an absolutely perfect new creation. By insisting on this point, John was seeking to refute a false conception about sin. Sin is not, nor ever can be, anything but satanic. It can never spring from what a Christian truly is at the level of his regenerate being.

3:10a. Literally, the first phrase of this verse is, "By this are manifest **the children of God** and **the children of the devil.**" The words "by this" probably refer back to the whole previous discussion. By sharply differentiating between sin and righteousness, John made plain the fundamental way in which God's children are manifest over against the children of the devil. The key to his idea is the word "manifest" in which the ideas presented in 2:29 and 3:1 are touched again. Because a child of God is sinless at the core of his being, he can never be "manifest" through sin as can a child of the devil. While an unsaved person can display his true nature through sin, a child of God cannot. When a Christian sins, he *conceals* who he really is rather than making it *manifest.* If the readers perceive someone doing real righteousness, then—but only then—can they perceive this action as a true product of new birth (2:29) and can thus behold God's love (3:1). This consideration is crucial to John's advancing argument.

C. Discerning love for the brethren (3:10b-23)

John now left behind the subject of new birth which he did not mention again until 4:7. The function of the section that begins here is to define righteousness primarily in terms of Christian brotherly love and to show how such love properly expresses itself.

1. WHAT LOVE IS NOT (3:10B-15)

3:10b. Rather than taking verse 10a as introductory to verse 10b, it is better to regard 10a as the conclusion of the previous paragraph and 10b as the beginning of a new one. The words **a child** in 10b are not in the Greek. Thus the statement would better read, **Anyone who does not do what is right is not . . . of God.** The Greek expression for "of God" (*ek tou theou*) need mean no more than that a person so described does not find the source of his actions in God. He is "not . . . of God" in what he does. A failure to perform righteousness and a failure to **love** one's **brother** can never be traced to God. John had already said that all sin can be traced to the devil (v. 8). John also used this phrase *ek tou theou* ("of God") seven other times (4:1-4, 6-7; 3 John 11).

By joining together the idea of righteousness (mentioned in 1 John 2:29–3:7) with love (not mentioned in vv. 2-9), John formed a bridge to a new discussion. He now considered love as the appropriate expression of the regenerate life of which he had been speaking. Love is righteousness in action.

3:11-12. John here made it plain that his admonitions were directed to Christians. **This is the message you** (Christians) **have heard from the beginning: We** (Christians) **should love one another.** But before telling his audience precisely what love is, he first told them what it is not. It is most certainly **not** the kind of action **Cain** exhibited toward **his brother** Abel. Cain **murdered** his brother (Gen. 4:8) and in that action he was of **the evil one** (*ek tou ponērou;* **belonged to** is misleading). The reason for this murder was Cain's jealous resentment of his brother's superior righteousness (Gen. 4:2-7). In saying this, John touched a sensitive nerve, since hatred toward another Christian is often prompted by a feeling of guilt about one's **own** life as compared with that person's. It is well to remember that such reactions are satanic, as John bluntly affirmed here.

3:13. Such reactions of hatred and murder (vv. 11-12) are also worldly, since **the world hates** Christians. That fact should **not** surprise the readers (called **brothers** only here in 1 John) at all, however. What else can the world be expected to do? It is hatred among believers that is so abnormal, and against which John was fundamentally warning. In that sense it is right to treat this verse as more or less parenthetical.

3:14. In contrast with the world, however, John stated, **We know that we have passed from death to life, because we love our brothers.** The first "we" of this statement is quite emphatic in the original and may mean "we, the apostles." But even if it does, the writer no doubt intended that the readers apply this comment to themselves. Love for one's brothers is evidence that he has entered God's sphere of life (cf. John 13:35).

The expression translated "passed from death to life" occurs elsewhere only in John 5:24 (there trans. "crossed over from death to life") where it refers to conversion. But a phrase which is used only twice in John's writing can hardly be said to have a fixed meaning. The context here must decide its significance. The statements of 1 John 3:14b-15 suggest that the spheres of "death" and "life" are here treated as experiential and determined by one's actions. If so, the issue of conversion is not in view here.

The statement, **Anyone who does not love** (the majority of the mss. add "a brother" or "his brother") **remains in death,** is considered under verse 15.

3:15. This verse is usually taken to mean that a true Christian cannot hate his fellow Christian, since hatred is the moral equivalent of murder. But this view cannot stand up under close scrutiny.

To begin with, John speaks of **anyone who hates his brother.** If John had believed that only an unsaved person can hate another Christian, the word "his" unnecessarily personalizes the relationship (cf. comments on 2:9). But it is an illusion to believe that a real Christian is incapable of hatred and murder. David was guilty of the murder of pious Uriah the Hittite (2 Sam. 12:9) and Peter warned his Christian readers, "If you suffer, it should not be as a murderer" (1 Peter 4:15; more lit., "Let none of you suffer as a murderer"). The view that 1 John 3:15 cannot refer to the saved is totally devoid of all realism. The solemn fact remains that hatred of some other believer is the spiritual equivalent of murder (Matt. 5:21-22), as a lustful eye is the spiritual equivalent of adultery (Matt. 5:28).

John insisted then that **no murderer has eternal life** abiding **in him.** The NIV does not translate the Greek participle *menousan* ("abiding"), which is a crucial word here. John does *not* say that someone who hates his brother does not *possess* eternal life, but rather that he does not have it *abiding* in him. But since for John, Christ Himself is eternal life (John 14:6; 1 John 1:2; 5:20), John's statement is saying that no murderer has *Christ* abiding in him. Thus once more the experience of "abiding" is what John had in view.

Hatred on the part of one Christian toward another is thus an experience of moral murder. As John had indicated in 3:14b, he held that a Christian who fails to love his brother "remains (*menei*) in death." He is thus experientially living in the same sphere in which the world lives (see v. 13). Because he is a murderer at heart he can make no real claim to the kind of intimate fellowship with God and Christ which the word "abide" suggests. Eternal life (i.e., Christ) is not at home in his heart so long as the spirit of murder is there. Such a person is disastrously out of touch with his Lord and he experiences only death. (Cf. Paul's statement, "For if you live according to the sinful nature, you will die" [Rom. 8:13].) John's words were surely grim. But no service is rendered to the church by denying their applicability to believers. The experience of the Christian church through the ages shows how urgently they are needed. Hate, unfortunately, is not confined to unsaved people.

2. WHAT LOVE IS (3:16-18)

3:16. In stark contrast with hatred stands the true character of Christian love. So far is it from the spirit of murder that its essence lies in giving one's life for others rather than taking lives. This was exemplified in **Jesus Christ** who **laid down His life for us.** With this as a model, Christians should be prepared to make similar sacrifices **for** their **brothers.**

3:17-18. Yet the opportunity to sacrifice one's life for another may not arise. But **material possessions** (as food and clothes) help sustain life and, **if** a Christian's love is real, he cannot see **his brother in need** without having **pity on him.** "Pity" (*splanchna*) suggests a deepseated emotional concern or affectionate sympathy (also used in Luke 1:78; 2 Cor. 6:12; 7:15; Phil. 1:8; 2:1; Phile. 7, 12, 20). The true test of love is not one's verbal profession of it (loving **with words or tongue**) but his willingness to help and thus to **love . . . with actions and in truth.**

3. WHAT LOVE DOES FOR BELIEVERS (3:19-23)

3:19-20. The statement, **This then is how we know that we belong to the truth,** probably refers back to verses 17-18. By practical acts of love in which the needs of others are met, Christians can have a basic assurance that they are participating experientially in the truth. (The NIV's "we belong to the truth" paraphrases the Gr. "we are of the truth"; cf. "of God" [v. 10] and "belonged to the evil one" [v. 12].)

The rest of verse 19 and all of verse 20 are difficult in the original, but probably should be translated, "And we shall persuade **our hearts** before Him that, if **our hearts condemn us,** God **is greater than our hearts,** and **knows** all things." It is precisely in the sphere of a believer's love for other Christians, in which Christ has set him so high a standard, that he may feel deeply his own

inadequacy and failure. But if his heart condemns him, he can remind himself that **God** takes account of those things which at the moment his heart ignores. If he has been engaged in the kind of practical acts of love which John enjoined, his guilt-ridden heart can be persuaded by realizing that God is well aware of his fundamental commitment to the truth. The passage clearly recalls Peter's response to the Lord's final query, "Do you love Me?" Peter replied, "Lord, You know all things; You know that I love You" (John 21:17).

3:21-22. Once a condemning heart has been silenced by resting on God's knowledge of all things, there comes a new **confidence before God.** "Confidence" here translates *parrēsia*, which John had not used since his thematic statement in 2:28 (cf. 4:17; 5:14). The halfway point in his argument had now been reached. As a result of active participation in the truth by real deeds of love, Christians can calm their disapproving **hearts** and achieve boldness in prayer, and their prayers will be answered because they, as believers, are consciously subject to God's will (they **obey His commands** [cf. 2:3] **and do what pleases Him**). This presumes, of course, that the requests themselves are made in subjection to God's will (5:14-15).

3:23. The writer had declared that a confident and effective prayer life is founded on obedience to God's "commands" (v. 22). Now those commands are summed up in a single **command** consisting of faith and **love.** The phrase **believe in the name of His Son** contains the epistle's first direct reference to faith. The Greek here contains no word for "in" so the expression could be rendered "believe the name of His Son." In this context it certainly includes the faith in Christ's name which true Christian prayer involves (see John 14:12-15; 16:24).

First John 3:23 furnishes a kind of climax to the paragraph beginning in verse 18. As a Christian actively engages in deeds of love (v. 18) and as he achieves boldness before God in prayer (v. 21), he is doing what God commands (cf. 2:3; 3:24; 5:2-3): living a life of confidence in the name of Christ which is undergirded by love (3:23; cf. v. 14; 4:7, 11, 21). Since faith and love, thus conceived, go together, this kind of life is seen as obedience to a single "command."

D. Discerning the indwelling God (3:24-4:16)

Since the thematic statement of 2:28, John's argument has passed through two stages: (1) the one born of God is manifested only through righteousness (2:29-3:10a), and (2) this righteousness takes the form of a Christlike love for the brethren that leads to boldness in prayer (3:10b-23). Now John showed that this kind of life is the manifestation of the indwelling God.

1. DISCERNING THE SPIRIT OF TRUTH (3:24-4:6)

3:24. Two new themes appear in this verse. The first theme is the epistle's first reference to God, or Christ, abiding in each obedient believer. **Those who obey His commands** (cf. 2:3; 3:23; 5:2-3) **live** (menei, "abide") **in Him, and He in them.** That the abiding life involves this mutuality is made plain in the Parable of the Vine and the Branches (John 15:4-5, 7).

The second new idea is the epistle's first of six explicit references to the Holy Spirit (cf. 1 John 4:2, 6, 13; 5:6, 8; cf. "the Holy One" in 2:20). The way a believer can verify that God **lives** (menei, "abides") **in** him is **by the** operation of God's **Spirit** in his life. John then showed that God's Spirit is the Spirit of both faith (4:1-6) and love (4:7-16)—the two aspects of the two-part "command" given in 3:23.

4:1-3. To begin with, **the Spirit of God** must be distinguished from false spirits. This is particularly necessary **because many false prophets have gone out into the world.** The touchstone by which these **spirits** (false prophets) are to be tested is their attitude toward the incarnate person of **Jesus Christ.** The failure to acknowledge (homologei, "confess"; cf. 1:9; 2:23; 4:15) **that** Jesus Christ **has come in the flesh** is precisely what exposes **the spirit of the antichrist, which** John had already warned his readers about (2:18-27; cf. 2 John 7).

4:4-6. Up to now, the writer assured his **dear children** (teknia; cf. comments on 2:12), the readers, that they had **overcome** these antichrists. The readers had successfully resisted the antichrists (false prophets) by means of **the One who is in** them (no doubt another reference to the Spirit; cf. 3:24; 4:2). Reliance on God is the secret of all victory whether over heresy or any other snare. The indwelling One—the Holy Spirit who indwells every believer (3:24; 4:13; Rom. 8:9) and is thus "the One who is in you"—**is mightier than the one who is in the world,** namely, Satan (cf. 1 John 5:19). He is called "the prince of this world" (John 12:31); "the god of this Age" (2 Cor. 4:4); and "the ruler of the kingdom of the air" (Eph. 2:2).

The antichrists **are from the world and . . . speak from the viewpoint of the world.** For this reason they get a good hearing from **the world.** It is always true that satanically inspired thought has a special appeal to worldly minds. But people who **are from God** (ek tou theou, "of God"; cf. 1 John 4:4, "from God"; v. 5, "from the world"; and 3:12, "belonged to the evil one") **listen to** the apostles. The pronouns which begin verses 4-6 (**You . . . They,** and **We**) are emphatic in the original and evidently mark off three groups: the readers, the antichrists, and the apostles. Each one who can be described as "from God" (i.e., actuated and influenced by God) and thus **knows God listens to** the apostolic voice. In the history of the church, apostolic doctrine has always been the means by which **the** Holy **Spirit of truth and the spirit of falsehood** can be effectively distinguished. True Christianity is apostolic Christianity.

2. DISCERNING THE GOD OF LOVE (4:7-16)

4:7-8. The writer now returned to the subject of **love** which, like faith in God's Son (v. 13), is a product of the Spirit. As a confession of the incarnate person of Christ marks one off as being actuated by God (i.e., "from God", vv. 4, 6) so does love, since **love comes from God.** Hence, one **who loves** (in the Christian sense of that term) **has been born of God** (cf. 2:29; 3:9; 5:1, 4, 18) **and** he **knows God.** Love stems from a regenerate nature and also from fellowship with God which issues in knowing Him (see 2:3-5). The absence of **love** is evidence that a person **does not know God.** Significantly, John did not say such a person is not born of God. In the negative statement only the last part of the positive one (in 4:7) is repeated. Since

God is love, intimate acquaintance with Him will produce love. Like light (1:5), love is intrinsic to the character and nature of God, and one who is intimately acquainted with God walks in His light (1:7).

4:9-11. If one wishes to know **how** God has demonstrated **His love,** he need only look at the fact that God **sent His One and only Son into the world that we might** obtain eternal life thereby ("One and only" translates *monogenē,* "only born one," which also is used in John 1:14, 18; 3:16.) Moreover, this **love** was **not** a response to man's **love,** but an initiative on God's part (1 John 4:10). By it the **Son** became **an atoning Sacrifice** (*hilasmon,* "propitiation"; see comments on 2:2) **for our sins.** Nothing less than God's love in Christ is the model for the **love** Christians should have toward **one another.**

Important to John's argument is his reference to God's love in 4:9 as His love **among us.** In verses 12-16 he showed how this love, experienced among Christians, can make God visible to them.

4:12-13. In His divine nature and essence, **God** has never been **seen** by any living man (cf. John's similar statement, John 1:18). Yet in the experience of mutual **love** among believers, this invisible **God** actually **lives in us and His love is made complete in us.** The term "lives" once again renders John's characteristic word (*menō*) for the abiding life. As in 1 John 2:5, the idea of God's love reaching completeness in a believer may suggest a deep and full experience of that love (cf. 4:17).

The statement in verse 13 is intimately related to the ideas just expressed. **We know that we live** (*menomen,* "we abide"**) in Him and He in us, because He has given us of His Spirit.** The mutual abiding of a believer in God and God in that believer (cf. John 15:4-7) is indicated by that believer's experience of the Spirit. The Greek for "of His Spirit" (*ek tou pneumatos*) suggests participation in the Spirit of God, literally, "He has given us *out of* His Spirit." The same construction occurs in 1 John 3:24. When a believer loves, he is drawing that love from God's Spirit (cf. Rom. 5:5), who is also the Source of his confession of Christ (1 John 4:2). Thus both the faith and the love enjoined in the dual "command" of 3:23 are products of the Spirit's operation in a

believer. A believer's Spirit-led obedience becomes the evidence that he is enjoying the mutual abiding relationship with God that John wrote about.

4:14. The apostle now reached a climactic point in his argument. He had just written that "if we love each other," then the God whom no one has seen abides "in us and His love is made complete in us." The result of this experience is that **we have seen and testify that the Father has sent His Son to be the Savior of the world.** Since the first person plural in verses 7-13 is clearly meant to include the readers, the "we" of this verse includes them as well. The indwelling God, whose presence is manifested in the midst of a loving Christian community, thus becomes in a sense truly visible to the eye of faith. Though no one "has seen" (*tetheatai,* "beheld") God (v. 12), believers who abide in Him (v. 13) "have seen" (*tetheametha,* "behold") the Son as He is manifested among loving Christians. Christians who behold this manifestation have in fact "seen" and can "testify" to the fundamental truth that "the Father has sent the Son to be the Savior of the world." This great truth can be put on display through the instrumentality of Christian love.

With these words, John reached the goal he had announced in the prologue (1:1-4), namely, that his readers might share the apostles' experience. The apostles had "seen" (*heōrakamen*) the "life which was with the Father and . . . appeared to us" (1:2). In a loving Christian community, the believers can see that too. The term "Life" in 1:2, though it refers to Christ incarnate, nevertheless was carefully chosen by the writer. What his readers could witness is the renewed manifestation of that Life in their fellow Christians. But, as he had argued ever since 2:29, the "life" which Christians possess by new birth is inherently sinless and can only be manifested through righteousness and Christlike love. But when that occurs, Christ whom the apostles saw in the flesh is, in a real but spiritual sense, "seen" again (4:14).

4:15-16. Under the circumstances just described, confession (cf. 1:9; 2:23; 4:3) **that Jesus is the Son of God** is a sign that the confessor enjoys a mutual abiding relationship with **God.** The section is rounded off by the assertion, **We know and rely on** (lit., "have come to believe") **the love God has for us.** Living in the atmosphere of mutual Christian love produces a personal knowledge of God's love and fresh experience of faith in that love. Since **God is love** (cf. v. 8), one who **lives in love lives** (*menei*, "abides") **in God** and has **God** abiding with **him.** The last part of verse 16 ought to be taken as the conclusion of the paragraph, rather than the start of a new one. John again affirmed the reality of the abiding experience enjoyed by all Christians who love.

E. The theme realized (4:17-19)

The writer now returned to the theme of boldness (*parrēsia*) at the Second Advent, which he had introduced at 2:28. At the midpoint of his argument, he had spoken of boldness in prayer (3:21-22), but now he went a step further. Loving Christians can even have boldness at the judgment seat of Christ when their Lord returns.

4:17. This verse might be rendered, literally, "In this respect love is made complete with **us,** namely, **that we** should have boldness in **the day of** judgment." The writer was not referring here to a final judgment in which the eternal destiny of each believer hangs in balance. There is no such **judgment** for a believer (John 5:24). But a believer's life will be assessed at the judgment seat of Christ (1 Cor. 3:12-15; 2 Cor. 5:10). Yet even on that solemn occasion, a believer may **have confidence** (*parrēsian*; cf. 1 John 2:28; 3:21; 5:14) that God will approve the quality of his life if, through **love,** that believer while **in this world** becomes **like Him.** An unloving Christian is *unlike* his Lord and may anticipate rebuke and loss of reward at the judgment seat. But a loving believer is one in whom the work of God's love has been **made complete** (cf. the same words in 2:5; 4:12), and the fruit of that is boldness before the One who will judge him. In this way he achieves the goal of confidence and no shame before Him, expressed in 2:28.

4:18-19. If a believer looks forward with trepidation to the judgment seat of Christ, it is because God's **love** has not yet reached completeness in Him. The words here rendered **perfect** are no different in force from the idea of

"completeness" expressed in 2:5 and 4:12. The matured experience of God's **love** (reached in the act of loving one another) is incompatible with **fear** and expels **fear** from the heart.

The words **fear has to do with punishment** are literally, "fear has punishment." Fear carries with it a kind of torment that is its own punishment. Ironically, an unloving believer experiences punishment precisely because he feels guilty and is afraid to meet his Judge. Such fear prohibits a completed love (one **who fears is not made perfect in love**). But a Christian who loves has nothing to fear and thus escapes the inner torment which a failure to love can bring. Nevertheless a believers' love is essentially derivative.

We love (the majority of mss. add "Him") **because He first loved us.** A believer who loves other believers also loves God, and in facing his Judge he is simply facing One whom he loves. There is no fear in such an experience; yet he recognizes that his love for God originated in God's love for him.

V. Conclusion (4:20–5:17)

The high watermark of the epistle was reached in 4:11-19. But the experience described there, with its astounding concept of boldness on the day of judgment, can be reached only in a most practical way. In his conclusion, John crystallized what he meant by love and how that love can be realized in one's life.

A. Love clarified (4:20–5:3a)

The brief but climactic statement of 4:19 mentioned love *for* God for the first time (following most Gr. mss.). But a claim to love God cannot be substituted for love for other believers. This furnished John with his point of departure.

4:20-21. Anyone who claims to **love God, yet hates his brother** makes a false claim: **he is a liar.** John often pointed up false claims by using the word "liar": 1:10; 2:4, 22; 4:20; 5:10 (cf. "lie" in 1:6). **Love** for the unseen **God** (cf. 4:12) can only be concretely expressed by **love** for one's visible Christian **brother.** Furthermore, God's **command** (v. 21; cf. 2:3; 3:23-24; 5:3) has joined together the two kinds of **love**—love for **God** and love for one's **brother.**

5:1-3a. If one asks who his Christian

brother or sister is, the answer is that **everyone who believes that Jesus is the Christ is born of God** (cf. "born of God" in 3:9; 4:7; 5:4, 18). Whether or not a believer exhibits an admirable life, he should be an object of his fellow Christian's love. This love does not spring from something lovable in the person himself, but from his paternity, since **everyone who loves the Father loves His child as well.** Moreover, **love** for God's **children** is not mere sentiment or verbal expression (cf. 3:18), but is inseparable from **loving God and** obeying **His commands** (5:2; cf. 2:3; 3:22, 24; 5:3).

If a further question is asked about what it means to **love . . . God,** the answer is, **to obey His commands.** Thus the apostle, by this series of statements, reduces love for God and one's fellow Christians to its fundamental character. A person who obeys God's commands is doing what is right, both toward God and toward his fellow believers and is thus loving both God and them. But it must be remembered that this includes the willingness to sacrifice for one's brother (cf. 3:16-17).

B. Love empowered (5:3b-15)

If love for God and one's fellow Christians is at its core obedience to God's commands, how can these be carried out? Are they beyond the capacity of a believer? In this section John pointed to faith as the secret of a victorious, obedient life.

5:3b-5. As a matter of fact, God's **commands are not burdensome** (cf. Matt. 11:30). This is because the principle of victory resides in **everyone born of God.** Every such person **has** already **overcome the world** (cf. 1 John 4:4). His **faith** in Christ, by which he was regenerated, constitutes a victory over the world system which is satanically blinded to the gospel (cf. 2 Cor. 4:3-4). **Who is it then that overcomes the world? Only he who believes that Jesus is the Son of God.** With these words, the writer affirmed that a believer is a world-conqueror by means of his faith in Christ. This suggests that such faith is the secret of his continuing victory and, for that reason, obedience to God's commands need not be burdensome.

5:6-8. But the object of this faith must always be **the One who came by**

water and blood—Jesus Christ. It is simplest to take the term "water" as a reference to the baptism of Jesus by which His public ministry was initiated (Matt. 3:13-17; Mark 1:9-11; Luke 3:21-22). "Blood" would then refer to His death, by which His earthly work was terminated. John's insistence that **He did not come by water only, but by water and blood,** suggests that he was refuting a false notion of the type held by Cerinthus (see *Introduction*). Cerinthus taught that the divine Christ descended on the man Jesus at His baptism and left Him before His crucifixion. Thus he denied that one Person, Jesus Christ, came by both water and blood. Cerinthus was doubtless not alone in such views, which John regarded as utterly false and contrary to the true testimony of the Holy **Spirit.** Indeed, **there are three that testify: the Spirit, the water, and the blood; and the three are in agreement.** The Spirit's witness may be thought of as coming through the prophets (including John the Baptist). The Spirit's witness, then, was augmented by the historical realities involved in "the water" and "the blood." Both the baptism and the crucifixion of Jesus are strongly attested historical facts (cf. John 1:32-34; 19:33-37). All three witnesses ("water" and "blood" are personified) "are in agreement" that a single divine Person, Jesus Christ, was involved in these events.

5:9-12. One therefore has no reason for not accepting **God's testimony** to the person of Christ. If **man's testimony** can be accepted when adequately attested (Deut. 19:15), God's testimony, being **greater,** ought also be accepted. The NIV's words, **because it is the testimony of God, which He has given about His Son,** are perhaps better taken as commencing a new thought which involves a slight ellipsis. It might be paraphrased "Here then is God's testimony about His Son (which we ought to accept because of its greatness)."

But before specifying the content of God's testimony (which is done in 1 John 5:11-12), John paused parenthetically to remark that accepting this testimony internalizes it for the one **who believes.** Each believer **has** God's truth **in his heart.** By contrast, **anyone who** disbelieves **God has made Him out to be a liar** (cf. 1:10). For John there was no middle ground, no suspension of opinion. One either believes or he impugns God's veracity.

Having said this, John returned to the content of **the testimony,** which is that **God has given us eternal life** (cf. 5:13, 20) **and this life is in His Son. He who has the Son has life; he who does not have the Son of God does not have life.** In the light of 2:25-26 (see comments there), John's statement of God's testimony is probably directed against a claim by some antichrists that the readers did not really have eternal life through God's Son. But God has directly affirmed that eternal life is precisely what He has given in His Son. To deny this is to call Him a liar.

5:13. John wrote **these things . . . so that** his believing readers would **know** that they had eternal life (cf. vv. 12, 20). The words "these things" are often wrongly taken to refer to the whole epistle. But similar expressions in 2:1, 26 refer to the immediately preceding material and the same is true here. What John had just written about God's testimony (5:9-12) aims to assure his readers that, despite anything the antichrists have said, believers do indeed possess eternal life. It may be pointed out, in fact, that the assurance of one's salvation always rests fundamentally and sufficiently on the direct promises that God makes to that believer. In other words, one's assurance rests on the testimony of God.

After the words **that you have eternal life,** most Greek manuscripts add the words found in the KJV: "and that ye may believe on **the name of the Son of God."** Perhaps this statement seemed redundant to some early scribe or editor and for that reason was eliminated from his manuscript. But it actually prepares the ground for the discussion about prayer which follows by inviting continued faith in God's Son on the part of those who already have received eternal life through Him. Prayer too is an expression of trust in the name of God's Son (see comments on 3:23).

5:14-15. One who believes in the name of Jesus Christ has an **assurance** (parrēsia) **in approaching God** in prayer (cf. 3:21). Requests made in accordance with God's will are heard by Him and a believer can be certain of receiving answers to them. Naturally, Christians

today discern God's will through the Scriptures and ask accordingly. But the unit of thought that commences with 5:3b has focused on the truth that God's commands are not a burden because faith in God's Son is the secret of spiritual victory over the world. In this context, then, it is natural to suppose that John was thinking especially, though not exclusively, of a Christian's right to **ask** God for help in keeping His commands. That kind of prayer is transparently **according to His will.** Thus in victorious living a Christian is relieved of any burden through prayer that is based on faith in the name of God's Son.

C. Love practiced (5:16-17)

But if a Christian's own needs may be met by prayerful reliance on the name of Jesus, what about the needs of other Christians? Extending his discussion of prayer, John once again wove together his dual theme of faith and love. A Christian who truly loves his brother and sister cannot be indifferent to their spiritual needs.

5:16. Verses 16-17 have been much discussed. But they should not have occasioned as much difficulty as they have. Sometimes a Christian may sin so seriously that God judges that sin with swift physical death: "a sin that leads to death." Ananias and Sapphira are cases in point (Acts 5:1-11). But most of the sins which one **sees** a Christian **brother commit** are not of such a nature, as their common occurrence shows. For these, a believer ought to **pray,** knowing that any sin—if continued in long enough—is a threat to a fellow Christian's life (cf. James 5:19-20; also cf. Prov. 10:27; 11:19; 13:14; 19:16). Thus the restoration of a brother may secure a prolonging of his physical life.

The words, **a sin that does not lead to death,** can be easily misunderstood. All sin ultimately leads to death, but the expression "that does not lead to death" (mē pros thanaton) should be understood in the sense, "not punished by death." The distinction is between sins for which death is a rapid consequence and sins for which it is not.

When a Christian sees another Christian sin in a way that is not fatal, **he** is instructed to pray for him **and God will give him life.** (The word "God" is not in the original, but it is properly supplied, as in the NIV.) However, John reminded his readers that **there is . . . sin that leads to** (i.e., "is punished by") **death.** There is no need for the word **a** before "sin." John was not likely thinking of only one kind of sin. The New Testament example cited earlier (Acts 5:1-11) was a flagrant violation of the sanctity of the Christian community. It is not necessary for a Christian to be absolutely sure which flagrant sins are punishable by swift death as long as he can recognize many which are not. He *is* commanded to pray regarding sins which are not punishable by swift death. Even for other sins, where a greater seriousness seems attached to them, Christians have the freedom to pray. John's words about fatal sin are, **I am not saying that he should pray about that.** But this clearly does not forbid prayer even in the most serious cases. But naturally in such cases believers will submit their prayers to the will of God. In contrast, with regard to sins not punished swiftly by death, Christians, on the basis of this verse, should be able to pray with confidence.

5:17. This verse affirms that there is genuine scope for the kind of prayer John enjoined in verse 16. **All wrongdoing** (*adikia*, "unrighteousness") **is sin,** but out of this broad spectrum **there is sin that does not lead** (swiftly) **to death.** This passage has suffered a great deal by the concentration of expositors on the question of what kind of sin is directly punished by death. John's emphasis, however, is on sin *not* thus punished. It is for this that a believer should pray. When he does so, he is demonstrating his love for his brother and is thus obeying the frequently repeated command of this letter to do so. At the same time, he is exercising faith in the name of God's Son, since his loving request for his brother is in Jesus' name. Prayer for one's sinning brother is therefore in obedience to the single two-pronged command of 3:23.

VI. Epilogue (5:18-21)

In a brief epilogue, the Apostle John sought to reinforce some of the basic truths in his epistle. The "we" which runs throughout the epilogue (six times) is probably fundamentally apostolic, as it was also in the prologue (1:1-4; cf. the "we" of John 21:24). But no doubt the writer hoped and expected that his readers could fully identify with the assertions he was making. Each verse in 1 John 5:18-20 begins with "we know" (*oidamen*).

5:18. As in 3:6, 9 (see comments there) the words **continue to** are not justified by the original. John was affirming that **anyone born of God** is a person whose true, inward nature is inherently sinless. (Cf. "born of God" in 2:29; 3:9; 4:7; 5:1, 4.)

The additional statement about **the one who was born of God** is not, as often suggested, a reference to Christ. John nowhere else referred to Christ in this way; and he was still writing about regenerate people. On this view, the word "himself" should be read in place of **him.** John thus affirmed that "the one who has been born of God *keeps himself*" (there is no word for **safe** in the original). This restates the truth of 3:9 in a slightly different form. A believer's new man (or "new self"; Eph. 4:24; Col. 3:10) is fundamentally impervious to sin and hence **the evil one** (cf. 1 John 2:13-14; 3:12), Satan, **does not touch him.**

5:19. A regenerate person's new nature is inherently sinless (v. 18) because God's "seed" is in him (3:9). Knowledge of this truth is coupled with the conviction that **we know that we are . . . of God** (in the Gr., **children** does not occur). This assurance (founded for each believer on God's testimony [5:9-13]) is accompanied by a realization that **the whole world is under the control of the evil one** (cf. v. 18). John was seeking in these summarizing statements to reinforce the readers' consciousness that they are distinct from the satanically controlled world system and basically free from its power. They need not listen to the worldly ideas advanced by the antichrists (3:7-8). Nor need they succumb to worldly desires (cf. 2:15-17).

5:20. Moreover, the coming of **the Son of God has** granted to believers an **understanding** which makes possible a knowledge of God. John and his circle were **in Him who is true** (and so were his readers as they continued to "abide"). But to abide in God is also to abide **in His Son Jesus Christ.** For that matter, Jesus Christ Himself **is the true God** (cf. John 1:1, 14) **and eternal life** (cf. 1 John 1:2; 2:25; 5:11-13). With this grand affirmation of the deity of Christ, John concluded his summary of apostolic truths which stand against the falsehoods of the antichrists.

5:21. That the final admonition of the letter should be, **Dear children** (*teknia*, "born-ones"; cf. 2:1, 12, 28; 3:7, 18; 4:4), **keep yourselves from idols,** has seemed surprising. But there is no need to take "idols" in a figurative sense. In the Greco-Roman world of John's day, any moral compromise with worldly perspectives was likely to lead to some involvement with idolatry, since idolatry permeated pagan life at every level. To adhere to "the true God and eternal life" (5:20)—and to seek to express one's basically sinless nature as a child of God—would necessarily mean avoiding idolatry and the moral laxness which went with it. The apostle's closing admonition was thus relevant to his initial readers.

BIBLIOGRAPHY

Barker, Glenn W. "1, 2, 3 John." In *The Expositor's Bible Commentary*, vol. 12. Grand Rapids: Zondervan Publishing House, 1981.

Brooke, A.E. *A Critical and Exegetical Commentary on the Johannine Epistles.* The International Critical Commentary. Edinburgh: T. & T. Clark, 1912.

Brown, Raymond E. *The Epistles of John.* The Anchor Bible. Garden City, N.Y.: Doubleday & Co., 1983.

Burdick, Donald W. *The Epistles of John.* Everyman's Bible Commentary. Chicago: Moody Press, 1970.

Dodd, C.H. *The Johannine Epistles.* New York: Harper & Row, 1946.

Marshall, I. Howard. *The Epistles of John.* The New International Commentary on the New Testament. Grand Rapids: Wm. B. Eerdmans Publishing Co., 1978.

Mitchell, John G. *Fellowship: Three Letters from John.* Portland, Ore.: Multnomah Press, 1974.

Pentecost, J. Dwight. *The Joy of Fellowship: A Study of First John.* Grand Rapids: Zondervan Publishing House, 1977.

Stott, John R.W. *The Epistles of John: An Introduction and Commentary.* The Tyndale New Testament Commentaries. Grand Rapids: Wm. B. Eerdmans Publishing Co., 1964.

Vaughan, Curtis. *1, 2, 3 John: A Study Guide.* Grand Rapids: Zondervan Publishing House, 1970.

Vine, W.E. *The Epistles of John: Light, Love, Life.* Grand Rapids: Zondervan Publishing House, 1970.

Westcott, Brooke Foss. *The Epistles of St. John: The Greek Text and Notes.* 1882. Reprint. Grand Rapids: Wm. B. Eerdmans Publishing Co., 1966.

Wiersbe, Warren W. *Be Real.* Wheaton, Ill.: SP Publications, Victor Books, 1972.

2 JOHN

Zane C. Hodges

INTRODUCTION

Second John is a brief epistle which could have been written on a single sheet of papyrus of standard size. The preservation of this brief letter is no doubt a tribute to its spirituality and inspiration.

Authorship. The authorship of 2 John has been traditionally assigned to the Apostle John. But the writer identifies himself only as "the elder." This title is not likely to refer to the office of an elder in a local church. It might simply be an affectionate designation (*presbyteros*, "the old man"; cf. 1 Tim. 5:1-2; 1 Peter 5:5; 3 John 1) by which the author was known to his readers. However, some ancient evidence exists that the term "elder" could be used to designate any apostle or other original witness to the life and teachings of the Lord Jesus. In view of the manifest similarity in style and content between 1 and 2 John, the arguments that point to apostolic authorship for the larger epistle carry force for the smaller one as well. There is no adequate reason for doubting the correctness of the traditional ascription of 2 John to the Apostle John.

Background. The letter is addressed "to the chosen lady and her children" (v. 1; cf. vv. 4-5). No personal names are found in it, and the suggestion that the recipient was named either Eklecta (from *eklektē*, the word rendered "chosen") or Kyria (the word rendered "lady") carries little conviction. In this respect 2 John stands in contrast with 3 John, which contains the personal names of three people. It has therefore been suggested that the apostolic writer adopted a literary form in 2 John, in which a particular Christian church is personified as "the chosen lady" and its members are called "her children." The personification of nations and cities as female personages is common in the Bible (cf. "the daughter of Zion"), and the Christian church is often referred to as "the bride of Christ" (cf. Eph. 5:22-33; 2 Cor. 11:2; Rev. 19:7).

The conclusion that 2 John is addressed to a church is further supported by the observation that in the Greek the writer drops the singular number for his pronouns after verse 5 and uses a singular again only in verse 13. Indeed, the general nature of the epistle's content is most appropriate to a community. Thus, while the possibility that a particular Christian woman is addressed cannot be totally excluded, it is preferable to treat the letter as addressed to a church. If so, the problems confronted by this church do not differ much from the ones confronted by the readers of 1 John. Here too the author warned against antichrists (2 John 7; cf. 1 John 2:18, 22). The error of which they were guilty was, as also in 1 John, a denial of the person of Christ (2 John 7; cf. 1 John 2:22-23; 4:1-3). The epistle likewise insists on obedience to God's commands, especially the command to love one another (2 John 5-6; cf. 1 John 2:3-9; 3:14-18, 23; 4:7, 11, 20-21).

Date. No independent data is available on which to base the date of the writing of 2 John. But the situation presupposed in this letter is similar to what evidently lies behind 1 John. This therefore makes possible a date approximately the same as that suggested for the larger epistle. On this assumption, 2 John may also belong in the period before the outbreak of the Jewish war against the Romans in Palestine, in A.D. 66. A date in the early 60s is thus the most probable guess.

OUTLINE

I. Preamble (vv. 1-3)
II. Body of the Epistle (vv. 4-11)

905

A. The truth practiced (vv. 4-6)
B. The truth protected (vv. 7-11)
III. Farewell (vv. 12-13)

COMMENTARY

I. Preamble (vv. 1-3)

The epistle begins in the way ancient letters usually began. The writer announced himself, stated the identity of the recipient(s), and offered a greeting. But, as noted in the *Introduction*, John did not specifically name "the chosen lady" and the text reads naturally if a church were addressed. The preamble stresses that "truth" and "love" are the two major concerns of this letter ("truth": vv. 1 [twice], 2-4; "love": vv. 1, 3, 5-6 [twice in v. 6]) and of 3 John.

Vv. 1-2. The elder (see "Authorship" in the *Introduction*) commenced his communication by asserting that he loved this church (**the chosen lady;** cf. "dear lady," v. 5) **and** its members (**her children;** cf. v. 4) **in the truth.** So in fact did **all who know the truth.** This seems to suggest that the church addressed was well known in Christian circles. (It is called "chosen" because it was composed of God's elect, i.e., Christians.) The love of John and others for this community of believers was founded and predicated on God's truth. It arose **because of the truth, which lives in us and will be with us forever.** Christian love is by no means mere sentimentalism or humanistic compassion, but is motivated by a knowledge of the truth which has been revealed in Christ. Truth is the basis of love. It is precisely this truth, on account of which the church is loved, that the church must be careful to guard.

V. 3. Instead of just wishing **grace, mercy, and peace** for his readers, John announced that they would be experiencing these things **in truth and love** (cf. v. 1). (Interestingly Paul and Peter in the greetings in their epistles include only grace and peace, except for 1 and 2 Tim., which include "grace, mercy, and peace." See the chart, "Paul's Introductions to His Epistles" at Rom. 1:1-7.) But the qualities of truth and love are precisely the ones John enjoined his readers to maintain. If they do maintain them, then they can expect to enjoy the "grace, mercy, and peace" which come **from God the Father and from Jesus Christ.** The fact that these blessings stem from both the Father and the Son affirms the deity of Christ. **The Father's Son** is an unusual expression (cf. "the Father and the Son" in 2 John 9). God's blessings—favor (*charis*), compassion (*eleos*), and inner harmony and tranquility (*eirēnē*)—are enjoyed in an atmosphere where "truth" and "love" are in control. John had written that truth "will be with us" (v. 2). Now he added that grace, mercy, and peace **will be with us.**

II. Body of the Epistle (vv. 4-11)

Getting to his point immediately, John expressed his concerns (a) that the church would continue to be obedient to God and (b) that the believers would resist all inroads by false teachers. These two objectives, of course, are inseparable.

A. The truth practiced (vv. 4-6)

V. 4. Evidently John had encountered members of this church (**some of your children;** cf. v. 1) somewhere and was delighted (**it has given me great joy;** cf. 3 John 3-4) to observe their obedience to the truth. He used their fidelity, which he had observed, as a positive starting point. What they were doing (**walking in the truth;** cf. 3 John 3-4) was precisely what **the Father commanded.** To walk in the truth is to be obedient to the truth God has made known. John wanted the whole church to do the same.

V. 5. In his final reference to the church under personification (until v. 13), John enjoined it as a **dear lady.** What he wrote to the church was not some **new** requirement **but one the church has had from the beginning** (cf. v. 6). (For the same idea, see 1 John 2:7.) It is nothing other than the command **that we love one another.** As in the larger epistle, the apostle encouraged his readers to follow the old ways as he sought to help them resist the innovations of the antichrists (2 John 7).

V. 6. But what does it mean to "love one another"? The answer: **This is love, that we walk in obedience to His commands.** As he had also done in 1 John 5:2-3a, John defined Christian love in terms of obedience to God. A Christian who truly seeks God's best for his brothers and sisters can only do so by obeying what God has commanded him to do. Love undirected by God's revealed will may easily degenerate into unwise, sentimental activity. Believers who are "walking in the truth" (2 John 4), that is, living in response to what God has revealed, love each other. Brotherly love is part of the truth God has revealed and commanded.

The latter part of verse 6 is difficult in the original. The NIV rendering could be essentially correct (though the words **in love** interpretively render the Gr. *en autē*, "in it"). An alternative rendering would be, "And this is the command, that you walk in it as you have heard from the beginning." Under this construction of the text, John was affirming that obeying God's commands meant adhering to what had been commanded in the form in which it was expressed **from the beginning.** Taken in this way, the writer's words were designed to warn against any "reinterpretation" of God's will, such as the antichrists might propose.

The movement from the plural "commands" (v. 6a) to the singular **command** (v. 6b) is natural for this author (cf. 1 John 3:22-23). The many specifics of God's will can be thought of as a single obligation.

B. The truth protected (vv. 7-11)

V. 7. This verse is more closely linked in thought with verse 6 than the English rendering suggests. A Greek conjunction meaning "because" (*hoti*) has been left untranslated. The reason for John's previous admonition is that **many deceivers, who do not acknowledge Jesus Christ as coming in the flesh, have gone out into the world.** As in the first epistle, the apostle expressed his concern that many false teachers had arisen (cf. 1 John 2:18; 4:1). These teachers were "deceivers" (*planoi*, "ones who lead astray"; cf. *planaō*, "lead astray," in 1 John 2:26; 3:7). Their very number (as well as a probable variety of erroneous ideas) made them a substantial threat to Christian churches such as this one. What bound the false teachers and their views together was their unbelief and rejection of Christ's Incarnation.

The present participle "coming" (in the phrase "coming in the flesh") focuses on the principle involved in the Incarnation: Jesus taking on (coming in) and continuing with a human nature (cf. 1 John 4:2). This truth about "Jesus Christ . . . coming in the flesh" is what the deceivers denied. Some taught that Jesus' body was not truly human; it only appeared that way. That, of course, contradicted the truth of the Incarnation, that Jesus Christ is both fully God and fully human (Col. 2:9).

Such a denial marks that person as a **deceiver** as well as an **antichrist.** (See comments on 1 John 2:18). The word **the** before "deceiver" and "antichrist" could be misunderstood. The English article "a" (rather than "the") is sometimes appropriate for rendering the Greek definite article when an unnamed individual is in view. John did not mean to say here that "any such person" is *the* unique, end-time figure known as the Antichrist.

V. 8. Because of the appearance of these deceivers, the readers needed to **watch out** for the disastrous spiritual effects which any compromise with their ideas could lead to. The danger is not loss of salvation, of course, but loss of reward. The NIV uses the second person verb (**you**) for all three of the statements in this verse. But "we" (following most mss.) is preferred: "that we lose not those things which we have wrought, but that we receive a full reward" (KJV). Early scribes and editors may have altered the "we" to "you" in these places to avoid the suggestion that the apostle could share in a loss of reward. But the author's touch was both delicate and humble. He regarded himself as a co-laborer with his readers and their loss would be shared by him if they did not effectively resist false doctrine. The antichrists were a threat to the work of the Lord in which he and they were mutually engaged. It should be noted that the phrase **be rewarded fully** shows that failure by the readers would not totally deprive them of reward. God would not forget what they had done for Him (cf. Heb. 6:10). But the fullness of their reward (cf. 1 Cor. 3:11-15) was threatened by the subversion of the antichrists.

V. 9. The danger is now spelled out clearly. **Anyone who runs ahead** (*pro-agōn*; most mss. read "turns aside," *parabainōn*) **and does not continue in the teaching of Christ does not have God.** These words suggest strongly that the apostle was thinking here of defection from the truth by those who had once held to it. The word "continue" renders the Greek verb *menō*, familiar because of its frequent use (23 times) in 1 John in reference to the "abiding" life. A person who "does not continue" in a thing has evidently once been in it. The New Testament writers were realists about the possibility of true Christians falling prey to heresy and warned against it (cf. comments on the Book of Heb.). John had just cautioned his readers about possible loss of reward (2 John 8). They were thus now (v. 9) cautioned not to "overstep" the boundaries of sound doctrine, but to "remain" where they were, to "continue in the teaching (*didachē*; cf. v. 10) of (i.e., about) Christ." To deviate from the truth is to leave God behind. God is not with a person who does so. What such a person does, he does without God. This, of course, does not suggest loss of salvation. Instead it points to a doctrinal deviation, with its accompanying disobedience.

In contrast with the defector from the truth, **whoever continues in the teaching has both the Father and the Son.** This says that God is with those who persist in the true doctrine about Christ. (Here may also be another subtle affirmation of the deity of Christ; cf. v. 3.) But John no doubt had more in mind than mere creedal orthodoxy. He used *menō*, his characteristic word in the Johannine Epistles for the life of fellowship with the Father and Son, for the second time in verse 9. The roots of its significance in these letters are in texts such as John 8:31 and 15:1-7. For John, a person who "continues in the teaching" is one who "abides" or "makes his home" there. His connection with the truth is vital and dynamic, so he has a dynamic relationship with God whose commands he obeys (cf. John 14:21-23 for another expression of this kind of relationship). "Abiding" and obedience are inseparable in Johannine thought.

Vv. 10-11. But "continuing" in the truth about Jesus Christ calls for a firm response against those who have become purveyors of false doctrine. Hence John added, **If anyone comes to you and does not bring this teaching, do not take him into your house or welcome him.** In the Greco-Roman world of John's day, a traveling philosopher or religious teacher was a familiar phenomenon. Christian preachers also traveled and relied on local believers for support and hospitality (3 John 5-8). But the readers of 2 John were urged to be discriminating. If someone "comes" to them (the implication is "in the role of a traveling teacher") without also bringing sound doctrine (*didachēn*), he should be refused help. The Greek verb for "bring" is *pherō* ("to carry"), which continues the travel motif. If the truth is not part of his "baggage," he should receive no hospitality from those who are loyal to that truth. (By contrast, hospitality *is* to be shown to true believers [3 John 5, 8].) But a deceiver is not even to be given a greeting of welcome, since to do so would be to share **in his wicked** (*ponērois*, "evil"; cf. "the evil one" [*to ponēron*], 1 John 2:13-14) **work.** "Welcome him" (2 John 10-11) is literally, "Say 'Greetings' to him." In Greek "greetings" here is *chairein*, related to *chairō*, "to rejoice, be glad." *Chairein* was used as a cordial address of welcome or farewell, something like "I am glad to see you" or "I wish you well" (cf. Acts 15:23; 23:26; James 1:1).

To some modern minds these instructions seem unduly rigid and harsh. A great part of the problem, however, lies in the modern inclination to be highly tolerant of religious differences. One must frankly face the fact that the New Testament writers did not share this spirit of toleration. Their commitment to the truth and their consciousness of the dangers of religious error called forth many stern denunciations of false teachers. Not surprisingly, this modern age, having a diminishing sense of the dangers of heresy, has lost its convictions about the truth.

But the passage ought not to be taken beyond the writer's intent. He was thinking about false teachers actively engaged in disseminating error. In this activity they are not to be helped at all. Even a word of greeting might tend to give them a sense of acceptance that could be misconstrued. The readers were to make plain from their aloofness that they in no way condoned the activities of these men. The same must be true today. But John did not directly address the question of how efforts should be made to win such people to a recognition of the truth. Yet it is clear that any such efforts must be conducted so that they are not confused with any form of approbation.

III. Farewell (vv. 12-13)

The author's farewell is similar to his words in 3 John 13 (cf. "I have much to write you"; "I do not want to use [do so with] pen and ink"; "I hope to visit [see] you"; "talk . . . face to face"). Like the format of the letter as a whole, such conclusions were probably conventional. But this in no way suggests that they were insincere.

V. 12. John indicated that he had **much to write to** them **but** preferred **face-to-face** communication. He anticipated a **visit** soon, when he would have more to say to them. Such a personal visit would make his **joy** (*chara*) **complete.** What he might have written if he had not been planning to see them can perhaps be surmised from the contents of 1 John. Indeed, in some respects, 2 John reads like a condensed version of the first epistle. It is likely that the author would

have amplified his admonitions in ways similar to what he had done in the larger letter.

V. 13. John gave farewell **greetings** from **the children of your chosen sister.** *If* this letter were written to an actual Christian woman, one would expect the greetings to come from her sister, not from her sister's children. Because of the anonymity of the references to people, once again it seems easiest to construe this as a greeting sent by the members ("children," cf. v. 1) of a "sister" church to the church to which John was writing (see the *Introduction*)—both "lady" churches having been "chosen" (elected) by God's sovereign grace. As such it gives testimony to the network of Christian interest and concern which united the members of different churches in the earliest years of the faith.

BIBLIOGRAPHY

See Bibliography on 1 John.

3 JOHN

Zane C. Hodges

INTRODUCTION

Third John is a personal letter written to a specific person, a man named Gaius. If, as seems probable, 2 John was written to a church, 3 John and Philemon are the only personal letters in the New Testament. The Pastoral Epistles (1 and 2 Tim., Titus), though addressed to individuals, were probably intended for public reading. Thus the Apostle John's epistle to Gaius is a precious fragment of early Christian correspondence. Its spiritual character is evident.

Authorship. As in 2 John, the writer called himself simply "the elder." In all probability this suggests not only his seniority (*presbyteros* means "old man") but also his authority as an eyewitness to the life of Christ. (See the *Introduction* to 2 John.) The style of the epistle is manifestly the same as that of both 1 and 2 John, and efforts to deny that a single author produced all three carry no conviction. The ancient opinion that the Apostle John wrote this letter, as well as the other two, may be readily accepted. The arguments that support apostolic authorship of 1 John carry over to this tiny epistle by virtue of the clear stylistic ties. Moreover, the self-confident authority of the writer of 3 John (cf. v. 10) also befits an apostle.

Background. Where Gaius (v. 1) lived is not specified. It is likely that he belonged to a church somewhere in Roman Asia (western Turkey). Tradition assigns the Apostle John a role in this area, as does the Book of Revelation. The writer seems to have been urging Gaius to show hospitality to Demetrius (v. 12) who was evidently a traveling Christian preacher (vv. 5-8). Demetrius was probably also the bearer of the letter.

The Apostle John apparently needed to appeal directly to Gaius for the support of Demetrius, since the church was dominated by a man named Diotrephes who did not extend a welcome to traveling brethren (vv. 9-10). Indeed, Diotrephes even sought to excommunicate those who offered such men their hospitality. If Gaius was a member of this same church, he might possibly have run a risk of incurring Diotrephes' wrath as well. But conceivably Gaius was a man of some means who could not be easily driven from the church. The suggestion that Gaius belonged to a different church than did Diotrephes does not seem probable in the light of verse 9 with its simple reference to "the church."

Diotrephes may possibly be an early (and unfavorable) example of a monarchical bishop. Out of the earliest ecclesiastical situation in which a body of elders of equal authority ruled the congregations, a system emerged in which one man assumed prominence over the other elders and became the "bishop" (though this title was originally synonymous with that of elder). This process must often have happened almost imperceptibly when a man of strong character gained ascendancy over the rest of the leadership. But in the church to which Gaius evidently belonged, the process had led to the prominence of a self-willed and authoritarian individual. Diotrephes' reasons for refusing to receive traveling brethren were not spelled out specifically by John. No doubt Diotrephes rationalized his conduct in some way. But the apostle made it plain that what Diotrephes did was wrong (cf. v. 11). He expected to correct the situation when he arrived (v. 10).

Date. As with 2 John, no independent data exists on which to base a date for the writing of 3 John. It is simplest to suggest a date for all three epistles sometime in the early 60s of the Christian era.

OUTLINE

COMMENTARY

I. Salutation (vv. 1-4)

V. 1. The elder (see "Authorship" under *Introduction*) briefly greeted the recipient of this letter affectionately. This salutation is unlike most New Testament Epistles, in that it lacks the usual wish for grace and peace. However, the farewell includes "Peace to you" (v. 14).

My dear friend translates the Greek *tō agapētō* ("the beloved"), related to the verb *agapō* (**I love**). The spirit of Christian love prevailed in the elder's attitude toward **Gaius.** It is precisely this same spirit which was to dictate Gaius' attitude toward traveling preachers such as Demetrius. Three times more the writer addressed Gaius with this same significant term of address (vv. 2, 5, 11).

Moreover, the apostle's love for Gaius was **in the truth,** that is, it was genuine and in accord with God's truth. In the same way Gaius was to express his Christian love by a hospitality that supported the truth (cf. v. 8). As in John's two earlier epistles, the thought of this letter is dominated by concern for truth and love in Christian experience ("truth": vv. 1, 3 [twice], 4, 8, 12; "true": v. 12; "love": vv. 1, 6).

V. 2. The elder was pleased with Gaius' spiritual condition and wished that he might get **along** equally **well** on a physical level. As verses 2-6 show, Gaius was evidently an outstanding spiritual man. The words **I pray that you may enjoy good health and that all may go well with you** are not a mere conventional expression of good wishes. The apostle was concerned for the temporal well-being of others, and not only for their spiritual welfare. He must surely have learned this from Jesus whose concern for people's physical troubles is attested in all four Gospels. Certainly this is a biblical warrant for Christians today to pray for the temporal needs of their spiritual peers.

V. 3. The elder was glad (cf. v. 4) **to have** learned from **some brothers** about Gaius' loyalty to the truth. The words, **tell about your faithfulness to the truth,** somewhat paraphrase the Greek which more literally reads, "witness to your truth." The apostle was saying he had heard that Gaius was a man of the truth. Quite possibly the "brothers" who brought this testimony to John had enjoyed Gaius' hospitality, the same thing which the writer apparently urged on behalf of Demetrius (v. 10). The words, **and how you continue to walk in the truth,** elaborate what the "brothers" had said about Gaius. Gaius' style of life (his "walk") was consistent with God's truth.

V. 4. Nothing made John happier (cf. v. 3) **than to hear that** his **children** were **walking in the truth.** This wording is similar to that in 2 John 4. It is possible that by referring to Gaius as one of his "children," John meant that Gaius was a convert of his (cf. Paul's use of this idea in 1 Cor. 4:14; Gal. 4:19; Phil. 2:22). On the other hand the elderly apostle may simply have thought of those to whom he ministered from a paternal perspective, with fatherly concern.

II. Body of the Epistle (vv. 5-12)

After praising the general conduct of Gaius, the writer moved directly to a matter that concerned him. Those who go forth to preach the truth need the support of Christians in the places where they travel. Unlike Diotrephes, Gaius gave this kind of assistance and the apostle wished to assure him that this was the proper course of action. This contrasts, interestingly, with the emphasis in 2 John 10-11 on *not* giving hospitality to false teachers.

A. Commendation of Gaius (vv. 5-8)

V. 5. Addressing Gaius again as "beloved" (**dear friend;** cf. vv. 1, 2, 11), the writer commended his hospitality to Christians who came his way. The NIV adopts a form of text in which **brothers** and **strangers** are equated. But many manuscripts read, "for the brothers and for strangers." Read in this way, the writer would refer to the traveling preachers as "the brothers," while also asserting that Gaius' hospitality did not stop there but extended also to "strangers" (probably esp. Christians) who happened to be in the vicinity. (Regarding Christian responsibility to entertain strangers, see Heb. 13:2.) About this course of conduct, the apostle declared, **You are faithful in what you are doing.** That is to say, such conduct is praiseworthy because it is an act of fidelity to the truth of God. Again, as in 2 John 1-2, love stems from truth.

V. 6. The report of Gaius' hospitality (**your love**) had reached **the church** where John now was. This may well have been the church at Jerusalem if the epistle was written before A.D. 66 (cf. *Introduction* to 1 John for a discussion of the possibility that the first epistle was written before that date). Undoubtedly, if this is so, Gaius would have been pleased to know that the highly respected Jerusalem congregation had heard of his service to the servants of God. But John now followed up this encouragement with an exhortation: **You will do well to send them on their way in a manner worthy of God.** The words "you will do well" are idiomatic in the original and virtually equal to "please." The verb for "send . . . on their way" (*propempsas*) no doubt carried in general usage the connotation of making adequate provisions for one's guests, both while they stayed and at the time of their departure. The force of the apostle's words was to enjoin on Gaius an openhanded generosity toward the traveling brethren. Nothing less than such generosity would be "worthy of God," who expressed His supreme generosity in the giving of His Son.

V. 7. The reason for such behavior (the verse begins in the Gr. with the untranslated "for," *gar*) is that those whom Gaius should help have gone out **for the sake of the Name.** The "Name" here is, of course, that of Jesus which was now exalted above every name (Phil. 2:9-11). To go out on behalf of that Name was a supreme honor (cf. Acts 5:41 for the honor of suffering for it). Naturally, it was inappropriate for those who did so to seek support from those who did not believe in or honor that Name. Thus the Lord's servants **went out, receiving no help from the pagans.** Even in the present day, there is something unseemly in a preacher of the gospel soliciting

funds from people to whom he offers God's free salvation.

V. 8. But the fact that faithful Christian preachers sought no help from the unsaved meant that Christians were under a special obligation to assist them. By extending the needed help (showing **hospitality to such men**), Christians such as Gaius could **work together for the truth.** This last phrase might be better rendered "be fellow workers with the truth" (NASB). The thought is of partnership with what the truth accomplishes in people's hearts and lives. It was a noble objective for Gaius to follow.

B. Condemnation of Diotrephes (vv. 9-11)

V. 9. Not everyone shared this worthy objective, however. John stated, **I wrote to the church, but Diotrephes, who loves to be first, will have nothing to do with us.** The simple reference to "the church" suggests strongly that this was the church to which Gaius belonged. It sounds as if Gaius may not have known about John's letter to the church. It may well be that Diotrephes had suppressed it and kept it from the church's attention. Diotrephes, John observed, was motivated by a love for preeminence in the church. He was not the last church leader to be so motivated. The temptation to use a role in the Christian assembly as a means of self-gratification remains a real one that all servants of God need to resist. As a result of his personal ambitions, Diotrephes resisted the apostle's wishes. The expression, "will have nothing to do with us," may also be translated, "does not welcome us as guests." The apostle was probably thinking of Diotrephes' refusal to accord hospitality to the traveling brethren (cf. v. 5) who came to the church (perhaps with the letter just mentioned), and he took Diotrephes' rejection of the brothers as a rejection of himself. Quite possibly Diotrephes did not present himself as a personal opponent of John, but in rejecting John's representatives he was rejecting John (cf. John 13:20).

V. 10. The writer, however, knew that he could deal with this matter in person. **So if I come, I will call attention to what he is doing.** This assertion should probably be taken as an understatement. The verb (*hypomnēsō*) means basically "to remind" or "to call to mind." Here the phrase might be translated, "I will call his works to mind" with the manifest implication that Diotrephes' works would be dealt with appropriately.

Diotrephes, the writer asserted, had been guilty of three things. First, he was **gossiping maliciously about us.** These words are literally "bringing false charges (*phlyarōn*, used only here in the NT) against us with evil (*ponērois*) words." No doubt that self-willed leader did his best to tear down the reputation of those whom he was not prepared to receive (as in v. 9, the "us" may refer chiefly to John's representatives).

But Diotrephes went beyond mere talk, wrong as that was. **Not satisfied with that, he refuses to welcome the brothers.** This was his second wrongdoing. His malicious prattle no doubt laid the groundwork for actual refusal of hospitality (in contrast with Gaius' hospitality). And, third, like many other ecclesiastical dictators since his time, Diotrephes did all he could to enforce his will on others: **He also stops those who want to do so and puts them out of the church.** Using his self-acclaimed authority, having a prominent position (v. 9), he forced other believers to be inhospitable or, if they weren't, even prevented them from gathering with the church.

Perhaps Gaius already knew most of these facts. It is likely that John was indirectly reminding him of the potential difficulties he faced in welcoming men who served the truth. But Gaius' obvious dedication to hospitality (vv. 5-6) suggests that he was a man of some means and probably in a good position to resist the authority of Diotrephes. He would be further encouraged by John's promise that he would deal with Diotrephes when he arrived.

V. 11. At any rate, Gaius was **not** to **imitate what is evil but what is good.** Diotrephes' behavior was to be avoided, not copied. One's conduct clearly reflects one's relationship with God. **Anyone who does what is good is from God.** The words "from God" translate the Greek phrase *ek tou theou*, which occurs a number of times in 1 John (e.g., 3:10; 4:1-4, 6-7). It suggests that the source of one's actions or attitudes is in God. Conversely, **anyone who does what is**

evil **has not seen God.** With this, the statement of 1 John 3:6 should be compared (see the discussion on that verse). The assertion should not be watered down. Evil never arises from a real spiritual perception of God but is always a product of darkness of heart and blindness toward Him. John was not questioning Diotrephes' salvation, but he *was* affirming that Diotrephes' conduct manifested real blindness toward God. Gaius was to be careful to shun such an experience as this.

C. Recommendation of Demetrius (v. 12)

V. 12. If Gaius would indeed "imitate what is . . . good" (cf. v. 11), he would extend hospitality to **Demetrius.** This is not explicitly requested, but seems the obvious implication of John's recommendation of Demetrius. In accordance with the Jewish law of witnesses (Deut. 19:15), the apostle adduced a threefold testimony to the character of Demetrius. (1) He was **well spoken of by everyone** who knew him. (2) He was also vouched for **by the truth itself.** Here the truth is personified as a "witness" and John no doubt meant that Demetrius' character and doctrine were in such conformity with that truth that the truth itself virtually spoke on his behalf. (3) As a third line of testimony, John wrote, **we also speak well of him, and you know that our testimony is true.** John himself could personally attest the worth of this man. Thus Gaius had no reason to hesitate showing Demetrius the kind of hospitality he had shown others. (The Demetrius of this letter is not to be confused with the Demetrius of Acts 19:24, an enemy of the gospel.)

III. Farewell (vv. 13-14)

Vv. 13-14a. John was now finished with what he wished to say in this short letter, but he still had **much to write** to Gaius. He *could* have said much more in writing, but (as he had also written in 2 John) he hoped to be able **soon** to communicate those things **face to face.**

V. 14b. The apostle wished Gaius **peace** and passed on **greetings** from **the friends here.** Similarly, he wanted Gaius to **greet the friends there by name.** The use of the term "friends" twice in these closing statements is perhaps one final reminder to Gaius that Christians in every place are or should be a network of friends who are ready to help one another whenever a need arises. It is part of the genius of Christianity that one can meet people whom he has never seen before, in places far from home, and discover through a shared faith an immediate bond of friendship.

BIBLIOGRAPHY

See Bibliography on 1 John.

JUDE

Edward C. Pentecost

INTRODUCTION

Authorship. The writer of the Epistle of Jude, the last of the "General Epistles," introduced his letter with one simple declaration about himself: "Jude, a servant of Jesus Christ, and a brother of James" (v. 1).

Who was this Jude? Three possibilities exist. The author may be either (a) Judas, a half brother of Christ, or (b) Judas, the apostle, or (c) Judas, a leader in the early church of Jerusalem. This latter Judas was sent to Antioch with Paul, Barnabas, and Silas (Acts 15:22). His surname was Barsabbas, indicating that he could have been a brother of Joseph Barsabbas, who was one of two "nominees" to replace Judas Iscariot (Acts 1:23). Thus he would have been known in the church. But little other evidence points to this individual as the author of this epistle.

As to whether he was the Apostle Jude, verse 17 in his letter seems to indicate that he did not consider himself to be an apostle, though modesty could have led him to write as he did. However, the important subject that he wrote about would probably have called for his identifying himself with the other apostles, for authority's sake, if he really was an apostle.

The most probable identification is that the author Jude was a half brother of Christ, a son of Joseph and Mary after Jesus. The term "servant" would be fitting, for though at first Jesus' brothers did not believe in Him (John 7:5), yet later they saw the resurrected Christ and were convinced (Acts 1:14). Among these was Judas, who did not consider himself worthy to call himself a "brother" but just a "servant" of Jesus Christ.

The James referred to by Jude as his brother was thus also a half brother of the Lord (Matt. 13:55; Mark 6:3), as well as a leader of the church at Jerusalem (Acts 15:13), and author of the epistle bearing his name (James 1:1).

Jude wrote with a heart of love and understanding, and with a note of concern and authority. He wanted to write on a joyful theme, "about the salvation we share" (Jude 3), but was compelled to write a much more somber epistle. His love for believers whom he saw endangered by encroaching adversaries moved him to turn from the more pleasant theme to sound a solemn warning.

Style. Jude wrote in a dynamic style, using many figures of speech (e.g., shepherds, clouds, and trees, v. 12; and waves and stars, v. 13).

Jude frequently wrote in triads, with some commentators discerning as many as 18 such series. Outstanding among them are his introduction: "Jude . . . servant . . . brother" (v. 1); his address: "to those . . . called . . . loved . . . kept" (v. 1); his greetings: "mercy, peace, and love" (v. 2); his description of the apostates: "godless men . . . change the grace of our Lord . . . deny Jesus Christ" (v. 4); his examples of other apostates who were judged: "people out of Egypt . . . angels . . . Sodom and Gomorrah and the surrounding towns" (vv. 5-7); his description of these heretical "dreamers": "pollute their own bodies . . . reject authority . . . slander celestial beings" (v. 8); his description elaborated: "taken the way of Cain . . . rushed for profit into Balaam's error . . . destroyed in Korah's rebellion" (v. 11).

Then Jude went beyond the triad, adding figure on figure, to emphasize his denouncement of the apostates. He called them "blemishes . . . [selfish] shepherds . . . clouds without rain . . . autumn trees without fruit . . . wild waves . . . wandering stars" (vv. 12-13).

In other trilogies Jude said these "grumblers and fault-finders" "follow their own evil desires . . . boast about themselves . . . and flatter others" (v. 16), and were characterized as those who "divide you . . . follow mere natural instincts . . . do not have the Spirit" (v. 19). Jude's readers were to "be merciful . . . snatch others from the fire . . . to others show mercy" (vv. 22-23).

Jude frequently referred to the Old Testament. He spoke of the Exodus (v. 5), the death of many Israelites in the wilderness (v. 5), Sodom and Gomorrah (v. 7), Moses' body (v. 9), Cain (v. 11), Balaam (v. 11), Korah (v. 11), Enoch (v. 14), and Adam (v. 14).

Date. Scholars disagree on the date of the writing of this book because Jude did not directly identify either the assembly he addressed the epistle to or the exact heretical group about whom he was writing. Most commentators, however, assign the date between A.D. 67 and 80. Jude was probably influenced by Peter, who wrote his second epistle about A.D. 67-68. (Peter predicted that false teachers *would* arise [2 Peter 2:1; 3:3], but Jude stated that they *have* "slipped in among you" [Jude 4].) And the antinomian Gnostic heresy (to which Jude may have been responding), was beginning to make its influence felt in the first century.

Purpose. One thought characterizes this epistle: beware of the apostates. In keeping with this warning, Jude proceeded to sound an exhortation to his readers to "contend for the faith" (v. 3). The heresy of Gnosticism had raised its head. "Here, in an undeveloped form, are all the main characteristics which went to make up later Gnosticism—emphasis on knowledge which was emancipated from the claims of morality; arrogance toward 'unenlightened' church leaders; interest in angelology; divisiveness; lasciviousness" (Michael Green, *The Second Epistle General of Peter and the General Epistle of Jude*, p. 39).

The incipient Gnostics against whom Jude warned were denying the lordship of Christ (v. 4), exercising sinful license (vv. 4, 8, 16), rebelling against authority (vv. 8, 11, 18), giving in to their own desires (vv. 16, 19), being concerned only with gain for themselves (vv. 11-12, 16), being divisive (v. 19), fault-finding (v. 16), and boasting (v. 16).

Gnosticism declared that the spirit was good and the material was evil. Therefore the spiritual was to be cultivated and fed, with freedom to pursue its good inclinations. In addition Gnostics felt free to give vent to the desires of the flesh. Thus the heart of this apostasy was that it turned the grace of God into license and lasciviousness. Jude wrote to warn of this dual apostasy of wrong conduct and false doctrine.

Original Readers. The tone of the letter demonstrates that the original recipients may have been Christian Jews of Palestine who were gathered into local fellowships. The references made to Old Testament incidents and to extrabiblical literature identified the recipients as people who would understand these references with no need for explanation. Egypt, Sodom and Gomorrah, Moses, Cain, Balaam, Korah, Enoch, Adam, and the fallen angels all point to a people familiar with Old Testament history and possibly apocryphal literature.

Application. The book is a solemn warning to Christians everywhere, since all are subject to the same doctrinal and practical errors. Though its theme regarding apostasy was specifically directed to first-century Jewish Christians, its message is applicable to all Christians. All believers need to avoid the pitfalls of denying Christ's lordship, promiscuously following the fleshly desires, rejecting authority, being divisive, and living for self.

OUTLINE

IV. Guidelines for Avoiding Apostasy (vv. 17-23)
   A. Remembering the teaching of the apostles (vv. 17-19)
   B. Nurturing themselves (vv. 20-21)
   C. Being merciful to others (vv. 22-23)
V. Victory over Apostasy (vv. 24-25)

COMMENTARY

I. Salutation (vv. 1-2)

V. 1. The author introduced himself simply as **Jude, a servant of Jesus Christ and a brother of James.** He made no appeal to his readers on the basis of his personal authority. He was satisfied with being identified as a "servant" (*doulos,* "bondslave") of Jesus Christ. (For a discussion of the identity of this Jude, see the *Introduction.*)

Jude's epistle was directed **to those who have been called, who are loved by God the Father, and kept by Jesus Christ.** This threefold description of the people of God is one of many triads in this letter. The first expression "to those who have been called" reflects on the past—God's sovereign call to salvation in His electing grace (cf. Rom. 1:6; 8:30; 1 Cor. 1:24; Eph. 4:4; 2 Peter 1:3). The phrase "who are loved by God the Father" refers to the present. The verbal form of "loved" indicates that God's love was manifested in the past but also continues in the present. His third description, "kept by Jesus Christ," expresses the most positive assurance regarding the future, for He preserves those who trust Him till His coming (1 Thes. 5:23; 2 Tim. 1:12; 1 Peter 1:5; Jude 24). The calling is the active work of the Holy Spirit; the love emanates from the Father (cf. 2 Cor. 13:14); and the keeping work is the ministry of the Son. Thus the entire Godhead is included in Jude's salutation. The knowledge of God's calling, loving, and keeping brings believers assurance and peace during times of apostasy.

Each of these points in Jude's address seem to be alluded to later in the epistle: the calling may be hinted at in the words "the salvation we share" (v. 3), the love of God is mentioned in verse 21, and the keeping power of Jesus may be implied in the words, "as you wait for the mercy of our Lord Jesus Christ to bring you to eternal life" (v. 21; cf. v. 24).

V. 2. The divine provisions of **mercy, peace, and love** included in Jude's greeting are needed by Christians living in the licentious atmosphere of apostate teaching. God's mercy can sustain them in times of difficulty (Heb. 4:16); His peace can give a subtle calmness when evil abounds (Rom. 15:13; Phil. 4:7); and His love can protect and assure believers in the face of peril (Rom. 5:5; 1 John 4:12, 15-16).

The nature of the salutation reflects the writer's attitude. Jude's choice of words introduces his deep-seated compassion and heartfelt concern for his readers. He longed for them to know in the fullest measure God's "mercy, peace, and love." Jude overflowed with love for the believers while warning them about those who were making their way into the church to destroy it, those who knew nothing of God's mercy, peace, or love.

II. Warnings concerning Apostates (vv. 3-4)

Vv. 3-4. Wishing **to write** of the more pleasant theme of **salvation,** Jude was forced by his concern to write on an urgent and abhorrent theme. Circumstances had arisen that demanded immediate action, thus presenting an emergency situation. Jude addressed himself to a recognized problem, and exhorted the believers to respond with positive determination.

Jude got directly to the point: **I . . . urge you to contend for the faith.** Then he proceeded to tell his readers why he was so concerned. Godless men had **secretly slipped in among** them. They had joined the assemblies of believers, pretending to belong with them when actually they were enemies.

Jude's words were written to those who shared faith and salvation. His words were a warning to the believers to beware of those apostates who had made their way into local assemblies and would destroy if possible the foundation of faith on which the church was built.

"The faith" that God had **once for all entrusted to the saints** is the body of truths taught by the apostles. The term "the faith," used also in Galatians 1:23 and 1 Timothy 4:1, refers to things believed. The false teachings of the apostates called for the believers to contend (*epagōnizesthai*, "agonize earnestly") with all diligence in defense of those truths, which ungodly men were trying to destroy. In effect Jude said, "Let us hold firmly to the faith we profess" (Heb. 4:14).

The intrusion of the libertines refers to outsiders who would poison the church and who should be rejected. These apostates were not followers of Christ who had erred, but intruders who did not belong and who sought to wreck the believers' faith.

The **condemnation** of these men, which **was written about long ago,** may refer to Old Testament prophecies (e.g., Isa. 8:19-22; Jer. 5:13-14). Their end is also predicted in the New Testament (e.g., 2 Thes. 2:6-10; 2 Peter 2:3).

Two characteristics identify these **godless** (*asebeis*, "irreverent"; cf. Jude 15) apostates: perverting God's **grace,** and rejecting God's Son.

Claiming liberty in Christ, they interpreted His grace as **license** to do what their flesh desired with no inhibitions. Their libertinism turned grace into barbarous licentiousness. These antinomians declared that since the flesh was not created by God, it was proper to give in to its desires. Not surprisingly, this perversion in practice was accompanied by a perversion in doctrine—a denial of the person and authority of **Jesus Christ.**

III. Warnings concerning the Peril of Apostasy (vv. 5-16)

Jude first warned his readers of the peril of apostasy by citing three examples from the past of apostates who were destroyed (vv. 5-7), and then by describing the upcoming judgment on present apostates (vv. 8-16).

A. Examples of apostates in the past (vv. 5-7)

1. EGYPT (V. 5)

V. 5. Egypt is mentioned as a reminder of the fact that most Israelites who left Egypt were not faithful. An entire generation perished in the wilderness because of their unbelief (cf. Heb. 3:16-19).

2. ANGELS (V. 6)

V. 6. Among the **angels** were those who had remained in their first abode and had been obedient to God. But others rebelled and left **their** first **positions of authority** and are now **in darkness, bound . . . for judgment on the Great Day.**

Jude's source of information for this statement is debated. Some feel that this may refer to Genesis 6:1-4, and that "the sons of God" who cohabited with "the daughters of men" on earth were the angels who left "their positions of authority" in disobedience to God. (But see the comments on Gen. 6:1-4.) Others feel Jude was making use of the apocryphal Book of Enoch. Since Jude did not identify his source, any decision is only conjecture. The way Jude referred to the angels gives reason to believe that this truth was well accepted by his readers and thus needed no further explanation.

3. SODOM AND GOMORRAH (V. 7)

V. 7. Jude's third illustration, of **Sodom and Gomorrah and the surrounding towns,** serves as a dreadful example of what happens to those who turn from God to follow their own lustful natures. The fate of the unbelievers in those two cities (Gen. 19:1-29) foreshadows the fate of those who deny God's truth and ignore His warnings. The punishment by fire on the perverse inhabitants of Sodom and Gomorrah illustrates the **eternal fire** of hell, which will be experienced by false teachers.

B. Actions of apostates in the present (vv. 8-16)

1. REJECTING AUTHORITY (VV. 8-10)

V. 8. Jude returned to the apostates within the church, altering the order of his historical references in verses 5-7. Those who **pollute their own bodies** are like Sodom and Gomorrah. "Pollute" is *miainousin*, literally, "defile, deprave" used elsewhere only in Titus 1:15 and Hebrews 12:15. Those who **reject authority** are like the unbelieving Israelites who rejected the authority of both Moses and Yahweh. Those who **slander celestial beings** recall the angels who abandoned their home. These three actions reveal their inner attitudes of physical immorality (cf. Rom. 1:24, 26-27; Eph. 4:19), intellectual insubordination, and spiritual irreverence. As **dreamers,** they are unrealistic in thinking their ways will bring satisfaction.

V. 9. The archangel Michael was sent to bury Moses' body, but according to Jewish tradition (the pseudepigraphical book, The Assumption of Moses), **the devil** argued with the angel about **the body,** apparently claiming the right to dispose of it. But Michael, though powerful and authoritative, **did not dare** dispute with Satan, so he left the matter in God's hands, saying, **The Lord rebuke you!** The false teachers Jude spoke of had no respect for authority or for angels. The apostates' slandering of celestial beings (v. 8) stands in arrogant contrast to the chief angelic being, Michael, who would not dare slander Satan, chief of the fallen angels.

V. 10. Whereas Michael did not dare accuse the devil, these apostates, by contrast spoke **abusively** against what **they** did **not understand.** This abusive speech may refer to their slandering of angels (v. 8). Their understanding was debased, for it followed only natural animal instinct. The apostates' only "reasoning" was like that of **unreasoning animals.** Rather than comprehending what was above them (the angels), they really understood only what was below them (the animals). Jude thus demolished their Gnostic claim to superior knowledge. And their understanding—polluting "their own bodies" (v. 8)—was, like the sin of Sodom, self-destructive.

2. WALKING IN ERROR (V. 11)

V. 11. Again Jude returned to one of his triads. The apostates erred in three respects so Jude said, **Woe to them!** **They have taken the way of Cain.** This may mean either that they, like Cain, (a) disobediently devised their own ways of worship, (b) were envious of others, or (c) hated others with a murderous spirit (cf. 1 John 3:12).

They have rushed for profit into Balaam's error. Balaam, under the guise of serving God, encouraged others to sin, while at the same time seeking to gain monetarily from their error (2 Peter 2:15-16; Num. 22:21-31). Similarly the false leaders of Jude's day, greedy for money, led others into sin without recognizing the danger of their actions.

They have been destroyed in Korah's rebellion. Korah led a revolt against Moses and Aaron, not acknowledging that God had delegated authority to them (Num. 16). So their rebellion was actually against God Himself. Likewise the men of whom Jude spoke (perhaps local church leaders) rebelled against God's authority and as a result would be destroyed suddenly. That destruction was so certain that Jude stated in the past tense that "they have been destroyed."

3. LEADING FALSELY (VV. 12-13)

V. 12. Jude pointed out how craftily the apostates had moved into the church. They had made their way into the **love feasts**—which were the closest celebrations of believers—meals (indicated by the words **eating with you**), which were probably followed by the Lord's Supper. Yet these false teachers, though participating outwardly, were inwardly denying the Lord (v. 4b). This is the most outrageous blasphemy possible. Such men were thus **blemishes** that marred the inner beauty of the church. Furthermore they were intruding (cf. "secretly slipped in among you," v. 4a) **without the slightest qualm** or inhibition. "Blemishes" is *spilades* ("stains"); cf. the verb form *espilōmenon* ("stained") in verse 23. In staining others (v. 12) they stained themselves (v. 23).

In addition these unbelievers had taken a shepherding role, but did not function as **shepherds.** Instead of feeding the flock of God, they selfishly would **feed only themselves.** How unthinkable for a shepherd not to feed his sheep—which was his major responsibility! Their leadership was false, for it was deceptive, hardened, and selfish.

As leaders, these apostates were **clouds without rain, blown along by the wind.** This is the first of four vivid comparisons from nature in verses 12-13. These men had no water for thirsty souls; they only pretended that they did. And they were soon gone, unstable as wind-driven clouds.

As leaders these apostates were spiritually dead. A tree in the **autumn** (the time of gathering fruit from fruit trees) without fruit appears (or is) dead, and a fruitless tree that is **uprooted** is dead forever—thus it is **twice dead.** The dead condition of apostate leaders was indicated by two things: (a) they did not bear spiritual fruit in others, and (b) they were without spiritual roots themselves, and thus faced judgment.

V. 13. Like **wild waves of the sea,** raging back and forth and producing only froth on the shore, these apostates spewed their foam with nothing solid, edifying, helpful, or nourishing. What they produced was only **shame,** which their actions caused.

Wandering stars (i.e., "shooting" stars), move across the sky, shining briefly, and then vanish without producing light or giving direction. Fixed stars help guide navigators, but wandering stars are useless to them. If any shipmaster would be stupid enough to follow one, he would be led astray. Similarly the prominence of apostate leaders is short-lived, useless, and false. They do lead unwary followers astray, pretending to be what they are not. They will therefore be swallowed up into the **blackest darkness** forever; eternal judgment is certain for them.

These apostates were not unfruitful believers, who would not receive rewards in heaven at the judgment seat of Christ. Instead they were impostors who would be judged according to their evil deeds.

4. PLEASING SELF (VV. 14-16)

Vv. 14-15. The judgment on apostates, already mentioned in verses 4-7, 13, was now confirmed by a reference to a pre-Flood prophecy made by **Enoch, the seventh from Adam** (Gen. 5:4-20). However, scholars have puzzled over the absence of any reference in the Old Testament to this prophecy attributed to Enoch. Since Jude's statement is similar to a passage in the apocryphal Book of Enoch (1:9)—written prior to 110 B.C. and thus probably known by the early Christians—many assume that Jude is quoting from that book. Others suggest that the difference between Jude's words and the Book of Enoch indicate that Jude received the information about Enoch directly from God, or that under divine inspiration he recorded an oral tradition. None of these views affects the doctrine of inspiration adversely. If Jude quoted the apocryphal book, he was affirming only the truth of that prophecy and not endorsing the book in its entirety (cf. Paul's quotation of the Cretan poet Epimenides, in Titus 1:12).

Enoch's prophecy pointed to the glorious return of Christ to the earth with **thousands upon thousands of His angels** (holy ones) (Matt. 24:30; 2 Thes. 1:10), when **His** purpose will be **to judge everyone** (2 Thes. 1:7-10) **and to convict all the ungodly** with unanswerable evidence that their actions, manners, and words have been **ungodly** (asebeis, "irreverent"; cf. Jude 4). Jude's fourfold use of this word **ungodly** reinforces his description of their nature. Rather than being true spiritual leaders, they had spoken **harsh words** (cf. "speak abusively" in v. 10) against Jesus Christ whom they denied.

V. 16. Here Jude described the apostates in a fourfold way. These descriptions justify Enoch's calling them "ungodly." (a) They were **grumblers and faultfinders** who faulted others but saw no flaws in themselves; (b) they lustfully followed **their own evil desires** (cf. vv. 8, 10, 18-19); (c) they bragged **about themselves** (the word hyperonka, used only here and in 2 Peter 2:18, means to be "puffed up" or "swollen"); and (d) they flattered **others,** currying favor only when it was to **their own** evil advantage to do so. Vocally discontented, sinfully self-centered, extravagantly egotistical, and deceptively flattering—such are apostates, then and today.

Thus in unflinching terms Jude clearly identified the apostates, while at the same time exposing their character in order to warn believers of their true nature and their final destiny. He was laying the groundwork to call his readers to action against these ungodly men and their practices.

IV. Guidelines for Avoiding Apostasy (vv. 17-23)

Having identified the apostates in expressive language, Jude gave the believers guidelines on how to avoid the apostates' errors. It is not enough to recognize false teachers; it is also necessary to avoid falling into their errors.

A. Remembering the teaching of the apostles (vv. 17-19)

Vv. 17-19. Jude told his readers to **remember what the apostles** had **foretold** about **scoffers.** At Ephesus, Paul warned of the "savage wolves" that would come in to destroy the flock and distort the truth (Acts 20:29-30). He sounded similar warnings of apostasy to Timothy (1 Tim. 4:1; 2 Tim. 3:1-5; 4:3-4). Peter had addressed the same issue (2 Peter 2:1-3; 3:3-4). The quotation in Jude 18 is a loose rendering of Peter's words in 2 Peter 3:3, and at the same time it summarized Paul's warnings.

As stated in Jude 18-19, these intruders (a) scoffed (cf. vv. 10-15), (b) followed **their own ungodly desires** (cf. v. 16) and **mere natural instincts** (cf. vv. 10, 16), and (c) sought to **divide** believers. Such men obviously did **not have the** Holy **Spirit** and thus were not born again (Rom. 8:9).

B. Nurturing themselves (vv. 20-21)

Vv. 20-21. In addition to remembering what the apostles had said about the apostates, Jude's readers were to give attention to themselves. Here is the heart of his message: **build yourselves up in your most holy faith . . . pray in the Holy Spirit, keep yourselves in God's love,** and **wait for** Christ's return. (The NIV seems to suggest three exhortations, but the Greek has four parallel participles: building, praying, keeping, expecting.) The evident contrast of these actions to the scoffers was introduced by the words **But you.** And for the third time Jude addressed his readers as **dear friends** (vv. 3, 17, 20).

Personal edification ("build yourselves up") comes from progressing in the knowledge of "your most holy faith." This "faith that was once for all entrusted to the saints" (v. 3) was the teaching of the apostles now recorded in the Scriptures, to be studied (Acts 20:32; 2 Tim. 2:15).

Praying in the Holy Spirit is not speaking in tongues, but is "praying out of hearts and souls that are indwelt, illuminated, and filled with the Holy Spirit" (George Lawrence Lawlor, *Translation and Exposition of the Epistle of Jude,* p. 127). It is praying in the power of the Holy Spirit (cf. Eph. 6:18).

Keeping oneself "in God's love" (Jude 21) does not indicate that salvation depends on one's own efforts, for that would contradict other Scripture passages (e.g., v. 24). Instead, a believer is nurtured as he is occupied with God's love for him, and is in fellowship with Him (cf. John 15:9-10, "remain in My love").

Waiting (*prosdechomenoi,* "looking expectantly") for the blessed hope, the return of Christ for His church, is a fourth means of personal nurture. Waiting for

that event is waiting **for the mercy of our Lord Jesus Christ** in the sense that the Rapture will be the consummating evidence of His mercy. Jude added that it will **bring you to eternal life,** that is, to enjoying never-ending life in God's own presence (cf. 1 Peter 1:5, 9, 13).

C. Being merciful to others (vv. 22-23)

Vv. 22-23. Because the words of the apostates were confusing, probably many believers were in **doubt** as to whether to follow them. Such persons, Jude wrote, should not be slandered or criticized. They should be dealt with in love and mercy—the same way in which the Lord dealt with them (cf. v. 21). They needed encouragement, not criticism. They needed to be built up, not torn down.

Others—those who are unsaved—were about to fall into the fire, the eternal fire of hell (cf. v. 7). Jude exhorted his readers to **snatch** them **from the fire and save them.**

To still others, a third group, believers should **show mercy.** But they were to do so in an attitude of **fear,** that is, caution, lest they become contaminated by the sin of "the most abandoned heretic" (Michael Green, *The Second Epistle General of Peter and the General Epistle of Jude,* p. 188). Such persons are so corrupt that the stench of death has polluted them and even their **clothing,** as it were, reeks with the odor of **corrupted flesh** (cf. comments on "stained" in v. 12).

In his short epistle, Jude gave seven commands to believers:

1. Earnestly contend for the faith (v. 3).
2. Remember the teaching and warning of the apostles (v. 17).
3. Build yourselves up in the most holy faith (v. 20).
4. Pray in the Holy Spirit (v. 20).
5. Keep yourselves in the love of God (v. 21).
6. Look for the mercy of the Lord to bring you to eternal life (v. 21).
7. Show mercy to Christians who are doubting, snatch unbelievers from the fire, and cautiously show mercy to the corrupt (vv. 22-23).

V. Victory over Apostasy (vv. 24-25)

Vv. 24-25. In this final paragraph Jude exploded with a most elevated doxology, answering the unexpressed question, "But who will deliver us from the apostates and the apostasy into which they lead the unsuspecting?" His proclamation was, praise be **to Him who is able to keep you from falling.** Victory over apostasy is found in Jesus Christ! He is the One who will "keep" believers. Christ will **present** believers to His Father **without fault and with great joy**—joy both for Himself and for them (Heb. 12:2; 1 Peter 1:8). Here is the greatest theme of victory to be sounded, the highest note of praise and adoration possible, and the greatest assurance for the redeemed. Jude attributes to God—to **the only God our Savior . . . glory, majesty, power, and authority,** which are all available to believers through the Victor, **Jesus Christ our Lord.** And this exalted position is true of God in eternity past, in the present, and for all eternity in the future.

Thus Jude fulfills his heart's desire of writing in the most joyful terms (Jude 3), for in Christ there is hope in victory, which gives believers joy and confidence.

BIBLIOGRAPHY

Bigg, Charles. *A Critical and Exegetical Commentary on the Epistles of St. Peter and St. Jude.* The International Critical Commentary. Edinburgh: T.&T. Clark, 1902.

Blum, Edwin A. "Jude." In *The Expositor's Bible Commentary*, vol. 12. Grand Rapids: Zondervan Publishing House, 1981.

Coder, S. Maxwell. *Jude.* Everyman's Bible Commentary. Chicago: Moody Press, 1967.

Green, Michael. *The Second Epistle General of Peter and the General Epistle of Jude: An Introduction and Commentary.* The Tyndale New Testament Commentaries. Grand Rapids: Wm. B. Eerdmans Publishing Co., 1968.

Ironside, H.A. *Exposition of the Epistle of Jude.* Rev. ed. New York: Loizeaux Brothers, n.d.

Lawlor, George Lawrence. *Translation and Exposition of the Epistle of Jude.* Nutley, N.J.: Presbyterian and Reformed Publishing Co., 1976.

Lenski, R.C.H. *The Interpretation of the Epistles of St. Peter, St. John and St. Jude.* Minneapolis: Augsburg Publishing House, 1966.

MacArthur, John, Jr. *Beware the Pretenders.* Wheaton, Ill.: Scripture Press Publications, Victor Books, 1980.

Manton, Thomas. *An Exposition on the Epistle of Jude.* Reprint. London: Banner of Truth Trust, 1978.

Mayor, Joseph B. *The Epistle of St. Jude and the Second Epistle of St. Peter.* London: Macmillan Co., 1907. Reprint. Minneapolis: Klock & Klock Christian Publishers, 1978.

Pettingill, William L. *Simple Studies in the Epistles of James, First and Second Peter, First, Second and Third John and Jude.* Findlay, Ohio: Fundamental Truth Publishers, n.d.

Plummer, Alfred. *The General Epistles of St. James and St. Jude.* The Expositor's Bible. New York: Hodder & Stoughton, n.d.

Sadler, M.F. *The General Epistles of James, Peter, John, and Jude.* 2d ed. London: George Bell & Sons, 1895.

Wand, J.W.C., ed. *The General Epistles of St. Peter and St. Jude.* London: Methuen & Co., 1934.

Wolff, Richard. *A Commentary on the Epistle of Jude.* Grand Rapids: Zondervan Publishing House, 1960.

REVELATION

John F. Walvoord

INTRODUCTION

Importance. The Book of Revelation is important because it is the last inspired book of the Bible to be written and is rightly positioned as the New Testament's final book. As the New Testament opens with the four Gospels relating to the first coming of Christ, so the Book of Revelation closes the New Testament with the general theme of the second coming of Christ. The Book of Revelation is also the climax of many lines of revelation running through both Testaments, and it brings to conclusion the revelation of many prophecies yet to be fulfilled.

The second coming of Christ and the years immediately preceding it are revealed in Revelation more graphically than in any other book of the Bible. The Book of Daniel describes in detail the period from Daniel's time to Christ's first coming and speaks briefly of the Tribulation and Christ's rule on earth. But the Book of Revelation amplifies the great end-time events with many additional details, culminating in the new heaven and the new earth.

Authorship. As the opening verses in Revelation plainly state, the book was written by John. From the first century to the present, orthodox Christians have almost unanimously agreed that he is the Apostle John. Dionysius was the first to dispute the Johannine authorship, and did so on the grounds that he disagreed with the book's theology and found many inaccuracies in its grammar. These objections were disregarded in the early church by most of the important fathers such as Justin Martyr, Irenaeus, Tertullian, Hippolytus, Clement of Alexandria, and Origen. (For a full discussion see John F. Walvoord, *The Revelation of Jesus Christ*, pp. 11-4.) Practically all scholars today who accept the divine inspiration of the Book of Revelation also accept John the Apostle as its author. However, Erasmus, Luther, and Zwingli questioned the Johannine authorship because it teaches a literal 1,000-year reign of Christ.

Date. Most evangelical scholars affirm that Revelation was written in A.D. 95 or 96. This is based on accounts of the early church fathers that the Apostle John had been exiled on Patmos Island during the reign of Domitian who died in A.D. 96. John was then allowed to return to Ephesus.

Because of a statement by Papias, an early church father, that John the Apostle was martyred before A.D. 70, the Johannine authorship has been questioned. However, the accuracy of this quotation from Papias has been seriously challenged by statements by Clement of Alexandria and Eusebius who affirm that the book was written by John on Patmos in A.D. 95 or 96.

Inspiration and Canonicity. Those accepting John the Apostle as the author universally recognize the divine inspiration of Revelation and its rightful place in the Bible. Because its style differs from that of other New Testament books, acceptance of Revelation by early Christians was delayed by a rising opposition to premillennialism. The doctrine of the literal 1,000-year reign of Christ was rejected by some church leaders in the third and fourth centuries. The evidence, however, shows that orthodox theologians readily accepted the book as genuinely inspired. Early fathers who recognized the book as Scripture include Irenaeus, Justin Martyr, Eusebius, Apollonius, and Theophilus, the bishop of Antioch. By the beginning of the third century the book was widely quoted as Scripture. The fact that the Book of

Revelation complements other inspired Scripture such as the Book of Daniel has confirmed its divine inspiration.

Style. Like the Old Testament Books of Daniel and Ezekiel, Revelation uses symbolic and apocalyptic forms of revelation extensively. The fact that symbols must be interpreted has led to many diverse interpretations. In most cases, however, the meaning of the symbolic revelation is found by comparing it with previous prophetic and apocalyptic revelation in the Old Testament. This has led many interpreters to view the Book of Revelation as presenting realistic predictions of the future. Its apocalyptic and symbolic character sharply contrasts with books of similar nature written outside the Bible which are classified as Pseudepigrapha. While many of these extrabiblical books are almost impossible to understand, Revelation, by contrast, presents a sensible view of the future in harmony with the rest of Scripture (cf. Walvoord, *Revelation*, pp. 23-30).

Interpretation. Because of its unusual character, Revelation has been approached from a number of interpretive principles, some of which raise serious questions concerning its value as divine authoritative revelation.

The allegorical or nonliteral approach. This form of interpretation was offered by the Alexandrian school of theology in the third and fourth centuries. It regards the entire Bible as an extensive allegory to be interpreted in a nonliteral sense. The allegorical interpretation of the Bible was later restricted largely to prophecy about the Millennium by Augustine (354–430), who interpreted Revelation as a chronicle of the spiritual conflict between God and Satan being fulfilled in the present Church Age. A liberal variation of this in modern times considers Revelation simply as a symbolic presentation of the concept of God's ultimate victory.

The preterist approach. A more respected approach is known as the preterist view which regards Revelation as a symbolic picture of early church conflicts which have been fulfilled. This view denies the future predictive quality of most of the Book of Revelation. In varying degrees this view combines the allegorical and symbolic interpretation with the concept that Revelation does not deal with specific future events. Still another variation of the preterist view regards Revelation as setting forth principles of divine dealings with man, without presenting specific events.

The historical approach. A popular view stemming from the Middle Ages is the historical approach which views Revelation as a symbolic picture of the total church history of the present Age between Christ's first and second comings. This view was advanced by Luther, Isaac Newton, Elliott, and many expositors of the postmillennial school of interpretation and has attained respectability in recent centuries. Its principal problem is that seldom do two interpreters interpret a given passage as referring to the same event. Each interpreter tends to find its fulfillment in his generation. Many have combined the historical interpretation with aspects of other forms of interpretation in order to bring out a devotional or spiritual teaching from the book. The preceding methods of interpretation tend to deny a literal future Millennium and also literal future events in the Book of Revelation.

The futuristic approach. The futuristic approach has been adopted by conservative scholars, usually premillenarians, who state that chapters 4–22 deal with events that are yet future today. The content of Revelation 4–18 describes the last seven years preceding the second coming of Christ and particularly emphasizes the Great Tribulation, occurring in the last three and one-half years before His coming.

Objections to this view usually stem from theological positions opposed to premillennialism. The charge is often made that the Book of Revelation would not have been a comfort to early Christians or understood by them if it were largely futuristic. Adherents of the futuristic school of interpretation insist, on the contrary, that future events described in Revelation bring comfort and reassurance to Christians who in the nature of their faith regard their ultimate victory as future. The futuristic interpretation, however, is demanding of the expositor as it requires him to reduce to tangible prophetic events the symbolic presentations which characterize the book.

Purpose. The purpose of the Book of Revelation is to reveal events which will take place immediately before, during, and following the second coming of Christ. In keeping with this purpose the book devotes most of its revelation to this subject in chapters 4–18. The Second Coming itself is given the most graphic portrayal anywhere in the Bible in chapter 19, followed by the millennial reign of Christ described in chapter 20. The eternal state is revealed in chapters 21–22. So the obvious purpose of the book is to complete the prophetic theme presented earlier in the prophecies of the Old Testament (e.g., Dan.) and the prophecies of Christ, especially in the Olivet Discourse (Matt. 24–25). Along with the predictive character of the Book of Revelation is extensive revelation in almost every important area of theology. In addition, many verses suggest practical applications of prophetic truths to a Christian's life. Specific knowledge and anticipation of God's future program is an incentive to holy living and commitment to Christ.

Application. In addition to passages that suggest practical application of prophetic truth, chapters 2–3 are especially important for they consist of messages to seven local churches which appropriately represent the entire church. The pointed message of Christ to each of these churches is the capstone to New Testament Epistles dealing with the practical life of those committed to the Christian faith. On the one hand believers are exhorted to holy living, and on the other hand unbelievers are warned of judgments to come. The book provides solid evidence that the righteous God will ultimately deal with human sin and bring to consummation the salvation of those who have trusted in Christ. A solemn warning is given to those who are unprepared to face the future. A day of reckoning, when every knee will bow to Christ (Phil. 2:10), is inevitable in the divine program. Because of its broad revelation of events to come as well as its pointed exhortation to righteousness, the book pronounces blessing on those "who

hear it and take to heart what is written in it, because the time is near" (Rev. 1:3).

OUTLINE

I. Introduction: "What You Have Seen" (chap. 1)
  A. Prologue (1:1-3)
  B. Salutation (1:4-8)
  C. The Patmos vision of Christ glorified (1:9-18)
  D. The command to write (1:19-20)
II. Letters to the Seven Churches: "What Is Now" (chaps. 2–3)
  A. The letter to the church in Ephesus (2:1-7)
  B. The letter to the church in Smyrna (2:8-11)
  C. The letter to the church in Pergamum (2:12-17)
  D. The letter to the church in Thyatira (2:18-29)
  E. The letter to the church in Sardis (3:1-6)
  F. The letter to the church in Philadelphia (3:7-13)
  G. The letter to the church in Laodicea (3:14-22)
III. The Revelation of the Future: "What Will Take Place Later" (chaps. 4–22)
  A. The vision of the heavenly throne (chap. 4)
  B. The seven-sealed scroll (chap. 5)
  C. The opening of the six seals: the time of divine wrath (chap. 6)
  D. Those who will be saved in the Great Tribulation (chap. 7)
  E. The opening of the seventh seal and the introduction of the seven trumpets (chaps. 8–9)
  F. The mighty angel and the little scroll (chap. 10)
  G. The two witnesses (11:1-14)
  H. The sounding of the seventh trumpet (11:15-19)
  I. The seven great personages of the end times (chaps. 12–15)
  J. The bowls of divine wrath (chap. 16)
  K. The fall of Babylon (chaps. 17–18)
  L. The song of hallelujah in heaven (19:1-10)
  M. The second coming of Christ (19:11-21)
  N. The millennial reign of Christ (20:1-10)

O. The judgment of the great white throne (20:11-15)
P. The new heaven and the new earth (21:1–22:5)
Q. The final word from God (22:6-21)

COMMENTARY

I. Introduction: "What You Have Seen" (chap. 1)

A. Prologue (1:1-3)

1:1. The opening words, **The revelation of Jesus Christ,** indicate the subject of the entire book. The word "revelation" is a translation of the Greek *apokalypsis*, meaning "an unveiling" or "a disclosure." From this word comes the English "apocalypse." The revelation was given to John to communicate to others, **His servants,** and it prophesies **what must soon take place,** rather than relating a historic presentation as in the four Gospels. The word "soon" (*en tachei*; cf. 2:16; 22:7, 12, 20) means that the action will be sudden when it comes, not necessarily that it will occur immediately. Once the end-time events begin, they will occur in rapid succession (cf. Luke 18:8; Acts 12:7; 22:18; 25:4; Rom. 16:20). The words, **He made it known,** are from the Greek verb *esēmanen*, meaning "to make known by signs or symbols," but the verb also includes communication by words. The angel messenger is not named but some believe he was Gabriel, who brought messages to Daniel, Mary, and Zechariah (cf. Dan. 8:16; 9:21-22; Luke 1:26-31). The reference to **John** as a **servant** (*doulos*, which normally means "slave") is the term used by Paul, James, Peter, and Jude (cf. Rom. 1:1; Phil. 1:1; Titus 1:1; James 1:1; 2 Peter 1:1; Jude 1) in speaking of their positions as God's servants.

1:2. John faithfully described what he saw as **the Word of God and the testimony of Jesus Christ.** What John saw was a communication from—and about—Jesus Christ Himself.

1:3. The prologue concludes with a blessing on each individual **who reads the** book as well as on **those who hear it and take to heart what is written in it.** The implication is that a reader will read this message aloud to an audience. Not only is there a blessing for the reader and the hearers, but there is also a blessing for those who respond in obedience.

John concluded his prologue with **the time is near.** The word "time" (*kairos*) refers to a period of time, that is, the time of the end (Dan. 8:17; 11:35, 40; 12:4, 9). The end time, as a time period, is mentioned in Revelation 11:18 and 12:12. In 12:14 the word "time" means a year (cf. Dan. 7:25); and the phrase "time, times, and half a time" means one year ("time") plus two years ("times") plus six months ("half a time"), totaling three and one-half years—the length of the time of "the end." Revelation 1:3 includes the first of seven beatitudes in the book (1:3; 14:13; 16:15; 19:9; 20:6; 22:7, 14).

The prologue presents concisely the basic facts underlying the entire book: its subjects, purpose, and angelic and human channels. It is most important to observe that the book was primarily intended to give a practical lesson to those who read and heed its contents.

B. Salutation (1:4-8)

1:4-6. This salutation—like Paul's salutations in his epistles and the salutation of John himself in 2 John—specifies the book's destination. The recipients of this message were **the seven churches in the** Roman **province of Asia** in Asia Minor (Rev. 1:11; chaps. 2 and 3). The words **grace and peace** concisely summarize both a Christian's standing before God and his experience. "Grace" speaks of God's attitude toward believers; "peace" speaks both of their standing with God and their experience of divine peace.

The salutation is unusual in that it describes God the Father as the One **who is, and who was, and who is to come** (cf. 1:8). **The seven spirits** probably refers to the Holy Spirit (cf. Isa. 11:2-3; Rev. 3:1; 4:5; 5:6), though it is an unusual way to refer to the third Person of the Trinity. Of the three Persons in the Trinity, **Jesus Christ** is here mentioned last, probably because of His prominence in this book. He is described as **the faithful Witness,** that is, the source of the revelation to be given; **the Firstborn from the dead** (cf. Col. 1:18), referring to His historic resurrection; **and the Ruler of the kings of the earth,** indicating His prophetic role after His second coming (chap. 19).

The Seven "Beatitudes" in Revelation

"Blessed is the one who reads the words of this prophecy, and blessed are those who hear it and take to heart what is written in it, because the time is near" (1:3).

"Then I heard a voice from heaven say, 'Write: "Blessed are the dead who die in the Lord from now on. "Yes,' says the Spirit, 'they will rest from their labor, for their deeds will follow them' " (14:13).

"Behold, I come like a thief! Blessed is he who stays awake and keeps his clothes with him, so that he may not go naked and be shamefully exposed" (16:15).

"Then the angel said to me, 'Write: "Blessed are those who are invited to the wedding supper of the Lamb!"' And he added, 'These are the true words of God' " (19:9).

"Blessed and holy are those who have part in the first resurrection. The second death has no power over them, but they will be priests of God and of Christ and will reign with Him for a thousand years" (20:6).

"Behold, I am coming soon! Blessed is he who keeps the words of the prophecy in this book" (22:7).

"Blessed are those who wash their robes, that they may have the right to the tree of life and may go through the gates into the city" (22:14).

Christ's resurrection was **from the dead.** As the "Firstborn," He is the first to be resurrected with an everlasting body, which is a token of other selective resurrections including those of saints who die in the Church Age (Phil. 3:11), the Tribulation martyrs (Rev. 20:5-6), and the wicked dead of all ages (20:12-13).

In His dying on the cross Christ **who loves us** is the One who **freed us from our sins by His blood** (some Gr. mss. have the word "washed" instead of "freed"). Believers are now **a kingdom and priests** with the purpose now and forever of serving God. This prompted John to express a benediction of praise and worship culminating with **Amen** (lit., "so be it").

1:7-8. Readers are exhorted to **look** for **He is coming.** This is His second coming which will be **with the clouds** (cf. Acts 1:9-11). **Every eye will see Him, even those who pierced Him.** Though the literal executioners and rejectors of Christ are now dead and will not be resurrected until after the Millennium, the godly remnant of Israel "will look on [Him], the One they have pierced" (Zech. 12:10). This godly remnant will represent the nation.

Christ's second coming, however, will be visible to the entire world including unbelievers, in contrast with His first coming at His birth in Bethlehem and in contrast with the future Rapture of the church, which probably will not be visible to the earth as a whole. The present tense of the expression "He is coming" (Rev. 1:7) points to the future Rapture of the church (John 14:3). John again appended the word **Amen.** The salutation closes with a reminder of Christ as the eternal One, **the Alpha and the Omega,** the first and last letters of the Greek alphabet (also used in Rev. 21:6; 22:13). He is further described as the One **who is, and who was, and who is to come** (cf. 4:8; 11:17), **the Almighty.** The Greek word for "Almighty" is *pantokratōr,* "the all-powerful One." It is used 10 times in the New Testament, 9 of them in Revelation (2 Cor. 6:18; Rev. 1:8; 4:8; 11:17; 15:3; 16:7, 14; 19:6, 15; 21:22). The major revelation of the entire book is referred to in these salutation verses.

C. The Patmos vision of Christ glorified (1:9-18)

The location of the dramatic revelation of Christ recorded in this book was the island of Patmos, a small island in the Aegean Sea southwest of Ephesus and between Asia Minor and Greece. According to several early church fathers (Irenaeus, Clement of Alexandria, and Eusebius), John was sent to this island as a prisoner following his effective pastorate at Ephesus. Victorinus, the first commentator on the Book of Revelation, stated that John worked as a prisoner in the mines on this small island. When the Emperor Domitian died in A.D. 96, his successor Nerva let John return to Ephesus. During John's bleak days on Patmos, God gave him the tremendous revelation embodied in this final book of the Bible.

1:9-11. This section begins with the expression **I, John.** This is the third reference to John as the human author in this chapter and the first of three times in the book when he referred to himself as **I** (cf. 21:2; 22:8). This contrasts with his reference to himself in 2 John 1 and 3 John 1 as an elder and his indication in John 21:24 that he was a disciple.

In these opening chapters addressed to the seven churches of Asia, John described himself as a **brother** who was **patient** in his **endurance** of **suffering.** His suffering had come because of his faithful proclamation of and faith in **the Word of God and the testimony of Jesus.** (Some Gr. texts add "Christ" after Jesus.) "The testimony of Jesus" means John's testimony *for* and *about* Jesus, not a testimony given *by* Jesus. Like many other well-known writers of Scripture (Moses, David, Isaiah, Ezekiel, Jeremiah, and Peter), John was writing from a context of suffering because of his commitment to the true God.

John's revelation occurred **on the Lord's Day** while he **was in the Spirit.** Some have indicated that "the Lord's Day" refers to the first day of the week. However, the word "Lord's" is an adjective and this expression is never used in the Bible to refer to the first day of the week. Probably John was referring to the day of the Lord, a familiar expression in both Testaments (cf. Isa. 2:12; 13:6, 9; 34:8; Joel 1:15; 2:1, 11, 31; 3:14; Amos 5:18, 20; Zeph. 1:7-8, 14, 18; 2:3; Zech. 14:1; Mal. 4:5; 1 Thes. 5:2; 2 Peter 3:10). "In the Spirit" could also be rendered "in [my] spirit" (cf. Rev. 4:2; 17:3; 21:10). That is, he was projected forward in his inner self in a vision, not bodily, to that future day of the Lord when God will pour out His judgments on the earth.

The stirring events beginning in Revelation 4 are the unfolding of the day of the Lord and the divine judgments related to it. The idea that the entire Book of Revelation was given to John in one 24-hour day seems unlikely, especially if he had to write it all down. Being transported prophetically into the future day of the Lord, he then recorded his experience.

Hearing **a loud voice like a trumpet,** John was instructed to write on a scroll what he saw and heard and send it to seven churches located in Asia Minor. This is the first of 12 commands in this book for John to write what he saw, a command which seems related to each preceding vision (cf. 1:19; 2:1, 8, 12, 18; 3:1, 7, 14; 14:13; 19:9; 21:5). One vision, however, was not to be recorded (10:4).

Each of these churches was an autonomous local church and the order of mention is geographical in a half-moon circle beginning at Ephesus on the coast, proceeding north to Smyrna and Pergamum, then swinging east and south to Thyatira, Sardis, Philadelphia, and Laodicea. (For more information on these seven churches see comments on chaps. 2–3).

1:12-16. Hearing **the voice** behind him, John **turned . . . to see** its source. What he **saw** was **seven golden lampstands.** Apparently these were individual lampstands rather than one lampstand with seven lamps as was true of a similar piece of furniture in the tabernacle and the temple.

Among the lampstands John saw **Someone "like a Son of Man,"** an expression used in Daniel 7:13 to refer to Christ. The description was that of a priest **dressed in a long robe . . . with a golden sash around his chest.** The whiteness of His hair corresponded to that of the Ancient of Days (cf. Dan. 7:9), a reference to God the Father. God the Son has the same purity and eternity as God the Father, as signified by the whiteness of **His head and hair.** The **eyes like blazing fire** described His piercing judgment of sin (cf. Rev. 2:18).

This concept is further enhanced by **His feet** which **were like bronze glowing** in a furnace (cf. 2:18). The bronze altar in the temple was related to sacrifice for sin and divine judgment on it. His voice was compared to the roar of rushing waters. His face glowed with a brilliance like the sun shining. John noticed that in His right hand He held seven stars, described in verse 20 as the angels or messengers of the seven churches. Significantly Christ held them in His right hand, indicating sovereign possession. Speaking of Christ's role as a Judge, John saw a sharp double-edged sword coming out of His mouth. This type of sword (rhomphaia, also referred to in 2:12, 16; 6:8; 19:15, 21) was used by the Romans in a stabbing action designed to kill. Jesus Christ was no longer a Baby in Bethlehem or a Man of sorrows crowned with thorns. He was now the Lord of glory.

1:17-18. John stated, When I saw Him, I fell at His feet as though dead. Paul was struck to the ground in a similar way when he saw Christ in His glory (Acts 9:4). Previously John had put his head on Jesus' breast (cf. John 13:25, KJV). But now John could not be this familiar with the Christ of glory.

John received reassurance from Christ in the words, Do not be afraid. Christ stated that He is the eternal One, the First and the Last (cf. Rev. 1:8; 2:8; 21:6; 22:13), and the resurrected One, the Living One, who though once dead is now alive forever and ever! Here Christ affirmed that He alone has the keys of death and hades that is, authority over death and the place of the dead (cf. John 5:21-26; 1 Cor. 15:54-57; Heb. 2:14; Rev. 20:12-14). Though the glorified Christ is to be revered, faithful believers like John can be sure they are accepted by the Son of God. The Christian's death and resurrection are both in His hands. This picture of Christ glorified contrasts with the portrayal of Christ as a Man in the four Gospels (cf. Phil. 2:6-8), except for His transfiguration (Matt. 17:2; Mark 9:2).

D. The command to write (1:19-20)

1:19-20. Following the revelation of Christ in glory, John was again commanded to write. The subject of his record has three tenses: (a) what he had already experienced: what you have seen; (b) the present experiences: what is now; and (c) the future: what will take place later. This appears to be the divine outline of Revelation. What John was told to write was first a record of his experience (chap. 1), now history. Then he was to write the present message of Christ to seven churches (chaps. 2-3). Finally, the main purpose of the book being prophetic, he was to introduce the events preceding, culminating in, and following the second coming of Christ (chaps. 4-22).

The chronological division of the Book of Revelation is much superior to many other outlines in which interpreters often seize on incidental phrases or manipulate the book to fit their peculiar schemes of interpretation. This outline harmonizes beautifully with the concept that most of Revelation (beginning in chap. 4) is future, not historic or merely symbolic, or simply statements of principles. It is significant that only a futuristic interpretation of Revelation 4-22 has any consistency. Interpreters following the allegorical approach to the book seldom agree among themselves on their views. This is also true of those holding to the symbolic and historical approaches.

In Revelation a symbol of vision is often presented first, and then its interpretation is given. So here the seven stars were declared to be the angels or messengers of the seven churches, and the seven lampstands are the seven churches themselves. The Book of Revelation, instead of being a hopeless jumble of symbolic vision, is a carefully written record of what John saw and heard, with frequent explanations of its theological and practical meanings.

Revelation, with assistance from such other symbolic books as Daniel and Ezekiel, was intended by God to be understood by careful students of the entire Word of God. Like the Book of Daniel, it will be better understood as history unfolds. Though timeless in its truth and application, it is a special comfort to those who need guidance in the days leading up to Christ's second coming.

Before unfolding the tremendous prophetic scenes of chapters 4-22, Christ first gave a personal message to each of the seven churches with obvious practical applications to His church today.

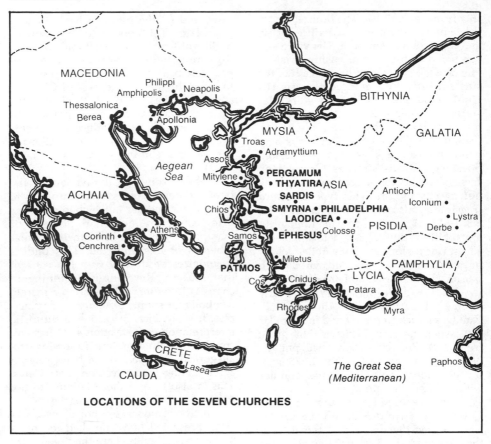

LOCATIONS OF THE SEVEN CHURCHES

II. Letters to the Seven Churches: "What Is Now" (chaps. 2–3)

As stated in Revelation 1:11 Christ sent a message to each of seven local churches in Asia Minor. The order of scriptural presentation was geographic. A messenger would naturally travel the route from the seaport Ephesus 35 miles north to another seaport Smyrna, proceed still farther north and to the east, to Pergamos, and then would swing further to the east and south to visit the other four cities (1:11).

There has been much debate as to the meaning of these messages for today. Obviously these churches were specially selected and providentially arranged to provide characteristic situations which the church has faced throughout its history. Just as Paul's epistles, though addressed to individual churches, are also intended for the entire church, so these seven messages also apply to the entire church today insofar as they are in similar situations. There were many other churches such as those at Colosse, Magnesia, and Tralles, some larger than the seven churches mentioned in Asia Minor, but these were not addressed.

As the contents of the letters are analyzed, it is clear that they are, first, messages to these historic local churches in the first century. Second, they also constitute a message to similar churches today. Third, individual exhortations to persons or groups in the churches make it clear that the messages are intended for individuals today. Fourth, some believe that the order of the seven churches follows the order of various eras in church history from the first century until now.

There are some remarkable similarities in comparing these letters to the seven churches to the movement of church history since the beginning of the apostolic church. For instance, Ephesus seems to characterize the apostolic church as a whole, and Smyrna seems to depict the church in its early persecutions. However, the Scriptures do not expressly authorize this interpretation, and it should be applied only where it fits naturally. After all, these churches all existed simultaneously in the first century.

Though each message is different, the letters have some similarities. In each one Christ declared that He knows their works; each one includes a promise to those who overcome; each one gives an exhortation to those hearing; and each letter has a particular description of Christ that related to the message which follows. Each letter includes a commendation (except the letter to Laodicea), a rebuke (except the letters to Smyrna and Philadelphia), an exhortation, and an encouraging promise to those heeding its message. In general these letters to the seven churches address the problems inherent in churches throughout church history and are an incisive and comprehensive revelation of how Christ evaluates local churches.

This portion of Scripture has been strangely neglected. While many turn to the epistles of Paul and other portions of the New Testament for church truth, often the letters to these seven churches, though coming from Christ Himself and being climactic in character, are completely ignored. This neglect has contributed to churches today not conforming to God's perfect will.

A. The letter to the church in Ephesus (2:1-7)

1. DESTINATION (2:1)

2:1. At the time this letter was written, **Ephesus** was a major city of Asia Minor, a seaport, and the location of the great temple of Artemis (cf. Acts 19:24, 27-28, 34-35), one of the seven wonders of the ancient world. Paul had visited Ephesus about A.D. 53, about 43 years before this letter in Revelation was sent to them. Paul remained in Ephesus for several years and preached the gospel so effectively "that all the Jews and Greeks who lived in the province of Asia heard the word of the Lord" (Acts 19:10). This large city was thoroughly stirred by Paul's message (Acts 19:11-41), with the result that the silversmiths created a riot because their business of making shrines of Artemis was threatened.

The church accordingly had a long history and was the most prominent one in the area. The pastor or messenger of the church was addressed as **the angel** (*angelos*). The word's principal use in the Bible is in reference to heavenly angels (William F. Arndt and F. Wilbur Gingrich, *A Greek-English Lexicon of the New Testament.* Chicago: University of Chicago Press, 1957, pp. 7-8). But it is also used to refer to human messengers (cf. Matt. 11:10; Mark 1:2; Luke 7:24, 27; 9:52).

Christ was holding **seven stars in His right hand** and walking **among the seven golden lampstands.** The "stars" were the angels or messengers of the churches and the "lampstands" were the seven churches (1:20).

2. COMMENDATION (2:2-3)

2:2-3. Christ commended those in the Ephesian church for their **hard work . . . perseverance,** their condemnation of **wicked men,** and their identification of **false** apostles. (False teachers were present in each of the first four churches; cf. vv. 2, 6, 9, 14-15, 20.) In addition they were commended for enduring **hardships** and **not** growing **weary** in serving God. In general this church had continued in its faithful service to God for more than 40 years.

3. REBUKE (2:4)

2:4. In spite of the many areas of commendation, the church in Ephesus was soundly rebuked: **Yet I hold this against you: you have forsaken your first love.** The order of words in the Greek is emphatic; the clause could be translated, "Your first love you have left." Christ used the word *agapēn,* speaking of the deep kind of love that God has for people. This rebuke contrasts with what Paul wrote the Ephesians 35 years earlier, that he never stopped giving thanks for them because of their faith in Christ and their love (*agapēn*) for the saints (Eph. 1:15-16). Most of the Ephesian Christians were now second-generation believers, and though they had retained purity of doctrine and life and had maintained a high level of service, they were lacking in deep devotion to Christ. How the church today needs to heed this same warning, that orthodoxy and service are not enough. Christ wants believers' hearts as well as their hands and heads.

4. EXHORTATION (2:5-6)

2:5-6. The Ephesians were first reminded to **remember the height from which you have fallen!** They were told to **repent** and to return to the love they had left. Similar exhortations concerning the need for a deep love for God are frequently found in the New Testament (Matt. 22:37; Mark 12:30; Luke 10:27; John 14:15, 21, 23; 21:15-16; James 2:5; 1 Peter 1:8). Christ stated that one's love for God should be greater than his love for his closest relatives, including his father, mother, son, and daughter (Matt. 10:37). Paul added that love for God should even be above one's love for his or her mate (1 Cor. 7:32-35). In calling the Ephesian believers to repentance Christ was asking them to change their attitude as well as their affections. They were to continue their service not simply because it was right but because they loved Christ. He warned them that if they did not respond, the light of their witness in Ephesus would be extinguished: **I will . . . remove your lampstand from its place.** The church continued and was later the scene of a major church council, but after the 5th century both the church and the city declined. The immediate area has been uninhabited since the 14th century.

One additional word of commendation was inserted. They were commended because they hated **the practices of the Nicolaitans.** There has been much speculation concerning the identity of the Nicolaitans, but the Scriptures do not specify who they were. They apparently were a sect wrong in practice and in doctrine (for further information see Henry Alford, *The Greek Testament*, 4: 563–65; Merrill C. Tenney, *Interpreting Revelation*, pp. 60-1; Walvoord, *Revelation*, p. 58).

5. PROMISE (2:7)

2:7. As in the other letters, Christ gave the Ephesian church a promise addressed to individuals who will hear. He stated, **To him who overcomes, I will give the right to eat from the tree of life, which is in the paradise of God.** The tree of life, first mentioned in Genesis 3:22, was in the Garden of Eden. Later it reappears in the New Jerusalem where it bears abundant fruit (Rev. 22:2). Those who eat of it will never die (Gen. 3:22). This promise should not be construed as reward for only a special group of Christians but a normal expectation for all Christians. "The paradise of God" is probably a name for heaven (cf. Luke 23:43; 2 Cor. 12:4—the only other NT references to paradise). Apparently it will be identified with the New Jerusalem in the eternal state.

This encouragement to true love reminded them again of God's gracious provision for salvation in time and eternity. Love for God is not wrought by legalistically observing commands, but by responding to one's knowledge and appreciation of God's love.

B. The letter to the church in Smyrna (2:8-11)

1. DESTINATION (2:8)

2:8. The second letter was addressed to **Smyrna,** a large and wealthy city 35 miles north of Ephesus. Like Ephesus, it was a seaport. In contrast to Ephesus, which today is a deserted ruin, Smyrna is still a large seaport with a present population of about 200,000. Christ described Himself as **the First and the Last, who died and came to life again.** Christ is portrayed as the eternal One (cf. 1:8, 17; 21:6; 22:13) who suffered death at the hands of His persecutors and then was resurrected from the grave (cf. 1:5). These aspects of Christ were especially relevant to the Christians at Smyrna who, like Christ in His death, were experiencing severe persecution.

The name of the city, Smyrna, means "myrrh," an ordinary perfume. It was also used in the anointing oil of the tabernacle, and in embalming dead bodies (cf. Ex. 30:23; Ps. 45:8; Song 3:6; Matt. 2:11; Mark 15:23; John 19:39). While the Christians of the church at Smyrna were experiencing the bitterness of suffering, their faithful testimony was like myrrh or sweet perfume to God.

2. COMMENDATION (2:9)

2:9. What a comfort it was to the Christians in Smyrna to know that Christ knew all about their sufferings: **I know your afflictions and your poverty—yet you are rich!** Besides suffering persecution, they were also enduring extreme poverty (*ptōcheian* in contrast with *penia*, the ordinary word for "poverty"). Though extremely poor, they were rich in the wonderful promises Christ had given them (cf. 2 Cor. 6:10; James 2:5). They were being persecuted not only by pagan Gentiles but also by hostile Jews and by Satan himself. Apparently the local Jewish synagogue was called the **synagogue of Satan** (cf. Rev. 3:9). (Satan is mentioned in four of the seven letters: 2:9, 13, 24; 3:9.) In the history of the church the most severe persecution has come from religionists.

3. REBUKE

Notable is the fact that there was no rebuke whatever for these faithful, suffering Christians. This is in striking contrast with Christ's evaluations of five of the other six churches, which He rebuked. Smyrna's sufferings, though extremely difficult, had helped keep them pure in faith and life.

4. EXHORTATION (2:10A)

2:10a. The word of Christ to these suffering Christians was an exhortation to have courage: **Do not be afraid** (lit., stop being afraid) **of what you are about to suffer.** Their severe trials were to continue. They would receive further **persecution** by imprisonment and additional suffering **for 10 days.** Some have taken these words "for 10 days" as a symbolic representation of the entire persecution of the church; others think it refers to 10 persecutions under Roman rulers. The most probable meaning is that it anticipated a limited period of time for suffering (cf. Walvoord, *Revelation*, pp. 61-2). Scott finds precedence in Scripture that 10 days means a limited period of time (Walter Scott, *Exposition of the Revelation of Jesus Christ*, p. 69). He cites Genesis 24:55; Nehemiah 5:18; Jeremiah 42:7; Daniel 1:12; Acts 25:6. Alford holds the same position, citing Numbers 11:19; 14:22; 1 Samuel 1:8; Job 19:3 (*The Greek Testament*, 4:567).

The problem of human suffering, even for a limited time, has always perplexed faithful Christians. Suffering can be expected for the ungodly, but why

should the godly suffer? The Scriptures give a number of reasons. Suffering may be (1) disciplinary (1 Cor. 11:30-32; Heb. 12:3-13), (2) preventive (as Paul's thorn in the flesh, 2 Cor. 12:7), (3) the learning of obedience (as Christ's suffering, Heb. 5:8; cf. Rom. 5:3-5), or (4) the providing of a better testimony for Christ (as in Acts 9:16).

5. PROMISE (2:10B-11)

2:10b-11. In their suffering the believers at Smyrna were exhorted, **Be faithful, even to the point of death.** While their persecutors could take their physical lives, it would only result in their receiving **the crown of life.** Apparently up to this time none had died, but this could be expected. Later Polycarp, having become the bishop of the church in Smyrna, was martyred, and undoubtedly others were also killed (cf. Robert Jamieson, A. R. Fausset, and David Brown, *A Commentary Critical, Experimental and Practical on the Old and New Testaments.* Grand Rapids: Wm. B. Eerdmans Publishing Co., 1945. 6:662). "The crown of life" is one of several crowns promised to Christians (cf. 1 Cor. 9:25; 1 Thes. 2:19; 2 Tim. 4:6-8; 1 Peter 5:4; Rev. 4:4). The crown of life is also mentioned in James 1:12. Believers are encouraged to be faithful by contemplating what awaits them after death, namely, eternal life.

As in all the letters, an exhortation is given to the individuals who will listen. The promise is given to overcomers, referring in general to all believers, assuring them that they **will not be hurt at all by the second death** (cf. Rev. 20:15).

The reassuring word of Christ to Smyrna is the word to all suffering and persecuted Christians. As stated in Hebrews 12:11, "No discipline seems pleasant at the time, but painful. Later on, however, it produces a harvest of righteousness and peace for those who have been trained by it."

C. The letter to the church in Pergamum (2:12-17)

1. DESTINATION (2:12)

2:12. The third church was in **Pergamum** or Pergamos, about 20 miles inland from Smyrna. Like Ephesus and Smyrna it was a wealthy city, but it was wicked.

People in its pagan cults worshiped Athena, Asclepius, Dionysus, and Zeus. Pergamum was famous for its university with a library of about 200,000 volumes, and for manufacturing parchment resulting in a paper called *pergamena*. The atmosphere of this city was adverse to any effective Christian life and testimony.

Anticipating Christ's rebuke for their being tolerant of evil and immorality, John described **Him** as the One **who has the sharp, double-edged sword** (also mentioned in 1:16; 2:16; 19:15, 21). The sword is a symbolic representation of the Word of God's twofold ability to separate believers from the world and to condemn the world for its sin. It was the sword of salvation as well as the sword of death.

2. COMMENDATION (2:13)

2:13. Following the same order as in the two preceding letters, commendation is given first. Christ recognized the difficulty of their situation. They lived **where Satan has his throne.** This may refer to the great temple of Asclepius, a pagan god of healing represented in the form of a serpent. Further recognition of Satan is indicated at the close of the verse. Pergamum was **where Satan lives.** The saints there were commended for being true, **even** when **Antipas** (which means "against all") was martyred. Nothing is known of this incident. The Christians at Pergamum had been true to God under severe testing but had compromised their testimony in other ways, as seen in the next two verses.

3. REBUKE (2:14-15)

2:14-15. They had been guilty of severe compromise by holding **the teaching of Balaam** and **the teaching of the Nicolaitans.** Balaam had been guilty of counseling King **Balak** to cause Israel **to sin** through intermarriage with heathen women and through idol-worship (cf. Num. 22–25; 31:15-16). Intermarriage with heathen women was a problem in Pergamum where any social contact with the world also involved worship of idols. Usually meat in the marketplace had been offered to idols earlier (cf. 1 Cor. 8).

They were also condemned for following the Nicolaitans' teaching. Earlier the Ephesian church had been commended for rejecting what appears to be a moral departure (cf. Rev. 2:6). Some Greek manuscripts add here that God hates the teaching of the Nicolaitans, as also stated in v. 6. Compromise with worldly morality and pagan doctrine was prevalent in the church, especially in the third century when Christianity became popular. So compromise with pagan morality and departure from biblical faith soon corrupted the church.

4. EXHORTATION (2:16)

2:16. Christ sharply rebuked the church with the abrupt command, **Repent therefore!** They were warned, **Otherwise, I will soon come to you and will fight against them with the sword of My mouth.** He promised that the judgment would come "soon" (*tachys*) which also means "suddenly" (cf. 1:1; 22:7, 12, 20). Christ would contend with them, using the sword of His mouth (cf. 1:16; 2:12; 19:15, 21). This again is the Word of God sharply judging all compromise and sin.

5. PROMISE (2:17)

2:17. The final exhortation to individuals, as in the messages to other churches, is again addressed to those who are willing to **hear.** Overcomers are promised **hidden manna** and **a white stone with a new name written on it.** The "hidden manna" may refer to Christ as the Bread from heaven, the unseen source of the believer's nourishment and strength. Whereas Israel received physical food, manna, the church receives spiritual food (John 6:48-51).

Scholars differ as to the meaning of the "white stone." Alford is probably right in saying that the important point is the stone's inscription which gives the believer "a new name," indicating acceptance by God and his title to glory (*The Greek Testament,* 4:572). This may be an allusion to the Old Testament practice of the high priest wearing 12 stones on his breastplate with the names of the 12 tribes of Israel inscribed on it. Though believers at Pergamum may not have had precious stones or gems of this world, they had what is far more important, acceptance by Christ Himself and assurance of infinite blessings to come. Taken as a whole, the message to the church in Pergamum is a warning against compromise in morals or teaching and against deviating from the purity of doctrine required of Christians.

D. The letter to the church in Thyatira (2:18-29)

1. DESTINATION (2:18)

2:18. Thyatira, 40 miles southeast of Pergamum, was a much smaller city. Thyatira was situated in an area noted for its abundant crops and the manufacture of purple dye. The church was small, but it was singled out for this penetrating letter of rebuke.

In keeping with what follows, Christ is introduced as **the Son of God, whose eyes are like blazing fire and whose feet are like burnished bronze.** This description of Christ is similar to that in 1:13-15, but here He is called the Son of God rather than the Son of Man. The situation required reaffirmation of His deity and His righteous indignation at their sins. The words "burnished bronze," which describe His feet, translate a rare Greek word *chalkolibanō*, also used in 1:15. It seems to have been an alloy of a number of metals characterized by brilliance when polished. The reference to His eyes being "like blazing fire" and the brilliant reflections of His feet emphasize the indignation and righteous judgment of Christ.

2. COMMENDATION (2:19)

2:19. Though much was wrong in the church at Thyatira, believers there were commended for their **love . . . faith . . . service, and perseverance** (cf. 2:2). And the Thyatira Christians were doing **more** as time went on (in contrast to the Ephesus church which did less). But despite these evidences of Christian life and testimony, the church at Thyatira had serious problems.

3. REBUKE (2:20-23)

2:20-23. Jesus' major condemnation concerned **that woman Jezebel,** who claimed to be **a prophetess** and taught believers to take part in the **sexual immorality** that accompanied pagan religion and to eat **food sacrificed to idols.** What was acceptable to that local society was abhorred by Christ. Their departure from morality had gone on for some time (v. 21). The church in Thyatira may have first heard the gospel from Lydia, converted through Paul's ministry (Acts 16:14-15). Interestingly now a woman, a self-claimed "prophetess," was influencing the church. Her name "Jezebel" suggests that she was corrupting the Thyatira church much like Ahab's wife Jezebel corrupted Israel (1 Kings 16:31-33). Christ promised sudden and immediate judgment, called her sin **adultery** and promised that all who followed her would **suffer intensely.** He also promised, **I will strike her children dead,** meaning that suffering would extend also to her followers. The judgment would be so dramatic that **all the churches** would **know that** Christ is the One **who searches hearts and minds.**

4. EXHORTATION (2:24-25)

2:24-25. After His condemnation, Christ extended a word of exhortation to the godly remnant who existed in the church in Thyatira, implying that the rest of the church was apostate. The remnant He called **the rest of you in Thyatira . . . you who do not hold to her teaching and have not learned Satan's so-called deep secrets.** On this godly remnant He imposed one simple instruction: **only hold on to what you have until I come.** Perhaps because the church was small, Christ did not command them to leave it but to remain as a godly testimony. Judgment on Jezebel and her followers would come soon and would purge the church. In modern times Christians who find themselves in apostate local churches can usually leave and join another fellowship, but this was impractical under the circumstances in Thyatira.

The parallels between Thyatira and other apostate churches throughout church history are clear. Some compare Thyatira to believers in the Middle Ages when Protestantism separated from Roman Catholicism and attempted a return to purity in doctrine and life. The prominence of Jezebel as a woman prophetess is sometimes compared to the unscriptural exaltation of Mary. The participation in idolatrous feasts can illustrate the false teaching that the Lord's Supper is another sacrifice of Christ. In spite of the apostasy of churches in the Middle Ages, there were churches then which, like the church of Thyatira, had some believers who were bright lights of faithfulness in doctrine and life.

5. PROMISE (2:26-29)

2:26-27. Christ promises believers who are faithful that they will join Him in His millennial **rule** (Ps. 2:8-9; 2 Tim. 2:12; Rev. 20:4-6). The word in verse 27 translated "rule" (*poimanei*) means "to shepherd," indicating that they will not simply be administering justice but will also, like a shepherd using his rod, be dealing with his sheep and protecting them as well. Though Psalm 2:9 refers to Christ's rule, John's quotation of it here relates the ruling (shepherding) to the believer who overcomes. Believers will have authority just as Christ does (1 Cor. 6:2-3; 2 Tim. 2:12; Rev. 3:21; 20:4, 6). Christ **received** this **authority from** His **Father** (cf. John 5:22).

2:28. In addition, the faithful will receive **the morning star,** which appears just before the dawn. The Scriptures do not explain this expression, but it may refer to participation in the Rapture of the church before the dark hours preceding the dawn of the millennial kingdom.

2:29. The letter to Thyatira closes with the familiar exhortation to **hear what the Spirit says to the churches.** Unlike the earlier letters, this exhortation follows rather than precedes the promise to overcomers, and this order is followed in the letters to the last three churches.

E. The letter to the church in Sardis (3:1-6)

1. DESTINATION (3:1A)

3:1a. The important commercial city of **Sardis** was located about 30 miles southeast of Thyatira, on an important trade route that ran east and west through the kingdom of Lydia. Important industries included jewelry, dye, and textiles, which had made the city wealthy. From a religious standpoint it was a center of pagan worship and site of a temple of Artemis, which ruins still remain (cf. comments on 2:1 regarding another temple of Artemis). Only a small village called Sart remains on the site of this once-important city. Archeologists have located the ruins of a Christian church building next to the temple. In addressing the message to the church Christ described Himself as the One **who holds the seven spirits of God and the seven stars,** similar to the description in 1:4. Here Christ said He holds them, speaking

of the Holy Spirit in relation to Himself (Isa. 11:2-5; cf. Rev. 5:6). As in 1:20 the seven stars, representing the pastors of the churches, were also in His hands (cf. 2:1).

2. COMMENDATION (3:1B)

3:1b. The only word of approval is in actuality a word of rebuke as Christ declared that they had **a reputation** for **being alive** and apparently were regarded by their contemporaries as an effective church.

3. REBUKE (3:1C, 2B)

3:1c, 2b. Christ quickly stripped away their reputation of being alive by declaring, **you are dead.** Like the Pharisees, their outer appearance was a facade hiding their lack of life (cf. Matt. 23:27-28). Christ added, **I have not found your deeds complete in the sight of My God.** They were falling far short of fulfilling their obligations as believers.

4. EXHORTATION (3:2A, 3)

3:2a, 3. They were exhorted to **wake up** from their spiritual slumber and to **strengthen** the few evidences of life they still had. He exhorted them to **remember . . . obey . . . and repent.** He warned them that if they did not heed this exhortation, He would **come** on them **like a thief,** that is, suddenly and unexpectedly.

5. PROMISE (3:4-6)

3:4-6. While this church as a whole was dead or dying, Christ recognized a godly remnant **in the Sardis** church who had **not soiled their clothes** with sin. He promised that true believers will **be dressed in white** (cf. v. 18), symbolic of the righteousness of God, that their names will remain in **the book of life,** and that He will acknowledge them as His own **before** His **Father and His angels.**

The statement that their names will not be erased from the book of life presents a problem to some. But a person who is truly born again remains regenerate, as John said elsewhere (John 5:24; 6:35-37, 39; 10:28-29). While this passage may imply that a name could be erased from the book of life, actually it only gives a positive affirmation that their names will not be erased (cf. Walvoord,

Revelation. pp. 82, 338). Six times John referred to the book of life (Rev. 3:5; 13:8 [cf. comments there]; 17:8; 20:12, 15; 21:27).

The letter also concludes with the exhortation to **hear what the Spirit says to the churches.** The letter to Sardis is a searching message to churches today that are full of activity and housed in beautiful buildings but are so often lacking in evidences of eternal life. Christ's word today is to "remember," "repent," and "obey," just as it was to the church in Sardis.

F. The letter to the church in Philadelphia (3:7-13)

1. DESTINATION (3:7)

3:7. The city of **Philadelphia** was 28 miles southeast of Sardis. It was located in an area noted for its agricultural products but afflicted with earthquakes which destroyed the city several times, most recently about A.D. 37. The city was named for a king of Pergamum, Attalus Philadelphus, who had built it. "Philadelphus" is similar to the Greek word *philadelphia,* meaning "brotherly love," which occurs seven times in the Bible (Rom. 12:10; 1 Thes. 4:9; Heb. 13:1; 1 Peter 1:22; 2 Peter 1:7[twice]; Rev. 3:7). Only here is it used of the city itself. Christian testimony continues in the city in this present century.

Christ described Himself as the One **who is holy and true, who holds the key of David,** and who is able to open or shut a door which no one else could open or shut. The holiness of Christ is a frequent truth in Scripture (1 Peter 1:15), and being holy He is worthy to judge the spiritual life of the Philadelphia church. "The key of David" seems to refer to Isaiah 22:22, where the key of the house of David was given to Eliakim who then had access to all the wealth of the king. Christ earlier had been described as the One who holds "the keys of death and hades" (Rev. 1:18). The reference here, however, seems to be to spiritual treasures.

2. COMMENDATION (3:8-9)

3:8. As in the messages to the other churches, Christ stated, **I know your deeds.** In keeping with the description of His authority to open and close doors (v. 7), He declared, **See, I have placed before you an open door that no one can shut.** There is no word of rebuke, though Christ said, **I know that you have little strength.** These words, however, become a basis for His commendation that **you have kept My word and have not denied My name.**

3:9. Christ referred to their enemies as the **synagogue of Satan** (cf. 2:9). They were Jews who opposed the believers' Christian testimony. False religion has always been a formidable antagonist against true Christian faith. The day will come, however, when all opponents of the faith will have to acknowledge the truth (cf. Isa. 45:23; Rom. 14:11; Phil. 2:10-11). Then Christ declared, **I will make them come and fall down at your feet and acknowledge that I have loved you.**

3. PROMISE (3:10-12)

3:10. The church in Philadelphia received no rebuke from Christ. Instead they were commended and given a promise because they had been willing to **endure patiently.** The promise was, **I will also keep you from the hour of trial that is going to come upon the whole world to test those who live on the earth.** This is an explicit promise that the Philadelphia church will not endure the hour of trial which is unfolded, beginning in Revelation 6. Christ was saying that the Philadelphia church would not enter the future time of trouble; He could not have stated it more explicitly. If Christ had meant to say that they would be preserved *through* a time of trouble, or would be *taken out* from within the Tribulation, a different verb and a different preposition would have been required.

Though scholars have attempted to avoid this conclusion in order to affirm posttribulationism, the combination of the verb "keep" (*tērein*) with the preposition "from" (*ek*) is in sharp contrast to the meaning of keeping the church "through" (*dia*), a preposition which is not used here. The expression "the hour of trial" (a time period) makes it clear that they would be kept *out of* that period. It is difficult to see how Christ could have made this promise to this local church if it were God's intention for the entire church to go through the Tribulation that will come on the entire world. Even though the church at Philadelphia would go to glory via death long before the time of trouble would come, if the church here is taken to be typical of the body of Christ standing true to the faith, the promise seems to go beyond the Philadelphia church to all those who are believers in Christ (cf. Walvoord, *Revelation*, pp. 86-8).

3:11. Additional promises were given. Christ promised, **I am coming soon,** a concept repeated often in the Book of Revelation. The thought is not simply that of coming soon but coming suddenly or quickly (cf. 1:1; 2:16). They were exhorted in the light of His coming to continue to **hold on to what** they **have.**

3:12. Everyone who is an overcomer will become **a pillar in the temple of . . . God.** This is of course symbolic of the permanent place in heaven for believers, referred to here as the temple of God. The entire New Jerusalem will be the ultimate temple (21:22). In contrast to earthly temples and earthly pillars which fall, believers will continue forever in the temple. Christ specified that He was referring to **the city of My God,** that is, the New Jerusalem (cf. 21:2). He repeated His promise: **I will also write on him My new name** (cf. 2:17; 14:1; 19:12). Because believers have identified with Christ by faith, He will identify Himself with them.

4. EXHORTATION (3:13)

3:13. The letter closed with the familiar appeal, **hear what the Spirit says to the churches.** The promise given to the Philadelphia church and the challenge to continue to be faithful is certainly God's Word to His whole church today.

G. *The letter to the church in Laodicea (3:14-22)*

1. DESTINATION (3:14)

3:14. The wealthy city of **Laodicea** was located on the road to Colosse about 40 miles southeast of Philadelphia. About 35 years before this letter was written, Laodicea was destroyed by an earthquake, but it had the wealth and ability to rebuild. Its main industry was wool cloth. There is no record that Paul ever visited this city, but he was concerned about it (Col. 2:1-2; 4:16).

In addressing the church Christ introduced Himself as **the Amen, the faithful and true Witness, the Ruler of**

God's creation. The word "Amen," meaning "so be it," refers to the sovereignty of God which is behind human events (cf. 2 Cor. 1:20; Rev. 1:6). In speaking of Himself as "the faithful and true Witness" Christ was repeating what He had said earlier (1:5; 3:7). As "the Ruler of God's creation" Christ existed before God's Creation and is sovereign over it (cf. Col 1:15, 18; Rev. 21:6). This description was in preparation for the stern word of rebuke which Christ would give the church in Laodicea.

2. REBUKE (3:15-17)

3:15-16. No word of commendation was extended to the Laodicean church. They were pictured as utterly abhorrent to Christ because they were **lukewarm.** This was addressed to the church and also to the messenger or the pastor whom some believe was Archippus (Col. 4:17). It is improbable, however, that Archippus, if he had been the pastor of the church, was still living. In referring to the church as "lukewarm" Christ had in mind that this was its permanent situation. In their feasts as well as in their religious sacrifices people in the ancient world customarily drank what was either hot or cold—never lukewarm. This rebuke would have been especially meaningful to this church, for water was piped to the city from Hierapolis, a few miles north. By the time the water reached Laodicea, it was lukewarm!

3:17. Their being lukewarm spiritually was evidenced by their being content with their material **wealth** and their being unaware of their spiritual poverty. Christ used strong words to describe them: **wretched, pitiful, poor, blind, and naked.**

3. EXHORTATION (3:18-19)

3:18-19. They were urged to buy not ordinary gold, but **refined** gold, referring to that which would glorify God and make them truly rich. Through its banking industry the city had material wealth. But the church lacked spiritual richness. Though they had beautiful clothes, they were urged to wear **white clothes** (cf. v. 4), symbolic of righteousness which would cover their spiritual **nakedness.** As wool was a major product of the area, Laodicea was especially

THE LETTERS TO THE SEVEN CHURCHES

	Christ	Commendation	Rebuke	Exhortation	Promise
Ephesus (2:1-7)	Holds the seven stars in His right hand and walks among the seven golden lampstands.	Deeds, hard work, perseverance. Does not tolerate wicked men. Endures hardships. Hates the practices of the Nicolaitans.	Has forsaken her first love.	Remember; repent; do the things you did at first.	Will eat from the tree of life.
Smyrna (2:8-11)	The First and the Last, who died and came to life again.	Suffers persecution and poverty.	—	Do not be afraid. Be faithful, even to the point of death.	Will receive a crown of life; will not be hurt by the second death.
Pergamum (2:12-17)	Has the sharp, double-edged sword.	Remains true to Christ; does not renounce her faith.	People there hold the teachings of Balaam and of the Nicolaitans.	Repent.	Will receive hidden manna and a white stone with a new name on it.
Thyatira (2:18-29)	The Son of God, whose eyes are like blazing fire and whose feet are like burnished brass.	Deeds, love, faith, service, perseverance, doing more than at first.	Tolerates Jezebel with her immorality and idolatry.	Repent; hold on to what you have.	Will have authority over the nations; the morning star.
Sardis (3:1-6)	Holds the seven spirits of God and the seven stars.	Deeds; reputation of being alive.	Dead.	Wake up! Strengthen what remains. Remember what you received, obey it, repent.	Will be dressed in white; will be acknowledged before My Father and His angels.
Philadelphia (3:7-13)	Holy and true, holds the key of David.	Deeds, keeps Christ's word and does not deny His name, endures patiently.	—	Hold on to what you have.	Those who overcome will be pillars in the temple; the name of God, of the New Jerusalem, and of Christ's new name, will be written on them.
Laodicea (3:14-22)	The Amen, the faithful and true Witness, the Ruler of God's creation.	—	Lukewarm, neither cold nor hot. Wretched, pitiful, poor, blind, and naked.	Buy from Christ refined gold, white clothes, and eye salve. Be earnest, and repent.	Overcomers will eat with Christ; will rule with Christ.

famous for a black garment made out of black wool. What they needed instead was pure white clothing.

Then Christ exhorted them to put **salve . . . on** their **eyes.** A medical school was located in Laodicea at the temple of Asclepius, which offered a special salve to heal common eye troubles of the Middle East. What they needed was not this medicine but spiritual sight. The church at Laodicea is typical of a modern church quite unconscious of its spiritual needs and content with beautiful buildings and all the material things money can buy. This is a searching and penetrating message. To all such the exhortation is **be earnest, and repent.** Christ rebuked them because He loved them, which love would also bring chastisement on this church.

4. PROMISE (3:20-22)

3:20-21. Dramatically Christ pictured Himself as standing outside and knocking on a **door.** In a familiar painting the latch is not shown but is assumed to be on the inside. The appeal is for those who hear to open the door. To them Christ promised, **I will go in and eat with him, and he with Me.** With Christ on the outside, there can be no fellowship or genuine wealth. With Christ on the inside, there is wonderful fellowship and sharing of the marvelous grace of God. This was an appeal to Christians rather than to non-Christians. This raises the important question concerning the extent of one's intimate fellowship with Christ. To those who respond, Christ promises to give the right to **sit with** Him on His **throne** and share His victory.

3:22. Once again the invitation to listen and respond is given: **He who has an ear, let him hear what the Spirit says to the churches.**

The letters to the seven churches are a remarkably complete treatment of problems that face the church today. The recurring dangers of losing their first love (2:4), of being afraid of suffering (2:10), doctrinal defection (2:14-15), moral departure (2:20), spiritual deadness (3:1-2), not holding fast (v. 11), and lukewarmness (vv. 15-16) are just as prevalent today as they were in first-century churches. Because these letters come from Christ personally, they take on significance as God's final word of exhortation to the church down through the centuries. The final appeal is to all individuals who will hear. People in churches today would do well to listen.

III. The Revelation of the Future: "What Will Take Place Later" (chaps. 4-22)

In keeping with the divine outline given in 1:19, God unfolded to John the details of the future, "what will take place later." This includes the stirring events leading up to the second coming of Christ (chaps. 4-18); then the Second Coming itself (chap. 19); then the aftermath, the millennial kingdom (chap. 20); and finally the New Jerusalem and the new heaven and new earth (chaps. 21-22). It is obvious that the central truth is the second coming of Christ in chapter 19, just as the central feature of the four Gospels was the first coming of Christ.

While many interpretations of the Book of Revelation have been suggested, the only views which provide a cogent understanding are those which consider the book, beginning with chapter 4, as referring to future events. Any other system of interpretation gets lost in a maze of conflicting opinions.

While the events portrayed in this futuristic section are not necessarily all in strict chronological order, they are all yet future. As such, they present a more graphic picture of the future, given in more detail, than is found in any other part of the Bible. Such a revelation is a fitting climax to all the biblical prophecies relating to human history, which are properly centered in the person and work of Jesus Christ.

The revelation of the future opens with a vision of heaven (chaps. 4-5). Beginning in chapter 6 the seven seals, as they are broken, constitute the main chronological movement of the Great Tribulation, leading up to the second coming of Christ. The seven trumpets give the details of events which will follow the breaking of the seventh seal. Likewise in chapter 16 the seven bowls of the wrath of God unfold the content of the seventh trumpet.

The order is climactic, and as the period approaches the second coming of Christ, events occur with increasing rapidity and greater devastation. Once Christ's second coming is revealed, the concluding chapters briefly summarize the wide expanse of future events— chapter 20 relating to the millennial kingdom, and chapters 21–22 describing the new heaven and the new earth.

It is obvious that the main purpose of the Book of Revelation is to present the second coming of Christ and accompanying events and to alert the people of God as well as the world as a whole to the importance of being prepared for God's coming judgment.

A. The vision of the heavenly throne (chap. 4)

1. THE INVITATION (4:1)

4:1. John saw the vision of the heavenly throne after he heard the revelation of the messages to the churches. The time sequence is indicated by the expression **after this** (*meta tauta*, in the NASB, "after these things").

John saw **a door . . . open in heaven** and heard a **voice** inviting him, **Come up here, and I will show you what must take place after this.** The words "what must take place after this" are similar to those in 1:19, "what will take place later." Whereas 1:19 indicates that the events *will* take place later, in 4:1b the Greek word *dei* is used, which means that the events *must* occur. This points not only to the future but also to the sovereign purpose of God. The similarity of the two expressions confirms the threefold chronological outline given in 1:19. Both the revelation and its fulfillment are chronologically subsequent to chapters 1–3.

2. THE HEAVENLY THRONE (4:2-3)

4:2-3. John stated that immediately he **was in the Spirit** (or "in [my] spirit"; cf. 1:10; 17:3) meaning that experientially he was taken up to heaven though his body was actually still on the island of Patmos. **In heaven** he saw a great **throne** with One **sitting on it** who **had the appearance of jasper and carnelian.** This jasper (cf. 21:18) is a clear stone in contrast to the opaque jasper stones known today; it may have resembled a diamond. The carnelian, also known as ruby (the NIV trans. it "ruby" in the OT), and sardius, were a ruby-red color. The jasper and the carnelian were the first and last of the 12 gemstones worn on the high priest's breast (cf. Ex. 28:17-21). Jasper and sardius were used in relation to the king of Tyre (Ezek. 28:13) and will be in the foundation of the New Jerusalem (Rev. 21:19-20). The throne's overall appearance was one of great beauty and color, enhanced by **a rainbow, resembling an emerald,** which **encircled the throne.** The green color of the emerald added further beauty to the scene.

3. THE 24 ELDERS (4:4)

4:4. Around the principal **throne** were **24** lesser **thrones** on which were **seated . . . 24 elders. They were dressed in white** and were wearing **crowns of gold on their heads.** The crowns were similar to those given victors in Greek games (*stephanos*), in contrast with the crown of a sovereign ruler (*diadēma*, "diadem"). The crowns seem to indicate that the elders had been judged and rewarded.

There has been much speculation on the identity of the elders. The two major views are (1) that they represent the church raptured prior to this time and rewarded in heaven, or (2) that they are angels who have been given large responsibilities. The number 24 is the number of representation, illustrated in the fact that in the Law of Moses there were 24 orders of the priesthood. (For further discussion of the identity of the 24 elders see the comments on 5:8-10.)

4. THE SEVEN SPIRITS OF GOD (4:5)

4:5. The impressive scene of heaven was enhanced by **flashes of lightning, rumblings, and peals of thunder.** Thunder is mentioned eight times in Revelation (4:5; 6:1; 8:5; 11:19; 14:2; 16:18; 19:6). John also saw **seven lamps** which **were blazing.** These seven lamps were said to be **the seven spirits of God.** These should be understood to represent the Holy Spirit rather than seven individual spirits or angels, with the concept of the sevenfold character of the Spirit (Isa. 11:2-3; cf. Rev. 1:4; 5:6). With God the Father seated on the throne and the Holy Spirit represented by the seven lamps, the stage was then set for the revelation (chap. 5) of Christ Himself as the slain Lamb.

14 Doxologies in the Book of Revelation

References	The One(s) Giving the Praise	The One(s) Receiving the Praise
4:8	4 living creatures	God the Father
4:11	24 elders	God the Father
5:9–10	24 elders and 4 living creatures	The Lamb (Christ)
5:12	Many angels	The Lamb
5:13	Every creature	God the Father and the Lamb
7:10	Tribulation martyrs	God the Father and the Lamb
7:12	Angels, 24 elders, and 4 living creatures	God the Father
11:16–18	24 elders	God the Father
15:3–4	Tribulation saints	God the Father and the Lamb
16:5–6	Angel	God the Father
16:7	"The altar"	God the Father
19:1–3	A great multitude	God the Father
19:4	24 elders and 4 living creatures	God the Father
19:6–8	A great multitude	God the Father

5. THE FOUR LIVING CREATURES (4:6-8)

4:6-8. A sea of glass, clear as crystal, was before the throne and reflected all the brilliant colors of the entire heavenly scene (cf. 15:2). **In the center** of the picture **four living creatures** were compared to **a lion . . . an ox . . . a man** and **a flying eagle. Each of the . . . creatures had six wings and was covered with eyes all around.** They were said to be continually praising God as the **holy . . . Almighty** (*pantokratōr*; cf. 1:8; 11:17; 15:3; 16:7, 14; 19:6, 15; 21:22), and eternal One (**who was, and is, and is to come;** cf. 1:8; 11:17). This is the first of 14 doxolo-gies in the Book of Revelation (see the chart).

Many interpretations have been given of the four living creatures. As the Holy Spirit was seen symbolically in the seven lamps, probably the four living creatures symbolically represent the attributes of God including His omni-science and omnipresence (indicated by the creatures being full of eyes)—with the four animals bringing out other attributes of God: the lion indicating majesty and omnipotence; the ox, typical of faithful labor and patience; man, indicating intelligence; and the eagle, the greatest bird, representing supreme sovereignty.

Another possible view is that they represent Christ as revealed in the four Gospels: in Matthew, the lion of the tribe of Judah; in Mark, the ox as the servant of Yahweh; in Luke, the incarnate human Jesus; and in John, the eagle as the divine Son of God. Another alternative is that the four living creatures are angels (cf. Isa. 6:2-3), who extol the attributes of God.

6. WORSHIP IN HEAVEN (4:9-11)

4:9-11. The worship by the four **living creatures** is attended by **the 24 elders** also worshiping the One **on the throne** and attributing to God **glory and honor and power** (cf. 5:12-13) and acknowledging that He is the Creator and Sustainer of the universe (cf. John 1:3; Eph. 3:9; Col. 1:16-17; Heb. 1:2-3; Rev. 10:6; 14:7). **They lay their crowns before the throne** in ascribing all glory to Him as the Sovereign.

B. The seven-sealed scroll (chap. 5)

1. THE SEVEN-SEALED SCROLL INTRODUCED (5:1)

5:1. All of chapter 4 is an introduction to the main point of chapters 4–5, that is, to introduce the **scroll** with its **seven seals.** The symbolic presentation showed a scroll or a rolled-up parchment with seven seals affixed to the side in such a way that if unrolled the seven seals would need to be broken one by one.

2. THE QUESTION, "WHO IS WORTHY?" (5:2-5)

5:2-5. John **saw a mighty angel** (cf. 10:1; 18:21) and heard him ask **in a loud voice, Who is worthy to break the seals and open the scroll?** This is the first of 20 times "loud voice" occurs in Revelation. The last is in 21:3. The Greek word rendered "scroll" is *biblion*, from which is derived the word "Bible." When **no one** was found to be worthy, John **wept and wept** (lit., "kept on shedding many tears"). **One** of the 24 **elders,** however, told him not to weep, and introduced him to **the Lion of the tribe of Judah, the Root of David** (cf. Isa. 11:1; Rev. 22:16). The elder informed John that He had **triumphed,** that is, had already achieved victory, and that He alone was **able to break the seals** and **open the scroll.**

3. THE LAMB (5:6-7)

5:6-7. Though introduced as a "Lion" (v. 5), what John **saw** was **a Lamb** that appeared to have been **slain** or sacrificed. Yet the Lamb was **standing in the center of the throne.** About Him were the 24 **elders** and **the four living creatures.** The Lamb **had seven horns and seven eyes.**

The Lion and the Lamb surely refer to Christ, with the Lamb referring to His first coming and His death and the Lion referring to His second coming and His sovereign judgment of the world. This is the only place in Revelation where Christ is called a Lion, whereas the word "Lamb" (*arnion*, "a small or young lamb") is found 27 times in Revelation and nowhere else in the New Testament. But two similar words for a sacrificial lamb are used in the New Testament: *arēn*, found only in Luke 10:3, and *amnos,* which occurs four times (John 1:29, 36; Acts 8:32; 1 Peter 1:19).

Since horns symbolize strength (1 Kings 22:11), the "seven horns" represent the authority and strength of a ruler (Dan. 7:24; Rev. 13:1). The "seven eyes" defined as **the seven spirits of God** (cf. Zech. 3:9; 4:10) symbolically represent the Holy Spirit (cf. Rev. 1:4, 4:5). Because He alone is worthy, the Lamb **took the scroll from the right hand of Him who sat on the throne** (cf. Dan. 7:9, 13-14).

4. THE WORSHIP OF THE LAMB (5:8-14)

5:8. When the scroll was **taken** by the Lamb, **the 24 elders fell down before the Lamb** in worship. Each elder **had a harp** and **golden bowls full of incense,** which was interpreted as **the prayers of the saints** (cf. Ps. 141:2). While the angels presented the prayers, they were not priests or mediators. Only the harp (lyre) and the trumpet are mentioned as musical instruments in heavenly worship in the Book of Revelation.

5:9-10. In **a new song** the 4 creatures and 24 elders ascribed worthiness to the Lamb **to take the scroll** and break the seals, stating that the Lamb had been **slain** and had **purchased men for God from every tribe and language and people and nation.** Those He purchased with His **blood** were made **a kingdom and priests to serve our God** (cf. 1:6), and to **reign on the earth.** "Purchased" is from the verb *agorazō*, "to redeem." (See the chart, "New Testament Words for Redemption," at Mark 10:45.)

A textual problem exists in these verses. The Greek text used by the KJV indicates that the new song is sung by those who themselves have been redeemed: "Thou . . . has redeemed *us* to God . . . and hast made *us* unto our God kings and priests, and *we* shall reign on the earth."

The NIV, however, reads, "You purchased *men* for God. . . . You have made *them* to be a kingdom and priests to serve our God, and *they* will reign on the earth." If the KJV is correct, the 24 elders must represent the church or saints in general. If their song is impersonal as in the NIV and they simply are singing that Christ is the Redeemer of all men, it opens the possibility that the 24 elders could be angels, though it does not expressly affirm it.

While scholars differ on this point, it would seem that since the elders are on thrones and are crowned as victors, they represent the church rather than angels. Angels have not been judged and rewarded at this point in the program of God. But angels soon join the creatures and the elders in praising the Lamb (5:11-12). The two different interpretations here should not mar the beauty of the picture and the wonder of this song of praise.

5:11-12. The elders were joined by the hosts of **angels** in heaven who added their words of praise **in a loud voice.** The words **they sang** are literally "they said" (*legontes*). This is in contrast to verse 9 where the 24 elders "sang" (*adousin*). In the angels' praise they ascribed **power and wealth and wisdom and strength and honor and glory and praise** to God.

5:13-14. Every creature in heaven and on earth and under the earth and on the sea and all that is in them joined the heavenly throng in words of praise to God. In this final act of praise the four . . . creatures said Amen, and the 24 elders fell prostrate in worship.

With the heavenly vision of chapters 4–5, the stage was set for the dramatic events to follow, the opening of the seven seals. It is clear from this revelation that heaven is real, not imagined. These two chapters reveal the indescribable glory and infinite majesty of the Godhead in heaven. The following chapters reveal this sovereign power of God expressed in judgment on a wicked world sunk in unprecedented depths of sin and blasphemy. Though believers today do not have the privilege of sharing John's vision or a similar one granted to Paul (2 Cor. 12:1-3), every believer can take the word pictures of Scripture here and anticipate the glory and the wonder of the heavenly scene that he will someday see with his own eyes.

C. The opening of the six seals: the time of divine wrath (chap. 6)

1. THE FIRST SEAL (6:1-2)

Five important questions must be answered before the events of chapter 6 can be understood: *Are the events which begin with the breaking of the first seal past or future?* Though many have tried to find fulfillment in the past (see *Introduction*), there are solid reasons for believing that the revelation concerns events yet future.

The vision in chapters 4–5 is described in 4:1 as "after this," that is, after the revelation to the seven churches which is described in 1:19 as "what is now," in contrast to "what will take place later." Since the scroll in 5:1 is "sealed," the clear implication is that the seals are broken at a time after chapter 5. All attempts to find fulfillment of the seals in history have failed to yield any uniform interpretation with no two commentators agreeing. Actually there is no sequence in history that clearly corresponds to these events. So it may be concluded that they are yet future.

A second question arises: *What is the relationship of the seals to the Rapture of the church?* In the letter to Thyatira the Rapture is pictured as yet future (2:25, 28) and the Rapture is in view in the letter to the church in Philadelphia (3:10-11). Beginning in chapter 6, however, there is no reference whatever to the churches or to the Rapture that is described in familiar passages (e.g., 1 Cor. 15:51-58; 1 Thes. 4:13-18). Since neither the Rapture nor the church are the subject of Revelation 6–18, many conclude that the Rapture of the church takes place before the events beginning in chapter 4 and thus precedes the Tribulation (for full discussion see Charles C. Ryrie, *Revelation*; Charles C. Ryrie, *The Final Count-*

down; and John F. Walvoord, *The Rapture Question*).

A third question: *What is the relationship of the seals to Daniel 9:27?* Israel's program, concluding in the 70th week of Daniel, is best understood as related to the scenes here described in Revelation. Though some have tried to find historic fulfillment of Daniel 9:27, nothing in history really corresponds to it; so it is better to consider the last seven years as the final period leading up to the Second Coming and therefore still future.

A fourth question: *Does Revelation deal with the entire seven years anticipated in Daniel 9:27 or only with the last three and one-half years, often referred to as "the Great Tribulation" or "a time of great distress"?* (Jer. 30:7; Dan. 12:1; Matt. 24:21) Because the Great Tribulation is specifically mentioned in Revelation 7:14 and the same period is called "the great day of their wrath" (6:17), there seems to be clear identification of Daniel 9:27 with the events of Revelation. Most expositors assume that the events beginning in Revelation 6 cover the whole seven-year period. The Book of Revelation, however, never uses a seven-year figure but frequently refers to three and one-half years or 42 months (11:2; 13:5). Because the events of chapter 6 and afterward seem to coincide with the Great Tribulation rather than with the time of peace in the first half of the seven years (1 Thes. 5:3), there are good reasons for concluding that these great events are compacted in the last three and one-half years before Christ's return to the earth. Certainly at least by the fourth seal (Rev. 6:7-8), the events described anticipate a time of unprecedented trouble.

A fifth question: *What is the relationship of the events of Revelation to Christ's sermon on the end times?* (Matt. 24–25) As J. Dwight Pentecost points out (*Things to Come*, pp. 280-82), the order of events in Revelation and the order of events in Matthew are strikingly similar: (a) war (Matt. 24:6-7; Rev. 6:3-4), (b) famine (Matt. 24:7; Rev. 6:5-6), (c) death (Matt. 24:7-9; Rev. 6:7-8), (d) martyrdom (Matt. 24:9-10, 16-22; Rev. 6:9-11), (e) the sun and the moon darkened with stars falling (Matt. 24:29; Rev. 6:12-14), (f) divine judgment (Matt. 24:32–25:26; Rev. 6:15-17). It should be obvious that the events of Revelation have their background in previous prophecies, which aids in interpreting John's symbolic revelation. The evidence points to the conclusion that it describes the final period (probably the final three and one-half years) climaxed by the second coming of Christ to set up His kingdom (for further discussion, see Walvoord, *Revelation*, pp. 123-28; also cf. comments on Matt. 24–25).

6:1-2. As John **watched** the events after the opening of **the first . . . seal** by **the Lamb,** he saw **a white horse** with a **rider** holding **a bow,** wearing a victor's **crown** (*stephanos*), and going forth to conquer. Because Christ in His second coming is pictured (19:11) as riding on a white horse, some have taken it that this rider in 6:2 also must refer to Christ, as the white horse is a symbol of victory. Roman generals after a victory in battle would ride a white horse in triumph with their captives following. The chronology, however, is wrong, as Christ returns to the earth **as a conqueror** not at the beginning of the Tribulation but at the end of the Tribulation. Also the riders on the other horses obviously relate to destruction and judgment which precede the second coming of Christ by some period of time.

A better interpretation is that the conqueror mentioned here is the future world ruler, sometimes referred to as Antichrist though Revelation does not use this term. He is probably the same person as the ruler of the people mentioned in Daniel 9:26. This ruler has a bow without an arrow, indicating that the world government which he establishes is accomplished without warfare (see comments on Rev. 13:4). The future world government begins with a time of peace but is soon followed by destruction (1 Thes. 5:3). In general, the seals, trumpets, and bowls of divine wrath signal the terrible judgments of God on the world at the end of the Age, climaxing in the second coming of Christ.

2. THE SECOND SEAL (6:3-4)

6:3-4. With the breaking of **the second seal** a **red** horse appeared with a **rider** empowered **to take peace from the earth** (cf. "the red dragon," 12:3; the "scarlet beast," 17:3). In contrast with the first rider who has a bow without an arrow this second rider carried **a large**

947

sword. This again was a picture of political power with the rider as the world ruler.

3. THE THIRD SEAL (6:5-6)

6:5-6. With the opening of **the third seal** a **black horse** was revealed with a **rider** carrying **a pair of scales in his hand.** At the same time **a voice** was heard from **among the four living creatures** saying, **A quart of wheat for a day's wages, and three quarts of barley for a day's wages, and do not damage the oil and the wine!** "A day's wages" refers to a silver coin, the Roman denarius, worth about 15 cents, which was the normal wage for a worker for an entire day. So this passage is saying that in that food shortage an entire day's work would be required to buy either a quart of wheat or three quarts of barley. If one bought wheat, it would be enough for one good meal; if he bought barley, it would be enough for three good meals but nothing would be left for buying oil or wine. Famine is the inevitable aftermath of war. This will be a major cause of death in the Great Tribulation. The black color of the horse speaks of famine and death.

4. THE FOURTH SEAL (6:7-8)

6:7-8. A **pale horse** was introduced when **the fourth seal** was **opened.** "Pale" is literally a pale green (cf. the same word used of vegetation in Mark 6:39; Rev. 8:7; 9:4). John stated that the rider's name was **Death and** that **hades was following close behind him.** Here is the aftermath of war, famine, and death. With war and famine people fall prey to a plague and the wild beasts of the earth. The startling fact is revealed that **a fourth of the earth,** or approximately a billion people by today's population figures, will be killed by these means. It should be obvious that this is not a trivial judgment but a major factor in the Great Tribulation, thus supporting the conclusion that the Great Tribulation has begun. The first four seals may be considered as a unit and a general description of the Great Tribulation as an unprecedented time of trouble (cf. Jer. 30:7; Dan. 12:1; Matt. 24:21-22).

5. THE FIFTH SEAL (6:9-11)

6:9. With the opening of **the fifth seal** John had another revelation of heaven itself and his attention was directed to **souls** pictured as **under the altar** and identified as those **who had been slain because of the Word of God and the testimony they had maintained.** (For "under the altar," see Ex. 29:12; Lev. 4:7.) These are obviously martyrs, mentioned in more detail in Revelation 7. This makes it clear that souls will be saved in the Great Tribulation, but many of them will be martyred.

6:10-11. They will cry out to the **Lord,** asking **how long** it will be before He will **avenge** them. In reply **each** is **given a white robe** and informed that the Tribulation is not over and that others must be martyred before God's judgment on the wicked and deliverance of the righteous occurs at the Second Coming. This passage shows that the time period is the Great Tribulation, but not its end.

Spirits without any substance could not wear robes. The fact that they will be given robes supports the concept that when believers die they are given temporary bodies in heaven which are later replaced by resurrection bodies at the time of resurrection (cf. 20:4).

6. THE SIXTH SEAL (6:12-17)

6:12-14. As **the sixth seal** opened, John recorded that **a great earthquake** occurred. More dramatic than the earthquake was the transformation of the heavens with **the sun** turning **black,** the **moon** turning **blood red,** and **stars** falling like **late figs from a fig tree.** The heavens appeared **like a scroll** being rolled up. At the same time, due to the earthquake, all the mountains and islands were moved from their places. Here again in the sequence of events, the end had not been reached as there was still another seal. But this was the most dramatic judgment thus far in this time of great distress before the Second Coming.

Many expositors have attempted to see a figurative fulfillment to this prophecy. It is preferable, however, to take this prediction literally. The trumpet and bowl judgments, to be revealed later in Revelation, also include great disturbances in the heavens and on the earth before Christ's second coming.

6:15-17. The practical effect of the judgment was fear in unbelievers from all walks of life. They called on **the mountains and the rocks** to fall on them and to **hide** them from God's **wrath.** Their fear was so great they would rather be killed by a falling mountain than to face the wrath of **the Lamb** and **Their wrath,** referring to the anger of the Triune God. Again this is not a picture of ordinary trouble but the period of greatest distress in world history.

Taken as a whole, chapter 6 is one of the most important and pivotal chapters in the entire book. It describes the first six seals and also introduces the seventh seal which consists of and introduces the seven trumpets and the seven bowls of the wrath of God in chapters 8–9; 16.

The contents of chapter 6 should put to rest the false teachings that God, being a God of love, could not judge a wicked world. It also raises the important question contained in the closing words of verse 17: **Who can stand?** Only those who have availed themselves of the grace of God before the time of judgment will be able to stand when God deals with the earth in this final period of great distress. Those who will be saved in the Great Tribulation are described in the next chapter.

D. Those who will be saved in the Great Tribulation (chap. 7)

1. THE SEALING OF THE 144,000 OF ISRAEL (7:1-8)

7:1-3. The question was raised in 6:17 whether any would be saved in the Tribulation. This is answered in this chapter, and two classes of the saved are mentioned specifically: (1) those who are saved in Israel, (2) those of all nations who, though saved spiritually, are martyred. **Four angels** were told to withhold judgment on **the earth** until the **servants of** . . . **God** were sealed (v. 3). The **seal on** their **foreheads** symbolizes protection and ownership and God's intention to protect the 12 tribes that are mentioned, much as He protected Noah from the Flood, Israel from the plagues of Egypt, and Rahab and her household in Jericho.

7:4-8. John heard the names of 12 **tribes** with **12,000** from each **tribe** . . . **sealed** and thus protected. The 12 tribes are not "lost" as some contend.

Attempts have been made to identify the 12 tribes here with the church, mostly to avoid the implication that this is literally **Israel.** The fact that specific tribes were mentioned and specific numbers

from each tribe were indicated would seem to remove this from the symbolic and to justify literal interpretation. If God intended these verses to represent Israel literally, He would have used this means. Nowhere else in the Bible do a dozen references to the 12 tribes mean the church. Obviously Israel will be in the Tribulation, and though men do not know the identification of each tribe today, certainly God knows.

Much speculation has arisen about why the tribe of Dan is omitted. Joseph and one of his two sons, Manasseh, are listed, but Ephraim, Joseph's other son, is omitted. Thus if Dan were included, there would have been 13 tribes. According to J.B. Smith, Scripture contains 29 lists of the tribes of Israel in the Old and New Testaments and in no case are more than 12 tribes mentioned (*A Revelation of Jesus Christ,* p. 130). The tribe omitted was usually Levi, from which the priesthood came. Inasmuch as it is normal to have only 12 and not 13 tribes, the omission of Dan is not significant. Perhaps Dan was omitted here because it was one of the first tribes to go into idolatry (Jud. 18:30; cf. 1 Kings 12:28-29). However, Dan is mentioned in Ezekiel 48:2 in the millennial land distribution.

The most important fact taught here is that God continues to watch over Israel even in the time of Israel's great distress. There is no justification whatever for spiritualizing either the number or the names of the tribes in this passage, to make them represent the church.

2. THE MULTITUDE OF MARTYRS (7:9-17)

7:9-12. Then John saw a **multitude** of people **from every nation, tribe, people, and language,** who were **standing before the throne** (i.e., before God the Father) **and in front of the Lamb** (i.e., God the Son). This is the same group mentioned in 6:9, but here they were **wearing white robes** and **holding palm branches,** apparently signifying righteous triumph. As this multitude ascribed salvation to God and to the Lamb, **all the angels,** the 24 **elders, and the 4 living creatures** joined them in worship as they did in 5:9-10.

7:13-17. One of the 24 elders asked about the origin of those who stood **in white robes. Is** it not significant that if the

24 elders represent the church these described here are a different group of the saved? When John indicated that he did not know the answer (v. 14a) the elder himself answered the question as to who this multitude was and where they came from: **These are they who have come out of the Great Tribulation; they have washed their robes and made them white in the blood of the Lamb.**

It seems evident that these "who have come out of the Great Tribulation" have been martyred and were then safe in heaven. They were given the special privilege of being before God's **throne** and serving **Him day and night in His temple.** They were protected by God Himself and never again would they experience **hunger . . . thirst,** or **scorching heat,** with the implication that this was their experience of suffering on earth. They were under the special shepherd-care of **the Lamb** and were drinking from **springs of living water.** The narration concludes with the comforting truth that all their tears would be wiped away.

The two groups seen by John were the 144,000 Israelites and a great multitude from every nation, including some Israelites who were not thus protected and who were martyred in the Great Tribulation. A natural explanation of these two groups is that neither represents the church, the body of Christ in the present Age, because both groups are distinguished from the 24 elders and neither group is clearly identified with the church in this present dispensation.

The events of this chapter, like those in other chapters to follow, do not advance the narrative but are a pause in the description of the events to spotlight a concentrated revelation on a special feature, in this case the answer to the question of 6:17, "Who can stand?"

Though the chapters of Revelation are not all in chronological sequence, chapter 7 depicts a scene in heaven which precedes the second coming of Christ to the earth. Those seen in heaven were said to "come out of the Great Tribulation" (v. 14). The chapter accordingly indicates how they will be marvelously blessed in heaven after their trials on earth. The 144,000 will appear again (14:1-5), and the multitude of martyrs who were killed for refusing to worship the beast appear again at the time of the resurrection in 20:4. That they are not millennial saints should be evident from the fact that they will be in heaven before God's throne, and will have been resurrected.

E. *The opening of the seventh seal and the introduction of the seven trumpets (chaps. 8–9)*

1. THE OPENING OF THE SEVENTH SEAL (8:1)

8:1. The opening of **the seventh seal** is a most important event, confirmed by the fact that **there was silence in heaven**

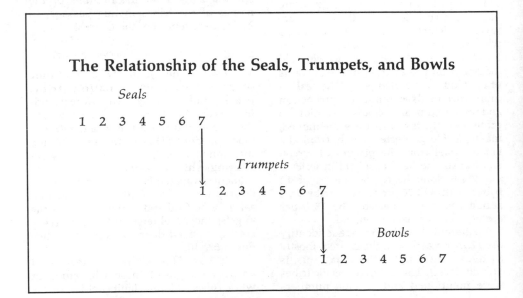

The Relationship of the Seals, Trumpets, and Bowls

Seals

1 2 3 4 5 6 7

Trumpets

1 2 3 4 5 6 7

Bowls

1 2 3 4 5 6 7

for about half an hour after it was opened. The contents of the seven trumpets indicate that they differ from the seven seals. W. Graham Scroggie states, "The trumpets, therefore, do not double back over all or some of the seals, but lie under the sixth seal, and proceed from it" (*The Great Unveiling*, p. 111). He also holds that the bowls of the wrath of God (chap. 16) "do not double back over the seal and trumpet judgments" (p. 112).

C.A. Blanchard holds the same position: "The series of three sevens are really included in one series of seven, that is, the seven trumpets are included under the seventh seal and the seven bowls are included under the seventh trumpet, so that we have in fact a single series in three movements" (*Light on the Last Days*, p. 58). The seventh seal accordingly is important because it actually includes all the events from 8:1 through 19:10.

2. THE SEVEN ANGELS AND THE SEVEN TRUMPETS (8:2)

8:2. As John observed the heavenly scene, he wrote that he saw the seven angels to whom were given seven trumpets. The fact that these are angels' trumpets distinguishes them from the trumpet of God (1 Cor. 15:52; 1 Thes. 4:16) and from other New Testament trumpets (Heb. 12:19; Rev. 1:10; 4:1).

3. THE GOLDEN CENSER (8:3-5)

8:3-5. Before the trumpets sounded, however, a dramatic introduction was given them by another angel, one in addition to the seven, who stood before the golden altar with a golden censer. In the Old Testament tabernacle a censer made of copper, probably heavy to handle, was used to carry coals from the brazen altar outside the tabernacle to the altar of incense inside. Later, in the temple, Solomon used censers made of gold (1 Kings 7:50; 2 Chron. 4:22).

This is the only reference to censers in the Book of Revelation, though golden bowls full of incense, which probably were not censers, are mentioned in Revelation 5:8. Like the golden bowls of 5:8, however, the golden censer offering incense here is symbolic of the prayers of all the saints.

This offering in heaven corresponds to the custom of offering incense on the altar of incense in both the tabernacle and the temple. The censer would hold the coals, and a separate vessel would carry the incense which was to be poured on the coals once the altar was reached. The resulting smoke was typical of prayer ascending before God.

In verse 5 the angel offered the incense on the coals before God, and then, taking the censer with the fire still in it, he threw it on the earth. As a result there were thunder, rumblings, flashes of lightning, and an earthquake. The picture is one of ominous anticipation.

4. THE FIRST TRUMPET (8:6-7)

8:6-7. As the first angel sounded his trumpet . . . hail and fire mixed with blood . . . was hurled down upon the earth, resulting in a third of the earth being burned up, including the trees and all the green grass. This devastating judgment, like that announced by most of the trumpets, primarily affected a third of the earth.

5. THE SECOND TRUMPET (8:8-9)

8:8-9. As the second . . . trumpet sounded, something like a huge mountain, all ablaze, was thrown into the sea. The result was that a third of the sea turned into blood, and this caused a third of the living creatures in the sea to die, and also a third of the ships were destroyed. It is best to interpret these events literally though the description of the sea being turned into blood may be the language of appearance as in the mention of blood after the first trumpet blast. Reference to blood as a divine judgment is found in the plagues of Egypt (cf. Ex. 7:14-22).

Obviously the results of these judgments are literal. The sea turned to blood results in the death of a third of the sea creatures, and the blazing mountain cast into the sea results in destruction of a third of the ships. The mountain is probably best understood as being a literal large body that fell from heaven. Since the results are literal, it is reasonable to take the judgments as literal also.

6. THE THIRD TRUMPET (8:10-11)

8:10-11. The judgment following the third . . . trumpet was similar to that of the second. But here the mass falling from heaven to earth was **a great star, blazing like a torch.** This fell **on a third of the rivers and on the springs of water;** in other words, waters other than the oceans.

The **star** was named **Wormwood.** Wormwood is a bitter desert plant mentioned only here in the New Testament. It is mentioned seven times in the Old Testament where it represents sorrow and bitter judgment (Deut. 29:18; Prov. 5:4; Jer. 9:15; 23:15; Lam. 3:15, 19; Amos 5:7).

Though many have attempted to interpret the third trumpet symbolically, it seems best to consider it as a large meteor or star falling on the earth from heaven and turning the water, as indicated, into bitterness so that people who drank it **died.** The contrast found in the Cross of Christ is symbolized in the sweetening of the waters of Marah (Ex. 15:23-25) and the turning of bitter judgment into sweet mercy, bringing life and hope. The third trumpet is another awesome judgment resulting in great loss of life.

7. THE FOURTH TRUMPET (8:12)

8:12. At the sound of **the fourth . . . trumpet** the light of the sky was reduced by one third. Without **a third of the sun** a third of the day was lacking normal light, and a third of the night was without light from **the moon** and **the stars.** Again the best interpretation is literal. Just as the first three trumpets dealt with a third of the earth, so the fourth trumpet dealt with a third of the heavens.

8. ANNOUNCEMENT OF THE FINAL THREE TRUMPETS (8:13)

8:13. Warning was given that the next three trumpets would be more severe and devastating than those which preceded them. The triple **woe** announced by **an eagle** warned of coming judgment. Eagles are also mentioned in 4:7 and 12:14.

9. THE FIFTH TRUMPET (9:1-11)

9:1-6. The events after the sounding of **the fifth . . . trumpet** are given considerable explanation, implying that this is a most important step in God's progressive and increasing judgments on the earth. Because of the **he** in verse 2 and

"king" in verse 11, the **star** that fell **to the earth** was a person rather than a fragment of a star (cf. Isa. 14:12-17; Luke 10:18). Even in modern terminology it is customary to speak of an unusual athlete or performer as a star. This star, probably representing Satan cast out of heaven at the beginning of the Great Tribulation (Rev. 12:9), **was given the key to the shaft of the Abyss** ("bottomless pit," KJV). The "Abyss" (*abyssos*) is the home of demons (cf. Luke 8:31; Rev. 9:11; 11:7; 17:8; 20:1, 3; in Rom. 10:7 it is translated "deep"). Satan will be confined for a thousand years in the Abyss during the reign of Christ on earth (Rev. 20:1-3).

Here the star (Satan) used his key to allow demons in the Abyss to come out and afflict the earth. Visually this event was represented as a great **smoke,** darkening the **sky** and **the sun. Out of the smoke** came creatures called **locusts** with the deadly sting of **scorpions.** While they were harmless to natural vegetation and trees, they stung **people who did not have the seal of God on their foreheads.**

In chapter 7 the 144,000 of Israel were sealed, and protection from the plague was extended to all who knew the Lord in that day (cf. Eph. 1:13-14; 2 Tim. 2:19). In the Old Testament locusts were a fearful plague, for they were able to reduce the land to starvation by eating up all green vegetation (Ex. 10:12-20; Joel 1:4-7). These locusts, however, did not eat vegetation, but had the power to torment people **for five months** (cf. Rev. 9:10). Thus they might be demons who appeared in the form of locusts. This is confirmed by the fact that they came from the Abyss, the home of demons (Luke 8:31). Their demonic control over people was such, however, that though the victims desired to die they could not take their own lives.

9:7-11. The description of **the locusts** compared to **horses prepared for battle** is awesome: **human faces . . . crowns of gold . . . women's hair . . . lions' teeth,** ironlike **breastplates,** and **wings** that sounded like horse-drawn **chariots rushing into battle.**

Obviously John was describing what he saw but did not interpret each characteristic. The picture is one of Satan's awesome supernatural power and the demon world especially in relation to unbelievers.

Unlike the previous judgments which apparently were short in time this judgment extended for five months (v. 10; cf. v. 5). This is important as it refutes clearly the notion that all these judgments will occur in a brief span of time immediately before the second coming of Christ.

The demons had a ruler **over them** whose **Hebrew** name **is Abaddon** and whose **Greek** name is **Apollyon.** Both words mean "destroyer." Though Satan is sometimes portrayed as an angel of light (2 Cor. 11:14), here Satan and his demons are seen for what they really are, destroyers of people. This judgment confirms what was already intimated in preceding judgments, that the Great Tribulation, as Christ described it, will be a time of "great distress, unequaled from the beginning of the world until now—and never to be equaled again" (Matt. 24:21).

10. THE SIXTH TRUMPET (9:12-21)

9:12. The fifth trumpet described as **the first woe** is now to be followed by the two final trumpets, also called "woes" (cf. 8:13).

9:13-15. The sixth . . . trumpet seems to relate to the final military conflict described in 16:12-16 (cf. Dan. 11:40-45). At the sounding of the sixth trumpet John **heard a voice coming from the horns of the golden altar that is before God.** The sixth angel was then instructed to **release the four angels . . . bound** by the **Euphrates** River. These **four angels** are clearly demons, as holy angels are not bound. The release of these four is minutely timed at a particular **hour and day and month and year,** and they **kill a third** of the world's population.

The fourth seal (Rev. 6:7-8) resulted in a fourth of the earth's people being killed. Here a third of the remainder were put to death. These two judgments alone, disregarding all intervening judgments, would account for the death of half the earth's population. This fact is to be taken literally as it confirms the statement by Daniel (Dan. 12:1) and the words of Christ (Matt. 24:21) that the Great Tribulation will be without precedent and would end in the death of all mankind if it were not stopped by His second coming (Matt. 24:22).

9:16. The loosing of the four angels (not the same as the four angels of 7:1) resulted in releasing an army of **200 million . . . mounted troops.** Most interpreters do not take the number literally, though there is good evidence that all other numbers in Revelation are literal. Even if taken symbolically, this figure clearly represents an overwhelming military force. Years ago Red China claimed to have an army of 200 million (cf. *Time,* May 21, 1965, p. 35).

Some interpreters say these millions are demons, but demons are not normally marshaled as a military force. The fact that John **heard** the **number,** as obviously he could not visually count 200 million men, seems to lend credence to the concept that this is literal and predicts that an army will come from the East crossing the dried-up Euphrates River (16:12).

Great dams have already been placed across the Euphrates River to divert water for irrigation so that at times the riverbed is dry or partially so. A large invasion from the East and North in the end times is predicted in Daniel 11:44.

9:17-19. The horses and their **riders** had **breastplates** of **red, dark blue, and yellow.** The lionlike **heads of the horses** imply something other than natural horses. Furthermore, John declared, **out of their mouths came fire, smoke, and sulfur.** Some have taken this as a picture of modern warfare including the use of armed vehicles such as tanks. Whether symbolic or literal, the passage certainly implies terrible destruction and an awesome invading force. The results are twice stated and include the death of **a third of mankind** (vv. 15, 18).

9:20-21. Though the judgment was devastating and obviously from God, it did not bring men to repentance, and they continued to worship **demons** and their representation in **idols** and kept on murdering and participating in the occult (**magic arts,** *pharmakeiōn,* from which is derived "pharmacies"; cf. Gal. 5:20; Rev. 18:23; 21:8; 22:15), **their sexual immorality,** and thievery.

The trumpet judgments clearly grew in a crescendo, becoming worse and more devastating. In spite of the clear evidence of God's power to judge the world, no evidence was given John that there would be any change of heart on the part of the great mass of humanity. Though the sixth judgment produced fear, it did not produce repentance.

F. The mighty angel and the little scroll (chap. 10)

1. THE INTRODUCTION OF THE ANGEL HOLDING THE SCROLL (10:1-4)

Chapter 7 dealt parenthetically with the 144,000 and the many martyrs, without advancing chronologically the events of the Great Tribulation. Similarly 10:1–11:14 give additional information as a background to the seal, trumpet, and bowl judgments.

Another angel was introduced, apparently not one of the seven angels sounding the trumpets. Some believe this angel was Christ, pointing to the angel mentioned in 8:3 as also probably a representation of Christ as a priest. But though Christ appeared frequently as the Angel of Jehovah in the Old Testament (e.g., Gen. 16:13; 24:7; 31:11, 13; Jud. 6:22), there is no evidence that this person was other than a mighty angel (cf. Rev. 5:2), perhaps Michael the archangel.

10:1-4. This **angel,** however, was pictured dramatically as **robed in a cloud,** having **a rainbow above his head,** his face brilliant with glory **like the sun,** and with **his legs . . . like fiery pillars.** John added that the angel held **a little scroll** and stood with **his right foot on the sea and his left foot on the land.** At the same time he shouted **like the roar of a lion.** The scene is certainly one to inspire awe, and when this angel **shouted, the voices of the seven thunders spoke.** John was forbidden to record **what the seven thunders** said. While Revelation is primarily designed to reveal and not to conceal God's purpose and future events, some revelation was kept hidden as illustrated by God's prohibiting John to write what "the voices" of the seven thunders said.

In contrast with the seven-sealed scroll (*biblion*) held by the Lamb (5:1), this angel held a small scroll (*biblaridion,* also used in 10:9-10). This scroll apparently contained the angel's written order for the mission he was about to fulfill.

2. THE ANNOUNCEMENT OF THE IMPENDING END (10:5-7)

10:5-7. The dramatic introduction of this angel (in vv. 1-4) was a preparation for the pronouncement which followed in verses 5-7. Solemnly swearing by God the eternal Creator, the angel declared, **There will be no more delay!** The KJV rendering, "There shall be time no longer," has been mistakenly interpreted as an abolishment of the present time system with its sequence of events. But this is not the thought of the passage, as the NIV translation is accurate. The clear reference to God as Creator (cf. 4:11; 14:7) answers evolutionary speculation as to the origin of the earth, and it also affirms the omnipotence of God in dealing with the world in judgment when the time is ripe.

Announcement was made that **the seventh . . . trumpet** would bring about the accomplishment of **the mystery of God.** This mystery had been previously announced to God's **prophets.** The reference, therefore, is not to hidden truth but to the fulfillment of many Old Testament passages which refer to the glorious return of the Son of God and the establishment of His kingdom of righteousness and peace on the earth. While God's purposes are not necessarily revealed in current events where Satan is allowed power and manifestation, the time will come when Satan no longer will be in power and the predictions of the Old Testament prophets will be fulfilled. Then all will know the Lord and the truth about Him (Jer. 31:34). Here again is evidence that the seventh trumpet introduces the seven bowl judgments of God's wrath described in Revelation 16.

3. THE EATING OF THE SCROLL (10:8-11)

10:8-11. John obeyed the angel's instruction to **eat** the scroll, and though it was **sweet** (like **honey**) in his **mouth,** it soured in his **stomach.** The angel then added that John would **prophesy again.**

What does this incident mean? Though no interpretation was given John, it is evident that in partaking of the book he was appropriating what the book states (cf. Jer. 15:16). The scroll seems to symbolize the Word of God and divine revelation in general, for John was told to deliver the Word faithfully.

To John the Word of God was indeed sweet with its revelation of the grace of God and its many precious promises that belong to believers. As such it sharply contrasted with his circumstances on Patmos Island. David stated, "The ordinances of the Lord are sure and altogether righteous. They are more precious than gold, than much pure gold; they are sweeter than honey, than honey from the comb" (Ps. 19:9-10). Though the Word is sweet to believers, it will be bitter to unbelievers when it brings divine judgment on them.

G. The two witnesses (11:1-14)

While it is clear that 11:1-14 continues the parenthetical section begun in 10:1, an amazing variation of interpretations of this portion of Scripture have been offered. Alford calls this chapter "one of the most difficult in the whole Apocalypse" (*The Greek Testament,* 4:655).

The best guideline to follow in interpreting this section is to take each fact literally. In line with this principle, a literal temple will be in existence during the Great Tribulation, and the city should be considered the literal city Jerusalem in keeping with its identification in 11:8. The time periods of 42 months (v. 2) and three and one-half days (vv. 9, 11) again should be considered literally. The earthquake will kill literally 7,000 individuals, and the two witnesses should be considered as two individual men.

1. THE MEASURING OF THE TEMPLE (11:1-2)

11:1-2. John **was given a reed,** a lightweight **rod,** to be used as a measuring instrument. John was instructed to **measure the temple** and **the altar** but not **the outer court,** meaning he was to measure the holy place and the holy of holies. While others could come into the outer court, only priests could enter into those two temple rooms. The explanation was given that this would be under the control of **the Gentiles** who would **trample on the holy city for 42 months.**

Why should John measure the temple? Measurement is usually taken of one's possessions, and the temple belonged to God. In a similar way the temple of Ezekiel 40 was measured and the New Jerusalem was measured (Rev. 21:15-17). The temple here will be constructed so that orthodox Jews can offer sacrifices according to the Mosaic Law in the period in the first half of the

seven-year period known as Daniel's 70th week. At the beginning of the 42-month Great Tribulation, however, the sacrifices will stop and the temple will be desecrated and become a shrine for the world ruler of the Great Tribulation who will put an idol in it and proclaim himself to be God (cf. Dan. 9:27; 12:11; 2 Thes. 2:4; Rev. 13:14-15).

John was also instructed, however, to count the worshipers who came to the temple. Here the thought seems to be that God will evaluate both the temple and those in it.

The tendency of some is to spiritualize the 42-month length of the Great Tribulation, but this should be taken as a literal period, as confirmed by the 1,260 days of 11:3 which are 42 months of 30 days each. From this it is also clear that "the times of the Gentiles" (Luke 21:24) will not end until the second coming of Christ to the earth to set up His kingdom. Though Jews may possess Jerusalem temporarily, as they have in this century, they will lose possession in the Great Tribulation.

Some believe that the 42 months refer to the first half of Daniel's 70th week (Dan. 9:27). While it is not clear, the evidence surrounding this passage in Revelation seems to refer to the final three and one-half years. This also seems to be confirmed by the fact that in the first half of the last seven years the Jews will actually possess the city of Jerusalem and worship in their temple, whereas here the context indicates that this is the period when Gentiles will tread down the Holy City, implying ill treatment of the Jews and desecration of the temple.

2. THE MINISTRY OF THE TWO WITNESSES (11:3-6)

11:3-6. It was revealed to John that the **two witnesses** would be empowered by God to serve as prophets for 1,260 days or 42 months. They would be **clothed in sackcloth** and would be called **two olive trees** and **two lampstands.**

Numerous and varied interpretations have been given concerning the two witnesses. Some have suggested that they are not literal individuals. However, in view of the fact that they die and are resurrected, the implication is that they are actual people.

Another problem is their identification. A common interpretation is that they are Moses and Elijah because the judgments inflicted by Moses and Elijah in the Old Testament are similar to those of these two witnesses (11:5-6). Further support is given the identification of Elijah because of the prediction (Mal. 4:5) that he will appear "before that great and dreadful day of the Lord comes." Christ said this prophecy of Elijah was partially fulfilled in His lifetime (Matt. 17:10-13; Mark 9:11-13; cf. Luke 1:17). And both Moses and Elijah were involved in the transfiguration (Matt. 17:3), which anticipated the Second Coming. But a problem with this suggested identity is that Moses had already died once. Some have identified the two witnesses as Enoch and Elijah inasmuch as they did not die but were translated (cf. Heb. 9:27).

While there is room for considerable discussion of these various views, the fact is that the passage does not identify the two witnesses, and they probably do not have historic identification.

The description of the two witnesses as olive trees and lampstands has an Old Testament background (Zech. 4:2-14). The two witnesses in this passage were Joshua the high priest and Zerubbabel the governor. Their connection to the lampstands was that they were empowered by the Holy Spirit, symbolized by the olive oil. In a similar way the two witnesses of Revelation 11 will be empowered by the Holy Spirit.

Like prophets of old the two witnesses will be able to do supernatural miracles, and fire will destroy those who will try to harm them (Rev. 11:5). Like Elijah they will have power to stop rain, and will have power like Moses to turn water into blood and to bring on plagues (v. 6). In the midst of the unbelief, apostasy, and satanic power of the Great Tribulation these two witnesses will be a threat to the entire wicked world for a literal period of 1,260 days.

3. THE DEATH OF THE TWO WITNESSES (11:7-10)

11:7-10. With the ministry of the two witnesses ended, God permitted **the beast that comes up from the Abyss** (cf. 9:1-2, 11; 17:8; 20:1, 3) to overcome them. The beast, that is, the Antichrist, is mentioned nine other times in Revelation (13:1; 14:9, 11; 15:2; 16:2; 17:3, 13; 19:20; 20:10). After the witnesses were killed, their bodies were left unburied in Jerusalem, **figuratively called Sodom and Egypt,** because of the people's apostasy and rejection of God.

For three and one-half days the whole world gloated over their dead **bodies.** This implies some worldwide display, now made possible by television. Their deaths were considered a great victory for the world ruler and Satan, and were celebrated by people **sending each other gifts.**

4. THE RESURRECTION OF THE TWO WITNESSES (11:11-12)

11:11-12. After three and one-half days in the street, however, suddenly the two witnesses were resurrected and **stood on their feet.** They responded to the invitation, **Come up here,** and **went up to heaven in a cloud, while their enemies looked on** with great fear.

5. THE RESULTING JUDGMENT OF GOD ON JERUSALEM (11:13-14)

11:13-14. At the same moment an **earthquake** occurred in Jerusalem with **a 10th of the city** collapsing and **7,000 people were killed.** In contrast with previous judgments where revolt and rebellion against God continued, **the survivors were terrified and gave glory to the God of heaven.** So ended **the second woe,** leaving only the seventh trumpet, the final and **third woe,** to come.

H. The sounding of the seventh trumpet (11:15-19)

11:15. Though the full results from the sounding of **the seventh . . . trumpet** are only introduced here and not brought to finality (as they will be in chap. 16), the introduction of the seventh trumpet itself is dramatic. As the trumpet sounded, voices were heard in heaven: **The kingdom of the world has become the kingdom of our Lord and of His Christ, and He will reign forever and ever.** (Cf. predictions of the earthly kingdom of Christ in Ezek. 21:26-27; Dan. 2:35, 44; 4:3; 6:26; 7:14, 26-27; Zech. 14:9.) The fact that this will be fulfilled at the Second Coming makes it clear that the period of the seventh trumpet chronologically reaches to Christ's return. Therefore the seventh trumpet introduces and includes the seven bowl judgments of the wrath of God revealed in chapter 16. In contrast with previous trumpets where a single voice was heard, here a mighty chorus from heaven joined in the proclamation.

11:16-18. After this announcement, **the 24 elders,** who appear frequently (4:4, 10; 5:5-6, 8, 11, 14; 7:11, 13; 11:16; 14:3; 19:4) and **who were seated on their thrones before God,** were seen by John as falling **on their faces** to worship **God.** Their song of praise indicates that the time had come for God to judge **the nations,** to judge **the dead,** and to reward God's **servants.**

God was described as the **Almighty** (*pantokratōr;* also used in 1:8; 4:8; 15:3; 16:7, 14; 19:6, 15; 21:22), eternal (**who is and who was;** cf. 1:8; 4:8), and possessing **power** (*dynamin*) (11:17). In general their hymn of praise anticipates the second coming of Christ and the establishment of His rule on earth.

11:19. The chapter closes with another dramatic incident. John wrote, **Then God's temple in heaven was opened.** At the same time John was able to look into the **temple** where he saw **the ark of His covenant.** This refers to the heavenly temple rather than to a temple on earth. The corresponding results in the earth, however, included **lightning . . . thunder, an earthquake, and a great hailstorm** (cf. 8:5).

The dramatic introduction of the events relating to the seventh trumpet concluded here and will be resumed in chapter 16. Chronologically the time was close to Christ's second coming.

I. The seven great personages of the end times (chaps. 12–15)

Though the seventh trumpet was recorded in 11:15 as sounding, the details of what will come out of the seventh trumpet are not revealed until chapter 16. Accordingly chapters 12–15 view the prophecies of the end time from another perspective and introduce the great personages who are involved in the second half of the seven-year period.

Many have pointed out that seven personages appear in chapters 12–13: (1) a woman clothed with the sun, representing Israel (12:1-2); (2) the red dragon with seven heads and 10 horns, representing Satan (12:3-4); (3) the male Child, representing Christ (12:5-6); (4) the archangel Michael, casting Satan out of heaven (12:7-12); (5) the offspring of the woman, persecuted by the dragon (12:13-17); (6) the beast out of the sea, the future world dictator (13:2-10); (7) the beast out of the earth, the false prophet (13:11-18). These chapters do not advance the narrative chronologically, but present events and situations that are concurrent with the soundings of the trumpets. Chronological progress of events resumes in chapter 16.

1. THE FIRST PERSONAGE: A WOMAN CLOTHED WITH THE SUN (12:1-2)

12:1-2. The first great personage to appear was **a woman clothed with the sun, with the moon under her feet and a crown of 12 stars on her head.** She was called **a great and wondrous sign** (*sēmeion mega,* lit., "a great sign"; cf. 13:13). Undoubtedly the sign provoked wonder, as indicated in the KJV and NIV, but the translation "a great sign" (NASB) is more accurate, since John did not use the Greek word for wonder (*teras*). This was the first of a series of events called "signs" or "miracles" (12:3; 13:13-14; 15:1; 16:14; 19:20). As signs they were symbols of something that God was about to reveal and usually contained an element of prophetic warning. Though this sign was seen in heaven, the events which followed obviously occurred on earth.

The woman symbolized Israel, as indicated by Genesis 37:9-11, where the sun and the moon referred to Jacob and Rachel, Joseph's parents. The stars in the woman's crown clearly related to the 12 sons of Jacob and identified the woman as Israel fulfilling the Abrahamic Covenant. J.B. Smith cites Isaiah 60:1-3, 20 as proof that the sun refers to Israel's future glory (*A Revelation of Jesus Christ,* p. 182).

Many commentaries are so intent on attempting to identify Israel as the church that they ignore these plain indications that the woman is Israel. Robert H. Mounce, for instance, makes the woman "the messianic community, the ideal Israel . . . the church (Rev. 12:17). The people of God are one throughout all redemptive history" (*The Book of Revela-*

tion, p. 236). While there is a unity of the people of God, this does not wipe out dispensational and racial distinctions.

The symbolism, while not referring specifically to Mary, the mother of Christ, points to Israel as the source of Jesus Christ. Thus it does not refer to the church. Wicked women are sometimes used to represent false religions, as in the case of Jezebel (2:20), the apostate church of the end time as a prostitute (17:1-7, 15, 18), and Israel as the unfaithful wife of Yahweh (Hosea 2:2-13). The church by contrast is pictured as the virgin bride (2 Cor. 11:2), the Lamb's wife (Rev. 19:7).

The woman was said to be **pregnant** and **about to give birth** (12:2). While in some sense this may be fulfilled in the birth of Christ to the Virgin Mary, the context seems to refer to the emerging nation of Israel in its suffering prior to the second coming of Christ. This is further supported by the verses which follow.

2. THE SECOND PERSONAGE: THE RED DRAGON WITH THE 7 HEADS AND 10 HORNS (12:3-4)

12:3-4. The second wonder (*semeion*, "sign"; cf. v. 1) **appeared in heaven,** though it actually related to scenes on earth. It was a great **red dragon,** having **7 heads and 10 horns, and 7 crowns on his heads.** From similar descriptions in Daniel 7:7-8, 24 and Revelation 13:1, this beast represented Satan's control over world empires in the Great Tribulation. Revelation 12:9 identifies the dragon as Satan. The color red might indicate the bloodshed related to this period. The 10 horns presented symbolically the 10 kings (see Dan. 7:24) who reigned simultaneously with the coming world ruler and who were mentioned both in Daniel 7:7 and Revelation 13:1.

The casting down of **a third of the stars out of the sky** seemed to imply satanic power which extended to the heavens and the earth. Satan was seen here to extend his power over those who opposed him spiritually or politically. The dragon's attempt to **devour** the newborn **Child** (12:4) seemed to point to Satan's attempts to destroy the Infant Jesus. Satanic opposition to Israel and especially to the messianic line is clear in both Testaments.

3. THE THIRD PERSONAGE: THE MALE-CHILD, CHRIST (12:5-6)

12:5-6. When the Child—described as **a Son, a male Child, who will rule all the nations with an iron scepter**—was born, He **was snatched up to God and to His throne.** The Child obviously is Jesus Christ (Ps. 2:9; Rev. 19:15). Alford states that "the Man-Child is the Lord Jesus Christ, *and none other*" (*The Greek Testament,* 4:668). The catching up of the Child referred to the Ascension, not to the later Rapture of the church though the same word for "snatched up" is used of the Rapture (1 Thes. 4:17; cf. Acts 8:39; 2 Cor. 12:2-4). The Rapture of the church would not constitute a deliverance of the Man-Child from Satan.

The deliverance itself took place when the woman **fled into the desert to a place prepared for her by God,** and she was preserved **for 1,260 days,** which was three and one-half years or 42 months of 30 days each. Matthew (24:16) referred to the flight of Israel at the beginning of the Great Tribulation (cf. Mark 13:14). References to both desert and mountains are not a contradiction as both were wilderness areas. In her desert hideout Israel was cared for perhaps as miraculously as Israel was in her wilderness journey from Egypt to the Promised Land.

The time period was 1,260 days, later described as "a time, times, and half a time" (cf. comments on Rev. 12:14). This action (vv. 5-6) followed what is described in verse 7 as a "war in heaven."

4. THE FOURTH PERSONAGE: SATAN CAST OUT OF HEAVEN (12:7-12)

12:7. Michael the archangel (cf. Jude 9) **and his angels** fought Satan **and his angels,** that is, demons. The time of this **war in heaven** was not indicated but the context refers to the end time. The efforts of some expositors to make this coincidental with the first coming of Christ, linking it with Luke 10:18, are not justified by the context in Revelation 12. Also Satan is most obviously active throughout the period of the Church Age (cf. Acts 5:3; 1 Cor. 5:5; 7:5; 2 Cor. 2:11; 11:14; 12:7; 1 Tim. 1:20; 1 Peter 5:8).

The concept that Satan is inactive in the present Age is a false conclusion based on an attempt to place the binding of Satan at the first coming of Christ (Rev. 20:1-3). However, the binding of Satan is still a future event that relates to the millennial kingdom.

12:8-9. The outcome of the war was that Satan **was hurled to the earth,** and his character was clearly revealed in the various titles ascribed to him: **the great dragon . . . that ancient serpent . . . the devil or Satan.** With him went the fallen **angels** of the demon world.

While the concept of Satan in heaven is difficult to comprehend, it is clear that he is now the accuser of saints (cf. Job 1:6; Rev. 12:10). Though Satan was defeated at the first coming of Christ (John 16:11), his execution was delayed and is in stages. Here (Rev. 12:8-9) he will be cast out of heaven in the middle of the Tribulation. Later he will be bound for the duration of the millennial kingdom (20:1-3). The devil will finally be thrown into the lake of burning sulfur (20:10) where the world ruler (Antichrist) and the false prophet will have been cast a thousand years earlier.

Satan and his activities in heaven and earth opposed Christ as Priest in heaven, as King in Satan's world rule in the Great Tribulation, and as the true Prophet by advancing the beast out of the earth (13:11), who was the false prophet (20:10). Satan was identified as that ancient serpent, alias the devil or Satan, and was declared to be the one who led the whole world astray. When he will be cast into the earth, all the fallen angels or demons will be cast down with him.

12:10-12. John then heard a hymn of praise uttered by **a loud voice in heaven.** Announcement was made of the coming demonstration of divine **salvation** and **power** with the advent of the millennial kingdom. Satan was characterized as the one who **accuses** believers **before our God day and night.** The principle by which he was overcome and cast out of heaven was **the blood of the Lamb** and **the word of their testimony.** Not only did Christ provide the victory, but also those who were martyred took part in that victory. Those in the heavens were called on to rejoice because of Satan's defeat, but the earth was warned that the devil was **filled with fury, because he** knew **that his time** was **short.** The devil knew that his time was limited to 1,260 days,

the period of the Great Tribulation. By no stretch of the imagination can these prophecies be spread to cover the whole Interadvent Age as some attempt to do.

5. THE FIFTH PERSONAGE: THE OFFSPRING OF THE WOMAN PERSECUTED BY THE DRAGON (12:13-17)

12:13-14. The woman introduced in verse 1 became the special object of Satan's persecution. She was given supernatural help symbolized by **the two wings of a great eagle** which enabled her to **fly to the place prepared for her in the desert.**

This hiding place was not clearly identified. Some suggest that it might be Petra, fortress capital of the Nabateans in Edom, south of the Dead Sea. This city has a narrow access which could easily be blocked but which opens up into a large canyon capable of caring for many thousands of people. Though Scripture is not specific, some believe the 144,000 of chapter 7 are to be preserved here. The Scriptures themselves speak of God's seal of protection on them.

The two wings probably do not refer to modern airplanes but rather to God's delivering power, and are a figure of speech taken from such Old Testament passages as Exodus 19:4 and Deuteronomy 32:11-12. The flight of Israel to a place of safety was also indicated in Matthew 24:16; Mark 13:14; and Luke 21:21.

Though Revelation 12:6, 14 referred to the refuge as a desert and the Synoptic passages referred to mountains, this is no contradiction as both desert and mountains are in a wilderness area. The length of time of her preservation was said to be **a time, times, and half a time.** This refers to the three and one-half years of the Great Tribulation with "a time" equaling one year, "times" equaling two years, and "half a time" indicating 6 months (cf. Dan. 7:25; 12:7 with the 42 months referred to in Rev. 11:2; 13:5). References to these specific time periods show that the Great Tribulation is *not* the entire present Age but the three and one-half years preceding the second coming of Christ.

12:15-17. Pursuing the woman, the devil as **the serpent** originated a flood to **sweep her away with the torrent,** but the earth swallowed up the water. Some have taken this as a literal flood, but since Israel could flee in every direction the contour of the Holy Land does not lend itself to such a flood. Probably the flood represents Satan's effort to exterminate Israel. This is thwarted by the rough terrain which provides hiding places. In some way God assists the Israelites so that they are not completely destroyed, though Zechariah 13:8 indicates that "two-thirds will be struck down and perish."

Though only one-third of Israel in the land is thus preserved (of which the 144,000 of Rev. 7 are a portion), Satan the dragon continues to war against the rest.

Revelation 12 introduces four important persons and one group of people living at the end time: Israel, Satan, Christ, the archangel, and the remnant of Israel. In Revelation 13 two important persons complete the scene.

6. THE SIXTH PERSONAGE: THE BEAST OUT OF THE SEA (13:1-10)

a. The beast out of the sea introduced (13:1-2)

13:1-2. Chapter 13 presents a most important personage of the end time—**a beast coming out of the sea.** His **10 horns and 7 heads, with 10 crowns on his horns,** depict the revived Roman Empire, which was also represented by the fourth beast of Daniel, which also had 10 horns (Dan. 7:7-8; cf. Rev. 13:3; 17:3, 7). In Revelation 13 and 17 the beast is the world ruler, whereas in Daniel 7 the little horn on the beast was the world ruler.

The fact that the beast comes out from the sea indicates that he is a Gentile, for the sea of humanity is involved as his source (cf. Rev. 17:15).

Many have said that the beast refers to some character in past history, but the context clearly refers to the final three and one-half years before Christ's second coming. Under the control of this central ruler in the Middle East during the Great Tribulation will be 10 nations (cf. Dan. 7:24, "The 10 horns are 10 kings"). (For discussion of various alternative views, see Walvoord, *Revelation*, pp. 198-99.)

In Revelation 13:2 the beast was seen to gather in the symbolism of the three preceding empires—Greece (**a leopard,** cf. Dan. 7:6), Medo-Persia (**a bear,** cf.

Dan. 7:5), and Babylon (**a lion,** cf. Dan. 7:4). The power of the beast was derived from Satan himself: **the dragon gave the beast his power and his throne and great authority.** This accords with Paul (2 Thes. 2:9) who referred to "the lawless one" (i.e., the Antichrist, this first beast of Rev. 13) as working "all kinds of counterfeit miracles [*dynamei*], signs [*sēmeiois*], and wonders [*terasin*]."

b. The fatal wound of the beast (13:3)

13:3. The seven **heads of the beast** seem to represent important rulers, and one of them, probably the seventh, suffered **a fatal wound** caused by a sword (v. 14), which was subsequently **healed,** causing astonishment in the entire world.

Many have attempted to identify this beast as someone in the past or present who is to become the final world ruler. Among the suggestions have been Nero, Judas Iscariot, Mussolini, Hitler, Stalin, Kissinger, and many others; but such men obviously do not fit the details of this yet-future ruler.

What is the meaning of the fatal wound that is healed? Two possibilities seem to fit this description. Alford, for instance, sees the deadly wound as the destruction of "the Roman pagan Empire" by "the Christian Roman Empire," thus making it a matter of history rather than prophecy (*The Greek Testament*, 4: 675). The revival of the Roman Empire would then be its miraculous healing. Another plausible explanation is that the final world ruler receives a wound which normally would be fatal but is miraculously healed by Satan. While the resurrection of a dead person seems to be beyond Satan's power, the healing of a wound would be possible for Satan, and this may be the explanation. The important point is that the final world ruler comes into power obviously supported by a supernatural and miraculous deliverance by Satan himself.

c. The worship of Satan and the beast (13:4-6)

13:4-6. The supernatural character of **the beast** makes him the object of worship along with Satan, the source of his power. It has always been Satan's purpose to receive the worship due to

God alone, as stated in Isaiah 14:14: "I will make myself like the Most High." This is Satan's final form of counterfeit religion in which he assumes the place of God the Father, and the beast or the world ruler assumes the role of King of kings as a substitute for Christ. This situation is probably introduced at the beginning of the last three and one-half years when the Great Tribulation begins.

Recognizing the supernatural character of Satan and the ruler, the question is raised, **Who is like the beast? Who can make war against him?** (Rev. 13:4) This apparently explains how the beast could become world ruler without a war. His blasphemous assumption of the role of God continues **for 42 months,** during which time he blasphemes **God** as well as heaven and **those who live in heaven.**

d. The worldwide power of the beast (13:7-8)

13:7-8. The beast becomes a worldwide ruler, for his authority extends **over every tribe, people, language, and nation.** As predicted in Daniel 7:23, he does "devour the whole earth, trampling it down and crushing it."

In addition to achieving political domination over the entire world, he also abolishes all other religions and demands that everyone worship him (cf. 2 Thes. 2:4). **All inhabitants of the earth** worship **the beast** except for those whose names are recorded **in the book of life.** In the expression **the Lamb that was slain from the Creation of the world,** the words "from the Creation of the world" seem, as in the NIV margin, to relate to the time in eternity past when the names were written in the book of life, rather than to Christ's crucifixion, since He was not crucified when the world was created. As Paul wrote, those who were saved were foreordained to salvation before Creation (cf. Eph. 1:4).

Some hold that the book of life originally contained the names of every living person to be born in the world, and that the names of the unsaved get blotted out when they die. This interpretation stems from Revelation 3:5, where Christ promised the believers in Sardis that their names would not be erased from the book of life, and from 22:19, where a

person who rejects the messages in the Book of Revelation is warned that "God will take away from him his share in the tree of life" (cf. "tree of life" in 2:7 and 22:2, 14 and "book of life" in 3:5; 17:8; 20:12, 15; 21:27). However, 13:8 probably means simply that those who are saved had their names written in the book of life in eternity past in anticipation of the death of Christ on the cross for them and that they will never be erased.

Taken together, verses 7 and 8 indicate the universal extent of the beast's political government as well as the final form of satanic religion in the Great Tribulation. Only those who come to Christ will be delivered from the condemnation that is involved.

e. The exhortation to hear (13:9-10)

13:9-10. In a format similar to the exhortation to the seven churches of Asia Minor (chaps. 2–3) this passage gave an invitation to individuals who would listen. The dream of many today, of a universal church and a universal religion, will be realized in the end time, but it will be satanic and blasphemous instead of involving worship of the true God. In such a situation, appeal can only be made to individuals who will turn from it to God. In every age God speaks to those who will hear, a concept mentioned frequently in the Gospels (Matt. 11:15; 13:9, 43; Mark 4:9, 23; Luke 8:8; 14:35).

In contrast with the invitation addressed to the seven churches where each exhortation was addressed "to the church," the mention of churches is notably absent here. This is another indication that the church has been raptured before the time of these events. Revelation, instead of being interpreted as addressed only to first-generation Christians facing persecution, is better understood as an exhortation to believers in all generations but especially those who will be living in the end time. Those who are willing to listen are reminded that their obedience to the Word of God may result in their **captivity** or martyrdom (Rev. 13:10), so the exhortation closes, **This calls for patient endurance** (hypomonē, "steadfastness, perseverance"; cf. 14:12) **and faithfulness on the part of the saints.**

7. THE SEVENTH PERSONAGE: THE BEAST
OUT OF THE EARTH (13:11-18)

a. Introduction of the beast out of the
earth (13:11-12)

13:11-12. In contrast with the first
beast who came "out of the sea" (v. 1),
the second beast came **out of the earth.**
He was similar to the first beast (thērion,
"a beast," was used of both personages).
However, while the first beast was a
Gentile, since he came from the entire
human race as symbolized by "the sea"
(v. 1), the second beast was a creature of
the earth. Some have taken this as a
specific reference to the Promised Land
and have argued that he was therefore a
Jew. There is no support for this in the
context as the word for "earth" is the
general word referring to the entire world
(gē). Actually his nationality and geographic origin are not indicated, and he is
apparently the one referred to as "the
false prophet" in 19:20 and 20:10. (For a
comprehensive discussion of the two
beasts see Alford, The Greek New Testament, 4:678-79.)

The second beast **had two horns like
a lamb, but he spoke like a dragon,** that
is, like Satan. From this it can be gathered
that he was a religious character whose
role was to support the political ruler, **the
first beast.** He had great **authority**
apparently derived from Satan and the
political ruler, and he **made the earth and
its inhabitants worship the first beast,**
the one **whose fatal wound had been
healed.**

The false religious system, which
was supported in this way imitated the
divine Trinity. Satan seeks to take the
place of God the Father; the first beast
assumes the place of Jesus Christ, the
Son, the King of kings; and the second
beast, the false prophet, has a role similar
to the Holy Spirit who causes Christians
to worship God. This is Satan's final
attempt to substitute a false religion for
true faith in Christ.

b. The miracles of the beast (13:13-15)

13:13-15. To induce people to worship the first beast, the second beast
performs **great and miraculous signs** (lit.,
"great signs," sēmeia megala; cf. "a great
. . . sign" in 12:1), including **fire . . . from
heaven.** People sometimes overlook the
fact that, while God can do supernatural
things, Satan within certain limitations

can also perform miracles, and he used
this **power** to the full in this situation to
induce people to worship Satan's substitute for Christ. Accordingly the second
beast **deceived the inhabitants of the
earth.**

In addition to causing fire to come
down from heaven, the second beast set
up an image of the first beast. The image
was probably set up in the first temple in
Jerusalem which was taken over from the
Jews. According to Paul (2 Thes. 2:4) the
first beast actually sat in God's temple at
times and received worship which properly belonged to God. Perhaps the beast's
image was placed in the same temple to
provide an object of worship when the
beast himself was not there.

This image was mentioned frequently (Rev. 13:14-15; 14:9, 11; 15:2;
16:2; 19:20; 20:4). Whether the image was
in the form of the world ruler, the first
beast, or merely some object of worship
is not clear, but it did seem to symbolize
the power of the first beast.

The fact that the second beast could
**give breath to the image of the first
beast,** even making it **speak,** has created
problems for expositors, for the Bible
does not seem to indicate that Satan has
the power to give life to an inanimate
object. Only God is the Creator. So
probably the beast's image is able to give
an *impression* of breathing and speaking
mechanically, like computerized talking
robots today. There might be a combination of natural and supernatural powers
to enable the beast out of the earth to
accomplish his purpose. It apparently was
quite convincing to people and induced
them to worship the image.

The command to **worship the image**
as well as the first beast was enforced by
killing those who **refused to** do so. But
there was a difference between the decree
to put them to death and its execution.
The problem of ferreting out everyone in
the entire earth who would not worship
the beast would naturally take time.
Hitler, in his attempt to exterminate the
Jews, took many months and never
completed his task. The multitude of
martyrs is referred to in 7:9-17.

c. The mark of the beast (13:16-18)

13:16-18. Enforcing his control over
the human race and encouraging worship
of the beast out of the sea, the second

beast required **everyone . . . to receive a mark on his right hand or on his forehead,** and without this evidence that he had worshiped the beast **no one could buy or sell.** The need to buy or sell such necessities as food and clothing would force each person in the entire world to decide whether to worship the beast or to bear the penalty. Apparently the great majority worshiped the beast.

There has been much speculation on the insignia or "mark" of the beast, but it could be any of several kinds of identification. Countless attempts have been made to interpret the number **666,** usually using the numerical equivalents of letters in the Hebrew, Greek, or other alphabets. As there probably have been hundreds of explanations continuing down to the present day, it is obvious that if the number refers to an individual it is not clear to whom it refers.

Probably the best interpretation is that the number six is one less than the perfect number seven, and the threefold repetition of the six would indicate that for all their pretensions to deity, Satan and the two beasts were just creatures and not the Creator. That six is **man's number** is illustrated in many instances in the Bible, including the fact that man should work six days and rest the seventh. (For further discussion of the many views cf. Mounce, *The Book of Revelation,* pp. 263-65; Smith, *A Revelation of Jesus Christ,* pp. 206-7; and Walvoord, *Revelation,* pp. 209-12.)

The practice of gematria, the attempt to find hidden meanings in numbers in Scripture, was prominent in the ancient world. Maybe John had in mind a particular person whom his close associates would be able to identify. Literature from the early church fathers, however, reveals the same confusion and variety of meanings that exist today, so probably it is best to leave this puzzle unsolved. Probably the safest conclusion is that of Thomas F. Torrance, "This evil trinity 666 apes the Holy Trinity 777, but always falls short and fails" (*The Apocalypse Today,* p. 86).

Chapter 13 is important because it introduces two of the main characters of Revelation: the beast out of the sea, the world dictator; and the beast out of the earth, the false prophet and chief supporter of the political ruler. There is no evidence that either of them is a Jew though some have identified one or the other as an apostate Jew based on the expression "the God of his fathers" (Dan. 11:37, KJV). However, the Hebrew word *'ĕlōhîm* is a general word for god, quite different from *Yahweh,* and there is no proof that in Daniel it refers to the God of Israel. In recent translations it is "gods" (cf. ASV, NASB, NEB, NIV, AND RSV). Thus while it has been popular to consider either the first or the second ruler of Revelation 13 as an apostate Jew, the supporting evidence is lacking. Both beasts are probably Gentiles inasmuch as this will be the final hour of the time of the Gentiles, when Gentiles will tramp underfoot the city of Jerusalem (Luke 21:24), and both rulers will persecute Jews as well as believing Gentiles.

Revelation 13, however, gives much insight into the character of the Great Tribulation. It will be a time of one world government and one world religion, with one world economic system. Those who will resist the ruler and refuse to worship him will be subject to execution, and the martyrs may outnumber the believers who survive. It will be Satan's final and ultimate attempt to cause the world to worship him and to turn them from the worship of the true God and Jesus Christ as their Savior.

This chapter also makes it clear that the postmillennial dream of a world getting better and better through Christian effort and gospel preaching is not supported in the Bible. Instead the final form of world religion will be apostate, satanic, and blasphemous. There are many indications today that the world is heading in this direction, with the corresponding conclusion that the coming of the Lord may be near.

8. THE RESULTING SCENE IN EARTH AND HEAVEN (CHAPS. 14–15)

a. The 144,000 on Mount Zion (14:1-5)

In chapters 14 and 15 various other details of the world scene in heaven and earth are introduced in preparation for the final series of seven bowl judgments in chapter 16 and the judgments in chapters 17–18.

14:1-2. First, another view is given of the **144,000** who were **standing on Mount Zion** with **the Lamb.** It is reasonable to conclude that this is the same group mentioned in 7:4-8, except that here they are in a later period of the Tribulation. Chronologically the vision anticipates the triumph of the 144,000 still intact at the time of Jesus Christ's return from heaven to earth. In contrast with many others who become martyrs, these people live through the period. But they are not the only ones to survive, as many Gentiles and Jews will turn to Christ in the end time and somehow escape martyrdom and be honored to welcome Christ at His return.

Again the scene in heaven is dramatic with a loud noise similar to **rushing waters . . . thunder,** and **harpists** (cf. "thunder" in 4:5; 6:1; 8:5; 11:19; 16:18; 19:6).

14:3-5. John wrote, **And they sang a new song before the throne and before the four living creatures and the elders.** These singers were apparently a heavenly group. They could be the multitude in white robes mentioned in 7:9-17. But there is no justification here for symbolizing Mount Zion as heaven. It is better to take the chorus as the 144,000 (cf. 14:1) who had not yet died and would still be on earth at the literal Mount Zion.

Reference to the purity of **the 144,000** could be recognition that during the difficult times of the Tribulation they could not have led normal married lives. Or it may refer to spiritual purity, often symbolized by virginity (cf. 2 Kings 19:21; Isa. 37:22; Jer. 18:13; 31:4, 21; Lam. 2:13; Amos 5:2). In 2 Corinthians 11:2 the concept of virginity is extended to the entire church, including both sexes.

Some people believe that the 144,000 will be evangelists in the Great Tribulation. But there is no indication that the 144,000 were preachers or prophets; their testimony was largely from their moral purity and the fact that they were not martyred like many others. **They follow the Lamb wherever He goes.** John further stated, **They were purchased from among men and offered as firstfruits to God and the Lamb.** The word "firstfruits" suggests that these converted Israelites precede many others who at the Lord's second coming will turn to Him (Zech. 12:10; Rom. 11:15, 26-27). They were also described as **blameless** (amōmoi, a word used of sacrificial animals without defect)

and as those who, living in a period of great satanic deception, were free from lying. The passage as a whole is a prophetic foreview of the triumph of the 144,000 when Christ returns.

b. The message of the three angels (14:6-12)

14:6-8. John was then given a vision of an angel carrying a message called **the eternal gospel.** The angel was commissioned to bring his message to every group of people **on the earth.** Because of the word "gospel," some have felt that this was a message of salvation or the good news of the coming kingdom. The context, however, seems to indicate otherwise, for the message is one of **judgment** and condemnation. The angel announced, **Fear God and give Him glory, because the hour of His judgment has come.** So the "eternal" message seems to be a message of God's righteousness and judgment rather than a message of salvation.

The first angel was followed by **a second angel** who announced that **Babylon the Great,** which intoxicated others with **her adulteries,** has **fallen.** This apparently is in anticipation of the description of that city (see comments on chap. 18).

14:9-12. A third angel followed with another judgment that worshipers of **the beast and his image** who receive **his mark** will be objects of God's wrath and will be destined for eternal torment along with Satan, the demon world, and all unsaved people. The everlasting character of this judgment is stated plainly in verse 11: **The smoke of their torment rises forever and ever,** and they will have **no rest.** Those who keep God's commandments and are faithful to Him will need **patient endurance** (v. 12; cf. 13:10). The doctrine of eternal punishment, though unpopular with liberal scholars and difficult to accept, is nevertheless clearly taught in the Bible. Jesus and the Apostle John say more on this subject than does all the rest of the Bible.

c. The blessing of the faithful saints (14:13)

14:13. After the solemn pronouncement of the third angel John **heard a voice from heaven** commanding him,

Write: Blessed are the dead who die in the Lord from now on. To this the Holy Spirit added the promise, they will rest from their labor, for their deeds will follow them.

This passage is often quoted in regard to God's general blessings on all Christians, but the context indicates that the blessing is especially for those who die in the Great Tribulation. For them it is a blessed release from persecution, torture, and trial and a deliverance into the glorious presence of the Lord.

d. The messages of the second group of three angels (14:14-20)

14:14-16. John in his vision next saw seated on **a white cloud** one **like a Son of Man** wearing **a crown of gold** and holding a **sharp sickle.** Though some have identified "a Son of Man" as an angel, it is more probable that it is Christ Himself who is frequently called "the Son of Man" (cf. 1:13). In the Book of Matthew alone this title is ascribed to Christ more than 25 times (Matt. 8:20; 9:6; 11:19; 12:8, 32; 13:41; etc.). The sickle in His hand suggests judgment. And this is supported by the messages of the three angels (Rev. 14:15-20).

An **angel** called out to Christ to **reap, because the harvest of the earth is ripe.** The ripeness is in the sense of withered or overripe (*exēranthē*). What follows is judgment as the **sickle** is **swung . . . over the earth.** Alford holds that verse 14 refers to the harvest of the saints, and that verses 15-16 describe judgment on the wicked (*The Greek New Testament,* 4: 691). But it is difficult to imagine a harvest of saints as being withered or overripe.

14:17-20. Another angel had a **sharp sickle,** and a fellow **angel** commanded him to **gather . . . clusters of grapes from the earth's vine, because its grapes are ripe.** Here a different word is used for ripe (*ēkmasan*), meaning "to be fully grown" or "in prime condition." The grapes were full of juice and ready for harvest. In obedience the angel **gathered the grapes and threw them into the great winepress of God's wrath. They were trampled** there **outside the city,** probably Jerusalem (cf. "the great city" in 11:8).

The custom was to produce grape juice by trampling on grapes in a winepress. The result here, however, is different. **Blood flowed out of the press rising as high as the horses' bridles for a distance of 1,600 stadia,** about 180 miles. While this distance may be literal and may designate the area of judgment as around the city of Jerusalem, it is of course impossible for the blood to reach a height where it would touch horses' bridles. What this affirms is a tremendous bloodletting in which blood is spattered as high as the bridles of horses. This is a graphic picture of a great slaughter (Isa. 63:1-3). Other Scriptures (e.g., Rev. 16:14; Dan. 11:40-45) make it clear that there will be a world war of tremendous scope underway at the time of the second coming of Christ, and this may be a partial fulfillment of these prophecies.

Taken as a whole, Revelation 14 on the one hand refers to the preservation of the 144,000 through the Great Tribulation. And on the other hand it graphically declares some of the terrible judgments that will be inflicted on the world which rejects Christ and follows Satan's substitute for the Lord.

William Kelly regards this chapter as an outline of major events at the end of the Age: (1) the appearance of the godly remnant of Israel; (2) a testimony to Gentiles; (3) the fall of Babylon; (4) the doom of the worshipers of the beast; (5) the blessedness of saints who are martyred; (6) the harvest; (7) the wrath of God on the world (*Lectures on the Book of Revelation,* p. 330).

e. The seven angels introduced (15:1-8)

15:1-2. With the background of the scene in heaven described in chapter 14, John then recorded more details of God's judgment. He wrote that he **saw in heaven another great and marvelous sign. Seven angels**—each having a plague which all together were described as **the seven last plagues**—were introduced as the final step in the outpouring of **God's wrath** on the earth. This final "sign" relates to the preceding great signs of the woman in 12:1 and the red dragon in 12:3. These seven angels should not be confused with the two groups of three angels in the preceding chapter (14:6-20) or with any other previous group of angels.

John also **saw what looked like a sea of glass mixed with fire.** This is probably the same sea that was described in 4:6. **Beside** this **sea** John saw the martyred dead, the same group described in 7:9-17.

15:3-4. The victorious saints **sang** with harps **the song of Moses . . . and the song of the Lamb.** These may be two separate songs, the first referring to God's faithfulness to Israel and the second referring to their present situation in the Great Tribulation. Some, like Walter Scott, refer the song of Moses to Exodus 15 where Israel triumphed over the Egyptians (*Exposition of Revelation*, p. 315). Others, such as J.B. Smith, suggest that this is the song of Deuteronomy 32, which gives a comprehensive review of God's faithfulness to Israel (*A Revelation of Jesus Christ*, pp. 224-25). In this song in Revelation 15:3-4 God is praised for His great deeds, justice, truth (cf. 16:7), glory, and holiness (see 4:8 for a chart of the 14 doxologies in Rev.). Then a prediction is made that **all** the **nations** will **worship** God.

This description of praise to God and prediction of universal worship is in keeping with many other Scriptures and relates, of course, to the second coming of Christ and worship of God by the entire world in the millennial kingdom (Pss. 2:8-9; 24:1-10; 66:1-4; 72:8-11; 86:9; Isa. 2:2-4; 9:6-7; 66:18-23; Jer. 10:7; Dan. 7:14; Zeph. 2:11; Zech. 14:9). The awful hour of wickedness and blasphemy against God, which will characterize the period leading up to the Second Coming, will be followed by a full vindication of God's judgment and holiness in the next period.

15:5-8. As John continued to look at the heavenly vision, he saw **the temple** described as **the tabernacle of Testimony.** The allusion to a temple **in heaven** seems to be the heavenly counterpart of the earthly temple. As it was opened, **the seven angels with** their **plagues** exited from it. The **clean, shining linen** of the angels indicates their purity, and the **golden sashes around their chests** point to the glory of God.

John saw **one of the four living creatures** give the **seven golden bowls filled with the wrath of God** to the seven angels. When this was done, **smoke** filled **the temple,** making it impossible for anyone to **enter** it **until the seven plagues** were poured out on the earth (cf. Ex. 40:34-35). Taken as a whole, Revelation 15:5-8 presents a fearful picture of impending divine judgment on a wicked world. The judgments which are to be poured out (chap. 16) fully justify this ominous introduction.

J. The bowls of divine wrath (chap. 16)

Chronologically this chapter is close to the time of the second coming of Christ, and the judgments described fall in rapid succession. Alford says, "There can then be no doubt here, not only that the series reaches on to the time of the end, but that the whole of it is to be placed close to the same time" (*The Greek Testament,* 4:696). Daniel indicated that these closing days of the Tribulation will be a time of world war (Dan. 11:36-45). World events are now pictured by John as rapidly coming to their climax.

1. THE FIRST BOWL (16:1-2)

16:1-2. John recorded that he **heard a loud voice from the temple** instructing **the seven angels** to **pour out the seven bowls of God's wrath on the earth.** This is undoubtedly the voice of God speaking from His heavenly temple. The adjective translated "loud" (*megalēs*) is frequently used in this chapter (v. 17 also refers to the loud voice). But the same Greek word is used in connection with intense heat (v. 9), the great river Euphrates (v. 12), the great day of God Almighty (v. 14), a severe earthquake (v. 18), the great city (v. 19), Babylon the Great (v. 19), huge hailstones (v. 21), and a terrible plague (v. 21). The judgments being poured out are greater, more severe, more intense than anything that has happened in the preceding events. When **the first angel . . . poured out his bowl** of wrath, it produced **ugly and painful sores** on those who had the beast's mark and **worshiped his image.**

The question has been raised as to whether the bowls of the wrath of God are chronologically subsequent to or identical with the seven trumpets of the angels. There is clearly much similarity between the trumpet judgments and the bowl judgments. They both deal with (a) the earth (8:7) or the land (16:2), (b) the sea (8:8; 16:3), (c) the rivers and springs of water (8:10; 16:4), and (d) the sun, moon, and stars (8:12) with only the sun mentioned in the bowl judgments (16:8-9). The fifth trumpet dealt with demon possession with the sun and sky darkened (9:1-3), which is similar to the fifth bowl in which darkness will cover the earth and sores will cause agony among men (16:10-11). The sixth trumpet deals with the river Euphrates (9:13-14), and the sixth bowl will dry up the Euphrates (16:12). The seventh trumpet implies that the Great Tribulation is coming to its end (11:15-19), and the seventh bowl of the wrath of God records a loud voice from heaven, saying, "It is done!" (16:17) with resulting destruction of the earth by earthquake and hail, which is also included in the seventh trumpet (11:18-19).

Similarities, however, do not prove identity, and a comparison of the trumpets with the bowls of God's wrath reveals striking differences even though the order of the judgments is the same. In the trumpet judgments, generally speaking, a third of the earth or heaven is afflicted, whereas in the bowl judgments the effects of the judgments are on the entire earth and are much more severe and final in character. Accordingly it seems best to follow the interpretation which has long been held in the church that the seven bowls are an expansion of the seventh trumpet, just as the seven trumpets are an expansion of the breaking of the seventh seal. The order is climactic and the judgments become more intensive and extensive as the time of the second coming of Christ approaches. All indications are that the bowl judgments fall with trip-hammer rapidity on a world that is reeling under previous judgments and a gigantic world war. Some bowl judgments are selective and extend only to the wicked (16:2, 8-11), and several affect parts of nature (sea, rivers, sun, etc.).

In the first bowl judgment people who followed the Antichrist received painful sores. Sores also come with the fifth bowl (vv. 10-11).

2. THE SECOND BOWL (16:3)

16:3. After the second trumpet blew (8:8-9), "a third of the sea turned into blood," killing "a third of the living creatures" and destroying "a third of the ships" (8:8-9). In **the second . . . bowl,** however, **every living thing in the sea died** (16:3). It is probable that the ocean here did not chemically correspond to

human blood, but that it looked like blood and had the same effect in killing everything. Just as in the second trumpet, the blood here is analogous to the first plague in Egypt (Ex. 7:20-25). As most of the earth's surface is covered by the seas, this is a worldwide, tremendous judgment.

3. THE THIRD BOWL (16:4-7)

16:4-7. Just as the third trumpet made "a third of the waters" bitter (8:11), so **the third . . . bowl** extends the judgment of the second bowl on the sea to **rivers and springs** and **they became blood** (16:4). John heard the angel in charge of the waters proclaim that God the Holy One is **just in** His **judgments** (v. 5). For God's work in turning the waters to blood is in response to the shedding of **the blood of . . . saints and prophets** (v. 6). This is echoed by a word from the altar declaring the judgment just (v. 7; cf. 15:3).

4. THE FOURTH BOWL (16:8-9)

16:8-9. This judgment focused the **intense heat** of the **sun.** In response people **cursed . . . God** and **refused to repent** (cf. v. 11). By contrast, the fourth trumpet (8:12) darkened a third of the heavens but did not include additional intense heat. It is clear from this and other prophecies that dramatic changes in climate will occur in the Great Tribulation.

5. THE FIFTH BOWL (16:10-11)

16:10-11. This judgment was directed toward the beast's **throne,** imposed **darkness** on the earth, and inflicted painful **sores** (cf. v. 2) on people. Again they **cursed . . . God** and **refused to repent.** This is the last reference in Revelation to a failure to repent (cf. 2:21; 9:21; 16:9; cf., however, 16:21). The fifth bowl is similar to the fifth trumpet (9:1-11) in that both will bring darkness, but the fifth trumpet has to do with demon possession rather than physical pain.

6. THE SIXTH BOWL (16:12-16)

16:12. According to John's revelation, **the sixth angel poured out his bowl and dried up the river Euphrates to prepare the way for the kings from the**

East. There has been endless speculation about "the kings from the East," with many expositors trying to relate them to some contemporary leaders of their generation. A survey of 100 commentaries of the Book of Revelation reveals at least 50 interpretations of the identity of the kings of the East. The simplest and best explanation, however, is that this refers to kings or rulers from the Orient or East who will participate in the final world war. In the light of the context of this passage indicating the near approach of the second coming of Christ and the contemporary world situation in which the Orient today contains a large portion of the world's population with tremendous military potential, any interpretation other than a literal one does not make sense. Alford states it concisely: "This is the only understanding of these words which will suit the context, or the requirement of this series of prophecies" (Alford, *The Greek Testament*, 4:700).

This is related to the **great river Euphrates** because this is the water boundary between the Holy Land and Asia to the east (cf. comments on 9:12-16). While the implication is that the water is dried up by an act of God, the fact is that dams have been built across the Euphrates River in this century to divert water for irrigation so that there are times even today when there is little or no water in the Euphrates. The Euphrates River is frequently mentioned in Scripture (e.g., Gen. 15:18; Deut. 1:7; 11:24; Josh. 1:4). The drying up of this river is also predicted in Isaiah 11:15.

16:13-16. John was then given a symbolic and comprehensive view of the preparation for the final bowl of God's wrath. He **saw three evil spirits that looked like frogs** coming out of the mouths of Satan (**the dragon**) and the two beasts (Antichrist [13:1-10] and the false prophet [13:11-18]). One need not speculate on the identity of the three frogs, for verse 14 explains that **they are spirits of demons performing miraculous signs.** These demons go throughout the world influencing kings to assemble **for the battle on the great day of God Almighty** ("Almighty" [*pantokratōr*] is also used in 1:8; 4:8; 11:17; 15:3; 16:7; 19:6, 15; 21:22).

While the meaning of this symbolic presentation is clear, there is a major problem involved in what the demons do. The coming world government in the Great Tribulation will be established by the power of Satan (13:2). Here, however, Satan, the world ruler, and the false prophet unite in inciting the nations of the world **to gather** for the final world war. Actually the war is a form of rebellion against the world ruler. Why then should satanic forces be let loose to destroy the world empire which has just been created?

The answer seems to be in the events which follow. Satan, knowing that the second coming of Christ is near, will gather all the military might of the world into the Holy Land to resist the coming of the Son of Man who will return to the Mount of Olives (Zech. 14:4). Though the nations may be deceived in entering into the war in hope of gaining world political power, the satanic purpose is to combat the armies from heaven (introduced in chap. 19) at the second coming of Christ.

The war is said to continue right up to the day of the Second Coming and involves house-to-house fighting in Jerusalem itself on the day of the Lord's return (Zech. 14:1-3). The reference to "the battle" (*ton polemon*, Rev. 16:14) is probably better translated "the war" (NASB). Thus it is better to speak of "the war of Armageddon" (see v. 16) rather than the "the battle of Armageddon." The war will be going on for some time, but the climax will come at Christ's second coming. "Armageddon" comes from the Greek *Harmagedōn*, which transliterates the Hebrew words for Mount (*har*) of Megiddo. That mountain is near the city of Megiddo and the plain of Esdraelon, the scene of many Old Testament battles.

Accordingly John heard the warning coming from Christ Himself: **Behold, I come like a thief! Blessed is he who stays awake and keeps his clothes with him, so that he may not go naked and be shamefully exposed.**

Christ's return is often compared to the coming of a thief. It implies suddenness and unpreparedness as far as unbelievers are concerned. Just as Christians are not to be surprised by the Rapture of the church (1 Thes. 5:4), so believers at the time of the Second Coming will be anticipating His return. Blessing is promised to the one who is prepared for the coming of the Lord by being attired in the righteousness or clothing which God Himself supplies.

Taken as a whole, the sixth bowl of the wrath of God is preparation for the final act of judgment before the Second Coming, and is the later stage of development related to the river Euphrates, anticipated earlier (Rev. 9:14). The time factor between the sixth trumpet and the sixth bowl is comparatively short.

7. THE SEVENTH BOWL (16:17-21)

16:17-20. The seventh angel then **poured out his bowl into the air.** John heard **a loud voice from the throne, saying, It is done!** A similar pronouncement followed the seventh trumpet (11:15-19). Here also John saw **lightning** flashes and heard **thunder,** which was followed by **a severe earthquake (16:18).** John was then informed that this will be the greatest earthquake of all time (other earthquakes are mentioned in 8:5 and 11:19), and the resulting description indicates that it will affect the whole earth with the possible exception of the land of Israel. **The great city** which **split into three parts** refers to the destruction of **Babylon.** The most important event, however, is that **the cities of the nations collapsed.** The huge earthquake will reduce to rubble all the cities of the nations (Gentiles). The stage is thus being set for the second coming of Christ. Obviously in the collapse of the world's cities there will be tremendous loss of life and destruction of what is left of the world empire.

Though Jerusalem is mentioned in 11:8 as "the great city, which is figuratively called Sodom and Egypt, where also their Lord was crucified," "the great city" here is specifically Babylon, as indicated in 16:19. God will give Babylon **the cup filled with the wine of the fury of His wrath,** that is, she will experience a terrible outpouring of His judgment. Some have suggested that this city is Rome, but is called Babylon because of its spiritual declension. While this has been debated at length by scholars (cf. J.A. Seiss, *The Apocalypse,* pp. 381-82, 397-420), it is preferable to view "Babylon" as the rebuilt city of Babylon located on the Euphrates River, which will be the capital of the final world government (cf. Walvoord, *Revelation,* pp. 240-41).

In addition to the terrible earthquake and probably because of it, John recorded, **Every island fled away and mountains could not be found.** These verses (vv. 18-20), if taken literally, indicate topographical changes in the earth which eventually will also include great changes in the Holy Land in preparation for Christ's millennial kingdom.

16:21. In addition to the earthquake, **huge hailstones of about 100 pounds each** fell on people. Such huge masses of ice supernaturally formed would destroy anything left standing from the earthquake and would no doubt kill or seriously injure those they hit. In spite of the severity of the judgment and its cataclysmic character the hardness of human hearts is revealed in the final sentence: **And they cursed God on account of the plague of hail, because the plague was so terrible.**

The question is sometimes raised why eternal punishment is eternal. The answer is that people in the hardness of their hearts will not change; they deserve eternal punishment because they are eternally unrepentant. With the final destruction coming from the seventh bowl of the wrath of God, the stage will then be set for the dramatic and climactic second coming of Christ, revealed in chapter 19. Before this event, however, a future detailed description is given of Babylon in chapters 17-18.

K. The fall of Babylon (chaps. 17-18)

Babylon—the source of so many heathen and pagan religions which have opposed the faith of Israel as well as the faith of the church—is here seen in its final judgment. These chapters do not fall chronologically within the scheme of the seals, trumpets, and bowls of the wrath of God, and expositors have had difficulty in determining precisely the meaning of the revelation in these chapters.

In general, however, in chapter 17 Babylon is seen in its religious character climaxing in a world religion which seems to fit the first half of the last seven years preceding Christ's second coming. Chapter 17 also records the destruction of Babylon by the 10 kings (v. 16).

Chapter 18, by contrast, seems to refer to Babylon as a political power and as a great city and as the seat of power of the great world empire which will dominate the second half of the last seven years before Christ's return. Babylon, referred to about 300 times in the Bible, is occasionally viewed as a satanic religious program opposing the true worship of God, but primarily it is viewed as a political power with a great city bearing the name Babylon as its capital. The end times bring together these two major lines of truth about Babylon and indicate God's final judgment on it.

1. RELIGIOUS BABYLON DESTROYED (CHAP. 17)

17:1-2. One of the seven angels (in chap. 16) **who had** one of **the seven bowls** invited John to witness **the punishment of the great prostitute, who sits on many waters.** This evil woman symbolizes the religious system of Babylon, and the waters symbolize "peoples, multitudes, nations, and languages" (v. 15). The angel informed John that **the kings of the earth** had **committed adultery** with the woman; in other words, they had become a part of the religious system which she symbolized (cf. 14:8).

17:3-5. John was then taken in **the Spirit** (or better, "in [his] spirit," i.e., in a vision, not bodily; cf. 1:10; 4:2) to **a desert** where he saw the **woman** herself. She was **sitting on a scarlet beast that was covered with blasphemous names.** The beast **had 7 heads and 10 horns.** The beast is an obvious reference to the world government (13:1). The 10 horns are later defined (17:12) as 10 kings who had "not yet received a kingdom." The 7 heads seem to refer to prominent rulers of the yet-future Roman Empire.

The woman was dressed in purple and scarlet, and was glittering with gold, precious stones, and pearls. Her adornment is similar to that of religious trappings of ritualistic churches today. While purple, scarlet, gold, precious stones, and pearls can all represent beauty and glory in relation to the true faith, here they reveal a false religion that prostitutes the truth.

In her hand the woman **held a golden cup . . . filled with abominable things and the filth of her adulteries** (cf. "the wine of her adulteries" in v. 2). This confirms previous indications that her

character and life are symbolic of false religion, confirmed by the words **written on her forehead:** MYSTERY BABYLON THE GREAT THE MOTHER OF PROSTITUTES AND OF THE ABOMINATIONS OF THE EARTH. The NASB and NIV are probably right in separating the word "mystery" from the title which follows because the word "mystery" is not a part of the title itself; it describes the title.

The Bible is full of information about Babylon as the source of false religion, the record beginning with the building of the tower of Babel (Gen. 10–11). The name "Babel" suggests "confusion" (Gen. 11:9). Later the name was applied to the city of Babylon which itself has a long history dating back to as early as 3,000 years before Christ. One of its famous rulers was Hammurabi (1728–1686 B.C.). After a period of decline Babylon again rose to great heights under Nebuchadnezzar about 600 years before Christ. Nebuchadnezzar's reign (605–562 B.C.) and the subsequent history of Babylon is the background of the Book of Daniel.

Babylon was important not only politically but also religiously. Nimrod, who founded Babylon (Gen. 10:8-12), had a wife known as Semiramis who founded the secret religious rites of the Babylonian mysteries, according to accounts outside the Bible. Semiramis had a son with an alleged miraculous conception who was given the name Tammuz and in effect was a false fulfillment of the promise of the seed of the woman given to Eve (Gen. 3:15).

Various religious practices were observed in connection with this false Babylonian religion, including recognition of the mother and child as God and of creating an order of virgins who became religious prostitutes. Tammuz, according to the tradition, was killed by a wild animal and then restored to life, a satanic anticipation and counterfeit of Christ's resurrection. Scripture condemns this false religion repeatedly (Jer. 7:18; 44:17-19, 25; Ezek. 8:14). The worship of Baal is related to the worship of Tammuz.

After the Persians took over Babylon in 539 B.C., they discouraged the continuation of the mystery religions of Babylon. Subsequently the Babylonian cultists moved to Pergamum (or Pergamos) where one of the seven churches of Asia

Minor was located (cf. Rev. 2:12-17). Crowns in the shape of a fish head were worn by the chief priests of the Babylonian cult to honor the fish god. The crowns bore the words "Keeper of the Bridge," symbolic of the "bridge" between man and Satan. This handle was adopted by the Roman emperors, who used the Latin title *Pontifex Maximus*, which means "Major Keeper of the Bridge." And the same title was later used by the bishop of Rome. The pope today is often called the *pontiff*, which comes from *pontifex*. When the teachers of the Babylonian mystery religions later moved from Pergamum to Rome, they were influential in paganizing Christianity and were the source of many so-called religious rites which have crept into ritualistic churches. Babylon then is the symbol of apostasy and blasphemous substitution of idol-worship for the worship of God in Christ. In this passage Babylon comes to its final judgment.

17:6. The woman symbolizing the apostate religious system, **was drunk with the blood of the saints.** This makes it clear that the apostate religious system of the first half of the last seven years leading up to Christ's second coming will be completely devoid of any true Christians. As a matter of fact the apostate church will attempt to kill all those who follow the true faith. John expressed his great astonishment at this revelation.

17:7-8. The angel explained the meaning **of the woman and of the beast** she was riding. **The beast . . . will come up out of the Abyss,** the home of Satan (11:7) and the place from which demons come (9:1-2, 11). This indicates that the power behind the ruler is satanic (cf. 13:4) and that Satan and the man he controls are closely identified. Their power is one. The fact that the beast **was, now is not, and will come up** in the future is another indication of what was introduced in 13:3. The supernatural survival and revival of both the world ruler and his empire will impress the world as being supernatural and will lead to worship of the beast and Satan. (On **the book of life** see comments on 3:5; 13:8. Also cf. 20:12, 15; 21:27.)

17:9-11. The angel informed John, **This calls for a mind with wisdom** (cf. 13:18). The truth that is being presented here symbolically requires spiritual insight to be understood, and the difficulty of correct interpretation is illustrated by the various ways it has been interpreted in the history of the church.

The angel informed John that the beast's **heads are seven hills on which the woman sits.** Many ancient writers, such as Victorinus, who wrote one of the first commentaries on the Book of Revelation, identified the seven hills as Rome, often described as "the city of seven hills." This identification has led to the conclusion this passage teaches that Rome will be the capital of the coming world empire. Originally Rome included seven small mountains along the Tiber River, and the hills were given the names Palatine, Aventine, Caelian, Equiline, Viminal, Quirimal, and Capitoline. Later, however, the city expanded to include the hill Janiculum and also a hill to the north called Pincian. While Rome is often referred to as having seven hills or mountains, different writers do not necessarily name the same seven mountains.

A close study of the passage does not support the conclusion that this refers to the city of Rome. Seiss, for instance, offers extensive evidence that the reference is to rulers rather than to physical mountains (*The Apocalypse*, pp. 391-94). This is supported by the text which explains, **They are also seven kings** (lit., "the seven heads are seven kings"). If the mountains represent kings, then obviously they are not literal mountains and refer not to a literal Rome but to persons.

This view is also supported by verse 10, **Five have fallen, one is, the other has not yet come; but when he does come, he must remain for a little while.** John was writing from his point of view in which five prominent kings of the Roman Empire had already come and gone, and one was then on the throne (probably Domitian, who caused the persecution which put John on the island of Patmos). The identity of the seventh king, the one to come after John's time, is unknown.

Verse 11 adds that the final world empire will be headed by **an eighth king. . . . The beast who once was, and now is not. . . . belongs to the seven and is going to his destruction.** The eighth king is obviously identical to the final world ruler, the man who heads up the final world empire destroyed by Christ at His second coming.

One possible explanation of the difference between the seventh and eighth beast is that the seventh beast itself is the Roman Empire marvelously revived in the end time, and the eighth beast is its final ruler. These verses show that in the end time, particularly during the first half of the last seven years, there will be an alliance between the Middle East ruler (the Antichrist) and the apostate world church of that time. This will come to a head, however, at the midpoint of the seven years, when that political power becomes worldwide.

17:12-14. Verse 12 explains that **the 10 horns . . . are 10 kings.** While many commentators have tried to identify 10 successive kings in the past, the passage itself indicates that they are contemporaneous kings who are heads of the countries which will form the original alliance in the Middle East that will support the future world ruler. They will receive authority **for one hour . . . as kings along with the beast.** While the 7 heads may be chronologically successive rulers of the Roman Empire who are singled out as prominent, the 10 horns by contrast are contemporaneous with each other, and as the text indicates they will receive political power for a brief time.

The 10 kings will unite their **power** to support **the beast** (v. 13), the Middle East ruler who will emerge in the end time and will make a covenant with Israel seven years before the second coming of Christ. Their antagonism to Christ is indicated throughout the entire seven years. And when Christ returns, these 10 kings will **war against** Him but will be defeated (v. 14). Interestingly Christ **the Lamb** is also the **Lord of lords and King of kings** (cf. 1 Tim. 6:15; Rev. 19:16).

17:15. Verse 1 stated that the woman "sits on many waters." These **waters** are now interpreted as **peoples, multitudes, nations, and languages.** This indicates that there will be one ecumenical world religious system, embracing all nations and languages.

17:16-18. The chapter closes with the dramatic destruction of the woman. **The beast** (the world ruler, the Antichrist) **and the 10 horns** (10 kings) **will hate the prostitute** and **will bring her to ruin.** While the exact time of this event is not given in this passage, it would seem to occur at the midpoint of the seven years when the beast will assume the role of world dictator by proclamation (Dan. 9:27; Matt. 24:15).

When the ruler in the Middle East takes on worldwide political power, he will also assume the place of God and demand that everyone worship him or else be killed (cf. Dan. 11:36-38; 2 Thes. 2:4; Rev. 13:8, 15). The world church movement, which characterizes the first half of the seven years leading up to the Second Coming, is thus brought to an abrupt end. It will be replaced by the final form of world religion which will be the worship of the world ruler, Satan's substitute for Christ.

This is part of God's sovereign purpose to bring evil leaders into judgment, **For God has put it into their hearts to accomplish His purpose by agreeing to give the beast their power to rule, until God's words are fulfilled.**

The final description of the woman is given in 17:18: **The woman you saw is the great city that rules over the kings of the earth.** The reference to the woman as a city is another link with ancient Babylon, this time regarded as a religious center for false religion. The apostate church represented by the woman was a combination of religious and political power. As stated in verse 5, the city and the woman are a "mystery," and are therefore a symbolic presentation. Verse 18, however, introduces the next chapter which seems to refer to Babylon more as a literal city than as a religious entity.

2. POLITICAL BABYLON DESTROYED (CHAP. 18)

18:1-3. Further revelation on the destruction of Babylon was made by **another angel coming down from heaven.** This contrasts with "one of the seven angels" mentioned in 17:1 and should not be confused with angelic representations of Christ. Angels do have great authority and often make pronouncements in the Book of Revelation. The power and glory of this angel was such that **the earth was illuminated by his splendor** (18:1).

The angel's message is summarized: **Fallen! Fallen is Babylon the Great!** The question has been raised as to whether or not this is another view of the same destruction mentioned in 17:16-17. A comparison of chapters 17 and 18 reveals that these are different events. The woman in chapter 17 was associated with the political power but was not the political power itself, and her destruction apparently brought no mourning from the earth. By contrast the destruction of Babylon in chapter 18 brings loud lamentation from the earth's political and economic powers. Instead of being destroyed and consumed by the 10 kings, here the destruction seems to come from an earthquake, and it is probable that this is an enlarged explanation of what was described in 16:19-21.

What is pictured here is a large prosperous city, the center of political and economic life. The judgment of God makes it a home for demons and a haunt for every evil spirit, a haunt for every unclean and detestable bird. For all the nations have drunk the maddening wine of her adulteries. This false religion is like a drug that drives men to madness. While it brought riches to merchants, it is now doomed for destruction.

18:4-8. Following the pronouncement of the angel, another voice from heaven instructed the people of God to leave the city so that they would escape the judgment to come on it (vv. 4-5). Babylon will receive torture and grief commensurate with her glory and luxury, in which she boasted that she was a queen (v. 7). Death, mourning, and famine, also fire, will come on the city in one day (v. 8).

18:9-20. When kings who were involved with the city see its destruction they will be grieved, and will cry, Woe! Woe, O great city, O Babylon, city of power! (v. 10) Merchants too will bemoan the city's downfall since they will no longer be able to carry on commerce with the city. The description in verses 12-13 indicates the great luxury and wealth of the city. This obviously refers to an economic and political situation rather than a religious one. The mourning of the merchants is similar to that of the kings: Woe! Woe, O great city . . . ! (v. 16)

Sea captains . . . sailors, and others in navigational occupations will lament in similar fashion: Woe! Woe, O great city . . . ! (v. 19) All three groups—kings, merchants, and sailors—speak of her destruction as sudden: in one hour (vv. 10, 17, 19). As the world mourns the destruction of Babylon, the saints are told to rejoice because God has judged her for the way she treated you (v. 20).

18:21-24. The final and violent destruction of the city is compared to throwing a large millstone . . . into the sea (v. 21). The lament follows that those who once characterized the city—harpists and musicians, flute players and trumpeters, and workmen of any trade (v. 22)—will not be seen in the city again. Nor will there be light and the joy of weddings (v. 23). The reason for her judgment is that by her magic spell (pharmakeia; cf. 9:21) all the nations were led astray from God (18:23; cf. 17:2), and she was guilty of murdering prophets and . . . saints (18:24; cf. 17:6).

The question remains as to what city is in view here. A common view is that it refers to the city of Rome, because of the prominence of Rome as the seat of the Roman Catholic Church and the capital of the ancient Roman Empire. Some find confirmation of this in the fact that the kings and sea merchants will be able to see the smoke of the burning of the city (18:9, 18).

Other evidence seems to point to the fact that it is Babylon itself, located on the Euphrates River, which in the end time will be converted into a ship-bearing river. When all the evidence is studied, the conclusion seems to point to Babylon being rebuilt as the capital of the world empire in the end time rather than to Rome in Italy. Bible expositors, however, continue to be divided on this question.

The events of chapter 17 will be fulfilled at the midpoint of the seven years, whereas the events of chapter 18 will occur at the end of the seven years, immediately before the second coming of Christ. The destruction of the city of Babylon is the final blow to the times of the Gentiles, which began when the Babylonian army attacked Jerusalem in 605 B.C. (cf. Luke 21:24).

With chapters 17 and 18 giving additional insight and information concerning the earth's major religious and political movements during that final seven years, the stage is now set for the climax of the Book of Revelation—the second coming of Christ (chap. 19).

L. The song of hallelujah in heaven (19:1-10)

1. THE HALLELUJAH OF THE MULTITUDES IN HEAVEN (19:1-3)

Revelation 4–18 dealt primarily with the events of the Great Tribulation. Beginning in chapter 19 there is a noticeable change. The Great Tribulation is now coming to its end and the spotlight focuses on heaven and the second coming of Christ. For the saints and angels it is a time of rejoicing and victory.

19:1. Beginning in chapter 19 a chronological development is indicated by the phrase **after this** (*meta tauta*). Literally this phrase means "after these things," and refers to the events of chapter 18. Accordingly John **heard what sounded like the roar** of many people **in heaven** praising God, obviously because of the judgment on Babylon. Interpreters have shown much confusion in understanding the order of the events in chapters 19–20; thus it is important to note that this praise in 19:1 follows Babylon's destruction in chapter 18.

The word "roar" (*phōnēn*) is literally a "sound," modified by the adjective "great" (*megalēn*). This loud noise is from **a great multitude,** the same phrase used in 7:9 where the "great multitude" refers to the martyred dead of the Great Tribulation. For them in particular the judgment of Babylon is a great triumph. The Greek word for **Hallelujah** is *hallēlouia,* sometimes translated "alleluiah." The word "hallelujah" is derived from the similar Hebrew word in the Old Testament. It occurs in the New Testament only four times, all of them in Revelation 19 (vv. 1, 3-4, 6). This is the biblical "Hallelujah Chorus."

19:2-3. In expressing their praise of God, God's glory and power resulting from and caused by His salvation are mentioned along with the fact that **His judgments** are **true and just.** The destruction of **the great prostitute** (cf. 17:1, 4) is a proper act of vengeance for her martyring the **servants** of God (17:6). The judgment that is wrought on her, however, is only the beginning of the eternal punishment of the wicked, indicated in the statement that **the smoke from her goes up forever and ever.**

2. THE HALLELUJAH OF THE 24 ELDERS (19:4-5)

19:4-5. The 24 elders and the 4 living creatures also sing a hallelujah chorus. This is another reminder that the 24 elders, representing the church of the present Age, are distinguished from the Tribulation saints, described in verse 1 as "a great multitude." The 4 living creatures, previously introduced in 4:6-8, seem to refer to angels who praise God. Still another voice of praise, apparently coming from an angel, also praised God and exhorted **all you His servants** (19:5) to join in this praise.

3. THE PROPHETIC PROCLAMATION OF THE WEDDING OF THE LAMB (19:6-9)

19:6-8. The fourth and final hallelujah of this chapter, according to John, sounded like a **multitude** of people, **rushing waters,** and loud **thunder.** Here the rejoicing is prophetic for what is about to happen rather than for the judgment just executed.

The second coming of Christ is anticipated in the words, **for our Lord God Almighty reigns.** John used the word "Almighty" (*pantokratōr;* also in 1:8; 4:8; 11:17; 15:3; 16:7, 14; 19:15; 21:22). Along with the exhortation to **rejoice,** announcement is made that **the wedding of the Lamb has come, and His bride has made herself ready.**

In Scripture, marriage is often used to describe the relationship of saints to God. In the Old Testament Israel is pictured, as in Hosea, as the unfaithful wife of Yahweh who is destined to be restored in the future kingdom. In the New Testament, marriage is also used to describe the relationship between Christ and the church, but the illustration contrasts with the Old Testament, for the church is regarded as a virgin bride waiting the coming of her heavenly bridegroom (2 Cor. 11:2).

The **fine linen** with which the bride will be adorned is explained as representing **the righteous acts of the saints** (Rev. 19:8). (In the OT the high priest's clothing included linen: Ex. 28:42; Lev. 6:10; 16:4, 23, 32.) While some think this refers to the fact that the saints are justified by faith, the plural expression "the righteous acts" seems to refer to the righteous deeds wrought by the saints through the grace of God. Though all this has been made possible by the grace of God, the emphasis here seems to be on the works of the bride rather than on her standing as one who has been justified by faith.

This is the last of 14 outbursts of praise to God in the Book of Revelation by saints, angels, the 24 elders, and/or the 4 living creatures. The hymns or shouts of praise are in 4:8, 11; 5:9-10, 12-13; 7:10, 12; 11:16-18; 15:3-4; 16:5-7; 19:1-4, 6-8 (see the chart near 4:8).

19:9. The angel who commanded John to write (14:13) commanded him again to record the message, **Blessed are those who are invited to the wedding supper of the Lamb!**

One of the false interpretations that has plagued the church is the concept that God treats all saints exactly alike. Instead, a literal interpretation of the Bible distinguishes different groups of saints, and here the bride is distinguished from those who are invited to the wedding supper. Instead of treating all alike, God indeed has a program for Israel as a nation and also for those in Israel who are saved. He also has a program for Gentiles in the Old Testament who come to faith in God. And in the New Testament He has a program for the church as still a different group of saints. Again in the Book of Revelation the Tribulation saints are distinguished from other previous groups. It is not so much a question of difference in blessings as it is that God has a program designed for each group of saints which corresponds to their particular relationship to His overall program. Here the church, described as a bride, will be attended by angels and by saints who are distinct from the bride.

Expositors have debated whether the wedding will be in heaven or on earth. While the difference is not that important, the interpretive problem can be resolved by comparing the wedding described here to weddings in the first century. A wedding normally included these stages: (1) the legal consummation of the marriage by the parents of the bride and of the groom, with the payment of the dowry; (2) the bridegroom coming to claim his bride (as illustrated in Matt. 25:1-13 in the familiar Parable of the 10 Virgins); (3) the wedding supper (as illustrated in John 2:1-11) which was a several-day feast following the previous phase of the wedding.

In Revelation 19:9 "the wedding supper" is phase 3. And the announcement coincides with the second coming of Christ. It would seem, therefore, that the wedding supper has not yet been observed. In fulfilling the symbol, Christ is completing phase 1 in the Church Age as individuals are saved. Phase 2 will be accomplished at the Rapture of the church, when Christ takes His bride to heaven, the Father's house (John 14:1-3). Accordingly it would seem that the beginning of the Millennium itself will fulfill the symbolism of the wedding supper (*gamos*). It is also significant that the use of the word "bride" in 19:7 (*gynē*, lit., "wife,") implies that phase 2 of the wedding will have been completed and that all that remains is the feast itself. (The word commonly used for "bride" is *nymphē*; cf. John 3:29; Rev. 18:23; 21:2, 9; 22:17.)

All this suggests that the wedding feast is an earthly feast, which also corresponds to the illustrations of weddings in the Bible (Matt. 22:1-14; 25:1-13), and thus will take place on earth at the beginning of the Millennium. The importance of the announcement and invitation to the wedding supper, repeated in Revelation 22:17, is seen in the angel's remarks, **These are the true words of God.**

4. THE COMMAND TO WORSHIP GOD (19:10)

19:10. So impressive was the scene in heaven with the four great hallelujahs and the announcement of the coming wedding feast that John once again fell down to worship the angel, as he had done before (1:17). Then, however, he was worshiping Christ, which was proper. But here the angel rebuked him, urging him to worship only God and not him since he was **a fellow servant** with John. The angel added, **For the testimony of Jesus is the spirit of prophecy,** that is, the very nature or purpose of prophecy is to testify of Jesus Christ and to bring glory to Him. In the present Age one of the special functions of the Holy Spirit is to glorify Christ and to inform believers of "what is yet to come" (John 16:13). The tremendous revelation in the first 10 verses of Revelation 19 is a fitting introduction to what is about to be revealed, the second coming of Jesus

Christ, the subject of the entire book (1:1).

M. The second coming of Christ (19:11-21)

As John saw heaven open, he saw prophetically Christ's second coming and the events which will follow it. The second coming of Christ is a prominent doctrine in Scripture (Pss. 2:1-9; 24:7-10; 96:10-13; 110; Isa. 9:6-7; Jer. 23:1-8; Ezek. 37:15-28; Dan. 2:44-45; 7:13-14; Hosea 3:4-5; Amos 9:11-15; Micah 4:7; Zech. 2:10-12; 12; 14:1-9; Matt. 19:28; 24:27-31; 25:6, 31-46; Mark 13:24-27; Luke 12:35-40; 17:24-37; 18:8; 21:25-28; Acts 1:10-11; 15:16-18; Rom. 11:25-27; 2 Thes. 2:8; 2 Peter 3:3-4; Jude 14-15; Rev. 1:7-8; 2:25-28; 16:15; 22:20). So this is obviously a major event in the divine program.

Conservative interpreters of the Bible almost universally recognize this as a yet-future event, as indicated in orthodox creeds throughout the history of the church. Just as the first coming of Christ was literal and was fulfilled in history, so the second coming of Christ which is yet future will be fulfilled in the same literal manner.

Among conservative interpreters, however, the question has been raised whether the Rapture of the church, as revealed in such major passages as 1 Thessalonians 4:13-18 and 1 Corinthians 15:51-58, is fulfilled at the time of the second coming of Christ to the earth or, as pretribulationists hold, is fulfilled as a separate event seven years before His formal second coming to the earth.

It should be noted that none of the many details given in Revelation 19:11-21 corresponds to the Rapture of the church. In Revelation Christ returns, but in none of the Rapture passages is He ever pictured as touching the earth, for the saints meet Him in the air (1 Thes. 4:17).

Most significant is the fact that in Revelation 19-20 there is complete silence concerning any translation of living saints. In fact the implication of the passage is that saints who are on earth when Christ returns will remain on earth to enter the millennial kingdom in their natural bodies. If the Rapture were included in the second coming of Christ to the earth, one would expect to find reference to such a major event in Revelation 19. But no such reference is to be found. For these and many other reasons chapter 19 is a confirmation of the teaching that the Rapture of the church is a separate earlier event and that there is no translation of the living at the time of His second coming to the earth. (For further discussion see John F. Walvoord, *The Rapture Question.*)

1. THE REVELATION OF THE RIDER ON THE WHITE HORSE (19:11-13)

19:11-13. As John gazed into **heaven,** he saw Christ on **a white horse.** Though some have identified this rider with the rider in 6:2, the context is entirely different. In 6:2 the rider is the world ruler of the Great Tribulation, while here the rider is a ruler who obviously comes from heaven itself. The white horse is a sign of His coming triumph. It was customary for a triumphant Roman general to parade on the Via Sacra, a main thoroughfare of Rome, followed by evidences of His victory in the form of booty and captives (cf. 2 Cor. 2:14). The white horse is thus a symbol of Christ's triumph over the forces of wickedness in the world, the details of which follow.

The horse's **rider is called Faithful and True** for, as John declared, **With justice He judges and makes war.** His piercing judgment of sin is indicated in the words, **His eyes are like blazing fire** (cf. Rev. 1:14), and His right to rule is evidenced by the **many crowns** He is wearing. **Written on Him** is a name **that no one but He Himself knows,** suggesting that Christ is the ineffable, indescribable One. But actual titles are given for Him. Revelation 19:13 says, **His name is the Word of God** (cf. John 1:1, 14; 1 John 1:1), and Revelation 19:16 states that the name of His robe and on His thigh is KING OF KINGS AND LORD OF LORDS (cf. 1 Tim. 6:15; Rev. 17:14). The rider obviously is Jesus Christ, returning to the earth in glory. That He is coming as Judge is further supported by the fact that **He is dressed in a robe dipped in blood** (19:13; cf. Isa. 63:2-3; Rev. 14:20).

2. THE COMING OF THE KING AND HIS ARMIES OF HEAVEN (19:14-16)

19:14-16. The drama of the scene is further enhanced by the multitude of the

armies of heaven described as **riding on white horses and dressed in fine linen, white and clean** (cf. v. 8). In Christ's mouth was **a sharp sword** (cf. 1:16; 2:12, 16; 19:21) which He would use **to strike down the nations.** The word for "sword" (*rhomphaia*) was used of an unusually long sword and sometimes used as a spear, thus indicating a piercing action. In addition to using the sword for striking down, He will use **an iron scepter** for ruling (cf. Ps. 2:9; Rev. 2:27). Christ is also described as the One who **treads the winepress of the fury of the wrath of God Almighty** (cf. 14:19-20; and cf. "Almighty" in 1:8; 4:8; 11:17; 15:3; 16:7, 14; 19:6; 21:22). This scene is a dramatic indication of the awfulness of the impending judgment. Matthew 24:30 indicates that those on earth will be witnesses of this impressive scene.

The scene on earth is the final stage of the great world war that will be under way for many weeks. With armies battling up and down the Holy Land for victory, on the very day of the return of Christ there will be house-to-house fighting in Jerusalem itself (Zech. 14:2). Combatants will have been lured to the battle site by demons sent by Satan to assemble the armies of the world to fight the armies of heaven (cf. Rev. 16:12-16).

3. THE DESTRUCTION OF THE WICKED (19:17-21)

19:17-18. The armies of earth are no match for the armies from heaven. The sharp sword in Christ's mouth (v. 15) is symbolic of His authoritative word of command that destroys earth's armies by divine power. Millions of men and their horses will be destroyed instantly. In keeping with this, John recorded that he **saw an angel standing in the sun,** who **cried in a loud voice to all** flying **birds** to **gather together for the great supper of God** to eat the carcasses of **kings, generals,** horsemen, and all people slain by Christ.

19:19-21. The beast and his **armies** will gather to fight against Christ and His army. The outcome of this battle— referred to in 16:14 as "the battle on the great day of God Almighty"—is summarized in 19:19-21. The world rulers—**the beast** and **the false prophet**—will both be **captured.** Their former **miraculous** demonic power will no longer be sufficient to save them. Both of them will be **thrown alive into the fiery lake of burning sulfur.**

The wicked who have died throughout the history of the world up to this point are in hades (Luke 16:23). The fiery lake, a different place, was prepared for the devil and his angels (Matt. 25:41), and will not be occupied by human beings until later (Rev. 20:14-15).

The armies themselves will be killed by Christ's sword (19:21; cf. 1:16; 2:12, 16; 19:15). The number of dead will be so great that the vultures will have more than they can eat. The defeat of the earth's wicked will then be complete, and will be finalized as later judgments search out the unsaved in other parts of the earth and also kill them (cf. Matt. 25:31-45).

The same inspired Word of God which so wonderfully describes the grace of God and the salvation which is equally plain about the judgment of all who reject the grace of God. The tendency of liberal interpreters of the Bible to emphasize passages dealing with the love of God and to ignore passages dealing with His righteous judgment is completely unjustified. The passages on judgment are just as inspired and accurate as those which develop the doctrines of grace and salvation. The Bible is clear that judgment awaits the wicked, and the second coming of Christ is the occasion for a worldwide judgment unparalleled in Scripture since the time of Noah's flood.

N. The millennial reign of Christ (20:1-10)

This chapter presents the fact that Christ will reign on earth for a thousand years. If this chapter is taken literally, it is relatively simple to understand what is meant. However, because many Bible interpreters have rejected the idea that there will be a reign of Christ on earth for a thousand years after His second coming, this chapter has been given an unusually large number of diverse interpretations, all designed to eliminate a literal millennial reign. In general there are three viewpoints, each with a number of variations.

The most recent view is what is known as *postmillennialism.* According to this view the thousand years represent the triumph of the gospel in the period *leading up to* the second coming of Christ. The return of Christ will follow the Millennium. Usually traced to Daniel Whitby, a controversial writer of the 17th century, this view has been advanced by other prominent scholars in the history of the church including Charles Hodge, A.H. Strong, David Brown, and more recently, Loraine Boettner. Basically it is an optimistic view that Christ will reign spiritually on earth through the work of the church and the preaching of the gospel. This view has largely been discarded in the 20th century, because many anti-Christian movements have prospered and the world has not progressed spiritually.

A second major view is *amillennialism,* which denies that there is any literal Millennium or reign of Christ on earth. The millennial reign of Christ is reduced to a spiritual reign in the hearts of believers. This reign is either over those on earth who put their trust in Him or over those in heaven. Both the amillennial and postmillennial views must interpret Revelation 20 in a nonliteral sense. Often there is wide difference among amillenarians in their interpretations of various passages in the Book of Revelation. Amillennialism historically had its first important advocate in Augustine who lived in the 4th and 5th centuries. Before Augustine, it is difficult to find one orthodox amillenarian. Modern advocates include such respected 20th-century theologians as Oswald Allis, Louis Berkhof, William Hendriksen, Abraham Kuyper, R.C.H. Lenski, and Gerhardus Vos.

A third form of interpretation is *premillennialism,* so named because it interprets Revelation 20 as referring to a literal thousand-year reign of Christ following His second coming. As the Second Coming occurs *before* the Millennium, it is therefore *pre*millennial. Twentieth-century advocates of this position include Lewis Sperry Chafer, Charles L. Feinberg, A.C. Gaebelein, H.A. Ironside, Alva McClain, William Pettingill, Charles C. Ryrie, C.I. Scofield, Wilbur Smith, and Merrill F. Unger. Other premillenarians can be found from the first century on, including Papias,

Justin Martyr, and many other early church fathers. Arguments for this position are based on the natural sequence of events in chapter 20 following chapter 19, viewing them as sequential and as stemming from the second coming of Christ. Many passages speak of the second coming of Christ being followed by a reign of righteousness on earth (Pss. 2; 24; 72; 96; Isa. 2; 9:6-7; 11–12; 63:1-6; 65–66; Jer. 23:5-6; 30:8-11; Dan. 2:44; 7:13-14; Hosea 3:4-5; Amos 9:11-15; Micah 4:1-8; Zeph. 3:14-20; Zech. 8:1-8; 14:1-9; Matt. 19:28; 25:31-46; Acts 15:16-18; Rom. 11:25-27; Jude 14-15; Rev. 2:25-28; 19:11–20:6).

It should be evident that one's interpretation of Revelation 20 is an important decision that serves as a watershed for various approaches to prophetic Scripture. The approach taken in this commentary is that the events in chapter 20 follow chronologically the events in chapter 19. Many also believe that chapters 21–22 follow in chronological order (for more detailed discussion of various views, see Walvoord's *Revelation,* pp. 282-90; and *The Millennial Kingdom.* Grand Rapids: Zondervan Publishing House, 1959, pp. 263-75).

1. THE BINDING OF SATAN (20:1-3)

20:1-3. Chapter 20 begins with the familiar phrase, **And I saw an angel** (cf. 7:2; 8:2; 10:1; 14:6; 18:1; 19:17). The "and" with which this chapter begins suggests that it continues the sequence of events begun in 19:1, which is introduced with the words "after this." In chapter 19 the Greek has "and" at the beginnings of 15 verses (but it is omitted in the NIV in vv. 4, 8, 10-11, 13-16, and 21 and is trans. "then" in vv. 5-6, 9, and 19 and "but" in v. 20). The use of the word "and" (*kai*) often indicates action that follows in logical and/or chronological sequence. Accordingly there is no reason why chapter 20 should not be considered as describing events which follow chapter 19. "And" (*kai*) continues throughout chapter 20, beginning each verse except verse 5. There is thus no linguistic or grammatical suggestion that these events are anything other than events following the second coming of Christ and occurring in sequence.

In addition to the grammar which connects these incidents, there is also the causal connection of the events which follow naturally from the fact that Christ will have returned to the earth. In chapter 19 these events include casting the beast and the false prophet into the lake of burning sulfur and destroying their armies. Having disposed of the world ruler and the false prophet as well as the armies, it would be only natural that Christ should then turn to Satan himself, as He does in chapter 20.

Accordingly John saw an angel descend from **heaven** holding **the key to the Abyss** and **a great chain.** The angel grabbed Satan, **the dragon** (cf. 12:3-4, 7, 9, 13, 16-17; 13:2, 4, 11; 16:13), **that ancient serpent** (12:9, 14-15), **bound him, and threw him into the Abyss, and locked** it, in order to prevent Satan's work of **deceiving the nations any more** for a **thousand years.**

An important interpretive question is whether Satan was bound at the first coming of Christ, as is commonly advanced by amillenarians, or will be bound at His second coming, as is held by premillenarians. Revelation 20:1-3 rather clearly contradicts the amillennial interpretation that Satan was bound at the first coming of Christ. Throughout the Scriptures Satan is said to exert great power not only against the world but also against Christians (Acts 5:3; 1 Cor. 5:5; 7:5; 2 Cor. 2:11; 11:14; 12:7; 1 Tim. 1:20). If there is still any question whether this is so, it should be settled by the exhortation of 1 Peter 5:8: "Be self-controlled and alert. Your enemy the devil prowls around like a roaring lion looking for someone to devour."

Amillenarians answer this by saying that Satan is limited by the power of God. But this has always been true, as illustrated in the Book of Job and elsewhere. To describe Satan's present situation as being locked in the Abyss and unable to deceive the nations for a period of a thousand years is simply not factually true today, and it requires extreme spiritualization of the literalness of this passage as well as other New Testament references to Satan's activities and present power. This same power of Satan is further revealed in the Great Tribulation when he empowers the world ruler

(Rev. 13:4). Satan will have been cast out of heaven at the beginning of the Great Tribulation and will then be more active than ever (Rev. 12:9, 13, 15, 17).

If Satan is actually deceiving the nations today, as the Scriptures and the facts of history indicate, then he is not now locked in the Abyss, and the thousand-year Millennium is still future. This interpretation is also supported by the final statement that after the thousand years, **he must be set free for a short time** (20:3). Here expositors again are at a loss to explain this except in a literal way, making possible a final satanic rebellion at the end of the millennial kingdom.

2. THE RESURRECTION AND REWARD OF THE MARTYRS (20:4-6)

20:4. Next in the series of revelations John recorded that he **saw thrones on which were seated those who had been given authority to judge.** In addition he **saw the souls of those who had been beheaded because of their** standing true to the Lord and His **Word** in the Great Tribulation. The fact that John could see them implies that they had received intermediate bodies in heaven and were awaiting their resurrections.

A distinction should be made between what John saw and what he received as revelation. Though he could see the souls, he was informed that they had been beheaded because they had refused to worship **the beast or his image** and would not receive **his mark.** What John saw was not all the souls in heaven but a particular generation of martyred dead who had been contemporaneous with the world ruler, the beast out of the sea (13:1). If the church were raptured prior to this event, as premillenarians teach, it would make sense to single out these martyred dead for resurrection. But if the church were not raptured, it would be most unusual to ignore all the martyrs of preceding generations, the church as a whole, and to specify this relatively small group.

John apparently was not told the identity of the individuals seated on the thrones. They evidently do not include the martyred dead themselves. Christ had predicted (Luke 22:29-30) that the 12 disciples would "eat and drink at My table in My kingdom and sit on thrones, judging the 12 tribes of Israel." As the disciples are also a part of the church, the body of Christ, it would be natural for them to sit on these thrones.

According to the Scriptures a series of judgments is related to Christ's return. The beast and the false prophet will be cast into the fiery lake (Rev. 19:20), Satan will be cast into the Abyss (20:1-3), and then the martyred dead of the Great Tribulation will be judged and rewarded (v. 4). In addition, Israel will be judged (Ezek. 20:33-38), and the Gentiles will be judged (Matt. 25:31-46). These judgments precede and lead up to the millennial kingdom.

John stated that these martyred dead **came to life and reigned with Christ a thousand years.** Their coming to life suggests that they will be given resurrected bodies. In addition to receiving the visual revelation, John was informed as to the meaning and character of the judgment that was here taking place.

20:5. John was also informed that **the rest of the dead did not come to life until the thousand years were ended.** This refers to the resurrection of the wicked dead, discussed later (vv. 11-15).

John stated that what he was seeing **is the first resurrection.** Posttribulationists refer to this as proof that the church will not be raptured before the Tribulation and that no resurrection has taken place prior to this point in fulfillment of God's prophetic program. It should be obvious, however, that in no sense could this be the number-one resurrection chronologically because historically Christ was the first to rise from the dead with a transformed, resurrected body. There was also the resurrection "of many" (Matt. 27:52-53) which took place when Christ died. In what sense then can this resurrection in Revelation 20:5 be "first"?

As the context which follows indicates, "the first resurrection" (vv. 5-6) contrasts with the last resurrection (vv. 12-13), which is followed by "the second death" (vv. 6, 14). It is first in the sense of *before.* All the righteous, regardless of when they are raised, take part in the resurrection which is first or before the final resurrection (of the wicked dead) at the end of the Millennium. This supports the conclusion that the resurrection of the

righteous is by stages. Christ was "the Firstfruits" (1 Cor. 15:23), which was preceded by the token resurrection of a number of saints (Matt. 27:52-53). Then will occur the Rapture of the church, which will include the resurrection of dead church saints and the translation of living church saints (1 Thes. 4:13-18). The resurrection of the two witnesses will occur in the Great Tribulation (Rev. 11:3, 11). Then the resurrection of the martyred dead of the Great Tribulation will occur soon after Christ returns to earth (20:4-5). To these may be added the resurrection of Old Testament saints which apparently will also occur at this time, though it is not mentioned in this text (cf. Isa. 26:19-21; Ezek. 37:12-14; Dan. 12:2-3).

20:6. All those who share in the resurrection of the righteous are said to be **blessed and holy,** and **the second death has no power over them, but they will be priests of God and of Christ and will reign with Him for a thousand years.** While all the righteous will be raised before the Millennium, individuals will retain their identities and their group identifications such as Gentile believers and believers in Israel in the Old Testament, the church of the New Testament, and saints of the Tribulation.

It should be noted that the term "a thousand years" occurs six times in chapter 20. This was not something that could be seen visually; John had to be informed of it and the vision had to be interpreted as relating to a period of a thousand years. While amillenarians and others have tended to view this as nonliteral, there is no evidence to support this conclusion. This is the only chapter in Revelation where a period of a thousand years is mentioned, and the fact that it is mentioned six times and is clearly described as a period of time before which and after which events take place lead to the conclusion that it means a literal thousand-year period.

Since other time designations in Revelation are literal (e.g., "42 months," 11:2; 13:5; "1,260 days," 11:3; 12:6) it is natural to take "a thousand years" literally also. If the term "a thousand years" designates a nonspecific but long period of time, the present Age between Christ's two advents, as amillenarians hold, then one would expect John to say simply that Christ would reign "a long time," in contrast to the "short time" of Satan's release (20:3).

Events which precede the thousand years are (a) the second coming of Christ, (b) the beast and the false prophet thrown into the fiery lake, (c) the armies destroyed, (d) Satan bound and locked in the Abyss, (e) thrones of judgment introduced, and (f) the martyred dead of the Tribulation resurrected. These events revealed in their proper sequence make it clear that the thousand-year period follows all these events, including the second coming of Christ. The conclusion that the Second Coming is premillennial is clearly supported by a normal, literal interpretation of this text.

3. THE FINAL DOOM OF SATAN (20:7-10)

Apart from frequent mention of the thousand years, no details are given concerning the reign of Christ on earth except that it is a time of great blessing. Many Old Testament passages supply additional information about the Millennium. The main point of the revelation here is that the Millennium follows the Second Coming.

20:7-8. John was told what would happen at the conclusion of **the thousand years. Satan will be released from** the Abyss, **his prison,** and will make a final attempt to induce nations—called **Gog and Magog**—to come and **battle** with him against Christ. Satan's release will produce a worldwide rebellion against the millennial reign of Christ. The armies will be so vast in numbers that they are said to be **like the sand on the seashore.**

Who are these who will follow Satan? Those who survive the Tribulation will enter the Millennium in their natural bodies, and they will bear children and repopulate the earth (Isa. 65:18-25). Under ideal circumstances in which all know about Jesus Christ (cf. Jer. 31:33-34), many will outwardly profess faith in Christ without actually placing faith in Him for salvation. The shallowness of their professions will become apparent when Satan is released. The multitudes who follow Satan are evidently those who have never been born again in the millennial kingdom.

The question has been raised as to whether this war is the same one discussed in Ezekiel 38-39, where Gog and Magog are also mentioned (Ezek. 38:2). These are two different battles, for in the war of Ezekiel 38-39 the armies come primarily from the north and involve only a few nations of the earth. But the battle in Revelation 20:7-9 will involve all nations, so armies will come from all directions.

Furthermore nothing in the context of Ezekiel 38-39 is similar to the battle in Revelation, as there is no mention of Satan or of millennial conditions. In Revelation 20:7 the context clearly places the battle at the end of the Millennium, whereas the Ezekiel battle takes place in connection with end-time events.

Why then is the expression "Gog and Magog" used by John? The Scriptures do not explain the expression. In fact it can be dropped out of the sentence without changing the meaning. In Ezekiel 38 Gog was the ruler and Magog was the people, and both were in rebellion against God and were enemies of Israel. It may be that the terms have taken on a symbolic meaning much as one speaks of a person's "Waterloo," which historically refers to the defeat of Napoleon at Waterloo, Belgium, but has come to represent any great disaster. Certainly the armies here come in the same spirit of antagonism against God that is found in Ezekiel 38.

20:9. The armies will surround **the camp of God's people, the city He loves.** This could mean only Jerusalem, which will be the capital of the world government of Christ throughout the millennial kingdom (cf. Isa. 2:1-5). The result is immediate judgment. **Fire** will come **down from heaven** and devour them.

In contrast with Ezekiel 38, there is no mention of earthquake, hail, or other disasters. The only similarity is that in both cases there is fire from heaven, a frequent method of divine judgment on the earth (cf. Gen. 19:24; Ex. 9:23-24; Lev. 9:24; 10:2; Num. 11:1; 16:35; 26:10; 1 Kings 18:38; 2 Kings 1:10, 12, 14; 1 Chron. 21:26; 2 Chron. 7:1, 3; Ps. 11:6; etc.).

20:10. After Satan's followers will be destroyed, he will be **thrown into the lake of burning sulfur.** Being cast into the lake that was prepared for him and his angels is the final judgment on Satan (cf. Matt. 25:41). Most significant as a support of the doctrine of eternal punishment is the concluding statement, **They will be tormented day and night forever and ever.** The word "they" includes the devil, the beast, and the false prophet. The lake of burning sulfur is not annihilation, for the beast and false prophet are still there a thousand years after they experienced their final judgment (Rev. 19:20).

O. The judgment of the great white throne (20:11-15)

1. THE RESURRECTION AND JUDGMENT OF THE WICKED DEAD (20:11-13)

20:11. The final five verses of chapter 20 introduce the judgment at the end of human history and the beginning of the eternal state. John wrote, **I saw a great white throne.** The events here described clearly follow the thousand years of verses 1-6. The great white throne apparently differs from the throne mentioned more than 30 times in Revelation beginning with 4:2. It apparently is located neither in heaven nor earth but in space, as suggested by the statement, **Earth and sky fled from His presence, and there was no place for them.** It is not indicated who sits on this throne, but probably it is Christ Himself as in 3:21 (cf. Matt. 19:28; 25:31; John 5:22; 2 Cor. 5:10—though the throne in these references is not necessarily the same throne as in Rev. 20:11). While Christ is now seated on the throne in heaven and will be seated on the Davidic throne on earth in the Millennium (Matt. 25:31), this white throne judgment is a special situation.

The question has been raised as to whether the earth and the starry heavens as they are today will be destroyed at this point in the future or will be simply restored to a new state of purity. Many references in the Bible suggest that the earth and the heavens, as now known, will be destroyed (cf. Matt. 24:35; Mark 13:31; Luke 16:17; 21:33; 2 Peter 3:10-13). This is confirmed by the opening statement of Revelation 21, "the first heaven and the first earth had passed away."

The present universe was created like a gigantic clock which is running down, and if left to itself, would ultimately come to a state of complete inactivity. Inasmuch as God created the universe and set it in motion for the purpose of enacting the drama of sin and redemption, it would seem proper to begin anew with a new heaven and a new earth suitable for His eternal purpose and built on a different principle. The new heaven and new earth described in chapter 21 has no similarity to the present earth and heaven.

20:12. The purpose of establishing the great white throne is to judge the dead. John wrote that **the dead, great and small,** stood **before the throne.** From other Scriptures it seems that all the righteous dead have been raised, including Old Testament saints, the dead of the Great Tribulation, and the church saints, the body of Christ (see comments on v. 5). Thus it may be assumed that verses 11-15 refer to the judgment of the wicked dead, who according to verse 5 would not be resurrected until after the thousand years and will have no part in what is called "the first resurrection."

At that judgment John saw **books . . . opened,** including a book called **the book of life.** The text does not state clearly what these books are, but the first opened books may refer to human works and "the book of life" is the record of those who are saved (cf. 3:5; 13:8; 17:8; 20:15; 21:27). The fact that these dead have not been raised before is evidence in itself that they do not have eternal life and that their judgment is a judgment of their works.

All final judgments deal with works, whether the works of Christians rewarded at the judgment seat of Christ or the works of the unsaved which are in view here. The question of who is saved is determined not in heaven but in life on earth. What is revealed here is the *confirmation* of one's destiny by means of God's written records.

Some view the book of life as the record of all the living and that when the unsaved die their names are deleted from it. A better view is that the book is the record of those who are saved whose names were "written in the book of life from the creation of the world" (17:8). Regardless of which view is taken, at this time only the saved are in the book of life.

20:13. In order for the wicked **dead to be judged . . . the sea . . . death, and hades** will give up their dead. Those who are unsaved at the time of death go immediately to a state of conscious punishment described in the Old Testament as sheol and in the New Testament as hades. Neither sheol nor hades ever refer to the *eternal* state and should not be considered equivalent to the English word "hell," which properly is the place of eternal punishment. The lake of fire (vv. 14-15) referred to as "the fiery lake of burning sulfur" (19:20) is the same as gehenna (cf. Matt. 5:22, 29-30; 10:28; 18:9; 23:15, 33; Mark 9:43, 45, 47; Luke 12:5; James 3:6) and is translated "hell" in the NIV and KJV with the word "fire" added in several passages. Actually gehenna was originally a name for the place of burning refuse, located in the Valley of Hinnom south of Jerusalem. The term, however, goes far beyond this geographic background and refers to eternal punishment.

The statement "death and hades gave up the dead" means that the physical bodies of the unsaved will be joined with their spirits which have been in hades. The mention of "the sea" giving up its dead makes it clear that regardless of how far a body has disintegrated, it will nevertheless be resurrected for this judgment.

2. THE LAKE OF FIRE (20:14-15)

20:14-15. Following the great white throne judgment **death and hades were thrown into the lake of fire. The lake of fire is the second death,** the final destination of the wicked. The doctrine of eternal punishment has always been a problem to Christians who enjoy the grace of God and salvation in Christ. The Bible is clear, however, that the punishment of the wicked is eternal. This is confirmed in verse 10, where the beast and the false prophet are still in the lake of fire after the thousand years of Christ's millennial reign. Though the wicked dead will receive resurrection bodies, they will be quite unlike the resurrection bodies of the saints. The former people will continue to be sinful but will be indestructible and will exist forever in the lake of fire.

Though many have attempted to find some scriptural way to avoid the doctrine of eternal punishment, as far as biblical revelation is concerned there are only two destinies for human souls; one is to be with the Lord and the other is to be forever separated from God in the lake of fire. This solemn fact is motivation for carrying the gospel to the ends of the earth whatever the cost, and doing everything possible to inform and challenge people to receive Christ before it is too late.

P. *The new heaven and the new earth (21:1–22:5)*

1. THE NEW HEAVEN AND THE NEW EARTH CREATED (21:1)

21:1. The opening verses of chapter 21 describe the creation of the new heaven and the new earth, which chronologically follows the thousand-year reign of Christ described in chapter 20. Chapter 21 begins with the familiar words **I saw,** an expression repeated in verse 2 (cf. v. 22, "I did not see"). This new creation is described as **a new heaven and a new earth.** That it is a totally new heaven and a new earth, and not the present heaven and earth renovated, is supported by the additional statement, **for the first heaven and the first earth had passed away** (also see comments on 20:11). An amazingly small amount of information is given about the new heaven and the new earth. But one major fact is stated in this verse: **there was no longer any sea.**

In contrast with the present earth, which has most of its surface covered by water, no large body of water will be on the new earth. The Bible is silent, however, on any features of the first heaven except the statement in 21:23 that there will be no sun or moon and, by implication, no stars. The new heaven refers not to the abode of God, but to the earth's atmosphere and planetary space.

No landmarks whatever are given concerning the new earth, and nothing is known of its characteristics, vegetation, color, or form. The implication, however, is that it is round and is the residence of all who are saved. A few other references are found in Scripture in relation to the new earth, including Isaiah 65:17; 66:22; and 2 Peter 3:10-13.

Because in some of these passages the Millennium is also discussed, expositors have often confused the eternal state with the Millennium. However, the principle is well established in Scripture that distant events are often telescoped together. Examples of this are Isaiah 61:1-2 (cf. Luke 4:17-19), which speaks of the first and second comings of Christ together, and Daniel 12:2, which mentions the resurrection of the righteous and of the wicked together even though, according to Revelation 20:5, they will be separated by a thousand years. Sometimes even the chronological order is reversed, as in Isaiah 65:17-25 (vv. 17-19 refer to the new heaven and new earth whereas vv. 20-25 clearly refer to the Millennium). End-time events are all also brought in close proximity in 2 Peter 3:10-13, where the beginning and the end of the day of the Lord are mentioned in the same passage.

Though expositors have differed on this point, the principle that clear passages should be used to explain obscure passages supports the conclusion that the second coming of Christ is followed by a thousand-year reign on earth, and this in turn is followed by a new heaven and new earth, the dwelling place of the saints for eternity. With the absence of any geographic identification and the absence of a sea, the new earth will obviously be entirely different. By contrast, the sea is mentioned many times in relation to the Millennium (e.g., Ps. 72:8; Isa. 11:9, 11; Ezek. 47:8-20; 48:28; Zech. 9:10; 14:8). The evidence is conclusive that the new heaven and new earth are not to be confused with the Millennium.

2. THE NEW JERUSALEM DESCRIBED (21:2-8)

21:2. John's attention was then directed to a specific feature of the new heaven and new earth, namely, **the Holy City, the New Jerusalem, coming down out of heaven from God, prepared as a bride beautifully dressed for her husband.** The New Jerusalem is called "the Holy City," in contrast with the earthly Jerusalem (which spiritually was compared to Sodom in 11:8). As early as 3:12 the New Jerusalem was described as "the city of My God, the New Jerusalem, which is coming down out of heaven from My God." The fact that the New Jerusalem comes down from heaven and that it is not said to be created at this

point has raised the question as to whether it has been in existence during the Millennium (see further discussion on this under 21:9).

Many expositors regard the promise of Christ in John 14:2, "I am going there to prepare a place for you," as referring to this city. The suggestion has been made that if the New Jerusalem is in existence during the millennial reign of Christ, it may have been suspended in the heavens as a dwelling place for resurrected and translated saints, who nevertheless would have immediate access to the earth to carry on their functions of ruling with Christ. J. Dwight Pentecost, for instance, quotes F.C. Jennings, William Kelly, and Walter Scott as supporting this concept of the New Jerusalem as a satellite city during the Millennium (*Things to Come.* Grand Rapids: Zondervan Publishing House, 1958, pp. 577-79). In the Millennium the New Jerusalem clearly does not rest on the earth, for there is an earthly Jerusalem and an earthly temple (Ezek. 40–48).

The New Jerusalem then will apparently be withdrawn from its proximity to the earth when the earth will be destroyed at the end of the Millennium, and then will come back after the new earth is created. Though this possibility of a satellite city has been disregarded by most commentators and must be considered as an inference rather than a direct revelation of the Bible, it does solve some problems of the relationship between the resurrected and translated saints to those still in their natural bodies in the Millennium, problems which otherwise are left without explanation.

Here, however, the New Jerusalem is described as it will be in the eternal state, and it is said to be "a bride beautifully dressed for her husband." Because the church is pictured in Scripture as a bride (2 Cor. 11:2), some have tried to identify the New Jerusalem's inhabitants as specifically the church saints, excluding saints of other dispensations. However, the use of marriage as an illustration is common in Scripture, not only to relate Christ to the church but also Yahweh to Israel. Though the city is compared to a beautifully dressed bride, it actually is a city, not a person or group of people.

21:3-4. Following this initial revelation of the New Jerusalem John wrote, I

heard a loud voice from the throne. This is the last of 20 times that the expression "a loud voice" is used in Revelation (first used in 5:2).

The final revelation from heaven states that God will then dwell **with men, that the saints will be His people** and He will **be their God.** In eternity saints will enjoy a new intimacy with God which is impossible in a world where sin and death are still present. The new order will be without sorrow. God **will wipe every tear from their eyes,** and death with its mourning, and pain with its crying will vanish, **for the old order of things** will have **passed away.**

Some have wondered if grief and sorrow will exist for a while in heaven and then be done away with here at the establishing of the new order. It is better to understand this passage as saying that heaven will have none of the features that so characterize the present earth.

21:5-6. The dramatic change to the new order is expressed in the words, **I am making everything new!** This revelation is **trustworthy and true,** and John was instructed to write down that fact. The One bringing about the change is Christ, who calls Himself **the Alpha and the Omega** (cf. 1:8; 22:13), the first and last letters of the Greek alphabet, interpreted by the phrase **the Beginning and the End.**

Those who are **thirsty** are promised that they will be able **to drink without cost from the spring of the water of life.** Apparently this refers not to physical thirst but to a desire for spiritual blessings.

21:7-8. Christ explained that **he who overcomes will inherit all this, and I will be his God and he will be My son.** This expresses the intimate relationship between the saints and God in the eternal state.

By contrast, **those who practice** the sins of the unbelieving world will be excluded from the New Jerusalem and will be destined for the fiery lake of burning sulfur. This judgment is a righteous punishment for their sins, eight of which are itemized here. He adds, **This is the second death.**

It should be obvious that this passage is not affirming salvation by works, but rather is referring to works as indicative of whether one is saved or not. Obviously many will be in heaven who before their conversions were indeed guilty of these sins but who turned from them in the day of grace in trusting Christ as their Savior. Though works are the evidence of salvation or lack of it, they are never the basis or ground of it. Similar lists of sins are found elsewhere in Revelation (cf. v. 27; 22:15).

3. THE NEW JERUSALEM AS THE BRIDE (21:9-11)

21:9-11. One of the angels of chapter 16 who had poured out a bowl of wrath on the earth then invited John to see the New Jerusalem as a bride. **Come, I will show you the bride, the wife of the Lamb.** Carried by **the Spirit** to a high **mountain,** John saw the New Jerusalem **coming down out of heaven from God,** shining with **the glory of God.**

Expositors have raised questions about the additional revelation of the New Jerusalem, beginning in verse 9. Some believe that this section is a recapitulation and pictures the New Jerusalem as it will be suspended over the earth during the millennial reign of Christ. A preferred interpretation, however, is that the passage continues to describe the New Jerusalem as it will be in the eternal state. Obviously the city would be much the same in either case, but various indications seem to relate this to the eternal state rather than to the Millennium.

The overall impression of the city as a gigantic brilliant **jewel** compared to **jasper, clear as crystal** indicates its great beauty. John was trying to describe what he saw and to relate it to what might be familiar to his readers. However, it is evident that his revelation transcends anything that can be experienced.

The jasper stone known today is opaque and not clear (cf. 4:3). It is found in various colors, and John apparently was referring to the beauty of the stone rather than to its particular characteristics. Today one might describe that city as a beautifully cut diamond, a stone not known as a jewel in the first century.

As in the earlier references to the New Jerusalem as a bride, here again is a city, not a person or group of people. This is confirmed by the description of the city which follows.

4. THE NEW JERUSALEM AS A CITY (21:12-27)

21:12-13. John saw a gigantic city, "square" in shape (v. 16), and surrounded by **a great, high wall with 12 gates.** The 12 gates bore **the names of the 12 tribes of Israel.** The number 12 is prominent in the city with 12 gates and 12 **angels** (v. 12), 12 tribes of Israel (v. 12), 12 foundations (v. 14), 12 apostles (v. 14), 12 pearls (v. 21), 12 kinds of fruit (22:2), with the wall 144 cubits—12 times 12 (21:17), and the height, width, and length, 12,000 stadia, about 1,400 miles (v. 16). The city has walls north, south, east, and west with **three gates** on each side (v. 13) and with an angel standing guard at each gate (v. 12).

This is an entirely different situation from the earthly Jerusalem in the Millennium. But if the names of the gates corresponded to the millennial Jerusalem described in Ezekiel 48:31-34, the north side from east to west would have the gates named Levi, Judah, and Reuben. On the west side from north to south were Naphtali, Asher, and Gad; on the south side from east to west, Simeon, Issachar, and Zebulun; and on the east side from north to south, Joseph, Benjamin, and Dan. In contrast to Revelation 7:5-8, where Dan is omitted and Joseph and Manasseh are included, Ezekiel mentioned Dan but not Manasseh.

21:14-16. The **12 foundations** to the city's **wall** bore **the names of the 12 apostles of the Lamb.** The apostles were part of the church, the body of Christ. Thus both the church and Israel will be in the city; the former are represented by the apostles' names on the foundations (v. 14), and the latter by the names of Israel's 12 tribes on the gates (v. 12). The distinction between Israel and the church is thus maintained. An **angel** measured **the city** with **a measuring rod of gold,** about 10 feet in length. The city is **12,000 stadia in length** and width, approximately 1,400 miles on each side. Tremendous as is the dimension of the city, the amazing fact is that it is also 1,400 miles **high.**

Commentators differ as to whether the city is a cube or a pyramid. The descriptions seem to favor the pyramid form.

21:17-18. Surrounding this huge city is a wall **144 cubits** or 216 feet thick. The reference to **man's measurement** simply means that though an angel is using the rod, he is using human dimensions.

As John gazed at **the wall,** he saw that it was **made of jasper,** and that **the city** was made **of pure gold, as pure as glass.** John was using the language of appearance, for apparently both the jasper and the gold differ from these metals as they are known today. In verse 11 the jasper is translucent, and in verses 18 and 21 the gold is clear like glass.

21:19-21. The decorations of the **foundations** (with the apostles' names inscribed on them) include 12 stones involving different colors. The color of the **jasper** is not indicated. The **sapphire** was probably blue; the **chalcedony** comes from Chalcedon, Turkey and is basically blue with stripes of other colors. The **emerald** is a bright green; the **sardonyx** is red and white; and the **carnelian,** called a "sardius" in the NASB, is usually ruby-red in color, though it sometimes has an amber or honey color. In 4:3 the carnelian stone is coupled with the jasper to reflect the glory of God. The **chrysolyte** is a golden color, probably different from the modern chrysolyte stone which is pale green. The **beryl** is a sea green; the **topaz** is a transparent yellow-green; the **chrysoprase** is also green; the **jacinth** is violet in color; and the **amethyst** is purple. The stones together provide a brilliant array of beautiful colors. The gates resemble huge, single **pearls,** and **the street of the city was of pure gold, like transparent glass** (cf. 21:18).

While the beauty of the city may have symbolic meaning, no clue is given as to the precise interpretation. Since it is reasonable to assume that the saints will dwell in the city, it is best to take the city as a literal future dwelling place of the saints and angels.

21:22-27. John declared that he **did not see a temple in the city** because **God** the Father **and the Lamb** (God the Son) **are its temple.** There will be no need for light from the **sun** or **moon** because **the glory of God** will provide the **light.** As John explained, **the Lamb is its lamp.**

From the fact that the nations (the Gentiles) will be in the city (vv. 24, 26)—as well as Israel and the church—it is evident that the city is the dwelling place of the saints of all ages, the angels, and

God Himself. The description of the heavenly Jerusalem in Hebrews 12:22-24 itemizes all those mentioned here and adds "the spirits of righteous men made perfect," which would include all other saints not specifically mentioned.

John learned that the gates of the city will never **be shut,** and because God's glory will be present continually **there will be no night there. The glory and honor of the nations will be** in the city, and everything that is **impure . . . shameful, or deceitful** will be excluded (cf. Rev. 21:8; 22:15). The inhabitants will be **only those whose names are written in the Lamb's book of life.** It is interesting that in the six references to the book of life in Revelation only this one calls it "the Lamb's" (cf. 3:5; 13:8; 17:8; 20:12, 15).

Though the description of the city does not answer all questions concerning the eternal state, the revelation given to John describes a beautiful and glorious future for all who put their trust in the living God.

5. THE RIVER OF THE WATER OF LIFE (22:1-2A)

22:1-2a. In the opening verses of chapter 22 additional facts are given about the New Jerusalem. **The angel showed** John **the river of the water of life, as clear as crystal, flowing from the throne of God and of the Lamb.** While this may be a literal river, its symbolism is clear. Out of the throne of God will flow pure water, symbolic of the holiness and purity of God and the city. This reference to a river should not be confused with similar millennial situations such as those in Ezekiel 47:1, 12 and Zechariah 14:8. These refer to literal rivers flowing from the temple and from Jerusalem and will be part of the millennial scene. The river in Revelation 22:1 will be part of the New Jerusalem in the new earth. The water flows **down the middle of the great street of the city.** This apparently refers to a main thoroughfare in the New Jerusalem coming from the throne of God with the river being a narrow stream in the middle of the street. The KJV attaches the phrase "in the midst of the street" to the next sentence rather than to the river.

It is significant also that the Lamb is pictured on the throne (mentioned also in

v. 3). This makes it clear that 1 Corinthians 15:24, which states that Christ "hands over the kingdom to God the Father after He has destroyed all dominion, authority, and power," does not mean that Christ's reign on the throne will end but that it will change its character. Christ is King of kings and Lord of lords (cf. Rev. 17:14; 19:16) for all eternity.

6. THE TREE OF LIFE (22:2B)

22:2b. As John contemplated the heavenly city, he saw **the tree of life, bearing 12 crops of fruit, yielding its fruit every month.** Interpreters have puzzled over this expression that the tree of life is **on each side of the river.** Some take this is as a group of trees. Others say that the river of life is narrow and that it flows on both sides of the tree. The tree of life was referred to in the Garden of Eden (Gen. 3:22, 24), where it was represented as perpetuating physical life forever. Adam and Eve were forbidden to eat of the fruit of this tree. Earlier in Revelation (2:7) the saints were promised the "right to eat from the tree of life, which is in the paradise of God."

While the literal and the symbolic seem to be combined in this tree, there is no reason why it could not be an actual tree with literal fruit. The practical effect would be to continue physical life forever. While the verse does not state that the fruit can be eaten, this is presumably the implication.

The tree's **leaves . . . are for the healing of the nations.** Based on this statement some have referred this situation back to the millennial times when there will be sickness and healing. However, another meaning seems to be indicated. The word "healing" (*therapeian*) can be understood as "health-giving." The English "therapeutic" is derived from this Greek word. Even though there is no sickness in the eternal state, the tree's fruit and leaves seem to contribute to the physical well-being of those in the eternal state.

7. THE THRONE OF GOD (22:3-4)

22:3-4. As if to remind the reader that healing as such is not necessary, John added, **No longer will there be any curse.** As the curse of Adam's sin led to illness requiring healing and death, so in the eternal state there will be no curse;

therefore no healing of illness is necessary.

As mentioned earlier, God and the Lamb are in the new city (21:22-23; 22:1). The New Jerusalem will be the temple of God (21:22), and the throne of God will also be in it. Then John wrote, **His servants will serve Him.** The highest joy and privilege of the saints in eternity will be to serve their blessed Lord, even though it is true that they will also reign with Him (2 Tim. 2:12; Rev. 5:10; 20:4-6). They will have a privileged place before the throne for **they will see His face.** The implication is that they are under the Lord's good favor and in His "inner circle." This intimacy is also indicated by the fact that **His name will be on their foreheads** (cf. 2:17; 3:12; 7:3; 14:1). Their freedom to be in the presence of God indicates that they will then be in their glorified bodies (cf. 1 John 3:2).

8. THE SAINTS' REIGN WITH GOD (22:5)

22:5. Once again John wrote that the glory and **light** of the New Jerusalem will be the presence of God, with no artificial illumination (cf. 21:23-24). And once again the statement is made that the servants of God will **reign** with Christ **forever** (cf. 20:6b).

Q. The final word from God (22:6-21)

1. THE CERTAINTY OF THE RETURN OF CHRIST (22:6-7)

22:6-7. Confirming both the truth and possibility of comprehending the prophecies previously given, the angel told John that the **words** of this book are **trustworthy and true.** The purpose of these communications is not to bewilder and confuse but to reveal many of **the things that must soon take place.**

This directly contradicts the point of view of many scholars that the Book of Revelation is an imponderable mystery for which no key is available today. This book is the Word of God and not the vague imaginations of John. In addition it is intended to describe future events. When taken in its literal, ordinary meaning, this is exactly what it does, even though much of Revelation is written in symbolic form. The Word of God was not given to be obscure. It was given to be understood by those taught by the Spirit.

The theme of Revelation is stated again in verse 7: **Behold, I am coming soon!** (cf. 1:7; 22:12, 20) Also He is coming quickly. The Greek word *tachy* may be translated "soon" (NIV) or "quickly" (NASB, ASV), and from the divine standpoint both are true. The coming of Christ is always soon from the standpoint of the saints' foreview of the future, and when it occurs, it will come suddenly or quickly. Accordingly a special blessing is pronounced on those who believe and heed the prophecy of the book. As stated earlier, this last book of the Bible, so neglected by the church and with its meanings confused by many expositors, contains more promises of blessing than any other book of Scripture. This reference to blessing is the sixth beatitude in the book (the seventh is in v. 14). The first blessing (in 1:3) is similar to this one in 22:7.

2. THE WORSHIP BY JOHN (22:8-9)

22:8-9. As this tremendous revelation was given to John, he once again **fell down to worship . . . the angel.** Again he was rebuked and reminded that angels should not be worshiped because, like the saints, they are fellow servants. John was commanded to **worship** the Lord, not angels (cf. 19:10).

3. THE COMMAND TO PROCLAIM THE PROPHECY OF THE BOOK (22:10-11)

22:10-11. Daniel was told that his prophecies would be "sealed until the time of the end" (Dan. 12:9). But John was told **not** to **seal up the words of** these prophecies. Again it should be emphasized that the viewpoint of some scholars that the Book of Revelation is an impenetrable puzzle is expressly contradicted by this and other passages. Revelation, both via its plain statements and its symbols, is designed to reveal facts and events relating to the second coming of Christ.

The exhortation which follows has puzzled some. Those who do **wrong** and are **vile** are encouraged to **continue** to do so, and those who do **right** and are **holy** are encouraged to **continue** to do so (Rev. 22:11). The point here is not to condone what is evil, but to point out that if people do not heed this prophecy, they will continue in their wickedness.

On the other hand those who do heed the prophecy will continue to do what is right. Relatively speaking, **the time** of the Lord's return **is near** and no major changes in mankind's conduct can be expected.

4. THE COMING JUDGMENT AND REWARD (22:12)

22:12. The words with which this verse begins: **Behold, I am coming soon!** are the same as those at the beginning of verse 7. In connection with His return, which will be "soon" (cf. vv. 7, 20), a **reward** is promised to His saints for what they have **done** for Christ. The reference is to the judgment seat of Christ (2 Cor. 5:10-11). The final judgments of both the wicked and the righteous will be judgments of works. This is the joyous expectation of those who are faithful and the fear of those who have not been faithful.

5. THE ETERNAL CHRIST (22:13)

22:13. Once again Christ is described as **the Alpha and the Omega** (first and last letters of the Gr. alphabet), **the First and the Last, the Beginning and the End.** Christ is before all Creation and He will continue to exist after the present creation is destroyed. He is the Eternal One (cf. 1:4, 8, 17; 2:8; 21:6).

6. THE COMING BLESSING AND JUDGMENT (22:14-15)

22:14-15. The last of the seven beatitudes of Revelation is bestowed on the saints, **those who wash their robes.** They have access to the New Jerusalem and its **tree of life** (cf. v. 19). The other six beatitudes are in 1:3; 14:13; 16:15; 19:9; 20:6; 22:7. In the manuscripts followed by the KJV, the expression "those who wash their robes" is translated "that do His commandments." In both cases the words accurately describe the righteous.

By contrast, judgment is pronounced on those who are unsaved; cf. Phil. 3:2): **those who practice magic arts** (cf. Rev. 9:21; 18:23; 21:8), **the sexually immoral, the murderers, the idolaters, and everyone who loves and practices falsehood.** As in the similar description of the unsaved in 21:8, 27, the wicked works which characterize the unsaved are described. Though some

saints have been guilty of these same practices, they have been washed in the blood of the Lamb and are acceptable to God. But those who refuse to come to the Lord receive the just reward for their sins. Though the world is excessively wicked, God will bring every sin into judgment. And the time for Christ's return may be drawing near, when this will be effected.

7. THE INVITATION OF THE SPIRIT AND THE BRIDE (22:16-17)

22:16-17. The entire Book of Revelation was delivered by Christ through His **angel** and is **for the churches.** Christ described Himself as **the Root and the Offspring of David, and the bright Morning Star.** Historically Christ comes from David (Matt. 1:1; cf. Isa. 11:11; Rev. 5:5). Prophetically His coming is like the morning star, the beginning of a bright new day. The Holy **Spirit** joined with **the bride,** the church, in extending an invitation to all who heed. Those who hear are encouraged to respond and also to extend the invitation to others. The wonderful promise is given that all those who are **thirsty** may **come** and will receive God's **free gift.**

This is the wonderful invitation extended to every generation up to the coming of Christ. Those who recognize their need and realize that Christ is the provider of salvation are exhorted to come while there is yet time before the judgment falls and it is too late. As the Scriptures make clear, the gift of eternal life (here called the **water of life;** cf. 22:1; John 7:37-39) is free. It has been paid for by the death of Christ on the cross and is extended to all who are willing to receive it in simple faith.

8. THE FINAL WARNING (22:18-19)

22:18-19. While on the one hand an invitation is extended to those who will listen, a word of warning is also given to those who reject the revelation of **this** final **book** of the Bible. A dual warning is given against adding to it or subtracting from it (cf. Deut. 4:2; 12:32; Prov. 30:6). How great will be the judgment of those who despise this book and relegate it to the mystical experiences of an old man, thereby denying that it is the inspired Word of God. Rejecting the Word of God is rejecting God Himself. And those who deny His promises of blessing and subtract from His truths will receive His judgment and will have no part in **the tree of life** or access to **the holy city** (cf. Rev. 22:14).

9. THE FINAL PRAYER AND PROMISE (22:20-21)

22:20-21. One further word of testimony was then given: **Yes, I am coming soon** (cf. vv. 7, 12). To this John replied in a brief prayer, **Amen. Come, Lord Jesus.**

With this tremendous revelation completed, a final word of benediction was pronounced. **The grace of the Lord Jesus be with God's people. Amen.** This expression, so common in other New Testament books, brings this final word from God to an end. For those who believe that Christ in His first coming provided salvation, there is the wonderful promise of His coming again to bring full and final deliverance. As the book began by introducing a revelation of Jesus Christ so it ends with the same thought that He is coming again.

Probably no other book of Scripture more sharply contrasts the blessed lot of the saints with the fearful future of those who are lost. No other book of the Bible is more explicit in its description of judgment on the one hand and the saints' eternal bliss on the other. What a tragedy that so many pass by this book and fail to fathom its wonderful truths, thereby impoverishing their knowledge and hope in Christ Jesus. God's people who understand and appreciate these wonderful promises can join with John in his prayer, "Come, Lord Jesus."

BIBLIOGRAPHY

Alford, Henry. *The Greek Testament*. Revised by Everett F. Harrison. 4 vols. in 2. Chicago: Moody Press, 1958.

Blanchard, Charles A. *Light on the Last Days*. Chicago: Bible Institute Colportage Association, 1913.

Ironside, H.A. *Lectures on the Book of Revelation*. New York: Loizeaux Brothers, 1930.

Kelly, William. *Lectures on the Book of Revelation*. London: W.H. Broom, 1874.

Mounce, Robert H. *The Book of Revelation*. The New International Commentary on the New Testament. Grand Rapids: Wm. B. Eerdmans Publishing Co., 1977.

Ryrie, Charles Caldwell. *Revelation*. Everyman's Bible Commentary. Chicago: Moody Press, 1968.

————. *The Final Countdown*. Wheaton, Ill.: Scripture Press Publications, Victor Books, 1982.

Scott, Walter. *Exposition of the Revelation of Jesus Christ*. London: Pickering and Inglis, n.d.

Scroggie, W.G. *The Great Unveiling*. Reprint. Grand Rapids: Zondervan Publishing House, 1979.

Seiss, Joseph A. *The Apocalypse*. Grand Rapids: Zondervan Publishing House, 1957.

Smith, J.B. *A Revelation of Jesus Christ*. Scottdale, Pa.: Herald Press, 1961.

Swete, Henry Barclay. *Commentary on Revelation*. 3d ed. London: Macmillan & Co., 1911. Reprint. Grand Rapids: Kregel Publications, 1978.

Tenney, Merrill C. *Interpreting Revelation*. Grand Rapids: Wm. B. Eerdmans Publishing Co., 1957.

Torrance, Thomas F. *The Apocalypse Today*. Greenwood, S.C.: Attic Press, 1960.

Walvoord, John F. *The Revelation of Jesus Christ*. Chicago: Moody Press, 1966.

————. *The Rapture Question*. Rev. ed. Grand Rapids: Zondervan Publishing House, 1979.

BIBLIOGRAPHY ON THE SEVEN CHURCHES IN REVELATION 2–3

Blaiklock, E.M. *The Seven Churches*. London: Marshall, Morgan & Scott, n.d.

Havner, Vance. *Repent or Else!* New York: Fleming H. Revell Co., 1958.

Loane, Marcus L. *They Overcame: An Exposition of the First Three Chapters of Revelation*. Grand Rapids: Baker Book House, 1981.

Morgan, G. Campbell. *A First Century Message to Twentieth Century Christians*. Westwood, N.J.: Fleming H. Revell Co., 1902.

Ramsay, W.M. *The Letters to the Seven Churches of Asia.* 4th ed. New York: Hodder and Stoughton, 1904. Reprint. Grand Rapids: Baker Book House, 1979.

Seiss, Joseph A. *Letters to the Seven Churches.* 1889. Reprint. Grand Rapids: Baker Book House, 1956.

Tatford, Frederick A. *The Patmos Letters.* Grand Rapids: Kregel Publications, 1969.

Trench, Richard Chenevix. *Commentary on the Epistles to the Seven Churches in Asia.* London: Macmillan & Co., 1867. Reprint. Minneapolis: Klock & Klock, 1978.

Yamauchi, Edwin M. *The Archaeology of New Testament Cities in Western Asia Minor.* Grand Rapids: Baker Book House, 1980. (Includes chapters on Ephesus, Pergamum, Sardis, and Laodicea.)